DATE DUE

DEMCO 38-296

Business Rankings Annual

ISSN 1043-7908

2 0 0 0

Business Rankings Annual

Lists of Companies, Products, Services, and Activities Compiled from a Variety of Published Sources.

Compiled by
Brooklyn Public Library
Business Library Staff

Detroit
San Francisco
London
Boston
Woodbridge, CT

Brooklyn Public Library, Business Library Staff

Susan Phillis, *Chief, Business Library*
Micki Trager, *Senior Librarian and In-House Editor*
Maud Andrew, Wendy Carribon, Deborah Crooke, Weina Lin, Danny Luce, Eileen McKee, Nancy O'Brien, Paul Otto, Bharathi Subramanian, and Florence Tenzer, *Contributing Librarians*

Gale Group Staff

Sheila M. Dow, *Editor and Project Coordinator*
Donna Craft, Terrance W. Peck, Amanda C. Quick, Brian Rabold, *Contributing Editors*
Paul Lewon, *Technical Training Specialist*

Erin E. Braun, *Managing Editor*

Mary Beth Trimper, *Composition Manager*
Evi Seoud, *Assistant Production Manager*
Nekita McKee, *Buyer*
Gary Leach, *Graphic Artist*

Theresa A. Rocklin, *Manager, Technical Support Services*
Charles Beaumont, *Sr. Programmer/Analyst*

Gale Group, Inc.
27500 Drake Rd.
Farmington Hills, MI 48331-3535

ISBN 0-7876-2432-2
ISSN 1043-7908

Printed in the United States of America

Contents

Preface

The staff of the Business Library of the Brooklyn Public Library answers over 175,000 reference questions each year, many of them requests for ranking information. To provide quick answers to questions in the highest interest subject areas, we have compiled *Business Rankings Annual*. Working from a bibliographic file we have built up over the years, we have culled thousands of items from periodicals, newspapers, financial services, directories, statistical annuals, and other printed material. The "top ten" from each of these rankings appears in this volume, grouped under standard subject headings for easy browsing. In addition to the standard entries, more than 1,000 additional entries, including foreign rankings, have been included to broaden the scope of the book's information for the 2000 edition.

Methods of Compilation

The Business Library subscribes to some 1,400 hundred periodicals and twenty newspapers, including the *Wall Street Journal* (three-star eastern edition) and *New York Times* (late edition). Every morning a team of librarians thumbs through the day's new arrivals looking for rankings. Other librarians check through new editions of statistical annuals and directories as they arrive. In fact, every member of the staff is constantly looking for ranking information when reading any publication. These sources have all contributed to a bibliographic card file citing over 10,000 rankings that has proved invaluable in answering patrons' inquiries. (Gale published a print version of this bibliographic file, along with a similar, though smaller, file on salaries under the title *Business Rankings and Salaries Index* in 1988.) For *Business Rankings Annual*, we have selected the lists that are most in demand by businesspeople, librarians, students, and the public; for each one, this volume typically provides at least the "top ten" on the list, along with important details about the ranking as described below. In order to represent as many publications as possible, we alternate sources of rankings from edition to edition. This volume draws most of its entries from serials and periodicals published between July, 1998, and the end of June, 1999.

Arrangement

Business Rankings Annual presents the lists grouped by subject, and subjects are arranged alphabetically. Most headings are taken from the Library of Congress (LC) subject headings, for example: Banks and Banking; Banks and Banking, International. However, when LC did not offer an appropriate or sufficiently up-to-date heading, we turned first to Wilson's *Business Periodicals Index* and then to the ABI/INFORM, a CD-ROM index from UMI, to find categories already in use in the field.

Broad subject categories like Advertising Agencies are subdivided. A primary method of subdivision is geographic;

unless otherwise indicated, a heading covers information about the United States. "International" indicates the source covers both U.S. and foreign aspects. Some categories are further divided for individual U.S. regions, states, and cities, as well as foreign countries. Other subdivisions reflect different facets of an industry. For example, the broad heading Automobile Industry and Trade has not only geographic subdivisions, but also categories for Automobile Industry and Trade -Advertising...-Export- Import Trade, and ...-Market Share. Cross-references have been included to help the user locate the exact subject term (for example: Business Climate, see Location of Industry). All of these subject terms appear in the Outline of Contents, where it is possible to scan the list of headings quickly to determine the exact form of the subject term that has been used.

Sample Entry

Each numbered item is explained below in the paragraph with the same number.

① **★1281★**
② **MOST ADMIRED COMPUTER SOFTWARE CORPORATIONS, 1997**

③ **Ranked by:** Scores (1-10) derived from a survey of senior executives, outside directors, and securities analysts.
④ **Remarks:** Respondents rated companies in their own industry on 8 attributes of reputation. Also notes previous year's rank.
⑤ **Number listed:** 7

1. Microsoft, with 8.26 points
2. Oracle Corp., 7.26
3. Computer Associates International, 7.08
⑥ 4. Computer Sciences, 6.97
5. Novell, 5.67
6. Sybase Inc., 5.63
7. Cognizant Corp., 5.60

⑦ **Source:** *Fortune,* America's Most Admired Corporations (annual), March 2, 1998 p. F-6

① **Sequential entry number**.
② **Ranking title** – A descriptive phrase identifying the contents of the list cited. These titles may be taken from the original source or, if need be, assigned by the rankings librarian to better categorize the list. In some instances, an asterisk will follow the title year, indicating the year of the source rather than the actual data year.
③ **Ranked by:** Indicates the criteria that establish the hierarchy, with specifics of date and units of measurement, if given.
④ **Remarks:** Provides additional details relating to the list from the source material.
⑤ **Number listed:** Notes the number of listees in the ranking source.
⑥ **Top 10 items on the list** – In many cases, the listing also includes data substantiating the rankings, as the scores in the above sample show.
⑦ **Source:** Gives complete bibliographic details. For periodicals, notes title, date, and page number. For serials, also gives frequency and publisher. For books, lists author/editor and publisher, as well.

Comprehensive Index

The reader can quickly locate all the rankings in which a given company, person, or product appears by consulting the Index. Look up Adolph Coors Co., for example, and see that there are *six* entries where it was in the top ten. And, another feature enhances the Index by also listing the subject under which each citation appears. The user will see that Adolph Coors Co.'s six entries appear under the following three subject headings: Beverage Industry; Beverage Industry—North America; and Food Industry and Trade. Thus, the Index provides an overview of the areas in which the companies, people, etc. are being ranked, and users can be more selective about looking up the entries that interest them. As always, every name in every list is indexed, not just those that are ranked first.

SIC Index

Business Rankings Annual cites entries in 2-, 3-, and 4-digit SIC categories as provided by the *Standard Industrial Classification Manual, 1987*, Executive Office of the President, Office of Management and Budget. Each SIC item is followed by a listing of subject headings pertaining to the specific SIC; entry numbers follow in sequence for easy reference. Arrangement is by SIC number, from least specific (major group heading) to most specific (industry number); thus TRANSPORTATION EQUIPMENT serves as the major group heading for the listings classified by *SIC 3710 Motor Vehicles and Motor Vehicle Equipment* and *SIC 3721 Aircraft*.

SIC to NAICS Conversion Guide

This guide is presented as a tool to classify listings in *Business Rankings Annual* by the North American Industry Classification System (NAICS) when a listing is present in the SIC Index. The NAICS was implemented in 1997 by the U.S. government as its new standard for economic data, replacing the primary SIC system. The new system will be implemented over several years by the respective North American governments; the conversion guide provided in this book reflects the U.S. version of the NAICS.

Bibliography

A complete listing of nearly 300 original sources used to compile *Business Rankings Annual* is provided in the Bibliography. Information cited includes:

- publication name
- publisher
- address, telephone, fax number, and URL
- frequency of publication
- price
- ISSN if applicable

Acknowledgments

Over the years many librarians have worked on the rankings file and to all of them we offer our thanks. Since the 1991 Edition, Micki Trager has been the primary force behind the compilation of *BRA* at the Brooklyn Public Library Business Library. Micki selects the data from a much larger file that has been created by the librarians as a reference resource, and manages the transformation of the data into standardized and categorized entries. She coordinates the herculean tasks of editing and proofreading with superb professional judgment and great good humor.

All of the librarians on the current staff of the Business Library are to be commended for their enthusiasm for the project and for their long hours spent in creating this book. On this, our last colaboration with Gale, our thanks to everyone who has ever worked on the rankings file in the Business Library, and special thanks to Joan M. Canning for her ongoing role in seeing the book to completion.

Susan Phillis
Chief
Brooklyn Public Library
Business Library

Outline of Contents

B

C

D

E

F

G

H

T

U

V

W

Y

Z

Business Rankings Annual

Accounting Firms

★1★
LARGEST U.S. ACCOUNTING FIRMS BY NUMBER OF EMPLOYEES, 1998
Ranked by: Number of employees. **Number listed:** 500

1. Andersen Worldwide/Arthur Andersen, with 37,419
2. Ernst & Young, 23,072
3. Deloitte & Touche, 19,764
4. KPMG Peat Marwick, 17,579
5. Coopers & Lybrand, 16,812
6. Price Waterhouse, 15,203
7. Grant Thornton, 2,900
8. McGladrey & Pullen, 2,896
9. BDO Seidman, 1,633
10. Crowe, Chizek & Co., 1,049

Source: *Emerson's Directory of Leading U.S. Accounting Firms*, Emerson Co., 1998, p. 291+.

★2★
TOP U.S. ACCOUNTING FIRMS BY FEE INCOME, 1998
Ranked by: Fee income, in millions of dollars. **Remarks:** Also notes percent change from previous year, previous year's figures, number of offices, number of partners, number of professional staff and year-end data. **Number listed:** 25

1. Andersen Worldwide, with $6,828 million
2. PricewaterhouseCoopers, $5,853
3. Ernst & Young, $5,545
4. Deloitte & Touche, $4,700
5. KPMG, $3,800
6. Grant Thornton, $336
7. McGladrey & Pullen, $296.1
8. BDO Seidman, $250
9. Crowe Chizek, $118.2
10. Plante & Moran, $104.7

Source: *Accountancy*, International Edition, February, 1999, p. 8.

★3★
TOP U.S. ACCOUNTING FIRMS BY NUMBER OF ENTITIES AUDITED, 1998*
Ranked by: Number of entities audited. **Remarks:** Also notes percentage of all Big-5 audited entities each firm represents. **Number listed:** 6

1. Coopers & Lybrand, with 206
2. Arthur Andersen, 188
3. Price Waterhouse, 172
4. KPMG Peat Marwick, 133
5. Ernst & Young, 90
6. Deloitte & Touche, 41

Source: *Issues in Accounting Education*, August, 1998, p. 697.

★4★
TOP U.S. ACCOUNTING FIRMS BY REVENUE, 1997
Ranked by: Revenue, in millions of dollars. **Remarks:** Also notes international affiliation, growth rate, number of offices, number of partners, number of professional staff and year-end date. **Number listed:** 5

1. PricewaterhouseCoopers, with $740 million
2. Andersen Worldwide, $449
3. KPMG, $359
4. Ernst & Young, $337
5. Deloitte & Touche Tohmatsu, $236

Source: *The Accountant*, August, 1998, p. 19.

Accounting Firms--Australia

★5★
TOP ACCOUNTING FIRMS IN AUSTRALIA, 1998
Ranked by: Fee income, in millions of Australian dollars (A$). **Remarks:** Also notes difference from previous year, percent change, number of offices, number of partners, number of professional staff and year-end data. **Number listed:** 25

1. PricewaterhouseCoopers, with $A720 million
2. Andersen Worldwide, $A449
3. KPMG, $A403
4. Ernst & Young, $A337
5. Deloitte Touche Tohmatsu, $A310
6. Horwath Australia, $A54
7. Pannell Kerr Forster, $A38.8
8. Grant Thornton, $A38.7
9. RSM, $A31.4
10. Moore Stephens Australia, $A30.6

Source: *Accountancy*, International Edition, November, 1998, p. 12.

Accounting Firms--Chicago Metropolitan Area

★6★

LARGEST ACCOUNTING FIRMS IN CHICAGO, 1997

Ranked by: Number of professional staff. **Remarks:** Also notes firm's address and phone number, managing partner, previous years' number of professionals, number of personnel audit/accounting, taxes, consulting and other. **Number listed:** 25

1. Arthur Andersen, with 2,102 professionals
2. Ernst & Young, 1,722
3. KPMG Peat Marwick, 1,368
4. Coopers & Lybrand, 1,263
5. Price Waterhouse, 1,100
6. Deloitte & Touche, 924
7. Altschuler, Melvoin & Glasser, 440
8. McGladrey & Pullen, 354
9. Grant Thornton, 264
10. Friedman, Eisenstein, Raemer & Schwartz, 246

Source: *Crain's Chicago Business*, Top Business Lists (annual), 1999, p. 127+.

Accounting Firms--China

★7★

LARGEST ACCOUNTING FIRMS IN CHINA, 1998*

Ranked by: Number of professional staff. **Remarks:** Also notes number of offices, number of partners and year-end data. **Number listed:** 12

1. Price Waterhouse, with 805 professionals
2. Coopers & Lybrand, 606
3. KPMG, 550
4. Arthur Andersen, 470
5. Deloitte & Touche Tohmatsu, 460
6. Horwath & Co., 450
7. Ernst & Young, 350
8. Moore Stephens, 282
9. BDO McCabe Lo & Co., 109
10. Beijing YongTuo, 108

Source: *Accountancy*, International Edition, June, 1998, p. 12.

Accounting Firms--Detroit Metropolitan Area

★8★

LARGEST ACCOUNTING FIRMS IN THE DETROIT METROPOLITAN AREA, 1998

Ranked by: Number of employees. **Remarks:** Also notes firms' address and phone number, previous years' number of employees, number of personnel audit/accounting, taxes, consulting, other and number of CPAs in the Detroit area. **Number listed:** 20

1. PricewaterhouseCoopers, with 906 employees
2. Andersen Worldwide, 894
3. Deloitte & Touche, 866
4. Plante & Moran, 634
5. Ernst & Young, 502
6. KPMG Peat Marwick, 244
7. Follmer, Rudzewicz & Co., 208
8. Doeren Mayhew & Co., 154
9. BDO Seidman, 144
10. Grant Thornton, 77

Source: *Crain's Detroit Business*, Crain's Book of Lists Detroit (annual), December 28, 1998, p. 142.

Accounting Firms--Florida

★9★

LARGEST ACCOUNTING FIRMS IN FLORIDA, 1998

Ranked by: Number of accounting professionals. **Remarks:** Also notes firm's address and phone number, number of CPAs, number of offices, managing partners and year established. **Number listed:** 24

1. Andersen Worldwide, with 1,288 professionals
2. Price Waterhouse, 800
3. KPMG Peat Marwick, 577
4. Ernst & Young, 515
5. Deloitte & Touche, 480
6. Coopers & Lybrand, 465
7. American Express Tax & Business Services, 160
8. Grant Thornton, 125
9. BDO Seidman, 100
10. Saltmarsh, Cleaveland & Gund, 91

Source: *Florida Trend*, TopRank Florida (annual), 1999, p. 88.

Accounting Firms--Ireland

★10★

TOP ACCOUNTING FIRMS IN IRELAND BY FEE INCOME, 1998

Ranked by: Fee income, in millions of Irish pounds. **Remarks:** Also notes difference from previous year, percent change, previous year's figures, number of offices, number of partners, number of professional staff and year-end data. **Number listed:** 16

1. PricewaterhouseCoopers, with IR£65 million
2. KPMG, IR£52.2
3. Arthur Andersen, IR£30
4. Ernst & Young, n/a
5. Deloitte & Touche, n/a
6. BDO Simpson Xavier, IR£14.5
7. Grant Thornton, IR£9
8. Chapman Food Mazars, IR£5.5
9. IFAC, IR£4.7
10. Bastow Charleton, IR£3.8

Source: *Accountancy*, International Edition, September, 1998, p. 12.

Accounting Firms--Long Island (NY)

★11★

LARGEST ACCOUNTING FIRMS IN LONG ISLAND, 1998

Ranked by: Number of professional staff. **Remarks:** Also notes partner's name and contact information, number of CPAs nationally and in Long Island and major clients. **Number listed:** 71

1. KPMG Peat Marwick, with 190 professionals
2. Margolin, Winer & Evans, 155

3. Deloitte & Touche, 135
4. PricewaterhouseCoopers, 120
5. Marks, Shron & Co., 108
6. Lopez, Edwards, Frank & Co., 106
7. Ernst & Young, 103
8. Marcum & Kliegman, 97
9. Arthur Andersen, 80
10. Albrecht, Viggiano, Zureck & Co., 67

Source: *Long Island Business News*, LI Book of Lists (annual), 1999, p. 46+.

Accounting Firms--Los Angeles County (CA)

★12★

LARGEST CERTIFIED PUBLIC ACCOUNTING FIRMS IN LOS ANGELES COUNTY, 1999

Ranked by: Number of accounting professionals in Los Angeles County. **Remarks:** Also notes contact information, number of CPAs, profile, accounting services, operations manager, and local executives. **Number listed:** 50

1. Deloitte & Touche, with 1,065 professionals
2. PricewaterhouseCoopers, 925
3. Arthur Andersen, 825
4. Ernst & Young, 700
5. KPMG Peat Marwick, 500
6. Gelfand, Rennergt & Feldman, 106
7. Grant Thornton, 86
7. Miller, Kaplan, Arase & Co., 86
9. BDO Seidman, 85
10. Nigro, Karlin & Segal, 85

Source: *Los Angeles Business Journal*, Book of Lists (annual), 1999, p. 20+.

Accounting Firms--Middle Western States

★13★

TOP ACCOUNTING FIRMS IN THE MIDDLE WESTERN STATES, 1998

Ranked by: Revenue, in millions of dollars. **Remarks:** Also includes percentage change from previous year, number of partners and professional staff and revenue breakdown. **Number listed:** 15

1. Baird, Kurtz & Dobson (MO), with $98 million
2. Larson Allen Weishair & Co. (MN), $59.1
3. Eide Bailly (ND), $33.5
4. Rubin, Brown, Gornstein & Co. (MO), $18.7
5. Kennedy & Co. (KS), $18.2
6. Lurie, Besikof, Lapidus & Co. (MN), $13
7. Grace & Co. (MO), $12.7
8. Olson, Thielen & Co. (MN), $11.7
9. Brady, Martz & Associates (ND), $10.6
10. Boulay, Heutmaker, Zibell & Co. (MN), $10.6

Source: *Practical Accountant*, Regional Rankings (annual), April, 1999, p. S11.

Accounting Firms--New England

★14★

TOP ACCOUNTING FIRMS IN NEW ENGLAND, 1998

Ranked by: Revenue, in millions of dollars. **Remarks:** Also includes percentage change from previous year, number of partners and professional staff and revenue breakdown. **Number listed:** 15

1. Berry, Dunn, McNeil & Parker (ME), with $18.1 million
2. Tofias, Fleishman, Shapiro & Co. (MA), $16.8
3. Blum Shapiro & Co. (CT), $14.1
4. Baker, Newman & Noyes (ME), $12.3
5. Carlin, Charron & Rosen (MA), $11.2
6. Vitale, Caturano & Co. (MA), $11.1
7. Freeley & Driscoll (MA), $9.5
8. Wolf & Co. (MA), $8.5
9. Kostin, Ruffkess & Co. (CT), $8.3
10. Whittlesey & Hadley (CT), $6.5

Source: *Practical Accountant*, Regional Rankings (annual), April, 1999, p. S5.

Accounting Firms--New Jersey

★15★

LARGEST CERTIFIED PUBLIC ACCOUNTING FIRMS IN NEW JERSEY, 1999

Ranked by: Number of CPAs. **Remarks:** Also notes contact information, number of staff, year founded, managing partner, and URL. **Number listed:** 24

1. PricewaterhouseCoopers, with 315 CPAs
2. Deloitte & Touche, 280
3. KPMG Peat Marwick, 244
4. J. H. Cohn, 175
5. Arthur Andersen, 125
6. Rothstein, Kass & Co., 87
7. Withum, Smith & Brown, 75
8. Amper, Politziner & Mattia, 71
9. Ernst & Young, 70
10. RD Hunter & Co., 50

Source: *New Jersey Business*, Book of Lists (annual), 1999, p. 12+.

Accounting Firms--New York Metropolitan Area

★16★

LARGEST ACCOUNTING FIRMS IN THE NEW YORK METROPOLITAN AREA, 1999

Ranked by: Number of area professionals. **Remarks:** Also notes contact information, managing partner, previous year's figures and number of offices. **Number listed:** 25

1. PricewaterhouseCoopers, with 7,004 professionals
2. Deloitte & Touche, 4,640
3. Ernst & Young, 3,500
4. KPMG Peat Marwick, 2,775
5. Arthur Andersen, 2,252
6. Constantin Associates, 593
7. BDO Seidman, 480
8. Grant Thornton, 435

9. Richard A. Eisner, 380
10. American Express Tax & Business Services, 377

Source: *Crain's New York Business*, March 22, 1999, p. 16+.

Accounting Firms--Northeastern States

★17★
TOP ACCOUNTING FIRMS IN THE NORTHEASTERN STATES, 1998
Ranked by: Revenue, in millions of dollars. **Remarks:** Also includes percentage change from previous year, number of partners and professional staff and revenue breakdown. **Number listed:** 15

1. Constantin Associates (NY), with $85.1 million
2. Eisner (NY), $69
3. Resnick Fedder & Silverman (MD), $46.9
4. David Berdon & Co. (NY), $41.1
5. M. R. Weiser & Co. (NY), $33
6. Anchim, Block & Anchim (NY), $31
7. JH Cohn (NY), $28.1
8. Parente, Randolph, Orlando & Assoc. (PA), $26.4
9. Edward Issacs & Co. (NY), $25.3
10. Mahoney Cohen & Co. (NY), $24.5

Source: *Practical Accountant*, Regional Rankings (annual), April, 1999, p. S6.

Accounting Firms--Philadelphia Metropolitan Area

★18★
LARGEST ACCOUNTING FIRMS IN THE PHILADELPHIA METROPOLITAN AREA, 1999
Ranked by: Number of local full-time employees. **Remarks:** Also notes total number of staff, local and total number of CPAs and consulting staff, hourly fees, specialization, clients and managing partner. **Number listed:** 24

1. PricewaterhouseCoopers, with 2,300 employees
2. Deloitte & Touche, 950
3. KPMG, 820
4. Arthur Andersen, 750
5. Ernst & Young, 721
6. ZA Business Services/Zelenkofske Axelrod, 199
7. BDO Seidman, 150
8. Grant Thornton, 140
9. Goldenberg Rosenthal, 120
10. Elko, Fischer, McCabe & Rudman, 108

Source: *Philadelphia Business Journal*, January 15-21, 1999, p. 19.

Accounting Firms--Southern States

★19★
TOP ACCOUNTING FIRMS IN THE SOUTHEASTERN STATES, 1998
Ranked by: Revenue, in millions of dollars. **Remarks:** Also includes percentage change from previous year, number of partners and professional staff and revenue breakdown. **Number listed:** 15

1. Cherry, Bekaert & Holland (VA), with $31 million
2. Dixon Odom (NC), $23.8
3. Elliott, Davis & Co. (SC), $18.5
4. Crisp Hughes Evans (NC), $17.4
5. Kaufman Rossin & Co. (FL), $16.3
6. Joseph Decosimo & Co. (TN), $16.1
7. Goodman & Co. (VA), $16
8. Rachlin Cohen & Holtz (FL), $14.7
9. Hyatt, Imler, Ott & Blount, Inc. (GA), $14
10. Mauldin & Jenkins (GA), $13.9

Source: *Practical Accountant*, Regional Rankings (annual), April, 1999, p. S7.

Accounting Firms--Southwestern States

★20★
TOP ACCOUNTING FIRMS IN THE SOUTHWESTERN STATES, 1998
Ranked by: Revenue, in millions of dollars. **Remarks:** Also includes percentage change from previous year, number of partners and professional staff and revenue breakdown. **Number listed:** 15

1. Mann Frankfort Stein & Lipp (TX), with $21.6 million
2. Weaver & Tidwell (TX), $12.9
3. Postlethwaite & Netterville (LA), $10.9
3. Lane Gorman Trubitt (TX), $10.9
5. Henry & Horne (AZ), $10
6. Toback & Co. (AZ), $8.7
7. Bourgeois Bennett (LA), $8.5
8. Heard, McElroy & Vestal (LA), $7.4
9. Broussard, Poche, Lewis & Breaux (LA), $7.3
10. Padgett, Stratemann & Co. (TX), $7.1

Source: *Practical Accountant*, Regional Rankings (annual), April, 1999, p. S13.

Accounting Firms--Western States

★21★
TOP ACCOUNTING FIRMS IN THE WESTERN STATES, 1998
Ranked by: Revenue, in millions of dollars. **Remarks:** Also includes percentage change from previous year, number of partners and professional staff and revenue breakdown. **Number listed:** 15

1. Moss Adams (WA), with $82 million
2. LeMaster & Daniels (WA), $19.8
3. Frank, Rimerman & Co. (CA), $16.8
4. Nigro, Karlin & Segal (CA), $16.6
5. RGL Gallagher (CA), $16
6. Stonefield Josphson (CA), $14
7. Yergen & Meyer (OR), $13.6
8. Singer, Lewak, Greenbaum & Goldstein (CA), $13
9. Vavrinek, Trine, Day & Co. (CA), $12.3
10. Miller, Kaplan, Arase & Co. (CA), $12.2

Source: *Practical Accountant*, Regional Rankings (annual), April, 1999, p. S15.

Acne--Therapy

★22★
TOP ACNE PRODUCTS BRANDS, 1998
Ranked by: Sales, in millions of dollars. **Remarks:** Also ranks by unit sales. **Number listed:** 10

1. Clearasil, with $70.8 million
2. Neutrogena, $52.7
3. Stridex, $18.8
4. Clean & Clear, $14.9
5. Noxzema, $13.2
6. Clear Logix, $5.5
7. Nature's Cure, $4.3
8. Oxy, $4.2
9. Aveeno, $4.1
10. Stiefel, $3.2

Source: *MMR*, May 3, 1999, p. 46.

Acquisition, Corporate

See: **Corporate Acquisitions and Mergers**

ADI (Areas of Dominant Influence)

See: **Metropolitan Areas Television**

Advertisements

See: **Advertising**

Advertisers

★23★
COMPANIES SPENDING THE MOST ON ADVERTISING, 1998
Ranked by: U.S. advertising expenditures, in millions of dollars. **Remarks:** Also notes percent change from previous year. **Number listed:** 10

1. General Motors Corp., with $2,121.5 million
2. Procter & Gamble, $1,725
3. DaimlerChrysler, $1,411.1
4. Phillip Morris Cos., $1,264.4
5. Ford Motor Co., $1,244.7
6. Time Warner, $1,206.6
7. Walt Disney Co., $1,066.4
8. PepsiCo, $1,041.7
9. Diageo, $830.6
10. McDonald's, $809.7

Source: *Advertising Age*, March 22, 1999, p. 6.

★24★
TOP ADVERTISING MEDIA, 1997
Ranked by: Measured ad spending, in millions of dollars. **Remarks:** Also notes figures from previous year, percent change and additional financial information. **Number listed:** 10

1. Newspapers, with $15,777.5 million
2. Network TV, $15,225.1
3. Spot TV, $14,534.6
4. Magazines, $12,701.1
5. Cable TV and networks, $5,781.9
6. Syndicated TV, $2,515
7. National Spot Radio, $1,684.2
8. National Newspaper, $1,650
9. Outdoor, $1,462.7
10. Sunday magazine, $1,016.6

Source: *Advertising Age*, Top 100 MegaBrands (annual), July 13, 1998, p. S2.

★25★
TOP AUTOMOBILE BRANDS SPENDING THE MOST ON ADVERTISING, 1997
Ranked by: U.S. advertising expenditures, in millions of dollars. **Remarks:** Also notes figures from previous year, percent change and additional financial information. **Number listed:** 10

1. Chevrolet cars & trucks, with $656.3 million
2. Ford cars & trucks, $569.9
3. Dodge cars & trucks, $551.8
4. Toyota cars & trucks, $453.8
5. Nissan cars & trucks, $347
6. Honda cars & trucks, $335.6
7. Chrysler cars & trucks, $301.3
8. GM cars, trucks & financial services, $279.3
9. Buick cars, $252.9
10. Jeep vehicles, $250.4

Source: *Advertising Age*, Top 100 MegaBrands (annual), July 13, 1998, p. S7.

★26★
TOP BRANDS SPENDING THE MOST ON ADVERTISING DURING ABC "20/20", 1997
Ranked by: Advertising spending ABC "20/20" television newsmagazine, in thousands of dollars. **Number listed:** 10

1. McDonald's Restaurant, with $5,328.6 thousand
2. Merrill Lynch Financial Services, $2,125.6
3. U.S. Postal Service, $1,871.3
4. Nissan AutomobilesAltima, $1,859.6
5. Sprint, $1,502.6
6. Discover Card, $1,479.5
7. Target Discount Stores, $1,295.5
8. MCI, $1,211.3
9. Sears Department Stores, $1,210.1
10. Home Depot Home Center, $1,131.4

Source: *American Demographics*, November, 1998, p. 34.

★27★
TOP BRANDS SPENDING THE MOST ON ADVERTISING DURING CBS "48 HOURS", 1997
Ranked by: Advertising spending CBS "48 Hours" television newsmagazine, in thousands of dollars. **Number listed:** 10

1. McDonald's Restaurant, with $860 thousand
2. Nissan Motor Corp., $670.7
3. Nissan AutomobilesAltima, $637.6
4. Chrysler Corp., $609.2
5. Campbell's, $583.3
6. True Value Hardware Stores, $572.2
7. Ultra Slim Fast, $511.2
8. U.S. Postal Service, $474.9
9. KFC Restaurant, $446.4
10. Zocor Cholesterol Rx, $398.2

Source: *American Demographics*, November, 1998, p. 34.

★28★
TOP BRANDS SPENDING THE MOST ON ADVERTISING DURING CBS "60 MINUTES", 1997
Ranked by: Advertising spending CBS "60 Minutes" television newsmagazine, in thousands of dollars. **Number listed:** 10
1. United Parcel Service, with $2,786.4 thousand
2. Dollar Rent-A-Car, $2,553.8
3. Nissan AutomobilesAltima, $1,629.4
4. Nissan Motor Corp., $1,621.8
5. Charles Schwab, $1,497
6. Merrill Lynch, $1,421.2
7. Wausau, $1,358.6
8. MCI Communications Corp., $1,353
9. Chrysler Corp., $1,263.1
10. U.S. Postal Service, $1,256.3

Source: *American Demographics*, November, 1998, p. 34.

★29★
TOP BRANDS SPENDING THE MOST ON ADVERTISING DURING NBC "DATELINE", 1997
Ranked by: Advertising spending NBC "Dateline" television newsmagazine, in thousands of dollars. **Number listed:** 10
1. Chrysler Corp., with $5,533 thousand
2. KFC Restaurant, $3,492
3. U.S. Postal Service, $3,381
4. Brita, $3,267
5. Nissan AutomobilesAltima, $3,099.5
6. Nissan Motor Corp., $2,864.5
7. McDonald's Restaurant, $2,689
8. Sprint, $2,081
9. Pizza Hut Restaurant, $2,039.5
10. Eveready Energizer Batteries, $2,009

Source: *American Demographics*, November, 1998, p. 34.

★30★
TOP CATEGORIES BY ADVERTISING EXPENDITURES, 1997
Ranked by: Advertising expenditures, in millions of dollars. **Remarks:** Also notes figures from previous year, percent change and additional financial information. **Number listed:** 10
1. Automotive, with $6,507.4 million
2. Retail, $3,404.3
3. Restaurants, $1,917.9
4. Telephone, $1,721.7
5. Food, $1,659.4
6. Drugs & Personal Care, $1,090.3
7. Financial Services, brokers & insurance, $980.0
8. Computers & Electronics, $841.6
9. Beer, $569.2
10. Imaging/office machines, $238.4

Source: *Advertising Age*, Top 100 MegaBrands (annual), July 13, 1998, p. S2.

★31★
TOP COMPANIES BY MEASURED AD SPENDING, 1997
Ranked by: Measured ad spending, in millions of dollars. **Remarks:** Also notes figures from previous year, percent change and additional financial information. **Number listed:** 10
1. General Motors Corp., with $2,226.9 million
2. Procter & Gamble, $1,703.1
3. Phillip Morris Cos., $1,319
4. Chrysler Corp., $1,311.8
5. Ford Motor Co., $973.1
6. Johnson & Johnson, $823.5
7. Time Warner, $779.1
8. Walt Disney Co., $746.3
9. Sears, Roebuck & Co., $734.1
10. Diageo, $685

Source: *Advertising Age*, Top 100 MegaBrands (annual), July 13, 1998, p. S2.

★32★
TOP MAJOR BRANDS SPENDING THE MOST ON ADVERTISING, 1997
Ranked by: U.S. advertising expenditures, in millions of dollars. **Remarks:** Also notes figures from previous year, percent change, additional financial information, marketing executives, and lead agencies. **Number listed:** 100
1. Sears stores, with $664.6 million
2. Chevrolet cars & trucks, $656.3
3. McDonald's restaurants, $580.5
4. Ford cars & trucks, $569.9
5. Dodge cars & trucks, $551.8
6. AT & T telephone services, $475.9
7. Toyota cars & trucks, $453.8
8. MCI telephone services, $435
9. Burger King restaurants, $427
10. Circuit City stores, $400.1

Source: *Advertising Age*, Top 100 MegaBrands (annual), July 13, 1998, p. S8.

★33★
TOP MOVIE STUDIOS SPENDING THE MOST ON ADVERTISING, 1997
Ranked by: U.S. advertising expenditures, in millions of dollars. **Remarks:** Also notes figures from previous year, percent change and top film in ad spending. **Number listed:** 10
1. Buena Vista Pictures, with $406.5 million
2. Warner Brothers, $243.9
3. Paramount Pictures, $238.9
4. 20th Century Fox Films, $212.3
5. Columbia Pictures, $169.3
6. Universal Pictures, $169.1
7. Miramax Films, $133.1
8. New Line Cinema Corp., $118.4
9. TriStar Pictures, $104.8
10. MGM/UA, $86.5

Source: *Advertising Age*, Top 100 MegaBrands (annual), July 13, 1998, p. S6.

Advertisers--Great Britain

★34★
TOP ADVERTISERS IN GREAT BRITAIN, 1998
Ranked by: Advertising expenditures in British Pounds. **Remarks:** Also notes figures from previous year, percent change and additional financial information. **Number listed:** 100
1. BT, with £105,015,866
2. Procter & Gamble, £99,137,797
3. Vauxhall Motors, £83,005,987
4. Renault (UK), £79,991,461
5. Ford Motor, £79,733,484
6. Kellogg, £67,098,394
7. Elida Faberge, £62,985,545
8. Central Office of Information, £60,202,414
9. L'Oreal, £57,897,362
10. Mars Confectionery, £54,126,098

Source: *Marketing*, February 25, 1999, p. 27+.

★35★
TOP TOUR OPERATORS BY ADVERTISING EXPENDITURES IN GREAT BRITAIN, 1997
Ranked by: Advertising expenditures, in thousands of British pounds. **Number listed:** 9

1. Thomson & Portland, with £13,004 thousand
2. Airtours, Aspro, Eurosites, Tradewinds, £8,304
3. Page & Moy, £3,447
4. Saga, £2,859
5. First Choice & Eclipse & Enterprise, £1,642
6. Unijet, £1,409
7. Titan Travel, £1,275
8. Kuoni, £883
9. BA Holidays, £688

Source: *Marketing*, November 26, 1998, p. 36.

Advertising

★36★
TOP ADVERTISING AND MARKETING COMPANIES BY REVENUE, 1998
Ranked by: Revenue, in millions of dollars. **Remarks:** Also notes profits and investment figures as well as number of employees. **Number listed:** 4

1. Omnicom Group, with $4,092 million
2. Interpublic Group, $3,969
3. Young & Rubicam, $1,522
4. True North Communications, $1,242

Source: *Fortune*, Fortune 500 Largest U.S. Corporations (annual), April 26, 1999, p. F-51.

★37★
TOP ADVERTISING EXECUTIVES, 1999
Ranked by: Influence in the advertising industry. **Remarks:** Also includes short biographies. **Number listed:** 100

1. William Bernbach
2. Marion Harper, Jr.
3. Leo Burnett
4. David Ogilvy
5. Rosser Reeves
6. John Wanamaker
7. William Paley
8. Maurice Saatchi and Charles Saatchi
9. Albert Lasker
10. Jay Chiat

Source: *Advertising Age*, The Advertising Century, March 29, 1999, p. 51+.

★38★
TOP BRANDING LEADERS, 1998
Ranked by: U.S. advertising budgets as a percent of U.S. revenues. **Number listed:** 12

1. Personal Care, with 13.3%
2. Fast Food, 11.9%
3. Food, 9.1%
4. Entertainment, 8%
5. Sneakers, 7.5%
6. Apparel, 6%
7. Soft Drinks, 4%
8. Computers, 2.9%
9. Retail, 2.5%
10. Telephone, 2.3%

Source: *Credit Card Management*, December, 1998, p. 32.

★39★
TOP GENERAL INDUSTRY CATEGORY SPENDERS FOR ADVERTISING AND PROMOTION, 1997
Ranked by: Expenditure on advertising and promotion, in billions of dollars. **Remarks:** Also notes SIC code. **Number listed:** 20

1. Motor Vehicles & Car Bodies, with $15.3 billion
2. Food & Kindred Products, $14.8
3. Telephone Communications, $11.9
4. Pharmaceutical preparations, $11.2
5. Cigarettes, $5.8
6. Department stores, $5.6
7. Soaps, Detergents, & Toilet Preparations, $4.7
8. Variety stores, $4.3
9. Computers & Office Equipment, $3.9
10. Beverages, $3.7

Source: *Graphic Arts Monthly*, Top Spenders on Advertising and Printing, February, 1999, p. 52.

★40★
TOP INDUSTRIES BY TOTAL U.S. ADVERTISING EXPENDITURES, 1997
Ranked by: Expenditure on advertising and promotion, in billions of dollars. **Remarks:** Also notes percent change from previous year. **Number listed:** 20

1. Automotive, Auto Accessories, Equipment & Supplies, with $13.32 billion
2. Retail, Department, and Discount Stores, $10.66
3. Movies & Media, $3.72
4. Toiletries and cosmetics, $3.64
5. Medicines & Proprietary Remedies, $3.54
6. Food & Food Products, $3.36
7. Financial Services, $3.33
8. Restaurants & Fast Food, $3.15
9. Airline & Cruise Travel, Hotels & Resorts, $2.81
10. Telecommunications, $2.57

Source: *Graphic Arts Monthly*, Top Spenders on Advertising and Printing, February, 1999, p. 52.

Advertising Agencies

★41★
ADVERTISING AGENCIES FOR TOP TITLES, 1999
Ranked by: Basis for determination of top titles not specified. **Number listed:** 24

1. *TV Guide* - In House
2. *People* - Y & R Advertising
3. *Sports Illustrated* - Fallon McElligott
4. *Time* - Fallon McElligott
5. *Reader's Digest* - D'Arcy Masius Benton & Bowles
6. *Newsweek* - Della Femina/Jerry & Partners
7. *Better Homes & Gardens* - In-house
8. *Parade* - Warwick Baker O'Neill
9. *PC Magazine* - Parners & Simons
10. *Business Week* - DraftWorldwide

Source: *Advertising Age*, March 8, 1999, p. S22.

★42★
LARGEST ADVERTISING AGENCIES BY NUMBER OF EMPLOYEES
Ranked by: Number of employees. **Remarks:** Also notes previous year's figures and percent change. **Number listed:** 30

1. DDB Needham Worldwide, with 2,057
2. Foote, Cone & Belding, 2,022
3. Lee Burnett USA, 1,942
4. J. Walter Thompson USA, 1,931
5. Y & R Advertising, 1,915
6. BBDO Worldwide, 1,709
7. McCann-Erickson Worldwide, 1,683
8. Grey Advertising, 1,584
9. Ogilvy & Mather Worldwide, 1,413
10. Bozell Worldwide, 1,378

Source: *Advertising Age*, December 7, 1998, p. S12.

★43★

TOP ADVERTISING AGENCIES BY INCREASE IN BILLINGS, 1998

Ranked by: Increase in billings. **Number listed:** 100

1. Grey Advertising, with $422,304
2. McCann-Erickson (IPG), $421,000
3. Young & Rubicam, $416,953
4. J. Walter Thompson (WPP), $411,600
5. Leo Burnett Co., $396,280
6. Foote, Cone & Belding (TN), $338,000
7. DDB Needham (OMC), $316,616
8. BBDO (OMC), $307,000
9. Ogilvy & Mather (WPP), $282,000
10. Saatchi & Saatchi, $250,000

Source: *Adweek Eastern Edition*, Agency Report Card (Annual), April 19, 1999, p. 100+.

★44★

TOP ADVERTISING AGENCIES BY NON-U.S. GROSS INCOME, 1998

Ranked by: Non-U.S. gross income, in millions of U.S. dollars ($). **Remarks:** Also notes previous year's rank, percent change from previous year, and volume. **Number listed:** 20

1. McCann-Erickson Worldwide, with $1,261.7 million
2. BBDO Worldwide, $1,070.3
3. DDB Needham Worldwide, $873.0
4. Young & Rubicam, $771.4
5. Euro RSCG Worldwide, $763.5
6. J. Walter Thompson Co., $761.9
7. Ogilvy & Mather Worldwide, $737.1
8. Publicis Worldwide, $688.0
9. Grey Advertising, $605.5
10. TBWA Worldwide, $587.0
11. Leo Burnett Co., $553.5

Source: *Advertising Age*, Agency Report (annual), April 19, 1999, p. S47.

★45★

TOP ADVERTISING AGENCIES BY U.S. GROSS INCOME, 1998

Ranked by: U.S. gross income, in millions of U.S. dollars ($). **Remarks:** Also notes previous year's rank, percent change from previous year, and volume. **Number listed:** 25

1. DDB Needham Worldwide, with $732.0 million
2. McCann-Erickson Worldwide, $690.3
3. BBDO Worldwide, $585.4
4. Young & Rubicam, $582.8
5. Grey Advertising, $555.2
6. Ammirati Puris Lintas, $514.8
7. J. Walter Thompson Co., $478.8
8. Leo Burnett Co., $396.3
9. Ogilvy & Mather Worldwide, $380.8
10. Euro RSCG Worldwide, $366.3

Source: *Advertising Age*, Agency Report (annual), April 19, 1999, p. S47.

★46★

TOP ADVERTISING AGENCIES BY WORLDWIDE GROSS INCOME, 1998

Ranked by: Worldwide gross income, in millions of U.S. dollars ($). **Remarks:** Also notes previous year's rank, percent change from previous year, and volume. **Number listed:** 25

1. McCann-Erickson Worldwide, with $1,952.0 million
2. BBDO Worldwide, $1,655.7
3. DDB Needham Worldwide, $1,605.0
4. Young & Rubicam, $1,354.2
5. J. Walter Thompson Co., $1,240.7
6. Grey Advertising, $1,160.7
7. Euro RSCG Worldwide, $1,129.8
8. Ogilvy & Mather Worldwide, $1,117.9
9. Ammirati Puris Lintas, $1,014.9
10. Leo Burnett Co., $949.8

Source: *Advertising Age*, Agency Report (annual), April 19, 1999, p. S47.

★47★

TOP ADVERTISING AGENCIES IN CABLE TV ADVERTISING, 1998

Ranked by: Media billings, in millions of U.S. dollars. **Remarks:** Includes previous year's figures, percentage change, total billings, and cable TV advertising as a percentage of the total. **Number listed:** 10

1. Euro RSCG Worldwide, with $366.9 million
2. Grey Advertising, $352.8
3. Leo Burnett CO., $328.5
4. D'Arcy Masius Benton & Bowles, $310.0
5. BBDO Worldwide, $308.6
6. J. Walter Thompson CO., $304.0
7. McCann-Erickson Worldwide, $294.5
8. Young & Rubicam Advertising, $278.4
9. Foote, Cone & Belding, $260.0
10. DDB Needham Worldwide, $226.3

Source: *Advertising Age*, Agency Report (annual), April 19, 1999, p. S14.

★48★

TOP ADVERTISING AGENCIES IN MAGAZINE ADVERTISING, 1998

Ranked by: Media billings, in millions of U.S. dollars. **Remarks:** Includes previous year's figures, percentage change, total billings, and consumer magazine advertising as a percent of total. **Number listed:** 10

1. Leo Burnett Co., with $935.9 million
2. Saatchi & Saatchi, $488.8
3. McCann-Erickson Worldwide, $454.2
4. J. Walter Thompson, $433.0
5. Young & Rubicam Advertising, $418.1
6. Ogilvy & Mather Worldwide, $413.8
7. Foote, Cone & Belding, $359.4
8. BBDO Worldwide, $343.4
9. DDB Needham Worldwide, $294.3
10. Euro RSCG Worldwide, $284.0

Source: *Advertising Age*, Agency Report (annual), April 19, 1999, p. S14.

★49★

TOP ADVERTISING AGENCIES IN NETWORK TV ADVERTISING, 1998

Ranked by: Media billings, in millions of U.S. dollars. **Remarks:** Includes previous year's figures, percentage change, total billings, and network TV advertising as a percentage of the total. **Number listed:** 10

1. D'Arcy, Masius Benton & Bowles, with $1,415.0 million
2. Young & Rubicam Advertising, $1,370.2
3. Euro RSCG Worldwide, $1,305.3
4. McCann-Erickson Worldwide, $1,205.1
5. BBDO Worldwide, $1,114.1
6. Ogilvy & Mather Worldwide, $1,055.4
7. J. Walter Thompson Co., $908.0
8. Foote, Cone & Belding, $840.0
9. Saatchi & Saatchi, $815.6
10. Leo Burnett Co., $722.4

Source: *Advertising Age*, Agency Report (annual), April 19, 1999, p. S14.

★50★
TOP ADVERTISING AGENCIES IN NEWSPAPER ADVERTISING, 1998
Ranked by: Media billings, in millions of U.S. dollars. **Remarks:** Includes previous year's figures, percentage change, total billings, and newspaper advertising as a percentage of the total. **Number listed:** 10
1. Bernard Hodes Group, with $595.2 million
2. TMP Worldwide, $526.8
3. Nationwide Advertising Service, $327.6
4. J. Walter Thompson Co., $286.0
5. McCann-Erickson Worldwide, $185.6
6. Allied Advertising, $161.9
7. DDB Needham Worldwide, $147.7
8. Ogilvy & Mather Worldwide, $138.5
9. Foote, Cone & Belding, $136.0
10. Young & Rubicam Advertising, $132.0

Source: *Advertising Age*, Agency Report (annual), April 19, 1999, p. S14.

★51★
TOP ADVERTISING AGENCIES IN RADIO ADVERTISING, 1998
Ranked by: Media billings, in millions of U.S. dollars. **Remarks:** Includes previous year's figures, percentage change, total billings, and spot radio advertising as a percentage of the total. **Number listed:** 10
1. BBDO Worldwide, with $232.5 million
2. Young & Rubicam Advertising, $179.1
3. DDB Needham Worldwide, $169.2
4. McCann-Erickson Worldwide, $139.8
5. Foote, Cone & Belding, $136.5
6. J. Walter Thompson Co., $134.0
7. Saatchi & Saatchi, $121.6
8. Bozell Worldwide, $114.6
9. Ogilvy & Mather Worldwide, $105.4
10. Campbell Mithum Esty, $95.6

Source: *Advertising Age*, Agency Report (annual), April 19, 1999, p. S14.

★52★
TOP ADVERTISING AGENCIES IN SPOT TV ADVERTISING, 1998
Ranked by: Media billings, in millions of U.S. dollars. **Remarks:** Includes previous year's figures, percentage change, total billings, and spot TV advertising as a percentage of the total. **Number listed:** 10
1. BBDO Worldwide, with $841.2 million
2. J. Walter Thompson Co., $705.0
3. Saatchi & Saatchi, $653.5
4. McCann-Erickson Worldwide, $643.7
5. Euro RSCG Worldwide, $623.0
6. Young & Rubicam Advertising, $585.9
7. TBWA Worldwide, $578.4
8. Foote, Cone & Belding, $530.9
9. Bozell Worldwide, $514.8
10. Grey Advertising, $490.6

Source: *Advertising Age*, Agency Report (annual), April 19, 1999, p. S14.

★53★
TOP ADVERTISING AGENCIES IN SYNDICATED TV ADVERTISING, 1998
Ranked by: Media billings, in millions of U.S. dollars. **Remarks:** Includes previous year's figures, percentage change, total billings, and syndicated TV advertising as a percentage of the total. **Number listed:** 10
1. D'Arcy Masius Benton & Bowles, with $292.0 million
2. Leo Burnett Co., $211.3
3. Euro RSCG Worldwide, $170.2
4. Foote, Cone & Belding, $122.0
5. McCann-Erickson Worldwide, $121.3
6. BBDO Worldwide, $113.2
7. Grey Advertising, $98.1
8. DDB Needham Worldwide, $89.1
9. J. Walter Thompson Co., $75.0
10. Young & Rubicam Advertising, $62.7

Source: *Advertising Age*, Agency Report (annual), April 19, 1999, p. S14.

★54★
TOP ADVERTISING AGENCIES IN YELLOW PAGES ADVERTISING, 1998
Ranked by: Media billings, in millions of U.S. dollars. **Remarks:** Includes previous year's figures, percentage change, total billings, and yellow pages advertising as a percentage of the total. **Number listed:** 10
1. TMP Worldwide, with $790.1 million
2. Berry Network, $157.3
3. Ketchum Directory Advertising, $143.0
4. Wahlstrom & Co., $137.4
5. DAC Group, $60.8
6. D'Arcy Masius Benton & Bowles, $55.4
7. Ruppman National Yellow Pages, $38.3
8. Bozell Yellow Pages, $34.4
9. Saatchi & Saatchi, $23.7
10. Grey Direct Marketing, $20.8

Source: *Advertising Age*, Agency Report (annual), April 19, 1999, p. S47.

★55★
TOP ADVERTISING AGENCIES SPECIALIZING IN HISPANIC MARKETING, 1997
Ranked by: Capitalized billings, in millions of dollars. **Remarks:** Also notes headquarters, percent Hispanic owned, previous year's figures and agency affiliation. **Number listed:** 10
1. Bravo Group, with $128 million
2. Mendoza, Dillon & Asociados, $76.7
3. FOVA, $67
4. Casanova Pendrill Publicidad, $50
5. Siboney USA, $47
6. Dieste & Partners, $43
7. La Agencia de Orci & Asociados, $42
8. Montemayor y Asociados, $35.5
9. IAC Advertising Group, $24
10. Valdes Zacky Associates, $20

Source: *Advertising Age*, August 24, 1998, p. S16.

★56★
TOP ADVERTISING AGENCY BRANDS BY GROSS INCOME, 1998
Ranked by: Gross volume, in millions of dollars. **Remarks:** Also notes location of headquarters, previous year's rank, percent change from previous year, and volume. **Number listed:** 660
1. Grey Advertising, with $422.3 million
2. J. Walter Thompson, $414.6
3. Leo Burnett Co., $380.2
4. McCann-Erickson Worldwide, $378.4
5. Young & Rubicam Advertising, $344.0
6. BBDO Worldwide, $336.6
7. DDB Needham Worldwide, $316.6
8. Foote, Cone & Belding, $298.0
9. Brann Worldwide, $287.6
10. Ogilvy & Mather Worldwide, $278.4

Source: *Advertising Age*, Agency Report (annual), April 19, 1999, p. S4+.

★57★
TOP BUSINESS-TO-BUSINESS ADVERTISING AGENCIES BY GROSS INCOME, 1997
Ranked by: Business-to-business gross income, in millions of dollars. **Remarks:** Also notes agency phone number, URL and percent change from previous year. **Number listed:** 208
1. TMP Worldwide, with $180.3 million
2. CommonHealth USA, $102.2
3. DDB Needham Worldwide, $68.27
4. Gage Marketing Group, $68.05
5. Carlson Marketing Group, $62.92
6. Lyons/Lavey/Nickel/Swift, $37.54
7. Torre Lazur McCarr Healthcare Worldwide, $31.70
8. Sudler & Hennessey, $28.91
9. Harrison & Star Business Group, $27.35
10. KPR, $26.77

Source: *Business Marketing*, Business-to-Business Agency Ranking, July, 1998, p. 20+.

★58★
TOP U.S. HEALTHCARE ADVERTISING AGENCY BRANDS, 1997
Ranked by: Gross income, in thousands of dollars. **Remarks:** Also notes previous year's figures and percentage change. **Number listed:** 20
1. CommonHealth, with $109,184 thousand
2. Nelson Communications, $107,074
3. Medicus Group International (D'Arcy Masius Benton & Bowles), $40,052.8
4. KPR (DDB Needham Worldwide), $37,953
5. Lyons/Lavey/Nickel/Swift, $37,541
6. Lowe McAdams Healthcare (Lowe Group), $37,486
7. Integrated Communications Corp. (Ammirati Puras Lintas), $36,914
8. Healthworld Corp., $35,300
9. Torre Lazur McCann Healthcare Worldwide (McCann-Erickson Worldwide), $31,700
10. Grey Healthcare Group, $31,609

Source: *Advertising Age*, March 15, 1999, p. S6.

Advertising Agencies--Argentina

★59★
TOP ADVERTISING AGENCIES IN ARGENTINA, 1998
Ranked by: Gross income, in thousands of U.S. dollars ($). **Remarks:** Also notes percent change from previous year and volume. **Number listed:** 21
1. McCann-Erickson SA de Publicidad, with $27,291 thousand
2. Young & Rubicam Argentina, $23,705
3. Pragma/FCB Publicidad, $22,865
4. J. Walter Thompson Buenos Aires, $19,057
5. Ratto/BBDO, $14,998
6. Bozell Vazquez SA de Publicidad, $14,505
7. Ogilvy & Mather, $9,674
8. Lautrec NAZCA Saatchi & Saatchi, $9,585
9. Agulla & Baccetti (Lowe), $8,702
10. Euro RSCG, $8,201

Source: *Advertising Age*, Agency Report (annual), April 19, 1999, p. S22.

Advertising Agencies--Australia

★60★
TOP ADVERTISING AGENCIES IN AUSTRALIA, 1998
Ranked by: Gross income, in thousands of U.S. dollars ($). **Remarks:** Also notes percent change from previous year and volume. **Number listed:** 32
1. Clemenger BBDO, with $79,221 thousand
2. Communications Group/G. Patterson Bates, $61,260
3. Young & Rubicam Australia, $35.934
4. DDB Needham Australia Worldwide, $33,199
5. Singleton Ad Agency, $29,693
6. McCann-Erickson Advertising, $28,428
7. Ammirati Puris Lintas, $24,957
8. J. Walter Thompson, $24,201
9. Leo Burnett Connaghan & May, $23,175
10. Publicis Mojopartners, $19,833

Source: *Advertising Age*, Agency Report (annual), April 19, 1999, p. S22.

Advertising Agencies--Austria

★61★
TOP ADVERTISING AGENCIES IN AUSTRIA, 1998
Ranked by: Gross income, in thousands of U.S. dollars ($). **Remarks:** Also notes percent change from previous year and volume. **Number listed:** 21
1. Demner Merlicek & Bergmann, with $17,600 thousand
2. Lowe GGK Wien/Salzburg, $15,417
3. Wirz Werbeagentur Gesellschaft, $13,570
4. Ammirati Puris Lintas, $12,317
5. Ogilvy & Mather, $10,719
6. Euro RSCG Group, $9,918
7. Team BBDO/Werbeagentur, $9,491
8. Saatchi & Saatchi, $8,939
9. McCann-Erickson, $8,270
10. Grey Group Austria, $8,070

Source: *Advertising Age*, Agency Report (annual), April 19, 1999, p. S22.

Advertising Agencies--Bahrain

★62★
TOP ADVERTISING AGENCIES IN BAHRAIN, 1998
Ranked by: Gross income, in thousands of U.S. dollars ($). **Remarks:** Also notes percent change from previous year and volume. **Number listed:** 6
1. Promoseven-Bahrain (McCann), with $7,643 thousand
2. Gulf Advertising (APL), $2,339
3. Memac (O&M), $1,632
4. DDB Bahrain, $344
5. MADCO Bahrain (Bates), $329
6. Publi-Graphics Group, $161

Source: *Advertising Age*, Agency Report (annual), April 19, 1999, p. S22.

Advertising Agencies--Bangladesh

★63★
TOP ADVERTISING AGENCIES IN BANGLADESH, 1998
Ranked by: Gross income, in thousands of U.S. dollars ($). **Remarks:** Also notes percent change from previous year and volume. **Number listed:** 4

1. Grey, with $492 thousand
2. Asiatic Marketing (JWT), $447
3. Unitrend (McCann), $422
4. Bitopi Advertising (Burnett), $297

Source: *Advertising Age*, Agency Report (annual), April 19, 1999, p. S22.

Advertising Agencies--Barbados

★64★
TOP ADVERTISING AGENCIES IN BARBADOS, 1998
Ranked by: Gross income, in thousands of U.S. dollars ($). **Remarks:** Also notes percent change from previous year and volume. **Number listed:** 2

1. Londsdale/Barbados (Y&R), with $1,150 thousand
2. McCann-Erickson, $1,132

Source: *Advertising Age*, Agency Report (annual), April 19, 1999, p. S22.

Advertising Agencies--Belarus

★65★
TOP ADVERTISING AGENCIES IN BELARUS, 1998
Ranked by: Gross income, in thousands of U.S. dollars ($). **Remarks:** Also notes percent change from previous year and volume. **Number listed:** 2

1. EuroStyle McCann-Erickson, with $33 thousand
2. Adel Saatchi & Saatchi, $30

Source: *Advertising Age*, Agency Report (annual), April 19, 1999, p. S22.

Advertising Agencies--Belgium

★66★
TOP ADVERTISING AGENCIES IN BELGIUM, 1998
Ranked by: Gross income, in thousands of U.S. dollars ($). **Remarks:** Also notes percent change from previous year and volume. **Number listed:** 28

1. HHD O & M, with $27,680 thousand
2. McCann-Erickson Co. (Belgium), $25,028
3. BBDO Belgium, $20,423
4. DDB/Belgium, $15,945
5. TBWA/GV Group, $13,000
6. Grey, $11,868
7. Euro RSCG United, $11,489
8. Ammirati Puris Lintas Belgium, $11,307
9. Young & Rubicam Belgium, $9,941
10. Publicis, $9,762

Source: *Advertising Age*, Agency Report (annual), April 19, 1999, p. S22.

Advertising Agencies--Bermuda

★67★
TOP ADVERTISING AGENCIES IN BERMUDA, 1998
Ranked by: Gross income, in thousands of U.S. dollars ($). **Remarks:** Also notes percent change from previous year and volume. **Number listed:** 2

1. AAC Saatchi & Saatchi, with $1,100 thousand
2. Aardvark Communications (FCB), $863

Source: *Advertising Age*, Agency Report (annual), April 19, 1999, p. S22.

Advertising Agencies--Black Agencies

★68★
LARGEST BLACK ADVERTISING AGENCIES, 1998
Ranked by: Billings, in millions of dollars. **Remarks:** Also lists chief executive, year started, and number of staff. **Number listed:** 20

1. Burrel Communications Group, Inc., with $173.872 million
2. Uniworld Group Inc., $160.355
3. Don Coleman Advertising, $137
4. Chisholm-Mingo Group Inc., $78.014
5. Carol H. Williams Advertising, $61
6. Muse Cordero Chen & Partners Inc., $55
7. Wimbley Group Inc., $45
8. Sykes Communication, $24.883
9. R. J. Dale Advertising & Public Relations, $24.5
10. E. Morris Communications Inc., $18.2

Source: *Black Enterprise*, June, 1999, p. 177.

Advertising Agencies--Bolivia

★69★
TOP ADVERTISING AGENCIES IN BOLIVIA, 1998
Ranked by: Gross income, in thousands of U.S. dollars ($). **Remarks:** Also notes percent change from previous year and volume. **Number listed:** 4

1. Nexus Comunicacion Total (McCann), with $1,537 thousand
2. Contacto Gullco (APL), $659
3. Fondo y Forma (JWT), $412
4. Grey, $339

Source: *Advertising Age*, Agency Report (annual), April 19, 1999, p. S22.

Advertising Agencies--Botswana

★70★
TOP ADVERTISING AGENCIES IN BOTSWANA, 1998
Ranked by: Gross income, in thousands of U.S. dollars ($). **Remarks:** Also notes percent change from previous year and volume. **Number listed:** 2

1. Horizon Saatchi & Saatchi, with $182 thousand
2. Ogilvy & Mather, $18

Source: *Advertising Age*, Agency Report (annual), April 19, 1999, p. S22.

Advertising Agencies--Brazil

★71★
TOP ADVERTISING AGENCIES IN BRAZIL, 1998
Ranked by: Gross income, in thousands of U.S. dollars ($). **Remarks:** Also notes percent change from previous year and volume. **Number listed:** 30

1. McCann-Erickson, with $121,881 thousand
2. DPZ-Dualibi, Petit, Zaragoza Propaganda, $71,221
3. DM9 DDB, $71,075
4. J. Walter Thompson, $70,506
5. Fischer America Comunicacao, $66,884
6. Salles/DMB&B, $64,171
7. Young & Rubicam do Brasil, $53,282
8. Giovanni, FCB, $52,370
9. Standard, O & M, $52,200
10. ALMAP/BBDO Comunicacoes, $51,145

Source: *Advertising Age*, Agency Report (annual), April 19, 1999, p. S22+.

Advertising Agencies--Bulgaria

★72★
TOP ADVERTISING AGENCIES IN BULGARIA, 1998
Ranked by: Gross income, in thousands of U.S. dollars ($). **Remarks:** Also notes percent change from previous year and volume. **Number listed:** 10

1. S Team Bates Saatchi & Saatchi, with $829 thousand
2. P.B.I./McCann-Erickson, $477
3. Ogilvy & Mather, $318
4. Swing Communication (APL), $200
5. Adia Advertising (Y&R), $180
6. Leo Burnett Advertising, $177
7. Lowe GGK, $163
8. DDB/Bulgaria, $156
9. Grey, $120
10. TBWA Sofia, $69
11. TBWA Sofia, $69

Source: *Advertising Age*, Agency Report (annual), April 19, 1999, p. S24.

Advertising Agencies--Cambodia

★73★
TOP ADVERTISING AGENCIES IN CAMBODIA, 1998
Ranked by: Gross income, in thousands of U.S. dollars ($). **Remarks:** Also notes percent change from previous year and volume. **Number listed:** 3

1. Bates Indochina, with $337 thousand
2. McCann-Erickson, $271
3. Grey, $49

Source: *Advertising Age*, Agency Report (annual), April 19, 1999, p. S24.

Advertising Agencies--Cameroon

★74★
TOP ADVERTISING AGENCIES IN CAMEROON, 1998
Ranked by: Gross income, in thousands of U.S. dollars ($). **Remarks:** Also notes percent change from previous year and volume. **Number listed:** 2

1. Nelson McCann, with $337 thousand
2. Synergie Saatchi & Saatchi, $96

Source: *Advertising Age*, Agency Report (annual), April 19, 1999, p. S24.

Advertising Agencies--Canada

★75★
TOP ADVERTISING AGENCIES IN CANADA, 1998
Ranked by: Gross income, in thousands of U.S. dollars ($). **Remarks:** Also notes percent change from previous year and volume. **Number listed:** 47

1. MacLaren McCann, with $57,168 thousand
2. Cossette Communication Marketing, $55,205
3. Y & R/Saint-Jaques Vallee, $45,444
4. BBDO Canada, $36,452
5. DDB Group, $32,208
6. Ogilvy & Mather, $28,251
7. Carlson Marketing Group, $22,886
8. Vickers & Benson, $22,641
9. FCB Canada, $21,249
10. Publicis BCP, $19,939

Source: *Advertising Age*, Agency Report (annual), April 19, 1999, p. S24.

★76★
TOP ADVERTISING AGENCIES IN CANADA, 1998
Ranked by: Gross revenues, in thousands of Canadian dollars (C$). **Remarks:** Also notes previous year's figures, office location, year established, number of employees, agency affiliation, subsidiaries and major clients. **Number listed:** 75

1. Cossette Communication Group Inc., with C$82,373,000 thousand
2. BBDO Canada Inc., C$61,921,698
3. Young & Rubicam Group of Cos. Ltd, C$60,735,352
4. MacLaren McCann Canada Inc., C$60,668,000
5. Wolf Group Integrated Communications, C$43,230,882
6. Mosaic Group Inc., C$40,640,000
7. Ogilvy & Mather, C$37,037,605
8. Palmer Jarvis DDB Inc., C$33,849,983
9. Publicis Canada Inc., C$31,728,714
10. Vickers & Benson Cos. Ltd., C$31,122,000

Source: *Marketing*, (Canada), June 28, 1999, p. 96+.

Advertising Agencies--Chicago (IL)

★77★
TOP ADVERTISNG AGENCIES IN CHICAGO, 1997
Ranked by: Billings, in millions. **Remarks:** Also notes contact information, last years figures, percent change, number of employees and top accounts. **Number listed:** 24
1. Leo Burnett Co., with $2,649.3 million
2. Foote Cone & Belding, $1,004
3. DDB Needham Chicago, $972
4. Frankel & Co., $519.1
5. J. Walter Thompson, $506
6. Ogilvy & Mather Chicago, $452
7. Euro RSCG Tatham, $448.4
8. Draftworldonline, $354.1
9. BBDO Chicago Inc., $271.5
10. Leap Group, $236.2

Source: *Crain's Chicago Business*, Top Business Lists (annual), 1999, p. 117+.

Advertising Agencies--Chile

★78★
TOP ADVERTISING AGENCIES IN CHILE, 1998
Ranked by: Gross income, in thousands of U.S. dollars ($). **Remarks:** Also notes percent change from previous year and volume. **Number listed:** 15
1. McCann-Erickson, with $14,970 thousand
2. BBDO de Chile, $13,775
3. Prolam/Young & Rubicam, $11,756
4. Leo Burnett/Santiago, $8,259
5. Ammirati Puris Lintas, $7,408
6. Lowe Porta, $6,082
7. Euro RSCG, $4,940
8. Northcote & Asociados (O & M), $4,847
9. Grey Chile, $4,579
10. J. Walter Thompson, $4,358

Source: *Advertising Age*, Agency Report (annual), April 19, 1999, p. S24.

Advertising Agencies--China

★79★
TOP ADVERTISING AGENCIES IN CHINA, 1998
Ranked by: Gross income, in thousands of U.S. dollars ($). **Remarks:** Also notes percent change from previous year and volume. **Number listed:** 55
1. Ogilvy & Mather (Hong Kong), with $25,351 thousand
2. McCann-Erickson Guangming, $20,128
3. Saatchi & Saatchi, $19,041
4. J. Walter Thompson (Hong Kong), $18,075
5. Denstu, Young & Rubicam, $16,214
6. Leo Burnett Co. (Hong Kong), $15,113
7. Ogilvy & Mather (Beijing), $15,272
8. Leo Burnett (Guangzhou), $15,113
9. J. Walter Thompson (Beijing), $12,480
10. Bozell Worldwide, $12,364

Source: *Advertising Age*, Agency Report (annual), April 19, 1999, p. S24.

Advertising Agencies--Colombia

★80★
TOP ADVERTISING AGENCIES IN COLOMBIA, 1998
Ranked by: Gross income, in thousands of U.S. dollars ($). **Remarks:** Also notes percent change from previous year and volume. **Number listed:** 19
1. McCann-Erickson Colombia, with $20,574 thousand
2. Lowe & Partners/SSPM, $10,881
3. Young & Rubicam Bogota, $8,515
4. Jaime Uribe & Asociados, $7,655
5. Leo Burnett Colombia, $6,579
6. J. Walter Thompson Bogota, $5,675
7. Sancho NAZCA Saatchi & Saatchi, $4,992
8. Publicidad Toro/DMB & B, $4,809
9. SSA Bates, $4,712
10. DDB Needham Worldwide/Colombia, $4,138

Source: *Advertising Age*, Agency Report (annual), April 19, 1999, p. S24+.

Advertising Agencies--Costa Rica

★81★
TOP ADVERTISING AGENCIES IN COSTA RICA, 1998
Ranked by: Gross income, in thousands of U.S. dollars ($). **Remarks:** Also notes percent change from previous year and volume. **Number listed:** 14
1. Garnier BBDO, with $3,688 thousand
2. McCann-Erickson Centroamericana, $3,006
3. Jimenez, Blanco & Quiros (Grey), $1,487
4. Asesores/Young & Rubicam, $1,281
5. Modernoble Publicidad (O & M), $1,097
6. DDB Needham Worldwide Costa Rica, $1,067
7. APCU (JWT), $853
8. Leo Burnett de Costa Rica, $640
9. TBWA Publicidad, $561
10. Consumer Excepcional NAZCA Saatchi & Saatchi, $526

Source: *Advertising Age*, Agency Report (annual), April 19, 1999, p. S26.

Advertising Agencies--Croatia

★82★
TOP ADVERTISING AGENCIES IN CROATIA, 1998
Ranked by: Gross income, in thousands of U.S. dollars ($). **Remarks:** Also notes percent change from previous year and volume. **Number listed:** 9
1. McCann-Erickson Croatia, with $1,644 thousand
2. Digitel (APL), $1,363
3. BBDO Zagreb, $1,049
4. S Team Bates Saatchi & Saatchi, $768
5. Futura DDB, $648
6. Ogilvy & Mather, $440
7. Grey, $415
8. Publicis, $400
9. TBWA Zagreb, $273

Source: *Advertising Age*, Agency Report (annual), April 19, 1999, p. S26.

Advertising Agencies--Cyprus

★83★
TOP ADVERTISING AGENCIES IN CYPRUS, 1998
Ranked by: Gross income, in thousands of U.S. dollars ($). **Remarks:** Also notes percent change from previous year and volume. **Number listed:** 4

1. Ogilvy & Mather, with $547 thousand
2. Pyramis DDB, $448
3. Gremona McCann-Erickson, $375
4. Innovation Advertising (Burnett), $234

Source: *Advertising Age*, Agency Report (annual), April 19, 1999, p. S26.

Advertising Agencies--Czech Republic

★84★
TOP ADVERTISING AGENCIES IN THE CZECH REPUBLIC, 1998
Ranked by: Gross income, in thousands of U.S. dollars ($). **Remarks:** Also notes percent change from previous year and volume. **Number listed:** 18

1. Leo Burnett Advertising, with $6,292 thousand
2. McCann-Erickson Prague, $6,253
3. Mark/BBDO, $6,133
4. Young & Rubicam Czech Republic, $5,470
5. Grey, $5,363
6. Euro RSCG, $4,017
7. Ammirati Puris Lintas Czech Republic, $3,811
8. Ark Communications (JWT), $3,738
9. Ogilvy & Mather, $3,444
10. Lowe GGK Praha, $2,645

Source: *Advertising Age*, Agency Report (annual), April 19, 1999, p. S26.

Advertising Agencies--Denmark

★85★
TOP ADVERTISING AGENCIES IN DENMARK, 1998
Ranked by: Gross income, in thousands of U.S. dollars ($). **Remarks:** Also notes percent change from previous year and volume. **Number listed:** 21

1. Grey Communications Group, with $41,033 thousand
2. McCann-Erickson AS (Denmark), $21,058
3. Bates Gruppen Denmark, $16,489
4. Young & Rubicam Copenhagen, $16,249
5. DDB Denmark, $14,977
6. SCAN-AD, $9,320
7. BBDO Denmark, $9,257
8. Ammirati Puris Lintas Denmark, $8,337
9. Ogilvy & Mather, $7,988
10. NP/3 Advertising, $6,685

Source: *Advertising Age*, Agency Report (annual), April 19, 1999, p. S26.

Advertising Agencies--Detroit Metropolitan Area

★86★
METRO DETROIT'S LARGEST ADVERTISNG AGENCIES, 1997
Ranked by: Gross revenu, in millions. **Remarks:** Also notes contact information, last years figures, percent change, number of employees and leading accounts. **Number listed:** 26

1. Campbell-Ewald Co., with $139.2 million
2. J. Walter Thompson, $116.3
3. Bozell Worldwide, $88.8
4. D'Arcy Masius, Benton & Bowles, $70.2
5. W.B. Doner & Co., $68.5
6. Ross Roy Communications, $60.6
7. Young & Rubicam Detroit, $49.7
8. BBDO Detroit, $46.3
9. McCann-Erickson Detroit, $42.5
10. Mars Advertising Co. Inc., $11.3

Source: *Crain's Detroit Business*, Crain's Book of Lists Detroit (annual), December 28, 1998, p. 126+.

Advertising Agencies--Dominican Republic

★87★
TOP ADVERTISING AGENCIES IN THE DOMINICAN REPUBLIC, 1998
Ranked by: Gross income, in thousands of U.S. dollars ($). **Remarks:** Also notes percent change from previous year and volume. **Number listed:** 9

1. McCann-Erickson, with $2,911 thousand
2. Young & Rubicam Damaris, $2,529
3. Leo Burnett Co., $2,083
4. Interamerica Ammirati Puris Lintas, $1,904
5. Cumbre NAZCA Saatchi & Saatchi, $1,141
6. Ogilvy & Mather, $974
7. El Taller Creativo (Grey), $895
8. Foote, Cone & Belding, $870
9. EPI Bates, $203

Source: *Advertising Age*, Agency Report (annual), April 19, 1999, p. S26.

Advertising Agencies--Eastern States

★88★
LEADING ADVERTISING AGENCIES IN THE EASTERN STATES, 1998
Ranked by: Revenue, in thousands of dollars. **Remarks:** Also notes billings and percent change from previous year. **Number listed:** 50

1. Grey Advertising (NY), with $371,300 thousand
2. Young & Rubicam (NY), $316,087
3. McCann-Erickson (NY), $216,000
4. Bates USA (NY), $191,400
5. Saatchi & Saatchi (NY), $178,000
6. Ogilvy & Mather (NY), $172,000
7. BBDO (NY), $167,616
8. Ammirati Puris Lintas (NY), $155,602
9. J. Walter Thompson (NY), $135,000

10. Foote, Cone & Belding (NY), $124,000

Source: *Adweek Eastern Edition*, Agency Report Card (annual), April 19, 1999, p. 102.

Advertising Agencies--Ecuador

★89★

TOP ADVERTISING AGENCIES IN ECUADOR, 1998

Ranked by: Gross income, in thousands of U.S. dollars ($). **Remarks:** Also notes percent change from previous year and volume. **Number listed:** 9

1. Norlop Thompson, with $4,886 thousand
2. DeMaruri Publicidad (Grey), $3,905
3. McCann-Erickson, $3,452
4. Veritas/Ogilvy & Mather, $1,200
5. Qualitat SA (Ammirati), $1,117
6. Publicitas Saatchi & Saatchi, $642
7. FCB Ecuador, $492
8. Bozell del Ecuador, $379
9. VIP Bates Publicidad, $307

Source: *Advertising Age*, Agency Report (annual), April 19, 1999, p. S26.

Advertising Agencies--Egypt

★90★

TOP ADVERTISING AGENCIES IN EGYPT, 1998

Ranked by: Gross income, in thousands of U.S. dollars ($). **Remarks:** Also notes percent change from previous year and volume. **Number listed:** 14

1. TN Communications Group (DDB), with $11,540 thousand
2. Look Advertising (Ammirati), $4,279
3. AMA, Leo Burnett, $2,451
4. Impact Advertising (BBDO), $1,937
5. TMI (JWT), $1,620
6. Promoseven WLL-Cairo (McCann), $948
7. Animation Advertising (Bozell), $782
8. MADCO Egypt (Bates), $660
9. Saatchi & Saatchi, $632
10. Publi-Graphics Group, $609

Source: *Advertising Age*, Agency Report (annual), April 19, 1999, p. S26.

Advertising Agencies--El Salvador

★91★

TOP ADVERTISING AGENCIES IN EL SALVADOR, 1998

Ranked by: Gross income, in thousands of U.S. dollars ($). **Remarks:** Also notes percent change from previous year and volume. **Number listed:** 11

1. Apex BBDO, with $3,731 thousand
2. Lemusimun Publicidade (Y & R), $2,879
3. Publicidad Comercial Ammirati Puris Lintas, $2,594
4. McCann-Erickson Centroamericana, $2,531
5. MB/Ogilvy & Mather, $1,729
6. J.M. Creativos (Grey), $1,382
7. RCM DDB Needham Worldwide, $1,259
8. APCU (JWT), $747
9. FCB El Salvador, $450
10. Publicidad Diaz (Burnett), $323

Source: *Advertising Age*, Agency Report (annual), April 19, 1999, p. S26.

Advertising Agencies--Estonia

★92★

TOP ADVERTISING AGENCIES IN ESTONIA, 1998

Ranked by: Gross income, in thousands of U.S. dollars ($). **Remarks:** Also notes percent change from previous year and volume. **Number listed:** 6

1. Bates Baltic Group, with $2,306 thousand
2. Division M/E Tallinn (McCann), $926
3. Inorek Marketing (Grey), $915
4. Kontuur-Leo Burnett, $894
5. Brand Sellers DDB Estonia, $862
6. Adel Saatchi & Saatchi, $604

Source: *Advertising Age*, Agency Report (annual), April 19, 1999, p. S26.

Advertising Agencies--Europe

★93★

TOP ADVERTISING AGENCIES IN EUROPE, 1997

Ranked by: Sales, in thousand of U.S. dollars ($). **Remarks:** Also notes previous year's rank, location of headquarters, industry code, and percent change in sales and in local currencies. **Number listed:** 100

1. WPP Group PLC, with $12,021,280 thousand
2. Havas SA, $8,101,571
3. Cordiant Communications Group PLC, $6,938,634
4. Aegis Group PLC, $6,025,239
5. Saatchi & Saatchi PLC, $3,264,104
6. Zenith Media Holdings Ltd., $2,820,254
7. Publicis Communication, $2,633,465
8. Interpublic Ltd., $2,571,545
9. Tempus Group PLC, $1,597,428
10. Publitalia 80 Concessionaria Pubblicita Spa, $1,520,632

Source: *Europe's 15,000 Largest Companies*, (annual), Dun & Bradstreet, 1999, p. 676+.

Advertising Agencies--Finland

★94★

TOP ADVERTISING AGENCIES IN FINLAND, 1998

Ranked by: Gross income, in thousands of U.S. dollars ($). **Remarks:** Also notes percent change from previous year and volume. **Number listed:** 18

1. Oy Likemainonta-McCann, with $17,030 thousand
2. Brand Sellers DDB/Finland, $13,021
3. Publicis Torma, $6,972
4. VPV Euro RSCG Oy, $6,520
5. Paltemaa Huttunen Santala TBWA, $6,265
6. BBDO Helsinki Oy, $6,167

7. Ammirati Puris Lintas Finland, $5,763
8. Komeetta Saatchi & Saatchi, $4,453
9. AS & Grey, $4,424
10. Kauppamainos Bozell, $4,100

Source: *Advertising Age*, Agency Report (annual), April 19, 1999, p. S26.

Advertising Agencies--Florida

★95★
LARGEST ADVERTISING AGENCIES IN FLORIDA, 1998
Ranked by: Number of full-time employees. **Remarks:** Also includes capitalized billings, number of Florida-based clients, percent billings, senior executives, and year founded. **Number listed:** 25

1. Paradigm Communications, with 123
2. Zimmerman & Partners Advertising Inc., 116
3. Yesawich, Pepperdine & Brown, 112
4. Cooper HMS Partners Advertising Inc., 93
5. William Cook Agency Inc., 90
6. Curtin & Pease/Peneco, 87
7. Tinsley Advertising Inc., 85
8. Harris Drury Cohen, 82
9. Beber Silverstein & Partners, 77
10. St. John & Partners Advertising and Public Relations, 76

Source: *Florida Trend*, TopRank Florida (annual), 1998, p. 69.

Advertising Agencies--France

★96★
TOP ADVERTISING AGENCIES IN FRANCE, 1998
Ranked by: Gross income, in thousands of U.S. dollars ($). **Remarks:** Also notes percent change from previous year and volume. **Number listed:** 38

1. Euro RSCG France, with $282,187 thousand
2. Publicis Conseil, $216,404
3. DDB France, $150,931
4. BDDP/TBWA, $139,600
5. Ogilvy & Mather, $80,807
6. BBDO Paris, $74,743
7. McCann-Erickson (France), $72,086
8. Young & Rubicam France, $63,437
9. Ammirati Puris Lintas France Group, $59,387
10. DMB & B, $40,228

Source: *Advertising Age*, Agency Report (annual), April 19, 1999, p. S26+.

Advertising Agencies--Germany

★97★
TOP ADVERTISING AGENCIES IN GERMANY, 1998
Ranked by: Gross income, in thousands of U.S. dollars ($). **Remarks:** Also notes percent change from previous year and volume. **Number listed:** 40

1. BBDO Group Germany, with $216,978 thousand
2. Grey Gruppe Deutschland, $113,216
3. Publicis, $106,488
4. Young & Rubicam, $80,866
5. J. Walter Thompson Frankfurt, $80,665
6. Ogilvy & Mather, $72,075
7. Ammirati Puris Lintas Deutschland, $71,069
8. McCann-Erickson Deutschland, $66,920
9. Springer & Jacoby, $61,384
10. DDB/Germany, $52,136
11. DMB&B GmbH, $45,881

Source: *Advertising Age*, Agency Report (annual), April 19, 1999, p. S30.

Advertising Agencies--Ghana

★98★
TOP ADVERTISING AGENCIES IN GHANA, 1998
Ranked by: Gross income, in thousands of U.S. dollars ($). **Remarks:** Also notes percent change from previous year and volume. **Number listed:** 6

1. STB & A (McCann), with $1,563 thousand
2. Ghana Advertising & Marketing (JWT), $326
3. Target Saatchi & Saatchi, $280
4. Insight Advertising (Grey), $194
5. ADS Limited (Burnett), $135
6. Media Majique & Research Systems (O & M), $44

Source: *Advertising Age*, Agency Report (annual), April 19, 1999, p. S30.

Advertising Agencies--Great Britain

★99★
TOP ADVERTISING AGENCIES IN GREAT BRITAIN, 1998
Ranked by: Gross income, in thousands of U.S. dollars ($). **Remarks:** Also notes percent change from previous year and volume. **Number listed:** 64

1. Abbott Mead Vickers/BBDO, with $201,000 thousand
2. Brann Worldwide (Snyder), $148,100
3. McCann-Erickson United Kingdom, $146,695
4. J. Walter Thompson London, $142,564
5. Ogilvy & Mather, $122,308
6. Young & Rubicam UK, $121,766
7. Bates Dorland, $115,293
8. DMB & B, $102,167
9. Lowe & Partners UK, $91,930
10. Grey Communications Group, $86,098

Source: *Advertising Age*, Agency Report (annual), April 19, 1999, p. S40.

Advertising Agencies--Greece

★100★
TOP ADVERTISING AGENCIES IN GREECE, 1998
Ranked by: Gross income, in thousands of U.S. dollars ($). **Remarks:** Also notes percent change from previous year and volume. **Number listed:** 25

1. Spot Thompson Athens, with $33,011 thousand

2. BBDO Group, $22,258
3. Bold Advertising (O & M), $14,748
4. McCann-Erickson Athens, $14,675
5. Olympic DDB, $13,033
6. Leo Burnett Co., $12,281
7. Ammirati Puris Lintas Athens, $10,274
8. Adel Saatchi & Saatchi, $7,081
9. Geo-Young & Rubicam, $6,053
10. Horizon (FCB), $5,530

Source: *Advertising Age*, Agency Report (annual), April 19, 1999, p. S30.

Advertising Agencies--Guatemala

★101★
TOP ADVERTISING AGENCIES IN GUATEMALA, 1998
Ranked by: Gross income, in thousands of U.S. dollars ($). **Remarks:** Also notes percent change from previous year and volume. **Number listed:** 13

1. Leo Burnett-Comunica, with $3,825 thousand
2. BBDO/Guatemala, $2,792
3. McCann-Erickson Centroamericana, $2,778
4. Eco Young & Rubicam, $1,632
5. Wurmser/O & M, $1,497
6. Publinac DDB, $1,331
7. Publicentro (APL), $1,220
8. APCU (JWT), $904
9. Jotabequ-Grey, $719
10. Creacion Saatchi & Saatchi, $708

Source: *Advertising Age*, Agency Report (annual), April 19, 1999, p. S30.

Advertising Agencies--Honduras

★102★
TOP ADVERTISING AGENCIES IN HONDURAS, 1998
Ranked by: Gross income, in thousands of U.S. dollars ($). **Remarks:** Also notes percent change from previous year and volume. **Number listed:** 10

1. McCann-Erickson Centroamericana, with $1,299 thousand
2. Calderon Publicidad (Burnett), $1,198
3. FCB Honduras, $1,085
4. Delfos Publicidad (Y & R), $870
5. Talento Grey, $826
6. Publicidad Comercial Ammirati Puris Lintas, $645
7. Adcom/DDB Needham, $599
8. Mass Nazca Saatchi & Saatchi, $542
9. Zeus/BBDO, $507
10. APCU (JWT), $318

Source: *Advertising Age*, Agency Report (annual), April 19, 1999, p. S30.

Advertising Agencies--Hungary

★103★
TOP ADVERTISING AGENCIES IN HUNGARY, 1998
Ranked by: Gross income, in thousands of U.S. dollars ($). **Remarks:** Also notes percent change from previous year and volume. **Number listed:** 19

1. McCann-Erickson Budapest, with $7,011 thousand
2. Young & Rubicam Hungary, $5,128
3. Lowe GGK Budapest, $4,650
4. Ogilvy & Mather, $4,485
5. Ammirati Puris Lintas Hungary, $4,301
6. BBDO Budapest, $3,516
7. DDB Hungary, $3,322
8. Saatchi & Saatchi, $2,525
9. Grey, $2,258
10. Leo Burnett Budapest, $2,180

Source: *Advertising Age*, Agency Report (annual), April 19, 1999, p. S30.

Advertising Agencies--India

★104★
TOP ADVERTISING AGENCIES IN INDIA, 1998
Ranked by: Gross income, in thousands of U.S. dollars ($). **Remarks:** Also notes percent change from previous year and volume. **Number listed:** 21

1. Hindustan Thompson, with $42,833 thousand
2. Ammirati Puris Lintas India, $28,951
3. Ogilvy & Mather, $18,456
4. Mudra Communications (DDB), $16,988
5. FCB-Ulka Advertising, $14,800
6. McCann-Erickson, $12,922
7. Rediffusion-Dy & R, $9,458
8. R.K. Swamy/BBDO, $7,782
9. Contract Advertising (JWT), $7,200
10. MAA Group (Bozell), $5,540

Source: *Advertising Age*, Agency Report (annual), April 19, 1999, p. S30+.

Advertising Agencies--Indonesia

★105★
TOP ADVERTISING AGENCIES IN INDONESIA, 1998
Ranked by: Gross income, in thousands of U.S. dollars ($). **Remarks:** Also notes percent change from previous year and volume. **Number listed:** 19

1. Adforce Jakarta (JWT), with $3,309 thousand
2. Ammirati Puris Lintas Indonesia, $3,119
3. Grafik/McCann-Erickson, $3,043
4. PT Indo-Ad (O & M), $1,442
5. PT Fortune Indonesia DDB, $1,029
6. Inter Admark (Dentsu), $832
7. PT Bates Mulia, $619
8. Pratama Bozell, $555
9. Euro RSCG Ad Work! Partnership, $528
10. PT Leo Burnett Kreasindo, $507

Source: *Advertising Age*, Agency Report (annual), April 19, 1999, p. S32.

Advertising Agencies--Interactive Departments

★106★
TOP INTERACTIVE ADVERTISING AGENCIES, 1998
Ranked by: Projected revenue, in thousands of dollars. **Remarks:** Also lists previous year's revenue. **Number listed:** 50
1. iXL (GA), with $100,000 thousand
2. Cambridge Technology (MA), $90,000
3. Agency.com (NY), $80,000
4. Grey New Technologies (NY), $75,000
5. Euro RSCG Worldwide (NY), $72,500
6. OgilvyOne (NY), $60,000
7. Think New Ideas (NY), $53,000
8. USWeb (CA), $50,000
9. TMP Worldwide (NY), $46,000
10. c2o Interactive Architects (TX), $45,000

Source: *Mediaweek*, January 18, 1999, p. 40.

Advertising Agencies, International

★107★
NON-U.S. CITIES WITH THE MOST LOCAL-SHOP ADVERTISING BILLINGS, 1998
Ranked by: Total local shop billings, in millions of U.S. dollars ($). **Remarks:** Also notes figures for 1997, percent change from previous year, shops reporting, top office in market by local volume, and volume. **Number listed:** 10
1. Tokyo, with $28,192.5 million
2. London, $18,625.3
3. Paris, $10,277.2
4. Sao Paulo, $5,907.5
5. Milan, $4,976.4
6. Frankfurt, $4,627.3
7. Duesseldorf, $4,123.6
8. Amsterdam, $3,482.2
9. Sydney, $3,456.9
10. Toronto, $3,168.4

Source: *Advertising Age*, Agency Report (annual), April 19, 1999, p. S16.

★108★
TOP ADVERTISING AGENCIES HOLDING COMPANIES WORLDWIDE, 1998
Ranked by: Revenue, in thousands of U.S. dollars ($). **Remarks:** Also notes previous year's rank, headquarters, billings and percent change. **Number listed:** 15
1. Omnicom Group, with $4,812,022 thousand
2. Interpublic Group of Companies, $4,402,478
3. WPP Group of Companies, $4,144,000
4. Dentsu, $1,809,600
5. Young & Rubicam, $1,659,000
6. Havas Advertising, $1,251,210
7. True North, $1,242,309
8. Grey Advertising, $1,190,600
9. Pulicis Communications, $1,011,645
10. Leo Burnett Co., $949,800

Source: *Adweek, Eastern Edition*, Agency Report Card (annual), April 19, 1999, p. 99.

★109★
TOP GLOBAL ADVERTISING AGENCIES, 1998
Ranked by: Gross income, in thousands of U.S. dollars ($). **Remarks:** Also notes headquarters, 1997 income and percent change and capitalized volume for 1997 and 1998. **Number listed:** 50
1. Omnicom Group, with $4,812.0 thousand
2. Interpublic Group of Cos., $4,304.5
3. WPP Group, $4,156.8
4. Dentsu, $1,786.0
5. Young & Rubicam, $1,659.9
6. Havas Advertising, $1,297.9
7. True North Communications, $1,242.3
8. Grey Advertising, $1,240.4
9. Leo Burnett Co., $949.8
10. Publicis, $930.0

Source: *Advertising Age*, Agency Report (annual), April 19, 1999, p. S18.

★110★
TOP INTERNATIONAL ADVERTISING AGENCY NETWORKS BASED IN THE U.S., 1998
Ranked by: Revenue, in thousands of U.S. dollars ($). **Remarks:** Also notes previous year's rank, headquarters, billings and percent change. **Number listed:** 15
1. Omnicom Group, with $4,812,022 thousand
2. McCann-Erickson World Group (IPG), $1,950,944
3. BBDO Worldwide (OMC), $1,868,314
4. DDB Needham Worldwide (OMC), $1,780,101
5. J. Walter Thompson (WPP), $1,233,000
6. Young & Rubicam, $1,209,609
7. Euro RSCG Worldwide (Havas), $1,151,624
8. Ogilvy & Mather Worldwide (WPP), $1,118,000
9. Grey Advertising, $1,002,300
10. Leo Burnett Co., $949,800

Source: *Adweek, Eastern Edition*, Agency Report Card (annual), April 19, 1999, p. 99.

Advertising Agencies--Ireland

★111★
TOP ADVERTISING AGENCIES IN IRELAND, 1998
Ranked by: Gross income, in thousands of U.S. dollars ($). **Remarks:** Also notes percent change from previous year and volume. **Number listed:** 10
1. Wilson Harnell Group (O & M), with $10,166 thousand
2. DDFH & B (JWT), $5,845
3. Quinn McDonnell Pattison/DMB & B, $4,909
4. Young Advertising (Burnett), $4,500
5. McCann-Erickson (Ireland), $3,818
6. Peter Owens Advertising & Marketing DDB, $2,976
7. Bates Ireland, $2,780
8. CDP Associates (Dentsu), $2,419
9. Saatchi & Saatchi, $1,281
10. Campbell Grey & Associates, $1,192

Source: *Advertising Age*, Agency Report (annual), April 19, 1999, p. S32.

Advertising Agencies--Israel

★112★
TOP ADVERTISING AGENCIES IN ISRAEL, 1998
Ranked by: Gross income, in thousands of U.S. dollars ($). **Remarks:** Also notes percent change from previous year and volume. **Number listed:** 16
1. Kesher-Barel & Associates (McCann), with $14,300 thousand

2. Gitab BBDO, $10,800
3. Adler, Chomski & Warshavsky (Grey), $10,656
4. Publicis Ariely, $10,485
5. Tamir Cohen (JWT), $7,163
6. Reuveni Pridan Advertising (Burnett), $6,000
7. Linial DDB, $4,465
8. Zarfatti Sternschuss Zamir (Euro RSCG), $4,000
8. Yehoshua TBWA, $4,000
10. Shimoni-Finkelstein FCB, $2,616

Source: *Advertising Age*, Agency Report (annual), April 19, 1999, p. S32.

Advertising Agencies--Italy

★113★
TOP ADVERTISING AGENCIES IN ITALY, 1998
Ranked by: Gross income, in thousands of U.S. dollars ($). **Remarks:** Also notes percent change from previous year and volume. **Number listed:** 35

1. Armando Testa Group, with $54,697 thousand
2. MCCann-Erickson Italiana, $49,721
3. Young & Rubicam Italia, $44,429
4. J. Walter Thompson Milan, $35,881
5. Barbella Gagliardi Saffirio/DMB &B, $34,969
6. Milano & Grey, $29,395
7. Euro RSCG Mezzano Costantini Mignani, $27,365
8. Publicis, $24,342
9. Saatchi & Saatchi, $23,907
10. Leo Burnett, $21,916

Source: *Advertising Age*, Agency Report (annual), April 19, 1999, p. S32.

Advertising Agencies--Ivory Coast

★114★
TOP ADVERTISING AGENCIES IN IVORY COAST, 1998
Ranked by: Gross income, in thousands of U.S. dollars ($). **Remarks:** Also notes percent change from previous year and volume. **Number listed:** 4

1. Nelson McCann-Ivory Coast, with $3,999 thousand
2. Ocean, Ogilvy & Mather, $1,394
3. Ammirati Puris Lintas, $719
4. Univers Saatchi & Saatchi, $496

Source: *Advertising Age*, Agency Report (annual), April 19, 1999, p. S32.

Advertising Agencies--Jamaica

★115★
TOP ADVERTISING AGENCIES IN JAMAICA, 1998
Ranked by: Gross income, in thousands of U.S. dollars ($). **Remarks:** Also notes percent change from previous year and volume. **Number listed:** 4

1. McCann-Erickson Jamaica, with $1,817 thousand
2. Dunlop Corbin Communications (JWT), $1,799
3. Grimax Advertising (Grey), $805
4. Lindo/FCB Communications, $702

Source: *Advertising Age*, Agency Report (annual), April 19, 1999, p. S32.

Advertising Agencies--Japan

★116★
TOP ADVERTISING AGENCIES IN JAPAN, 1998
Ranked by: Gross income, in thousands of U.S. dollars ($). **Remarks:** Also notes percent change from previous year and volume. **Number listed:** 67

1. Dentsu, with $1,389,075 thousand
2. Hakuhodo, $668,450
3. Asatsu-DK, $268,610
4. Daiko Advertising, $168,650
5. Tokyu Agency, $164,756
6. McCann-Erickson (Japan), $131,291
7. Yomiko Advertising, $98,791
8. BBDO/I&S, $89,462
9. Asahi Advertising, $74,634
10. Dentsu Young & Rubicam, $61,182

Source: *Advertising Age*, Agency Report (annual), April 19, 1999, p. S32.

Advertising Agencies--Jordan

★117★
TOP ADVERTISING AGENCIES IN JORDAN, 1998
Ranked by: Gross income, in thousands of U.S. dollars ($). **Remarks:** Also notes percent change from previous year and volume. **Number listed:** 3

1. Afkar Promoseven Jordan (McCann), with $639 thousand
2. Intermarkets Jordan, $515
3. Publi-Graphics Group, $198

Source: *Advertising Age*, Agency Report (annual), April 19, 1999, p. S32.

Advertising Agencies--Kazakhstan

★118★
TOP ADVERTISING AGENCIES IN KAZAKHSTAN, 1998
Ranked by: Gross income, in thousands of U.S. dollars ($). **Remarks:** Also notes percent change from previous year and volume. **Number listed:** 4

1. Ogilvy & Mather, with $869 thousand
2. Styx Advertising Agency, $459
3. DMB&B Tengri, $315
4. McCann-Erickson, $202

Source: *Advertising Age*, Agency Report (annual), April 19, 1999, p. S34.

Advertising Agencies--Kenya

★119★
TOP ADVERTISING AGENCIES IN KENYA, 1998
Ranked by: Gross income, in thousands of U.S. dollars ($). **Remarks:** Also notes percent change from previous year and volume. **Number listed:** 6

1. Scanad Marketing (APL), with $2,838 thousand

2. McCann-Erickson Kenya, $1,872
3. Ayton Young & Rubicam, $1,309
4. Ogilvy & Mather, $1,181
5. Century Advertising (Grey), $753
6. MCL/Saatchi & Saatchi, $375

Source: *Advertising Age*, Agency Report (annual), April 19, 1999, p. S34.

Advertising Agencies--Korea, South

★120★
TOP ADVERTISING AGENCIES IN SOUTH KOREA, 1998
Ranked by: Gross income, in thousands of U.S. dollars ($). **Remarks:** Also notes percent change from previous year and volume. **Number listed:** 19

1. Cheil Communications, with $103,647 thousand
2. LG Ad, $36,000
3. Diamond Ad, $27,775
4. Daehong Communications, $17,179
5. McCann-Erickson (South Korea), $8,778
6. SangAm Communications (Grey), $6,482
7. Cheil Bozell, $6,300
8. Seoul DMB & B, $4,490
9. TBWA Korea, $4,248
10. Phoenix Communications (Dentsu), $3,677

Source: *Advertising Age*, Agency Report (annual), April 19, 1999, p. S37.

Advertising Agencies--Kuwait

★121★
TOP ADVERTISING AGENCIES IN KUWAIT, 1998
Ranked by: Gross income, in thousands of U.S. dollars ($). **Remarks:** Also notes percent change from previous year and volume. **Number listed:** 9

1. Intermarkets Kuwait, with $3,800 thousand
2. TMI (JWT), $2,003
3. Impact & Echo (BBDO), $1,851
4. Publi-Graphics Group, $1,661
5. Memac (O&M), $1,382
6. Al Siham Promoseven Kuwait (McCann), $1,179
7. Team/Young & Rubicam, $1,025
8. MADCO Kuwait (Bates), $944
9. CSS & Grey, $508

Source: *Advertising Age*, Agency Report (annual), April 19, 1999, p. S34.

Advertising Agencies--Latvia

★122★
TOP ADVERTISING AGENCIES IN LATVIA, 1998
Ranked by: Gross income, in thousands of U.S. dollars ($). **Remarks:** Also notes percent change from previous year and volume. **Number listed:** 5

1. Metro Advertising (Burnett), with $828 thousand
2. Brand Sellers DDB Baltics Latvia, $784
3. Division M/E Latvia (McCann), $342
4. Adel Saatchi & Saatchi, $295
5. Grey, $246

Source: *Advertising Age*, Agency Report (annual), April 19, 1999, p. S34.

Advertising Agencies--Lebanon

★123★
TOP ADVERTISING AGENCIES IN LEBANON, 1998
Ranked by: Gross income, in thousands of U.S. dollars ($). **Remarks:** Also notes percent change from previous year and volume. **Number listed:** 14

1. CSS & Grey, with $3,440 thousand
2. H & C Leo Burnett, $3,166
3. Publi-Graphics Group, $3,055
4. Impact/BBDO Sal, $2,607
5. MADCO Lebanon (Bates), $1,889
6. Team/Young & Rubicam, $1,588
7. TMI (JWT), $1,526
8. BD&A (Saatchi & Saatchi), $1,361
9. Intermarkets Lebanon, $1,300
10. Pimo Group (Ammirati), $905

Source: *Advertising Age*, Agency Report (annual), April 19, 1999, p. S34.

Advertising Agencies--Lithuania

★124★
TOP ADVERTISING AGENCIES IN LITHUANIA, 1998
Ranked by: Gross income, in thousands of U.S. dollars ($). **Remarks:** Also notes percent change from previous year and volume. **Number listed:** 5

1. Dvyniu Ratas & Leo Burnett, with $333 thousand
2. Brand Sellers DDB, $194
3. Asta Dizainas M/E (McCann), $186
4. Adel Saatchi & Saatchi, $175
5. Grey, $48

Source: *Advertising Age*, Agency Report (annual), April 19, 1999, p. S34.

Advertising Agencies--Los Angeles County (CA)

★125★
LARGEST ADVERTISING AGENCIES IN LOS ANGELES COUNTY, 1997
Ranked by: Billings in Los Angeles County, in millions of dollars. **Remarks:** Also includes profile, creative director, top local executive, clients and other financial figures. **Number listed:** 25

1. TBWA/Chiat/Day Inc., with $925 million
2. Rubin Postaer & Associates, $504.8
3. Saatchi & Saatchi/Pacific, $496
4. DDB Needham Worldwide, $319.7
5. BBDO West, $310
6. Ogilvy & Mather, $288
7. Grey Advertising Inc., $281.9
7. Team One Advertising, $281.9
9. Suissa Miller Advertising Inc., $240

10. Dailey & Associates, $225

Source: *Los Angeles Business Journal*, Book of Lists (annual), 1999, p. 60+.

Advertising Agencies--Macedonia

★126★
TOP ADVERTISING AGENCIES IN MACEDONIA, 1998
Ranked by: Gross income, in thousands of U.S. dollars ($). **Remarks:** Also notes percent change from previous year and volume. **Number listed:** 4

1. S Team Bates Saatchi & Saatchi, with $288 thousand
2. Grey Skopje, $231
3. Idea Plus DDB Skopje, $132
4. I & G Group/McCann Macedonia, $106

Source: *Advertising Age*, Agency Report (annual), April 19, 1999, p. S34.

Advertising Agencies--Malawi

★127★
TOP ADVERTISING AGENCIES IN MALAWI, 1998
Ranked by: Gross income, in thousands of U.S. dollars ($). **Remarks:** Also notes percent change from previous year and volume. **Number listed:** 3

1. Graphic McCann, with $412 thousand
2. Impact Saatchi & Saatchi, $104
3. Top Advertising Agency (O&M), $15

Source: *Advertising Age*, Agency Report (annual), April 19, 1999, p. S34.

Advertising Agencies--Malaysia

★128★
TOP ADVERTISING AGENCIES IN MALAYSIA, 1998
Ranked by: Gross income, in thousands of U.S. dollars ($). **Remarks:** Also notes percent change from previous year and volume. **Number listed:** 25

1. McCann-Erickson (Malaysia), with $8,838 thousand
2. Bates Malaysia, $7,688
3. Leo Burnett Co., $4,451
4. Ogilvy & Mather, $4,387
5. Ammirati Puris Lintas Malaysia, $3,666
6. Dentsu, Young & Rubicam, $3,333
7. Naga DDB, $2,735
8. Publicis Wet Desert, $2,431
9. FCB Malaysia, $2,368
10. Batey Ads Malaysia, $2,153

Source: *Advertising Age*, Agency Report (annual), April 19, 1999, p. S34.

Advertising Agencies--Mauritius

★129★
TOP ADVERTISING AGENCIES IN MAURITIUS, 1998
Ranked by: Gross income, in thousands of U.S. dollars ($). **Remarks:** Also notes percent change from previous year and volume. **Number listed:** 2

1. Grey, with $146 thousand
2. P&P Link Saatchi & Saatchi, $121

Source: *Advertising Age*, Agency Report (annual), April 19, 1999, p. S34.

Advertising Agencies--Media Departments

★130★
TOP MEDIA SERVICES COMPANIES BY BILLINGS OUTSIDE THE U.S., 1998
Ranked by: Billings, in millions of U.S. dollars ($). **Remarks:** Includes billings for 1997 and percent change. **Number listed:** 10

1. MindShare, with $10,079.0 million
2. McCann-Erickson/Universal McCann, $9,084.9
3. Carat Group, $8,386.0
4. Optimum Media Directories, $7,864.3
5. Media Edge, $6,783.0
6. MediaCom, $6,380.0
7. Starcom/Leo Burnett Co., $4,387.5
8. CIA Group, $4,280.0
9. Western Initiative Media Worldwide, $4,000.0
10. Zenith Media Services, $3,981.0

Source: *Advertising Age*, Agency Report (annual), April 19, 1999, p. S12.

★131★
TOP MEDIA SERVICES COMPANIES BY CABLE TV BILLINGS, 1998
Ranked by: Billings, in millions of U.S. dollars ($). **Remarks:** Includes billings for 1997, percent change, 1998 total volume and media percentage. **Number listed:** 10

1. MediaCom, with $352.8 million
2. Western Initiative Media Worldwide, $344.0
3. Starcom Worldwide, $328.5
4. SFM Media (Media Planning Group), $328.0
5. MediaVest, $310.0
6. TN Media, $300.0
7. McCann-Erickson/Universal McCann, $294.5
8. Media Edge, $281.8
9. Optimum Media, $226.3
10. Zenith Media Services, $160.0

Source: *Advertising Age*, Agency Report (annual), April 19, 1999, p. S14.

★132★
TOP MEDIA SERVICES COMPANIES BY MAGAZINE BILLINGS, 1998
Ranked by: Billings, in millions of U.S. dollars ($). **Remarks:** Includes billings for 1997, percent change, 1998 total volume and media percentage. **Number listed:** 10

1. Starcom Worldwide, with $935.9 million
2. McCann-Erickson/Universal McCann, $464.2
3. Media Edge, $440.4
4. Optimum Media, $294.7
5. MediaCom, $281.9
6. Carat North America, $201.0
7. Advanswers, $177.0

8. Western Initiative Media Worldwide, $163.0
9. SFM Media (Media Planning Group), $87.0
10. Zenith Media Services, $86.0

Source: *Advertising Age*, Agency Report (annual), April 19, 1999, p. S14.

★133★
TOP MEDIA SERVICES COMPANIES BY NETWORK TV BILLINGS, 1998
Ranked by: Billings, in millions of U.S. dollars ($). **Remarks:** Includes billings for 1997, percent change, 1998 total volume and media percentage. **Number listed:** 10

1. MediaVest, with $1,569.5 million
2. Media Edge, $1,353.7
3. McCann-Erickson/Universal McCann, $1,205.1
4. TN Media, $800.0
5. Zenith Media Services, $740.0
6. Starcom Worldwide, $722.4
7. Optimum Media, $592.4
8. MediaCom, $554.5
9. Western Initiative Media Worldwide, $553.0
10. Botway Group, $521.0

Source: *Advertising Age*, Agency Report (annual), April 19, 1999, p. S14.

★134★
TOP MEDIA SERVICES COMPANIES BY NEWSPAPER BILLINGS, 1998
Ranked by: Billings, in millions of U.S. dollars ($). **Remarks:** Includes billings for 1997, percent change, 1998 total volume and media percentage. **Number listed:** 10

1. Western Initiative Media Worldwide, with $1,100.0 million
2. Empower MediaMarketing, $190.0
3. McCann-Erickson/Universal McCann, $185.6
4. Optimum Media, $147.7
5. MediaCom, $123.3
6. Media Edge, $119.2
7. PubliGroupe, $103.0
8. Zenith Media Services, $85.0
9. Starcom Worldwide, $83.6
10. Carat North America, $71.0

Source: *Advertising Age*, Agency Report (annual), April 19, 1999, p. S14.

★135★
TOP MEDIA SERVICES COMPANIES BY RADIO BILLINGS, 1998
Ranked by: Billings, in millions of U.S. dollars ($). **Remarks:** Includes billings for 1997, percent change, 1998 total volume and media percentage. **Number listed:** 10

1. Western Initiative Media Worldwide, with $407.0 million
2. TN Media, $340.0
3. Zenith Media Services, $229.0
4. Carat North America, $192.0
5. Media Edge, $172.0
6. Optimum Media, $169.2
7. McCann-Erickson/Universal McCann, $139.8
8. Horizon Media, $113.0
9. J.L. Media, $96.6
10. MediaCom, $92.3

Source: *Advertising Age*, Agency Report (annual), April 19, 1999, p. S14.

★136★
TOP MEDIA SERVICES COMPANIES BY SPOT TV BILLINGS, 1998
Ranked by: Billings, in millions of U.S. dollars ($). **Remarks:** Includes billings for 1997, percent change, 1998 total volume and media percentage. **Number listed:** 10

1. Western Initiative Media Worldwide, with $1,485.0 million
2. TN Media, $1,000.0
3. McCann-Erickson/Universal McCann, $742.4
4. Zenith Media Services, $655.0
5. Media Edge, $644.0
6. MediaCom, $490.6
7. MediaVest, $322.2
8. Optimum Media, $288.7
9. SFM Media (Media Planning Group), $265.0
10. Starcom Worldwide, $243.5

Source: *Advertising Age*, Agency Report (annual), April 19, 1999, p. S14.

★137★
TOP MEDIA SERVICES COMPANIES BY SYNDICATED TV BILLINGS, 1998
Ranked by: Billings, in millions of U.S. dollars ($). **Remarks:** Includes billings for 1997, percent change, 1998 total volume and media percentage. **Number listed:** 10

1. MediaVest, with $292.0 million
2. Starcom Worldwide, $211.3
3. Botway Group, $175.0
4. SFM Media (Media Planning Group), $160.0
5. McCann-Erickson/Universal McCann, $121.3
6. TN Media, $100.0
7. MediaCom, $98.1
8. Zenith Media Services, $95.0
8. Carat North America, $95.0
10. Optimum Media, $89.1

Source: *Advertising Age*, Agency Report (annual), April 19, 1999, p. S14.

★138★
TOP MEDIA SERVICES COMPANIES BY U.S. BILLINGS, 1998
Ranked by: Billings, in millions of U.S. dollars ($). **Remarks:** Includes billings for 1997 and percent change. **Number listed:** 40

1. Western Initiative Media Worldwide, with $4,600.0 million
2. McCann-Erickson/Universal McCann, $4,121.5
3. Media Edge, $3,494.4
4. Starcom Worldwide, $2,912.5
5. Optimum Media, $2,700.0
6. TN Media, $2,540.0
7. MediaVest, $2,517.7
8. Zenith Media Services, $2,119.0
9. MediaCom, $2,098.6
10. SFM Media (Media Planning Group), $1,365.0

Source: *Advertising Age*, Agency Report (annual), April 19, 1999, p. S12.

★139★
TOP MEDIA SERVICES COMPANIES BY WORLDWIDE BILLINGS BY PARENT, 1998
Ranked by: Billings, in millions of U.S. dollars ($). **Remarks:** Includes billings for 1997 and percent change. **Number listed:** 10

1. Interpublic Group of Cos., with $22,041.4 million
2. Omnicom Group, $11,558.9
3. Young & Rubicam Inc., $10,277.4
4. WPP Group, $10,202.0
5. Aegis Group, $9,600.0

6. Grey Advertising, $8,478.6
7. Leo Burnett Co., $7,300.0
8. Saatchi & Saatchi/Cordiant, $6,100.0
9. True North Communications, $5,700.0
10. Havas Advertising, $5,325.6

Source: *Advertising Age*, Agency Report (annual), April 19, 1999, p. S12.

★140★
TOP MEDIA SERVICES COMPANIES BY WORLDWIDE BILLINGS, 1998
Ranked by: Billings, in millions of U.S. dollars ($). **Remarks:** Includes billings for 1997 and percent change. **Number listed:** 10

1. McCann-Erickson/Universal McCann, with $13,206.4 million
2. Optimum Media Directories, $10,564.3
3. Media Edge, $10,277.4
4. MindShare, $10,079.0
5. Carat Group, $9,600.0
6. Western Initiative Media Worldwide, $8,600.0
7. MediaCom, $8,478.6
8. Starcom/Leo Burnett Co., $7,300.0
9. Zenith Media Services, $6,100.0
10. TN Media, $5,700.0

Source: *Advertising Age*, Agency Report (annual), April 19, 1999, p. S12.

Advertising Agencies--Mexico

★141★
TOP ADVERTISING AGENCIES IN MEXICO, 1998
Ranked by: Gross income, in thousands of U.S. dollars ($). **Remarks:** Also notes percent change from previous year and volume. **Number listed:** 21

1. McCann-Erickson Mexico, with $27,806 thousand
2. Young & Rubicam, $16,301
3. Publicidad Ferrer y Asociados, $14,394
4. Leo Burnett Co., $13,813
5. BBDO Mexico, $12,529
6. J. Walter Thompson Mexico City, $10,718
7. Panamer/Graficoncepto (O & M), $9,517
8. Betancourt Barba Euro RSCG, $8,454
9. Bozell, $8,039
10. Ammirati Puris Lintas Mexico, $7,117

Source: *Advertising Age*, Agency Report (annual), April 19, 1999, p. S34.

Advertising Agencies--Middle Western States

★142★
LEADING ADVERTISING AGENCIES IN THE MIDDLE WESTERN SATES, 1998
Ranked by: Revenue, in thousands of dollars. **Remarks:** Also notes percent change from previous year and total billings. **Number listed:** 50

1. Leo Burnett Co. (IL), with $396,280 thousand
2. J. Walter Thompson (MI), $151,000
3. Campbell-Ewald Co. (MI), $131,638
4. DDB Needham (IL), $126,771
5. Bozell (MI), $109,000
6. Foote, Cone & Belding (IL), $97,500
7. Campbell Mithun Esty (MN), $90,700
8. J. Walter Thompson (IL), $68,000
9. Fallon McElligott (MN), $62,821
10. D'Arcy Masius Benton & Bowles (MI), $58,589

Source: *Adweek Eastern Edition*, Agency Report Card (annual), April 19, 1999, p. 103.

Advertising Agencies--Morocco

★143★
TOP ADVERTISING AGENCIES IN MOROCCO, 1998
Ranked by: Gross income, in thousands of U.S. dollars ($). **Remarks:** Also notes percent change from previous year and volume. **Number listed:** 3

1. Klem Euro RSCG, with $1,868 thousand
2. Fortune Promoseven-McCann Lorin, $1,301
3. Grey Casablanca, $160

Source: *Advertising Age*, Agency Report (annual), April 19, 1999, p. S34.

Advertising Agencies--Mozambique

★144★
TOP ADVERTISING AGENCIES IN MOZAMBIQUE, 1998
Ranked by: Gross income, in thousands of U.S. dollars ($). **Remarks:** Also notes percent change from previous year and volume. **Number listed:** 3

1. Intermark Saatchi & Saatchi, with $390 thousand
2. F & F McCann, $141
3. Pangolim Publicidade (Ogilvy & Mather), $13

Source: *Advertising Age*, Agency Report (annual), April 19, 1999, p. S34.

Advertising Agencies--Myanmar

★145★
TOP ADVERTISING AGENCIES IN MYANMAR, 1998
Ranked by: Gross income, in thousands of U.S. dollars ($). **Remarks:** Also notes percent change from previous year and volume. **Number listed:** 2

1. Sann Aung Imaging (McCann), with $300 thousand
2. Leo Burnett/Yangon, $223

Source: *Advertising Age*, Agency Report (annual), April 19, 1999, p. S34.

Advertising Agencies--Namibia

★146★
TOP ADVERTISING AGENCIES IN NAMIBIA, 1998
Ranked by: Gross income, in thousands of U.S. dollars ($). **Remarks:** Also notes percent change from previous year and volume. **Number listed:** 3

1. Advantage McCann, with $250 thousand

2. DV8 Saatchi & Saatchi, $75
3. The Agency (O & M), $26

Source: *Advertising Age*, Agency Report (annual), April 19, 1999, p. S34.

Advertising Agencies--Netherlands

★147★
TOP ADVERTISING AGENCIES IN THE NETHERLANDS, 1998
Ranked by: Gross income, in thousands of U.S. dollars ($). **Remarks:** Also notes percent change from previous year and volume. **Number listed:** 28

1. BBDO Nederland, with $54,809 thousand
2. PMS & vW/Y & R, $46,454
3. Publicis, $39,752
4. TBWA Netherlands, $37,971
5. Ogilvy & Mather, $30,677
6. PPGH (JWT), $29,438
7. Result DDB, $26,692
8. Grey, $20,752
9. McCann-Erickson, $18,733
10. Ammirati Puris Lintas Netherlands, $18,615

Source: *Advertising Age*, Agency Report (annual), April 19, 1999, p. S34.

Advertising Agencies--New England

★148★
LEADING ADVERTISING AGENCIES IN NEW ENGLAND, 1998
Ranked by: Revenue, in thousands of dollars. **Remarks:** Also notes percent change from previous year and total billings. **Number listed:** 50

1. Hill, Holliday, Connors, Cosmopulos (MA), with $92,000 thousand
2. Arnold Communications (MA), $86,000
3. Mullen (MA), $38,160
4. Ingalls (MA), $17,164
5. Holland Mark Martin Edmund (MA), $17,011
6. Mintz & Hoke (CT), $11,130
7. North Castle Partners (CT), $9,620
8. Heater Advertising (MA), $9,490
9. RDW Group (RI), $9,400
10. Allen & Gerritsen (MA), $7,650
11. D'Arcy Masius Benton & Bowles (MI), $5,589

Source: *Adweek Eastern Edition*, Agency Report Card (annual), April 19, 1999, p. 104.

Advertising Agencies--New Jersey

★149★
LARGEST ADVERTISING AGENCIES IN NEW JERSEY, 1997
Ranked by: Number of employees. **Remarks:** Also includes contact information, previous year's billings, year founded and top officer. **Number listed:** 25

1. Common Health, with 448 employees
2. Integrated Communications, 287
3. Dugan Valva Contess, 255
4. The Gillespie Organization, 130
5. The Sawtooth Group, 115
6. Gianettino & Meredith, 90
6. Hastings Health Care, 90
8. QLM Marketing Inc., 75
9. The Starr Group, 72
10. The Cherenson Group, 70

Source: *New Jersey Business*, Book of Lists (annual), 1999, p. 4.

Advertising Agencies--New York (NY)

★150★
LARGEST ADVERTISING AGENCIES IN NEW YORK, 1998
Ranked by: Local office billings, in millions of dollars. **Remarks:** Also notes gross income, number of staff, top officer and additional units. **Number listed:** 25

1. Young & Rubicam, with $3,933.3 million
2. Grey Advertising Inc., $2,844.8
3. McCann-Erickson, $2,655.8
4. Bates USA, $2,332.4
5. Ogilvy & Mather, $2,200
6. BBDO, $1,798
7. Saatchi & Saatchi, $1,767.1
8. D'Arcy Masuis Benton & Bowles, $1,335.7
9. Foote Cone & Belding, $1,300
10. Ammirati Puris Lintas, $1,280.3

Source: *Crain's New York Business*, June 28, 1999, p. 28+.

Advertising Agencies--New Zealand

★151★
TOP ADVERTISING AGENCIES IN NEW ZEALAND, 1998
Ranked by: Gross income, in thousands of U.S. dollars ($). **Remarks:** Also notes percent change from previous year and volume. **Number listed:** 17

1. Clemenger BBDO/Colenso, with $22,592 thousand
2. Saatchi & Saatchi, $11,484
3. Ammirati Puris lintas New Zealand, $5,876
4. Ogilvy & Mather, $5,712
5. Young & Rubicam New Zealand, $5,408
6. DDB Needham New Zealand, $5,392
7. McCann-Erickson (New Zealand), $5,070
8. Publicis Mojopartners, $4,566
9. FCB, $3,156
10. Grey Advertising, $2,566

Source: *Advertising Age*, Agency Report (annual), April 19, 1999, p. S34+.

Advertising Agencies--Nicaragua

★152★
TOP ADVERTISING AGENCIES IN NICARAGUA, 1998
Ranked by: Gross income, in thousands of U.S. dollars ($). **Remarks:** Also notes percent change from previous year and volume. **Number listed:** 7
1. Cuadra Cardenal (McCann), with $1,215 thousand
2. Imagen Publicidad (Grey), $1,061
3. J.B. & Asociados (Y & R), $1,050
4. BBDO/Nicaragua, $534
5. GAP Publicidad (FCB), $431
6. Publicidad Cuadra Chamberlain (Burnett), $302
7. APCU (JWT), $200

Source: *Advertising Age*, Agency Report (annual), April 19, 1999, p. S36.

Advertising Agencies--Nigeria

★153★
TOP ADVERTISING AGENCIES IN NIGERIA, 1998
Ranked by: Gross income, in thousands of U.S. dollars ($). **Remarks:** Also notes percent change from previous year and volume. **Number listed:** 5
1. LTC (JWT), with $1,553 thousand
2. STB McCann, $1,030
3. MC & A Saatchi & Saatchi, $944
4. Rosabel Advertising (Burnett), $735
5. Prima Garnet Communications (O&M), $33

Source: *Advertising Age*, Agency Report (annual), April 19, 1999, p. S36.

Advertising Agencies--Norway

★154★
TOP ADVERTISING AGENCIES IN NORWAY, 1998
Ranked by: Gross income, in thousands of U.S. dollars ($). **Remarks:** Also notes percent change from previous year and volume. **Number listed:** 16
1. JBR McCann, with $20,290 thousand
2. Bates-Gruppen, $19,045
3. Leo Burnett/Oslo, $18,086
4. GCG Norway (Grey), $11,647
5. Ogilvy & Mather, $10,098
6. DMB & B, $7,551
7. New Deal DDB, $5,894
8. Publicis, $4,552
9. BBDO, $3,418
10. Young & Rubicam/(BM) Norway, $3,416

Source: *Advertising Age*, Agency Report (annual), April 19, 1999, p. S36.

Advertising Agencies--Pakistan

★155★
TOP ADVERTISING AGENCIES IN PAKISTAN, 1998
Ranked by: Gross income, in thousands of U.S. dollars ($). **Remarks:** Also notes percent change from previous year and volume. **Number listed:** 11
1. Interflow Communications (O & M), with $2,570 thousand
2. Orient McCann, $1,752
3. Asiatic Advertising (JWT), $1,337
4. R-Lintas, $1,243
5. Blazon Advertising (Grey), $654
6. Manhattan Communications (Burnett), $621
7. MCM Advertising, $470
8. IAL Saatchi & Saatchi, $292
9. Wahedna/DMB & B, $283
10. Publicic, $200

Source: *Advertising Age*, Agency Report (annual), April 19, 1999, p. S36.

Advertising Agencies--Panama

★156★
TOP ADVERTISING AGENCIES IN PANAMA, 1998
Ranked by: Gross income, in thousands of U.S. dollars ($). **Remarks:** Also notes percent change from previous year and volume. **Number listed:** 12
1. Publitres/FCB, with $3,705 thousand
2. BB & M Ammirati Puris Lintas, $3,400
3. Cerebro/Young & Rubicam, $2,416
4. Conte/McCann-Erickson (Panama), $2,184
5. Campagnani/BBDO, $1,690
6. Publicidad Interamericana (Grey), $1,450
7. Leo Burnett Panama, $1,100
8. Fergo Nazca Saatchi & Saatchi, $1,046
9. APCU (JWT), $736
10. InterAd Bozell, $599

Source: *Advertising Age*, Agency Report (annual), April 19, 1999, p. S36.

Advertising Agencies--Paraguay

★157★
TOP ADVERTISING AGENCIES IN PARAGUAY, 1998
Ranked by: Gross income, in thousands of U.S. dollars ($). **Remarks:** Also notes percent change from previous year and volume. **Number listed:** 6
1. Mass Publicidad (Burnett), with $991 thousand
2. McCann-Erickson Co. (Paraguay), $824
3. Almirall y Compania Publicidad (Ammirati), $533
4. J. Walter Thompson Asuncion, $220
5. Euro RSCG Paraguay, $103
6. Nivel Publicidad (FCB), $79

Source: *Advertising Age*, Agency Report (annual), April 19, 1999, p. S36.

Advertising Agencies--Peru

★158★
TOP ADVERTISING AGENCIES IN PERU, 1998
Ranked by: Gross income, in thousands of U.S. dollars ($). **Remarks:** Also notes percent change from previous year and volume. **Number listed:** 16

1. Properu Publicidad Ammirati Puris Lintas, with $8,564 thousand
2. Creativity-Young & Rubicam Asociados, $6,856
3. J. Walter Thompson Lima, $5,456
4. Mayo/FCB Publicidad, $4,612
5. McCann-Erickson Publicidad (Peru), $4,599
6. Interandina TBWA, $2,965
7. Bozell Borobio, $2,505
8. BBDO Peru, $2,246
9. Pragma/DMB & B, $2,173
10. Intercom DDB, $1,797

Source: *Advertising Age*, Agency Report (annual), April 19, 1999, p. S36.

Advertising Agencies—Philadelphia Metropolitan Area

★159★
LARGEST ADVERTISING AGENCIES IN THE PHILADELPHIA AREA, 1997
Ranked by: Number of local full-time employees. **Remarks:** Also notes contact information, number of local and total accounts, local and total gross income, percent of income for advertising public relations, major clients, special services and creative director. **Number listed:** 25

1. Tierney & Partners Inc., with 190 employees
2. Devon Direct Marketing & Advertising Inc., 151
3. Vox Medica Inc., 117
4. Earle Palmer Brown, 114
5. Dudnyk Advertising & Public Relations, 82
6. Al Paul Lefton Co. Inc., 75
7. The Weightman Group, 72
8. The Star Group, 70
9. Kingswood Advertising Inc., 65
10. Dorland Sweeney Jones Inc., 62

Source: *Philadelphia Business Journal*, Book of Lists (annual), December 28, 1999, p. 139.

Advertising Agencies--Philippines

★160★
TOP ADVERTISING AGENCIES IN THE PHILIPPINES, 1998
Ranked by: Gross income, in thousands of U.S. dollars ($). **Remarks:** Also notes percent change from previous year and volume. **Number listed:** 16

1. McCann-Erickson Philippines, with $12,699 thousand
2. J. Walter Thompson Manila, $10,221
3. Ammirati Puris Lintas Philippines, $6,500
4. Publicis Philippines, $6,218
5. Ama-DDB Philippines, $4,025
6. Campaigns & grey, $3,892
7. Ogilvy & Mather, $3,483
8. Ace Advertising Saatchi & Saatchi, $3,469
9. Jimenez/DMB & B, $3,290
10. Hemisphere-Leo Burnett, $3,249

Source: *Advertising Age*, Agency Report (annual), April 19, 1999, p. S36.

Advertising Agencies--Poland

★161★
TOP ADVERTISING AGENCIES IN POLAND, 1998
Ranked by: Gross income, in thousands of U.S. dollars ($). **Remarks:** Also notes percent change from previous year and volume. **Number listed:** 20

1. ITI McCann-Erickson (Poland), with $11,308 thousand
2. DMB & B, $10,814
3. J. Walter Thompson Parintex, $9,169
4. Leo Burnett Warsaw, $8,929
5. Corporate Profiles DDB, $8,526
6. Ammirati Puris Lintas Warszawa, $8,489
7. Euro RSCG Poland, $7,654
8. Grey, $7,500
9. Ogilvy & Mather, $7,161
10. Young & Rubicam Poland, $6,230

Source: *Advertising Age*, Agency Report (annual), April 19, 1999, p. S36.

Advertising Agencies--Portugal

★162★
TOP ADVERTISING AGENCIES IN PORTUGAL, 1998
Ranked by: Gross income, in thousands of U.S. dollars ($). **Remarks:** Also notes percent change from previous year and volume. **Number listed:** 22

1. McCann-Erickson Portugal Publicidade, with $20,576 thousand
2. Young & Rubicam Portugal, $14,040
3. Euro RSCG, $11,363
4. J. Walter Thompson Lisbon, $10,795
5. Publicis, $10,084
6. Ammirati Puris Lintas Lisbon, $7,593
7. Guerreiro DDB, $7,526
8. TBWA-EPG Publicidade, $6,907
9. Ogilvy & Mather, $6,088
10. BBDO Portugal, $4,923

Source: *Advertising Age*, Agency Report (annual), April 19, 1999, p. S36.

Advertising Agencies--Puerto Rico

★163★
TOP ADVERTISING AGENCIES IN PUERTO RICO, 1998
Ranked by: Gross income, in thousands of U.S. dollars ($). **Remarks:** Also notes percent change from previous year and volume. **Number listed:** 17

1. De la Cruz Group, with $10,732 thousand

2. Young & Rubicam Puerto Rico, $10,277
3. MFPW (JWT), $10,237
4. FCB, $9,508
5. Premier Maldonado & Associates (Bozell), $8,800
6. Lopito, Ileana & Howle (O & M), $8,693
7. Badillo NAZCA Saatchi & Saatchi, $7,871
8. McCann-Erickson Corp SA (Puerto Rico), $7,606
9. Ballori & Farre, Inc., $6,900
10. West Indies & Grey, $5,881

Source: *Advertising Age*, Agency Report (annual), April 19, 1999, p. S36.

Advertising Agencies--Romania

★164★
TOP ADVERTISING AGENCIES IN ROMANIA, 1998
Ranked by: Gross income, in thousands of U.S. dollars ($). **Remarks:** Also notes percent change from previous year and volume. **Number listed:** 15

1. B.V. McCann-Erickson Advertising, with $3,030 thousand
2. Ogilvy & Mather, $2,384
3. Focus Advertising (Publicis), $2,285
4. Bates Centrade Saatchi & saatchi, $2,241
5. Graffiti/BBDO, $2,133
6. Ammirati Puris Lintas, $2,084
7. OFC International/DMB & B, $2,021
8. Tempo Advertising, $1,658
9. Leo Burnett & Target Advertising, $1,306
10. Scala/J. Walter Thompson, $1,089

Source: *Advertising Age*, Agency Report (annual), April 19, 1999, p. S37.

Advertising Agencies--Russia (Republic)

★165★
TOP ADVERTISING AGENCIES IN RUSSIA, 1998
Ranked by: Gross income, in thousands of U.S. dollars ($). **Remarks:** Also notes percent change from previous year and volume. **Number listed:** 15

1. BBDO Moscow, with $9,981 thousand
2. Adventa-Ammirati Puris Lintas/Initiative, $7,858
3. McCann-Erickson (Russia), $6,632
4. Grey, $6,434
5. DMB & B Moscow, $5,729
6. Navigator DDB, $4,257
7. Ogilvy & Mather, $4,102
8. Ark Thompson, $4,066
9. Young & Rubicam/Sovero, $3,532
10. Leo Burnett Moradpour, $3,301

Source: *Advertising Age*, Agency Report (annual), April 19, 1999, p. S37.

Advertising Agencies--Saudi Arabia

★166★
TOP ADVERTISING AGENCIES IN SAUDI ARABIA, 1998
Ranked by: Gross income, in thousands of U.S. dollars ($). **Remarks:** Also notes percent change from previous year and volume. **Number listed:** 14

1. Afkar Promoseven Jeddah/Riyadh (McCann), with $9,424 thousand
2. TMI (JWT), $9,253
3. Publi-Graphics Group, $6,986
4. Intermarkets Saudi Arabia, $4,600
5. Team/Young & Rubicam, $3,935
6. Arabian Central Establishment (BBDO), $3,666
7. Promoaction DDB, $3,150
8. Arab Centre for Marketing & Advertising, $3,073
9. Targets-Leo Burnett Advertising, $2,417
10. Akeel Saatchi & Saatchi, $2,111

Source: *Advertising Age*, Agency Report (annual), April 19, 1999, p. S37.

Advertising Agencies--Senegal

★167★
TOP ADVERTISING AGENCIES IN SENEGAL, 1998
Ranked by: Gross income, in thousands of U.S. dollars ($). **Remarks:** Also notes percent change from previous year and volume. **Number listed:** 2

1. McCann-Erickson Senegal, with $1,039 thousand
2. Ocean, Ogilvy & Mather, $132

Source: *Advertising Age*, Agency Report (annual), April 19, 1999, p. S37.

Advertising Agencies--Singapore

★168★
TOP ADVERTISING AGENCIES IN SINGAPORE, 1998
Ranked by: Gross income, in thousands of U.S. dollars ($). **Remarks:** Also notes percent change from previous year and volume. **Number listed:** 28

1. Denstu, Young & Rubicam, with $16,330 thousand
2. Ogilvy & Mather, $11,282
3. McCann-Erickson, $10,518
4. Batey Ads Singapore, $10,317
5. Euro RSCG Partnership, $8,753
6. Saatchi & Saatchi, $8,051
7. DDB Singapore, $6,144
8. Publicis Eureka, $4,676
9. TBWA Singapore, $4,333
10. Leo Burnett Co., $4,082

Source: *Advertising Age*, Agency Report (annual), April 19, 1999, p. S37.

Advertising Agencies--Slovakia

★169★
TOP ADVERTISING AGENCIES IN THE SLOVAK REPUBLIC, 1998
Ranked by: Gross income, in thousands of U.S. dollars ($). **Remarks:** Also notes percent change from previous year and volume. **Number listed:** 11

1. Soria & Grey, with $5,134 thousand
2. Mark/BBDO Bratislva, $3,902
3. Creo/Young & Rubicam, $1,777
4. Ogilvy & Mather, $1,083
5. Lowe GGK Bratislava, $852
6. Wiktor/Leo Burnett, $797
7. Publicis, $500
8. TBWA/Hager, $440
9. DDB Bratislava, $435
10. FCB Slovakia, $342

Source: *Advertising Age*, Agency Report (annual), April 19, 1999, p. S37.

Advertising Agencies--Slovenia

★170★
TOP ADVERTISING AGENCIES IN SLOVENIA, 1998
Ranked by: Gross income, in thousands of U.S. dollars ($). **Remarks:** Also notes percent change from previous year and volume. **Number listed:** 10

1. Pristop (Grey), with $4,285 thousand
2. Futura (DDB), $2,056
3. Studio Marketing (JWT), $1,771
4. Publicis Virgo, $1,000
5. Mayer & Co. (APL), $718
6. S Team Bates Saatchi & Saatchi, $672
7. Lowe Avanta Ljubljana, $641
8. Votan Leo Burnett, $421
9. Ogilvy & Mather, $229
10. McCann-Erickson Slovenia, $188

Source: *Advertising Age*, Agency Report (annual), April 19, 1999, p. S37.

Advertising Agencies--South Africa

★171★
TOP ADVERTISING AGENCIES IN SOUTH AFRICA, 1998
Ranked by: Gross income, in thousands of U.S. dollars ($). **Remarks:** Also notes percent change from previous year and volume. **Number listed:** 23

1. O & M Rightford, with $29,756 thousand
2. TBWA Hunt Lascaris, $27,800
3. Lindsay Smithers/FCB, $23,320
4. Herdbouys McCann-Erickson, $13,080
5. Jupiter, $11,773
6. Sonnenberg Murphy Leo Burnett, $10,162
7. Y & R South Africa, $7,903
8. Publicis, $6,449
9. Berry Bush, $6,300
10. Grey Holdings, $6,261

Source: *Advertising Age*, Agency Report (annual), April 19, 1999, p. S37.

Advertising Agencies--Southern States

★172★
TOP ADVERTISING AGENCIES IN THE SOUTHERN STATES, 1998
Ranked by: Revenue, in thousands of dollars. **Remarks:** Also includes percentage change from previous year and total billings. **Number listed:** 50

1. The Martin Agency (VA), with $54,385 thousand
2. Long Haymes Carr (NC), $32,375
3. WestWayne (GA), $25,711
4. Zimmerman & Partners Advertising (FL), $22,640
5. McKinney & Silver (NC), $20,894
6. BBDO South (GA), $20,800
7. Fitzgerald & Co. (GA), $20,700
8. Arnold Communications (VA), $20,436
9. Eisner & Associates (MD), $18,720
10. J. Walter Thompson (GA), $18,200

Source: *Adweek Eastern Edition*, Agency Report Card (annual), April 19, 1999, p. 106.

Advertising Agencies--Southwestern States

★173★
TOP ADVERTISING AGENCIES IN THE SOUTHWESTERN STATES, 1998
Ranked by: Revenue, in thousands of dollars. **Remarks:** Also includes percentage change from previous year and total billings. **Number listed:** 50

1. Tamerlin McClain (TX), with $61,000 thousand
2. GSD&M (TX), $56,140
3. The Richards Group(TX), $54,100
4. DDB Needham (TX), $24,739
5. Publicis (TX), $24,000
6. Ackerman McQueen (OK), $22,614
7. Fogarty Klein & Partners (TX), $21,777
8. Bromley, Aguilar & Associates (TX), $14,818
9. McCann-Erickson (TX), $13,800
10. Bates Southwest (TX), $11,200

Source: *Adweek Eastern Edition*, Agency Report Card (annual), April 19, 1999, p. 108.

Advertising Agencies--Spain

★174★
TOP ADVERTISING AGENCIES IN SPAIN, 1998
Ranked by: Gross income, in thousands of U.S. dollars ($). **Remarks:** Also notes percent change from previous year and volume. **Number listed:** 25

1. McCann-Erickson (Spain), with $45,463 thousand
2. Bassat, O & M, $43,747
3. BBDO Espana, $41,777
4. J. Walter Thompson Madrid, $35,687
5. Grey Espana, $35,074
6. Publicis, $34,774
7. Young & Rubicam, $32,755
8. Bates Spain, $31,005
9. FCB Tapsa, $29,117
10. Tandem DDB, $25,998

Source: *Advertising Age*, Agency Report (annual), April 19, 1999, p. S37.

Advertising Agencies--Sri Lanka

★175★
TOP ADVERTISING AGENCIES IN SRI LANKA, 1998
Ranked by: Gross income, in thousands of U.S. dollars ($). **Remarks:** Also notes percent change from previous year and volume. **Number listed:** 7

1. Thompson Lanka, with $1,140 thousand
2. Grant Advertising (McCann), $1,013
3. LDB Lintas, $987
4. Minds Lanka (Bozell), $425
5. Grey, $312
6. Masters Advertising (DDB), $274
7. Bates Strategic Alliance, $267

Source: *Advertising Age*, Agency Report (annual), April 19, 1999, p. S37+.

Advertising Agencies--Sweden

★176★
TOP ADVERTISING AGENCIES IN SWEDEN, 1998
Ranked by: Gross income, in thousands of U.S. dollars ($). **Remarks:** Also notes percent change from previous year and volume. **Number listed:** 19

1. Hall & Cederquist/Y & R, with $19,833 thousand
2. Grey Communications, $17,730
3. McCann-Erickson AB (Sweden), $17,655
4. Icon Medialab International, $16,657
5. Lowe Brindfors, $15,856
6. Ogilvy & Mather 2, $14,429
7. BBDO Sweden, $9,569
8. Bates Sweden, $7,725
9. Paradiset DDB, $7,137
10. Liberg Thompson, $6,766

Source: *Advertising Age*, Agency Report (annual), April 19, 1999, p. S38.

Advertising Agencies--Switzerland

★177★
TOP ADVERTISING AGENCIES IN SWITZERLAND, 1998
Ranked by: Gross income, in thousands of U.S. dollars ($). **Remarks:** Also notes percent change from previous year and volume. **Number listed:** 23

1. Advico Young & Rubicam, with $34,505 thousand
2. McCann-Erickson (Switzerland), $26,478
3. Publicis, $23,520
4. Wirz Werbeberatung, $17,283
5. Seiler DDB, $16,503
6. Fisch, Meier Direct (Ammirati), $11,992
7. Euro RSCG, $11,689
8. Impuls TBWA, $9,008
9. Lowe GGK, $7,830
10. Grey, $6,943

Source: *Advertising Age*, Agency Report (annual), April 19, 1999, p. S38.

Advertising Agencies--Taiwan

★178★
TOP ADVERTISING AGENCIES IN TAIWAN, 1998
Ranked by: Gross income, in thousands of U.S. dollars ($). **Remarks:** Also notes percent change from previous year and volume. **Number listed:** 22

1. Ogilvy & Mather, with $19,393 thousand
2. Dentsu Taipei, $14,905
3. J. Walter Thompson Taipei, $12,791
4. Denstu, Young & Rubicam, $11,686
5. McCann-Erickson Communications Group, $9,410
6. Hwa Wei & Grey, $7,183
7. HY Marketing (Hakuhodo), $5,828
8. DDB Needham Worldwide, $5,724
9. Kuo Hua Inc. (Dentsu), $5,482
10. Leo Burnett Co., $4,997

Source: *Advertising Age*, Agency Report (annual), April 19, 1999, p. S38.

Advertising Agencies--Tazania

★179★
TOP ADVERTISING AGENCIES IN TANZANIA, 1998
Ranked by: Gross income, in thousands of U.S. dollars ($). **Remarks:** Also notes percent change from previous year and volume. **Number listed:** 3

1. Advert International (McCann), with $603 thousand
2. Multimedia Saatchi & Saatchi, $116
3. M&M Communications (O&M), $22

Source: *Advertising Age*, Agency Report (annual), April 19, 1999, p. S38.

Advertising Agencies--Thailand

★180★
TOP ADVERTISING AGENCIES IN THAILAND, 1998
Ranked by: Gross income, in thousands of U.S. dollars ($). **Remarks:** Also notes percent change from previous year and volume. **Number listed:** 23

1. Ammirati Puris Lintas Thailand, with $17,551 thousand
2. J. Walter Thompson Bangkok, $14,092
3. Ogilvy & Mather, $11,178
4. McCann-Erickson (Thailand), $7,054
5. Leo Burnett Limited, $5,474
6. Denstu, Young & Rubicam, $4,939
7. Denstu (Thailand), $4,196
8. Saatchi & Saatchi, $2,842
9. Prakit Publicis, $2,414
10. Thai Hakuhodo, $1,902

Source: *Advertising Age*, Agency Report (annual), April 19, 1999, p. S38.

Advertising Agencies--Trinidad and Tobago

★181★
TOP ADVERTISING AGENCIES IN TRINIDAD AND TOBAGO, 1998
Ranked by: Gross income, in thousands of U.S. dollars ($). **Remarks:** Also notes percent change from previous year and volume. **Number listed:** 5
1. McCann-Erickson (Trinidad), with $3,222 thousand
2. Lonsdale Saatchi & Saatchi, $1,414
3. Hernandez/FCB, $1,108
4. Valdez & Torry Advertising (Grey), $1,084
5. Inglefeld, Ogilvy & Mather, $826

Source: *Advertising Age*, Agency Report (annual), April 19, 1999, p. S38.

Advertising Agencies--Tunisia

★182★
TOP ADVERTISING AGENCIES IN TUNISIA, 1998
Ranked by: Gross income, in thousands of U.S. dollars ($). **Remarks:** Also notes percent change from previous year and volume. **Number listed:** 2
1. KNRG Saatchi & Saatchi, with $355 thousand
2. Fortune Promoseven McCann, $282

Source: *Advertising Age*, Agency Report (annual), April 19, 1999, p. S38.

Advertising Agencies--Turkey

★183★
TOP ADVERTISING AGENCIES IN TURKEY, 1998
Ranked by: Gross income, in thousands of U.S. dollars ($). **Remarks:** Also notes percent change from previous year and volume. **Number listed:** 46
1. Cenajans Grey, with $14,459 thousand
2. Pars/McCann-Erickson Group, $13,981
3. Young & Rubicam Turkey, $11,260
4. Guzel Sanatiar/Bates, $10,033
5. Penajans DMB & B, $7,981
6. Manajans Thompson, $6,445
7. BBDO Group, $6,208
8. Ammirati Puris Lintas Turkey, $6,055
9. Lowe Adam, $5,912
10. Medina/Turgul DDB/Turkey, $5,342

Source: *Advertising Age*, Agency Report (annual), April 19, 1999, p. S38.

Advertising Agencies--Uganda

★184★
TOP ADVERTISING AGENCIES IN UGANDA, 1998
Ranked by: Gross income, in thousands of U.S. dollars ($). **Remarks:** Also notes percent change from previous year and volume. **Number listed:** 2
1. MCL, with $213 thousand
2. Ogilvy & Mather, $18

Source: *Advertising Age*, Agency Report (annual), April 19, 1999, p. S38.

Advertising Agencies--Ukraine

★185★
TOP ADVERTISING AGENCIES IN THE UKRAINE, 1998
Ranked by: Gross income, in thousands of U.S. dollars ($). **Remarks:** Also notes percent change from previous year and volume. **Number listed:** 15
1. Provid/BBDO, with $2,200 thousand
2. Leo Burnett Co., $1,899
3. Linea 12 McCann-Erickson, $1,856
4. Young & Rubicam, $1,400
5. Meridian Advertising (Ammirati), $1,233
6. Ark Communications (JWT), $1,195
7. Image DDB Ukraine, $1,182
8. Grey, $1,140
9. Visage (Publicis), $1,000
10. DMB & B Kiev, $751

Source: *Advertising Age*, Agency Report (annual), April 19, 1999, p. S38+.

Advertising Agencies--United Arab Emirates

★186★
TOP ADVERTISING AGENCIES IN THE UNITED ARAB EMIRATES, 1998
Ranked by: Gross income, in thousands of U.S. dollars ($). **Remarks:** Also notes percent change from previous year and volume. **Number listed:** 18
1. Impact/BBDO, with $16,393 thousand
2. Intermarkets UAE, $9,300
3. Team/Young & Rubicam, $9,167
4. Fortune Promoseven-Dubai (McCann), $8,866
5. Memac (O&M), $8,250
6. Radius/Leo Burnett, $7,769
7. Publi-Graphics Group, $6,093
8. Impact/BBDO for Publicity & Advertising, $5,709
9. TMI (JWT), $5,409
10. MADCO Gulf (Bates), $5,005

Source: *Advertising Age*, Agency Report (annual), April 19, 1999, p. S40.

Advertising Agencies--Uruguay

★187★
TOP ADVERTISING AGENCIES IN URUGUAY, 1998
Ranked by: Gross income, in thousands of U.S. dollars ($). **Remarks:** Also notes percent change from previous year and volume. **Number listed:** 15
1. Vice Versa/Y & R, with $5,538 thousand
2. Corporacion/Thompson, $4,083
3. Punto Publicidad (O & M), $3,993
4. McCann-Erickson (Uruguay), $3,436
5. Impetu (Ammirati), $2,750

6. Slogan DDB, $1,774
7. EFPZ Publicidad (FCB), $1,530
8. Ginkgo Saatchi & Saatchi, $1,501
9. Camara TBWA, $1,452
10. Euro RSCG Norton, $1,231

Source: *Advertising Age*, Agency Report (annual), April 19, 1999, p. S40.

Advertising Agencies--Uzbekistan

★188★
TOP ADVERTISING AGENCIES IN UZBEKISTAN, 1998
Ranked by: Gross income, in thousands of U.S. dollars ($). **Remarks:** Also notes percent change from previous year and volume. **Number listed:** 3

1. DMB&B Turon, with $242 thousand
2. McCann-Erickson, $123
3. Grey, $118

Source: *Advertising Age*, Agency Report (annual), April 19, 1998, p. S40.

Advertising Agencies--Venezuela

★189★
TOP ADVERTISING AGENCIES IN VENEZUELA, 1998
Ranked by: Gross income, in thousands of U.S. dollars ($). **Remarks:** Also notes percent change from previous year and volume. **Number listed:** 19

1. J.M.C. Creatividad Orientada/Y & R, with $13,760 thousand
2. J. Walter Thompson Caracas, $11,544
3. Leo Burnett-Venezuela, $10,296
4. Concept (Lowe), $6,756
5. ARS/DMB & B, $6,264
6. McCann-Erickson Publicidad, $6,224
7. Vapro Publicidad (Bozell), $5,180
8. Roberto Eliaschev y Asociados (APL), $4,655
9. BBDO Venezuela, $4,473
10. AW NAZCA Saatchi & Saatchi, $4,252

Source: *Advertising Age*, Agency Report (annual), April 19, 1999, p. S40.

Advertising Agencies--Vietnam

★190★
TOP ADVERTISING AGENCIES IN VIETNAM, 1998
Ranked by: Gross income, in thousands of U.S. dollars ($). **Remarks:** Also notes percent change from previous year and volume. **Number listed:** 6

1. McCann-Erickson Vietnam, with $1,287 thousand
2. Vietnam Advertising (DDB), $1,005
3. Ogilvy & Mather, $810
4. Saatchi & Saatchi, $650
5. Leo Burnett Worldwide, $461
6. Grey, $203

Source: *Advertising Age*, Agency Report (annual), April 19, 1999, p. S40.

Advertising Agencies--Western States

★191★
TOP ADVERTISING AGENCIES IN THE WESTERN STATES, 1998
Ranked by: Revenue, in thousands of dollars. **Remarks:** Also includes percentage change from previous year and total billings. **Number listed:** 50

1. TBWA/Chiat/Day (CA), with $150,080 thousand
2. Foote, Cone & Belding (CA), $88,500
3. The Goldberg Moser O'Neill (CA), $67,500
4. Publicis & Hal Riney (CA), $63,200
5. Wieden & Kennedy (OR), $60,200
6. Rubin Postaer & Associates (CA), $56,400
7. McCann-Erickson (CA), $55,200
8. Saatchi & Saatchi (CA), $51,600
9. Grey Advertising (CA), $42,203
10. Team One Advertising (CA), $41,500

Source: *Adweek Eastern Edition*, Agency Report Card (annual), April 19, 1999, p. 109.

Advertising Agencies--Yugoslavia

★192★
TOP ADVERTISING AGENCIES IN YUGOSLAVIA, 1998
Ranked by: Gross income, in thousands of U.S. dollars ($). **Remarks:** Also notes percent change from previous year and volume. **Number listed:** 6

1. S Team Bates Saatchi & Saatchi, with $829 thousand
2. I & F Group/McCann, $604
3. Ogilvy & Mather, $397
4. Idea Plus DDB Belgrade, $382
5. Grey Belgrade, $125
6. Studio Marketing (JWT), $61

Source: *Advertising Age*, Agency Report (annual), April 27, 1998, p. S40.

Advertising Agencies--Zambia

★193★
TOP ADVERTISING AGENCIES IN ZAMBIA, 1998
Ranked by: Gross income, in thousands of U.S. dollars ($). **Remarks:** Also notes percent change from previous year and volume. **Number listed:** 5

1. Young & Rubicam (Zambia), with $317 thousand
2. Fleerfoot McCann, $211
3. D&C Saatchi & Saatchi, $84
4. MG Studios (Ammirati), $70
5. Goman Advertising (O & M), $20

Source: *Advertising Age*, Agency Report (annual), April 19, 1999, p. S40.

Advertising Agencies--Zimbabwe

★194★
TOP ADVERTISING AGENCIES IN ZIMBABWE, 1998
Ranked by: Gross income, in thousands of U.S. dollars ($). **Remarks:** Also notes percent change from previous year and volume. **Number listed:** 8

1. Barker McCormac, O & M, with $2,238 thousand
2. Michael Hogg/Y & R, $1,138
3. Ammirati Puris Lintas Zimbabwe, $913
4. Upton & Fulton, McCann, $733
5. Dicomm Advertising (Grey), $393
6. DDH & M (JWT), $334
7. Linsell Saatchi & Saatchi, $280
8. Yon Broembsen Marson Leo Burnett, $195

Source: *Advertising Age*, Agency Report (annual), April 19, 1999, p. S40.

Advertising--Appeal to Hispanics

★195★
TOP ADVERTISERS CULTIVATING THE HISPANIC MARKET, 1997
Ranked by: Media expenditures, in millions of dollars. **Remarks:** Also notes previous year's expenditures. **Number listed:** 50

1. Procter & Gamble, with $40 million
2. AT & T Corp., $18
3. Sears, Roebuck & Co., $15
3. General Motors Corp., $15
5. MCI Communications Corp., $14
6. McDonald's, $13.9
7. Anheuser-Busch Cos., $12.5
7. Philip Morris, $12.5
9. Colgate-Palmolive Co., $12
10. Ford Motor Co., $12

Source: *Advertising Age*, August 24, 1998, p. S14.

Advertising--Canada

★196★
TOP ADVERTISING CATEGORIES IN CANADA, 1997
Ranked by: Ad spending, in millions of Canadian dollars (C$). **Remarks:** Also notes figures for previous two years. **Number listed:** 25

1. Retail, with C$879.2 million
2. Automotive, C$655.6
3. Business Equipment & Services, C$475.7
4. Food, C$426.6
5. Financial & Insurance Services, C$343
6. Entertainment, C$269.7
7. Travel & Transportation, C$211.4
8. Local Automotive Dealers, C$203.8
9. Restaurants, Catering Services, Night Clubs, C$191.9
10. Cosmetics & Toiletries, C$151.4

Source: *Marketing*, Top 25 Advertising Categories, December 14, 1998, p. 36.

Advertising Expenditures

★197★
TOP BRANDS ADVERTISING ON CABLE TELEVISION, 1998
Ranked by: Advertising expenditures, in millions of dollars. **Number listed:** 20

1. Sprint, with $53,964.3 million
2. McDonald's, $46,442.7
3. Burger King, $44,425.1
4. 10-10-32, $37,909.4
5. 1-800-Collect, $29,540.5
6. Time Life, $20,865.7
7. Blockbuster Video, $19,302.4
8. AT & T, $19,181.6
9. American Express Card, $19,116.7
10. MCI WorldCom, $16,146.9

Source: *Mediaweek*, March 1, 1999, p. 24.

★198★
TOP BRANDS AND THEIR AD SPENDING ON NBC'S DATELINE, 1997
Ranked by: Ad spending, in thousands of dollars. **Number listed:** 10

1. Chrysler Corp., with $5,533,000 thousand
2. Kentucky Fried Chicken, $3,492,000
3. U.S. Postal Service, $3,381,000
4. Brita, $3,267,000
5. Nissan Automobiles-Altima, $3,099,500
6. Nissan Motor, $2,864,500
7. McDonald's Restaurants Ltd., $2,689,000
8. Sprint, $2,081,000
9. Pizza Hut Restaurant, $2,039,500
10. Eveready Energizer Batteries, $2,009,000

Source: *American Demographics*, October, 1998, p. 34.

Advertising, Magazine

★199★
TOP ADVERTISERS IN SUNDAY MAGAZINES, 1997
Ranked by: Expenditures, in millions of dollars. **Remarks:** Also notes previous year's expenditures and percent change. **Number listed:** 25

1. National Syndications, with $92.3 million
2. Roll International, $73.2
3. Bradford Exchange, $35.5
4. Chrysler Corp., $26.9
5. Bose Corp., $22.9
6. Sony, $22.7
7. Merck & Co. Inc., $21.7
8. Elizabeth Kaye Inc., $21.3
9. Bertelsmann, $20.5
10. Philip Morris, $18.2

Source: *Advertising Age*, 100 Leading National Advertisers (annual), September 28, 1998, p. S28.

★200★
TOP INDUSTRIAL CATEGORIES FOR BUSINESS MAGAZINE ADVERTISING, 1997
Ranked by: U.S. advertising expenditures, in millions of dollars. **Remarks:** Also notes previous year's figures and percent change. **Number listed:** 6

1. Technology, with $3,507 million
2. Health Care & Pharmaceutical, $920
3. Business & Finance, $474

4. Manufacturing, Processing & Industrial, $433
5. Business Travel, $361
6. Architecture & Construction, $284

Source: *Folio*, November 1, 1998, p. 17.

★201★
TOP INDUSTRIAL CATEGORIES FOR MAGAZINE ADVERTISING, 1998
Ranked by: U.S. advertising expenditures, in millions of dollars. **Remarks:** Also notes percent change from previous year. **Number listed:** 12

1. Automotive, Auto Accessories, Equipment, & Supplies, with $1,510,000 million
2. Direct-Response Companies, $1,130,000
3. Toiletries & Cosmetics, $1,100,000
4. Business & Consumer Services, $1,070,000
5. Office equipment, Computers & Stationery, $928
6. Apparel, Footwear & Accessories, $760
7. Drugs and remedies, $758
8. Food and Food Products, $730
9. Travel, Hotels & Resorts, $570
10. Retail, $454

Source: *Graphic Arts Monthly*, Top Spenders on Advertising and Printing, February, 1999, p. 53.

★202★
TOP MAGAZINE ADVERTISERS, 1997
Ranked by: Magazine advertising expenditures, in millions of dollars. **Remarks:** Also notes previous year's figures and percent change. **Number listed:** 25

1. General Motors Corp., with $588.4 million
2. Procter & Gamble, $363.4
3. Philip Morris, $345.4
4. Chrysler Corp., $327.9
5. Ford Motor Corp., $284.8
6. Time Warner, $180.1
7. Toyota Motor, $149.1
8. Johnson & Johnson, $140.8
9. Unilever, $131.1
10. L'Oreal, $104.3

Source: *Advertising Age*, 100 Leading National Advertisers (annual), September 28, 1998, p. S28.

★203★
TOP MAGAZINES FOR MOST AD PAGES, 1998
Ranked by: Number of ad pages. **Remarks:** Also notes dollar equivalent and percent change from previous year. **Number listed:** 25

1. *PC Magazine*, with 5,385.84 pages
2. *Forbes*, 4,733.7
3. *Business Week*, 4,167.3
4. *People*, 4,038.08
5. *Fortune*, 3,898.59
6. *Bride's*, 3,669.82
7. *TV Guide*, 3,087.72
8. *Modern Bride*, 2,983.62
9. *The Economist*, 2,841
10. *Time*, 2,837.09

Source: *Advertising Age*, January 18, 1999, p. 16.

Advertising, Newspaper

★204★
COMPANIES SPENDING THE MOST ON NATIONAL NEWSPAPER ADVERTISING, 1998
Ranked by: National newspaper advertising expenditures, in millions of dollars. **Number listed:** 15

1. IBM Corp., with $44.35 million
2. Federated Department Stores, $41.97
3. Time Warner, $37.11
4. General Motors Corp., $36
5. Compaq Computer Corp., $34.72
6. DaimlerChrysler, $31.94
7. Ford Motor Co., $29.26
8. Citigroup, $25.83
9. Walt Disney Co., $24.56
10. Charles Schwab & Co., $23.95

Source: *Advertising Age*, April 20, 1999, p. 54.

★205★
COMPANIES SPENDING THE MOST ON NATIONAL NEWSPAPER ADVERTISING, 1997
Ranked by: National newspaper advertising expenditures, in millions of dollars. **Remarks:** Also notes previous year's figures and percent change. **Number listed:** 25

1. IBM Corp., with $32 million
2. Compaq Computer Corp., $28.4
3. General Motors Corp., $26.2
4. Ford Motor Co., $25.9
5. Charles Schwab Corp., $25.2
6. BMW, $21.9
7. Hewlett-Packard Co., $21.7
8. FMR Corp., $19.5
9. Dow Jones & Co., $17.4
10. Merrill Lynch & Co., $17

Source: *Advertising Age*, 100 Leading National Advertisers (annual), September 28, 1998, p. S32.

★206★
COMPANIES SPENDING THE MOST ON NEWSPAPER ADVERTISING, 1997
Ranked by: Newspaper advertising expenditures, in millions of dollars. **Remarks:** Also notes previous year's figures and percent change. **Number listed:** 25

1. Federated Department Stores, with $446.9 million
2. May Department Stores, $358.8
3. Circuit City Stores, $293
4. Sears, Roebuck & Co., $227.1
5. Dillard's, $215.8
6. Dayton Hudson Corp., $189.4
7. J.C. Penney Co., $159.1
8. Time Warner, $134.5
9. Kmart, $109.4
10. Walt Disney Co., $109.3

Source: *Advertising Age*, 100 Leading National Advertisers (annual), September 28, 1998, p. S30.

★207★
TOP ADVERTISERS IN DAILY NEWSPAPERS, 1998
Ranked by: Daily newspaper advertising expenditures, in millions of dollars. **Number listed:** 15

1. Ford Motor Co., with $529.82 million
2. Federated Department Stores, $437.23
3. General Motors Corp., $408
4. May Department Stores, $382.7
5. DaimlerChrysler, $342.63
6. Circuit City Stores, $314.32
7. Toyota Motor Sales USA, $276.24
8. Sears, Roebuck & Co., $228.6
9. Dayton Hudson Corp., $207.24
10. Dillard, $201.65

Source: *Advertising Age*, April 20, 1999, p. 54.

★208★
TOP ADVERTISERS IN SUNDAY MAGAZINES, 1998
Ranked by: Expenditures, in millions of dollars. **Number listed:** 15

1. National Syndications, with $126.68 million
2. Roll International, $63.92
3. Bose Corp., $37.61
4. Bertelsmann, $25.87
5. Bradford Exchange, $22
6. Sony, $20.49
7. DaimlerChrysler, $20.43
8. Eli Lilly & Co., $19.56
9. Procter & Gamble, $16.75
10. American Home Products, $16.43

Source: *Advertising Age*, April 20, 1999, p. 54.

Advertising, Outdoor

★209★
TOP INDUSTRY CATEGORIES FOR OUTDOOR ADVERTISING, 1998
Ranked by: Expenditures, in millions of dollars. **Remarks:** Also notes percent of total revenue and percent change. **Number listed:** 7

1. Local Services & Amusements, with $190 million
2. Public Transportation, Hotels & Resorts, $176.6
3. Retail, $162.7
4. Miscellaneous Merchandise, $161.7
5. Restaurants, $158.1
6. Media & Advertising, $143.5
7. Automotive Dealers & services, $120.3

Source: *Advertising Age*, April 19, 1999, p. 48.

★210★
TOP INDUSTRY CATEGORIES FOR OUTDOOR ADVERTISING, 1999
Ranked by: Expenditures, in millions of dollars. **Remarks:** Also notes percent change from previous year. **Number listed:** 10

1. Cigarettes, Tobacco & Accessories, with $123 million
2. Business & Consumer Services, $84
3. Retail, $82
4. Entertainment & Amusements, $64
5. Miscellaneous/General Retail, $50
6. Automotive, Auto Accessories, $47
7. Travel, Hotels & Resorts, $39
8. Beer & Wine, $36
9. Publishing & media, $34
10. Insurance & Real Estate, $23

Source: *Signs of the Times*, May, 1999, p. 124.

★211★
TOP OUTDOOR ADVERTISERS, 1997
Ranked by: Advertising expenditures, in millions of dollars. **Remarks:** Also notes previous year's figures and percent change. **Number listed:** 25

1. Philip Morris, with $76.4 million
2. RJR Nabisco, $42.1
3. B.A.T. Industries, $32.6
4. McDonald's, $18.8
5. U.S. Dairy Producers, Processors, $17.1
6. Seagram, $16.7
7. General Motors Corp., $14.7
8. Cendant Corp., $14.6
9. Anheuser-Busch Cos., $13
10. Diageo, $12.7

Source: *Advertising Age*, 100 Leading National Advertisers (annual), September 28, 1998, p. S34.

★212★
TOP U.S. OUTDOOR ADVERTISING COMPANIES, 1999
Ranked by: U.S. gross revenue, in millions of dollars. **Remarks:** Also notes percent of out-of-home total. **Number listed:** 5

1. Outdoor Systems, with $750 million
2. Clear Channel/Universal, $595
3. Lamar, $325
4. TDIndustries, $246
5. Chancellor, $236

Source: *Advertising Age*, April 19, 1999, p. 50.

Aerospace Industries

★213★
LARGEST COMPANIES IN THE AEROSPACE INDUSTRY, 1998
Ranked by: Revenue, in millions of dollars. **Remarks:** Also includes profit and investment figures as well as number of employees. **Number listed:** 13

1. Boeing, with $56,154 million
2. Lockheed Martin, $26,266
3. United Technologies, $25,715
4. AlliedSignal, $15,128
5. Textron, $11,549
6. Northrop Grumman, $8,902
7. General Dynamics, $4,970
8. B.F. Goodrich, $3,951
9. Gulfstream Aerospace, $2,428
10. Sundstrand, $2,005

Source: *Fortune*, Fortune 500 Largest U.S. Corporations (annual), April 26, 1999, p. F-51+.

★214★
MOST ADMIRED AEROSPACE CORPORATIONS, 1998
Ranked by: Scores (1-10) derived from a survey of senior executives, outside directors, and securities analysts. **Remarks:** Respondents rated companies in their own industry on 8 attributes of reputation. Also notes previous year's rank. **Number listed:** 10

1. AlliedSignal, with 7.28 points
2. United Technologies, 7.18
3. Lockheed Martin, 6.92
4. Textron, 6.67
5. Sundstrand, 6.59
5. General Dynamics, 6.59
7. Gulfstream Aerospace, 6.57
8. Boeing, 6.42
9. B.F. Goodrich, 6.33
10. Northrop Grumman, 6.26

Source: *Fortune*, America's Most Admired Corporations (annual), March 1, 1999, p. F2.

★215★
TOP AEROSPACE AND DEFENSE COMPANIES IN THE S&P 500, 1998
Ranked by: Companies are listed, not ranked. **Remarks:** Figures are provided in nine areas: by market value - one-year, three year and February 1999 returns; by sales - percent change last 12 months, percent average change over three years, and recent 12 months' sales in millions of dollars; by profitability - percent change last 12 months, percent average change over three years, and recent 12 months' profit in millions of dollars. **Number listed:** 6

1. General Dynamics
2. United Technologies
3. B. F. Goodrich
4. Boeing
5. Lockheed Martin
6. Northrop Grumman

Source: *Business Week*, Business Week 50: Top Companies of the S&P 500 (annual), March 29, 1999, p. 142.

★216★
TOP GOVERNMENT, MILITARY & AEROSPACE COMPANIES, 1998
Ranked by: Segment revenue, in millions of dollars. **Number listed:** 20

1. Lockheed Martin, with $7,069 million
2. Raytheon, $6,555.2
3. TRW, $4,157.3
4. Northrop Grumman, $4,098.4
5. Litton Industries, $2,812.5
6. AlliedSignal, $2,108.5
7. The Boeing Co., $2,061
8. Honeywell, $2,006.9
9. Rockwell International, $1,740.9
10. Motorola, $1,489.7

Source: *Electronic Business*, July, 1998, p. 97.

★217★
TOP R&D SPENDERS IN THE AEROSPACE INDUSTRY, 1997
Ranked by: Spending, in millions of dollars. **Number listed:** 10

1. Boeing Co., with $1,887 million
2. Lockheed Martin Corp., $794.8
3. Raytheon, $411.1
4. Northrop Grumman, $271.7
5. Trinity Industries, $120
6. B.F. Goodrich Co., $104.8
7. Lear Corp., $92.2
8. Brunswick, $90.9
9. Sundstrand, $72.6
10. Litton Industries, $71.8

Source: *R & D Magazine*, Giants of R & D (annual), October, 1998, p. S14.

Aerospace Industries, International

★218★
WORLD'S LARGEST COMPANIES IN THE AEROSPACE INDUSTRY BY REVENUE, 1997
Ranked by: Revenue, in millions of dollars. **Remarks:** Also notes profits and profits as a percent of revenues and assets. **Number listed:** 8

1. Boeing (U.S.), with $45,800 million
2. Lockheed Martin (U.S.), $28,069
3. United Technologies (U.S.), $24,713
4. AlliedSignal (U.S.), $14,472
5. British Aerospace (Great Britain), $11,904
6. Textron (U.S.), $10,544
7. Aerospatiale (France), $9,767
8. Northrop Grumman (U.S.), $9,153

Source: *Fortune*, The Global 500: World's Biggest Corporations (annual), August 3, 1998, p. F-15.

Affiliated Corporations--Detroit Metropolitan Area

★219★
LEADING DIVISIONS, AFFILIATES AND SUBSIDIARIES IN THE DETROIT METROPOLITAN AREA, 1997
Ranked by: Revenue, in millions of dollars. **Remarks:** Also notes contact information, revenue from previous year's local and parent company, number of local and worldwide employees, and business description. **Number listed:** 20

1. Johnson Controls Inc. Automotive Systems Group, with $9,300 million
2. TRW, automotive operations, $7,000
3. DuPont Automotive, $4,000
4. Ameritech Michigan, $3,384.8
5. UT Automotive Inc., $2,900
6. Textron Automotive Co. Inc., $2,200
7. NBD Bank, $2,114
8. Farmer Jack Supermarkets, $1,450
9. AlliedSignal Friction Materials, $1,000
10. General Dynamics Land Systems Inc., $1,000

Source: *Crain's Detroit Business*, October 19, 1998, p. 26.

Agricultural Banking

See: **Agricultural Credit**

Agricultural Credit

★220★
LARGEST AGRICULTURAL BANKS, 1997
Ranked by: Total agricultural loans, in thousands of dollars. **Remarks:** Also notes loans secured by farm land, other loans to farmers, total loans and leases, and farm loans as percentage of total loans. **Number listed:** 100

1. Wells Fargo Bank (CA), with $1,913,633 thousand
2. Bank of America National Trust & Savings Association (CA), $1,833,000
3. U.S. Bank (MN), $1,405,144
4. NationsBank (NC), $996,513
5. Keybank (OH), $860,008
6. Sanwa Bank of California (CA), $831,347
7. First Union (NC), $480,771
8. Norwest Bank of South Dakota (SD), $365,017
9. First Security Bank (UT), $348,117
10. Corestates Bank (PA), $307,143

Source: *Agri Finance*, July, 1998, p. 10+.

★221★
TOP AGRICULTURAL CREDIT UNION LENDERS, 1998
Ranked by: Total agricultural loans, in millions of dollars. **Remarks:** Also notes total assets. **Number listed:** 20

1. Wabash County Farm Bureau Credit Union (IN), with $54.9 million
2. Melrose Credit Union (MN), $38.3
3. First Community Credit Union (ND), $35.7
4. Town & Country Credit Union (ND), $31.3
5. Western Cooperative Credit Union (ND), $25.8
6. Benson County Co-op Credit Union (ND), $25.5

7. Lake Region Credit Union (ND), $20.7
8. Houston Milk Producers FCU (TX), $16.3
9. Heartland Credit Union (WI), $13.8
10. Community Credit Union (ND), $13.2

Source: *Credit Union Magazine*, May, 1999, p. 17.

★222★
TOP FARM CREDIT SYSTEM ASSOCIATIONS, 1998
Ranked by: Gross loans outstanding, in thousands of dollars. **Remarks:** Also notes real estate, non-real estate and other loans. **Number listed:** 100

1. Farm Credit System of the Midlands (NE), with $4,515,715 thousand
2. Farm Credit System of Mid-America (KY), $4,482,925
3. Northwest Farm Credit System (WA), $2,473,199
4. First Pioneer Farm Credit (CT), $1,118,560
5. Ag Star Farm Credit System (MN), $986,005
6. Farm Credit System of Fargo/West Central Minnesota (MN), $917,649
7. Pacific Coast Farm Credit Services (CA), $709,339
8. Valley Production Credit Association (CA), $660,226
9. First South Production Credit Association (MS), $607,776
10. Farm Credit System of Michigan's Heartland (MI), $557,618

Source: *Ag Lender*, November, 1998, p. 10+.

Agriculture--Asia

★223★
TOP COMPANIES IN AGRICULTURE, FISHING, FORESTRY AND PLANTATIONS, 1999
Ranked by: Sales, in thousands of U.S. dollars ($). **Remarks:** Also notes profits as a percentage of sales and activity codes. **Number listed:** 66

1. Sumitomo Forestry Co. Ltd. (Japan), with $5,342,275 thousand
2. Nippon Suisan Kaisma Ltd. (Japan), $3,571,032
3. Osaka Uoichiba Co. Ltd. (Japan), $3,518,151
4. Sime Darby Bhd (Malaysia), $3,483,432
5. Nichiro Gyogyo Kaisha Ltd. (Japan), $1,806,197
6. Perlis Plantations Bhd (Malaysia), $1,560,386
7. Kyokuyo Co. Ltd. (Japan), $1,317,529
8. Pokka Corp. (Japan), $855,157
9. Hoko Fishing Co. (Japan), $741,893
10. Chubu Suisan Co. Ltd. (Japan), $557,043

Source: *Asia's 7,500 Largest Companies*, (annual), Dun & Bradstreet, 1999, p. 71+.

Agriculture--Europe

★224★
TOP COMPANIES IN AGRICULTURE, FORESTRY AND FISHING IN THE EEC, 1999
Ranked by: Financial size, in millions of ECUs. **Remarks:** Also notes overall rank and number of employees. **Number listed:** 26

1. Dalgety Ltd. (Great Britain), with ECUs6,120 million
2. Associated Co-Operative Creameries Ltd. (Great Britain), ECUs888
3. Lohmann & Co. (Germany), ECUs864
4. Grampian Country Food Group Ltd. (Great Britain), ECUs692
5. Bernhard Matthews PLC (Great Britain), ECUs548
6. Marshall Food Group (Great Britain), ECUs349
7. KWS Kleinwanzilebener Saatzucht AG Vorm (Germany), ECUs299
8. Linton Park PLC (Great Britain), ECUs273
9. Sovereign Food Group Ltd. (Great Britain), ECUs243
10. Moy Park Ltd. (Great Britain), ECUs207

Source: *Dun's Europa*, (annual), 1999, vol. 4, p. 227.

Air Cargo

See: **Air Freight Service**

Air Cleaners and Cleaning

★225★
BEST-SELLING AIR CLEANERS, 1998
Ranked by: Market share, in percent. **Number listed:** 7

1. Holmes, with 38%
2. Honeywell, 19%
3. Rival (Bionaire), 10%
4. Duracraft, 8%
5. Sunbeam, 6%
6. Hunter, 4%
7. Others, 15%

Source: *Appliance Manufacturer*, April, 1999, p. 20.

Air Conditioning Industry

★226★
BEST-SELLING CENTRAL RESIDENTIAL AIR CONDITIONERS, 1998
Ranked by: Market share, in percent. **Number listed:** 9

1. United Technologies, with 21%
2. Goodman, 17%
3. American Standard, 13%
4. Rheem, 12%
5. Lennox, 10%
6. International Comfort Products, 9%
7. York, 6%
8. Nortex, 5%
9. Others, 7%

Source: *Appliance Manufacturer*, April, 1999, p. 20.

★227★
BEST-SELLING ROOM AIR CONDITIONERS, 1998
Ranked by: Market share, in percent. **Number listed:** 10

1. Fedders, with 27%
2. Whirlpool, 23%
3. Electrolux, 20%
4. Matsushita, 7%
5. Goodman, 6%
6. Friedrich, 5%
7. LG Electronics, 4%
7. United Technologies, 4%

9. Samsung, 2%
10. Sharp, 2%

Source: *Appliance Manufacturer*, April, 1999, p. 20.

Air Couriers

See: **Air Freight Service**

Air Freight Service

★228★
TOP AIRLINES BY DOMESTIC FREIGHT TON MILES, 1998
Ranked by: Freight ton miles, in thousands. **Remarks:** Also ranks by international and total freight ton miles. **Number listed:** 50

1. Federal Express, with 4,651 thousand
2. United Parcel Service, 2,845
3. Lufthansa, 1,062
4. Korean Airlines, 1,033
5. Air France, 943
6. Japan Airlines, 870
7. Singapore Airlines, 753
8. United Airlines, 668
9. British Airways, 662
10. Cathay Pacific, 580

Source: *World Air Transport Statistics*, (annual), International Air Transport Association, 1999, p. 46.

★229★
TOP AIRLINES BY FREIGHT TON MILES, 1997
Ranked by: Freight ton miles, in millions. **Remarks:** Also ranks by passengers, revenue passenger miles and total operating revenues. **Number listed:** 25

1. Federal Express, with 6,176.8 million
2. United Parcel Service, 3,682.5
3. United Airlines, 2,221.8
4. Northwest Airlines, 1,951.8
5. American Airlines, 1,645.7
6. Delta Airlines, 1,241.6
7. Polar Air Cargo, 1,191.5
8. Emery Worldwide, 970.6
9. Evergreen International, 668.5
10. Airborne Express, 577.8

Source: *Air Transport World*, (annual), Air Transport Association, 1999, p. 15.

Air Freight Service--Asia

★230★
MOST ADMIRED SHIPPING AND TRANSPORT COMPANIES IN ASIA, 1999
Ranked by: Scores (1-10) derived from a survey of chief executives and corporate board members. **Remarks:** Respondents rated companies in 8 attributes including quality of management, products and services, contribution to the local economy, being a good employer, potential for growth, being honest and ethical, potential for future profit, and ability to cope with the changing economic environment. Also notes previous year's score and overall rank **Number listed:** 11

1. DHL, with 7.34 points
2. Federal Express, 7.28
3. Saha Union, 7.06
4. Natsteel Electronics, 6.79
5. United Parcel Service, 6.66
6. Berli Jucker, 6.4
7. East Asiatic, 6.35
8. Keppel Corp., 6.25
9. Hanjin Shipping Co., 6.09
10. Sumitomo Corp., 6.03

Source: *Asian Business*, May, 1999, p. 29.

Air Freight Service, International

★231★
TOP MEMBERS OF THE INTERNATIONAL AIR TRANSPORT ASSOCIATION BY SCHEDULED INTERNATIONAL FREIGHT TONNE-KILOMETERS FLOWN, 1998
Ranked by: Scheduled international freight tonne-kilometers flown, in millions. **Number listed:** 50

1. British Airways, with 112,365 million
2. United Airlines, 75,170
3. Lufthansa, 70,051
4. Air France, 65,955
5. Japan Airlines, 62,018
6. American Airlines, 58,288
7. Singapore Airlines, 57,737
8. KLM, 57,271
9. Northwest Airlines, 48,319
10. Qantas Airways, 42,731

Source: *World Air Transport Statistics*, (annual), International Air Transport Association, 1999, p. 47.

★232★
TOP MEMBERS OF THE INTERNATIONAL AIR TRANSPORT ASSOCIATION BY SCHEDULED INTERNATIONAL FREIGHT TONNES CARRIED, 1998
Ranked by: Scheduled international freight tonnes carried, in thousands. **Number listed:** 50

1. Federal Express, with 1,131 thousand
2. Lufthansa, 1,004
3. Air France, 907
4. Korean Air Lines, 795
5. Singapore Airlines, 753
6. British Airways, 656
7. Cathay Pacific, 580
8. Japan Airlines, 543
9. ELM, 537
10. EAT, 424

Source: *World Air Transport Statistics*, (annual), International Air Transport Association, 1999, p. 46.

★233★
TOP MEMBERS OF THE INTERNATIONAL AIR TRANSPORT ASSOCIATION BY TOTAL SCHEDULED FREIGHT TONNE-KILOMETERS FLOWN, 1998
Ranked by: Total scheduled freight tonne-kilometers flown, in millions. **Number listed:** 50

1. United Airlines, with 200,421 million
2. American Airlines, 175,249
3. Delta Airlines, 166,154
4. British Airways, 116,001
5. Northwest Airlines, 107,402

6. Continental Airlines, 79,778
7. Japan Airlines, 78,813
8. Lufthansa, 75,438
9. Air France, 74,598
10. US Airways, 66,389

Source: *World Air Transport Statistics*, (annual), International Air Transport Association, 1999, p. 47.

★234★
TOP MEMBERS OF THE INTERNATIONAL AIR TRANSPORT ASSOCIATION BY TOTAL SCHEDULED FREIGHT TONNES CARRIED, 1998
Ranked by: Total scheduled freight tonnes carried, in thousands. **Number listed:** 50

1. Federal Express, with 4,651 thousand
2. United Parcel Service, 2,845
3. Lufthansa, 1,062
4. Korean Air Lines, 1,033
5. Air France, 943
6. Japan Airlines, 870
7. Singapore Airlines, 753
8. United Airlines, 668
9. British Airways, 662
10. Cathay Pacific, 580

Source: *World Air Transport Statistics*, (annual), International Air Transport Association, 1999, p. 46.

Air Travel

★235★
TOP DOMESTIC AIRLINE MARKETS, 1997
Ranked by: Number of passengers, outbound plus inbound, in thousands. **Number listed:** 30

1. New York/Los Angeles, with 3,725 thousand
2. New York/Miami, 3,093
3. New York/Chicago, 2,980
4. New York/Boston, 2,689
5. Honolulu/Kahului, Maui, 2,620
6. New York/San Francisco, 2,609
7. New York/Orlando, 2,454
8. New York/Washington, 2,398
9. Dallas/Fort Worth/Houston, 2,219
10. Los Angeles/Las Vegas, 2,111

Source: *Air Transport*, (annual), Air Transport Association, 1998, p. 13.

Airlines

★236★
MOST ADMIRED AIRLINES, 1998
Ranked by: Scores (1-10) derived from a survey of survey of senior executives, outside directors and securities analysts. **Remarks:** Respondents rated companies in their own industry on 8 attributes of reputation. Also notes previous year's rank. **Number listed:** 10

1. Southwest Airlines, with 7.21 points
2. AMR, 6.87
3. Continental Airlines, 6.72
4. UAL, 6.36
5. Alaska Air Group, 5.91
5. Delta Air Lines, 5.91
7. US Airways Group, 5.83
8. Northwest Airlines, 4.98
9. America West Holdings, 4.9
10. Trans World Airlines, 4.53

Source: *Fortune*, America's Most Admired Corporations (annual), March 1, 1999, p. F2.

★237★
TOP AIRLINE COMPANIES BY REVENUE, 1998
Ranked by: Revenue, in millions of dollars. **Remarks:** Also includes profit and investment figures as well as number of employees. **Number listed:** 10

1. American Airlines, with $19,205 million
2. United Airlines, $17,561
3. Delta Airlines, $14,138
4. Northwest Airlines, $9,045
5. US Airways Group, $8,688
6. Continental Airlines, $7,951
7. Southwest Airlines, $4,164
8. Trans World Airlines, $3,259
9. America West Holdings, $2,032
10. Alaska Air Group, $1,898

Source: *Fortune*, Fortune 500 Largest U.S. Corporations (annual), April 26, 1999, p. F-52.

★238★
TOP AIRLINES BY AVAILABLE SEAT MILES, 1998
Ranked by: Available seat miles, in thousands. **Number listed:** 10

1. UAL Corp., with 173,890,760 thousand
2. AMR Corp., 155,217,721
3. Delta Airlines, 142,154,000
4. Northwest Airlines, 91,310,675
5. Continental Airlines, 74,727,000
6. US Airways, 56,723,000
7. Southwest Airlines, 47,543,515
8. Trans World Airlines, 34,641,162
9. America West Holdings, 24,307,000
10. Alaska Air Group, 16,807,000

Source: *Business Travel News*, Business Travel Survey (annual), May 31, 1999, p. 36.

★239★
TOP AIRLINES BY NET PROFIT, 1998
Ranked by: Net profits, in thousands of dollars. **Number listed:** 10

1. AMR Corp., with $1,314,000 thousand
2. UAL Corp., $1,310,000
3. Delta Airlines, $1,100,000
4. US Airways, $538,000
5. Southwest Airlines, $433,431
6. Continental Airlines, $383,000
7. Comair, $128,769
8. Alaska Air Group, $124,400
9. America West Holdings, $108,571
10. Atlantic Southeast, $66,137

Source: *Business Travel News*, Business Travel Survey (annual), May 31, 1999, p. 36.

★240★
TOP AIRLINES BY NUMBER OF PASSENGERS, 1997
Ranked by: Number of passengers, in thousands. **Number listed:** 25

1. Delta Airlines, with 103,133 thousand
2. United Airlines, 84,203
3. American Airlines, 81,083
4. US Airways, 58,659
5. Southwest Airlines, 55,946
6. Northwest Airlines, 54,650
7. Continental Airlines, 38,756
8. Trans World Airlines, 23,370

9. America West Holdings, 18,294
10. Alaska Air Group, 12,245

Source: *Air Transport World*, (annual), Air Transport Association, 1999, p. 15.

★241★
TOP AIRLINES BY REVENUE PASSENGER MILES, 1998
Ranked by: Revenue passenger miles, in billions. **Number listed:** 10

1. United Airlines, with 123.3 billion
2. American Airlines, 108.3
3. Delta Airlines, 102.6
4. Northwest Airlines, 67.6
5. Continental Airlines, 49.7
6. US Airways, 41.1
7. Southwest Airlines, 29.7
8. Trans World Airlines, 25
9. America West Holdings, 16.2
10. Alaska Air Group, 11

Source: *Aviation Week & Space Technology*, January 18, 1999, p. 50.

★242★
TOP AIRLINES BY REVENUE PASSENGER MILES, 1997
Ranked by: Revenue passenger miles, in millions. **Number listed:** 25

1. United Airlines, with 121,350 million
2. American Airlines, 106,936
3. Delta Airlines, 99,624
4. Northwest Airlines, 71,998
5. Continental Airlines, 44,072
6. US Airways, 41,578
7. Southwest Airlines, 28,359
8. Trans World Airlines, 25,099
9. America West Holdings, 16,171
10. Alaska Air Group, 10,362

Source: *Air Transport World*, (annual), Air Transport Association, 1999, p. 15.

★243★
TOP AIRLINES BY SALES, 1999
Ranked by: Total sales, in billions of dollars. **Remarks:** Also notes parent company and location, lead advertising agency and media expenditures. **Number listed:** 10

1. American Airlines, with $19 billion
2. United Airlines, $17
3. Delta Airlines, $14
4. Northwest Airlines, $9
4. US Airways, $9
6. Continental Airlines, $8
7. Southwest Airlines, $4
8. Trans World Airlines, $3
9. America West Holdings, $2
10. Alaska Air Group, $2

Source: *Brandweek*, Superbrands: America's Top 2,000 Brands (annual), June 21, 1999, p. S70.

★244★
TOP AIRLINES BY TOTAL OPERATING REVENUE, 1997
Ranked by: Total operating revenues, in millions of dollars. **Number listed:** 25

1. United Airlines, with $17,335 million
2. American Airlines, $15,856
3. Delta Airlines, $14,204
4. Federal Express, $12,730
5. Northwest Airlines, $9,984
6. US Airways, $8,501
7. Continental Airlines, $6,361
8. Southwest Airlines, $3,817
9. Trans World Airlines, $3,328
10. America West Holdings, $1,887

Source: *Air Transport World*, (annual), Air Transport Association, 1999, p. 15.

★245★
TOP AIRLINES WEB SITES, 1999
Ranked by: Number of unique visitors in a given month, in thousands. **Number listed:** 10

1. Southwest Airlines, with 1,903 thousand
2. American Airlines, 1,635
3. Delta Airlines, 1,299
4. United Airlines, 1,130
5. Northwest Airlines, 1,100
6. Continental Airlines, 967
7. US Airways, 871
8. Trans World Airlines, 568
9. America West Airlines, 384
10. AirTran Airways, 222

Source: *Mediaweek*, May 17, 1999, p. 60.

★246★
TOP IATA AIRLINES BY DOMESTIC SCHEDULED FREIGHT TONNES CARRIED,1998
Ranked by: Domestic scheduled freight tonnes carried, in thousands. **Number listed:** 50

1. Federal Express, with 3,520 thousand
2. United Parcel Service, 2,483
3. All Nippon Airways Co. Ltd., 392
4. Japan Airlines, 327
5. United Airlines, 313
6. Delta Airlines, 290
7. Korean Airlines, 239
8. China Southern Airlines, 236
9. Northwest Airlines, 219
10. American Airlines, 218

Source: *World Air Transportation Statistics*, (annual), International Air Transport Association, 1999, p. 46.

★247★
TOP IATA AIRLINES BY SCHEDULED PASSENGER-KILOMETERS FLOWN,1998
Ranked by: Scheduled passenger-kilometers flown, in millions. **Number listed:** 50

1. Delta Airlines, with 126,266 million
2. United Airlines, 125,251
3. American Airlines, 116,961
4. Northwest Airlines, 59,083
5. US Airways, 59,058
6. Continental Airlines, 57,049
7. All Nippon Airlines, 33,732
8. Trans World Airlines, 31,819
9. America West Airlines, 25,512
10. Japan Airlines, 16,796

Source: *World Air Transportation Statistics*, (annual), International Air Transport Association, 1999, p. 47.

★248★
TOP IATA DOMESTIC AIRLINES, 1998
Ranked by: Scheduled domestic passengers carried, in thousands. **Number listed:** 50

1. Delta Airlines, with 97,948 thousand
2. United Airlines, 75,302
3. American Airlines, 64,151
4. US Airways, 56,310
5. Northwest Airlines, 41,921
6. All Nippon Airlines, 38,075
7. Continental Airlines, 34,789

8. Trans World Airlines, 22,606
9. Japan Airlines, 20,204
10. Japan Air System, 19,174

Source: *World Air Transportation Statistics*, (annual), International Air Transport Association, 1999, p. 45.

★249★
TOP U.S. AIRLINES BY REVENUE, 1998
Ranked by: Revenue, in thousands of dollars. **Number listed:** 10

1. UAL Corp., with $17,600,000 thousand
2. AMR Corp., $17,449,000
3. Delta Airlines, $14,402,000
4. Northwest Airlines, $9,044,800
5. US Airways, $8,556,000
6. Continental Airlines, $7,951,000
7. Southwest Airlines, $4,163,980
8. Trans World Airlines, $3,259,147
9. America West Holdings, $2,023,284
10. Alaska Air Group, $1,566,300

Source: *Business Travel News*, Business Travel Survey (annual), May 31, 1999, p. 36.

★250★
TOP U.S. AIRLINES BY REVENUE PASSENGER MILES, 1998
Ranked by: Revenue passenger miles, in thousands of dollars. **Number listed:** 10

1. UAL Corp., with $124,500,000 thousand
2. AMR Corp., $108,898,345
3. Delta Airlines, $103,342,000
4. Northwest Airlines, $66,738,274
5. Continental Airlines, $53,910,000
6. US Airways, $41,253,000
7. Southwest Airlines, $31,419,110
8. Trans World Airlines, $24,488,021
9. America West Holdings, $16,374,000
10. Alaska Air Group, $11,283,000

Source: *Business Travel News*, Business Travel Survey (annual), May 31, 1999, p. 36.

Airlines--Asia

★251★
MOST ADMIRED AIRLINES IN ASIA, 1999
Ranked by: Scores (1-10) derived from a survey of chief executives and corporate board members. **Remarks:** Respondents rated companies in 8 attributes including quality of management, products and services, contribution to the local economy, being a good employer, potential for growth, being honest and ethical, potential for future profit, and ability to cope with the changing economic environment. Also notes previous year's score and overall rank **Number listed:** 10

1. Singapore Airlines, with 8.84 points
2. KLM, 7.65
3. British Airways, 7.18
4. Cathay Pacific, 7.07
5. Swiss Air, 6.89
6. Thai Airways, 6.75
7. All Nippon, 6.48
8. Lufthansa, 6.42
9. United Airlines, 6.31
10. Qantas, 6.29

Source: *Asian Business*, May, 1999, p. 28.

Airlines--Detroit Metropolitan Area

★252★
TOP AIRLINES SERVING THE DETROIT AREA, 1997
Ranked by: Total passengers boarded. **Remarks:** Also notes contact information, number domestic and international passengers, number of local employees, tons of enplaned mail and cargo and previous year's figures. **Number listed:** 12

1. Northwest Airlines, with 11,209,935
2. Mesaba Airlines, 762,563
3. Southwest Airlines, 445,727
4. American Airlines, 445,092
5. United Airlines, 356,562
6. Delta Airlines, 354,494
7. US Airways, 266,362
8. Continental Airlines, 258,748
9. Trans World Airlines, 236,587
10. American Trans Air, 180,386

Source: *Crain's Detroit Business*, August 17, 1998, p. 13.

Airlines--Florida

★253★
TOP AIRLINES SERVING FLORIDA, 1997
Ranked by: Total number of enplanements. **Remarks:** Also notes number of Florida cities served, number of full-time Florida employees, primary hubs, senior Florida executive and contact information. **Number listed:** 19

1. Delta Airlines, with 11,112,692 enplanements
2. American Airlines, 9,955,700
3. US Airways & US Airways Express, 7,680,358
4. Northwest Airlines, 2,569,302
5. Southwest Airlines, 2,300,000
6. United Airlines, 2,240,000
7. American Eagle, 1,469,220
8. Trans World Airlines, 1,275,197
9. Kiwi International, 1,000,000
10. American Trans Air, 900,000

Source: *Florida Trend*, TopRank Florida (annual), 1998, p. 51.

Airlines--Food Service

★254★
LEADING AIRPORT/AIRLINE FOODSERVICE PROVIDERS, 1997
Ranked by: Food and beverage sales, in millions of dollars. **Remarks:** Also notes number of contracts or sites and number of production kitchens. **Number listed:** 6

1. LSG-Sky Chefs (TX), with $1,602.8 million
2. Dobbs International Services (TN), $800
3. Host Marriott Services Corp. (MD), $269.3
4. CA One (NY), $184
5. Anton Airfood, $30
6. United Airlines, $20

Source: *Restaurants and Institutions*, September 15, 1998, p. 90.

Airlines, International

★255★
LARGEST AIRLINES WORLDWIDE BY INTERNATIONAL PASSENGER-KILOMETERS FLOWN,1998
Ranked by: Scheduled international passenger-kilometers flown, in millions. **Number listed:** 50
1. British Airways, with 112,365 million
2. United Airlines, 75,170
3. Lufthansa, 70,051
4. Air France, 65,955
5. Japan Airlines, 62,018
6. American Airlines, 58,288
7. Singapore Airlines, 57,737
8. KLM, 57,271
9. Northwest Airlines, 48,319
10. Qantas Airways, 42,731

Source: *World Air Transportation Statistics*, (annual), International Air Transport Association, 1999, p. 47.

★256★
LARGEST AIRLINES WORLDWIDE BY INTERNATIONAL SCHEDULED FREIGHT TONNES CARRIED,1998
Ranked by: International scheduled freight tonnes carried, in thousands. **Number listed:** 50
1. Federal Express, with 1,131 thousand
2. Lufthansa, 1,004
3. Air France, 907
4. Korean Airlines, 795
5. Singapore Airlines, 753
6. British Airways, 656
7. Cathay Pacific, 580
8. Japan Airlines, 543
9. KLM, 537
10. EAT, 424

Source: *World Air Transportation Statistics*, (annual), International Air Transport Association, 1999, p. 46.

★257★
LARGEST AIRLINES WORLDWIDE BY INTERNATIONAL SCHEDULED PASSENGERS CARRIED, 1998
Ranked by: Scheduled international passengers carried, in thousands. **Number listed:** 50
1. British Airways, with 30,092 thousand
2. Lufthansa, 24,752
3. Air France, 18,190
4. American Airlines, 17,301
5. KLM, 14,920
6. SAS, 12,482
7. Singapore Airlines, 12,329
8. United Airlines, 11,498
9. Japan Airlines, 11,158
10. Swiss Air, 10,959

Source: *World Air Transportation Statistics*, (annual), International Air Transport Association, 1999, p. 45.

★258★
WORLD'S LARGEST AIRLINE COMPANIES BY REVENUE, 1997
Ranked by: Revenue, in millions of dollars. **Remarks:** Also notes profits, profits as a percent of revenue and profits as a percent of assets. **Number listed:** 9
1. American Airlines (U.S.), with $18,570 million
2. United Airlines (U.S.), $17,378
3. British Airways (Great Britain), $14,191
4. Delta Air Lines (U.S.), $13,590
5. Lufthansa Group (Germany), $13,354
6. Japan Airlines (Japan), $12,884
7. Northwest Airlines (U.S.), $10,226
8. Air France Group (France), $10,186
9. Sepi (Spain), $9,916

Source: *Fortune*, The Global 500: World's Biggest Corporations (annual), August 3, 1998, p. F-15.

★259★
WORLD'S LEADING AIRLINES BY FLEET SIZE, 1997
Ranked by: Number of aircraft. **Number listed:** 25
1. American Airlines, with 641 thousand
2. Federal Express, 616
3. United Airlines, 575
4. Delta Airlines, 559
5. Northwest Airlines, 406
6. US Airways Group, 352
7. Continental Airlines, 327
8. British Airways, 268
9. Southwest Airlines, 261
10. Lufthansa, 217

Source: *Air Transport World*, Top 25 Airlines (annual), July, 1998, p. 63.

★260★
WORLD'S LEADING AIRLINES BY FREIGHT TONNE-KILOMETERS, 1997
Ranked by: Freight tonne-kilometers, in thousands. **Number listed:** 25
1. Federal Express, with $9,306,211 thousand
2. Lufthansa Cargo, $6,548,000
3. Korean Airlines, $5,718,702
4. United Parcel Service, $5,376,491
5. Air France, $5,011,000
6. Singapore Airlines, $4,760,144
7. Japan Airlines, $4,174,350
8. KLM, $3,860,642
9. Cathay Pacific, $3,567,253
10. Northwest Airlines, $3,332,888

Source: *Air Transport World*, Top 25 Airlines (annual), July, 1998, p. 63.

★261★
WORLD'S LEADING AIRLINES BY NET PROFIT, 1997
Ranked by: Net profit, in thousands. **Number listed:** 25
1. American Airlines, with $1,303,000 thousand
2. KLM, $1,102,000
3. US Airways Group, $1,025,000
4. British Airways, $962,800
5. UAL Corp., $949,000
6. Delta Airlines, $934,000
7. Northwest Airlines, $596,500
8. Singapore Airlines, $569,200
9. Lufthansa, $464,000
10. Federal Express, $458,197

Source: *Air Transport World*, Top 25 Airlines (annual), July, 1998, p. 63.

★262★
WORLD'S LEADING AIRLINES BY NUMBER OF EMPLOYEES, 1997
Ranked by: Number of employees, in thousands. **Number listed:** 25
1. Federal Express, with 94,000 thousand
2. United Airlines, 91,779
3. American Airlines, 90,600
4. Delta Airlines, 65,454
5. British Airways, 53,060

6. Northwest Airlines, 50,000
7. Lufthansa, 45,000
8. Continental Airlines, 40,000
9. Air France, 38,800
10. US Airways Group, 38,500

Source: *Air Transport World*, Top 25 Airlines (annual), July, 1998, p. 63.

★263★
WORLD'S LEADING AIRLINES BY NUMBER OF PASSENGERS, 1997
Ranked by: Number of passengers, in thousands. **Number listed:** 25

1. Delta Airlines, with $103,295 thousand
2. United Airlines, $84,245
3. American Airlines, $81,139
4. US Airways Group, $58,659
5. Northwest Airlines, $54,650
6. Southwest Airlines, $50,400
7. Continental Airlines, $41,210
8. All Nippon, $40,697
9. British Airways, $34,159
10. Lufthansa, $33,340

Source: *Air Transport World*, Top 25 Airlines (annual), July, 1998, p. 63.

★264★
WORLD'S LEADING AIRLINES BY OPERATING PROFIT, 1997
Ranked by: Operating profit, in thousands. **Number listed:** 25

1. Delta Airlines, with $1,628,000 thousand
2. American Airlines, $1,560,000
3. UAL Corp., $1,259,000
4. Northwest Airlines, $1,157,000
5. Federal Express, $901,060
6. British Airways, $836,640
7. Continental Airlines, $716,000
8. US Airways Group, $584,000
9. Southwest Airlines, $524,326
10. Singapore Airlines, $467,000

Source: *Air Transport World*, Top 25 Airlines (annual), July, 1998, p. 63.

★265★
WORLD'S LEADING AIRLINES BY OPERATING REVENUE, 1997
Ranked by: Operating revenue, in thousands. **Number listed:** 25

1. UAL Corp., with $17,378,000 thousand
2. American Airlines, $16,903,000
3. British Airways, $14,342,000
4. Delta Airlines, $13,946,000
5. Lufthansa, $12,800,000
6. Federal Express, $12,730,235
7. Northwest Airlines, $10,226,000
8. Air France, $9,772,700
9. Japan Airlines, $9,603,984
10. US Airways Group, $8,514,000

Source: *Air Transport World*, Top 25 Airlines (annual), July, 1998, p. 63.

★266★
WORLD'S LEADING AIRLINES BY REVENUE PASSENGER KILOMETERS, 1997
Ranked by: Revenue passenger kilometers, in millions. **Number listed:** 25

1. United Airlines, with 195,372 million
2. American Airlines, 172,166
3. Delta Airlines, 160,398
4. Northwest Airlines, 115,898
5. British Airways, 98,405
6. Japan Airlines, 79,063
7. Continental Airlines, 77,081
8. Lufthansa, 68,267
9. US Airways, 66,901
10. Air France, 63,182

Source: *Air Transport World*, Top 25 Airlines (annual), July, 1998, p. 63.

Airlines--Los Angeles County (CA)

★267★
BUSIEST AIRLINES SERVING LOS ANGELES COUNTY, 1997
Ranked by: Number of passengers carried. **Remarks:** Also notes previous year's figures, market share, headquarters, top local executives and contact information. **Number listed:** 25

1. United Airlines, with 14,742,841
2. Southwest Airlines, 9,242,491
3. Delta Airlines, 6,245,958
4. American Airlines, 5,848,448
5. Northwest Airlines, 2,453,453
6. Alaska Airlines, 2,192,017
7. Continental Airlines, 2,023,605
8. America West Airlines, 2,014,584
9. US Airways, 1,462,886
10. Skywest, 1,244,582

Source: *Los Angeles Business Journal*, Book of Lists (annual), 1999, p. 94.

Airlines--New York (NY)

★268★
NEW YORK'S BUSIEST AIRLINES, 1997-1998
Ranked by: Total passenger arrivals and departures. **Remarks:** Combined results at JFK, La Guardia and Newark airports. **Number listed:** 50

1. Continental Airlines, with 15,948,237
2. American Airlines, 11,973,518
3. Delta Airlines, 9,460,552
4. United Airlines, 5,899,645
5. US Airways, 5,009,064
6. Trans World Airlines, 4,498,990
7. Northwest Airlines, 2,723,715
8. Delta Shuttle, 2,056,729
9. Continental Express, 1,981,668
10. British Airways, 1,509,207

Source: *Crain's New York Business*, 1999, p. 34.

Airplanes, Jet

★269★
TOP ADVERTISING AGENCIES IN SYRIA, 1998
Ranked by: Gross income, in thousands of U.S. dollars ($). **Remarks:** Also notes percent change from previous year and volume. **Number listed:** 3

1. TMI (JWT), with $961 thousand
2. Intermarkets Syria, $275

3. Publi-Graphics Group, $108

Source: *Advertising Age*, Agency Report (annual), April 19, 1999, p. S38.

Airports

★270★
AIRPORT CARGO TRAFFIC IN U.S. AIRPORTS, 1997
Ranked by: Metric tons of cargo, in thousands. **Number listed:** 20

1. Memphis, with 2,233 thousand tons
2. Los Angeles, 1,873
3. Miami, 1,766
4. New York Kennedy, 1,668
5. Chicago O'Hare, 1,407
6. Louisville, 1,346
7. Anchorage, 1,260
8. Newark, 1,043
9. Atlanta, 865
10. Dayton, 813

Source: *Air Transport World*, (annual), Air Transport Association, 1999, p. 19.

★271★
TOP U.S. AIRPORTS BY DEPARTING PASSENGERS
Ranked by: Number of departing passengers. **Number listed:** 25

1. Hartsfield International, Atlanta, with 32,676,994 passengers
2. O'Hare International, Chicago, 31,122,795
3. Dallas/Ft. Worth International, 27,255,967
4. Los Angeles International, 22,595,903
5. San Francisco International, 16,857,888
6. Denver International, 16,005,647
7. Wayne County, Detroit, 14,773,407
8. Phoenix Sky Harbor International, 14,650,380
9. McCarran International, Las Vegas, 14,011,012
10. Lambert-St. Louis Municipal, 13,955,770

Source: *Philadelphia Business Journal*, July 31, 1998, p. 14.

★272★
TOP U.S. AIRPORTS, 1997
Ranked by: Total number of passengers, arriving and departing, in thousands. **Number listed:** 20

1. Chicago O'Hare, with 70,385 thousand
2. Atlanta, 68,206
3. Dallas/Ft. Worth, 60,489
4. Los Angeles, 60,143
5. San Francisco, 40,494
6. Denver, 34,969
7. Miami, 34,533
8. Detroit, 31,542
9. New York Kennedy, 31,355
10. Newark, 30,916

Source: *Air Transport World*, (annual), Air Transport Association, 1999, p. 19.

Airports--Florida

★273★
TOP AIRPORTS IN FLORIDA, 1998
Ranked by: Number of commercial passengers. **Remarks:** Also includes contact information, number of gates, airport code, year opened governing body, and director. **Number listed:** 20

1. Miami International Airport, with 34,533,268 passengers
2. Orlando International Airport, 27,305,149
3. Tampa International Airport, 13,370,630
4. Fort Lauderdale-Hollywood International Airport, 12,277,411
5. Palm Beach International Airport, 5,820,869
6. Southwest Florida International Airport, 4,447,865
7. Jacksonville International Airport, 4,300,000
8. Sarasota Bradenton International Airport, 1,631,214
9. Pensacola Regional Airport, 1,159,368
10. Orlando Sanford Airport, 1,034,584

Source: *Florida Trend*, TopRank Florida (annual), 1999, p. 100.

Airports--North America

★274★
TOP NORTH AMERICAN AIRPORTS, 1997
Ranked by: Total number of passengers. **Remarks:** Also notes percent change from previous year. **Number listed:** 50

1. Chicago (ORD), with 70,385,073 passengers
2. Atlanta (ATL), 68,205,769
3. Dallas/Ft. Worth (DFW), 60,488,713
4. Los Angeles (LAX), 60,142,588
5. San Francisco (SFO), 40,493,959
6. Denver (DEN), 34,969,021
7. Miami (MIA), 34,533,268
8. Detroit (DTW), 31,541,650
9. New York (JFK), 31,355,268
10. Newark (EWR), 30,915,587

Source: *Travel Industry World Yearbook: The Big Picture*, (annual), Child & Waters, Inc., 1998, p. 163.

Airports--Western States

★275★
AIRPORT CARGO TRAFFIC IN THE WESTERN STATES, 1997
Ranked by: Metric tons of cargo. **Remarks:** Also notes world rank and percent change from previous year. **Number listed:** 11

1. Los Angeles (CA), with 1,872,862 metric tons
2. Anchorage (AK), 1,259,827
3. San Francisco (CA), 780,029
4. Oakland (CA), 678,083
5. Honolulu (HI), 500,830
6. Denver (CO), 437,203
7. Ontario (CA), 418,804
8. Seattle (WA), 393,786
9. Phoenix (AZ), 314,860
10. Vancouver (BC), 260,773

Source: *Air Cargo World*, February, 1999, p. 28.

All Terrain Vehicles

★276★
TOP STATES FOR ALL TERRAIN VEHICLE RETAIL SALES, 1997
Ranked by: Also notes ten largest growth states for ATVs. **Number listed:** 20
1. Texas
2. North Carolina
3. Louisiana
4. Kentucky
5. Arkansas
6. Mississippi
7. Pennsylvania
8. Georgia
9. Tennessee
10. Michigan

Source: *Agri Marketing*, February, 1999, p. 46.

Allergy

★277★
BEST SELLING ALLERGY AND SINUS REMEDIES, 1998
Ranked by: Sales, in millions of dollars. **Remarks:** Also notes unit sales. **Number listed:** 10
1. Tylenol, with $257.3 million
2. Robitussin, $206.7
3. Benadryl, $165.2
4. Sudafed, $161.7
5. Nyquil, $136.6
6. Alka-Seltzer, $119.7
7. Dimetapp, $92.4
8. Theraflu, $57.4
9. F 44, $57.3
10. Triaminic, $55.8

Source: *MMR*, May 3, 1999, p. 50.

American Stock Exchange

★278★
BEST PERFORMING AMEX COMPANIES BY INCREASE IN STOCK PRICE, 1998
Ranked by: Percent increase in stock price. **Remarks:** Also notes closing stock price and net change. **Number listed:** 10
1. Alba-Waldensian, with 723.1%
2. Price Communications, 372.2%
3. InfoCure, 249.3%
4. Westower, 210.6%
5. Softnet Systems, 164.7%
6. FFP Marketing, 160%
7. Jan Bell Marketing, 157.5%
8. Envirotest Systems, 138.9%
9. Audio Book, 138.5%
10. Stillwater Mining, 137%

Source: *Barron's*, January 4, 1999, p. 30.

★279★
FASTEST GROWING AMEX COMPANIES, 1998
Ranked by: Five-year annual EPS growth, in percent. **Remarks:** Also lists stock symbol, recent share price, last 12 month's EPS, industry and headquarters location. **Number listed:** 35
1. Pre-Paid Legal Services, with 94%
2. Balchem Corp., 82%
3. Thermo Cardiosystems Inc., 75%
4. Alliance Bancorp of Nebraska, 61%
5. Thermo Ecotek Corp., 59%
6. PMC Financial Corp., 53%
7. Gencor Industries Inc., 52%
8. Top Air Manufacturing, 48%
9. Diodes Inc., 46%
10. Premier Bancshares, 45%

Source: *Equities*, July/August, 1998, p. 39.

★280★
LARGEST COMPANIES ON THE AMEX, 1998
Ranked by: Market value, in millions of dollars. **Remarks:** Also notes total assets, revenues, income and earnings for latest 12 months, return on equity, book value and industry. **Number listed:** 100
1. Viacom Inc., with $25,739.6 million
2. British-American Tobacco PLC, $13,746.3
3. Cablevision Systems Corp., $7,564
4. Imperial Oil Ltd., $6,998.4
5. Hasbro, Inc., $4,725.8
6. Starwood Financial Trust, $4,716.7
7. Forest Laboratories, $4,338.1
8. Untied States Cellular Corp., $3,320.6
9. Keane, Inc., $2,800.3
10. Telephone & Data Systems, Inc., $2,748.5

Source: *Equities*, AMEX 100 (annual), January/February, 1999, p. 10.

★281★
LARGEST LISTED COMPANIES ON THE AMEX, 1997
Ranked by: Market value, in millions of dollars. **Number listed:** 20
1. B.A.T. Industries, with $29,122.1 million
2. Viacom Inc., $14,596.8
3. Imperial Oil, $9,690
4. EdperBrascan Corp., $5,062.8
5. Hasbro, Inc., $4,218.5
6. Thermo Instrument Systems Inc., $4,188.4
7. Nabors Industries, $3,188.9
8. Canadian Occidental Petroleum, $3,090.8
9. First Empire State Corp., $3,068.1
10. Keane, Inc., $2,675.5

Source: *SSB Guide to World Equity Markets*, (annual), Euromoney Publications, 1998, p. 537.

★282★
MOST ACTIVE OPTIONS BY TOTAL CONTRACTS TRADED, 1997
Ranked by: Number of contracts traded. **Remarks:** Also notes stock symbol and daily average. **Number listed:** 50
1. Intel Corp., with 14,358,643 contracts
2. Philip Morris, 4,822,699
3. Telecommunications Brasileiras S.A., 4,190,379
4. Motorola, 2,543,936
5. Office Depot, 2,455,737
6. Ascend Communications, 2,274,814
7. Chase Manhattan Corp., 1,871,212
8. Morgan Stanley High Technology 35 Index, 1,759,454
9. Iomega Corp., 1,707,381
10. Seagate Technology, 1,370,060

Source: *American Stock Exchange Fact Book*, (annual), American Stock Exchange, 1998, p. 40.

★283★
MOST ACTIVELY TRADED ISSUES ON THE AMEX, 1997
Ranked by: Trading volume, in millions of shares. **Number listed:** 20
1. Standard & Poor's Depository Receipts, with 801.4 million
2. Viacom Inc., 223.1
3. Trans World Airlines, 222.8
4. Harken Energy Corp., 214.5
5. Echo Bay Mines, 188.7
6. JTS Corp., 177
7. Nabors Industries, 172.9
8. Hasbro, Inc., 159.1
9. Royal Oak Mines, Inc., 140.9
10. Grey Wolf Industries, 132.9

Source: *SSB Guide to World Equity Markets*, (annual), Euromoney Publications, 1998, p. 538.

★284★
TOP AMEX LEADERS BY MARKET VALUE, 1997
Ranked by: Market value, in millions of dollars. **Number listed:** 10
1. B.A.T. Industries, with $29,122 million
2. Viacom Inc., $14,597
3. Imperial Oil Ltd., $9,690
4. EdperBrascan Corp., $5,063
5. Hasbro, Inc., $4,219
6. Thermo Instrument Systems Inc., $4,188
7. Nabors Industries, Inc., $3,189
8. Canadian Occidental Petroleum Ltd., $3,091
9. First Empire State Corp., $3.068
10. Keane, Inc., $2,675

Source: *American Stock Exchange Fact Book*, (annual), American Stock Exchange, 1998, p. 2.

★285★
TOP AMEX LEADERS BY NET INCOME, 1997
Ranked by: Net income, in millions of dollars. **Number listed:** 10
1. B.A.T. Industries, with $2,272 million
2. Imperial Oil Ltd., $558
3. Hasbro, Inc., $215
4. EdperBrascan Corp., $198
5. First Empire State Corp., $176
6. FINA, Inc., $161
7. Courtaulds PLC, $158
8. Tubos de Acero De Mexico, $155
9. Thermo Instrument Systems Inc., $141
10. BHC Communications, Inc., $125

Source: *American Stock Exchange Fact Book*, (annual), American Stock Exchange, 1998, p. 2.

★286★
TOP AMEX LEADERS BY PRICE GAIN, 1997
Ranked by: Percent price gain. **Remarks:** Also notes stock symbol. **Number listed:** 10
1. Cognitronics Corp., with 448.2%
2. Aerosonic Corp., 250%
3. Andrea Electronics Corp., 226.1%
4. General Employment Enterprises, Inc., 221.4%
5. Halter Marine Group, Inc., 215.0%
6. Cablevision Systems Corp., 212.7%
7. U.S.B. Holding Co., Inc., 210.6%
8. United Capital Corp., 202.9%
9. Virco Manufacturing Corp., 194.7%
10. ZEVEX International, Inc., 183%

Source: *American Stock Exchange Fact Book*, (annual), American Stock Exchange, 1998, p. 2.

★287★
TOP AMEX LEADERS BY SALES, 1997
Ranked by: Sales, in millions of dollars. **Number listed:** 10
1. B.A.T. Industries, with $38,249 million
2. Viacom Inc., $13,005
3. Imperial Oil Ltd., $6,966
4. EdperBrascan Corp., $4,907
5. Quebecor Inc., $4,841
6. FINA, Inc., $4,336
7. Giant Food, Inc., $4,022
8. NFC PLC, $3,887
9. The Turner Corp., $3,587
10. Courtaulds PLC, $3,392

Source: *American Stock Exchange Fact Book*, (annual), American Stock Exchange, 1998, p. 2.

★288★
TOP AMEX LEADERS BY SHARE VOLUME, 1997
Ranked by: Share volume, in millions of shares. **Remarks:** Also notes stock symbol. **Number listed:** 10
1. Viacom Inc., with 223.1 million shares
2. Trans World Airlines, 222.8
3. Harken Energy Corp., 214.5
4. Echo Bay Mines Ltd., 188.7
5. JTS Corp., 177
6. Nabors Industries, 172.9
7. Hasbro, Inc., 159.1
8. Royal Oak Mines, Inc., 140.6
9. Grey Wolf Industries, 132.9
10. IVAX Corp., 132.5

Source: *American Stock Exchange Fact Book*, (annual), American Stock Exchange, 1998, p. 2.

★289★
TOP AMEX LEADERS BY SHAREHOLDERS' EQUITY, 1997
Ranked by: Shareholders' equity, in millions of dollars. **Number listed:** 10
1. Viacom Inc., with $12,785 million
2. B.A.T. Industries, $9,294
3. Imperial Oil Ltd., $3,159
4. EdperBrascan Corp., $2,842
5. Telephone & Data Systems, Inc., $1,997
6. BHC Communications, Inc., $1,752
7. Hasbro, Inc., $1,635
8. United States Cellular Corp., $1,571
9. Wesco Financial Corp., $1,530
10. FINA, Inc., $1,298

Source: *American Stock Exchange Fact Book*, (annual), American Stock Exchange, 1998, p. 3.

★290★
TOP AMEX LEADERS BY SHARES OUTSTANDING, 1997
Ranked by: Shares outstanding, in millions of shares. **Remarks:** Also notes stock symbol. **Number listed:** 10
1. B.A.T. Industries, with 1,553 million shares
2. Courtaulds PLC, 407
3. Viacom Inc., 284
4. EdperBrascan Corp., 279
5. Hanover Direct, Inc., 200
6. The First Australia Prime Income Fund, Inc., 195
7. JTS Corp., 169
8. Grey Wolf Industries, 164
9. Imperial Oil Ltd., 152
10. Royal Oak Mines, Inc., 141

Source: *American Stock Exchange Fact Book*, (annual), American Stock Exchange, 1998, p. 2.

★291★
TOP AMEX LEADERS BY TOTAL ASSETS, 1997
Ranked by: Total assets, in millions of dollars. **Number listed:** 10
1. B.A.T. Industries, with $80,357 million
2. Viacom Inc., $29,054
3. First Empire State Corp., $13,675
4. EdperBrascan Corp., $7,289
5. Imperial Oil Ltd., $7,211
6. ARM Financial Group, Inc., $6,231
7. Quebecor Inc., $5,346
8. Cablevision Systems Corp., $4,873
9. Telephone & Data Systems, Inc., $4,661
10. MAXXAM Inc., $4,048

Source: *American Stock Exchange Fact Book*, (annual), American Stock Exchange, 1998, p. 3.

★292★
WORST PERFORMING AMEX COMPANIES BY INCREASE IN STOCK PRICE, 1998
Ranked by: Percent decrease in stock price. **Remarks:** Also notes closing stock price and net change. **Number listed:** 10
1. Oncor, with -97.3%
2. Phonetel Technologies, -96.3%
3. Millenia, -95.7%
4. Milestone Scientific, -93.2%
5. Cotton Value Resource, -92.5%
6. Saba Pete, -91.9%
7. Hondo Oil, -90.4%
8. NetMed, -90.3%
9. Strategia, -90.2%
10. Excel Maritime, -90%

Source: *Barron's*, January 4, 1999, p. 30.

Amman Financial Market

★293★
LARGEST LISTED COMPANIES ON THE AMMAN FINANCIAL MARKET, 1997
Ranked by: Market capitalization, in millions of Jordanian dinar (JD). **Remarks:** Ten largest accounted for 69.6% of total market capitalization. **Number listed:** 20
1. Arab Bank, with JD1,430 million
2. Arab Potash, JD517.4
3. Jordan Cement Factories, JD182.5
4. Jordan Phosphate Mines, JD136.2
5. The Housing Bank, JD130
6. Jordon National Bank, JD74.8
7. Jordan Petroleum Refinery, JD66.8
8. Cairo Amman Bank, JD54.8
9. Zara For Investment, JD52
10. Arab International Hotels, JD44.5

Source: *SSB Guide to World Equity Markets*, (annual), Euromoney Publications, 1998, p. 292.

★294★
MOST ACTIVELY TRADED SHARES ON THE AMMAN FINANCIAL MARKET, 1997
Ranked by: Value traded, in millions of Jordanian dinar (JD). **Number listed:** 20
1. Arab Bank, with JD69.1 million
2. Jordan Cement Factories, JD35.3
3. Jordan Kuwait Bank, JD26.3
4. The Housing Bank, JD81.8
5. Jordan National Bank, JD16.7
6. Jordan Electric Power, JD8.7
7. Arab Pharmaceutical Manufacturing, JD8.6
8. Jordan Phosphate Mines, JD8.1
9. Bank of Jordan, JD7.8
9. Arab Potash, JD7.8

Source: *SSB Guide to World Equity Markets*, (annual), Euromoney Publications, 1998, p. 293.

Amsterdam Stock Exchange

★295★
LARGEST LISTED COMPANIES ON THE AMSTERDAM STOCK EXCHANGE, 1997
Ranked by: Market value, in millions of guilders. **Number listed:** 20
1. Royal Dutch Petroleum Co., with f238,660 million
2. Unilever Cert, f80,021
2. Dordtsche Petroleum Mij, f80,021
4. ING Group Cert, f71,510
5. ABN AMRO Holding N.V., f56,260
6. Aegon, f52,603
7. Philips Electronics, f42,155
8. KPN, f39,951
9. Ahold, f27,628
10. AkzoNobel, f24,923

Source: *SSB Guide to World Equity Markets*, (annual), Euromoney Publications, 1998, p. 353.

Amusement Parks

★296★
TOP FLORIDA AMUSEMENT/THEME PARKS, 1997
Ranked by: Attendance. **Number listed:** 10
1. Magic Kingdom, (FL), with 17,000,000 attendees
2. Disneyland, (CA), 14,250,000
3. Epcot, (FL), 11,796,750
4. Disney-MGM Studios, (FL), 10,473,450
5. Universal Studios Florida, 8,900,000
6. Universal Studios Hollywood, (CA), 5,400,000
7. Sea World, (FL), 4,900,000
8. Busch Gardens, (FL), 4,200,000
9. Sea World, (CA), 3,990,000
10. Six Flags, (NJ), 3,700,000

Source: *Florida Trend*, September, 1998, p. 20.

Amusement Parks--Europe

★297★
TOP EUROPEAN AMUSEMENT/THEME PARKS, 1998
Ranked by: Attendance. **Number listed:** 10
1. Disneyland Paris (France), with 12,500,000 attendees
2. Blackpool Pleasure Beach (England), 6,600,000
3. Tivoli Gardens (Denmark), 2,766,000
4. De Efteling (Netherlands), 2,700,000
4. Port Aventura (Spain), 2,700,000
4. Gardaland (Italy), 2,700,000
4. Europa Park (Germany), 2,700,000
8. Liseberg (Sweden), 2,500,000

8. Alton Towers (England), 2,500,000
10. Phantasialand (Germany), 2,100,000

Source: *Amusement Business*, Amusement Business Annual Year-End Issue, December 28, 1998, p. 81.

Amusement Parks, International

★298★
TOP AMUSEMENT/THEME PARKS WORLDWIDE, 1998
Ranked by: Attendance. **Number listed:** 50

1. Tokyo Disneyland (Japan), with 16,686,000 attendees
2. Magic Kingdom at Walt Disney World (U.S.), 15,640,000
3. Disneyland (U.S.), 13,680,000
4. Disneyland Paris (France), 12,500,000
5. Epcot Center at Walt Disney World (U.S.), 10,596,750
6. Disney-MGM Studios Theme Park at Walt Disney World (U.S.), 9,473,750
7. Universal Studios Florida (U.S.), 8,900,000
8. Everland (South Korea), 7,326,000
9. Blackpool (England), 6,600,000
10. Disney's Animal Kingdom at Walt Disney World (U.S.), 6,000,000

Source: *Amusement Business*, Amusement Business Annual Year-End Issue, December 28, 1998, p. 84.

Amusement Parks--Latin America

★299★
TOP SOUTH/CENTRAL AMERICAN AMUSEMENT/ THEME PARKS,1998
Ranked by: Attendance. **Number listed:** 10

1. Chapultapec (Mexico), with 2,700,000 attendees
2. Playcenter (Brazil), 2,100,000
2. Reino Aventura (Mexico), 2,100,000
4. Beto Carrero (Brazil), 1,900,000
5. Selva Magica (Mexico), 1,800,000
6. Terra Encantada (Brazil), 1,600,000
7. Parque de la Costa (Argentina), 1,500,000
8. Parque de la Monica (Brazil), 1,200,000
9. Divertido (Mexico), 1,100,000
10. Parque du Gugu (Brazil), 720,000

Source: *Amusement Business*, Amusement Business Annual Year-End Issue, December 28, 1998, p. 86.

Amusement Parks--North America

★300★
TOP NORTH AMERICAN AMUSEMENT/THEME PARKS
Ranked by: Attendance. **Remarks:** Also includes previous year's rank, percent change and comments. **Number listed:** 50

1. Magic Kingdom at Walt Disney World (FL), with 15,640,000 attendees
2. Disneyland (CA), 13,680,000
3. Epcot Center at Walt Disney World (FL), 10,596,750
4. Disney-MGM Studios at Walt Disney World (FL), 9,473,750
5. Universal Studios Florida, 8,900,000
6. Disney's Animal Kingdom at Walt Disney World (FL), 6,000,000
7. Universal Studios Hollywood (CA), 5,100,000
8. SeaWorld Florida, 4,900,000
9. Busch Gardens Tampa Bay (FL), 4,200,000
10. SeaWorld California, 3,700,000

Source: *Amusement Business*, Amusement Business Annual Year-End Issue, December 28, 1998, p. 90+.

Amusement Parks--Pacific Region

★301★
TOP ASIA/PACIFIC RIM AMUSEMENT/THEME PARKS, 1998
Ranked by: Attendance. **Number listed:** 10

1. Tokyo Disneyland(Japan), with 16,686,000 attendees
2. Everland (South Korea), 7,326,000
3. Lotte World (Korea), 5,800,000
4. Yokohama (Japan), 5,737,000
5. Huis Ten Bosch (Japan), 4,130,000
6. Suzuka Circuit (Japan), 3,238,000
7. Nagashima Spa Land (Japan), 3,200,000
8. Kurashiki Tivoli Park (Japan), 2,986,000
9. Ocean Park (Hong Kong), 2,950,000
10. Seoul Land (South Korea), 2,800,000

Source: *Amusement Business*, Amusement Business Annual Year-End Issue, December 28, 1998, p. 80.

Analgesics

★302★
BEST SELLING INTERNAL ANALGESIC BRANDS, 1998
Ranked by: Total sales, in millions of dollars. **Remarks:** Also notes lead agency and media expenditures. **Number listed:** 5

1. Private Label, with $644 million
2. Tylenol, $541.8
3. Advil, $366.6
4. Aleve, $149.3
5. Excedrin, $125.4

Source: *Brand Week*, Superbrands: America's Top 2,000 Brands, June 21, 1999, p. S58.

Analysts, Security

See: **Financial Analysts**

Annuities

See also: **Variable Annuities**

★303★
LARGEST UNDERWRITERS OF INDIVIDUAL ANNUITIES SOLD THROUGH BANKS, 1998
Ranked by: Premiums, in millions of dollars. **Remarks:** Also notes previous year's figures. **Number listed:** 10

1. Hartford, with $3,808 million
2. American General Life Cos., $2,043
3. Nationwide, $2,035
4. Allstate, $1,014
5. Safeco, $964
6. Aegon, $706
7. Transamerica, $657
8. GE Companies, $653
9. Keyport, $643
10. American Skandia, $633

Source: *National Underwriter Life & Health*, April 19, 1999, p. 1.

Antacids

★304★
BEST SELLING INTERNAL ANTACIDS BY SALES, 1998
Ranked by: Total sales, in millions of dollars. **Remarks:** Also notes lead agency and media expenditures. **Number listed:** 5

1. Pepcid AC, with $224.6 million
2. Tums, $182
3. Private Label, $171.8
4. Zantac, $170.8
5. Mylanta, $132.7

Source: *Brand Week*, Superbrands: America's Top 2,000 Brands, June 21, 1999, p. S58.

Apartment Houses

★305★
LARGEST U.S. MULTIFAMILY MANAGERS BY NUMBER OF APARTMENTS MANAGED, 1999
Ranked by: Number of apartments managed. **Remarks:** Also notes headquarters location, CEO and previous year's figures. **Number listed:** 50

1. Apartment Investor & Management Co., with 347,692 apartments
2. Equity Residential Properties Trust, 201,665
3. Lincoln Property Co. - Residential, 103,395
4. Pinnacle Realty Management Co., 92,055
5. United Dominion Realty Trust, Inc., 83,034
6. Archstone Communities, 69,582
7. Camden Property Trust, 56,636
8. Sentinel Real Estate, 56,509
9. Conam Management Corp., 45,250
10. Avalonbay Communities, Inc., 44,724

Source: *National Real Estate Investor Supplement*, March, 1999, p. 4+.

★306★
LARGEST U.S. MULTIFAMILY OWNERS BY NUMBER OF APARTMENTS WITH OWNERSHIP INTEREST, 1999
Ranked by: Number of apartments with ownership interest. **Remarks:** Also notes headquarters location, CEO and previous year's figures. **Number listed:** 50

1. Apartment Investor & Management Co., with 223,329 apartments
2. Equity Residential Properties Trust, 192,558
3. Related Capital Co., 137,817
4. Boston Capital Partners, Inc., 95,741
5. United Dominion Realty Trust, Inc., 86,748
6. Boston Financial, 86,000
7. Archstone Communities, 69,582
8. Sunamerica Affordable Housing Partners, Inc., 67,000
9. Whitehall Real Estate, 66,297
10. Lefrak Organization, 62,000

Source: *National Re al Estate Investor Supplement*, March, 1999, p. 2+.

Apparel Industry

See: **Clothing Trade**

Apparel Stores

See: **Clothing Stores**

Appliances, Household

See: **Household Appliances**

Application Specific Integrated Circuits

★307★
TOP APPLICATION SPECIFIC CIRCUIT SUPPLIERS, 1998
Ranked by: Total sales, in millions of dollars. **Remarks:** Also notes other sales figures. **Number listed:** 10

1. Lucent Technologies, with $1,735 million
2. IBM Micro, $1,685
3. LSI Logic, $1,470
4. NEC, $1,255
5. Fujitsu, $715
6. Altera, $665
7. Texas Instruments, $655
8. Xilinx, $638
9. Toshiba, $560
10. VLSI Technology, $440

Source: *Electronic News*, January 18, 1999, p. 16.

Application Specific Integrated Circuits, International

★308★
TOP APPLICATION SPECIFIC CIRCUIT SUPPLIERS WORLDWIDE, 1997
Ranked by: Total sales, in millions of dollars. **Remarks:** Also notes market share. **Number listed:** 16

1. NEC, with $1,863 million
2. IBM, $1,541
3. Lucent Technologies, $1,486
4. Fujitsu, $1,248
5. LSI Logic, $1,182
6. Texas Instruments, $886
7. VLSI Technology, $667
8. Toshiba, $660
9. Altera, $631
10. Xilinx, $612

Source: *Electronic Business*, March, 1999, p. 76.

Architectural Firms

★309★
LARGEST ARCHITECTURAL/ENGINEERING FIRMS, 1997
Ranked by: Billings, in millions of dollars. **Remarks:** Also includes narrative profile of firms. **Number listed:** 60

1. Hellmuth, Obata & Kassabaum Inc., with $186 million
2. Ellerbe Becket, $68.2
3. Leo A. Daly, $63.7
4. SmithGroup, $59.16
5. DLR Group, $56.9
6. RTKL Associates Inc., $54.39
7. Perkins & Will, $53.42
8. HNTB Corp., $52.03
9. HKS Inc., $49.37
10. A. Epstein & Sons International Inc., $44.46

Source: *Building Design & Construction*, Design/Construct 300 (annual), July, 1998, p. 20+.

★310★
TOP ARCHITECTS IN COMMERCIAL, INDUSTRIAL AND INSTITUTIONAL BUILDING, 1997
Ranked by: Billings for design and planning services performed internally, in millions of dollars. **Remarks:** Also includes narrative profile of firms. **Number listed:** 50

1. Gensler, with $109.5 million
2. NBBJ, $59.4
3. The Hiller Group, $43.75
4. Thompson, Ventulett, Stainback & Associates, $27.7
5. Zimmer Gunsul Frasca Partnership, $26
6. Callison Architecture Inc., $24.1
7. Corgan Associates, $23.37
8. Smallwood, Reynolds, Stewart, Stewart & Associates, $22.37
9. VOA Associates, $20.47
10. Ehrlich-Rominger Architects, $20.07

Source: *Building Design & Construction*, Design/Construct 300 (annual), July, 1998, p. 12+.

★311★
TOP ARCHITECTURAL FIRMS DESIGNING HEALTHCARE FACILITIES, 1998
Ranked by: Firm fees, in thousands of dollars. **Remarks:** Also notes square feet of facilities, percent change from previous year, number of architects, number of engineers, and number of years in business. **Number listed:** 131

1. Design Group, with $278,400 thousand
2. NBBJ, $46,000
3. HLM Design, $45,700
4. HKS Architects, $42,720
5. HDR Architecture, $40,800
6. Perkins & Will, $40,370
7. Ellerbe Becket, $39,850
8. Gresham, Smith & Partners, $26,800
9. Earl Swensson Associates, $24,900
10. Cannon, $21,800

Source: *Modern Healthcare*, March 22, 1999, p. 24+.

★312★
TOP DESIGNERS/BUILDERS OF HEALTHCARE FACILITIES BY DOLLAR VOLUME, 1998
Ranked by: Dollar volume, in thousands of dollars. **Remarks:** Also notes square feet of facilities, percent change from previous year, number of architects, number of engineers, and number of years in business. **Number listed:** 12

1. Marshall Erdman & Associates, with $207,000 thousand
2. ADP Marshall, $203,500
3. HBE Corp., $187,800
4. Haskell Co., $80,200
5. BBL Medical Facilities, $44,000
6. Cooper Medical Buildings, $33,830
7. Summit Healthcare Facilities, $21,700
8. Simmonds Healthcare Facilities, $20,445
9. Commons Medical, $13,050
10. Monitor Builders, $10,500

Source: *Modern Healthcare*, March 22, 1999, p. 34.

Architectural Firms--Detroit Metropolitan Area

★313★
LARGEST ARCHITECTURAL FIRMS IN THE DETROIT METROPOLITAN AREA, 1997
Ranked by: Local revenue, in millions of dollars. **Remarks:** Also notes number of registered architects, staff, dollar value of projects, notable projects, local executives and contact information. **Number listed:** 25

1. SmithGroup, with $81.3 million
2. Giffels Associates Inc., $43
3. Ghafari Associates Inc., $36.3
4. Albert Kahn Associates Inc., $33.5
5. Harley Ellington Design, $28.5
6. Hobbs & Black Associates, $13.2
7. BEI Associates Inc., $13.2
8. TMP Associates Inc., $13
9. SSOE Inc. Architects & Engineers, $12.5
10. JGA Inc., $10.4

Source: *Crain's Detroit Business*, Crain's Book of Lists Detroit (annual), December 28, 1998, p. 118.

Architectural Firms--Florida

★314★
LARGEST ARCHITECTURAL FIRMS IN FLORIDA, 1999
Ranked by: Number of architects in Florida. **Remarks:** Also notes number of engineers, employees, and offices in Florida, specialty areas, year founded, senior Florida executive and contact information. **Number listed:** 23

1. Spillis Candela & Partners Inc., with 41 architects
2. Helman Hurley Charvat Peacock Architects Inc., 37
3. Hellmuth Obata & Kassabaum Inc., 35
4. Sverdrup Corp., 22
5. KBJ Architects Inc., 21
6. Harvard Jolly Clees Toppe Architects PA, 20
6. The Haskell Co., 20
8. Heery International Inc., 19
8. Reynolds Smith & Hills Inc., 19
10. Fugelberg Koch, 18

Source: *Florida Trend*, TopRank Florida (annual), 1999, p. 89.

Architectural Firms--Los Angeles County (CA)

★315★
LARGEST ARCHITECTURAL FIRMS IN LOS ANGELES COUNTY, 1998
Ranked by: Billings, in millions of dollars. **Remarks:** Also notes previous year's billings, services current projects, top local executive and contact information. **Number listed:** 25

1. Daniel, Mann, Johnson & Mendenhall (DMJM), with $66 million
2. Gensler, $24
3. MCG Architects, $23.9
4. Hellmuth Obata & Kassabaum Inc., $22.1
5. Jerde Partnership International, $19.6
6. HNTB Corp., $17.5
7. Leidenfrost/Horowitz & Associates, $17.3
8. Langdon-Wilson Architecture Planning Interiors, $17
9. Johnson Fain Partners, $16
10. RTKL Associates Inc., $15.6

Source: *Los Angeles Business Journal*, March 15, 1999, p. 44+.

Architectural Firms—Philadelphia Metropolitan Area

★316★
LARGEST ARCHITECTURAL FIRMS IN THE GREATER PHILADELPHIA AREA, 1998
Ranked by: Local billings, in millions of dollars. **Remarks:** Also lists number of local architects, engineers, interior designers, staff and top executives, areas of specialization and notable projects. **Number listed:** 25

1. Kling Lindquist, with $45 million
2. Ewing Cole Cherry Brott, $28
3. Vitetta Group, $21.4
4. Granary Associates, $17.9
5. Ballinger, $15.2
6. BLM Group, $10.1
6. The Hiller Group, $10.1
8. Francis Cauffman Foley Hoffmann, $9.8
9. Wallace Roberts & Todd, $9.6
10. Daroff Design Inc. and DDI Architects, $8.2

Source: *Philadelphia Business Journal*, February 26-March 4, 1999, p. 19.

Arms Trade

See: **Defense Industries--Export-Import Trade**

Art Exhibits

★317★
TOP ART EXHIBITS IN THE U.S., 1998
Ranked by: Number of visitors. **Remarks:** Excludes shows at the Museum of Modern Art in New York, the Art Institute of Chicago and the History Museum in Washington. **Number listed:** 10

1. Monet in the 20th Century, Museum of Fine Arts Boston, with 565,992 visitors
2. The Private Collection of Edgar Degas, Metropolitan Museum of Art, 528,267
3. Van Gogh's van Goghs, National Gallery of Art, 480,496
4. Gianni Versace, Metropolitan Museum of Art, 410,357
5. Delacroix: The Late Work, Philadelphia Museum of Art, 305,883
6. Art of the Motorcycle, Solomon R. Guggenheim Museum, 301,037
7. Alexander Calder, San Francisco Museum of Modern Art, 300,000
8. China: 5,000 Years, Solomon R. Guggenheim Museum, 299,950
9. Alexander Calder, National Gallery of Art, 288,709
10. Indian Carpets of the Mughal Era, Metropolitan Museum of Art, 284,064

Source: *The New York Times*, February 1, 1999, p. E3.

Asian Americans

★318★
LEADING ASIAN/PACIFIC ISLANDER METROPOLITAN AREAS, 1998
Ranked by: Asian and Pacific Islander population, in thousands. **Number listed:** 321

1. Los Angeles - Long Beach, CA, with 1,275.1 thousand
2. New York, NY, 767.1
3. Honolulu, HI, 563.2
4. San Francisco, CA, 453.2
5. Oakland, CA, 385.5
6. San Jose, CA, 369.3
7. Orange County, CA, 358.5
8. Chicago, IL, 354.1
9. Washington, DC, 299.7
10. San Diego, CA, 295

Source: *Sales & Marketing Management*, Survey of Buying Power (annual), August, 1998, p. 12.

Aspirin

See: **Analgesics**

Associations, Institutions, etc.--Florida

★319★
TOP BUSINESS AND PROFESSIONAL ASSOCIATIONS IN FLORIDA, 1999
Ranked by: Total number of members. **Remarks:** Also includes annual budget, annual dues, type of industry represented and senior executive. **Number listed:** 25

1. Florida Association of Realtors, with 60,000 members
2. The Florida Bar, 56,441
3. Florida Education Association, 43,000
4. Florida Institute of Certified Public Accountants, 18,434
5. Florida Medical Association, 16,000
6. Florida Home Builders Association, 13,973
7. National Federation of Independent Business, 13,000
8. Florida Citrus Mutual, 11,681
9. Florida United Business Association, 9,500
10. Associated Industries of Florida, 9,200

Source: *Florida Trend*, TopRank Florida, 1999, p. 83.

Athens Stock Exchange

★320★
LARGEST LISTED COMPANIES ON THE ATHENS STOCK EXCHANGE, 1997
Ranked by: Market value, in millions of drachma (Dr). **Number listed:** 20

1. Hellenic Telecommunications, with Dr2,640,236 million
2. Hellenic Bottling Co., Dr686,423
3. Alpha Credit Bank, Dr656,370
4. National Bank of Greece, Dr564,420
5. Ergo Bank, Dr372,285
6. Heracles Cement, Dr297,644
7. Titan Cement Co., Dr268,217
8. Commercial Bank of Greece, Dr238,221
9. National Mortgage Bank, Dr208,802
10. Intracom, Dr197,910

Source: *SSB Guide to World Equity Markets*, (annual), Euromoney Publications, 1998, p. 213.

★321★
MOST ACTIVELY TRADED SHARES ON THE ATHENS STOCK EXCHANGE, 1997
Ranked by: Trading value, in millions of drachma (Dr). **Number listed:** 20

1. Hellenic Telecommunications, with Dr1,007,357 million
2. National Bank of Greece, Dr437,462
3. Alpha Credit Bank, Dr425,846
4. Ergo Bank, Dr238,870
5. National Mortgage Bank, Dr221,612
6. Commercial Bank of Greece, Dr208,715
7. Hellenic Bottling Co., Dr137,446
8. Heracles Cement, Dr134,560
9. Titan Cement Co., Dr134,187
10. Intracom, Dr125,153

Source: *SSB Guide to World Equity Markets*, (annual), Euromoney Publications, 1998, p. 213.

Athletes--Salaries, Pensions, etc.

★322★
HIGHEST PAID MALE ATHLETES, 1998
Ranked by: Salaries, winnings and other income, in millions of dollars. **Number listed:** 12

1. Michael Jordan, with $69 million
2. Michael Schumacher, $38
3. Sergie Federov, $29.8
4. Tiger Woods, $26.8
5. Dale Earnhardt, $24.1
6. Grant Hill, $21.6
7. Oscar De La Hoya, $18.5
8. Patrick Ewing, $18.3
9. Arnold Palmer, $18.1
10. Gary Sheffield, $17.2

Source: *Forbes*, Super 40 (annual), March 22, 1999, p. 220+.

Athletic Shoes

★323★
BEST-SELLING ATHLETIC FOOTWEAR BRANDS, 1999
Ranked by: Total sales, in billions of dollars. **Remarks:** Also notes lead agency and media expenditures. **Number listed:** 8

1. Nike, with $3.25 billion
2. Reebok, $1.05
3. Adidas, $.95
4. New Balance, $.35
5. Fila, $.24
6. Keds, $.2
7. Converse, $.17
8. K-Swiss, $.15

Source: *Brandweek*, Superbrands: America's Top 2,000 Brands (annual), June 21, 1999, p. S50.

★324★
TOP ATHLETIC FOOTWEAR BRANDS BY PERCENT SHARE OF MARKET, 1997
Ranked by: Percent share of market. **Remarks:** Also notes measured advertising and previous year's figures. **Number listed:** 10

1. Nike, with 47%
2. Reebok, 15.2%
3. Adidas, 6.1%
4. Fila, 6%
5. Converse, 3.5%
6. New Balance, 3.3%
7. Keds, 2.2%
7. Airwalk, 2.2%
9. Asics, 1.6%
10. Foot-Joy, 1.5%

Source: *Advertising Age*, September 28, 1998, p. S20.

Australian Stock Exchange

★325★
LARGEST LISTED COMPANIES ON THE AUSTRALIAN STOCK EXCHANGE, 1997
Ranked by: Market value, in millions of Australian dollars (A$). **Number listed:** 20
1. National Australia Bank, with $A30,267 million
2. News Corporation, $A29,913
3. BHP, $A29,101
4. Westpac Banking Corp., $A18,717
5. Commonwealth Bank, $A16,729
6. ANZ Banking Corp., $A15,285
7. Telstra, $A13,794
8. Rio Tinto, $A11,500
9. Coco-Cola Amatil, $A9,703
10. Coles Myer, $A8,451

Source: *SSB Guide to World Equity Markets*, (annual), Euromoney Publications, 1998, p. 57.

★326★
MOST ACTIVELY TRADED SHARES ON THE AUSTRALIAN STOCK EXCHANGE, 1997
Ranked by: Turnover value, in millions of Australian dollars (A$). **Number listed:** 20
1. BHP, with $A21,296 million
2. National Australia Bank, $A15,886
3. News Corporation, $A12,054
4. ANZ Banking Corp., $A8,672
5. Westpac Banking Corp., $A8,658
6. Rio Tinto, $A7,664
7. Western Mining Corp., $A7,417
8. Commonwealth Bank, $A6,867
9. Telstra, $A4,601
10. Fosters Brewing, $A4,435

Source: *SSB Guide to World Equity Markets*, (annual), Euromoney Publications, 1998, p. 57.

Automated Teller Machines

★327★
TOP BANK HOLDING COMPANIES BY AUTOMATED TELLER MACHINES, 1998
Ranked by: Total number of ATMs owned. **Remarks:** Also notes number of ATMs inside bank offices and outside bank offices, previous year's figures and percent change. **Number listed:** 50
1. Banc One Corp. (OH), with 8,432 ATMs
2. BankAmerica Corp. (CA), 7,850
3. NationsBank Corp. (NC), 6,938
4. U.S. Bancorp (MN), 4,874
5. Wells Fargo & Co. (CA), 4,427
6. First Union Corp. (NC), 3,613
7. PNC Bank Corp. (PA), 2,593
8. KeyCorp (OH), 2,511
9. Fleet Financial Group (MA), 2,498
10. National City Corp. (OH), 2,048

Source: *American Banker*, December 1, 1998, p. 10A+.

Automated Teller Machines--North America

★328★
LARGEST AUTOMATED TELLER MACHINE OWNERS, 1999
Ranked by: Total number of ATMs owned. **Remarks:** Also notes POS terminal vendors. **Number listed:** 336
1. BankAmerica Corp. (CA), with 87,706 ATMs
2. Banc One Corp. (OH), 7,323
3. NationsBank Corp. (NC), 6,700
4. EDS Corp., 5,957
5. Royal Bank of Canada, 4,827
6. Wells Fargo & Co. (CA), 4,400
7. U.S. Bancorp (MN), 3,701
8. CIBC (Toronto, ON), 3,276
9. CitiCorp (NY), 3,200
9. Card Capture Services Inc. (OR), 3,200

Source: *Card Industry Directory*, Faulkner & Gray, 1999, p. 355+.

Automobile Dealers

★329★
LEADING AUTOMOBILE DEALER GROUPS, 1998
Ranked by: Total new retail units sold. **Remarks:** Also notes total used units, total fleet units, total number of dealerships, average new retail units per dealership and group revenue in all departments. **Number listed:** 100
1. AutoNation Inc., with 286,179 units
2. United Auto Group Inc., 77,403
3. Asbury Automotive Group, 68,000
4. V.T. Inc., 64,296
5. Hendrick Automotive Group, 55,667
6. Group 1 Automotive Inc., 39,822
7. Sonic Automotive Inc., 37,674
8. Planet Automotive, 37,674
9. Bill Heard Enterprises Inc., 27,895
10. Penske Automotive Group, 24,514

Source: *Automotive News*, April 19, 1999, p. 34+.

★330★
LEADING HISPANIC AUTOMOBILE DEALERS, 1998
Ranked by: Revenue, in millions of dollars. **Number listed:** 10
1. Burt Automotive Network, with $837.53 million
2. Ancira Enterprises Inc., $449
3. Tory Ford, $291.65
4. Lloyd A. Wise Cos., $216.7
5. Manchester Financial Corp., $101.4
6. Mack Sales of South Florida Inc., $97.44
7. Gus Machado Ford Inc., $94.26
8. Lou Sobh Pontiac Buick GMC, $87.82
9. Paul Young Co., $66.16
10. Metro Ford Inc., $64

Source: *Hispanic Business*, Hispanic Business 500 (annual), June, 1999, p. 92.

★331★
LEADING METROPOLITAN AREAS FOR AUTOMOBILE SALES, 1998
Ranked by: Automobile sales, in thousands of dollars. **Number listed:** 321
1. Chicago, IL, with $18,462,045 thousand
2. Los Angeles Long Beach, CA, $16,463,850
3. Detroit, MI, $13,093,936

4. Philadelphia, PA, $12,666,651
5. Houston, TX, $10,940,119
6. Washington, DC, $10,487,980
7. Atlanta, GA, $9,795,116
8. Dallas, TX, $9,728,012
9. Fort Lauderdale, FL, $8,388,574
10. Minneapolis-St.Paul, MN, $7,893,827

Source: *Sales & Marketing Management*, Survey of Buying Power (annual), August, 1998, p. 21.

★332★
LEADING PUBLIC DEALERSHIPS, 1997
Ranked by: Revenue from new and used car sales, in millions of dollars. **Remarks:** Also notes previous year's figures, measured advertising, and sales for specific makes. **Number listed:** 9

1. Republic Industries (FL), with $10,305.6 million
2. United Auto Group Inc. (NY), $2,087.1
3. Sonic Automotive Inc. (GA), $949.2
4. Group1 Automotive Inc. (TX), $902.3
5. Sunbelt Automotive (GA), $688
6. Cross-Continent Auto Retailers (TX), $549.5
7. Lithia Motors (OR), $419.7
8. Home Town Auto Retailers (CN), $240.2
9. Smart Choice Automotive Group (FL), $70.9

Source: *Advertising Age*, September 28, 1998, p. S12.

Automobile Dealers--Detroit Metropolitan Area

★333★
LEADING AUTOMOBILE DEALERS IN THE DETROIT METROPOLITAN AREA, 1998
Ranked by: Revenue, in millions of dollars. **Remarks:** Also include previous year's sales, percent change, number of dealerships, total local employees, new vehicles sold, used vehicles, sold and new vehicles leased. **Number listed:** 20

1. Don Massey Cadillac Group, with $979.9 million
2. Mel Farr Automotive Group, $588.1
3. Troy Motors Inc., $437.9
4. The Suburban Collection, $374
5. Tamaroff Automotive Group, $284
6. Bob Saks Motor Mall of Farmington Hills, $179.1
7. Stewart Management Group Inc., $167.7
8. Snethkamp Automotive Group, $166.4
9. The AutoHahn Network, $121.4
10. Art Moran Pontiac-GMC Inc., $111

Source: *Crain's Detroit Business*, May 10, 1999, p. 16.

Automobile Dealers--Los Angeles County (CA)

★334★
LARGEST NEW AUTO DEALERSHIPS IN LOS ANGELES COUNTY, 1997
Ranked by: Revenue, in millions of dollars. **Remarks:** Also notes previous year's figures number of vehicles sold, services, profile and top local executive. **Number listed:** 25

1. Longo Toyota, with $504 million
2. Galpin Ford, $409.1
3. Norm Reeves Honda, $181.5
4. Don Kott Ford, $143
5. Magic Ford, $143
6. Toyota of Cerritos, $135.6
7. Vista Ford, $118.5
8. Gunderson Chevrolet, $117.7
9. Universal City Nissan, $116.2
10. Longo Lexus, $110.7

Source: *Los Angeles Business Journal*, Book of Lists (annual), 1999, p. 153.

Automobile Engines--Emissions

★335★
CLEANEST RUNNING AUTOMOBILES, 1998
Ranked by: Score (out of 100). **Remarks:** Also notes engine type. **Number listed:** 10

1. General Motors EV1, with 56 points
2. Honda Civic CXCNG, 49
2. Toyota RAV4 EV, 49
4. Chevrolet S10 EV, 42
5. Ford Ranger EV, 41
6. Honda EV Plus, 39
7. Chevrolet Metro, 38
8. Ford Crown Victoria CNG, 36
9. Suzuki Swift, 35
9. Chrysler Epic EV, 35

Source: *Electric Perspectives*, July/August, 1998, p. 8.

Automobile Industry and Trade

See also: **Motor Vehicles**

★336★
AUTOMOTIVE INDUSTRY CORPORATIONS SPENDING THE MOST ON RESEARCH AND DEVELOPMENT, 1997
Ranked by: Research and development expenditures, in millions of dollars. **Number listed:** 10

1. General Motors, with $8,413.6 million
2. Ford Motor Co., $6,538
3. Chrysler Corp., $1,710.7
4. TRW, $1,152.7
5. Caterpillar Inc., $523.4
6. ITT Industries Inc., $516.1
7. Deere & Co., $421.9
8. Cummins Engine, $252.1
9. Case Corp., $203.9
10. Genuine Parts Co., $201.9

Source: *R & D*, October, 1998, p. S14.

★337★
CUSTOMER SATISFACTION WITH AUTOMOBILE DEALERS, 1998
Ranked by: Customer satisfactions scores. **Remarks:** Industry average is 120. Also notes change from previous year. **Number listed:** 21

1. Saturn, with 144 points
2. Cadillac, 143
3. Lexus, 142
4. Land Rover, 140
5. Volvo, 139
6. BMW, 138
6. Jaguar, 138
6. Mercedes, 138
9. Lincoln, 136
10. Infiniti, 134

Source: *Automotive News*, July 16, 1998, p. 6.

★338★

HIGHEST QUALITY AUTOMOBILE BRANDS, 1999

Ranked by: Number of problems per 100 vehicles. **Remarks:** Industry average is 167 problems per 100 vehicles. **Number listed:** 33

1. Jaguar, with 110 problems
2. Buick, 114
3. Infiniti, 118
4. Acura, 124
5. BMW, 125
6. Lexus, 131
7. Toyota, 135
8. Honda, 137
9. Cadillac, 139
10. Chrysler, 148

Source: *Automotive News*, May 10, 1999, p. 6.

★339★

MOST DEPENDABLE VEHICLES AFTER FIVE YEARS, 1998

Ranked by: Number of problems per 100 vehicles after five years. **Remarks:** Industry average is 399. **Number listed:** 19

1. Lexus, with 167 problems
2. Cadillac, 234
3. Infiniti, 273
4. Mercedes-Benz, 278
5. Acura, 281
6. Buick, 290
7. Lincoln, 312
8. Toyota, 313
9. Audi, 316
10. Oldsmobile, 317

Source: *Medical Economics*, August 10, 1998, p. 22.

★340★

TOP AUTOMOTIVE COMPANIES BY LIGHT VEHICLE MARKET SHARE, 1997

Ranked by: Market share percentage. **Remarks:** Also notes previous year's figures. **Number listed:** 12

1. General Motors, with 31.1%
2. Ford Motor Co., 25%
3. Chrysler, 15.2%
4. Toyota, 8.1%
5. Honda, 6.2%
6. Nissan, 4.8%
7. Mazda, 1.5%
8. Mitsubishi Corp., 1.3%
9. VW/Audi, 1.1%
10. Subaru, 0.9%

Source: *Ward's Automotive Yearbook*, (annual), Ward's Communication Inc., 1998, p. 216.

★341★

TOP AUTOMOTIVE COMPANIES IN THE S&P 500, 1998

Ranked by: Each company is ranked by eight criteria: one-year total return, three-year total return, on-year sales growth, three-year average annual sales growth, one-year profit growth, three-year annual average profit growth, net profit margins, and return on equity, with additional weight given to a company's sales. A company's composite rank is calculated using the sum of all of its ranks. **Remarks:** Overall scores not provided. **Number listed:** 7

1. Ford Motor
2. Navistar International
3. Paccar
4. Dana
5. General Motors
6. Goodyear Tire & Rubber
7. Cooper Tire & Rubber

Source: *Business Week*, Business Week 50: Top Companies of the S & P 500 (annual), March 29, 1999, p. 142.

★342★

TOP FACTORS SHAPING NEW CAR CHOICES, 1998

Ranked by: Survey results percentages. **Number listed:** 8

1. Appearance, with 74%
2. Functionality, 71%
3. Features/Options, 69%
4. Good reputation, 63%
5. High Quality, 51%
6. Best Value, 47%
7. Low Price, 25%
7. Luxury Features, 25%

Source: *Adweek*, September 14, 1998, p. 36.

★343★

TOP FAMILY SEDAN BRANDS

Ranked by: Number of units sold. **Remarks:** Also notes company name, lead agency and media expenditures. **Number listed:** 5

1. Toyota Camry, with 429,575 units
2. Honda Accord, 401,071
3. Ford Taurus, 371,074
4. Honda Civic, 334,562
5. Chevy Malibu, 223,703

Source: *Brandweek*, Superbrands: America's Top 2,000 Brands (annual), June 21, 1999, p. S22.

★344★

TOP GENERAL AUTOMOTIVE BRANDS

Ranked by: Number of units sold. **Remarks:** Also notes company name, lead agency and media expenditures. **Number listed:** 10

1. Ford, with 3,239,467 units
2. Chevrolet, 2,413,433
3. Dodge, 1,442,777
4. Toyota, 1,204,765
5. Honda, 899,208
6. Nissan, 557,879
7. Pontiac, 536,469
8. Jeep, 459,294
9. GMC, 446,472
10. Mercury, 410,186

Source: *Brandweek*, Superbrands: America's Top 2,000 Brands (annual), June 21, 1999, p. S20.

★345★

TOP LUXURY AUTOMOBILE BRANDS, 1999

Ranked by: Number of units sold. **Remarks:** Also notes company name, lead agency and media expenditures. **Number listed:** 5

1. Cadillac Deville, with 102,022 units
2. Lincoln Town Car, 97,547
3. Cadillac Seville, 39,009
4. Lincoln Continental, 35,210
5. Buick Park Avenue, 31,220

Source: *Brandweek*, Superbrands: America's Top 2,000 Brands (annual), June 21, 1999, p. S20.

★346★

TOP SUB-COMPACT CAR MODELS, 1999

Ranked by: Number of units sold. **Remarks:** Also notes company name, lead agency and media expenditures. **Number listed:** 5

1. Ford Escort, with 291,936 units
2. Toyota Corolla, 283,898
3. Chevy Cavalier, 256,099
4. Saturn, 231,522

5. Dodge/Plymouth Neon, 196.497

Source: *Brandweek*, Superbrands: America's Top 2,000 Brands (annual), June 21, 1999, p. S22.

★347★
TOP U.S. CAR SALES, 1997

Ranked by: Number of units sold. **Remarks:** Also notes market share and percent change from previous year. **Number listed:** 10

1. Toyota Camry, with 397,156 units
2. Honda Accord, 384,609
3. Ford Taurus, 357,162
4. Honda Civic, 315,546
5. Chevy Cavalier, 302,161
6. Ford Escort, 283,898
7. Saturn, 250,810
8. Chevy Lumina, 228,451
9. Toyota Corolla, 218,461
10. Pontiac Grand Am, 204,078

Source: *Ward's Automotive Yearbook*, (annual), Ward's Communication Inc., 1998, p. 216.

★348★
TOP U.S. LUXURY CAR MODELS BY MARKET SHARE, 1997

Ranked by: Market share percentage. **Remarks:** Also notes measured advertising and previous year's figures. **Number listed:** 10

1. Cadillac DeVille, with 4.8%
2. Lincoln Town Car, 4.3%
3. Mercedes-Benz E Class, 2%
4. BMW 5 Series, 1.5%
5. Lincoln Continental, 1.4%
5. Cadillac Seville, 1.4%
7. Oldsmobile Aurora, 1.2%
8. Cadillac Eldorado, 1%
9. Lexus LS 400, .9%
10. BMW 7 Series, .9%

Source: *Advertising Age*, September 28, 1998, p. S12.

Automobile Industry and Trade--Export-Import Trade

★349★
TOP IMPORTED LUXURY AUTOMOBILE BRANDS, 1999

Ranked by: Number of units sold. **Remarks:** Also notes company name, lead agency and media expenditures. **Number listed:** 5

1. Mercedes-Benz, with 170,245 units
2. Lexus, 156,260
3. BMW, 131,559
4. Acura, 110,392
5. Volvo, 101,172

Source: *Brandweek*, Superbrands: America's Top 2,000 Brands (annual), June 21, 1999, p. S20.

Automobile Industry and Trade, International

★350★
GLOBAL AUTO INDUSTRY AVERAGE PRODUCTION, 1998-2005

Ranked by: Average production percentage. **Number listed:** 6

1. Asia-Pacific, with 31%
2. North America, 28%
2. Western Europe, 28%
4. Eastern Europe, 7%
5. South America, 5%
6. Middle East & Africa, 1%

Source: *Automotive Industries*, May, 1999, p. 15.

Automobile Leasing and Rental Companies

★351★
TOP CAR RENTAL COMPANIES BY NUMBER OF LOCATIONS, 1998

Ranked by: Number of locations. **Remarks:** Does not include Enterprise Rent-A-Car. **Number listed:** 8

1. Hertz, with $6,100 thousand
2. Avis, $4,394
3. Budget, $3,206
4. Dollar, $2,505
5. National, $1,698
6. Thrifty, $1,214
7. Alamo, $546
8. Advantage, $112

Source: *Business Travel News*, Business Travel Survey (annual), May 31, 1999, p. 52.

★352★
TOP CAR RENTAL COMPANIES BY NUMBER OF VEHICLES IN FLEET, 1998

Ranked by: Number of vehicles in fleet. **Remarks:** Does not include Enterprise Rent-A-Car. **Number listed:** 8

1. Avis, with $503,000 thousand
2. Hertz, $431,000
3. Budget, $265,000
4. National, $250,000
5. Dollar, $148,692
6. Alamo, $130,000
7. Advantage, $111,000
8. Thrifty, $63,800

Source: *Business Travel News*, Business Travel Survey (annual), May 31, 1999, p. 52.

★353★
TOP CAR RENTAL COMPANIES BY SYSTEMWIDE REVENUE, 1998

Ranked by: Revenue, in thousands of dollars. **Remarks:** Does not include Enterprise Rent-A-Car. **Number listed:** 8

1. Hertz, with $4,238,300 thousand
2. Avis, $3,556,399
3. Budget, $2,900,000
4. National, $1,509,412
5. Alamo, $1,400,000
6. Dollar, $789,600
7. Thrifty, $637,400
8. Advantage, $85,000

Source: *Business Travel News*, Business Travel Survey (annual), May 31, 1999, p. 52.

★354★
TOP RENTAL CAR AGENCIES BY SALES, 1999
Ranked by: Total sales, in billions of dollars. **Remarks:** Also notes company name, lead agency and media expenditures. **Number listed:** 5
1. Enterprise, with $4.1 billion
1. Hertz, $4.1
3. Alamo National, Car Temps, $3.5
4. Budget, $2.6
5. Avis, $2.3

Source: *Brandweek*, Superbrands: America's Top 2,000 Brands (annual), June 21, 1999, p. S70.

Automobile Parts

★355★
TOP AUTOMOTIVE BRANDS ACCORDING TO DISCOUNT SHOPPERS, 1998
Ranked by: Percent of discount shoppers naming brand as favorite. **Number listed:** 11
1. Penzoil, with 19%
2. Valvoline, 16%
3. Quaker State, 13%
4. Fram, 11%
5. Castrol, 8%
6. AC Delco, 6%
7. Champion, 5%
8. Havoline, 4%
9. Armor All, 3%
9. Michelin, 3%
9. Turtle Wax, 3%

Source: *Discount Store News*, Top Brands Consumer Survey (annual), September 17, 1998, p. 28.

Automobile Parts, International

★356★
WORLD'S LARGEST CORPORATIONS IN THE MOTOR VEHICLES AND PARTS INDUSTRY BY REVENUE, 1997
Ranked by: Revenue, in millions of dollars. **Remarks:** Also notes profits and profits as a percent of revenues and assets. **Number listed:** 25
1. General Motors (U.S.), with $178,174 million
2. Ford Motor (U.S.)
3. 153,627
4. Toyota Motor (Japan), $95,137
5. Daimler-Benz (Germany), $71,561
6. Daewoo (Korea), $71,526
7. Volkswagen (Germany), $65,328
8. Chrysler (U.S.), $61,147
9. Nissan Motor (Japan), $53,478
10. Fiat (Italy), $52,569
11. Honda Motor (Japan), $48,876

Source: *Fortune*, The Global 500: World's Biggest Corporations (annual), August 3, 1998, p. F-22+.

Automobile Parts--North America

★357★
TOP AUTOMOBILE PARTS SUPPLIERS TO NORTH AMERICA, 1998
Ranked by: Total Original Equipment Manufacturer (OEM) parts sales, in millions of U.S. dollars ($). **Remarks:** Also notes worldwide sales, North American and worldwide sales for previous year, types of products, contact information and executive officer. **Number listed:** 150
1. Delphi Automotive Systems, with $20,635 million
2. Visteon Automotive Systems, $14,489
3. Johnson Controls Inc., $5,590
4. Dana Corp., $5,542
5. Lear Corp., $5,369
6. Magna International, $3,780
7. TRW, $3,528
8. Robert Bosch Corp., $3,458
9. Eaton Corp., $2,380
10. Cummins Engine Co., $2,344

Source: *Automotive News*, Top 150 OEM Parts Suppliers (annual), April 12, 1999, p. 21+.

Automobile Plants--Production

★358★
TOP CAR ASSEMBLY PLANTS, 1998
Ranked by: Hours per vehicle assembled. **Number listed:** 10
1. Nissan Smyrna, with 16.55 hours
2. Toyota Cambridge, 17.14
3. Ford Atlanta, 17.83
4. Ford Chicago, 18.97
5. GM Oshawa #1, 20.18
6. Toyota Georgetown #1, 20.51
7. Ford St. Thomas, 20.82
8. Ford Wayne, 21.05
9. Honda East Liberty, 21.16
10. GM Oshawa #2, 21.84

Source: *Ward's Auto World*, August, 1998, p. 24.

Automobile Service Stations

★359★
LEADING METROPOLITAN AREAS FOR GASOLINE SERVICE STATION SALES, 1998
Ranked by: Sales, in thousands of dollars. **Number listed:** 321
1. Los Angeles - Long Beach, CA, with $4,011,528 thousand
2. Chicago, IL, $2,965,338
3. Washington, DC, $2,206,732
4. Philadelphia, PA, $2,120,000
5. Detroit, MI, $2,079,937
6. Boston-Lawrence-Lowell-Brockton, MA, $2,018,578
7. Minneapolis-St.Paul, MN, $2,013,036
8. Dallas, TX, $1,937,275
9. Atlanta, GA, $1,840,033
10. Riverside-San Bernadino, CA, $1,829,684

Source: *Sales & Marketing Management*, Survey of Buying Power (annual), August, 1998, p. 27.

Automobile Theft

★360★
MOST FREQUENTLY STOLEN VEHICLES, 1997
Ranked by: Frequency of theft. **Remarks:** Specific figures not provided. Also notes previous year's ranking. **Number listed:** 10

1. Honda Accord
2. Toyota Camry
3. Oldsmobile Cutlass
4. Honda Civic
5. Ford Mustang
6. Toyota Corolla
7. Chevrolet Full-size pickup
8. Nissan Maxima
9. Jeep Grand Cherokee
10. Ford F-150 Series pickup

Source: *Medical Economics*, December 14, 1998, p. 29.

Automobiles--Painting and Finishing--North America

★361★
MOST POPULAR COLORS FOR FULL-SIZE/INTERMEDIATE CARS, 1998
Ranked by: Percentage of North American made vehicles manufactured. **Remarks:** Also notes previous year's figures. **Number listed:** 10

1. Medium/Dark Green, with 16.4%
2. White, 15.6%
3. Light Brown, 14.1%
4. Silver, 11%
5. Black, 8.9%
6. Medium Red, 6.5%
7. Medium/Dark Blue, 6%
8. Dark Red, 4.9%
9. Light Blue, 3.8%
10. White Metallic, 3.2%

Source: *Ward's Auto World*, March, 1999, p. 30.

★362★
MOST POPULAR COLORS FOR LUXURY CARS, 1998
Ranked by: Percentage of North American made vehicles manufactured. **Remarks:** Also notes previous year's figures. **Number listed:** 10

1. Light Brown, with 17.7%
2. White Metallic, 12.3%
2. Black, 12.3%
4. White, 11.3%
5. Medium/Dark Green, 10%
6. Silver, 9.2%
7. Medium Red, 7.5%
8. Medium/Dark Grey, 5.3%
9. Medium/Dark Blue, 4.8%
9. Gold, 4.8%

Source: *Ward's Auto World*, March, 1999, p. 30.

★363★
MOST POPULAR COLORS FOR SPORT/COMPACT CARS, 1998
Ranked by: Percentage of North American made vehicles manufactured. **Remarks:** Also notes previous year's figures. **Number listed:** 10

1. Medium/Dark Green, with 15.9%
2. Black, 15%
3. White, 14.7%
4. Silver, 10.4%
5. Bright Red, 9.5%
6. Light Brown, 7.0%
7. Medium Red, 6.4%
8. Medium/Dark Blue, 5.3%
9. Teal/Aqua, 4%
10. Purple, 3.4%

Source: *Ward's Auto World*, March, 1999, p. 30.

★364★
MOST POPULAR COLORS FOR TRUCKS, SUVS AND VANS, 1998
Ranked by: Percentage of North American made vehicles manufactured. **Remarks:** Also notes previous year's figures. **Number listed:** 10

1. White, with 22.5%
2. Medium/Dark Green, 15.5%
3. Black, 11.5%
4. Medium Red, 7.2%
5. Bright Red, 7.1%
6. Silver, 6.2%
7. Light Brown, 6.1%
8. Medium/Dark Blue, 4.7%
9. Dark Red, 4.5%
10. Medium/Dark Brown, 3.2%

Source: *Ward's Auto World*, March, 1999, p. 30.

Automobiles—Theft

See: **Automobile Theft**

Automotive Electronics

★365★
TOP AUTOMOTIVE ELECTRONICS COMPANIES
Ranked by: Segment revenue, in millions of dollars. **Number listed:** 5

1. General Motors Co. (Delco Electronics), with $5,500 million
2. Ford Motor Co., $3,840.7
3. Chrysler, $1,834
4. TRW, $1,039.3
5. Harman International Industries, $968.2

Source: *Electronic Business*, Top 200 (annual), July, 1998, p. 95.

Baby Care Products

★366★
TOP BABY CARE PRODUCTS, 1998
Ranked by: Sales, in millions of dollars. **Number listed:** 10

1. Desitin, with $27.3 million
2. Balmex, $10.0
3. A & D, $6.4
4. Daily Care, $5.8
5. A & D Medicated, $4.3

6. Johnson's, $3.9
7. Blistex Dyprotex, $1.0
8. Diaparene, $0.7
8. Johnson's Ultra Sensitive, $0.7
10. Dr. Smith's, $0.5

Source: *MMR*, November 2, 1998, p. 42.

Baby Foods

See: **Infants' Food**

Baby Wipes

★367★

TOP BABY WIPES, 1998

Ranked by: Sales, in millions of dollars. **Number listed:** 8

1. Huggies, with $222.2 million
2. Pampers Baby Fresh, $139.8
3. Chubs, $32.8
4. Luvs, $22.8
5. Kidfresh, $10.6
6. Diaparene, $3.5
7. Drypers, $1.4
8. Wash A Bye, $0.8

Source: *Mass Market Retailer*, November 2, 1998, p. 42.

Baked Goods

★368★

TOP DONUT COMPANIES, 1998

Ranked by: Dollar sales, in thousands of dollars. **Number listed:** 10

1. Entenmann's, with $106,304,824 thousand
2. Hostess, $89,456,720
3. Dolly Madison, $43,638,840
4. Krispy Kreme, $36,387,776
5. Break Cake, $13,042,997
6. Freihofer, $12,524,086
7. Metz, $12,214,810
8. Merita, $12,045,647
9. Little Debbie, $11,947,614
10. Private Label, $80,863,080

Source: *Milling and Baking News (annual)*, July 28, 1998, p. 34.

★369★

TOP SELLING SNACK PIES, 1998

Ranked by: Sales, in millions of dollars. **Remarks:** Figures are for 52-week period ending July 26, 1998. **Number listed:** 10

1. Hostess, with $12.26 million
2. Private Label, $11.7
3. Table Talk, $7.77
4. Tastykake, $7.13
5. Home Run Pie, $5.7
6. Entenmann's, $3.9
7. JJS, $3.27
8. Drake, $3.05
9. Cutie Pie, $2.9
10. Aunt Fanny's, $2.89

Source: *Automatic Merchandiser*, October, 1998, p. 62.

★370★

TOP SNACK CAKE BRANDS ACCORDING TO *AUTOMATIC MERCHANDISER*, 1998

Ranked by: Sales, in millions of dollars. **Remarks:** Figures are for 52-week period ending July 26, 1998. **Number listed:** 10

1. Little Debbie, with $207.7 million
2. Hostess, $205.1
3. Tastykake, $60.3
4. Drake, $60.2
5. Private Label, $36.3
6. Nabisco Snackwells, $16.3
7. Entenmann's, $12.5
8. Betty Crocker Sweet Rewards, $10.4
9. Break Cake, $10.06
10. Dolly Madison, $9.6

Source: *Automatic Merchandiser*, October, 1998, p. 62.

★371★

TOP SNACK CAKE BRANDS ACCORDING TO *MILLING & BAKING NEWS*, 1998

Ranked by: Dollar sales. **Remarks:** Figures are for 52-week period ending May 31, 1998. **Number listed:** 10

1. Little Debbie, with $208,674,672 thousand
2. Hostess, $205,685,536
3. Tastykake, $59,488,644
4. Drake, $51,392,340
5. Nabisco SnackWell's, $18,727,976
6. Entenmann's, $12,968,566
7. Betty Crocker Sweet Rewards, $11,902,501
8. Break Cake, $10,132,863
9. Dolly Madison, $9,360,187
10. Private Label, $35,601,040

Source: *Milling and Baking News (annual)*, July 28, 1998, p. 32.

Bakers and Bakeries

★372★

LEADING IN-STORE BAKERIES OF SUPERMARKET CHAINS, 1997

Ranked by: Total number of in-store bakeries. **Remarks:** Also notes total number of stores. **Number listed:** 100

1. Winn-Dixie Stores Inc., with $1,172 stores
2. Safeway, $1,054
3. Kroger Co., $995
4. Food Lion Inc., $892
5. American Stores, $807
6. Great A & P Tea Co. Inc., $758
7. Albertson's Inc., $700
8. Publix Supermarkets Inc., $480
9. Wal-Mart Supercenters, $450
10. Supervalu, $322

Source: *Bakery Production and Marketing*, Bakery Red Book (annual), July 15, 1998, p. 49.

★373★

TOP BAKERS IN THE U.S. AND CANADA, 1996

Ranked by: Sales, in millions of U.S. dollars ($). **Remarks:** Also notes number of plants, employees, and routes, as well as regional breakdown of total sales. **Number listed:** 95

1. Nabisco Biscuit Co., with $3,700 millions
2. Interstate Brands Corp, $3,300
3. Keebler Co., $2,100
4. The Earthgrains Co., $1,719
5. Bestfoods Baking Co., $1,600
6. Weston Foods, $1,500 (CAN)

7. Flowers Industries Inc., $1,400
8. Sara Lee Bakery, $1,000
9. McKee Foods Corp., $830
10. Pepperidge Farm Inc., $700

Source: *Bakery Production and Marketing*, Bakery Red Book (annual), July 15, 1998, p. 40+.

Bank Acquisitions and Mergers

★374★
TOP BANK AND THRIFT DEALS BY ANNOUNCED VALUE, 1998
Ranked by: Announced value, in millions of dollars. **Remarks:** Also, notes other financial details. **Number listed:** 25

1. Citicorp (seller), Travelers Group (buyer), with $82,536 million
2. BankAmerica (seller), NationsBank Corp. (buyer), $66,624
3. Norwest Corp. (seller), Wells Fargo & Co. (buyer), $31,171
4. First Chicago/NBD (seller), Bank One Corp. (buyer), $29,482
5. HF Ahmanson & Co. (seller), Washington Mutual (buyer), $9,907
6. Crestar Financial (seller), SunTrust Banks Inc. (buyer), $9,606
7. Bankers Trust Corp. (seller), Deutsche Bank AG (buyer), $9,417
8. Firstar Corp. (seller), Star Banc Corp. (buyer), $7,357
9. First Commercial (seller), Regions Financial (buyer), $2,705
10. Magna Group (seller), Union Planters Corp. (buyer), $2,239

Source: *Banking Strategies*, M & A Forum (annual), 1999, p. 68+.

★375★
TOP BANK AND THRIFT DEALS BY DEAL VALUE, 1998
Ranked by: Deal value, in millions of dollars. **Remarks:** Also notes other financial details. **Number listed:** 150

1. Citicorp (seller), Travelers Group Inc. (buyer), with $74,313.4 million
2. BankAmerica Corp. (seller), NationsBank Corp. (buyer), $62,029.2
3. Wells Fargo & Co. (seller), Northwest Corp. (buyer), $34,521.6
4. First Chicago NBD Corp. (seller), Banc One Corp. (buyer), $29,807.5
5. Bankers Trust Corp. (seller), Deutsche Bank AG (buyer), $10,282.4
6. H. F. Ahmanson & Co. (seller), Washington Mutual Inc. (buyer), $9,894.4
7. Crestar Financial Corp. (seller), SunTrust Banks Inc. (buyer), $9,606.3
8. Firstar Corp. (seller), Sun Banc Corp. (buyer), $7,228.6
9. First Commercial Corp. (seller), Regions Financial Corp. (buyer), $2,715.4
10. Golden State Bancorp Inc. (seller), California Federal Bank (buyer), $2,700.0

Source: *American Banker*, February 1, 1999, p. 14A+.

★376★
TOP M & A ADVISORS FOR ALL ANNOUNCED DEPOSITORY INSTITUTIONS, 1999
Ranked by: Announced value, in millions of dollars. **Remarks:** Also notes other financial details. **Number listed:** 113

1. Goldman, Sachs & Co., with $142,828.7 million
2. Merrill Lynch & Co., $102,686.7
3. NationsBanc Montgomery Securities LLC, $62,575.0
4. Credit Suisse First Boston Corp., $55,420.1
5. Morgan Stanley Dean Witter & Co., $50,227.1
6. Lazard Freres & Co. L.L.C., $29,807.5
7. Lehman Brothers, $22,397.4
8. Keefe Bruyette & Woods Inc., $8,729.7
9. Sandler O'neill & Partners L. P., $6,289.7
10. J.P. Morgan Securities, $3,990.8

Source: *U.S. Banker*, M & A Rankings (annual), March, 1999, p. 76+.

★377★
TOP M & A ADVISORS FOR ALL ANNOUNCED THRIFT DEALS, 1997
Ranked by: Announced value, in millions of dollars. **Remarks:** Also notes other financial details. **Number listed:** 54

1. Credit Suisse First Boston Corp., with $12,711.9 million
2. Lehman Brothers, $12,702.9
3. Goldman (Sachs & Co.), $3,780.7
4. Saloman Smith Barney Inc., $3,515.4
5. Keefe (Bruyette & Woods Inc.), $3,227.8
6. Sandler O'neill & Partners L. P., $2,991.6
7. Merrill Lynch & Co., $1,848.7
8. Hovde Financial Inc., $658.0
9. Wallach Co., $530.1
10. Ryan Inc. (Beck & Company), $477.9

Source: *U.S. Banker*, M & A Rankings (annual), March, 1999, p. 84.

★378★
TOP M & A ADVISORS FOR ANNOUNCED DEALS OF ALL COMMERCIAL BANKS, 1997
Ranked by: Announced value, in millions of dollars. **Remarks:** Also notes other financial details. **Number listed:** 98

1. Goldman Sachs & Co., with $139,048.0 million
2. Merrill Lynch & Co., $100,838.0
3. NationsBanc Montgomery Securities LLC, $62,575.0
4. Morgan Stanley Dean Witter & Co., $49,972.4
5. Credit Suisse First Boston Corp., $42,708.2
6. Lazard Freres & Co. L.L.C., $29,807.5
7. Lehman Brothers, $9,694.5
8. Keefe Bruyette & Woods Inc., $5,501.9
9. J.P. Morgan Securities, $3,990.8
10. Sandler O'neill & Partners L. P., $3,298.1

Source: *U.S. Banker*, M & A Rankings (annual), March, 1999, p. 80+.

Bank Credit Cards

★379★
LARGEST MERCHANT ACQUIRERS BY SALES, 1997-1998
Ranked by: Volume of sales, in U.S. dollars. **Remarks:** Also notes contact information; top executives; volume of credit and debit transactions; number of clients, locations, and EDC terminals; percent electronic capture; and figures from previous year. **Number listed:** 67

1. Chase Merchant Services, with $93,916,000,000 dollar volume
2. National City Bank, $74,000,000,000
3. Paymentech Inc., $45,989,873,000
4. BA Merchant Services Inc., $33,900,045,000
5. U.S. Bancorp, $21,262,000,000
6. Fifth Third Bank, $21,185,000,000
7. First National Bank of Omaha, $16,719,000,000
8. Banc One Payment Services LLC, $16,341,287,000
9. Wells Fargo Bank, $15,944,000,000
10. Nova Information Systems Inc., $14,980,000,000

Source: *Faulkner & Gray*, Card Industry Directory, 1999, p. 408+.

★380★
TOP COMPANIES IN MANAGED BANK CREDIT CARD LOANS, 1997-1998
Ranked by: Managed car loans, in millions of dollars. **Remarks:** Also notes company type and location, as well as other financial figures. **Number listed:** 50

1. Citicorp, with $54,6660.0 million
2. MBNA Corp., $48,961.0
3. Banc One Corp., $39,605.7
4. Morgan Stanley Dean Whitter & Co., $35,804.0
5. Chase Manhattan Corp., $34,049.0
6. Household International, $17,360.0
7. First Chicago NBDCorp., $17,216.0
8. American Express Co., $13,360.2
9. Fleet Financial Group Inc., $13,232.9
10. Capital One Financial Corp., $13,134.1

Source: *American Banker*, (annual), September 22, 1998, p. 10.

Bank Debit Cards--North America

★381★
LEADING DEBIT CARD ISSUERS, 1998
Ranked by: Number of debit cards. **Remarks:** Also notes contact information, total cards, comparisons for ATM and POS activity, figures from previous year, and debit card managers. **Number listed:** 340

1. Bank of America, with $16,686,000 debit cards
2. NationsBank Corp., $11,000,000
3. Wells Fargo Bank, $10,950,000
4. Citicorp, $5,600,000
5. Banc One Corp., $5,422,835
6. CIBC, $5,300,000
7. First Union National Bank, $3,800,000
7. Chase Manhattan Bank NA, $3,800,000
9. Caisses Populaires et deconomie Desjardins, $3,478,900
10. Norwest Bank, $3,237,651

Source: *Faulkner & Gray*, Card Industry Directory, 1999, p. 241+.

Bank Holding Companies

★382★
LEADING BANK HOLDING COMPANIES BY ASSETS, 1998
Ranked by: Total assets, in millions of dollars. **Remarks:** Also notes figures from previous year, percent change, net income, total deposits, number of banks, number of thrifts, and number of employees. **Number listed:** 50

1. Citigroup Inc., with $667,400 million
2. BankAmerica Corp., $617,679
3. Chase Manhattan Corp., $365,875
4. Banc One Corp., $261,496
5. J.P. Morgan & Co. Inc., $261,067
6. First Union Corp., $237,363
7. Wells Fargo & Co., $202,475
8. Bankers Trust Corp., $133,115
9. Fleet Financial Group Inc., $104,382
10. SunTrust Banks Inc., $93,170

Source: *American Banker*, March 25, 1999, p. 8+.

★383★
LEADING BANK HOLDING COMPANIES BY NET INCOME, 1998
Ranked by: Net income, in millions of dollars. **Remarks:** Also notes figures from previous year, change in rank, profitability ratio figures, and other performance ratio figures. **Number listed:** 9

1. Citigroup Inc., with $5,807.0 million
2. Chase Manhattan Corp., $3,782.0
3. BankAmerica Corp., $3,441.0
4. Banc One Corp., $3,108.0
5. First Union Corp., $2,891.0
6. Wells Fargo & Co., $1,950.0
7. Fleet Financial Group Inc., $1,532.0
8. U.S. Bancorp, $1,327.4
9. Bank of New York Co., $1,193.0

Source: *American Banker*, Top 50 U.S. Bank Holding Companies (annual), March 25, 1999, p. 11.

Bank Holding Companies--Detroit Metropolitan Area

★384★
TOP BANK HOLDING COMPANIES IN THE DETROIT METROPOLITAN AREA, 1997
Ranked by: Assets, in millions of dollars. **Remarks:** Also notes contact information, performance figures, and figures from previous year. **Number listed:** 15

1. Comerica Inc., with $36,292.4 million
2. NBD Bank, $21,900.0
3. Michigan National Corp./Independence One Capital Management Corp., $9,311.2
4. Great Lakes National Bank, $2,214.6
5. Republic Bancorp Inc., $1,872.9
6. Old Kent Financial Corp., $1,755.3
7. Franklin Bank N.A., $503.9
8. First State Financial Corp., $474.9
9. Capitol Bancorp Ltd., $285.1
10. Oxford Bank, $252.7

Source: *Crain's Detroit Business*, Crain's Book of Lists Detroit (annual), December 28, 1998, p. 144.

Bank Loans

★385★
TOP SMALL BUSINESS LENDERS, 1998
Ranked by: Overall, in millions of dollars. **Number listed:** 10

1. Wells Fargo & Co., with $5,751 million

2. Banc One Corp., $4,262
3. NationsBank Corp., $4,078
4. First Union Corp., $3,851
5. Norwest Corp., $3,758
6. Chase Manhattan Corp., $3,724
7. American Express, $3,505
8. KeyCorp., $3,464
9. U.S. Bancorp., $3,316
10. Fleet Financial Group, $3,227

Source: *U.S. Banker*, November 2, 1998, p. 12.

Bankers--Salaries, Pensions, etc.

★386★
HIGHEST PAID BANK EXECUTIVES, 1997
Ranked by: Annual compensation, in U.S. dollars. **Remarks:** Also notes title, age, bank name, figures from previous year and percent change. **Number listed:** 50

1. J. Carter Bacot, with $8,494,743
2. Gerry B. Cameron, $7,661,357
3. John B. McCoy, $6,956,961
4. Frank N. Newman, $6,660,700
5. Walter V. Shipley, $6,195,417
6. A. B. Krongard, $5,866,700
7. Thomas G. Lambrecque, $5,705,417
8. David A. Coulter, $5,677,089
9. Thomas A. Renyl, $5,632,771
10. Mayo A. Shattuck, $5,566,700

Source: *American Banker*, July 9, 1998, p. 11.

Bankruptcy

★387★
LARGEST COMPANIES FILING FOR CHAPTER 11, BY EMPLOYEES, 1997
Ranked by: Employee count. **Remarks:** Also notes bankruptcy date and company description. **Number listed:** 10

1. Flagstar Companies Inc., with $93,000
2. Montgomery Ward Holding Corp., $63,200
3. Payless Cashways Inc., $16,700
4. Harvard Industries Inc., $6,990
5. Guy F. Atkinson Co., $6,500
6. Farm Fresh Inc., $6,300
7. Levitz Furniture Inc., $5,018
8. JPS Textile Group Inc., $4,000
9. MobileMedia Corp., $3,370
10. AMRE Inc., $3,095

Source: *New Generation Research*, Bankruptcy Yearbook & Almanac (annual), 1997, p. 55.

★388★
LARGEST COMPANIES FILING FOR CHAPTER 11, BY LIABILITIES, 1997
Ranked by: Liabilities, in millions of dollars. **Remarks:** Also notes bankruptcy date and company description. **Number listed:** 10

1. Montgomery Ward Holdings Corp., with $4,179 million
2. Flagstar Companies Inc., $2,818
3. MobileMedia Corp., $1,056
4. Levitz Furniture Inc., $1,002
5. Payless Cashways Inc., $985
6. Harvard Industries Inc., $680
7. Alliance Entertainment Corp., $524
8. Stratosphere Corp., $396
9. JPS Textile Group Inc., $373
10. Consolidated Hydro Inc., $291

Source: *New Generation Research*, Bankruptcy Yearbook & Almanac (annual), 1997, p. 55.

★389★
LARGEST COMPANIES FILING FOR CHAPTER 11, BY REVENUE, 1997
Ranked by: Revenue, in millions of dollars. **Remarks:** Also notes bankruptcy date & company description. **Number listed:** 10

1. Montgomery Ward Holdings Corp., with $6,620 million
2. Payless Cashways Inc., $2,651
3. Flagstar Companies Inc., $2,542
4. Levitz Furniture Inc., $967
5. Harvard Industries Inc., $825
6. Alliance Entertainment Corp., $691
7. Guy F. Atkinson Co., $468
8. JPS Textile Group Inc., $449
9. Grossman's Inc., $386
10. RDM Sports Group Inc., $367

Source: *New Generation Yearbook*, Bankruptcy Yearbook & Almanac (annual), 1997, p. 55.

★390★
LARGEST PUBLIC BANKRUPTCIES IN HISTORY, EXCLUDING PRIMARILY FINANCIAL COMPANIES, THROUGH 1998
Ranked by: Assets, in millions of dollars. **Remarks:** Also notes bankruptcy date. **Number listed:** 35

1. Texaco Inc., with $35,892 million
2. Federated Deptartment Stores, $7,913
3. Continental Airlines Holdings., $7,656
4. Olympia & York Developments Ltd., $7,023
5. Penn Central, $6,851
6. Maxwell Communication Corp., $6,352
7. LTV, $6,307
8. Columbia Gas System, $6,196
9. Montgomery Ward Holding Corp., $4,879
10. R.H. Macy & Co. Inc., $4,812

Source: *New Generation Research*, Bankruptcy Yearbook & Almanac (annual), 1998, p. 62.

★391★
LARGEST PUBLIC BANKRUPTCIES IN HISTORY, THROUGH 1998
Ranked by: Assets, in millions of dollars. **Remarks:** Also notes bankruptcy date. **Number listed:** 40

1. Texaco Inc., with $35,892 million
2. Financial Corp. of America, $33,864
3. MCorp, $20,228
4. First Executive Corp., $15,193
5. Gibraltar Financial Corp., $15,011
6. HomeFed Corp., $13,885
7. Imperial Corp. of America, $12,263
8. First Capital Holdings, $9,675
9. Baldwin-United, $9,383
10. Southmark Corp., $9,161

Source: *New Generation Research*, Bankruptcy Yearbook & Almanac (annual), 1998, p. 60.

Banks, Agricultural

See: **Agricultural Credit**

Banks and Banking

★392★

BANKS WITH THE HIGHEST RETURN ON EQUITY, 1998

Ranked by: Return on equity, in percent. **Number listed:** 10

1. MBNA Corp., with $40.17%
2. U.S. Trust Corp., $26.20%
3. Bank of New York, $24.23%
4. First Tennessee National Corp., $22.73%
5. Comerica Inc., $22.54%
6. National Commerce Bancorp, $22.01%
7. U.S. Bancorp, $21.94%
8. Wilmington Trust Corp., $21.70%
9. Mellon Bank Corp., $20.55%
10. First BanCorp, $20.54%

Source: *U.S Banker*, U.S. Banker Top 100 (annual), May, 1999, p. 45.

★393★

BANKS WITH THE HIGHEST RETURN ON EQUITY, 1998

Ranked by: Return on equity, in percent. **Number listed:** 20

1. MBNA Corp., with $36.91%
2. Irwin Financial Corp., $26.30%
3. U.S. Trust Corp., $25.89%
4. HSBC Americas Inc., $24.93%
5. Bank of New York Co. Inc., $24.25%
6. Comerica Inc., $23.20%
7. First Tennessee National Corp., $22.73%
8. U.S. Bancorp, $22.16%
9. National Commerce Bancorp, $22.15%
10. Wilmington Trust Corp., $21.70%

Source: *Top Performers (annual)*, ABA Banking Journal, June, 1999, p. 36+.

★394★

BANKS WITH THE LOWEST RETURN ON EQUITY, 1998

Ranked by: 15-year return on equity, in percent. **Number listed:** 10

1. Republic Security Financial Corp., with $-5.43%
2. Bankers Trust Corp., $-0.78%
3. Sky Financial Group, $4.68%
4. HUBCO Inc., $4.75%
5. Union Planters Corp., $7.70%
6. Republic New York Corp., $7.84%
7. UMB Financial Corp., $8.34%
8. J.P. Morgan & Co., $8.57%
9. The Colonial BancGroup Inc., $8.59%
10. BancWest Corp., $8.86%

Source: *U.S. Banker*, U.S. Banker Top 100 (annual), May, 1999, p. 48.

★395★

BEST EARNING MID-SIZED BANKS, 1998

Ranked by: Return on equity, in percent. **Number listed:** 5

1. Bank of Commerce, with 26.39%
2. Westernbank Puerto Rico, 23.19%
3. Greater Bay Bancorp, 22.31%
4. Great Southern Bancorp, 21.08%
5. Irwin Financial Corp., 20.23%

Source: *U.S. Banker*, Top 200 Mid-Sized Banks (annual), June, 1999, p. 58.

★396★

LEADING BANKS BY CAPITAL, 1998

Ranked by: Capital, in millions of U.S. dollars ($). **Remarks:** Also lists capital percentage change, as well as dollar amount, rank, and percentage change for size, soundness, profits, and performance, and rank among top banks of the world. **Number listed:** 200

1. Citigroup, with $41,889 million
2. BankAmerica Corp., $36,877
3. Chase Manhattan Corp., $24,121
4. Banc One Corp., $19,654
5. First Union Corp., $13,592
6. Wells Fargo & Co., $12,424
7. J.P. Morgan & Co., $11,242
8. Fleet Financial, $7,384
9. SunTrust Banks Inc., $6,561
10. National City Corp., $6,401

Source: *The Banker*, Top 200 U.S. Banks (annual), June, 1999, p. 35+.

★397★

LEADING BANKS BY MARKET PENETRATION, 1998*

Ranked by: Market penetration, in percent. **Number listed:** 10

1. Citicorp, with 16.2%
2. Discover, 16.1%
3. BankAmerica, 9.3%
4. NationsBank, 9.0%
5. Chase, 8.8%
6. BancOne, 8.2%
7. MBNA, 6.4%
8. Wells Fargo, 5.3%
9. FCNBD, 5.2%
10. First USA Bank, 5.1%

Source: *Future Banker*, July, 1998, p. 45.

★398★

LEADING BANKS IN AGRICULTURE LOANS, 1998

Ranked by: Value of agriculture loans, in thousands of dollars. **Remarks:** Also notes percentage and dollar change from previous year. **Number listed:** 25

1. Bank of America National Trust & Savings Association, with $2,161,000 thousand
2. Wells Fargo Bank, $2,078,000
3. U.S. Bank NA, $1,336,405
4. NationsBank, $1,295,000
5. Sanwa Bank of California, $838,109
6. KeyBank, $827,945
7. First Union National Bank, $817,145
8. Regions Bank, $582,361
9. Union Planters National Bank, $541,250
10. First Security Bank, $366,723

Source: *Sheshunoff Bank Quarterly*, December 31, 1998, p. I.48.

★399★

LEADING BANKS IN ASSETS, 1998

Ranked by: Assets, in thousands of dollars. **Remarks:** Also notes percentage and dollar change from previous year. **Number listed:** 25

1. NationsBank, with $317,127,000 thousand
2. Citibank, $300,895,000
3. Chase Manhattan Bank, $296,717,000
4. Bank of America National Trust & Savings Association, $257,479,000
5. First Union National Bank, $222,483,323

6. Morgan Guaranty Trust Co., $175,827,034
7. Bankers Trust Co., $104,558,000
8. Wells Fargo Bank, $87,262,000
9. Fleet National Bank, $75,601,000
10. First National Bank of Chicago, $74,200,906

Source: *Sheshunoff Bank Quarterly*, December 31, 1998, p. I.42.

★400★
LEADING BANKS IN BROKERED DEPOSITS, 1998
Ranked by: Brokered deposits, in thousands of dollars. **Remarks:** Also notes percentage and dollar change from previous year. **Number listed:** 25

1. Greenwood Trust Co., with $4,826,816 thousand
2. MBNA America Bank, $3,393,054
3. Bankers Trust Co., $3,336,000
4. La Salle National Bank, $3,190,727
5. Bank of America National Trust & Savings Association, $1,815,000
6. First Tennessee Bank, $1,616,800
7. Providian National Bank, $1,533,363
8. Merrill Lynch Bank & Trust Co., $1,506,927
9. Fleet National Bank, $1,374,000
10. Harris Trust & Savings Bank, $1,251,993

Source: *Sheshunoff Bank Quarterly*, December 31, 1998, p. I.50.

★401★
LEADING BANKS IN COMMERCIAL REAL ESTATE LOANS, 1998
Ranked by: Value of commercial real estate loans, in thousands of dollars. **Remarks:** Also notes percentage and dollar change from previous year. **Number listed:** 25

1. First Union National Bank, with $17,651,698 thousand
2. NationsBank, $15,284,000
3. Wells Fargo Bank, $11,844,000
4. Bank of America National Trust & Savings Association, $10,055,000
5. Southtrust Bank, $7,742,036
6. U.S. Bank NA, $7,625,527
7. KeyBank, $7,303,218
8. Wachovia Bank, $6,818,746
9. Manufacturers & Traders Trust Co., $4,834,837
10. Fleet National Bank, $4,252,000

Source: *Sheshunoff Bank Quarterly*, December 31, 1998, p. I.49.

★402★
LEADING BANKS IN CONSTRUCTION LOANS, 1998
Ranked by: Value of construction loans, in thousands of dollars. **Remarks:** Also notes percentage and dollar change from previous year. **Number listed:** 25

1. NationsBank, with $4,976,000 thousand
2. Southtrust Bank, $3,526,376
3. KeyBank, $3,437,522
4. U.S. Bank NA, $3,046,307
5. First Union National Bank, $2,108,622
6. Regions Bank, $2,106,149
7. Wachovia Bank, $2,044,258
8. Wells Fargo Bank, $1,885,000
9. Bank of America National Trust & Savings Association, $1,836,000
10. Branch Banking & Trust Co., $1,607,663

Source: *Sheshunoff Bank Quarterly*, December 31, 1998, p. I.49.

★403★
LEADING BANKS IN CORRESPONDENT BALANCES, 1998
Ranked by: Correspondent balances, in thousands of dollars. **Remarks:** Also notes percentage and dollar change from previous year. **Number listed:** 25

1. Bank of America National Trust & Savings Association, with $2,472,000 thousand
2. NationsBank, $1,996,000
3. First Union National Bank, $1,857,474
4. Bank One, $1,724,749
5. Wells Fargo Bank, $1,287,000
6. Chase Manhattan Bank, $919,000
7. Mellon Bank, $741,484
8. Norwest Bank, $731,628
9. U.S. Bank NA, $653,049
10. Union Bank of California, $620,085

Source: *Sheshunoff Bank Quarterly*, December 31, 1998, p. I.51.

★404★
LEADING BANKS IN CREDIT CARD LOANS, 1998
Ranked by: Value of credit card loans, in thousands of dollars. **Remarks:** Also notes percentage and dollar change from previous year. **Number listed:** 25

1. Chase Manhattan Bank, with $15,619,683 thousand
2. Citibank, $14,145,000
3. Greenwood Trust Co., $13,974,356
4. MBNA America Bank, $12,307,070
5. Citibank South Dakota, $11,729,388
6. American Express Centurion, $11,093,3535
7. FCC National Bank, $9,927,940
8. NationsBank, $7,859,668
9. Citibank (Nevada) NA, $7,565,648
10. First USA Bank NA, $6,351,033

Source: *Sheshunoff Bank Quarterly*, December 31, 1998, p. I.51.

★405★
LEADING BANKS IN FEE INCOME, 1998
Ranked by: Fee Income, in thousands of dollars. **Remarks:** Also notes percentage and dollar change from previous year. **Number listed:** 25

1. Citibank, with $5,895,000 thousand
2. NationsBank, $5,416,000
3. First Union National Bank, $4,916,816
4. Chase Manhattan Bank, $4,499,000
5. Bank of America National Trust & Savings Association, $4,389,000
6. MBNA America Bank, $3,227,800
7. Wells Fargo Bank, $2,390,000
8. Bankers Trust Co., $2,362,000
9. First USA Bank, $2,273,379
10. Bank One, $2,140,758

Source: *Sheshunoff Bank Quarterly*, December 31, 1998, p. I.46.

★406★
LEADING BANKS IN FIDUCIARY INCOME, 1998
Ranked by: Fiduciary income, in thousands of dollars. **Remarks:** Also notes percentage and dollar change from previous year. **Number listed:** 25

1. State Street Bank & Trust Co., with $1,493,857 thousand
2. Chase Manhattan Bank, $1,283,000
3. Bank of New York, $1,073,984
4. Bankers Trust Co., $919,000
5. Mellon Bank, $834,251
6. First Union National Bank, $823,227
7. Citibank, $674,000

8. NationsBank, $657,000
9. PNC Bank Corp., $636,629
10. Northern Trust Corp., $522,947

Source: *Sheshunoff Bank Quarterly*, December 31, 1998, p. I.46.

★407★

LEADING BANKS IN FOREIGN LOANS, 1998

Ranked by: Value of foreign loans, in thousands of dollars. **Remarks:** Also notes percentage and dollar change from previous year. **Number listed:** 25

1. Citibank, with $123,629,000 thousand
2. Bank of America National Trust & Savings Association, $39,371,000
3. Chase Manhattan Bank, $38,153,000
4. Morgan Guaranty Trust Co. of New York, $20,499,925
5. Bank of New York, $20,222,271
6. BankBoston, $13,646,657
7. Bankers Trust Co., $9,407,000
8. First National Bank of Chicago, $5,635,668
9. First Union National Bank, $3,562,596
10. Republic National Bank of New York, $3,530,813

Source: *Sheshunoff Bank Quarterly*, December 31, 1998, p. I.48.

★408★

LEADING BANKS IN HOME EQUITY LOANS, 1998

Ranked by: Value of home equity loans, in thousands of dollars. **Remarks:** Also notes percentage and dollar change from previous year. **Number listed:** 25

1. NationsBank, with $7,161,000 thousand
2. Bank of America National Trust & Savings Association, $6,561,000
3. First Union National Bank, $6,504,809
4. Wells Fargo Bank, $4,284,000
5. KeyBank, $3,223,082
6. Fleet National Bank, $2,096,000
7. Bank One, $1,900,754
8. U.S. Bank NA, $1,770,161
9. Chase Manhattan Bank, $1,650,000
10. Wachovia Bank, $1,546,621

Source: *Sheshunoff Bank Quarterly*, December 31, 1998, p. I.52.

★409★

LEADING BANKS IN INCOME, 1998

Ranked by: Income, in thousands of dollars. **Remarks:** Also notes percentage and dollar change from previous year. **Number listed:** 25

1. NationsBank, with $4,029,000 thousand
2. First Union National Bank, $2,639,128
3. Chase Manhattan Bank, $2,458,000
4. Citibank, $1,700,000
5. U.S. Bank NA, $1,180,160
6. Bank of New York, $1,060,285
7. KeyBank, $1,020,676
8. Fleet National Bank, $1,012,000
9. PNC Bank Corp., $1,008,240
10. Bank of America National Trust & Savings Association, $983,000

Source: *Sheshunoff Bank Quarterly*, December 31, 1998, p. I.42.

★410★

LEADING BANKS IN IRA DEPOSITS, 1998

Ranked by: IRA deposits, in thousands of dollars. **Remarks:** Also notes percentage and dollar change from previous year. **Number listed:** 25

1. First Union National Bank, with $8,102,394 thousand
2. NationsBank, $7,673,000
3. Bank of America National Trust & Savings Association, $3,851,000
4. Chase Manhattan Bank, $3,218,000
5. Wells Fargo Bank, $2,735,000
6. PNC Bank Corp., $2,698,184
7. Fleet National Bank, $2,593,000
8. Wachovia Bank, $2,478,502
9. KeyBank, $2,384,867
10. U.S. Bank NA, $2,336,260

Source: *Sheshunoff Bank Quarterly*, December 31, 1998, p. I.50.

★411★

LEADING BANKS IN NET CHARGE-OFFS, 1998

Ranked by: Net charge-offs, in thousands of dollars. **Remarks:** Also notes percentage and dollar change from previous year. **Number listed:** 25

1. Citibank NA, with $1,429,000 thousand
2. Bank of America National Trust & Savings Association, $888,000
3. Chase Manhattan Bank, $867,324
4. Greenwood Trust Co., $827,480
5. American Express Centurion, $720,914
6. Chase Manhattan Bank, $622,000
7. Citibank South Dakota NA, $590,429
8. First Union National Bank, $588,458
9. NationsBank, $460,000
10. PNC Bank Corp., $442,480

Source: *Sheshunoff Bank Quarterly*, December 31, 1998, p. I.43.

★412★

LEADING BANKS IN NONPERFORMING AGRICULTURAL LOANS, 1998

Ranked by: Value by nonperforming agricultural loans, in thousands of dollars. **Remarks:** Also notes percentage and dollar change from previous year. **Number listed:** 25

1. KeyBank, with $40,791 thousand
2. Wells Fargo Bank, $18,000
3. First National Bank of Holdrege (NE), $12,412
4. NationsBank, $11,000
5. U.S. Bank NA, $10,937
6. First Security Bank, $8,799
7. First National Bank ND, $6,320
8. Norwest Bank (El Paso, TX), $5,822
9. Norwest Bank (MN South), $4,886
10. Bank One-Arizona, $4,760

Source: *Sheshunoff Bank Quarterly*, December 31, 1998, p. I.45.

★413★

LEADING BANKS IN NONPERFORMING COMMERCIAL AND ALL OTHER LOANS, 1998

Ranked by: Value of nonperforming commercial and all other loans, in thousands of dollars. **Remarks:** Also notes percentage and dollar change from previous year. **Number listed:** 25

1. Citibank, with $1,231,000 thousand
2. Chase Manhattan Bank, $1,018,000
3. Bank of America National Trust & Savings Association, $515,000
4. NationsBank, $495,000
5. First Union National Bank, $278,332
6. Bankers Trust Co., $248,000
7. KeyBank, $233,688
8. PNC Bank Corp., $197,944
9. U.S. Bank NA, $167,523

10. BankBoston NA, $167,405

Source: *Sheshunoff Bank Quarterly*, December 31, 1998, p. I.45.

★414★
LEADING BANKS IN NONPERFORMING CONSUMER LOANS, 1998

Ranked by: Value of nonperforming consumer loans, in thousands of dollars. **Remarks:** Also notes percentage and dollar change from previous year. **Number listed:** 25

1. Citibank, with $1,456,000 thousand
2. Greenwood Trust Co., $740,957
3. Bank One-Arizona NA, $483,870
4. Chase Manhattan Bank, $338,631
5. Citibank-New York State, $275,582
6. MBNA America Bank, $217,627
7. American Express Centurion, $196,506
8. Citibank South Dakota NA, $188,044
9. Fleet National Bank, $168,000
10. FCC National Bank, $165,338

Source: *Sheshunoff Bank Quarterly*, December 31, 1998, p. I.44.

★415★
LEADING BANKS IN NONPERFORMING LOANS, 1998

Ranked by: Value of nonperforming loans, in thousands of dollars. **Remarks:** Also notes percentage and dollar change from previous year. **Number listed:** 25

1. Citibank, with $3,767,000 thousand
2. NationsBank, $1,481,000
3. Chase Manhattan Bank, $1,408,000
4. First Union National Bank, $991,278
5. Bank of America National Trust & Savings Association, $905,000
6. Greenwood Trust Co., $742,334
7. PNC Bank Corp., $545,491
8. Bank One-Arizona NA, $536,306
9. KeyBank, $519,593
10. Wells Fargo Bank, $451,000

Source: *Sheshunoff Bank Quarterly*, December 31, 1998, p. I.43.

★416★
LEADING BANKS IN NONPERFORMING REAL ESTATE LOANS, 1998

Ranked by: Value of nonperforming real estate loans, in thousands of dollars. **Remarks:** Also notes percentage and dollar change from previous year. **Number listed:** 25

1. Citibank, with $1,080,000 thousand
2. NationsBank, $835,000
3. First Union National Bank, $581,064
4. Bank of America National Trust & Savings Association, $353,000
5. Wells Fargo Bank, $287,000
6. GreenPoint Bank, $274,856
7. Chase Manhattan Bank, $270,000
8. Union Planters National Bank, $267,405
9. PNC Bank Corp., $247,808
10. KeyBank, $202,403

Source: *Sheshunoff Bank Quarterly*, December 31, 1998, p. I.44.

★417★
LEADING BANKS IN 1-4 FAMILY RESIDENTIAL REAL ESTATE LOANS, 1998

Ranked by: Value of residential real estate loans, in thousands of dollars. **Remarks:** Also notes percentage and dollar change from previous year. **Number listed:** 25

1. NationsBank, with $49,696,000 thousand
2. First Union National Bank, $40,088,468
3. Chase Manhattan Bank, $31,365,000
4. Bank of America National Trust & Savings Association, $28,286,000
5. PNC Bank Corp., $18,616,598
6. Norwest Bank, $15,443,266
7. Washington MSB, $15,180,824
8. Fleet National Bank, $13,327,000
9. Wells Fargo Bank, $11,937,000
10. KeyBank, $10,429,954

Source: *Sheshunoff Bank Quarterly*, December 31, 1998, p. I.52.

★418★
LEADING BANKS IN SALARY EXPENSE, 1998

Ranked by: Salary expense, in thousands of dollars. **Remarks:** Also notes percentage and dollar change from previous year. **Number listed:** 25

1. Citibank, with $5,291,000 thousand
2. Chase Manhattan Bank, $4,187,000
3. Bank of America National Trust & Savings Association, $3,792,000
4. NationsBank, $3,707,000
5. First Union National Bank, $2,990,913
6. Bankers Trust Co., $1,897,000
7. Wells Fargo Bank, $1,674,000
8. Morgan Guaranty Trust Co. of New York, $1,529,730
9. BankBoston, $1,359,148
10. PNC Bank Corp., $1,175,148

Source: *Sheshunoff Bank Quarterly*, December 31, 1998, p. I.47.

★419★
LEADING BANKS IN SERVICE CHARGE INCOME, 1998

Ranked by: Service charge income, in thousands of dollars. **Remarks:** Also notes percentage and dollar change from previous year. **Number listed:** 25

1. NationsBank, with $1,863,000 thousand
2. Bank of America National Trust & Savings Association, $1,335,000
3. First Union National Bank, $1,223,474
4. Wells Fargo Bank, $817,000
5. U.S. Bank NA, $416,926
6. Wachovia Bank, $333,741
7. Fleet National Bank, $328,000
8. PNC Bank Corp., $307,642
9. KeyBank, $302,076
10. Citibank, $298,000

Source: *Sheshunoff Bank Quarterly*, December 31, 1998, p. I.47.

★420★
LEAST EFFICIENT BANKS, 1998

Ranked by: Efficiency ratio, in percent. **Number listed:** 10

1. Bankers Trust New York Corp., with $95.37%
2. J.P. Morgan & Co., $76.75%
3. U.S. Trust Corp., $76.50%
4. Citigroup, $75.10%
5. State Street Corp., $74.60%
6. UMB Financial Corp., $72.81%
7. First Tennessee National Corp., $71.48%
8. Republic Security Financial Corp., $70.55%
9. The Colonial BancGroup Inc., $69.88%
10. First Citizens BancShares Inc., $69.44%

Source: *U.S. Banker*, U.S. Banker Top 100 (annual), May, 1999, p. 48.

★421★

MOST ADMIRED MONEY CENTER BANKS, 1998

Ranked by: Scores (1-10) derived from a survey of senior executives, outside directors and securities analysts. **Remarks:** Respondents rated companies in their own industry on 8 attributes of reputation. Also notes previous year's rank. **Number listed:** 7

1. Citicorp, with $7.39 points
2. Chase Manhattan, $7.26
3. J.P. Morgan & Co., $7.16
4. First Chicago NBD, $6.81
5. Bank of New York, $6.64
6. Republic New York, $6.44
7. Bankers Trust, $5.56

Source: *Fortune*, America's Most Admired Corporations (annual), March, 1999, p. F-1.

★422★

MOST EFFICIENT BANKS, 1998

Ranked by: Efficiency ratio, in percent. **Number listed:** 10

1. North Fork Bancorp, with $35.03%
2. MBNA Corp., $40.36%
3. Fifth Third Bancorp, $41.49%
4. First BanCorp, $43.50%
5. Westamerica Bancorp, $44.11%
6. Charter One Financial Inc., $46.44%
7. Valley National Bancorp, $46.78%
8. Mercantile Bankshares Corp., $46.85%
9. U.S. Bancorp, $49.06%
10. National Commerce Bancorp, $49.49%

Source: *U.S. Banker*, U.S. Banker Top 100 (annual), May, 1999, p. 45.

★423★

MOST EFFICIENT BANKS, 1998

Ranked by: Efficiency ratio, in percent. **Number listed:** 10

1. Queens County Bancorp, with $36.51%
2. North Fork Bancorp, $37.10%
3. Hamilton Bancorp, $39.27%
4. GBC Bancorp, $39.66%
5. Cathay Bancorp, $40.53%
6. BSB Bancorp, $41.19%
7. Mississippi Valley Bancshares, $42.10%
8. T R Financial, $42.76%
9. S & T Bancorp, $43.75%
10. Frontier Financial, $43.77%

Source: *ABA Banking Journal*, Top Performers (annual), June, 1999, p. 42.

★424★

MOST EFFICIENT MID-SIZED BANKS, 1998

Ranked by: Efficiency ratio, in percent. **Number listed:** 5

1. Bank of Granite, with $37.86%
2. Hamilton Bancorp, $38.15%
3. Westernbank Puerto Rico, $38.88%
4. GBC Bancorp, $39.54%
5. Cathay Bancorp, $40.37%

Source: *U.S. Banker*, Top 200 Mid-Sized Banks (annual), June, 1999, p. 58.

★425★

TOP BANKS BY ASSETS, 1998

Ranked by: Total assets, in millions of dollars. **Remarks:** Also notes other figures on performance and profitability. **Number listed:** 100

1. Citicorp, with $668,641 million
2. BankAmerica Corp., $617,679
3. Chase Manhattan Corp., $365,875
4. Bank One Corp., $261,496
5. J.P. Morgan & Co., $261,067
6. First Union Corp., $237,363
7. Wells Fargo & Co., $202,475
8. Bankers Trust Corp., $133,115
9. Fleet Financial Group, $104,382
10. SunTrust Banks Inc., $93,170

Source: *U.S. Banker*, U.S. Banker (annual), May, 1999, p. 46.

★426★

TOP BANKS BY MARKET CAPITAL, 1998

Ranked by: Year end price per share times outstanding shares, in billions of dollars. **Number listed:** 50

1. Citicorp Inc., with $112.1 billion
2. BankAmerica Corp., $103.7
3. Wells Fargo & Co., $65.7
4. Banc One Corp., $60.1
5. First Union Corp., $59.7
6. Chase Manhattan Corp., $59.4
7. Bank of New York Co. Inc., $31.1
8. U.S. Bancorp, $25.8
9. Fleet Financial Group Inc., $25.5
10. SunTrust Banks Inc., $24.6

Source: *Banking Strategies*, Top 50 Banking Companies (annual), March, 1999, p. 16+.

★427★

TOP BANKS BY NONINTEREST INCOME, 1998

Ranked by: Compares income to total revenue, in percent. **Remarks:** Also notes rank, ROA, location, and total assets. **Number listed:** 10

1. Irwin Financial Corp., with $66.57
2. MBNA Corp., $62.15%
3. U.S. Trust Corp., $60.18%
4. Investors Financial Services Corp., $53.34%
5. Mellon Bank Corp., $49.95%
6. State Street Corp., $47.17%
7. First Tennessee National Corp., $46.40%
8. Synovus Financial Corp., $42.16%
9. Northern Trust Corp., $41.59%
10. Bank of New York Co. Inc., $37.52

Source: *ABA Banking Journal*, Top Performers (annual), June, 1999, p. 40.

★428★

TOP BANKS BY PERFORMANCE RANKING OVER 25 BILLION, 1998

Ranked by: Composite score. **Remarks:** The composite score was calculated by weighing the scores in 7 categories: total assets, NPA ratio, net charge-off ratio, return on equity, efficiency ratio, leverage ratio, and tier one capital. Lower composite score is best. **Number listed:** 33

1. MBNA Corp., with 123
2. Bank of New York, 133
3. Summit Bancorp, 137
4. Comerica Inc., 151
4. Fifth Third Bancorp, 151
6. Northern Trust Corp., 165
6. UnionBanCal Corp., 165
8. BB&T Financial Corp., 173
9. State Street Corp., 209
10. SunTrust Banks Inc., 219

Source: *U.S. Banker*, U.S. Banker Top 100 (annual), May, 1999, p. 43.

★429★

TOP BANKS BY PERFORMANCE RANKING UNDER 25 BILLION, 1999

Ranked by: Composite Score. **Remarks:** The composite score was calculated by weighing the scores in 7 categories: total assets, NPA ratio, net charge-off ratio, return on equity, efficiency ratio, leverage ratio, and tier one capital. **Number listed:** 67

1. National Commerce Bancorp, with $87
2. North Fork Bancorp, $88
3. Mercantile Bankshares Corp., $95
4. Westamerica Bancorp, $107
5. Valley National Bancorp, $113
6. CCB Financial Corp., $118
7. One Valley Bancorp, $142
7. Trustmark Corp., $142
9. Fulton Financial Corp., $144
10. National Bancorp of Alaska Inc., $159

Source: *U.S. Banker*, U.S. Banker Top 100 (annual), May, 1999, p. 42+.

★430★

TOP BANKS IN CAPITAL STRENGTH, 1998

Ranked by: Leverage ratio, in percent. **Remarks:** Also notes tier one capital and tier one rank. **Number listed:** 10

1. National Bancorp of Alaska Inc., with 14.24%
2. Mercantile Bankshares Corp., 12.51%
3. MBNA Corp., 11.34%
4. Synovus Financial Corp., 10.76%
5. Whitney Holding Corp., 10.39%
5. Fifth Third Bancorp., 10.39%
7. Valley National Bancorp, 10.12%
8. Fulton Financial Corp., 9.93%
9. Trustmark Corp., 9.88%
10. Marshall & Ilsley Corp., 9.86%

Source: *U.S. Banker*, U.S. Banker Top 100 (annual), May, 1999, p. 48.

★431★

TOP BANKS IN THE GENERATION X MARKET, 1998*

Ranked by: Market share, in percent. **Number listed:** 10

1. Citicorp, with 16.2%
2. Discover, 16.1%
3. BankAmerica, 9.3%
4. NationsBank, 9.0%
5. Chase, 8.8%
6. BancOne, 8.2%
7. MBNA, 6.4%
8. Wells Fargo, 5.3%
9. FCNBD, 5.2%
10. First USA Bank, 5.1%

Source: *Future Banker*, July, 1998, p. 45.

★432★

TOP BANKS IN THE S&P 500, 1999

Ranked by: Each company is ranked by eight criteria: one-year total return, three-year total return, one-year sales growth, three-year average annual sales growth, one-year profit growth, three-year average annual sales growth, one-year profit growth, net profit margins, and return on equity, with additional weight given to its sales. **Remarks:** A company's composite rank is calculated using the sum of its individual ranks. Overall scores not provided. **Number listed:** 33

1. MBNA
2. BB & T
3. State Street Corp.
4. U.S. Bancorp
5. Firstar
6. First Union
7. Bank One
8. Wachovia
9. Northern Trust
10. Mellon Bank

Source: *Business Week*, Business Week 50: Top Companies of the S & P 500 (annual), March 29, 1999, p. 142+.

★433★

TOP BANKS WITH TOTAL ASSETS BETWEEN $100 MILLION AND $1 BILLION, 1998

Ranked by: 5-year return on assets, in percent. **Remarks:** Also notes total assets, 5-year return on equity, efficiency ratio, rank from previous year, and other economic measures. **Number listed:** 50

1. Beneficial National Bank (Wilmington, DE), with 4.32%
2. First Bank of Oak Park (IL), 3.89%
3. Brighton Bank (Salt Lake City, UT), 3.62%
4. First Premier Bank (Sioux Falls, SD), 3.50%
5. Guardian State Bank (Salt Lake City, UT), 3.46%
6. U.S. National Bank of Galveston (TX), 3.43%
7. Cosmopolitan Bank & Trust (Chicago, IL), 3.04%
8. First Bank & Trust Co. of Illinois (Palatine, IL), 2.81%
9. Citizens 1st Bank (Tyler, TX), 2.66%
10. Fireside Thrift Co. (Newark, CA), 2.62%

Source: *ABA Banking Journal*, Banking's Top Performers (annual), July, 1998, p. 36.

★434★

TOP BANKS WITH TOTAL ASSETS GREATER THAN $1 BILLION, 1998

Ranked by: 5-year return on assets, in percent. **Remarks:** Also notes total assets, 5-year return on equity, efficiency ratio, rank from previous year, and other economic measures. **Number listed:** 50

1. Northern Trust Bank of Florida (Miami, FL), with 2.37%
2. Bank One of Wisconsin (Milwaukee, WI), 2.32%
3. Park National Bank (Newark, OH), 2.06%
4. National Bank of Arizona (Tucson, AZ), 2.03%
5. Mercantile Bank NA (Hartford, IL), 2.01%
6. Colorado Community First National Bank (Fort Morgan, CO), 1.96%
7. First National Bank of Southwestern Ohio (Hamilton, OH), 1.90%
8. BB&T South Carolina (Greenville, SC), 1.87%
9. Norwest Bank Iowa NA (Des Moines, IA), 1.86%
9. Fifth Third Bank of Norwest Ohio NA (Toledo, OH), 1.86%

Source: *ABA Banking Journal*, Banking's Top Performers (annual), July, 1998, p. 40.

★435★

TOP BANKS WITH TOTAL ASSETS LESS THAN $100 MILLION, 1998

Ranked by: 5-year return on assets, in percent. **Remarks:** Also notes total assets, 5-year return on equity, efficiency ratio, rank from previous year, and other economic measures. **Number listed:** 50

1. First Coleman National Bank (Coleman, TX), with 3.31%
2. Lakeside Bank of Salina (OK), 2.86%
3. First State Bank (Keene, TX), 2.74%
4. Bank of Locust Grove (OK), 2.68%
5. Security Bank of Southwest Missouri (Cassville, MO), 2.67%
6. Miami Valley Bank (Quincy, OH), 2.65%
7. First Bank & Trust (New Orleans, LA), 2.64%
8. First State Bank (Idaho Springs, CO), 2.62%
9. Martell State Bank (Martell, NE), 2.56%
10. Liberty National Bank (Longwood, FL), 2.51%

Source: *ABA Banking Journal*, Banking's Top Performers (annual), July, 1998, p. 30+.

★436★
TOP COMMERCIAL BANKS BY REVENUE, 1998
Ranked by: Revenue, in millions of dollars. **Remarks:** Also includes profits, profits as a percentage of revenue, assets and stockholders' equity, earning per share, total return to investors, and number of employees. **Number listed:** 44

1. BankAmerica Corp., with $50,777 million
2. Chase Manhattan Corp., $32,379
3. Bank One Corp., $25,595
4. First Union Corp., $21,543
5. Wells Fargo, $20,482
6. J.P. Morgan & Co., $18,425
7. Bankers Trust Corp., $12,048
8. Fleet Financial Group, $10,002
9. National City Corp., $8,071
10. PNC Bank, $7,936

Source: *Fortune*, Fortune 500 Largest U.S. Corporations (annual), April 26, 1999, p. F-54.

★437★
TOP MID-SIZED BANKS, 1998
Ranked by: Six criteria were used to rank the 200 mid-sized banks according to their year-end performance: Non- performing assets ratio, net charge-off ratio, return on equity, efficiency ratio, leverage ratio and tier one capital ratio. **Remarks:** Also notes total assets. **Number listed:** 200

1. Frontier Financial Corp., with 93 points
2. First of Long Island Corp., 128
3. Park National Corp., 150
4. Merchants New York Bancorp, 163
5. Tompkins County Trust Co. Inc., 164
6. Glacier Bancorp Inc., 168
7. Central Coast Bancorp, 169
8. Mississippi Valley Bancshares, 175
9. Mahoning National Bancorp, 178
10. Bank of Commerce, 179

Source: *U.S. Banker*, Top 200 Mid-Sized Banks (annual), June, 1999, p. 61.

★438★
TOP U.S. BANKS, 1998
Ranked by: Capital, in millions of dollars. **Remarks:** Also notes size, soundness, profitability, and performance figures, as well as rank worldwide. **Number listed:** 154

1. Chase Manhattan Corp., with $22,594 million
2. Citicorp, $21,211
3. BankAmerica Corp., $17,292
4. NationsBank, $13,599
5. J.P. Morgan & Co., $11,854
6. First Union Corp., $10,203
7. Banc One Corp., $8,909
8. First Chicago NBD Corp., $8,540
9. Bankers Trust New York Corp., $6,431
10. Fleet Financial, $6,159

Source: *World Top 1,000 (annual)*, Summer, July, 1998, p. 201+.

Banks and Banking—Acquisitions and Mergers

See: **Bank Acquisitions and Mergers**

Banks and Banking--Africa

★439★
AFRICA'S LARGEST BANKS, 1997
Ranked by: Capital, in millions of U.S. dollars ($). **Remarks:** Also lists capital percentage change, as well as dollar amount, rank, and percentage change for size, soundness, profits, and performance, and rank among the top banks of the world. **Number listed:** 100

1. Stanbic, with $2,091 million
2. ABSA Group, $1,665
3. Nedcor, $1,409
4. First National Bank Holdings, $1,156
5. Investec Group, $958
5. NBS Boland Bank, $958
7. First Bank of Nigeria, $343
8. United Bank of Africa, $243
9. Mauritius Commercial Bank, $190
10. Kenya Commercial Bank, $156
10. Union Bank of Nigeria, $150

Source: *The Banker*, Top 100 African Banks-By Country (annual), December, 1998, p. 69.

Banks and Banking--Algeria

★440★
LARGEST BANKS IN ALGERIA BY CAPITAL, 1996
Ranked by: Capital, by millions of U.S. dollars ($). **Remarks:** Also notes capital percentage change, as well as dollar amount, rank and percentage change for size, soundness, profits, and performance; and rank among the world's top 1,000 banks. **Number listed:** 3

1. Banque Exterieure d'Algerie, with $557 million
2. Credit Populaire d'Algerie, $275
3. Banque Nationale d'Algerie, $188

Source: *The Banker*, World Top 1,000 Banker (annual), Summer, July, 1997, p. 175.

Banks and Banking--Andorra

★441★
LARGEST BANKS IN ANDORRA, 1997
Ranked by: Capital, in millions of U.S. dollars ($). **Remarks:** Also notes capital percentage change, as well as dollar amount, rank and percentage change for size, soundness, profits, and performance, and rank among the world's top 1,000 banks. **Number listed:** 3

1. Credit Andorra, with $315 million
2. Banc International d'Andorra, $238
3. Banc Agricol i Comercial d'Andorra, $185

Source: *The Banker*, World Top 1,000 (annual), Summer, July, 1998, p. 175.

Banks and Banking--Arab

★442★
LARGEST ARAB FINANCIAL INSTITUTIONS, 1997
Ranked by: Capital, in millions of U.S. dollars ($). **Remarks:** Also lists capital percentage change, as well as dollar amount, rank, and percentage change for size, soundness, profits, and performance, and rank among the top banks of the world. **Number listed:** 100

1. National Commercial Bank, with $2,076 million
2. Arab Banking Corporation, $2,046
3. Riyad Bank, $2,013
4. Al Rajhi Banking & Investment Corp., $1,376
5. Arab Bank, $1,260
6. Saudi American Bank, $1,222
7. National Bank of Kuwait, $1,215
8. Gulf Investment Corp., $1,123
9. National Bank of Dubai, $990
10. National Bank of Egypt, $916

Source: *The Banker*, Top 100 Arab Financial Institutions (annual), November, 1998, p. 78.

Banks and Banking--Arab--Algeria

★443★
LARGEST ARAB BANKS IN ALGERIA, 1996
Ranked by: Capital, in millions of U.S. dollars ($). **Remarks:** Also lists capital percentage change, as well as dollar amount, rank, and percentage change for size, soundness, profits, and performance, and rank among the top banks of the world. **Number listed:** 3

1. Banque Extereure d'Algerie, with $557 million
2. Credit Polulaire d'Algerie, $275
3. Banque Nationale d'Algerie, $188

Source: *The Banker*, Top 100 Arab Financial Institutions (annual), November, 1998, p. 80.

Banks and Banking--Arab--Bahrain

★444★
LARGEST ARAB BANKS IN BAHRAIN, 1997
Ranked by: Capital, in millions of U.S. dollars ($). **Remarks:** Also lists capital percentage change, as well as dollar amount, rank, and percentage change for size, soundness, profits, and performance, and rank among the top banks of the world. **Number listed:** 13

1. Arab Banking Corp., with $2,046 million
2. Gulf International Bank, $694
3. Investcorp, $591
4. Bank of Bahrain & Kuwait, $262
5. National Bank of Bahrain, $247
6. United Gulf Bank, $224
7. Bahrain International Bank, $218
8. Faysal Islamic Bank of Bahrain, $145
9. Bahrain Middle East Bank, $119
10. Al-Ahli Commercial Bank, $113

Source: *The Banker*, Top 100 Arab Financial Institutions (annual), November, 1998, p. 80.

Banks and Banking--Arab--Egypt

★445★
LARGEST ARAB BANKS IN EGYPT, 1997
Ranked by: Capital, in millions of U.S. dollars ($). **Remarks:** Also lists capital percentage change, as well as dollar amount, rank, and percentage change for size, soundness, profits, and performance, and rank among the top banks of the world. **Number listed:** 13

1. National Bank of Egypt, with $916 million
2. Banque Misr, $469
3. Arab International Bank, $356
4. Commercial International Bank, $320
5. Banque du Caire, $317
6. Bank of Alexandria, $305
7. Misr International Bank, $164
8. Faisal Islamic Bank of Egypt, $144
9. Arab African International Bank, $140
10. Suez Canal Bank, $130

Source: *The Banker*, Top 100 Arab Financial Institutions (annual), November, 1998, p. 80.

Banks and Banking--Arab--Jordan

★446★
LARGEST ARAB BANKS IN JORDAN, 1997
Ranked by: Capital, in millions of U.S. dollars ($). **Remarks:** Also lists capital percentage change, as well as dollar amount, rank, and percentage change for size, soundness, profits, and performance, and rank among the top banks of the world. **Number listed:** 3

1. Arab Bank, with $1,260 million
2. Housing Bank, $303
3. Jordan National Bank, $99

Source: *The Banker*, Top 100 Arab Financial Institutions (annual), November, 1998, p. 80.

Banks and Banking--Arab--Kuwait

★447★
LARGEST ARAB BANKS IN KUWAIT, 1997
Ranked by: Capital, in millions of U.S. dollars ($) **Remarks:** Also lists capital percentage change, as well as dollar amount, rank, and percentage change for size, soundness, profits, and performance, and rank among top banks in the world. **Number listed:** 8

1. National Bank of Kuwait, with $1,215 million
2. Gulf Investment Corp., $1,123
3. Gulf Bank, $550
4. Commercial Bank of Kuwait, $500
5. Burgan Bank, $493
6. Kuwait Finance House, $459
7. Al-Ahli Bank of Kuwait, $444
8. Bank of Kuwait & the Middle East, $359

Source: *The Banker*, Top 100 Arab Financial Institutions (annual), November, 1998, p. 80+.

Banks and Banking--Arab--Lebanon

★448★
LARGEST ARAB BANKS IN LEBANON, 1997
Ranked by: Capital, in millions of U.S. dollars ($). **Remarks:** Also lists capital percentage change, as well as dollar amount, rank, and percentage change for size, soundness, profits, and performance, and rank among the top banks of the world. **Number listed:** 7

1. Banque de la Mediterranee, with $314 million
2. Byblos Bank, $222
3. Banque Audi, $165
4. Banque du Liban & d'Outre Mer, $133
5. Fransabank, $103
6. Credit Libanais, $68
7. Bank of Beirut & the Arab Countries, $57

Source: *The Banker*, Top 100 Arab Financial Institutions (annual), November, 1998, p. 82.

Banks and Banking--Arab--Libya

★449★
LARGEST ARAB BANKS IN LIBYA, 1997
Ranked by: Capital, in millions of U.S. dollars ($). **Remarks:** Also lists capital percentage change, as well as dollar amount, rank, and percentage change for size, soundness, profits, and performance, and rank among the top of the world. **Number listed:** 4

1. Libyan Arab Foreign Bank, with $698 million
2. Sahara Bank, $647
3. National Commercial Bank, $269
4. Jamahiriya Bank, $110

Source: *The Banker*, Top Arab Financial Institutions (annual), November, 1998, p. 82.

Banks and Banking--Arab--Morocco

★450★
LARGEST ARAB BANK IN MOROCCO, 1997
Ranked by: Capital, in millions of U.S. dollars ($) **Remarks:** Also lists capital percentage change, as well as dollar amount, rank, and percentage change for size, soundness, profits, and performance, and rank among the top banks of the world. **Number listed:** 5

1. Credit Populaire du Maroc, with $564 million
2. Banque Marocaine du Commerce Exterieur, $351
3. Banque Commerciale du Maroc, $350
4. Wafabank, $233
5. Credit du Maroc, $139

Source: *The Banker*, Top 100 Arab Financial Institutions (annual), November, 1998, p. 82.

Banks and Banking--Arab--Oman

★451★
LARGEST ARAB BANKS IN OMAN, 1997
Ranked by: Capital, in millions of U.S. dollars ($) **Remarks:** Also lists capital percentage change, as well as dollar amount, rank, and percentage change for size, soundness, profits, and performance, and rank among top banks of the world. **Number listed:** 6

1. Oman International Bank, with $165 million
2. National Bank of Oman, $124
3. Commercial Bank of Oman, $107
4. Bank Muscat Al Ahli Al Omani SAOG (Muttrah), $78
5. Oman Arab Bank, $69
6. Bank of Oman, Bahrain & Kuwait, $63

Source: *The Banker*, Top 100 Financial Institutions (annual), November, 1998, p. 82.

Banks and Banking--Arab--Qatar

★452★
LARGEST ARAB BANKS IN QATAR, 1997
Ranked by: Capital, in millions of U.S. dollars ($). **Remarks:** Also lists capital percentage change, as well as dollar amount, rank, and percentagechange for size, soundness, profits, and performance, and rank among the top banks of the world. **Number listed:** 5

1. Qatar National Bank, with $797 million
2. Commercial Bank of Qatar, $118
3. Doha Bank, $93
4. Qatar Islamic Bank, $70
5. Al-Ahli of Qatar, $53

Source: *The Banker*, Top 100 Arab Financial Institutions (annual), November, 1998, p. 82+.

Banks and Banking--Arab--Saudi Arabia

★453★
LARGEST ARAB BANKS IN SAUDI ARABIA, 1997
Ranked by: Capital, in millions of U.S. dollars ($). **Remarks:** Also lists capital percentage change, as well as dollar amount, rank, and percentage change for size, soundness, profits, and performance, and rank among the top banks of the world. **Number listed:** 11

1. National Commercial Bank, with $2,076 million
2. Riyad Bank, $2,013
3. Al Rajhi Banking & Investment Corp., $1,376
4. Saudi British Bank, $1,222
5. United Saudi Bank, $848
6. Saudi British Bank, $787
7. Al Bank Al Saudi Al Fransi, $782
8. Arab National Bank, $773
9. Saudi Investment Bank, $365
10. Saudi Hollandi Bank, $352

Source: *The Banker*, Top Arab Financial Institutions (annual), November, 1998, p. 84.

Banks and Banking--Arab--Tunisia

★454★
LARGEST ARAB BANKS IN TUNISIA, 1997
Ranked by: Capital, in millions of U.S. dollars ($). **Remarks:** Also lists capital percentage change, as well as dollar amount

rank, and percentage change for size, soundness, profits, and performance, and rank among the top banks of the world. **Number listed:** 5

1. Banque Nationale Agricole, with $300 million
2. Banque du Sud, $113
3. Societe Tunisienne de Banque, $97
4. Banque Internationale Arabe de Tunisie, $74
5. Banque de Tunisie, $54

Source: *The Banker*, Top 100 Arab Financial Institutions (annual), November, 1998, p. 84.

Banks and Banking--Arab--United Arab Emirates

★455★

LARGEST ARAB BANKS IN THE UNITED ARAB EMIRATES, 1997

Ranked by: Capital, in millions of U.S. dollars ($). **Remarks:** Also lists capital percentage change, as well as dollar amount, rank, and percentage change for size, soundness, profits, and performance, and rank among the top banks of the world. **Number listed:** 16

1. National Bank of Dubai, with $990 million
2. Abu Dhabi Commercial Bank, $693
3. Emirates Bank International, $667
4. National Bank of Abu Dhabi, $629
5. MashreqBank, $528
6. Arab Bank for Investment & Foreign Trade, $293
7. Commercial Bank of Dubai, $232
8. Dubai Islamic Bank, $156
9. Union National Bank, $153
10. National Bank of Fujairah, $126

Source: *The Banker*, Top 100 Arab Financial Institutions (annual), November, 1998, p. 84.

Banks and Banking--Argentina

★456★

LARGEST BANKS IN ARGENTINA BY MARKET SHARE, 1998*

Ranked by: Loan market share, in percent. **Number listed:** 10

1. De la Nacion Argentina, with 11.78%
2. De la Provincia de Buenos Aires, 10.45%
3. De Galicia Buenos Aires, 7.68%
4. Rio de la Plata, 5.89%
5. Hipotecario Nacional, 4.95%
6. Bankboston, 4.92%
7. Citibank, 4.42%
8. Bansud, 3.66%
9. Frances del Rio de la Plata, 3.61%
10. HSBC Banco Roberts, 3.04%

Source: *LatinFinance*, Top 50 Latin Banks (annual), October, 1998, p. 60.

★457★

LARGEST BANKS IN ARGENTINA, 1998*

Ranked by: Capital, in millions of U.S. dollars ($). **Remarks:** Also lists capital percent change, as well as dollar amount, rank, and percentage change for size, soundness, profits, and performance, and rank among the top banks of the world. **Number listed:** 8

1. Banco de la Nacion Argentina, with $2,002 million
2. Banco de la Provincia de Buenos Aires, $1,223
3. Banco Rio de la Plata, $917
4. Banco de Galicia y Buenos Aires, $895
5. Banco Frances del Rio de la Plata, $639
6. Banco Bansud, $382
7. Banco de la Ciudad de Buenos Aires, $194
8. Banco de la Provincia de Cordoba, $193

Source: *The Banker*, World Top 1,000 (annual), July, 1998, p. 175.

★458★

LEADING BANKS IN ARGENTINA BY DEPOSIT MARKET SHARE, 1998*

Ranked by: Deposit market share, in percent. **Number listed:** 10

1. De la Nacion Argentina, with 13.59%
2. De la Provincia de Buenos Aires, 11.80%
3. De Galicia Buenos Aires, 8.60%
4. Citibank, 5.79%
5. Rio de la Plata, 5.33%
6. Bankboston, 4.33%
7. Frances del Rio de la Plata, 4.00%
8. HSBC Banco Roberts, 3.07%
9. Nazionale del Lavoro, 2.63%
10. De la Ciudad de Buenos Aires, 2.44%

Source: *LatinFinance*, Top 50 Latin Banks (annual), October, 1998, p. 60.

★459★

LEADING BANKS IN ARGENTINA BY EFFICIENCY, 1998*

Ranked by: Efficiency ratio, in percent. **Number listed:** 10

1. De Inversion y Comercio Exterior, with 20.40%
2. Del Sol, 34.92%
3. Hipotecario Nacional, 37.45%
4. Of America, 42.38%
5. De la Republic Oriental del Uruguay, 43.76%
6. Saenz, 52.35%
7. Roela, 56.92%
8. Banco Julio S.A., 62.33%
9. Corp. Metrop. de Finanzas, 62.36%
10. Nuevo Banco Industrial de Azul, 63.63%

Source: *LatinFinance*, Top 50 Latin Banks (annual), October, 1998, p. 60.

★460★

LEADING BANKS IN ARGENTINA BY EQUITY, 1998*

Ranked by: Return on equity, in percent. **Number listed:** 10

1. Del Sol, with 54.50%
2. De Salta, 45.61%
3. De Prevision Social, 35.87%
4. De Corrientes, 34.49%
5. Social de Cordoba, 27.93%
6. De San Juan, 26.67%
7. De Santiago del Estero, 26.35%
8. Del Tucuman, 25.53%
9. Provincia de Tierra del Fuego, 22.57%
10. Citibank, 20.54%

Source: *LatinFinance*, Top 50 Latin Banks, October, 1998, p. 60.

★461★

TOP BANKS IN ARGENTINA BY ASSETS, 1998*

Ranked by: Assets, in thousands of U.S. dollars ($). **Number listed:** 10

1. De la Nacion Argentina, with $15,289,007 thousand
2. De la Provincia de Buenos Aires, $11,913,269
3. De Galicia Buenos Aires, $11,484,677
4. Rio de la Plata, $8,972,109

5. Bankboston, $6,455,914
6. Citibank, $5,887,864
7. Frances del Rio de la Plata, $5,310,225
8. Hipotecario Nacional, $3,767,006
9. Bansud, $3,709,455
10. HSBC Banco Roberts, $3,538,384

Source: *LatinFinance*, Top 50 Latin Banks (annual), October, 1998, p. 60.

Banks and Banking--Asia

★462★
LARGEST BANKS IN ASIA BY ASSETS, 1997
Ranked by: Assets, in thousands of U.S. dollars ($). **Number listed:** 200

1. Bank of Tokyo Mitsubishi Ltd. (Tokyo), with $625,524,214 thousand
2. Sumitomo Bank (Tokyo), $450,822,821
3. Sakura Bank (Tokyo), $409,578,256
4. Sanwa Bank (Osaka), $397,893,884
5. Dai-Ichi Kangyo Bank (Tokyo), $397,776,609
6. Fuji Bank Ltd. (Tokyo), $389,721,766
7. Norinchukin Bank (Tokyo), $351,597,732
8. Industrial Bank of Japan Ltd. (Tokyo), $325,225,082
9. China Construction Bank, $256,072,666
10. Bank of China, $253,656,886

Source: *Dun & Bradstreet*, Asia's 7500 Largest Companies (annual), 1999, p. 296+.

★463★
MOST ADMIRED BANKS AND FINANCE COMPANIES IN ASIA, 1999
Ranked by: Survey results. **Number listed:** 10

1. HSBC, with 8.84
2. Hang Seng Bank, 7.85
3. DBS Bank, 7.80
4. Standard Chartered, 7.77
5. Citibank, 7.63
6. Shinhan Bank, 7.51
7. American Insurance Group, 7.47
8. Public Bank, 7.30
9. American Express, 7.13
10. Bank of America, 7.10

Source: *Asian Business*, Most Admired Companies in Asia (annual), May, 1999, p. 28.

Banks and Banking--Australia

★464★
LARGEST BANKS IN AUSTRALIA, 1997
Ranked by: Capital, in millions of U.S. dollars ($). **Remarks:** Also lists capital percentage change, as well as dollar amount, rank, and percentage change for size, soundness, profits, and performance, and rank among the world's top 1,000 banks. **Number listed:** 7

1. National Australia Bank, with $7,552 million
2. Commonwealth Bank Group, $5,567
3. ANZ Banking Group, $5,032
4. Westpac Banking Corp., $5,026
5. St George Bank, $1,382
6. Colonial State Bank, $864
7. Macquarie Bank, $385

Source: *World Top 1,000 Banker*, (annual), Summer, July, 1998, p. 175.

Banks and Banking--Austria

★465★
LARGEST BANKS IN AUSTRIA, 1997
Ranked by: Capital, in millions of U.S. dollars ($). **Remarks:** Also lists capital percentage change, as well as dollar amount, rank, and percentage change for size, soundness, profits, and performance, and rank among the world's top 1,000 banks. **Number listed:** 20

1. Bank Austria, with $4,241 million
2. Erste Bank, $1,712
3. Raiffeisen Zentralbank Osterreich, $1,045
4. Bank fur Arbeit and Wirtschaft, $841
5. PSK Banking Group, $820
6. OsterreichischeVolksbanken, $437
7. Raiffeisenlandesbank Niederosterreich-Wien, $396
8. Oberbank, $370
9. Raiffeisenlandesbank Oberosterreich, $353
10. Landes-Hypothekenbank Tirol, $262

Source: *World Top 1,000 Banker*, (annual), Summer, July, 1998, p. 175+.

Banks and Banking--Bahrain

★466★
LARGEST BANKS IN BAHRAIN, 1997
Ranked by: Capital, in millions of U.S. dollars ($). **Remarks:** Also lists capital percentage change, as well as dollar amount, rank, and percentage change for size, soundness, profits, and performance, and rank among the world's top 1,000 banks. **Number listed:** 6

1. Arab Banking Corp., with $2,046 million
2. Investcorp, $591
3. Bank of Bahrain & Kuwait, $262
4. National Bank of Bahrain, $247
5. United Gulf Bank, $224
6. Bahrain International Bank, $218

Source: *World Top 1,000 Banker*, (annual), Summer, July, 1998, p. 176.

Banks and Banking--Bangladesh

★467★
TOP BANKS IN BANGLADESH, 1999
Ranked by: Assets, in million of U.S. dollars ($). **Remarks:** Also lists location, previous rank, balance against local currency, paid-up capital, and balance sheet date. **Number listed:** 13

1. Sonali Bank, with $3,863 million
2. Agrani Bank, $2,312
3. Bangladesh Krishi Bank, $1,166
4. National Bank Ltd., $611
5. Islami Bank Bangladesh Ltd., $590
6. International Finance Investment & Commerce Bank Ltd., $491

7. Uttara Bank Ltd., $441
8. Arab Bangladesh Bank Ltd., $336
9. United Commercial Bank Ltd., $280
10. Eastern Bank Ltd., $264

Source: *Bankers' Almanac World Ranking*, (annual), 1999, p. 112.

Banks and Banking--Belarus

★468★
TOP BANKS IN BELARUS, 1999
Ranked by: Assets, in millions of U.S. dollars ($). **Remarks:** Also lists location, previous rank, balance against local currency, paid-up capital, and balance sheet date. **Number listed:** 6

1. Belarusbank, with $692 million
2. Belagroprombank, $387
3. Belarussian Joint Stock Commercial Bank for Industry & Construction, $282
4. Belvnesheconombank, $207
5. Priorbank, $133
6. Belgazprombank, $18

Source: *Bankers' Almanac World Ranking*, (annual), 1999, p. 112.

Banks and Banking--Belgium

★469★
LARGEST BANKS IN BELGIUM, 1997
Ranked by: Capital, in millions of U.S. dollars ($). **Remarks:** Also lists capital percentage change, as well as dollar amount, rank, and percentage change for size, soundness, profits, and performance, and rank among the world's top 1,000 banks. **Number listed:** 8

1. Generale Bank, with $4,176 million
2. Kredietbank, $3,588
3. Bank Brussels Lambert, $2,877
4. ASLK-CGER Bank, $2,464
5. CERA Bank, $2,120
6. BACOB Bank, $1,770
7. Anhyp, $489
8. IPPA Bank, $158

Source: *World Top 1,000 Banker*, (annual), Summer, July, 1998, p. 176.

Banks and Banking--Bermuda

★470★
TOP BANKS IN BERMUDA, 1997
Ranked by: Assets, in millions of U.S. ($). **Remarks:** Also lists location, previous rank, balance against local ccurrency, paid-up capital, and balance sheet date. **Number listed:** 3

1. Bank of Burmuda Ltd., with $9,911 million
2. Bank of N. T. Butterfield & Son Ltd., $4,429
3. Bermuda Commercial Bank Ltd., $405

Source: *Bankers' Almanac World Ranking*, (annual), 1999, p. 114.

Banks and Banking--Black Banks

★471★
LARGEST BLACK-OWNED BANKS, 1998
Ranked by: Total assets, in millions of U.S. dollars ($). **Remarks:** Also notes rank of previous year, chief executive, year founded, number of employees, and total capital, deposits, and loans. **Number listed:** 25

1. Carver Bancorp Inc., with $420.492 million
2. Highland Community Bank, $290.000
3. Industrial Bank N. A., $269.553
4. Independence Federal Savings Bank, $267.389
5. Seaway National Bank of Chicago, $254.433
6. Citizens Trust Bank, $205.663
7. Harbor Bank of Maryland, $184.723
8. Liberty Bank & Trust Co., $177.789
9. Fanily Savings Bank FSB, $175.000
10. City National Bank of New Jersey, $165.000

Source: *D. C. Green Minorities*, Black Enterprise, June, 1999, p. 212.

Banks and Banking--Botswana

★472★
TOP BANKS IN BOTSWANA, 1999
Ranked by: Assets, in millions of U.S. dollars ($). **Remarks:** Also lists location, previous rank, balance against local currency, paid-up capital, and balance sheet date. **Number listed:** 3

1. Barclays Bank of Botswana Ltd., with $412 million
2. Stanbic Bank Botswana Ltd., $112
3. National Development Bank, $45

Source: *Bankers' Almanac World Ranking*, (annual), 1999, p. 115.

Banks and Banking--Brazil

★473★
BRAZIL'S LARGEST BANKS BY DEPOSIT MARKET SHARE, 1998
Ranked by: Deposit market share, in percent. **Number listed:** 10

1. CEF, with 21.43%
2. Brasil, 19.74%
3. Bradesco, 8.82%
4. Itau, 6.56%
5. Banespa, 5.14%
6. Nossa Caixa, 3.82%
7. Real (Grupo), 3.10%
8. HSBC Bamerindus, 2.37%
9. Unibanco, 2.30%
10. Safra Republic Holdings, 1.41%

Source: *LatinFinance*, Top 50 Latin Banks, October, 1998, p. 60.

★474★
BRAZIL'S LARGEST BANKS BY RETURN ON EQUITY, 1998
Ranked by: Return on equity, in percent. **Number listed:** 10

1. Fininvest, with 62.12%
2. Banespa, 51.83%
3. Ford, 42.37%

4. Patrimonio, 41.50%
5. Exprinter Losan, 34.45%
6. FICSA, 34.25%
7. Credibel, 33.52%
8. Volkswagen, 33.49%
9. A. J. Renner, 32.94%
10. Marka, 31.51%

Source: *LatinFinance*, Top 50 Latin Banks, October, 1998, p. 60.

★475★
LEADING BANKS IN BRAZIL BY EFFICIENCY, 1998
Ranked by: Efficiency, in (EOGOR) percent. **Number listed:** 10

1. American Express, with 10.77%
2. Classico, 12.85%
3. Theca, 13.27%
4. Itabanco, 16.11%
5. Multi Banco, 20.61%
6. Guanabara, 21.66%
7. Investcred, 23.24%
8. Volkswagen, 25.61%
9. Exterior de Espana, 27.98%
10. Ford/Liberal, 31.05%

Source: *LatinFinance*, Top 50 Latin Banks (annual), October, 1998, p. 60.

★476★
TOP BANKS IN BRAZIL BY LOAN MARKET SHARE, 1998
Ranked by: Loan market share, in percent. **Number listed:** 10

1. CEF, with 22.63%
2. Brasil, 19.78%
3. Bradesco, 9.28%
4. Itau, 6.12%
5. Unibanco, 4.39%
6. Real (Grupo), 2.87%
7. BCN, 2.01%
8. Banespa, 1.98%
9. BNB, 1.35%
10. Citigroup (Grupo), 1.31%

Source: *LatinFinance*, Top 50 Latin Banks (annual), October, 1998, p. 60.

★477★
TOP BANKS IN BRAZIL BY RETURN ON ASSETS, 1998
Ranked by: Return on assets, in percent. **Number listed:** 10

1. Exprinter Losan, with 17.00%
2. Theca, 15.16%
3. Investcred, 14.39%
4. Boreal, 12.52%
5. American Express, 12.28%
6. A. J. Renner, 11.24%
7. FICSA, 10.74%
8. OK Investimentos, 10.41%
9. Exterior de Espana, 10.17%
10. Liberal, 9.88%

Source: *LatinFinance*, Top 50 Latin banks (annual), October, 1998, p. 60.

★478★
TOP BANKS IN BRAZIL, 1998
Ranked by: Assets, in thousands of U.S. dollars ($). **Number listed:** 10

1. CEF, with $99,646,003 thousand
2. Brasil, $97,246,058
3. Bradesco, $55,108,520
4. Banespa, $52,142,248
5. Itau, $41,419,605
6. Unibanco, $25,124,274
7. Real (Grupo), $16,770,371
8. Safra Republic Holdings, $13,143,280
9. BCN, $12,334,452
10. Nossa Caixa, $11,685,140

Source: *LatinFinance*, Top 50 Latin Banks (annual), October, 1998, p. 60.

Banks and Banking--Burkina Faso

★479★
LARGEST BANKS IN BURKINA FASO, 1998
Ranked by: Capital, in millions of U.S. dollars ($). **Remarks:** Also notes location, as well as capital percentage change, and dollar amount, rank, and percentage change for assets. **Number listed:** 2

1. Caisse Nationale de Credit Agricole du Burkina, with $11 million
1. Banque Internationale pour le Commerce, I' Industrie & I' Agriculture, $11

Source: *The Banker*, Top 100 African Banks - By Country (annual), December, 1998, p. 69.

Banks and Banking--Burundi

★480★
TOP BANKS IN BURUNDI, 1999
Ranked by: Assets, in millions of U.S. ($). **Remarks:** Also lists location, previous rank, balance against local currency, paid-up capital, and balance sheet date. **Number listed:** 3

1. Banque de Credit de Bujumbura SARL, with $90 million
2. Banque Commerciale du Burundi SM, $74
3. Banque Nationale pour le Developpement Economique Societe, $27

Source: *Bankers' Almanac World Ranking*, (annual), 1999, p. 119.

Banks and Banking--Cameroon

★481★
LARGEST BANKS IN CAMEROON
Ranked by: Capital, in millions of U.S. dollars ($). **Remarks:** Also notes location, as well as capital percentage change, and dollar amount, rank, and percentage change for assets. **Number listed:** 2

1. Credit Foncier du Cameroon, with $15 million
2. Societe Generale Banques au Cameroon, $10

Source: *The Banker*, Top 100 African Banks - By Country (annual), December, 1998, p. 69.

Banks and Banking--Canada

★482★
CANADA'S LARGEST BANKS BY CAPITAL, 1997
Ranked by: Capital, in millions of U.S. dollars ($). **Remarks:** Also notes capital percentage change, as well as dollar amount, rank, and percentage change for size, soundness, profits, and performance, and rank among world's top 1,000 banks. **Number listed:** 8

1. Canadian Imperial Bank of Commerce, with $7,429 million
2. Royal Bank of Canada, $7,309
3. Scotiabank, $6,820
4. Bank of Montreal, $6,140
5. Toronto-Dominion Bank, $4,921
6. Desjardins Group, $2,558
7. National Bank of Canada, $2,186
8. Laurentian Bank of Canada, $379

Source: *World Top 1,000 Banker*, (annual), Summer, July, 1998, p. 178.

Banks and Banking--Cayman Islands

★483★
TOP BANKS IN THE CAYMAN ISLANDS, 1999
Ranked by: Assets, in millions of U.S. dollars ($). **Remarks:** Also notes capital percentage change, as well as dollar amount, rank, and percentage change for size, soundness, profits, and performance, and rank among world's top 1,000 banks. **Number listed:** 5

1. Cayman National Bank Ltd., with $500 million
2. Ansbacher Holdings (Cayman) Ltd., $413
3. Ambroveneto International Bank Ltd., $175
3. Trade & Commerce Bank, $175
4. Deutsche Girozentrale Overseas Ltd., $7.76

Source: *Bankers' Almanac World Ranking*, (annual), 1999, p. 120.

Banks and Banking--Central Europe

★484★
TOP CENTRAL EUROPEAN BANKS, 1999
Ranked by: Capital, in millions of U.S. dollars ($). **Remarks:** Also notes location, as well as percent change from previous year, and dollar amount, rank, and percentage change of assets. **Number listed:** 100

1. Komercni Banka, with $970 million
2. Bank Handlowy & Warszawie, $718
3. Bank Pekao SA, $665
4. Ceska Sporitelna, $631
5. Powszechna Kasa Oszczedosci, $503
6. Ceskoslovenska obchodnib Banka, $437
7. BIG Bank Gdanski, $366
8. Beogradska Banka, $358
9. Banca Comerciala Romana, $338
10. Vseobecna Uverova Banka, $337

Source: *The Banker*, Top 100 Central Europeans (annual), April, 1999, p. 42.

Banks and Banking--Channel Islands

★485★
TOP BANKS IN THE CHANNEL ISLANDS, 1999
Ranked by: Assets, in millions of U.S. dollars ($). **Remarks:** Also lists location, previous rank, balance against local currency, paid-up capital, and balance sheet date. **Number listed:** 47

1. Royal Bank of Scotland International Ltd., with $8,895 million
2. British Bank of the Middle East, $7,182
3. Midland Bank Offshore Ltd., $5,705
4. Republic National Bank of New York, $5,506
5. Deutsche Morgan Grenfell (CI) Ltd., $3,740
6. Royal Bank of Canada (Channel Islands) Ltd., $3,312
7. Standard Chartered Bank (CI) Ltd., $2,503
8. Credit Suisse (Guernsey) Ltd., $1,953
9. HSBC Private Bank (Jersey) Ltd., $1,905
10. AIB Bank (CI) Ltd., $1,892

Source: *Bankers' Almanac World Ranking*, (annual), 1999, p. 120+.

Banks and Banking--Chicago (IL)

★486★
LARGEST BANKS IN CHICAGO, 1997-1998
Ranked by: Assets, in millions of dollars. **Remarks:** Also notes percent change from previous year, earnings, breakdown between loan types, and total loans. **Number listed:** 25

1. First National Bank of Chicago, with $58,137.7 million
2. Northern Trust Corp., $20,140.9
3. LaSalle National Bank, $19,148.1
4. Harris Trust & Savings Bank, $15,731.7
5. American National Bank & Trust Co., $9,259.7
6. LaSalle Bank, $6,011.2
7. First of America Bank-Illinois, $5,778.5
8. TCF National Bank-Illinois, $3,270.5
9. Firstar Bank-Illinois, $2,702.6
10. Corus Bank, $2,140.5

Source: *Crain's Chicago Business*, Top Business Lists (annual), 1999, p. 69.

Banks and Banking--Chicago Metropolitan Area

★487★
CHICAGO BANKS WITH THE HIGHEST RETURN ON AVERAGE ASSETS, 1999
Ranked by: Return on average assets, in percent. **Remarks:** Also notes figures from previous year, return on equity, equity capital as a percentage of assets, net income, average capital, and total assets. **Number listed:** 259

1. First Bank of Oak Park, with 4.07%
2. First Bank & Trust Co. of Illinois, 3.76%
3. First Bank USA, 3.73%
4. Bank of Palatine, 3.37%
5. Cosmopolitan Bank & Trust, 3.14%
6. First National Bank of La Grange, 3.06%
7. Howard Savings Bank, 3.04%

8. State Bank of Illinois, 2.64%
9. Bronson-Gore Bank, 2.31%
10. State Bank of Countryside, 2.30%

Source: *Crain's Chicago Business*, Top Business Lists (annual), 1999, p. 57+.

Banks and Banking--Chile

★488★
LARGEST BANKS IN CHILE, 1998
Ranked by: Capital, in millions of U.S. dollars ($). **Remarks:** Also notes capital percentage change, as well as dollar amount, rank, and percentage change for size, soundness, profits, and performance, and rank among world's top 1,000 banks. **Number listed:** 6

1. Banco Santiago, with $799 million
2. Banco de Chili, $635
3. Banco del Estado de Chili, $573
4. Banco de A. Edwards, $272
5. Banco de Credito & Inversiones, $242
6. Banco Sud Americano, $196

Source: *World Top 1,000 Banker*, (annual), Summer, July, 1998, p. 178.

★489★
LEADING BANKS IN CHILE BY EFFICIENCY, 1998
Ranked by: Efficiency, in (OEONI)percent. **Number listed:** 10

1. Of America, with 24.67%
2. Of Tokyo, 29.73%
3. Do Estado de Sao Paulo, 41.61%
4. Do Brasil, 42.74%
5. Chase Manhattan, 47.05%
6. American Express, 48.17%
7. ABN Ambro Holding N.V., 49.16%
8. De la Nacion Argentina, 50.36%
9. Security, 57.81%
10. De Chili, 63.01%

Source: *LatinFinance*, Top 50 Latin Banks, October, 1998, p. 60+.

★490★
LEADING BANKS IN CHILE BY LOAN MARKET SHARE, 1998
Ranked by: Loan market share, in percent. **Number listed:** 10

1. Santiago, with 16.97%
2. Del Estado, 12.88%
3. Santander, 12.41%
4. De Chili, 11.59%
5. De A. Edwards, 7.80%
6. De Credito e Inversiones, 7.63%
7. Sud Americano, 5.53%
8. BHIF, 5.18%
9. Del Desarrollo, 4.06%
10. Coorpbanca, 3.57%

Source: *LatinFinance*, Top 50 Latin Banks, October, 1998, p. 60+.

★491★
LEADING BANKS IN CHILE BY MARKET SHARE, 1998
Ranked by: Deposit market share, in percent. **Number listed:** 10

1. Del Estado, with 16.25%
2. Santiago, 14.13%
3. Santander, 12.88%
4. De Chili, 11.14%
5. De Credito e Inversiones, 9.07%
6. De A. Edwards, 7.55%
7. Sud Americano, 5.13%
8. BHIF, 4.16%
9. Coorpbanca, 4.07%
10. Del Desarrollo, 3.27%

Source: *LatinFinance*, Top 50 Latin Banks (annual), October, 1998, p. 60+.

★492★
TOP BANKS IN CHILE BY ASSETS, 1998
Ranked by: Total assets, in thousands of U.S. dollars ($). **Number listed:** 10

1. Santiago, with $10,797,106 thousand
2. Del Estado, $10,780,373
3. Santander, $9,922,057
4. De Chili, $7,646,459
5. De Credito e Inversiones, $6,019,222
6. Sud Americano, $4,921,475
7. De A. Edwards, $4,712,057
8. Citibank, $3,782,590
9. BHIF, $3,203,192
10. Bankboston, $2,969,371

Source: *LatinFinance*, Top 50 Latin Banks (annual), October, 1998, p. 60+.

★493★
TOP BANKS IN CHILE BY RETURN ON EQUITY, 1998
Ranked by: Return on equity, in percent. **Number listed:** 10

1. Of America, with 25.08%
2. De Credito e Inversiones, 22.03%
3. De Chili, 21.14%
4. BHIF, 17.84%
5. De A. Edwards, 16.44%
6. Security, 15.53%
7. Santiago, 14.74%
8. Internacional, 14.71%
9. Del Desarrollo, 11.98%
10. BICE, 10.60%

Source: *LatinFinance*, Top 50 Latin Banks (annual), October, 1998, p. 60+.

★494★
TOP BANKS IN CHILE WITH THE HIGHEST RETURN ON ASSETS, 1998
Ranked by: Return on assets, in percent. **Number listed:** 10

1. Of Tokyo, with 3.17%
2. De Chile, 2.13%
3. Do Brasil, 1.60%
4. De La Nacion Argentina, 1.47%
5. Internacional, 1.36%
6. Of America, 1.31%
7. Santiago, 1.28%
8. De Credito e Inversiones, 1.14%
9. De A. Edwards, 1.11%
10. Security, 1.08%

Source: *LatinFinance*, Top 50 Latin Banks (annual), October, 1998, p. 60+.

Banks and Banking--China

★495★
LARGEST BANKS IN CHINA, 1997
Ranked by: Capital, in millions of U.S. dollars ($). **Remarks:** Also notes capital percentage change, as well as dollar amount,

rank, and percentage change for size, soundness, profits, and performance, and rank among world's top 1,000 banks. **Number listed:** 6

1. Industrial & Commercial Bank of China, with $11,698 million
2. Bank of China, $10,594
3. China Construction Bank, $5,988
4. Agricultural Bank of China, $4,802
5. Bank of Communications, $2,824
6. China Merchants Bank, $637

Source: *World Top 1,000 Banker*, (annual), Summer, July, 1998, p. 178.

Banks and Banking--Colombia

★496★

LARGEST BANKS IN COLOMBIA, 1997

Ranked by: Capital, in millions of U.S. dollars ($). **Remarks:** Also notes capital percentage, as well as dollar amount, rank, and percentage change for size, soundness, profits, and performance, and rank among world's top 1,000 banks. **Number listed:** 3

1. BBV-Banco Ganadero, with $466 million
2. Banco de Occidente, $226
3. Banco de Bogota, $160

Source: *The Banker*, World Top 1,000 (annual), Summer, July, 1998, p. 178.

★497★

LEADING BANKS IN COLOMBIA BY DEPOSIT MARKET SHARE, 1998

Ranked by: Deposit market share, in percent. **Number listed:** 10

1. Ganadero, with 9.32%
2. Davivienda, 9.21%
3. Colombia, 7.93%
4. Bogota, 7.67%
5. Bancafe, 7.34%
6. Caja de Credito Agrario, 6.14%
7. Industrial Colombiano, 5.65%
8. Popular, 5.64%
9. Santander, 5.12%
10. Citibank, 3.40%

Source: *LatinFinance*, Top 50 Latin Banks (annual), July, 1998, p. 62.

★498★

LEADING BANKS IN COLOMBIA BY RETURN ON ASSETS, 1998

Ranked by: Return on assets, in percent. **Number listed:** 10

1. Occidente, with 3.68%
2. Bogota, 3.51%
3. Caja Social, 3.49%
4. Citibank, 2.80%
5. Popular, 2.22%
6. Superior, 2.15%
7. Industrial Colombiano, 1.79%
8. Anglo Colombiano, 1.71%
9. Colombia, 1.48%
10. Ganadero, 1.38%

Source: *LatinFinance*, Top 50 Latin Banks (annual), October, 1998, p. 62.

★499★

TOP BANKS IN COLOMBIA BY EFFICIENCY, 1998

Ranked by: Efficiency, in (OEONI percent). **Number listed:** 10

1. Bankboston SA, with 47.36%
2. Occidente, 54.80%
3. Citibank, 56.70%
4. Bogota, 57.36%
5. Bank of America, 58.89%
6. Industrial Colombiano, 58.91%
7. Ganadero, 68.03%
8. Real de Colombia, 68.56%
9. Popular, 70.96%
10. Standard & Chartered, 72.51%

Source: *LatinFinance*, Top 50 Latin Banks (annual), October, 1998, p. 62.

★500★

TOP BANKS IN COLOMBIA, BY MARKET SHARE, 1998

Ranked by: Loan market share, in percent. **Number listed:** 10

1. Ganadero, with 11.35%
2. Davivienda, 8.57%
3. Colombia, 7.93%
4. Bogota, 7.67%
5. Bancafe, 7.51%
6. Caja de Credito Agrario, 6.14%
7. Industrial Colombiano, 5.65%
8. Popular, 5.64%
9. Santander, 5.12%
10. Citibank, 3.40%

Source: *LatinFinance*, Top 50 Latin Banks (annual), October, 1998, p. 62.

★501★

TOP BANKS IN COLOMBIA BY RETURN ON EQUITY, 1998

Ranked by: Return on equity, in percent. **Number listed:** 10

1. Caja Social, with 26.29%
2. Occidente, 22.31%
3. Citibank, 18.86%
4. Bogota, 16.20%
5. Anglo Colombiano, 13.92%
6. Popular, 12.91%
7. Colpatria, 12.26%
8. Industrial Colombiano, 11.60%
9. Superior, 11.16%
10. Colombia, 10.63%

Source: *LatinFinance*, Top 50 Latin Banks (annual), October, 1998, p. 62.

★502★

TOP BANKS IN COLOMBIA, 1998

Ranked by: Assets, in thousands of U.S. ($). **Number listed:** 10

1. Ganadero, with $3,551,312 thousand
2. Colombia, $2,882,591
3. Bogota, $2,799,115
4. Bancafe, $2,481,284
5. Davivienda, $2,369,489
6. Industrial Colombiano, $2,322,973
7. Caja de Credito Agrario, $2,016,108
8. Santander, $1,760,777
9. Popular, $1,668,237
10. Occidente, $1,377,070

Source: *LatinFinance*, Top 50 Latin Banks (annual), October, 1998, p. 62.

Banks and Banking--Congo (Republic)

★503★
TOP BANKS IN CONGO (REPUBLIC)
Ranked by: Assets, in millions of U.S. dollars ($). **Remarks:** Also lists location, previous rank, balance against local currency, paid-up capital, and balance sheet data. **Number listed:** 3
1. Banque Commerciale du Congo SARL, with $104 million
2. Citibank NA Congo, $17
3. Stanbic Bank Congo sarl, $9.41

Source: *Bankers' Almanac World Ranking*, (annual), 1999, p. 125.

Banks and Banking--Correspondent Banks

★504★
PRO FORMA RANKING OF CORRESPONDENT BALANCES, 1998
Ranked by: Thousands of dollars. **Remarks:** Also lists location and percentage change from previous year. **Number listed:** 25
1. BankAmerica Corp., with $4,300,965 thousand
2. Chase Manhattan Corp., $3,898,341
3. Wells Fargo & Co., $3,549,924
4. Banc One Corp., $3,332,076
5. Citigroup Inc., $2,612,441
6. Fleet Financial Group, $1,336,782
7. Bank of New York Co., $1,286,850
8. Bankers Trust Corp., $1,016,500
9. First Union Corp., $814,518
10. SunTrust Banks Inc., $802,616

Source: *American Banker*, December 17, 1998, p. 8.

★505★
TOP CORRESPONDENT BANK HOLDING COMPANIES, 1998
Ranked by: Balances, in thousands of dollars. **Remarks:** Also lists location, and percent change from previous year. **Number listed:** 50
1. Chase Manhattan Corp., with $3,898,341 thousand
2. BankAmerica Corp., $2,949,250
3. Citicorp, $2,612,441
4. Wells Fargo & Co., $2,107,141
5. Banc One Corp., $1,801,173
6. First Chicago NBD, $1,530,903
7. Norwest Corp., $1,442,783
8. NationsBank Corp., $1,351,715
9. Fleet Financial Group, $1,336,782
10. Bank of New York Co., $1,286,850

Source: *American Banker*, December 17, 1998, p. 8.

Banks and Banking--Croatia

★506★
LARGEST BANKS IN CROATIA, 1997
Ranked by: Capital, in millions of U.S. dollars ($). **Remarks:** Also notes capital percentage change, as well as dollar amount, rank, and percentage change for size, soundness, profits, and performance, and rank among the world's top 1,000 banks. **Number listed:** 2
1. Zagrebacka Banka, with $330 million
2. Privredna Banka Zagreb, $287

Source: *The Banker*, Europe Top 500 (annual), September, 1998, p. 64.

Banks and Banking--Cyprus

★507★
TOP BANKS IN CYPRUS, 1998
Ranked by: Assets, in millions of U.S. dollars ($). **Remarks:** Also lists location, previous rank, balance against local currency, paid-up capital, and balance sheet date. **Number listed:** 17
1. Bank of Cyprus Ltd., with $6,750 million
2. Cyprus Popular Bank Ltd., $5,081
3. Hellenic Bank Ltd., $1,963
4. Co-operative Central Bank Ltd., $1,064
5. Lombard NatWest Bank Ltd., $583
6. Turkish Bank Ltd., $353
7. Cyprus Development Bank Ltd., $210
8. Credit Suisse First Boston, $181
9. Cyprus Turkish Co-operative Central Bank Ltd., $165
10. Limassol Turkish Cooperative Bank Ltd.

Source: *Bankers' Almanac World Ranking*, (annual), 1999, p. 131.

Banks and Banking--Czech Republic

★508★
LARGEST BANKS IN THE CZECH REPUBLIC, 1998
Ranked by: Capital, in millions of U.S. dollars ($). **Remarks:** Also notes capital percentage change, as well as dollar amount, rank, and percentage change for size, soundness, profits, and performance, and rank among the world's top 1,000 banks. **Number listed:** 4
1. Komercni Banka, with $970 million
2. Ceska Sporitelna, $631
3. Ceskoslovenska Obchodni Banka, $437
4. Investicni a Postovni Banks, $221

Source: *The Banker*, European Top 500, September, 1998, p. 64.

Banks and Banking--Denmark

★509★
LARGEST BANKS IN DENMARK, 1997
Ranked by: Capital, in millions of U.S. ($). **Remarks:** Also notes capital percentage change, as well as dollar amount, rank, and percentage change for size, soundness, profits, and performance, and rank among world's top 1,000 banks. **Number listed:** 7
1. Den Danske Bank, with $3,932 million
2. Unidanmark Group, $2,679
3. Bikuben Girobank, $1,188
4. Jyske Bank, $681
5. Sydbank, $376
6. Spar Nord Bank, $246
7. Arbejdernes Landsbank, $177

Source: *The Banker*, World Top 1,000 Banker (annual), Summer, July, 1998, p. 179.

Banks and Banking--Detroit Metropolitan Area

★510★
LARGEST COMMERCIAL BANKS IN THE DETROIT METROPOLITAN AREA, 1997
Ranked by: Assets, in thousands of dollars. **Remarks:** Also notes chief executive officer and other financial figures. **Number listed:** 25
1. Comerica Bank, with $28,936,210 thousand
2. NBD Bank, $21,946,700
3. Michigan National Bank, $9,583,916
4. Great Lakes National Bank, $2,228,809
5. Republic Bancorp Inc., $1,375,808
6. Franklin Bank N. A., $501,969
7. First State Bank in East Detroit, $474,867
8. Oxford Bank, $252,704
9. First National Bank in Howell, $225,358
10. Charter National Bank, $222,261

Source: *Crain's Detroit Business*, Crain's Book of Lists Detroit (annual), December 28, 1998, p. 148.

Banks and Banking--Djibouti

★511★
TOP BANKS IN THE REPUBLIC OF DJIBOUTI
Ranked by: Assets, in millions of U.S. dollars ($). **Remarks:** Also lists location, previous rank, balance against local currency, paid-up capital, and balance sheet date. **Number listed:** 2
1. Banque pour le Commerce et I'Industrie-Mer Rouge, with $195 million
2. Banque Indosuez Mer Rouge, $125

Source: *Bankers' Almanac World Ranking*, (annual), 1999, p. 133.

Banks and Banking--Dominican Republic

★512★
TOP BANKS IN THE DOMINICAN REPUBLIC, 1997
Ranked by: Assets, in millions of U.S. ($). **Remarks:** Also notes location; previous rank; balance against local currency; paid-up capital; and balance sheet data. **Number listed:** 3
1. Banco de Reservas de la Republica, with $1,498 million
2. Banco Popular Dominicano, $872
3. Banco Dominicano del Progreso SA, $126

Source: *Bankers' Almanac World Ranking*, (annual), 1999, p. 134.

Banks and Banking--Ecuador

★513★
LARGEST BANKS IN ECUADOR, 1998
Ranked by: Return on assets, in percent. **Number listed:** 10
1. Comercial Manabi, with 11.58%
2. Internacional, 4.47%
3. Centro Mundo, 4.34%
4. Bolivariano, 3.65%
5. Produbanco, 3.18%
6. Lloyds Bank, 2.81%
7. Cofiec, 2.75%
8. Pichincha, 2.67%
9. Machala, 2.44%
10. Citibank, 2.41%

Source: *LatinFinance*, Top 50 Latin Banks (annual), October, 1998, p. 62.

★514★
TOP BANKS IN ECUADOR
Ranked by: Assets, in thousands of U.S. dollars ($). **Number listed:** 10
1. Progreso, with $1,709,996 thousand
2. Filanbanco, $1,066,832
3. Pichincha, $946,969
4. Pacifico, $887,645
5. Popular, $768,870
6. De Guayaquil, $483,920
7. Previsora, $375,978
8. Prestamos, $322,114
9. Produbanco, $283,224
10. Continental, $228,794

Source: *LatinFinance*, Top 50 Latin Banks (annual), October, 1998, p. 62.

★515★
TOP BANKS IN ECUADOR BY EFFICIENCY, 1998
Ranked by: Efficiency, in OEONI percent. **Number listed:** 10
1. Comercial de Manabi, with 51.63%
2. Cofiec, 63.78%
3. Aserval, 67.95%
4. Internacional, 69.19%
5. Progreso, 70.30%
6. Produbanco, 70.67%
7. Lloyds Bank, 71.14%
8. Finagro, 72.55%
9. Bolivariano, 73.35%
10. Citibank, 73.53%

Source: *LatinFinance*, Top 50 Latin Banks, October, 1998, p. 62.

★516★
TOP BANKS IN ECUADOR, 1998
Ranked by: Assets, in millions of U.S. dollars ($). **Remarks:** Also lists location, previous rank, balance against local currency, paid-up capital, and balance sheet date. **Number listed:** 4
1. Banco del Pacifico SA, with $1,897 million
2. Filanbanco SA, $981
3. Banco Popular del Ecuador, $303
4. Produbanco, $208

Source: *Bankers' Almanac World Ranking*, (annual), 1999, p. 134.

★517★
TOP BANKS IN ECUADOR, 1998
Ranked by: Deposit market share, in percent. **Number listed:** 10
1. Progreso, with 17.82%
2. Filanbanco, 14.45%
3. Pacifico, 10.10%
4. Pichincha, 9.26%
5. Prestamos, 4.04%
6. De Guayaquil, 4.02%
7. Previsora, 3.85%
8. Popular, 3.69%
9. Produbanco, 2.98%
10. Austro, 2.41%

Source: *LatinFinance*, Top 50 Latin Banks (annual), October, 1998, p. 62.

Banks and Banking--Egypt

★518★

LARGEST BANKS IN EGYPT, 1997

Ranked by: Capital, in millions of U.S. dollars ($). **Remarks:** Also notes capital percentage change, as well as dollar amount, rank, and percentage change for size, soundness, profits, and performance, and rank among world's top 1,000 banks. **Number listed:** 7

1. National Bank of Egypt, with $916 million
2. Banque Misr, $469
3. Arab International Bank, $329
4. Commercial Bank, $320
5. Banque du Caire, $317
6. Bank of Alexandria, $305
7. Misr International Bank, $164

Source: *The Banker*, World Top 1,000 Banker (annual), Summer, July, 1998, p. 179.

Banks and Banking--Estonia

★519★

TOP BANKS IN ESTONIA BY ASSETS, 1997

Ranked by: Assets, in millions of U.S dollars ($). **Number listed:** 11

1. Bank of Estonia, with $837 million
2. Hansabank Ltd., $668
3. Eesti Uhispank, $658
4. Tallinna Pank, $209
5. Estonian Forexbank, $176
6. Eesti Maapank, $86
7. Estonian Investment Bank, $85
8. EVEA Bank, $55
9. Estonian Credit Bank, $51
10. ERA Pank, $46

Source: *Bankers' Almanac World Ranking*, (annual), 1999, p. 139.

Banks and Banking--Ethiopia

★520★

LARGEST BANKS IN ETHIOPIA, 1997

Ranked by: Capital, in millions of U.S. dollars ($). **Remarks:** Also notes capital percentage change, as well as dollar amount, rank, and percentage change for size, soundness, profits, and performance, and rank among world's top 1,000 banks. **Number listed:** 2

1. Commercial Bank of Ethiopia, with $130 million
2. Construction & Business Bank, $9

Source: *The Banker*, Top 100 African Banks-By Country, December, 1998, p. 69.

Banks and Banking--Europe

★521★

LARGEST BANKS IN EUROPE BY ASSETS ACCORDING TO EUROPE'S 15,000 LARGEST COMPANIES, 1997

Ranked by: Assets, in thousands of U.S. dollars ($). **Remarks:** Also includes 1996 ranking, as well as asset percentage change and percentage change in local currency. **Number listed:** 300

1. Deutsche Bank (Frankfurt am Main, Germany), with $494,469,866 thousand
2. HSBC Holdings (London, England), $472,436,489
3. Credit Agricole (Paris, France), $416,655,332
4. ABN AMRO Bank (Amsterdam, Netherlands), $414,202,733
5. Union Bank of Switzerland (Zurich), $396,577,863
6. Barclays Bank (London, England), $387,095,018
7. Dresdner Bank (Frankfurt am Main, Germany), $313,148,995
8. Banque National de Paris (Paris, France), $310,191,009
9. National Westminster Bank (London, England), $305,846,255
10. Swiss Bank Corp. (Basle), $301,392,474

Source: *Dun & Bradstreet*, Europe's 15,000 Largest Companies (annual), 1999, p. 648+.

★522★

LARGEST BANKS IN EUROPE BY CAPITAL, 1997

Ranked by: Capital, in millions of U.S. dollars ($). **Remarks:** Also notes capital percentage change, and dollar amount rank, and percentage change for assets. **Number listed:** 500

1. HSBC Holdings (London, England), with $27,392 million
2. Credit Agricole (Paris, France), $22,280
3. Deutsche Bank (Frankfurt, Germany), $17,371
4. ABN AMRO Bank (Amsterdam, Netherlands), $15,864
5. Union Bank of Switzerland (Zurich), $13,570
6. Barclays Bank (London, England), $13,020
7. Credit Suisse Group (Zurich, Switzerland), $12,984
8. Rabobank Nederland (Utecht, Netherlands), $12,680
9. National Westminster Bank (London, England), $12,342
10. Halifax (West Yorkshire, UK), $11,955

Source: *The Banker*, Europe Top 500 (annual), September, 1998, p. 55+.

★523★

LARGEST BANKS IN EUROPE BY CORE CAPITAL, 1997

Ranked by: Core capital, in millions of U.S. dollars ($). **Remarks:** Also notes tier-1 ratio, as well as total-capital ratio. **Number listed:** 48

1. HSBC Holdings, with $26,528.6 million
2. Credit Agricole, $21,269.5
3. Deutsche Bank, $17,709.2
4. ABN AMRO Bank, $16,287.5
5. Union Bank of Switzerland, $15,041.5
6. Credit Suisse Group, $13,958.6
7. National Westminster Bank, $13,442.1
8. Barclays, $13,083.2
9. Rabobank, $12,680.5
10. Int'Le Nederlanden Group, $11,986.5

Source: *Institutional Investor*, World's Largest Banks (annual), August, 1998, p. 134.

★524★
TOP BANKS IN EUROPE BY MARKET CAPITALIZATION, 1999
Ranked by: Market capitalization, in billions of U.S. dollars ($). **Number listed:** 10
1. HSBC, with $82.9 billion
2. Lloyds TSB, $80.3
3. UBS, $71.6
4. ING, $50.9
5. BNP/SG/Paribas, $50.0
6. Credit Suisse, $46.2
7. Barclays, $43.3
8. Fortis, $42.1
9. Santander/BCH, $38.1
10. NatWest, $37.5

Source: *Financial Times*, March 11, 1999, p. 13.

Banks and Banking--Finland

★525★
LARGEST BANKS IN FINLAND, 1997
Ranked by: Capital, in millions of U.S. dollars ($). **Remarks:** Also notes capital percentage change, as well as dollar amount, rank, and percentage change for size, soundness, profits, and performance, and rank among world's top 1,000 banks. **Number listed:** 3
1. Merita, with $2,576 million
2. Okobank, $1,023
3. Postipankki, $835

Source: *The Banker*, World Top 1,000 Banks (annual), Summer, July, 1998, p. 179.

Banks and Banking--Florida

★526★
TOP BANKS IN FLORIDA BY DEPOSITS, 1998
Ranked by: Deposits, in thousands of dollars. **Remarks:** Also notes location, percent share of Florida bank holding company deposits, number of Florida offices, and number of banks. **Number listed:** 50
1. Barnett Banks Inc. (Jacksonville), with $34,028,958 thousand
2. First Union Corp. of Florida (Jacksonville), $32,290,341
3. SunTrust Banks of Florida (Orlando), $19,350,511
4. NationsBank Corp. (Tampa), $19,215,527
5. SouthTrust Bancorporation (Birmingham, AL), $6,749,924
6. AmSouth Bancorporation (Birmingham, AL), $5,028,142
7. Northern Trust of Florida (Miami), $2,064,335
8. Colonial Bancgroup (Montgomery, AL), $2,012,261
9. Ocean Bancshares Inc. (Miami), $1,973,557
10. Huntington Bancshares (Columbus, OH), $1,585,780

Source: *Florida Trend*, TopRank Florida (annual), 1999, p. 16.

Banks and Banking, Foreign

★527★
TOP FOREIGN EMERGING-MARKETS BANKS, 1998
Ranked by: Basis for ranking not specified. **Number listed:** 300
1. United Overseas Bank (Singapore)
2. Shanghai Commercial & Savings Bank (Taiwan)
3. Banco Rio de la Plata (Argentina)
4. Liu Chong Hing Bank (Hong Kong)
5. Bank of Bahrain & Kuwait (Bahrain)
6. Banco Popular Dominicano (Dominican Republic)
7. Budapest Bank (Hungary)
8. Oversea-Chinese Banking Corp. (Singapore)
9. Banco Santiago (Chile)
10. Royal Bank of Trinidad & Tobago Ltd. (Trinidad & Tobago)

Source: *Euromoney*, October, 1998, p. 48+.

Banks and Banking, Foreign--Chicago (IL)

★528★
LARGEST FOREIGN BANK BRANCHES IN CHICAGO, 1997-1998
Ranked by: Total assets, in millions of dollars. **Remarks:** Also notes contact information for Chicago branch, CEO, previous year's figures, and country of parent company. **Number listed:** 25
1. ABN AMBRO Bank, with $19,557.2 million
2. Bank of Montreal, $16,643.4
3. Bank of Tokyo-Mitsubishi Bank, $2,646.6
4. Sumitomo Bank, $2,491.7
5. Fuji Bank Ltd., $2,363.1
6. Industrial Bank of Japan, $2,235.7
7. Banque Nationale de Paris, $1,914.2
8. Banca di Roma, $1,874.8
9. Sanwa Bank, $1,473.7
10. Dai-ichi Kangyo Bank, $1,166.1

Source: *Crain's Chicago Business*, Top Business Lists (annual), 1999, p. 71.

Banks and Banking, Foreign--New York (NY)

★529★
LARGEST FOREIGN BANK AGENCIES IN NEW YORK, 1997-1998
Ranked by: Total assets, in thousands of dollars. **Remarks:** Also notes contact information, CEO, previous year's figures, license date, and location of parent company. **Number listed:** 25
1. Canadian Imperial Bank of Commerce, with $28,147,000 thousand
2. Bank of Nova Scotia, $8,946,000
3. International Commercial Bank of China, $3,204,000
4. Banco Nacional de Mexico, $1,694,000
5. Development Bank of Singapore, $1,199,000
6. Banco Totta & Acores, $915,000
7. Banco Atlantico, $850,000
8. Credit Local de France, $793,000
9. Hanil Bank, $769,000

10. First Commercial Bank, $664,000

Source: *Crain's New York Business*, Largest Foreign Banks in New York, September 21, 1998, p. 49.

★530★
LARGEST FOREIGN BANK BRANCHES IN NEW YORK, 1997-1998
Ranked by: Total assets, in thousands of dollars. **Remarks:** Also notes contact information for New York branch, CEO, previous year's figures, license date, and location of parent company. **Number listed:** 25

1. Societe Generale, with $66,133,000 thousand
2. Deutsche Bank, $42,687,000
3. Bank of Tokyo-Mitsubishi, $31,230,000
4. Credit Lyonnais, $25,619,000
5. Union Bank of Switzerland, $24,335,000
6. Barclays Bank, $22,849,000
7. Bayerische Landesbank Girozentrale, $22,458,000
8. Westdeutsche Landsbank Girozentrale, $21,114,000
9. Industrial Bank of Japan, $18,847,000
10. Fuji Bank, $15,577,000

Source: *Crain's New York Business*, Largest Foreign Banks in New York, September 21, 1998, p. 49.

Banks and Banking, Foreign--United States

★531★
TOP FOREIGN AGENCIES IN THE U.S. IN COMMERCIAL AND INDUSTRIAL LOANS, 1997-1998
Ranked by: Total commercial and industrial loans, in millions of dollars. **Remarks:** Also notes branch location, and figures and rank from previous year. **Number listed:** 25

1. Bank of Nova Scotia (Atlanta), with $5,382.6 million
2. Bank of Nova Scotia (New York), $4,617.5
3. Dai-Ichi Kangyo Bank, $2,071.6
4. Fuji Bank Ltd. (Houston), $2,023.4
5. Societe Generale, $1,959.8
6. Fuji Bank Ltd. (Los Angeles), $1,927.1
7. Industrial Bank of Japan, $1,884.6
8. Canadian Imperial Bank of Commerce, $1,802.6
9. Union Bank of Switzerland, $1,581.9
10. Lloyds Bank PLC (Miami), $1,553.1

Source: *American Banker*, (annual), February 18, 1999, p. 17.

★532★
TOP FOREIGN BANK BRANCHES IN THE U.S. IN COMMERCIAL AND INDUSTRIAL LOANS, 1997-1998
Ranked by: Total commercial and industrial loans, in millions of dollars. **Remarks:** Also notes branch location, and figures and rank from previous year. **Number listed:** 25

1. Credit Lyonnais, with $9,867.6 million
2. Bank of Tokyo Mitsubishi, $9,636.1
3. Bank of Montreal, $8,564.7
4. Societe Generale, $6,563.5
5. Sumitomo Bank, $6,188.7
6. Fuji Bank Ltd., $5,790.3
7. Union Bank of Switzerland, $5,470.5
8. Dai-Ichi Kangyo Bank, $5,072.7
9. Credit Suisse First Boston, $4,810.6
10. Sakura Bank, $4,745.9

Source: *American Banker*, (annual), February 18, 1999, p. 17.

★533★
TOP FOREIGN BANKS IN THE U.S. IN COMMERCIAL AND INDUSTRIAL LOANS, 1997-1998
Ranked by: Total commercial and industrial loans, in millions of dollars. **Remarks:** Also notes number of offices, figures from previos year, and percentage changed. **Number listed:** 25

1. Bank of Tokyo-Mitsubishi Ltd., with $29,349 million
2. ABN AMRO Bank, $16,372
3. Bank of Montreal, $14,194
4. Fuji Bank Ltd., $13,482
5. Bank of Nova Scotia, $12,370
6. Industrial Bank of Japan, $11,918
7. Credit Lyonnais, $11,891
8. Sumitoma Bank, $11,491
9. Societe Generale, $10,788
10. Sanwa Bank, $8,359

Source: *American Banker*, (annual), February 18, 1999, p. 15.

★534★
TOP FOREIGN BANKS IN U.S. COMMERCIAL BANK ASSETS, 1997-1998
Ranked by: Total assets in U.S. commercial banking offices, in millions of U.S. dollars ($). **Remarks:** Also notes number of offices, figures from previous year, and percentage changed. **Number listed:** 25

1. Bank of Tokyo-Mitsubishi Ltd., with $74,002 million
2. Societe Generale, $70,605
3. UBS Corp., $70,247
4. ABN AMRO Bank, $50,046
5. Deutsche Bank, $49,842
6. Industrial Bank of Japan, $40,689
7. Bank of Montreal, $40,208
8. HSBC Holdings, $37,031
9. Sumitomo Bank, $27,519
10. Canadian Imperial Bank of Commerce, $26,347

Source: *American Banker*, (annual), February 18, 1999, p. 15.

Banks and Banking--France

★535★
LARGEST BANKS IN FRANCE, 1997
Ranked by: Capital, in millions of U.S. dollars ($). **Remarks:** Also notes capital percentage change, as well as dollar amount, rank, and percentage change for size, soundness, profits, and performance, and rank among world's top 1,000 banks. **Number listed:** 19

1. Credit Agricole, with $22,280 million
2. Banque Nationale de Paris, $11,521
3. Groupe Caissed'Epargne, $10,971
4. Societe Generale, $9,745
5. Compagnie Financiere de Paribas, $8,538
6. Credit Mutuel, $7,852
7. Credit Lyonnais, $7,131
8. Groupe Banques Populaires, $5,427
9. Natexis, $2,903
10. Union Europeenne de CIC, $2,851

Source: *World Top 1,000 Banker*, (annual), Summer, July, 1998, p. 179+.

Banks and Banking--French Polynesia

★536★
LARGEST BANKS IN FRENCH POLYNESIA, 1999
Ranked by: Total assets, in millions of U.S. dollars ($). **Remarks:** Also notes location, previous rank, balance against local currency, paid-up capital, and balance sheet date. **Number listed:** 2

1. Banque de Tahiti, with $690 million
2. Banque Paribas Polynesie, $109

Source: *Bankers' Almanac World Ranking*, (annual), 1999, p. 146.

Banks and Banking--Gabon

★537★
LARGEST BANKS IN GABON, 1998
Ranked by: Capital, in millions of U.S. dollars ($). **Remarks:** Also notes capital percentage change, as well as dollar amount, rank, and percentage change for size, soundness, profits, and performance, and rank among top 1,000 banks. **Number listed:** 2

1. Banque Int. pour le Comm. & I'Ind. du Gabon, with $38 million
2. Union Gabonaise de Banque, $25

Source: *The Banker*, Top 100 African Banks-By Country (annual), December, 1998, p. 69.

Banks and Banking--Germany

★538★
LARGEST BANKS IN GERMANY BY CAPITAL, 1997
Ranked by: Capital, in millions of U.S. dollars ($). **Remarks:** Also notes capital percentage change, as well as dollar amount, rank, and percentage change for size, soundness, profits, and performance, and rank among world's top 1,000 banks. **Number listed:** 82

1. Deutsche Bank, with $17,371 million
2. Dresdner Bank, $10,456
3. Commerzbank, $8,829
4. Bayerische Vereinsbank, $8,729
5. Westdeutsche Landesbank Giro, $7,792
6. Bayerische Landesbank, $5,946
7. Kreditanstalt fur Wiederaufbau, $5,607
8. Bayerische Hypotheken & Wechsel Bank, $5,208
9. Bankgesellschaft Berlin, $4,480
10. DG Bank, $3,619

Source: *World Top 1,000 Banker*, (annual), Summer, July, 1998, p. 180+.

Banks and Banking--Ghana

★539★
LARGEST BANKS IN GHANA, 1998
Ranked by: Capital, in millions of U.S. dollars ($). **Remarks:** Also notes capital percentage change, as well as dollar amount, rank, and percentage change for size, soundness, profits, and performance, and rank among world's top 1,000 banks. **Number listed:** 3

1. Ghana Commercial Bank, with $43 million
2. Social Security Bank, $33
3. Ghana Cooperative Bank, $6

Source: *The Banker*, Top 100 African Banks-By Country (annual), December, 1998, p. 69.

Banks and Banking--Great Britain

★540★
LARGEST BANKS IN GREAT BRITAIN, 1997
Ranked by: Capital, in millions of U.S. dollars ($). **Remarks:** Also notes capital percentage change, as well as dollar amount, rank, and percentage change for size, soundness, profits, and performance, and rank among world's top 1,000 banks. **Number listed:** 32

1. HSBC Holdings, with $27,392 million
2. Barclays Bank, $13,020
3. National Westminster Bank, $12,342
4. Halifax, $11,955
5. Lloyds TSB, $10,408
6. Abbey National, $8,067
7. Royal Bank of Scotland, $5,012
8. Bank of Scotland, $4,486
9. Standard Chartered, $4,189
10. Woolwich, $3,138

Source: *The Banker*, World Top 1,000 Banker (annual), Summer, July, 1998, p. 205.

Banks and Banking--Greece

★541★
LARGEST BANKS IN GREECE, 1997
Ranked by: Capital, in millions of U.S. dollars ($). **Remarks:** Also notes capital percentage change, as well as dollar amount, rank, and percentage change for size, soundness, profits, and rank among world's top 1,000 banks. **Number listed:** 9

1. Greek Post Office Savings Bank, with $1,537 million
2. National Bank of Greece, $1,389
3. Alpha Credit Bank, $951
4. Agricultural Bank of Greece, $753
5. Commercial Bank of Greece, $700
6. Ergobank, $489
7. National Mortgage Bank of Greece, $328
8. Ionian & Popular Bank of Greece, $312
9. Cretabank, $156

Source: *The Banker*, World Top 1,000 Banker, Summer, July, 1998, p. 183.

★542★
TOP BANKS IN GREECE BY ASSETS, 1998
Ranked by: Assets, in millions of U.S. dollars ($). **Remarks:** Also notes market share, in percent. **Number listed:** 10

1. National Bank of Greece, with $12,300 million
2. Alpha Credit, $3,400
3. Commercial Bank, $3,300
4. Ionian Bank, $2,200
5. Ergo Bank, $1,400
6. EFG Eurobank, $685
7. Cretabank, $406
8. General Bank, $394

9. Xiosbank, $332
10. Bank of Piraeus, $312

Source: *Financial Times*, July 16, 1998, p. 3.

Banks and Banking--Guatemala

★543★
LARGEST BANKS IN GUATEMALA BY ASSETS, 1999
Ranked by: Assets, in millions of U.S. dollars ($). **Remarks:** Also lists location, previous rank, balance against local currency, paid-up capital, and balance sheet date. **Number listed:** 5

1. Banco de Cafe, with $300 million
2. Banco Internacional, $202
3. Banco Agricola Mercantil, $181
4. Banco de Construccion, $162
5. Banco de Ejercito, $143

Source: *The Banker*, Bankers' Almanac World Ranking (annual), 1999, p. 162.

Banks and Banking--Guinea

★544★
LARGEST BANKS IN GUINEA, 1998
Ranked by: Capital, in millions of U.S. dollars ($). **Remarks:** Also notes capital percentage change, as well as dollar amount, rank, and percentage change for size, soundness, profits, and performance, and rank among world's top 1,000 banks. **Number listed:** 2

1. Banque Int. Pour le Comm. & I'Ind. Guinee, with $11
2. Societe Generale de Banques en Guinee, $6

Source: *The Banker*, Top 100 African Banks-By Country (annual), December, 1998, p. 69.

Banks and Banking--Haiti

★545★
LARGEST BANKS IN HAITI, 1999
Ranked by: Assets, in millions of U.S. dollars ($). **Remarks:** Also lists location, previous rank, balance against local currency, paid-up capital, and balance sheet date. **Number listed:** 2

1. Banque de I'Union Haitienne SA, with $89 million
2. Banque de Promotion Commerciale et Industrielle SA, $85

Source: *Bankers' Almanac World Ranking*, (annual), 1999, p. 162.

Banks and Banking--Honduras

★546★
LARGEST BANKS IN HONDURAS, 1999*
Ranked by: Assets, in millions of U.S. dollars ($). **Remarks:** Also lists location, previous rank, balance against local curren cy, paid-up capital, and balance sheet date. **Number listed:** 3

1. Banco Atlantida SA, with $243 million
2. Banco Hondureno del Cafe, $63
3. Banco de Honduras, $28

Source: *Bankers' Almanac World Ranking*, (annual), 1999, p. 162.

Banks and Banking--Hong Kong

★547★
LARGEST BANKS IN HONG KONG BY ASSETS, 1999
Ranked by: Assets, in millions of U.S. dollars ($). **Remarks:** Also lists location, previous rank, balance against local currency, paid-up capital, and balance sheet date. **Number listed:** 49

1. Hong Kong & Shanghai Banking Corp., with $190,417 million
2. Hang Seng Bank, $51,194
3. Bank of East Asia, $17,241
4. Dao Heng Bank Ltd., $16,195
5. Sin Hua Bank, $10,888
6. Nanyang Commercial Bank Ltd., $10,360
7. Shanghai Commercial Bank, $6,641
8. Wing Hang Bank Ltd., $6,375
9. Wing Hang Bank Ltd., $6,117
10. HSBC Investment Bank Asia Ltd., $6,072

Source: *Bankers' Almanac World Ranking*, (annual), 1999, p. 163+.

★548★
LARGEST BANKS IN HONG KONG BY CAPITAL, 1997
Ranked by: Capital, in millions of U.S. dollars ($). **Remarks:** Also notes capital percentage change, as well as dollar amount, rank, and percentage change for size, soundness, profits, and performance, and rank among world's top 1,000 banks. **Number listed:** 20

1. Bank of East Asia, with $1,534 million
2. Sin Hua Bank, $1,281
3. Nanyang Commercial Bank Ltd., $1,142
4. Kwangtung Provincial Bank, $929
5. Po Sang Bank, $912
6. Kincheng Banking Corp., $801
7. Shanghai Commercial Bank, $714
8. Hua Chiao Commercial Bank, $657
9. Ka Wah Bank, $586
10. China & South Sea Bank, $557

Source: *The Banker*, World Top 1,000 Banker (annual), Summer, July, 1998, p. 183.

Banks and Banking--Iceland

★549★
TOP BANKS IN ICELAND, 1999
Ranked by: Assets, in millions of U.S. dollars ($). **Remarks:** Also lists location, previous rank, balance against local currency, paid-up capital, and balance sheet date. **Number listed:** 4

1. Landsbanki Islands, with $1,720 million
2. Islandsbanki HF, $1,125
3. Bunadarbanki Islands, $931
4. Icebank Ltd., $232

Source: *Bankers' Almanac World Ranking*, (annual), 1999, p. 165.

Banks and Banking--Independent Banks

★550★
TOP LARGE COMMUNITY BANKS BY RETURN ON AVERAGE ASSETS, 1998
Ranked by: Return on average assets, in percent. **Remarks:** Also notes return on average equity, nonperforming assets, total assets, net income, efficiency ratio, and average salary per employee. **Number listed:** 75

1. First National Bank of Keystone, with 7.24%
2. Brighton Bank (Salt Lake City, UT), 4.91%
3. Kentucky Farmers Bank (Cattlesburg, KY.), 4.60%
4. First Bank & Trust Co. of Illinois (Palatine, IL), 4.56%
5. First Credit Bank (Los Angeles, CA), 4.48%
6. Bank of San Francisco (California), 3.93%
7. First Security Bank (Sleepy Eye, MN), 3.56%
8. Pueblo Bank & Trust Co. (Pueblo, CO), 3.41%
9. Miami Valley Bank (Quincy, OH), 3.40%
10. Bank of Newport (Newport, OR), 3.34%

Source: *American Banker*, Top Community Banks (annual), June 8, 1999, p. 9+.

★551★
TOP SMALL COMMUNITY BANKS BY RETURN ON AVERAGE ASSETS, 1998
Ranked by: Return on average assets, in percent, for banks with assets less than $100 million. **Remarks:** Also notes return on average equity, nonperforming assets, total assets, net income, efficiency ratio, and average salary per employee. **Number listed:** 50

1. Tri-State Bank & Trust Co. (Haughton, LA), with 5.91%
2. First State Bank (Idaho Springs, CO), 4.67%
3. State Bank of Delano (MN), 4.37%
4. Security National Bank of Quanah (TX), 4.30%
5. Avery County Bank (Newland, NC), 4.13%
6. Central Bank of Kansas City (MO), 4.05%
7. American National Bank (Parma, OH), 4.02%
8. First Security Bank (Lake Benton, MN), 3.96%
9. Wilmott State Bank (Wilmot, SD), 3.91%
10. First Coleman National Bank (Coleman, TX), 3.89%

Source: *American Banker*, Top Community Banks (annual), June 8, 1999, p. 10.

★552★
TOP SMALL COMMUNITY BANKS, 1998
Ranked by: Composite score for banks with assets less than $368 million. **Remarks:** The composite score was calculated by weighing the scores in 6 categories: total assets, leverage cap, NPA ratio, ROA, return on equity, and efficiency. **Number listed:** 190

1. Button Gwinnett Fin Corp., with 48 points
2. WCN Bancorp Inc., 93
3. Penns Woods Bancorp Inc., 112
4. VRB Bancorp, 120
5. O.A.K. Financial Corp., 123
6. Home Port Bancorp Inc., 132
7. Cascade Bancorp, 150
8. First Keystone Corp., 152
9. Merit Holding Corp., 172
10. First McMinnville Corp., 175

Source: *U.S. Banker*, Community Banking Ranking (annual), July, 1998, p. 70+.

Banks and Banking--India

★553★
LARGEST BANKS IN INDIA BY ASSETS, 1999
Ranked by: Assets, in millions of U.S. dollars ($). **Remarks:** Also lists location,, previous rank, balance against local currency, paid-up capital, and balance sheet date. **Number listed:** 41

1. State Bank of India, with $43,616 million
2. Industrial Development Bank of India, $15,178
3. Bank of Baroda, $11,605
4. Bank of India, $10,577
5. Canara Bank, $9,939
6. Punjab National Bank, $9,768
7. Central Bank of India, $7,357
8. Union Bank of India, $6,242
9. Indian Overseas Bank, $5,426
10. Syndicate Bank, $4,882

Source: *Reed Business Information*, Bankers' Almanac World Ranking (annual), 1999, p. 166+.

★554★
LARGEST BANKS IN INDIA BY CAPITAL, 1997
Ranked by: Capital, in millions of U.S. dollars ($). **Remarks:** Also notes capital percentage change, as well as dollar amount, rank, and percentage change for size, soundness, profits, and performance, and rank among world's top 1,000 banks. **Number listed:** 10

1. State Bank of India, with $1,885 million
2. Bank of Baroda, $554
3. United Bank of India, $506
4. Canara Bank, $484
5. Bank of India, $469
6. Punjab National Bank, $267
7. Oriental Bank of Commerce, $262
8. Union Bank of India, $237
9. Andhra Bank, $180
10. Maharashtra State Co-operative Bank, $166

Source: *The Banker*, World Top 1,000 Banker (annual), Summer, July, 1998, p. 183+.

Banks and Banking--Indonesia

★555★
LARGEST BANKS IN INDONESIA BY ASSETS, 1999
Ranked by: Assets, in millions of U.S. dollars ($). **Remarks:** Also lists location, previous rank, balance against local currency, paid-up capital, and balance sheet date. **Number listed:** 44

1. PT Bank Central Asia, with $15,279 million
2. PT Bank Rakyat Indonesia (Persero), $14,566
3. PT Bank Dagang Negara (Persero), $13,696
4. PT Bank Ekspor Impor Indonesia (Persero), $10,921
5. PT Bank Negara Indonesia (Persero), $10,405
6. PT Bank Danamon Indonesia, $9,378
7. PT Bank Dagang Nasional Indonesia, $7,048
8. PT Bank Bumi Daya (Persero), $6,196
9. PT Bank Tabungan Negara (Persero), $4,809
10. PT Bank Internasional Indonesia, $4,495

Source: *Reed Business Information*, Bankers' Almanac World Ranking (annual), 1999, p. 167+.

★556★
LARGEST BANKS IN INDONESIA BY CAPITAL, 1997
Ranked by: Capital, in millions of U.S. dollars ($). **Remarks:** Also notes capital percentage change, as well as dollar amount, rank, and percentage change for size, soundness, profits, and

performance, and rank among world's top 1,000 banks. **Number listed:** 13

1. Bank Central Asia, with $745 million
2. Bank BNI, $706
3. Bank Rakyat Indonesia, $698
4. Bank Ekspor Impor Indonesia, $593
5. Bank Dagang Nasional Indonesia, $416
6. Bank Internasional Indonesia, $410
7. Bank Dagang Negara, $325
8. Bank Danamon Indonesia, $315
9. Bank Bumi Daya (Persero), $286
10. Bank BTN, $235

Source: *The Banker*, World Top 1,000 Banker (annual), Summer, July, 1998, p. 184.

Banks and Banking, International

★557★

BANKS WORLDWIDE WITH THE GREATEST ASSET DECLINES, 1997

Ranked by: Decrease in assets, in percent. **Number listed:** 10

1. Daiwa Bank Ltd. (Japan), with -40.92%
2. Credit Lyonnais (France), -19.76%
3. Nippon Credit Bank Ltd. (Japan), -19.46%
4. Long-Term Credit Bank of Japan (Japan), -18.67%
5. Toyo Trust & Banking Co. Ltd. (Japan), -17.35%
6. Compagnie Financiere de Paribas (France), -16.17%
7. Yasuda Trust & Banking Co. Ltd. (Japan), -15.64%
8. Istituto Bancario San Paola di Torino (Italy), -15.53%
9. Credtio Italiano (Italy), -13.33%
10. Shoko Chukin Bank (Japan), -13.06%

Source: *American Banker*, December 31, 1997, p. 23.

★558★

BANKS WORLDWIDE WITH THE HIGHEST ASSET INCREASES, 1997

Ranked by: Increase in assets, in percent. **Number listed:** 10

1. Bank Austria (Vienna), with 77.99%
2. Dexia Belgium (Brussels), 72.30%
3. ING Bank (Netherlands), 71.93%
4. Svenska Handelsbanken (Sweden), 66.66%
5. Landsbank Schleswig-Holstein Girozentrale (Germany), 43.93%
6. NationsBank Corp. (U.S.), 43.09%
7. Banco do Brasil (Brazil), 29.11%
8. Cassa di Risparmio delle Provincie Lombarde (Italy), 28.83%
9. Banca di Roma (Italy), 28.34%
10. Banco Central Hispanoamericano (Spain), 26.51%

Source: *American Banker*, December 31, 1997, p. 23.

★559★

LEADING BANKS WORLDWIDE BY MARKET CAPITALIZATION, 1997

Ranked by: Market Capitalization, in millions of U.S. dollars ($). **Number listed:** 50

1. UBS Corp. (Switzerland), with $85,752 million
2. Lloyds TSB (United Kingdom), $75,985
3. NationsBank Corp. (U.S.), $73,850
4. Citicorp (U.S.), $67,390
5. HSBC Holdings Plc. (United Kingdom), $66,121
6. Chase Manhattan Corp. (U.S.), $64,302
7. Credit Suisse Group (Switzerland), $59,485
8. BankAmerica Corp. (U.S.), $59,060
9. First Union Corp. (U.S.), $58,693
10. Bank of Tokyo-Mitsubishi Ltd. (Japan), $49,666

Source: *American Banker*, August 6, 1998, p. 24.

★560★

TOP BANKS WORLDWIDE BY DEPOSITS, 1997

Ranked by: Deposits, in millions of U.S. dollars ($). **Number listed:** 100

1. Deutsche Bank AG (Germany), with $488,231.9 million
2. Bank of Tokyo-Mitsubishi Ltd. (Japan), $404,387.6
3. HSBC Holdings Plc. (United Kingdom), $332,677.6
4. ABN AMRO Holding N.V., $332,101.3
5. Societe Generale (France), $310.330.3
6. Westdeutsche Landsbank Girozentrale (Germany), $308,547.0
7. Credit Agricole Mutual (France), $300,212.1
8. Credit Suisse Group (Switzerland), $291,581.0
9. Sumitomo Bank (Japan), $289,374.0
10. Sanwa Bank (Japan), $284,071.1

Source: *American Banker*, August 6, 1998, p. 22.

★561★

TOP BANKS WORLDWIDE BY OVERSEAS BUSINESS VOLUME, 1997-1998

Ranked by: Overseas business volume, in percent. **Remarks:** Also notes assets, income, and staff figures. **Number listed:** 50

1. American Express Bank (U.S.), with 79.98%
2. Standard Chartered (United Kingdom), 74.00%
3. Credit Suisse Group (Switzerland), 73.00%
4. Union Bank of Switzerland (Switzerland), 68.40%
5. Swiss Bank Corp. (Switzerland), 67.20%
6. HSBC Holdings (United Kingdom), 65.00%
7. Citicorp (U.S.), 63.00%
8. Bank Austria-Creditanstalt (Austria), 57.35%
9. ABN AMBRO Bank (Netherlands), 57.09%
10. Cie Financiere de Paribas (France), 55.05%

Source: *The Banker*, Global Banking (annual), February, 1999, p. 40+.

★562★

WORLD'S LARGEST BANKING COMPANIES BY ASSETS, 1997

Ranked by: Assets, in millions of U.S. dollars ($). **Remarks:** Also notes 1996 asset figure and rank, and equity capital data. **Number listed:** 200

1. Bank of Tokyo-Mitsubishi Ltd. (Japan), with $691,920.3 million
2. Deutsche Bank (Germany), $580,069.0
3. Sumitomo Bank (Japan), $483,730.4
4. Credit Suisse Group (Switzerland), $473,829.8
5. HSBC Holdings (United Kingdom), $471,037.8
6. Dai-lchi Kangyo Bank Ltd. (Japan), $433,102.9
7. Sanwa Bank Ltd. (Japan), $427,979.6
8. Credit Agricole Mutual (France), $419,763.2
9. Fuji Bank Ltd. (Japan), $414,173.0
10. ABN AMRO Holding N.V., $412,771.9

Source: *American Banker*, August 6, 1998, p. 20.

★563★

WORLD'S LARGEST BANK'S BY SHAREHOLDER EQUITY, 1998

Ranked by: Shareholder equity in millions of U.S. dollars ($). **Remarks:** Also notes equity and asset growth, net income, income growth, and percentage of ROAE. **Number listed:** 200

1. Bank of America (U.S.), with $45,938 million
2. Citigroup (U.S.), $42,708
3. HSBC Holdings (United Kingdom), $30,587
4. Credit Agricole Group (France), $26,426
5. Chase Manhattan (U.S.), $23,838

6. Industrial & Commercial Bank of China (China), $22,213
7. UBS (Switzerland), $21,104
8. Deutsche Bank (Germany), $20,952
9. Wells Fargo (U.S.), $20,759
10. Bank One (U.S.), $20,560

Source: *Euromoney*, (annual), June, 1999, p. 209+.

★564★
WORLD'S LARGEST COMMERCIAL AND SAVINGS BANKING COMPANIES BY REVENUE, 1997
Ranked by: Revenue, in millions of dollars. **Remarks:** Also notes profits and profits and a percent of revenues and assets. **Number listed:** 68

1. Credit Suisse (Switzerland), with $48,242 million
2. Deutsche Bank (Germany), $40,792
3. HSBC Holdings (Great Britain), $37,474
4. Bank of Tokyo-Mitsubishi (Japan), $34,750
5. Citicorp (U.S.), $34,697
6. Credit Agricole (France), $34,015
7. Chase Manhattan Corp. (U.S.), $30,381
8. ABN AMRO Holding N.V., $28,946
9. Gan (France), $28,937
10. Societe Generale, $28,725

Source: *Fortune*, The Global 500: World's Biggest Corporations (annual), August 3, 1998, p. F-15+.

★565★
WORLD'S LEADING BANKS BY CAPITAL, 1997
Ranked by: Capital, in millions of U.S. dollars ($). **Remarks:** Also notes assets, capital to assets ratio, profit, and performance figures. **Number listed:** 1000

1. HSBC Holdings (United Kingdom), with $27,392 million
2. Chase Manhattan Corp. (U.S.), $22,594
3. Credit Agricole (France), $22,280
4. Citicorp (U.S.), $21,211
5. Bank of Tokyo-Mitsubishi (Japan), $18,585
6. Deutsche Bank (Germany), $17,371
7. BankAmerica Corp. (U.S.), $17,292
8. ABN AMRO Bank (Netherlands), $15,864
9. Sumitomo Bank (Japan), $14,757
10. Dai-Ichi Kangyo Bank (Japan), $14,458

Source: *The Banker*, World Top 1,000 (annual), Summer, July, 1998, p. 131+.

★566★
WORLD'S TOP BANKS BY CORE CAPITAL, 1997
Ranked by: Core capital, in millions of U.S. dollars ($). **Remarks:** Also notes fiscal year end, and assets, profits, and employee figures. **Number listed:** 100

1. Chase Manhattan Bank (U.S.), with $26,622.0 million
2. HSBC Holdings (United Kingdom), $26,528.6
3. NationsBank Corp. (U.S.), $25,247.0
4. BankAmerica Corp. (U.S.), $24,081.0
5. Citicorp (U.S.), $22,904.0
6. Credit Agricole (France), $21,269.5
7. Bank of Tokyo-Mitsubishi (Japan), $18,661.7
8. Deutsche Bank(Germany), $17,709.2
9. ABN AMRO Bank (Netherlands), $16,287.5
10. Wells Fargo & Co. (U.S.), $15,532.1

Source: *Institutional Investor*, World's 100 Largest Banks (annual), August, 1998, p. 128+.

Banks and Banking--Iran

★567★
LARGEST BANKS IN IRAN, 1997
Ranked by: Capital, in millions of U.S. dollars ($). **Remarks:** Also notes capital percentage change, as well as dollar amount, rank, and percentage change for size, soundness, profits, and performance, and rank among world's top 1,000 banks. **Number listed:** 5

1. Bank Melli Iran, with $656 million
2. Bank Saderat Iran, $519
3. Bank Mellat, $351
4. Bank Tejarat, $328
5. Bank Sepah, $219

Source: *The Banker*, World Top 1,000 Banker (annual), Summer, July, 1998, p. 185.

Banks and Banking--Ireland

★568★
LARGEST BANKS IN IRELAND, 1997
Ranked by: Capital, in millions of U.S. dollars ($). **Remarks:** Also notes capital percentage change, as well as dollar amount, rank, and percentage change for size, soundness, profits, and performance, and rank among world's top 1,000 banks. **Number listed:** 3

1. Allied Irish Banks, with $2,910 million
2. Bank of Ireland, $2,153
3. Anglo Irish Bank Corp., $310

Source: *The Banker*, World Top 1,000 Banker (annual), Summer, July, 1998, p. 184.

Banks and Banking--Isle of Man

★569★
TOP BANKS ON THE ISLE OF MAN, 1997
Ranked by: Assets, in millions of U.S. dollars ($). **Remarks:** Also lists location, previous rank, balance against local currency, paid-up capital, and balance sheet date. **Number listed:** 13

1. NatWest Offshore Ltd., with $3,216 million
2. Bank of Ireland (Isle of Man) Ltd., $1,015
3. Ulster Bank (Isle of Man) Ltd., $547
4. Cater Allen Bank (Isle of Man) Ltd., $430
5. Royal Bank of Canada, $347
6. Standard Bank Isle (Isle of Man) Ltd., $325
7. Bank of Bermuda (Isle of Man) Ltd., $317
8. Celtic Bank Ltd., $226
9. Singer & Friedlander (Isle of Man) Ltd., $204
10. Allied Dunbar Bank International Ltd., $177

Source: *Reed Business Information Services*, Bankers' Almanac World Ranking (annual), 1999, p. 169+.

Banks and Banking--Israel

★570★
LARGEST BANKS IN ISRAEL, 1997
Ranked by: Capital, in millions of U.S. dollars ($). **Remarks:** Also notes capital percentage change, as well as dollar amount,

rank, and percentage change for size, soundness, profits, and performance, and rank among world's top 1,000 banks. **Number listed:** 5

1. Bank Hapoalim, with $2,843 million
2. Bank Leumi le-Isreal, $2,484
3. Isreal Discount Bank, $1,320
4. First International Bank of Isreal, $665
5. United Mizrahi Bank, $614

Source: *The Banker*, World Top 1,000 Banker (annual), Summer, July, 1998, p. 184.

Banks and Banking--Italy

★571★

LARGEST BANKS IN ITALY, 1997

Ranked by: Capital, in millions of U.S. dollars ($). **Remarks:** Also notes capital percentage change, as well as dollar amount rank, and percentage change for size, soundness, profits, and performance, and rank among world's top 1,000 banks. **Number listed:** 68

1. Cariplo, with $5,946 million
2. Banca di Roma, $5,374
3. Instituto Bancario San Paolo di Torino, $5,339
4. Banca Commerciale, $4,717
5. Istituto Mobiliare Italiana, $4,101
6. Credito Italiano, $4,100
7. Banca Monte dei Paschi di Siena, $3,996
8. BNL-Banca Nazionale del Lavoro, $3,680
9. Cariverona Banca, $2,221
10. Rolo Banca, $1,876

Source: *The Banker*, World Top 1,000 Banker (annual), Summer, July, 1998, p. 184+.

Banks and Banking--Ivory Coast

★572★

LARGEST BANKS IN THE IVORY COAST, 1997

Ranked by: Capital, in millions of U.S. dollars ($). **Remarks:** Also notes capital percentage change, as well as dollar amount, rank, and percentage change for size, soundness, profits, and performance, and rank among world's top 1,000 banks. **Number listed:** 4

1. Societe Generale de Banques en Cote d'Ivoire, with $55 million
2. Banque Int. pour le Comm. & I'Ind. Cote d'Ivoire, $50
3. Societe Ivoirienne de Banque, $17
4. Banque Atlantique de Cote d'Ivoire, $11

Source: *The Banker*, Top 100 African Banks-By Country (annual), December, 1998, p. 69.

Banks and Banking--Jamaica

★573★

TOP BANKS IN JAMAICA, 1997

Ranked by: Assets, in millions of U.S. dollars ($). **Remarks:** Also lists location, previous rank, balance against local currency, paid-up capital, and balance sheet date. **Number listed:** 4

1. Bank of Nova Scotia Jamaica Ltd., with $1,588 million
2. National Commercial Bank Jamaica Ltd., $1,178
3. CIBC Jamaica Ltd., $280
4. Citizens Bank Ltd., $224

Source: *Reed Information Services*, Bankers' Almanac World Ranking (annual), 1999, p. 181.

Banks and Banking--Japan

★574★

TOP JAPANESE BANKS BY ASSETS, 1997

Ranked by: Assets, in millions of U.S. dollars ($). **Remarks:** Also lists location, previous rank, balance against local currency, paid-up capital, and balance sheet date. **Number listed:** 141

1. Bank of Tokyo-Mitsubishi Ltd., with $666,085 million
2. Sumitomo Bank, $493,878
3. Sakura Bank, $442,555
4. Dai-Ichi Kangyo Bank Ltd., $429,803
5. Fuji Bank Ltd., $421,099
6. Sanwa Bank, $404,407
7. Norinchukin Bank, $379,906
8. Industrial Bank of Japan Ltd., $351,410
9. Asahi Bank Ltd., $276,977
10. Tokai Bank, $257,579

Source: *Reed Business Information Services*, Banker's Almanac World Ranking (annual), 1999, p. 181+.

★575★

TOP JAPANESE BANKS BY CAPITAL, 1998

Ranked by: Capital, in millions of U.S. dollars ($). **Remarks:** Also notes capital percentage change, as well as dollar amount, rank, and percentage change for size, soundness, profits, and performance, and rank among world's top 1,000 banks. **Number listed:** 100

1. Bank of Tokyo-Mitsubishi, with $18,585 million
2. Sumitomo Bank, $14,757
3. Dai-Ichi Kangyo Bank, $14,458
4. Sanwa Bank, $13,805
5. Fuji Bank, $13,705
6. Sakura Bank, $12,873
7. Norinchukin Bank, $11,640
8. Industrial Bank of Japan, $10,939
9. Tokai Bank, $8,929
10. Long-Term Credit Bank of Japan, $7,712

Source: *The Banker*, Top 100 Japanese Banks (annual), January, 1999, p. 33+.

★576★

TOP JAPANESE BANKS BY CORE CAPITAL, 1998

Ranked by: Core capital, in millions of U.S. dollars ($). **Remarks:** Also lists rank, tier-1 ratio, and total-capital ratio. **Number listed:** 25

1. Bank of Tokyo-Mitsubishi, with $18,661.7 million
2. Sumitomo Bank, $15,107.3
3. Dai-Ichi kangyo Bank, $14,990.8
4. Fuji Bank, $14,313.1
5. Sanwa Bank, $14,132.1
6. Sakura Bank, $13,301.9
7. Industrial Bank of Japan, $11,205.3
8. Tokai Bank, $9,238.5
9. Long-Term Credit Bank, $7,896.4
10. Asahi Bank, $7,408.3

Source: *Institutional Investor*, World's Largest Banks (annual), August, 1998, p. 134.

Banks and Banking--Jordan

★577★
TOP BANKS IN JORDAN
Ranked by: Assets, in millions of U.S. dollars ($). **Remarks:** Also lists location, previous rank, balance against local currency, paid-up capital, and balance sheet date. **Number listed:** 14

1. Arab Bank, with $16,808 million
2. Housing Bank, $1,904
3. Jordan National Bank, $1,067
4. Cairo Amman Bank, $987
5. Jordan Islamic Bank for Finance & Investment, $917
6. Bank of Jordan, $753
7. Jordan Kuwait Bank, $429
8. Jordan Investment & Finance Bank, $355
9. Arab Jordan Investment Bank, $352
10. Union Bank for Savings & Investment, $260

Source: *Reed Business Information Services*, Bankers' Almanac World Ranking (annual), 1999, p. 187.

★578★
TOP BANKS IN JORDAN, 1997
Ranked by: Capital, in millions of U.S. dollars ($). **Remarks:** Also notes capital percentage change, as well as dollar amount, rank, and percentage change for size, soundness, profits, and performance, and rank among world's top 1,000 banks. **Number listed:** 2

1. Arab Bank, with $1,260 million
2. Housing Bank, $303

Source: *The Banker*, World Top 1,000 Banker (annual), Summer, July, 1998, p. 190.

Banks and Banking--Kazakhstan

★579★
TOP BANKS IN KAZAKHSTAN, 1998
Ranked by: Assets, in millions of U.S. dollars ($). **Remarks:** Also lists location, previous rank, balance against local currency, paid-up capital, and balance sheet date. **Number listed:** 7

1. Halyk Savings Bank of Kazakstan, with $492 million
2. Kazkommertsbank, $464
3. ABN AMRO Holding N.V., $102
4. Centercredit, $57
5. Eurasian Bank, $54
6. Bank Caspiyskiy, $33
7. Kazkommerts Ziraat International, $13

Source: *Reed Business Information*, Bankers' Almanac World Ranking (annual), 1999, p. 187.

Banks and Banking--Kenya

★580★
LARGEST BANKS IN KENYA, 1997
Ranked by: Capital, in millions of U.S. dollars ($). **Remarks:** Also notes capital percentage change, as well as dollar amount, rank, and percentage change for size, soundness, profits, and performance, and rank among world's top 1,000 banks. **Number listed:** 8

1. Kenya Commercial Bank, with $156 million
2. National Bank of Kenya, $39
3. Co-operative Bank of Kenya, $25
4. Diamond Trust of Kenya, $23
4. CFC Bank, $23
6. Commercial Bank of Africa, $14
7. Trust Bank, $13
8. Consolidated Bank of Kenya, $11

Source: *The Banker*, Top 100 African Banks-By Country, December, 1998, p. 69+.

Banks and Banking--Korea, South

★581★
LARGEST BANKS IN SOUTH KOREA, 1997
Ranked by: Capital, in millions of U.S. dollars ($). **Remarks:** Also notes capital percentage change, as well as dollar amount, rank, and percentage change for size, soundness, profits, and performance, and rank among world's top 1,000 banks. **Number listed:** 20

1. Korea Exchange Bank, with $1,240 million
2. Shinhan Bank, $1,110
3. Hanil Bank, $1,061
4. Cho Hung Bank, $1,027
5. Kookmin Bank, $890
6. Commercial Bank of Korea, $887
7. Korea Long-Term Credit Bank, $768
8. Housing & Commercial Bank Korea, $638
9. Daegu Bank, $476
10. Seoul Bank, $428

Source: *World Top 1,000 Banker*, (annual), Summer, July, 1998, p. 190.

Banks and Banking--Kuwait

★582★
LARGEST BANKS IN KUWAIT
Ranked by: Capital, in millions of U.S. dollars ($). **Remarks:** Also notes capital percentage change, as well as dollar amount, rank, and percentage change for size, soundness, profits, and performance, and rank among world's top 1,000 banks. **Number listed:** 8

1. National Bank of Kuwait, with $1,215 million
2. Gulf Investment Corp., $1,123
3. Gulf Bank, $550
4. Commercial Bank of Kuwait, $500
5. Burgan Bank, $493
6. Kuwait Finance House, $459
7. Al-Ahli Bank of Kuwait, $444
8. Bank of Kuwait & the Middle East, $359

Source: *The Banker*, World Top 1,000 Banker (annual), Summer, July, 1998, p. 190.

Banks and Banking--Latin America

★583★
LARGEST BANKS IN LATIN AMERICA BY CAPITAL, 1997
Ranked by: Capital, in millions of U.S. dollars ($). **Remarks:** Also notes capital percentage change, as well as dollar amount, rank, and percentage change for size, soundness, profits, and rank among world's top 1,000 banks. **Number listed:** 100

1. Banco do Brasil, with $5,562 million
2. Banco Bradesco, $5,481
3. Banco Itau, $3,893
4. Banco do Estado de Sao Paulo, $3,522
5. Unibanco-Uniao de Bancos Brasileiros, $2,357
6. Banco de la Nacion Argentina, $2,002
7. Banamex, $1,790
8. Bancomer, $1,659
9. Banco Real, $1,581
10. Banco de la Provincia de Buenos Aires, $1,223

Source: *100 Top Latin America Banks*, (annual), August, 1998, p. 56+.

★584★
LEADING BANKS IN LATIN AMERICA BY CORE CAPITAL, 1998
Ranked by: Core capital, in millions of U.S. dollars ($). **Remarks:** Also lists tier-1 ratio, total-capital ratio, and world rank. **Number listed:** 25

1. Banco Bradesco, with $5,479 million
2. Banco do Brasil, $5,376.6
3. Banco Itau, $3,970.9
4. Uniao Bancos Brasileiros, $2,758.2
5. Banco Nacional de Mexico, $2,721.7
6. Bancomer, $2,253.8
7. Banco de la Nacion Argentina, $2,001.6
8. Banco Provincial, $1,977.7
9. Banco de la Provincia de Buenos Aires, $1,223.0
10. Banco de Galicia y Buenos Aires, $1,037.5

Source: *Institutional Investor*, World's Largest Banks (annual), August, 1998, p. 134.

★585★
LEADING BANKS IN LATIN AMERICA BY GROUP SHAREHOLDERS' EQUITY, 1997
Ranked by: Shareholders' equity, in millions of U.S. ($). **Remarks:** Also notes location, fiscal period, percentage equity growth, total assets, percentage income growth, percentage return on equity, and dollar rate differential. **Number listed:** 50

1. Banco Bradesco, with $5,479 million
2. Banco do Brasil, $5,377
3. Banco Itau, $3,971
4. Banco do Estando de Sao Paulo, $3,521
5. Banco Nacional de Mexico, $2,896
6. Banco Hipotecario Nacional, $2,767
7. Unibanco Uniao de Bancos Brasileiros, $2,758
8. Bancomer, $2,276
9. Banco de la Nacion Argentina, $1,934
10. Banco Real, $1,581

Source: *Euromoney*, Latin America 50 (annual), September, 1998, p. 146+.

★586★
TOP BANKS IN LATIN AMERICA BY ASSET GROWTH, 1997-1998
Ranked by: Asset growth year-on-year, in percent. **Number listed:** 60

1. Banco Excel Economico, with 1.50%
2. Banco Bozano Simonsen, 1.19%
3. Banco Multibanco, 0.63%
4. Banco del Pichincha, 0.54%
5. Banco Votorantim, 0.53%
6. Banco Bradesco, 0.48%
7. Banco Credicoop Cooperative, 0.44%
7. Banco Rio de la Plata, 0.44%
7. Banco Mercantil, 0.44%
9. BAC International Bank, 0.42%
10. Banco de Galicia & Buenos Aires, 0.40%
10. BanCrecer, 0.40%

Source: *Euromoney*, Latin America 50 (annual), September, 1998, p. 148.

★587★
TOP BANKS IN LATIN AMERICA BY CAPITAL GROWTH, 1997-1998
Ranked by: Capital growth year-on-year, in percent. **Number listed:** 60

1. Banco Multibanco, with 2.17%
2. Banco Votorantim, 0.78%
3. Banco Mercantil, 0.76%
4. Banco General de Negocios, 0.59%
5. Corpbanca, 0.58%
6. Bance do Nordeste do Brasil, 0.51%
7. Banco del Progreso, 0.50%
7. Banco do Estado de Sao Paulo, 0.50%
9. Banco Santiago, 0.47%
10 Banco de Galicia & Buenos Aires, 0.44%

Source: *Euromoney*, Latin America 50 (annual), September, 1998, p. 148.

★588★
TOP BANKS IN LATIN AMERICA BY PROFIT GROWTH, 1997-1998
Ranked by: Profit growth year-to-year, in percent. **Number listed:** 60

1. Corpbanca, with 7.97%
2. Banco Multibanco, 5.43%
3. Banco Credicoop Cooperative, 4.39%
4. BanCrecer, 3.45%
5. Banco Rio de la Plata, 2.16%
6. Banco Bansud, 1.92%
7. Nossa Caixa Nosso Banco, 1.61%
8. Banco del Centro, 1.35%
9. Banco Inversion & Comercio Exterior, 1.01%
10. Banco de la Nacion, 0.88%

Source: *Euromoney*, Latin America 50 (annual), September, 1998, p. 149.

★589★
TOP BANKS IN LATIN AMERICA BY RETURN ON EQUITY, 1997-1998
Ranked by: Return on equity, in percent. **Number listed:** 60

1. Banco do Estado de Sao Paulo, with 63.96%
2. Banco Mercantil, 47.53%
3. Banco Provincial, 45.15%
4. Banco Volkswagen, 38.03%
5. Banco Rio de la Plata, 37.19%
6. Banco General Motors, 35.68%
7. Corp Banca, 34.14%
8. Banco Pactual, 27.40%
9. Banco de Chili, 27.08%
10. Banco Bozano Simonsen, 26.66%

Source: *Euromoney*, Latin American 50 (annual), September, 1998, p. 149.

★590★
TOP BANKS IN LATIN AMERICA, 1998
Ranked by: Assets, in thousands of U.S. dollars ($). **Number listed:** 50

1. CEF, with $99,646,003 thousand
2. Brasil, $97,246,058
3. Bradesco, $55,108,520
4. Banespa, $52,142,248
5. Itau, $41,419,605
6. Banamex, $31,154,447
7. Bancomer, $27,115,829
8. Unibanco, $25,124,274
9. Serfin, $17,930,014

10. Real, $16,770,371

Source: *LatinFinance*, Top 50 Latin Banks (annual), October, 1998, p. 59.

Banks and Banking--Latvia

★591★
LARGEST BANKS IN LATIVA, 1997
Ranked by: Assets, in millions of U.S. dollars ($). **Remarks:** Also lists location, previous rank, balance against local currency, paid-up capital, and balance sheet date. **Number listed:** 13

1. Latvijas Banka, with $1,160 million
2. Parex Bank, $301
3. Rigas Komercbanka, $246
4. Latvijas Krajbanka, $142
5. Saules Banka, $112
6. Latvijas Zemes Banka, $103
7. Trasta Komercbanka, $75
8. Latvijas Kapital-Banka, $56
9. A/S Vereinsbank Riga, $38
10. Multibanka, $31

Source: *Reed business Information*, Bankers' Almanac World Ranking (annual), 1999, p. 191.

Banks and Banking--Lebanon

★592★
TOP BANKS IN LEBANON, 1999
Ranked by: Assets, in millions of U.S. dollars ($). **Remarks:** Also lists location, previous rank, balance against local currency, paid-up capital, and balance sheet date. **Number listed:** 38

1. Banque du Liban et d'Outre-Mer SAL, with $3,830 million
2. Banque de la Mediterranee SAL, $3,601
3. Banque Audi SAL, $2,672
4. Banque Libano-Francaise SAL, $2,167
5. Fransabank SAL, $1,847
6. Byblos Bank SAL, $1,430
7. Societe Generale Libano Europeenne, $1,238
8. Credit Libanais SAL, $898
9. Banque Saradar SAL, $797
10. Bank of Beirut & the Arab Countries SAL, $782

Source: *Reed Business Information Services*, Bankers' Almanac World Ranking (annual), 1999, p. 191+.

★593★
TOP BANKS IN LEBANON, 1997
Ranked by: Capital, in millions of U.S. dollars ($). **Remarks:** Also notes capital percentage change, as well as dollar amount, rank, and percentage change for size, soundness, profits, and performance, and rank among world's top 1,000 banks. **Number listed:** 4

1. Banque de la Mediterranee, with $314 million
2. Byblos Bank, $222
3. Banque Audi, $165
4. Banque du Liban et d'Outre- Mer, $162

Source: *The Banker*, World Top 1,000 (annual), Summer, July, 1998, p. 190.

Banks and Banking--Lesotho

★594★
TOP BANKS IN LESOTHO, 1999
Ranked by: Assets, in millions of U.S. dollars ($). **Remarks:** Also lists location, previous rank, balance against local currency, paid-up capital, and balance sheet date. **Number listed:** 2

1. Central Bank of Lesotho, with $508 million
2. Standard Bank Lesotho Ltd., $62

Source: *Reed Business Information Services*, Bankers' Almanac World Ranking (annual), 1999, p. 195.

Banks and Banking--Libya

★595★
LARGEST BANKS IN LIBYA, 1997
Ranked by: Capital, in millions of U.S. dollars ($). **Remarks:** Also notes capital percentage change, as well as dollar amount, rank, and percentage change for size, soundness, profits, and performance, and rank among world's top 1,000 banks. **Number listed:** 3

1. Libyan Arab Foreign Bank, with $751 million
2. Sahara Bank, $647
3. National Commercial Bank, $269

Source: *The Banker*, World Top 1,000 Banker (annual), Summer, July, 1998, p. 192.

Banks and Banking--Liechtenstein

★596★
LARGEST BANKS IN LIECHTENSTEIN, 1997
Ranked by: Capital, in millions of U.S. dollars ($). **Remarks:** Also notes capital percentage change, as well as dollar amount, rank, and percentage change for size, soundness, profits, and performance, and rank among world's top 1,000 banks. **Number listed:** 3

1. LGT Bank in Liechtenstein, with $670 million
2. Liechtensteinische Landesbank, $573
3. Verwaltungs & Privat-Bank, $557

Source: *The Banker*, World Top 1,000, Summer, July, 1998, p. 204.

Banks and Banking--Lithuania

★597★
LARGEST BANKS IN LITHUANIA BY ASSETS, 1999
Ranked by: Assets, in millions of U.S. dollars ($). **Remarks:** Also lists location, previous rank, balance against local currency, paid-up capital, and balance sheet date. **Number listed:** 6

1. Lithuanian Savings Bank, with $460 million
2. Vilniaus Bankas, $451
3. Lietuvos Zemes Ukio Bankas, $363
4. Bankas Hermis, $288
5. Litimpeks Bankas, $54
6. Medicinos Bankas, $17

Source: *Reed Business Information*, Bankers' Almanac World Ranking (annual), 1999, p. 196.

Banks and Banking--Luxembourg

★598★
LARGEST BANKS IN LUXEMBOURG, 1997
Ranked by: Capital, in millions of U.S. dollars ($). **Remarks:** Also notes capital percentage change, as well as dollar amount, rank, and percentage change for size, soundness, profits, and performance, and rank among world's top 1,000 banks. **Number listed:** 4
1. Banque Internationale a Luxembourg, with $897 million
2. Banque Generale du Luxembourg, $815
3. Kredietbank Luxembourgeoise, $749
4. Banque et Caisse d'Epargne de l'Etat, $725

Source: *The Banker*, World Top 1,000 Banker (annual), Summer, July, 1998, p. 192.

Banks and Banking--Macedonia

★599★
TOP BANKS IN MACEDONIA REPUBLIC, 1999
Ranked by: Assets, in millions of U.S. dollars ($). **Remarks:** Also lists location, previous rank, balance against local currency, paid-up capital, and balance sheet date. **Number listed:** 6
1. Stopanska Banka AD, with $340 million
2. Komercijanlna Bank AD Skopje, $182
3. Stopanska Banka AD, $44
4. Tutunska Banka AD Skopje, $33
5. Ohridska Banka AD Skopje, $27
6. Kreditna Banka AD Skopje, $16

Source: *Bankers' Almanac World Ranking*, (annual), 1999, p. 203.

Banks and Banking--Madagascar

★600★
LARGEST BANKS IN MADAGASCAR, 1998
Ranked by: Capital, in millions of U.S. dollars ($). **Remarks:** Also notes capital percentage change, as well as dollar amount rank, and percentage change in assets. **Number listed:** 2
1. Banque Malgache de l'Ocean Indien, with $20 million
2. BNI-Credit Lyonnais Madagascar, $12

Source: *The Banker*, Top 100 African Banks-by Country (annual), December, 1998, p. 70.

Banks and Banking--Malawi

★601★
LEADING BANKS IN MALAWI BY ASSETS, 1999
Ranked by: Assets, in millions of U.S. dollars ($). **Remarks:** Also notes location, total assets, paid-up capital, and balance sheet data. **Number listed:** 2
1. National Bank of Malawi (Blantyre), with $255 million
2. Commercial Bank of Malawi (Blantyre), $183

Source: *Bankers' Almanac World Ranking*, (annual), 1999, p. 203.

★602★
LEADING BANKS IN MALAWI BY CAPITAL, 1998
Ranked by: Capital, in millions of U.S. dollars ($). **Remarks:** Also lists percentage change for capital percentage change, as well as dollar amount, rank, percentage for size, soundness, profits, and performance. **Number listed:** 3
1. Malawi Savings Bank, with $22 million
2. National Bank of Malawi, $21
3. Commercial Bank of Malawi, $12

Source: *The Banker*, Top 100 African Banks-By Country (annual), December, 1998, p. 70.

Banks and Banking--Malaysia

★603★
LARGEST BANKS IN MALAYSIA, 1997
Ranked by: Capital, in millions of U.S. dollars ($). **Remarks:** Also lists capital percentage change, as well as dollar amount, rank, percentage change for size, soundness, profits, and performance. **Number listed:** 16
1. Maybank, with $3,293 million
2. Bank Bumiputra Malaysia, $1,121
3. AMMB Holdings, $1,022
4. Public Bank, $991
5. Sime Bank Berhad, $782
6. RHB Bank Berhad, $727
7. Bank of Commerce (Malaysia), $432
8. Hong Leong Bank, $406
9. Perwira Affin Bank, $337
10. Southern Bank Berhad, $286

Source: *The Banker*, World Top 1,000 Banker (annual), Summer, July, 1998, p. 192.

Banks and Banking--Malta

★604★
TOP BANKS IN MALTA, 1997
Ranked by: Assets, in millions of U.S. dollars ($). **Remarks:** Also lists location, previous rank, balance against local currency, paid-up capital, and balance sheet data. **Number listed:** 6
1. Mid-Med Bank Ltd. (Qormi), with $2,879 million
2. Bank of Valletta (Sliema), $2,665
3. Central Bank of Malta (Valletta), $1,822
4. Bank of Valletta International Ltd. (Valletta), $379
5. Lombard Bank Malta (Valletta), $189
6. APS Bank Ltd. (Floriana), $187

Source: *Bankers' Almanac World Ranking*, (annual), 1999, p. 206.

Banks and Banking--Mauritania

★605★
LARGEST BANKS IN MAURITANIA, 1998
Ranked by: Capital, in millions of U.S. dollars ($). **Remarks:** Also lists capital percentage changes, as well as dollar amount, rank, percentage change for size, soundness, profits, and performance. **Number listed:** 2

1. Banque Mauritanie Pour le Commerce International, with $15 million
2. Banque Nationale de Mauritanie, $10

Source: *The Banker*, Top 100 African Banks-By Country (annual), December, 1998, p. 70.

Banks and Banking--Mauritius

★606★

LARGEST BANKS IN MAURITIUS, 1998

Ranked by: Capital, in millions of U.S. dollars ($). **Remarks:** Also lists capital percentage change, as well as dollar amount, rank, and percentage change for size, soundness, profits, and performance. **Number listed:** 4

1. Mauritius Commercial Bank, with $190 million
2. State Bank of Mauritius, $119
3. Delphis Bank, $9
4. Indian Ocean International Bank, $8

Source: *The Banker*, Top 100 African Banks-By Country (annual), December, 1998, p. 70.

Banks and Banking--Mexico

★607★

LARGEST BANKS IN MEXICO BY LOAN MARKET SHARE, 1997

Ranked by: Loan market share, in percent. **Number listed:** 10

1. Bancomer, with 24.52%
2. Banamex, 21.38%
3. Serfin, 14.74%
4. Bital, 7.70%
5. Santander Mexicano, 6.53%
6. Bilbao Vizcaya, 5.89%
7. Promex, 3.41%
8. Centro, 2.99%
9. Mercantil del Norte, 2.93%
10. Banpais, 2.82%

Source: *LatinFinance*, Top 50 Latin Banks (annual), October, 1998, p. 62+.

★608★

LARGEST BANKS IN MEXICO, 1998

Ranked by: Capital, in millions of U.S. dollars ($). **Remarks:** Also lists capital percentage change, dollar amount rank, percentage change for size, soundness, profits, and performance. **Number listed:** 9

1. Banamex, with $1,790 million
2. Bancomer, $1,659
3. Banca Serfin, $912
4. Bital, $542
5. Confia, $331
6. Banco Mercantil del Norte, $313
7. Banco del Atlantico, $272
8. Banco Promex, $233
9. Banco Inverlat, $224

Source: *The Banker*, World Top 1,000 Banker, Summer, July, 1998, p. 192+.

★609★

LEADING BANKS IN MEXICO BY DEPOSIT MARKET SHARE, 1998

Ranked by: Deposit market share, in percent. **Number listed:** 10

1. Banamex, with 24.85%
2. Bancomer, 22.08%
3. Serfin, 14.87%
4. Bital, 7.43%
5. Bilbao Vizcaya, 7.26%
6. Santander Mexicano, 6.49%
7. Promex, 4.25%
8. Mercantil del Norte, 2.53%
9. Banpais, 2.05%
9. Centro, 2.05%

Source: *LatinFinance*, Top 50 Latin Banks (annual), October, 1998, p. 62+.

★610★

LEADING BANKS IN MEXICO BY RETURN ON ASSETS, 1998*

Ranked by: Return on assets, in percent. **Number listed:** 10

1. Inbursa, with 5.31%
2. Republic National Bank of New York, 3.42%
3. Centro, 2.56%
4. Chase Manhattan, 2.52%
5. J. P. Morgan, 1.63%
6. Banregio, 1.17%
7. Banamex, 1.15%
8. Invex, 1.05%
9. Bilbao Vizcaya, 1.02%
10. Interacciones, 0.65%

Source: *LatinFinance*, Top 50 Latin Banks (annual), October, 1998, p. 62+.

★611★

LEADING BANKS IN MEXICO BY RETURN ON EQUITY, 1998

Ranked by: Return on equity, in percent. **Number listed:** 10

1. Centro, with 20.75%
2. Bilbao Vizcaya, 17.39%
3. Inbursa, 15.36%
4. Chase Manhattan, 13.12%
5. Banamex, 12.99%
6. Interacciones, 11.42%
7. Invex, 7.93%
8. J. P. Morgan, 7.54%
9. Republic National Bank of New York, 6.97%
10. Bancomer, 6.03%

Source: *LatinFinance*, Top 50 Latin Banks (annual), October, 1998, p. 62+.

★612★

TOP BANKS IN MEXICO BY EFFICIENCY, 1997

Ranked by: Efficiency, in OEONI percent. **Number listed:** 10

1. Imbursa, with 11.17%
2. Chase Manhattan, 55.59%
3. Invex, 62.61%
4. Bilbao Vizcaya, 79.57%
5. Banamex, 79.70%
6. J. P. Morgan, 79.83%
7. Centro, 81.98%
8. Interacciones, 84.99%
9. Mifel, 90.71%
10. Bancomer, 94.09%

Source: *LatinFinance*, Top 50 Latin Banks (annual), October, 1998, p. 62+.

★613★

TOP BANKS IN MEXICO, 1998

Ranked by: Assets, in thousands of U.S. dollars ($). **Number listed:** 10

1. Banamex, with $31,154,447 thousand
2. Bancomer, $27,115,829
3. Serfin, $17,930,014

4. Bital, $9,181,322
5. Santander Mexicano, $8,018,811
6. Bilbao Vizcaya, $7,820,842
7. Promex, $4,754,795
8. Mercantil del Norte, $3,670,103
9. Banpais, $2,765,084
10. Centro, $2,654,753

Source: *LatinFinance*, Top 50 Latin Banks (annual), October, 1998, p. 62+.

Banks and Banking--Monaco

★614★
TOP BANKS IN MONACO, 1999
Ranked by: Assets, in millions of U.S. dollars ($). **Remarks:** Also lists location, previous rank, balance against local currency, paid-up capital, and balance sheet data. **Number listed:** 8

1. Credit Foncier de Monaco (Monte Carlo), with $2,564 million
2. Compagnie Monegasque de Banque (Monte Carlo), $2,224
3. Banque du Gothard, $1,491
4. Societe de Banque Suisse (Monaco), $1,214
5. Credit Commercial de France, $492
6. Societe Monegasque de Banque Privee, $480
7. ABC Banque Internationale de Monaco, $372
8. KB Luxembourg (Monaco), $100

Source: *Bankers' Almanac World Ranking*, (annual), 1999, p. 208.

Banks and Banking--Mongolia

★615★
TOP BANKS IN MONGOLIA, 1999
Ranked by: Assets, in millions of U.S. dollars ($). **Remarks:** Also lists location, previous rank, balance against local currency, paid-up capital, and balance sheet data. **Number listed:** 2

1. Trade & Development Bank of Mongolia, with $82 million
2. Golomt Bank of Mongolia, $13

Source: *Bankers' Almanac World Ranking*, (annual), 1999, p. 208.

Banks and Banking--Morocco

★616★
LARGEST BANKS IN MOROCCO, 1997
Ranked by: Capital, in millions of U.S. dollars ($). **Remarks:** Also lists capital percentage change, as well as dollar amount, rank, percentage change for size, soundness, profits, and performance, and rank among the world's top 1,000 banks. **Number listed:** 4

1. Credit Populaire du Maroc, with $572 million
2. Banque Commerciale du Maroc, $374
3. Banque Marocaine du Commerce Exterieur, $351
4. Wafabank, $233

Source: *The Banker*, World Top 1,000 (annual), Summer, July, 1998, p. 193.

Banks and Banking--Mozambique

★617★
TOP BANKS IN MOZAMBIQUE, 1999
Ranked by: Assets, in millions of U.S. dollars ($). **Remarks:** Also lists location, previous rank, balance against local currency, paid-up capital, and balance sheet date. **Number listed:** 2

1. Banco Standard Totta de Mozambique SARL, with $126 million
2. Banco Internacional de Mocambique SARL, $100

Source: *Bankers' Almanac World Ranking*, (annual), 1999, p. 210.

Banks and Banking--Mutual Fund Business

★618★
TOP BANKS AND THRIFTS THAT MANAGE INSTITUTIONAL MUTUAL FUND ASSETS, 1997-1998
Ranked by: Total proprietary institutional fund assets, in millions of dollars. **Remarks:** Also notes breakdown of fund assets by type, total number of portfolios, breakdown of portfolios by type, and total fund assets as of September 30, 1998 and December 31, 1997. **Number listed:** 25

1. PNC Bank Corp., with $46,523.7 million
2. BankOne Corp., $44,426.3
3. BankAmerica Corp., $43,926.7
4. Mellon Bank Corp., $34,696.9
5. U.S. Bancorp, $23,300.0
6. Chase Manhattan, $22,474.0
7. First Union Corp., $20,816.4
8. Wells Fargo & Co., $20,157.2
9. Bankers Trust Corp., $15,240.4
10. SunTrust Banks Inc., $14,979.8

Source: *American Banker*, (annual), February 12, 1999, p. 8A.

★619★
TOP BANKS AND THRIFTS THAT MANAGE MUTUAL FUND ASSETS, 1997
Ranked by: Year-end total assets, in percent. **Number listed:** 10

1. Mellon Bank Corp., with 16.8%
2. PNC Bank Corp., 16.3%
3. First Union Corp., 12.1%
4. Summit Bancorp, 10.5%
5. Wells Fargo & Co., 9.6%
6. SunTrust Banks Inc., 7.5%
7. AmSouth BanCorp., 7.3%
8. Regions Financial Corp., 6.1%
9. Citizens Financial Group, 5.8%
10. Harris Bankcorp, 5.8%

Source: *Banking Strategies*, November/December, November, 1998, p. 80.

★620★
TOP BANKS AND THRIFTS THAT MANAGE MUTUAL FUND ASSETS, 1997-1998
Ranked by: Total Proprietary fund assets, in millions of dollars. **Remarks:** Also notes breakdown of fund assets by type, and total fund assets as of September 30, 1998 and December 31, 1997. **Number listed:** 100

1. Mellon Bank Corp., with $109,730.0 million
2. First Union Corp., $68,165.5
3. BankAmerica Corp., $66,011.1
4. BankOne Corp., $55,139.1
5. PNC Bank Corp., $52,580.9

6. Wells Fargo & Co., $51,743.8
7. Chase Manhattan Corp., $42,600.3
8. U.S. Bancorp, $30,332.0
9. Bankers Trust Corp., $27,735.1
10. Northern Trust Corp., $20,854.5

Source: *American Banker*, (annual), February 12, 1999, p. 6A+.

★621★
TOP BANKS AND THRIFTS THAT MANAGE RETAIL FUND ASSETS, 1997-1998
Ranked by: Total proprietary retail fund assets, in millions of dollars. **Remarks:** Also notes breakdown of fund assets by type, total number of portfolios, breakdown of portfolios by type, and total fund assets as of September 30, 1998 and December 31, 1997. **Number listed:** 25

1. Mellon Bank Corp., with $75,033.1 million
2. First Union Corp., $47,349.1
3. Wells Fargo & Co., $31,586.6
4. BankAmerica Corp., $22,084.4
5. Chase Manhattan Corp., $20,126.3
6. KeyCorp, $14,646.6
7. Fleet Financial Group, $14,300.3
8. State Street Corp., $13,009.0
9. Bankers Trust Corp., $12,494.7
10. Bank One Corp., $10,712.8

Source: *American Banker*, (annual), February 12, 1999, p. 8A.

★622★
TOP EQUITY FUNDS MANAGED BY BANKS AND THRIFTS, 1997-1998
Ranked by: Total return, in millions of dollars. **Remarks:** Also notes bank name, investment objective, fund assets, 4th quarter returns, and returns for the previous 3, 5, and 10 years. **Number listed:** 50

1. Munder Net Net Fund A, with $97.83 million
2. Northern Technology, $82.99
3. Exceisior Large Cap Growth Fund, $67.04
4. WM Growth Fund A, $57.10
5. WM Growth Fund B, $55.87
6. Ark Funds-Capital Growth Institutional, $52.20
7. Robertson Stephens Info Age A, $50.14
8. Nations Marsico Focused Equity Inv A, $49.80
9. Nations Marsico Focused Equity Pr A, $49.34
10. Nations Marsico Focused Equity Inv B, $48.01

Source: *American Banker*, (annual), February 12, 199, p. 9A.

★623★
TOP INTERNATIONAL BOND FUNDS MANAGED BY BANKS AND THRIFTS, 1998
Ranked by: Total return, in millions of dollars. **Remarks:** Also notes bank name, fund assets, 4th quarter returns for 1998, plus return figures for 3, 5, and 10 years. **Number listed:** 10

1. STI Classic International Equity Index Trust, with $26.56 million
2. Dreyfus Premier Worldwide Growth A, $25.62
3. Chase Vista European Shares A, $25.58
4. Dreyfus Premier Worldwide Growth B, $25.15
5. Dreyfus Premier Worldwide Growth C, $24.82
6. BJB International Equity A, $24.67
7. Northern Institutional International Growth A, $24.28
8. First American-International Y, $22.65
9. ABN AMRO International Equity Trust, $22.58
10. First American-International A, $22.37

Source: *American Banker*, (annual), February 12, 1999, p. 9A.

★624★
TOP MIXED FUNDS MANAGED BY BANKS AND THRIFTS, 1998
Ranked by: Total return, in millions of dollars. **Remarks:** Also notes bank name, investment objective, fund assets, 4th quarter returns, and returns for the previous 3, 5, and 10 years. **Number listed:** 25

1. Stagecoach Index Allocation A, with $26.56 million
2. Stagecoach Index Allocation C, $25.62
3. Stagecoach Index Allocation A, $25.58
4. Chase Balanced Fund, $25.15
5. Stagecoach LifePath 2040 A, $24.82
6. Stagecoach Asset Allocation B, $24.67
7. Stagecoach LifePath 2040 B, $24.28
8. Norwest Advantage-Growth Bal, $22.65
9. Dreyfus Premier Balanced Fund R, $22.58
10. Northern Institutional Balanced A, $22.37

Source: *American Banker*, (annual), February 12, 1999, p. 11A.

★625★
TOP TAX-EXEMPT BOND FUNDS MANAGED BY BANKS AND THRIFTS, 1998
Ranked by: Total return, in millions of dollars. **Remarks:** Also notes bank name, fund assets, 4th quarter returns for 1997, plus return figures for 3, 5, and 10 years. **Number listed:** 25

1. CitiFunds National Tax Free, with $10.06 million
2. STI Classic Inv Grade T/E Tr, $7.07
3. Stagecoach CA Tax Free Bond 1, $6.87
4. CitiFunds NY Tax Free Income, $6.82
5. Stagecoach CA Tax Free Bond A, $6.81
6. Dreyfus Basic Municipal Bond Fund, $6.79
7. STI Classic Inv Grade T/E Inv, $6.73
8. Dreyfus Basic Interm Municiapal Bond, $6.71
9. Dreyfus NY Tax Exempt Bond, $6.70
10. Boston 1784 Funds-CT Tax-Ex Inc A, $6.67

Source: *American Banker*, (annual), February 12, 1999, p. 11A.

★626★
TOP TAXABLE BOND FUNDS MANAGED BY BANKS AND THRIFTS, 1998
Ranked by: Total return, in millions of dollars. **Remarks:** Also notes bank name, fund assets, 4th quarter returns for 1998, plus return figures for 3, 5, and 10 years. **Number listed:** 50

1. Dreyfus Lifetime Income Rest, with $12.04 million
2. Dreyfus UST Long-Term, $10.84
3. Excelsior Short-Term Government, $10.05
4. Pacific Capital Divers Fixed, $9.78
5. Galaxy II-US Treasury Idx Inv, $9.76
6. BB&T Interm US Government Bond Tr, $9.58
7. Norwest Advantage-Intrm Gov Inc I, $9.55
8. Galazy High Quality Bond Institutional, $9.42
9. AmSouth-Bond Fund Premier, $9.40
10. First Omaha Fixed Income Fund, $9.36

Source: *American Banker*, (annual), February 12, 1999, p. 10A.

Banks and Banking--Namibia

★627★
TOP BANKS IN NAMIBIA, 1998
Ranked by: Assets, in millions of U.S. dollars ($). **Remarks:** Also lists location, previous rank, balance against local currency, paid-up capital, and balance sheet data. **Number listed:** 4

1. First National Bank of Namibia Ltd., with $575 million
2. Bank of Namibia, $435
3. The Commercial Bank of Namibia, $321
4. Bank Windhoek Ltd., $318

Source: *Bankers' Almanac World Ranking*, (annual), 1999, p. 210.

Banks and Banking--Nepal

★628★
TOP BANKS IN NEPAL, 1998
Ranked by: Assets, in millions of U.S. dollars ($). **Remarks:** Also lists location, previous rank, balance against local currency, paid-up capital, and balance sheet data. **Number listed:** 3

1. Nepal Grindlays Bank Ltd., with $177 million
2. Nepal Arab Bank Ltd., $173
3. Nepal Indosuez Bank Ltd., $48

Source: *Bankers' Almanac World Ranking*, (annual), 1999, p. 210.

Banks and Banking--Netherlands

★629★
LARGEST BANKS IN THE NETHERLANDS, 1997
Ranked by: Capital, in millions of U.S. dollars ($). **Remarks:** Also lists location, previous rank, balance against local currency, paid-up capital, and balance sheet data. **Number listed:** 13

1. ABN AMRO Bank, with $15,864 million
2. Robobank Nederland, $12,680
3. ING Bank Group, $8,730
4. Bank Nederlandse Gemeenten, $1,751
5. Fortis Bank Nederland, $1,738
6. SNS Bank Nederland, $815
7. Nationale Investeringsbank, $755
8. Nederlandse Waterschapsbank, $636
9. F.Van Lanschot Bankiers, $318
10. Friesland Bank, $239

Source: *The Banker*, World Top 1,000 Banker (annual), Summer, July, 1998, p. 193.

Banks and Banking--Netherlands Antilles

★630★
TOP BANKS IN THE NETHERLANDS ANTILLES, 1997
Ranked by: Assets, in millions of U.S. dollars ($). **Remarks:** Also lists location, previous year's rank, balance against local currency, paid-up capital, and balance sheet data. **Number listed:** 3

1. Rabobank Curacao NV (Curacao), with $1,900 million
2. Maduro & Curiel's Bank NV (Willemstad), $1,275
3. Orco Bank NV (Willemstad), $53

Source: *Reed Business Information*, Bankers' Almanac World Ranking (annual), 1999, p. 213.

Banks and Banking--New Caledonia

★631★
TOP BANKS IN NEW CALEDONIA, 1999
Ranked by: Assets, in millions of U.S. dollars ($). **Remarks:** Also lists location, previous rank, balance against local currency, paid-up capital, and balance sheet data. **Number listed:** 2

1. Societe Generale Caledonienne de Banque (Noumea), with $378 million
2. Bank of Hawaii-Nouvelle Caledonie (Noumea), $257

Source: *Reed Business Information*, Bankers' Almanac World Ranking (annual), 1999, p. 213.

Banks and Banking--New Jersey

★632★
LARGEST COMMERCIAL BANKS IN NEW JERSEY, 1998
Ranked by: Total deposits, in thousands of U.S. dollars. **Remarks:** Also notes contact information, total assets, and chief executive. **Number listed:** 25

1. First Union Corp., with $140,000,000,000 thousand
2. Fleet Bank NA, $78,000,000,000
3. PNC Bank, $47,000,000,000
4. Bank of New York, $43,379,000,000
5. Mellon PSFS, $32,953,000,000
6. Summit Bank, $22,360,864,000
7. Valley National Bancorp, $4,345,000,000
8. Trustcompany Bank, $2,381,000,000
9. HUBCO Inc., $2,315,607,000
10. Commerce Bank, $2,192,173,000

Source: *New Jersey Business*, Book of Lists (annual), 1999, p. 6.

Banks and Banking--New York Metropolitan Area

★633★
LARGEST BANKS IN THE NEW YORK METROPOLITAN AREA, 1999
Ranked by: Total assets, in millions of dollars. **Remarks:** Also notes contact information, total earnings, breakdown between loan types, total loans, nonperforming loans, and figures from previous year. **Number listed:** 25

1. Citibank NA, with $668,641.0 million
2. Chase Manhattan Bank, $365,875.0
3. Morgan Guaranty Trust Co. of New York, $175,827.0
4. Bankers Trust Co., $133,115.0
5. Bank of New York, $63,141.0
6. Republic National Bank of New York, $46,460.0
7. European American Bank, $14,150.0
8. North Fork Bank, $10,680.0
9. Hudson United Bank, $6,779.0
10. Bank of Yokyo-Mitsubishi Trust Co., $4,376.0

Source: *Crain's New York Business*, (annual), April 19, 1999, p. 65+.

Banks and Banking--New Zealand

★634★
TOP BANKS IN NEW ZEALAND,1999
Ranked by: Assets, in millions of U.S. dollars. **Remarks:** Also lists location, previous rank, balance against local currency, paid-up capital, and balance sheet data. **Number listed:** 6

1. Bank of New Zealand (Wellington), with $15,111 million
2. ANZ Banking Group (New Zealand), $13,607
3. National Bank of New Zealand Ltd. (Wellington), $12,613
4. ASB Bank Ltd. (Auckland), $7,460
5. Countrywide Banking Corp., $4,977
6. Bankers Trust New Zealand Ltd. (Auckland), $1,958

Source: *Reed Business Information*, Bankers' Almanac World Ranking (annual), 1999, p. 213.

Banks and Banking--Nigeria

★635★
LARGEST BANKS IN NIGERIA BY CAPITAL, 1997
Ranked by: Capital, in millions of U.S. dollars ($). **Remarks:** Also lists capital percentage change, as well as dollar amount, rank, percentage change for size, soundness, profits, and performance. **Number listed:** 30

1. First Bank of Nigeria, with $343 million
2. United Bank for Africa, $243
3. Union Bank of Nigeria, $150
4. Citibank Nigeria, $133
5. Afribank Nigeria, $132
6. NAL Merchant Bank, $95
7. Investmant Banking & Trust Co., $89
8. Diamondbank, $77
9. FSB International Bank, $63
10. Wema Bank, $62

Source: *The Banker*, Top 100 African Banks-By Country (annual), December, 1998, p. 70+.

Banks and Banking--North America

★636★
LARGEST BANKS IN NORTH AMERICA, 1998
Ranked by: Core capital, in millions of dollars. **Remarks:** Also notes rank worldwide, tier one ratio, and total capital ratio. **Number listed:** 25

1. Chase Manhattan Bank, with $26,622.0 million
2. NationsBank Corp., $25,247.0
3. BankAmerica Corp., $24,081.0
4. Citicorp, $22,904.0
5. Wells Fargo & Co., $15,532.1
6. J. P. Morgan & Co., $13,704.4
7. First Union Corp., $13,022.7
8. Banc One Corp., $10,418.0
9. First Chicago NBD Corp., $9,954.0
10. Bankers Trust New York, $9,054.0

Source: *Institutional Investor*, World's Largest Banks (annual), August, 1998, p. 134.

Banks and Banking--Norway

★637★
LARGEST BANKS IN NORWAY, 1997
Ranked by: Capital, in millions of U.S. dollars ($). **Remarks:** Also lists capital percentage change, as well as dollar amount, rank, percentage change for size, soundness, profits, and performance, and rank among world's top 1,000 banks. **Number listed:** 9

1. Den Norske Bank Group, with $1,972 million
2. Christiania Bank, $1,481
3. Union Bank of Norway, $912
4. Postbanken, $523
5. Fokus Bank, $316
6. Sparebanken Rogaland, $229
7. Sparebanken Nord Norge, $210
8. Sparebanken Midt-Norge, $202
9. Sparebanken Hedmark, $186

Source: *The Banker*, World Top 1,000 Banker (annual), Summer, July, 1998, p. 193.

Banks and Banking--Oman

★638★
LEADING BANKS IN OMAN BY ASSETS, 1999
Ranked by: Assets, in millions of U.S. dollars ($). **Remarks:** Also lists location, previous rank, balance against local currency, paid-up capital, and balance sheet data. **Number listed:** 7

1. Bank Muscat Al Ahli Al Omani SAOG (Muttrah), with $1,601 million
2. Oman International Bank SAOG (Muscat), $1,536
3. National Bank of Oman Ltd. SAOG (Muscat), $1,520
4. Commercial Bank of Oman Ltd. SAOG (Ruwi), $861
5. Oman Arab Bank SAOC (Ruwi), $702
6. Bank Dhofar Al Omani Al Fransi SAOC (Ruwi), $600
7. Oman Development Bank SAOG (Muscat), $161

Source: *Reed Business Information*, Bankers' Almanac World Ranking (annual), 1999, p. 216.

Banks and Banking--Papua New Guinea

★639★
TOP BANKS IN PAPUA NEW GUINEA, 1999
Ranked by: Assets, in millions of U.S. dollars ($). **Remarks:** Also lists location, previous rank, balance against local currency, paid-up capital, and balance sheet data. **Number listed:** 4

1. Papua New Guinea Banking Corp. (Port Moresby), with $780 million
2. Australia & New Zealand Banking Group (Port Moresby), $322
3. Bank of South Pacific Ltd. (Port Moresby), $220
4. Bank of Hawaii (PNG) Ltd. (Port Moresby), $75

Source: *Reed Business Information*, Bankers' Almanac World Ranking (annual), 1999, p. 218.

Banks and Banking--Peru

★640★
LARGEST BANKS IN PERU BY DEPOSIT MARKET SHARE, 1997
Ranked by: Deposit market share, in percent. **Number listed:** 10
1. Credito, with 27.40
2. Wiese, 15.96
3. Continental, 15.68
4. De La Nacion, 7.09
5. Interbank, 6.33
6. Latino, 4.32
7. Lima, 3.68
8. Santander, 2.99
9. Bancosur, 2.82
10. Nuevo Mundo, 2.07

Source: *LatinFinance*, Top 50 Latin Banks (annual), October, 1998, p. 65.

★641★
LARGEST BANKS IN PERU BY RETURN ON EQUITY, 1998
Ranked by: Return on equity, in percent. **Number listed:** 10
1. Del Trabajo, with 35.86
2. Interbank, 20.72
3. Nuevo Mundo, 20.19
4. Del Progresso, 18.59
5. Credito, 18.16
6. InterAmericano, 17.26
7. Orion, 16.56
8. Lima, 15.70
9. Continental, 14.78
10. Exebandes, 12.44

Source: *LatinFinance*, Top 50 Latin banks (annual), October, 1998, p. 65.

★642★
LARGEST BANKS IN PERU, 1997
Ranked by: Capital, in millions of U.S. dollars ($). **Remarks:** Also lists capital percentage change, as well as dollar amount, rank, percentage change for size, soundness, profits, and performance, and rank among the world's top 1,000 banks. **Number listed:** 4
1. Banco de Credito del Peru, with $528 million
2. Banco Wiese, $263
3. Banco de la Nacion, $217
4. Banco Continental, $198

Source: *The Banker*, World Top 1,000 (annual), Summer, July, 1998, p. 194.

★643★
LEADING BANKS IN PERU BY LOAN MARKET SHARE, 1997
Ranked by: Loan market share, in percent. **Number listed:** 10
1. Credito, with 21.96
2. Wiese, 17.60
3. Continental, 12.63
4. Interbank, 7.08
5. De la Nacion, 6.83
6. Bancosur, 4.51
7. Latino, 4.11
8. Lima, 4.06
9. Santander, 3.80
10. Nuevo Mundo, 2.29

Sourcc: *LatinFinance*, Top 50 Latin Banks (annual), October, 1998, p. 65.

★644★
LEADING BANKS IN PERU BY RETURN ON ASSETS, 1997
Ranked by: Return on assets, in percent. **Number listed:** 10
1. Del Trabajo, with 3.95
2. Orion, 2.34
3. Extebandes, 1.93
4. Interbank, 1.64
5. Credito, 1.62
5. Del Progresso, 1.62
7. Nuevo Mundo, 1.53
8. InterAmericano, 1.36
9. Continental, 1.32
10. Lima, 1.31

Source: *LatinFinance*, Top 50 Latin Banks (annual), October, 1998, p. 65.

★645★
TOP BANKS BY EFFICIENCY, 1998
Ranked by: Efficiency, in OEONI percent. **Number listed:** 10
1. Exebandes, with 60.47
2. Nuevo Mundo, 65.64
3. Del Progresso, 66.09
4. InterAmericano, 67.38
5. Continental, 71.57
6. Sud Americano, 71.95
7. Credito, 72.64
8. Interbank, 76.00
9. Lima, 76.10
10. Del Trabajo, 77.36

Source: *LatinFinance*, Top 50 Latin Banks (annual), October, 1998, p. 65.

★646★
TOP BANKS IN PERU, 1998
Ranked by: Assets, in thousands of U.S. dollars ($). **Number listed:** 10
1. Credito, with $5,637,867 thousand
2. Wiese, $3,930,048
3. Continental, $3,105,489
4. De La Nacion, $2,771,011
5. Interbank, $1,610,382
6. Santander, $977,139
7. Bancosur, $922,749
8. Lima, $919,255
9. Latino, $908,366
10. Nuevo Mundo, $508,626

Source: *LatinFinance*, Top 50 Latin Banks (annual), October, 1998, p. 65.

Banks and Banking--Philadelphia Metropolitan Area

★647★
LARGEST COMMERCIAL BANKS IN THE PHILADELPHIA METROPOLITAN AREA, 1996-1997
Ranked by: Local deposits, in dollars. **Remarks:** Also notes holding company contact information and CEO, total assets, net income, net loans, total deposits, and number of local and total offices. **Number listed:** 25
1. First Union Corp., with $25,722,534 dollar
2. PNC Bank Corp., $10,291,706
3. Mellon Bank Corp., $8,45,424
4. Commerce Bancorp Inc., $2,370,188
5. Summit Bancorp, $2,153,355
6. Keystone Financial Inc., $914,078

7. JeffBanks Inc., $819,299
8. Univest Corp. of Pennsylvania, $789,796
9. Harleysville National Corp., $779,921
10. Prime Bancorp Inc., $660,642

Source: *Philadelphia Business Journal*, Book of Business Lists (annual), December 25, 1998, p. 29.

Banks and Banking--Philippines

★648★
LARGEST BANKS IN THE PHILIPPINES, 1997
Ranked by: Capital, in millions of U.S. dollars ($). **Remarks:** Also lists capital percentage change as well as dollar amount, rank, percentage change for size, soundness, profits, and performance, and rank among world's top 1,000 banks. **Number listed:** 14

1. Metrobank, with $961 million
2. Bank of the Philippine Islands, $618
3. Philippine Commercial International Bank, $525
4. Philippine National Bank, $482
5. Far East Bank & Trust Co., $433
6. Equitable Banking Corp., $373
7. Land Bank Philippines, $339
8. Development Bank of the Philippines, $336
9. United Coconut Planters Bank, $327
10. Rizal Commercial Banking Corp., $241

Source: *The Banker*, World Top 1,000 Banker (annual), Summer, July, 1999, p. 194.

Banks and Banking--Poland

★649★
LARGEST BANKS IN POLAND BY CAPITAL, 1997
Ranked by: Capital, in millions of U.S. dollars ($). **Remarks:** Notes percentage change in tier-1 capital and information about size of assets, soundness and profitability. **Number listed:** 13

1. Bank Pekao, with $900 million
2. Bank Handlowy w Warszawie, $718
3. Powszechna Kasa Oszczednosci BP, $503
4. Bank Slaski, $305
5. BIG Bank Gdanski, $293
6. Powszechny Bank Kredytowy, $269
7. Bank Przemyslowo Handlowy, $238
8. Bank Rozwoju Eksportu, $201
9. Bank Gospodarki Zywnosciowej, $199
10. Bank Zachodni SA Wroclaw, $128

Source: *The Banker*, Europe Top 500 (annual), September, 1998, p. 71.

Banks and Banking--Portugal

★650★
LARGEST BANKS IN PORTUGAL, 1997
Ranked by: Capital, in millions of U.S. dollars ($). **Remarks:** Also lists capital percentage change, as well as dollar amount, rank, percentage change for size, soundness, profits, and performance, and rank among the world's top 1,000 banks. **Number listed:** 9

1. Caixa Geral de Depositos, with $2,408 million
2. Banco Pinto & Sotto Mayer, $1,512
3. Banker Comercial Portugues, $1,200
4. Banco Espirito Santo e Comercial de Lisboa, $1,074
5. Banco Totta & Acores, $874
6. BPI-SGPS, $632
7. Banco Mello, $334
8. Banco Internacional do Funchal , $223
9. Credito Predial Poetugues, $201

Source: *The Banker*, World Top 1,000 Banker (annual), Summer, July, 1998, p. 194.

Banks and Banking--Qatar

★651★
TOP BANKS IN QATAR, 1999
Ranked by: Assets, in millions of U.S. dollars ($). **Remarks:** Also lists location, previous rank, balance against local currency, paid-up capital, and balance sheet data. **Number listed:** 5

1. Qatar National Bank (Doha), with $5,026 million
2. Doha Bank Ltd., $1,132
3. Commercial Bank of Qatar (Doha), $997
4. Qatar Islamic Bank (Doha), $834
5. Al-Ahli Bank of Qatar (Doha), $555

Source: *Reed Business Information*, Bankers' Alamanac World Ranking (annual), 1999, p. 224.

Banks and Banking—Regional

See: **Regional Banks**

Banks and Banking--Romania

★652★
LARGEST BANKS IN ROMANIA BY CAPITAL, 1998
Ranked by: Capital, in millions of U.S. dollars ($). **Remarks:** Notes percentage change in tier-1 capital and information about size of assets, soundness, and profitability. **Number listed:** 3

1. Banca Comerciala Romana, with $338 million
2. Romanian Bank for Development, $244
3. Banca Romana De Comert Exterior, $132

Source: *The Banker*, Europe Top 500 (annual), September, 1998, p. 71.

Banks and Banking--Russia (Republic)

★653★
LARGEST BANKS IN RUSSIA BY CAPITAL, 1997
Ranked by: Capital, in millions of U.S. dollars ($). **Remarks:** Also lists capital percentage change, as well as dollar amount, rank, percentage change for size, soundness, profits, and performance, and rank among the world's top 1,000 banks. **Number listed:** 12

1. Sberbank, with $2,752 million
2. Vneshtorgbank-Bank for Foreign Trade, $1,023

3. United Export Import Bank, $826
4. SBS-Agro (Stolichny Bank of Savings), $466
5. International Co. of Finance & Investment, $320
6. Rossiyskiy Kredit Bank, $314
7. Bank Menatep, $305
8. Tokobank, $287
9. Inkombank, $261
10. Bank Imperial, $210

Source: *The Banker*, World Top 1,000 (annual), Summer, July, 1998, p. 196.

Banks and Banking--Rwanda

★654★
LARGEST BANKS IN RWANDA, 1998
Ranked by: Capital, in millions of U.S. dollars ($). **Remarks:** Also lists capital percentage change, as well as dollar amount, rank, percentage change for size, soundness, profits, and performance, and rank among the world's top 1,000 banks. **Number listed:** 2

1. Banque Commerciale du Rwanda, with $6 million
2. Banque de Kigali, $5

Source: *The Banker*, Top African Banks-By Country (annual), December, 1998, p. 71.

★655★
TOP BANKS IN RWANDA, 1999
Ranked by: Assets, in millions of U.S. dollars ($). **Remarks:** Also lists location, previous rank balance against local currency, paid-up capital, and balance sheet data. **Number listed:** 2

1. Banque Commerciale du Rwanda SA (Kigali), with $83 million
2. Banque de Kigali (Kigali), $79

Source: *The Banker*, Bankers' Almanac World Ranking (annual), 1999, p. 233.

Banks and Banking--Saudi Arabia

★656★
LARGEST BANKS IN SAUDI ARABIA, 1998
Ranked by: Capital, in millions of U.S. dollars ($). **Remarks:** Also lists capital percentage change, as well as dollar amount, rank, percentage change for size, soundness, profits, and performance, and rank among the world's top 1,000 banks. **Number listed:** 10

1. National Commercial Bank, with $2,076 million
2. Riyad Bank, $2,013
3. Al Rajhi Banking & Investment Corp., $1,376
4. Saudi American Bank, $1,222
5. United Saudi Bank, $848
6. Saudi British Bank, $787
7. Al Bank Al Saudi Al Fransi, $782
8. Arab National Bank, $773
9. Saudi Investment Bank, $365
10. Saudi Hollandi Bank, $352

Source: *The Banker*, World Top 1,000 Banker, Summer, July, 1998, p. 196.

Banks and Banking--Senegal

★657★
LARGEST BANKS IN SENEGAL, 1998
Ranked by: Capital, in millions of U.S. dollars ($). **Remarks:** Also lists capital percentage change, as well as dollar amount, rank, percentage change for size, soundness, profits, and performance. **Number listed:** 3

1. Societe Generale de Banques au Senegsal, with $12 million
2. Banque Int. Pour le Comm. & I'Ind. du Senegal, $11
3. Banque de l'Habitat du Senegal, $6

Source: *The Banker*, Top 500 African Banks-By Country, December, 1998, p. 71.

Banks and Banking--Serbia

★658★
LARGEST BANKS IN SERBIA, 1998
Ranked by: Capital, in millions of U.S. dollars ($). **Remarks:** Notes percentage change in tier-1 capital and information about size of assets, soundness, and profitability. **Number listed:** 3

1. Beogradska Banka, with $358 C
2. Jugobanka DD Beograd, $245
3. Vojvodjanska Banka, $23

Source: *The Banker*, Europe Top 500 (annual), September, 1998, p. 72.

Banks and Banking--Seychelles

★659★
TOP BANKS IN SEYCHELLES, 1999
Ranked by: Assets, in millions of U.S. dollars ($). **Remarks:** Also lists location, previous rank, balance against local currency, paid-up capital, and balance sheet data. **Number listed:** 2

1. Seychelles International Mercantile Banking Corp. Ltd. (Victoria), with $138 million
2. Development Bank of Seychelles (Victoria), $39

Source: *Reed Business Information*, Bankers' Almanac World Ranking (annual), 1999, p. 235.

Banks and Banking--Sierra Leone

★660★
TOP BANKS IN SIERRA LEONE, 1999
Ranked by: Assets, in millions of U.S. dollars ($). **Remarks:** Also lists location, previous rank, balance against local currency, paid-up capital, and balance sheet data. **Number listed:** 2

1. Standard Chartered Bank Sierra Leone Ltd. (Freetown), with $29 million
2. Sierra Leone Commercial Bank Ltd. (Freetown), $24

Source: *Reed Business Information*, Bankers' Almanac World Ranking (annual), 1999, p. 235.

Banks and Banking--Singapore

★661★
LARGEST BANKS IN SINGAPORE, 1997
Ranked by: Capital, in millions of U.S. dollars ($). **Remarks:** Also lists location, previous rank, balance against local currency, paid-up capital, and balance sheet data. **Number listed:** 6
1. Oversea-Chinese Banking Corp., with $4,363 million
2. DBS Bank, $4,325
3. United Overseas Bank, $3,179
4. Overseas Union Bank, $2,412
5. Tat Lee Bank, $1,013
6. Keppel Bank of Singapore, $929

Source: *The Banker*, World Top 1,000 Banker (annual), Summer, July, 1998, p. 196.

Banks and Banking--Slovakia

★662★
LARGEST BANKS IN SLOVAKIA, 1997
Ranked by: Capital in millions of U.S. dollars ($). **Remarks:** Notes percentage change in tier-1 capital and information about size of assets, soundness, and profitability. **Number listed:** 2
1. Vseobecna Uverova Banka, with $337 million
2. Slovenska sporitel'na, $186

Source: *The Banker*, World Top 1,000 (annual), Summer, July, 1998, p. 196.

Banks and Banking--Slovenia

★663★
LARGEST BANKS IN SLOVENIA, 1997
Ranked by: Capital, in millions of U.S. dollars ($). **Remarks:** Notes percentage change in tier-1 capital and information about size of assets, soundness, and profitability. **Number listed:** 4
1. Nova Ljubljanska Banka, with $225 million
2. SKB Banka DD, $139
3. Nova Kreditna Banka Maribor, $81
4. Gorenjska Banka DD Kranj, $80

Source: *The Banker*, Europe Top 500 (annual), September, 1997, p. 76.

Banks and Banking--South Africa

★664★
LARGEST BANKS IN SOUTH AFRICA, 1998
Ranked by: Capital, in millions of U.S. dollars ($). **Remarks:** Also lists capital percentage change, as well as dollar amount, rank, and percentage change for assets. **Number listed:** 11
1. Stanbic, with $2,091 million
2. ABSA Group, $1,665
3. Nedcor, $1,409
4. First National Bank Holdings, $1,156
5. Investec Group, $958
5. NBS Boland Bank, $958
7. Rand Merchant Bank, $95
8. Saambou Bank, $77
9. Mercantile Lisbon Bank Holdings Ltd., $65
10. Fidelity Bank, $61

Source: *The Banker*, Top 100 African Banks-By Country (annual), December, 1998, p. 71.

Banks and Banking--Spain

★665★
LARGEST BANKS IN SPAIN, 1997
Ranked by: Capital, in millions of U.S. dollars ($). **Remarks:** Also lists capital percentage change, as well as dollar amount, rank, percentage change for size, soundness, profits, and performance, and rank among the world's top 1,000 banks. **Number listed:** 41
1. Banco Santander, with $7,952 million
2. Banco Bilbao Vizcaya, $6,800
3. Argentaria, $5,069
4. Banco Central Hispanoamericano, $3,454
5. Caja de Ahorros y Pen. de Barcelona, $3,366
6. Caja de Madrid, $2,877
7. Banco Popular Espanol, $2,191
8. Banco Sabadell, $1,027
9. Bankinter, $879
10. Caja Gipuzkoa Sebastian (Kutxa), $837

Source: *The Banker*, World Top 1,000 Banker (annual), Summer, July, 1998, p. 198.

Banks and Banking--Sri Lanka

★666★
TOP BANKS IN SRI LANKA, 1999
Ranked by: Assets, in millions of U.S. dollars ($). **Remarks:** Also lists location, previous rank, balance against local currency, paid-up capital, and balance sheet data. **Number listed:** 9
1. Bank of Ceylon (Colombo), with $2,372 million
2. People's Bank (Colombo), $1,872
3. Hatton National Bank Ltd. (Colombo), $851
4. Seylan Bank Ltd. (Colombo), $580
5. Commercial Bank of Ceylon Ltd. (Colombo), $448
6. National Development Bank of Sri Lanka (Colombo), $351
7. DFCC Bank Ltd. (Colombo), $305
8. Sampath Bank (Colombo), $298
9. Union Bank of Colombo Ltd. (Colombo), $57

Source: *Reed Business Information*, Bankers' Alamanac World Ranking (annual), 1999, p. 243.

Banks and Banking--Sudan

★667★
TOP BANKS IN SUDAN, 1999
Ranked by: Assets, in millions of U.S. dollars ($). **Remarks:** Also lists location, previous rank, balance against local currency, paid-up capital, and balance sheet data. **Number listed:** 5
1. El Nilein Industrial Development Bank (Khartoum), with $1,160 million
2. Tadamon Islamic Bank (Khartoum), $530
3. Omdurman National Bank (Khartoum), $418

4. Saudi Sudanese Bank (Khartoum), $327
5. Al Baraka Bank (Sudan), $218

Source: *Reed Business Information*, Bankers' Almanac World Ranking (annual), 1999, p. 243.

Banks and Banking--Suriname

★668★
TOP BANKS IN SURINAME, 1999
Ranked by: Assets, in millions of U.S. dollars ($). **Remarks:** Also lists location, previous rank, balance against local currency, paid-up capital, and balance sheet data. **Number listed:** 2

1. De Surinaamsche Bank NV (Paramaribo), with $111 million
2. Handels-Krediet-en Industriebank NV (Paramaribo), $53

Source: *Reed Business Information*, Bankers' Almanac World Ranking (annual), 1999, p. 243.

Banks and Banking--Sweden

★669★
LARGEST BANKS IN SWEDEN, 1997
Ranked by: Capital, in millions of U.S. dollars ($). **Remarks:** Also lists capital percentage change, as well as dollar amount, rank, percentage change for size, soundness, profits, and performance, and rank among world's top 1,000 banks. **Number listed:** 4

1. Svenska Handelsbanken, with $3,288 million
2. Skandinaviska Enskilda Banken, $3,161
3. Foreningsbanken, $2,753
4. Nordbanken, $2,092

Source: *The Banker*, World Top 1,000 Banker (annual), Summer, July, 1998, p. 199.

Banks and Banking--Switzerland

★670★
LARGEST BANKS IN SWITZERLAND, 1997
Ranked by: Capital, in millions of U.S. dollars ($). **Remarks:** Also lists capital percentage change, as well as dollar amount, rank, percentage change for size, soundness, profits, and performance, and rank among the world's top 1,000 banks. **Number listed:** 31

1. Union Bank of Switzerland, with $13,570 million
2. Credit Suisse Group, $12,984
3. Swiss Bank Corp., $6,371
4. Zurcher Kantonalbank, $2,356
5. Schweizer Verband der Raiffeisenbanken, $1,725
6. Banque Cantonale Vaudoise, $1,402
7. Union Bancaire Privee, $935
8. Julius Baer Group, $928
9. Luzerner Kantonalbank, $735
10. Berner Kantonalbank, $704

Source: *The Banker*, World Top 1,000 Banker (annual), Summer, July, 1998, p. 199.

Banks and Banking--Taiwan

★671★
LARGEST BANKS IN TAIWAN, 1997
Ranked by: Capital, in millions of U.S. dollars ($). **Remarks:** Also lists capital percentage change, as well as dollar amount, rank, percentage change for size, soundness, profits, and performance, and rank among world's top 1,000 banks. **Number listed:** 37

1. Bank of Taiwan, with $3,277 million
2. Land Bank of Taiwan, $1,520
3. First Commercial Bank, $1,512
4. Taiwan Cooperative Bank, $1,457
5. Hua Nan Commercial Bank, $1,426
6. Taipeibank, $1,286
7. Chang Hwa Commercial Bank, $1,268
8. Taiwan Business Bank, $1,195
9. International Commercial Bank of China, $1,132
10. Chinatrust Commercial Bank, $1,100

Source: *The Banker*, World Top 1,000 Banker (annual), Summer, July, 1998, p. 202.

Banks and Banking--Tanzania

★672★
TOP BANKS IN TANZANIA, 1999
Ranked by: Assets, in millions of U.S. dollars ($). **Remarks:** Also lists location, previous rank, balance against local currency, paid-up capital, and balance sheet data. **Number listed:** 4

1. Stanbic Bank Tanzania Ltd. (Dar es), with $110 million
2. Tanzania Investment Bank (Dar es), $12
3. Greenland Bank Tanzania Ltd., $8.97
4. National Bank of Commerce Ltd. (Dar es Salaam), $7.08

Source: *Reed business Information*, Bankers' Almanac World Ranking (annual), 1999, p. 253.

Banks and Banking--Thailand

★673★
LARGEST BANKS IN THAILAND, 1997
Ranked by: Capital, in millions of U.S. dollars ($). **Remarks:** Also lists capital percentage change, as well as dollar amount, rank, percentage change for size, soundness, profits, and performance, and rank among world's top 1,000 banks. **Number listed:** 9

1. Bangkok Bank, with $2,138 million
2. Thai Farmers Bank, $1,269
3. First Bangkok City Bank, $1,027
4. Siam Commercial Bank, $970
5. Krung Thai Bank, $969
6. Bank of Ayudhya, $641
7. Thai Military Bank, $488
8. Siam City Bank, $246
9. Thai Danu Bank, $174

Source: *The Banker*, World Top 1,000 Banker (annual), Summer, July, 1998, p. 201.

Banks and Banking--Togo

★674★
TOP BANKS IN TOGO, 1998
Ranked by: Capital, in millions of U.S. dollars ($). **Remarks:** Also lists capital percentage change, as well as dollar amount, rank, percentage change for size, soundness, profits, and performance, and rank among world's top 1,000 banks. **Number listed:** 2

1. Ecobank Transnational, with $33 million
2. Union Togolaise de Banque, $8

Source: *Top 100 African Banks-By Country*, (annual), December, 1998, p. 171.

Banks and Banking--Trinidad and Tobago

★675★
TOP BANKS IN TRINIDAD AND TOBAGO, 1998
Ranked by: Assets, in millions of U.S. dollars ($). **Remarks:** Also lists location, previous rank, balance against local currency, paid-up capital, and balance sheet data. **Number listed:** 5

1. Republic Bank Ltd. (Port of Spain), with $1,919 million
2. Royal Bank of Trinidad & Tobago Ltd. (Port of Spain), $1,904
3. Scotiabank Trinidad & Tobago Ltd. (Port of Spain), $658
4. First Citizens Bank Ltd. (Port of Spain), $528
5. Citibank Trinidad & Tobago Ltd. (Port of Spain), $128

Source: *Reed Business Information*, Bankers' Almanac World Ranking (annual), 1999, p. 254.

Banks and Banking—Trust Departments

★676★
TOP BANKING COMPANIES IN DISCRETIONARY TRUST ASSETS, 1998
Ranked by: Managed trust assets, in thousands of dollars. **Remarks:** Also notes gross trust income and rank from previous year. **Number listed:** 50

1. State Street Corp., with $397,553,397 thousand
2. Bankers Trust Corp., $319,377,812
3. Mellon Bank Corp., $304,461,000
4. J. P. Morgan & Co. Inc., $251,485,000
5. Northern Trust Corp., $203,111,792
6. Chase Manhattan Corp., $165,752,000
7. PNC Bank Corp., $147,960,403
8. NationsBank Corp., $128,536,679
9. Citicorp, $113,100,000
10. Bank of New York Co. Inc., $103,480,000

Source: *American Banker*, July 21, 1998, p. 10.

★677★
TOP BANKING COMPANIES IN TRUST INCOME, 1997
Ranked by: Gross trust revenue, in thousands of dollars. **Remarks:** Also notes total operating income, and figures and rank from previous year. **Number listed:** 50

1. J. P. Morgan & Co. Inc., with $1,439,000 thousand
2. Mellon Bank Corp., $1,311,000
3. Chase Manhattan Corp., $1,307,000
4. State Street Corp., $1,252,000
5. Bankers Trust Corp., $1,059,000
6. Bank of New York Co. Inc., $971,000
7. Northern Trust Corp., $689,200
8. NationsBank Corp., $648,000
9. Citicorp, $624,600
10. PNC Bank Corp., $603,000

Source: *American Banker*, July 21, 1998, p. 12.

★678★
TOP CONCENTRATED TRUST COMPANIES, 1998
Ranked by: Ratios of trust revenues to net revenues, in percent. **Number listed:** 10

1. U.S. Trust Corp., with 76.4%
2. State Street Corp., 56.4%
3. Northern Trust Corp., 52.9%
4. Mellon Bank Corp., 38.6%
5. Wilmington Trust Corp., 31.1%
6. J. P. Morgan & Co. Inc., 25.4%
7. Bankers Trust Corp., 19.0%
8. UMB Financial Corp., 17.4%
9. Riggs National Corp., 16.7%
10. PNC Bank Corp., 15.5%

Source: *Banking Strategies*, December, 1998, p. 144.

★679★
TOP CORPORATE TRUST ACCOUNTS, 1997
Ranked by: Number of accounts. **Number listed:** 5

1. Chase Manhattan Corp., with 341,190
2. Wells Fargo & Co., 46,512
3. Bankers Trust New York Corp., 24,227
4. U.S. Bancorp, 24,182
5. State Street Corp., 20,527

Source: *American Banker*, July 21, 1998, p. 13.

★680★
TOP INSTITUTIONAL TRUST & EMPLOYEE BENEFIT ACCOUNTS, 1997
Ranked by: Number of accounts. **Number listed:** 5

1. Fidelity Management Trust Co., with 5,386,322
2. UMB Financial Corp., 25,715
3. Northern Trust Corp., 20,276
4. Banc One Corp., 16,043
5. NationsBank Corp., 14,300

Source: *American Banker*, July 21, 1998, p. 13.

★681★
TOP INSTITUTIONAL TRUST OTHER ACCOUNTS, 1997
Ranked by: Number of accounts. **Number listed:** 5

1. State Street Corp., with 40,066
2. Bank of New York Co. Inc., 39,074
3. Bankers Trust New York Corp., 21,444
4. BankAmerica Corp., 19,868
5. Northern Trust Corp., 16,590

Source: *American Banker*, July 21, 1998, p. 13.

★682★
TOP PERSONAL TRUST ACCOUNTS, 1997
Ranked by: Number of accounts, in millions of dollars. **Number listed:** 5

1. NationsBank Corp., with $126,227 million
2. Wells Fargo & Co., $61,739
3. PNC Bank Corp., $37,823
4. Bank One Corp., $26,182
5. First Union Corp., $25,272

Source: *American Banker*, July 21, 1998, p. 13.

Banks and Banking--Tunisia

★683★
TOP BANKS IN TUNISIA, 1999
Ranked by: Assets, in millions of U.S. dollars ($). **Remarks:** Also lists location, previous rank, balance against local currency, paid-up capital, and balance sheet data. **Number listed:** 10

1. Banque Nationale Agricole (Tunis), with $2,459 million
2. Societe Tunisienne de Banque (Tunis), $2,389
3. Banque Internationale Arabe de Tunisie (Tunis), $1,695
4. Union Internationale de Banques (Tunis), $1,106
5. Banque de Tunisie (Tunis), $986
6. Amen Bank (Tunis), $973
7. Banque de Developpement Economique de Tunisie (Ariana), $817
8. Banque Nationale de Developpement Touristique (Tunis), $577
9. Tunis International Bank (Tunis), $153
10. Banque Arabe Tuniso-Libyenne de Developpement et de Commerce Exterieur (Tunis), $142

Source: *Bankers' Almanac World Ranking*, (annual), Reed Business Information, 1999, p. 254+.

Banks and Banking--Turkey

★684★
LARGEST BANKS IN TURKEY BY CAPITAL, 1997
Ranked by: Capital, in millions of U.S. dollars ($). **Remarks:** Also lists capital percentage change, as well as dollar amount, rank, percentage change for size, soundness, profits, and performance, and rank among world's top 1,000 banks. **Number listed:** 8

1. Turkiye Is Bankasi, with $779 million
2. Akbank, $752
3. Turkiye Garanti Bankasi, $632
4. Yapi ve Kredi Bankasi, $617
5. Turkiye Halk Bankski, $472
6. TC Ziraat Bankasi, $300
7. VakifBank, $189
8. Pamukbank, $159

Source: *The Banker*, World Top 1,000 (annual), Summer, July, 1998, p. 201.

Banks and Banking--Uganda

★685★
TOP BANKS IN UGANDA, 1999
Ranked by: Assets, in millions of U.S. dollars ($). **Remarks:** Also lists location, previous rank, balance against local currency, paid-up capital, and balance sheet data. **Number listed:** 11

1. Uganda Commercial Bank Ltd. (Kampala), with $183 million
2. Standard Chartered Bank Uganda Ltd. (Kampala), $79
3. Barclays Bank of Uganda Ltd. (Kampala), $74
3. Stancic Bank Uganda Ltd. (Kampala), $74
5. Bank of Baroda (Uganda) Ltd. (Kampala), $70
6. Greenland Bank Ltd. (Kampala), $49
7. Orient Bank Ltd. (Kampala), $46
7. Crane Bank Ltd. (Kampala), $46
9. Nile Bank Ltd. (Kampala), $30
10. Gold Trust Bank Ltd. (Kampala), $23

Source: *Reed Business Information*, Bankers' Almanac World Ranking (annual), 1999, p. 257+.

Banks and Banking--Ukraine

★686★
TOP BANKS IN THE UKRAINE, 1999
Ranked by: Assets, in millions of U.S. dollars ($). **Remarks:** Also lists location, previous rank, balance against local currency, paid-up capital, and balance sheet data. **Number listed:** 21

1. Bank Ukraina (Kiev), with $1,529 million
2. Prominvestbank of Ukraine (Kiev), $757
3. UKREXIMBANK (Kiev), $484
4. AVAL Bank (Kiev), $427
5. Ukrainian Innovation Bank (Kiev), $158
6. First Ukrainian International Bank (Donetsk), $141
7. Ukrainian Credit Bank (Kiev), $82
8. VABank (Kiev), $71
9. ENERGOBANK (Kiev), $53
10. Inkombank-Ukraina (Kiev), $50

Source: *Reed Business Information*, Bankers' Almanac World Ranking (annual), 1999, p. 258.

Banks and Banking--United Arab Emirates

★687★
LARGEST BANKS IN THE UNITED ARAB EMIRATES, 1997
Ranked by: Capital, in millions of U.S. dollars ($). **Remarks:** Also lists capital percentage change, as well as dollar amount, rank, percentage change for size, soundness, profits, and performance, and rank among the world's top 1,000 banks. **Number listed:** 9

1. National Bank of Dubai, with $990 million
2. Abu Dhabi Commercial Bank, $693
3. Emirates Bank International, $667
4. National Bank of Abu Dhabi, $629
5. MashreqBank, $528
6. Arab Bank for Investment & Foreign Trade, $293
7. Commercial Bank of Dubai, $232
8. Dubai Islamic Bank, $156
9. Union National Bank, $153

Source: *The Banker*, World Top 1,000 Banker (annual), Summer, July, 1998, p. 204+.

Banks and Banking--Uruguay

★688★
TOP BANKS IN URUGUAY, 1999
Ranked by: Assets, in millions of U.S. dollars ($). **Remarks:** Also lists location, previous rank, balance against local currency, paid-up capital, and balance sheet data. **Number listed:** 7

1. Banco de la Republica Oriental del Uruguay (Montevideo), with $4,466 million

2. Banco Comercial SA (Montevideo), $1,304
3. Banco de Credito (Montevideo), $493
4. Banco de Montevideo SA (Montevideo), $436
5. Banco la Caja Obrera SA (Montevideo), $355
6. Banco Surinvest SA (Montevideo), $288
7. HSBC Banco Roberts Uruguay SAIFE Montevideo, $217

Source: *Reed Business Information*, Bankers' Almanac World Ranking (annual), 1999, p. 282.

Banks and Banking--Venezuela

★689★
LARGEST BANKS IN VENEZUELA BY MARKET SHARE, 1998
Ranked by: Loan market share, in percent. **Number listed:** 10

1. Provincial, with 20.68%
2. Mercantil, 17.38%
3. Venezuela, 8.41%
4. Union, 7.76%
5. Caribe, 5.08%
6. Corp Banca, 3.92%
7. Interbank, 3.56%
8. Banesco, 3.39%
9. Exterior, 3.35%
10. Citibank, 3.32%

Source: *LatinFinance*, Top 50 Latin Banks (annual), October, 1998, p. 65.

★690★
LEADING BANKS IN VENEZUELA BY ASSETS, 1998
Ranked by: Return on assets, in percent. **Number listed:** 10

1. ING Bank, with 7.39%
2. Noroco, 3.67%
3. Citibank, 3.45%
4. Interbank, 3.28%
5. Exterior, 2.97%
6. Plaza, 2.89%
7. Corp Banca, 2.87%
8. Tequendama, 2.85%
9. Industrial de Venezuela, 2.78%
10. Banfocoro, 2.58%

Source: *LatinFinance*, Top 50 Latin Banks (annual), October, 1998, p. 65.

★691★
LEADING BANKS IN VENEZUELA BY EFFICIENCY, 1998
Ranked by: Efficiency, in OEONI percent. **Number listed:** 10

1. Bancoex, with 26.48%
2. ING Bank, 43.05%
3. Plaza, 49.08%
4. Interbank, 55.02%
5. Exterior, 55.02%
6. Venezolano de Credito, 59.45%
7. Citibank, 60.18%
8. Lara, 60.72%
9. Noroco, 62.31%
10. Occidental de Descuento, 62.36%

Source: *LatinFinance*, Top 50 Latin Banks (annual), October, 1998, p. 65.

★692★
LEADING BANKS IN VENEZUELA BY MARKET SHARE, 1997
Ranked by: Deposit market share, in percent. **Number listed:** 10

1. Provincial, with 21.57%
2. Mercantil, 13.48%
3. Venezuela, 9.48%
4. Union, 8.28%
5. Corp Banca, 4.44%
6. Industrial de Venezuela, 4.40%
7. Banesco, 4.23%
8. Caribe, 4.15%
9. Interbank, 3.35%
10. Lara, 2.79%

Source: *LatinFinance*, Top 50 Latin Banks (annual), October, 1998, p. 65.

★693★
TOP BANKS IN VENEZUELA BY EQUITY, 1998
Ranked by: Return on equity, in percent. **Number listed:** 10

1. ING Bank, with 55.49%
2. Interbank, 32.07%
3. Sofitasa, 29.59%
4. Orinoco, 27.41%
5. Occidente, 27.06%
6. Occidental de Descuento, 26.51%
7. Noroco, 24.64%
8. Exterior, 24.05%
9. Citibank, 23.86%
10. Union, 23.83%

Source: *LatinFinance*, Top 50 Latin Banks (annual), October, 1998, p. 65.

★694★
TOP BANKS IN VENEZUELA, 1998
Ranked by: Assets, in thousands of dollars. **Number listed:** 10

1. Provincial, with $4,108,123 thousand
2. Mercantil, $2,656,028
3. Venezuela, $1,973,361
4. Union, $1,487,462
5. Industrial de Venezuela, $1,081,951
6. Corp Banca, $924,533
7. Caribe, $802,583
8. Banesco, $793,200
9. Interbank, $640,318
10. Lara, $505,025

Source: *LatinFinance*, Top 50 Latin Banks (annual), October, 1998, p. 65.

★695★
TOP BANKS IN VENEZUELA, 1997
Ranked by: Capital, in millions of U.S. dollars ($). **Remarks:** Also lists location, previous rank, balance against local currency, paid-up capital, and balance sheet data. **Number listed:** 2

1. Banco Provincial-Banco Universal, with $412 million
2. Banco Mercantil, $287

Source: *The Banker*, World Top 1,000 Banker (annual), Summer, July, 1998, p. 205.

Banks and Banking--Vietnam

★696★
TIO BANKS IN VIETNAM, 1999
Ranked by: Assets, in millions of U.S. dollars ($). **Remarks:** Also lists location, previous rank, balance against local currency, paid-up capital, and balance sheet data. **Number listed:** 3

1. Industrial & Commercial Bank of Vietnam (Hanoi), with $2,205 million

2. Bank for Foreign Trade of Vietnam (Hanoi), $2,012
3. Vietnam Export-Import Commercial Joint-Stock Bank (ho Chi Minh City), $283

Source: *Reed Business Information*, Bankers' Almanac World Ranking (annual), 1999, p. 283.

Banks and Banking--Western Samoa

★697★
TOP BANKS IN WESTERN SAMOA, 1999
Ranked by: Assets, in millions of U.S. dollars ($). **Remarks:** Also lists location, previous rank, balance against local currency, paid-up capital, and balance sheet data. **Number listed:** 2

1. ANZ Bank (Samoa) Ltd. (Apia), with $57 million
2. Pacific Commercial Bank Ltd. (Apia), $21

Source: *Reed Business Information*, Bankers' Almanac World Ranking (annual), 1999, p. 233.

Banks and Banking--Yemen Arab Republic

★698★
TOP BANKS IN THE YEMEN ARAB REPUBLIC, 1999
Ranked by: Assets, in millions of U.S. dollars ($). **Remarks:** Also lists location, previous rank, balance against local currency, paid-up capital, balance sheet data. **Number listed:** 4

1. Yemen Bank for Reconstruction & Development (Sana's), with $389 million
2. National Bank of Yemen (Aden), $213
3. International Bank of Yemen YSC (Sana's), $92
4. Yemen Commercial Bank (Sana's), $91

Source: *Reed Business Information*, Bankers' Almanac World Ranking (annual), 1999, p. 283.

Banks and Banking--Zambia

★699★
LARGEST BANKS IN ZAMBIA BY ASSETS, 1998
Ranked by: Assets, in millions of U.S. dollars ($). **Remarks:** Also lists location, previous rank, balance against local currency, paid-up capital, and balance sheet data. **Number listed:** 7

1. Zambia National Commercial Bank Ltd. (Lusaka), with $166 million
2. Barclays Bank of Zambia Ltd. (Lusaka), $151
3. Standard Chartered Bank Zambia Ltd. (Lusaka), $109
4. Stanbic Bank of Zambia (Lusaka), $76
5. Development Bank of Zambia (Lusaka), $63
6. Citibank Zambia Ltd. (Lusaka), $41
7. Indo-Zambia Bank Ltd. (Lusaka), $23

Source: *Reed Business Information*, Bankers' Almanac World Ranking (annual), 1999, p. 285.

★700★
LARGEST BANKS IN ZAMBIA BY CAPITAL, 1998
Ranked by: Capital, in millions of U.S. dollars ($). **Remarks:** Also lists capital percentage change as well as, dollar amount, rank, and percentage change for size, soundness, profits, and performance, and rank among top 1,000 banks. **Number listed:** 2

1. Barclays Bank of Zambia, with $14 million
2. Zambia National Commercial Bank, $12

Source: *The Banker*, Top 1,000 Banks-By Country, December, 1998, p. 71.

Banks and Banking--Zimbabwe

★701★
LARGEST BANKS IN ZIMBABWE, 1997
Ranked by: Capital, in millions of U.S. dollars ($). **Remarks:** Also lists capital percentage change, as well as dollar amount, rank, and percentage change for size, soundness, profits and performance, and rank among top 100 banks in Africa. **Number listed:** 5

1. Zimbabwe Financial Holdings (Finhold), with $44 million
2. Barclays Bank of Zimbabwe, $30
3. National Merchant Bank of Zimbabwe, $19
4. FMB Holdings, $15
5. Merchant Bank of Central Africa, $11

Source: *The Banker*, Top 100 African Banks-By Country (annual), December, 1998, p. 71.

Barbeque Grills

★702★
BEST-SELLING OUTDOOR GAS GRILLS, 1998
Ranked by: Market share, in percent. **Number listed:** 5

1. Bradley (Char-Broil), with 40%
2. Sunbeam, 28%
3. Weber-Stephen, 8%
4. Ducane, 2%
4. Others, 2%

Source: *Appliance Manufacturer*, April, 1999, p. 21.

Baseball

★703★
BASEBALL TEAMS WITH THE HIGHEST DOLLAR VALUE, 1998
Ranked by: Current value, in millions of dollars. **Remarks:** Also notes percent change from previous year, revenue, operating income and principal owner. **Number listed:** 30

1. New York Yankees, with $491 million
2. Cleveland Indians, $359
3. Atlanta Braves, $357
4. Baltimore Orioles, $351
5. Colorado Rockies, $311
6. Arizona Diamondbacks, $291
7. Texas Rangers, $281
8. Los Angeles Dodgers, $270
9. Boston Red Sox, $256
10. New York Mets, $249

Source: *Forbes*, May 31, 1999, p. 114.

Basketball

★704★
BASKETBALL TEAMS WITH THE HIGHEST DOLLAR VALUE, 1997-1998
Ranked by: Current value, in millions of dollars. **Remarks:** Also notes revenue, operating income and principal owner. **Number listed:** 29

1. Chicago Bulls, with $303 million
2. New York Knicks, $296
3. Los Angeles Lakers, $268
4. Portland Trail Blazers, $245
5. Phoenix Suns, $235
6. Washington Wizards, $207
7. Detroit Pistons, $206
8. Utah Jazz, $200
9. Philadelphia 76ers, $196
10. Boston Celtics, $176

Source: *Forbes*, December 14, 998, p. 130.

Bath Products

★705★
BEST-SELLING BATH PRODUCTS, 1998
Ranked by: Unit sales, in millions. **Number listed:** 10

1. Vaseline Intensive Care, with 11.7 million units
2. Calgon, 4.7
3. Lander, 4.6
4. Mr. Bubble, 4.3
5. Appearance, 3.6
6. Delagar, 2.2
7. Cabot, 2.0
8. Sesame Street, 1.9
9. Sarah Michaels, 1.6
9. Village Naturals, 1.6

Source: *MMR*, October 5, 1998, p. 48.

Bedding

★706★
TOP MATTRESSES STORES BY SALES, 1997
Ranked by: Sales, in millions of dollars. **Remarks:** Also notes percentage of total sales. **Number listed:** 25

1. Helig-Myers (VA), with $500 million
2. Sears HomeLife (IL), $111.4
3. Sleepy's/Kleinsleep (NY), $105.5
4. Levitz (FL), $83.7
5. Mattress Giant (TX), $83
6. Art Van Furniture (MI), $77.8
7. Dial-A-Mattress (NY), $68
8. Rooms To Go (FL), $62.5
9. Berkshire Hathaway (NE), $57.1
10. J.C. Penney, $53.7

Source: *HFN*, December 7, 1998, p. 23.

Best Managed Companies

See: **Management**

Best Sellers

★707★
LONGEST RUNNING FICTION HARDCOVER BESTSELLERS, 1998
Ranked by: Numbers of weeks on the *Publishers Weekly* best seller list. **Remarks:** Also notes author, publisher, and number of weeks on previous year's list. **Number listed:** 12

1. Memoirs of a Geisha, with 49 weeks
2. Cold Mountain, 34
3. The Street Lawyer, 29
4. Message in a Bottle, 28
5. Summer Sisters, 24
5. I know This Much is True, 24
7. A Widow for One Year, 21
8. Black and Blue, 20
9. Rainbow Six, 19
10. Paradise, 18

Source: *Publishers Weekly*, January 4, 1999, p. 62.

★708★
LONGEST RUNNING NONFICTION HARDCOVER BESTSELLERS, 1998
Ranked by: Numbers of weeks on the *Publishers Weekly* best seller list. **Remarks:** Also notes author, publisher, and number of weeks on previous year's list. **Number listed:** 18

1. Tuesdays with Morrie, with 51 weeks
2. Angela's Ashes, 41
3. The 9 Steps to Financial Freedom, 39
3. Freedom, 39
5. In the Meantime, 36
6. The Millionaire Next Door, 35
7. Sugar Busters, 32
8. Simple Abundance, 32
9. Conversations with God, Book 1, 27
10. Talking to Heaven, 21
10. Midnight in the Garden of Good and Evil, 21

Source: *Publishers Weekly*, January 4, 1999, p. 62.

★709★
LONGEST RUNNING PAPERBACK MASS MARKET BESTSELLERS, 1998
Ranked by: Numbers of weeks on the *Publishers Weekly* best seller list. **Remarks:** Also notes author, publisher, and number of weeks on previous year's list. **Number listed:** 8

1. Dr. Atkins' New Diet Revolution, with 51 weeks
2. The Notebook, 45
3. Into Thin Air, 36
4. The Perfect Storm, 28
5. Protein Power, 25
6. She's Come Undone, 22
7. The Partner, 19
8. The Horse Whisperer, 17

Source: *Publishers Weekly*, January 4, 1999, p. 63.

★710★
LONGEST RUNNING TRADE PAPERBACK BESTSELLERS, 1998
Ranked by: Numbers of weeks on the *Publishers Weekly* best seller list. **Remarks:** Also notes author, publisher, and number of weeks on previous year's list. **Number listed:** 16

1. Don't Sweat the Small Stuff..., with 51 weeks
2. Chicken Soup for the Teenage Soul, 49
3. Divine Secrets of the Ya-Ya Sisterhood, 45
4. Under the Tuscan Sun, 41
5. A Child Called "It", 33
6. The BeanieBaby Handbook, 30
7. The Color of Water, 27
8. Don't Sweat the Small Stuff with Your Family, 24
8. The God of Small Things, 24
10. Into the Wild, 21

Source: *Publishers Weekly*, January 4, 1999, p. 63.

Beverage Industry

★711★

LEADING BEVERAGE CATEGORIES BY CONSUMPTION VOLUME, 1997

Ranked by: Volume, in millions of gallons. **Remarks:** Also notes annual compound growth rate, per capita consumption and figures from previous years. **Number listed:** 11

1. Soft Drinks, with 14,889 million gallons
2. Coffee, 7,854
3. Milk, 6,494
4. Beer, 5,935
5. Bottled Water, 3,038
6. Tea, 1,788
7. Juices, 1,702
8. Powdered Drinks, 1,365
9. Wine, 506
10. Distilled Spirits, 330

Source: *Adams Liquor Handbook*, (annual), Adams Media, Inc., 1998, p. 302.

★712★

LEADING BEVERAGE CATEGORIES BY PER CAPITA CONSUMPTION, 1997

Ranked by: Number of gallons per person. **Remarks:** Also notes annual compound growth rate, volume consumption and figures from previous years. **Number listed:** 11

1. Soft Drinks, with 55.6 gallons
2. Coffee, 29.3
3. Milk, 24.3
4. Beer, 22.2
5. Bottled Water, 11.4
6. Tea, 6.7
7. Juices, 6.4
8. Powdered Drinks, 5.1
9. Wine, 1.9
10. Distilled Spirits, 1.2

Source: *Adams Liquor Handbook*, (annual), Adams Media, Inc., 1998, p. 302.

★713★

LEADING BEVERAGE CATEGORIES BY SALES, 1998

Ranked by: Sales, in millions of dollars. **Number listed:** 4

1. Single-Serve Bottled Juices, with $3,500 million
2. Canned Fruit Drinks, $932
3. Aseptic Juice Drink, $500
4. Canned and Bottled Tea Brands, $494

Source: *Dairy Field*, April, 1999, p. 20.

★714★

MOST ADMIRED BEVERAGE CORPORATIONS, 1998

Ranked by: Scores (1-10) derived from a survey of senior executives, outside directors, and securities analysts. **Remarks:** Respondents rated companies in their own industry on 8 attributes of reputation. Also notes previous year's rank. **Number listed:** 9

1. Coca-Cola, with 8.39 points
2. Anheuser-Busch, 7.38
3. Coca-Cola Enterprises, 7.14
4. Adolph Coors, 6.72
5. PepsiCo, 6.55
6. Brown-Forman, 6.28
7. Joseph E. Seagram & Sons, 6.13
8. Canandaigua Brands, 5.56
9. Whitman, 5.22

Source: *Fortune*, America's Most Admired Corporations (annual), March 1, 1999, p. F-3.

★715★

TOP BEVERAGE BRANDS ACCORDING TO DISCOUNT SHOPPERS, 1998

Ranked by: Percent of discount Shoppers naming brand as best. **Number listed:** 10

1. Coke, with 48%
2. Pepsi, 39%
3. Dr. Pepper, 8%
3. 7-Up, 8%
5. Mountain Dew, 4%
5. A & W, 4%
7. Sprite, 3%
8. Canada Dry, 2%
8. Diet-Rite, 2%
10. RC, 1%

Source: *Discount Store News*, Top Brands Survey (annual), September 7, 1998, p. 26.

★716★

TOP BEVERAGE CATEGORIES BY MARKET SHARE, 1998

Ranked by: Market share, in percent. **Number listed:** 8

1. Single Serve Fruit Beverages, with 27.6%
2. Sport Beverages, 19.6%
3. Retail Water, 19.5%
4. Ready to Drink Teas, 17.4%
5. Sparkling Water, 5.8%
6. Premium Sodas, 4.7%
7. Functional Beverages, 2.9%
8. Ready to Drink Coffee, 2.6%

Source: *U.S. Distribution Journal*, January/February, 1999, p. 42.

★717★

TOP BEVERAGE CATEGORIES BY PER CAPITA CONSUMPTION, 1998

Ranked by: Number of gallons per person. **Number listed:** 8

1. Soft Drinks, with 54.5 gallons
2. Beer, 21.9
3. Fruit Beverages, 15
4. Bottled Water, 12.1
5. Ready to Drink Teas, 2.5
6. Sport Drinks, 2
7. Wine, 1.9
8. Spirits, 1.2

Source: *U.S. Distribution Journal*, March/April, 1999, p. 58.

★718★

TOP BEVERAGE COMPANIES WORLDWIDE BY SALES, 1998

Ranked by: Sales, in millions of U.S. dollars ($). **Remarks:** Also notes sales and rank from previous year. **Number listed:** 100

1. Coca-Cola Co. (Atlanta, GA), with $18,813 million
2. Diageo (London, England), $18,153

3. Nestle SA (Vevey, Switzerland), $13,078
4. PepsiCo (Purchase, NY), $11,373
5. Anheuser-Busch Inc. (St. Louis, MO), $8,570
6. The Seagram Co. (Montreal, Canada), $4,670
7. Miller Brewing Co. (Milwaukee, WI), $4,105
8. Cadbury Schweppes (London, England), $3,215
9. Danone Group (Paris, France), $3,120
10. Coors Brewing Co. (Golden, CO), $1,900

Source: *Beverage Industry*, Top 100 (annual), June, 1999, p. 22+.

★719★
TOP BEVERAGE CORPORATIONS BY REVENUE, 1998
Ranked by: Revenue, in millions of dollars. **Remarks:** Also notes profits, profits as a percentage of revenue, assets and stockholders' equity, earnings per share, total return to investors, and number of employees. **Number listed:** 8

1. PepsiCo, with $22,348 million
2. Coca-Cola, $18,813
3. Coca-Cola Enterprises, $13,414
4. Anheuser-Busch, $11,246
5. Adolph Coors, $1,900
6. Whitman, $1,845
7. Brown-Forman, $1,669
8. Canandaigua Brands, $1,213

Source: *Fortune*, Fortune 500 Largest U.S. Corporations (annual), April 26, 1999, p. F-52+.

★720★
TOP FLAVORS USED IN THE BEVERAGE INDUSTRY, 1999
Ranked by: Percent of respondents. **Number listed:** 20

1. Orange, with 87.3%
2. Lemon, 80%
3. Grape, 75.3%
4. Strawberry, 72.7%
5. Lime, 70.7%
6. Cherry, 65.3%
7. Apple, 64.7%
8. Cola, 63.3%
9. Cranberry, 62.7%
9. Grapefruit, 62.7%
9. Raspberry, 62.7%
9. Root Beer, 62.7%

Source: *Beverage Industry*, February, 1999, p. 27.

Beverage Industry, International

★721★
WORLD'S LARGEST BEVERAGE CORPORATIONS BY REVENUE, 1997
Ranked by: Revenue, in millions of dollars. **Remarks:** Also notes profits and profits as a percent of revenues and assets. **Number listed:** 5

1. PepsiCo, with $29,292 million
2. Coca-Cola, $18,868
3. Seagram, $12,560
4. Coca-Cola Enterprises, $11,278
5. Anheuser-Busch, $11,066

Source: *Fortune*, The Global 500: World's Biggest Corporations (annual), August 3, 1998, p. F-17.

Beverage Industry--North America

★722★
BIGGEST BEVERAGE COMPANIES IN NORTH AMERICA BY DEBT TO EQUITY RATIO, 1997
Ranked by: Long-term debt to equity ratio, in percent. **Number listed:** 10

1. Genesse, with 0.00%
1. Lion Brewery, 0.00%
1. Pyramid Brewing Co., 0.00%
4. American Craft Brewing International, 0.25%
5. Odwalla, 2.4%
6. Brown-Forman, 8.77%
7. Coca-Cola Co., 10.96%
8. Clearly Canadian, 13.32%
9. Boston Beer, 14.03%
10. Independence Brewing, 14.2%

Source: *Beverage World*, Top 50 (annual), July, 1998, p. 52.

★723★
BIGGEST BEVERAGE COMPANIES IN NORTH AMERICA BY NUMBER OF EMPLOYEES, 1997
Ranked by: Number of employees worldwide. **Number listed:** 10

1. Philip Morris, with 152,000 employees
2. PepsiCo, 142,000
3. Bass, 83,461
4. Coca-Cola Enterprises, 56,000
5. Cadbury Schweppes, 42,911
6. The Seagram Co., 30,000
7. Coca-Cola Co., 29,500
8. Panamerican Beverages, 28,000
9. Fortune Brands, 25,000
10. Anheuser-Busch Cos., 24,326

Source: *Beverage World*, Top 50 (annual), July, 1998, p. 50.

★724★
BIGGEST BEVERAGE COMPANIES IN NORTH AMERICA BY PROFIT GROWTH, 1997
Ranked by: Annual profit growth, in percent. **Remarks:** Also notes 1996 and 1997 net income. **Number listed:** 10

1. Saratoga Beverage, with 647.62%
2. The Seagram Co., 253.52%
3. Hansen Natural, 250.14%
4. Fresh Juice, 247.15%
5. Cadbury Schweppes, 205.11%
6. Vermont Pure, 184.21%
7. Coors Brewing Co., 89.43%
8. Aqua Penn, 87.68%
9. Canandaigua Wine, 80.93%
10. Coca-Cola Enterprises, 59.43%

Source: *Beverage World*, Top 50 (annual), July, 1998, p. 50.

★725★
BIGGEST BEVERAGE COMPANIES IN NORTH AMERICA BY PROFIT PER EMPLOYEE, 1997
Ranked by: Profit per employee, in thousands of U.S. dollars ($). **Remarks:** Also notes net income and number of employees worldwide. **Number listed:** 10

1. Coca-Cola Co., with $169.53 thousand
2. Anheuser-Busch, $84.4
3. Philip Morris, $76.73
4. Robert Mondavi, $61.75
5. Canandaigua Wine, $46.82
6. Brown-Forman, $38.27
7. Saratoga Beverage, $37.83
8. Boston Beer, $37.57
9. Hansen Natural, $35.51

10. Seagram, $31.1

Source: *Beverage World*, Top 50 (annual), July, 1998, p. 52.

★726★

BIGGEST BEVERAGE COMPANIES IN NORTH AMERICA BY PROFITS, 1997

Ranked by: Net income, in thousands of U.S. dollars ($). **Number listed:** 10

1. Philip Morris, with $6,310,000 thousand
2. Coca-Cola Co., $4,129,000
3. Cadbury Schweppes, $1,802,600
4. PepsiCo, $1,491,000
5. Anheuser-Busch Cos., $1,179,200
6. The Seagram Co., $502,200
7. Bass, $404,000
8. Kirin Brewery, $206,156
9. Panamerican Beverages, $173,835
10. Brown-Forman, $169,000

Source: *Beverage World*, Top 50 (annual), July, 1998, p. 50.

★727★

BIGGEST BEVERAGE COMPANIES IN NORTH AMERICA BY RETURN ON SALES, 1997

Ranked by: Return on sales, in percent. **Remarks:** Also notes total revenue and net income. **Number listed:** 10

1. Cadbury Schweppes, with 26.15%
2. Coca-Cola Co., 21.88%
3. Saratoga Beverage, 12.84%
4. Anheuser-Busch Cos., 10.66%
5. Chalone Wine Group, 9.54%
6. Robert Mondavi, 9.38%
7. Brown-Forman, 9.18%
8. Philip Morris Cos., 8.76%
9. Coca-Cola FEMSA, 7.7%
10. Aqua Penn, 7.33%

Source: *Beverage World*, Top 50 (annual), July, 1998, p. 52.

★728★

BIGGEST BEVERAGE COMPANIES IN NORTH AMERICA BY REVENUE, 1997

Ranked by: Sales, in millions of U.S. dollars ($). **Number listed:** 10

1. Philip Morris, with $72,055,000 million
2. PepsiCo, $20,917,000
3. Coca-Cola Co., $18,868,000
4. The Seagram Co., $12,560,000
5. Kirin Brewery, $12,046,240
6. Coca-Cola Enterprises, $11,278,000
7. Anheuser-Busch Cos., $11,066,200
8. Bass, $8,487,000
9. Cadbury Schweppes, $6,892,500
10. Quaker Oats, $5,015,700

Source: *Beverage World*, Top 50 (annual), July, 1998, p. 50.

★729★

BIGGEST BEVERAGE COMPANIES IN NORTH AMERICA BY SALES GROWTH, 1997

Ranked by: Annual sales growth, in percent. **Remarks:** Also notes revenue. **Number listed:** 10

1. American Craft Brewing International, with 327.8%
2. Fresh Juice, 107.35%
3. Frederick Brewing, 78.95%
4. Vermont Pure Holdings, 48.88%
5. Saratoga Beverage, 43.34%
6. Coca-Cola Enterprises, 42.38%
7. Culligan Water, 36.31%
8. Aqua Penn, 34.61%
9. Independence Brewing, 29.98%
10. Northland Cranberries, 25.97%

Source: *Beverage World*, Top 50 (annual), July, 1998, p. 50.

★730★

BIGGEST BEVERAGE COMPANIES IN NORTH AMERICA BY SALES, 1997

Ranked by: Sales, in millions of U.S. dollars ($). **Remarks:** Also notes location, principal subsidiaries, product categories and rank from previous year. **Number listed:** 50

1. Coca-Cola Co., with $18,868 million
2. Coca-Cola Enterprises, $11,278
3. PepsiCo, $10,541
4. Anheuser-Busch Cos., $10,253.5
5. The Seagram Co., $6,967
6. Philip Morris, $4,201
7. Cadbury Schweppes, $3,202.9
8. Panamerican Beverages Co., $2,510.2
9. Southern Wine & Spirits of America, $2,365
10. Adolph Coors Co., $1,822.2

Source: *Beverage World*, Top 50 (annual), July, 1998, p. 44+.

★731★

BIGGEST BEVERAGE COMPANIES IN NORTH AMERICA BY SALES PER EMPLOYEE, 1997

Ranked by: Sales per employee, in thousands of U.S. dollars ($). **Remarks:** Also notes total revenue and number of employees worldwide. **Number listed:** 10

1. Clearly Canadian, with $1,595.17 thousand
2. Kirin Brewery, $1,435.61
3. Hansen Natural, $812.4
4. Coca-Cola Co., $639.59
5. Boston Beer, $625.34
6. Atlantic Premium, $581.75
7. Cott, $508.55
8. Canandaigua Wine, $485.12
9. Philip Morris, $474.05
10. Anheuser-Busch, $454.91

Source: *Beverage World*, Top 50 (annual), July, 1998, p. 50.

★732★

BIGGEST BEVERAGE COMPANIES IN NORTH AMERICA BY SHAREHOLDER EQUITY, 1997

Ranked by: Common equity, in thousands of U.S. dollars ($). **Number listed:** 10

1. Philip Morris, with $14,920,000 thousand
2. Seagram, $9,422,000
3. Coca-Cola Co., $7,311,000
4. PepsiCo, $6,936,000
5. Bass, $6,088,000
6. Anheuser-Busch, $4,041,800
7. Fortune Brands, $4,005,800
8. Panamerican Beverages, $1,937,770
9. Coca-Cola Enterprises, $1,782,000
10. Coors Brewing Co., $736,568

Source: *Beverage World*, Top 50 (annual), July, 1998, p. 52.

★733★

BIGGEST BEVERAGE COMPANIES IN NORTH AMERICA BY TWO-YEAR TOTAL RETURN EQUITY, 1997

Ranked by: Two-year total return, in percent. **Remarks:** Also notes stock prices as of March 31, 1996 and March 31, 1998. **Number listed:** 10

1. Coca-Cola Enterprises, with 257.82%
2. Hansen Natural, 252.17%
3. Vermont Pure, 180%
4. Coca-Cola FEMSA, 172.96%
5. Atlantic Premium, 125%
5. National Beverage, 125%
7. Triarc, 107.92%
8. Coors Brewing Co., 103.56%
9. Panamerican Beverages, 101.14%

10. Vina Concha y Toro, 98.81%

Source: *Beverage World*, Top 50 (annual), July, 1998, p. 53.

Beverages & Tobacco

See: **Beverage Industry Tobacco Industry**

Billionaires

★734★
AMERICA'S RICHEST PEOPLE, 1998
Ranked by: Net worth, in billions of dollars. **Remarks:** Also provides biographical information and select short articles. Financial data is not provided for all listees. **Number listed:** 400

1. Bill Gates, with $58 billion
2. S. Robson Walton, $55
3. Warren Buffett, $29
4. Paul Allen, $22
5. Michael Dell, $13
6. Steven Ballmer, $12
7. Helen Robson Walton, $(not provided)
8. Jim C. Walton, $(not provided)
9. John T. Walton, $(not provided)
10. Alice Lousie Walton, $(not provided)

Source: *Forbes*, 400 Richest People in America (annual), October 12, 1998, p. 166+.

Billionaires, International

★735★
WORLD'S RICHEST PEOPLE
Ranked by: Net worth in billions of U.S. dollars ($). **Remarks:** Also provides brief descriptive information. **Number listed:** 10

1. Bill Gates, with $51 billion
2. Prince Alwaleed Bin Talal Bin Abdulaziz Alsaud, $13.3
3. Philip F. Anschutz, $8.8
4. Hasso Plattner, $6.9
5. Francois Pinault, $6.6
6. Rupert Murdoch, $5.3
7. Robert Kuok, $4.7
8. Lorenzo Zambrano, $2.9
9. Masayoshi Son, $2.2
10. Vladimir Patanin, $1.6

Source: *Forbes*, World's Billionaires, July 6, 1998, p. 190+.

Biometric Identification Systems

★736★
TOP INDUSTRIES BY BIOMETRIC SPENDING
Ranked by: Industries spending the most on biometric identification systems, by percent. **Number listed:** 4

1. Law Enforcement, with 50%
2. Financial Services, 30%
3. Security, 12%
4. Other, 8%

Source: *Red Herring*, September, 1998, p. 22.

Biotechnology Industries

★737★
TOP BANKS IN TURKEY BY ASSETS, 1999
Ranked by: Assets, in millions of U.S. dollars ($). **Remarks:** Also lists location, previous rank, balance against local currency, paid-up capital, and balance sheet data. **Number listed:** 44

1. Turkiye Cumhuriyeti Ziraat Bankasi (Ankara), with $14,926 million
2. Turkiye Garanti Bankasi AS (Istanbul), $7,920
3. Turkiye Halk Bankski AS (Ankara), $7,413
4. Turkiye Is Bankasi AS (Ankara), $6,514
5. Yapi ve Kredi Bankasi AS (Levent), $5,801
6. Akbank TAS (Istanbul), $5,647
7. Turkiye Emlak Bankasi AS (Istanbul), $5,435
8. Turkiye Vakiflar Bankasi TAO (Ankara), $4,716
9. Pamukbank TAS (Istanbul), $3,812
10. Turkiye Ihracat Kredi Bankasi AS (Bakanliklar), $2,610

Source: Bankers' Almanac World Ranking (annual), 1999, p. 255+.

★738★
TOP BIOTECHNOLOGY COMPANIES BY SALES, 1998
Ranked by: Sales, in millions of dollars. **Remarks:** Also notes profits and profit margins, per share data and assets. **Number listed:** 13

1. Amgen, with $2,718 million
2. Genetech, $1,062
3. Chiron, $737
4. Genzyme General, $709
5. Alza, $585
6. Biogen, $558
7. Life Technologies, $364
8. Centocor, $338
9. Immunex, $243
10. Gensia Sicor, $179

Source: *Chemical Week*, Chemical Week 300 (annual), May 12, 1999, p. 50.

★739★
TOP RESEARCH & DEVELOPMENT SPENDERS IN THE BIOMEDICAL/BIOTECHNOLOGY INDUSTRY, 1997
Ranked by: Research and development expenses, in millions of dollars. **Remarks:** Also notes overall rank in research and development expenses. **Number listed:** 10

1. Baxter International, with $725.4 million
2. Medtronic, $349.3
3. Guidant Corp., $259.6
4. Boston Scientific Corp., $224.1
5. Becton Dickinson & Co., $181.8
6. St. Jude Medical Co., $111.4
7. CR Bard Inc., $85.5
8. Imagyn Medical Technologies, $85.3
9. Marquette Medical Systems, $73
10. U.S. Surgical Corp, $71.4

Source: *R & D*, Giants of R & D (annual), October, 1998, p. S14.

Biotechnology Industries—Philadelphia Metropolitan Area

★740★

LARGEST PHARMACEUTICAL/BIOTECHNOLOGY COMPANIES IN THE PHILADELPHIA AREA, 1998

Ranked by: Number of local employees. **Remarks:** Also notes contact information, total number of employees, business description, products, chief executive officer, personnel administrator and year founded. **Number listed:** 25

1. SmithKline Beecham, with 7,200 local employees
2. Merck & Co. Inc., 7,000
3. Wyeth-Ayerst Global Pharmaceuticals, 6,425
4. Zeneca Pharmaceuticals, 3,500
5. Rhone-Poulenc Rorer Inc., 2,000
6. DuPont Merck Pharmaceutical Co., 1,767
7. McNeil Consumer Products Co., 1,200
8. Astra Merck Inc., 600
9. Teva Pharmaceuticals USA, 572
10. Sanofi Research, 480

Source: *Philadelphia Business Journal*, Book of Lists (annual), December 25, 1998, p. 83.

Black Automobile Dealers

★741★

TOP BLACK AUTOMOBILE DEALERS, 1998

Ranked by: Gross sales, in millions of dollars. **Remarks:** Also notes location, chief executive, year founded, number of employees, type of dealership and rank form previous year. **Number listed:** 20

1. Mel Farr Automotive Group (MI), with $596.6 million
2. Chicago Truck Center (IL), $224.0
3. Family Automotive Group (CA), $192.0
4. March/Hodge Holding Co. (CT), $184.0
5. Martin Automotive Group (KY), $159.259
6. S & J Enterprises (NC), $158.0
7. Southgate Automotive Group (MI), $136.325
8. 32 Ford Lincoln Mercury (OH), $122.012
9. Armstrong Holdings (FL), $116.0
10. Avis Ford Inc. (MI), $109.437

Source: *Black Enterprise*, Top 100 Black Businesses (annual), June, 1999, p. 141+.

Black Business Enterprise—Detroit Metropolitan Area

★742★

LEADING DETROIT AREA BLACK-OWNED BUSINESSES, 1997

Ranked by: Revenue, in millions of dollars. **Remarks:** Also notes contact information, previous year's revenue, percent change, local employees, name of majority owner and business description. **Number listed:** 20

1. Mel Farr Automotive Group, with $573.1 million
2. The Bing Group, $183.4
3. Avis Ford Inc., $112.7
4. Barden Cos. Inc., $110
5. Wesley International Inc., $93
6. Thomas Madison Inc., $90
7. The Bartech Group, $62
8. Bradley Automotive Group, $52.8
9. Exemplar Manufacturing Co., $52
10. Regal Plastics Co., $48.1

Source: *Crain's Detroit Business*, Crain's Book of Lists Detroit (annual), December 28, 1998, p. 50.

Black Business Enterprises

★743★

TOP BLACK INDUSTRIAL/SERVICE COMPANIES, 1998

Ranked by: Sales, in millions of dollars. **Remarks:** Also notes location, chief executive, year founded, number of employees, type of business and rank form previous year. **Number listed:** 100

1. The Philadelphia Coca Cola Bottling Co., with $389.0 million
2. Johnson Publishing Co., $371.945
3. TLC Beatrice International Holdings Inc., $322.0
4. Active Transportation, $250.0
5. The Bing Group, $232.0
6. World Wide Technology Inc., $201.0
7. FUCI Metals USA Inc., $200.0
8. Granite Broadcasting Corp., $193.934
9. H. J. Russell & Co., $184.436
10. BET Holdings II Inc., $178.0

Source: *Black Enterprise*, Top 100 Black Businesses (annual), June, 1999, p. 109+.

Black Colleges and Universities

★744★

TOP COLLEGES AND UNIVERSITIES FOR BLACKS, 1998-1999

Ranked by: DayStar Rating. **Remarks:** Also notes survey scores in academic and social categories, 1996-97 tuition, room & board and student population. **Number listed:** 50

1. Spelman College (GA), with 4,144 points
2. Morehouse College (GA), 4,106
3. Florida A & M University (FL), 4,046
4. Clark Atlanta University (GA), 3,959
5. Howard University (DC), 3,957
6. Xavier University (LA), 3,951
7. Hampton University (VA), 3,915
7. Tuskegee University (AL), 3,915
9. North Carolina A & T University (NC), 3,893
10. Stanford University (CA), 3,842

Source: *Black Enterprise*, January, 1999, p. 74.

Black Investment Banking

★745★

TOP BLACK INVESTMENT BANKING COMPANIES, 1998

Ranked by: Value of senior-managed issues, in millions of dollars. **Remarks:** Also notes location, chief executive, year founded, value of co-managed issues and rank form previous year. **Number listed:** 15

1. Siebert Brandford Shank & Co. LLC, with $2,503.375 million
2. Utendahl Capital Partners LP, $1,640
3. The Williams Capital Group, $1,541.279
4. Apex Securities, a division of Rice Financial Products Co., $976
5. SBK-Brooks Investment Corp., $826.079
6. Jackson Securities, $749
7. Blaylock & Partners LP, $678.44
8. M. R. Beal & Co., $530
9. Pryor, McClendon, Counts & Co. Inc., $427.2
10. Walton Johnson & Co., $360.380

Source: *Black Enterprise*, Top 100 Black Businesses (annual), June, 1999, p. 202.

Black Periodicals

★746★
TOP AFRICAN-AMERICAN MAGAZINES, 1998
Ranked by: Circulation, in thousands. **Number listed:** 5

1. Ebony, with 1,800 thousand copies
2. Essence, 1,090
3. Jet, 950
4. Vibe, 550
5. Black Enterprise, 335

Source: *Discount Store News*, October 26, 1998, p. 112.

Blacks--Population

★747★
LEADING METROPOLITAN AREAS IN BLACK POPULATION, 1998
Ranked by: Population, in thousands. **Number listed:** 321

1. New York, NY, with $2,523.1 thousand people
2. Chicago, IL, $1,538
3. Washington, DC, $1,174
4. Los Angeles - Long Beach, CA, $1,065.6
5. Detroit, MI, $1,030.8
6. Philadelphia, PA, $996.1
7. Atlanta, GA, $957.1
8. Houston, TX, $729.7
9. Baltimore, MD, $684.9
10. Dallas, TX, $495.7

Source: *Sales & Marketing Management*, Survey of Buying Power (annual), August, 1998, p. 13.

★748★
METROPOLITAN AREAS WITH THE LARGEST BLACK POPULATION, 1996
Ranked by: Population, in thousands. **Number listed:** 20

1. New York, NY, with 2,539.4 thousand
2. Chicago, IL, 1,538.3
3. Washington, DC, 1,159.5
4. Los Angeles - Long Beach, CA, 1,083.1
5. Detroit, MI, 1,002.5
6. Philadelphia, PA, 996
7. Atlanta, GA, 923.3
8. Houston, TX, 718.8
9. Baltimore, MD, 674.9
10. Dallas, TX, 485.9

Source: *Adams Liquor Handbook*, (annual), Adams Media Inc., 1998, p. 286.

Blank Video Tapes

★749★
BEST BLANK VIDEO CASSETTE BRANDS ACCORDING TO DISCOUNT SHOPPERS
Ranked by: Percent of discount shoppers naming brand as best. **Number listed:** 10

1. Maxell, with 17%
2. Scotch/3M, 15%
3. Sony, 14%
3. Kodak, 14%
5. TDK, 13%
6. Fuji, 10%
6. Memorex, 10%
8. Polaroid, 7%
9. BASF, 6%
10. JVC, 4%

Source: *Discount Store News*, Top Brand Consumer Survey Part III (annual), September 7, 1998, p. 22.

Blenders (Cookery)

★750★
BEST-SELLING BLENDERS, 1998
Ranked by: Market share, in percent. **Remarks:** Also notes 1993 market share. **Number listed:** 6

1. Hamilton Beach/Proctor-Silex, with 55%
2. Sunbeam-Oster, 28%
3. Braun, 6%
4. Appliance Corp. (Betty Crocker), 5%
5. Waring, 4%
6. Black & Decker, 2%

Source: *Appliance Manufacturer*, April, 1999, p. 21.

Boards of Directors

See: **Corporations--Directors**

Boats and Boating

★751★
STATES WITH HIGHEST BOAT SALES, 1998
Ranked by: Spending on boats, in millions of dollars. **Remarks:** Also notes spending on marine accessories. **Number listed:** 20

1. Florida, with $475.7 million
2. Michigan, $334.3
3. Texas, $302.4
4. Minnesota, $300
5. California, $293
6. Wisconsin, $232.9
7. Louisiana, $195
8. New York, $178.1
9. North Carolina, $170.5
10. South Carolina, $167.3

Source: *Boating Industry*, February, 1999, p. 13.

Bolsa de Madrid

★752★
LARGEST LISTED COMPANIES ON THE MADRID STOCK EXCHANGE, 1997
Ranked by: Market value, in billions of Spanish pesetas. **Number listed:** 20
1. Telefonica, with Ptas4,086.7 billion
2. BBV, Ptas3,334.4
3. Endesa, Ptas2,813.3
4. Santander, Ptas2,438.9
5. Repsol, Ptas1,950
6. Iberdrola, Ptas1,807.6
7. BCH, Ptas1,215.5
8. Popular, Ptas1,179.8
9. Gas Natural, Ptas1,179.1
10. Argentaria, Ptas1,135.6

Source: *SSB Guide to World Equity Markets*, (annual), Euromoney Publications, 1998, p. 455.

★753★
MOST ACTIVELY TRADED SHARES ON THE MADRID STOCK EXCHANGE, 1997
Ranked by: Trading value, in millions of Spanish pesetas. **Number listed:** 20
1. Telefonica, with Ptas4,018,019 million
2. Endesa, Ptas2,265,572
3. Repsol, Ptas1,873,936
4. BBV, Ptas1,391,861
5. Iberdrola, Ptas1,358,929
6. Santander, Ptas1,261,417
7. Argenaria, Ptas763,974
8. Popular, Ptas669,918
9. BCH, Ptas519,036
10. Banesto, Ptas381,918

Source: *SSB Guide to World Equity Markets*, (annual), Euromoney Publications, 1998, p. 455+.

Bombay Stock Exchange

★754★
LARGEST LISTED COMPANIES ON THE BOMBAY STOCK EXCHANGE, 1997
Ranked by: Market value, in billions of Indian Rupees (Rs). **Number listed:** 20
1. Oil & Natural Gas Commission, with Rs406.39 billion
2. Hindustan Levers, Rs275.55
3. Indian Oil Corp., Rs270.2
4. Mahanager Telephone Nigam, Rs154.8
5. ITC, Rs151.79
6. State Bank of India, Rs128.03
7. Gas Authority of India, Rs103.8
8. Hindustan Petroleum Corp., Rs102.22
9. Videsh Sanchar Nigam, Rs85.1
10. Bharat Heavy Electricals, Rs84.93

Source: *SSB Guide to World Equity Markets*, (annual), Euromoney Publications, 1998, p. 235.

★755★
MOST ACTIVELY TRADED SHARES ON THE BOMBAY STOCK EXCHANGE, 1997
Ranked by: Turnover value, in billions of Indian Rupees (Rs). **Number listed:** 20
1. ITC, with Rs433.95 billion
2. Reliance Industries, Rs414.04
3. State Bank, Rs352.32
4. Tata Iron & Steel, Rs111.43
5. Tata Tea, Rs80.03
6. Tata Engineering & Locomotive, Rs66.94
7. Castrol Industries, Rs43.13
8. Mahanager Telephone Nigam, Rs37.95
9. Associated Cement Companies, Rs36.67
10. Larsen & Toubro, Rs25.24

Source: *SSB Guide to World Equity Markets*, (annual), Euromoney Publications, 1998, p. 235.

Bond Funds

★756★
BEST CORPORATE BONDS, 1998
Ranked by: Return, in percent. **Remarks:** Also notes phone number, assets, returns over three, five and ten years and other financial data. **Number listed:** 10
1. Vanguard Bond Index Long Term, with 12%
2. USAA Income Strategy, 11.2%
3. CG Capital Markets Long-Term Bond, 10.7%
4. Calvert Fund Strategic Income A, 10.5%
5. Vanguard Intermediate-Term Bond Index, 10.1%
6. Federated Managed Income Select, 10%
6. Stagecoach LifePath Opportunity A, 10%
8. Metropolitan West Total Return Bond, 9.9%
8. Fremont Bond Fund, 9.9%
10. Wright Total Return, 9.6%

Source: *U.S. News & World Report*, Best Mutual Funds (annual), February 1, 1999, p. 85.

★757★
BEST CORPORATE INTERMEDIATE BONDS, 1998
Ranked by: Scores are ranked by an overall performance index (OPI) that relies on a formula measuring relative results over one, three, five and ten years. **Remarks:** Also notes phone number, assets and other financial data. **Number listed:** 13
1. Harbor Bond, with 88.9
2. Hotchkis & Wiley Total Return, 85.9
3. Fremont Bond Fund, 85.8
4. Vanguard Bond Index Total Bond, 85.7
5. Vanguard Bond Index Intermediate Term, 82.3
6. Clvoer Fixed Income, 81.1
7. Invesco Income Select Income, 78.6
8. Dodge & Cox Income, 78.3
9. Calvert Fund Income, 77.7
10. Eaton Vance Prime Rate Reserve, 77.4

Source: *U.S. News & World Report*, Best Mutual Funds (annual), February 1, 1999, p. 82.

★758★
BEST CORPORATE LONG-TERM BONDS, 1998
Ranked by: Scores are ranked by an overall performance index (OPI) that relies on a formula measuring relative results over one, three, five and ten years. **Remarks:** Also notes phone number, assets and other financial data. **Number listed:** 6
1. Vanguard Bond Index Long Term, with 85.3
2. Vanguard Fixed Long-Term Corporate, 82.9
3. Forum Investors Bond, 77.5
4. SmithBarney Investment Grade Bond A, 73.9
5. Strong Corporate Bond, 73.1
6. HighMark Bond Fund, 70.2

Source: *U.S. News & World Report*, Best Mutual Funds (annual), February 1, 1999, p. 82.

★759★
BEST CORPORATE SHORT-TERM BONDS, 1998
Ranked by: Scores are ranked by an overall performance index (OPI) that relies on a formula measuring relative results over one, three, five and ten years. **Remarks:** Also notes phone number, assets and other financial data. **Number listed:** 5
1. Pilgrim Prime Rate, with 81.1
2. Hotchkis & Wiley Low Duration, 74.8
3. Van Kampen Prime Rate Income Trust, 72.6
4. Vanguard Bond Index Short Term, 71.7
5. CCB Bond Fund, 71.1
6. FPA New Income, 70.9

Source: *U.S. News & World Report*, Best Mutual Funds (annual), February 1, 1999, p. 82.

★760★
BEST GLOBAL BONDS BY OPI, 1998
Ranked by: Scores are ranked by an overall performance index (OPI) that relies on a formula measuring relative results over one, three, five and ten years. **Remarks:** Also notes phone number, assets and other financial data. **Number listed:** 10
1. Payden & Rygel Global Fixed R, with 92.3
2. Goldmann Sachs Global Income A, 89.1
3. Janus Flexible Income, 83.1
4. PaineWebber Pace Global Fixed Income, 82.3
5. Prudential Global Total Return A, 82.1
6. Morgan Stanley Dean Witter World Wide B, 81
7. Morgan Stanley Dean Witter Global Short Term, 80.8
8. Lord Abbett Global Income A, 793
9. Prudential International Global Income A, 77.7
10. SmithBarney World Global Government A, 74.6

Source: *U.S. News & World Report*, Best Mutual Funds (annual), February 1, 1999, p. 81.

★761★
BEST GLOBAL BONDS BY RETURN, 1998
Ranked by: Return, in percent. **Remarks:** Also notes phone number, assets, returns over three, five and ten years and other financial data. **Number listed:** 5
1. PaineWebber Pace Global Fixed, with 18.6%
2. American Century-Benham International, 17.9%
3. CG Capital Markets International Fixed Income, 17.6%
4. T. Rowe Price International Bond, 15%
4. Van Eck Chubb Global Income A, 15%

Source: *U.S. News & World Report*, Best Mutual Funds (annual), February 1, 1999, p. 85.

★762★
BEST GOVERNMENT BONDS, 1998
Ranked by: Return, in percent. **Remarks:** Also notes phone number, assets, returns over three, five and ten years and other financial data. **Number listed:** 10
1. American Century-Benham Target 2025, with 21.6%
2. Rydex U.S. Government Bond, 15.8%
3. Wasatch-Hosington U.S. Treasuries, 14.6%
3. American Century-Benham Target 2010, 14.6%
5. American Century-Benham Target 2015, 14.5%
6. Vanguard Admiral Long Treasury, 13.2%
7. Vanguard Fixed Long Term Treasury, 13.1%
8. PaineWebber U.S. Government Income A, 12.9%
9. T. Rowe Price U.S. Treasury Long, 12.8%
9. American Century-Benham Long Treasury, 12.8%

Source: *U.S. News & World Report*, Best Mutual Funds (annual), February 1, 1999, p. 85.

★763★
BEST GOVERNMENT LONG-TERM BONDS, 1998
Ranked by: Scores are ranked by an overall performance index (OPI) that relies on a formula measuring relative results over one, three, five and ten years. **Remarks:** Also notes phone number, assets and other financial data. **Number listed:** 5
1. Wasatch-Hosington U.S. Treasury, with 93.5
2. American Century-Benham Target 2015, 88.9
3. American Century-Benham Target 2010, 88.2
4. Vanguard Long-Term Treasury, 87.8
5. American Century-Benham Target 2020, 85.2

Source: *U.S. News & World Report*, Best Mutual Funds (annual), February 1, 1999, p. 81.

★764★
BEST GOVERNMENT MEDIUM-TERM BONDS, 1998
Ranked by: Scores are ranked by an overall performance index (OPI) that relies on a formula measuring relative results over one, three, five and ten years. **Remarks:** Also notes phone number, assets and other financial data. **Number listed:** 15
1. American Century-Benham Target 2005, with 84.8
2. Vanguard Fixed GMNA, 84
3. USAA GNMA, 83.6
4. Federated Government 5-10 Years I, 83.4
5. State Street Research Government Income A, 83.1
6. Vanguard Admiral Intermediate Treasury, 82.4
7. T. Rowe Price U.S. Treasury Intermediate, 82.3
8. Galaxy Funds II U.S. Treasury Retail A, 82.1
9. Vanguard Fixed Intermediate Treasury, 80.8
10. Fidelity Spartan Government Income, 79.9

Source: *U.S. News & World Report*, Best Mutual Funds (annual), February 1, 1999, p. 81.

★765★
BEST GOVERNMENT SHORT-TERM BONDS, 1998
Ranked by: Scores are ranked by an overall performance index (OPI) that relies on a formula measuring relative results over one, three, five and ten years. **Remarks:** Also notes phone number, assets and other financial data. **Number listed:** 10
1. Lexington GNMA Income, with 80.8
2. Montgomery Short Duration Government R, 71.3
3. Monterey PIA Short-Term Government Securities, 71
4. Vanguard Admiral Short-Term Treasury, 68.2
5. Oppenheimer Limited-Term Government A, 67.9
6. SSgA Intermediate Fund, 65.9
7. Vanguard Fixed Short-Term Treasury, 65.8
8. Gradison Government Income, 65.1
9. Vanguard Fixed Short-Term Federal, 64.1
10. SEI Daily Income Short Government A, 63.2

Source: *U.S. News & World Report*, Best Mutual Funds (annual), February 1, 1999, p. 81.

★766★
BEST HIGH YIELD BONDS BY OPI, 1998
Ranked by: Scores are ranked by an overall performance index (OPI) that relies on a formula measuring relative results over one, three, five and ten years. **Remarks:** Also notes phone number, assets and other financial data. **Number listed:** 10
1. Vanguard High-Yield Corporate, with 74.6
2. Columbia High Yield, 73.3
3. Northeast Investors Trust, 73.2
4. Lord Abbett Bond Debenture A, 71.4
5. Colonial High-Yield Securities A, 71.2
6. Idex Income Plus A, 70.5
6. Eaton Vance Income Fund Boston, 70.5
8. Fidelity Capital and Income, 69.9
9. Safeco High-Yield Bond, 69

10. Nicholas Income, 68.8

Source: *U.S. News & World Report*, Best Mutual Funds (annual), February 1, 1999, p. 81.

★767★
BEST HIGH-YIELD BONDS BY RETURN, 1998
Ranked by: Return, in percent. **Remarks:** Also notes phone number, assets, returns over three, five and ten years and other financial data. **Number listed:** 5

1. Strong Short-Term High-Yield Bond, with 8.4%
2. Brinson High-Yield Bond I, 7.7%
3. Conseco High Yield A, 6.6%
4. Payden & Rygel High Income R, 6.3%
4. Columbia High Yield, 6.3%

Source: *U.S. News & World Report*, Best Mutual Funds (annual), February 1, 1999, p. 85.

★768★
BEST MUNICIPAL BONDS, 1998
Ranked by: Return, in percent. **Remarks:** Also notes phone number, assets, returns over three, five and ten years and other financial data. **Number listed:** 10

1. CitiFunds National Tax-Free Income, with 10.1%
2. United Municipal High Income A, 6.8%
2. Dreyfus Basic Municipal Bond, 6.8%
2. Eaton Vance Municipal Bond, 6.8%
5. STI Classic Investment Grade Tax-Exempt, 6.7%
5. Dreyfus Basic Intermediate Municipal, 6.7%
5. Strong Municipal Bond, 6.7%
5. Delaware National High Yield A, 6.7%
5. Colonial Tax Exempt A, 6.7%
5. Van Kampen High-Yield Municipal A, 6.7%

Source: *U.S. News & World Report*, Best Mutual Funds (annual), February 1, 1999, p. 85.

★769★
BEST MUNICIPAL HIGH YIELD BONDS, 1998
Ranked by: Scores are ranked by an overall performance index (OPI) that relies on a formula measuring relative results over one, three, five and ten years. **Remarks:** Also notes phone number, assets and other financial data. **Number listed:** 5

1. United Municipal High Income A, with 99.9
2. Van Kampen High-Yield Municipal A, 98.8
3. Delaware National High Yield A, 98.3
4. Scudder High-Yield Tax Free, 90.4
5. T. Rowe Price Tax-Free High Yield, 87.4

Source: *U.S. News & World Report*, Best Mutual Funds (annual), February 1, 1999, p. 82.

★770★
BEST MUNICIPAL INTERMEDIATE BONDS, 1998
Ranked by: Scores are ranked by an overall performance index (OPI) that relies on a formula measuring relative results over one, three, five and ten years. **Remarks:** Also notes phone number, assets and other financial data. **Number listed:** 5

1. CitiFunds National Tax-Free Income, with 96.8
2. Sit Tax-Free Income Fund, 95.3
3. Dreyfus Basic Intermediate Municipal, 92.2
4. STI Classic Investment Grade Tax Exempt, 91.4
5. USAA Intermediate Term, 90.1

Source: *U.S. News & World Report*, Best Mutual Funds (annual), February 1, 1999, p. 82.

★771★
BEST MUNICIPAL LONG-TERM BONDS, 1998
Ranked by: Scores are ranked by an overall performance index (OPI) that relies on a formula measuring relative results over one, three, five and ten years. **Remarks:** Also notes phone number, assets and other financial data. **Number listed:** 15

1. Dreyfus Basic Municipal Bond, with 97.9
2. T. Rowe Price Summit Municipal Income, 97.5
3. Vanguard Municipal High Yield, 94.8
4. Norwest Advantage Tax-Free Income A, 93.9
5. Vanguard Municipal Long Term, 91.2
6. SmithBarney Municipal National A, 89.5
7. USAA Tax Exempt Long Term, 89.4
8. Vanguard Municipal Insured Long Term, 98.1
9. Excelsior Long-Term Tax Exempt, 87.7
10. Safeco Muni Bond, 87.1

Source: *U.S. News & World Report*, Best Mutual Funds (annual), February 1, 1999, p. 82.

Bonds

★772★
HIGH YIELD BOND OWNERSHIP
Ranked by: Percentage. **Number listed:** 7

1. Insurance Companies, with 23%
2. High Yield Mutual Funds, 21%
3. Pension Funds, 18%
4. Investment-Grade Funds, 12%
5. Equity & Income Funds, 11%
6. CBO/Other, 10%
7. Foreign-Owned, 5%

Source: *Financial Management*, Summer, 1998, p. 20.

★773★
LARGEST CORPORATE BOND LISTINGS, 1998
Ranked by: Principal amount, in thousands of dollars. **Number listed:** 48

1. Sprint Capital, with $2,500,000 thousand
2. Hewlett Packard, $2,000,000
2. Tennessee Valley Authority, $2,000,000
4. Freddie Mac, $1,458,730
5. Freddie Mac, $1,458,720
6. General Motors Acceptance Corp., $1,250,000
7. InterAmerican Development, $1,000,000
7. InterAmerican Development, $1,000,000
7. Tennessee Valley Authority, $1,000,000
7. Tennessee Valley Authority, $1,000,000
11. General Motors Acceptance Corp., $750,000
12. International Business Machines, $700,000
13. BellSouth Capital Funding, $500,000

Source: *New York Stock Exchange Fact Book*, 1998, p. 86.

★774★
MOST ACTIVE BONDS ON THE NEW YORK STOCK EXCHANGE, 1998
Ranked by: Par value of reported volume, in thousands of dollars. **Number listed:** 48

1. Penn Traffic, with $332,795 thousand
2. Service Merchandise, $266,876
3. Stone Container, $229,032
4. Hills Stores, $147,601
5. General Motors Acceptance Corp., $141,980
6. General Motors Acceptance Corp., $116,750
7. Del Webb Corp., $113,497
8. General Motors Acceptance Corp., $94,510
9. RJR Nabisco Inc., $72,320
10. General Motors Acceptance Corp., $64,270

Source: *New York Stock Exchange Fact Book*, (annual), 1998, p. 85.

Bonds--Argentina

★775★
TOP ISSUERS OF BONDS IN ARGENTINA
Ranked by: Principal amount, in millions of U.S. dollars ($). **Remarks:** Also notes market share percentage. **Number listed:** 10

1. Chase Manhattan Corp., with $661.33 million
2. JP Morgan, $600
3. Warburg Dillon Read, $575
4. ING Barings, $325
5. Deutsche Morgan Grenfell, $268.56
6. BT Alex Brown International, $120
7. Banca Commerciale Italiana, $111.33
8. Goldman Sachs & Co., $100
9. Banco Central Hispano SA, $95
10. Bear, Stearns Cos., $80

Source: *Latin Finance*, March, 1999, p. 75.

Bonds--Brazil

★776★
TOP ISSUERS OF BONDS IN BRAZIL
Ranked by: Principal amount, in millions of U.S. dollars ($). **Remarks:** Also notes market share percentage. **Number listed:** 10

1. Lehman Brothers, with $1,500 million
2. Chase Manhattan Corp., $455.03
3. Merrill Lynch & Co., $275
4. Goldman Sachs & Co., $250
5. Barclays Capital, $230
6. Deutsche Morgan Grenfell, $218.56
7. Banco Portugues De Investimento SA, $174.13
8. Banco Bozano Simonsen SA, $125
9. Westdeutsche Landesbank Girozentrale, $109.77
10. Bear, Stearns Cos., $100

Source: *Latin Finance*, March, 1999, p. 75.

Bonds--Latin America

★777★
TOP ISSUERS OF BONDS IN LATIN AMERICA
Ranked by: Principal amount, in millions of U.S. dollars ($). **Remarks:** Also notes market share percentage. **Number listed:** 15

1. Lehman Brothers, with $1,500 million
2. Chase Manhattan Corp., $1,446.12
3. BT Alex Brown International, $725.84
4. Warburg Dillon Read, $675
5. J. P. Morgan, $600
5. Morgan Stanley & Co. Inc., $600
7. Goldman Sachs & Co., $350
8. Merrill Lynch & Co., $330
9. ING Barings, $325
10. Deutsche Morgan Grenfell, $268.56

Source: *Latin Finance*, March, 1999, p. 75.

Bonds--Mexico

★778★
TOP ISSUERS OF BONDS IN MEXICO
Ranked by: Principal amount, in millions of U.S. dollars ($). **Remarks:** Also notes market share percentage. **Number listed:** 4

1. BT Alex. Brown, with $605.84 million
2. Chase Manhattan Corp., $339.75
3. Bank of America, $50
3. Credit Suisse First Boston, $50

Source: *Latin Finance*, March, 1999, p. 75.

Bonds--Panama

★779★
TOP ISSUERS OF BONDS IN PANAMA
Ranked by: Principal amount, in millions of U.S. dollars ($). **Remarks:** Also notes market share percentage. **Number listed:** 2

1. Merrill Lynch & Co., with $55 million
2. Prudential Securities Inc., $25

Source: *Latin Finance*, March, 1999, p. 75.

Books

★780★
BEST BUSINESS BOOKS, 1998
Ranked by: Books are listed, not ranked. Also notes author. **Number listed:** 10

1. Burn Rate
2. Competing on Internet Time
3. The Corrosion of Character
4. Gain
5. The House of Rothschild
6. I'd Like to Buy the World a Coke
7. The Profit Zone
8. Prosperity
9. Titan
10. The Weightless World

Source: *Business Week*, December 14, 1998, p. 15.

Bottled Water

★781★
BEST-SELLING BOTTLED WATER BY DOLLAR SALES, 1997
Ranked by: Specific figures not provided. **Number listed:** 8

1. Evian
2. Aquafina
3. Poland Spring
4. Crystal Geyser
5. Naya
6. Arrowhead
7. Dannon
8. Aqua Penn

Source: *U.S. Distribution Journal*, January/February, 1999, p. 42.

★782★
BEST-SELLING FLAVORED WATER IN CONVENIENCE STORES, 1997
Ranked by: Market share, in percent. **Number listed:** 11
1. Meridian Clear, with 47%
2. Clearly Canadian, 27.4%
3. Geyser, 7.5%
4. Crystal Bay, 4.8%
5. Kwencher, 4.2%
6. Saratoga Splash, 2.9%
7. Glacier Ridge, 1.7%
8. Glacier Peak, 1%
9. Time Out, 0.9%
9. Xtreme, 0.9%
11. Other, 1.9%

Source: *Convenience Store News*, July 6, 1998, p. 44.

★783★
LEADING BOTTLED WATER BRANDS BY MARKET SHARE, 1997
Ranked by: Market share, in percent. **Remarks:** Also notes figures for previous two years. **Number listed:** 11
1. Poland Spring, with 7.5%
2. Arrowhead, 6.7%
3. Evian, 4.7%
4. Sparkletts, 4.6%
5. Hinckley & Schmitt, 3.1%
6. Zephyrhills, 2.8%
7. Ozarka, 2.7%
8. Deer Park, 2.5%
9. Alpine Spring, 2.4%
10. Aquafina, 2.3%
11. All Others, 60.7%

Source: *Discount Merchandiser*, April, 1999, p. 110.

★784★
TOP SELLING BOTTLED WATER, 1998
Ranked by: Sales, in millions of dollars. **Remarks:** Also notes market share, one-year growth, and three-year growth. **Number listed:** 10
1. Poland Spring, with $350.9 million
2. Arrowhead, $283.2
3. Sparkletts, $205
4. Evian, $200.7
5. Aquafina, $165
6. Zephyrhills, $134.4
7. Hinckley & Schmitt, $128.6
8. Deer Park, $123.6
9. Ozarka, $122.8
10. Crystal Geyser, $113.1

Source: *Beverage World*, April, 1999, p. 60.

Bottled Water--Great Britain

★785★
TOP WATER COOLER COMPANIES IN THE UNITED KINGDOM, 1997
Ranked by: Market share, in percent. **Number listed:** 7
1. Ionics UK, with 17.6%
2. Sparkling Spring, 17.2%
3. Numbers 6-10, 13.3%
4. Braebourne, 6.1%
5. Hollywell Spring, 3.3%
6. Crystal Springs, 4.5%
7. Others, 38%

Source: *Bottled Water Reporter*, June/July, 1998, p. 47.

Bottling Plants--North America

★786★
TOP BOTTLING COMPANIES, 1997
Ranked by: Sales, in millions of dollars. **Remarks:** Also notes contact information, key executives, percentage of franchises company sales, and number of plants. **Number listed:** 25
1. Coca-Cola Enterprises, with $11,278 million
2. Pepsi-Cola Bottling Co., $7,156
3. Pepsi-Cola General Bottlers, $1,557.5
4. Coca-Cola Bottling Co., $935
5. Honcikman Affiliates, $870
6. Coca-Cola Bottling Co. Consolidated, $802.1
7. Dr. Pepper Bottling Co. of Texas, $709
8. Beverage America now American Bottling Co., $492.9
9. Delta Beverage Group, $450
10. Coca-Cola Bottling Co. United, $449

Source: *Beverage World*, Top 25 Bottlers in North America (annual), September, 1998, p. 62+.

Bourbon--Export-Import Trade

★787★
LEADING IMPORTERS OF U.S. BOURBON, 1997
Ranked by: Proof gallons, in thousands. **Remarks:** Also notes figures for previous two years. **Number listed:** 5
1. Australia, with 3,436.4 thousand gallons
2. Germany, 2,643.3
3. Japan, 2,587.9
4. United Kingdom, 1,678.5
5. France, 747.3
6. Other, 3,525.7

Source: *Adams Liquor Handbook*, (annual), Adams Media, Inc., 1998, p. 219.

Bourse de Bruxelles

★788★
LARGEST LISTED COMPANIES ON THE BRUSSELS STOCK EXCHANGE, 1997
Ranked by: Market value, in billions of Belgian Francs (BFr). **Number listed:** 20
1. Electrabel, with BFr466 billion
2. Fortis AG, BFr322
3. Petrofina, BFr320
4. Tractebel, BFr273
5. Generale de Banque, BFr266
6. Generale Belgiqe, BFr239
7. Kredietbank, BFr202
8. BBL, BFr198
9. Solvay, BFr196
10. Dexia CC, BFr183

Source: *SSB Guide to World Equity Markets*, (annual), Euromoney Publications, 1998, p. 81.

★789★
MOST ACTIVELY TRADED SHARES ON THE BRUSSELS STOCK EXCHANGE, 1997
Ranked by: Trading value, in billions of Belgian Francs (BFr). **Number listed:** 20

1. Petrofina, with BFr78.7 billion
2. Fortis AG, BFr66
3. Electrabel, BFr64
4. BBL, BFr62.8
5. Dexia CC, BFr60.1
6. UCB, BFr55.9
7. Kredietbank, BFr55.2
8. Solvay, BFr54.4
9. Generale de Banque, BFr53.8
10. Delhaize, BFr42.3

Source: *SSB Guide to World Equity Markets*, (annual), Euromoney Publications, 1998, p. 82.

Bourse de Paris

★790★
LARGEST LISTED COMPANIES ON THE PARIS STOCK EXCHANGE, 1997
Ranked by: Market value, in billions of French Francs (Fr). **Number listed:** 20

1. France Telecom, with Fr218.3 billion
2. Elf Aquitaine, Fr192.6
3. Total, Fr159.5
4. L'Oreal, Fr159.2
5. Axa, Fr154.3
6. Alcatel Altsthom, Fr124.5
7. Carrefour, Fr120.8
8. Eaux, Fr112.6
9. Rhone-Poulenc, Fr97.2
10. LVMH, Fr87.5

Source: *SSB Guide to World Equity Markets*, (annual), Euromoney Publications, 1998, p. 188.

★791★
MOST ACTIVELY TRADED SHARES ON THE PARIS STOCK EXCHANGE, 1997
Ranked by: Average daily turnover, in millions of French Francs (Fr). **Number listed:** 20

1. Elf Aquitaine, with Fr599.1 million
2. Alcatel Altsthom, Fr502.5
3. Axa, Fr407.4
4. Total, Fr386.0
5. Carrefour, Fr360.2
6. Eaux, Fr356.8
7. LVMH, Fr323.1
8. Societe Generale, Fr319.8
9. Rhone-Poulenc, Fr267.6
10. L'Oreal, Fr256.1

Source: *SSB Guide to World Equity Markets*, (annual), Euromoney Publications, 1998, p. 188.

Brand Name Goods

★792★
BRANDS WITH THE HIGHEST ADVERTISING EXPENDITURES, 1998
Ranked by: Advertising expenditures, in millions of dollars. **Remarks:** Also notes figure from previous year and percent change. **Number listed:** 2000

1. McDonald's Restaurant, with $569,192.9 million
2. Burger King Restaurant, $404,594.9
3. Circuit City Stores, $403,590.4
4. Valassis Coupons, $287,237.5
5. News America FSI, $254,168.1
6. Home Depot Home Center, $215,241.1
7. Best Buy Electronics Store, $203,995.8
8. Taco Bell Restaurant, $202,781.4
9. Wendy's Restaurant, $187,264.4
10. Sprint Long Distance Residential, $171,337.3

Source: *Brandweek*, Superbrands: America's Top 2,000 Brands, June 21, 1999, p. S74+.

★793★
MOVIE STUDIOS SPENDING THE MOST ON ADVERTISING, 1997
Ranked by: U.S. advertising expenditures, in millions of dollars. **Remarks:** Also notes figures from previous year, percent change, and top film in ad spending. **Number listed:** 10

1. Buena Vista Pictures, with $406.5 million
2. Warner Brothers, $243.9
3. Paramount Pictures, $238.9
4. 20th Century Fox Films, $212.3
5. Columbia Pictures, $169.3
6. Universal Pictures, $169.1
7. Miramax Films, $133.1
8. New LineCinema, $118.4
9. TriStar Pictures, $104.8
10. MGM/UA, $86.5

Source: *Advertising Age*, Top 100 MegaBrands (annual), July 13, 1998, p. S6.

★794★
TOP ADVERTISING MEDIA, 1997
Ranked by: Measured ad spending, in millions of dollars. **Remarks:** Also notes figures from previous year, percent change and additional financial information. **Number listed:** 10

1. Newspapers, with $15,777.5 million
2. Network TV, $15,225.1
3. Spot TV, $14,534.6
4. Magazines, $12,701.1
5. Cable TV and networks, $5,781.9
6. Syndicated TV, $2,515
7. National Spot Radio, $1,684.2
8. National Newspaper, $1,650
9. Outdoor, $1,462.7
10. Sunday magazine, $1,016.6

Source: *Advertising Age*, Top 100 MegaBrands (annual), July 13, 1998, p. S2.

★795★
TOP AUTOMOBILE BRANDS SPENDING THE MOST ON ADVERTISING, 1997
Ranked by: U.S. advertising expenditures, in millions of dollars. **Remarks:** Also notes figures from previous year, percent change, and additional financial information. **Number listed:** 10

1. Chevrolet cars & trucks, with $656.3 million
2. Ford cars & trucks, $569.9
3. Dodge cars & trucks, $551.8
4. Toyota cars & trucks, $453.8
5. Nissan cars & trucks, $347
6. Honda cars & trucks, $335.6
7. Chrysler cars & trucks, $301.3
8. GM cars, trucks & financial services, $279.3
9. Buick cars, $252.9
10. Jeep vehicles, $250.4

Source: *Advertising Age*, Top 100 MegaBrands (annual), July 13, 1998, p. S7.

★796★
TOP BRAND NAME CEOS, 1998
Ranked by: Basis for ranking not specified. **Number listed:** 10

1. Bill Gates, Microsoft Corp.
2. Michael Eisner, The Walt Disney Co.
3. Louis V. Gerstner Jr., IBM Corp.
4. Larry Ellison, Oracle Systems Corp.
5. Jack Welch, General Electric Co.
6. Lew Platt, Hewlett-Packard Co.
7. Michael Dell, Dell computer Corp.
8. Sanford I. Weill, Travelers Group
9. Peter Bijur, Texaco Inc.
10. John Chambers, Cisco Systems, Inc.

Source: *Electronic Business*, July, 1998, p. 24.

★797★
TOP CATEGORIES BY ADVERTISING EXPENDITURES, 1997
Ranked by: Advertising expenditures, in millions of dollars. **Remarks:** Also notes figures from previous year, percent change and additional financial information. **Number listed:** 10

1. Automotive, with $6,507.4 million
2. Retail, $3,404.3
3. Restaurants, $1,917.9
4. Telephone, $1,721.7
5. Food, $1,659.4
6. Drugs & Personal Care, $1,090.3
7. Financial Services, brokers & insurance, $980.0
8. Computers & Electronics, $841.6
9. Beer, $569.2
10. Imaging/office machines, $238.4

Source: *Advertising Age*, Top 100 MegaBrands (annual), July 13, 1998, p. S2.

★798★
TOP COMPANIES BY MEASURED AD SPENDING, 1997
Ranked by: Measured ad spending, in millions of dollars. **Remarks:** Also notes figures from previous year, percent change, and additional financial information. **Number listed:** 10

1. General Motors Corp., with $2,226.9 million
2. Procter & Gamble, $1,703.1
3. Phillip Morris Cos., $1,319
4. Chrysler Corp., $1,311.8
5. Ford Motor Co., $973.1
6. Johnson & Johnson, $823.5
7. Time Warner, $779.1
8. Walt Disney Co., $746.3
9. Sears, Roebuck & Co., $734.1
10. Diageo, $685

Source: *Advertising Age*, Top 100 MegaBrands (annual), July 13, 1998, p. S2.

★799★
TOP ICE CREAM BRANDS, 1997-1998
Ranked by: Sales, in millions of dollars. **Number listed:** 10

1. Store Brands, with $823.5 million
2. Breyers, $406.5
3. Dreyers Edy's Grand, $365.6
4. Blue Bell, $180.2
5. Haagen-Dazs, $157.2
6. Ben & Jerry's, $120.4
7. Healthy Choice, $102
8. Dreyers Edy's Grand Light, $87.7
9. Turkey Hill, $78.6
10. Wells Bluebunny, $68.5

Source: *U.S. Distribution Journal*, July/August, 1998, p. 54.

★800★
TOP MAJOR BRANDS SPENDING THE MOST ON ADVERTISING, 1997
Ranked by: U.S. advertising expenditures, in millions of dollars. **Remarks:** Also notes figures from previous year, percent change, additional financial information, marketing executives, and lead agencies. **Number listed:** 100

1. Sears stores, with $664.6 million
2. Chevrolet cars & trucks, $656.3
3. McDonald's restaurants, $580.5
4. Ford cars & trucks, $569.9
5. Dodge cars & trucks, $551.8
6. AT & T telephone services, $475.9
7. Toyota cars & trucks, $453.8
8. MCI telephone services, $435
9. Burger King restaurants, $427
10. Circuit City stores, $400.1

Source: *Advertising Age*, Top 100 MegaBrands (annual), July 13, 1998, p. S8.

Brandy

★801★
LEADING BRANDS OF DOMESTIC BRANDY, 1997
Ranked by: Sales, in thousands of 9-liter cases. **Remarks:** Also notes supplier, figures from previous five years, and percent change. **Number listed:** 11

1. E & J, with 1,900 thousand cases
2. Christian Brothers, 1,260
3. Paul Masson Brandy, 600
4. Korbel, 375
5. Coronet Brandy, 175
6. Mr. Boston Brandy, 87
7. J. Bavet, 85
8. Aristocrat Brandy, 75
9. Almaden, 69
10. Phillips Brandy, 50

Source: *Adams Liquor Handbook*, (annual), Adams Media, Inc., 1998, p. 174.

★802★
METROPOLITAN AREAS WITH THE HIGHEST CONSUMPTION OF BRANDY AND COGNAC, 1997
Ranked by: Consumption, in thousands of 9-liter cases. **Remarks:** Also notes market share. **Number listed:** 50

1. Chicago, IL, with 452.8 thousand cases
2. Los Angeles-Long Beach, CA, 380.4
3. Minneapolis-St. Paul, MN, 307.2
4. Washington, DC, 272.3
5. Detroit, MI, 214
6. Milwaukee-Waukesha, WI, 206.8
7. Atlanta, GA, 187.1
8. New York, NY, 155
9. Baltimore, MD, 129
10. Orange County, CA, 127

Source: *Adams Liquor Handbook*, (annual), Adams Media, Inc., 1998, p. 176.

★803★
STATES WITH THE HIGHEST CONSUMPTION OF BRANDY AND COGNAC, 1997
Ranked by: Consumption in 9-liter cases. **Remarks:** Also notes figures from previous year. **Number listed:** 51

1. California, with 1,287,200 cases
2. Wisconsin, 607,530
3. Illinois, 593,270

4. Minnesota, 421,690
5. Michigan, 409,140
6. New York, 365,480
7. Florida, 351,990
8. Texas, 323,860
9. Georgia, 316,000
10. Maryland, 245,620

Source: *Adams Liquor Handbook*, (annual), Adams Media, Inc., 1998, p. 171.

★804★
STATES WITH THE HIGHEST CONSUMPTION OF BRANDY AND COGNAC PER CAPITA, 1997
Ranked by: Consumption in 9-liter cases per thousand adults. **Remarks:** Also notes figures from previous year. **Number listed:** 51

1. District of Columbia, with 237.2 cases
2. Wisconsin, 167.4
3. Minnesota, 129.8
4. Nevada, 89
5. Illinois, 72.1
6. Maryland, 67.9
7. Delaware, 66.8
8. North Dakota, 66.7
9. Michigan, 61
10. Georgia, 60.8

Source: *Adams Liquor Handbook*, (annual), Adams Media, Inc., 1998, p. 172.

Brandy--Advertising

★805★
MOST ADVERTISED BRANDY AND COGNAC IN MAGAZINES, 1997
Ranked by: Advertising expenditures, in thousands of dollars. **Remarks:** Also notes expenditures from previous year. **Number listed:** 5

1. Hennessy, with $3,661 thousand
2. Remy Martin, $3,123.4
3. Paul Masson Brandy, $334.7
4. Hine, $36.6
5. E & J Brandy, $35.7

Source: *Adams Liquor Handbook*, (annual), Adams Media, Inc., 1998, p. 178.

★806★
MOST ADVERTISED BRANDY AND COGNAC IN OUTDOOR ADVERTISING, 1997
Ranked by: Advertising expenditures, in thousands of dollars. **Remarks:** Also notes expenditures from previous year. **Number listed:** 7

1. Hennessy, with $479.9 thousand
2. Remy Martin, $133.5
3. Martell, $72.9
4. Korbel, $64.7
5. Remy Amerique, $54.7
6. Presidente, $31.7
7. Don Pedro, $7.4

Source: *Adams Liquor Handbook*, (annual), Adams Media, Inc., 1998, p. 178.

★807★
MOST ADVERTISED BRANDY AND COGNAC, 1997
Ranked by: Advertising expenditures, in thousands of dollars. **Remarks:** Also notes expenditures from previous year. **Number listed:** 12

1. Hennessy, with $4,140.9 thousand
2. Remy Martin, $3,256.9
3. Martell, $411.6
4. Paul Masson Brandy, $334.7
5. Korbel, $64.7
6. Remy Amerique, $54.7
7. Hine, $36.6
8. E & J Brandy, $35.7
9. Presidente, $31.7
10. Don Pedro, $7.4

Source: *Adams Liquor Handbook*, (annual), Adams Media, Inc., 1998, p. 178.

Brandy--Export-Import Trade

★808★
LEADING IMPORTERS OF BRANDY, 1997
Ranked by: Proof gallons, in thousands. **Remarks:** Also notes figures from the previous two years. **Number listed:** 5

1. Japan, with 174 thousand gallons
2. United Kingdom, 67.4
3. Canada, 41.8
4. Bahamas, 30.3
5. Brazil, 19.8
6. Other, 88.5

Source: *Adams Liquor Handbook*, (annual), Adams Media, Inc., 1998, p. 219.

Bratislava Stock Exchange

★809★
LARGEST LISTED COMPANIES ON THE BRATISLAVA STOCK EXCHANGE, 1997
Ranked by: Market value, in millions of U.S. dollars ($). **Remarks:** Also notes industry sector. **Number listed:** 20

1. Slovnaft, with $419 million
2. VSV, $324
3. Slovakofarma, $233
4. VUB, $150
5. Nafta, $124
6. Slovenska poistovna, $49
7. ZSNP, $36
8. Vahostav, $19
8. Povazske strojarne, $19
10. Chemolak, $13

Source: *SSB Guide to World Equity Markets*, (annual), Euromoney Publications, 1998, p. 437.

★810★
MOST ACTIVELY TRADED SHARES ON THE BRATISLAVA STOCK EXCHANGE, 1997
Ranked by: Market value, in millions of koruna (Kcs). **Remarks:** Also notes number of shares. **Number listed:** 20

1. VSV, with Din11,776 million
2. VUB, Din8,814
3. Slovnaft, Din8,226
4. Nafta, Din4,180
5. Slovakofarma, Din3,609
6. Drotovna, Din2,229
7. Slovenska poistovna, Din1,920
8. JcaP, Din1,458
9. Chemolak, Din816

10. ISK, Din694

Source: *SSB Guide to World Equity Markets*, (annual), Euromoney Publications, 1998, p. 437.

Breath Fresheners

★811★

BEST SELLING BREATH FRESHENER BRANDS, 1998

Ranked by: Unit sales, in millions. **Remarks:** Also notes market share. **Number listed:** 10

1. Sweet Breath, with 18.8 million units
2. Binaca, 4.9
3. Breath Asure, 3.8
4. Orablast, 1.4
5. Ice Drops, .9
6. Breath Asure D, .5
7. Sweet Breath Sorbet, .4
7. Puretek Breath Relief, .4
9. Crystal Breath, .3
10. Yow, .2

Source: *MMR*, November 2, 1998, p. 37.

Brewing Industry

★812★

LEADING BRANDS OF IMPORTED BEER, 1997

Ranked by: Sales, in millions of 2.25-gallon cases. **Remarks:** Also notes figures for previous years and percent change. **Number listed:** 11

1. Corona Extra, with 39.4 million cases
2. Heineken, 39.3
3. Molson Ice, 11.5
4. Labatt Blue, 9.3
5. Beck's, 7.4
6. Guinness Stout, 7.1
7. Foster's Lager, 6.8
8. Tecate, 6
9. Molson Golden, 5.9
10. Bass Ale, 5.8
11. Others, 56.8

Source: *Adams Liquor Handbook*, (annual), Adams Media, Inc., 1998, p. 305.

★813★

LEADING BRANDS OF LIGHT BEER, 1998

Ranked by: 2.25-Liter cases, in thousands. **Remarks:** Also notes brewer/supplier, previous year's data and percent change. **Number listed:** 10

1. Bud Light, with 349,250 thousand cases
2. Miller Light, 218,000
3. Coors Light, 210,000
4. Natural Light, 99,000
5. Busch Light, 65,000
6. Michelob Light, 33,900
7. Keystone Light, 27,250
8. Milwaukee's Best Light, 27,000
9. Old Milwaukee Light, 11,000
9. Miller Genuine Draft Light, 11,000

Source: *Beverage Dynamics*, March, 1999, p. 40.

★814★

LEADING BREWERS IN THE U.S. BY SALES VOLUME, 1997

Ranked by: Sales, in millions of 2.25-gallon cases. **Remarks:** Also notes figures for previous year and percent change. **Number listed:** 5

1. Annheuser-Busch, with 1,255.6 million cases
2. Miller Brewing Co., 552.2
3. Coors Brewing, 286.6
4. Stroh Brewery Co., 203.1
5. Pabst Brewing Co., 58.2

Source: *Adams Liquor Handbook*, (annual), Adams Media, Inc., 1998, p. 304.

★815★

TOP BREWERS BY MARKET SHARE, 1998

Ranked by: Market share, in percent. **Number listed:** 6

1. Anheuser-Busch, with 50.9% Barrels
2. Miller Brewing Co., 22.5%
3. Coors Brewing Co., 11.4%
4. Stroh Brewery Co., 8.8%
5. Pabst Brewing Co., 2.2%
6. All Others, 4.2%

Source: *Modern Brewery Age*, MBA Statistical Survey (annual), March 23, 1998, p. 12.

★816★

TOP BREWERS BY SALES, 1998

Ranked by: Sales of 31-gallon barrels. **Number listed:** 10

1. Anheuser-Busch, with 94,200,000 Barrels
2. Miller Brewing Co., 41,700,000
3. Coors Brewing Co., 21,187,000
4. Stroh Brewery Co., 16,251,000
5. Pabst Brewing Co., 4,000,000
6. Genessee Brewing Co., 1,500,000
7. Botston Beer Co., 1,150,000
8. Latrobe Brewing Co., 1,020,000
9. Pearl Brewing Co., 900,000
10. D. G. Yuengling & Son, 631,170

Source: *Modern Brewery Age*, MBA Statistical Survey (annual), March 23, 1998, p. 10.

★817★

TOP BREWERS BY TEN-YEAR GAIN OR LOSS, 1998

Ranked by: Ten-year gain or loss in percent. **Number listed:** 10

1. Botston Beer Co., with 2,775%
2. D. G. Yuengling & Son, 400.1%
3. Latrobe Brewing Co., 87.7%
4. Pearl Brewing Co., 44%
5. Coors Brewing Co., 28.4%
6. Anheuser-Busch, 20%
7. Miller Brewing Co., 2.5%
8. Genessee Brewing Co., -4%
9. Stroh Brewery Co., -20.8%
10. Pabst Brewing Co., -32.8%

Source: *Modern Brewery Age*, MBA Statistical Survey (annual), March 23, 1998, p. 19.

★818★

TOP COMMERCIAL BREWERS BY PRODUCTION SHARE OF U.S. SALES, 1998

Ranked by: Production share of U.S. Sales, in percent. **Remarks:** Also notes location, number of barrels, variant amount and previous year's figures. **Number listed:** 243

1. Anheuser-Busch, with 50.89%
2. Miller Brewing Co., 22.53%
3. Coors Brewing Co., 11.45%
4. Stroh Brewery Co., 8.78%
5. Pabst Brewing Co., 2.16%

6. Genessee Brewing Co., 0.81%
7. Botston Beer Co., 0.62%
8. Latrobe Brewing Co., 0.55%
9. Pearl Brewing Co., 0.49%
10. D. G. Yuengling & Son, 0.34%

Source: *Modern Brewery Age*, MBA Statistical Survey (annual), March 23, 1998, p. 16+.

★819★
TOP SELLING BEERS BY NUMBER OF BARRELS, 1998
Ranked by: Number of barrels shipped, in millions. **Remarks:** Also notes media expenditures. **Number listed:** 10

1. Budweiser, with 35 million barrels
2. Bud Light, 25.6
3. Miller Lite, 15.8
4. Coors Light, 13.8
5. Busch, 8.2
6. Natural Light, 7.4
7. Miller Genuine Draft, 5.3
8. Miller High Life, 4.9
8. Busch Light, 4.9
10. Corona Extra, 3.9

Source: *Brandweek*, Superbrands: America's Top 2,000 Brands, June 21, 1999, p. S24.

Brewing Industry--Export-Import Trade

★820★
BIGGEST BEER EXPORTERS, 1998
Ranked by: Dollar value, in millions of U.S. dollars ($). **Remarks:** Also notes percent of total market. **Number listed:** 10

1. Netherlands, with $833.7 million
2. Germany, $625
3. USA, $340.7
4. United Kingdom, $262.9
5. Mexico, $232.5
6. Belgium, $231.5
7. Denmark, $204
8. Canada, $197.9
9. Ireland, $139
10. France, $116

Source: *Nightclub & Bar*, August, 1998, p. 69.

★821★
TOP BRANDS OF IMPORTED BEER BY BARRELS SOLD, 1997
Ranked by: Number of 31-gallon barrel sold. **Remarks:** Also notes market share, percentage change, variance figures, and figures from previous four years. **Number listed:** 25

1. Corona, with 2,852,000
2. Heineken, 2,851,550
3. Molson, 1,500,968
4. Labatt, 943,000
5. Beck's, 668,830
6. Foster's, 548,710
7. Guinness Stout, 509,879
8. Tecate, 439,000
9. Bass Ale, 415,669
10. Amstel, 398,320

Source: *Modern Brewery Age*, July 10, 1998, p. 9.

★822★
TOP BRANDS OF IMPORTED BEER BY IMPORT MARKET SHARE, 1997
Ranked by: Import market share, in percent. **Number listed:** 11

1. Heineken, with 20.1%
1. Corona, 20.1%
3. Molson, 10.6%
4. Beck's, 4.7%
5. Labatt, 6.7%
6. Guinness Stout, 3.6%
7. Foster's, 3.9%
8. Tecate, 3.1%
9. Bass Ale, 2.9%
10. Amstel, 2.8%
11. All Others, 21.5%

Source: *Modern Brewery Age*, July 10, 1998, p. 10.

Brewing Industry, Foreign

★823★
FASTEST GROWING BEER MARKETS, 1991-1997
Ranked by: Percent growth from 1991-1997. **Number listed:** 10

1. Vietnam, with 366.7%
2. Thailand, 195.4%
3. Tanzania, 193.6%
4. Singapore, 171.9%
5. China, 127.5%
6. India, 108.9%
7. Paraguay, 103%
8. Tunisia, 95%
9. Turkey, 83.2%
10. Israel, 68.5%

Source: *Modern Brewery Age*, March 29, 1999, p. 3.

★824★
MOST RAPIDLY DECLINING BEER MARKETS, 1991-1997
Ranked by: Percent decline from 1991-1997. **Number listed:** 10

1. Nigeria, with -44.2%
2. The Congo, -42.2%
3. Bulgaria, -40.2%
4. Zambia, -39.9%
5. Romania, -35.1%
6. Kenya, -33.3%
7. Democratic Republic of Congo, -28.7%
8. Cameroon, -27.7%
9. Zimbabwe, -23.3%
10. Hungary, -22.2%

Source: *Modern Brewery Age*, March 29, 1999, p. 3.

Broadcasting Industry

★825★
TOP PUBLISHING AND BROADCASTING COMPANIES IN THE S&P 500, 1998
Ranked by: Each company is ranked by eight criteria: one-year total return, three-year total return, on-year sales growth, three-year average annual sales growth, one-year profit growth, three-year annual average profit growth, net profit margins, and return on equity, with additional weight given to a company's sales. A company's composite rank is calculated using the sum of all of its ranks. **Remarks:** Overall scores not provided. **Number listed:** 13

1. Gannett

2. Comcast
3. McGraw-Hill
4. Tribune
5. Clear Channel Communications
6. New York Times
7. Meredith
8. Time Warner
9. Knight-Ridder
10. Mediaone Group

Source: *Business Week*, Business Week 50: Top Companies of the S & P 500 (annual), March 29, 1999, p. 162.

Brokers

★826★

LEADING BROKERS BY CUSTOMER EQUITY, 1998

Ranked by: Customer equity, in millions of dollars. **Remarks:** Also notes figures and rank from previous year, secured amount, adjusted net capital and non-U.S. customer equity. **Number listed:** 40

1. Merrill Lynch Futures Inc., with $3,856.05 million
2. Goldman, Sachs & Co., $3,793.23
3. Salomon Smith Barney, $3,172.27
4. Morgan Stanley Dean Witter, $2,814.11
5. Bear, Stearns Securities Corp., $1,965.21
6. Prudential Securities Inc., $1,807.04
7. J. P. Morgan Futures Inc., $1,755
8. E. D. & F. Man International Inc., $1,546.04
9. Refco Inc., $1,531.52
10. Carr Futures Inc., $1,434.08

Source: *Futures*, December, 1998, p. 72.

★827★

MOST ADMIRED SECURITIES FIRMS, 1998

Ranked by: Scores (1-10) derived from a survey of senior executives, outside directors, and securities analysts. **Remarks:** Respondents rated companies in their own industry on 8 attributes of reputation. Also notes previous year's rank. **Number listed:** 10

1. Merrill Lynch, with 7.58 points
2. Morgan Stanley Dean Witter, 7.29
3. Charles Schwab, 7.24
4. Travelers Group, 6.67
5. Equitable, 6.43
6. Bear Stearns, 6.31
7. A. G. Edwards, 6.29
8. Franklin Resources, 6
9. PaineWebber Group, 5.77
10. Lehman Brothers Holdings Inc., 5.67

Source: *Fortune*, America's Most Admired Corporations (annual), March 1, 1999, p. F-1.

★828★

SECURITIES INDUSTRY ASSOCIATION BROKERAGE FIRMS WITH THE MOST EMPLOYEES, 1998

Ranked by: Number of employees. **Number listed:** 50

1. Merrill Lynch & Co., with 56,600 employees
2. Morgan Stanley Dean Witter & Co., 47,000
3. Salomon Smith Barney Holdings, 34,400
4. Prudential Securities Inc., 16,967
5. PaineWebber Group, 16,627
6. A. G. Edwards, Inc., 12,810
7. The Charles Schwab Corp., 12,700
8. Credit Suisse First Boston, 12,000
9. Edward Jones, 11,000
10. The Goldman Sachs Group, 10,899

Source: *Securities Industry Yearbook*, (annual), Securities Industry Association, 1998, p. 46+.

★829★

SECURITIES INDUSTRY ASSOCIATION BROKERAGE FIRMS WITH THE MOST INSTITUTIONAL REGISTERED REPRESENTATIVES, 1998

Ranked by: Number of institutional registered representatives. **Number listed:** 50

1. Morgan Stanley Dean Witter & Co., with 2,000 representatives
2. Chase Securities, Inc., 1,230
3. J. P. Morgan Securities, 1,007
4. Salomon Smith Barney Holdings, 878
5. Merrill Lynch & Co., 852
6. Citicorp Securities Inc., 704
7. SBC Warburg Dillon Read, Inc., 677
8. The Goldman Sachs Group, 650
9. Deutsche Bank Securities, Inc., 614
10. ING Baring Furman Selz LLC, 500

Source: *Securities Industry Yearbook*, (annual), Securities Industry Association, 1998, p. 49.

★830★

SECURITIES INDUSTRY ASSOCIATION BROKERAGE FIRMS WITH THE MOST OFFICES, 1998

Ranked by: Number of offices. **Number listed:** 50

1. Edward Jones, with 3,840 offices
2. First Chicago NBD Investment Services, Inc., 612
3. A. G. Edwards, Inc., 592
4. Merrill Lynch & Co., 565
5. Salomon Smith Barney Holdings, 483
6. Morgan Stanley Dean Witter & Co., 448
7. Citicorp Investment Services, 380
8. Prudential Securities Inc., 294
9. PaineWebber Group, 289
10. The Charles Schwab Corp., 272

Source: *Securities Industry Yearbook*, (annual), Securities Industry Association, 1998, p. 44+.

★831★

SECURITIES INDUSTRY ASSOCIATION BROKERAGE FIRMS WITH THE MOST REGISTERED REPRESENTATIVES, 1998

Ranked by: Number of registered representatives. **Number listed:** 50

1. Merrill Lynch & Co., with 15,327 representatives
2. Morgan Stanley Dean Witter & Co., 12,000
3. Salomon Smith Barney Holdings, 11,197
4. Prudential Securities Inc., 6,702
5. PaineWebber Group, 6,320
6. A. G. Edwards, Inc., 6,241
7. Fidelity Brokerage, 5,177
8. The Charles Schwab Corp., 4,944
9. Edward Jones, 3,954
10. NationsBanc Montgomery Securities LLC, 1,720

Source: *Securities Industry Yearbook*, (annual), Securities Industry Association, 1998, p. 47.

★832★

SECURITIES INDUSTRY ASSOCIATION BROKERAGE FIRMS WITH THE MOST RETAIL REGISTERED REPRESENTATIVES, 1998

Ranked by: Number of retail registered representatives. **Number listed:** 50

1. Merrill Lynch & Co., with 14,475 representatives
2. Salomon Smith Barney Holdings, 1,319

3. Morgan Stanley Dean Witter & Co., 10,000
4. Prudential Securities Inc., 6,473
5. PaineWebber Group, 6,249
6. A. G. Edwards, Inc., 6,169
7. The Charles Schwab Corp., 4,915
8. Fidelity Brokerage, 4,702
9. Edward Jones, 3,954
10. American Express Financial Advisors, 1,503

Source: *Securities Industry Yearbook*, (annual), Securities Industry Association, 1998, p. 48.

★833★
TOP BROKER-DEALER INSURERS BY PERCENT CHANGE IN REVENUE, 1999*
Ranked by: Change in revenue, in percent. **Number listed:** 10

1. John Hancock Distributors, with 60.2%
2. Washington Square Securities, 42.3%
3. MONY Securities, 28.1%
4. NYLIFE Securities Inc., 26.9%
5. Intersecurities, 21.6%
6. Transamerica Financial, 20.3%
7. New England Securities, 19%
8. Lutheran Brotherhood Securities, 18.1%
9. 1717 Capital Management, 17.8%
10. MML Investors Services, 16.7%

Source: *Financial Planning*, Annual Broker Dealer Survey, June, 1999, p. 184.

★834★
TOP BROKER-DEALER INSURERS BY TOTAL REVENUE, 1999*
Ranked by: Total revenue, in millions of U.S. dollars. **Number listed:** 10

1. MML Investors Services, with $216,907,996 million
2. NYLIFE Securities Inc., $197,289,516
3. John Hancock Distributors, $179,693,912
4. Intersecurities, $118,708,001
5. Lutheran Brotherhood Securities, $81,708,001
6. Washington Square Securities, $78,717,000
7. New England Securities, $68,834,000
8. 1717 Capital Management, $59,532,478
9. MONY Securities, $41,911,755
10. Transamerica Financial, $31,465,000

Source: *Financial Planning*, Annual Broker Dealer Survey, June, 1999, p. 158.

★835★
TOP BROKERAGE FIRMS BY REVENUE, 1998
Ranked by: Revenue, in millions of dollars. **Remarks:** Also notes profits, profits as a percentage of revenue, assets and stockholders' equity, earnings per share, total return to investors, and number of employees. **Number listed:** 7

1. Merrill Lynch, with $35,853 million
2. Morgan Stanley Dean Witter, $31,131
3. Lehman Brothers Holdings, $19,894
4. Bear Stearns, $7,980
5. PaineWebber Group, $7,250
6. Charles Schwab, $3,388
7. A. G. Edwards, $2,004

Source: *Fortune*, Fortune 500 Largest U.S. Corporations (annual), April 26, 1999, p. F-68.

★836★
TOP FULL-SERVICE BROKERAGES, 1998
Ranked by: Overall ranking. **Remarks:** Ranked in stock research, range of services, breadth of products, commissions and fees, mutual funds, account information and 'staying out of trouble.' The overall ranking double-weights stock research, range of services and breadth of products. **Number listed:** 8

1. A. G. Edwards
2. Merrill Lynch
3. PaineWebber
4. Salomon Smith Barney
5. Everen Securities
6. Prudential
7. Moran Stanley Dean Witter
8. Edwards Jones

Source: *SmartMoney*, December, 1998, p. 125.

★837★
TOP GENERAL SECURITIES INSURERS, 1999*
Ranked by: Total general securities revenue, in U.S. dollars. **Remarks:** Also notes percentage change in revenue, revenue per representative, payout per representative, total number of trades, total volume of trades, and percentage from equities and bonds. **Number listed:** 10

1. MML Investors Services, with $4,325,839
2. New England Securities, $3,751,000
3. MONY Securities, $2,712,698
4. Intersecurities, $1,707,634
5. NYLIFE Securities Inc., $1,289,900
6. Washington Square Securities, $1,177,000
7. John Hancock Distributors, $816,125
8. Transamerica Financial, $730,000
9. 1717 Capital Management, $681,216
10. Lutheran Brotherhood Securities, $290,875

Source: *Financial Planning*, Annual Broker Dealer Survey, June, 1999, p. 164.

★838★
TOP INSURERS BY PAYOUT PER REPRESENTATIVE, 1999*
Ranked by: Payout per representative, in U.S. dollars. **Remarks:** Also notes total payout, percentage payout and representatives-generated revenue per representative. **Number listed:** 10

1. Intersecurities, with $66,641
2. Lutheran Brotherhood Securities, $44,286
3. John Hancock Distributors, $41,166
4. MML Investors Services, $37,861
5. Transamerica Financial, $34,988
6. 1717 Capital Management, $33,901
7. Washington Square Securities, $31,331
8. NYLIFE Securities Inc., $24,542
9. MONY Securities, $16,624
10. New England Securities, $14,098

Source: *Financial Planning*, Annual Broker Dealer Survey, June, 1999, p. 182.

★839★
TOP INSURERS BY SERVICES PROVIDED, 1999*
Ranked by: Items are listed, not ranked. **Remarks:** Respondents answered eight questions regarding offering no-load mutual funds, charging a percentage on assets, charging a ticket, paying raep's education cos, approval of financial plans, offering real-time quotes, wire transferring mutual fund orders, and networking. **Number listed:** 10

1. 1717 Capital Management
2. Intersecurities
3. John Hancock Distributors
4. Lutheran Brotherhood Securities
5. MML Investors Services
6. MONY Securities
7. New England Securities
8. NYLIFE Securities Inc.
9. Transamerica Financial
10. Washington Square Securities

Source: *Financial Planning*, Annual Broker Dealer Survey, June, 1999, p. 160.

★840★
TOP LARGE-SIZED BROKER-DEALERS BY PAYOUT PER REPRESENTATIVE, 1999*
Ranked by: Payout per representative, in U.S. dollars. **Remarks:** Large-sized is defined as having more than 300 representatives. Also notes total payout, percentage payout and representatives-generated revenue per representative. **Number listed:** 30

1. Commonwealth Financial Network, with $142,332
2. LPL Financial Services, $131,086
3. Raymond James Financial Services, $126,013
4. First Allied Securities, Inc., $114,098
5. Mutual Service Corp., $108,505
6. IFG Network Securities, $101,881
7. Securities America, $100,002
8. Nathan & Lewis Securities, $97,677
9. Investacorp, $94,231
10. Royal Alliance Associates, $88,779

Source: *Financial Planning*, Annual Broker Dealer Survey, June, 1999, p. 182.

★841★
TOP LARGE-SIZED BROKER-DEALERS BY PERCENT CHANGE IN REVENUE, 1999*
Ranked by: Chang in revenue, in percent. **Remarks:** Large-sized is defined as having more than 300 representatives. Also notes net change in revenues. **Number listed:** 30

1. SII Investments, with 70.1%
2. VESTAX Securities, 65.8%
3. Investors Capital, 63.7%
4. Locust Street Securities, 53.4%
5. Sentra Securities, 40.6%
6. First Allied Securities, 36.8%
7. LPL Financial Services, 35.8%
8. Mutual Service Corp., 34.9%
9. Securities America, 33%
10. Commonwealth Financial Network, 31.2%

Source: *Financial Planning*, Annual Broker Dealer Survey, June, 1999, p. 184.

★842★
TOP LARGE-SIZED BROKER-DEALERS BY SERVICES PROVIDED, 1999*
Ranked by: Items are listed, not ranked. **Remarks:** Large-sized is defined as having more than 300 representatives. Respondents answered eight questions regarding offering no-load mutual funds, charging a percentage on assets, charging a ticket, paying reps' education costs, approval of financial plans, offering real-time quotes, wire transferring mutual fund orders, and networking. **Number listed:** 30

1. Advantage Capital
2. Cadaret, Grant & Co.
3. Capital Analysts
4. Carillon Investments
5. Commonwealth Financial Network
6. Corporate Securities Group
7. FFP Securities
8. Financial Service Corp.
9. First Allied Securities
10. First Montauk Securities

Source: *Financial Planning*, Annual Broker Dealer Survey, June, 1999, p. 160.

★843★
TOP LARGE-SIZED BROKER-DEALERS BY TOTAL REVENUE, 1999*
Ranked by: Total revenue, in U.S. dollars. **Remarks:** Large-sized is defined as having more than 300 representatives. Also notes breakdown of types by revenue and percentage. **Number listed:** 30

1. LPL Financial Services, with $480,375,539
2. Raymond James Financial Services, $450,126,689
3. Royal Alliance Associates, $355,769,000
4. Mutual Service Corp., $204,542,891
5. FNIC, $193,212,000
6. Financial Service Corp., $190,290,000
7. SunAmerica Securities, $174,253,000
8. Securities America, $140,432,862
9. Nathan & Lewis Securities, $104,384,600
10. Commonwealth Financial Network, $102,350,684

Source: *Financial Planning*, Annual Broker Dealer Survey, June, 1999, p. 158.

★844★
TOP LARGE-SIZED LIMITED PARTNERSHIP BROKER-DEALERS, 1999*
Ranked by: Total limited partnership revenue, in millions of U.S. dollars. **Remarks:** Large-sized is defined as having more than 300 representatives. Also notes total sales, percentage change in revenue and sales, revenue per representative, and payout per representative. **Number listed:** 30

1. LPL Financial Services, with $8,081,413 million
2. IFG Network Securities, $4,924,000
3. Commonwealth Financial Group, $3,948,380
4. Financial Service Corp., $3,434,000
5. SunAmerica Securities, $3,156,000
6. Royal Alliance Associates, $2,892,000
7. FFP Securities, $2,225,137
8. Mutual Service Corp., $1,999,132
9. SII Investments, $1,432,504
10. Cadaret, Grant & Co., $1,194,964

Source: *Financial Planning*, Annual Broker Dealer Survey, June, 1999, p. 178.

★845★
TOP LARGE-SIZED MANAGED ASSETS BROKER-DEALERS, 1999*
Ranked by: Managed Assets revenue, in millions of U.S. dollars. **Remarks:** Large-sized is defined as having more than 300 representatives. Also notes percentage change in revenue and in asset base, revenue per representative, discretionary and proprietary assets, assets managed by a third party and total advisory asset base. **Number listed:** 30

1. Raymond James Financial Services, with $101,090,971 million
2. LPL Financial Services, $96,098,100
3. Royal Alliance Associates, $51,388,000
4. Financial Service Corp., $19,507,000
5. FNIC, $13,805,000
6. Commonwealth Financial Network, $12,853,015
7. FFP Securities, $11,684,877
8. Mutual Service Corp., $11,0161,455
9. SunAmerica Securities, $10,933,000
10. Securities America, $9,232,304

Source: *Financial Planning*, Annual Broker Dealer Survey, June, 1999, p. 174.

★846★
TOP LARGE-SIZED MUTUAL FUNDS BROKER-DEALERS, 1999*
Ranked by: Total mutual funds revenue, in millions of U.S. dollars. **Remarks:** Large-sized is defined as having more than 300 representatives. Also notes total sales, percentage change in revenue and sales, revenue per representative, and payout per representative. **Number listed:** 30

1. Royal Alliance Associates, with $159,019,000 million
2. LPL Financial Services, $153,161,677
3. Raymond James Financial Services, $117,850,071
4. FNIC, $100,029,000

5. SunAmerica Securities, $75,024,000
6. Financial Service Corp., $74,737,000
7. Mutual Service Corp., $58,207,224
8. Securities America, $51,085,629
9. Commonwealth Financial Network, $47,836,884
10. Nathan & Lewis Securities, $44,015,000

Source: *Financial Planning*, Annual Broker Dealer Survey, June, 1999, p. 162.

★847★
TOP LARGE-SIZED TRADITIONAL INSURANCE BROKER-DEALERS, 1999*
Ranked by: Traditional insurance revenue, in U.S. dollars. **Remarks:** Large-sized is defined as having more than 300 representatives. Also notes first-year premiums, percent change in revenue and first year premiums, revenue per representative, and payout per representative. **Number listed:** 30

1. Financial Service Corp., with $4,352,000
2. LPL Financial Services, $3,860,562
3. Nathan & Lewis Securities, $3,741,000
4. FNIC, $2,066,000
5. Raymond James Financial Services, $1,725,169
6. First Allied Securities, $1,657,500
7. Advantage Capital, $1,615,000
8. Securities America, $1,125,000
9. SunAmerica Securities, $1,021,000
10. Multi-Financial Securities, $970,000

Source: *Financial Planning*, Annual Broker Dealer Survey, June, 1999, p. 172.

★848★
TOP LARGE-SIZED VARIABLE ANNUITIES BROKER-DEALERS, 1999*
Ranked by: Variable annuities revenue, in U.S. dollars. **Remarks:** Large-sized is defined as having more than 300 representatives. Also notes total revenue and sales, percentage change in revenue and sales, revenue per representative, and payout per representative. **Number listed:** 30

1. LPL Financial Services, with $97,908,708
2. Royal Alliance Associates, $78,928,000
3. SunAmerica Securities, $54,838,000
4. Raymond James Financial Services, $53,472,339
5. FNIC, $48,190,000
6. Financial Service Corp., $44,780,000
7. Securities America, $34,219,660
8. Mutual Service Corp., $33,071,364
9. Locust Street Securities, $26,488,782
10. FFP Securities, $22,157,607

Source: *Financial Planning*, Annual Broker Dealer Survey, June, 1999, p. 166.

★849★
TOP LIMITED PARTNERSHIP INSURERS, 1999*
Ranked by: Total limited partnership revenue, in millions of U.S. dollars. **Remarks:** Also notes total sales, percentage change in revenue and sales, revenue per representative, and payout per representative. **Number listed:** 7

1. MML Investors Services, with $1,018,739 million
2. Intersecurities, $910,000
3. Washington Square Securities, $498,000
4. MONY Securities, $157,552
5. New England Securities, $122,000
6. John Hancock Distributors, $101,167
7. Transamerica Financial, $60,000

Source: *Financial Planning*, Annual Broker Dealer Survey, June, 1999, p. 178.

★850★
TOP MANAGED ASSETS INSURERS, 1999*
Ranked by: Managed assets revenue, in U.S. dollars. **Remarks:** Also notes percentage change in revenue and in asset base, revenue per representative, assets managed by a third party and total advisory asset base. **Number listed:** 9

1. New England Securities, with $4,001,000
2. 1717 Capital Management, $3,502,752
3. Intersecurities, $3,016,000
4. Washington Square Securities, $1,419,000
5. MONY Securities, $947,667
6. MML Investors Services, $703,453
7. Transamerica Financial, $426,000
8. NYLIFE Securities Inc., $190,995
9. Lutheran Brotherhood Securities, $4,011

Source: *Financial Planning*, Annual Broker Dealer Survey, June, 1999, p. 174.

★851★
TOP MEDIUM-SIZED BROKER-DEALERS BY PAYOUT PER REPRESENTATIVE, 1999*
Ranked by: Payout per representative, in U.S. dollars. **Remarks:** Medium-sized is defined as having 300 or fewer representatives. Also notes total payout, percentage payout and representatives-generated revenue per representative. **Number listed:** 12

1. D. E. Frey & Co., with $257,730
2. Associated Securities, $207,257
3. Spelman & Co., $139,351
4. Cambridge Investment Research, $89,907
5. Lincoln Investment Planning, $85,351
6. VSR Financial Services, $79,406
7. H. Beck/Capital Financial, $69,843
8. Northeast Securities, $55,274
9. The Investment Center, $54,724
10. Polaris Financial Services, $44,358

Source: *Financial Planning*, Annual Broker Dealer Survey, June, 1999, p. 182.

★852★
TOP MEDIUM-SIZED BROKER-DEALERS BY PERCENT CHANGE IN REVENUE, 1999*
Ranked by: Change in revenue, in percent. **Remarks:** Medium-sized is defined as having 300 or fewer representatives. **Number listed:** 14

1. Cambridge Investment Research, with 77.1%
2. Sky Investments, 56.9%
3. AUL Equity Sales Corp., 49%
4. Brecek & Young Advisors, 48.5%
5. H. Beck/Capital Financial, 26.2%
6. VSR Financial Services, 19%
7. Polaris Financial Services, 18.3%
8. The Investment Center, 15.2%
9. Associated Securities, 14.4%
10. Northeast Securities, 7.6%

Source: *Financial Planning*, Annual Broker Dealer Survey, June, 1999, p. 184.

★853★
TOP MEDIUM-SIZED BROKER-DEALERS BY SERVICES PROVIDED, 1999*
Ranked by: Items are listed, not ranked. **Remarks:** Medium-sized is defined as having 300 or fewer representatives. Respondents answered eight questions regarding offering no-load mutual funds, charging a percentage on assets, charging a ticket, paying reps' educational costs, approval of financial plans, offering real-time quotes, wite transferring mutual fund orders, and networking. **Number listed:** 14

1. Associated Securities
2. AUL Equity Sales Corp.

3. Brecek & Young Advisors
4. Cambridge Investment Research
5. D. E. Frey & Co.
6. H. Beck/Capital Financial
7. Lincoln Investment Planning
8. Northeast Securities
9. Polaris Financial Services
10. Sky Investments

Source: *Financial Planning*, Annual Broker Dealer Survey, June, 1999, p. 160.

★854★
TOP MEDIUM-SIZED BROKER-DEALERS BY TOTAL REVENUE, 1999*

Ranked by: Total revenue, in millions of U.S. dollars. **Remarks:** Medium-sized is defined as having 300 or fewer representatives. Also notes breakdown of types by revenue and percentage. **Number listed:** 14

1. Associated Securities, with $49,698,671 million
2. Lincoln Investment Planning, $43,571,840
3. D. E. Frey & Co., $36,984,822
4. H. Beck/Capital Financial, $23,877,199
5. Spelman & Co., $22,957,758
6. The Investment Center, $18,063,000
7. Northeast Securities, $17,531,085
8. VSR Financial Services, $17,083,804
9. Polaris Financial Services, $15,784,757
10. Cambridge Investment Research, $14,700,000

Source: *Financial Planning*, Annual Broker Dealer Survey, June, 1999, p. 158.

★855★
TOP MEDIUM-SIZED GENERAL SECURITIES BROKER-DEALERS, 1999*

Ranked by: Total general securities revenue, in U.S. dollars. **Remarks:** Medium-sized is defined as having 300 or fewer representatives. Also notes percentage change in revenue, revenue per representative, payout per representative, total number of trades, total volume of trades, and percentage from equities and bonds. **Number listed:** 14

1. D. E. Frey & Co., with $16,057,128
2. Northeast Securities, $10,680,288
3. Spelman & Co., $7,067,514
4. The Investment Center, $6,225,671
5. VSR Financial Services, $3,722,056
6. Associated Securities, $3,252,433
7. Sky Investments, $2,346,345
8. H. Beck/Capital Financial, $1,695,118
9. Lincoln Investment Planning, $1,004,355
10. Polaris Financial Services, $833,428

Source: *Financial Planning*, Annual Broker Dealer Survey, June, 1999, p. 164.

★856★
TOP MEDIUM-SIZED LIMITED PARTNERSHIP BROKER-DEALERS, 1999*

Ranked by: Total limited partnership revenue, in millions of U.S. dollars. **Remarks:** Medium-sized is defined as having 300 or fewer representative. Also notes total sales, percentage change in revenue and sales, revenue per representative, and payout per representative. **Number listed:** 8

1. H. Beck/Capital Financial, with $6,573,309 million
2. VSR Financial Services, $3,218,214
3. Associated Securities, $1,162,311
4. Spelman & Co., $447,465
5. Cambridge Investment Research, $382,000
6. D.E. Frey & Co., $16,400
7. Polaris Financial Services, $4,800
8. Northeast Securities, $4,595

Source: *Financial Planning*, Annual Broker Dealer Survey, June, 1999, p. 178.

★857★
TOP MEDIUM-SIZED MANAGED ASSETS BROKER-DEALERS, 1999*

Ranked by: Managed asset revenue, in millions of U.S. dollars. **Remarks:** Medium-sized is defined as having 300 or fewer representatives. Also notes percentage change in revenue and in asset base, revenue per representative, discretionary and proprietary assets, assets managed by a third party and total advisory asset base. **Number listed:** 10

1. Lincoln Investment Planning, with $15,586,012 million
2. Associated Securities, $5,171,450
3. Cambridge Investment Research, $4,410,000
4. D. E. Frey & Co., $4,356,570
5. Spelman & Co., $2,090,000
6. The Investment Center, $851,169
7. H. Beck/Capital Financial, $795,571
8. VSR Financial Services, $756,000
9. Polaris Financial Services, $735,253
10. Brecek & Young Advisors, $529,341

Source: *Financial Planning*, Annual Broker Dealer Survey, June, 1999, p. 174.

★858★
TOP MEDIUM-SIZED MUTUAL FUNDS BROKER-DEALERS, 1999*

Ranked by: Total mutual funds revenue, in millions of U.S. dollars. **Remarks:** Medium-sized is defined as having 300 or fewer representatives. Also notes total sales, percentage change in revenue and sales, revenue per representative, and payout per representative. **Number listed:** 14

1. Lincoln Investment Planning, with $20,390,680 million
2. Associated Securities, $19,999,360
3. H. Beck/Capital Financial, $8,548,461
4. D. E. Frey & Co., $7,706,780
5. The Investment Center, $6,705,164
6. Polaris Financial Services, $6,103,090
7. Spelman & Co., $5,882,391
8. Cambridge Investment Research, $5,466,000
9. VSR Financial Services, $5,229,458
10. Northeast Securities, $3,343,262

Source: *Financial Planning*, Annual Broker Dealer Survey, June, 1999, p. 162.

★859★
TOP MEDIUM-SIZED TRADITIONAL INSURANCE BROKER-DEALERS, 1999*

Ranked by: Traditional insurance revenue, in U.S. dollars. **Remarks:** Medium-sized is defined as having 300 or fewer representatives. Also notes first-year premiums, percent change in revenue and first year premiums, revenue per representative, and payout per representative. **Number listed:** 9

1. Associated Securities, with $3,060,366
2. Polaris Financial Services, $2,005,623
3. Brecek & Young Advisors, $585,540
4. Lincoln Investment Planning, $367,700
5. Sky Investments, $232,012
6. Cambridge Investment Research, $98,000
7. The Investment Center, $89,475
8. VSR Financial Services, $86,336
9. Spelman & Co., $7,360

Source: *Financial Planning*, Annual Broker Dealer Survey, June, 1999, p. 172.

★860★
TOP MEDIUM-SIZED VARIABLE ANNUITIES BROKER-DEALERS, 1999*
Ranked by: Variable annuities revenue, in millions of U.S. dollars. **Remarks:** Medium-sized is defined as having 300 or fewer representatives. Also notes total revenue and sales, percentage change in revenue and sales, revenue per representative, and payout per representative. **Number listed:** 12
1. Associated Securities, with $9,811,784 million
2. H. Beck/Capital Financial, $4,750,794
3. D. E. Frey & Co., $4,423,981
4. Polaris Financial Services, $3,773,220
5. Brecek & Young Advisors, $3,596,442
6. Sky Investments, $3,498,906
7. Spelman & Co., $3,023,811
8. Cambridge Investment Research, $2,650,000
9. VSR Financial Services, $2,592,759
10. Lincoln Investment Planning, $2,410,093

Source: *Financial Planning*, Annual Broker Dealer Survey, June, 1999, p. 166.

★861★
TOP MEDIUM-SIZED VARIABLE LIFE BROKER-DEALERS, 1999*
Ranked by: Total variable life revenue, in U.S. dollars. **Remarks:** Medium-sized is defined as having 300 or fewer representatives. Also notes percent change in revenues, first-year premiums, change in first-year premiums, revenues per representative and payout per representative. **Number listed:** 10
1. Associated Securities, with $1,886,392
2. H. Beck/Capital Financial, $1,270,238
3. Polaris Financial Services, $1,037,240
4. VSR Financial Services, $774,461
5. The Investment Center, $714,380
6. Brecek & Young Advisors, $487,520
7. Cambridge Investment Research, $411,000
8. Lincoln Investment Planning, $289,515
9. Sky Investments, $281,248
10. Spelman & Co., $204,619

Source: *Financial Planning*, Annual Broker Dealer Survey, June, 1999, p. 168.

★862★
TOP MUTUAL FUND INSURERS, 1999*
Ranked by: Total mutual funds revenue, in millions of U.S. dollars. **Remarks:** Also notes total sales, percentage change in revenue and sales, revenue per representative, and payout per representative. **Number listed:** 10
1. MML Investors Services, with $82,967,698 million
2. NYLIFE Securities Inc., $70,487,397
3. John Hancock Distributors, $54,803,752
4. New England Securities, $53,426,000
5. Washington Square Securities, $336,529,000
6. MONY Securities, $32,481,131
7. Intersecurities, $30,890,573
8. 1717 Capital Management, $19,084,191
9. Transamerica Financial, $13,620,000
10. Lutheran Brotherhood Securities, $10,966,247

Source: *Financial Planning*, Annual Broker Dealer Survey, June, 1999, p. 162.

★863★
TOP SECURITIES INDUSTRIES ASSOCIATION BROKERS HEADQUARTERED OUTSIDE NEW YORK BY CAPITAL POSITION, 1998
Ranked by: Capital position, in thousands of dollars. **Remarks:** Capital position is defined as the sum of ownership equity and subordinated debt. **Number listed:** 402
1. NationsBanc Montgomery Securities LLC, with $1,838,530 thousand
2. The Charles Schwab Corp., $1,506,166
3. A. G. Edwards, Inc., $1,414,148
4. SBC Warburg Dillon Read, Inc., $1,412,211
5. Fidelity Brokerage, $683,075
6. Zions First National Bank, $575,861
7. Legg Mason Inc., $574,217
8. Edward Jones, $491,449
9. Raymond James Financial Inc., $444,893
10. ABN AMRO Inc., $415,709

Source: *Securities Industry Yearbook*, (annual), Securities Industry Association, 1998, p. 28+.

★864★
TOP SECURITIES INDUSTRIES ASSOCIATION FIRMS BY CAPITAL POSITION, 1998
Ranked by: Capital position, in thousands of dollars. **Remarks:** Capital position is defined as the sum of ownership equity and subordinated debt. **Number listed:** 430
1. Merrill Lynch & Co., with $51,419,000 thousand
2. Morgan Stanley Dean Witter & Co., $39,747,000
3. Salomon Smith Barney Holdings, $27,592,000
4. Lehman Brothers Holdings Inc., $24,784,000
5. The Goldman Sachs Group, $21,774,000
6. The Bear Stearns Cos., Inc., $14,789,047
7. PaineWebber Group, $5,911,342
8. Donaldson, Lufkin & Jenrette, Inc., $4,513,347
9. Credit Suisse First Boston, $3,736,126
10. BT Alex. Brown, $2,360,000

Source: *Securities Industry Yearbook*, (annual), Securities Industry Association, 1998, p. 6+.

★865★
TOP VARIABLE ANNUITIES INSURERS, 1999*
Ranked by: Variable annuities revenue, in millions U.S. dollars. **Remarks:** Also notes total revenue and sales, percentage change in revenue and sales, revenue per representative, and payout per representative. **Number listed:** 9
1. John Hancock Distributors, with $123,063,409 million
2. NYLIFE Securities Inc., $75,096,390
3. Intersecurities, $40,199,779
4. Washington Square Securities, $36,582,000
5. Lutheran Brotherhood Securities, $36,468,833
6. MML Investors Services, $34,158,143
7. Transamerica Financial, $11,500,000
8. 1717 Capital Management, $6,219,615
9. MONY Securities, $4,257,436

Source: *Financial Planning*, Annual Broker Dealer Survey, June, 1999, p. 166.

★866★
TOP VARIABLE LIFE INSURERS, 1999*
Ranked by: Total variable life revenue, in U.S. dollars. **Remarks:** Also notes percent change in revenues, first-year premiums, change in first-year premiums, revenues per representative and payout per representative. **Number listed:** 8
1. MML Investors Services, with $79,429,771
2. NYLIFE Securities Inc., $42,349,387
3. 1717 Capital Management, $27,341,773
4. Intersecurities, $17,632,000
5. Lutheran Brotherhood Securities, $11,648,026
6. Transamerica Financial, $3,300,000
7. Washington Square Securities, $993,000
8. MONY Securities, $847,888

Source: *Financial Planning*, Annual Broker Dealer Survey, June, 1999, p. 168.

Brokers--Asia

★867★
ASIA'S BEST BROKERS BY ASSETS UNDER MANAGEMENT, 1998
Ranked by: Points, based on votes cast by over 100 international institutional investors active in the Asian equity markets from five continents. **Remarks:** Also notes previous year's rank. **Number listed:** 10

1. Jardine Fleming, with 1,691.27 points
2. CLSA, 1,447.99
3. Warburg Dillon Read, 1,335.79
4. Merrill Lynch, 1,176,76
5. ING Barings, 851.35
6. HSBC Securities, 797.72
7. ABN Amro, 692.57
8. Credit Suisse First Boston, 392.54
9. Indosuez WI Carr, 337.65
10. Goldman Sachs, 275.05

Source: *Asiamoney*, Asiamoney's Stockbrokers' Poll (annual), October, 1998, p. 22.

★868★
ASIA'S BEST BROKERS FOR REGIONAL ECONOMISTS, 1998
Ranked by: Points, based on votes cast by over 100 international institutional investors active in the Asian equity markets from five continents. Also notes previous year's rank. **Number listed:** 5

1. Jim Walker, CLSA, with 128 points
2. Sigmon Ogus, Warburg Dillon Read, 76
3. Michael Taylor, Indosuez WI Carr, 33
4. Angus Armstrong, Deutsche Securities, 12
5. Manu Bhaskaran, SG Securities

Source: *Asiamoney*, Asiamoney's Stockbrokers' Poll (annual), October, 1998, p. 20.

★869★
ASIA'S BEST BROKERS FOR REGIONAL SECTORAL RESEARCH, 1998
Ranked by: Points, based on votes cast by over 100 international institutional investors active in the Asian equity markets from five continents. **Number listed:** 20

1. Goldman Sachs, with 155 points
2. Jardine Fleming, 108
3. Merrill Lynch, 107
4. Morgan Stanley Dean Witter, 95
5. Deutsche Securities, 71
6. HSBC Securities, 59
7. Salomon Smith Barney, 58
8. Warburg Dillon Read, 53
9. CLSA, 47
10. ABN Amro, 29

Source: *Asiamoney*, Asiamoney's Stockbrokers' Poll (annual), October, 1998, p. 20.

★870★
ASIA'S BEST BROKERS FOR REGIONAL STRATEGISTS, 1998
Ranked by: Points, based on votes cast by over 100 international institutional investors active in the Asian equity markets from five continents. Also notes previous year's rank. **Number listed:** 5

1. Russel Napier, CLSA, with 101 points
2. David Scott, Indosuez WI Carr, 69
3. Paul Shulte, ING Barings, 27
4. Jim Walker, CLSA, 15
5. Andrew Houston, Jardine Fleming, 13

Source: *Asiamoney*, Asiamoney's Stockbrokers' Poll (annual), October, 1998, p. 20.

★871★
ASIA'S BEST BROKERS IN SECTORAL RESEARCH, 1998
Ranked by: Points, based on votes cast by over 100 international institutional investors active in the Asian equity markets from five continents. **Remarks:** Also notes previous year's rank. **Number listed:** 20

1. Jardine Fleming, with 2,358.55 points
2. CLSA, 2,175.88
3. Warburg Dillon Read, 1,506.6
4. Merrill Lynch, 1,500.65
5. ING Barings, 1,271.8
6. ABN Amro, 1,188.43
7. HSBC Securities, 950.25
8. Indosuez WI Carr, 696.17
9. SG Securities, 529.88
10. Goldman Sachs, 580.27

Source: *Asiamoney*, Asiamoney's Stockbrokers' Poll (annual), October, 1998, p. 19.

★872★
ASIA'S BEST BROKERS, 1998
Ranked by: Points, based on votes cast by over 100 international institutional investors active in the Asian equity markets from five continents. **Remarks:** Also notes previous year's rank. **Number listed:** 20

1. Jardine Fleming, with 2,250.55 points
2. CLSA, 2,128.88
3. Warburg Dillon Read, 1,453.6
4. Merrill Lynch, 1,393.65
5. ING Barings, 1,255.8
6. ABN Amro, 1,549.43
7. HSBC Securities, 891.25
8. Indosuez WI Carr, 685.17
9. SG Securities, 518.88
10. Goldman Sachs, 425.27

Source: *Asiamoney*, Asiamoney's Stockbrokers' Poll (annual), October, 1998, p. 19.

★873★
ASIA'S TOP EQUITY SALESPEOPLE, 1998
Ranked by: Points, based on votes cast by over 100 international institutional investors active in the Asian equity markets from five continents. **Number listed:** 6

1. Garth Fox, CLSA, with 32 points
2. Scott Mackie, Indosuez WI Carr, 15
3. Anton Periquet, Deutsche Securities Asia, 14
4. Patrick Ying, Merrill Lynch, 13
4. Jain Pickett, Indosuez WI Carr, 13
4. Damien Dwerryhouse, CLSA, 13

Source: *Asiamoney*, Asiamoney's Stockbrokers' Poll (annual), October, 1998, p. 22.

Brokers--Australia

★874★
TOP AUSTRALIAN BROKERAGE FIRMS, 1998
Ranked by: Points, based on votes cast by over 100 international institutional investors active in the Asian equity markets from five continents. **Remarks:** Also notes three highest scorers in the categories of overall research, specialist research, sales, execution. Also notes previous year's rank. **Number listed:** 3

1. JB Were, with 94.3 points
2. Warburg Dillon Read, 92.49
3. Ord Minnett, 73.14

Source: *Asiamoney*, Asiamoney's Stockbrokers' Poll (annual), October, 1998, p. 25.

Brokers--China

★875★

TOP CHINESE BROKERAGE FIRMS, 1998

Ranked by: Points, based on votes cast by over 100 international institutional investors active in the Asian equity markets from five continents. **Remarks:** Also notes three highest scorers in the categories of overall research, specialist research, sales, execution. Also notes previous year's rank. **Number listed:** 3

1. CLSA, with 347.99 points
2. Jardine Fleming, 129.26
3. ABN AMRO Asia, 117.1

Source: *Asiamoney*, Asiamoney's Stockbrokers' Poll (annual), October, 1998, p. 25.

Brokers--Hong Kong

★876★

TOP HONG KONG BROKERAGE FIRMS, 1998

Ranked by: Points, based on votes cast by over 100 international institutional investors active in the Asian equity markets from five continents. **Remarks:** Also notes three highest scorers in the categories of overall research, specialist research, sales, execution. Also notes previous year's rank. **Number listed:** 3

1. CLSA, with 400.86 points
2. Jardine Fleming, 288.88
3. Warburg Dillon Read, 206.08

Source: *Asiamoney*, Asiamoney's Stockbrokers' Poll (annual), October, 1998, p. 25.

Brokers--India

★877★

TOP INDIAN KONG BROKERAGE FIRMS, 1998

Ranked by: Points, based on votes cast by over 100 international institutional investors active in the Asian equity markets from five continents. **Remarks:** Also notes three highest scorers in the categories of overall research, specialist research, sales, execution. Also notes previous year's rank. **Number listed:** 3

1. CLSA, with 191.3 points
2. Jardine Fleming, 132.48
3. Warburg Dillon Read, 108.33

Source: *Asiamoney*, Asiamoney's Stockbrokers' Poll (annual), October, 1998, p. 25.

Brokers--Indonesia

★878★

TOP INDONESIAN BROKERAGE FIRMS, 1998

Ranked by: Points, based on votes cast by over 100 international institutional investors active in the Asian equity markets from five continents. **Remarks:** Also notes three highest scorers in the categories of overall research, specialist research, sales, execution. Also notes previous year's rank. **Number listed:** 3

1. Jardine Fleming, with 206.38 points
2. CLSA, 141.22
3. ING Barings, 124.79

Source: *Asiamoney*, Asiamoney's Stockbrokers' Poll (annual), October, 1998, p. 25.

Brokers, International

★879★

TOP GLOBAL BROKERAGE FIRMS BY EXECUTION COSTS, 1997

Ranked by: Basis points, difference versus Elkins/McSherry universe. **Remarks:** Encompasses firms that traded more than $355 million. Ranking based on the Elkins/McSherry Co. analysis of total trading cost, consisting of execution commissions and fees added to a calculation of trading effectiveness called ''market impact.'' Also notes number of countries firm traded in and dollar amount of principal traded. **Number listed:** 20

1. Nesbitt Burns, with 50.2 basis points
2. RBC Dominion Securities, 42.6
3. CIBC Wood Gundy, 38
4. ABN Amro, 24.3
5. J.B. Were & Son, 23.5
6. Instinet Corp., 17.6
7. ING Baring Furman Selz, 13.5
8. Schroder Wertheim, 8.8
9. Robert Fleming, 8.3
10. Jefferies & Co., 6.8

Source: *Institutional Investor*, November, 1998, p. 55.

★880★

TOP NYSE BROKERAGE FIRMS BY EXECUTION COSTS, 1997

Ranked by: Basis points, difference versus Elkins/McSherry universe. **Remarks:** Encompasses firms that traded more than $934 million. Based on the Elkins/McSherry Co. analysis of total trading cost, consisting of execution commissions and fees added to a calculation of trading effectiveness called ''market impact.'' Also notes dollar amount of principal traded. **Number listed:** 20

1. BancAmerica Roberston Stephens, with 44.3 basis points
2. A. G. Edwards & Sons, 27.6
3. Weeden & Co., 20.9
4. HSBC Securities, 19.7
5. Goldman, Sachs & Co., 18.9
6. Bear Stearns Cos., 18
7. ING Baring Furman Selz, 17.1
8. Credit Suisse First Boston, 16.7
9. Lehman Brothers, 15.4
10. Merrill Lynch & Co., 14.8

Source: *Institutional Investor*, November, 1998, p. 55.

★881★
TOP U.S. OVER THE COUNTER BROKERAGE FIRMS BY EXECUTION COSTS, 1997
Ranked by: Basis points, difference versus Elkins/McSherry universe. **Remarks:** Encompasses firms that traded more than $175 million. Based on the Elkins/McSherry Co. analysis of total trading cost, consisting of execution commissions and fees added to a calculation of trading effectiveness called ''market impact.'' Also notes dollar amount of principal traded. **Number listed:** 20

1. Instinet Corp., with 60.9 basis points
2. Levesque Beaubien Geoffrion, 59
3. Merrill Lynch & Co., 50.6
4. Lehman Brothers, 50.3
5. ING Baring Furman Selz, 50.1
6. ITG Posit, 47.9
7. A. G. Edwards & Sons, 44.6
8. CIBC Oppenheimer, 42.5
9. Goldman, Sachs & Co., 37.9
10. Credit Suisse First Boston, 36.1

Source: *Institutional Investor*, November, 1998, p. 55.

★882★
WORLD'S LARGEST BROKERAGE FIRMS BY REVENUE, 1997
Ranked by: Revenue, in millions of dollars. **Remarks:** Also notes profits and profits as a percent of revenues and assets. **Number listed:** 3

1. Merrill Lynch (U.S.), with $31,731 million
2. Morgan Stanley Dean Witter, $27,132
3. Lehman Brothers Holdings, $16,883

Source: *Fortune*, The Global 500: World's Biggest Corporations (annual), August 3, 1998, p. F-24.

Brokers--Japan

★883★
TOP JAPANESE BROKERAGE FIRMS, 1998
Ranked by: Points, based on votes cast by over 100 international institutional investors active in the Asian equity markets from five continents. **Remarks:** Also notes three highest scorers in the categories of overall research, specialist research, sales, execution. Also notes previous year's rank. **Number listed:** 3

1. Nomura, with 211.5 points
2. Jardine Fleming, 110.17
3. Morgan Stanley Dean Witter, 103.04

Source: *Asiamoney*, Asiamoney's Stockbrokers' Poll (annual), October, 1998, p. 25.

Brokers--Korea, South

★884★
TOP SOUTH KOREAN BROKERAGE FIRMS, 1998
Ranked by: Points, based on votes cast by over 100 international institutional investors active in the Asian equity markets from five continents. **Remarks:** Also notes three highest scorers in the categories of overall research, specialist research, sales, execution. Also notes previous year's rank. **Number listed:** 3

1. Warburg Dillon Read, with 211.24 points
2. ING Barings, 187.45
3. Jardine Fleming, 180.32

Source: *Asiamoney*, Asiamoney's Stockbrokers' Poll (annual), October, 1998, p. 27.

Brokers--Los Angeles County (CA)

★885★
LARGEST BROKERAGE FIRMS IN LOS ANGELES COUNTY, 1998
Ranked by: Number of full-time licensed securities brokers. **Remarks:** Also notes contact information, services, profile and top local executive. **Number listed:** 25

1. Morgan Stanley Dean Witter, with 666 brokers
2. Salomon Smith Barney, 549
3. SunAmerica Financial Network, 463
4. Merrill Lynch, 450
5. PaineWebber, 381
6. Prudential Securities Inc., 268
7. Financial Network Investment Corp., 177
8. Crowell Weedon & Co., 134
9. Jefferies Group Inc., 90
10. Everen Securities, 87

Source: *Los Angeles Business Journal*, Book of Lists (annual), January 18, 1999, p. 32.

Brokers--Malaysia

★886★
TOP MALAYSIAN BROKERAGE FIRMS, 1998
Ranked by: Points, based on votes cast by over 100 international institutional investors active in the Asian equity markets from five continents. **Remarks:** Also notes three highest scorers in the categories of overall research, specialist research, sales, execution. Also notes previous year's rank. **Number listed:** 3

1. Jardine Fleming, with 188.54 points
2. Merrill Lynch, 178.94
3. ING Barings, 180.32

Source: *Asiamoney*, Asiamoney's Stockbrokers' Poll (annual), October, 1998, p. 27.

Brokers--New Zealand

★887★
TOP NEW ZEALAND BROKERAGE FIRMS, 1998
Ranked by: Points, based on votes cast by over 100 international institutional investors active in the Asian equity markets from five continents. **Remarks:** Also notes three highest scorers in the categories of overall research, specialist research, sales, execution. Also notes previous year's rank. **Number listed:** 3

1. Warburg Dillon Read, with 57.9 points
2. Ord Minnett, 52.9
3. Merrill Lynch, 48.76

Source: *Asiamoney*, Asiamoney's Stockbrokers' Poll (annual), October, 1998, p. 27.

Brokers--Pakistan

★888★
TOP PAKISTAN BROKERAGE FIRMS, 1998
Ranked by: Points, based on votes cast by over 100 international institutional investors active in the Asian equity markets from five continents. **Remarks:** Also notes three highest scorers in the categories of overall research, specialist research, sales, execution. Also notes previous year's rank. **Number listed:** 3

1. Jardine Fleming, with 51.29 points
2. CLSA, 36.8
3. HSBC Securities, 36.34

Source: *Asiamoney*, Asiamoney's Stockbrokers' Poll (annual), October, 1998, p. 27.

Brokers--Philippines

★889★
TOP PHILIPPINE BROKERAGE FIRMS, 1998
Ranked by: Points, based on votes cast by over 100 international institutional investors active in the Asian equity markets from five continents. **Remarks:** Also notes three highest scorers in the categories of overall research, specialist research, sales, execution. Also notes previous year's rank. **Number listed:** 3

1. Jardine Fleming, with 188.54 points
2. Merrill Lynch, 178.84
3. ING Barings, 175.49

Source: *Asiamoney*, Asiamoney's Stockbrokers' Poll (annual), October, 1998, p. 27.

Brokers--Singapore

★890★
TOP SINGAPORE BROKERAGE FIRMS, 1998
Ranked by: Points, based on votes cast by over 100 international institutional investors active in the Asian equity markets from five continents. **Remarks:** Also notes three highest scorers in the categories of overall research, specialist research, sales, execution. Also notes previous year's rank. **Number listed:** 3

1. CLSA, with 279.22 points
2. Jardine Fleming, 209.01
3. Merrill Lynch, 184.46

Source: *Asiamoney*, Asiamoney's Stockbrokers' Poll (annual), October, 1998, p. 27.

Brokers--Sri Lanka

★891★
TOP SRI LANKA BROKERAGE FIRMS, 1998
Ranked by: Points, based on votes cast by over 100 international institutional investors active in the Asian equity markets from five continents. **Remarks:** Also notes three highest scorers in the categories of overall research, specialist research, sales, execution. Also notes previous year's rank. **Number listed:** 3

1. CLSA, with 272.78 points
2. Jardine Fleming, 249.99
3. ABN AMRO Asia, 139.38

Source: *Asiamoney*, Asiamoney's Stockbrokers' Poll (annual), October, 1998, p. 28.

Brokers--Taiwan

★892★
TOP TAIWAN BROKERAGE FIRMS, 1998
Ranked by: Points, based on votes cast by over 100 international institutional investors active in the Asian equity markets from five continents. **Remarks:** Also notes three highest scorers in the categories of overall research, specialist research, sales, execution. Also notes previous year's rank. **Number listed:** 3

1. ABN AMRO Asia, with 202.86 points
2. Warburg Dillon Read, 193.89
3. ING Barings, 180.78

Source: *Asiamoney*, Asiamoney's Stockbrokers' Poll (annual), October, 1998, p. 28.

Brussels Stock Exchange

See: **Bourse de Bruxelles**

Budapest Stock Exchange

★893★
LARGEST LISTED COMPANIES ON THE BUDAPEST STOCK EXCHANGE, 1997
Ranked by: Market capitalization, in billions of Hungarian forints (Ft). **Number listed:** 10

1. Matav Rt., with Ft1,124.41 billion
2. MOL, Ft487.08
3. Richter, Ft431.05
4. OTP, Ft207.82
5. Egis, Ft99.66
6. TVK, Ft82.32
7. BorsodChem, Ft75.11
8. Graboplast, Ft56.28
9. Raba Rt, Ft50.97
10. Danubius, Ft49.6

Source: *SSB Guide to World Equity Markets*, (annual), Euromoney Publications, 1998, p. 228.

Bucks County (PA)--Industries

★894★
LARGEST PRIVATE EMPLOYERS IN BUCKS COUNTY, PENNSYLVANIA, 1998
Ranked by: Number of full-time employees. **Remarks:** Also notes contact information, previous year's rank, number of part-time employees, number of offices, description of business, local CEO and total revenue. **Number listed:** 25

1. Woods Services, with 1,238 employees
2. Charming Shoppes Inc., 1,100
2. Rohm & Haas Co., 1,100
4. Union Fidelity Life Insurance Co., 934
5. U.S. Steel Fairless Works, 850
6. Saint Mary Medical Center, 815
7. Penn Engineering & Manufacturing Corp., 701
8. Ametek Inc., 700
9. Grand View Hospital, 670
10. Waste Management Inc., 614

Source: *Philadelphia Business Journal*, Book of Business Lists (annual), December 28, 1998, p. 97.

Buenos Aires Stock Exchange

★895★
LARGEST LISTED COMPANIES ON THE BUENOS AIRES STOCK EXCHANGE, 1997
Ranked by: Market value, in millions of U.S. dollars ($). **Number listed:** 10

1. YPF, with $11,896.1 million
2. Telefonica de Argentina, $8,840.7
3. Telecom Argentina, $7,087.5
4. Perez Companc, $6,010.5
5. Siderca, $2,780
6. Banco Galicia y Buenos Aires, $2,025.9
7. Banco Rio de la Plata, $2,010
8. Transportation Gas del Sur, $1,803.5
9. CEI Citicorp Holdings, $1,632.2
10. Banco Frances, $1,600.4

Source: *SSB Guide to World Equity Markets*, (annual), Euromoney Publications, 1998, p. 48.

★896★
MOST ACTIVELY TRADED SHARES THE BUENOS AIRES STOCK EXCHANGE, 1997
Ranked by: Trading value, in millions of U.S. dollars ($). **Number listed:** 10

1. Telefonica de Argentina, with $12,994.2 million
2. YPF, $8,405.2
3. Telecom Argentina, $7,087.5
4. Perez Companc, $3,225.7
5. Telecom, $2,014.1
6. Acindar, $1,121.3
7. CEI Citicorp Holdings, $873.8
8. Banco de Galicia, $866.4
9. Siderca, $814.9
10. Banco Frances, $736

Source: *SSB Guide to World Equity Markets*, (annual), Euromoney Publications, 1998, p. 48.

Building Contractors

See: **Contractors**

Building Materials Industry

★897★
MOST ADMIRED BUILDING MATERIALS AND GLASS CORPORATIONS, 1998
Ranked by: Scores (1-10) derived from a survey of senior executives, outside directors, and securities analysts. **Remarks:** Respondents rated companies in their own industry on 8 attributes of reputation. Also notes previous year's rank. **Number listed:** 6

1. Corning, with 8.24 points
2. Armstong World Industries, 6.89
3. USG, 5.66
4. Ownes-Illinois, 5.62
5. Owens Corning, 5.45
6. Johns Manville, 5.14

Source: *Fortune*, America's Most Admired Corporations (annual), March 1, 1999, p. F-4.

★898★
TOP CORPORATIONS IN THE BUILDING MATERIALS INDUSTRY, BY REVENUE, 1998
Ranked by: Revenue, in millions of dollars. **Remarks:** Also notes profits, profits as a percentage of revenue, assets and stockholders' equity, earnings per share, total return to investors, and number of employees. **Number listed:** 8

1. Owens-Illinois, with $5,450 million
2. Owens Corning, $5,009
3. Corning, $3,689
4. USG, $3,130
5. Armstrong World Industries, $2,746
6. Johns Manville, $1,781
7. Vulcan Materials, $1,776
8. Southdown, $1,185

Source: *Fortune*, Fortune 500 Largest U.S. Corporations (annual), April 26, 1999, p. F-553.

Building Materials Industry, International

★899★
WORLD'S LARGEST BUILDING MATERIALS COMPANIES BY REVENUE, 1997
Ranked by: Revenue, in millions of dollars. **Remarks:** Also notes profits, and profits as a percent of revenues and assets. **Number listed:** 2

1. Saint-Gobain (France), with $18,347 million
2. Asahi Glass (Japan), $10,971

Source: *Fortune*, The Global 500: World's Biggest Corporations (annual), August 3, 1998, p. F-17.

Bus Lines

★900★
LARGEST NORTH AMERICAN BUS TRANSIT SYSTEMS, 1998
Ranked by: Fleet size. **Remarks:** Also notes location, previous year's rank, number of each type of motorcoach and change in fleet size from previous year. **Number listed:** 100

1. MTA New York City Transit, with 4,209 buses
2. New Jersey Transit Corp., 3,097
3. Los Angeles County MTA, 2,589

4. Chicago Transit Authority, 1,882
5. Montreal Urban Community Transit Corp., 1,636
6. Toronto Transit Commission, 1,608
7. Southeastern Pennsylvania Transportation Authority, 1,361
8. Washington Metropolitan Area Transit Authority, 1,336
9. Metropolitan Transit Authority of Harris County, TX, 1,281
10. King County Metro, 1,276

Source: *Metro Magazine*, Largest 100 Transit Bus Fleets (annual), September/October, 1998, p. 46.

Business Climate

See: **Location of Industry**

Business Consultants

★901★
TOP MANAGEMENT CONSULTANTS, 1998
Ranked by: Global revenue, in millions of U.S. dollars ($). **Remarks:** Also notes fiscal year end, U.S. revenue and percent growth in both global revenue and U.S. revenue. **Number listed:** 10

1. Andersen Consulting, with $5,726 million
2. CSC, $3,000
3. Ernst & Young, $2,680
4. Coopers & Lybrand, $2,400
5. Deloitte & Touche, $2,300
6. McKinsey & Co., $2,200
7. KPMG Peat Marwick, $2.011
8. Cap Gemini, $1,648
9. Price Waterhouse, $1,400
10. Mercer Consulting Group, $1,338

Source: *Chemical Week*, August 5, 1998, p. 54.

Business Consultants--Chicago (IL)

★902★
LARGEST MANAGEMENT CONSULTANTS IN THE CHICAGO METROPOLITAN AREA, 1998
Ranked by: Number of full-time consultants. **Remarks:** Also notes contact information, top local executive, figures for previous year, revenue and specialty breakdown. **Number listed:** 25

1. Andersen Consulting, with 4,074 consultants
2. PricewaterhouseCoopers, 1,679
3. CSC Consulting Group, 1,436
4. Arthur Andersen LLP, 1,348
5. Ernst & Young LLP, 1,266
6. Interim Technology, 1,050
7. KPMG Peat Marwick LLP, 962
8. Whittman-Hart Inc., 900
9. Deloitte & Touche Consulting Group, 801
10. Interactive Business Systems Inc., 700

Source: *Crain's Chicago Business*, Top Business Lists (annual), 1999, p. 119.

Business Consultants--Long Island (NY)

★903★
LARGEST TECHNICAL CONSULTANTS IN LONG ISLAND, 1998
Ranked by: Number of local employees. **Remarks:** Also notes contact information, top executive and specialty areas. **Number listed:** 54

1. Interim Technology Staffing Solutions Group, with 200 employees
2. IMI Systems, 185
3. Custom Computer Specialists, 145
4. Integrated Systems Group, 140
5. TSR, 100
6. Interworks Systems, 85
7. Contemporary Computer Services, 60
7. Sheridan Consulting Group, 60
9. IDP Computer Services, 53
10. Computer Enterprises, 40

Source: *Long Island Business News*, LI Book of Lists (annual), 1999, p. 134.

Business Consultants--Los Angeles County (CA)

★904★
LARGEST MANAGEMENT CONSULTANTS IN LOS ANGELES COUNTY, 1997
Ranked by: Number of consultants. **Remarks:** Also notes contact information, top local executive, figures for previous year, consulting revenues, services and preferred industries. **Number listed:** 25

1. Deloitte & Touche Consulting Group LLC, with 863 consultants
2. Andersen Consulting LLP, 807
3. IBM Global Services, 800
4. M2 Inc., 750
5. PricewaterhouseCoopers LLP, 751
6. Ernst & Young, 500
7. Arthur Andersen, 340
8. KPMG Peat Marwick, 278
9. Source Consulting, 218
10. Tower Perrin, 196

Source: *Los Angeles Business Journal*, 1999, p. 56.

Business Consultants--Mexico

★905★
SPECIALIZATION AREAS OF MEXICAN CONSULTING FIRMS, 1998
Ranked by: Specialization area in percent. **Number listed:** 5

1. Planning, with 35%
2. Project Administration, 28%
3. Technology, 17%
4. Management, 12%
5. Finance, 8%

Source: *Business Mexico*, August, 1998, p. 36.

Business--Forms, Blanks, etc.

★906★
TOP BUSINESS FORMS DISTRIBUTORS BY ELECTRONIC-FORMS SALES, 1998
Ranked by: Electronic form sales, in thousands of dollars. **Remarks:** Also notes location and total sales figures. **Number listed:** 32

1. SFI, with $2,552 thousand
2. Southern Systems, $2,439
3. American Business Forms, $1,615
4. Precept, $1,579
5. FormsTronics, $1,270
6. The Graphics & Technology Group, $1,245
7. Marudas Print Service & Promotional Products, $942
8. Altec, $924
9. Print Technologies & Services, $692
10. Voluforms, $669

Source: *Business Forms, Labels & Systems*, November 20, 1998, p. 32.

★907★
TOP BUSINESS FORMS DISTRIBUTORS BY FORMS SALES, 1998
Ranked by: Form sales, in thousands of dollars. **Remarks:** Also notes location and total sales figures. **Number listed:** 32

1. American Business Forms, with $87,210 thousand
2. SFI, $70,180
3. Precept, $63,180
4. GBS, $54,961
5. Data Supplies, $42,530
6. BNB Systems, $16,254
7. Great American Business Products, $13,950
8. Data Source, $12,818
9. PSI Group, $12,100
10. Creative Printed Solutions, $11,120

Source: *Business Forms, Labels & Systems*, November 20, 1998, p. 32.

★908★
TOP BUSINESS FORMS DISTRIBUTORS BY LABEL SALES, 1998
Ranked by: Label sales, in thousands of dollars. **Remarks:** Also notes location and total sales figures. **Number listed:** 34

1. Precept, with $30,010 thousand
2. American Business Forms, $16,150
3. GBS, $15,555
4. SFI, $11,484
5. FORMost Graphic Communication, $5,946
6. Land Mark Printing, $3,887
7. Premiere Forms, $2,722
8. Merrill Corp. Resource Management Division, $2,649
9. Data Supplies, $2,617
10. Southern Systems, $2,439

Source: *Business Forms, Labels & Systems*, November 20, 1998, p. 34.

★909★
TOP BUSINESS FORMS DISTRIBUTORS BY NON-FORM SALES, 1998
Ranked by: Non-form sales, in thousands of dollars. **Remarks:** Also notes location and total sales figures. **Number listed:** 20

1. American Business Forms, with $24,225 thousand
2. SFI, $17,864
3. Data Supplies, $17,012
4. Precept, $15,795
5. BNB Systems, $9,481
6. Teutberg Business Forms, $9,329
7. Merrill Corp. Resource Management Division, $5,298
8. BC Graphics, $4,692
9. Applied Graphics, $4,674
10. Eagle Division of Forms Plus, $4,620

Source: *Business Forms, Labels & Systems*, November 20, 1998, p. 28.

★910★
TOP BUSINESS FORMS DISTRIBUTORS BY TOTAL SALES, 1998
Ranked by: Total sales, in thousands of dollars. **Remarks:** Also notes location, previous year's rank and sales, principal officer, number of employees, number of locations and year founded. **Number listed:** 200

1. American Business Forms, with $161,500 thousand
2. Precept, $157,952
3. SFI, $127,600
4. ProForma, $118,000
5. GBS Corporation, $103,700
6. Data Supplies, $65,431
7. Jerome Group, $28,300
8. BNB Systems, $27,090
9. Merrill Corp. Resource Management Division, $26,492
10. The Graphics & Technology Group, $24,911

Source: *Business Forms, Labels & Systems*, November 20, 1998, p. 36.

★911★
TOP BUSINESS FORMS MANUFACTURERS BY COMMERCIAL PRINTING SALES, 1998
Ranked by: Printing sales, in thousands of dollars. **Remarks:** Also notes location and total sales. **Number listed:** 20

1. Braceland Inc., with $34,018 thousand
2. Hippographics, $14,000
3. CST/Star Forms, $10,200
4. Champion Business Forms, $9,512
5. Des Plaines Publishing, $8,077
6. BFP Print Communications, $7,200
7. EPX, $6,400
8. Interform Solutions, $5,311
9. Web Express Printing, $5,280
10. Arthur Blank & Co., $4,600

Source: *Business Forms, Labels & Systems*, October 20, 1998, p. 30.

★912★
TOP BUSINESS FORMS MANUFACTURERS BY FORM SALES, 1998
Ranked by: Form sales, in thousands of dollars. **Remarks:** Also notes location and total sales. **Number listed:** 20

1. CST/Star Forms, with $244,800 thousand
2. Tanskrit, $75,750
3. Poser, $73,050
4. Adams Business Forms, $61,750
5. Datagraphic, $59,868
6. Continuous Forms & Charts, $48,500
7. Calibrated Forms, $45,251
8. Northstar Computer Forms, $41,710
9. Sovereign Business Forms, $39,008
10. DSFI Distributor's Stock Forms, $37,100

Source: *Business Forms, Labels & Systems*, October 20, 1998, p. 28.

★913★
TOP BUSINESS FORMS MANUFACTURERS BY LABEL SALES, 1998
Ranked by: Label sales, in thousands of dollars. **Remarks:** Also notes location and total sales. **Number listed:** 20
1. Arthur Blank & Co., with $4,600 thousand
2. Wright Business Graphics, $3,493
3. Printgraphics, $1,956
4. Bernadette Business Forms, $1,579
5. Hano Document Printers, $1,487
6. Cal Snap & Tab, $1,211
7. Crabar Business Systems, $1,200
8. Stylecraft Printing, $1,195
9. MRM, $953
10. Calibrated Forms, $923

Source: *Business Forms, Labels & Systems*, October 20, 1998, p. 36.

★914★
TOP BUSINESS FORMS MANUFACTURERS BY TOTAL SALES, 1998
Ranked by: Total sales, in thousands of dollars. **Remarks:** Also notes location, previous year's sales and rank, principal officer, number of employees, number of locations and year founded. **Number listed:** 100
1. CST/Star Forms, with $255,000 thousand
2. Ennis Business Forms, $154,348
3. Poser, $121,750
4. Tanskrit, $101,000
5. GBF Graphics, $82,700
6. Hippographics, $70,000
7. Adams Business Forms, $65,000
8. Datagraphic, $60,473
9. Label Art, $56,203
10. Discount Labels, $53,971

Source: *Business Forms, Labels & Systems*, October 20, 1998, p. 38+.

Business Journals, International

★915★
TOP BUSINESS PUBLICATIONS WORLDWIDE, 1998
Ranked by: Circulation. **Number listed:** 10
1. *Money* (U.S.), with 1,942,000 copies
2. *China Tax Policy* (China), 1,380,000
3. *Stern* (Germany), 1,115,000
4. *Kiplinger's Personal Finance* (U.S.), 1,100,000
5. *Der Spiegel* (Germany), 1,045,000
6. *Business Week* (U.S.), 915,000
7. *Nations's Business* (U.S.), 858,000
8. *Kamerkrant Landelijk* (Netherlands), 788,000
9. *Frobes* (U.S.), 783,000
10. *Fortunr* (U.S.), 763,000

Source: *Business Marketing*, November 1, 1998, p. 8.

Business Machines

See: **Office Equipment Industry**

Business Schools and Colleges

★916★
BEST BUSINESS SCHOOLS, 1998
Ranked by: Overall score in a survey of business schools. Ranking is derived from consideration of three factors: reputation, student selectivity and placement success. **Remarks:** Also notes average GMAT score, acceptance rate, median starting salary and percent employed three months after graduation. **Number listed:** 49
1. Stanford University, with 100 points
2. Harvard University, 98
2. Northwestern University, 98
2. University of Pennsylvania, 98
5. Massachusetts Institute of Technology, 95
6. University of Chicago, 94
7. Columbia University, 93
7. University of Michigan - Ann Arbor, 93
9. Duke University, 91
10. University of California - Los Angeles, 90

Source: *U.S News & World Report*, America's Best Graduate and Professional Schools (annual), March 29, 1999, p. 86.

★917★
BUSINESS SCHOOLS WITH THE BEST ACCOUNTING DEPARTMENTS, 1998
Ranked by: Overall score in a survey of business schools. Ranking is derived from consideration of three factors: reputation, student selectivity and placement success. Specific figures not provided. **Number listed:** 10
1. University of Chicago
2. University of Pennsylvania
3. Stanford University
4. University of Texas - Austin
5. University of Illinois - Urbana Champaign
6. University of Michigan - Ann Arbor
7. New York University
8. Harvard University
9. University of Southern California
10. Northwestern University

Source: *U.S News & World Report*, America's Best Graduate and Professional Schools (annual), March 29, 1999, p. 87.

★918★
BUSINESS SCHOOLS WITH THE BEST ENTREPRENEURSHIP DEPARTMENTS, 1998
Ranked by: Overall score in a survey of business schools. Ranking is derived from consideration of three factors: reputation, student selectivity and placement success. Specific figures not provided. **Number listed:** 10
1. Babson College
2. University of Pennsylvania
3. Harvard University
4. Stanford University
5. University of California - Los Angeles
6. University of Southern California
7. Northwestern University
8. University of Southern California
9. University of Michigan - Ann Arbor
10. University of Texas - Austin

Source: *U.S News & World Report*, America's Best Graduate and Professional Schools (annual), March 29, 1999, p. 87.

★919★
BUSINESS SCHOOLS WITH THE BEST FINANCE DEPARTMENTS, 1998
Ranked by: Overall score in a survey of business schools. Ranking is derived from consideration of three factors: reputa-

tion, student selectivity and placement success. Specific figures not provided. **Number listed:** 10

1. University of Pennsylvania
2. University of Chicago
3. New York University
4. Stanford University
5. Massachusetts Institute of Technology
6. Columbia University
7. Northwestern University
8. Harvard University
9. University of California - Los Angeles
10. University of Michigan - Ann Arbor

Source: *U.S News & World Report*, America's Best Graduate and Professional Schools (annual), March 29, 1999, p. 87.

★920★

BUSINESS SCHOOLS WITH THE BEST GENERAL MANAGEMENT DEPARTMENTS, 1998

Ranked by: Overall score in a survey of business schools. Ranking is derived from consideration of three factors: reputation, student selectivity and placement success. Specific figures not provided. **Number listed:** 10

1. Harvard University
2. Stanford University
3. Northwestern University
4. University of Michigan - Ann Arbor
5. University of Pennsylvania
6. Dartmouth College
7. University of Virginia
8. Duke University
9. Columbia University
10. University of California - Los Angeles

Source: *U.S News & World Report*, America's Best Graduate and Professional Schools (annual), March 29, 1999, p. 87.

★921★

BUSINESS SCHOOLS WITH THE BEST INTERNATIONAL BUSINESS DEPARTMENTS, 1998

Ranked by: Overall score in a survey of business schools. Ranking is derived from consideration of three factors: reputation, student selectivity and placement success. Specific figures not provided. **Number listed:** 10

1. Thunderbird Graduate School
2. University of South Carolina
3. University of Pennsylvania
4. Columbia University
5. New York University
6. Harvard University
7. University of California - Los Angeles
8. University of Michigan - Ann Arbor
9. Stanford University
10. University of California - Berkeley

Source: *U.S News & World Report*, America's Best Graduate and Professional Schools (annual), March 29, 1999, p. 87.

★922★

BUSINESS SCHOOLS WITH THE BEST MANAGEMENT INFORMATION SYSTEMS DEPARTMENTS, 1998

Ranked by: Overall score in a survey of business schools. Ranking is derived from consideration of three factors: reputation, student selectivity and placement success. Specific figures not provided. **Number listed:** 11

1. Massachusetts Institute of Technology
2. Carnegie Mellon University
3. University of Minnesota - Twin Cities
4. University of Texas - Austin
5. University of Arizona
6. Stanford University
7. University of Pennsylvania
8. New York University
9. Harvard University
9. University of California - Los Angeles
9. University of Michigan - Ann Arbor

Source: *U.S News & World Report*, America's Best Graduate and Professional Schools (annual), March 29, 1999, p. 87.

★923★

BUSINESS SCHOOLS WITH THE BEST MARKETING DEPARTMENTS, 1998

Ranked by: Overall score in a survey of business schools. Ranking is derived from consideration of three factors: reputation, student selectivity and placement success. Specific figures not provided. **Number listed:** 10

1. Northwestern University
2. University of Pennsylvania
3. Harvard University
3. Stanford University
5. University of Michigan - Ann Arbor
6. Duke University
7. University of California - Los Angeles
8. Columbia University
9. University of California - Berkeley
9. University of Chicago

Source: *U.S News & World Report*, America's Best Graduate and Professional Schools (annual), March 29, 1999, p. 87.

★924★

BUSINESS SCHOOLS WITH THE BEST NONPROFIT ORGANIZATIONS DEPARTMENTS, 1998

Ranked by: Overall score in a survey of business schools. Ranking is derived from consideration of three factors: reputation, student selectivity and placement success. Specific figures not provided. **Number listed:** 10

1. Yale University
2. Harvard University
3. Stanford University
4. Northwestern University
5. University of California - Berkeley
6. University of Pennsylvania
7. Case Western Reserve University
8. Columbia University
9. Cornell University
10. University of Michigan - Ann Arbor

Source: *U.S News & World Report*, America's Best Graduate and Professional Schools (annual), March 29, 1999, p. 87.

★925★

BUSINESS SCHOOLS WITH THE BEST PART-TIME MBA DEPARTMENTS, 1998

Ranked by: Overall score in a survey of business schools. Ranking is derived from consideration of three factors: reputation, student selectivity and placement success. Specific figures not provided. **Number listed:** 10

1. New York University
2. University of Chicago
3. Northwestern University
4. University of Michigan - Ann Arbor
5. DePaul University
6. Georgia State University
6. University of California - Los Angeles
8. University of California - Berkeley
9. Babson College
10. University of Southern California

Source: *U.S News & World Report*, America's Best Graduate and Professional Schools (annual), March 29, 1999, p. 87.

★926★
BUSINESS SCHOOLS WITH THE BEST PRODUCTIONS/OPERATIONS MANAGEMENT DEPARTMENTS, 1998
Ranked by: Overall score in a survey of business schools. Ranking is derived from consideration of three factors: reputation, student selectivity and placement success. Specific figures not provided. **Number listed:** 10
1. Massachusetts Institute of Technology
2. Carnegie Mellon University
3. Purdue University - West Lafayette
4. Harvard University
5. Stanford University
6. University of Pennsylvania
7. University of Michigan - Ann Arbor
8. Northwestern University
9. Indiana University - Bloomington
10. University of Chicago

Source: *U.S News & World Report*, America's Best Graduate and Professional Schools (annual), March 29, 1999, p. 87.

★927★
BUSINESS SCHOOLS WITH THE BEST QUANTITATIVE ANALYSIS DEPARTMENTS, 1998
Ranked by: Overall score in a survey of business schools. Ranking is derived from consideration of three factors: reputation, student selectivity and placement success. Specific figures not provided. **Number listed:** 10
1. Massachusetts Institute of Technology
2. University of Chicago
3. Carnegie Mellon University
4. University of Pennsylvania
5. University of California - Berkeley
6. Northwestern University
7. University of Michigan - Ann Arbor
7. Indiana University - Bloomington
9. Columbia University
10. Purdue University - West Lafayette

Source: *U.S News & World Report*, America's Best Graduate and Professional Schools (annual), March 29, 1999, p. 87.

★928★
TOP BUSINESS SCHOOLS ACCORDING TO *BUSINESS WEEK*, 1999
Ranked by: Overall score in a survey of graduates and recruiters. Specific figures not provided. **Remarks:** Also notes previous year's ran, results of corporate poll and graduatc poll, annual tuition, percentage of applicants accepted, percentage of women, international and minority students enrolled, median pay pre- and post-MBA, percentage of graduates earning more than $100,000, average number of job offers per graduate and comments. **Number listed:** 25
1. University of Pennsylvania
2. Northwestern University
3. University of Chicago
4. University of Michigan - Ann Arbor
5. Harvard University
6. Columbia University
7. Duke University
8. Cornell University
9. Stanford University
10. Dartmouth College

Source: *Business Week*, The Best B-Schools, October 19, 1998, p. 88.

★929★
TOP MBA PROGRAMS IN HISPANIC ENROLLMENT, 1998
Ranked by: Number of Hispanic graduate students. **Remarks:** Also notes contact information, total graduate enrollment, percent Hispanic graduate enrollment, total MBA degrees earned by overall and by Hispanic students and percent of MBAs earned by Hispanic students. **Number listed:** 10
1. Florida International University, with 382
2. Pepperdine University, 226
3. Golden State University, 205
4. Saint Thomas University, 200
5. University of Miami, 199
6. Nova Southeastern University, 163
7. Our Lady of the Lake University, 131
8. University of Southern California, 105
9. University of Texas at San Antonio, 98
10. University of Maryland at College Park, 96

Source: *Hispanic Business*, September, 1998, p. 28+.

Business Schools and Colleges—Los Angeles County (CA)

★930★
LARGEST MBA PROGRAMS IN LOS ANGELES COUNTY, 1998
Ranked by: Enrollment, full time equivalents. **Remarks:** Also notes contact information, full-time and part-time enrollment, campus locations, types of programs offered, number of graduates and top local official. **Number listed:** 15
1. University of Southern California Marshall School of Business, with 869
2. Anderson Graduate School of Management, UCLA, 848
3. California State Polytechnic University, 675
4. University of Phoenix, 647
5. Pepperdine's Graziadio School, 605
6. University of La Verne, 363
7. Peter F. Drucker Graduate School of Management, 305
8. Keller Graduate School of Management, 288
9. Loyola Marymount University, 269
10. California State University, Long Beach, 230

Source: *Los Angeles Business Journal*, May 17, 1999, p. 51.

Business Schools and Colleges—Philadelphia Metropolitan Area

★931★
LARGEST MBA PROGRAMS IN THE PHILADELPHIA METROPOLITAN AREA, 1997-1998
Ranked by: Total Enrollment. **Remarks:** Also notes contact information, percentage of students working full-time, average student age, credit hours required, average completion time for program, public or private status, tuition per credit hours, fees per semester, areas of specialization. **Number listed:** 14
1. Pennsylvania State University Great Valley, with 1,700 students
2. Saint Joseph's University, 1,098
3. Temple University, The Fox School, 1,058
4. La Salle University, 922
5. Drexel University, 795
6. University of Pennsylvania, The Wharton School, 765
7. Villanova University, 625
8. Widener University, 537

9. Allentown College of St. Francis de Sales, 450
10. Philadelphia College of Textile and Science, 383

Source: *Philadelphia Business Journal*, October/November, 1998, p. 16.

Business-to-Business Advertising

★932★
TOP ADVERTISERS IN CONSUMER MAGAZINES, 1997
Ranked by: Total spending, in millions of dollars. **Number listed:** 5

1. Microsoft, with $48.1 million
2. Hewlett-Packard Co., $36.3
3. IBM Corp., $32.5
4. Compaq Computer Corp., $31
5. Packard Bell NEC, $22.1

Source: *Business Marketing*, Top 100 (annual), September, 1998, p. 24.

★933★
TOP ADVERTISERS IN TRADE MAGAZINES, 1997
Ranked by: Total spending, in millions of dollars. **Number listed:** 5

1. Compaq Computer Corp., with $102.9 million
2. IBM Corp., $90.8
3. Microsoft, $69
4. Hewlett-Packard Co., $66.6
5. 3Com Corp., $50.7

Source: *Business Marketing*, Top 100 (annual), September, 1998, p. 24.

★934★
TOP ADVERTISERS ON CABLE TV, 1997
Ranked by: Total spending, in millions of dollars. **Number listed:** 5

1. AT & T, with $30 million
2. American Express Co., $18.6
3. MCI Communications Corp., $18.2
4. Sprint, $15.2
5. Microsoft, $15.1

Source: *Business Marketing*, Top 100 (annual), September, 1998, p. 24.

★935★
TOP ADVERTISERS ON NETWORK TV, 1997
Ranked by: Total spending, in millions of dollars. **Number listed:** 5

1. AT & T, with $83.2 million
2. MCI Communications Corp., $50.9
3. Sprint, $42
4. IBM Corp., $40.1
5. United Parcel Service of America, $34.5

Source: *Business Marketing*, Top 100 (annual), September, 1998, p. 24.

★936★
TOP ADVERTISERS ON SPOT TV, 1997
Ranked by: Total spending, in millions of dollars. **Number listed:** 5

1. MCI Communications Corp., with $37.3 million
2. Sprint, $32.6
3. AT & T, $29.8
4. Bell Atlantic Corp., $21.1
5. BellSouth, $19.9

Source: *Business Marketing*, Top 100 (annual), September, 1998, p. 24.

★937★
TOP BUSINESS-TO-BUSINESS ADVERTISERS, 1997
Ranked by: Total spending, in thousands of dollars. **Remarks:** Also notes breakdown for spending in various media, as well as rank form previous year and percent change. **Number listed:** 100

1. AT & T, with $210,377.3 thousand
2. IBM Corp., $199,776.5
3. Microsoft, $176,693.1
4. Compaq Computer Corp., $172,480.9
5. MCI Communications Corp., $168,734.3
6. Hewlett-Packard Co., $127,614.9
7. Sprint, $115,223.8
8. American Express Co., $76,730.2
9. Canon, $76,499.3
10. 3Com Corp., $75,991.8

Source: *Business Marketing*, Top 100 (annual), September, 1998, p. 20+.

★938★
TOP BUSINESS-TO-BUSINESS ADVERTISING CATEGORIES, 1997
Ranked by: Percent of total spending. **Number listed:** 11

1. High-Technology, with 50.2%
2. Telecommunications, 20.4%
3. Copiers/Printers, 5.9%
4. Business Travel, 5.3%
5. Package Delivery, 4.2%
6. Automotive, 2.1%
7. Associations, 1.8%
8. Pharmaceuticals, 1.6%
9. Media, 1.5%
10. Heavy Industry, .9%
11. Other, 6%

Source: *Business Marketing*, Top 100 (annual), September, 1998, p. 24.

★939★
TOP MEDIA FOR BUSINESS-TO-BUSINESS ADVERTISING, 1997
Ranked by: Spending by category, in millions of dollars. **Remarks:** Also notes percent change from previous year. **Number listed:** 12

1. Trade Magazines, with $1,272.99 million
2. Consumer Magazines, $582.6
3. Network TV, $575.4
4. Spot TV, $282.7
5. Cable TV, $209.6
6. National Newspapers, $199
7. Local Newspapers, $180.7
8. National Spot Radio, $199
9. Syndicated TV, $39.4
10. Network Radio, $29.9

Source: *Business Marketing*, Top 100 (annual), September, 1998, p. 24.

Business-to-Business Marketing

★940★
COMPANIES WITH THE BEST BUSINESS-TO-BUSINESS WEB SITES, 1998
Ranked by: Score, based on staff size, age of site and functionality. **Remarks:** Also notes URL, industry and comments. **Number listed:** 200

1. Marshall Industries, with A grade
2. Cisco Systems, A

3. Bay Networks, A
4. Dell Computer Corp., A
5. Compaq Computer Corp., A
6. Federal Express Corp., A
7. IBM Corp., A
8. W.W. Grainger, A
9. 3Com Corp., A
10. First Union Corp., A

Source: *Business Marketing*, NetMarketing 200 (annual), August, 1999, p. 32.

★941★
TOP SPENDING CATEGORIES FOR BUSINESS-TO-BUSINESS MARKETERS, 1999
Ranked by: Spending, in percent. **Number listed:** 10

1. Advertising, with 24%
2. Sales Promotions, 18.7%
3. Trade shows, 17.3%
4. Sales Force Management, 10.9%
5. Direct Marketing, 7.8%
6. Online, 5.8%
7. Market Research, 4.2%
8. Premiums/Incentives, 3.7%
9. Public Relations, 3.5%
10. Other, 3.8%

Source: *Business Marketing*, May, 1999, p. 1.

Business Travel

★942★
CORPORATIONS SPENDING THE MOST ON BUSINESS TRAVEL, 1997
Ranked by: U.S. air volume, in millions of dollars. **Number listed:** 100

1. IBM Corp., with $400 million
2. Lockheed Martin, $305
3. General Electric, $275
4. Andersen Worldwide, $270
5. Raytheon, $220
6. Hewlett-Packard, $210
7. Boeing, $200
8. Motorola, $181
9. General Motors, $175
10. Lucent Technologies, $174

Source: *Business Travel News*, Corporate Travel 100, July 6, 1998, p. 4.

Business Women

See: **Women Executives**

Cable Television

★943★
TOP BASIC CABLE PRIME TIME NETWORKS, 1999
Ranked by: Rankings based on Nielsen Ratings. **Number listed:** 10

1. USA, with 2.3
2. TNT, 2.1
3. NICK, 2.0
4. TBS, 1.9
5. ESPN, 1.6
5. LIFE, 1.6
7. TOON, 1.5
8. A & E, 1.3
9. FAM, 1.2
9. DISC, 1.2

Source: *Broadcasting & Cable*, January 4, 1999, p. 65.

★944★
TOP MEDIA COMPANIES BY CABLE TV REVENUE, 1998
Ranked by: Total cable TV revenue, in millions of dollars. **Remarks:** Also notes 1996 rank, cable revenue for 1996 with percent change from 1996 to 1997, and cable revenue as a percentage of total revenue. **Number listed:** 25

1. Time Warner, with $10,060.0 million
2. Tele-Communications, $6,429.0
3. MediaOne Group, $2,323.0
4. Viacom Inc., $2,273.6
5. Comcast Corp., $2,073.0
6. Walt Disney Co., $1,950.0
7. Cablevision Systems Corp., $1,949.4
8. Cox Enterprises, $1,610.4
9. News Corp. Ltd., $1,200.0
10. Discovery Communications, $756.0

Source: *Advertising Age*, August 17, 1998, p. 56.

Cable Television--Advertising

★945★
COMPANIES ADVERTISING THE MOST ON CABLE TELEVISION, 1998
Ranked by: Network expenditures, in millions of dollars. **Number listed:** 20

1. Procter & Gamble, with $241,510.4 million
2. General Motors Corp., $169,368.1
3. MCI WorldCom, $135,452.1
4. Philip Morris, $120,654.6
5. Diageo, $86,288.2
6. Time Warner, $86,201.2
7. Kellogg Co., $79,768.4
8. Daimler Chrysler AG, $78,876.9
9. Mattel, $77,157.3
10. Unilever, $71,067.6

Source: *Mediaweek*, March 1, 1999, p. 26.

★946★
COMPANIES ADVERTISING THE MOST ON CABLE TELEVISION, 1997
Ranked by: Network expenditures, in millions of dollars. **Remarks:** Also notes previous year's figures and percent change. **Number listed:** 25

1. Procter & Gamble, with $238.7 million
2. General Motors Corp., $174.8
3. Time Warner, $105.7
4. Phillip Morris Co., $100.8
5. Kellogg Co., $86.8
6. Diageo, $84.1
7. Unilever, $76.9
8. Johnson & Johnson, $76.3
9. Mattel, $74.6
10. Chrysler Corp., $68.0

Source: *Advertising Age*, 100 Leading National Advertisers (annual), Fall, September 28, 1998, p. 542.

★947★
LEADING CABLE ADVERTISING CATEGORIES, 1998
Ranked by: Advertising expenditures, in millions of dollars. **Remarks:** Also notes previous year's figures and percent change. **Number listed:** 10

1. Automotive, automotive access & equipment, with $648,331.00 million
2. Medicines & proprietary remedies, $440,532.00
3. Financial services, $423,949.00
4. Telecommunications, $348,460.00
5. Media & advertising, $318,819.00
6. Games, toys & hobbycraft, $300,332.00
7. Retail, $273,271.00
8. Computers & software, $248,564.00
9. Restaurants, $220,732.00
10. Prepared foods, $218,577.00

Source: *Mediaweek*, Cable Television Advertising (annual), April 12, 1999, p. 38.

★948★
LEADING MEDIA AND ADVERTISING COMPANIES ADVERTISING ON CABLE TELEVISION, 1998
Ranked by: Sales, in millions of dollars. **Number listed:** 5

1. Time Warner, with $51,468.70 million
2. Walt Disney Co., $43,988.60
3. National Amusements Inc., $40,089.10
4. News Corp Ltd., $22,462.20
5. Sony, $20,674.30

Source: *Mediaweek*, April 12, 1999, p. 38.

★949★
LEADING RESTAURANTS ADVERTISING ON CABLE T.V., 1998
Ranked by: Sales, in millions of dollars. **Number listed:** 5

1. McDonald's, with $51,094.30 million
2. Diageo Plc., $50,429.30
3. Tricon Global Restaurants, $28,579.70
4. Darden Restaurants, $16,403.20
5. Wendy's International, $15,591.80

Source: *Mediaweek*, April 12, 1999, p. 38.

★950★
LEADING RETAIL COMPANIES ADVERTISING ON CABLE TELEVISION, 1998
Ranked by: Sales, in millions of dollars. **Number listed:** 5

1. The Gap, with $21,430.50 million
2. National Amusements Inc., $20,368.10
3. Home Depot Inc., $17,563.80
4. Auto Zone Inc., $17,022.30
5. Walgreen, $15,702.70

Source: *Mediaweek*, April 12, 1999, p. 38.

★951★
TOP AUTOMOTIVE, ACCESSORIES AND EQUIPMENT CABLE TELEVISION ADVERTISERS, 1998
Ranked by: Sales, in millions of dollars. **Number listed:** 5

1. General Motors Corp., with $175,806 million
2. Daimler/Chrysler AG, $85,228.80
3. Ford Motor Co., $62,507.70
4. Toyota Motor, $39,451.80
5. Honda Motor Co. Ltd., $33,969.50

Source: *Mediaweek (annual)*, April 12, 1999, p. 38.

★952★
TOP CABLE T.V. CATEGORIES, 1998
Ranked by: Sales, in millions of dollars. **Number listed:** 7

1. Long Distance, with $238.0 million
2. National restaurants, $218.2
3. Motion pictures, $201.0
4. Cars, domestic, $144.0
5. Credit cards, $138.0
6. Cereals, $136.4
7. Prescription medications, $133.0

Source: *Advertising Age*, May 10, 1999, p. 16.

★953★
TOP COMPUTER AND SOFTWARE COMPANIES ADVERTISING ON CABLE TELEVISION, 1998
Ranked by: Sales, in millions of dollars. **Number listed:** 5

1. Microsoft, with $25,626.20 million
2. Gateway Inc., $20,263.80
3. IBM Corp., $15,509.60
4. America Online Inc., $15,182.10
5. Dell Computer Corp., $14,340.20

Source: *Mediaweek*, April 12, 1999, p. 38.

★954★
TOP FINANCIAL INSTITUTIONS ADVERTISING ON CABLE TELEVISION, 1998
Ranked by: Sales, in millions of dollars. **Number listed:** 5

1. American Express Co., with $58,277.00 million
2. Visa USA Inc., $26,129.00
3. Countrywide Home Loans Inc., $19,176.60
4. Mastercard International Inc., $18,975.80
5. First USA Bank, $18,550.90

Source: *Mediaweek*, April 12, 1999, p. 38.

★955★
TOP GAMES, TOYS AND HOBBYCRAFT USING CABLE TELEVISON FOR ADVERTISING, 1998
Ranked by: Sales, in millions of dollars. **Number listed:** 5

1. Mattel, with $83,140.50 million
2. Hasbro Inc., $75,752.80
3. Nintendo Co. Ltd., $24,741.80
4. Sony, $16,533.80
5. MacAndrews & Forbes Holdings, $13,076.40

Source: *Mediaweek*, April 12, 1999, p. 38.

★956★
TOP MANUFACTURERS OF PREPARED FOODS ADVERTISING ON CABLE T.V., 1998
Ranked by: Sales, in millions of dollars. **Number listed:** 5

1. Kellogg Co., with $54,087.20 million
2. Philip Morris, $46,606.00
3. General Mills Inc., $42,619.80
4. Campbell Soup Co., $19,814.60
5. Quaker Oats Co., $9,524.70

Source: *Mediaweek*, April 12, 1999, p. 38.

★957★
TOP MEDICINE AND PROPRIETARY REMEDIES ADVERTISING ON CABLE TELEVISION, 1998
Ranked by: Sales, in millions of dollars. **Number listed:** 5

1. Glaxo Wellcome PLC, with $40,223.10 million
2. Johnson & Johnson, $40,209.50
3. Merck & Co. Inc., $33,268.00
4. American Home Corp., $30,935.00
5. SmithKline Beecham, $27,594.00

Source: *Mediaweek*, April 12, 1999, p. 38.

★958★
TOP TELECOMMUNICATION COMPANIES ADVERTISING ON CABLE TELEVISION, 1998
Ranked by: Sales, in millions of dollars. **Number listed:** 5

1. MCI WorldCom, with $153,298.80 million
2. Sprint, $68,841.20
3. AT & T, $45,285.30
4. Nextel Communications Inc., $9,820.50
5. Quintel Corp., $8,017.60

Source: *Mediaweek*, April 12, 1999, p. 38.

Cable Television--New York Metropolitan Area

★959★
NEW YORK CITY'S TOP CABLE COMPANIES, 1998
Ranked by: Number of subscribers. **Remarks:** Also notes 1997 figures, contact information, parent company, top executive, year service started, number of channels available, and data pertaining to basic cable service. **Number listed:** 5

1. Time Warner Cable of New York City, with $889,995 subscribers
2. Cablevision of NYC (Bronx-Brooklyn), $504,423
3. RCN Corp., $249,360
4. Staten Island Cable, $106,238
5. Queens Inner Unity Cable Systems, $103,767

Source: *Crain's New York Business (annual)*, September 28, 1998, p. 22.

Cafeterias

See: **Restaurants**

California--Industries

★960★
TOP CALIFORNIA COMPANIES BY EMPLOYEES, 1997
Ranked by: Number of employees. **Number listed:** 100

1. Safeway, with $147,000 employees
2. Hewlett-Packard Co., $121,900
3. Seagate Technology, $111,000
4. Walt Disney Co., $108,000
5. BankAmerica Corp., $77,000
6. Tenet Healthcare Corp., $71,400
7. Intel Corp., $63,700
8. ABM Industries Inc., $52,000
8. Northrop Grumman, $52,000
9. Pinkerton's Inc., $47,000
10. Rockwell International, $45,000

Source: *Database Publishing Company*, California Manufacturers Register (annual), 1999, p. 18+.

★961★
TOP PUBLIC CORPORATIONS IN CALIFORNIA, 1997
Ranked by: Revenue, in millions of dollars. **Remarks:** Also notes 1996 rank and percentage change. **Number listed:** 100

1. Hewlett-Packard, with $44,416.0 million
2. Chevron Corp., $41,950.0
3. Intel Corp., $25,070.0
4. Safeway, $23,795.0
5. Walt Disney Co., $22,534.0
6. Atlantic Richfield, $19,272.0
7. McKesson Corp., $17,479.0
8. BankAmerica Corp., $17,457.0
9. Ingram Micro Inc., $16,581.0
10. PG & E Corp., $16,387.0

Source: *Database Publishing Company*, California Manufacturers Register (annual), 1999, p. 16+.

Call Centers

★962★
CALL CENTER COSTS, 1998*
Ranked by: Workstations in market, in percent. **Number listed:** 3

1. Personnel, with 65%
2. Telecom, 20%
3. Overhead & Equipment, 15%

Source: *Communications News*, October, 1998, p. 66.

Camcorders

★963★
BEST-SELLING CAMCORDERS, 1998
Ranked by: Market share, in percent. **Remarks:** Also notes 1993 market share. **Number listed:** 8

1. Sony, with 31%
2. Thomson, 21%
3. Matsushita, 18%
4. JVC, 15%
5. Sharp, 7%
6. Hitachi, 4%
7. Canon, 2%
7. NAP, 2%

Source: *Appliance Manufacturer*, April, 1999, p. 22.

★964★
TOP CAMCORDER BRANDS BY MARKET SHARE, 1998
Ranked by: Market share, in percent. **Number listed:** 10

1. RCA, with 57.60%
2. Panasonic, 13.70%
3. General Electric, 7.20%
4. Philips/Magnavox, 5.80%
5. Sharp, 5.00%
6. Hitachi, 3.60%
6. JVC, 3.60%
7. Samsung, 1.40%
8. Sears, 1.80%
9. Goldstar, 1.10%
10. Others, 2.10%

Source: *Dealerscope Consumer Electronics Marketplace*, August, 1998, p. 20.

Camden County (NJ)--Industries

★965★
LARGEST EMPLOYERS IN CAMDEN COUNTY, NJ, 1998
Ranked by: Number of employees. **Number listed:** 25

1. The Cooper Health System, with $3,096 employees
2. West Jersey Health System, $2,606
3. Kennedy Health System, $1,567
4. Our Lady of Lourdes Medical Center, $1,488
5. Arch America, $1,400
6. Campbell Soup Co., $1,300
7. Bancroft, $976
8. Alliance Data Systems, $974
9. L-3 Communications Systems-East, $850

10. Cigna Corp., $713

Source: *Philadelphia Business Journal*, Book of Business Lists (annual), December 25, 1998, p. 101.

Cameras

★966★
TOP CAMERA BRANDS ACCORDING TO DISCOUNT SHOPPERS, 1998
Ranked by: Percentage of discount shoppers naming brand as best. **Remarks:** Figures may total more than 100% due to multiple responses. Also notes figures for previous year. **Number listed:** 10

1. Kodak, with 36%
2. Canon, 29%
3. Olympus, 13%
4. Pentax, 7%
5. Polaroid, 6%
6. Minolta, 5%
7. Sony, 4%
7. Vivitar, 4%
8. Duracell, 2%
8. Nikon, 2%

Source: *Discount Store News*, Top Brand Consumer Survey-Pt.II (annual), September 7, 1998, p. 26.

Campaign Funds

★967★
TOP HIGH-TECH CAMPAIGN CONTRIBUTORS
Ranked by: Donations are for the first 18 months of the 1997-1998 election cycle. **Remarks:** Donations include "soft money" and contributions from political action committees and individuals. **Number listed:** 10

1. Microsoft, with $574,099 million
2. Kleiner Perkins Caufield & Byers, $328,863
3. EDS Corp., $280,646
4. Oracle, $275,663
5. Gateway 2000, $174,554
6. Cisco Systems, $134,000
7. IDX Systems Corp., $133,750
8. JD Edwards, $118,500
9. Sterling Software Inc., $107,800
10. CDB Infotek, $103,000

Source: *High Technology Industry*, CQ Weekly, October 31, 1998, p. 2959.

Candy Industry

★968★
BEST-SELLING NON-CHOCOLATE CANDY BY MARKET SHARE, 1997
Ranked by: Market share, in percent. **Number listed:** 10

1. Skittles Bite Size Candies, with 12%
2. Starburst Fruit Chews, 11%
3. GummiSavers, 10%
4. Mentos, 9%
5. Airheads, 8%
6. Starburst Fruit Twists, 5%
7. Y&S Twizzlers, 4%
8. Reese's Pieces, 3%
8. Private Label, 3%
8. Tootsie Roll, 3%

Source: *Candy Industry*, July, 1998, p. A12.

★969★
BEST-SELLING NON-CHOCOLATE CANDY, 1998
Ranked by: Sales, in millions of dollars. **Number listed:** 8

1. Skittles, with $30.2 million
2. Payday, $24.7
3. Starburst, $23.9
4. Snak-Stop, $21.4
5. Jolly Rancher, $21.3
6. Reese's Pieces, $19.9
7. LifeSaver's Gummi, $18.7
8. Sathers Gummi, $15.9

Source: *Candy Industry*, July, 1998, p. A16.

★970★
LEADING NON-CHOCOLATE BARS CANDY BY MARKET SHARE, 1997
Ranked by: Market share, in percent. **Number listed:** 5

1. M&M/Mars, with 29%
2. Van Melle, 17%
3. LifeSavers, 13%
4. Hershey Chocolate USA, 12%
5. Tootsie Roll Industries, 4%

Source: *Candy Industry*, July, 1998, p. A12.

★971★
TOP CANDY AND SNACK BRANDS ACCORDING TO DISCOUNTERS, 1998*
Ranked by: Percentage of discounters naming brand as best. **Remarks:** Figures may total more than 100% due to multiple responses. Also notes figures for previous year. **Number listed:** 10

1. M&M/Mars, with 19%
2. Hershey, 13%
3. Frito-Lay, 12%
4. Little Debbie, 11%
5. Nabisco, 6%
6. Kit Kat, 4%
6. Pringles, 4%
6. Reese's, 4%
7. Planter's, 3%
7. Brach's, 3%

Source: *Discount Store News*, Top Brands Survey (annual), September 7, 1998, p. 28.

★972★
TOP CANDY BRANDS IN GREAT BRITAIN, 1998
Ranked by: Sales, in millions of British pounds. **Remarks:** Also notes ad spending. **Number listed:** 10

1. Kit Kat(Nestle), with £163.7 millions
2. Mars Bar(Mars), £132.4
3. Twix(Mars), £88.6
4. Snickers(Mars), £75.5
5. Nestle Aero, £60.5
6. Bounty(Mars), £42.1
7. Cadbury's Crunchie, £37.4
8. Cadbury's Time Out, £36.0
9. Milky Way(Mars), £30.9
10. Cadbury's Caramel, £30.5

Source: *Marketing*, February 11, 1999, p. 25.

Candy, mints

★973★
LEADING BRANDS OF PLAIN MINTS, 1997
Ranked by: Market share, in percent. **Number listed:** 10

1. LifeSavers, with 34%
2. Mentos, 14%
3. Brach's Plain Mints, 11%
4. Brock's Plain Mints, 9%
5. Private label, 8%
6. Farley's Plain Mints, 4%
6. Sathers Plain Mints, 4%
8. Richardson After Dinner Mints, 3%
9. Hershey's TasteTations Mints, 2%
10. Necco Canada Mints, 1%

Source: *Candy Industry*, July, 1998, p. A13.

★974★
LEADING BREATH FRESHENER BRANDS, 1997
Ranked by: Market share, in percent. **Number listed:** 10

1. Tic Tac, with 29%
2. BreathSavers, 28%
3. Altoids, 14%
4. Certs, 12%
5. Certs Cool Mints, 7%
6. Certs Extra, 6%
7. Velamints, 1%
7. Smint, 1%
7. Ricola Pearls, 1%
7. Certs Fresh Fruit, 1%

Source: *Candy Industry*, July, 1998, p. A13.

★975★
LEADING BREATH FRESHENER COMPANIES, 1997
Ranked by: Market share, in percent. **Number listed:** 5

1. Ferrero USA, with 29%
2. LifeSavers, 28%
3. Adams, 26%
4. Callard & Bowser Suchard, 14%
5. Ragold, 1%

Source: *Candy Industry*, July, 1998, p. A13.

★976★
LEADING MINT/HARD ROLL BRANDS BY CANDY & TOBACCO DISTRIBUTOR SALES, 1998
Ranked by: Sales, in millions of dollars. **Remarks:** Also notes 1997 rank and sales. **Number listed:** 10

1. LifeSavers Roll, with $56.3 million
2. Tic Tac, $43.5
3. Breath Savers, $43.2
4. Certs, $36.8
5. Mentos, $24.1
6. Altoids, $18.5
7. Certs Cool Mint Drops, $12.0
8. Certs Extra Flavor, $9.3
9. Certs Fresh Fruit, $8.0
10. Smint, $2.5

Source: *Candy Industry*, July, 1998, p. A17.

★977★
LEADING PLAIN MINT COMPANIES, 1997
Ranked by: Market share, in percent. **Number listed:** 5

1. LifeSavers, with 34%
2. Brach, Brock, 20%
3. Van Melle, 14%
4. Private label, 8%
4. Favorite Brands, 8%

Source: *Candy Industry*, July, 1998, p. A13.

Capital Equipment Industry

See: **Industrial Equipment Industry**

Captive Insurance Companies--Barbados

★978★
BARBADOS' LARGEST CAPTIVE MANAGERS, 1998
Ranked by: Gross premium volume, in millions of U.S. dollars ($). **Remarks:** Also notes 1997 premium volume, 1997 and 1998 captives, and 1997 and 1998 staff. **Number listed:** 6

1. MIMS International Ltd. (Barbados), with $376.0 million
2. Merchant Corporate Management Ltd., $210.0
3. Aon Insurance Managers Ltd. (Barbados), $162.0
4. IAS Ltd. (Barbados), $160.0
5. J & H Marsh & McLennan Ltd. (Barbados), $84.0
6. Mutual Risk Management Ltd. (Barbados), $53.0

Source: *Business Insurance (annual)*, April 12, 1999, p. 41.

Captive Insurance Companies--Bermuda

★979★
BERMUDA'S LARGEST CAPTIVE MANAGERS, 1998
Ranked by: Premium volume, in millions of U.S. dollars ($). **Remarks:** Also notes 1997 premium volume, 1997 and 1998 captives, and 1997 and 1998 staff. **Number listed:** 10

1. J & H Marsh & McLennan Management Ltd., with $2,767 million
2. Aon Insurance Managers Ltd., $1,643
3. Mutual Risk Captive Group Ltd., $1,403
4. Skandia International Risk Management Inc., $309
5. International Risk Management Ltd., $290
6. Pinehurst Management Co. Ltd., $200
7. Becher & Carlson Management Ltd., $174
8. Symphony Management Ltd., $150
9. AIG Insurance Management Services Ltd., $147
10. Atlantic Security Ltd., $145

Source: *Business Insurance (annual)*, April 12, 1999, p. 16.

Captive Insurance Companies--Cayman Islands

★980★
CAYMAN ISLANDS' LARGEST CAPTIVE MANAGERS, 1998
Ranked by: Premium volume, in millions of U.S. dollars ($). **Remarks:** Also notes 1997 premium volume, 1997 and 1998 captives, and 1997 and 1998 staff. **Number listed:** 10

1. J & H McLennan Management Ltd., with $817.0 million
2. International Risk Management Ltd., $461.3
3. Midland BankTrust Corp. Ltd./HSBC Insurance Management, $220.0
3. Willis Corroon Management Ltd., $220.0
4. Aon Insurance Managers Ltd., $170.0
5. Mutual Risk Management Ltd., $109.0
6. Cayside Insurance Management Ltd., $57.4

7. Britannia Insurance Management Ltd., $38.0
8. Chandler Insurance Management Ltd., $27.9
9. Crusader International Management Ltd., $21.5

Source: *Business Insurance*, April 12, 1999, p. 24.

Captive Insurance Companies--Hawaii

★981★
HAWAII'S LARGEST CAPTIVE MANAGERS, 1998
Ranked by: Gross premium volume, in millions of dollars. **Remarks:** Also notes 1997 premium volume, number of captives in 1997 and 1998, and number of staff members. **Number listed:** 7

1. J & H Marsh & McLennan Management Inc., with $118.1 million
2. Hawaii Captive Insurance Management Inc., $76.8
3. Becher & Carlson Risk Management Inc., $55.6
4. Aon Insurance Managers, $10.5
5. Willis Corroon Management Ltd., $5.4
6. IAS Insurance Management, $3.6
7. 50th State Risk Management Services Inc., $2.2

Source: *Business Insurance (annual)*, April 12, 1999, p. 49.

★982★
HAWAII'S LARGEST CAPTIVES, 1998
Ranked by: Gross premium volume. **Remarks:** Specific figures not provided. **Number listed:** 10

1. Transamerica Pacific Insurance Co. Ltd.
2. Nissan Motor Insurance Corp.
3. Meridian Pacific insurance Co. Inc.
4. Entertainment Risk Management Insurance Co. Inc.
5. F. L. Insurance Corp.
6. Sutter Insurance Services Corp.
7. Medical Professional Liability Insurance Co. Inc.
8. National Liberty Insurance Co. Inc.
9. California Healthcare Insurance Co.
10. Attorneys Insurance Mutual Risk Retention Group

Source: *Business Insurance (annual)*, April 12, 1999, p. 53.

Captive Insurance Companies--Vermont

★983★
LEADING VERMONT-BASED GROUP CAPTIVES, 1998
Ranked by: Gross written premiums. **Remarks:** Also notes net premiums and net income. **Number listed:** 20

1. Attorneys' Liability Assurance Society Inc., with $251,134,697 million
2. Controlled Risk Insurance Co. of Vermont Inc., $39,794,170
3. United Educators Insurance Risk Retention Group Inc., $39,588,206
4. ICI Mutual Insurance Co., $35,511,547
5. MCIC Vermont Inc., $34,104,163
6. American Excess Insurance Exchange, $32,884,936
7. Housing Authority Risk Retention Group, $22,435,070
8. NCL Mutual Insurance Co., $18,756,682
9. Ophthalmic Mutual Insurance Co., $14,242,578
10. Housing Authority Property Insurance Inc., $12,004,121

Source: *Business Insurance*, April 12, 1999, p. 32.

★984★
VERMONT'S LARGEST CAPTIVE MANAGERS, 1998
Ranked by: Premium volume, in millions of dollars. **Remarks:** Also notes 1997 volume and captive and staff figures for 1997 and 1998. **Number listed:** 10

1. J & H Marsh & McLennan Management Inc., with $1,459.2 million
2. IRMG/American Risk Management Corp., $652.9
3. Aon Insurance Managers, $434.8
4. Yankee Captive Management Co., $304.8
5. Sedgwick ManagementServices US Ltd., $144.6
6. AIG Insurance Management Services Inc., $141.0
7. SB & T Captive Management Co., $109.7
8. Vermont Insurance Management Inc., $97.3
9. Willis Corroon Management Ltd. (Vermont), $36.9
10. Skandia International Risk Management Inc. (Vermont), $31.1

Source: *Business Insurance*, April 12, 1999, p. 32.

Caracas Stock Exchange

★985★
LARGEST LISTED COMPANIES ON THE CARACAS STOCK EXCHANGE, 1997
Ranked by: Market value, in millions of Venezuelan bolivars. **Number listed:** 20

1. Electricidad de Caracas, with Bs1,279.8 million
2. CANTV, Bs1,060.8
3. Banco Provincial, Bs658.9
4. Banco de Venezuela, Bs355.0
5. Sivensa, Bs321.9
6. Vencemos, Bs288.6
7. Mercantil A, Bs280.5
8. Mercantil B, Bs191.7
9. Mavesa, Bs190.7
10. Banco Union, Bs180.0

Source: *Euromoney Publications*, SSB Guide to World Equity Markets (annual), 1998, p. 552.

★986★
MOST ACTIVELY TRADED STOCKS ON THE CARACAS STOCK EXCHANGE, 1997
Ranked by: Trading value, in millions of Venezuelan bolivars. **Number listed:** 20

1. Electricidad de Caracas, with Bs1,107.0 million
2. CANTV, Bs208.1
3. Banco Provincial, Bs162.0
4. Sivensa, Bs158.1
5. Fondo de Valores Immobiliarios, Bs130.0
6. Vencemos, Bs97.4
7. Corimon, Bs95.1
8. Mavesa, Bs62.0
9. Banco Union, Bs61.2
10. Sudamtex, Bs47.7

Source: *Euromoney Publications*, SSB Guide to World Equity Markets (annual), 1998, p. 552.

Careers

See: **Occupations**

Carnivals

★987★
LEADING CARNIVAL COMPANIES PLAYING AT FAIRS, 1998
Ranked by: Cumulative attendance. **Remarks:** Also notes 1997 ranking, number of fairs worked, and specific fairs played. **Number listed:** 22

1. Conklin Shows, with $7,521,589 people
2. Ray Cammack Shows, $5,577,777
3. Strates Shows, $2,645,986
4. Murphy Bros. Enterprises, $2,571,328
5. Reithoffer Shows, $2,503,340
6. Funtastic Shows, $1,918,569
7. Farrow Shows, $1,863,959
8. Butler Amusements, $1,846,303
9. Wade Shows, $1,657,303
10. Bill Hames Shows, $1,504,441

Source: *Amusement Business*, Amusement Business (annual), December 28, 1998, p. 198.

Carpet Industry

★988★
LEADING USES OF NEEDLEPUNCHED CARPETS, 1997
Ranked by: Usage, in percent. **Number listed:** 3

1. Car interiors, with 70%
2. Exhibition carpets, 9%
3. General-use carpets, 4%

Source: *Nonwomens Industry*, November, 1998, p. 29.

Carriers--North America

★989★
LARGEST NORTH AMERICAN PRIVATE BUS LINE OPERATORS, 1998
Ranked by: Fleet size. **Remarks:** Also notes location, number of each type of motorcoach, and rank from previous year. **Number listed:** 50

1. Laidlaw Transit Services, with 4,768 coaches
2. Coach USA Inc., 4,596
3. Greyhound Lines Inc., 2,188
4. ATC/Vancom Inc., 1,241
5. Global Passenger Services LLC, 902
6. Academy Bus Tours Inc., 585
7. Ryder-ATE, 450
8. Pacific Western Transportation Ltd., 416
9. Martz Group, 405
10. Holland America Line-Westours Inc., 319

Source: *Metro Magazine*, Largest Private Motorcoach Fleets (annual), January/February, 1999, p. 36+.

Casablanca Stock Exchange

★990★
LARGEST LISTED COMPANIES ON THE CASABLANCA STOCK EXCHANGE
Ranked by: Market capitalization, in Moroccan dirhans. **Number listed:** 20

1. ONA, with Dh14,500 million
2. BCM, Dh11,726
3. BMCE, Dh8,356
4. SNI, Dh8,267
5. Lafarge Climents, Dh6,622
6. Samir, Dh6,605
7. Societe Brasseries du Maroc, Dh6,076
8. Lesieur, Dh5,620
9. Wafabank, Dh5,620
10. Credit du Maroc, Dh5,464

Source: *Euromoney Publications*, SSB Guide to World Equity Markets (annual), 1998, p. 349.

★991★
MOST ACTIVELY TRADED COMPANIES ON THE CASABLANCA STOCK EXCHANGE, 1997
Ranked by: Turnover value, in millions of Moroccan dirhams. **Number listed:** 20

1. BMCE, with Dh5,473 million
2. ONA, Dh3,819
3. BCM, Dh2,421
4. SNI, Dh2,074
5. Samir, Dh1,740
6. Wafabank, Dh1,553
7. BNDE, Dh981
8. Brasseries du Maroc, Dh917
9. Sonasid, Dh778
10. CIOR, Dh727

Source: *Euromoney Publications*, SSB Guide to World Equity Markets (annual), 1998, p. 349.

Casinos--France

★992★
LARGEST CASINOS IN FRANCE BY NUMBER, 1999
Ranked by: Number of casinos. **Number listed:** 9

1. Partouche, with 20 casinos
2. Tranchant, 15
3. Barriere, 13
3. EDC, 13
4. Emeraude, 7
4. Molifor, 7
5. SPIC/ACCOR, 5
6. SFC, 3
7. Independent Groups, 82

Source: *International Gaming and Wagering Business*, January, 1999, p. 8.

Cat Food

See: **Pet Food**

Catalogs

★993★
LEADING U.S. MAIL ORDER CATALOG BUSINESSES IN WORLDWIDE SALES, 1998*
Ranked by: Worldwide mail order sales, in millions of dollars. **Remarks:** Also notes sales segment. **Number listed:** 25
1. Dell Computer Corp., with $8,471.5 million
2. Gateway 2000, $5,035.2
3. J. C. Penney, $3,500.0
4. Hewlett-Packard Direct Marketing Division, $2,125.0
5. Micro Warehouse, $1,706.0
6. Micron Electronics, $1,528.3
7. Fingerhut Catalog, $1,480.0
8. W. W. Grainger, $1,380.0
9. Viking Office Products, $1,286.3
10. Caremark, $1,211.0

Source: *Direct Marketing (annual)*, September, 1998, p. 27+.

★994★
MAIL ORDER CATALOG REQUEST FREQUENCIES, 1998
Ranked by: Survey results, in percent. **Number listed:** 5
1. Daily, with $59%
2. Weekly, $25%
3. Biweekly, $11%
4. monthly, $2%
5. Other, $3%

Source: *Catalog Age*, September, 1998, p. 16.

★995★
TOP CATALOGERS, 1997
Ranked by: Mail order sales, in millions of dollars. **Remarks:** Also notes contact information, 1996 sales, and market segment. **Number listed:** 100
1. Dell Computer Corp., with $11,946.33 million
2. Gateway 2000, $6,293.68
3. J. C. Penney, $3,880
4. International Business Machines, $3,000
5. Micro Warehouse, $2,126
6. Fingerhut Cos., $1,530
7. Spiegel, $1,522
8. Henry Schein, $1,518.1
9. Viking Office Products, $1,382.9
10. Brylane, $1,278.96

Source: *Catalog Age*, The Catalog Age 100 (annual), August, 1998, p. 60+.

Celebrities

★996★
TOP CELEBRITIES FOR 1998
Ranked by: Power, measuring income for 1997, and media attention including: web mentions, press clips, magazine covers, and TV/radio mentions. **Number listed:** 100
1. Michael Jordan
2. Oprah Winfrey
3. Leonardo DiCaprio
4. Jerry Seinfeld
5. Steven Spielberg
6. Spice Girls
7. Harrison Ford
8. Robin Williams
9. Celine Dion
10. Rolling Stones

Source: *Forbes*, Celebrity 100 (annual), March, March 22, 1999, p. 203+.

Cellular Radio Service Companies

★997★
LEADING CELLULAR TELEPHONES IN CHINA BY MARKET SHARE, 1997
Ranked by: Market share, in percent. **Number listed:** 5
1. Ericsson, with 35%
2. Motorola, 26%
3. Nokia, 22%
4. Siemens, 9%
5. Others, 8%

Source: *Far Eastern Economic Review*, July 3, 1998, p. 11.

Cellular Telephone Equipment Industry

★998★
LEADING CELLULAR PHONE MANUFACTURERS BY MARKET SHARE, 1998*
Ranked by: Market share, in percent. **Number listed:** 7
1. Motorola, with 41.0%
2. Nokia, 22.0%
3. Ericsson, 11.0%
4. Sony, 5.0%
5. Audiovox, 4.0%
5. NEC, 4%
5. Qualcomm, 4%

Source: *Advertising Age*, September 28, 1999, p. S18.

Cellular Telephone Systems

See: **Cellular Radio Service Companies**

Cellular Telephones

★999★
TOP U.S. CELLULAR PHONE SERVICES, 1997
Ranked by: Total subscribers, in million of dollars. **Number listed:** 10
1. AT & T Wireless, with $7.0 million
2. Air Touch Communications, $6.6
3. Bell Atlantic Mobile, $5.4
4. SBC Communications, $5.2
5. GTE Moblenet, $4.5
6. BellSouth Mobility, $4.1
7. 360 Communications, $3.2
7. Ameritech Cellular, $3.2
8. U.S. Cellular, $1.7
9 Comcast Corp., $0.8

Source: *Advertising Age*, September 28, 1998, p. S18.

Cement Industry

★1000★
LEADING CEMENT COMPANIES IN INDIA, 1998*
Ranked by: Capacity, in millions of tons per year. **Number listed:** 5

1. Associated Cement Companies, with 11.00 million tons
2. Larsen & Toubro, 10.65
3. Grasim Industries, 7.45
4. Gujarat Ambuja, 6.50
5. India Cements, 5.80

Source: *Financial Times*, July 19, 1998, p. 17.

Cereal Products

★1001★
BEST-SELLING BRANDS OF COLD CEREAL, 1999
Ranked by: Sales, in millions of dollars. **Remarks:** Also notes unit sales. **Number listed:** 9

1. Cheerios (General Mills), with $341.8 million
2. Frosted Flakes (Kellogg), $284.4
3. Honey Nut Cheerios (General Mills), $218.7
4. Frosted Mini Wheats (Kellogg), $215.8
5. Corn Flakes (Kellogg), $210.7
6. Raisin Bran (Kellogg), $206.6
7. Lucky Charms (General Mills), $156.0
8. Rice Krispies (Kellogg), $147.7
9. Cinnamon Toast Crunch (General Mills), $143.1

Source: *Brand Week*, Superbrands: America's Top 2,000 Brands, 1999, June 21, 1999, p. S46.

★1002★
TOP-SELLING CEREAL BRANDS, 1998-1999
Ranked by: Sales, in millions of dollars. **Remarks:** Also notes percent change from 1998 and unit sales. **Number listed:** 10

1. Cheerios (General Mills), with $341.796 million
2. Frosted Flakes (Kellogg), $284.362
3. Honey Nut Cheerios (General Mills), $218.772
4. Frosted Mini-Wheats (Kellogg), $215.836
5. Corn Flakes (Kellogg), $210.750
6. Raisin Bran (Kellogg), $206.583
7. Lucky Charms (General Mills), $156.048
8. Quaker Oats, $155.485
9. Rice Krispies (Kellogg), $147.698
10. Private Label, $554.117

Source: *Milling and Baking News*, May 25, 1999, p. 31.

★1003★
TOP 10 READY-TO-EAT CEREAL BRANDS, 1998*
Ranked by: Market share, in percent. **Number listed:** 10

1. Cheerios (General Mills), with 9.8
2. Frosted Flakes (Kellogg), 4.2
3. Corn Flakes (Kellogg), 4.1
4. Frosted Mini-Wheats (Kellogg), 3.0
5. Rice Krispies (Kellogg), 2.9
6. Raisin Bran (Kellogg), 2.6
7. Froot Loops (Kellogg), 2.3
8. Lucky Charms (General Mills), 2.1
9. Special K (Kellogg), 2.0
10. Corn Pops (Kellogg), 1.8

Source: *Advertising Age*, September 28, 1998, p. 510.

Chain Stores, Apparel

See: **Clothing Stores**

Chain Stores, Food

See: **Grocery Trade**

Chain Stores, Grocery

See: **Supermarkets--Chain and Franchise Operations**

Chain Stores, Hotel

See: **Hotels and Motels--Chain and Franchise Operations**

Chain Stores, Restaurants

See: **Restaurants--Chain and Franchise Operations**

Chain Stores, Supermarkets

See: **Supermarkets--Chain and Franchise Operations**

Chambers of Commerce--Florida

★1004★
FLORIDA'S LEADING CHAMBERS OF COMMERCE, 1999
Ranked by: Number of members. **Remarks:** Also notes contact information, senior executive, operating budget, and miscellaneous organizational information. **Number listed:** 25

1. Greater Miami Chamber, with 7,200 members
2. Florida Chamber, 4,519
3. Greater Orlando Chamber, 4,500
4. Jacksonville Chamber, 4,000
5. Chamber South, 2,500
5. Greater Tampa Chamber, 2,500
6. St. Petersburg Area Chamber, 2,428
7. Lakeland Area Chamber, 2,113
8. Greater Fort Lauderdale Chamber, 2,000
8. Naples Area Chamber, 2,000
9. Greater Boca Raton Chamber, 1,945
10. Gainesville Area Chamber, 1,856

Source: *Florida Trend*, TopRank Florida (annual), 1999, p. 85.

Champagne

★1005★
TOP MARKETS FOR CHAMPAGNE AND SPARKLING WINE CONSUMPTION, 1997
Ranked by: Sales, in thousands of 9-liter cases. **Remarks:** Also notes 1996 figures, percent change, and share figures. **Number listed:** 51
1. California, with 3,063,100 cases
2. Illinois, 1,299,800
3. New York, 1,140,800
4. Florida, 895,100
5. Texas, 607,000
6. Michigan, 593,500
7. New Jersey, 545,400
8. Massachusetts, 372,800
9. Pennsylvania, 369,300
10. Ohio, 266,700

Source: *Adams Wine Handbook (annual)*, Adams Media, Inc., 1998, p. 67.

★1006★
TOP METROPOLITAN AREAS FOR CHAMPAGNE AND SPARKLING WINE SALES, 1997
Ranked by: Sales, in thousands of 9-liter cases. **Remarks:** Also notes market share. **Number listed:** 50
1. Los Angeles-Long Beach, CA, with 1,036.80 cases
2. Chicago, IL, 988.9
3. New York, NY, 581.2
4. Orange County, CA, 318.6
5. San Diego, CA, 291.7
6. Riverside-San Bernardino, CA, 288.7
7. Oakland, CA, 263.3
8. Detroit, MI, 261.3
9. Boston-Lawrence-Lowell-Brockton, MA, 254.9
10. Washington, DC, 245.9

Source: *Adams Wine Handbook*, (annual), Adams Media, Inc., 1998, p. 63.

★1007★
TOP PER CAPITA MARKETS FOR CHAMPAGNE AND SPARKLING WINE, 1997
Ranked by: 9-liter cases sold, per thousand adults. **Remarks:** Also notes 1996 figures. **Number listed:** 51
1. District of Columbia, with 376
2. Illinois, 235
3. California, 208
4. Hawaii, 200
5. New Hampshire, 167
6. New Jersey, 141
7. Connecticut, 139
8. Michigan, 132
9. New York, 131
10. Florida, 125

Source: *Adams Wine Handbook (annual)*, Adams Media, Inc., 1998, p. 66.

Champagne--Advertising

★1008★
CHAMPAGNE AND SPARKLING WINE BRANDS WITH THE HIGHEST CABLE TELEVISION ADVERTISING EXPENDITURES, 1997
Ranked by: Spot radio advertising expenditures, in thousands of dollars. **Remarks:** Also notes 1996 figures. **Number listed:** 13
1. Korbel, with $3,421.0 thousand
2. Moet & Chandon, $1,301.3
3. Ballatore, $1,291.5
4. Tott's, $1,076.4
5. Veuve Clicquot, $287.7
6. Martini & Rossi Asti, $232.1
7. Freixenet, $190.9
8. Domaine Chandon, $74.7
9. Louis Roederer, $49.0
10. Great Western, $45.8

Source: *Adams Wine Handbook*, (annual), Adams Media, Inc., 1998, p. 75.

Champagne--Export-Import Trade

★1009★
LEADING BRANDS OF IMPORTED CHAMPAGNE AND SPARKLING WINE, 1997
Ranked by: Sales, in thousands of cases. **Remarks:** Also notes supplier, country of origin, and sales figures for 1993-1996. **Number listed:** 21
1. Freixenet, with 750 cases
2. Moet & Chandon, 680
3. Martini & Rossi Asti, 630
4. Veuve Clicquot/La Grande Dame, 318
5. G. H. Mumm, 170
6. Perrier-Jouet, 100
7. Codorniu, 90
8. Piper Heidsieck, 65
9. Taittinger, 61
10. Gancia Asti, 56

Source: *Adams Wine Handbook (annual)*, Adams Media, Inc., 1998, p. 71.

★1010★
TOP METROPOLITAN AREAS FOR IMPORTED CHAMPAGNE AND SPARKLING WINE SALES, 1997
Ranked by: Sales, in thousands of 9-liter cases. **Remarks:** Also notes market share. **Number listed:** 10
1. Chicago, IL, with 305.7 cases
2. New York, NY, 241
3. Los Angeles-Long Beach, CA, 115.6
4. Boston/Lawrence/Lowell/Brockton, MA, 110
5. Detroit, MI, 94
6. Washington, DC, 90.1
7. Nassau-Suffolk, NY, 89.3
8. Philadelphia, PA, 78.2
9. Newark, NJ, 54.3
10. Orange County, CA, 49.4

Source: *Adams Wine Handbook (annual)*, Adams Media, Inc., 1998, p. 63.

Charge Accounts (Retail Trade)

★1011★
LARGEST RETAIL CREDIT CARD PROGRAMS, 1998
Ranked by: Amount of outstanding debt, in millions of dollars. **Remarks:** Also notes contact information, executive officer, interest income, bad-debt reserve, accounts, and cardholder APR for 1997 and 1998. **Number listed:** 49

1. Sears Merchandise Group, with $27,150,000,000 million
2. General Electric Capital Retailer Financial Services, $16,000,000,000
3. J. C. Penney, $5,242,000,000
4. Household Retailer Services, $4,375,000,000
5. Beneficial National Bank, $3,748,969,000
6. Dayton Hudson, $2,424,000,000
7. Banc One Private Label Credit Services, $2,350,374,000
8. Federated Department Stores, $2,222,000,000
9. May Department Stores, $2,167,000,000
10. SPS Payment Systems, $1,876,000,000

Source: *Faulkner & Gray*, Card Industry Directory, 1999, p. 384+.

Charitable Contributions

★1012★
CHARITABLE CONTRIBUTIONS FOR 1998
Ranked by: Uses of contributions, in billions of dollars. **Number listed:** 9

1. Religion, with $76.06 billion
2. Education, $24.56
3. Gifts to Foundations, $16.64
4. Health, $16.89
5. Human Services, $16.08
6. Public/Society Benefit, $10.86
7. Arts/Culture/Humanities, $10.53
8. Environment/Wildlife, $5.25
9. International Affairs, $2.14

Source: *The Non-Profit Times*, June, 1999, p. 6.

★1013★
SOURCES OF CONTRIBUTIONS, 1997
Ranked by: Sources, in billions of dollars. **Number listed:** 4

1. Individuals, with $109.26 billion
2. Foundations, $13.37
3. Bequests, $12.63
4. Corporations, $8.20

Source: *Financial Planning*, July, 1998, p. 103.

Cheese

★1014★
BEST-SELLING AMERICAN CHEESE BRANDS, 1998
Ranked by: Sales, in millions of dollars. **Remarks:** Also notes annual growth from previous year and market share. **Number listed:** 10

1. Private Label, with $429.7 million
2. Kraft Velveeta, $351.6
3. Kraft Singles, $327.6
4. Kraft, $170.5
5. Kraft Deluxe, $148.3
6. Borden, $135.8
7. Kraft Free, $61.1
8. Kraft Velveeta Light, $45.9
9. Land O'Lakes, $24.4
10. Crystal Farms, $13.2

Source: *Dairy Field*, February, 1999, p. 38.

★1015★
BEST-SELLING COTTAGE CHEESE BRANDS, 1998
Ranked by: Sales, in millions of dollars. **Remarks:** Also notes percent change from previous year. **Number listed:** 10

1. Private Label, with $287.6 million
2. Knudsen, $61.0
3. Breakstone, $51.9
4. Light n' Lively, $24.2
5. Dean's, $19.3
6. Friendship, $18.8
7. Light n' Lively Free, $13.5
8. Prairie Farms, $11.4
9. Knudsen Free, $10.4
10. Kemps, $9.7

Source: *Dairy Field*, August, 1998, p. 20.

★1016★
BEST-SELLING NATURAL SHREDDED CHEESE BRANDS, 1998
Ranked by: Sales, in millions of dollars. **Remarks:** Also notes annual growth from previous year and market share. **Number listed:** 9

1. Private Label, with $559.9 million
2. Kraft, $401.2
3. Sargento, $178.7
4. Healthy Choice, $43.3
5. Crystal Farms, $39.2
6. Sorrento, $20.0
7. Churny Provincia, $16.9
8. Kraft Free, $16.7
9. Sargento Double Cheese, $12.7

Source: *Dairy Field*, April, 1999, p. 17.

Chemical Industries

★1017★
BIGGEST CHEMICAL PRODUCERS, 1998
Ranked by: Sales, in millions of dollars. **Remarks:** Also notes 1997 rank, percent change, profits, assets, and return-related data. **Number listed:** 75

1. DuPont, with $26,202.0 million
2. Dow Chemical, $17,710.0
3. Exxon, $10,504.0
4. General Electric, $6,633.0
5. Union Carbide, $5,659.0
6. Huntsman, $5,200.0
7. ICI Americas, $4,900.0
8. Praxair, $4,833.0
9. BASF, $4,800.0
10. Eastman Chemical, $4,481.0

Source: *Chemical & Engineering News*, June 28, 1999, p. 41+.

★1018★
CHEMICAL/PETROCHEMICAL/MATERIALS CORPORATIONS SPENDING THE MOST ON RESEARCH AND DEVELOPMENT, 1997
Ranked by: Research and development expenditures, in millions of dollars. **Number listed:** 10

1. Du Pont De Nemours, with $2,526.5 million
2. Monsanto, $933.6
3. Dow Chemical, $768.6
4. Exxon Corp., $529.8
5. Goodyear Tire & Rubber Co., $386.9
6. PPG Industries Inc., $250.6
7. Corning Inc., $246.4
8. Mobil Corp., $237.1
9. Rohm & Haas Co., $201.6
10. Shell Oil Co., $200.0

Source: *Research & Development*, Giants of R & D (annual), October 28, 1998, p. S-14.

★1019★
LEADING DIVERSIFIED CHEMICAL CORPORATIONS, 1998

Ranked by: Sales, in millions of dollars. **Number listed:** 12

1. DuPont, with $24,767 million
2. AlliedSignal, $15,128
3. PPG Industries, $7,510
4. FMC, $4,378
5. Englehard, $4,172
6. BF Goodrich, $3,951
7. Mallinckrodt, $2,367
8. Sequa, $1,802
9. Vulcan Materials, $1,776
10. Cabot, $1,648

Source: *Chemical Week*, Chemical Week 300 (annual), April, May 12, 1999, p. 49+.

★1020★
LEADING INDUSTRIAL AND SYNTHETIC MATERIALS CORPORATIONS, 1998

Ranked by: Sales, in millions of dollars. **Number listed:** 19

1. Dow Chemical, with $18,441 million
2. Monsanto, $8,648
3. Union Carbide, $5,659
4. Air Products & Chemicals, $4,919
5. Praxair, $4,833
6. Eastman Chemical, $4,481
7. Rohm & Haas Co., $3,720
8. Nova Chemicals, $2,075
9. Millennium Chemicals, $1,597
10. Airgas, Inc., $1,448

Source: *Chemical Week*, Chemical Week 300 (annual), April, May 12, 1999, p. 49.

★1021★
MULTI-INDUSTRY COMPANIES WITH CHEMICAL PROCESS OPERATIONS, 1998

Ranked by: Sales, in millions of dollars. **Number listed:** 12

1. General Electric, with $100,469 million
2. Johnson's Controls, $12,587
3. Tenneco, $7,597
4. ITT Industries, $4,493
5. Allegheny Teledyne, $3,923
6. Armstrong World Industries, $2,746
7. Viad, $2,542
8. Aeroquip-Vickers, $2,150
9. Agway, $1,563
10. Hexcel, $1,089

Source: *Chemical Week*, Chemical Week 300 (annual), April, May 12, 1999, p. 51+.

★1022★
TOP CHEMICAL COMPANIES IN THE S & P 500, 1998

Ranked by: Each company is ranked by 8 criteria: one-year total return, three-year total return, one-year sales growth, three-year average annual sales growth, one-year profit growth, three-year average annual profit growth, net profit margins, and return on equity, with additional weight given to a company's sales. A company's composite rank is calculated using the sum of all its ranks. **Remarks:** Overall score not provided. **Number listed:** 13

1. Air Products & Chemicals
2. Rohm & Haas Co.
3. Praxair
4. DuPont
5. Dow Chemical
6. International Flavors & Fragrances
7. Morton International
8. Union Carbide
9. Monsanto
10. Eastman Chemical

Source: *Business Week*, Business Week 50: Top Companies of the S & P 500 (annual), March 29, 1999, p. 144.

★1023★
TOP CORPORATIONS IN THE CHEMICALS INDUSTRY, 1998

Ranked by: Revenue, in millions of dollars. **Remarks:** Also notes profits, profits as a percentage of revenue, assets and stockholders' equity, earnings per share, total return to investors, and number of employees. **Number listed:** 37

1. E.I. Du Pont de Nemours, with $39,130 million
2. Dow Chemical, $18,441
3. Monsanto, $8,648
4. PPG Industries, $7,510
5. Union Carbide, $5,659
6. Sherwin-Williams, $4,934
7. Air Products & Chemicals, $4,934
8. Praxair, $4,833
9. Eastman Chemical, $4,481
10. FMC, $4,378

Source: *Fortune*, Fortune 500 Largest U.S. Corporations (annual), April 26, 1999, p. F-53.

★1024★
WORLD'S MOST ADMIRED CHEMICAL COMPANIES, 1998

Ranked by: Scores (1-10) derived from a survey of senior executives, outside directors, and securities analysts. **Remarks:** Respondents rated companies in their own industry on 8 attributes of reputation. **Number listed:** 10

1. DuPont, with 7.85 points
2. Dow Chemical, 7.02
3. Monsanto, 6.79
4. PPG Industries, 6.55
5. Bayer, 6.54
6. BASF, 6.39
7. Union Carbide, 5.97
8. Sherwin-Williams, 5.94
9. FMC, 5.46
10. Occidental Petroleum, 5.05

Source: *Fortune*, America's Most Admired Corporations (annual), March 1, 1999, p. F-5.

Chemical Industries--Acquisitions and Mergers

★1025★
LEADING MERGER AND ACQUISITIONS ADVISERS FOR CHEMICAL INDUSTRY COMPANIES, 1999*

Ranked by: Value of deals, in millions of dollars. **Remarks:** Also notes number of deals. **Number listed:** 24

1. J.P. Morgan, with $200,583 million

2. Goldman Sachs, $172,033
3. Merrill Lynch, $106,547
4. Morgan Stanley Dean Witter, $98,886
5. Credit Suisse First Boston, $78,171
6. Lazard-Freres, $28,844
7. Paribas, $16,800
8. Deutsche Bank, $14,095
9. CCF Charterhouse, $13,172
10. Salomon Smith Barney, $10,852

Source: *Chemical Week*, March 31, 1999, p. 32.

Chemical Industries--Asia

★1026★
ASIA'S LARGEST QUOTED COMPANIES IN CHEMICALS, PLASTICS, AND PETROLEUM, 1999*
Ranked by: Sales, in thousands of U.S. dollars. **Remarks:** Also notes profit as percentage of sales, as well as country, and activity codes. **Number listed:** 100

1. Japan Energy Corp., with $14,716,235 thousand
2. Mitsubishi Chemical, $12,975,261
3. Showa Shell Sekiyu KK, $11,886,729
4. Fuji Photo Film Co. Ltd., $10,314,827
5. Asahi Chemical Industry Co. Ltd., $9,593,375
6. SK, $9,028,115
7. Mitsubishi Oil, $8,592,110
8. POSCOChemical, $8,156,105
9. Toray Industries Inc., $8,141,564
10. Sekisui Chemical Co. Ltd., $8,083,547

Source: *Dun & Bradstreet*, Asia's 7500 Largest Companies (annual), 1999, p. 75+.

Chemical Industries--Canada

★1027★
LEADING CHEMICAL COMPANIES IN CANADA, 1997
Ranked by: Sales in millions of Canadian dollars (C$). **Remarks:** Also notes sales in 1996, as well as the headquarters location, and ownership. **Number listed:** 19

1. Nova Chemicals, with C$3,360 million
2. Potash Corp. Saskatchewan, C$2,358
3. Dow Chemical Canada, C$2,271
4. DuPont Canada, C$2,012
5. Agrium Ltd., C$1,955
6. Bayer, C$1,309
7. Methanex Corp., C$1,134
8. Imperial Oil Ltd., C$992
9. ICI Canada, C$890
10. PPG Canada, C$779

Source: *Chemical Week*, July 22, 1998, p. 28.

Chemical Industries--Europe

★1028★
LARGEST EUROPEAN COMPANIES IN CHEMICAL AND ALLIED PRODUCTS
Ranked by: Financial size, in millions of ECUs. **Remarks:** Also lists country and number of employees. **Number listed:** 229

1. BASF, with ECUs28.288 million
2. Bayer, ECUs27.895
3. Hoechst, ECUs26.422
4. Imperial Chemical Industries PLC, ECUs16.322
5. Glaxo Wellcome PLC, ECUs11.775
6. SmithKline Beecham, ECUs11.052
7. Henkel KG Auf Aktien, ECUs10.175
8. Zeneca Group PLC, ECUs7.664
9. DSM NV, ECUs5.580
10. B.O.C Group PLC, ECUs5.426

Source: *Dun & Bradstreet*, Duns Europa (annual), 1999, p. 241+.

Chemical Industries, International

★1029★
LARGEST WORLDWIDE CHEMICAL COMPANIES, 1997
Ranked by: Chemical sales, in millions of U.S. dollars ($). **Remarks:** Also notes total sales, net profit, capital, and R & D figures, as well as employee data. **Number listed:** 187

1. DuPont (U.S.), with $24,100 million
2. BASF (Germany), $20,000
3. Dow Chemical (U.S.), $19,056
4. Bayer (Germany), $18,471
5. ICI (U.K.), $18,134
6. Shell (U.K./Netherlands), $14,831
7. Hoechst (Germany), $14,309
8. Unilever (U.K./Netherlands), $12,582
9. Exxon (U.S.), $12,195
10. Mitsubishi Chemical (Japan), $11,671

Source: *Chemical Week*, Billion-Dollar Club (annual), December 16, 1998, p. 23+.

★1030★
WORLD'S LARGEST CHEMICAL CORPORATIONS BY REVENUE, 1997
Ranked by: Revenue, in millions of dollars. **Remarks:** Also notes profits and profits and a percent of revenues and assets. **Number listed:** 16

1. E.I. Du Pont de Nemours (U.S.), with $41,304 million
2. BASF (Germany), $32,178
3. Bayer (Germany), $31,731
4. Hoechst (Germany), $30,055
5. Dow Chemical (U.S.), $20,018
6. Imperial Chemical Industries (Great Britain), $18,121
7. Rhone-Poulenc (France), $15,413
8. Mitsubishi Chemical (Japan), $14,122
9. Montedison (Italy), $13,897
10. Norsk Hydro (Norway), $13,585

Source: *Fortune*, The Global 500: World's Biggest Corporations (annual), August 3, 1998, p. F-17.

★1031★
WORLD'S LARGEST CHEMICAL PRODUCERS, 1997
Ranked by: Chemical sales, in millions of U.S. dollars ($). **Remarks:** Also notes total sales and chemical operating profits. **Number listed:** 50

1. BASF Germany (Germany), with $27,046.9 million
2. DuPont (U.S.), $21,295.0
3. Bayer (Germany), $19,178.2
4. Dow Chemical (U.S.), $19,056.0
5. Hoechst (Germany), $16,293.8
6. Shell (U.K./Netherlands), $14,251.6
7. ICI (U.K.), $13,349.2

8. Exxon (U.S.), $14,024.0
9. Akzo Nobel (Netherlands), $9,997.9
10. Elf Aquitaine (Norway), $9,954.3

Source: *Chemical & Engineering News (annual)*, July 20, 1998, p. 38.

Chemical Patents

★1032★
COUNTRIES HOLDING THE MOST U.S. CHEMICAL PATENTS, 1997
Ranked by: Patents issued, in percent. **Remarks:** Also notes number of patents issued from 1987 to 1996. **Number listed:** 17

1. U.S., with 25.9%
2. Japan, 13.1%
3. Germany, 7.7%
4. China, 6.8%
5. U.K., 5.5%
6. France, 4.6%
7. Russia, 4.5%
8. Canada, 2.8%
8. Italy, 2.8%
9. India, 2.3%
10. Spain, 2.0%

Source: *Chemical & Engineering News*, Facts & Figures for Chemical R & D (annual), October 19, 1998, p. 81.

Chemical Research--Expenditures

★1033★
CORPORATIONS SPENDING THE MOST ON CHEMICAL RESEARCH AND DEVELOPMENT, 1997
Ranked by: Research and development expenditures, in millions of dollars. **Remarks:** Also notes expenditures for 1987 to 1996 and expenditures as a percentage of sales. **Number listed:** 16

1. Dow Chemical, with $785 million
2. Rohm & Haas Co., $200
3. Union Carbide, $157
4. Air Products & Chemicals, $114
5. International Flavors & Fragrances, $94
6. Lubrizol, $88
7. Praxair, $79
8. Witco Corp., $72
9. Solutia, $60
10. Morton International, $59

Source: *Chemical Engineering News*, Facts & Figures for Chemical R & D (annual), October 19, 1998, p. 66.

★1034★
UNIVERSITIES SPENDING THE MOST ON CHEMICAL ENGINEERING RESEARCH AND DEVELOPMENT, 1996
Ranked by: Research and development expenditures, in thousands of dollars. **Remarks:** Also notes spending for 1986 to 1995 and one- and ten-year annual change. **Number listed:** 25

1. Massachusetts Institute of Technology, with $17,788 thousand
2. Texas A & M University, $11,074
3. University of Minnesota, $10,973
4. North Carolina State University, $10,758
5. Case Western Reserve University, $9,198
6. University of Texas at Austin, $7,515
7. New Mexico State University, $6,971
8. Michigan State University, $6,739
9. University of Wisconsin, $6,367
10. University of Oklahoma, $6,238

Source: *Chemical & Engineering News*, Facts & Figures for Chemical R & D (annual), October 19, 1998, p. 73.

★1035★
UNIVERSITIES SPENDING THE MOST ON CHEMICAL RESEARCH AND DEVELOPMENT, 1996
Ranked by: Research and development expenditures, in thousands of dollars. **Remarks:** Also notes spending for 1986 to 1995. **Number listed:** 50

1. California Institute of Technology, with $15,599 thousand
2. Massachusetts Institute of Technology, $14,856
3. University of California, Berkeley, $14,277
4. University of Illinois at Urbana-Champaign, $12,956
5. University of Wisconsin, $12,910
6. University of Pennsylvania, $12,855
7. University of Colorado, $12,701
8. Pennsylvania State University, $12,670
9. Texas A & M University, $12,478
10. Stanford University, $12,253

Source: *Chemical & Engineering News*, Facts & Figures for Chemical R & D (annual), October 19, 1998, p. 71.

★1036★
UNIVERSITIES WITH THE MOST FEDERAL SUPPORT FOR CHEMICAL ENGINEERING RESEARCH AND DEVELOPMENT, 1996
Ranked by: Federal funds received, in thousands of dollars. **Remarks:** Also notes funding for 1986-1995 and 1- and ten-year annual change. **Number listed:** 50

1. Massachusetts Institute of Technology, with $13,735 thousand
2. California Institute of Technology, $12,478
3. University of Pennsylvania, $12,181
4. Stanford University, $12,171
5. University of California, Berkeley, $12,050
6. Harvard University, $10,608
7. University of Colorado, $9,442
8. University of California, Los Angeles, $9,338
9. University of Wisconsin, $9,318
10. Cornell University, $8,805

Source: *Chemical & Engineering News*, Facts & Figures for Chemical R & D (annual), October 19, 1998, p. 72.

★1037★
UNIVERSITIES WITH THE MOST FEDERAL SUPPORT FOR CHEMICAL RESEARCH AND DEVELOPMENT, 1996
Ranked by: Federal funds received, in thousands of dollars. **Remarks:** Also notes funding for 1986 to 1995 and one- and ten-year annual change. **Number listed:** 25

1. Massachusetts Institute of Technology, with $10,443 thousand
2. University of Minnesota, $8,141
3. New Mexico State University, $6,305
4. Case Western Reserve University, $5,841
5. North Carolina State University, $4,810
6. University of California at San Diego, $4,637
7. Johns Hopkins University, $4,605
8. University of Texas at Austin, $4,187
9. Stanford University, $3,961
10. University of Tulsa, $3,409

Source: *Chemical & Engineering News*, Facts & Figures for Chemical R & D (annual), October 19, 1998, p. 73.

Chemical Specialties Industry

★1038★
TOP SPECIALTY CHEMICAL COMPANIES, 1997
Ranked by: Sales, in billions of dollars. **Number listed:** 10
1. ICI, with $8.9 billion
2. Clariant, $6.6
3. Rhodia, $6.4
4. Ciba, $5.2
5. Rohm & Haas Co., $4.0
6. Morton International, $2.3
7. Witco, $2.2
8. Crompton & Knowles, $1.9
9. Hercules, $1.8
10. Engelhard, $1.5

Source: *Chemical Market Place*, August 24, 1998, p. FR4.

Chester County (PA)--Industries

★1039★
LARGEST EMPLOYERS IN CHESTER COUNTY PA, 1998*
Ranked by: Number of full-time local employees. **Remarks:** Also notes contact information, executive officers, total number of employees, revenue, and number of offices. **Number listed:** 25
1. The Vanguard Group, with 5,800 employees
2. Shared Medical Systems Corp., 3,200
3. QVC Inc., 2,205
4. Lukens Inc., 2,000
5. Providian, 1,400
6. Unisys Corp., 1,200
7. The Devereux Foundation, 1,017
8. Johnson Matthey Investments Inc., 1,006
9. DecisionOne Corp., 1,000
10. Brandywine Health System, 828

Source: *Philadelphia Business Journal*, Book of Business Lists (annual), December 25, 1998, p. 99.

Chewing Gum

★1040★
BEST SELLING REGULAR GUM BRANDS, 1997
Ranked by: Sales, in billions of dollars. **Remarks:** Also notes unit sales and percent sales by supermarkets, discounters, and drugstores. **Number listed:** 10
1. Wrigley's Doublemint Gum, with $12 billion
2. Wrigley's Winterfresh Gum, $11
3. Wrigley's Freedent, $9
4. Wrigley's Big Red, $8
5. Wrigley's Juicyfruit Gum, $7
5. Wrigley's Spearmint, $7
7. Adams Bubbleicious, $5
7. LifeSavers Bubble Gum, $5
9. Adams Cinn-A-Burst, $4
10. Adams Dentyne, $3

Source: *Candy Industry*, July, 1998, p. A7.

★1041★
BEST-SELLING SUGAR-FREE CHEWING GUM BRANDS, 1997
Ranked by: Market share, in percent. **Number listed:** 10
1. Wrigley's Extra, with 34%
2. Adams Trident, 25%
3. LifeSavers Care-Free, 17%
4. LifeSavers Ice Breakers, 11%
5. Dentyne, 4%
6. Stick-Free, 3%
6. Bubble Yum, 3%
8. Dentyne, 2%
9. Topps Bozooka, 0%
10. Biotene, 0%

Source: *Candy Industry*, July, 1998, p. A17.

Chicago (IL)--Industries

★1042★
CHICAGO'S TOP EMPLOYERS, 1997
Ranked by: Number of Chicago employees. **Remarks:** Also notes contact information, executive officer, total number of employees, revenue and earnings. **Number listed:** 35
1. U.S. Government, with 67,733 employees
2. Chicago Public Schools, 44,727
3. City of Chicago, 41,113
4. Jewel-Osco, 38,796
5. Cook County, 26,730
6. U.S. Postal Service, 25,550
7. Motorola, 25,500
8. Ameritech Corp., 22,000
9. State of Illinois, 20,419
10. United Airlines, 19,242

Source: *Crain's Chicago Business*, Top Business Lists (annual), 1999, p. 171+.

★1043★
FASTEST-GROWING PUBLIC COMPANIES IN CHICAGO, 1997
Ranked by: Compound annual growth rate, in percent. **Remarks:** Also notes revenue for 1997 and 1992, percent change, net earnings, and number of employees. **Number listed:** 50
1. Accumed International Inc., with 312.5%
2. American Disposal Services Inc., 287.7%
3. Leap Group Inc., 201.1%
4. BAB Holdings Inc., 195.0%
5. Great Lakes Reit Inc., 146.4%
6. USN Communications Inc., 144.7%
7. Amerin Corp., 140.4%
8. Platinum Entertainment Inc., 135.6%
9. Anicom Inc., 131.4%
10. Career Education Corp., 122.6%

Source: *Crain's Chicago Business*, Top Business Lists (annual), 1999, p. 51+.

Chief Executive Officers

★1044★
TOP BRAND-NAME CHIEF EXECUTIVE OFFICERS, 1998
Ranked by: Number of times mentioned in the media, percentage change in company's revenue and profit. **Number listed:** 10
1. Bill Gates (Microsoft Corp.)
2. Michael Eisner (Walt Disney Co.)
3. Louis V. Gerstner Jr. (IBM Corp.)

4. Larry Ellison (Oracle Systems Corp.)
5. Jack Welch (General Electric Co.)
6. Lew Platt (Hewlett-Packard Co.)
7. Michael Dell (Dell Computer Corp.)
8. Sanford I. Weill (Travelers Group)
9. Peter Bijur (Texaco Inc.)
10. John Chambers (Cisco Systems Inc.)

Source: *Electronic Business*, July, 1998, p. 24.

Chief Executive Officers--Salaries, Pensions, etc.

★1045★
BEST-PAID CHIEF EXECUTIVE OFFICERS IN THE DETROIT METROPOLITAN AREA, 1997
Ranked by: Total compensation, including options and grants. **Remarks:** Also notes age, total pay, and various financial data. **Number listed:** 50

1. Richard Manoogian (Masco Corp.), with $19,744,001 thousand
2. David Brandon (Valassis Communications Inc.), $12,176,530
3. Robert Eaton (Chrysler Corp.), $11,378,105
4. Alex Trotman (Ford Motor Co.), $10,690,885
5. Kenneth Way (Lear Corp.), $7,947,691
6. John Smith Jr. (General Motors Corp.), $7,120,715
7. Floyd Hall (Kmart Corp.), $6,120,543
8. Robert Burgess (Pulte Corp.), $5,058,867
9. Eugene Miller (Comerica Inc.), $3,651,929
10. Alfred Glancy III (MCN Energy Group Inc.), $3,540,390

Source: *Crain's Detroit Business*, Crain's Book of Lists Detroit (annual), December 28, 1999, p. 132+.

★1046★
HIGHEST-PAID CHIEF EXECUTIVE OFFICERS IN THE NEW YORK METROPOLITAN AREA, 1998
Ranked by: Total compensation. **Remarks:** Also notes short-term, long-term compensation, revenue of firm, and total pay as a percentage of revenue. **Number listed:** 100

1. Sandord I. Weill (Citigroup Inc.), with $167,095.4 thousand
2. Linda J. Wachner (Warnaco Group Inc.), $91,198.1
3. Henry R. Silverman (Cendant Corp.), $63,959.1
4. Charles A Heimbold Jr. (Bristol-Myers Squibb Co.), $56,337.6
5. Philip J. Purcell (Morgan Stanley Dean Witter & Co.), $53,397.4
6. Reuben Mark (Colgate-Palmolive Co.), $46,581.9
7. Louis V. Gerstner Jr. (IBM Corp.), $46,526.0
8. W. C. Steere Jr. (Pfizer Inc), $38,401.5
9. Maurice R. Greenberg (American International Group Inc.), $31,207.8
10. Charles B. Wang (Computer Associates International Inc.), $30,015.4

Source: *Crain's New York Business*, Fortunate 100, June 21, 1999, p. 42+.

★1047★
HIGHEST-PAID CHIEF EXECUTIVE OFFICERS, 1997
Ranked by: Total pay, in thousands of dollars. **Remarks:** Includes salary, bonus, and long-term compensation. **Number listed:** 20

1. Michael Eisner (Walt Disney), with $575,592 thousand
2. Mel Karmazin (CBS), $201,934
3. Sanford I. Weill (Walt Disney), $167,093
4. Stephen Case (America Online), $159,233
5. Craig Barrett (Intel), $116,511
6. John Welch (General Electric), $83,664
7. Henry Schacht (Lucent Technologies), $67,037
8. L. Dennis Kozlowski (Tyco International), $65,264
9. Henry Silverman (Cendant), $63,882
10. M. Douglas Ivester (Coca-Cola), $57,332

Source: *Business Week*, (annual), May, April 19, 1999, p. 72+.

Chief Financial Officers

★1048★
FAVORITE PASTIME OF CHIEF FINANCIAL OFFICERS, 1998
Ranked by: Pastime cited, in percent. **Number listed:** 9

1. Golf, with 21%
2. Reading, 14%
3. Team sports, 10%
4. Exercise, 9%
5. Movies or theater, 9%
6. Music, 5%
7. Surfing the Internet, 4%
8. Tennis, 3%
9. Fishing or hunting, 2%

Source: *Journal of Accountancy*, July, 1998, p. 18.

Chief Financial Officers--Salaries, Pensions, etc.

★1049★
BIGGEST WORRIES OF CHIEF FINANCIAL OFFICERS, 1998
Ranked by: Reason cited, in percent. **Number listed:** 6

1. Finding qualified staff, with 27%
2. Sustaining growth, 22%
3. Keeping pace with competitors, 20%
4. Meeting customer demands, 14%
5. Complying with government regulations, 12%
6. Others, 2%

Source: *Management Review*, October, 1998, p. 8.

★1050★
HIGHEST-PAID CHIEF FINANCIAL OFFICERS, 1998
Ranked by: Compensation. **Number listed:** 25

1. Scott Sullivan (WorldCom), with $19,250,000 thousand
2. Earl L. Mason (Compaq Computer), $16,157,500
3. Robert G. Scott (Morgan Stanley Dean Witter), $12,669,311
4. Donald K. Peterson (Lucent Technologies), $10,591,316
5. James G. Stewart (Cigna), $9,457,400
6. Barry D. Romeril (Xerox), $9,010,438
7. Harry Kavetas (Eastman Kodak), $8,859,771
8. Lawrence R. Ricciardi (IBM), $7,957,200
9. Louis C. Camerilli (Philip Morris), $6,686,832
10. Teresa Beck (American Stores), $5,560,444

Source: *CFO*, November, 1998, p. 53.

★1051★
HIGHEST-PAID CHIEF FINANCIAL OFFICERS, 1997
Ranked by: Total remuneration. **Remarks:** Also notes total salary, bonus, other compensation and percent change from 1996 total. **Number listed:** 100

1. Rollin M. Dick (Conseco), with $38,807.50 thousand
2. Thomas J. Meredith (Dell Computer), $21,339.41
3. Gerald F. Taylor (Applied Materials), $18,519.94
4. M. S. Kaufman (MBNA), $11,532.35
5. Robert S. Woodruff (Quest Communication International), $9,723.03
6. Scott D. Sullivan (WorldCom), $9,581.31
7. Jeffrey O. Henley (Oracle), $7,758.24
8. James R. Elsesser (Ralston Purina), $7,617.28
9. Lennert J. Leader (America Online), $7,553.68
10. H. R. Bingham (Cadence Design Systems), $7,386.46

Source: *Global Finance*, CFO Compensation Survey (annual), August, 1998, p. 19+.

Chief Financial Officers—Salaries, Pensions, etc.--Great Britain

★1052★
HIGHEST-PAID CHIEF FINANCIAL OFFICERS IN GREAT BRITIAN, 1997
Ranked by: Total compensation, in thousands of British pounds. **Number listed:** 20

1. Robert McCullough (Amvescap), with £925.0 thousand
2. Peter Wood (Standard Chartered), £828.0
3. Hugh Collum (SmithKline Beecham), £803.0
4. Ian Duncan (Tomkins), £774.0
5. John Coombe (Glaxo Wellcome), £773.0
6. Hans Eggerstedt (Unilever), £717.6
7. Anthony Percival (Kingfisher), £659.0
8. Christopher Bull (Rio Tinto), £572.0
9. John Buchanan (British Petroleum), £565.0
10. Michael Davis (Billiton), £561.0

Source: *Accountancy International*, January, 1999, p. 14.

Child Care Centers

★1053★
LEADING CHILD CARE CENTERS, 1997
Ranked by: Percentage of child care centers. **Number listed:** 5

1. Independent, nonprofit, with 35%
2. Independent, for-profit, 29%
3. Group, nonprofit, 22%
4. Public Schools, 8%
5. Chains, 6%

Source: *New York Times*, July 26, 1998, p. 8BU.

Children's Clothing

See: **Clothing and Dress--Children**

Chocolate Industry

★1054★
BEST-SELLING CHOCOLATE BRAND, 1998
Ranked by: Sales, in millions of dollars. **Remarks:** Also notes 1997 sales and rank. **Number listed:** 10

1. Snickers Original, with $133.8 million
2. Reese's Peanut Butter Cups, $114.4
3. M & M Peanut, $85.1
4. M & M Plain, $80.8
5. Kit Kat, $58.2
6. Hershey Almond, $53.2
7. Butterfinger Bar, $46.6
8. Hershey Milk, $45.9
9. Twix Caramel, $37.6
10. Milky Way Original, $36.1

Source: *Candy Industry*, July, 1998, p. A16.

★1055★
BEST-SELLING SNACK-SIZE CHOCOLATE BARS, 1997
Ranked by: Sales, in millions of dollars. **Remarks:** Also notes unit sales. **Number listed:** 11

1. Snickers, with $103.0 million
2. Reese's, $94.0
3. Kit Kat, $71.0
4. Milky Way, $46.0
5. Butterfinger, $40.0
5. Three Musketeers, $40.0
7. M & Ms, $36.0
8. Nestle Crunch, $34.0
9. Peter Paul Almond Joy, $23.0
9. Baby Ruth, $23.0
11. Twix, $22.0

Source: *Discount Merchandiser*, October, 1998, p. 52.

★1056★
BEST-SELLING SNACK-SIZE CHOCOLATE BARS, 1997
Ranked by: Market share, in percent. **Number listed:** 10

1. M & M Chocolate Candies, with 16%
2. Hershey's Chocolate Bar, 10%
3. Reese's Peanut Butter Cups, 9%
4. Snickers, 8%
5. York Peppermint Patty, 4%
5. Butterfinger, 4%
6. Nestle Crunch, 3%
6. Three Musketeers, 3%
6. Russell Stover Chocolate Bars, 3%
7. Reese's Nutrageous, 2%

Source: *Candy Industry*, July, 98, p. A12.

★1057★
BEST-SELLING SNACK-SIZE CHOCOLATE CANDY, 1997
Ranked by: Sales, in millions of dollars. **Remarks:** Also notes unit sales. **Number listed:** 11

1. M & Ms, with $212.0 million
2. Hershey's, $148.0
3. Hershey's Kisses, $96.0
4. Snickers, $79.0
5. Reese's, $75.0
6. Hershey's Nuggets, $56.0
7. York Peppermint Patty, $44.0
8. Hershey's Sweet Escapes, $38.0
9. Private Label, $28.0
10. Milky Way, $25.0

Source: *Discount Merchandiser*, October, 1998, p. 52.

★1058★
BEST-SELLING 3.5 OZ. CHOCOLATE CANDY BAR, 1997
Ranked by: Sales, in millions of dollars. **Remarks:** Also notes unit sales. **Number listed:** 10
1. M & Ms, with $121.0 million
2. Hersey's, $77.0
3. Reese's, $64.0
4. Snickers, $63.0
5. York Peppermint Patty, $27.0
6. Butterfinger, $25.0
7. Nestle Crunch, $22.0
8. Three Musketeers, $21.0
9. Russell Stover, $19.0
10. Peter Paul Almond Joy, $18.0

Source: *Discount Merchandiser*, October, 1998, p. 52.

★1059★
LEADING CHOCOLATE BAR COMPANIES BY MARKET SHARE, 1997
Ranked by: Market share, in percent. **Number listed:** 3
1. Hershey Chocolate, with 40%
2. M & M/Mars, 33%
3. Nestle Chocolate, 15%

Source: *Candy Industry*, July, 1998, p. A12.

Chocolate Industry--Great Britain

★1060★
BEST-SELLING BOXED CHOCOLATES IN GREAT BRITAIN, 1998
Ranked by: Market share, in percent. **Remarks:** Also notes value sales. **Number listed:** 10
1. Cadbury's Roses, with 14.4%
2. Nestle Quality Street, 12%
3. Mars Celebrations, 8.1%
4. Cadbury's Milk Tray, 7.6%
5. Ferrere Rocher, 5.6%
6. Terry's All Gold, 4.5%
7. After Eight (Nestle), 4.4%
8. Dairy Box (Nestle), 3.6%
9. Black Magic (Nestle), 2.8%
10. Matchmaker's, 2.1%

Source: *Marketing*, February 11, 1999, p. 25.

Cigarette Industry

See also: **Tobacco Industry**

★1061★
TOP CIGARETTE BRANDS, 1998
Ranked by: Total sales, in units. **Remarks:** Also lists company name and location, lead agency, and media expenditures. **Number listed:** 10
1. Marlboro, with 162.5 units
2. Newport, 32.1
3. Doral, 30.8
4. GPC, 26.1
5. Winston, 23.8
6. Basic, 23.4
7. Camel, 22.9
8. Kool, 15.8
9. Salem, 14.7
10. Virginia Slims, 10.9

Source: *Brandweek*, Superbrands: America's Top 2,000 Brands, June 21, 1999, p. 27.

Cigarette Industry--Export-Import Trade--Japan

★1062★
TOP CIGARETTE BRANDS IN JAPAN, 1997-1998
Ranked by: Unit sales, in millions. **Number listed:** 10
1. Mild Seven, with 33,191 million
2. Mild Seven Lights, 32,979
3. Mild Seven Super Lights, 32,574
4. Seven Stars, 23,181
5. Caster Mild, 20,066
6. Cabin Mild Box, 10,717
7. Frontier Lights Box, 8,783
8. Lark Milds Box, 6,022
9. Hope, 5,973
10. Hi-Lite, 4,720

Source: *Tobacco International*, November, 1998, p. 26.

★1063★
TOP IMPORTED CIGARETTE BRANDS IN JAPAN, 1997-1998
Ranked by: Number of units imported, in millions. **Number listed:** 9
1. Lark Milds Box, with 6,022 million
2. Parliament 100 Box, 3,712
3. Philip Morris Super Lights Box, 3,432
4. Virginia Slims Lights Menthol, 3,291
5. Kent Milds King Size Box, 2,952
6. Kent 1, 2,668
7. Philip Morris Super Light 100 Box, 2,482
8. Philip Morris One KS Box, 2,406
9. Next King Size Box, 2,374

Source: *Tobacco International*, November, 1998, p. 27.

Cigars--Europe

★1064★
EUROPEAN CIGAR CONSUMPTION, 1997
Ranked by: Million units. **Number listed:** 14
1. France, with 1,571 million
2. Germany, 1,200
3. United Kingdom, 1,023
4. Spain, 831
5. Belgium/Luxembourg, 613
6. Netherlands, 442
7. Italy, 183
8. Denmark, 182
9. Sweden, 71
10. Finland, 63

Source: *Tobacco Invternational*, December, 1998, p. 23.

Cities and Towns

See also: **Metropolitan Areas**

★1065★

BEST MASS TRANSIT SYSTEMS IN U.S., 1999*

Ranked by: Study results by the Transportation Center at the University of North Carolina as Charlotte. **Remarks:** Transit systems in 135 urban areas were ranked according to 12 different measures such as service levels, operating costs and per-passenger revenue. **Number listed:** 10

1. Santa Monica, CA
2. Champaign-Urbana, IL
3. Tucson, AZ
4. Las Vegas, NV
5. Springfield, MA
6. Santa Barbara, CA
7. Newport News, VA
8. El Paso, TX
9. Los Angeles, CA
10. Richmond, VA

Source: *Governing*, February, 1999, p. 96.

★1066★

CITIES WITH THE HIGHEST AVERAGE INCOME PER HOUSEHOLD, 1998*

Ranked by: Average income per household. **Number listed:** 250

1. Hanover, NH, with $124,149 dollars
2. Toms River, NJ, $119,549
3. Greenwich, CT, $101,652
4. East Brunswick, NJ, $92,197
5. Falls Church, VA, $90,896
6. Palm Beach, FL, $89,521
7. Parsippany, NJ, $88,772
8. Cherry Hill, NJ, $86,278
9. Palo Alto, CA, $82,989
10. Lanham, MD, $82,744

Source: *Editor & Publisher Market Guide*, (annual), 1998, p. I-31+.

★1067★

CITIES WITH THE HIGHEST GASOLINE SALES, 1998*

Ranked by: Sales, in thousands of dollars. **Number listed:** 250

1. Los Angeles, CA, with $1,728,497 thousand
2. New York City, NY, $1,468,576
3. Houston, TX, $1,230,259
4. Indianapolis, IN, $862,268
5. Chicago, IL, $832,029
6. Dallas, TX, $724,187
7. Phoenix, AZ, $713,099
8. San Antonio, TX, $659,780
9. San Diego, CA, $604,697
10. Jacksonville, FL, $531,162

Source: *Editor & Publisher Market Guide*, (annual), 1998, p. I-35+.

★1068★

CITIES WITH THE HIGHEST MEDIAN HOME PRICE, 1999

Ranked by: Median home price. **Remarks:** Also notes population. **Number listed:** 250

1. Jupiter Island, FL, with $1,700,000 dollars
2. Aspen, CO, $1,620,000
3. Atherton, CA, $1,537,500
4. Hillsborough, CA, $1,250,000
5. Belvedere, CA, $1,225,000
6. Mountain Village, CO, $1,206,500
7. Rolling Hills, CA, $1,205,000
8. Snowmass Village, CO, $1,120,150
9. Los Altos Hills, CA, $1,102,000
10. Rancho Santa Fe, CA, $1,100,000

Source: *Worth*, June, 1999, p. 115.

★1069★

CITIES WITH THE HIGHEST SPENDING FOR TOURISM, 1999*

Ranked by: Reinvesting of tax dollars in travel and tourism, in percent. **Number listed:** 10

1. Reno, NV, with 77.8%
2. Houston, TX, 67.6%
3. Riverside, CA, 60.6%
4. Las Vegas, NV, 59.8%
5. Dallas, TX, 57.7%
6. Detroit, MI, 57.1%
7. San Antonio, TX, 54.7%
8. Indianapolis, IN, 54.6%
9. St. Louis, MO, 51.4%
10. Austin, TX, 50.0%

Source: *Travelware*, February, 1999, p. 16.

★1070★

CITIES WITH THE HIGHEST WAGE, 1998*

Ranked by: Wages, in dollars. **Number listed:** 10

1. New York City, NY, with $45,028
2. San Jose, CA, $44,819
3. San Francisco, CA, $40,016
4. Middlesex/Somerset/Hunterdon, NJ, $39,631
5. New Haven/Bridgeport/Stamford/Danbury/Waterbury, CT, $39,488
6. Newark, NJ, $38,886
7. Trenton, NJ, $37,598
8. Jersey City, NJ, $36,833
9. Washington DC/MD/VA/WV, $36,383
10. Kokomo, IN, $34,779

Source: *Site Selection*, August/September, September, 1998, p. 620.

★1071★

CITIES WITH THE LARGEST FOOD SALES, 1998*

Ranked by: Food sales, in thousands of dollars. **Number listed:** 250

1. New York City, NY, with $8,046,416 thousand
2. Los Angeles, CA, $5,310,313
3. Houston, TX, $3,880,761
4. Chicago, IL, $2,991,650
5. Phoenix, AZ, $2,360,696
6. Philadelphia, PA, $2,265,259
7. San Antonio, TX, $2,038515
8. Dallas, TX, $1,882,926
9. San Diego, CA, $1,761,785
10. Indianapolis, IN, $1,713,444

Source: *Editor & Publisher Market Guide*, (annual), 1998, p. I-33+.

★1072★

CITIES WITH THE LARGEST HOTEL MARKETS, 1998

Ranked by: Number of rooms. **Remarks:** Also notes number of hotels. **Number listed:** 10

1. Las Vegas, NV, with 105,347 rooms
2. Los Angeles, CA, 93,000
3. Orlando, FL, 89,000
4. Chicago, IL, 73,400
5. Washington, DC, 64,716
6. Atlanta, GA, 64,583
7. New York, NY, 61,000
8. San Francisco, CA, 55,000

9. Anaheim, CA, 48,000
10. Dallas, TX, 47,834

Source: *Crain's New York Business*, April 5, 1999, p. 20.

★1073★
CITIES WITH THE LARGEST LUMBER/HARDWARE SALES, 1998*

Ranked by: Sales, in thousands of dollars. **Number listed:** 250

1. New York City, NY, with $1,303,338 thousand
2. Los Angeles, CA, $1,238,279
3. Houston, TX, $972,349
4. Indianapolis, IN, $714,822
5. Chicago, IL, $596,361
6. Phoenix, AZ, $553,374
7. San Diego, CA, $538,737
8. Dallas, TX, $470,312
9. Jacksonville, FL, $460,592
10. Austin, TX, $439,889

Source: *Editor & Publisher Market Guide*, (annual), 1998, p. I-32+.

★1074★
CITIES WITH THE LARGEST POPULATION, 1998*

Ranked by: Population estimates. **Number listed:** 250

1. New York City, NY, with 7,860,003 people
2. Los Angeles, CA, 3,829,886
3. Chicago, IL, 2,763,884
4. Houston, TX, 1,852,063
5. Philadelphia, PA, 1,459,602
6. San Diego, CA, 1,325,472
7. Phoenix, AZ, 1,196,451
8. Dallas, TX, 1,107,729
9. San Antonio, TX, 1,065,661
10. San Jose, CA, 957,485

Source: *Editor & Publisher Market Guide*, (annual), 1998, p. I-30.

★1075★
CITIES WITH THE LARGEST TOTAL RETAIL SALES, 1998*

Ranked by: Sales, in thousands of dollars. **Number listed:** 250

1. New York City, NY, with $48,454,337 thousand
2. Los Angeles, CA, $29,776,655
3. Houston, TX, $25,815,042
4. Chicago, IL, $19,852,259
5. Dallas, TX, $13,814,786
6. Phoenix, AZ, $12,248,100
7. Indianapolis, IN, $11,443,641
8. San Diego, CA, $11,268,247
9. San Antonio, CA, $11,121,729
10. Philadelphia, PA, $10,886,787

Source: *Editor & Publisher Market Guide*, (annual), 1998, p. I-32+.

★1076★
CITIES WITH THE LOWEST WAGES, 1998*

Ranked by: Wages, in thousands of dollars. **Number listed:** 10

1. Jacksonville, NC, with $17,534 thousand
2. Yuma, AZ, $18,213
3. Myrtle Beach, SC, $18,551
4. McAllen-Edinburg-Mission, TX, $18,928
5. Brownsville-Harlingen-San Benito, TX, $19,056
6. Visalia/Tulare/Portersville, CA, $19,768
7. Yakima, WA, $19,056
8. Laredo, TX, $20,388
9. Grand Forks, ND/MN, $20,476
10. Enid, OK, $20,629

Source: *Site Selection*, August/September, September, 1998, p. 620.

★1077★
CITIES WITH THE MOST APPAREL SALES, 1998*

Ranked by: Sales, in thousands of dollars. **Number listed:** 250

1. New York City, NY, with $4,975,243 thousand
2. Los Angeles, CA, $1,819,686
3. Houston, TX, $1,420,681
4. Chicago, IL, $1,383,063
5. San Francisco, CA, $944,227
6. Philadelphia, PA, $895,745
7. Dallas, TX, $867,427
8. San Diego, CA, $720,943
9. Honolulu, HI, $656,748
10. San Antonio, CA, $639,320

Source: *Editor & Publisher Market Guide*, (annual), 1998, p. I-35+.

★1078★
CITIES WITH THE MOST AUTOMOBILE SALES, 1998*

Ranked by: Sales, in thousands of dollars. **Number listed:** 250

1. Houston, TX, with $7,768,198 thousand
2. Los Angeles, CA, $5,119,400
3. New York City, NY, $4,447,203
4. Dallas, TX, $3,696,191
5. Phoenix, AZ, $3,397,406
6. San Antonio, TX, $2,859,923
7. Indianapolis, IN, $2,729,834
8. Memphis, TN, $2,716,527
9. Jacksonville, FL, $2,518,977
10. Fort Lauderdale, FL, $2,517,421

Source: *Editor & Publisher Market Guide*, (annual), 1998, p. I-34+.

★1079★
CITIES WITH THE MOST DISPOSABLE INCOME, 1998*

Ranked by: Disposable income, in thousands of dollars. **Number listed:** 250

1. New York City, NY, with $177,765,246 thousand
2. Los Angeles, CA, $56,925,539
3. Chicago, IL, $45,483,421
4. Philadelphia, PA, $30,678,148
5. Houston, TX, $29,752,671
6. San Francisco, CA, $24,611,721
7. Phoenix, AZ, $22,601,435
8. San Diego, CA, $20,517,000
9. San Jose, CA, $19,810,845
10. Dallas, TX, $19,575,328

Source: *Editor & Publisher Market Guide*, (annual), 1998, p. I-30+.

★1080★
CITIES WITH THE MOST DRUG SALES, 1998*

Ranked by: Drug sales, in thousands of dollars. **Number listed:** 250

1. New York City, NY, with $2,786,707 thousand
2. Chicago, IL, $1,357,902
3. Los Angeles, CA, $1,247,504
4. Houston, TX, $808,811
5. Philadelphia, PA, $797,974
6. Indianapolis, IN, $504,666
7. Phoenix, AZ, $453,745
8. San Diego, CA, $435,839
9. San Francisco, CA, $360,323
10. Honolulu, HI, $353,343

Source: *Editor & Publisher Market Guide*, (annual), 1998, p. I-37+.

★1081★
CITIES WITH THE MOST FOOD AND DRINK SALES, 1997*
Ranked by: Food and drink sales, in thousands of dollars. **Number listed:** 250
1. New York City, NY, with $6,693,549 thousand
2. Los Angeles, CA, $3,671,398
3. Chicago, IL, $2,999,386
4. Houston, TX, $2,838,426
5. Dallas, TX, $1,736,974
6. San Francisco, CA, $1,564,097
7. San Diego, CA, $1,468,265
8. Honolulu, HI, $1,344,561
9. San Antonio, TX, $1,336,654
10. Philadelphia, PA, $1,325,870

Source: *Editor & Publisher Market Guide*, (annual), 1998, p. I-37.

★1082★
CITIES WITH THE MOST FOREIGN VISITORS, 1998
Ranked by: Number of foreign visitors, in millions. **Number listed:** 10
1. New York, NY, with 5 million
2. Los Angeles, CA, 3.9
3. Miami, FL, 3.3
4. San Francisco, CA, 2.9
5. Orlando, FL, 2.8
6. Honolulu, HI, 2.5
7. Las Vegas, NV, 2.1
8. Washington, DC, 1.4
9. Boston, MA, 1.1
9. Chicago, IL, 1.1

Source: *EXPO*, March, 1999, p. 50.

★1083★
CITIES WITH THE MOST FURNITURE SALES, 1998*
Ranked by: Sales, in thousands of dollars. **Number listed:** 250
1. New York City, NY, with $3,846,000 thousand
2. Los Angeles, CA, $2,416,030
3. Houston, TX, $1,833,172
4. Chicago, IL, $1,163,510
5. San Diego, CA, $883,876
6. Dallas, TX, $798,228
7. Phoenix, AZ, $753,187
8. Indianapolis, IN, $675,105
9. San Francisco, CA, $673,306
10. Philadelphia, PA, $630,917

Source: *Editor & Publisher Market Guide*, (annual), 1998, p. I-36+.

★1084★
CITIES WITH THE MOST GENERAL MERCHANDISE SALES, 1998*
Ranked by: General Merchandise sales, in thousands of dollars. **Number listed:** 250
1. New York City, NY, with $4,473,313 thousand
2. Houston, TX, $3,194,704
3. Los Angeles, CA, $3,050,680
4. Honolulu, HI, $1,998,619
5. Columbus, OH, $1,811,603
6. Chicago, IL, $1,793,754
7. Dallas, TX, $1,711,445
8. San Antonio, TX, $1,570,440
9. Indianapolis, IN, $1,567,267
10. Phoenix, AZ, $1,451,299

Source: *Editor & Publisher Market Guide*, (annual), 1998, p. I-33.

★1085★
CITIES WITH THE MOST HOTEL ROOMS, 1999*
Ranked by: Number of rooms. **Number listed:** 10
1. Las Vegas, with 105,347 rooms
2. Los Angeles, 93,000
3. Orlando, FL, 89,000
4. Chicago, 73,400
5. Hawaii, 71,025
6. Washington, DC, 64,716
7. Atlanta, 64,583
8. New York, 61,000
9. San Francisco, 55,000
10. Anaheim, CA, 48,000

Source: *Expo*, March, 1999, p. 47.

★1086★
CITIES WITH THE MOST LOCAL-SHOP ADVERTISING BILLINGS, 1998
Ranked by: Total local shop billings, in millions of U.S. dollars ($). **Remarks:** Also notes figures for 1997, percent change from previous year, shops reporting, top office in market by local volume, and volume. **Number listed:** 25
1. New York, with $44,568.1 million
2. Chicago, $13,881.4
3. Los Angeles, $8,279.4
4. Detroit, $8,164.4
5. Minneapolis, $5,077.9
6. San Francisco, $5,068.1
7. Boston, $4,621.2
8. Dallas, $2,965.9
9. New Jersey, $2,187.7
10. Philadelphia, $1,715.3

Source: *Advertising Age*, Agency Report (annual), April 19, 1999, p. S16.

★1087★
CITIES WITH THE MOST TRAFFIC ACCIDENTS, 1992-1996
Ranked by: Fatal red-light accidents, per 100,000. **Remarks:** Figures are for cities with populations greater than 200,000. **Number listed:** 10
1. Phoenix, AZ, with 8.11
2. Mesa, AZ, 7.08
3. Memphis, TN, 5.45
4. Tucson, AZ, 5.11
5. St. Petersburg, FL, 4.95
6. Dallas, TX, 4.89
6. Fresno, CA, 4.89
8. Birmingham, AL, 4.80
9. Albuquerque, NM, 4.77
10. Louisville, KY, 4.40

Source: *Governing*, July, 1998, p. 13.

★1088★
FASTEST GROWING U.S. CITIES, 1990-1997
Ranked by: Measuring the net migration in the 59 metro areas with over 1 million people, from 1990 to 1997. **Number listed:** 5
1. Las Vegas, NV
2. Atlanta, GA
3. Phoenix, AZ
4. Austin, TX
5. Raleigh-Durham, NC

Source: *Business Week*, May 10, 1999, p. 6.

★1089★
LEAST LIVABLE U.S. CITIES, 1990-1997
Ranked by: Rankings based on net migration in the 59 metro areas with over 1 million people, from 1990-1997. **Number listed:** 5

1. Orange County, CA
2. Miami, FL
3. San Jose, CA
4. New York, NY
5. Los Angeles, CA

Source: *Business Week*, May 10, 999, p. 6.

★1090★
MOST AFFLUENT U.S. MICRO-CITIES, 1998*
Ranked by: Per-capita income, in dollars. **Number listed:** 10

1. Vero Beach, FL, with $28,977
2. Torrington, CT, $25,912
3. Key West, FL, $25,160
4. Concord, NH, $24,734
5. Carcon City, NV, $24,422
6. Newport, RI, $22,465
7. Columbus, IN, $22,464
8. Salem, KS, $21,785
9. Elko, NV, $21,785
10. Muscatine, IA, $21,742

Source: *GSB*, August, 1998, p. 13.

★1091★
TOP CITIES FOR INFORMATION TECHNOLOGY EMPLOYMENT, 1999
Ranked by: Based on survey results. **Remarks:** Also includes metro population, meidan house cost, top IT jobs and salaries, and reason for selection. **Number listed:** 10

1. Boston, MA
2. Chicago, IL
3. Atlanta, GA
4. Washington, DC
5. New York, NY
6. San Francisco, CA
7. Seattle, WA
8. Las Vegas, NV
9. St. Louis, MO
10. Austin, TX

Source: *Computerworld*, Top 10 IT Job Markets (annual), January 11, 1999, p. 64+.

★1092★
WORST MASS TRANSIT SYSTEMS IN U.S., 1999*
Ranked by: Study results by the Transportation Center at the University of North Carolina as Charlotte. **Remarks:** Transit systems in 135 urban areas were ranked according to 12 different measures such as service levels, operating costs and per-passenger revenue. **Number listed:** 10

1. Oklahoma City, OK
2. Jackson, MS
3. Birmingham, AL
4. Youngstown, OH
5. Suffolk County, NY
6. Riverside, CA
7. West Palm Beach, FL
8. New York, NY
9. Lexington, KY
10. Greenville, SC

Source: *Governing*, February, 1999, p. 96.

Claims Administrators

★1093★
LARGEST CLAIMS ADMINISTRATORS SERVING SELF-INSURERS, 1998
Ranked by: Claims paid for self-insurers, in dollars. **Remarks:** Also notes estimated gross revenues from claims services, and self-insured clients for 1998. **Number listed:** 10

1. ESIS Inc., with $2,806,947,262
2. Sedgwick Claims Management, $2,556,452,000
3. Harrington Benefit Services, $2,250,000,000
4. RSKCo, $1,965,000,000
5. Gallagher Bassett Services Inc., $1,916,420,000
6. TPA Inc., $1,860,000,000
7. Crawford & Co., $1,800,000,000
8. CoreScore Inc., $1,623,300,000
9. Brokerage Concepts Inc., $1,412,000,000
10. GAB Robins North America Inc., $1,000,000,0000

Source: *Business Insurance*, February 15, 1999, p. 3.

Cleaning Products Industry

★1094★
BEST HOUSEHOLD CLEANER BRANDS ACCORDING TO DISCOUNT SHOPPERS, 1998*
Ranked by: Percent of discount shoppers naming brand as best. **Remarks:** Figures may total more than 100% due to multiple responses. **Number listed:** 10

1. Tide, with 41%
2. Lysol, 15%
3. Clorox, 13%
4. Dawn, 12%
5. Comet, 9%
6. Colgate Palmolive, 7%
6. Downey, 7%
6. Windex, 7%
6. Cascade, 7%
6. Pine Sol, 7%

Source: *Discount Store News*, September 7, 1998, p. 27.

★1095★
LEADING BRANDS OF LAUNDRY DETERGENT, 1998
Ranked by: Total sales, in millions of dollars. **Remarks:** Also notes company name, location, lead agency, and media expenditures. **Number listed:** 10

1. Tide, with $1,712.3 million
2. Cheer, $332.0
3. All, $308.7
4. Wisk, $300.7
5. Purex, $261.4
6. Gain, $240.2
7. Surf, $231.5
8. Arm & Hammer, $203.3
9. Era, $158.1
10. Xtra, $142.4

Source: *Brandweek (supplement)*, Superbrands: America's Top 2,000 Brands, June 21, 1999, p. S56.

★1096★
LEADING HOUSEHOLD CLEANER BRANDS, 1998
Ranked by: Total sales, in millions of dollars. **Remarks:** Also notes company name, location, lead agency, and media expenditures. **Number listed:** 10

1. Pine Sol, with $141.3 million

2. Lysol All Purpose, $100.9
3. Clorox Clean-Up, $54.0
4. Formula 409, $53.1
5. Mr. Clean, $35.5
6. Fantastic, $34.7
7. Murphy's Oil Soap, $26.1
8. Spic & Span, $24.1
9. Private Label, $17.6
10. Xtra Pine, $12.8

Source: *Brandweek (Supplement)*, Superbrands: America's Top 2,000 Brands, June 21, 1999, p. S56.

Clearinghouse (Banking)

★1097★
TOP CLEARING FIRMS, 1999*
Ranked by: Number of brokerages served. **Number listed:** 7

1. Bear Sterns, with 354
2. Pershing, 326
3. National Financial, 215
4. Interrra Clearing, 170
5. Southwest Securities, 157
6. Correspondent Services, 124
7. U.S. Clearing, 122

Source: *American Banker*, January 29, 1999, p. 8.

Closely Held Corporations

★1098★
FASTEST-GROWING PRIVATE COMPANIES IN THE U.S., 1993-1997
Ranked by: Sales growth, in percent, from 1993-1997. **Remarks:** Also notes 1993 and 1997 sales, profit range, number of employees, year founded, and location. **Number listed:** 20

1. Justice Technology, with 26,899%
2. Power Lift, 16,988%
3. NexCycle, 14,332%
4. Heritage Communities, 13,991%
5. Adams Golf, 12,684%
6. Commercial Financial Services, 12,277%
7. Cybertech International, 11,682%
8. Charter Communications, 10,761%
9. Jade Systems, 10,432%
10. Gaiam, 9,653%

Source: *Inc. 500*, America's Fastest Growing Private Companies (annual), October 20, 1998, p. 81+.

★1099★
FASTEST-GROWING PRIVATELY HELD INNER-CITY COMPANIES IN THE U.S., 1993-1997
Ranked by: Sales growth from 1993 to 1997, in percent. **Remarks:** Also notes number of employees, 1997 revenues, and compound annual growth from 1993 to 1997. **Number listed:** 100

1. Pac-Van, with 19,265%
2. Shore.Net, 8,712%
3. Roundhouse, 5,425%
4. Tucker Technology, 3,330%
5. Construct Two Group, 2,964%
6. Thermagon, 2,662%
7. Baja Printing, 1,363%
8. TCG, 1,109%
9. Envios R. D./Pronto Envios, 1,060%
10. YMLA, 1,021%

Source: *Inner City 100*, (annual), May, 1999, p. 81+.

★1100★
LARGEST PRIVATE COMPANIES, 1998
Ranked by: Revenue, in millions of dollars. **Remarks:** Also notes profit range, assets, number of employees, and fiscal year-end. **Number listed:** 500

1. Cargill, with $51,400 million
2. Koch Industries, $36,200
3. United Parcel Service, $22,458
4. Goldman Sachs & Co., $20,433
5. Continental Grain, $15,000
5. PricewaterhouseCoopers, $15,000
7. Mars, $14,500
8. Andersen Worldwide, $13,700
9. Bechtel Group Inc., $11,300
10. Publix Super Markets, $11,224
11. KPMG Peat Marwick, $10,600

Source: *Forbes*, Largest Private Companies in the U.S. (annual), November 30, 1998, p. 203+.

Closely Held Corporations--Chicago (IL)

★1101★
LEADING PRIVATE COMPANIES IN CHICAGO, 1997
Ranked by: Revenues, in millions of dollars. **Remarks:** Also notes location, executive, percent change, number of employees, and business type. **Number listed:** 303

1. Marmon Group, with $6,000.0 million
2. Montgomery Ward & Co., $5,400.0
3. Alliant Foodservice Inc., $5,200.0
4. Kemper Insurance Cos., $4,147.1
5. Topco Associates Inc., $3,900.0
6. Truserv Corp., $3,332.0
7. Hyatt Hotels Corp., $3,100.0
8. ACE Hardware Corp., $2,900.0
9. Shurfine International Inc., $1,712.0
10. Hyatt International Corp., $1,700.0

Source: *Crain's Chicago Business*, Top Business Lists (annual), 1999, p. 11+.

Closely Held Corporations--Colorado

★1102★
LEADING PRIVATE FIRMS IN COLORADO, 1997
Ranked by: Revenue. **Remarks:** Also notes 1996 rank and business description. **Number listed:** 250

1. CH2M Hill, with $1,236,000,000
2. Security Life of Denver, $1,037,442,000
3. Hensel Phelps Construction Co., $955,000,000
4. Gray Line Worldwide, $950,000,000
5. Centura Health, $894,000,000
6. Burt Automotive Network, $866,557,988
7. Courtesy Auto Group, $714,547,387
8. Symbios Inc., $620,000,000
9. PCL Construction Services Inc., $558,000,000
10. Blue Cross Blue Shield of Colorado & Nevada, $550,000,000

Source: *Colorado Business*, Colorado's Private 250 (annual), September, 1998, p. 28+.

Closely Held Corporations—Detroit Metropolitan Area

★1103★
LEADING PRIVATE FIRMS IN THE DETROIT METROPOLITAN AREA, 1997
Ranked by: Revenue, in millions of dollars. **Remarks:** Also notes contact information, chief executive officer, 1996 revenue, and employee data. **Number listed:** 200

1. Penske Corp., with $5,800.0 million
2. American Axle & Manufacturing Inc., $2,159.0
3. Questor Management Co., $1,900.0
4. Guardian Industries Corp., $1,750.0
5. Stroh Brewery Co., $1,450.0
6. Becker Group Inc., $1,400.0
7. Flint Ink Corp., $1,216.0
8. Peregrine Inc., $1,200.0
9. Domino's Pizza Inc., $1,045.0
10. Citizens Corp., $992.4

Source: *Crain's Detroit Business*, Crain's Book of Lists Detroit (annual), December 28, 1998, p. 4+.

Closely Held Corporations--Florida

★1104★
LEADING PRIVATE COMPANIES IN FLORIDA, 1997
Ranked by: Revenue, in thousands of dollars. **Remarks:** Also notes contact information, top executive, previous year's revenue, and number of employees. **Number listed:** 200

1. Publix Supermarkets Inc., with $11,200,000 thousands
2. J M Family Enterprises Inc., $5,400,000
3. George E. Warren Corp., $2,602,072
4. Southern Wine & Spirits of America, $2,200,000
5. Ed Morse Automotive Group, $1,862,220
6. Adventist Health System, $1,767,108
7. Mortgage Investors Corp., $1,360,000
8. Purity Wholesale Grocers Inc., $1,200,000
9. Carnival Hotels & Casinos, $1,100,000
10. Mark III Industries Inc., $900,000

Source: *Florida Trend*, TopRank Florida (annual), 1999, p. 128+.

Closely Held Corporations--Long Island (NY)

★1105★
LEADING PRIVATE FIRMS IN THE LONG ISLAND NEW YORK AREA, 1997
Ranked by: Revenue, in thousands of dollars. **Remarks:** Also notes contact information, chief executive officer, 1996 revenue, and number of employees. **Number listed:** 50

1. Quality King Distributors, with $1,300,000 thousands
2. P C Richard & Son, $550,000
3. Harold Levinson Associates, $459,00
4. Bellco Drug, $458,000
5. Fortunoff, $400,000
6. Robert Plan, $311,233
7. Overseas Military Sales, $311,000
8. 1-800-FLOWERS, $300,000
9. Vytra Healthcare, $299,866
10. Banfi Vintners, $251,000

Source: *Long Island Business*, LI Book of Lists (annual), 1999, p. 34.

Closely Held Corporations--Los Angeles County (CA)

★1106★
FASTEST-GROWING PRIVATE COMPANIES IN LOS ANGELES COUNTY, 1995-1997
Ranked by: Percentage growth in revenue, from 1995 to 1997. **Remarks:** Also notes rank, revenue in millions, number of employees, company description, profile, and executive. **Number listed:** 100

1. Platinum Capital Group, with 773%
2. Market Scan Information Systems, 640%
3. Nova Development, 594%
4. Travelers Telecom, 430%
5. New Age Electronics, Inc., 414%
6. Justice Technology Corp., 394%
7. Store of Knowledge Inc., 340%
8. Cook Inlet Energy Supply, 321%
9. Tecstar Inc., 260%
10. CIM Vision International Corp., 242%

Source: *Los Angeles Business Journal*, November 16, 1998, p. 60+.

★1107★
LEADING PRIVATE FIRMS IN THE CALIFORNIA LOS ANGELES COUNTY AREA, 1997
Ranked by: Revenue, in millions of dollars. **Remarks:** Also notes contact information, profile, company description, controlling stakeholder(s). **Number listed:** 100

1. Certified Grocers of California, with $1,927 million
2. Consolidated Electrical Distributors, $1,900
3. Roll International, $1,510
4. Parsons Corp., $1,263
5. Sunkist Growers Inc., $1,070
6. J. F. Shea Co., $1,025
7. A-Mark Precious Metals Inc., $1,000
8. California Milk Producers, $958
9. Trader Joe's Co., $922
10. PMC Global Inc., $849

Source: *Los Angeles Business Journal*, (annual), October 25, 1998, p. 47+.

Closely Held Corporations—New York Metropolitan Area

★1108★
TOP PRIVATELY HELD COMPANIES IN THE NEW YORK AREA, 1998
Ranked by: Revenue, in millions of dollars. **Remarks:** Also notes rank, contact information, top executive, previous year's revenue, number of employees, and business description. **Number listed:** 200

1. Goldman Sachs Group, with $20,433 million
2. Continental Grain Co., $15,000
3. Trump Organization, $6,900
4. Wakefern Food Corp., $3,500
5. Lefrak Organization, $2,810

6. Advance Publications, $2,700
6. Rosenthal & Rosenthal Inc., $2,700
8. Entex Information Systems, $2,500
8. Renco Group Inc., $2,500
10. MacAndrews & Forbes Holdings, $2,457
11. Neuman Distributors Inc., $2,400
12. Hearst Corp., $2,375

Source: *Crain's New York Business*, The Private 200, November 30, 1998, p. 46+.

Closely Held Corporations—Philadelphia Metropolitan Area

★1109★
FASTEST GROWING PRIVATE COMPANIES IN THE PHILADELPHIA METROPOLITAN AREA, 1995-1997
Ranked by: Percentage growth in revenue, from 1995 to 1997. **Remarks:** Also notes location, contact information, previous revenue, profitability, start-up capital, number of employees, company description, top executive, and year founded. **Number listed:** 25

1. ESPS, with 8,350%
2. V-Span Inc., 4,049.51%
3. Omicron Systems Inc., 2,236.94%
4. Networks Around the World Inc., 1,759.22%
5. Polaris Consulting & Information, 1,196.61%
6. Cybertech International, 948.90%
7. Protech Systems Inc., 854.57%
8. e-Tech Solutions, 767.33%
9. Fidelity Commercial Real Estate, 587.67%
10. U.S. Interactive Inc., 547.91%

Source: *Philadelphia Business Journal*, Book of Lists (annual), December 25, 1998, p. 9.

★1110★
LARGEST PRIVATELY HELD FIRMS IN THE GREATER PHILADELPHIA AREA, 1997
Ranked by: Revenue, in millions of dollars. **Remarks:** Also notes previous year's rank, contact information, number of employees, business description, majority owner(s), and chief executive officer. **Number listed:** 50

1. Aramark Corp., with $6,300 million
2. Keystone Foods Corp., $2,800
3. Helman Enterprises, $1,380
4. Amkor Electronics Inc., $1,200
5. Berwind Group, $1,158
6. Day & Zimmermann Inc., $1,000
7. Asplundh Tree Expert Co., $935
8. Travel One, $916
9. Wawa Inc., $838
10. WWF Paper, $825

Source: *Philadelphia Business Journal*, Book of Business Lists (annual), December 25, 1998, p. 105+.

Clothes Dryers

★1111★
BEST SELLING GAS AND ELECTRIC DRYERS, 1998
Ranked by: Market share, in percent. **Number listed:** 5

1. Whirlpool, with 35.2%
2. GEA, 30.3%
3. Maytag, 18.6%
4. Electrolux, 10.1%
5. Goodman, 5.2%

Source: *Appliance Manufacturer*, April, 1999, p. 19.

Clothing and Dress--Children

★1112★
BEST CHILDREN'S APPAREL BRANDS ACCORDING TO DISCOUNT SHOPPERS, 1998*
Ranked by: Percent of discount shoppers naming brand as best. **Remarks:** Also notes 1997 figures. Figures may total more than 100% due to multiple responses. **Number listed:** 10

1. OshKosh, with 18%
2. Hanes, 15%
3. Levi's, 10%
4. Fruit of the Loom, 6%
4. Wrangler, 6%
4. Luvs, 6%
7. Reebok, 5%
8. Pampers, 5%
9. Nike, 5%
10. Huggies, 4%

Source: *Discount Store News*, September 7, 1998, p. 20.

★1113★
TOP CHILDREN'S WEAR RETAILERS, 1998
Ranked by: Sales, in millions of dollars. **Remarks:** Also notes rank, location, store type, and number of stores. **Number listed:** 100

1. Wal-Mart, with $4,800 million
2. Kmart, $2,300
3. J. C. Penney, $1,860
4. Target, $1,450
5. Sears, $1,400
6. Federated Department Stores, $1,260
7. May Company, $1,000
8. J. C. Penney-Catalog, $830
9. TJX, $800
10. Kids ''R'' Us, $770

Source: *Children's Business*, Focus 100 (annual), May, 1999, p. 12+.

Clothing and Dress--Men

★1114★
BEST MEN'S APPAREL BRANDS ACCORDING TO DISCOUNT SHOPPERS, 1998*
Ranked by: Percent of discount shoppers naming brand as best. **Remarks:** Also notes 1997 figures. Figures may total more than 100% due to multiple responses. **Number listed:** 10

1. Hanes, with 33%
2. Levi's, 24%
3. Fruit of the Loom, 14%
4. Wrangler, 11%
5. Arrow, 6%
6. Dickies, 5%
7. Lee, 3%
8. BVD, 2%
8. Jockey, 2%
8. Wilson, 2%

Source: *Discount Store News*, September 7, 1998, p. 23.

★1115★
TOP METROPOLITAN AREAS BY APPAREL AND ACCESSORIES STORES, 1998*
Ranked by: Sales, in thousands of dollars. **Number listed:** 321
1. New York, NY, with $5,786,224 thousand
2. Chicago, IL, $4,002,839
3. Los Angeles - Long Beach, CA, $3,533,955
4. Washington, DC, $2,939,655
5. Philadelphia, PA, $2,771,123
6. Boston-Lawrence-Lowell-Brockton, MA, $2,624,665
7. Atlanta, GA, $2,126,508
8. Detroit, MI, $2,027,739
9. Orange County, CA, $1,889,614
10. Nassau - Suffolk, NY, $1,808,373

Source: *Survey of Buying Power*, (annual), August, 1998, p. 20.

Clothing and Dress--Women

★1116★
BEST WOMEN'S APPAREL BRANDS ACCORDING TO DISCOUNTERS, 1998*
Ranked by: Percent of discounters naming brand as best. **Remarks:** Also notes 1997 figures. Figures may total more than 100% due to multiple responses. **Number listed:** 9
1. Hanes, with 24%
2. Playtex, 7%
3. Levi's, 6%
3. Lee, 6%
5. Fruit of the Loom, 4%
5. Jaclyn Smith, 4%
7. Chic, 3%
7. No Response, 3%
7. Cherokee, 3%

Source: *Discount Store News*, September 7, 1999, p. 20.

Clothing Stores

★1117★
LEADING WOMEN'S AND GIRL'S APPAREL IN THE METROPOLITAN AREAS, 1998*
Ranked by: Sales, in thousands of dollars. **Number listed:** 321
1. Chicago, IL, with $4,747,177 thousand
2. New York, NY, $4,305,282
3. Los Angeles-Long Beach, CA, $3,477,932
4. Philadelphia, PA, $2,930,021
5. Boston/Lawrence/Lowell/Brockton, MA, $2,698,562
6. Washington, DC, $2,672,408
7. Atlanta, GA, $2,260,769
8. Detroit, MI, $2,259,829
9. Houston, TX, $2,068,812
10. Dallas, TX, $1,809,744

Source: *Sales & Marketing Management*, (annual), August, 1998, p. 193.

★1118★
TOP DISCOUNT AND APPAREL RETAILERS IN THE S & P 500, 1998
Ranked by: Each company is ranked by 8 criteria: one-year sales growth, three-year total return, one-year sales growth, three-year average annual sales growth, one-year profit growth, three-year average annual profit growth, net profit margins, and return on equity, with additional weight given to a company's sales. **Remarks:** Overall score not provided. **Number listed:** 22
1. The Gap
2. Home Depot
3. TJX
4. Wal-Mart Stores
5. Lowe's
6. Dayton Hundon
7. Kohl's
8. Limited
9. Staples
10. Cosco

Source: *Business Week*, Business Week 50: Top Companies of the S & P 500 (annual), March 29, 1999, p. 146+.

★1119★
TOP OFF-PRICE APPAREL CHAINS, 1997
Ranked by: Sales, in millions of dollars. **Remarks:** Also notes location, 1996 sales and percent change, number of stores, and average store size. **Number listed:** 29
1. T. J. Max, with $3,549 million
2. Marshalls, $3,265
3. Ross Stores, $1,989
4. Burlington Coat Factory, $1,777
5. Goody's Family Clothing, $972
6. Kids "R" Us, $795
7. Stein Mart, $793
8. Men's Werehouse, $631
9. Dress Barn, $555
10. Filene's Basement, $554

Source: *Discount Store News*, Discount Industry Annual Report (annual), July, July 13, 1998, p. 83.

Clothing Trade

★1120★
APPAREL SALES BY CATEGORY, 1998*
Ranked by: Sales, in billions of dollars. **Number listed:** 9
1. Men's, with $11.25 billion
2. Ladies', $10.84
3. Shoes, $4.50
4. Other, $3.67
5. Intimates, $3.52
6. Infant/Toddler, $3.35
7. Boys', $3.13
8. Girls', $2.96
9. Accessories, $2.40

Source: *Discount Trade News*, August 10, 1998, p. 50.

★1121★
MOST ADMIRED APPAREL CORPORATIONS, 1998
Ranked by: Scores (1-10) derived from a survey of senior executives, outside directors and securities analysts. **Remarks:** Respondents rated companies in their own industry on 8 attributes of reputation. **Number listed:** 10
1. Liz Claiborne, with 6.82
2. VF Corp., 6.69
3. Nike, 6.65
4. Jones Apparel Group, 6.24
5. Kellwood, 5.58
6. Russell, 5.55
6. Warnaco Group, 5.55
8. Reebok International, 4.98
9. Nine West Group, 4.70

10. Fruit of the Loom, 4.27

Source: *Fortune*, America's Most Admired Corporations (annual), December/January, March 1, 1999, p. F-3.

★1122★
TOP APPAREL BRANDS, 1998
Ranked by: Sales, in billions of dollars. **Remarks:** Also notes company name and location, lead agency, and media expenditures. **Number listed:** 10

1. Hanes, Champion, Leggs, with $7.3 billion
2. Levi's, Dockers, Slates, $6.0
3. Lee, Wrangler, Vanity Fair, $5.5
4. Liz Claiborne, Dana Buchman, Elisabeth, $2.5
5. Fruit of the Loom, BVD, Gitano, $2.2
6. Warner's, Olga, Calvin Klein Lingerie, $2.0
7. Melrose, Prophesy, Sag Harbor, $1.8
8. Jones New York, $1.7
9. Nike, $1.6
10. Polo, $1.5

Source: *Brandweek (supplement)*, Superbrands: America's Top 2,000 Brands, June 21, 1999, p. S16.

★1123★
TOP CORPORATIONS IN THE APPAREL INDUSTRY, 1998
Ranked by: Sales, in dollars. **Remarks:** Also notes earnings and employee data. **Number listed:** 100

1. The Gap, with $9,054,462,000
2. Sara Lee Branded Apparel, $7,317,000,000
3. Levi Strauss & Co., $6,000,000,000
4. VF Corp., $5,478,800,000
5. Calvin Klein Inc., $5,400,000,000
6. Nike Inc. (apparel only), $2,991,000,000
7. Polo/Ralph Lauren Corp., $2,640,000,000
8. Liz Claiborne, $2,535,268,000
9. Fruit of the Loom, $2,170,300,000
10. Warnaco Group Inc., $1,950,300,000

Source: *Apparel Industry Magazine*, AIM 100 (annual), June, 1999, p. A-4+.

★1124★
TOP CORPORATIONS IN THE APPAREL INDUSTRY, 1998
Ranked by: Revenue, in millions of dollars. **Remarks:** Also notes profits, profits as a percentage of revenue, assets and stockholders' equity, earnings per share, total return to investors, and number of employees. **Number listed:** 13

1. Nike, with $9,553 million
2. VF Corp., $5,479
3. Reebok International, $3,225
4. Liz Claiborne, $2,535
5. Fruit of the Loom, $2,170
6. Warnaco Group, $1,950
7. Nine West Group, $1,917
8. Kellwood, $1,782
9. Jones Apparel Group, $1,685
10. Pillowtex, $1,510

Source: *Fortune*, Fortune 500 Largest U.S. Corporations (annual), April 26, 1999, p. F-52.

Clothing Trade--Europe

★1125★
TOP APPAREL COMPANIES IN EUROPE, 1999*
Ranked by: Financial size, in millions of ECU's. **Remarks:** Also notes number of employees and overall rank among European businesses. **Number listed:** 61

1. Courtaulds Textiles PLC (U.K.), with ECUs1.233 million
2. William Baird PLC (U.K.), ECUs882
3. SAI Automotive AG (Germany), ECUs862
4. Baird Textile Holdings Ltd. (U.K.), ECUs785
5. Levi Strauss & Co. Europe SA (Belgium), ECUs760
6. Klaus Steilmann GmbH & Co. KG, ECUs659
7. Escada AG (Germany), ECUs624
8. Hugo Boss AG, ECUs576
9. Adler Modemaekte GmbH (Germany), ECUs563
10. Laura Ashley Holdings PLC (U.K.), ECUs508

Source: *Dun & Bradstreet*, Duns Europa (annual), 1999, p. 237.

Coal Industry

★1126★
LARGEST COAL MINES IN THE U.S., 1998*
Ranked by: Coal produced, in millions of short tons. **Remarks:** Also includes type of mine and company. **Number listed:** 29

1. Black Thunder, WY, with 39.3 million tons
2. North Antelope, WY, 28.6
3. Rochelle, WY, 26.2
4. Jacobs Ranch, WY, 24.5
5. Caballo, WY, 22.0
6. Belle Ayr, WY, 20.0
7. Eagle Butte, WY, 15.6
7. Freedom, ND, 15.6
9. Caballo Rojo, WY, 13.1
10. Rawhide, WY, 12.0
10. Cordero, WY, 12.0

Source: *DCBuff: Coal*, Keystone Coal Industry Manual (annual), McGraw-Hill, 1998, p. 16.

★1127★
LARGEST COAL PRODUCERS IN THE U.S., 1998*
Ranked by: Coal produced, in millions of short tons. **Remarks:** Also notes percent of total U.S. production. **Number listed:** 29

1. Peabody Group, with 156.7 million tons
2. Cyprus Amax Coal Co., 75.4
3. CONSOL Coal Group, 71.6
4. ARCO Coal Co., 50.9
5. Arch Coal Co., 47.4
6. Kennecott Energy Co., 45.1
7. A. T. Massey Coal Co., 31.9
8. Zeigler Coal Holding Co., 31.4
9. Kerr-McGee Coal Corp., 31.3
10. Texas Utilities Mining Co., 29.2

Source: *DCBuff: Coal*, Keystone Coal Industry Manual (annual), McGraw-Hill, 1998, p. 16.

★1128★
STATES PRODUCING THE MOST COAL, 1997
Ranked by: Coal produced in thousands of short tons. **Remarks:** Also notes 1996 production and percent change. **Number listed:** 10

1. Wyoming, with 281,647 thousand tons
2. West Virginia, 172,954
3. Kentucky, 155,859
4. Pennsylvania, 73,232
5. Texas, 53,722
6. Illinois, 41,956
7. Montana, 41,016
8. Virginia, 36,389

9. Indiana, 34,515
10. Ohio, 30,654

Source: *Coal Age*, August, 1998, p. 10.

★1129★

TOP COAL PRODUCERS BY MARKET SHARE, 1999*

Ranked by: Market share, in percent. **Number listed:** 10

1. Peabody Holding, with 13.8%
2. Arch Coal Co., 9.7%
3. Kennecott Energy Co., 9.6%
4. CONSOL energy, 7.6%
5. Cyprus Amax Coal Co., 6.1%
6. AB Holding, 4.4%
7. A. T. Massey Coal Co., 3.4%
8. Texas Utilities Mining Co., 2.5%
9. North American Coal, 2.3%
10. PacifiCorp, 2.0%

Source: *Coal Age*, May, 1999, p. 8.

Coffee Industry

★1130★

BEST-SELLING DRIP COFFEEMAKERS, 1998

Ranked by: Market share, in percent. **Remarks:** Also notes 1993 market share. **Number listed:** 11

1. Hamilton Beach/Proctor-Silex, with 30%
2. Signature Brands USA, 28%
3. Black & Decker, 11%
4. Betty Crocker, 7%
4. Braun, 7%
6. Krups, 6%
7. West Bend, 5%
8. Bunn-O-Matic, 2%
9. Regal Ware, 2%
10. Melitta, 1%
11. Others, 1%

Source: *Appliance Manufacturer*, April, 1999, p. 22.

★1131★

BEST-SELLING PERCOLATOR COFFEEMAKERS, 1998

Ranked by: Market share, in percent. **Number listed:** 6

1. Betty Crocker, with 40%
2. Regal Ware, 31%
3. West Bend, 15%
4. Presto, 8%
5. Faberware, 5%
6. Rival, 1%

Source: *Appliance Manufacturer*, April, 1999, p. 22.

Cold (Disease)--Care and Treatment

★1132★

BEST-SELLING COUGH AND COLD REMEDIES, 1998

Ranked by: Total sales, in millions of dollars. **Remarks:** Also notes dollar share, unit sales, and unit sale. **Number listed:** 5

1. Private Label, with $703.8 million
2. Tylenol, $257.3
3. Robitussin, $206.7
4. Benadryl, $165.2
5. Sudafed, $161.7

Source: *Brandweek (supplement)*, Superbrands: America's Top 2,000 Brands, June 21, 1999, p. S58.

★1133★

BEST-SELLING COUGH AND SORE THROAT DROP BRANDS, 1998

Ranked by: Sales, in millions of dollars. **Remarks:** Also notes dollar share, unit sales, and unit share. **Number listed:** 10

1. Halls, with $121.0 million
2. Cold-Eeze, $70.8
3. Ricola, $42.6
4. Robitussin, $30.4
4. Luden's, $30.4
6. Halls Zinc Defense, $17.2
7. Sucrets, $17.1
8. Halls Plus, $14.5
9. Celestial Seasonings, $14.2
10. N'Ice, $12.8

Source: *MMR*, August 24, 1998, p. 41.

★1134★

BEST-SELLING NASAL SPRAY BRANDS, 1998

Ranked by: Sales, in millions of dollars. **Remarks:** Also notes dollar share, unit sales, and unit share. **Number listed:** 10

1. Afrin, with $54.7 million
2. Four Way, $20.5
3. Sinex, $20.3
4. Neo-Synephrine, $14.9
5. Vicks Inhaler, $11.2
6. Dristan, $8.2
7. Ocean, $6.3
8. Ayr, $5.4
9. Duration, $4.2
10. Benzodrex, $3.4

Source: *MMR*, May 3, 1999, p. 49.

★1135★

TOP COUGH AND COLD BRANDS, 1998

Ranked by: Sales, in millions of dollars. **Remarks:** Also notes dollar share, unit sales, and unit share. **Number listed:** 10

1. Tylenol, with $252.9 million
2. Robitussin, $210.3
3. Sudafed, $161.5
4. Benedryl, $161.0
5. Nyquil, $139.0
6. Alka-Seltzer, $116.0
7. Dimetapp, $96.0
8. Formula 44, $59.7
9. Theraflu, $59.1
10. Triaminic, $55.4

Source: *MMR*, August 24, 1998, p. 42.

Colleges and Universities

See also: **Business Schools and Colleges**

★1136★

LEADING NATIONAL LIBERAL ARTS COLLEGES

Ranked by: Composite score in academic reputation, graduation and retention rank, student selectivity rank, financial resources rank, alumni giving rank, and freshman retention rank. **Remarks:** Also notes individual score in each category. **Number listed:** 39

1. Amherst College, with 100.0
2. Swarthmore College, 99.0
3. Williams College, 97.0

4. Wellesley College, 95.0
5. Haverford College, 93.0
5. Pomona College, 93.0
7. Bowdoin College, 91.0
7. Middlebury College, 91.0
9. Carleton College, 90.0
9. Wesleyan College, 90.0
10. Davidson College, 89.0
10. Grinnell College, 89.0

Source: *U.S. News & World Report*, America's Best Colleges (annual), August 31, 1998, p. 90.

★1137★
LEADING NATIONAL UNIVERSITIES, 1999
Ranked by: Composite score in academic reputation, graduation and retention rank, student selectivity rank, financial resources rank, alumni giving rank, and freshman retention rank. **Remarks:** Also notes individual score in each category. **Number listed:** 50

1. Harvard University, with 100.0
1. Princeton University, 100.0
1. Yale University, 100.0
4. Massachusetts Institute of Technology, 98.0
4. Stanford University, 98.0
6. Cornell University, 97.0
6. Duke University, 97.0
6. University of Pennsylvania, 97.0
9. California Institute of Technology, 96.0
10. Brown University, 95.0
10. Columbia University, 95.0
10. Dartmouth College, 95.0

Source: *U.S. News & World Report*, America's Best Colleges (annual), August 31, 1998, p. 84.

★1138★
LEADING UNIVERSITIES IN THE MIDWEST
Ranked by: Composite score in academic reputation, graduation and retention rank, student selectivity rank, financial resources rank, alumni giving rank, and freshman retention rank. **Remarks:** Also notes individual score in each category. **Number listed:** 14

1. Creighton University, with $100.0 points
2. Valparaiso University, $97.0
3. Drake University, $96.0
3. University of Dayton, $96.0
4. John Carroll University, $96.0
5. Bradley University, $93.0
6. Butler University, $92.0
7. Xavier University, $91.0
8. University of St. Thomas, $90.0
9. Baldwin-Wallace College, $89.0
10. Calvin College, $88.0

Source: *U.S. New & World Report*, America's Best Colleges (annual), August 31, 1998, p. 94.

★1139★
LEADING UNIVERSITIES IN THE NORTH
Ranked by: Composite score in academic reputation, graduation and retention rank, student selectivity rank, financial resources rank, alumni giving rank, and freshman retention rank. **Remarks:** Also notes individual score in each category. **Number listed:** 15

1. Villanova University, with 100.0
2. Providence College, 94.0
3. College of New Jersey, 91.0
3. Fairfield University, 91.0
3. Loyola College, 91.0
3. SUNY College of Arts & Sciences, 91.0
3. University of Scranton, 91.0
8. Ithaca College, 90.0
8. Quinnipiac College, 90.0
10. Rochester Institute of Technology, 90.1
11. Hood College, 89.0
11. St. Michael's College, 89.0

Source: *U.S. New & World Report*, America's Best Colleges (annual), August 31, 1998, p. 94.

★1140★
TOP COLLEGE MERCHANDISE SALES, 1997-1998
Ranked by: Merchandise sold between July 1997 and March 1998. **Remarks:** Specific figures not given. **Number listed:** 10

1. Michigan
2. North Carolina
3. Penn State
4. Nebraska
5. Florida
6. Kentucky
7. Tennessee
8. Florida State
9. Alabama
10. Wisconsin

Source: *Potentials In Marketing*, August, 1998, p. 5.

Colleges and Universities--Florida

★1141★
LARGEST PUBLIC UNIVERSITIES IN FLORIDA BY NUMBER OF FLORIDA STUDENTS, 1998
Ranked by: Number of Florida students. **Remarks:** Also notes tuition, number of full-time faculty, number of graduates, operating budget, chief administrator, and year founded. **Number listed:** 10

1. University of Florida, with 28,378 students
2. Florida State University, 20,366
3. University of South Florida, 15,199
4. University of Central Florida, 14,769
5. Florida International University, 12,480
6. Florida A & M University, 8,164
7. Florida Atlantic University, 7,848
8. University of North Florida, 5,186
9. University of West Florida, 3,969
10. Florida Gulf Coast University, 1,532

Source: *Florida Trend*, TopRank Florida (annual), 1999, p. 53.

★1142★
LARGEST PUBLIC UNIVERSITIES IN FLORIDA BY NUMBER OF FULL-TIME STUDENTS, 1999
Ranked by: Number of full-time students. **Remarks:** Also notes tuition, number of full-time faculty, number of graduates, number of campuses, operating budget, chief administrator, and year founded. **Number listed:** 25

1. University of Miami, with 7,451 students
2. Florida Metropolitian University, 4,948
3. Nova Southeastern University, 3,976
4. Embry-Riddle Aeronautical University, 3,898
5. Saint Leo College, 2,916
6. Bethune-Cookman College, 2,343
7. University of Tampa, 2,321
8. Stetson University, 1,840
9. Barry University, 1,775
10. Florida Memorial College, 1,740

Source: *Florida Trend*, TopRank Florida (annual), 1999, p. 55+.

Colleges and Universities--Gifts, Legacies, etc.

★1143★
WEALTHIEST EDUCATIONAL INSTITUTIONS, 1998
Ranked by: Market value of endowments, in billions. **Number listed:** 10
1. Harvard University, with $12.8 billion
2. University of Texas, $7.6
3. Yale University, $6.6
4. Princeton University, $5.6
5. Stanford University, $Not Available
6. Emory University, $5.0
7. University of California, $3.9
8. Massachusetts Institute of Technology, $3.7
9. Columbia University, $3.4
10. Washington University, $3.5

Source: *New York Times*, October 21, 1998, p. B9.

Colleges and Universities--Los Angeles County (CA)

★1144★
LARGEST COLLEGES AND UNIVERSITIES IN LOS ANGELES COUNTY, 1997-1998
Ranked by: Average full-time equivalent enrollment for 1997 and 1998. **Remarks:** Also notes contact information, profile, local executive, faculty, budget, and additional enrollment figures. **Number listed:** 25
1. University of California, Los Angeles, with 32,050 students
2. University of Southern California, 24,670
3. Mt. San Antonio College, 24,050
4. California State University - Long Beach, 20,229
5. California State University - Northridge, 20,022
6. Pasadena City College, 18,960
7. Santa Monica College, 15,777
8. Cerritos College, 14,747
9. Long Beach City College, 14,424
10. California State Polytechnic University, 14,249

Source: *Los Angeles Business Journal*, Book of Lists (annual), 1999, p. 116.

Colleges and Universities--New Jersey

★1145★
LARGEST COLLEGES AND UNIVERSITIES IN NEW JERSEY, 1999*
Ranked by: Total enrollment. **Remarks:** Also notes contact information, year founded, degrees offered, president, and number of full-time faculty. **Number listed:** 45
1. Rutgers (The State University of New Jersey), with 48,341 students
2. Bergen Community College, 13,000
3. Montclair State University, 12,808
4. Camden County College, 11,935
5. Brookdale Community College, 11,868
6. Kean University, 11,778
7. Raritan Valley Community College, 11,573
8. Middlesex County College, 9,800
9. Seton Hall University, 9,500
10. Rowan University, 9,367

Source: *New Jersey Business*, Book of Lists (annual), 1999, p. 14+.

Colleges and Universities--Research

★1146★
TOP UNIVERSITIES IN RESEARCH AND DEVELOPMENT SPENDING, 1996
Ranked by: Total R & D expenditures, in millions of dollars. **Remarks:** Also notes expenditures in individual departments. **Number listed:** 50
1. Johns Hopkins University, with $798.7 million
2. University of Michigan, $468.9
3. University of Wisconsin, $412.5
4. University of Washington, $406.5
5. Massachusetts Institute of Technology, $380.7
6. University of California at San Diego, $371.6
7. Texas A & M University, $367.0
8. University of California, Los Angeles, $354.6
9. University of Minnesota, $341.2
10. Cornell University, $339.6

Source: *Chemical & Engineering News*, Facts & Figures for Chemical R & D (annual), October 19, 1998, p. 74.

★1147★
UNIVERSITIES SPENDING THE MOST ON CHEMICAL RESEARCH AND DEVELOPMENT, 1996
Ranked by: Expenditures, in thousands of dollars. **Remarks:** Also notes 1986 and 1992-1995 expenditures. **Number listed:** 50
1. California Institute of Technology, with $15,599 thousand
2. Massachusetts Institute of Technology, $14,856
3. University of California, Berkley, $14,277
4. University of Illinois at Urbana-Champaign, $12,956
5. University of Wisconsin, $12,910
6. University of Pennsylvania, $12,855
7. University of Colorado, $12,701
8. Pennsylvania State University, $12,670
9. Texas A & M University, $12,478
10. Stanford University, $12,253

Source: *Chemical & Engineering News*, Facts & Figures for Chemical R & D (annual), October 19, 1998, p. 71.

★1148★
UNIVERSITIES WITH THE MOST SUPPORT FOR CHEMICAL RESEARCH AND DEVELOPMENT, 1996
Ranked by: Amount received, in thousands of dollars. **Remarks:** Also notes funding for previous years. **Number listed:** 50
1. Massachusetts Institute of Technology, with $13,735 thousand
2. California Institute of Technology, $12,478
3. University of Pennsylvania, $12,181
4. Stanford University, $12,171
5. University of California, Berkley, $12,050
6. Harvard University, $10,608
7. University of Colorado, $9,442
8. University of California, Los Angeles, $9,338
9. University of Wisconsin, $9,318
10. Cornell University, $8,667

Source: *Chemical & Engineering News*, Facts & Figures for Chemical R & D (annual), October 19, 1998, p. 72.

Colombo Stock Exchange

★1149★
LARGEST LISTED COMPANIES ON THE COLOMBO STOCK EXCHANGE, 1997
Ranked by: Market value, in millions of Sri Lankan rupees (CRs). **Number listed:** 20

1. John Keells Holding, with CRs11,192 million
2. National Development Bank, CRs7,704
3. DFCC Bank, CRs6,407
4. Hatton National Bank, CRs5,600
5. Hayley's, CRs5,280
6. Ceylon Tobacco, CRs4,616
7. Commercial Bank, CRs4,125
8. Commercial Bank, CRs2,668
9. Sampath Bank, CRs2,500
10. Lion Brewery, CRs2,355

Source: *Euromoney Publications*, Guide to World Equity Markets (annual), 1998, p. 462.

★1150★
MOST ACTIVELY TRADED SHARES ON THE COLOMBO STOCK EXCHANGE, 1997
Ranked by: Turnover value, in millions of Sri Lankan rupees (CRs). **Remarks:** Also notes percentage of total. **Number listed:** 20

1. DFFC, with CRs1,993 million
2. John Keells Holdings, CRs1,660
3. NDB, CRs1,622
4. Sampath Bank, CRs1,290
5. Hayley's Ltd., CRs721
6. Asia Capital, CRs673
7. Commercial Bank, CRs524
8. Ceylon Brewery, CRs461
9. Ceylon Grain Elevators, CRs433
10. Aitken Spence, CRs371

Source: *Guide to World Equity Markets (annual)*, 1998, p. 463.

Color Television

★1151★
BEST-SELLING COLOR TELEVISON BRANDS, 1998
Ranked by: Market share, in percent. **Number listed:** 12

1. Thomson, with 22%
2. NAP, 14%
3. Zenith, 12%
4. Sony, 9%
5. Sanyo Fisher, 6%
5. Sharp, 6%
7. Matsushita, 5%
7. Toshiba, 5%
9. Mitsubishi, 3%
9. Samsung, 3%
11. Emerson, 2%
12. Others, 13%

Source: *Consumer Electronics*, 1999, p. 22.

Commercials

See: **Radio Advertising Television Advertising**

Commodity Funds

★1152★
TOP-PERFORMING FUTURES' PUBLIC FUNDS, 1998
Ranked by: Rate of return, in percent. **Remarks:** Also notes trading advisor. Some are non-U.S. funds. **Number listed:** 10

1. Oxford Future Fund, with 142.66%
2. AHL Gtd. Real Time Trading, 64.96%
3. Hasenbichler Commodities AG, 55.51%
4. AHL Commodity, 54.23%
5. AHL Gtd. Capital Markets Ltd., 52.56%
6. Athena Gtd. Futures, 48.18%
7. PB International Futures Fund F, 47.90%
8. AHL Diversified Gtd., 46.24%
9. AHL Diversified Guaranteed II, 45.67%
10. AHL Commodity Markets, 45.06%

Source: *Futures*, March, 1999, p. 83.

★1153★
WORST-PERFORMING FUTURES' PUBLIC FUNDS, 1998
Ranked by: Rate of return, in percent. **Number listed:** 10

1. Equilibrium Fund (905) Can., with -60.88%
2. Morgan Stanley Tangible Asset Fund, -34.30%
3. Stonehedge Ltd., -27.43%
4. Gaia Hedge II Ltd., -18.54%
5. Gaia FX Ltd., -11.62%
6. Dearborn Street Fund, -10.63%
7. PB Capital Return III, -10.12%
8. PB Capital Return II, -7.69%
9. Green Way Investments Ltd., -7.02%
10. Green Way Ltd., -6.56%

Source: *Futures*, March, 1999, p. 83.

Community Banks

See: **Banks and Banking--Independent Banks**

Companies

See: **Corporations**

Competition, International

★1154★
WORLD COMPETITIVENESS IN EUROPE, 1998*
Ranked by: Overall Competitiveness. **Number listed:** 10

1. United States
2. Singapore
3. Hong Kong
4. Netherlands
5. Finland
6. Norway
7. Switzerland
8. Denmark
9. Luxembourg
10. Canada

Source: *Business Facilities*, December, 1998, p. 24.

★1155★
WORLD'S MOST ECONOMICALLY COMPETITIVE COUNTRIES, 1999*
Ranked by: Countries rated on 8 economic and political factors. **Remarks:** Specific figures not provided. **Number listed:** 10
1. United States
2. Singapore
3. Finland
4. Luxembourg
5. Netherlands
6. Switzerland
7. Hong Kong
8. Denmark
9. Germany
10. Canada

Source: *IndustryWeek*, May 17, 1999, p. 13.

Computer Industry

See also: **Microcomputers**

★1156★
BEST COMPUTER HARDWARE BRANDS ACCORDING TO DISCOUNT SHOPPERS, 1999*
Ranked by: Percent of discount shoppers naming brand as best. **Remarks:** Also notes 1997 figures. Figures may total more than 100% due to multiple responses. **Number listed:** 8
1. Packard Bell, with 24%
2. IBM, 13%
3. 3M, 11%
4. Apple, 7%
5. Nintendo/Game boy, 3%
6. Sony, 2%
6. Microsoft, 2%
8. Seagate Technology, 1%

Source: *Discount Store News*, Top Brands Survey (annual), September 7, 1999, p. 22.

★1157★
COMPUTERS/SOFTWARE/OFFICE/ EQUIPMENT COMPANIES SPENDING THE MOST ON RESEARCH AND DEVELOPMENT, 1998*
Ranked by: Research and Development expenditures, in millions of dollars. **Number listed:** 10
1. IBM, with $4,327.2 million
2. Hewlett-Packard, $3,134.9
3. Cisco Systems, $1,316.4
4. Xerox, $1,088.7
5. Digital Equipment, $984.9
6. Sun Microsystems, $882.8
7. Compaq, $801.5
8. Seagate Technology, $574.7
9. Silicon Graphics Inc., $526.4
10. Apple Computer, $484.7

Source: *Research & Development*, Giants of R & D (annual), October, 1998, p. S-14.

★1158★
LEADING METROPOLITIAN SUPPLIERS OF COMPUTER HARDWARE AND SOFTWARE, 1998*
Ranked by: Supply sales, in millions of dollars. **Number listed:** 321
1. Chicago, IL, with $789,368 million
2. Wasington, DC, $740,326
3. Los Angeles - Long Beach, CA, $718,254
4. Phoenix - Mesa, AZ, $641,752
5. Dallas, TX, $550,805
6. New York, NY, $480,869
7. Houston, TX, $369,851
8. Minneapolis - St. Paul, MN, $369,752
9. Detroit, MI, $352,645
10. Orange County, CA, $348,606

Source: *Survey of Buying Power & Media Markets (annual)*, Sales & Marketing Management, August, 1998, p. 200.

★1159★
MOST ADMIRED COMPUTER AND DATA SERVICES CORPORATIONS, 1998
Ranked by: Scores (1-10) derived from a survey of senior executives, outside directors and securities analysts. **Remarks:** Respondents rated companies in their own industry on 8 attributes of reputation. Also notes previous year's rank. **Number listed:** 10
1. Automatic Data Processing, with 7.12
2. America Online, Inc., 6.92
3. Equifax, 6.89
4. Computer Sciences, 6.44
5. Comdisco, 6.09
6. First Data, 5.89
7. Unisys, 5.75
8. Electronic Data Systems, 5.50
9. Micro Warehouse, 5.35
10. Dun & Bradstreet, 5.29

Source: *Fortune*, America's Most Admired Corporations (annual), December/January, March 1, 1999, p. F-6.

★1160★
TOP COMPUTER AND OFFICE EQUIPMENT COMPANIES IN THE S & P 500, 1999
Ranked by: Based on S & P ranking. Overall scores not provided. **Remarks:** Each company is ranked by eight criteria: one-year total return, three-year total return, nine-year sales growth, three-year average annual sales growth, one-year profit growth, three-year average annual profit growth, net profit margins, and return on equity, with additional weight given to a company's sales. A company's composite rank is calculated using the sum of all its ranks. **Number listed:** 37
1. Microsoft
2. Dell Computer
3. Oracle
4. EMC
5. Compuware
6. America Online
7. Cisco Systems
8. BMC Software
9. Sun Microsystems
10. Gateway 2000

Source: *Business Week*, Top Companies of the S & P 500 (annual), March 29, 1999, p. 160+.

★1161★
TOP COMPUTER HARDWARE COMPANIES BY SEGMENT REVENUE, 1998*
Ranked by: Segment revenue, in millions of dollars. **Number listed:** 20
1. IBM, with $25,907.6 million
2. Compaq Computer, $24,584.0
3. Hewlett-Packard, $16,310.4
4. Dell Computer, $8,628.9
5. Sun Microsystems, $6,905.0
6. Gateway 2000, $6,042.0
7. Apple Computer, $4,897.5
8. Digital Equipment, $3,918.5
9. NCR, $3,116.6

10. Silicon Graphics Inc., $3,100.0

Source: *Electronic Business*, Top 200 (annual), July, 1998, p. 95.

★1162★
TOP COMPUTER HARDWARE COMPANIES, 1998
Ranked by: Total sales, in billions of dollars. **Number listed:** 10

1. IBM, with $81.6 billion
2. Hewlett-Packard, $47.0
3. Compaq, $31.1
4. Intel, $26.2
5. Dell, $18.2
6. Sun Microsystems, $9.7
7. Cisco Systems, $8.4
8. Gateway, $7.4
9. Unisys, $7.2
10. Apple, $5.9

Source: *Brandweek (supplement)*, Superbrands: America's Top 2,000 Brands, June 21, 1999, p. S32.

★1163★
TOP COMPUTER LOBBYING SPENDERS, 1997
Ranked by: Lobby expenditures, in millions of dollars. **Number listed:** 11

1. IBM, with $5.2 million
2. EDS, $2.2
3. Texas Instruments, $2.0
4. Microsoft, $1.9
5. Business Software Alliance, $1.0
6. Oracle, $0.9
7. America Online, $0.8
8. Netscape Communications, $0.7
8. Computer Systems Policy Project, $0.7
10. Intel, $0.6
10. Software Publishers Association, $0.6

Source: *Red Herring*, December, 1998, p. 64.

★1164★
TOP CORPORATIONS IN THE COMPUTER AND OFFICE EQUIPMENT INDUSTRY, 1998
Ranked by: Revenue, in millions of dollars. **Remarks:** Also notes profits, profits as a percentage of revenue, assets and stockholders' equity, earnings per share, total return to investors, and number of employees. **Number listed:** 12

1. International Business Machines, with $81,667 million
2. Hewlett-Packard, $47,061
3. Compaq Computer, $31,169
4. Xerox, $20,019
5. Dell Computer, $18,243
6. Sun Microsystems, $9,791
7. Gateway 2000, $7,468
8. NCR, $6,505
9. Apple Computer, $5,941
10. Pitney Bowes, $4,334

Source: *Fortune*, Fortune 500 Largest U.S. Corporations (annual), April 26, 1999, p. F-55.

★1165★
TOP PERIPHERALS COMPANIES BY SEGMENT REVENUE, 1998*
Ranked by: Segment revenue, in millions of dollars. **Number listed:** 20

1. Hewlett-Packard, with $14,164.3 million
2. Seagate Technology, $7,806.4
3. Quantum Technology Services Inc., $6,083.0
4. IBM, $4,710.5
5. Western Digital, $4,214.6
6. EMC, $2,937.9
7. Intel, $2,507.0
8. Storage Technology, $2,144.7
9. Lexmark International Group, $2,019.7
10. Iomega, $1,740.0

Source: *Electronic Business*, Top 200 (annual), July, 1998, p. 97.

Computer Industry, International

★1166★
WORLD'S LARGEST CORPORATIONS IN THE COMPUTER AND OFFICE EQUIPMENT INDUSTRY BY REVENUE, 1997
Ranked by: Revenue, in millions of dollars. **Number listed:** 9

1. International Business Machines, with $78,508 million
2. Hewlett-Packard, $42,895
3. Fujitsu, $40,613
4. Compaq Computer, $24,584
5. Canon, $22,813
6. Xerox, $18,166
7. Digital Equipment, $13,047
8. Dell Computer, $12,327
9. Ricoh, $11,432

Source: *Fortune*, The Global 500: World's Biggest Corporations (annual), August 3, 1998, p. F-17.

Computer Industry--Long Island (NY)

★1167★
TOP COMPUTER DEALERS IN THE LONG ISLAND METROPOLITAN AREA, BY EMPLOYEES, 1999*
Ranked by: Number of employees. **Remarks:** Also lists location, contact information, number of stores, brands carried and related services. **Number listed:** 55

1. IBM, with 320 employees
2. Sandata, 240
3. Manchester Equipment, 239
4. U.S. Computer Group, 220
5. Custom Computer Specialists, 150
5. ISG, 150
7. Comp USA, 120
8. Vomittag Associates, 90
9. Hewlett-Packard, 88
10. Contemporary Computer Services, 73
11. Rent-A-PC, 65

Source: *Long Island Business*, LI Book of Lists (annual), 1999, p. 118+.

Computer Networks--Gateways

★1168★
LARGEST STAND-ALONE GATEWAYS COMPUTER NETWORKS, 1997
Ranked by: Market share, in percent. **Number listed:** 7

1. VocalTec Communications, with 34%
2. Micom Communications, 18%

2. Others, 18%
4. Vienna Systems, 12%
5. Clarent, 8%
6. Lucent Technologies, 5%
7. NetSpeak, 5%

Source: *Telephony*, November 16, 1998, p. 36.

Computer Peripherals Equipment Industry

★1169★
MOST ADMIRED COMPUTER PERIPHERALS CORPORATIONS, 1998
Ranked by: Scores (1-10) derived from a survey of senior executives, outside directors and securities ananysts. **Remarks:** Respondents rated companies in their own industry on 8 attributes of reputation. Also notes previous year's rank. **Number listed:** 8

1. EMC, with 7.59
2. Storage Technology, 6.73
3. Lexmark International Group, 6.71
4. Seagate Technology, 6.58
5. Quantum Technology Services Inc., 6.46
6. Imation, 5.98
7. Western Digital, 5.57
8. Iomega, 5.30

Source: *Fortune*, America's Most Admired Corporations (annual), March 1, 1999, p. F-6.

Computer Services Industry

See: **Computer Software Industry**

Computer Software Industry

★1170★
BEST COMPUTER ENTERTAINMENT SOFTWARE BRANDS ACCORDING TO DISCOUNT SHOPPERS, 1998*
Ranked by: Percent of discount shoppers naming brand as best. **Remarks:** Also notes 1997 figures. **Number listed:** 7

1. Microsoft, with 39%
2. Nintendo/Game Boy, 11%
3. IBM, 9%
4. Sony, 8%
5. Quicken, 5%
6. Sega Genesis, 4%
7. 3M, 2%

Source: *Discount Store News*, Top Brands Survey (annual), September 7, 1998, p. 28.

★1171★
BEST-SELLING SOFTWARE BRANDS, 1998
Ranked by: Sales, in billions of dollars. **Number listed:** 5

1. Microsoft Windows, with $14.40 billion
2. NetWare, $1.08
3. McAfee VirusScan, $0.99
4. Adobe PageMaker, etc., $0.89
5. AutoDesk, Auto Cad, $0.74

Source: *Brandweek (supplement)*, Superbrands: America's Top 2,000 Brands, June 21, 1999, p. S32.

★1172★
MOST ADMIRED COMPUTER SOFTWARE CORPORATIONS, 1998
Ranked by: Scores (1-10) derived from a survey of senior executives, outside directors and securities ananysts. **Remarks:** Respondents rated companies in their own industry on 8 attributes of reputation. Also notes previous year's rank. **Number listed:** 5

1. Microsoft, with 7.73
2. Oracle, 6.95
3. Computer Associates International, 6.58
4. Novell, 5.86
5. Sybase, 4.77

Source: *Fortune*, America's Most Admired Corporations (annual), March 1, 1999, p. F-6.

★1173★
SOFTWARE COMPANIES SPENDING THE MOST ON RESEARCH AND DEVELOPMENT, 1997
Ranked by: Research and development expenditures, in millions of dollars. **Number listed:** 20

1. Microsoft, with $2,141 million
2. Computer Associates International Inc., $1,505.3
3. Oracle, $778.4
4. NCR, $446.0
5. Automatic Data Processing, $319.2
6. Unisys Corp., $300
7. Novell, $276.2
8. Platinum Technology Inc., $267.9
9. Netscape Communications, $226.2
10. Learning Company Inc., $205.5

Source: *Research & Development*, Giants of R & D (annual), October, 1998, p. S-15.

★1174★
TOP COMPUTER SOFTWARE/SERVICES COMPANIES BY SEGMENT REVENUE, 1998*
Ranked by: Segment revenue, in millions of dollars. **Number listed:** 20

1. IBM, with $39,254.0 million
2. Electronic Data Systems, $15,235.6
3. Microsoft, $13,089.0
4. Digital Equipment, $7,837.1
5. Oracle, $6,303.2
6. Computer Sciences, $6,267.0
7. General Electric Co., $4,899.8
8. Computer Associates International, $4,457.0
9. Hewlett-Packard, $4,292.2
10. Unisys, $4,180.7

Source: *Electronic Business*, Top 200 (annual), July, 1998, p. 95.

★1175★
TOP CORPORATIONS IN THE COMPUTER SOFTWARE INDUSTRY, 1998
Ranked by: Revenue, in millions of dollars. **Remarks:** Also notes profits and investment figures as well as number of employees. **Number listed:** 5

1. Microsoft, with $14,484 million
2. Oracle, $7,144
3. Computer Associates International, $4,719
4. Peoplesoft, $1,314
5. Cadence Design Systems, $1,216

Source: *Fortune*, Fortune 500 Largest U.S. Corporations (annual), April 26, 1999, p. F-55.

★1176★
WORLD'S LEADING SOFTWARE VENDORS FOR DATABASE MANAGEMENT, 1999*
Ranked by: Market share, in percent. **Number listed:** 6
1. Oracle, with 40.4%
2. IBM, 17.8%
3. Informix, 5.7%
4. Microsoft, 5.1%
5. Sybase, 4.4%
6. Others, 26.6%

Source: *ComputerWorld*, May 10, 1999, p. 4.

Computer Software Industry--Export-Import--India

★1177★
LEADING SOFTWARE EXPORTERS IN INDIA, 1997-1998
Ranked by: Total sales, in millions of rupees. **Number listed:** 20
1. TataConsultancy Services, with Rs9,491 million
2. HCL Corp., Rs7,309
3. Wipro, Rs3,889
4. Pentafour Software &Exports, Rs2,717
5. NIIT, Rs2,583
6. Infosys Technologies, Rs2,472
7. Satyam Computers Services, Rs1,781
8. Tata Infotech, Rs1.723
9. Patni Computer Systems, Rs1,375
10. Tata IBM, Rs1,204

Source: *Financial Times*, December 2, 1998, p. III.

Computer Software Industry, International

★1178★
LARGEST COMPANIES WORLDWIDE DOMINATING THE SOFTWARE MARKETPLACE, 1997
Ranked by: Market share, in percent. **Number listed:** 11
1. SAP, with 31%
2. Oracle, 14%
3. PeopleSoft, 7%
4. J. D. Edwards, 6%
4. Bean Co., 6%
6. Systems Software Associates Inc., 4%
7. JBA Software Products Ltd., 3%
8. Intentia A. B., 2%
8. QAD Inc., 2%
8. Lawson Software, 2%
10. Other, 23%

Source: *Purchasing*, July 16, 1998, p. 113.

Computer Software Industry--Long Island (NY)

★1179★
LARGEST SOFTWARE DEVELOPERS IN LONG ISLAND, 1999
Ranked by: Number of employees. **Remarks:** Also notes location, contact information, and major software products. **Number listed:** 82
1. Computer Association International, with 2,000 employees
2. Global Computer Supplies, 350
3. Sandata, 240
3. Volt Information Sciences, 240
5. Anchor Computer, 120
5. Computer Concepts, 120
7. Camp Systems International, 100
7. TSR, 100
9. Interworks Systems, 85
9. Mentortech, 85
10. Infosys International, 60
10. Vomittag Associates, 60

Source: *Long Island Business News*, LI Book of Lists (annual), 1999, p. 130+.

Computer Software Publishers

See: **Computer Software Industry**

Computer Stores

★1180★
LEADING U.S. COMPUTER RETAILERS BY PRODUCT SALES, 1997
Ranked by: Product sales. **Remarks:** Also notes company location, type of business, and number of units. **Number listed:** 100
1. CompUSA Inc., with $5,290,000,000
2. Best Buy, $3,259,620,000
3. Office Depot Inc., $2,418,480,000
4. Circuit City Stores Inc., $2,217,699,250
5. Computer City, $1,903,700,000
6. Micro Electronics Inc., $1,300,000,000
7. Staples, $1,295,258,750
8. Computer Discount Warehouse, $1,276,000,000
9. Office Max Inc., $1,016,669,880
10. Sears Merchandise Group, $874,280,000

Source: *Chain Store Guide/Business Guides Inc.*, Directory of Computer Retailers, Dealers, & Distributors (annual), 1999, p. a19+.

★1181★
TOP U.S. COMPUTER DEALERS, 1997
Ranked by: Product sales. **Number listed:** 20
1. ASCII Group Inc., with $5,990,000,000
2. MicroAge, $4,446,308,000
3. Inacom Corp., $3,896,302,000
4. Computerland Corp., $1,100,000,000
5. Corporate Software & Technology Inc., $850,000,000
6. Elcom Services Group Inc., $760,000,000
7. Government Technology Services Inc., $486,400,000

8. Pomeroy Computer Resources, $485,413,000
9. SARCOM Inc., $400,000,000
10. Hartford Computer Group Inc., $350,000,000

Source: *Chain Store Guide/Business Guides Inc.*, Directory of Computer, Retailers, Dealers & Distributors (annual), 1999, p. a20.

Concerts

★1182★
TOP CONCERT TOURS, 1998
Ranked by: Gross ticket sales. **Number listed:** 10

1. The Rolling Stones, with $193,351,265
2. U2, $45,086,058
3. Elton John, $40,040,779
4. Yanni, $38,185,482
5. Garth Brooks, $34,883,676
6. George Strait, $32,948,832
7. Janet Jackson, $32,279,900
8. Eric Clapton, $29,877,575
9. Celine Dion, $29,781,703
10. Shania Twain, $27,083,481

Source: *Amusement Business*, Amusement Business (annual), December, December 29, 1998, p. 16.

★1183★
TOP CONCERTS, 1998
Ranked by: Gross ticket sales. **Remarks:** Also notes total capacity shows, ticket scale, promoter, and venue. **Number listed:** 100

1. The Rolling Stones, with $14,819,850
2. The Rolling Stones/Dave Matthews Band, $11,094,308
3. The Rolling Stones/Pearl Jam, $10,955,527
4. The Rolling Stones, $10,025,470
5. U2, $8,668,840
6. Luis Miguel, $6,766,336
7. The Rolling Stones/Fiona Apple, $6,395,815
8. U2, $6,103,065
9. The Rolling Stones, $5,317,800
10. U2, $4,595,225

Source: *Amusement Business*, Amusement Business (annual), December, December 29, 1998, p. 17+.

★1184★
TOP COUNTRY MUSIC CONCERTS, 1998
Ranked by: Gross ticket sales. **Remarks:** Also notes total attendance, capacity, and number of shows. **Number listed:** 10

1. Garth Brooks, with $34,883,676
2. George Strait, $32,948,832
3. Shania Twain, $27,083,481
4. Reba McEntire/Brooks & Dunn, $10,485,248
5. Alan Jackson, $7,168,362
6. LeAnn Rimes/Bryan White, $5,687,082
7. Tim McGraw, $3,174,172
8. Clint Black, $2,909,188
9. Brooks & Dunn, $2,461,646
10. Clay Walker, $2,375,595

Source: *Amusement Business*, Amusement Business (annual), December, December 29, 1998, p. 16.

Conference Rooms—Los Angeles Metropolitan Area (CA)

★1185★
LARGEST CONFERENCE ROOMS IN THE LOS ANGELES METROPOLITAN AREA, 1999*
Ranked by: Total square feet. **Number listed:** 25

1. Los Angeles Convention Center, with 867,000 square feet
2. Long Beach Convention & Entertainment Center, 306,000
3. Westin Bonaventure Hotel & Suites, 100,000
3. Century Plaza Hotel & Tower, 100,000
5. Queen Mary Hotel, 85,000
5. Pasadena Center, 85,000
7. Regal Biltmore Hotel, 70,000
8. Hilton Los Angeles Airport, 55,000
9. Shrine Auditorium & Expo Center, 54,000
10. Beverly Hilton, 53,000
10. Museum of Flying, 53,000
11. Hilton Burbank Airport & Convention Center, 50,000
11. Omni Los Angeles Hotel & Center, 50,000

Source: *Los Angeles Business Journal*, Book of Lists (annual), 1999, p. 100.

Conglomerate Corporations

See: **Diversified Corporations**

Construction Industry

See also: **Contractors Prefabricated Building Industry**

★1186★
BUILDERS WITH THE GREATEST DECREASE IN NUMBER OF CLOSINGS, 1997
Ranked by: Decrease in number of closings, in percent. **Remarks:** Specific figures not provided. **Number listed:** 10

1. Town & Country Homes, with -28% closings
2. Hunt Building Corp., -22%
3. Rottlund Co., -19%
4. Landstar Development Corp., -10%
5. Cambridge Cos., -9%
5. Jones Co., -9%
7. G. L. Homes of Florida Corp., -8%
8. Arthur Rutenberg Homes, -7%
9. Lakewood Homes, -6%
9. John Wieland Homes & Neighborhoods, -6%

Source: *Builder*, Builder 100, May, 1999, p. 102.

★1187★
BUILDERS WITH THE GREATEST DECREASE IN REVENUE, 1997
Ranked by: Decrease in revenue, in percent. **Remarks:** Specific figures not provided. **Number listed:** 9

1. Town & Country Homes, with -23%
2. Rottlund Co., -11%
3. Landstar Development Corp., -10%
4. Hunt Building Co., -9%
5. Jim Walter Homes, -3%
5. Lakewood Homes, -3%

7. Arvida/JMB Partners, -2%
7. Cambridge Cos., -2%
7. Rhode Homes, -2%

Source: *Builder*, Builder 100, May, 1999, p. 102.

★1188★
BUILDERS WITH THE GREATEST INCREASE IN NUMBER OF CLOSINGS, 1997
Ranked by: Increase in number of closings, in percent. **Number listed:** 10

1. H. R. Horton, with 171%
2. Newmark Home Corp., 130%
3. WL Homes, 89%
4. WCI, 76%
5. Western Pacific Housing, 75%
6. Shea Homes, 57%
7. Elliot Homes, 55%
8. American West Homes, 54%
9. Fortress Group, 49%
10. Choice Homes, 43%

Source: *Builder*, Builder 100, May, 1999, p. 99.

★1189★
BUILDERS WITH THE GREATEST INCREASE IN REVENUE, 1997
Ranked by: Increase in revenue, in percent. **Number listed:** 10

1. WCI, with 269%
2. Brookfield Properties Corp., 192%
3. D. R. Horton, 162%
4. WL Homes, 158%
5. Western Pacific Housing, 129%
6. Newmark Home Corp., 123%
7. American West Homes, 77%
8. Shea Homes, 62%
9. Fortress Group, 58%
10. Elliott Homes, 56%

Source: *Builder*, Builder 100, May, 1999, p. 99.

★1190★
LARGEST HOUSING CONSTRUCTION COMPANIES BY CLOSING, 1997
Ranked by: Number of closings. **Number listed:** 100

1. Pulte Home Corp., with 20,359 closings
2. Kaufman & Broad Home Corp., 15,213
3. D. R. Horton, 15,168
4. Centex Corp., 13,759
5. Lennar Corp., 10,777
6. Ryland Group, 8,994
7. U.S. Home Corp., 8,258
8. NVR, 7,622
9. Beazer Homes USA, 6,471
10. M.D.C. Holdings Inc., 6,293

Source: *Builder*, Builder 100, May, 1999, p. 104+.

★1191★
LARGEST HOUSING CONSTRUCTION COMPANIES BY GROSS REVENUE, 1997
Ranked by: Gross revenue, in millions of dollars. **Number listed:** 100

1. Centex Corp., with $4,749 million
2. Pulte Home Corp., $3,005
3. Kaufman & Broad Home Corp., $2,449
4. D. R. Horton, $2,421
5. Lennar Corp., $2,417
6. Ryland Group, $1,766
7. Shea Homes, $1,621
8. NVR, $1,560
9. U.S. Home Corp., $1,500
10. Del Webb Corp., $1,274

Source: *Builder*, Builder 100, May, 1999, p. 134+.

★1192★
LEADING BUILDERS OF ATTACHED FOR-SALE HOMES, 1998
Ranked by: Number of units built. **Number listed:** 10

1. Pulte Home Corp., with 7,323 units
2. NVR, 3,049
3. D. R. Horton, 1,820
4. U.S. Home Corp., 1,782
5. Hunt Building Corp., 1,240
6. Hovnanian Enterprises, 1,228
7. Centex Corp., 952
8. Pasquinelli Construction Co., 740
9. Rottlund Co., 661
10. Brookfield Properties Corp., 647

Source: *Builder*, Builder 100, May, 1999, p. 99.

★1193★
LEADING BUILDERS OF DETACHED FOR-SALE HOMES, 1997
Ranked by: Number of units built. **Number listed:** 10

1. Kaufman & Broad Home Corp., with 15,213 units
2. D. R. Horton, 13,348
3. Pulte Home Corp., 13,036
4. Centex Corp., 12,807
5. Lennar Corp., 9,633
6. Ryland Group, 8,994
7. U.S. Home Group, 6,476
8. Beazer Homes USA, 6,471
9. Del Webb Corp., 6,281
10. M.D.C. Holdings Inc., 5,992

Source: *Builder*, Builder 100, May, 1999, p. 99.

★1194★
LEADING BUILDERS OF RENTAL HOUSING, 1997
Ranked by: Number of units built. **Number listed:** 10

1. A. G. Spanos Cos., with 11,260 units
2. JPI, 9,935
3. Lincoln Property Co., 9,213
4. Trammell Crow Residential, 8,758
5. Colson & Colson Construction Co., 5,125
6. Picerne Real Estate Group, 3,621
7. Clark Realty Builders, 2,822
8. Post Properties, 2,742
9. Simpson Housing, 2,582
10. Brisben Cos., 2,512

Source: *Builder*, Builder 100, May, 1999, p. 142+.

★1195★
LEADING CONSTRUCTION COMPANIES OF MANUFACTURED HOUSING, 1998
Ranked by: Gross revenue, in millions of dollars. **Remarks:** Also notes total factory-built units. **Number listed:** 25

1. Champion Enterprises Inc., MI, with $1,898,596,000 million
2. Fleetwood Enterprises Inc., CA, $1,547,925,000
3. Oakwood Homes, $1,404,432,000
4. Clayton Homes Inc., TN, $880,856,000
5. Palm Harbor Homes Inc., TX, $637,268,000
6. Cavalier Homes Inc., AL, $603,369,040
7. Skyline Corp., IN, $532,894,000
8. American Homestar Corp., TX, $513,939,000
9. Southern Energy Homes, AL, $306,964,000
10. Horton Homes Inc., GA, $305,000,000

Source: *Giants*, Professional Builder. Annual Report of the 400 Housing Giants (annual), April, 1999, p. 108.

★1196★
MOST ADMIRED ENGINEERING AND CONSTRUCTION CORPORATIONS, 1998
Ranked by: Scores (1-10) derived from a survey of senior executives, outside directors, and securities analysts. **Remarks:** Respondents rated companies in their own industry on 8 attributes of reputation. Also notes previous year's rank. **Number listed:** 10

1. Jacobs Engineering Group, with 6.80
2. Halliburton, 6.66
3. Pulte, 6.31
4. Turner, 6.29
5. Centex, 6.13
6. Emcor, 5.90
7. Fluor, 5.89
8. Kaufman & Broad Home, 5.81
9. Fleetwood Enterprises, 5.75
10. Foster Wheeler, 5.72

Source: *Fortune*, America's Most Admired Corporations (annual), December/January, March 1, 1999, p. F-4.

★1197★
TOP CONSTRUCTION FIRMS BY HOUSING REVENUE, 1998
Ranked by: Housing revenue. **Remarks:** Also notes closings, starts, and total revenue. **Number listed:** 400

1. Pulte Corp., MI, with $2,948,202,000 million
2. Centex Corp., TX, $2,562,747,638
3. Kaufman & Broad Home Corp., CA, $2,378,958,000
4. D. R. Horton Inc., TX, $2,363,600,000
5. Lennar Corp., FL, $2,089,762,000
6. Ryland Group Inc., MD, $1,664,300,000
7. NVR, $1,504,700,000
8. U.S. Home Corp., TX, $1,445,334,555
9. Shea Homes, CA, $1,245,170,000
10. M.D.C. Holdings Inc. (CO), $1,218,659,000

Source: *Giants*, Professional Builder. Annual Report of the 400 Housing Giants (annual), April, 1999, p. 70+.

★1198★
TOP CONSTRUCTION FIRMS BY NUMBER OF HOUSING CLOSINGS, 1998
Ranked by: Number of for-sale housing closings. **Number listed:** 100

1. Pulte Corp., with 20,359 closings
2. Kaufman & Broad Home Corp., 15,213
3. D. R. Horton Inc., 15,168
4. Centex Corp., 14,063
5. Lennar Corp., 10,777
6. Lincoln Property Co., 9,213
7. Ryland Group, 8,994
8. Trammell Crow Residential, 8,758
9. U.S. Home Corp., 8,258
10. A. G. Spanos Cos., 7,630

Source: *Giants*, Professional Builder. Annual Report of the 400 Housing Giants (annual), April, 1999, p. 98.

★1199★
TOP CONSTRUCTION FIRMS BY TOTAL REVENUE, 1998
Ranked by: Total revenue. **Number listed:** 400

1. Centex Corp., with $4,445,588,638 million
2. Pulte Corp., $2,948,202,000
3. Kaufman & Broad Home Corp., $2,449,362,000
4. D. R. Horton Inc., $2,446,000,000
5. Lennar Corp., $2,416,865,000
6. Ryland Group, $1,765,500,000
7. Shea Homes, $1,620,734,000
8. Trammell Crow Residential, $1,617,300,000
9. NVR, $1,559,800,000
10. U.S. Home Corp., $1,497,648,555

Source: *Giants*, Professional Builder. Annual Report of the 400 Housing Giants (annual), April, 1999, p. 100+.

★1200★
TOP CONSTRUCTION MANAGEMENT FIRMS FOR HEALTHCARE FACILITIES, 1997
Ranked by: Dollar volume, in thousands. **Remarks:** Also notes figures for previous year. **Number listed:** 19

1. CRSS Construction, with $782,000 thousand
2. Turner Corp., $727,884
3. Bovis, $655,200
4. Centex Construction Group, $557,100
5. McCarthy, $554,000
6. Beers Construction Co., $356,700
7. Barton Malow Co., $257,600
8. Walbridge Aldinger, $188,480
9. Power Contracting & Engineering Co., $133,800
10. J. E. Dunn Construction Co., $127,236

Source: *Modern Healthcare*, Modern Healthcare Design & Construction Survey (annual), March, 1999, p. 32.

★1201★
TOP HOUSING AND REAL ESTATE COMPANIES IN THE S & P 500, 1997
Ranked by: Each company is ranked by eight criteria, with additional weight given to a company's sales. A company's composite is calculated using the sum of all its ranks. **Number listed:** 8

1. Centex
2. Masco
3. Kaufman & Broad Home Corp.
4. Pulte
5. PPG Industries
6. Fleetwood Enterprises
7. Sherwin-Williams
8. Owens Corning

Source: *Business Week*, Top Companies on the S & P 500 (annual), March 29, 1999, p. 154.

Construction Industry--Albuquerque (NM)

★1202★
LARGEST HOME BUILDERS IN ALBUQUERQUE, 1998
Ranked by: Number of single-family permits. **Remarks:** Also notes market share and division head. **Number listed:** 5

1. Artistic Homes, with 498 permits
2. Kaufman & Broad Home Corp., 397
3. AMREP Southwest, 390
4. Sivage-Thomas Homes, 334
5. Longford Homes, 321

Source: *Builder*, May, 1999, p. 238.

Construction Industry--Asia

★1203★
LARGEST ASIAN COMPANIES IN THE CONSTRUCTION INDUSTRY, 1998
Ranked by: Sales, in thousands of U.S. dollars ($). **Remarks:** Includes profit as a percentage of sales and activity codes. **Number listed:** 100

1. Samsung (ROK), with $24,955,937 thousand
2. Daewoo (ROK), $20,150,230
3. Kajima Corp. (Japan), $14,512,971
4. Taisei Corp. (Japan), $13,702,080
5. Shimizu (Japan), $13,150,396
6. Obayashi Corp. (Japan), $11,133,944
7. Sekisui House (Japan), $10,911,070
8. Kumagai Gumi Corp. (Japan), $8,490,374
9. Daiwa House Industry Co. Ltd. (Japan), $8,007,402
10. Fujita Corp. (Japan), $5,503,121

Source: *Dun & Bradstreet*, Asia's 7500 Largest Companies (annual), 1999, p. 85+.

★1204★
MOST ADMIRED PROPERTY/CONSTRUCTION COMPANIES IN ASIA, 1999
Ranked by: Score. **Remarks:** Also notes previous year's rank, overall rank, and change in rank. **Number listed:** 10

1. Ayala Corp., with 7.60
2. Sun Hung Kai Properties, 7.34
3. Cheung Kong, 7.11
4. NTT, 7.03
5. ABB Asea Brown Boveri, 6.99
6. Bechtel, 6.72
7. Henderson Land, 6.24
8. Cathay Construction, 6.17
9. Kuok Philippines Properties, Inc., 5.92
10. Ricoh, 5.75

Source: *Asian Business*, Most Admired Companies in Asia (annual), May, 1999, p. 29.

Construction Industry--Baltimore Metropolitan Area

★1205★
LARGEST HOME BUILDERS IN THE BALTIMORE METROPOLITAN AREA, 1998
Ranked by: Number of new home building permits. **Remarks:** Also notes market share. **Number listed:** 5

1. Ryan Homes/NVR, with 619 permits
2. Ryland Group, 239
3. Patriot Homes, 208
4. Pulte Home Corp., 199
5. NV Homes/NVR, 172

Source: *Builder*, May, 1999, p. 228.

Construction Industry--Boston Metropolitan Area

★1206★
LARGEST HOME BUILDERS IN THE BOSTON METROPOLITIAN AREA, 1998
Ranked by: Number of new home building permits. **Remarks:** Also notes market share. **Number listed:** 5

1. Pulte Home Corp., with 184 permits
2. Toll Brothers, 110
3. Modern Continental Enterprises, 96
4. Commons Development Group, 72
5. Robert M. Hicks, 58

Source: *Builder*, May, 1999, p. 234.

Construction Industry--Charlotte (NC)

★1207★
LARGEST HOME BUILDERS IN THE CHARTLOTTE AREA, 1998
Ranked by: Number of new home building pemits. **Remarks:** Also notes market share. **Number listed:** 5

1. Pulte Home Corp., with 657 permits
2. Torrey Homes/D. R. Horton, 519
3. Squires Homes/Beazer Homes USA, 512
4. Ryland Group, 466
5. Ryan Homes/NVR, 458

Source: *Builder*, May, 1999, p. 220.

Construction Industry--Chicago (IL)

★1208★
LARGEST HOME BUILDERS IN THE CHICAGO AREA, 1998
Ranked by: Number of new home building permits. **Remarks:** Also notes market share. **Number listed:** 5

1. Cambridge Homes, with 604 permits
2. Sundance Homes, 411
3. Lakewood Homes, 405
4. Kimball Hill Homes, 390
5. Town & Country Homes, 361

Source: *Builder*, May, 1999, p. 218.

Construction Industry--Cincinnati (OH)

★1209★
LARGEST HOME BUILDERS IN THE CINCINNATI AREA, 1998
Ranked by: Number of new home building permits. **Remarks:** Also notes market share. **Number listed:** 5

1. M/I Schottenstein Homes, with 316 permits
2. Dress Co., 310
3. Zaring National Corp., 288
4. Crossmann Communities, 233
5. Fischer Homes, 181

Source: *Builder*, May, 1999, p. 230.

Construction Industry—Dallas/Ft. Worth Metropolitan Area

★1210★
LARGEST HOME BUILDERS IN THE DALLAS/FT. WORTH METROPOLITIAN AREA, 1998
Ranked by: Number of new home building permits. **Remarks:** Also notes market share. **Number listed:** 5

1. Centex Corp., with 1,245 permits
2. Highland Homes, 1,209
3. Choice Homes, 1,121
4. Pulte Home Corp., 827
5. Lennar Corp., 685

Source: *Builder*, May, 1999, p. 218.

Construction Industry--Denver (CO)

★1211★
LARGEST HOME BUILDERS IN DENVER AREA, 1998
Ranked by: Number of new home building permits. **Remarks:** Also notes market share. **Number listed:** 5

1. Richmond American Homes, with 2,049 permits
2. Melody Homes/Schuler Homes, 1,143
3. Kaufman & Broad Home Corp., 1,118
4. U.S. Home Corp., 909
5. Continental Homes/D. R. Horton, 666

Source: *Builder*, May, 1999, p. 222.

Construction Industry--Detroit Metropolitan Area

★1212★
LARGEST HOME BUILDERS IN THE DETROIT METROPOLITAN AREA, 1998
Ranked by: Number of new home building permits. **Remarks:** Also notes market share. **Number listed:** 5

1. Pulte Home Corp., with 834 permits
2. MJC Cos., 504
3. Tri Mount-Vincenti Cos., 432
4. Crosswinds Communities, 381
5. Silverman Cos., 287

Source: *Builder*, May, 1999, p. 220.

Construction Industry--District of Columbia

★1213★
LARGEST HOME BUILDERS IN THE WASHINGTON AREA, 1998
Ranked by: Number of new home building permits. **Remarks:** Also notes market share. **Number listed:** 5

1. Ryan Homes/NVR, with 1,413 permits
2. Richmond American Homes, 754
3. NV Homes/NVR, 515
4. Washington Homes, 487
5. Winchester Homes, 395

Source: *Builder*, May, 1999, p. 218.

Construction Industry--Europe

★1214★
TOP CONSTRUCTION COMPANIES IN EUROPE
Ranked by: Financial size, in millions of ECUs. **Remarks:** Also notes country, employees, and rank. **Number listed:** 249

1. Kvaerner PLC (United Kingdom), with ECUs6.954 million
2. BICC PLC (United Kingdom), ECUs6.107
3. Philipp Holzmann AG (Germany), ECUs5.784
4. Rentokil Initial PLC (United Kingdom), ECUs4.149
5. Tarmac PLC (United Kingdom), ECUs4.091
6. Bilfinger & Berger Bau AG (Germany), ECUs3.563
7. Hochtief AG (Germany), ECUs3.433
8. Va Technologie Aktiengesellschaft (Austria), ECUs2.768
9. Balfour Beatty Ltd. (United Kingdom), ECUs2.756
10. ACS Actividades de Construccion y Servicios S.A. (Spain), ECUs2.151

Source: *Dun & Bradstreet*, Duns Europa (annual), 1999, p. 228+.

Construction Industry--Florida

★1215★
TOP CONSTRUCTION FIRMS IN FLORIDA, 1997
Ranked by: Revenue. **Remarks:** Also notes number of full-time employees, senior exec, location of corporate headquarters, and year founded. **Number listed:** 25

1. Centex Rooney Construction Co., with $340,900,000
2. WCI Communities, $300,000,000
3. Clark Construction Group Inc., $270,000,000
4. Hubbard Construction Co., $217,000,000
5. Arthur Rutenberg Homes Inc., $180,000,000
6. Bovis Construction Corp., $169,500,000
7. Summit Contractors Inc., $168,200,000
8. WELBRO Building Corp., $165,340,000
9. G. L. Homes, $162,000,000
10. Turner Construction Co., $161,187,000

Source: *Florida Trend*, TopRank Florida (annual), 1999, p. 37.

Construction Industry--Houston Metropolitan Area

★1216★
LARGEST HOME BUILDERS IN THE HOUSTON METROPOLITAN AREA, 1998
Ranked by: Number of new home building permits. **Remarks:** Also notes market share. **Number listed:** 5

1. MHI, with 1,210 permits
2. Perry Homes, 1,102
3. Royce Homes, 1,059
4. Village Builders, 991
5. Ryland Group, 779

Source: *Builder*, May, 1999, p. 220.

Construction Industry--Indianapolis (IN)

★1217★
LARGEST HOME BUILDERS IN THE INDIANAPOLIS AREA, 1998
Ranked by: Number of new home building permits. **Remarks:** Also notes market share. **Number listed:** 5

1. Crossmann Communities, with 1,838 permits
2. Davis Homes, 841
3. C. P. Morgan, 797
4. Ryland Group, 639
5. Dura Builders, 527

Source: *Builder*, May, 1999, p. 224.

Construction Industry--Las Vegas (NV)

★1218★
LARGEST HOME BUILDERS IN THE LAS VEGAS AREA, 1998
Ranked by: Number of new home building permits. **Remarks:** Also notes market share. **Number listed:** 5

1. Lewis Homes Group of Cos., with 1,873 permits
2. Kaufman & Broad Home Corp., 1,359
3. Del Webb Corp., 1,192
4. Pulte Home Corp., 1,109
5. Pardee Construction/Weyerhaeuser Real Estate Co., 783

Source: *Builder*, May, 1999, p. 220.

Construction Industry--Long Island (NY)

★1219★
TOP RESIDENTIAL BUILDERS IN LONG ISLAND, 1998
Ranked by: Number of units completed and under construction. **Number listed:** 22

1. Holiday Organization, with 337 units
2. Klar Organization, 312
3. Park Ridge Estates, 205
4. Emmy Building, 95
5. Klein & Eversoil, 60
6. Homeworks, 58
7. Country View Properties, 50
8. LI Housing Partnership, 49
9. Clifton Commons at Farmingdale, 35
10. Metro Group, 22

Source: *Long Island Business News*, LI Book of Lists (annual), 1999, p. 102.

Construction Industry--Los Angeles County (CA)

★1220★
LARGEST HOME BUILDERS IN THE LOS ANGELES COUNTY AREA, 1998
Ranked by: Number of new home building permits. **Remarks:** Also notes market share. **Number listed:** 5

1. Kaufman & Broad Home Corp., with 273 permits
2. S & S Construction, 245
3. Centex Corp., 234
4. Shea Homes, 216
5. Pacific Bay Homes, 214

Source: *Builder*, May, 1999, p. 234.

Construction Industry--Memphis (TN)

★1221★
LARGEST HOME BUILDERS IN THE MEMPHIS AREA, 1998
Ranked by: Number of new home building permits. **Remarks:** Also notes market share. **Number listed:** 5

1. Bowden Building Co., with 424 permits
2. Summit Homes, 136
3. Vintage Homes, 136
4. Paragon Properties/Crossmann Communities, 94
5. FaxonGillis Homes, 92

Source: *Builder*, May, 1999, p. 232.

Construction Industry--Miami

★1222★
LARGEST HOME BUILDERS IN THE MIAMI AREA, 1998
Ranked by: Number of new home building permits. **Remarks:** Also notes market share. **Number listed:** 5

1. Lennar Corp., with 558 permits
2. Caribe Group, 313
3. Shoma Homes, 232
4. Continental Homes/D. R. Horton, 194
5. Adrian Homes, 177

Source: *Builder*, May, 1999, p. 238.

Construction Industry—Minneapolis/St. Paul Metropolitan Area

★1223★
LARGEST HOME BUILDERS IN THE MINNEAPOLIS/ST. PAUL METROPOLITAN AREA, 1998
Ranked by: Number of new home building permits. **Remarks:** Also notes market share. **Number listed:** 5

1. Rottlund Co., with 731 permits
2. Pulte Home Corp., 520
3. Orrin Thompson Homes, 514
4. Joe Miller Homes/D. R. Horton, 369
5. Centex Corp., 333

Source: *Builder*, May, 1999, p. 220.

Construction Industry--Nashville (TN)

★1224★
LARGEST HOME BUILDERS IN THE NASHVILLE AREA, 1998
Ranked by: Number of new home building permits. **Remarks:** Also notes market share. **Number listed:** 5

1. Fox Ridge Homes, with 468 permits
2. Philips Builders/Beazer Homes USA, 452
3. Pulte Home Corp., 351
4. Zaring National Corp., 238
5. Jerry Butler Builder, 204

Source: *Builder*, May, 1999, p. 224.

Construction Industry--New Jersey

★1225★
TOP CONSTRUCTION COMPANIES IN NEW JERSEY BY EMPLOYEES, 1999*
Ranked by: Number of employees. **Remarks:** Also notes contact information, total revenues, year established, chief executive officer, and URL address. **Number listed:** 17

1. Foster Wheeler, with 12,000 employees
2. Gilbane Building Co., 150
3. Morse Diesel International, 682
4. Sordoni Skanska Construction Co., 600
5. Kajima Construction Services, 400
6. Torcon Inc., 170
7. Barr & Barr Inc. Builders, 283
8. C. Raimondo & Sons Construction Co., 250
9. Turner Construction Co., 130
10. Conectiv Services, 500

Source: *New Jersey Business*, Book of Lists (annual), 1999, p. 18.

Construction Industry--Orlando (FL)

★1226★
LARGEST BUILDERS IN THE ORLANDO AREA, 1998
Ranked by: Number of new home building permits. **Remarks:** Also notes market share. **Number listed:** 5

1. Centex Corp., with 651 permits
2. Maronda Homes, 534
3. American Heritage Homes, 510
4. Engle Homes, 483
5. Morrison Homes, 370

Source: *Builder*, May, 1999, p. 222.

Construction Industry—Philadelphia Metropolitan Area

★1227★
LARGEST CONSTRUCTION PROJECTS UNDERWAY IN THE GREATER PHILADELPHIA AREA, 1998
Ranked by: Project cost, in millions of dollars. **Remarks:** Also notes start/completion dates, owner, general contractor/construction manager, architectural firm, and engineering firm. **Number listed:** 25

1. Frankford Elevated reconstruction project, with $733 million
2. New International Terminal, $325
3. Regional Performing Arts Center, $245
4. Philadelphia International Airport Runway 8-26, $221
5. Children's Hospital of Philadelphia-renovations, $150
5. Hospital of the University of Pennsylvania-renovations, $150
7. Sansom Common, $90
8. Walt Whitman Bridge rechecking, $74
9. New Computer Terminal (Terminal F), $65
10. Loews Philadelphia Hotel, $54.4

Source: *Philadelphia Business Journal*, Book of Business Lists (annual), December 25, 1998, p. 61.

★1228★
LARGEST HOME BUILDERS IN THE PHILADELPHIA METROPOLITAN AREA, 1998
Ranked by: Number of new home building permits. **Remarks:** Also notes market share. **Number listed:** 5

1. Toll Brothers, with 859 permits
2. Ryan Homes/NVR, 433
3. Homes on Parade, 396
4. Hovnanian Enterprises, 333
5. Quaker Group, 324

Source: *Builder*, May, 1999, p. 222.

★1229★
LARGEST HOUSING CONSTRUCTION COMPANIES IN THE PHILADELPHIA AREA BY CLOSINGS, 1997
Ranked by: Number of closings. **Number listed:** 25

1. Toll Brothers, with 780 closings
2. Orleans Corp., 562
3. David Cutler Group, 424
4. K. Hovnanian Cos., 309
5. Pulte Home Corp., 294
6. Realen Homes, 256
7. Quaker Group, 243
8. DeLuca Enterprises Inc., 218
9. Trafaigar House Property Inc., 198
10. Iacobucci Organization, 197

Source: *Philadelphia Business Journal*, Book of Business Lists (annual), 1999, p. 59.

Construction Industry--Phoenix (AZ)

★1230★
LARGEST HOME BUILDERS IN THE PHOENIX AREA, 1998
Ranked by: Number of new home building permits. **Remarks:** Also lists market share. **Number listed:** 5

1. Shea Homes, with 2,748 permits
2. Continental Homes/D. R. Horton, 2,234
3. Beazer Homes USA, 1,490
4. Del Webb Corp., 1,244
5. Kaufman & Broad Home Corp., 1,239

Source: *Builder*, May, 1999, p. 217.

Construction Industry--Portland (OR)

★1231★
LARGEST HOME BUILDERS IN THE PORTLAND AREA, 1998
Ranked by: Number of new home building permits. **Remarks:** Also notes market share. **Number listed:** 5

1. Arbor Custom Homes, with 601 permits
2. Marshall Grimburg Group, 522
3. Centex Corp., 403
4. New Tradition Homes, 315
5. Aho Construction, 302

Source: *Builder*, May, 1999, p. 224.

Construction Industry--Richmond (VA)

★1232★
LARGEST HOME BUILDERS IN THE RICHMOND AREA, 1998
Ranked by: Number of new home building permits. **Remarks:** Also notes market share. **Number listed:** 5
1. Ryan Homes/NVR, with 259 permits
2. Teal Homes/Centex Corp., 151
2. Eagle Construction, 151
4. Tomac, 138
5. Parker Lancaster Corp., 133

Source: *Builder*, May, 1999, p. 236.

Construction Industry--St. Louis (MO)

★1233★
LARGEST HOME BUILDERS IN THE ST. LOUIS AREA, 1998
Ranked by: Number of new home building permits. **Remarks:** Also notes market share. **Number listed:** 5
1. Whittaker Homes/Fortress Group, with 556 permits
2. Jones Co., 423
3. McBride & Son, 270
4. Mayer Homes, 243
5. Taylor Morley Homes, 192

Source: *Builder*, May, 1999, p. 224.

Construction Industry--Salt Lake City (UT)

★1234★
LARGEST HOME BUILDERS IN THE SALT LAKE CITY AREA, 1998
Ranked by: Number of new home building permits. **Remarks:** Also notes market share. **Number listed:** 5
1. Ivory Homes, with 520 permits
2. Woodside Homes, 261
3. Perry Homes, 179
4. Kaufman & Broad Home Corp., 156
5. Mark Higley Construction, 142

Source: *Builder*, May, 1999, p. 230.

Construction Industry--San Diego Metropolitan Area

★1235★
LARGEST HOME BUILDERS IN THE SAN DIEGO METROPOLITAN AREA, 1998
Ranked by: Number of new home building permits. **Remarks:** Also notes market share. **Number listed:** 5
1. Pardee Construction/Weyerhaeuser Real Estate Co., with 877 permits
2. Kaufman & Broad Home Corp., 741
3. Shea Homes, 505
4. Lemar Corp., 402
5. Standard Pacific Corp., 316

Source: *Builder*, May, 1999, p. 228.

Construction Industry--Seattle (WA)

★1236★
LARGEST HOME BUILDERS IN THE SEATTLE AREA, 1998
Ranked by: Number of new home building permits. **Remarks:** Also notes market share. **Number listed:** 5
1. Centex Corp., with 291 permits
2. Murray Franklin Cos., 206
3. D.L.B. Johnson Construction, 200
4. Stafford Homes, 197
5. Geonerco, 167

Source: *Builder*, May, 1999, p. 226.

Construction Project Management

★1237★
LARGEST COMMERCIAL, INSTITUTIONAL AND INDUSTRIAL BUILDING CONSTRUCTION MANAGERS, 1997
Ranked by: Fees earned, in millions of dollars. **Remarks:** Also notes previous year's ranking. **Number listed:** 10
1. Bovis Inc., with $2,020.90 million
2. Gilbane Building Co., $1,790.42
3. Sverdrup Corp., $1,183.32
4. Heery International Inc., $1,120.00
5. 3/D/International Inc., $1,059.00
6. Tishman Realty & Construction Co., $936.88
7. URS Greiner Woodward-Clyde, $931.00
8. Parsons Brinckerhoff Inc., $837.00
9. Barton Malow Co., $756.00
10. H & N/McClier, $558.36

Source: *Building Design & Construction*, Design/Construct 300 (annual), July, 1998, p. 30+.

★1238★
TOP AT-RISK CONSTRUCTION MANAGEMENT FIRMS, 1998
Ranked by: Revenue, in millions of dollars. **Remarks:** Also notes domestic/international revenue split, 1997 rank. **Number listed:** 100
1. Kellogg Brown & Root, with $3,11.0 million
2. Turner Corp., $2,619.8
3. Bovis Construction Corp., $1,935.9
4. Structure Tone Inc., $1,488.2
5. Skanska, $1,408.0
6. DPR Construction Inc., $1,165.5
7. Foster Wheeler Corp., $1,163.6
8. Gilbane Building Co., $1,137.8
9. Fluor Daniel Inc., $1,097.0
10. Morse Daniel International, $892.0

Source: *ENR*, Top CM Firms (annual), June 14, 1999, p. 58.

★1239★
TOP DESIGN-BUILD CONSTRUCTION MANAGEMENT FIRMS, 1998
Ranked by: Revenue, in millions of dollars. **Remarks:** Also notes domestic/international revenue split, 1997 ranking. **Number listed:** 100
1. Bechtel Group Inc., with $8,309.0 million
2. Fluor Daniel Inc., $4,816.0
3. McDermott International Inc., $2,067.8
4. Kellogg Brown & Root, $1,978.0
5. Jacobs Sverdrup, $1,548.0
6. Raytheon Engineers & Contractors, $1,482.0

7. Black & Veatch, $1,463.0
8. ABB Lummus Global Inc., $1,079.6
9. Opus Group of Companies, $806.3
10. Foster Wheeler Corp., $790.2

Source: *ENR*, Top CM Firms (annual), June 14, 1999, p. 50.

★1240★
TOP MANAGEMENT-FOR-FEE CONSTRUCTION MANAGEMENT FIRMS, 1998
Ranked by: Revenue, in millions of dollars. **Remarks:** Also notes domestic/international revenue split, 1997 ranking. **Number listed:** 100

1. Parsons Corp., with $850.4 million
2. Bechtel Group Inc., $729.0
3. Kellogg Brown & Root, $669.0
4. Foster Wheeler Corp., $479.0
5. Jacobs Sverdrup, $365.0
6. Fluor Daniel Inc., $362.0
7. CH2M Hill Inc., $343.7
8. Morrison Knudsen Corp., $264.0
9. Turner Corp., $212.5
10. O'Brien-Kreitzberg Inc., $180.7

Source: *ENR*, Top CM Firms (annual), June 14, 1999, p. 54.

Consumer Credit

★1241★
MOST ADMIRED CONSUMER CREDIT CORPORATIONS, 1998
Ranked by: Scores (1-10) derived from a survey of senior executives, outside directors and securities analysts. **Remarks:** Respondents rated companies in their own industry on 8 attributes of reputation. Also notes previous year's rank. **Number listed:** 5

1. American Express, with 7.44
2. MBNA, 7.36
3. Capital One Financial, 7.05
4. SLM Holdings, 6.47
5. Household International, 6.35

Source: *Fortune*, America's Most Admired Corporations (annual), March 1, 1999, p. F-1.

Consumer Electronics

See: **Home Electronics**

Consumer Goods

★1242★
TOP CONSUMER PRODUCTS COMPANIES IN THE S & P 500, 1998
Ranked by: Overall score; each company is ranked by eight criteria: one-year total return, three-year total return, one-year sales growth, three-year average annual sales growth, one-year profit growth, three-year average annual profit growth, net profit margins, and return on equity, with additional weight given to a company's sales. A company's composite rank is calculated using the sum. **Remarks:** Overall score not provided. **Number listed:** 27

1. Maytag
2. Clorox
3. Ecolab
4. Anheuser-Busch
5. Colgate-Palmolive
6. Procter & Gamble
7. Pepsi-Cola
8. Coca-Cola Enterprises
9. Gillette
10. Brown-Forman

Source: *Business Week*, Top Companies on the S & P 500 (annual), March 29, 1999, p. 144+.

★1243★
TOP R & D SPENDERS IN CONSUMER GOODS INDUSTRY, 1997
Ranked by: R & D expenditures, in millions of dollars. **Number listed:** 13

1. Procter & Gamble, with $1,324.5 million
2. Eastman Kodak Co., $1,223.4
3. Conagra Inc., $530.1
4. Coca-Cola Co., $319
5. Gillette Co., $218.2
6. Kimberly-Clark, $216.5
7. Anheuser-Busch Cos. Inc., $212
8. Whirlpool, $188.0
9. RJR Nabisco Holdings Corp., $181.0
10. Colgate-Palmolive Co., $169.9

Source: *Research & Development*, Giants of R & D (annual), October, 1998, p. S-14.

Consumer Products

See: **Consumer Goods**

Container Industry

★1244★
TOP CONTAINER AND PACKAGING COMPANIES IN THE S&P 500, 1999
Ranked by: Each company is ranked by eight criteria: one-year total return, three-year total return, one-year sales growth, three-year average annual sales growth, one-year profit growth, three-year average annual profit growth, net profit margins, and return on equity, with addtional weight given to a company's sales. A company's composite rank is calculated using the sum of each ranking. **Remarks:** Overall score not provided. **Number listed:** 6

1. Avery Dennison
2. Ball
3. Bemis
4. Temple-Inland
5. Owens-Illinois
6. Crown Cork & Seal

Source: *Business Week*, Business Week 50: Top Companies of the S&P 500 (annual), March 29, 1999, p. 146.

Contract Manufacturers

★1245★
TOP CONTRACT MANUFACTURERS, 1997
Ranked by: Segment revenue, in millions of dollars. **Number listed:** 5
1. SCI Systems, with $6,389 million
2. IBM, $4,710.5
3. Solectron, $4,023.4
4. Hewlett-Packard, $1,287.7
5. Jabil Circuit, $1,094.5

Source: *Electronic Business*, Contract Manufacturers Top 200 (annual), July, 1998, p. 97.

Contractors

See also: **Industry**

★1246★
LARGEST CONTRACTORS BY NEW CONTRACT REVENUE, 1998
Ranked by: New contracts revenue, in millions of U.S. dollars. **Number listed:** 100
1. The Bechtel Group Inc., with $12,513.00 million
2. Fluor Daniel Inc., $6,388.00
3. Kellogg Brown & Root, $5,983.00
4. Foster Wheeler Corp., $5,269.00
5. Jacobs Sverdrup, $4,776.00
6. Skanska (USA) Inc., $4,755.00
7. The Turner Corp., $4,302.00
8. CENTEX Construction Group, $4,294.60
9. Morrison Knudsen Corp., $4,021.00
10. Bovis Construction Corp., $2,865.00

Source: *ENR*, ENR Top 400 Contractors (annual), May 31, 1999, p. 76.

★1247★
LARGEST CONTRACTORS BY REVENUE, 1998
Ranked by: Revenue, in millions of dollars. **Remarks:** Also note international revenue, new contracts, and market share. **Number listed:** 400
1. Bechtel Group Inc., with $9,771.0 million
2. Fluor Daniel Inc., $9,640.0
3. Kellogg Brown & Root, $6,835.0
4. CENTEX Construction Group, $3,748.1
5. The Turner Corp., $3,699.0
6. Foster Wheeler Corp., $3,072.1
7. Skanska (USA) Inc., $3,028.0
8. Peter Kiewit Sons Inc., $2,996.2
9. Gilbane Building Co., $2,248.6
10. Bovis Construction Corp., $2,213.8

Source: *ENR*, ENR Top 400 Contractors (annual), May 31, 1999, p. 79+.

★1248★
LARGEST CONTRACTORS WORKING ABROAD BY INTERNATIONAL REVENUE, 1998
Ranked by: International revenue, in millions of dollars. **Number listed:** 50
1. The Bechtel Group Inc., with $6,022.0 million
2. Fluor Daniel Inc., $5,343.0
3. Kellogg Brown & Root, $4,772.0
4. Foster Wheeler Corp., $2,204.8
5. McDermott International Inc., $1,219.1
6. Raytheon Engineers & Constructors, $902.0
7. PCL Enterprises Inc., $825.0
8. Black & Veatch, $819.0
9. ABB Lummus Global Inc., $695.1
10. Parsons Corp., $525.1

Source: *ENR*, ENR Top 400 Contractors (annual), May 31, 1999, p. 122.

★1249★
LARGEST GENERAL BUILDING CONTRACTORS, 1998
Ranked by: Domestic revenue, in millions of dollars. **Number listed:** 50
1. CENTEX Construction Group, with $3,721.20 million
2. The Turner Corp., $3,644.66
3. Skanska (USA) Inc., $2,240.00
4. Bovis Construction Corp., $1,998.50
5. Gilbane Building Co., $1,580.30
6. Structure Tone Inc., $1,287.60
7. The Clark Construction Group Inc., $1,278.50
8. The Whiting-Turner Contraction Co., $1,260.50
9. J.A. Jones Inc., $1,132.00
10. DPR Construction Inc., $1,058.00

Source: *ENR*, ENR Top 400 Contractors (annual), May 31, 1999, p. 114.

★1250★
LARGEST HAZARDOUS WASTE CONTRACTORS, 1998
Ranked by: Revenue. **Remarks:** Specific figures not included. **Number listed:** 20
1. The Bechtel Group Inc.
2. The IT Group
3. Fluor Daniel Inc.
4. Morrison Knudsen Corp.
5. Jacobs Sverdrup
6. ICF Kaiser International Inc.
7. Foster Wheeler Corp.
8. Earth Tech Inc.
9. Kellogg Brown & Root
10. Raytheon Engineers & Constructors

Source: *ENR*, ENR Top 400 Contractors (annual), May 31, 1999, p. 75.

★1251★
LARGEST HEAVY CONTRACTORS, 1998
Ranked by: Domestic revenue, in millions of dollars. **Number listed:** 50
1. Bechtel Group Inc., with 2,002.0 million
2. Peter Kiewit Sons Inc., 1,995.8
3. The IT Group, 802.0
4. Granite Construction Inc., 758.0
5. Morrison Knudsen Corp., 717.0
6. Fluor Daniel Inc., 697.0
7. Skanska (USA) Inc., 615.0
8. Tutor-Saliba Corp., 581.3
9. Modern Continental Construction Co. Inc., 521.8
10. The Walsh Group, 405.0

Source: *ENR*, ENR Top 400 Contractors (annual), May 31, 1999, p. 118.

★1252★
LARGEST INDUSTRIAL PETROCHEMICAL CONTRACTORS, 1998
Ranked by: Revenue. **Remarks:** Specific figures not included. **Number listed:** 20
1. Kellogg Brown & Root
2. Bechtel Group Inc.
3. Fluor Daniel Inc.
4. Foster Wheeler Corp.

5. McDermott International Inc.
6. Jacobs Sverdrup
7. ABB Lummus Global Inc.
8. Parsons Corp.
9. Raytheon Engineers & Constructors
10. Chicago Bridge & Iron Co.

Source: *ENR*, ENR Top 400 Contractors (annual), May 31, 1999, p. 75.

★1253★
LARGEST POWER CONTRACTORS, 1998
Ranked by: Revenue. **Remarks:** Specific figure not included. **Number listed:** 20

1. Bechtel Group Inc.
2. Black & Veatch
3. Raytheon Engineers & Constructors
4. Fluor Daniel Inc.
5. Foster Wheeler Corp.
6. Stone & Webster
7. Peter Kiewit Sons Inc.
8. NEPCO
9. Morrison Knudsen Corp.
10. McDermott International Inc.

Source: *ENR*, ENR Top 400 Contractors (annual), May 31, 1999, p. 75.

★1254★
LARGEST SPECIALTY CONTRACTORS, 1997
Ranked by: Revenue, in million of dollars. **Remarks:** Also includes company contact information and current projects. **Number listed:** 20

1. EMCOR Group Inc., with $897 million
2. The Poole and Kent Organization, $379.9
3. Limbach Constructors Inc., $258.6
4. MMC Corp., $255.78
5. Air Conditioning Co. Inc., $167
6. Shambaugh & Son Inc., $156
7. Harmon Ltd., $150
8. Murphy Co., $131.95
9. TDIndustries, $128.06
10. Fisk Electric Co., $120.93

Source: *Building Design & Construction*, Design/Construct 300 (annual), July, 1998, p. 68+.

★1255★
LARGEST TRANSPORTATION CONTRACTORS, 1998
Ranked by: Revenue. **Remarks:** Specific figures not included. **Number listed:** 20

1. Peter Kiewit Sons
2. Bechtel Group Inc.
3. Granite Construction Inc.
4. Tutor-Saliba Corp.
5. Skanska (USA) Inc.
6. Modern Continental Construction Co. Inc.
7. Morrison Knudsen Corp.
8. Balfour Beatty Construction Corp.
9. The Lane Construction Corp.
10. The Walsh Group

Source: *ENR*, ENR Top 400 Contractors (annual), May 31, 1999, p. 75.

★1256★
LARGEST VOLUME CONTRATORS, 1997
Ranked by: Volume of business, in millions of dollars. **Remarks:** Also includes company contact information and current projects. **Number listed:** 70

1. The Turner Corp., with $3,081.24 million
2. Fluor Daniel Inc., $2,108.88
3. BE&K Inc., $1,760
4. Bovis Inc., $1,464.2
5. Centex Construction Group, $974.07
6. Morse Diesel International, $973
7. Hensel Phelps Construction Co., $945.95
8. DPR Construction Inc., $895
9. Sordoni Skanska Construction Co., $892.80
10. The Whiting-Turner Contracting Co., $872.34

Source: *Building Design & Construction*, Design/Construct 300 (annual), July, 1998, p. 34+.

★1257★
LEADING ASBESTOS ABATEMENT CONTRACTORS, 1997
Ranked by: Revenue, in millions of dollars. **Remarks:** Also notes percentage change. **Number listed:** 20

1. NSC corp., with $100.8 million
2. LVI Environmental Services Group, $86.5
3. PDG Environmental Inc., $25.0
4. Specialty Systems Inc. & Affiliates, $20.2
5. Philip Services Corp., $20.0
6. Performance Contracting Group Inc., $14.0
7. Spray Systems Environmental Inc., $13.9
8. Centimark Corp., $10.5
9. IREX Contracting Group, $10.3
10. Anco Industries Inc., $10.2

Source: *ENR*, Top 600 Specialty Contractors (annual), October 12, 1998, p. 68.

★1258★
LEADING CONCRETE CONTRACTORS, 1997
Ranked by: Revenue, in millions of dollars. **Remarks:** Also notes percentage change. **Number listed:** 20

1. Baker Concrete Construction Inc., with $202.0 million
2. Ceco Concrete Construction Corp., $105.9
3. Miller & Long Co. Inc., $90.3
4. Capform Inc., $70.7
5. The Western Group, $62.0
6. Structural Preservation Systems Inc., $61.4
7. T.A.S. Construction Inc., $56.5
8. McHugh Concrete Construction, $56.0
9. Strescon Industries Inc., $44.1
10. Bomel Construction Co., $43.8

Source: *ENR*, Top 600 Specialty Contractors (annual), October 12, 1998, p. 58.

★1259★
LEADING DEMOLITION/WRECKING CONTRACTORS, 1997
Ranked by: Revenue, in millions of dollars. **Remarks:** Also notes percentage change. **Number listed:** 20

1. Penhall International Inc., with $79.8 million
2. Philip Services Corp., $40.0
3. Cleveland Wrecking Co., $38.7
4. Bierlein Demolition Contractors, $34.7
5. North American Site Developers Inc., $31.8
6. Diamond Dismantling Inc., $29.7
7. Mainline Contracting Corp., $24.3
8. Mercer Wrecking Recycling Corp., $24.0
9. Concrete Cutting & Breaking Inc., $23.2
10. Midwest Steel Co. Inc., $22.0

Source: *ENR*, Top 600 Specialty Contractors (annual), October 12, 1998, p. 68.

★1260★
LEADING ELECTRICAL CONTRACTORS, 1997
Ranked by: Revenue, in millions of dollars. **Remarks:** Also notes percentage change. **Number listed:** 50

1. EMCOR Group Inc., with $1,053.5 million
2. Building One Electrical Inc., $591.7

3. Integrated Electrical Services Inc., $558.0
4. MYR Group Inc., $409.7
5. SASCO Group, $381.8
6. Mass. Electric Construction Co., $272.7
7. Motor City Electric Co., $176.3
8. Quanta Services Inc., $173.8
9. Rosendin Electric Inc., $168.0
10. Cupertino Electric Inc., $157.0

Source: *ENR*, Top 600 Specialty Contractors (annual), October 12, 1998, p. 54.

★1261★

LEADING EXCAVATION/FOUNDATION CONTRACTORS, 1997

Ranked by: Revenue, in millions of dollars. **Remarks:** Also notes percentage change. **Number listed:** 20

1. Ryan Inc., with $79.9 million
2. Hayward Baker Inc., $79.2
3. Malcolm Drilling Co. Inc., $76.9
4. McKinney Drilling Co., $63.4
5. Philip Services Corp., $60.0
6. Independence Excavating Inc., $58.9
7. AGRA Foundations Inc., $57.2
8. Case Foundation Co., $53.8
9. The Beaver Excavating Co., $51.5
10. Berkel & Co. Contractors inc., $50.0

Source: *ENR*, Top 600 Specialty Contractors (annual), October 12, 1998, p. 60.

★1262★

LEADING GLAZING/CURTAIN WALL CONTRACTORS, 1997

Ranked by: Revenue, in millions of dollars. **Remarks:** Also notes percentage change. **Number listed:** 20

1. Harmon Ltd., with $88.7 million
2. Walters & Wolf, $62.7
3. Harmon Inc., $60.8
4. Flour City Architectural Metals Inc., $35.2
5. MTH Industries, $21.3
6. Cartner Glass Systems Inc., $20.5
7. Masonry Arts Inc., $19.5
8. Elward Construction Co., $17.5
9. Zephyr Aluminum Inc., $14.9
10. Ajay Glass & Mirror Co. Inc., $13.9

Source: *ENR*, Top 600 Specialty Contractors (annual), October 12, 1998, p. 65.

★1263★

LEADING MASONRY CONTRACTORS, 1997

Ranked by: Revenue, in millions of dollars. **Remarks:** Also notes percentage change. **Number listed:** 20

1. The Western Group, with $46.6 million
2. Seedorff Masonry Inc., $35.0
3. Pyramid Masonry Contractors Inc., $33.5
4. Dee Brown Inc., $32.5
5. J.D. Long Masonry Inc., $29.7
6. Sun Valley Masonry Inc., $28.8
7. WASCO Inc., $25.6
8. Leonard Masonry Inc., $24.7
9. Masonry Arts Inc., $20.3
10. John J. Smith Masonry Co., $19.8

Source: *ENR*, Top 600 Specialty Contractors (annual), October 12, 1998, p. 58.

★1264★

LEADING MECHANICAL CONTRACTORS, 1997

Ranked by: Revenue, in millions of dollars. **Remarks:** Also notes percentage change. **Number listed:** 50

1. EMCOR Group Inc., with $858.4 million
2. The Kinetics Group Inc., $430.0
3. Poole and Kent Org., $379.9
4. MMC Corp., $269.2
5. Limbach Constructors Inc., $258.6
6. Comfort Systems USA, $240.0
7. Scott Co. of California, $220.0
8. Philip Services Corp., $220.0
9. Air Conditioning Co. Inc., $168.0
10. Southland Industries, $156.4

Source: *ENR*, Top 600 Specialty Contractors (annual), October 12, 1998, p. 57.

★1265★

LEADING PAINTING CONTRACTORS, 1997

Ranked by: Revenue, in millions of dollars. **Remarks:** Also notes percentage change. **Number listed:** 20

1. Cannon Sline Inc., with $44.7 million
2. J.L. Manta Inc., $33.4
3. Techno Coatings Inc., $32.6
4. Protherm Services Group LLC, $30.0
5. M.L. McDonald Co. Inc., $29.2
6. Swanson & Youngdale Inc., $26.9
7. Robison-Prezioso Inc., $21.1
8. F.D. Thomas Inc., $18.5
9. Ascher Brothers Co. Inc., $17.9
10. Multiple Plant Services Inc., $16.5

Source: *ENR*, Top 600 Specialty Contractors (annual), October 12, 1998, p. 66.

★1266★

LEADING ROOFING CONTRACTORS, 1997

Ranked by: Revenue, in millions of dollars. **Remarks:** Also notes percentage change. **Number listed:** 20

1. Centimark Corp., with $188.3 million
2. The Hartford Roofing Co. Inc., $58.5
3. Birdair Inc., $42.0
4. W.R. Kelso Co. Inc., $39.2
5. Baker Roofing Co., $32.8
6. Seyforth Roofing Co. Inc., $31.1
7. Schreiber Corp., $28.8
8. Western Roofing Services, $27.6
9. The Campbell Companies, $27.2
10. General Roofing Industries Inc., $26.8

Source: *ENR*, Top 600 Specialty Contractors (annual), October 12, 1998, p. 63.

★1267★

LEADING SHEET METAL CONTRACTORS, 1997

Ranked by: Revenue, in millions of dollars. **Remarks:** Also notes percentage change. **Number listed:** 20

1. Kirk & Blum, with $64.6 million
2. Hill Mechanical Group, $52.5
3. Comfort Systems USA, $45.0
4. Apex Industries Inc., $43.0
5. EMCOR Group Inc., $39.0
6. Crown Corr Inc., $34.3
7. Martin Petersen Co. Inc., $27.5
8. Cal-Air Inc., $27.0
9. Anson Industries Inc., $25.6
10. Holaday-Parks Inc., $25.1

Source: *ENR*, Top 600 Specialty Contractors (annual), October 12, 1998, p. 63.

★1268★

LEADING SPECIALTY CONTRACTORS, 1997

Ranked by: Revenue, in millions of dollars. **Remarks:** Also notes new contract figures and market share data. **Number listed:** 600

1. EMCOR Group Inc., with $1,950.9 million
2. Philip Services Corp., $900.0
3. Building One Electrical Inc., $636.3

4. Integrated Electrical Services Inc., $558.0
5. MYR Group Inc., $431.3
6. The Kinetics Group Inc., $430.0
7. Henkels & McKoy Inc., $428.0
8. SASCO Group, $381.8
9. Poole and Kent Org., $379.9
10. Performance Contracting Group Inc., $350.1

Source: *ENR*, Top 600 Specialty Contractors (annual), October 12, 1998, p. 71+.

★1269★
LEADING STEEL ERECTION CONTRACTORS, 1997
Ranked by: Revenue, in millions of dollars. **Remarks:** Also notes percentage change. **Number listed:** 20

1. Midwest Steel Co. Inc., with $143.0 million
2. Schuff Steel Co., $138.2
3. The Williams Group Inc., $60.4
4. The Broad Group, $59.4
5. National Riggers & Erectors Inc., $43.0
6. Adams & Smith Inc., $38.5
7. Allstate Steel Co. Inc., $36.5
8. Sowles Co., $35.5
9. J.L. Davidson Co. Inc., $34.8
10. Interstate Iron Works Corp., $34.4

Source: *ENR*, Top 600 Specialty Contractors (annual), October 12, 1998, p. 60.

★1270★
LEADING UTILITY CONTRACTORS, 1997
Ranked by: Revenue, in millions of dollars. **Remarks:** Also notes percentage change. **Number listed:** 20

1. Henkels & McCoy Inc., with $342.4 million
2. Insituform Technologies Inc., $320.6
3. Quanta Services Inc., $97.8
4. UTILX Corp., $77.6
5. Kearney Development Co. Inc., $59.5
6. RCI Construction Group, $44.5
7. Garney Companies Inc., $44.0
8. Davis H. Elliot Co. Inc., $42.3
9. Kimmins Contracting Corp., $38.4
10. Super Excavators Inc., $24.6

Source: *ENR*, Top 600 Specialty Contractors (annual), October 12, 1998, p. 65.

★1271★
LEADING WALL/CEILING CONTRACTORS, 1997
Ranked by: Revenue, in millions of dollars. **Remarks:** Also notes percentage change. **Number listed:** 20

1. Cannon Sline Inc., with $44.7 million
2. J.L. Manta Inc., $33.4
3. Techno Coatings Inc., $32.6
4. Protherm Services Group LLC, $30.0
5. M.L. McDonald Co. Inc., $29.2
6. Swanson & Youngdale Inc., $26.9
7. Robison-Prezioso Inc., $21.1
8. F.D. Thomas Inc., $18.5
9. Ascher Brothers Co. Inc., $17.9
10. Multiple Plant Services Inc., $16.5

Source: *ENR*, Top 600 Specialty Contractors (annual), October 12, 1998, p. 66.

★1272★
TOP HISPANIC CONSTRUCTION COMPANIES, 1998
Ranked by: Revenue, in millions of dollars. **Number listed:** 10

1. MasTec Inc., with $1,005.10 million
2. Related Group of Florida, $297.00
3. Rosendin Electric Inc., $206.00
4. AJ Contracting Co., Inc., $183.18
5. Corella Companies, $98.90
6. Electric Machinery Enterprises Inc., $91.00
7. Crossland Construction Co. Inc., $73.26
8. Capo Group, $72.5
9. GSE Construction Co. Inc., $37.75
10. Kfoury Construction Group Inc., $35.00

Source: *Hispanic Business*, The 1999 Hispanic Business 500 (annual), June, 1999, p. 94.

Contractors--China

★1273★
TOP CONTRACTORS IN CHINA, 1997
Ranked by: International revenue. **Remarks:** Specific figures not provided. **Number listed:** 10

1. China State Construction Engineering Corp.
2. China Railway Construction Corp.
3. Bei Jing Chang Cheng Construction Corp.
4. China Harbour Engineering Co.
5. China Petroleum Engineering Construction Corp.
6. Beijing Urban Construction Group Co.
7. China Road & Bridge Corp.
8. China Metallurgical Construction (Group) Corp.
9. Sinopec Engineering Inc.
10. China Jilin International Econ. & Tech. Corp.

Source: *ENR*, Top 225 International Contractors (annual), August 17, 1998, p. 70.

Contractors--Detroit Metropolitan Area

★1274★
LEADING GENERAL CONTRACTORS IN METROPOLITAN DETROIT, 1998
Ranked by: Revenue, in millions of dollars. **Remarks:** Also notes contact information, 1997 revenue, value of new contracts, number of employees, and number of projects started. **Number listed:** 20

1. Barton Malow Co., with $785.0 million
2. Walbridge Aldinger Co., $675.0
3. A.J. Etkin Construction Co., $222.0
4. George W. Auch Co., $198.1
5. Ellis-Don Michigan Inc., $160.0
6. J.S. Alberici Construction Co. Inc., $158.0
7. Silverman Construction Co., $110.0
7. Turner Construction Co., $110.0
9. DeMaria Building Co. Inc., $109.2
10. Roncelli Inc., $109.0

Source: *Crain's Detroit Business*, March 1, 1999, p. 13.

Contractors, Foreign--Africa

★1275★
LARGEST CONTRACTORS IN AFRICA, 1997
Ranked by: International revenue. **Remarks:** Specific figures not provided. **Number listed:** 10

1. Bouygues S.A.
2. Groupe GTM
3. Bilfinger & Berger Bau AG
4. The M.W. Kellogg Co.

5. Bechtel Group Inc.
6. JGC Corp.
7. TECHNIP
8. Snamprogetti S.P.A.
9. CEGELEC
10. SGE

Source: *ENR*, Top 225 International Contractors (annual), August 17, 1998, p. 44.

Contractors, Foreign--Asia

★1276★
LARGEST FOREIGN CONTRACTORS IN ASIA, 1997
Ranked by: International revenue. **Remarks:** Specific figures not provided. **Number listed:** 10

1. Bechtel Group Inc.
2. The Kvaerner Group
3. Fluor Daniel Inc.
4. Toyo Engineering Corp.
5. Hyundai Engineering & Construction Co. Ltd.
6. Bilfinger & Berger Bau AG
7. Bouygues S.A.
8. Nishimatsu Construction Co. Ltd.
9. China State Construction Engineering Corp.
10. JGC Corp.

Source: *ENR*, Top 225 International Contractors (annual), August 17, 1998, p. 44.

Contractors, Foreign--Canada

★1277★
LARGEST FOREIGN CONTRACTORS IN CANADA, 1997
Ranked by: International revenue. **Remarks:** Specific figures not provided. **Number listed:** 10

1. The Kvaerner Group
2. Bouygues S.A.
3. Ellis-Don Construction Inc.
4. McDermott International Inc.
5. Groupe GTM
6. Kiewit Construction Group Inc.
7. KTI Corp.
8. J.S. Alberici Construction Co. Inc.
9. Fluor Daniel Inc.
10. Bechtel Group Inc.

Source: *ENR*, Top 225 International Contractors (annual), August 17, 1998, p. 44.

Contractors, Foreign--Europe

★1278★
LARGEST FOREIGN CONTRACTORS IN EUROPE, 1997
Ranked by: International revenue. **Remarks:** Specific figures not provided. **Number listed:** 10

1. The Kvaerner Group
2. SGE
3. Bouygues S.A.
4. Groupe GTM
5. Brown & Root Inc.
6. CEGELEC
7. Fluor Daniel Inc.
8. Skanska AB
9. Foster Wheeler Corp.
10. STRABAG AG

Source: *ENR*, Top 225 International Contractors (annual), August 17, 1998, p. 44.

Contractors, Foreign--Latin America

★1279★
LARGEST FOREIGN CONTRACTORS IN LATIN AMERICA, 1997
Ranked by: International revenue. **Remarks:** Specific figures not provided. **Number listed:** 10

1. Bechtel Group Inc.
2. Fluor Daniel Inc.
3. Odebrecht SA
4. IMPREGILO SPA
5. Techint Group of Construction
6. Dragados y Construcciones S.A.
7. The Kvaerner Group
8. The M.W. Kellogg Co.
9. CEGELEC
10. Grupo Tribasa S.A. de C.V.

Source: *ENR*, Top 225 International Contractors (annual), August 17, 1998, p. 44.

Contractors, Foreign--Middle East

★1280★
LARGEST FOREIGN CONTRACTORS IN THE MIDDLE EAST, 1997
Ranked by: International revenue. **Remarks:** Specific figures not provided. **Number listed:** 10

1. Consolidated Contractors International Co. SAL
2. Bechtel Group Inc.
3. Fluor Daniel Inc.
4. JGC Corp.
5. Joannou & Paraskevaides (Overseas) Ltd.
6. Ansaldo SPA
7. Ballast Nedam International BV
8. TECHNIP
9. Foster Wheeler Corp.
10. The Kvaerner Group

Source: *ENR*, Top 225 International Contractors (annual), August 17, 1998, p. 44.

Contractors, Foreign--United States

★1281★
TOP FOREIGN CONTRACTORS IN THE U.S. BY DOLLAR AMOUNT OF CONTRACTS, 1997
Ranked by: Amount of contracts. **Remarks:** Specific figures not provided. **Number listed:** 10

1. Skanska AB

2. Bovis Construction Group
3. Philipp Holzmann AG
4. The Kvaerner Group
5. AMEC PLC
6. PCL Constructors Inc.
7. Kajima Corp.
8. Obayashi Corp.
9. Fletcher Construction
10. Bouygues S.A.

Source: *ENR*, Top 225 International Contractors (annual), August 17, 1998, p. 44.

Contractors--France

★1282★
LARGEST CONTRACTORS IN FRANCE, 1997
Ranked by: International revenue. **Remarks:** Specific figures not provided. **Number listed:** 10

1. Bouygues S.A.
2. SGE
3. Groupe GTM
4. EIFFAGE
5. CEGELEC
6. TECHNIP
7. SOLETANCHE/BACHY
8. Sade-Compagnie Generale de Travaux D'Hydraulique
9. Prezioso Group
10. Groupe EGIS

Source: *ENR*, Top 225 International Contractors (annual), August 17, 1998, p. 70.

Contractors, International

★1283★
LEADING INTERNATIONAL BUILDING PROJECT CONTRACTORS, 1997
Ranked by: Dollar value of foreign contracts. **Remarks:** Specific figures not provided. **Number listed:** 10

1. Skanska AB
2. Bovis Construction Group
3. SGE
4. Bouygues S.A.
5. Bilfinger & Berger Bau AG
6. China State Construction Engineering Corp.
7. AMEC PLC
8. Fletcher Construction
9. Groupe GTM
10. Dongah Construction Ind. Co. Ltd.

Source: *ENR*, Top 225 International Contractors (annual), August 17, 1998, p. 46.

★1284★
LEADING INTERNATIONAL CONTRACTORS BY TOTAL REVENUE, 1997
Ranked by: Total revenue, in millions of U.S. dollars. **Remarks:** Total revenue includes both domestic and international contract revenue. **Number listed:** 225

1. Taisei Corp., with $12,208.0 million
2. Kajima Corp., $12,167.0
3. Obayashi Corp., $11,071.0
4. Bouygues S.A., $10,971.0
5. Fluor Daniel Inc., $10,798.0
6. Takenaka, $10,312.1
7. Bechtel Group Inc., $9,662.0
8. The Kvaerner Group, $9,614.0
9. SGE, $8,917.0
10. Philipp Holzmann AG, $8,043.0

Source: *ENR*, Top 225 International Contractors (annual), August 17, 1998, p. 72+.

★1285★
LEADING INTERNATIONAL CONTRACTORS, 1997
Ranked by: International revenue, in millions of U.S. dollars. **Number listed:** 225

1. The Kvaerner Group, with $7,605.0 million
2. Bechtel Group Inc., $6,347.0
3. Fluor Daniel Inc., $4,940.0
4. Bouygues S.A., $4,478.0
5. Skanska AB, $3,363.0
6. Groupe GTM, $3,191.0
7. SGE, $3,109.0
8. Philipp Holzmann AG, $3,040.0
9. Bilfinger & Berger Bau AG, $2,747.0
10. Bovis Construction Group, $2,156.0

Source: *ENR*, Top 225 International Contractors (annual), August 17, 1998, p. 49+.

★1286★
LEADING INTERNATIONAL HAZARDOUS WASTE PROJECT CONTRACTORS, 1997
Ranked by: Dollar value of foreign contracts. **Remarks:** Specific figures not provided. **Number listed:** 10

1. CEGELEC
2. The Kvaerner Group
3. NCC AB
4. Foster Wheeler Corp.
5. Philipp Holzmann AG
6. Hyundai Engineering & Construction Co. Ltd.
7. Bechtel Group Inc.
8. Morrison Knudsen Corp.
9. Samsung Engineering Co. Ltd.
10. Pitt-Des Moines Inc.

Source: *ENR*, Top 225 International Contractors (annual), August 17, 1998, p. 46.

★1287★
LEADING INTERNATIONAL INDUSTRIAL/ PETROLEUM PROJECT CONTRACTORS, 1997
Ranked by: Dollar value of foreign contracts. **Remarks:** Specific figures not provided. **Number listed:** 10

1. The Kvaerner Group
2. Bechtel Group Inc.
3. Fluor Daniel Inc.
4. TECHNIP
5. JGC Corp.
6. Brown & Root Inc.
7. The M.W. Kellogg Co.
8. Foster Wheeler Corp.
9. ABB Lummus Global Inc.
10. Toyo Engineering Corp.

Source: *ENR*, Top 225 International Contractors (annual), August 17, 1998, p. 46.

★1288★
LEADING INTERNATIONAL MANUFACTURING PROJECT CONTRACTORS, 1997
Ranked by: Dollar value of foreign contracts. **Remarks:** Specific figures not provided. **Number listed:** 10

1. Obayashi Corp.
2. Kajima Corp.
3. Taikisha Ltd.

4. Philipp Holzmann AG
5. Ansaldo SPA
6. The Kvaerner Group
7. Hyundai Engineering & Construction Co. Ltd.
8. Hoffman Corp.
9. Bouygues S.A.
10. J.S. Alberici Construction Co. Inc.

Source: *ENR*, Top 225 International Contractors (annual), August 17, 1998, p. 46.

★1289★
LEADING INTERNATIONAL POWER PROJECT CONTRACTORS, 1997
Ranked by: Dollar value of foreign contracts. **Remarks:** Specific figures not provided. **Number listed:** 10

1. Bechtel Group Inc.
2. CEGELEC
3. Black & Veatch
4. Toyo Engineering Corp.
5. Foster Wheeler Corp.
6. Hyundai Engineering & Construction Co. Ltd.
7. Raytheon Engineers & Constructors International
8. Nishimatsu Construction Co. Ltd.
9. Ansaldo SPA
10. Fluor Daniel Inc.

Source: *ENR*, Top 225 International Contractors (annual), August 17, 1998, p. 46.

★1290★
LEADING INTERNATIONAL SEWER/WASTE PROJECT CONTRACTORS, 1997
Ranked by: Dollar value of foreign contracts. **Remarks:** Specific figures not provided. **Number listed:** 10

1. Bechtel Group Inc.
2. Toa Corp.
3. Skanska AB
4. Costain Group PLC
5. Odebrecht SA
6. CEGELEC
7. Hyundai Engineering & Construction Co. Ltd.
8. Aoki Corp.
9. Fomento de Construcciones y Contratas SA
10. NCC AB

Source: *ENR*, Top 225 International Contractors (annual), August 17, 1998, p. 46.

★1291★
LEADING INTERNATIONAL TRANSPORTATION PROJECT CONTRACTORS, 1997
Ranked by: Dollar value of foreign contracts. **Remarks:** Specific figures not provided. **Number listed:** 10

1. Bouygues S.A.
2. Groupe GTM
3. Bilfinger & Berger Bau AG
4. SGE
5. Ansaldo SPA
6. Ballast Nedam International BV
7. Penta-Ocean Construction Co. Ltd.
8. Hyundai Engineering & Construction Co. Ltd.
9. China Harbour Engineering Co.
10. IMPREGILO SPA

Source: *ENR*, Top 225 International Contractors (annual), August 17, 1998, p. 46.

★1292★
LEADING INTERNATIONAL WATER PROJECT CONTRACTORS, 1997
Ranked by: Dollar value of foreign contracts. **Remarks:** Specific figures not provided. **Number listed:** 10

1. IMPREGILO SPA
2. Philipp Holzmann AG
3. Odebrecht SA
4. Skanska AB
5. Dongah Construction Ind. Co. Ltd.
6. SGE
7. Groupe GTM
8. Wayss & Freytag AG
9. SOLETANCHE/BACHY
10. Dick Corp.

Source: *ENR*, Top 225 International Contractors (annual), August 17, 1998, p. 46.

Cookies and Crackers

★1293★
TOP SNACK CRACKER BRANDS, 1997
Ranked by: Market share in supermarkets, in percent. **Number listed:** 10

1. Ritz (RJR Nabisco), with 16.2%
2. Cheez-it Sunshine, 8.9%
3. Wheat Thins (RJR Nabisco), 7.6%
4. Honey Maid (RJR Nabisco), 7.4%
5. Goldfish (Pepperidge Farm), 7.3%
6. Triscuit (RJR Nabisco), 7.1%
7. Private Label, 6.9%
8. Townhouse (Keebler), 4.9%
9. Cheese Nips (RJR Nabisco), 3.8%
10. SnackWells (RJR Nabisco), 2.4%

Source: *Distribution Channels*, March, 1999, p. 55.

Cooperative Societies, Foreign

★1294★
COMPANIES IN MALAYSIA WITH THE BEST LONG-TERM VISION BY MANAGEMENT, 1998
Ranked by: Scores (1-7) based on a survey response of over 4,000 professionals throughout Asia. **Remarks:** Specific figures not provided. **Number listed:** 5

1. YTL Corp.
2. Hong Leong Group
3. Genting
4. Sime Darby
5. Golden Hope Plantations

Source: *Far Eastern Economic Review*, Review 200 (annual), December 31, 1998, p. 75.

★1295★
COMPANIES IN MALAYSIA WITH THE HIGHEST QUALITY OF PRODUCTS AND SERVICES, 1998
Ranked by: Scores (1-7) based on a survey response of over 4,000 professionals throughout Asia. **Remarks:** Specific figures not provided. **Number listed:** 5

1. UMW Toyota Motor
2. Malaysia Airlines
3. New Straits Times Press
4. Public Bank
5. Sime Darby

Source: *Far Eastern Economic Review*, Review 200 (annual), December 31, 1998, p. 75.

★1296★
COMPANIES IN MALAYSIA WITH THE MOST FINANCIAL SOUNDNESS, 1998
Ranked by: Scores (1-7) based on a survey response of over 4,000 professionals throughout Asia. **Remarks:** Specific figures not provided. **Number listed:** 5
1. Genting
2. Petronas
3. Maybank
4. YTL Corp.
5. Magnum

Source: *Far Eastern Economic Review*, Review 200 (annual), December 31, 1998, p. 75.

★1297★
COMPANIES IN MALAYSIA WITH THE MOST INNOVATIVE RESPONSES TO CUSTOMER NEEDS, 1998
Ranked by: Scores (1-7) based on a survey response of over 4,000 professionals throughout Asia. **Remarks:** Specific figures not provided. **Number listed:** 5
1. Arab-Malaysian Merchant Bank
2. Hong Leong Bank
3. Rashid Hussain
4. UMW Toyota Motor
5. Edaran Otomobil Nasional

Source: *Far Eastern Economic Review*, Review 200 (annual), December 31, 1998, p. 75.

★1298★
LEADING COMPANIES IN MALAYSIA, 1998
Ranked by: Scores (1-7) based on a survey response of over 4,000 professionals throughout Asia. **Remarks:** Respondents rated companies on their quality of services/products offered and financial soundness. **Number listed:** 10
1. Genting, with 5.94
2. Maybank, 5.45
3. Petronas, 5.43
4. YTL Corp., 5.37
5. Hong Leong Group, 5.16
6. Public Bank, 5.13
7. Hong Leong Bank, 4.94
8. Telekom Malaysia, 4.69
9. Golden Hope Plantations, 4.63
10. New Straits Times Press, 4.60

Source: *Far Eastern Economic Review*, Review 200 (annual), December 31, 1998, p. 48.

★1299★
MOST EMULATED COMPANIES IN MALAYSIA, 1998
Ranked by: Scores (1-7) based on a survey response of over 4,000 professionals throughout Asia. **Remarks:** Specific figures not provided. **Number listed:** 5
1. Genting
2. YTL Corp.
3. Sime Darby
4. Maybank
5. Petronas

Source: *Far Eastern Economic Review*, Review 200 (annual), December 31, 1998, p. 75.

Cordials (Liquor)

See: **Liqueurs**

Corporate Acquisitions and Mergers

★1300★
ACQUISITION LEADERS, 1998
Ranked by: Number of acquisitions announced. **Remarks:** Also notes product lines and businesses acquired. **Number listed:** 21
1. Century Business Services Inc., with 65 acquisitions
2. General Electric Co., 42
3. IKON Office Solutions Inc., 28
3. Republic Industries, 28
3. Superior Services Inc., 28
3. United Rentals Inc., 28
7. Comfort Systems USA Inc., 27
8. Metals USA Inc., 22
9. Consolidated Graphics Inc., 21
9. Cumulus Media Inc., 21
10. U.S.A. Floral Products Inc., 20

Source: *Mergerstat Review (annual)*, 1998, p. 48.

★1301★
BIGGEST CANCELLATIONS OF ACQUISITION DEALS, 1998
Ranked by: Price offered, in millions of dollars. **Remarks:** Also notes year announced. **Number listed:** 5
1. American Home Products (buyer), Monsanto Co. (seller), with $33,274.5 million
2. GTE Corp. (buyer), MCI Communications Corp. (seller), $27,674.0
3. Private Group, led by Shearson Lehman (buyer), RJR Nabisco (seller), $25,237.6
4. Bank of New York Co. Inc. (buyer), Mellon Bank Corp. (seller), $23,294.8
5. Private Group, led by Kirk Kerkorian and Lee Iacocca (buyer), C hrysler Corp. (seller), $19,528.0

Source: *Mergerstat Review (annual)*, 1998, p. 214.

★1302★
BIGGEST CORPORATE ACQUISITIONS IN HISTORY, 1998
Ranked by: Price offered, in millions of dollars. **Remarks:** Also notes year announced. **Number listed:** 100
1. Exxon Corp. (buyer), Mobil Corp. (seller), with $7,213.4 million
2. SBC Communications (buyer), Ameritech Corp. (seller), $61,388.0
3. British Petroleum Co. PLC-UK (buyer), Amoco Corp. (seller), $56,482.0
4. Bell Atlantic Corp. (buyer), GTE Corp. (seller), $52,845.8
5. NationsBank Corp. (buyer), BankAmerica Corp. (seller), $43,158.3
6. WorldCom Inc. (buyer), MCI Communications Corp. (seller), $42,459.2
7. AT & T (buyer), Tele-Communications Inc. (seller), $37,017.3
8. Travelers Group Inc. (buyer), Citicorp (seller), $36,031.6
9. Norwest Corp. (buyer), Wells Fargo & Co. (seller), $31,660.2
10. Daimler Benz AG-Germany (buyer), Chrysler Corp. (seller), $31,156.0

Source: *Mergerstat Review (annual)*, 1998, p. 216+.

★1303★
CORPORATE ACQUISITIONS QUALIFYING FOR THE *MERGERSTAT REVIEW* $ BILLION CLUB, 1998
Ranked by: Amount of acquisition, in millions of dollars. **Number listed:** 200

1. Exxon Corp. (buyer), Mobil Corp. (seller), with $77,213.4 million
2. SBC Communications (buyer), Ameritech Corp. (seller), $61,388.0
3. British Petroleum Co. PLC-UK (buyer), Amoco Corp. (seller), $56,482.0
4. Bell Atlantic Corp. (buyer), GTE Corp. (seller), $52,845.8
5. NationsBank Corp. (buyer), BankAmerica Corp. (seller), $43,158.3
6. AT & T (buyer), Tele-Communications Inc. (seller), $37,017.3
7. Travelers Group Inc. (buyer), Citicorp (seller), $36,031.6
8. Norwest Corp. (buyer), Wells Fargo & Co. (seller), $31,660.2
9. Daimler Benz AG-Germany (buyer), Chrysler Corp. (seller), $31,156.0
10. Berkshire Hathaway (buyer), General RE Corp. (seller), $20,947.2

Source: *Mergerstat Review (annual)*, 1998, p. 195+.

★1304★

CORPORATE ACQUISITIONS QUALIFYING FOR THE *MERGERSTAT REVIEW* $1 BILLION CLUB, 1998

Ranked by: Amount of acquisition, in millions of dollars. **Number listed:** 200

1. Exxon Corp. (buyer), Mobil Corp. (seller), with $77,213.4 million
2. SBC Communications (buyer), Ameritech Corp. (seller), $61,388.0
3. British Petroleum Co. PLC-UK (buyer), Amoco Corp. (seller), $56,482.0
4. Bell Atlantic Corp. (buyer), GTE Corp. (seller), $52,845.8
5. NationsBank Corp. (buyer), BankAmerica Corp. (seller), $43,158.3
6. AT & T (buyer), Tele-Communications Inc. (seller), $37,017.3
7. Travelers Group Inc. (buyer), Citicorp (seller), $36,031.6
8. Norwest Corp. (buyer), Wells Fargo & Co. (seller), $31,660.2
9. Daimler Benz AG-Germany (buyer), Chrysler Corp. (seller), $31,156.0
10. Berkshire Hathaway Inc. (buyer), General RE Corp. (seller), $20,947.2

Source: *Mergerstat Review (annual)*, 1998, p. 195+.

★1305★

HIGHEST P/E OFFERED ACQUISITION TRANSACTIONS, 1998

Ranked by: P/E ratio offered, in percent. **Number listed:** 5

1. Stolt Comex Seaway Ltd. (buyer), Ceanic Corp. (seller), with 99.6%
2. Silicon Valley Research Inc. (buyer), Quality IC (seller), 95.0%
3. Corporate Family Solutions (buyer), Bright Horizons Inc. (seller), 94.5%
4. Exel Ltd. (buyer), Intercargo Corp. (seller), 92.5%
5. BMC Industries Inc. (buyer), Monsanto Co. (Orcolite Eyeglass Lens Unit) (seller), 91.2%

Source: *Mergerstat Review (annual)*, 1998, p. 21.

★1306★

HIGHEST PREMIUM OFFERED TRANSACTIONS, 1998

Ranked by: Premium offered, in percent. **Number listed:** 5

1. Fabri-Centers of America Inc. (buyer), House of Fabrics Inc. (seller), with 99.5%
2. General Motors Corp. (buyer), US Satellite Broadcasting Co. (seller), 99.2%
3. Network Associates Inc. (buyer), Trusted Information Systems Inc. (seller), 97.4%
4. Sanmina Corp. (buyer), Altron Inc. (seller), 94.8%
5. Hercules Inc. (buyer), BetzDearborn Inc. (seller), 94.6%

Source: *Mergerstat Review (annual)*, 1998, p. 27.

★1307★

INDUSTRY SECTORS WITH THE GREATEST NUMBER OF ACQUISITION TRANSACTIONS, 1998

Ranked by: Number of transactions. **Remarks:** Also notes transactions for 1994-1998 and 5-year totals. **Number listed:** 50

1. Computer Software, Supplies & Services, with 963 transactions
2. Miscellaneous Services, 896
3. Wholesale & Distribution, 583
4. Banking & Finance, 435
5. Leisure & Entertainment, 338
6. Brokerage, Investment & Management Consulting, 331
7. Health Services, 329
8. Retail, 303
9. Insurance, 248
10. Communications, 243

Source: *Mergerstat Review (annual)*, 1998, p. 56.

★1308★

LARGEST ACQUISITIONS OF PRIVATELY OWNED SELLERS, 1998

Ranked by: Price offered, in millions of dollars. **Remarks:** Also notes year announced. **Number listed:** 5

1. U.S. West Inc. (buyer), Continental Cablevision Inc. (seller), with $5,132.6 million
2. General Motors Corp. (buyer), Hughes Aircraft Co. (seller), $5,025.0
3. Simon DeBartolo Group (buyer), Corporate Property Investor s (seller), $4,530
4. Marcus Cable Co. (buyer), Charter Communications (seller), $4,500.0
5. Federated Department Stores Inc. (buyer), R.H. Macy & Co. Inc. (seller), $4,100.0

Source: *Mergerstat Review (annual)*, 1998, p. 212.

★1309★

LARGEST CANCELLATIONS OF ACQUISITION DEALS, 1998

Ranked by: Price offered, in millions of dollars. **Remarks:** Also notes year announced. **Number listed:** 5

1. American Home Products (buyer), Monsanto co. (seller), with $33,274.5 million
2. GTE Corp. (buyer), MCI Communications Corp. (seller), $27,674.0
3. Private Group, led by Shearson Lehman (buyer), RJR Nabisco (seller), $25,237.6
4. Bank of New York Co. Inc. (buyer), Mellon Bank Corp. (seller), $23,294.8
5. Private Group, led by Kirk Kerkorian and Lee Iacocca (buyer), C hrysler Corp. (seller), $19,528.0

Source: *Mergerstat Review (annual)*, 1998, p. 214.

★1310★

LARGEST CORPORATE ACQUISITONS AND MERGERS BY INDUSTRY, 1998

Ranked by: Industry total, in billions of dollars. **Number listed:** 16

1. Banks, with $295 billion
2. Telecom/Cellular, $203

3. Media, $138
4. All other, $130
5. Oil & Gas, $119
6. High Tech, $110
6. Nonbank Financial, $110
8. Real Estate/Hotel, $103
9. Retail, $66
9. Transportation, $66

Source: *CFO*, January, 1999, p. 28.

★1311★
LARGEST STATUTORY MERGERS, 1998
Ranked by: Price offered, in millions of dollars. **Remarks:** Also notes year announced. **Number listed:** 5

1. Travelers Group Inc. (buyer), Citicorp (seller), with $36,031 million
2. Beechham Group PLC-UK (buyer), SmithKline Beckman Corp. (seller), $16,082.4
3. KeyCorp (buyer), Society Corp. (seller), $7,800.0
4. Upjohn Co. (buyer), Pharmacia AB-Sweden (seller), $7,000.0
5. Columbia Healthcare Corp. (buyer), HCA-Hospital Corp. of America (seller), $5,700.0

Source: *Mergerstat Review (annual)*, 1998, p. 211.

★1312★
LEADING INDUSTRY SECTORS IN CORPORATE ACQUISITIONS AND MERGERS BY DOLLAR VALUE OFFERED, 1998
Ranked by: Value of deal, in millions of dollars. **Remarks:** Also notes values for 1993-1997. **Number listed:** 50

1. Banking & Finance, with $213,980.4 million
2. Communications, $170,311.3
3. Oil & Gas, $154,124.7
4. Electric, Gas, Water & Sanitary Services, $65,469.2
5. Insurance, $65,105.8
6. Broadcasting, $57,257.7
7. Computer Software, Supplies & Services, $52,678.1
8. Drugs, Medical Supplies & Services, $43,259.9
9. Retail, $38,774.5
10. Autos & Trucks, $31,495.0

Source: *Mergerstat Review (annual)*, 1998, p. 57.

★1313★
LEADING INDUSTRY SECTORS IN CORPORATE ACQUISITIONS AND MERGERS BY NUMBER OF TRANSACTIONS OVER $100 MILLION, 1998
Ranked by: Total number of transactions exceeding $100 million. **Remarks:** Also notes total number of transactions for 1993-1997 and 5-year totals. **Number listed:** 50

1. Banking & Finance, with 78 transactions
2. Computer Software, Supplies & Services, 69
3. Miscellaneous Services, 54
4. Communications, 50
5. Brokerage, Investment & Management Consulting, 46
6. Electric, Gas, Water & Sanitary Services, 43
7. Drugs, Medical Supplies & Equipment, 41
8. Retail, 40
9. Leisure & Entertainment, 36
10. Insurance, 35

Source: *Mergerstat Review (annual)*, 1998, p. 58.

★1314★
LOWEST P/E OFFERED ACQUISITION TRANSACTIONS, 1998
Ranked by: P/E ratio offered, in percent. **Number listed:** 5

1. Inland Steel Industries Inc. (buyer), Ryerson Tull Inc. (seller), with $1.0% million
2. Lion Gate LLC (buyer), Besicorp Group Inc. (seller), $1.2%
3. Trans World Entertainment Corp. (buyer), Camelot Music Holdings Inc. (seller), $1.6%
4. Life Re Corp. (buyer), Loewen Group International Inc. (Eagan Holding Co.) (seller), $1.7%
5. Dan River Inc. (buyer), Bibb Co. (seller), $2.0%

Source: *Mergerstat Review (annual)*, 1998, p. 21.

★1315★
LOWEST PREMIUM OFFERED TRANSACTIONS, 1998
Ranked by: Premium offered, in percent. **Number listed:** 5

1. Fortis AG (buyer), John Alden Financial Corp. (seller), with 0.0%
2. CCA Prison Realty Trust (buyer), Corrections Corp. of America (seller), 0.1%
3. Commercial Federal Corp. (buyer), First Colorado Bancorp Inc. (seller), 0.2%
4. International Verifact Inc. (buyer), Checkmate Electronics Inc. (seller), 0.6%
5. Corporate Family Solutions (buyer), Bright Horizons Inc. (seller), 0.6%

Source: *Mergerstat Review (annual)*, 1998, p. 27.

★1316★
MOST ACQUISITIONS BY TOP FIRMS IN THE GAS/PROPANE INDUSTRY, 1998
Ranked by: Number of acquisitions. **Remarks:** Also notes gallons. **Number listed:** 18

1. Cornerstone Propane (Watsonville, CA), with 20 acquisitions
2. Independent Propane (Irvine, TX), 14
3. MFA (Columbia, MO), 13
4. All-Star Propane (Lebanon, MO), 10
4. AmeriGas (Valley Forge, PA), 10
6. Heritage Propane (Tulsa, OK), 8
7. Star Gas (Stamford, CT), 7
8. Atmos Propane (Franklin, TN), 5
8. Suburban Propane (Whippany, NJ), 5
8. Aeropres Propane (Shreveport, LA), 5

Source: *LP/Gas*, February, 1999, p. 18.

★1317★
STATES WITH THE HIGHEST NUMBER OF CORPORATE BUYERS, 1998
Ranked by: Number of corporate buyers. **Remarks:** Also notes number and state ranking for 1994-1997 and 5-year total. **Number listed:** 51

1. California, with 918 corporate buyers
2. New York, 719
3. Texas, 695
4. Florida, 522
5. Illinois, 343
6. Ohio, 335
7. Pennsylvania, 315
8. New Jersey, 292
9. Georgia, 233
10. Massachusetts, 231

Source: *Mergerstat Review (annual)*, 1998, p. 80.

★1318★
STATES WITH THE HIGHEST NUMBER OF CORPORATE SELLERS, 1998
Ranked by: Number of corporate sellers. **Remarks:** Also notes number and state ranking for 1994-1997 and 5-year total. **Number listed:** 51

1. California, with 1,015 sellers
2. Texas, 532
3. New York, 527

4. Florida, 429
5. Illinois, 299
6. Pennsylvania, 267
7. Massachusetts, 257
8. New Jersey, 256
9. Georgia, 228
10. Ohio, 227

Source: *Mergerstat Review (annual)*, 1998, p. 79.

★1319★
TOP REASONS FOR CORPORATION ACQUISITION & MERGER FAILURE, 1998*
Ranked by: Percent. **Number listed:** 7

1. Poor communication, with 22%
2. Poor management, 21%
3. Cultural differences, 19%
4. Poor integration strategies, 16%
5. Business issues, 10%
6. Lack of employee support, 7%
7. Other, 5%

Source: *Financial Times*, October 16, 1998, p. VI.

Corporate Acquisitions and Mergers--Eastern Europe

★1320★
TOP CENTRAL AND EASTERN EUROPEAN MERGER & ACQUISITION DEALS, 1998*
Ranked by: Value of deal, in millions of U.S. dollars. **Remarks:** Also notes target and acquirer nation, status of deal, and target and acquirer advisors. **Number listed:** 10

1. Sibirskaya Neftyyana (target), Yukosneftegaz (acquirer), with $4,849.5 million
2. Amur Steel Joint Stock (target), Amur Steel Joint Stock (acquirer), $762.3
3. Sibirskaya Neftyyana (target), Soc National Elf Aquitaine (acquirer), $528
4. Petrotel (target), Lukoil Europe (acquirer), $300
5. Harvardsky Prumyslovy (target), Harvard Capital Management (acquirer), $286.3
6. Octomobilcific (target), Sevket Demirel Holding Group (acquirer), $180
7. Kolomensky (target), Kransky Oklyabr (acquirer), $166
8. Pannon (target), Investor Group (acquirer), $160
9. Zywiec Brewery (Heineken) (target), Heineken (Heineken Holding) (acquirer), $141.2
10. Zywiec Brewery (Heineken) (target), Heineken (Heineken Holding) (acquirer), $126.1

Source: *Financial Times*, October 16, 1998, p. IV.

Corporate Acquisitions and Mergers—International Aspects

★1321★
COUNTRIES IN WHICH THE U.S. SPENT THE MOST TO ACQUIRE CORPORATIONS, 1998
Ranked by: Value of purchases, in millions of U.S. dollars. **Remarks:** Also notes figures for 1994-1997. **Number listed:** 50

1. United Kingdom, with $83,515.1 million
2. Germany, $47,981.4
3. Canada, $18,452.6
4. France, $14,895.0
5. Scotland, $8,039.8
6. Netherlands, $6,893.6
7. Sweden, $4,782
8. Switzerland, $2,328.8
9. Japan, $1,851.6
10. Ireland, $1,241.5

Source: *Mergerstat Review (annual)*, 1999, p. 85.

★1322★
COUNTRIES PURCHASING THE GREATEST NUMBER OF U.S. COMPANIES, 1998
Ranked by: Number of transactions. **Remarks:** Also notes number of transactions for 1994-1997 and 5-year total. **Number listed:** 50

1. Canada, with 518 transactions
2. United Kingdom, 394
3. Germany, 142
4. Netherlands, 131
5. France, 124
6. Switzerland, 74
7. Japan, 64
8. Sweden, 51
9. Ireland, 44
10. Australia, 43

Source: *Mergerstat Review (annual)*, 1999, p. 84.

★1323★
COUNTRIES SELLING THE MOST COMPANIES TO U.S. BUYERS, 1998
Ranked by: Number of transactions. **Remarks:** Also notes number of transactions for 1994-1997 and 5-year total. **Number listed:** 50

1. United Kingdom, with 267 transactions
2. Canada, 214
3. Germany, 112
4. France, 83
5. Australia, 46
6. Netherlands, 45
7. Italy, 36
8. Brazil, 32
9. Japan, 26
10. South Korea, 25

Source: *Mergerstat Review (annual)*, 1999, p. 86+.

★1324★
COUNTRIES SPENDING THE MOST TO ACQUIRE U.S. CORPORATIONS, 1998
Ranked by: Value of purchases, in millions of U.S. dollars. **Remarks:** Also notes figures for 1994-1997. **Number listed:** 50

1. United Kingdom, with $39,243.5 million
2. Canada, $16,215.1
3. Germany, $6,690.7
4. Australia, $4,496.1
5. Switzerland, $4,851.3
6. Brazil, $3,834.0
7. France, $3,830.6
8. Netherlands, $2,668.0
9. Israel, $1,719.2
10. South Korea, $1,504.5

Source: *Mergerstat Review (annual)*, 1999, p. 88+.

★1325★
INDUSTRIES ATTRACTING THE MOST FOREIGN BUYERS, 1998
Ranked by: Number of transactions. **Remarks:** Also notes number of transactions for 1994-1997 and 5-year total. **Number listed:** 50

1. Computer Software, Supplies & Services, with 82 transactions
2. Miscellaneous Services, 47
3. Wholesale & Distribution, 32
4. Brokerage, Investment & Management Consulting, 26
5. Leisure & Entertainment, 24
5. Insurance, 24
7. Drugs, Medical Supplies & Equipment, 23
8. Industrial & Farm Equipment & Machinery, 22
9. Electrical Equipment, 19
10. Electronics, 18
10. Food Processing, 18

Source: *Mergerstat Review (annual)*, 1999, p. 73.

★1326★
INDUSTRIES IN WHICH FOREIGN BUYERS SPENT THE MOST MONEY ON ACQUISITIONS, 1998
Ranked by: Value of purchases, in millions of U.S. dollars. **Remarks:** Also notes figures for 1994-1997. **Number listed:** 50

1. Oil & Gas, with $56,596.0 million
2. Autos & Trucks, $31,180.5
3. Electric, Gas, Water & Sanitary Services, $17,187.7
4. Publishing & printing, $9,268.8
5. Banking & Finance, $8,914.0
6. Communications, $8,356.3
7. Office Equipment & Computer Hardware, $6,954.2
8. Drugs, Medical Supplies & Equipment, $6,766.4
9. Computer Software, Supplies & Services, $5,736.7
10. Insurance, $5,130.1

Source: *Mergerstat Review (annual)*, 1999, p. 74.

★1327★
INDUSTRIES IN WHICH FOREIGN SELLERS SPENT THE MOST MONEY ON ACQUISITIONS, 1998
Ranked by: Value of purchases, in millions of U.S. dollars. **Remarks:** Also notes figures for 1994-1997. **Number listed:** 50

1. Electric, Gas, Water & Sanitary Services, with $14,035.2 million
2. Miscellaneous Services, $6,889.1
3. Communications, $6,701.1
4. Drugs, Medical Supplies & Equipment, $6,122.0
5. Oil & Gas, $5,405.1
6. Insurance, $4,633.0
7. Publishing & printing, $4,019.4
8. Food Processing, $3,912.6
9. Computer Software, Supplies & Services, $3,792.7
10. Packaging & Containers, $3,730.1

Source: *Mergerstat Review (annual)*, 1999, p. 76.

★1328★
LARGEST ACQUISITIONS OF FOREIGN COMPANIES BY U.S. BUYERS, 1998
Ranked by: Price offered, in millions of U.S. dollars. **Remarks:** Also notes year deal was announced. **Number listed:** 5

1. Texas Utilities (buyer), Energy Group PLC-UK (seller), with $7,327.4 million
2. Merrill Lynch & Co. (buyer), Mercury Asset Management Group PLC-UK (seller), $5,230.0
3. Tyco International Ltd. (buyer), ADT Ltd.-Bermuda (seller), $5,111.4
4. Amoco Corp. (buyer), Dome Petroleum Ltd.-Canada (seller), $4,180.0
5. Exxon Corp. (buyer), Texaco Canada Inc.-Canada (seller), $4,149.6

Source: *Mergerstat Review (annual)*, 1999, p. 213.

★1329★
LARGEST ACQUISITIONS OF U.S. COMPANIES BY FOREIGN BUYERS, 1998
Ranked by: Price offered, in millions of U.S. dollars. **Remarks:** Also notes year deal was announced. **Number listed:** 5

1. British Petroleum Co. PLC-UK (buyer), Amoco Corp. (seller), with $56,481.97 million
2. Daimler Benz AG-Germany (buyer), Chrysler Corp. (seller), $31,155.96
3. Deutsche Bank AG-Germany (buyer), Bankers Trust New York Corp. (seller), $8,863.36
4. British Petroleum Co. PLC-UK (buyer), Standard Oil Co. (seller), $7,762.20
5. Scottish Power PLC-UK (buyer), PacificCorp (seller), $7,760.43

Source: *Mergerstat Review (annual)*, 1999, p. 212.

Corporate Growth

See: **Growth Companies**

Corporate Philanthropy

See: **Charitable Contributions**

Corporations

★1330★
CITIES WITH THE MOST FORTUNE 500 COMPANY HEADQUARTERS, 1998
Ranked by: Total number of company headquarters. **Number listed:** 15

1. New York, NY, with 46 headquarters
2. Chicago, IL, 14
3. Houston, TX, 13
4. Atlanta, GA, 11
4. St. Louis, MO, 11
6. Dallas, TX, 9
6. Pittsburgh, PA, 9
6. San Francisco, CA, 9
9. Cleveland, OH, 7
9. Philadelphia, PA, 7

Source: *Fortune*, Fortune 500 Largest U.S. Corporations (annual), April 26, 1999, p. F-33.

★1331★
COMPANIES WITH THE GREATEST GROWTH IN EARNINGS PER SHARE, 1988-1998
Ranked by: Annual growth rate, in percent. **Remarks:** Also notes Fortune 500 revenue rank. **Number listed:** 50

1. Dell Computer, with 51.3%
2. Sunoco, 47.6%

3. Charles Schwab, 47.2%
4. Microsoft, 39.1%
5. Best Buy, 33.8%
6. Oracle, 32.6%
7. Dollar General, 31.8%
7. PaineWebber Group, 31.8%
9. PacifiCare Health Systems, 31.5%
10. Starwood Hotels & Resorts, 30.8%

Source: *Fortune*, Fortune 500 Largest U.S. Corporations (annual), April 26, 1999, p. F-31.

★1332★
COMPANIES WITH THE GREATEST RETURN TO INVESTORS, 1988-1998
Ranked by: Return to investors, in percent. **Remarks:** Also notes Fortune 500 revenue rank. **Number listed:** 50

1. Dell Computer, with 79.7%
2. EMC, 69%
3. Charles Schwab, 63.4%
4. Microsoft, 57.5%
5. Conseco, 47%
6. Best Buy, 46%
7. Intel, 44.8%
8. Home Depot, 44.8%
9. United HealthCare Corp., 44.1%
10. Applied Materials, 40.8%

Source: *Fortune*, Fortune 500 Largest U.S. Corporations (annual), April 26, 1999, p. F-31.

★1333★
COMPANIES WITH THE GREATEST RETURN TO INVESTORS, 1998
Ranked by: Return to investors, in percent. **Remarks:** Also notes Fortune 500 revenue rank. **Number listed:** 50

1. Dell Computer, with 248.5%
2. Best Buy, 232.9%
3. Apple Computer, 211.9%
4. EMC, 209.8%
5. Lucent Technologies, 175.9%
6. Allegiance, 165.6%
7. Lexmark International, 164.5%
8. Cisco Systems, 149.7%
9. Unisys, 148.2%
10. The Gap, 138.4%

Source: *Fortune*, Fortune 500 Largest U.S. Corporations (annual), April 26, 1999, p. F-31.

★1334★
COMPANIES WITH THE HIGHEST RETURN ON ASSETS, 1998
Ranked by: Profit, as a percentage of assets. **Remarks:** Also notes Fortune 500 revenue rank. **Number listed:** 50

1. Limited, with 45.1%
2. Ryerson Tull, 41%
3. Times Mirror, 33.6%
4. ITT Industries, 30.5%
5. Schering-Plough, 22.4%
6. Dell Computer, 21.2%
7. The Gap, 20.8%
8. Microsoft, 20.1%
9. Ralston Purina, 19.9%
10. Bristol-Myers Squibb, 19.3%

Source: *Fortune*, Fortune 500 Largest U.S. Corporations (annual), April 26, 1999, p. F-30.

★1335★
COMPANIES WITH THE HIGHEST RETURN ON REVENUE, 1998
Ranked by: Profits, as a percentage of Revenue. **Remarks:** Also notes Fortune 500 revenue rank. **Number listed:** 50

1. Times Mirror, with 43.1%
2. Microsoft, 31%
3. Tele-Communications, 26.4%
4. Starwood Hotels & Resorts, 26%
5. Computer Associates International, 24.8%
6. Intel, 23.1%
7. Pfizer, 22.8%
8. Limited, 22%
9. Schering-Plough, 21.7%
10. Ameritech Corp., 21%

Source: *Fortune*, Fortune 500 Largest U.S. Corporations (annual), April 26, 1999, p. F-30.

★1336★
COMPANIES WITH THE HIGHEST RETURN ON STOCKHOLDERS' EQUITY, 1998
Ranked by: Profits as a percentage of equity. **Remarks:** Also notes Fortune 500 revenue rank. **Number listed:** 50

1. General Mills, with 221.8%
2. U.S. West Inc., 199.7%
3. Quaker Oats, 164.7%
4. Hilton Hotels, 158.8%
5. ITT Industries, 117.9%
6. Times Mirror, 105.6%
7. Ralston Purina, 100.5%
8. Ryerson Tull, 97.8%
9. Avon Products, 94.7%
10. Ford Motor, 94.3%

Source: *Fortune*, Fortune 500 Largest U.S. Corporations (annual), April 26, 1999, p. F-30.

★1337★
CORPORATE LEADERS IN ASSET GROWTH, 1998
Ranked by: Asset growth, in percent. **Number listed:** 5

1. Sprint, with 789%
2. Lyondell Chemical, 492%
3. Qwest Communications, 477%
4. Federal-Mogul, 452%
5. KN Energy, 317%

Source: *Forbes*, Forbes 500s (annual), April 19, 1999, p. 286.

★1338★
CORPORATE LEADERS IN ASSETS, 1998
Ranked by: Assets, in millions of dollars. **Remarks:** Includes percent change from previous year and previous year rank. **Number listed:** 50

1. Citigroup, with $668,641 million
2. BankAmerica, $617,679
3. Fannie Mae, $485,014
4. Chase Manhattan, $365,875
5. General Electric, $355,935
6. Freddie Mac, $321,421
7. Morgan Stanley Dean Witter & Co., $317,590
8. Merrill Lynch, $299,804
9. Bank One, $261,496
10. J. P. Morgan & Co, $261,067

Source: *Forbes*, Forbes 500s (annual), April 19, 1999, p. 286.

★1339★
CORPORATE LEADERS IN MARKET VALUE, 1998
Ranked by: Market value, in millions of dollars. **Remarks:** Includes percent change from previous year and previous year rank. **Number listed:** 50

1. Microsoft, with $404,228 million
2. General Electric, $351,255
3. Wal-Mart Stores, $214,338
4. Merck, $197,983
5. Intel, $196,028
6. Pfizer, $181,529
7. Exxon, $179,521

8. Coca-Cola, $171,607
9. AT & T, $170,857
10. Cisco Systems, $164,910

Source: *Forbes*, Forbes 500s (annual), April 19, 1999, p. 288.

★1340★
CORPORATE LEADERS IN MARKET VALUE, 1998
Ranked by: Market value growth, in percent. **Number listed:** 5

1. CMGI, with 1,191%
2. Amazon.com, 1,030%
3. Yahoo, 824%
4. Infoseek, 821%
5. Network Solutions, 767%

Source: *Forbes*, Forbes 500s (annual), April 19, 1999, p. 288.

★1341★
CORPORATE LEADERS IN PROFIT GROWTH, 1998
Ranked by: Profit growth, in percent. **Number listed:** 5

1. Eastman Kodak, with 27,700%
2. Sonoco Products, 7,237%
3. ITT Industries, 1,248%
4. Limited, 845%
5. Primark, 647%

Source: *Forbes*, Forbes 500s (annual), April 19, 1999, p. 282.

★1342★
CORPORATE LEADERS IN PROFITS, 1998
Ranked by: Net profits, in millions of dollars. **Remarks:** Includes percent change from previous year and previous year rank. **Number listed:** 50

1. General Electric, with $9,296.0 million
2. AT & T, $6,535.0
3. Exxon, $6,440.0
4. Microsoft, $6,360.0
5. IBM, $6,328.0
6. Intel, $6,068.0
7. Ford Motor, $5,939.0
8. Citigroup, $5,807.0
9. Philip Morris, $5,372.0
10. Merck, $5,248.2

Source: *Forbes*, Forbes 500s (annual), April 19, 1999, p. 282.

★1343★
CORPORATE LEADERS IN SALES GROWTH, 1998
Ranked by: Sales growth, in percent. **Number listed:** 5

1. Avista, with 183%
2. Fred Meyer, 172%
3. Flowers Industries, 161%
4. Federal-Mogul, 147%
5. MCI WorldCom, 141%

Source: *Forbes*, Forbes 500s (annual), April 19, 1999, p. 280.

★1344★
CORPORATE LEADERS IN SALES, 1998
Ranked by: Sales, in millions of dollars. **Remarks:** Includes percent change from previous year and previous year rank. **Number listed:** 50

1. General Motors, with $161,315 million
2. Ford Motor, $142,666
3. Wal-Mart Stores, $137,634
4. Exxon, $100,697
5. General Electric, $100,469
6. IBM, $81,667
7. Citigroup, $76,431
8. Philip Morris, $57,813
9. Boeing, $56,154
10. AT & T, $53,223

Source: *Forbes*, Forbes 500s (annual), April 19, 1999, p. 280.

★1345★
CORPORATE LOSERS IN ASSET GROWTH, 1998
Ranked by: Asset loss, in percent. **Number listed:** 5

1. KeySpan Energy, with -42%
2. Textron, -26%
3. Browning-Ferris Industries, -24%
4. Ashland, -23%
5. Tricon Global Restaurants, -21%

Source: *Forbes*, Forbes 500s (annual), April 19, 1999, p. 286.

★1346★
CORPORATE LOSERS IN MARKET VALUE, 1998
Ranked by: Market value loss, in percent. **Number listed:** 5

1. Service Corp. International, with -65%
2. PeopleSoft, -63%
3. HealthSouth, -59%
4. Cendant, -56%
5. Mattel, -49%

Source: *Forbes*, Forbes 500s (annual), April 19, 1999, p. 288.

★1347★
CORPORATE LOSERS IN PROFIT GROWTH, 1998
Ranked by: Profit loss, in percent. **Number listed:** 5

1. Texas Instruments, with -78%
2. Texaco Inc., -77%
3. Atlantic Richfield, -76%
4. Phillips Petroleum, -75%
5. Xerox, -73%

Source: *Forbes*, Forbes 500s (annual), April 19, 1999, p. 282.

★1348★
CORPORATE LOSERS IN SALES GROWTH, 1998
Ranked by: Sales loss, in percent. **Number listed:** 5

1. MedPartners, with -58%
2. Consol Natural Gas, -52%
3. ITT Industries, -48%
4. Ryerson Tull, -45%
4. Atlantic Richfield, -45%

Source: *Forbes*, Forbes 500s (annual), April 19, 1999, p. 280.

★1349★
***FORBES* SUPER 100 CORPORATIONS, 1998**
Ranked by: Combination of sales, net profits, assets, and market value. **Remarks:** Specific figures not provided. **Number listed:** 100

1. General Electric
2. Citigroup
3. BankAmerica
4. Exxon
5. International Business Machines
6. Ford Motor
7. American International Group
8. AT & T
9. Chase Manhattan
10. Wal-Mart Stores

Source: *Forbes*, Forbes 500s (annual), April 19, 1999, p. 275.

★1350★
INDUSTRIES WITH THE HIGHEST INCREASE IN PROFITS, 1998
Ranked by: Increase in profits, in percent. **Number listed:** 38

1. Specialty retailers, with 39.1%
2. Engineering & construction, 35.9%
3. Mail, package and freight delivery, 26.8%
4. Commercial banks, 22.4%
5. Pharmaceuticals, 21.1%
6. Hotels, casinos, resorts, 18.8%
7. Computer and data services, 17.9%
8. Motor vehicles and parts, 17.1%
9. Diversified financials, 16.9%

10. Computer peripherals, 15%

Source: *Fortune*, Fortune 500 Largest U.S. Corporations (annual), April 26, 1999, p. F-26.

★1351★
INDUSTRIES WITH THE HIGHEST INCREASE IN REVENUE, 1998
Ranked by: Increase in revenue, in percent. **Number listed:** 38

1. Hotels, casinos, resorts, with 206.8%
2. Pipelines, 30.4%
3. Diversified financials, 16.5%
4. Securities, 16.3%
5. Commercial banks, 15.8%
6. Metal products, 15%
7. Telecommmunications, 13.8%
7. Specialty retailers, 13.8%
9. Motor vehicles and parts, 13.6%
10. General merchandise, 13.1%

Source: *Fortune*, Fortune 500 Largest U.S. Corporations (annual), April 26, 1999, p. F-25.

★1352★
INDUSTRIES WITH THE HIGHEST RETURN ON ASSETS, 1998
Ranked by: Return on assets, in percent. **Number listed:** 38

1. Pharmaceuticals, with 16.8%
2. Soaps & cosmetics, 11.1%
3. Beverages, 9.3%
4. Publishing & printing, 8.6%
5. Computers and office equipment, 7.3%
6. Mail, package and freight delivery, 7.2%
7. Computer peripherals, 7%
8. Hotels, casinos, resorts, 6.9%
9. Metal products, 6.7%
10. Food, 6.6%

Source: *Fortune*, Fortune 500 Largest U.S. Corporations (annual), April 26, 1999, p. F-27.

★1353★
INDUSTRIES WITH THE HIGHEST RETURN ON EQUITY, 1998
Ranked by: Return on equity, in percent. **Number listed:** 38

1. Pharmaceuticals, with 39.4%
2. Soaps & cosmetics, 35.8%
3. Beverages, 30.2%
4. Building materials, glass, 26.2%
5. Airlines, 24.6%
6. Hotels, casinos, resorts, 22.5%
7. Telecommunications, 22.3%
8. Publishing & printing, 22%
9. Food, 20.1%
10. Diversified financials, 19.8%

Source: *Fortune*, Fortune 500 Largest U.S. Corporations (annual), April 26, 1999, p. F-27.

★1354★
INDUSTRIES WITH THE HIGHEST RETURN ON REVENUE, 1998
Ranked by: Return on revenue, in percent. **Number listed:** 38

1. Pharmaceuticals, with 18.5%
2. Commercial banks, 13.2%
3. Telecommunications, 11.9%
4. Publishing & printing, 11.8%
5. Diversified financials, 10.1%
6. Beverages, 9.9%
7. Railroads, 9.2%
8. Insurance, property and casualty, 8.6%
9. Soaps & cosmetics, 8%
10. Insurance, life & health, 7.2%

Source: *Fortune*, Fortune 500 Largest U.S. Corporations (annual), April 26, 1999, p. F-27.

★1355★
INDUSTRIES WITH THE HIGHEST RETURN TO INVESTORS, 1988-1998
Ranked by: Return to investors, in percent. **Number listed:** 38

1. Securities, with 28.2%
2. Soaps & cosmetics, 26.3%
3. Computer peripherals, 26.1%
4. Pharmaceuticals, 25.7%
5. Insurance, life & health, 23.1%
6. Computers and office equipment, 22.9%
7. Health care, 22.6%
8. Beverages, 22.5%
9. Commercial banks, 22%
10. Food service, 21.4%

Source: *Fortune*, Fortune 500 Largest U.S. Corporations (annual), April 26, 1999, p. F-26.

★1356★
INDUSTRIES WITH THE HIGHEST REVENUE PER EMPLOYEE, 1998
Ranked by: Revenue per employee. **Number listed:** 38

1. Pipelines, with 1,681,145
2. Petroleum refining, 676,840
3. Insurance, life and health, 669,942
4. Securities, 596,710
5. Wholesalers, 551,800
6. Electric & gas utilities, 546,987
7. Insurance, property & casualty, 496,315
8. Health care, 429,599
9. Diversified financials, 409,933
10. Computers and office equipment, 372,275

Source: *Fortune*, Fortune 500 Largest U.S. Corporations (annual), April 26, 1999, p. F-25.

★1357★
INDUSTRIES WITH THE HIGHEST TOTAL RETURN TO INVESTORS, 1998
Ranked by: Return to investors, in percent. **Number listed:** 38

1. Food and drug stores, with 65.1%
2. Food service, 61.8%
3. Telecommunications, 61.5%
4. Computer peripherals, 57.1%
5. Computers and office equipment, 56.3%
6. Pharmaceuticals, 50.9%
7. Entertainment, 45.1%
8. Soaps & cosmetics, 37.4%
9. Mail, package and freight delivery, 31.4%
10. Specialty retailers, 27.3%

Source: *Fortune*, Fortune 500 Largest U.S. Corporations (annual), April 26, 1999, p. F-26.

★1358★
LEADING COMPANIES IN REVENUE GROWTH, 1998
Ranked by: Revenue increase from 1997, in percent. **Remarks:** Also notes Fortune 500 revenue rank and 1998 revenue figures. **Number listed:** 50

1. Starwood Hotels & Resorts, with 417.6%
2. Waste Management, 386%
3. Firstar Corp., 247%
4. U.S. Foodservice, 225.5%
5. Host Marriott, 206.8%
6. Avista Corp., 182.9%
7. Fred Meyer, 171.5%
8. Sempra Energy, 149.2%
9. Federal-Mogul, 147.4%

10. MCI WorldCom, 140.5%

Source: *Fortune*, Fortune 500 Largest U.S. Corporations (annual), April 26, 1999, p. F-28.

★1359★

LEADING CORPORATIONS BY PROFIT GROWTH, 1998

Ranked by: Profit increase from 1997, in percent. **Remarks:** Also notes Fortune 500 revenue rank and 1998 profit figures. **Number listed:** 50

1. Eastman Kodak, with 27,700%
2. Best Buy, 5,305.5%
3. Starwood Hotels & Resorts, 3,196.4%
4. United Stationers, 2,418.1%
5. NCR, 1,642.9%
6. ITT Industries, 1,317.7%
7. CBS, 951.5%
8. Limited, 844.7%
9. Enron, 569.5%
10. Times Mirror, 466.2%

Source: *Fortune*, Fortune 500 Largest U.S. Corporations (annual), April 26, 1999, p. F-29.

★1360★

LEADING CORPORATIONS BY PROFITS, 1998

Ranked by: Net profits, in millions of dollars. **Remarks:** Also notes previous year's rank and percentage change. **Number listed:** 50

1. Ford Motor, with $22,071 million
2. General Electric, $9,296
3. AT&T, $6,398
4. Exxon, $6,370
5. IBM, $6,328
6. Intel, $6,068
7. Citigroup, $5,807
8. Philip Morris, $5,372
9. Merck, $5,248.2
10. BankAmerica Corp., $5,165

Source: *Fortune*, Fortune 500 Largest U.S. Corporations (annual), April 26, 1999, p. F-29.

★1361★

LEAST ADMIRED CORPORATIONS IN EMPLOYEE TALENT, 1998

Ranked by: Scores (1-10) derived from a survey of senior executives, outside directors, and securities analysts. **Remarks:** Respondents rated companies in their own industry on 8 attributes of reputation. Also notes previous year's rank. **Number listed:** 3

1. MedPartners, with with 3.41 points
2. Shoney's, 3.40
3. Trump Hotels & Casinos, 2.87

Source: *Fortune*, America's Most Admired Corporations (annual), March 1, 1999, p. 70.

★1362★

LEAST ADMIRED CORPORATIONS IN FINANCIAL SOUNDNESS, 1998

Ranked by: Scores (1-10) derived from a survey of senior executives, outside directors, and securities analysts. **Remarks:** Respondents rated companies in their own industry on 8 attributes of reputation. Also notes previous year's rank. **Number listed:** 3

1. MedPartners, with with 2.60 points
2. Trump Hotels & Casinos, 2.40
3. Oxford Health Plans, 2.19

Source: *Fortune*, America's Most Admired Corporations (annual), March 1, 1999, p. 71.

★1363★

LEAST ADMIRED CORPORATIONS IN INNOVATIVENESS, 1998

Ranked by: Scores (1-10) derived from a survey of senior executives, outside directors, and securities analysts. **Remarks:** Respondents rated companies in their own industry on 8 attributes of reputation. Also notes previous year's rank. **Number listed:** 3

1. Trump Hotels & Casinos, with with 3.83 points
2. Fruit of the Loom, 3.81
3. Shoney's, 3.51

Source: *Fortune*, America's Most Admired Corporations (annual), March 1, 1999, p. 70.

★1364★

LEAST ADMIRED CORPORATIONS IN LONG-TERM INVESTMENT VALUE, 1998

Ranked by: Scores (1-10) derived from a survey of senior executives, outside directors, and securities analysts. **Remarks:** Respondents rated companies in their own industry on 8 attributes of reputation. Also notes previous year's rank. **Number listed:** 3

1. Shoney's, with with 3.16 points
2. MedPartners, 3.07
3. Trump Hotels & Casinos, 2.42

Source: *Fortune*, America's Most Admired Corporations (annual), March 1, 1999, p. 71.

★1365★

LEAST ADMIRED CORPORATIONS IN QUALITY OF MANAGEMENT, 1998

Ranked by: Scores (1-10) derived from a survey of senior executives, outside directors, and securities analysts. **Remarks:** Respondents rated companies in their own industry on 8 attributes of reputation. Also notes previous year's rank. **Number listed:** 3

1. Oxford Health Plans, with with 3.92 points
2. Cabletron Systems, 3.42
3. Trump Hotels & Casinos, 3.25

Source: *Fortune*, America's Most Admired Corporations (annual), March 1, 1999, p. 70.

★1366★

LEAST ADMIRED CORPORATIONS IN QUALITY OF PRODUCTS/SERVICES, 1998

Ranked by: Scores (1-10) derived from a survey of senior executives, outside directors, and securities analysts. **Remarks:** Respondents rated companies in their own industry on 8 attributes of reputation. Also notes previous year's rank. **Number listed:** 3

1. Viad, with with 4.31 points
2. U.S. Industries, 4.24
3. Shoney's, 3.99

Source: *Fortune*, America's Most Admired Corporations (annual), March 1, 1999, p. 70.

★1367★

LEAST ADMIRED CORPORATIONS IN SOCIAL RESPONSIBILITY, 1998

Ranked by: Scores (1-10) derived from a survey of senior executives, outside directors, and securities analysts. **Remarks:** Respondents rated companies in their own industry on 8 attributes of reputation. Also notes previous year's rank. **Number listed:** 3

1. Shoney's, with with 3.76 points
2. MedPartners, 3.74
3. Trump Hotels & Casinos, 3.50

Source: *Fortune*, America's Most Admired Corporations (annual), March 1, 1999, p. 71.

★1368★
LEAST ADMIRED CORPORATIONS IN USE OF CORPORATE ASSETS, 1998
Ranked by: Scores (1-10) derived from a survey of senior executives, outside directors, and securities analysts. **Remarks:** Respondents rated companies in their own industry on 8 attributes of reputation. Also notes previous year's rank. **Number listed:** 3
1. MedPartners, with with 3.41 points
2. Oxford Health Plans, 3.15
3. Trump Hotels & Casinos, 2.75

Source: *Fortune*, America's Most Admired Corporations (annual), March 1, 1999, p. 71.

★1369★
MOST ADMIRED CORPORATIONS IN EMPLOYEE TALENT, 1998
Ranked by: Scores (1-10) derived from a survey of senior executives, outside directors, and securities analysts. **Remarks:** Respondents rated companies in their own industry on 8 attributes of reputation. Also notes previous year's rank. **Number listed:** 3
1. Microsoft, with with 8.59 points
2. Cisco Systems, 8.58
3. Coca-Cola, 8.33

Source: *Fortune*, America's Most Admired Corporations (annual), March 1, 1999, p. 70.

★1370★
MOST ADMIRED CORPORATIONS IN FINANCIAL SOUNDNESS, 1998
Ranked by: Scores (1-10) derived from a survey of senior executives, outside directors, and securities analysts. **Remarks:** Respondents rated companies in their own industry on 8 attributes of reputation. Also notes previous year's rank. **Number listed:** 3
1. Microsoft, with with 9.56 points
2. Intel, 9.46
3. Cisco Systems, 9.42

Source: *Fortune*, America's Most Admired Corporations (annual), March 1, 1999, p. 71.

★1371★
MOST ADMIRED CORPORATIONS IN INNOVATIVENESS, 1998
Ranked by: Scores (1-10) derived from a survey of senior executives, outside directors, and securities analysts. **Remarks:** Respondents rated companies in their own industry on 8 attributes of reputation. Also notes previous year's rank. **Number listed:** 3
1. Enron, with with 9.18 points
2. Mirage Resorts, 8.50
3. Herman Miller, 8.43

Source: *Fortune*, America's Most Admired Corporations (annual), March 1, 1999, p. 70.

★1372★
MOST ADMIRED CORPORATIONS IN LONG-TERM INVESTMENT VALUE, 1998
Ranked by: Scores (1-10) derived from a survey of senior executives, outside directors, and securities analysts. **Remarks:** Respondents rated companies in their own industry on 8 attributes of reputation. Also notes previous year's rank. **Number listed:** 3
1. General Electric, with with 8.79 points
2. Coca-Cola, 8.77
3. Cisco Systems, 8.63

Source: *Fortune*, America's Most Admired Corporations (annual), March 1, 1999, p. 71.

★1373★
MOST ADMIRED CORPORATIONS IN QUALITY OF MANAGEMENT, 1998
Ranked by: Scores (1-10) derived from a survey of senior executives, outside directors, and securities analysts. **Remarks:** Respondents rated companies in their own industry on 8 attributes of reputation. Also notes previous year's rank. **Number listed:** 3
1. Philip Morris, with with 9.12 points
2. General Electric, 9.09
3. Cisco Systems, 8.89

Source: *Fortune*, America's Most Admired Corporations (annual), March 1, 1999, p. 70.

★1374★
MOST ADMIRED CORPORATIONS IN QUALITY OF PRODUCTS/SERVICES, 1998
Ranked by: Scores (1-10) derived from a survey of senior executives, outside directors, and securities analysts. **Remarks:** Respondents rated companies in their own industry on 8 attributes of reputation. Also notes previous year's rank. **Number listed:** 3
1. Mirage Resorts, with with 8.84 points
2. Corning, 8.78
3. Toyota Motor Sales USA, 8.72

Source: *Fortune*, America's Most Admired Corporations (annual), March 1, 1999, p. 70.

★1375★
MOST ADMIRED CORPORATIONS IN SOCIAL RESPONSIBILITY, 1998
Ranked by: Scores (1-10) derived from a survey of senior executives, outside directors, and securities analysts. **Remarks:** Respondents rated companies in their own industry on 8 attributes of reputation. Also notes previous year's rank. **Number listed:** 3
1. Corning, with with 8.56 points
2. Du Pont, 8.09
3. Herman Miller, 8.04

Source: *Fortune*, America's Most Admired Corporations (annual), March 1, 1999, p. 71.

★1376★
MOST ADMIRED CORPORATIONS IN USE OF CORPORATE ASSETS, 1998
Ranked by: Scores (1-10) derived from a survey of senior executives, outside directors, and securities analysts. **Remarks:** Respondents rated companies in their own industry on 8 attributes of reputation. Also notes previous year's rank. **Number listed:** 3
1. Cisco Systems, with with 8.63 points
2. Berkshire Hathaway, 8.45
3. Coca-Cola, 8.34

Source: *Fortune*, America's Most Admired Corporations (annual), March 1, 1999, p. 71.

★1377★
MOST ADMIRED CORPORATIONS, 1998
Ranked by: Scores (1-10) derived from a survey of senior executives, outside directors, and securities analysts. **Remarks:** Respondents rated companies in their own industry on 8 attributes of reputation. Also notes previous year's rank. **Number listed:** 10
1. General Electric
2. Coca-Cola
3. Microsoft
4. Dell Computers
5. Berkshire Hathaway
6. Wal-Mart Stores
7. Southwest Airlines

8. Intel
9. Merck
10. Walt Disney

Source: *Fortune*, America's Most Admired Corporations (annual), March 1, 1999, p. 71.

★1378★
STATES WITH THE MOST FORTUNE 500 COMPANY HEADQUARTERS, 1998
Ranked by: Total number of company headquarters. **Number listed:** 40

1. New York, with 59 headquarters
2. California, 56
3. Illinois, 39
4. Texas, 36
5. Ohio, 27
5. Pennsylvania, 27
7. New Jersey, 24
8. Virginia, 18
9. Connecticut, 16
9. Massachusetts, 16

Source: *Fortune*, Fortune 500 Largest U.S. Corporations (annual), April 26, 1999, p. F-33.

★1379★
TOP COMPANIES BY ASSETS, 1998
Ranked by: Assets, in millions of dollars. **Remarks:** Also notes Fortune 500 revenue rank. **Number listed:** 50

1. Citigroup, with $668,641 million
2. BankAmerica Corp., $617,679
3. Fannie Mae, $485,014
4. Chase Manhattan Corp., $365,875
5. General Electric, $355,935
6. Freddie Mac, $321,421
7. Morgan Stanley Dean Witter, $317,590
8. Merrill Lynch, $299,804
9. Prudential Insurance Co. of America, $279,422
10. Bank One Corp., $261,496

Source: *Fortune*, Fortune 500 Largest U.S. Corporations (annual), April 26, 1999, p. F-32.

★1380★
TOP COMPANIES BY MARKET VALUE, 1998
Ranked by: Market value, in millions of dollars. **Remarks:** Also notes Fortune 500 revenue rank. **Number listed:** 50

1. Microsoft, with $418,579 million
2. General Electric, $360,251
3. Wal-Mart Stores, $212,850
4. Merck, $198,868
5. Intel, $196,616
6. Pfizer, $182,211
7. AT & T, $180,156
8. Exxon, $178,913
9. Coca-Cola, $169,350
10. Cisco Systems, $166,616

Source: *Fortune*, Fortune 500 Largest U.S. Corporations (annual), April 26, 1999, p. F-32.

★1381★
TOP COMPANIES BY NUMBER OF EMPLOYEES, 1998
Ranked by: Total number of employees. **Remarks:** Also notes Fortune 500 revenue rank. **Number listed:** 50

1. Wal-Mart Stores, with 910,000 employees
2. General Motors, 594,000
3. Ford Motor, 345,175
4. United Parcel Service, 333,000
5. Sears Roebuck, 324,000
6. General Electric, 293,000
7. IBM, 291,067
8. McDonald's, 284,000
9. Kmart, 278,525
10. Columbia/HCA Healthcare, 260,000

Source: *Fortune*, Fortune 500 Largest U.S. Corporations (annual), April 26, 1999, p. F-32.

★1382★
TOP CORPORATIONS BY REVENUE, 1997
Ranked by: Revenue, in millions of dollars. **Number listed:** 500

1. General Motors, with $161,315 million
2. Ford Motor, $144,416
3. Wal-Mart Stores, $139,208
4. Exxon, $100,697
5. General Electric, $100,469
6. IBM, $81,667
7. Citigroup, $76,431
8. Philip Morris, $57,813
9. Boeing, $56,154
10. AT & T, $53,588

Source: *Fortune*, Fortune 500 Largest U.S. Corporations (annual), April 26, 1999, p. F-1.

Corporations--Alabama

★1383★
TOP CORPORATIONS IN ALABAMA, 1998
Ranked by: Revenue, in millions of dollars. **Remarks:** Also notes profits, contact information, number of employees, and CEO. **Number listed:** 7

1. MedPartners, with $7,003.6 million
2. SCI Systems, $6,805.9
3. Saks, $6,219.9
4. HealthSouth, $4,006.1
5. Sonat, $3,709.8
6. Regions Financial Corp., $3,072.5
7. SouthTrust Corp., $2,943.3

Source: *Fortune*, Fortune 500 Largest U.S. Corporations (annual), April 26, 1999, p. F-33+.

Corporations--Arizona

★1384★
TOP CORPORATIONS IN ARIZONA, 1998
Ranked by: Revenue, in millions of dollars. **Remarks:** Also notes profits, contact information, number of employees, and CEO. **Number listed:** 3

1. Avnet, with $5,916.3 million
2. MicroAge, $5,520
3. Phelps Dodge, $3,063.4

Source: *Fortune*, Fortune 500 Largest U.S. Corporations (annual), April 26, 1999, p. F-34.

Corporations--Arkansas

★1385★
TOP CORPORATIONS IN ARKANSAS, 1998
Ranked by: Revenue, in millions of dollars. **Remarks:** Also notes profits, contact information, number of employees, and CEO. **Number listed:** 4

1. Wal-Mart Stores, with $139,208 million
2. Dillard's, $8,012
3. Tyson Foods Inc., $7,414.1
4. Alltel, $5,194

Source: *Fortune*, Fortune 500 Largest U.S. Corporations (annual), April 26, 1999, p. F-34.

Corporations--Australia

★1386★
MOST VALUABLE CORPORATIONS IN AUSTRALIA, 1998
Ranked by: Market value as of May 29, 1998, in millions of U.S. dollars. **Remarks:** Also notes overall rank, share price, percentage change from previous year, price rates, sales, profits, assets, equity, and industry code. **Number listed:** 12

1. Telstra, with $30,278 million
2. News Corp. Ltd., $21,802
3. National Australia Bank, $19,828
4. Broken Hill Proprietary, $17,500
5. Westpac Banking, $12,243
6. Commonwealth Bank of Australia, $10,865
7. Australia & New Zealand Banking Group, $10,825
8. Coca-Cola Amatil, $6,237
9. Lend Lease, $5,333
10. Coles Myer, $5,171

Source: *Business Week*, Business Week Global 1,000, July 13, 1998, p. 54.

★1387★
MOST VALUABLE CORPORATIONS IN AUSTRALIA, 1998
Ranked by: Market value as of May 29, 1998, in millions of U.S. dollars. **Remarks:** Also notes overall rank, share price, percentage change from previous year, price rates, sales, profits, assets, equity, and industry code. **Number listed:** 12

1. Telstra, with $30,278 million
2. News Corp. Ltd., $21,802
3. National Australia Bank, $19,828
4. Broken Hill Proprietary, $17,500
5. Westpac Banking, $12,243
6. Commonwealth Bank of Australia, $10,865
7. Australia & New Zealand Banking Group, $10,825
8. Coca-Cola Amatil, $6,237
9. Lend Lease, $5,333
10. Coles Myer, $5,171

Source: *Business Week*, Business Week Global 1,000, July 13, 1998, p. 54.

★1388★
TOP CORPORATIONS IN AUSTRALIA, 1997
Ranked by: Revenue, in millions of U.S. dollars ($). **Remarks:** Also notes overall rank, type of business, net income, assets, market value, stock price, percentage yield, and number of employees. **Number listed:** 11

1. Broken Hill Proprietary, with $16,464 million
2. Coles Myer, $14,974
3. National Australia Bank, $12,446
4. Woolworths, $12,191
5. News Corp. Ltd., $11,264
6. ANZ Banking, $9,117
7. Westpac Banking Group, $7,920
8. Rio Tinto, $7,715
9. Commonwealth Bank Group, $7,533
10. Qantas Airways, $6,212

Source: *Forbes*, Forbes Foreign Rankings (annual), July 27, 1998, p. 120.

Corporations--Austria

★1389★
LARGEST COMPANIES IN AUSTRIA, 1999
Ranked by: Sales, in thousands of U.S. dollars. **Number listed:** 100

1. OMV AG, with $6,588,716 thousand
2. Renault Oesterreich Automobilvertriebs AG, $3,835,343
3. Porsche Holding OHG, $3,705,760
4. Siemens Matsushita Components OHG, $1,967,941
5. Siemens AG Oesterreich, $1,840,977
6. Wiener Stadtwerke, $1,711,150
7. Opel Austria AG, $1,491,826
8. Leykam-Muerztaler Papier Und Zellstoff AG, $1,388,668
9. Shell Austria AG, $1,325,186
10. Metro International AG, $1,229,963

Source: *Europe's 15,000 Largest Companies (annual)*, Dun & Bradstreet, 1999, p. 71.

★1390★
LEADING COMPANIES IN AUSTRIA, 1998
Ranked by: Market cap. **Remarks:** Also notes price, price earnings ratio, and sector. **Number listed:** 13

1. Bank Austria, with 48.7
2. Verbund, 29.1
3. Erste Bank, 28.5
4. OMV, 27.7
5. Wienerberger, 20.9
6. EVN, 18.3
7. Generall, 17.9
8. Austria Tabak, 16.9
9. VA Tech, 14.9
10. VA Stahl, 9.5

Source: *Financial Times*, December 11, 1998, p. FIII.

★1391★
TOP CORPORATIONS IN AUSTRIA, 1997
Ranked by: Revenue, in millions of U.S. dollars ($). **Remarks:** Also notes overall rank, type of business, net income, assets, market value, stock price, percentage yield, and number of employees. **Number listed:** 2

1. Bank Austria Group, with $8,421 million
2. OMV Group, $6,803

Source: *Forbes*, Forbes Foreign Rankings (annual), July 27, 1998, p. 154.

Corporations--Belgium

★1392★
TOP CORPORATIONS IN BELGIUM BY MARKET VALUE, 1998
Ranked by: Market value as of May 29, 1998, in millions of dollars. **Remarks:** Also notes overall rank, share price, percentage change from previous year, price rates, sales, profits, assets, equity, and industry code. **Number listed:** 15

1. Electrabel, with $13,679 million

2. Societe Generale de Belgique, $12,585
3. Generale de Banque, $12,112
4. Fortis AG, $11,987
5. Tractebel, $11,195
6. Kredietbank, $10,571
7. Petrofina, $9,625
8. Almanij, $7,187
9. Groupe UCB, $6,951
10. Royale Belge, $6,194

Source: *Business Week*, Global 1,000 (annual), July 13, 1998, p. 54.

★1393★
TOP CORPORATIONS IN BELGIUM BY SALES, 1999
Ranked by: Sales, in thousands of U.S. dollars. **Number listed:** 100

1. Electrabel SA, with $8,489,075 thousand
2. Solvay SA, $7,631,041
3. Petrofina SA, $4,966,984
4. Belgacom SA, $3,628,996
5. GB Unic SA, $3,148,911
6. Volvo Cars Europe Industry NV, $2,797,859
7. Delhaize Freres Et Cie-Le Lion Sa, $2,666,249
8. Societe Nationale des Chemins de Fer Belges, $2,033,272
9. Volkswagen Bruxelles SA, $2,004,814
10. Fina Europe SA, $1,868,351

Source: *Europe's 15,000 Largest Companies (annual)*, Dun & Bradstreet, 1999, p. 72.

★1394★
TOP CORPORATIONS IN BELGIUM, 1997
Ranked by: Revenue, in millions of U.S. dollars ($). **Remarks:** Also notes overall rank, type of business, net income, assets, market value, stock price, percentage yield, and number of employees. **Number listed:** 12

1. Fortis Group, with $23,695 million
2. Delhaize Le Lion Group, $14,217
3. PetroFina, $13,819
4. Dexla, $12,872
5. Tractebel, $10,856
6. Generale Bank Group, $10,309
7. Solvay Group, $8,693
8. Arbed, $8,013
9. Kredietbank, $7,788
10. GIB Group, $6,029

Source: *Forbes*, Forbes Foreign Rankings (annual), July 27, 1998, p. 122.

Corporations--Brazil

★1395★
TOP CORPORATIONS IN BRAZIL, 1997
Ranked by: Revenue, in millions of U.S. dollars ($). **Remarks:** Also notes overall rank, type of business, net income, assets, market value, stock price, percentage yield, and number of employees. **Number listed:** 10

1. Banco do Brasil, with $20,304 million
2. Petrobras-Petroleo Brasil, $18,045
3. Banespa Group, $17,347
4. Telebras, $14,661
5. Banco Bradesco Group, $12,662
6. Banco Itau Group, $7,719
7. Unibanco Group, $7,659
8. Eletrobras, $5,981
9. Distrib Produtos Petroleo, $5,115
10. Vale do Rio Doce, $4,874

Source: *Forbes*, Forbes Foreign Rankings (annual), July 27, 1998, p. 122.

Corporations--California

★1396★
TOP CORPORATIONS IN CALIFORNIA, 1998
Ranked by: Revenue, in millions of dollars. **Remarks:** Also notes profits, contact information, number of employees, and CEO. **Number listed:** 56

1. Hewlett-Packard, with $47,061 million
2. Chevron, $26,801
3. Intel, $26,273
4. Safeway, $24,484.2
5. Walt Disney, $22,976
6. Ingram Micro, $22,034
7. McKesson HBOC, $20,857.3
8. Wells Fargo, $20,482
9. PG&E Corp., $19,942
10. Bergen Brunswig, $13,720

Source: *Fortune*, Fortune 500 Largest U.S. Corporations (annual), April 26, 1999, p. F-34+.

Corporations--Canada

★1397★
TOP CANADIAN CORPORATIONS BY RETURN TO INVESTORS, 1999
Ranked by: Percent change, for three years. **Number listed:** 50

1. Rogers Communications Inc., with 265.17
2. Shaw Communications Inc., 175.81
3. Globelle Corp., 123.64
4. Celestica Inc., 123.42
5. SMK Speedy International Inc., 97.22
6. Groupe Videotron Itee, 82.35
7. Rogers Cantel Mobile Communications Inc., 58.71
8. Onex Corp., 47.97
9. Quebecor Printing Inc., 47.01
10. Groupe Cantrex Inc., 42.05

Source: *Canadian Business*, Performance 2,000 (annual), June 25, 1999, p. 71.

★1398★
TOP CANADIAN CORPORATIONS BY SALES, 1999
Ranked by: Sales, in millions of dollars. **Number listed:** 2000

1. General Motors of Canada Ltd., with C$31,800.0 million
2. BCE Inc., C$27,454.0
3. Ford Motor Co. of Canada Ltd., C$26,469.0
4. Nortel Networks Corp., C$26,190.6
5. Chrysler Canada Ltd., C$20,712.0
6. Canadian Imperial Bank of Commerce, C$19,804.0
7. Royal Bank of Canada, C$19,761.0
8. Bank of Montreal, C$17,239.0
9. TransCanada Pipelines, C$17,228.0
10. Bank of Nova Scotia, C$15,949.0

Source: *Canadian Business*, Performance 2,000 (annual), June 25, 1999, p. 72+.

★1399★
TOP CANADIAN GROWTH LEADERS BY PERCENT CHANGE IN SALES, 1999

Ranked by: Percent change, for three years. **Remarks:** Also notes sales in millions. **Number listed:** 50

1. Telesystem International Wireless Inc., with 7,514.2%
2. RGA Life Reinsurance Co. of Canada, 1,944.4%
3. Newcourt Credit Group Inc., 1,526.1%
4. Philip Services Corp., 825.3%
5. American Eco Corp., 780.9%
6. CGI Group Inc., 666.3%
7. Magellan Aerospace Corp., 565.4%
8. Precision Drilling Corp., 459.9%
9. Goran Capital Inc., 407.8%
10. Onex Corp., 399.2%

Source: *Canadian Business*, Performance 2,000 (annual), June 25, 1999, p. 70.

★1400★
TOP CORPORATIONS IN CANADA BY MARKET VALUE, 1998

Ranked by: Market value as of May 29, 1998, in millions of U.S. dollars. **Remarks:** Also notes overall rank, share price, percentage change from previous year, price rates, sales, profits, assets, equity, and industry code. **Number listed:** 31

1. Northern Telecom, with $33,796 million
2. Bell Canada Enterprises, $29,418
3. Royal Bank of Canada, $18,885
4. Thomson Corp., $17,158
5. Seagram, $15,172
6. Bank of Montreal, $14,746
7. Canadian Imperial Bank of Commerce, $14,064
8. Toronto-Dominion Bank, $13,348
9. Bank of Nova Scotia, $13,153
10. Canadian Pacific, $9,791

Source: *Business Week*, Global 1,000 (annual), July 13, 1998, p. 56+.

★1401★
TOP CORPORATIONS IN CANADA, 1997

Ranked by: Revenue, in millions of U.S. dollars ($). **Remarks:** Also notes overall rank, type of business, net income, assets, market value, stock price, percentage yield, and number of employees. **Number listed:** 21

1. BCE Inc., with $23,971 million
2. Royal Bank of Canada, $12,809
3. Canadian Imperial Bank, $12,288
4. Seagram, $11,752
5. Bank of Montreal, $10,572
6. TransCanada PipeLines, $10,286
7. George Weston, $10,054
8. Bank of Nova Scotia, $9,593
9. Thomson Corp., $8,766
10. Onex, $8,098

Source: *Forbes*, Forbes Foreign Rankings (annual), July 27, 1998, p. 124.

Corporations—Charitable Contributions

See: **Charitable Contributions**

Corporations--Colorado

★1402★
COLORADO'S TOP PUBLIC COMPANIES, 1998

Ranked by: Revenue, in thousands. **Remarks:** Also notes city, business, description, an gross and net revenue. **Number listed:** 150

1. U.S. West Inc., with $12,378,000 thousand
2. Tele-Communications, $7,351,000
3. KN Energy Inc., $4,387,843
4. Corporate Express Inc., $3,752,591
5. New Century Energies, $3,610,905
6. Ball Corp., $2,896,400
7. MediaOne Group, $2,882,000
8. Cyprus Amax Minerals Co., $2,566,000
9. Storage Technology, $2,258,222
10. Quest Communications International, $2,242,700

Source: *Colorado's Business Magazine*, Colorado's Top Public Companies (annual), June, 1999, p. 26+.

★1403★
TOP CORPORATIONS IN COLORADO, 1998

Ranked by: Revenue, in millions of dollars. **Remarks:** Also notes profits, contact information, number of employees, and CEO. **Number listed:** 6

1. U.S. West Inc., with $12,378 million
2. Tele-Communications, $7,351
3. Corporate Express, $4.474.6
4. KN Energy, $4,387.8
5. New Century Energies, $3,610.9
6. Ball, $2,896.4

Source: *Fortune*, Fortune 500 Largest U.S. Corporations (annual), April 26, 1999, p. F-36.

Corporations--Connecticut

★1404★
TOP CORPORATIONS IN CONNECTICUT, 1998

Ranked by: Revenue, in millions of dollars. **Remarks:** Also notes profits, contact information, number of employees, and CEO. **Number listed:** 16

1. General Electric, with $100,469 million
2. United Technologies, $25,715
3. Aetna, $20,604.1
4. Xerox, $20,019
5. Hartford Financial Services, $15,022
6. Tosco, $12,021.5
7. Tenneco, $7,605
8. Nevco Evans, $7,421
9. Union Carbide, $5,659
10. Champion International, $5,653

Source: *Fortune*, Fortune 500 Largest U.S. Corporations (annual), April 26, 1999, p. F-36.

Corporations--Delaware

★1405★
TOP CORPORATIONS IN DELAWARE, 1998

Ranked by: Revenue, in millions of dollars. **Remarks:** Also notes profits, contact information, number of employees, and CEO. **Number listed:** 3

1. E.I. Du Pont de Nemours, with $39,130 million
2. MBNA, $5,195.1
3. Conectiv, $3,071.6

Source: *Fortune*, Fortune 500 Largest U.S. Corporations (annual), April 26, 1999, p. F-36.

Corporations--Denmark

★1406★
LARGEST CORPORATIONS IN DENMARK BY SALES, 1997
Ranked by: Sales, in thousands of U.S. dollars. **Number listed:** 100

1. Filial af Delta Air Lines, Inc. USA Delta Airlines, with $9,857,083 million
2. Scandinavian Airlines System, $4,745,435
3. Nykredit Holding AS, $4,524,036
4. A.P. Moeller Gruppen, $4,175,830
5. Unidanmark A/S, $3,217,923
6. FLS Industries A/S, $2,853,001
7. Danisco AS, $2,489,567
8. Tele Danmark, $2,434,363
9. ISS International Service System Aktieselskab, $2,254,433
10. The East Asiatic Company Ltd., $2,111,636

Source: *Dun & Bradstreet*, Europe's 15,000 Largest Companies (annual), 1999, p. 75.

★1407★
MOST VALUABLE CORPORATIONS IN DENMARK BY MARKET VALUE, 1998
Ranked by: Market value as of May 29, 1998, in millions of U.S. dollars. **Remarks:** Also note overall rank, share price, percentage change from previous year, price rates, sales, profits, assets, equity, and industry code. **Number listed:** 8

1. Tele Danmark, with $12,267 million
2. Novo-Nordisk, $11,820
3. Dampskibsselskabet AF 1912, $9,859
4. Dampskibsselskabet Svenborg, $9,765
5. Den Danske Bank, $6,585
6. Ratin, $5,243
7. Carlsberg, $4,453
8. Unidanmark, $4,302

Source: *Business Week*, Global 1,000 (annual), July 13, 1998, p. 57.

★1408★
TOP CORPORATIONS IN DENMARK, 1997
Ranked by: Revenue, in millions of U.S. dollars ($). **Remarks:** Also notes overall rank, type of business, net income, assets, market value, stock price, percentage yield, and number of employees. **Number listed:** 2

1. SAS, with $5,099 million
2. Den Danske Bank, $4,947

Source: *Forbes*, Forbes Foreign Rankings (annual), July 27, 1998, p. 154.

Corporations--Directors

★1409★
MOST COMMON NETWORK SOURCES FOR DIRECTORS, 1998*
Ranked by: By percent. **Number listed:** 8

1. Industry network, with 54%
2. Professional network, 48%
3. Dining club, 30%
4. Boardroom forum, 24%
5. Business school course, 12%
6. Benchmarking group, 9%
6. Local network, 9%
8. Other, 6%

Source: *Director*, October, 1998, p. 73.

Corporations--District of Columbia

★1410★
TOP CORPORATIONS IN DISTRICT OF COLUMBIA, 1998
Ranked by: Revenue, in millions of dollars. **Remarks:** Also notes profits, contact information, number of employees, and CEO. **Number listed:** 3

1. Fannie Mae, with $31,498.8 million
2. U.S. Office Products, $3,604.3
3. Danaher, $2,910

Source: *Fortune*, Fortune 500 Largest U.S. Corporations (annual), April 26, 1999, p. F-37.

Corporations--Europe

★1411★
EUROPE'S LARGEST CORPORATIONS BY SALES, 1997
Ranked by: Sales, in thousands of U.S. dollars. **Remarks:** Also notes previous year's rank. **Number listed:** 500

1. Royal Dutch Petroleum Co., with $134,129,295 thousand
2. BP Amoco PLC, $71,692,510
3. Daimler-Benz AG, $69,224,330
4. Volkswagen AG, $63,194,754
5. Siemens AG, $59,670,758
6. Nestle SA, $48,062,345
7. Unilever NV, $46,844,112
8. The Shell Transport & Trading Co. Plc, $45,922,137
9. Fiat Spa, $43,992,730
10. Veba AG, $42,448,102

Source: *Europe's 15,000 Largest Companies (annual)*, Dun & Bradstreet, 1999, p. 29+.

★1412★
EUROPE'S LEADING CORPORATIONS BY PROFITS, 1997
Ranked by: Profits, in thousands of U.S. dollars. **Number listed:** 500

1. Royal Dutch Petroleum Co., with $17,758,294 thousand
2. Unilever NV, $7,640,388
3. Wellcome Foundation Ltd., $6,636,753
4. BP Amoco PLC, $6,014,516
5. BT Plc, $5,310,128
6. The Shell Transport & Trading Co Plc, $5,262,289
7. ENI SpA, $4,990,628
8. Glaxo Wellcome Plc, $4,430,880
9. Deutsche Telekom AG, $4,015,625
10. Diageo Plc, $3,906,301

Source: *Europe's 15,000 Largest Companies (annual)*, Dun & Bradstreet, 1999, p. 39+.

★1413★
EUROPE'S TOP CORPORATIONS BY EMPLOYEES, 1997
Ranked by: Number of employees. **Number listed:** 500
1. Siemens AG, with 360,000 employees
2. Daimler-Benz AG, 300,068
3. Poste, 290,839
4. Unilever NV, 287,000
5. Volkswagen AG, 279,892
6. Deutsche Bahn AG, 268,273
7. Deutsche Post AG, 266,823
8. Philips Electronics NV, 264,685
9. Fiat Spa, 237,426
10. Nestle SA, 225,808

Source: *Europe's 15,000 Largest Companies (annual)*, Dun & Bradstreet, 1999, p. 59+.

★1414★
EUROPE'S TOP CORPORATIONS BY PROFITABILITY, 1997
Ranked by: Profits as a percentage of sales. **Number listed:** 500
1. Wellcome Foundation Ltd., with 1,364.7%
2. Amorim & Irmao SA, 566.6%
3. Coca-Cola Holdings (UK) Ltd., 480.0%
4. British American Tobacco Investments Ltd., 288.4%
5. BG North Sea Holdings Ltd., 191.8%
6. Glaxo Group Ltd., 144.8%
7. Renault Portuguesa-Soc Ind e Comercial SA, 133.9%
8. Castrol Ltd., 125.8%
9. Antofagasta Holdings Plc, 125.2%
10. Millennium Overseas Holdings Ltd., 122.7%

Source: *Europe's 15,000 Largest Companies (annual)*, Dun & Bradstreet, 1999, p. 49+.

★1415★
EUROPE'S TOP INDUSTRIAL CORPORATIONS BY SALES, 1997
Ranked by: Sales, in thousands of U.S. dollars ($). **Remarks:** Also notes previous year's rank, industry code, percentage change in sales, and percentage change in local currencies. **Number listed:** 500
1. Royal Dutch Petroleum Co., with $134,129,295 thousand
2. BP Amoco PLC, $71,692,510
3. Daimler-Benz AG, $69,224,330
4. Volkswagen AG, $63,194,754
5. Siemens AG, $59,670,758
6. Nestle SA, $48,062,345
7. Unilever NV, $46,844,112
8. Fiat Spa, $43,992,730
9. Veba AG, $42,448,102
10. Elf Aquitaine, $42,386,452

Source: *Europe's 15,000 Largest Companies (annual)*, Dun & Bradstreet, 1999, p. 92+.

★1416★
LARGEST EMPLOYERS IN EUROPE, 1997
Ranked by: Number of employees. **Remarks:** Also notes overall rank and financial size. **Number listed:** 5000
1. National Health Service, with 1,000,000 employees
2. Ministry of Defence, 400,000
3. Siemens AG, 382,000
4. Deutsche Bahn AG, 306,241
5. Min Education Nat, ENS SUP ET, 300,000
6. Deutsche Post AG, 292,027
7. Daimler-Benz AG, 290,029
8. Unilever Plc, 287,000
9. Volkswagen AG, 274,575
10. Deutsche Telekom AG, 236,812

Source: *Duns Europa (annual)*, Dun & Bradstreet, 1998, vol. 4, p. 163+.

★1417★
LARGEST EUROPEAN CORPORATIONS BY LOSS, 1997
Ranked by: Losses, in thousands of U.S. dollars ($). **Number listed:** 100
1. SNCF-Ste National des Chemins de Fers Francais, with $2,763,985 thousand
2. Bourgela, $1,848,104
3. British Gas Trading Ltd., $1,457,123
4. Magnox Electric Plc, $1,344,440
5. Eurotunnel Sa, $967,881
6. Ing C. Olivetti & Co. Spa, $865,097
7. Rhone-Poulenc SA, $831,874
8. Centrica Plc, $710,986
9. The Brent Walker Group Plc, $684,592
10. Kloeckner-Humboldt-Deutz AG, $662,220

Source: *Europe's 15,000 Largest Companies (annual)*, Dun & Bradstreet, 1999, p. 89+.

★1418★
TOP COMPANIES IN EUROPE BY SALES, 1997
Ranked by: Sales, in millions of ECUs. **Remarks:** Also notes overall rank and number of employees. **Number listed:** 5000
1. Citroen Nederland BV, with 285.239 million
2. British Petroleum Co. Plc, 64.128
3. Volkswagen AG, 57.432
4. Bank Austria Aktiengesellschaft, 54.660
5. Siemens AG, 54.229
6. Daimler-Benz AG, 53.929
7. Creditanstalt AG, 51.254
8. Unilever Plc, 43.922
9. Jacobs Suchard-Pavlides Chocolate Ind S.A., 43.639
10. Veba AG, 41.950

Source: *Duns Europa (annual)*, Dun & Bradstreet, 1999, vol. 4, p. 53+.

Corporations--Finland

★1419★
FINLAND'S TOP CORPORATIONS BY SALES, 1997
Ranked by: Sales, in thousands of U.S. dollars ($). **Number listed:** 100
1. Neste Oy, with $10,192,991 thousand
2. Nokia AB Oy, $7,240,636
3. Repola Ltd., $6,112,952
4. Kesko Oy, $5,391,485
5. Enso-Gutzeit Oy, $5,388,704
6. Metsaliitto Group, $4,801,421
7. Kymmene Oy, $3,966,633
8. Outokumpu Oy, $3,508,820
9. Metra, $2,816,815
10. Metsa-Serla Oy, $2,701,451

Source: *Europe's 15,000 Largest Companies*, Dun & Bradstreet, 1999, p. 85.

★1420★
TOP CORPORATIONS IN FINLAND BY MARKET, 1998
Ranked by: Market value, in millions of U.S. dollars. **Remarks:** Also notes overall rank, share price, percentage change from previous year, price rates, sales, profits, assets, equity, and industry code. **Number listed:** 3

1. Nokia, with $39,481 million
2. UPM-Kymmene, $8,037
3. Merita-Nordbanken, $5,236

Source: *Business Week*, Global 1,000 (annual), July 13, 1998, p. 57.

★1421★
TOP CORPORATIONS IN FINLAND BY MARKET VALUE, 1998
Ranked by: Market value, in millions of U.S. dollars. **Remarks:** Also notes overall rank, share price, percentage change from previous year, price rates, sales, profits, assets, equity, and industry code. **Number listed:** 3

1. Nokia, with $52,754 million
2. UPM-Kymmene, $8,037
3. Merita-Nordbanken, $5,236

Source: *Business Week*, Global 1,000 (annual), July 13, 1998, p. 57.

★1422★
TOP CORPORATIONS IN FINLAND, 1997
Ranked by: Revenue, in millions of U.S. dollars ($). **Remarks:** Also notes overall rank, type of business, net income, assets, market value, stock price, percentage yield, and number of employees. **Number listed:** 6

1. Nokia, with $10,134 million
2. Merita-Nordbanken, $9,318
3. UPM-Kymmene, $8,906
4. Neste, $8,795
5. Kesko Group, $6,708
6. Enso, $5,637

Source: *Forbes*, Forbes Foreign Rankings (annual), July 27, 1998, p. 126.

Corporations--Florida

★1423★
TOP CORPORATIONS IN FLORIDA, 1998
Ranked by: Revenue, in millions of dollars. **Remarks:** Also notes profits, contact information, number of employees, and CEO. **Number listed:** 11

1. Republic Industries, with $17,487.3 million
2. Winn-Dixie Stores Inc., $13,617.5
3. Publix Super Markets, $12,067.1
4. Tech Data, $11,529
5. Office Depot, $8,997.7
6. CHS Electronics, $8,545.8
7. FPL Group, $6,661
8. Ryder System, $5,188.7
9. Harris, $3,939.1
10. Florida Progress, $3,620.3

Source: *Fortune*, Fortune 500 Largest U.S. Corporations (annual), April 26, 1999, p. F-37.

Corporations, Foreign

See also: **Corporations, International**

★1424★
LARGEST PUBLIC FOREIGN CORPORATIONS, 1997
Ranked by: Revenue, in millions of U.S. dollars ($). **Remarks:** Also notes type of business and number of employees. **Number listed:** 25

1. Mitsui & Co. (Japan), with $142,754 million
2. Mitsubishi Corp. (Japan), $128,982
3. Royal Dutch/Shell Group (Netherlands), $128,108
4. Itochu (Japan), $126,691
5. Marubeni (Japan), $111,173
6. Sumitomo (Japan), $102,443
7. Toyota Motor (Japan), $95,181
8. Nissho Iwai (Japan), $81,932
9. Nippon Tel & Tel (Japan), $77,019
10. AXA-UAP (France), $76,869

Source: *Forbes*, Forbes Foreign Rankings (annual), July 27, 1998, p. 117.

Corporations, Foreign--Asia

★1425★
COMPANIES IN INDONESIA WITH THE HIGHEST QUALITY OF PRODUCTS AND SERVICES, 1998
Ranked by: Scores (1-7) based on a survey response of over 4,000 professionals throughout Asia. **Remarks:** Specific figures not provided. **Number listed:** 5

1. Toyota Astra Motor
2. Astra International
3. Asahimas Flat Glass
4. United Tractors
5. Indosat

Source: *Far Eastern Economic Review*, Review 200 (annual), December 31, 1998, p. 69.

★1426★
FOREIGN COMPANIES IN ASIA WITH THE BEST LONG-TERM VISION BY MANAGEMENT, 1998
Ranked by: Scores (1-7) based on a survey response of over 4,000 professionals throughout Asia. **Remarks:** Specific figures not provided. **Number listed:** 10

1. Microsoft
2. Intel
3. General Electric
4. Citibank
5. Coca-Cola
6. IBM
7. Walt Disney
8. Royal Dutch/Shell Group
9. Merrill Lynch
10. Boeing

Source: *Far Eastern Economic Review*, Review 200 (annual), December 31, 1998, p. 46.

★1427★
FOREIGN COMPANIES IN ASIA WITH THE HIGHEST QUALITY OF PRODUCTS AND SERVICES, 1998
Ranked by: Scores (1-7) based on a survey response of over 4,000 professionals throughout Asia. **Remarks:** Specific figures not provided. **Number listed:** 10

1. Rolex
2. Daimler-Benz
3. BMW
4. Rolls-Royce Motor Cars
5. 3M
6. Hewlett-Packard
7. Xerox
8. Volvo
9. Nestle

10. Microsoft

Source: *Far Eastern Economic Review*, Review 200 (annual), December 31, 1998, p. 46.

★1428★

FOREIGN COMPANIES IN ASIA WITH THE MOST FINANCIAL SOUNDNESS, 1998

Ranked by: Scores (1-7) based on a survey response of over 4,000 professionals throughout Asia. **Remarks:** Specific figures not provided. **Number listed:** 10

1. Hongkong Bank
2. Citibank
3. Bank of America
4. Deutsche Bank
5. Chase Manhattan Bank
6. Coca-Cola
7. Microsoft
8. Exxon
9. American Express
10. Royal Dutch/Shell Group

Source: *Far Eastern Economic Review*, Review 200 (annual), December 31, 1998, p. 46.

★1429★

FOREIGN COMPANIES IN ASIA WITH THE MOST INNOVATIVE RESPONSES TO CUSTOMER NEEDS, 1998

Ranked by: Scores (1-7) based on a survey response of over 4,000 professionals throughout Asia. **Remarks:** Specific figures not provided. **Number listed:** 10

1. Microsoft
2. McDonald's
3. Ericsson
4. Citibank
5. Nike
6. Walt Disney
7. Hewlett-Packard
8. Compaq Computer
9. Federal Express
10. American Express

Source: *Far Eastern Economic Review*, Review 200 (annual), December 31, 1998, p. 46.

★1430★

LEADING FOREIGN COMPANIES IN ASIA, 1998

Ranked by: Scores (1-7) based on a survey response of over 4,000 professionals throughout Asia. **Remarks:** Respondents rated companies on their quality of services/products offered and financial soundness. **Number listed:** 90

1. Microsoft, with 6.37 a score of
2. Coca-Cola, 6.06
3. Citibank, 5.87
4. Intel, 5.86
5. McDonald's, 5.83
6. Walt Disney, 5.74
7. IBM, 5.68
7. BMW, 5.68
9. General Electric, 5.67
10. Daimler-Benz, 5.65

Source: *Far Eastern Economic Review*, Review 200 (annual), December 31, 1998, p. 49.

★1431★

MOST EMULATED FOREIGN COMPANIES IN ASIA, 1998

Ranked by: Scores (1-7) based on a survey response of over 4,000 professionals throughout Asia. **Remarks:** Specific figures not provided. **Number listed:** 10

1. Microsoft
2. Coca-Cola
3. McDonald's
4. Walt Disney
5. Intel
6. IBM
7. Citibank
8. Daimler-Benz
9. Boeing
10. BMW

Source: *Far Eastern Economic Review*, Review 200 (annual), December 31, 1998, p. 46.

Corporations, Foreign--Detroit Metropolitan Area

★1432★

LEADING DETROIT-AREA FOREIGN-OWNED DIVISIONS, AFFILIATES, AND SUBSIDIARIES BY REVENUE, 1997

Ranked by: Revenue, in millions of dollars. **Remarks:** Also notes top local executive, relationship to parent company, 1996 revenue and 1997 percent change, number of employees local/ worldwide, business description. **Number listed:** 20

1. Volkswagen of America Inc., with $4,100.0 million
2. Siemens Automotive, $3,000.0
3. Denso International America Inc., $2,700.0
3. Robert Bosch Corp.-Automotive, $2,700.0
5. Thyssen Inc. N,A., $2,500.0
6. Yazaki North America Inc., $2,200.0
7. The Budd Co., $1,800.0
8. Bundy Corp., $1,230.0
9. Valeo Inc., $800.0
10. Takata Inc., $700.0

Source: *Crain's Detroit Business*, Crain's International, October 12, 1998, p. 14.

Corporations, Foreign--Long Island (NY)

★1433★

TOP FOREIGN AFFILIATED/OWNED FIRMS ON LONG ISLAND, 1999*

Ranked by: Number of employees. **Remarks:** Also notes product/service, parent company name and country. **Number listed:** 37

1. EAB, with 2,083 employees
2. Canon USA, 795
3. Olympus America, 750
4. Altana Inc., 500
5. HSBC Bank USA, 443
6. Lufthansa, 440
7. Henlopen Mfg., 400
7. Konica Graphic Imaging International, 400
9. Nikon, 350
10. Red Wing Products, 230

Source: *Long Island Business News (annual)*, -May 27, 1999, May 21, 1999, p. 14A.

Corporations--France

★1434★
FRANCE'S TOP CORPORATIONS BY MARKET VALUE, 1998
Ranked by: Market value as of May 29, 1998, in millions of U.S. dollars. **Remarks:** Also notes overall rank, share price, percentage change from previous year, price rates, sales, profits, assets, equity, and industry code. **Number listed:** 51

1. France Telecom, with $56,011 million
2. Elf Aquitanine, $38,123
3. Axa-UAP, $37,782
4. Alcatel, $34,916
5. L'Oreal, $33,573
6. Total, $30,345
7. Vivendi, $27,188
8. Carrefour, $23,512
9. Suez Lyonnaise Des Eaux, $21,544
10. Rhone-Poulenc, $20,122

Source: *Business Week*, Global 1,000 (annual), July 13, 1998, p. 57+.

★1435★
FRANCE'S TOP CORPORATIONS BY SALES, 1997
Ranked by: Sales, in thousands of U.S. dollars. **Number listed:** 100

1. Elf Aquitaine, with $42,386,452 thousand
2. Renault, $34,653,732
3. Total, $31,849,092
4. Suez Lyonnaise Des Eaux, $31,738,253
5. Peugeot SA, $31,132,389
6. Electricite De France, $31,084,887
7. Alcatel Alsthom, $30,979,548
8. Carrefour, $28,212,910
9. Vivendi, $27,854,059
10. France Telecom, $26,123,139

Source: *Europe's 15,000 Largest Companies (annual)*, Dun & Bradstreet, 1999, p. 77.

★1436★
TOP CORPORATIONS IN FRANCE, 1997
Ranked by: Revenue, in millions of U.S. dollars ($). **Remarks:** Also notes overall rank, type of business, net income, assets, market value, stock price, percentage yield, and number of employees. **Number listed:** 43

1. AXA-UAP, with $76,869 million
2. Elf Aquitaine Group, $43,570
3. Renault, $35,621
4. Total Group, $32,738
5. Suez Lyonnaise Group, $32,625
6. Peugeot Groupe, $32,002
7. Alcatel Alsthom, $31,845
8. Carrefour Group, $29,001
9. GAN-Assur Nationales, $28,935
10. Societe Generale Group, $28,723

Source: *Forbes*, Forbes Foreign Rankings (annual), July 27, 1998, p. 126+.

Corporations--Georgia

★1437★
TOP CORPORATIONS IN GEORGIA, 1998
Ranked by: Revenue, in millions of dollars. **Remarks:** Also notes profits, contact information, number of employees, and CEO. **Number listed:** 15

1. Home Depot, with $30,219 million
2. United Parcel Service, $24,788
3. BellSouth, $23,123
4. Coca-Cola, $18,813
5. Delta Air Lines, $14,138
6. Coca-Cola Enterprises, $13,414
7. Georgia-Pacific, $13,233
8. Southern, $11,403
9. SunTrust Banks Inc., $7,392.1
10. AFLAC, $7,104.2

Source: *Fortune*, Fortune 500 Largest U.S. Corporations (annual), April 26, 1999, p. F-37.

Corporations--Germany

★1438★
GERMANY'S TOP CORPORATIONS BY SALES, 1997
Ranked by: Sales, in thousands of U.S. dollars ($). **Number listed:** 100

1. Daimler-Benz AG, with $69,224,330 thousand
2. Volkswagen AG, $63,194,754
3. Siemens AG, $59,670,758
4. Veba AG, $42,448,102
5. RWE AG, $40,254,464
6. Deutsche Telekom AG, $37,696,428
7. Rewe Group, $34,363,839
8. Bayerische Motoren Werke Group AG BMW, $33,147,321
9. Edeka Group, $31,718,750
10. Metro AG, n/a

Source: *Europe's 15,000 Largest Companies (annual)*, Dun & Bradstreet, 1999, p. 74.

★1439★
MOST VALUABLE CORPORATIONS IN GERMANY, 1998
Ranked by: Market value as of May 29, 1998, in millions of U.S. dollars. **Remarks:** Also notes overall rank, share price, percentage change from previous year, price rates, sales, profits, assets, equity, and industry code. **Number listed:** 46

1. Allianz, with $77,412 million
2. Deutsche Telekom, $73,640
3. SAP, $55,593
4. Daimler-Benz, $52,105
5. Deutsche Bank, $45,920
6. Mannesmann, $38,037
7. Muenshener Rueck., $37,311
8. Siemens, $37,062
9. Bayer, $34,944
10. Veba, $32,686

Source: *Business Week*, Global 1,000 (annual), July 13, 1998, p. 58.

★1440★
TOP CORPORATIONS IN GERMANY, 1997
Ranked by: Revenue, in millions of U.S. dollars ($). **Remarks:** Also notes overall rank, type of business, net income, assets, market value, stock price, percentage yield, and number of employees. **Number listed:** 41

1. Daimler-Benz Group, with $71,536 million
2. Volkswagen Group, $65,306
3. Siemens Group, $63,731
4. Allianz Worldwide, $55,397
5. Veba Group, $43,866
6. Deutsche Bank Group, $40,778
7. Deutsche Telekom, $38,956

8. RWE Group, $38,243
9. BMW-Bayerische Motor, $34,679
10. Metro, $32,778

Source: *Forbes*, Forbes Foreign Rankings (annual), July 27, 1998, p. 130+.

Corporations--Great Britain

★1441★

GREAT BRITAIN'S TOP CORPORATIONS BY SALES, 1997

Ranked by: Sales, in thousands of U.S. dollars. **Number listed:** 100

1. BP Amoco PLC, with $71,692,510 thousand
2. The Shell Transport & Trading Co Plc, $45,922,137
3. BAT Industries PLC, $34,759,155
4. Shell International Petroleum Co. Ltd., $33,380,897
5. Diageo Plc, $29,194,985
6. Tesco PLC, $27,139,557
7. BP International Ltd., $26,552,282
8. BT Plc, $25,800,065
9. Tesco Stores Ltd., $23,944,242
10. J. Sainsbury Plc, $23,919,498

Source: *Europe's 15,000 Largest Companies (annual)*, Dun & Bradstreet, 1999, p. 78.

★1442★

MOST VALUABLE CORPORATIONS IN GREAT BRITAIN, 1998

Ranked by: Market value as of May 29, 1998, in millions of U.S. dollars. **Remarks:** Also notes overall rank, share price, percentage change from previous year, price rates, sales, profits, assets, equity, and industry code. **Number listed:** 115

1. Glaxo Wellcome, with $96,070 million
2. British Petroleum, $78,275
3. Lloyds TSB, $73,372
4. Shell Transport & Trading, $67,257
5. HSBC Holdings, $66,261
6. British Telecommunications, $66,261
7. SmithKline Beecham, $60,888
8. Barclays Bank, $40,700
9. Diageo, $40,169
10. Zeneca Group, $38,521

Source: *Business Week*, Global 1,000 (annual), July 13, 1998, p. 55+.

★1443★

TOP COMPANIES IN GREAT BRITAIN BY SALES TURNOVER, 1997

Ranked by: Sales turnover, in millions of British pounds. **Number listed:** 3808

1. British Petroleum Co. PLC, with 43,460 million
2. Unilever PLC, 29,766
3. BAT Industries PLC, 23,376
4. Diageo PLC, 17,698
5. Tesco PLC, 16,452
6. British Telecommunications PLC, 15,640
7. J Sainsbury PLC, 14,500
8. Tesco Stores Ltd., 12,973
9. Imperial Chemical Industries PLC, 11,062
10. Sainsbury's Supermarkets Ltd., 10,836

Source: *British Business Rankings*, (annual), Dun & Bradstreet, 1999, p. 397+.

★1444★

TOP CORPORATIONS IN GREAT BRITAIN, 1997

Ranked by: Revenue, in millions of U.S. dollars ($). **Remarks:** Also notes overall rank, type of business, net income, assets, market value, stock price, percentage yield, and number of employees. **Number listed:** 70

1. Royal Dutch/Shell Group, with $128,108 million
2. British Petroleum, $71,175
3. Unilever, $48,479
4. HSBC Group, $48,404
5. Prudential, $27,797
6. Tesco, $26,049
7. British Telecom, $25,671
8. J. Sainsbury, $23,800
9. Lloyds TSB, $22,307
10. B.A.T. Industries, $21,904

Source: *Forbes*, Forbes Foreign Rankings (annual), July 27, 1998, p. 150+.

Corporations--Hong Kong

★1445★

COMPANIES IN HONG KONG WITH THE BEST LONG-TERM VISION BY MANAGEMENT, 1998

Ranked by: Scores (1-7) based on a survey response of over 4,000 professionals throughout Asia. **Remarks:** Specific figures not provided. **Number listed:** 5

1. Cheung Kong
2. Hutchison Whampoa
3. Sun Hung Kai Properties
4. Swire Pacific
5. Hongkong Telecom

Source: *Far Eastern Economic Review*, Review 200 (annual), December 31, 1998, p. 63.

★1446★

COMPANIES IN HONG KONG WITH THE HIGHEST QUALITY OF PRODUCTS AND SERVICES, 1998

Ranked by: Scores (1-7) based on a survey response of over 4,000 professionals throughout Asia. **Remarks:** Specific figures not provided. **Number listed:** 5

1. Mandarin Oriental
2. Shangri-La Asia
3. Cathay Pacific Airways
4. Hongkong Telecom
5. Mass Transit Railway Corp.

Source: *Far Eastern Economic Review*, Review 200 (annual), December 31, 1998, p. 63.

★1447★

COMPANIES IN HONG KONG WITH THE MOST FINANCIAL SOUNDNESS, 1998

Ranked by: Scores (1-7) based on a survey response of over 4,000 professionals throughout Asia. **Remarks:** Specific figures not provided. **Number listed:** 5

1. Hang Seng Bank
2. China Light & Power
3. Cheung Kong
4. Hong Kong & China Gas
5. Hongkong Electric

Source: *Far Eastern Economic Review*, Review 200 (annual), December 31, 1998, p. 63.

★1448★
COMPANIES IN HONG KONG WITH THE MOST INNOVATIVE RESPONSES TO CUSTOMER NEEDS, 1998
Ranked by: Scores (1-7) based on a survey response of over 4,000 professionals throughout Asia. **Remarks:** Specific figures not provided. **Number listed:** 5
1. Giordano Holdings
2. Hongkong Telecom
3. Cathay Pacific Airways
4. Dickson Concepts
5. Mass Transit Railway Corp.

Source: *Far Eastern Economic Review*, Review 200 (annual), December 31, 1998, p. 63.

★1449★
LEADING COMPANIES IN HONG KONG, 1998
Ranked by: Scores (1-7) based on a survey response of over 4,000 professionals throughout Asia. **Number listed:** 10
1. Mass Transit Railway Corp., with 5.70 a score of
2. Hongkong Telecom, 5.64
3. Cheung Kong, 5.52
4. Cathay Pacific Airways, 5.40
5. Hang Seng Bank, 5.33
6. China Light & Power, 5.23
7. Sun Hung Kai Properties, 5.22
8. Hutchison Whampoa, 5.21
9. Swire Pacific, 5.14
10. Kowloon-Canton Railway Corp., 4.99

Source: *Far Eastern Economic Review*, Review 200 (annual), December 31, 1998, p. 48.

★1450★
LEADING QUOTED CORPORATIONS IN HONG KONG BY SALES, 1997
Ranked by: Sales, in thousands of U.S. dollars. **Number listed:** 100
1. First Pacific Company Ltd., with $8,093,566 thousand
2. Hutchison Whampoa Ltd., $5,756,222
3. Cathay Pacific Airways Ltd., $3,956,289
4. Sun Hung Kai Properties, $3,738,510
5. Swire Pacific, $3,163,663
6. CLP Holdings, $2,788,650
7. New World Development Co. Ltd., $2,578,746
8. Henderson Land Development Co. Ltd., $2,448,492
9. CITIC Pacific Ltd., $2,168,491
10. Orient Overseas (International) Ltd., $1,683,194

Source: *Asia's 7,500 Largest Companies*, (annual), Dun & Bradstreet, 1999, p. 62.

★1451★
MOST EMULATED COMPANIES IN HONG KONG, 1998
Ranked by: Scores (1-7) based on a survey response of over 4,000 professionals throughout Asia. **Remarks:** Specific figures not provided. **Number listed:** 5
1. Cathay Pacific Airways
2. Cheung Kong
3. Mandarin Oriental
4. Sun Hung Kai Properties
5. Giordano Holdings

Source: *Far Eastern Economic Review*, Review 200 (annual), December 31, 1998, p. 63.

★1452★
TOP CORPORATIONS IN HONG KONG, 1997
Ranked by: Revenue, in millions of U.S. dollars ($). **Remarks:** Also notes overall rank, type of business, net income, assets, market value, stock price, percentage yield, and number of employees. **Number listed:** 3
1. Jardine Matheson, with $11,522 million
2. First Pacific, $8,308
3. Hutchison Whampoa, $5,759

Source: *Forbes*, Forbes Foreign Rankings (annual), July 27, 1998, p. 154.

Corporations--Idaho

★1453★
TOP CORPORATIONS IN IDAHO, 1998
Ranked by: Revenue, in millions of dollars. **Remarks:** Also notes profits, contact information, number of employees, and CEO. **Number listed:** 3
1. Albertson's, with $16,005.1 million
2. Boise Cascade, $6,162.1
3. Micron Technology, $3,011.9

Source: *Fortune*, Fortune 500 Largest U.S. Corporations (annual), April 26, 1999, p. F-38.

Corporations--Illinois

★1454★
TOP CORPORATIONS IN ILLINOIS, 1998
Ranked by: Revenue, in millions of dollars. **Remarks:** Also notes profits, contact information, number of employees, and CEO. **Number listed:** 39
1. State Farm Insurance Co., with $48,113.9 million
2. Sears Roebuck, $41,322
3. Motorola, $29,398
4. Allstate, $25,879
5. Bank One Corp., $25,595
6. Caterpillar, $20,977
7. Sara Lee, $20,011
8. UAL, $17,561
9. Ameritech Corp., $17,154
10. Archer Daniels Midland, $16,108.6

Source: *Fortune*, Fortune 500 Largest U.S. Corporations (annual), April 26, 1999, p. F-38+.

Corporations--India

★1455★
COMPANIES IN INDIA WITH THE BEST LONG-TERM VISION BY MANAGEMENT, 1998
Ranked by: Scores (1-7) based on a survey response of over 4,000 professionals throughout Asia. **Remarks:** Specific figures not provided. **Number listed:** 5
1. Reliance Industries
2. Hindustan Lever
3. Larsen & Toubro
4. Tata Engineering & Locomotive
5. Ranbaxy Laboratories

Source: *Far Eastern Economic Review*, Review 200 (annual), December 31, 1998, p. 67.

★1456★
COMPANIES IN INDIA WITH THE HIGHEST QUALITY OF PRODUCTS AND SERVICES, 1998
Ranked by: Scores (1-7) based on a survey response of over 4,000 professionals throughout Asia. **Remarks:** Specific figures not provided. **Number listed:** 5

1. Titan Watches
2. Larson & Toubro
3. Hindustan Lever
4. MRF Ltd.
5. Brooke Bond Lipton India

Source: *Far Eastern Economic Review*, Review 200 (annual), December 31, 1998, p. 67.

★1457★
COMPANIES IN INDIA WITH THE MOST FINANCIAL SOUNDNESS, 1998
Ranked by: Scores (1-7) based on a survey response of over 4,000 professionals throughout Asia. **Remarks:** Specific figures not provided. **Number listed:** 5

1. Reliance Industries
2. Hindustan Lever
3. Bajaj Auto
4. Larsen & Toubro
5. ITC Ltd.

Source: *Far Eastern Economic Review*, Review 200 (annual), December 31, 1998, p. 67.

★1458★
COMPANIES IN INDIA WITH THE MOST INNOVATIVE RESPONSES TO CUSTOMER NEEDS, 1998
Ranked by: Scores (1-7) based on a survey response of over 4,000 professionals throughout Asia. **Remarks:** Specific figures not provided. **Number listed:** 5

1. Titan Watches
2. Hindustan Lever
3. BPL Ltd.
4. MRF Ltd.
5. Videocon International

Source: *Far Eastern Economic Review*, Review 200 (annual), December 31, 1998, p. 67.

★1459★
LEADING COMPANIES IN INDIA, 1998
Ranked by: Scores (1-7) based on a survey response of over 4,000 professionals throughout Asia. **Remarks:** Respondents rated companies on their quality of services/products offered, long-term management vision, response to customer needs, and financial soundness. **Number listed:** 10

1. Hindustan Lever, with 6.52 a score of
2. Reliance Industries, 6.41
3. Larsen & Toubro, 6.09
4. Titan Watches, 5.78
5. MRF Ltd., 5.77
6. Tata Engineering & Locomotive, 5.62
7. ITC Ltd., 5.60
8. Bajaj Auto, 5.59
9. Brooke Bond Lipton India, 5.51
10. Ranbaxy Laboratories, 5.48

Source: *Far Eastern Economic Review*, Review 200 (annual), December 31, 1998, p. 48.

★1460★
MOST EMULATED COMPANIES IN INDIA, 1998
Ranked by: Scores (1-7) based on a survey response of over 4,000 professionals throughout Asia. **Remarks:** Specific figures not provided. **Number listed:** 5

1. Hindustan Lever
2. Reliance Industries
3. Larson & Toubro
4. Titan Watches
5. MRF Ltd.

Source: *Far Eastern Economic Review*, Review 200 (annual), December 31, 1998, p. 67.

Corporations--Indiana

★1461★
TOP CORPORATIONS IN INDIANA, 1998
Ranked by: Revenue, in millions of dollars. **Remarks:** Also notes profits, contact information, number of employees, and CEO. **Number listed:** 7

1. Eli Lilly, with $10,051.3 million
2. Conseco, $7,716
3. Bindley Western, $7,623.1
4. Cummins Engine, $6,266
5. Lincoln National, $6,087.1
6. Anthem Insurance, $5,878.2
7. Nipsco Industries, $2,932.8

Source: *Fortune*, Fortune 500 Largest U.S. Corporations (annual), April 26, 1999, p. F-39.

Corporations--Indonesia

★1462★
COMPANIES IN INDONESIA WITH THE BEST LONG-TERM VISION BY MANAGEMENT, 1998
Ranked by: Scores (1-7) based on a survey response of over 4,000 professionals throughout Asia. **Remarks:** Specific figures not provided. **Number listed:** 5

1. Astra International
2. Toyota Astra Motor
3. Indosat
4. United Tractors
5. Freeport Indonesia

Source: *Far Eastern Economic Review*, Review 200 (annual), December 31, 1998, p. 69.

★1463★
COMPANIES IN INDONESIA WITH THE MOST FINANCIAL SOUNDNESS, 1998
Ranked by: Scores (1-7) based on a survey response of over 4,000 professionals throughout Asia. **Remarks:** Specific figures not provided. **Number listed:** 5

1. Freeport Indonesia
2. Gudang Garam
3. Bank Negara Indonesia
4. HM Sampoerna
5. Bank Bali

Source: *Far Eastern Economic Review*, Review 200 (annual), December 31, 1998, p. 69.

★1464★
COMPANIES IN INDONESIA WITH THE MOST INNOVATIVE RESPONSES TO CUSTOMER NEEDS, 1998
Ranked by: Scores (1-7) based on a survey response of over 4,000 professionals throughout Asia. **Remarks:** Specific figures not provided. **Number listed:** 5

1. Bank Bali
2. Astra International

3. Bank Central Asia
4. HM Sampoerna
5. Matahari Putra Prima

Source: *Far Eastern Economic Review*, Review 200 (annual), December 31, 1998, p. 69.

★1465★
LARGEST QUOTED COMPANIES IN INDONESIA, 1997
Ranked by: Sales, in thousands of U.S. dollars. **Number listed:** 99

1. Astra International Pt, with $2,008,993 thousand
2. Telekomunikasi Indonesia, $747,930
3. Sinar Mas Multiartha, $519,579
4. HM Sampoerna, $393,756
5. Indah Kiat Pulp & Paper Corp. Pt, $373.196
6. Indofood Sukses Makmur, $357,669
7. Hanjaya Mandala Sampoerna, $299,513
8. Polysindo Eka Perkasa, $275.383
9. Matahari Putra Prima, $268,598
10. Pabrik Kertas Tijwi Kimia, $255,754

Source: *Asia's 7,500 Largest Companies*, (annual), Dun & Bradstreet, 1999, p. 63.

★1466★
LEADING COMPANIES IN INDONESIA, 1998
Ranked by: Scores (1-7) based on a survey response of over 4,000 professionals throughout Asia. **Remarks:** Respondents rated companies on their quality of services/products offered and financial soundness. **Number listed:** 10

1. Astra International, with 5.38 a score of
2. Indosat, 5.33
3. Toyota Astra Motor, 5.30
4. Gudang Garam, 5.25
5. Freeport Indonesia, 5.17
6. Bank Bali, 5.08
7. Sampoerna, 5.06
8. United Tractors, 4.84
9. Indofood, 4.83
10. Bank Negara Indonesia, 4.72

Source: *Far Eastern Economic Review*, Review 200 (annual), December 31, 1998, p. 48.

★1467★
MOST EMULATED COMPANIES IN INDONESIA, 1998
Ranked by: Scores (1-7) based on a survey response of over 4,000 professionals throughout Asia. **Remarks:** Specific figures not provided. **Number listed:** 5

1. Astra International
2. Toyota Astra Motor
3. Freeport Indonesia
4. Indosat
5. Indofood

Source: *Far Eastern Economic Review*, Review 200 (annual), December 31, 1998, p. 69.

Corporations, International

★1468★
CORPORATIONS WITH THE HIGHEST SHARE-PRICE GAIN, 1998
Ranked by: Change in share price, in percent. **Number listed:** 10

1. Alitalia, with 566%
2. Banca Intesa, 416%
3. Yahoo, 409%
4. Olivetty, 286%
5. Credito Italiano, 276%
6. Unisys, 257%
7. Cablevision Systems, 239%
8. Capital One Financial, 211%
9. America Online, 202%
10. Banca Commerciale Italiana, 198%

Source: *Business Week*, Global 1,000 (annual), July 13, 1998, p. 52.

★1469★
LARGEST CORPORATIONS WORLDWIDE, 1997
Ranked by: Composite score based on best three out of four rankings in sales, profits, assets, and market value. Specific figures not provided. **Remarks:** Also notes type of business and number of employees. **Number listed:** 50

1. General Electric
2. HSBC Group
3. Royal Dutch/Shell Group
4. Ford Motor
5. General Motors
6. Exxon
7. Toyota Motor
8. International Business Machines
9. Travelers Group
10. Citicorp

Source: *Forbes*, Forbes Foreign Rankings (annual), July 27, 1998, p. 118.

★1470★
LEADING CORPORATIONS WORLDWIDE BY MARKET VALUE, 1998
Ranked by: Market value, in billions of U.S. dollars. **Remarks:** Also notes 1997 rank. **Number listed:** 100

1. General Electric, with $271.64 billion
2. Microsoft, $208.98
3. Royal Dutch/Shell Group, $195.68
4. Coca-Cola, $193.53
5. Exxon, $172.50
6. Merck, $139.85
7. Pfizer, $133.03
8. NTT, $130.91
9. Wal-Mart Stores, $123.47
10. Intel, $121.16

Source: *Business Week*, Global 1,000 (annual), July 13, 1998, p. 53.

★1471★
LEADING CORPORATIONS WORLDWIDE BY RETURN ON EQUITY, 1998
Ranked by: Return on equity, in percent. **Number listed:** 10

1. Northwest Airlines, with 633.7%
2. WPP Group, 521.9%
3. America Online, 454.7%
4. Reuters Group, 274.5%
5. Britannic Assurance, 216.4%
6. US Airways Group, 141.9%
7. Dell Computer, 139.9%
8. Pearson, 132.0%
9. Avon Products, 122.6%
10. UST, 103.0%

Source: *Business Week*, Global 1,000 (annual), July 13, 1998, p. 52.

★1472★
LEADING EMERGING-MARKET CORPORATIONS WORLDWIDE BY MARKET VALUE, 1998
Ranked by: Market value, in millions of U.S. dollars. **Number listed:** 100

1. Gazprom, with $32,906 million
2. Telebras, $32,759
3. China Telecom, $20,676
4. Telefonos de Mexico, $19,999
5. Eletrobras, $18,101
6. Petrobras, $17,871
7. Taiwan Semiconductor Mfg., $14,595
8. Hellenic Telecommunications Organization, $13,334
9. Cathay Life Insurance, $12,748
10. Telecomunicacoes de Sao Paulo, $12,257

Source: *Business Week*, Global 1,000 (annual), July 13, 1998, p. 89+.

★1473★
TOP MANUFACTURING COMPANIES BY REVENUE, 1998
Ranked by: Revenue, in millions of U.S. dollars. **Remarks:** Also notes industry description, earnings per share, profit margin, and profit growth. **Number listed:** 100

1. DaimlerChrysler AG, with $154,476 million
2. General Motors Corp., $154,018
3. Ford Motor Co., $144,416
4. Toyota Motor, $102,939
5. Exxon Corp., $100,697
6. General Electric Co., $100,330
7. Royal Dutch/Shell Group, $93,692
8. IBM Corp., $81,667
9. Volkswagen AG, $80,457
10. Hitachi Ltd., $74,190

Source: *IndustryWeek*, IndustryWeek 1,000, June 7, 1999, p. 59+.

★1474★
WORLD'S LARGEST INDUSTRIAL CORPORATIONS BY ASSETS, 1997
Ranked by: Assets, in millions of dollars. **Remarks:** Also notes overall rank, revenue, profits, stockholders' equity, and number of employees. **Number listed:** 500

1. Bank of Tokyo-Mitsubishi (Japan), with $690,461.7 million
2. Deutsche Bank (Germany), $579,992.2
3. Sumitomo Bank (Japan), $482,707.2
4. Credit Suisse (Switzerland), $472,768
5. HSBC Holdings (Great Britain), $471,256.4
6. Barclays Bank (Great Britain), $451,948.1
7. Dai-Ichi Kangyo Bank (Japan), $432,189.5
8. Sanywa Bank (Japan), $427,077.4
9. Credit Agricole (France), $417,973.9
10. Fuji Bank (Japan), $413,296.2

Source: *Fortune*, The Global 500: World's Biggest Corporations (annual), August 3, 1998, p. F-1+.

★1475★
WORLD'S LARGEST INDUSTRIAL CORPORATIONS BY INCREASE IN PROFITS, 1996-1997
Ranked by: Increase in profits, in percent. **Remarks:** Also notes overall rank and profits. **Number listed:** 50

1. Texas Instruments, with 2,765.1% percent
2. CBS, 1,730%
3. IRI, 926.5%
4. Bankgesellschaft Berlin, 876.7%
5. Thyssen, 518.9%
6. France Telecom, 518.4%
7. Goodyear Tire, 449.4%
8. Delta Air Lines, 447.4%
9. Mitsubishi Trust & Banking Corp., 434.2%
10. Credit Lyonnais, 358.7%

Source: *Fortune*, The Global 500: World's Biggest Corporations (annual), August 3, 1998, p. F-13.

★1476★
WORLD'S LARGEST INDUSTRIAL CORPORATIONS BY INCREASE IN REVENUE, 1996-1997
Ranked by: Increase in revenue, in percent. **Remarks:** Also notes overall rank and revenue. **Number listed:** 50

1. Republic Industries, with 335.7% percent
2. Duke Energy, 242.8%
3. Morgan Stanley Dean Witter, 200.5%
4. Bell Atlantic, 130.8%
5. Boeing, 101.9%
6. AXA, 94.3%
7. NGC, 84.3%
8. SBC Communications, 78.8%
9. Travelers Group, 76.2%
10. Credit Suisse, 74.5%

Source: *Fortune*, The Global 500: World's Biggest Corporations (annual), August 3, 1998, p. F-12.

★1477★
WORLD'S LARGEST INDUSTRIAL CORPORATIONS BY NUMBER OF EMPLOYEES, 1997
Ranked by: Number of employees. **Remarks:** Also notes overall rank, revenue, profits, assets, and stockholders' equity. **Number listed:** 500

1. U.S. Postal Service (U.S.), with $898,384 million
2. Wal-Mart Stores (U.S.), $825,000
3. General Motors (U.S.), $608,000
4. Siemens (Germany), $386,000
5. Ford Motor (U.S.), $363,892
6. Rao Gazprom (Russia), $362,200
7. Hitachi (Japan), $331,494
8. United Parcel Service (U.S.), $331,000
9. Daimler-Benz (Germany), $300,068
10. Sears Roebuck (U.S.), $296,000

Source: *Fortune*, The Global 500: World's Biggest Corporations (annual), August 3, 1998, p. F-1+.

★1478★
WORLD'S LARGEST INDUSTRIAL CORPORATIONS BY PROFITS, 1997
Ranked by: Profits, in millions of dollars. **Remarks:** Also notes previous years' rank, percent change from previous year, and other data. **Number listed:** 500

1. Exxon (U.S.), with $8,460 million
2. General Electric (U.S.), $8,203
3. Royal Dutch/Shell Group (Britain/Netherlands), $7,758.2
4. Intel (U.S.), $6,945
5. Ford Motor (U.S.), $6,920
6. General Motors (U.S.), $6,698
7. Philip Morris (U.S.), $6,310
8. International Business Machines (U.S.), $6,093
9. HSBC Holdings (Great Britain), $5,496
10. Unilever (Britain/Netherlands), $5,463.2

Source: *Fortune*, The Global 500: World's Biggest Corporations (annual), August 3, 1998, p. F-1+.

★1479★
WORLD'S LARGEST INDUSTRIAL CORPORATIONS BY RETURN ON ASSETS, 1997
Ranked by: Profits as a percentage of assets. **Remarks:** Also notes overall rank. **Number listed:** 50

1. Coca-Cola, with 24.4% percent
2. Intel, 24%
3. Microsoft, 24%
4. Dell Computer, 22.1%
5. Glaxo Wellcome, 21.8%
6. Bristol-Myers Squibb, 21.4%
7. Merck, 17.9%
8. Abbott Laboratories, 17.4%

9. Unilever, 17.2%
10. Texas Instruments, 16.6%

Source: *Fortune*, The Global 500: World's Biggest Corporations (annual), August 3, 1998, p. F-14.

★1480★
WORLD'S LARGEST INDUSTRIAL CORPORATIONS BY RETURN ON REVENUE, 1997
Ranked by: Profits as a percentage of revenues. **Remarks:** Also notes overall rank. **Number listed:** 50

1. Microsoft, with 30.4% percent
2. Petronas, 28.4%
3. Intel, 27.7%
4. Sepi, 25.6%
5. Telebras, 24.7%
6. Glaxo Wellcome, 23.2%
7. Coca-Cola, 21.9%
8. Merck, 19.5%
9. Bristol-Myers Squibb, 19.2%
10. Cable & Wireless, 18.4%

Source: *Fortune*, The Global 500: World's Biggest Corporations (annual), August 3, 1998, p. F-14.

★1481★
WORLD'S LARGEST INDUSTRIAL CORPORATIONS BY REVENUE, 1997
Ranked by: Revenue, in millions of dollars. **Remarks:** Also notes previous years' rank, percent change from previous year, and other data. **Number listed:** 500

1. General Motors (U.S.), with $178,174 million
2. Ford Motor (U.S.), $153,627
3. Mitsui (Japan), $142,688.3
4. Mitsuibishi (Japan), $128,922.3
5. Royal Dutch/Shell Group (Britain/Netherlands), $128,141.7
6. Itochu (Japan), $126,631.9
7. Exxon (U.S.), $122,379
8. Wal-Mart Stores (U.S.), $119,299
9. Marubeni (Japan), $111,121.2
10. Sumitomo (Japan), $102,395.2

Source: *Fortune*, The Global 500: World's Biggest Corporations (annual), August 3, 1998, p. F-1+.

★1482★
WORLD'S LARGEST INDUSTRIAL CORPORATIONS BY STOCKHOLDERS' EQUITY, 1997
Ranked by: Stockholders' equity, in millions of dollars. **Remarks:** Also notes overall rank, revenue, profits, assets, and number of employees. **Number listed:** 500

1. Rao Gazprom (Russia), with $73,447.9 million
2. Royal Dutch/Shell Group (Britain/Netherlands), $59,981.8
3. Toyota Motor (Japan), $45,158.2
4. Exxon (U.S.), $43,660
5. State Farm Insurance Co. (U.S.), $37,635.4
6. Nippon Telegraph & Telephone (Japan), $35,989.7
7. Electricite de France (France), $35,220.1
8. Japan Postal Service (Japan), $34,981.8
9. PDVSA (Venezuela), $34,555
10. General Electric (U.S.), $34,438

Source: *Fortune*, The Global 500: World's Biggest Corporations (annual), August 3, 1998, p. F-1+.

Corporations--Iowa

★1483★
TOP CORPORATIONS IN IOWA, 1998
Ranked by: Revenue, in millions of dollars. **Remarks:** Also notes profits, contact information, number of employees, and CEO. **Number listed:** 2

1. Principal Financial Group, with $7,697.4 million
2. Maytag, $4,069.3

Source: *Fortune*, Fortune 500 Largest U.S. Corporations (annual), April 26, 1999, p. F-39.

Corporations--Ireland

★1484★
LARGEST COMPANIES IN IRELAND, 1997
Ranked by: Sales, in thousands of U.S. dollars ($). **Number listed:** 100

1. Intel Ireland Ltd., with $4,703,534 thousand
2. Jefferson Smurfit Group Plc, $3,697,464
3. CRH Plc, $3,460,438
4. Avonmore Waterford Group Plc, $1,880,604
5. Fyffes Plc, $1,878,862
6. Irish Dairy Board Co-operative Ltd., $1,869,126
7. Kerry Group Plc, $1,757,772
8. Bord Telecom Eireann PLC, $1,737,505
9. Dunnes Stores Ltd., $1,639,110
10. Electricity Supply Board, $1,560,639

Source: *Europe's 15,000 Largest Companies (annual)*, Dun & Bradstreet, 1999, p. 80.

★1485★
MOST VALUABLE CORPORATIONS IN IRELAND, 1998
Ranked by: Market value as of May 29, 1998, in millions of U.S. dollars. **Remarks:** Also notes overall rank, share price, percentage change from previous year, price rates, sales, profits, assets, equity, and industry code. **Number listed:** 4

1. Allied Irish Banks, with $11,339 million
2. Bank of Ireland, $9,203
3. Elan, $7,238
4. CRH, $5,550

Source: *Business Week*, Global 1,000 (annual), July 13, 1998, p. 60.

Corporations--Italy

★1486★
ITALY'S LARGEST COMPANIES BY SALES, 1997
Ranked by: Sales, in thousands of U.S. dollars ($). **Number listed:** 100

1. Fiat Spa, with $43,992,730 thousand
2. ENI SpA, $33,491,793
3. Agip Petroli Spa, $22,808,822
4. Enel SpA, $16,950,163
5. Telecom Italia Spa, $16,683,491
6. Fiat Auto Spa, $16,672,588
7. Ferruzzi Finanziaria Spa, $15,107,059
8. Italiana Petroli Spa, $10,589,538
9. EFIBANCA-ente Finanziario Interbancario SpA, $8,067,573

10. Snam Spa, $7,886,511

Source: *Europe's 15,000 Largest Companies (annual)*, Dun & Bradstreet, 1999, p. 79.

★1487★
MOST VALUABLE COMPANIES IN ITALY, 1998
Ranked by: Market value as of May 29, 1998, in millions of U.S. dollars. **Remarks:** Also notes overall rank, share price, percentage change from previous year, price rates, sales, profits, assets, equity, and industry code. **Number listed:** 24

1. ENI, with $56,424 million
2. Telecom Italia, $51,301
3. TIM, $44,943
4. Assicurazioni Generali, $33,062
5. Fiat Group, $21,291
6. Credito Italiano, $16,113
7. Istituto Bancario San Paolo di Torino, $12,888
8. Istituto Nazionale Delle Assicurazioni, $12,470
9. Banca Intesa, $12,050
10. Banca di Roma, $10,963

Source: *Business Week*, Global 1,000 (annual), July 13, 1998, p. 60.

★1488★
TOP CORPORATIONS IN ITALY, 1997
Ranked by: Revenue, in millions of U.S. dollars ($). **Remarks:** Also notes overall rank, type of business, net income, assets, market value, stock price, percentage yield, and number of employees. **Number listed:** 12

1. Fiat Group, with $52,590 million
2. ENI, $35,651
3. Generali Group, $26,759
4. Telecom Italia, $25,140
5. Montedison Group, $13,903
6. Sanpaolo Bank Group, $11,876
7. Banca Commerciale Italiana, $9,925
8. Banca di Roma, $9,379
9. Credito Italiano, $9,126
10. Finmeccanica, $8,973

Source: *Forbes*, Forbes Foreign Rankings (annual), July 27, 1998, p. 132.

Corporations--Japan

★1489★
COMPANIES IN JAPAN WITH THE BEST LONG-TERM VISION BY MANAGEMENT, 1998
Ranked by: Scores (1-7) based on a survey response of over 4,000 professionals throughout Asia. **Remarks:** Specific figures not provided. **Number listed:** 5

1. Sony
2. Kyocera
3. Honda Motor
4. Toyota Motor
5. Mitsubishi Corp.

Source: *Far Eastern Economic Review*, Review 200 (annual), December 31, 1998, p. 72.

★1490★
COMPANIES IN JAPAN WITH THE HIGHEST QUALITY OF PRODUCTS AND SERVICES, 1998
Ranked by: Scores (1-7) based on a survey response of over 4,000 professionals throughout Asia. **Remarks:** Specific figures not provided. **Number listed:** 5

1. Canon
2. Toyota Motor
3. Sony
4. Fuji Photo Film
5. NEC

Source: *Far Eastern Economic Review*, Review 200 (annual), December 31, 1998, p. 72.

★1491★
COMPANIES IN JAPAN WITH THE MOST FINANCIAL SOUNDNESS, 1998
Ranked by: Scores (1-7) based on a survey response of over 4,000 professionals throughout Asia. **Remarks:** Specific figures not provided. **Number listed:** 5

1. Toyota Motor
2. Bank of Tokyo-Mitsubishi
3. Nippon Telegraph & Telephone
4. Sony
5. Hitachi

Source: *Far Eastern Economic Review*, Review 200 (annual), December 31, 1998, p. 72.

★1492★
COMPANIES IN JAPAN WITH THE MOST INNOVATIVE RESPONSES TO CUSTOMER NEEDS, 1998
Ranked by: Scores (1-7) based on a survey response of over 4,000 professionals throughout Asia. **Remarks:** Specific figures not provided. **Number listed:** 5

1. Sony
2. Honda Motor
3. Sega
4. Nintendo
5. Sharp

Source: *Far Eastern Economic Review*, Review 200 (annual), December 31, 1998, p. 72.

★1493★
LARGEST CORPORATIONS IN JAPAN BY MARKET CAPITAL, 1998
Ranked by: Market capital, in billions of Japanese yen. **Number listed:** 50

1. Nippon Telegraph & Telephone, with ¥18,139,680 billion
2. Toyota Motor, ¥13,041,687
3. Bank of Tokyo-Mitsubishi, ¥6,662,523
4. Sony, ¥4,787,605
5. Honda Motor, ¥4,599,234
6. Matsushita Elcctric Industrial, ¥4,583,741
7. Sumitomo Bank, ¥4,067,675
8. Seven-Eleven Japan, ¥3,698,023
9. Tokyo Electric Power, ¥3,585,098
10. Sanwa Bank, ¥3,583,800

Source: *Asian Business*, July, 1998, p. 36.

★1494★
LARGEST QUOTED COMPANIES IN JAPAN BY SALES, 1997
Ranked by: Sales, in thousands of U.S. dollars ($). **Number listed:** 100

1. Mitsui & Co., with $131,103,869 thousand
2. Mitsubishi Corp., $119,069,318
3. Itochu Corp., $116,351,107
4. Marubeni Corp., $102,099,678
5. Sumitomo Corp., $94,082,073
6. Toyota Motor, $87,413,151
7. Nissho Iwai Corp., $75,245,112
8. Nippon Telegraph & Telephone, $70,733,630
9. Hitachi Ltd., $63,000,254
10. Matsushita Electric Industrial Co. Ltd., $59,061,841

Source: *Asia's 7,500 Largest Companies*, (annual), Dun & Bradstreet, 1999, p. 64.

★1495★
LEADING COMPANIES IN JAPAN, 1998
Ranked by: Scores (1-7) based on a survey response of over 4,000 professionals throughout Asia. **Remarks:** Respondents rated companies on their quality of services/products offered and financial soundness. **Number listed:** 10
1. Sony, with 6.46 a score of
2. Toyota Motor, 6.16
3. Honda Motor, 6.06
4. Canon, 5.75
5. Fuji Photo Film, 5.73
6. Matsushita Electric Industrial, 5.55
7. NEC, 5.31
7. Fujitsu, 5.31
9. Kyocera, 5.21
10. Nippon Telegraph & Telephone, 5.18

Source: *Far Eastern Economic Review*, Review 200 (annual), December 31, 1998, p. 48.

★1496★
MOST EMULATED COMPANIES IN JAPAN, 1998
Ranked by: Scores (1-7) based on a survey response of over 4,000 professionals throughout Asia. **Remarks:** Specific figures not provided. **Number listed:** 5
1. Sony
2. Toyota Motor
3. Honda Motor
4. Matsushita Electric Industrial
5. Canon

Source: *Far Eastern Economic Review*, Review 200 (annual), December 31, 1998, p. 72.

★1497★
MOST VALUABLE CORPORATIONS IN JAPAN, 1998
Ranked by: Market value as of May 29, 1998, in millions of U.S. dollars. **Remarks:** Also notes overall rank, share price, percentage change from previous year, price rates, sales, profits, assets, equity, and industry code. **Number listed:** 116
1. Nippon Telegraph & Telephone, with $130,911 million
2. Toyota Motor, $94,345
3. Bank of Tokyo-Mitsubishi, $48,077
4. Sony, $34,382
5. Honda Motor, $33,192
6. Matsushita Electric Industrial, $33,080
7. Sumitomo Bank, $29,356
8. Seven-Eleven Japan, $26,688
9. Tokyo Electric Power, $25,873
10. Sanwa Bank, $25,426

Source: *Business Week*, Global 1,000 (annual), July 13, 1998, p. 60.

★1498★
TOP CORPORATIONS IN JAPAN, 1997
Ranked by: Revenue, in millions of U.S. dollars ($). **Remarks:** Also notes overall rank, type of business, net income, assets, market value, stock price, percentage yield, and number of employees. **Number listed:** 168
1. Mitsui & Co., with $142,754 million
2. Mitsubishi Corp., $128,982
3. Itochu, $126,691
4. Marubeni, $111,173
5. Sumitomo, $102,443
6. Toyota Motor, $95,181
7. Nissho Iwai, $81,932
8. Nippon Tel & Tel, $77,019
9. Hitachi, $68,599
10. Matsushita Electric Indl., $64,310

Source: *Forbes*, Forbes Foreign Rankings (annual), July 27, 1998, p. 134+.

Corporations--Kansas

★1499★
TOP CORPORATIONS IN KANSAS, 1998
Ranked by: Revenue, in millions of dollars. **Remarks:** Also notes profits, contact information, number of employees, and CEO. **Number listed:** 2
1. Sprint, with $17,134.3 million
2. Yellow, $3,112.1

Source: *Fortune*, Fortune 500 Largest U.S. Corporations (annual), April 26, 1999, p. F-39.

Corporations--Kentucky

★1500★
TOP CORPORATIONS IN KENTUCKY, 1998
Ranked by: Revenue, in millions of dollars. **Remarks:** Also notes profits, contact information, number of employees, and CEO. **Number listed:** 6
1. Humana, with $9,781 million
2. Tricon Global Restaurants, $8,468
3. Ashland, $6,933
4. LG & E Energy, $5,528.7
5. Vencor, $3.132.4
6. Lexmark International, $3,020.6

Source: *Fortune*, Fortune 500 Largest U.S. Corporations (annual), April 26, 1999, p. F-39+.

Corporations--Korea, South

★1501★
COMPANIES IN SOUTH KOREA WITH THE BEST LONG-TERM VISION BY MANAGEMENT, 1998
Ranked by: Scores (1-7) based on a survey response of over 4,000 professionals throughout Asia. **Remarks:** Specific figures not provided. **Number listed:** 5
1. Daewoo Corp.
2. Daewoo Heavy Industries
3. Daewoo Electronics
4. Hyundai Corp.
5. Daewoo Motor

Source: *Far Eastern Economic Review*, Review 200 (annual), December 31, 1998, p. 83.

★1502★
COMPANIES IN SOUTH KOREA WITH THE HIGHEST QUALITY OF PRODUCTS AND SERVICES, 1998
Ranked by: Scores (1-7) based on a survey response of over 4,000 professionals throughout Asia. **Remarks:** Specific figures not provided. **Number listed:** 5
1. Samsung Electronics
2. Lotte Shopping
3. Hyundai Motor
4. Asian Airlines
5. Samsung Display Devices

Source: *Far Eastern Economic Review*, Review 200 (annual), December 31, 1998, p. 83.

★1503★
COMPANIES IN SOUTH KOREA WITH THE MOST FINANCIAL SOUNDNESS, 1998
Ranked by: Scores (1-7) based on a survey response of over 4,000 professionals throughout Asia. **Remarks:** Specific figures not provided. **Number listed:** 5
1. Korea Electric Power
2. Kookmin Bank
3. Shinhan Bank
4. Pohang Iron & Steel Co.
5. Samsung Fire & Marine Insurance

Source: *Far Eastern Economic Review*, Review 200 (annual), December 31, 1998, p. 83.

★1504★
COMPANIES IN SOUTH KOREA WITH THE MOST INNOVATIVE RESPONSES TO CUSTOMER NEEDS, 1998
Ranked by: Scores (1-7) based on a survey response of over 4,000 professionals throughout Asia. **Remarks:** Specific figures not provided. **Number listed:** 5
1. Daewoo Motor
2. Daewoo Electronics
3. LG Electronics
4. LG Information & Communications
5. Asiana Airlines

Source: *Far Eastern Economic Review*, Review 200 (annual), December 31, 1998, p. 83.

★1505★
LARGEST QUOTED COMPANIES IN SOUTH KOREA, 1997
Ranked by: Sales, in thousands of U.S. dollars. **Number listed:** 100
1. Samsung, with $24,955,937 thousand
2. Daewoo, $20,150,230
3. Samsung Electronics, $15,497,272
4. LG International, $13,079,311
5. KEPCO, $11,007,973
6. Hyundai Motor Co. Ltd., $9,787,662
7. Korea Electric Power Co. Ltd., $9,717,163
8. SK, $9,028,115
9. POSCO Chemical, $8,156,105
10. LG Electronics, $7,754,930

Source: *Europe's 15,000 Largest Companies (annual)*, Dun & Bradstreet, 1999, p. 65.

★1506★
LEADING COMPANIES IN SOUTH KOREA, 1998
Ranked by: Scores (1-7) based on a survey response of over 4,000 professionals throughout Asia. **Remarks:** Respondents rated companies on their quality of services/products offered and financial soundness. **Number listed:** 10
1. Pohang Iron & Steel Co., with 6.16 a score of
2. Hyundai Motor, 5.98
3. Samsung Electronics, 5.96
4. Samsung Life Insurance, 5.49
5. SK Telecom, 5.47
6. Samsung, 5.45
7. Hyundai Heavy Industries, 5.37
8. Lotte Shopping, 5.34
9. Korea Telecom, 5.25
10. Samsung Fire & Marine Insurance, 5.23

Source: *Far Eastern Economic Review*, Review 200 (annual), December 31, 1998, p. 48.

★1507★
MOST EMULATED COMPANIES IN SOUTH KOREA, 1998
Ranked by: Scores (1-7) based on a survey response of over 4,000 professionals throughout Asia. **Remarks:** Specific figures not provided. **Number listed:** 5
1. Samsung
2. Korean Air
3. Pohang Iron & Steel Co.
4. Hyundai Corp.
5. Hyundai Heavy Industries

Source: *Far Eastern Economic Review*, Review 200 (annual), December 31, 1998, p. 83.

★1508★
TOP CORPORATIONS IN SOUTH KOREA, 1997
Ranked by: Revenue, in millions of U.S. dollars ($). **Remarks:** Also notes overall rank, type of business, net income, assets, market value, stock price, percentage yield, and number of employees. **Number listed:** 26
1. Daewoo, with $33,500 million
2. Samsung, $31,257
3. Hyundai, $26,324
4. Samsung Electronics, $19,411
5. LG International, $16,399
6. SK, $15,480
7. LG Electronics, $14,720
8. Korea Electric Power, $13,788
9. Hyundai Motor, $12,420
10. Pohang Iron and Steel, $12,108

Source: *Forbes*, Forbes Foreign Rankings (annual), July 27, 1998, p. 144+.

Corporations--Maine

★1509★
TOP CORPORATIONS IN MAINE, 1998
Ranked by: Revenue, in millions of dollars. **Remarks:** Also notes profits, contact information, number of employees, and CEO. **Number listed:** 2
1. UNUM, with $4,630.8 million
2. Hannaford Bros., $3,323.6

Source: *Fortune*, Fortune 500 Largest U.S. Corporations (annual), April 26, 1999, p. F-40.

Corporations--Malaysia

★1510★
LARGEST QUOTED COMPANIES IN MALAYSIA, 1999*
Ranked by: Sales, in thousands of U.S. dollars. **Number listed:** 100
1. Sime Darby Bhd, with $3,483,432 thousand
2. Tenaga Nasional Berhad, $2,635,734
3. Edaran Otomobil Nasional Bhd, $1,994,100
4. Telekom Malaysia Bhd, $1,885,938
5. Malaysia Airline System Bhd, $1,706,713
6. Perlis Plantations Bhd, $1,560,386
7. Amsteel Corp. Bhd, $1,464,062
8. Perusahaan Otomobil Nasional Bhd, $1,374,319
9. Berjaya Group Bhd, $1,343,383

10. United Engineers Bhd, $1,130,350

Source: *Asia's 7,500 Largest Companies*, (annual), Dun & Bradstreet, 1999, p. 66.

★1511★
TOP COMPANIES IN MALAYSIA BY MARKET CAPITAL, 1999*
Ranked by: Market capital, in millions of U.S. dollars. **Remarks:** Also notes performance and operating details. **Number listed:** 50

1. Telekom Malaysia, with $5,878.8 millions
2. Tenega Nasional, $4,119.7
3. Malayan Banking, $3,610.7
4. Petronas Gas, $3,604.3
5. Sime Darby, $2,166.9
6. YTL Power International, $1,666.3
7. Genting, $1,492.2
8. Rothmans Malaysia, $1,487.6
9. Malaysian International Shipping, $1,440.5
10. YTL Corporation, $1,393.7

Source: *Asian Business*, April, 1999, p. 38.

Corporations--Maryland

★1512★
TOP CORPORATIONS IN MARYLAND, 1998
Ranked by: Revenue, in millions of dollars. **Remarks:** Also notes profits, contact information, number of employees, and CEO. **Number listed:** 10

1. Lockheed Martin, with $26,266 million
2. Marriott International, $7,968
3. Sodexho Marriott Services, $6,704
4. U.S. Foodservice, $5,506.9
5. Black & Decker, $4,559.9
6. Giant Food, $4,230.6
7. Host Marriott, $3,519
8. Hechinger, $3,449.2
9. BG & E, $3,358.1
10. Integrated Health Services, $2,972.6

Source: *Fortune*, Fortune 500 Largest U.S. Corporations (annual), April 26, 1999, p. F-40.

Corporations--Massachusetts

★1513★
TOP CORPORATIONS IN MASSACHUSETTS, 1998
Ranked by: Revenue, in millions of dollars. **Remarks:** Also notes profits, contact information, number of employees, and CEO. **Number listed:** 16

1. Raytheon, with $19,530 million
2. Liberty Mutual Group, $13,166
3. Massachusetts Mutual Life Insurance, $10,668.1
4. Gilette, $10,056
5. Fleet Financial Group, $10,002
6. John Hancock Mutual Life, $8,911.7
7. TJX, $7,949.1
8. BankBoston Corp., $7,609
9. Staples, $7,123.2
10. Harcourt General, $4,235.3

Source: *Fortune*, Fortune 500 Largest U.S. Corporations (annual), April 26, 1999, p. F-40+.

Corporations--Mexico

★1514★
TOP CORPORATIONS IN MEXICO, 1997
Ranked by: Revenue, in millions of U.S. dollars ($). **Remarks:** Also notes overall rank, type of business, net income, assets, market value, stock price, percentage yield, and number of employees. **Number listed:** 2

1. Telefonos de Mexico, with $7,673 million
2. Grupo Financiero Bancomer, $5,510

Source: *Forbes*, Forbes Foreign Rankings (annual), July 27, 1998, p. 154.

★1515★
TOP MEXICAN COMPANIES, 1999*
Ranked by: Score. **Remarks:** Companies are scored by a combination of five indicators: assets, sales, operating profit, market capitalization and number of employees. **Number listed:** 100

1. Telefonos de Mexico, with 499 points
2. Grupo Carso, 481
3. Cementos Mexicanos, 476
4. Fomento Economico Mexicano, 473
5. Cifra, 472
6. Alfa, 471
7. Grupo Modelo, 469
8. Grupo Industrial Bimbo, 457
9. Grupo Televisa, 451
10. Grupo Mexico, 444

Source: *Business Mexico*, Business Mexico 100 (annual), June, 1999, p. 36.

Corporations--Michigan

★1516★
TOP CORPORATIONS IN MICHIGAN, 1998
Ranked by: Revenue, in millions of dollars. **Remarks:** Also notes profits, contact information, number of employees, and CEO. **Number listed:** 14

1. General Motors, with $161,315 million
2. Ford Motor, $144,416
3. Kmart, $33,674
4. Dow Chemical, $18,441
5. Whirlpool, $10,323
6. Lear, $9,059.4
7. Kellogg, $6,762.1
8. CMS Energy, $5,141
9. Federal-Mogul, $4,468.7
10. Masco, $4,345

Source: *Fortune*, Fortune 500 Largest U.S. Corporations (annual), April 26, 1999, p. F-41.

Corporations--Minnesota

★1517★
TOP CORPORATIONS IN MINNESOTA, 1998
Ranked by: Revenue, in millions of dollars. **Remarks:** Also notes profits, contact information, number of employees, and CEO. **Number listed:** 13

1. Dayton Hudson, with $30,951 million
2. United HealthCare Corp., $17,355
3. Supervalu, $17,201.4

4. Minnesota Mining & Manufacturing, $15,021
5. St. Paul Cos., $9,108.4
6. NWA, $9,044.8
7. Honeywell, $8,426.7
8. Best Buy, $8,358.2
9. U.S. Bancorp, $7,664
10. General Mills, $6,033

Source: *Fortune*, Fortune 500 Largest U.S. Corporations (annual), April 26, 1999, p. F-41+.

Corporations--Mississippi

★1518★
TOP CORPORATIONS IN MISSISSIPPI, 1998
Ranked by: Revenue, in millions of dollars. **Remarks:** Also notes profits, contact information, number of employees, and CEO. **Number listed:** 1

1. MCI WorldCom, with $17,678 million

Source: *Fortune*, Fortune 500 Largest U.S. Corporations (annual), April 26, 1999, p. F-42.

Corporations--Missouri

★1519★
TOP CORPORATIONS IN MISSOURI, 1998
Ranked by: Revenue, in millions of dollars. **Remarks:** Also notes profits, contact information, number of employees, and CEO. **Number listed:** 15

1. Emerson Electric, with $13,447.2 million
2. May Department Stores, $13,413
3. Utilicorp United, $12,563.4
4. Anheuser-Busch, $11,245.8
5. Farmland Industries, $8,775
6. Monsanto, $8,648
7. Ralston Purina, $5,577
8. Genamerica, $3,913.9
9. Graybar Electric, $3,744.1
10. Clark USA, $3,668.2

Source: *Fortune*, Fortune 500 Largest U.S. Corporations (annual), April 26, 1999, p. F-42.

Corporations--Nebraska

★1520★
TOP CORPORATIONS IN NEBRASKA, 1998
Ranked by: Revenue, in millions of dollars. **Remarks:** Also notes profits, contact information, number of employees, and CEO. **Number listed:** 6

1. ConAgra, with $23,840.5 million
2. Berkshire Hathaway, $13,832
3. IBP, $12,848.6
4. Inacom, $4,258.4
5. Mutual of Omaha Insurance, $3,820.1
6. Peter Kiewit Sons, $3,403

Source: *Fortune*, Fortune 500 Largest U.S. Corporations (annual), April 26, 1999, p. F-42+.

Corporations--Netherlands

★1521★
MOST VALUABLE CORPORATIONS IN THE NETHERLANDS, 1998
Ranked by: Market value as of May 29, 1998, in millions of U.S. dollars. **Remarks:** Also notes overall rank, share price, percentage change from previous year, price rates, sales, profits, assets, equity, and industry code. **Number listed:** 24

1. Royal Dutch Petroleum Co., with $122,312 million
2. ING Groep, $64,084
3. Unilever NV, $50,918
4. Aegon, $46,499
5. Philips Electronics, $34,756
6. ABN AMRO Holding N.V., $34,185
7. Koninklijke PTT Nederland, $26,420
8. Koninklijke Ahold, $17,612
9. Akzo Nobel, $14,918
10. Heineken, $12,065

Source: *Business Week*, Global 1,000 (annual), July 13, 1998, p. 66.

★1522★
NETHERLANDS' TOP CORPORATIONS BY SALES, 1997
Ranked by: Sales, in thousands of U.S. dollars. **Number listed:** 100

1. Royal Dutch Petroleum Co. (Shell), with $134,129,295 thousand
2. Unilever NV, $46,844,112
3. Philips Electronics NV, $38,002,872
4. Koninklijke Ahold NV, $25,041,339
5. Internationale Nederlanden Groep NV, $24,258,195
6. SV Holdings NV, $14,837,724
7. Akzo Nobel NV, $11,942,161
8. Nederlandse Gasunie NV, $9,282,460
9. GEC Alsthom NV, $9,085,352
10. Koninklijke KPN NV, $7,939,486

Source: *Europe's 15,000 Largest Companies (annual)*, Dun & Bradstreet, 1999, p. 82.

★1523★
TOP CORPORATIONS IN THE NETHERLANDS, 1997
Ranked by: Revenue, in millions of U.S. dollars ($). **Remarks:** Also notes overall rank, type of business, net income, assets, market value, stock price, percentage yield, and number of employees. **Number listed:** 18

1. Royal Dutch/Shell Group, with $128,108 million
2. Unilever, $48,479
3. Philips Group, $39,181
4. ING Group, $38,724
5. ABN AMRO Holding N.V., $28,940
6. Ahold, $25,916
7. Fortis Group, $23,695
8. Aegon Insurance Group, $16,045
9. Royal KPN, $15,285
10. Akzo Nobel Group, $12,326

Source: *Forbes*, Forbes Foreign Rankings (annual), July 27, 1998, p. 144.

Corporations--New Jersey

★1524★
TOP CORPORATIONS IN NEW JERSEY, 1998
Ranked by: Revenue, in millions of dollars. **Remarks:** Also notes profits, contact information, number of employees, and CEO. **Number listed:** 24

1. Prudential of America Group, with $34,427 million
2. Lucent Technologies, $30,147
3. Merck, $26,898.2
4. Johnson & Johnson, $23,657
5. AlliedSignal, $15,128
6. American Home Products, $13,462.7
7. Toys "R" Us, $11,200
8. Warner-Lambert, $10,213.7
9. BestFoods, $8,374
10. Ingersoll-Rand, $8,291.5

Source: *Fortune*, Fortune 500 Largest U.S. Corporations (annual), April 26, 1999, p. F-43.

Corporations--New York

★1525★
TOP CORPORATIONS IN NEW YORK, 1998
Ranked by: Revenue, in millions of dollars. **Remarks:** Also notes profits, contact information, number of employees, and CEO. **Number listed:** 59

1. IBM, with $81,667 million
2. Citigroup, $76,431
3. Philip Morris, $57,813
4. AT & T, $53,588
5. TIAA-CREF, $35,889.1
6. Merrill Lynch, $35,853
7. American International Group, $33,296
8. Chase Manhattan Corp., $32,379
9. Texaco Inc., $31,707
10. Bell Atlantic, $31,565.9

Source: *Fortune*, Fortune 500 Largest U.S. Corporations (annual), April 26, 1999, p. F-43+.

Corporations--New York Metropolitan Area

★1526★
LEADING VENTURE CAPITAL FIRMS IN THE NEW YORK METROPOLITAN AREA, 1999
Ranked by: Amount invested, in millions of dollars. **Remarks:** Also notes contact information, number of deals, assets, and key industries. **Number listed:** 25

1. Chase Capital Partners, with $1,800.0 million
2. Sprout Group, $171.3
3. Patricof & Co. Ventures Inc., $146.0
4. Venrock Associates, $83.4
5. Morgan Stanley Dean Witter Venture Partners, $78.7
6. BCI Advisors, $67.7
7. Excelsior Private Equity Fund II, $46.3
8. Victory Ventures, $43.6
9. Waller Sutton Management Group, $36.0
10. Sentinel Capital Partners, $33.6

Source: *Crain's New York Business*, January 18, 1999, p. 54.

Corporations--North Carolina

★1527★
TOP CORPORATIONS IN NORTH CAROLINA, 1998
Ranked by: Revenue, in millions of dollars. **Remarks:** Also notes profits, contact information, number of employees, and CEO. **Number listed:** 9

1. BankAmerica Corp., with $50,777 million
2. First Union Corp., $21,543
3. Duke Energy, $17,610
4. Lowe's, $12,244.9
5. Wachovia Corp., $5,913.8
6. VF Corp., $5,478.8
7. Nucor, $4,151.2
8. Carolina Power & Light, $3,130
9. BB & T Corp., $3,009.2

Source: *Fortune*, Fortune 500 Largest U.S. Corporations (annual), April 26, 1999, p. F-45.

Corporations--Norway

★1528★
LARGEST CORPORATIONS IN NORWAY BY SALES, 1997
Ranked by: Sales, in thousands of U.S. dollars ($). **Number listed:** 100

1. Den Norske Stats Oljeselskap AS Statoil, with $11,345,824 thousand
2. Kvaerner AS, $7,956,466
3. Orkla ASA, $3,352,432
4. Storebrand Konsern, $3,464,115
5. Telenor Konsern, $3,012,310
6. Aker AS, $2,841,109
7. ABB Konsernet I Norge, $2,825,959
8. Norsk Hydro Produksjon AS, $2,696,269
9. Esso Norge AS, $1,818,527
10. Norske Skogindustrier AS, $1,802,358

Source: *Europe's 15,000 Largest Companies (annual)*, Dun & Bradstreet, 1999, p. 81.

★1529★
MOST VALUABLE CORPORATIONS IN NORWAY, 1998
Ranked by: Market value as of May 29, 1998, in millions of U.S. dollars. **Remarks:** Also notes overall rank, share price, percentage change from previous year, price rates, sales, profits, assets, equity, and industry code. **Number listed:** 2

1. Norsk Hydro, with $10,401 million
2. Orkla, $4,422

Source: *Business Week*, Global 1,000 (annual), July 13, 1998, p. 66.

★1530★
TOP CORPORATIONS IN NORWAY, 1997
Ranked by: Revenue, in millions of U.S. dollars ($). **Remarks:** Also notes overall rank, type of business, net income, assets, market value, stock price, percentage yield, and number of employees. **Number listed:** 3

1. Norsk Hydro, with $13,596 million
2. Kvaerner, $10,315
3. SAS, $5,099

Source: *Forbes*, Forbes Foreign Rankings (annual), July 27, 1998, p. 154.

Corporations--Ohio

★1531★
TOP CORPORATIONS IN OHIO, 1998
Ranked by: Revenue, in millions of dollars. **Remarks:** Also notes profits, contact information, number of employees, and CEO. **Number listed:** 27
1. Procter & Gamble, with $37,154 million
2. Kroger, $28,203.3
3. Cardinal Health, $15,918.1
4. Federated Department Stores, $15,833
5. Nationwide Insurance Enterprise, $13,105
6. Dana, $12,838.7
7. Goodyear Tire, $12,648.7
8. TRW, $11,886
9. Limited, $9,346.9
10. National City Corp., $8,070.8

Source: *Fortune*, Fortune 500 Largest U.S. Corporations (annual), April 26, 1999, p. F-46.

Corporations--Oklahoma

★1532★
TOP CORPORATIONS IN OKLAHOMA, 1998
Ranked by: Revenue, in millions of dollars. **Remarks:** Also notes profits, contact information, number of employees, and CEO. **Number listed:** 3
1. Fleming, with $15,069.3 million
2. Phillips Petroleum, $11,845
3. Williams, $7,658.3

Source: *Fortune*, Fortune 500 Largest U.S. Corporations (annual), April 26, 1999, p. F-46.

Corporations--Oregon

★1533★
TOP CORPORATIONS IN OREGON, 1998
Ranked by: Revenue, in millions of dollars. **Remarks:** Also notes profits, contact information, number of employees, and CEO. **Number listed:** 4
1. Fred Meyer, with $14,878.8 million
2. Nike, $9,553.1
3. Pacificorp, $9,442.5
4. Willamette Industries, $3,700.3

Source: *Fortune*, Fortune 500 Largest U.S. Corporations (annual), April 26, 1999, p. F-47.

Corporations--Pennsylvania

★1534★
TOP CORPORATIONS IN PENNSYLVANIA, 1998
Ranked by: Revenue, in millions of dollars. **Remarks:** Also notes profits, contact information, number of employees, and CEO. **Number listed:** 27
1. USX, with $24,754 million
2. Cigna, $21,437
3. Alcoa, $15,489.4
4. Rite Aid, $11,375.1
5. H.J. Heinz, $9,209.3
6. Amerisource Health, $8,575.4
7. Crown Cork & Seal, $8,300
8. PNC Bank, $7,936
9. PPG Industries, $7,510
10. Unisource, $7,417.3

Source: *Fortune*, Fortune 500 Largest U.S. Corporations (annual), April 26, 1999, p. F-47.

Corporations--Philadelphia Metropolitan Area

★1535★
LARGEST VENTURE CAPITAL FIRMS IN THE PHILADELPHIA AREA, 1998*
Ranked by: Total capital raised, in millions of dollars. **Remarks:** Also notes contact information, size of investment, sources of capital, and managing partner. **Number listed:** 25
1. Nassau Capital LLC, with $1,500 million
2. Patricof & Co. Ventures Inc., $1,200
3. First Union Capital Partners, $750
4. TL Ventures, $540
5. Domain Associates, $450
6. SCP Private Equity Partners LP, $265
7. Mellon Ventures, Inc., $250
8. Bachow & Associates Inc., $225
9. Edison Venture Fund LP, $210
10. Hillman Medical Ventures/Rock Hill Ventures Inc., $150

Source: *Book of Business Lists*, (annual), Philadelphia Business Journal, December 25, 1998, p. 34.

Corporations--Philippines

★1536★
COMPANIES IN THE PHILIPPINES WITH THE BEST LONG-TERM VISION BY MANAGEMENT, 1998
Ranked by: Scores (1-7) based on a survey response of over 4,000 professionals throughout Asia. **Remarks:** Specific figures not provided. **Number listed:** 5
1. Ayala Corp.
2. Jollibee Foods
3. San Miguel Corp.
4. Shoemart
5. ABS-CBN Broadcasting Corp.

Source: *Far Eastern Economic Review*, Review 200 (annual), December 31, 1998, p. 78.

★1537★
COMPANIES IN THE PHILIPPINES WITH THE HIGHEST QUALITY OF PRODUCTS AND SERVICES, 1998
Ranked by: Scores (1-7) based on a survey response of over 4,000 professionals throughout Asia. **Remarks:** Specific figures not provided. **Number listed:** 5
1. San Miguel Corp.
2. Jollibee Foods
3. Pure Foods Corp.
4. RFM Corp.
5. ABS-CBN Broadcasting Corp.

Source: *Far Eastern Economic Review*, Review 200 (annual), December 31, 1998, p. 78.

★1538★
COMPANIES IN THE PHILIPPINES WITH THE MOST FINANCIAL SOUNDNESS, 1998
Ranked by: Scores (1-7) based on a survey response of over 4,000 professionals throughout Asia. **Remarks:** Specific figures not provided. **Number listed:** 5
1. Bank of the Philippine Islands
2. Ayala Corp.
3. Metropolitan Bank & Trust
4. Far East Bank & Trust
5. Manila Electric Co.

Source: *Far Eastern Economic Review*, Review 200 (annual), December 31, 1998, p. 78.

★1539★
COMPANIES IN THE PHILIPPINES WITH THE MOST INNOVATIVE RESPONSES TO CUSTOMER NEEDS, 1998
Ranked by: Scores (1-7) based on a survey response of over 4,000 professionals throughout Asia. **Remarks:** Specific figures not provided. **Number listed:** 5
1. Jollibee Foods
2. Smart Communications
3. ABS-CBN Broadcasting Corp.
4. Shoemart
5. San Miguel Corp.

Source: *Far Eastern Economic Review*, Review 200 (annual), December 31, 1998, p. 78.

★1540★
LARGEST QUOTED COMPANIES IN THE PHILIPPINES, 1999*
Ranked by: Sales, in thousands of U.S. dollars. **Number listed:** 100
1. San Miguel Corp., with $2,193,497 thousand
2. Philippine Long Distance Telephone Co., $919,133
3. Ayala Corp., $803,896
4. RFM Corp., $352,522
5. Ayala Land Inc., $318,745
6. Bacnotan Consolidated Industries Inc., $313,301
7. Universal Robina Corporation, $279,860
8. DMCI Holdings, $250,083
9. C & P Homes, $242,858
10. Metro Pacific Corp., $239,194

Source: *Asia's 7,500 Largest Companies*, (annual), Dun & Bradstreet, 1999, p. 67.

★1541★
LEADING COMPANIES IN THE PHILIPPINES, 1998
Ranked by: Scores (1-7) based on a survey response of over 4,000 professionals throughout Asia. **Remarks:** Respondents rated companies on their quality of services/products offered and financial soundness. **Number listed:** 10
1. Jollibee Foods, with 6.30 a score of
2. Ayala Corp., 6.10
3. ABS-CBN Broadcasting Corp., 5.97
4. Shoemart, 5.95
5. Bank of the Philippine Islands, 5.87
6. San Miguel Corp., 5.68
7. Metropolitan Bank & Trust, 5.39
8. Manila Electric Co., 5.33
9. Smart Communications, 5.33
9. Pure Foods Corp., 5.11

Source: *Far Eastern Economic Review*, Review 200 (annual), December 31, 1998, p. 48.

★1542★
MOST EMULATED COMPANIES IN THE PHILIPPINES, 1998
Ranked by: Scores (1-7) based on a survey response of over 4,000 professionals throughout Asia. **Remarks:** Specific figures not provided. **Number listed:** 5
1. Jollibee Foods
2. San Miguel Corp.
3. Shoemart
4. Ayala Corp.
5. ABS-CBN Broadcasting Corp.

Source: *Far Eastern Economic Review*, Review 200 (annual), December 31, 1998, p. 78.

Corporations--Portugal

★1543★
MOST VALUABLE CORPORATIONS IN PORTUGAL, 1998
Ranked by: Market value as of May 29, 1998, in millions of U.S. dollars. **Remarks:** Also notes overall rank, share price, percentage change from previous year, price rates, sales, profits, assets, equity, and industry code. **Number listed:** 4
1. Electricidade De Portugal, with $15,785 million
2. Portugal Telecom, $9,997
3. Banco Comercial Portugues, $6,318
4. Banco Espirito Santo e Comercial de Lisboa, $4,140

Source: *Business Week*, Global 1,000 (annual), July 13, 1998, p. 66.

★1544★
PORTUGAL'S TOP CORPORATIONS BY SALES, 1999*
Ranked by: Sales, in thousands of U.S. dollars. **Number listed:** 100
1. Petrogal-Petroleos De Portugal SA, with $4,385,081 thousand
2. Portugal Telecom SA, $2,123,750
3. Rede Electrica Nacional SA, $1,628,586
4. Electricidade Do Norte SA, $1,134,672
5. Tabaqueira-Empresa Industrial De Tabacos SA, $1,107,549
6. Transportes Aereos Portugueses SA, $1,080,349
7. Companhia Portuguesa De Producao De Elecricadade, $1,063,122
8. BP Portuguesa SA, $1,039,776
9. Shell Portuguesa SA, $835,152
10. Modelo Continente Hipermercados SA, $633,187

Source: *Europe's 15,000 Largest Companies (annual)*, Dun & Bradstreet, 1999, p. 83.

Corporations--Rhode Island

★1545★
TOP CORPORATIONS IN RHODE ISLAND, 1998
Ranked by: Revenue, in millions of dollars. **Remarks:** Also notes profits, contact information, number of employees, and CEO. **Number listed:** 3
1. CVS, with $15,273.6 million
2. Textron, $11,549
3. Hasbro, $3,304.5

Source: *Fortune*, Fortune 500 Largest U.S. Corporations (annual), April 26, 1999, p. F-48.

Corporations--Singapore

★1546★
COMPANIES IN SINGAPORE WITH THE BEST LONG-TERM VISION BY MANAGEMENT, 1998
Ranked by: Scores (1-7) based on a survey response of over 4,000 professionals throughout Asia. **Remarks:** Specific figures not provided. **Number listed:** 5
1. Singapore Airlines
2. Creative Technology
3. Development Bank of Singapore
4. Singapore Telecom
5. DBS Land

Source: *Far Eastern Economic Review*, Review 200 (annual), December 31, 1998, p. 81.

★1547★
COMPANIES IN SINGAPORE WITH THE HIGHEST QUALITY OF PRODUCTS AND SERVICES, 1998
Ranked by: Scores (1-7) based on a survey response of over 4,000 professionals throughout Asia. **Remarks:** Specific figures not provided. **Number listed:** 5
1. Singapore Airlines
2. Shangri-La Hotels
3. Singapore MRT
4. Asia Pacific Breweries
5. Cycle & Carriage

Source: *Far Eastern Economic Review*, Review 200 (annual), December 31, 1998, p. 81.

★1548★
COMPANIES IN SINGAPORE WITH THE MOST FINANCIAL SOUNDNESS, 1998
Ranked by: Scores (1-7) based on a survey response of over 4,000 professionals throughout Asia. **Remarks:** Specific figures not provided. **Number listed:** 5
1. Development Bank of Singapore
2. Singapore Airlines
3. Oversea-Chinese Banking Corp.
4. Singapore Telecom
5. United Overseas Bank

Source: *Far Eastern Economic Review*, Review 200 (annual), December 31, 1998, p. 81.

★1549★
COMPANIES IN SINGAPORE WITH THE MOST INNOVATIVE RESPONSES TO CUSTOMER NEEDS, 1998
Ranked by: Scores (1-7) based on a survey response of over 4,000 professionals throughout Asia. **Remarks:** Specific figures not provided. **Number listed:** 5
1. Creative Technology
2. Singapore Airlines
3. Singapore Telecom
4. Shangri-La Hotels
5. Singapore MRT

Source: *Far Eastern Economic Review*, Review 200 (annual), December 31, 1998, p. 81.

★1550★
LARGEST COMPANIES IN SINGAPORE BY SALES, 1999*
Ranked by: Sales, in thousands of U.S. dollars. **Number listed:** 100
1. Singapore Airlines, with $4,674,069 thousands
2. Singapore Telecommunications, $2,990,741
3. Keppel Corp. Ltd., $2,086,414
4. Fraser & Neave Ltd., $1,665,658
5. Neptune Orient Lines Ltd., $1,617,186
6. Natsteel Ltd., $1,615,086
7. City Developments Ltd., $1,494,886
8. Asia Pulp & Paper Co. Ltd., $1,444,577
9. Sembawang Corp. Ltd., $1,180,332
10. Singapore Petroleum Co. Ltd., $1,080,665

Source: *Asia's 7,500 Largest Companies*, (annual), Dun & Bradstreet, 1999, p. 68.

★1551★
LEADING COMPANIES IN SINGAPORE, 1998
Ranked by: Scores (1-7) based on a survey response of over 4,000 professionals throughout Asia. **Remarks:** Respondents rated companies on their quality of services/products offered and financial soundness. **Number listed:** 10
1. Singapore Airlines, with 6.46
2. Singapore MRT, 5.44
3. Creative Technology, 5.41
4. Development Bank of Singapore, 5.27
5. Singapore Telecom, 5.20
6. Shangri-La Hotels, 5.00
7. Singapore Press Holdings, 4.91
8. United Overseas Bank, 4.89
9. Oversea-Chinese Banking Corp., 4.85
10. Asia Pacific Breweries, 4.81

Source: *Far Eastern Economic Review*, Review 200 (annual), December 31, 1998, p. 48.

★1552★
MOST EMULATED COMPANIES IN SINGAPORE, 1998
Ranked by: Scores (1-7) based on a survey response of over 4,000 professionals throughout Asia. **Remarks:** Specific figures not provided. **Number listed:** 5
1. Singapore Airlines
2. Creative Technology
3. Shangri-La Hotels
4. Singapore Telecom
5. Singapore MRT

Source: *Far Eastern Economic Review*, Review 200 (annual), December 31, 1998, p. 81.

★1553★
MOST VALUABLE CORPORATIONS IN SINGAPORE, 1998
Ranked by: Market value as of May 29, 1998, in millions of U.S. dollars. **Remarks:** Also notes overall rank, share price, percentage change from previous year, price rates, sales, profits, assets, equity, and industry code. **Number listed:** 4
1. Singapore Telecommunications, with $21,499 million
2. Singapore Airlines, $7,125
3. Development Bank of Singapore, $5,555
4. OCBC Overseas Chinese Bank, $4,820

Source: *Business Week*, Global 1,000 (annual), July 13, 1998, p. 68.

Corporations--South Africa

★1554★
TOP CORPORATIONS IN SOUTH AFRICA, 1997
Ranked by: Revenue, in millions of U.S. dollars ($). **Remarks:** Also notes overall rank, type of business, net income, assets, market value, stock price, percentage yield, and number of employees. **Number listed:** 5
1. South African Breweries, with $6,676 million
2. Smith (CG), $6,401
3. AMIC-Anglo American, $6,050

4. Liberty Holdings, $6,001
5. Standard Bank Investment, $4,962

Source: *Forbes*, Forbes Foreign Rankings (annual), July 27, 1998, p. 154.

Corporations--Spain

★1555★
MOST VALUABLE CORPORATIONS IN SPAIN, 1998
Ranked by: Market value as of May 29, 1998, in millions of U.S. dollars. **Remarks:** Also notes overall rank, share price, percentage change from previous year, price rates, sales, profits, assets, equity, and industry code. **Number listed:** 11

1. Telefonica, with $45,854 million
2. Banco Bilbao Vizcaya, $34,025
3. Banco de Santander, $28,930
4. Endesa, $24,950
5. Repsol, $16,694
6. Iberdrola, $14,895
7. Banco Central, $12,094
8. Argentaria, Corp. Bancaria de Espana, $10,452
9. Gas Natural SDG, $10,219
10. Banco Popular Espanol, $8,800

Source: *Business Week*, Global 1,000 (annual), July 13, 1998, p. 68.

★1556★
SPAIN'S TOP CORPORATIONS BY SALES, 1999*
Ranked by: Sales, in thousands of U.S. dollars. **Number listed:** 100

1. Repsol SA, with $21,140,494 thousand
2. Telefonica SA, $15,567,206
3. Repsol Petroleo SA, $9,387,351
4. Repsol Comercial de Productos Petroliferos SA, $9,009,413
5. Empresa Nacional De Electricidad SA, $8,447,918
6. Compania Espanola de Petroleos SA, $6,588,274
7. Tabacalera, SA, $5,951,482
8. Iberdrola SA, $5,403,708
9. SEAT SA, $5,098,214
10. El Corte Ingles SA, $4,989,137

Source: *Europe's 15,000 Largest Companies (annual)*, Dun & Bradstreet, 1999, p. 76.

★1557★
TOP CORPORATIONS IN SPAIN, 1997
Ranked by: Revenue, in millions of U.S. dollars ($). **Remarks:** Also notes overall rank, type of business, net income, assets, market value, stock price, percentage yield, and number of employees. **Number listed:** 9

1. Repsol, with $16,522 million
2. Telefonica, $16,140
3. Banco Santander, $15,093
4. Banco Bilbao Vizcaya, $12,645
5. Endesa Group, $8,506
6. Cepsa-Cia Espanola de Pet, $7,121
7. Banco Central Hispanoamer, $6,727
8. Argentaria, $6,039
9. Iberdrola, $5,533

Source: *Forbes*, Forbes Foreign Rankings (annual), July 27, 1998, p. 145.

Corporations--Sweden

★1558★
MOST VALUABLE CORPORATIONS IN SWEDEN, 1998
Ranked by: Market value as of May 29, 1998, in millions of U.S. dollars. **Remarks:** Also notes overall rank, share price, percentage change from previous year, price rates, sales, profits, assets, equity, and industry code. **Number listed:** 22

1. L. M. Ericsson, with $55,624 million
2. Astra, $32,854
3. ABB AB, $15,117
4. Volvo, $14,071
5. Hennes & Mauritz, $11,624
6. Investor, $11,116
7. Foereningssparbanken, $10,582
8. Svenska Handelsbanken, $9,989
9. Skandinaviska Enskilda Banken, $9,803
10. Nordbanken Holding, $9,066

Source: *Business Week*, Global 1,000 (annual), July 13, 1998, p. 68.

★1559★
SWEDEN'S TOP CORPORATIONS BY SALES, 1999*
Ranked by: Sales, in thousands of U.S. dollars. **Number listed:** 100

1. Volvo, with $19,712,510 thousand
2. Telefonaktiebolaget LM Ericsson, $15,686,493
3. Electrolux AB, $13,894,502
4. Volvo Personvagnar AB, $10,549,338
5. Svenska Cellulosa Aktiebolaget SCA, $6,998,408
6. Volvo Lastvagnar AB, $6,322,251
7. Skanska AB, $5,996,362
8. Stora Kopparbergs Berglags AB, $5,704,451
9. Telia AB, $5,570,432
10. ICA Handlarnas AB, $5,112,924

Source: *Europe's 15,000 Largest Companies (annual)*, Dun & Bradstreet, 1999, p. 84.

★1560★
TOP CORPORATIONS IN SWEDEN, 1997
Ranked by: Revenue, in millions of U.S. dollars ($). **Remarks:** Also notes overall rank, type of business, net income, assets, market value, stock price, percentage yield, and number of employees. **Number listed:** 16

1. ABB Group, with $31,021 million
2. Volvo Group, $24,042
3. L.M. Ericsson, $21,970
4. Electrolux Group, $14,800
5. Skandia Insurance, $9,497
6. Merita Nordbanken, $9,318
7. Svenska Handelsbanken, $8,342
8. SCA-Svenska Cellulosa, $7,675
9. Skanska, $7,184
10. Forenings Sparbanken, $7,049

Source: *Forbes*, Forbes Foreign Rankings (annual), July 27, 1998, p. 148.

Corporations--Switzerland

★1561★
MOST VALUABLE CORPORATIONS IN SWITZERLAND, 1998
Ranked by: Market value as of May 29, 1998, in millions of U.S. dollars. **Remarks:** Also notes overall rank, share price,

percentage change from previous year, price rates, sales, profits, assets, equity, and industry code. **Number listed:** 20

1. Novartis, with $116,174 million
2. Roche Holding, $98,901
3. Nestle, $84,399
4. Credit Suisse Group, $58,592
5. UBS, $43,186
6. Swiss RE, $33,747
7. Zurich Insurance Group, $29,342
8. Swiss Bank Corp., $28,764
9. ABB AG, $15,720
10. Clariant, $9,512

Source: *Business Week*, Global 1,000 (annual), July 13, 1998, p. 68.

★1562★
SWITZERLAND'S TOP CORPORATIONS BY SALES, 1998
Ranked by: Sales, in thousands of U.S. dollars. **Number listed:** 99

1. Nestle SA, with $48,062,345 thousand
2. Glencore International AG, $39,824,224
3. ABB Asea Brown Boveri AG, $31,342,351
4. Novartis AG, $21,408,953
5. F Hoffmann-La Roche AG, $12,885,883
6. Migros-Genossenschafts-Bund, $11,847,020
7. PTT, $10,439,439
8. Krafts Jacobs Suchard AG, $8,788,794
9. SairGroup AG, $8,672,068
10. Coop Switzerland AG, $8,184,564

Source: *Europe's 15,000 Largest Companies (annual)*, Dun & Bradstreet, 1999, p. 73.

★1563★
TOP CORPORATIONS IN SWITZERLAND, 1997
Ranked by: Revenue, in millions of U.S. dollars ($). **Remarks:** Also notes overall rank, type of business, net income, assets, market value, stock price, percentage yield, and number of employees. **Number listed:** 16

1. Credit Suisse Group, with $48,641 million
2. Nestle, $48,230
3. ABB Group, $31,021
4. Zurich Insurance Group, $26,456
5. Novartis Group, $21,484
6. UBS, $19,393
7. Swiss Bank Corp., $16,424
8. Swiss Reinsurance Group, $14,415
9. Roche Group, $12,931
10. Adecco, $7,877

Source: *Forbes*, Forbes Foreign Rankings (annual), July 27, 1998, p. 150.

Corporations--Taiwan

★1564★
COMPANIES IN TAIWAN WITH THE BEST LONG-TERM VISION BY MANAGEMENT, 1998
Ranked by: Scores (1-7) based on a survey response of over 4,000 professionals throughout Asia. **Remarks:** Specific figures not provided. **Number listed:** 5

1. Acer
2. Taiwan Semiconductor Manufacturing Co.
3. Evergreen Marine
4. Formosa Plastics
5. President Enterprises

Source: *Far Eastern Economic Review*, Review 200 (annual), December 31, 1998, p. 85.

★1565★
COMPANIES IN TAIWAN WITH THE HIGHEST QUALITY OF PRODUCTS AND SERVICES, 1998
Ranked by: Scores (1-7) based on a survey response of over 4,000 professionals throughout Asia. **Remarks:** Specific figures not provided. **Number listed:** 5

1. EVA Airways
2. Taiwan Semiconductor Manufacturing Co.
3. Evergreen Marine
4. Acer
5. Nan Ya Plastics

Source: *Far Eastern Economic Review*, Review 200 (annual), December 31, 1998, p. 85.

★1566★
COMPANIES IN TAIWAN WITH THE MOST FINANCIAL SOUNDNESS, 1998
Ranked by: Scores (1-7) based on a survey response of over 4,000 professionals throughout Asia. **Remarks:** Specific figures not provided. **Number listed:** 5

1. Cathay Life Insurance
2. Taiwan Power
3. Chinese Petroleum
4. Taiwan Cement
5. Taiwan Sugar Corp.

Source: *Far Eastern Economic Review*, Review 200 (annual), December 31, 1998, p. 85.

★1567★
COMPANIES IN TAIWAN WITH THE MOST INNOVATIVE RESPONSES TO CUSTOMER NEEDS, 1998
Ranked by: Scores (1-7) based on a survey response of over 4,000 professionals throughout Asia. **Remarks:** Specific figures not provided. **Number listed:** 5

1. EVA Airways
2. President Enterprises
3. Acer Peripherals Inc.
4. Acer
5. Chinatrust Commercial Bank

Source: *Far Eastern Economic Review*, Review 200 (annual), December 31, 1998, p. 85.

★1568★
LARGEST COMPANIES IN TAIWAN BY SALES, 1998
Ranked by: Sales, in thousands of U.S. dollars. **Number listed:** 100

1. Nan Ya Plastics Corp., with $2,948,142 thousand
2. China Steel Corp., $2,735,271
3. Hotai Motor Co. Ltd., $1,798,165
4. China Air Lines, $1,736,359
5. Yue Loong Motor, $1,439,390
6. Formosa Chemicals & Fibre Corp., $1,401,057
7. Taiwan Semiconductor Mfg., $1,365,925
8. Inventec, $1,268,583
9. Formosa Plastics Corp., $1,243,587
10. Yulon Motor Co. Ltd., $1,103,000

Source: *Asia's 7,500 Largest Companies*, (annual), Dun & Bradstreet, 1999, p. 69.

★1569★
LEADING COMPANIES IN TAIWAN, 1998
Ranked by: Scores (1-7) based on a survey response of over 4,000 professionals throughout Asia. **Remarks:** Respondents rated companies on their quality of services/products offered and financial soundness. **Number listed:** 10

1. Taiwan Semiconductor Manufacturing Co., with 6.05

2. Acer, 6.03
3. Evergreen Marine, 5.81
4. Formosa Plastics, 5.66
4. EVA Airways, 5.66
6. President Enterprises, 5.53
7. Nan Ya Plastics, 5.44
8. Cathay Life Insurance, 5.07
8. Far Eastern Textile, 5.07
10. Chinatrust Commercial Bank, 5.00

Source: *Far Eastern Economic Review*, Review 200 (annual), December 31, 1998, p. 48.

★1570★
MOST EMULATED COMPANIES IN TAIWAN, 1998
Ranked by: Scores (1-7) based on a survey response of over 4,000 professionals throughout Asia. **Remarks:** Specific figures not provided. **Number listed:** 5

1. Taiwan Semiconductor Manufacturing Co.
2. Formosa Plastics
3. Acer
4. President Enterprises
5. Evergreen Marine

Source: *Far Eastern Economic Review*, Review 200 (annual), December 31, 1998, p. 85.

Corporations--Tennessee

★1571★
TOP CORPORATIONS IN TENNESSEE, 1998
Ranked by: Revenue, in millions of dollars. **Remarks:** Also notes profits, contact information, number of employees, and CEO. **Number listed:** 7

1. Columbia/HCA Healthcare, with $18,881 million
2. FDX, $15,872.8
3. Eastman Chemical, $4,481
4. Provident Companies, $3,904
5. Service Merchandise, $3,327.3
6. AutoZone, $3,242.9
7. Dollar General, $3,221

Source: *Fortune*, Fortune 500 Largest U.S. Corporations (annual), April 26, 1999, p. F-48.

Corporations--Texas

★1572★
TOP CORPORATIONS IN TEXAS, 1998
Ranked by: Revenue, in millions of dollars. **Remarks:** Also notes profits, contact information, number of employees, and CEO. **Number listed:** 36

1. Exxon, with $100,697 million
2. Enron, $31,260
3. Compaq Computer, $31,169
4. J.C. Penney, $30,678
5. SBC Communications, $28,777
6. GTE, $25,473
7. AMR, $19,205
8. Dell Computer, $18,243
9. Halliburton, $17,353.1
10. Electronic Data Systems, $16,891

Source: *Fortune*, Fortune 500 Largest U.S. Corporations (annual), April 26, 1999, p. F-48+.

Corporations--Thailand

★1573★
COMPANIES IN THAILAND WITH THE BEST LONG-TERM VISION BY MANAGEMENT, 1998
Ranked by: Scores (1-7) based on a survey response of over 4,000 professionals throughout Asia. **Remarks:** Specific figures not provided. **Number listed:** 5

1. Charoen Pokphand Group
2. Shinawatra Group
3. Thai Farmers Bank
4. Telecom Asia Corporation
5. Nation Publishing Group

Source: *Far Eastern Economic Review*, Review 200 (annual), December 31, 1998, p. 87.

★1574★
COMPANIES IN THAILAND WITH THE HIGHEST QUALITY OF PRODUCTS AND SERVICES, 1998
Ranked by: Scores (1-7) based on a survey response of over 4,000 professionals throughout Asia. **Remarks:** Specific figures not provided. **Number listed:** 5

1. Dusit Thani
2. Thai Airways International
3. Siam Cement
4. Nation Publishing Group
5. Srithai Superware

Source: *Far Eastern Economic Review*, Review 200 (annual), December 31, 1998, p. 87.

★1575★
COMPANIES IN THAILAND WITH THE MOST FINANCIAL SOUNDNESS, 1998
Ranked by: Scores (1-7) based on a survey response of over 4,000 professionals throughout Asia. **Remarks:** Specific figures not provided. **Number listed:** 5

1. Bangkok Bank
2. Krung Thai Bank
3. Thai Farmers Bank
4. Petroleum Authority of Thailand
5. Electricity Generating Authority of Thailand

Source: *Far Eastern Economic Review*, Review 200 (annual), December 31, 1998, p. 87.

★1576★
COMPANIES IN THAILAND WITH THE MOST INNOVATIVE RESPONSES TO CUSTOMER NEEDS, 1998
Ranked by: Scores (1-7) based on a survey response of over 4,000 professionals throughout Asia. **Remarks:** Specific figures not provided. **Number listed:** 5

1. Grammy Entertainment
2. Dusit Thani
3. Serm Suk
4. Nation Publishing Group
5. Saha Pathanapibul

Source: *Far Eastern Economic Review*, Review 200 (annual), December 31, 1998, p. 87.

★1577★
LARGEST QUOTED COMPANIES IN THAILAND, 1998
Ranked by: Sales, in thousands of U.S. dollars. **Number listed:** 100

1. Thai Airways International, with $2,402,633 thousand
2. Thai Oil Co. Ltd., $1,690,516
3. Seagate Technology, $883,824
4. Siam Makro Pcl, $874,458

5. MMC Sittipol Co. Ltd., $873,284
6. Thai Petrochemical Industry Co., $839,012
7. Bangkok Produce Merchandising Co. Ltd., $586,611
8. Siam Nissan Automobile Co. Ltd., $564,495
9. Finance One Pcl, $484,334
10. Charoen Pokphand Feedmill Public Ltd., $464,142

Source: *Asia's 7,500 Largest Companies*, (annual), Dun & Bradstreet, 1999, p. 70.

★1578★
LEADING COMPANIES IN THAILAND, 1998
Ranked by: Scores (1-7) based on a survey response of over 4,000 professionals throughout Asia. **Remarks:** Respondents rated companies on their quality of services/products offered and financial soundness. **Number listed:** 10

1. Charoen Pokphand Group, with 5.82 a score of
2. Thai Farmers Bank, 5.65
3. Bangkok Bank, 5.58
4. Siam Cement, 5.54
5. Shinawatra Group, 5.38
6. Dusit Thani, 5.33
7. Petroleum Authority of Thailand, 5.30
8. Grammy Entertainment, 5.18
9. Thai Airways International, 5.14
10. Nation Publishing Group, 5.11

Source: *Far Eastern Economic Review*, Review 200 (annual), December 31, 1998, p. 48.

★1579★
MOST EMULATED COMPANIES IN THAILAND, 1998
Ranked by: Scores (1-7) based on a survey response of over 4,000 professionals throughout Asia. **Remarks:** Specific figures not provided. **Number listed:** 5

1. Charoen Pokphand Group
2. Siam Cement
3. Dusit Thani
4. Shinawatra Group
5. Grammy Entertainment

Source: *Far Eastern Economic Review*, Review 200 (annual), December 31, 1998, p. 87.

Corporations--Utah

★1580★
TOP CORPORATIONS IN UTAH, 1998
Ranked by: Revenue, in millions of dollars. **Remarks:** Also notes profits, contact information, number of employees, and CEO. **Number listed:** 2

1. American Stores, with $19,866.7 million
2. Autoliv, $3,488.7

Source: *Fortune*, Fortune 500 Largest U.S. Corporations (annual), April 26, 1999, p. F-49.

Corporations--Virginia

★1581★
TOP CORPORATIONS IN VIRGINIA, 1998
Ranked by: Revenue, in millions of dollars. **Remarks:** Also notes profits, contact information, number of employees, and CEO. **Number listed:** 18

1. Mobil, with $47,678 million
2. Freddie Mac, $18,048
3. CSX, $9,898
4. Circuit City Group, $8,870.8
5. US Airways Group, $8,688
6. Fort James, $7,301.1
7. Columbia Energy Group, $6,568.2
8. Dominion Resources, $6,086.2
9. Reynolds Metals, $5,859
10. Gannett, $5,121.3

Source: *Fortune*, Fortune 500 Largest U.S. Corporations (annual), April 26, 1999, p. F-49+.

Corporations--Washington

★1582★
TOP CORPORATIONS IN WASHINGTON, 1998
Ranked by: Revenue, in millions of dollars. **Remarks:** Also notes profits, contact information, number of employees, and CEO. **Number listed:** 10

1. Boeing, with $56,154 million
2. Costco Companies, $24,269.9
3. Microsoft, $14,484
4. Washington Mutual, $12,745.6
5. Weyerhaeuser, $10,766
6. Paccar, $7,894.8
7. Safeco, $6,452.1
8. Nordstrom, $5,027.9
9. Avista Corp., $3,684
10. Airborne Freight, $3,074.5

Source: *Fortune*, Fortune 500 Largest U.S. Corporations (annual), April 26, 1999, p. F-50.

Corporations--Wisconsin

★1583★
TOP CORPORATIONS IN WISCONSIN, 1998
Ranked by: Revenue, in millions of dollars. **Remarks:** Also notes profits, contact information, number of employees, and CEO. **Number listed:** 9

1. Northwestern Mutual Life, with $14,644.9 million
2. Johnson Controls, $12,586.8
3. Manpower, $8,814.3
4. Case, $6,149
5. American Family Insurance Group, $4,002.6
6. Kohl's, $3,681.8
7. Firstar Corp., $3,501.6
8. Aid Association for Lutherans, $3,217.9
9. Shopko, $2,993.8

Source: *Fortune*, Fortune 500 Largest U.S. Corporations (annual), April 26, 1999, p. F-50.

Corrugated Boxes

★1584★
LARGEST PRODUCERS OF CORRUGATED BOXES BY NUMBER OF PLANTS, 1997
Ranked by: Total number of plants. **Remarks:** Also notes number of corrugated plants and sheet plants. **Number listed:** 18

1. Stone Container, with 80 plants
2. Tenneco Packaging, 66
3. Jefferson Smurfit, 49
4. Georgia-Pacific, 35
5. Weyerhaeuser, 45
6. Inland Paperboard, 35
7. Willamette, 31
8. Union Camp, 25
9. International Paper, 33
10. Gaylord Container, 14

Source: *Paperboard Packaging*, January, 1999, p. 24.

Corruption in Politics--International Aspects

★1585★
COUNTRIES POLITICAL PRACTICES, FROM CLEAN TO CORRUPT, 1999*
Ranked by: Score, from 10 to O. **Remarks:** 10 indicates highly clean; 0 highly corrupt. **Number listed:** 70

1. Denmark, with 10.0 a score of
2. Finland, 9.6
3. Sweden, 9.5
4. New Zealand, 9.4
5. Iceland, 9.3
6. Canada, 9.2
7. Singapore, 9.1
8. Netherlands, 9.0
8. Norway, 9.0
10. Switzerland, 8.9

Source: *World Trade*, January, 1999, p. 61.

Cosmetics Industry

See also: **Perfumes Personal Care Products**

★1586★
BEST COSMETICS BRANDS ACCORDING TO DISCOUNT SHOPPERS, 1998
Ranked by: Percent of discount shoppers naming brand as favorite. **Remarks:** Figures may total more than 100% due to multiple responses. **Number listed:** 10

1. Cover Girl, with 36%
2. Revlon, 23%
3. Maybelline, 18%
4. L'Oreal, 10%
5. Oil of Olay, 6%
6. Almay, 5%
6. Max Factor, 5%
8. Avon, 4%
9. Cutex, 2%
9. Estee Lauder, 2%

Source: *Discount Store News*, Top Brands Consumer Survey--Part II (annual), September 9, 1998, p. 28.

★1587★
BEST SELLING COLOR COSMETICS BRANDS, 1998
Ranked by: Total sales, in millions of dollars. **Remarks:** Also notes company name, location, lead agency, and media expenditures. **Number listed:** 5

1. Revlon, with $618.5 million
2. Cover Girl, $566.7
3. Maybelline, $490.0
4. L'Oreal, $366.0
5. Almay, $217.0

Source: *Brandweek*, Superbrands: America's Top 2,000 Brands, June 21, 1999, p. 534.

★1588★
BEST-SELLING ETHNIC COSMETICS BRANDS, 1998
Ranked by: Sales, in millions of dollars. **Remarks:** Also notes percent change from previous year, percent of dollar share, and percent of ACV. **Number listed:** 8

1. Black Radiance, with $3.9 million
2. Tropez, $3.7
3. Posner, $2.7
4. Cover Girl, $2.3
5. Black Opal, $2.0
6. Maybelline Shades of You, $1.7
7. Wet 'n' Wild, $0.5
8. Zuri, $0.4

Source: *Drug Store News*, August 3, 1998, p. 54.

★1589★
BEST-SELLING FACIAL COSMETICS BRANDS, 1998
Ranked by: Sales, in millions of dollars. **Remarks:** Also notes unit volume. **Number listed:** 10

1. Cover Girl, with $309.0 million
2. Revlon, $193.2
3. Maybelline, $112.2
4. L'Oreal, $97.3
5. Almay, $71.2
6. Max Factor, $67.5
7. Coty, $14.0
8. Physicians Formula, $11.5
9. Cornsilk, $11.0
10. jane, $8.5

Source: *MMR*, May 3, 1999, p. 23.

★1590★
BEST-SELLING TEEN FACIAL COSMETICS BRANDS, 1998
Ranked by: Sales, in millions of dollars. **Number listed:** 10

1. Revlon, with $615.3 million
2. Cover Girl, $582.1
3. Maybelline, $473.2
4. L'Oreal, $351.2
5. Almay, $216.6
6. Max Factor, $136.1
7. Sally Hansen, $93.1
8. Wet 'n' Wild, $70.4
9. Bonne Bell, $50.2
10. jane, $35.9

Source: *Drug Store News*, December 14, 1998, p. 15.

Cosmetics Industry, International

★1591★
TOP GLOBAL BEAUTY PRODUCTS PRODUCERS, 1997
Ranked by: Sales, in billions of dollars. **Remarks:** Also notes chief brands. **Number listed:** 5

1. L'Oreal, with $9.6 billion
2. Unilever, $7.2
3. Procter & Gamble, $7.1
4. Shiseido, $4.6
5. Estee Lauder, $3.4

Source: *Marketing*, April 29, 1999, p. 14.

★1592★
WORLD'S LARGEST SOAP AND COSMETICS CORPORATIONS BY REVENUE, 1997

Ranked by: Revenue, in millions of dollars. **Number listed:** 3

1. Procter & Gamble (U.S.), with $35,764 million
2. L'Oreal (France), $11,843
3. Colgate-Palmolive (U.S.), $9,057

Source: *Fortune*, The Global 500: World's Biggest Corporations (annual), August 3, 1998, p. F-24.

Counties

★1593★
FASTEST-GROWING COUNTIES, 1997*

Ranked by: 1996-97 population growth, in percent. **Remarks:** Notes counties with 10,000 or more persons in 1997. **Number listed:** 10

1. Douglas, CO, with 12.9%
2. Lincoln, SD, 9.9%
3. Forsyth, GA, 9.5%
4. Park, CO, 8.9%
5. Nye, NV, 8.3%
6. Elbert, CO, 8.0%
7. Paulding, GA, 7.7%
7. Loudoun, VA, 7.7%
9. Henry, GA, 7.5%
9. Collin, TX, 7.5%

Source: *Real Estate Outlook*, July, 1998, p. 8.

★1594★
LARGEST U.S. COUNTIES BY APPAREL SALES, 1998

Ranked by: Apparel sales, in thousands of dollars. **Number listed:** 250

1. Los Angeles, CA, with $4,433,526 thousand
2. New York, NY, $3,152,915
3. Cook, IL, $3,143,700
4. Dade, FL, $1,859,458
5. Harris, TX, $1,780,899
6. Orange, CA, $1,554,614
7. Dallas, TX, $1,338,741
8. San Diego, CA, $1,327,486
9. Nassau, NY, $1,170,896
10. King, WA, $1,110,488

Source: *Editor & Publisher Market Guide (annual)*, Editor & Publisher Co., 1998, p. I-27+.

★1595★
LARGEST U.S. COUNTIES BY AUTOMOBILE SALES, 1998

Ranked by: Automobile sales, in thousands of dollars. **Number listed:** 250

1. Los Angeles, CA, with $19,442,944 thousand
2. Cook, IL, $11,197,649
3. Harris, TX, $9,987,649
4. Broward, FL, $8,629,530
5. Dallas, TX, $7,865,956
6. Maricopa, AZ, $7,472,586
7. Orange, CA, $6,885,167
8. Dade, FL, $6,653,029
9. San Diego, CA, $5,782,183
10. Oakland, MI, $5,274,218

Source: *Editor & Publisher Market Guide (annual)*, Editor & Publisher Co., 1998, p. I-26.

★1596★
LARGEST U.S. COUNTIES BY DISPOSABLE INCOME, 1998

Ranked by: Disposable income, in thousands of dollars. **Number listed:** 250

1. Los Angeles, CA, with $198,194,326 thousand
2. Cook, IL, $129,262,178
3. Harris, TX, $75,260,116
4. Orange, CA, $65,646,267
5. San Diego, CA, $57,398,773
6. Maricopa, AZ, $53,166,324
7. Dallas, TX, $52,326,194
8. New York, NY, $47,923,874
9. King, WA, $47,539,721
10. Queens, NY, $46,647,905

Source: *Editor & Publisher Market Guide (annual)*, Editor & Publisher Co., 1998, p. I-22.

★1597★
LARGEST U.S. COUNTIES BY DRUG SALES, 1998

Ranked by: Drug sales, in thousands of dollars. **Number listed:** 250

1. Los Angeles, CA, with $3,304,760 thousand
2. Cook, IL, $3,007,184
3. Dade, FL, $1,288,050
4. Harris, TX, $1,183,173
5. Cuyahoga, OH, $1,058,618
6. Wayne, MI, $1,014,897
7. Maricopa, AZ, $1,013,732
8. Orange, CA, $1,011,999
9. New York, NY, $983,190
10. San Diego, CA, $956,550

Source: *Editor & Publisher Market Guide (annual)*, Editor & Publisher Co., 1998, p. I-29.

★1598★
LARGEST U.S. COUNTIES BY FOOD/DRINK SALES, 1998

Ranked by: Food/drink sales, in thousands of U.S. dollars. **Number listed:** 250

1. Los Angeles, CA, with $9,159,851 thousand
2. Cook, IL, $5,752,510
3. New York, NY, $4,248,407
4. Harris, TX, $3,703,257
5. Orange, CA, $3,159,018
6. Dallas, TX, $2,892,308
7. San Diego, CA, $2,813,536
8. Maricopa, AZ, $2,620,427
9. Dade, FL, $2,301,483
10. King, WA, $2,243,167

Source: *Editor & Publisher Market Guide (annual)*, Editor & Publisher Co., 1998, p. I-28+.

★1599★
LARGEST U.S. COUNTIES BY FOOD SALES, 1998

Ranked by: Food sales, in thousands of dollars. **Number listed:** 250

1. Los Angeles, CA, with $14,251,580 thousand
2. Cook, IL, $8,117,537
3. Harris, TX, $6,271,088
4. Maricopa, AZ, $4,767,169
5. Orange, CA, $4,360,303
6. San Diego, CA, $4,226,197
7. Dallas, TX, $3,571,448
8. Dade, FL, $3,531,810
9. King, WA, $3,156,338
10. Wayne, MI, $2,825,556

Source: *Editor & Publisher Market Guide (annual)*, Editor & Publisher Co., 1998, p. I-25+.

★1600★
LARGEST U.S. COUNTIES BY FURNITURE SALES, 1998
Ranked by: Furniture sales, in thousands of dollars. **Number listed:** 250
1. Los Angeles, CA, with $5,901,944 thousand
2. Cook, IL, $3,428,631
3. Harris, TX, $2,364,957
4. New York, NY, $2,084,998
5. Orange, CA, $2,084,928
6. Dade, FL, $1,979,012
7. Dallas, TX, $1,769,254
8. San Diego, CA, $1,737,954
9. Santa Clara, CA, $1,613,583
10. Maricopa, AZ, $1,545,091

Source: *Editor & Publisher Market Guide (annual)*, Editor & Publisher Co., 1998, p. I-28+.

★1601★
LARGEST U.S. COUNTIES BY GASOLINE SALES, 1998
Ranked by: Gasoline sales, in thousands of dollars. **Number listed:** 250
1. Los Angeles, CA, with $4,629,275 thousand
2. Cook, IL, $2,430,335
3. Harris, TX, $1,825,688
4. Maricopa, AZ, $1,494,674
5. Dallas, TX, $1,473,298
6. Orange, CA, $1,466,962
7. San Diego, CA, $1,424,122
8. Wayne, MI, $1,232,336
9. Dade, FL, $1,210,306
10. San Bernardino, CA, $979,607

Source: *Editor & Publisher Market Guide (annual)*, Editor & Publisher Co., 1998, p. I-26+.

★1602★
LARGEST U.S. COUNTIES BY GENERAL MERCHANDISE SALES, 1998
Ranked by: General merchandise sales, in thousands of dollars. **Number listed:** 250
1. Los Angeles, CA, with $10,144,416 thousand
2. Cook, IL, $5,860,622
3. Harris, TX, $4,967,479
4. Orange, CA, $3,701,731
5. Maricopa, AZ, $3,554,502
6. Dallas, TX, $3,403,925
7. San Diego, CA, $3,298,761
8. Wayne, MI, $2,707,587
9. Oakland, MI, $2,704,366
10. Dade, FL, $2,700,316

Source: *Editor & Publisher Market Guide (annual)*, Editor & Publisher Co., 1998, p. I-24+.

★1603★
LARGEST U.S. COUNTIES BY INCOME PER HOUSEHOLD, 1998
Ranked by: Income per household. **Number listed:** 250
1. Skagway-Yakutat-Angoon, AK, with $142,105
2. Aleutians West, AK, $135,399
3. Bristol Bay, AK, $130,078
4. Sherman, TX, $104,581
5. Fairfield, CT, $101,887
6. Westchester, NY, $98,029
7. Marin, CA, $97,888
8. Somerset, NJ, $92,760
9. Bergen, NJ, $91,296
10. Falls Church, VA, $90,896

Source: *Editor & Publisher Market Guide (annual)*, Editor & Publisher Co., 1998, p. I-23.

★1604★
LARGEST U.S. COUNTIES BY LUMBER/HARDWARE SALES, 1998
Ranked by: Lumber/hardware sales, in thousands of dollars. **Number listed:** 250
1. Los Angeles, CA, with $3,745,814 thousand
2. Cook, IL, $2,195,771
3. Harris, TX, $1,456,815
4. Orange, CA, $1,375,141
5. San Diego, CA, $1,340,832
6. Maricopa, AZ, $1,306,778
7. Suffolk, NY, $1,114,397
8. Dade, FL, $1,094,637
9. Dallas, TX, $1,029,007
10. King, WA, $995,475

Source: *Editor & Publisher Market Guide (annual)*, Editor & Publisher Co., 1998, p. I-24+.

★1605★
LARGEST U.S. COUNTIES BY POPULATION, 1998
Ranked by: Estimated population. **Number listed:** 250
1. Los Angeles, CA, with 9,283,453
2. Cook, IL, 5,198,128
3. Harris, TX, 3,224,981
4. Maricopa, AZ, 2,730,354
5. San Diego, CA, 2,722,411
6. Orange, CA, 2,673,941
7. Kings, NY, 2,223,785
8. Dade, FL, 2,089,940
9. Wayne, MI, 2,052,174
10. Dallas, TX, 2,034,656

Source: *Editor & Publisher Market Guide (annual)*, Editor & Publisher Co., 1998, p. I-21+.

★1606★
LARGEST U.S. COUNTIES BY TOTAL RETAIL SALES, 1998
Ranked by: Total retail sales, in thousands of dollars. **Number listed:** 250
1. Los Angeles, CA, with $82,991,235 thousand
2. Cook, IL, $52,248,284
3. Harris, TX, $36,208,363
4. Orange, CA, $27,923,574
5. Maricopa, AZ, $26,939,668
6. Dallas, TX, $26,713,769
7. San Diego, CA, $25,262,427
8. Dade, FL, $24,821,695
9. New York, NY, $23,137,822
10. Broward, FL, $20,455,788

Source: *Editor & Publisher Market Guide (annual)*, Editor & Publisher Co., 1998, p. I-23+.

★1607★
U.S. COUNTIES WITH HIGH CAPITATION RATES, 1998
Ranked by: AAPCC rate (Adjusted Average Per Capita Cost), a prospective estimate of Medicare cost levels in the fee-for-service sector of the geographic area. **Remarks:** Also notes number of eligibles, enrollees, and penetration. **Number listed:** 50
1. Richmond, NY, with $782.70
2. Dade, FL, $763.19
3. Bronx, NY, $742.80
4. New York, NY, $727.38
5. Kings, NY, $719.48
6. Philadelphia, PA, $718.33

7. Montgomery, TX, $678.67
8. Queens, NY, $672.02
9. Broward, FL, $663.37
10. Wayne, MI, $651.45

Source: *Journal of Compensation and Benefits*, July/August, 1998, p. 43.

Country Credit Risk

★1608★
COUNTRIES WITH THE BEST CREDIT RISK RATING, 1998
Ranked by: Overall credit-risk ratings score. Ratings tabulated using analytical, credit, and market indicators. **Remarks:** Also notes change from previous year. **Number listed:** 180

1. Luxembourg, with 98.90 a score of
2. United States, 97.85
3. Germany, 97.06
4. Netherlands, 96.92
5. Austria, 96.79
6. Switzerland, 96.43
7. France, 95.87
8. Norway, 95.83
9. United Kingdom, 95.01
10. Ireland, 94.87

Source: *Euromoney*, September, 1998, p. 203+.

Country Credit Risk--Africa

★1609★
AFRICAN COUNTRIES WITH THE BEST CREDIT-RISK RATINGS AS OF MARCH, 1998
Ranked by: Credit-risk ratings. **Remarks:** Also notes 6-month and one-year changes in ratings, plus regional and global rankings. **Number listed:** 35

1. Mauritius, with 53.7 a rating of
2. Botswana, 53.5
3. Tunisia, 50.3
4. South Africa, 45.8
5. Morocco, 43.2
6. Namibia, 37.3
7. Ghana, 29.5
8. Seychelles, 29.1
9. Swaziland, 28.5
10. Libya, 28.1

Source: *Institutional Investor-International Edition*, March, 1999, p. 126.

Country Credit Risk--Asia

★1610★
ASIAN COUNTRIES WITH THE BEST CREDIT-RISK RATINGS AS OF MARCH, 1999
Ranked by: Credit-risk ratings. **Remarks:** Also notes 6-month and one-year changes in ratings, plus regional and global rankings. **Number listed:** 22

1. Japan, with 86.5 a rating of
2. Singapore, 81.3
3. Taiwan, 75.5
4. Australia, 74.3
5. New Zealand, 73.1
6. Hong Kong, 61.8
7. China, 57.2
8. South Korea, 52.7
9. Malaysia, 51.0
10. Thailand, 46.9

Source: *Institutional Investor-International Edition*, March, 1999, p. 130.

Country Credit Risk--Europe, Eastern

★1611★
EASTERN EUROPEAN COUNTRIES WITH THE BEST CREDIT-RISK RATINGS AS OF MARCH, 1999
Ranked by: Credit-risk ratings. **Remarks:** Also notes 6-month and one-year changes in ratings, plus regional and global rankings. **Number listed:** 19

1. Czech Republic, with 59.7 a rating of
2. Slovenia, 58.4
3. Poland, 56.7
4. Hungary, 55.9
5. Estonia, 42.8
6. Slovakia, 41.3
7. Croatia, 39.0
8. Latvia, 38.0
9. Lithuania, 36.1
10. Romania, 31.2

Source: *Institutional Investor-International Edition*, March, 1999, p. 128.

Country Credit Risk--Europe, Western

★1612★
WESTERN EUROPEAN COUNTRIES WITH THE BEST CREDIT-RISK RATINGS AS OF MARCH, 1999
Ranked by: Credit-risk ratings. **Remarks:** Also notes 6-month and one-year changes in ratings, plus regional and global rankings. **Number listed:** 20

1. Switzerland, with 92.7 a rating of
2. Germany, 92.5
3. Netherlands, 91.7
4. France, 90.8
5. United Kingdom, 90.2
6. Luxembourg, 89.9
7. Austria, 88.7
8. Norway, 86.8
9. Denmark, 84.7
10. Belgium, 83.5

Source: *Institutional Investor-International Edition*, March, 1999, p. 128.

Country Credit Risk, International

★1613★
COUNTRIES WITH THE BEST CREDIT-RISK RATINGS AS OF MARCH, 1999
Ranked by: Credit-risk ratings. **Remarks:** Also notes 6-month and one-year changes in ratings, plus regional and global rankings. **Number listed:** 118

1. Switzerland, with 92.7 a rating of
2. Germany, 92.5
3. United States, 92.2
4. Netherlands, 91.7
5. France, 90.8
6. United Kingdom, 90.2
7. Luxembourg, 89.9
8. Austria, 88.7
9. Norway, 86.8
10. Japan, 86.5

Source: *Institutional Investor-International Edition*, March, 1999, p. 124.

Country Credit Risk--Latin America

★1614★
LATIN AMERICAN COUNTRIES WITH THE BEST CREDIT-RISK RATINGS AS OF MARCH, 1999
Ranked by: Credit-risk ratings. **Remarks:** Also notes 6-month and one-year changes in ratings, plus regional and global rankings. **Number listed:** 23

1. Chile, with 61.8 a rating of
2. Uruguay, 46.5
3. Colombia, 44.5
4. Barbados, 43.5
5. Trinidad & Tobago, 43.3
6. Argentina, 42.7
7. Panama, 39.9
8. Costa Rica, 38.4
9. Brazil, 37.4
10. Peru, 35.0

Source: *Institutional Investor-International Edition*, March, 1999, p. 127.

Country Credit Risk--Middle East

★1615★
MIDDLE EASTERN COUNTRIES WITH THE BEST CREDIT-RISK RATINGS AS OF MARCH, 1999
Ranked by: Credit-risk ratings. **Remarks:** Also notes 6-month and one-year changes in ratings, plus regional and global rankings. **Number listed:** 14

1. United Arab Emirates, with 62.5 a rating of
2. Cyprus, 57.3
3. Kuwait, 56.5
4. Saudi Arabia, 54.4
5. Israel, 54.3
6. Oman, 53.3
7. Qatar, 51.7
8. Bahrain, 50.7
9. Egypt, 44.4
10. Jordan, 37.3

Source: *Institutional Investor-International Edition*, March, 1999, p. 127.

Country Credit Risk--North America

★1616★
NORTH AMERICAN COUNTRIES WITH THE BEST CREDIT-RISK RATINGS AS OF MARCH, 1999
Ranked by: Credit-risk ratings. **Remarks:** Also notes 6-month and one-year changes in ratings, plus regional and global rankings. **Number listed:** 3

1. United States, with 92.2 a rating of
2. Canada, 83.0
3. Mexico, 46.0

Source: *Institutional Investor-International Edition*, March, 1999, p. 126.

Credit Cards

See also: **Bank Credit Cards Charge Accounts (Retail Trade) Gasoline Credit Cards**

★1617★
LARGEST CREDIT CARD ISSUERS BY AMOUNT OF RECEIVABLES OUTSTANDING, 1998
Ranked by: Receivables outstanding, in millions of dollars. **Remarks:** Also notes other financial and card data for 1997 and 1998. **Number listed:** 300

1. Citicorp, with $48,200,000,000
2. MBNA America, $44,507,000,000
3. Banc One Corp./First USA Bank, $38,548,817,000
4. Morgan Stanley, Dean Witter & Co., $36,000,000,000
5. The Chase Manhattan Corp., $32,536,089,581
6. First Chicago NBD Corp., $18,098,101,067
7. Household Credit Services Inc., $17,314,186,000
8. AT&T Universal Card Services Corp., $15,300,000,000
9. American Express Centurion Bank, $14,722,300,000
10. Capital One Financial Corp., $13,620,701,000

Source: *Card Industry Directory*, Faulkner & Gray, 1999, p. 63+.

★1618★
LARGEST CREDIT CARD ISSUERS, 1998
Ranked by: U.S. volume, in billions of dollars. **Remarks:** Also notes growth rate as well as figures for 1997. **Number listed:** 4

1. Visa, with $475.6 billion
2. MasterCard, $275.6
3. American Express, $165.6
4. Discover/Novus, $58.0

Source: *Credit Card Management*, CCM's Credit Card Industry Annual Report, May, 1999, p. 53.

★1619★
LEADING CREDIT CARDS BY MARKET SHARE, 1998
Ranked by: Percent of market share. **Number listed:** 5

1. Visa, with 50%
2. MasterCard, 25%
3. American Express, 18%

4. Discover, 6%
5. Diner's Club, 1%

Source: *Wall Street Journal*, October 8, 1998, p. A3.

★1620★
LEADING CREDIT CARDS BY TOTAL SALES, 1999*
Ranked by: Total sales, in billions of dollars. **Remarks:** Also notes company name, location, lead agency, and media expenditures. **Number listed:** 5

1. Visa, with $610.3 billion
2. MasterCard, $310.7
3. American Express, $165.6
4. Discover, etc., $58.0
5. Citibank, n/a

Source: *BrandWeek*, Superbrands: America's Top 2,000 Brands, June 21, 1999, p. 536.

★1621★
TOP RETAIL CARD ISSUERS, 1997
Ranked by: Outstanding amount, in billions of dollars. **Remarks:** Also notes number of cards issued, and amount of active accounts. **Number listed:** 9

1. Sears Roebuck, with $28.94 billion
2. GE Capital, $15.71
3. J.C. Penney, $5.24
4. Household International, $4.37
5. Beneficial Corp., $3.51
6. Dayton Hudson, $2.42
7. Banc One, $2.35
8. Federated Department Stores, $2.22
9. May Department Stores, $2.16
10. SPS Transaction Services, $1.90

Source: *American Banker*, September 4, 1998, p. 6.

Credit Unions

★1622★
CREDIT UNIONS WITH THE LARGEST DEPOSIT GROWTH, 1996-97
Ranked by: Deposit growth as a percentage of assets. **Number listed:** 20

1. University FCU (Austin, TX), with 16.0%
2. 1st Security CU (Green Bay, WI), 15.3%
3. Alliance CU (Davenport, IA), 15.0%
4. VF Credit Association FCU (Greensboro, NC), 13.5%
5. Freedom FCU (Rocky Mount, NC), 13.2%
6. White Sands FCU (Las Cruces, NM), 11.5%
7. Pelkie-Copper Community CU (Pelkie, MI), 11.3%
8. Burlington Colorado Southern CU (Wheat Ridge, CO), 10.4%
9. Butte FCU (Biggs, CA), 10.3%
10. Lassen County FCU (Susanville, CA), 10.0%

Source: *Credit Union Magazine*, October, 1998, p. 22.

★1623★
LEADING CREDIT UNIONS BY CAPITAL TO ASSETS, 1998
Ranked by: Percentage of capital to assets. **Remarks:** Ranks credit unions with assets greater than $10 million as of June 30, 1998. **Number listed:** 100

1. Middle Village (NY), with 64.28%
2. Memphis Municipal Employees (TN), 43.68%
3. Riverview (OH), 41.61%
4. Lyell (NY), 41.58%
5. Progressive (NY), 40.73%
6. Boise Employees (MN), 39.28%
7. Guadalupe Parish (CO), 37.46%
8. GT & R Employees N.C. (NC), 36.31%
9. Ohio Teamsters (OH), 34.02%
10. Pannonia (PA), 33.44%

Source: *Callahan's Credit Union Directory (annual)*, Callahan & Associates, 1999, p. 58.

★1624★
LEADING CREDIT UNIONS BY PERCENT LOANS TO SHARES, 1998
Ranked by: Percent of loans to shares. Ranks credit unions with assets greater than $10 million as of June 30, 1998. **Number listed:** 100

1. Middle Village (NY), with 196.82%
2. Progressive (NY), 163.33%
3. Melrose (NY), 121.79%
4. Memphis Municipal Employees (TN), 117.93%
5. Southwest Airlines Employees (TX), 117.31%
6. Ohio Teamsters (OH), 116.65%
7. Government of Guam (GU), 112.61%
8. Boise Employees (MN), 112.13%
9. University of Iowa Community (IA), 111.77%
10. Governmental Employees (WI), 111.01%

Source: *Callahan's Credit Union Directory (annual)*, Callahan & Associates, 1999, p. 43.

★1625★
LEADING CREDIT UNIONS BY REAL ESTATE LOAN CONCENTRATION, 1998
Ranked by: Percentage of real estate loans to total loans. Ranks credit unions with assets greater than $10 million as of June 30, 1998. **Number listed:** 100

1. Polish & Slavic (NY), with 96.30%
2. Credit Union Central Falls (RI), 85.57%
3. Luso (MA), 95.51%
4. Self Reliance NY (NY), 95.00%
5. Ukrainian Orthodox (NY), 94.71%
6. Suma Yonkers (NY), 93.63%
7. Emsbla (WI), 93.59%
8. Self Reliance (NJ), 92.50%
9. Ukrainian Selfreliance (PA), 92.35%
10. Park Square (RI), 91.25%

Source: *Callahan's Credit Union Directory (annual)*, Callahan & Associates, 1999, p. 46.

★1626★
LEADING CREDIT UNIONS BY SHARES PER MEMBER, 1998
Ranked by: Dollar amount of shares per member. Ranks credit unions with assets greater than $10 million as of June 30, 1998. **Number listed:** 100

1. Lufthansa (NY), with $26,945
2. Self-Help (NC), $26,324
3. Progressive (NY), $25,085
4. IDB-IIC (DC), $25,070
5. PASB WHO (DC), $24,690
6. Star One (CA), $23,717
7. United Nations (NY), $23,622
8. League of Mutual Taxi Owners (NY), $23,112
9. Self Reliance NY (NY), $21,850
10. Bank Fund Staff (DC), $20,523

Source: *Callahan's Credit Union Directory (annual)*, Callahan & Associates, 1999, p. 42.

★1627★
LEADING CREDIT UNIONS BY TOTAL ASSETS, 1998
Ranked by: Total assets, in dollars. Ranks credit unions with assets greater than $10 million as of June 30, 1998. **Number listed:** 200
1. Navy (VA), with $10,439,889,960
2. State Employees (NC), $5,328,164,910
3. Boeing Employees (WA), $3,082,260,680
4. Pentagon (VA), $2,911,765,560
5. United Airlines Employees (IL), $2,591,805,810
6. The Golden 1 (CA), $2,174,043,640
7. American Airlines Employees (TX), $2,171,262,450
8. Orange County Teachers (CA), $2,004,723,381
9. Suncoast Schools (FL), $1,864,942,743
10. Hughes Aircraft Employees (CA), $1,753,907,530

Source: *Callahan's Credit Union Directory (annual)*, Callahan & Associates, 1999, p. 36+.

★1628★
LEADING CREDIT UNIONS BY TOTAL MEMBERS, 1998
Ranked by: Total number of members. Ranks credit unions with assets greater than $10 million as of June 30, 1998. **Remarks:** Also notes average share balance. **Number listed:** 100
1. Navy (VA), with 1,728,420 members
2. State Employees (NC), 686,990
3. Pentagon (VA), 403,910
4. The Golden 1 (CA), 334,040
5. Security Service (TX), 332,711
6. Pennsylvania State Employees (PA), 247,674
7. Boeing Employees (WA), 242,674
8. San Antonio, TX, 240,919
9. Municipal (NY), 238,178
10. America First CU (UT), 237,681

Source: *Callahan's Credit Union Directory (annual)*, Callahan & Associates, 1999, p. 40.

★1629★
TOP AGRICULTURAL LENDERS, 1998
Ranked by: Average loans, in millions of dollars. **Remarks:** Also notes assets. **Number listed:** 20
1. Wabash County Farm Bureau (IN), with $54.9 million
2. Melrose Credit Union (MN), $38.3
3. First Community CU (Jamestown, ND), $35.7
4. Town & Country Credit Union (Minot, ND), $31.3
5. Western Cooperative Credit Union (Williston, ND), $25.8
6. Benson County Co-op Credit Union, $25.5
7. Lake Region CU (Devils Lake, ND), $20.7
8. Houston Milk Producers FCU, $16.3
9. Heartland CU (Madison, WI), $13.8
10. Community CU (New Rockford, ND), $13.2

Source: *Credit Union Magazine*, May, 1999, p. 17.

Credit Unions--Detroit Metropolitan Area

★1630★
LARGEST CREDIT UNIONS IN METROPOLITAN DETROIT, 1997
Ranked by: Assets, in millions of dollars. **Remarks:** Also notes 1996 assets, percent change, number of members, net income, and total loans for both 1996 and 1997. **Number listed:** 25
1. Dearborn Federal Credit Union, with $1,001.8 million
2. Credit Union One, $451.7
3. USA Federal Credit Union, $327.8
4. Detroit Edison Credit Union, $324.0
5. Macomb Schools and Government Credit Union, $262.1
6. Detroit Teachers Credit Union, $261.6
7. T&C Federal Credit Union, $249.2
8. Detroit Municipal Credit Union, $247.6
9. Wayne Out County Teachers Credit Union, $246.8
10. Telcom Credit Union, $191.0

Source: *Crain's Detroit Business*, August 16, 1998, p. 18.

Credit Unions--Florida

★1631★
TOP CREDIT UNIONS IN FLORIDA, 1999
Ranked by: Total assets, in millions of dollars. **Remarks:** Also notes loan amounts, capital/asset ratio, number of members, number of locations, senior executive, and year founded. **Number listed:** 25
1. Suncoast Schools Federal Credit Union, with $1,783.2 million
2. Jax Navy Federal Credit Union, $1,355.4
3. Eastern Financial Federal Credit Union, $1,049.0
4. Space Coast Credit Union, $606.4
5. GTE Federal Credit Union, $645.4
6. Eglin Federal Credit Union, $549.3
7. Fairwinds Federal Credit Union, $494.9
8. MacDill Federal Credit Union, $511.1
9. Tyndall Federal Credit Union, $425.9
10. Tropical Federal Credit Union, $408.4

Source: *TopRank Florida (annual)*, 1999, p. 25.

Crime and Criminals--Canada

★1632★
AVERAGE COST OF PROPERTY CRIMES IN CANADA, 1998*
Ranked by: Cost of crime, in dollars. **Number listed:** 5
1. Motor vehicle theft, with $6,649
2. Fraud, $3,531
3. Robbery, $2,857
4. Breaking and entering, $2,309
5. Vandalism, $646.52

Source: *CA Magazine*, November, 1998, p. 13.

Cruise Lines--Florida

★1633★
BIGGEST CRUISE LINES IN FLORIDA, 1997
Ranked by: Number of passengers. **Remarks:** Also notes contact information, executive officer, gross tonnage of largest ship, fleet size, and origination ports. **Number listed:** 10
1. Carnival Cruise Lines, with 1,945,000 passengers
2. Royal Caribbean International, 1,285,000
3. Norwegian Cruise Line, 507,304

4. Princess Cruises, 460,000
5. Holland America Line Westours, 440,291
6. Celebrity Cruises, 348,088
7. Premier Cruises, 293,000
8. Royal Olympic Cruises, 125,000
9. Cunard Line Limited, 113,000
10. Cape Canaveral Cruise Line, 80,262

Source: *TopRank Florida (annual)*, Florida Trend, 1999, p. 17.

Dairy Industry

★1634★
TOP BUTTER BRANDS ACCORDING TO *DAIRY FIELD*, 1999
Ranked by: Sales, in millions of dollars. **Remarks:** Also notes annual growth and market share percentage. **Number listed:** 10

1. Private Label, with $1,148.9 million
2. Land O'Lakes, $373.7
3. Challenge, $46.3
4. Breakstone, $29.5
5. Keller's, $21.6
6. Land O'Lakes Light, $19.6
7. Hotel Bar, $18.7
8. Crystal Farms, $15.6
9. Tillamook, $12.5
10. Grassland, $9.2

Source: *Dairy Field*, Top 10 Butter Brands (annual), May, 1999, p. 24.

★1635★
TOP DAIRY COMPANIES ACCORDING TO *DAIRY FIELD*, 1997
Ranked by: Sales, in billions of dollars. **Remarks:** Also notes number of plants and locations. **Number listed:** 100

1. Kraft Foods (Northfield, IL), with $4.2 billion
2. Dairy Farmers of America (Kansas City, MO), $2.25
3. Dean Foods Co. (Franklin Park, IL), $2.1
4. Suiza Foods Corp. (Dallas, TX), $1.7
5. Land O'Lakes Inc. (Arden Hills, MN), $1.8
6. The Kroger Co. (Cincinnati, OH), $1.4
6. Schreiber Foods Inc. (Green Bay, WI), $1.4
8. Prairie Farms Dairy Inc. (Carlinville, IL), $1.2
9. Saputo Group (Montreal, CAN), $1.2
9. Leprino Foods (Denver, CO), $1.2

Source: *Dairy Field*, Top 100 U.S. Dairy Companies (annual), July, 1998, p. 24+.

★1636★
TOP REFRIGERATED BUTTER BRANDS IN U.S. SUPERMARKETS, 1998
Ranked by: Sales, in millions of dollars. **Remarks:** Also notes percent change from previous year. **Number listed:** 10

1. Private Label, with $404.3 million
2. Land O'Lakes, $305.8
3. Challenge, $38
4. Breakstone, $23.6
5. Land O'Lakes Light, $19
6. Kellers, $16.1
7. Crystal Farms, $13
8. Hotel Bar, $12
9. Tillamook, $11.2
10. Grassland, $9

Source: *Dairy Field*, Top Refrigerated Butter Brands, August, 1998, p. 36.

★1637★
TOP REFRIGERATED DIP BRANDS IN U.S. SUPERMARKETS, 1998
Ranked by: Sales, in millions of dollars. **Remarks:** Also notes percent change from previous year and other financial figures. **Number listed:** 10

1. T. Marzetti, with $50.2 million
2. Private Label, $44.3
3. Dean's, $32.7
4. Kraft, $20.6
5. Heluva Good, $13.2
6. Calavo, $6.2
7. Rite Tribe of the Two Sheiks, $6.1
8. Rite, $5.7
9. Imo, $5.3
10. Bison, $4.7

Source: *Dairy Field*, August, 1998, p. 21.

★1638★
TOP SOUR CREAM BRANDS IN U.S. SUPERMARKETS, 1998
Ranked by: Sales, in millions of dollars. **Remarks:** Also notes percent change from previous year and other financial figures. **Number listed:** 10

1. Private Label, with $152.1 million
2. Breakstone, $74.5
3. Knudson (Hampshire), $38.2
4. Daisy, $25.3
5. Land O'Lakes, $16.6
6. Daisy Light, $13.2
7. Land O'Lakes Light, $11.2
8. Naturally Yours, $10
9. Knudsen Nice N'Light, $8.9
10. Dean's, $8.6

Source: *Dairy Field*, August, 1998, p. 21.

Dairy Industry--Europe

★1639★
TOP EUROPEAN DAIRY COMPANIES, 1997
Ranked by: Dairy Sales, in billions of dollars. **Remarks:** Also notes total sales. **Number listed:** 20

1. Nestle SA (Switzerland), with $16 billion
2. Unilever (United Kingdom/Netherlands), $10
3. Friesland Coberco (Netherlands), $5
3. Danone SA (France), $5
3. Besnier (France), $5
6. MD Foods (Denmark), $4
7. Capina Melkunie BV (Netherlands), $3
7. Sodiaal (France), $3
7. Unigate PLC (United Kingdom), $3
10. Avonmore Waterford Group (Ireland), $2.7

Source: *Dairy Foods*, Top 20 Dairy Companies in Europe (annual), July, 1998, p. 16.

★1640★
TOP EUROPEAN DAIRY PROCESSORS, 1998
Ranked by: Milk volume, in billions of liters. **Remarks:** Also notes company type, co-op or private. **Number listed:** 10

1. Bresnier (France), with 6.54 billion liters
2. Friesland (Netherlands), 5.9
3. Campina (Netherlands), 4.7
4. Bongrain (France), 3.7
5. MD Foods (Denmark), 3.3
5. Avonmore Waterford (Ireland), 3.3
7. Nestle (Multinational), 2.9

8. Sodiaal (France), 2.7
9. Danone (France), 2.2
10. Aria (Sweden), 2.1

Source: *Dairy Foods*, January, 1999, p. 76.

Dairy Industry--North America

★1641★
TOP U.S. AND CANADIAN DAIRY COMPANIES, 1997
Ranked by: Dairy sales, in millions of dollars. **Remarks:** Also notes previous year results and key brands. **Number listed:** 80

1. Kraft Foods, with $4.2 million
2. Land O'Lakes, $1.81
3. Dean Foods Co., $1.781
4. Suiza Foods Corp., $1.740
5. Mid-America Dairymen Inc., $1.7
6. Parmalat Canada Ltd., $1.4
7. Kroger Dairy Division, $1.3
8. Associated Milk Producers Inc., $1.22
9. Leprino Foods, $1.150
10. Schreiber Foods Inc., $1.1

Source: *Dairy Foods*, Top 80 U.S. and Canadian Dairy Companies (annual), July, 1998, p. 11+.

Death--Causes

★1642★
LEADING CAUSES OF DEATH FOR MEN IN THE U.S., 1995
Ranked by: Number of deaths. **Number listed:** 10

1. Diseases of the Heart, with 362,714 deaths
2. Malignant neoplasms, 281,611
3. Cerebrovascular Disease, 61,563
4. Unintentional injuries, 61,401
5. Chronic obstructive pulmonary disease, 53,983
6. Pneumonia and influenza, 37,787
7. HIV, 35,950
8. Diabetes, 26,124
9. Suicide, 25,369
10. Homicide and legal intervention, 17,740

Source: *Drug Store News*, July 20, 1998, p. 24.

★1643★
LEADING CAUSES OF FATALITIES IN THE WORKPLACE, 1996
Ranked by: Number of fatalities. **Number listed:** 7

1. Transportation, with 2,556 deaths
2. Violence, 1,144
3. Object/Equipment contact, 1,005
4. Falls, 684
5. Harmful substances, 523
6. Fires and Explosives, 184
7. Other, 16

Source: *Nation's Business*, September, 1998, p. 22.

★1644★
TOP CAUSES OF DEATH FOR MEN, 1998
Ranked by: Percentage of deaths. **Number listed:** 10

1. Accidental Death, with 20.2%
2. HIV, 17.4%
3. Diseases of the Heart, 11.7%
4. Suicide, 10.1%
5. Cancer, 9.9%
6. Homicide, 7.2%
7. Chronic Liver Conditions, 3.0%
8. Cerebrovascular Disease, 1.8%
9. Diabetes, 1.5%
10. Pneumonia, 1.2%

Source: *National Underwriter Life & Health*, April 26, 1999, p. 7.

★1645★
TOP CAUSES OF DEATH FOR WOMEN, 1998
Ranked by: Percentage of deaths. **Number listed:** 10

1. Cancer, with 25.4%
2. Accidental Death, 14.5%
3. Diseases of the Heart, 10.2%
4. HIV, 9.0%
5. Suicide, 5.2%
6. Homicide, 4.5%
7. Cerebrovascular Disease, 3.5%
8. Chronic Liver Conditions, 2.6%
9. Diabetes, 2.2%
10. Pneumonia, 1.7%

Source: *National Underwriter Life & Health*, April 26, 1999, p. 7.

Defense Contracts, International

★1646★
TOP DEFENSE CONTRACTORS WORLDWIDE, 1999*
Ranked by: Defense sales, in billions of dollars. **Number listed:** 12

1. Lockheed Martin (U.S.), with $18.5 billion
2. British Aerospace, Marconi (United Kingdom), $16.93
3. Boeing (U.S.), $13.78
4. Northrop Grumman (USA), $8.2
5. Raytheon (U.S.), $6.27
6. Thomson CSF (France), $4.18
7. Aerospatiale Matra (France), $4.16
8. TRW (U.S.), $3.8
9. General Dynamics (U.S.), $3.65
10. United Technologies (U.S.), $3.31

Source: *Interavia*, February, 1999, p. 11.

Defense Industries

★1647★
TOP AEROSPACE AND DEFENSE COMPANIES IN THE S&P 500, 1998
Ranked by: Each company is ranked by eight criteria: one-year total return, three-year total return, one-year sales growth, three-year average annual sales growth, one-year profit growth, three-year average annual profit growth, net profit margins, and return on equity, with additional weight given to a company's sales. A company's composite rank is calculated using the sum of all its ranks. **Remarks:** Overall score not provided. **Number listed:** 6

1. General Dynamics
2. United Technologies
3. B.F. Goodrich
4. Boeing
5. Lockheed Martin

6. Northrop Grumman

Source: *Business Week*, Business Week 50: Top Companies of the S&P 500 (annual), March 29, 1999, p. 142.

★1648★
TOP U.S. DEFENSE CONTRACTORS, 1997
Ranked by: Total value of contracts with Department of Defense, in billions of dollars. **Number listed:** 10

1. Lockheed Martin, with $12.4 billion
2. Boeing, $10.9
3. Raytheon, $6.5
4. Northrop Grumman, $4.1
5. GEC, Tracor, $2.2
6. General Dynamics, $2.1
7. United Technologies, $1.9
8. Litton Industries, $1.8
9. Science Applications International Corp., $1.1
10. ITT, $9

Source: *Financial Times*, December 9, 1998, p. 23.

Defense Industries--Export-Import Trade

★1649★
TOP DEFENSE EXPORTERS, 1996
Ranked by: Exports, in billions of dollars. **Remarks:** Also includes world market share. **Number listed:** 10

1. U.S., with $23.5 billion
2. United Kingdom, $6.1
3. Russia, $3.3
4. France, $3.2
5. Sweden, $1.2
6. Germany, $.83
7. Israel, $.68
8. China, $.60
9. Canada, $.46
10. Netherlands, $.34

Source: *Defense News*, February 8, 1999, p. 6.

★1650★
TOP DEFENSE IMPORTERS, 1996
Ranked by: Imports, in billions of dollars. **Remarks:** Also includes world market share. **Number listed:** 10

1. Saudi Arabia, with $9.8 billion
2. Japan, $2.4
3. Taiwan, $2
4. Egypt, $1.8
5. Kuwait, $1.7
6. China, $1.5
6. United Kingdom, $1.5
8. Turkey, $1.4
9. Australia, $1.3
10. South Korea, $1.1

Source: *Defense News*, February 8, 1999, p. 6.

Defense Industries, International

★1651★
WORLD'S LEADING DEFENSE FIRMS BY DEFENSE REVENUE, 1997
Ranked by: Defense revenue, in millions of dollars. **Remarks:** Also notes principal line of business, total revenue, and net income. **Number listed:** 100

1. Lockheed Martin (U.S.), with $18,500 million
2. Boeing (U.S.), $13,775
3. British Aerospace PLC (United Kingdom), $10,091
4. Northrop Grumman (U.S.), $8,200
5. Raytheon (U.S.), $6,270
6. General Electric Co. (United Kingdom), $5,773.6
7. Thomson CSF (France), $4,184.1
8. TRW (U.S.), $3,800
9. General Dynamics (U.S.), $3,650
10. United Technologies (U.S.), $3,311

Source: *Defense News*, Top 100 Firms (annual), July 20, 1998, p. 12.

Dehumidifiers

★1652★
BEST-SELLING DEHUMIDIFIERS, 1998
Ranked by: Market share, in percent. **Number listed:** 8

1. Whirlpool, with 25%
2. MCD, 20%
3. Electrolux, 18%
4. GEA, 5%
4. Holmes, 5%
6. Royal Sovereign, 2%
6. Sanyo Fisher, 2%
8. Others, 23%

Source: *Appliance Manufacturer*, (annual), April, 1999, p. 20.

Delaware County (PA)--Industries

★1653★
LARGEST EMPLOYERS IN DELAWARE COUNTY, PA, 1998
Ranked by: Number of local full-time employees. **Remarks:** Also notes local and total part-time employees, revenue, number of local offices, business description, and CEO. **Number listed:** 25

1. Crozar-Keystone Health System, with 6,831 employees
2. Boeing Defense & Space Group, 6,450
3. Mercy Health System of Southeastern Pennyslvania, 4,505
4. Wyeth-Ayerst Laboratories Inc., 3,300
5. Villanova University, 1,550
6. Sun Co. Inc., 1,500
6. The Franklin Mint, 1,500
8. Elwyn Inc., 1,308
9. Arco Chemical Co., 1,020
10. Paco Energy Co., 993

Source: *Philadelphia Business Journal*, Book of Business Lists (annual), December 25, 1998, p. 100.

Dental Care Industry--Advertising

★1654★
LEADING ADVERTISERS IN DENTAL PUBLICATIONS, 1998
Ranked by: Market shares of expenditures, in percent. **Remarks:** Also notes rank and market share for 1996 and 1997 and percent change from previous years. **Number listed:** 12

1. Dentsply International Inc., with 4.43%
2. Ivoclar North American, 2.73%
3. Ultradent Products Inc., 2.54%
4. Discus Dental Inc., 2.35%
5. Jeneric/Pentron Inc., 2.19%
6. Bisco Dental Products, 2.04%
7. Kerr Manufacturing Co., 1.97%
8. Den-Mat Corp., 1.92%
9. GC America Inc., 1.83%
10. Colgate Palmolive Co., 1.63%

Source: *Medical Marketing & Media*, Healthcare Advertising Review (annual), April, 1998, p. 57.

★1655★
MOST ADVERTISED DENTAL PRODUCTS/ SERVICES, 1998
Ranked by: Market share, in percent. **Remarks:** Also notes rank and market share for 1996 and 1997 and percent change from previous years. **Number listed:** 12

1. Colgate Total Toothpaste (Colgate Palmolive Co.), with 1.16%
2. Crest Extra Whitening Toothpaste (Proctor & Gamble), .77%
3. Trex Trophy Dental Digital X-Ray System (Trex Medical), .73%
4. Alert Amalgam Restoration Treatment (Jeneric/ Pentron Inc.), .70%
5. Fuji Plus Glass Ionomer Cement (GC America Inc.), .66%
6. Sonic Plaque Removal Instruments (Optiva Corp.), .65%
7. Vicoprofen (Knoll Pharmaceutical Co.), .64%
8. Opalescence Tooth Whitening Family (Ultradent Products Inc.), .63%
9. Universal Adhesive System (Bisco Dental Products), .62%
10. Dpa-300 Digital Still Recorder (Sony), .57%

Source: *Medical Marketing & Media*, Healthcare Advertising Review (annual), April, 1998, p. 57.

Dental Care Products

★1656★
BEST-SELLING TOOTHPASTE BRANDS, 1998
Ranked by: Sales, in millions of dollars. **Remarks:** Also notes media expenditures and advertising agencies. **Number listed:** 5

1. Colgate, with $477.5 million
2. Crest, $410
3. Aquafresh, $169.5
4. Mentadent, $164.2
5. Arm & Hammer, $94.8

Source: *Superbrands*, America's Top 2000 Brands, June 21, 1999, p. S52.

Dental Health Maintenance Organizations--Florida

★1657★
TOP DENTAL PLANS IN FLORIDA, 1999*
Ranked by: Number of members in Florida. **Remarks:** Also notes number of Florida providers, employees, offices, year founded, and senior Florida executive. **Number listed:** 13

1. Oral Health Services Inc. (Miami), with 1,000,000 members
2. MetLife (Tampa), 700,000
3. American Dental Plan Inc. (Gainesville), 599,374
4. Cigna Dental Care (Plantation), 416,968
5. Prudential Health Care Plan Inc. (Atlanta, GA), 373,381
6. Protective Dental Care (Jacksonville), 215,860
7. The Dental Concern/Humana (Louisville, KY), 197,500
8. Signature Dental Plan (Schaumburg, IL), 178,664
9. Guardian Life Insurance Co. of America (Tampa), 172,650
10. International Dental Plans (Hollywood, FL), 150,000

Source: *Florida Trend*, TopRank Florida (annual), 1999, p. 64.

Deodorants and Antiperspirants

★1658★
BEST-SELLING DEODORANT BRANDS RANKED BY MARKET SHARE, 1998
Ranked by: Percent of market share. **Remarks:** Also notes sales and unit sales. **Number listed:** 10

1. Secret, with 15.1%
2. Right Guard, 10.2%
3. Mennen, 8.8%
4. Degree, 7.6%
5. Sure, 7.1%
6. Arrid, 6.4%
7. Ban, 6.2%
8. Old Spice, 5.3%
9. Lady Mennen, 5.1%
10. Soft 'n' Dri, 4.3%

Source: *Drug Store News*, August 24, 1998, p. 121.

★1659★
BEST-SELLING DEODORANT BRANDS RANKED BY SALES, 1998
Ranked by: Sales, in millions of dollars. **Remarks:** Also notes unit sales. **Number listed:** 10

1. Secret, with $233.4 million
2. Right Guard, $157.3
3. Mennen, $135.5
4. Degree, $117.2
5. Sure, $109.3
6. Arrid, $98.4
7. Ban, $96
8. Old Spice, $81.5
9. Lady Mennen, $78.9
10. Soft 'n' Dri, $67

Source: *Drug Store News*, August 24, 1998, p. 121.

Department Stores

★1660★
TOP DEPARTMENT STORES RANKED BY FURNITURE AND BEDDING SALES, 1997
Ranked by: Sales of furniture and bedding, in millions of dollars. **Remarks:** Also notes previous year results, percent change, furniture and bedding sales as a percent of total sales, and total number of stores. **Number listed:** 25

1. JC Penney, with $747,000,000 million

2. Rich's Lazarus Goldsmith's, $176.3
3. Macy's East, $143.3
4. Daytons Hudson's Marshall Field's, $131
5. Macy's West, $121.2
6. Dillard's, $110
7. Hecht's, $92
8. Bloomingdale's, $89.6
9. The Bon Marche, $84.8
10. Burdines, $83.5

Source: *Furniture/Today*, Furniture/Today (annual), July 27, 1998, p. 17.

★1661★
TOP DISCOUNT DEPARTMENT STORE, 1997
Ranked by: Sales, in millions of dollars. **Remarks:** Also notes 1996 sales, percent change, number of stores, and average store size. **Number listed:** 28

1. Wal-Mart, with $58,002 million
2. Kmart, $27,559
3. Target, $20,368
4. Dollar General, $2,627
5. Shopko, $2,577
6. Caldor, $2,497
7. Ames, $2,325
8. Family Dollar Stores, $1,995
9. Hills Stores, $1,768
10. Bradlees, $1,392

Source: *Discount Store News*, Discount Industry Annual Report, July 13, 1998, p. 77.

Department Stores--Men's Departments

★1662★
TOP METROPOLITAN AREAS RANKED BY MEN'S AND BOY'S CLOTHING SALES, 1998*
Ranked by: Sales, in millions of dollars. **Number listed:** 321

1. Chicago, IL, with $2,341,142 million
2. New York, NY, $2,173,841
3. Los Angeles-Long Beach, CA, $1,899,368
4. Washington, DC, $1,459,842
5. Philadelphia, PA, $1,331,731
6. Detroit, MI, $1,229,373
7. Atlanta, GA, $1,158,770
8. Boston-Lawrence-Lowell-Brockton, MA, $1,119,831
9. Dallas, TX, $1,055,883
10. Houston, TX, $1,003,467

Source: *S&MM*, Survey of Buying Power (annual), August, 1998, p. 194.

Detroit Metropolitan Area--Industries

★1663★
LARGEST EMPLOYERS IN DETROIT, 1998
Ranked by: Full-time employees. **Remarks:** Also notes top local executive, previous year results, and Michigan totals. **Number listed:** 25

1. City of Detroit, with 17;302 employees
2. Detroit Public Schools, 17,286
3. Detroit Medical Center, 13,987
4. Chrysler Corp., 12,571
5. U.S. Government, 11,735
6. Henry Ford Health System, 8,247
7. General Motors Corp., 7,307
8. St. John Health System, 5,974
9. American Axle & Manufacturing Inc., 4,824
10. Wayne County Government, 4,693

Source: *Crain's Detroit Business*, August 3, 1998, p. 29.

★1664★
TOP PUBLICLY HELD COMPANIES IN THE DETROIT AREA, 1997
Ranked by: Revenues, in millions of dollars. **Remarks:** Also notes figures for 1996, type of industry, net income, stock price high and low, and ticker symbol. **Number listed:** 92

1. General Motors, with $178,174 million
2. Ford Motor Co., $153,627
3. Chrysler Corp., $61,147
4. Kmart, $32,183
5. Lear Corp., $7,342.9
6. CMS Energy Corp., $4,787
7. Kelly Services Inc., $3,852.9
8. DTE Energy Co., $3,764
9. Masco, $3,760
10. Meritor Automotive Corp., $3,309

Source: *Detroit Crain's Business*, August 31, 1998, p. 9+.

Dhaka Stock Exchange

★1665★
LARGEST LISTED COMPANIES ON THE DHAKA STOCK EXCHANGE, 1997
Ranked by: Capitalization, in millions of dollars. **Number listed:** 20

1. Singer Bangladesh, with $6,244,400 million
2. BTC Ltd., $5,209,200
3. Beximco Pharma, $3,550,180
4. Shinepukur, $2,549,480
5. Chittagong Cement, $2,145,630
6. Square Pharma, $2,050,250
7. BOC Ltd., $1,780,840
8. Glaxo, $1,640,610
9. Padma Oil Co. Ltd., $1,580,940
10. Bata Shoe, $1,490,570

Source: *Euromoney Publications*, SSB Guide to World Equity Markets (annual), 1998, p. 76.

Diapers, Infants

★1666★
TOP DIAPER AND TRAINING PANTS BRANDS, 1998
Ranked by: Sales, in U.S. dollars. **Remarks:** Also notes unit sales. **Number listed:** 9

1. Huggies, with $1.6 billion
2. Pampers, $991.7
3. Luvs, $467.2
4. Drypers, $131.5
5. Fitti, $28.9
6. Cuddles, $3.7
7. Comfees, $2.5
8. Snuggems, $2.1
9. Baby's Choice, $800

Source: *Mass Market Retailer*, November 2, 1999, p. 41.

★1667★
TOP DISPOSABLE DIAPER BRANDS, 1998
Ranked by: Total sales, in millions of dollars. **Remarks:** Also notes lead agency and media expenditures. **Number listed:** 5
1. Huggies, with $1,563.7 million
2. Pampers, $1,009.7
3. Private Label, $624.9
4. Luvs, $475.5
5. Drypers, $134.5

Source: *Brandweek*, America's Top 2,000 Brands, June 21, 1999, p. S56.

Diet

★1668★
TOP DIET AIDS, 1998
Ranked by: Sales, in millions of dollars. **Remarks:** Also notes unit sales, market share and percent change. **Number listed:** 10
1. Ultra Slim Fast, with $368.3 million
2. Ensure, $146.8
3. Ensure Plus, $89.2
4. Private Label, $62.2
5. Boost, $53.6
6. Nestle Sweet Success, $50.6
7. Pedia Sure Weight, $33.5
8. Slim Fast Jump Start, $29.7
9. Slim Fast, $24.6
10. Ensure Light, $19.7

Source: *Supermarket Business*, October, 1998, p. 69.

★1669★
TOP DIET/WEIGHT LOSS CANDY AND TABLET BRANDS, 1998
Ranked by: Sales, in millions of dollars. **Remarks:** Also notes percent change from previous year, market share, and unit sales. **Number listed:** 10
1. Dexatrim, with $39.1 million
2. Private Label, $16.9
3. Acutrim, $8.2
4. Ultra Chroma Slim, $7
5. Great American Nutrition, $6.7
6. Diet System Six, $6.1
7. PhenCal 106, $6
8. Chroma Slim Plus, $4.5
9. Sundown, $4.4
10. Schiff, $3.7

Source: *Drug Store News*, February 1, 1999, p. 24.

Direct Mail Advertising

★1670★
TOP SPENDERS FOR DIRECT MAIL MATERIALS
Ranked by: Expenditures, in billions of dollars. **Remarks:** Also notes projected growth rate. **Number listed:** 20
1. Miscellaneous Retail, with $8.82 billion
2. Business Services, $8.57
3. General Merchandise Stores, $7.97
4. Communications, $6.89
5. Wholesale trade, $6.45
6. Transportation, except Airlines, $5.22
7. Publishing & printing, $5.15
8. Depository Institutions, $4.7
9. Transportation Equipment, $4.44
10. Electrical Machinery, $3.95

Source: *Graphic Arts Monthly*, Top Spenders on Advertising & Printing (annual), February, 1999, p. 53.

Direct Marketing Agencies

★1671★
TOP DIRECT MARKETING AGENCIES, 1998
Ranked by: Direct Marketing revenue, in thousands of dollars. **Remarks:** Also notes U.S. agency revenue. **Number listed:** 10
1. Brann Worldwide, with $287,580 thousand
2. Draft Worldwide, $142,641
3. Rapp Collins Worldwide, $126,148
4. Bronnercom, $124,200
5. Wunderman Cato Johnson, $120,495
6. Harte-Hanks/DiMark, $90,538
7. Grey Direct Marketing, $82,740
8. OgilvyOne Worldwide, $77,200
9. Carlson Marketing Group, $75,757
10. MRM/Gillespie, $48,600

Source: *Advertising Age*, Top Agencies by U.S. Marketing Revenue (annual), May 17, 1999, p. 51.

★1672★
TOP DIRECT MARKETING AGENCIES RANKED BY MARKETING SERVICES REVENUE, 1998
Ranked by: Revenue, in thousands of dollars. **Remarks:** Also notes previous year ranking, and total agency revenue. **Number listed:** 205
1. Brann Worldwide, with $287,580 thousand
2. Carlson Marketing Group, $254,096
3. Ha-Lo, $212,800
4. Draft Worldwide, $180,558
5. Wunderman Cato Johnson, $140,110
6. Rapp Collins Worldwide, $126,148
7. Bronnercom, $124,200
8. CommonHealth, $107,940
9. Alcone Marketing Group, $107,250
10. Cyrk-Simon, $106,171

Source: *Advertising Age*, Top Agencies by U.S. Marketing Revenue (annual), May 17, 1999, p. 52.

★1673★
TOP DIRECT RESPONSE AGENCIES BY BILLINGS, 1998
Ranked by: Total billings, in 1998. **Remarks:** Also notes revenue. **Number listed:** 10
1. Draft Worldwide, with $1,337,452 million
2. Wunderman Cato Johnson, $1,035,950
3. Bronner Slosberg Humphrey, $848,414
4. Rapp Collins Worldwide, $803,000
5. Blau Marketing Technologies, $694,947
6. OgilvyOne, $591,386
7. Grey Direct, $368,100
8. Devon Direct, $290,000
9. Targetbase Marketing, $291,000
10. Customer Dev. Corp., $240,405

Source: *Adweek, Eastern Edition*, Agency Report Card (annual), April 19, 1999, p. 99.

★1674★
TOP MARKETING SERVICES SHOPS BY NON-U.S. REVENUE, 1998
Ranked by: Non-U.S. marketing services revenue, in thousands of dollars. **Remarks:** Also notes direct marketing and sales promotion revenue. **Number listed:** 10
1. Wunderman Cato Johnson, with $182,859 thousand
2. OgilvyOne Worldwide, $155,000
3. Brann Worldwide, $148,100
4. Rapp Collins Worldwide, $146,194
5. Bates/141 Worldwide, $107,400
6. Grey Direct Marketing Group, $77,860
7. Carlson Marketing Group, $76,251
8. Draft Worldwide, $58,344
9. MRM Worldwide, $57,000
10. Momentum, $40,700

Source: *Advertising Age*, Top Agencies by U.S. Marketing Revenue (annual), May 17, 1999, p. 54.

★1675★
TOP SALES PROMOTION AGENCIES, 1998
Ranked by: Sales Promotion Revenue, in thousands of dollars. **Remarks:** Also notes U.S. agency revenue. **Number listed:** 10
1. Carlson Marketing Group, with $178,339 thousand
2. Ha-Lo, $168,000
3. Alcone Marketing Group, $107,250
4. Cyrk-Simon, $106,171
5. CommonHealth, $88,872
6. Frankel & Co., $87,934
7. HMG Worldwide, $70,000
8. Spar Group, $69,023
9. TLP, $63,665
10. Integer Group, $59,057

Source: *Advertising Age*, Top Agencies by U.S. Marketing Revenue (annual), May 17, 1999, p. 51.

Direct Marketing Agencies--Great Britain

★1676★
TOP DIRECT MARKETERS BY TURNOVER, 1998
Ranked by: Turnover, in billions of British pounds. **Remarks:** Also notes gross profit and previous year results. **Number listed:** 72
1. WWAV Rapp Collins, with £71,370,000 pounds
2. Tequila Payne Stracey, n/a
3. OgilvyOne Worldwide London, £39,004,0000
4. Barraclough Hall Woolston Gray, £29,336,000
5. Joshua, £37,721,000
6. Evans Hunt Scott, £48,157,000
7. IMP, £36,289,000
8. Claydon Heeley, £26,805,000
9. KLP Euro RSCG, £26,810,000
10. McCann-Erickson Manchester, £49,358,000

Source: *Marketing*, Direct Marketing League Table (annual), March 11, 1999, p. 36+.

★1677★
TOP HYBRID DIRECT MARKETING AGENCIES, 1998
Ranked by: Gross profit, in British pounds. **Remarks:** Also notes previous year profits and turnover. **Number listed:** 10
1. Brann, with £40,522,000 pounds
2. Wunderman Cato Johnson, £28,300,000
3. Carlson, £24,754,000
4. Colleagues, £9,000,000
5. Advertising Research Marketing, £5,155,000
6. MBO, £5,085,000
7. Tri-Direct, £2,828,000
8. Eclipse Marketing Services, £1,557,000
9. UKAMS, £1,400,000
10. Response Advertising Media, £335,000

Source: *Marketing*, Direct Marketing League Tables (annual), March 11, 1999, p. 36.

★1678★
TOP LARGEST AGENCIES RANKED BY GROWTH, 1998
Ranked by: Percent change in gross profit from 1997 to 1998. **Remarks:** Also notes gross profit for both years. **Number listed:** 10
1. Black Cat, with 87.99%
2. Lowe Direct, 75.00%
3. Claydon Heeley, 65.64%
4. Perspectives, 56.37%
5. GGT Direct Advertising, 51.65%
6. Clarke Hooper Consulting, 49.90%
7. Momentum Integrated Comms, 35.00%
8. MBO, 34.03%
9. Communicator, 32.91%
10. The Haygarth Group, 31.46%

Source: *Marketing*, Direct Marketing League Tables (annual), March 11, 1999, p. 35.

★1679★
TOP SMALL AGENCIES RANKED BY GROWTH, 1998
Ranked by: Percent change in gross profit from 1997 to 1998. **Remarks:** Also notes gross profit for both years. **Number listed:** 10
1. Millennnium ADMP, with 160.00%
2. The Opus Group, 101.51%
3. WWAV Rapp Collins West, 86.05%
4. Wilson Harvey, 85.40%
5. Red Fish, 72.45%
6. Milton PDM, 69.98%
7. Manifesto, 66.54%
8. Ffwd Precision Marketing, 64.92%
9. CMB, 61.13%
10. Ohe Direct Agency, 58.37%

Source: *Marketing*, Direct Marketing League Tables (annual), March 11, 1999, p. 35.

Direct Response Advertising

★1680★
LEADING DIRECT RESPONSE AGENCIES, 1997
Ranked by: Revenue, in millions of dollars. **Number listed:** 20
1. Wunderman Cato Johnson, with $280.5 million
2. Rapp Collins Worldwide, $258.1
3. OgilvyOne Worldwide, $195.1
4. DIMAC Direct, $188.5
5. DraftWorldwide, $142.8
6. Bronner Slosberg Humphrey/Strategic Interactive Group, $101.3
7. FCB Direct, $83.7
8. Grey Direct Marketing Group, $82.5
9. DiMark, $75.5
9. Blau Marketing Technologies, $75.5

Source: *Business Marketing*, August, 1998, p. 6.

Disasters

★1681★
MOST EXPENSIVE CATASTROPHES, 1999*
Ranked by: Estimated insured losses, in billions of dollars. **Number listed:** 10
1. Hurricane Andrew Aug. '92, with $16.5 billion
2. Northridge Earthquake Jan. '94, $12.5
3. Hurricane Hugo Sept. '89, $4.2
4. Hurricane Opal Oct. '95, $2.1
5. Blizzard of 1993, Mar. '93, $1.7
5. Oakland Fire Oct. '91, $1.7
7. Hurricane Iniki Sept.'92, $1.6
8. Texas Hailstorm, May '95, $1.1
9. Loma Prieta Earthquake Oct. '89, $1.0
9. California Brush Fires, Oct./Nov. '93, $1.0

Source: *ENR*, April 26, 1999, p. I-22.

Discount Brokers

★1682★
TOP DISCOUNT BROKERS, 1999*
Ranked by: Firms are ranked in nine different categories to arrive at the overall rankings, ''web reliability'' was double-weighted. **Remarks:** Specific figures are not provided. **Number listed:** 21
1. Muriel Siebert
2. Waterhouse Securities
3. Quick & Reilly
4. Bidwell
5. Charles Schwab
6. National Discount Brokers
7. Accutrade
8. T. Rowe Price
9. Ameritrade
10. Jack White

Source: *Smart Money*, Top Discount Brokers (annual), June, 1999, p. 119.

Discount Stores

★1683★
LARGEST DISCOUNT CHAINS BY SALES, 1998
Ranked by: Sales, in billions of dollars. **Number listed:** 10
1. Wal-Mart, with $137.6 billion
2. Kmart, $33.7
3. Target, $23.1
4. Zellers, $4.50
5. Shopko, $2.98
6. Ames, $2.51
7. Caldor, $2.48
8. Hills, $1.75
9. Bradlees, $1.34
10. Pamida, $672.4

Source: *MMR*, Annual Report of the Mass Market Industries, May 3, 1999, p. 65.

★1684★
LARGEST DISCOUNT CHAINS BY SALES, 1997
Ranked by: Sales, in millions of dollars. **Remarks:** Also notes store count and earnings. **Number listed:** 150
1. Wal-Mart Stores, with $58,002 million
2. Kmart, $27,559
3. Wal-Mart Supercenter, $25,775
4. Sears Merchandise Group, $22,839
5. Costco, $21,484
6. Sam's Club, $20,668
7. Target, $20,368
8. Best Buy, $8,358
9. Circuit City, $7,997
10. Meijer, $7,950

Source: *Discount Store News*, Discount Industry Annual Report, July 13, 1998, p. 63+.

★1685★
LARGEST DISCOUNT CHAINS BY STORE COUNT, 1998
Ranked by: Number of Stores. **Number listed:** 10
1. Wal-Mart, with 3,601 stores
2. Kmart, 2,161
3. Target, 851
4. Ames, 456
5. Zellers, 341
6. Hills, 155
7. Pamida, 148
8. Shopko, 147
9. Caldor, 145
10. Rose's, 107

Source: *MMR*, Annual Report of the Mass Market Industries, May 3, 1999, p. 65.

★1686★
LARGEST MASS MARKET RETAILER BY SALES, 1998
Ranked by: Sales, in billions of dollars. **Number listed:** 10
1. Wal-Mart, with $137.6 billion
2. Kmart, $33.7
3. Kroger, $28.2
4. Safeway, $24.5
5. Target, $23.1
6. American Stores, $19.9
7. Ahold USA, $16.2
8. Albertson's, $16.0
9. Walgreens, $15.3
9. CVS, $15.3

Source: *MMR*, Annual Report of the Mass Market Industries, May 3, 1999, p. 62.

★1687★
LARGEST MASS MARKET RETAILERS BY STORE COUNT, 1998
Ranked by: Number of stores. **Number listed:** 10
1. CVS, with 4,122 stores
2. Rite Aid, 3,821
3. Wal-Mart, 3,601
4. Eckerd, 2,756
5. Walgreens, 2,647
6. Kmart, 2,161
7. American Stores, 1,580
8. Kroger, 1,410
9. Medicine Shoppe, 1,266
10. Food Lion, 1,207

Source: *MMR*, Annual Report of the Mass Market Industries, May 3, 1999, p. 62.

★1688★
LEADING MASS MERCHANDISERS BY PHARMACY SALES, 1998
Ranked by: Pharmacy sales, in millions of dollars. **Remarks:** Also notes 1997 pharmacy sales, percent of 1998 sales from

pharmacy, and number of stores with pharmacies. **Number listed:** 11

1. Wal-Mart, with $5,500 million
2. Kmart, $1,700
3. Shopko, $348
4. Meijer Inc., $276
5. Target, $270
6. Costco Wholesale, $215
7. Fred's Inc., $160
8. Bi-Mart Corp., $63
9. Pamida, $49
10. Fedco, $27

Source: *Drug Store News*, Annual Report of the Drug Industry, April 26, 1999, p. 68.

★1689★
TOP DISCOUNT AND FASHION RETAILERS IN THE S&P 500, 1998
Ranked by: Each company is ranked by eight criteria; one-year total return, three-year total return, one-year sales growth, three-year average annual sales growth, one-year profit growth, three-year average annual profit growth, net profit margins, and return on equity, with additional weight given to a company's sales. A company's composite score is calculated using the sum of all its ranks. **Remarks:** Overall score not provided. **Number listed:** 22

1. The Gap
2. Home Depot
3. TJX
4. Wal-Mart Stores
5. Lowe's
6. Dayton Hudson
7. Kohl's
8. Limited
9. Staples
10. Costco

Source: *Business Week*, Business Week 50: Top Companies of the S&P 500 (annual), March 29, 1999, p. 146.

Discount Stores--North America

★1690★
TOP NORTH AMERICAN DISCOUNT STORES, 1997
Ranked by: Sales, in million of dollars. **Remarks:** Also notes sales and earnings figures for previous year. **Number listed:** 40

1. Wal-Mart Stores, with $117,958 million
2. Sears, $41,269
3. Kmart, $32,183
4. Dayton Hudson, $27,757
5. Home Depot, $24,156
6. Costco, $21,484
7. American Stores Co., $19,139
8. Walgreen, $13,363
9. CVS, $12,738
10. Rite Aid Corp., $11,400

Source: *Discount Store News*, Discount Industry Annual Report, July 13, 1998, p. 74.

Dishwashing Machines

★1691★
BEST-SELLING DISHWASHERS, 1998
Ranked by: Market share, in percent. **Remarks:** Also notes 1993 market share. **Number listed:** 4

1. Whirlpool, with 39%
2. GEA, 37%
3. Maytag, 18%
4. Electrolux, 6%

Source: *Appliance Manufacturer*, April, 1999, p. 19.

Distilling Industry

See: **Liquor Industry**

Diversified Corporations

★1692★
CONGLOMERATES SPENDING THE MOST ON RESEARCH AND DEVELOPMENT, 1997
Ranked by: R&D expenditures, in millions of dollars. **Number listed:** 10

1. General Electric Co., with $1,498.7 million
2. United Technologies Corp., $1,185.4
3. Minnesota Mining & Manufacturing Co., $1,001.6
4. Rockwell International, $729.7
5. Philip Morris, $539.9
6. AlliedSignal Inc., $350.9
7. Textron, $219.6
8. Thermo Electron, $191.3
9. FMC Corp., $182
10. Sunstrand, $72.6

Source: *Research and Development*, Giants of R&D (annual), October, 1998, p. S-14.

★1693★
LEADING CONGLOMERATES IN THE S&P 500, 1998
Ranked by: Each company is ranked by eight criteria; one-year total return, three-year total return, one-year sales growth, three-year average annual sales growth, one-year profit growth, three-year average annual profit growth, net profit margins, and return on equity, with additional weight given to a company's sales. A company's composite score is calculated using the sum of all its ranks. **Remarks:** Overall score not provided. **Number listed:** 10

1. General Electric
2. AlliedSignal
3. Textron
4. TRW
5. EG&G
6. Harcourt General
7. Pall
8. Allegheny Teledyne
9. Tenneco
10. Ikon Office Solutions

Source: *Business Week*, Business Week 50: Top Companies of the S&P 500 (annual), March 29, 1999, p. 144.

Diversified Corporations--Asia

★1694★
MOST ADMIRED CONGLOMERATES IN ASIA, 1999
Ranked by: Scores (1-10) derived from a survey of chief executives, CEOs, and corporate board members. **Remarks:** Respondents rated companies in 8 attributes including quality of management, products and services, contribution to the local economy, being a good employer, potential for growth, being honest and ethical, potential for future profit, and ability to cope with the changing economic environment. Also notes previous year's score and overall rank. **Number listed:** 10

1. Genting, with 8.07%
2. Samsung, 7.78%
3. Hyundai, 7.44%
4. Charoen Pokphand, 7.41%
5. Swire Pacific, 7.33%
6. Cycle & Carriage, 7.30%
7. Hutchison Whampoa, 7.29%
8. Astra International, 6.88%
9. Perlis Plantations, 6.83%
10. LG Group, 6.78%

Source: *Asian Business*, Most Admired Companies in Asia (annual), May, 1999, p. 28.

Dog Food

See: **Pet Food**

Drug Industry

★1695★
LEADING CHEMICAL PROCESS COMPANIES BY PHARMACEUTICAL SALES, 1998
Ranked by: Sales, in millions of dollars. **Remarks:** Also notes 1998 profits and profit ratios, and per share data. **Number listed:** 16

1. Merck, with $26,898 million
2. Johnson & Johnson, $23,657
3. Bristol-Myers Squibb, $18,284
4. Pfizer, $13,544
5. American Home Products, $13,463
6. Abbott Laboratories, $12,478
7. Warner-Lambert, $10,214
8. Eli Lilly, $9,237
9. Schering-Plough, $8,077
10. Phamacia & Upjohn, $6,893

Source: *Chemical Week*, Chemical Week 300 (annual), May 12, 1999, p. 53.

★1696★
LEADING THERAPEUTIC TYPES, 1998
Ranked by: Sales, in millions of dollars. **Remarks:** Also notes previous year rank and percent growth. **Number listed:** 20

1. Anti-Ulcerants, with $6,215 million
2. Specific Neurotransmitter Modulators, $5,638
3. Cholesterol Reducers Rx Statins, $4,596
4. Calcium-channel blockers, $3,825
5. Cytostatics, $3,683
6. Ace Inhibitors, Alone, $2,634
7. Other Antipsychotics, $2,257
8. Cephalosporins, $2,235
9. Erythropoietins, $2,133
10. Seizure disorders, $2,079

Source: *Medical Marketing & Media*, May, 1999, p. 58.

★1697★
MOST ADMIRED PHARMACEUTICAL CORPORATIONS, 1998
Ranked by: Scores (1-10) derived from a survey of senior executives, outside directors and securities analysts. **Remarks:** Respondents rated companies in their own industry on 8 attributes of reputation. Also notes previous year's rank. **Number listed:** 10

1. Pfizer
2. Merck
3. Johnson & Johnson
4. Eli Lilly
5. Bristol-Myers Squibb
6. Schering-Plough
7. Warner-Lambert
8. Abbott Laboratories
9. American Home Products
10. Pharmacia & Upjohn

Source: *Fortune*, America's Most Admired Corporations (annual), March 1, 1999, p. F-5.

★1698★
PHARMACEUTICAL COMPANIES SPENDING THE MOST ON RESEARCH AND DEVELOPMENT, 1997
Ranked by: Research and Development expenditures, in millions of dollars. **Remarks:** Also notes domestic R&D ranking. **Number listed:** 15

1. Johnson & Johnson, with $2,167.8 million
2. Pfizer, $1,939.5
3. Merck, $1,678.0
4. American Home Products, $1,623.0
5. Bristol-Myers Squibb, $1,383.3
6. Eli Lilly, $1,378.5
7. Abbott Laboratories, $1,308.2
8. Pharmacia & Upjohn, $1,307.6
9. Schering-Plough, $841.4
10. Warner-Lambert, $667.1

Source: *Research and Development*, Giants of R&D (annual), October, 1998, p. S-15.

★1699★
RX PHARMACEUTICAL PRESCRIPTION LEADERS, 1998
Ranked by: Total prescriptions dispensed, in millions. **Remarks:** Also notes percent growth or decline. **Number listed:** 20

1. Premarin, with 46.8 million
2. Synthroid, 38.8
3. Hydrocodone w/APAP, 29.4
4. Trimox, 28.5
5. Prilosec, 26.7
6. Albuterol, 26.0
7. Lipitor, 24.9
8. Prozac, 24.8
9. Lanoxin, 24.2
10. Norvasc, 23.4

Source: *Medical Marketing & Media*, May, 1999, p. 62.

★1700★
TOP CORPORATIONS IN THE PHARMACEUTICALS INDUSTRY, 1998
Ranked by: Revenue, in millions of dollars. **Remarks:** Also notes profits and investment figures as well as number of employees. **Number listed:** 12

1. Merck, with $26,898 million

2. Johnson & Johnson, $23,657
3. Bristol-Myers Squibb, $18,284
4. Pfizer, $14,704
5. American Home Products, $13,463
6. Abbott Laboratories, $12,478
7. Warner-Lambert, $10,214
8. Eli Lilly, $10,051
9. Schering-Plough, $8,077
10. Pharmacia & Upjohn, $6,893

Source: *Fortune*, Fortune 500 Largest U.S. Corporations (annual), April 26, 1999, p. F-66.

★1701★

TOP CORPORATIONS IN THE PHARMACEUTICALS INDUSTRY, 1997

Ranked by: Revenue, in billions of dollars. **Remarks:** Also notes percent change from previous year. **Number listed:** 15

1. Merck, with $5.6 billion
2. Glaxo Wellcome, $5.5
2. Bristol-Myers Squibb, $5.5
4. Pfizer, $5.1
5. Eli Lilly, $4.8
6. American Home Products, $4.4
7. Johnson & Johnson, $4.1
8. Schering-Plough, $3.6
8. Novartis, $3.6
10. SmithKline Beecham, $3.4

Source: *Chemical Market Reporter*, November 23, 1998, p. FR4.

★1702★

TOP HEALTHCARE COMPANIES IN THE S&P 500, 1998

Ranked by: Each company is ranked by eight criteria; one-year total return, three-year total return, one-year sales growth, three-year average annual sales growth, one-year profit growth, three-year average annual profit growth, net profit margins, and return on equity, with additional weight given to a company's sales. A company's composite score is calculated using the sum of all its ranks. **Remarks:** Overall scores not provided. **Number listed:** 36

1. Schering-Plough
2. Warner-Lambert
3. Merck
4. Eli Lilly
5. Bristol-Myers Squibb
6. Amgen
7. Walgreen
8. Pfizer
9. CVS
10. Abbott Laboratories

Source: *Business Week*, Business Week 50: Companies of the S&P 500 (annual), March 29, 1999, p. 152+.

★1703★

TOP OVER-THE-COUNTER DRUGS THAT WERE PREVIOUSLY PRESCRIPTION DRUGS, 1998

Ranked by: Sales, in percent of the top 21 over-the-counter products. **Remarks:** This list is comprised of switched products alone. **Number listed:** 9

1. Advil, with 9%
2. Pepcid AC, 7%
3. Aleve, 4%
3. Benadryl, 4%
5. Motrin IB, 3%
5. Tagamet HB, 3%
5. Zantac 75, 3%
5. Imodium AD, 3%
5. Rogaine, 3%

Source: *Drug Topics*, July 20, 1998, p. 71.

★1704★

TOP PRESCRIPTIONS BY SALES VOLUME, 1998

Ranked by: Sales volume, in millions of dollars. **Remarks:** Also notes percent growth or decline. **Number listed:** 20

1. Prilosec, with $2,933 million
2. Prozac, $2,181
3. Lipitor, $1,544
4. Zocor, $1,481
5. Epogen, $1,455
6. Zoloft, $1,392
7. Prevacid, $1,245
8. Paxil, $1,190
9. Claritin, $1,150
10. Norvasc, $1,086

Source: *Medical Marketing & Media*, May, 1999, p. 62.

★1705★

TOP THERAPEUTIC PHARMACEUTICALS, 1998

Ranked by: Number of prescriptions. **Remarks:** Also notes 1997 rank and percent growth or decline. **Number listed:** 20

1. Codeine & Comb, non injectable, with 103.1 million
2. Calcium-channel blockers, 91.5
3. Ace Inhibitors, 83.5
4. Anti-Ulcerants, 81.4
5. Specific Neurotransmitter Modulators, 77.4
6. Antiarithirtics, Plain, 76.9
7. Beta Blockers, 71.9
8. O/C Estrogen/Progesterone, 68.7
9. Cholesterol Reducers Rx Statins, 67.9
10. Oral Diabetes, 64.2

Source: *Medical Marketing & Media*, May, 1999, p. 58.

Drug Industry--Advertising

★1706★

TOP ADVERTISERS IN PHARMACY PUBLICATIONS, 1998

Ranked by: Market share of advertising expenditures, in percent. **Remarks:** Also notes percent change from previous year. **Number listed:** 12

1. Pfizer Laboratories, with 4.80%
2. Astra Pharmaceuticals, 2.44%
3. Schering Corp., 1.66%
4. Roxane Laboratories Inc., 1.52%
5. Merck, 1.38%
6. Eli Lilly, 1.32%
7. Forest Pharmaceuticals, 1.25%
8. Zeneca Pharmaceuticals Group, 1.24%
9. Procter & Gamble, 1.20%
10. ESI Lederle, 1.13%

Source: *Medical Marketing & Media*, Healthcare Advertising Review (annual), April, 1999, p. 62.

Drug Industry, International

★1707★

LEADING BIO-TECH DRUGS, 1997

Ranked by: Worldwide sales, in millions of dollars. **Remarks:** Also notes biological basis and use. **Number listed:** 15

1. Epogen, with $1,161 million
2. Neupogen, $1,056
3. Procrit, $1,000

4. Humulin, $936
5. Intron-A, $598
6. Engerix-B, $584
7. Cerezyme, $333
8. Activase, $261
9. Humatrope, $260
10. ReoPro, $254

Source: *C&EN*, August 10, 1998, p. 30.

★1708★
TOP BRANDED PHARMACEUTICALS, 1998
Ranked by: Worldwide sales, in millions of dollars. **Remarks:** Also notes company, market share and previous year results. **Number listed:** 10

1. Zocor, with $3,926 million
2. Losec, $3,083
3. Prozac, $2,651
4. Vasotec, $2,499
5. Prilosec, $2,480
6. Norvasc, $2,408
7. Claritin, $1,926
8. Zantac, $1,850
9. Paxil, $1,667
10. Augmentin, $1,606

Source: *Chemical Market Reporter*, January 4, 1999, p. 18.

★1709★
TOP PHARMACEUTICAL COMPANIES WORLDWIDE BY MARKET VALUE, 1997
Ranked by: Market value, in billions of dollars. **Number listed:** 13

1. Merck, with $187.3 billion
2. Pfizer, $150.2
3. Novartis, $130.0
4. Bristol-Myers Squibb, $128.5
5. Glaxo Wellcome, $116.1
6. Johnson & Johnson, $107.2
7. Eli Lilly, $95.6
8. Schering-Plough, $80.4
9. Abbott Laboratories, $75.9
10. American Home Products, $70.1

Source: *Financial Times*, December 9, 1998, p. 21.

★1710★
WORLD'S LARGEST PHARMACEUTICALS COMPANIES BY REVENUE, 1997
Ranked by: Revenue, in millions of dollars. **Number listed:** 10

1. Merck (U.S.), with $23,637 million
2. Johnson & Johnson (U.S.), $22,629
3. Novartis (Switzerland), $21,494
4. Bristol-Myers Squibb (U.S.), $16,701
5. American Home Products (U.S.), $14,196
6. Glaxo Wellcome (Great Britain), $13,072
7. Roche Holding (Switzerland), $12,937
8. SmithKline Beecham (Great Britain), $12,769
9. Pfizer (U.S.), $12,504
10. Abbott Laboratories (U.S.), $11,883

Source: *Fortune*, The Global 500: World's Biggest Corporations (annual), August 3, 1998, p. F-23+.

Drug Industry--New Jersey

★1711★
LARGEST PHARMACEUTICAL COMPANIES IN NEW JERSEY, 1998
Ranked by: Number of local employees. **Remarks:** Also notes contact information, year founded, CEO, and internet address and description of business. **Number listed:** 25

1. Johnson & Johnson, with 13,000 employees
2. Bristol-Myers Squibb, 8,000
3. Merck, 5,263
4. Schering-Plough, 5,147
5. American Home Products, 4,069
6. Novartis Pharmaceuticals Corp., 3,500
7. Hoffman La-Roche, 3,000
8. Warner-Lambert, 2,700
9. Janssen Pharmaceuticals, 1,100
10. Organon Inc., 1,010

Source: *New Jersey Business*, Book of Lists (annual), 1999, p. 36.

Drug Industry--Philadelphia Metropolitan Area

★1712★
TOP PHARMACEUTICAL COMPANIES IN PHILADELPHIA, 1998
Ranked by: Number of local employees. **Remarks:** Also notes contact information, description of business, products, CEO, and year founded. **Number listed:** 25

1. SmithKline Beecham, with 7,200 employees
2. Merck, 7,000
3. Wyeth-Ayerst Global Pharmaceuticals, 6,425
4. Zeneca Pharmaceuticals, 3,500
5. Rhone-Poulenc Rorer Inc., 2,000
6. DuPont Merck Pharmaceutical Co., 1,767
7. McNeil Consumer Products Co., 1,200
8. Astra/Merck Inc., 600
9. Teva Pharmaceuticals USA, 572
10. Sanofi Research, 480

Source: *Philadelphia Business Journal*, Book of Lists (annual), December 25, 1998, p. 83.

Drug Stores

★1713★
LEADING METROPOLITAN AREAS RANKED BY DRUGSTORE SALES, 1998*
Ranked by: Sales, in millions of dollars. **Number listed:** 321

1. Chicago, IL, with $4,176,813 million
2. New York, NY, $3,296,918
3. Philadelphia, PA, $2,528,913
4. Detroit, MI, $2,108,681
5. Los Angeles-Long Beach, CA, $1,790,639
6. Boston-Lawrence-Lowell-Brockton, MA, $1,665,487
7. Washington, DC, $1,590,241
8. Cleveland-Lorain-Elyria, OH, $1,552,867
9. Nassau-Suffolk, $1,400,114
10. Houston, TX, $1,397,102

Source: *Sales & Marketing Management*, August, 1998, p. 23.

★1714★
MOST ADMIRED FOOD AND DRUG STORES, 1998.
Ranked by: Scores (1-10) derived form a survey of senior executives, outside directors and securities analysts. **Remarks:** Respondents rated companies in their own industry on 8 attributes of reputation. Also notes previous year's rank. **Number listed:** 10

1. Safeway, with 7.49 points
2. Publix Super Markets, 7.48
3. Walgreen, 7.27
4. Albertson's, 7.21
5. Kroger, 7.04
6. CVS, 6.53
7. Food Lion, 5.70
8. Winn-Dixie Stores Inc., 5.65
9. American Stores, 5.26
10. A&P, 4.51

Source: *Fortune*, America's Most Admired Corporations (annual), March 1, 1999, p. F-3.

★1715★
TOP OVER-THE-COUNTER PRIVATE LABEL CATEGORIES IN DRUG STORES, 1997
Ranked by: Drug sales, in millions of dollars. **Number listed:** 10

1. Vitamins, with $358.9 million
2. Internal Analgesics, $226.5
3. Cold/allergy sinus tablets/lozenges, $162.2
4. Laxatives, $92.3
5. First Aid Treatments, $90.0
6. Adult Incontinence, $71.1
7. Feminine Needs, $48.1
8. Cold/allergy/sinus liquid, $47.3
9. Cough Syrup, $44.3
10. Antacids, $42.6

Source: *Drug Store News*, November 9, 1998, p. 54.

Drug Stores--Chain and Franchise Operations

★1716★
BUSIEST PHARMACIES RANKED BY AVERAGE SALES PER STORE, 1998
Ranked by: Sales, in thousands of dollars. **Remarks:** Also notes average store size. **Number listed:** 43

1. Navarro Discount Pharmacies, Inc., with $12,000 thousand
2. Marc's, $11,063
3. Phar-Mor Inc., $10,385
4. Discount Drug Mart, $8,720
5. Longs Drug Stores, $8,574
6. Price-Less Drug Stores, $8,375
7. Big A Drug Stores, $7,857
8. Texas Drug Warehouse, $6,555
9. Drug Emporium, $6,304
10. Walgreen, $6,005

Source: *Drug Store News*, Annual Report of the Drug Industry, April 26, 1999, p. 60.

★1717★
LARGEST DRUG STORE CHAINS BY NUMBER OF STORES, 1998
Ranked by: Number of stores. **Number listed:** 50

1. CVS Corp., with 4,122 stores
2. Rite Aid Corp., 3,821
3. Eckerd Corp., 2,748
4. Walgreen, 2,549
5. American Drug Stores, 1,146
6. Medicine Shoppe International, 1,065
7. Longs Drug Stores, 381
8. Brooks Pharmacy, 251
9. Drug Emporium, 197
10. Kerr Drug Inc., 157

Source: *Drug Store News*, Annual Report of the Drug Industry, April 26, 1999, p. 54.

★1718★
LARGEST 24-HOUR DRUG STORE CHAINS, 1998
Ranked by: Number of 24-hour stores. **Remarks:** Also notes percent of locations. **Number listed:** 14

1. Walgreen, with 500 stores
2. Rite Aid Corp., 285
3. CVS Corp., 206
4. Eckerd Corp., 160
5. Drug Emporium Inc., 24
6. Duane Reade Inc., 9
7. Farmacias El Amal, 8
8. Brooks Pharmacy, 6
9. Phar-Mor Inc., 5
10. Longs Drug Stores, 2

Source: *Drug Store News*, Annual Report of the Drug Industry, April 26, 1999, p. 58.

★1719★
LEADING DRUG STORE CHAINS BY PRESCRIPTION SALES, 1998
Ranked by: Sales, in millions of dollars. **Remarks:** Also notes 1997 Rx sales and 1998 percent of sales from pharmacy. **Number listed:** 50

1. CVS Corp., with $8,536 million
2. Walgreen, $7,650
3. Eckerd Corp., $6,665
4. Rite Aid Corp., $6,365
5. American Drug Stores, $2,900
6. Medicine Shoppe International, $1,294
7. Longs Drug Stores, $1,210
8. Brooks Pharmacy, $428
9. Drug Emporium, $384
10. Genovese Drug Stores, $340

Source: *Drug Store News*, Annual Report of the Drug Industry, April 26, 1999, p. 62+.

★1720★
LEADING DRUG STORE CHAINS BY SALES VOLUME, 1998
Ranked by: Sales, in millions of dollars. **Remarks:** Also notes previous year sales and percent change. **Number listed:** 50

1. Walgreen, with $15,306 million
2. CVS Corp., $15,273
3. Rite Aid Corp., $12,732
4. Eckerd Corp., $10,325
5. American Drug Stores, $6,500
6. Longs Drug Stores, $3,267
7. Medicine Shoppe International, $1,362
8. Drug Emporium Inc., $1,242
9. Phar-Mor Inc., $1,101
10. Genovese Drug Stores Inc., $830

Source: *Drug Store News*, Annual Report of the Drug Industry, April 26, 1999, p. 52+.

★1721★
TOP DRUG STORE CHAIN BY DOLLAR VOLUME ACCORDING TO *MASS MARKET RETAILER*
Ranked by: Dollar volume, in billions of dollars. **Number listed:** 20

1. Walgreens, with $15.3 billion
1. CVS, $1.5

3. Rite Aid, $12.7
4. Eckerd, $10.30
5. American Drug Stores, $6.09
6. Longs, $3.27
7. SDM, $2.79
8. Jean Coutu, $1.40
9. Medicine Shoppe, $1.31
10. Phar-Mor, $1.10

Source: *Mass Market Retailers*, Annual Report of the Mass Market Industries, May 3, 1999, p. 115.

★1722★
TOP DRUG STORE CHAINS BY STORE COUNT ACCORDING TO *MASS MARKET RETAILER*
Ranked by: Number of stores. **Number listed:** 20

1. CVS, with 4,122 stores
2. Rite Aid, 3,975
3. Eckerd, 2,756
4. Walgreens, 2,647
5. Medicine Shoppe, 1,266
6. American Drug Stores, 1,056
7. SDM, 824
8. Jean Coutu, 496
9. Longs, 381
10. Katz Enterprises, 298

Source: *Mass Market Retailers*, Annual Report of the Mass Market Industries, May 3, 1999, p. 115.

Drugs, Prescription

See: **Prescriptions**

Drugstores

See: **Drug Stores**

Elderly--Housing

★1723★
TOP MANAGERS OF SENIOR HOUSING, 1998
Ranked by: Units managed. **Remarks:** Also notes previous year's rank, location of headquarters, CEO and number of properties managed. **Number listed:** 25

1. Colson & Colson/Holiday Retirement Corp., with 24,504 units
2. Professional Community Management, 19,731
3. Marriott Senior Living Services, 18,400
4. Life Care Services Corp., 16,381
5. Alternative Living Services Inc., 12,304
6. Emeritius Corp., 10,649
7. American Retirement Corp., 9,933
8. ARV Assisted Living Inc., 9,127
9. Senior Lifestyle Corp., 8,107
10. Grand Court Lifestyles Inc., 5,720

Source: *National Real Estate Investor*, Top 25 Senior Housing Owners & Managers (annual), October, 1998, p. A3.

★1724★
TOP OWNERS OF SENIOR HOUSING, 1998
Ranked by: Units owned. **Remarks:** Also notes previous year's rank, location of headquarters, CEO and number of properties owned. **Number listed:** 25

1. Colson & Colson/Holiday Retirement Corp., with 23,706 units
2. Prometheus Senior Quarters, 13,626
3. Alternative Living Services Inc., 11,579
4. Health Care REIT Inc., 10,211
5. Emeritius Corp., 9,561
6. Meditrust Corp., 7,518
7. Nationwide Health Properties Inc., 7,397
8. Host Marriott Corp., 7,216
9. Senior Lifestyle Corp., 7,206
10. ARV Assisted Living Inc., 7,137

Source: *National Real Estate Investor*, Top 25 Senior Housing Owners & Managers (annual), October, 1998, p. A2.

Electric Appliances, Domestic

See: **Household Appliances**

Electric Irons

★1725★
BEST-SELLING IRONS, 1998
Ranked by: Market share, in percent. **Remarks:** Also notes 1993 market share. **Number listed:** 5

1. Black & Decker, with 38%
2. Hamilton Beach/Procter-Silex, 36%
3. Sunbeam-Oster, 13%
4. Rowenta, 5%
5. Others, 8%

Source: *Appliance Manufacturer*, April, 1999, p. 22.

Electric Power

★1726★
TOP ELECTRIC POWER BOND COUNSEL, 1998
Ranked by: Amount, in thousands of dollars. **Remarks:** Also notes number of issues. **Number listed:** 10

1. Willkie Farr & Gallagher, with $1,202,800 thousand
2. Orrick, Herrington & Sutcliffe, $951,020
3. Brown & Wood, $706,200
4. Hawkins, Delafield & Wood, $584,400
5. Oliver, Maner & Gray, $397,800
6. Fulbright & Jaworksi, $386,300
7. Curls, Brown & Roushon, $375,700
8. Ochoa & Sillas, $374,500
9. O'Melveny & Myers, $334,900
10. McNair Law Firm, $302,700

Source: *Bond Buyer Yearbook*, (annual), 1998, p. 177.

★1727★
TOP ELECTRIC POWER ISSUERS, 1998
Ranked by: Amount, in thousands of dollars. **Remarks:** Also notes number of issues. **Number listed:** 25

1. Washington Public Power Supply System, with $1,202,800 thousand
2. Puerto Rico Electric Power Authority, $694,300
3. Jacksonville Electric Authority, FL, $466,620
4. Municipal Electric Authority of Georgia, $397,800
5. Southern California Public Power Authority, $375,700
6. Sacramento Municipal Utility District, CA, $374,500
7. Chelan County Public Utility District, WA, $334,900
8. M-S-R Public Power Agency, CA, $314,200
9. Piedmont Municipal Power Agency, SC, $302,700
10. Salt River Project, AZ, $256,000

Source: *Bond Buyer Yearbook*, (annual), 1998, p. 177.

Electric Shavers

★1728★

BEST-SELLING SHAVERS FOR MEN, 1998

Ranked by: Market share, in percent. **Remarks:** Also notes 1993 market share. **Number listed:** 5

1. Norelco, with 55%
2. Remington, 22%
3. Braun, 15%
4. Wahl, 5%
5. Matsushita, 3%

Source: *Appliance Manufacturer*, April, 1999, p. 21.

★1729★

BEST-SELLING SHAVERS FOR WOMEN, 1998

Ranked by: Market share, in percent. **Remarks:** Also notes 1993 market share. **Number listed:** 5

1. Remington, with 34%
2. Norelco, 30%
3. Matsushita, 25%
4. Conair, 5%
5. Others, 6%

Source: *Appliance Manufacturer*, April, 1999, p. 22.

Electric Toasters

★1730★

BEST-SELLING ELECTRIC TOASTERS, 1998

Ranked by: Market share, in percent. **Remarks:** Also notes 1993 market share. **Number listed:** 7

1. Hamilton Beach/Proctor-Silex, with 60%
2. Toastmaster, 17%
3. Rival, 5%
4. Appliance Corp. (Betty Crocker), 2%
5. Black & Decker, 2%
6. Sunbeam-Oster, 1%
7. Others, 13%

Source: *Appliance Manufacturer*, April, 1999, p. 22.

Electric Utilities

★1731★

MOST ADMIRED ELECTRIC AND GAS UTILITIES, 1998

Ranked by: Scores (1-10) derived from a survey of senior executives, outside directors, and securities analysts. **Remarks:** Respondents rated companies in their own industry on 8 attributes of reputation. Also notes previous year's rank. **Number listed:** 11

1. Duke Energy, with 7.89 points
2. Southern, 7.31
3. FPL Group, 7.22
4. Edison International, 6.84
5. PG & E, 6.76
6. Texas Utilities, 6.63
7. Dominion Resources, 6.24
8. Consolidated Edison, 6.04
9. Utilicorp United, 5.89
10. Unicom, 5.67

Source: *Fortune*, America's Most Admired Corporations (annual), March 1, 1999, p. F-4.

Electronic Funds Transfer Systems--North America

★1732★

LEADING ELECTRONIC FUNDS TRANSFER NETWORKS, 1998

Ranked by: Monthly switch volume. **Remarks:** Also notes ATM and POS volume, terminals in network, terminal driven, debit cards, contact names, network membership and previous year's data. **Number listed:** 41

1. Interac Association, with 123,228,628 switches
2. MAC, 116,059,000
3. Star System, 71,045,876
4. HONOR Technologies, 64,609,571
5. NYCE Corp., 41,800,000
6. TransAlliance, 41,543,639
7. Pulse EFT Association, 27,963,720
8. Interlink, 21,400,000
9. Xpress 24, 19,335,767
10. Instant Cash, 18,495,255

Source: *Card Industry Directory*, Faulkner & Gray, 1999, p. 456+.

★1733★

LEADING ELECTRONIC FUNDS TRANSFER PROCESSORS, 1998

Ranked by: Number of transactions processed. **Remarks:** Also notes terminals driven, clients and market, executive officers and previous year's data. **Number listed:** 24

1. Midwest Payment Systems Inc., with 220,000,000 transactions
2. Banc One Payment Services LLC, 215,020,000
3. Deluxe Electronic Payment Systems, 201,400,000
4. Electronic Payment Services, Inc., 189,076,123
5. First Data Corp., 150,000,000
6. EDS Corp., 125,000,000
7. Bank of America, 90,948,000
8. Mellon Bank Network Services, 53,563,119
9. Wells Fargo Bank, 48,085,000
10. M & I Data Services Inc., 44,234,291

Source: *Card Industry Directory*, Faulkner & Gray, 1999, p. 444+.

Electronic Industries

★1734★
BEST-PERFORMING ELECTRONICS COMPANIES BY DEBT ON EQUITY, 1997
Ranked by: Debt to equity, in percent. **Remarks:** Also notes top 200 average. **Number listed:** 10
1. Anacomp, with 1,775.9%
2. Beckman Coulter, 1,468.5%
3. Ascend Communications, 574.9%
4. Xerox, 253.8%
5. Berg Electronics, 252.6%
6. Mangnetex, 238.6%
7. GTE, 222.6%
8. Lockheed Martin, 220.3%
9. Pioneer-Standard Electronics Inc., 174.5%
10. ITT Industries, 160.9%

Source: *Electronic Business*, Top 200 (annual), July, 1998, p. 81.

★1735★
BEST-PERFORMING ELECTRONICS COMPANIES BY 5-YEAR ANNUAL REVENUE GROWTH, 1997
Ranked by: 5-year annual revenue growth, in percent. **Remarks:** Also notes top 200 average. **Number listed:** 10
1. CHS Electronics, with 126.4%
2. Smart Modular Technologies, 117.7%
3. Network Associates, 113.8%
4. Glenayre Technologies, 96%
5. Peoplesoft, 91.6%
6. Bay Networks, 89.8%
7. Qualcomm, 81.1%
8. Cisco Systems, 80.1%
9. S3 Inc., 7.2%
10. BTG, 69.3%

Source: *Electronic Business*, Top 200 (annual), July, 1998, p. 76.

★1736★
BEST-PERFORMING ELECTRONICS COMPANIES BY FOREIGN REVENUE, 1997
Ranked by: Foreign revenue, in percent. **Remarks:** Top 200 average is 43.7%. **Number listed:** 10
1. Read-Rite, with 98.0%
2. Texas Instruments, 67.0%
2. Molex, 67.0%
4. Digital Equipment, 66.0%
4. Stratus Computer, 66.0%
6. Kla-Tencor, 65.0%
7. Applied Materials, 63.0%
8. Scientific Atlanta, 63.0%
9. Perkin-Elmer, 62.0%
9. Cirrus Logic, 62.0%

Source: *Electronic Business*, Top 200 (annual), July, 1998, p. 81.

★1737★
BEST-PERFORMING ELECTRONICS COMPANIES BY NET INCOME AS A PERCENT OF REVENUE, 1997
Ranked by: Net income as a percent of revenue, in percent. **Remarks:** Also notes top 200 average. **Number listed:** 10
1. Ciena, with 30.7%
2. Microsoft, 29.7%
3. Intel, 27.7%
4. Altera, 26.9%
5. Computer Associates International, 24.7%
6. BMC Software, 22.5%
7. Tellabs, 21.9%
8. Xilinx, 20.7%
9. Adobe Systems, 20.5%
10. Cabletron Systems, 18.6%

Source: *Electronic Business*, Top 200 (annual), July, 1998, p. 79.

★1738★
BEST-PERFORMING ELECTRONICS COMPANIES BY NET INCOME PER EMPLOYEE, 1997
Ranked by: Net income per employee, in millions of dollars. **Remarks:** Also notes top 200 average. **Number listed:** 10
1. Microsoft, with $155.4 million
2. Ciena, $134.4
3. Altera, $122.9
4. Intel, $109
5. Cisco Systems, $95.3
6. BMC Software, $90.4
7. Xilinx, $86.5
8. EMC, $85.5
9. Adobe Systems, $69.1
10. Tellabs, $64.5

Source: *Electronic Business*, Top 200 (annual), July, 1998, p. 79.

★1739★
BEST-PERFORMING ELECTRONICS COMPANIES BY RETURN ON ASSETS, 1997
Ranked by: Return on assets, in percent. **Remarks:** Also notes top 200 average. **Number listed:** 10
1. Ciena, with 25.3%
2. Intel, 24.0%
3. Microsoft, 24.0%
4. Tellabs, 22.3%
5. Medtronic, 22.0%
6. Computer Associates International, 20.6%
7. Western Digital, 20.5%
8. Applied Magnetics, 20.1%
9. Cabletron Systems, 20.0%
10. Adobe Systems, 19.9%

Source: *Electronic Business*, Top 200 (annual), July, 1998, p. 76.

★1740★
BEST-PERFORMING ELECTRONICS COMPANIES BY RETURN ON EQUITY, 1997
Ranked by: Return on equity, in percent. **Remarks:** Also notes top 200 average. **Number listed:** 10
1. Dell Computer, with 64.3%
2. Ciena, 61.3%
3. Applied Magnetics, 50.5%
4. Western Digital, 49.8%
5. Parametric Technology, 40.2%
6. Corning, 39.9%
7. Oracle, 39.3%
8. Microsoft, 39.1%
9. Intel, 38.4%
10. GTE, 36.3%

Source: *Electronic Business*, Top 200 (annual), July, 1998, p. 79.

★1741★
BEST-PERFORMING ELECTRONICS COMPANIES BY REVENUE PER EMPLOYEE, 1997
Ranked by: Revenue per employee, in thousands of dollars. **Remarks:** Also notes top 200 average. **Number listed:** 10
1. Merisel, with $1,760.4 thousand
2. Tech Data, $1,390.5
3. Ingram Micro, $1,381.8
4. CHS Electronics, $1,116.5
5. Government Technology Services, $937.2

6. Marshall Industries, $846.1
7. Quantum Technology Services Inc., $833.8
8. Bell Microproducts, Inc., $818.6
9. Arrow Electronics, Inc., $792.2
10. Elcom International, $763.2

Source: *Electronic Business*, Top 200 (annual), July, 1998, p. 76.

★1742★
BEST-PERFORMING SMALL ELECTRONICS COMPANIES BY 3-YEAR ANNUAL REVENUE GROWTH, 1998
Ranked by: 3-year annual revenue growth, in percent. **Remarks:** Also notes revenue, net income and net income as a percent of revenue. **Number listed:** 20

1. PC-Tel, with 448%
2. Broadcom, 222%
3. RF Micro Devices, 199%
4. Quadrant International, 196%
5. Carrier Access, 184%
6. Engineering Animation, 117%
7. Sapient, 94%
8. Axent Technologies, 90%
9. Visio, 69%
10. Legato Systems, 69%

Source: *Electronic Business*, April, 1999, p. 56+.

★1743★
LEADING COMPANIES BY ELECTRONICS SALES, 1997
Ranked by: Electronics sales, in millions of dollars. **Remarks:** Also notes total sales, net profits, and profits as a percentage of sales. **Number listed:** 200

1. IBM, with $78,508 million
2. Hewlett-Packard, $42,922
3. Motorola, $29,794
4. Lucent Technologies, $27,16
5. Intel, $25,070
6. Compaq Computer, $24,584
7. Ingram Micro, $16,581.5
8. Electronic Data Systems, $15,235.6
9. Xerox, $13,526
10. Microsoft, $13,098

Source: *Electronic Business*, Top 200 (annual), July, 1998, p. 86+.

★1744★
MOST ADMIRED ELECTRONICS AND ELECTRICAL EQUIPMENT CORPORATIONS, 1998
Ranked by: Scores (1-10) derived from a survey of senior executives, outside directors, and securities analysts. **Remarks:** Respondents rated companies in their own industry on 8 attributes of reputation. Also notes previous year's rank. **Number listed:** 10

1. General Electric, with 8.21 points
2. Lucent Technologies, 7.78
3. Emerson Electric, 7.28
4. Honeywell, 6.68
5. Motorola, 6.39
6. Raytheon, 6.22
7. Siemens, 6.17
8. Whirlpool, 6.07
9. Rockwell International, 5.95
10. Eaton, 5.93

Source: *Fortune*, America's Most Admired Corporations (annual), March 1, 1999, p. F-6.

★1745★
TOP CORPORATIONS IN THE ELECTRONICS INDUSTRY, 1998
Ranked by: Revenue, in millions of dollars. **Remarks:** Also notes profits and investment figures as well as number of employees. **Number listed:** 37

1. General Electric, with $100,469 million
2. Lucent Technologies, $30,147
3. Motorola, $29,398
4. Raytheon, $19,530
5. Emerson Electric, $13,447
6. Whirlpool, $10,323
7. Honeywell, $8,427
8. Rockwell International, $8,025
9. SCI Systems, $6,806
10. Eaton, $6,625

Source: *Fortune*, Fortune 500 Largest U.S. Corporations (annual), April 26, 1999, p. F-56.

★1746★
TOP ELECTRICAL AND ELECTRONICS COMPANIES IN THE S&P 500, 1998
Ranked by: Each company is ranked by eight criteria: one-year total return, three-year total return, one-year sales growth, three-year average annual sales growth, one-year profit growth, three-year annual average profit growth, net profit margins, and return on equity, with additional weight given to a company's sales. A company's composite rank is calculated using the sum of all of its ranks. **Remarks:** Overall scores not provided. **Number listed:** 26

1. Solectron
2. Intel
3. Emerson Electric
4. Honeywell
5. Raytheon
6. Perkin-Elmer
7. Texas Instruments
8. Cooper Industries
9. General Instrument
10. Thermo Electron

Source: *Business Week*, Business Week 50: Top Companies of the S & P 500 (annual), March 29, 1999, p. 148.

★1747★
TOP ELECTRONICS COMPANIES IN NON-COMPUTER RELATED SERVICES BY SEGMENT REVENUE, 1997
Ranked by: Segment Revenue, in millions of dollars. **Number listed:** 10

1. Northrop Grumman, with $1,024.6 million
2. EG & G, $466.8
3. Diebold, $429.4
4. Pitney Bowes, $410.1
5. Qualcomm, $398.9
6. Bell & Howell, $191.6
7. Anacomp, $171.6
8. Teradyne, $126.6
9. Volt Information Sciences, $69.2
10. Picturetel, $46.6

Source: *Electronic Business*, Top 200 (annual), July, 1998, p. 95.

★1748★
TOP ELECTRONICS COMPANIES IN OTHER COMPONENTS BY SEGMENT REVENUE, 1997
Ranked by: Segment revenue, in millions of dollars. **Number listed:** 20

1. AMP, with $5,745 million
2. Corning, $2,466
3. Motorola, $2,383.5

4. Anixter International, $2,244.2
5. Molex, $1,602.6
6. Hewlett-Packard, $1,287.7
7. AVX, $1,263.2
8. Texas Instruments, $1,170
9. Vishay Intertechnology, $1,125.2
10. Thomas & Betts, $893.9

Source: *Electronic Business*, Top 200 (annual), July, 1998, p. 97.

★1749★
TOP ELECTRONICS COMPANIES INITIAL PUBLIC OFFERINGS, 1997-1998
Ranked by: Amount raised, in millions of dollars. **Remarks:** Does not include internet service providers. **Number listed:** 50

1. Amkor Technologies Inc., with $388 million
2. J.D. Edwards & Co., $363.4
3. Celestica Inc., $360.5
4. Hypercom Corp., $180
5. L-3 Communications Holdings Inc., $132
6. Arm Holdings PLC, $114.1
7. Stoneridge Inc., $102.4
8. Software Systems Inc., $100.1
9. Excel Switching Corp., $94.5
10. QAD Inc., $8.3

Source: *Electronic Business*, September, 1998, p. 52.

★1750★
TOP INSTRUMENT, TEST & MEASUREMENT COMPANIES BY SEGMENT REVENUE, 1997
Ranked by: Segment revenue, in millions of dollars. **Number listed:** 10

1. Hewlett-Packard, with $4,292.2 million
2. Thermo Electron, $1,866.5
3. Perkin-Elmer, $1,414.3
4. Kla-Tencor, $1,167.3
5. Terdyne, $1,051
6. Tektronix, $894.6
7. Varian Associates, $536
8. Fluke, $441
9. Hubbell, $400.7
10. EG & G, $280.1

Source: *Electronic Business*, Top 200 (annual), July, 1998, p. 97.

★1751★
TOP RESEARCH AND DEVELOPMENT SPENDERS BY COST, 1997
Ranked by: Research and development costs, in millions of dollars. **Number listed:** 100

1. IBM, with $4,877 million
2. Hewlett-Packard, $3,078
3. Lucent Technologies, $3,023
4. Motorola, $2,748
5. Intel, $2,347
6. Microsoft, $1,925
7. Texas Instruments, $1,536
8. Xerox, $1,079
9. Digital Equipment, $1,014
10. Sun Microsystems, $848.9

Source: *Electronic Business*, Top 100 R & D, November, 1998, p. 70+.

★1752★
TOP RESEARCH & DEVELOPMENT SPENDERS IN THE ELECTRONICS INDUSTRY, 1997
Ranked by: Research and development expenses, in millions of dollars. **Remarks:** Also notes overall rank in research and development expenses. **Number listed:** 15

1. Schlumberger, with $484.4 million
2. Honeywell Inc., $441.7
3. AMP Inc., $322.2
4. EMC Corp., $218.8
5. Storage Technology, $208.3
6. Adaptec Inc., $178.5
7. Halliburton Co., $163.4
8. Western Digital Corp., $162.8
9. Lexmark International Group Inc., $131.1
10. S3 Inc., $95.1

Source: *R & D*, Giants of R & D (annual), October, 1998, p. S15.

★1753★
TOP U.S. VENTURE CAPITAL ROUNDS IN ELECTRONICS, 1998
Ranked by: Fund amount, in millions of dollars. **Remarks:** Also notes location, description and URL. **Number listed:** 30

1. Starmedia, with $88 million
2. Avici Systems, $52.3
3. Somera Communications, $51.8
4. Commerce One, $34.4
5. Talk City, $34
6. Unwired Planet, $33
6. U.S. Internetworking, $33
8. Argon Networks, $26.5
9. Nexabit Networks, $25
9. Pros Strategic Solutions, $25
9. Teralogic, $25
12. Sharewave, $23.7

Source: *Electronic Business*, March, 1999, p. 66.

★1754★
WORST-PERFORMING ELECTRONICS COMPANIES BY 5-YEAR ANNUAL REVENUE GROWTH, 1997
Ranked by: 5-year annual revenue growth, in percent. **Number listed:** 5

1. Novell, with -7.8%
2. Wang Laboratories, -7.7%
3. Eastman Kodak, -6.4%
4. Litton Industries, -6.0%
4. Anacomp, -6.0%

Source: *Electronic Business*, Top 200 (annual), July, 1998, p. 76.

★1755★
WORST-PERFORMING ELECTRONICS COMPANIES BY NET INCOME AS A PERCENT OF REVENUE, 1997
Ranked by: Net income as a percent of revenue, in percent. **Number listed:** 5

1. Informix, with -53.9%
2. Zenith Electronics, -25.5%
3. Sterling Software Inc., -23.3%
4. Beckman Coulter, -22.1%
5. Netscape Communications, -21.6%

Source: *Electronic Business*, Top 200 (annual), July, 1998, p. 79.

★1756★
WORST-PERFORMING ELECTRONICS COMPANIES BY NET INCOME PER EMPLOYEE, 1997
Ranked by: Net income per employee, in thousands of dollars. **Number listed:** 5

1. Apple Computer, with $-102.7 thousand
2. Informix, $-102.3
3. Ascend Communications, $-67.5
4. Novellus Systems, $-53.9
5. Diamon Multimedia Systems, $-52.8

Source: *Electronic Business*, Top 200 (annual), July, 1998, p. 79.

★1757★
WORST-PERFORMING ELECTRONICS COMPANIES BY RETURN ON ASSETS, 1997
Ranked by: Return on assets, in percent. **Number listed:** 5
1. Informix, with -63.4%
2. Zenith Electronics, -56.7%
3. Apple Computer, -24.7%
4. Novellus Systems, -19.4%
5. Netscape Communications, -18.3%

Source: *Electronic Business*, Top 200 (annual), July, 1998, p. 76.

★1758★
WORST-PERFORMING ELECTRONICS COMPANIES BY RETURN ON EQUITY, 1997
Ranked by: Return on equity, in percent. **Number listed:** 5
1. Anacomp, with -186.0%
2. Informix, -113%
3. Beckman Coulter, -110%
4. Apple Computers, -64.1%
5. Unisys, -60.7%

Source: *Electronic Business*, Top 200 (annual), July, 1998, p. 79.

★1759★
WORST-PERFORMING ELECTRONICS COMPANIES BY REVENUE PER EMPLOYEE, 1997
Ranked by: Revenue per employee, in thousands of dollars. **Number listed:** 5
1. Volt Information Sciences, with $38.1 thousand
2. Read-Rite, $50.3
3. Kemet, $51.9
4. Applied Magnetics, $58.2
5. Hutchinson Technology, $63.1

Source: *Electronic Business*, Top 200 (annual), July, 1998, p. 76.

Electronic Industries--Acquisitions and Mergers

★1760★
TOP ELECTRONICS MERGERS AND ACQUISITIONS, 1998
Ranked by: Value of the deal, in millions of dollars. **Remarks:** Also notes target and acquirer business descriptions, date announced and date effective. **Number listed:** 50
1. HBO & Co. (target), McKesson (acquirer), with $13,828.9 million
2. AMP (target), Tyco International (acquirer), $11,610.2
3. Bay Networks (target), Northern Telecom (acquirer), $9,009
4. Digital Equipment (target), Compaq Computer (acquirer), $8,680.5
5. DSC Communications (target), Alcatel Alsthom CGE (acquirer), $5,085.7
6. Netscape Communications (target), America Online (acquirer), $4,095.8
7. General Signal (target), SPX (acquirer), $2,171.5
8. Berg Electronics (target), Framatome Connectors International (acquirer), $1,852.8
9. Seagate Technology (target), Veritas Software (acq uirer), $1,592.3
10. Tracor (target), General Electric (acquirer), $1,384.8

Source: *Electronic Business*, January, 1999, p. 48.

Electronic Industries--Distributors

★1761★
LEADING ELECTRONICS DISTRIBUTIONS COMPANIES BY SALES, 1998
Ranked by: Sales, in millions of dollars. **Number listed:** 25
1. Arrow Electronics, Inc., with $8,300 million
2. Avnet, Inc., $6,200
3. VEBA Electronics, $4,400
4. Future Electronics, $2,200
4. Pioneer-Standard Electronics, Inc., $2,200
6. Marshall Industries, $1,700
7. Premier-Farnell PLC, $1,200
8. Bell Microproducts, Inc., $841
9. Bell Industries Inc., $800
10. Kent Electronics Corp., $626

Source: *Electronic News*, December 7, 1998, p. 4.

★1762★
LEADING NORTH AMERICAN ELECTRONICS COMPONENT DISTRIBUTORS BY NORTH AMERICAN REVENUE, 1998
Ranked by: North American revenue, in millions of U.S dollars ($). **Remarks:** Also notes total revenue, percent change in revenue from previous year, public/private status, independent/franchise status, percentage of North American, European and Asian revenue and URL. **Number listed:** 25
1. Arrow Electronics, Inc. (Melville, NY), with $5,340.8 million
2. Avnet, Inc. (Phoenix, AZ), $4,870.5
3. VEBA Electronics (Santa Clara, CA), $2,150
4. Pioneer-Standard Electronics, Inc. (Cleveland, OH), $2,133.4
5. Future Electronics (Pointe Claire, Quebec, Canada), $1,870
6. Marshall Industries (El Monte, CA), $1,700
7. Premier-Farnell PLC (Wetherby, West Yorkshire), $780
8. Bell Microproducts, Inc. (San Jose, CA), $661
9. Kent Electronics Corp. (Sugar Land, TX), $622.4
10. Savoir Technology Group (Campbell, CA), $593

Source: *Electronic Business*, April, 1999, p. 72+.

★1763★
TOP ELECTRONICS DISTRIBUTION COMPANIES BY SEGMENT REVENUE, 1997
Ranked by: Segment revenue, in millions of dollars. **Number listed:** 11
1. Ingram Micro, with $16,581.5 million
2. Arrow Electronics, Inc., $7,763.9
3. Tech Data, $7,056.6
4. Avnet, Inc., $5,523.9
5. CHS Electronics, $4,756.4
6. Merisel, $4,049
7. Pioneer-Standard Electronics, Inc., $1,643.2
8. Marshall Industries, $1,304.6
9. Bell Industries Inc., $719.5
10. Bell Microproducts, Inc., $55.37

Source: *Electronic Business*, Top 200 (annual), July, 1998, p. 95.

Electronic Industries--Distributors--North America

★1764★
LEADING NORTH AMERICAN ELECTRONICS COMPANIES IN ACTIVE COMPONENT SALES, 1998
Ranked by: Active component sales, in millions of U.S. dollars ($). **Remarks:** Also notes percentage of sales and previous year's sales. **Number listed:** 10

1. Arrow Electronics, Inc., with $3,103.6 million
2. Avnet, Inc., $2,651
3. VEBA Electronics, $1,725
4. Marshall Industries, $1,128.6
5. Bell Industries Inc., $260.1
6. Bell Microproducts Inc., $246.9
7. All American, $220
8. Reptron Electronics, Inc., $205.9
9. Nu Horizons Electronics Corp., $193.7
10. Interface Electronics Corp., $90.8

Source: *Purchasing*, Top 100 Electronics Distributors (annual), May 20, 1999, p. 60.

★1765★
LEADING NORTH AMERICAN ELECTRONICS COMPANIES IN COMPUTER PRODUCTS SALES, 1998
Ranked by: Computer products sales, in millions of U.S. dollars ($). **Remarks:** Also notes percentage of sales and previous year's sales. **Number listed:** 10

1. Arrow Electronics, Inc., with $1,819.4 million
2. Avnet, Inc., $1,301.4
3. VEBA Electronics, $575
4. Bell Microproducts Inc., $452.7
5. Marshall Industries, $256.5
6. Bell Industries, Inc., $130.1
7. Kent Electronics Corp., $80.9
8. Richardson Electronics, Ltd., $15.9
9. Interface Electronics Corp., $12.1
10. The Genie Group, $9.2

Source: *Purchasing*, Top 100 Electronics Distributors (annual), May 20, 1999, p. 60.

★1766★
LEADING NORTH AMERICAN ELECTRONICS COMPANIES IN INTERCONNECT SALES, 1998
Ranked by: Interconnect sales, in millions of U.S. dollars ($). **Remarks:** Also notes percentage of sales and previous year's sales. **Number listed:** 10

1. Avnet, Inc., with $433.8 million
2. Kent Electronics Corp., $205.4
3. Richey Electronics, Inc., $172.6
4. The D.A.C. Group, $137
5. Anixter Inc., $128
6. TTI, Inc., $103
7. Accu-Tech Corp., $90
8. Sager Electronics, $70.5
9. A.E. Petsche Co. Inc., $54.5
10. Powell Electronics, Inc., $51.8

Source: *Purchasing*, Top 100 Electronics Distributors (annual), May 20, 1999, p. 60.

★1767★
LEADING NORTH AMERICAN ELECTRONICS COMPANIES IN PASSIVE/EM SALES, 1998
Ranked by: Passive EM sales, in millions of U.S. dollars ($). **Remarks:** Also notes percentage of sales and previous year's sales. **Number listed:** 10

1. Avnet, Inc., with $433.8 million
2. Arrow Electronics, Inc., $428.1
3. TTI, Inc., $345
4. Marshall Industries, $222.3
5. Sager Electronics, $156.6
6. Bell Industries, Inc., $136.9
7. Digi-Key Corp., $123.1
8. Kent Electronics, Inc., $99.6
9. Reptron Electronics, Inc., $96.9
10. Advacom Inc., $88.1

Source: *Purchasing*, Top 100 Electronics Distributors (annual), May 20, 1999, p. 60.

★1768★
LEADING NORTH AMERICAN ELECTRONICS DISTRIBUTORS BY SALES GROWTH, 1998
Ranked by: Sales growth, in percent. **Remarks:** Also notes total sales and number of employees. **Number listed:** 10

1. Bell Microproducts, Inc., with 54.1%
2. Priebe Electronics, 40%
3. ESCO LLC, 35.1%
4. Pioneer-Standard Electronics, Inc., 33.3%
5. Marshall Industries, 29.5%
6. The D.A.C. Group, 29.4%
7. Accu-Tech Corp., 25%
7. Metuchen Capacitors, Inc., 25%
9. Universal Semiconductor Inc., 23.5%
10. Airtechnics Inc., 22.5%

Source: *Purchasing*, Top 100 Electronics Distributors (annual), May 20, 1999, p. 60.

★1769★
LEADING NORTH AMERICAN ELECTRONICS DISTRIBUTORS BY SALES PER EMPLOYEE, 1998
Ranked by: Sales per employee, in U.S. dollars ($). **Remarks:** Also notes total sales and number of employees. **Number listed:** 10

1. The Genie Group, with $3,833,333.3
2. Interface Electronics Corp., $2,240,470.7
3. Marshall Industries, $1,219,686.2
4. Arrow Electronics, Inc., $897,835.6
5. Airtechnics Inc., $890,909.1
6. VEBA Electronics, $851,851.9
7. Reptron Electronics, Inc., $841,111.1
8. Bell Microproducts, Inc., $823,000
9. Dependable Component Supply Corp., $806,666.7
10. Pioneer-Standard Electronics, Inc., $800,000

Source: *Purchasing*, Top 100 Electronics Distributors (annual), May 20, 1999, p. 60.

★1770★
LEADING NORTH AMERICAN INDEPENDENT ELECTRONICS DISTRIBUTORS BY SALES, 1998
Ranked by: Sales, in millions of U.S. dollars ($). **Remarks:** Also notes percent change from previous year, sales per employee, number of employees and breakdown of sales by type. **Number listed:** 15

1. Smith & Associates, with $423 million
2. NECX, $240
3. Classic Components Corp., $178
4. America II Electronics, $175
5. Real World The Technology Trading Co., $155
6. Advanced MP Technology, $102
7. American IC Exchange, $95.3
8. West Coast Engineering, $45
9. Blue Fin Technologies, $40
10. IMS Inc., $32.2

Source: *Purchasing*, Top 100 Electronics Distributors (annual), May 20, 1999, p. 60.

★1771★
TOP NORTH AMERICAN ELECTRONICS DISTRIBUTORS BY SALES, 1998
Ranked by: Sales, in millions of U.S. dollars ($). **Remarks:** Also notes percent change from previous year, sales per employee, number of employees and breakdown of sales by type. **Number listed:** 100

1. Arrow Electronics, Inc., with $5,351.1 million
2. Avnet Inc., $4,820
3. Future Electronics, $2,570
4. VEBA Electronics, $2,300
5. Pioneer-Standard Electronics, Inc., $2,000
6. Marshall Industries, $1,710
7. Bell Microproducts Inc., $823
8. Premier-Farnell PLC, $760
9. Bell Industries, Inc., $684
10. Kent Electronics Corp., $622.4

Source: *Purchasing*, Top 100 Electronics Distributors (annual), May 20, 1999, p. 58.

Electronic Industries, Foreign

★1772★
TOP FOREIGN COMPANIES BY ELECTRONICS REVENUE, 1997
Ranked by: Electronics revenue, in millions of U.S. dollars ($). **Number listed:** 150

1. Matsushita Electric Industrial Co., with $55,712.3 million
2. NEC Corp., $39,906.8
3. Phillips Electronics N.V., $37,737.2
4. Fujitsu Ltd., $36,378.5
5. Sony Corp., $35,385
6. Toshiba Corp., $35,240.8
7. Siemens AG, $29,508.8
8. Hitachi Ltd., $27,494
9. Alcatel Alsthsom, $26,443
10. Canon, $21,238.7

Source: *Electronic Business*, Top 200 (annual), July, 1998, p. 84.

Electronic Industries, International

★1773★
WORLD'S LARGEST ELECTRONICS CORPORATIONS BY REVENUE, 1997
Ranked by: Revenue, in millions of dollars. **Number listed:** 25

1. General Electric (U.S.), with $90,840 million
2. Hitachi (Japan), $68,567
3. Matshushita Elec. Indl. (Japan), $64,281
4. Siemens (Germany), $63,755
5. Sony (Japan), $55,033
6. Toshiba (Japan), $44,467
7. NEC (Japan), $39,927
8. Royal Philips Electronics (Netherlands), $39,188
9. ABB Asea Brown Boveri (Switzerland), $31,265
10. Mitsubishi Electronics (Japan), $30,967

Source: *Fortune*, The Global 500: World's Biggest Corporations (annual), August 3, 1998, p. F-18.

Employee Benefit Consultants

★1774★
LARGEST EMPLOYEE BENEFIT CONSULTANTS, 1998
Ranked by: Estimated benefit consulting revenue, in millions of dollars. **Number listed:** 10

1. Hewitt Associates LLC, with $731 million
2. William M. Mercer Inc., $608
3. Towers Perrin, $589
4. PricewaterhouseCoopers Global HR Solutions, $413
5. Watson Wyatt Worldwide, $344
6. Aon Consulting Inc., $302
7. Buck Consultants Inc., $252
8. Deloitte & Touche Human Capital Advisory Services, $173
9. The Segal Co., $103
10. ASA Inc., $100

Source: *Business Insurance*, December 14, 1998, p. 4.

Employee Benefit Consultants--Chicago (IL)

★1775★
LARGEST EMPLOYEE BENEFIT CONSULTANTS IN CHICAGO, 1997
Ranked by: Number of consulting professionals. **Remarks:** Also notes contact information, head of employee benefits, previous year's figures, total number of Chicago staff, total number of benefits consultants in the U.S., percent change from previous year and services offered. **Number listed:** 25

1. Hewitt Associates LLC, with 190 consultants
2. Aon Consulting, 134
3. Towers Perrin, 84
4. Lincoln Financial Advisors, 60
5. Fringe Benefits Management Co., 38
6. Poe & Brown, 31
7. Sedgwick Noble Lowndes, 29
8. Coopers & Lybrand, 27
9. William M. Mercer Inc., 26
10. Davis Baldwin Inc., 20

Source: *Crain's Chicago Business*, Top Business Lists (annual), 1999, p. 129+.

Employee Benefit Consultants--Florida

★1776★
LARGEST EMPLOYEE BENEFIT CONSULTANTS IN FLORIDA, 1999
Ranked by: Number of full-time consulting professionals. **Remarks:** Also notes contact information, number of Florida offices, number of clients in Florida and in total, percentage of revenue from fee-for-service, percent revenue from commissions, senior Florida executives. **Number listed:** 24

1. Hewitt Associates, with 2,673 consultants
2. William M. Mercer Inc., 552
3. Towers Perrin, 282
4. Coopers & Lybrand LLP, 195
5. Watson Wyatt Worldwide, 177
6. Aon Consulting Inc., 171
7. KPMG Peat Marwick, 139

8. Arthur Andersen LLP, 109
9. Price Waterhouse LLP, 100
10. Ernst & Young LLP, 94

Source: *Florida Trend*, TopRank Florida(annual), 1999, p. 96.

Employee Benefit Consultants, International

★1777★
WORLD'S LARGEST EMPLOYEE BENEFIT CONSULTANTS, 1998
Ranked by: Worldwide consulting revenues, in millions of U.S. dollars ($). **Remarks:** Also notes previous year's revenue, percent change and number of offices in the U.S. and worldwide. **Number listed:** 10

1. William M. Mercer Inc., with $1,266 million
2. Hewitt Associates LLC, $765
3. Towers Perrin, $757
4. PricewaterhouseCoopers Global HR Solutions, $622
5. Watson Wyatt Worldwide, $593
6. Aon Consulting Worldwide, $520
7. Buck Consultants, $327
8. Deloitte & Touche Human Capital Advisory Services, $206
9. Ernst & Young LLP Human Resource Services, $160
10. Arthur Andersen LLP Human Capital Services, $145

Source: *Business Insurance*, December 14, 1998, p. 3.

Employee Benefit Consultants—New York Metropolitan Area

★1778★
LARGEST EMPLOYEE BENEFIT CONSULTANTS IN THE NEW YORK METROPOLITAN AREA, 1999
Ranked by: Number of professional employees. **Remarks:** Also notes contact information, previous year's figures and services offered. **Number listed:** 25

1. PricewaterhouseCoopers Kwasha HR Solutions, with 1,750 professionals
2. Buck Consultants, 780
3. Towers Perrin, 644
4. Ernst & Young, 515
5. William M. Mercer Inc., 434
6. Deloitte & Touche, 332
7. Segal Co., 277
8. ASA Inc., 257
9. Arthur Andersen, 200
10. Aon Consulting Inc., 167

Source: *Crain's New York Business*, March 29, 1999, p. 60+.

Employee Benefit Consultants—Philadelphia Metropolitan Area

★1779★
LARGEST EMPLOYEE BENEFIT CONSULTANTS IN THE PHILADELPHIA METROPOLITAN AREA, 1998
Ranked by: Number of local benefits consulting professionals. **Remarks:** Also notes total number of benefits consulting professionals, total number of employees, percent revenue by fees commission, contact names, sample of local clients, hourly cost range and areas of specialty. **Number listed:** 24

1. Brokerage Concepts Inc., with 194 professionals
2. Towers Perrin, 178
3. Karr Barth Associates Inc., 165
4. William M. Mercer Inc., 140
5. Aon Consulting Inc., 130
6. PricewaterhouseCoopers, 84
7. Hay Group, 40
8. Kistler-Tiffany Cos., 40
9. Commerce National Insurance, 32
10. Mid America Group Inc., 32

Source: *Philadelphia Business Journal*, Book of Business Lists (annual), December 25, 1998, p. 69.

Employee Fringe Benefits

★1780★
LEADING EMPLOYEE INCENTIVES BY EMPLOYEE USE, 1998
Ranked by: Employee use of benefits during the past 12 months, in percent. **Number listed:** 8

1. Flexible Work Arrangements, with 30%
2. Family/Unpaid Leave, 18%
3. Long-term Care Insurance, 17%
4. Workplace Seminars, 13%
5. Employee Assistance Programs, 12%
6. Child Care Resource & Referral, 4%
7. Elder Care Resource & Referral, 2%
8. On-site/Employer Sponsored Child or Adult Care Centers, 2%

Source: *R & D Magazine*, September, 1998, p. S5.

★1781★
LEADING EMPLOYEE INCENTIVES, 1998
Ranked by: Employers offering incentives, in percent. **Number listed:** 12

1. Medical Insurance, with 92%
2. Vacation, 86%
3. 401K Plan, 71%
4. Pension Plan, 64%
5. Disability Insurance, 61%
6. Education Reimbursement, 45%
7. Profit Sharing, 28%
8. Performance Bonus, 25%
9. Stock Options, 21%
10. Company Car, 5%

Source: *R & D Magazine*, September, 1998, p. S5.

Employee Motivation

★1782★
TOP WAYS TO PRAISE EMPLOYEES, 1999
Ranked by: Managers citing incentives, in percent. **Number listed:** 11

1. Job Responsibilities, with 94%
2. Salary, 89%
3. Culture and values, 85%
4. Benefits Packages, 83%
5. Advancement Opportunities, 78%
6. Success/Stability of Organization, 77%

7. Long-term Rewards, 65%
8. Relationships with their co-workers, 64%
9. Ease of Commute, 56%
10. Diversity/Affirmative Action Policy, 26%

Source: *Bottom Line/Business*, July, 1999, p. 12.

Employee Retention

★1783★
TOP METHODS FOR RETAINING FRONT-LINE EMPLOYEES, 1998
Ranked by: Methods cited for retaining front-line employees, in percent. **Number listed:** 10

1. More Careful Selection in Hiring, with 57%
2. Better Compensation & Benefits, 50%
3. Tuition Reimbursement, 47%
4. Improved Training Programs, 45%
5. Better Orientation Programs, 39%
6. Adoption of a casual Dress Code, 38%
7. Flexible Hours & Schedules, 33%
8. Providing Health Insurance, 29%
9. Exit Interviews, 28%
10. Profit-Sharing, 17%

Source: *Compensation & Benefits Review*, September/October, 1998, p. 10.

★1784★
TOP METHODS FOR RETAINING MIDDLE MANAGERS, 1998
Ranked by: Methods cited for retaining middle managers, in percent. **Number listed:** 10

1. Better Compensation & Benefits, with 61%
2. More Careful Selection in Hiring, 54%
3. Tuition Reimbursement, 41%
4. Stock Options, 32%
5. Adoption of a casual Dress Code, 31%
6. Exit Interviews, 28%
7. Flexible Hours & Schedules, 25%
8. Profit-Sharing, 23%
9. Better Orientation Programs, 22%
10. Retention Bonuses, 20%

Source: *Compensation & Benefits Review*, September/October, 1998, p. 10.

Employee Stock Ownership Plans

★1785★
LARGEST AMERICAN FIRMS WITH MAJORITY OWNERSHIP HELD BY EMPLOYEES, 1998
Ranked by: Number of employees. **Number listed:** 12

1. Publix Super Markets, with 103,000 employees
2. United Airlines, 77,900
3. Science Applications International Corp., 25,000
4. Dynacorp, 18,000
5. Lifetouch, 15,000
6. AECOM, 7,500
7. CH2M Hill, 7,020
8. Journal Communications, 6,500
9. Graybar Electric, 6,300
10. W. L. Gore & Associates, 6,000

Source: *Working Woman*, December/January, 1999, p. 32.

Employees

★1786★
MOST PRODUCTIVE WORKING DAYS, 1998
Ranked by: Response of corporate executives, in percent. **Number listed:** 5

1. Tuesday, with 51%
2. Monday, 17%
3. Wednesday, 15%
4. Thursday, 5%
5. Don't Know, 11%

Source: *Success*, October, 1998, p. 14.

★1787★
TYPES OF EMPLOYEES COMPANIES HAVE DIFFICULTY FINDING AND HIRING, 1998
Ranked by: Incidence among companies with serious problems. **Number listed:** 7

1. Experienced Professionals or Technicians, with 54%
2. Skilled Information Technology Personnel, 43%
3. Experienced Sales & Marketing Executives, 33%
4. Production/Semi-skilled Workers, 27%
5. Entry-Level Workers, 25%
6. Administrative Support, 21%
7. Top-Level Managers/Executives, 15%

Source: *Black Enterprise*, February, 1999, p. 34.

Employees--Transfer

★1788★
NEEDS OF TRANSFEREES, 1998
Ranked by: Transferee needs, in percent. **Number listed:** 5

1. Moving or Finding Facilities for Elderly Parents, with 49%
2. Unmarried Partners of Relocated Employees, 47%
3. Education/School Finding for Children, 43%
4. Single Parent Concerns, 27%
5. Divorced Transferees Requiring Legal Assistance to Alter Custody Agreements, 6%

Source: *HRFOCUS*, September, 1998, p. 4.

Employment

★1789★
FASTEST GROWING JOBS, 1999
Ranked by: Projected percentage increase. **Number listed:** 10

1. E-Commerce CFO, with 158%
2. Internet CEO, 133%
3. Chief Technology Officer, 119%
4. VP, E-Commerce, 108%
5. M & A Investment Banker, 87%
6. Y2K Consultant, 82%
7. VP, Online Community, 76%
8. CEO, Network Integration Services, 61%
9. VP, Data Warehousing, 58%
10. New Generation VP of Human Resources, 51%

Source: *Management Review*, June, 1999, p. 11.

★1790★
LEADING CITIES FOR INFORMATION TECHNOLOGY JOBS, 1998
Ranked by: Results of *Computerworld's* annual salary, skills and hiring surveys. Overall scores not provided. **Remarks:** Also includes metro population of city, median housing cost, and top IT jobs and salaries for the area. **Number listed:** 10
1. Boston, MA
2. Chicago, IL
3. Atlanta, GA
4. Washington, DC
5. New York, NY
6. San Francisco, CA
7. Seattle, WA
8. Las Vegas, NV
9. St. Louis, MO
10. Austin, TX

Source: *Computerworld*, Top 10 Job Markets (annual), January 11, 1999, p. 64+.

Energy Consumption

★1791★
STATES WITH THE HIGHEST ENERGY CONSUMPTION PER CAPITA
Ranked by: Per capita energy consumption, in millions of BTUs. **Number listed:** 10
1. Alaska, with 1,139 million BTUs
2. Louisiana, 879
3. Wyoming, 846
4. Texas, 559
5. North Dakota, 546
6. Kentucky, 459
7. Alabama, 455
8. West Virginia, 449
9. Indiana, 447
10. Montana, 435

Source: *Governing*, February, 1999, p. 97.

★1792★
STATES WITH THE LOWEST ENERGY CONSUMPTION PER CAPITA
Ranked by: Per capita energy consumption, in millions of BTUs. **Number listed:** 10
1. Vermont, with 256 million BTUs
2. Florida, 248
2. New Hampshire, 248
4. Massachusetts, 246
4. Arizona, 246
6. Connecticut, 240
6. California, 240
8. Rhode Island, 237
9. Hawaii, 216
10. New York, 215

Source: *Governing*, February, 1999, p. 97.

Engineering Construction Companies

★1793★
LARGEST ENGINEERING/ARCHITECTURAL FIRMS, 1997
Ranked by: Billings, in millions of dollars. **Remarks:** Also includes narrative profile of firms. **Number listed:** 50
1. Sverdrup Corp., with $242.4 million
2. URS Greiner Woodward-Clyde, $235.25
3. Lockwood Greene, $221.2
4. Daniel, Mann, Johnson, Mendenhall (DMJM), $81.9
5. Homes & Navar, $79.1
6. McClier, $55.57
7. SSOE Inc., $49.4
8. Carter-Burgess, $45
9. Giffels Associates Inc., $42
10. The Benham Group, $38.87

Source: *Building Design & Construction*, Design/Construct 300 (annual), July, 1998, p. 58+.

★1794★
LARGEST ENGINEERING FIRMS, 1997
Ranked by: Billings, in millions of dollars. **Remarks:** Also includes narrative profile of firms. **Number listed:** 50
1. Fluor Daniel Inc., with $448.2 million
2. Jacobs Engineering Group Inc., $338.36
3. B E & K, $264
4. Dames & Moore, $229.2
5. Raytheon Engineers & Constructors, $153,84
6. Bechtel Group Inc., $108.75
7. CDI Engineering Group, $89.76
8. Burns & Roe Enterprises, $56
9. Simons Engineering Inc., $54.08
10. Syska & Hennessy, $46.55

Source: *Building Design & Construction*, Design/Construct 300 (annual), July, 1998, p. 48+.

★1795★
LARGEST QUOTED COMPANIES IN ENGINEERING, ELECTRICAL, AND TRANSPORTATION EQUIPMENT, 1998
Ranked by: Sales, in thousands of U.S. dollars ($). **Remarks:** Also notes profits as a percentage of sales and activity codes. **Number listed:** 100
1. Toyota Motor, with $87,413,151 thousand
2. Hitachi Ltd., $63,000,254
3. Matsushita Electric Industrial Co., $59,061,841
4. Sony, $50,565,044
5. Nissan Motor, $49,136,504
6. Honda Motor Co. Ltd., $44,908,218
7. Toshiba Corp., $40,857,020
8. Fujitsu Ltd., $37,315,733
9. NEC Corp., $36,685,044
10. Mitsubishi Motors, $27,968,293

Source: *Asia's 7,500 Largest Companies*, (annual), Dun & Bradstreet, 1999, p. 77+.

★1796★
LEADING DESIGN FIRMS IN ENGINEERING/ CONSTRUCTION, 1998
Ranked by: Total billings, in millions of dollars. **Remarks:** Also notes type of firm, international billings and percent of billings in specific markets. **Number listed:** 500
1. Fluor Daniel Inc. (CA), with $1,698 million
2. Bechtel Group Inc. (CA), $1,209
3. Jacobs Sverdrup (CA), $1,094
4. Kellogg Brown & Root (TX), $1,084
5. Parsons Corp. (CA), $944
6. URS Greiner Woodward-Clyde (CA), $925
7. Foster Wheeler Corp. (NJ), $917.7
8. CH2M Hill Cos. Ltd. (CO), $773.6
9. Parsons Brinckerhoff Inc. (NY), $742.7
10. ABB Lummus Global Inc. (NJ), $710.1

Source: *ENR*, Top 500 Design Firms (annual), April 19, 1999, p. 63+.

★1797★
LEADING DESIGN FIRMS IN GENERAL BUILDING, 1998
Ranked by: Billings, unspecified. **Remarks:** Top 20 billed $2.3 billion. **Number listed:** 20
1. Hellmuth, Obata & Kassabaum (HOK)
2. Gensler
3. URS Greiner Woodward-Clyde
4. Jacobs Sverdrup
5. NBBJ
6. Parsons Corp.
7. Holmes & Narver
8. Daniel, Mann, Johnson & Mendenhall
9. Law Engineering & Environmental Services
10. RTKL Associates Inc.

Source: *ENR*, Top 500 Design Firms (annual), April 19, 1999, p. 54.

★1798★
LEADING DESIGN FIRMS IN HAZARDOUS WASTE, 1998
Ranked by: Billings, unspecified. **Remarks:** Top 20 billed $3.7 billion. **Number listed:** 20
1. ICF Kaiser International
2. The IT Group
3. Earth Tech
4. Tetra Tech
5. ERM Group
6. Dames & Moore Group
7. CH2M Hill Cos. Ltd.
8. Fluor Daniel Inc.
9. URS Greiner Woodward-Clyde
10. Duke Engineering & Services

Source: *ENR*, Top 500 Design Firms (annual), April 19, 1999, p. 57.

★1799★
LEADING DESIGN FIRMS IN INDUSTRIAL PROCESS/PETROLEUM INDUSTRY, 1998
Ranked by: Billings, unspecified. **Remarks:** Top 20 billed $7.2 billion. **Number listed:** 20
1. Fluor Daniel Inc.
2. Kellogg Brown & Root
3. Bechtel Group Inc.
4. ABB Lummus Global
5. Jacobs Sverdrup
6. Foster Wheeler Corp.
7. Raytheon Engineers & Constructors International
8. Parsons Corp.
9. CDI Engineering Group Inc.
10. McDermott International Inc.

Source: *ENR*, Top 500 Design Firms (annual), April 19, 1999, p. 54.

★1800★
LEADING DESIGN FIRMS IN MANUFACTURING, 1998
Ranked by: Billings, unspecified. **Remarks:** Top 20 billed $779 million. **Number listed:** 20
1. CH2M Hill Cos. Ltd.
2. Lockwood Greene Engineers Inc.
3. General Physics Corp.
4. Dames & Moore Group
5. Morrison Knudsen Corp.
6. Lester B. Knight & Associates
7. Professional Service Industries Inc.
8. Day & Zimmerman International Inc.
9. Law Engineering & Environmental Services
10. Fluor Daniel Inc.

Source: *ENR*, Top 500 Design Firms (annual), April 19, 1999, p. 57.

★1801★
LEADING DESIGN FIRMS IN THE POWER INDUSTRY, 1998
Ranked by: Billings, unspecified. **Remarks:** Top 20 billed $2.1 billion. **Number listed:** 20
1. Sargent & Lundy LLC
2. Duke Engineering & Services
3. Stone & Webster
4. Bechtel Group Inc.
5. Raytheon Engineers & Constructors International
6. Black & Veatch
7. Burns & Row Enterprises Inc.
8. Parsons Corp.
9. Parsons Brinckerhoff Inc.
10. Foster Wheeler Corp.

Source: *ENR*, Top 500 Design Firms (annual), April 19, 1999, p. 54.

★1802★
LEADING DESIGN FIRMS IN THE SEWERAGE/ SOLID WASTE INDUSTRY, 1998
Ranked by: Billings, unspecified. **Remarks:** Top 20 billed $1.5 billion. **Number listed:** 20
1. Montgomery Watson Inc.
2. Earth Tech
3. CH2M Hill Cos. Ltd.
4. Camp Dresser & McKee Inc.
5. Aqua Alliance Inc./Metcalf & Eddy
6. Malcom Pirnie Inc.
7. Brown & Caldwell
8. Black & Veatch
9. HDR Inc.
10. Parsons Corp.

Source: *ENR*, Top 500 Design Firms (annual), April 19, 1999, p. 57.

★1803★
LEADING DESIGN FIRMS IN THE TRANSPORTATION INDUSTRY, 1998
Ranked by: Billings, unspecified. **Remarks:** Top 20 billed $3.1 billion. **Number listed:** 20
1. Parsons Brinckerhoff Inc.
2. URS Greiner Woodward-Clyde
3. The Louis Berger Group
4. HNTB Corp.
5. Parsons Corp.
6. Daniel, Mann, Johnson & Mendenhall
7. Frederic R. Harris Inc.
8. Dames & Moore Group
9. Jacobs Sverdrup
10. ICF Kaiser International Inc.

Source: *ENR*, Top 500 Design Firms (annual), April 19, 1999, p. 54.

★1804★
LEADING DESIGN FIRMS IN WATER SUPPLY, 1998
Ranked by: Billings, unspecified. **Remarks:** Top 20 billed $9.71 million. **Number listed:** 20
1. Montgomery Watson Inc.
2. Black & Veatch
3. CH2M Hill Cos. Ltd.
4. Camp Dresser & McKee Inc.
5. Earth Tech
6. Malcom Pirnie Inc.
7. Ogden Environmental & Energy
8. URS Greiner Woodward-Clyde

9. Law Engineering & Environmental Services Inc.
10. Hazara Engineering Co.

Source: *ENR*, Top 500 Design Firms (annual), April 19, 1999, p. 57.

★1805★
TOP CORPORATIONS IN THE ENGINEERING CONSTRUCTION INDUSTRY, 1998
Ranked by: Revenue, in millions of dollars. **Remarks:** Also notes profits and investment figures as well as number of employees. **Number listed:** 23

1. Halliburton, with $17,353 million
2. Fluor, $13,505
3. Foster Wheeler, $4,597
4. Turner Corp., $4,130
5. Centex, $3,975
6. Peter Kiewit Sons, $3,403
7. Fleetwood Enterprises, $3,051
8. Pulte, $2,873
9. Kaufman & Broad Home, $2,449
10. Lennar Corp., $2,417

Source: *Fortune*, Fortune 500 Largest U.S. Corporations (annual), April 26, 1999, p. F-57.

★1806★
TOP "PURE" DESIGNERS, 1998
Ranked by: Basis for ranking not specified. **Remarks:** "Pure" Designers are those with no construction capability. Notes type of firm. **Number listed:** 100

1. URS Greiner Inc.
2. Parsons Brinckerhoff Inc.
3. Duke Engineering & Services, Inc.
4. Tetra Tech
5. The Louis Berger Group
6. Law & Engineering Environmental Services
7. Hellmuth, Obata & Kassabaum Inc.
8. Sargent & Lundy LLC
9. Daniel, Mann, Johnson, Mendenhall
10. HDR Inc.

Source: *ENR*, Top 500 Design Firms (annual), April 19, 1999, p. 60.

Engineering Construction Companies--Florida

★1807★
FLORIDA'S TOP ENGINEERING FIRMS
Ranked by: Number of licensed engineers. **Remarks:** Also notes number of employees, total number of offices, headquarters location, year founded, Florida senior executive and contact information. **Number listed:** 24

1. PBS & J, with 223 engineers
2. Kimley-Horn & Associates Inc., 111
3. URS Greiner Inc., 97
4. CH2M Hill Inc., 95
5. Camp Dresser & McKee Inc., 83
6. Reynolds Smith & Hills Inc., 82
7. Dames & Moore Group, 79
8. Black & Veatch, 69
9. Parsons Brinckerhoff Quade & Douglas Inc., 56
10. Law Engineering & Environmental Services Inc., 55

Source: *Florida Trend*, TopRank Florida (Annual), 1999, p. 92.

Engineering Construction Companies, Foreign—Africa

★1808★
TOP DESIGN FIRMS IN AFRICA, 1997
Ranked by: Billings, unspecified. **Remarks:** Top 10 billed $532.5 million U.S. ($). **Number listed:** 10

1. SNC-Lavalin International Inc.
2. The Louis Berger Group
3. Dar Al-Handasah Consultants
4. Foster Wheeler Corp.
5. Brown & Root Inc.
6. Tactebel Engineering
7. Law Engineering & Environmental Services, Inc.
8. Groupe EGIS
9. NEDECO
10. Nethconsult

Source: *ENR*, Top International Design Firms (annual), July 20, 1998, p. 34.

Engineering Construction Companies, Foreign--Asia

★1809★
TOP DESIGN FIRMS IN ASIA, 1997
Ranked by: Billings, unspecified. **Remarks:** Top 10 billed $1,908 million U.S. ($). **Number listed:** 10

1. Bechtel Group Inc.
2. Toyo Engineering Corp.
3. The Kvaerner Group
4. Maunsell
5. Foster Wheeler Corp.
6. SNC-Lavalin International Inc.
7. Mott MacDonald
8. Black & Veatch
9. ABB Lummus Global Inc.
10. Ove Arup Partnership

Source: *ENR*, Top International Design Firms (annual), July 20, 1998, p. 34.

Engineering Construction Companies, Foreign—Canada

★1810★
TOP DESIGN FIRMS IN CANADA, 1997
Ranked by: Billings, unspecified. **Remarks:** Top 10 billed $337.5 million U.S. ($). **Number listed:** 10

1. McDermott International Inc.
2. Fluor Daniel Inc.
3. Golder Associates Corp.
4. Stone & Webster
5. Bechtel Group Inc.
6. CH2M Hill Cos. Ltd.
7. KTI Corp.
8. Jaakko Poyry Group
9. The Kvaerner Group
10. Korea Power Engineering Co. Ltd.

Source: *ENR*, Top International Design Firms (annual), July 20, 1998, p. 34.

Engineering Construction Companies, Foreign—Europe

★1811★
TOP DESIGN FIRMS IN EUROPE, 1997
Ranked by: Billings, unspecified. **Remarks:** Top 10 billed $2,748.4 million U.S. ($). **Number listed:** 10

1. Brown & Root Inc.
2. The Kvaerner Group
3. Foster Wheeler Corp.
4. Nethconsult
5. ABB Lummus Global Inc.
6. Jaakko Poyry Group
7. Fugro N.V.
8. Fluor Daniel Inc.
9. Groupe EGIS
10. ARCADIS NV

Source: *ENR*, Top International Design Firms (annual), July 20, 1998, p. 34.

Engineering Construction Companies, Foreign—Latin America

★1812★
TOP DESIGN FIRMS IN LATIN AMERICA, 1997
Ranked by: Billings, unspecified. **Remarks:** Top 10 billed $633.9 million U.S. ($). **Number listed:** 10

1. Bechtel Group Inc.
2. Jaakko Poyry Group
3. SNC-Lavalin International Inc.
4. AGRA Inc.
5. Fluor Daniel Inc.
6. The Louis Berger Group
7. Black & Veatch
8. Harza Engineering Co.
9. Raytheon Engineers & Constructors International
10. Foster Wheeler Corp.

Source: *ENR*, Top International Design Firms (annual), July 20, 1998, p. 34.

Engineering Construction Companies, Foreign—Middle East

★1813★
TOP DESIGN FIRMS IN THE MIDDLE EAST, 1997
Ranked by: Billings, unspecified. **Remarks:** Top 10 billed $720.2 million U.S. ($). **Number listed:** 10

1. Bechtel Group Inc.
2. Dar Al-Handasah Consultants
3. Parsons Corp.
4. ABB Lummus Global Inc.
5. Foster Wheeler Corp.
6. Mott MacDonald
7. Black & Veatch
8. Hyundai Engineering Co. Ltd.
9. SNC-Lavalin International Inc.
10. Nethconsult

Source: *ENR*, Top International Design Firms (annual), July 20, 1998, p. 34.

Engineering Construction Companies, Foreign—United States

★1814★
TOP DESIGN FIRMS IN THE UNITED STATES, 1997
Ranked by: Billings, unspecified. **Remarks:** Top 10 billed $1,241.8 million (U.S.$). **Number listed:** 10

1. The Kvaerner Group
2. Phillip Holzmann AG
3. ARCADIS NV
4. Nethconsult
5. Furgo N.V.
6. Dar Al-Handasah Consultants
7. AGRA Inc.
8. Simons International Corp.
9. Sandwell International Inc.
10. GROUPE SYSTRA

Source: *ENR*, Top International Design Firms (annual), July 20, 1998, p. 34.

Engineering Construction Companies, International

★1815★
LEADING INTERNATIONAL DESIGN FIRMS IN GENERAL BUILDING, 1998
Ranked by: Billings, unspecified. **Remarks:** Top 10 billed $836.3 million (U.S.$). **Number listed:** 10

1. Nethconsult
2. Furgo N.V.
3. Philip Holzmann AG
4. Ove Arup Partnership
5. Hellmuth, Obata & Kassabaum (HOK)
6. Dar Al-Handasah Consultants
7. Skimmer, Owing & Merrill LLP
8. AGRA Inc.
9. Parsons Brinckerhoff Inc.
10. RTKL Associates Inc.

Source: *ENR*, Top International Design Firms (annual), July 20, 1998, p. 35.

★1816★
LEADING INTERNATIONAL DESIGN FIRMS IN HAZARDOUS WASTE, 1998
Ranked by: Billings, unspecified. **Remarks:** Top 10 billed $374.9 million (U.S.$). **Number listed:** 10

1. ARCADIS NV
2. ERM Group
3. Dames & Moore Group
4. URS Greiner Woodward-Clyde
5. CH2M Hill Cos. Ltd.
6. SNC-Lavalin International Inc.
7. Philipp Holzmann AG
8. International Technology Corp.
9. COWI
10. Montgomery Watson Inc.

Source: *ENR*, Top International Design Firms (annual), July 20, 1998, p. 35.

★1817★
LEADING INTERNATIONAL DESIGN FIRMS IN INDUSTRIAL PROCESS/PETROLEUM INDUSTRY, 1998
Ranked by: Billings, unspecified. **Remarks:** Top 10 billed $4,246.8 million (U.S.$). **Number listed:** 10

1. The Kvaerner Group
2. Bechtel Group Inc.
3. Foster Wheeler Corp.
4. ABB Lummus Global
5. Brown & Root Inc.
6. Fluor Daniel Inc.
7. SNC-Lavalin International Inc.
8. Nethconsult
9. Furgo N.V.
10. Jaakko Poyry Group

Source: *ENR*, Top International Design Firms (annual), July 20, 1998, p. 35.

★1818★
LEADING INTERNATIONAL DESIGN FIRMS IN MANUFACTURING, 1998
Ranked by: Billings, unspecified. **Remarks:** Top 10 billed $814.4 million (U.S.$). **Number listed:** 10

1. The Kvaerner Group
2. Day & Zimmerman International Inc.
3. CH2M Hill cos. Ltd.
4. SNC-Lavalin International Inc.
5. Ove Arup Partnership
6. Samsung Engineering Co. Ltd.
7. ENSR
8. Lockwood Greene Engineers Inc.
9. Kajima Corp.
10. Fluor Daniel Inc.

Source: *ENR*, Top International Design Firms (annual), July 20, 1998, p. 35.

★1819★
LEADING INTERNATIONAL DESIGN FIRMS IN THE POWER INDUSTRY, 1998
Ranked by: Billings, unspecified. **Remarks:** Top 10 billed $905.3 million (U.S.$). **Number listed:** 10

1. Stone & Webster
2. Black & Veatch
3. Bechtel Group Inc.
4. Jaakko Poyry Group
5. Sargent & Lundy LLC
6. Toyo Engineering Corp.
7. Foster Wheeler Corp.
8. Electrowatt Engineering Services Ltd.
9. Raytheon Engineers & Constructors International
10. McDermott International Inc.

Source: *ENR*, Top International Design Firms (annual), July 20, 1998, p. 35.

★1820★
LEADING INTERNATIONAL DESIGN FIRMS IN THE SEWERAGE/SOLID WASTE INDUSTRY, 1998
Ranked by: Billings, unspecified. **Remarks:** Top 10 billed $398.5 million (U.S.$). **Number listed:** 10

1. Montgomery Watson Inc.
2. Dar Al-Handasah Consultants
3. Black & Veatch
4. CH2M Hill Cos.
5. Groupe EGIS
6. Hyder Consulting Ltd.
7. The Louis Berger Group
8. Scott Wilson
9. Camp Dresser & McKee Inc.
10. Dorsch Consult Ingenieur GmbH

Source: *ENR*, Top International Design Firms (annual), July 20, 1998, p. 35.

★1821★
LEADING INTERNATIONAL DESIGN FIRMS IN THE TRANSPORTATION INDUSTRY, 1998
Ranked by: Billings, unspecified. **Remarks:** Top 10 billed $1,263.9 million (U.S.$). **Number listed:** 10

1. The Louis Berger Group
2. GROUPE SYSTRA
3. Manusell
4. Brown & Root Inc.
5. Nethconsult
6. SNC-Lavalin International Inc.
7. Groupe EGIS
8. NEDECO
9. Dar Al-Handasah Consultants
10. Pacific Consultants International Group

Source: *ENR*, Top International Design Firms (annual), July 20, 1998, p. 35.

★1822★
LEADING INTERNATIONAL DESIGN FIRMS IN WATER SUPPLY, 1998
Ranked by: Billings, unspecified. **Remarks:** Top 10 billed $594.3 million (U.S.$). **Number listed:** 10

1. Black & Veatch
2. SNC-Lavalin International Inc.
3. NEDECO
4. Brown & Root Inc.
5. ARCADIS NV
6. Groupe EGIS
7. Montgomery Watson Inc.
8. Dar Al-Handasah Consultants
9. Mott MacDonald
10. Nippon Koei Co. Ltd.

Source: *ENR*, Top International Design Firms (annual), July 20, 1998, p. 35.

★1823★
TOP INTERNATIONAL DESIGN FIRMS, 1998
Ranked by: International billings, in millions of U.S. dollars ($). **Remarks:** Also notes type of firm, international billings as a percentage of total billings and percentage of billings in specific markets. **Number listed:** 200

1. The Kvaerner Group (England), with $925 million
2. Bechtel Group Inc. (USA), $828
3. Brown & Root Inc. (USA), $734
4. Nethconsult (Netherlands), $646.8
5. Foster Wheeler Corp. (USA), $629.6
6. SNC-Lavalin International Inc. (Canada), $599
7. ABB Lummus Global Inc. (USA), $526.4
8. Fugro N.V. (Netherlands), $471
9. Jaakko Poyry Group (Finland), $413
10. Fluor Daniel Inc. (USA), $407

Source: *ENR*, Top 500 Design Firms (annual), July 20, 1998, p. 38+.

★1824★
WORLD'S LARGEST ENGINEERING/ CONSTRUCTION COMPANIES BY REVENUE, 1997
Ranked by: Revenue, in millions of dollars. **Number listed:** 10

1. Vivendi (France), with $28,634 million
2. Bouygues (France), $16,406
3. Kajima (Japan), $15,795
4. Taisei Corp. (Japan), $14,913
5. Shimizu (Japan), $14,312
6. Fluor (U.S.), $14,299
7. Takenaka (Japan), $12,663
8. Obayashi (Japan), $12,118
9. Sekisui House (Japan), $11,950

10. Kumagai Gumi (Japan), $9,241

Source: *Fortune*, The Global 500: World's Biggest Corporations (annual), August 3, 1998, p. F-18+.

Engineering Construction Companies—Long Island (NY)

★1825★

LARGEST ENGINEERING FIRMS AND CONSULTANTS IN LONG ISLAND, 1998

Ranked by: Number of professional engineers. **Remarks:** Also notes number of architects, services provided and notable Long Island projects. **Number listed:** 27

1. Greenman-Pedersen, with 76 engineers
2. Liro-Kassner, 35
3. Lockwood, Kessler & Bartlett, 30
4. Shah Associates, 29
5. Dvirka & Bartilucci Consulting Engineers, 27
6. Cashin Associates, 22
7. Gibbons, Esposito & Boyce, 20
8. H2M Group, 18
8. Sidney B. Bowne & Son, 18
10. ERM Northeast, 16

Source: *Long Island Business News*, LI Book of Lists (annual), 1999, p. 66.

Engineering Schools

★1826★

AMERICA'S BEST AEROSPACE ENGINEERING SCHOOLS, 1998

Ranked by: Results of reputational survey of engineering deans by *U.S. News & World Report*. Overall scores not provided. **Number listed:** 10

1. Massachusetts Institute of Technology
2. California Institute of Technology
3. Stanford University
4. University of Michigan - Ann Arbor
5. Georgia Institute of Technology
6. Purdue University
7. University of Illinois - Urbana-Champaign
8. University of Texas - Austin
9. Princeton University
10. Virginia Tech

Source: *U.S News & World Report*, America's Best Graduate and Professional Schools (annual), March 29, 1999, p. 106.

★1827★

AMERICA'S BEST BIOMEDICAL ENGINEERING SCHOOLS, 1998

Ranked by: Results of reputational survey of engineering deans by *U.S. News & World Report*. Overall scores not provided. **Number listed:** 10

1. Johns Hopkins University
2. University of California - San Diego
3. Massachusetts Institute of Technology
4. Duke University
5. University of Washington
6. University of Pennsylvania
7. Case Western Reserve University
8. Georgia Institute of Technology
9. University of California - Berkeley
10. University of Michigan - Ann Arbor

Source: *U.S News & World Report*, America's Best Graduate and Professional Schools (annual), March 29, 1999, p. 106.

★1828★

AMERICA'S BEST CHEMICAL ENGINEERING SCHOOLS, 1998

Ranked by: Results of reputational survey of engineering deans by *U.S. News & World Report*. Overall scores not provided. **Number listed:** 10

1. Massachusetts Institute of Technology
2. University of California - Berkeley
3. University of Minnesota - Twin Cities
4. California Institute of Technology
5. University of Wisconsin - Madison
6. Stanford University
7. University of Delaware
8. University of Illinois - Champaign Urbana
9. University of Texas - Austin
10. Princeton University

Source: *U.S News & World Report*, America's Best Graduate and Professional Schools (annual), March 29, 1999, p. 106.

★1829★

AMERICA'S BEST CIVIL ENGINEERING SCHOOLS, 1998

Ranked by: Results of reputational survey of engineering deans by *U.S. News & World Report*. Overall scores not provided. **Number listed:** 10

1. University of Illinois - Champaign Urbana
2. University of California - Berkeley
3. Massachusetts Institute of Technology
4. University of Texas - Austin
5. Purdue University - West Lafayette
6. Stanford University
7. University of Michigan - Ann Arbor
8. Georgia Institute of Technology
9. Cornell University
10. Northwestern University

Source: *U.S News & World Report*, America's Best Graduate and Professional Schools (annual), March 29, 1999, p. 106.

★1830★

AMERICA'S BEST COMPUTER ENGINEERING SCHOOLS, 1998

Ranked by: Results of reputational survey of engineering deans by *U.S. News & World Report*. Overall scores not provided. **Number listed:** 10

1. Massachusetts Institute of Technology
2. Stanford University
3. University of California - Berkeley
4. University of Illinois - Champaign Urbana
5. Carnegie Mellon University
6. University of Texas - Austin
7. University of Michigan - Ann Arbor
8. Cornell University
9. University of Washington
10. Princeton University

Source: *U.S News & World Report*, America's Best Graduate and Professional Schools (annual), March 29, 1999, p. 106.

★1831★

AMERICA'S BEST ELECTRICAL/ELECTRONIC ENGINEERING SCHOOLS, 1998

Ranked by: Results of reputational survey of engineering deans by *U.S. News & World Report*. Overall scores not provided. **Number listed:** 10

1. Massachusetts Institute of Technology
2. Stanford University
3. University of Illinois - Champaign Urbana

4. University of California - Berkeley
5. University of Michigan - Ann Arbor
6. California Institute of Technology
7. Georgia Institute of Technology
8. Purdue University - West Lafayette
9. Cornell University
10. University of Texas - Austin

Source: *U.S News & World Report*, America's Best Graduate and Professional Schools (annual), March 29, 1999, p. 106.

★1832★
AMERICA'S BEST ENGINEERING SCHOOLS, 1998
Ranked by: Results of reputational survey of engineering deans by *U.S. News & World Report*. **Remarks:** Also notes average quantitative and analytic GRE score, acceptance rate, ratio of Ph.D. students to faculty, percentage of faculty who are members of the National Academy of Engineering, engineering research expenditures and number of Ph.D.s granted. **Number listed:** 50

1. Massachusetts Institute of Technology, with 100 points
2. Stanford University, 91
3. Georgia Institute of Technology, 86
3. University of Michigan - Ann Arbor, 86
5. University of California - Berkeley, 84
6. University of Illinois - Urbana-Champaign, 79
7. California Institute of Technology, 77
8. Carnegie Mellon University, 76
9. Purdue University, 74
10. University of Texas - Austin, 72

Source: *U.S News & World Report*, America's Best Graduate and Professional Schools (annual), March 29, 1999, p. 104.

★1833★
AMERICA'S BEST ENVIRONMENTAL ENGINEERING SCHOOLS, 1998
Ranked by: Results of reputational survey of engineering deans by *U.S. News & World Report*. Overall scores not provided. **Number listed:** 10

1. Stanford University
2. University of Michigan - Ann Arbor
3. University of Illinois - Champaign Urbana
4. University of Texas - Austin
5. University of California - Berkeley
6. California Institute of Technology
7. Johns Hopkins University
8. Massachusetts Institute of Technology
9. Georgia Institute of Technology
10. University of North Carolina-Chapel Hill

Source: *U.S News & World Report*, America's Best Graduate and Professional Schools (annual), March 29, 1999, p. 106.

★1834★
AMERICA'S BEST INDUSTRIAL/MANUFACTURING ENGINEERING SCHOOLS, 1998
Ranked by: Results of reputational survey of engineering deans by *U.S. News & World Report*. Overall scores not provided. **Number listed:** 10

1. Georgia Institute of Technology
2. Purdue University - West Lafayette
3. University of Michigan - Ann Arbor
4. Pennsylvania State University - University Park
5. Stanford University
6. Texas A & M University College Station
7. University of California - Berkeley
8. University of Wisconsin - Madison
9. Virginia Tech
10. Northwestern University

Source: *U.S News & World Report*, America's Best Graduate and Professional Schools (annual), March 29, 1999, p. 106.

★1835★
AMERICA'S BEST MATERIALS AND METALLURGICAL ENGINEERING SCHOOLS, 1998
Ranked by: Results of reputational survey of engineering deans by *U.S. News & World Report*. Overall scores not provided. **Number listed:** 10

1. Massachusetts Institute of Technology
2. Stanford University
3. University of California - Berkeley
4. University of Michigan - Ann Arbor
5. University of Illinois - Champaign Urbana
6. Purdue University - West Lafayette
7. Georgia Institute of Technology
8. California Institute of Technology
9. Cornell University
10. University of Minnesota - Twin Cities

Source: *U.S News & World Report*, America's Best Graduate and Professional Schools (annual), March 29, 1999, p. 106.

★1836★
AMERICA'S BEST NUCLEAR ENGINEERING SCHOOLS, 1998
Ranked by: Results of reputational survey of engineering deans by *U.S. News & World Report*. Overall scores not provided. **Number listed:** 10

1. Massachusetts Institute of Technology
2. University of Illinois - Champaign Urbana
3. University of Michigan - Ann Arbor
4. University of California - Berkeley
5. University of Wisconsin - Madison
6. Pennsylvania State University - University Park
7. North Carolina State University
8. Texas A & M University - Main Campus
9. Purdue University - West Lafayette
10. University of Florida

Source: *U.S News & World Report*, America's Best Graduate and Professional Schools (annual), March 29, 1999, p. 106.

★1837★
AMERICA'S BEST PETROLEUM ENGINEERING SCHOOLS, 1998
Ranked by: Results of reputational survey of engineering deans by *U.S. News & World Report*. Overall scores not provided. **Number listed:** 10

1. Texas A & M University - College Station
2. University of Texas - Austin
3. Stanford University
4. Colorado School of Mines
5. University of Oklahoma
6. University of Tulsa
7. Louisiana State University - Baton Rouge
8. Pennsylvania State University - University Park
9. Texas Tech University
10. New Mexico Institute of Mining and Technology

Source: *U.S News & World Report*, America's Best Graduate and Professional Schools (annual), March 29, 1999, p. 106.

Entertainers--Salaries, Pensions, etc.

★1838★
RICHEST ENTERTAINERS, 1998
Ranked by: Gross income, in millions of dollars. **Number listed:** 40

1. Jerry Seinfeld, with $267 million
2. Larry David, $242
3. Steven Spielberg, $175

4. Oprah Winfrey, $125
5. James Cameron, $115
6. Tim Allen, $77
7. Michael Chrichton, $65
8. Harrison Ford, $58
9. Rolling Stones, $57
10. Master P, $56.5

Source: *Forbes*, Entertainers Making the Most Money (annual), March 22, 1999, p. 208+.

Entertainment Industries

★1839★
MOST ADMIRED ENTERTAINMENT CORPORATIONS, 1998
Ranked by: Scores (1-10) derived from a survey of senior executives, outside directors, and securities analysts. **Remarks:** Respondents rated companies in their own industry on 8 attributes of reputation. Also notes previous year's rank. **Number listed:** 5

1. Walt Disney, with 7.41 points
2. Time Warner, 7.22
3. Viacom Inc., 6.56
4. News America Publishing, 5.88
5. CBS, 5.2

Source: *Fortune*, America's Most Admired Corporations (annual), March 1, 1999, p. F-5.

★1840★
TOP CORPORATIONS IN THE ENTERTAINMENT INDUSTRY, 1998
Ranked by: Revenue, in millions of dollars. **Remarks:** Also notes profits and investment figures as well as number of employees. **Number listed:** 8

1. Walt Disney, with $22,976 million
2. Time Warner, $14,582
3. Viacom Inc., $12,096
4. CBS, $9,061
5. USA Networks, $2,634
6. Clear Channel Communications, $1,351
7. Chancellor Media, $1,274
8. Metro-Goldwyn-Mayer, $1,241

Source: *Fortune*, Fortune 500 Largest U.S. Corporations (annual), April 26, 1999, p. F-58.

Entertainment Industries, International

★1841★
WORLD'S LARGEST ENTERTAINMENT CORPORATIONS BY REVENUE, 1997
Ranked by: Revenue, in millions of dollars. **Number listed:** 5

1. Walt Disney (U.S.), with $22,473 million
2. Viacom Inc. (U.S.), $13,505
3. Time Warner (U.S.), $13,294
4. News Corp. Ltd. (Australia), $11,262
5. CBS (U.S.), $9,632

Source: *Fortune*, The Global 500: World's Biggest Corporations (annual), August 3, 1998, p. F-19.

Entrepreneurs

★1842★
TOP WAYS ENTREPRENEURS RELIEVE STRESS, 1999*
Ranked by: Percentage. **Number listed:** 8

1. Go for a walk, with 17%
2. Exercise, 7%
3. Meditate, 6%
4. Leave the office, 5%
4. Listen to music, 5%
4. Talk to others, 5%
7. Read, 4%
7. Go to lunch, 4%

Source: *Business Start-Ups*, March, 1999, p. 8.

Environmental Consultants

★1843★
TOP ENVIRONMENTAL RISK MANAGEMENT CONSULTANTS, 1998
Ranked by: Environmental consulting revenue, in millions of dollars. **Remarks:** Also notes percentage of total revenue, total number of clients, and total number of professional staff. **Number listed:** 10

1. Dames & Moore Group, with $350 million
2. Environmental Resources Management, $232
3. URS Greiner Woodward Clyde, $161.2
4. IT Corp., $75
5. QST Environmental Inc., $36.6
6. Professional Service Industries Inc., $34
7. Clayton Group Services, $30.8
8. Terracon, $28.1
9. EMG, $15.8
10. GAI Consultants Inc., $11.5

Source: *Business Insurance*, Top Environmental Risk Management Consultants (annual), May 24, 1999, p. 24.

Environmental Services Firms

★1844★
LEADING ALL-ENVIRONMENTAL SERVICE FIRMS, 1997
Ranked by: Revenue, in millions of dollars. **Remarks:** All-environmental firms are defined as having 100% environmental revenue. **Number listed:** 20

1. Philip Environmental Services Group, with $1,750 million
2. Montgomery Watson Inc., $482
3. Camp Dresser & McKee Inc., $377
4. ERM Group, $280
5. Roy F. Weston Inc., $238
6. ENSR Corp., $220
7. Heritage Environmental Services, Inc., $155
8. Malcolm Pirnie Inc., $150
9. Danis Environmental Industries Inc., $144.8
10. EMCON, $139.3

Source: *ENR*, July 6, 1998, p. 39.

★1845★
LEADING ENVIRONMENTAL SERVICE FIRMS BY FEDERAL GOVERNMENT REVENUE, 19 97
Ranked by: Revenue, unspecified. **Remarks:** Top 20 billed $4.89 billion. **Number listed:** 20
1. ICF Kaiser International Inc.
2. Bechtel Group Inc.
3. International Technology Corp.
4. Fluor Daniel Inc.
5. CH2M Hill Cos.
6. Morrison Knudsen Corp.
7. Foster Wheeler Corp.
8. Science Applications International Corp.
9. Battelle Memorial Institute
10. Roy F. Weston Inc.

Source: *ENR*, July 6, 1998, p. 40.

★1846★
LEADING ENVIRONMENTAL SERVICE FIRMS BY INTERNATIONAL REVENUE, 1997
Ranked by: Non-U.S. revenue, in millions of U.S. dollars ($). **Remarks:** Top 20 billed $4.78 billion. **Number listed:** 20
1. Bechtel Group Inc., with $1,402.4 million
2. U.S. Filter Corp., $611.1
3. Foster Wheeler Corp., $452.4
4. Philip Environmental Services, $437.5
5. Black & Veatch, $374.1
6. Ionics Inc., $163.8
7. Montgomery Watson Inc., $149.2
8. Dick Corp., $117.6
9. Kvaerner PLC, $116
10. CH2M Hill Cos., $102

Source: *ENR*, July 6, 1998, p. 48.

★1847★
LEADING ENVIRONMENTAL SERVICE FIRMS BY NEW CONTRACTS, 1997
Ranked by: New contracts, in millions of dollars. **Number listed:** 46
1. Foster Wheeler Corp., with $2,140 million
2. Bechtel Group Inc., $1,429.8
3. International Technology Corp., $1,400
4. CH2M Hill Cos., $1,027.3
5. Montgomery Watson Inc., $813
6. Black & Veatch, $785
7. Morrison Knudsen Corp., $668
8. Fluor Daniel Inc., $650
9. Parsons Infrastructure & Technology Group, $562.2
10. Science Applications International Corp., $549

Source: *ENR*, July 6, 1998, p. 39.

★1848★
LEADING ENVIRONMENTAL SERVICE FIRMS BY PRIVATE CLIENT REVENUE, 1997
Ranked by: Revenue, unspecified. **Remarks:** Top 20 billed $8.94 billion. **Number listed:** 20
1. U.S. Filter Corp.
2. Philip Environmental Service Group
3. Bechtel Group Inc.
4. Foster Wheeler Corp.
5. Fluor Daniel Inc.
6. International Technology Corp.
7. Black & Veatch
8. ERM Group
9. Ionics Inc.
10. CH2M Hill Cos.

Source: *ENR*, July 6, 1998, p. 40.

★1849★
LEADING ENVIRONMENTAL SERVICE FIRMS BY STATE/LOCAL GOVERNMENT REVENUE, 1997
Ranked by: Revenue, unspecified. **Remarks:** Top 20 billed $3.33 billion. **Number listed:** 20
1. U.S. Filter Corp.
2. Black & Veatch
3. CH2M Hill Cos.
4. Camp Dresser & McKee Inc.
5. Montgomery Watson Inc.
6. Bechtel Group Inc.
7. Dick Corp.
8. PCL Enterprises Inc.
9. Foster Wheeler Corp.
10. Pizzagalli Construction Co.

Source: *ENR*, July 6, 1998, p. 40.

★1850★
LEADING ENVIRONMENTAL SERVICE FIRMS IN CONSTRUCTION/REMEDIATION, 1997
Ranked by: Revenue, unspecified. **Remarks:** Top 20 billed $5.46 billion. **Number listed:** 20
1. Bechtel Group Inc.
2. International Technology Corp.
3. Foster Wheeler Corp.
4. ICF Kaiser International Inc.
5. Black & Veatch
6. Morrison Knudsen Corp.
7. Fluor Daniel Inc.
8. Davis Environmental Industries Inc.
9. PCL Enterprises Inc.
10. Pizzagalli Construction Co.

Source: *ENR*, July 6, 1998, p. 42.

★1851★
LEADING ENVIRONMENTAL SERVICE FIRMS IN DESIGN/CONSULTING, 1997
Ranked by: Revenue, unspecified. **Remarks:** Top 20 billed $5.12 billion. **Number listed:** 20
1. Bechtel Group Inc.
2. CH2M Hill Cos.
3. Montgomery Watson Inc.
4. Black & Veatch
5. ICF Kaiser International Inc.
6. Foster Wheeler Corp.
7. Camp Dresser & McKee Inc.
8. URS Greiner Woodward-Clyde
9. Science Applications International Corp.
10. ERM Group

Source: *ENR*, July 6, 1998, p. 42.

★1852★
LEADING ENVIRONMENTAL SERVICE FIRMS IN ENVIRONMENTAL COMPLIANCE, 1997
Ranked by: Revenue, unspecified. **Remarks:** Top 30 billed $884.4 million. **Number listed:** 20
1. Dames & Moore Group
2. Foster Wheeler Corp.
3. ERM Group
4. Battelle Memorial Institute
5. Radian International LLC
6. ICF Kaiser International Inc.
7. Roy F. Weston Inc.
8. ENSR Corp.
9. International Technology Corp.
10. Tetra Tech

Source: *ENR*, July 6, 1998, p. 47.

★1853★
LEADING ENVIRONMENTAL SERVICE FIRMS IN HAZARDOUS WASTE, 1997
Ranked by: Revenue, unspecified. **Remarks:** Top 30 billed $5.91 billion. **Number listed:** 30
1. Bechtel Group Inc.
2. International Technology Corp.
3. Foster Wheeler Corp.
4. Philip Environmental Services Group
5. Fluor Daniel Inc.
6. CH2M Hill Cos.
7. ICF Kaiser International Inc.
8. Roy F. Weston Inc.
9. URS Greiner Woodward-Clyde
10. Black & Veatch

Source: *ENR*, July 6, 1998, p. 45.

★1854★
LEADING ENVIRONMENTAL SERVICE FIRMS IN NUCLEAR WASTE, 1997
Ranked by: Revenue, unspecified. **Remarks:** Top 30 billed $2.51 billion. **Number listed:** 20
1. Bechtel Group Inc.
2. ICF Kaiser International Inc.
3. Fluor Daniel Inc.
4. Morrison Knudsen Corp.
5. CH2M Hill Cos.
6. International Technology Corp.
7. Battelle Memorial Institute
8. BNFL Inc.
9. Science Applications International Corp.
10. Parson Infrastructure & Technology Group

Source: *ENR*, July 6, 1998, p. 45.

★1855★
LEADING ENVIRONMENTAL SERVICE FIRMS IN SOLID WASTE, 1997
Ranked by: Revenue, unspecified. **Remarks:** Top 30 billed $1.91 billion. **Number listed:** 20
1. Philip Environmental Services Group
2. Foster Wheeler Corp.
3. EMCON
4. Bechtel Group Inc.
5. Rust Environmental & Infrastructure
6. CH2M Hill Cos.
7. Black & Veatch
8. ICF Kaiser International Inc.
9. SCS Engineers
10. Thermo Remediation Inc.

Source: *ENR*, July 6, 1998, p. 47.

★1856★
LEADING ENVIRONMENTAL SERVICE FIRMS IN WASTEWATER TREATMENT, 1997
Ranked by: Revenue, unspecified. **Remarks:** Top 30 billed $3.09 billion. **Number listed:** 20
1. U.S. Filter Corp.
2. CH2M Hill Cos.
3. Montgomery Watson Inc.
4. Foster Wheeler Corp.
5. Black & Veatch
6. ICF Kaiser International Inc.
7. Camp Dresser & McKee Inc.
8. Danis Environmental Industries Inc.
9. M.A. Mortenson Co.
10. Metcalf & Eddy

Source: *ENR*, July 6, 1998, p. 45.

★1857★
LEADING ENVIRONMENTAL SERVICE FIRMS IN WATER QUALITY, 1997
Ranked by: Revenue, unspecified. **Remarks:** Top 30 billed $3.94 billion. **Number listed:** 20
1. U.S. Filter Corp.
2. Bechtel Group Inc.
3. Black & Veatch
4. Ionics Inc.
5. CH2M Hill Cos.
6. Montgomery Watson Inc.
7. Camp Dresser & McKee Inc.
8. Dick Corp.
9. Foster Wheeler Corp.
10. EARTH TECH

Source: *ENR*, July 6, 1998, p. 45.

★1858★
LEADING ENVIRONMENTAL SERVICE FIRMS, 1997
Ranked by: Environmental revenue, in millions of dollars. **Remarks:** Also notes percentage of environmental services revenue, percentage of international revenue, type of firm, markets served, and client types. **Number listed:** 200
1. U.S. Filter Corp. (CA), with $2,910 million
2. Bechtel Group Inc. (CA), $2,191.2
3. Philip Environmental Services Group (Ontario, Canada), $1,750
4. Foster Wheeler Corp. (NJ), $1,131
5. CH2M Hill Cos. (CO), $927.1
6. ICF Kaiser International Inc. (VA), $885
7. International Technology Corp. (PA), $874
8. Fluor Daniel Inc. (CA), $793
9. Black & Veatch, $706
10. Montgomery Watson Inc., $482

Source: *ENR*, July 6, 1998, p. 51.

★1859★
TOP POLLUTION CONTROL AND ENVIRONMENTAL SERVICES COMPANIES BY SALES, 1998
Ranked by: Sales, in millions of dollars. **Remarks:** Also notes profits and profit margins, per share data and assets. **Number listed:** 13
1. Browning-Ferris, with $4,746 million
2. Laidlaw, $3,690
3. Safety-Kleen, $1,186
4. Pall, $1,087
5. IT Group, $442
6. Tetra Tech, $239
7. Clean Harbors, $197
8. Oil Dri, $160
9. Roy F. Weston, $140
10. C.H. Heist, $136

Source: *Chemical Week*, Chemical Week 300 (annual), May 12, 1999, p. 53.

Environmental Services Firms--Long Island (NY)

★1860★
LARGEST ENVIRONMENTAL CONSULTANTS IN LONG ISLAND, 1998
Ranked by: Number of employees. **Remarks:** Also notes contact information and specialty areas. **Number listed:** 30
1. Fenley & Nicol Environmental, with 85 employees
2. ERM Northeast, 68

3. Roux Associates, 56
4. Fanning Phillips & Molnar, 52
5. Gannett Fleming Engineers & Architects, 50
6. Cameron Engineering & Associates, 45
7. Geraghty & Miller, 40
8. Environmental Testing Lab, 28
9. Environmental Planning & Management, 26
10. Catapano Engineering, 23

Source: *Long Island Business News*, LI Book of Lists (annual), 1999, p. 123+.

Environmental Services Firms—Los Angeles County (CA)

★1861★
LARGEST ENVIRONMENTAL SERVICES FIRMS IN LOS ANGELES COUNTY, 1997
Ranked by: Number of Los Angeles County environmental employees. **Remarks:** Also notes revenue from previous year, services offered, types of clients, profile, top local executive and contact information. **Number listed:** 25

1. Waste Management Inc., with 720 employees
2. Parsons Corp., 467
3. Jacobs Engineering Group Inc., 410
4. TEG/LVI Environmental Services Inc., 350
5. Impco Technologies Inc., 260
6. Montgomery Watson Inc., 375
7. Dames & Moore Group, 191
8. Earth Technology Corp., 180
9. Mintie Corp., 127
10. A. Q. Management & Control, 110

Source: *Los Angeles Business Journal*, Book of Lists, 1999, p. 44.

Equipment Leasing

See: **Leasing and Renting of Equipment**

ESOP

See: **Employee Stock Ownership Plans**

Eurobonds

★1862★
TOP ISSUERS OF JUMBO PFANDBRIEFE, 1998
Ranked by: Total volume, in millions of Deutsche mark (DM). **Remarks:** Also notes number of issues and average issue size. **Number listed:** 10

1. DePfa-Bank, with DM44,500 million
2. Allgemeine HypothekenBank, DM28,250
3. Hypothekenbank in Essen, DM37,000
4. Deutsche Hyp, DM32,250
5. Rheinhyp, DM29,500
6. HypoVereinsbank, DM27,000
7. Frankfurter Hypo Centralboden, DM21,250
8. West LB, DM19,750
9. DG Hyp, DM14,250
10. Westfalische Hypothekenbank

Source: *Global Finance*, December, 1998, p. 72.

Executive Search Consultants

★1863★
LEADING EXECUTIVE SEARCH FIRMS FOR THE INSURANCE INDUSTRY, 1997
Ranked by: U.S. revenues, in millions of dollars. **Remarks:** Also notes 1-year growth rate, number of recruiters, number of researchers, revenues for search team member and number of offices. **Number listed:** 10

1. Korn/Ferry International, with $157.2 million
2. Heidrick & Struggles, $154
3. SpencerStuart, $131.1
4. Russell Reynolds Associates, $94.1
5. LAI, $58
6. A. T. Kearney Executive Search, $36.9
7. Ray & Berndtson, $36.3
8. Egon Zehnder International, $29.4
9. Ward Howell International, $26.5
10. DHR International, $23

Source: *Best's Review*, December, 1998, p. 31.

Executive Search Consultants--Chicago (IL)

★1864★
LEAD EXECUTIVE SEARCH FIRMS IN CHICAGO, 1997
Ranked by: Fee revenues, in millions of dollars. **Remarks:** Also notes previous year's figures, U.S. fees, number of professional recruiters in Chicago and the U.S., number of searches performed in Chicago and in the U.S. and head of Chicago office and contact information, **Number listed:** 22

1. SpencerStuart, with $21.1 million
2. Heidrick & Struggles, $16
3. LAI, $9.4
4. Ray & Berndtson, $9.3
5. Korn/Ferry International, $8.6
6. Egon Zehnder International, $7.4
7. DHR International, $7
8. Witt/Kieffer Ford Hadleman Lloyd Corp., $6.8
9. Heidrick Partners Inc., $4.5
10. Lynch Miller Moore Inc., $4.4

Source: *Crain's Chicago Business*, Top Business Lists (annual), 1999, p. 179+.

Executive Search Consultants—Los Angeles County (CA)

★1865★
LARGEST CONTINGENCY EXECUTIVE SEARCH FIRMS IN LOS ANGELES COUNTY, 1998
Ranked by: Los Angeles County revenue, in millions of dollars. **Remarks:** Also notes profile, annual salary, industries in

which executives are placed, location, marketing contact and top local executive. **Number listed:** 15

1. Source Services/Romac International, with $6.9 million
2. Ryan, Miller & Associates, $4.5
3. Search West Inc., $4.3
4. The Culver Group, $4.1
5. Technical Connections Inc., $4
6. AccountPros/Human Resources International, $3.9
7. Search Associates Inc., $3.1
8. Independent Resources Systems, $3
9. Transquest Technologies, $2.1
10. Century Group, $2

Source: *Los Angeles Business Journal*, March 29, 1999, p. 34.

★1866★
LARGEST RETAINED EXECUTIVE SEARCH FIRMS IN LOS ANGELES COUNTY, 1998
Ranked by: Los Angeles County revenue, in millions of dollars. **Remarks:** Also notes profile, annual salary, industries in which executives are placed, location and top local executive. **Number listed:** 15

1. Heidrick & Struggles, with $12 million
2. SpencerStuart, $5.6
3. Cornerstone International Group, $5.2
4. HRCS Inc., $4.5
5. Bench International, $3.8
6. Wingate Dunross Inc., $3.5
7. Cfour Partners ITP Worldwide, $3.4
8. The Wentworth Co. Inc., $3.3
9. DHR International Inc., $3.1
10. Morgan Samuels Co. Inc., $3.1

Source: *Los Angeles Business Journal*, March 29, 1999, p. 31.

Executive Search Consultants—New York Metropolitan Area

★1867★
LARGEST EXECUTIVE SEARCH FIRMS IN THE NEW YORK METROPOLITAN AREA, 1997
Ranked by: Number of New-York area recruiters. **Remarks:** Also notes contact information, total number of recruiters in the U.S., U.S. and New York billings, number of New York searches, year founded and selected areas of specialization. **Number listed:** 26

1. Korn/Ferry International, with 95 recruiters
2. Solomon Page Group Ltd., 59
3. Johnson Smith & Knisely, 41
4. A-L Associates Inc., 40
5. Russell Reynolds Associates, 38
6. Sullivan & Co., 28
7. Kenzer Corp., 26
7. Viscusi Group Inc., 26
9. Howard-Sloan Search Inc., 25
10. LAI Ward Howell, 24

Source: *Crain's New York Business*, New York's Largest Executive Recruiters, August 24, 1998, p. 12+.

Executive Search Consultants—Philadelphia Metro Area

★1868★
LARGEST EXECUTIVE SEARCH FIRMS IN THE PHILADELPHIA METROPOLITAN AREA.
Ranked by: Number of local placements. **Remarks:** Also notes previous year's figures, number of local recruiters/consultants, minimum compensation level for executives placed, fees charged, industries served, other services, year locally established, and top local executive. **Number listed:** 24

1. Diversified Search Inc., with 137 local placements
2. Kily, Owen & McGovern Inc., 64
3. Empire International, 61
4. Heidrick & Struggles Inc., 52
5. PCD Partners, 45
6. SpencerStuart, 42
7. F-O-R-T-U-N-E of Abington, 40
8. Howard Fischer Associates, 37
9. Howe & Associates Inc., 31
10. Tyler & Co., 28

Source: *Philadelphia Business Journal*, June 18-24, 1998, p. 20.

Executives--Employment

★1869★
FASTEST GROWING EXECUTIVE POSITIONS, 1998
Ranked by: Predicted growth, in percent. **Number listed:** 10

1. Brand Name CEO, with 300%
2. Chief Financial Officer, 227%
3. Vice President - Electronic Commerce, 210%
4. Principals/Senior Managers/Consulting/System Integration, 205%
5. Chief Information Officer, 179%
6. Vice President-Development, Internet Company, 163%
7. Vice President-Supply Chain Management, 154%
8. Vice President-Out-Sourcing, 133%
9. Financial Portfolio Manager, 127%
10. CEO, traditional IT Company, 104%

Source: *Business Marketing*, July, 1999, p. 14.

Executives--Salaries, Pensions, etc.

★1870★
EXECUTIVES WHO GAVE SHAREHOLDERS THE LEAST FOR THEIR PAY, 1996-1998
Ranked by: Relative index, based on pay and total shareholder return. **Remarks:** Also notes total pay and shareholder return. **Number listed:** 5

1. Michael Eisner (Walt Disney), with .3
2. Sanford I. Weill (Citigroup), .5
3. Ray Irani (Occidental Petroleum), .8
4. Anthony O'Reilly (H.J. Heinz), 1.8
5. John Welch(General Electric), 2

Source: *Business Week*, Annual Survey of Executive Compensation, April 19, 1999, p. 74.

★1871★
EXECUTIVES WHO GAVE SHAREHOLDERS THE MOST FOR THEIR PAY, 1996-1998

Ranked by: Relative index, based on pay and total shareholder return. **Remarks:** Also notes total pay and shareholder return. **Number listed:** 5

1. Richard Fairbank (Capital One Financial), with 376
2. Bill Gates (Microsoft), 373
3. James Sinegal (Costco), 319
4. Edward Fritzky (Immunex), 313
5. Warren Buffett(Berkshire Hathaway), 259

Source: *Business Week*, Annual Survey of Executive Compensation, April 19, 1999, p. 74.

★1872★
EXECUTIVES WHOSE COMPANIES PERFORMED BEST RELATIVE TO THEIR PAY, 1996-1998

Ranked by: Relative index, based on pay and average return on equity. **Remarks:** Also notes total pay and average return on equity. **Number listed:** 5

1. Dane Miller (Biomet), with 30
2. Warren Buffett (Berkshire Hathaway), 29
2. Stephen Sanger (General Mills), 29
4. Bill Gates (Microsoft), 27
4. Richard Fairbank(Capital One Financial), 27

Source: *Business Week*, Annual Survey of Executive Compensation, April 19, 1999, p. 74.

★1873★
EXECUTIVES WHOSE COMPANIES PERFORMED WORST RELATIVE TO THEIR PAY, 1996-1998

Ranked by: Relative index, based on pay and average return on equity. **Remarks:** Also notes total pay and average return on equity. **Number listed:** 5

1. Jeffery Bezos (Amazon.com), with -0.5
2. Nolan Archibald (Black & Decker), -0.4
3. Stephen Case (America Online), -0.2
4. Michael Eisner (Walt Disney), 0.1
5. Sanford I. Weill (Citigroup), 0.1

Source: *Business Week*, Annual Survey of Executive Compensation, April 19, 1999, p. 74.

★1874★
HIGHEST PAID ADVERTISING EXECUTIVES, 1997

Ranked by: Total compensation. **Remarks:** Also notes salary and bonus, previous year's figures and percent change from previous year. **Number listed:** 25

1. Ed Meyer(Grey), with $3,050,000
2. Keith Reinhard(Omnicom), $2,503,000
3. John Wren(Omnicom), $2,475,000
4. Martin Sorrell(WPP), $2,374,000
5. Fred Meyer(Omnicom), $2,315,000
6. Phil Geier(Interpublic), $2,235,000
7. Bruce Crawford(Omnicom), $1,985,000
8. Chuck Peebler(True North), $1,941,000
9. Gene Beard(Interpublic), $1,883,000
10. Leo-Arthur Kelmenson(True North), $1,880,000

Source: *Adweek*, September 7, 1998, p. 36.

★1875★
HIGHEST PAID CHIEF EXECUTIVES, 1998

Ranked by: Total pay, in millions of dollars. **Remarks:** Also notes long-term compensation and salary plus bonus. **Number listed:** 20

1. Michael Eisner (Walt Disney), with $575,592 million
2. Mel Karmazin (CBS), $201,934
3. Sandord I. Weill (Citigroup), $167,093
4. Stephen Case (America Online), $159,223
5. Craig Barrett (Intel), $116,511
6. John Welch (General Electric), $83,664
7. Henry Schacht (Lucent Technologies), $67.037
8. L. Dennis Kozlowksi (Tyco International), $65,264
9. Henry Silverman (Cendant), $63,882
10. M. Douglas Ivester (Coca-Cola), $57,322

Source: *Business Week*, Annual Survey of Executive Compensation, April 19, 1999, p. 74.

★1876★
HIGHEST PAID DISCOUNT STORE EXECUTIVES, 1997

Ranked by: Total cash compensation. **Remarks:** Also notes title, salary and bonus, previous year's figures, percent change in cash compensation, percent change in stock price and potential realizable value at 5% or grant present value. **Number listed:** 50

1. Robert Ulrich(Dayton-Hudson), with $4,285,024
2. Floyd Hall(Kmart), $3,015,600
3. David Fuente(Office Depot), $2,640,000
4. William Kelley(Consolidated Stores), $2,550,000
5. Bernard Cammarata(TJX Cos.), $2,333,313
6. David Glass(Wal-Mart), $2,265,846
7. Michael Glazer(Consolidated Stores), $1,800,000
8. Donald Soderquist(Wal-Mart), $1,661,700
9. Richard Schulze(Best Buy), $1,586,750
10. James Halpin(CompUSA), $1,581,395

Source: *Discount Store News*, September 21, 1998, p. 21.

★1877★
HIGHEST PAID EXECUTIVES IN THE GAMING INDUSTRY, 1998

Ranked by: Total compensation, in thousands of dollars. **Remarks:** Also notes salary, bonus, worth of long-term stock options, value of in-the-money options and tenure as CEO. **Number listed:** 61

1. Neil D. Nicastro (WMS Industries, Inc.), with $14,922 thousand
2. Frank J. Fertitta, III (Station Casinos, Inc.), $8,755
3. Guy B. Snowden (GTECH Holdings Corp.), $4,762
4. Anthony A. Marnell, II (Rio Hotel & Casino), $4,651
5. M. Micky Arison (Carnival), $4,496
6. Joseph A. Corazzi (Las Vegas Entertainment Network), $4,096
7. Stephen A. Wynn (Mirage Resorts), $3,754
8. Philip G. Satre (Harrah's Entertainment Inc.), $3,400
9. Nicholas L. Ribis (Trump Hotels & Casino Resorts), $2,759
10. Howard A Goldberg (Players International, Inc.), $2,649

Source: *International Gaming & Wagering Business*, Executive Salary Update (annual), September, 1998, p. 25.

★1878★
HIGHEST PAID EXECUTIVES OF COMPANIES OWNING HMOS, 1997

Ranked by: Annual compensation, exclusive of unexercised stock options. **Number listed:** 25

1. Stephen Wiggins(Oxford Health Plans, Inc.), with $30,725,093
2. Wilson Taylor(Cigna Corp.), $12,456,169
3. William McGuire(United Healthcare Corp.), $8,607,743
4. James Stewart(Cigna Corp.), $7,306,921
5. Robert Smoler(Oxford Health Plans, Inc.), $6,918,509
6. Gerald Isom(Cigna Corp.), $5,73,691
7. Ronald Compton(Aetna), $5,383,148
8. H. Edward Hanway(Cigna Corp.), $5,282,734
9. Donald Levinson(Cigna Corp.), $5,177,026

10. Eugene Froelich(Maxicare Healthplans Inc.), $4,720,483

Source: *National Underwriter Life Health Financial Services Edition*, September 28, 1998, p. 1.

★1879★

HIGHEST PAID NEWSPAPER EXECUTIVES, 1997

Ranked by: Total compensation. **Remarks:** Also notes previous year's figures. **Number listed:** 21

1. Robert M. Jelenic (Journal Register Co.), with $11,578,029
2. Richard J. Harrington (Thomson Corp.), $3,962,438
3. Conrad M. Black (Hollinger International), $3,027,304
4. Marke H. Willes (Times Mirror Co.), $2,951,072
5. John J. Curley (Gannett Co.), $2,232,161
6. John W. Madigan (Tribune Co.), $1,931,127
7. P. Anthony Ridder (Knight Ridder), $1,549,762
8. Larry Franklin (Harte-Hank Communications), $1,514,800
9. Michael E. Pulitzer (Pulitzer Publishing Co.), $1,511,038
10. Arthur Ochs Sulzberger (New York Times Co.), $1,427,581

Source: *Editor & Publisher*, December 12, 1998, p. 6.

★1880★

HIGHEST PAID NON-CEOS, 1998

Ranked by: Total pay, in thousands of dollars. **Remarks:** Also notes long-term compensation and salary plus bonus. **Number listed:** 10

1. John McCartney (3Com), with $78,450 thousand
2. Leslie Vadasz (Intel), $55,894
3. Robert Luciano (Schering-Plough), $53,976
4. Charles Cawley (MBNA), $53,681
5. Richard Vague (Bank One), $43,275
6. James Dimon (Citigroup), $37,164
7. Charles Rice (BankAmerica), $32,236
8. Terrence Larsen (First Union), $29,374
9. Mark Swartz (Tyco International), $29,032
10. William Shanahan (Colgate-Palmolive), $27,724

Source: *Business Week*, Annual Survey of Executive Compensation, April 19, 1999, p. 74.

★1881★

TECHNOLOGY'S RICHEST EXECUTIVES, 1998

Ranked by: Estimated worth in billions of dollars. **Remarks:** Also notes age, position, type of business, location and holdings. **Number listed:** 100

1. Bill Gates (Microsoft), with $58.73 billion
2. Paul Allen (Microsoft), $16.98
3. Steve Ballmer (Microsoft), $12.99
4. Michael Dell (Dell Computer), $12.69
5. Gordon Moore (Intel), $7.62
6. Larry Ellison (Oracle), $6
7. Ted Waitt (Gateway), $3.69
8. William Hewlett (Hewlett-Packard), $3.41
9. Jeff Bezos (Amazon.com), $2.14
10. David Duffield (PeopleSoft), $1.89

Source: *Forbes*, Forbes ASAP, October 5, 1998, p. 51+.

★1882★

TOP PAID U.S. ELECTRONICS EXECUTIVES, 1998

Ranked by: Total compensation, based on a combination of salary, bonus and other compensation. **Remarks:** Also notes age, salary, bonus and other compensation. **Number listed:** 40

1. Craig R. Barrett (Intel), with $116,840,147
2. John McCartney (3Com), $78,452,969
3. Henry B. Schacht (Lucent Technologies), $67,097,584
4. Leslie L. Vadasz (Intel), $56,067,638
5. Scott G. McNealy (Sun Microsystems), $46,808,122
6. L.V. Gerstner, Jr. (IBM), $42,380,556
7. Morton L. Topfer (Dell Computer), $40,172,080
8. Albert W. Duffield (Peoplesoft), $35,769,669
9. Peter Karmanos, Jr. (Compuware), $24,104,943
10. Ross W. Manire (3Com), $23,537,804

Source: *Electronic Business*, June, 1999, p. 58.

★1883★

WEALTHIEST FINANCIAL SERVICES EXECUTIVES, 1998

Ranked by: Total beneficial ownership, in thousands of dollars. **Remarks:** Also notes previous year's figures. **Number listed:** 80

1. Warren Buffett(Berkshire Hathaway), with $37,447,957 thousand
2. Maurice Greenberg(American International Group), $2,361,214
3. Alfred Lerner(MBNA Corp.), $2,265,502
4. Edmond Safra(Republic New York Corp.), $1,931,315
5. Charles Schwab(Charles Schwab Corp.), $1,577,085
6. Laurence Tisch(Loews Corp.), $1,546,412
6. Preston Tisch(Loews Corp.), $1,546,412
8. Charles Munger(Berkshire Hathaway), $1,440,029
9. Patrick Ryan(Aon Corp.), $1,392,744
10. Charles B. Johnson(Franklin Resources), $1,274,910

Source: *Institutional Investor*, August, 1998, p. 52.

Executives--Salaries, Pensions, etc.--Chicago (IL)

★1884★

HIGHEST PAID FORTUNE-100 EXECUTIVES IN THE CHICAGO AREA, 1997

Ranked by: Total compensation, in thousands of dollars. **Remarks:** Also notes salary, bonus, and long-term incentives and company revenue, net income and shareholder return. **Number listed:** 52

1. William Farley(Fruit of the Loom Inc.), with $22,541,7 thousand
2. Robert S. Morrison(Quaker Oats Co.), $14,042.2
3. William L. Davis(R.R. Donnelley & Sons Co.), $13,773.8
4. Arthur C. Martinez(Sears, Roebuck & Co.), $10,420.3
5. Timothy H. Callahan(Equity Office Properties Trust), $9,699.5
6. John W. Madigan (Tribune Co.), $8,187.8
7. William F. Aldinger(Household International), $7,999
8. Michael R. Quinlan(McDonald's Corp.), $7,832.7
9. Duane L. Burnham(Abbott Laboratories), $7,806.5
10. John H. Bryan(Sara Lee Corp.), $7,475.4

Source: *Crain's Chicago Business*, Top Business Lists (annual), 1999, p. 87+.

Executives—Salaries, Pensions, etc.--Detroit Metropolitan Area

★1885★

HIGHEST PAID NON-CEOS IN THE DETROIT METROPOLITAN AREA, 1997

Ranked by: Total compensation, including options and grants, change revenue and net income. **Remarks:** Also notes previous year's compensation, percent change, revenue and net income. **Number listed:** 50

1. Robert Lutz(Chrysler Corp.), with $16,621,226
2. Robert Rossiter(Lear Corp.), $7,410,226
3. Edward Hagenlocker(Ford Motor Co.), $5,604,265
4. Richard Mosteller(Masco Corp.), $5,107,000
5. Kenneth Whipple(Ford Motor Co.), $4,749,822
6. Warren Flick(Kmart Corp.), $4,530,148
7. Gary Valade(Chrysler Corp.), $4,186,316
8. Jacques Nasser(Ford Motor Co.), $4,122,533
9. Thomas Denomme(Chrysler Corp.), $3,951,2777
10. L.R. Hughes(General Motors Corp.), $3,824,117

Source: *Crain's Detroit Business*, Crain's Book of Lists Detroit, December 28, 1998, p. 136+.

Executives—Salaries, Pensions, etc.--Los Angeles County (CA)

★1886★

HIGHEST PAID PUBLIC COMPANY EXECUTIVES IN LOS ANGELES COUNTY, 1998

Ranked by: Total compensation, in thousands of dollars. **Remarks:** Also notes base salary, bonus, company revenue, net income, shareholders equity, return on equity and compensation as a percent of net income. **Number listed:** 100

1. Stephen F. Bollenbach (Hilton Hotels Corp.), with $27,294 thousand
2. Charles G. Betty (EarthLink Network), $23,456
3. Linda J. Wachner (Authentic Fitness Corp.), $19,678
4. Bruce Karatz (Kaufman & Broad), $15,484
5. William S. Heys (EarthLink Network), $13,167
6. Richard B Handler (Jefferies Group), $11,705
7. James A. McIntyre (Fremont General Corp.), $11,370
8. Louis J. Rampino (Fremont General Corp.), $10,174
9. Mark Hughes (Herbalife), $9,874
10. Brinton O.C. Young (EarthLink Network), $8,520

Source: *Los Angeles Business Journal*, May 31, 1999, p. 14.

Executives—Salaries, Pensions, etc.--Philadelphia Metropolitan Area

★1887★

HIGHEST PAID CHIEF EXECUTIVES IN THE PHILADELPHIA AREA, 1998

Ranked by: Total cash compensation. **Remarks:** Also notes contact information, age, salary, bonus, cash and equity grants package, sales number of employees, ratio of stock holdings package, company and industry performance over five-year period and change in pay. **Number listed:** 100

1. Wilson H. Taylor(Cigna Corp.), with $3,270,200
2. Lawrence A. Weinbach(Unisys Corp.), $3,192,000
3. Robert Toll(Toll Brothers Inc.), $2,689,851
4. J. Lawrence Wilson(Rohm & Haas Co.), $1,939,210
5. Robert H. Campbell(SunCo Inc.), $1,581,140
6. Dorrit J. Bern(Charming Shoppes Inc.), $1,570,000
7. William J. Avery(Crown Cork & Seal Co. Inc.), $1,282,500
8. James J. Maguire(Philadelphia Consolidated Holdings), $1,275,000
9. Alan B. Miller(Universal Health Services Inc.), $1,207,000
10. John H. Lynch(Knoll Inc.), $1,149,996

Source: *Philadelphia Business Journal*, Book of Business Lists (annual), December 25, 1998, p. 87+.

Exhibitions and Fairs--North America

★1888★

TOP NORTH AMERICAN FAIRS, 1998

Ranked by: Attendance. **Remarks:** Also notes previous year's attendance and 1999 dates. **Number listed:** 50

1. State Fair of Texas (Dallas), with 3,480,000 attendees
2. Houston Livestock Show & Rodeo (TX), 1,769,359
3. Canadian National Exhibition (Ontario, Canada), 1,768,000
4. Minnesota State Fair (St. Paul), 1,689,034
5. State Fair of Oklahoma (Oklahoma City), 1,657,303
6. Eastern States Exposure (West Springfield, MA), 1,254,523
7. Los Angeles County Fair (Pomona, CA), 1,251,951
8. Western Washington Fair (Pallyup, WA), 1,229,007
9. Del Mar Fair (CA), 1,164,360
10. Calgary Stampede (Alberta, Canada), 1,124,271

Source: *Amusement Business*, Amusement Business Annual Year-end Issue, December 28, 1998, p. 98+.

Export-Import Trade

★1889★

LARGEST U.S. EXPORT MARKETS, 1997

Ranked by: Export value, in millions of U.S. dollars ($). **Number listed:** 10

1. Canada, with $151,451 million
2. Mexico, $71,378
3. Japan, $65.673
4. United Kingdom, $36,435
5. South Korea, $25,067
6. Germany, $24,467
7. Taiwan, $20,388
8. Netherlands, $19,822
9. Singapore, $17,727
10. France, $15,982

Source: *Nation's Business*, August, 1998, p. 20.

★1890★

LEADING COUNTRIES OF ORIGIN FOR U.S. IMPORTS, 1997

Ranked by: Dollar value, in thousands of U.S. dollars ($). **Remarks:** Also notes previous year's figures and percent change. **Number listed:** 10

1. India, with $230,730 thousand
2. China, $171,319

3. Canada, $138,660
4. Pakistan, $70,391
5. United Kingdom, $63,738
6. Belgium, $59,314
7. Turkey, $39,522
8. Mexico, $26,667
9. Netherlands, $22,309
10. Egypt, $21,124

Source: *HFN*, August 10, 1998, p. 10.

★1891★
LEADING DESTINATIONS OF U.S. EXPORTS, 1997
Ranked by: Dollar value, in thousands of U.S. dollars ($). **Remarks:** Also notes previous year's figures and percent change. **Number listed:** 10

1. Canada, with $352,086 thousand
2. Mexico, $72,269
3. Japan, $45,034
4. United Kingdom, $44,848
5. Hong Kong, $35,484
6. Singapore, $30,483
7. Saudi Arabia, $29,369
8. United Arab Emirates, $17,418
9. Chile, $15,755
10. Australia, $15,182

Source: *HFN*, August 10, 1998, p. 10.

★1892★
TOP U.S. EXPORT COMMODITIES, 1997
Ranked by: Dollar value, in millions of U.S. dollars ($). **Number listed:** 10

1. Semiconductors, with $41,745.5 million
2. Aircraft and associated equipment, $40,766.0
3. Motor Vehicle Parts and accessories, $28,895.9
4. Computers, $28,158.9
5. Telecommunications Equipment, $22,744.6
6. Parts for computers and Office equipment, $22,355.9
7. All Motor Vehicles, $17,329.6
8. Measuring, Checking and Analyzing Instruments, $17,055.9
9. Nonelectric Engines and Motors, $11,778.8
10. Specialized Industrial Machinery, $11,191.8

Source: *World Trade*, November, 1998, p. 51.

★1893★
TOP U.S. EXPORTERS OF BULK CARGO, 1998
Ranked by: Metric tons. **Remarks:** Also notes commodities exported. **Number listed:** 25

1. Cargill, with 20,808,554.46 metric tons.
2. Continental Grain Exports, 14,257,129.87
3. Alfred C. Toepfer International, 7,468,595.65
4. AMCI Exports, 7,317,908.26
5. Consol Sales, 7,239,514.20
6. Zen Noh Grain, 7,025,569.41
7. Louis Dreyfus, 6,893,232.15
8. Mitsui & Co., 6,574,259.04
9. Marubeni, 5,815,959.11
10. Massey Coal Exports, 5,646,241.94

Source: *World Trade*, November, 1998, p. 51.

★1894★
TOP U.S. EXPORTERS OF CONTAINERIZED GOODS, 1997
Ranked by: Twenty-foot container equivalents (TEUs). **Remarks:** Also notes commodities exported. **Number listed:** 25

1. Weyerhaeuser, with 92,233.72 TEUs
2. American Chung Nam, 60,920.41
3. Philip Morris, 48,736.12
4. Westvaco, 43,067.49
5. Pacific Forest Resources, 41,449.22
6. General Electric, 38,599.21
7. IBP, 30,974.71
8. Dow Chemical, 29,789.21
9. Chrysler, 29,273.90
10. General Motors, 29,241.32

Source: *World Trade*, November, 1998, p. 52.

★1895★
TOP U.S. EXPORTS TO CHINA, 1998
Ranked by: Basis for ranking not specified. **Number listed:** 10

1. Power-generation Equipment
2. Air and spacecraft
3. Electrical Machinery
4. Fertilizer
5. Medical Instruments
6. Cotton, Yarn and Fabric
7. Plastics and articles
8. Oil Seeds
9. Paper and paperboard
10. Mineral Oils

Source: *Metal Center News*, January, 1999, p. 45.

Export-Import Trade--Africa

★1896★
LARGEST U.S. EXPORT MARKETS IN AFRICA, 1997
Ranked by: Export value, in billions of U.S. dollars ($). **Number listed:** 14

1. South Africa, with $3.1 billion
2. Egypt, $3
3. Nigeria, $.8
4. Algeria, $.6
5. Morocco, $.5
6. Ghana, $.3
6. Angola, $.3
8. Tunisia, $.2
9. Cameroon, $.1
10. Ethiopia, $.1

Source: *World Trade*, November, 1998, p. 36.

Export-Import Trade--Asia

★1897★
TOP U.S. CONTAINERIZED EXPORTS TO ASIA, 1998
Ranked by: Forty-foot equivalent units (FEUs). **Remarks:** Also notes previous year's figures and percent change. **Number listed:** 9

1. Other Forest Products, with 4,581 FEU
2. Resin/Chemical, 4,043
3. Waste Paper, 3,349
4. Refrigerated Products, 2,492
5. Machinery, 1,751
6. Metals, 1,283
7. Hay, 1,100
8. Cotton, 1,053
9. Meat, 777

Source: *Better Investing*, September, 1998, p. 16.

★1898★
TOP U.S. CONTAINERIZED IMPORTS FROM ASIA, 1998
Ranked by: Forty-foot equivalent units (FEUs). **Remarks:** Also notes previous year's figures and percent change. **Number listed:** 10

1. Electrical Goods, with 8,324 FEU
2. Furniture, 2,616
3. Footwear, 2,532
4. Auto Parts, 2,474
5. Toys & Games, 2,396
6. Apparel, 2,067
7. Canned Food/Beverages, 1,661
8. Tires, 1,130
9. Fiber/Fabric, 1,112
10. Hand Tools, 1,001

Source: *Better Investing*, September, 1998, p. 16.

Export-Import Trade--California

★1899★
CALIFORNIA'S TOP EXPORT DESTINATIONS, 1997
Ranked by: Export value, in millions of U.S. dollars ($). **Remarks:** Also notes percent of total and change from previous year. **Number listed:** 10

1. Japan, with $17,460 million
2. Mexico, $12,082
3. Canada, $11,426
4. South Korea, $7,046
5. Taiwan, $6,991
6. Singapore, $5,674
7. United Kingdom, $5,414
8. Hong Kong, $4,153
9. Germany, $4,108
10. Netherlands, $3,411

Source: *Knitting Times*, February, 1999, p. 20.

Export-Import Trade--Detroit Metropolitan Area

★1900★
LEADING EXPORTERS IN SOUTHEAST MICHIGAN, 1997
Ranked by: Export revenue, in millions of dollars. **Remarks:** Also notes total revenue, previous year's figures, number of employees in southeast Michigan, number of employees worldwide and type of business. **Number listed:** 20

1. General Motors Corp., with $20,500 million
2. Chrysler Corp., $10,200
3. Ford Motor Co., $1,608
4. Detroit Diesel Corp., $752
5. Federal-Mogul Corp., $332.9
6. Compuware Corp., $313.3
7. Hayes Lemmerz International Inc., $175
8. Freduenberg-NOK Group Cos., $100
9. The Stroh Brewery Co., $95
10. MascoTech, $71

Source: *Crain's Detroit Business*, August 17, 1998, p. 12.

Export-Import Trade--Florida

★1901★
FLORIDA'S TOP EXPORT DESTINATIONS, 1998
Ranked by: Export value. **Remarks:** Also notes percent change from previous year. **Number listed:** 50

1. Brazil, with $3,399,909,731
2. Venezuela, $2,241,478,473
3. Columbia, $1,655,260,551
4. Argentina, $1,476,084,197
5. Dominican Republic, $1,225,648,200
6. Honduras, $802,880,659
7. Costa Rica, $791,607,137
8. Chile, $656,952,925
9. Guatemala, $570,539,266
10. United Kingdom, $536,740,860

Source: *Florida Trend*, TopRank Florida, 1999, p. 102.

★1902★
FLORIDA'S TOP IMPORT ORIGINS, 1998
Ranked by: Import value in millions of dollars. **Remarks:** Also notes percent change from previous year. **Number listed:** 50

1. Japan, with $2,088,782,050
2. Dominican Republic, $1,189,808,758
3. Brazil, $1,139,864,842
4. Germany, $1,056,966,809
5. Honduras, $899,091,073
6. Colombia, $783,836,203
7. Mainland China, $749,935,500
8. Mexico, $699,688,969
9. Costa Rica, $651,361,384
10. Italy, $580,907,899

Source: *Florida Trend*, TopRank Florida, 1999, p. 102.

Eye Make-up Products

★1903★
BEST-SELLING EYE-MASCARA BRANDS, 1998
Ranked by: Sales, in millions of dollars. **Remarks:** Also notes unit volume. **Number listed:** 10

1. Maybelline, with $129.1 million
2. L'Oreal, $85.2
3. Cover Girl, $66
4. Almay, $52
5. Max Factor, $24.3
6. Revlon, $24.2
7. Wet 'n' Wild, $2.3
8. jane, $2.2
9. Naturisitics, $1.5
10. Physician's Formula, $1.4

Source: *MMR*, May 3, 1999, p. 33.

★1904★
BEST-SELLING EYE-PENCIL BRANDS, 1998
Ranked by: Sales, in millions of dollars. **Remarks:** Also notes unit volume. **Number listed:** 10

1. Maybelline, with $43.8 million
2. Cover Girl, $41.8
3. Revlon, $28
4. L'Oreal, $22.7
5. Almay, $18.6
6. Wet 'n' Wild, $8.2
7. jane, $4
8. Max Factor, $3.9

9. Nat Robbins, $3.5
10. Artmatic, $2.6

Source: *MMR*, May 3, 1999, p. 33.

Facial Tissue

See: **Tissue Paper**

Factories

★1905★
TOP STATES FOR NEW MANUFACTURING FACILITIES AND EXPANSIONS, 1998
Ranked by: Number of facilities/expansions. **Number listed:** 10

1. Michigan, with 1,722
2. California, 1,673
3. Ohio, 1,153
4. North Carolina, 1,044
5. New York, 1,025
6. Texas, 926
7. Virginia, 462
8. Illinois, 448
9. Florida, 430
10. Minnesota, 402

Source: *Site Selection & Industrial Development*, March, 1999, p. 184.

★1906★
TOP STATES FOR NEW MANUFACTURING PLANTS, 1998
Ranked by: Number of plants. **Number listed:** 11

1. California, with 296 plants
2. Michigan, 260
3. Ohio, 202
4. New York, 157
5. North Carolina, 139
6. Texas, 121
7. Illinois, 106
8. Pennsylvania, 85
9. Minnesota, 71
10. Florida, 66
10. South Carolina, 66

Source: *Site Selection & Industrial Development*, March, 1999, p. 190.

Farm Management

★1907★
LARGEST FARM MANAGEMENT FIRMS BY TOTAL ACRES MANAGED, 1998
Ranked by: Total acres managed. **Remarks:** Also notes contact name and phone number. **Number listed:** 10

1. NationsBank (TX), with 2,114,346 acres
2. Banc One Farm and Ranch Management (TX), 1,600,000
3. Farmers National Co. (NE), 1,079,315
4. Texas Pacific Land Trust (TX), 1,067,000
5. Norwest Bank (NE), 1,063,790
6. U.S. Bank, NA (ND), 740,000
7. Am South Bank (AL), 558,480
8. Hall and Hall, Inc. (MT), 530,925
9. Capital Agricultural Property Services, Inc. (IL), 451,366
10. North-east Agri Service (CO), 425,000

Source: *Ag Lender*, November, 1998, p. 3.

Fast Food Restaurants

★1908★
TOP METROPOLITAN AREAS IN FAST FOOD SALES, 1997
Ranked by: Sales, in thousands of dollars. **Number listed:** 321

1. Chicago, IL, with $2,743,164 thousand
2. Los Angeles-Long Beach, CA, $2,372,862
3. Atlanta, GA, $1,901,478
4. Washington, DC, $1,706,528
5. Detroit, MI, $1,652,022
6. Houston, TX, $1,477,401
7. New York, NY, $1,400,532
8. Phoenix-Mesa, AZ, $1,372,277
9. Dallas, TX, $1,224,295
10. Philadelphia, PA, $1,123,944

Source: *Restaurant Business*, Restaurant Growth Index (annual), October 1, 1998, p. 68.

★1909★
TOP METROPOLITAN AREAS IN PER CAPITA FAST FOOD SALES, 1997
Ranked by: Sales per capita. **Number listed:** 321

1. Myrtle Beach, SC, with $847
2. Greenville, SC, $686
3. Flagstaff, AZ, $684
4. Wilmington, NC, $660
5. Albuquerque, NM, $648
5. Sioux Falls, SD, $648
7. Rapid City, SD, $639
8. Fayetteville, NC, $637
   Cheyenne, WY, $606
   Columbus, OH, $596

Source: *Restaurant Business*, Restaurant Growth Index (annual), October 1, 1998, p. 73.

Fast Food Restaurants—Chain and Franchise Operations

★1910★
LEADING CHICKEN RESTAURANT CHAINS BY SALES, 1997
Ranked by: Sales, in millions of dollars. **Remarks:** Also notes *Restaurant and Institutions* ranking in their individual menu category. **Number listed:** 14

1. Kentucky Fried Chicken, with $8,200 million
2. Popeye's Chicken & Biscuits, $847
3. Churchs Chicken, $720
4. Chick-fil-A, $672
5. El Pollo Loco, $235
6. Bojangles' Restaurants, $229.1
7. Lee's Famous Recipe Chicken, $136.5
8. Mrs. Winner's, $113.4
9. Buffalo Wild Wings, $82

10. Pudgie's Famous Chicken, $82.9

Source: *Restaurant & Institutions*, July 15, 1998, p. 102.

★1911★
LEADING FAST FOOD RESTAURANTS, 1998
Ranked by: Total sales, in billions of dollars. **Remarks:** Also includes lead advertising agency and media expenditures. **Number listed:** 10

1. McDonald's, with $18.1 billion
2. Burger King, $8.5
3. Taco Bell, $5
4. Wendy's, $4.9
5. Pizza Hut, $4.8
6. Kentucky Fried Chicken, $4.2
7. Subway, $3.1
8. Dairy Queen, $2.7
9. Domino's Pizza, $2.5
10. Hardee's, $2.3

Source: *Brandweek*, Superbrands: America's Top 2,000 Brands (annual), June 21, 1999, p. S42.

★1912★
LEADING FAST FOOD TAKE-OUT RESTAURANT CHAINS BY ESTIMATED TAKE-OUT SALES, 1998
Ranked by: Estimated take-out sales, in thousands. **Remarks:** Also notes segment, units, and total sales. **Number listed:** 17

1. McDonald's, with $9,494,368 thousand
2. Burger King, $4,041,708
3. Pizza Hut, $3,196,050
4. Kentucky Fried Chicken, $2,730,000
5. Taco Bell, $2,651,473
6. Domino's Pizza, $2,277,000
7. Wendy's, $2,142,023
8. Subway, $2,106,000
9. Dairy Queen, $1,952,162
10. Hardee's, $1,613,873

Source: *Convenience Store News*, Top 100 Take-out Leaders (annual), October 11, 1998, p. 172+.

★1913★
LEADING SWEET/SNACKS RESTAURANT CHAINS BY SALES, 1997
Ranked by: Sales, in millions of dollars. **Remarks:** Also notes *Restaurant and Institutions* ranking in their individual menu category. **Number listed:** 12

1. Dairy Queen, with $2,540 million
2. Dunkin' Donuts, $2,229.5
3. Baskin-Robbins, $800
4. Tim Hortons, $772
5. Starbucks, $596.2
6. TCBY, $300
7. Haagen-Dazs Ice Cream Cafe, $260
8. Braum's Ice Cream & Dairy, $222.5
9. Krispy Kreme Doughnuts, $202
10. Carvel Ice Cream Bakery, $150

Source: *Restaurant & Institutions*, July 15, 1998, p. 102.

Fertilizer Industry

★1914★
LEADING FERTILIZER PRODUCING CHEMICAL COMPANIES BY SALES, 1998
Ranked by: Sales, in millions of dollars. **Remarks:** Also notes percentage change from 1997, net income, profit margin, capital ratios, shareholder returns, price and assets. **Number listed:** 8

1. Farmland Industries, with $8,775 million
2. IMC Global, $2,696
3. Terra Industries, $2,552
4. Potash Corp. Of Saskatchewan, $2,308
5. Scotts, $1,116
6. Phosphate Resource, $687
7. Mississippi Chemical, $519
8. Terra Nitrogen, $249

Source: *Chemical Week*, Chemical Week 300 (annual), May 12, 1999, p. 51.

Fiber Optic Cables, International

★1915★
LEADING CAUSES OF FIBER OPTIC CABLE FAILURE, 1998*
Ranked by: Percentage of total occurances. **Number listed:** 8

1. dig-ups, with 58.1%
2. Vehicle, 7.5%
3. Process or craft error, 6.9%
4. Power line, 4.4%
5. Rodent, 3.8%
6. Sabotage, 2.5%
7. Fire, 1.9%
8. Firearm, 1.3%

Source: *Telephony*, November 16, 1998, p. 16.

Filling Stations

See: **Automobile Service Stations**

Finance Companies

★1916★
TOP FINANCE COMPANIES BY NET INCOME, 1997
Ranked by: Net income, in thousands of dollars. **Remarks:** Also notes total assets and percentage change from previous year. **Number listed:** 25

1. General Electric Capital Services (CT), with $3,256,000 thousand
2. General Motors Acceptance Corp. (MI), $1,301,100
3. Associates First Capital Corp. (TX), $1,031,700
4. Ford Motor Credit Company (MI), $1,030,800
5. Household International Inc. (IL), $685,600
6. Chrysler Financial Corp. (MI), $419,000
7. Transamerica Finance Group Inc. (CA), $380,005
8. International Lease Finance Co. (CA), $338,685
9. CIT Group Holdings Inc. (NY), $310,100
10. Green Tree Financial Corp. (MN), $301,396

Source: *American Banker*, September 12, 1998, p. 8.

★1917★
TOP FINANCE COMPANIES BY TOTAL ASSETS, 1997
Ranked by: Total assets, in thousands of dollars. **Remarks:** Also notes total assets and percentage change from previous year. **Number listed:** 25

1. General Electric Capital Services (CT), with $255,408,000 thousand
2. Ford Motor Credit Company (MI), $121,973,000
3. General Motors Acceptance Corp. (MI), $109,319,300
4. Associates First Capital Corp. (TX), $57,232,700
5. Household International Inc. (IL), $30,302,600
6. CIT Group Holdings Inc. (NY), $20,464,100
7. Toyota Motor Credit Corp. (CA), $19,830,000
8. Chrysler Financial Corp. (MI), $19,321,000
9. Beneficial Corp. (DE), $17,645,100
10. Sears Roebuck Acceptance Corp. (DE), $16,716,000

Source: *American Banker*, September 12, 1998, p. 8.

★1918★
TOP FINANCE COMPANIES BY TOTAL CAPITAL FUNDS, 1997
Ranked by: Total capital funds, in thousands of dollars. **Remarks:** Also notes total capital funds and percentage change from previous year, total equity capital, total assets, percentage of assets change from previous year, net income, percentage of net income change from previous year and number of employees. **Number listed:** 25

1. General Electric Capital Services (CT), with $18,235,000 thousand
2. Ford Motor Credit Company (MI), $9,684,000
3. General Motors Acceptance Corp. (MI), $8,756,100
4. Commercial Credit Company (MD), $7,804,400
5. Associates First Capital Corp. (TX), $6,519,000
6. Household International Inc. (IL), $4,516,200
7. Chrysler Financial Corp. (MI), $3,297,000
8. CIT Group Holdings Inc. (NY), $2,982,900
9. International Lease Finance Co. (CA), $2,517,188
10. Sears Roebuck Acceptance Corp. (DE), $2,162,000

Source: *American Banker*, September 12, 1998, p. 8.

Financial Analysts

★1919★
LEADING INVESTMENT RESEARCH COMPANIES, 1998
Ranked by: Total number of positions on the All-America Fixed Income Research Team. **Remarks:** Also notes previous year's ranking, number of analysts from each firm that made the first, second, and third All-America Research Teams, and the numbers of runners-up for 1997 and 1998. **Number listed:** 20

1. Merrill Lynch & Co., with 32 positions
2. Salomon Smith Barney, 28
3. Bear Stearns, 26
4. Lehman Brothers, 24
5. Donaldson, Lufkin & Jenrette, 18
5. Goldman, Sachs & Co., 18
7. Morgan Stanley Dean Witter, 14
8. J. P. Morgan, 10
9. Chase Securities, 9
10. Grantchester Securities, 7

Source: *Institutional Investor*, All-America Fixed-Income Research Team (annual), August, 1998, p. 67.

★1920★
TOP BROKERAGE FIRMS BY COMPLETION PERCENTAGES, 1998
Ranked by: Completion percentage, arrived at by dividing the number of a firm's places on the All-America Research Team by its total number of equity analysts. **Remarks:** Also notes specific figures for the AART places and the number of analysts. **Number listed:** 20

1. Goldman Sachs, with 81.7%
2. Merrill Lynch, 74.7%
3. Donaldson, Lufkin & Jenrette, 73.1%
4. Sanford C. Bernstein & Co., 63.2%
5. Salomon Smith Barney, 60.8%
6. PaineWebber, 57.1%
7. Bear Stearns, 55.9%
8. Morgan Stanley Dean Witter, 54.5%
9. Schroder Group, 50%
10. J. P. Morgan, 39%

Source: *Institutional Investor*, All-America Research Team (annual), October, 1998, p. 100.

★1921★
TOP BROKERAGE FIRMS BY NUMBER OF POSITIONS ON ALL-AMERICA RESEARCH TEAM, 1998
Ranked by: Total positions on the All-America Research Team. **Remarks:** Also notes 1997 rank and total number of positions as well as number of analysts on the first, second, third and runner-up teams. **Number listed:** 20

1. Merrill Lynch, with 57 positions
2. Goldman Sachs, 50
2. Morgan Stanley Dean Witter, 50
4. Salomon Smith Barney, 46
5. Donaldson, Lufkin & Jenrette, 38
6. Credit Suisse First Boston, 27
7. Paine Webber, 25
8. Lehman Brothers, 21
9. Bear Stearns, 19
10. J. P. Morgan, 16

Source: *Institutional Investor*, All-America Research Team (annual), October, 1998, p. 99.

★1922★
TOP BROKERAGE FIRMS BY WEIGHTED VALUE OF NUMBER OF POSITIONS ON THE ALL-AMERICA RESEARCH TEAM, 1998
Ranked by: Weighted value of total positions on the All-America Research Team by assigning a value of 4 to a first-team position, 3 to a second-team position, 2 to a third-team position and 1 to a runner-up team position. **Number listed:** 15

1. Morgan Stanley Dean Witter, with 137 weighted value
2. Merrill Lynch, 127
3. Salomon Smith Barney, 116
4. Goldman Sachs, 109
5. Donaldson, Lufkin & Jenrette, 85
6. Credit Suisse First Boston, 59
7. PaineWebber, 51
8. Bear Stearns, 41
8. Lehman Brothers, 41
10. Sanford C. Bernstein & Co., 33

Source: *Institutional Investor*, All-America Research Team (annual), October, 1998, p. 100.

★1923★
TOP FINANCIAL ANALYSTS FOR HIGH-GRADE SECURITIES IN BASIC INDUSTRIES, 1998
Ranked by: Results of research undertaken by staff of *Institutional Investor*. **Remarks:** Includes reason for selection. **Number listed:** 3

1. William Reed (Merrill Lynch)
2. Katherine Oakley (Goldman Sachs)
3. John Kollar (Bear Stearns)

Source: *Institutional Investor*, All-America Fixed-Income Research Team (annual), August, 1998, p. 72.

★1924★

TOP FINANCIAL ANALYSTS FOR HIGH-GRADE SECURITIES IN FINANCE COMPANIES, 1998

Ranked by: Results of research undertaken by staff of *Institutional Investor.* **Remarks:** Includes reason for selection. **Number listed:** 5

1. Mark Girolamo (Deutsche Bank Securities)
2. Jean Sievert (Salomon Smith Barney)
3. Ann Maysek (Bear Stearns)
4. Vincent Breitenbach (Lehman Brothers)
4. Matthew Burnell (Merrill Lynch)

Source: *Institutional Investor*, All-America Fixed-Income Research Team (annual), August, 1998, p. 74.

★1925★

TOP FINANCIAL ANALYSTS FOR HIGH-GRADE SECURITIES IN MANUFACTURING, 1998

Ranked by: Results of research undertaken by staff of *Institutional Investor.* **Remarks:** Includes reason for selection. **Number listed:** 7

1. James Drury (Bear Stearns)
2. Anja King (Lehman Brothers)
3. Katherine Oakley (Goldman Sachs)
4. Mark Altherr (Salomon Smith Barney)
4. Brian Jacoby (J. P. Morgan)
4. Kevin Morley (Credit Suisse First Boston)
4. Stephen Penwell (Morgan Stanley Dean Witter)

Source: *Institutional Investor*, All-America Fixed-Income Research Team (annual), August, 1998, p. 75.

★1926★

TOP FINANCIAL ANALYSTS FOR HIGH-GRADE SECURITIES IN REAL ESTATE INVESTMENT TRUSTS, 1998

Ranked by: Results of research undertaken by staff of *Institutional Investor.* **Remarks:** Includes reason for selection. **Number listed:** 4

1. John Forrey (Merrill Lynch)
2. Kris Grimm (Lehman Brothers)
3. David Havens (Warburg Dillon Read)
4. Van Hesser (Goldman Sachs)

Source: *Institutional Investor*, All-America Fixed-Income Research Team (annual), August, 1998, p. 76.

★1927★

TOP FINANCIAL ANALYSTS FOR HIGH-GRADE SECURITIES IN RETAILING, 1998

Ranked by: Results of research undertaken by staff of *Institutional Investor.* **Remarks:** Includes reason for selection. **Number listed:** 4

1. Eric Miller (Merrill Lynch)
2. Margaret Cannella (Citicorp Securities)
3. Jan Dillow (Goldman Sachs)
4. Matthew Clark (Morgan Stanley Dean Witter)

Source: *Institutional Investor*, All-America Fixed-Income Research Team (annual), August, 1998, p. 76+.

★1928★

TOP FINANCIAL ANALYSTS FOR HIGH-GRADE SECURITIES IN SOVEREIGNS, 1998

Ranked by: Results of research undertaken by staff of *Institutional Investor.* **Remarks:** Includes reason for selection. **Number listed:** 4

1. Peter Petas (Deutsche Bank Securities)
2. Scott MacDonald (Donaldson, Lufkin & Jenrette)
3. Joseph Taylor (Merrill Lynch)
4. John Paulsen (J. P. Morgan)

Source: *Institutional Investor*, All-America Fixed-Income Research Team (annual), August, 1998, p. 77.

★1929★

TOP FINANCIAL ANALYSTS FOR HIGH-GRADE SECURITIES IN THE CONSUMER PRODUCTS INDUSTRY, 1998

Ranked by: Results of research undertaken by staff of *Institutional Investor.* **Remarks:** Includes reason for selection. **Number listed:** 7

1. Margaret Cannella (Citicorp Securities)
2. Jan Dillow (Goldman Sachs)
3. James Drury (Bear Stearns)
4. Matthew Clark (Morgan Stanley Dean Witter)
4. Amy Eadon-Judd (J. P. Morgan)
4. Vincent Fea (Chase Securities)
4. Eric Miller (Merrill Lynch)

Source: *Institutional Investor*, All-America Fixed-Income Research Team (annual), August, 1998, p. 72+.

★1930★

TOP FINANCIAL ANALYSTS FOR HIGH-GRADE SECURITIES IN THE ELECTRIC UTILITIES INDUSTRY, 1998

Ranked by: Results of research undertaken by staff of *Institutional Investor.* **Remarks:** Includes reason for selection. **Number listed:** 5

1. Daniel Scotto (Bear Stearns)
2. Terran Miller (Donaldson, Lufkin & Jenrette)
3. Leo Kelser (Merrill Lynch)
4. Helen Clement (Warburg Dillon Read)
4. Kevin Roach (Morgan Stanley Dean Witter)

Source: *Institutional Investor*, All-America Fixed-Income Research Team (annual), August, 1998, p. 73.

★1931★

TOP FINANCIAL ANALYSTS FOR HIGH-GRADE SECURITIES IN THE ENERGY INDUSTRY, 1998

Ranked by: Results of research undertaken by staff of *Institutional Investor.* **Remarks:** Includes reason for selection. **Number listed:** 3

1. Paul Tice (Deutsche Bank Securities)
2. Varkki Chacko (Goldman Sachs)
3. Mark Pibl (Merrill Lynch)

Source: *Institutional Investor*, All-America Fixed-Income Research Team (annual), August, 1998, p. 73+.

★1932★

TOP FINANCIAL ANALYSTS FOR HIGH-GRADE SECURITIES IN THE INSURANCE INDUSTRY, 1998

Ranked by: Results of research undertaken by staff of *Institutional Investor.* **Remarks:** Includes reason for selection. **Number listed:** 4

1. Donna Halverstadt (Goldman Sachs)
2. Thomas Walsh (Lehman Brothers)
3. John Forrey (Merrill Lynch)
4. Jean Sievert (Salomon Smith Barney)

Source: *Institutional Investor*, All-America Fixed-Income Research Team (annual), August, 1998, p. 74+.

★1933★

TOP FINANCIAL ANALYSTS FOR HIGH-GRADE SECURITIES IN THE INTERNATIONAL BANKING INDUSTRY, 1998

Ranked by: Results of research undertaken by staff of *Institutional Investor.* **Remarks:** Includes reason for selection. **Number listed:** 4

1. Charles Mounts (Warburg Dillon Read)
2. Allerton Smith (Donaldson, Lufkin & Jenrette)
3. John Raymond (Lehman Brothers)
4. Ethan Heisler (Salomon Smith Barney)

Source: *Institutional Investor*, All-America Fixed-Income Research Team (annual), August, 1998, p. 71.

★1934★
TOP FINANCIAL ANALYSTS FOR HIGH-GRADE SECURITIES IN THE MEDIA AND ENTERTAINMENT INDUSTRY, 1998
Ranked by: Results of research undertaken by staff of *Institutional Investor.* **Remarks:** Includes reason for selection. **Number listed:** 5
1. Stevyn Schutzman (Salomon Smith Barney)
2. Marion Boucher Soper (Bear Stearns)
3. Amy Richards (Goldman Sachs)
4. Douglas Colandrea (Morgan Stanley Dean Witter)
4. George King (Credit Suisse First Boston)

Source: *Institutional Investor*, All-America Fixed-Income Research Team (annual), August, 1998, p. 75+.

★1935★
TOP FINANCIAL ANALYSTS FOR HIGH-GRADE SECURITIES IN THE TELECOMMUNICATIONS INDUSTRY, 1998
Ranked by: Results of research undertaken by staff of *Institutional Investor.* **Remarks:** Includes reason for selection. **Number listed:** 4
1. Marion Boucher Soper (Bear Stearns)
2. Robert Waldman (Salomon Smith Barney)
3. Amy Richards (Goldman Sachs)
4. Robert Schiffman (Donaldson, Lufkin & Jenrette)

Source: *Institutional Investor*, All-America Fixed-Income Research Team (annual), August, 1998, p. 77+.

★1936★
TOP FINANCIAL ANALYSTS FOR HIGH-GRADE SECURITIES IN THE TRANSPORTATION INDUSTRY, 1998
Ranked by: Results of research undertaken by staff of *Institutional Investor.* **Remarks:** Includes reason for selection. **Number listed:** 6
1. Lawrence Taylor (Donaldson, Lufkin & Jenrette)
2. Daniel Ward (Deutsche Bank Securities)
3. Eileen Dowling (Merrill Lynch)
4. Jan Dillow (Goldman Sachs)
4. Claire Kendrick (Prudential Securities)
4. John Kollar (Bear Stearns)

Source: *Institutional Investor*, All-America Fixed-Income Research Team (annual), August, 1998, p. 78.

★1937★
TOP FINANCIAL ANALYSTS FOR HIGH-GRADE SECURITIES IN THE U.S. BANKING INDUSTRY, 1998
Ranked by: Results of research undertaken by staff of *Institutional Investor.* **Remarks:** Includes reason for selection. **Number listed:** 4
1. Allerton Smith (Donaldson, Lufkin & Jenrette)
2. Marc Hellman (Lehman Brothers)
3. Jay Weintraub (Merrill Lynch)
4. Ethan Heisler (Salomon Smith Barney)

Source: *Institutional Investor*, All-America Fixed-Income Research Team (annual), August, 1998, p. 71+.

★1938★
TOP FINANCIAL ANALYSTS FOR HIGH-YIELD SECURITIES IN BUILDING, 1998
Ranked by: Results of research undertaken by staff of *Institutional Investor.* **Remarks:** Includes reason for selection. **Number listed:** 3
1. Michael Kender (Salomon Smith Barney)
2. Kevin Eng (Grantchester Securities)
3. Robert Crowley (BancBoston Securities)

Source: *Institutional Investor*, All-America Fixed-Income Research Team (annual), August, 1998, p. 80.

★1939★
TOP FINANCIAL ANALYSTS FOR HIGH-YIELD SECURITIES IN CONSUMER PRODUCTS, 1998
Ranked by: Results of research undertaken by staff of *Institutional Investor.* **Remarks:** Includes reason for selection. **Number listed:** 5
1. Evan Ratner (Donaldson, Lufkin & Jenrette)
2. Steven Ruggiero (Chase Securities)
3. Sally Dessloch (J. P. Morgan)
4. Kevin Eng (Grantchester Securities)
4. Kenneth Goldberg (Merrill Lynch)

Source: *Institutional Investor*, All-America Fixed-Income Research Team (annual), August, 1998, p. 81.

★1940★
TOP FINANCIAL ANALYSTS FOR HIGH-YIELD SECURITIES IN GENERAL INDUSTRIAL MANUFACTURING, 1998
Ranked by: Results of research undertaken by staff of *Institutional Investor.* **Remarks:** Includes reason for selection. **Number listed:** 5
1. David Bitterman (Bear Stearns)
2. Thomas Klamka (Donaldson, Lufkin & Jenrette)
3. Jeffrey Harlib (Credit Suisse First Boston)
4. Kevin Eng (Grantchester Securities)
4. Michael Kender (Salomon Smith Barney)

Source: *Institutional Investor*, All-America Fixed-Income Research Team (annual), August, 1998, p. 84.

★1941★
TOP FINANCIAL ANALYSTS FOR HIGH-YIELD SECURITIES IN HEALTH CARE, 1998
Ranked by: Results of research undertaken by staff of *Institutional Investor.* **Remarks:** Includes reason for selection. **Number listed:** 6
1. Treacy Gaffney (Salomon Smith Barney)
2. Kathleen Lamb (Donaldson, Lufkin & Jenrette)
3. David Waill (Merrill Lynch)
4. Andrew Berg (Bear Stearns)
4. Susannah Gray (Chase Securities)
4. David K. Peterson (NationsBanc Montgomery Securities)

Source: *Institutional Investor*, All-America Fixed-Income Research Team (annual), August, 1998, p. 83.

★1942★
TOP FINANCIAL ANALYSTS FOR HIGH-YIELD SECURITIES IN RETAILING, 1998
Ranked by: Results of research undertaken by staff of *Institutional Investor.* **Remarks:** Includes reason for selection. **Number listed:** 3
1. Clare Schiedermayer (Merrill Lynch)
2. Christine Fasano (Donaldson, Lufkin & Jenrette)
3. Shelley Ben-Nathan (Bear Stearns)

Source: *Institutional Investor*, All-America Fixed-Income Research Team (annual), August, 1998, p. 86+.

★1943★
TOP FINANCIAL ANALYSTS FOR HIGH-YIELD SECURITIES IN SUPERMARKETS, 1998
Ranked by: Results of research undertaken by staff of *Institutional Investor.* **Remarks:** Includes reason for selection. **Number listed:** 4
1. Theodore Bernstein (Grantchester Securities)
2. Christina Boni (Donaldson, Lufkin & Jenrette)
3. Howard Goldberg (Salomon Smith Barney)
4. Kenneth Goldberg (Merrill Lynch)

Source: *Institutional Investor*, All-America Fixed-Income Research Team (annual), August, 1998, p. 87.

★1944★
TOP FINANCIAL ANALYSTS FOR HIGH-YIELD SECURITIES IN TELECOMMUNICATIONS, 1998
Ranked by: Results of research undertaken by staff of *Institutional Investor.* **Remarks:** Includes reason for selection. **Number listed:** 3
1. Les Levi (Chase Securities)
2. Robert Waldman (Salomon Smith Barney)
3. Mark Grotevant (TD Securities, U.S.)

Source: *Institutional Investor*, All-America Fixed-Income Research Team (annual), August, 1998, p. 87+.

★1945★
TOP FINANCIAL ANALYSTS FOR HIGH-YIELD SECURITIES IN TEXTILES AND APPAREL, 1998
Ranked by: Results of research undertaken by staff of *Institutional Investor.* **Remarks:** Includes reason for selection. **Number listed:** 4
1. Clare Schiedermayer (Merrill Lynch)
2. Sally Dessloch (J. P. Morgan)
3. Jeffrey Stewart (First Union Capital Markets)
4. Evan Mann (NationsBanc Montgomery Securities)

Source: *Institutional Investor*, All-America Fixed-Income Research Team (annual), August, 1998, p. 88.

★1946★
TOP FINANCIAL ANALYSTS FOR HIGH-YIELD SECURITIES IN THE AUTO SUPPLIES MANUFACTURING INDUSTRY, 1998
Ranked by: Results of research undertaken by staff of *Institutional Investor.* **Remarks:** Includes reason for selection. **Number listed:** 3
1. David Bitterman (Bear Stearns)
2. Michael Kender (Salomon Smith Barney)
3. Kevin Eng (Grantchester Securities)

Source: *Institutional Investor*, All-America Fixed-Income Research Team (annual), August, 1998, p. 84.

★1947★
TOP FINANCIAL ANALYSTS FOR HIGH-YIELD SECURITIES IN THE CHEMICALS INDUSTRY, 1998
Ranked by: Results of research undertaken by staff of *Institutional Investor.* **Remarks:** Includes reason for selection. **Number listed:** 4
1. David Troyer (Donaldson, Lufkin & Jenrette)
2. Steven Cohen (Salomon Smith Barney)
3. Mark Hughes (Chase Securities)
4. Paul Greenberg (Bear Stearns)

Source: *Institutional Investor*, All-America Fixed-Income Research Team (annual), August, 1998, p. 80.

★1948★
TOP FINANCIAL ANALYSTS FOR HIGH-YIELD SECURITIES IN THE ENERGY INDUSTRY, 1998
Ranked by: Results of research undertaken by staff of *Institutional Investor.* **Remarks:** Includes reason for selection. **Number listed:** 7
1. Erik Dybesland (Bear Stearns)
2. Thomas Parker (Chase Securities)
3. J. Robert Chambers (Lehman Brothers)
4. Varkki Chacko (Goldman Sachs)
4. Mark Kellstrom (Jefferies & Co.)
4. Adam Leight (Donaldson, Lufkin & Jenrette)
4. Christy Parsons (Merrill Lynch)

Source: *Institutional Investor*, All-America Fixed-Income Research Team (annual), August, 1998, p. 82.

★1949★
TOP FINANCIAL ANALYSTS FOR HIGH-YIELD SECURITIES IN THE GAMING INDUSTRY, 1998
Ranked by: Results of research undertaken by staff of *Institutional Investor.* **Remarks:** Includes reason for selection. **Number listed:** 3
1. Raz Kafri (Grantchester Securities)
2. Richard Byrne (Merrill Lynch)
3. Thomas Shandell (Bear Stearns)

Source: *Institutional Investor*, All-America Fixed-Income Research Team (annual), August, 1998, p. 83.

★1950★
TOP FINANCIAL ANALYSTS FOR HIGH-YIELD SECURITIES IN THE MEDIA/CABLE AND SATELLITE INDUSTRY, 1998
Ranked by: Results of research undertaken by staff of *Institutional Investor.* **Remarks:** Includes reason for selection. **Number listed:** 4
1. Les Levi (Chase Securities)
2. Oren Cohen (Bear Stearns)
3. Mark Grotevant (TD Securities, U.S.)
4. Stevyn Schutzman (Salomon Smith Barney)

Source: *Institutional Investor*, All-America Fixed-Income Research Team (annual), August, 1998, p. 85.

★1951★
TOP FINANCIAL ANALYSTS FOR HIGH-YIELD SECURITIES IN THE METALS AND MINING INDUSTRY, 1998
Ranked by: Results of research undertaken by staff of *Institutional Investor.* **Remarks:** Includes reason for selection. **Number listed:** 5
1. John Hudson (Goldman Sachs)
2. Richard Miller (BancBoston Securities)
3. Kenneth Silver (Grantchester Securities)
4. Peter Dell'Orto (Salomon Smith Barney)
4. Brett Levy (BT Alexander Brown Securities)

Source: *Institutional Investor*, All-America Fixed-Income Research Team (annual), August, 1998, p. 85+.

★1952★
TOP FINANCIAL ANALYSTS FOR HIGH-YIELD SECURITIES IN THE PAPER AND FOREST PRODUCTS INDUSTRY, 1998
Ranked by: Results of research undertaken by staff of *Institutional Investor.* **Remarks:** Includes reason for selection. **Number listed:** 4
1. Bruce Klein (Donaldson, Lufkin & Jenrette)
2. Paul Greenberg (Bear Stearns)
3. Sharyl Van Winkle (Merrill Lynch)
4. William Hoffmann (TD Securities, U.S.)

Source: *Institutional Investor*, All-America Fixed-Income Research Team (annual), August, 1998, p. 86.

★1953★
TOP FINANCIAL ANALYSTS FOR MUNICIPALS IN UTILITIES, 1998
Ranked by: Results of research undertaken by staff of *Institutional Investor.* **Remarks:** Includes reason for selection. **Number listed:** 2
1. Gary Krellenstein (Lehman Brothers)
2. Christopher Mauro (Merrill Lynch)

Source: *Institutional Investor*, All-America Fixed-Income Research Team (annual), August, 1998, p. 90.

★1954★
TOP FINANCIAL ANALYSTS FOR STRATEGY AND ECONOMICS/GENERALIST, 1998
Ranked by: Results of research undertaken by staff of *Institutional Investor.* **Remarks:** Includes reason for selection. **Number listed:** 3
1. Jack Malvey (Lehman Brothers)
2. Thomas Sowanick (Merrill Lynch)
3. Krishna Memani (Morgan Stanley Dean Witter)

Source: *Institutional Investor*, All-America Fixed-Income Research Team (annual), August, 1998, p. 99.

★1955★
TOP FINANCIAL ANALYSTS FOR STRATEGY AND ECONOMICS IN ASSET-BACKED SECURITIES/ MORTGAGE BASED, 1998
Ranked by: Results of research undertaken by staff of *Institutional Investor.* **Remarks:** Includes reason for selection. **Number listed:** 4
1. Tracy van Eck (Bear Stearns)
2. Arthur Chu & team (Lehman Brothers)
3. Dan Castro & team (Merrill Lynch)
4. Charles Schorin (Morgan Stanley Dean Witter)

Source: *Institutional Investor*, All-America Fixed-Income Research Team (annual), August, 1998, p. 97+.

★1956★
TOP FINANCIAL ANALYSTS FOR STRATEGY AND ECONOMICS IN ASSET-BACKED SECURITIES/NON-MORTGAGE BASED, 1998
Ranked by: Results of research undertaken by staff of *Institutional Investor.* **Remarks:** Includes reason for selection. **Number listed:** 5
1. Tracy van Eck (Bear Stearns)
2. Dan Castro & team (Merrill Lynch)
3. Paul Jablansky & team (Salomon Smith Barney)
4. Charles Schorin (Morgan Stanley Dean Witter)
4. Beth Starr & team (Lehman Brothers)

Source: *Institutional Investor*, All-America Fixed-Income Research Team (annual), August, 1998, p. 98.

★1957★
TOP FINANCIAL ANALYSTS FOR STRATEGY AND ECONOMICS IN EMERGING MARKETS, 1998
Ranked by: Results of research undertaken by staff of *Institutional Investor.* **Remarks:** Includes reason for selection. **Number listed:** 4
1. Joyce Chang (Merrill Lynch)
2. Jose Luis Daza & team (J. P. Morgan)
3. Lawrence Brainard & team (Chase Securities)
4. Paulo Leme & team (Goldman Sachs)

Source: *Institutional Investor*, All-America Fixed-Income Research Team (annual), August, 1998, p. 98+.

★1958★
TOP FINANCIAL ANALYSTS FOR STRATEGY AND ECONOMICS IN GOVERNMENT, 1998
Ranked by: Results of research undertaken by staff of *Institutional Investor.* **Remarks:** Includes reason for selection. **Number listed:** 3
1. Janet Showers (Salomon Smith Barney)
2. Douglas Johnston & team (Lehman Brothers)
3. Gerald Lucas & team (Merrill Lynch)

Source: *Institutional Investor*, All-America Fixed-Income Research Team (annual), August, 1998, p. 99+.

★1959★
TOP FINANCIAL ANALYSTS FOR STRATEGY AND ECONOMICS IN HIGH-GRADE CORPORATES, 1998
Ranked by: Results of research undertaken by staff of *Institutional Investor.* **Remarks:** Includes reason for selection. **Number listed:** 3
1. Dennis Adler (Salomon Smith Barney)
2. Krishna Memani (Morgan Stanley Dean Witter)
3. Jack Malvey (Lehman Brothers)

Source: *Institutional Investor*, All-America Fixed-Income Research Team (annual), August, 1998, p. 100.

★1960★
TOP FINANCIAL ANALYSTS FOR STRATEGY AND ECONOMICS IN HIGH-YIELD MARKET ECONOMICS, 1998
Ranked by: Results of research undertaken by staff of *Institutional Investor.* **Remarks:** Includes reason for selection. **Number listed:** 2
1. Martin Fridson (Merrill Lynch)
2. Sam DeRosa-Farag (Donaldson, Lufkin & Jenrette)

Source: *Institutional Investor*, All-America Fixed-Income Research Team (annual), August, 1998, p. 100.

★1961★
TOP FINANCIAL ANALYSTS FOR STRATEGY AND ECONOMICS IN MORTGAGE-BACKED SECURITIES, 1998
Ranked by: Results of research undertaken by staff of *Institutional Investor.* **Remarks:** Includes reason for selection. **Number listed:** 6
1. Laurie Goodman (Paine Webber)
2. Ravi Mattu & team (Lehman Brothers)
3. Peter Niculescu & team (Goldman Sachs)
4. Alexander Crawford (Morgan Stanley Dean Witter)
4. Robert Kulason & team (Salomon Smith Barney)
4. W. Scott Simon & team (Bear Stearns)

Source: *Institutional Investor*, All-America Fixed-Income Research Team (annual), August, 1998, p. 101.

★1962★
TOP FINANCIAL ANALYSTS FOR STRATEGY AND ECONOMICS IN MUNICIPALS, 1998
Ranked by: Results of research undertaken by staff of *Institutional Investor.* **Remarks:** Includes reason for selection. **Number listed:** 3
1. George Friedlander (Salomon Smith Barney)
2. Christopher Dillon (J. P. Morgan)
3. Philip Fischer (Merrill Lynch)

Source: *Institutional Investor*, All-America Fixed-Income Research Team (annual), August, 1998, p. 101.

★1963★
TOP FINANCIAL ANALYSTS IN ACCOUNTING AND TAX POLICY, 1998
Ranked by: Results of research undertaken by staff of *Institutional Investor.* **Remarks:** Includes reason for selection. **Number listed:** 4
1. Patricia McConnell (Bear Stearns)
2. Gabrielle Napolitano (Goldman Sachs)
3. David Hawkins (Merrill Lynch)
4. Robert Willens (Lehman Brothers)

Source: *Institutional Investor*, All-America Research Team (annual), October, 1998, p. 180+.

★1964★
TOP FINANCIAL ANALYSTS IN ASSET-BACKED/ PREPAYMENTS, 1998
Ranked by: Results of research undertaken by staff of *Institutional Investor.* **Remarks:** Includes reason for selection. **Number listed:** 5

1. Gyan Sinha (Bear Stearns)
2. Arthur Chu & team (Lehman Brothers)
3. Christopher Flanagan & team (Merrill Lynch)
4. Paul Jablansky & team (Salomon Smith Barney)
4. Charles Schorin (Morgan Stanley Dean Witter)

Source: *Institutional Investor*, All-America Fixed-Income Research Team (annual), August, 1998, p. 90.

★1965★
TOP FINANCIAL ANALYSTS IN CONVERTIBLES, 1998
Ranked by: Results of research undertaken by staff of *Institutional Investor.* **Remarks:** Includes reason for selection. **Number listed:** 3

1. Anand Iyer (Morgan Stanley Dean Witter)
2. T. Anne Cox & team (Merrill Lynch)
3. Ravi Suria & team (Paine Webber)

Source: *Institutional Investor*, All-America Research Team (annual), October, 1998, p. 183.

★1966★
TOP FINANCIAL ANALYSTS IN ECONOMICS, 1998
Ranked by: Results of research undertaken by staff of *Institutional Investor.* **Remarks:** Includes reason for selection. **Number listed:** 4

1. Ed Hyman (ISI Group)
   Stephen Slifer (Lehman Brothers)
   Paul McCulley (Warburg Dillon Read)
   Edward Yardeni (Deutsche Bank Securities)

Source: *Institutional Investor*, All-America Fixed-Income Research Team (annual), August, 1998, p. 102.

★1967★
TOP FINANCIAL ANALYSTS IN EQUITY DERIVATIVES, 1998
Ranked by: Results of research undertaken by staff of *Institutional Investor.* **Remarks:** Includes reason for selection. **Number listed:** 3

1. Joanne Hill (Goldman Sachs)
2. Eric Sorensen & team (Salomon Smith Barney)
3. Joseph Mezrich & team (Morgan Stanley Dean Witter)

Source: *Institutional Investor*, All-America Research Team (annual), October, 1998, p. 185.

★1968★
TOP FINANCIAL ANALYSTS IN MORTGAGE-BACKED/ADJUSTABLE SECURITIES, 1998
Ranked by: Results of research undertaken by staff of *Institutional Investor.* **Remarks:** Includes reason for selection. **Number listed:** 4

1. Jeffrey Biby (Lehman Brothers)
2. Satish Mansukhani (Bear Stearns)
3. Laurie Goodman & team (Paine Webber)
4. Alan Brazil & team (Goldman Sachs)

Source: *Institutional Investor*, All-America Fixed-Income Research Team (annual), August, 1998, p. 91.

★1969★
TOP FINANCIAL ANALYSTS IN MORTGAGE-BACKED/AGENCY SECURITIES, 1998
Ranked by: Results of research undertaken by staff of *Institutional Investor.* **Remarks:** Includes reason for selection. **Number listed:** 4

1. Laurie Goodman (Paine Webber)
2. Robert Kulason & team (Salomon Smith Barney)
3. Jeffrey Biby & team (Lehman Brothers)
4. Alan Brazil & team (Goldman Sachs)

Source: *Institutional Investor*, All-America Fixed-Income Research Team (annual), August, 1998, p. 96.

★1970★
TOP FINANCIAL ANALYSTS IN MORTGAGE-BACKED/COMMERCIAL SECURITIES, 1998
Ranked by: Results of research undertaken by staff of *Institutional Investor.* **Remarks:** Includes reason for selection. **Number listed:** 4

1. Howard Esaki (Morgan Stanley Dean Witter)
2. James Titus & team (Donaldson, Lufkin & Jenrette)
3. Haejin Baek & team (Lehman Brothers)
4. Patrick Corcoran (J. P. Morgan)

Source: *Institutional Investor*, All-America Fixed-Income Research Team (annual), August, 1998, p. 91.

★1971★
TOP FINANCIAL ANALYSTS IN MORTGAGE-BACKED/CREDIT SECURITIES, 1998
Ranked by: Results of research undertaken by staff of *Institutional Investor.* **Remarks:** Includes reason for selection. **Number listed:** 4

1. Laurie Goodman (Paine Webber)
2. Bruce Alpern & team (Donaldson, Lufkin & Jenrette)
3. Peter DiMartino (Salomon Smith Barney)
4. Steven Abrahams & team (Morgan Stanley Dean Witter)

Source: *Institutional Investor*, All-America Fixed-Income Research Team (annual), August, 1998, p. 92.

★1972★
TOP FINANCIAL ANALYSTS IN MORTGAGE-BACKED/NON-AGENCY SECURITIES, 1998
Ranked by: Results of research undertaken by staff of *Institutional Investor.* **Remarks:** Includes reason for selection. **Number listed:** 6

1. Laurie Goodman (Paine Webber)
2. Bruce Alpern & team (Donaldson, Lufkin & Jenrette)
3. Akiva Dickstein & team (Lehman Brothers)
4. Steven Abrahams & team (Morgan Stanley Dean Witter)
4. Peter DiMartino (Salomon Smith Barney)
4. Dale Westhoff & team (Bear Stearns)

Source: *Institutional Investor*, All-America Fixed-Income Research Team (annual), August, 1998, p. 97.

★1973★
TOP FINANCIAL ANALYSTS IN MORTGAGE-BACKED/PASS-THROUGH SECURITIES, 1998
Ranked by: Results of research undertaken by staff of *Institutional Investor.* **Remarks:** Includes reason for selection. **Number listed:** 5

1. W. Scott Simon (Bear Stearns)
2. Laurie Goodman & team (Paine Webber)
3. Akiva Dickstein & team (Lehman Brothers)
4. Alan Brazil & team (Goldman Sachs)
4. Robert Kulason & team (Salomon Smith Barney)

Source: *Institutional Investor*, All-America Fixed-Income Research Team (annual), August, 1998, p. 92.

★1974★
TOP FINANCIAL ANALYSTS IN MORTGAGE-BACKED/PREPAYMENTS, 1998
Ranked by: Results of research undertaken by staff of *Institutional Investor.* **Remarks:** Includes reason for selection. **Number listed:** 4

1. Dale Westhoff (Bear Stearns)
2. Gregg Patruno & team (Goldman Sachs)
3. Lakhbir Hayre & team (Salomon Smith Barney)

4. Andrew Sparks & team (Lehman Brothers)

Source: *Institutional Investor*, All-America Fixed-Income Research Team (annual), August, 1998, p. 96.

★1975★
TOP FINANCIAL ANALYSTS IN PORTFOLIO STRATEGY, 1998
Ranked by: Results of research undertaken by staff of *Institutional Investor.* **Remarks:** Includes reason for selection. **Number listed:** 5

1. Abby Joseph Cohen (Goldman Sachs)
2. Edward Kerschner (Paine Webber)
3. Michael Goldstein (Sanford C. Bernstein)
4. Jeffrey Applegate (Lehman Brothers)
4. Greg Smith (Prudential Securities)

Source: *Institutional Investor*, All-America Research Team (annual), October, 1998, p. 185+.

★1976★
TOP FINANCIAL ANALYSTS IN QUANTITATIVE RESEARCH, 1998
Ranked by: Results of research undertaken by staff of *Institutional Investor.* **Remarks:** Includes reason for selection. **Number listed:** 4

1. Richard Bernstein (Merrill Lynch)
2. Michael Goldstein (Sanford C. Bernstein)
3. Claudia Mott (Prudential Securities)
4. Eric Sorensen (Salomon Smith Barney)

Source: *Institutional Investor*, All-America Research Team (annual), October, 1998, p. 186.

★1977★
TOP FINANCIAL ANALYSTS IN SMALL COMPANIES, 1998
Ranked by: Results of research undertaken by staff of *Institutional Investor.* **Remarks:** Includes reason for selection. **Number listed:** 3

1. Claudia Mott (Prudential Securities)
2. L. Keith Mullins (Salomon Smith Barney)
3. Satya Pradhuman (Merrill Lynch)

Source: *Institutional Investor*, All-America Research Team (annual), October, 1998, p. 186+.

★1978★
TOP FINANCIAL ANALYSTS IN TECHNICAL ANALYSIS, 1998
Ranked by: Results of research undertaken by staff of *Institutional Investor.* **Remarks:** Includes reason for selection. **Number listed:** 5

1. Alan Shaw (Salomon Smith Barney)
2. Ralph Acampora (Prudential Securities)
3. Stephen Shobin (Lehman Brothers)
4. Richard McCabe (Merrill Lynch)
4. Edward Nicoski (Piper Jaffray Cos)

Source: *Institutional Investor*, All-America Research Team (annual), October, 1998, p. 187.

★1979★
TOP FINANCIAL ANALYSTS IN THE ADVERTISING AGENCIES AND MARKETING SERVICES INDUSTRIES, 1998
Ranked by: Results of research undertaken by staff of *Institutional Investor.* **Remarks:** Includes reason for selection. **Number listed:** 3

1. Lauren Rich Fine (Merrill Lynch)
2. Susan Decker (Donaldson, Lufkin & Jenrette)
3. William Bird (Salomon Smith Barney)

Source: *Institutional Investor*, All-America Research Team (annual), October, 1998, p. 113.

★1980★
TOP FINANCIAL ANALYSTS IN THE AEROSPACE AND DEFENSE ELECTRONICS INDUSTRY, 1998
Ranked by: Results of research undertaken by staff of *Institutional Investor.* **Remarks:** Includes reason for selection. **Number listed:** 9

1. George Shapiro (Salomon Smith Barney)
2. Pierre Chao (Morgan Stanley Dean Witter)
3. Cai von Rumohr (SG Cowen)
4. Peter Aseritis (Credit Suisse First Boston)
4. Steven Binder (Bear Stearns)
4. Byron Callan (Merrill Lynch)
4. Joseph Campbell (Lehman Brothers)
4. Jack Modzelewski (Paine Webber)
4. Howard Rubel (Goldman Sachs)

Source: *Institutional Investor*, All-America Research Team (annual), October, 1998, p. 113+.

★1981★
TOP FINANCIAL ANALYSTS IN THE AIRFREIGHT INDUSTRY, 1998
Ranked by: Results of research undertaken by staff of *Institutional Investor.* **Remarks:** Includes reason for selection. **Number listed:** 5

1. Kevin Murphy (Morgan Stanley Dean Witter)
2. Gregory Burns (Gerard Klauer Mattison & Co.)
3. Paul Schlesinger (Donaldson, Lufkin & Jenrette)
4. Jeffrey Kauffman (Merrill Lynch)
4. Gary Yablon (Schroeder & Co.)

Source: *Institutional Investor*, All-America Research Team (annual), October, 1998, p. 114.

★1982★
TOP FINANCIAL ANALYSTS IN THE AUTO INDUSTRY, 1998
Ranked by: Results of research undertaken by staff of *Institutional Investor.* **Remarks:** Includes reason for selection. **Number listed:** 7

1. Stephen Girsky (Morgan Stanley Dean Witter)
2. David Bradley (J. P. Morgan)
3. Jack Krinan (Salomon Smith Barney)
4. John Casesa (Schroeder & Co.)
4. Nicholas Lobaccaro (Merrill Lynch)
4. Wendy Beale Needham (Donaldson, Lufkin & Jenrette)
4. Michael Ward (Paine Webber)

Source: *Institutional Investor*, All-America Research Team (annual), October, 1998, p. 115.

★1983★
TOP FINANCIAL ANALYSTS IN THE AUTO PARTS INDUSTRY, 1998
Ranked by: Results of research undertaken by staff of *Institutional Investor.* **Remarks:** Includes reason for selection. **Number listed:** 5

1. Stephen Girsky (Morgan Stanley Dean Witter)
2. Wendy Beale Needham (Donaldson, Lufkin & Jenrette)
3. Matthew Stover (Paine Webber)
4. John Casesa (Schroeder & Co.)
4. Darren Kimball (Merrill Lynch)

Source: *Institutional Investor*, All-America Research Team (annual), October, 1998, p. 115+.

★1984★
TOP FINANCIAL ANALYSTS IN THE BANKING/ MONEY CENTERS INDUSTRY, 1998
Ranked by: Results of research undertaken by staff of *Institutional Investor.* **Remarks:** Includes reason for selection. **Number listed:** 5

1. Judah Kraushaar (Merrill Lynch)
2. Robert Albertson (Goldman Sachs)
3. Thomas Hanley (Warburg Dillon Read)
4. Diane Glossman (Lehman Brothers)
4. Ronald Mandle (Sanford C. Bernstein)

Source: *Institutional Investor*, All-America Research Team (annual), October, 1998, p. 116.

★1985★

TOP FINANCIAL ANALYSTS IN THE BANKING/ REGIONAL INDUSTRY, 1998

Ranked by: Results of research undertaken by staff of *Institutional Investor.* **Remarks:** Includes reason for selection. **Number listed:** 9

1. Michael Mayo (Credit Suisse First Boston)
2. Henry Dickson (Salomon Smith Barney)
3. Lori Appelbaum (Goldman Sachs)
4. Sandra Flannigan (Merrill Lynch)
4. Thomas Hanley (Warburg Dillon Read)
4. Ruchi Madan (Paine Webber)
4. Diane Merdian (NationsBanc Montgomery Securities)
4. Catherine Murray (J. P. Morgan)
4. Moshe Orenbuch (Sanford C. Bernstein)

Source: *Institutional Investor*, All-America Research Team (annual), October, 1998, p. 116+.

★1986★

TOP FINANCIAL ANALYSTS IN THE BEVERAGE INDUSTRY, 1998

Ranked by: Results of research undertaken by staff of *Institutional Investor.* **Remarks:** Includes reason for selection. **Number listed:** 6

1. Andrew Conway (Morgan Stanley Dean Witter)
2. William Pecoriello (Sanford C. Bernstein)
3. Michael Branca (Lehman Brothers)
4. Marc I. Cohen (Goldman Sachs)
4. Emanuel Goldman (Paine Webber)
4. Caroline Levy (Schroeder & Co.)

Source: *Institutional Investor*, All-America Research Team (annual), October, 1998, p. 119.

★1987★

TOP FINANCIAL ANALYSTS IN THE BROADCASTING/CABLE INDUSTRY, 1998

Ranked by: Results of research undertaken by staff of *Institutional Investor.* **Remarks:** Includes reason for selection. **Number listed:** 5

1. Richard Bilotti (Morgan Stanley Dean Witter)
2. Jessica Reif Cohen (Merrill Lynch)
3. Raymond Katz (Bear Stearns)
4. Barry Kaplan (Goldman Sachs)
4. Dennis Leibowitz (Donaldson, Lufkin & Jenrette)

Source: *Institutional Investor*, All-America Research Team (annual), October, 1998, p. 119+.

★1988★

TOP FINANCIAL ANALYSTS IN THE BROADCASTING/RADIO & TELEVISION INDUSTRY, 1998

Ranked by: Results of research undertaken by staff of *Institutional Investor.* **Remarks:** Includes reason for selection. **Number listed:** 7

1. Frank Bodenchak (Morgan Stanley Dean Witter)
2. Andrew Marcus (BT Alex. Brown)
3. Richard Rosenstein (Goldman Sachs)
4. Harry DeMott III (Credit Suisse First Boston)
4. Niraj Gupta (Schroeder & Co.)
4. Jessica Reif Cohen (Merrill Lynch)
4. Paul Sweeney (Salomon Smith Barney)

Source: *Institutional Investor*, All-America Research Team (annual), October, 1998, p. 120.

★1989★

TOP FINANCIAL ANALYSTS IN THE BROKERAGE AND ASSET MANAGEMENT INDUSTRY, 1998

Ranked by: Results of research undertaken by staff of *Institutional Investor.* **Remarks:** Includes reason for selection. **Number listed:** 4

1. Sallie Krawcheck (Sanford C. Bernstein)
2. Richard Strauss (Goldman Sachs)
3. Joan Solotar (Donaldson, Lufkin & Jenrette)
4. James Hanbury (Schroeder & Co.)

Source: *Institutional Investor*, All-America Research Team (annual), October, 1998, p. 120+.

★1990★

TOP FINANCIAL ANALYSTS IN THE BUILDING INDUSTRY, 1998

Ranked by: Results of research undertaken by staff of *Institutional Investor.* **Remarks:** Includes reason for selection. **Number listed:** 3

1. David Dwyer (Salomon Smith Barney)
2. Ivy Zelman (Credit Suisse First Boston)
3. Gregory Nejmeh (Donaldson, Lufkin & Jenrette)

Source: *Institutional Investor*, All-America Research Team (annual), October, 1998, p. 123.

★1991★

TOP FINANCIAL ANALYSTS IN THE BUSINESS SERVICES INDUSTRY, 1998

Ranked by: Results of research undertaken by staff of *Institutional Investor.* **Remarks:** Includes reason for selection. **Number listed:** 6

1. David Togut (Morgan Stanley Dean Witter)
2. Judith Scott (Robert W. Baird & Co.)
3. James Kissane (Bear Stearns)
4. Gregory Gould (Goldman Sachs)
4. Stephen McClellan (Merrill Lynch)
4. Adam Waldo (Morgan Stanley Dean Witter)

Source: *Institutional Investor*, All-America Research Team (annual), October, 1998, p. 123+.

★1992★

TOP FINANCIAL ANALYSTS IN THE CHEMICALS/ AGRICULTURAL INDUSTRY, 1998

Ranked by: Results of research undertaken by staff of *Institutional Investor.* **Remarks:** Includes reason for selection. **Number listed:** 5

1. Donald Carson (J. P. Morgan)
2. Charles LoCastro (Donaldson, Lufkin & Jenrette)
3. Avi Nash (Goldman Sachs)
4. Douglas Groh (Merrill Lynch)
4. Robert Koort (Deutsche Bank Securities)

Source: *Institutional Investor*, All-America Research Team (annual), October, 1998, p. 125.

★1993★

TOP FINANCIAL ANALYSTS IN THE CHEMICALS/ MAJOR INDUSTRY, 1998

Ranked by: Results of research undertaken by staff of *Institutional Investor.* **Remarks:** Includes reason for selection. **Number listed:** 6

1. Avi Nash (Goldman Sachs)
2. William Young (Donaldson, Lufkin & Jenrette)
3. John Roberts (Merrill Lynch)
4. Donald Carson (J. P. Morgan)
4. J. Jeffrey Cianci (Bear Stearns)

4. Leslie Ravitz (Morgan Stanley Dean Witter)

Source: *Institutional Investor*, All-America Research Team (annual), October, 1998, p. 125+.

★1994★

TOP FINANCIAL ANALYSTS IN THE CHEMICALS/ SPECIALTY INDUSTRY, 1998

Ranked by: Results of research undertaken by staff of *Institutional Investor.* **Remarks:** Includes reason for selection. **Number listed:** 4

1. Kimberly Ritrievi (Goldman Sachs)
2. Robert Ottenstein (Paine Webber)
3. David Manlowe (BT Alex. Brown)
4. Mark Gulley (Morgan Stanley Dean Witter)

Source: *Institutional Investor*, All-America Research Team (annual), October, 1998, p. 126.

★1995★

TOP FINANCIAL ANALYSTS IN THE COMMERCIAL REAL ESTATE INVESTMENT TRUSTS (REITS) INDUSTRY, 1998

Ranked by: Results of research undertaken by staff of *Institutional Investor.* **Remarks:** Includes reason for selection. **Number listed:** 7

1. Eric Hemel (Merrill Lynch)
2. Jonathan Litt (Paine Webber)
3. Steven Hash (Lehman Brothers)
4. David Kostin (Goldman Sachs)
4. Lawrence Raiman (Donaldson, Lufkin & Jenrette)
4. David Sherman (Salomon Smith Barney)
4. Gregory Whyte (Morgan Stanley Dean Witter)

Source: *Institutional Investor*, All-America Research Team (annual), October, 1998, p. 164.

★1996★

TOP FINANCIAL ANALYSTS IN THE COMPUTER SERVICES INDUSTRY, 1998

Ranked by: Results of research undertaken by staff of *Institutional Investor.* **Remarks:** Includes reason for selection. **Number listed:** 6

1. David Togut (Morgan Stanley Dean Witter)
2. Stephen McClellan (Merrill Lynch)
3. James Kissane (Bear Stearns)
4. Patrick Burton (Lehman Brothers)
4. Gregory Gould (Goldman Sachs)
4. Mark Wolfenberger (Credit Suisse First Boston)

Source: *Institutional Investor*, All-America Research Team (annual), October, 1998, p. 126+.

★1997★

TOP FINANCIAL ANALYSTS IN THE COSMETICS AND PERSONAL CARE PRODUCTS INDUSTRY, 1998

Ranked by: Results of research undertaken by staff of *Institutional Investor.* **Remarks:** Includes reason for selection. **Number listed:** 6

1. Holly Becker (Salomon Smith Barney)
2. Heather Hay (Merrill Lynch)
3. Amy Low Chasen (Goldman Sachs)
4. Alice Beebe Longley (Donaldson, Lufkin & Jenrette)
4. Andrew Shore (Paine Webber)
4. Carol Warner (Prudential Securities)

Source: *Institutional Investor*, All-America Research Team (annual), October, 1998, p. 128.

★1998★

TOP FINANCIAL ANALYSTS IN THE DATA NETWORKING INDUSTRY, 1998

Ranked by: Results of research undertaken by staff of *Institutional Investor.* **Remarks:** Includes reason for selection. **Number listed:** 7

1. William Rabin (J. P. Morgan)
2. George Kelly (Morgan Stanley Dean Witter)
3. Paul Weinstein (Credit Suisse First Boston)
4. Joseph Bellace (Merrill Lynch)
4. Paul Johnson (BancBoston Robertson Stephens)
4. Christopher Stix (SG Cowen)
4. Peter Swartz (Salomon Smith Barney)

Source: *Institutional Investor*, All-America Research Team (annual), October, 1998, p. 128+.

★1999★

TOP FINANCIAL ANALYSTS IN THE DOMESTIC OIL INDUSTRY, 1998

Ranked by: Results of research undertaken by staff of *Institutional Investor.* **Remarks:** Includes reason for selection. **Number listed:** 5

1. James Clark (Credit Suisse First Boston)
2. Douglas Terreson (Morgan Stanley Dean Witter)
3. Michael Mayer (Schroeder & Co.)
3. Paul Ting (Salomon Smith Barney)
4. Frank Knuettel (Paine Webber)

Source: *Institutional Investor*, All-America Research Team (annual), October, 1998, p. 156+.

★2000★

TOP FINANCIAL ANALYSTS IN THE EDUCATIONS SERVICES INDUSTRY, 1998

Ranked by: Results of research undertaken by staff of *Institutional Investor.* **Remarks:** Includes reason for selection. **Number listed:** 4

1. Gregory Cappelli (Credit Suisse First Boston)
2. Gerald Odening (Salomon Smith Barney)
3. Peter Appert (BT Alex. Brown)
4. Howard Block (BancBoston Robertson Stephens)

Source: *Institutional Investor*, All-America Research Team (annual), October, 1998, p. 131.

★2001★

TOP FINANCIAL ANALYSTS IN THE ELECTRIC UTILITIES INDUSTRY, 1998

Ranked by: Results of research undertaken by staff of *Institutional Investor.* **Remarks:** Includes reason for selection. **Number listed:** 4

1. Steven Fleishman (Merrill Lynch)
2. Kit Konolige (Morgan Stanley Dean Witter)
3. Jonathan Raleigh (CIBC Oppenheimer)
4. Ernest Liu (Goldman Sachs)

Source: *Institutional Investor*, All-America Research Team (annual), October, 1998, p. 131+.

★2002★

TOP FINANCIAL ANALYSTS IN THE ELECTRICAL EQUIPMENT INDUSTRY, 1998

Ranked by: Results of research undertaken by staff of *Institutional Investor.* **Remarks:** Includes reason for selection. **Number listed:** 3

1. Jennifer Murphy (Morgan Stanley Dean Witter)
2. Robert Cornell (Lehman Brothers)
3. Jeffrey Sprague (Salomon Smith Barney)

Source: *Institutional Investor*, All-America Research Team (annual), October, 1998, p. 132.

★2003★

TOP FINANCIAL ANALYSTS IN THE ELECTRONICS/CONNECTORS AND OTHER COMPONENTS INDUSTRY, 1998

Ranked by: Results of research undertaken by staff of *Institutional Investor.* **Remarks:** Includes reason for selection. **Number listed:** 3

1. Mark Hassenberg (Donaldson, Lufkin & Jenrette)
2. Jerry Labowitz (Merrill Lynch)

3. Shelby Fleck (Morgan Stanley Dean Witter)

Source: *Institutional Investor*, All-America Research Team (annual), October, 1998, p. 132+.

★2004★

TOP FINANCIAL ANALYSTS IN THE ELECTRONICS/MANUFACTURING SERVICES INDUSTRY, 1998

Ranked by: Results of research undertaken by staff of *Institutional Investor.* **Remarks:** Includes reason for selection. **Number listed:** 7

1. Shelby Fleck (Morgan Stanley Dean Witter)
2. James Savage (BT Alex. Brown)
3. J. Keith Dunne (BancBoston Robertson Stephens)
4. Todd Bakar (Hambrecht & Quist)
4. John Dean (Salomon Smith Barney)
4. Paul Fox (NationsBanc Montgomery Securities)
4. Jerry Labowitz (Merrill Lynch)

Source: *Institutional Investor*, All-America Research Team (annual), October, 1998, p. 134.

★2005★

TOP FINANCIAL ANALYSTS IN THE ELECTRONICS/SEMICONDUCTOR CAPITAL EQUIPMENT INDUSTRY, 1998

Ranked by: Results of research undertaken by staff of *Institutional Investor.* **Remarks:** Includes reason for selection. **Number listed:** 6

1. Gunnar Miller (Goldman Sachs)
2. Jay Deahna (Morgan Stanley Dean Witter)
3. Elliott Rogers (Credit Suisse First Boston)
4. Brett Hodess (NationsBanc Montgomery Securities)
4. Robert Maire (Donaldson, Lufkin & Jenrette)
4. Edward White, Jr. (Lehman Brothers)

Source: *Institutional Investor*, All-America Research Team (annual), October, 1998, p. 137 +.

★2006★

TOP FINANCIAL ANALYSTS IN THE ELECTRONICS/SEMICONDUCTORS INDUSTRY, 1998

Ranked by: Results of research undertaken by staff of *Institutional Investor.* **Remarks:** Includes reason for selection. **Number listed:** 5

1. Thomas Kurlak (Merrill Lynch)
2. Mark Edelstone (Morgan Stanley Dean Witter)
3. James Barlage (Salomon Smith Barney)
4. G. Scott Nirenberski (Credit Suisse First Boston)
4. Drew Peck (SG Cowen)

Source: *Institutional Investor*, All-America Research Team (annual), October, 1998, p. 134+.

★2007★

TOP FINANCIAL ANALYSTS IN THE ENGINEERING AND CONSTRUCTION INDUSTRY, 1998

Ranked by: Results of research undertaken by staff of *Institutional Investor.* **Remarks:** Includes reason for selection. **Number listed:** 4

1. Tobias Levkovich (Salomon Smith Barney)
2. Jeanne Gallagher Terrile (Merrill Lynch)
3. Marc Sulam (Donaldson, Lufkin & Jenrette)
4. John McGinty (Credit Suisse First Boston)

Source: *Institutional Investor*, All-America Research Team (annual), October, 1998, p. 137+.

★2008★

TOP FINANCIAL ANALYSTS IN THE ENTERTAINMENT INDUSTRY, 1998

Ranked by: Results of research undertaken by staff of *Institutional Investor.* **Remarks:** Includes reason for selection. **Number listed:** 4

1. Jessica Reif Cohen (Merrill Lynch)
2. David Londoner (Schroeder & Co.)
3. Richard Simon (Goldman Sachs)
4. Jill Krutick (Salomon Smith Barney)

Source: *Institutional Investor*, All-America Research Team (annual), October, 1998, p. 138.

★2009★

TOP FINANCIAL ANALYSTS IN THE ENVIRONMENTAL SERVICES INDUSTRY, 1998

Ranked by: Results of research undertaken by staff of *Institutional Investor.* **Remarks:** Includes reason for selection. **Number listed:** 4

1. Marc Sulam (Donaldson, Lufkin & Jenrette)
2. Mari Bari (Deutsche Bank Securities)
3. Michael Hoffman (Credit Suisse First Boston)
4. William Genco (Merrill Lynch)

Source: *Institutional Investor*, All-America Research Team (annual), October, 1998, p. 138+.

★2010★

TOP FINANCIAL ANALYSTS IN THE FOOD INDUSTRY, 1998

Ranked by: Results of research undertaken by staff of *Institutional Investor.* **Remarks:** Includes reason for selection. **Number listed:** 4

1. John McMillin (Prudential Securities)
2. Nomi Ghez (Goldman Sachs)
3. William Leach (Donaldson, Lufkin & Jenrette)
4. Erika Gritman Long (J. P. Morgan)

Source: *Institutional Investor*, All-America Research Team (annual), October, 1998, p. 139.

★2011★

TOP FINANCIAL ANALYSTS IN THE GAMING INDUSTRY, 1998

Ranked by: Results of research undertaken by staff of *Institutional Investor.* **Remarks:** Includes reason for selection. **Number listed:** 4

1. W. Bruce Turner (Salomon Smith Barney)
2. Jason Ader (Bear Stearns)
3. Joseph Coccimiglio (Prudential Securities)
4. David Anders (Credit Suisse First Boston)

Source: *Institutional Investor*, All-America Research Team (annual), October, 1998, p. 139+.

★2012★

TOP FINANCIAL ANALYSTS IN THE HEALTH CARE/BIOTECHNOLOGY INDUSTRY, 1998

Ranked by: Results of research undertaken by staff of *Institutional Investor.* **Remarks:** Includes reason for selection. **Number listed:** 4

1. Maykin Ho (Goldman Sachs)
2. Eric Hecht (Merrill Lynch)
3. Meirav Chovav (Salomon Smith Barney)
4. David Molowa (Bear Stearns)

Source: *Institutional Investor*, All-America Research Team (annual), October, 1998, p. 140.

★2013★

TOP FINANCIAL ANALYSTS IN THE HEALTH CARE/FACILITIES INDUSTRY, 1998

Ranked by: Results of research undertaken by staff of *Institutional Investor.* **Remarks:** Includes reason for selection. **Number listed:** 4

1. John Hindelong (Donaldson, Lufkin & Jenrette)
2. A. J. Rice (Bear Stearns)
3. Deborah Lawson (Goldman Sachs)
4. Joseph Chiarelli (J. P. Morgan)

Source: *Institutional Investor*, All-America Research Team (annual), October, 1998, p. 140+.

★2014★
TOP FINANCIAL ANALYSTS IN THE HEALTH CARE/INFORMATION TECHNOLOGY INDUSTRY, 1998
Ranked by: Results of research undertaken by staff of *Institutional Investor.* **Remarks:** Includes reason for selection. **Number listed:** 3
1. Raymond Falci (Bear Stearns)
2. Marie Rossi (Morgan Stanley Dean Witter)
3. Steven Halper (Donaldson, Lufkin & Jenrette)

Source: *Institutional Investor*, All-America Research Team (annual), October, 1998, p. 142.

★2015★
TOP FINANCIAL ANALYSTS IN THE HEALTH CARE/MANAGED CARE INDUSTRY, 1998
Ranked by: Results of research undertaken by staff of *Institutional Investor.* **Remarks:** Includes reason for selection. **Number listed:** 5
1. Miriam Cutler Willard (Donaldson, Lufkin & Jenrette)
2. Gary Frazier (BT Alex. Brown)
3. Kenneth Abramowitz (Sanford C. Bernstein)
4. Todd Richter (Morgan Stanley Dean Witter)
4. Roberta Walter (Merrill Lynch)

Source: *Institutional Investor*, All-America Research Team (annual), October, 1998, p. 142+.

★2016★
TOP FINANCIAL ANALYSTS IN THE HEALTH CARE/MEDICAL SUPPLIES AND TECHNOLOGY INDUSTRY, 1998
Ranked by: Results of research undertaken by staff of *Institutional Investor.* **Remarks:** Includes reason for selection. **Number listed:** 5
1. Glenn Reicin (Morgan Stanley Dean Witter)
2. Frederick Wise (Bear Stearns)
3. Daniel Lemaitre (SG Cowen)
4. Lawrence Keusch (Goldman Sachs)
4. Michael Weinstein (J. P. Morgan)

Source: *Institutional Investor*, All-America Research Team (annual), October, 1998, p. 144.

★2017★
TOP FINANCIAL ANALYSTS IN THE HEALTH CARE/PHARMACEUTICALS INDUSTRY, 1998
Ranked by: Results of research undertaken by staff of *Institutional Investor.* **Remarks:** Includes reason for selection. **Number listed:** 8
1. Paul Brooke (Morgan Stanley Dean Witter)
2. Jami Rubin (Schroeder & Co.)
3. Joseph Riccardo (Bear Stearns)
4. Christina Heuer (Salomon Smith Barney)
4. Steve Scala (SG Cowen)
4. Carl Seiden (J. P. Morgan)
4. Steven Tighe (Merrill Lynch)
4. Richard Victor (Merrill Lynch)

Source: *Institutional Investor*, All-America Research Team (annual), October, 1998, p. 144+.

★2018★
TOP FINANCIAL ANALYSTS IN THE HOUSEHOLD PRODUCTS INDUSTRY, 1998
Ranked by: Results of research undertaken by staff of *Institutional Investor.* **Remarks:** Includes reason for selection. **Number listed:** 6
1. Holly Becker (Salomon Smith Barney)
2. Heather Hay (Merrill Lynch)
3. Carol Warner (Prudential Securities)
4. Amy Low Chasen (Goldman Sachs)
4. Alice Beebe Longley (Donaldson, Lufkin & Jenrette)
4. Andrew Shore (Paine Webber)

Source: *Institutional Investor*, All-America Research Team (annual), October, 1998, p. 146.

★2019★
TOP FINANCIAL ANALYSTS IN THE INTERNATIONAL OIL INDUSTRY, 1998
Ranked by: Results of research undertaken by staff of *Institutional Investor.* **Remarks:** Includes reason for selection. **Number listed:** 4
1. Paul Ting (Salomon Smith Barney)
2. James Clark (Credit Suisse First Boston)
3. Douglas Terreson (Morgan Stanley Dean Witter)
4. Michael Mayer (Schroeder & Co.)

Source: *Institutional Investor*, All-America Research Team (annual), October, 1998, p. 157.

★2020★
TOP FINANCIAL ANALYSTS IN THE INTERNET AND NEW MEDIA INDUSTRY, 1998
Ranked by: Results of research undertaken by staff of *Institutional Investor.* **Remarks:** Includes reason for selection. **Number listed:** 6
1. Mary Meeker (Morgan Stanley Dean Witter)
2. Jamie Kiggen (Donaldson, Lufkin & Jenrette)
3. Michael Parekh (Goldman Sachs)
4. Keith Benjamin (BancBoston Robertson Stephens)
4. Alan Braverman (Deutsche Bank Securities)
4. Jonathan Cohen (Merrill Lynch)

Source: *Institutional Investor*, All-America Research Team (annual), October, 1998, p. 149+.

★2021★
TOP FINANCIAL ANALYSTS IN THE LIFE INSURANCE INDUSTRY, 1998
Ranked by: Results of research undertaken by staff of *Institutional Investor.* **Remarks:** Includes reason for selection. **Number listed:** 4
1. Michael Blumstein (Morgan Stanley Dean Witter)
2. Vanessa Wilson (Donaldson, Lufkin & Jenrette)
3. Eric Berg (CIBC Oppenheimer)
4. Joan Zief (Goldman Sachs)

Source: *Institutional Investor*, All-America Research Team (annual), October, 1998, p. 146+.

★2022★
TOP FINANCIAL ANALYSTS IN THE LODGING INDUSTRY, 1998
Ranked by: Results of research undertaken by staff of *Institutional Investor.* **Remarks:** Includes reason for selection. **Number listed:** 4
1. Michael Rietbrock (Salomon Smith Barney)
2. John Rohs (Schroeder & Co.)
3. Jason Ader (Bear Stearns)
4. Steven Kent (Goldman Sachs)

Source: *Institutional Investor*, All-America Research Team (annual), October, 1998, p. 150.

★2023★
TOP FINANCIAL ANALYSTS IN THE MACHINERY INDUSTRY, 1998
Ranked by: Results of research undertaken by staff of *Institutional Investor.* **Remarks:** Includes reason for selection. **Number listed:** 5
1. Tobias Levkovich (Salomon Smith Barney)
2. John McGinty (Credit Suisse First Boston)
3. Gary McManus (J. P. Morgan)
4. Lisa Shalett (Sanford C. Bernstein)

4. Karen Ubelhart (Goldman Sachs)

Source: *Institutional Investor*, All-America Research Team (annual), October, 1998, p. 150+.

★2024★

TOP FINANCIAL ANALYSTS IN THE MULTI-INDUSTRY SECTOR, 1998

Ranked by: Results of research undertaken by staff of *Institutional Investor.* **Remarks:** Includes reason for selection. **Number listed:** 5

1. Phua Young (Lehman Brothers)
2. Jack Blackstock (Donaldson, Lufkin & Jenrette)
3. Jennifer Murphy (Morgan Stanley Dean Witter)
4. Jack Kelly (Goldman Sachs)
4. Jack Modzelewski (Paine Webber)

Source: *Institutional Investor*, All-America Research Team (annual), October, 1998, p. 152.

★2025★

TOP FINANCIAL ANALYSTS IN THE MULTIFAMILY REAL ESTATE INVESTMENT TRUSTS (REITS) INDUSTRY, 1998

Ranked by: Results of research undertaken by staff of *Institutional Investor.* **Remarks:** Includes reason for selection. **Number listed:** 3

1. Steven Hash (Lehman Brothers)
2. Jonathan Litt (Paine Webber)
3. Eric Hemel (Merrill Lynch)

Source: *Institutional Investor*, All-America Research Team (annual), October, 1998, p. 164+.

★2026★

TOP FINANCIAL ANALYSTS IN THE NATURAL GAS INDUSTRY, 1998

Ranked by: Results of research undertaken by staff of *Institutional Investor.* **Remarks:** Includes reason for selection. **Number listed:** 5

1. Curt Launer (Donaldson, Lufkin & Jenrette)
2. Donald Dufresne (Salomon Smith Barney)
3. Ronald Barone (Paine Webber)
4. David Fleischer (Goldman Sachs)
4. John Olsen (Merrill Lynch)

Source: *Institutional Investor*, All-America Research Team (annual), October, 1998, p. 152+.

★2027★

TOP FINANCIAL ANALYSTS IN THE NONFERROUS METALS INDUSTRY, 1998

Ranked by: Results of research undertaken by staff of *Institutional Investor.* **Remarks:** Includes reason for selection. **Number listed:** 7

1. John Tumazos (Sanford C. Bernstein)
2. R. Wayne Atwell (Morgan Stanley Dean Witter)
3. J. Clarence Morrison (Prudential Securities)
4. Leanne Baker (Salomon Smith Barney)
4. Thomas McNamara (CIBC Oppenheimer)
4. Anthony Rizzuto Jr. (Bear Stearns)
4. Daniel Roling (Merrill Lynch)

Source: *Institutional Investor*, All-America Research Team (annual), October, 1998, p. 155.

★2028★

TOP FINANCIAL ANALYSTS IN THE NONLIFE INSURANCE INDUSTRY, 1998

Ranked by: Results of research undertaken by staff of *Institutional Investor.* **Remarks:** Includes reason for selection. **Number listed:** 7

1. Weston Hicks (Sanford C. Bernstein)
2. Alice Schroeder (Paine Webber)
3. Thomas Cholnoky (Goldman Sachs)
4. Jay Cohen (Merrill Lynch)
4. Ronald Frank (Salomon Smith Barney)
4. Charles Gates (Credit Suisse First Boston)
4. G. Alan Zimmermann (Morgan Stanley Dean Witter)

Source: *Institutional Investor*, All-America Research Team (annual), October, 1998, p. 149.

★2029★

TOP FINANCIAL ANALYSTS IN THE OIL AND GAS EXPLORATIONS AND PRODUCTION INDUSTRY, 1998

Ranked by: Results of research undertaken by staff of *Institutional Investor.* **Remarks:** Includes reason for selection. **Number listed:** 5

1. John Herrlin, Jr. (Merrill Lynch)
2. David Bradshaw (Donaldson, Lufkin & Jenrette)
3. Phillip Pace (Credit Suisse First Boston)
4. Thomas Driscoll (Salomon Smith Barney)
4. Donald Textor (Goldman Sachs)

Source: *Institutional Investor*, All-America Research Team (annual), October, 1998, p. 157+.

★2030★

TOP FINANCIAL ANALYSTS IN THE OIL SERVICES AND EQUIPMENT INDUSTRY, 1998

Ranked by: Results of research undertaken by staff of *Institutional Investor.* **Remarks:** Includes reason for selection. **Number listed:** 5

1. Gordon Hall (Credit Suisse First Boston)
2. John Lovoi (Morgan Stanley Dean Witter)
3. Arvind Sanger (Donaldson, Lufkin & Jenrette)
4. Geoffrey Kieburtz (Salomon Smith Barney)
4. Kevin Simpson (Merrill Lynch)

Source: *Institutional Investor*, All-America Research Team (annual), October, 1998, p. 158.

★2031★

TOP FINANCIAL ANALYSTS IN THE PACKAGING INDUSTRY, 1998

Ranked by: Results of research undertaken by staff of *Institutional Investor.* **Remarks:** Includes reason for selection. **Number listed:** 4

1. Daniel Khoshaba (BT Alex. Brown)
2. George Staphos (Salomon Smith Barney)
3. Cornelius Thornton (Goldman Sachs)
4. Joel Tiss (Lehman Brothers)

Source: *Institutional Investor*, All-America Research Team (annual), October, 1998, p. 158+.

★2032★

TOP FINANCIAL ANALYSTS IN THE PAPER AND FOREST PRODUCTS INDUSTRY, 1998

Ranked by: Results of research undertaken by staff of *Institutional Investor.* **Remarks:** Includes reason for selection. **Number listed:** 7

1. Chip Dillon (Salomon Smith Barney)
2. Richard Schneider (Paine Webber)
3. Sherman Chao (Merrill Lynch)
4. Matthew Berler (Morgan Stanley Dean Witter)
4. Peter Ruschmeier (Donaldson, Lufkin & Jenrette)
4. Mark Weintraub (Goldman Sachs)
4. William Wigder (Credit Suisse First Boston)

Source: *Institutional Investor*, All-America Research Team (annual), October, 1998, p. 159.

★2033★

TOP FINANCIAL ANALYSTS IN THE PC HARDWARE INDUSTRY, 1998

Ranked by: Results of research undertaken by staff of *Institutional Investor.* **Remarks:** Includes reason for selection. **Number listed:** 4

1. Michael Kwatinetz (Credit Suisse First Boston)

2. Richard Schutte (Goldman Sachs)
3. Andrew Neff (Bear Stearns)
4. Donald Young (Paine Webber)

Source: *Institutional Investor*, All-America Research Team (annual), October, 1998, p. 159+.

★2034★
TOP FINANCIAL ANALYSTS IN THE PC SOFTWARE INDUSTRY, 1998
Ranked by: Results of research undertaken by staff of *Institutional Investor*. **Remarks:** Includes reason for selection. **Number listed:** 3

1. Richard Sherlund (Goldman Sachs)
2. Michael Kwatinetz (Credit Suisse First Boston)
3. Mary Meeker (Morgan Stanley Dean Witter)

Source: *Institutional Investor*, All-America Research Team (annual), October, 1998, p. 160.

★2035★
TOP FINANCIAL ANALYSTS IN THE PHOTOGRAPHY AND ELECTRONIC IMAGING INDUSTRY, 1998
Ranked by: Results of research undertaken by staff of *Institutional Investor*. **Remarks:** Includes reason for selection. **Number listed:** 5

1. B. Alexander Henderson (Prudential Securities)
2. Jonathan Rosenzweig (Salomon Smith Barney)
3. Rebecca Runkle (Morgan Stanley Dean Witter)
4. Ty Govatos (Donaldson, Lufkin & Jenrette)
4. Jack Kelly (Goldman Sachs)

Source: *Institutional Investor*, All-America Research Team (annual), October, 1998, p. 160+.

★2036★
TOP FINANCIAL ANALYSTS IN THE PUBLISHING INDUSTRY, 1998
Ranked by: Results of research undertaken by staff of *Institutional Investor*. **Remarks:** Includes reason for selection. **Number listed:** 4

1. William Drewry (Paine Webber)
2. Kevin Gruneich (Bear Stearns)
3. Lauren Rich Fine (Merrill Lynch)
4. Douglas Arthur (Morgan Stanley Dean Witter)

Source: *Institutional Investor*, All-America Research Team (annual), October, 1998, p. 163.

★2037★
TOP FINANCIAL ANALYSTS IN THE RAILROAD INDUSTRY, 1998
Ranked by: Results of research undertaken by staff of *Institutional Investor*. **Remarks:** Includes reason for selection. **Number listed:** 4

1. James Valentine (Morgan Stanley Dean Witter)
2. Gary Yablon (Schroeder & Co.)
3. Scott Flower (Paine Webber)
4. James Higgins (Donaldson, Lufkin & Jenrette)

Source: *Institutional Investor*, All-America Research Team (annual), October, 1998, p. 163+.

★2038★
TOP FINANCIAL ANALYSTS IN THE RESTAURANT INDUSTRY, 1998
Ranked by: Results of research undertaken by staff of *Institutional Investor*. **Remarks:** Includes reason for selection. **Number listed:** 4

1. Howard Penney (Morgan Stanley Dean Witter)
2. Janice Meyer (Donaldson, Lufkin & Jenrette)
3. Peter Oakes (Merrill Lynch)
4. Stacy Jamar (Salomon Smith Barney)

Source: *Institutional Investor*, All-America Research Team (annual), October, 1998, p. 167+.

★2039★
TOP FINANCIAL ANALYSTS IN THE RETAIL FOOD AND DRUG CHAINS INDUSTRY, 1998
Ranked by: Results of research undertaken by staff of *Institutional Investor*. **Remarks:** Includes reason for selection. **Number listed:** 3

1. Edward Comeau (Donaldson, Lufkin & Jenrette)
2. John Heinbockel (Goldman Sachs)
3. Debra Levin (Morgan Stanley Dean Witter)

Source: *Institutional Investor*, All-America Research Team (annual), October, 1998, p. 168+.

★2040★
TOP FINANCIAL ANALYSTS IN THE RETAIL REAL ESTATE INVESTMENT TRUSTS (REITS) INDUSTRY, 1998
Ranked by: Results of research undertaken by staff of *Institutional Investor*. **Remarks:** Includes reason for selection. **Number listed:** 4

1. Jonathan Litt (Paine Webber)
2. Eric Hemel (Merrill Lynch)
3. Steven Hash (Lehman Brothers)
4. Andrew Jones (Morgan Stanley Dean Witter)

Source: *Institutional Investor*, All-America Research Team (annual), October, 1998, p. 167.

★2041★
TOP FINANCIAL ANALYSTS IN THE RETAILING/BROADLINES INDUSTRY, 1998
Ranked by: Results of research undertaken by staff of *Institutional Investor*. **Remarks:** Includes reason for selection. **Number listed:** 6

1. Daniel Barry (Merrill Lynch)
2. Michael Exstein (Credit Suisse First Boston)
3. Jeffrey Feiner (Lehman Brothers)
4. Gary Balter (Donaldson, Lufkin & Jenrette)
4. Richard Church (Salomon Smith Barney)
4. Bruce Missett (Morgan Stanley Dean Witter)

Source: *Institutional Investor*, All-America Research Team (annual), October, 1998, p. 168.

★2042★
TOP FINANCIAL ANALYSTS IN THE RETAILING/HARDLINES INDUSTRY, 1998
Ranked by: Results of research undertaken by staff of *Institutional Investor*. **Remarks:** Includes reason for selection. **Number listed:** 3

1. Peter Caruso (Merrill Lynch)
2. David Bolotsky (Goldman Sachs)
3. Gary Balter (Donaldson, Lufkin & Jenrette)

Source: *Institutional Investor*, All-America Research Team (annual), October, 1998, p. 169.

★2043★
TOP FINANCIAL ANALYSTS IN THE RETAILING/SOFTLINES INDUSTRY, 1998
Ranked by: Results of research undertaken by staff of *Institutional Investor*. **Remarks:** Includes reason for selection. **Number listed:** 4

1. Sharon Pearson (Morgan Stanley Dean Witter)
2. Dana Telsey (Bear Stearns)
3. Richard Baum (Goldman Sachs)
4. Dana Eisman Cohen (Donaldson, Lufkin & Jenrette)

Source: *Institutional Investor*, All-America Research Team (annual), October, 1998, p. 169+.

★2044★

TOP FINANCIAL ANALYSTS IN THE SATELLITE INDUSTRY, 1998

Ranked by: Results of research undertaken by staff of *Institutional Investor.* **Remarks:** Includes reason for selection. **Number listed:** 7

1. Thomas Watts (Merrill Lynch)
2. Robert Kaimowitz (ING Baring Furman Selz)
3. Mark Crossman (CIBC Oppenheimer)
4. John Bensche (Lehman Brothers)
4. Vijay Jayant (Bear Stearns)
4. Dennis Leibowitz (Donaldson, Lufkin & Jenrette)
4. Doug Shapiro (Deutsche Bank Securities)

Source: *Institutional Investor*, All-America Research Team (annual), October, 1998, p. 170.

★2045★

TOP FINANCIAL ANALYSTS IN THE SAVINGS & LOAN AND GSE INDUSTRY, 1998

Ranked by: Results of research undertaken by staff of *Institutional Investor.* **Remarks:** Includes reason for selection. **Number listed:** 6

1. Jonathan Gray (Sanford C. Bernstein)
2. Bruce Harting (Lehman Brothers)
3. Thomas O'Donnell (Salomon Smith Barney)
4. David Dusenbury (Credit Suisse First Boston)
4. Jerry Gitt (Merrill Lynch)
4. Vivek Juneja (J. P. Morgan)

Source: *Institutional Investor*, All-America Research Team (annual), October, 1998, p. 170+.

★2046★

TOP FINANCIAL ANALYSTS IN THE SERVER AND ENTERPRISE HARDWARE INDUSTRY, 1998

Ranked by: Results of research undertaken by staff of *Institutional Investor.* **Remarks:** Includes reason for selection. **Number listed:** 4

1. Steven Milunovich (Merrill Lynch)
2. Laura Conigliaro (Goldman Sachs)
3. John Jones (Salomon Smith Barney)
4. Donald Young (Paine Webber)

Source: *Institutional Investor*, All-America Research Team (annual), October, 1998, p. 172.

★2047★

TOP FINANCIAL ANALYSTS IN THE SERVER AND ENTERPRISE SOFTWARE INDUSTRY, 1998

Ranked by: Results of research undertaken by staff of *Institutional Investor.* **Remarks:** Includes reason for selection. **Number listed:** 4

1. Charles Phillips, Jr. (Morgan Stanley Dean Witter)
2. Richard Sherlund (Goldman Sachs)
3. Christopher Shilakes (Merrill Lynch)
4. Andrew Brosseau (SG Cowen)

Source: *Institutional Investor*, All-America Research Team (annual), October, 1998, p. 172+.

★2048★

TOP FINANCIAL ANALYSTS IN THE SPECIALTY FINANCE INDUSTRY, 1998

Ranked by: Results of research undertaken by staff of *Institutional Investor.* **Remarks:** Includes reason for selection. **Number listed:** 6

1. Susan Roth (Donaldson, Lufkin & Jenrette)
2. Robert Hottensen, Jr. (Goldman Sachs)
3. Thomas Facciola (Lehman Brothers)
4. Steven Eisman (CIBC Oppenheimer)
4. Michael Freudenstein (J. P. Morgan)
4. Gary Gordon (Paine Webber)
4. Michael Hughes (Merrill Lynch)

Source: *Institutional Investor*, All-America Research Team (annual), October, 1998, p. 175.

★2049★

TOP FINANCIAL ANALYSTS IN THE STEEL INDUSTRY, 1998

Ranked by: Results of research undertaken by staff of *Institutional Investor.* **Remarks:** Includes reason for selection. **Number listed:** 3

1. Anthony Carpet (Goldman Sachs)
2. Michelle Galanter Applebaum (Salomon Smith Barney)
3. Michael Gambardella (J. P. Morgan)

Source: *Institutional Investor*, All-America Research Team (annual), October, 1998, p. 175+.

★2050★

TOP FINANCIAL ANALYSTS IN THE TECHNICAL SOFTWARE INDUSTRY, 1998

Ranked by: Results of research undertaken by staff of *Institutional Investor.* **Remarks:** Includes reason for selection. **Number listed:** 7

1. Laura Conigliaro (Goldman Sachs)
2. Jennifer Smith (BancBoston Robertson Stephens)
3. Erach Desai (Credit Suisse First Boston)
4. John Barr (Needham & Co.)
4. Kevin McCarthy (Donaldson, Lufkin & Jenrette)
4. Raj Seth (SG Cowen)
4. Doug van Dorsten (Hambrecht & Quist)

Source: *Institutional Investor*, All-America Research Team (annual), October, 1998, p. 176.

★2051★

TOP FINANCIAL ANALYSTS IN THE TELECOM EQUIPMENT INDUSTRY, 1998

Ranked by: Results of research undertaken by staff of *Institutional Investor.* **Remarks:** Includes reason for selection. **Number listed:** 7

1. Joseph Bellace (Merrill Lynch)
2. Alex Cena (Salomon Smith Barney)
3. Nikos Theodosopoulos (Warburg Dillon Read)
4. Gregory Geiling (J. P. Morgan)
4. Mary Henry (Goldman Sachs)
4. Steven Levy (Lehman Brothers)
4. James Parmelee (Credit Suisse First Boston)

Source: *Institutional Investor*, All-America Research Team (annual), October, 1998, p. 176+.

★2052★

TOP FINANCIAL ANALYSTS IN THE TEXTILES, APPAREL AND FOOTWEAR INDUSTRY, 1998

Ranked by: Results of research undertaken by staff of *Institutional Investor.* **Remarks:** Includes reason for selection. **Number listed:** 5

1. Faye Landes (Salomon Smith Barney)
2. Josephine Esquivel (Morgan Stanley Dean Witter)
3. Dennis Rosenberg (Credit Suisse First Boston)
4. Brenda Gall (Merrill Lynch)
4. Carol Pope Murray (J. P. Morgan)

Source: *Institutional Investor*, All-America Research Team (annual), October, 1998, p. 177.

★2053★

TOP FINANCIAL ANALYSTS IN THE TOBACCO INDUSTRY, 1998

Ranked by: Results of research undertaken by staff of *Institutional Investor.* **Remarks:** Includes reason for selection. **Number listed:** 4

1. Gary Black (Sanford C. Bernstein)
2. Martin Feldman (Salomon Smith Barney)

3. Marc I. Cohen (Goldman Sachs)
4. David Adelman (Morgan Stanley Dean Witter)

Source: *Institutional Investor*, All-America Research Team (annual), October, 1998, p. 177.

★2054★
TOP FINANCIAL ANALYSTS IN THE TRUCKING INDUSTRY, 1998
Ranked by: Results of research undertaken by staff of *Institutional Investor.* **Remarks:** Includes reason for selection. **Number listed:** 6

1. Gary Yablon (Schroeder & Co.)
2. James Valentine (Morgan Stanley Dean Witter)
3. Anthony Gallo (BT Alex. Brown)
4. Jeffrey Kauffman (Merrill Lynch)
4. Douglas Rockel (ING Baring Furman Selz)
4. Paul Schlesinger (Donaldson, Lufkin & Jenrette)

Source: *Institutional Investor*, All-America Research Team (annual), October, 1998, p. 178.

★2055★
TOP FINANCIAL ANALYSTS IN THE WIRELESS TELECOM SERVICES INDUSTRY, 1998
Ranked by: Results of research undertaken by staff of *Institutional Investor.* **Remarks:** Includes reason for selection. **Number listed:** 4

1. Linda Runyon Mutschler (Merrill Lynch)
2. John Bensche (Lehman Brothers)
3. Thomas Lee (Salomon Smith Barney)
4. Steven Yanis (NationsBanc Montgomery Securities)

Source: *Institutional Investor*, All-America Research Team (annual), October, 1998, p. 178+.

★2056★
TOP FINANCIAL ANALYSTS IN THE WIRELINE TELECOM SERVICES INDUSTRY, 1998
Ranked by: Results of research undertaken by staff of *Institutional Investor.* **Remarks:** Includes reason for selection. **Number listed:** 7

1. Jack Grubman (Salomon Smith Barney)
2. Daniel Reingold (Merrill Lynch)
3. Frank Governali (Credit Suisse First Boston)
4. Stephanie Georges Comfort (Morgan Stanley Dean Witter)
4. William Deatherage (Bear Stearns)
4. Simon Flannery (J. P. Morgan)
4. Richard Klugman (Goldman Sachs)

Source: *Institutional Investor*, All-America Research Team (annual), October, 1998, p. 180.

★2057★
TOP FINANCIAL ANALYSTS IN WASHINGTON RESEARCH, 1998
Ranked by: Results of research undertaken by staff of *Institutional Investor.* **Remarks:** Includes reason for selection. **Number listed:** 4

1. Mark Melcher (Prudential Securities)
2. Thomas Gallagher & team (Lehman Brothers)
3. Edward Garlich & team (Schwab Washington Research Group)
4. Leslie Alperstein & team (HSBC Washington Analysis)

Source: *Institutional Investor*, All-America Research Team (annual), October, 1998, p. 187+.

Financial Analysts--Asia

★2058★
INVESTMENT FIRMS WITH THE MOST ANALYSTS ON THE ALL-ASIA RESEARCH TEAM, 1999
Ranked by: Total number of positions on the All-Asia Research Team. **Remarks:** Also notes previous year's rank, total team positions for both years, total first-, second-, and third-team positions for both years, and runners-up for both years. Excludes Japan. **Number listed:** 11

1. Merrill Lynch, with 18 positions
2. Warburg Dillon Read, 16
3. Jardine Fleming Securities, 14
4. CLSA Global Emerging Markets, 10
5. Morgan Stanley Dean Witter, 8
6. Goldman Sachs (Asia), 7
7. ING Barings, 6
8. Deutsche Securities (Asia), 4
8. Indosuez W.I. Carr Securities, 4
10. Salomon Smith Barney, 3

Source: *Institutional Investor-International Edition*, All-Asia Research Team (annual), April, 1999, p. 72.

★2059★
TOP FINANCIAL ANALYSTS COVERING AIRLINES IN ASIA, 1999
Ranked by: Results of research undertaken by editorial staff of *Institutional Investor.* **Remarks:** May also cite runners-up, if applicable. Includes reason for selection. Excludes Japan. **Number listed:** 4

1. Viktor Shvets (Deutsche Securities Asia)
2. Jean-Louis Morisot (Goldman Sachs Asia)
3. Timothy Ross (Warburg Dillon Read)
4. Wendy Wong & team (Merrill Lynch)

Source: *Institutional Investor*, All-Asia Research Team (annual), April, 1999, p. 85.

★2060★
TOP FINANCIAL ANALYSTS COVERING BANKS IN ASIA, 1999
Ranked by: Results of research undertaken by editorial staff of *Institutional Investor.* **Remarks:** May also cite runners-up, if applicable. Includes reason for selection. Excludes Japan. **Number listed:** 4

1. Roy Ramos (Goldman Sachs)
2. Keith Irving & team (Merrill Lynch)
3. Todd Martin & team (Warburg Dillon Read)
4. Andrew Brown & team (Deutsche Securities Asia)

Source: *Institutional Investor*, All-Asia Research Team (annual), April, 1999, p. 85.

★2061★
TOP FINANCIAL ANALYSTS COVERING ECONOMICS IN ASIA, 1999
Ranked by: Results of research undertaken by editorial staff of *Institutional Investor.* **Remarks:** May also cite runner-up, in applicable. Includes reason for selection. Excludes Japan. **Number listed:** 6

1. Jim Walker (CLSA Global Emerging Markets)
2. Simon Ogus & team (Warburg Dillon Read)
3. Stephen Roach & team (Morgan Stanley Dean Witter)
4. Sun Bae Kim & team (Goldman Sachs, Asia)
4. Michael Taylor team (Indosuez W.I. Carr Securities)
4. James Winder & team (Merrill Lynch)

Source: *Institutional Investor*, All-Asia Research Team (annual), April, 1999, p. 88.

★2062★

TOP FINANCIAL ANALYSTS COVERING EQUITY STRATEGY IN ASIA, 1999

Ranked by: Results of research undertaken by editorial staff of *Institutional Investor*. **Remarks:** May also cite runners-up, if applicable. Includes reason for selection. Excludes Japan. **Number listed:** 6

1. Stewart Paterson (CLSA Global Emerging Markets)
2. David Scott & team (Indosuez W.I. Carr Securities)
3. Daniel Fineman & team (Jardine Fleming Securities)
4. Peter Churchouse (Morgan Stanley Dean Witter)
4. Ian MncLennan & team (Warburg Dillon Read)
4. Paul Schulte & team (ING Barings)

Source: *Institutional Investor*, All-Asia Research Team (annual), April, 1999, p. 89.

★2063★

TOP FINANCIAL ANALYSTS COVERING FIXED INCOME/CORPORATES IN ASIA, 1999

Ranked by: Results of research undertaken by editorial staff of *Institutional Investor*. **Remarks:** May also cite runners-up, if applicable. Includes reason for selection. Excludes Japan. **Number listed:** 3

1. Chris Francis (Merrill Lynch)
2. Fan Jiang & team (Goldman Sachs Asia)
3. John Woods & team (HSBC Securities)

Source: *Institutional Investor*, All-Asia Research Team (annual), April, 1999, p. 89.

★2064★

TOP FINANCIAL ANALYSTS COVERING FIXED INCOME/STRATEGY IN ASIA, 1999

Ranked by: Results of research undertaken by editorial staff of *Institutional Investor*. **Remarks:** May also cite runners-up, if applicable. Includes reason for selection. Excludes Japan. **Number listed:** 6

1. William Belchere (Merrill Lynch)
2. Ronald Leven & team (J. P. Morgan)
3. John Woods & team (HSBC Securities)
4. Carson Cole & team (BT Alex. Brown)
4. Fan Jiang & team (Goldman Sachs Asia)
4. Simon Ogus & team (Warburg Dillon Read)

Source: *Institutional Investor*, All-Asia Research Team (annual), April, 1999, p. 90.

★2065★

TOP FINANCIAL ANALYSTS COVERING POWER IN ASIA, 1999

Ranked by: Results of research undertaken by editorial staff of *Institutional Investor*. **Remarks:** May also cite runners-up, if applicable. Includes reason for selection. Excludes Japan. **Number listed:** 4

1. Hilary Judis (Goldman Sachs Asia)
2. Anne Kao (Morgan Stanley Dean Witter)
3. Michelle Ring & team (CLSA Global Emerging Markets)
4. Alice Hui & team (Indosuez W.I. Carr Securities)

Source: *Institutional Investor*, All-Asia Research Team (annual), April, 1999, p. 86.

★2066★

TOP FINANCIAL ANALYSTS COVERING PROPERTY IN ASIA, 1999

Ranked by: Results of research undertaken by editorial staff of *Institutional Investor*. **Remarks:** May also cite runners-up, if applicable. Includes reason for selection. Excludes Japan. **Number listed:** 3

1. Franklin Lam (Warburg Dillon Read)
2. Peter Churchouse & team (Morgan Stanley Dean Witter)
3. John So (Jardine Fleming Securities)

Source: *Institutional Investor*, All-Asia Research Team (annual), April, 1999, p. 86.

★2067★

TOP FINANCIAL ANALYSTS COVERING PULP AND PAPER IN ASIA, 1999

Ranked by: Results of research undertaken by editorial staff of *Institutional Investor*. **Remarks:** May also cite runners-up, if applicable. Includes reason for selection. Excludes Japan. **Number listed:** 1

1. Charles Spencer (Morgan Stanley Dean Witter)

Source: *Institutional Investor*, All-Asia Research Team (annual), April, 1999, p. 87.

★2068★

TOP FINANCIAL ANALYSTS COVERING TECHNOLOGY IN ASIA, 1999

Ranked by: Results of research undertaken by editorial staff of *Institutional Investor*. **Remarks:** May also cite runners-up, if applicable. Includes reason for selection. Excludes Japan. **Number listed:** 6

1. Lily Wu (Salomon Smith Barney)
2. Gurinder Kalra & team (Morgan Stanley Dean Witter)
3. Bernard Tan & team (Merrill Lynch)
4. Bhavin Shah & team (Credit Suisse First Boston)
   Lucas Ward & team (Goldman Sachs Asia)
   Peter Wolff & team (ING Barings)

Source: *Institutional Investor*, All-Asia Research Team (annual), April, 1999, p. 87.

★2069★

TOP FINANCIAL ANALYSTS COVERING TELECOMMUNICATIONS IN ASIA, 1999

Ranked by: Results of research undertaken by editorial staff of *Institutional Investor*. **Remarks:** May also cite runners-up, if applicable. Includes reason for selection. Excludes Japan. **Number listed:** 1

1. Craig Irvine (Merrill Lynch)

Source: *Institutional Investor*, All-Asia Research Team (annual), April, 1999, p. 87+.

Financial Analysts--Australia

★2070★

TOP FINANCIAL ANALYSTS COVERING AUSTRALIA, 1999

Ranked by: Results of research undertaken by editorial staff of *Institutional Investor*. **Remarks:** May cite runners-up if applicable. Includes reason for selection. **Number listed:** 5

1. Justin Arter (J.B. Were & Son)
2. Mark Fulton & team (Salomon Smith Barney)
3. Richard Beaurepaire & team (Deutsche Securities Asia)
4. Tony Brennan & team (Warburg Dillon Read)
4. Michael Brown & team (Merrill Lynch)
4. Geoff Warren & team (Ord Minnett Securities)

Source: *Institutional Investor-International Edition*, All-Asia Team (annual), April, 1999, p. 77.

Financial Analysts--China

★2071★
TOP FINANCIAL ANALYSTS COVERING CHINA, 1999
Ranked by: Results of research undertaken by editorial staff of *Institutional Investor.* **Remarks:** May cite runners-up if applicable. Includes reason for selection. **Number listed:** 4
1. Jing Ulrich (CLSA Global Emerging Markets)
2. Kenneth Ho & team (Jardine Fleming Securities)
3. Kalina Ip & team (ABN Amro Asia)
4. Vincent Chan (Warburg Dillon Read)

Source: *Institutional Investor-International Edition,* All-Asia Research Team (annual), April, 1999, p. 77.

Financial Analysts--Czech Republic

★2072★
TOP FINANCIAL ANALYSTS COVERING THE CZECH REPUBLIC, 1999
Ranked by: Results of research undertaken by editorial staff of *Institutional Investor.* **Remarks:** May cite runners-up if applicable. Includes reason for selection. **Number listed:** 3
1. Miroslave Nosal (Merrill Lynch)
2. David Pejcha & team (Credit Suisse First Boston)
3. Michal Rizek & team (CA IB Securities)

Source: *Institutional Investor-International Edition,* All-Asia Research Team (annual), April, 1999, p. 110.

Financial Analysts--Europe

★2073★
INVESTMENT FIRMS WITH THE MOST POSITIONS ON THE ALL-EUROPE RESEARCH TEAM, 1999
Ranked by: Total number of positions investment firm has on team. **Remarks:** Also notes previous year's rank, total team positions for both years, total first-, second-, and third-team positions for both years, and runners up for both years. **Number listed:** 16
1. Merrill Lynch, with 52 positions
2. Warburg Dillon Read, 45
3. Morgan Stanley Dean Witter, 37
4. Goldman Sachs International, 25
5. BT Alex. Brown, 23
6. Credit Suisse First Boston, 16
7. Schroeder Securities, 10
8. Deutsche Bank Securities, 9
8. HSBC Securities, 9
10. ABN Amro, 7
10. Dresdner Kleinwort Benson, 7

Source: *Institutional Investor-International Edition,* All-Europe Research Team (annual), February, 1999, p. 67.

★2074★
TOP FINANCIAL ANALYSTS IN ECONOMICS/ DEVELOPED EUROPEAN MARKETS, 1999
Ranked by: Results of research undertaken by editorial staff of *Institutional Investor.* **Remarks:** May cite runners-up if applicable. Includes reason for selection. **Number listed:** 4
1. Thomas Mayer (Goldman Sachs International)
2. David Bowers & team (Merrill Lynch)
3. Joachim Fels & team (Morgan Stanley Dean Witter)
4. Darren Winder & team (Warburg Dillon Read)

Source: *Institutional Investor-International Edition,* All-Europe Research Team (annual), February, 1999, p. 107.

★2075★
TOP FINANCIAL ANALYSTS IN EQUITY STRATEGY/DEVELOPED EUROPEAN MARKETS, 1999
Ranked by: Results of research undertaken by editorial staff of *Institutional Investor.* **Remarks:** May cite runners-up if applicable. Includes reason for selection. **Number listed:** 4
1. Richard Davidson (Morgan Stanley Dean Witter)
2. David Bowers & team (Merrill Lynch)
3. Michael Young & team (Goldman Sachs International)
4. Julian Edwards & team (Warburg Dillon Read)

Source: *Institutional Investor-International Edition,* All-Europe Research Team (annual), February, 1999, p. 108.

★2076★
TOP FINANCIAL ANALYSTS IN EUROBONDS, 1999
Ranked by: Results of research undertaken by editorial staff of *Institutional Investor.* **Remarks:** May cite runners-up if applicable. Includes reason for selection. **Number listed:** 3
1. Andy Evans (Warburg Dillon Read)
2. Rick Deutsch & team (Merrill Lynch)
3. Gary Jenkins (Barclays Capital)

Source: *Institutional Investor-International Edition,* All-Europe Research Team (annual), February, 1999, p. 109.

★2077★
TOP FINANCIAL ANALYSTS IN THE AUTOMOBILE INDUSTRY, 1999
Ranked by: Results of research undertaken by editorial staff of *Institutional Investor.* **Remarks:** May cite runners-up if applicable. Includes reason for selection. **Number listed:** 6
1. Nick Snee (J. P. Morgan)
2. Stephen Reitman & team (Merrill Lynch)
3. Gregory Melich & team (Morgan Stanley Dean Witter)
4. Steve Haggerty & team (Schroeder Securities)
4. Keith Hayes & team (Goldman Sachs International)
4. John Lawson & team (Salomon Smith Barney)

Source: *Institutional Investor-International Edition,* All-Europe Research Team (annual), February, 1999, p. 94.

★2078★
TOP FINANCIAL ANALYSTS IN THE BANKING INDUSTRY, 1999
Ranked by: Results of research undertaken by editorial staff of *Institutional Investor.* **Remarks:** May cite runners-up if applicable. Includes reason for selection. **Number listed:** 6
1. Susan Leadem (Goldman Sachs International)
2. Alan Broughton & team (Morgan Stanley Dean Witter)
3. Gabriel Besson & team (Warburg Dillon Read)
4. Stuart Graham & team (J. P. Morgan)
4. Marc Rubinstein & team (Schroeder Securities)
4. Christopher Williams & team (Fox-Pitt, Kelton)

Source: *Institutional Investor-International Edition,* All-Europe Research Team (annual), February, 1999, p. 94.

★2079★
TOP FINANCIAL ANALYSTS IN THE BEVERAGE INDUSTRY, 1999
Ranked by: Results of research undertaken by editorial staff of *Institutional Investor.* **Remarks:** May cite runners-up if applicable. Includes reason for selection. **Number listed:** 2
1. John Wakely (Lehman Brothers)

2. Sylvain Massot (Morgan Stanley Dean Witter)

Source: *Institutional Investor-International Edition*, All-Europe Research Team (annual), February, 1999, p. 96.

★2080★
TOP FINANCIAL ANALYSTS IN THE BUILDING INDUSTRY, 1999
Ranked by: Results of research undertaken by editorial staff of *Institutional Investor.* **Remarks:** May cite runners-up if applicable. Includes reason for selection. **Number listed:** 2

1. Sandrine Naslin (Warburg Dillon Read)
2. Emilio Alvarez (Morgan Stanley Dean Witter)

Source: *Institutional Investor-International Edition*, All-Europe Research Team (annual), February, 1999, p. 96.

★2081★
TOP FINANCIAL ANALYSTS IN THE CHEMICALS INDUSTRY, 1999
Ranked by: Results of research undertaken by editorial staff of *Institutional Investor.* **Remarks:** May cite runners-up if applicable. Includes reason for selection. **Number listed:** 3

1. Charles Brown (Goldman Sachs)
2. Campbell Gillies & team (BT Alex. Brown)
3. Peter Houghton & team (J. P. Morgan)

Source: *Institutional Investor-International Edition*, All-Europe Research Team (annual), February, 1999, p. 98.

★2082★
TOP FINANCIAL ANALYSTS IN THE ENGINEERING AND MACHINERY INDUSTRY, 1999
Ranked by: Results of research undertaken by editorial staff of *Institutional Investor.* **Remarks:** May cite runners-up if applicable. Includes reason for selection. **Number listed:** 3

1. Chris Heminway (Lehman Brothers)
2. Gideon Franklin & team (Morgan Stanley Dean Witter)
3. Olaf Toelke & team (Merrill Lynch)

Source: *Institutional Investor-International Edition*, All-Europe Research Team (annual), February, 1999, p. 98.

★2083★
TOP FINANCIAL ANALYSTS IN THE FOOD INDUSTRY, 1999
Ranked by: Results of research undertaken by editorial staff of *Institutional Investor.* **Remarks:** May cite runners-up if applicable. Includes reason for selection. **Number listed:** 2

1. Kieran Mahon (Schroeder Securities)
2. Sylvain Massot & team (Morgan Stanley Dean Witter)

Source: *Institutional Investor-International Edition*, All-Europe Research Team (annual), February, 1999, p. 99.

★2084★
TOP FINANCIAL ANALYSTS IN THE INSURANCE INDUSTRY, 1999
Ranked by: Results of research undertaken by editorial staff of *Institutional Investor.* **Remarks:** May cite runners-up if applicable. Includes reason for selection. **Number listed:** 4

1. Mark Cathcart BT Alex. Brown
2. Bob Yates & team Fox-Pitt, Kelton
3. Rob Procter & team Morgan Stanley Dean Witter
4. Robin Mitra & team Merrill Lynch

Source: *Institutional Investor-International Edition*, All-Europe Research Team (annual), February, 1999, p. 99.

★2085★
TOP FINANCIAL ANALYSTS IN THE LUXURY GOODS INDUSTRY, 1999
Ranked by: Results of research undertaken by editorial staff of *Institutional Investor.* **Remarks:** May cite runners-up if applicable. Includes reason for selection. **Number listed:** 2

1. Claire Kent (Morgan Stanley Dean Witter)
2. Jacques-Franck Dossin (Goldman Sachs International)

Source: *Institutional Investor-International Edition*, All-Europe Research Team (annual), February, 1999, p. 99+.

★2086★
TOP FINANCIAL ANALYSTS IN THE MEDIA AND ENTERTAINMENT INDUSTRY, 1999
Ranked by: Results of research undertaken by editorial staff of *Institutional Investor.* **Remarks:** May cite runners-up if applicable. Includes reason for selection. **Number listed:** 2

1. Rebecca Winnington-Ingram (Morgan Stanley Dean Witter)
2. Neil Blackley & team (Merrill Lynch)

Source: *Institutional Investor-International Edition*, All-Europe Research Team (annual), February, 1999, p. 100.

★2087★
TOP FINANCIAL ANALYSTS IN THE OIL AND GAS INDUSTRY, 1999
Ranked by: Results of research undertaken by editorial staff of *Institutional Investor.* **Remarks:** May cite runners-up if applicable. Includes reason for selection. **Number listed:** 4

1. Anthony Ling (Schroeder Securities)
2. Fergus MacLeod & team (BT Alex. Brown)
3. Gavin White (Warburg Dillon Read)
4. Susan Graham & team (Merrill Lynch)

Source: *Institutional Investor-International Edition*, All-Europe Research Team (annual), February, 1999, p. 100+.

★2088★
TOP FINANCIAL ANALYSTS IN THE PAN-EUROPEAN BANKING INDUSTRY, 1999
Ranked by: Results of research undertaken by editorial staff of *Institutional Investor.* **Remarks:** May cite runners-up if applicable. Includes reason for selection. **Number listed:** 4

1. Susan Leadem (Goldman Sachs International)
2. Alan Broughton & team (Morgan Stanley Dean Witter)
3. Anik Sen & team (Warburg Dillon Read)
4. Christopher Williams & team (Fox-Pitt, Kelton)

Source: *Institutional Investor-International Edition*, All-Europe Research Team (annual), February, 1999, p. 73.

★2089★
TOP FINANCIAL ANALYSTS IN THE PAN-EUROPEAN CHEMICALS INDUSTRY, 1999
Ranked by: Results of research undertaken by editorial staff of *Institutional Investor.* **Remarks:** May cite runners-up if applicable. Includes reason for selection. **Number listed:** 4

1. Charles Brown (Goldman Sachs International)
2. Peter Houghton & team (J. P. Morgan)
3. Penny Tattersall & team (Credit Suisse First Boston)
4. Campbell Gillies & team (BT Alex. Brown)

Source: *Institutional Investor-International Edition*, All-Europe Research Team (annual), February, 1999, p. 73.

★2090★
TOP FINANCIAL ANALYSTS IN THE PAN-EUROPEAN FOOD INDUSTRY, 1999
Ranked by: Results of research undertaken by editorial staff of *Institutional Investor.* **Remarks:** May cite runners-up if applicable. Includes reason for selection. **Number listed:** 3

1. Sylvain Massot (Morgan Stanley Dean Witter)
2. Mark Lynch & team (Warburg Dillon Read)
3. Kieran Mahon & team (Schroeder Securities)

Source: *Institutional Investor-International Edition*, All-Europe Research Team (annual), February, 1999, p. 74.

★2091★
TOP FINANCIAL ANALYSTS IN THE PAN-EUROPEAN INSURANCE INDUSTRY, 1999
Ranked by: Results of research undertaken by editorial staff of *Institutional Investor.* **Remarks:** May cite runners-up if applicable. Includes reason for selection. **Number listed:** 6
1. Rob Yates (Fox-Pitt, Kelton)
2. Rogin Mitra & team (Merrill Lynch)
3. Rob Procter & team (Morgan Stanley Dean Witter)
4. Mark Cathcart & team (BT Alex. Brown)
4. Stephen Dias & team (Goldman Sachs International)
4. Richard Urwick (Schroeder Securities)

Source: *Institutional Investor-International Edition*, All-Europe Research Team (annual), February, 1999, p. 74.

★2092★
TOP FINANCIAL ANALYSTS IN THE PAN-EUROPEAN MEDIA INDUSTRY, 1999
Ranked by: Results of research undertaken by editorial staff of *Institutional Investor.* **Remarks:** May cite runners-up if applicable. Includes reason for selection. **Number listed:** 5
1. Neil Blackley (Merrill Lynch)
2. Rebecca Winnington-Ingram & team (Morgan Stanley Dean Witter)
3. Guy Lamming & team (Goldman Sachs International)
4. Mark Beilby (Deutsche Bank Securities)
4. Colin Tennant (Warburg Dillon Read)

Source: *Institutional Investor-International Edition*, All-Europe Research Team (annual), February, 1999, p. 75.

★2093★
TOP FINANCIAL ANALYSTS IN THE PAN-EUROPEAN OIL AND GAS INDUSTRY, 1999
Ranked by: Results of research undertaken by editorial staff of *Institutional Investor.* **Remarks:** May cite runners-up if applicable. Includes reason for selection. **Number listed:** 3
1. Fergus MacLeod (BT Alex. Brown)
2. Susan Graham & team (Merrill Lynch)
3. Gavin White & team (Warburg Dillon Read)

Source: *Institutional Investor-International Edition*, All-Europe Research Team (annual), February, 1999, p. 75.

★2094★
TOP FINANCIAL ANALYSTS IN THE PAN-EUROPEAN PAPER INDUSTRY, 1999
Ranked by: Results of research undertaken by editorial staff of *Institutional Investor.* **Remarks:** May cite runners-up if applicable. Includes reason for selection. **Number listed:** 3
1. Mads Asprem (Morgan Stanley Dean Witter)
2. Thomas Brodin (Salomon Smith Barney)
3. Hakan Ostling (Goldman Sachs International)

Source: *Institutional Investor-International Edition*, All-Europe Research Team (annual), February, 1999, p. 76.

★2095★
TOP FINANCIAL ANALYSTS IN THE PAN-EUROPEAN PHARMACEUTICALS INDUSTRY, 1999
Ranked by: Results of research undertaken by editorial staff of *Institutional Investor.* **Remarks:** May cite runners-up if applicable. Includes reason for selection. **Number listed:** 5
1. Mark Tracey (Goldman Sachs International)
2. James McKean & team (Morgan Stanley Dean Witter)
3. Janet Dyson & team (Merrill Lynch)
4. Stewart Adkins & team (Lehman Brothers)
4. Vikram Sahu (Credit Suisse First Boston)

Source: *Institutional Investor-International Edition*, All-Europe Research Team (annual), February, 1999, p. 76.

★2096★
TOP FINANCIAL ANALYSTS IN THE PAN-EUROPEAN TECHNOLOGY INDUSTRY, 1999
Ranked by: Results of research undertaken by editorial staff of *Institutional Investor.* **Remarks:** May cite runners-up if applicable. Includes reason for selection. **Number listed:** 4
1. Charles Elliott (Goldman Sachs International)
2. Angela Dean & team (Morgan Stanley Dean Witter)
3. Rennie McArthur Miller & team (Deutsche Bank Securities)
4. Neil Barton & team (Merrill Lynch)

Source: *Institutional Investor-International Edition*, All-Europe Research Team (annual), February, 1999, p. 77.

★2097★
TOP FINANCIAL ANALYSTS IN THE PAN-EUROPEAN TELECOMMUNICATIONS SERVICES INDUSTRY, 1999
Ranked by: Results of research undertaken by editorial staff of *Institutional Investor.* **Remarks:** May cite runners-up if applicable. Includes reason for selection. **Number listed:** 4
1. Christopher McFadden (Merrill Lynch)
2. Patrick Earle & team (Warburg Dillon Read)
3. Michael Armitage (Morgan Stanley Dean Witter)
4. Francis Woollen & team (Goldman Sachs International)

Source: *Institutional Investor-International Edition*, All-Europe Research Team (annual), February, 1999, p. 77.

★2098★
TOP FINANCIAL ANALYSTS IN THE PAN-EUROPEAN TRANSPORTATION INDUSTRY, 1999
Ranked by: Results of research undertaken by editorial staff of *Institutional Investor.* **Remarks:** May cite runners-up if applicable. Includes reason for selection. **Number listed:** 5
1. Andrew Barker (Warburg Dillon Read)
2. Richard Hannah & team (BT Alex. Brown)
3. Guy Kekwick (Goldman Sachs International)
4. Clive Anderson (Merrill Lynch)
4. Martin Borghetto (Morgan Stanley Dean Witter)

Source: *Institutional Investor-International Edition*, All-Europe Research Team (annual), February, 1999, p. 78.

★2099★
TOP FINANCIAL ANALYSTS IN THE PAN-EUROPEAN UTILITIES INDUSTRY, 1999
Ranked by: Results of research undertaken by editorial staff of *Institutional Investor.* **Remarks:** May cite runners-up if applicable. Includes reason for selection. **Number listed:** 5
1. Michael Sayers (Morgan Stanley Dean Witter)
2. Chris Rowland & team (Merrill Lynch)
3. Isabelle Hayen & team (Goldman Sachs International)
4. Nick Pink (Warburg Dillon Read)
4. John Willis (BT Alex. Brown)

Source: *Institutional Investor-International Edition*, All-Europe Research Team (annual), February, 1999, p. 78.

★2100★
TOP FINANCIAL ANALYSTS IN THE PAPER AND PACKAGING INDUSTRY, 1999
Ranked by: Results of research undertaken by editorial staff of *Institutional Investor.* **Remarks:** May cite runners-up if applicable. Includes reason for selection. **Number listed:** 3
1. Hakan Ostling (Goldman Sachs International)
2. Thomas Brodin (Salomon Smith Barney)
3. Mads Asprem & team (Morgan Stanley Dean Witter)

Source: *Institutional Investor-International Edition*, All-Europe Research Team (annual), February, 1999, p. 103.

★2101★
TOP FINANCIAL ANALYSTS IN THE PHARMACEUTICALS INDUSTRY, 1999
Ranked by: Results of research undertaken by editorial staff of *Institutional Investor.* **Remarks:** May cite runners-up if applicable. Includes reason for selection. **Number listed:** 4
1. Mark Tracey (Goldman Sachs International)
2. Janet Dyson (Merrill Lynch)
3. James McKean & team (Morgan Stanley Dean Witter)
4. Johanna Walton & team (Lehman Brothers)

Source: *Institutional Investor-International Edition*, All-Europe Research Team (annual), February, 1999, p. 103+.

★2102★
TOP FINANCIAL ANALYSTS IN THE RETAILING INDUSTRY, 1999
Ranked by: Results of research undertaken by editorial staff of *Institutional Investor.* **Remarks:** May cite runners-up if applicable. Includes reason for selection. **Number listed:** 4
1. Keith Wills (Goldman Sachs International)
2. Didier Rabattu & team (Deutsche Bank Securities)
3. Eric Tibi & team (Warburg Dillon Read)
4. Toby Radford (J. P. Morgan)

Source: *Institutional Investor-International Edition*, All-Europe Research Team (annual), February, 1999, p. 104.

★2103★
TOP FINANCIAL ANALYSTS IN THE STEEL INDUSTRY, 1999
Ranked by: Results of research undertaken by editorial staff of *Institutional Investor.* **Remarks:** May cite runners-up if applicable. Includes reason for selection. **Number listed:** 3
1. Jeremy Fletcher (Credit Suisse First Boston)
2. Terry Sinclair (Salomon Smith Barney)
3. Alan Coats & team (Merrill Lynch)

Source: *Institutional Investor-International Edition*, All-Europe Research Team (annual), February, 1999, p. 105.

★2104★
TOP FINANCIAL ANALYSTS IN THE TECHNOLOGY INDUSTRY, 1999
Ranked by: Results of research undertaken by editorial staff of *Institutional Investor.* **Remarks:** May cite runners-up if applicable. Includes reason for selection. **Number listed:** 4
1. Charles Elliott (Goldman Sachs International)
2. Angela Dean & team (Morgan Stanley Dean Witter)
3. Neil Barton & team (Merrill Lynch)
4. Rennie McArthur Miller & team (Deutsche Bank Securities)

Source: *Institutional Investor-International Edition*, All-Europe Research Team (annual), February, 1999, p. 105.

★2105★
TOP FINANCIAL ANALYSTS IN THE TELECOMMUNICATIONS EQUIPMENT INDUSTRY, 1999
Ranked by: Includes reason for selection. **Remarks:** May cite runners-up if applicable. **Number listed:** 3
1. Richard Kramer (Goldman Sachs International)
2. Neil Barton & team (Merrill Lynch)
3. Angela Dean & team (Morgan Stanley Dean Witter)

Source: *Institutional Investor-International Edition*, All-Europe Research Team (annual), February, 1999, p. 106.

★2106★
TOP FINANCIAL ANALYSTS IN THE TELECOMMUNICATIONS SERVICES INDUSTRY, 1999
Ranked by: Results of research undertaken by editorial staff of *Institutional Investor.* **Remarks:** May cite runners-up if applicable. Includes reason for selection. **Number listed:** 5
1. Patrick Earle (Warburg Dillon Read)
2. Christopher McFadden & team (Merrill Lynch)
3. Michael Armitage & team (Morgan Stanley Dean Witter)
4. James Golob & team (Deutsche Bank Securities)
4. Douglas Wight & team (Salomon Smith Barney)

Source: *Institutional Investor-International Edition*, All-Europe Research Team (annual), February, 1999, p. 106.

★2107★
TOP INVESTMENT FIRMS IN CONTINENTAL COUNTRIES, 1999
Ranked by: Results of research undertaken by editorial staff of *Institutional Investor.* **Number listed:** 4
1. Warburg Dillon Read
2. Credit Suisse First Boston
2. Merrill Lynch
3. ABN Amro
4. CA IB Securities
4. Deutsche Bank Securities
4. ING Barings

Source: *Institutional Investor*, All-Europe Research Team (annual), February, 1999, p. 69.

★2108★
TOP INVESTMENT FIRMS IN CONTINENTAL SECTORS, 1999
Ranked by: Results of research undertaken by editorial staff of *Institutional Investor.* **Number listed:** 4
1. Morgan Stanley Dean Witter
2. Merrill Lynch
3. Goldman Sachs International
4. Warburg Dillon Read

Source: *Institutional Investor*, All-Europe Research Team (annual), February, 1999, p. 69.

★2109★
TOP INVESTMENT FIRMS IN PAN-EUROPEAN SECTORS, 1999
Ranked by: Results of research undertaken by editorial staff of *Institutional Investor.* **Number listed:** 5
1. Goldman Sachs International
1. Morgan Stanley Dean Witter
3. Merrill Lynch
4. Warburg Dillon Read
5. BT Alex. Brown

Source: *Institutional Investor*, All-Europe Research Team (annual), February, 1999, p. 68.

★2110★
TOP INVESTMENT FIRMS IN STRATEGY AND ECONOMICS, 1999
Ranked by: Results of research undertaken by editorial staff of *Institutional Investor.* **Number listed:** 3
1. Merrill Lynch
2. Warburg Dillon Read
3. Goldman Sachs International
3. Morgan Stanley Dean Witter

Source: *Institutional Investor*, All-Europe Research Team (annual), February, 1999, p. 69.

★2111★
TOP INVESTMENT FIRMS IN U.K. SECTORS, 1999
Ranked by: Results of research undertaken by editorial staff of *Institutional Investor.* **Number listed:** 4
1. Merrill Lynch
2. Warburg Dillon Read
3. BT Alex. Brown
4. Credit Suisse First Boston
4. Morgan Stanley Dean Witter

Source: *Institutional Investor*, All-Europe Research Team (annual), February, 1999, p. 68.

Financial Analysts--France

★2112★
TOP FINANCIAL ANALYSTS COVERING FRANCE, 1999
Ranked by: Results of research undertaken by editorial staff of *Institutional Investor.* **Remarks:** May cite runners-up if applicable. Includes reason for selection. **Number listed:** 5
1. Bruno Renard (Credit Agricole Indosuez Cheuvreux)
2. Alain Galene & team (SG Securities)
3. Patrick Legland & team (Paribas Capital Markets)
4. Alain Kayayan & team (Exane)
4. Mark Mills & team (Warburg Dillon Read)

Source: *Institutional Investor-International Edition*, All-Europe Research Team (annual), February, 1999, p. 110.

Financial Analysts--Germany

★2113★
TOP FINANCIAL ANALYSTS COVERING GERMANY, 1999
Ranked by: Results of research undertaken by editorial staff of *Institutional Investor.* **Remarks:** May cite runners-up if applicable. Includes reason for selection. **Number listed:** 3
1. Hans-Dieter Klein (Deutsche Bank Equity Research)
2. Roger Hirst & team (Kleinwort Benson Research)
3. Bernd Janssen & team (Warburg Dillon Read)

Source: *Institutional Investor-International Edition*, All-Europe Research Team (annual), February, 1999, p. 111.

Financial Analysts--Great Britain

★2114★
TOP FINANCIAL ANALYSTS IN ECONOMICS IN GREAT BRITAIN, 1999
Ranked by: Results of research undertaken by editorial staff of *Institutional Investor.* **Remarks:** May cite runners-up if applicable. Includes reason for selection. **Number listed:** 6
1. David Walton (Goldman Sachs International)
2. Paul Turnbull & team (Merrill Lynch)
3. Darren Winder (Warburg Dillon Read)
4. Kevin Gardiner & team (Morgan Stanley Dean Witter)
4. Stephen King & team (HSBC Securities)
4. David Owen & team (Dresdner Kleinwort Benson)

Source: *Institutional Investor-International Edition*, All-Europe Research Team (annual), February, 1999, p. 107+.

★2115★
TOP FINANCIAL ANALYSTS IN EQUITY STRATEGY IN GREAT BRITAIN, 1999
Ranked by: Results of research undertaken by editorial staff of *Institutional Investor.* **Remarks:** May cite runners-up if applicable. Includes reason for selection. **Number listed:** 5
1. Philip Wolstencroft (Merrill Lynch)
2. Robert Semple & team (BT Alex. Brown)
3. Mark Tinker & team (Warburg Dillon Read)
4. Richard Davidson & team (Morgan Stanley Dean Witter)
4. Michael Young & team (Goldman Sachs International)

Source: *Institutional Investor-International Edition*, All-Europe Research Team (annual), February, 1999, p. 109.

★2116★
TOP FINANCIAL ANALYSTS IN THE BANKING INDUSTRY IN GREAT BRITAIN, 1999
Ranked by: Results of research undertaken by editorial staff of *Institutional Investor.* **Remarks:** May cite runners-up if applicable. Includes reason for selection. **Number listed:** 4
1. Richard Coleman (Merrill Lynch)
2. William de Winton & team (ABN Amro)
3. Michael Lever & team (HSBC Securities)
4. Mark Eady (BT Alex. Brown)

Source: *Institutional Investor-International Edition*, All-Europe Research Team (annual), February, 1999, p. 80.

★2117★
TOP FINANCIAL ANALYSTS IN THE BEVERAGE INDUSTRY IN GREAT BRITAIN, 1999
Ranked by: Results of research undertaken by editorial staff of *Institutional Investor.* **Remarks:** May cite runners-up if applicable. Includes reason for selection. **Number listed:** 5
1. Mark Puleikis (Merrill Lynch)
2. John Spicer & team (Warburg Dillon Read)
3. Charles Winston & team (HSBC Securities)
4. Graeme Eadie & team (BT Alex. Brown)
4. Alexandra Oldroyd (Morgan Stanley Dean Witter)

Source: *Institutional Investor-International Edition*, All-Europe Research Team (annual), February, 1999, p. 80+.

★2118★
TOP FINANCIAL ANALYSTS IN THE BREWERIES, PUBS AND RESTAURANTS INDUSTRY IN GREAT BRITAIN, 1999
Ranked by: Results of research undertaken by editorial staff of *Institutional Investor.* **Remarks:** May cite runners-up if applicable. Includes reason for selection. **Number listed:** 4
1. Graeme Eadie (BT Alex. Brown)
2. John Spicer & team (Warburg Dillon Read)
3. Charles Winston (HSBC Securities)
4. Mark Puleikis & team (Merrill Lynch)

Source: *Institutional Investor-International Edition*, All-Europe Research Team (annual), February, 1999, p. 81.

★2119★
TOP FINANCIAL ANALYSTS IN THE BUILDING INDUSTRY IN GREAT BRITAIN, 1999
Ranked by: Results of research undertaken by editorial staff of *Institutional Investor.* **Remarks:** May cite runners-up if applicable. Includes reason for selection. **Number listed:** 3
1. Mark Stockdale (Warburg Dillon Read)
2. Kevin Cammack & team (Merrill Lynch)
3. Robert Donald & team (Schroeder Securities)

Source: *Institutional Investor-International Edition*, All-Europe Research Team (annual), February, 1999, p. 81.

★2120★
TOP FINANCIAL ANALYSTS IN THE CHEMICALS INDUSTRY IN GREAT BRITAIN, 1999
Ranked by: Results of research undertaken by editorial staff of *Institutional Investor.* **Remarks:** May cite runners-up if applicable. Includes reason for selection. **Number listed:** 6
1. Robyn Coombs (Merrill Lynch)
2. Lucas Herrmann (BT Alex. Brown)
3. Peter Clark (Warburg Dillon Read)
4. Andrew Benson (Schroeder Securities)
4. Charles Brown (Goldman Sachs International)
4. Andrew Scott & team (Credit Suisse First Boston)

Source: *Institutional Investor-International Edition,* All-Europe Research Team (annual), February, 1999, p. 82.

★2121★
TOP FINANCIAL ANALYSTS IN THE DISTRIBUTORS INDUSTRY IN GREAT BRITAIN, 1999
Ranked by: Results of research undertaken by editorial staff of *Institutional Investor.* **Remarks:** May cite runners-up if applicable. Includes reason for selection. **Number listed:** 1
1. Andrew Ripper (Merrill Lynch)

Source: *Institutional Investor-International Edition,* All-Europe Research Team (annual), February, 1999, p. 82.

★2122★
TOP FINANCIAL ANALYSTS IN THE ELECTRICITY INDUSTRY IN GREAT BRITAIN, 1999
Ranked by: Results of research undertaken by editorial staff of *Institutional Investor.* **Remarks:** May cite runners-up if applicable. Includes reason for selection. **Number listed:** 5
1. Nick Pink (Warburg Dillon Read)
2. Simon Williams (Deutsche Bank Securities)
3. Ian Graham & team (Merrill Lynch)
4. James Hutton-Mills & team (Morgan Stanley Dean Witter)
4. Anthony White & team (Dresdner Kleinwort Benson)

Source: *Institutional Investor-International Edition,* All-Europe Research Team (annual), February, 1999, p. 82+.

★2123★
TOP FINANCIAL ANALYSTS IN THE ELECTRONIC AND ELECTRICAL EQUIPMENT INDUSTRY IN GREAT BRITAIN, 1999
Ranked by: Results of research undertaken by editorial staff of *Institutional Investor.* **Remarks:** May cite runners-up if applicable. Includes reason for selection. **Number listed:** 4
1. Andrew Clifton (Merrill Lynch)
2. Andrew Bryant & team (BT Alex. Brown)
3. Edwin Lloyd (HSBC Securities)
4. Neil Steer (Warburg Dillon Read)

Source: *Institutional Investor-International Edition,* All-Europe Research Team (annual), February, 1999, p. 84.

★2124★
TOP FINANCIAL ANALYSTS IN THE ENGINEERING INDUSTRY IN GREAT BRITAIN, 1999
Ranked by: Results of research undertaken by editorial staff of *Institutional Investor.* **Remarks:** May cite runners-up if applicable. Includes reason for selection. **Number listed:** 5
1. Charles Burrows (HSBC Securities)
2. Paul Compton & team (Merrill Lynch)
3. Paul Ruddle & team (Warburg Dillon Read)
4. Tim Bennett (Morgan Stanley Dean Witter)
4. Colin Fell & team (Dresdner Kleinwort Benson)

Source: *Institutional Investor-International Edition,* All-Europe Research Team (annual), February, 1999, p. 84+.

★2125★
TOP FINANCIAL ANALYSTS IN THE FOOD INDUSTRY IN GREAT BRITAIN, 1999
Ranked by: Results of research undertaken by editorial staff of *Institutional Investor.* **Remarks:** May cite runners-up if applicable. Includes reason for selection. **Number listed:** 5
1. Alan Erskine (BT Alex. Brown)
2. Martin Dolan & team (Merrill Lynch)
3. Mark Lynch & team (Warburg Dillon Read)
4. Darren Chadwick & team (Dresdner Kleinwort Benson)
4. Claire Kent & team (Morgan Stanley Dean Witter)

Source: *Institutional Investor-International Edition,* All-Europe Research Team (annual), February, 1999, p. 85.

★2126★
TOP FINANCIAL ANALYSTS IN THE INSURANCE INDUSTRY IN GREAT BRITAIN, 1999
Ranked by: Results of research undertaken by editorial staff of *Institutional Investor.* **Remarks:** May cite runners-up if applicable. Includes reason for selection. **Number listed:** 4
1. Steven Bird (Merrill Lynch)
2. David Nisbet & team (BT Alex. Brown)
3. Ben Cohen & team (Warburg Dillon Read)
4. Jonathan Sheehan & team (Dresdner Kleinwort Benson)

Source: *Institutional Investor-International Edition,* All-Europe Research Team (annual), February, 1999, p. 85.

★2127★
TOP FINANCIAL ANALYSTS IN THE LEISURE AND HOTELS INDUSTRY IN GREAT BRITAIN, 1999
Ranked by: Results of research undertaken by editorial staff of *Institutional Investor.* **Remarks:** May cite runners-up if applicable. Includes reason for selection. **Number listed:** 5
1. Mark Finnie (BT Alex. Brown)
2. Julian Easthope & team (Warburg Dillon Read)
3. Bruce Jones & team (Merrill Lynch)
4. Max Dolding & team (HSBC Securities)
4. Simon Johnson (Credit Suisse First Boston)

Source: *Institutional Investor-International Edition,* All-Europe Research Team (annual), February, 1999, p. 86.

★2128★
TOP FINANCIAL ANALYSTS IN THE MEDIA INDUSTRY IN GREAT BRITAIN, 1999
Ranked by: Results of research undertaken by editorial staff of *Institutional Investor.* **Remarks:** May cite runners-up if applicable. Includes reason for selection. **Number listed:** 5
1. Neil Blackley (Merrill Lynch)
2. Richard Dale & team (Salomon Smith Barney)
3. Neill Junor & team (BT Alex. Brown)
4. Vighnesh Padiachy (Morgan Stanley Dean Witter)
4. Colin Tennant & team (Warburg Dillon Read)
4. Patrick Wellington (Schroeder Securities)

Source: *Institutional Investor-International Edition,* All-Europe Research Team (annual), February, 1999, p. 86.

★2129★
TOP FINANCIAL ANALYSTS IN THE OIL/ EXPLORATION AND PRODUCTION INDUSTRY IN GREAT BRITAIN, 1999
Ranked by: Results of research undertaken by editorial staff of *Institutional Investor.* **Remarks:** May cite runners-up if applicable. Includes reason for selection. **Number listed:** 4
1. Fergus MacLeod (BT Alex. Brown)
2. Iain Reid (Warburg Dillon Read)
3. Jonathan Wright (Merrill Lynch)

4. Gordon Hall & team (Credit Suisse First Boston)

Source: *Institutional Investor-International Edition*, All-Europe Research Team (annual), February, 1999, p. 89.

★2130★

TOP FINANCIAL ANALYSTS IN THE OIL/ INTEGRATED INDUSTRY IN GREAT BRITAIN, 1999

Ranked by: Results of research undertaken by editorial staff of *Institutional Investor*. **Remarks:** May cite runners-up if applicable. Includes reason for selection. **Number listed:** 4

1. Fergus MacLeod (BT Alex. Brown)
2. Alan MacDonald & team (Warburg Dillon Read)
3. Susan Graham & team (Merrill Lynch)
4. Rod Maclean & team (ABN Amro)

Source: *Institutional Investor-International Edition*, All-Europe Research Team (annual), February, 1999, p. 89.

★2131★

TOP FINANCIAL ANALYSTS IN THE PHARMACEUTICALS INDUSTRY IN GREAT BRITAIN, 1999

Ranked by: Results of research undertaken by editorial staff of *Institutional Investor*. **Remarks:** May cite runners-up if applicable. Includes reason for selection. **Number listed:** 4

1. Steve Plag (Credit Suisse First Boston)
2. James Culverwell & team (Merrill Lynch)
3. Duncan Moore (Morgan Stanley Dean Witter)
4. Anthony Colletta & team (ABN Amro)

Source: *Institutional Investor-International Edition*, All-Europe Research Team (annual), February, 1999, p. 90.

★2132★

TOP FINANCIAL ANALYSTS IN THE PROPERTY INDUSTRY IN GREAT BRITAIN, 1999

Ranked by: Results of research undertaken by editorial staff of *Institutional Investor*. **Remarks:** May cite runners-up if applicable. Includes reason for selection. **Number listed:** 3

1. Alec Pelmore (Merrill Lynch)
2. Alan Carter & team (Credit Suisse First Boston)
3. Roger Moore & team (Warburg Dillon Read)

Source: *Institutional Investor-International Edition*, All-Europe Research Team (annual), February, 1999, p. 90.

★2133★

TOP FINANCIAL ANALYSTS IN THE RETAILING/ FOOD INDUSTRY IN GREAT BRITAIN, 1999

Ranked by: Results of research undertaken by editorial staff of *Institutional Investor*. **Remarks:** May cite runners-up if applicable. Includes reason for selection. **Number listed:** 5

1. Andrew Fowler (Morgan Stanley Dean Witter)
2. David McCarthy (BT Alex. Brown)
3. Sara Carter (Merrill Lynch)
4. James Edwardes-Jones & team (Credit Suisse First Boston)
4. Andrew Kasoulis (Warburg Dillon Read)

Source: *Institutional Investor-International Edition*, All-Europe Research Team (annual), February, 1999, p. 91.

★2134★

TOP FINANCIAL ANALYSTS IN THE RETAILING/ GENERAL INDUSTRY IN GREAT BRITAIN, 1999

Ranked by: Results of research undertaken by editorial staff of *Institutional Investor*. **Remarks:** May cite runners-up if applicable. Includes reason for selection. **Number listed:** 3

1. Andrew Hughes (Warburg Dillon Read)
2. Nicholas Hawkins & team (Merrill Lynch)
3. Tony Shiret & team (Credit Suisse First Boston)

Source: *Institutional Investor-International Edition*, All-Europe Research Team (annual), February, 1999, p. 91.

★2135★

TOP FINANCIAL ANALYSTS IN THE SUPPORT SERVICES INDUSTRY IN GREAT BRITAIN, 1999

Ranked by: Results of research undertaken by editorial staff of *Institutional Investor*. **Remarks:** May cite runners-up if applicable. Includes reason for selection. **Number listed:** 3

1. Andrew Ripper (Merrill Lynch)
2. Paul Morland & team (BT Alex. Brown)
3. Mark Shepperd & team (Warburg Dillon Read)

Source: *Institutional Investor-International Edition*, All-Europe Research Team (annual), February, 1999, p. 92.

★2136★

TOP FINANCIAL ANALYSTS IN THE TELECOMMUNICATIONS INDUSTRY IN GREAT BRITAIN, 1999

Ranked by: Results of research undertaken by editorial staff of *Institutional Investor*. **Remarks:** May cite runners-up if applicable. Includes reason for selection. **Number listed:** 4

1. Mark Lambert (Merrill Lynch)
2. Paul Marsch (Morgan Stanley Dean Witter)
3. Patrick Earle & team (Warburg Dillon Read)
4. Jane Bidmead (Dresdner Kleinwort Benson)

Source: *Institutional Investor-International Edition*, All-Europe Research Team (annual), February, 1999, p. 92.

★2137★

TOP FINANCIAL ANALYSTS IN THE TRANSPORTATION INDUSTRY IN GREAT BRITAIN, 1999

Ranked by: Results of research undertaken by editorial staff of *Institutional Investor*. **Remarks:** May cite runners-up if applicable. Includes reason for selection. **Number listed:** 5

1. Clive Anderson (Merrill Lynch)
2. Peter Hyde & team (Credit Suisse First Boston)
3. Richard Hannah & team (BT Alex. Brown)
4. Andrew Barker & team (Warburg Dillon Read)
4. Matthew Owen & team (HSBC Securities)

Source: *Institutional Investor-International Edition*, All-Europe Research Team (annual), February, 1999, p. 93.

★2138★

TOP FINANCIAL ANALYSTS IN THE WATER INDUSTRY IN GREAT BRITAIN, 1999

Ranked by: Results of research undertaken by editorial staff of *Institutional Investor*. **Remarks:** May cite runners-up if applicable. Includes reason for selection. **Number listed:** 3

1. William Dale (Warburg Dillon Read)
2. Robert Miller-Bakewell & team (Merrill Lynch)
3. Richard Smith & team (Deutsche Bank Securities)

Source: *Institutional Investor-International Edition*, All-Europe Research Team (annual), February, 1999, p. 93.

Financial Analysts--Hong Kong

★2139★

TOP FINANCIAL ANALYSTS COVERING HONG KONG, 1999

Ranked by: Results of research undertaken by editorial staff of *Institutional Investor*. **Remarks:** May cite runners-up if applicable. Includes reason for selection. **Number listed:** 4

1. Dio Wong (CLSA Global Emerging Markets)
2. Colin Bradbury & team (Jardine Fleming Securities)
3. Simon Rogers & team (Warburg Dillon Read)
4. Adrian Faure & team (Merrill Lynch)

Source: *Institutional Investor-International Edition*, All-Asia Research Team (annual), April, 1999, p. 78.

Financial Analysts--Hungary

★2140★
TOP FINANCIAL ANALYSTS COVERING HUNGARY, 1999
Ranked by: Results of research undertaken by editorial staff of *Institutional Investor.* **Remarks:** May cite runners-up if applicable. Includes reason for selection. **Number listed:** 4
1. Spencer Jakab (Credit Suisse First Boston)
2. Thomas Chadwick & team (Merrill Lynch)
3. Katalin Dani & team (CA IB Securities)
4. Norbert Toth & team (ING Barings)

Source: *Institutional Investor-International Edition,* All-Europe Research Team (annual), February, 1999, p. 112.

Financial Analysts--India

★2141★
TOP FINANCIAL ANALYSTS COVERING INDIA, 1999
Ranked by: Results of research undertaken by editorial staff of *Institutional Investor.* **Remarks:** May cite runners-up if applicable. Includes reason for selection. **Number listed:** 4
1. Vineet Nagrani (Morgan Stanley Dean Witter)
2. Andrew Holland & team (DSP Merrill Lynch)
3. Nitin Anandkar & team (Jardine Fleming Securities)
4. Ratnesh Kumar & team (CLSA Global Emerging Markets)

Source: *Institutional Investor-International Edition,* All-Asia Research Team (annual), April, 1999, p. 78+.

Financial Analysts--Indonesia

★2142★
TOP FINANCIAL ANALYSTS COVERING INDONESIA, 1999
Ranked by: Results of research undertaken by editorial staff of *Institutional Investor.* **Remarks:** May cite runners-up if applicable. Includes reason for selection. **Number listed:** 6
1. Peter Sutton (CLSA Global Emerging Markets)
2. Stephan Hasjim & team (Warburg Dillon Read)
3. Charles Whitworth & team (Jardine Fleming Securities)
4. Irwan Junus & team (Indosuez W.I. Carr Securities)
4. Laksono Widodo & team (ING Barings)
4. Alex Wreksoremboko & team (Merrill Lynch)

Source: *Institutional Investor-International Edition,* All-Asia Research Team (annual), April, 1999, p. 79.

Financial Analysts--Ireland

★2143★
TOP FINANCIAL ANALYSTS COVERING IRELAND, 1999
Ranked by: Results of research undertaken by editorial staff of *Institutional Investor.* **Remarks:** May cite runners-up if applicable. Includes reason for selection. **Number listed:** 2
1. Robert Kelleher (Davy Stockbrokers)
2. John Conroy & team (NCB Stockbrokers)

Source: *Institutional Investor-International Edition,* All-Europe Research Team (annual), February, 1999, p. 112.

Financial Analysts--Italy

★2144★
TOP FINANCIAL ANALYSTS COVERING ITALY, 1999
Ranked by: Results of research undertaken by editorial staff of *Institutional Investor.* **Remarks:** May cite runners-up if applicable. Includes reason for selection. **Number listed:** 4
1. Roberto Condulmari (Giubergia Warburg)
2. Stefano Alberti & team (Intermobiliare Securities)
3. Gianpaolo Trasi & team (Banca IMI)
4. Marco Cipelletti & team (Cia. Italiana Mobiliare)

Source: *Institutional Investor-International Edition,* All-Europe Research Team (annual), February, 1999, p. 113.

Financial Analysts--Japan

★2145★
JAPANESE INVESTMENT FIRMS WITH THE MOST ANALYSTS ON THE ALL-ASIA RESEARCH TEAM, 1999
Ranked by: Total number of positions investment firm has on team. **Remarks:** Also notes previous year's rank, total team positions for both years, total first-, second-, and third-team positions for both years, and runners-up for both years. **Number listed:** 12
1. Nomura, with 23 positions
2. Morgan Stanley Dean Witter, 19
3. Merrill Lynch Japan, 17
4. Goldman Sachs (Japan), 12
5. Nikko Salomon Smith Barney, 11
6. Daiwa Institute of Research, 8
7. Warburg Dillon Read, 6
8. Deutsche Bank Securities, 5
8. Dresdner Kleinwort Benson (Asia), 5
8. HSBC Securities (Japan), 5

Source: *Institutional Investor-International Edition,* All-Asia Research Team (annual), April, 1999, p. 92.

★2146★
TOP FINANCIAL ANALYSTS IN ECONOMICS IN JAPAN, 1999
Ranked by: Results of research undertaken by editorial staff of *Institutional Investor.* **Remarks:** May also cite runners-up, if applicable. Includes reason for selection. **Number listed:** 4
1. Robert Alan Feldman (Morgan Stanley Dean Witter)
2. Richard Koo (Nomura)
3. Kazuhide Uekusa (Nomura)
4. Tetsufumi Yamakawa (Goldman Sachs Japan)

Source: *Institutional Investor-International Edition,* All-Asia Research Team (annual), April, 1999, p. 109.

★2147★
TOP FINANCIAL ANALYSTS IN EQUITY STRATEGY IN JAPAN, 1999
Ranked by: Results of research undertaken by editorial staff of *Institutional Investor.* **Remarks:** May also cite runners-up, if applicable. Includes reason for selection. **Number listed:** 4

1. Chisato Haganuma (Nomura)
2. Alexander Kinmont (Morgan Stanley Dean Witter)
3. Kathy Matsui (Goldman Sachs Japan)
4. Ryoji Musha (Deutsche Securities)

Source: *Institutional Investor-International Edition*, All-Asia Research Team (annual), April, 1999, p. 109.

★2148★
TOP FINANCIAL ANALYSTS IN FINANCIALS/ BANKS IN JAPAN, 1999
Ranked by: Results of research undertaken by editorial staff of *Institutional Investor*. **Remarks:** May also cite runners-up, if applicable. Includes reason for selection. **Number listed:** 3

1. Yoshinobu Yamada (Merrill Lynch Japan)
2. Yukiko Ohara (Morgan Stanley Dean Witter)
3. David Atkinson (Goldman Sachs Japan)

Source: *Institutional Investor-International Edition*, All-Asia Research Team (annual), April, 1999, p. 102.

★2149★
TOP FINANCIAL ANALYSTS IN FINANCIALS/ OTHER IN JAPAN, 1999
Ranked by: Results of research undertaken by editorial staff of *Institutional Investor*. **Remarks:** May also cite runners-up, if applicable. Includes reason for selection. **Number listed:** 3

1. Shin Maeda (Nomura)
2. Ayako Sato (Warburg Dillon Read)
3. Hideyasu Ban (Morgan Stanley Dean Witter)

Source: *Institutional Investor-International Edition*, All-Asia Research Team (annual), April, 1999, p. 102.

★2150★
TOP FINANCIAL ANALYSTS IN FIXED-INCOME STRATEGY IN JAPAN, 1999
Ranked by: Results of research undertaken by editorial staff of *Institutional Investor*. **Remarks:** May also cite runners-up, if applicable. Includes reason for selection. **Number listed:** 2

1. Atsushi Mizuno (Deutsche Securities)
2. Masuhisa Kobayashi (Merrill Lynch Japan)

Source: *Institutional Investor-International Edition*, All-Asia Research Team (annual), April, 1999, p. 110.

★2151★
TOP FINANCIAL ANALYSTS IN QUANTITATIVE RESEARCH IN JAPAN, 1999
Ranked by: Results of research undertaken by editorial staff of *Institutional Investor*. **Remarks:** May also cite runners-up, if applicable. Includes reason for selection. **Number listed:** 4

1. Fumiyuki Takahashi (Morgan Stanley Dean Witter)
2. Patrick Mohr (Merrill Lynch Japan)
3. Takashi Ito (Nomura)
4. Takeshi Kurosawa (Nikko Salomon Smith Barney)

Source: *Institutional Investor-International Edition*, All-Asia Research Team (annual), April, 1999, p. 110+.

★2152★
TOP FINANCIAL ANALYSTS IN SMALL AND OTC COMPANIES IN JAPAN, 1999
Ranked by: Results of research undertaken by editorial staff of *Institutional Investor*. **Remarks:** May also cite runners-up, if applicable. Includes reason for selection. **Number listed:** 4

1. Tadashi Ohta (Jardine Fleming Securities Asia)
2. Noboru Terashima (Goldman Sachs Japan)
3. Kiyohisa Hirano (Daiwa Institute of Research)
4. Mahendra Negi (Merrill Lynch Japan)

Source: *Institutional Investor-International Edition*, All-Asia Research Team (annual), April, 1999, p. 106.

★2153★
TOP FINANCIAL ANALYSTS IN TECHNICAL ANALYSIS IN JAPAN, 1999
Ranked by: Results of research undertaken by editorial staff of *Institutional Investor*. **Remarks:** May also cite runners-up, if applicable. Includes reason for selection. **Number listed:** 2

1. Hidenobu Sasaki (Nikko Salomon Smith Barney)
2. Tatsuo Kurokawa (Nomura)

Source: *Institutional Investor-International Edition*, All-Asia Research Team (annual), April, 1999, p. 111.

★2154★
TOP FINANCIAL ANALYSTS IN THE AUTOMOBILE INDUSTRY IN JAPAN, 1999
Ranked by: Results of research undertaken by editorial staff of *Institutional Investor*. **Remarks:** May also cite runners-up, if applicable. Includes reason for selection. **Number listed:** 4

1. Noriyuki Matsushima (Nikko Salomon Smith Barney)
2. Koji Endo (Schroders Japan)
3. Takaki Nakanishi (Merrill Lynch Japan)
4. Seiji Sugiura (Nomura)

Source: *Institutional Investor-International Edition*, All-Asia Research Team (annual), April, 1999, p. 95.

★2155★
TOP FINANCIAL ANALYSTS IN THE AUTOMOBILE PARTS INDUSTRY IN JAPAN, 1999
Ranked by: Results of research undertaken by editorial staff of *Institutional Investor*. **Remarks:** May also cite runners-up, if applicable. Includes reason for selection. **Number listed:** 4

1. Koichi Sugimoto (Nomura)
2. Shinji Kakiuchi (Daiwa Institute of Research)
3. Kunihiko Shiohara (ING Baring Securities Japan)
4. Koji Endo (Schroders Japan)

Source: *Institutional Investor-International Edition*, All-Asia Research Team (annual), April, 1999, p. 95.

★2156★
TOP FINANCIAL ANALYSTS IN THE BASIC MATERIALS/CHEMICALS INDUSTRY IN JAPAN, 1999
Ranked by: Results of research undertaken by editorial staff of *Institutional Investor*. **Remarks:** May also cite runners-up, if applicable. Includes reason for selection. **Number listed:** 4

1. Toshihiko Ginbayashi (Morgan Stanley Dean Witter)
2. Takao Kanai (Dresdner Kleinwort Benson Asia)
3. Tommy Tang (Merrill Lynch Japan)
4. Yuichi Fujimoto (Deutsche Securities)

Source: *Institutional Investor-International Edition*, All-Asia Research Team (annual), April, 1999, p. 96.

★2157★
TOP FINANCIAL ANALYSTS IN THE BASIC MATERIALS/ENERGY INDUSTRY IN JAPAN, 1999
Ranked by: Results of research undertaken by editorial staff of *Institutional Investor*. **Remarks:** May also cite runners-up, if applicable. Includes reason for selection. **Number listed:** 3

1. Toshinori Ito (HSBC Securities Japan)
2. Lalita Gupta (Deutsche Securities)
3. Masaru Okawa (Nomura)

Source: *Institutional Investor-International Edition*, All-Asia Research Team (annual), April, 1999, p. 96.

★2158★
TOP FINANCIAL ANALYSTS IN THE BASIC MATERIALS/METALS INDUSTRY IN JAPAN, 1999
Ranked by: Results of research undertaken by editorial staff of *Institutional Investor*. **Remarks:** May also cite runners-up, if applicable. Includes reason for selection. **Number listed:** 4

1. Toru Nagai (Morgan Stanley Dean Witter)

2. Kenichiro Yoshida (Nikko Salomon Smith Barney)
3. Makoto Hiranuma (Nomura)
4. Atsushi Yamaguchi (Jardine Fleming Securities Asia)

Source: *Institutional Investor-International Edition*, All-Asia Research Team (annual), April, 1999, p. 97.

★2159★
TOP FINANCIAL ANALYSTS IN THE BASIC MATERIALS/PAPER INDUSTRY IN JAPAN, 1999
Ranked by: Results of research undertaken by editorial staff of *Institutional Investor.* **Remarks:** May also cite runners-up, if applicable. Includes reason for selection. **Number listed:** 5

1. Shinsuke Iwasa (Nomura)
2. William Gallagher (Schroders Japan)
3. Takato Watabe (Daiwa Institute of Research)
4. Eiichi Katayama (Nomura)
4. Chiharu Shima (Paribas Capital Markets)

Source: *Institutional Investor-International Edition*, All-Asia Research Team (annual), April, 1999, p. 97.

★2160★
TOP FINANCIAL ANALYSTS IN THE BASIC MATERIALS/TEXTILES INDUSTRY IN JAPAN, 1999
Ranked by: Results of research undertaken by editorial staff of *Institutional Investor.* **Remarks:** May also cite runners-up, if applicable. Includes reason for selection. **Number listed:** 3

1. Shuichi Nishimura (Nomura)
2. Takato Watabe (Daiwa Institute of Research)
3. Tommy Tang (Merrill Lynch Japan)

Source: *Institutional Investor-International Edition*, All-Asia Research Team (annual), April, 1999, p. 98.

★2161★
TOP FINANCIAL ANALYSTS IN THE BROADCASTING INDUSTRY IN JAPAN, 1999
Ranked by: Results of research undertaken by editorial staff of *Institutional Investor.* **Remarks:** May also cite runners-up, if applicable. Includes reason for selection. **Number listed:** 4

1. Tomoyasu Kato (Nomura)
2. Paul Smith (HSBC Securities Japan)
3. Hironori Tanaka (Morgan Stanley Dean Witter)
4. Kota Nakako (Warburg Dillon Read)

Source: *Institutional Investor-International Edition*, All-Asia Research Team (annual), April, 1999, p. 98.

★2162★
TOP FINANCIAL ANALYSTS IN THE COMPUTER SOFTWARE INDUSTRY IN JAPAN, 1999
Ranked by: Results of research undertaken by editorial staff of *Institutional Investor.* **Remarks:** May also cite runners-up, if applicable. Includes reason for selection. **Number listed:** 5

1. Mitsuko Morita (Morgan Stanley Dean Witter)
2. Naoko Ito (Goldman Sachs Japan)
3. Yasuo Imanaka (Commerz Securities Japan)
4. Mahendra Negi (Merrill Lynch Japan)
4. Hiroyuki Ono (Nomura)

Source: *Institutional Investor-International Edition*, All-Asia Research Team (annual), April, 1999, p. 99.

★2163★
TOP FINANCIAL ANALYSTS IN THE ELECTRONICS/COMPONENTS INDUSTRY IN JAPAN, 1999
Ranked by: Results of research undertaken by editorial staff of *Institutional Investor.* **Remarks:** May also cite runners-up, if applicable. Includes reason for selection. **Number listed:** 5

1. Hisanori Shimoi (Nikko Salomon Smith Barney)
2. Eisaku Ohmori (Dresdner Kleinwort Benson Asia)
3. Hiroshi Takada (ABN Amro Securities Japan)
4. Fumihide Goto (Daiwa Institute of Research)
4. Takatoshi Yamamoto (Morgan Stanley Dean Witter)

Source: *Institutional Investor-International Edition*, All-Asia Research Team (annual), April, 1999, p. 99+.

★2164★
TOP FINANCIAL ANALYSTS IN THE ELECTRONICS/CONSUMER INDUSTRY IN JAPAN, 1999
Ranked by: Results of research undertaken by editorial staff of *Institutional Investor.* **Remarks:** May also cite runners-up, if applicable. Includes reason for selection. **Number listed:** 4

1. Takatoshi Yamamoto (Morgan Stanley Dean Witter)
2. Kiyotaka Teranishi (Goldman Sachs Japan)
3. Hitoshi Kuriyama (Merrill Lynch Japan)
4. Masami Fujino (Jardine Fleming Securities Asia)

Source: *Institutional Investor-International Edition*, All-Asia Research Team (annual), April, 1999, p. 100.

★2165★
TOP FINANCIAL ANALYSTS IN THE ELECTRONICS/INDUSTRIAL INDUSTRY IN JAPAN, 1999
Ranked by: Results of research undertaken by editorial staff of *Institutional Investor.* **Remarks:** May also cite runners-up, if applicable. Includes reason for selection. **Number listed:** 3

1. Hideki Wakabayashi (Dresdner Kleinwort Benson Asia)
2. Takatoshi Yamamoto (Morgan Stanley Dean Witter)
3. Fumiaki Sato (Deutsche Securities)

Source: *Institutional Investor-International Edition*, All-Asia Research Team (annual), April, 1999, p. 100+.

★2166★
TOP FINANCIAL ANALYSTS IN THE ELECTRONICS/PRECISION INSTRUMENTS INDUSTRY IN JAPAN, 1999
Ranked by: Results of research undertaken by editorial staff of *Institutional Investor.* **Remarks:** May also cite runners-up, if applicable. Includes reason for selection. **Number listed:** 3

1. Hiroshi Yoshihara (Nikko Salomon Smith Barney)
2. Kimihide Takano (Dresdner Kleinwort Benson Asia)
3. Noriko Oki (Morgan Stanley Dean Witter)

Source: *Institutional Investor-International Edition*, All-Asia Research Team (annual), April, 1999, p. 101.

★2167★
TOP FINANCIAL ANALYSTS IN THE FOOD AND BEVERAGE INDUSTRY IN JAPAN, 1999
Ranked by: Results of research undertaken by editorial staff of *Institutional Investor.* **Remarks:** May also cite runners-up, if applicable. Includes reason for selection. **Number listed:** 5

1. Shuichi Shibanuma (Merrill Lynch Japan)
2. Masaaki Yamaguchi (Nomura)
3. Tsutomu Matsuno (Daiwa Institute of Research)
4. Taizo Demura (Morgan Stanley Dean Witter)
4. Yuji Fujimori (Goldman Sachs Japan)

Source: *Institutional Investor-International Edition*, All-Asia Research Team (annual), April, 1999, p. 102+.

★2168★
TOP FINANCIAL ANALYSTS IN THE MACHINERY INDUSTRY IN JAPAN, 1999
Ranked by: Results of research undertaken by editorial staff of *Institutional Investor.* **Remarks:** May also cite runners-up, if applicable. Includes reason for selection. **Number listed:** 4

1. Hidehiko Hoshino (Jardine Fleming Securities Asia)
2. Fumihiko Nakazawa (Merrill Lynch Japan)
3. Katsushi Saito (Nomura)
4. Masayuki Mochizuki (Morgan Stanley Dean Witter)

Source: *Institutional Investor-International Edition*, All-Asia Research Team (annual), April, 1999, p. 103.

★2169★

TOP FINANCIAL ANALYSTS IN THE PHARMACEUTICALS AND HEALTH CARE INDUSTRY IN JAPAN, 1999

Ranked by: Results of research undertaken by editorial staff of *Institutional Investor.* **Remarks:** May also cite runners-up, if applicable. Includes reason for selection. **Number listed:** 5

1. Yoshihiko Yamamoto (Nikko Salomon Smith Barney)
2. Mayo Mita (Morgan Stanley Dean Witter)
3. Shigeru Mishima (Warburg Dillon Read)
4. Shunji Katayama (Goldman Sachs Japan)
4. Masatake Miyoshi (Merrill Lynch Japan)

Source: *Institutional Investor-International Edition*, All-Asia Research Team (annual), April, 1999, p. 103+.

★2170★

TOP FINANCIAL ANALYSTS IN THE REAL ESTATE AND HOUSING INDUSTRY IN JAPAN, 1999

Ranked by: Results of research undertaken by editorial staff of *Institutional Investor.* **Remarks:** May also cite runners-up, if applicable. Includes reason for selection. **Number listed:** 6

1. Takashi Hashimoto (Nikko Salomon Smith Barney)
2. Junichi Shiomoto (Goldman Sachs Japan)
3. Rie Murayama (Goldman Sachs Japan)
4. Yoshihiro Hashimoto (Merrill Lynch Japan)
4. Etsusuki Masuda (HSBC Securities Japan)
4. Keiko Otsuki (Morgan Stanley Dean Witter)

Source: *Institutional Investor-International Edition*, All-Asia Research Team (annual), April, 1999, p. 104.

★2171★

TOP FINANCIAL ANALYSTS IN THE RETAILING/ GENERAL INDUSTRY IN JAPAN, 1999

Ranked by: Results of research undertaken by editorial staff of *Institutional Investor.* **Remarks:** May also cite runners-up, if applicable. Includes reason for selection. **Number listed:** 4

1. Masahiro Matsuoka (Warburg Dillon Read)
2. Yukihiro Moroe (Goldman Sachs Japan)
3. Masafumi Shouda (Nomura)
4. Michinori Shimizu (Morgan Stanley Dean Witter)

Source: *Institutional Investor-International Edition*, All-Asia Research Team (annual), April, 1999, p. 104+.

★2172★

TOP FINANCIAL ANALYSTS IN THE RETAILING/ SPECIALTY INDUSTRY IN JAPAN, 1999

Ranked by: Results of research undertaken by editorial staff of *Institutional Investor.* **Remarks:** May also cite runners-up, if applicable. Includes reason for selection. **Number listed:** 4

1. Eizo Uchikura (Goldman Sachs Japan)
2. Takayuki Suzuki (Merrill Lynch Japan)
3. Masahiro Matsuoka (Warburg Dillon Read)
4. Keiichi Nakabayashi (Warburg Dillon Read)

Source: *Institutional Investor-International Edition*, All-Asia Research Team (annual), April, 1999, p. 105.

★2173★

TOP FINANCIAL ANALYSTS IN THE SHIPBUILDING AND PLANT ENGINEERING INDUSTRY IN JAPAN, 1999

Ranked by: Results of research undertaken by editorial staff of *Institutional Investor.* **Remarks:** May also cite runners-up, if applicable. Includes reason for selection. **Number listed:** 3

1. Akira Sato (Nomura)
2. Minoru Kawahara (Nikko Salomon Smith Barney)
3. Mitsutoshi Murakata (Kokusai Securities)

Source: *Institutional Investor-International Edition*, All-Asia Research Team (annual), April, 1999, p. 105+.

★2174★

TOP FINANCIAL ANALYSTS IN THE TELECOMMUNICATIONS INDUSTRY IN JAPAN, 1999

Ranked by: Results of research undertaken by editorial staff of *Institutional Investor.* **Remarks:** May also cite runners-up, if applicable. Includes reason for selection. **Number listed:** 3

1. Eric Gan (Goldman Sachs Japan)
2. Kiyohisa Ota (Merrill Lynch Japan)
3. Makio Inui (Nikko Salomon Smith Barney)

Source: *Institutional Investor-International Edition*, All-Asia Research Team (annual), April, 1999, p. 106+.

★2175★

TOP FINANCIAL ANALYSTS IN THE TRANSPORTATION INDUSTRY IN JAPAN, 1999

Ranked by: Results of research undertaken by editorial staff of *Institutional Investor.* **Remarks:** May also cite runners-up, if applicable. Includes reason for selection. **Number listed:** 6

1. Naoto Hashimoto (Nomura)
2. Naoko Matsumoto (Merrill Lynch Japan)
3. Masahiro Kubo (Daiwa Institute of Research)
4. Laurent Del Grande (Dresdner Kleinwort Benson Asia)
4. Douglas Hayashi (HSBC Securities Japan)
4. Tomokazu Soejima (Morgan Stanley Dean Witter)

Source: *Institutional Investor-International Edition*, All-Asia Research Team (annual), April, 1999, p. 108.

★2176★

TOP FINANCIAL ANALYSTS IN TRADING COMPANIES IN JAPAN, 1999

Ranked by: Results of research undertaken by editorial staff of *Institutional Investor.* **Remarks:** May also cite runners-up, if applicable. Includes reason for selection. **Number listed:** 3

1. Kenichiro Yoshida (Nikko Salomon Smith Barney)
2. Tomoyasu Kato (Nomura)
3. Matt Aizawa (Merrill Lynch Japan)

Source: *Institutional Investor-International Edition*, All-Asia Research Team (annual), April, 1999, p. 107.

★2177★

TOP FINANCIAL ANALYSTS IN UTILITIES IN JAPAN, 1999

Ranked by: Results of research undertaken by editorial staff of *Institutional Investor.* **Remarks:** May also cite runners-up, if applicable. Includes reason for selection. **Number listed:** 3

1. Naoto Hashimoto (Nomura)
2. Paul Smith (HSBC Securities Japan)
3. Masanori Maruo (Daiwa Institute of Research)

Source: *Institutional Investor-International Edition*, All-Asia Research Team (annual), April, 1999, p. 108.

Financial Analysts--Korea (South)

★2178★

TOP FINANCIAL ANALYSTS COVERING SOUTH KOREA, 1999

Ranked by: Results of research undertaken by editorial staff of *Institutional Investor.* **Remarks:** May cite runners-up if applicable. Includes reason for selection. **Number listed:** 3

1. Stephen Marvin (Jardine Fleming Securities)
2. Richard Samuelson & team (Warburg Dillon Read)
3. Hunsoo Kim & team (Merrill Lynch)

Source: *Institutional Investor-International Edition*, All-Asia Research Team (annual), April, 1999, p. 82.

Financial Analysts--Malaysia

★2179★
TOP FINANCIAL ANALYSTS COVERING MALAYSIA, 1999
Ranked by: Results of research undertaken by editorial staff of *Institutional Investor.* **Remarks:** May cite runners-up if applicable. Includes reason for selection. **Number listed:** 5
1. Amar Gill (CLSA Global Emerging Markets)
2. Leong Fee Yee & team (Warburg Dillon Read)
3. Stephen Weller & team (Jardine Fleming Securities)
4. Richard Jones & team (ING Barings)
4. Yeoh Keat Seng & team (Merrill Lynch)

Source: *Institutional Investor-International Edition*, All-Asia Research Team (annual), April, 1999, p. 79.

Financial Analysts--Netherlands

★2180★
TOP FINANCIAL ANALYSTS COVERING THE NETHERLANDS, 1999
Ranked by: Results of research undertaken by editorial staff of *Institutional Investor.* **Remarks:** May cite runners-up if applicable. Includes reason for selection. **Number listed:** 4
1. Frans Van Schaik (ABN Amro)
2. Herman van Everdigen & team (Kempen & Co.)
3. Thibaud de Guerre & team (ING Barings)
4. Roel Gooskens & team (Van Meer James Capel)

Source: *Institutional Investor-International Edition*, All-Europe Research Team (annual), February, 1999, p. 113+.

Financial Analysts--New Zealand

★2181★
TOP FINANCIAL ANALYSTS COVERING NEW ZEALAND, 1999
Ranked by: Results of research undertaken by editorial staff of *Institutional Investor.* **Remarks:** May cite runners-up if applicable. Includes reason for selection. **Number listed:** 6
1. Doug Smaill (J.B. Were & Son)
2. Andrew Bascand & team (BT Alex. Brown)
3. Michael Brown & team (Merrill Lynch)
4. Tony Brennan & team (Warburg Dillon Read)
4. Ewen Griffiths & team (Ord Minnett Securities NZ)
4. Stephen Hudson & team (Salomon Smith Barney)

Source: *Institutional Investor-International Edition*, All-Asia Research Team (annual), April, 1999, p. 80.

Financial Analysts--Philippines

★2182★
TOP FINANCIAL ANALYSTS COVERING THE PHILIPPINES, 1999
Ranked by: Results of research undertaken by editorial staff of *Institutional Investor.* **Remarks:** May also cite runners-up, if applicable. Includes reason for selection. **Number listed:** 3
1. Joven Babaan (Jardine Fleming Securities)
2. Alexander Pomento & team (Merrill Lynch)
3. Xen Gladstone & team (ING Barings)

Source: *Institutional Investor-International Edition*, All-Asia Research Team (annual), April, 1999, p. 81.

Financial Analysts--Poland

★2183★
TOP FINANCIAL ANALYSTS COVERING POLAND, 1999
Ranked by: Results of research undertaken by editorial staff of *Institutional Investor.* **Remarks:** May also cite runners-up, if applicable. Includes reason for selection. **Number listed:** 3
1. Andrzej Nowaczek (Credit Suisse First Boston)
2. Stephen Pettyfer & team (Merrill Lynch)
3. Andreas Madej & team (ABN Amro)

Source: *Institutional Investor-International Edition*, All-Europe Research Team (annual), February, 1999, p. 115.

Financial Analysts--Russia

★2184★
TOP FINANCIAL ANALYSTS COVERING RUSSIA, 1999
Ranked by: Results of research undertaken by editorial staff of *Institutional Investor.* **Remarks:** May also cite runners-up, if applicable. Includes reason for selection. **Number listed:** 4
1. Julia Baeva (Credit Suisse First Boston)
2. Par Mellstrom & team (Brunswick Warburg)
3. John-Paul Smith & team (Morgan Stanley Dean Witter)
4. Dan Lubash & team (Merrill Lynch)

Source: *Institutional Investor-International Edition*, All-Europe Research Team (annual), February, 1999, p. 115.

Financial Analysts--Scandinavia

★2185★
TOP FINANCIAL ANALYSTS COVERING SCANDINAVIA, 1999
Ranked by: Results of research undertaken by editorial staff of *Institutional Investor.* **Remarks:** May also cite runners-up, if applicable. Includes reason for selection. **Number listed:** 3
1. Ulf Stromsten (Alfred Berg)
2. Fredrik Nygren & team (Enskilda Securities)
3. Tommy Erixon (D. Carnegie)

Source: *Institutional Investor-International Edition*, All-Europe Research Team (annual), February, 1999, p. 114.

Financial Analysts--Singapore

★2186★
TOP FINANCIAL ANALYSTS COVERING SINGAPORE
Ranked by: Results of research undertaken by editorial staff of *Institutional Investor.* **Remarks:** May also cite runners-up, if applicable. Includes reason for selection. **Number listed:** 4

1. Jason Wee (CLSA Global Emerging Markets)
2. Olivier Stocker & team (Jardine Fleming Securities)
3. Tan Sin Mui & team (Merrill Lynch)
4. Lim Chung Chun & team (ING Barings)

Source: *Institutional Investor-International Edition*, All-Asia Research Team (annual), April, 1999, p. 81+.

Financial Analysts--South Africa

★2187★
TOP FINANCIAL ANALYSTS COVERING SOUTH AFRICA, 1999
Ranked by: Results of research undertaken by editorial staff of *Institutional Investor*. **Remarks:** May also cite runners-up, if applicable. Includes reason for selection. **Number listed:** 4

1. Murray Winckler (Deutsche Bank Securities)
2. Francois Gouws & team (Warburg Dillon Read)
3. Jerome O'Regan & team (Fleming Martin Securities)
4. John Morris & team (Merrill Lynch)

Source: *Institutional Investor-International Edition*, All-Europe Research Team (annual), February, 1999, p. 116.

Financial Analysts--Spain

★2188★
TOP FINANCIAL ANALYSTS COVERING SPAIN, 1999
Ranked by: Results of research undertaken by editorial staff of *Institutional Investor*. **Remarks:** May also cite runners-up, if applicable. Includes reason for selection. **Number listed:** 4

1. Alberto Sanchez (Santander Investment)
2. Mark Giacopazzi & team (Schroeder & Co.)
3. Juan Luis Perez & team (AB Asesores)
4. Javier Echanove & team (Warburg Dillon Read)

Source: *Institutional Investor-International Edition*, All-Europe Research Team (annual), February, 1999, p. 117.

Financial Analysts--Switzerland

★2189★
TOP FINANCIAL ANALYSTS COVERING SWITZERLAND, 1999
Ranked by: Results of research undertaken by editorial staff of *Institutional Investor*. **Remarks:** May also cite runners-up, if applicable. Includes reason for selection. **Number listed:** 5

1. Andreas Vogler (Warburg Dillon Read)
2. Mirko Sangiorgio & team (Pictet & Cie.)
3. Hans Kaufman & team (Bank Julius Baer)
4. Thomas Pfyl & team (Bank J. Vontobel & Co.)
4. Theresia Tolxdorff & team (Credit Suisse First Boston)

Source: *Institutional Investor-International Edition*, All-Europe Research Team (annual), February, 1999, p. 117.

Financial Analysts--Taiwan

★2190★
TOP FINANCIAL ANALYSTS COVERING TAIWAN, 1999
Ranked by: Results of research undertaken by editorial staff of *Institutional Investor*. **Remarks:** May also cite runners-up, if applicable. Includes reason for selection. **Number listed:** 4

1. Daniel Hellberg (Warburg Dillon Read)
2. Peter Kurz & team (Merrill Lynch)
3. Jonathan Ross & team (ABN Amro Asia)
4. Jeffrey Toder & team (Jardine Fleming Securities)

Source: *Institutional Investor-International Edition*, All-Asia Research Team (annual), April, 1999, p. 82+.

Financial Analysts--Thailand

★2191★
TOP FINANCIAL ANALYSTS COVERING THAILAND, 1999
Ranked by: Results of research undertaken by editorial staff of *Institutional Investor*. **Remarks:** May also cite runners-up, if applicable. Includes reason for selection. **Number listed:** 4

1. Daniel Tabbush (CLSA Global Emerging Markets)
2. Scott Christensen & team (Jardine Fleming Securities)
3. Timothy Taylor & team (Warburg Dillon Read)
4. Asoke Wongcha-um & team (Merrill Lynch Phatra Securities Co.)

Source: *Institutional Investor-International Edition*, All-Asia Research Team (annual), April, 1999, p. 83.

Financial Companies

See: **Financial Institutions**

Financial Institutions

★2192★
TOP DIVERSIFIED FINANCIAL COMPANIES, 1998
Ranked by: Revenue, in millions of dollars. **Remarks:** Also notes profits and investment figures as well as number of employees. **Number listed:** 16

1. Citigroup, with $76,431 million
2. Fannie Mae, $31,499
3. American Express, $19,132
4. Freddie Mac, $18,048
5. Household International, $8,708
6. Marsh & McLennan, $7,190
7. AON, $6,493
8. SLM Holdings, $3,065
9. First American Financial, $2,877
10. Capital One Financial, $2,600

Source: *Fortune*, Fortune 500 Largest U.S. Corporations (annual), April 26, 1999, p. F-56.

★2193★
TOP FINANCIAL SERVICES/SECURITIES BRANDS BY TOTAL ASSETS, 1998
Ranked by: Total assets, in billions of dollars. **Remarks:** Also notes company name and location, advertising agency and media expenditures. **Number listed:** 5
1. Citigroup, with $76.4 billion
2. Bank of America, $51.7
3. Merrill Lynch, $35.8
4. MSDW, $31.1
5. Prudential Insurance, $27

Source: *Brandweek*, Superbrands: America's Top 2,000 Brands (annual), June 21, 1999, p. S40.

Financial Institutions--Asia

★2194★
LARGEST QUOTED INVESTMENT COMPANIES IN ASIA, 1997
Ranked by: Assets, in thousands of dollars. **Remarks:** Also notes previous year's rank and percentage of change. **Number listed:** 50
1. Korea Long-Term Credit Ltd., with $20,841,796 thousand
2. Daiichi Housing Loan Co. Ltd. (Korea), $14,848,862
3. Tokyo Leasing Co. Ltd. (Japan), $10,017,994
4. Central Leasing Co. Ltd. (Japan), $6,135,464
5. The Industrial Finance Corporation of Thailand (Thailand), $5,703,648
6. Mbf Capital Bhd. (Malaysia), $5,544,648
7. J. P. Morgan Securities Asia Ltd., $4,472,123
8. Affin Holdings Bhd. (Malaysia), $4,296,654
9. Hong Leong Finance Ltd., $3,513,464
10. Malaysian Industrial Development Finance Bhd. (Malaysia), $3,331,052

Source: *Asia's 7,500 Largest Companies.*, (annual), Dun & Bradstreet, 1999, p. 306.

Financial Institutions, International

★2195★
WORLD'S LARGEST DIVERSIFIED FINANCIAL COMPANIES BY REVENUE, 1997
Ranked by: Revenue, in millions of dollars. **Number listed:** 4
1. Travelers Group (U.S.), with $37,609 million
2. Fannie Mae (U.S.), $27,777
3. American Express (U.S.), $17,760
4. Federal Home Loan Mortgage (U.S.), $14,399

Source: *Fortune*, The Global 500: World's Biggest Corporations (annual), August 3, 1998, p. F-18.

Financial Planning

★2196★
TOP FINANCIAL PLANNING SERVICES OFFERED BY EMPLOYERS, 1999
Ranked by: Employers offering benefit, in percent. **Number listed:** 9
1. Any, with 40% percent
2. Retirement planning, 33%
3. Investment advice, 16%
4. Comprehensive planning, 9%
5. Credit or debt management, 8%
6. Tax planning, 5%
7. College planning, 3%
7. Estate planning, 3%
9. None, 60%

Source: *Employee Benefit Plan Review*, April, 1999, p. 31.

★2197★
TOP REASON WHY EMPLOYERS DON'T OFFER FINANCIAL PLANNING SERVICES, 1999
Ranked by: Results of employers surveyed, in percent. **Number listed:** 7
1. Can't administer effectively, with 19% percent
2. Costs, 15%
3. Not important, 9%
4. Employee privacy, 7%
4. Lack of interest among employees, 7%
4. Not firm's responsibility, 7%
7. Firm feel legal or fiduciary responsibility, 6%

Source: *Employee Benefit Plan Review*, April, 1999, p. 31.

Financial Services

★2198★
TOP HISPANIC-OWNED FINANCIAL SERVICES COMPANIES, 1998
Ranked by: Revenue, in millions of dollars. **Number listed:** 10
1. International Bancshares Corp., with $367.87 million
2. IFS Financial Corp., $305
3. Hamilton Bancorp Inc., $142.62
4. TELACU Industries Inc., $100
5. United PanAm Financial Corp., $96.41
6. VPM Funding Co., $79
7. Century Finance USA LLC, $41
8. R.F.G. Financial Services, $32
9. Valor Insurance & Financial Services, $18.98
10. Menendez Financial & Insurance Services, $17.20

Source: *Hispanic Business*, Hispanic Business 500 (annual), June, 1999, p. 96.

★2199★
TOP NON-BANK FINANCIAL SERVICE COMPANIES IN THE S&P 500, 1998
Ranked by: Each company in ranked by eight criteria: one year total return, three-year total return, one-year sales growth, three-year average annual sales growth, one-year profit growth, three-year average annual profit growth, net profit margins, and return on equity, with additional weight given to a company's sales. A company's composite rank is calculated using the sum of all its ranks. **Remarks:** Overall score not provided. **Number listed:** 37
1. Morgan Stanley Dean Witter
2. Capital One Financial
3. Charles Schwab
4. Marsh & McLennan
5. Freddie Mac
6. Washington Mutual
7. Fannie Mae
8. American International Group
9. Progressive

10. Aon

Source: *Business Week*, Business Week 50: Top Companies of the S & P 500 (annual), March 29, 1999, p. 158.

Fish Industry

★2200★

LEADING U.S. FISHING PORTS BY VALUE, 1997

Ranked by: Value, in millions of dollars. **Number listed:** 10

1. Dutch Harbor, AK, with $122.6 million
2. New Bedford, MA, $103.2
3. Kodiak, AK, $88.6
4. Empire-Venice, LA, $57.8
5. Key West, FL, $54.9
6. Honolulu, HI, $53.7
7. Point Judith, RI, $47.6
8. Brownsville-Post Isabel, TX, $46.1
9. Portland, ME, $43.2
10. Dulac-Chauvin, LA, $42.1

Source: *National Fisherman*, November, 1998, p. 16.

Flavoring Essences Industry

★2201★

TOP FLAVORS USED IN BEVERAGES, 1999

Ranked by: Results of survey, in percent. **Number listed:** 13

1. Orange, with 87.3% percent
2. Lemon, 80%
3. Grape, 75.3%
4. Strawberry, 72.7%
5. Lime, 70.7%
6. Cherry, 65.3%
7. Apple, 64.7%
8. Cola, 63.3%
9. Cranberry, 62.7%
10. Grapefruit, 62.7%

Source: *Beverage Industry*, February, 1999, p. 27.

Fleets, Motor Vehicle

See: **Motor Vehicle Fleets**

Floor Coverings

★2202★

LARGEST DISTRIBUTORS OF FLOOR COVERINGS, 1997

Ranked by: Sales, in millions of dollars. **Remarks:** Also notes 1996 sales, branch offices, and chief executives. **Number listed:** 25

1. LD Brinkman, with $355 million
2. J.J. Haines & Co., Inc., $170
3. Florstar Sales Inc., $143
4. Hoboken Floors, $115
5. ProSource Wholesale Floorcoverings, $110
6. William M. Bird & Co., Inc., $105
7. Ohio Valley Flooring, $104
8. BPI, $92
9. Bayard Sales Corp., $91
10. Misco Shawnee, Inc., $88

Source: *Floorings*, September, 1998, p. 23+.

Floor Polishers

See: **Floor Polishing Machines**

Floor Polishing Machines

★2203★

BEST-SELLING FLOOR POLISHERS, 1998

Ranked by: Market share, in percent. **Remarks:** Also notes 1993 market share. **Number listed:** 3

1. Hoover, with 71% percent
2. Thorne Electric, 20%
3. Electrolux, 10%

Source: *Appliance Manufacturer*, April, 1999, p. 21.

Florida--Industries

★2204★

FLORIDA'S LARGEST EMPLOYERS, 1997

Ranked by: Number of employees. **Number listed:** 5

1. Winn-Dixie Stores Inc., with 136,000
2. Darden Restaurants, 114,582
3. Wackenhut Corp., 56,000
3. Republic Industries, 56,000
5. Ryder System, 42,342

Source: *Florida Trend*, Florida's Top 250 Companies (annual), July, 1998, p. 60.

★2205★

FLORIDA'S LARGEST PRIVATE EMPLOYERS, 1998

Ranked by: Number of employees. **Number listed:** 16

1. Publix Super Markets, with 22,508 employees
2. GTE Florida, 10,050
3. Kash n' Karry, 8,500
4. GTE Data Services, 7,000
5. St. Joseph's Hospital, 5,000
6. TECO Energy, 3,735
7. Busch Gardens, 3,300
8. Citigroup, 3,000
9. Tampa General Hospital, 3,000
10. Caspers Co., 2,850

Source: *Florida Trend*, June, 1999, p. 17.

★2206★

FLORIDA'S LARGEST PUBLIC COMPANIES BY INCREASE IN REVENUE, 1997

Ranked by: Increase in revenue from 1996 to 1997, in percent. **Number listed:** 5

1. BMJ Medical Management, with 1,086.2% percent
2. Vision Twenty-One, 488.6%
3. Budget Group, 264.8%
4. IMC Mortgage Co., 263.7%

5. Extended Stay America, 237%

Source: *Florida Trend*, Florida's Top 250 Companies (annual), July, 1998, p. 60.

★2207★
FLORIDA'S LARGEST PUBLIC COMPANIES BY REVENUE, 1997
Ranked by: Revenue, in thousands of dollars. **Remarks:** Also note percent change from 1996, type of business, and senior executive. **Number listed:** 250

1. Winn-Dixie Stores Inc., with $13,218,715 thousand
2. Republic Industries, $10,305,600
3. Tech Data, $7,056,619
4. Office Depot Inc., $6,717,514
5. FPL Group Inc., $6,369,000
6. Ryder System, $4,893,905
7. CHS Electronics Inc., $4,756,383
8. Harris Corp., $3,834,600
9. Florida Progress Corp., $3,315,600
10. Darden Restaurants Inc., $3,171,800

Source: *Florida Trend*, Florida's Top 250 Companies (annual), July, 1998, p. 61.

★2208★
FLORIDA'S MOST PROFITABLE PUBLIC COMPANIES, 1997
Ranked by: Profits, in thousands of dollars. **Number listed:** 5

1. Carnival Corp., with $666,050 thousand
2. FPL Group, $618,000
3. Republic Industries, $439,700
4. Paxson Communications Corp., $214,690
5. Harris Corp., $207,500

Source: *Florida Trend*, Florida's Top 250 Companies (annual), July, 1998, p. 60.

★2209★
FLORIDA'S PUBLIC COMPANIES LOSING THE MOST REVENUE, 1997
Ranked by: Decrease in revenue from 1996 to 1997, in percent. **Number listed:** 5

1. Boca Research, with -54.3%
2. Atlantic Gulf Communities, -44.8%
3. Encore Computer Corp., -38.1%
4. Empire of Carolina, -33.2%
5. Echelon International, -30.2%

Source: *Florida Trend*, Florida's Top 250 Companies (annual), July, 1998, p. 60.

★2210★
FLORIDA'S PUBLIC COMPANIES WITH THE HIGHEST PROFIT LOSSES, 1997
Ranked by: Losses, in thousands of dollars. **Number listed:** 5

1. Intermedia Communications, with $241,123 thousand
2. Ivax Corp., $233,254
3. Forcenergy, $134,818
4. U.S. Diagnostic, $116,712
5. JumboSports, $111,297

Source: *Florida Trend*, Florida's Top 250 Companies (annual), July, 1998, p. 60.

Flour

★2211★
LEADING FLOUR FREE TRADE BY CUSTOMER TYPE, 1998*
Ranked by: Market share, in percent. **Number listed:** 9

1. Large plant, with 16.8% percent
2. Food manufacturers, 16.4%
3. Small businesses, 16%
4. Biscuit/contract, 11.6%
5. In-store bakeries, 10.1%
6. Small plant, 5.7%
7. Retail bakeries, 5.3%
8. Wholesalers, 2.1%
9. Other, 16%

Source: *Milling & Baking*, November 3, 1998, p. 1.

Food Chain Stores

See: **Grocery Trade**

Food Industry and Trade

★2212★
CONSUMER/FOOD COMPANIES SPENDING THE MOST ON RESEARCH AND DEVELOPMENT, 1997
Ranked by: Expenditures on research and development, in millions of dollars. **Number listed:** 13

1. Procter & Gamble, with $1324.5 million
2. Eastman Kodak Co., $1223.4
3. ConAgra Inc., $530.1
4. Coca-Cola Co., $319
5. Gilette Co., $218.2
6. Kimberly-Clark, $216.5
7. Anheuser-Busch Inc., $212
8. Whirlpool, $188
9. RJR Nabisco Holdings Corp., $181
10. Colgate-Palmolive Co., $169.9

Source: *R & D Magazine*, Giants of R & D (annual), October, 1998, p. S-14.

★2213★
LEADING FACTORS IN CONSUMER JUDGEMENT OF FOOD QUALITY, 1999*
Ranked by: Consumer survey results, in percent. **Number listed:** 12

1. Prepared as ordered, with 28% percent
2. Taste/flavor, 20%
3. Temperature, 17%
4. Prepared as per menu, 7%
5. Freshness, 6%
6. Texture, 5%
6. Consistency, 5%
8. Portion size, 4%
9. Presentation, 3%
10. Aroma, 2%

Source: *Restaurants and Institutions*, February 15, 1999, p. 46.

★2214★
MOST ADMIRED FOOD MANUFACTURERS, 1998
Ranked by: Scores (1-10) derived from a survey of senior executives, outside directors, and securities analysts. **Remarks:**

Respondents rated companies in their own industry on 8 attributes of reputation. Also notes previous year's rank. **Number listed:** 10

1. Nestle USA Inc., with 7.37 points
2. Sara Lee, 7.20
3. Campbell Soup, 7.03
4. H.J. Heinz, 6.71
5. ConAgra, 6.62
6. Bestfoods, 6.34
7. RJR Nabisco Holdings Corp., 6.03
8. IBP, 5.62
9. Farmland Industries, 5.51
10. Archer Daniels Midland, 5

Source: *Fortune*, America's Most Admired Corporations (annual), March 1, 1999, p. F-3.

★2215★
MOST POPULAR GROCERY AND CANNED FOOD BRANDS ACCORDING TO DISCOUNT SHOPPERS, 1998
Ranked by: Percentage of discount shoppers naming brand as preferred. **Remarks:** Also notes demographic profile of shoppers surveyed. **Number listed:** 10

1. Campbell's, with 23% percent
2. Del Monte, 15%
3. Libby's, 14%
4. Starkist, 9%
5. Folgers, 8%
6. Bush, 6%
6. Kellogg's, 6%
6. Hunt's, 6%
6. Green Giant, 6%
10. Prego, 2%

Source: *Discount Store News*, Top Brands Survey (annual), September 7, 1998, p. 26.

★2216★
TOP CORPORATIONS IN THE FOOD INDUSTRY, 1998
Ranked by: Revenue, in millions of dollars. **Remarks:** Also notes profits and investment figures as well as number of employees. **Number listed:** 36

1. ConAgra, with $23,841 million
2. Sara Lee, $20,011
3. RJR Nabisco Holdings Corp., $17,037
4. Archer Daniels Midland, $16,109
5. IBP, $12,849
6. H.J. Heinz, $9,209
7. Farmland Industries, $8,775
8. BestFoods, $8,374
9. Campbell Soup, $7,505
10. Tyson Foods Inc., $7,414

Source: *Fortune*, Fortune 500 Largest U.S. Corporations (annual), April 26, 1999, p. F-58.

★2217★
TOP CORPORATIONS IN THE FOOD SERVICES INDUSTRY, 1998
Ranked by: Revenue, in millions of dollars. **Remarks:** Also notes profits and investment figures as well as number of employees. **Number listed:** 14

1. McDonald's, with $12,421 million
2. Tricon Global Restaurants, $8,468
3. Nebco Evans, $7,421
4. Darden Restaurants, $3,287
5. Advantica, $1,962
6. Wendy's International, $1,948
7. CKE Restaurants, $1,892
8. Performance Food Group, $1,623
9. Brinker International, $1,574
10. Host Marriott Services, $1,378

Source: *Fortune*, Fortune 500 Largest U.S. Corporations (annual), April 26, 1999, p. F-58+.

★2218★
TOP FOOD AND DAIRY COMPANIES WITH CHEMICAL PROCESS OPERATIONS, 1998
Ranked by: Sales, in millions of dollars. **Remarks:** Also notes percent change from previous year, net income, profit margin, capital ratios, shareholder returns, price and assets. **Number listed:** 4

1. ConAgra, with $23,841 million
2. Archer-Daniels-Midland, $16,109
3. Bestfoods, $8,374
4. Midwest Grain Products, $223

Source: *Chemical Week*, Chemical Week 300 (annual), May 12, 1999, p. 51.

★2219★
TOP FOOD AND DRUG STORE CORPORATIONS, 1998
Ranked by: Revenue, in millions of dollars. **Remarks:** Also notes profits and investment figures as well as number of employees. **Number listed:** 26

1. Kroger, with $28,203 million
2. Safeway, $24,484
3. American Stores, $19,867
4. Albertson's, $16,005
5. Walgreen, $15,307
6. CVS, $15,274
7. Fred Meyer, $14,879
8. Winn-Dixie Stores Inc., $13,617
9. Publix Super Markets, $12,067
10. Rite Aid, $11,375

Source: *Fortune*, Fortune 500 Largest U.S. Corporations (annual), April 26, 1999, p. F-59.

★2220★
TOP FOOD COMPANIES BY SALES, 1997-1998
Ranked by: Sales, in millions of dollars. **Number listed:** 100

1. Philip Morris, with $31,527 million
2. ConAgra Inc., $28,840
3. Cargill Inc., $21,400
4. PepsiCo, $20,917
5. Coca-Cola Co., $18,800
6. Archer Daniels Midland Co., $16,109
7. Mars Inc., $14,000
8. IBP Inc., $13,258.8
9. Anheuser-Busch Cos. Inc., $12,832.4
10. Sara Lee, $10,800

Source: *Food Processing*, Top 100 Food Companies (annual), December, 1998, p. 22+.

★2221★
TOP FOOD COMPANIES IN THE S&P 500, 1998
Ranked by: Each company in ranked by eight criteria: one year total return, three-year total return, one-year sales growth, three-year average annual sales growth, one-year profit growth, three-year average annual profit growth, net profit margins, and return on equity, with additional weight given to a company's sales. A company's composite rank is calculated using the sum of all its ranks. **Remarks:** Overall score not provided. **Number listed:** 22

1. Safeway
2. General Mills
3. Sysco
4. Albertson's
5. William Wrigley Jr.
6. H.J. Heinz
7. Fred Meyer

8. Sara Lee
9. American Stores
10. Kroger

Source: *Business Week*, Business Week 50: Top Companies of the S & P 500 (annual), March 29, 1999, p. 150.

★2222★
TOP NATURAL FOOD PRODUCTS, 1998
Ranked by: Ranked by percentage change in sales in natural product stores and mainstream supermarkets. **Remarks:** Actual sales and percentages not provided. **Number listed:** 10

1. Non-dairy beverages
2. Chips/pretzels/snacks
3. Cold cereals
4. Frozen entrees/pizzas/convenience foods
5. Yogurt/kefir
6. Shelf-stable juice/functional drinks
7. Teas
8. Carbonated beverages/single-serve drinks
9. Condiments
10. Frozen/refrigerated meat alternatives

Source: *Progressive Grocer*, September, 1998, p. 78.

Food Industry and Trade--Asia

★2223★
LARGEST QUOTED COMPANIES IN FOOD, BEVERAGE, AND TOBACCO IN ASIA, 1999*
Ranked by: Sales, in thousands of dollars. **Remarks:** Also notes profits as a percentage of sales and activity codes. **Number listed:** 100

1. Japan Tobacco, with $26,923,046 million
2. Kirin Brewery Co. Ltd., $11,265,523
3. Asahi Breweries Ltd., $9,829,760
4. Snow Brand Milk Products Co., $9,334,461
5. Maruha Corp., $7,321,744
6. Nippon Meat Packers Inc., $6,455,681
7. Ajinomoto Co. Inc., $6,257,223
8. Yamazaki Baking Co. Ltd., $5,160,306
9. Sapporo Breweries Ltd., $4,932,185
10. Meiji Milk Products Co. Ltd., $4,633,600

Source: *Asia's 7,500 Largest Companies*, (annual), Dun & Bradstreet, 1999, p. 73+.

★2224★
TOP ASIA/PACIFIC FOOD AND BEVERAGE COMPANIES, 1998
Ranked by: Food and beverage sales, in millions of dollars. **Remarks:** Also notes total sales and net profit. Top nine are in Japan. **Number listed:** 50

1. Kirin Brewery Co. Ltd., with $12,807 million
2. Asahi Breweries Ltd., $7,636
3. Suntory Ltd., $6,955
4. Taiyo, $6,250
5. Ajinomoto Co. Inc., $5,532
6. Sapporo Breweries Ltd., $5,375
7. Nippon Meat Packers Inc., $4,892
8. Yamazaki Baking, $4,868
9. Snow Brand Milk Products Co., $4,727
10. Coca-Cola Amatil Ltd. (Australia), $3,705

Source: *Prepared Foods*, The Global 250 Food Companies Report, July, 1998, p. 28.

Food Industry and Trade--Europe

★2225★
TOP EUROPEAN FOOD AND BEVERAGE COMPANIES, 1997
Ranked by: Food and beverage sales, in millions of dollars. **Remarks:** Also notes total sales and net profit. **Number listed:** 50

1. Nestle SA (Switzerland), with $45,149 million
2. Unilever (United Kingdom/Netherlands), $24,268
3. Diageo (United Kingdom), $20,.749
4. Danone (France), $13,331
5. Eridania Beghin Say (France), $8,676
6. Cadbury Schweppes PLC (United Kingdom), $8,511
7. Associated British Foods (United Kingdom), $6,926
8. Tate & Lyle PLC (United Kingdom), $6,657
9. Heineken NV (Netherlands), $6,238
10. Besnier SA (France), $4,579

Source: *Prepared Foods*, The Global 250 Food Companies (annual), July, 1998, p. 24.

★2226★
TOP FOOD AND KINDRED PRODUCTS COMPANIES IN THE EEC, 1999*
Ranked by: Sales, in millions of European Currency Units (ECUs). **Remarks:** Also notes number of employees and overall rank. **Number listed:** 400

1. Grand Metropolitan PLC (United Kingdom), with ECUs12.061 million
2. Bass PLC (United Kingdom), ECUs7.752
3. Wittington Investments Ltd. (United Kingdom), ECUs7.724
4. Associated British Foods PLC (United Kingdom), ECUs7.677
4. ABF Investments PLC (United Kingdom), ECUs7.677
6. Tchibo Holding AG (Denmark), ECUs7.356
7. Diageo PLC (United Kingdom), ECUs6.979
8. Tomkins PLC (United Kingdom), ECUs6.771
9. Yate & Lyle PLC (United Kingdom), ECUs6.422
10. Cadbury Schweppes PLC (United Kingdom), ECUs6.226

Source: *Dun's Europe (annual)*, Dun & Bradstreet, 1999, p. 231+.

Food Industry and Trade, International

★2227★
WORLD'S LARGEST FOOD CORPORATIONS BY REVENUE, 1997
Ranked by: Revenue, in millions of dollars. **Number listed:** 13

1. Univlever (Great Britain/Netherlands), with $48,761 million
2. Nestle (Switzerland), $47,030
3. ConAgra (U.S.), $24,002
4. Diageo (Great Britain), $21,217
5. Sara Lee (U.S.), $19,734
6. RJR Nabisco (U.S.), $17,057
7. Groupe Danone (France), $15,160
8. Archer Daniels Midland (U.S.), $13,853
9. IBP (U.S.), $13,259
10. Snow Brand Milk Products Co. (Japan), $10,159

Source: *Fortune*, The Global 500: World's Biggest Corporations (annual), August 3, 1998, p. F-19.

Food Industry and Trade--Latin America

★2228★
LARGEST LATIN AMERICAN FOOD COMPANIES BY MARKET CAP, 1998
Ranked by: Market capital, in millions of dollars. **Remarks:** Also notes other financial data. **Number listed:** 13
1. Moderna Empresas (Mexico), with $2,759.87 million
2. Bimbo (Mexico), $2,190.34
3. Gmaseca (Mexico), $687.32
4. Maseca (Mexico), $660,17
5. Parmalat (Brazil), $443.38
6. Bachoco Industrias UBL (Mexico), $413.57
7. Molinos Rio (Argentina), $333.26
8. Sadia (Brazil), $291.29
9. Sigma Grupo (Mexico), $243.27
10. Bagley ORD (Argentina), $241.32

Source: *Latin Finance*, November, 1998, p. 38.

★2229★
TOP LATIN AMERICAN FOOD AND BEVERAGE COMPANIES, 1996
Ranked by: Food and beverage sales, in millions of dollars. **Remarks:** Also notes previous year's figures. **Number listed:** 50
1. Brahma (Brazil), with $4,877 million
2. Antarctica Paulista (Brazil), $3,143
3. Sadia (Brazil), $3,000
4. Ceval Alimentos (Brazil), $2,795
5. FEMSA (Mexico), $2,483
6. PANAMCO (Mexico), $1,993
7. Bimbo (Mexico), $1,920
8. Brupo Modelo (Mexico), $1,504
9. Gruma (Mexico), $1,398
10. Parmalat Brasil (Brazil), $1,050

Source: *Prepared Foods*, The Global 250 Food Companies (annual), July, 1998, p. 34.

Food Industry and Trade--North America

★2230★
LARGEST U.S./CANADIAN PRIVATE FOOD AND BEVERAGE COMPANIES, 1997
Ranked by: Food and beverages sales, in millions of dollars. **Remarks:** Also includes location and previous year's sales. **Number listed:** 40
1. Cargill Inc. (MN), with $20,400 million
2. Mars Inc. (VA), $13,500
3. Dairy Farmers of America (MO), $6,900
4. Farmland Industries Inc. (MO), $3,559
5. McCain Food Ltd. (Ontario, Canada), $3,032
6. Perdue Farms Inc. (MD), $2,417
7. Keystone Foods Corp. (PA), $2,200
7. Land O'Lakes Inc. (MN), $2,200
9. Borden Inc. and Affiliates (OH), $1,990
10. Stroh Brewery Co. (MI), $1,600

Source: *Prepared Foods*, The Global 250 Food Companies Report (annual), July, 1998, p. 14.

★2231★
LARGEST U.S./CANADIAN PUBLIC FOOD AND BEVERAGE COMPANIES, 1997
Ranked by: Food and beverage sales, in millions of dollars. **Remarks:** Also includes previous year's rank, location, previous year's sales, operating income, net change, and company's internet address. **Number listed:** 60
1. Philip Morris, with $34,524 million
2. PepsiCo, $20,917
3. Coca-Cola Co., $18,868
4. ConAgra Inc., $18,233
5. IBP Inc., $13,529
6. Sara Lee, $10,427
7. Anheuser-Busch Companies Inc., $10,254
8. H.J. Heinz Co., $9,357
9. Nabisco, $8,734
10. Bestfoods, $8,400

Source: *Prepared Foods*, The Global 250 Food Companies Report (annual), July, 1998, p. 16.

Food Processing Plants

★2232★
TOP MEAT AND POULTRY PROCESSING COMPANIES, 1999
Ranked by: Sales, in millions of dollars. **Remarks:** Also notes previous year's rank, number of plants and employees, chief officer and type of operations. **Number listed:** 160
1. ConAgra, with $24,219 million
2. IBP, $12,800
3. Excel Corp., $9,000
4. Tyson Foods Inc., $7,450
5. Sara Lee Packaged Meats, $4,300
6. Smithfield Foods, Inc., $3,867
7. Refrigerated Food and Livestock Production Group, $3,700
8. Hormel Foods Corp., $3,261
9. Perdue Farms Inc., $2,500
10. Oscar Mayer Food Division, $2,200

Source: *National Provisioner*, The Provisioner Top 200 (annual), May, 1999, p. 28+.

Food Processors

★2233★
BEST-SELLING FOOD PROCESSORS, 1998
Ranked by: Market share, in percent. **Remarks:** Also notes 1993 market share. **Number listed:** 10
1. Hamilton Beach/Proctor-Silex, with 44% percent
2. Cuisinart, 20%
3. Black & Decker, 9%
4. Braun, 5%
4. KitchenAid, 5%
4. Sunbeam-Oster, 5%
7. Regal Ware, 4%
8. Betty Crocker, 1%
8. West Bend, 1%
10. Others, 6%

Source: *Appliance Manufacturer*, April, 1999, p. 22.

Food Service

★2234★
LEADING CONVENIENCE STORE COMPANIES BY SALES OF FOOD SERVICE UNITS, 1998*
Ranked by: Sales, in millions of dollars. **Remarks:** Also notes *Restaurant and Institutions 400* rank. **Number listed:** 5

1. 7-Eleven Convenience Stores, with $2,174 million
2. Wawa Food Markets, $356
3. Casey's General Store, $177.3
4. Circle K, $140
5. Speedway, $132

Source: *Restaurants & Institutions*, Restaurants & Institutions 400 (annual), July 15, 1998, p. 103.

★2235★
LEADING FOOD SERVICE CONTRACT-MANAGEMENT COMPANIES IN NORTH AMERICA, 1997
Ranked by: Food and beverage sales, in millions of dollars. **Remarks:** Also notes number of total U.S. accounts. **Number listed:** 13

1. Sodexho Marriott Services (MD), with $4,200 million
2. Aramark (PA), $3,700
3. Compass Group (NC), $1,900
4. Delaware North (NY), $1,224
5. Wood Co. (PA), $430
6. Restaura (AZ), $406
7. Restaurant Associates (NY), $300
8. Fine Host Corp. (CT), $275
9. ServiceMaster (IL), $255
10. Bon Appetit (CA), $185

Source: *Restaurants & Institutions*, Institutional Giants (annual), September 15, 1998, p. 64.

★2236★
LEADING FOOD SERVICE PARENT COMPANIES BY SALES VOLUME, 1997
Ranked by: Sales volume, in millions of dollars. **Remarks:** Also notes specific restaurants and combined number of units. **Number listed:** 15

1. Tricon Global Restaurants, with $20,400 million
2. Grand Metropolitan PLC, $10,060
3. Wendy's International, $5,998
4. CKE Restaurants Inc., $4,391.5
5. Advantica, $3,353.6
6. Darden Restaurants, $3,300
7. Allied Domecq PLC, $3,151.7
8. Starwood Hotels and Resorts, $3,015.4
9. International Dairy Queen, $2,612.2
10. Carlson Restaurants Worldwide Inc., $2,430

Source: *Restaurants & Institutions*, Restaurants & Institutions 400 (annual), July 15, 1998, p. 60.

★2237★
LEADING MILITARY FOOD SERVICE ORGANIZATIONS, 1997
Ranked by: Food and beverage purchases, in millions of dollars. **Remarks:** Also notes food and beverage sales, bases/sites served and whether or not a chain brand. **Number listed:** 11

1. U.S. Army Center of Excellence, Subsistence (VA), with $411.8 million
2. Naval Supply Systems Command (VA), $241
3. Army & Air Force Exchange Service (TX), $120
4. U.S. Air Force APF Food Operations (TX), $98.9
5. U.S. Air Force Clubs (TX), $82
6. U.S. Marine Corps Food Service Section (DC), $75.8
7. U.S. Navy MWR Division (TN), $50.9
8. U.S. Army community & Family Support Centers (VA), $50.4
9. U.S. Coast Guard (DC), $27.3
10. U.S. Marine Corps MWR Support Activity (VA), $19.7

Source: *Restaurants & Institutions*, Institutional Giants (annual), September 15, 1998, p. 92.

★2238★
LEADING RECREATIONAL FOOD SERVICE COMPANIES, 1997
Ranked by: Food and beverage sales, in millions of dollars. **Remarks:** Also notes number of properties and type of business. **Number listed:** 9

1. Walt Disney Co. (CA), with $1,018 million
2. Carnival Cruise Lines (FL), $331
3. Club Corp. International (TX), $270
4. AMC Entertainment (MO), $251
5. Volume Services (SC), $234
6. Harrah's (TN), $230
7. Sportservice (NY), $220
8. Mirage Resorts (NV), $218.9
9. Royal Caribbean Cruises (FL), $150

Source: *Restaurants & Institutions*, Institutional Giants (annual), September 15, 1998, p. 86.

★2239★
LEADING SELF-OPERATED BUSINESS AND INDUSTRY DINING SERVICE COMPANIES, 1997
Ranked by: Food and beverage purchases, in millions of dollars. **Remarks:** Also notes units, transactions per day, and customer base. **Number listed:** 9

1. Motorola, with $17.4 million
2. J.P. Morgan & Co., $6
3. Abbott Laboratories, $5
4. Aetna Life & Casualty, $4
5. Pharmacia & Upjohn, $3.5
5. Honeywell, $3.5
7. The Limited, $2.7
8. Steelcase, $2
9. Hallmark Cards, $1.4

Source: *Restaurants & Institutions*, Institutional Giants (annual), September 15, 1998, p. 84.

★2240★
MOST ADMIRED FOOD SERVICES CORPORATIONS, 1998
Ranked by: Scores (1-10) derived from a survey of senior executives, outside directors, and securities analysts. **Remarks:** Respondents rated companies in their own industry on 8 attributes of reputation. Also notes previous year's rank. **Number listed:** 10

1. McDonald's, with 7.01 points
2. Brinker International, 6.99
3. Outback Steakhouse, 6.82
4. Wendy's International, 6.68
5. Host Marriott Services, 6.16
6. Darden Restaurants, 6.01
7. Performance Food Group, 4.93
8. Advantica, 4.66
9. Viad, 4.25
10. Shoney's, 3.61

Source: *Fortune*, America's Most Admired Corporations (annual), March 1, 1999, p. F-3.

★2241★
TOP CORPORATIONS IN THE FOREST PRODUCTS INDUSTRY, 1998
Ranked by: Revenue, in millions of dollars. **Remarks:** Also notes profits and investment figures as well as number of employees. **Number listed:** 21
1. International Paper, with $19,500 million
2. Georgia-Pacific, $13,223
3. Kimberly-Clark, $12,298
4. Weyerhaeuser, $10,766
5. Fort James, $7,301
6. Boise Cascade, $6,162
7. Champion International, $5,653
8. Mead, $4,579
9. Union Camp, $4,503
10. Smurfit-Stone Container, $3,794

Source: *Fortune*, Fortune 500 Largest U.S. Corporations (annual), April 26, 1999, p. F-59.

Food Service--Distributors

★2242★
LEADING FOOD SERVICE DISTRIBUTORS, 1998
Ranked by: Food service sales in dollars. **Remarks:** Also notes headquarters location. **Number listed:** 25
1. Sysco, with $15,327,536,000
2. AmeriServe Food Distribution Inc., $9,081,000,000
3. Alliant Foodservice Inc., $6,100,000,000
4. US Foodservice, $6,000,000,000
5. Sam's Club, $3,450,000,000
6. Martin-Brower Co. L.L.C., $2,853,000,000
7. PYA/Monarch Inc., $2,700,000,000
8. MBM Corp., $2,000,000,000
9. Multifood Distribution Group, $1,900,000,000
10. Gordon Food Service Inc., $1,700,000,000

Source: *Directory of Food Service Distributors (annual)*, 1999, p. 14.

★2243★
LEADING FOOD SERVICE EQUIPMENT AND SUPPLIES DISTRIBUTORS, 1998
Ranked by: Equipment and supplies sales, in millions of dollars. **Remarks:** Also includes previous year's sales. **Number listed:** 100
1. Edward Don & Co., with $364 million
2. The Wasserstrom Co., $200
3. Franke Contract Group, $130.99
4. Superior Products Manufacturing Co., $107
5. Stainless Inc., $105
6. Cassidy's Ltd., $100
7. Hubert Co., $78.7
8. Food Service Supplies, $77.63
9. The Boelter Companies, $70
10. Marstan Industries Inc., $67.69

Source: *Foodservice Equipment & Supplies*, March, 1999, p. 24+.

★2244★
TOP BROADLINE FOOD SERVICE EQUIPMENT AND SUPPLIES DISTRIBUTORS, 1998
Ranked by: Equipment and supplies sales, in millions of dollars. **Remarks:** Also notes previous year's sales. **Number listed:** 10
1. Sysco, with $776.29 million
2. U.S. Foodservice, $542.22
3. Alliant, $150.53
4. Gordon Food Service Inc., $45.5
5. Reinhart Institutional Foods, $43.1
6. Lady Baltimore Foods Inc., $41.33
7. Clark Foodservice, $32
8. Maines Paper & Food Service Inc., $19.37
9. Shamrock Foods Co., $18.9
10. Foodservices of America, $17.61

Source: *Foodservice Equipment & Supplies*, March, 1999, p. 25.

Food Service--Take-Out Service

★2245★
LEADING CONVENIENCE STORE COMPANIES BY TAKE-OUT SALES, 1998*
Ranked by: Estimated take-out sales, in thousands of dollars. **Remarks:** Also notes non-gas sales, estimated percent of take-out sales and rank by percent. **Number listed:** 20
1. Southland Corp., with $1,300,000 thousand
2. Wawa, $203,000
3. Casey's, $180,000
4. Tosco, $120,000
5. Dillon, $95,000
6. Emro, $85,000
7. Total, $67,000
8. Crown Central, $66,000
9. Ultramar Diamond Shamrock, $62,000
10. Sheetz, $59,000

Source: *Convenience Store News*, Top 20 C-Stores for Takeout (annual), October 11, 1998, p. 176.

★2246★
LEADING TAKE-OUT CHAIN STORES, 1998
Ranked by: Estimated take-out sales, in thousands of dollars. **Remarks:** Also notes segment, units, and total sales. **Number listed:** 100
1. McDonald's, with $9,494,368 thousand
2. Burger King, $4,041,708
3. Pizza Hut, $3,196,050
4. Kentucky Fried Chicken, $2,730,000
5. Taco Bell, $2,651,473
6. Domino's Pizza, $2,277,000
7. Wendy's, $2,142,023
8. Subway, $2,106,000
9. Dairy Queen, $1,952,162
10. Hardee's, $1,613,873

Source: *Convenience Store News*, Top 100 Takeout Leaders (annual), October 11, 1998, p. 172+.

Foot Care Products

★2247★
BEST-SELLING ATHLETE'S FOOT MEDICATION, 1998
Ranked by: Sales, in millions of dollars. **Remarks:** Also notes percent change, market share, and unit sales. **Number listed:** 8
1. Lotrimin AF, with $56.6 million
2. Tinactin, $42.6
3. Desenex, $32.3
4. Private Label, $28.4
5. Dr. Scholl, $27.7

6. Micatin, $16
7. Johnson Odor Eaters, $9.6
8. Freeman Bare Foot, $7.7

Source: *Discount Merchandiser*, December, 1998, p. 51.

★2248★
BEST-SELLING FOOT CARE DEVICE BRANDS, 1998
Ranked by: Sales, in millions of dollars. **Remarks:** Also notes change from previous year, dollar share type, unit sales, unit sales change from previous year, and unit share type. **Number listed:** 10

1. Dr. Scholl, with $114.9 million
2. Dr. Scholl Dynastep, $22.8
3. Dr. Scholl Maximum Comfort, $17.5
4. Dr. Scholl Air Pillow, $17.5
5. Private Label, $15.9
6. Dr. Scholl Flexo, $9.7
7. Dr. Scholl Advanced Pain Relief, $9.3
8. Dr. Scholl One Step, $9.2
9. Dr. Scholl Double Air Pillow, $7.9
10. Sof Comfort, $7.4

Source: *Discount Merchandiser*, December, 1998, p. 51.

★2249★
LEADING ATHLETE'S FOOT MEDICATION VENDORS, 1998
Ranked by: Sales, in millions of dollars. **Remarks:** Also notes brands, percent change from previous year, percent of market share, unit sales, unite sales change, and unit share. **Number listed:** 5

1. Schering-Plough, with $134.4 million
2. Novartis, $31.6
3. Private Label, $27.2
4. Pharmacia & Upjohn, $18
5. Combe Inc., $14

Source: *Drug Store News*, September 7, 1998, p. 63.

★2250★
LEADING FOOT CARE DEVICE VENDORS, 1998
Ranked by: Sales, in millions of dollars. **Remarks:** Also notes percent change from previous year, dollar share type, and unit sales. **Number listed:** 8

1. Schering-Plough, with $236.9 million
2. Private Label, $15.9
3. ProFoot Care, $13.6
4. Combe Inc., $10.5
5. Implus Corp., $10
6. Johnson & Johnson, $6.9
7. Footsply, $5.8
8. Spenco Medical Corp., $4.3
9. LaLoren Inc., $2.1
10. Del Labs Inc., $1.8

Source: *Discount Merchandiser*, December, 1998, p. 51.

★2251★
LEADING MANUFACTURERS OF FOOT CARE DEVICES, 1998
Ranked by: Sales, in millions of dollars. **Remarks:** Also notes percent change from previous year, percent of market share, unit sales, and unit share. **Number listed:** 5

1. Schering-Plough, with $232.7 million
2. Private Label, $15.5
3. ProFoot Care, $13.5
4. Combe Inc., $10.7
5. Implus Corp., $9

Source: *Drug Store News*, September 7, 1998, p. 63.

Football

★2252★
LEADING FOOTBALL TEAMS BY CURRENT VALUE, 1997
Ranked by: Current value, in millions of dollars. **Remarks:** Also notes revenues, operating income, debt/value, and principal owners. **Number listed:** 30

1. Dallas Cowboys, with $413 million
2. Washington Redskins, $403
3. Carolina Panthers, $365
4. Tampa Bay Buccaneers, $346
5. Miami Dolphins, $340
6. Baltimore Ravens, $329
7. Seattle Seahawks, $324
8. Tennessee Oilers, $322
9. St. Louis Rams, $322
10. Denver Broncos, $320

Source: *Forbes*, December 14, 1998, p. 132.

Foreign Exchange

★2253★
LEADING FOREIGN EXCHANGE RESERVES, 1997
Ranked by: Share of reserves, in percent. **Number listed:** 7

1. Dollar, with 57.1%
2. Deutsche Mark, 12.8%
3. European Currency Unit (ECU), 5.0%
4. Yen, 4.9%
5. Pound Sterling, 2.4%
6. French Franc, 1.2%
7. Other, 15.6%

Source: *Economist*, November 14, 1998, p. 90.

Forest Products Industry

★2254★
MOST ADMIRED FOREST AND PAPER PRODUCTS CORPORATIONS, 1998
Ranked by: Scores (1-10) derived from a survey of senior executives, outside directors, and securities analysts. **Remarks:** Respondents rated companies in their own industry on 8 attributes of reputation. Also notes previous year's rank. **Number listed:** 10

1. Kimberly-Clark, with 7.26 points
2. Weyerhaeuser, 6.56
3. Mead, 6.4
4. International Paper, 5,98
5. Union Camp, 5.96
6. Fort James, 5.72
7. Georgia-Pacific, 5.27
8. Champion International, 5.07
9. Boise Cascade, 4.5
10. Stone Container, 4.1

Source: *Fortune*, America's Most Admired Corporations (annual), March 1, 1999, p. F-5.

★2255★
TOP CORPORATIONS IN THE FURNITURE INDUSTRY, 1998
Ranked by: Revenue, in millions of dollars. **Remarks:** Also notes profits and investment figures as well as number of employees. **Number listed:** 6

1. Leggett & Platt, with $3,370 million
2. Steelcase, $2,760
3. Lifestyle Furniture International, $2,002
4. Furniture Brands International, $1,960
5. Herman Miller, $1,719
6. Hon Industries, $1,696

Source: *Fortune*, Fortune 500 Largest U.S. Corporations (annual), April 26, 1999, p. F-60.

★2256★
TOP PAPER AND FOREST PRODUCTS COMPANIES IN THE S&P 500, 1998
Ranked by: Each company is ranked by eight criteria: one-year total return, three-year return, one-year sales growth, three-year average annual sales growth, one-year profit growth, three-year average annual profit growth, net profit margins, and return on equity, with additional weight given to a company's sales. A company's composite rank is calculated using the sum of all its ranks. **Remarks:** Overall score not provided. **Number listed:** 13

1. Kimberly-Clark
2. Fort James
3. Georgia-Pacific Group
4. Williamette Industries
5. Weyerhaeuser
6. International Paper
7. Union Camp
8. Boise Cascade
9. Mead
10. Potlatch

Source: *Business Week*, Business Week 50: Top Companies of the S & P 500 (annual), March 29, 1999, p. 162.

Forest Products Industry, International

★2257★
WORLD'S LARGEST FOREST PRODUCTS CORPORATIONS BY REVENUE, 1997
Ranked by: Revenue, in millions of dollars. **Number listed:** 6

1. International Paper (U.S.), with $20,096 million
2. Georgia-Pacific (U.S.), $13,094
3. Kimberly-Clark (U.S.), $12,547
4. Weyerhaeuser (U.S.), $11,210
5. Oji Paper (Japan), $10,987
6. UPM-Kymmene (Finland), $10,211

Source: *Fortune*, The Global 500: World's Biggest Corporations (annual), August 3, 1998, p. F-20.

Forwarding Companies--Los Angeles County (CA)

★2258★
LARGEST CUSTOMS BROKERS/FREIGHT FORWARDERS IN LOS ANGELES COUNTY, 1997
Ranked by: Number of employees in Los Angeles County. **Remarks:** Also notes shipping volume, business volume, services, company profile, parent company, and top local executive. **Number listed:** 15

1. Air Express International Corp., with 256 employees
2. Fritz Cos. Inc., 250
3. Interstate Consolidation Inc., 157
4. Nippon Express USA Inc., 126
5. Dependable Hawaiian Express/DHX Inc., 85
6. Danzas Corp., 80
7. Circle International Inc., 76
8. Global Transportation Services Inc., 60
9. L.E. Coppersmith Inc., 56
10. O'Neill & Whitaker Inc., 49

Source: *Los Angeles Business Journal*, Book of Lists (annual), 1999, p. 39.

Foundations, Charitable and Educational

See also: **Nonprofit Institutions**

★2259★
LARGEST FOUNDATIONS BY ASSETS ACCORDING TO *FOUNDATION DIRECTORY*, 1998
Ranked by: Assets. **Remarks:** Also includes total giving amount. **Number listed:** 100

1. Lilly Endowment Inc., with 11,459,588,283
2. Ford Foundation, 9,597,907,967
3. David and Lucile Packard Foundation, 8,991,300,000
4. W.K. Kellogg Foundation, 7,588,408,314
5. J. Paul Getty Trust, 7,389,565,432
6. Robert Wood Johnson Foundation, 6,734,918,302
7. Pew Charitable Trusts, 4,522,480,597
8. John D. And Catherine T. MacArthur Foundation, 4,030,139,783
9. Robert W. Woodruff Foundation, Inc., 3,680,536,964
10. Rockefeller Foundation, 3,094,733,452

Source: *Foundation Directory*, 1999, p. 11.

★2260★
LARGEST FOUNDATIONS BY TOTAL GIVING, 1998
Ranked by: Amount given. **Remarks:** Also includes assets. **Number listed:** 100

1. Ford Foundation, with 390,558,686
2. W.K. Kellogg Foundation, 255,259,633
3. Lilly Endowment Inc., 254,113,476
4. Robert Wood Johnson Foundation, 241,543,631
5. Pew Charitable Trusts, 211,879,645
6. David and Lucile Packard Foundation, 173,074,000
7. John D. And Catherine T. MacArthur Foundation, 156,976,932
8. Andrew W. Mellon Foundation, 118,541,000
9. Rockefeller Foundation, 99,262,759
10. Annenberg Foundation, 97,190,186

Source: *Foundation Directory*, 1999, p. 12.

Foundations, Charitable and Educational—Detroit Metropolitan Area

★2261★
LARGEST CHARITABLE TRUSTS AND FOUNDATIONS IN THE DETROIT METROPOLITAN AREA, 1997
Ranked by: Assets, in millions of dollars. **Remarks:** Also notes top executive, type, purpose, grant range and grant limitations. **Number listed:** 10

1. Kresge Foundation, with $2,103 million
2. Skillman Foundation, $512.7
3. Herrick Foundation, $248.3
4. Community Foundation for Southeastern Michigan, $187
5. McGregor Fund, $170.7
6. Hudson-Webber Foundation, $148
7. Richard and Jane Manoogian Foundation, $119.8
8. Louis Manoogian Simone Foundation, $99.5
9. Earhart Foundation, $88.5
10. Carls Foundation, $65

Source: *Crain's Detroit Business (annual)*, 1998, p. 8.

Foundations, Charitable and Educational--Florida

★2262★
TOP FOUNDATIONS IN FLORIDA, 1999
Ranked by: Assets, in millions of dollars. **Remarks:** Also notes largest grant awards and recipients, geographic preference, senior officers, and contact information. **Number listed:** 50

1. John S. & James L. Knight Foundation, with $1,055.8 million
2. Arthur S. De Moss Foundation, $322
3. Jessie Ball duPont Fund, $231.8
4. Arthur Vining Davis Foundations, $187.4
5. Quantum Foundation Inc., $140
6. Venice Foundation, $137.7
7. Health Foundation of South Florida, $129.4
8. Koch Foundation Inc., $125.7
9. Arison Foundation Inc., $100
10. Chatlos Foundation Inc., $93.2

Source: *Florida Trend*, TopRank Florida (annual), 1999, p. 106+.

401(k) Plan

★2263★
BEST 401(K) PLANS, 1998
Ranked by: Overall score arrived at by a point system in six categories: enrollment/vesting, company contributions, investment choices, investment performance, service, and monitoring. **Remarks:** Also notes scores in each category and general comments. **Number listed:** 10

1. American Stores, with 84.6 points
2. Merrill Lynch, 83.9
3. Freddie Mac, 75.4
4. American Express, 75.2
5. Chrysler, 72.8
6. Eastman Kodak, 71.7
7. Ford Motor, 69.8
8. Tenet Healthcare Corp., 69.6
9. 3M, 69.3
10. First Union, 67.3

Source: *Smart Money*, August, 1998, p. 119.

★2264★
TOP 401 (K) PLAN PROVIDERS, 1997
Ranked by: Assets, in billions of dollars. **Remarks:** Also notes percentage change from previous year. **Number listed:** 20

1. Fidelity Investments, with $175.2 billion
2. Vanguard Group, $87.3
3. State Street Global, $85.2
4. Barclays Global Investors, $49
5. Merrill Lynch, $45.2
6. Bankers Trust, $42.9
7. UAM, $35.1
8. T. Rowe Price, $32.2
9. Putnam Investments, $31.3
10. Principal Financial Group, $29.3

Source: *Life and Health*, Financial Services Edition (annual), October 26, 1998, p. 4.

★2265★
TOP 401 (K) PROVIDERS, INSURANCE COMPANIES, 1997
Ranked by: Assets, in billions of dollars. **Remarks:** Also notes current and previous years number of plans. **Number listed:** 10

1. Principal Financial Group, with $29.3 billion
2. Prudential Investments, $27
3. Cigna Retirement & Investment Services, $26.2
4. MetLife Defined Contribution Group, $21.2
5. Aetna Retirement Services, $19.5
6. Manulife Financial, $18
7. New York Life/Mainstay Funds, $17.1
8. Mass Mutual, $12
9. Nationwide Financial Services Inc., $8.1
10. Equitable, $6.5

Source: *National Underwriter*, October 26, 1998, p. 1.

★2266★
WORST 401(K) PLANS, 1998
Ranked by: Overall score arrived at by a point system in six categories: enrollment/vesting, company contributions, investment choices, investment performance, service, and monitoring. **Remarks:** Also notes scores in each category and general comments. **Number listed:** 10

1. Coca-Cola, with 36.8 points
2. Advantica, 35.5
3. Walgreen, 33.7
4. AMR Corp., 32.3
5. Kroger, 28.4
6. May Department Stores, 26.6
7. Safeway, 24.5
8. PepsiCo, 23.9
9. Tricon Global Restaurants, 22.7
10. J.C. Penney, 22

Source: *Smart Money*, August, 1998, p. 119.

Franchises (Retail Trade)

★2267★
FASTEST GROWING FRANCHISES, 1997-1998
Ranked by: Number of new franchises. **Remarks:** Also notes total number of franchises, location, contact information and description. **Number listed:** 101

1. Yogen Fruz Worldwide, with 1,161 new franchises
2. McDonald's, 925
3. Jani-King, 753
4. 7-Eleven Convenience Stores, 730
5. Jackson Hewitt Tax Service, 540
6. Kentucky Fried Chicken, 503
7. Subway, 481
8. Century Small Business Solutions, 428
9. Wendy's International, 391
10. CleanNet USA Inc., 364

10. Taco Bell Corp., 364

Source: *Entrepreneur*, 101 Fastest Growing Franchises (annual), February, 1999, p. 164+.

★2268★
LEADING FRANCHISES, 1999
Ranked by: Based on seven criteria: long-term stability, comprehensive support services, franchisors-franchisee communications, franchisor-franchisee relationships, franchisee success rate, low start-up costs, and long-term potential. Specific figures are not provided. **Remarks:** Also notes number of units, fees, royalty and contact information. **Number listed:** 100

1. Travel Network
2. Molly Maid
3. Novus Windshield Repair
4. Primrose Schools
5. One Hour Martinizing
6. Cousins Subs
7. Pak Mail
8. American Leak Detection
9. Children's Orchard
10. Great Clips

Source: *Income Opportunities*, Platinum 200 (annual), March, 1999, p. 24+.

★2269★
TOP FRANCHISES, 1998
Ranked by: Each company was ranked by four major criteria: financial performance, corporate growth, management and stability, relationship between franchisor and franchisees and opportunities to expand. Specific figures are not provided. **Remarks:** Also notes business, number of locations, and initial fee. **Number listed:** 100

1. ServiceMaster
2. Sylvan Learning Centers
3. Stanley Steemer Carpet Cleaner
4. MRI/Management Recruiters
5. Mr. Rooter
6. Padgett Business Services
7. Taco John's Restaurants
8. MAACO Auto Painting & Bodyworks
9. Dunkin' Donuts
10. Aaron's Rental Purchase

Source: *Success*, Franchise Gold 100 (annual), November, 1998, p. 76+.

★2270★
TOP FRANCHISES, 1999
Ranked by: Results of a survey. **Remarks:** Specific figures not provided. **Number listed:** 10

1. Yogen Fruz Worldwide
2. McDonald's
3. Subway
4. Wendy's
5. Jackson Hewitt Tax Service
6. Kentucky Fried Chicken
7. Mail Boxes Etc.
8. TCBY Treats
9. Taco Bell
10. Jani-King

Source: *Entrepreneur*, Entrepreneur annual Franchise 500, January, 1999, p. 209.

★2271★
TOP NEW FRANCHISES, 1994-1999
Ranked by: Order of their ranking in *Entrepreneur's* annual Franchise 500 listing. **Remarks:** Also includes contact information, description of business, and when franchising began. **Number listed:** 50

1. Curves for Women
2. Ace America's Cash Express Inc.
3. Cash Converters USA Inc.
4. Home Instead Senior Care
5. House Doctors
6. MaxCare Professional Cleaning
7. Budget Blinds Inc.
8. Mad Scientist Group
9. Millicare Environmental Services
10. Frullati Cafe & Bakery

Source: *Entrepreneur*, 50 Top New Franchises (annual), April, 1999, p. 150+.

Franchises (Retail Trade)--Florida

★2272★
TOP FRANCHISORS BY NUMBER OF FRANCHISES IN FLORIDA, 1998
Ranked by: Number of franchises in Florida. **Remarks:** Also notes number of franchises outside Florida, number of co-owned units in and outside of Florida, total initial investment, contact information, type of business and year established. **Number listed:** 25

1. Burger King, with 385 franchises
2. Anago International Inc., 192
3. Arby's Inc., 150
4. Miami Subs Inc., 119
5. Pinch-A-Penny, 108
6. Service One Janitorial, 69
6. Sonny's Real Pit Bar B-Q, 69
8. Abbey Carpet Co. Inc., 62
8. I CLEAN Tampa Bay, 62
10. LedgerPlus, 54

Source: *Florida Trend*, TopRank Florida (annual), 1999, p. 108.

Franchises (Retail Trade)--Michigan, Southern

★2273★
LEADING FRANCHISES IN SOUTHEAST MICHIGAN, 1997
Ranked by: Estimated systemwide sales, in millions of dollars. **Remarks:** Also notes previous year's sales, percent change, number of outlets, number of company-owned outlets, franchise fee, and type of business. **Number listed:** 20

1. Domino's Pizza Inc., with $3,200 million
2. Little Caesar Enterprises Inc., $1,780
3. Elias Bros. Corp., $750
4. A & W Restaurants, $282
5. Pro Golf America Inc., $224
6. American Speedy Printing Centers Inc., $185
7. Sav-Mor Drug Stores, $161
8. Hungry Howies Pizza and Subs INC.., $157
9. Ziebart International Corp., $150
10. Tastee-Freez International Inc., $114

Source: *Crain's Detroit Business*, Crain's Book of Lists Detroit (annual), December 28, 1998, p. 72.

Frankfurt Stock Exchange

★2274★
LARGEST LISTED COMPANIES ON THE FRANKFURT STOCK EXCHANGE, 1997
Ranked by: Market value, in billions of Deutsche Marks (DM). **Number listed:** 20
1. Allianz AG Holding, with DM118.44 billion
2. Deutsche Telekom AG, DM87.45
3. Daimler Benz AG, DM69.23
4. Siemens AG, DM63.92
5. Veba AG, DM59.06
6. Bayer AG, DM51.06
7. Dresdner Bank AG, DM42.98
8. BASF AG, DM40.73
9. Hoechst AG, DM40.19
10. RWE AG, DM34.01

Source: *SSB Guide to World Equity Markets (annual)*, Euromoney Publications, 1997, p. 199.

Frankfurters

★2275★
LEADING FRANKFURTER BRANDS, 1998
Ranked by: Sales, in millions of dollars. **Remarks:** Also notes market share, unit sales, and sales comparison with previous year. **Number listed:** 23
1. Hygrade Ball Park, with $221,873,216 million
2. Oscar Mayer, $183,342,944
3. Private label, $116,050,448
4. Bar-S, $65,456,024
5. Bryan, $50,770,468
6. Armour, $47,605,688
7. Oscar Mayer Bun Length, $42,605,688
8. Eckrich, $41,067,864
9. Kahn, $39,580,780
10. Hebrew National, $37,189.328

Source: *National Provisioner*, July, 1998, p. 36.

Fraud

★2276★
LEADING MANAGERIAL EXPLANATIONS FOR FRAUD, 1998
Ranked by: Percent of reason given in a survey. **Number listed:** 6
1. Poor internal controls, with 48%
2. Weak ethics policy, 39%
3. Industry type, 20%
4. Lack of duty segregation, 17%
5. Collusion with third parties, 15%
6. Collusion with members, 14%

Source: *Ivey Business Quarterly*, Winter, 1998, p. 70.

★2277★
LEADING ORGANIZATIONAL RESPONSES TO FRAUD, 1998
Ranked by: Percent of reason given, in a survey. **Number listed:** 6
1. Dismissed employee, with 41%
2. Kept it quiet, 27%
3. Initiated formal investigation, 21%
4. Informed law enforcement, 18%
5. Permitted employee to resign, 16%
6. Other, 21%

Source: *Ivey Business Quarterly*, Winter, 1998, p. 70.

Freezers, Home

See: **Home Freezers**

Frozen Dinners

★2278★
BEST-SELLING FROZEN DINNERS AND ENTREES, 1998
Ranked by: Sales, in millions of dollars. **Remarks:** Also notes lead agency and media expenditures. **Number listed:** 6
1. Stouffer's, with $746.6 million
2. Lean Cuisine, $518.8
3. Healthy Choice, $432.2
4. Banquet, $393.3
5. Swanson, $351.6
6. Budget Gourmet, $200.8

Source: *Brandweek*, Superbrands: America's Top 2,000 Brands (annual), June 21, 1999, p. 546.

★2279★
BEST-SELLING FROZEN DINNERS BY MARKET SHARE, 1998
Ranked by: Market share, in percent. **Number listed:** 6
1. Nestle, with 26.4%
2. ConAgra, 19.8%
3. Heinz, 9.3%
4. Vlasic, 9%
5. Tyson, 1.5%
6. Other, 34%

Source: *New York Times*, July 25, 1998, p. D1.

★2280★
TOP FROZEN DINNER AND ENTREES, 1998
Ranked by: Sales, in millions of dollars. **Remarks:** Also notes change from previous year, market share, units, and unit share. **Number listed:** 7
1. Stouffer's, with $558.8 million
2. Healthy Choice, $402.1
3. Stouffer's Lean Cuisine, $307.8
4. Marie Callender's, $221.3
5. Weight Watchers Smart Ones, $170.5
6. Swanson, $167.2
7. Banquet, $147.4

Source: *Supermarket Business*, February, 1999, p. 36.

Frozen Yogurt

★2281★
BEST-SELLING FROZEN YOGURT, 1998
Ranked by: Sales, in millions of dollars. **Number listed:** 10
1. Dreyer's/Edy's, with $52.5 million
2. Ben & Jerry's, $36.3

3. Turkey Hill, $21.1
4. Haagen-Dazs, $20.2
5. Breyer's, $17.4
6. Kemps, $16.2
7. Mayfield, $7.5
8. Blue Bell, $6.7
9. Wells' Blue Bunny, $5.9
10. Private label, $54.1

Source: *Dairy Foods*, March, 1999, p. 74.

Fruit Drinks

★2282★
BEST-SELLING BOTTLED FRUIT DRINKS, 1998
Ranked by: Sales, in millions of dollars. **Remarks:** Also notes unit sales. **Number listed:** 10

1. Hi-C, with $71.5 million
2. Hawaiian Punch, $69.8
3. Kool-Aid Bursts, $54.9
4. Squeezit, $48
5. Tropicana Twister, $44.6
6. Snapple, $40.7
7. Mondo Fruit Squeezers, $30.7
8. Fruitopia, $28.7
9. Ocean Spray Mauna Lai, $22.3
10. Sunny Delight, $21.9

Source: *MMR*, August 3, 1998, p. 14.

★2283★
BEST-SELLING FRUIT DRINK MIXES, 1998
Ranked by: Volume, in millions of dollars. **Remarks:** Also notes percent change from previous year, dollars share percent, unit sales, and percent change in unit sales from previous year. **Number listed:** 10

1. Kool-Aid, with $209.6 million
2. Crystal Light, $93.1
3. Country Time, $72.1
4. Kool-Aid Mega Mountain Twists, $53.4
5. Kool-Aid Island Twists, $46.4
6. Private Label, $38.4
7. Crystal Light Tropical Passions, $37.4
8. CountryTime Lemonade N' Berry Sippers, $24.2
9. Crystal Light Teas, $11.9
10. Flavor Aid, $10.9

Source: *Beverage Industry*, July, 1998, p. 10.

Fruit Juices

★2284★
BEST-SELLING CHILLED JUICES, 1998
Ranked by: Market share, in percent. **Number listed:** 4

1. Tropicana, with 39.8% percent
2. Minute Maid, 19.3%
3. Citrus World, 8.7%
4. Private Label, 22.5%
5. Other, 9.7%

Source: *Wall Street Journal*, July 21, 1998, p. B1.

★2285★
BEST-SELLING FROZEN CONCENTRATES, 1998
Ranked by: Market share, in percent. **Number listed:** 4

1. Minute Maid, with 44.7% percent
2. Tropicana, 5.4%
3. Private label, 39.4%
4. Other, 10.5%

Source: *Wall Street Journal*, July 21, 1998, p. B1.

Furnaces

★2286★
BEST-SELLING RESIDENTIAL GAS FURNACES, 1998
Ranked by: Market share, in percent. **Remarks:** Also notes 1993 market share. **Number listed:** 9

1. United Technologies, with 23% percent
2. Goodman, 17%
3. Lennox, 13%
4. Rheem, 12%
5. American Standard, 11%
5. International Comfort Products, 11%
7. York, 6%
8. Nortek, 4%
9. Duacne, 3%

Source: *Appliance Manufacturer*, April, 1999, p. 20.

Furniture Industry

★2287★
LEADING FURNITURE MANUFACTURERS BY VALUE OF SHIPMENTS, 1998
Ranked by: Shipments, in millions of dollars. **Remarks:** Also includes previous year's figures and percent change. **Number listed:** 25

1. Furniture Brands International, with $1,960.3 million
2. LifeStyle Furnishings International, $1,744.7
3. La-Z-Boy, $1,244
4. Klaussner, $725
5. Ashley, $651
6. Ethan Allen, $610.8
7. Ladd, $571.1
8. Sauder, $530
9. Bassett, $397.6
10. Bush Furniture, $384.3

Source: *Furniture/Today*, Top 25 Furniture Manufacturers (annual), May 10, 1999, p. 9.

★2288★
MOST ADMIRED FURNITURE CORPORATIONS, 1998
Ranked by: Scores (1-10) derived from a survey of senior executives, outside directors and securities analysts. **Remarks:** Respondents rated companies in their own industry on 8 attributes of reputation. Also notes previous year's rank. **Number listed:** 4

1. Herman Miller, with 8.09 points
2. Leggett & Platt, 7.73
3. Hon Industries, 7.42
4. Furniture Brands International, 6.67

Source: *Fortune*, America's Most Admired Corporations (annual), March 1, 1999, p. F-3.

★2289★
READY-TO-ASSEMBLE (RTA) FURNITURE ITEMS PURCHASED MOST, 1998
Ranked by: Sales volume, in percent. **Number listed:** 7

1. Entertainment, with 27% percent
2. Home office, 25%
3. Bedroom, 11%
3. Bookcases, 11%
5. Storage, 10%
6. Tables, 6%
7. Other, 9%

Source: *Furniture/Today*, November 9, 1998, p. 9.

★2290★
TOP DEPARTMENT STORES BY SALES OF FURNITURE AND BEDDING, 1997

Ranked by: Estimated sales, in millions of dollars. **Remarks:** Also notes sales and percent change from previous year, furniture and bedding sales as a percent of store's total sales, and total number of stores. **Number listed:** 25

1. J.C. Penney, with $747 million
2. Rich's Lazarus Goldsmith's, $176.3
3. Macy's East, $143.3
4. Dayton's Hudson's Marshall Field's, $131
5. Macy's West, $121.2
6. Dillard's, $110
7. Hecht's, $92
8. Bloomingdale's, $89.6
9. The Bon Marche, $84.8
10. Burdines, $83.5

Source: *Furniture/Today*, July 27, 1998, p. 17+.

★2291★
TOP FURNITURE COMPANIES BY BEDDING SALES, 1997

Ranked by: Bedding sales, in millions of dollars. **Remarks:** Also notes percentage of total sales. **Number listed:** 25

1. Heilig-Meyers, with $500 million
2. Sears HomeLife, $111.4
3. Sleepy's/Kleinsleep, $105.5
4. Levitz, $83.7
5. Mattress Giant, $83
6. Art Van Furniture, $77.8
7. Dial-A-Mattress, $68
8. Rooms To Go, $62.5
9. Berkshire Hathaway, $57.1
10. J.C. Penney, $53.7

Source: *HFN*, December 7, 1998, p. 23.

★2292★
TOP GROWTH LEADERS IN FURNITURE SALES, 1997-1998

Ranked by: Revenue increase, in percent. **Remarks:** Also notes increase in millions of dollars. **Number listed:** 10

1. Bernhardt, with 35.9% percent
2. Rowe Price-Fleming, 34.2%
3. Bush Furniture, 27.1%
4. Sherrill, 25.4%
5. Ashley, 22.8%
6. Ethan Allen, 17.3%
7. Hooker, 17.1%
8. Stanley, 16.7%
9. La-Z-Boy, 15.8%
10. O'Sullivan, 13%

Source: *Furniture/Today*, Top 25 Furniture Manufacturers (annual), May 10, 1999, p. 8.

★2293★
TOP RENTAL DEALERS BY FURNITURE REVENUE, 1998

Ranked by: Estimated revenues, in millions of dollars. **Remarks:** Also notes previous year's revenue, percent change from previous year and number of stores. **Number listed:** 10

1. Renters Choice, with $1,418 million
2. Aaron's Rental Purchase, $292.8
3. Home Choice, $260
4. Rent-Way, $175
5. Rentavision, $103
6. Rainbow Rentals, $66.4
7. Shastar, $11.1
8. Appliance & Furniture RentAll, $8.4
9. Ace TV Rentals, $24
10. Bestway Rental, $25

Source: *Furniture/Today*, Top 10 Rental Dealers (annual), August 10, 1998, p. 23+.

Furniture Industry--Europe

★2294★
TOP FURNITURE AND FIXTURES COMPANIES IN THE EEC, 1999

Ranked by: Sales, in millions of European Currency Units (ECUs). **Remarks:** Also notes overall rank and number of employees. **Number listed:** 63

1. Bertrand Faure (France), with ECUs862 million
2. Keiper GmbH & Co. (Germany), ECUs686
3. Bertrand Faure Equipements SA (France), ECUs592
4. Wagon Industrial Holdings PLC (United Kingdom), ECUs571
5. Industrie Natuzzi SpA (Italy), ECUs467
6. Newmond PLC (United Kingdom), ECUs396
7. Nobia Nordisk Bygginterior AB (Sweden), ECUs390
8. Wagon Industrial Ltd. (United Kingdom), ECUs381
9. DFS Furniture Co. PLC (United Kingdom), ECUs375
10. Hygena Ltd. (United Kingdom), ECUs359

Source: *Duns Europa (annual)*, Dun & Bradstreet, 1999, p. 238+.

Furniture Industry--Export-Import Trade

★2295★
COUNTRIES THAT EXPORTED THE MOST FURNITURE TO THE U.S., 1998

Ranked by: Value of exports, in millions of dollars. **Remarks:** Also notes previous year's figures and percentage change. **Number listed:** 10

1. China, with $1,839.4 million
2. Canada, $1,765.1
3. Italy, $847.9
4. Taiwan, $793
5. Mexico, $741.9
6. Malaysia, $398.2
7. Indonesia, $340.4
8. Philippines, $221.2
9. Thailand, $191.7
10. United Kingdom, $139.2

Source: *Furniture/Today*, May 3, 1999, p. 28.

Furniture Stores

★2296★
FURNITURE STORES WITH THE GREATEST GROWTH BY NET SALES INCREASES, 1997-1998
Ranked by: Net sales increases, in millions of dollars. **Number listed:** 10
1. Heilig-Meyers, with $330.1 million
2. Pier 1 Imports, $216.4
3. Rooms To Go, $120
4. Ethan Allen, $117.5
5. La-Z-Boy, $86.9
6. Breuners, $73.9
7. Jordan's Furniture, $69.2
8. Bassett Furniture Direct, $62.3
9. Select Comfort, $61.8
10. Havertys, $50.3

Source: *Furniture/Today*, Top Growth Leaders (annual), June 27, 1999, p. 9.

★2297★
FURNITURE STORES WITH THE GREATEST GROWTH IN NUMBER OF UNITS, 1997-1998
Ranked by: Number of new units. **Remarks:** Also includes previous year's figures. **Number listed:** 10
1. Select Comfort, with 64 units
2. Sleepy's, 44
3. Mattress Firm, 36
4. Pier 1 Imports, 31
5. Mattress Giant, 30
6. Restoration Hardware, 23
6. Sleep Train, 23
8. Bassett Furniture Direct, 17
9. Norwalk, 16
9. Rockaway Bedding, 16

Source: *Furniture/Today*, Top Growth Leaders (annual), June 27, 1999, p. 9.

★2298★
TOP CASUAL FURNITURE RETAILERS, 1998
Ranked by: Sales, in millions of dollars. **Remarks:** Also notes sales from previous year, type of retailer, number of stores, and contact information. **Number listed:** 100
1. M. Fortunoff, with $30-35 million
2. Seasonal Concepts, $23.6
3. Paddock Pools, $19.963
4. Treasure Island, $16.5
5. Harrow's, $15.75
6. American Sales, $14.5
7. Namco, $13.5
8. Leader's Casual Furniture, $12
9. The Chair King, $11.861
10. United Consumers Club, Inc., $10.5

Source: *Casual Living*, Top 100 Retailers Report (annual), September, 1998, p. 70+.

★2299★
TOP CONVENTIONAL FURNITURE STORES, 1998
Ranked by: Furniture, bedding and decorative accessories sales, in millions of dollars. **Remarks:** Also notes number of units, previous year's figures and percentage change. **Number listed:** 10
1. Heilig-Meyers, with $2,060 million
2. Ethan Allen, $962.2
3. Rooms To Go, $705
4. Levitz, $703.9
5. HomeLife, $644
6. La-Z-Boy, $593.1
7. Havertys, $540.3
8. Value City, $511.2
9. Art Van, $490
10. Berkshire Hathaway furniture division, $426

Source: *Furniture/Today*, Top 100 (annual), May 24, 1999, p. S-7.

★2300★
TOP FURNITURE RETAILERS BY ESTIMATED SALES IN FURNITURE AND BEDDING, 1997
Ranked by: Estimated furniture and bedding sales, in millions of dollars. **Remarks:** Also notes number of units with furniture and bedding, previous year's figures and percentage change. **Number listed:** 25
1. Heilig-Meyers, with $1,693.9 million
2. Levitz, $839.1
3. Office Depot, $779.2
4. J.C. Penney, $747
5. Federated Department Stores, $742.9
6. Sears, $737
7. Ethan Allen, $735.9
8. Wal-Mart, $673
9. Rooms To Go, $549.9
10. Montgomery Ward, $547.3

Source: *Furniture/Today*, Top 25 Retailers (annual), August 31, 1998, p. 9+.

★2301★
TOP FURNITURE RETAILERS BY SALES, 1997
Ranked by: Estimated sales, in millions of dollars. **Remarks:** Also notes previous year's figures and percentage change. **Number listed:** 100
1. Heilig-Meyers, with $1,729.9 million
2. Levitz, $856.2
3. Sears HomeLife, $650
4. Rooms To Go, $585
5. Pier 1 Imports, $563.7
6. Havertys, $490
7. Value City, $475
8. Art Van, $440
9. Ikea, $423.2
10. Berkshire Hathaway furniture division, $386

Source: *Furniture/Today*, Top 100 Furniture Retailers (annual), December 28, 1998, p. 48+.

★2302★
TOP FURNITURE STORE SPECIALISTS, 1998
Ranked by: Furniture, bedding and decorative accessories sales, in millions of dollars. **Remarks:** Also notes number of units, previous year's figures and percentage change. **Number listed:** 10
1. Pier 1 Imports, with $780.1 million
2. Ikea, $458
3. Bombay Co., $316.8
4. Select Comfort, $246.3
5. Crate & Barrel, $194
6. Slumberland, $192.5
7. This End Up, $154.9
8. Sleepy's, $152
9. Jennifer Convertibles, $142
10. Krause's Custom Crafted Furniture, $130.6

Source: *Furniture/Today*, Top 100 (annual), May 24, 1999, p. S7.

★2303★
TOP FURNITURE STORES BY FURNITURE, BEDDING AND DECORATIVE ACCESSORIES SALES, 1998
Ranked by: Furniture, bedding and decorative accessories sales, in millions of dollars. **Remarks:** Also notes previous

year's figures and percentage change, number of units, and selling space. **Number listed:** 100

1. Heilig-Meyers, with $2,060 million
2. Ethan Allen, $962.2
3. Pier 1 Imports, $780.1
4. Rooms To Go, $705
5. Levitz, $703.9
6. HomeLife, $644
7. La-Z-Boy, $593.1
8. Havertys, $540.3
9. Value City, $511.2
10. Art Van, $490

Source: *Furniture/Today*, Top 100 (annual), May 24, 1999, p. S-16+.

★2304★
TOP FURNITURE STORES BY FURNITURE, BEDDING AND DECORATIVE ACCESSORIES SALES, 1998
Ranked by: Furniture, bedding and decorative accessories sales, in millions of dollars. **Remarks:** Also notes previous year's figures and percentage change, number of units, and selling space. **Number listed:** 100

1. Heilig-Meyers, with $2,060 million
2. Ethan Allen, $962.2
3. Pier 1 Imports, $780.1
4. Rooms To Go, $705
5. Levitz, $703.9
6. HomeLife, $644
7. La-Z-Boy, $593.1
8. Havertys, $540.3
9. Value City, $511.2
10. Art Van, $490

Source: *Furniture/Today*, Top 100 (annual), May 24, 1999, p. S-16+.

★2305★
TOP FURNITURE STORES BY SALES PER SQUARE FEET, 1998
Ranked by: Furniture, bedding and decorative accessories sales, per square feet. **Number listed:** 10

1. Jordan's Furniture, with 964 per sq. ft.
2. Rooms To Go, 600
3. Walter E. Smithe Furniture, 509
4. This End Up, 485
5. Domain, 475
6. The RoomStore, 442
7. Furnitureland South, 408
8. Walker Furniture, 407
9. Room & Board, 372
10. Robb & Stucky, 350

Source: *Furniture/Today*, Top 100 (annual), May 24, 1999, p. S10.

★2306★
TOP METROPOLITAN STATISTICAL AREAS BY FURNITURE, HOME FURNISHINGS, AND APPLIANCE STORE SALES, 1998
Ranked by: Sales, in thousands of dollars. **Number listed:** 321

1. Chicago, IL, with $5,776,235 thousand
2. Los Angeles-Long Beach, CA, $4,705,268
3. Washington, DC, $4,148,899
4. New York, NY, $3,836,205
5. Detroit, MI, $2,841,600
6. Atlanta, GA, $2,563,668
7. Philadelphia, PA, $2,251,748
8. Dallas, TX, $2,159,753
9. Nassau-Suffolk, NY, $2,084,613
10. Houston, TX, $2,057,005

Source: *Sales & Marketing Management*, Survey of Buying Power & Media Markets (annual), August, 1998, p. S16.

Garbage Disposers

★2307★
BEST-SELLING DISPOSERS, 1998
Ranked by: Market share, in percent. **Remarks:** Also notes 1993 market share. **Number listed:** 3

1. In-Sink-Erator, with 70%
2. Anaheim, 24%
3. Watertown Metal Products, 6%

Source: *Appliance Manufacturer*, April, 1999, p. 19.

Gas Industry

★2308★
OIL COMPANIES WITH THE GREATEST U.S. RESERVES, 1997
Ranked by: Reserves, in millions of barrels. **Number listed:** 20

1. Exxon Corp., with 9,689 million barrels
2. Amoco Corp., 9,097
3. Burlington Resources Inc., 5,884
4. Shell Oil Co., 5,143
5. Chevron Corp., 4,991
6. Atlantic Richfield, 4,988
7. Texaco Inc., 4,022
8. Mobil Corp., 3,931
9. Phillips Petroleum Co., 3,790
10. BP (U.S.), 3,224

Source: *Oil & Gas Journal*, Oil & Gas Journal 200 (annual), September 7, 1998, p. 65.

Gas Industry, International

★2309★
LEADING PETROLEUM COMPANIES IN RESERVES, 1997
Ranked by: Reserves, in millions of barrels. **Number listed:** 20

1. Exxon Corp., with 42,129 million barrels
2. Amoco Corp., 21,456
3. Mobil Corp., 16,956
4. Chevron Corp., 9,963
5. Atlantic Richfield, 8,472
6. Unocal Corp., 6,550
7. Phillips Petroleum Co., 6,521
8. Burlington Resources Inc., 6,418
9. Texaco Inc., 6,242
10. Conoco Inc., 6,165

Source: *Oil & Gas Journal*, Oil & Gas Journal 200 (annual), September 7, 1998, p. 65.

Gas Pipelines

★2310★
GAS-PIPELINE COMPANIES WITH THE MOST MILES OF PIPELINE, 1997
Ranked by: Miles of pipeline. **Number listed:** 10
1. Northern Natural Gas Co., with 16,424 miles
2. Tennessee Gas Pipeline Co., 15,257
3. Columbia Gas Transmission Corp., 11,249
4. Transcontinental Gas Pipe Line Corp., 10,245
5. Natural Gas Pipeline of America, 9,856
6. El Paso Natural Gas Co., 9,856
7. ANR Pipeline Co., 9,564
8. Texas Eastern Transmission Corp., 9,270
9. Koch Gateway Pipeline Co., 7,781
10. Southern Natural Gas Co., 7,394

Source: *Oil & Gas Journal*, August 31, 1998, p. 35.

★2311★
INTERSTATE LIQUIDS PIPELINE COMPANIES WITH THE MOST MILES OF PIPELINE, 1997
Ranked by: Miles of pipeline. **Number listed:** 10
1. Koch Pipelines Inc., with 17,601 miles
2. Mid-America Pipeline Co., 11,497
3. Amoco Pipeline Co., 10,408
4. Williams Pipe Line Co., 7,107
5. Mobil Pipe Line Co., 6,257
6. Exxon Pipeline Co., 6,130
7. Conoco Pipe Line Co., 5,393
8. Colonial Pipeline Co., 5,353
9. Shell Pipe Line Corp., 5,322
10. Texaco Pipeline Inc., 4,996

Source: *Oil & Gas Journal*, August 31, 1998, p. 35.

★2312★
LEADING GAS-PIPELINE COMPANIES BY NET INCOME, 1997
Ranked by: Net income, in thousands of dollars. **Number listed:** 10
1. Natural Gas Pipeline of America, with $210,677 thousand
2. El Paso Natural Gas Co., $191,474
3. Columbia Gas Transmission Corp., $145,253
4. MidAmerican Energy Holdings Co., $125,941
5. Texas Eastern Transmission Corp., $125,441
6. Transcontinental Gas Pipe Line Corp., $123,609
7. CNG Transmission Corp., $117,456
8. Northern Natural Gas Co., $116,475
9. ANR Pipeline Co., $114,218
10. Southern Natural Gas Co., $105,407

Source: *Oil & Gas Journal*, August 31, 1998, p. 35.

★2313★
LEADING INTERSTATE LIQUIDS PIPELINE COMPANIES BY TRUNKLINE TRAFFIC, 1997
Ranked by: Trunkline traffic, in millions of barrel-miles. **Number listed:** 10
1. Colonial Pipeline Co., with 691,441 million
2. Lakehead Pipe Line Co. L.P., 392,002
3. BP Pipelines Inc. (Alaska), 194,936
4. Explorer Pipeline Co., 132,794
5. Plantation Pipe Line Co., 131,206
6. Shell Pipe Line Corp., 119,722
7. Exxon Pipeline Co., 105,838
8. TE Products Pipeline Co. L.P., 106,863
9. Amoco Pipeline Co., 95,118
10. Marathon Pipe Line Co., 86,269

Source: *Oil & Gas Journal*, August 31, 1998, p. 35.

★2314★
TOP GAS-PIPELINE COMPANIES BY VOLUMES MOVED FOR FEE, 1997
Ranked by: Volume, in millions of cubic feet (cf). **Number listed:** 10
1. Transcontinental Gas Pipe Line Corp., with 2,606,297 million cf
2. Tennessee Gas Pipeline Co., 1,942,217
3. ANR Pipeline Co., 1,798,601
4. Natural Gas Pipeline of America, 1,664,131
5. Northern Natural Gas Co., 1,593,445
6. Columbia Gas Transmission Corp., 1,295,810
7. Texas Eastern Transmission Corp., 1,300,276
8. El Paso Natural Gas Co., 1,275,208
9. Great Lakes Gas Transmission Co., 1,638,896
10. PG & E Gas Transmission, 969,257

Source: *Oil & Gas Journal*, August 31, 1998, p. 35.

★2315★
TOP INTERSTATE LIQUIDS PIPELINE COMPANIES BY INCOME, 1997
Ranked by: Income, in thousands of dollars. **Number listed:** 20
1. Exxon Pipeline Co., with $211,922 thousand
2. Shell Pipe Line Corp., $149,658
3. Colonial Pipeline Co., $146,797
4. Amoco Pipeline Co., $116,693
5. Koch Pipelines Inc., $90,764
6. Chevron Pipe Line Co., $89,339
7. Lakehead Pipe Line Co. L.P., $79,166
8. SFPP L.P., $71,763
9. TE Products Pipeline Co. L.P., $66,865
10. Mobil Pipe Line Co., $66,699

Source: *Oil & Gas Journal*, August 31, 1998, p. 35.

Gas Producers

★2316★
TOP PETROLEUM COMPANIES BY U.S. GAS PRODUCTION, 1997
Ranked by: Gas production, in billions of cubic feet (bcf). **Number listed:** 20
1. Amoco Corp., with 847 bcf
2. Exxon Corp., 831
3. Chevron Corp., 675
4. Texaco Inc., 643
5. Shell Oil Co., 630
6. Burlington Resources Inc., 583
7. Mobil Corp., 423
8. Union Pacific Resources Group Inc., 407
9. Atlantic Richfield, 389
10. Unocal Corp., 383

Source: *Oil & Gas Journal*, Oil & Gas Journal 200 (annual), September 7, 1998, p. 65.

★2317★
TOP PETROLEUM COMPANIES BY WORLDWIDE GAS PRODUCTION, 1997
Ranked by: Gas production, in billions of cubic feet (bcf). **Number listed:** 20
1. Exxon Corp., with 2,582 bcf
2. Mobil Corp., 1,663
3. Amoco Corp., 1,498
4. Chevron Corp., 886
5. Texaco Inc., 839
6. Unocal Corp., 721

7. Shell Oil Co., 706
8. Atlantic Richfield, 697
9. Burlington Resources, 609
10. Phillips Petroleum Co., 541

Source: *Oil & Gas Journal*, Oil & Gas Journal 200 (annual), September 7, 1998, p. 65.

Gas Stations

See: **Automobile Service Stations**

Gas Utilities--Florida

★2318★
LEADING GAS UTILITIES IN FLORIDA, 1998
Ranked by: Number of customers. **Remarks:** Also notes number of employees, total revenue, type of ownership, senior executive, and year founded. **Number listed:** 10

1. Peoples Gas System, with 237,654 customers
2. City Gas Co. of Florida, 98,000
3. Energy Services of Pensacola, 47,952
4. Florida Public Utilities Co., 45,508
5. Okaloosa Gas District, 29,675
6. Gainesville Regional Utilities, 25,000
7. City of Tallahassee Gas Operations, 16,329
8. Clearwater Gas, 13,328
9. Sunrise Gas System, 9,600
10. Lake Apopka Natural Gas District, 9,000

Source: *Florida Trend*, TopRank Florida (annual), 1999, p. 105.

Gases, International

★2319★
BEST-SELLING ELECTRONIC AND SPECIALTY GASES WORLDWIDE, 1997
Ranked by: Market share, in percent. **Number listed:** 6

1. Air Products, with 22%
2. Air Liquide, 21%
3. BOC, 18%
4. Nippon Sanso, 17%
5. Praxair, 7%
6. Others, 15%

Source: *Chemical Week*, July 15, 1998, p. 27.

Gasoline Credit Cards

★2320★
TOP OIL CARD PROGRAMS, 1998
Ranked by: Number of customer accounts. **Remarks:** Also notes number of cards, charge volume, contact information, and executives. **Number listed:** 17

1. Mobil Oil Credit Corp., with 8,200,000 accounts
2. Chevron Co. U.S.A., 7,400,000
3. Citgo Petroleum Corp., 5,474,975
4. Tosco, 4,500,000
5. Shell Oil Co., 3,500,000
6. BP America, 2,190,000
7. Phillips 66 Co., 1,800,000
8. Sun Co. Inc., 1,482,000
9. Gulf Oil, 1,000,000
10. Conoco Inc., 940,000

Source: *Card Industry Directory*, Faulkner & Gray, 1999, p. 401+.

General Merchandise

See: **Retail Trade**

Generic Drugs

★2321★
LEADING GENERIC DRUG MANUFACTURERS, 1997
Ranked by: Sales, in millions of dollars. **Remarks:** Also notes market share percent and percent change from previous year. **Number listed:** 20

1. Apothecon, with $845.3 million
2. Mylan, $588.6
3. Abbot Hospital Products, $622.9
4. Teva Pharmaceuticals, $525.1
5. Watson Laboratories, $384
6. Schein Pharmaceuticals, $353.6
7. Geneva Pharmaceuticals, $342.3
8. Roxane Laboratories Inc., $311.6
9. Zenith Goldline, $300.1
10. Barr Labs, $297.6

Source: *Drug Store News*, February 24, 1998, p. CP36.

★2322★
LEADING GENERICS THERAPEUTIC CATEGORIES, 1997
Ranked by: Sales, in millions of dollars. **Remarks:** Also notes market share percent and percent of change from previous year. **Number listed:** 15

1. Antibiotics, broad and medium spectrum, with $652.5 million
2. Bronchodialatros, general, $439.5
3. Analgesics, narcotic, $425.9
4. Calcium-channel blockers, $382.1
5. Systemic anti-arthritis, $356.9
6. Anti-Ulcerants, $338.7
7. Adrenergic blockers, $325.4
8. Cytostatics, $260.1
9. Corticoids, pain, $251.7
10. Seizure disorders, $247.5

Source: *Drug Store News*, August 24, 1998, p. CP36.

★2323★
TOP GENERIC DRUG COMPANIES, 1998
Ranked by: Sales, in millions of dollars. **Number listed:** 12

1. Apothecon, with $844.4 million
2. Mylan, $623.2
3. Teva, $559.3
4. Abbott Hospital, $551.8
5. Watson, $439.2
6. Schein Pharmaceuticals, $432.7
7. Geneva, $341.4
8. Ivax, $322.4

9. Roxane Laboratories Inc., $311.6
10. Barr, $297.8

Source: *Drug Topics Supplement*, August, 1998, p. 10.

★2324★
TOP GENERIC DRUGS, 1998
Ranked by: Total retail units sold, in thousands. **Number listed:** 200

1. Hydrocodone/APAP, with 51,587 thousand
2. Trimox, 29,928
3. Furosemide Oral, 27,151
4. Atenolol, 27,143
5. Cephalexin, 24,996
6. Albuterol Aerosol, 24,344
7. Propoxyphene-N/APAP, 24,220
8. Amoxicillin, 23,898
9. Acetaminophen w/Codeine, 23,232
10. Alprazolam, 22,123

Source: *Drug Topics*, March 15, 1999, p. 38.

★2325★
TOP NEW AND REFILL GENERIC PRESCRIPTION DRUGS, 1998
Ranked by: Total number of new or refilled prescriptions dispensed in community pharmacies, in thousands. **Remarks:** Also notes overall rank and 1997 overall rank. **Number listed:** 50

1. Trimox (Apothecon), with 31,281 thousand
2. Hydrocodone/APAP (Watson Lab), 30,747
3. Albuterol Aerosol (Warrick), 18,272
4. Amoxicillin (Teva Pharm), 17m432
5. Cephalexin (Teva Pharm), 16,271
6. Acetaminophen w/Codeine (Teva Pharm), 16,271
7. Ibuprofen (Greenstone), 13,491
8. Furosemide Oral (Mylan), 13,099
9. Trimethoprim/Sulfa (Teva Pharm), 12,317
10. Propoxyphene-N/APAP (Mylan), 11,217

Source: *American Druggist*, Top 200 Rx Drugs (annual), February, 1999, p. 48.

Gifts (In Business)

★2326★
MOST IMPORTANT FACTORS IN DECIDING WHERE TO SHOP FOR A HOLIDAY GIFT, 1998
Ranked by: Survey results, in percent. **Number listed:** 4

1. Price, with 40%
2. Convenience, 29%
3. Selection, 23%
4. Service, 8%

Source: *HFN*, November 2, 1998, p. 6.

Gin

★2327★
STATES CONSUMING THE MOST GIN, 1997
Ranked by: Consumption, in 9-liter cases. **Remarks:** Also notes 1996 consumption, change in percent, and market share and cumulative share in percent. **Number listed:** 51

1. California, with 1,237,510 9-liter cases
2. Florida, 857,620
3. Georgia, 705,140
4. New York, 646,110
5. Illinois, 555,590
6. Texas, 499,980
7. New Jersey, 443,400
8. North Carolina, 380,240
9. Michigan, 378,850
10. Maryland, 361,540

Source: *Adams Liquor Handbook*, Adams Media, Inc., 1998, p. 115.

★2328★
STATES WITH THE GREATEST PER CAPITA CONSUMPTION OF GIN BY ADULTS, 1997
Ranked by: Consumption, in 9-liter cases per 1,000 adults. **Remarks:** Also notes 1996 consumption and rank. **Number listed:** 51

1. District of Columbia, with 254.7 9-liter cases
2. New Hampshire, 162.9
3. Georgia, 135.7
4. Delaware, 132.9
5. South Carolina, 122.4
6. Maryland, 99.9
7. Nevada, 98.5
8. Alabama, 91
9. Mississippi, 90.9
10. Louisiana, 82.6

Source: *Adams Liquor Handbook*, Adams Media, Inc., 1998, p. 116.

★2329★
TOP GIN BRANDS, 1997
Ranked by: Sales, in thousands of 9-liter cases. **Remarks:** Also notes country of origin, supplier, and 1992-1996 sales figures. **Number listed:** 14

1. Seagram's Gin, with 3,170 thousand cases
2. Gordon's Gin, 1,115
3. Gilbey's Gin, 721
4. Fleischmann's Gin, 407
5. Burnetts White Satin Gin, 365
6. Barton Gin, 346
7. McCormick Gin, 186
8. Crystal Palace Gin, 172
9. Seagram's Lime Twist, 150
10. Booth's Hi & Dry, 100

Source: *Adams Liquor Handbook*, Adams Media, Inc., 1998, p. 118.

★2330★
TOP METROPOLITAN AREAS FOR GIN SALES, 1997
Ranked by: Sales, in thousands of 9-liter cases. **Remarks:** Also notes market share in percent. **Number listed:** 50

1. Atlanta, GA, with 431 thousand cases
2. Chicago, IL, 426.1
3. Washington, DC, 389.8
4. Los Angeles-Long Beach, CA, 328.7
5. New York, NY, 283.1
6. Boston-Lawrence-Lowell-Brockton, MA, 198.5
7. Detroit, MI, 176.4
8. Philadelphia, PA, 175.9
9. Baltimore, MD, 170.8
10. Tampa-St. Petersburg-Clearwater, FL, 137.3

Source: *Adams Liquor Handbook*, Adams Media, Inc., 1998, p. 117.

★2331★
TOP SUPPLIERS OF GIN BY MARKET SHARE, 1997
Ranked by: Market share, in percent. **Number listed:** 6

1. Seagram Americas, with 29.1%
2. Schieffelin & Somerset, 11.9%
3. United Distillers USA, 10.7%

4. Barton Inc., 9.5%
5. Jim Bean Brands, 7%
6. Others, 31.8%

Source: *Adams Liquor Handbook*, Adams Media, Inc., 1998, p. 119.

Gin--Advertising

★2332★

GIN BRANDS WITH THE HIGHEST MAGAZINE ADVERTISING EXPENDITURES, 1997

Ranked by: Magazine advertising expenditures, in thousands of dollars. **Remarks:** Also notes 1996 figures. **Number listed:** 5

1. Bombay Sapphire, with $5,359.9 thousand
2. Tanqueray, $4,456.9
3. Seagram's Gin, $3,863.9
4. Beefeater, $2,776.9
5. Tanqueray Malacca, $613.6

Source: *Adams Liquor Handbook*, Adams Media, Inc., 1998, p. 121.

★2333★

GIN BRANDS WITH THE HIGHEST OUTDOOR ADVERTISING EXPENDITURES, 1997

Ranked by: Outdoor advertising expenditures, in thousands of dollars. **Remarks:** Also notes 1996 figures. **Number listed:** 4

1. Seagram's Gin, with $651.3 thousand
2. Gordon's Gin, $414.4
3. Beefeater, $129.9
4. Tanqueray Malacca, $36.3

Source: *Adams Liquor Handbook*, Adams Media, Inc., 1998, p. 121.

★2334★

GIN BRANDS WITH THE HIGHEST TOTAL ADVERTISING EXPENDITURES, 1997

Ranked by: Total advertising expenditures, in thousands of dollars. **Remarks:** Also notes 1996 figures. **Number listed:** 7

1. Bombay Sapphire, with $5,359.9 thousand
2. Seagram's Gin, $5,126
3. Tanqueray, $4,456.9
4. Beefeater, $2,906.8
5. Tanqueray Malacca, $649.9
6. Gordon's Gin, $414.4
7. Bombay, $374

Source: *Adams Liquor Handbook*, Adams Media, Inc., 1998, p. 121.

Gin--Export-Import Trade

★2335★

COUNTRIES EXPORTING THE MOST GIN TO THE U.S., 1997

Ranked by: Proof gallons, in thousands. **Remarks:** Also notes 1995 and 1996 figures. **Number listed:** 10

1. United Kingdom, with 5,075.9 thousand gallons
2. Canada, 30.9
3. Netherlands, 26.9
4. Germany, 8.5
5. Denmark, 4.6
6. France, 2.3
7. Ireland, .7
7. Spain, .7
9. Czech Republic, .1

Others, .2

Source: *Adams Liquor Handbook*, Adams Media, Inc., 1998, p. 223.

★2336★

COUNTRIES IMPORTING THE MOST U.S. GIN, 1997

Ranked by: Proof gallons, in thousands. **Remarks:** Also notes 1995 and 1996 figures. **Number listed:** 6

1. Iceland, with 61.6 thousand gallons
2. Canada, 43.3
3. Belgium, 36
4. Netherlands Antilles, 23.8
5. Japan, 21.1
6. Other, 76.4

Source: *Adams Liquor Handbook*, Adams Media, Inc., 1998, p. 219.

Glass

★2337★

LEADING CHEMICAL PROCESS COMPANIES PRODUCING GLASS, CEMENT, LIME, ABRASIVES, AND REFRACTORIES BY SALES, 1998

Ranked by: Sales, in millions of dollars. **Remarks:** Also notes change from 1997 in percent, net income, profit margin, capital ratios, shareholder returns, price and assets. **Number listed:** 11

1. Owens-Illinois, with $5,306 million
2. Owens Corning, $5,009
3. Corning, $3,484
4. USG, $3,130
5. Ball, $2,896
6. John Manville, $1,781
7. Texas Industries, $1,214
8. Southdown, $1,185
9. Lancaster Colony, $1,009
10. Global Industrial Technologies, $496

Source: *Chemical Week*, Chemical Week 300 (annual), May 12, 1999, p. 51.

Glassware

★2338★

BEST-SELLING CRYSTAL STEMWARE PATTERNS, 1998

Ranked by: Market share, in percent. **Remarks:** Also notes price and 1997 rank. **Number listed:** 25

1. Lismore (Waterford), with 4.83%
2. Stephanie (Mikasa), 3.8%
3. Lady Anne (Gorham), 3.71%
4. Arctic Lights (Mikasa), 3.62%
5. Park Lane (Mikasa), 3.48%
6. Araglin (Waterford), 2.94%
7. French Countryside (Mikasa), 2.67%
8. Debut Gold (Lenox), 2.55%
9. Flame D'Amore (Mikasa), 2.43%
10. Hanover Gold (Marquis by Waterford), 2.18%

Source: *HFN*, August 24, 1998, p. 30.

★2339★
BEST-SELLING GLASS BEVERAGEWARE PATTERNS, 1998
Ranked by: Ranked by sales, figures not given. **Remarks:** Also notes average price and 1997 rank. **Number listed:** 20

1. Georgia (Indiana Glass Coke)
2. Tartan (Anchor Hocking)
3. Essex (Anchor Hocking)
4. Michelangelo (Luigi Bormioli)
5. Diamond Cut (Anchor Glass Co.)
6. Impulse (Libbey)
7. Savannah (Anchor Hocking)
8. Tartan Seamist (Anchor Hocking)
9. Napa (Libbey)
10. Rigoletto (LuigiBormioli)

Source: *HFN*, January 4, 1999, p. 53.

★2340★
BEST-SELLING TYPES OF GLASSWARE, 1998
Ranked by: Market share, in percent. **Number listed:** 5

1. Beverageware, with 47%
2. Serveware, tabletop accessories, 21.1%
3. Ovenware, 15.3%
4. Storageware, 8.1%
5. Decorative accessories, 8.5%

Source: *HFN*, August 3, 1998, p. 48.

★2341★
TOP NEW CRYSTAL STEMWARE PATTERNS, 1998
Ranked by: Market share, in percent. **Remarks:** Also notes price. **Number listed:** 10

1. Debut Platinum (Lennox), with .57%
2. Isabelle Green (Villeroy & Boch), .13%
3. Kensington Gold (Mikasa), .1%
4. Overture (Mikasa), .09%
5. Nadine Blue (Villeroy & Boch), .08%
6. Overture (Waterford), .07%
7. Lismore Platinum (Waterford), .06%
7. Kensington Frost (Mikasa), .06%
9. Sonesta (Marquis by Waterford), .04%
10. Linette (Durand), .03%

Source: *HFN*, August 24, 1998, p. 30.

★2342★
TOP-SELLING CRYSTAL BEVERAGEWARE PATTERNS, 1998
Ranked by: Ranked by sales, figures not given. **Remarks:** Also notes average price and 1997 rank. **Number listed:** 20

1. Lismore (Waterford)
2. Lady Anne (Gorham)
3. Love (Waterford)
4. Arctic Lites (Mikasa)
5. Longchamp (Cristal d'Arque)
6. Marquis Vintage (Waterford)
7. Araglin (Waterford)
8. Prosperity (Waterford)
9. Parklane (Mikasa)
10. Stephanie (Mikasa)

Source: *HFN*, January 4, 1999, p. 53.

Glazing

★2343★
LEADING GLAZING CONTRACTORS, 1998
Ranked by: Gross sales, in millions of dollars. **Remarks:** Also notes location, 1996 and 1997 gross sales, and number of employees. **Number listed:** 50

1. Harmon, Ltd., with $85 million
2. Harmon, Inc., $79.8
3. LBL SkySystems Corp., $40
4. Flour City Architectural Metals, Inc., $32.2
5. Trainor Glass Co., $30.35
6. Haley-Greer, Inc., $30.3
7. Architectural Glass & Aluminum Co. Inc., $30.2
8. Cartner Glass Systems, Inc., $25.2
9. W&W Glass Systems, Inc., $23.2
10. MTH Industries, $22.3

Source: *Glass Magazine*, Annual Survey of America's Top Glazing Contractors (annual), June, 1999, p. 26+.

Global Custodians, International

★2344★
TOP GLOBAL CUSTODIANS BY TOTAL GLOBAL CUSTODY ASSETS, 1998
Ranked by: Total global custody assets, in millions of dollars. **Remarks:** Also notes separate figures for individual assets. **Number listed:** 25

1. Chase Manhattan Bank, with $1,592,000 million
2. Bank of New York, $924,000
3. Citibank, $890,000
4. Deutsche Bank, $805,000
5. State Street Corp., $705,100
6. Bankers Trust Co., $485,000
7. Paribas, $421,000
8. ABN Amro Bank, $357,100
9. Brown Brothers Harriman & Co., $295,080
10. Royal Trust Corp. of Canada, $234,853

Source: *Institutional Investor*, Top 25 (annual), September, 1998, p. 201.

Gloucester County (NJ)--Industries

★2345★
LARGEST EMPLOYERS IN GLOUCESTER COUNTY, NJ, 1998
Ranked by: Number of full-time employees. **Remarks:** Also notes contact information, number of offices, and top executive. **Number listed:** 25

1. Sony Music Inc., with 850 employees
2. Underwood-Memorial Hospital, 797
3. Mobil Oil Corp., 750
4. Kennedy Health System, 481
5. Compucom Systems Inc., 450
6. Delaware Valley Wholesale Florists, Inc., 400
7. Coastal Eagle Point Oil Co., 387
8. Rapidforms Inc., 375
9. VWR Scientific Products Corp., 350
10. Tenneco Packaging, 300

Source: *Philadelphia Business Journal*, Book of Business Lists (annual), December 25, 1998, p. 103.

Going Private (Securities)

★2346★
LARGEST PRIVATIZATION DEALS, 1983-1998
Ranked by: Purchase price, in millions of dollars. **Remarks:** Also notes year of deal, price/earnings ratio, and premium offered over market. **Number listed:** 20

1. RJR Nabisco, with $24,561.6 million
2. Beatrice Companies, $5,361.6
3. Safeway, $4,198.4
4. Borg-Warner Corp., $3,798.6
5. Southland Corp., $3,723.3
6. Owens-Illinois, $3,631.9
7. Hospital Corp. of America, $3,602.1
8. Fort Howard Paper Co., $3,574.2
9. NWA, $3,524.5
10. R.H. Macy & Co. Inc., $3,484.7

Source: *Mergerstat Review (annual)*, Houlihan Lokey Howard & Zukin, 1999, p. 43.

★2347★
LARGEST PRIVATIZATION TRANSACTIONS OF ALL-TIME
Ranked by: Price offered, in millions of dollars. **Remarks:** Also notes year of deal. **Number listed:** 5

1. Kohlberg Kravis Roberts & Co. buyer, RJR Nabisco seller, with $24,561.6 million
2. Kohlberg Kravis Roberts & Co. buyer, Beatrice Companies seller, $5,361.6
3. SSI Holdings Corp. (buyer), Safeway Stores Inc. (seller), $4,198.4
4. Private group, led by Merrill Lynch Capital Partners (buyer), org-Warner Corp. (seller), $3,798.6
5. Private group, led by John & Jere Thompson (buyer), Southland Corp. (seller), $3,723.3

Source: *Mergerstat Review (annual)*, Houlihan Lokey Howard & Zukin, 1999, p. 213.

Gold as an Investment

★2348★
LEADING GOLD BAR HOARDING COUNTRIES IN LATIN AMERICA, 1996
Ranked by: Gold bar hoards, in metric tons. **Remarks:** Also notes gold bar hoards from 1987 to 1995. **Number listed:** 4

1. Brazil, with -13.5 metric tons
2. Colombia, 3.4
3. Venezuela, 1
4. Argentina, .8

Source: *Gold 1997*, Gold Fields Mineral Services, 1997, p. 69.

★2349★
LEADING GOLD BAR HOARDING COUNTRIES IN THE FAR EAST, 1996
Ranked by: Gold bar hoards, in metric tons. **Remarks:** Also notes gold bar hoards from 1987 to 1995. **Number listed:** 11

1. Vietnam, with 30.3 metric tons
2. Thailand, 26.7
3. Japan, 25
4. Burma, Laos & Cambodia, 5.5
5. South Korea, 4.5
6. Hong Kong, -2.5
7. Indonesia, -1.8
8. Taiwan, .5
9. Philippines, .1
10. Malaysia, 0

Source: *Gold 1997*, Gold Fields Mineral Services, 1997, p. 69.

★2350★
LEADING GOLD BAR HOARDING COUNTRIES IN THE INDIAN SUB-CONTINENT, 1996
Ranked by: Gold bar hoards, in metric tons. **Remarks:** Also notes gold bar hoards from 1987 to 1995. **Number listed:** 3

1. India, with 95 metric tons
2. Pakistan & Afghanistan, 1.3
3. Sri Lanka, .5

Source: *Gold 1997*, Gold Fields Mineral Services, 1997, p. 69.

★2351★
LEADING GOLD BAR HOARDING COUNTRIES IN THE MIDDLE EAST, 1996
Ranked by: Gold bar hoards, in metric tons. **Remarks:** Also notes gold bar hoards from 1987 to 1995. **Number listed:** 8

1. Arabian Gulf States, with 3.2 metric tons
2. Iran, 2
3. Saudi Arabia & Yemen, 1
4. Iraq, Syria & Jordan, .5
4. Kuwait, .5
6. Turkey, .4
6. Israel, .4
8. Lebanon, 0

Source: *Gold 1997*, Gold Fields Mineral Services, 1997, p. 69.

Gold, International

★2352★
LEADING AFRICAN COUNTRIES IN GOLD FABRICATION IN CARAT JEWELRY, EXCEPT SCRAP, 1996
Ranked by: Gold use in carat jewelry, except the use of scrap, by metric ton. **Remarks:** Also notes gold usage in carat jewelry from 1987 to 1995. **Number listed:** 7

1. South Africa, with 4.6 metric tons
2. Morocco, 4
2. Libya, 4
4. Zimbabwe, 3
5. Tunisia, 1.8
6. Algeria, .5
7. Other, 2.6

Source: *Gold 1997*, Gold Fields Mineral Services, 1997, p. 52+.

★2353★
LEADING AFRICAN COUNTRIES IN GOLD FABRICATION IN CARAT JEWELRY, 1996
Ranked by: Gold use in carat jewelry, by metric ton. **Remarks:** Also notes gold usage in carat jewelry from 1987 to 1995. **Number listed:** 7

1. Morocco, with 9 metric tons
2. Libya, 5
3. South Africa, 4.6
4. Algeria, 3
4. Zimbabwe, 3
6. Tunisia, 1.8
7. Other, 3.9

Source: *Gold 1997*, Gold Fields Mineral Services, 1997, p. 48+.

★2354★
LEADING CONSUMER GOLD MARKETS, 1997
Ranked by: Gold offtake, in tons. **Remarks:** Also notes percent change from 1996. **Number listed:** 11

1. India, with 737 tons
2. United States, 377
3. China, 214
4. Turkey, 202
5. Saudi Arabia, 199
6. Gulf States, 142
6. Taiwan, 142
8. Japan, 130
9. South Korea, 114
9. Italy, 114

Source: *SA Banker*, November 3, 1998, vol. 95, p. 32.

★2355★

LEADING EUROPEAN COUNTRIES IN GOLD FABRICATION IN CARAT JEWELRY, EXCLUDING SCRAP, 1996

Ranked by: Gold use in carat jewelry, except use of scrap, by metric ton. **Remarks:** Also notes gold usage in carat jewelry from 1987 to 1995. **Number listed:** 22

1. Italy, with 409 metric tons
2. Germany, 33.8
3. France, 29.2
4. Spain, 28.5
5. United Kingdom & Ireland, 26.4
6. Switzerland, 25.3
7. Portugal, 15.1
8. Greece, 12.3
9. Poland, 3.2
10. Czech & Slovak Republics, 2.8

Source: *Gold 1997*, Gold Fields Mineral Services, 1997, p. 52.

★2356★

LEADING EUROPEAN COUNTRIES IN GOLD FABRICATION IN CARAT JEWELRY, 1996

Ranked by: Gold use in carat jewelry, by metric ton. **Remarks:** Also notes gold usage in carat jewelry from 1987 to 1995. **Number listed:** 22

1. Italy, with 439 metric tons
2. Germany, 37.2
3. Spain, 30
3. France, 30
5. United Kingdom & Ireland, 28.4
6. Switzerland, 25.3
7. Portugal, 15.4
8. Greece, 13.2
9. Poland, 5.6
10. Czech & Slovak Republics, 3.7

Source: *Gold 1997*, Gold Fields Mineral Services, 1997, p. 48.

★2357★

LEADING FAR EASTERN COUNTRIES IN GOLD FABRICATION IN CARAT JEWELRY, EXCEPT SCRAP, 1996

Ranked by: Gold use in carat jewelry, except the use of scrap, by metric ton. **Remarks:** Also notes gold usage in carat jewelry from 1987 to 1995. **Number listed:** 11

1. Indonesia, with 117.5 metric tons
2. Taiwan, 84.1
3. Malaysia, 75.7
4. Hong Kong, 71.2
5. Thailand, 62
6. Japan, 61.9
7. South Korea, 50.7
8. Singapore, 14.3
9. Vietnam, 13.3
10. Burma, Laos & Cambodia, 9.9

Source: *Gold 1997*, Gold Fields Mineral Services, 1997, p. 52+.

★2358★

LEADING FAR EASTERN COUNTRIES IN GOLD FABRICATION IN CARAT JEWELRY, 1996

Ranked by: Gold use in carat jewelry, by metric ton. **Remarks:** Also notes gold usage in carat jewelry from 1987 to 1995. **Number listed:** 11

1. Indonesia, with 132 metric tons
2. Taiwan, 91
3. Malaysia, 79.5
4. Hong Kong, 79
5. Japan, 74
6. Thailand, 71
7. South Korea, 61
8. Singapore, 19
9. Vietnam, 16.5
10. Burma, Laos & Cambodia, 11

Source: *Gold 1997*, Gold Fields Mineral Services, 1997, p. 48+.

★2359★

LEADING GOLD FABRICATION COUNTRIES IN AFRICA, 1996

Ranked by: Gross usage of gold, in metric tons. **Remarks:** Also notes gold usage from 1987 to 1995. **Number listed:** 7

1. South Africa, with 10.2 metric tons
2. Morocco, 9
3. Libya, 5
4. Algeria, 3
4. Zimbabwe, 3
6. Tunisia, 1.8
7. Other, 3.9

Source: *Gold 1997*, Gold Fields Mineral Services, 1997, p. 45.

★2360★

LEADING GOLD FABRICATION COUNTRIES IN EUROPE, 1996

Ranked by: Gross usage of gold, in metric tons. **Remarks:** Also notes gold usage from 1987 to 1995. **Number listed:** 22

1. Italy, with 449.8 metric tons
2. Germany, 69.3
3. France, 44.2
4. Switzerland, 41.8
5. United Kingdom & Ireland, 40.1
6. Sapin, 31.7
7. Austria, 21.6
8. Portugal, 15.6
9. Greece, 13.2
10. Netherlands, 8.3

Source: *Gold 1997*, Gold Fields Mineral Services, 1997, p. 44.

★2361★

LEADING GOLD FABRICATION COUNTRIES IN LATIN AMERICA, 1996

Ranked by: Gross usage of gold, in metric tons. **Remarks:** Also notes gold usage from 1987 to 1995. **Number listed:** 11

1. Brazil, with 27.6 metric tons
2. Mexico, 25.2
3. Peru, 8
4. Dominican Republic, 7.4
5. Bolivia, 6.6
6. Chile, 6.3
7. Columbia, 3.5
8. Argentina, 2.7
9. Ecuador, 2.5
10. Venezuela, 1.3

Source: *Gold 1997*, Gold Fields Mineral Services, 1997, p. 44.

★2362★
LEADING GOLD FABRICATION COUNTRIES IN NORTH AMERICA, 1996
Ranked by: Gross usage of gold, in metric tons. **Remarks:** Also notes gold usage from 1987 to 1995. **Number listed:** 2
1. United States, with 245.5 metric tons
2. Canada, 25.4

Source: *Gold 1997*, Gold Fields Mineral Services, 1997, p. 44.

★2363★
LEADING GOLD FABRICATION COUNTRIES IN THE FAR EAST, 1996
Ranked by: Gross usage of gold, in metric tons. **Remarks:** Also notes gold usage from 1987 to 1995. **Number listed:** 11
1. Japan, with 187.5 metric tons
2. Indonesia, 132
3. Taiwan, 99
4. Hong Kong, 83.9
5. South Korea, 80.9
6. Malaysia, 79.5
7. Thailand, 75.5
8. Singapore, 22
9. Vietnam, 16.5
10. Burma, Laos & Cambodia, 11

Source: *Gold 1997*, Gold Fields Mineral Services, 1997, p. 45.

★2364★
LEADING GOLD FABRICATION COUNTRIES IN THE INDIAN SUB-CONTINENT, 1996
Ranked by: Gross usage of gold, in metric tons. **Remarks:** Also notes gold usage from 1987 to 1995. **Number listed:** 5
1. India, with 454.8 metric tons
2. Pakistan & Afghanistan, 43.6
3. Bangladesh & Nepal, 11
4. Sri Lanka, 4.4
5. Mauritius, .5

Source: *Gold 1997*, Gold Fields Mineral Services, 1997, p. 44.

★2365★
LEADING GOLD FABRICATION COUNTRIES IN THE MIDDLE EAST, 1996
Ranked by: Gross usage of gold, in metric tons. **Remarks:** Also notes gold usage from 1987 to 1995. **Number listed:** 9
1. Saudi Arabia & Yemen, with 162.3 metric tons
2. Turkey, 157.6
3. Egypt, 69.2
4. Arabian Gulf States, 45.9
5. Iran, 36.1
6. Iraq, Syria, & Jordan, 33.4
7. Israel, 24.7
8. Kuwait, 23.9
9. Lebanon, 10.7

Source: *Gold 1997*, Gold Fields Mineral Services, 1997, p. 44.

★2366★
LEADING INDIAN SUB-CONTINENTAL COUNTRIES IN GOLD FABRICATION IN CARAT JEWELRY, EXCEPT SCRAP, 1996
Ranked by: Gold use in carat jewelry, except the use of scrap, by metric ton. **Remarks:** Also notes gold usage in carat jewelry from 1987 to 1995. **Number listed:** 5
1. India, with 317.8 metric tons
2. Pakistan & Afghanistan, 32.9
3. Bangladesh & Nepal, 9.5
4. Sri Lanka, 3.8
5. Mauritius, .5

Source: *Gold 1997*, Gold Fields Mineral Services, 1997, p. 52.

★2367★
LEADING INDIAN SUB-CONTINENTAL COUNTRIES IN GOLD FABRICATION IN CARAT JEWELRY, 1996
Ranked by: Gold use in carat jewelry, by metric ton. **Remarks:** Also notes gold usage in carat jewelry from 1987 to 1995. **Number listed:** 5
1. India, with 427.8 metric tons
2. Pakistan & Afghanistan, 42.9
3. Bangladesh & Nepal, 11
4. Sri Lanka, 4.4
5. Mauritius, .5

Source: *Gold 1997*, Gold Fields Mineral Services, 1997, p. 48.

★2368★
LEADING LATIN AMERICAN COUNTRIES IN GOLD FABRICATION IN CARAT JEWELRY, EXCEPT SCRAP, 1996
Ranked by: Gold use in carat jewelry, except the use of scrap, by metric ton. **Remarks:** Also notes gold usage in carat jewelry from 1987 to 1995. **Number listed:** 11
1. Brazil, with 18.4 metric tons
2. Mexico, 13.7
3. Peru, 7.7
4. Dominican Republic, 7.4
5. Bolivia, 6.5
6. Chile, 6.3
7. Colombia, 2.3
8. Ecuador, 2.2
9. Venezuela, .3
10. Argentina, 0

Source: *Gold 1997*, Gold Fields Mineral Services, 1997, p. 52.

★2369★
LEADING LATIN AMERICAN COUNTRIES IN GOLD FABRICATION IN CARAT JEWELRY, 1996
Ranked by: Gold use in carat jewelry, by metric ton. **Remarks:** Also notes gold usage in carat jewelry from 1987 to 1995. **Number listed:** 11
1. Brazil, with 23 metric tons
2. Mexico, 22.2
3. Peru, 8
4. Dominican Republic, 7.4
5. Bolivia, 6.6
6. Chile, 6.3
7. Colombia, 3.2
8. Argentina, 2.4
8. Ecuador, 2.4
10. Venezuela, 1.2

Source: *Gold 1997*, Gold Fields Mineral Services, 1997, p. 48.

★2370★
LEADING MIDDLE EASTERN COUNTRIES IN GOLD FABRICATION IN CARAT JEWELRY, EXCEPT SCRAP, 1996
Ranked by: Gold use in carat jewelry, except the use of scrap, by metric ton. **Remarks:** Also notes gold usage in carat jewelry from 1987 to 1995. **Number listed:** 9
1. Turkey, with 91.7 metric tons
2. Saudi Arabia & Yemen, 71.8
3. Egypt, 35.8
4. Arabian Gulf States, 34.8
5. Iran, 22.1
6. Iraq, Syria & Jordan, 18.4
7. Israel, 17.9
8. Kuwait, 10.2
9. Lebanon, 9.9

Source: *Gold 1997*, Gold Fields Mineral Services, 1997, p. 52.

★2371★
LEADING MIDDLE EASTERN COUNTRIES IN GOLD FABRICATION IN CARAT JEWELRY, 1996
Ranked by: Gold use in carat jewelry, by metric ton. **Remarks:** Also notes gold usage in carat jewelry from 1987 to 1995. **Number listed:** 9
1. Saudi Arabia & Yemen, with 159.3 metric tons
2. Turkey, 140.7
3. Egypt, 69
4. Arabian Gulf States, 41.9
5. Iraq, Syria & Jordan, 32.4
6. Iran, 31.1
7. Israel, 23.9
8. Kuwait, 23.7
9. Lebanon, 10.7

Source: *Gold 1997*, Gold Fields Mineral Services, 1997, p. 48.

★2372★
LEADING NORTH AMERICAN COUNTRIES IN GOLD FABRICATION IN CARAT JEWELRY, EXCEPT SCRAP, 1996
Ranked by: Gold use in carat jewelry, except the use of scrap, by metric ton. **Remarks:** Also notes gold usage in carat jewelry from 1987 to 1995. **Number listed:** 2
1. United States, with 134.4 metric tons
2. Canada, 13.9

Source: *Gold 1997*, Gold Fields Mineral Services, 1997, p. 52.

★2373★
LEADING NORTH AMERICAN COUNTRIES IN GOLD FABRICATION IN CARAT JEWELRY, 1996
Ranked by: Gold use in carat jewelry, by metric ton. **Remarks:** Also notes gold usage in carat jewelry from 1987 to 1995. **Number listed:** 2
1. United States, with 152.4 metric tons
2. Canada, 17.7

Source: *Gold 1997*, Gold Fields Mineral Services, 1997, p. 48.

★2374★
WORLD LEADERS IN GOLD FABRICATION IN DENTISTRY, 1996
Ranked by: Gold use in dentistry, in metric tons. **Remarks:** Also notes gold use in dentistry from 1987 to 1995. **Number listed:** 27
1. Japan, with 19.5 metric tons
2. Germany, 15.2
3. United States, 11.5
4. Switzerland, 4.2
5. Italy, 4.1
6. South Korea, 3.2
7. Netherlands, 2.3
8. Brazil, 1
9. Austria, .8
10. France, .4

Source: *Gold 1997*, Gold Fields Mineral Services, 1997, p. 61.

★2375★
WORLD LEADERS IN GOLD FABRICATION IN ELECTRONICS, 1996
Ranked by: Gold use in electronics, in metric ton. **Remarks:** Also notes electronics gold usage from 1987 to 1995. **Number listed:** 20
1. Japan, with 78.8 metric tons
2. United States, 51
3. South Korea, 11.6
4. Germany, 8.9
5. United Kingdom & Ireland, 6.8
6. Taiwan, 6.5
7. France, 6.3
8. Switzerland, 6.2
9. Netherlands, 3.1
10. Singapore, 2.6

Source: *Gold 1997*, Gold Fields Mineral Services, 1997, p. 60.

★2376★
WORLD LEADERS IN GOLD FABRICATION IN MEDALS AND IMITATION COINS, 1996
Ranked by: Gold use in medal and imitation coins, in metric tons. **Remarks:** Also notes gold use in medal and imitation coins from 1987-1995. **Number listed:** 21
1. Turkey, with 14.8 metric tons
2. India, 7
3. Arabian Gulf States, 4
4. Saudi Arabia & Yemen, 3
5. Pakistan & Afghanistan, .7
6. Iraq, Syria & Jordan, .5
6. Italy, .5
6. South Korea, .5
9. Switzerland, .4
9. Japan, .4
9. Thailand, .4

Source: *Gold 1997*, Gold Fields Mineral Services, 1997, p. 63.

★2377★
WORLD LEADERS IN GOLD FABRICATION IN OFFICIAL COINS, 1996
Ranked by: Gold usage in official coins, in metric tons. **Remarks:** Also notes gold usage in official coins from 1987-1995. **Number listed:** 27
1. Austria, with 18.1 metric tons
2. United States, 11
3. Canada, 7.3
4. Australia, 6.2
5. Iran, 5
6. United Kingdom & Ireland, 3.1
7. Thailand, 2.2
8. Mexico, 1.8
8. Turkey, 1.8
10. South Africa, 1

Source: *Gold 1997*, Gold Fields Mineral Services, 1997, p. 64.

★2378★
WORLD LEADERS IN GOLD FABRICATION IN OTHER INDUSTRIAL AND DECORATIVE APPLICATIONS, 1996
Ranked by: Gold use, in metric tons. **Remarks:** Also notes gold usage in other industrial and decorative applications from 1987 to 1995. **Number listed:** 28
1. United States, with 19.6 metric tons
2. India, 19
3. Japan, 14.7
4. Germany, 7.7
5. France, 6.9
6. Switzerland, 5.6
7. Italy, 5.1
8. South Korea, 4.6
9. Hong Kong, 3.8
10. South Africa, 3.5

Source: *Gold 1997*, Gold Fields Mineral Services, 1997, p. 62.

Gold Mines and Mining, International

★2379★
LEADING GOLD PRODUCERS WORLDWIDE, 1996
Ranked by: Gold production, in metric tons. **Remarks:** Also notes gold production and rank in 1987. **Number listed:** 15

1. South Africa, with 495 metric tons
2. United States, 329
3. Australia, 289
4. Canada, 164
5. China, 145
6. Russia, 130
7. Indonesia, 92
8. Uzbekistan, 71
9. Peru, 65
10. Brazil, 64

Source: *Gold 1997*, Gold Fields Mineral Service, 1997, p. 18.

★2380★
LEADING GOLD PRODUCING COMPANIES WORLDWIDE, 1996
Ranked by: Gold production, in tonnes. **Remarks:** Also notes gold output in 1995. **Number listed:** 15

1. Anglo American (South Africa), with 226 tonnes
2. Barrick Gold (Canada), 98
3. GFSA (South Africa), 94
4. Newmont (United States), 71
5. RTZ-CRA (United Kingdom), 60
5. Placer Dome (Canada), 60
7. Homestake (United States), 54
8. Gencor (South Africa), 53
8. Freeport-McMoRan (United States), 53
10. Randgold (South Africa), 47

Source: *Gold 1997*, Gold Fields Mineral Services, 1997, p. 20.

Golf Courses

★2381★
GREATEST GOLF COURSES IN THE U.S., 1998
Ranked by: Ranking criteria not given. **Number listed:** 10

1. Pine Valley Golf Course (Pine Valley, NJ)
2. Augusta National Golf Course (Augusta, GA)
3. Cypress Point Club (Pebble Beach, CA)
4. Pebble Beach Golf Links (Pebble Beach, CA)
5. Shinnecock Hills Golf Course (Southampton, NY)
6. Winged Foot Golf Course (West) (Mamaroneck, NY)
7. Oakmont Country Club (Oakmont, PA)
8. Merion Golf Course (East) (Ardmore, PA)
9. Pinehurst Country Club (Pinehurst, NC)
10. Oaklands Hills Country Club (South) (Bloomfield Hills, MI)

Source: *Incentive*, October, 1998, p. 60.

★2382★
STATES WITH THE MOST GOLF COURSES, 1998
Ranked by: Total number of golf courses. **Number listed:** 5

1. Florida, with 1,170 golf courses
2. California, 942
3. Michigan, 906
4. New York, 838
4. Texas, 838

Source: *Hotel and Management*, September 7, 1998, p. 32.

Granola Bars

★2383★
BEST-SELLING GRANOLA BARS, 1998
Ranked by: Sales, in billions of dollars. **Remarks:** Also notes total granola bar sales. **Number listed:** 11

1. Kellogg's Nutri-Grain Bars, with $150.4 billion
2. Quaker Chewy, $120.3
3. Kellogg's Rice Krispies Treats, $102.8
4. Nabisco SnackWell's, $80
5. Store brands, $54.5
6. Kudos, $46.5
7. Nature Valley Granola Bars, $37.5
8. Sunbelt Granola Bars, $33.7
9. Power Bar, $30.4
10. Golden Grahams Treats, $28.8

Source: *Food Processing*, September, 1998, p. 70.

Gravel Industry

See: **Sand and Gravel Industry**

Grills, Barbeque

See: **Barbeque Grills**

Grocery Store Chains

See: **Grocery Trade Supermarkets--Chain and Franchise Operations**

Grocery Trade

See also: **Supermarkets**

★2384★
TOP GROCERY WHOLESALE COMPANIES BY SALES INCREASE, 1998
Ranked by: Sales increase, in percent. **Number listed:** 10

1. Nash Finch, with 41.9%
2. C & S Wholesale, 39.6%
3. Buzzuto's, 35.6%
4. Associated Grocers of Florida, 13.9%
5. Wakefern Food Corp., 12.2%
6. Associated Grocers of the South, 11.2%
7. Fairway Foods, 11.1%
8. Affiliated Foods Southwest, 10%
9. Dearborn Wholesale Grocers, 8.2%
10. Affiliated Foods (NE), 7.1%

Source: *U.S. Distribution Journal*, September, 1998, p. 70.

★2385★
TOP GROCERY WHOLESALE COMPANIES BY SALES, 1998
Ranked by: Sales, in millions of dollars. **Remarks:** Also notes location, chief executive, previous year's data, and trading area. **Number listed:** 50

1. Supervalue, with $17,200 million
2. Fleming Cos., $12,781
3. C & S Wholesale Grocers Inc., $5,054
4. Wakefern Food Corp., $4,600
5. Nash Finch, $3,503
6. Associated Wholesale Grocers Inc., $3,200
7. Richfood, $3,021
8. Penn Traffic Co., $3,010
9. Roundy's, $2,611
10. Spartan Stores, $2,489

Source: *U.S. Distribution Journal*, September, 1998, p. 68.

★2386★
TOP GROCERY WHOLESALE COMPANIES BY SALES PER DELIVERY PER WEEK, 1998

Ranked by: Sales, per delivery, per week. **Number listed:** 10

1. Wakefern Food Corp., with $34,208
2. Schultz Sav-O Stores, $29,856
3. Roundy's, $29,024
4. Associated Wholesalers (PA), $27,826
5. Associated Food Stores (UT), $25,272
6. Copps Distributing, $22,682
7. Associated Wholesale Grocers (KS), $22,386
8. Piggly Wiggly Carolina, $22,115
9. J.B. Gottstein, $21,769
10. Nash Finch, $21,006

Source: *U.S. Distribution Journal*, September, 1998, p. 70.

★2387★
TOP GROCERY WHOLESALE COMPANIES BY SALES PER FULL-TIME EMPLOYEE, 1998

Ranked by: Sales per full-time employee, in thousands. **Number listed:** 10

1. Schultz Sav-O Stores, with $2,046 thousand
2. Super Store Industries, $1,928
3. Central Grocers Cooperative, $1,696
4. Hale Halsell, $1,527
5. Wakefern Food Corp., $1,533
6. J.B. Gottstein, $1,489
7. C & S Wholesale, $1,264
8. Affiliated Foods (NE), $1,235
9. Fairway Foods, $1,230
10. Mitchell Grocery Corp., $1,121

Source: *U.S. Distribution Journal*, September, 1998, p. 70.

★2388★
TOP GROCERY WHOLESALE COMPANIES BY SALES PER RETAIL LOCATION, 1998

Ranked by: Sales per retail location, in thousands. **Number listed:** 10

1. Wakefern Food Corp., with $25,698 thousand
2. Penn Traffic, $6,020
3. Giant Eagle, $5,806
4. Piggly Wiggly Carolina, $5,750
5. Mid-Mountain Foods, $5,457
6. Copps Corp., $5,279
7. Twin County Grocers, $5,020
8. Fleming, $4,123
9. Super Store Industries, $4,017
10. Key Food Stores, $3,896

Source: *U.S. Distribution Journal*, September, 1998, p. 70.

★2389★
TOP GROCERY WHOLESALE COMPANIES BY SALES PER SQUARE FOOT, 1998

Ranked by: Sales per warehouse square feet, in dollars. **Number listed:** 10

1. Wakefern Food Corp., with $1,876
2. Hale Halsell, $1,554
3. Penn Traffic, $1,483
4. Krasdale, $1,357
5. Associated Wholesale (KS), $1,356
6. Professional Food Systems, $1,288
7. Mitchell Grocery Corp., $1,182
8. C & S Wholesale, $1,175
9. Spartan Stores, $1,133
10. Richfood, $1,007

Source: *U.S. Distribution Journal*, September, 1998, p. 70.

★2390★
TOP GROCERY WHOLESALE COMPANIES BY STOCK MERCHANDISING UNITS (SKU), 1998

Ranked by: Total SKUs. **Number listed:** 10

1. C & S Wholesale, with 53,000 SKUs
2. Twin County Grocers, 47,000
3. Associated Wholesalers (PA), 44,000
4. Certified Grocers of California, 41,300
5. Richfood, 37,000
6. Associated Grocers, Seattle (WA), 36,000
7. Roundy's, 35,000
7. Associated Wholesale (KS), 35,000
9. United Grocers, Portland, 32,313
10. Affiliated Foods (TX), 32,000

Source: *U.S. Distribution Journal*, September, 1998, p. 70.

★2391★
TOP GROCERY WHOLESALE COMPANIES BY WAREHOUSE SQUARE FEET, 1998

Ranked by: Warehouse square feet, in thousands. **Number listed:** 10

1. Fleming, with 24,958 square feet
2. Supervalu, 20,000
3. Nash Finch, 6,971
4. C & S Wholesale, 4,300
5. Certified Grocers of California, 3,851
6. Roundy's, 3,126
7. Richfood, 3,000
8. Wakefern Food Corp., 2,452
9. Associated Wholesale (KS), 2,361
10. Spartan Stores, 2,197

Source: *U.S. Distribution Journal*, September, 1998, p. 70.

★2392★
TOP METROPOLITAN STATISTICAL AREAS BY GROCERY & OTHER FOOD SALES, 1998

Ranked by: Grocery and other food sales, in thousands. **Number listed:** 300

1. Los Angeles-Long Beach, CA, with $10,662,529 thousand
2. Chicago, IL, $9,093,047
3. New York, NY, $7,049,788
4. Washington, DC, $6,521,262
5. Philadelphia, PA, $6,149,561
6. Boston-Lawrence-Lowell-Brockton, MA, $6,026,328
7. Detroit, MI, $5,801,179
8. Atlanta, GA, $5,457,774
9. Houston, TX, $5,186,488
10. Phoenix-Mesa, AZ, $4,132,724

Source: *Sales & Marketing Management*, 1998, p. 191.

Group Medical Practice--New York Metropolitan Area

★2393★
LARGEST PHYSICIAN GROUPS IN NEW YORK, BY TOTAL DOCTORS, 1998
Ranked by: Total number of doctors. **Remarks:** Also notes number of board-certified doctors, practice administrator, revenue, 1997 hospital in-patient admissions, outpatient visits, managed care contracts, and total capitated lives. **Number listed:** 16

1. Columbia College of Physicians & Surgeons Faculty Practice, with 803 doctors
2. Mount Sinai Faculty Practice Associates, 693
3. Cornell Physician Organization, 533
4. Queens-Long Island Medical Group, 366
5. Memorial Sloan-Kettering Cancer Center, 355
6. New York Medical Group, 226
7. NCMC Faculty Practice Plan, 210
8. TJH Medical Services, 142
9. Kingsboro Medical Group, 96
10. Central Brooklyn Medical Group, 78

Source: *Crain's New York Business (annual)*, October 26, 1998, p. 22.

Growth Companies

★2394★
FASTEST-GROWING COMPANIES BY MARKET CAPITALIZATION, 1998
Ranked by: Market value, in millions of dollars. **Number listed:** 10

1. Dell Computer, with $74,905 million
2. Airtouch Communications, $34,417
3. Waste Management, $29,447
4. CompuWare, $10,032
5. Ascend Communications, $8,811
6. TJX, $8,425
7. PeopleSoft, $7,933
8. Republic Industries, $7,908
9. Biogen, $3,979
10. Qualcomm, $3,720

Source: *Fortune*, Fortune Fast 100 (annual), September 28, 1998, p. 232.

★2395★
FASTEST-GROWING COMPANIES BY REVENUE GROWTH, 1995-1998
Ranked by: Average annual revenue increase from 1995 to 1998, in percent. **Number listed:** 10

1. Republic Industries, with 407%
2. York Research, 324%
3. Ascend Communications, 179%
4. Rainforest Cafe, 175%
5. U.S. Office Products, 164%
6. SLI, 130%
7. CHS Electronics, 124%
8. Accustaff, 121%
9. Modtech, 118%
10. Qualcomm, 117%

Source: *Fortune*, Fortune Fast 100 (annual), September 28, 1998, p. 232.

★2396★
FASTEST-GROWING COMPANIES BY STOCK PERFORMANCE, 1998
Ranked by: One-year stock price increase, in percent. **Number listed:** 10

1. Dell Computer, with 177%
2. Gencor Industries, 161%
3. Stewart Information Services, 140%
4. Fidelity National Financial, 131%
5. National RV Holdings, 120%
6. Salton/Maxim Housewares, 114%
7. TJX, 94%
8. KV Pharmaceutical, 90%
9. Compuware, 77%
10. Rent-Way, 75%

Source: *Fortune*, Fortune Fast 100 (annual), September 28, 1998, p. 232.

★2397★
FASTEST-GROWING COMPANIES, 1998
Ranked by: Earnings per share annual growth rate over three years, in percent. **Remarks:** Also notes net income, revenue, stock valuation, and type of business. **Number listed:** 100

1. Noble Drilling, with 394%
2. Funco, 276%
3. Marine Drilling, 268%
4. Vitesse Semiconductor, 227%
5. Central Garden & Pet, 206%
6. Jabil Circuit, 200%
6. Cliffs Drilling, 200%
8. Pairgain Technologies, 187%
9. RMI Titanium, 180%
10. Sanmina Corp., 179%

Source: *Fortune*, Fortune Fast 100 (annual), September 28, 1998, p. 237+.

★2398★
FASTEST-GROWING, PRIVATELY HELD INNER CITY COMPANIES BY SALES GROWTH, 1993-1997
Ranked by: Sales increase, from 1993-1997, in percent. **Remarks:** Also notes contact information, type of business, 1997 revenue, number of employees, and compound annual growth. **Number listed:** 100

1. Pac-Van, with 19,265% increase
2. Shore.Net, 8,712%
3. Roundhouse, 5,425%
4. Tucker Technology, 3,330%
5. Construct Two Group, 2,964%
6. Thermagon, 2,662%
7. Baja Printing, 1,363%
8. TCG, 1,109%
9. Envios, R.D./Pronto Envios, 1,060%
10. YMLA, 1,021%

Source: *Inc.*, The Inner City 100 (annual), May, 1999, p. 81+.

★2399★
LEADING HIGH-TECH COMPANIES BY EMPLOYMENT GROWTH, 1997
Ranked by: Employment growth, in percent. **Remarks:** Also notes type of business, contact information, number of employees, sales volume and CEO. **Number listed:** 100

1. PowerQuest Corp., with 200%
2. Slenna Imaging Inc., 143%
3. Citrix Systems Inc., 110%
4. Etec Systems Inc., 100%
4. Arterial Vascular Engineering Inc., 100%
4. Universal Avionics Systems Corp., 100%
7. E-TEK Dynamics Inc., 98%
8. FLIR Systems Inc., 86%
9. PAREXEL International Corp., 85%

10. Visio Corp., 81%

Source: *World Trade*, The World Trade 100 (annual), October, 1998, p. 51+.

★2400★
TOP SMALL GROWTH COMPANIES BY EARNINGS GROWTH, 1999

Ranked by: Average annual growth, in percent. **Number listed:** 5

1. Brass Eagle, with 1620.2%
2. LHS Group, 286.7%
3. Cotielligent, 232.4%
4. Funco, 229.1%
5. QLogic, 225.1%

Source: *Business Week*, Growth Companies (annual), May 31, 1999, p. 87.

★2401★
TOP SMALL GROWTH COMPANIES BY EARNINGS, 1999

Ranked by: Earnings, in millions of dollars. **Number listed:** 5

1. Linear Technology, with $189.6 million
2. Centex Const. Prods., $77.3
3. Citrix Systems, $74.6
4. Kaydon, $69
5. Anchor Gaming, $68.6

Source: *Business Week*, Growth Companies (annual), May 31, 1999, p. 86.

★2402★
TOP SMALL GROWTH COMPANIES BY MARKET VALUE, 1999

Ranked by: Market value, in millions of dollars. **Number listed:** 5

1. Linear Technology, with $8,360 million
2. VISX, $3,750
3. Citrix Systems, $3,663
4. Total System Services, $3,590
5. Vitesse Semiconductor, $3,560

Source: *Business Week*, Growth Companies (annual), May 31, 1999, p. 87.

★2403★
TOP SMALL GROWTH COMPANIES BY PROFITABILITY, 1997-1999

Ranked by: Average annual rate on invested capital, in percent. **Number listed:** 5

1. Specialty Equipment, with 47.5%
2. Plantronics, 44.7%
3. Landauer, 44.7%
3. Duff & Phelps Credit Rating, 44.1%
5. Metro Information, 42.6%

Source: *Business Week*, Growth Companies (annual), May 31, 1999, p. 87.

★2404★
TOP SMALL GROWTH COMPANIES BY SALES GROWTH, 1999

Ranked by: Average annual sales growth, in percent. **Number listed:** 5

1. Friede Goldman, with 186.5%
2. Citrix Systems, 159.5%
3. Brass Eagle, 159.3%
4. Advanced Tech. Products, 149.4%
5. International Network Services, 122.1%

Source: *Business Week*, Growth Companies (annual), May 31, 1999, p. 86.

★2405★
TOP SMALL GROWTH COMPANIES BY SALES, 1999

Ranked by: Sales, in millions of dollars. **Number listed:** 5

1. Linear Technology, with $498.2 million
2. Specialty Equipment, $495.6
3. Wet Seal, $485.4
4. RemedyTemp, $465
5. Friede Goldman International, $459.3

Source: *Business Week*, Growth Companies (annual), May 31, 1999, p. 86.

Growth Companies--Los Angeles County (CA)

★2406★
FASTEST-GROWING PRIVATE COMPANIES IN LOS ANGELES COUNTY, 1998

Ranked by: Revenue growth, in percent. **Remarks:** Also notes contact information, revenue, number of employees, type of business, and top local executive. **Number listed:** 100

1. Platinum Capital Group, with 773% growth
2. Market Scan Information Systems, 640%
3. Nova Development, 594%
4. Travelers Telecom, 430%
5. New Age Electronics, Inc., 414%
6. Justice Technology Corp., 394%
7. Store of Knowledge Inc., 340%
8. Cook Inlet Energy Supply, 321%
9. Tecstar Inc., 260%
10. CIM Vision International Corp., 242%

Source: *Los Angeles Business Journal (annual)*, November 16, 1998, p. 60+.

Growth Companies--New York Metropolitan Area

★2407★
FASTEST-GROWING COMPANIES IN THE NEW YORK METROPOLITAN AREA, 1998

Ranked by: Revenue growth rate, in percent. **Remarks:** Also notes contact information, revenue figures and rank, net income figures, price/earnings ratio, return on equity, and number of employees. **Number listed:** 50

1. Comforce Corp., with 852.4%
2. Metromedia International Group, 529.4%
3. Headway Corporate Resources Inc., 260.4%
4. IDT Corp., 249.4%
5. Niagara Corp., 246.9%
6. NTL Inc., 229.5%
7. Delta Financial Corp., 83.1%
8. Caribiner International Inc., 79.5%
9. ContiFinancial Corp., 75.1%
10. GT Interactive Software Corp., 73.4%

Source: *Crain's New York Business*, Fastest Growing Companies (annual), October 19, 1998, p. 68+.

Growth Companies--Philadelphia Metropolitan Area

★2408★
FASTEST-GROWING PRIVATELY HELD COMPANIES IN THE PHILADELPHIA METROPOLITAN AREA, 1995-1997
Ranked by: Revenue growth rate from 1995 to 1997, in percent. **Remarks:** Also notes contact information, revenue figures, profitability, start-up capital, number of employees, type of business, top executive and year founded. **Number listed:** 25

1. ESPS, with 8,350.93% growth
2. V-Span Inc., 4,049.51%
3. Omicron Systems Inc., 2,236.94%
4. Networks Around the World Inc., 1,759.22%
5. Polaris Consulting & Information, 1,196.61%
6. Cybertech International, 948.90%
7. Protech Systems Inc., 854.57%
8. e-Tech Solutions, 767.33%
9. Fidelity Commercial Real Estate, 587.67%
10. US Interactive Inc., 547.91%

Source: *Philadelphia Business Journal*, Book of Lists (annual), December 25, 1998, p. 9.

Hair Care Products

★2409★
BEST-SELLING HAIR-COLORING BRANDS, 1998
Ranked by: Sales, in millions of dollar. **Remarks:** Also notes percentage change from previous year. **Number listed:** 8

1. L'Oreal Preference, with $158.6 million
2. Clairol Nice 'N Easy, $122.7
3. L'Oreal Excellence, $108.3
4. Just for Men, $72.1
5. Clairol Natural Instincts, $67.9
6. Clairol Hydrience, $62.3
7. Clairol Loving Care, $45.0
8. Clairol Ultress, $43.7

Source: *Advertising Age*, February 15, 1999, p. 4.

★2410★
LEADING ETHNIC HAIR CARE BRANDS, 1998*
Ranked by: Sales, in millions of dollars. **Remarks:** Includes percentage of dollar share. **Number listed:** 22

1. Optimum Care Kit, No-Lye, Regular, with $2.31 million
2. Optimum Care Kit, No-Lye, Super, $1.63
3. Dark & Lovely Creme, Relaxer, Regular, $1.62
4. Gentle Treatment, Relaxer, Regular, $1.61
5. Dark & Lovely Creme, Relaxer Plus, $1.36
6. African Pride No-Lye, Relaxer, Regular, $1.27
7. Soft & Beautiful, Relaxer, Regular, $1.13
8. Gentle Treatment, Relaxer, Super, $1.04
9. Fabu-laxer Relaxer Regular, $0.86
9. Luster's Pink Oil, Moisturizer Relaxer, Regular, $0.86
10. Revlon Realistic Kit, Regular, $0.71

Source: *Drug Store News*, August 3, 1998, p. 41.

★2411★
LEADING MANUFACTURERS OF HAIR SETTERS, 1998
Ranked by: Market share, in percent. **Number listed:** 5

1. Remington, with 36%
2. Conair, 27%
3. Helen of Troy, 18%
4. Windmere, 9%
5. Others, 10%

Source: *Appliance Manufacturer*, April, 1999, p. 21.

Hair Dryers

★2412★
LEADING MANUFACTURERS OF HAND-HELD HAIR DRYERS, 1998
Ranked by: Market share, in percent. **Number listed:** 5

1. Conair, with 40%
2. Helen of Troy, 30%
3. Windmere, 11%
4. Remington, 2%
5. Others, 17%

Source: *Appliance Manufacturer*, April, 1999, p. 21.

Hamburgers

★2413★
HAMBURGER RESTAURANTS MOST POPULAR WITH CUSTOMERS
Ranked by: Percent of respondents rating chain above average or excellent. **Remarks:** Also notes scores based on food quality, menu variety, value, service, atmosphere, cleanliness, and convenience. **Number listed:** 14

1. In-N-Out Burger, with 42%
2. Sonic Drive-In, 40%
3. Wendy's, 39%
4. Steak 'n Shake, 35%
5. McDonald's, 32%
6. Burger King, 31%
7. Whataburger, 29%
8. Checkers, 27%
8. White Castle, 27%
8. Jack In The Box, 27%
8. Carl's Jr., 27%

Source: *Restaurants & Institutions*, Choice in Chains (annual), March 1, 1999, p. 90.

★2414★
LEADING HAMBURGER RESTAURANTS, 1997
Ranked by: Sales, in millions of dollars. **Remarks:** Includes rank in 400. **Number listed:** 20

1. McDonald's, with $33,628.0 million
2. Burger King, $9,800.0
3. Wendy's, $5,226.0
4. Hardee's, $3,526.0
5. Jack In The Box, $1,300.0
6. Sonic Drive-In, $1,191.8
7. Carl's Jr., $703.0
8. Whataburger, $530.0
9. White Castle, $384.7
10. Checkers Drive-In Restaurants, $310.3

Source: *Restaurants & Institutions*, Restaurants & Institutions 400 (annual), July 15, 1998, p. 102.

Hardware Industry

★2415★
BEST HARDWARE BRANDS ACCORDING TO DISCOUNT SHOPPERS, 1998
Ranked by: Percent of discount shoppers naming brand as best. **Remarks:** Includes demographic profile. **Number listed:** 9

1. Stanley, with 14%
2. General Electric, 13%
3. Black & Decker, 12%
4. Sherwin Williams, 5%
4. Skil, 5%
6. Benjamin Moore, 4%
7. Glidden, 3%
8. DuPont, 2%
8. Kwik Set, 2%

Source: *Discount Store News*, September 7, 1998, p. 20.

Hardware Stores

★2416★
GEOGRAPHIC AREAS WITH THE HIGHEST BUILDING MATERIAL AND HARDWARE STORE SALES, 1998*
Ranked by: Sales, in thousands of dollars. **Number listed:** 321

1. Chicago, IL, with $3,165,357 thousand
2. Los Angeles-Long Beach, CA, $3,071,499
3. Washington, DC, $2,305,903
4. Atlanta, GA, $2,256,870
5. Philadelphia, PA, $2,128,732
6. Nassau-Suffolk, NY, $2,014,830
7. San Diego, CA, $1,777,876
8. New York, NY, $1,763,533
9. Detroit, MI, $1,706,203
10. Minneapolis-St. Paul, MN, $1,691,023

Source: *Sales & Marketing Management*, Survey of Buying Power (annual), August, 1998, p. 22.

Health and Beauty Aid Products

See: **Personal Care Products**

Health Care Industry

★2417★
LEADING HEALTHCARE GENERAL CONTRACTORS, 1998
Ranked by: Volume, in thousands of dollars. **Remarks:** Includes square footage completed for 1998 and 1997, volume for 1997, percent change, firm fees, number of architects and engineers, number of years, number of states and percentage of work. **Number listed:** 15

1. M. A. Mortenson, with $404,300 thousand
2. Brasfield & Gorrie, $180,600
3. R. J. Griffin & Co., $158,000
4. Robins & Morton Group, $146,639
5. Pepper Cos., $127,935
6. Clark Construction Group, $119,100
7. Rodgers Builders, $87,394
8. T. U. Parks Construction Co., $45,424
9. J. S. Alberici Construction Co., $42,820
10. Brice Building Co., $40,864

Source: *Modern Healthcare*, March 22, 1999, p. 36.

★2418★
LEADING HEALTHCARE PROGRAM MANAGEMENT CONTRACTORS, 1998
Ranked by: Volume, in thousands of dollars. **Remarks:** Includes square footage completed for 1998 and 1997, volume for 1997, percent change, firm fees, number of architects and engineers, number of years, number of states and percentage of work. **Number listed:** 4

1. W. R. Adams Co., with $470,000 thousand
2. META Associates, $208,450
3. American Heatlh Facilities Development, $205,000
4. Beam & Associates, $39,500

Source: *Modern Healthcare*, March 22, 1999, p. 33.

★2419★
MOST ADMIRED HEALTH CARE CORPORATIONS, 1998
Ranked by: Scores (1-10) derived from a survey of senior executives, outside directors and securities analysts. **Remarks:** Respondents rated companies in their own industry on 8 attributes of reputation. Also notes previous year's rank. **Number listed:** 10

1. WellPoint Health Networks, with 6.65
2. United HealthCare Corp., 6.60
3. Tenet Healthcare Corp., 6.41
4. PacifiCare Health Systems, 5.92
5. Allegiance, 5.83
6. Humana, 5.63
7. Columbia/HCA Healthcare, 4.82
8. Foundation Health, 4.31
9. Oxford Health Plans, 3.99
10. MedPartners, 3.61

Source: *Fortune*, American's Most Admired Corporations (annual), March 1, 1999, p. F-2.

★2420★
TOP HEALTH CARE COMPANIES IN THE S&P 500, 1998
Ranked by: Each company is ranked by 8 criteria: one-year total return, three-year total return, one-year sales growth, three-year average annual sales growth, one-year profit growth, three-year average annual profit growth, net profit margins, and return on equity, with additional weight given to a company's sales. A company's composite rank is calculated using the sum of all its ranks. **Remarks:** Overall score not provided. **Number listed:** 36

1. Schering-Plough
2. Warner-Lambert
3. Merck
4. Eli Lilly
5. Bristol-Myers Squibb
6. Amgen
7. Walgreen
8. Pfizer
9. CVS
10. Abbott Laboratories

Source: *Business Week*, Business Week 50: Top Companies of the S&P 500 (annual), March 29, 1999, p. 152+.

★2421★
TOP HEALTH CARE COMPANIES, 1998
Ranked by: Revenue, in millions of dollars. **Remarks:** Includes percentage change in revenue from 1997, 1998 adjusted income, percentage change in adjusted income from 1997, share price as of 12/31/98, percentage change in share price from 12/31/97, market cap as of 12/31/98 and type of market. **Number listed:** 250

1. Merck, with $26,898 million
2. Johnson & Johnson, $23,657
3. Columbia/HCA Healthcare Corp., $18,681
4. Bristol-Myers Squibb, $18,284
5. McKesson HBOC, $18,153
6. United HealthCare Corp., $17,355
7. Aetna U.S. Healthcare, $15,020
8. Rhone-Poulenc, $14,711
9. Bergen Brunswig Corp., $13,720
10. Pfizer, $13,544

Source: *Hospitals & Health Networks*, Health Care 250 (annual), April, 1999, p. 39+.

★2422★
TOP HEALTH CARE COMPANIES, 1998
Ranked by: Revenue, in millions of dollars. **Remarks:** Also notes profits and investment figures as well as number of employees. **Number listed:** 35

1. Cigna, with $21,437 million
2. Aetna, $20,604
3. Columbia/HCA Healthcare, $18,681
4. United HealthCare Corp., $17,355
5. Tenet Healthcare Corp., $9,895
6. Humana, $9,781
7. PacifiCare Health Systems, $9,521
8. Foundation Health System, $8,896
9. MedPartners, $7,004
10. Wellpoint Health Networks, $6,573

Source: *Fortune*, Fortune 500 Largest U.S. Corporations (annual), April 26, 1999, p. F-60+.

Health Care Industry--Detroit

★2423★
LEADING GROUP HEALTH CARE PLANS IN DETROIT, 1998
Ranked by: Revenue, in millions of dollars. **Remarks:** Also notes 1997 data, percent change, total number of enrolled members, and number of enrolled members in various plans. **Number listed:** 20

1. Blue Cross and Blue Shield of Michigan/Blue Care Network, with $8,379.5 million
2. Health Alliance Plan, $992.4
3. Aetna U.S. Healthcare, $492.0
4. M-Care Inc., $296.0
5. Mercy Health Plans, $276.8
6. Comprehensive Health Services Inc., $240.0
7. Delta Dental Plan of Michigan, $207.0
8. SelectCare Inc., $187.8
9. OmniCare Health Plan, $148.8
10. Total Health Care Inc., $84.8

Source: *Crain's Detroit Business*, June 28, 1999, p. 17.

Health Clubs, Spas, etc.--Los Angeles County (CA)

★2424★
TOP HEALTH AND FITNESS CLUBS IN L. A. COUNTY
Ranked by: Number of members in L. A. County. **Remarks:** Includes number of member nationwide, number of locations, number of instructors, amenities, fees and corporate headquarters. **Number listed:** 15

1. Bally Total Fitness, with 380,000 members
2. 24 Hour Fitness, 326,993
3. YMCA of Metropolitan Los Angeles, 219,178
4. Spectrum Clubs, 75,000
5. Bodies in Motion, 14,000
6. Marina Athletic Club, 10,000
7. The Sports Club L.A., 8,500
8. Easton Gym, 5,000
9. Mid Valley Athletic Club, 3,500
10. Meridian Sports Clubs, 3,000
10. Power House Gym, 3,000
10. The Los Angeles Athletic Club, 3,000

Source: *Los Angeles Business Journal*, January 4, 1999, p. 24.

Health Food Industry

See: **Food Industry and Trade**

Health Maintenance Organizations

★2425★
HIGHEST PAID EXECUTIVES OF PUBLIC COMPANIES OWNING HMOS, 1997
Ranked by: Annual compensation, in dollars. **Number listed:** 25

1. Stephen Wiggins (Chairman & CEO, Oxford Health Plans, Inc.), with $30,735,093
2. Wilson Taylor, (Chairmand and CEO, CIGNA Corporation), $12,456,169
3. William McGuire, CEO (United HealthCare Corporation), $8,607,743
4. James Stewart (Executive Vice President, CIGNA Corporation), $7,306,921
5. Robert Smoler (Executive Vice President, Oxford Health Plans, Inc.), $6,918,509
6. Gerald Isom (President, Property & Casualty, CIGNA Corporation), $5,737,691
7. Ronald Compton (former Chairman and CEO, Aetna), $5,383,148
8. H. Edward Hanway (President, CIGNA Healthcare, CIGNA Corporation), $5,282,734
9. Donald Levinson, Executive Vice President (CIGNA Corporation), $5,177,026
10. Eugene Froelich (Executive Vice President, Maxicare Health Plan, Inc.), $4,720,483

Source: *National Underwriter*, Life and Health/Financial Services Edition, September 28, 1998, p. 1.

★2426★
LARGEST HMO DOCTOR NETWORKS, 1998*
Ranked by: Number of primary care physicians as of June 30, 1998. **Number listed:** 10

1. CIGNA HealthCare, with 81,385
2. Humana, 73,500
3. Aetna U.S. Healthcare, 55,000
4. UnitedHealth Group, 52,022
5. Prudential Health Care Plan Inc., 40,746
6. PacifiCare Health Systems, 20,359
7. California Care HMO, 20,247
8. Health Net, 12,052
9. Oxford Health Plans, 11,706
10. Physicians Health Services, 8,759

Source: *Business Insurance*, December 28, 1998, p. 1.

★2427★
LARGEST HMOS BY ENROLLMENT
Ranked by: Total enrollment as of June 30, 1998. **Number listed:** 10

1. Kaiser Foundation Health Plan Inc., with 8,853,782
2. CIGNA HealthCare, 6,376,987
3. Aetna U.S. Healthcare, 6,228,000
4. UnitedHealth Group, 6,060,674
5. Humana, 3,827,600
6. PacifiCare Health Systems, 3,523,116
7. Prudential Health Care Plan Inc., 2,762,434
8. Health Net, 2,301,205
9. Oxford Health Plans Inc., 1,800,271
10. CaliforniaCare HMO, 1,639,311

Source: *Business Insurance*, December 28, 1998, p. 1.

★2428★
LARGEST MEDICARE HMOS, 1998*
Ranked by: Number of Medicare enrollees as of June 30, 1998. **Number listed:** 5

1. PacifiCare Health Systems, with 978,850
2. Kaiser Foundation Health Plan Inc., 582,053
3. Aetna U.S. Healthcare, 520,000
4. Humana, 501,000
5. UnitedHealth Group, 427,000

Source: *Business Insurance*, December 28, 1998, p. 1.

★2429★
LARGEST MULTIPLAN HMOS
Ranked by: Enrollment, in millions. **Remarks:** Includes number of HMOs and tax status. **Number listed:** 10

1. Blue Cross and Blue Shield Plans, with 17.2 million
2. Kaiser Foundation Health Plan, Oakland, CA, 8.0
3. Aetna U.S. Healthcare, Hartford, CT, 5.9
4. United HealthCare Corp, Minneapolis, MN, 5.6
5. CIGNA Healthcare, Bloomfield, CT, 5.0
6. Prudential HealthCare, Roseland, NJ, 4.6
7. PacifiCare Health Systems, Cypress, CA, 3.7
8. Foundation Health Systems, Woodland Hills, CA, 3.6
9. Humana Health Care Plans, Louisville, KY, 2.2
10. Oxford Health Plans, Norwalk, CT, 1.8

Source: *Business & Health*, October, 1998, p. 12.

★2430★
STRONGEST HMOS IN THE U.S.
Ranked by: Weiss safety rating, based on analysis of a company's capital, five-year historical profitability, liquidity, and stability. **Remarks:** Includes company's state location. **Number listed:** 10

1. Total Health Care Inc., with A
2. Blue Shield of Calif., A-
2. Fallon Community Health Plan, A-
2. Partners National Health Plans of NC, A-
2. Total Health Care Plan Inc., A-
6. Health Alliance Plan of Mich., B
6. Kaiser Foundation Health Plan Inc., B
6. Kaiser Foundation Health Plan Colorado, B
6. Kaiser Foundation Health Plan Mid-Atlantic States, B
6. United HealthCare of the Midwest, Inc., B

Source: *Insurance Advocate*, September 5, 1998, p. 24.

★2431★
TOP MEDICARE RISK HMO PLANS, 1999*
Ranked by: Enrollment. **Remarks:** Includes parent/affiliation and state. **Number listed:** 10

1. PacifiCare of California Inc., with 599,806
2. Kaiser Foundation Health Plan Inc., 406,244
3. Humana Medical Plan Inc., 264,610
4. Health Net, 149,970
5. Aetna U.S. Healthcare, 147,449
6. Keystone Health Plan West Inc., 137,868
7. Oxford Health Plans Inc., 122,472
8. Health Options Inc., 119,533
9. Keystone Health Plan East Inc., 112,515
10. UnitedHealthcare of Florida Inc., 104,870

Source: *Best's Review*, April, 1999, p. 47.

★2432★
WEAKEST HMOS IN THE U.S.
Ranked by: Weiss safety rating, based on analysis of a company's capital, five-year historical profitability, liquidity, and stability. **Remarks:** Includes company's state location. **Number listed:** 10

1. Physicians Health Services of NJ Inc., with E
2. Beacon Health Plans Inc., E-
2. Certus HealthCare LLC, E-
2. CHA HMO Inc., E-
2. DayMed Health Maintenance Plan Inc., E-
2. Emerald HMO Inc., E-
2. Horizon Health Plan Inc., E-
2. Integrity Health Plan of Mississippi, E-
2. North Medical Community Health Plan, E-
2. PriorityPlus of California Inc., E-

Source: *Insurance Advocate*, September 5, 1998, p. 24.

Health Maintenance Organizations--Chicago (IL)

★2433★
CHICAGO'S LARGEST HMOS, 1998
Ranked by: Enrollment. **Remarks:** Also notes percent change from previous year, year founded, number of primary care physicians, number of affiliated hospitals, and specific data available to employers. **Number listed:** 18

1. Blue Cross Blue Shield of Illinois HMOs, with 722,463
2. Humana Health Plans, 383,935
3. Rush Prudential Health Plans, 357,773
4. United Healthcare of Illinois Inc., 332,700
5. First Commonwealth Inc., 291,000
6. CIGNA Healthcare of Illinois Inc., 214,674
7. Aetna U.S. Healthcare of Illinois Inc., 74,512
8. American Health Care Providers Inc., 61,362
9. Principal Health Care of Illinois, 54,077
10. Rockford Health Plans Inc., 43,130

Source: *Crain's Chicago Business*, Top Business Lists (annual), June 30, 1998, p. 155+.

Health Maintenance Organizations—Detroit Metropolitan Area

★2434★
LEADING HMOS IN THE DETROIT METROPOLITAN AREA, 1997
Ranked by: Revenue, in thousands of dollars. **Remarks:** Also notes previous year's figures, net income, net worth, and enrollment figures. **Number listed:** 21

1. Blue Cross and Blue Shield of Michigan Inc., with $7,730.7 thousand
2. Health Alliance Plan, $911.8
3. Delta Dental Plan of Michigan, $560.7
4. Aetna U.S. Healthcare, $456.0
5. Comprehensive Health Services Inc., $266.3
6. Mercy Health Plans, $263.4
7. M-Care Inc., $205.8
8. OmniCare Health Plan, $158.6
9. Claimspro Health Claims Services Inc., $157.0
10. SelectCare Inc., $121.2

Source: *Crain's Detroit Business*, Crain's Book of Lists Detroit (annual), December 28, 1998, p. 98+.

Health Maintenance Organizations--Florida

★2435★
FLORIDA'S LARGEST HMOS, 1998
Ranked by: Enrollment. **Remarks:** Also notes number of physicians, affiliated hospitals, counties served, accrediting organizations, senior executives, and year licensed. **Number listed:** 25

1. Humana Inc., with 772,581
2. Prudential Health Care Plan Inc., 700,765
3. United HealthCare of Florida, 698,987
4. Health Options Inc., 691,377
5. CIGNA HealthCare of Florida, 451,199
6. AvMed Health Plan, 376,000
7. HIP Health Plan of Florida, 167,253
8. Aetna U.S. Healthcare, 167,000
9. Foundation Health, 137,750
10. Neighborhood Health Partnership, 126,553

Source: *Florida Trend*, TopRank Florida (annual), 1999, p. 62.

Health Maintenance Organizations—Los Angeles County (CA)

★2436★
LARGEST HMOS SERVING LOS ANGELES COUNTY, 1998
Ranked by: Number of members in southern California. **Remarks:** Also notes figures for enrollment in California, companywide enrollment, number of hospitals and physicians affiliated with California, revenue, Medicare/Medicaid enrollee mix, company profile, structure, and top local executive. **Number listed:** 15

1. Kaiser Permanente, with 2,630,211
2. PacifiCare of California, 1,500,000
3. American Specialty Health Plans, 1,300,000
4. Health Net, 790,340
5. CaliforniaCare (Blue Cross), 752,487
6. CIGNA HealthCare of California, 430,663
7. Prudential Health Care Plan Inc., 350,539
8. Aetna U.S. Healthcare of California, 281,425
9. Blue Shield of California HMO, 270,076
10. L.A. Care Health Plan, 268,000

Source: *Los Angeles Business Journal*, Book of Lists (annual), 1999, p. 108.

Health Maintenance Organizations--Medicare

★2437★
TOP COUNTIES IN MEDICARE MANAGED CARE PENETRATION, 1998
Ranked by: 1998 AAPCC Rate, in dollars. **Remarks:** Adjusted Average Per Capita Cost (AAPCC) is a prospective estimate of Medicare cost levels in the fee-for-service sector of the geographic area. **Number listed:** 50

1. Richmond, NY, with $782.70
2. Dade, FL, $763.19
3. Bronx, NY, $742.80
4. New York, NY, $727.38
5. Kings, NY, $719.48
6. Philadelphia, PA, $718.33
7. Montgomery, TX, $678.67
8. Queens, NY, $672.02
9. Broward, FL, $663.37
10. Wayne, MI, $651.45

Source: *Journal of Compensation and Benefits*, July, 1998, p. 43.

Health Maintenance Organizations--New York (NY)

★2438★
LARGEST HMOS IN NEW YORK CITY, 1998
Ranked by: Number of enrollees in New York City. **Remarks:** Also notes figures for enrolled members in New York area. **Number listed:** 15

1. Oxford Health Plans Inc., with 852,000
2. HIP Health Plan of New York, 647,425
3. Aetna U.S. Healthcare, 460,000
4. Empire Blue Cross Blue Shield, 254,838
5. Cigna HealthCare, 151,871
6. Physicians Health Services, 142,316
7. United HealthCare Corp., 109,663
8. Prudential HealthCare of New York Inc., 55,081
9. HealthFirst Inc., 52,972
10. MetroPlus Health Plan, 52,161

Source: *Crain's New York Business*, August 31, 1998, p. 22.

★2439★
LARGEST PPOS IN NEWYORK CITY, 1998
Ranked by: Number of subscribers in New York City. **Remarks:** Also notes figures for enrolled members in New York area. **Number listed:** 15

1. MagnaCare, with 1,054,700
2. Group Health Inc., 795,044
3. MultiPlan Inc., 699,075
4. Empire Blue Cross Blue Shield, 622,321
5. United HealthCare Corp., 549,610
6. Davis Vision, 497,221
7. Select Providers Inc., 325,000

8. Cigna HealthCare, 300,282
9. First Health Network, 218,485
10. Dental Health Alliance, 188,800

Source: *Crain's New York Business*, August 31, 1998, p. 24.

Healthcare Systems

See: **Multihospital Systems**

Health Maintenance Organizations—Philadelphia Metropolitan Area

★2440★
LARGEST HMOS IN THE PHILADELPHIA METROPOLITAN AREA, 1997
Ranked by: Number of local commercial members. **Remarks:** Also notes total number of members, number of Medicare/Medicaid members, year licensed, parent company, and local administrator. **Number listed:** 18

1. Aetna U.S. Healthcare, with 859,983
2. Keystone Health Plan East, 489,639
3. AmeriHealth HMO Inc., 49,918
4. Cigna Healthcare Inc., 34,208
5. HIP Health Plan of New Jersey, 32,316
6. QualMed Plans for Health, 29,580
7. Prudential Health Care Plan Inc., 28,291
8. Horizon Blue, 23,852
9. Oxford Health Plans Inc., 7,932
10. First Option Health Plan of New Jersey, Inc., 6,467

Source: *Philadelphia Business Journal*, Book of Business Lists (annual), December 25, 1998, p. 81.

Heaters

★2441★
BEST-SELLING ELECTRIC ROOM HEATERS, 1998
Ranked by: Market share, in percent. **Number listed:** 8

1. Holmes, with 40%
2. Honeywell/Duracraft, 15%
3. Rival (Patton), 13%
4. Arvin (HeatStream), 9%
5. DeLonghi, 7%
6. Lakewood, 6%
7. Marvin, 2%
8. Others, 8%

Source: *Appliance Manufacturer*, (annual), April, 1999, p. 20.

Heating and Cooling Industry

See: **Air Conditioning Industry**

Heating Pads

See: **Household Appliances**

Heat Pumps

★2442★
BEST-SELLING CENTRAL RESIDENTIAL HEAT PUMPS, 1998
Ranked by: Market share, in percent. **Number listed:** 9

1. United Technologies, with 24%
2. Goodman, 16%
3. American Standard, 14%
4. Rheem, 12%
5. Lennox, 10%
5. York, 10%
7. International Comfort Products, 9%
8. Nortek (Nordyne), 4%
9. Others, 1%

Source: *Appliance Manufacturer*, (annual), April, 1999, p. 20.

Helsinki Stock Exchange

★2443★
LARGEST LISTED COMPANIES ON THE HELSINKI STOCK EXCHANGE, 1997
Ranked by: Market value, in thousands of Finnish marks (FM). **Number listed:** 20

1. Nokia Oyj, with FM116,265 million
2. UPM-Kymmene Oyj, FM29,472
3. Merita Oyj, FM24,673
4. Enso Oyj, FM13,165
5. Neste Oy, FM13,005
6. Vakuutusosakeyhtio Sampo, FM10,719
7. Orion-yhtyma Oyj, FM10,076
8. Vakuutusosakeyhtio Pohjola, FM8,305
9. Outokumpu Oyj, FM8,281
10. Raisio Yhtyma Oyj, FM7,783

Source: *SSB Guide to World Equity Markets*, (annual), Euromoney Publications, 1998, p. 180.

★2444★
MOST ACTIVELY TRADED SHARE ON THE HELSINKI STOCK EXCHANGE, 1997
Ranked by: Turnover, in thousands of Finnish marks (FM). **Number listed:** 20

1. Nokia Oyj A, with FM69,148,339 thousand
2. UPM-Kymmene Oyj, FM18,581,699
3. Nokia Oyj K, FM8,712,239
4. Merita Oy A, FM8,419,760
5. Enso Oyj R, FM5,197,736
6. Valmet Oyj, FM4,639,696
7. Raisio Yhtyma Oyj (Free share), FM4,373,518
8. Rauma Oy, FM4,227,171
9. Outokumpu Oyj A, FM3,952,781
10. Vakuutusosakeyhtio Sampo A, FM3,930,593

Source: *SSB Guide to World Equity Markets*, (annual), Euromoney Publications, 1998, p. 180+.

Herbs

★2445★
BEST-SELLING HERBAL REMEDIES IN THE NORTH AMERICAN MARKET, 1998
Ranked by: Estimated sales, in millions of dollars. **Remarks:** Includes bulk price per kg. **Number listed:** 10

1. Ginseng, with $416 million
2. Garlic, $302
3. Echinacea, $276
4. St. John's Wort, $128
5. Kava kava, $106
6. Saw palmetto, $62
7. Valerian, $44
8. Goldenseal, $24
9. Evening primrose, $21
10. Black cohosh, $17

Source: *Chemical Market Reporter*, September 28, 1998, p. 12.

★2446★
LEADING USES FOR HERBAL REMEDIES, 1997
Ranked by: Market share, in percent. **Remarks:** Data taken from Prevention Magazine. **Number listed:** 10

1. Colds, with 59%
2. Burns, 45%
3. Headaches, 22%
4. Allergies, 21%
5. Rashes, 18%
5. Insomnia, 18%
7. PMS, 17%
8. Depression, 7%
8. Diarrhea, 7%
10. Menopause, 4%

Source: *The New York Times*, February 9, 1999, p. F7.

Herbs--Europe

★2447★
TOP EUROPEAN BOTANICALS, 1997
Ranked by: Annual turnover, in millions of dollars. **Number listed:** 10

1. Ginkgo, with $350 million
2. St. John's Wort, $250
2. Saw palmetto, $250
4. Valerian, $200
4. Ginseng, $200
4. Garlic, $200
7. Echinacea, $180
8. Horse chestnut, $150
9. Black cohosh, $100
9. Vitex agnus castus, $100

Source: *Chemical Market Reporter*, July 13, 1998, p. FR4.

High Technology Industry

★2448★
HIGHEST PAID EXECUTIVES IN THE HIGH-TECH INDUSTRY, 1997
Ranked by: Estimated wealth, in billions of dollars. **Remarks:** Also notes company, location, type of business, and holdings. **Number listed:** 100

1. Bill Gates (Microsoft), with $58.73 billion
2. Paul Allen (Microsoft), $16.98
3. Steve Ballmer (Microsoft), $12.99
4. Michael Dell (Dell Computer), $12.69
5. Gordon Moore (Intel), $7.62
6. Larry Ellison (Oracle), $6.00
7. Ted Waitt (Gateway), $3.69
8. William Hewlett (Hewlett-Packard), $3.41
9. Jeff Bezos (Amazon.com), $2.14
10. David Duffield (PeopleSoft), $1.89

Source: *Forbes ASAP*, Technology's 100 Wealthiest (annual), October 5, 1998, p. 51+.

★2449★
LEADING HISPANIC-OWNED HIGH-TECH COMPANIES, 1997
Ranked by: Revenue, in millions of dollars. **Remarks:** Also notes CEO, products and services, and number of employees. **Number listed:** 50

1. Government Micro Resources Inc. (Manassas, VA), with $122.00 million
2. McBride and Associates Inc. (Albuquerque, NM), $89.05
3. Gonzalez Design Group (Madison Heights, MI), $80.80
4. Force 3 Inc. (Crofton, MD), $80.00
5. UniBoring Co Inc. (Howell, MI), $78.00
6. Collazo Enterprises Inc. (Huntsville, AL), $76.90
7. International Data Products Corp. IDP (Gaithersburg, MD), $74.00
7. Sherikon Inc. (Chantilly, VA), $74.00
9. Pacific Access Technology Holdings Inc. (Rancho Cordova, CA), $60.00
10. Tech. & Mgmt. Svcs. Corp. (Calverton, MD), $53.00
10. Tri-Cor Industries Inc. (Alexandria, VA), $53.00

Source: *Hispanic Business*, Hispanic High Tech Companies (annual), July/August, 1998, p. 24.

★2450★
LEADING U.S. HIGH-TECH EXPORTERS BY EMPLOYEMENT GROWTH, 1997
Ranked by: Employment growth, in percent. **Remarks:** Includes location, phone number, website, description of operations, number of employees, 1997 sales volume and CEO. **Number listed:** 100

1. PowerQuest Corporation, with 200%
2. Sienna Imaging Inc., 143%
3. Citrix Systems Inc., 110%
4. Etec Systems Inc., 100%
4. Arterial Vascular Engineering Inc., 100%
4. Universal Avionics Systems Corp., 100%
7. E-TEK Dynamics Inc., 98%
8. FLIR Systems Inc., 86%
9. PAREXEL International Corp., 85%
10. Visio Corp., 81%

Source: *World Trade*, World Trade 100 (annual), October, 1998, p. 51+.

★2451★
TOP CONVERTIBLE TECH UNDERWRITERS (PUBLIC + 144A) EXCLUDING BIOTECH AND COMMUNICATIONS, 1998
Ranked by: Proceeds, in millions of dollars. **Remarks:** Includes market share, number of issues, and figures for 1997. **Number listed:** 15

1. Bear, Stearns, with $14,344.1 million
2. Merrill Lynch, $2,366.8
3. Morgan Stanley Dean Witter, $2,298.7
4. Donaldson, Lufkin & Jenrette, $1,200.0
5. Goldman, Sachs, $825.0

6. Salomon Smith Barney, $770.0
7. Bank of America, $190.0
8. Lazard Houses, $125.0
9. Prudential Securities Inc., $100.0
10. Deutsche Bank, $90.0

Source: *Investment Dealers' Digest*, February 8, 1999, p. 23.

★2452★
TOP CYBERSTATES, 1996
Ranked by: Number of high-tech workers per 1,000 private-sector workers. **Number listed:** 10

1. New Hampshire, with 84
2. Colorado, 78
3. Massachusetts, 76
4. California, 65
5. Vermont, 59
6. Minnesota, 57
7. New Jersey, 56
8. Virginia, 55
9. Arizona, 54
10. Oregon, 53

Source: *Area Development*, September, 1998, p. 42.

★2453★
TOP HIGH-TECH CAMPAIGN CONTRIBUTORS, 1997-98
Ranked by: Amount contributed for the first 18 months of the 1997-98 election cycle, in dollars. **Remarks:** Includes breakdown between Democrats and Republicans. **Number listed:** 10

1. Microsoft, with $574,099
2. Kleiner Perkins Caufield & Byers, $328,863
3. EDS Corp., $280,646
4. Oracle, $275,663
5. Gateway 2000, $174,554
6. Cisco Systems, $134,000
7. IDX Systems Corp., $133,750
8. JD Edwards, $118,500
9. Sterling Software Inc., $107,800
10. CDB Infotek, $103,000

Source: *CQ Weekly*, October 31, 1998, p. 2959.

★2454★
TOP HIGH-TECH EMPLOYMENT STATES, 1996
Ranked by: Employment. **Remarks:** Includes percent change from 1995. **Number listed:** 10

1. California, with 723,976
2. Texas, 343,075
3. New York, 307,510
4. Illinois, 198,899
5. Massachusetts, 197,491
6. Florida, 184,456
7. New Jersey, 168,059
8. Pennsylvania, 151,366
9. Virginia, 137,596
10. Ohio, 125,356

Source: *New Jersey Business*, July, 1998, p. 6.

★2455★
TOP M&A ADVISERS ON ANNOUNCED U.S. TARGET TECHNOLOGY DEALS, 1998
Ranked by: Proceeds, in millions of dollars. **Remarks:** Includes market share, number of issues, and figures for 1997. **Number listed:** 15

1. Morgan Stanley Dean Witter, with $59,198.2 million
2. Goldman, Sachs, $37,253.7
3. Credit Suisse First Boston, $34,370.6
4. Merrill Lynch, $29,873.1
5. Donaldson, Lufkin & Jenrette, $29,145.7
6. Lehman Brothers, $26,654.3
7. Bear, Stearns, $14,344.1
8. Gleacher NatWest/Hawkpoint, $14,004.8
9. Peter J. Solomon Co. Ltd., $13,994.5
10. Lazard Houses, $12,417.8

Source: *Investment Dealers' Digest*, February 8, 1999, p. 24.

★2456★
TOP TECH IPO UNDERWRITERS, 1998
Ranked by: Proceeds, in millions of dollars. **Remarks:** Includes market share, number of issues and figures for 1997. **Number listed:** 15

1. Morgan Stanley Dean Witter, with $1,116.9 million
2. Goldman, Sachs, $755.5
3. Salomon Smith Barney, $700.5
4. BankBoston, $298.3
5. Deutsche Bank, $228.8
6. Bankers Trust, $225.5
7. Merrill Lynch, $150.4
8. Bank of America, $139.8
9. Lehman Brothers, $105.6
10. Hambrecht & Quist, $97.3

Source: *Investment Dealers' Digest*, February 8, 1999, p. 20.

★2457★
TOP TECH UNDERWRITERS FOR STRAIGHT DEBT ISSUES EXCLUDING BIOTECH AND COMMUNICATIONS, 1998
Ranked by: Proceeds, in millions of dollars. **Remarks:** Includes market share, number of issues, and figures for 1997. **Number listed:** 15

1. Merrill Lynch, with $6,475.30 million
2. Morgan Stanley Dean Witter, $4,761.20
3. Goldman, Sachs, $3,298.50
4. Salomon Smith Barney, $2,009.50
5. Credit Suisse First Boston, $1,897.10
6. Lehman Brothers, $1,841.80
7. Chase Manhattan Corp., $1,743.00
8. J. P. Morgan, $1,380.30
9. Bear, Stearns, $1,155.80
10. Donaldson, Lufkin & Jenrette, $189.5

Source: *Investment Dealers' Digest*, February 8, 1999, p. 22.

High Technology Industry--Canada

★2458★
TOP HIGH TECHNOLOGY COMPANIES IN CANADA ACCORDING TO CANADIAN BUSINESS
Ranked by: Sales, in millions of Canadian dollars (C$). **Remarks:** Also notes the primary exchange, percentage change from one year, earnings per share, share price as of May 14, 1999, and the parent company. **Number listed:** 100

1. BCE Inc., with C$27,454,000 million
2. Nortel Networks Corp., C$26,224,887
3. BCT. TELUS, C$5,850,000
4. Teleglobe Inc., C$5,050,196
5. Celestica Inc., C$4,842,013
6. Rogers Communications Inc., C$2,839,229
7. Mitel Corp., C$1,976,374
8. Newbridge Networks Corp., C$1,620,620
9. CAE Inc., C$1,614,382
10. ATI Technologies Inc., C$1,156,921

Source: *Canadian Business*, June 11, 1999, p. 101+.

High Technology Industry—Detroit Metropolitan Area

★2459★
TOP TECHNOLOGY-BASED COMPANIES IN THE DETROIT METROPOLITAN AREA, 1997
Ranked by: Revenue, in millions of dollars. **Remarks:** Also notes figures for previous year, percent change, contact information, number of employees, and type of business. **Number listed:** 24

1. Philips Display Components, with $547.0 million
2. Fanuc Robotics North America Inc., $370.0
3. Eaton Corp. - Innovation Center division, $130.0
4. Phillips Service Industries Inc., $87.0
5. Becton Dickinson Microbiology Systems, $85.0
6. ISI Norgren Inc., $81.0
7. ERIM International Inc., $72.9
8. Perceptron Inc., $65.1
9. Medar Inc., $41.0
10. Vector Research Inc., $40.6

Source: *Crain's Detroit Business*, Crain's Book of Lists Detroit (annual), December 28, 1998, p. 80.

High Technology Industry--Long Island (NY)

★2460★
FASTEST-GROWING TECHNOLOGY COMPANIES ON LONG ISLAND, 1993-1997
Ranked by: Growth, in percent. **Remarks:** Includes 1993 and 1997 revenues. **Number listed:** 50

1. Netsmart Technologies Inc., with 13,728.07%
2. Boundless, 3,392.22%
3. Computer Concepts, 785.06%
4. Applied Theory Communications, 596.74%
5. Nastech Pharmaceutical, 539.86%
6. Comverse Technology, 337.89%
7. Veeco Instruments, 283.35%
8. Global Payment Technologies, 268.67%
9. Nu Horizons Electronics Corp., 257.99%
10. Allied Digital Technologies, 251.85%

Source: *Long Island Business*, LI Book of Lists (annual), 1999, p. 138.

★2461★
TOP HIGH TECH FIRMS BY NUMBER OF EMPLOYEES
Ranked by: Number of employees. **Remarks:** Includes CEO or President, phone and fax numbers, web address and e-mail. **Number listed:** 37

1. Bell Atlantic, with 5,700 employees
2. Keyspan Energy, 5,000
3. Northrop Grumman, 4,178
4. Brookhaven National Laboratory, 3,200
5. Cablevision Systems, 2,100
6. Computer Assoc Intl, 2,000
7. Photocircuits, 1,850
8. Symbol Technologies, 1,800
9. Ademco Group, 1,500
9. Estee Lauder, 1,500

Source: *Long Island Business*, LI Book of Lists (annual), 1999, p. 125.

Hispanic American Business Enterprises

★2462★
FASTEST-GROWING HISPANIC-OWNED COMPANIES BY REVENUE GROWTH, 1998
Ranked by: Revenue growth from 1997 to 1998, in percent. **Remarks:** Includes revenue figures for 1997 and 1998. **Number listed:** 10

1. United PanAm Financial Group, with 221.37%
2. MARISA Industries Inc., 198.06%
3. Harvard Manufacturing Texas, 154.55%
4. Quantum Technology Services Inc., 116.67%
5. Sandoval Dodge, 112.08%
6. Corporate Systems Group Inc., 111.54%
7. Century Finance USA LLC, 105.21%
8. Leticia Inc., 98.04%
9. Cal Inc., 96.72%
10. Hedges Construction Co., 95.55%

Source: *Hispanic Business*, Hispanic Business 500 (annual), June, 1999, p. 54.

★2463★
FASTEST-GROWING HISPANIC-OWNED EXPORTERS, 1998
Ranked by: Growth from 1996 to 1997, in percent. **Remarks:** Includes export sales for 1996 and 1997. **Number listed:** 50

1. GTC Inc., with 1,059%
2. Mack Sales of South Florida Inc., 159%
3. HUSCO International Inc., 88%
4. Gus Machado Ford Inc., 60%
5. South Cone Inc., 59%
6. North American Trade Corp., 53%
7. Farma International, 44%
8. Offshore Traders Inc., 30%
9. Alrod International Inc., 28%
10. Carfel Inc., 24%

Source: *Hispanic Business*, Top 50 Exporters (annual), November, 1998, p. 32.

★2464★
INDUSTRIES WITH THE MOST HISPANIC-OWNED EXPORTERS, 1998
Ranked by: Number of companies. **Remarks:** Includes total 1997 export sales. **Number listed:** 8

1. Wholesale, with 24
2. Service, 8
3. Manufacturing, 7
4. Transportation, 3
4. Automotive, 3
6. Finance, 2
6. Retail, 2
8. Construction, 1

Source: *Hispanic Business*, Top 50 Exporters (annual), November, 1998, p. 32.

★2465★
STATES WITH MOST HISPANIC-OWNED EXPORT COMPANIES, 1998
Ranked by: Number of companies. **Remarks:** Includes total 1997 export sales. **Number listed:** 50

1. Florida, with 29
2. California, 6
3. Texas, 5
4. Virginia, 3
5. Washington, DC, 2
6. Wisconsin, 1
6. Alabama, 1
6. Maryland, 1
6. New Jersey, 1

6. Michigan, 1

Source: *Hispanic Business*, Top 50 Exporters (annual), November, 1998, p. 32.

★2466★
TOP HISPANIC-OWNED COMPANIES, 1998
Ranked by: Revenue, in millions of dollars. **Remarks:** Includes CEO, type of business, number of employees and year started. **Number listed:** 500

1. MasTec Inc., with $1,005.10 million
2. Burt Automotive Network, $837.53
3. Goya Foods Inc., $653.00
4. Ancira Enterprises Inc., $449.00
5. International Bancshares Corp., $367.87
6. IFS Financial Corp., $305.00
7. Related Group of Florida, $297.00
8. Sedano's Supermarkets, $294.00
9. Troy Ford, $291.65
10. Lloyd A. Wise Cos., $216.70

Source: *Hispanic Business*, Hispanic Business 500 (annual), June, 1999, p. 60+.

★2467★
TOP HISPANIC-OWNED EXPORTERS BY EXPORT SALES, 1998
Ranked by: Export sales, in millions of dollars. **Remarks:** Includes CEO, number of employees, number of Hispanic employees, 1997 revenue, percent from 1997 exports, 1997 export sales, 1996 export sales, 1996-97 export sales growth, products and services and destination. **Number listed:** 50

1. Precision Trading Corp., with $150.23 million
2. HUSCO International Inc., $65.00
3. Alrod International Inc., $41.00
4. Collazo Enterprises Inc., $40.26
5. Hamilton Bancorp Inc., $38.35
6. Mack Sales of South Florida Inc., $34.29
7. Plastec USA Inc., $34.26
8. Albert Rebel & Associates Inc., $32.70
9. Northwestern Meat Inc., $32.00
10. Tire Group International Inc., $31.00

Source: *Hispanic Business*, Top 50 Exporters (annual), November, 1998, p. 34.

★2468★
TOP HISPANIC-OWNED HIGH TECH BUSINESSES, 1997
Ranked by: Revenue, in millions of dollars. **Remarks:** Includes CEO, location, high-tech product/service and number of employees. **Number listed:** 50

1. Government Micro Resources Inc., with $122.00 million
2. McBride and Associates Inc., $89.05
3. Gonzalez Design Group, $80.80
4. Force 3 Inc., $80.00
5. UniBoring Co. Inc., $78.00
6. Collazo Enterprises Inc., $76.90
7. International Data Products Corp. (IDP), $74.38
8. Sherikon Inc., $74.00
9. Pacific Access Technology Holdings Inc., $60.00
10. Tech. & Mgmt. Svcs. Corp., $53.00
10. Tri-Cor Industries Inc., $53.00

Source: *Hispanic Business*, Hispanic High Tech Companies (annual), July/August, 1998, p. 24.

Hispanic American Business Enterprises—Detroit Metropolitan Area

★2469★
LEADING HISPANIC-OWNED BUSINESSES IN THE DETROIT METROPOLITAN AREA, 1997
Ranked by: Revenue, in millions of dollars. **Remarks:** Includes revenue for 1996, percent change, number of employees, percent Hispanic ownership, and type of business. **Number listed:** 15

1. Troy Ford, with $388.1 million
2. Mexican Industries in Michigan Inc., $167.4
3. Gonzalez Design Group, $80.8
4. Uni Boring Co. Inc., $78.1
5. Scion Steel Inc., $45.0
6. Ideal Steel and Builders' Supplies Inc., $25.0
7. Aztec Manufacturing Corp., $24.0
8. CSI Cardenas Inc., $23.0
9. ASG Renaissance, $19.4
10. PMA Consultants L.L.C., $12.2

Source: *Crain's Detroit Business*, Crain's Book of Lists Detroit (annual), December 28, 1998, p. 48.

Hispanic Market

★2470★
TOP HISPANIC MARKETS, 1998
Ranked by: Specific ranking figures not available. **Remarks:** Data taken from FMI, Profile of the U.S. Hispanic Grocery Shopper. **Number listed:** 10

1. Los Angeles
2. New York
3. Miami
4. San Francisco
5. Chicago
6. Houston
7. San Antonio
8. Dallas/Fort Worth
9. San Diego
10. Fresno

Source: *Distribution Channels*, January/February, 1999, p. 141.

★2471★
TOP RESPONSES OF HISPANIC CONSUMERS TO DIRECT MAIL
Ranked by: Percentage of Hispanic consumers with given response. **Remarks:** Survey conducted by Simmons Market Research of 1,700 Hispanic consumers on behalf of Draft Worldwide, Chicago. **Number listed:** 9

1. believe marketers should make an effort to understand/respect His panic consumers, with 79%
2. are loyal to brands they like, 77%
3. always read their direct mail, 72%
4. direct mail sent to homes is in English, 60%
5. think marketers take advantage of Hispanic consumers, 55%
6. are loyal to marketers they know support Hispanic communities, 54%
7. repondents speak only Spanish in their homes, 52%
8. get only 10 pieces of direct mail a year, 40%
9. want to receive more direct mail, 39%

Source: *Advertising Age*, August 24, 1998, p. S6.

Hispanics--Population

★2472★
LEADING HISPANIC METROPOLITAN AREAS
Ranked by: Hispanic origin population, in thousands. **Number listed:** 50

1. Los Angeles-Long Beach, with 4,235.8 thousand
2. New York, 2,188.1
3. Miami, 1,189.7
4. Chicago, 1,119.2
5. Riverside-San Bernardino, 1,021.7
6. Houston, 965.9
7. San Antonio, 813.7
8. Orange County, CA, 779.2
9. San Diego, 721.9
10. Phoenix-Mesa, 588.2

Source: *Sales & Marketing Management*, Survey of Buying Power (annual), August, 1998, p. 14.

★2473★
LEADING PLACES OF ORIGIN FOR U.S. HISPANICS
Ranked by: Market share, in percent. **Number listed:** 5

1. Mexico, with 64%
2. Central and South America, 15%
3. Puerto Rico, 10%
4. Cuba, 5%
5. Other, 6%

Source: *Distribution Channels*, January/February, 1999, p. 142.

★2474★
METROPOLITAN AREAS WITH THE LARGEST HISPANIC POPULATION, 1996
Ranked by: Population, in thousands. **Remarks:** Also notes percent of total metropolitan and U. S. populations. **Number listed:** 20

1. Los Angeles-Long Beach, with 4,044.5 thousand
2. New York, 2,265.4
3. Miami, 1,165.0
4. Chicago, 1,069.3
5. Riverside-San Bernardino, 981.1
6. Houston, 904.9
7. San Antonio, 773.4
8. Orange County, CA, 740.8
9. San Diego, 680.9
10. Phoenix-Mesa, 544.1

Source: *Adams Liquor Handbook*, (annual), Adams Media Inc., 1998, p. 286.

★2475★
TOP HISPANIC POPULATED STATES, 1999
Ranked by: Population, in thousands. **Number listed:** 10

1. California, with 11,090.4 thousand
2. Texas, 6,235.9
3. New York, 2,868.4
4. Florida, 2,333.6
5. Illinois, 1,284.4
6. Arizona, 1,116.8
7. New Jersey, 1,026.3
8. New Mexico, 759.5
9. Colorado, 600.0
10. Massachusetts, 368.5
11. Other areas, 4,680.3

Source: *Telephony*, May 17, 1999, p. 112.

Hockey

★2476★
LEADING NATIONAL HOCKEY LEAGUE TEAMS, 1998*
Ranked by: Current value, in millions of dollars. **Remarks:** Includes revenue, operating income, debt/value ratio and principal owners. **Number listed:** 26

1. New York Rangers, with $195 million
2. Philadelphia Flyers, $187
3. Boston Bruins, $185
4. Detroit Red Wings, $184
5. Washington Capitals, $178
6. Chicago Blackhawks, $170
7. Montreal Canadiens, $167
8. St. Louis Blues, $154
9. Colorado Avalanche, $138
10. New Jersey Devils, $125

Source: *Forbes*, December 14, 1998, p. 134.

Holding Companies

★2477★
TOP HOLDING AND OTHER INVESTMENT COMPANIES IN EUROPE
Ranked by: Financial size, in millions of European Currency Units (ECUs). **Remarks:** Also notes number of employees and overall rank among European businesses. **Number listed:** 58

1. Metro AG, with S31.455 million
2. Thyssen AG, S20.668
3. Auchan, S6.489
4. Schickedanz Holding-Stiftung & Co. KG, S6.100
5. Deutsche Babcock AG, S4.540
6. Heraeus Holding GMbH, S3.458
7. Porsche Holding Gesellschaft M.B.H., S3.402
8. BML Vermogensverwaltungs Aktiengesellschaft, S3.171
9. Bunge Corporation Ltd., S3.071
10. Landesbeteiligungen Baden-Wuerttemberg GMbH, S2.827

Source: *Dun & Bradstreet*, Dun's Europa (annual), 1999, p. 288+.

Home Building Industry

See: **Construction Industry**

Home Electronics

★2478★
BEST CONSUMER ELECTRONICS BRANDS ACCORDING TO DISCOUNT SHOPPERS
Ranked by: Percent of discount shoppers naming brand as best. **Number listed:** 10

1. Sony, with 21%
2. Panasonic, 11%
3. Kodak, 8%

3. Duracell, 8%
3. General Electric, 8%
3. Zenith, 8%
7. Nintendo, 7%
7. Magnavox, 7%
7. AT&T, 7%
10. RCA, 6%

Source: *Discount Store News*, Top Brands Consumer Survey, Part II (annual), September 7, 1998, p. 22.

★2479★
BEST-SELLING CD PLAYER BRANDS, 1998
Ranked by: Market share, in percent. **Number listed:** 10

1. Sony, with 36%
2. Pioneer, 13%
3. Matsushita, 11%
4. Kenwood, 8%
5. Sanyo Fisher, 7%
6. JVC, 6%
6. NAP, 6%
8. Thomson, 5%
9. Sharp, 4%
10. Others, 4%

Source: *Appliance Manufacturer*, (annual), April, 1999, p. 22.

★2480★
TOP CONSUMER ELECTRONICS BRANDS
Ranked by: Total sales, in billions of dollars. **Remarks:** Also notes company location, lead agency, and media expenditures. **Number listed:** 5

1. Sony, with $10.6 billion
2. Philips, Magnavox, $8.2
3. Panasonic, $8.1
4. Hitachi, $6.9
5. RCA, ProScan, GE, $4.1

Source: *Brandweek*, Superbrands: America's Top 2,000 Brands (annual), June 21, 1999, p. 533.

★2481★
TOP CONSUMER ELECTRONICS CHAINS, 1997
Ranked by: Sales, in millions of dollars. **Remarks:** Also notes 1996 sales, percent change, number of stores, and average store size. **Number listed:** 12

1. Best Buy, with $8,358 million
2. Circuit City, $7,997
3. Radio Shack, $3,300
4. Nobody Beats The Wiz, $950
5. The Good Guys, $891
6. Sun Television and Appliances, $508
7. Rex Stores, $411
8. BrandsMart USA, $375
9. J & R Music World, $315
10. Tops Appliance, $294

Source: *Discount Store News*, Discount Industry Annual Report, July 13, 1998, p. 84.

★2482★
TOP CONSUMER ELECTRONICS COMPANIES BY SEGMENT REVENUE
Ranked by: Segement revenue, in millions of dollars. **Number listed:** 5

1. Zenith Electronics, with $1,173.1 million
2. Eastman Kodak, $919.2
3. Audiovox, $536.2
4. Recoton, $502.0
5. Harman Intl. Industries, $498.7

Source: *Electronic Business*, Top 200 (annual), July, 1998, p. 95.

★2483★
TOP CONSUMER ELECTRONICS RETAILERS, 1997
Ranked by: Revenue, in millions of dollars. **Remarks:** Includes store type and corporate location. Figures for Sears and KMart are estimates. **Number listed:** 25

1. Circuit City, with $5,837.5 million
2. Best Buy, $5,500.0
3. Comp USA, $5,070.0
4. Sears, $3,437.9
5. Radio Shack, $3,119.2
6. Office Depot, $3,083.3
7. Kmart, $2,869.0
8. Staples, $2,719.5
9. Wal-Mart, $2,500.0
10. Office Max Inc., $1,920.0

Source: *HFN*, July 20, 1998, p. 84.

Home Equity Loans

★2484★
TOP BANKS AND THRIFT COMPANIES IN HOME EQUITY LOANS AND LINES OF CREDIT, 1998
Ranked by: Amount of loans, in thousands of dollars as of 6/30/98. **Remarks:** Also includes home equity open-end revolving lines of credit, home equity permanent closed-end loans and percent nonperforming open-end revolving lines of credit as well as figures for 6/30/97. **Number listed:** 100

1. First Union Corp., with $12,934,482 thousand
2. NationsBank Corp., $12,751,526
3. BankAmerica Corp., $10,182,540
4. Banc One Corp., $9,319,405
5. Wells Fargo & Co., $6,145,601
6. U.S. Bancorp, $5,854,130
7. Chase Manhattan Corp., $5,689,612
8. KeyCorp, $5,233,395
9. PNC Bank Corp., $5,167,882
10. National City Corp., $4,545,914

Source: *American Banker*, Top 100 Bank and Thrift Companies in Home Equity Loans and Lines of Credit (annual), November 3, 1998, p. 14+.

★2485★
TOP INSTITUTIONS IN HOME EQUITY ASSET DECLINE, 1998
Ranked by: Percent change in total open-end lines and permanent closed-end loans as of 6/30/98. **Number listed:** 10

1. Bank of New York Co., with -43.36%
2. Sanwa Bank, -35.24%
3. Wilmington Trust Corp., -35.15%
4. Bank of Tokyo-Mitsubishi, -14.44%
5. Ohio Savings Financial Corp., -14.37%
6. BankAmerica Corp., -11.63%
7. America First CU, -11.36%
8. Webster Financial Corp., -10.97%
9. Trustco Bank Corp., -10.78%
10. First of America Bank Corp., -9.79%

Source: *American Banker*, Top 100 Bank and Thrift Companies in Home Equity Loans and Lines of Credit (annual), November 3, 1998, p. 15.

★2486★
TOP INSTITUTIONS IN HOME EQUITY ASSET GROWTH, 1998
Ranked by: Percent change in total open-end lines and permanent closed-end loans as of 6/30/98. **Number listed:** 10

1. Bank United Corp., with 172.43%

2. Crestar Financial Corp., 99.06%
3. Colonial BancGroup, 95.29%
4. Charter One Financial, 87.16%
5. H. F. Ahmanson & Co., 76.08%
6. Provident Bankshares, 58.89%
7. Republic New York Corp., 51.20%
8. Peoples Mutual, 46.44%
9. SouthTrust Corp., 44.96%
10. One Valley Bancorp, 42.95%

Source: *American Banker*, Top 100 Bank and Thrift Companies in Home Equity Loans and Lines of Credit (annual), November 3, 1998, p. 15.

Home Freezers

★2487★
BEST-SELLING FREEZERS, 1998
Ranked by: Market share, in percent. **Remarks:** Also notes 1993 market share. **Number listed:** 4

1. Electrolux, with 69%
2. W. C. Wood, 30%
3. Sanyo Fisher, 1%
4. Others, 0%

Source: *Appliance Manufacturer*, April, 1999, p. 19.

Home Furnishings Industry

★2488★
TOP HOME FURNISHINGS RETAILERS, 1997
Ranked by: Home furnishings revenue, in millions of dollars. **Remarks:** Also notes number of stores, store type, 1997 total retail revenue and percent change from 1996.. **Number listed:** 200

1. Wal-Mart, with $16,956.46 million
2. Sears, $12,677.90
3. Circuit City, $7,560.00
4. Kmart, $6,399.59
5. Best Buy, $6,250.00
6. Home Depot, $6,039.00
7. CompUSA, $5,070.00
8. Target, $4,888.30
9. J.C. Penney, $4,109.35
10. Radio Shack, $3,112.17

Source: *HFN*, Top 200 Home Goods Retailers (annual), July 20, 1998, p. 11+.

★2489★
TOP SUPERMARKET RETAILERS OF HOME FURNISHINGS, 1997
Ranked by: Home furnishings sales, in millions of dollars. **Remarks:** Includes percent change from previous year. **Number listed:** 15

1. Fred Meyer, with $642.96 million
2. Albertson's, $383.43
3. American Stores, $251.61
4. Supervalu, $238.39
5. Ahold USA, $198.18
6. Kroger Co., $183.05
7. Safeway, $170.76
8. A&P, $142.22
9. Food Lion, $141.28
10. Publix, $135.23

Source: *Supermarket News*, September 7, 1998, p. 54.

Home Health Care--Equipment and Supplies

★2490★
MOST PROFITABLE HOME MEDICAL EQUIPMENT COMPANIES BY GROSS REVENUE, 1998
Ranked by: Gross revenue, in millions of dollars. **Remarks:** Also notes locations, top officer, number of branches and employees, private/public status, and distribution of revenue percentage. **Number listed:** 58

1. Olsten Health Services, with $1,320 million
2. Apria Healthcare Group, $988.90
3. Integrated Health Services, $854.51
4. Lincare Holdings, $464.89
5. Coram Healthcare, $449.00
6. American Homepatient, $414.00
7. Pediatric Services of America, $337.82
8. Staff Builders, $326.10
9. Nursefinders, $205.00
10. Home Health Corp. of America, $198.20

Source: *Homecare*, HME 58 (annual), December, 1998, p. 46+.

Home Health Care Services—Detroit Metropolitan Area

★2491★
TOP HOME HEALTH CARE COMPANIES IN THE DETROIT METROPOLITAN AREA, 1998
Ranked by: Total net revenue, in millions of dollars. **Remarks:** Also notes contact information, top local executive, 1996 revenue, number of local employees, number of patients, and services provided. **Number listed:** 20

1. Arcadia Health Services Inc., with $62.3 million
2. Henry Ford at Home, $52.0
3. Olsten Health Care Services, $33.2
4. Visiting Nurse Association of Southeast Michigan, $27.4
5. Beaumont Home Health Services, $24.3
6. Personal Home Care Services Inc., $18.4
7. Oakwood Home Care Services, $15.9
8. St. John Home Health Care, $14.6
9. Metrostaff Home Health Care, $11.5
10. Renaissance Home Health Care Inc., $10.7

Source: *Crain's Detroit Business*, Crain's Book of Lists (annual), December 28, 1998, p. 102.

Home Improvement Centers

★2492★
TOP HOME CENTER/HARDWARE/SPECIALTY HOME IMPROVEMENT COMPANIES, 1998
Ranked by: Sales, in dollars. **Remarks:** Includes headquarters' location, 1997 sales, 1996 sales, number of stores and page number. **Number listed:** 200

1. Home Depot, with $30,219,000,000
2. Lowe's Cos., $12,244,900,000
3. Menard Inc., $4,000,000,000
4. Hechinger Investment Company of Delaware Inc., $3,444,400,000
5. Payless Cashways Inc., $1,906,862,000

6. 84 Lumber Co., $1,650,000,000
7. Carolina Holdings Inc., $1,600,000,000
8. HomeBase Inc., $1,442,341,000
9. Sears Hardware Stores, $1,373,071,000
10. Eagle Hardware & Garden Inc., $1,085,658,000

Source: *Chain Store Guides*, Directory of Home Center Operators & Hardware Chains (annual), 1999, p. a18+.

Home Textiles

See: **Household Linens**

Hong Kong Stock Exchange

★2493★

LARGEST LISTED COMPANIES ON THE HONG KONG STOCK EXCHANGE, 1997

Ranked by: Market value, in billions of Hong Kong dollars. **Number listed:** 20

1. HSBC Holdings, with HK$582.32 billion
2. HK Telecommunications, HK$189.59
3. Hutchison Whampoa, HK$188.27
4. China Telecom, HK$156.68
5. Hang Seng Bank, HK$143.65
6. Sun Hung Kai Properties, HK$129.03
7. Cheung Kong Holdings, HK$116.60
8. China Light & Power Co., HK$106.99
9. CITIC Pacific, HK$65.52
10. Swire Pacific, HK$63.97

Source: *SSB Guide to World Equity Markets (annual)*, Euromoney Publications, 1998, p. 220.

★2494★

MOST ACTIVELY TRADED SHARE ON THE HONG KONG STOCK EXCHANGE, 1997

Ranked by: Trading value, in billions of Hong Kong dollars. **Number listed:** 20

1. HSBC Holdings, with HK$268.65 billion
2. Cheung Kong Holdings, HK$126.42
3. CNPC, HK$94.71
4. Sun Hung Kai Properties, HK$93.72
5. Hutchison Whampoa, HK$93.34
6. Hong Kong Telecom, HK$92.58
7. CITIC Pacific, HK$84.91
8. China Merchants Holdings, HK$72.95
9. Hang Seng Bank, HK$66.54
10. Henderson Land Development, HK$57.33

Source: *SSB Guide to World Equity Markets (annual)*, Euromoney Publications, 1998, p. 220.

Hospital Management Companies

★2495★

LARGEST HEALTHCARE FACILITY CLINICAL DIAGNOSTIC EQUIPMENT MAINTENANCE CONTRACTORS, 1997

Ranked by: Number of healthcare clients. **Remarks:** Also notes number of 1996 clients and percent change. **Number listed:** 5

1. COHR, with with 451 clients
2. ServiceMaster Healthcare Management Services, 367
3. Hospital Shared Services, 186
4. Modern Biomedical Services, 153
5. Novare Services, 66

Source: *Modern Healthcare*, Contract Management Survey (annual), August 31, 1998, p. 48.

★2496★

LARGEST HEALTHCARE FACILITY CONTRACT MANAGERS BY REVENUE, 1997

Ranked by: Healthcare revenue, in millions of dollars. **Remarks:** Also notes number of 1996 clients and percent change. **Number listed:** 5

1. Sodexho Marriott Services, with $2,900.0 million
2. Aramark, $392.0
3. Medaphis Corp., $378.0
4. EmCare, $313.0
5. Morrison Health Care, $250.0

Source: *Modern Healthcare*, Contract Management Survey (annual), August 31, 1998, p. 48.

★2497★

LARGEST HEALTHCARE FACILITY CONTRACT MANAGERS, 1997

Ranked by: Number of healthcare clients. **Remarks:** Also notes number of 1996 clients and percent change. **Number listed:** 20

1. Medaphis Corp., with 7,300 clients
2. Allegiance Healthcare, 4,200
3. Service Master Healthcare Managements Services, 2,619
4. Sodexho Marriott Services, 1,860
5. Healthcare Services Group, 1,067
6. Aramark, 535
7. COHR, 466
8. Owen Healthcare, 426
9. EmCare, 382
10. Team Health, 346

Source: *Modern Healthcare*, Contract Management Survey (annual), August 31, 1998, p. 44.

★2498★

LARGEST HEALTHCARE FACILITY EMERGENCY DEPARTMENT CONTRACTORS, 1997

Ranked by: Number of healthcare clients. **Remarks:** Also notes number of 1996 clients and percent change. **Number listed:** 5

1. EmCare, with with 382 clients
2. Team Health, 254
3. MedAmerica, 60
4. California Emergency Physicians Medical Group, 44
5. Janzen, Johnston & Rockwell Emergency Medicine Management Services, 17

Source: *Modern Healthcare*, Contract Management Survey (annual), August 31, 1998, p. 48.

★2499★

LARGEST HEALTHCARE FACILITY FOOD SERVICE CONTRACTORS, 1997

Ranked by: Number of healthcare clients. **Remarks:** Also notes number of 1996 clients and percent change. **Number listed:** 5

1. Sodexho Marriott Services, with with 910 clients
2. Aramark, 384
3. Morrison Health Care, 303
4. Wood Co., 240
5. ServiceMaster Healthcare Management Services, 235

Source: *Modern Healthcare*, Contract Management Survey (annual), August 31, 1998, p. 46.

★2500★
LARGEST HEALTHCARE FACILITY HOUSEKEEPING CONTRACTORS, 1997
Ranked by: Number of healthcare clients. **Remarks:** Also notes number of 1996 clients and percent change. **Number listed:** 5

1. Healthcare Services Group, with 1,045 clients
2. ServiceMaster Healthcare Management Services, 543
3. Sodexho Marriott Services, 430
4. Professional Services, 97
5. Crothall Healthcare, 89

Source: *Modern Healthcare*, Contract Management Survey (annual), August 31, 1998, p. 48.

★2501★
LARGEST HEALTHCARE FACILITY PHARMACY SERVICES CONTRACTORS, 1997
Ranked by: Number of healthcare clients. **Remarks:** Also notes number of 1996 clients and percent change. **Number listed:** 5

1. ServiceMaster Healthcare Management Services, with with 410 clients
2. Owen Healthcare, 387
3. MedManagement, 104
4. PharmaSource Healthcare, 73
5. Pharmacy Systems, 42

Source: *Modern Healthcare*, Contract Management Survey (annual), August 31, 1998, p. 48.

★2502★
LARGEST HEALTHCARE FACILITY REHABILITATION/PHYSICAL THERAPY CONTRACTORS, 1997
Ranked by: Number of healthcare clients. **Remarks:** Also notes number of 1996 clients and percent change. **Number listed:** 5

1. RehabCare Group, with 138 clients
2. GNA, 136
3. Milestone Healthcare, 87
4. ServiceMaster Healthcare Management Services, 50
5. RCSA, 22

Source: *Modern Healthcare*, Contract Management Survey (annual), August 31, 1998, p. 48.

★2503★
LARGEST HOSPITAL DEPARTMENT MANAGEMENT CONTRACTS, 1997
Ranked by: Number of hospital clients. **Remarks:** Also notes number of 1996 clients, number of 1996 and 1997 contractors, and percent change. **Number listed:** 20

1. Food service, with 1,756 clients
2. Housekeeping, 1,116
3. Clinical/diagnostic equipment maintenance, 1,094
4. Collections, 821
5. Emergency, 763
6. Pharmacy, 733
7. Laundry, 539
8. Plant operations, 431
9. Accounts receivable, 300
10. Rehabilitation/physical therapy, 250

Source: *Modern Healthcare*, Contract Management Survey (annual), August 31, 1998, p. 43.

Hospitals

See also: **Multihospital Systems Nursing Homes Psychiatric Hospitals**

★2504★
LEADING ADVERTISERS IN HOSPITAL PUBLICATIONS, 1998
Ranked by: Market share of ad expenditures, in percent. **Remarks:** Also notes rank and market share for previous years, as well as percent change. **Number listed:** 12

1. Team Health, with 1.15%
2. Kimberly-Clark Corporation, 1.12%
3. Multiplan Inc., 1.11%
4. People Soft, 1.09%
5. Implementation Specialists For Healthcare Inc., 1.07%
6. Tempus Software, 0.98%
7. 3M Healthcare, 0.95%
8. Kodak, 0.94%
9. Dupont Flooring Systems, 0.93%
9. HBE Medical Buildings, 0.93%
11. Olympus America, 0.92%

Source: *Medical Marketing & Media*, Healthcare Advertising Review (annual), April, 1999, p. 57.

★2505★
MOST ADVERTISED HOSPITAL PRODUCTS AND SERVICES IN HOSPITAL PUBLICATIONS, 1998
Ranked by: Market share of ad dollars, in percent. **Remarks:** Also notes rank and market share for previous years, as well as percent change. **Number listed:** 12

1. Team Health Ad (Team Health), with 1.15%
2. Multiplan Network (Multiplan Inc.), 1.11%
3. People Soft Software (People Soft), 1.09%
4. Service/ISH Services (Imp. Specialists for Healthcare Inc.), 1.05%
5. HBE Medical Buildings (HBE Medical Buildings), 0.93%
6. Marshall Erdman and Associates Inc. (Marshall Erdman Assoc), 0.90%
7. Olympus America Financial Services (Olympus America), 0.87%
8. Lawson Software Company Ad (Lawson Software), 0.83%
9. St. Paul Medical Services (St. Paul Fire and Marine Insurance Co.), 0.74%
10. Interserv 2000 Systems (Aramark), 0.69%

Source: *Medical Marketing & Media*, Healthcare Advertising Review (annual), April, 1999, p. 57.

★2506★
STATES WITH THE BEST HOSPITAL QUALITY-OF-CARE, 1997
Ranked by: Specific figures not provided. **Remarks:** Data taken from Center for Healthcare Industry Performance Studies. **Number listed:** 5

1. Arizona
2. Colorado
3. Washington
4. Oregon
5. Florida

Source: *Crain's New York Business*, April 5, 1999, p. 4.

★2507★
STATES WITH THE WORST HOSPITAL QUALITY-OF-CARE, 1997
Ranked by: Specific figures not provided. **Remarks:** Data taken from Center for Healthcare Industry Performance Studies. **Number listed:** 5
1. Maine
2. New Jersey
3. New Hampshire
4. New York
5. Hawaii

Source: *Crain's New York Business*, April 5, 1999, p. 4.

★2508★
TOP HOSPITALS FOR CANCER TREATMENT AND CARE ,1998
Ranked by: U.S. News points index. **Remarks:** Index is overall measure of quality for care; one-third is ''reputational'' score, one-third is ''mortality rate'', and one-third is for data that vary by specialty. Top hospitals in each specialty receive score of 100. **Number listed:** 42
1. Memorial Sloan-Kettering Cancer Center (New York, NY), with 100.0
2. University of Texas, M.D. Anderson Cancer Center (Houston), 94.7
3. Johns Hopkins Hospital (Baltimore), 58.7
4. Mayo Clinic (Rochester, MN), 48.3
5. Dana-Farber Cancer Institute (Boston), 48.1
6. Duke University Medical Center (Durham, NC), 33.9
7. Stanford University Hospital (Stanford, CA), 31.1
8. University of Washington Medical Center (Seattle), 29.6
9. University of Chicago Hospitals, 28.6
10. UCLA Medical Center (Los Angeles), 25.9

Source: *U.S. News & World Report*, America's Best Hospitals (annual), July 27, 1998, p. 67.

★2509★
TOP HOSPITALS FOR CARDIOLOGY AND CARDIAC SURGERY ,1998
Ranked by: U.S. News points index. **Remarks:** Index is overall measure of quality for care; one-third is ''reputational'' score, one-third is ''mortality rate'', and one-third is for data that vary by specialty. Top hospitals in each specialty receive score of 100. **Number listed:** 42
1. Cleveland Clinic, with 100.0
2. Mayo Clinic (Rochester, MN), 94.3
3. Massachusetts General Hospital (Boston), 60.9
4. Duke University Medical Center (Durham, NC), 53.9
5. Texas Heart Institute-St. Luke's Episcopal Hospital (Houston), 52.2
6. Brigham and Women's Hospital (Boston), 50.1
7. Emory University Hospital (Atlanta), 47.0
8. Johns Hopkins Hospital (Baltimore), 43.7
9. Stanford University Hospital (Stanford, CA), 43.2
10. Barnes-Jewish Hospital (St. Louis), 34.6

Source: *U.S. News & World Report*, America's Best Hospitals (annual), July 27, 1998, p. 68.

★2510★
TOP HOSPITALS FOR ENDOCRINOLOGY, 1998
Ranked by: U.S. News points index. **Remarks:** Index is overall measure of quality for care; one-third is ''reputational'' score, one-third is ''mortality rate'', and one-third is for data that vary by specialty. Top hospitals in each specialty receive score of 100. **Number listed:** 42
1. Mayo Clinic (Rochester, MN), with 100.0
2. Massachusetts General Hospital (Boston), 91.6
3. Johns Hopkins Hospital (Baltimore), 48.1
4. Barnes-Jewish Hospital (St. Louis), 39.7
5. Brigham and Women's Hospital (Boston), 35.5
6. University of Chicago Hospitals, 35.4
7. University of Virginia Health Sciences Center (Charlottesville), 33.3
8. UCLA Medical Center (Los Angeles), 28.8
9. Duke University Medical Center (Durham, NC), 27.9
10. Beth Israel Deaconess Medical Center (Boston), 25.9

Source: *U.S. News & World Report*, America's Best Hospitals (annual), July 27, 1998, p. 69.

★2511★
TOP HOSPITALS FOR GASTROENTEROLOGY, 1998
Ranked by: U.S. News points index. **Remarks:** Index is overall measure of quality for care; one-third is ''reputational'' score, one-third is ''mortality rate'', and one-third is for data that vary by specialty. Top hospitals in each specialty receive score of 100. **Number listed:** 42
1. Mayo Clinic (Rochester, MN), with 100.0
2. Cleveland Clinic, 52.2
2. Johns Hopkins Hospital (Baltimore), 52.2
4. Massachusetts General Hospital (Boston), 51.5
5. Mount Sinai Medical Center (New York), 44.0
6. University of Chicago Hospitals, 36.7
7. UCLA Medical Center (Los Angeles), 35.0
8. University of California, San Francisco Medical Center, 34.8
9. Duke University Medical Center (Durham, NC), 30.5
10. Brigham and Women's Hospital (Boston), 28.7

Source: *U.S. News & World Report*, America's Best Hospitals (annual), July 27, 1998, p. 73.

★2512★
TOP HOSPITALS FOR GERIATRICS, 1998
Ranked by: U.S. News points index. **Remarks:** Index is overall measure of quality for care; one-third is ''reputational'' score, one-third is ''mortality rate'', and one-third is for data that vary by specialty. Top hospitals in each specialty receive score of 100. **Number listed:** 42
1. UCLA Medical Center (Los Angeles), with 100.0
2. Mount Sinai Medical Center (New York), 80.5
3. Johns Hopkins Hospital (Baltimore), 77.4
4. Duke University Medical Center (Durham, NC), 67.5
5. Massachusetts General Hospital (Boston), 66.9
6. Mayo Clinic (Rochester, MN), 47.6
7. University of Michigan Medical Center (Ann Arbor), 39.5
8. Beth Israel Deaconess Medical Center (Boston), 36.6
9. Cleveland Clinic, 32.4
10. St. Louis University Hospital, 31.6

Source: *U.S. News & World Report*, America's Best Hospitals (annual), July 27, 1998, p. 77.

★2513★
TOP HOSPITALS FOR GYNECOLOGY, 1998
Ranked by: U.S. News points index. **Remarks:** Index is overall measure of quality for care; one-third is ''reputational'' score, one-third is ''mortality rate'', and one-third is for data that vary by specialty. Top hospitals in each specialty receive score of 100. **Number listed:** 42
1. Johns Hopkins Hospital (Baltimore), with 100.0
2. Mayo Clinic (Rochester, MN), 79.8
3. Massachusetts General Hospital (Boston), 72.1
4. University of Texas, M.D. Anderson Cancer Center (Houston), 70.9
5. Brigham and Women's Hospital (Boston), 61.1
6. Memorial Sloan-Kettering Cancer Center (New York), 56.7
7. Duke University Medical Center (Durham, NC), 52.5
8. UCLA Medical Center (Los Angeles), 43.0

9. Columbia-Presbyterian Medical Center (New York), 39.4
10. Northwestern Memorial Hospital (Chicago), 38.9

Source: *U.S. News & World Report*, America's Best Hospitals (annual), July 27, 1998, p. 78.

★2514★
TOP HOSPITALS FOR NEUROLOGY AND NEUROSURGERY, 1998

Ranked by: U.S. News points index. **Remarks:** Index is overall measure of quality for care; one-third is ''reputational'' score, one-third is ''mortality rate'', and one-third is for data that vary by specialty. Top hospitals in each specialty receive score of 100. **Number listed:** 42

1. Mayo Clinic (Rochester, MN), with 100.0
2. Massachusetts General Hospital (Boston), 93.3
3. Johns Hopkins Hospital (Baltimore), 82.7
4. Columbia-Presbyterian Medical Center (New York), 63.1
5. University of California, San Francisco Medical Center, 55.8
6. Cleveland Clinic, 42.3
7. UCLA Medical Center (Los Angeles), 40.5
8. Duke University Medical Center (Durham, NC), 34.2
9. Hospital of the University of Pennsylvania (Philadelphia), 32.9
10. New York Hospital-Cornell Medical Center, 31.5

Source: *U.S. News & World Report*, America's Best Hospitals (annual), July 27, 1998, p. 81.

★2515★
TOP HOSPITALS FOR OPHTHALMOLOGY, 1998

Ranked by: Reputational score, in percent. **Number listed:** 17

1. University of Miami (Bascom Palmer Eye Institute), with 74.4%
2. Johns Hopkins Hospital (Wilmer Eye Institute) (Baltimore), 72.5%
3. Wills Eye Hospital (Philadelphia), 61.5%
4. Massachusetts Eye and Ear Infirmary (Boston), 48.8%
5. UCLA Medical Center (Jules Stein Eye Institute) (Los Angeles), 28.1%
6. University of Iowa Hospitals and Clinics (Iowa City), 21.2%
7. University of California, San Francisco Medical Center, 10.8%
8. Los Angeles County-USC Medical Center (Doheny Eye Institute), 10.3%
9. Duke University Medical Center (Durham, NC), 8.7%
10. Mayo Clinic (Rochester, MN), 7.6%

Source: *U.S. News & World Report*, America's Best Hospitals (annual), July 27, 1998, p. 91.

★2516★
TOP HOSPITALS FOR ORTHOPEDICS, 1998

Ranked by: U.S. News points index. **Remarks:** Index is overall measure of quality for care; one-third is ''reputational'' score, one-third is ''mortality rate'', and one-third is for data that vary by specialty. Top hospitals in each specialty receive score of 100. **Number listed:** 42

1. Mayo Clinic (Rochester, MN), with 100.0
2. Hospital for Special Surgery (New York), 93.8
3. Massachusetts General Hospital (Boston), 67.5
4. Johns Hopkins Hospital (Baltimore), 45.0
5. Cleveland Clinic, 35.2
6. Duke University Medical Center (Durham, NC), 32.8
7. University of Washington Medical Center (Seattle), 29.3
8. University of Iowa Hospitals and Clinics (Iowa City), 27.1
9. UCLA Medical Center (Los Angeles), 26.9
10. Brigham and Women's Hospital (Boston), 24.7

Source: *U.S. News & World Report*, America's Best Hospitals (annual), July 27, 1998, p. 82.

★2517★
TOP HOSPITALS FOR OTOLARYNGOLOGY, 1998

Ranked by: U.S. News points index. **Remarks:** Index is overall measure of quality for care; one-third is ''reputational'' score, one-third is ''mortality rate'', and one-third is for data that vary by specialty. Top hospitals in each specialty receive score of 100. **Number listed:** 42

1. Johns Hopkins Hospital (Baltimore), with 100.0
2. University of Iowa Hospitals and Clinics (Iowa City), 84.2
3. University of Michigan Medical Center (Ann Arbor), 60.4
4. Barnes-Jewish Hospital (St. Louis), 56.4
5. University of Pittsburgh Medical Center, 55.5
6. UCLA Medical Center (Los Angeles), 53.7
7. Mayo Clinic (Rochester, MN), 51.0
8. University of Washington Medical Center (Seattle), 42.6
9. University of Texas, M.D. Anderson Cancer Center (Houston), 42.3
10. University of California, San Francisco Medical Center, 42.1

Source: *U.S. News & World Report*, America's Best Hospitals (annual), July 27, 1998, p. 85.

★2518★
TOP HOSPITALS FOR PEDIATRICS, 1998

Ranked by: Reputational score, in percent. **Number listed:** 24

1. Children's Hospital (Boston), with 48.6%
2. Children's Hospital of Philadelphia, 37.7%
3. Johns Hopkins Hospital (Baltimore), 28.4%
4. Childrens Hospital (Los Angeles), 13.5%
5. Children's National Medical Center (Washington, DC), 11.3%
6. Children's Hospital of Pittsburgh, 11.2%
7. Children's Memorial Hospital (Chicago), 11.0%
8. Children's Hospital Medical Center (Cincinnati), 10.9%
9. Columbia-Presbyterian Medical Center (New York), 10.5%
10. University Hospitals of Cleveland (Rainbow Babies & Children's Hospital), 10.2%

Source: *U.S. News & World Report*, America's Best Hospitals (annual), July 27, 1998, p. 91.

★2519★
TOP HOSPITALS FOR PSYCHIATRY, 1998

Ranked by: Reputational score, in percent. **Number listed:** 17

1. Massachusetts General Hospital (Boston), with 24.3%
2. C. F. Menninger Memorial Hospital (Topeka, KS), 23.4%
3. McLean Hospital (Belmont, MA), 19.4%
4. Johns Hopkins Hospital (Baltimore), 13.5%
5. New York Hospital-Cornell Medical Center, 11.8%
6. Mayo Clinic (Rochester, MN), 9.4%
7. UCLA Neuropsychiatric Hospital (Los Angeles), 9.3%
8. Columbia-Presbyterian Medical Center (New York), 8.9%
9. Sheppard and Enoch Pratt Hospital (Baltimore), 8.3%

10. Yale-New Haven Hospital (New Haven, CT), 8.0%

Source: *U.S. News & World Report*, America's Best Hospitals (annual), July 27, 1998, p. 91.

★2520★
TOP HOSPITALS FOR PULMONARY DISEASE, 1998

Ranked by: U.S. News points index. **Remarks:** Index is overall measure of quality for care; one-third is ''reputational'' score, one-third is ''mortality rate'', and one-third is for data that vary by specialty. Top hospitals in each specialty receive score of 100. **Number listed:** 42

1. National Jewish Center (Denver), with 100.0
2. Mayo Clinic (Rochester, MN), 75.9
3. Barnes-Jewish Hospital (St. Louis), 51.4
4. Johns Hopkins Hospital (Baltimore), 47.0
5. Massachusetts General Hospital (Boston), 40.5
6. University of California, San Francisco Medical Center, 40.4
7. University Hospital (Denver), 37.3
8. Duke University Medical Center (Durham, NC), 34.2
9. Cleveland Clinic, 28.2
10. UCLA Medical Center (Los Angeles), 24.5

Source: *U.S. News & World Report*, America's Best Hospitals (annual), July 27, 1998, p. 86.

★2521★
TOP HOSPITALS FOR REHABILITATION, 1998

Ranked by: Reputational score, in percent. **Number listed:** 21

1. Rehabilitation Institute of Chicago, with 58.1%
2. University of Washington Medical Center (Seattle), 33.0%
3. TIRR (Texas Institute for Rehabilitation and Research) (Houston), 28.0%
4. Kessler Institute for Rehabilitation (West Orange, NJ), 26.2%
4. Craig Hospital (Englewood, CO), 26.2%
6. Mayo Clinic (Rochester, MN), 20.5%
7. New York University Medical Center (Rusk Institute), 14.8%
8. Ohio State University Medical Center (Columbus), 13.1%
9. Los Angeles County-Rancho Los Amigos Med. Ctr. (Downey, CA), 12.1%
10. Thomas Jefferson University Hospital (Philadelphia), 12.0%

Source: *U.S. News & World Report*, America's Best Hospitals (annual), July 27, 1998, p. 91.

★2522★
TOP HOSPITALS FOR RHEUMATOLOGY, 1998

Ranked by: U.S. News points index. **Remarks:** Index is overall measure of quality for care; one-third is ''reputational'' score, one-third is ''mortality rate'', and one-third is for data that vary by specialty. Top hospitals in each specialty receive score of 100. **Number listed:** 42

1. Mayo Clinic (Rocheseter, MN), with 100.0
2. Johns Hopkins Hospital (Baltimore), 76.7
3. Hospital for Special Surgery (New York), 72.0
4. Brigham and Women's Hospital (Boston), 60.9
5. University of Alabama Hospital at Birmingham, 60.0
6. UCLA Medical Center (Los Angeles), 58.3
7. Massachusetts General Hospital (Boston), 54.9
8. Cleveland Clinic, 53.6
9. University of Michigan Medical Center (Ann Arbor), 40.9
10. Duke University Medical Center (Durham, NC), 39.3

Source: *U.S. News & World Report*, America's Best Hospitals (annual), July 27, 1998, p. 88.

★2523★
TOP HOSPITALS FOR UROLOGY, 1998

Ranked by: U.S. News points index. **Remarks:** Index is overall measure of quality for care; one-third is ''reputational'' score, one-third is ''mortality rate'', and one-third is for data that vary by specialty. Top hospitals in each specialty receive score of 100. **Number listed:** 42

1. Johns Hopkins Hospital (Baltimore), with 100.0
2. Mayo Clinic (Rochester, MN), 65.8
3. UCLA Medical Center (Los Angeles), 51.7
4. Cleveland Clinic, 46.9
5. Duke University Medical Center (Durham, NC), 39.0
6. Massachusetts General Hospital (Boston), 37.4
7. Stanford University Hospital (Stanford, CA), 33.0
8. Barnes-Jewish Hospital (St. Louis), 32.8
9. Memorial Sloan-Kettering Cancer Center (New York), 30.2
10. University of Texas, M.D. Anderson Cancer Center (Houston), 29.0
10. Methodist Hospital (Houston), 29.0

Source: *U.S. News & World Report*, America's Best Hospitals (annual), July 27, 1998, p. 90.

★2524★
U.S. NEWS & WORLD REPORT ''HONOR ROLL'' HOSPITALS, 1998

Ranked by: Points. **Remarks:** To be named to the U.S. News & World Report ''Honor Roll'', hospitals had to rank high in six out of seventeen specialties. **Number listed:** 42

1. Johns Hopkins Hospital (Baltimore), with with 30 points
2. Mayo Clinic (Rochester), 26
3. Massachusetts General Hospital (Boston), 24
4. Duke University Medical Center (Durham), 22
5. UCLA Medical Center (Los Angeles), 21
6. Cleveland Clinic (Cleveland), 20
7. Stanford University Hospital (Stanford), 15
8. Brigham and Women's Hospital (Boston), 14
9. Barnes-Jewish Hospital (St. Louis), 13
9. University of California, San Francisco Medical Center, 13

Source: *U.S. News & World Report*, America's Best Hospitals (annual), July 27, 1998, p. 51.

Hospitals--Chicago (IL)

★2525★
LARGEST HOSPITALS IN CHICAGO BY NET PATIENT REVENUE, 1997

Ranked by: Net patient revenue, in millions of dollars. **Remarks:** Also notes CEO, percent change from 1996 revenue, number of beds, number of inpatient days, and average occupancy percentages. **Number listed:** 23

1. University of Chicago Hospitals, with $483.3 million
2. Rush-Presbyterian-St. Luke's Medical Center, $482.7
3. Northwestern Memorial Hospital, $414.8
4. Loyola University Medical Center, $356.4
5. Lutheran General Hospital, $333.8
6. Christ Hospital and Medical Center, $332.5
7. MacNeal Memorial Hospital Assn., $254.4
8. Cook County Hospital, $238.0
9. University of Illinois at Chicago Medical Center, $220.4
10. Evanston Hospital, $219.0

Source: *Crain's Chicago Business*, Top Business Lists (annual), 1999, p. 167+.

Hospitals--Detroit Metropolitan Area

★2526★
LARGEST HOSPITALS IN THE DETROIT METROPOLITAN AREA, 1997
Ranked by: Gross revenue, in millions of dollars. **Remarks:** Includes revenue for 1996, percent change, licensed-bed capacity, number of full-time equivalent employees, total patient days, average occupancy percentage and number of hospitals, ambulatory facilities. **Number listed:** 15

1. Mercy Health Services, with $2,398.8 million
2. Henry Ford Health System, $1,940.0
3. The Detroit Medical Center, $1,593.8
4. St. John Health System, $915.9
5. University of Michigan Health System, $896.0
6. William Beaumont Hospital, $873.7
7. Oakwood Healthcare Inc., $559.7
8. Providence Hospital and Medical Centers, $334.8
9. MCG Telesis, $162.1
10. Botsford General Hospital, $159.1

Source: *Crain's Detroit Business*, August 24, 1998, p. 14.

Hospitals--Florida

★2527★
TOP FOR-PROFIT FLORIDA HOSPITALS BY NUMBER OF LICENSED BEDS, 1998
Ranked by: Number of licensed beds. **Remarks:** Also notes number of physicians and employees, average length of stay and occupancy rate, number of 1997 admissions, chief administrator and year founded. **Number listed:** 25

1. Cedars Medical Center (Miami), with with 575 beds
2. West Florida Regional Medical Center (Pensacola), 531
3. Manatee Memorial Hospital & Health System (Bradenton), 512
4. Florida Medical Center (Fort Lauderdale), 459
5. New Port Richey Hospital (New Port Richey), 414
6. Kendall Medical Center (Miami), 412
7. Aventura Hospital and Medical Center (Aventura), 407
8. Southwest Florida Regional Medical Center (Fort Meyers), 400
9. North Ridge Medical Center (Fort Lauderdale), 391
10. Blake Medical Center (Bradenton), 383

Source: *Florida Trend*, TopRank Florida (annual), 1999, p. 74.

★2528★
TOP NOT-FOR-PROFIT FLORIDA HOSPITALS BY NUMBER OF LICENSED BEDS, 1998
Ranked by: Number of licensed beds. **Remarks:** Also notes number of physicians and employees, average length of stay and occupancy rate, number of 1997 admissions, chief administrator and year founded. **Number listed:** 25

1. Jackson Memorial Hospital (Miami), with with 1,567 beds
2. St. Joseph's Hospitals (Tampa), 883
3. Tampa General Hospital (Tampa), 877
4. Lakeland Regional Medical Center (Lakeland), 851
5. Sarasota Memorial Hospital (Sarasota), 850
6. Florida Hospital Orlando (Orlando), 840
7. Tallahassee Memorial Healthcare (Tallahassee), 770
8. Broward General Medical Center (Fort Lauderdale), 744
9. Mount Sinai Medical Center (Miami Beach), 707
10. Morton Plant Hospital (Clearwater), 697

Source: *Florida Trend*, TopRank Florida (annual), 1999, p. 73+.

Hospitals--Food Service

★2529★
LEADING SELF-OPERATED HEALTHCARE FOOD SERVICES, 1997
Ranked by: Food and beverage purchases, in millions of dollars. **Remarks:** Includes volume retail f/s ops, number of nonpatient transactions per year and occupancy. **Number listed:** 10

1. Continuum Health Partners (New York), with $6.2 million
2. Florida Hospital (Orlando), $5.8
3. Massachusetts General Hospital (Boston), $4.4
4. Baptist Memorial Hospital (Memphis), $4.3
5. New York University Medical Center (New York), $3.8
6. New York-Presbyterian Hospital (New York), $3.2
6. Carolinas Medical Center (Charlotte), $3.2
8. UCSF Stanford Health Care (San Francisco), $2.9
9. Cook County Hospital (Chicago), $2.5
10. St. Vincent Medical Center (Little Rock), $2.2

Source: *Restaurants & Institutions*, Institutional Giants, September 15, 1998, p. 70.

Hospitals--Los Angeles County (CA)

★2530★
LARGEST HOSPITALS IN LOS ANGELES COUNTY BY NUMBER OF BEDS, 1998
Ranked by: Number of licensed beds. **Remarks:** Includes previous year's number of beds, occupancy rates for 1997 and 1996, profile, number of employees, hospital specialty, marketing contact and CEO. **Number listed:** 25

1. L. A. County-USC Medical Center, with 1,779
2. Metropolitan State Hospital, 1,327
3. Lanterman State Hospital & Developmental Center, 1,286
4. VA Medical Center-West Los Angeles, 932
5. Cedars-Sinai Medical Center, 877
6. Long Beach Memorial Medical Center, 760
7. UCLA Medical Center, 668
8. Kaiser Permanente Medical Center-Los Angeles, 613
9. Huntington Memorial Hospital, 589
10. VA Medical Center-Long Beach, 558

Source: *Los Angeles Business Journal*, Book of Lists (annual), 1999, p. 110.

Hospitals--New Jersey

★2531★
TOP HEALTHCARE SYSTEMS IN NEW JERSEY BY TOTAL ADMISSIONS, 1998
Ranked by: Total admissions. **Remarks:** Also notes number of beds, number of employees, payroll, occupancy, and CEO. **Number listed:** 20

1. St. Barnabas Health Care System, with 183,300
2. Atlantic Health System, 92,786
3. West Jersey Health System, 48,383
4. Hackensack University Medical Center, 47,747
5. Meridian Health System, 46,896
6. Solaris Health Systems, 42,000
7. St. Peter's Medical Center, 40,959
8. The Valley Hospital, 37,149
9. Liberty Healthcare System, 34,026
10. St. Joseph's Hospital and Medical Center, 28,815

Source: *New Jersey Business*, Book of Lists (annual), 1999, p. 30.

Hospitals--New York (NY)

★2532★
TOP HOSPITALS IN NEW YORK CITY BY OPERATING EXPENSES, 1997
Ranked by: Operating expenses, in millions of dollars. **Remarks:** Includes operating expenses for 1996, number of beds, employees, ambulatory care visits, deliveries, inpatient days, medical/surgical occupancy rate and inpatient discharges. **Number listed:** 25

1. New York and Presbyterian Hospital, with $1,484 million
2. Mount Sinai Hospital, $851
3. Beth Israel Medical Center, $826
4. Montefiore Medical Center, $823
5. Memorial Sloan-Kettering Cancer Center, $727
6. Catholic Medical Centers of Brooklyn and Queens Inc., $620
7. Long Island Jewish Medical Center, $566
8. St. Luke's-Roosevelt Hospital Center, $546
9. Kings County Hospital Center, $462
10. Saint Vincents Hospital and Medical Center, $432

Source: *Crain's New York Business*, Top Business Lists (annual), 1999, p. 68+.

Hospitals--Philadelphia Metropolitan Area

★2533★
LARGEST HOSPITAL GROUPS IN THE PHILADELPHIA AREA BY OPERATING REVENUE, 1998
Ranked by: Operating revenue, in millions of dollars. **Remarks:** Also notes CEOs, total licensed beds, subsidiary hospitals' beds, occupancy rates, FTE's, operating revenue, inpatient admissions, and division CEOs. **Number listed:** 25

1. Jefferson Health System, with $1,742.9 million
2. University of Pennsylvania Health System, $1,086.2
3. Allegheny Health, Education and Research Foundation, $1,027.2
4. Temple University Health System, $674.3
5. Crozer-Keystone Health System, $494
6. Virtua Health, $406.7
7. The Cooper Health System, $376.6
8. Children's Hospital of Philadelphia, $317.0
9. Abington Memorial Hospital, $280.2
10. Mercy Health System, $231.5

Source: *Philadelphia Business Journal*, Book of Business Lists (annual), December 25, 1998, p. 77+.

Hotel Management Companies

★2534★
TOP HOTEL MANAGEMENT COMPANIES BY NUMBER OF ROOMS MANAGED, 1998
Ranked by: Number of rooms managed. **Remarks:** Includes previous year's rank, number of rooms managed previous year, properties managed current and previous years and revenues current and previous years. **Number listed:** 50

1. MeriStar Hotels & Resorts, with 45,191 rooms
2. Interstate Hotels Management, 35,214
3. Bristol Hotels & Resorts, 31,767
4. Lodgian, 27,000
5. Prime Hospitality Corp., 24,516
6. Westmont Hospitality Group, 23,500
7. Tharaldson Enterprises, 18,515
8. Ocean Hospitalities, 12,705
9. UniHost, 12,500
10. Remington Hotel Corp., 12,462

Source: *Hotel & Motel Management*, Top 25 Management Companies (annual), March 1, 1999, p. 39.

★2535★
TOP MANAGEMENT COMPANIES BY NUMBER OF ROOMS MANAGED, 1998*
Ranked by: Total number of rooms managed. **Remarks:** Also notes properties owned and managed and properties managed for other owners. **Number listed:** 50

1. Patriot American, with 110,602 rooms
2. Starwood Hotels & Resorts, 109,961
3. MeriStar Hotels & Resorts, 45,087
4. Bristol Hotels & Resorts, 32,900
5. Westmont Hospitality, 23,500
6. Prime Hospitality Corp., 23,362
7. Lane Hospitality, 18,905
8. Tharaldson Enterprises, 17,996
9. Winegardner & Hammons, 17,571
10. Servico, 17,057

Source: *Lodging Hospitality*, Lodgings 400 Top Performer (annual), August, 1998, p. 53.

Hotels and Motels

★2536★
CITIES WITH THE MOST MEETINGS AND CONVENTIONS HELD AT HOTELS, 1999*
Ranked by: Number of hotel rooms. **Number listed:** 10

1. Las Vegas, with 105,347 rooms
2. Los Angeles, 93,000
3. Orlando, 89,000
4. Chicago, 73,400
5. Washington, 64,716
6. Atlanta, 64,583
7. New York, 61,000
8. San Francisco, 55,000
9. Anaheim, 48,000
10. Dallas, 47,834

Source: *Crain's New York Business*, April 5, 1999, p. 20.

★2537★
GEOGRAPHIC AREAS WITH THE MOST HOTEL ROOMS, 1999*
Ranked by: Number of rooms. **Number listed:** 10

1. Las Vegas, with 105,347 rooms
2. Los Angeles, 93,000

3. Orlando, FL, 89,000
4. Chicago, 73,400
5. Hawaii, 71,025
6. Washington, DC, 64,716
7. Atlanta, 64,583
8. New York, 61,000
9. San Francisco, 55,000
10. Anaheim, CA, 48,000

Source: *Expo*, March, 1999, p. 47.

★2538★
LARGEST HOTEL EXHIBIT HALLS, 1999*
Ranked by: Size of hall, in square feet. **Remarks:** Includes city where located. **Number listed:** 10

1. Opryland Hotal Convention Center, with 600,000
2. MGM Grand Hotel & Conference Center, 210,000
3. Concord Resort Hotel, 177,347
4. Adam's Mark Hotel Dallas, 177,032
5. Las Vegas Hilton Hotel, 171,730
6. Orlando World Center Marriott Resort, 150,000
7. Radisson Centre/Radisson Mart Plaza Hotel Complex, 148,000
8. Walt Disney World Dolphin Hotel, 147,175
9. Wyndham Anatole Dallas, 145,000
10. Reno Hilton, 140,000

Source: *Expo*, March, 1999, p. 47.

★2539★
TOP CENTER-CITY HOTELS NATIONWIDE BY SALES PER ROOM
Ranked by: Sales per room, in dollars. **Remarks:** Includes location, number of rooms/suites, total sales and average occupancy. **Number listed:** 100

1. The Lowell Hotel, with $256,459
2. The Rittenhouse Hotel, $186,296
3. Four Season Hotel, $173,611
4. La Valencia Hotel, $126,240
5. Rihga Royal Hotel, $122,600
6. The Royalton, $110,686
7. Hotel Inter-Continental, $109,971
8. The Lombardy, $106,060
9. The Carlton, $100,000
10. Brown Palace Hotel, $98,756

Source: *Lodging Hospitality*, Lodgings 400 Top Performers, August, 1998, p. 33+.

★2540★
TOP CORPORATIONS IN THE HOTEL, CASINO, RESORT INDUSTRY, 1998
Ranked by: Revenue, in millions of dollars. **Remarks:** Also notes profits and investment figures as well as number of employees. **Number listed:** 9

1. Marriott International, with $7,968 million
2. Starwood Hotels & Resorts, $4,832
3. Hilton Hotels, $4,064
4. Host Marriott, $3,519
5. Patriot American Hospitality, $2,056
6. Harrah's Entertainment, $2,004
7. Mirage Resorts, $1,524
8. Circus Circus Entertainment, $1,480
9. Trump Hotels & Casinos, $1,404

Source: *Fortune*, Fortune 500 Largest U.S. Corporations (annual), April 26, 1999, p. F-61.

★2541★
TOP HIGHWAY/AIRPORT HOTELS NATIONWIDE BY SALES PER ROOM, 1998*
Ranked by: Sales per room, in dollars. **Remarks:** Includes location, number of rooms/suites, total sales and average occupancy. **Number listed:** 100

1. Harris Ranch Inn, with $103,333
2. Hanover Inn, $81,934
3. Doubletree Hotel, $75,387
4. DFW Lakes Hilton, $67,190
5. Crystal Gateway Marriott, $64,562
6. Miami International Airport Hotel, $61,673
7. Regal Alaskan Hotel, $60,193
8. Sheraton at Woodbridge Pl., $59,289
9. Miami Airport Hilton, $58,000
10. Best Western Lake Lucille Inn, $55,759

Source: *Lodging Hospitality*, Lodgings 400 Top Performers, August, 1998, p. 45+.

★2542★
TOP HOTEL COMPANIES BY SYSTEMWIDE REVENUE, 1998
Ranked by: Systemwide revenue, in thousands of dollars. **Remarks:** Includes number of hotels and number of rooms. **Number listed:** 25

1. Bass Hotels & Resorts, with $10,000,000 thousand
2. Marriott International, $8,000,000
3. Cendant, $7,000,000
4. Best Western, $6,800,000
5. Carlson Hospitality, $5,600,000
6. Promus, $5,100,000
7. Accor, $3,705,340
8. Hyatt Hotels, $3,400,000
9. Starwood, $3,333,000
10. Choice, $3,100,000

Source: *Business Travel News*, Business Travel Survey (annual), May 31, 1999, p. 70.

★2543★
TOP RESORT HOTELS NATIONWIDE BY SALES PER ROOM
Ranked by: Sales per room, in dollars. **Remarks:** Includes location, number of rooms/suites, total sales and average occupancy. **Number listed:** 100

1. Auberge du Soleil, with $280,769
2. Timberline Lodge, $207,129
3. Rancho Valencia Resort, $185,142
4. Turnberry Isle Resort & Club, $158,852
5. Resort at Longboat Key Club, $155,414
6. Four Seasons Resort & Club, $154,062
7. Ponte Vedra Inn/Club, $146,396
8. Salish Lodge & Spa, $142,019
9. Silverado C.C. & Resort, $137,931
10. Kona Village Resort, $128,952

Source: *Lodging Hospitality*, Lodgings 400 Top Performers, August, 1998, p. 37+.

★2544★
TOP SOURCES OF REVENUE FOR THE LODGING INDUSTRY, 1997
Ranked by: Market share, in percent. **Remarks:** Data taken from Smith Travel Research. **Number listed:** 5

1. Rooms, with 73%
2. Food & Beverage, 20.6%
3. Telecommunications, 2.5%
3. Minor Profit Centers, 2.5%
5. Rentals & Other Income, 1.4%

Source: *Hotel & Motel Management*, July 20, 1998, p. 1.

★2545★
TOP SUBURBAN HOTELS NATIONWIDE BY SALES PER ROOM
Ranked by: Sales per room, in dollars. **Remarks:** Includes location, number of rooms/suites, total sales and average occupancy. **Number listed:** 100

1. Eagle Lodge, with $132,942

2. Townsend Hotel, $128,433
3. Hayes Conference Center, $106,813
4. Ritz-Carlton, $92,960
5. Woodmark Hotel, $90,141
6. Olde Mill Inn, $78,873
7. Somerset Hills Hilton, $78,741
8. Golden Plough Inn, $78,592
9. Don Shula's Hotel & Golf Club, $78,398
10. Ashman Court Hotel, $77,670

Source: *Lodging Hospitality*, Lodgings 400 Top Performers, August, 1998, p. 41+.

Hotels and Motels--Asia

★2546★

BEST HOTELS IN THE ASIA-PACIFIC AREA, 1998

Ranked by: Survey of executives from 23 countries rating hotels on a score of 1-100. **Remarks:** Scores were averaged. To qualify for ranking hotels had to receive a substantial number of favorable reviews and have a minimum score of 75.7. Also notes previous year's ranking and global rank. **Number listed:** 17

1. Raffles (Singapore), with 88.4
2. Four Seasons (Singapore), 87.8
3. Oriental (Bangkok), 87.6
4. Regent (Hong Kong), 87.0
4. Peninsula (Hong Kong), 87.0
6. Island Shangri-La (Hong Kong), 84.7
6. Ritz-Carlton Millenia (Singapore), 84.7
8. Mandarin Oriental (Hong Kong), 83.8
9. Okura (Tokyo), 83.6
10. Shangri-La (Bangkok), 83.1

Source: *Institutional Investor*, Best Hotels Worldwide list (annual), September, 1998, p. 183.

★2547★

LARGEST ASIAN HOTEL AND RESTAURANT COMPANIES

Ranked by: Sales, in thousands of U.S. dollars ($). **Remarks:** Includes profits as a percentage of sales and activity codes. **Number listed:** 97

1. New World Development Co. Ltd. (Hong Kong), with $2,578,746 thousand
2. Skylark Co. Ltd. (Japan), $2,183,869
3. Dia Kenetsu Co. Ltd. (Japan), $1,855,950
4. Genting Bhd (Malaysia), $1,005,868
5. Resorts World Bhd (Malaysia), $799,799
6. Denny's Japan Co. Ltd. (Japan), $778,592
7. Royal Co. Ltd. (Japan), $719,244
8. Fujita Kanko Inc. (Japan), $714,708
9. CDL Hotels International Ltd. (Hong Kong), $656,821
10. Uehara Sei Shoji Co. Ltd. (Japan), $619,154

Source: *Asia's 7,500 Largest Companies*, (annual), E.L.C. Publishing, Ktd., 1999, p. 91+.

★2548★

MOST ADMIRED HOTELS IN ASIA, 1999

Ranked by: Scores (1-10) based on a survey response of over 4,000 professionals throughout Asia. **Remarks:** Respondents were asked to rate companies on their quality of services/products offered, long-term management vision, response to customer needs, and financial soundness. **Number listed:** 11

1. Hotel Shilla, with 7.70
2. Hyatt Hotels, 7.45
3. Mandarin Oriental, 7.27
4. Shangri-La Hotels, 7.21
5. Dusit Thani Hotel, 7.19
6. Peninsula Group, 7.13
7. Lotte, 7.05
8. Marriott, 7.00
9. Hilton International, 6.93
10. Westin Hotels, 6.67

Source: *Asian Business*, Most Admired Companies in Asia (annual), May, 1999, p. 28.

Hotels and Motels--Canada

★2549★

CITIES IN CANADA WITH THE MOST HOTEL ROOMS, 1998*

Ranked by: Number of rooms. **Number listed:** 10

1. Toronto, with 32,000 rooms
2. Montreal, 24,308
3. Vancouver, BC, 18,000
4. Quebec City, 12,000
5. Edmonton, AB, 11,416
6. Ottawa, 9,350
7. Calgary, AB, 8,700
8. Halifax, NS, 5,000
9. Winnipeg, MB, 3,000
10. London, ON, 2,700

Source: *Expo*, September, 1998, p. 36.

★2550★

LARGEST HOTEL CHAINS IN CANADA, 1998*

Ranked by: Approximate number of rooms. **Remarks:** Data taken from Lyle Hall, KPMG, Toronto. **Number listed:** 18

1. Choice Hotels Canada, with 19,500 rooms
2. Holiday Inn, 15,000
3. Best Western, 13,700
4. Canadian Pacific, 11,000
5. Travelodge, 8,100
6. Ramada, 7,900
7. Sheraton, 6,600
8. Days Inn, 6,500
9. Delta, 6,300
10. Radisson Hotels, 4,300

Source: *Hotel and Motel Management*, July 6, 1998, p. 15.

Hotels and Motels--Chain and Franchise Operations

★2551★

BEST BUDGET HOTEL CHAIN AND FRANCHISE OPERATIONS, 1999*

Ranked by: Overall weighted average score (1-10) based on 6 specific factors. **Remarks:** Also notes percent usage rate. **Number listed:** 5

1. Econo Lodges of America, with 6.77
2. Microtel, 6.66
3. Thrifty Inn, 6.55
4. Motel 6, 6.03
5. Knights Inn, 5.88

Source: *Business Travel News*, U.S. Hotel Chain Survey (annual), February 22, 1999, p. 54.

★2552★
BEST DELUXE HOTEL CHAIN AND FRANCHISE OPERATIONS, 1999*

Ranked by: Overall weighted average score (1-10) based on 14 specific factors. **Remarks:** Also notes percent usage rate. **Number listed:** 7

1. Four Seasons/Regent, with 8.75
2. Ritz-Carlton, 8.67
3. Luxury Collection/St. Regis, 8.39
4. Shangri-La Hotels & Resorts, 8.29
5. Mandarin Oriental, 8.08
6. Peninsula Group, 7.98
7. Fairmont, 7.84

Source: *Business Travel News*, U.S. Hotel Chain Survey (annual), February 22, 1999, p. 46.

★2553★
BEST ECONOMY-PRICED HOTEL CHAIN AND FRANCHISE OPERATIONS, 1999*

Ranked by: Overall weighted average score (1-10) based on 6 specific factors. **Remarks:** Also notes percent usage rate. **Number listed:** 6

1. Holiday Inn Express, with 7.98
2. Fairfield Inns, 7.95
3. Ramada Limited, 7.63
4. Red Roof Inns, 7.30
5. Days Inn, 6.86
6. Travelodge, 6.62

Source: *Business Travel News*, U.S. Hotel Chain Survey (annual), February 22, 1999, p. 54.

★2554★
BEST EXTENDED STAY HOTEL CHAIN AND FRANCHISE OPERATIONS, 1999*

Ranked by: Overall weighted average score (1-10) based on 9 specific factors. **Remarks:** Also notes percent usage rate. **Number listed:** 7

1. Residence Inn, with 8.00
2. Homewood Suites, 7.89
3. Summerfield Suites, 7.70
4. Extended Stay America, 7.62
5. Hawthorn Suites, 7.60
6. Towneplace Suites by Marriott, 7.43
7. Lexington Hotel Suites, 6.94

Source: *Business Travel News*, U.S. Hotel Chain Survey (annual), February 22, 1999, p. 50.

★2555★
BEST MID-PRICED HOTEL CHAIN AND FRANCHISE OPERATIONS WITH FOOD AND BEVERAGE, 1999*

Ranked by: Overall weighted average score (1-10) based on 12 specific factors. **Remarks:** Score for each factor and usage rate also provided. **Number listed:** 15

1. Four Points by Sheraton, with 7.97
2. Courtyard by Marriott, 7.92
3. Hilton Garden Inn, 7.85
4. Club Hotels by Doubletree, 7.72
5. Outrigger Hotels & Resorts, 7.63
6. Red Lion Hotels, 7.62
7. Holiday Inn Select, 7.60
8. Holiday Inn Hotels, 7.56
9. Clarion Hotels, 7.49
10. Novotel, 7.44

Source: *Business Travel News*, U.S. Hotel Chain Survey (annual), February 22, 1999, p. 50.

★2556★
BEST MID-PRICED HOTEL CHAIN AND FRANCHISE OPERATIONS WITHOUT FOOD AND BEVERAGE, 1999*

Ranked by: Overall weighted average score (1-10) based on 14 specific factors. **Remarks:** Also notes percent usage rate. **Number listed:** 8

1. Hampton Suites, with 7.60
2. Country Inns & Suites, 7.48
3. Signature Inns, 7.35
4. Amerisuites, 7.34
5. La Quinta Inns, 7.26
5. Drury Inn, 7.26
7. Clubhouse Inns of America, 7.00
8. Comfort Inns, 6.99

Source: *Business Travel News*, U.S. Hotel Chain Survey (annual), February 22, 1999, p. 50.

★2557★
BEST UPPER UPSCALE HOTEL CHAIN AND FRANCHISE OPERATIONS, 1999*

Ranked by: Overall weighted average score (1-10) based on 14 specific factors. **Remarks:** Also notes percent usage rate. **Number listed:** 10

1. Peabody Hotels, with 8.00
2. Forte/Le Meridien Hotels, 7.89
3. Inter-Continental Hotels, 7.85
4. Swissotels Worldwide, 7.83
5. Nikko Hotels, 7.75
5. Loews Hotels, 7.75
7. Kempinski Hotels, 7.74
8. Conrad International, 7.63
9. Pan Pacific Hotels & Resorts, 7.57
10. Helmsley Hotels, 7.49

Source: *Business Travel News*, U.S. Hotel Chain Survey (annual), February 22, 1999, p. 46.

★2558★
BEST UPSCALE HOTEL CHAIN AND FRANCHISE OPERATIONS, 1999*

Ranked by: Overall weighted average score (1-10) based on 14 specific factors. **Remarks:** Also notes percent usage rate. **Number listed:** 15

1. Hyatt Hotels, with 8.30
2. Westin Hotels & Resorts, 8.26
3. Doubletree Guest Suites, 8.25
4. Renaissance Hotels & Resorts, 8.20
4. Walt Disney World Resorts, 8.20
6. Marriott Hotels & Resorts, 8.17
7. Hilton Hotels, 8.15
8. Embassy Suites, 8.11
8. Hilton International, 8.11
10. Wyndham Hotels & Resorts, 8.08

Source: *Business Travel News*, U.S. Hotel Chain Survey (annual), February 22, 1999, p. 46.

★2559★
LEADING HOTEL FRANCHISES/CHAINS BY TOTAL SALES, 1998

Ranked by: Sales, in billions of dollars. **Remarks:** Also notes location, lead agency, and media expenditures. **Number listed:** 10

1. Holiday Inn, Crowne Plaza, etc., with $10.0 billion
2. Marriott Courtyard, $7.9
3. Hilton Inns, $7.7
4. Radisson Hotels, $6.6
5. Ramada, Howard Johnson, Days Inn, Super 8, $5.3
6. Sheraton, Westin, $4.7
7. Hyatt, $3.3
8. Embassy, Hampton Inn, $1.1

9. Red Roof Inns, $0.4
10. La Quinta Inns, $0.3

Source: *Brandweek*, Superbrands: America's Top 2,000 Brands (annual), June 21, 1999, p. S70.

★2560★
MOST ADMIRED HOTEL, CASINO AND RESORT CORPORATIONS, 1998
Ranked by: Scores (1-10) derived from a survey of senior executives, outside directors and securities analysts. **Remarks:** Respondents rated companies in their own industry on 8 attributes of reputation. Also notes previous year's rank. **Number listed:** 9

1. Mirage Resorts, with 7.76
2. Marriott International, 7.44
3. Host Marriott, 6.70
4. Harrah's Entertainment, 6.60
5. Promus Hotel Corp., 6.50
6. Hilton Hotels, 5.75
7. Starwood Hotels & Resorts, 5.32
8. Circus Circus Enterprises, 4.90
9. Trump Hotels & Casino Resorts, 3.20

Source: *Fortune*, America's Most Admired Corporations (annual), March 1, 1999, p. F-5.

★2561★
TOP HOTEL COMPANIES BY NUMBER OF GUESTROOMS, 1998
Ranked by: Total number of guestrooms. **Remarks:** Includes number of properties. **Number listed:** 100

1. Cendant Corp., with 516,262 rooms
2. Bass Hotels & Resorts, 443,891
3. Marriott Hotels, Resorts & Suites, 313,600
4. Best Western International, 301,820
5. Choice Hotels International, 287,444
6. Promus Hotel Corp., 186,920
7. Starwood Hotels & Resorts, 133,000
8. Patriot American Hospitality, 105,000
9. Carlson Hospitality Worldwide, 103,497
10. Hilton Hotels Corp., 103,151

Source: *Hotel & Motel Management*, Top 100 Hotel Companies (annual), September 21, 1998, p. 49.

★2562★
TOP U.S. HOTEL CHAINS, 1998*
Ranked by: Number of U.S. rooms. **Remarks:** Includes number of properties, status of properties and foreign properties. **Number listed:** 50

1. Holiday Inn Hotels/Select/Sunspree, with 234,527 rooms
2. Best Western Hotels, 187,457
3. Days Inns of America, 153,585
4. Ramada, 121,490
5. Comfort Inns, 107,900
6. Super 8, 102,204
7. Marriott Hotels, Resorts & Suites, 100,800
8. Hilton Inns/Hotels, 93,888
9. Motel 6, 85,000
10. Hampton Inns/Inn & Suites, 83,249

Source: *Lodging Hospitality*, Lodgings 400 Top Performers (annual), August, 1998, p. 49+.

Hotels and Motels—Chain and Franchise Operations--California

★2563★
TOP HOTEL FRANCHISES IN CALIFORNIA, 1998*
Ranked by: Number of new projects. **Remarks:** Includes number of new rooms. **Number listed:** 8

1. Marriott International, with 28
2. Extended Stay America, 26
3. Homestead Village, 14
3. Choice Hotels International, 14
5. Hilton Hotel Corp., 13
5. Bass Hotels & Resorts, 13
7. Promus Hotel Corp., 10
7. Prime Hospitality Corp., 10

Source: *Hotel & Motel Management*, November 2, 1998, p. 13.

Hotels and Motels—Chain and Franchise Operations--Europe, Western

★2564★
BEST HOTELS IN EUROPE, 1998
Ranked by: Survey of executives from 23 countries rating hotels on a score of 1 to 100. **Remarks:** Scores were averaged. To qualify for ranking, hotels had to receive a substantial number of favorable reviews and a minimum score of 75.7. Also notes previous year's ranking and global rank. **Number listed:** 28

1. Ritz (Paris), with 88.5
2. Lanesborough (London), 88.2
3. Claridge's (London), 86.9
4. Connaught (London), 85.8
5. Amstel Inter-Continental (Amsterdam), 85.6
6. Bristol (Paris), 84.8
7. Ciragan Palace Kempinski (Istanbul), 83.8
7. Hassler (Rome), 83.8
9. Four Seasons (London), 83.7
10. Dorchester (London), 83.0

Source: *Institutional Investor*, Best Hotels Worldwide list (annual), September, 1998, p. 183.

★2565★
BIGGEST LUXURY AND UPSCALE HOTEL CHAINS IN EUROPE, 1999*
Ranked by: Number of rooms. **Remarks:** Includes number of properties. **Number listed:** 11

1. Holiday Inn, with 20,258 rooms
2. Sheraton, 18,257
3. Hilton International, 16,834
4. Radisson SAS, 16,747
5. Inter-Continental, 13,559
6. Gran Melia/Melia, 12,460
7. Meridien, 10,041
8. Marriott, 9,714
9. Sofitel, 9,271
10. Kempinski, 4,917

Source: *Business Travel News*, May 3, 1999, p. 18.

★2566★
LARGEST HOTELS AND RESTAURANTS IN EUROPE, 1997
Ranked by: Sales, in thousands of U.S. dollars ($). **Remarks:** Also notes previous year's rank, headquarters' location, industry codes, change in sales between 1996 1nd 1997, and change in local currencies. **Number listed:** 100

1. Compass Group Plc (Great Britain), with $6,951,171 thousand
2. Granada Group Plc (Great Britain), $6,649,620
3. Accor (France), $5,296,931
4. Whitebread Plc (Great Britain), $5,275,816
5. Sodexho Alliance (France), $4,916,412
6. The Rank Organisation PLC (Great Britain), $4,312,108
7. Forte Plc (Great Britain), $2,951,171
8. Allied Domecq Retailing Ltd. (Great Britain), $2,727,317
9. Bass Taverns Ltd. (Great Britain), $2,134,938
10. McDonald's Deutschland (Germany), $1,888,392

Source: *Europe's 1,000 Largest Companies (annual)*, E.L.C. Publishing Ltd., 1999, p. 682+.

Hotels and Motels--Design and Construction

★2567★
TOP LODGING DESIGN FIRMS BY PROJECT FEES, 1997
Ranked by: Project fees. **Remarks:** Also notes total fees received, percent of fees from renovations, international business, and other data. **Number listed:** 25

1. Wimberly Allison Tong Goo, with $42,300,000
2. Hirsch Bedner Assoc., $23,450,000
3. Wilson & Associates, $22,100,000
4. Arthur Schuster, $16,000,000
5. DiLeonardo International, $14,500,000
6. Brennan Beer Gorman Monk, $12,700,000
7. RTKL Associates Inc., $7,600,000
8. Daroff Design, $6,000,000
9. Concepts 4, $3,400,000
10. BSW International, $4,800,000

Source: *Hotel & Motel Management*, Top 25 Design Firms (annual), November 2, 1998, p. 56.

Hotels and Motels--Florida

★2568★
TOP HOTELS AND RESORTS IN FLORIDA, 1999*
Ranked by: Total guest rooms and suites. **Remarks:** Also notes rates, manager, year opened, and speical features. **Number listed:** 50

1. Disney's All-Star Resorts Music/Sports (Lake Buena Vista), with 3,840 rooms
2. Walt Disney World Swan and Dolphin (Lake Buena Vista), 2,267
3. Disney's Caribbean Beach Resort (Lake Buena Vista), 2,112
4. Disney's Dixie Landings Resort (Lake Buena Vista), 2,048
5. Orlando World Center Marriott (Orlando), 1,503
6. Caribe Royale Resort Suites (Orlando), 1,338
7. Omni Rosen Hotel (Orlando), 1,334
8. Fontainebleu Hilton Resort and Towers (Miami Beach), 1,206
9. Orlando Marriott International Drive (Orlando), 1,064
10. Disney's Contemporary Resort (Lake Buena Vista), 1,041

Source: *Florida Trend*, TopRank Florida (annual), 1999, p. 40+.

Hotels and Motels--Food Service

★2569★
TOP FOODSERVICE/RESTAURANT OPERATIONS IN HOTELS, 1997
Ranked by: Sales, in millions of dollars. **Number listed:** 23

1. ITT Sheraton, with $2,150.0 million
2. Holiday Inn Worldwide, $1,950.0
3. Hilton Hotels, $1,756.5
4. Marriott Lodging Group, $1,300.0
5. Radisson Hotels, $1,139.0
6. Hyatt Hotels, $954.0
7. Westin Hotels & Resorts, $865.4
8. Inter-Continental, $739.3
9. Ramada Franchise & Hotels, $540.0
10. Four Seasons Hotels & Resorts, $528.0

Source: *Restaurants & Institutions*, Restaurants & Institutions 400 (annual), July 15, 1998, p. 100.

Hotels and Motels, International

★2570★
BEST HOTELS WORLDWIDE, 1998
Ranked by: Survey of executives from 23 countries rating hotels on a score of 1 to 100. **Remarks:** Scores were averaged. To qualify for ranking, hotels had to receive a substantial number of favorable reviews and have a minimum score of 75.7. Also notes previous year's ranking and score. **Number listed:** 75

1. Mansion on Turtle Creek (Dallas), with 89.0
2. Ritz (Paris), 88.5
2. Beverly Hills (Los Angeles), 88.5
4. Raffles (Singapore), 88.4
5. Lanesborough (London), 88.2
6. Four Seasons (Singapore), 87.8
7. Oriental (Bangkok), 87.6
8. Four Seasons (Philadelphia), 87.4
9. Four Seasons (New York), 87.3
11. Regent (Hong Kong), 87.0
11. Peninsula (Hong Kong), 87.0

Source: *Institutional Investor*, September, 1998, p. 182.

★2571★
TOP INTERNATIONAL HOTEL COMPANIES BY COUNTRY REPRESENTATION, 1998
Ranked by: Number of countries where present. **Number listed:** 10

1. Bass Hotels & Resorts, with 87
2. Accor, 79
3. Best Western, 72
4. Starwood, 71
5. Marriott International, 52
5. Hilton International, 52
7. Forte, 51
8. Golden Tulip, 50
9. Carlson Hospitality, 49
10. Hyatt, 38

Source: *Hotel and Motel Management*, March 1, 1999, p. 24.

★2572★
TOP INTERNATIONAL HOTEL COMPANIES BY NUMBER OF GUESTROOMS, 1998
Ranked by: Number of guestrooms, in thousands. **Number listed:** 10

1. Cendant, with 515 thousand

2. Bass Hotels & Resorts, 458
3. Choice, 321
4. Marriott International, 310
5. Best Western, 301
6. Accor, 289
7. Starwood, 195
8. Promus, 189
9. Hilton Corp., 103
10. Hyatt, 82

Source: *Hotel & Motel Management*, March 1, 1999, p. 24.

Hotels and Motels--Los Angeles County (CA)

★2573★
LARGEST HOTELS IN LOS ANGELES COUNTY BY NUMBER OF SLEEPING ROOMS, 1999*
Ranked by: Number of rooms. **Remarks:** Also notes rates, amenities, employees, year built, property owner, contact phone numbers, and general manager. **Number listed:** 50

1. Westin Bonaventure Hotal and Suites, with with 1,354 rooms
2. Los Angeles Airport Hilton & Towers, 1,234
3. Century Plaza Hotel & Tower, 1,046
4. Los Angeles Airport Marriott, 1,010
5. Omni Los Angeles Hotel & Center, 900
6. Sheraton Gateway Hotel Los Angeles Airport, 804
7. Furama Hotel Los Angeles, 765
8. Westin Los Angeles Airport, 721
9. Regal Biltmore Hotel, 683
10. Hacienda Hotel, 630

Source: *Los Angeles Business Journal*, Book of Lists (annual), 1999, p. 96+.

Hotels and Motels--Meeting Facilities--Florida

★2574★
TOP HOTEL MEETING CENTERS IN FLORIDA BY TOTAL MEETING AND EXHIBIT SPACE, 1999*
Ranked by: Square feet of meeting and exhibit space. **Remarks:** Also notes number of meeting & hotel rooms, largest room, miles from airport, and general manager. **Number listed:** 45

1. Walt Disney World Swan and Dolphin (Lake Buena Vista), with 305,000
2. Marriott's Orlando World Center (Orlando), 200,000
3. Fountainebleau Hilton Resort & Towers (Miami Beach), 190,000
4. Renaissance Orlando Resort (Orlando), 185,000
5. Radisson Mart Plaza Hotel (Miami), 150,000
6. Boca Raton Resort & Club (Boca Raton), 136,759
7. Omni Rosen Hotel (Orlando), 135,000
8. Hyatt Regency Miami (Miami), 110,000
9. Disney's Coronado Springs Resort (Lake Buena Vista), 95,000
10. Buena Vista Palace Resort & Spa (Lake Buena Vista), 90,000
10. Orlando Mariott Downtown (Orlando), 90,000

Source: *Florida Trend*, TopRank Florida (annual), 1999, p. 46+.

Hotels and Motels--New Jersey

★2575★
TOP HOTELS IN NEW JERSEY BY NUMBER OF GUEST ROOMS, 1999*
Ranked by: Number of guest rooms. **Remarks:** Also notes number of meeting rooms & largest, and general manager. **Number listed:** 25

1. Tropicana Casino and Resort (Atlantic City), with 1,624
2. Trump Plaza Hotel & Casino (Atlantic City), 1,404
3. Bally's Park Place Casino Resort (Atlantic City), 1,268
4. Trump Taj Mahal Casino (Atlantic City), 1,250
5. Harrah's Atlantic City (Atlantic City), 1,174
6. Caesars Atlantic City (Atlantic City), 1,114
7. Trump Marina (Atlantic City), 728
8. Atlantic City Hilton Casino Resort (Atlantic City), 717
9. Resorts Casino Hotel (Atlantic City), 662
10. Newark Airport Marriott (Newark), 590

Source: *New Jersey Business*, Book of Lists (annual), 1999, p. 32+.

Hotels and Motels--Philadelphia Metropolitan Area

★2576★
LARGEST HOTELS IN THE PHILADELPHIA-AREA BY NUMBER OF ROOMS, 1998
Ranked by: Number of rooms. **Remarks:** Includes banquet capacity, exhibit space, single-room rate, dining room capacity, number of full-time employees, occupancy rate, owner, general manager and personnel director. **Number listed:** 25

1. Philadelphia Marriott Hotel, with with 1,200 rooms
2. Wyndham Franklin Plaza Hotel, 758
3. Adam's Mark Hotel Dallas, 515
4. Sheraton Valley Forge Hotel and Convention Center, 488
5. Crowne Plaza Philadelphia, Center City, 445
6. Doubletree Hotel Philadelphia, 428
7. Philadelphia Airport Marriott, 419
8. Hilton at Cherry Hill, 408
9. Sheraton University City Hotel, 374
10. Four Seasons Hotel Philadelphia, 371

Source: *Philadelphia Business Journal*, Book of Business Lists (annual), December 25, 1998, p. 121.

Household Appliances

★2577★
BEST-SELLING APPLIANCE BRANDS, 1998
Ranked by: Sales, in billions of dollars. **Remarks:** Also notes location, lead agency, and media expenditures. **Number listed:** 5

1. Whirlpool, with $10.3 billion
2. GE Appliances, $5.6
3. Maytag, $3.4
4. Frigidaire, n/a

5. Amana, n/a

Source: *Brandweek,* Superbrands: America's Top 2,000 Brands, June 21, 1999, p. S17.

★2578★
BEST-SELLING CAN OPENERS, 1998
Ranked by: Market share, in percent. **Remarks:** Also notes 1993 market share. **Number listed:** 8

1. Hamilton Beach/Proctor-Silex, with 31%
2. Rival, 28%
3. Sunbeam-Oster, 14%
4. Black & Decker, 11%
5. Appliance Corp. Betty Crocker, 8%
6. Presto, 4%
7. Farberware, 1%
8. Others, 3%

Source: *Appliance Manufacturer*, April, 1999, p. 21.

★2579★
BEST-SELLING MIXERS, 1998
Ranked by: Market share, in percent. **Remarks:** Also notes 1993 market share. **Number listed:** 10

1. Hamilton Beach/Proctor Silex, with 36%
2. Black & Decker, 12%
3. West Bend, 9%
4. KitchenAid, 6%
5. Rival, 5%
6. Sunbeam-Oster, 3%
6. Toastmaster, 3%
8. Waring, 2%
9. Appliance Corp. Betty Crocker, 1%
10. Others, 22%

Source: *Appliance Manufacturer*, April, 1999, p. 22.

★2580★
GEOGRAPHIC AREAS WITH THE LARGEST MAJOR HOUSEHOLD APPLIANCE SALES
Ranked by: Sales, in thousands of dollars. **Number listed:** 321

1. Los Angeles-Long Beach, CA, with $761,677 thousand
2. Chicago, IL, $723,104
3. New York, NY, $532,367
4. Washington, DC, $468,973
5. Detroit, MI, $436,592
6. Philadelphia, PA, $404,652
7. Houston, TX, $351,573
8. Phoenix-Mesa, AZ, $349,958
9. Atlanta, GA, $323,131
10. San Diego, CA, $321,261

Source: *Sales & Marketing Management*, Survey of Media Markets (annual), August, 1998, p. 200.

★2581★
TOP HOUSEHOLD APPLIANCE RETAILERS, 1997
Ranked by: Revenue, in millions of dollars. **Remarks:** Includes store type. Revenue for Sears is an estimate. **Number listed:** 25

1. Sears (Hoffman Estates, IL), with $5,100.0 million
2. Circuit City (Richmond, VA), $1,199.5
3. Best Buy (Eden Prairie, MN), $756.0
4. Montgomery Ward (Chicago, IL), $643.7
5. Lowe's (Wilkesboro, NC), $611.0
6. Wal-Mart (Bentonville, AR), $386.0 estimated
7. Costco (Issaquah, WA), $270.0
8. P.C. Richard & Son (Farmingdale, NY), $230.0 estimated
9. ABC Warehouse (Pontiac, MI), $215.0 estimated
10. Heilig-Meyers (Richmond, VA), $132.29

Source: *HFN*, July 20, 1998, p. 84.

★2582★
TOP MAJOR APPLIANCE MANUFACTURERS, 1998
Ranked by: Market share, in percent. **Remarks:** Includes brand information. **Number listed:** 5

1. Whirlpool, with 35.2%
2. GEA, 30.3%
3. Maytag, 18.6%
4. Electrolux, 10.1%
5. Goodman, 5.2%

Source: *Metal Center News*, May, 1999, p. 74.

Household Appliances, International

★2583★
TOP WORLDWIDE MAJOR APPLIANCE DEMANDS, 1996
Ranked by: Market share of demand. **Remarks:** Total demand is 220 million units. **Number listed:** 6

1. Refrigeration, with 32.1%
2. Ranges & Ovens, 22.1%
3. Clothes washers, 20.0%
4. Microwave ovens, 14.7%
5. Dishwashers, 5.9%
6. Clothes dryers, 5.3%

Source: *Appliance Manufacturer*, February, 1999, p. G-4.

Household Cleaning Products Industry

See: **Cleaning Products Industry**

Household Income

See: **Income**

Household Linens

★2584★
BEST HOUSEHOLD LINEN BRANDS ACCORDING TO CONSUMERS, 1998
Ranked by: Percent of consumers naming brand as best. **Remarks:** Includes demographic profile of those surveyed. **Number listed:** 4

1. Cannon, with 59%
2. Burlington, 5%
3. Martex, 4%
3. St. Mary's, 4%

Source: *Discount Store News*, Top Brand Consumer Survey-Pt. II (annual), September 7, 1998, p. 25.

★2585★
COMPANIES WITH THE HIGHEST HOME TEXTILE SHIPMENT DOLLARS, 1997
Ranked by: Home textile shipments, in millions of dollars. **Number listed:** 6

1. WestPoint Stevens, with $1,670 million

2. Springs Industries, $1,662
3. Pillowtex, $1,630
4. Burlington, $307
5. Crown Crafts, $306
6. Dan River, $256

Source: *ATI*, October, 1998, p. 46.

Household Products

See: **Housewares**

Households

★2586★
GEOGRAPHIC AREAS WITH THE GREATEST NUMBER OF HOUSEHOLDS, 1998*
Ranked by: Number of houses, thousands. **Number listed:** 317

1. New York, with 3,257.5 thousand
2. Los Angeles-Long Beach, 3,146.1
3. Chicago, 2,813.1
4. Philadelphia, 1,822.6
5. Washington, 1,712.6
6. Detroit, 1,677.3
7. Boston-Lawrence-Lowell-Brockton, MA, 1,450.0
8. Houston, 1,382.1
9. Atlanta, 1,373.1
10. Dallas, 1,174.4

Source: *Sales & Marketing Management*, Survey of Buying Power (annual), August, 1998, p. 15.

Housewares

★2587★
BEST HOUSEWARE BRANDS ACCORDING TO CONSUMERS, 1998
Ranked by: Percent of consumers naming brand as best. **Remarks:** Includes demographic profile of those surveyed. **Number listed:** 10

1. Black & Decker, with 18%
2. Mr. Coffee, 15%
3. Rubbermaid, 11%
4. Corning/Corelle/Visions, 9%
5. Proctor-Silex, 6%
5. T-Fal, 6%
7. Anchor Hocking, 4%
8. Ekco, 3%
8. Hefty/Mobil, 3%
10. Oster, 2%

Source: *Discount Store News*, Top Brand Consumer Survey-Pt. II (annual), September 7, 1998, p. 22.

★2588★
TOP HOUSEWARES BY SALES, 1998*
Ranked by: Sales, in billions of dollars. **Number listed:** 15

1. Electrics, with $10.4 billion
2. Tabletop, $7.8
3. Cookware & bakeware, $7.6
4. Decorative accessories, $6.5
5. Space organizers, $4.3
6. Cleaning products, $3.7
7. Furniture, $3.6
8. Kitchen tools & accessories, $3.2
9. Outdoor & hardware, $2.9
10. Bathroom & personal, $2.7

Source: *Potentials*, November, 1998, p. 17.

Housing

★2589★
METROPOLITAN AREAS WITH THE GREATEST NUMBER OF NEW RESIDENTIAL PERMITS, 1998*
Ranked by: Number of permits. **Remarks:** Includes percent change from previous year. **Number listed:** 15

1. Atlanta, with 32,348 permits
2. Phoenix/Mesa, 28,245
3. Houston, 26,729
4. Dallas, 23,589
5. Washington, DC, 21,389
6. Las Vegas, 20,244
7. Chicago, 18,979
8. Orlando, 14,232
9. Denver, 13,099
10. Portland/Vancouver, 10,461

Source: *Professional Builder*, October, 1998, p. 15.

★2590★
TOP HOUSING AND REAL ESTATE COMPANIES IN THE S&P 500 BY INDUSTRY AVERAGE, 1998
Ranked by: Industry average. **Remarks:** Industry average includes totals from market value, 1-year and 3-year returns; sales volumes, percent change from 1997 and 3-year average change; profitability change from 1997 and 3-year average change; also notes Fortune 500 ranking. **Number listed:** 8

1. Centex
2. Masco
3. Kaufman & Broad Home
4. Pulte
5. PPG Industries
6. Fleetwood Enterprises
7. Sherwin-Williams
8. Owens Corning

Source: *Business Week*, Business Week 50: Top Companies of the S&P 500 (annual), March 29, 1999, p. 154.

★2591★
TOP MOTIVATIONS FOR BUYING ANOTHER HOME
Ranked by: Response, in percent. **Number listed:** 7

1. Moving up to bigger and/or better home, with 38.0%
2. Retirement, 25.1%
3. To downsize when we become empty nesters, 17.2%
4. Buying for the first time, 11.6%
5. Relocating for job, 10.2%
6. To better accommodate older relative(s), 5.1%
7. Vacation/second home, 4.7%

Source: *Professional Builder*, May, 1999, p. 51.

Housing Authorities--Securities

★2592★
TOP BOND COUNSEL FIRMS, 1997
Ranked by: Amount issued, in thousands of dollars. **Remarks:** Also notes number of issues. **Number listed:** 10

1. California, with $1,167,000 thousand
2. California Housing Finance Agency, $1,064,900
3. New York State Housing Finance Agency, $746,000
4. Alaska Housing Finance Corp., $742,300
5. Pennsylvania Housing Finance Agency, $528,400
6. New York State Mortgage Agency, $448,100
7. Ohio Housing Finance Agency, $408,200
8. South Dakota Housing Development Authority, $330,700
9. Connecticut Housing Finance Authority, $325,100
10. Maryland Community Dev. Administration, $323,700

Source: *Bond Buyer Yearbook*, (annual), 1998, p. 145.

★2593★
TOP BOND ISSUERS, 1997
Ranked by: Amount issued, in thousands of dollars. **Remarks:** Also notes number of issues. **Number listed:** 25

1. Orrick Herrington & Sutcliffe, with $2,971,700 thousand
2. Hawkins, Delafield & Wood, $2,694,300
3. Kutak Rock, $1,838,900
4. Ballard Spahr Andrews & Ingersoll, $974,900
5. Wohlforth, Argetsinger, Johnson & Brecht, $742,300
6. Dorsey & Whitney, $723,900
7. Peck, Shaffer & Williams, $643,100
8. Pamela S. Jue, $597,100
9. Daniel E. Lungren, $566,600
10. Gilmore & Bell, $423,700

Source: *Bond Buyer Yearbook*, (annual), 1998, p. 145.

Humidifiers

★2594★
BEST-SELLING HUMIDIFIERS, 1998
Ranked by: Market share, in percent. **Remarks:** Also notes 1993 market share. **Number listed:** 7

1. Holmes, with 44%
2. Honeywell/Duracraft, 30%
3. Rival (Bionaire), 8%
4. Lasko, 4%
5. Bemis, 2%
5. Kaz, 2%
7. Others, 10%

Source: *Appliance Manufacturer*, April, 1999, p. 20.

Hypermarkets

★2595★
TOP SUPERCENTER/HYPERMARKET CHAINS, 1997
Ranked by: Sales, in millions of dollars. **Remarks:** Also notes sales for 1996, percent change, number of stores, and average store size. **Number listed:** 14

1. Wal-Mart Supercenter, with $25,775 million
2. Meijer, $7,950
3. Fred Meyer, $5,481
4. Super Kmart Centers, $4,325
5. Fedco, $594
6. bigg's, $530
7. SuperTarget, $525
8. Smitty's, $410
9. Big Bear Plus, $210
10. Holiday Mart (DAIEI), $150

Source: *Discount Store News*, Discount Industry Annual Report, July 13, 1998, p. 79.

Ice Cream, Ices, etc.

★2596★
BEST-SELLING FROZEN DAIRY PRODUCT TYPES, 1998
Ranked by: Market share, in percent. **Number listed:** 7

1. Regular fat Ice cream, with 75.5%
2. Reduced, light & low-fat ice cream, 10.3%
3. Frozen yogurt, 6.0%
4. Nonfat ice cream, 3.6%
5. Sherbet, 3.5%
6. Sorbet, 0.5%
7. Other, 0.6%

Source: *Dairy Foods*, Annual Ice Cream Report, March, 1999, p. 68.

★2597★
LEADING BRANDS OF SHERBET/SORBET/ICES, 1998
Ranked by: Sales, in millions of dollars. **Remarks:** Figures are for the 52 weeks ending Dec. 6, 1998. **Number listed:** 10

1. Haagen-Dazs, with $28.7 million
2. Dreyer's/Edy's Whole Fruit, $16.9
3. Ben & Jerry's, $13.2
4. Dreyer's/Edy's, $10.5
5. Blue Bell, $8.9
6. Kemps, $6.8
7. Breyer's, $4.2
8. Wells' Blue Bunny, $3.0
9. Prairie Farms, $2.5
10. Private label, $53.8

Source: *Dairy Foods*, March, 1999, p. 70.

★2598★
LEADING ICE CREAM BRANDS, 1998
Ranked by: Sales, in millions of dollars. **Remarks:** Figures are for the 52 weeks ending Dec. 6, 1998. **Number listed:** 10

1. Breyer's, with $443.9 million
2. Dreyer's/Edy's, $374.9
3. Blue Bell, $199.2
4. Haagen-Dazs, $167.9
5. Ben & Jerry's, $137.8
6. Healthy Choice, $99.6
7. Turkey Hill, $85.6
8. Dreyer's/Edy's Grand Light, $82.3
9. Wells' Blue Bunny, $81.7
10. Private label, $855.2

Source: *Dairy Foods*, March, 1999, p. 69.

★2599★
STATES WITH THE HIGHEST PRODUCTION OF ICE CREAM AND RELATED PRODUCTS, 1996
Ranked by: Production, in millions of gallons. **Number listed:** 6

1. California, with 172.5 million gallons
2. Indiana, 89.4

3. Ohio, 68.5
4. Illinois, 61.5
5. Michigan, 53.2
6. Texas, 51.7

Source: *Facts & Figures on Ice Cream and Related Products*, The Latest Scoop (annual), 1997, p. 26.

★2600★
TOP FROZEN NOVELTY BRANDS, 1998
Ranked by: Sales, in millions of dollars. **Remarks:** Also notes annual growth and dollar share. **Number listed:** 10

1. Klondike, with $106.8 million
2. Popsicle, $99.9
3. Drumstick, $90.5
4. Haagen Dazs, $54.4
5. Dole Fruit & Juice, $46.7
6. Eskimo Pie, $43
7. Dove Bar, $39.9
8. Blue Bell, $36.4
8. Wells' Blue Bunny, $36.4
10. Private label, $278

Source: *Dairy Field*, March, 1999, p. 18.

★2601★
TOP FROZEN NOVELTY BRANDS, 1997-1998
Ranked by: Sales, in millions of dollars. **Remarks:** Figures are for 52 weeks ending May 24, 1998. Also includes percent change from previous year, dollar share, unit sales and percent change in unit sales from previous year. **Number listed:** 10

1. Klondike, with $98.5 million
2. Drumstick, $93.2
3. Popsicle, $92.8
4. Haagen Dazs, $59.4
5. Dole Fruit & Juice, $46.0
6. Eskimo Pie, $44.2
7. Dove Bar, $38.3
8. Blue Bell, $33.2
9. Wells' Blue Bunny, $32.6
10. Private Label, $263.9

Source: *Dairy Field*, August, 1998, p. 30.

★2602★
TOP ICE CREAM BRANDS, 1998
Ranked by: Sales, in millions of dollars. **Remarks:** Also notes percentage change from previous year, dollar share, unit sales and percent change in unit sales from previous year. **Number listed:** 10

1. Breyers, with $408.7 million
2. Dreyer's/Edy's, $363.4
3. Blue Bell, $181.9
4. Haagen Dazs, $157.0
5. Ben & Jerry's, $122.7
6. Healthy Choice, $100.7
7. Dreyer's/Edy's Grand Light, $86.6
8. Turkey Hill, $80.0
9. Wells' Blue Bunny, $70.2
10. Private label, $824.4

Source: *Dairy Field*, August, 1998, p. 30.

Immigrants in the United States

★2603★
STATES WITH THE HIGHEST CONCENTRATION OF IMMIGRANTS, 1997
Ranked by: Market share, in percent. **Remarks:** Includes number of immigrants out of total of 25.8 million. **Number listed:** 7

1. California, with 31.3%
2. New York, 14%
3. Florida, 9.1%
4. Texas, 8.4%
5. New Jersey, 4.7%
6. Illinois, 4.3%
7. All other, 28.2%

Source: *Southwest Economy*, Federal Reserve Bank of Dallas, July/August, 1998, p. 2.

Income

★2604★
METROPOLITAN AREAS WITH THE HIGHEST BUYING POWER INDEX, 1998*
Ranked by: Buying power index. **Number listed:** 321

1. Chicago, IL, with 3.1921
2. Los Angeles-Long Beach, CA, 3.1168
3. New York, NY, 3.1093
4. Washington, DC, 2.0505
5. Philadelphia, PA, 2.0330
6. Detroit, MI, 1.7247
7. Boston-Lawrence-Lowell-Brockton, MA, 1.6316
8. Houston, TX, 1.5372
9. Atlanta, GA, 1.4946
10. Dallas, TX, 1.3160

Source: *Sales & Marketing Management*, Survey of Buying Power (annual), August, 1998, p. B-30.

★2605★
METROPOLITAN AREAS WITH THE HIGHEST MEDIAN HOUSEHOLD EBI (EFFECTIVE BUYING INCOME), 1998*
Ranked by: Effective buying income (EBI), in dollars. **Number listed:** 321

1. Bridgeport-Stamford-Norwalk-Danbury, CT, with $60,374
2. Middlesex-Somerset-Hunterdon, NJ, $54,492
3. San Jose, CA, $54,407
4. Nassau-Suffolk, NY, $52,697
5. Washington, DC, $49,977
6. Trenton, NJ, $48,502
7. Newark, NJ, $46,959
8. Seattle-Bellevue-Everett, WA, $46,567
9. Portsmouth-Rochester, NY, $46,428
10. Bergen-Passaic, NJ, $46,394

Source: *Sales & Marketing Management*, Survey of Buying Power (annual), August, 1998, p. B-17.

★2606★
METROPOLITAN AREAS WITH THE MOST HOUSEHOLDS WITH EBI (EFFECTIVE BUYING INCOME) OF $50,000 AND OVER, 1998*
Ranked by: Effective buying income (EBI), in thousands of dollars. **Number listed:** 317

1. New York, NY, with $162,080,888 thousand
2. Chicago, IL, $153,409,545
3. Los Angeles-Long Beach, CA, $142,050,140
4. Washington, DC, $101,698,562
5. Philadelphia, PA, $96,689,382
6. Boston-Lawrence-Lowell-Brockton, MA, $79,251,497
7. Detroit, MI, $77,020,474
8. Houston, TX, $70,843,638
9. Atlanta, GA, $65,908,314

10. Dallas, TX, $61,925,415

Source: *Sales & Marketing Management*, Survey of Buying Power (annual), August, 1998, p. B-22.

★2607★

METROPOLITAN AREAS WITH THE MOST HOUSEHOLDS WITH EBI (EFFECTIVE BUYING INCOME) OF $150,000 AND OVER, 1998*

Ranked by: Effective buying income (EBI), in thousands of dollars. **Number listed:** 315

1. New York, NY, with $274.1 thousand
2. Los Angeles, CA, $118.2
3. Chicago, IL, $100.5
4. San Francisco-Oakland-San Jose, CA, $82.0
5. Philadelphia, PA, $74.4
6. Washington, DC, $62.0
7. Boston, MA, $58.1
8. Dallas-Ft. Worth, TX, $54.9
9. Houston, TX, $49.7
10. Seattle-Tacoma, WA, $41.1

Source: *Sales & Marketing Management*, Survey of Buying Power (annual), August, 1998, p. B-18.

★2608★

STATES WITH THE HIGHEST INCOME, 1998*

Ranked by: Average income, in dollars. **Remarks:** Includes percent change from previous year. **Number listed:** 10

1. Connecticut, with $36,263
2. New Jersey, $32,654
3. Massachusetts, $31,524
4. New York, $30,752
5. Delaware, $29,022
6. Maryland, $28,969
7. Illinois, $28,202
8. New Hampshire, $28,047
9. Colorado, $27,051
10. Minnesota, $26,797

Source: *New Jersey Business*, July, 1998, p. 60.

★2609★

TOP CITIES BY DISPOSABLE INCOME, 1998

Ranked by: Disposable income, in thousands of dollars. **Number listed:** 250

1. New York City, NY, with $177,765,246 thousand
2. Los Angeles, CA, $56,925,539
3. Chicago, IL, $45,483,421
4. Philadelphia, PA, $30,678,148
5. Houston, TX, $29,752,671
6. San Francisco, CA, $24,611,721
7. Phoenix, AZ, $22,601,435
8. San Diego, CA, $20,517,000
9. San Jose, CA, $19,810,845
10. Dallas, TX, $19,575,328

Source: *Editor & Publisher Market Guide*, (annual), Editor & Publisher Co., 1998, p. I-30+.

★2610★

TOP CITIES BY INCOME PER HOUSEHOLD, 1998

Ranked by: Income per household, in dollars. **Number listed:** 250

1. Hanover, NH, with $124,149
2. Toms River, NJ, $119,549
3. Greenwich, CT, $101,652
4. East Brunswick, NJ, $92,197
5. Falls Church, VA, $90,896
6. Palm Beach, FL, $89,521
7. Parsippany, NJ, $88,772
8. Cherry Hill, NJ, $86,278
9. Palo Alto, CA, $82,989
10. Lanham, MD, $82,744

Source: *Editor & Publisher Market Guide*, (annual), Editor & Publisher Co., 1998, p. I-31+.

★2611★

TOP COUNTIES BY DISPOSABLE INCOME, 1998

Ranked by: Disposable income, in thousands of dollars. **Number listed:** 10

1. Los Angeles, CA, with $198,194,326 thousand
2. Cook, IL, $129,262,178
3. Harris, TX, $75,260,116
4. Orange, CA, $65,646,267
5. San Diego, CA, $57,398,773
6. Maricopa, AZ, $53,166,324
7. Dallas, TX, $52,326,194
8. New York, NY, $47,923,874
9. King, WA, $47,539,721
10. Queens, NY, $46,647,905

Source: *Editor & Publisher Market Guide*, (annual), Editor & Publisher Co., 1998, p. I-22+.

★2612★

TOP COUNTIES BY INCOME PER HOUSEHOLD, 1998

Ranked by: Income per household, in dollars. **Number listed:** 10

1. Skagway-Yakutat-Angoon, AK, with $142,105
2. Aleutians West, AK, $135,399
3. Bristol Bay, AK, $130,078
4. Sherman, TX, $104,581
5. Fairfield, CT, $101,887
6. Westchester, NY, $98,029
7. Marin, CA, $97,888
8. Somerset, NJ, $92,760
9. Bergen, NJ, $91,296
10. Falls Church, VA, $90,896

Source: *Editor & Publisher Market Guide*, (annual), Editor & Publisher Co., 1998, p. I-23.

★2613★

TOP COUNTIES IN TOTAL RETAIL SALES, 1998

Ranked by: Retail sales, in thousands of dollars. **Number listed:** 250

1. Los Angeles, CA, with $82,991,235 thousand
2. Cook, IL, $52,248,284
3. Harris, TX, $36,208,363
4. Orange, CA, $27,923,574
5. Maricopa, AZ, $26,939,668
6. Dallas, TX, $26,713,769
7. San Diego, CA, $25,262,427
8. Dade, FL, $24,821,695
9. New York, NY, $23,137,822
10. Broward, FL, $20,455,788

Source: *Editor & Publisher Market Guide*, (annual), Editor & Publisher Co., 1998, p. I-23+.

★2614★

TOP METROPOLITAN AREAS BY DISPOSABLE INCOME, 1998

Ranked by: Disposable income, in thousands of dollars. **Number listed:** 315

1. New York, NY, with $210,972,180 thousand
2. Los Angeles-Long Beach, CA, $198,194,326
3. Chicago, IL, $189,539,009
4. Boston-Worcester-Lawrence-Lowell-Brockton, MA-NH, $149,049,377
5. Washington, DC-MD-VA-WV, $124,594,025
6. Philadelphia, PA-NJ, $122,712,595
7. Detroit, MI, $110,654,991
8. Houston, TX, $88,111,636

9. Atlanta, GA, $81,444,470
10. Dallas, TX, $74,350,798

Source: *Editor & Publisher Market Guide*, (annual), Editor & Publisher Co., 1998, p. I-11+.

★2615★
TOP METROPOLITAN AREAS BY INCOME PER HOUSEHOLD, 1998
Ranked by: Income per household, in dollars. **Number listed:** 315

1. New Haven-Bridgeport-Stamford-Waterbury-Danbury, CT, with $84,211
2. Nassau-Suffolk, NY, $82,569
3. San Francisco, CA, $82,402
4. Bergen-Passaic, NJ, $82,067
5. Trenton, NJ, $80,805
6. Newark, NJ, $78,551
7. San Jose, CA, $78,311
8. Middlesex-Somerset-Hunterdon, NJ, $76,896
9. West Palm Beach-Boca Raton, FL, $75,357
10. Honolulu, HI, $75,316

Source: *Editor & Publisher Market Guide*, (annual), Editor & Publisher Co., 1998, p. I-12.

Incubators (Entrepreneurship)

★2616★
AREAS WITH THE MOST BUSINESS INCUBATORS, 1999*
Ranked by: Market share, in percent. **Number listed:** 3

1. Urban areas, with 45%
2. Rural areas, 36%
3. Suburbs, 19%

Source: *New York Times*, January 17, 1999, p. BU7.

★2617★
LEADING FOCUS FOR BUSINESS INCUBATORS, 1999*
Ranked by: Share, in percent. **Number listed:** 6

1. Technology, with 25%
2. General manufacturing, 10%
3. Service, 6%
4. Minority-owned business, 5%
5. Other specific industries, 9%
6. Other or no specific focus, 45%

Source: *New York Times*, January 17, 1999, p. BU7.

Independent Practice Associations—New York Metropolitan Area

★2618★
LARGEST INDEPENDENT PRACTICE ASSOCIATIONS IN THE NEW YORK AREA, 1998
Ranked by: Number of doctors as of June 1, 1998. **Remarks:** Includes address, phone number, practice administrator, number of board-certified doctors, revenues, 1997 hospital inpatient admissions, 1997 outpatient visits, managed care contracts and total capitated lives as of June 1, 1998. **Number listed:** 15

1. Columbia-Cornell Care LLC, with 1,759 doctors
2. Benchmark Physician Organization LLC, 1,666
3. New York Servitas IPA Inc., 1,097
4. Montefiore IPA Integrated Provider Association Inc., 1,093
5. Mount Sinai Independent Practice Association Inc., 841
6. South Shore-Rockaways IPA Inc., 794
7. Metropolitan Physicians Practice Association IPA Inc., 650
7. University Physicians Network IPA, 650
9. New York Hospital Queens-Independent Physicians Association, 600
10. University Physicians of Brooklyn, 523

Source: *Crain's New York Business*, October 26, 1998, p. 23.

Indiana--Industries

★2619★
TOP MANUFACTURERS IN INDIANA, 1999*
Ranked by: Number of employees. **Remarks:** Includes city, SIC code and entry number. **Number listed:** 200

1. Inland Steel Co., with 11,500 employees
2. Delphi Delco Electronics Systems, 10,000
3. USS-USX Corp/Gary Works, 8,000
4. Chrysler Corp., 7,000
5. Naval Surface Warfare Center, 6,666
6. Bethlehem Steel Corp., 6,000
6. Lilly, Eli & Co., 6,000
6. Rolls-Royce Allison, 6,000
9. Delphi Energy & Engine Management Systems, 4,500
10. General Motors Corp., 4,000

Source: *Harris Indiana Industrial Directory (annual)*, Harris Publishing Co., 1999, p. 22+.

Industrial Development Bonds

★2620★
LEADING INDUSTRIAL DEVELOPMENT BOND COUNSEL, 1997
Ranked by: Value of bond issues, in thousands of dollars. **Remarks:** Also notes number of issues. **Number listed:** 10

1. Orrick Herrington & Sutcliffe, with $458,600 thousand
2. Chapman and Cutler, $431,400
3. Jones Hall, $323,700
4. Whitman Breed Abbott & Morgan, $322,900
5. Hawkins, Delafield & Wood, $269,800
6. Brown & Wood, $211,300
7. Nossaman, Guthner, Knox & Elliott, $191,800
8. Katten Muchin & Zavis, $189,700
9. Albert, Bates, Whitehead & McGaugh, $187,000
10. Robinson & Pearman, $172,000

Source: *Bond Buyer Yearbook*, (annual), 1998, p. 169.

★2621★
LEADING INDUSTRIAL DEVELOPMENT BOND ISSUERS, 1997
Ranked by: Value of bond issues, in thousands of dollars. **Remarks:** Also notes number of issues. **Number listed:** 25

1. New York City Industrial Development Agency, with $320,800 thousand
2. New Jersey Economic Development Authority, $314,300

3. Pima County Industrial Development Auth., AZ, $247,500
4. Chicago, IL, $221,800
5. Los Angeles Community Redevelopment Agency, CA, $172,000
6. United Nations Development Corp., NY, $161,800
7. Puerto Rico Industrial Development Co., $149,900
8. Industry Urban Development Agency, CA, $144,900
9. Philadelphia Industrial Development Authority, PA, $140,700
10. Hoffman Estates, IL, $118,400

Source: *Bond Buyer Yearbook*, (annual), 1998, p. 169.

Industrial Distributors--North America

★2622★
LEADING NORTH AMERICAN INDUSTRIAL DISTRIBUTORS, 1998
Ranked by: Total sales, in billions of dollars. **Remarks:** Also notes executive officer, number of branches and employees, and includes a descriptive paragraph. **Number listed:** 100

1. W.W. Grainger, Inc., with $4.3 billion
2. Graybar Electric Co., $3.74
3. WESCO Distribution, $3.02
4. Hughes Supply, $2.53
5. Motion Industries, Inc., $2.04
6. G.E. Supply, $1.9
7. Airgas, Inc., $1.56
8. Applied Industrial Technologies, Inc., $1.49
9. Premier Farnell Plc, $1.17
10. Westburne Inc., $.762

Source: *Industrial Distribution*, Top 100 (annual), June, 1999, p. 78+.

Industrial Equipment Industry

★2623★
MOST ADMIRED INDUSTRIAL AND FARM EQUIPMENT CORPORATION, 1998
Ranked by: Scores (1-10) derived from a survey of senior executives, outside directors and securities analysts. **Remarks:** Respondents rated companies in their own industry on 8 attributes of reputation. Also notes previous year's rank. **Number listed:** 10

1. Caterpillar, with 7.5
2. Deere, 7.12
3. Black & Decker, 6.64
4. Ingersoll-Rand, 6.61
5. Parker Hannifin, 6.38
6. Dover, 6.19
7. Cummins Engine, 6.15
7. American Standard, 6.15
9. Case, 5.89
10. Dresser Industries, 5.70

Source: *Fortune*, America's Most Admired Corporations (annual), March 1, 1999, p. F-2.

Industrial Equipment Industry, International

★2624★
WORLD'S LARGEST INDUSTRIAL AND FARM EQUIPMENT COMPANIES BY REVENUE, 1997
Ranked by: Revenue, in millions of dollars. **Number listed:** 8

1. Mitsubishi Heavy Industries (Japan), with $25,222 million
2. Thyssen (Germany), $24,298
3. Mannesmann (Germany), $22,554
4. Iri (Italy), $22,232
5. Caterpillar (U.S.), $18,925
6. BTR (Great Britain), $13,254
7. Deere (U.S.), $12,791
8. Komatsu (Japan), $8,994

Source: *Fortune*, The Global 500: World's Biggest Corporations (annual), August 3, 1998, p. F-20.

Industrial Parks--Florida

★2625★
LARGEST INDUSTRIAL PARKS IN FLORIDA, 1998
Ranked by: Total square footage. **Remarks:** Also notes contact information, number of buildings, total acreage, rent range, and year established. **Number listed:** 25

1. Orlando Central Park Inc., with 8,900,000
2. Gratigny Central Industrial Park, 8,000,000
3. Imeson International Industrial Park, 6,500,000
4. Sunshine State Industrial Park, 5,063,860
5. Regency Industrial Park, 4,300,000
6. Miami International Commerce Center, 3,470,771
7. Gran Park, 3,250,000
8. Vista Center Corporate Park, 3,100,000
9. Westside Industrial Park, 3,000,000
10. Pelmad Industrial Park, 2,700,000

Source: *Florida Trend*, TopRank Florida (annual), 1999, p. 29.

Industrial Parks--Philadelphia Metropolitan Area

★2626★
LARGEST INDUSTRIAL PARKS IN THE PHILADELPHIA METROPOLITAN AREA, 1998
Ranked by: Total square footage. **Remarks:** Also notes contact information, number of buildings, rent range, percent occupied use, major tenants, and year established. **Number listed:** 50

1. Pureland Industrial Complex, with 10,300,000
2. Northeast Philadelphia Industrial Park, 7,600,000
3. King of Prussia Business Park, 6,500,000
4. Philadelphia Naval Business Center, 5,000,000
5. Fort Washington Office Center, 4,987,415
6. Penn Warner Industrial Park, 4,200,000
7. Great Valley Corporate Center, 4,000,000
8. Bucks County Business Park, 3,500,000
9. Valley Forge Corporate Center, 3,100,000
10. Mid Atlantic Corporate Center, 2,900,000

Source: *Philadelphia Business Journal*, Book of Business Lists (annual), December 25, 1998, p. 48+.

Industrials

See: **Mutual Funds--Europe**

Industries

See: **Industry**

Industries, Manufacturing

See: **Manufacturing Industries**

Industry

★2627★
INDUSTRIES SPENDING THE MOST ON INFORMATION TECHNOLOGY, 1999*
Ranked by: Share of total information technology spending, in percent. **Number listed:** 7

1. Retail trade, with 17%
2. Banking/finance, 12%
3. Architecture/engineering/construction, 8%
4. Wholesale trade, 7%
4. Manufacturing, 7%
6. Other services, 24%
7. All others, 25%

Source: *Business Communications*, April, 1999, p. 8.

★2628★
TOP GENERAL INDUSTRY CATEGORY SPENDERS ON ADVERTISING AND PROMOTION, 1997
Ranked by: Advertising and promotion expenditures, in billions of dollars. **Remarks:** Includes SIC code. **Number listed:** 20

1. Motor vehicles and car bodies, with $15.3 billion
2. Food and kindred products, $14.8
3. Telephone communications, except radio-telephone, $11.9
4. Pharmaceutical preparations, $11.2
5. Cigarettes, $5.8
6. Department stores, $5.6
7. Soaps, detergents and toilet preparations, $4.7
8. Variety stores, $4.3
9. Computers and office equipment, $3.9
10. Beverages, $3.7

Source: *Graphic Arts Monthly*, Top Spenders on Advertising and Printing (annual), February, 1999, p. 52.

★2629★
TOP INDUSTRIES BY TOTAL U.S. ADVERTISING EXPENDITURES, 1997
Ranked by: Advertising expenditures, in billions of dollars. **Remarks:** Includes percent change from 1996 to 1997. **Number listed:** 20

1. Automotive, auto accessories, equipment and supplies, with $13.32 billion
2. Retail, department, and discount stores, $10.66
3. Movies and media, $3.72
4. Toiletries and cosmetics, $3.64
5. Medicines and proprietary remedies, $3.54
6. Food and food products, $3.36
7. Financial Services, $3.33
8. Restaurants and fast food, $3.15
9. Airline and cruise travel, hotels and resorts, $2.81
10. Telecommunications, $2.57

Source: *Graphic Arts Monthly*, Top Spenders on Advertising and Printing (annual), February, 1999, p. 52.

★2630★
TOP INDUSTRIES RECEIVING VENTURE CAPITAL, 1998
Ranked by: Amount invested, in billions of dollars. **Remarks:** Includes percent of total. **Number listed:** 3

1. Software and information, with $4.55 billion
2. Communications, $3.95
3. Health care, $1.10

Source: *Entrepreneur*, May, 1999, p. 38.

Industry, International

★2631★
WORLD'S LARGEST INDUSTRIES BY ASSETS, 1997
Ranked by: Assets, in millions of dollars. **Remarks:** Also notes total number of companies in each industry, profits, assets, stockholders' equity, and number of employees. **Number listed:** 45

1. Banks, commercial and savings, with $17,372,718 million
2. Insurance, stock life and health, $2,375,456
3. Insurance, mutual life and health, $1,782,715
4. Insurance, property and casualty, $1,476,487
5. Motor vehicles and parts, $1,257,833
6. Diversified financials, $1,092,828
7. Electronics and electrical equipment, $969,969
8. Telecommunications, $869,711
9. Petroleum refining, $864,312
10. Securities, $746,811

Source: *Fortune*, The Global 500: World's Biggest Corporations (annual), August 3, 1998, p. F-27.

★2632★
WORLD'S LARGEST INDUSTRIES BY NUMBER OF EMPLOYEES, 1997
Ranked by: Number of employees in industry. **Remarks:** Also notes total number of companies in each industry, profits, assets, stockholders' equity, and number of employees. **Number listed:** 45

1. Electronics and electrical equipment, with 3,656,120 employees
2. Motor vehicles and parts, 2,879,083
2. Banks, commercial and savings, 2,879,083
4. Food and drug stores, 2,782,912
5. Telecommunications, 2,384,667
6. General merchandise, 2,380,587
7. Mail, package and freight delivery, 2,287,173
8. Food, 1,146,006
9. Petroleum refining, 1,077,912
10. Chemicals, 968,841

Source: *Fortune*, The Global 500: World's Biggest Corporations (annual), August 3, 1998, p. F-27.

★2633★
WORLD'S LARGEST INDUSTRIES BY PROFITS, 1997
Ranked by: Profits, in millions of dollars. **Remarks:** Also notes total number of companies in each industry, profits, as-

sets, stockholders' equity, and number of employees. **Number listed:** 45

1. Petroleum refining, with $54,928 million
2. Banks, commercial and savings, $49,353
3. Telecommunications, $40,371
4. Motor vehicles and parts, $33,564
5. Pharmaceuticals, $24,463
6. Electronics and electrical equipment, $21,458
7. Insurance, property and casualty, $19,241
8. Computers and office equipment, $14,877
9. Food, $13,354
10. Insurance, stock life and health, $13,132

Source: *Fortune*, The Global 500: World's Biggest Corporations (annual), August 3, 1998, p. F-27.

★2634★
WORLD'S LARGEST INDUSTRIES BY REVENUE, 1997
Ranked by: Revenue, in millions of dollars. **Remarks:** Also notes total number of companies in each industry, profits, assets, stockholders' equity, and number of employees. **Number listed:** 45

1. Banks, commercial and savings, with $1,243,155 million
2. Motor vehicles and parts, $1,150,812
3. Trading, $1,013,106
4. Petroleum refining, $945,174
5. Electronics and electrical equipment, $782,434
6. Telecommunications, $534,222
7. Food and drug stores, $486,405
8. Insurance, stock life and health, $425,851
9. Insurance, mutual life and health, $410,825
10. General merchandise, $373,322

Source: *Fortune*, The Global 500: World's Biggest Corporations (annual), August 3, 1998, p. F-27.

★2635★
WORLD'S LARGEST INDUSTRIES BY STOCKHOLDERS' EQUITY, 1997
Ranked by: Stockholders' equity, in millions of dollars. **Remarks:** Also notes total number of companies in each industry, profits, assets, stockholders' equity, and number of employees. **Number listed:** 45

1. Banks, commercial and savings, with $686,105 million
2. Petroleum refining, $363,941
3. Telecommunications, $291,179
4. Electronics and electrical equipment, $234,695
5. Motor vehicles and parts, $234,318
6. Insurance, property and casualty, $171,081
7. Utilities, gas and electric, $150,078
8. Insurance, stock life and health, $134,686
9. Chemicals, $99,120
10. Energy, $91,444

Source: *Fortune*, The Global 500: World's Biggest Corporations (annual), August 3, 1998, p. F-27.

Infants' Food

★2636★
BABY FOOD INDUSTRY, 1998
Ranked by: Sales, in dollars. **Number listed:** 5

1. Gerber Baby Products, with $546,105,216 dollar
2. Heinz USA, $100,459,136
3. Beech-Nut Corp., $97,505,680
4. Nabisco Foods Group, $8,845,624
5. Nestle USA, $839,405

Source: *U.S. Distribution Journal*, May/June, November 3, 1999, p. 66.

Information Technology

★2637★
TOP CITIES FOR INFORMATION TECHNOLOGY JOBS, 1999*
Ranked by: Survey score. **Remarks:** Survey score determined by annual salary, skills and hiring. Includes metro population and median house cost. **Number listed:** 10

1. Boston, MA
2. Chicago, IL
3. Atlanta, GA
4. Washington, DC
5. New York, NY
6. San Francisco, CA
7. Seattle, WA
8. Las Vegas, NV
9. St. Louis, MO
10. Austin, TX

Source: *Computerworld*, Top 10 IT Job Markets (annual), January 11, 1999, p. 64+.

Information Technology, International

★2638★
TOP INFORMATION SERVICE PROVIDERS BASED ON REVENUE FROM ALL SERVERS, 1998*
Ranked by: Percentage of worldwide vendor totals based on a total revenue estimate of $49.0 billion. **Number listed:** 6

1. IBM, with 29.8%
2. HP, 10.9%
3. Compaq, 6.7%
4. Sun, 6.6%
5. Fujitsu, 4.4%
6. Unisys, 3.6%

Source: *Electronic Business*, December, 1998, p. 66.

★2639★
TOP INFORMATION TECHNOLOGY SERVICE PROVIDERS, 1997
Ranked by: Worldwide revenue, in billions of dollars. **Remarks:** Includes market share. **Number listed:** 15

1. IBM, with $25.7 billion
2. Electronic Data Systems, $15.2
3. Fujitsu, $8.9
4. Compaq, $7.9
5. Andersen Consulting, $6.6
6. Hewlett-Packard, $6.1
7. Computer Sciences (CSC), $5.9
8. First Data, $5.8
9. Unisys, $4.2
10. Automatic Data Processing (ADP), $4.1

Source: *Electronic Business*, December, 1998, p. 66.

★2640★
WORLD'S FASTEST GROWING INFORMATION TECHNOLOGY COMPANIES, 1999*
Ranked by: Revenue growth, in percent. **Number listed:** 10

1. XOOM.COM, with 615.9%

2. eBay, 577.8%
3. Earthweb, 508.5%
4. Infospace.com, 451.3%
5. At Home, 443.1%
6. Inktomi, 325.3%
7. Exodus, 324.3%
8. Amazon.com, 272.5%
9. Qwest Communications, 267.5%
10. Go2net, 221.8%

Source: *Business Week*, Top 100 IT Companies (annual), June 21, 1999, p. 120.

★2641★
WORLD'S LARGEST INFORMATION TECHNOLOGY COMPANIES BY RETURN ON INVESTMENT, 1999*
Ranked by: Revenue growth, in percent. **Number listed:** 10

1. XOOM.COM, with 615.9%
2. eBay, 577.8%
3. Infospace.com, 451.3%
4. At Home, 443.1%
5. Inktomi, 325.3%
6. Exodus, 324.3%
7. Amazon.com, 272.5%
8. Go2net, 258.7%
9. Qwest Communications, 267.5%
10. MCI WorldCom, 203.5%

Source: *Business Week*, Top 100 IT Companies (annual), June 21, 1999, p. 121.

★2642★
WORLD'S LARGEST INFORMATION TECHNOLOGY COMPANIES BY REVENUE, 1999*
Ranked by: Revenue, in millions of dollars. **Number listed:** 10

1. IBM, with $84,366 million
2. Lucent Technologies, $32,750
3. British Telecom, $30,346
4. SBC Communications, $29,239
5. France Telecom, $28,763
6. Intel, $27,375
7. NTT, $25,986
8. GTE, $25,467
9. MCI WorldCom, $24,357
10. BellSouth, $23,670

Source: *Business Week*, Top 100 IT Companies (annual), June 21, 1999, p. 120.

★2643★
WORLD'S LARGEST INFORMATION TECHNOLOGY COMPANIES, 1999*
Ranked by: Combined factors of revenue, revenue growth, return on equity, shareholder return and profits. **Remarks:** Also notes sector, country, revenue, revenue growth, return on equity, shareholder return and profits. **Number listed:** 100

1. America Online
2. Dell Computer
3. Solectron
4. Vodafone Group
5. Cisco Systems
6. EMC
7. MCI WorldCom
8. Inktomi
9. Sun Microsystems
10. Microsoft

Source: *Business Week*, Top 100 IT Companies (annual), June 21, 1999, p. 152+.

★2644★
WORLD'S MOST PROFITABLE INFORMATION TECHNOLOGY COMPANIES BY RETURN ON EQUITY, 1999*
Ranked by: Return on equity, in percent. **Number listed:** 10

1. U.S. West Inc., with 159.9%
2. Vodafone Group, 108.6%
3. Quanta Computer, 74.0%
4. Cap Gemini, 63.6%
5. Giga-Byte Technology, 58.0%
6. Dell Computer, 56.4%
7. Lexmark International Group, 52.5%
8. Arima Computer, 49.0%
9. Asustek Computer, 46.0%
10. Cable & Wireless, 41.6%

Source: *Business Week*, Top 100 IT Companies (annual), June 21, 1999, p. 121.

Infrastructure (Economics)

★2645★
STATES WITH THE HIGHEST TRANSPORTATION FUNDS, 1998*
Ranked by: Transportation funds, in billions of dollars. **Number listed:** 10

1. California, with $2.407 billion
2. Texas, $1.888
3. New York, $1.351
4. Pennsylvania, $1.306
5. Florida, $1.209
6. Ohio, $.897
7. Illinois, $.885
8. Michigan, $.825
9. New Jersey, $.676
10. Virginia, $.671

Source: *Metal Center*, July, 1998, p. 31.

Institutional Investments

★2646★
TOP SOURCES OF EQUITY FUNDS, 1999*
Ranked by: Market share, in percent. **Remarks:** Includes equity figures. **Number listed:** 6

1. REITs, with 41.4%
2. Pension Funds, 34.7%
3. Life companies, 12.2%
4. Foreign investors, 10.5%
5. Commercial banks, 0.8%
6. Savings associations, 0.4%

Source: *Journal of Property Management*, January/February, 1999, p. 22.

Instrument Industry

★2647★
MOST ADMIRED SCIENTIFIC, PHOTOGRAPHIC AND CONTROL EQUIPMENT CORPORATIONS, 1998
Ranked by: Scores (1-10) derived from a survey of senior executives, outside directors and securities analysts. **Remarks:**

Respondents rated companies in their own industry on 8 attributes of reputation. Also notes previous year's rank. **Number listed:** 10

1. Medtronic, with 7.70
2. Minnesota Mining & Manufacturing, 7.65
3. Eastman Kodak, 6.59
4. Baxter International, 6.34
5. Thermo Electron, 6.13
6. Becton Dickinson, 6.12
7. Bausch & Lomb, 5.90
8. Tektronix, 5.76
9. Polaroid, 5.58
10. Boston Scientific, 5.54

Source: *Fortune*, America's Most Admired Corporations (annual), March 1, 1999, p. F-6.

Instrument Industry--Europe

★2648★
TOP MEASURING, ANALYZING, AND CONTROLLING INSTRUMENT MANUFACTURE RS IN EUROPE, 1999*
Ranked by: Sales, in millions of European Currency Units (ECUs). **Remarks:** Also notes number of employees and overall rank among European businesses. **Number listed:** 53

1. Xerox Ltd. (UK), with ECUs3.593 million
2. Williams PLC (UK), ECUs3.288
3. Hewlett-Packard Ltd. (UK), ECUs2.962
4. Carl Zeiss (DE), ECUs2.586
5. Agfa-Gevaert AG (DE), ECUs1.613
6. Asea Brown Boveri Ltd. (UK), ECUs1.355
7. APV Ltd. (UK), ECUs1.139
8. Mannesmann Vdo AG (DE), ECUs1.081
9. Kodak AG (DE), ECUs.876
10. Jenoptik AG (DE), ECUs.858

Source: *Dun's Europa*, (annual), Dun & Bradstreet, 1999, p. 259+.

Insurance, Accident

★2649★
LARGEST ACCIDENT & HEALTH COMPANIES, 1997
Ranked by: Dollar amount of current premiums written. **Remarks:** Includes prior rank, percent increase over prior year, dollar amount of premiums earned, loss ratio, expense ratio and underwriting gain. **Number listed:** 300

1. Blue Cross & Blue Shield of MI, with $6,657,678,239
2. Prudential Insurance Co. of America, $6,271,672,882
3. American Family Life Columbus, $5,411,871,168
4. Highmark, Inc., $4,946,358,838
5. Empire BC & BS, $3,081,846,560
6. Guardian Life Insurance Co. of Amer, $2,461,387,237
7. Principal Mutual Life Insurance Co., $2,290,101,548
8. Continental Assurance Co., $2,276,023,056
9. Connecticut General Life Insurance, $2,196,617,919
10. Metropolitan Life Insurance Co., $2,135,189,776

Source: *Best's Review Life/Health*, Accident & Health Premiums (annual), October, 1998, p. 62+.

Insurance, Automobile

★2650★
LEADING AUTO INSURANCE COMPANIES, 1997
Ranked by: Earned premiums, in thousands of dollars. **Remarks:** Also notes 1996 figures. **Number listed:** 20

1. State Farm Mutual Auto Insurance Co., with $24,085,022 thousand
2. Allstate Insurance Co., $14,189,095
3. Farmers Insurance Exchange, $4,263,136
4. Nationwide Mutual Insurance Co., $2,964,407
5. Government Employees Insurance Co., $2,809,172
6. United Services Auto Association, $2,279,395
7. American Family Mutual Insurance, $2,019,813
8. Liberty Mutual Insurance Co., $1,926,249
9. Progressive Casualty Insurance Co., $1,696,392
10. Calif. State Auto Association Inter-Insurance, $1,418,257

Source: *National Underwriter*, Property & Casualty/Risk & Benefits Management Edition (annual), August 17, 1998, p. 17.

★2651★
LEADING MUTUAL INSURANCE COMPANIES, 1997
Ranked by: Earned premiums, in thousands of dollars. **Remarks:** Also notes 1996 figures and percent change. **Number listed:** 10

1. State Farm Mutual Auto Insurance Co., with $24,085,022 thousand
2. Nationwide Mutual Insurance Co., $2,964,407
3. American Family Mutual Insurance, $2,019,813
4. Liberty Mutual Insurance Co., $1,926,249
5. Auto-Owners Insurance Co., $855,302
6. Employers Insurance of Wausau & Mutual Co., $784,134
7. Amico Mutual Insurance Co., $663,209
8. Lumbermens Mutual Casualty, $616,442
9. Nationwide Mutual Fire Insurance Co., $540,287
10. Sentry Insurance, $511,033

Source: *National Underwriter*, Property & Casualty/Risk & Benefits Management Edition (annual), August 17, 1998, p. 17.

★2652★
LEADING RECIPROCAL INSURANCE COMPANIES, 1997
Ranked by: Earned premiums, in thousands of dollars. **Remarks:** Also notes 1996 figures and percent change. **Number listed:** 10

1. Farmers Insurance Exchange, with $4,263,136 thousand
2. United Services Auto Association, $2,279,395
3. California State Auto Association Inter-Insurance, $1,418,257
4. Erie Insurance Exchange, $1,264,075
5. Inter-Insurance Exchange of the Automobile Club, $969,390
6. Auto Club Insurance Association, $861,107
7. Truck Insurance Exchange, $536,296
8. Fire Insurance Exchange, $499,096
9. California Casualty Indemnity Exchange, $103,455
10. Farmers Automobile Insurance Association, $84,079

Source: *National Underwriter*, Property & Casualty/Risk & Benefits Management Edition (annual), August 17, 1998, p. 17.

★2653★
LEADING STOCK INSURANCE COMPANIES, 1997
Ranked by: Earned premiums, in thousands of dollars. **Remarks:** Also notes 1996 figures and percent change. **Number listed:** 10

1. Allstate Insurance Co., with $14,189,095 thousand

2. Government Employees Insurance Co., $2,809,172
3. Progressive Casualty Insurance Co., $1,696,392
4. USAA Casualty Insurance Co., $1,304,325
5. Metropolitan Property and Casualty Insurance Co., $923,763
6. Southern Farm Bureau Casualty Insurance Co., $824,602
7. State Farm Indemnity Co., $801,484
8. Travelers Casualty & Surety Co., $789,368
9. Continental Casualty Co., $783,220
10. Hartford Fire Insurance Co., $782,907

Source: *National Underwriter*, Property & Casualty/Risk & Benefits Management Edition (annual), August 17, 1998, p. 17.

★2654★

LEADING WAYS AUTO INSURANCEURERS DISTRIBUTE BODILY-INJURY PREMIUMS, 1998*

Ranked by: Share, in percent. **Number listed:** 7

1. Attorney's fees, with 28.4%
2. Pain and suffering awards, 16.9%
3. Commissions/sales expenses on policies, 15.5%
4. Medical bills/lost wages, 14.8%
5. Fraudulent and excessive claims, 12.6%
6. Other overhead, 10.1%
7. State taxes and fees, 2.3%

Source: *Nation's Business*, August, 1998, p. 76.

★2655★

LEADING WRITERS OF AUTOMOBILE INSURANCE, 1997

Ranked by: Premiums written, in thousands of dollars. **Remarks:** Also notes change from previous year, market share and adjusted loss ratios for current and previous two years, and percentage of total company premiums. **Number listed:** 100

1. State Farm Group, with $9,422,882 thousand
2. Allstate Insurance Group, $5,640,869
3. Farmers Insurance Group, $2,572,000
4. Nationwide Group, $1,694,462
5. Progressive Group, $1,621,765
6. USAA Group, $1,405,111
7. Berkshire Hathaway, $1,274,314
8. American Family Insurance Group, $843,487
9. Travelers Property/Casualty Group, $824,065
10. Liberty Mutual, $794,786

Source: *Best's Review Property/Casualty Edition*, October, 1998, p. 32+.

★2656★

LEADING WRITERS OF COMMERCIAL AUTOMOBILE INSURANCE, 1997

Ranked by: Premiums written, in thousands of dollars. **Remarks:** Also notes change from previous year, market share and adjusted loss ratios for current and previous two years, and percentage of total company premiums. **Number listed:** 100

1. CNA Insurance Group, with $1,008,834 thousand
2. Travelers Property/Casualty Group, $947,740
3. Zurich Insurance Group-U.S., $842,130
4. State Farm Group, $671,227
5. Liberty Mutual, $620,929
6. American International Group, $588,045
7. Old Republic General Group, $494,414
8. St. Paul Cos., $466,426
9. Nationwide Group, $456,283
10. Progressive Group, $441,283

Source: *Best's Review Property/Casualty Edition*, October, 1998, p. 35+.

★2657★

LEADING WRITERS OF PRIVATE PASSENGER AUTOMOBILE INSURANCE, 1997

Ranked by: Premiums written, in thousands of dollars. **Remarks:** Also notes change from previous year, market share and adjusted loss ratios for current and previous two years, and percentage of total company premiums. **Number listed:** 100

1. State Farm Group, with $23,522,216 thousand
2. Allstate Insurance Group, $14,168,329
3. Farmers Insurance Group, $6,864,839
4. Nationwide Group, $4,495,611
5. Progressive Group, $4,270,247
6. USAA Group, $3,548,760
7. Berkshire Hathaway, $3,455,529
8. American Family Insurance Group, $2,042,231
9. Liberty Mutual, $1,950,918
10. Travelers Property/Casualty Group, $1,934,970

Source: *Best's Review Property/Casualty Edition*, October, 1998, p. 38+.

★2658★

STATES WITH THE HIGHEST AUTOMOBILE RESIDUAL MARKET AS A PERCENT OF THE TOTAL WRITTEN INSURANCE PREMIUMS BY LINE, 1996

Ranked by: Total written premiums, in thousands of dollars. **Remarks:** Includes % PPNF liability, % PPNF physical damage, % comm. liability, % comm. physical damage and % total. **Number listed:** 51

1. New York, with $1,329,832 thousand
2. Massachusetts, $680,448
3. North Carolina, $577,530
4. South Carolina, $493,534
5. New Jersey, $343,893
6. Michigan, $197,576
7. Maryland, $183,595
8. Texas, $181,094
9. California, $147,522
10. Pennsylvania, $138,699

Source: *AIPSO Facts*, Automobile Insurance Plans Service Office, 1998, p. 219+.

★2659★

STATES WITH THE HIGHEST RESIDUAL MARKET WRITTEN INSURANCE PREMIUM VOLUME, 1996

Ranked by: Written premium volume, in thousands of dollars. **Remarks:** Includes % PPNF liability, % PPNF physical damage, & comm. liability and % comm. physical damage. **Number listed:** 51

1. New York, with $1,321,325 thousand
2. North Carolina, $621,636
3. Massachusetts, $607,461
4. South Carolina, $493,578
5. New Jersey, $320,585
6. Michigan, $197,576
7. Maryland, $183,595
8. Texas, $174,735
9. California, $147,153
10. Pennsylvania, $138,456

Source: *AIPSO Facts*, Automobile Insurance Plans Service Office, 1998, p. 217.

Insurance, Automobile--Reinsurance

★2660★
LEADING AUTOMOBILE RE-INSURERS, 1997
Ranked by: Total auto assumptions from nonaffiliates, in dollars. **Remarks:** Includes private passenger and commercial auto liabilities, auto physical damage, and total auto assumptions and percent total auto assumptions to all lines assumed. **Number listed:** 16

1. American Re-Insurance, with $403,180,374
2. Constitution Reinsurance Corp., $271,267,657
3. General Reinsurance Corp., $236,686,514
4. Transatlantic Reinsurance, $208,643,201
5. SCOR Reinsurance Co., $202,028,999
6. Kemper Reinsurance Co., $141,278,686
7. Zurich Reinsurance (NA) Inc., $112,728,408
8. Dorinco Reinsurance Co., $105,653,370
9. Underwriters Reinsurance Co., $103,103,868
10. TIG Reinsurance Co., $97,594,586

Source: *Best's Review*, Property/Casualty edition, October, 1998, p. 48.

Insurance Brokers

★2661★
LARGEST COMMERCIAL INSURANCE BROKERS BY ESTIMATED RETAIL BROKERAGE REVENUE, 1997
Ranked by: Estimated retail brokerage revenue, in millions of dollars. **Remarks:** Includes percent change. **Number listed:** 20

1. Marsh & McLennan Cos. Inc., with $1,712.0 million
2. Aon Corp., $1,356.5
3. Sedgwick Group PLC, $442.3
4. Willis Corroon Group PLC, $396.4
5. Arthur J. Gallagher & Co., $274.8
6. Acordia Inc., $214.1
7. USI Insurance Services Corp., $155.7
8. Hilb, Rogal & Hamilton Co., $125.3
9. Norwest Insurance Inc., $113.7
10. Lockton Cos. Inc., $90.6

Source: *Business Insurance*, (annual), July 20, 1998, p. 10.

★2662★
TOP COMMERCIAL INSURANCE BROKERS, 1997
Ranked by: U. S. brokerage revenue, in dollars. **Number listed:** 100

1. Marsh & McLennan Cos. Inc., with $2,260,194,800
2. Aon Corp., $2,257,808,000
3. Sedgwick Group PLC, $643,062,420
4. Willis Corroon Group PLC, $600,752,880
5. Arthur J. Gallagher & Co., $417,264,300
6. Acordia Inc., $308,561,724
7. USI Insurance Services Corp., $236,200,000
8. Hilb, Rogal & Hamilton Co., $161,757,821
9. Norwest Insurance Inc., $126,900,000
10. Poe & Brown Inc., $124,365,000

Source: *Business Insurance*, (annual), July 20, 1998, p. 3.

Insurance Brokers--Acquisitions and Mergers

★2663★
TOP BROKERS IN MERGERS AND ACQUISITIONS, 1997
Ranked by: Revenue, in thousands of dollars. **Remarks:** Includes number of acquisitions for 1996, 1997, and 1998. **Number listed:** 10

1. J&H Marsh & McLennan Cos. Inc., with $2,620,195 thousand
2. Aon Corp., $2,257,808
3. Sedgwick Group PLC, $643,062
4. Willis Corroon Group PLC, $600,753
5. Arthur J. Gallagher & Co., $417,264
6. Acordia Inc., $308,562
7. USI Insurance Services Corp., $236,200
8. Hilb, Rogal & Hamilton Co., $161,758
9. Norwest Insurance Inc., $126,900
10. Poe & Brown Inc., $124,365

Source: *Best's Review*, April, 1999, p. 82.

Insurance Brokers, International

★2664★
TOP WORLD BUSINESS INSURANCE BROKERS, 1997
Ranked by: Brokerage revenue, in dollars. **Remarks:** Includes revenue for 1996, percent change, number of employees in 1997 and 1996 and percent change. **Number listed:** 20

1. Marsh & McLennan Cos. Inc., with $4,396,300,000
2. Aon Corp., $4,031,800,000
3. Sedgwick Group PLC, $1,549,548,000
4. Willis Corroon Group PLC, $1,133,496,000
5. Arthur J. Gallagher & Co., $463,627,000
6. Jardine Lloyd Thompson Group PLC, $394,889,040
7. Acordia Inc., $311,364,000
8. Lambert Fenchurch Group PLC, $252,628,268
9. Forbes Group Ltd., $249,100,000
10. Gras Savoye & Cie., $244,230,750

Source: *Business Insurance*, (annual), July 20, 1998, p. P1.

Insurance Brokers--Los Angeles County (CA)

★2665★
LARGEST INSURANCE BROKERS IN LOS ANGELES COUNTY, 1997
Ranked by: Los Angeles county revenue, in millions of dollars. **Remarks:** Also notes contact information, figures from previous year, number of employees, types of Insuranceurers, major lines written, number of offices, year established, and top executive. **Number listed:** 15

1. J&H Marsh & McLennan Co., with $121 million
2. Aon Risk Services of Southern Calif., $53.5
3. Keenan & Associates, $24.7
4. Total Financial & Insurance Services, $24
5. TriWest Insurance Services Inc., $16.4
6. Lockton Insurance Brokers Inc., $12.5
7. Willis Corroon Corp. of Los Angeles, $12
8. Petersen International Underwriters, $11.8
9. Sander A. Kessler & Associates Inc., $9.9

10. Bolton/RGV Insurance Brokers, $9.6

Source: *Los Angeles Business Journal*, Book of Lists (annual), 1999, p. 46.

Insurance Business--Detroit Metropolitan Area

★2666★

LEADING BUSINESS INSURANCE AGENCIES IN THE DETROIT METROPOLITAN AREA, 1997

Ranked by: Revenue, in millions of dollars. **Remarks:** Includes 1996 revenue, premium volume, number of Detroit area employees, total U.S. employees, revenue source as percent of retail and as percent with sale, comp. as a percent of commissions and fees and investment income. **Number listed:** 15

1. Meadowbrook Insurance Group Inc., with $50.0 million
2. J&H Marsh & McLennan of Michigan, $44.0
3. Aon Risk Services Inc. of Michigan, $24.0
4. Willis Corroon Corp., $20.5
5. Proctor Homer Warren Inc., $19.6
6. Sedgwick of Michigan, $15.0
7. Kelter-Thorner Inc., $14.9
8. Gallagher ABOW Inc., $9.4
9. The Allied Cos. Inc., $8.1
10. First of America Insurance Group, $6.3

Source: *Crain's Detroit Business*, Crain's Book of Lists Detroit (annual), December 28, 1998, p. 158.

Insurance Companies

★2667★

TOP 401K PROVIDERS, 1997

Ranked by: 401K assets, in billions of dollars. **Remarks:** Includes number of plans below 100, 100-999, 1,000-4,999, and about 5,000, number of plans for 1996, 1995 and 1994. **Number listed:** 10

1. Principal Financial Group, with $29.3 billion
2. Prudential Investments, $27.0
3. Cigna Retirement & Investment Services, $26.2
4. MetLife Defined Contribution Group, $21.2
5. Aetna Retirement Services, $19.5
6. Manulife Financial, $18.0
7. New York Life/Mainstay Funds, $17.1
8. Mass Mutual, $12.0
9. Nationwide Financial Services Inc., $8.1
10. Equitable, $6.5

Source: *National Underwriter*, October 26, 1998, p. 1.

★2668★

TOP STOCK INSURANCEURERS, 1997

Ranked by: Revenue, in thousands of dollars. **Remarks:** Includes year 2000 costs. **Number listed:** 60

1. Citigroup Inc. (includes Travelers Group), with $37,509,000 thousand
2. American International Group Inc., $27,246,032
3. Allstate, $24,949,000
4. Cigna Corp., $20,038,000
5. Aetna Inc., $18,540,200
6. CNA Financial Corp., $17,072,000
7. Hartford Financial Services Group Inc., $13,305,000
8. Berkshire Hathaway, $10,430,000
9. Travelers Property/Casualty Group, $9,911,000
10. Equitable Cos., $9,666,100

Source: *Best's Review*, January, 1999, p. 51.

Insurance Companies--Black Companies

★2669★

TOP BLACK-OWNED INSURANCE COMPANIES, 1998

Ranked by: Assets, in millions of dollars. **Remarks:** Also notes rank from previous year, chief executive, year founded, number of staff, statutory reserves, Insurance in force, and premium and net investment income. **Number listed:** 1

1. North Carolina Mutual Life Insurance Co., with $210.151 million
2. Atlanta Life Insurance Co., $196.017
3. Golden State Mutual Life Insurance Co., $102.288
4. Booker T. Washington Insurance Co., $44.432
5. Protective Industrial Insurance Co., $17.950
6. Winnfield Life Insurance Co., $12.145
7. Universal Life Insurance Co., $9.249
8. Williams-Progressive Life & Accident Insurance Co., $8.749
9. Golden Circle Life Insurance Co., $7.113
10. Reliable Life Insurance Co., $4.642

Source: *Black Enterprise*, June, 1999, p. 220.

Insurance Companies, International

★2670★

STANDARD & POOR'S TOP GLOBAL BUSINESS INSURERS, 1998*

Ranked by: Net premiums written, in millions of dollars. **Remarks:** Includes country where located, year written, adjusted shareholder funds and rating as of 10/22/98. **Number listed:** 200

1. Tokio Marine & Fire, with $10,714 million
2. Lloyd's of London, $9,940
3. American International Group, $9,770
4. CNA (Continental Casualty/Continental Insurance Group), $9,623
5. Farmers Insurance Co. Inc. and subsidiary cos., $9,114
6. Nationwide Insurance Co. and subsidiary cos., $8,375
7. Travelers Insurance Group (Aetna), $7,905
8. Yasuda Fire & Marine Insurance Co. Ltd., $7,615
9. Royal & Sun Alliance Insurance PLC, $6,355
10. Zurich Versicherung AG, $6,174

Source: *Business Insurance*, Standard & Poor's Top Global Business insurers (annual), November 9, 1998, p. 58+.

Insurance Companies--Mexico

★2671★

TOP INSURANCE FIRMS IN MEXICO, 1997

Ranked by: Sales, in millions of pesos. **Remarks:** Includes market share. **Number listed:** 10

1. Comercial America, with MP10,221 million

2. Grupo Nacional Provincial, MP8,132
3. Monterrey Aetna, MP3,763
4. Inbursa, MP2,427
5. Tepeyac, MP1,433
6. Genesis, MP1,242
7. Bancomer, MP912
8. AIG MexiCo., MP646
9. Aba/Seguros, MP627
10. Atlas, MP617

Source: *Business Mexico*, September, 1998, p. 38.

Insurance Companies--New York Metropolitan Area

★2672★
LARGEST INSURANCE COMPANIES IN THE NEW YORK METROPOLITAN AREA, 1997
Ranked by: Assets, in millions of dollars. **Remarks:** Also notes contact information, executive officer, premium volume, number of employees, and selected subsidiaries. **Number listed:** 25

1. Travelers Group, with $386,555.0 million
2. TIAA-CREF, $213,448.2
3. Metropolitan Life Insurance Co., $201,907.0
4. American International Group Inc., $163,970.7
5. Equitable Cos., $151,437.6
6. New York Life Insurance Co., $84,067.0
7. Guardian Life Insurance Co. of America, $22,088.9
8. Mutual Life Insurance Co. of New York, $16,575.9
9. Reliance Group Holdings Inc., $11,332.5
10. MBIA Inc., $9,810.8

Source: *Crain's New York Business*, July 20, 1998, p. 16+.

Insurance Companies--South Africa

★2673★
TOP INSURANCE COMPANIES IN SOUTH AFRICA, 1999*
Ranked by: Number of premiums. **Number listed:** 10

1. Santam Ltd., with 2,382,802
2. Mutual & Federal, 2,311,682
3. Guardian National, 1,806,240
4. South African Eagle, 1,403,980
5. Aegis Insurance Co., 1,103,017
6. Sanlam Health, 1,060,385
7. Commercial Union of S.A., 1,031,749
8. Hollard Insurance Co., 1,006,300
9. Allianz Insurance Ltd., 627,050
10. Protea Assurance Co., 605,455

Source: *Best's Review*, March, 1999, p. 41.

Insurance, Health

★2674★
LARGEST HEALTH INSURANCE COMPANIES BY NON-CANCELLABLE PREMIUMS, 1997
Ranked by: Premiums earned less dividends, in thousands of dollars. **Remarks:** Also notes number of incurred claims. **Number listed:** 150

1. Paul Revere Life Insurance Co., with $817,780 thousand
2. American Life Insurance Co., $706,713
3. Provident Life & Accident Insurance, $495,224
4. Northwestern Mutual Life Insurance, $432,576
5. Combined Insurance Co. of America, $307,033
6. Massachusetts Mutual Life Insurance, $280,912
7. Equitable Life Assr. Society of the US, $130,329
8. Guardian Life Insurance Co. of America, $108,175
9. New York Life Insurance Co., $101,561
10. Lincoln National Life Insurance Co., $77,137

Source: *National Underwriter*, Life & Health Statistical Review (annual), July 20, 1998, p. 32.

★2675★
LARGEST HEALTH INSURANCE COMPANIES IN GROUP HEALTH PREMIUMS, 1997
Ranked by: Premiums earned less dividends, in thousands of dollars. **Remarks:** Also notes number of incurred claims. **Number listed:** 250

1. Prudential Insurance Co. of America, with $6,131,214 thousand
2. National Heritage Insurance Co., $3,344,310
3. Guardian Life Insurance Co. of America, $2,325,844
4. Continental America Co., $2,272,061
5. Principal Mutual Life Insurance Co., $2,243,295
6. Connecticut General Life Insurance, $2,128,028
7. Metropolitan Life Insurance Co., $2,034,377
8. Aetna Life Insurance Co., $2,022,721
9. Blue Cross & Blue Shield of TX, $2,013,373
10. United Healthcare Insurance Co., $1,986,682

Source: *National Underwriter*, Life & Health Statistical Review (annual), July 20, 1998, p. 31+.

★2676★
LARGEST HEALTH INSURANCE COMPANIES IN GUARANTEED RENEWABLES, 1997
Ranked by: Premiums earned less dividends, in thousands of dollars. **Remarks:** Also notes number of incurred claims. **Number listed:** 100

1. American Family Life Association Columbus, with $5,388,542 thousand
2. Bankers Life & Casualty Co., $811,628
3. American Travellers Life Insurance Co., $512,192
4. Physicians Mutual Insurance Co., $460,580
5. Colonial Life & Accident Insurance Co., $443,176
6. General Electric Capital Assurance Co., $423,728
7. United American Insurance Co., $409,723
8. Combined Insurance Co. of America, $306,596
9. Mutual of Omaha Insurance Co., $263,705
10. Wellmark, $242,781

Source: *National Underwriter*, Life & Health Statistical Review (annual), July 20, 1998, p. 32.

★2677★
LARGEST HEALTH INSURANCE COMPANIES, 1997
Ranked by: Premiums earned, in thousands of dollars. **Remarks:** Also notes number of incurred claims. **Number listed:** 300

1. Prudential Insurance Co. of America, with $6,223,409 thousand
2. American Family Life Association Columbus, $5,397,470
3. National Heritage Insurance Co., $3,344,310
4. Guardian Life Insurance Co. of America, $2,453,846
5. Principal Mutual Life Insurance Co., $2,293,293
6. Continental America Co., $2,275.038
7. Connecticut General Life Insurance, $2,171,259
8. Metropolitan Life Insurance Co., $2,064,393
9. Aetna Life Insurance Co., $2,039,530

10. Blue Cross & Blue Shield of TX, $2,013,373

Source: *National Underwriter*, Life & Health Statistical Review (annual), July 20, 1998, p. 30+.

★2678★
LARGEST HEALTH INSURANCE INDIVIDUAL LEADERS, 1997
Ranked by: Premiums earned, in thousands of dollars. **Remarks:** Also notes number of incurred claims. **Number listed:** 150

1. American Farm Life Association Columbus, with $5,388,634 thousand
2. Bankers Life & Casualty Co., $852,047
3. Paul Revere Life Insurance Co., $821,191
4. American Life Insurance Co., $780,055
5. Combined Insurance Co. of America, $770,892
6. Mutual of Omaha Insurance Co., $706,837
7. Provident Life & Accident Insurance, $532,077
8. American Travellers Life Insurance Co., $516,723
9. Fortis Insurance Co., $509,561
10. Physicians Mutual Insurance Co., $484,543

Source: *National Underwriter*, Life & Health Statistical Review (annual), July 20, 1998, p. 32.

★2679★
TOP LIFE/HEALTH INSURANCE COMPANIES, 1997
Ranked by: Dollar amount of premiums written. **Remarks:** Includes prior year rank, percent increase over prior year, premiums earned, loss ratio, expense ratio and underwriting gain. **Number listed:** 320

1. Blue Cross & Blue Shield of MI, with $6,657,678,239
2. Prudential Insurance Co. of America, $6,271,672,882
3. American Family Life Columbus, $5,411,871,168
4. Highmark, Inc., $4,946,358,838
5. Empire BC & BS, $3,081,846,560
6. Guardian Life Insurance Co. of America, $2,461,387,237
7. Principal Mutual Life Insurance Co., $2,290,101,548
8. Continental Assurance Company, $2,273,023,056
9. Connecticut General Life Insurance, $2,196,617,919
10. Metropolitan Life Insurance Co., $2,135,189,776

Source: *Best's Review*, October, 1998, p. 62+.

Insurance, Homeowners

★2680★
TOP BUYERS OF HOMEOWNERS MULTIPERIL REINSURANCE ASSUMED FROM NONAFFILIATES 1998*
Ranked by: Homeowners multiperil assumed from nonaffiliates, in dollars. **Remarks:** Includes total all lines assumed from nonaffiliates and total homeowners multiperil assumed to all lines assumed. **Number listed:** 22

1. Constitution Reinsurance Corporation, with $128,825,098
2. Transatlantic Reinsurance, $68,035,227
3. Dorinco Reinsurance Company, $60,934,786
4. Everest Reinsurance Company, $45,549,985
5. Risk Capital Resinsurance, $37,230,270
6. General Reinsurance Corporation, $37,024,217
7. Employers Reinsurance Corporation, $32,316,782
8. AXA Reinsurance Company, $32,242,263
9. First Excess & Reinsurance Corporation, $30,735,186
10. Vesta Fire Insurance Corporation, $29,932,580

Source: *Best's Review*, November, 1998, p. 58.

★2681★
TOP BUYERS OF HOMEOWNERS MULTIPERIL REINSURANCE, 1998*
Ranked by: Homeowners multiperil ceded to nonaffiliates, in dollars. **Remarks:** Includes total all lines ceded to nonaffiliates and total homeowners multiperil ceded to all lines ceded. **Number listed:** 20

1. Farmers Insurance Exchange, with $245,776,349
2. State Farm Fire & Casualty, $127,844,313
3. Clarendon National Insurance, $110,011,076
4. United States F&G Co., $104,722,123
5. Travelers Indem Co., $92,680,891
6. Allstate Florida Insurance, $89,798,679
7. Great American Insurance Co., $78,455,164
8. Fire Insurance Exchange, $77,954,410
9. Amer Bankers Insurance, $73,668,461
10. Clarendon Select Insurance, $68,376,112

Source: *Best's Review*, November, 1998, p. 58.

★2682★
TOP HEALTH INSURANCE COMPANIES IN FLORIDA, 1997
Ranked by: Health premium, in dollars. **Remarks:** Includes Florida or regional headquarters. **Number listed:** 25

1. Blue Cross & Blue Shield of Florida, with $1,504,154,877
2. Prudential Insurance Co. of America, $470,923,236
3. Humana Health Insurance Co. of Florida Inc., $311,884,379
4. Principal Mutual Life Insurance Co., $215,044,233
5. United Wisconsin Life Insurance Co., $153,574,866
6. Aetna Life Insurance Co., $134,928,457
7. John Alden Life Insurance Co., $115,947,759
8. Continental Assurance Co., $104,118,101
9. Unum Life Insurance Co. of America, $94,603,646
10. Metropolitan Life Insurance Co., $84,211,435

Source: *Florida Trend*, August, 1998, p. 88.

Insurance, Liability

★2683★
STANDARD & POOR'S LISTS LEADING PROVIDERS OF MEDICAL MALPRACTICE INSURANCE, 1997
Ranked by: Direct premiums written, in millions of dollars. **Remarks:** Includes percent growth, market share and rating. **Number listed:** 50

1. CNA Insurance Group, with $409.1 million
2. St. Paul Cos., $402.7
3. MLMIC Group, $329.8
4. Health Care Indemnity Inc., $265.7
5. Medical Protective, $230.7
6. American International Group Inc., $214.2
7. Doctors' Co. Insurance Group, $202.8
8. Illinois State Medical InterInsurance Exchange, $196.1
9. MMI Cos. Group, $167.0
10. Medical Inter-Insurance Exchange, $162.5

Source: *Business Insurance*, April 19, 1999, p. 35.

Insurance, Life

★2684★

LEADING LIFE INSURANCE COMPANIES BY CREDIT INSURANCE IN FORCE, 1997

Ranked by: Current issued insurance, in thousands of dollars. **Remarks:** Includes percent change over prior year and prior rank. **Number listed:** 100

1. CUNA Mutual Insurance Society, with $41,713,136 thousand
2. American Bankers Life of FL, $19,393,521
3. Union Security Life Insurance Co., $14,940,597
4. Union Fidelity Life, $10,798,153
5. USLIFE Credit Life, $9,796,317
6. Associates Financial Life, $8,854,111
7. Combined Insurance Company of America, $8,681,835
8. Life Reassurance Corp of America, $8,616,648
9. RGA Reinsurance Company, $6,916,046
10. American National Insurance Co., $6,429,143

Source: *Best's Review*, 100 Leading Life Companies (annual), July, 1998, p. 45.

★2685★

LEADING LIFE INSURANCE COMPANIES BY CREDIT INSURANCE ISSUED, 1997

Ranked by: Current issued insurance, in thousands of dollars. **Remarks:** Includes percent change over prior year and prior rank. **Number listed:** 100

1. CUNA Mutual Insurance Society, with $25,697,661 thousand
2. American Bankers Life of FL, $10,604,695
3. Union Security Life Insurance Co., $9,260,904
4. USLIFE Credit Life, $6,066,406
5. Union Fidelity Life, $4,550,321
6. American Heritage Life, $4,344,593
7. Associates Financial Life, $4,216,118
8. American National Insurance Co., $4,067,452
9. Protective Life Insurance Co., $3,392,334
10. Caribbean American Life, $3,246,152

Source: *Best's Review*, 100 Leading Life Companies (annual), July, 1998, p. 44.

★2686★

LEADING LIFE INSURANCE COMPANIES BY GROUP INSURANCE IN FORCE, 1997

Ranked by: Current issued Insurance, in thousands of dollars. **Remarks:** Includes percent change over prior year and prior rank. **Number listed:** 100

1. Metropolitan Life Insurance Co., with $1,135,499,040 thousand
2. Prudential Insurance Co. of America, $544,997,760
3. Connecticut General Life Insurance, $425,162,153
4. Aetna Life Insurance Co., $284,051,749
5. Sun Life Assurance Company of CN, $265,706,874
6. UNUM Life Insurance Co. of Amer, $213,545,169
7. Hartford L & A Insurance Co., $190,489,844
8. John Hancock Mutual Life, $190,196,000
9. Canada Life Assurance Co., $169,660,389
10. ReliaStar Life Insurance Co., $138,690,229

Source: *Best's Review*, 100 Leading Life Companies (annual), July, 1998, p. 43.

★2687★

LEADING LIFE INSURANCE COMPANIES BY GROUP INSURANCE ISSUED, 1997

Ranked by: Current issued insurance, in thousands of dollars. **Remarks:** Includes percent change over prior year and prior rank. **Number listed:** 100

1. Metropolitan Life Insurance Co., with $60,728,529 thousand
2. Kemper Investors Life Insurance Co., $59,338,505
3. Sun Life Assurance Company of CN, $56,533,759
4. UNUM Life Insurance Co. of Amer, $44,501,074
5. Hartford L & A Insurance Co., $38,321,776
6. Prudential Insurance Co. of America, $34,491,943
7. Canada Life Assurance Co., $33,314,317
8. Connecticut General Life Insurance, $24,580,439
9. ReliaStar Life Insurance Co., $23,722,748
10. Aetna Life Insurance Co., $20,984,288

Source: *Best's Review*, 100 Leading Life Companies (annual), July, 1998, p. 42.

★2688★

LEADING LIFE INSURANCE COMPANIES BY INDUSTRIAL INSURANCE IN FORCE, 1997

Ranked by: Current issued insurance, in thousands of dollars. **Remarks:** Includes percent change over prior year and prior rank. **Number listed:** 85

1. Prudential Insurance Co. of America, with $3,753,091 thousand
2. Metropolitan Life Insurance Co., $3,589,887
3. American General L & A, $2,308,891
4. Liberty National Life Insurance Co., $1,002,842
5. United Insurance Co. of America, $826,072
6. Western & Southern Life Insurance Co., $721,820
7. Monumental Life Insurance Co., $528,045
8. RGA Reinsurance Company, $499,517
9. Security Industrial Insurance Co., $410,497
10. Life Insurance Co. of Georgia, $403,015

Source: *Best's Review*, 100 Leading Life Companies (annual), July, 1998, p. 46.

★2689★

LEADING LIFE INSURANCE COMPANIES BY INDUSTRIAL INSURANCE ISSUED, 1997

Ranked by: Current issued insurance, in thousands of dollars. **Remarks:** Includes percent change over prior year and prior rank. **Number listed:** 14

1. Security Industrial Insurance Co., with $78,137 thousand
2. Universal Life Insurance Co., $52,092
3. Family Guaranty Life Insurance Co., $7,983
4. Protective Industrial Insurance Co. (AL), $2,680
5. Pierce National Life, $2,658
6. Home Mutual Life Insurance Co., $2,646
7. Continental Life Insurance Co. - PA, $1,285
8. Life & Health Insurance Co. of America, $396
9. Provident American L/H, $348
10. American Industries Life, $294

Source: *Best's Review*, 100 Leading Life Companies (annual), July, 1998, p. 46+.

★2690★

LEADING LIFE INSURANCE COMPANIES BY ORDINARY INSURANCE IN FORCE, 1997

Ranked by: Current issued Insurance, in thousands of dollars. **Remarks:** Includes percent change over prior year and prior rank. **Number listed:** 100

1. Northwestern Mutual Life Insurance Co., with $485,275,611 thousand
2. Metropolitan Life Insurance Co., $417,015,816
3. Transamerica Occidental Life, $398,535,311
4. Prudential Insurance Co. of America, $380,454,040
5. Primerica Life Insurance Co., $334,098,793
6. State Farm Life Insurance Co., $311,550,042
7. New York Life Insurance Co., $302,157,271
8. Equitable Life Assurance Society, $275,750,738
9. RGA Reinsurance Company, $230,501,331

10. First Colony Life Insurance Co., $202,937,768

Source: *Best's Review*, 100 Leading Life Companies (annual), July, 1998, p. 41.

★2691★
LEADING LIFE INSURANCE COMPANIES BY ORDINARY INSURANCE ISSUED, 1997
Ranked by: Current issued Insurance, in thousands of dollars. **Remarks:** Includes percent change over prior year and prior rank. **Number listed:** 100

1. Northwestern Mutual Life Insurance Co., with $81,071,895 thousand
2. Hartford Life Insurance Co., $68,982,934
3. Valley Forge Life Insurance Co., $61,380,325
4. State Farm Life Insurance Co., $52,279,350
5. First Colony Life Insurance Co., $45,102,822
6. Primerica Life Insurance Co., $43,883,313
7. Prudential Insurance Co. of America, $40,461,980
8. New York Life Insurance Co., $39,199,786
9. Metropolitan Life Insurance Co., $37,518,837
10. Transamerica Occidental Life, $32,232,731

Source: *Best's Review*, 100 Leading Life Companies (annual), July, 1998, p. 40.

★2692★
LEADING LIFE INSURANCE COMPANIES BY TOTAL INSURANCE IN FORCE, 1997
Ranked by: Current issued insurance, in thousands of dollars. **Remarks:** Includes percent change over prior year and prior rank. **Number listed:** 100

1. Metropolitan Life Insurance Co., with $1,556,104,759 thousand
2. Prudential Insurance Co. of America, $933,737,148
3. Connecticut General Life Insurance, $542,866,330
4. Northwestern Mutual Life Insurance Co., $485,911,183
5. New York Life Insurance Co., $434,570,424
6. Transamerica Occidental Life, $425,146,832
7. Sun Life Assurance Company of CN, $407,105,093
8. Primerica Life Insurance Co., $334,098,793
9. State Farm Life Insurance Co., $324,115,357
10. Aetna Life Insurance Co., $294,372,926

Source: *Best's Review*, 100 Leading Life Companies (annual), July, 1998, p. 38.

★2693★
LEADING LIFE INSURANCE COMPANIES BY TOTAL INSURANCE ISSUED , 1997
Ranked by: Current issued insurance, in thousands of dollars. **Remarks:** Includes percent change over prior year and prior rank. **Number listed:** 100

1. Metropolitan Life Insurance Co., with $98,247,366 thousand
2. Hartford Life Insurance Co., $88,402,548
3. Northwestern Mutual Life Insurance, $81,071,895
4. Prudential Insurance Co. of America, $75,659,630
5. Sun Life Assurance Company of CN, $73,439,329
6. Valley Forge-Life Insurance Co., $61,380,485
7. Kemper Investors Life Insurance Co., $60,034,464
8. State Farm Life Insurance Co., $53,217,011
9. New York Life Insurance Co., $51,539,353
10. First Colony Life Insurance Co., $45,104,291

Source: *Best's Review*, 100 Leading Life Companies (annual), July, 1998, p. 39.

★2694★
MOST ADMIRED LIFE INSURANCE CORPORATIONS, 1998
Ranked by: Scores (1-10) derived from a survey of senior executives, outside directors and securities analysts. **Remarks:** Respondents rated companies in their own industry on 8 attributes of reputation. Also notes previous year's rank. **Number listed:** 10

1. Northwestern Mutual Life, with 7.39
2. New York Life, 6.65
3. Principal Financial Group, 6.44
4. TIAA-CREF, 6.31
5. Massachusetts Mutual Life, 6.08
6. Cigna, 6.03
7. American General, 5.84
8. Metropolitan Life, 5.81
9. Aetna, 5.43
10. Prudential Insurance Co. of America, 5.16

Source: *Fortune*, America's Most Admired Corporations (annual), March 1, 1999, p. F-1.

★2695★
TOP CORPORATIONS IN MUTUAL LIFE AND HEALTH INSURANCE, 1998
Ranked by: Revenue, in millions of dollars. **Remarks:** Also notes profits and investment figures as well as number of employees. **Number listed:** 12

1. TIAA-CREF, with $35,889 million
2. New York Life, $19,849
3. Northwestern Mutual Life, $14,645
4. Massachusetts Mutual Life Insurance, $10,668
5. John Hancock Mutual Life, $8,912
6. Guardian Life of America, $7,974
7. Pacific Life, $4,153
8. Mutual of Omaha Insurance Co., $3,820
9. Aid Association for Lutherans, $3,218
10. Lutheran Brotherhood, $3,027

Source: *Fortune*, Fortune 500 Largest U.S. Corporations (annual), April 26, 1999, p. F-62.

★2696★
TOP CORPORATIONS IN STOCK LIFE AND HEALTH INSURANCE, 1998
Ranked by: Revenue, in millions of dollars. **Remarks:** Also notes profits and investment figures as well as number of employees. **Number listed:** 23

1. Prudential of America Group, with $34,427 million
2. Metropolitan Life, $26,735
3. American General, $10,251
4. Conseco, $7,716
5. Principal Financial Group, $7,697
6. AFLAC, $7,104
7. Transamerica, $6,429
8. Lincoln National, $6,087
9. Unum, $4,631
10. Genamerica, $3,914

Source: *Fortune*, Fortune 500 Largest U.S. Corporations (annual), April 26, 1999, p. F-62+.

★2697★
TOP LIFE/HEALTH INSURANCE COMPANIES BY NET PREMIUMS WRITTEN, 1997
Ranked by: Current premiums, in dollars. **Remarks:** Includes percent change over prior year and prior rank. **Number listed:** 100

1. Metropolitan Life Insurance Co., with $20,568,907,108
2. Prudential Insurance Co. of America, $18,957,681,699
3. Connecticut General Life Insurance, $13,125,201,454
4. Principal Mutual Life Insurance Co., $12,710,851,098
5. Nationwide Life Insurance Co., $10,159,051,422
6. New York Life Insurance Co., $8,495,489,126
7. Equitable Life Assurance Society, $7,861,644,810

8. Hartford Life Insurance Co., $7,540,291,595
9. John Hancock Mutual Life, $7,317,564,708
10. Northwestern Mutual Life Insurance, $7,294,047,132

Source: *Best's Review*, 100 Leading Life Companies (annual), July, 1998, p. 31.

★2698★

TOP LIFE/HEALTH MUTUALS BY DIRECT PREMIUMS WRITTEN, 1998

Ranked by: Direct premiums written, in thousand of dollars. **Remarks:** Includes admitted assets. **Number listed:** 10

1. Metropolitan Life, with $17,338,574 thousand
2. Prudential Insurance Co., $12,314,283
3. John Hancock Mutual, $6,438,056
4. New York Life, $6,420,781
5. Northwestern Mutual, $6,285,807
6. Mass Mutual, $5,705,497
7. Guardian Life, $3,313,944
8. Minnesota Life Insurance, $1,609,233
9. Blue Cross/Blue Shield of Texas, $1,393,445
10. Phoenix Home Life, $1,340,992

Source: *Best's Review*, March, 1999, p. 55.

★2699★

TOP LIFE INSURANCE COMPANIES BY ADMITTED ASSETS, 1997

Ranked by: Admitted assets, in thousands of dollars. **Number listed:** 300

1. Prudential Insurance Co. of America, with $193,987,388 thousand
2. Metropolitan Life Insurance Co., $172,443,904
3. Teachers Insurance & Annuity Assoc., $93,795,318
4. Equitable Life Assurance Society of the US, $74,945,044
5. Northwestern Mutual Life Insurance Co., $71,076,086
6. Connecticut General Life Insurance Co., $69,705,294
7. New York Life Insurance Co., $65,274,905
8. Principal Mutual Life Insurance Co., $63,956,608
9. Hartford Life Insurance Co., $62,823,886
10. Lincoln National Life Insurance Co., $58,369,091

Source: *National Underwriter Life & Health/Financial Services*, Life & Health Statistical Review (annual), July 20, 1998, p. 23.

★2700★

TOP LIFE INSURANCE COMPANIES BY ANNUITY PREMIUMS, 1997

Ranked by: Annuity premiums, in thousands of dollars. **Number listed:** 300

1. Nationwide Life Insurance Co., with $4,817,631 thousand
2. Teachers Insurance & Annuity Assoc., $4,251,331
3. Lincoln National Life Insurance Co., $3,683,646
4. Jackson National Life Insurance Co., $3,255,317
5. IDS Life Insurance Co., $2,683,273
6. Allmerica Financial Life & Annuity, $2,306,033
7. American General Annuity Insurance Co., $2,021,434
8. Metropolitan Life Insurance Co., $1,999,405
9. ITT Hartford Life & Annuity Insurance Co., $1,980,332
10. Travelers Insurance Co. Life Dept., $1,965,398

Source: *National Underwriter Life & Health/Financial Services*, Life & Health Statistical Review (annual), July 20, 1998, p. 27+.

★2701★

TOP LIFE INSURANCE COMPANIES BY GROUP LIFE PREMIUMS, 1997

Ranked by: Group life premiums, in thousands of dollars. **Number listed:** 250

1. Metropolitan Life Insurance Co., with $4,008,027 thousand
2. Kemper Investors Life Insurance Co., $2,675,658
3. Connecticut General Life Insurance Co., $2,136,685
4. Prudential Insurance Co. of America, $1,658,018
5. Hartford Life Insurance Co., $1,338,797
6. Aetna Life Insurance Co., $908,066
7. Minnesota Mutual Life Insurance Co., $552,626
8. UNUM Life Insurance Co. of America, $521,363
9. Unicare Life & Health Insurance Co., $512,823
10. ReliaStar Life Insurance Co., $461,188

Source: *National Underwriter Life & Health/Financial Services*, Life & Health Statistical Review (annual), July 20, 1998, p. 28.

★2702★

TOP LIFE INSURANCE COMPANIES BY IN-FORCE GROUP LIFE, 1997

Ranked by: In-force group life, in thousands of dollars. **Number listed:** 250

1. Metropolitan Life Insurance Co., with $1,135,499,040 thousand
2. Prudential Insurance Co. of America, $544,997,760
3. Connecticut General Life Insurance Co., $425,162,153
4. Southwest Life & Health Insurance Co., $336,510,500
5. Aetna Life Insurance Co., $284,051,749
6. Unum Life Insurance Co. of America, $213,545,169
7. Hartford Life & Accident Insurance Co., $190,489,844
8. John Hancock Mil Life Insurance Co., $190,196,000
9. ReliaStar Life Insurance Co., $138,690,229
10. New York Life Insurance Co., $132,348,884

Source: *National Underwriter Life & Health/Financial Services*, Life & Health Statistical Review (annual), July 20, 1998, p. 29+.

★2703★

TOP LIFE INSURANCE COMPANIES BY IN-FORCE INDIVIDUAL LIFE, 1997

Ranked by: In-force individual life, in thousands of dollars. **Number listed:** 250

1. Northwestern Mutual Life Insurance Co., with $485,275,611 thousand
2. Metropolitan Life Insurance Co., $417,015,824
3. Transamerica Occidental Life, $398,535,311
4. Prudential Insurance Co. of America, $380,454,040
5. Primerica Life Insurance Co., $334,098,793
6. State Farm Life Insurance Co., $311,550,042
7. New York Life Insurance Co., $302,157,271
8. Equitable Life Assr. Society of the US, $275,750,738
9. RGA Reinsurance Company, $230,501,331
10. First Colony Life Insurance Co., $202,937,768

Source: *National Underwriter Life & Health/Financial Services*, Life & Health Statistical Review (annual), July 20, 1998, p. 28+.

★2704★

TOP LIFE INSURANCE COMPANIES BY IN-FORCE TOTAL, 1997

Ranked by: In-force total, in thousands of dollars. **Number listed:** 250

1. Metropolitan Life Insurance Co., with $1,556,104,759 thousand

2. Prudential Insurance Co. of America, $933,737,148
3. Connecticut General Life Insurance Co., $542,866,330
4. Northwestern Mutual Life Insurance Co., $485,911,183
5. New York Life Insurance Co., $434,570,424
6. Transamerica Occidental Life, $425,146,832
7. Southwest Life & Health Insurance Co., $356,521,500
8. Primerica Life Insurance Co., $334,098,793
9. State Farm Life Insurance Co., $324,115,357
10. Aetna Life Insurance Co., $294,372,926

Source: *National Underwriter Life & Health/Financial Services*, Life & Health Statistical Review (annual), July 20, 1998, p. 30.

★2705★
TOP LIFE INSURANCE COMPANIES BY INDIVIDUAL LIFE PREMIUMS, 1997
Ranked by: Individual life premiums, in thousands of dollars. **Number listed:** 250

1. Northwestern Mutual Life Insurance Co., with $5,861,661 thousand
2. Metropolitan Life Insurance Co., $5,156,697
3. Prudential Insurance Co. of America, $5,129,945
4. New York Life Insurance Co., $3,942,496
5. Hartford Life Insurance Co., $3,210,947
6. Massachusetts Mutual Life Insurance Co., $2,692,539
7. Guardian Life Insurance Co. of America, $2,314,541
8. State Farm Life Insurance Co., $2,057,269
9. Equitable Life Assr. Society of the US, $1,975,631
10. Connecticut General Life Insurance Co., $1,450,620

Source: *National Underwriter Life & Health/Financial Services*, Life & Health Statistical Review (annual), July 20, 1998, p. 26+.

★2706★
TOP LIFE INSURANCE COMPANIES BY NET GAIN, 1997
Ranked by: Net gain, in thousands of dollars. **Number listed:** 300

1. Charter National Life Insurance Co., with $1,267,834 thousand
2. Teachers Insurance & Annuity Assoc., $1,113,712
3. Prudential Insurance Co. of America, $828,974
4. AGC Life, $626,225
5. Travelers Insurance Co. Life Dept., $551,001
6. Connecticut General Life Insurance Co., $548,122
7. Aetna Life Insurance Co., $478,226
8. John Hancock Mutual Life Insurance Co., $467,269
9. Equitable Life Assr. Society of the US, $455,796
10. American General Life Insurance Co., $452,826

Source: *National Underwriter Life & Health/Financial Services*, Life & Health Statistical Review (annual), July 20, 1998, p. 26.

★2707★
TOP LIFE INSURANCE COMPANIES BY NET INVESTMENT INCOME, 1997
Ranked by: Net investment income, in thousands of dollars. **Number listed:** 300

1. Prudential Insurance Co. of America, with $8,467,529 thousand
2. Metropolitan Life Insurance Co., $8,264,000
3. Teachers Insurance & Annuity Assoc., $6,823,042
4. Northwestern Mutual Life Insurance Co., $4,132,633
5. New York Life Insurance Co., $4,010,102
6. Connecticut General Life Insurance Co., $2,948,862
7. Equitable Life Assr. Society of the US, $2,927,743
8. John Hancock Mutual Life Insurance Co., $2,856,033
9. Massachusetts Mutual Life Insurance Co., $2,836,319
10. Principal Mutual Life Insurance Co., $2,799,007

Source: *National Underwriter Life & Health/Financial Services*, Life & Health Statistical Review (annual), July 20, 1998, p. 24+.

★2708★
TOP LIFE INSURANCE COMPANIES BY NET OPERATIONAL GAIN, 1997
Ranked by: Net operational gain, in thousands of dollars. **Number listed:** 250

1. Charter National Life Insurance Co., with $1,267,898 thousand
2. Teachers Insurance & Annuity Assoc., $1,137,906
3. Connecticut General Life Insurance Co., $838,930
4. Travelers Insurance Co. Life Dept., $750,878
5. Equitable Life Assr. Society of the US, $635,794
6. Northwestern Mutual Life Insurance Co., $630,570
7. American Family Life Association Columbus, $612,751
8. Prudential Insurance Co. of America, $598,337
9. AGC Life Insurance Co., $587,333
10. Massachusetts Mutual Life Insurance, $584,495

Source: *National Underwriter Life & Health/Financial Services*, Life & Health Statistical Review (annual), July 20, 1998, p. 25+.

★2709★
TOP LIFE INSURANCE COMPANIES BY PREMIUM INCOME, 1997
Ranked by: Premium income, in thousands of dollars. **Number listed:** 300

1. Metropolitan Life Insurance Co., with $20,568,907 thousand
2. Prudential Insurance Co. of America, $18,957,682
3. Connecticut General Life Insurance Co., $13,125,201
4. Principal Mutual Life Insurance Co., $12,710,851
5. Nationwide Life Insurance Co., $10,159,051
6. New York Life Insurance Co., $8,495,489
7. Equitable Life Assr. Society of the US, $7,843,147
8. Hartford Life Insurance Co., $7,540,292
9. John Hancock Mutual Life Insurance Co., $7,317,565
10. Northwestern Mutual Life Insurance Co., $7,294,047

Source: *National Underwriter Life & Health/Financial Services*, Life & Health Statistical Review (annual), July 20, 1998, p. 23+.

Insurance, Life--Detroit Metropolitan Area

★2710★
LEADING LIFE INSURANCE COMPANIES IN THE DETROIT METROPOLITAN AREA, 1997
Ranked by: Assets, in millions of dollars. **Remarks:** Also notes contact information, executive officer, types of Insurance in force, net income, capital and surplus, and previous year's figures. **Number listed:** 7

1. Alexander Hamilton Life Insurance Co. of America, with $5,507.2 million
2. Royal Maccabees Life Insurance Co., $1,998.9
3. American Community Mutual Insurance Co., $182.9
4. Auto Club Life Insurance Co., $156.6
5. Vista Life Insurance Co., $56.9

6. Mutual of Detroit Insurance Co., $54.5
7. Liberty Union Life Assurance Co., $4.7

Source: *Crain's Detroit Business*, Crain's Book of Lists Detroit (annual), December 28, 1998, p. 160.

Insurance, Life--Florida

★2711★
TOP LIFE INSURANCE COMPANIES IN FLORIDA, 1997

Ranked by: Life insurance premiums, in dollars. **Remarks:** Includes Florida or regional headquarters. **Number listed:** 25

1. Hartford Life Insurance Co., with $563,966,840
2. Kemper Investors Life Insurance Co., $534,588,882
3. Metropolitan Life Insurance Co., $324,098,592
4. Prudential Insurance Co. of America, $304,416,061
5. Northwestern Mutual Life Insurance Co., $226,624,797
6. Equitable Life Assurance Society of the U.S., $133,041,401
7. New York Life Insurance Co., $115,851,817
8. Connecticut General Life Insurance Co., $111,824,556
9. Masschusetts Mutual Life Insurance Co., $102,051,219
10. State Farm Life Insurance Co., $102,023,793

Source: *Florida Trend*, TopRank Florida (annual), 1999, p. 59.

Insurance, Life, International

★2712★
WORLD'S LARGEST MUTUAL PROPERTY AND CASUALTY INSURANCE COMPANIES BY REVENUE, 1996

Ranked by: Revenue, in millions of U.S. dollars ($). **Number listed:** 2

1. Nippon Life (Japan), with $72,575 million
2. Dai-Ichi Mutual Life (Japan), $49,145

Source: *Fortune*, Global 500 (annual), August 4, 1997, p. F21+.

Insurance, Life--Japan

★2713★
TOP LIFE INSURANCE COMPANIES IN JAPAN, 1998*

Ranked by: Assets, in billions of yen. **Remarks:** Includes Moody's rating, S&P rating, real hidden capital gains, cumulative back-spread losses and capital gains less spread losses. **Number listed:** 16

1. Nippon, with ¥42,210 billion
2. Daichi, ¥28,670
3. Sumitomo, ¥23,716
4. Mejii, ¥17,046
5. Asahi, ¥12,176
6. Mitsui, ¥10,902
7. Yasuda, ¥9,476
8. Taiyo, ¥6,826
9. Daido, ¥5,346
10. Kyoei, ¥5,246

Source: *Euromoney*, October, 1998, p. 56.

Insurance, Long-term Care

★2714★
LEADING INSURANCE COMPANIES IN LONG-TERM CARE PREMIUM REVENUE, 1996

Ranked by: Long-term care insurance premium revenue, in millions of dollars. **Number listed:** 10

1. ConseCo., with $567 million
2. GE Capital, $485
3. John Hancock, $192
4. CNA, $185
5. Aegon, $148
6. Travelers, $128
7. Penn Treaty, $120
8. Prudential, $83
9. IDS Life, $73
10. Fortis, $68

Source: *National Underwriter*, Life & Health/Financial Services ed., August 10, 1998, p. 3.

Insurance, Malpractice

★2715★
LEADING WRITERS OF MEDICAL MALPRACTICE INSURANCE, 1997

Ranked by: Premiums written, in thousands of dollars. **Remarks:** Also notes change from previous year and market share. **Number listed:** 20

1. CNA Insurance Group, with $408,539 thousand
2. St. Paul Cos., $401,363
3. MLMIC Group, $329,798
4. Health Care Indemnity, $265,746
5. Medical Protective, $230,710
6. American International Group, $208,251
7. Doctors' Co. Insurance Group, $203,726
8. Illinois State Medical Exchange, $196,101
9. MMI Cos. Group, $167,044
10. Medical Inter-Insurance Exchange, $163,858

Source: *Best's Review*, Property/Casualty ed., May, 1999, p. 66.

Insurance, Property and Casualty

★2716★
FASTEST-GROWING PROPERTY/CASUALTY INSURERS, 1997

Ranked by: Percentage growth in new premiums written. **Number listed:** 10

1. Centurion Insurance Group, with 150.5%
2. Risk Capital Reinsurance (NE), 99.7%
3. Amer Road Insurance Co., MI, 85.1%
4. Dorinco Reinsurance Co., MI, 79.2%
5. Paula Insurance Co., California, 59.2%
6. Health Services Group, 58.9%

7. Great Lakes Insurance Co., Ohio, 58.8%
8. QualChoice Health Plan, 47.2%
9. Amerisafe Insurance Group, 44.3%
10. Financial Securities Asr. Group, 42.8%

Source: *Best's Review*, Property/Casualty Insurance ed., July, 1998, p. 33.

★2717★
MOST ADMIRED PROPERTY AND CASUALTY INSURANCE CORPORATIONS, 1998
Ranked by: Scores (1-10) derived from a survey of senior executives, outside directors and securities analysts. **Remarks:** Respondents rated companies in their own industry on 8 attributes of reputation. Also notes previous year's rank. **Number listed:** 11

1. Berkshire Hathaway, with 7.86
2. USAA, 7.33
3. American International Group, 7.18
4. State Farm, 7.02
5. Allstate, 6.91
6. Chubb, 6.71
7. Hartford Financial Services Group, 6.66
8. Nationwide Insurance Enterprise, 6.32
9. Liberty Mutual Insurance Group, 6.23
10. St. Paul, 6.06

Source: *Fortune*, America's Most Admired Corporations (annual), March 1, 1999, p. F-1.

★2718★
SLOWEST-GROWING PROPERTY/CASUALTY INSURERS, 1997
Ranked by: Percentage decrease in new premiums written. **Number listed:** 10

1. Vesta Insurance Group Inc., with -40.0%
2. Riscorp Inc. Group, -35.9%
3. Coregis Group, -32.2%
4. American Express Group, -29.7%
5. PSM Insurance Cos., -28.9%
6. Empire Insurance Group, -21.3%
7. Royal & Sun Alliance Insurance PLC, -20.7%
8. HCC Insurance Holdings Group, -20.2%
9. ProMutual Group, -17.6%
10. Constit Reinsurance Corp. NY, -17.5%

Source: *Best's Review*, Property/Casualty Insurance ed., July, 1998, p. 33.

★2719★
TOP CORPORATIONS IN MUTUAL PROPERTY AND CASUALTY INSURANCE, 1998
Ranked by: Revenue, in millions of dollars. **Remarks:** Also notes profits and investment figures as well as number of employees. **Number listed:** 5

1. State Farm Insurance Co., with $48,114 million
2. Liberty Mutual Group, $13,166
3. Auto-Owners Insurance, $2,199
4. Sentry Insurance, $1,367
5. Harleysville Mutual Insurance, $1,181

Source: *Fortune*, Fortune 500 Largest U.S. Corporations (annual), April 26, 1999, p. F-63.

★2720★
TOP CORPORATIONS IN STOCK PROPERTY AND CASUALTY INSURANCE, 1998
Ranked by: Revenue, in millions of dollars. **Remarks:** Also notes profits and investment figures as well as number of employees. **Number listed:** 27

1. American International Group, with $33,296 million
2. Allstate, $25,879
3. Loews, $20,713
4. Hartford Financial Services, $15,022
5. Berkshire Hathaway, $13,832
6. Nationwide Insurance Enterprise, $13,105
7. St. Paul Cos., $9,108
8. USAA, $7,687
9. Safeco, $6,452
10. Chubb, $6,350

Source: *Fortune*, Fortune 500 Largest U.S. Corporations (annual), April 26, 1999, p. F-63.

★2721★
TOP GROUP PROPERTY AND CASUALTY INSURANCE COMPANIES BY NET PREMIUMS WRITTEN, 1997
Ranked by: Premiums, in thousands of dollars. **Number listed:** 400

1. State Farm, IL, with $34,841,764 thousand
2. Allstate Insurance Group, $18,128,635
3. American International Group, $10,883,751
4. CNA Insurance Group, $9,861,974
5. Farmers Insurance Group, $9,113,791
6. Nationwide Corp., $8,280,945
7. Travelers Insurance Group, $7,904,810
8. Liberty Mutual Insurance Group, $5,920,920
9. Hartford Fire & Casualty Group, $5,768,823
10. Zurich American Insurance Group, $4,960,126

Source: *National Underwriter*, Property & Casualty ed., July 27, 1998, p. 15+.

★2722★
TOP LLOYD'S PROPERTY AND CASUALTY INSURANCE COMPANIES BY PREMIUMS, 1997
Ranked by: Premiums, in thousands of dollars. **Number listed:** 10

1. State Farm Lloyds, with $793,034 thousand
2. National Lloyds Insurance Co., $27,262
3. Underwriters Lloyds, $25,826
4. Cedar Hill Assurance Company, $22,919
5. Service Lloyds Insurance Co., $19,185
6. Underwriters Lloyds, London, $15,785
7. Nationwide Lloyds, $14,458
8. American National Lloyds Insurance Co., $11,891
9. Metropolitan Lloyds Insurance Co. Texas, $6,758
10. Continental Lloyds Insurance Co., $5,670

Source: *National Underwriter*, Property & Casualty ed., July 27, 1998, p. 16.

★2723★
TOP PROPERTY AND CASUALTY GROUP AND INDIVIDUAL INSURANCE COMPANIES BY NET PREMIUMS WRITTEN, 1997
Ranked by: Premiums, in thousands of dollars. **Number listed:** 20

1. State Farm Group, with $34,841,764 thousand
2. Allstate Insurance Group, $18,128,635
3. American International Group, $10,883,751
4. CNA Insurance Group, $9,861,974
5. Farmers Insurance Group, $9,113,791
6. Nationwide Group, $8,280,945
7. Travelers Insurance Group, $7,904,810
8. Liberty Mutual, $5,920,920
9. Hartford Financial Servers Group, $5,768,823
10. Zurich America Group, $4,960,126

Source: *National Underwriter*, Property & Casualty ed., July 27, 1998, p. 10+.

★2724★
TOP PROPERTY AND CASUALTY INSURANCE COMPANIES BY PREMIUMS, 1997
Ranked by: Premiums, in thousands of dollars. **Number listed:** 50

1. State Farm Mutual Auto Insurance Co., with $25,222,883 thousand
2. Allstate Insurance Company, $18,117,314
3. State Farm Fire & Casualty, $8,004,456
4. Farmers Insurance Exchange, $5,639,910
5. Continental Casualty Co., $5,494,093
6. Nationwide Mutual Insurance Co., $5,069,003
7. Liberty Mutual Insurance Co., $4,559,575
8. Federal Insurance Company, $3,676,579
9. St. Paul Fire & Marine Insurance Co., $3,432,508
10. United Services Auto Association, $3,173,095

Source: *National Underwriter*, Property & Casualty ed., July 27, 1998, p. 10.

★2725★
TOP PROPERTY AND CASUALTY INSURANCE GROUPS, 1997

Ranked by: Net income. **Remarks:** Also notes realized capital gains, federal income tax, pretax operating income, pretax rate of return, after-tax return on equity and combined ratio. **Number listed:** 100

1. State Farm Group, with $3,580,573
2. Allstate Insurance Group, $2,519,576
3. Berkshire Hathaway Insurance Group, $2,124,342
4. The Hartford Insurance Group, $2,089,853
5. Nationwide Group, $1,873,034
6. American International Group, $1,251,675
7. Travelers Property Casualty Group, $1,132,723
8. CNA Insurance Group, $903,375
9. General Re Group, $903,077
10. St. Paul Cos., $900,926

Source: *Best's Review*, Property/Casualty Insurance Edition, December, 1998, p. 42+.

★2726★
TOP PROPERTY AND CASUALTY MUTUAL INSURANCE COMPANIES BY PREMIUMS, 1997

Ranked by: Premiums, in thousands of dollars. **Number listed:** 300

1. State Farm Mutual Auto Insurance Co., with $25,222,883 thousand
2. Nationwide Mutual Insurance Co., $5,069,003
3. Liberty Mutual Insurance Co., $4,559,575
4. American Family Mutual Insurance, $3,035,293
5. Lumbermens Mutual Casualty, $2,382,327
6. Auto-Owners Insurance Co., $1,477,186
7. Employers Insurance of Wausau & Mutual Co., $1,329,763
8. Nationwide Mutual Fire Insurance Co., $923,867
9. Amica Mutual Insurance Company, $869,494
10. Federated Mutual Insurance Co., $780,258

Source: *National Underwriter*, Property & Casualty ed., July 27, 1998, p. 11+.

★2727★
TOP PROPERTY AND CASUALTY RECIPROCAL INSURANCE COMPANIES BY PREMIUMS, 1997

Ranked by: Premiums, in thousands of dollars. **Number listed:** 40

1. Farmers Insurance Exchange, with $5,639,910 thousand
2. United Services Auto Association, $3,173,095
2. Erie Insurance Exchange, $3,173,095
4. California State Auto Association Inter-Insurance, $1,592,756
5. Interinsurance Exchange of the Automobile Club, $1,081,068
6. Auto Club Insurance Association, $955,964
7. Truck Insurance Exchange, $709,324
8. Fire Insurance Exchange, $660,093
9. Doctors Co. an Interinsurance Exchange, $217,815
10. Farmers Automobile Insurance Association, $150,756

Source: *National Underwriter*, Property & Casualty ed., July 27, 1998, p. 16.

★2728★
TOP PROPERTY AND CASUALTY STOCK INSURANCE COMPANIES BY PREMIUMS, 1997

Ranked by: Premiums, in thousands of dollars. **Number listed:** 750

1. Allstate Insurance Company, with $18,117,314 thousand
2. State Farm Fire & Casualty, $8,004,456
3. Continental Casualty Co., $5,494,093
4. Federal Insurance Company, $3,676,579
5. St. Paul Fire & Marine Insurance Co., $3,432,508
6. Government Employees Insurance Co., $2,922,534
7. National Union Fire Insurance Co. of Pittsburgh, $2,911,276
8. American Home Assurance Company, $2,848,410
9. General Reinsurance Corp., $2,541,050
10. American Re-Insurancey, $2,491,723

Source: *National Underwriter*, Property & Casualty ed., July 27, 1998, p. 12+.

★2729★
TOP PROPERTY/CASUALTY INSURERS BY CHANGE IN NET INCOME, 1998

Ranked by: Change in net income, in percent. **Remarks:** Includes figures for corporate and property/casualty operations regarding percent increase/decrease 1997-1998, consolidated revenue, combined ratio for 1997 and 1998, net premiums written, pretax underwriting income (loss), pretax investment income, and policyholders surplus. **Number listed:** 18

1. General Reinsurance Corp., with 139.4 %
2. Hartford Steam Boiler, 102.7%
3. Argonaut Insurance Co., 44.4%
4. Reliance Insurance Group, 42.3%
5. CIGNA Corp., 19.0%
6. Fremont General Corp., 16.5%
7. American International Group Inc., 13.0%
8. Travelers Property/Casualty Group, 8.6%
8. Old Republic International, 8.6%
10. Sentry Insurance, 2.6%

Source: *Business Insurance*, March 23, 1998, p. 24.

★2730★
TOP PROPERTY/CASUALTY MUTUAL INSURANCE GROUPS, 1999*

Ranked by: Net premiums written, in thousands of dollars. **Remarks:** Includes policyholders' surplus. **Number listed:** 10

1. State Farm Mutual Auto Insurance Co., with $18,824,217 thousand
2. Nationwide Mutual Insurance Co., $3,930,531
3. Liberty Mutual Insurance Co., $3,553,631
4. American Family Mutual Insurance, $2,506,040
5. Lumbermens Mutual Cos., $1,588,690
6. Auto-Owners Insurance Co., $1,173,289
7. Employers Insurance Wausau, $1,031,386
8. Nationwide Mutual Fire, $716,371
9. Anthem Insurance Cos. Inc., $688,035
10. Amica Mutual Insurance, $675,481

Source: *Best's Review*, March, 1999, p. 55.

★2731★
TOP PUBLICLY TRADED PROPERTY/CASUALTY INSURERS, 1997

Ranked by: Earned premiums, in thousand of dollars. **Remarks:** Includes stock market symbol. **Number listed:** 10

1. American International Group, with $22,346,680 thousand
2. Allstate, $20,106,000
3. CNA, $13,362,000
4. Hartford Financial Services, $10,323,000
5. Travelers Property/Casualty Group, $7,225,000
6. Chubb, $5,157,400
7. St. Paul, $4,616,460
8. Progressive, $4,189,500
9. SAFECO, $3,106,800
10. Reliance Group, $2,810,760

Source: *Insurance Advocate*, January 9, 1999, p. 29.

Insurance, Property and Casualty--California

★2732★
LARGEST PROPERTY/CASUALTY INSURANCE COMPANIES IN CALIFORNIA, 1997
Ranked by: Property/casualty premium volume, in millions of dollars. **Remarks:** Also notes contact information, premium volume earned, rating grades, California market share, writer, major business lines, headquarters, top local executive, and figures from previous year. **Number listed:** 25

1. State Farm Group, with $3,544.5 million
2. Farmers Insurance Group of Cos., $3,250.2
3. Allstate Insurance Group, $1,764.2
4. California State Auto Association, $1,557.2
5. American International Group, $1,254.5
6. Allianz Group, $1,210.8
7. Auto Club, $1,093.7
8. Mercury General Corp., $998.4
9. CNA Insurance Cos., $994.3
10. 20th Century Insurance Group, $901.8

Source: *Los Angeles Business Journal*, Book of Lists (annual), 1999, p. 55.

Insurance, Property and Casualty--Florida

★2733★
TOP PROPERTY AND CASUALTY INSURANCEURERS IN FLORIDA, 1997
Ranked by: Property and casualty insurance premiums. **Remarks:** Includes Florida or regional headquarters. **Number listed:** 25

1. State Farm Mutual Auto Insurance Co., with $1,767,128,943
2. State Farm Fire & Casualty, $948,677,368
3. Allstate Insurance Co., $900,690,242
4. Allstate Indemnity Co., $491,925,406
5. Nationwide Mutual Fire Insurance Co., $430,349,285
6. United Services Automobile Association, $288,178,709
7. National Union Fire Insurance Co. of Pittsburgh, $285,531,832
8. Progressive Consumers Insurance Co., $276,900,032
9. FCCI Mutual Insurance Co., $273,053,296
10. Progressive Express Insurance Co., $261,635,225

Source: *Florida Trend*, TopRank Florida (annual), 1999, p. 65.

Insurance, Property and Casualty, International

★2734★
WORLD'S LARGEST MUTUAL PROPERTY AND CASUALTY INSURANCE COMPANIES BY REVENUE, 1997
Ranked by: Revenue, in millions of dollars. **Number listed:** 2

1. State Farm Insurance Co. (U.S.), with $43,957 million
2. Liberty Mutual Group (U.S.), $11,670

Source: *Fortune*, The Global 500: World's Biggest Corporations (annual), August 3, 1998, p. F-21.

Insurance, Property and Casualty—Los Angeles County (CA)

★2735★
LARGEST PROPERTY AND CASUALTY INSURANCE COMPANIES IN LOS ANGELES COUNTY, 1997
Ranked by: Direct statewide property/casualty premium volume, in millions of dollars. **Remarks:** Includes premium volume earned, rating grades, California market share, writer, headquarters and top local executive. **Number listed:** 25

1. State Farm Group, with $3,544.5 million
2. Farmers Insurance Group of Cos., $3,250.2
3. Allstate Insurance Group, $1,764.2
4. California State Auto Association, $1,557.2
5. American International Group, $1,254.5
6. Allianz Group, $1,210.8
7. Auto Club, $1,093.7
8. Mercury General Corp., $998.4
9. CNA Insurance Cos., $994.3
10. 20th Century Insurance Group, $901.8

Source: *Los Angeles Business Journal*, July 13, 1998, p. 41+.

Insurance—Reinsurance

See: **Reinsurance**

Insurance--Surety and Fidelity

★2736★
LEADING WRITERS OF FIDELITY INSURANCE, 1997
Ranked by: Direct premiums, in thousands of dollars. **Remarks:** Also notes change from previous year, market share and adjusted loss ratios for current and previous two years, and percentage of total company premiums. **Number listed:** 100

1. CUNA Mutual Group, with $131,520 thousand
2. Chubb Group of Insurance Cos., $127,962
3. American International Group, $101,436
4. Travelers Property/Casualty Group, $96,730
5. CNA Insurance Group, $65,379
6. Zurich Insurance Group-U.S., $53,721
7. St. Paul Cos., $36,885

8. Hartford Insurance Group, $33,900
9. Reliance Insurance Group, $33,352
10. USF&G Group, $16,313

Source: *Best's Review*, Property/Casualty ed., September, 1998, p. 74+.

★2737★
LEADING WRITERS OF SURETY INSURANCE, 1997
Ranked by: Direct premiums, in thousands of dollars. **Remarks:** Also notes change from previous year, market share and adjusted loss ratios for current and previous two years, and percentage of total company premiums. **Number listed:** 100

1. American International Group, with $223,913 thousand
2. CNA Insurance Group, $218,129
3. Reliance Insurance Group, $192,983
4. Zurich Insurance Group-U.S., $183,024
5. United States F&G Group, $175,375
6. Travelers Property/Casualty Group, $144,917
7. St. Paul Cos., $134,738
8. Safeco Insurance Cos., $105,481
9. Allianz of America, $101,446
10. Amwest Insurance Group, $82,055

Source: *Best's Review*, Property/Casualty ed., September, 1998, p. 73+.

Insurance, Title--Florida

★2738★
TOP TITLE UNDERWRITERS IN FLORIDA, 1997
Ranked by: Total Florida income, in thousands of dollars. **Number listed:** 12

1. Attorney's Title Insurance Fund Inc., with $164,721 thousand
2. Commonwealth Land Title Insurance Co., $79,620
3. First American Title Insurance Co., $76,235
4. Chicago Title Insurance Co., $74,131
5. American Pioneer Title Insurance Co., $49,341
6. Lawyers Title Insurance Corp., $41,926
7. Stewart Title Co., $41,411
8. Fidelity National Title Insurance Co. of NY, $37,287
9. Old Republic National Title Insurance Co., $23,593
10. Ticor Title Insurance Co., $14,918

Source: *Florida Trend*, TopRank Florida, 1999, p. 64.

Insurance, Title--Los Angeles County (CA)

★2739★
LARGEST TITLE COMPANIES IN LOS ANGELES COUNTY, 1997
Ranked by: Total mortgages Insuranceured, in billions of dollars. **Remarks:** Includes market share, number of mortgages Insuranceured, refinance mortgages Insuranceured, sales mortgages Insuranceured, grant deeds issued, profile and top local executive. **Number listed:** 15

1. First American Title Co. of Los Angeles, with $6.4 billion
2. Fidelity National Title Insurance Co., $4.9
3. Chicago Title Insurance Co., $4.3
4. Commonwealth Land Title Co., $2.9
5. Stewart Title Co., $2.4
6. Old Republic Title Co., $2.3
7. North American Title Co., $2.2
8. Lawyers Title Co., $2
9. Investors Title Co., $1.7
9. Southland Title Corp., $1.7
11. Equity Title Co., $1.6

Source: *Los Angeles Business Journal*, Book of Lists (annual), 1999, p. 90.

Insurance, Workers' Compensation

See: **Workers' Compensation**

Interior Decoration

★2740★
TOP DECORATING MOTIFS IN TODAY'S HOMES, 1998*
Ranked by: Type of decorating as percent of total home decorating. **Number listed:** 5

1. Traditional, with 40%
2. Country, 19%
3. Contemporary/Modern, 18%
4. Eclectic, 9%
5. Other, 14%

Source: *Flooring*, July, 1998, p. 39.

Interior Designers--Los Angeles County (CA)

★2741★
LARGEST COMMERCIAL INTERIOR DESIGN FIRMS IN LOS ANGELES COUNTY, 1997
Ranked by: Billings, in millions of dollars. **Remarks:** Also notes contact information, profile, current projects, specialties, industries served, and top local executive. **Number listed:** 25

1. Gensler, with $14.2 million
2. Hirsch Bedner Associates, $8.9
3. Cole Martinez Curtis and Associates, $6
3. ISI, $6
3. HLW International, $6
6. Interior Architects Inc., $4.6
7. DMJM Rottet, $4.5
8. Hellmuth Obata & Kassabaum Interiors, $4.3
9. C&J Partners Inc., $3.7
10. Texeira Inc., $3.5

Source: *Los Angeles Business Journal*, Book of Lists (annual), 1999, p. 40.

International Reserves

★2742★
TOP WORLD FOREIGN-EXCHANGE RESERVES, 1998*
Ranked by: Market share, in percent. **Number listed:** 7

1. Dollar, with 57.1%
2. German mark, 12.8%

3. ECU, 5%
4. Yen, 4.9%
5. Sterling, 3.4%
6. French franc, 1.2%
7. Other, 15.6%

Source: *Economist*, November 14, 1998, p. 20.

Internet

★2743★
TOP INTERNET CELEBRITIES, 1998
Ranked by: Specific ranking information not given. **Remarks:** The most mentioned celebrities on the internet, after the release of the Starr report. **Number listed:** 10

1. President Clinton
2. Pamela Anderson
3. Madonna
4. Cindy Crawford
5. Gillian Anderson
6. Demi Moore
7. Jenny McCarthy
8. Monica Lewinsky
9. Bill Gates
10. Michael Jordan

Source: *Computerworld*, October 5, 1998, p. 90.

Internet Access Providers--Canada

★2744★
TOP INTERNET SERVICE PROVIDERS IN CANADA, 1999*
Ranked by: Specific ranking information not given. **Number listed:** 10

1. Sympatico
2. PSINet
3. Sprint
4. AOL Canada
5. Internet Direct
6. Netcom
7. Shaw@Home
8. TotalNet
9. MSN
10. Rogers@Home

Source: *Marketing*, January 25, 1999, p. 20.

Internet Access Providers--Great Britain

★2745★
TOP INTERNET SERVICE PROVIDERS IN THE UNITED KINGDOM, 1998
Ranked by: Dial-up account, in thousands of dollars. **Remarks:** Includes number of users. **Number listed:** 6

1. CompuServe, with $410.0 thousand
2. AOL, $385.0
3. Demon, $185.0
4. MSN, $130.0
5. BT Internet, $118.5
6. Others, $771.2

Source: *Financial Times*, October 27, 1998, p. 10.

Internet Access Providers--New Jersey

★2746★
TOP INTERNET ACCESS PROVIDERS IN NEW JERSEY, 1999*
Ranked by: Number of employees. **Remarks:** Includes address, phone and fax numbers, price per month, tech support, year founded, president and URL address. **Number listed:** 11

1. AT&T, with 118,000
2. OPENIX, Open Internet Exchange, 75
3. IBS Interactive Inc., 56
4. InterPow, LLC, 50
4. The Recom Group, Inc., 50
6. Planet Access Networks, Inc., 40
7. Cyber Warrior Inc., 35
8. US Online, 30
9. Cyber ENET-Kaps, Inc., 25
9. WEBSPAN, 25
10. Cybernex, 24

Source: *New Jersey Business*, Book of Lists (annual), 1999, p. 39.

Internet Advertising

★2747★
TOP INTERNET ADVERTISERS, 1998
Ranked by: Advertising expenditures, in millions of dollars. **Remarks:** Includes 1997 rank. **Number listed:** 10

1. Microsoft, with $34.8 million
2. IBM Corp., $28.5
3. Compaq Computer Corp., $16.1
4. General Motors Corp., $12.7
5. Excite, $12.3
6. Infoseek Corp., $9.3
7. AT & T, $9.2
8. Hewlett-Packard Co., $8.0
9. Barnes & Noble, $7.6
9. Datek Securities, $7.6

Source: *Advertising Age*, May 3, 1999, p. s18.

Internet--Investment Information

★2748★
LEADING OPERATORS OF FAVORITE FINANCIAL MANAGEMENT SITES, 1999*
Ranked by: Percentage of on line investors who use company's site most often. **Number listed:** 8

1. America Online, with 32.5%
2. Intuit, 13.5%
3. Yahoo, 10.8%
4. Charles Schwab, 6.1%
5. Fidelity, 3.5%
6. Microsoft, 2.9%
7. Nasdaq, 2.6%
8. Other, 28.5%

Source: *American Banker*, April 28, 1999, p. 16.

Internet Search Engines

★2749★
TOP INTERNET SEARCH ENGINES BY INTERNET USERS, 1998*
Ranked by: Percentage of internet users. **Remarks:** Includes percent non-internet users. **Number listed:** 8
1. America Online, with 60%
2. Netscape, 45%
3. Yahoo!, 44%
4. Microsoft, 43%
5. Excite, 11%
6. Alta Vista, 10%
7. Infoseek, 8%
8. Lycos, 7%

Source: *Business Week*, September 7, 1998, p. 72.

Internet Shopping

★2750★
FASTEST-GROWING ON-LINE BUSINESS TRANSACTIONS, 1998
Ranked by: Total on-line users, in percent. **Number listed:** 5
1. E-commerce, with 60%
2. Banking, 19%
3. Bill Payment, 12%
4. Investing, 9%
5. Haven't done transaction, 34%

Source: *Bank Systems & Technology*, September 11, 1998, p. 11.

★2751★
TOP CONSUMER PURCHASES THROUGH INTERNET ON-LINE STORES, 1997
Ranked by: Market share, in percent. **Number listed:** 5
1. Computer products, with 35%
2. Travel, 26%
3. Books & music, 7%
4. Gifts & flowers, 6%
5. Other, 26%

Source: *INC*, October, 1998, p. 19.

★2752★
TOP FEATURES COMPANIES OFFER TO THEIR INTERNET CUSTOMERS, 1998*
Ranked by: Percentage of companies conducting electronic commerce offering named feature. **Number listed:** 6
1. Link to manufacturer's Web sites, with 67%
2. Receive quotes, 64%
3. Access product availability, 44%
3. Receive order confirmation/shipping data, 44%
5. See specific customer pricing, 36%
6. Check on completed delivery, 28%

Source: *Industrial Distribution*, October, 1998, p. 70.

★2753★
TOP INTERNET SHOPPING SITES, 1999*
Ranked by: Ranked by Media Metrix. **Remarks:** Exact ranking figure not given. **Number listed:** 10
1. Bluemountainarts.com
2. AOL Shopping Channel
3. Amazon.com
4. eBay.com
5. Cnet Software Download Services
6. Barnesandnoble.com
7. Cdnow.com
8. Columbiahouse.com
9. Musicblvd.com
10. Valupage.com

Source: *National Real Estate Investor*, May, 1999, p. 78.

Internet Users

★2754★
TOP RESEARCH USES OF THE INTERNET, 1998*
Ranked by: Usage, in percent. **Number listed:** 10
1. Find technical information, with 90%
2. Find new product information, 83%
3. Communicate via email, 73%
4. Find science/technical news, 61%
5. Find business information, 54%
6. Find technical info from science journals, 52%
7. Research other organizations, 51%
8. Download software, 49%
8. Source/purchase equipment, 49%
10. Find conference information, 40%

Source: *R&D Magazine*, November, 1998, p. 21.

Intranets

★2755★
TOP REASON WHY INTRANETS ARE BOOMING, 1999*
Ranked by: Reason, in percent. **Number listed:** 7
1. Aggressive growth, with 37%
2. Distributed personnel, 22%
3. Leverage investment, 8%
3. Information overload, 8%
5. Product complexity, 7%
6. Increased competition, 5%
7. Other, 13%

Source: *Business Travel*, June 7, 1999, p. 14.

Investment Advisers

★2756★
TOP FINANCIAL ADVISERS ELECTRIC POWER, 1997
Ranked by: Amount handled, in thousands of dollars. **Remarks:** Also notes number of issues. **Number listed:** 10
1. Public Financial Management Inc., with $2,005,900 thousand
2. Public Resources Advisory Group, $780,820
3. Sutro & Co., $721,900
4. O'Brien Partners Inc., $619,100
5. Seagraves & Hein Capital Advisors, $442,000
6. Lazard Freres & Co., $280,900
7. Morgan Stanley Dean Witter, $214,600
8. Dunlap & Associates Inc., $166,200
9. Dougherty Summit Securities LLC, $147,900
10. Seattle-Northwest Securities Corp., $131,200

Source: *Bond Buyer Yearbook*, (annual), 1998, p. 177.

★2757★
TOP FINANCIAL ADVISERS ENVIRONMENTAL BONDS, 1997
Ranked by: Amount handled, in thousands of dollars. **Remarks:** Also notes number of issues. **Number listed:** 10
1. Lamont Financial Services Corp., with $1,108,900 thousand
2. O'Brien Partners Inc., $614,200
3. Samuel A. Ramirez & Co., $591,900
4. First Southwest Co., $453,400
5. Public Resources Advisory Group, $417,900
6. Public Financial Management Inc., $384,500
7. Florida Municipal Advisors Inc., $300,500
8. Seasongood & Mayer, $290,000
9. Municipal Advisory Partners Inc., $211,400
10. James T. Cavanaugh & Associates, $195,000

Source: *Bond Buyer Yearbook*, (annual), 1998, p. 161.

★2758★
TOP FINANCIAL ADVISERS FOR DEVELOPMENT, 1997
Ranked by: Amount handled, in thousands of dollars. **Remarks:** Also notes number of issues. **Number listed:** 10
1. The Knight Group, with $187,000 thousand
2. DLCO Financial, $144,900
3. R.V. Norene & Associates Inc., $134,600
4. Stone & Youngberg, $106,000
5. Public Financial Management Inc., $92,200
6. Sutter Securities Inc., $92,000
7. Stephens McCarthy Kuenzel & Caldwell, $85,800
8. Rideau Lyons & Co., $80,000
8. First Albany Corp., $80,000
10. Seattle-Northwest Securities Corp., $78,300

Source: *Bond Buyer Yearbook*, (annual), 1998, p. 169.

★2759★
TOP FINANCIAL ADVISERS FOR EDUCATION, 1997
Ranked by: Amount handled, in thousands of dollars. **Remarks:** Also notes number of issues. **Number listed:** 10
1. Public Financial Management Inc., with $1,756,100 thousand
2. First Southwest Co., $1,603,300
3. Stauder, Barch & Associates Inc., $1,431,900
4. Dain Rauscher Inc., $1,073,800
5. A.C. Advisory Inc., $1,000,000
6. Municipal Advisory Partners Inc., $752,600
7. Evensen Dodge Inc., $631,500
8. C.M. de Crinis & Co., $617,400
8. Annette Yee & Co., $617,400
10. Springsted Inc., $582,800

Source: *Bond Buyer Yearbook*, (annual), 1998, p. 113.

★2760★
TOP FINANCIAL ADVISERS FOR HOUSING, 1997
Ranked by: Amount handled, in thousands of dollars. **Remarks:** Also notes number of issues. **Number listed:** 10
1. O'Brien Partners Inc., with $2,610,200 thousand
2. CGMS Inc., $1,929,000
3. Evensen Dodge Inc., $1,853,500
4. Dain Rauscher Inc., $363,700
5. Seasongood & Mayer, $339,400
6. Wheat First Butcher Singer, $237,700
7. Commonwealth Capital Partners, $235,100
8. Public Resources Advisory Group, $188,000
9. MG McMahon & Co., $146,700
10. Springsted Inc., $97,700

Source: *Bond Buyer Yearbook*, (annual), 1998, p. 145.

★2761★
TOP FINANCIAL ADVISERS FOR TAXABLE ISSUES, 1997
Ranked by: Amount handled, in thousands of dollars. **Remarks:** Also notes number of issues. **Number listed:** 10
1. Public Resources Advisory Group, with $3,222,900 thousand
2. Public Financial Management Inc., $667,500
3. P.G. Corbin & Co., $507,500
4. O'Brien Partners Inc., $381,500
5. Evenson Dodge Inc., $371,100
6. Ponder & Co., $356,200
7. Seagraves & Hein Capital Advisors, $163,400
8. CGMS Inc., $156,800
9. Salomon Smith Barney Holdings, $144,700
10. Dain Rauscher Inc., $107,300

Source: *Bond Buyer Yearbook*, (annual), 1998, p. 185.

★2762★
TOP FINANCIAL ADVISERS FOR UTILITIES, 1997
Ranked by: Amount handled, in thousands of dollars. **Remarks:** Also notes number of issues. **Number listed:** 10
1. O'Brien Partners Inc., with $2,195,400 thousand
2. First Southwest Co., $1,956,100
3. Estrada Hinojosa & Co., $1,631,700
4. Samuel A. Ramirez & Co., $1,525,600
5. Dain Rauscher Inc., $1,480,500
6. Public Financial Management Inc., $1,218,400
7. Robert W. Baird & Co., $743,700
8. Carnegie Morgan Partners, $704,400
9. Public Resources Advisory Group, $609,800
10. P.G. Corbin & Co., $533,400

Source: *Bond Buyer Yearbook*, (annual), 1998, p. 137.

★2763★
TOP FINANCIAL ADVISERS HEALTHCARE, 1997
Ranked by: Amount handled, in thousands of dollars. **Remarks:** Also notes number of issues. **Number listed:** 10
1. Ponder & Co., with $4,076,700 thousand
2. Public Financial Management Inc., $897,300
3. First Southwest Co., $715,200
4. Killarney Advisors Inc., $471,700
5. C.M. de Crinis & Co., $428,700
6. P.G. Corbin & Co., $393,900
7. Kaufman Hall & Associaties Inc., $367,500
8. A.H. Williams & Co., $334,000
9. Price Waterhouse & Co., $226,600
10. M.E. Allison & Co., $210,400

Source: *Bond Buyer Yearbook*, (annual), 1998, p. 121.

★2764★
TOP FINANCIAL ADVISERS, 1997
Ranked by: Amount handled, in thousands of dollars. **Remarks:** Also notes number of issues. **Number listed:** 100
1. Public Resources Advisory Group, with $20,042,500 thousand
2. Public Financial Management Inc., $11,143,000
3. O'Brien Partners Inc., $8,834,500
4. First Southwest Co., $6,934,200
5. Evensen Dodge Inc., $5,777,300
6. P.G. Corbin & Co., $5,102,300
7. Ponder & Co., $4,231,400
8. Dain Rauscher Inc., $4,003,400
9. Estrada Hinojosa & Co., $2,478,100
10. Samuel A. Ramirez & Co., $2,117,500

Source: *Bond Buyer Yearbook*, (annual), 1998, p. 46+.

★2765★
TOP FINANCIAL ADVISERS PUBLIC FACILITIES, 1997
Ranked by: Amount handled, in thousands of dollars. **Remarks:** Also notes number of issues. **Number listed:** 10
1. Public Financial Management Inc., with $1,490,800 thousand
2. O'Brien Partners Inc., $609,500
3. Tucker Anthony Inc., $593,800
4. Kitahata & Co., $472,600
5. Municipal Advisory Partners Inc., $420,000
6. Seattle-Northwest Securities Corp., $338,500
7. Evensen Dodge Inc., $307,200
8. Fidelity Financial Services L.C., $228,500
9. Morgan Stanley Dean Witter, $216,900
10. First Southwest Co., $168,400

Source: *Bond Buyer Yearbook*, (annual), 1998, p. 153.

★2766★
TOP FINANCIAL ADVISERS TRANSPORTATION, 1997
Ranked by: Amount handled, in thousands of dollars. **Remarks:** Also notes number of issues. **Number listed:** 10
1. Public Resources Advisory Group, with $5,266,500 thousand
2. Evensen Dodge Inc., $2,013,900
3. Columbia Equity Financial Corp., $1,764,400
4. P.G. Corbin & Co., $1,585,900
5. Public Financial Management Inc., $1,264,900
6. O'Brien Partners Inc., $1,250,900
7. Piper Jaffray Inc., $1,072,700
8. First Albany Corp., $1,069,000
9. Cambridge Partners LLC, $934,100
10. First Southwest Co., $886,700

Source: *Bond Buyer Yearbook*, (annual), 1998, p. 129.

★2767★
TOP INVESTMENT ADVISERS BY ASSETS, 1999*
Ranked by: Assets, in thousands of dollars. **Number listed:** 2595
1. Barclays Global Investors, with $615,498,846 thousand
2. Fidelity Management & Research Company, $558,100,000
3. State Street Global Advisors, $459,408,137
4. Vanguard Group, $400,547,057
5. UBS Brinson, $387,000,000
6. Prudential Insurance Co., $365,150,779
7. J.P. Morgan Investment Management Inc., $316,193,000
8. Merrill Lynch Asset Management, $300,999,999
9. Capital Research & Management Co., $296,485,354
10. Putnam Investments, $294,056,318

Source: *Directory of Registered Investment Advisers*, Money Market Directories, Inc., 1999, p. 1675+.

Investment Banking

★2768★
TOP INVESTMENT BANKS ACCORDING TO CFOS AT S&P 500 FIRMS, 1998*
Ranked by: Percent who ranked firm as best. **Number listed:** 10
1. Goldman Sachs, with 22.5%
2. Morgan Stanley Dean Witter, 17.8%
3. Merrill Lynch, 14.8%
4. Salomon Smith Barney, 8.4%
5. J.P. Morgan, 7.7%
6. Credit Suisse First Boston, 6.4%
7. Lehman Brothers, 6.1%
8. Bear Stearns, 4.8%
9. Lazard Freres, 2.2%
10. Warburg Dillon Read, 1.5%

Source: *American Banker*, July 23, 1998, p. 29.

Investment Banking--Chicago (IL)

★2769★
LARGEST INVESTMENT BANKERS IN ILLINOIS, 1998
Ranked by: Number of banking professionals in Chicago. **Remarks:** Also notes contact information, chief investment bankers, value of mergers and acquisitions, and various financial figures. **Number listed:** 18
1. Merrill Lynch & Co., with 58
2. ABN Amro Inc., 55
3. William Blair & Co. LLC, 47
4. Credit Suisse First Boston Corp., 40
5. Donaldson Lufkin & Jenrette Securities Corp., 39
5. BT Alex. Brown, 39
7. Robert W. Baird & Co., 31
8. Salomon Smith Barney, 30
9. Houlihan Lokey Howard & Zukin, 24
10. Morgan Stanley Dean Witter & Co., 22

Source: *Crain's Chicago Business*, Top Business Lists (annual), 1999, p. 77+.

Investment Management Firms

★2770★
THE LARGEST TAX-EXEMPT ASSET MANAGERS
Ranked by: Tax exempt assets under management, in millions of dollars. **Number listed:** 105
1. Barclays Global Investors, with $462,566 million
2. State Street Global Advisors, $386,899
3. Fidelity Investments, $349,654
4. Bankers Trust Co., $228,153
5. J.P. Morgan Investment Management, $183,377
6. Mellon Bank Corp., $181,600
7. Capital Group, $176,580
8. Pimco Advisors Holdings, $157,200
9. Morgan Stanley Dean Witter, $153,895
10. Northern Trust, $153,593

Source: *Institutional Investor*, Institutional Investor 300, July, 1998, p. 108.

★2771★
TOP HOLDERS OF CASH AND EQUIVALENT POSITIONS
Ranked by: Holders of cash, in millions of dollars. **Number listed:** 100
1. Merrill Lynch & Co., with $194,888 million
2. Barclays Global Investors, $149,128
3. Capital Group, $116, 132
4. Franklin Group of Funds, $92,314
5. Brinson Partners, $82,000
6. State Street Global Advisors, $79,803
7. J.P. Morgan Investment Management, $59,392

8. Morgan Stanley Dean Witter, $53,924
9. Fidelity Investments, $50,770
10. Bankers Trust Co., $46,873

Source: *Institutional Investor*, Institutional Investor 300, 1997, p. 110.

★2772★

TOP INSTITUTIONS BY ASSETS WHEN ALL ASSETS ARE INCLUDED-INSTITUTIONS AND CLIENTS

Ranked by: Assets, in millions of dollars. **Number listed:** 10

1. Fidelity Investments, with $625,864 million
2. Barclays Global Investors, $504,600
3. Merrill Lynch & Co., $446,279
4. State Street Global Advisors, $398,682
5. Prudential Insurance Co., $370,000
6. Capital Group, $343,526
7. Metropolitan Life, $330,300
8. Mellon Bank Corp., $318,612
9. Bankers Trust Co., $317,753
10. Equitable Cos., $274,084

Source: *Institutional Investor*, Institutional Investor 300, July, 1998, p. 112.

★2773★

TOP INSTITUTIONS RANKED BY DEFINED-CONTRIBUTION PLAN, 1997

Ranked by: Assets, millions of dollars. **Number listed:** 10

1. Fidelity Investments, with $222.1 million
2. TIAA-CREF, $209.6
3. Merrill Lynch & Co., $105.1
4. Vanguard Group, $105.0
5. State Street Global Advisors, $90.0
6. Barclays Global Investors, $59.1
7. American Express Retirement Services, $39.7
8. Metropolitan Life, $39.1
9. Prudential Investments, $35.8
10. Principle Financial Groups, $35.6

Source: *Institutional Investor*, Institutional Investor 300, July, 1998, p. 112.

★2774★

TOP INSTITUTIONS RANKED BY DOMESTIC EQUITIES ASSETS

Ranked by: Equity Assets, in millions of dollars. **Number listed:** 10

1. Fidelity Investments, with $402,763 million
2. Barclays Global Investors, $264,160
3. State Street Global Advisors, $169,399
4. Capitol Group, $161,598
5. Bankers Trust Co., $157,272
6. Putnam Investments, $140,178
7. Mellon Bank Corp., $125,125
8. United Asset Management Corp., $122,359
9. Equitable Cos., $118,582
10. Vanguard Group, $107,652

Source: *Institutional Investor*, Institutional Investor 300, July, 1998, p. 113.

★2775★

TOP INSTITUTIONS RANKED BY DOMESTIC FIXED INCOME ASSETS, 1997

Ranked by: Income Assets, in millions dollars. **Number listed:** 10

1. Prudential Insurance Co., with $148,303 million
2. Morgan Stanley Dean Witter, $104,101
3. Scudder Kemper Investments, $101,920
4. Pimco Advisors Holdings, $94,125
5. Equitable Cos., $83,067
6. Metropolitan Life, $80,123
7. Merrill Lynch & Co., $74,692
8. J.P. Morgan Investment Management, $70,268
9. Fidelity Investments, $65,262
10. Mellon Bank Corp., $64,340

Source: *Institutional Investor*, Institutional Investor 300, July, 1998, p. 113.

★2776★

TOP INTERMEDIARY MANAGERS RANKED BY ASSETS, 1998

Ranked by: Assets, in millions of dollars. **Number listed:** 10

1. SEI Investments, with $36,100 million
2. Frank Russell Co., $34,200
3. Common Fund, $19,100
4. Diversified Investment Advisors, $19,000
5. Primco Capital Management, $18,825
6. Dwight Asset Management Co., $8,651
7. Morley Capital Management, $7,500
8. Strategic Investment Management, $5,651
9. Certus Asset Advisors, $5,008
10. ICMA Retirement Corp., $4,671

Source: *Institutional Investor*, Institutional Investor 300, July, 1998, p. 114.

★2777★

TOP MONEY MANAGERS, 1997

Ranked by: Total assets under management, in millions of dollars. **Remarks:** Also notes previous year's rank, previous year's assets, tax-exempt assets under management, and 1997 portfolio mix. **Number listed:** 300

1. Fidelity Investments, with $625,864 million
2. Barclays Global Investors, $485,771
3. Merrill Lynch & Co., $446,279
4. State Street Global Advisors, $398,682
5. Capital Group, $343,226
6. Bankers Trust Co., $317,753
7. Mellon Bank Corp., $313,431
8. Prudential Insurance Co., $298,286
9. .Morgan Stanley Dean Witter, $268,649
10. Equitable Cos., $262,837

Source: *Institutional Investor*, Institutional Investor 300, July, 1998, p. 88+.

★2778★

TOP OVERLAY MANAGERS RANKED BY ASSETS, 1997

Ranked by: Asset Managers, in millions of dollars. **Number listed:** 10

1. J.P. Morgan, with $23,364 million
2. Pareto Partners, $19,894
3. Standish, Ayer & Wood, $12,000
4. State Street Global Advisors, $11,616
5. BEA Associates, $8,789
6. First Quadrant, $7,526
7. Bridewater Associates, $7,417
8. Rampart Investment Management Co., $6,614
9. Bankers Trusts Co., $4,482
10. Clifton Group, $3,800

Source: *Institutional Investor*, Institutional Investor 300, July, 1998, p. 114.

Investment Management Firms--Rating

★2779★
FIRMS WITH MOST NEW NET ACTIVE DOMESTIC FIXED-INCOME, 1998
Ranked by: Domestic fixed income, in millions of dollars. **Number listed:** 10
1. Pacific Investments Mgmt., with $16,897 million
2. Morgan Stanley Dean Witter, $12,885
3. Western Asset Mgmt., $7,437
4. Chase Manhattan Bank, $7,329
5. Standish, Ayer & Wood, $5,283
6. State Street Global, $4,834
7. BlackRock, $4,476
8. Northern Trust Global Investments, $3,394
9. Mellon Bond Associates, $3,352
10. Morgan Grenfell Asset Mgmt., $2,795

Source: *Pensions & Investments*, Scorecard for Pensions Managers (annual), March 8, 1999, p. 23.

★2780★
FIRMS WITH THE MOST NEW NET ACTIVE DOMESTIC EQUITY, 1998
Ranked by: Active domestic equity, in millions of dollars. **Number listed:** 10
1. Putnam Investments, with $5,482 million
2. J.P. Morgan Investment, $4,994
3. Barrow, Hanley, Mewhinney & Strauss, $3,799
4. Mellon Equity Associates, $3,087
5. MFS Investments Mgmt., $2,650
6. American Century Investments, $2,637
7. Institutional Capital, $2,520
8. Boston Partners, $2,475
9. Goldman, Sachs, $2,155
10. LSV Asset Mgmt., $2,118

Source: *Pensions & Investments*, Scorecard for Pensions Managers (annual), March 8, 1999, p. 23.

★2781★
LARGEST GIC PROVIDERS, 1998
Ranked by: Tax-exempt assets, in millions of dollars. **Number listed:** 16
1. Principle Capital, with $15,857 million
2. New York Life, $11,958
3. Prudential Insurance Co., $8,838
4. State Street Research, $8,127
5. Metropolitan, $8,045
6. Travelers Insurance Co., $5,564
7. Continental Assurance, $4,500
8. Pacific Life Insurance, $3,000
9. Aetna, $1,546
10. AIG Global, $1,314

Source: *Pensions & Investments*, Largest Money Managers (annual), May, 1999, p. 92.

★2782★
LARGEST INVESTMENT MANAGEMENT FIRMS IN NORTH AMERICA BY ASSETS, 1999*
Ranked by: Assets, in thousands of dollars. **Number listed:** 2595
1. Barclays Global Investors, with $615,498,846 thousand
2. Fidelity Management & Research Company, $558,100,000
3. State Street Global Advisors, $459,408,137
4. Vanguard Group, $400,547,057
5. UBS Brinson, $387,000,000
6. Prudential Insurance Co., $365,150,779
7. J.P. Morgan Investment Management Inc., $316,193,000
8. Merrill Lynch Asset Management, $300,999,999
9. Capital Research & Management Co., $296,485,354
10. Putnam Investments, $294,056,318

Source: *Money Market Directories*, Directory of Registered Investment Advisors, 1999, p. 1675+.

★2783★
LARGEST MANAGERS OF DEDICATED/ IMMUNIZED BOND STRATEGIES, 1998
Ranked by: Dedicated/immunized bonds, in millions of dollars. **Number listed:** 25
1. Prudential Insurance Co., with $29,171 million
2. PIMCO, $12,846
3. State Street Research, $5,990
4. T. Rowe Price, $3,935
5. Fiduciary Asset Mgmt., $2,040
6. Brundage Story & Rose, $1,368
7. Hartford Investment, $912
8. Mellon Bond, $825
9. Barrow Hanley, $803
10. Aetna, $750

Source: *Pensions & Investments*, Largest Money Managers (annual), May, 1999, p. 96.

★2784★
LARGEST MANAGERS OF DEFINED CONTRIBUTION ASSETS, 1998
Ranked by: Defined contributions assets, in millions of dollars. **Number listed:** 25
1. Fidelity Investments, with $287,000 million
2. TIAA-CREF, $245,177
3. State Street Global, $134,224
4. Barclays Global Investors, $78,257
5. Vanguard Group, $67,468
6. Prudential Insurance Co., $57,600
7. Bankers Trust, $43,575
8. Capital Research, $43,500
9. Metropolitan Life, $40,000
10. Merrill Lynch, $39,100

Source: *Pensions & Investments*, Largest Money Managers (annual), Green Pensions, May, 1999, p. 90.

★2785★
LARGEST MANAGERS OF ENHANCED DOMESTIC INDEXED BONDS, 1998
Ranked by: Enhanced domestic indexed bonds, in millions of dollars. **Number listed:** 25
1. State Street Global, with $20,297 million
2. Ryan Labs, $11,270
3. Lincoln Capital, $9,836
4. Firstar, $6,295
5. Aetna, $5,236
6. T. Rowe Price, $4,495
7. Brundage Story & Rose, $3,549
8. BlackRock, $2,448
9. Morgan Stanley Dean Witter, $2,370
10. PIMCO, $1,057

Source: *Pensions & Investments*, Largest Money Managers (annual), May, 1999, p. 50.

★2786★
LARGEST MANAGERS OF ENHANCED DOMESTIC INDEXED EQUITY, 1998
Ranked by: Enhanced domestic indexed equity, in millions of dollars. **Number listed:** 25
1. TIAA-CREF, with $81,800 million
2. Barclays Global Investors, $21,563
3. Dimensional Fund Advisor, $15,669

4. PIMCO, $14,761
5. UBS Brinson, $5,293
6. Prudential Insurance Co., $4,705
7. TradeStreet, $4,339
8. American Express, $4,385
9. Mellon Capital, $3,546
10. Atena, $2,645

Source: *Pensions & Investments*, Largest Money Managers (annual), May, 1999, p. 50.

★2787★
LARGEST MANAGERS OF HIGH-YIELD BONDS, 1998
Ranked by: High-yield bonds, in millions of dollars. **Number listed:** 25

1. Loomis Sayles, with $5,710 million
2. Oaktree Capital, $4,573
3. PIMCO, $3,643
4. TIAA-CREF, $2,540
5. Credit Suisse Asset, $2,099
6. American General, $1,881
7. Prudential Insurance Co., $1,478
8. Legg Mason Inc., $1,269
9. Putnam Investments, $1,232
10. MacKay-Shields Financial Corp., $1,100

Source: *Pensions & Investments*, Largest Money Managers (annual), May, 1999, p. 98.

★2788★
LARGEST MANAGERS OF MUTUAL FUND ASSETS, 1998
Ranked by: Mutual fund assets, in millions of dollars. **Remarks:** Also notes value of equities and bonds. **Number listed:** 25

1. Fidelity Investments, with $694,900 million
2. Vanguard Group, $434,699
3. Capital Research, $273,000
4. Merrill Lynch, $244,400
5. Putnam Investments, $228,624
6. Franklin Advisers, $152,000
7. Wellington, $146,024
8. SSBiti, $129,953
9. Allinace Capital, $118,538
10. Dreyfus, $118,478

Source: *Pensions & Investments*, Largest Money Managers (annual), May, 1999, p. 64.

★2789★
LARGEST MANAGERS OF PASSIVE DOMESTIC INDEXED BONDS, 1998
Ranked by: Passive domestic indexed bonds, in millions of dollars. **Number listed:** 25

1. Barclays Global Investors, with $35,730 million
2. Mellon Capital, $9,762
3. State Street Global, $8,616
4. Mellon Bond, $7,628
5. Lincoln Capital, $5,455
6. Vanguard Group, $5,053
7. Hartford Investments, $4,712
8. Bankers Trust, $3,575
9. Prudential Insurance Co., $2,779
10. PanAgora, $1,783

Source: *Pensions & Investments*, Largest Money Managers (annual), May, 1999, p. 48.

★2790★
LARGEST MANAGERS OF PASSIVE DOMESTIC INDEXED EQUITY, 1998
Ranked by: Passive domestic indexed equity, in millions of dollars. **Number listed:** 25

1. Barclays Global Investors, with $264,020 million
2. Bankers Trust, $138,213
3. State Street Global, $129, 137
4. Vanguard Group, $54,478
5. Mellon Capital, $45,590
6. Northern Trust, $33,152
7. Alliance Capital, $18,664
8. Munder Capital, $11,758
9. Prudential Insurance Co., $7,499
10. Wilshire Asset, $7,481

Source: *Pensions & Investments*, Largest Money Managers (annual), May, 1999, p. 48.

★2791★
LARGEST MANAGERS OF PASSIVE INTERNATIONAL INDEXED SECURITIES, 1998
Ranked by: Indexed international securities, in millions of dollars. **Remarks:** Also notes value of equities and bonds. **Number listed:** 20

1. State Street Global, with $56,752 million
2. Barclays Global Investors, $40, 483
3. Bankers Trust, $21,324
4. Munder Capital, $3,135
5. Alliance Capital, $2,708
6. Axe-Houghton, $1,974
7. Mellon Capital, $1,488
8. PanAgora, $1,331
9. Prudential Insurance, $1,099
10. Vanguard Group, $1,053

Source: *Pensions & Investments*, Largest Money Managers (annual), May, 1999, p. 46.

★2792★
LARGEST MANAGERS OF PRIVATE EQUITY, 1998
Ranked by: Private equity, in millions of dollars. **Number listed:** 19

1. UBS Brinson, with $7,930 million
2. Abbott Capital Mgmt., $3,027
3. Horsley Bridge, $2,000
4. GE Investments, $1,754
5. First Reserve, $1,600
6. INVESCO, $1,000
7. Oaktree Capital, $680
8. Fortsmann-Leff International, $608
9. Prudential Insurance Co., $537
10. TCW, $265

Source: *Pensions & Investments*, Largest Managers Issue (annual), May, 1999, p. 100.

★2793★
LARGEST MANAGERS OF PRIVATELY PLACED BONDS, 1998
Ranked by: Privately placed bonds, in millions of dollars. **Number listed:** 13

1. TIAA-CREF, with $14,371 million
2. Principle Capital, $12,975
3. Prudential Insurance Co., $9,832
4. American General, $7,619
5. CIGNA, $6,437
6. Massachusetts Mutual Life, $2,104
7. John Hancock Mutual, $1,335
8. Fiduiary Capital Management, $974
9. Allmerica, $329
10. Capital Consultants, $206

Source: *Pensions & Investments*, Largest Money Managers (annual), May, 1999, p. 94.

★2794★

LARGEST MANAGERS OF VENTURE CAPITAL, 1998

Ranked by: Venture capital, in millions of dollars. **Number listed:** 9

1. Weiss Peck & Greer, with $214 million
2. T. Rowe Price, $205
3. Rothschild International Asset Mgmt., $204
4. Alliance Capital, $179
4. Prudential Insurance Co., $179
6. Pioneer Investments, $120
7. Advantus Capital, $107
8. QCI Asset, $7
9. UMB Bank, $1

Source: *Pensions & Investments*, Largest Money Managers (annual), May, 1999, p. 104.

★2795★

LARGEST MANAGERS, RANKED BY U.S. INSTITUTIONAL, TAX EXEMPT ASSETS MANAGED INTERNALLY, 1998

Ranked by: U.S. institutional, tax-exempt assets managed internally, in millions of dollars. **Number listed:** 100

1. State Street Global, with $403,030 million
2. Barclays Global Investors, $398;378
3. Fidelity Investments, $319,100
4. TIAA-CREF, $245,177
5. Bankers Trust, $230,236
6. Northern Trust, $154,858
7. J.P. Morgan, $150,422
8. PIMCO, $130,898
9. Prudential Insurance Co., $119,221
10. Alliance Capital, $112,956

Source: *Pensions & Investments*, Largest Money Managers (annual), May, 1999, p. 42.

★2796★

LARGEST MONEY MANAGERS ON WALL STREET, 1998

Ranked by: Tax exempt assets, in millions of dollars. **Number listed:** 6

1. J.P. Morgan Investment, with $121,409 million
2. Morgan Stanley Asset, $112,204
3. Merrill Lynch Asset, $72,600
4. Sanford C. Bernstein & Co., $47,594
5. Legg Mason Inc., $39,430
6. Goldman Sachs, $29,301

Source: *Investment Dealers' Digest*, September 7, 1998, p. 20.

★2797★

LARGEST OVERLAY MANGERS OF U.S. INSTITUTIONAL TAX-EXEMPT ASSETS, 1998

Ranked by: Tax-exempt assets, millions of dollars. **Remarks:** Also nots value of internal assets. **Number listed:** 48

1. J.P. Morgan Investment Management, with $27,638 million
2. Pareto Partners, $19,486
3. Standish, Ayer & Wood, $16,350
4. State Street Global, $14,316
5. First Quardrant, $6,851
6. Bridgewater Associates, $5,544
7. Clifton Group, $4,474
8. Credit Suisse Asset, $4,304
9. Record Treasury, $3,634
10. Northern Light, $3,538

Source: *Pensions & Investments*, Largest Money Managers (annual), May, 1999, p. 52.

★2798★

LARGEST TAX-EXEMPT ASSET MANAGERS, 1998

Ranked by: Assets, in millions of dollars. **Number listed:** 250

1. State Street Global, with $405,332 million
2. Barclays Global, $398,378
3. Fidelity Investments, $319,100
4. TIAA-CREF, $245,177
5. Bankers Trust, $230,236
6. Northern Trust, $165,096
7. J.P. Morgan Investment, $150,422
8. Vanguard Group, $141,522
9. PIMCO, $130,898
10. Prudential Insurance Co., $119,221

Source: *Pensions & Investments*, Largest Money Managers (annual), Green Pensions, May, 1999, p. 26.

★2799★

MANAGERS, HANDLING MOST NEW BUSINESS PASSED TO SUBADVISORS, 1998

Ranked by: New business passed to subadvisors, in millions of dollars. **Number listed:** 10

1. Northern Trust Global Investments, with $4,169 million
2. Commonfund, $1,600
3. Diversified Investment Advisors, $1,300
4. American United Life, $907
5. Frank Russell, $900
6. Munder Capital Mgmt., $799
7. Pacific Life, $533
8. CIGNA Retirement & Investment, $500
9. Lend Lease Real Estate, $438
10. Trust Fund Advisors, $293

Source: *Pensions & Investments*, Scorecard for Pensions Managers (annual), March 8, 1999, p. 24.

★2800★

MANAGERS, HANDLING MOST NEW GROSS NON-U.S. PENSION BUSINESS, 1998

Ranked by: New gross pension business, in millions of dollars. **Number listed:** 10

1. Barclays Global Investors, with $23,475 million
2. UBS Brinson, $19,146
3. State Street Global, $16,783
4. J.P. Morgan Investment, $12,729
5. Goldman, Sachs, $6,534
6. Chase Manhattan Bank, $6,085
7. Dresdner RCM Global Investors, $2,440
8. Bridgewater Associates, $2,017
9. Putnam Investments, $1,815
10. First Quadrant, $1,485

Source: *Pensions & Investments*, Scorecard for Pensions Managers (annual), March 8, 1999, p. 24.

★2801★

MANAGERS, HANDLING MOST NEW INDEXED BUSINESS, 1998

Ranked by: New indexed business, in millions of dollars. **Number listed:** 10

1. State Street Global, with $21,852 million
2. Northern Trust Global Corp., $6,408
3. Bank of New York, $2,452
4. Lincoln Capital Management, $1,619
5. Metropolitan Life, $1,288
6. World Asset Management, $799
7. Amalgamated Bank of N.Y., $698
8. Conning Asset Mgmt.., $525
9. Putnam Investments, $439
10. Mellon Bond Associates, $270

Source: *Pensions & Investments*, Scorecard for Pensions Managers (annual), March 8, 1999, p. 26.

★2802★
MANAGERS, HANDLING MOST NEW STABLE VALUE BUSINESS, 1998
Ranked by: New stable value, in millions of dollars. **Number listed:** 10
1. J.P. Morgan Investment, with $2,953 million
2. Pacific Investment Management, $924
3. American Express Financial, $592
4. Galliard Capital Mgmt., $518
5. Putnam Investments, $498
6. State Street Global, $337
7. American Century Investments, $160
8. Mentor Investment Group, $149
9. Forstmann-Leff International, $140
10. Standish, Ayer & Wood, $100

Source: *Pensions & Investments*, Scorecard for Pensions Managers (annual), March 8, 1999, p. 24.

★2803★
MANAGERS, HANDLING $1 BILLION TO $10 BILLION, WITH THE LARGEST NET DOLLAR GAIN, 1998
Ranked by: Net dollar gain, in millions of dollars. **Number listed:** 10
1. LSV Asset Mgmt., with $2,102 million
2. U.S. Trust Co. of New York, $2,100
3. Bridgewater Associates, $2,005
4. AXA Rosenberg Investment, $1,932
5. Conning Asset Mgmt., $1,912
6. Delaware International Advisors, $1,861
7. Westpeak Investment Advisors, $1,778
8. Starwood Capital Group, $1,620
9. Seix Investment Advisors, $1,408
10. Scottish Widows, $1,319

Source: *Pensions & Investments*, Scorecard for Pensions Managers (annual), March 8, 1999, p. 23.

★2804★
MANAGERS, HANDLING $1 BILLION TO $10 BILLION, WITH THE MOST NEW DOMESTIC BALANCED BUSINESS, 1998
Ranked by: New domestic balanced business, in millions of dollars. **Number listed:** 10
1. ASB Capital, with $356 million
2. Chicago Equity Partners, $179
3. Crestar Asset Mgmt., $154
4. Heitman Capital Mgmt., $114
5. Rorer Asset Mgmt., $78
6. Carl Domino Assoiciates, $73
7. Bear Stearns Asset Mgmt., $64
8. J&W Seligman, $60
9. Westwood Mgmt., $57
10. Legg Masson Capital Management, $51

Source: *Pensions & Investments*, Scorecard for Pensions Managers (annual), March 8, 1999, p. 24.

★2805★
MANAGERS, HANDLING $1 BILLION TO $10 BILLION, WITH THE MOST NEW DOMESTIC EQUITY BUSINESS, 1998
Ranked by: New domestic equity business, in millions of dollars. **Number listed:** 10
1. LSV Asset Mgmt., with $2,118 million
2. AXA Rosenberg Investment, $1,916
3. Westpeak Investment Advisors, $1,778
4. Atlanta Capital Mgmt., $1,230
5. Paradigm Asset Management, $1,000
6. Trinity Investment Management, $958
7. Legg Mason Capital Mgmt., $930
8. Chartwell Investment Partners, $853
9. J&W Seligman, $823
10. Aronson & Partners, $781

Source: *Pensions & Investments*, Scorecard for Pensions Managers (annual), March 8, 1999, p. 23.

★2806★
MANAGERS, HANDLING $1 BILLION TO $10 BILLION, WITH THE MOST NEW DOMESTIC FIXEDINCOME BUSINESS, 1998
Ranked by: New domestic fixed-income business, in millions of dollars. **Number listed:** 10
1. Seix Investment Advisors, with $1,408 million
2. John Hancock Funds, $1,401
3. Metropolitan West , $1,275
4. Bradford & Marzec, $1,221
5. Conning Asset Mgmt., $1,028
6. Starwood Capital Group, $935
7. Back Bay Advisors, $878
8. Talplin, Canida & Habacht, $626
9. Conseco Capital Mgmt., $598
10. Calvert Asset Mgmt., $587

Source: *Pensions & Investments*, Scorecard for Pensions Managers (annual), March 8, 1999, p. 23.

★2807★
MANAGERS, HANDLING $1 BILLION TO $10 BILLION, WITH THE MOST NEW INTERNATIONAL/GLOBAL BUSINESS, 1998
Ranked by: New international/global business, in millions of dollars. **Number listed:** 10
1. Delaware International Advisers, with $1,861 million
2. Scottish Widows, $1,319
3. Silchester International, $1,011
4. Global Asset Mgmt., $988
5. Marvin & Palmer Associates, $703
6. Sprucegrove Investments, $596
7. Acadian Assset Mgmt., $560
8. Montgomery Assset Mgmt., $535
9. Oechsle International, $465
10. Bridgewater Associates, $455

Source: *Pensions & Investments*, Scorecard for Pensions Managers (annual), March 8, 1999, p. 24.

★2808★
MANAGERS, HANDLING $1 BILLION TO $10 BILLION, WITH THE MOST REAL ESTATE BUSINESS, 1998
Ranked by: New real estate business, in millions of dollars. **Number listed:** 10
1. Westbrook Partners, with $1,242 million
2. Allegis Realty Investors, $842
3. Sentinel Real Estate, $798
4. Starwood Capital Group, $685
5. O'Connor Group, $640
6. Lowe Enterprises Investment, $598
7. LaSalle Advisors Capital, $487
8. TA Associates Realty, $370
9. Walton Street Capital, $292
10. Kennedy Associates, $253

Source: *Pensions & Investments*, Scorecard for Pensions Managers (annual), March 8, 1999, p. 24.

★2809★
MANAGERS, HANDLING OVER A $10 BILLION WITH THE MOST NEW DOMESTIC EQUITY BUSINESS, 1998
Ranked by: New domestic equity business, in millions of dollars. **Number listed:** 10
1. State Street Global, with $11,096 million
2. Putnam Investments, $6,028

3. J.P. Morgan Investments, $4,994
4. Northern Trust Global Investments, $4,890
5. Barrow, Hanley, Mewhinney & Strauss, $3,799
6. Mellon Equity Associates, $3,142
7. MFS Investment Management, $2,650
8. American Century Investments, $2,637
9. Institutional Capital, $2,520
10. Boston Partners, $2,475

Source: *Pensions & Investments*, Scorecard for Pensions Managers (annual), March 8, 1999, p. 23.

★2810★

MANAGERS, HANDLING OVER $10 BILLION, WITH LARGEST NET DOLLAR GAIN, 1998

Ranked by: Net dollar gain, in millions of dollars. **Number listed:** 10

1. State Street Global, with $31,750 million
2. Pacific Investments Management, $18,346
3. J.P. Morgan Investment, $15,643
4. Morgan Stanley Dean Witter, $12,716
5. Northern Trust Global Investments, $9,922
6. Putnam Investments, $8,860
7. Chase Manhattan Bank, $8,281
8. Western Asset Mgmt., $7,437
9. Standish, Ayer & Wood, $6,762
10. BlackRock, $5,037

Source: *Pensions & Investments*, Scorecard for Pensions Managers (annual), March 8, 1999, p. 23.

★2811★

MANAGERS, HANDLING OVER $10 BILLION WITH THE MOST NEW DOMESTIC BALANCED BUSINESS, 1998

Ranked by: New domestic balanced business, in millions of dollars. **Number listed:** 10

1. State Street Global, with $1,463 million
2. Norwest Investment Management, $299
3. Key Asset Mgmt., $258
4. Putnam Investments, $248
5. Mellon Equity Associates, $246
6. Allied Investment Advisors, $212
7. MFS Investment Management, $86
8. Aeltus Investment Mgmt., $70
9. Standish, Ayer & Wood, $57
10. Boston Partners, $52

Source: *Pensions & Investments*, Scorecard for Pensions Managers (annual), March 8, 1999, p. 24.

★2812★

MANAGERS, HANDLING OVER $10 BILLION, WITH THE MOST NEW INTERNATIONAL/GLOBAL BUSINESS, 1998

Ranked by: New international/global business, in millions of dollars. **Number listed:** 10

1. State Street Global, with $13,555 million
2. Bank of Ireland Asset Mgmt. (U.S.), $2,278
3. Lazard Asset Mgmt., $1,686
4. Morgan Stanley Dean Witter, $1,628
5. Dresdner RCM Global Investor, $1,570
6. Putnam Investments, $1,516
7. Schroder Capital Mgmt. International, $1,277
8. Standish, Ayer & Wood, $835
9. Chase Manhattan Bank, $644
10. American Century Investment, $579

Source: *Pensions & Investments*, Scorecard for Pensions Managers (annual), March 8, 1999, p. 24.

★2813★

MANAGERS HANDLING OVER $10 BILLION WITH THE MOST NEW NET DOMESTIC FIXED-INCOME BUSINESS, 1998

Ranked by: New net domestic fixed-income business, in millions of dollars. **Number listed:** 10

1. Pacific Investments Mgmt., with $16,978 million
2. Morgan Stanley Dean Witter, $12,885
3. Western Asset Mgmt., $7,437
4. Chase Manhattan Bank, $7,329
5. Standish, Ayer & Wood, $5,283
6. State Street Global, $4,994
7. Northern Trust Global Investments, $4,818
8. BlackRock, $4,476
9. Mellon Bond Associates, $3,622
10. Morgan Grenfell Asset Mgmt., $2,795

Source: *Pensions & Investments*, Scorecard for Pensions Managers (annual), March 8, 1999, p. 23.

★2814★

MANAGERS, HANDLING OVER $10 BILLION, WITH THE MOST REAL ESTATE BUSINESS, 1998

Ranked by: New real estate business, in millions of dollars. **Number listed:** 7

1. J.P. Morgan Investment, with $5,242 million
2. Metropolitan Life, $460
3. Lend Lease Rosen Real Estate, $72
4. American Century Investments, $66
5. State Street Global, $55
6. INVESCO, $8
7. Key Asset Mgmt., $5

Source: *Pensions & Investments*, Scorecard for Pensions Managers (annual), March 8, 1999, p. 24.

★2815★

MANAGERS, HANDLING $250 MILLION TO $1 BILLION, WITH THE LARGEST NET GAIN, 1998

Ranked by: Net dollar gain, in millions of dollars. **Number listed:** 10

1. Colonial Advisory Services, with $626 million
2. Trias Capital Mgmt., $545
3. Transwestern Investments Co., $422
4. Financial Mgt. Advisors, $384
5. Lend Lease Rosen Real Estate Securities, $338
6. Mastholm Asset Mgmt., $321
7. Chadwick, Saylor, $305
8. Santander Global Advisors, $288
9. Allegiance Capital, $281
10. Pzena Investment Mgmt., $274

Source: *Pensions & Investments*, Scorecard for Pensions Managers (annual), March 8, 1999, p. 23.

★2816★

MANAGERS, HANDLING $250 MILLION TO $ 1 BILLION, WITH THE MOST NEW DOMESTIC BALANCED BUSINESS, 1998

Ranked by: New domestic balanced business, in millions of dollars. **Number listed:** 10

1. Martin & Co., with $50 million
2. Lowe, Brockenbrough, $42
3. Meridan Management, $17
4. Ferguson, Wellman, Rudd, Purdy & Van Winkle, $14
5. Starbuck, Tisdale, $7
5. Holland Capital, $7
5. SSI Investment Mgmt., $7
8. Edgar Lomax, $6
9. Westcap Investor, $5

10. Towneley Capital, $4

Source: *Pensions & Investments*, Scorecard for Pensions Managers (annual), March 8, 1999, p. 24.

★2817★

MANAGERS, HANDLING $250 MILLION TO $1 BILLION, WITH THE MOST NEW DOMESTIC FIXEDINCOME BUSINESS, 1998

Ranked by: New domestic fixed-income business, in millions of dollars. **Number listed:** 10

1. Colonial Advisory Services, with $626 million
2. Trias Capital Mgmt., $545
3. Financial Advisors, $386
4. Allegiance Capital, $281
5. Hughes Capital Mgmt., $212
6. Legg Mason Real Estate, $130
7. Longfellow Investments, $127
8. Sage Advisory Services, $124
9. McKee Investment Mgmt., $100
10. Martin, $96

Source: *Pensions & Investments*, Scorecard for Pensions Managers (annual), March 8, 1999, p. 23.

★2818★

MANAGERS, HANDLING $250 MILLION TO $1 BILLION, WITH THE MOST NEW DOMESTIC NEW DOMESTIC EQUITY BUSINESS, 1998

Ranked by: New domestic equity business, in millions of dollars. **Number listed:** 10

1. Lend Lease Rosen Real Estate Securities, with $338 million
2. Pzena Investment Mgmt., $274
3. Eaglc Asset Mgmt., $237
4. Smith Asset Mgmt., $230
5. Sallus Capital Mgmt., $225
6. New Amsterdam Partners, $169
7. Edgar Lomax, $138
8. Kern Capital Mgmt., $126
9. Arnhold & Bleichroeder, $109
10. Edgewood Mgmt., $100

Source: *Pensions & Investments*, Scorecard for Pensions Managers (annual), March 8, 1999, p. 23.

★2819★

MANAGERS, HANDLING $250 MILLION TO $1 BILLION, WITH THE MOST NEW INTERNATIONAL/GLOBAL BUSINESS, 1998

Ranked by: New international/global business, in millions of dollars. **Number listed:** 10

1. Mastholm Asset Management, with $321 million
2. Santander Global Advisors, $288
3. Berger Associates, $261
4. Jacobs Asset Management, $180
5. SG Pacific Assset, $167
6. Foreign & Colonial Emerging Markets, $141
7. Gartmore Global Partners, $62
8. Newport Pacific Management, $30
9. Sit/Kim International, $20
10. Arnhold & S. Bleichroeder, $18

Source: *Pensions & Investments*, Scorecard for Pensions Managers (annual), March 8, 1999, p. 24.

★2820★

MANAGERS, HANDLING $250 MILLION TO $1 BILLION, WITH THE MOST REAL ESTATE BUSINESS, 1998

Ranked by: New real estate business, in millions of dollars. **Number listed:** 10

1. Transwestern Investments Co., with $422 million
2. Chadwick, Saylor, $305
3. Urdang & Associates Real Estate, $227
4. Boston Financial, $226
5. Timberland Investment Services, $150
6. Kensington Realty Advisors, $103
7. Hart Advisers, $90
8. American Realty Advisors, $74
9. Legg Mason Real Estate, $49
10. Dalton, Greiner, Hartman, Maher, $6

Source: *Pensions & Investments*, Scorecard for Pensions Managers (annual), March 8, 1999, p. 24.

★2821★

MANAGERS, HANDLING UNDER $250 MILLION, WITH THE LARGEST NET GAIN, 1998

Ranked by: Net dollar gain, in millions of dollars. **Number listed:** 10

1. Lend Lease Hyperion Capital, with $181 million
2. Emerald Advisors, $147
3. Oakbrook Investments, $103
4. SEB Asset Mgmt. America, $85
5. Groupama Asset Mgmt., $72
6. Alpha Capital Mgmt., $65
6. Rockhaven Asset Mgmt., $65
8. M.A. Weatherbie, $56
9. Gratry, $55
10. LM Capital Mgmt., $48

Source: *Pensions & Investments*, Scorecard for Pensions Managers (annual), March 8, 1999, p. 23.

★2822★

MANAGERS, HANDLING UNDER $250 MILLION, WITH THE MOST NEW DOMESTIC BALANCED BUSINESS, 1998

Ranked by: New domestic balanced business, in millions of dollars. **Number listed:** 7

1. Alpha Capital Mgmt., with $25 million
2. Stuyvesant Capital Mgmt., $14
3. Wilbanks, Smith & Thomas, $8
4. Marshall & Sullivan, $7
5. Groupama Asset Mgmt., $4
6. J.W. Burns, $2
6. Leonetti& Asssociates, $2

Source: *Pensions & Investments*, Scorecard for Pensions Managers (annual), March 8, 1999, p. 24.

★2823★

MANAGERS, HANDLING UNDER $250 MILLION, WITH THE MOST NEW DOMESTIC EQUITY BUSINESS, 1998

Ranked by: New domestic equity business, in millions of dollars. **Number listed:** 10

1. Emerald Advisors, with $147 million
2. Oakbrook Investments, $103
3. Groupama Asset Mgmt., $68
4. Rockhaven Asset Mgmt., $65
5. M.A. Weatherbie, $56
6. Constitution Research & Mgmt., $34
7. Mazama Capital Mgmt., $31
8. Alpha Capital Mgmt., $27
8. Stafford Capital Mgmt., $27
10. Ironwood Capital Mgmt., $25

Source: *Pensions & Investments*, Scorecard for Pensions Managers (annual), March 8, 1999, p. 23.

★2824★

MANAGERS, HANDLING UNDER $250 MILLION, WITH THE MOST NEW DOMESTIC FIXED-INCOME BUSINESS, 1998

Ranked by: New domestic fixed-income business, in millions of dollars. **Number listed:** 8

1. Lend Lease Hyperion Capital, with $181 million
2. SEB Asset Mgmt. America, $81
3. LM Capital Mgmt., $48
4. Greystone Capital Mgmt., $37
5. Caywood-School Capital Mgmt., $15
6. Alpha Capital Mgmt., $14
7. Eastover Capital Mgmt., $2
7. Wilbanks, Smith & Thomas, $2

Source: *Pensions & Investments*, Scorecard for Pensions Managers (annual), March 8, 1999, p. 23.

★2825★
MANAGERS, HANDLING UNDER $250 MILLION, WITH THE MOST NEW INTERNATIONAL/GLOBAL BUSINESS, 1998
Ranked by: New international/global business, in millions of dollars. **Number listed:** 2

1. Gratry, with $55 million
2. Irish Life Investment, $16

Source: *Pensions & Investments*, Scorecard for Pensions Managers (annual), March 8, 1999, p. 24.

★2826★
MANAGERS, HANDLING UNDER $250 MILLION, WITH THE MOST REAL ESTATE BUSINESS, 1998
Ranked by: New real estate business, in millions of dollars. **Number listed:** 1

1. Hancock Agricultural, with $33 million

Source: *Pensions & Investments*, Scorecard for Pensions Managers (annual), March 8, 1999, p. 24.

★2827★
MOST NEW NET PRIVATE-EQUITY, 1998
Ranked by: New net private equity, in millions of dollars. **Number listed:** 6

1. Lazard Freres Real Estate, with $640 million
2. UBS Brinson, $638
3. Abbott Capital Mgmt., $294
4. State Street Global, $250
5. Goldman, Sachs, $76
6. McKinley Capital Mgmt., $36

Source: *Pensions & Investments*, Scorecard for Pensions Managers (annual), March 8, 1999, p. 24.

★2828★
TOP HYBRID DEBT MANAGERS, 1998
Ranked by: Hybrid debt assets, in millions of dollars. **Number listed:** 10

1. LaSalle Advisors Capital, with $905 million
2. J.P. Morgan Investment, $316
3. Urdang & Associates, $219
4. AFL-CIO Building Investment, $201
4. Heitman Capital Mgmt., $201
6. L.J. Melody, $144
7. ASB Capital Mgmt., $128
8. GE Capital Investment, $107
9. Capri Capital, $86
10. Lend Lease Rosen Real Estate, $55

Source: *Pensions & Investments*, October 5, 998, p. 21.

★2829★
TOP INDEPENDENT REAL ESTATE ADVISORS, 1999
Ranked by: Tax-Exempt Funds, thousands of dollars. **Number listed:** 71

1. Lend and Lease Real Estate Investments, with $14,920,500 thousand
2. LaSalle Advisors Capital Management, Inc., $11,522,500
3. The RREEF Funds, $8,877,325
4. Heltman Capital Management Corp., $7,748,000
5. Clarion Partners, $6,176,075
6. AEW Capital Management, $5,558,651
7. Allegis Realty Investors, $4,724,998
8. Corporate Property Investors, $4,250,000
9. Westbrook Partners L.L.C., $4,200,000
10. CB Richard Ellis Investors, $3,693,959

Source: *Money Market Directory of Pension Funds and Their Investment Managers*, (annual), Money Market Directories, 1999, p. 1827.

★2830★
TOP INVESTMENT ADVISORS WITH $200 BILLION TO $20 BILLION IN ASSETS UNDER MANAGEMENT, 1998
Ranked by: Asset under management, in millions of dollars. **Number listed:** 30

1. T. Rowe Price, with $126,055 millions
2. Wellington Management Company, LLP, $125,080.0
3. PIMCO Advisors LP, $100,706.0
4. Templeton International, $94,903.8
5. Federated Investors, $90,625.0
6. MFS Asset Management, Inc., $70,147.6
7. Sanford C. Bernstein & Co., $69,844.2
8. Chancellor Capital Management, Inc., $61,799
9. Miller, Anderson & Sherrerd, $60,023.3
10. RCM Capital Management, LLC, $59,863.0

Source: *USBanker*, November, 1998, p. 44.

★2831★
TOP INVESTMENT COUNSEL FIRMS, 1999
Ranked by: Tax Exempt Funds, thousands of dollars. **Number listed:** 1240

1. Barclays Global Investors, with $526,191,474 thousand
2. State Street Global Advisors, $419,013,826
3. Fidelity Management & Research Co., $308,200,000
4. UBS Brinson, $268,977,00
5. J.P. Morgan Investment Management Inc., $215,541,000
6. Vanguard Group, $202,239,050
7. Pacific Investment Management, $125,623,000
8. Alliance Capital Management Company, $117,633,000
9. Capital Research & Management Co., $110,000,000
10. INVESCO, $98,935,719

Source: *Money Market Directory of Pension Funds and Their Investment Managers*, (annual), Money Market Directories, 1999, p. 1809.

★2832★
TOP MANAGERS ASSIGNING ASSETS TO OTHERS BY TOTAL EXTERNAL, 1998
Ranked by: Total External Assets, in millions of dollars. **Number listed:** 10

1. Vanguard Group, with $170,855 million
2. SEI Investments, $50,000
3. Frank Russell, $41,458
4. Dreyfus, $35,283
5. Aetna, $25,643
6. American General, $24,338
7. Diversified Investments, $23,000
8. Commonfund Group, $21,900
9. CIGNA, $19,025
10. Pacific Life, $16,318

Source: *Pensions & Investments*, Largest Money Managers (annual), May, 1999, p. 54.

★2833★
TOP MANAGERS BY TOTAL ASSETS , 1998
Ranked by: Assets, in million of dollars. **Number listed:** 250

1. Fidelity Investments, with $785,600 million

2. Barclays Global, $615,457
3. State Street Global, $495,100
4. Vanguard Group, $447,546
5. Morgan Stanley Dean Witter, $386,000
6. Bankers Trust, $361,000
7. Prudential Insurance Co., $334,243
8. SSBCiti, $327,025
9. J.P. Morgan, $316,193
10. UBS Brinson, $297,648

Source: *Pensions & Investments*, Largest Money Managers (annual), May, 1999, p. 40.

★2834★
TOP MANAGERS OF CONVERTIBLE SECURITIES, 1998
Ranked by: Convertible securities, in millions of dollars. **Number listed:** 25

1. Loomis Sayles, with $2,735 million
2. Oaktree Capital, $1,624
3. Capital Guardian, $1,398
4. Froley Revy Investments, $1,270
5. TCW, $1,066
6. Palisades Capital, $783
7. SSBCiti, $752
8. Acadian Asset Mgmt., $647
9. Nicholas-Applegate, $615
10. Calamos Asset, $597

Source: *Pensions & Investments*, Largest Money Managers (annual), May, 1999, p. 102.

★2835★
TOP MANAGERS OF MORTGAGE-BACKED SECURITIES, 1998
Ranked by: Mortgage-backed securities, in millions of dollars. **Number listed:** 25

1. TIAA-CREF, with $21,286 million
2. American General, $11,169
3. Barclays Global Investors, $8,127
4. Standish, Ayer & Wood, $7,489
5. New York Life, $4,921
6. Dodge & Cox, $4,815
7. Massachusetts Mutual Life, $4,777
8. Smith Breeden, $4,624
9. State Street Global, $3,671
9. Loomis Sayles, $3,671

Source: *Pensions & Investments*, Largest Money Managers (annual), May, 1999, p. 60.

★2836★
TOP MORTGAGE MANAGERS, 1998
Ranked by: Mortgage debt assets, in millions of dollars. **Number listed:** 25

1. TIAA-CREF, with $19,922 million
2. Principal Capital, $9,127
3. TCW, $8,816
4. CIGNA, $6,554
5. Prudential Insurance Co., $6,072
6. Starwood Capital Group, $2,000
7. John Hancock Mutual, $1,711
8. Bradford & Marzec, $1,573
9. New York & Life, $1,534
10. Union Labor Life, $1,199

Source: *Pensions & Investments*, Largest Money Managers (annual), May, 1999, p. 62.

★2837★
TOP REAL ESTATE EQUITY MANAGERS, 1998
Ranked by: Real estate equity assets, in millions of dollars. **Number listed:** 10

1. Lend Lease Rosen Real Estate, with $12,448 million
2. Prudential Real Estate Investors, $8,859
3. Heitman Capital Mgmt., $8,677
4. TIAA-CREF, $8,219
5. RREEF Funds, $7,495
6. J.P. Morgan Investment, $5,653
7. AEW Capital Mgmt., $4,869
8. Allegis Realty Investors, $4,707
9. LaSalle Advisors Capital, $3,855
10. INVESCO Realty Advisors, $3,613

Source: *Pensions & Investments*, October 5, 1998, p. 21.

★2838★
TOP REAL ESTATE EQUITY MANAGERS, 1998
Ranked by: Real estate equity assets, in millions of dollars. **Number listed:** 25

1. Lend Lease Rosen Real Estate, with $11,728 million
2. Prudential Insurance Co., $7,140
3. TIAA-CREF, $6,877
4. RREEF Funds, $6,815
5. Heitman Capital, $5,985
6. Allegis Realty Investors, $5,270
7. Westbrook Partners, $4,530
8. LaSalle Advisors Capital, $4,020
9. TA Associates Realty, $3,631
10. Sentinel Real Estate, $3,613

Source: *Pensions & Investments*, Largest Money Managers (annual), May, 1999, p. 56.

★2839★
TOP REAL ESTATE INVESTMENT ADVISORS BY TAX-EXEMPT ASSETS, 1998
Ranked by: Total tax-exempt assets, in millions of dollars. **Remarks:** Also notes breakdown between types of tax-exempt and taxable assets. **Number listed:** 50

1. TIAA-CREF, with $34,385 million
2. Lend Lease Investment Management, $13,844
3. J. P. Morgan Investment Management, $12,747
4. Prudential Real Estate Investors, $10,340
5. Heitman Capital Management, $9,645
6. RREEF-Funds, $8,877
7. LaSalle Advisors Capital Management, $7,724
8. AEW Capital Mgmt., $6,235
9. Westbrook Partners, $5,776
10. Allegis Realty Investors, $4,725

Source: *Pensions & Investments*, October 5, 998, p. 22.

★2840★
TOP REIT MANAGERS, 1998
Ranked by: REIT assets, in millions of dollars. **Number listed:** 10

1. LaSalle Advisors Capital, with $2,710 million
2. Westbrook Partners, $2,247
3. Morgan Stanley/Miller Anderson, $1,901
4. TIAA-CREF, $1,873
5. Cohen & Steers Capital, $1,398
6. RREEF Funds, $1,382
7. Clarion/CRA, $1,352
8. E.I.I. Realty Secruities, $1,296
9. Fidelity Investments, $963
10. INVESCO Realty Advisors, $812

Source: *Pensions & Investments*, October 5, 1998, p. 21.

★2841★
TOP REITS MANAGERS, 1998
Ranked by: REIT assets, millions of dollars. **Number listed:** 25

1. Advisors Capital, with $2,274 million
2. TIAA-CREF, $2,271
3. RREEF Funds, $2,247
4. Clarion Partners, $1,306

5. E.I.I. Realty, $1,287
6. Morgan Stanley Dean Witter, $945
7. Aetna, $786
8. INVESCO, $714
9. Heitman Capital, $693
10. Lend Lease Rosen Real Estate, $609

Source: *Pensions & Investments*, Largest Money Managers (annual), May, 1999, p. 58.

★2842★

TOP U.S. BANKS & TRUST COMPANIES, 1999

Ranked by: Tax-Exempt Funds, thousands of dollars. **Number listed:** 93

1. Bankers Trust Co., with $263,676,580 thousand
2. The Northern Trust Co., $163,326,660
3. Capital Guardian Trust Co., $76,029,963
4. First Chicago NBD, $46,765,000
5. First Capital Group, $37,800,000
6. Fiduciary Trust Co. International, $30,760,000
7. Fleet Investment Advisors, $30,401,000
8. Wilmington Trust Co., $19,016,204
9. Wachovia Asset Management, $16,608,000
10. The Bank of New York, $13,396,725

Source: *Money Market Directory of Pension Funds and Their Investment Managers*, (annual), Money Market Directories, 1999, p. 1823.

★2843★

TOP U.S. INSURANCE COMPANIES, 1999

Ranked by: Tax-Exempt Funds, thousands of dollars. **Number listed:** 29

1. Teachers Insurance & Annuity Assoc. College Retirement Equities Fund, with $236,000,000 thousand
2. Prudential Insurance Co. of America, $166,296,870
3. The Principal Financial Group, $50,000,000
4. Massachusetts Mutual Life Insurance Co., $49,583,000
5. Lincoln National Life Insurance Co., $30,814,000
6. New York Life Insurance Co., $24,000,000
7. Aid Association for Lutherans, $15,100,000
8. Nationwide Insurance Group, $12,790,300
9. Pacific Life Insurance, $8,945,410
10. Continental Assurance Co., $7,700,000

Source: *Money Market Directory of Pension Funds and Their Investment Managers*, (annual), Money Market Directories, 1999, p. 1825.

Investment Management Firms--Rating--Canada

★2844★

LARGEST INVESTMENT MANAGERS RANKED BY TAX-EXEMPTED FUNDS UNDER MANAGEMENT IN CANADA, 1999

Ranked by: Tax-exempt funds, in millions of dollars. **Number listed:** 48

1. Caisse de depot et placement du (Montreal, Quebec), with C$44,800,000 thousands
2. Phillips, Hager & North, Investment Mgmt., Ltd. (Vancouver, BC), C$16,158,115
3. Perigee Investment Counsel, Inc. (Toronto, OT), C$12,323,000
4. Jarislowsky, Fraser Limited (Montreal, Quebec), C$10,122,000
5. Sceptre Investment Counsel, Ltd. (Toronto, OT), C$9,426,973
6. RT Capital Management Inc. (Toronto, OT), C$9,109658
7. Beutel, Goodman & Co., Ltd. (Toronto, OT), C$7,649,000
8. McLean, Budden, Ltd. (Toronto, OT), C$7,081,690
9. Knight, Bain, Seath & Holbrook Capital Management, Inc. (Toronto, OT), C$7,029,543
10. Canagex, Inc (Toronto, OT), C$6,476,500

Source: *Money Market Directories*, Money Market Directory of Pension Funds and Their Investment Managers (annual), 1999, p. 1829.

★2845★

LARGEST MONEY MANAGERS IN THE CHICAGO AREA, 1998

Ranked by: Total assets managed, in billions in dollars. **Number listed:** 14

1. Brinson Partners Inc., with $286.0 billion
2. Northern Trust Global Investments, $228.7
3. Scudder Kemper Investments, $91.3
4. Van Kampen Investment Advisory Corp., $58.6
5. Lincoln Capital Management, $57.2
6. First Chicago NBD Investment Management Co., $56.1
7. PPM America Inc., $44.0
8. John Nuveen Co., $40.0
9. Bank of America, $29.4
10. Stein Roe & Farnham, $29.1

Source: *Crain's Chicago Business*, Top Business Lists (annual), 1999, p. 81+.

Investment Management Firms—Rating--Detroit Metropolitan Area

★2846★

LEADING MONEY MANAGERS IN THE DETROIT METROPOLITAN AREA, 1998

Ranked by: Assets under managementt, in millions of dollars. **Remarks:** Also notes contact information, figures for previous year and percent change, total amount of tax-exempt accounts, minimum account requirements, asset mix, and number of portfolio manager/analysts. **Number listed:** 20

1. First Chicago NBD Institutional Investment Management, with $52,601.0 million
2. Munder Capital Management, $40,339.0
3. World Assset Management, $14,416.4
4. Comerica Private Banking, $9,738.8
5. Loomis, Sayles & Co. L.P., $9,115.0
6. Michigan National Corp./Independence One Capital Management Corp., $2,865.0
7. Wilson, Kemp & Associates Inc., $1,670.1
8. Key Asset Advisors, $660.0
9. Beacon Investment Co., $564.7
10. Jay A. Fishman Ltd., $418.2

Source: *Crain's Detroit Business*, Crain's Book of Lists Detroit (annual), December 28, 1998, p. 152.

Investment Management Firms--Rating--Europe

★2847★
LARGEST EUROPEAN INVESTMENT FUND MANAGERS BY ASSET GROWTH, 1997
Ranked by: Increase in assets, in percent. **Remarks:** Also lists assets in local currency. **Number listed:** 98

1. Henderson Investor, with 249.5%
2. Credit Rolo Gestioini, 173.0%
3. Banque Populaire Asset Management, 138%
4. Zurich Group, 118.2%
5. UBS, 111.0%
6. Credit Suisse Group, 106.2%
7. Aberdeen Asset Managers, 101.4%
8. Bank of Ireland Asset Management, 100.5%
9. Sanpaolo Fondi, 98.1%
10. Bayerische Hypo- und Vereinsbank, 88.8%

Source: *Institutional Investor*, The Euro 100 (annual), October, 1998, p. 124+.

★2848★
TOP EUROPEAN INVESTMENT FUND MANAGERS, 1997
Ranked by: Total assets, in millions of U.S. dollars ($). **Remarks:** Also notes domestic equities, foreign equities, domestic fixed income foreign fixed income, property, cash, and other assets. **Number listed:** 11

1. UBS, with $734,600 million
2. Credit Suisse Group, $591,800
3. AXA Group, $531,000
4. Barclays Global Investors, $485,747
5. Zurich Group, $288,700
6. Deutsche Bank, $279,040
7. Amvescap, $257,239
8. Allianz AG Holding, $212,360
9. Dresdner Bank Group, $202,715
10. Prudential Portfolio Managers, $195,130

Source: *Institutional Investor*, The Euro 100 (annual), October, 1998, p. 115+.

Investment Management Firms--Rating, Foreign

★2849★
LEADING INVESTMENT MANAGERS OUTSIDE THE U.S., 1997
Ranked by: Total management assets, in millions of U.S. dollars ($). **Remarks:** Also notes domestic management, as well as foreign management. **Number listed:** 17

1. Kampo, with $821.57 million
2. Groupe Axa, $529.26
3. UBS, $485.50
4. Barclays Global Investors, $485.36
5. Credit Suisse, $334.50
6. Swiss Bank Corp., $334.00
7. Nippon Life, $316.69
8. Deutsche Bank Group, $235.42
9. Zenkyoren, $232.44
10. Allianz Group, $226.24

Source: *Euromoney*, Intersec 250 (annual), September, 1998, p. 70.

Investment Management Firms--Rating, International

★2850★
LARGEST MANAGERS OF ACTIVE U.S. ASSETS INVESTED ABOARD, 1998
Ranked by: Tax-exempt assets, in millions of U.S. dollars ($). **Remarks:** Also notes equities and bonds figures. **Number listed:** 25

1. Capital Guardian, with $44,811 million
2. Morgan Stanley Dean Witter, $36,836
3. Schroders, $26,447
4. UBS Brinson, $23,292
5. TIAA-CREF, $19,914
6. Rowe Price-Fleming, $16,369
7. Putnam Investments, $15,520
8. Bank of Ireland, $15,386
9. Scudder Kemper, $15,120
10. Grantham Mayo Van Otterloo, $13,065

Source: *Pensions & Investments*, Largest Money Managers (annual), May 17, 1998, p. 44.

★2851★
TOP GLOBAL ACCOUNT MANAGERS, 1998
Ranked by: Assets, in millions of U.S. dollars ($). **Number listed:** 53

1. UBS Brinson, with $13,608 million
2. Morgan Stanley/Miller Anderson, $10,016
3. Barclays Global Investors, $7,681
4. First Quadrant, $7,658
5. Prudential Insurance Co., $7,635
6. Putnam Investments, $6,690
7. Capital Guardian Trust, $5,947
8. Scudder Kemper Investments, $5,850
9. TIAA-CREF, $5,800
10. State Street Global Advisors, $5,114

Source: *Pensions & Investments*, International Money Managers (annual), July 13, 1998, p. 20.

★2852★
TOP GLOBAL INVESTMENT MANGAERS BY EXECUTION COSTS RANKED BY DIFFERENCES VS. E/M UNIVERSE
Ranked by: Execution costs ranked by difference vs. EM/ universe, in basis points. **Remarks:** Also notes principle traded in millions of U.S. dollars ($). **Number listed:** 20

1. Phillips & Drew, with 84.1 basis points
2. Mercury Asset Management, 54.7
3. Genesis Asset Managers, 41.7
4. Grantham, Mayo, Van Otterloo & Co., 39.8
5. Sanford C. Bernstein & Co., 34.0
6. Capital Research & Management Co., 29.6
7. Templeton Investment Mgmt. Co., 24.2
8. Bank of Ireland, 18.1
9. Schudder Kemper Investments, 17.2
10. Marathon Asset Mgmt., 16.8

Source: *Institutional Investor*, November, 1998, p. 55.

★2853★
TOP INTERNATIONAL ACCOUNT MANAGERS, 1998
Ranked by: Tax exempt assets, in millions of U.S. dollars ($). **Number listed:** 50

1. State Street Global Advisors, with $57,657 million
2. Barclays Global Investors, $38,703
3. Capital Guardian Trust, $37,850
4. Morgan Stanley/Miller Anderson, $27,333
5. Schroders, $23,571
6. UBS Brinson, $19,527

7. J.P. Morgan Investment Mgmt., $17,284
8. Bankers Trust, $15,282
9. Scudder Kemper Investments, $13,153
10. Rowe Price-Fleming, $13,112

Source: *Pensions & Investments*, International Money Managers (annual), July 13, 1998, p. 18.

★2854★
TOP MANAGERS OF INTERNATIONAL/GLOBAL OVERLAY STRATEGIES, 1998
Ranked by: Total overlay, in millions of U.S. dollars ($). **Remarks:** Also notes, underlying assets managed internally. **Number listed:** 21

1. Pareto Partners, with $16,003 million
2. State Global Advisors, $14,876
3. J.P. Morgan Investment Mgmt., $14,588
4. Bankers Trust, $7,206
5. First Quadrant, $6,234
6. Bridgewater Associates, $4,313
7. Record Treasury Management, $4,071
8. Rothschild International Asset Mgmt., $3,424
9. BEA Associates, $3,241
10. Standish, Ayer & Wood, $2,726

Source: *Pensions & Investments*, International Money Managers (annual), July 13, 1998, p. 26.

★2855★
TOP MONEY MANAGERS WORLDWIDE BY ASSETS, 1998
Ranked by: Assets, in millions of U.S. dollars ($). **Number listed:** 179

1. State Street Global Advisors, with $63,090 million
2. Barclays Global Investors, $46,384
3. Capital Guardian Trust, $43,797
4. Morgan Stanley/Miller Anderson, $37,349
5. UBS Brinson, $33,135
6. Schroders, $24,116
7. Scudder Kemper Investments, $19,003
8. Bankers Trust, $18,906
9. J.P. Morgan Investment Mgmt., $18,868
10. Putnam Investments, $17,631

Source: *Pensions & Investment*, International Money Managers (annual), July 13, 1998, p. 17.

★2856★
TOP MONEY MANAGERS WORLDWIDE BY ASSETS, 1997
Ranked by: Assets, in millions of U.S. dollars ($). **Number listed:** 500

1. Kampo, with $785,517 million
2. Fidelity Investments, $635,000
3. Groupe AXA, $531,000
4. Barclays Global Investors, $485,771
5. Merrill Lynch Asset Management, $446,279
6. Union Bank of Switzerland, $431,250
7. State Street Global Advisors, $398,682
8. Prudential Insurance Co. (America), $370,000
9. Swiss Bank Corp., $368,000
10. Vanguard Group, $348,436

Source: *Pensions & Investments*, P&I/Watson World 500, July 27, 1998, p. 16+.

★2857★
TOP NYSE INVESTMENT MANAGERS BY EXECUTION COSTS RANKED BY DIFFERENCE VS. E/M UNIVERSE, 1998
Ranked by: Execution costs ranked by difference vs. EM/ universe, in basis points. **Remarks:** Also notes principle traded in millions of U.S. dollars ($). **Number listed:** 20

1. Barrow, Hanley, Mewhinney & Strauss, with 52.7 basis points
2. Ark Asset Mgmt., 41.6
3. Alliance Capital Management Co., 33.4
4. Trinity Investment Mgmt. Corp., 29.9
5. First Quadrant, 25.6
6. Goldman Sachs Asset Mgmt., 25.0
7. Capital Research & Mgmt., 24.5
8. Miller Anderson & Sherrerd, 20.1
9. J.P. Morgan, 19.8
10. CIBC Oppenheimer, 18.6

Source: *Institutional Investor*, November, 1998, p. 55.

★2858★
TOP U.S. OTC INVESTMENT MANAGERS, 1998
Ranked by: Execution costs ranked by difference vs. EM/ universe, in basis points. **Remarks:** Also notes principle traded in millions of U.S. dollars ($). **Number listed:** 20

1. Alliance Capital Management Co., with 84.2 basis points
2. Wellington Management Co., 79.2
3. Peregrine Capital Management, 76.5
4. Capital Research & Managment Co., 65.3
5. Ark Asset Management Co., 64.6
6. Massachusetts Financial Services, 62.4
7. Chancellor LGT Asset Management, 49.1
8. Numeric Investors, 41.0
9. First Quadrant, 40.0
10. Mellon Capital Management, 34.1

Source: *Institutional Investor*, November, 1998, p. 55.

Investment Management Firms—Rating--Los Angeles County (CA)

★2859★
LEADING INVESTMENT MANAGEMENT FIRMS IN LOS ANGLES COUNTY, 1998
Ranked by: Assets managed, in billions of dollars. **Remarks:** Also notes contact information, products offered, minimum separate account requirements, foreign assets managed, staff figures, key executives, and figures for previous year. **Number listed:** 25

1. Capital Research & Management Co., with $296.5 billion
2. Capital Guardian Trust Co., $81.3
3. TCW Group, $54.5
4. Dimensional Fund Advisors Inc., $27.9
5. First Quadrant LP, $26.7
5. Payden & Rygel, $26.7
7. Boston Co. Asset Management Inc., $22.3
8. Provident Investment Counsel Inc., $20.4
9. HighMark Capital Management Inc., $17.7
10. Hotchkis & Wiley, $14.4

Source: *Los Angeles Business Journal*, (annual), June 14, 1999, p. 54.

Investment Management Firms—Rating--Philadelphia Metropolitan Area

★2860★
LARGEST INVESTMENT MANAGERS IN THE PHILADELPHIA METROPOLITAN AREA, 1998
Ranked by: Institutional assets under management, in millions of dollars. **Remarks:** Also notes contact information, number of institutional clients, number of employees, number of offices, largest equity, holdings, type of organization, CEO, CIO, and year founded. **Number listed:** 25

1. The Vanguard Group, with $280,000 million
2. Miller, Anderson & Sherrerd, $126,600
3. SEI Investments, $124,000
4. Legg Mason Inc., $50,000
5. Mellon Bond Associates, $47,000
6. Wellington Management Co. LLP, $43,320
7. Delaware Investments, $26,100
8. Pilgrim Baxter & Associates, $16,395
9. Morgan Grenfell Capital Mgmt., $7,681
10. The Glenmede Trust Co., $6,500

Source: *Book of Business Lists*, (annual), Philadelphia Business Journal, 1999, p. 27.

Investment Trusts

See: **Mutual Funds**

Investments, Foreign--China

★2861★
TOP COUNTRIES INVESTING IN CHINA, 1997
Ranked by: Investments, in billions of U.S. dollars ($). **Number listed:** 5

1. Hong Kong, with $18.2 billion
2. United States, $4.9
3. Japan, $3.4
4. Taiwan, $2.8
5. Others, $22.4

Source: *Metal Center News*, January, 1999, p. 43.

Investments, Foreign--Great Britain

★2862★
TOP FOREIGN JOBS SAFEGUARDED IN THE UNITED KINGDOM, 1997-1998
Ranked by: Total number of jobs safeguarded. **Number listed:** 9

1. United States, with 40,509
2. France, 7,161
3. Germany, 5,786
4. Switzerland, 5,472
5. Netherlands, 3,461
6. Canada, 3,320
7. Japan, 2,568
8. Taiwan, 1,085
9. Sweden, 467
10. Denmark, 235

Source: *Financial Times*, July 16, 1998, p. 7.

Investments, Foreign--United States

★2863★
COUNTRIES WITH THE HIGHEST STAKE IN LARGE U.S. BUSINESSES, 1997
Ranked by: Revenue, in billions of U.S. dollars ($). **Remarks:** Also notes number of investments. **Number listed:** 15

1. United Kingdom, with $174 billion
2. Germany, $113
3. Netherlands, $104
3. Japan, $104
5. Switzerland, $60
6. Canada, $44
7. France, $34
8. Belgium, $19
9. Sweden, $18
10. Venezuela, $14

Source: *Forbes*, Forbes Foreign Rankings (annual), July 27, 1998, p. 166.

★2864★
TOP FOREIGN INVESTORS IN THE U.S., 1997
Ranked by: Revenue, in millions of U.S. dollars ($). **Remarks:** Also notes U.S. investments, percent owned, type of industry, net income, and assets. **Number listed:** 100

1. Royal Dutch/Shell Group, with $28,268 million
2. British Telecommunications, $19,653
3. Sony, $18,825
4. Diageo Plc, $18,000
5. British Petroleum Plc, $16,765
6. Toyota Motor, $15,600 estimated
7. Royal Ahold NV, $14,291
8. Petroleos de Venezuela SA, $13,645
9. Matshushita Electric Industrial, $13,593
10. BG Plc, $13,378

Source: *Forbes*, Forbes Foreign Rankings (annual), July 27, 1998, p. 167+.

IPO's (Initial Public Offerings)

See: **Securities--Initial Public Offerings**

Irish Stock Exchange

★2865★
LARGEST LISTED COMPANIES ON THE IRISH STOCK EXCHANGE, 1997
Ranked by: Market value, in millions of dollars of Irish pounds. **Number listed:** 20

1. AIB, with IR£5,790 million
2. Bank of Ireland, IR£5,544
3. Elan Corporation, IR£3,558
4. CRH, IR£3,154
5. Smurfit, IR£2,155
6. Irish Life, IR£1,271
7. Kerry Group, IR£1,231

8. Independent Newspaper, IR£955
9. NIE, IR£861
10. Avonmore, IR£752

Source: *Euromoney Publications*, SSB Guide to World Equity Markets (annual), 1998, p. 252.

★2866★
MOST ACTIVELY TRADED SHARES ON THE IRISH STOCK EXCHANGE, 1997
Ranked by: Turnover value, in millions of Irish pounds. **Number listed:** 20

1. Bank of Ireland, with IR£4,178.66 million
2. AIB, IR£3,977.82
3. CRH, IR£2,455.35
4. Smurfit, IR£1,965.33
5. Irish Life, IR£1,278.96
6. Tullow Oil, IR£1,153.83
7. Greencore, IR£1,095.343
8. Dana Petroleum, IR£670.27
9. Independent Newspapers, IR£515.27
10. Irish Permanent, IR£450.10

Source: *Euromoney Publications*, SSB Guide to World Equity Markets (annual), 1998, p. 252.

Iron Oxides

★2867★
LEADING WORLDWIDE CONSUMERS OF IRON OXIDE, 1996
Ranked by: World market share, in percent. **Number listed:** 5

1. Europe, with 47%
2. North America, 24%
3. Asia-Pacific, 15%
4. Africa, 8%
5. Central/South America, 6%

Source: *Chemical Market Reporter*, September 3, 1998, p. 12.

Irons

See: **Electric Irons**

Istanbul Stock Exchange

★2868★
LARGEST LISTED COMPANIES ON THE ISTANBUL STOCK EXCHANGE, 1997
Ranked by: Market value, in billions of Turkish lira. **Number listed:** 20

1. T Is Bank, with 1,898,738 billion
2. Akbank, 912,500
3. Koc Holding, 637,500
4. Tupras, 702,669
5. Sabanci Holding, 637,500
6. Yapy kredi Bankasi, 474,525
7. T Garanti Bankasi, 410,000
8. Turk Hava Yollari, 365,000
9. Petrol Ofisi, 346,500
10. Petkim, 337,500

Source: *Euromoney Publications*, SSB Guide to World Equity Markets (annual), 1997, p. 510.

★2869★
MOST ACTIVELY TRADED SHARES ON THE ISTANBUL STOCK EXCHANGE, 1997
Ranked by: Volume, in millions of shares. **Number listed:** 20

1. Eregli Dernir Celik, with 500,211 million
2. Cukurova Elektrik, 470,397
3. Dogan Holding, 441,808
4. Tupras, 321,924
5. T Is Bank, 272,192
6. Sabanci Holding, 267,242
7. Aktas Elekritk, 248,472
8. Tofas Fobrika, 225,510
9. Ihlas Holding, 192,171
10. Alcatel Teletas, 187,649

Source: *Euromoney Publications*, SSB Guide to World Equity Markets (annual), 1998, p. 510.

Italian Stock Exchange

★2870★
HIGHEST CAPITALIZATION COMPANIES ON THE ITALIAN STOCK EXCHANGE, 1997
Ranked by: Makret value, in billions of Italian lira. **Number listed:** 20

1. Eni, with Lr80,904.0 billion
2. Telecom Italia, Lr75,548.2
3. Telecom Italia Mobile, Lr62,231.2
4. Generali, Lr38,339.2
5. Fiat, Lr24,054.2
6. Credito Italiano, Lr15,794.8
7. INA, Lr14,472.0
8. San Paolo Torino, Lr13,849.8
9. Banco Amborsiano Veneto, Lr12,621.5
10. IMI, Lr12,585.0

Source: *Euromoney Publications*, SSB Guide to World Equity Markets (annual), 1998, p. 268.

★2871★
MOST ACTIVELY TRADED SHARES ON THE ITALIAN STOCK EXCHANGE, 1997
Ranked by: Market value, in billions of Italian lira. **Number listed:** 20

1. Eni, with Lr38,261.8 billion
2. Telecom Italia, Lr36,255.2
3. Generali, Lr22,263.5
4. Telecom Italia Mobile, Lr19,734.5
5. Fiat, Lr17,570.4
6. Credito Italiano, Lr12,839
7. Telecom Italia Rsp, Lr11,373.0
8. Banca Commerciale Italiana, Lr10,185.0
9. Telecom Italia, Lr9,844.6
10. Montedison, Lr8,709.1

Source: *Euromoney Publications*, SSB Guide to World Equity Markets (annual), 1998, p. 268.

Jakarta Stock Exchange

★2872★
MOST ACTIVELY TRADED SHARES ON THE JAKARTA STOCK EXCHANGE, 1997
Ranked by: Total trading volume, in billions of Indonesian Rupiah. **Number listed:** 20
1. Telekomunikasi Indonesia, with Rp10,479.21 billion
2. Astra International, Rp5,950.01
3. Bank Negara Indonesia Tbk, Rp5,115.32
4. Bank International Indonesia, Rp4,661.16
5. HM Sampoerna, Rp3,615.55
6. Matahari Puta Prima Tbk, Rp2,695.24
7. Bakrieland Development Tbk, Rp2,641.27
8. Putra Surya Multidana Tbk, Rp2,588.37
9. Gudang Garam, Rp2,563.49
10. Bimantara Citra, Rp2.512.57

Source: *Euromonay Publications*, SSB Guide to World Markets (annual), 1998, p. 244.

★2873★
TOP LARGEST COMPANIES ON THE JAKARTA STOCK EXCHANGE, 1997
Ranked by: Total trading volume, in billions of Indonesian Rupiah. **Number listed:** 20
1. HM Shmpoerna, with Rp38,733.3 billion
2. Indosat Tbk, Rp27,601.1
3. Gudang Garam, Rp24,076.3
4. Telekomunikasi Indonesia, Rp12,694.9
5. Schering Plough Indonesia, Rp10,111.5
6. Tigaraksa Satria, Rp6,783.0
7. Semen Gresik, Rp6,205.2
8. Aneka Kimia Raya, Rp5,272.7
9. Unilever Indonesia, Rp5,250.0
10. Astra International Tbk, Rp4,609.0

Source: *Euromoney Publications*, SSB Guide to World Equity Markets (annual), 1998, p. 244.

Jamaica Stock Exchange

★2874★
LARGEST LISTED COMPANIES ON THE JAMAICA STOCK EXCHANGE, 1997
Ranked by: Market value, in millions of Jamaican dollars. **Number listed:** 20
1. Telecom Jamaica, with J$18,927.41 million
2. CIBC Holdings, J$16,951.92
3. Bank of Nova Scotia, J$12,879.92
4. Carreras Group, J$7,281.60
5. Grace Kenndy, J$2,957.78
6. Desnoes and Geddes, J$2,427.68
7. Lascelles, J$2,256.00
8. NCB Group, J$2,121.52
9. CIBC (Jamaica), J$1,546.67
10. Jamaica Flour Mills, J$1,536.00

Source: *Ecromoney Publications*, SSB Guide to World Equity Markets (annual), 1998, p. 276.

★2875★
MOST TRADED ISSUES ON THE JAMAICAN STOCK EXCHANGE, 1997
Ranked by: Value, in millions of Jamaican dollars. **Number listed:** 20
1. Jamaica Flour Mills, with J$1,561.33 million
2. CIBC (Jamaica), J$526.24
3. Bank of Nova Scotia, J$426.84
4. Telecom Jamaica, J$331.29
5. Carreras, J$292.87
6. Kingston Wharves, J$267.39
7. Grace Kennedy, J$257.86
8. Citizens Bank, J$196.11
9. Lascelles, J$138.55
10. Pegasus Hotels, J$94.18

Source: *Euromoney Publications*, SSB Guide to World Equity markets (annual), 1998, p. 276.

Johannesburg Stock Exchange

★2876★
MOST ACTIVELY TRADED SHARES ON THE JOHANNESBURG STOCK EXCHANGE, 1997
Ranked by: Trading value, in millions of South African rand. **Number listed:** 20
1. De Beers Consol Mines, with R10,092 million
2. Sasol, R9,319
3. SA Breweris Ord, R7,814
4. Richemont Securities Dr, R6,867
5. Anglo Am Corp SA Ord, R6,442
6. Liberty Life Assn. Ord, R4,990
7. Barlow Ord, R4,805
8. Gencor, R3,616
9. Rembrandt Group, R3,456
10. First Nat Bank Hldgs, R3,396

Source: *Euromoney Publication*, SSB Guide to World Equity Markets (annual), 1998, p. 447.

★2877★
TOP LARGEST COMPANIES ON THE JOHANNESBURG STOCK EXCHANGE,1997
Ranked by: Market value, in millions of South African rand. **Number listed:** 20
1. Anglo Am Corp Sa Ord, with R45,989 million
2. S A Brewerie Ltd Ord, R41,877
3. De Beers Consol Mines, R37,640
4. Liberty Life Assn. Ord, R32,939
5. Sasol, R30,799
6. Richemont Securities Dr, R27,666
7. Billiton, R26,725
8. Standard Bnk Invcorp Ord, R25,785
9. Nedcor, R24,805
10. First Nat Bank Hldgs, R18,828

Source: *Euromoney Publications*, SSB Guide to World Equity Markets (annual), 1998, p. 446+.

Karachi Stock Exchange

★2878★
MOST ACTIVELY TRADED SHARES ON THE KARACHI STOCK EXCHANGE, 1997
Ranked by: Traded volume, in millions of shares. **Number listed:** 20
1. Hub Power, with PRs3,621.97 million
2. Pakistan Telecommunication Co, PRs3,531.74
3. ICI Pak, PRs2,716.80
4. Dewan Salman Fiber, PRs674.83
5. FFC Jordan, PRs671.15
6. Japan Power, PRs256.07

7. Dhan Fibre, PRs256.07
8. Southern Electric, PRs133.00
9. Sui Northern Gas Co, PRs105.94
10. Karachi Electric, PRs95.41

Source: *Euromoney Publications*, SSB Guide to World Equity markets (annual), 1998, p. 384.

★2879★
TOP LISTED COMPANIES ON THE KARACHI STOCK EXCHANGE, 1997
Ranked by: Market value, in billions of Pakisani rupees. **Number listed:** 20

1. PTC, with PRs164,735.10 billion
2. Hub Power Company, PRs66,304.95
3. Pakistan State Oil Company Limited, PRs30,977.07
4. Fauji Fertilizer Company Limited, PRs22,620.07
5. ICI Pakistan Limited, PRs15,269.69
6. Engro Chemical Pakistan Limited, PRs10,000.64
7. Sui Southern Gas Company Limited, PRs9,889.38
8. Sui Northern Gas Pipelines Limited, PRs7,677.57
9. Muslim Commercial Bank Limited, PRs7,191.14
10. Shell Pak, PRs6,574.84

Source: *Euromoney Publications*, SSB Guide To World Equity Markets (annual), 1998, p. 383.

Kentucky--Industries

★2880★
LARGEST KENTUCKY MANUFACTURERS, 1998
Ranked by: Establishment ranked by employees. **Number listed:** 200

1. General Electric Co (DH), with 8,500 employees
2. Toyota Motor manufacturing KY, 7,600
3. Lexmark International Inc. (HQ), 6,000
4. Ford Motor Co., 4,500
5. Ford Motor Co., 3,700
6. Fruit of the Loom, 3,100
7. Philip Morris U.S.A., 2,412
8. Matsushita Home Appliance Corp. (HQ), 2,000
9. Lockheed Martin Utility Services, 1,980
10. Publisher Printing Co. (HQ), 1,800

Source: *Dept. of Economic Development*, Kentucky Directory Of Manufacturers (annual), 1198, p. 30+.

Knives

★2881★
BEST-SELLING ELECTRIC KNIVES, 1998
Ranked by: Market shares, in percent. **Number listed:** 5

1. Hamilton Beach/Proctor-Silex, with 36%
2. Black & Decker, 30%
3. Toastmaster, 12%
4. Presto, 6%
5. Sunbeam-Oster, 3%

Source: *Appliance Manufacturer*, (annual), 1, 999, p. 22.

Korea Stock Exchange

★2882★
LARGEST LISTED COMPANIES ON THE KOREAN STOCK EXCHANGE, 1997
Ranked by: Market value, in millions of Korean won (W). **Number listed:** 55

1. Korea Electric Power, with W9,863,011 million
2. Pohang Iron & Steel, W4,310,011
3. Samsung Electronics, W3,996,910
4. SK Telecom, W2,767,439
5. Daewoo Heavy Industry, W1,761,991
6. Hyundai Electronics, W1,204,000
7. LG Electronics, W1,199,142
8. Dacom Corporation, W1,151,228
9. LG Semiconductor, W1,149,390
10. Yukong, W992,112

Source: *Euromoney Publications*, SSB Guide to World Equity Markets (annual), 1998, p. 303.

★2883★
MOST ACTIVELY TRADED SHARES ON THE KOREAN STOCK EXCHANGE, 1997
Ranked by: Trading value, in billions of Korean won (W). **Remarks:** Also notes percent of market total. **Number listed:** 20

1. Korea Electric Power, with W3,924.33 billion
2. Pohang Iron & Steel, W3,784.24
3. Samsung Electronics, W3,536,63
4. LG Electronics, W1,543.26
5. LG Semicon, W1,511.72
6. Daewoo Securities, W1,501.77
7. LG Information & Communications, W1,491.86
8. Kookmin Bank, W1,481.59
9. Hyundal Electronics, W1,466.94
10. SK Telecom, W1,429.20

Source: *Euromoney Publications*, SSB Guide to World Equity Markets (annual), 1998, p. 303.

Kuala Lumpur Stock Exchange

★2884★
LARGEST LISTED COMPANIES ON THE KUALA LUMPUR STOCK EXCHANGE, 1997
Ranked by: Market value, in millions of Malaysian ringgits. **Number listed:** 20

1. Telekom, with M$34,484.9 million
2. TND, M$25,729.84
3. PGas, M$15,959.36
4. Maybank, M$12,920.57
5. Sime Darby, M$8,698.78
6. Rothmans International Ltd., M$8,637.28
7. Resorts, M$7,151.57
8. Genting, M$6,846.42
9. YTL, M$6,376.06
10. KLK, M$5,951.89

Source: *Euromoney Publication*, SSB Guide to World Equity Markets (annual), 1, 998, p. 328+.

★2885★
MOST ACTIVELY TRADED SHARES ON THE KUALA LUMPUR STOCK EXCHANGE, 1997
Ranked by: Volume, in thousand of shares. **Remarks:** Also notes value in thousands of shares. **Number listed:** 20

1. MBF Capital, with M$1,671,767 thousand shares
2. Renong, M$1,443,985

3. Klih, M$1,344,037
4. Rekapac, M$1,221,921
5. Suria, M$999,110
6. Sime Darby, M$996,665
7. Aokam, M$884,004
8. Anson, M$786,729
9. CP Bhd, M$775,012
10. Tai Ping, M$749,611

Source: *Euromoney Publications*, SSB Guide to World Equity markets (annual), 1998, p. 329.

Labor Supply

★2886★
LEADING METROPOLITAN AREAS IN LABOR QUALITY, 1998
Ranked by: Scores are based on the Labor Quality index. **Remarks:** Statistical information in unemployment, educational attainment, labor organization representation, and total employment compensation was used to evaluate metropolitan areas and create an index. **Number listed:** 8

1. Austin-San Marcos, TX, with 8.28
2. Oklahoma City, OK, 7.70
3. Enid, OK, 7.47
4. San Antonio, TX, 7.41
5. Lexington, KY, 7.14
6. Albuquerque, NM, 7.00
7. Amarillo, TX, 6.91
8. Wichita, KS, 6.68
9. Salt Lake City-Ogden, UT, 6.56
10. Tulsa, OK, 6.56

Source: *Business Facilities*, April, 1999, p. 8.

★2887★
TOP ASSIGNMENT WORKERS BY FUNCTION, 1998*
Ranked by: Survey results, in percent. **Remarks:** Survey respondents represent 76 companies in a cross-section of industries. **Number listed:** 7

1. Production, Distribution, Assembly, with 37%
2. Clerical, Office Automation, 26%
3. Customer Service, Teleservices, 12%
4. Information Systems, 8%
4. Technical, 8%
4. Professional, 8%
7. Other, 1%

Source: *Distribution Supply*, September, 1998, p. 66.

Labor Unions--Detroit Metropolitan Area

★2888★
LARGEST UNIONS IN THE DETROIT METROPOLITAN AREA, 1997
Ranked by: Gross receipts in dollars. **Remarks:** Also notes gross receipts from previous year, percent change, assets, number of members, and groups represented. **Number listed:** 20

1. United Food & Commercial Workers 876, with $8,769,644
2. Operating Engineers Local 324, $8,081,176
3. UAW Local 600, $7,741,027
4. Electrical Workers Local 58, $6,065,920
5. Teamsters Local 337, $5,242,642
6. Iron Workers Local 25, $4,791,876
7. Service Employees International Local 79, $4,011,768
8. UAW Local 900, $3,772,372
9. Plumbers Local 653, $3,617,390
10. UAW Local 653, $3,109,136

Source: *Crain's Detroit Business*, Crain's Book of Lists Detroit (annual), December 28, 1998, p. 64.

Languages

★2889★
MOST POPULAR NON-ENGLISH INTERNET LANGUAGES, 1998*
Ranked by: Frequency of use, in percent. **Number listed:** 8

1. Spanish, with 24%
2. Japanese, 22%
3. German, 13%
4. French, 10%
5. Chinese, 6%
6. Dutch, 4%
6. Italian, 4%
6. Swedish, 4%

Source: *Bank Marketing*, November, 1998, p. 52.

★2890★
MOST WIDELY SPOKEN LANGUAGES WORLDWIDE, 1998*
Ranked by: Language. **Number listed:** 10

1. Mandarin
2. English
3. Russian
4. Spanish
5. Hindi
6. Arabic
7. Portuguese
8. Bengali
9. German
10. Japanese

Source: *Management Review*, December, 1998, p. 47.

Law Firms

★2891★
LARGEST LAW FIRMS, 1998
Ranked by: Total number of lawyers. **Remarks:** Also notes location of home office and rank for previous year. **Number listed:** 700

1. Baker & McKenzie, with 2,294 lawyers
2. Jones, Day, Reavis & Pogue, 1,199
3. Skadden, Arps, Slate, Meagher & Flom, 1,187
4. Morgan, Lewis & Bockius, 915
5. Latham & Watkins, 823
6. Sidley & Austin, 805
7. White & Case, 791
8. Mayer, Brown & Platt, 748.5
9. Gibson, Dunn & Crutcher, 672
10. Foley & Lardner, 668

Source: *Law and Business*, Lawyers Almanac (annual), 1999, p. A-1+.

★2892★
TOP LEGAL ADVISORS OF ALL ANNOUNCED DEALS INVOLVING U.S. TARGETS, 1998
Ranked by: Amount, in millions of dollars. **Remarks:** Also notes percentage and number of issues, as well as figures from previous year. **Number listed:** 15

1. Simpson Thacher & Bartlett, with $610,649.3 million
2. Skadden, Arps, Slate, Meagher & Flom, $545,803.3
3. Dewey Ballantine LLP, $472,613.6
4. Wachtell Lipton Rosen & Katz, $431,502.8
5. Shearman & Sterling, $412,902.9
6. Sullivan & Cromwell, $363.301.3
7. Davis Polk & Wardwell, $291,104.7
8. Cleary, Gottlieb, Steen & Hamilton, $287,253.1
9. Debevoise & Plimpton, $229,319.6
10. Richards, Layton & Finger, $216,701.5

Source: *Investment Dealers' Digest*, M&A Rankings (annual), January 18, 1999, p. 25.

★2893★
TOP LEGAL ADVISORS OF ALL COMPLETED DEALS INVOLVING U.S. TARGETS, 1998
Ranked by: Amount, in millions of dollars. **Remarks:** Also notes percentage and number of issues, as well as figures from previous year. **Number listed:** 15

1. Simpson Thacher & Bartlett, with $483,768.6 million
2. Wachtell Lipton Rosen & Katz, $349,986.3
3. Shearman & Sterling, $333,508.7
4. Skadden, Arps, Slate, Meagher & Flom, $313,460.2
5. Sullivan & Cromwell, $312,548.0
6. Morris, Nichols, Arsht & Tunnell, $210,005.0
7. Davis Polk & Wardwell, $207,421.2
8. Fried, Frank, Harris, Shriver & Jacobson, $158,386.6
9. Richards, Layton & Finger, $151,543.4
10. Cravath, Swaine & Moore, $143,711.1

Source: *Investment Dealers' Digest*, M&A Rankings (annual), January 18, 1999, p. 25.

Law Firms--Chicago (IL)

★2894★
LARGEST LAW FIRMS IN CHICAGO, 1998
Ranked by: Number of attorneys. **Remarks:** Also notes contact information, total from previous year, details of Chicago office staff and of U.S. staff, Chicago partners' specialties, and base salary for associates just hired from law school. **Number listed:** 35

1. Mayer, Brown & Platt, with 415 attorneys
2. Sidley & Austin, 397
3. Winston & Strawn, 347
4. Kirkland & Ellis, 325
5. Katten Muchin & Zavis, 305
6. Jenner & Block, 298
7. McDermott Will & Emery, 285
8. Lord Bissell & Brook, 265
9. Rudnick & Wolfe, 260
10. Schiff Hardin & Waite, 214

Source: *Crain's Chicago Business*, Top Business Lists (annual), 1998, p. 123+.

Law Firms--Detroit Metropolitan Area

★2895★
LARGEST LAW FIRMS IN THE DETROIT METROPOLITAN AREA, 1998
Ranked by: Number of attorneys. **Remarks:** Also notes contact information, total from previous year, leading executive, breakdown of new job titles, state and worldwide figures, and representative clients. **Number listed:** 23

1. Dykema Gossett P.L.L.C., with 184 attorneys
2. Miller Canfield Paddock & Stone plc, 175
3. Honigman Miller Schwartz & Cohn, 155
4. Dickinson Wright P.L.L.C., 128
5. Butzel Long, 125
6. Plunkett & Cooney P.C., 119
7. Bodman, Longley & Dahling L.L.P., 102
8. Clark Hill plc, 96
9. Kitch, Drutchas, Wagner & Kenney P.C., 91
10. Sommers, Schwartz, Silver & Schwartz P.C., 82

Source: *Crain's Detroit Business*, February 1, 1999, p. 23.

Law Firms--Florida

★2896★
LARGEST LAW FIRMS IN FLORIDA, 1999*
Ranked by: Number of lawyers. **Remarks:** Also notes contact information, number of employees and number of offices in Florida, hourly rate range, first year salary range, managing partner, and year founded. **Number listed:** 24

1. Holland & Knight LLP, with 379 lawyers
2. Greenberg Traurig, 250
3. Akerman Senterfitt & Edison PA, 180
4. Carlton Fields, 160
5. Steel Hector & Davis LLP, 153
6. Fowler White Gillen Boggs Villareal & Banker PA, 150
7. Broad & Cassel, 142
8. Gunster Yoakley Valdes-Fauli & Stewart PA, 140
9. Ruden McClosky Smith Schuster & Russell PA, 130
10. Foley & Lardner, 128

Source: *Florida Trend*, TopRank Florida (annual), 1999, p. 90.

Law Firms, International

★2897★
WORLD'S LARGEST LAW FIRMS, 1998
Ranked by: Number of lawyers. **Number listed:** 6

1. Baker & McKenzie (U.S.), with 2,325 lawyers
2. Linklaters & Alliance (Europe), 1,900
3. Clifford Chance (United Kingdom), 1,880
4. Skadden, Arps, Slate, Meagher & Flom (U.S.), 1,200
5. Jones Day Reavis & Pogue (U.S.), 1,100
5. Freshfields (United Kingdom), 1,100

Source: *Financial Times*, July 24, 1998, p. 1.

Law Firms--Long Island (NY)

★2898★
LARGEST LAW FIRMS IN LONG ISLAND, 1999*
Ranked by: Number of attorneys in Long Island. **Remarks:** Also notes contact information, managing partner, year founded, number of attorneys nationwide, and number of employees. **Number listed:** 66
1. Rivkin, Radler & Kremer, with 136 attorneys
2. Farrell Fritz, 63
3. Siben & Siben, 61
4. Certilman Balin Adler & Hyman, 58
5. Cullen & Dykman, 52
6. Meltzer, Lippe, Goldstein, Wolf & Schlissel PC, 50
6. Ruskin, Moscou, Evans & Faltischek, 50
8. L'Abbate, Balkan, Colavita & Contini LLP, 46
9. Berkman, Henoch, Peterson & Peddy PC, 43
9. Jaspan, Schlesinger, Silverman, & Hoffman LLP, 43

Source: *Long Island Business News*, 1999, p. 74+.

Law Firms--Los Angeles Metropolitan Area

★2899★
LARGEST LAW FIRMS IN LOS ANGELES COUNTY, 1998
Ranked by: Number of attorneys in Los Angeles county offices. **Remarks:** Also notes number of partners, figures from previous year, specialties, number of offices, year established, headquarters location, executive director and managing partner. **Number listed:** 50
1. O'Melveny & Myers LLP, with 327 attorneys
2. Latham & Watkins, 258
3. Gibson, Dunn & Crutcher, 219
4. Paul, Hastings, Janofsky & Walker LLP, 188
5. Irell & Manella LLP, 174
6. Sheppard, Mulin, Richter & Hampton LLP, 161
7. Troop Steuber Pasich Reddick & Tobey LLP, 144
8. Manatt, Phelps & Phillips LLP, 141
9. Skadden, Arps, Slate, Meagher & Flom, 134
10. Loeb & Loeb LLP, 133

Source: *Los Angeles Business Journal*, February 8, 1999, p. 35.

Law Firms--New Jersey

★2900★
LARGEST LAW FIRMS IN NEW JERSEY, 1999*
Ranked by: Number of attorneys in New Jersey. **Remarks:** Also notes contact information, year founded, total New Jersey staff, managing partner, and partial specialties. **Number listed:** 25
1. McCarter & English, with 227 attorneys
2. Pitney, Hardin, Kipp & Szuch, 151
2. Riker, Danzig, Scherer, Hyland & Perretti LLP, 151
4. Sills, Cummis, Zuckerman, Radin, Tischman, Epstein & Gross, 140
5. Crummy, Del Deo, Dolan, Griffinger & Vecchione P.C., 130
6. Wilentz, Goldman & Spitzer, 128
7. Lowenstein Sandler, 125
8. Shanley & Fisher P.C., 115
9. Archer & Greiner P.C., 87
9. Carpenter, Bennett & Morrissey, 87

Source: *New Jersey Business*, Book of Lists (annual), 1999, p. 34.

Law Firms--New York (State)

★2901★
LARGEST LAW FIRMS IN THE NEW YORK METROPOLITAN AREA, 1998
Ranked by: Number of lawyers in New York area. **Remarks:** Also notes contact information, senior partner, figures from previous year, total number of lawyers firmwide, and a breakdown of lawyers by specialty. **Number listed:** 25
1. Skadden, Arps, Slate, Meagher & Flom, with 652 lawyers
2. Simpson Thacher & Bartlett, 488
3. Davis Polk & Wardell, 475
4. Shearman & Sterling, 467
5. Sullivan & Cromwell, 404
6. Weil Gotshal & Manges, 399
7. Paul Weiss Rifkind Wharton & Garrison, 368
8. Proskauer Rose, 363
9. Cravath Swaine & Moore, 343
10. Debevoise & Plimpton, 333

Source: *Crain's New York Business*, November 23, 1998, p. 38.

Law Firms--Philadelphia Metropolitan Area

★2902★
LARGEST LAW FIRMS IN THE PHILADELPHIA METROPOLITAN AREA, 1998
Ranked by: Number of attorneys in the Philadelphia area. **Remarks:** Also notes contact information, total number of attorneys, staff figures, fee range, managing partner, branch offices, and types of law practiced. **Number listed:** 25
1. Dechert Price & Rhoads, with 259 attorneys
2. Blank Rome Comisky & McCauley, 241
3. Pepper Hamilton, 233
4. Morgan, Lewis & Bocklus, 229
5. Cozen & O'Connor, 200
6. Ballard Spahr Andrews & Ingersoll, 191
7. Duane Morris & Heckscher, 186
8. Drinker Biddle & Reath, 185
9. White & Williams, 175
10. Wolf Block Schorr & Solis-Cohen, 173

Source: *Philadelphia Business Journal*, Book of Business Lists (annual), December 25, 1998, p. 67.

Law Schools

★2903★
AMERICA'S BEST LAW SCHOOLS FOR CLINICAL TRAINING, 1998
Ranked by: Overall score in a survey of law schools. Ranking is derived from consideration of 12 factors including reputation, selectivity, placement success, faculty resources, overall

rank, and specialty ranking. See magazine for further discussion of factors. **Remarks:** Overall score not provided. **Number listed:** 10

1. Georgetown University
2. New York University
3. American University
4. University of Maryland
5. University of New Mexico
6. Yale University
7. CUNY-Queens College
8. University of Chicago
9. University of California, Los Angeles
10. Northwestern University

Source: *U.S. News & World Report*, America's Best Graduate and Professional Schools (annual), March 29, 1999, p. 95.

★2904★
AMERICA'S BEST LAW SCHOOLS FOR DISPUTE RESOLUTION, 1998
Ranked by: Overall score in a survey of law schools. Ranking is derived from consideration of 12 factors including reputation, selectivity, placement success, faculty resources, overall rank, and specialty ranking. See magazine for further discussion of factors. **Remarks:** Overall score not provided. **Number listed:** 10

1. Harvard University
1. Ohio State University
1. Pepperdine University
1. University of Missouri-Columbia
5. Willamette University
6. Hamline University
7. Georgetown University
8. Northwestern University
9. University of Texas-Austin
10. New York University

Source: *U.S. News & World Report*, America's Best Graduate and Professional Schools (annual), March 29, 1999, p. 95.

★2905★
AMERICA'S BEST LAW SCHOOLS FOR ENVIRONMENTAL LAW, 1998
Ranked by: Overall score in a survey of law schools. Ranking is derived from consideration of 12 factors including reputation, selectivity, placement success, faculty resources, overall rank, and specialty ranking. See magazine for further discussion of factors. **Remarks:** Overall score not provided. **Number listed:** 10

1. Vermont Law School
2. Lewis & Clark College
3. Pace University
4. George Washington University
5. Tulane University
6. University of California, Berkley
7. Georgetown University
7. University of Colorado at Boulder
9. University of Maryland
10. New York University

Source: *U.S. News & World Report*, America's Best Graduate and Professional Schools (annual), March 29, 1999, p. 95.

★2906★
AMERICA'S BEST LAW SCHOOLS FOR HEALTH LAW, 1998
Ranked by: Overall score in a survey of law schools. Ranking is derived from consideration of 12 factors including reputation, selectivity, placement success, faculty resources, overall rank, and specialty ranking. See magazine for further discussion of factors. **Remarks:** Overall score not provided. **Number listed:** 10

1. University of Houston
2. St. Louis University
3. University of Maryland
4. Loyola University Chicago
5. DePaul University
6. Widener University
7. Seton Hall University
8. Boston University
8. Case Western Reserve University
10. Indiana University-Indianapolis

Source: *U.S. News & World Report*, America's Best Graduate and Professional Schools (annual), March 29, 1999, p. 95.

★2907★
AMERICA'S BEST LAW SCHOOLS FOR INTELLECTUAL PROPERTY, 1998
Ranked by: Overall score in a survey of law schools. Ranking is derived from consideration of 12 factors including reputation, selectivity, placement success, faculty resources, overall rank, and specialty ranking. See magazine for further discussion of factors. **Remarks:** Overall score not provided. **Number listed:** 10

1. Franklin Pierce Law Center
1. University of California, Berkeley
3. Columbia University
3. George Washington University
5. New York University
5. University of Texas-Austin
7. University of Houston
8. Stanford University
9. Yeshiva University
10. Santa Clara University

Source: *U.S. News & World Report*, America's Best Graduate and Professional Schools (annual), March 29, 1999, p. 95.

★2908★
AMERICA'S BEST LAW SCHOOLS FOR INTERNATIONAL LAW, 1998
Ranked by: Overall score in a survey of law schools. Ranking is derived from consideration of 12 factors including reputation, selectivity, placement success, faculty resources, overall rank, and specialty ranking. See magazine for further discussion of factors. **Remarks:** Overall score not provided. **Number listed:** 10

1. New York University
2. Columbia University
3. Harvard University
4. Georgetown University
4. Yale University
6. George Washington University
7. University of Michigan
8. American University
9. University of Virginia
10. University of Iowa

Source: *U.S. News & World Report*, America's Best Graduate and Professional Schools (annual), March 29, 1999, p. 95.

★2909★
AMERICA'S BEST LAW SCHOOLS FOR TAX LAW, 1998
Ranked by: Overall score in a survey of law schools. Ranking is derived from consideration of 12 factors including reputation, selectivity, placement success, faculty resources, overall rank, and specialty ranking. See magazine for further discussion of factors. **Remarks:** Overall score not provided. **Number listed:** 11

1. New York University
2. Georgetown University
3. University of Florida
4. Harvard University
5. University of Miami

6. University of Texas-Austin
7. University of Virginia
8. Yale University
9. Boston University
10. Stanford University
10. University of Chicago

Source: *U.S. News & World Report*, America's Best Graduate and Professional Schools (annual), March 29, 1999, p. 95.

★2910★
AMERICA'S BEST LAW SCHOOLS FOR TRIAL ADVOCACY, 1998
Ranked by: Overall score in a survey of law schools. Ranking is derived from consideration of 12 factors including reputation, selectivity, placement success, faculty resources, overall rank, and specialty ranking. See magazine for further discussion of factors. **Remarks:** Overall score not provided. **Number listed:** 10

1. Temple University
2. Northwestern University
3. Emory University
4. Stetson University
5. New York University
6. Georgetown University
6. Harvard University
8. South Texas College of Law
8. University of Notre Dame
8. William Mitchell College of Law

Source: *U.S. News & World Report*, America's Best Graduate and Professional Schools (annual), March 29, 1999, p. 95.

★2911★
AMERICA'S BEST LAW SCHOOLS, 1998
Ranked by: Overall score in a survey of law schools. Ranking is derived from consideration of 6 factors: student selectivity, placement, graduation rates, instructional resources, research, and academic reputation. Factors are then weighted, totaled, and a final ranking achieved. See magazine for further discussion of methodology. **Remarks:** Also notes LSAT score percentile, acceptance rate, bar passage rate, and percent employed 9 months after graduation. **Number listed:** 50

1. Yale University, with 100 points
2. Harvard University, 93
2. Stanford University, 93
4. New York University, 89
5. Columbia University, 87
6. University of Chicago, 86
7. University of Virginia, 84
8. Duke University, 82
8. University of Michigan, 82
10. Cornell University, 81

Source: *U.S. News & World Report*, America's Best Graduate and Professional Schools (annual), March 29, 1999, p. 94.

★2912★
TOP LAW SCHOOLS FOR HISPANICS, 1998
Ranked by: Hispanic graduate enrollment. **Remarks:** Also notes total graduate enrollment, percent of Hispanic enrollment, and degrees earned by Hispanics. **Number listed:** 10

1. Loyola Marymount University, with 278 enrolled
2. University of Miami, 241
3. University of Texas-Austin, 145
4. Texas Southern University, 138
5. Fordham University, 117
6. St. Thomas University, 111
7. Georgetown University, 110
8. New York Law School, 108
9. South Texas College of Law, 106
10. University of California, Los Angeles, 102

Source: *Hispanic Business*, Top 10 Law Schools for Hispanics (annual), September, 1998, p. 34+.

Lawn Care Products

★2913★
BEST LAWN AND GARDEN BRANDS ACCORDING TO DISCOUNT STORE SHOPPERS, 1997
Ranked by: Percent of discount shoppers naming brand as favorite. **Number listed:** 6

1. Scotts, with 30%
2. Miracle-Gro, 11%
3. Ortho, 6%
4. Burpee, 5%
5. Murray, 3%
6. Hyponex, 2%

Source: *Discount Store News*, Top Brands Survey (annual), October 20, 1998, p. 28.

Lawn Care Services

★2914★
BEST-SELLING LEAF BLOWERS, 1998
Ranked by: Market Share, in percent. **Number listed:** 4

1. Frigidaire (Weed Eater), with 35%
2. Toro, 34%
3. Black & Decker, 29%
4. Others, 2%

Source: *Appliance Manufacturer*, April, 1999, p. 21.

★2915★
BEST-SELLING STRING TRIMMERS, 1998
Ranked by: Market share, in percent. **Number listed:** 5

1. Frigidaire (Weed Eater), with 44%
2. Toro, 27%
3. Black & Decker, 24%
4. Ryobi, 3%
5. Others, 2%

Source: *Appliance Manufacturer*, April, 1999, p. 21.

Leasing and Renting of Equipment

★2916★
LEADING COMPANIES IN THE RENTAL INDUSTRY, 1998
Ranked by: Rental volume, in millions of dollars. **Remarks:** Also notes location, top officer, number of outlets, and editorial comments. **Number listed:** 100

1. United Rentals, with $895.0 million
2. Hertz Equipment Rental Corp., $603.1
3. Rental Service Corp., $404.2
4. Prime Equipment, $391.6
5. Initial Plant Services, $228.0
6. Neff Rental, $179.0
7. National Equipment Services, $165.9
8. Nationsrent, $150.1
9. Brambles Equipment Services, $134.5

10. American Equipment Co., $127.0

Source: *Rental Equipment Register*, May, 1999, p. 49+.

Leather Industry--Europe

★2917★
TOP LEATHER AND LEATHER PRODUCTS COMPANIES IN EUROPE, 1999*
Ranked by: Sales, in million of European Currency Units (ECUs). **Remarks:** Also notes number of employees and overall rank among European businesses. **Number listed:** 31

1. Adidas AG, with ECUs2,437 million
2. C&J Clark Holdings Ltd., ECUs1,073
3. C&J Clark Int'l Ltd., ECUs823
4. Salamander AG, ECUs750
5. Hermes Sellier, ECUs385
6. R Griggs Group Ltd., ECUs365
7. Grampian Holdings Plc, ECUs360
8. R Griggs & Co. Ltd, ECUs302
9. The Hartstone Group Plc, ECUs287
10. Erich Rohde KG Schuhfabriken, ECUs177

Source: *Dun & Bradstreet*, Duns Europa (annual), 1999, p. 246.

Leisure

★2918★
AMERICA'S TOP LEISURE-TIME ACTIVITIES, 1997
Ranked by: Percentage of survey respondents naming activity. **Number listed:** 6

1. Watching TV, with 96%
1. Listening to Music, 91%
1. Reading, 91%
4. Watching Videotapes, 88%
5. Computer Games, 44%
6. Surfing the Internet, 35%

Source: *Cable World*, January 25, 1998, p. 6.

★2919★
TOP LEISURE-TIME ACTIVITIES ACCORDING TO CHIEF FINANCIAL OFFICERS, 1998
Ranked by: Survey of 1,400 U.S. men and women Chief Financial Officers. **Number listed:** 10

1. Golf, with 21%
2. Reading, 14%
3. Team Sports, 10%
4. Exercise, 9%
4. Movies, Theater, 9%
4. Adventure Sports, 9%
7. Music, 5%
8. Surfing the Internet, 4%
9. Tennis, 3%
10. Fishing, Hunting, 2%

Source: *Journal of Accountancy*, July, 1998, p. 18.

★2920★
TOP LEISURE-TIME COMPANIES OF THE S&P 500, 1998
Ranked by: Each company is ranked by eight criteria: one-year total return, three-year total return, one-year sales growth, three-year average annual sales growth, one-year profit growth, three-year average annual profit growth, net profit margins, and return on equity, with additional weight give to a company's sales. A company's composite rank is calculated using the sum of all its ranks. **Remarks:** Overall scores not provided. **Number listed:** 18

1. Carnival
2. McDonald's
3. Darden Restaurants
4. Walt Disney
5. Eastman Kodak
6. Hasbro
7. King World Productions
8. Harrah's Entertainment
9. Marriott International
10. Brunswick

Source: *Business Week*, Business Week 50: Top Companies of the S&P 500 (annual), March 29, 1999, p. 154.

Less than Truckload Shipments

See: **Trucking Industry--Small Shipments**

Letters of Credit

★2921★
LEADING LETTER OF CREDIT BANKS, 1998
Ranked by: Market share, in percent. **Number listed:** 9

1. Chase Manhattan, with 14.4%
2. First Union, 10.8%
3. Bank of America, 10.2%
4. Bank of New York, 6.5%
5. BankBoston, 6.3%
6. NationsBank, 3.5%
7. FNB Chicago, 2.0%
8. Republic New York, 1.9%
9. Comerica Bank, 1.5%

Source: *Banking Strategies*, January, 1999, p. 59.

★2922★
LEADING LETTER OF CREDIT BANKS WORLDWIDE FOR TAXABLE ISSUES, 1997
Ranked by: Value of bond issues, in thousands of U.S. dollars ($). **Number listed:** 10

1. Chase Manhattan Bank, with $118,500 thousand
2. Canadian Imperial Bank of Commerce, $86,200
3. KredietBank N.V., $47,800
4. Wachovia Bank, $46,500
5. First Chicago NBD, $45,300
6. Banque Nationale de Paris, $43,300
7. Commerzbank Aktiengesellschaft, $35,000
7. Banc One Investment Management & Trust Group, $35,000
9. Michigan National Bank (Detroit), $24,000
10. NationsBank, $21,900

Source: *Bond Buyer Yearbook (annual)*, 1998, p. 185.

★2923★
LEADING LETTER OF CREDIT BANKS WORLDWIDE FOR THE EDUCATION INDUSTRY, 1997
Ranked by: Value of bond issues, in thousands of U.S. dollars ($). **Number listed:** 10

1. Student Loan Marketing Association, with $303,600 thousand

2. Banque Nationale de Paris, $99,900
3. Commerzbank Aktiengesellschaft, $91,400
4. First Chicago NBD, $68,200
5. Union Bank, $64,900
6. NationsBank, $59,300
7. Canadian Imperial Bank of Commerce, $57,500
8. PNC Bank, $55,500
9. Allied Irish Investment Bank, $54,100
10. Banc One Investment Management & Trust Group, $51,500

Source: *Bond Buyer Yearbook (annual)*, 1998, p. 113.

★2924★
LEADING LETTER OF CREDIT BANKS WORLDWIDE FOR THE ENVIRONMENTAL INDUSTRY, 1997
Ranked by: Value of bond issues, in thousands of U.S. dollars ($). **Number listed:** 10

1. Canadian Imperial Bank of Commerce, with $399,900 thousand
2. Chase Manhattan Bank, $237,600
3. KredietBank N.V., $168,600
4. Deutsche Morgan Grenfell, $148,600
5. Union Bank of Switzerland, $133,300
6. Barclays Bank, $98,500
7. Toronto-Dominion Bank, $70,000
8. First Trust, $68,900
9. Wachovia Bank, $45,000
10. Bank of America, $40,000

Source: *Bond Buyer Yearbook (annual)*, 1998, p. 161.

★2925★
LEADING LETTER OF CREDIT BANKS WORLDWIDE FOR THE HEALTHCARE INDUSTRY, 1997
Ranked by: Value of bond issues, in thousands of U.S. dollars ($). **Number listed:** 10

1. Bank of America, with $317,900 thousand
2. Canadian Imperial Bank of Commerce, $275,000
3. First Trust, $226,000
4. First Chicago NBD, $213,900
5. Sun Trust Bank, $187,300
6. Toronto-Dominion Bank, $150,000
7. First Union National Bank, $95,200
8. KredietBank N.V., $85,500
9. Banque Paribas, $67,200
10. ABN Amro Bank, $63,400

Source: *Bond Buyer Yearbook (annual)*, 1998, p. 121.

★2926★
LEADING LETTER OF CREDIT BANKS WORLDWIDE FOR THE HOUSING INDUSTRY, 1997
Ranked by: Value of bond issues, in thousands of U.S. dollars ($). **Number listed:** 10

1. Fleet Bank, with $194,400 thousand
2. Chase Manhattan Bank, $123,200
3. Key Bank/Society National Bank, $117,900
4. Bayerische Hypotheken, $107,300
5. Commerzbank Aktiengesellschaft, $85,800
6. First Trust, $76,900
6. Credit Suisse, $76,900
8. Landesbank hessen-Thuringen, $75,000
9. Bank of America, $57,400
10. Banc One Investment Management & Trust Group, $35,200

Source: *Bond Buyer Yearbook (annual)*, 1998, p. 145.

★2927★
LEADING LETTER OF CREDIT BANKS WORLDWIDE FOR THE INDUSTRIAL DEVELOPMENT INDUSTRY, 1997
Ranked by: Value of bond issues, in thousands of U.S. dollars ($). **Number listed:** 10

1. Wachovia Bank, with $109,800 thousand
2. Chase Manhattan Bank, $105,500
3. ABN Amro Bank, $102,300
4. Banc One Investment Management & Trust Group, $88,100
5. Credit Local De France-CAECL, $77,800
6. PNC Bank, $74,800
7. Corestates Bank, $67,600
8. NationsBank, $52,500
9. Bank of America, $51,400
10. Sumitomo Trust & Banking, $44,500

Source: *Bond Buyer Yearbook (annual)*, 1998, p. 169.

★2928★
LEADING LETTER OF CREDIT BANKS WORLDWIDE FOR THE PUBLIC FACILITIES INDUSTRY, 1997
Ranked by: Value of bond issues, in thousands of U.S. dollars ($). **Number listed:** 10

1. Bank of America, with $177,000 thousand
2. Canadian Imperial Bank of Commerce, $89,600
3. First Trust, $45,300
4. KredietBank N.V., $33,700
5. Commerzbank A.G., $18,000
6. First Chicago NBD, $14,900
7. AmSouth Bank, $12,000
8. American National Bank & Trust of Chicago, $9,300
9. Chase Manhattan Bank, $6,000
10. Harris Trust & Savings Bank, $5,500

Source: *Bond Buyer Yearbook (annual)*, 1998, p. 153.

★2929★
LEADING LETTER OF CREDIT BANKS WORLDWIDE FOR THE TRANSPORTATION INDUSTRY, 1997
Ranked by: Value of bond issues, in thousands of U.S. dollars ($). **Number listed:** 10

1. Bayerische Landesbank Girozentrale, with $327,100 thousand
2. Westdeutsche Landesbank Girozentrale, $221,200
3. Union Bank of Switzerland, $160,000
4. Bank of America, $115,000
5. Canadian Imperial Bank of Commerce, $108,800
6. Bankers Trust Co., $102,000
7. Bank of Nova Scotia, $100,000
8. First Trust, $72,100
9. Toronto-Dominion Bank, $65,300
10. Credit Local De France-CAECL, $50,000

Source: *Bond Buyer Yearbook (annual)*, 1998, p. 129.

★2930★
LEADING LETTER OF CREDIT BANKS WORLDWIDE FOR THE UTILITIES INDUSTRY, 1997
Ranked by: Value of bond issues, in thousands of U.S. dollars ($). **Number listed:** 10

1. Morgan Guaranty Trust Co., with $115,900 thousand
1. Bayerische Landesbank Girozentrale, $115,900
1. Credit Suisse, $115,900
1. Wachovia Bank, $115,900
5. Bank of Montreal Trust, $98,500
6. Bayerische Vereinsbank, $77,500
7. State Street Bank & Trust Co., $31,000
8. Candian Imperial Bank of Commerce, $20,700
9. Banque Nationale de Paris, $12,000

Wilmington Trust Co., $5,400
Source: *Bond Buyer Yearbook (annual)*, 1998, p. 137.

Life Care Communities

★2931★
TOP REASONS RESIDENTS LEAVE ASSISTED LIVING, 1998*
Ranked by: Percentage of survey results. **Number listed:** 7

1. Need more care, with 42%
2. Death, 16%
3. Other, 13%
4. Moved in with family, 10%
6. Financial hardships, 7%
6. Seasonal/snowbird, 6%
6. Moved to another facility, 6%

Source: *Hospitals & Health Networks*, July 20, 1998, p. 26.

Lima Stock Exchange

★2932★
LARGEST LISTED COMPANIES ON THE LIMA STOCK EXCHANGE, 1997
Ranked by: Market value, in million of U.S. dollars ($). **Remarks:** Also notes market value in millions of Peruvian sol (S). **Number listed:** 20

1. Telefonica del Peru (B), with $3,331.91 million
2. Credicorp, $1,544.43
3. Banco de Credito, $925.55
4. Cementos Lima, $638.54
5. Backus, $577.95
6. Buenaventura (A), $491.63
7. Edegel B, $354.16
8. Backus (E), $321.43
9. Alicorp, $251.66
10. Luz del Sur (B), $228.24

Source: *Euromoney Publications*, SSB Guide to World Equity Markets (annual), 1998, p. 393.

★2933★
MOST ACTIVELY TRADED SHARES ON THE LIMA STOCK EXCHANGE, 1997
Ranked by: Turnover value, in millions of U.S. dollars ($). **Number listed:** 20

1. Telefonica del Peru, with $1,998.71 million
2. Buenaventura(A), $1,083.15
3. Credicorp, $684.53
4. Backus (E), $615.62
5. Minsur (E), $427.68
6. Cementos Lima, $353.95
7. Luz del Sur (B), $352.25
8. Tele 2000, $310.76
9. Volcan (E), $279.47
10. Buenaventura (B), $252.97

Source: *Euromoney Publications*, SSB Guide to World Equity Markets (annual), 1998, p. 393+.

Lime

★2934★
LEADING INDUSTRIES IN U.S. LIME CONSUMPTION, 1995
Ranked by: Percentage of use. **Number listed:** 7

1. Metallurgy, with 33%
2. Environmental, 27%
3. Other, 15%
4. Construction, 8%
5. PCC, 7%
6. Pulp & Paper, 6%
7. Sugar, 4%

Source: *Chemical Market Reporter*, September 21, 1998, p. 20.

★2935★
LEADING LIME PLANT IN THE U.S., 1997
Ranked by: Total output. **Number listed:** 10

1. St. Genevieve (plant), Mississippi Lime Co. (company)
2. Maysville Division, Dravo Lime Co.
3. Black River Division, Dravo Lime Co.
4. Montevallo/Alabaster, Chemical Lime Co.
5. Martin Marietta Magnesia Specialties
6. Buffinton, Marblehead Lime Co.
7. Longview Division, Dravo Lime Co.
8. St. Genevieve Plant, Chemical Lime Co.
9. Pilot Peak, Continental Lime Inc.
10. South Chicago, Marblehead Lime Co.

Source: *Mineral Industry Surveys*, September, 1998, p. 1.

Linens, Household

See: **Household Linens**

Lipstick

★2936★
LEADING LIPSTICK BRANDS, 1998
Ranked by: Sales, in million of dollars. **Remarks:** Also notes unit volume. **Number listed:** 10

1. Revlon, with $227.0 million
2. L'Oreal, $105.0
3. Maybelline, $78.3
4. Cover Girl, $66.4
5. Almay, $54.1
6. Bonnie Bell, $43.2
7. Wet 'n' Wild, $30.2
8. Max Factor, $25.6
9. Naturistics, $15.0
10. jane, $13.0

Source: *MMR*, May 3, 1999, p. 28.

Liqueurs

★2937★
LEADING BRANDS OF DOMESTIC U.S. CORDIALS AND LIQUEURS, 1997
Ranked by: Sales, in thousands of 9-liter cases. **Remarks:** Also notes sales for 1992 through 1996, percent change from previous year, and supplier. **Number listed:** 18
1. DeKuyper, with 2,291 thousand cases
2. Southern Comfort, 1,198
3. Hiram Walker Cordials, 1,043
4. Arrow Cordials, 469
5. Jacquin Cordials, 385
6. Leroux, 374
7. Bols Cordials, 320
8. Gaetano Cordials, 310
9. Philips Cordials, 265
10. Boston Cordials, 192

Source: *Adams Liquor Handbook*, (annual), Adams Media, Inc., 1998, p. 190.

★2938★
METROPOLITAN AREAS WITH THE MOST CORDIAL AND LIQUEUR SALES, 1997
Ranked by: Sales, in thousands of 9-liter cases. **Remarks:** Also notes market share. **Number listed:** 50
1. Boston-Lawrence-Lowell-Brockton, MA, with 631.2 cases
2. Chicago, IL, 578.5
3. New York, NY, 509.1
4. Detroit, MI, 429.4
5. Los Angeles-Long Beach, CA, 429.0
6. Minneapolis-St. Paul, MN, 328.7
7. Philadelphia, PA, 288.7
8. Washington, DC, 267.7
9. Las Vegas, 219.2
10. Denver, 212.9

Source: *Adams Liquor Handbook*, (annual), Adams Media, Inc., 1998, p. 189.

★2939★
STATES WITH THE HIGHEST CORDIAL AND LIQUEUR CONSUMPTION, 1997
Ranked by: Consumption, in 9-liter cases. **Remarks:** Also notes previous year's sales, percent change, and cumulative sharc. **Number listed:** 51
1. California, with 1,615,510 cases
2. New York, 1,070,390
3. Florida, 907,120
4. Massachusetts, 846,120
5. Michigan, 817,970
6. Illinois, 778,600
7. Pennsylvania, 716,770
8. New Jersey, 697,200
9. Texas, 664,740
10. Wisconsin, 597,350

Source: *Adams Liquor Handbook*, (annual), Adams Media, Inc., 1998, p. 187.

★2940★
STATES WITH THE HIGHEST CORDIAL AND LIQUEUR CONSUMPTION PER 1000 ADULTS, 1997
Ranked by: Consumption, in 9-liter cases per thousand adults. **Remarks:** Also notes previous year consumption and rank. **Number listed:** 51
1. New Hampshire, with 329.8 cases
2. Nevada, 236.4
3. Maine, 221.4
4. Massachusetts, 189.0
5. Wyoming, 166.1
6. Wisconsin, 164.6
7. Rhode Island, 162.5
8. Alaska, 156.0
9. Delaware, 144.3
10. North Dakota, 143.6

Source: *Adams Liquor Handbook*, (annual), Adams Media, Inc., 1998, p. 188.

★2941★
TOP SUPPLIERS OF CORDIALS AND LIQUEURS, 1997
Ranked by: Market share, in percent. **Number listed:** 6
1. Jim Beam Brands, with 18.8%
2. Hiram Walker, 18.7%
3. IDV North America, 17.7%
4. Brown-Forman Beverages, 7.5%
5. William Grant, 3.4%
6. Others, 33.9%

Source: *Adams Liquor Handbook*, (annual), Adams Media, Inc., 1998, p. 192.

Liqueurs--Advertising

★2942★
MOST-ADVERTISED CORDIAL AND LIQUEUR BRANDS, 1997
Ranked by: Total advertising expenditures, in thousands of dollars. **Remarks:** Also notes expenses for previous year. **Number listed:** 30
1. Grand Marnier, with $4,998.8 thousand
2. Southern Comfort, $4,574.6
3. Baileys, $4,125.7
4. Kahlua Royale Cream, $3,498.6
5. B&B, $3,345.6
6. Di Saronno Amaretto, $2,979.2
7. Romana Sambuca, $1,929.7
8. Campari, $1,315.2
9. Frangelico, $1,017.9
10. Alize, $871.9

Source: *Adams Liquor Handbook*, (annual), Adams Media, Inc., 1998, p. 194.

Liqueurs--Export-Import Trade

★2943★
LEADING IMPORTERS OF U.S. CORDIALS, 1997
Ranked by: Proof gallons, in thousands. **Remarks:** Also notes figures for the previous two years. **Number listed:** 5
1. Canada, with 143.5 thousand gallons
2. Japan, 122.8
3. Mexico, 63.7
4. Netherlands, 50.5
5. Australia, 28.9
6. Others, 173.5

Source: *Adams Liquor Handbook*, (annual), Adams Media, Inc., 1998, p. 219.

Liquor Industry

See also: **Brandy Gin Liqueurs Rum Scotch Vodka**

★2944★

LEADING BRANDS OF BLENDED WHISKEY, 1997

Ranked by: Sales, in thousands of 9-liter cases. **Remarks:** Also notes sales for 1992 through 1996, percent change from previous year, and supplier. **Number listed:** 12

1. 7 Crown, with 2,800 thousand cases
2. Kessler, 958
3. Calvert Extra, 232
4. Fleischmann's Preferred, 227
5. Beam's 8 Star, 202
6. Old Thompson, 187
7. McCormick Blends, 184
8. Kentucky Deluxe, 167
9. Heaven Hill Blended Whiskey, 155
10. Philadelphia, 125

Source: *Adams Liquor Handbook*, (annual), Adams Media, Inc., 1998, p. 62.

★2945★

LEADING BRANDS OF CANADIAN WHISKEY, 1997

Ranked by: Sales, in thousands of 9-liter cases. **Remarks:** Also notes sales for 1992 through 1996, percent change from previous year, and supplier. **Number listed:** 10

1. Canadian Mist, with 2,770 thousand cases
2. Black Velvet, 1,845
3. Windsor Supreme, 1,377
4. Lord Calvert, 747
5. Canadian LTD, 664
6. G & W Rich & Rare, 352
7. Canadian Hunter, 320
8. Canada House, 189
9. McMasters, 120
10. Harwood Canadian, 90

Source: *Adams Liquor Handbook*, (annual), Adams Media, Inc., 1998, p. 76.

★2946★

LEADING BRANDS OF DISTILLED SPIRITS, 1997

Ranked by: Sales, in thousands of 9-liter cases. **Remarks:** Also notes liquor category, supplier, figures from previous year, and percent change. **Number listed:** 140

1. Bacardi, with 6,600 thousand cases
2. Smirnoff, 5,787
3. Absolut, 3,440
4. Jim Beam, 3,339
5. Seagram's Gin, 3,170
6. Jack Daniel's Black, 3,120
7. 7 Crown, 2,800
8. Canadian Mist, 2,770
9. Jose Cuervo, 2,686
10. Popov, 2,577

Source: *Adams Liquor Handbook*, (annual), Adams Media, Inc., 1998, p. 22+.

★2947★

LEADING BRANDS OF PREPARED COCKTAILS, 1997

Ranked by: Sales, in thousands of 9-liter cases. **Remarks:** Also notes sales for 1992 through 1996, percent change from previous year, and supplier. **Number listed:** 18

1. TGI Friday's, with 1,262 thousand cases
2. Jack Daniel's Country Cooler, 1,130
3. Club Cocktails, 493
4. Jose Cuervo Authentic Margarita, 383
5. Chi-Chi's, 325
6. Kahlua Drinks to Go, 324
7. Jose Cuervo Margaritas-Cooler, 251
8. Heublein Cocktails, 204
9. Bacardi Breezer, 185
10. Seagram's Gin & Juice, 140

Source: *Adams Liquor Handbook*, (annual), Adams Media, Inc., 1998, p. 206.

★2948★

LEADING BRANDS OF STRAIGHT WHISKEY, 1997

Ranked by: Sales, in thousands of 9-liter cases. **Remarks:** Also notes sales for 1992 through 1996, percent change from previous year, and supplier. **Number listed:** 18

1. Jim Beam, with 3,339 thousand cases
2. Jack Daniel's Black, 3,120
3. Early Times, 965
4. Evan Williams, 910
5. Ancient Age/AAA, 600
6. Ten High, 561
7. Old Crow, 534
8. Wild Turkey, 464
9. Heaven Hill Bourbon, 310
10. Maker's Mark, 227

Source: *Adams Liquor Handbook*, (annual), Adams Media, Inc., 1998, p. 48.

★2949★

LEADING SELLING BRANDS OF LIQUOR, 1997

Ranked by: Sales, in millions of dollars. **Remarks:** Also notes type of liquor. **Number listed:** 50

1. Bacardi, with $430 million
2. Absolut, $381
3. Jack Daniel's Black, $346
4. Smirnoff, $343
5. Crown Royal, $310
6. Jim Beam, $225
7. Jose Cuervo 1800, $202
8. Hennessy, $197
9. Dewar's, $196
10. 7 Crown, $193

Source: *Adams Liquor Handbook*, (annual), Adams Media, Inc., 1998, p. 209.

★2950★

METROPOLITAN AREAS WITH HIGHEST BLENDED WHISKEY SALES, 1997

Ranked by: Sales, in thousands of 9-liter cases. **Remarks:** Also notes market share. **Number listed:** 50

1. Los Angeles-Long Beach, CA, with 174.0 thousand cases
2. Chicago, IL, 154.4
3. New York, NY, 142.6
4. Detroit, MI, 133.9
5. Milwaukee-Waukesha, WI, 132.1
6. Philadelphia, 123.7
7. Boston-Lawrence-Lowell-Brockton, 121.0
8. Atlanta, GA, 103.9
9. Houston, TX, 84.8
10. Washington, DC, 84.1

Source: *Adams Liquor Handbook*, (annual), Adams Media, Inc., 1998, p. 61.

★2951★

METROPOLITAN AREAS WITH THE HIGHEST CANADIAN WHISKEY SALES, 1997

Ranked by: Sales, in thousands of 9-liter cases. **Remarks:** Also notes market share. **Number listed:** 50

1. Chicago, IL, with 494.4 thousand cases
2. Minneapolis-St. Paul, MN, 421.4
3. Detroit, MI, 418.2

4. Atlanta, GA, 370.5
5. Seattle-Bellevue-Everett, WA, 304.3
6. Los Angeles-Long Beach, CA, 292.6
7. Washington, DC, 252.4
8. New York, NY, 231.8
9. Houston, TX, 217.6
10. Boston-Lawrence-Lowell-Brockton, MA, 203.8

Source: *Adams Liquor Handbook*, (annual), Adams Media, Inc., 1998, p. 78.

★2952★
METROPOLITAN AREAS WITH THE HIGHEST DISTILLED SPIRIT SALES, 1997
Ranked by: Sales, in thousands of 9-liter cases. **Remarks:** Also notes market share. **Number listed:** 50
1. Chicago, IL, with 4,701.1 thousand cases
2. Los Angeles-Long Beach, CA, 4,410.0
3. New York, NY, 4,030.5
4. Washington, DC, 3,261.5
5. Boston-Lawrence-Lowell-Brockton, MA, 2,758.2
6. Detroit, MI, 2,632.5
7. Atlanta, GA, 2,469.6
8. Minneapolis-St. Paul, MN, 2,224.7
9. Philadelphia, PA, 2,159.0
10. Phoenix, AZ, 1,774.5

Source: *Adams Liquor Handbook*, (annual), Adams Media, Inc., 1998, p. 31.

★2953★
METROPOLITAN AREAS WITH THE HIGHEST IRISH WHISKEY SALES, 1997
Ranked by: Sales, in thousands of 9-liter cases. **Remarks:** Also notes market share. **Number listed:** 50
1. New York, NY, with 19.6 thousand cases
2. Los Angeles-Long Beach, CA, 19.3
3. Washington, DC, 10.6
4. Boston-Lawrence-Lowell-Brockton, MA, 10.0
5. Chicago, IL, 9.7
6. Nassau-Suffolk, NY, 7.8
7. Philadelphia, PA, 7.2
8. Orange County, CA, 6.4
9. San Diego, CA, 5.8
10. Riverside-San Bernardino, CA, 5.7

Source: *Adams Liquor Handbook*, (annual), Adams Media, Inc., 1998, p. 105.

★2954★
METROPOLITAN AREAS WITH THE HIGHEST PREPARED COCKTAIL SALES, 1997
Ranked by: Sales, in thousands of 9-liter cases. **Remarks:** Also notes market share. **Number listed:** 25
1. Chicago, IL, with 330.5 thousand cases
2. Los Angeles-Long Beach, CA, 228.0
3. Boston-Lawrence-Lowell-Brockton, MA, 121.6
4. St. Louis, Mo, 108.6
5. Philadelphia, PA, 99.3
6. Washington, DC, 98.1
7. Phoenix, AZ, 82.0
8. New Orleans, LA, 76.2
9. Orange County, CA, 74.7
10. Cleveland-Lorain-Elyria, OH, 73.2

Source: *Adams Liquor Handbook*, (annual), Adams Media, Inc., 1998, p. 197.

★2955★
METROPOLITAN AREAS WITH THE HIGHEST STRAIGHT WHISKEY SALES, 1997
Ranked by: Sales, in thousands of 9-liter cases. **Remarks:** Also notes market share. **Number listed:** 50
1. Washington, DC, with 448.7 thousand cases
2. Los Angeles-Long Beach, CA, 401.5
3. Chicago, IL, 324.4
4. Atlanta, GA, 212.7
5. Houston, TX, 211.0
6. Dallas, TX, 175.7
7. St. Louis, MO, 174.7
8. Denver, CO, 166.7
9. Phoenix, AZ, 166.3
10. Baltimore, MD, 163.2

Source: *Adams Liquor Handbook*, (annual), Adams Media, Inc., 1998, p. 47.

★2956★
STATES WITH THE HIGHEST CONSUMPTION OF BLENDED WHISKEY, 1997
Ranked by: Consumption, in 9-liter cases. **Remarks:** Also notes figures from previous year, percent change, 1997 share, and cumulative share. **Number listed:** 51
1. California, with 651,310 cases
2. Texas, 403,970
3. Wisconsin, 390,280
4. Florida, 314,630
5. New York, 313,150
6. Pennsylvania, 266,020
7. Michigan, 259,120
8. Illinois, 231,550
9. New Jersey, 203,730
10. Ohio, 201,740

Source: *Adams Liquor Handbook*, (annual), Adams Media, Inc., 1998, p. 59.

★2957★
STATES WITH THE HIGHEST CONSUMPTION OF BLENDED WHISKEY PER CAPITA, 1997
Ranked by: Consumption, in 9-liter cases per thousand adults. **Remarks:** Also notes figures from previous year. **Number listed:** 51
1. Wisconsin, with 107.5 cases
2. Mississippi, 89.7
3. New Hampshire, 81.7
4. Nevada, 73.3
5. Oregon, 48.6
6. Delaware, 48.1
7. Louisiana, 47.6
8. Maine, 44.9
9. Oklahoma, 43.9
10. Indiana, 41.8

Source: *Adams Liquor Handbook*, (annual), Adams Media, Inc., 1998, p. 60.

★2958★
STATES WITH THE HIGHEST CONSUMPTION OF CANADIAN WHISKEY, 1997
Ranked by: Consumption, in 9-liter cases. **Remarks:** Also notes figures from previous year, percent change, 1997 share, and cumulative share. **Number listed:** 51
1. California, with 1,159,140 cases
2. Florida, 1,061,040
3. Texas, 1,009,520
4. Michigan, 776,350
5. Illinois, 679,330
6. Georgia, 611,320
7. Minnesota, 595,250
8. Washington, 587,670
9. New York, 545,620
10. Ohio, 512,710

Source: *Adams Liquor Handbook*, (annual), Adams Media, Inc., 1998, p. 73.

★2959★
STATES WITH THE HIGHEST CONSUMPTION OF CANADIAN WHISKEY PER CAPITA, 1997
Ranked by: Consumption, in 9-liter cases per thousand adults. **Remarks:** Also notes figures from previous year. **Number listed:** 51

1. South Dakota, with 331.9 cases
2. North Dakota, 295.5
3. Alaska, 275.3
4. New Hampshire, 230.6
5. Wyoming, 225.7
6. Nevada, 199.8
7. Minnesota, 183.2
8. Montana, 171.8
9. South Carolina, 161.7
10. Washington, 149.6

Source: *Adams Liquor Handbook*, (annual), Adams Media, Inc., 1998, p. 74.

★2960★
STATES WITH THE HIGHEST CONSUMPTION OF DISTILLED SPIRITS, 1997
Ranked by: Consumption, in 9-liter cases. **Remarks:** Also notes figures from previous year, percent change, 1997 share, and cumulative share. **Number listed:** 51

1. California, with 16,006,400 cases
2. Florida, 10,211,100
3. New York, 8,630,340
4. Texas, 7,432,830
5. Illinois, 6,537,890
6. Michigan, 5,247,900
7. New Jersey, 5,020,650
8. Pennsylvania, 4,541,620
9. Georgia, 4,366,700
10. Ohio, 3,975,040

Source: *Adams Liquor Handbook*, (annual), Adams Media, Inc., 1998, p. 20.

★2961★
STATES WITH THE HIGHEST CONSUMPTION OF DISTILLED SPIRITS PER CAPITA, 1997
Ranked by: Consumption, in 9-liter cases per thousand adults. **Remarks:** Also notes figures from previous year. **Number listed:** 51

1. New Hampshire, with 2,007.9 cases
2. District of Columbia, 1,895.0
3. Nevada, 1,731.4
4. Delaware, 1,201.7
5. Alaska, 1098.6
6. Wisconsin, 1,052.6
7. Minnesota, 1,009.7
8. Wyoming, 988.0
9. Colorado, 978.4
10. Florida, 961.6

Source: *Adams Liquor Handbook*, (annual), Adams Media, Inc., 1998, p. 21.

★2962★
STATES WITH THE HIGHEST CONSUMPTION OF IRISH WHISKEY, 1997
Ranked by: Consumption, in 9-liter cases. **Remarks:** Also notes figures from previous year, percent change, 1997 share, and cumulative share. **Number listed:** 51

1. California, with 62,270 cases
2. New York, 39,570
3. New Jersey, 17,780
4. Illinois, 13,840
5. Pennsylvania, 13,830
6. Massachusetts, 12,450
7. Florida, 11,640
8. Texas, 10,220
9. Washington, 9,930
10. Maryland, 8,460

Source: *Adams Liquor Handbook*, (annual), Adams Media, Inc., 1998, p. 103.

★2963★
STATES WITH THE HIGHEST CONSUMPTION OF PREPARED COCKTAILS, 1997
Ranked by: Consumption, in 9-liter cases. **Remarks:** Also notes figures from previous year, percent change, 1997 share, and cumulative share. **Number listed:** 51

1. California, with 774,920 cases
2. Illinois, 415,790
3. Ohio, 349,640
4. Florida, 336,600
5. Texas, 288,560
6. Pennsylvania, 224,120
7. Missouri, 207,510
8. New Jersey, 207,270
9. Louisiana, 201,640
10. Massachusetts, 173,150

Source: *Adams Liquor Handbook*, (annual), Adams Media, Inc., 1998, p. 203.

★2964★
STATES WITH THE HIGHEST CONSUMPTION OF PREPARED COCKTAILS PER CAPITA, 1997
Ranked by: Consumption, in 9-liter cases. **Remarks:** Also notes figures from previous year. **Number listed:** 50

1. New Hampshire, with 73.3 cases
2. Iowa, 70.3
3. Louisiana, 69.1
4. Alaska, 62.3
5. Nevada, 58.5
6. Delaware, 55.2
7. Missouri, 55.1
8. Arkansas, 52.0
9. Illinois, 50.5
10. Colorado, 47.1

Source: *Adams Media*, Adams Liquor Handbook (annual), 1998, p. 51.

★2965★
STATES WITH THE HIGHEST CONSUMPTION OF STRAIGHT WHISKEY, 1997
Ranked by: Consumption, in 9-liter cases. **Remarks:** Also notes figures from previous year, percent change, 1997 share, and cumulative share. **Number listed:** 51

1. California, with 1,463,720 cases
2. Texas, 931,240
3. Florida, 796,710
4. North Carolina, 542,770
5. Virginia, 541,840
6. Kentucky, 497,870
7. Illinois, 482,170
8. Ohio, 428,040
9. Tennessee, 407,890
10. Georgia, 396,440

Source: *Adams Liquor Handbook*, (annual), Adams Media, Inc., 1998, p. 45.

★2966★
STATES WITH THE HIGHEST CONSUMPTION OF STRAIGHT WHISKEY PER CAPITA, 1997
Ranked by: Consumption, in 9-liter cases per thousand adults. **Remarks:** Also notes figures from previous year. **Number listed:** 51

1. Kentucky, with 180.1 cases
2. District of Columbia, 150.9

3. Nevada, 124.4
4. Mississippi, 120.6
5. Louisiana, 116.0
6. Arkansas, 115.6
7. Virginia, 112.6
8. New Hampshire, 112.3
9. Colorado, 111.3
10. Wyoming, 107.9

Source: *Adams Liquor Handbook*, (annual), Adams Media, Inc., 1998, p. 46.

Liquor Industry--Advertising

★2967★
LEADING LIQUOR BRANDS IN MAGAZINE ADVERTISING, 1997
Ranked by: Magazine advertising expenditures, in thousands of dollars. **Remarks:** Also notes market share. **Number listed:** 10

1. Absolut, with $27,013.9 thousand
2. Bacardi, $21,727.3
3. Smirnoff, $12,363.3
4. Jack Daniel's Black, $12,012.4
5. Dewar's, $9,127.9
6. Stolichnaya, $7,662.9
7. Jim Beam, $6,704.1
8. Captain Morgan, $6,195.0
9. Jonnie Walker Black, $5,402.1
10. Bombay Sapphire, $5,359.9

Source: *Adams Liquor Handbook*, (annual), Adams Media, Inc., 1998, p. 239.

★2968★
LEADING LIQUOR BRANDS IN NEWSPAPER ADVERTISING, 1997
Ranked by: Newspaper advertising expenditures, in thousands of dollars. **Remarks:** Also notes market share. **Number listed:** 10

1. The Macallan, with $1,035.0 thousand
2. Romana Sambuca, $932.3
3. Dewar's, $800.1
4. Chambord, $514.8
5. Absolut, $207.1
6. Stolichnaya, $182.4
7. Chivas Regal, $177.7
8. J&B, $171.2
9. Fleischmann's Vodka, $156.7
10. Crown Royal, $146.7

Source: *Adams Liquor Handbook*, (annual), Adams Media, Inc., 1998, p. 240.

★2969★
LEADING LIQUOR BRANDS IN OUTDOOR ADVERTISING, 1997
Ranked by: Outdoor advertising expenditures, in thousands of dollars. **Remarks:** Also notes market share. **Number listed:** 10

1. Captain Morgan, with $2,825.4 thousand
2. Crown Royal, $1,352.0
3. Jack Daniel's, $1,336.3
4. Bacardi, $1,134.3
5. Smirnoff, $866.3
6. Sauza, $829.6
7. Jonnie Walker Red, $811.0
8. Grand Marnier, $736.6
9. Canadian Mist, $673.2
10. Seagram's Gin, $651.3

Source: *Adams Liquor Handbook*, (annual), Adams Media, Inc., 1998, p. 241.

★2970★
MOST ADVERTISED LIQUOR BRANDS, 1997
Ranked by: Total advertising expenditures, in thousands of dollars. **Remarks:** Also notes figures from previous two years, 1997 share, and cumulative share. **Number listed:** 50

1. Absolut, with $27,731.3 thousand
2. Bacardi, $24,487.1
3. Jack Daniel's Black, $13,425.9
4. Smirnoff, $13,309.6
5. Dewar's, $10,156.4
6. Captain Morgan, $9,060.4
7. Stolichnaya, $7,845.3
8. Jim Beam, $6,949.2
9. Chivas Regal, $5,975.7
10. Bombay/Sapphire, $5,733.9

Source: *Adams Liquor Handbook*, (annual), Adams Media, Inc., 1998, p. 234.

★2971★
MOST ADVERTISED PREPARED COCKTAILS, 1997
Ranked by: Total advertising expenditures, in thousands of dollars. **Remarks:** Also notes breakdown of media and figures from previous year. **Number listed:** 7

1. Kahlua Drinks to Go, with $1,782.7 thousand
2. Seagram's Gin & Juice, $244.9
3. TGI Fridays Frozen Drinks, $119.8
4. Jack Daniel's Country Cocktail, $51.2
5. Soco Rocks Rts Cocktails, $40.7
6. Southern Comfort Cocktails, n/a
7. Bacardi Breezer, n/a

Source: *Adams Liquor Handbook*, (annual), Adams Media, Inc., 1998, p. 197.

Liquor Industry--Advertising--Boston (MA)

★2972★
LIQUOR BRANDS MOST FREQUENTLY ADVERTISED IN BOSTON NEWSPAPERS, 1997
Ranked by: Number of appearances. **Remarks:** Also notes percent share of total ads. **Number listed:** 10

1. Barcardi, with 1,599 appearances
2. Kahlua, 1,299
3. Canadian Club, 1,105
4. Smirnoff, 1,079
5. Seagram's 7 Crown, 1,039
6. Dewar's, 977
7. Canadian Mist, 968
8. Absolut, 957
9. Seagram's V.O., 947
10. Beefeater, 912

Source: *Adams Liquor Handbook*, (annual), Adams Media, Inc., 1998, p. 243.

Liquor Industry--Advertising--Chicago (IL)

★2973★
LIQUOR BRANDS MOST FREQUENTLY ADVERTISED IN CHICAGO NEWSPAPERS, 1997
Ranked by: Number of appearances. **Remarks:** Also notes percent share of total ads. **Number listed:** 10

1. Smirnoff, with 1,711 appearances
2. Absolut, 1,386
3. Bacardi, 1,198
4. Christian Brothers, 1,174
5. Jim Beam, 835
6. Seagram's 7 Crown, 817
7. Canadian Club, 806
8. Jack Daniel's, 794
9. J&B, 753
10. Baileys, 719

Source: *Adams Liquor Handbook*, (annual), Adams Media, Inc., 1998, p. 243.

Liquor Industry--Advertising--Dallas (TX)

★2974★
LIQUOR BRANDS MOST FREQUENTLY ADVERTISED IN DALLAS/FT. WORTH NEWSPAPERS, 1997
Ranked by: Number of appearances. **Remarks:** Also notes percent share of total ads. **Number listed:** 10

1. Jack Daniel's, with 410 appearances
2. Crown Royal, 318
3. Jim Beam, 286
4. Smirnoff, 262
5. Bacardi, 248
6. Dewar's, 241
7. Seagram's 7 Crown, 237
8. Jose Cuervo, 230
9. Canadian Club, 229
10. J&B, 223

Source: *Adams Liquor Handbook*, (annual), Adams Media, Inc., 1998, p. 243.

Liquor Industry--Advertising--Houston (TX)

★2975★
LIQUOR BRANDS MOST FREQUENTLY ADVERTISED IN HOUSTON NEWSPAPERS, 1997
Ranked by: Number of appearances. **Remarks:** Also notes percent share of total ads. **Number listed:** 10

1. Jack Daniel's, with 720 appearances
2. Wild Turkey, 432
3. Canadian Mist, 425
4. Bacardi, 419
5. Jim Beam, 411
5. Smirnoff, 411
7. Jose Cuervo, 405
8. Seagram's 7 Crown, 383
9. Canadian Club, 378
10. Windsor Supreme, 370

Source: *Adams Liquor Handbook*, (annual), Adams Media, Inc., 1998, p. 243.

Liquor Industry--Advertising--Los Angeles (CA)

★2976★
LIQUOR BRANDS MOST FREQUENTLY ADVERTISED IN LOS ANGELES NEWSPAPERS, 1997
Ranked by: Number of appearances. **Remarks:** Also notes percent share of total ads. **Number listed:** 10

1. Smirnoff, with 201 appearances
2. Bacardi, 171
3. Jose Cuervo, 157
4. Seagram's 7 Crown, 150
5. Jack Daniel's, 143
6. E&J, 128
7. Christian Brothers, 105
8. Seagram's V.O., 95
9. Absolut, 89
10. Presidente Brandy, 87

Source: *Adams Liquor Handbook*, (annual), Adams Media, Inc., 1998, p. 243.

Liquor Industry--Advertising--Miami (FL)

★2977★
LIQUOR BRANDS MOST FREQUENTLY ADVERTISED IN MIAMI NEWSPAPERS, 1997
Ranked by: Number of appearances. **Remarks:** Also notes percent share of total ads. **Number listed:** 10

1. Absolut, with 1,884 appearances
2. Canadian Club, 1,579
3. Bacardi, 1,473
4. Crown Royal, 1,370
5. Beefeater, 1,331
6. Chivas Regal, 1,329
7. Captain Morgan, 1,293
8. Jack Daniel's, 1,269
9. Smirnoff, 1,144
10. Kahlua, 1,137

Source: *Adams Liquor Handbook*, (annual), Adams Media, Inc., 1998, p. 244.

Liquor Industry--Advertising--New York (NY)

★2978★
LIQUOR BRANDS MOST FREQUENTLY ADVERTISED IN NEW YORK NEWSPAPERS, 1997
Ranked by: Number of appearances. **Remarks:** Also notes percent share of total ads. **Number listed:** 10

1. Bacardi, with 1,198 appearances
2. Absolut, 670
3. Smirnoff, 598
4. Dewar's, 486
5. Beefeater, 434
6. Jack Daniels, 426
7. Jonnie Walker Red, 404
8. Tanqueray Gin, 364
9. Gordon's Vodka, 359
10. Seagram's 7 Crown, 328

Source: *Adams Liquor Handbook*, (annual), Adams Media, Inc., 1998, p. 244.

Liquor Industry--Advertising--San Francisco (CA)

★2979★
LIQUOR BRANDS MOST FREQUENTLY ADVERTISED IN SAN FRANCISCO NEWSPAPERS, 1997
Ranked by: Number of appearances. **Remarks:** Also notes percent share of total ads. **Number listed:** 10

1. E&J, with 444 appearances
2. Bacardi, 386
3. Jose Cuervo, 351
4. Seagram's 7 Crown, 346
5. Smirnoff, 342
6. Absolut, 304
7. Kahlua, 261
8. Christian Brothers, 239
9. Wolfschmidt, 229
10. Jack Daniel's, 209

Source: *Adams Liquor Handbook*, (annual), Adams Media, Inc., 1998, p. 244.

Liquor Industry--Advertising--Washington, D.C.

★2980★
LIQUOR BRANDS MOST FREQUENTLY ADVERTISED IN DISTRICT OF COLUMBIA NEWSPAPERS, 1997
Ranked by: Number of appearances. **Remarks:** Also notes percent share of total ads. **Number listed:** 10

1. Bacardi, with 698 appearances
2. Courvoisier, 544
3. Hennessy, 468
4. Bombay Gin, 426
5. Jack Daniel's, 376
6. Smirnoff, 369
7. J&B, 365
8. Stolichnaya, 362
9. Jose Cuervo, 350
10. Beefeater, 345

Source: *Adams Liquor Handbook*, (annual), Adams Media, Inc., 1998, p. 244.

Liquor Industry--Export-Import Trade

★2981★
LEADING IMPORTERS OF U.S. OTHER WHISKEY, 1997
Ranked by: Thousands of proof gallons. **Remarks:** Also notes previous year figures. **Number listed:** 5

1. Canada, with 156.8 thousand
2. Japan, 143.8
3. Taiwan, 137.4
4. Mexico, 137.0
5. Netherlands, 93.2

Source: *Jobson's Media*, Jobson's Liquor Handbook (annual), 1998, p. 219.

★2982★
LEADING IMPORTERS OF U.S. SPIRITS, 1997
Ranked by: Thousands of proof gallons. **Remarks:** Also notes previous year figures. **Number listed:** 5

1. CIS, with 48,403.0 thousand
2. Netherlands, 36,023.0
3. Mexico, 13,368.5
4. Korea, 12,180.2
5. Ukraine, 5,208.5

Source: *Jobson's Media*, Jobson's Liquor Handbook (annual), 1998, p. 219.

★2983★
LEADING IMPORTERS OF U.S. WHISKEY, 1997
Ranked by: Thousands of proof gallons. **Remarks:** Also notes previous year figures. **Number listed:** 5

1. Australia, with 3,436.4 thousand
2. Japan, 2,731.7
3. Germany, 2,643.3
4. United Kingdom, 1,678.5
5. France, 747.3

Source: *Jobson's Media*, Jobson's Liquor Handbook (annual), 1998, p. 219.

Lisbon Stock Exchange

★2984★
LARGEST LISTED COMPANIES ON THE LISBON STOCK EXCHANGE, 1996
Ranked by: Market value in millions of Portuguese escudos (Esc). **Number listed:** 20

1. Portugal Telecom, with Esc1,117,636 million
2. EDP, Esc618,838
3. BCP, Esc564,600
4. BES, Esc478,504
5. Telecel, Esc421,615
6. BPI, Esc348,818
7. Modelo Continente, Esc302,940
8. Sonae Investimentos, Esc297,760
9. BPA, Esc279,400
10. Cimpor, Esc263,390

Source: *Euromoney Publications*, SSB Guide to World Equity Markets (annual), 1998, p. 411.

★2985★
MOST ACTIVELY TRADED SHARES ON THE LISBON STOCK EXCHANGE, 1996
Ranked by: Turnover, in millions of Portuguese escudos (Esc). **Number listed:** 20

1. Portugal Telecom, with Esc692,198 million
2. EDP, Esc446,148
3. BCP, Esc312,992
4. Cimpor, Esc285,910
5. Telecel, Esc240,688
6. BES, Esc161,935
7. Sonae Investimentos, Esc150,396
8. BPI, Esc124,434
9. BTA, Esc122,265
10. Jeronimo Martins, Esc91,630

Source: *Euromoney Publications*, SSB Guide to World Equity Markets (annual), 1998, p. 411.

Ljubljana Stock Exchange

★2986★
LARGEST LISTED COMPANIES ON THE LJUBLJANA STOCK EXCHANGE, 1997
Ranked by: Market value, in millions of U.S. dollars ($). **Number listed:** 10
1. Krka, with $385.6 million
2. Lek, $325.4
3. Petrol, $200.0
4. Mercator, $84.1
5. Istrabenz, $80.6
6. Luka Koper, $79.2
7. SKB Bank, $73.9
8. BTC, $61.3
9. Radenska, $45.1
10. Droga, $44.0

Source: *Euromoney Publications*, SSB Guide to World Equity Markets (annual), 1998, p. 442.

★2987★
MOST ACTIVELY TRADED SHARES ON THE LJUBLJANA STOCK EXCHANGE, 1997
Ranked by: Turnover, in millions of Deutsche Marks (DM). **Number listed:** 10
1. Krka, with DM17,567 million
2. Lek, DM17,443
3. Mercator, DM9,636
4. SKB Bank, DM7,480
5. Petrol, DM6,809
6. Kolinska, DM2,980
7. Luka Koper, DM2,092
8. Terme Eate, DM2,042
9. Istrabenz, DM1,718
10. Droga, DM1,709

Source: *Euromoney Publications*, SSB Guide to World Equity Markets (annual), 1998, p. 442.

Lloyd's of London

★2988★
LARGEST CORPORATE MEMBER'S OF LLOYD'S, 1998
Ranked by: Capacity, in millions of British pounds. **Number listed:** 10
1. Limit PLC, with £677 million
2. Ace, £303
3. Terra Nova, £234
4. Cox Insurance, £227
5. CLM Insurance Fund, £224
6. Brockbank/X.L. Mid Ocean, £210
7. Charman/ACE, £188
8. Angerstein Underwriting Trust, £181
8. Duncanson & Holt, £181
10. Wellington, £166

Source: *Business Insurance*, Lloyd's of London (annual), 1998, p. 10.

Lobbyists

★2989★
LEADING LOBBYISTS IN WASHINGTON DC, 1998
Ranked by: Lobbyists with the most clout. **Number listed:** 25
1. American Association of Retired Persons
2. American Israel Public Affairs Committee
3. National Federation of Independent Business
4. National Rifle Association of America
5. AFL-CIO
6. Association of Trial Lawyers of America
7. Christian Coalition
8. Credit Union National Association
9. National Right to Life Committee
10. American Medical Association

Source: *Fortune*, December 7, 1998, p. 137.

★2990★
TOP COMPUTER LOBBYING SPENDERS, 1997
Ranked by: Lobby expenditures, in millions of dollars. **Number listed:** 10
1. IBM, with $5.2 million
2. EDS, $2.2
3. Texas Instruments, $2.0
4. Microsoft, $1.9
5. Business Software Alliance, $1.0
6. Oracle, $.9
7. America Online, $.8
8. Netscape, $.7
8. Computer Systems Policy Project, $.7
10. Intel, $.6

Source: *Red Herring*, December, 1998, p. 64.

Lobbyists--Detroit Metropolitan Area

★2991★
LEADING LOBBY FIRMS IN DETROIT, 1998
Ranked by: Number of Detroit-based business clients. **Remarks:** Also notes previous year figures, contact information, total number of clients, lobbying expenditures, and representative clients. **Number listed:** 14
1. Karoub Associates, with 49 clients
2. Governmental Consultant Services, 40
2. Muchmore Harrington Smalley & Associates, 40
4. Cawthorne, McCollough & Canavagh, 25
4. Scotes, Kindsvatter & Associates, 25
6. Dykema Gossett P.L.L.C., 24
7. Cusmano, Kandler & Reed, Inc., 20
8. Public Affairs Associates Inc., 18
9. Kheder & Associates, 17
10. Michigan Legislative Consultants, 16

Source: *Crain's Detroit Business*, November 16, 1998, p. 23.

Local Area Network Industry

★2992★
MOST ADMIRED ELECTRONICS AND NETWORKS CORPORATIONS, 1998
Ranked by: Scores (1-10) derived from a survey of senior executives, outside directors and securities analysts. **Remarks:** Respondents rated companies in their own industry on 8 attri-

butes of reputation. Also notes previous year rank. **Number listed:** 4

1. Cisco Systems, with 8.32 points
2. 3Com, 6.78
3. Bay Networks, 5.92
4. Cabletron Systems, 4.35

Source: *Fortune*, America's Most Admired Corporations (annual), March 1, 1999, p. F-6.

Local Transit

★2993★
BEST URBAN TRANSIT SYSTEMS, 1999*
Ranked by: Results of survey. **Remarks:** Survey included 12 measures such as service levels, operating costs, and per-passenger revenue. **Number listed:** 135

1. Santa Monica, CA
2. Champaign-Urbana, IL
3. Tucson, AZ
4. Las Vegas, NV
5. Springfield, MA
6. Santa Barbara, CA
7. Newport News, VA
8. El Paso, TX
9. Los Angeles, CA
10. Richmond, VA

Source: *Governing*, February, 1999, p. 96.

★2994★
LARGEST TRANSIT AGENCIES, 1996
Ranked by: Number of unlinked passenger trips. **Remarks:** Number of trips not provided. **Number listed:** 35

1. Metropolitan Transportation Authority (New York, NY)
2. Regional Transportation Authority (Chicago, IL)
3. Los Angeles County Metropolitan Transportation Authority
4. Southeastern Pennsylvania Transportation Authority
5. Washington Metropolitan Area Transit Authority (Washington, DC)
6. Massachusetts Bay Transportation Authority
7. New Jersey Transit Corporation
8. San Francisco Municipal Railway
9. Metropolitan Atlanta Rapid Transit Authority
10. Mass Transit Administration of Maryland

Source: *Transit Fact Book*, 1998, p. 67+.

★2995★
WORST URBAN TRANSIT SYSTEMS, 1999*
Ranked by: Results of survey. **Remarks:** Survey included 12 measures such as service levels, operating costs, and per-passenger revenue. **Number listed:** 135

1. Oklahoma City, OK
2. Jackson, MS
3. Birmingham, AL
4. Youngstown, OH
5. Suffolk County, NY
6. Riverside, CA
7. West Palm Beach, FL
8. New York, NY
9. Lexington, KY
10. Greenville, SC

Source: *Governing*, February, 1999, p. 96.

Location of Industry

★2996★
TOP CITIES FOR INFORMATION TECHNOLOGY JOBS, 1998
Ranked by: Results of survey based on annual salary, skill, and hiring results. **Remarks:** Also notes metro population, housing prices, and top IT jobs and salaries. **Number listed:** 10

1. Boston, MA
2. Chicago, IL
3. Atlanta, GA
4. Washington, DC
5. New York, NY
6. San Francisco, CA
7. Seattle, WA
8. Las Vegas, NV
9. St. Louis, MO
10. Austin, TX

Source: *Computer World*, January 11, 1999, p. 64+.

★2997★
TOP FACTORS IN SITE SELECTION, 1998
Ranked by: Percent of respondents naming factor as important. **Remarks:** Also notes previous year results. **Number listed:** 23

1. Highway accessibility, with 91.5%
2. Availability of skilled labor, 88.0%
3. Occupancy or construction costs, 85.7%
4. Labor costs, 84.8%
5. Availability of telecommunications services, 82.0%
6. Availability of land, 81.1%
7. State and local incentives, 80/9%
8. Energy availability and costs, 78.9%
9. Environmental regulations, 78.6%
10. Tax exemptions, 77.9%

Source: *Area Development*, December, 1998, p. 47.

London Stock Exchange

★2998★
LARGEST LISTED COMPANIES ON THE LONDON STOCK EXCHANGE, 1997
Ranked by: Market value, in millions of British pounds. **Number listed:** 20

1. Glaxo Wellcome, with £51,433.6 million
2. British Petroleum, £47,159.2
3. Shell Transport & Trading, £43,751.4
4. HSBC, £40,987.5
5. Lloyds TSB, £40,556.9
6. SmithKline Beecham, £34,415.3
7. British Telecommunications, £30,254.0
8. Barclays, £24,350.1
9. Diageo, £22,011.5
10. Halifax, £19,176.4

Source: *Euromoney Publications*, SSB Guide to World Equity Markets (annual), 1998, p. 524.

★2999★
MOST ACTIVELY TRADED SHARES ON THE LONDON STOCK EXCHANGE, 1997
Ranked by: Turnover value, in millions of British pounds. **Number listed:** 20

1. HSBC, with £48,267.4 million
2. British Telecommunications, £39,977.4
3. Shell Transport & Trading, £25,879.0

4. British Petroleum, £25,247.0
5. Glaxo Wellcome, £24,313.1
6. Lloyds TSB, £20,788.2
7. SmithKline Beecham, £19,761.5
8. Barclays, £19,462.1
9. National Westminster Bank, £15,448.4
10. BAT Industries, £14,764.4

Source: *Euromoney Publications*, SSB Guide to World Equity Markets (annual), 1998, p. 525.

Long Island (NY)--Industries

★3000★
TOP LONG ISLAND-BASED PUBLIC FIRMS, 1997
Ranked by: Revenue, in thousands of dollars. **Remarks:** Also notes contact information, fiscal year-end date, previous year rank, percent change, net income. **Number listed:** 57

1. Kimko Reality Corp., with $198,929 thousand
2. Manchester Equipment, $187,801
3. Morton's Restaurant Group, $172,725
4. Aceto, $169,387
5. Acclaim Entertainment, $165,411
5. Veeco Instruments, $165,411
7. Standard Microsystems, $155,747
8. Jaco Electronics, $155,098
9. Reckson Associates Reality, $153,395
10. Hirsch International, $152,477

Source: *Long Island Business*, October 2, 1998, p. 40+.

Looms, International

★3001★
LEADING LOOMING/WEAVING MACHINE PRODUCERS RANKED BY UNITS SOLD, 1998
Ranked by: Number of units sold. **Number listed:** 8

1. Tsudakoma, with 7,350 units
2. Picanol, 4,900
3. Sulzer Textil, 4,160
4. Somet, 2,900
5. Toyoda, 2,620
6. Varnatex, 2,500
7. Nissan, 2,400
8. Dornier, 1,750

Source: *Textile World*, April, 1999, p. 39.

★3002★
LEADING LOOMING/WEAVING MACHINES PRODUCERS, 1998
Ranked by: Sales, in millions of Swiss Francs (CHF). **Number listed:** 8

1. Sulzer Textil, with SFr747 million
2. Picanol, SFr461
3. Tsudakoma, SFr306
4. Dornier, SFr260
5. Somet, SFr247
6. Varnatex, SFr192
7. Toyoda, SFr114
8. Nissan, SFr106

Source: *Textile World*, April, 1999, p. 39.

Los Angeles County (CA)--Industries

★3003★
MOST PROFITABLE PUBLIC COMPANIES IN LOS ANGELES COUNTY (CA), 1998
Ranked by: Return on equity, in percent. **Remarks:** Also notes 1998 revenues and net income, 1997 net income, and description of company. **Number listed:** 50

1. Hilton Hotels Corp., with 95.2%
2. Natrol Inc., 50.3%
3. Guitar Center Inc., 47.8%
4. Newhall Land & Farm, 44.6%
5. Laser-Pacific Media Corp., 40.4%
6. Gemstar International Group, 37.4%
7. Herbalife International, 33.5%
8. Macneal-Schwendler Corp., 33.2%
9. Vertel Corp., 32.8%
10. Tarrant Apparel Group, 31.1%

Source: *Los Angles Business Journal (annual)*, April 26, 1999, p. 32+.

★3004★
TOP PRIVATE SECTOR EMPLOYERS IN LOS ANGELES COUNTY, 1998
Ranked by: Number of employees in L.A. County. **Remarks:** Also notes contact information, total employees, core business, parent company, and top executive. **Number listed:** 25

1. The Boeing Co., with 29,300 employees
2. Kaiser Permanente, 17,530
3. Northrop Grumman, 14,200
4. Tenet Healthcare Corp., 14,000
5. Walt Disney Co., 12,150
6. TRW Space & Electronics Group, 11,200
7. GTE California Inc., 10,600
8. SBC Communications, 10,000
8. Hughes Electronics Corp., 10,000
10. ABM Industries Inc., 8,200

Source: *Los Angeles Business Journal (annual)*, July 27, 1998, p. 13.

Lotteries

★3005★
TOP LOTTERIES BY FEWEST CENTS SPENT TO GENERATE ONE GOVERNMENT DOLLAR, 1998
Ranked by: Fewest cents spent. **Number listed:** 38

1. Pennsylvania, with $.207
2. New Jersey, $.213
3. Michigan, $.253
4. Maryland, $.254
5. Florida, $.265
6. New York, $.282
7. Ohio, $.286
8. Connecticut, $.290
9. Illinois, $.306
10. Massachusetts, $.317

Source: *International Gaming & Wagering Business*, Annual Study on Performance, April, 1999, p. 39.

★3006★
TOP LOTTERIES BY FEWEST CENTS SPENT TO GENERATE ONE SALES DOLLAR, 1998
Ranked by: Fewest cents spent. **Number listed:** 38

1. Massachusetts, with $.077
2. New Jersey, $.084

3. Pennsylvania, $.088
4. Connecticut, $.093
5. Maryland, $.095
6. Ohio, $.102
7. Illinois, $.108
8. New York, $.109
9. Michigan, $.110
10. Vermont, $.114

Source: *International Gaming & Wagering Business*, Annual Study on Performance, April, 1999, p. 39.

★3007★
TOP LOTTERIES BY FISCAL 1998 PRIZES AS A PERCENT OF TOTAL SALES
Ranked by: Prizes as a percent of sales. **Number listed:** 38

1. Massachusetts, with 68.9%
2. Oregon, 62.8%
3. Washington, 61.5%
4. Minnesota, 60.3%
5. Kentucky, 59.8%
6. Connecticut, 58.9%
6. Colorado, 58.9%
8. Idaho, 58.4%
9. Vermont, 58.2%
10. South Dakota, 58.0%

Source: *International Gaming & Wagering Business*, Annual Study on Performance, April, 1999, p. 39.

★3008★
TOP LOTTERIES BY GOVERNMENT REVENUE AS A PERCENT OF GROSS REVENUE, 1998
Ranked by: Government revenue as a percent of gross revenue. **Number listed:** 38

1. Michigan, with 95.2%
1. Wisconsin, 95.2%
3. Florida, 89.3%
4. New Jersey, 84.5%
5. Pennsylvania, 84.2%
5. Washington, 82.7%
7. Ohio, 82.3%
8. Maryland, 79.7%
9. Illinois, 79.6%
10. New York, 78.4%

Source: *International Gaming & Wagering Business*, Annual Study on Performance, April, 1999, p. 38+.

★3009★
TOP LOTTERIES BY GOVERNMENT REVENUE AS A PERCENT OF SALES, 1998
Ranked by: Government revenue as a percent of sales. **Number listed:** 38

1. Florida, with 44.8%
2. Michigan, 43.3%
3. Pennsylvania, 42.7%
4. Wisconsin, 41.0%
5. New Jersey, 39.5%
6. New York, 38.8%
7. Maryland, 37.3%
8. Louisiana, 36.6%
9. District of Columbia, 35.9%
10. Ohio, 35.7%

Source: *International Gaming & Wagering Business*, Annual Study on Performance, April, 1999, p. 38+.

★3010★
TOP LOTTERIES BY GOVERNMENT REVENUE AS A PERCENT OF STATE PERSONAL INCOME, 1998
Ranked by: Government revenue as a percent of state personal income. **Number listed:** 38

1. District of Columbia, with .421%
2. Massachusetts, .385%
3. Georgia, .294%
4. Michigan, .278%
4. Ohio, .278%
6. New York, .264%
7. Maryland, .260%
8. Florida, .240%
9. New Jersey, .237%
10. Texas, .225%

Source: *International Gaming & Wagering Business*, Annual Study on Performance, April, 1999, p. 38+.

Lotteries, International

★3011★
COUNTRIES WITH THE MOST LOTTERY SALES, 1998
Ranked by: Lottery sales, in billions of U.S. dollars ($). **Number listed:** 9

1. U.S., with $36.7 billion
2. Italy, $12.3
3. United Kingdom, $9.9
4. Spain, $9.7
5. Germany, $9.4
6. France, $6.1
7. Japan, $6.0
8. Canada, $5.1
9. Malaysia, $2.1

Source: *International Wagering Business*, May, 1999, p. 39.

★3012★
WORLD REGIONS WITH THE HIGHEST LOTTERY SALES, 1998
Ranked by: Lottery sales, in millions of U.S. dollars ($). **Remarks:** Also notes market share. **Number listed:** 6

1. Europe, with $61,246.6 million
2. North America, $42,825.6
3. Asia/Middle East, $13,390.7
4. Central/South America/Caribbean, $4,114.9
5. Australia/New Zealand, $2,334.8
6. Africa, $272.8

Source: *International Wagering Business*, May, 1999, p. 42.

★3013★
WORLD'S MOST POPULAR LOTTERY GAMES BY SALES, 1998
Ranked by: Lottery sales, in billions of U.S. dollars ($). **Remarks:** Also notes market share. **Number listed:** 6

1. Lotto/Spiel, with $50.4 billion
2. Instant, $21.8
3. Draw Passive, $17.5
4. Sports/Toto, $5.3
5. Keno, $3.1
6. Other, $5.6

Source: *International Wagering Business*, May, 1999, p. 42.

★3014★
WORLD'S TOP GROSSING LOTTERY ORGANIZATIONS, 1998
Ranked by: Sales, in billions of U.S. dollars ($). **Number listed:** 10

1. The U.K. National Lottery (United Kingdom), with $9.1 billion
2. Amministrazione Autonoma del Monopoli di Stato (Italy), $8.1

3. Organismo Nacional de Loterias y Apuestas (Spain), $7.0
4. La Francaise des Jeux (France), $6.1
5. Dai-Ichi Kangyo Bank Lottery (Japan), $6.0
6. New York State Lottery (U.S.), $3.9
7. Massachusetts State Lottery (U.S.), $3.2
8. Texas State Lottery (U.S.), $3.1
9. Organizacion Nacional de Ciegos de Espana (Spain), $2.6
10. Sisal Sport Italia (Italy), $2.4

Source: *International Wagering Business*, May, 1999, p. 39.

Lubrication and Lubricants

★3015★
LEADING MOTOR OIL BRANDS, 1998
Ranked by: Market share, in percent. **Number listed:** 6

1. Pennzoil, with 21.5%
2. Quaker State, 14.5%
3. Valvoline, 14.4%
4. Castrol, 13.2%
5. Havoline, 11.3%
6. All Others, 25.1%

Source: *Wall Street Journal*, July 1, 1998, p. B4.

★3016★
TOP SYNTHETIC LUBRICANTS, 1996
Ranked by: Market share, in percent. **Number listed:** 5

1. Poly-olefins, with 48%
2. Polyalkylene glycols, 23%
3. Polyol esters, 16%
4. Diesters, 8%
5. Phosphate esters, 5%

Source: *C&EN*, September 7, 1998, p. 21.

Lumber Trade--Europe

★3017★
TOP LUMBER AND WOOD PRODUCTS COMPANIES IN EUROPE, 1999*
Ranked by: Sales, in millions of European Currency Units (ECUs). **Remarks:** Also notes number of employees and overall rank among European businesses. **Number listed:** 43

1. Preglejka AS, with ECUs13.367 million
2. Unibank A/S, ECUs2.561
3. The Rugby Group PLC, ECUs1.571
4. Glunz AG, ECUs971
5. Fritz Egger Gesellschaft MBH & Co., ECUs922
6. Finnforest OY, ECUs660
7. The Davis Service Group PLC, ECUs601
8. Enso Timber OY Ltd, ECUs571
9. Schauman Wood OY, ECUs522
10. Hornitex-Weke Gebr, Kuennemeyer Gmbh & Co. Kg, ECUs471

Source: *Dun & Bradstreet*, Duns Europa (annual), 1999, p. 238+.

Luxembourg Stock Exchange

★3018★
LARGEST LISTED COMPANIES ON THE LUXEMBOURG STOCK EXCHANGE, 1997
Ranked by: Market value, in millions of Luxembourg francs (LFr). **Number listed:** 20

1. Vendome Luxury Group, with LFr203,700.0 million
2. Safra Republic Holdings, LFr141,063.9
3. Minorco, LFr139.886.7
4. Audiofina, LFr92,175.4
5. Banque Generale du Luxembourg, LFr77,207.5
6. Exor Group, LFr69,407.3
7. Kredietbank SA Luxembourg, LFr66,622.2
8. Millicom International Cellular, LFr63,874.3
9. Banque International a Luxembourg, LFr62,491.0
10. Quinsa, LFr45,314.2

Source: *Euromoney Publications*, SSB Guide to World Equity Markets (annual), 1998, p. 321.

★3019★
MOST ACTIVELY TRADED SHARES ON THE LUXEMBOURG STOCK EXCHANGE, 1997
Ranked by: Trading value, in millions of Luxembourg francs (LFr). **Remarks:** Also notes number of trades. **Number listed:** 15

1. Banque International a Luxembourg, with LFr3,315.00 million
2. Banque Generale du Luxembourg, LFr2,506.08
3. Arbed, LFr1,527.69
4. Audiofina, LFr1,270.61
5. Kredietbank SA Luxembourg (priv), LFr1,250.15
6. Socfinasia, LFr1,228.47
7. Luxempart, LFr1,219.41
8. Quinsa, LFr1,176.48
9. Intercultures, LFr1,077.32
10. Kredietbank SA Luxembourg (ord), LFr1,072.36

Source: *Euromoney Publications*, SSB Guide to World Equity Markets (annual), 1998, p. 321.

Machinery

★3020★
TOP ELECTRICAL AND ELECTRONIC MACHINERY COMPANIES IN EUROPE, 1999*
Ranked by: Sales, in millions of European Currency Units (ECUs). **Remarks:** Also notes number of employees and overall rank among European businesses. **Number listed:** 187

1. The General Electric Co. Plc, with ECUs9,586 million
2. EMI Group Plc, ECUs4,883
3. Motorola, ECUs4,608
4. Bosch-Siemens Hausgeraete GMBH, ECUs4,449
5. Siebe Plc, ECUs4,434
6. Hewlett Packard GMBH, ECUs4,221
7. Den Danske Bank A/S, ECUs3,668
8. Sony United Kingdom Ltd., ECUs3,265
9. GEC Marconi Ltd., ECUs2,871
10. Schneider Electric, ECUs2,811

Source: *Dun & Bradstreet*, Duns Europa (annual), 1999, p. 255+.

★3021★
TOP NON-ELECTRICAL MACHINERY COMPANIES IN EUROPE, 1999*
Ranked by: Sales, in millions of European Currency Units (ECUs). **Remarks:** Also notes number of employees and overall rank among European businesses. **Number listed:** 272
1. Mannesmann AG, with ECUs19,827 million
2. Fried Krupp AG Hoesch - Krupp, ECUs12,190
3. IBM United Kingdom Holdings, ECUs7,552
4. IBM United Kingdom Ltd., ECUs7,246
5. Thyssen Industrie AG, ECUs5,779
6. IBM Deutschland GMBH, ECUs5,786
7. Compaq Computer Manufacturing Ltd., ECUs5,753
8. IBM Deutschland Information Systeme GMBH, ECUs4,712
9. Linde AG, ECUs4,463
10. Hewlett Packard Holding GMBH, ECUs4,221

Source: *Dun & Bradstreet*, Duns Europa (annual), 1999, p. 252+.

Madrid Stock Exchange
See: **Bolsa de Madrid**

Magazine Advertising
See: **Advertising, Magazine**

Mail Order Business

★3022★
TOP U.S. MAIL ORDER BUSINESSES, 1998*
Ranked by: Worldwide sales through mail order, in millions of dollars. **Remarks:** Also notes sales segment. **Number listed:** 25
1. Dell Computer Corp., with $8,471.5 million
2. United Services Automobile Association, $7,464.0
3. Time Warner, $6,997.2
4. Tele-Communications, $6,645.1
5. Gateway 2000, $5,035.2
6. J.C. Penney, $4,540.0
7. AARP, $4,416.3
8. Comcast, $3,706.9
9. Berkshire Hathaway, $3,326.5
10. Cendant, $3,259.6

Source: *Direct Marketing*, September, 1998, p. 24+.

★3023★
TOP U.S. MAIL ORDER CATALOG BUSINESSES, 1998*
Ranked by: Worldwide sales through mail order, in millions of dollars. **Remarks:** Also notes sales segment. **Number listed:** 25
1. Dell Computer Corp., with $8,471.5 million
2. Gateway 2000, $5,035.2
3. J.C. Penney, $3,500.0
4. Hewlett Packard Direct Marketing Division, $2,125.0
5. Micro Warehouse, $1,706.0
6. Micron Electronics, $1,528.3
7. Fingerhut Catalog, $1,480.0
8. W.W. Grainger, $1,380.0
9. Viking Office Products, $1,286.3
10. Caremark, $1,211.0

Source: *Direct Marketing*, September, 1998, p. 27+.

Mail Order Business, International

★3024★
WORLD'S LEADING MAIL ORDER COMPANIES, 1997
Ranked by: Mail order sales, in millions of U.S. dollars ($). **Remarks:** Also notes type of service offered. **Number listed:** 25
1. Otto Versand (Germany), with $11,100 million
2. Dell Computer Corp. (U.S.), $8,472
3. United Services Automobile Association (U.S.), $7,464
4. Time Warner (U.S.), $6,997
5. Tele-Communications (U.S.), $6,645
6. Quelle (Germany), $5,960
7. Gateway 2000 (U.S.), $5,035
8. J.C. Penney (U.S.), $4,540
9. AARP (U.S.), $4,416
10. Comcast (U.S.), $3,707

Source: *Direct Marketing*, September, 1998, p. 31.

Management

★3025★
TOP SKILLS NEEDED BY MANAGERS FOR ORGANIZATIONAL SUCCESS ACCORDING TO HUMAN RESOURCE DIRECTORS, 1999*
Ranked by: Skills are listed, not ranked. **Remarks:** Survey of human resource directors of Fortune 1,000 firms. **Number listed:** 10
1. interpersonal
2. listening
3. persuasion and motivation
4. presentation
5. small-group communication
6. advising
7. interviewing
8. conflict management
9. writing
10. reading

Source: *Training and Development*, February, 1999, p. 10.

Management Buyouts

★3026★
LARGEST UNIT MANAGEMENT BUYOUTS COMPLETED/PENDING, 1998
Ranked by: Purchase price, in millions of dollars. **Number listed:** 18
1. Wesco Distribution Inc. (buyer), Clayton Dubilier & Rice Inc. (seller), with $1,100.0 million

2. Deutsche Woolworth GMBH (buyer), Venator Group Inc. (seller), $552.0
3. Hebdo Mag International (buyer), Cendant Corp. (seller), $503.7
4. Alaska Telephone Co. (buyer), Century Telephone Enterprises Inc. (seller), $415.0
5. Shoppers Food Warehouse Corp. (buyer), Dart Group Corp. (seller), $360.0
6. Commercial Laundry Business (buyer), Raytheon Co. (seller), $358.0
7. MCG Credit Corp. (buyer), First Union Corp. (seller), $220.0
8. Ajax Magnethermic Corp. (buyer), BBA Group Plc (seller), $135.0
8. Britton Group Plastics (buyer), ACX Technologies (seller), $135.0
10. United Commercial Bank (buyer), Salim Group (seller), $120.0

Source: *Mergerstat Review (annual)*, 1999, p. 34.

★3027★
LARGEST UNIT MANAGEMENT BUYOUTS ON RECORD, 1998
Ranked by: Price offered, in millions of dollars. **Number listed:** 5

1. Private group, led by Kohlberg Kravis Roberts & Co. (buyer), Allied Corp. (seller), with $1,700.0 million
2. Private group led by management (buyer), Mobile Corp. (seller), $1,500.0
3. Private group led by division management (buyer), Exxon Corp. (seller), $1,350.0
4. Private group led by Ford Motor Co. and Hertz management (buyer), Allegis Corp. (seller), $1,300.0
5. Private group led by Kohlberg Kravis Roberts & Co. (buyer), City Investing Co. (seller), $1,251.0

Source: *Mergerstat Review (annual)*, 1999, p. 34.

Management Consultants

See: **Business Consultants**

Manufacturers

★3028★
TOP INTERNATIONAL MANUFACTURING FACILITIES BY FLOOR AREA, 1998
Ranked by: Floor area, in thousands of square feet. **Remarks:** Also notes type of industry and square meters. **Number listed:** 20

1. Hino Auto Body Ltd. (Japan), with 2,240 square feet
2. Navistar International (Mexico), 863
3. Multi-Marques (Canada), 440
4. Case Corp. (Brazil), 400
5. Japan Fiber Coating (Japan), 340
6. Enerflex Manufacturing (Canada), 328
7. Caltex Tianjin Lubricating Oil (China), 322
8. Solectron (Brazil), 300
9. Tech Data (France), 278
10. Solectron (Romania), 266

Source: *Site Selection & Industrial Development*, March, 1999, p. 218.

★3029★
TOP INTERNATIONAL MANUFACTURING FACILITIES BY INVESTMENT, 1998
Ranked by: Investments, in millions of dollars. **Remarks:** Also notes type of industry. **Number listed:** 20

1. Alcan Aluminium (Canada), with $1,600 million
1. Jetpa Holdings (Turkey), $1,600
1. Motorola/Siemens (Germany), $1,600
4. Motorola (China), $1,300
5. Royal Philips Electronics (Taiwan), $1,200
6. Lucent Technologies/Chartered Semiconductor (Singapore), $1,000
7. Nan Ya Technology Corp. (Taiwan), $870
8. Ford Motor Co. (Brazil), $700
8. Volkswagen AG (Germany), $700
10. Fiat Auto S.p.A. (Argentina), $600
10. PSA Peugeot Citroen (Brazil), $600

Source: *Site Selection & Industrial Development*, March, 1999, p. 218.

★3030★
TOP INTERNATIONAL MANUFACTURING FACILITIES BY NUMBER OF EMPLOYEES, 1998
Ranked by: Number of employees. **Remarks:** Also notes type of industry. **Number listed:** 20

1. Dell Computer (Ireland), with 3,000 employees
2. Xerox (Ireland), 2,200
3. Daewoo Motor Polska (Poland), 2,000
3. NEC Computer Storage Philippines, 2,000
5. Cadence Design Systems (UK/Scotland), 1,895
6. Boston Scientific (Ireland), 1,000
7. Hino Auto Body Ltd. (Japan), 800
8. Bosch Corp. (Hungary), 700
9. Wacker Siltronic AG (Singapore), 600
10. General Electric Capital Services (Ireland), 515

Source: *Site Selection & Industrial Development*, March, 1999, p. 218.

Manufacturing Industries

★3031★
LEADING LOOMING/WEAVING MACHINES PRODUCERS RANKED BY REVENUE PER EMPLOYEE, 1998
Ranked by: Sales per employee, in thousands of Swiss Francs (CHF). **Number listed:** 8

1. Varmatex, with 519 thousand
2. Somet, 507
3. Toyoda, 392
4. Picanol, 371
5. Sulzer Textil, 319
6. Tsudakoma, 289
7. Dornier, 277
8. Nissan, 241

Source: *Textile World*, April, 1999, p. 39.

★3032★
MANUFACTURERS SPENDING THE MOST ON RESEARCH AND DEVELOPMENT, 1997
Ranked by: Research and development expenditures, in millions of dollars. **Number listed:** 15

1. Emergingson Electric Co., with $459 million
2. Eaton Corp., $396.8
3. Cirrus Logic Inc., $309.1
4. Johnson Controls Inc., $237.6
5. Ingersoll Rand Co., $222.2

6. Baker Hughes, $162.9
7. Dresser Industries Inc., $121.1
8. Raychem Corp., $119.7
9. American Standard, $111.1
10. Hadco Corp., $98.4

Source: *Research & Development*, Giants of R&D (annual), October, 1998, p. S-15.

★3033★
TOP HISPANIC-OWNED MANUFACTURING COMPANIES, 1998
Ranked by: Revenue, in millions of dollars. **Number listed:** 10

1. Goya Foods Inc., with $653.00 million
2. Supreme International Corp., $190.70
3. Mexican Industries in Michigan Inc., $162.12
4. HUSCO International Inc., $150.00
5. Avanti/Case-Hoyt, $145.00
6. Lopez Foods Inc., $138.30
7. Complas Inc., $130.00
8. Ruiz Food Products Inc., $92.70
9. UniBoring Co. Inc., $88.20
10. All American Containers Inc., $72.48

Source: *Hispanic Business*, Hispanic Business 500 (annual), June, 1999, p. 98.

★3034★
TOP MANUFACTURING COMPANIES ON THE S&P 500, 1998
Ranked by: Each company is ranked by eight criteria: one-year total return, three-year total return, one-year sales growth, three-year average annual sales growth, one-year profit growth, three-year average annual profit growth, net profit margins, and return on equity, with additional weight given to a company's sales. A company's composite rank is calculated using the sum of all its ranks. **Remarks:** Overall score not provided. **Number listed:** 33

1. Ingersoll-Rand
2. Illinois Tool Works
3. Johnson Controls
4. Tyco International
5. Danaher
6. Newell
7. Caterpillar
8. Crane
9. Parker Hannifin
10. Briggs & Stratton

Source: *Business Week*, Business Week 50: Top Companies of the S&P 500 (annual), March 29, 1999, p. 154.

Manufacturing Industries--Asia

★3035★
MOST ADMIRED LIGHT MANUFACTURING COMPANIES IN ASIA, 1999
Ranked by: Scores. **Remarks:** Also notes score in 1998, overall ranking in 1999, and rise or fall in rank. **Number listed:** 10

1. Sony, with 8.59
2. Taiwan Semiconductor Manufacturing Co., 8.27
2. Creative Technology, 8.27
4. Hewlett Packard, 8.12
5. IBM, 7.81
6. Matsushita Electrical, 7.70
7. Acer, 7.69
8. Siemens, 7.60
9. General Electric, 7.50
10. Compaq Computer, 7.34

Source: *Asian Business*, Most Admired Companies in Asia (annual), May, 1999, p. 29.

Manufacturing Industries--Europe

★3036★
TOP MISCELLANEOUS MANUFACTURING INDUSTRIES IN EUROPE, 1999*
Ranked by: Sales, in millions of European Currency Units (ECUs). **Remarks:** Also notes number of employees and overall rank. **Number listed:** 31

1. Tefal (France), with ECUs515 million
2. Ericsson Radio Access AB (Switzerland), ECUs403
3. Dunlop Slazenger Group Ltd. (United Kingdom), ECUs335
4. Saloman SA (France), ECUs330
5. Asprey Group Ltd. (United Kingdom), ECUs320
6. Groz-Beckert KG (Germany), ECUs227
7. Heinz Kettler GMBH & Co. (Germany), ECUs223
8. NSM AG (Germany), ECUs197
9. Dunlop Slazenger International Ltd. (United Kingdom), ECUs158
10. Schwann-Stabilo Schwanhaeusser GMBH & Co. (Germany), ECUs155

Source: *Dun & Bradstreet*, Duns Europa, 1999, p. 260.

★3037★
TOP STONE, CLAY, GLASS, AND CONCRETE COMPANIES IN EUROPE, 1999*
Ranked by: Sales, in millions of European Currency Units (ECUs). **Remarks:** Also notes number of employees and overall rank. **Number listed:** 102

1. RMC Group Plc (United Kingdom), with ECUs5.912 million
2. Pilkington Plc (United Kingdom), ECUs4.307
3. Redland Plc (United Kingdom), ECUs3.508
4. Heidelberger Zement AG (Germany), ECUs3.283
5. CRH Plc (Ireland), ECUs3.096
6. Blue Circle Industries Plc (United Kingdom), ECUs2.860
7. Schott Glass (Germany), ECUs2.776
8. BPB Plc (United Kingdom), ECUs2.044
9. Dyckerhoff AG (Germany), ECUs1.505
10. Pilkington Deutschland GMBH (Germany), ECUs1.009

Source: *Dun & Bradstreet*, Duns Europa, 1999, p. 247+.

Manufacturing Industries, International

★3038★
TOP INTERNATIONAL MANUFACTURING COMPANIES, 1999
Ranked by: Revenues, in millions of U.S. dollars ($). **Remarks:** Also notes net income, profit margin and growth, earnings per share, total equity, debt to equity ratio, and primary industry. **Number listed:** 50

1. Daimler Chrysler AG (Germany), with $154,475 million
2. General Motors Corp. (U.S.), $154,018
3. Ford Motor Corp. (U.S.), $144,415
4. Toyota Motor (Japan), $102,939

5. Exxon Corp. (U.S.), $100,597
6. General Electric Co. (U.S.), $100,330
7. Royal Dutch/Shell Group (Netherlands), $93,692
8. IBM Corp. (U.S.), $81,667
9. Volkswagen AG (Germany), $80,457
10. Hitachi Ltd., $74,190

Source: *Industryweek*, Industryweek 1000 (annual), June 4, 1999, p. 59+.

Margarine

★3039★
TOP MARGARINE/SPREADS BRANDS RANKED BY MARKET SHARE, 1998
Ranked by: Market share, in percent. **Number listed:** 10

1. I Can't Believe It's Not Butter, with 16.0%
2. Shedds Country Crock, 15.4%
3. Blue Bonnet, 8.9%
4. Parkay, 8.7%
5. Private label, 8.1%
6. Fleischmann's, 6.3%
7. Imperial, 5.5%
8. I Can't Believe It's Not Butter Light, 5.3%
9. Land O'Lakes, 4.8%
10. Brummel & Brown, 3.8%

Source: *Dairy Field*, May, 1999, p. 24.

★3040★
TOP MARGARINE/SPREADS BRANDS RANKED BY SALES, 1998
Ranked by: Sales, in millions of dollars. **Number listed:** 10

1. I Can't Believe It's Not Butter, with $206.4 million
2. Shedds Country Crock, $198.3
3. Blue Bonnet, $115.3
4. Parkay, $112.3
5. Private label, $103.9
6. Fleischmann's, $81.5
7. Imperial, $70.7
8. I Can't Believe It's Not Butter Light, $68.1
9. Land O'Lakes, $61.7
10. Brummel & Brown, $48.5

Source: *Dairy Field*, May, 1999, p. 24.

Market Research Firms

★3041★
TOP GLOBAL RESEARCH ORGANIZATIONS, 1997
Ranked by: Total research revenues, in millions of U.S. dollars ($). **Remarks:** Also notes 1996 ranking, headquarters information, number of full time employees, percent change, and revenues generated outside of home country. **Number listed:** 25

1. AC Nielson Corp. (U.S.), with $1,391.6 million
2. Cognizant Corp. (U.S.), $1,339.1
3. The Kantar Group (United Kingdom), $539.8
4. Taylor Nelson Sofres (United Kingdom), $463.4
5. Information Resources Inc. (U.S.), $456.3
6. GfK Holding AG (Germany), $311.7
7. Westat Inc. (U.S.), $182.0
8. Infratest Burke AG (Germany), $174.7
9. NFO Worldwide (U.S.), $190.0
10. The Abitron Co. (U.S.), $165.2

Source: *Marketing News*, Honomichl Global 25 (annual), August 17, 1998, p. H4.

★3042★
TOP MARKET RESEARCH FIRMS, 1998
Ranked by: Total research revenue, in millions of dollars. **Remarks:** Also notes contact information, percent change from 1997, and percent and revenue from outside U.S. **Number listed:** 50

1. AC Nielsen Corp., with $1,425.4 million
2. IMS Health Inc., $1,084.0
3. Information Resources Inc., $511.3
4. Nielsen Media Research Inc., $401.9
5. NFO Worldwide Inc., $275.4
6. Westat Inc., $205.4
7. The Arbitron Co., $194.5
8. Maritz Marketing Research Inc., $169.1
9. The Kantar Group, $150.6
10. The NPD Group Inc., $138.5

Source: *Marketing News*, The Homomichl 50 (annual), June 4, 1999, p. H4.

Market Research Firms--Great Britain

★3043★
TOP BUSINESS-TO-BUSINESS QUANTITATIVE RESEARCH FIRMS, 1997
Ranked by: Total business-to-business quantitative research expenditures, in British pounds. **Remarks:** Also notes figures for face-to-face, telephone, and postal research. **Number listed:** 30

1. NOP Research Group, with £8,091,000
2. Research International, £7,847,000
3. Taylor Nelson Sofres, £5,239,000
4. Opinion Research Corp., £3,014,000
5. Total Research, £2,603,000
6. Romtec, £2,109,000
7. BMRB International, £2,036,000
8. The Research Business International, £1,682,000
9. BPRI, £1,514,000
10. IFF Research, £1,405,000

Source: *Marketing*, September 24, 1998, p. 53.

★3044★
TOP CONSUMER QUANTITATIVE RESEARCH FIRMS, 1997
Ranked by: Total consumer quantitative, in British pounds. **Remarks:** Also notes face-to-face, telephone, and postal results. **Number listed:** 30

1. NOP Research Group, with £35,062,000
2. Research International, £32,958,000
3. Taylor Nelson Sofres, £21,829,000
4. BMRB International, £11,927,000
5. Infratest Burke Group, £10,653,000
6. Simon Godfrey Associates, £8,473,000
7. MBL Group, £7,346,000
8. The Research Business International, £18,194,000
9. Marketing Sciences, £3,435,000
10. FDS International, £3,080,000

Source: *Marketing*, September 24, 1998, p. 52+.

★3045★
TOP CONTINUOUS AND SYNDICATED RESEARCH FIRMS, 1997
Ranked by: Total continuous and syndicated research expenditures, in British pounds. **Remarks:** Also notes figures for consumer and business research. **Number listed:** 25

1. Taylor Nelson Sofres, with £41,912,000
2. Millward Brown, £27,788,000

3. BMRB International, £13,964,000
4. IRI Infoscan, £13,776,000
5. NOP Research Group, £13,485,000
6. GfK Marketing Services, £9,361,000
7. IPSOS RSL, £3,836,000
8. MBL Group, £3,756,000
9. Isis Research, £2,588,000
10. Audits & Surveys Europe, £2,395,000

Source: *Marketing*, September 24, 1998, p. 56.

★3046★
TOP MARKET RESEARCH FIRMS RANKED BY TURNOVER, 1997
Ranked by: Turnover, in British pounds. **Remarks:** Also notes 1996 turnover, percent change, current staff figurres, as well as previous staf figures. **Number listed:** 90

1. Taylor Nelson Sofres, with £87,316,000
2. NOP Research Group, £67,427,000
3. Research International, £52,314,000
4. Millward Brown, £47,910,000
5. BMRB International, £29,091,000
6. IPSOS-RSL, £25,572,000
7. The Research Business International, £18,688,000
8. MORI, £18,194,000
9. The MBL Group, £15,084,000
10. Infratest Burke Group, £14,017,000

Source: *Marketing*, September 24, 1998, p. 46+.

★3047★
TOP MYSTERY-SHOPPING RESEARCH FIRMS, 1997
Ranked by: Total Mystery Shopping research expenditures. **Remarks:** Also notes figures for consumer and business research. **Number listed:** 10

1. NOP Research Group, with £5,394,000
2. Research International, £1,869,000
3. The Research Business International, £1,046,000
4. WHF (Southern), £985,000
5. BPRI, £505,000
6. Marketing Sciences, £497,000
7. Aba Quality Monitoring, £496,000
8. MSS Marketing Research, £423,000
9. Sample Surveys, £300,000
10. IPSOS-RSL, £256,000

Source: *Marketing*, September 24, 1998, p. 58.

★3048★
TOP QUALITATIVE RESEARCH FIRMS, 1997
Ranked by: Total qualitative research expenditures, in British pounds. **Remarks:** Also notes figures for consumer and business research. **Number listed:** 40

1. Research International, with £10,463,000
2. The Research Business International, £10,092,000
3. Taylor Nelson Sofres, £6,985,000
4. NOP Research Group, £5,394,000
5. The Added Value Company, £4,461,000
6. Pegram Walters Group, £4,009,000
7. Hauck Research International, £3,887,000
8. MBL Group, £3,877,000
9. Isis Research, £3,019,000
10. Davies Riley-Smith Maclay, £2,772,000

Source: *Marketing*, September 24, 1998, p. 55.

★3049★
TOP QUANTITATIVE RESEARCH FIRMS, 1997
Ranked by: Total quantitative research expenditures, in British pounds. **Remarks:** Also notes turnover. **Number listed:** 15

1. NOP Research Group, with £43,153,000
2. Research International, £40,805,000
3. Taylor Nelson Sofres, £39,292,000
4. IPSOS-RSL, £20,458,000
5. Millward Brown, £18,206,000
6. MORI, £14,373,000
7. BMRB International, £13,964,000
8. Infratest Burke Group, £11,634,000
9. Simon Godfrey Associates, £8,473,000
10. MBL Group, £7,451,000

Source: *Marketing*, September 24, 1998, p. 53.

Mass Media

★3050★
LEADING MEDIA COMPANIES BY MEDIA REVENUE, 1997
Ranked by: Media revenue, in dollars. **Remarks:** Includes newspaper, magazine, TV & radio, cable TV and other media revenue. **Number listed:** 100

1. Time Warner, with $13,269.9
2. Walt Disney Co., $6,898.0
3. Tele-Communications, $6,420.0
4. News Corp. Ltd., $5,550.7
5. CBS Corp., $5,461.0
6. NBC TV, $5,153.0
7. Gannett Co., $4,497.7
8. Advance Publications, $3,668.7
9. Cox Enterprises, $3,310.0
10. New York Times Co., $2,886.4

Source: *Advertising Age*, 100 Leading Media Companies (annual), August 17, 1998, p. 54.

★3051★
TOP MEDIA MARKETS RANKED BY BUYING POWER INDEX, 1998*
Ranked by: Buying Power Index (BPI). **Number listed:** 210

1. New York, NY, with 7.6233 BPI
2. Los Angeles, CA, 5.3051
3. Chicago, IL, 3.5583
4. Philadelphia, PA, 2.9543
5. San Francisco-Oakland-San Jose, CA, 2.7786
6. Boston, MA, 2.4453
7. Washington, DC, 2.2697
8. Dallas-Ft. Worth, TX, 2.0950
9. Detroit, MI, 1.9371
10. Houston, TX, 1.7912

Source: *Sales & Marketing Management*, Sales & Marketing Management Survey of Buying Power (annual), August, 1998, p. 51.

★3052★
TOP MEDIA MARKETS RANKED BY HOUSEHOLDS, 1998*
Ranked by: Households, in thousands. **Number listed:** 210

1. New York, NY, with 6,918.6 thousand
2. Los Angeles, CA, 5,192.5
3. Chicago, IL, 3,187.6
4. Philadelphia, PA, 2,668.3
5. San Francisco-Oakland-San Jose, CA, 2,423.3
6. Boston, MA, 2,199.5
7. Washington, DC, 1,959.2
8. Dallas-Ft. Worth, TX, 1,946.1
9. Detroit, MI, 1,853.5
10. Atlanta, GA, 1,701.6

Source: *Sales & Marketing Management*, Sales & Marketing Management Survey of Buying Power (annual), August, 1998, p. 36.

★3053★
TOP MEDIA MARKETS RANKED BY POPULATION, 1998*
Ranked by: Population, in thousands. **Number listed:** 210
1. New York, NY, with 19,083.8 thousand
2. Los Angeles, CA, 15,853.3
3. Chicago, IL, 8,863.5
4. Philadelphia, PA, 7,276.1
5. San Francisco-Oakland-San Jose, CA, 6,590.7
6. Boston, MA, 5,852.1
7. Washington, DC, 5,276.6
8. Dallas-Ft. Worth, TX, 5,220.5
9. Detroit, MI, 4,968.3
10. Houston, TX, 4,673.9

Source: *Sales & Marketing Management*, Sales & Marketing Management Survey of Buying Power (annual), August, 1998, p. 31.

★3054★
TOP MEDIA MARKETS RANKED BY TOTAL EFFECTIVE BUYING INCOME, 1998*
Ranked by: Total effective buying income, in thousands. **Number listed:** 210
1. New York, NY, with 379,188,780 thousand
2. Los Angeles, CA, 237,772,240
3. Chicago, IL, 169,168,055
4. Philadelphia, PA, 138,686,779
5. San Francisco-Oakland-San Jose, CA, 134,654,474
6. Boston, MA, 114,669,942
7. Washington, DC, 110,919,526
8. Dallas-Ft. Worth, TX, 96,383,540
9. Detroit, MI, 86,275,294
10. Houston, TX, 82,314,576

Source: *Sales & Marketing Management*, Sales & Marketing Management Survey of Buying Power (annual), August, 1998, p. 37.

★3055★
TOP MEDIA MARKETS RANKED BY TOTAL RETAIL SALES, 1998*
Ranked by: Retail sales, in thousands. **Number listed:** 210
1. New York, NY, with 161,414,661 thousand
2. Los Angeles, CA, 121,379,597
3. Chicago, IL, 83,190,272
4. Philadelphia, PA, 71,312,320
5. San Francisco-Oakland-San Jose, CA, 64,561,442
6. Boston, MA, 60,163,724
7. Washington, DC, 52,505,609
8. Dallas-Ft. Worth, TX, 52,505,609
9. Detroit, MI, 50,005,563
10. Atlanta, GA, 47,595,813

Source: *Sales & Marketing Management*, Sales & Marketing Management Survey of Buying Power (annual), August, 1998, p. 40.

Materials

★3056★
CHEMICAL, PETROCHEMICAL AND MATERIALS COMPANIES WITH THE HIGHEST RESEARCH AND DEVELOPMENT EXPENDITURES, 1997
Ranked by: Research and development expenditures, in millions of dollars. **Number listed:** 10
1. Du Pont, with $2,526.5 million
2. Monsanto, $933.6
3. Dow Chemical, $768.6
4. Exxon Corp., $529.8
5. Goodyear Tire & Rubber Co., $386.9
6. PPG Industries Inc., $250.6
7. Corning Inc., $246.4
8. Mobil Corp., $237.1
9. Rohm & Haas Co., $201.6
10. Shell Oil Co., $200.0

Source: *Research & Development*, Giants of R&D (annual), October, 1998, p. S-14.

Meat Industry--North America

★3057★
BIGGEST LOSERS IN THE MEAT AND POULTRY COMPANIES BY LOST SALES IN PERCENT, 1997
Ranked by: Lost sales, in percent. **Remarks:** Also notes sales for previous year. **Number listed:** 7
1. Champion Boxed Beef, with -87%
2. Bob Evans Farms Inc., -36%
3. Gerber Agri Inc., -25%
4. H&M Food Systems, -16%
5. Norbest Inc., -10%
6. L&H Packing Co., -9%
7. Goodmark Foods Inc., -5%

Source: *Meat & Poultry*, Top 100 (annual), July, 1998, p. 38.

★3058★
BIGGEST LOSERS IN THE MEAT AND POULTRY INDUSTRY BY LOST SALES IN DOLLARS, 1997
Ranked by: Lost sales, in millions of dollars. **Remarks:** Also notes sales for previous year. **Number listed:** 9
1. Cargill Meat Sector, with $-200 million
2. Tyson Foods Inc., $-100
3. Champion Boxed Beef Co., $-65
4. Bob Evans Farms Inc., $-57
5. H&M Food Systems, $-33
6. Gerber Agri Inc., $-30
7. Thorn Apple Valley Inc., $-27
8. L&H Packing Co., $-15
8. Norbest, Inc., $-15

Source: *Meat & Poultry*, Top 100 (annual), July, 1998, p. 40.

★3059★
FASTEST GROWING MEAT AND POULTRY COMPANIES BY INCREASE IN DOLLAR SALES, 1997
Ranked by: Growth in sales, in millions of dollars. **Remarks:** Also notes sales for previous year. **Number listed:** 9
1. Smithfield Foods, Inc., with $1,486 million
2. ConAgra Inc., $1,323
3. IBP Inc., $761
4. Gold Kist, $500
5. Seaboard Corp., $381
6. Colorado Boxed Beef Co., $360
7. Hormel Foods Corp., $157
8. Greater Omaha Packing, $144
9. Pilgrim's Pride Corp., $139

Source: *Meat & Poultry*, Top 100 (annual), July, 1998, p. 38.

★3060★
FASTEST GROWING MEAT AND POULTRY COMPANIES BY PERCENT GROWTH IN SALES, 1997
Ranked by: Growth in sales, in percent. **Remarks:** Also notes sales for previous year. **Number listed:** 9
1. Colorado Boxed Beef Co., with 54%

2. Smithfield Foods Inc., 38%
3. Seaboard Corp., 34%
4. Greater Omaha Packaging, 32%
5. Maple Lodge Farms Ltd., 30%
6. Buckhead Beef Co. Inc., 23%
6. Fletcher's Fine Foods Ltd., 23%
8. Gold Kist, 20%
9. Rose Packaging Co. Inc., 18%

Source: *Meat & Poultry*, Top 100 (annual), July, 1998, p. 38.

★3061★
LARGEST MEAT AND POULTRY COMPANIES, 1997
Ranked by: Sales, in millions of dollars. **Remarks:** Also notes contact information and CEO, sales for previous year, fiscal year ending date, number of plants, employees, and subsidiaries. **Number listed:** 100

1. ConAgra Inc., with $16,510 million
2. IBP Inc., $13,300
3. Cargill Meat Sector, $9,000
4. Tyson Foods Inc., $6,400
5. Sara Lee Packaged Meats, $4,300
6. Smithfield Foods, Inc., $3,870
7. Farmland Foods Inc., $3,700
8. Hormel Foods Inc., $3,256
9. Gold Kist Inc., $2,500
9. Oscar Mayer Foods Corp., $2,500

Source: *Meat & Poultry*, Top 100 (annual), July, 1998, p. 24+.

Mechanical Contractors

See: **Contractors**

Medical Advertising

★3062★
LEADING MEDICAL/SURGICAL PRODUCT TYPES BY SHARE OF ADVERTISING DOLLARS, 1998
Ranked by: Market share of advertising dollars, in percent. **Remarks:** Includes 1996 and 1997 figures, and percent change. **Number listed:** 25

1. Calcium Blocking Agents, with 7.19%
2. Antihypertensives, 6.01%
3. Cholesterol Reducers/Rx, 4.49%
4. Antidepressants, 3.92%
5. Quinolones-Systemic, 3.82%
6. Diabetes-Oral, 3.52%
7. Anthistamines, 2.87%
8. Antispasmotics, 2.49%
8. Ethical Drugs, 2.49%
10. Antiarthritics, 2.08%

Source: *Medical Marketing & Media*, Healthcare Advertising Review (annual), May, 1999, p. 64.

★3063★
MOST HEAVILY ADVERTISED MEDICAL/ SURGICAL PRODUCTS, 1998
Ranked by: Market share, in percent. **Remarks:** Includes company name, 1996 and 1997 figures, and percent change. **Number listed:** 25

1. Trovan, with 2.10%
2. Norvasc, 2.04%
3. Viagra, 1.63%
4. Avapro, 1.42%
5. Cozaar & Hyzaar, 1.38%
6. Singulair, 1.37%
7. Lipitor, 1.32%
8. Prozac, 1.31%
9. Tiazac, 1.28%
10. Prevacid, 1.11%

Source: *Medical Marketing & Media*, Healthcare Advertising Review (annual), May, 1999, p. 61.

★3064★
TOP ADVERTISERS IN THE MEDICAL/SURGICAL FIELD, 1998
Ranked by: Market share of advertising dollars, in percent. **Remarks:** Includes 1996 and 1997 figures, and percent change. **Number listed:** 25

1. Pfizer Laboratories, with 8.47%
2. Merck, 6.38%
3. Forest Pharmaceuticals, 3.91%
4. Astra Pharmaceuticals, 3.67%
5. Hoechst Marion Roussel Inc., 3.52%
6. Novartis Inc., 3.35%
7. Wyeth-Ayerst, 3.18%
8. Schering Corp., 2.92%
9. Bristol-Myers Squibb, 2.90%
10. Eli Lilly & Co., 2.89%

Source: *Medical Marketing & Media*, Healthcare Advertising Review (annual), May, 1999, p. 62.

Medical Colleges

★3065★
TOP MEDICAL COLLEGES, 1998
Ranked by: Ranking derived from consideration of the following factors: student selectivity, placement, graduation rates, instructional resources, research and academic reputation. Factors are then weighted, totaled, and a final ranking achieved. **Number listed:** 48

1. Harvard University, with 100.0
2. Johns Hopkins University, 72.0
3. University of Pennsylvania, 68.0
4. Washington University in St. Louis, 64.0
5. Yale University, 63.0
6. Duke University, 62.0
6. University of California-San Francisco, 62.0
8. Columbia University, 61.0
9. University of Washington, 60.0
10. Stanford University, 57.0

Source: *U.S. News & World Report*, America's Best Graduate and Professional Schools (annual), March 29, 1999, p. 82.

★3066★
TOP MEDICAL COLLEGES SPECIALIZING IN AIDS, 1998
Ranked by: Ranking derived from consideration of the following factors: student selectivity, placement, graduation rates, instructional resources, research and academic reputation. Factors are then weighted, totaled, and a final ranking achieved by medical school deans and senior faculty. **Remarks:** Overall scores not provided. **Number listed:** 11

1. University of California-San Francisco
2. Harvard University
3. Johns Hopkins University
4. University of California, Los Angeles
5. University of Washington
6. University of Alabama-Birmingham
7. Columbia University

8. University of California at San Diego
9. University of Colorado
9. New York University

Source: *U.S. News & World Report*, America's Best Graduate and Professional Schools (annual), March 29, 1999, p. 84.

★3067★
TOP MEDICAL COLLEGES SPECIALIZING IN DRUGS/ALCOHOL ABUSE, 1998
Ranked by: Ranking derived from consideration of the following factors: student selectivity, placement, graduation rates, instructional resources, research and academic reputation. Factors are then weighted, totaled, and a final ranking achieved by medical school deans and senior faculty. **Remarks:** Overall scores not provided. **Number listed:** 11

1. Columbia University
2. University of California-San Francisco
2. Yale University
4. Harvard University
5. University of Pennsylvania
6. Johns Hopkins University
7. University of California, Los Angeles
7. University of Washington
9. Brown University
10. University of California at San Diego

Source: *U.S. News & World Report*, America's Best Graduate and Professional Schools (annual), March 29, 1999, p. 84.

★3068★
TOP MEDICAL COLLEGES SPECIALIZING IN FAMILY MEDICINE, 1998
Ranked by: Ranking derived from consideration of the following factors: student selectivity, placement, graduation rates, instructional resources, research and academic reputation. Factors are then weighted, totaled, and a final ranking achieved by medical school deans and senior faculty. **Remarks:** Overall scores not provided. **Number listed:** 10

1. University of Washington
2. University of Missouri
3. University of North Carolina-Chapel Hill
4. Oregon Health Sciences University
5. University of Colorado Health Sciences Center
6. Case Western Reserve University
7. Michigan State University
7. University of California-San Francisco
7. University of New Mexico
10. University of Wisconsin

Source: *U.S. News & World Report*, America's Best Graduate and Professional Schools (annual), March 29, 1999, p. 84.

★3069★
TOP MEDICAL COLLEGES SPECIALIZING IN GERIATRICS, 1998
Ranked by: Ranking derived from consideration of the following factors: student selectivity, placement, graduation rates, instructional resources, research and academic reputation. Factors are then weighted, totaled, and a final ranking achieved by medical school deans and senior faculty. **Remarks:** Overall scores not provided. **Number listed:** 10

1. Harvard University
2. Mount Sinai School of Medicine
3. University of California, Los Angeles
4. Johns Hopkins University
5. Duke University
6. University of Washington
7. Wake Forest University
8. University of Michigan
9. Yale University
10. University of Pennsylvania

Source: *U.S. News & World Report*, America's Best Graduate and Professional Schools (annual), March 29, 1999, p. 84.

★3070★
TOP MEDICAL COLLEGES SPECIALIZING IN INTERNAL MEDICINE, 1998
Ranked by: Ranking derived from consideration of the following factors: student selectivity, placement, graduation rates, instructional resources, research and academic reputation. Factors are then weighted, totaled, and a final ranking achieved by medical school deans and senior faculty. **Remarks:** Overall scores not provided. **Number listed:** 10

1. Harvard University
2. Johns Hopkins University
3. University of California-San Francisco
4. Duke University
5. Washington University
6. University of Pennsylvania
7. University of Washington
8. University of Texas-Southwestern
9. University of Michigan
10. Stanford University

Source: *U.S. News & World Report*, America's Best Graduate and Professional Schools (annual), March 29, 1999, p. 84.

★3071★
TOP MEDICAL COLLEGES SPECIALIZING IN PEDIATRICS, 1998
Ranked by: Ranking derived from consideration of the following factors: student selectivity, placement, graduation rates, instructional resources, research and academic reputation. Factors are then weighted, totaled, and a final ranking achieved by medical school deans and senior faculty. **Remarks:** Overall scores not provided. **Number listed:** 11

1. Harvard University
2. University of Pennsylvania
3. Johns Hopkins University
4. University of California-San Francisco
5. Washington University in St. Louis
6. University of Cincinnati
6. University of Washington
8. Baylor College of Medicine
9. Yale University
10. Duke University

Source: *U.S. News & World Report*, America's Best Graduate and Professional Schools (annual), March 29, 1999, p. 84.

★3072★
TOP MEDICAL COLLEGES SPECIALIZING IN PRIMARY CARE, 1998
Ranked by: Ranking derived from consideration of the following factors: student selectivity, placement, graduation rates, instructional resources, research and academic reputation. Factors are then weighted, totaled, and a final ranking achieved. **Number listed:** 48

1. University of Washington, with 100.0
2. Harvard University, 82.0
3. Mayo Medical School, 80.0
4. Oregon Health Sciences University, 79.0
5. University of Massachusetts at Worcester, 76.0
6. University of Iowa, 75.0
7. Case Western Reserve University, 74.0
8. University of California-San Francisco, 72.0
8. University of North Carolina-Chapel Hill, 72.0
10. University of New Mexico, 71.0

Source: *U.S. News & World Report*, America's Best Graduate and Professional Schools (annual), March 29, 1999, p. 83.

★3073★
TOP MEDICAL COLLEGES SPECIALIZING IN RURAL MEDICINE, 1998
Ranked by: Ranking derived from consideration of the following factors: student selectivity, placement, graduation rates, instructional resources, research and academic reputation. Factors are then weighted, totaled, and a final ranking achieved by medical school deans and senior faculty. **Remarks:** Overall scores not provided. **Number listed:** 10

1. University of Washington
2. University of New Mexico
3. East Tennessee State University
4. University of Minnesota-Duluth
5. East Carolina University
5. University of North Carolina-Chapel Hill
7. University of Iowa
8. Michigan State University
9. Oregon Health Sciences University
9. University of North Dakota

Source: *U.S. News & World Report*, America's Best Graduate and Professional Schools (annual), March 29, 1999, p. 84.

★3074★
TOP MEDICAL COLLEGES SPECIALIZING IN WOMEN'S HEALTH, 1998
Ranked by: Ranking derived from consideration of the following factors: student selectivity, placement, graduation rates, instructional resources, research and academic reputation. Factors are then weighted, totaled, and a final ranking achieved by medical school deans and senior faculty. **Remarks:** Overall scores not provided. **Number listed:** 12

1. Harvard University
2. University of California-San Francisco
3. University of Pennsylvania
4. University of Washington
5. Duke University
6. Johns Hopkins University
7. University of Pittsburgh
8. Northwestern University
8. University of Texas-Southwestern
10. Stanford University

Source: *U.S. News & World Report*, America's Best Graduate and Professional Schools (annual), March 29, 1999, p. 84.

Medical Laboratories

★3075★
MOST ADVERTISED LAB/PATHOLOGY PRODUCTS/ SERVICES IN LAB/PATHOLOGY JOURNALS, 1998
Ranked by: Market share of ad expenditures, in percent. **Remarks:** Also notes 1996 and 1997 expenditure percentage and rank, and percent changes. **Number listed:** 12

1. Roche Diag & Boehringer Mannheim Now One(Roche Diagnostic Systems), with 1.99%
2. Hospital Blood Glucose Management Systems (Lifescan Inc.), 1.53%
3. Dimensional Rxl Clinical Chemistry Systems (Dade Behring Inc.), 1.52%
4. Cobas Amplicor/Automated PCR (Roche Diagnostic Systems), 1.38%
5. Advia 120/Hematology System with unifluidics Tech (Bayer Diagnostic Division), 1.31%
6. Acscentaur/Automated Chemiluminescence (Chiron Diagnostics), 1.29%
7. Advia Approach (Bayer Diagnostic Division), 1.26%
8. Inova/Autoimmune Disease Diagnostic (Inova Diagnostics Inc.), 1.13%
9. Vitros Systems/Family of Lab Products (Ortho-Clinical Diagnostics), 1.09%
10. Vitros ECI Immunodiagnostic System (Ortho-Clinical Diagnostics), 1.02%

Source: *Medical Marketing & Media*, Healthcare Advertising Review (annual), April, 1999, p. 58.

★3076★
TOP ADVERTISERS IN LAB/PATHOLOGY PUBLICATIONS, 1998
Ranked by: Market share of expenditures, in percent. **Remarks:** Also notes 1996 and 1997 expenditure percentage and rank, and percent changes. **Number listed:** 12

1. Roche Diagnostic Systems, with 7.94%
2. Bayer Diagnostics Division, 5.02%
3. Abbott Diagnostics, 4.82%
4. Sigma Diagnostics, 3.59%
5. Lifescan Inc., 2.85%
6. Ortho-Cinical Diagnostics, 2.79%
7. Dade Behring Inc., 2.53%
8. Beckman Coulter, 2.38%
9. Becton Dickinson, 2.37%
10. Inova Diagnostics Inc., 2.26%

Source: *Medical Marketing & Media*, Healthcare Advertising Review (annual), April, 1999, p. 58.

Medical Radiology

★3077★
MOST ADVERTISED RADIOLOGY PRODUCTS/ SERVICES IN RADIOLOGY JOURNALS, 1998
Ranked by: Share of ad dollars, in percent. **Remarks:** Also notes 1996 and 1997 expenditure percentage and rank, and percent changes. **Number listed:** 12

1. Venue Suite(Picker International), with 2.24%
2. Visipaque Injection (Nycomed Amersham Inc.), 1.59%
3. Omniscan Injection (Nycomed Amersham Inc.), 1.47%
4. Upa-d3digital Print Server (SONY), 1.35%
5. Airis II Imaging System (Hitachi Medical Corp.), 1.25%
6. Trexmed/f/pmt6000/digispot2000/m-iv (Trex Medical), 1.24%
7. Dry View Laser Imager (Imation), .89%
8. EUB-525 Ultrasound System (Hitachi Medical Corp.), 1.11%
9. Kodak DS Digital Science Media Imaging System (Kodak), .99%
10. SONY Medical Imaging Products (SONY), .91%

Source: *Medical Marketing & Media*, Healthcare Advertising Review (annual), April, 1999, p. 62.

★3078★
TOP ADVERTISERS IN RADIOLOGY JOURNALS, 1998
Ranked by: Market share of expenditures, in percent. **Remarks:** Also notes 1996 and 1997 expenditure percentage and rank, and percent changes. **Number listed:** 12

1. Nycomed Amersham Inc., with 5.57%
2. Siemens Medical Systems Inc., 4.53%
3. GE Medical Systems Inc., 3.62%
4. Picker International, 3.30%
5. Hitachi Medical Corp., 2.77%

6. Fuji Medical Systems USA Inc., 2.36%
7. Kodak, 2.35%
8. Sony, 2.26%
9. Trex Medical, 2.24%
10. Bracco Diagnostics, 1.90%

Source: *Medical Marketing & Media*, Healthcare Advertising Review (annual), April, 1999, p. 62.

Medical Supplies

★3079★
TOP MEDICAL EQUIPMENT COMPANIES, 1997*
Ranked by: Segment revenue, in millions of dollars. **Number listed:** 10

1. Medtronic, with $1,862.1 million
2. Hewlett-Packard, $1,287.7
3. Beckman Coulter, $1,198.0
4. Varian Associates, $478.0
5. Acuson, $437.8
6. Imation, $341.8
7. Eastman Kodak, $306.4
8. Thermo Electron, $140.5
9. Diebold, $61.3
10. Polaroid, $45.1

Source: *Electronic Business*, Top 200 (annual), July, 1997, p. 95.

Men's Clothing

See: **Clothing and Dress--Men**

Mergers

See: **Corporate Acquisitions and Mergers**

Messengers--Los Angeles County (CA)

★3080★
TOP MESSENGER SERVICES COMPANIES IN LOS ANGELES COUNTY, 1999*
Ranked by: Number of Los Angeles county full-time delivery employees. **Number listed:** 25

1. Century Express, with 255 employees
2. Express Network Inc., 210
3. Jet Delivery Inc., 200
4. State Courier Service, 190
5. Procourier, 187
6. Southern California Messengers, 160
7. Accurate Express Messenger Services, 140
7. L.A. Express/NICA, 140
9. UCI Distribution Plus, 120
10. The Go Between, 107

Source: *Los Angeles Business Journal*, May 31, 1999, p. 32+.

Metal Industry

★3081★
TOP CORPORATIONS IN THE METALS INDUSTRY, 1998
Ranked by: Revenue, in millions of dollars. **Remarks:** Also notes profits and investment figures as well as number of employees. **Number listed:** 18

1. Alcoa, with $15,489 million
2. Reynolds Metals, $5,859
3. Bethlehem Steel, $4,478
4. LTV, $4,273
5. Nucor, $4,151
6. Ryerson Tull, $4,093
7. Allegheny Teledyne, $3,923
8. Phelps Dodge, $3,063
9. Maxxam, $2,573
10. AK Steel Holding, $2,394

Source: *Fortune*, Fortune 500 Largest U.S. Corporations (annual), April 26, 1999, p. F-64+.

Metal Industry--Europe

★3082★
TOP PRIMARY METAL COMPANIES IN EUROPE, 1999*
Ranked by: Sales, in millions of European Currency Units, (ECUs). **Remarks:** Also notes number of employees and overall rank among European businesses. **Number listed:** 111

1. Viag AG (Germany), with ECUs21.529 million
2. British Steel (United Kingdom), ECUs10.659
3. Thyssen Stahl AG (Germany), ECUs6.295
4. Sollac (France), ECUs5.171
5. Salzgitter AG Stahl & Technologie (Germany), ECUs3.400
6. Vaw Aluminium AG (Germany), ECUs2.941
7. Thyssen Krupp Stahl AG (Germany), ECUs2.810
8. Union Miniere SA (Belgium), ECUs2.684
9. Cookson Group Plc (United Kingdom), ECUs2.539
10. Aceralia Corporacion Siderurgica S.A. (Spain), ECUs2.351

Source: *Dun & Bradstreet*, Duns Europa (annual), 1999, vol. 4, p. 248+.

Metal Industry, International

★3083★
WORLD'S LARGEST METAL COMPANIES BY REVENUE, 1997
Ranked by: Revenue, in millions of dollars. **Number listed:** 13

1. Nippon Steel (Japan), with $25,063 million
2. NKK (Japan), $15,758
3. Krupp (Germany), $14,478
4. Alcoa (U.S.), $13,482
5. Kobe Steel (Japan), $12,506
6. Usinor (France), $12,337
7. Pohang Iron & Steel (South Korea), $12,091
8. Sumitomo Metal Industries (Japan), $11,970
9. British Steel (Great Britain), $11,408

10. Metallgesellschaft (Germany), $10,831

Source: *Fortune*, The Global 500: World's Biggest Corporations (annual), August 3, 1998, p. F-22.

Metal Products

★3084★
MOST ADMIRED METAL PRODUCTS CORPORATIONS, 1998

Ranked by: Scores (1-10) derived from a survey of senior executives, outside directors and securities analysts. **Remarks:** Respondents rated companies in their own industry on 8 attributes of reputation. Also notes previous year's rank. **Number listed:** 10

1. Fortune Brands, with 6.94 points
2. Tyco International, 5.98
3. Illinois Tool Works, 5.64
4. Newell, 4.94
5. Danaher, 4.86
6. Masco, 4.63
7. Ball, 4.60
8. Stanley Works, 4.56
9. Crown Cork & Seal, 4.47
10. U.S. Industries, 4.10

Source: *Fortune*, America's Most Admired Corporations (annual), March 1, 1999, p. F-4.

★3085★
TOP CORPORATIONS IN THE METAL PRODUCTS INDUSTRY, 1998

Ranked by: Revenue, in millions of dollars. **Remarks:** Also notes profits and investment figures as well as number of employees. **Number listed:** 15

1. Gillette, with $10,056 million
2. Crown Cork & Seal, $8,300
3. ITW, $5,648
4. Fortune Brands, $4,797
5. Masco, $4,345
6. Newell, $3,720
7. U.S. Industries, $3,362
8. Danaher, $2,910
9. Ball, $2,896
10. Stanley Works, $2,729

Source: *Fortune*, Fortune 500 Largest U.S. Corporations (annual), April 26, 1999, p. F-64.

Metal Products--Europe

★3086★
TOP COMPANIES IN FABRICATED METAL PRODUCTS EXCEPT MACHINERY AND TRANSPORTATION IN EUROPE, 1999*

Ranked by: Sales, in millions of European Currency Units (ECUs). **Remarks:** Also notes number of employees and overall rank among European businesses. **Number listed:** 162

1. TI Group Plc (United Kingdom), with ECUs2.514 million
2. Adolf Wuerth GMBH & Co. KG (Germany), ECUs2.470
3. Glynwed International Plc (United Kingdom), ECUs1.831
4. Buderus AG (Germany), ECUs1.651
5. The Laird Group Plc (United Kingdom), ECUs1.561
6. Diehl GMBH & Co. (Germany), ECUs1.365
7. Chubb Security Ltd. (United Kingdom), ECUs1.271
8. Framatome (France), ECUs1.232
9. Mckechnie Plc (United Kingdom), ECUs959
10. Heywood Williams Group Plc (United Kingdom), ECUs933

Source: *Dun & Bradstreet*, Duns Europa (annual), 1999, p. 249+.

Metal Products, International

★3087★
WORLD'S LARGEST METAL PRODUCTS CORPORATIONS BY REVENUE, 1997

Ranked by: Revenue, in millions of dollars. **Number listed:** 3

1. Pechiney (France), with $12,133 million
2. Sumitomo Electric Industries (Japan), $10,567
3. Gillette (U.S.), $10,062

Source: *Fortune*, The Global 500: World's Biggest Corporations (annual), August 3, 1998, p. F-22.

Metal Service Centers

★3088★
TOP MARKETS FOR METAL CENTERS, 1998

Ranked by: Percentage served by top 100. **Number listed:** 15

1. Construction, with 91%
2. Commercial Equipment, 80%
3. Electrical Equipment, 74%
4. Automotive, 73%
5. Machinery, 71%
6. Agriculture, 65%
7. Appliances, 59%
8. Mining/lumbering, 49%
8. Rail, 49%
10. Oil & Gas, 47%

Source: *Purchasing*, Top 100 (annual), May 5, 1999, p. 40B4.

★3089★
TOP METAL SERVICE CENTER BY SALES, 1998

Ranked by: Sales, in billions of dollars. **Remarks:** Also notes operating subsidiaries, warehouse space, delivery fleet, products, processing services and stocking regions. **Number listed:** 100

1. Ryerson Tull, with $2.8 billion
2. Thyssen Inc., $2.5
3. Metals USA Inc., $1.5
4. Reliance Steel & Aluminum Co., $1.35
5. MacSteel Service Centers USA, $1.2
5. Russell Metals Inc., $1.2
5. Samuel Son & Co., $1.2
8. Carpenter Steel Service Centers, $1.18
9. North American Metals Distribution Group, $1.16
10. Preussag North America Inc., $1.12

Source: *Purchasing*, Top 100 (annual), May 5, 1999, p. 40B14.

★3090★
TOP PRE-PRODUCTION PROCESSING SERVICES, 1998
Ranked by: Percentage offered by top 100. **Number listed:** 13
1. Cut-to-length, with 84%
2. Shearing, 70%
3. Cutting & Sawing, 60%
4. Slitting, 59%
5. Leveling, 58%
6. Blanking, 49%
7. Bending, 25%
8. Roll-forming, 22%
8. Welding, 22%
10. Heat-treating, 18%

Source: *Purchasing*, Top 100 (annual), May 5, 1999, p. 40B7.

Metals

★3091★
MOST ADMIRED METAL MANUFACTURING CORPORATIONS, 1998
Ranked by: Scores (1-10) derived from a survey of senior executives, outside directors and securities analysts. **Remarks:** Respondents rated companies in their own industry on 8 attributes of reputation. Also notes previous year's rank. **Number listed:** 10
1. Alcoa, with 7.45 score
2. Nucor, 6.90
3. Phelps Dodge, 6.36
4. Allegheny Teledyne, 6.23
5. Reynolds Metals, 6.11
6. AK Steel Holding, 5.97
7. Bethlehem Steel, 5.25
8. LTV, 4.99
9. Maxxam, 4.94
10. Inland Steel Industries, 4.92

Source: *Fortune*, America's Most Admired Corporations (annual), March 1, 1999, p. F-4.

★3092★
TOP METALS AND MINING COMPANIES ON THE S&P 500, 1998
Ranked by: Each company is ranked by eight criteria: one-year total return, three-year total return, one-year sales growth, three-year average annual sales growth, one-year profit growth, three-year average annual profit growth, net profit margins, and return on equity, with additional weight given to a company's sales. A company's composite rank is calculated using the sum of all its ranks. **Remarks:** Overall scores not provided. **Number listed:** 18
1. Alcoa
2. Engelhard
3. Nucor
4. Barrick Gold
5. USX-U.S. Steel Group
6. Placer Dome
7. Alcan Aluminum
8. Freeport-McMoran Copper & Gold
9. Reynolds Metals
10. Worthington Industries

Source: *Business Week*, Business Week 50: Top Companies of the S&P 500 (annual), March 29, 1999, p. 156+.

Metals--Asia

★3093★
LARGEST ASIAN COMPANIES MANUFACTURING FERROUS AND NON-FERROUS METALS, 1999*
Ranked by: Sales, in thousands of U.S. dollars ($). **Remarks:** Includes profit as a percentage of sales, activity codes, as well as the country. **Number listed:** 100
1. NKK Corp., with $14,478,794 thousand
2. Kobe Steel Ltd., $11,490,793
3. Sumitomo Metal Industries, $10,998,630
4. Sumitomo Electric Industries, $9,708,697
5. Kawasaki Steel Corp., $9,309,812
6. Mitsubishi Materials Corp., $8,952,155
7. Furukawa Electric Co. Ltd., $5,982,357
8. Nippon Light Metal Co. Ltd., $4,662,717
9. Hitachi Metals Ltd., $3,504,124
10. Nisshin Steel Co. Ltd., $3,463,031

Source: *Asia's 7,500 Largest Companies*, (annual), 1999, p. 79+.

Metals, International

★3094★
TOP WORLDWIDE EXPLORATION SPENDING BY REGION, 1998
Ranked by: Exploration expenditures, in millions of U.S. dollars ($). **Number listed:** 7
1. Latin America, with $814.1 million
2. Australia, $494.6
3. Africa, $494.3
4. Canada, $308
5. Pacific/Southeast Asia, $265.7
6. U.S., $242.7
7. Rest of world, $209.5

Source: *The Mining Record*, October 28, 1998, p. 16.

Metals--North America

★3095★
TOP NORTH AMERICAN METALS COMPANIES BY CHANGE IN NET PROFIT FROM 1995 TO 1996
Ranked by: Change in net profit form 1995 to 1996, in dollars. **Remarks:** Also notes top 50 rank and 1996 net profit/loss. **Number listed:** 50
1. U.S. Steel Group of USX Corp., with $729,000,000
2. Olin Corp., $236,000,000
3. Alcan Aluminum, $147,000,000
4. Noranda Inc., $67,589,000
5. Timken Co., $26,587,000
6. Essex International, $16,900,000
7. Cominco Ltd., $16,131,452
8. Rouge Steel Co., $12,967,000
9. Englehard Corp., $12,900,000
10. Carpenter Technology Corp., $12,656,000

Source: *Metal Statistics*, Top 50 Metals Companies (annual), 1998, p. XXIX.

★3096★
TOP NORTH AMERICAN METALS COMPANIES BY CORPORATE PROFITS, 1997
Ranked by: Net profit/loss, in dollars. **Remarks:** Also notes top 50 rank and 1996 net profit/loss. **Number listed:** 50
1. Aluminum Co. of America, with $805,000,000
2. U.S. Steel Group of USX Corp., $773,000,000
3. Alcan Aluminium Ltd., $485,000,000
4. Newmont Mining Co., $440,000,000
5. Phelps Dodge Corp., $408,500,000
6. Nucor Corp., $294,482,440
7. Bethlehem Steel Corp., $280,700,000
8. Allegheny-Teledyne, $267,000,000
9. National Steel Corp., $213,500,000
10. Freeport-McMoRan Copper & Gold Inc., $208,541,000

Source: *Metal Statistics*, Top 50 Metals Companies (annual), 1998, p. XXV.

★3097★
TOP NORTH AMERICAN METALS COMPANIES BY INCREASE IN TOTAL ASSETS, 1997
Ranked by: Return on assets, in percent. **Remarks:** Also notes top 50 rank and 1997 total assets and net profit/loss. **Number listed:** 50
1. Bethlehem Steel Corp., with 21.5140%
2. Algoma Steel Inc., 17.8734%
3. Freeport-McMoran Copper & Gold Inc., 12.7536%
4. Newmont Mining, 12.1809%
5. U.S. Steel Group of USX Corp., 11.5477%
6. Allegheny-Teledyne, 10.2515%
7. Quanex Corp., 10.0895%
8. Nucor Corp., 9.8674%
9. Essex International, 9.7245%
10. National Steel Corp., 8.7022%

Source: *Metal Statistics*, Top 50 Metals Companies (annual), 1998, p. XXX.

★3098★
TOP NORTH AMERICAN METALS COMPANIES BY RETURN ON ASSETS, 1997
Ranked by: Return on assets. **Remarks:** Also notes top 50 rank and 1996 net profit/loss. **Number listed:** 50
1. Barrick Gold Corp., with 0.890
2. Rouge Steel Co., 0.466
3. Olin Corp., 0.212
4. Allegheny-Teledyne, 0.178
5. U.S. Steel Group of USX Corp., 0.143
6. Cominco Ltd., 0.113
7. Phelps Dodge Corp., 0.096
8. Nucor Corp., 0.095
9. Alumax Inc., 0.076
10. Cyprus Amax Minerals Co., 0.073

Source: *Metal Statistics*, Top 50 Metals Companies (annual), 1998, p. XXVIII.

★3099★
TOP NORTH AMERICAN METALS COMPANIES BY SALES GROWTH IN PERCENT, 1997
Ranked by: Sales growth, in percent. **Remarks:** Also notes 1996 and 1997 sales. **Number listed:** 50
1. Newmont Mining Co., with 204.66%
2. Reliance Steel & Aluminum Co., 147.03%
3. Birmingham Steel Corp., 130.98%
4. Essex International, 130.90%
5. Kennecott Corp., 127.68%
6. Cyprus Amax Minerals Co., 124.63%
7. Ivaco Inc., 119.59%
8. Ryerson Tull, 116.52%
9. Nucor Corp., 114.74%
10. Russell Metals Inc., 113.50%

Source: *Metal Statistics*, Top 50 Metals Companies (annual), 1998, p. XXVII.

★3100★
TOP NORTH AMERICAN METALS COMPANIES BY SALES GROWTH, 1997
Ranked by: Sales growth, in dollars. **Remarks:** Also notes top 50 rank and 1996 sales. **Number listed:** 50
1. Newmont Mining Co., with $804,300,000
2. Nucor Corp., $537,300,000
3. Inland Steel Industries Inc., $462,800,000
4. Ryerson Tull, $395,400,000
5. Cyprus Amax Minerals Co., $384,000,000
6. Essex International, $372,300,000
7. Reynolds Metals, $347,000,000
8. LTV, $311,500,000
9. Reliance Steel & Aluminum Co., $307,543,000
10. Aluminum Co. of America, $264,000,000

Source: *Metal Statistics*, Top 50 Metals Companies (annual), 1998, p. XXVI.

★3101★
TOP NORTH AMERICAN METALS COMPANIES BY SALES, 1997
Ranked by: Metal sales, in dollars. **Remarks:** Also notes 1996 ranking. **Number listed:** 50
1. Aluminum Co. of America, with $8,240,000,000
2. Alcan Aluminium Ltd., $7,021,700,000
3. U.S. Steel Group of USX Corp., $6,793,000,000
4. Reynolds Metals, $5,738,000,000
5. Inland Steel Industries Inc., $5,046,800,000
6. Bethlehem Steel Corp., $4,631,200,000
7. LTV, $4,446,000,000
8. Nucor Corp., $4,184,497,854
9. Noranda Inc., $4,135,000,000
10. National Steel Corp., $3,139,700,000

Source: *Metal Statistics*, Top 50 Metals Companies (annual), 1998, p. XXIV.

Metropolitan Areas

See also: **Cities and Towns**

★3102★
LEADING METROPOLITAN COMMUTER RAILROADS, 1999*
Ranked by: Cost of projects under way and planned, in millions of dollars. **Number listed:** 50
1. Amtrak, with $5,400 million
2. Massachusetts Bay Corp., $2,800
3. Metro-Dade Transit Agency, $2,731
4. Bay Area Rapid Transit District, $2,645
5. Central Puget Sound Regional Transit Authority, $2,400
6. MTA New York City Transit, $2,356
7. San Francisco Municipal Railway, $2,200
8. Orange County Transportation Authority, $1,917
9. Tren Urbano, $1,718
10. New Jersey Transit Corp., $1,500

Source: *Metro Magazine*, Metro Rail Survey (annual), June, 1999, p. 34+.

★3103★
LEAST-LIVABLE LARGE METROPOLITAN AREAS, 1998
Ranked by: Rational index rank. **Remarks:** Rational index ranks metro areas according to the tendency of Americans to choose to migrate into them. **Number listed:** 59
1. Chicago, IL
2. Bergen-Passaic, NJ
3. Hartford, CT
4. San Francisco, CA
5. Newark, NJ
6. Orange County, CA
7. Miami, FL
8. San Jose, CA
9. New York, NY
10. Los Angeles, CA

Source: *Federal Reserve Bank of St. Louis: Regional Economist*, April, 1999, p. 11.

★3104★
MOST-LIVABLE LARGE METROPOLITAN AREAS, 1998
Ranked by: Rational index rank. **Remarks:** Rational index ranks metro areas according to the tendency of Americans to choose to migrate into them. **Number listed:** 59
1. Las Vegas, NV
2. Atlanta, GA
3. Phoenix, AZ
4. Austin, TX
5. Raleigh-Durham, NC
6. West Palm Beach, FL
7. Orlando, FL
8. Fort Lauderdale, FL
9. Portland, OR
10. Charlotte, NC

Source: *Federal Reserve Bank of St. Louis: Regional Economist*, April, 1999, p. 11.

★3105★
MOST POPULOUS METROPOLITAN AREAS, 1998
Ranked by: Population estimate, in thousands. **Number listed:** 321
1. Los Angeles-Long Beach, CA, with 9,602.0 thousand
2. New York, NY, 8,766.7
3. Chicago, IL, 7,842.5
4. Philadelphia, PA, 4,954.4
5. Washington, DC, 4,623.2
6. Detroit, MI, 4,482.8
7. Houston, TX, 3,872.4
8. Boston-Lawrence-Lowell-Brockton, MA, 3,869.3
9. Atlanta, GA, 3,682.1
10. Dallas, TX, 3,149.1

Source: *Sales & Media Market*, S&MM Survey of Buying Power (annual), August, 1998, p. 10.

★3106★
TOP METROPOLITAN AREAS BY HOUSING PERMITS, 1998
Ranked by: Number of permits. **Remarks:** Also notes percent change from previous year. **Number listed:** 15
1. Atlanta, GA, with 32,348 permits
2. Phoenix-Mesa, AZ, 28,245
3. Houston, TX, 26,729
4. Dallas, TX, 23,589
5. Washington, DC, 21,389
6. Las Vegas, NV, 20,244
7. Chicago, IL, 18,979
8. Orlando, FL, 14,232
9. Denver, CO, 13,099
10. Portland-Vancouver, OR, 10,461

Source: *Professional Builder*, October, 1998, p. 15.

★3107★
TOP METROPOLITAN AREAS BY LABOR SUPPLY, 1999*
Ranked by: Labor quality index. **Remarks:** Labor index is derived from statistical information in unemployment, educational attainment, labor organization representation, and total employment compensation. Scores range from 8.28 (high) to 3.23 (low). **Number listed:** 10
1. Austin-San Marcos, TX, with 8.28
2. Oklahoma City, OK, 7.70
3. Enid, OK, 7.47
4. San Antonio, TX, 7.41
5. Lexington, KY, 7.14
6. Albuquerque, NM, 7.00
7. Amarillo, TX, 6.91
8. Wichita, KS, 6.68
9. Salt Lake City-Ogden, UT, 6.56
9. Tulsa, OK, 6.56

Source: *Business Facilities*, April, 1999, p. 8.

★3108★
TOP METROPOLITAN AREAS BY MEDIAN AGE, 1998
Ranked by: Median age. **Number listed:** 321
1. Punta Gorda, FL, with 53.2 thousand
2. Sarasota-Bradenton, FL, 47.8
3. Fort Myers-Cape Coral, FL, 43.6
4. Ocala, FL, 42.8
5. Naples, FL, 42.5
6. Daytona Beach, FL, 41.9
7. West Palm Beach-Boca Raton, FL, 41.8
8. Fort Pierce-Port. St. Lucie, FL, 41.7
9. Barnstable-Yarmouth, FL, 41.3
10. Tampa-St. Petersburg-Clearwater, FL, 40.7

Source: *Sales & Media Market*, S&MM Survey of Buying Power (annual), August, 1998, p. 11.

★3109★
TOP METROPOLITAN AREAS WITH THE LARGEST REAL ESTATE INVESTMENT TRUSTS, 1998
Ranked by: Value of properties, in millions. **Remarks:** Also notes number of properties. **Number listed:** 20
1. Chicago, IL, with $16,943 million
2. Atlanta, GA, $16,692
3. Washington, DC, $15,630
4. Los Angeles, CA, $12,426
5. Dallas/Fort Worth, TX, $12,183
6. Houston, TX, $8,951
7. Midtown Manhattan, NY, $8,832
8. Boston, MA, $8,604
9. Orange County, FL, $7,382
10. Philadelphia, PA, $7,255

Source: *CB Richard Ellis Global Research & Consulting: North American Index Fourth Quarter*, 1998, p. 14.

★3110★
TOP METROPOLITAN STATISTICAL AREAS BY APPAREL SALES, 1998
Ranked by: Apparel Sales, in thousands of dollars. **Number listed:** 315
1. New York, NY, with $5,736,575 thousand
2. Chicago, IL, $4,662,710
3. Los Angeles-Long Beach, CA, $4,433,526
4. Boston-Worcester-Lawrence-Lowell-Brockton, MA, $3,716,715
5. Washington, DC, Maryland, Virginia, West Virginia, $3,321,431

6. Philadelphia, PA, $2,710,766
7. Detroit, MI, $2,411,940
8. Nassau-Suffolk, NY, $1,961,592
9. Houston, TX, $1,923,857
10. Miami, FL, $1,859,458

Source: *Editor & Publisher Market Guide (annual)*, Editor & Publisher Co., 1998, p. I-16+.

★3111★
TOP METROPOLITAN STATISTICAL AREAS BY AUTOMOBILE SALES, 1998
Ranked by: Automobile Sales, in thousands of dollars. **Number listed:** 315

1. Chicago, IL, with $19,498,323 thousand
2. Los Angeles-Long Beach, CA, $19,442,944
3. Detroit, MI, $13,991,556
4. Boston-Worcester-Lawrence-Lowell-Brockton, MA, $12,667,210
5. Washington, DC, Maryland, Virginia, West Virginia, $12,474,222
6. Philadelphia, PA, $12,030,667
7. Houston, TX, $11,228,901
8. Dallas, TX, $9,859,060
9. Atlanta, GA, $9,596,514
10. Fort Lauderdale, FL, $8,692,530

Source: *Editor & Publisher Market Guide (annual)*, Editor & Publisher Co., 1998, p. I-16+.

★3112★
TOP METROPOLITAN STATISTICAL AREAS BY DISPOSABLE INCOME, 1998
Ranked by: Disposable income, in thousands of dollars. **Number listed:** 315

1. New York, NY, with $210,972,180 thousand
2. Los Angeles-Long Beach, CA, $198,194,326
3. Chicago, IL, $189,539,009
4. Boston-Worcester-Lawrence-Lowell-Brockton, MA, $149,049,377
5. Washington, DC, Maryland, Virginia, West Virginia, $124,594,025
6. Philadelphia, PA, $122,712,595
7. Detroit, MI, $110,654,991
8. Houston, TX, $88,111,636
9. Atlanta, GA, $81,444,470
10. Dallas, TX, $74,350,798

Source: *Editor & Publisher Market Guide (annual)*, Editor & Publisher Co., 1998, p. I-11+.

★3113★
TOP METROPOLITAN STATISTICAL AREAS BY DRUG SALES, 1998
Ranked by: Drug Sales, in thousands of dollars. **Number listed:** 315

1. Chicago, IL, with $4,294,931 thousand
2. New York, NY, $3,366,372
3. Los Angeles-Long Beach, CA, $3,304,760
4. Boston-Worcester-Lawrence-Lowell-Brockton, MA, $2,270,656
5. Philadelphia, PA, $2,434,270
6. Detroit, MI, $2,411,540
7. Washington, DC, Maryland, Virginia, West Virginia, $1,797,555
8. Cleveland-Lorain-Elyria, OH, $1,522,755
9. Nassau-Suffolk, NY, $1,376,086
10. Houston, TX, $1,293,412

Source: *Editor & Publisher Market Guide (annual)*, Editor & Publisher Co., 1998, p. I-20+.

★3114★
TOP METROPOLITAN STATISTICAL AREAS BY FOOD SALES, 1998
Ranked by: Food Sales, in thousands of dollars. **Number listed:** 315

1. Los Angeles-Long Beach, CA, with $14,251,580 thousand
2. Chicago, IL, $12,119,404
3. Boston-Worcester-Lawrence-Lowell-Brockton, MA, $10,597,939
4. New York, NY, $10,441,444
5. Washington, DC, Maryland, Virginia, West Virginia, $8,947,519
6. Philadelphia, PA, $8,892,890
7. Houston, TX, $7,094,782
8. Detroit, MI, $6,568,329
9. Atlanta, GA, $5,599,250
10. Nassau-Suffolk, NY, $5,242,776

Source: *Editor & Publisher Market Guide (annual)*, Editor & Publisher Co., 1998, p. I-15+.

★3115★
TOP METROPOLITAN STATISTICAL AREAS BY FURNITURE SALES, 1998
Ranked by: Furniture Sales, in thousands of dollars. **Number listed:** 315

1. Los Angeles-Long Beach, CA, with $5,901,944 thousand
2. Chicago, IL, $5,341,401
3. New York, NY, $4,711,361
4. Washington, DC, Maryland, Virginia, West Virginia, $4,043,589
5. Boston-Worcester-Lawrence-Lowell-Brockton, MA, $3,153,059
6. Detroit, MI, $2,932,266
7. Philadelphia, PA, $2,753,403
8. Houston, TX, $2,468,702
9. Atlanta, GA, $2,165,165
10. Nassau-Suffolk, NY, $2,152,220

Source: *Editor & Publisher Market Guide (annual)*, Editor & Publisher Co., 1998, p. I-19+.

★3116★
TOP METROPOLITAN STATISTICAL AREAS BY GASOLINE SALES, 1998
Ranked by: Gasoline Sales, in thousands of dollars. **Number listed:** 315

1. Los Angeles-Long Beach, CA, with $4,629,275 thousand
2. Chicago, IL, $4,283,529
3. Boston-Worcester-Lawrence-Lowell-Brockton, MA, $3,252,825
4. Washington, DC, Maryland, Virginia, West Virginia, $3,103,893
5. Detroit, MI, $2,982,437
6. Philadelphia, PA, $2,485,504
7. Atlanta, GA, $2,304,357
8. Menneapolis-St. Paul, MN, Wisconsin, $2,155,699
9. Houston, TX, $2,131,699
10. New York, NY, $2,105,411

Source: *Editor & Publisher Market Guide (annual)*, Editor & Publisher Co., 1998, p. I-15+.

★3117★
TOP METROPOLITAN STATISTICAL AREAS BY GENERAL MERCHANDISE, 1998
Ranked by: General merchandise sales, in thousands of dollars. **Number listed:** 315

1. Los Angeles-Long Beach, CA, with $10,144,416 thousand

2. Chicago, IL, $9,158,147
3. Detroit, MI, $7,578,144
4. Boston-Worcester-Lawrence-Lowell-Brockton, MA, $7,003,012
5. New York, NY, $5,853,851
6. Washington, DC, Maryland, Virginia, West Virginia, $5,807,817
7. Philadelphia, PA, $5,615,686
8. Houston, TX, $5,502,096
9. Atlanta, GA, $4,969,475
10. Dallas, TX, $4,652,695

Source: *Editor & Publisher Market Guide (annual)*, Editor & Publisher Co., 1998, p. I-14+.

★3118★
TOP METROPOLITAN STATISTICAL AREAS BY INCOME PER HOUSEHOLD, 1998
Ranked by: Income per household, in dollars. **Number listed:** 315

1. New Haven-Bridgeport-Stamford-Waterbury-Danbury, CT, with $84,211
2. Nassau-Suffolk, NY, $82,569
3. San Francisco, CA, $82,402
4. Bergen-Passaic, NJ, $82,067
5. Trenton, NJ, $80,805
6. Newark, NJ, $78,551
7. San Jose, CA, $78,311
8. Middlesex-Somerset-Hunterdon, NJ, $76,896
9. West Palm Beach-Boca Raton, FL, $75,357
10. Honolulu, HI, $75,357

Source: *Editor & Publisher Market Guide (annual)*, Editor & Publisher Co., 1998, p. I-12+.

★3119★
TOP METROPOLITAN STATISTICAL AREAS BY LUMBER/HARDWARE SALES, 1998
Ranked by: Lumber/hardware sales, in thousands of dollars. **Number listed:** 315

1. Chicago, IL, with $3,979,791 thousand
2. Los Angeles-Long Beach, CA, $3,745,814
3. Boston-Worcester-Lawrence-Lowell-Brockton, MA, $3,060,295
4. Detroit, MI, $2,525,364
5. Washington, DC, Maryland, Virginia, West Virginia, $2,332,763
6. Philadelphia, PA, $2,210,677
7. Minneapolis-St. Paul, MN, Wisconsin, $2,141,909
8. Atlanta, GA, $2,043,627
9. Nassau-Suffolk, NY, $2,000,876
10. New York, NY, $1,960,330

Source: *Editor & Publisher Market Guide (annual)*, Editor & Publisher Co., 1998, p. I-13+.

★3120★
TOP METROPOLITAN STATISTICAL AREAS BY POPULATION, 1998
Ranked by: Population estimate. **Number listed:** 315

1. Los Angeles-Long Beach, CA, with 9,283,453
2. New York, NY, 8,686,864
3. Chicago, IL, 8,007,663
4. Boston-Worcester-Lawrence-Lowell-Brockton, MA, 5,956,777
5. Philadelphia, PA, 5,036,263
6. Washington, DC, Maryland, Virginia, West Virginia, 4,739,956
7. Detroit, MI, 4,411,964
8. Houston, TX, 3,951,299
9. Atlanta, GA, 3,811,978
10. Dallas, TX, 3,181,759

Source: *Editor & Publisher Market Guide (annual)*, Editor & Publisher Co., 1998, p. I-10+.

★3121★
TOP METROPOLITAN STATISTICAL AREAS BY TOTAL RETAIL SALES, 1998
Ranked by: Total Retail Sales, in thousands of dollars. **Number listed:** 315

1. Los Angeles-Long Beach, CA, with $82,991,235 thousand
2. Chicago, IL, $81,078,114
3. New York, NY, $61,268,828
4. Boston-Worcester-Lawrence-Lowell-Brockton, MA, $61,231,327
5. Washington, DC, Maryland, Virginia, West Virginia, $52,770,999
6. Philadelphia, PA, $51,788,786
7. Detroit, MI, $49,684,936
8. Houston, TX, $40,308,343
9. Atlanta, GA, $37,267,513
10. Dallas, TX, $34,756,498

Source: *Editor & Publisher Market Guide (annual)*, Editor & Publisher Co., 1998, p. I-13+.

Mexican Food

★3122★
LEADING MEXICAN FOOD CHAINS, 1999*
Ranked by: Satisfaction index score. **Remarks:** Includes rating in food quality, menu variety, value, service, atmosphere, cleanliness, and convenience. **Number listed:** 2

1. Chi-Chi's, with 46 index
2. Taco Bell, 33

Source: *Restaurants & Institutions*, Choice in Chains (annual), March 1, 1999, p. 90.

★3123★
TOP MEXICAN FOOD COMPANIES, 1997
Ranked by: Sales, in millions of dollars. **Number listed:** 23

1. Taco Bell, with $4,900.0 million
2. Chi-Chi's, $245.8
3. Del Taco, $239.0
4. El Torito, $228.4
5. Don Pablo's, $196.5
6. Taco John's Restaurants, $174.0
7. Chevys Mexican Restaurants, $169.7
8. El Chico, $139.9
9. Taco Cabana, $135.0
10. Rio Bravo Cantina, $128.2

Source: *Restaurants & Institutions*, Restaurants & Institutions 400 (annual), July 15, 1998, p. 102.

Mexico Stock Exchange

★3124★
LARGEST LISTED COMPANIES ON THE MEXICO STOCK EXCHANGE, 1997
Ranked by: Market value, in billions of U.S. dollars ($). **Number listed:** 20

1. Telmex, with $18.34 billion
2. Cifra, $11.66

3. Cemex, $6.75
4. Kimber, $6.44
5. Gcarso, $6.10
6. Banacci, $4.74
7. Gmodelo, $4.42
8. Televisa, $4.41
9. Femsa, $4.31
10. Alfa, $4.06

Source: *Euromoney Publications*, SSB Guide to World Equity Markets (annual), 1998, p. 343.

★3125★
MOST ACTIVELY TRADED ISSUES ON THE MEXICO STOCK EXCHANGE, 1997
Ranked by: Trading value, in millions of U.S. dollars ($). **Remarks:** Also notes stock volume. **Number listed:** 20

1. Telmex, with $6,736.4 million
2. Alfa (A), $2,270.8
3. Femsa (B), $2,522.1
4. GCarso (A1), $2,382.9
5. Cemex (B), $2,040.5
6. Cemex Cpo, $1,831.9
7. Cifra (V), $1,689.3
8. Kimber (A), $1,644.2
9. Banacci (B), $1,618.2
10. Cifra (C), $1,269.2

Source: *Euromoney Publications*, SSB Guide to World Equity Markets (annual), 1998, p. 343.

Microbreweries

★3126★
TOP U.S. MICRO- AND PUB-BREWERIES, 1998
Ranked by: Number of 31-gallon barrels sold. **Number listed:** 10

1. Great Lakes Beer Co., with 15,000 barrels
2. Anderson Valley Brewing Co., 14,906
3. Schirf Brewing Co., 14,185
4. Flying Dog Brewing Co., 14,000
5. Sprecher Brewing Co., 13,650
6. Hale's Ales, 13,043
7. Humboldt Brewing Co., 12,500
8. Lagunitas Brewing Co., 11,958
9. Capital Brewery, 11,027
10. Uinta Brewing Co., 10,718
11. North Coast Brewing Co., 9,817

Source: *Modern Brewery Age*, Micro & Specialty Beer Report (annual), May 10, 1999, p. 13.

★3127★
TOP U.S. REGIONAL BREWERS, 1998
Ranked by: Number of 31-gallon barrels sold. **Number listed:** 11

1. Genesee Brewing Co., with 1,500,000 barrels
2. Latrobe Brewing Co., 1,020,000
3. D.C. Yuengling Brewing Co., 637,170
4. Pittsburgh Brewing Co., 350,000
5. Matt Brewing Co., 251,000
6. Spoetzl Brewing Co., 241,476
7. Minnesota Brewing Co., 200,000
8. Anchor Brewing Co., 99,118
9. Jones Brewing Co., 46,100
10. August Schell Brewing Co., 41,000

Source: *Modern Brewery Age*, Micro & Specialty Beer Report (annual), May 10, 1999, p. 13.

★3128★
TOP U.S. SPECIALTY BREWERS, 1998
Ranked by: Number of 31-gallon barrels sold. **Number listed:** 30

1. Boston Beer, with 1,150,000 barrels
2. Sierra Nevada Brewing Co., 382,050
3. Pete's Brewing Co., 239,516
4. Redhook Ale Brewery, 202,500
5. Widmer Bros. Brewing Co., 117,000
6. Pyramid Brewing Co., 105,900
7. New Belgium Brewing Co., 104,835
8. Anchor Brewing Co., 99,118
9. Deschutes Brewing Co., 77,245
10. Full Sail Brewing Co., 66,337

Source: *Modern Brewery Age*, Micro & Specialty Beer Report (annual), May 10, 1999, p. 10.

Microcomputers

See also: **Computer Industry**

★3129★
TOP U.S. PERSONAL COMPUTER VENDORS, 1998
Ranked by: Market share, in percent. **Number listed:** 5

1. Compaq, with 16.7%
2. Dell, 13.2%
3. Packard Bell NEC, 8.4%
4. IBM, 8.2%
5. Gateway, 7.8%
6. Others, 45.7%

Source: *Appliance Manufacturer*, April, 1999, p. 23.

Microwave Ovens

★3130★
TOP MICROWAVE OVEN MANUFACTURERS, 1998
Ranked by: Market share, in percent. **Number listed:** 9

1. Sharp, with 31%
2. Samsung, 21%
3. Matsushita, 14%
4. Sanyo Fisher, 10%
5. LG Electronics, 9%
6. Whirlpool, 5%
7. Daewoo, 3%
8. Goodman, 2%
9. Others, 5%

Source: *Appliance Manufacturer*, April, 1999, p. 19.

Military Bases--Stores, Shopping Centers, etc.

★3131★
TOP DECA VENDORS AT MILITARY BASES, 1997
Ranked by: Payment to vendors, in dollars. **Number listed:** 326

1. Kraft Foods, with $338,215,103
2. AAFES, $276,793,371
3. Procter & Gamble, $264,932,710
4. ConAgra, $154,661,065
5. Nabisco Foods, $109,880,708

6. General Mills, $102,158,749
7. Umex, $101,032,789
8. Nestle USA Inc., $95,101,943
9. Campbell Soup, $90,987,617
10. Pillsbury, $88,907,850

Source: *Military Market*, October, 1998, p. 90.

★3132★
TOP VENDORS AT MILITARY BASES, 1998
Ranked by: Volume, in dollars. **Number listed:** 171

1. Eurpac, with $46,283,289
2. Philip Morris, $41,787,733
3. Buck Petroleum, $36,785,800
4. Brown & Williamson, $26,185,125
5. Citgo Petroleum Corp., $22,274,886
6. BP Oil Co., $14,733,820
7. Sony, $14,614,989
8. Compaq Computer Corp., $14,222,708
9. Levi Strauss & Co., $13,651,729
10. Coca-Cola, $12,852,258

Source: *Military Market*, June, 1999, p. 40.

Milk

★3133★
LEADING REFRIGERATED SKIM/LOW FAT MILK BRANDS, 1998
Ranked by: Sales, in millions of dollars. **Remarks:** Also notes annual growth and market share. **Number listed:** 10

1. Private label, with $3,992.4 million
2. Lactaid 100, $114.1
3. Dean's, $104.6
4. Mayfield Farms, $71.6
5. Land O'Lakes, $69.6
6. Kemps, $64.2
7. Prairie Farms, $57.1
8. Garelick Farms, $47.1
9. Anderson Erickson, $45.9
10. Sealtest, $45.6

Source: *Dairy Field*, February, 1999, p. 38.

★3134★
LEADING REFRIGERATED WHOLE MILK BRANDS, 1998
Ranked by: Sales, in millions of dollars. **Remarks:** Also notes annual growth and market share. **Number listed:** 10

1. Private label, with $1,896 million
2. Borden, $56.4
3. Lehigh Valley, $44.9
4. Dean's, $30.9
5. Mayfield Farms, $28.5
6. Tuscan Farms, $21.6
7. Plains, $21.3
8. Farmland, $20.8
9. Prairie Farms, $18.2
10. Garelick Farms, $17.7

Source: *Dairy Field*, February, 1999, p. 38.

Milk, International

★3135★
LEADING WORLD SKIM MILK POWDER USAGE, 1998
Ranked by: Percent of usage. **Number listed:** 8

1. Condensed Milk, with 30%
2. UHT/Fluid, 26%
3. Ice Cream, 18%
4. Cultured Products & Yogurt, 9%
5. Confectionery, 5%
5. Bakery, 5%
7. Cheese, 4%
8. Other products, 3%

Source: *Dairy Foods*, January, 1999, p. 15.

Mineral Industry

See: **Mining Industry**

Mining Industry

★3136★
MOST ADMIRED MINING AND CRUDE OIL PRODUCTION CORPORATIONS, 1998
Ranked by: Scores (1-10) derived from a survey of senior executives, outside directors and securities analysts. **Remarks:** Respondents rated companies in their own industry on 8 attributes of reputation. Also notes previous year's rank. **Number listed:** 10

1. Burlington Resources, with 6.72 points
2. Apache, 6.69
3. Unocal, 6.40
4. Vulcan Materials, 6.27
5. Newmont Mining, 6.13
6. Cyprus Amax Minerals, 5.93
7. Freeport-McMoran Copper & Gold, 5.75
8. Asarco, 5.60
9. Union Pacific Resources, 5.45
10. Oryx Energy, 4.90

Source: *Fortune*, America's Most Admired Corporations (annual), March 1, 1999, p. F-4.

★3137★
TOP CORPORATIONS IN THE MINING AND CRUDE-OIL PRODUCTION INDUSTRY, 1998
Ranked by: Revenue, in millions of dollars. **Remarks:** Also notes profits and investment figures as well as number of employees. **Number listed:** 10

1. Occidental Petroleum, with $6,596 million
2. Unocal, $5,379
3. Cyprus Amax Minerals, $2,558
4. Asarco, $2,233
5. Union Pacific Resources, $2,181
6. Freeport-McMoran Copper & Gold, $1,757
7. Burlington Resources, $1,637
8. Newmont Mining, $1,475
9. Plains Resources, $1,294
10. Global Marine, $1,162

Source: *Fortune*, Fortune 500 Largest U.S. Corporations (annual), April 26, 1999, p. F-65.

★3138★
TOP METALS & MINING COMPANIES IN THE S&P 500, 1998
Ranked by: Each company is ranked by eight criteria: one-year total return, three-year total return, one-year sales growth, three-year average annual sales growth, one-year profit growth, three-year average annual profit growth, net profit margins, and return on equity, with additional weight given to a company's sales. A company's composite rank is calculated using the sum of all its ranks. **Remarks:** Overall score not provided. **Number listed:** 18

1. Alcoa
2. Englehard
3. Nucor
4. Barrick Gold
5. USX-U.S. Steel Group
6. Placer Dome
7. Alcan Aluminum
8. Freeport-McMoran Copper & Gold
9. Reynolds Metals
10. Worthington Industries

Source: *Business Week*, Business Week 50: Top Companies of the S&P 500 (annual), March 29, 1999, p. 156+.

Mining Industry--Europe

★3139★
TOP MINING COMPANIES IN EUROPE, 1999*
Ranked by: Sales, in million of European Currency Units (ECUs). **Remarks:** Also notes number of employees and overall rank among European businesses. **Number listed:** 40

1. Rag AG (Germany), with ECUs12.648 million
2. Shell UK Ltd. (United Kingdom), ECUs10.669
3. Gaz de France (France), ECUs8.215
4. BG Plc (United Kingdom), ECUs7.895
5. Billiton Plc (United Kingdom), ECUs7.799
6. Esso UK Plc (United Kingdom), ECUs7.696
7. OMV Aktiengesellschaft, ECUs5.984
8. Conoco UK Ltd. (United Kingdom), ECUs4.484
9. Burmah Castrol PLC (United Kingdom), ECUs4.332
10. AMEC PLC (United Kingdom), ECUs4.093

Source: *Duns Europa (annual)*, Dun & Bradstreet, 1999, vol. 4, p. 227.

Mining Industry, International

★3140★
WORLD'S LARGEST CRUDE OIL MINING COMPANIES BY REVENUE, 1997
Ranked by: Revenue, in millions of dollars. **Number listed:** 3

1. Pemex (Mexico), with $28,566 million
2. Broken Hill Proprietary (Australia), $17,540
3. Rag AG (Germany), $14,403

Source: *Fortune*, The Global 500: World's Biggest Corporations (annual), August 3, 1998, p. F-22.

Minivans

★3141★
TOP BRAND MINIVANS AND UTILITY VEHICLES, 1998
Ranked by: Total unit sales, in thousands. **Remarks:** Also notes media expenditures. **Number listed:** 10

1. F-Series (Ford), with 787,522 thousand
2. C-K (Chevy), 454,311
3. Explorer (Ford), 431,488
4. Ram (Dodge), 410,130
5. Ranger (Ford), 328,136
6. Caravan (Dodge), 293,819
7. Grand Cherokee (Jeep), 229,135
8. S-10 Pickup (Chevy), 228,093
9. Expedition (Ford), 225,703
10. S-Series (Chevy), 192,314

Source: *Brand Week*, Superbrands: America's Top 2,000 Brands, June 21, 1999, p. 522.

Minority Broadcasting Stations

★3142★
TOP HISPANIC RADIO STATIONS, 1998
Ranked by: Estimated ad billings, in millions of dollars. **Remarks:** Includes format, location, owner, percent Hispanic-owned and 1997 gross billings. **Number listed:** 10

1. KLVE-FM, KTNQ-AM, KSCA-FM, with $64.66 million
2. WSKQ-FM, WPAT-FM, $36.00
3. WAMR-FM, WRTO-FM, WQBA-AM, WAQI-AM, $32.00
4. WRMA-FM, WXDJ-FM, WCMQ-AM, WCMQ-FM, $25.50
5. WOJO-FM, WIND-AM, WLXX-AM, $19.00
6. KCOR-FM, KROM-FM, KXTN-FM, $16.87
7. KKHJ-AM, KBUE-FM, KWIZ-AM, $16.55
8. KLAT-AM, KLTO-FM, KOVE-FM, KRTX-FM, $15.33
9. KQQK-FM, KXTJ-FM, KEYH-AM, $14.00
10. KLAX-FM, KXED-AM, $13.10

Source: *Hispanic Business*, Top 10 Hispanic Radio Stations by Ad Billings (annual), December, 1998, p. 62.

Minority Business Enterprises

★3143★
LEADING AFRICAN AMERICAN-OWNED COMPANIES, 1998
Ranked by: Sales, in millions of dollars. **Remarks:** Also notes business and previous year's rank. **Number listed:** 10

1. Philadelphia Coca-Cola Bottling Co., with $389 million
2. Johnson Publishing, $372
3. TLC Beatrice International Holdings Inc., $322
4. Active Transportation, $250
5. Bing Group, $232
6. World Wide Technology, $201
7. FUCI Metals USA, $200
8. Granite Broadcasting, $194

9. H.J. Russell & Co., $184
10. BET Holdings II Inc., $178

Source: *Wall Street Journal*, May 10, 1999, p. b1.

Minority Business Enterprises--Chicago (IL)

★3144★

TOP MINORITY-OWNED COMPANIES IN CHICAGO, 1997

Ranked by: Revenue, in millions of dollars. **Remarks:** Also notes contact information, top executive, minority group of ownership, year founded, number of employees, and description of business. **Number listed:** 25

1. Johnson Publishing Co., with $361.1 million
2. Harpo Entertainment Group, $150.0
3. American Healthcare Providers Inc., $122.6
4. Sayers Computer Source, $72.7
5. Reliant Industries Inc., $68.3
6. Flying Food Group, $58.0
7. Electro Wire Inc., $48.0
8. Landmark Ford of Niles, $42.0
9. Strathmore Printing Co., $33.2
10. Capsonic Group, $32.0

Source: *Crain's Chicago Business*, Top Business Lists (annual), 1999, vol. 21, p. 49+.

Minority Business Enterprises—Detroit Metropolitan Area

★3145★

LEADING BLACK-OWNED BUSINESSES IN THE DETROIT METROPOLITAN AREA, 1998

Ranked by: Revenue, in millions of dollars. **Remarks:** Includes 1997 revenue, percent change, number of local employees for 1999 and 1998, percent black-owned and type of business. **Number listed:** 20

1. Mel Farr Automotive Group, with $588.1 million
2. The Bing Group, $234.0
3. Barden Cos. Inc., $143.5
4. La-Van Hawkins Food Group LLC, $136.3
5. Thomas Madison Inc., $110.0
6. Avis Ford Inc., $109.4
7. Exemplar Manufacturing Co., $106.0
8. Wesley Industries Inc., $95.0
9. The Bartech Group, $76.5
10. American Basic Industries Inc., $70.0

Source: *Crain's Detroit Business*, Crain's Book of Lists Detroit (annual), May 17, 1999, p. 19.

Minority Business Enterprises--Colorado

★3146★

TOP MINORITY-OWNED COMPANIES IN COLORADO, 1997

Ranked by: Revenue, in dollars. **Remarks:** Also notes contact information, ethnicity and description, and previous year's revenue. **Number listed:** 100

1. The Burt Automotive Network, with $866,557,988
2. Space Mark Inc., $68,700,000
3. Productive Data Systems, $48,504,964
4. TSN Inc., $47,555,700
5. Native American Systems Inc., $41,500,000
6. 3SI, $25,000,000
7. Adams McClure Inc., $20,100,000
8. Excel Professional Services Inc., $20,000,000
9. Capital Packaging Corp., $16,000,000
9. Micro-Tel Inc., $16,000,000

Source: *Colorado Business*, Top 100 (annual), July, 1998, p. 28+.

Minority Business Enterprises--Florida

★3147★

TOP MINORITY-OWNED BUSINESSES IN FLORIDA, 1999*

Ranked by: Number of full-time employees. **Remarks:** Also notes 1997 revenue, type of business, owners and year founded. **Number listed:** 25

1. Farm Stores, with 1,177 employees
2. Gator Industries Inc., 850
3. Electric Machinery Enterprises Inc., 600
4. AIB Financial Group Inc., 491
5. Physicians Healthcare Plans Inc., 425
6. Avanti Press/Case-Hoyt Corp., 400
7. El Dorado Furniture Group, 330
8. Community Asphalt Corp., 280
9. Spillis Candela & Partners Inc., 225
10. Borrell Inc., 212

Source: *Florida Trend*, TopRank Florida (annual), 1999, p. 113.

Minority Business Enterprises--Long Island (NY)

★3148★

TOP MINORITY-OWNED FIRMS IN LONG ISLAND, 1999*

Ranked by: Number of employees. **Remarks:** Also notes contact information, year founded and products/services. **Number listed:** 26

1. Utopia Home Care, with 575 employees
2. Tishcon, 150
3. Sirina Fire Protection, 110
4. Air Industries Machining, 100
5. Shah Associates, 98
6. New York Business Systems, 60
7. Eastern Business Systems, 47
8. Captree Chemical, 40
8. RS Industries, 40
10. Palanker Chevrolet, 36

Source: *Long Island Business*, Long Island's Book of Lists (annual), 1999, p. 32.

Minority Business Enterprises—Los Angeles County (CA)

★3149★
LARGEST MINORITY-OWNED BUSINESSES IN LOS ANGELES COUNTY, 1997
Ranked by: Company-wide revenue, in millions of dollars. **Remarks:** Also notes 1996 revenues, majority ownership, profile, type of business, sales contact and top local executive. **Number listed:** 25

1. ViewSonic Corp., with $823 million
2. K.V. Mart Co., $238.5
3. NovaQuest InfoSystems, $190
4. Panda Management Co. Inc., $171.2
5. Tokal Bank of California, $138
6. Koos Manufacturing Inc., $130.2
7. Cathay Bancorp., $119
8. General Bank, $117.5
9. TELACU, $100
10. Board Ford Inc., $89.8

Source: *Los Angeles Business Journal*, Book of Lists (annual), 1999, p. 170.

Minority Business Enterprises—New York Metropolitan Area

★3150★
LARGEST BLACK- AND HISPANIC-OWNED FIRMS IN THE NEW YORK CITY AREA, 1997
Ranked by: Revenue, in millions of dollars. **Remarks:** Also notes contact information, top executive, nature of business, 1996 revenues, number of employees and year founded. **Number listed:** 25

1. TLC Beatrice International Holdings Inc., with $1,400 million
2. Goya Foods Inc., $620
3. AJ Contracting Co., Inc., $279
4. Granite Broadcasting Corp., $181.1
5. UniWorld Group Inc., $175
6. Gaseteria Oil Corp., $116
7. Essence Communications Inc., $104.8
8. Condal Distributors Inc., $88.5
9. Anpesil Distributors Inc., $75
10. Dial-A-Mattress Operating Inc., $70

Source: *Crain's New York Business*, July 27, 1998, p. 16+.

Minority Business Enterprises—Philadelphia Metropolitan Area

★3151★
LARGEST MINORITY-OWNED BUSINESSES IN THE PHILADELPHIA METROPOLITAN AREA, 1999*
Ranked by: Number of local full-time employees. **Remarks:** Also notes contact information, 1997 revenue, description of company, and local head. **Number listed:** 24

1. Philadelphia Coca-Cola Bottling Co., with 950 employees
2. Davis-Giovinazzo Construction Co., 220
3. Shepard-Patterson & Associates Inc., 150
4. L. Washington & Associates Inc., 101
5. Fabric Development, 95
5. J&B Software Inc., 95
7. A. Pomerantz & Co., 77
8. United Bank of Philadelphia, 75
9. The Philadelphia Tribune, 62
10. Rehab Option Inc., 54

Source: *Philadelphia Business Journal*, Book of Business Lists (annual), 1999, p. 119.

Mobile Home Parks

★3152★
LARGEST OWNERS OF MANUFACTURED HOME COMMUNITIES, 1999
Ranked by: Number of sites owned. **Remarks:** Includes state or province, number of sites owned/managed, number of communit tes or provinces and 1998 rank. **Number listed:** 150

1. Chateau Communities
2. Manufactured Home Communities
3. Sun Communities
4. Lautrec Ltd.
5. Clayton Homes
6. CWS Community Trust
7. Uniprop
8. The Bloch Organization
9. National Home Communities
10. Bessire & Casenhiser

Source: *Manufactured Home Merchandiser*, January, 1999, p. 42+.

Money Managers

See: **Investment Management Firms**

Montgomery County (PA)--Industries

★3153★
LARGEST MONTGOMERY COUNTY PRIVATE-SECTOR EMPLOYEES, 1999*
Ranked by: Number of county employees. **Remarks:** Includes address, revenue, number of offices, description of business and top executive. **Number listed:** 25

1. Merck & Co. Inc., with 7,000 employees
2. The Prudential Insurance Co. of America, 5,000
3. SmithKline Beecham, 4,625
4. Lockheed Martin Corp., 4,600
5. Aetna U.S. Healthcare, 3,065
6. Main Line Health Inc., 2,871
7. Unisys Corp., 2,200
8. Abington Memorial Hospital, 2,132
9. Rhone-Poulenc Rorer Inc., 2,000
10. Visteon Automotive Systems, 1,750

Source: *Philadelphia Business Journal*, Book of Business Lists (annual), 1999, p. 98.

Montreal Exchange

★3154★
LARGEST LISTED COMPANIES ON THE MONTREAL EXCHANGE, 1997
Ranked by: Market value, in millions of Canadian dollars (C$). **Number listed:** 20
1. Northern Telecom, with C$33,469 million
2. BCE Inc., C$31,473
3. Royal Bank of Canada, C$25,065
4. Thomson Corp., C$23,196
5. Canadian Imperial Bank of Commerce, C$20,122
6. Bank of Nova Scotia, C$17,933
7. Bank of Montreal, C$17,730
8. Seagram, C$16,627
9. Toronto-Dominion Bank, C$16,543
10. Imperial Oil Ltd., C$13,864

Source: *Euromoney Publications*, SSB Guide to World Equity Markets (annual), 1998, p. 116.

★3155★
MOST ACTIVELY TRADED SHARES ON THE MONTREAL EXCHANGE, 1997
Ranked by: Trading value, in millions of Canadian dollars (C$). **Number listed:** 20
1. Bombardier Inc. Class B, with C$2,296 million
2. BCE Inc., C$2,169
3. Bank of Montreal, C$2,164
4. Royal Bank of Canada, C$2,080
5. Biochem Pharma Inc., C$1,643
6. Canadian Imperial Bank of Commerce, C$1,568
7. Bank of Nova Scotia, C$1,441
8. National Bank of Canada, C$1,341
9. Toronto-Dominion Bank, C$1,316
10. Alcan Aluminum, C$1,171

Source: *Euromoney Publications*, SSB Guide to World Equity Markets (annual), 1998, p. 117.

Mortgage Banks

★3156★
TOP BANKS IN MORTGAGE-BACKED SECURITIES HOLDINGS
Ranked by: Mortgage-backed securities as of Sept. 30, 1998, in millions of dollars. **Remarks:** Also notes percent change, market value of MBS as a percent of book value, MBS pass-through, and total securities. **Number listed:** 50
1. Chase Manhattan Corp., with $35,016.7 million
2. BankAmerica Corp., $31,173.1
3. First Union Corp., $23,459.2
4. Norwest Corp., $16,005.4
5. Republic New York, $12,549.7
6. ABN AMRO Americas, $7,908.7
7. Fleet Financial Group, $7,525.2
8. Banc One Corp., $6,720.3
9. Fifth Third Bancorp, $6,000.5
10. Mellon Bank Corp., $5,060.7

Source: *American Banker*, Top 50 Mortgage Investments (annual), January 21, 1999, p. 11.

★3157★
TOP BANKS IN TOTAL MORTGAGE INVESTMENTS
Ranked by: Total mortgage investments as of Sept. 30, 1998, in thousands of dollars. **Remarks:** Also notes percent change, mortage-backed securities, collateralized mortgage obligations and home mortgage loans. **Number listed:** 50
1. BankAmerica Corp., with $127,478 thousand
2. Chase Manhattan Corp., $76,020
3. First Union Corp., $67,225
4. Norwest Corp., $36,872
5. Banc One Corp., $29,295
6. ABN AMRO Americas, $26,316
7. Fleet Financial Group, $24,333
8. PNC Bank Corp., $21,539
9. National City Corp., $20,954
10. Citicorp, $18,442

Source: *American Banker*, Top 50 Mortgage Investments (annual), January 21, 1999, p. 10.

★3158★
TOP RESIDENTIAL ORIGINATORS, 1998
Ranked by: Volume, in millions of dollars. **Remarks:** Includes location, 1997 volume, percent change and market share. **Number listed:** 50
1. Norwest Mortgage Inc., with $109,450 million
2. Countrywide Credit Industries Inc., $88,505
3. Chase Manhattan Mortgage, $82,988
4. Bank of America Mortgage, $62,228
5. Washington Mutual Savings, $37,286
6. Fleet Mortgage, $35,861
7. North American Mortgage, $30,810
8. ABN-AMRO Mortgage, $28,942
9. HomeSide Lending Inc., $26,886
10. Cendent Mortgage, $26,009

Source: *U.S. Banker*, April, 1999, p. 85.

★3159★
TOP RESIDENTIAL SERVICERS, 1998
Ranked by: Volume, in millions of dollars. **Remarks:** Includes location, 1997 volume, percent change and market share. **Number listed:** 50
1. Bank of America Mortgage, with $249,661 million
2. Norwest Mortgage Inc., $247,316
3. Countrywide Credit Industries Inc., $208,559
4. Chase Manhattan Mortgage, $206,347
5. GMAC Mortgage, $139,608
6. Fleet Mortgage, $120,098
7. HomeSide Lending Inc., $118,797
8. Washington Mutual Savings, $105,965
9. First Nationwide Mortgage, $86,355
10. GE Capital Mortgage Services, $83,273

Source: *U.S. Banker*, April, 1999, p. 86.

Mortgage Brokers

★3160★
TOP WOMEN MORTGAGE BROKERS, 1998
Ranked by: Sales volume achieved, in millions of dollars. **Remarks:** Also notes firm and location. **Number listed:** 12

1\. Terri Caffery, with $113.2 million
2\. Susan Suminski, $110.8
3\. Mary Bane, $62
3\. Mary Glavin, $62
5\. Judy Blackburn, $60
6\. Laurie Vree, $50
7\. Tamera Blaylock, $46
8\. Kathy Motlach, $38
9\. Sherry Windfield, $33
9\. Brenda Harden, $33

Source: *US Banker*, March, 1999, p. 92.

Mortgage Companies

See: **Mortgage Banks**

Mortgage Loans

See: **Mortgages**

Mortgage Origination

★3161★
TOP ORIGINATORS OF MORTGAGES, 1998
Ranked by: Origination of residential mortgage loans, in millions of dollars. **Remarks:** Also notes 1997 figures, percent change, market share and origination volume. **Number listed:** 100

1. Norwest Mortgage Inc., with $109,450 million
2. Countrywide Credit Industries Inc., $88,505
3. Chase Manhattan Mortgage, $82,988
4. Bank of America Mortgage, $62,228
5. Washington Mutual Savings, $37,286
6. Fleet Mortgage, $35,861
7. North American Mortgage, $30,810
8. ABN-AMRO Mortgage, $28,942
9. HomeSide Lending Inc., $26,886
10. Cendent Mortgage, $26,009

Source: *American Banker*, Top 100 (annual), April 19, 1999, p. 16A.

Mortgages

★3162★
TOP SERVICERS OF RESIDENTIAL MORTGAGES FOR INVESTORS, 1998
Ranked by: Mortgages serviced as of Dec. 31, 1998, in millions of dollars. **Remarks:** Includes location, 1997 figures, percent change and market share. **Number listed:** 50

1. Bank of America Mortgage, with $249,661 million
2. Norwest Mortgage Inc., $247,316
3. Countrywide Credit Industries Inc., $208,559
4. Chase Manhattan Mortgage, $206,347
5. GMAC Mortgage, $139,608
6. Fleet Mortgage, $120,098
7. HomeSide Lending Inc., $118,797
8. Washington Mutual Savings, $105,965
9. First Nationwide Mortgage, $86,355
10. GE Capital Mortgage Services, $83,273

Source: *American Banker*, April 19, 1999, p. 14A+.

Mortgages--Florida

★3163★
TOP MORTGAGE LENDERS IN FLORIDA, 1997
Ranked by: Residential loan amount, in dollars. **Remarks:** Also notes number of loans, average loan amount and market share. **Number listed:** 25

1. Barnett Bank Florida NA, with $3,047,187,893
2. NationsBank, $1,887,591,311
3. Chase Manhattan Mortgage, $1,739,314,548
4. Barnett Banks, $1,362,363,816
5. First Union Mortgage Co., $1,161,786,166
6. Norwest Mortgage Inc., $1,096,630,353
7. Countrywide Home Loans Inc., $1,018,171,596
8. Nationsbanc Mortgage, $808,923,079
9. CTX Mortgage Co., $751,994,657
10. First Union National Bank Florida, $684,117,643

Source: *Florida Trend*, TopRank Florida (annual), 1999, p. 22.

Motels

See: **Hotels and Motels**

Motion Picture Distributors—Los Angeles County (CA)

★3164★
LARGEST MOTION PICTURE DISTRIBUTION COMPANIES, 1998
Ranked by: Total U.S. and Canadian box office receipts, in millions of dollars. **Remarks:** Also notes top movie, box-office dollars, company, for whom the company distributes and top executive. **Number listed:** 10

1. Buena Vista Pictures Distribution Inc., with $1,108.9 million
2. Paramount Pictures, $1,045.4
3. Warner Bros. Domestic Theatrical Distribution, $756.8
4. Sony Pictures Releasing, $747.7
5. Twentieth Century Fox, $721.8
6. New Line Cinema Corp., $537.5
7. DreamWorks Pictures, $467.2
8. Miramax Films, $393.9
9. Universal Pictures Distribution, $392.1
10. MGM/UA, $182.2

Source: *Los Angeles Business Journal (annual)*, February 15, 1999, p. 36.

Motion Picture Industry

★3165★
TOP MOTION PICTURE STUDIOS, 1998
Ranked by: Total sales, in billions of dollars. **Remarks:** Also notes location, lead agency, and media expenditures. **Number listed:** 8

1. Buena Vista, with $1.11 billion
2. Paramount, $1.05
3. Warner Bros., $.76
4. Sony, $.74
5. 20th Century Fox Films, $.72
6. New Line/Fine Line, $.54
7. DreamWorks SKG, $.47
8. Miramax Films, $.40

Source: *Brand Week*, Superbrands: America's Top 2,000 Brands (annual), June 21, 1999, p. S38.

Motion Picture Theaters

★3166★
TOP ELEMENTS ON MOVIE WEB SITES, 1999*
Ranked by: Survey results, in percent. **Remarks:** Elements were ranked as ''very important'' by respondents who browse movie web sites. **Number listed:** 5

1. Show Times, with 59%
2. Plot, 55%
3. Video & Sound Clips, 32%
3. Reviews, 32%
5. Still Photos, 26%

Source: *Brandweek*, February 8, 1999, p. 46.

Motion Picture Theaters--Los Angeles County (CA)

★3167★
TOP MOVIE THEATER COMPLEXES IN LOS ANGELES COUNTY, 1998
Ranked by: Number of seats. **Remarks:** Also notes number of screens, owner, top grossing movie, promotional/specialty programs and top executive. **Number listed:** 25

1. Universal City Cinemas at Universal CityWalk, with 6,000 seats
2. Pacific Theaters Winnetka 20, 5,900
3. Pacific's Lakewood Center, 5,500
4. AMC Covina 30 Theaters, 4,940
5. AMC Norwalk 20 Theaters, 4,545
6. AMC Burbank 14 Theaters, 4,350
7. Magic Johnson Theaters, 4,100
8. AMC Puente Hills 20 Theaters, 4,048
9. Edwards West Covina Stadium 18 Theater, 4,008
10. AMC Rolling Hills 20 Theaters, 4,000

Source: *Los Angeles Business Journal*, December 21, 1998, p. 17+.

Motor Vehicle Fleets

★3168★
TOP LIMOUSINE COMPANIES IN THE U.S., 1999
Ranked by: Number of limousines. **Remarks:** Includes contact. **Number listed:** 10

1. American Limousine, with 230 limousines
2. Bell Trans, 217
3. My Chauffeur, 90
4. Indy Connection, 81
5. O'Hare Midway, 80
6. Altantic Limousine, 76
7. Carey New York/Manhattan International, 72
8. A-1 Airport, 70
9. Dav-El New York, 66
10. Dav-El Boston, 62

Source: *Limousine & Chauffeur*, Top 50 Livery Companies, March, 1999, p. 54+.

★3169★
TOP LIVERY COMPANIES IN THE U.S., 1999
Ranked by: Number of vehicles in fleet. **Remarks:** Includes contact and breakdown number of limos, sedans, vans and buses. **Number listed:** 50

1. Carey New York/Manhattan International, with 483 vehicles
2. Bell Trans, 358
3. American Limousine, 334
4. A-1 Limousine, 259
5. Empire International, 225
6. A-1 Airport Limousine Service, 199
7. King Limousine Service, 173
8. Dav-El New York, 166
9. Garden State Limousine, 152
10. Air Brook Limousine, 151

Source: *Limousine & Chauffeur*, Top 50 Livery Companies, March, 1999, p. 50+.

Motor Vehicles

★3170★
MOST ADMIRED MOTOR VEHICLES AND PARTS CORPORATIONS, 1998
Ranked by: Scores (1-10) derived from a survey of senior executives, outside directors and securities analysts. **Remarks:** Respondents rated companies in their own industry on 8 attributes of reputation. Also notes previous year's rank. **Number listed:** 9

1. Ford Motor, with 7.25 points
2. Daimler-Benz NA, 7.22
3. Toyota Motor Sales USA, 7.19
4. Chrysler, 7.04
5. American Honda Motor, 6.53
6. Johnson Controls, 6.40
7. Dana, 6.17
8. TRW, 6.04
9. General Motors, 5.33

Source: *Fortune*, America's Most Admired Corporations (annual), March 1, 1999, p. F-2.

★3171★
TOP CORPORATIONS IN THE MOTOR VEHICLES AND PARTS INDUSTRY, 1998
Ranked by: Revenue, in millions of dollars. **Remarks:** Also notes profits and investment figures as well as number of employees. **Number listed:** 20

1. General Motors, with $161,315 million
2. Ford Motor, $144,416
3. Dana, $12,839
4. Johnson Controls, $12,587
5. TRW, $11,886
6. Lear, $9,059
7. Paccar, $7,895
8. Navistar International, $7,885
9. Tenneco, $7,605
10. Federal-Mogul, $4,469

Source: *Fortune*, Fortune 500 Largest U.S. Corporations (annual), April 26, 1999, p. F-65.

Motorcycle Industry

★3172★
TOP MOTORCYCLE BRANDS IN THE U.S., 1998
Ranked by: Market share, in percent. **Number listed:** 6

1. Honda, with 27.3%
2. Harley Davidson, 26.6%

3. Yamaha, 15.8%
4. Kawasaki, 12.6%
5. Suzuki, 12.3%
6. Others, 5.4%

Source: *New York Times*, May 15, 1999, p. c1.

Motorcycle Industry--Europe

★3173★
TOP MOTORCYCLE BRANDS IN EUROPE, 1998
Ranked by: Market share, in percent. **Number listed:** 7

1. Honda, with 24.1%
1. Yamaha, 24.1%
3. Suzuki, 19.1%
4. Kawasaki, 10.5%
5. BMW, 9.4%
6. Ducati, 4.1%
7. Harley Davidson, 3.9%
8. Other, 6.4%

Source: *New York Times*, May 15, 1999, p. c1.

Motorcycle Industry--Great Britain

★3174★
TOP MOTORCYCLE COMPANIES IN GREAT BRITAIN, 1998
Ranked by: Number of units sold. **Number listed:** 10

1. Honda (CBR900RR), with 3,832 units
2. Kawasaki (ZX6R), 3,558
3. Honda (CBR600), 3,340
4. Yamaha (YZF-R1), 3,146
5. Honda (VFR800), 3,143
6. Peugeot (Speedfight 100), 3,131
7. Suzuki (GSF600), 2,722
8. Kawasaki (ZX9R), 2,516
9. Suzuki (GSXR600), 2,386
10. Yamaha (YZF600), 2,198

Source: *Dealernews*, March, 1999, p. 34.

Motorcycle Industry--International

★3175★
TOP COUNTRIES IN MUSIC AND SOUND PRODUCING, 1998*
Ranked by: Sales volume, in millions of U.S. dollars ($). **Number listed:** 11

1. Japan, with $6,743 million
2. U.S., $4,354
3. Korea, $659
4. Germany, $376
5. United Kingdom, $332
6. Taiwan, $257
7. Hong Kong, $235
8. Austria, $165
9. France, $159
10. Italy, $137

Source: *Music Trades*, Global 200 (annual), December 20, 1998, p. 83.

★3176★
WORLD'S LARGEST MUSIC AND SOUND COMPANIES, 1998*
Ranked by: Sales, in U.S. dollars ($). **Remarks:** Also notes employee count and chief executive. **Number listed:** 200

1. Yamaha Corp. (Japan), with $3,476,816,000
2. Kawai Musical Instrument Ltd. (Japan), $778,713,000
3. Roland Corp. (Japan), $520,000,000
4. Harman Int. (U.S.), $475,000,000
5. Telex Audio (U.S.), $362,900,000
6. Peavey Electronics (U.S.), $325,000,000
7. Samick Corp. (Korea), $285,000,000
8. Young Chang (Korea), $280,896,000
9. Steinway Musical Instruments (U.S.), $277,800,000
10. Yamano Music Co. (Japan), $262,500,000

Source: *Music Trades*, Global 200 (annual), December, 1998, p. 84+.

Mousses, Hair

See: **Hair Care Products**

Moving and Storage Companies

★3177★
TOP HOUSEHOLD GOODS MOVERS, 1997
Ranked by: Revenue, in thousands of dollars. **Remarks:** Also notes 1996 revenue, percent change, net income/loss, operating ratio, net profit margin, tonnage and mileage. **Number listed:** 7

1. United Van Lines, with $730,261 thousand
2. North American Van Lines, $642,052
3. Allied Van Lines, $486,222
4. Atlas Van Lines, $348,410
5. Mayflower Transit, $337,273
6. Bekins Van Lines Co., $207,838
7. Graebel Van Lines, $171,510

Source: *Transport Topics*, Annual Report, August 10, 1998, p. 21.

Multihospital Systems

★3178★
LARGEST CATHOLIC MULTI-HEALTHCARE SYSTEMS, 1998
Ranked by: Number of staffed U.S. acute-care beds. **Remarks:** Includes 1997 figures and number of hospitals. **Number listed:** 10

1. Catholic Health Initiatives, with 11,877 beds
2. Daughters of Charity National Health System, 10,249
3. Catholic Health East, 8,493
4. Mercy Health Services, 6,578
5. Catholic Healthcare West, 6,419
6. Marian Health System, 5,852
7. Catholic Healthcare Network, 4,176
8. Sisters of Mercy Health System, 3,928
9. Catholic Healthcare Partners, 3,698

10. SSM Health Care, 3,448

Source: *Modern Healthcare*, Modern Healthcare Multi-Units Providers Survey (annual), May 24, 1999, p. 26.

★3179★
LARGEST FOR-PROFIT MULTI-HEALTHCARE SYSTEMS, 1998

Ranked by: Number of U.S. hospitals. **Remarks:** Includes 1997 figures. **Number listed:** 11

1. Columbia/HCA Healthcare Corp., with 308 hospitals
2. Quorum Health Group, 251
3. U.S. Department of Veteran Affairs, 172
4. Tenet Healthcare Corp., 132
5. Catholic Health Initiatives, 71
6. Province Healthcare, 64
7. Universal Health Services, 61
8. Daughters of Charity National Health System, 56
9. Community Health Systems, 46
10. Catholic Healthcare West, 37

Source: *Modern Healthcare*, Modern Healthcare Multi-Units Providers Survey (annual), May 24, 1999, p. 25.

★3180★
LARGEST HOSPITAL CONTRACT MANAGERS, 1998

Ranked by: Number of staffed U.S. acute-care beds. **Remarks:** Includes 1997 figures and number of hospitals. **Number listed:** 10

1. Quorum Health Group, with 20,897 beds
2. Province Healthcare, 3,695
3. Carolinas HealthCare System, 1,070
4. Jewish Hospitals Healthcare Services, 680
5. Genesis Health System, 618
6. Mercy Health Services, 613
7. St. Joseph Health System, 554
8. Adventist Health System, 411
9. Orlando Regional Healthcare System, 347
10. Sioux Valley Hospitals & Health System, 320

Source: *Modern Healthcare*, Modern Healthcare Multi-Units Providers Survey (annual), May 24, 1999, p. 25.

★3181★
LARGEST MULTI-HEALTHCARE SYSTEMS, 1998

Ranked by: Net patient revenue, in millions of dollars. **Remarks:** Includes 1997 revenue. **Number listed:** 10

1. U.S. Department of Veteran Affairs, with $20,027.1 million
2. Columbia/HCA Healthcare Corp., $18,681.0
3. Tenet Healthcare Corp., $8,821.0
4. Catholic Health Initiatives, $4,587.3
5. New York City Health & Hospitals Corp., $3,834.5
6. Daughters of Charity National Health System, $3,767.4
7. Catholic Healthcare West, $3,301.3
8. New York Presbyterian Healthcare Network, $3,238.0
9. Sisters of Mercy Health Systems, $2,169.2
10. North Shore-Long Island Jewish Health System, $2,164.9

Source: *Modern Healthcare*, Modern Healthcare Multi-Units Providers Survey (annual), May 24, 1999, p. 23.

★3182★
LARGEST MULTI-HEALTHCARE SYSTEMS OPERATING FREESTANDING OUTPATIENT FACILITIES, 1998

Ranked by: Number of facilities on and off campus. **Remarks:** Includes 1997 figures and percent change. **Number listed:** 25

1. HealthSouth Corp., with 1,851 facilities
2. U.S. Department of Veteran Affairs, 551
3. Mercy Health Services, 263
4. Marian Health System, 182
5. Beverly Enterprises, 181
6. Mariner Post-Acute Network, 144
7. Detroit Medical Center, 138
8. Iowa Health System, 116
9. Rush System for Health, 115
10. Sisters of St. Joseph Health System, 111

Source: *Modern Healthcare*, Modern Healthcare Multi-Units Providers Survey (annual), May 24, 1999, p. 50.

★3183★
LARGEST NON-CATHOLIC RELIGIOUS MULTI-HEALTHCARE SYSTEMS, 1998

Ranked by: Number of staffed U.S. acute-care beds. **Remarks:** Includes 1997 figures. **Number listed:** 10

1. Adventist Health System, with 3,698 beds
2. Texas Health Resources, 2,878
3. Adventist Health, 2,693
4. Advocate Health Care, 2,107
5. OhioHealth, 2,023
6. Baylor Health Care System, 1,370
7. Methodist Health Care System, 1,297
8. Baptist/St. Vincent's Health System, 1,265
9. Saint Luke's-Shawnee Mission Health System, 1,036
10. Baptist Health System, 981

Source: *Modern Healthcare*, Modern Healthcare Multi-Units Providers Survey (annual), May 24, 1999, p. 28.

★3184★
LARGEST NON-PROFIT MULTI-HEALTHCARE SYSTEMS, 1998

Ranked by: Number of staffed U.S. acute-care beds. **Remarks:** Includes 1997 figures. **Number listed:** 10

1. U.S. Department of Veteran Affairs, with 23,176 beds
2. Catholic Health Initiatives, 11,877
3. Daughters of Charity National Health System, 10,249
4. Catholic Health East, 8,493
5. Mercy Health Services, 6,578
6. Catholic Healthcare West, 6,419
7. Marian Health System, 5,852
8. New York Presbyterian Healthcare Network, 5,721
9. Sutter Health, 5,145
10. New York City Health & Hospitals Corp., 4,834

Source: *Modern Healthcare*, Modern Healthcare Multi-Units Providers Survey (annual), May 24, 1999, p. 24.

★3185★
LARGEST PUBLIC MULTI-HEALTHCARE SYSTEMS, 1998

Ranked by: Number of staffed U.S. acute-care beds. **Remarks:** Includes 1997 figures and number of hospitals. **Number listed:** 10

1. U.S. Department of Veteran Affairs, with 23,176 beds
2. New York City Health & Hospitals Corp., 4,834
3. Carolinas Healthcare System, 3,029
4. Los Angeles County Health Services Department, 1,910
5. LSUMC-Health Care Services Division, 1,423
6. North Broward Hospital District, 1,225
7. Memorial Healthcare System, 1,127
8. West Tennessee Healthcare, 896
9. Harris County Hospital District, 830
10. Cook County Bureau of Health Services, 827

Source: *Modern Healthcare*, Modern Healthcare Multi-Units Providers Survey (annual), May 24, 1999, p. 26.

★3186★
LARGEST SECULAR NON-PROFIT MULTI-HEALTHCARE SYSTEMS, 1998
Ranked by: Number of staffed U.S. acute-care beds. **Remarks:** Includes 1997 figures. **Number listed:** 10
1. New York Presbyterian Healthcare Network, with 5,721 beds
2. Sutter Health, 5,145
3. North Shore-Long Island Jewish Health System, 4,331
4. BJC Health System, 3,275
5. Northwestern Healthcare, 2,834
6. Continuum Health Partners, 2,513
7. Promina Health System, 2,495
8. Rush System for Health, 2,386
9. Detroit Medical Center, 2,121
10. Henry Ford Health System, 2,117

Source: *Modern Healthcare*, Modern Healthcare Multi-Units Providers Survey (annual), May 24, 1999, p. 25.

Multinational Corporations

★3187★
LEADING U.S. MULTINATIONAL CORPORATIONS, 1997
Ranked by: Foreign revenue, in millions of U.S. dollars ($). **Remarks:** Also notes total revenue and foreign revenue as a percentage of total, foreign and total net profit, and foreign and total assets. **Number listed:** 100
1. Exxon, with $92,540 million
2. General Motors, $51,046
3. Ford Motor, $46,991
4. IBM, $45,845
5. Mobil, $35,606
6. Texaco Inc., $33,292
7. General Electric, $26,981
8. Hewlett-Packard, $23,819
9. Chevron, $23,055
10. Citicorp, $21,566

Source: *Forbes*, Forbes Foreign Rankings (annual), July 27, 1998, p. 163+.

Municipal Bonds

★3188★
LARGEST MUNICIPAL ISSUES, 1947-1997
Ranked by: Amount, in thousands of dollars. **Number listed:** 82
1. California (7/20/94), with $4,000,000 thousand
2. New Jersey Economic Division (6/26/97), $2,803,042
3. New Jersey Turnpike Authority (11/21/85), $2,000,000
4. Los Angeles County, CA (10/13/94), $1,965,230
5. New Jersey (12/18/92), $1,804,564
6. Massachusetts Turnpike Authority (9/25/97), $1,764,382
7. Puerto Rico (4/2/87), $1,621,614
8. New Jersey Turnpike Authority (11/22/91), $1,618,850
9. North Carolina East Municipal Power Agency (1/15/93), $1,614,620
10. San Joaquin Hills, CA Transportation Corridor (9/26/97), $1,448,274

Source: *Bond Buyer Yearbook (annual)*, 1998, p. 26.

★3189★
LARGEST MUNICIPAL ISSUES, 1997
Ranked by: Amount of issue, in thousands of dollars. **Number listed:** 20
1. New Jersey Economic Development Authority (6/26), with $2,803,042 thousand
2. Massachusetts Turnpike Authority (9/25), $1,764,382
3. San Joaquin Hills, CA Transportation Corridor (9/26), $1,448,274
4. California, GOs (12/10), $1,116,970
5. New York City, GOs (12/11), $1,033,948
6. New York City, GOs (4/11), $1,023,415
7. California, GOs, $1,000,000
8. Puerto Rico Infrastructure Finance Authority (11/20), $936,420
9. Port Authority of New York & New Jersey Airports (4/25), $934,100
10. New York City GOs (10/30), $862,230

Source: *Bond Buyer Yearbook (annual)*, 1998, p. 26.

★3190★
LEADING MANAGERS OF ALL MUNICIPAL ISSUES WITH FULL CREDIT TO BOOK MANAGER, 1998
Ranked by: Value of issues, in millions of dollars. **Remarks:** Includes market share percentage and number of issues. **Number listed:** 15
1. Salomon Smith Barney, with $36,012.5 million
2. PaineWebber, $27,510.2
3. Goldman Sachs, $22,858.0
4. Merrill Lynch, $21,507.9
5. Bear, Sterns, $19,528.8
6. Lehman Brothers, $16,961.0
7. Morgan Stanley Dean Witter, $14,363.3
8. J.P. Morgan, $9,530.2
9. Bank of America, $6,146.4
10. First Union Capital Markets, $5,773.2

Source: *Investment Dealers Digest*, Municipal Rankings (annual), January 11, 1999, p. 39.

★3191★
LEADING MANAGERS OF ALL MUNICIPAL TAX-EXEMPT NEGOTIATED BOND ISSUES WITH FULL CREDIT TO BOOK MANAGER, 1998
Ranked by: Value of issues, in millions of dollars. **Remarks:** Includes market share percentage and number of issues. **Number listed:** 15
1. Salomon Smith Barney, with $27,584.4 million
2. PaineWebber, $21,307.0
3. Bear, Sterns, $17,240.9
4. Goldman Sachs, $17,130.0
5. Merrill Lynch, $13,036.7
6. Lehman Brothers, $10,125.5
7. Morgan Stanley Dean Witter, $9,831.8
8. J.P. Morgan, $6,834.6
9. A.G. Edwards & Sons, $4,191.4
10. Dain Rauscher, $3,473.2

Source: *Investment Dealers Digest*, Municipal Rankings (annual), January 11, 1999, p. 39.

★3192★
LEADING MANAGERS OF ALL TAX-EXEMPT MUNICIPAL BOND ISSUES WITH FULL CREDIT TO BOOK MANAGER, 1998
Ranked by: Value of issues, in millions of dollars. **Remarks:** Includes market share percentage and number of issues. **Number listed:** 15
1. Salomon Smith Barney, with $34,433.8 million
2. PaineWebber, $24,815.0
3. Goldman Sachs, $21,874.3
4. Merrill Lynch, $20,477.7
5. Bear, Sterns, $18,759.5
6. Lehman Brothers, $15,800.9
7. Morgan Stanley Dean Witter, $14,166.3
8. J.P. Morgan, $8,907.4
9. Bank of America, $5,605.9
10. First Union Capital Markets, $5,403.2

Source: *Investment Dealers Digest*, Municipal Rankings (annual), January 11, 1999, p. 39.

★3193★
LEADING MANAGERS OF MUNICIPAL TAX-EXEMPT REVENUE BOND ISSUES WITH FULL CREDIT TO BOOK MANAGER, 1998
Ranked by: Value of issues, in millions of dollars. **Remarks:** Includes market share percentage and number of issues. **Number listed:** 15
1. Salomon Smith Barney, with $24,879.1 million
2. PaineWebber, $18,257.3
3. Goldman Sachs, $16,492.6
4. Bear, Sterns, $15,769.7
5. Merrill Lynch, $14,732.9
6. Lehman Brothers, $11,187.5
7. Morgan Stanley Dean Witter, $8,915.5
8. J.P. Morgan, $6,610.9
9. A.G. Edwards & Sons, $2,654.1
10. Bank of America, $2,628.6

Source: *Investment Dealers Digest*, Municipal Rankings (annual), January 11, 1999, p. 38.

★3194★
LEADING MANAGERS OF TAX-EXEMPT COMPETITIVE MUNICIPAL BOND ISSUES WITH FULL CREDIT TO BOOK MANAGER, 1998
Ranked by: Value of issues, in millions of dollars. **Remarks:** Includes market share percentage and number of issues. **Number listed:** 15
1. Merrill Lynch, with $7,441.0 million
2. Salomon Smith Barney, $6,849.4
3. Lehman Brothers, $5,675.5
4. Goldman Sachs, $4,744.3
5. Morgan Stanley Dean Witter, $4,334.5
6. PaineWebber, $3,508.0
7. Bank of America, $3,443.7
8. Prudential Securities Inc., $2,533.9
9. First Union Capital Markets, $2,108.4
10. J.P. Morgan, $2,072.9

Source: *Investment Dealers Digest*, Municipal Rankings (annual), January 11, 1999, p. 38.

★3195★
LEADING MANAGERS OF TAX-EXEMPT GENERAL OBLIGATION MUNICIPAL BOND ISSUES WITH FULL CREDIT TO BOOK MANAGER, 1998
Ranked by: Value of issues, in millions of dollars. **Remarks:** Includes market share percentage and number of issues. **Number listed:** 15
1. Salomon Smith Barney, with $9,554.7 million
2. PaineWebber, $6,557.7
3. Merrill Lynch, $5,774.8
4. Goldman Sachs, $5,381.7
5. Morgan Stanley Dean Witter, $5,250.8
6. Lehman Brothers, $4,613.4
7. Bear, Sterns, $2,989.8
8. Bank of America, $2,977.3
9. First Union Capital Markets, $2,946.1
10. Dain RauscherInc., $2,544.8

Source: *Investment Dealers Digest*, Municipal Rankings (annual), January 11, 1999, p. 38.

★3196★
LEADING MUNICIPAL HEALTHCARE BOND COUNSELS, 1997
Ranked by: Value of issue, in thousands of dollars. **Remarks:** Also notes number of issues. **Number listed:** 10
1. Orrick Herrington & Sutcliffe, with $2,117,800 thousand
2. Vinson & Elkins, $2,004,000
3. Jones Day Reavis & Pogue, $1,914,800
4. Hawkins Delafield & Wood, $1,545,000
5. Brown & Wood, $1,084,800
6. Squire Sanders & Dempsey, $992,900
7. Foley Lardner Weissburg & Aronson, $949,400
8. Fulbright & Jaworski, $822,300
9. Peck, Shaffer & Williams, $807,800
10. Quarles & Brady, $610,500

Source: *Bond Buyer Yearbook (annual)*, 1998, p. 121.

★3197★
LEADING MUNICIPAL HEALTHCARE BOND ISSUERS, 1997
Ranked by: Value of bond issue, in thousands of dollars. **Remarks:** Also notes number of issues. **Number listed:** 25
1. New York State Dormitory Authority, with $1,698,200 thousand
2. Illinois Health Facilities Authority, $1,337,000
3. Harris County Health Facilities Development Corp., $1,273,700
4. Wisconsin Health & Educational Facilities Authority, $784,600
5. California Health Facilities Financing Authority, $669,700
6. New Jersey Healthcare Facilities Finance Authority, $526,200
7. Indiana Health Facility Financing Authority, $521,400
8. Maryland Health & Higher Education Facilities Authority, $506,500
8. Massachusetts Health & Education Facilities Authority, $506,500
10. Tarrant County Health Facilities Development Corp., $475,700

Source: *Bond Buyer Yearbook (annual)*, 1998, p. 121.

★3198★
LEADING SHORT-TERM BOND COUNSELS, 1997
Ranked by: Value of issue, in thousands of dollars. **Remarks:** Also notes number of issues. **Number listed:** 50
1. Orrick Herrington & Sutcliffe, with $5,600,600 thousand
2. Brown & Wood, $4,119,900
3. Vinson & Elkins, $3,192,000
4. Yava D. Scott, $2,900,000
5. Hawkins Delafield & Wood, $2,712,500
6. Dickinson Wright Moon Van Dusen & Freeman, $2,230,000
7. O'Melvaney & Myers, $1,926,900
8. Squire Sanders & Dempsey, $1,455,300
9. Wilkie Farr & Gallagher, $1,240,300

10. Nixon Hargrave Devans & Doyle, $1,014,300

Source: *Bond Buyer Yearbook (annual)*, 1998, p. 55.

★3199★

TOP BOND COUNSELS FOR ENVIRONMENTAL FACILITIES ISSUES, 1997

Ranked by: Amount of issue, in thousands of dollars. **Remarks:** Also notes number of issues. **Number listed:** 10

1. Hawkins Delafield & Wood, with $1,003,000 thousand
2. Squire Sanders & Dempsey, $726,100
3. Chapman & Cutler, $679,700
4. Orrick Herrington & Sutcliffe, $655,600
5. McCall, Parkhurst & Horton, $501,300
6. Leslie M. Lava, $489,000
7. Nixon Hargrave Devans & Doyle, $381,700
8. Potter Anderson & Corroon, $365,000
9. Ballard Spahr Andrews & Ingersoll, $353,900
10. King & Spalding, $310,200

Source: *Bond Buyer Yearbook (annual)*, 1998, p. 161.

★3200★

TOP BOND COUNSELS FOR MUNICIPAL ISSUES, 1997

Ranked by: Amount of issue, in thousands of dollars. **Remarks:** Also notes number of issues. **Number listed:** 100

1. Orrick Herrington & Sutcliffe, with $15,551,900 thousand
2. Hawkins Delafield & Wood, $15,135,200
3. Brown & Wood, $13,116,700
4. Chapman & Cutler, $7,093,800
5. Fulbright & Jaworski, $6,615,200
6. Squire Sanders & Dempsey, $6,555,200
7. Kutak Rock, $5,490,800
8. Vinson & Elkins, $5,035,300
9. Preston Gates & Ellis, $4,172,700
10. Nixon Hargrave Devans & Doyle, $3,720,300

Source: *Bond Buyer Yearbook (annual)*, 1998, p. 48+.

★3201★

TOP BOND ISSUERS FOR ENVIRONMENTAL FACILITIES, 1997

Ranked by: Value of issue, in thousands of dollars. **Remarks:** Also notes number of issues. **Number listed:** 25

1. New York State Environmental Facilities Corp., with $823,400 thousand
2. California Pollution Control Financing Authority, $627,300
3. Delaware Economic Development Authority, $365,000
4. Palm Beach County Solid Waste Authority, $300,500
5. Delaware County Industrial Development Authority, $277,900
6. Farmington, NM, $270,400
7. Ohio Water Development Authority, $266,000
8. Hempstead Industrial Development Agency, $245,700
9. Illinois Development Finance Authority, $207,900
10. Ocean County Utilities Authority, $195,000

Source: *Bond Buyer Yearbook (annual)*, 1998, p. 161.

★3202★

TOP COUNSELS FOR PUBLIC FACILITIES BONDS, 1997

Ranked by: Value of issue, in thousands of dollars. **Remarks:** Also notes number of issues. **Number listed:** 10

1. Orrick Herrington & Sutcliffe, with $1,004,800 thousand
2. O'Melveny & Myers, $994,100
3. Squire Sanders & Dempsey, $723,600
4. Brown & Wood, $644,300
5. Hawkins Delafield & Wood, $633,100
6. Dickinson Wright Moon Van Dusen & Freeman, $567,100
7. Lofton De Lancie & Nelson, $449,100
8. Holland & Knight, $423,600
9. Chapman & Cutler, $387,000
10. Preston Gates & Ellis, $376,700

Source: *Bond Buyer Yearbook (annual)*, 1998, p. 153.

★3203★

TOP ISSUERS FOR PUBLIC FACILITIES BONDS, 1997

Ranked by: Amount of issue, in thousands of dollars. **Remarks:** Also notes number of issues. **Number listed:** 25

1. Michigan State Building Authority, with $593,800 thousand
2. Puerto Rico Public Buildings Authority, $565,000
3. Anaheim Public Finance Authority, $510,400
4. Los Angeles County Public Works Finance Authority, $510,200
5. San Francisco, CA, $449,100
6. Ohio Building Authority, $347,000
7. King County, WA, $326,000
8. Marian County Convention & Recs Facilities Authority, $249,400
9. New Jersey Building Authority, $224,600
10. Florida, $202,600

Source: *Bond Buyer Yearbook (annual)*, 1998, p. 153.

★3204★

TOP TAXABLE BOND COUNSELS, 1997

Ranked by: Amount of issue, in thousands of dollars. **Remarks:** Also notes number of issues. **Number listed:** 10

1. Blank Rome Comisky & McCauley, with $2,864,700 thousand
2. Riker, Danzig, Scherer, Hyland, & Perretti LLP, $2,803,000
3. Brown & Wood, $902,000
4. Hawkins Delafield & Wood, $789,400
5. Orrick Herrington & Sutcliffe, $627,800
6. Preston Gates & Ellis, $596,900
7. Sherman & Howard, $419,900
8. Fulbright & Jaworski, $374,700
9. McNair Law Firm, $350,500
10. Curls Brown & Roushon, $345,700

Source: *Bond Buyer Yearbook (annual)*, 1998, p. 185.

★3205★

TOP TAXABLE BOND ISSUERS, 1997

Ranked by: Value of bond issues, in thousands of dollars. **Remarks:** Also notes number of issues. **Number listed:** 25

1. New Jersey Economic Development Authority, with $2,975,100 thousand
2. New York City, $1,035,300
3. Oakland,CA, $436,300
4. Denver School District No. 1, CO, $384,200
5. Southern California Public Power Authority, $345,700
6. South Carolina Student Loan Corp., $335,300
7. California Housing Finance Agency, $282,700
8. Missouri Higher Education Loan Authority, $189,000
9. Virginia Housing Development Authority, $172,700
10. Chelan County Public Utility District No. 1, $151,300

Source: *Bond Buyer Yearbook (annual)*, 1998, p. 185.

Municipal Bonds--Insurance

★3206★
LEADING BOND INSURANCE COMPANIES, 1997
Ranked by: Value of bond issues, in thousands of dollars. **Remarks:** Also notes number of issues. **Number listed:** 7
1. MBIA Insurance Corp., with $44,416,500 thousand
2. Ambac Assurance Corp., $25,795,100
3. Financial Guaranty Insurance Co., $20,398,100
4. Financial Security Assurance, $15,665,400
5. Asset Guaranty Insurance Co., $270,000
6. Connie Lee Insurance Co., $163,400
7. American Capital Access, $13,200

Source: *Bond Buyer Yearbook (annual)*, 1998, p. 59.

★3207★
LEADING DEVELOPMENT BOND INSURANCE COMPANIES, 1997
Ranked by: Value of bond issues, in thousands of dollars. **Remarks:** Also notes number of issues. **Number listed:** 5
1. MBIA Insurance Corp., with $893,500 thousand
2. Ambac Assurance Corp., $679,100
3. Financial Security Assurance, $150,200
4. Financial Guaranty Insurance Co., $100,700
5. Asset Guaranty Insurance Co., $26,000

Source: *Bond Buyer Yearbook (annual)*, 1998, p. 169.

★3208★
LEADING EDUCATION BOND INSURANCE COMPANIES, 1997
Ranked by: Value of bond issues, in thousands of dollars. **Remarks:** Also notes number of issues. **Number listed:** 6
1. MBIA Insurance Corp., with $6,818,200 thousand
2. Ambac Assurance Corp., $6,565,100
3. Financial Guaranty Assurance, $6,285,500
4. Financial Security Insurance Co., $4,353,700
5. Connie Lee Insurance Co., $25,000
6. Asset Guaranty Insurance Co., $13,500

Source: *Bond Buyer Yearbook (annual)*, 1998, p. 113.

★3209★
LEADING ELECTRIC POWER BOND INSURANCE COMPANIES, 1997
Ranked by: Value of bond issues, in thousands of dollars. **Remarks:** Also notes number of issues. **Number listed:** 4
1. MBIA Insurance Corp., with $2,430,700 thousand
2. Ambac Assurance Corp., $1,080,400
3. Financial Security Assurance, $878,300
4. Financial Guaranty Insurance Co., $248,020

Source: *Bond Buyer Yearbook (annual)*, 1998, p. 177.

★3210★
LEADING ENVIRONMENTAL BOND INSURANCE COMPANIES, 1997
Ranked by: Value of bond issues, in thousands of dollars. **Remarks:** Also notes number of issues. **Number listed:** 4
1. MBIA Insurance Corp., with $1,700,700 thousand
2. Ambac Assurance Corp., $1,077,900
3. Financial Guaranty Assurance, $156,800
4. Financial Security Insurance Co., $40,800

Source: *Bond Buyer Yearbook (annual)*, 1998, p. 161.

★3211★
LEADING HEALTH CARE BOND INSURANCE COMPANIES, 1997
Ranked by: Value of bond issues, in thousands of dollars. **Remarks:** Also notes number of issues. **Number listed:** 6
1. MBIA Insurance Corp., with $8,882,600 thousand
2. Ambac Assurance Corp., $3,196,500
3. Financial Security Assurance, $1,767,200
4. Asset Guaranty Insurance Co., $128,000
5. Connie Lee Insurance Co., $104,600
6. Financial Guaranty Insurance Co., $37,500

Source: *Bond Buyer Yearbook (annual)*, 1998, p. 121.

★3212★
LEADING HOUSING BOND INSURANCE COMPANIES, 1997
Ranked by: Value of bond issues, in thousands of dollars. **Remarks:** Also notes number of issues. **Number listed:** 4
1. MBIA Insurance Corp., with $1,989,100 thousand
2. Ambac Assurance Corp., $1,039,800
3. Financial Security Assurance, $498,600
4. American Capital Access, $13,200

Source: *Bond Buyer Yearbook (annual)*, 1998, p. 145.

★3213★
LEADING PUBLIC FACILITIES BOND INSURANCE COMPANIES, 1997
Ranked by: Value of bond issues, in thousands of dollars. **Remarks:** Also notes number of issues. **Number listed:** 5
1. MBIA Insurance Corp., with $2,365,100 thousand
2. Ambac Assurance Corp., $2,002,000
3. Financial Guaranty Assurance, $1,102,500
4. Financial Security Insurance Co., $1,064,000
5. Asset Guaranty Insurance Co., $26,600

Source: *Bond Buyer Yearbook (annual)*, 1998, p. 153.

★3214★
LEADING TAXABLE ISSUES BOND INSURANCE COMPANIES, 1997
Ranked by: Value of bond issues, in thousands of dollars. **Remarks:** Also notes number of issues. **Number listed:** 4
1. MBIA Insurance Corp., with $3,273,500 thousand
2. Financial Security Assurance, $1,801,700
3. Ambac Assurance Corp., $1,377,900
4. Financial Guaranty Insurance Co., $146,600

Source: *Bond Buyer Yearbook (annual)*, 1998, p. 185.

★3215★
LEADING TRANSPORTATION BOND INSURANCE COMPANIES, 1997
Ranked by: Value of bond issues, in thousands of dollars. **Remarks:** Also notes number of issues. **Number listed:** 5
1. MBIA Insurance Corp., with $8,001,500 thousand
2. Financial Guaranty Insurance Co., $2,651,800
3. Financial Security Assurance, $2,550,600
4. Ambac Assurance Corp., $1,940,800
5. Connie Lee Insurance Co., $8,500

Source: *Bond Buyer Yearbook (annual)*, 1998, p. 129.

★3216★
LEADING UTILITIES BOND INSURANCE COMPANIES, 1997
Ranked by: Value of bond issues, in thousands of dollars. **Remarks:** Also notes number of issues. **Number listed:** 5
1. Financial Guaranty Insurance Co., with $5,071,300 thousand
2. MBIA Insurance Corp., $3,855,000
3. Ambac Assurance Corp., $2,311,700
4. Financial Security Assurance, $1,101,800
5. Asset Guaranty Insurance Co., $31,400

Source: *Bond Buyer Yearbook (annual)*, 1998, p. 137.

Municipalities

See: **Cities and Towns**

Museums

★3217★

TOP MUSEUM ART EXHIBITS, 1998

Ranked by: Attendance. **Number listed:** 10

1. Boston Museum of Fine Arts (Monet in the 20th Century), with 565,992 attendees
2. Metropolitan Museum of Art (The Private Collection of Edgar Degas), 528,267
3. National Gallery of Art (Van Gogh's van Gogh's), 480,496
4. Metropolitan Museum of Art (Gianni Versace), 410,357
5. Philadelphia Museum of Art (Delacroix: The Late Work), 305,883
6. Solomon R. Guggenheim Museum (Art of the Motorcycle), 301,037
7. San Francisco Museum of Modern Art (Alexander Calder), 300,000
8. Solomon R. Guggenheim Museum (China: 5,000 Years), 299,950
9. National Gallery of Art (Alexander Calder), 288,709
10. Metropolitan Museum of Art (Indian Carpets of the Mughal Era), 284,064

Source: *The New York Times*, February 1, 1999, p. E3.

Music Industry

★3218★

LARGEST MUSIC RETAILERS BY SALES, 1997

Ranked by: Sales, in dollars. **Remarks:** Includes 1996 sales and percent change, number of employees, store fronts and products carried. **Number listed:** 200

1. Guitar Center Inc., with $296,700,000
2. Sam Ash Music Corp., $198,000,000
3. Musicians Friend Wholesale, $83,000,000
4. Brook Mays/H&H, $66,690,000
5. Schmitt Music Company, $50,780,000
6. Hermes Music, $50,080,000
7. Mars Inc./Ace Music, $49,875,000
8. Thoroughbred Music, $48,000,000
9. Washington Music Center, $44,257,000
10. J.W. Pepper, $40,350,000
11. Fletcher Music Centers, $40,067,000

Source: *Music Trades*, Top 100 Music Retailers (annual), May, 1998, p. 90+.

★3219★

LARGEST MUSIC RETAILERS BY SALES PER EMPLOYEE, 1997

Ranked by: Sales per employee, in dollars. **Remarks:** Includes 1996 sales and percent change, and number of employees. **Number listed:** 200

1. Fields Piano & Organ, with $1,092,850
2. Steinway Hall of Dallas, $676,923
3. DJ's Music, $637,000
4. Steve Weiss Music, $615,000
5. Piano Superstore, $611,538
6. Steinway Piano Gallery, $610,857
7. Rudy's Music Stop, $600,000
8. Sound Deals Inc., $582,142
9. Rolls Music, $567,857
10. Keyboard Concepts, $546,666
11. Medley Music Corp., $504,166

Source: *Music Trades*, Top 100 Music Retailers (annual), May, 1998, p. 116+.

★3220★

LARGEST MUSIC RETAILERS BY SALES PER STORE, 1997

Ranked by: Sales, in dollars. **Remarks:** Includes 1996 sales and percent change, and store count. **Number listed:** 200

1. Washington Music Center, with $44,257,000
2. Pro Sound & Stage Lighting, $32,000,000
3. Sweetwater Sound Inc., $31,282,000
4. Victor's House of Music, $29,400,000
5. Manny's Music Store, $28,500,000
6. Full Compass, $21,000,000
7. Musicians Friend Wholesale, $20,750,000
8. Cascio Music Co., $17,750,000
9. West L.A. Music, $14,587,000
10. Veneman Music, $14,500,000
11. Hermes Music, $12,520,000

Source: *Music Trades*, Top 100 Music Retailers (annual), May, 1998, p. 104+.

★3221★

TOP MUSIC SUPPLIERS, 1998

Ranked by: Sales, in dollars. **Remarks:** Also notes employees and top executive. **Number listed:** 100

1. Yamaha Corp. of America, with $795,000,000
2. Harman International, $453,000,000
3. Telex Audio, $345,000,000
4. Peavey Electronics, $300,000,000
5. Steinway Musical Instruments, $293,251,000
6. Shure Brothers, $220,000,000
7. Fender Musical Instruments, $200,735,000
8. Roland Corp., $175,000,000
9. Baldwin Piano & Organ, $134,290,000
10. Kaman Music Corp., $118,300,000

Source: *Music Trades*, America's 100, April, 1999, p. 120+.

Mutual Funds

★3222★

AMERICA'S MOST POPULAR MUTUAL FUNDS, 1998

Ranked by: Net assets, in billions of dollars. **Remarks:** Also notes M-Star rating and risk, and 12-month, 5-year, and 10-year load adjusted return. **Number listed:** 20

1. Fidelity Magellan, with $76.3 billion
2. Vanguard 500 Index, $64.7
3. Fidelity Growth & Income, $46.0
4. Washington Mutual Investors, $44.7
5. Investment Comp of America, $41.8
6. Fidelity Contrafund, $34.8
7. Vanguard Windsor II, $29.6
8. American Century C Ultra, $27.2
9. Vanguard Wellington, $24.9
10. Fidelity Puritan, $24.8

Source: *Your Money*, February/March, 1999, p. 52.

★3223★
BEST AGGRESSIVE GROWTH MID CAP STOCK FUNDS FOR THE FUTURE
Ranked by: OPI (overall performance index) that relies on a formula that measures relative results over 1, 3, 5, and 10 years. **Remarks:** Includes trading style, downside volatility grade, overall volatility grade, 1998 return and down-market grade, 10-, 5-, and 3-year returns, growth of $1,000 in three years, expense ratio, assets and phone number. **Number listed:** 10

1. Janus Twenty, with 90.7
2. Analytic Enhanced Equity A, 86.2
3. Janus Mercury Fund, 82.2
4. Value Line Leverage Growth, 81.2
5. Spectra Fund, 79.7
6. Northern Select Equity, 78.9
7. Rydex Nova, 77.9
8. Rydex OTC, 76.9
8. Oppenheimer Capital Appreciation, 76.9
10. Ariel Appreciation Fund, 75.7

Source: *U.S. News & World Report*, Best Mutual Funds (annual), February 1, 1999, p. 76.

★3224★
BEST AGGRESSIVE GROWTH SMALL CAP STOCK FUNDS FOR THE FUTURE
Ranked by: OPI (overall performance index) that relies on a formula that measures relative results over 1, 3, 5, and 10 years. **Remarks:** Includes trading style, downside volatility grade, overall volatility grade, 1998 return and down-market grade, 10-, 5-, and 3-year returns, growth of $1,000 in three years, expense ratio, assets and phone number. **Number listed:** 10

1. Oppenheimer Enterprise, with 71.5
2. Robertson Stephens Emerging Growth, 63.8
3. Royce Total Return, 59.6
4. Safeco Growth, 58.5
5. Fasciano Fund, 56.9
6. Wachovia Special Value A, 55.9
7. Dreyfus Growth & Value Emerging Leaders, 55.7
8. Lord Abbett Developing Growth, 55.4
9. Wasatch Micro-Cap Fund, 54.8
10. UAM FMA Small Company, 53.6

Source: *U.S. News & World Report*, Best Mutual Funds (annual), February 1, 1999, p. 76.

★3225★
BEST AGGRESSIVE GROWTH STOCK FUNDS, 1998
Ranked by: Return, in percent. **Remarks:** Includes OPI, trading style, downside volatility grade, overall volatility grade, 1998 return and down-market grade, 10-, 5-, and 3-year returns, growth of $1,000 in three years, expense ratio, assets and phone number. **Number listed:** 10

1. UltraOTC ProFund, with 185.3%
2. Potomac OTC, 104.2%
3. Dreyfus Technology Growth, 98.4%
4. Munder NetNet A, 98.1%
5. Fidelity Select Computers, 95.5%
6. Rydex OTC, 86.5%
7. Transamerica Premier, 84.1%
8. Northern Technology, 83.0%
9. Flag Investment Communications A, 81.7%
10. Transamerica Premier Small Co., 80.3%

Source: *U.S. News & World Report*, Best Mutual Funds (annual), February 1, 1999, p. 84.

★3226★
BEST BALANCED STOCK FUNDS FOR THE FUTURE
Ranked by: OPI (overall performance index) that relies on a formula that measures relative results over 1, 3, 5, and 10 years. **Remarks:** Includes trading style, downside volatility grade, overall volatility grade, 1998 return and down-market grade, 10-, 5-, and 3-year returns, growth of $1,000 in three years, expense ratio, assets and phone number. **Number listed:** 20

1. Oppenheimer Quest Balanced Value, with 83.8
2. Janus Balanced, 82.0
3. IDEX Balanced A, 78.6
4. Transamerica Premier Balanced, 77.4
5. Pax World, 77.3
6. Dreyfus Premier Balanced A, 75.4
7. Mentor Balanced A, 74.5
8. McM Balanced, 74.3
9. Alleghany Montag & Caldwell Balanced, 74.2
9. Flag Investors Value Builder, 74.2

Source: *U.S. News & World Report*, Best Mutual Funds (annual), February 1, 1999, p. 79.

★3227★
BEST BALANCED STOCK FUNDS, 1998
Ranked by: Return, in percent. **Remarks:** Includes OPI, trading style, downside volatility grade, overall volatility grade, 1998 return and down-market grade, 10-, 5-, and 3-year returns, growth of $1,000 in three years, expense ratio, assets and phone number. **Number listed:** 5

1. Berger Balanced, with 34.4%
2. Janus Balanced, 31.2%
3. IDEX Balanced A, 30.8%
3. Provident Inv. Counsel Pinnacle Balanced, 30.8%
5. Transamerica Premier Balanced, 29.3%

Source: *U.S. News & World Report*, Best Mutual Funds (annual), February 1, 1999, p. 85.

★3228★
BEST EQUITY INCOME STOCK FUNDS FOR THE FUTURE
Ranked by: OPI (overall performance index) that relies on a formula that measures relative results over 1, 3, 5, and 10 years. **Remarks:** Includes trading style, downside volatility grade, overall volatility grade, 1998 return and down-market grade, 10-, 5-, and 3-year returns, growth of $1,000 in three years, expense ratio, assets and phone number. **Number listed:** 15

1. American Century Income & Growth, with 85.1
2. Cutler Equity Income, 79.4
3. United Income A, 78.5
4. Vanguard Equity Income, 77.7
5. Strong Equity Income, 76.5
6. One Group Income Equity A, 74.8
7. Fidelity Equity Income II, 74.2
8. Pioneer Equity Income A, 72.3
8. Huntington Income Equity Inv., 72.3
10. First American Equity Income Retail A, 71.0

Source: *U.S. News & World Report*, Best Mutual Funds (annual), February 1, 1999, p. 79.

★3229★
BEST EQUITY INCOME/UTILITIES STOCK FUNDS, 1998
Ranked by: Return, in percent. **Remarks:** Includes OPI, trading style, downside volatility grade, overall volatility grade, 1998 return and down-market grade, 10-, 5-, and 3-year returns, growth of $1,000 in three years, expense ratio, assets and phone number. **Number listed:** 10

1. Fidelity Select Utilities Growth, with 43.2%
2. Janus Equity Income, 40.3%
3. Icom Telecom & Utilities, 30.0%
4. Fidelity Utilities Fund, 28.5%
5. Value Line Income, 27.8%
6. American Century Income & Growth, 27.7%
7. American Century Utilities, 27.4%
8. Merrill Lynch Global Utility A, 24.9%
9. INVESCO Strategy Utilities, 24.3%

10. United Income A, 24.0%

Source: *U.S. News & World Report*, Best Mutual Funds (annual), February 1, 1999, p. 84.

★3230★
BEST EQUITY MUTUAL FUNDS, 1999
Ranked by: Total return, in percent. **Number listed:** 50

1. Amerindo Technology D, with 98.90%
2. Internet, 86.20%
3. Van Wagoner Emerging Growth, 77.37%
4. Van Wagoner Post -Venture, 76.99%
5. Monument Internet, 76.47%
6. Van Wagoner Technology, 76.34%
7. Lexington Troika Dialog Russia, 65.91%
8. Fidelity Japan Small Companies, 51.66%
9. Warbug Pincus Japan, 50.23%
10. Matthews Korea I, 44.85%

Source: *Business Week*, The Best (annual), June 14, 1999, p. 154.

★3231★
BEST GEOGRAPHIC SECTOR STOCK FUNDS FOR THE FUTURE
Ranked by: OPI (overall performance index) that relies on a formula that measures relative results over 1, 3, 5, and 10 years. **Remarks:** Includes trading style, downside volatility grade, overall volatility grade, 1998 return and down-market grade, 10-, 5-, and 3-year returns, growth of $1,000 in three years, expense ratio, assets and phone number. **Number listed:** 4

1. Merrill EuroFund B, with 99.9
2. Vanguard International Equity European, 98.0
3. T. Rowe Price European Stock Fund, 96.6
4. Invesco European, 92.4

Source: *U.S. News & World Report*, Best Mutual Funds (annual), February 1, 1999, p. 78.

★3232★
BEST GLOBAL EQUITY STOCK FUNDS FOR THE FUTURE
Ranked by: OPI (overall performance index) that relies on a formula that measures relative results over 1, 3, 5, and 10 years. **Remarks:** Includes trading style, downside volatility grade, overall volatility grade, 1998 return and down-market grade, 10-, 5-, and 3-year returns, growth of $1,000 in three years, expense ratio, assets and phone number. **Number listed:** 9

1. New Perspective, with 93.2
2. Janus Worldwide, 91.5
3. Dreyfus Premier Worldwide Growth A, 91.4
4. AIM Global Growth & Income, 90.4
5. Capital World Growth & Income, 87.9
6. MFS Global Total Return A, 86.6
7. Index Global A, 86.5
8. Eaton Vance Worldwide Health A, 85.1
9. Putnam Global Growth, 84.3

Source: *U.S. News & World Report*, Best Mutual Funds (annual), February 1, 1999, p. 78.

★3233★
BEST GLOBAL EQUITY STOCK FUNDS, 1998
Ranked by: Return, in percent. **Remarks:** Includes OPI, trading style, downside volatility grade, overall volatility grade, 1998 return and down-market grade, 10-, 5-, and 3-year returns, growth of $1,000 in three years, expense ratio, assets and phone number. **Number listed:** 5

1. Montgomery Global Communications, with 55.0%
2. INVESCO Specialty Worldwide Communications, 41.0%
3. Nicholas-Applegate Worldwide Growth, 37.1%
4. Gabelli Global Telecommunications, 34.8%
5. Montgomery Global Opportunities, 32.8%

Source: *U.S. News & World Report*, Best Mutual Funds (annual), February 1, 1999, p. 84.

★3234★
BEST GROWTH & INCOME STOCK FUNDS FOR THE FUTURE
Ranked by: OPI (overall performance index) that relies on a formula that measures relative results over 1, 3, 5, and 10 years. **Remarks:** Includes trading style, downside volatility grade, overall volatility grade, 1998 return and down-market grade, 10-, 5-, and 3-year returns, growth of $1,000 in three years, expense ratio, assets and phone number. **Number listed:** 10

1. Fidelity Growth & Income, with 88.8
2. Vanguard 500 Index, 88.3
2. SsgA Growth & Income, 88.3
4. MAP Equity Fund L, 88.0
4. Regions Growth Fund R, 88.0
6. Capital Exchange Fund, 87.3
7. Fidelity Fund, 87.2
8. Janus Growth & Income, 85.6
9. Pioneer, 85.4
10. Reynolds Blue Chip Growth, 85.3

Source: *U.S. News & World Report*, Best Mutual Funds (annual), February 1, 1999, p. 78.

★3235★
BEST GROWTH & INCOME STOCK FUNDS, 1998
Ranked by: Return, in percent. **Remarks:** Includes OPI, trading style, downside volatility grade, overall volatility grade, 1998 return and down-market grade, 10-, 5-, and 3-year returns, growth of $1,000 in three years, expense ratio, assets and phone number. **Number listed:** 10

1. Reynolds Blue Chip Growth, with 54.1%
2. Strong Blue Chip 100 Fund, 43.9%
3. Marsico Growth % Income, 43.4%
4. Regions Growth Fund B, 41.5%
5. Pegasus Growth Fund A, 37.9%
6. Rightime Midcap, 37.2%
7. Alleghany Chicago Growth & Income, 35.5%
8. Janus Growth & Income, 34.9%
9. SsgA Growth & Income, 34.7%
9. PBHG Large Cap Value, 34.7%

Source: *U.S. News & World Report*, Best Mutual Funds (annual), February 1, 1999, p. 84.

★3236★
BEST GROWTH & INCOME VALUE STOCK FUNDS FOR THE FUTURE
Ranked by: OPI (overall performance index) that relies on a formula that measures relative results over 1, 3, 5, and 10 years. **Remarks:** Includes trading style, downside volatility grade, overall volatility grade, 1998 return and down-market grade, 10-, 5-, and 3-year returns, growth of $1,000 in three years, expense ratio, assets and phone number. **Number listed:** 15

1. Massachusetts Investors Trust, with 87.5
2. Ameristock Mutual Fund, 86.9
3. Firstar Growth & Income Institutional, 86.5
4. Safeco Equity, 85.9
5. Devon Fund A, 85.2
6. Washington Mutual Investors, 85.1
7. Vanguard Growth & Income, 82.8
8. Investment Company of America, 82.0
9. Van Kampen Comstock Fund A, 80.6
9. T. Rowe Price Dividend Growth, 80.6

Source: *U.S. News & World Report*, Best Mutual Funds (annual), February 1, 1999, p. 78.

★3237★
BEST INTERNATIONAL EQUITY STOCK FUNDS FOR THE FUTURE
Ranked by: OPI (overall performance index) that relies on a formula that measures relative results over 1, 3, 5, and 10 years. **Remarks:** Includes trading style, downside volatility grade, overall volatility grade, 1998 return and down-market grade, 10-, 5-, and 3-year returns, growth of $1,000 in three years, expense ratio, assets and phone number. **Number listed:** 12
1. UMB Scout Worldwide, with 88.8
2. Putnam International Voyager A, 84.8
3. United International Growth, 84.5
4. BT Investment International Equity, 84.2
5. Aetna International Fund A, 82.5
6. Artisan International, 82.3
7. STI Classic International Equity Index, 82.1
8. Harbor International Growth, 81.3
9. Tweedy Brown Global Value, 80.9
10. EuroPacific Growth L, 80.6

Source: *U.S. News & World Report*, Best Mutual Funds (annual), February 1, 1999, p. 78.

★3238★
BEST INTERNATIONAL EQUITY STOCK FUNDS, 1998
Ranked by: Return, in percent. **Remarks:** Includes OPI, trading style, downside volatility grade, overall volatility grade, 1998 return and down-market grade, 10-, 5-, and 3-year returns, growth of $1,000 in three years, expense ratio, assets and phone number. **Number listed:** 5
1. Matthews Korea, with 96.2%
2. Montgomery Global Long Short A, 53.4%
3. Bartlett Europe A, 41.9%
4. AIM European Development A, 40.6%
5. INVESCO International European, 32.9%

Source: *U.S. News & World Report*, Best Mutual Funds (annual), February 1, 1999, p. 84.

★3239★
BEST LONG-TERM GROWTH LARGE CAP STOCK FUNDS FOR THE FUTURE
Ranked by: OPI (overall performance index) that relies on a formula that measures relative results over 1, 3, 5, and 10 years. **Remarks:** Includes trading style, downside volatility grade, overall volatility grade, 1998 return and down-market grade, 10-, 5-, and 3-year returns, growth of $1,000 in three years, expense ratio, assets and phone number. **Number listed:** 20
1. Vanguard U.S. Growth, with 92.6
2. Vanguard Growth Index, 90.8
3. Fidelity Dividend Growth, 90.4
4. ISG Large Cap Equity A, 90.2
5. Dreyfus Appreciation, 89.7
6. Fidelity Destination Plan I, 89.3
7. One Group Large Company Growth, 89.1
8. Accessor Growth Portfolio, 88.6
9. Massachusetts Investors Growth Stock A, 88.5
10. Wilshire Target Large Company Growth, 87.9

Source: *U.S. News & World Report*, Best Mutual Funds (annual), February 1, 1999, p. 76.

★3240★
BEST LONG-TERM GROWTH MID CAP STOCK FUNDS FOR THE FUTURE
Ranked by: OPI (overall performance index) that relies on a formula that measures relative results over 1, 3, 5, and 10 years. **Remarks:** Includes trading style, downside volatility grade, overall volatility grade, 1998 return and down-market grade, 10-, 5-, and 3-year returns, growth of $1,000 in three years, expense ratio, assets and phone number. **Number listed:** 10
1. Weitz Value, with 90.4
2. Weitz Hickory, 86.2
3. Salomon Brothers Capital O, 76.2
4. First Eagle Fund of America, 75.9
5. Fidelity New Millenium, 71.8
6. Gabelli Value Fund L, 71.1
7. Hodges Fund, 70.7
8. WM Northwest Fund, 70.0
9. Waddell & Reed Growth, 69.6
10. Fidelity Export & Multinational, 69.3

Source: *U.S. News & World Report*, Best Mutual Funds (annual), February 1, 1999, p. 76.

★3241★
BEST LONG-TERM GROWTH STOCK FUNDS, 1998
Ranked by: Return, in percent. **Remarks:** Includes OPI, trading style, downside volatility grade, overall volatility grade, 1998 return and down-market grade, 10-, 5-, and 3-year returns, growth of $1,000 in three years, expense ratio, assets and phone number. **Number listed:** 10
1. Berger Select, with 72.3%
2. Excelsior Large Cap Growth, 67.0%
3. IDEX Growth A, 64.0%
4. Reynolds Opportunity, 59.1%%
5. Managers Capital Appreciation, 57.3%
6. WM Growth Fund, 57.1%
7. Janus Olympus, 57.0%
8. Marsico Focus, 51.3%
9. Alger Growth Fund, 50.0%
10. Alliance Premier Growth A, 49.3%

Source: *U.S. News & World Report*, Best Mutual Funds (annual), February 1, 1999, p. 84.

★3242★
BEST TOTAL RETURN STOCK FUNDS FOR THE FUTURE
Ranked by: OPI (overall performance index) that relies on a formula that measures relative results over 1, 3, 5, and 10 years. **Remarks:** Includes trading style, downside volatility grade, overall volatility grade, 1998 return and down-market grade, 10-, 5-, and 3-year returns, growth of $1,000 in three years, expense ratio, assets and phone number. **Number listed:** 15
1. Vanguard Asset Allocation, with 85.2
2. PaineWebber Tactical Allocation, 82.2
3. Value Line Asset Allocation, 81.2
4. Preferred Asset Allocation, 80.8
5. Stagecoach Index Allocation, 76.0
6. Alleghany Chicago Trust Balanced, 75.6
7. Guardian Asset Allocation A, 73.6
8. Stagecoach Asset Allocation, 73.1
9. Smith Barney Concert Social Awareness, 71.8
10. Pacific Horizon Asset Allocation A, 71.1

Source: *U.S. News & World Report*, Best Mutual Funds (annual), February 1, 1999, p. 79.

★3243★
BEST TOTAL RETURN STOCK FUNDS, 1998
Ranked by: Return, in percent. **Remarks:** Includes OPI, trading style, downside volatility grade, overall volatility grade, 1998 return and down-market grade, 10-, 5-, and 3-year returns, growth of $1,000 in three years, expense ratio, assets and phone number. **Number listed:** 5
1. Flex-fund Muirfield Fund, with 30.6%
2. Purisima Total Return, 29.7%
3. PaineWebber Tactical Allocation A, 27.8%
4. SmithBarney Concert Social Awareness, 27.6%
5. Preferred Asset Allocation, 27.1%

Source: *U.S. News & World Report*, Best Mutual Funds (annual), February 1, 1999, p. 84.

★3244★
TOP AGGRESSIVE GROWTH MUTUAL FUNDS BY ONE-YEAR RETURN, 1998
Ranked by: One year return, in percent. **Remarks:** Also notes 3- and 5-year return, net assets, exp. ratio, max load, beta, std. deviation and CDA rating. **Number listed:** 75
1. ProFunds Ultra OTC Fund Investor, with 185.35%
2. Rydex Series-OTC Fund, 86.48%
3. Transamerica Premier Aggressive Growth, 84.07%
4. IDEX Aggressive Growth A, 48.90%
5. ProFunds-Ultra Bull Fund Investor, 42.95%
6. Value Line Leveraged Growth, 39.63%
7. Delaware Aggressive Growth A, 36.46%
8. Delaware Aggressive Growth C, 35.46%
9. Delaware Aggressive Growth A, 35.40%
9. Van Kampen Aggressive Growth A, 35.40%

Source: *Financial Planning*, Mutual Funds Survey (annual), February, 1999, p. 144.

★3245★
TOP AGGRESSIVE GROWTH MUTUAL FUNDS, 1998
Ranked by: One year annualized return, in percent. **Remarks:** Includes 3- and 5-year returns, sales charge, minimum investment, risk, 1st quarter 1999 percentage, M-star rating and phone number. **Number listed:** 25
1. Janus Olympus, with 66.5%
2. Transamerica Prem Agg Gr Inv, 59.7%
3. Van Wagoner Emerging Growth, 56.8%
4. Fidelity Aggressive Growth, 48.8%
5. Alger Capital Appreciation B, 47.4%
6. Idex Alger Aggressive Growth A, 46.7%
7. Fidelity New Millenium, 40.0%
8. Van Kampen Agg Growth A, 39.9%
9. Quaker Aggressive Growth, 37.5%
9. Pin Oak Aggressive Stock, 37.5%

Source: *Your Money*, Top 400 (annual), June/July, 1999, p. 48.

★3246★
TOP AGGRESSIVE GROWTH MUTUAL FUNDS, 1998
Ranked by: Three year return, in percent. **Remarks:** Also notes 1 and 5-year return. **Number listed:** 75
1. Rydex Series-OTC Fund, with 33.40%
2. Caldwell & Orkin Mkt. Opportunity, 30.84%
3. Dreyfus Gr & Value-Aggressive Val, 27.75%
4. First Eagle Fund of America, 23.06%
5. Delaware-Aggressive Growth A, 22.85%
6. Morgan Stanley Inst. Aggr Eq A, 22.31%
7. Delaware-Aggressive Growth B, 20.09%
8. Star Growth Equity Fund B, 19.29%
9. Value Line Leveraged Growth, 17.23%
10. Putnam Cap Appreciation A, 17.19%

Source: *Financial Planning*, Equity Fund Survey (annual), December, 1998, p. 149.

★3247★
TOP ASSET ALLOCATION MUTUAL FUNDS, 1998
Ranked by: One year annualized return, in percent. **Remarks:** Includes 3- and 5-year returns, sales charge, minimum investment, risk, 1st quarter 1999 percentage, M-star rating and phone number. **Number listed:** 25
1. Flex-funds Muirfield, with 31.3%
2. Flex-Partners Tact Asset, 30.2%
3. Eastcliff Total Return, 29.8%
4. Rightime MidCap, 22.4%
5. Preferred Asset Allocation, 19.6%
6. Smith Barney Conc Alc Sos B, 18.6%
7. Purisima Total Return, 18.3%
7. Alleghany/Chicago Trust, 18.3%
9. Rightime Blue Chip, 18.1%
10. Stagecoach Index Allocation A, 17.0%

Source: *Your Money*, Top 400 (annual), June/July, 1999, p. 54.

★3248★
TOP BALANCED DOMESTIC MUTUAL FUNDS BY ONE-YEAR RETURN, 1998
Ranked by: One year return, in percent. **Remarks:** Also notes 3- and 5-year return, net assets, exp. ratio, max load, beta, std. deviation and CDA rating. **Number listed:** 34
1. Alger Fund-Balanced, with 32.49%
2. Janus Balanced Fund, 31.92%
3. Prov Inv Counsel Pinnacle Balanced, 31.12%
4. IDEX Balanced A, 30.80%
5. Transamerica Premier Balanced, 29.30%
6. Phoenix-Engemann Balanced Return A, 29.12%
7. Oppenheimer/Quest Balanced Val A, 28.17%
8. Oppenheimer/Quest Balanced Val B, 27.48%
9. Oppenheimer/Quest Balanced Val C, 27.45%
10. MainStay Total Return A, 26.93%

Source: *Financial Planning*, Mutual Funds Survey (annual), February, 1999, p. 150.

★3249★
TOP BALANCED/LIFESTYLE/ASSET ALLOCATION MUTUAL FUNDS BY FIVE-YEAR RETURN, 1998
Ranked by: Five year return, in percent. **Number listed:** 25
1. Vanguard Asset Allocation, with 21.0%
2. Vanguard Wellington, 17.2%
3. Vanguard Balanced Index, 17.1%
4. INVESCO Total Return, 16.5%
5. Fidelity Asset Mgr. Growth, 16.2%
5. George Putnam A, 16.2%
7. Fidelity Puritan, 15.7%
8. T. Rowe Balanced, 15.5%
9. Capital Research America Balanced, 15.3%
10. Dodge & Cox Balanced, 15.1%

Source: *Pensions & Investments*, Special Report: Mutual Funds (annual), May 3, 1999, p. 27.

★3250★
TOP BALANCED/LIFESTYLE/ASSET ALLOCATION MUTUAL FUNDS MOST USED BY DEFINED CONTRIBUTION PLANS, 1998
Ranked by: Assets, in millions of dollars. **Number listed:** 25
1. Fidelity Puritan, with $12,143 million
2. Vanguard Wellington, $11,523
3. Fidelity Asset Manager, $5,117
4. Dodge & Cox Balanced, $3,985
5. Merrill Lynch Capital, $3,450
6. Fidelity Balanced, $3,319
7. Fidelity Asset Manager Growth, $2,310
8. Capital Research American Balanced, $2,234
9. MFS Total Return, $2,139
10. INVESCO Total Return, $2,054

Source: *Pensions & Investments*, Special Report: Mutual Funds (annual), May 3, 1999, p. 22.

★3251★
TOP BALANCED MUTUAL FUNDS, 1998
Ranked by: One year annualized return, in percent. **Remarks:** Includes 3- and 5-year returns, sales charge, minimum investment, risk, 1st quarter 1999 percentage, M-star rating and phone number. **Number listed:** 25
1. Alger Balanced B, with 30.7%
2. Idex JCC Balanced A, 29.5%
3. Janus Balanced, 28.2%
4. Berger Balanced, 25.9%
5. Leonetti Balanced, 23.4%
6. Phoenix-Engemann, 23.3%
7. Tranamerica Prem Bal Inv, 21.5%

8. Riverfront Balanced Inv A, 21.3%
9. Pax World, 20.2%
10. MainStay Total Return B, 18.9%

Source: *Your Money*, Top 400 (annual), June/July, 1999, p. 48.

★3252★

TOP BALANCED MUTUAL FUNDS, 1998

Ranked by: Three year return, in percent. **Remarks:** Also notes 1 and 5-year return. **Number listed:** 75

1. IDEX Balanced A, with 19.19%
2. Janus Balanced Fund, 18.41%
3. Dreyfus Premier Balanced, 18.35%
4. Montag & Caldwell Balanced, 18.33%
5. Dreyfus Premier Balanced Fd A, 18.05%
6. Pax World Fund, 18.03%
7. Mairs & Power Balanced Fund, 17.76%
8. BlackRock Balanced Inst, 17.65%
9. BlackRock Balanced Svc, 17.30%
10. Flag Investors Value Builder A, 16.85%

Source: *Financial Planning*, Equity Fund Survey (annual), December, 1998, p. 157.

★3253★

TOP CORPORATE BOND MUTUAL FUNDS, 1998

Ranked by: One year annualized return, in percent. **Remarks:** Includes 3- and 5-year returns, sales charge, minimum investment, risk, 1st quarter 1999 percentage, M-star rating and phone number. **Number listed:** 25

1. Calvert Income A, with 11.4%
2. Metropolitan West Total Return Bond, 8.9%
3. Crabbe Huson Contrarian Inc. A, 8.2%
4. Harbor Bond, 8.1%
5. Fremont Bond, 8.0%
6. Monetta Intermediate Bond, 7.7%
6. USAA Income Strategy, 7.7%
8. Van Kampen Sen Floating Rate, 7.6%
9. WPG Core Bond, 7.0%
9. EV Adv Senior Floating Rate, 7.0%

Source: *Your Money*, Top 400 (annual), June/July, 1999, p. 54+.

★3254★

TOP CORPORATE HIGH-YIELD MUTUAL FUNDS BY ONE-YEAR RETURN, 1998

Ranked by: One year return, in percent. **Remarks:** Also notes 3- and 5-year return, net assets, exp. ratio, max load, beta, std. deviation and CDA rating. **Number listed:** 34

1. Strong Short-Term HY Bond, with 8.38%
2. Phoenix Seneca Bond X, 7.63%
3. Endowments Bond Portfolio, 7.47%
4. SteinRoe Intermediate Bond, 6.38%
5. Payden & Rygel High Income R, 6.34%
6. PIMCO High Yield Fund, 6.29%
7. Columbia High Yield Fund, 6.26%
8. PIMCO High Yield Fund A, 6.18%
9. PIMCO High Yield Fund Inst., 5.93%
10. BT Pyramid-Preserve Plus, 5.76%

Source: *Financial Planning*, Mutual Funds Survey (annual), February, 1999, p. 152.

★3255★

TOP CORPORATE HIGH YIELD MUTUAL FUNDS, 1998

Ranked by: One year annualized return, in percent. **Remarks:** Includes 3- and 5-year returns, sales charge, minimum investment, risk, 1st quarter 1999 percentage, M-star rating and phone number. **Number listed:** 25

1. Strong Short-Term High Yield Bond, with 7.7%
2. Brinson High Yield, 7.5%
3. Columbia High Yield, 5.2%
4. Payden & Rygel, 5.1%
5. Fidelity Capital & Income, 4.9%
6. Legg Mason High Yield, 4.3%
7. ASAF Federated, 4.1%
7. Vanguard High Yield Corp, 4.1%
9. Fidelity High Income, 3.9%
10. Idex AEGON Income Plus A, 3.6%

Source: *Your Money*, Top 400 (annual), June/July, 1999, p. 56.

★3256★

TOP DOMESTIC GROWTH MUTUAL FUNDS, 1998

Ranked by: Three year return, in percent. **Remarks:** Also notes 1 and 5-year return. **Number listed:** 75

1. Janus Fd Inc.-Twenty, with 30.68%
2. Legg Mason Value Trust Navig, 30.52%
3. Weitz Series-Hickory Fund, 29.52%
4. Legg Mason Value Trust Prim, 29.32%
5. Sequoia Fund, 28.57%
6. Vanguard Growth Index Fund, 26.67%
7. MFS Mass Investors Growth Stock A, 26.63%
8. MFS Mass Investors Growth Stock B, 25.64%
9. Reynolds Blue Chip Growth, 25.55%
10. Weitz Series-Value, 25.36%

Source: *Financial Planning*, Equity Fund Survey (annual), December, 1998, p. 150.

★3257★

TOP EMERGING MARKETS MUTUAL FUNDS BY ONE-YEAR RETURN, 1998

Ranked by: One year return, in percent. **Remarks:** Also notes 3- and 5-year return, net assets, exp. ratio, max load, beta, std. deviation and CDA rating. **Number listed:** 34

1. Oakmark International Small Cap Fund, with 9.20%
2. DFA Emerging Markets, -9.43%
3. Montgomery Emerging Asia R, -14.72%
4. SsgA Emerging Markets, -15.94%
5. Dreyfus Emerging Market Fund, -18.01%
6. Templeton Inst-Emerging Markets, -18.03%
7. STI Classic Emerging Markets Tr, -18.19%
8. Vanguard Emerging Markets Stock Index, -18.21%
9. Templeton Developing Markets Adv, -18.47%
10. Templeton Developing Markets A, -18.72%

Source: *Financial Planning*, Mutual Funds Survey (annual), February, 1999, p. 150.

★3258★

TOP EMERGING MARKETS MUTUAL FUNDS, 1998

Ranked by: Three year return, in percent. **Remarks:** Also notes 1 and 5-year return. **Number listed:** 75

1. BT Investment-Latin America, with .51%
2. Evergreen Emerging Mkts Growth Y, .49%
3. Fidelity Latin America Fund, -1.59%
4. Nicholas-Applegate Emerging Cos I, -2.78%
5. Nicholas-Applegate Emerging Cos Q, -2.97%
6. Nicholas-Applegate Emerging Cos A, -3.56%
7. Evergreen Latin America Fund B, -3.75%
8. Calvert New Africa Fund, -3.84%
9. Nicholas-Applegate Emerging Cos B, -3.95%
10. Nicholas-Applegate Emerging Cos C, -3.96%

Source: *Financial Planning*, Equity Fund Survey (annual), December, 1998, p. 153.

★3259★

TOP EQUITY FUNDS BY FIVE-YEAR RETURN, 1998

Ranked by: Five year return, in percent. **Number listed:** 50

1. Janus Twenty, with 36.1%
2. Fidelity Div. Growth, 28.8%
3. MFS Mass. Investors Growth A, 28.3%
4. T. Rowe Science & Tech., 27.9%
5. Vanguard U.S. Growth, 27.8%

6. Fidelity Aggressive Growth, 27.1%
7. Dreyfus Appreciation, 26.7%
8. Vanguard PRIMECAP, 27.8%
9. Putnam Investors A, 26.4%
10. Vanguard Inst'l Index, 26.3%

Source: *Pensions & Investments*, Special Report: Mutual Funds (annual), May 3, 1999, p. 23.

★3260★
TOP EQUITY FUNDS BY ONE-YEAR RETURN, 1998
Ranked by: One year return, in percent. **Number listed:** 50

1. Janus Twenty, with 79.9%
2. Fidelity Aggressive Growth, 48.8%
3. T. Rowe Science & Tech., 39.2%
4. Janus Fund, 35.1%
5. Fidelity Adv. Equity Growth, 33.3%
6. Prudential Jenn. Growth A, 32.8%
7. Fidelity OTC, 30.0%
8. American Century Select, 29.5%
9. AIM Value A, 28.7%
10. American Century Ultra, 28.0%

Source: *Pensions & Investments*, Special Report: Mutual Funds (annual), May 3, 1999, p. 24.

★3261★
TOP EQUITY INCOME MUTUAL FUNDS BY ONE-YEAR RETURN, 1998
Ranked by: One year return, in percent. **Remarks:** Also notes 3- and 5-year return, net assets, exp. ratio, max load, beta, std. deviation and CDA rating. **Number listed:** 75

1. MFS Strategic Growth A, with 45.20%
2. MFS Strategic Growth B, 44.15%
3. MFS Strategic Growth C, 44.11%
4. Janus Equity Income Fund, 40.05%
5. PBHG Advison, 28.90%
6. Arch Fd-Equity Index, 28.19%
7. Value Line Income Fund, 27.83%
8. Dreyfus Premier Large Co. Stock R, 26.46%
9. Dreyfus Premier Large Co. Stock A, 26.23%
10. Chase Equity Income Fund, 26.20%

Source: *Financial Planning*, Mutual Funds Survey (annual), February, 1999, p. 143.

★3262★
TOP EQUITY INCOME MUTUAL FUNDS, 1998
Ranked by: One year annualized return, in percent. **Remarks:** Includes 3- and 5-year returns, sales charge, minimum investment, risk, 1st quarter 1999 percentage, M-star rating and phone number. **Number listed:** 25

1. Janus Equity-Income, with 39.0%
2. Value Line Income, 28.3%
3. Ameristock, 20.0%
4. Centura Large-Cap, 16.1%
5. GE Value Equity, 15.2%
6. Rockhaven Premier Dividend, 14.6%
7. Dreyfus Premier, 14.1%
8. Strong Equity Income, 13.4%
9. Fidelity Equity-Income II, 12.3%
10. Federated Equity, 10.2%

Source: *Your Money*, Top 400 (annual), June/July, 1999, p. 48+.

★3263★
TOP EQUITY MUTUAL FUNDS BY FIVE-YEAR RISK ADJUSTED RETURN, 1998
Ranked by: Five year return, in percent. **Number listed:** 52

1. Janus Twenty, with 36.1%
2. Fidelity Division Growth, 28.8%
3. MFS Mass. Investors Growth A, 28.3%
4. T. Rowe Science & Tech, 27.9%
5. Vanguard U.S. Growth, 27.8%
6. Fidelity Aggressive Growth, 27.1%
7. Dreyfus Appreciation, 26.7%
7. Vanguard PRIMECAP, 26.7%
9. Putnam Investors A, 26.4%
10. Vanguard Institutional Index, 26.3%

Source: *Pensions & Investments*, Special Report: Mutual Funds (annual), May 3, 1999, p. 23.

★3264★
TOP EQUITY MUTUAL FUNDS MOST USED BY DEFINED CONTRIBUTION PLANS, 1998
Ranked by: Assets, in millions of dollars. **Number listed:** 100

1. Fidelity Magellan, with $52,758 million
2. Fidelity Growth & Income, $25,320
3. Vanguard 500 Index, $20,599
4. Fidelity Contrafund, $20,346
5. Fidelity Equity Income, $16,384
6. Fidelity Spartan U.S. Equity Index, $13,397
7. Vanguard Institutional Index, $10,734
8. Fidelity Advisor Growth Opportunity, $10,553
9. Fidelity Blue Chip Growth, $9,886
10. Vanguard Windsor, $8,573

Source: *Pensions & Investments*, Special Report: Mutual Funds (annual), May 3, 1999, p. 21.

★3265★
TOP FIXED-INCOME FUNDS BY FIVE-YEAR RETURN, 1998
Ranked by: Five year return, in percent. **Number listed:** 50

1. Fidelity High Income, with 12.1%
2. MAS High Yield Inst., 11.0%
3. Federated High Inc. A, 10.1%
3. MainStay High Yield Corp. B, 10.1%
3. Strong Corp. Bond, 10.1%
6. Fidelity Capital & Inc., 9.9%
7. Vanguard High Yield Corp, 9.8%
8. Federated High Yield, 9.7%
9. Cap. Res. America High Income, 9.4%
10. Vanguard Long Term Treasury, 9.3%

Source: *Pensions & Investments*, Special Report: Mutual Funds (annual), May 3, 1999, p. 25.

★3266★
TOP FIXED INCOME FUNDS BY ONE-YEAR RETURN, 1998
Ranked by: One year return, in percent. **Number listed:** 50

1. PIMCO Total Return Inst'l, with 7.6%
2. Payden & Rygel Total Return, 7.2%
3. Fidelity Spartan Invst. Growth, 6.8%
4. Fidelity Bond Index, 6.7%
5. Vanguard Total Bond Mkt Inst'l, 6.6%
5. BGI/Masterworks Index, 6.6%
7. Vanguard Long-term Treasury, 6.5%
7. Vanguard Total Bond Market, 6.5%
9. Firstar IMMDEX Inst'l, 6.4%
9. PIMCO Low Dur. Inst'l, 6.4%

Source: *Pensions & Investments*, Special Report: Mutual Funds (annual), May 3, 1999, p. 26.

★3267★
TOP FIXED-INCOME MUTUAL FUNDS MOST USED BY DEFINED CONTRIBUTION PLANS, 1998
Ranked by: Assets, in millions of dollars. **Number listed:** 100

1. PIMCO Total Return, with $2,848 million
2. Fidelity Interm. Bond, $2,291
3. Vanguard Total Market Index, $1,957
4. Cap. Res. Bond Fund of America, $1,950
5. T. Rowe Spectrum Inc., $1,164
6. Fidelity Invst. Grade, $1,095

7. MAS Funds, $995
8. Fidelity U.S. Bond Index, $983
9. Fidelity Government Sector, $759
10. Putnam Income, $727

Source: *Pensions & Investments*, Special Report: Mutual Funds (annual), May 3, 1999, p. 21.

★3268★

TOP GENERAL BOND INVESTMENT GRADE MUTUAL FUNDS BY ONE-YEAR RETURN, 1998

Ranked by: One year return, in percent. **Remarks:** Also notes 3- and 5-year return, net assets, exp. ratio, max load, beta, std. deviation and CDA rating. **Number listed:** 34

1. Potomac OTC Plus Fund, with 104.22%
2. Janus Twenty, 73.39%
3. PBHG Large Cap 20, 69.76%
4. Excelsior Large Cap Growth Fund, 67.04%
5. IDEX Growth Fund T, 64.09%
6. IDEX Growth Fund A, 64.00%
7. IDEX Growth Fund C, 63.79%
8. IDEX Growth Fund B, 63.75%
9. ASAF Janus Capital Growth A, 59.91%
10. ASAF Janus Capital Growth B, 59.16%

Source: *Financial Planning*, Mutual Funds Survey (annual), February, 1999, p. 152.

★3269★

TOP GOVERNMENT-BOND MUTUAL FUNDS, 1998

Ranked by: One year annualized return, in percent. **Remarks:** Includes 3- and 5-year returns, sales charge, minimum investment, risk, 1st quarter 1999 percentage, M-star rating and phone number. **Number listed:** 25

1. API Treasuries Trust, with 8.5%
2. American Cent Target 2025 I, 8.4%
3. American Cent Target 2025 I, 7.7%
4. American Cent Target 2025 I, 7.5%
5. California Investment U.S. Government., 7.4%
6. Vanguard Admiral Long Term, 7.1%
7. Vanguard Admiral Interm-Term, 7.0%
8. Dreyfus U.S. Treasuries Long Term, 6.9%
9. Safeco Interm-Term U.S., 6.8%
10. T. Rowe Price U.S. Treasury, 6.7%

Source: *Your Money*, Top 400 (annual), June/July, 1999, p. 56+.

★3270★

TOP GROWTH & INCOME MUTUAL FUNDS BY ONE-YEAR RETURN, 1998

Ranked by: One year return, in percent. **Remarks:** Also notes 3- and 5-year return, net assets, exp. ratio, max load, beta, std. deviation and CDA rating. **Number listed:** 75

1. One Group-Large Co. Growth Fidelity, with 44.71%
2. One Group-Large Co. Growth Investment, 44.33%
3. Strong Blue Chip 100 Fund, 43.93%
4. Marsico Growth & Income Fund, 43.40%
5. One Group-Large Co. Growth B, 43.24%
6. American Performance Growth Equity, 42.25%
7. IPS Millenium Fund, 39.55%
8. Nations Marsico Gr & Inc Pr A, 38.42%
9. Nations Marsico Gr & Inc Pr B, 37.92%
10. PBHG Advisor Enhanced Equity, 37.90%

Source: *Financial Planning*, Mutual Funds Survey (annual), February, 1999, p. 141.

★3271★

TOP GROWTH & INCOME MUTUAL FUNDS, 1998

Ranked by: One year annualized return, in percent. **Remarks:** Includes 3- and 5-year returns, sales charge, minimum investment, risk, 1st quarter 1999 percentage, M-star rating and phone number. **Number listed:** 25

1. IPS Millenium, with 45.6%
2. Noah, 44.9%
3. Strong Total Returns, 33.0%
4. Janus Growth & Income, 32.2%
5. Marsico Growth & Income, 31.4%
6. Quaker Core Equity, 31.2%
7. Citizens Index, 29.5%
8. Bridgeway Ultra-Large 35 Index, 29.4%
9. Newpoint Equity, 26.8%
10. Value Line U.S. Multinational Co., 26.7%

Source: *Your Money*, Top 400 (annual), June/July, 1999, p. 50.

★3272★

TOP GROWTH & INCOME MUTUAL FUNDS, 1998

Ranked by: Three year return, in percent. **Remarks:** Also notes 1- and 5-year return. **Number listed:** 75

1. Ameristock Mutual Fund, with 26.85%
2. Nationwide Fund, 25.04%
3. Janus Fd Inc.-Growth & Income, 24.82%
4. PBHG Advisor Enhanced Equity A, 23.75%
5. SsgA Growth & Income, 23.62%
6. One Group-Large Co. Growth Fid., 23.57%
7. SunAmerica Growth & Income A, 23.37%
8. WPG Growth & Income, 23.34%
9. Firstar Growth & Income Inst., 23.12%
9. One Group-Large Co. Growth Inv., 23.12%

Source: *Financial Planning*, Equity Fund Survey (annual), December, 1998, p. 152.

★3273★

TOP GROWTH-DOMESTIC MUTUAL FUNDS BY ONE-YEAR RETURN, 1998

Ranked by: One year return, in percent. **Remarks:** Also notes 3- and 5-year return, net assets, exp. ratio, max load, beta, std. deviation and CDA rating. **Number listed:** 75

1. Potomac OTC Plus Fund, with 104.22%
2. Janus Twenty, 73.39%
3. PBHG Large Cap 20, 69.76%
4. Excelsior Large Cap Growth Fund, 67.04%
5. IDEX Growth Fund T, 64.09%
6. IDEX Growth Fund A, 64.00%
7. IDEX Growth Fund C, 63.79%
8. IDEX Growth Fund B, 63.75%
9. ASAF Janus Capital Growth A, 59.91%
10. ASAF Janus Capital Growth B, 59.16%

Source: *Financial Planning*, Mutual Funds Survey (annual), February, 1999, p. 142.

★3274★

TOP GROWTH MUTUAL FUNDS, 1998

Ranked by: One year annualized return, in percent. **Remarks:** Includes 3- and 5-year returns, sales charge, minimum investment, risk, 1st quarter 1999 percentage, M-star rating and phone number. **Number listed:** 25

1. ProFunds UltraOTC Inv, with 136.4%
2. Berkshire Capital Growth & Value, 123.9%
3. Potomac OTC Plus, 87.4%
4. Van Wagoner Post-Venture, 86.3%
5. Janus Twenty, 79.9%
6. Millennium Growth, 79.5%
7. Rydex OTC Inv, 73.7%
8. Excelsior Large Cap Growth, 68.0%
9. Janus Mercury, 65.1%
10. WM Growth A, 63.3%

Source: *Your Money*, Top 400 (annual), June/July, 1999, p. 48.

★3275★

TOP INTERNATIONAL EQUITY MUTUAL FUNDS BY ONE-YEAR RETURN, 1998

Ranked by: One year return, in percent. **Remarks:** Also notes 3- and 5-year return, net assets, exp. ratio, max load, beta, std. deviation and CDA rating. **Number listed:** 75

1. Matthews Korea Fund I, with 96.15%
2. Bartlett Europe Fund A, 41.99%
3. AIM European Development A, 40.62%
4. AIM European Development B, 39.51%
5. Nicholas-Applegate Int Sm Cap Growth I, 36.34%
6. Nicholas-Applegate Int Sm Cap Growth Q, 35.96%
7. Nicholas-Applegate Int Sm Cap Growth A, 35.57%
8. Nicholas-Applegate Int Sm Cap Growth B, 34.80%
9. INVESCO European Fund, 32.93%
10. Lipper Prime Europe Equity Prem, 32.29%

Source: *Financial Planning*, Mutual Funds Survey (annual), February, 1999, p. 146.

★3276★

TOP INTERNATIONAL/GLOBAL EQUITY FUNDS BY FIVE-YEAR RETURN, 1998

Ranked by: Five year return, in percent. **Number listed:** 25

1. Janus Worldwide, with 21.1%
2. Vanguard European Index, 19.3%
3. Capital Resources New Perspective, 18.3%
3. Capital Research New Perspective, 18.3%
5. Fidelity Europe, 17.7%
6. Capital Research Capital World, 16.7%
7. Putnam Global Growth A, 15.5%
8. Putnam International Growth A, 14.8%
9. Templeton World A, 14.5%
10. Oppenheimer Global A, 14.2%

Source: *Pensions & Investments*, Special Report: Mutual Funds (annual), May 3, 1999, p. 27.

★3277★

TOP INTERNATIONAL/GLOBAL MUTUAL FUNDS MOST USED BY DEFINED CONTRIBUTION PLANS, 1998

Ranked by: Assets, in millions of dollars. **Number listed:** 25

1. Capital Research EuroPacific Growth, with $5,211 million
2. Templeton Foreign, $4,403
3. Janus Worldwide, $4,306
4. Capital Research New Perspective, $3,443
5. T. Rowe International Stock, $2,572
6. Vanguard International Growth, $2,474
7. Fidelity Overseas, $2,304
8. Putnam Global Growth, $1,322
9. Capital Research SMALLCAP World, $1,170
10. Templeton World, $1,041

Source: *Pensions & Investments*, Special Report: Mutual Funds (annual), May 3, 1999, p. 23.

★3278★

TOP INTERNATIONAL MUTUAL FUNDS, 1998

Ranked by: Three year return, in percent. **Remarks:** Also notes 1 and 5-year return. **Number listed:** 75

1. Scudder Greater Europe Growth, with 23.10%
2. Bartlett Europe Fund A, 22.61%
3. INVESCO European Fund, 19.47%
4. Vanguard Europe Stock Index Fund, 19.11%
5. Wright EquiFund Netherlands, 18.75%
6. Wright EquiFund Belgium, 18.28%
7. Price European Stock, 17.62%
8. AmCent-20th Century, 16.99%
9. Fidelity European Cap Apprec, 16.91%
10. Fidelity Europe, 16.77%

Source: *Financial Planning*, Equity Fund Survey (annual), December, 1998, p. 158.

★3279★

TOP INTERNATIONAL STOCK MUTUAL FUNDS, 1998

Ranked by: One year annualized return, in percent. **Remarks:** Includes 3- and 5-year returns, sales charge, minimum investment, risk, 1st quarter 1999 percentage, M-star rating and phone number. **Number listed:** 25

1. Fidelity Japan Small Co., with 83.4%
2. Matthews Korea I, 41.6%
3. Newport Japan Opport A, 38.1%
4. Japan, 35.8%
5. Deutsche Japanese Equity A, 34.2%
6. Fidelity Japan, 30.7%
7. T. Rowe Price Japan, 27.6%
8. Artisan International, 22.3%
9. Warburg Pincus Adv Japan Growth, 21.8%
10. Fidelity Pacific Basin, 21.7%

Source: *Your Money*, Top 400 (annual), June/July, 1999, p. 52.

★3280★

TOP MANAGERS OF MUTUAL FUNDS ASSETS MANAGED FOR DEFINED CONTRIBUTION PLANS, 1998

Ranked by: Assets, in millions of dollars. **Number listed:** 25

1. Fidelity Investments, with $248,400 million
2. Vanguard Group, $104,495
3. Capital Research & Management Co., $42,834
4. Merrill Lynch, $39,100
5. Putnam Investments, $31,400
6. T. Rowe Price, $29,760
7. American Century Investments, $27,200
8. MFS Investment Management, $16,450
9. Franklin Templeton, $14,512
10. Janus, $13,828

Source: *Pensions & Investments*, Special Report: Mutual Funds (annual), May 3, 1999, p. 22.

★3281★

TOP MID-CAP MUTUAL FUNDS BY ONE-YEAR RETURN, 1998

Ranked by: One year return, in percent. **Remarks:** Also notes 3- and 5-year return, net assets, exp. ratio, max load, beta, std. deviation and CDA rating. **Number listed:** 34

1. TCW/DW Mid-Cap Equity Trust B, with 62.71%
2. Norwest Advantage-Large Co. Growth, 48.01%
3. Citizens Emergingging Growth, 42.71%
4. Rightime Midcap Fund, 37.16%
5. MAS Mid Cap Growth Instl, 37.10%
6. MAS Mid Cap Growth Adv, 36.74%
7. Van Kampen Emergingging Growth A, 34.73%
8. Janus Enterprise Fund, 33.75%
9. Van Kampen Emergingging Growth B, 33.66%
10. Van Kampen Emergingging Growth C, 33.65%

Source: *Financial Planning*, Mutual Funds Survey (annual), February, 1999, p. 148.

★3282★

TOP MID-CAP MUTUAL FUNDS, 1998

Ranked by: Three year return, in percent. **Remarks:** Also notes 1 and 5-year return. **Number listed:** 75

1. MAS Mid Cap Value, with 22.43%
2. Norwest Advantage, 21.59%
3. Warburg Pincus Cap App Com, 21.39%
4. Warburg Pincus Cap App Adv, 20.85%
5. Ariel Appreciation Fund, 20.73%
6. MAS Mid Cap Growth, 18.95%

7. Kemper Value A, 18.70%
8. Dreyfus Premier Midcap Stock R, 17.56%
9. Dreyfus Premier Midcap Stock A, 17.24%
10. Wachovia Equity Fund A, 16.60%

Source: *Financial Planning*, Equity Fund Survey (annual), December, 1998, p. 155.

★3283★
TOP MONEY MARKET FUNDS USED MOST BY DEFINED CONTRIBUTION PLANS, 1998
Ranked by: Assets, in millions of dollars. **Number listed:** 25

1. Fidelity FMMT Ret. Money Market, with $8,612 million
2. Vanguard Prime Money Market, $4,810
3. Fidelity Inst'l Money Market, $3,592
4. Fidelity FMMT Ret. Goverment, $3,482
5. Capital Resources Cash Management America, $1,112
6. SsgA Money Market, $1,053
7. Vanguard Federal Money Market, $1,049
8. Putnam Money Market, $958
9. Vanguard Treasury Money Market, $910
10. Merrill Lynch, $753

Source: *Pensions & Investments*, Special Report: Mutual Funds (annual), May 3, 1999, p. 24.

★3284★
TOP MULTI-ASSET GLOBAL MUTUAL FUNDS, 1998
Ranked by: One year annualized return, in percent. **Remarks:** Includes 3- and 5-year returns, sales charge, minimum investment, risk, 1st quarter 1999 percentage, M-star rating and phone number. **Number listed:** 25

1. Montgomery Global, with 38.9%
2. Fidelity Asset Manager: Growth, 12.1%
3. Vanguard Global Asset Allocation, 10.7%
4. Fidelity Global Balanced, 10.1%
5. Smith Barney International Balanced A, 10.0%
6. Fidelity Asset Manager, 9.8%
7. Van Eck Global Balanced A, 9.5%
8. IDS Global Balanced A, 9.4%
9. API Capital Income, 6.4%
10. Oppenheimer Global A, 6.3%

Source: *Your Money*, Top 400 (annual), June/July, 1999, p. 48.

★3285★
TOP MUNICIPAL-BOND--NATIONAL MUTUAL FUNDS, 1998
Ranked by: One year annualized return, in percent. **Remarks:** Includes 3- and 5-year returns, sales charge, minimum investment, risk, 1st quarter 1999 percentage, M-star rating and phone number. **Number listed:** 25

1. CitiFunds National Tax-Free A, with 8.3%
2. Executive Investors Ins T/E, 7.5%
2. American Cent Hi-Yield Municipal Inv., 7.5%
4. Heartland Hi-Yield Municipal Bond, 7.3%
5. First Investors Ins Intrm. T/E A, 6.7%
6. Delaware National Hi-Yield A, 6.4%
6. Dreyfus Basic Municipal Bond, 6.4%
6. Mason Street Municpal Bond A, 6.4%
9. Lord Abbett National T/F Inc A, 6.3%
9. Colonial Tax-Exempt A, 6.3%

Source: *Your Money*, Top 400 (annual), June/July, 1999, p. 58.

★3286★
TOP SMALL-CAP MUTUAL FUNDS BY ONE-YEAR RETURN, 1998
Ranked by: One year return, in percent. **Remarks:** Also notes 3- and 5-year return, net assets, exp. ratio, max load, beta, std. deviation and CDA rating. **Number listed:** 34

1. Transamerica Premier Small Co., with 76.06%
2. Pin Oak Aggressive Stock, 49.20%
3. Fidelity Emerging Growth, 43.28%
4. Fidelity OTC Portfolio, 40.38%
5. United New Concepts Fund A, 38.70%
6. Oppenheimer Enterprises Fund A, 34.81%
7. Oppenheimer Enterprises Fund C, 33.88%
8. Oppenheimer Enterprises Fund B, 33.81%
9. One Group-Growth Opportunity Fidelity, 30.38%
10. One Group-Growth Opportunity Investment, 30.06%

Source: *Financial Planning*, Mutual Funds Survey (annual), February, 1999, p. 148.

★3287★
TOP SMALL-CAP MUTUAL FUNDS, 1998
Ranked by: Three year return, in percent. **Remarks:** Also notes 1 and 5-year return. **Number listed:** 75

1. Dreyfus Growth & Value-Emerging Leaders, with 26.08%
2. State Street Aurora Fund A, 23.30%
3. State Street Aurora Fund B, 22.36%
4. State Street Aurora Fund C, 22.33%
5. Longleaf Partners, 19.28%
6. Wachovia Special Values Fund A, 18.41%
7. Accessor Fd-Small-Mid Cap Port, 18.26%
8. Phoenix-Engemann Sm & Mid Cap A, 18.01%
9. Eclipse Equity Fund, 17.51%
10. Nations Disciplined Equity Pr A, 17.43%

Source: *Financial Planning*, Equity Fund Survey (annual), December, 1998, p. 154.

★3288★
TOP SMALL COMPANY MUTUAL FUNDS, 1998
Ranked by: One year annualized return, in percent. **Remarks:** Includes 3- and 5-year returns, sales charge, minimum investment, risk, 1st quarter 1999 percentage, M-star rating and phone number. **Number listed:** 25

1. TCW/DW Mid-Cap Equity B, with 80.9%
2. Transamerica Pren Sm Co Inv, 62.4%
3. Schroder Micro Cap Inv, 43.9%
4. Robertson Stephens Emg Gr A, 38.5%
5. Van Wagoner Micro-Cap, 38.4%
6. Kobrick Emerging Growth, 29.7%
7. Jundt U.S. Emerging Growth A, 23.5%
8. Oppenheimer Enterprise A, 23.3%
9. SunAmerica Small Co Growth A, 22.2%
10. Janus Venture, 20.9%

Source: *Your Money*, Top 400 (annual), June/July, 1999, p. 48.

★3289★
TOP SPECIALIZED MUTUAL FUNDS, 1998
Ranked by: Three year return, in percent. **Remarks:** Also notes 1 and 5-year return. **Number listed:** 75

1. Pilgrim America Bank & Thrift A, with 29.19%
2. Fidelity Select-Health Care, 27.22%
3. Vanguard Specialized Health, 27.08%
4. Flag Investors Communications A, 25.61%
5. Fidelity Select-Reg Banks, 25.28%
6. Flag Investors Communications D, 25.18%
7. Flag Investors Communications B, 24.66%
8. SmithBarney Telecom-Income, 24.58%
9. Fidelity Select-Insurance, 23.88%
10. Davis Financial A, 23.87%

Source: *Financial Planning*, Equity Fund Survey (annual), December, 1998, p. 156.

★3290★
TOP SPECIALTY STOCK MUTUAL FUNDS, 1998
Ranked by: One year annualized return, in percent. **Remarks:** Includes 3- and 5-year returns, sales charge, minimum invest-

ment, risk, 1st quarter 1999 percentage, M-star rating and phone number. **Number listed:** 25

1. Internet, with 343.2%
2. Amerindo Technology D, 164.5%
3. Munder NetNet A, 141.1%
4. Van Wagoner Technology, 115.0%
5. WWW Internet, 96.8%
6. Dreyfus Technology Growth, 96.1%
7. Fidelity Sel Computers, 91.4%
8. Fidelity Sel Developing Comm, 82.0%
9. Northern Technology, 80.0%
10. Firsthand Technology Leaders, 79.1%

Source: *Your Money*, Top 400 (annual), June/July, 1999, p. 53.

★3291★
TOP WORLD STOCK MUTUAL FUNDS, 1998
Ranked by: One year annualized return, in percent. **Remarks:** Includes 3- and 5-year returns, sales charge, minimum investment, risk, 1st quarter 1999 percentage, M-star rating and phone number. **Number listed:** 25

1. Pilgrims Worldwide Growth A, with 33.6%
2. Citizens Global Equity, 26.0%
3. Maxus Laureate, 23.4%
4. Deutsche Top 50 World A, 22.3%
5. Warburg Pincus Glb Post Venture, 20.2%
6. New Perspective, 17.9%
7. Janus Worldwide, 15.4%
8. Putnam Global Growth A, 15.1%
9. Dreyfus Premier Worldwide, 14.1%
10. Idex JCC Global A, 13.7%

Source: *Your Money*, Top 400 (annual), June/July, 1999, p. 52+.

★3292★
TOP WORLDWIDE BOND MUTUAL FUNDS, 1998
Ranked by: One year annualized return, in percent. **Remarks:** Includes 3- and 5-year returns, sales charge, minimum investment, risk, 1st quarter 1999 percentage, M-star rating and phone number. **Number listed:** 25

1. Guinness Flight Global Government., with 11.2%
2. Managers Global Bond, 11.1%
3. Strong International Bond, 11.0%
4. American Cent International Bond, 10.1%
5. Northern International Fixed-Income, 9.7%
6. Scudder International Bond, 9.1%
7. Payden & Rygel Global, 9.0%
8. Scudder Global Bond, 8.3%
8. Alliance North American Government., 8.3%
10. Vontoble International Bond, 7.9%

Source: *Your Money*, Top 400 (annual), June/July, 1999, p. 58.

★3293★
WEIRDEST FUND NAMES, 1998
Ranked by: Unusual fund names. **Number listed:** 10

1. Bullfinch Unrestricted
2. Delaware Pooled Labor Select International Equity
3. Fleming Fledging
4. Gabelli Global Interactive Coach Potato
5. Grand Prix
6. Hennessy Leveraged Dogs
7. Morgan FunShares
8. Noah
9. Pelican
10. World Sand Hill Portfolio Manager

Source: *Mutual Funds*, November, 1998, p. 61.

★3294★
WORST EQUITY MUTUAL FUNDS, 1999
Ranked by: Total return, in percent. **Number listed:** 50

1. Profunds Ultrashort OTC Investments, with -29.91%
2. American Heritage, -26.32%
3. Franklin Global Health Care A, -19.45%
4. Potomac OTC/Short, -18.09%
5. Fidelity Select Medical Delivery, -16.70%
6. U.S. Global Investors World Gold, -16.10%
7. Parkstone Small Cap Investments A, -15.26%
8. Fairport Midwest Growth, -15.06%
9. Rydex Arktos Investments, -14.59%
10. Growth Fund of Spain A, -14.52%

Source: *Business Week*, The Best (annual), June 14, 1999, p. 155.

Mutual Funds--Europe

★3295★
TOP EUROPEAN INVESTMENT TRUSTS, 1997-1998
Ranked by: Value of 1,000 European Currency Units (ECUs) invested over one year, from August 29, 1997 to August 29, 1998. **Number listed:** 12

1. Henderson Eurotrusts Units, with ECUs1,363.84
2. Perpetual European, ECUs1,335.48
3. Fleming European Fledging, ECUs1,315.07
4. Gartmore European, ECUs1,291.40
5. Foreign & Colonial Eurotrust, ECUs1,289.74
6. Charter European, ECUs1,203.66
7. Fleming Continental European, ECUs1,182.23
8. TR European Growth, ECUs1,181.95
9. Fidelity European Values, ECUs1,123.09
10. Aberdeen European, ECUs1,084.18

Source: *Investors Chronicle*, September, 1998, p. 38.

★3296★
TOP EUROPEAN INVESTMENT TRUSTS, 1993-1998
Ranked by: Value of 1,000 European Currency Units (ECUs) invested over five years, from August 31, 1993 to August 31, 1998. **Number listed:** 11

1. TR European Growth, with ECUs3,403.95
2. Gartmore European, ECUs2,361.01
3. Charter European, ECUs2,229.32
4. Foreign & Col Eurotrust, ECUs2,132.71
5. Fleming European Fledging, ECUs2,074.07
6. Henderson Eurotrust Units, ECUs2,054.76
7. Fidclity Europcan Values, ECUs1,941.44
8. Perpetual European, ECUs1,920.78
9. Fleming Continental European, ECUs1,822.70
10. Martin Currie European, ECUs1,727.47

Source: *Investors Chronicle*, September, 1998, p. 38.

Mutual Funds--Great Britain

★3297★
BEST PERFORMING GROWTH & INCOME UNIT TRUSTS IN THE UNITED KINGDOM, 1997-1998
Ranked by: Value of 1,000 British pounds invested over one year, from Sept. 30, 1997 to Sept. 30, 1998. **Number listed:** 10

1. Newton Income, with £1,105.05
2. CF Quantock Inc., £1,064.77
3. Royal Bank of Scot Income, £1,039.56
4. CF Net PEP Tracker, £1,036.65
5. Edinburgh UK Growth, £1,034.73
6. BWD Balanced Portfolio, £1,023.75

7. Five Arrows GI UK Equity Income A, £1,021.60
8. Family Asset, £1,021.33
9. Five Arrows GI UK Major Cos A, £1,019.78
10. Fidelity Growth & Income, £1,018.46

Source: *Investor's Chronicle*, November 6, 1998, p. 48.

★3298★
BEST PERFORMING INCOME & GROWTH INVESTMENT TRUSTS IN THE UNITED KINGDOM, 1997-1998
Ranked by: Value of 1,000 British pounds invested over 1 year, from Sept. 30, 1997 to Sept. 30, 1998. **Number listed:** 10

1. Fleming Income & Capital Units, with £1,144.91
2. Gartmore Br Income & Growth Units, £1,103.67
3. Dunedin Income Growth, £1,102.00
4. Merchants, £1,090.60
5. Temple Bar, £1,018.70
6. Foreign & Colonial Income Growth, £999.48
7. City of London, £991.63
8. Murray Income, £971.42
9. Investors Capital Units, £963.41
10. Lowland, £963.12

Source: *Investor's Chronicle*, November 6, 1998, p. 50.

★3299★
TOP ECOLOGY UNIT TRUSTS IN THE UNITED KINGDOM, 1999*
Ranked by: Percent change, over one year. **Number listed:** 5

1. TSB Environmental Investor, with 19.39%%
2. NPI Global Care, 12.65%
3. CIS Environmental, 11.35%
4. Jupiter Ecology, -0.44%
5. Clerical Med Evergreen, -0.79%

Source: *Investors Chronicle*, January 22, 1999, p. 99.

★3300★
TOP ETHICAL UNIT TRUSTS IN THE UNITED KINGDOM, 1999*
Ranked by: Percent change, over one year. **Number listed:** 5

1. NPI Global Care Income, with 13.96%
2. Henderson Ethical, 13.03%
3. FPAM Exempt Ethical, 12.47%
4. Equitable Ethical, 2.04%
5. Family Charities Ethical, 0.91%

Source: *Investors Chronicle*, January 22, 1999, p. 99.

★3301★
TOP INCOME INVESTMENT TRUSTS IN THE UNITED KINGDOM BY HIGH INCOME, 1998
Ranked by: Three-year percent change, in U.K. income growth. **Number listed:** 5

1. Aberdeen High Income, with 96.65%
2. M&G Recovery Geared Unit, 96.42%
3. Dartmoor, 95.07%
4. Shires Income, 86.88%
5. Glasgow Income, 85.47%

Source: *Investors Chronicle*, January 22, 1999, p. 22.

★3302★
TOP INCOME INVESTMENT TRUSTS IN THE UNITED KINGDOM BY INCOME & RESIDUAL CAP, 1998
Ranked by: Three-year percent change, in U.K. income growth. **Number listed:** 5

1. J Fry Utilities (2003), with 261.97%
2. J Fry Euro Utilities (2004), 194.22%
3. Henderson Eurotrust (2002), 149.53%
4. SR Pan-European (2001), 123.00%
5. Edinburgh Income (2000), 120.91%

Source: *Investors Chronicle*, January 22, 1999, p. 22.

★3303★
TOP INCOME INVESTMENT TRUSTS IN THE UNITED KINGDOM BY INCOME SHARES, 1998
Ranked by: Three-year percent change, in income shares. **Number listed:** 5

1. Rights & Issues Inc. (2001), with 88.78%
2. Jove Inc. (2004), 85.55%
3. M&G Recovery Inc. (2002), 69.78%
4. Framlington I&C Inc. (2008), 55.6%
5. Jupiter Geared Inc. (1999), 53.8%

Source: *Investors Chronicle*, January 22, 1999, p. 108.

★3304★
TOP INCOME INVESTMENT TRUSTS IN THE UNITED KINGDOM, 1998
Ranked by: Three year percent change, in U.K. income growth. **Number listed:** 5

1. Dunedin Income Growth, with 72.51%
2. Temple Bar, 66.71%
3. Fleming Inc. & Cap Units, 66.05%
4. Merchants, 64.67%
5. City of London, 63.06%

Source: *Investors Chronicle*, January 22, 1999, p. 22.

★3305★
TOP INVESTMENT TRUSTS IN THE UNITED KINGDOM, 1997-1998
Ranked by: Value of 1,000 British pounds invested over 1 year, from Nov. 28, 1997, to Nov. 30, 1998. **Number listed:** 20

1. Jove Gap, with £3,036.36
2. Johnson Fry Utilities, £2,419.42
3. Second St. David's Capital, £2,102.04
4. Finsbury Income & Growth Capital, £1,821.43
5. Aberdeen Preferred Income, £1,769.73
6. Jupiter Split Capital, £1,758.87
7. Johnson Fry European Utilities, £1,729.00
8. Fulcrum Cap, £1,696.00
9. Martin Currie Inc., £1,621,62
10. Edinburgh Income, £1,574.90

Source: *Investor's Chronicle*, December 4, 1998, p. 58.

★3306★
TOP PERFORMING INVESTMENT TRUSTS IN THE UNITED KINGDOM, 1997-1998
Ranked by: Value of 1,000 British pounds invested over 1 year, from June 30, 1997 to June 30, 1998. **Number listed:** 20

1. BFS Income & Growth, with £6,698.95
2. St. Davids 2nd Residual, £6,521.74
3. Jove Cap, £6,200.00
4. Framlington Dual Cap, £3,421.43
5. Scottish National Cap, £3,383.26
6. M&G Recovery Cap, £2,987.50
7. Finsbury Income & Growth Cap, £2,837.21
8. Schroder Split Fund Cap, £2,752.38
9. Fulcrum Cap, £2,722.89
10. M&G Recovery, £2,331.90

Source: *Investor's Chronicle*, August 7, 1998, p. 47.

★3307★
TOP PERFORMING UNIT TRUSTS IN THE UNITED KINGDOM, 1997-1998
Ranked by: Value of 1,000 British pounds invested over 1 year, from June 30, 1997 to June 30, 1998. **Number listed:** 20

1. Exeter Capital Growth, with £1,713.97
2. Baring German Growth, £1,623.84
3. Royal London European Growth, £1,621.30
4. INVESCO European Growth, £1,616.25
5. Jupiter Financial Opportunity, £1,590.04
6. GT UK Smaller Cos Acc, £1,588.32

7. Dresdner RCM European Special, £1,586.86
8. INVESCO European Small Cos, £1,582.67
9. Baring UK Smaller Cos, £1,573.45
10. Baring European Growth, £1,544.08

Source: *Investor's Chronicle*, August 7, 1998, p. 47.

★3308★
TOP UNIT TRUSTS IN THE UNITED KINGDOM, 1997-1998
Ranked by: Value of 1,000 British pounds invested over 1 year, from Nov. 28, 1997, to Nov. 30, 1998. **Number listed:** 20

1. Baring German Growth, with £1,718.60
2. Newton European, £1,550.95
3. CF Odey European Acc, £1,504.43
4. Jupiter Financial Opportunity, £1,486.31
5. OM Paribas French Equities, £1,484.31
6. Gartmore European, £1,481.75
7. Jupiter UK Growth, £1,472.74
8. CGU PPT Europe Growth, £1,468.04
9. INVESCO European Growth, £1,456.44
10. INVESCO European Small Cos, £1,453.07

Source: *Investor's Chronicle*, December 4, 1998, p. 58.

★3309★
WORST PERFORMING INVESTMENT TRUSTS IN THE UNITED KINGDOM, 1997-1998
Ranked by: Value of 1,000 British pounds invested over 1 year, from Nov. 28, 1997, to Nov. 30, 1998. **Number listed:** 20

1. F&C Latin America, with £691.61
2. Commodities Trust, £685.99
3. Govett Emerging Markets, £685.04
4. Morgan Grenfell Latin America, £682.86
5. Prelude, £682.69
6. INVESCO Enterprise, £679.92
7. New Zealand, £670.26
8. Tea Plantations, £655.17
9. Fleming Chinese, £654.47
10. Murray Emerging Economies, £648.62

Source: *Investor's Chronicle*, December 4, 1998, p. 58.

★3310★
WORST PERFORMING UNIT TRUSTS IN THE UNITED KINGDOM, 1997-1998
Ranked by: Value of 1,000 British pounds invested over 1 year, from Nov. 28, 1997, to Nov. 30, 1998. **Number listed:** 20

1. Old Mutual Latin America, with £765.45
2. Five Arrows Ptf Emerging Markets, £756.02
3. Baille Gifford Emerging Markets Growth, £743.94
4. NPI Latin America, £738.84
5. Martin Currie Emerging Markets, £737.92
6. Investec GF Asian Smaller Cos, £736.95
7. Save & Prosper Southern Africa, £720.46
8. Mercury Emerging Markets, £719.48
9. Aberdeen Prolific Latin America, £719.41
10. Perpetual Latin America, £714.70

Source: *Investor's Chronicle*, December 4, 1998, p. 58.

Mutual Funds--Management

★3311★
TOP FUND MANAGERS, 1999*
Ranked by: Rating scale. **Remarks:** Also notes objective, fund started date, manager, and 1- and 3-year return. **Number listed:** 100

1. Morgan Stanley Aggressive Equity Inst'l A, with 16.6 points
2. Janus Overseas, 14.9
3. Salomon Brothers Capital, 11.7
4. State Steet Research Aurora, 11.5
5. Oakmark Fund, 11.4
6. Lord Abbett Developing Growth A, 11.0
7. BT Investment International Equity, 10.8
8. Scout Worldwide, 9.5
9. Weitz Partners Value, 8.8
9. GAM International Class A, 8.8

Source: *Barron's*, July 20, 1998, p. 36.

Mutual Funds--New York Metropolitan Area

★3312★
LARGEST MUTUAL FUND COMPANIES IN THE NEW YORK AREA, 1998
Ranked by: Total assets, in millions of dollars. **Remarks:** Also notes assets by category, 12-month flows, and total funds. **Number listed:** 14

1. Smith Barney Advisors Inc., with $100,660.5 million
2. Morgan Stanley Dean Witter, $92,134.7
3. Dreyfus, $90,950.1
4. OppenheimerFunds Inc., $82,753.8
5. Prudential Securities Inc., $57,408.7
6. Alliance Fund Distributors, $50,050.1
7. BlackRock Funds, $49,894.84
8. Goldman Sachs Asset Management, $46,357.9
9. Chase Manhattan Bank, $38,601.3
10. PaineWebber Inc., $37,030.1

Source: *Crain's New York Business*, (annual), November 16, 1998, p. 45+.

Nail Polish

★3313★
TOP BRANDS OF NAIL POLISH, 1998
Ranked by: Sales, in millions of dollars. **Number listed:** 10

1. Revlon, with $94.6 million
2. Maybelline, $51.5
3. Sally Hansen, $50.0
4. L'Oreal, $29.0
5. Cover Girl, $23.5
6. Wet 'n' Wild, $19.4
7. Almay, $11.6
8. Naturistics, $6.6
9. jane, $5.2
10. Max Factor, $4.6

Source: *MMR*, May 3, 1999, p. 25.

Nairobi Stock Exchange

★3314★
LARGEST LISTED COMPANIES ON THE NAIROBI STOCK EXCHANGE, 1997
Ranked by: Market value, in millions of U.S. dollars ($). **Number listed:** 20

1. Barclays Bank, with $251.5 million
2. Bamburi Cement, $223.7
3. Kenya Power & Lighting, $161.5
4. Kenya Commercial Bank, $146.9
5. Standard Chartered Bank, $128.9
6. Brooke Bond Kenya, $91.4
7. Firestone East Africa, $74.2
8. BAT Kenya, $63.8
9. Kenya Airways, $58.9
10. Kenya Breweries, $54.0

Source: *Euromoney*, SSB Guide to World Equity Markets (annual), 1998, p. 297.

★3315★
MOST ACTIVELY TRADED SHARES ON THE NAIROBI STOCK EXCHANGE, 1997
Ranked by: Turnover value, in millions of U.S. dollars ($). **Number listed:** 20

1. Kenya Power & Lighting, with $15.64 million
2. Kenya Commercial Bank, $14.94
3. Barclays Bank, $8.80
4. Kenya Airways, $5.85
5. Sasini, $5.82
6. NIC Bank, $5.39
7. Firestone, $5.04
8. Uchumi, $4.92
9. Kenya Breweries, $4.47
10. Bamburi, $3.27

Source: *Euromoney*, SSB Guide to World Equity Markets (annual), 1998, p. 297.

Natural Foods

★3316★
USE FREQUENCY OF NATURAL OR ORGANIC FOODS, 1998
Ranked by: Results of a consumer survey. **Number listed:** 5

1. Never, with 34%
2. 1 to 3 Times a Month, 27%
3. Less Than Once a Month, 19%
4. At Least One a Month, 17%
5. Not Sure, 3%

Source: *Supermarket Business*, November, 1998, p. 16.

Natural Gas—Pipelines

See: **Gas Pipelines**

Negotiation in Business

★3317★
TOP NEGOTIATION MISTAKES, 1998*
Ranked by: Listed by John Patrick Dolan, author of *Negotiate Like The Pros*. **Number listed:** 13

1. Wanting something too much
2. Believing that the other side has all of the power
3. Failing to recognize your own strengths
4. Getting hung up on one issue
5. Failing to see more than one option
6. Approaching negotiations with a win-lose mentality
7. Short term thinking that ruins long term relationships
8. Trying to squeeze out too much
9. Accepting opinions, statements, and feeling as facts
10. Accepting positions as final

Source: *Restaurant Hospitality*, November, 1998, p. 74.

New Jersey—Industries

★3318★
TOP EMPLOYERS IN NEW JERSEY, 1997
Ranked by: Number of employees. **Remarks:** Also notes contact information, revenue, and top executive. **Number listed:** 100

1. Wakefern Food Corp., with 34,669 employees
2. AT & T, 28,900
3. UPS, 18,000
4. Bell Atlantic Corp., 17,651
5. Lucent Technologies, 17,500
6. The Prudential Insurance Co., 17,405
7. Pathmark Stores Inc., 16,022
8. Johnson & Johnson, 11,000
9. Merrill Lynch & Co., 10,566
10. Public Service Enterprise Group, 10,400

Source: *New Jersey Business*, Book of Lists (annual), 1999, p. 22+.

New Products

★3319★
BEST SELLING NEW NONFOOD PRODUCTS, 1997
Ranked by: Sales, in millions of dollars. **Number listed:** 10

1. Nicoderm, with $243.6 million
2. Pampers Baby Fresh, $133.6
3. Dixie Everyday, $118.4
4. Biore Pore Perfect, $106.3
5. Colgate Whitening, $64.3
6. Crest Multicare, $58.2
7. Bounty Rise & Reuse, $57.6
8. Playtex Gentle Glide, $56.3
9. Clairol Hydrience, $54.7
10. Osteo Bi Flex 450, $54.1

Source: *MMR*, December 14, 1998, p. 14.

New York Metropolitan Area--Industries

★3320★
NEW YORK CITY'S LARGEST EMPLOYERS, 1998
Ranked by: Number of New York City employees. **Remarks:** Also notes contact information, revenue figures, and top executive. **Number listed:** 25

1. Mount Sinai NYU Health, with 35,432 employees
2. Citigroup Inc., 25,693
3. Bell Atlantic Corp., 24,400
4. New York Presbyterian Healthcare Network, 24,000
5. Chase Manhattan Corp., 19,300
6. Continuum Health Partners Inc., 15,500
7. Consolidated Edison Inc., 12,153

8. Time Warner, 11,800
9. Morgan Stanley Dean Witter & Co., 10,818
10. Columbia University, 10,031

Source: *Crain's New York Business*, May 24, 1999, p. 33.

★3321★
TOP COMPANIES IN THE NEW YORK METROPOLITAN AREA BY REVENUE, 1998
Ranked by: Revenue, in millions of dollars. **Remarks:** Also notes contact information, revenue figures and number of employees. **Number listed:** 500

1. International Business Machines Corp., with $81,667 million
2. Citigroup Inc., $76,431
3. Philip Morris, $57,813
4. AT & T, $53,223
5. Merrill Lynch & Co., $35,715
6. American International Group Inc., $33,239
7. Chase Manhattan Corp., $32,379
8. Texaco Inc., $31,707
9. Bell Atlantic Corp., $31,565
10. Morgan Stanley Dean Witter & Co., $31,131

Source: *Crain's New York Business*, May 31, 1999, p. 47+.

New York Stock Exchange

★3322★
BEST PERFORMERS ON THE NEW YORK STOCK EXCHANGE, 1998
Ranked by: Percent change. **Remarks:** Also notes closing price and net change. **Number listed:** 10

1. America Online, with 585.6%
2. Sonic Automotive Inc., 258.4%
3. Nokia Corp., 246.6%
4. National Media, 242.0%
5. Best Buy, 232.9%
6. EMC, 209.8%
7. Ann Taylor Stores, 194.9%
8. Group 1 Auto, 186.9%
9. Brooke Group, 182.6%
10. Mossimo, 182.4%

Source: *Barron's*, January 4, 1999, p. 30.

★3323★
FASTEST GROWING COMPANIES ON THE NEW YORK STOCK EXCHANGE, 1998*
Ranked by: Growth rate over a five year period, in percent. **Remarks:** Also notes share information, type of industry, and headquarters location. **Number listed:** 279

1. Santa Fe International Corp., with 169%
2. Thomas & Betts, 144%
3. International Business Machines, 131%
4. Ha Lo Industries, 98%
5. Imperial Bancorp, 95%
6. Delta Financial Corp., 94%
7. Texas Industries, 87%
8. Varco International Inc., 83%
9. Precision Castparts Corp., 81%
10. Confinancial Corp., 77%

Source: *Equities*, July, 1998, p. 35+.

★3324★
LARGEST NEW YORK STOCK EXCHANGE BLOCK TRANSACTION BY SHARE VOLUME, 1998
Ranked by: Number of shares. **Remarks:** Also notes NYSE symbol. **Number listed:** 10

1. Amoco, with 52,671,000 shares
2. Chrysler, 27,573,300
3. Infinity Broadcasting, 24,076,000
4. Conoco, 20,342,400
5. Fox Entertainment, 19,300,000
6. Cendent, 17,758,100
7. America Online, 16,772,500
8. Amoco, 13,059,000
9. Media One Group, 11,167,700
10. Carnival Corp., 10,362,100

Source: *New York Stock Exchange*, New York Stock Exchange Fact Book (annual), 1998, p. 17.

★3325★
LEADING COMPANIES ON THE NEW YORK STOCK EXCHANGE, 1998
Ranked by: Market value, in millions of dollars. **Remarks:** Also notes listed shares. **Number listed:** 50

1. General Electric Co., with $379,045 million
2. Coca-Cola Co., $231,052
3. Merck & Co., $219,172
4. Exxon Corp., $218,129
5. Wal-Mart Stores, $187,308
6. International Business Machines, $181,090
7. Pfizer Inc., $173,019
8. Philip Morris, $150,119
9. Bristol-Myers Squibb, $146,204
10. AT & T, $136,825

Source: *New York Stock Exchange Fact Book*, (annual), New York Stock Exchange, 1998, p. 40.

★3326★
LEADING COMPANIES ON THE NEW YORK STOCK EXCHANGE, 1997
Ranked by: Market value, in millions of dollars. **Number listed:** 20

1. General Electric, with $287,823 million
2. Coca-Cola, $222,963
3. Exxon Corp., $176,967
4. Merck & Co. Inc., $174,002
5. Philip Morris, $116,447
6. Pfizer, $113,018
7. Bristol-Myers Squibb, $112,547
8. Johnson & Johnson, $102,737
8. International Business Machines, $102,737
10. AT & T, $101,796

Source: *Euromoney*, SSB Guide to World Equity Markets (annual), 1998, p. 536.

★3327★
MOST ACTIVELY TRADED SHARES ON THE NEW YORK STOCK EXCHANGE BY SHARE VOLUME, 1998
Ranked by: Share volume, in millions of shares. **Remarks:** Also includes previous year ranking. **Number listed:** 50

1. Compaq Computer, with 2,868.4 million
2. Philip Morris, 1,457.4
3. Cendant Corp., 1,436.1
4. Lucent Technologies, 1,167.1
5. AT & T, 1,165.7
6. America Online, 1,159.2
7. General Electric, 1,031.8
8. Micron Technology, 911.0
9. International Business Machines, 905.9
10. Boeing Co., 866.5

Source: *New York Stock Exchange*, New York Stock Exchange Fact Book (annual), 1998, p. 14.

★3328★
MOST ACTIVELY TRADED SHARES ON THE NEW YORK STOCK EXCHANGE, 1997
Ranked by: Trading value, in millions of dollars. **Number listed:** 20
1. International Business Machines, with $104,348 million
2. Compaq Computer, $92,652
3. Telecom Brasil, $79,465
4. General Electric, $64,765
5. Merck, $61,813
6. Philip Morris, $60,530
7. Citicorp, $58,846
8. Chase Manhattan New, $58,406
9. Texas Instruments, $46,799
10. Coca-Cola, $46,459

Source: *Euromoney*, SSB Guide to World Equity Markets (annual), 1998, p. 532.

★3329★
TOP SHARE VOLUME DAYS IN NEW YORK STOCK EXCHANGE HISTORY, 1998*
Ranked by: Share volume. **Number listed:** 10
1. September 1, 1998, with 1,204.9 million shares
2. October 28, 1997, 1,195.8
3. October 8, 1998, 1,109.5
4. October 7, 1998, 964.5
5. August 27, 1998, 934.7
6. August 31, 1998, 914.7
7. September 23, 1998, 897.5
8. October 2, 1998, 897.3
9. September 2, 1998, 891.6
10. October 1, 1998, 886.7

Source: *Wall Street Journal*, October 9, 1998, p. C1.

★3330★
WORST PERFORMERS ON THE NEW YORK STOCK EXCHANGE, 1998
Ranked by: Percent change. **Remarks:** Also notes closing price and net change. **Number listed:** 10
1. Philip Services Corp., with -98.3%
2. Penncorp Financial, -97.2%
3. Complete Management, -96.9%
4. CML Group, -94.8%
5. PHP Hither, -94.6%
6. So Pac Fd Corp., -93.8%
7. Texfi Industries, -93.0%
8. FirstPlus Financial, -92.8%
9. EA Industries, -90.9%
10. Zenith Electronics, -90.8%

Source: *Barron's*, January 4, 1999, p. 30.

New Zealand Stock Exchange

★3331★
LEADING COMPANIES LISTED ON THE NEW ZEALAND STOCK EXCHANGE, 1997
Ranked by: Market value, in New Zealand dollars (NZ$). **Number listed:** 20
1. Telecom Corp. of New Zealand, with NZ$14,634.2 million
2. Carter Holt Harvey, NZ$4,601.9
3. Brierley Investments, NZ$3,295.4
4. Lion Nathan, NZ$2,144.0
5. Fletcher Challenge Energy, NZ$2,105.6
6. Fletcher Challenge Paper, NZ$1,536.8
7. Fletcher Challenge Building, NZ$1,226.5
8. Fletcher Challenge Forests, NZ$1,165.3
9. Independent Newspapers, NZ$1,109.7
10. Wilson & Horton, NZ$1,033.1

Source: *Euromoney*, SSB Guide to World Equity Markets (annual), 1998, p. 361.

★3332★
MOST ACTIVELY TRADED SHARES ON THE NEW ZEALAND STOCK EXCHANGE, 1997
Ranked by: Turnover value, in millions of New Zealand dollars (NZ$). **Number listed:** 20
1. Telecom Corp. of New Zealand, with NZ$3,562.3 million
2. Fletcher Challenge Energy, NZ$1,169.3
3. Fletcher Challenge Paper, NZ$1,117.4
4. Lion Nathan, NZ$1,031.0
5. Carter Holt Harvey, NZ$1,030.7
6. Brierley Investments, NZ$1,004.9
7. Air New Zealand B, NZ$798.9
8. Fletcher Challenge Forests, NZ$633.4
9. Fletcher Challenge Building, NZ$608.4
10. Telstra, NZ$286.4

Source: *Euromoney*, SSB Guide to World Equity Markets (annual), 1998, p. 361.

Newspaper Publishers and Publishing

★3333★
TOP NEWSPAPER PUBLISHERS, 1997
Ranked by: Revenue, in millions of dollars. **Remarks:** Also notes 1996 revenue. **Number listed:** 20
1. Gannet Co., with $3,582.0 million
2. Knight Ridder, $2,770.0
3. New York Times Co., $2,557.1
4. Advance Publications, $2,385.7
5. Times Mirror, $2,196.1
6. Dow Jones & Co., $1,601.0
7. Tribune Co., $1,437.0
8. Cox Enterprises, $1,050.0
9. McClatchy Co., $998.9
10. Hearst Corp., $949.8

Source: *Advertising Age*, August 17, 1998, p. S10.

Newspapers—Advertising

See: **Advertising, Newspaper**

Newspapers--Editions

★3334★
TOP DAILY NEWSPAPERS, 1998
Ranked by: Daily circulation. **Number listed:** 25
1. *The Wall Street Journal*, with 1,740,450 papers
2. *USA Today*, 1,653,428
3. *Los Angeles Times*, 1,067,540
4. *The New York Times*, 1,066,658
5. *The Washington Post*, 759,122
6. *Daily News*, 723,143

7. *Chicago Tribune A*, 651,687
8. *Newsday*, 572,444
9. *Houston Chronicle B.*, 550,763
10. *Dallas Morning News A.*, 504,357

Source: *Advertising Age*, November 9, 1998, p. 36.

Newspapers--Editions--Detroit Metropolitan Area

★3335★
LARGEST DAILY NEWSPAPERS IN THE DETROIT AREA, 1998
Ranked by: Daily circulation. **Remarks:** Also notes previous year circulation. **Number listed:** 6

1. *Detroit Free Press*, with 383,638 papers
2. *The Detroit News*, 246,302
3. *The Oakland Press*, 83,694
4. *The Macomb Daily*, 58,370
5. *The Ann Arbor News*, 57,825
6. *The Daily Tribune*, 21,012

Source: *Crain's Detroit Business*, Crain's Book of Lists Detroit (annual), December 28, 1998, p. 124.

★3336★
LARGEST WEEKLY NEWSPAPER COMPANIES IN THE DETROIT AREA, 1997
Ranked by: Total circulation. **Remarks:** Also notes contact information, 1996 circulation figures, and newspapers published. **Number listed:** 15

1. HomeTown Communications Network, with 348,718 papers
2. C&G Publishing, 329,817
3. Heritage Newspapers, 232,198
4. Metro Times, Inc., 106,605
5. Voice Communications Corp., 65,287
6. The Michigan Citizen, 52,193
7. Anteebo Publishers, 50,271
8. SCN Communications Group, 49,710
9. Michigan Community Newspapers, 48,000
10. The Michigan Chronicle, 45,217

Source: *Crain's Detroit Business*, Crain's Book of List Detroit (annual), December 28, 1998, p. 124.

Newspapers--Editions--Florida

★3337★
LARGEST DAILY NEWSPAPERS IN FLORIDA, 1998
Ranked by: Daily circulation. **Remarks:** Also notes contact information, number of employees, parent company, year founded, and publisher. **Number listed:** 42

1. *St.Petersburg Times*, with 366,212 papers
2. *Miami Herald*, 353,348
3. *Sun-Sentinel*, 273,967
4. *Orlando Sentinel*, 267,737
5. *Tampa Tribune*, 249,760
6. *Palm Beach Post*, 187,943
7. *Florida Times-Union*, 175,574
8. *Sarasota Herald Tribune*, 120,773
9. *Daytona Beach News-Journal*, 102,406
10. *News-Press*, 99,161

Source: *Florida Trend*, TopRank Florida (annual), 1999, p. 67+.

Newspapers--Editions--Los Angeles County (CA)

★3338★
LARGEST DAILY NEWSPAPERS IN LOS ANGELES COUNTY, 1998
Ranked by: Daily Circulation. **Remarks:** Also notes contact information, parent company, year founded, and top executive. **Number listed:** 10

1. *Los Angeles Times*, with 1,095,007 papers
2. *Investor's Business Daily*, 248,728
3. *Daily News*, 200,463
4. *Press-Telegram*, 106,485
5. *La Opinion*, 102,183
6. *Daily Breeze*, 101,538
7. *San Gabriel Valley Tribune*, 58,582
8. *Pasadena Star-News*, 42,051
9. *Antelope Valley Press*, 39,413
10. *Daily Variety*, 27,941

Source: *Los Angeles Business Journal*, Book of Lists (annual), 1999, p. 66.

Newspapers--Editions--New York Metropolitan Area

★3339★
LARGEST NEW YORK DAILY NEWSPAPERS BY CIRCULATION, 1998
Ranked by: Daily Circulation. **Remarks:** Also notes contact information, publisher, editor, 1997 circulation figures, number of employees, and ad rates. **Number listed:** 9

1. *The New York Times*, with 1,110,143 papers
2. *Daily News*, 727,089
3. *Newsday*, 571,283
4. *New York Post*, 432,707
5. *The Star-Ledger*, 405,333
6. *The Record*, 145,185
7. *Gannett Suburban Newspapers*, 113,886
8. *Staten Island Advance*, 69,231
9. *Jersey Journal*, 50,386

Source: *Crain's New York Business*, September 28, 1998, p. 21.

Nonferrous Metal Industries

★3340★
LEADING NONFERROUS METALS AND FERROALLOYS COMPANIES BY SALES, 1998
Ranked by: Sales, in millions of dollars. **Remarks:** Also notes 1998 profits and profit ratios and share data. **Number listed:** 11

1. Alcoa, with $15,340 million
2. Alcan Aluminum, $7,789
3. Reynolds Metals, $5,859
4. Phelps Dodge, $3,063
5. Asarco, $2,233
6. Inco, $1,766
7. Kennametal, $1,678
8. Newmont Mining, $1,454
9. Cominco, $1,062

10. Homestake Mining, $803

Source: *Chemical Week*, Chemical Week 300 (annual), May 12, 1999, p. 52.

Nonprofit Institutions

See also: **Foundations, Charitable and Educational**

★3341★

TOP COMMUNITY FOUNDATIONS RANKED BY REVENUE, 1997

Ranked by: Total revenue. **Remarks:** Also notes previous year results and government support. **Number listed:** 33

1. New York Community Trust, with $311,120,195
2. Cleveland Foundation, $284,963,799
3. United Jewish Appeal, $175,194,011
4. Greater Kansas City Community Foundation, $110,902,840
5. Jewish Community/Federation of Cleveland, $94,939,853
6. Boston Foundation, $89,913,733
7. Jewish Federation of Metro Detroit, $87,538,844
8. California Community Foundation, $73,058,555
9. The San Francisco Foundation, $60,372,096
10. Communities Foundation of Texas, $59,575,220

Source: *Nonprofit Times*, NPT 100 (annual), November, 1998, p. 36.

★3342★

TOP CONSERVATION ORGANIZATIONS RANKED BY TOTAL REVENUE, 1997

Ranked by: Total revenue. **Remarks:** Also notes 1996 and 1995 income and sources of income. **Number listed:** 5

1. The Nature Conservancy, with $421,353,191
2. Wildlife Conservation Society, $121,583,427
3. National Wildlife Federation, $101,933,311
4. Ducks Unlimited Inc., $88,536,352
5. World Wildlife Fund, $85,133,471

Source: *Nonprofit Times*, NPT 100 (annual), November, 1998, p. 50.

★3343★

TOP CULTURAL ORGANIZATIONS RANKED BY TOTAL REVENUE, 1997

Ranked by: Total revenue. **Remarks:** Also notes 1996 and 1995 income and sources of income. **Number listed:** 9

1. Smithsonian Institution, with $380,706,500
2. The Metropolitan Museum of Art, $328,830,085
3. Metropolitan Opera Association, $183,021,000
4. National Gallery of Art, $164,576,528
5. Art Institute of Chicago, $161,077,137
6. American Museum of Natural History, $147,359,182
7. Museum of Modern Art, $139,942,027
8. Colonial Williamsburg Foundation, $136,126,743
9. J.F. Kennedy Center for the Performing Arts, $125,223,964

Source: *Nonprofit Times*, NPT 100 (annual), November, 1998, p. 48.

★3344★

TOP EDUCATIONAL ORGANIZATIONS RANKED BY TOTAL REVENUE, 1997

Ranked by: Total revenue. **Remarks:** Also notes 1996 and 1995 income and sources of income. **Number listed:** 6

1. United Negro College Fund, with $98,590,300
2. Citizen's Scholarship Fund of America, $95,590,300
3. Junior Achievement Inc., $91,453,864
4. American Society for Technion-Israel Institute of Technology, $85,971,789
5. Cold Spring Harbor Laboratory, $74,741,221
6. Population Council, $67,380,023

Source: *Nonprofit Times*, NPT 100 (annual), November, 1998, p. 50.

★3345★

TOP HEALTH ORGANIZATIONS RANKED BY TOTAL REVENUE, 1997

Ranked by: Total revenue. **Remarks:** Also notes 1996 and 1995 income and sources of income. **Number listed:** 19

1. Shriners Hospitals for Children, with $1,393,689,000
2. American Cancer Society, $540,530,000
3. National Easter Seal Society, $483,688,000
4. American Heart Association, $398,669,000
5. ALSAC-St.Jude's Children's Research Hospital, $335,680,432
6. City of Hope, $249,275,133
7. March of Dimes, $167,172,000
8. American Lung Association, $156,309,000
9. Fox Chase Cancer Center, $143,334,421
10. American Diabetes Association, $115,752,698

Source: *Nonprofit Times*, NPT 100 (annual), November, 1998, p. 44.

★3346★

TOP HUMAN SERVICE ORGANIZATIONS RANKED BY TOTAL REVENUE, 1997

Ranked by: Total revenue. **Remarks:** Also notes 1996 and 1995 income and sources of income. **Number listed:** 25

1. The National Council of YMCA's, with $2,859,886,000
2. Salvation Army, $2,500,000,000
3. Catholic Charities USA, $2,218,938,135
4. American Red Cross, $1,933,848,803
5. Goodwill Industries International, $1,360,000,000
6. Boy Scouts of America, $648,630,000
7. YWCA of the USA, $636,208,666
8. Girl Scouts of the USA, $605,294,000
9. Planned Parenthood Federation of America, $530,900,000
10. Boys & Girls Club of America, $529,755,178

Source: *Nonprofit Times*, NPT 100 (annual), November, 1998, p. 38.

★3347★

TOP IN-KIND ORGANIZATIONS RANKED BY TOTAL REVENUE, 1997

Ranked by: Total revenue. **Remarks:** Also notes 1996 and 1995 income and sources of income. **Number listed:** 9

1. Fidelity Investments Charitable Gift Fund, with $519,216,867
2. Second Harvest, $402,530,011
3. Gifts in Kind International, $292,677,884
4. Larry Jones International Ministries, $163,858,949
5. Americares Foundation, $157,201,697
6. Map International, $148,047,220
7. National Association for Exchange of Independent Resources, $113,185,821
8. Project HOPE, $109,141,000
9. Christian Aid Ministries, $104,710,163

Source: *Nonprofit Times*, NPT 100 (annual), November, 1998, p. 46.

★3348★

TOP NONPROFIT ORGANIZATIONS RANKED BY INCOME, 1997

Ranked by: Income, in dollars. **Remarks:** Also notes 1996 income and sources of income. **Number listed:** 100

1. The National Council of YMCA's, with $2,859,886,000
2. Salvation Army, $2,500,000,000
3. Catholic Charities USA, $2,218,938,135
4. American Red Cross, $1,933,848,803
5. Shriners Hospitals for Children, $1,393,689,000
6. Goodwill Industries International, $1,360,000,000
7. Boy Scouts of America, $648,630,000
8. YWCA of the USA, $636,208,666
9. Girl Scouts of the USA, $605,294,000
10. American Cancer Society, $540,530,000

Source: *Nonprofit Times*, NPT 100 (annual), November, 1998, p. 40+.

★3349★
TOP RELIEF ORGANIZATIONS RANKED BY TOTAL REVENUE, 1997
Ranked by: Total revenue. **Remarks:** Also notes 1996 and 1995 income and sources of income. **Number listed:** 10

1. CARE, with $362,526,000
2. Habitat for Humanity, $357,510,000
3. World Vision, $348,357,000
4. Catholic Relief Services, $218,562,000
5. Save the Children, $131,291,113
6. Christian Children's Fund, $117,756,064
7. Inernational Rescue Committee, $82,619,356
8. US Committee for UNICEF, $67,026,000
9. Compassion International, $66,783,452
10. Children International, $65,496,007

Source: *Nonprofit Times*, NPT 100 (annual), November, 1998, p. 52.

★3350★
TOP RELIGIOUS ORGANIZATIONS RANKED BY TOTAL REVENUE, 1997
Ranked by: Total revenue. **Remarks:** Also notes 1996 and 1995 income and sources of income. **Number listed:** 9

1. Campus Crusade for Christ, with $266,587,000
2. The Christian and Missionary Alliance, $126,049,716
3. American Bible Study, $118,942,137
4. Billy Graham Evangelistic Association, $108,074,687
5. Focus on the Family, $103,886,009
6. Wycliffe Bible Translators, $99,077,000
7. Young Life, $77,578,450
8. The Navigators, $69,240,000
9. Promise Keepers, $68,089,484

Source: *Nonprofit Times*, NPT 100 (annual), November, 1998, p. 46.

Nonprofit Institutions--Detroit Metropolitan Area

★3351★
LARGEST NONPROFIT ORGANIZATIONS IN THE DETROIT METROPOLITAN AREA, 1998
Ranked by: Operating budget for 1999, in millions of dollars. **Remarks:** Also notes contact information, top executive, and 1997 results. **Number listed:** 25

1. Barbara Ann Karmanos Cancer Institute, with $185.0 million
2. Macomb-Oakland Regional Center, $147.4
3. Wayne Community Living Services, $126.4
4. Lutheran Social Services of Michigan, $96.0
5. Focus: HOPE, $67.5
6. United Way Community Services, $63.0
7. Hospice of Michigan, $48.8
8. American Red Cross, $37.9
9. Detroit Institute of Arts, $37.1
10. Henry Ford Museum & Greenfield Village, $34.0

Source: *Crain's Detroit Business*, Crain's Book of Lists Detroit (annual), December 28, 1998, p. 68.

Nonprofit Institutions—New York Metropolitan Area (NY)

★3352★
LARGEST NONPROFIT ORGANIZATIONS IN THE NEW YORK METROPOLITAN AREA, 1997
Ranked by: Operating budget, in millions of dollars. **Remarks:** Also notes income and fund-raising expense figures, number of employees, and year-end date. **Number listed:** 25

1. United Jewish Appeal, with $186.9 million
2. Metropolitan Opera Association, $163.2
3. March of Dimes Birth Defects Foundation, $160.6
4. American Lung Association, $144.0
5. Metropolitan Museum of Art, $116.6
6. National Multiple Sclerosis Society, $103.2
7. Institute of International Education, $102.8
8. United Way of New York City, $102.5
9. Thirteen/WNET, $99.6
10. New York Foundling Hospital, $85.0

Source: *Crain's New York Business*, December 21, 1998, p. 12+.

Nonwoven Fabrics Industry--Brazil

★3353★
BRAZILIAN NONWOVEN PRODUCTION, 1997
Ranked by: Percentage of types in production. **Number listed:** 6

1. Needlepunch, with 40%
2. Sponbond, 33%
3. Chemical Bond, 13%
4. Thermal Bond, 9%
5. Melt Blown, 3%
6. Stitchbond, 2%

Source: *Nonwovens Industry*, December, 1998, p. 47.

Nonwoven Fabrics Industry--Export-Import Trade

★3354★
BIGGEST EXPORTERS OF ROLL GOODS TO THE U.S., 1998
Ranked by: Total weight of roll goods, in millions of kilograms. **Number listed:** 10

1. Canada, with 15.6 million
2. Israel, 11.0
3. Italy, 4.4
4. Japan, 4.3
5. Luxembourg, 4.0
6. Mexico, 3.3
7. United Kingdom, 2.6

8. Germany, 2.2
9. France, 2.0
10. Finland, 1.04

Source: *Nonwovens Industry*, May, 1999, p. 21.

Nonwoven Fabrics Industry, International

★3355★
BIGGEST IMPORTERS OF U.S. PRODUCED NONWOVEN ROLL GOODS, 1998
Ranked by: Total weight of nonwoven roll goods, in millions of kilograms. **Number listed:** 10

1. Mexico, with 35.2 million
2. Canada, 31.5
3. U.K., 12.4
4. Japan, 5.2
5. Belgium, 4.6
6. Netherlands, 3.9
7. Honduras, 3.8
8. Germany, 2.9
9. Australia, 2.3
10. China, 2.2

Source: *Nonwovens Industry*, May, 1999, p. 21.

★3356★
LEADING NONWOVENS PRODUCERS WORLDWIDE, 1998*
Ranked by: Worldwide roll goods sales, in millions of U.S. dollars ($). **Remarks:** Also notes U.S. sales. **Number listed:** 40

1. Freudenberg, with $1.37 billion
2. DuPont, $1.04
3. BBA, $842
4. PGI, $622
5. Kimberly-Clark, $578
6. Johns Manville/Hoechst, $410
7. Dexter Nonwovens, $300
8. Japan Vilene, $227
9. Akzo Nobel, $180
10. Amoco Fabrics & Fibers, $154

Source: *Nonwoven Industry*, September, 1998, p. 36.

Nuclear Reactors, International

★3357★
LEADERS IN GLOBAL NUCLEAR ENERGY, 1999*
Ranked by: Number of nuclear reactors. **Number listed:** 16

1. U.S., with 107 reactors
2. France, 59
3. Japan, 54
4. Britain, 35
5. Russia, 29
6. Germany, 20
7. Canada, 16
7. Ukraine, 16
9. South Korea, 12
9. Sweden, 12

Source: *New York Times*, March 7, 1999, p. 10WK.

Nursing

★3358★
LEADING ADVERTISERS IN NURSING PUBLICATIONS, 1998
Ranked by: Market share, in percent. **Remarks:** Also notes previous years' ranks and market share. **Number listed:** 12

1. Florida, with 4.63%
2. Nurses Service Organization, 4.00%
3. California, 3.33%
4. Texas, 2.76%
5. North Carolina, 2.67%
6. Johnson & Johnson Medical Division, 2.10%
7. Trav Corp., 1.99%
7. Medical Express, 1.99%
9. Becton Dickinson, 1.96%
10. Cross Country Healthcare, 1.82%

Source: *Medical Marketing & Media*, Healthcare Advertising Review (annual), April, 1999, p. 58.

★3359★
MOST ADVERTISED PRODUCTS AND SERVICES IN NURSING PUBLICATIONS, 1998
Ranked by: Market share, in percent. **Remarks:** Also notes previous years' ranks and market share. **Number listed:** 12

1. Nursinsur/Liability Insurance for Nurses, with 4.00%
2. American Mobile Nurses Recruitment, 2.00%
3. Travcorps Recruitment, 1.99%
3. Medical Express Recruitment, 1.99%
5. Cross Country Staffing Recruitment, 1.82%
6. Contract Management Services by Tx, 1.77%
7. Star-Med Recruitment, 1.74%
7. Army Reserve Med/Nat. Guard, 1.40%
9. Graceland College Recruitment, 1.13%
10. J.C. Penney Uniforms Catalog, .99%

Source: *Medical Marketing & Media*, Healthcare Advertising Review (annual), April, 1999, p. 58.

Nursing Homes

★3360★
LARGEST HEALTHCARE SYSTEMS OPERATING TWO OR MORE SKILLED-NURSING FACILITIES, 1998
Ranked by: Total number of staffed beds. **Remarks:** Also notes number of facilities. **Number listed:** 72

1. U.S. Department of Veteran Affairs, with 14,831 beds
2. Catholic Healthcare Network, 3,919
3. Catholic Health Initiatives, 3,340
4. Catholic Health East, 3,169
5. Fairview Health Services, 2,958
6. Adventist Health System, 2,250
7. Tenet Healthcare Corp., 2,233
8. Mercy Health Services, 2,052
9. Lutheran Health Services, 1,950
10. Daughters of Charity National Health System, 1,899

Source: *Modern Healthcare*, Modern Healthcare Multi-Unit Providers Survey (annual), May 24, 1999, p. 72.

★3361★
LARGEST LONG-TERM CARE SYSTEMS OPERATING SKILLED-NURSING FACILITIES, 1998
Ranked by: Total number of U.S. beds. **Remarks:** Also notes number of facilities. **Number listed:** 39

1. Beverly Enterprises, with 62,293 beds
2. Mariner Post-Acute Network, 50,471
3. Sun Healthcare Group, 44,491
4. Integrated Health Services, 42,825
5. HCR Manor Care, 39,630
6. Vancor, 38,362
7. Genesis Health Ventures, 34,917
8. Life Care Centers of America, 26,989
9. Extendicare Health Services, 21,734
10. ServiceMaster Diversified Health Services, 18,572

Source: *Modern Healthcare*, Modern Healthcare Multi-Unit Providers Survey (annual), May 24, 1999, p. 57.

Nursing Homes--Long Island (NY)

★3362★
LEADING NURSING HOMES RANKED BY NUMBER OF BEDS IN LONG ISLAND, NEW YORK, 1998
Ranked by: Number of beds. **Remarks:** Also notes contact information, number of full time nurses, and room rates. **Number listed:** 26

1. A. Holly Patterson Geriatric Center, with 889 beds
2. United Presbyterian Residence, 672
3. Parker Jewish Institute for Health Care & Rehabilitation, 527
4. Our Lady of Consolation, 450
5. Lutheran Center For The Aging, 353
6. LI State Veterans Homes, 350
7. Woodmere Rehab & HCC, 336
8. Broadlawn Manor Nursing Care, 320
9. Carillon Nursing & Rehab, 315
10. Gurwin Jewish Geriatric Center of LI, 300

Source: *Long Island Business News*, LI Book of Lists (annual), 1999, p. 113+.

Occupations

★3363★
OCCUPATIONS WITH THE FASTEST EMPLOYMENT GROWTH, 1996-2006
Ranked by: Expected employment growth, in percent. **Number listed:** 5

1. Database Administrators, Computer Support Specialists, other Computer Scientists, with 118%
2. Computer Engineers, 109%
3. System Analysts, 103%
4. Personal and Home-Care Aides, 85%
4. Physical & Corrective Therapy Assistants & Aides, 85%

Source: *Bureau of Labor Statistics*, American Demographics, May, 1999, p. 23.

Off Price Stores

See: **Discount Stores**

Office Buildings--Florida

★3364★
LARGEST OFFICE BUILDINGS IN FLORIDA, 1998*
Ranked by: Leasable square feet. **Remarks:** Also notes contact information, property manager, number of floors, and major tenants. **Number listed:** 25

1. First Union Financial Center, with 1,150,000 square feet
2. Miami Center, 782,685
3. BellSouth Tower, 780,000
3. Two Prudential Plaza, 780,000
4. Barnett Plaza, 766,136
5. Tampa City Center, 735,050
6. Barnett Tower, 677,667
7. Independent Square, 675,000
8. Barnett Center, 656,000
9. SunTrust Center, 640,385
10. One Biscayne Tower, 605,237

Source: *Florida Trend*, TopRank Florida (annual), January, 1998, p. 31.

Office Buildings--Philadelphia (PA)

★3365★
LARGEST OFFICE BUILDINGS IN PHILADELPHIA, 1999
Ranked by: Rented square feet. **Remarks:** Also notes contact information, rent, occupancy, owner, leasing agent, and principal tenants. **Number listed:** 13

1. Centre Square, with 1,850,000 square feet
2. Mellon Bank Center, 1,327,689
3. Two Liberty Place, 1,257,000
4. One Liberty Place, 1,200,000
4. Bell Atlantic Tower, 1,200,000
5. The Wanamaker Building, 1,074,487
6. Two Commerce Square, 953,276
7. One Commerce Square, 942,866
8. 1818 Market Street, 941,314
9. Fidelity Building, 892,282
10. Penn Mutual Towers, 850,000

Source: *Philadelphia Business Journal*, Book of Business Lists (annual), December 25, 1999, p. 39.

Office Equipment and Supplies Stores

★3366★
LEADING OFFICE SUPPLY COMPANIES, 1997
Ranked by: Sales, in millions of dollars. **Number listed:** 4

1. Office Depot, with $6,718 million
2. Staples, $5,181
3. Office Max Inc., $3,765
4. Arvey Paper & Supplies, $80

Source: *Discount Store News*, Discount Industry Annual Report (annual), July 13, 1998, p. 86.

Office Equipment Industry

★3367★
MOST ADMIRED COMPUTER AND OFFICE EQUIPMENT CORPORATIONS, 1998
Ranked by: Composite score (1-10). **Number listed:** 10
1. IBM, with 7.49 points
2. Hewlett-Packard, 7.42
3. Dell Computer Corp., 7.35
4. Sun Microsystems, 7.06
5. Compaq Computer, 6.98
6. Xerox, 6.88
7. Gateway 2000, 6.46
8. Canon U.S.A., 5.71
9. Apple Computer, 5.37
10. NCR, 5.03

Source: *Fortune (annual)*, March 1, 1999, p. F-6.

★3368★
TOP OFFICE EQUIPMENT AND COMPUTER COMPANIES IN THE S & P 500, 1999
Ranked by: Each company is ranked by eight criteria; one-year sales growth, three-year average annual sales growth, one-year profit growth, three-year average annual profit growth, net profit margins, and return on equity, with additional weight given to a company's sales. A company's composite rank is calculated using the sum of all its ranks. **Remarks:** Overall score not provided. **Number listed:** 35
1. Microsoft
2. Dell Computer
3. Oracle
4. EMC
5. Compuware
6. America Online
7. Cisco Systems
8. BMC Software
9. Sun Microsystems
10. Gateway 2000

Source: *Business Week*, Business Week 50: Top Companies of the S & P 500 (annual), March 29, 1999, p. 160+.

★3369★
TOP OFFICE EQUIPMENT COMPANIES BY SEGMENT REVENUE, 1998*
Ranked by: Segment revenue, in millions of dollars. **Number listed:** 4
1. Xerox, with $13,526.0 million
2. Pitney Bowes, $2,460.3
3. Eastman Kodak, $912.2
4. Texas Instruments, $487.5

Source: *Electronic Business*, Top 200 (annual), July, 1998, p. 95.

Office Equipment Industry, International

★3370★
WORLD'S LARGEST OFFICE EQUIPMENT CORPORATIONS BY REVENUE, 1997
Ranked by: Revenue, in millions of dollars. **Number listed:** 9
1. International Business Machines (U.S.), with $78,508 million
2. Hewlett-Packard (U.S.), $42,895
3. Fujitsu (Japan), $40,613
4. Compaq Computer (U.S.), $24,584
5. Canon (Japan), $22,813
6. Xerox (U.S.), $18,166
7. Digital Equipment (U.S.), $13,047
8. Dell Computer (U.S.), $12,327
9. Ricoh (Japan), $11,432

Source: *Fortune*, The Global 500: World's Biggest Corporations (annual), August 3, 1998, p. F-17.

Office Furniture

★3371★
U.S. OFFICE FURNITURE BY MARKET SHARE, 1998
Ranked by: Market share, in percent. **Number listed:** 5
1. HON Industries, with 11.7%
2. Haworth, 11.1%
3. Knoll, 6.9%
4. Kimball Industries, 3.9%
5. Other, 34.6%

Source: *Barron's*, April 5, 1999, p. 26.

★3372★
VARIOUS OFFICE FURNITURE DISTRIBUTION CHANNELS, 1998*
Ranked by: Total sales, in percent. **Number listed:** 7
1. Aligned contract office furniture dealers, with 52.9%
2. Non-aligned contract office furniture dealers, 16.1%
3. Office products ''mega'' dealers, 8.4%
4. Mail order, direct, all other, 6.7%
5. Superstores/warehouse clubs/ other mass merchants, 6.3%
6. Wholesalers, 5.9%
7. Federal government, 3.7%

Source: *Furniture Today*, Soho Today, Fall, 1998, p. 4.

Offices--Leasing and Renting--Europe

★3373★
EUROPEAN RETURNS ON OFFICE SPACE, 1998
Ranked by: Annual gross returns, in percent. **Number listed:** 9
1. Stockholm, with 24.7
2. London-WE, 21.7
3. Barcelona, 21.0
4. Budapest, 20.0
5. London (Downtown), 17.3
6. Luxembourg, 16.1
7. Dublin, 16.0
8. Amsterdam, 14.7
9. Madrid, 14.2

Source: *Real Estate Forum*, August, 1998, p. 67.

Offices--Leasing and Renting--Foreign

★3374★
WORLD'S MOST EXPENSIVE PRIME OFFICE SPACE, 1999
Ranked by: Square feet, in U.S. dollars, per year. **Number listed:** 10

1. Tokyo (Inner Central), with $137.53
2. London (City), $120.45
3. Mumbai, Bombay India, $97.79
4. Hong Kong, $88.91
5. Paris, $70.99
6. Moscow, $69.95
7. New Delhi, India, $62.80
8. Edinburgh, Scotland, $56.56
9. Manchester, England, $54.60
10. Glasgow, Scotland, $54.07

Source: *Site Selection*, May, 1999, p. 320.

Offices--Leasing and Renting, International

★3375★
LEADING GLOBAL MARKET OFFICE SPACE RENT, 1998
Ranked by: Square footage, in U.S. dollars, per year. **Number listed:** 10

1. Tokyo (Inner Central), with $137.53
2. London (City), $120.45
3. Bombay, $97.79
4. Hong Kong, $88.91
5. Paris, $70.99
6. Moscow, $69.95
7. New Delhi, $62.80
8. Edinburgh, $56.56
9. Manchester, $54.60
10. Glasgow, $54.07

Source: *Real Estate Forum*, March, 1999, p. 320.

★3376★
TOP GLOBAL PRIME OFFICE RENT OR LEASE SPACE, 1999
Ranked by: Square footage, in U.S. dollars, per year. **Number listed:** 10

1. Harare (Zimbabwe), with $4.23
2. Durban (South Africa), $7.96
3. Bangkok (Thailand), $12.27
4. Johannesburg (South Africa), $13.08
5. Kuala Lumpur (Maylasia), $13.58
6. El Paso (TX), $14.40
7. Albuquerque (NM), $14.44
8. Gaborone (Botswana), $14.89
9. Jakarta (Indonesia), $14.98
10. Tulsa (Oklahoma), $15.08

Source: *Site Selection*, May, 1999, p. 320.

★3377★
WORLD'S MOST EXPENSIVE SHOPPING DISTRICTS, 1998
Ranked by: Square footage, in U.S. dollars, per year. **Number listed:** 11

1. New York, with $550
2. Hong Kong, $542
3. London, $468
4. Paris, $432
5. Moscow, $325
6. Sydney, $292
7. Munich, $233
8. Athens, $217
9. Zurich, $187
10. Tokyo, $36

Source: *Business Mexico*, February, 1999, p. 25.

Offices—Leasing and Renting--Philadelphia Metropolitan Area

★3378★
TOP LEASING TRANSACTIONS IN METROPOLITAN PHILADELPHIA, 1997-1998
Ranked by: Square footage leased. **Remarks:** Also notes location and owner/tenant representatives. **Number listed:** 25

1. Sun Co. Inc., with 375,000 square feet
2. Hartford Fire Insurance Co., 265,083
3. Wolf, Block, Schorr & Sells-Cohen, 138,000
4. Astra Pharmaceuticals, 113,749
5. PNC Bank, 108,208
6. Keystone Mercy Health Plan, 106,231
7. Lockheed Martin Corp., 86,331
8. Icon Clinical Research, 80,000
9. Associate Credit Card Services, 79,184
10. Cendant Corp., 75,000

Source: *Philadelphia Business Journal*, Book of Business Lists (annual), December 25, 1998, p. 45+.

Oil Companies

See: **Petroleum Industry**

On-Line Investing

See: **Internet--Investment Information**

Ophthalmology

★3379★
LEADING ADVERTISED OPTOMETRY PRODUCTS AND SERVICES, 1998
Ranked by: Market share, in percent. **Remarks:** Also notes previous year's rank and market share. **Number listed:** 12

1. Xalatan Solution, with 3.46%
2. Cosopt Ophthalmic Solution, 3.24%
3. Alphagen/Ophthalmic Solution, 3.03%
4. Ocuflox/Ophthalmic Solution, 1.89%
5. Voltaren Ophthalmic Solution, 1.61%
6. Lotemax/Ophthalmic Corticosteroid, 1.53%
7. Trusopt/Ophthalmic Solution, 1.52%
8. Milenium Microsurgical System, 1.46%
9. Acrysof Acrylic Foldable Iol, 1.40%
10. Timoptic-XE, 1.36%

Source: *Medical Marketing & Media*, Healthcare Advertising Review (annual), April, 1999, p. 60.

★3380★
TOP ADVERTISERS IN OPTOMETRY PUBLICATIONS, 1998
Ranked by: Market share, in percent. **Remarks:** Also notes previous years' rank and market share. **Number listed:** 12

1. Merck, with 6.12%
2. Allergan Inc., 5.43%
3. Alcon Laboratories Inc., 5.07%
4. Allergan Pharmaceuticals, 4.99%

5. Pharmacia & Upjohn Inc., 4.47%
6. Chiron Vision, 3.47%
7. Novartis Inc., 3.37%
8. Storz Ophthalmics Inc., 3.24%
9. Alcon Surgical, 2.79%
10. Bausch & Lomb Pharmaceutical Products, 2.55%

Source: *Medical Marketing & Media*, Healthcare Advertising Review (annual), April, 1999, p. 62.

Options (Contracts)

★3381★

TOP U.S. OPTIONS CONTRACTS WITH VOLUME OVER 1000,000, 1997

Ranked by: Contract volume. **Remarks:** Also notes voule for previous year and percentage of total volume. **Number listed:** 50

1. Intel Corp. (INQ), with $14,358,643 contracts
2. Philip Morris, $4,822,699
3. Telecomunicacoes Brasileiras SA (TBR), $4,190,379
4. Motorola, $2,543,936
5. Office Depot, $2,455,737
6. Ascend Communications, $2,274,814
7. Chase Manhattan Corp. (CMB), $1,871,212
8. Morgan Stanley High-Technology 35 Index (MSH), $1,759,454
9. Iomega Corp. (IOM), $1,707,381
10. Seagate Technology (SEG), $1,370,060

Source: *American Stock Exchange Fact Book*, (annual), American Stock Exchange, 1998, p. 40+.

Organic Foods

See: **Natural Foods**

OSHA

See: **United States Occupational Safety and Health Administration**

Oslo Stock Exchange

★3382★

LARGEST LISTED COMPANIES ON THE OSLO STOCK EXCHANGE, 1997

Ranked by: Market value, in millions of Norwegian krone (NKr). **Number listed:** 20

1. Norsk Hydro, with NKr82,352 million
2. Orkla, NKr30,726
3. Den norske Bank, NKr22,289
4. Saga Petroleum, NKr16,893
5. Petroleum Geo-Services, NKr16,703
6. Charter Bank & Kr., NKr16,424
7. Kvaerner, NKr16,058
8. Storebrand, NKr15,465
9. Bergesen D.Y., NKr13,114
10. Aker RGI, NKr9,989

Source: *Euromoney Publications*, Guide to World Equity Markets (annual), 1998, p. 372.

★3383★

MOST ACTIVELY TRADED SHARES ON THE OSLO STOCK EXCHANGE, 1997

Ranked by: Trading value, in millions of Norwegian krones (NKr). **Number listed:** 20

1. Norsk Hydro, with NKr25,440 million
2. Nycomed A, NKr17,352
3. Kvaerner A, NKr12,323
4. Nycomed B, NKr12,014
5. Orkla, NKr11,081
6. Storebrand Ord., NKr10,456
7. Fokus Bank, NKr10,168
8. Den norske Bank, NKr9,609
9. Petroleum Geo-Services, NKr8,026
10. NCL Holding, NKr7,445

Source: *Euromoney Publications*, Guide to World equity Markets (annual), 1998, p. 372+.

Outsourcing

★3384★

TOP CORPORATIONS IN THE DIVERSIFIED OUTSOURCING SERVICE INDUSTRY, 1998

Ranked by: Revenue, in millions of dollars. **Remarks:** Also notes profits and investment figures as well as number of employees. **Number listed:** 12

1. Sodexho Marriott Services, with $6,704 million
2. Aramark, $6,377
3. ServiceMaster, $4,724
4. Viad, $2,542
5. Staff Leasing, $2,376
6. Wackenhut, $1,755
7. Ogden, $1,692
8. Administaff, $1,683
9. ABM Industries Inc., $1,502
10. Borg-Warner Security, $1,461

Source: *Fortune*, Fortune 500 Largest U.S. Corporations (annual), April 26, 1999, p. F-56.

★3385★

TOP REASONS TO OUTSOURCE, 1998*

Ranked by: Basis for ranking not specified. **Number listed:** 10

1. Accelerates reengineering benefits which aim for dramatic improvements in cost, quality, service and speed.
2. Gives access to world class capabilities.
3. Cash infusion: outsourcing often involves the transfer of assets from the customer to the provider.
4. Frees resources for other purposes; an organization can redirect its people and other resources to activities that serve the customer.
5. Eliminates difficult-to-manage functions.
6. Shifts company focus to the customer.
7. Frees up capital funds: outsourcing can reduce the need to invest capital funds to non-core business functions.
8. Reduces operating costs. Companies that try to do everything themselves often incur high research, development, marketing and deployment expenses.

9. Reduces risk. Vendors make investments on behalf of many clients; shared investment spreads risk.
10. Provides access to resources not available internally.

Source: *Managing Office Technology*, September, 1998, p. 17.

Outsourcing--Great Britain

★3386★
LEADING OUTSOURCING PROVIDERS IN GREAT BRITIAN, 1997
Ranked by: Revenue, in millions of British pounds. **Remarks:** Also notes previous years' revenue and 1996-97 growth, in percent. **Number listed:** 15

1. EDS, with £660 million
2. Computer Sciences Corp., £306
3. IBM, £280
4. ICL, £235
5. CAP Gemini/Hoskyns, £224
6. Sema, £196
7. Andersen Consulting, £150
8. Capita, £139
9. Digital, £84
10. FI Group, £71

Source: *Investors Chronicle*, September 4, 1998, p. 14.

Over-the-Counter Markets

★3387★
FASTEST-GROWING NASDAQ COMPANIES BY RETURN ON EQUITY, 1998*
Ranked by: Five-year annual EPS growth, in percent. **Remarks:** Also notes share information. **Number listed:** 303

1. CHS Electronics Inc., with 140%
2. Metris Companies Inc., 118%
3. Coherent Communication Systems, 114%
4. Micrel Inc., 108%
5. II-VI Inc., 103%
5. Tollgrade Communications, 103%
6. S C B Computer Technology Inc., 100%
7. Zygo Corp., 96%
8. Powerwave Technology Inc., 92%
8. Mayflower Co-op Bank MA, 92%
8. American Woodmark Corp., 92%
9. First International Bancorp Inc., 89%
10. Datastream Systems Inc., 88%

Source: *Equities 1998*, July/August, 1998, p. 25+.

★3388★
LARGEST LISTED COMPANIES ON THE NASDAQ, 1997
Ranked by: Market value, in millions of dollars. **Number listed:** 20

1. Microsoft, with $156,005 million
2. Intel, $114,830
3. Cisco Systems, $56,442
4. Dell Computer, $27,972
5. WorldCom, $27,442
6. MCI Communications Corp., $23,797
7. Oracle Corp., $21,877
8. Washington Mutual, $16,411
9. Sun Microsystems, $14,938
10. Amgen, $14,246

Source: *Euromoney Publications*, Guide to World Equity Markets (annual), 1998, p. 537.

★3389★
LEADING OVER-THE-COUNTER STOCKS, BY MARKET SHARE, 1998
Ranked by: Market value, in millions of dollars. **Number listed:** 1000

1. Microsoft, with $272,131.7 million
2. Intel, $143,205.2
3. Cisco Systems, $99,249.6
4. Dell Computer, $68,734.6
5. WorldCom, $54,571.6
6. Tele-Communications, $44,648.5
7. MCI Communications Corp., $38,870.3
8. Oracle, $25,796.2
9. Amgen, $18,658.1
10. Sun Microsystems, $17,898.8

Source: *Equities*, Annual NASDAQ 1,000 (annual), September, 1998, p. 7+.

★3390★
MOST ACTIVELY TRADED SHARES ON THE NASDAQ MARKET, 1997
Ranked by: Trading volume, in millions of shares. **Number listed:** 20

1. Cisco Systems, with 5,386.6 million shares
2. Ascend Communications, 3,892.0
3. Intel, 3,887.9
4. Dell Computer, 3,719.0
5. Tele-Communications, 2,456.3
6. 3Com, 2,200.4
7. Microsoft, 2,097.9
8. Oracle, 1,970.2
9. Applied Materials, 1,804.2
10. WorldCom, 1,784.8

Source: *Euromoney Publications*, Guide to World Equity Markets (annual), 1998, p. 537+.

★3391★
NASDAQ BEST PERFORMERS, 1998
Ranked by: Change in price of stock, in percent. **Remarks:** Also notes price as of December 31, 1998 and net change. **Number listed:** 10

1. Amazon.com, with 996.4%
2. Network Solutions, 897.1%
3. Metromedia Fiber, 705.9%
4. New Era Network, 682.2%
5. CMGI, 604.1%
6. Yahoo, 584.3%
7. MySoftware, 468.8%
8. Colt Telecom ADR, 461.9%
9. MindSpring Entertainment, 444.8%
10. Energis ADS, 441.2%

Source: *Barron's*, (annual), January 4, 1999, p. 130.

★3392★
NASDAQ WORST PERFORMERS, 1998
Ranked by: Change in price stock, in percent. **Remarks:** Also notes price as of December 31, 1998 and net change. **Number listed:** 10

1. FPA Med Management, with -99%
1. Stormedia, -99%
3. First Ent Financial, -98%
3. Nexar Technology, -98%
3. Hayes, -98%
6. Wilshire Financial, -97%
6. IMC Manufacturing, -97%
6. PacAm MoneyCenter, -97%

6. Martin Color, -97%
6. CellPro, -97%

Source: *Barron's*, (annual), January 4, 1999, p. 130.

Package Express Service

★3393★
MOST ADMIRED MAIL PACKAGE AND FREIGHT DELIVERY CORPORATIONS, 1998
Ranked by: Scores (1-10) derived from a survey of senior executives, outside directors and securities analysts. **Remarks:** Respondents rated companies in their own industry on 8 attributes of reputation. Also notes previous year's rank. **Number listed:** 6

1. United Parcel Service, with 8.18
2. FDX, 7.55
3. Air Express International, 6.20
4. Airborne Freight, 5.95
5. Fritz, 4.94
6. Pittston, 4.69

Source: *Fortune*, America's Most Admired Corporations (annual), March 1, 1999, p. F-2.

★3394★
TOP CORPORATIONS IN THE MAIL, PACKAGE DELIVERY AND FREIGHT DELIVERY INDUSTRY, 1998
Ranked by: Revenue, in millions of dollars. **Remarks:** Also notes profits and investment figures as well as number of employees. **Number listed:** 6

1. United Parcel Service, with $24,788 million
2. FDX, $15,873
3. Pittston, $3,747
4. Airborne Freight, $3,075
5. AEI, $1,513
6. Fritz Companies, $1,300

Source: *Fortune*, Fortune 500 Largest U.S. Corporations (annual), April 26, 1999, p. F-63+.

★3395★
TOP PACKAGE CARRIERS, 1997
Ranked by: Revenue, in thousands of dollars. **Remarks:** Also notes 1996 revenue and percent change, net income (loss), operating ratio, net profit margin, tonnage and mileage for 1996 and 1997. **Number listed:** 2

1. United Parcel Service, with $15,730,318 thousand
2. RPS Inc., $1,581,754

Source: *Transport Topics*, Annual Report, August 10, 1998, p. 22.

Package Tours--Great Britain

★3396★
LEADING TOUR OPERATOR ADVERTISERS IN THE MAIN MEDIA IN GREAT BRITAIN, 1997
Ranked by: Rates, in thousands of British pounds. **Remarks:** Includes percentage. **Number listed:** 11

1. Thomson & Portland, with £13,004 thousand
2. Airtours, Aspro, Eurosites, Tradewinds, £8,304
3. Page & Moy, £3,447
4. Saga, £2,859
5. First Choice & Eclipse & Enterprise, £1,642
6. Unijet, £1,409
7. Titan Travel, £1,275
8. Kuoni, £883
9. BA Holidays, £688
10. Crystal Holidays, £673

Source: *Marketing*, November 26, 1998, p. 36.

Packaging

★3397★
TOP CONTAINER AND PACKAGING COMPANIES IN THE S&P 500, 1998
Ranked by: Each company is ranked by 8 criteria: one-year total return, three-year total return, one-year sales growth, three-year average annual sales growth, one-year profit growth, three-year average annual profit growth, net profit margins, and return on equity, with additional weight given to a company's sales. A company's composite rank is calculated using the sum of all its ranks. **Remarks:** Overall score not provided. **Number listed:** 6

1. Avery Dennison
2. Ball
3. Bemis
4. Temple-Inland
5. Owens-Illinois
6. Crown Cork & Seal

Source: *Business Week*, Business Week 50: Top Companies of the S&P 500 (annual), March 29, 1999, p. 146.

Packaging Industry

See: **Container Industry**

Pain Relievers

See: **Analgesics**

Paint Industry

★3398★
LEADING CHEMICAL PROCESS INDUSTRIES BY SALES OF PAINTS AND COATINGS, 1998
Ranked by: Sales, in millions of dollars. **Remarks:** Includes percent change from 1997, net income, profit margin, capital ratios, shareholder returns, prices and assets. **Number listed:** 7

1. Sherwin-Williams, with $4,934 million
2. RPM, $1,615
3. Valspar, $1,155
4. Benjamin Moore, $711
5. Lilly Industries, $619
6. McWhorter Technologies, $455
7. Hitox, $12

Source: *Chemical Week*, Chemical Week 300 (annual), May 12, 1999, p. 52.

★3399★
TOP USES FOR PAINT*
Ranked by: Share of total usage, in percent. **Number listed:** 5
1. Architectural, with 37%
2. Original equipment manufacturer, 30%
3. Special purpose, 27%
4. Powder, 5%
5. Radiation cured, 1%

Source: *C&EN*, October 12, 1998, p. 43.

Panama Stock Exchange

★3400★
LARGEST LISTED COMPANIES ON THE PANAMA STOCK EXCHANGE, 1997
Ranked by: Market value, in millions of U.S. dollars ($). **Number listed:** 10
1. Empresa General de Inversiones, with $497.22 million
2. Banco del Istmo, $342.00
3. Cerveceria Nacional, $239.44
4. Grupo Assa, $222.00
5. Primer Banco de Ahorros, $149.73
6. Capitales Nacionales, $142.09
7. Coca Cola de Panama, $103.77
8. Banco Disa, $44.00
9. Banco Internacional de Panama, $66.00
10. Conase, $65.04

Source: *SSB Guide to World Equity Markets*, (annual), Euromoney Publications, 1998, p. 389.

★3401★
MOST ACTIVELY TRADED SHARE ON THE PANAMA STOCK EXCHANGE, 1997
Ranked by: Turnover, in thousands of U.S. dollars ($). **Number listed:** 10
1. Interamerica's Fund Ltd., with $13.356 thousand
2. Banco del Istmo, $8.231
3. IDS Holding Corp., $7.668
4. Cerveceria Nacional, $6.674
5. Empresa General de Inversiones, $5.575
6. Capitales Nacionales, $2.093
7. Primer Banco de Ahorros, $1.548
8. Union Nacional de Empresas, $1.319
9. Coca-Cola de Panama, $1.095
10. Grupo Assa, $0.957

Source: *SSB Guide to World Equity Markets*, (annual), Euromoney Publications, 1998, p. 389.

Paper Box Industry

★3402★
LARGEST FOLDING CARTON MANUFACTURERS IN THE U.S., 1998
Ranked by: Number of plants. **Number listed:** 19
1. Rock-Tenn, with with 23 plants
2. Jefferson Smurfit, 18
3. James River/Fort James, 12
4. Simkins Industries, 8
5. Field Container, 7
5. Green Bay Packaging, 7
7. Mebane Packaging Group, 6
7. Dopaco, 6
9. Tenneco Packaging, 5
9. Mead Packaging, 5
9. Gulf States Paper, 5

Source: *Paperboard Packaging*, January, 1999, p. 28.

Paper Box Industry--Europe

★3403★
TOP CARTON CONVERTERS IN EUROPE*
Ranked by: Thousands of tons. **Number listed:** 10
1. MM Karton, with 275 thousand tons
2. Van Genechten, 210
3. FCP-ECA, 180
4. LBW/MCA, 140
5. Field, 100
6. Mead, 90
7. Riverwood, 70
8. Wall, 65
8. CPC, 65
10. Amcor, 60

Source: *Paperboard Packaging*, January, 1999, p. 10.

Paper Box Industry, International

★3404★
TOP GLOBAL PRODUCERS OF CARTON BOARD*
Ranked by: Thousands of tons. **Number listed:** 10
1. IP, with 2,410 thousand tons
2. Stora-Enso, 2,240
3. MM Karton, 1,980
4. Jefferson Smurfit, 1,100
5. Riverwood, 965
6. Westvaco, 960
7. Newark, 944
8. Asian P&P, 900
9. Honshu, 865
9. Mead, 865

Source: *Paperboard Packaging*, January, 1999, p. 10.

Paper Industry

★3405★
LEADING PULP, PAPER, AND PACKAGING COMPANIES, 1998
Ranked by: Sales, in millions of dollars. **Remarks:** Includes percent change from 1997, net income, profit margin, capital ratios, shareholder returns, prices and assets. **Number listed:** 22
1. International Paper, with $19,541 million
2. Georgia-Pacific, $13,223
3. Kimberly-Clark, $12,298
4. Weyerhaeuser, $10,766
5. Fort James, $7,301
6. Boise Cascade, $6,162
7. Champion International, $5,653
8. Union Camp, $4,503

9. Mead, $3,772
10. Willamette Industries, $3,700

Source: *Chemical Week*, Chemical Week 300 (annual), May 12, 1999, p. 55+.

★3406★
TOP FUEL COMPANIES IN THE S&P 500, 1998
Ranked by: Each company is ranked by 8 criteria: one-year total return, three-year total return, one-year sales growth, three-year average annual sales growth, one-year profit growth, three-year average annual profit growth, net profit margins, and return on equity, with additional weight given to a company's sales. A company's composite rank is calculated using the sum of all its ranks. **Remarks:** Overall score not provided. **Number listed:** 24

1. Helmerich & Payne
2. Schlumberger
3. Coastal
4. Exxon
5. Chevron
6. USX-Marathon Group
7. Rowan
8. Mobil
9. Sunoco
10. Halliburton

Source: *Business Week*, Business Week 50: Top Companies of the S&P 500 (annual), March 29, 1999, p. 150+.

★3407★
TOP PAPER AND FOREST PRODUCTS COMPANIES IN THE S&P 500, 1998
Ranked by: Each company is ranked by 8 criteria: one-year total return, three-year total return, one-year sales growth, three-year average annual sales growth, one-year profit growth, three-year average annual profit growth, net profit margins, and return on equity, with additional weight given to a company's sales. A company's composite rank is calculated using the sum of all its ranks. **Remarks:** Overall score not provided. **Number listed:** 13

1. Kimberly-Clark
2. Fort James
3. Georgia-Pacific Group
4. Willamette Industries
5. Weyerhaeuser
6. International Paper
7. Union Camp
8. Boise Cascade
9. Mead
10. Potlatch

Source: *Business Week*, Business Week 50: Top Companies of the S&P 500 (annual), March 29, 1999, p. 162.

Paper Industry--Asia

★3408★
LARGEST ASIAN PAPER, PRINTING, AND PUBLISHING COMPANIES
Ranked by: Sales, in thousands of U.S. dollars ($). **Remarks:** Includes profits as a percentage of sales and activity codes. **Number listed:** 100

1. Oji Paper Co. Ltd., with $10,095,082 thousand
2. Dai Nippon Printing Co. Ltd., $10,004,520
3. Toppan Printing, $9,611,863
4. Nippon Paper Industries, $7,769,932
5. Softbank, $3,842,544
6. Honshu Paper Co. Ltd., $3,519,326
7. Daishowa Paper Manufacturing Co. Ltd., $2,774,603
8. Kokuyo Co. Ltd., $2,374,386
9. Daio Paper Corp., $2,312,155
10. Rengo Co. Ltd., $2,134,049

Source: *Asia's 7,500 Largest Companies*, (annual), E.L.C. Publishing, Ktd., 1999, p. 83+.

Paper Industry--Europe

★3409★
TOP PAPER AND ALLIED PRODUCT COMPANIES IN EUROPE
Ranked by: Financial size, in millions of European Currency Units (ECUs). **Remarks:** Also notes number of employees and overall rank among European businesses. **Number listed:** 88

1. UPM-KYMMENE OYJ, with ECUs8.409 million
2. Enso Oyj, ECUs4.882
3. Arjo Wiggins Appleton PLC, ECUs4.820
4. Jefferson Smurfit Group PLC, ECUs3.308
5. Mo Och Domsjo AB, ECUs2.579
6. Pwa Papierwerke Waldhof-Aschaffenburg AG, ECUs2.536
7. FPB Holding AG, ECUs2.416
8. David S. Smith (Holdings) PLC, ECUs1.741
9. G. Haindl'sche Papierfabriken KG auf Aktien, ECUs1.439
10. Enso Fine Papers Oy, ECUs1.237

Source: *Dun & Bradstreet*, Dun's Europa (annual), 1999, p. 239+.

Paper Industry--North America

★3410★
TOP NEWSPRINT PRODUCERS IN NORTH AMERICA*
Ranked by: Annual capacity, in thousands of metric tons. **Remarks:** Includes capacity share. **Number listed:** 10

1. Abitibi-Consolidated Inc., with 3,643 thousand tons
2. Bowater Inc., 2,727
3. Donohue Inc., 2,259
4. Kruger Inc., 963
5. Fletcher Challenge Canada, 735
6. Smurfit Newsprint Corp., 708
7. North Pacific Paper Corp., 698
8. Tembec Inc., 473
9. Southeast Paper Mfg. Co., 445
10. Pacifica Papers Ltd., 441

Source: *Pulp & Paper*, December, 1998, p. 13.

★3411★
TOP PRODUCERS OF PULP AND PAPER IN NORTH AMERICA, 1998*
Ranked by: Annual capacity, in thousands of metric tons. **Remarks:** Includes market share. **Number listed:** 10

1. Weyerhaeuser, with 2,180 thousand
2. Georgia-Pacific, 1,705
3. Stone Container, 1,135
4. International Paper, 1,095
5. Parsons & Whittemore, 1,090
6. Avenor, 845
7. Champion, 765
8. Fletcher Challenge Canada, 720

9. Canfor, 660
10. Skeena Cellulose, 420

Source: *Pulp & Paper*, August, 1998, p. 11.

Paris Stock Exchange

See: **Bourse de Paris**

Part-Time Employment

★3412★
COMPANIES WITH THE BEST PART-TIME JOBS*
Ranked by: Companies are ranked by several criteria including medical, vacation pay, holiday pay, retirement plan, discounts/privileges and other benefits. **Remarks:** Includes types of available part-time jobs. **Number listed:** 13

1. UPS
2. Wal-Mart
3. Starbucks
4. Alaska Airlines
5. Kmart
6. The Home Depot
7. Walgreens
8. Nordstrom
9. Hilton Hotels
10. Dayton Hudson

Source: *Your Money*, October/November, 1998, p. 77.

Participation Loans

★3413★
TOP LOAN SYNDICATORS WITH FULL CREDIT TO ADMINISTRATIVE SYNDICATION DOCUMENTATION AGENTS, 1998
Ranked by: Loans, in millions of dollars. **Remarks:** Includes market share and number of deals. **Number listed:** 20

1. Bank of America, with $443,847.9 million
2. Chase Manhattan Corp., $441,538.7
3. Salomon Smith Barney, $237,176.3
4. J.P. Morgan, $215,755.0
5. BANK ONE Corp., $98,498.2
6. Bankers Trust, $88,344.7
7. Bank of New York, $78,872.6
8. First Union Corp., $52,694.6
9. Scotiabank, Bank of Nova Scotia, $49,540.0
10. Toronto-Dominion Bank, $43,195.5

Source: *Investment Dealers' Digest*, (annual), February 1, 1999, p. 16.

★3414★
TOP LOAN SYNDICATORS WITH FULL CREDIT TO BOOK MANAGERS, 1998
Ranked by: Loans, in millions of dollars. **Remarks:** Includes market share and number of deals. **Number listed:** 20

1. Chase Manhattan Corp., with $271,166.0 million
2. Bank of American Corp., $173,551.5
3. J.P. Morgan, $106,477.0
4. Salomon Smith Barney, $86,560.0
5. BANK ONE Corp., $51,585.0
6. Bankers Trust, $42,716.2
7. Bank of New York, $25,153.2
8. Lehman Brothers, $23,219.1
9. First Union Corp., $20,647.5
10. Toronto-Dominion Bank, $19,683.6

Source: *Investment Dealers' Digest*, (annual), February 1, 1999, p. 15.

★3415★
TOP LOAN SYNDICATORS WITH FULL CREDIT TO EACH AGENT, 1998
Ranked by: Loans, in millions of dollars. **Remarks:** Includes market share and number of deals. **Number listed:** 20

1. Bank of America, with $616,720.1 million
2. Chase Manhattan Corp., $504,458.4
3. Salomon Smith Barney, $315,875.7
4. Bank One Corp., $285,626.4
5. J.P. Morgan, $253,635.2
6. Scotiabank, Bank of Nova Scotia, $245,132.3
7. Bank of New York, $230,128.3
8. First Union Corp., $181,650.6
9. Fleet Financial Group Inc., $177,856.3
10. ABN AMRO, $177,702.8

Source: *Investment Dealers' Digest*, (annual), February 1, 1999, p. 17.

Participation Loans--Argentina

★3416★
TOP ARRANGERS OF CORPORATE LOANS IN ARGENTINA, 1998
Ranked by: Amount of loans, in millions of U.S. dollars ($). **Remarks:** Includes number of issues and market share. **Number listed:** 10

1. BankAmerica Corp., with $979.65 million
2. Societe Generale, $716.76
3. ING Barings, $618.75
4. Dresdner Bank AG, $594.94
5. Citigroup Inc., $523.25
6. Banco Santander, $511.81
7. Merrill Lynch & Co., $508.23
8. Barclays, $501.67
9. Deutsche Bank AG, $465.53
10. Chase Manhattan Bank, $437.90

Source: *Latin Finance*, March, 1999, p. 78.

Participation Loans--Brazil

★3417★
TOP ARRANGERS OF CORPORATE LOANS IN BRAZIL, 1998
Ranked by: Loan amount, in millions of U.S. dollars ($). **Remarks:** Includes number of issues and market share. **Number listed:** 10

1. Chase Manhattan Bank, with $1,963.48 million
2. BankAmerica Corp., $1,887.26
3. Citigroup Inc., $471.72
4. J. P. Morgan & Co., $438.48
5. Warburg Dillon Read, $428.33
6. WestLB, $426.29
7. ABN AMRO Holding N.V., $356.76
8. Dresdner Bank AG, $338.48

9. Deutsche Bank AG, $276.29
10. BT Alex. Brown, $250.00

Source: *Latin Finance*, March, 1999, p. 78.

Participation Loans--Chile

★3418★
TOP ARRANGERS OF CORPORATE LOANS IN CHILE, 1998
Ranked by: Loan amount, in millions of U.S. dollars ($). **Remarks:** Includes number of issues and market share. **Number listed:** 10

1. Chase Manhattan Bank, with $406.63 million
2. Barclays, $373.50
3. Dresdner Bank AG, $162.25
4. Citigroup Inc., $92.88
5. Paribas, $80.67
6. Banco Central-Hispanoamericano SA, $67.92
7. J.P. Morgan & Co., $67.25
8. Banque Nationale de Paris, $62.50
9. Royal Bank of Canada, $57.92
10. HSBC, $36.67
10. Societe Generale, $36.67

Source: *Latin Finance*, March, 1999, p. 78.

Participation Loans--Latin America

★3419★
TOP ARRANGERS OF CORPORATE LOANS IN LATIN AMERICA, 1998
Ranked by: Loan amount, in millions of U.S. dollars ($). **Remarks:** Includes number of issues and market share. **Number listed:** 15

1. BankAmerica Corp., with $4,694.25 million
2. Chase Manhattan Bank, $4,027.48
3. Citigroup Inc., $3,138.63
4. ING Barings, $1,854.54
5. Barclays, $1,805.29
6. Dresdner Bank AG, $1,799.63
7. Societe Generale, $1,284.19
8. WestLB, $1,243.29
9. Deutsche Bank AG, $1,229.18
10. Warburg Dillon Read, $1,178.00

Source: *Latin Finance*, March, 1999, p. 78.

Participation Loans--Mexico

★3420★
TOP ARRANGERS OF CORPORATE LOANS IN MEXICO, 1998
Ranked by: Loan amount, in millions of U.S. dollars ($). **Remarks:** Includes number of issues and market share. **Number listed:** 10

1. BankAmerica Corp., with $1,153,51 million
2. Citigroup Inc., $879.67
3. ING Barings, $563.00
4. Chase Manhattan Bank, $488.50
5. Warburg Dillon Read, $454.50
6. Barclays, $449.67
7. Bancomer SA, $357.33
8. Bank of Montreal, $323.00
9. Paribas, $317.33
10. J.P. Morgan & Co., $306.33

Source: *Latin Finance*, March, 1999, p. 78.

Participation Loans--Venezuela

★3421★
TOP ARRANGERS OF CORPORATE LOANS IN VENEZUELA, 1998
Ranked by: Loan amount, in millions of U.S. dollars ($). **Remarks:** Includes number of issues and market share. **Number listed:** 10

1. Banco Santander, with $342.88 million
2. ING Barings, $336.11
3. Dresdner Bank AG, $329.27
4. Chase Manhattan Bank, $327.05
5. Deutsche Bank AG, $244.44
6. J.P. Morgan & Co., $200.00
7. WestLB, $167.32
8. BankAmerica Corp., $162.83
9. Paribas, $159.32
10. Merrill Lynch & Co., $150.00

Source: *Latin Finance*, March, 1999, p. 78.

Pasta

★3422★
LEADING CHANNELS OF DISTRIBUTION FOR DRY PASTA, 1996
Ranked by: Production, in thousands of pounds. **Remarks:** Includes market share. **Number listed:** 3

1. Retail, with 1,657,321 thousand pounds
2. Industrial, 637,782
3. Food service, 336,323

Source: *Milling & Baking News*, October 27, 1998, p. 28.

Patents

★3423★
CHEMICAL COMPANIES GRANTED THE MOST PATENTS, 1997
Ranked by: Number of patents issued. **Remarks:** Also includes number of patents issued to these companies in each year from 1987-1997. **Number listed:** 16

1. Dupont, with 318 patents
2. Dow Chemical, 163
3. American Cyanamid, 107
4. Monsanto, 97
5. Dow Corning, 88
6. PPG Industries, 74
7. W.R. Grace, 73
8. Air Products & Chemicals, 71
9. Rohm & Haas Co., 63
10. Hercules, 35
10. International Specialty Products, 35

Source: *Chemical & Engineering News*, Facts & Figures for Chemical R & D (annual), October 19, 1998, p. 67.

★3424★
DRUG COMPANIES GRANTED THE MOST PATENTS, 1997
Ranked by: Number of patents issued. **Remarks:** Also includes number of patents issued to these companies in each year from 1987-1997. **Number listed:** 9

1. Eli Lilly, with 222 patents
2. Abbott Laboratories, 189
3. Merck, 161
4. Bristol-Myers Squibb, 134
5. Pfizer, 102
6. Warner-Lambert, 87
7. Hoffmann-La Roche, 79
8. American Home Products, 34
9. Pharmacia & Upjohn, 21

Source: *Chemical & Engineering News*, Facts & Figures for Chemical R & D (annual), October 19, 1998, p. 67.

Pens

★3425★
LEADING BRANDS OF PENS BY PRICE PER PEN*
Ranked by: Price, in dollars. **Remarks:** Price on Bic Round Stic is for a pack of 10 pens. **Number listed:** 4

1. Parker Duofold, with $185.00
2. Waterman LeMan Rhapsody, $165.00
2. Mont Blanc, $165.00
4. Cross Townsend, $75.00
5. Bic Round Stic, $3.15

Source: *ABA Journal*, September, 1998, p. 16.

★3426★
TOP MANUFACTURERS OF PENS*
Ranked by: Market share, in percent. **Number listed:** 11

1. Sanford, with 18.8%
2. Papermate, 14.3%
3. Binney & Smith, 11.4%
4. Bic, 11.1%
5. Pentel, 8.8%
5. Pilot, 8.8%
7. Pentech, 5.8%
8. Rose Art, 4.1%
9. Avery Dennison, 3.1%
10. Zebra, 1.5%
11. Other, 12.2%

Source: *Discount Store News*, February 22, 1999, p. 41.

Pension Plans

See also: **Trade Unions--Pension Plans**

★3427★
TOP CORPORATE PENSION FUNDS*
Ranked by: Assets, in millions of dollars. **Number listed:** 10

1. General Motors, with $87,000 million
2. General Electric, $58,739
3. IBM, $52,657
4. Ford Motor, $50,700
5. Lucent Technologies, $49,828
6. Boeing, $49,500
7. Bell Atlantic, $47,357
8. Lockheed Martin, $35,215
9. SBC Communications, $31,106
10. DuPont, $30,655

Source: *Pensions & Investments*, Top 1,000 Funds (annual), January 25, 1999, p. 39.

★3428★
TOP CORPORATE TAX-EXEMPT PENSION FUNDS, 1999
Ranked by: Assets, in thousands of dollars. **Number listed:** 7059

1. General Motors Investment Management, with $95,498,827 thousand
2. General Electric Investment Corporation, $59,485,000
3. IBM Corp., $57,641,000
4. Ford Motor Company, $56,400,000
5. Bell Atlantic Asset Management Co., $55,096,778
6. Lucent Technologies Inc., $51,020,000
7. Boeing Company, $47,200,000
8. Lockheed Martin Investment Management, $36,214,000
9. SBC Communications Inc., $33,998,371
10. E.I. DuPont de Nemours & Co., $31,488,034

Source: *Money Market Directories*, Money Market Directory of Pension Funds and Their Investment Managers (annual), 1999, p. 1369+.

★3429★
TOP DEFINED BENEFIT PENSION FUNDS*
Ranked by: Assets, in millions of dollars. **Number listed:** 10

1. California Employees, with $133,449 million
2. New York Common, $99,739
3. California Teachers, $82,600
4. Florida State Board, $77,525
5. New York State Teachers, $71,077
6. Texas Teachers, $69,464
7. General Motors, $67,000
8. New Jersey, $62,614
9. New York City Retirement, $55,160
10. Wisconsin Investment, $50,197

Source: *Pensions & Investments*, Top 1,000 Funds (annual), January 25, 1999, p. 38.

★3430★
TOP DEFINED CONTRIBUTION PENSION FUNDS*
Ranked by: Assets, in millions of dollars. **Number listed:** 10

1. Federal Retirement Thrift, with $64,452 million
2. United Nations, $21,174
3. General Motors, $20,000
4. General Electric, $19,735
5. Procter & Gamble, $19,560
6. Boeing, $17,150
7. Ford Motor, $15,700
8. IBM, $14,969
9. DuPont, $13,722
10. Lucent, $13,637

Source: *Pensions & Investments*, Top 1,000 Funds (annual), January 25, 1999, p. 38.

★3431★
TOP ENDOWMENT TAX-EXEMPT PENSION FUNDS*
Ranked by: Assets, in thousands of dollars. **Number listed:** 762

1. Texas Permanent School Fund, with $18,200,000 thousand
2. Harvard University, $12,800,000
3. University of Texas System, $11,211,000
4. New Mexico State Permanent Fund, $9,800,000
5. Massachusetts Institute of Technology, $7,049,511
6. Yale University, $6,745,775

7. Stanford University, $5,215,834
8. Trustees of Princeton University, $5,100,000
9. Emory University, $4,764,000
10. University of California, $4,300,000

Source: *Money Market Directories*, Money Market Directory of Pension Funds and Their Investment Managers (annual), 1999, p. 1449+.

★3432★
TOP GOVERNMENT TAX-EXEMPT PENSION FUNDS*
Ranked by: Assets, in thousands of dollars. **Number listed:** 917

1. California Public Employees' Retirement Systems (CALPERS), with $143,620,626 thousand
2. New York State Common Retirement Fund, $104,669,000
3. New York City Retirement Systems, $89,439,055
4. Florida State Board of Administration, $89,404,930
5. California State Teachers' Retirement System, $87,216,000
6. New York State Teachers' Retirement System, $76,950,000
7. Teacher Retirement System of Texas, $71,373,000
8. Federal Retirement Thrift Investment Board, $67,000,000
9. Wisconsin Investment Board, $59,845,000
10. New Jersey Division of Investment, $59,439,000

Source: *Money Market Directories*, Money Market Directory of Pension Funds and Their Investment Managers (annual), 1999, p. 1449+.

★3433★
TOP MISCELLANEOUS PENSION FUNDS*
Ranked by: Assets, in millions of dollars. **Number listed:** 10

1. Federal Retirement Thrift, with $64,452 million
2. University of California, $37,372
3. United Nations Joint Staff, $21,174
4. United Methodist, $9,915
5. Illinois State Universities, $8,988
6. World Bank, $8,637
7. Federal Reserve, $7,425
8. Southern Baptist, $6,066
9. Presbyterian Church, $5,585
10. National Rural Electric, $5,107

Source: *Pensions & Investments*, Top 1,000 Funds (annual), January 25, 1999, p. 39.

★3434★
TOP PENSION FUNDS WITH ASSETS IN MORTGAGE-BACKED SECURITIES*
Ranked by: Assets, in millions of dollars. **Number listed:** 61

1. Texas Teachers, with $7,275 million
2. Ohio Employees, $6,406
3. California Teachers, $6,206
4. Florida State Board, $5,954
5. New York Common, $5,383
6. Indiana Employees, $4,870
7. North Carolina, $4,417
8. Texas Employees, $4,350
9. Texas County & District, $3,752
10. South Carolina, $3,399

Source: *Pensions & Investments*, Top 1,000 Funds (annual), January 25, 1999, p. 40.

★3435★
TOP PENSION FUNDS WITH DEFINED BENEFIT ASSETS IN BUY-OUT/ACQUISITIONS*
Ranked by: Assets, in millions of dollars. **Number listed:** 45

1. New York Common, with $2,867 million
2. Oregon Employees, $2,821
3. Washington State Board, $2,520
4. Lucent Technologies, $2,343
5. IBM, $1,775
6. General Electric, $1,519
7. Michigan Retirement, $1,480
8. California Teachers, $1,304
9. Wisconsin Investment, $1,053
10. Colorado Employees, $842

Source: *Pensions & Investments*, Top 1,000 Funds (annual), January 25, 1999, p. 64.

★3436★
TOP PENSION FUNDS WITH DEFINED BENEFIT ASSETS IN DISTRESSED DEBT*
Ranked by: Assets, in millions of dollars. **Number listed:** 18

1. Virginia Retirement, with $199 million
2. Louisiana Teachers, $87
3. Los Angeles Fire & Police, $70
4. Chrysler, $56
5. Delta Air Lines, $50
6. Northwest Airlines, $36
7. Goodyear Tire & Rubber, $27
8. Los Angeles County, $26
9. Tenneco, $22
10. United Airlines, $20

Source: *Pensions & Investments*, Top 1,000 Funds (annual), January 25, 1999, p. 64.

★3437★
TOP PENSION FUNDS WITH DEFINED BENEFIT ASSETS IN EMERGING MARKETS*
Ranked by: Assets, in millions of dollars. **Remarks:** Includes equity and debt. **Number listed:** 100

1. Ohio Teachers, with $3,024 million
2. New York Common, $1,347
3. DuPont, $1,012
4. IBM, $977
5. California Teachers, $950
6. Bell Atlantic, $832
7. General Electric, $820
8. Florida State Board, $813
9. Virginia Retirement, $804
10. California Employees, $751

Source: *Pensions & Investments*, Top 1,000 Funds (annual), January 25, 1999, p. 70.

★3438★
TOP PENSION FUNDS WITH DEFINED BENEFIT ASSETS IN INDEXED EQUITIES AND INDEXED BONDS*
Ranked by: Assets, in millions of dollars. **Remarks:** Includes domestic equity, domestic bonds, international equity and international bonds. **Number listed:** 120

1. California Employees, with $64,316 million
2. California Teachers, $60,018
3. New York State Teachers, $41,105
4. Texas Teachers, $38,475
5. Florida State Board, $35,850
6. New York Common, $35,015
7. New York City Retirement, $27,428
8. New York City Teachers, $21,103
9. Washington State Board, $16,812
10. Wisconsin Investment, $15,310

Source: *Pensions & Investments*, Top 1,000 Funds (annual), January 25, 1999, p. 52.

★3439★
TOP PENSION FUNDS WITH DEFINED BENEFIT ASSETS IN INTERNATIONAL INVESTMENTS*
Ranked by: Assets, in millions of dollars. **Remarks:** Includes active equity, indexed equity, active bonds and indexed bonds. **Number listed:** 75
1. California Employees, with $28,369 million
2. California Teachers, $16,599
3. New Jersey, $11,465
4. Wisconsin Board, $10,648
5. IBM, $9,157
6. New York Common, $8,902
7. Ohio Teachers, $8,325
8. New York State Teachers, $7,673
9. Oregon Employees, $6,183
10. Maryland Retirement, $6,028

Source: *Pensions & Investments*, Top 1,000 Funds (annual), January 25, 1999, p. 46.

★3440★
TOP PENSION FUNDS WITH DEFINED BENEFIT ASSETS IN NON-INVESTMENT GRADE BONDS*
Ranked by: Assets, in millions of dollars. **Number listed:** 44
1. Pennsylvania Employees, with $1,250 million
2. Florida Board, $1,051
3. Oregon Employees, $865
4. Connecticut Retirement, $840
5. General Electric, $679
6. Los Angeles County, $652
7. Teamsters Central States, $589
8. Tennessee Valley Authority, $560
9. Massachusetts PRIM, $517
10. Delta Air Lines, $500

Source: *Pensions & Investments*, Top 1,000 Funds (annual), January 25, 1999, p. 60.

★3441★
TOP PENSION FUNDS WITH DEFINED BENEFIT ASSETS IN OIL & GAS*
Ranked by: Assets, in millions of dollars. **Number listed:** 18
1. Teamsters Central States, with $366 million
2. Minnesota State Board, $157
3. BellSouth, $123
4. Delta Air Lines, $100
5. AT&T, $86
6. San Francisco City & County, $77
7. GTE, $71
8. Virginia Retirement, $55
9. American Airlines, $52
10. USX, $48

Source: *Pensions & Investments*, Top 1,000 Funds (annual), January 25, 1999, p. 64.

★3442★
TOP PENSION FUNDS WITH DEFINED BENEFIT ASSETS IN PRIVATE EQUITY*
Ranked by: Assets, in millions of dollars. **Remarks:** Includes domestic and international. **Number listed:** 48
1. California Employees, with $3,635 million
2. Michigan Retirement, $1,759
3. General Electric, $1,535
4. Bell Atlantic, $1,324
5. Florida State Board, $1,256
6. California Teachers, $509
7. SBC Communications, $506
8. Louisiana Teachers, $476
9. DuPont, $457
10. AT&T, $433

Source: *Pensions & Investments*, Top 1,000 Funds (annual), January 25, 1999, p. 58.

★3443★
TOP PENSION FUNDS WITH DEFINED BENEFIT ASSETS IN REAL ESTATE EQUITY*
Ranked by: Assets, in millions of dollars. **Number listed:** 109
1. California Employees, with $6,070 million
2. Ohio Teachers, $4,153
3. Michigan Retirement, $3,098
4. Florida State Board, $3,022
5. Pennsylvania Public School, $2,807
6. Lucent Technologies, $2,799
7. New York Common, $2,688
8. New York State Teachers, $2,630
9. Illinois Teachers, $2,457
10. Los Angeles County, $2,256

Source: *Pensions & Investments*, Top 1,000 Funds (annual), January 25, 1999, p. 62.

★3444★
TOP PENSION FUNDS WITH DEFINED BENEFIT ASSETS IN VENTURE CAPITAL*
Ranked by: Assets, in millions of dollars. **Number listed:** 69
1. Lucent Technologies, with $1,108 million
2. Minnesota Board, $1,098
3. Connecticut Trust Funds, $835
4. Washington State Board, $779
5. Bell Atlantic, $736
6. California Employees, $673
7. AT&T, $445
8. Virginia Retirement, $421
9. Pennsylvania Employees, $416
10. Colorado Employees, $394

Source: *Pensions & Investments*, Top 1,000 Funds (annual), January 25, 1999, p. 60.

★3445★
TOP PENSION FUNDS WITH DEFINED BENEFIT INDEXED ASSETS MANAGED INTERNALLY*
Ranked by: Assets, in millions of dollars. **Remarks:** Includes equity and bonds. **Number listed:** 35
1. California Employees, with $49,939 million
2. New York Teachers, $38,561
3. New York Common, $30,905
4. California Teachers, $27,863
5. Florida State Board, $22,067
6. IBM, $13,053
7. Colorado Employees, $10,020
8. Michigan Retirement, $6,754
9. Ohio Teachers, $6,069
10. Kentucky Retirement, $5,483

Source: *Pensions & Investments*, Top 1,000 Funds (annual), January 25, 1999, p. 50.

★3446★
TOP PENSION FUNDS WITH DEFINED CONTRIBUTION ASSETS IN INDEXED EQUITIES AND INDEXED BONDS*
Ranked by: Assets, in millions of dollars. **Remarks:** Includes equity and bonds. **Number listed:** 81
1. Federal Retirement Thrift, with $38,118 million
2. Boeing, $9,335
3. IBM, $7,939
4. New York City Teachers, $5,984
5. United Methodist Church, $2,663
6. Bell Atlantic, $2,391
7. Shell Oil, $2,115
8. Philip Morris, $1,960
9. Ford Motor, $1,873
10. Lucent Technologies, $1,800

Source: *Pensions & Investments*, Top 1,000 Funds (annual), January 25, 1999, p. 54.

★3447★
TOP PENSION FUNDS WITH DEFINED CONTRIBUTION ASSETS IN INTERNATIONAL INVESTMENTS*
Ranked by: Assets, in millions of dollars. **Remarks:** Includes equity and bonds. **Number listed:** 36

1. United Nations Joint Staff, with $11,228 million
2. American Airlines, $998
2. United Methodist Church, $998
4. New York City Teachers, $832
5. Evangelical Lutheran Church, $739
6. IBM, $684
7. American Stores, $660
8. Southern Baptist Convention, $567
9. AT&T, $461
10. Motorola, $369

Source: *Pensions & Investments*, Top 1,000 Funds (annual), January 25, 1999, p. 48.

★3448★
TOP PENSION FUNDS WITH DEFINED CONTRIBUTION INTERNALLY MANAGED ASSETS*
Ranked by: Assets, in millions of dollars. **Number listed:** 32

1. Federal Retirement Thrift, with $26,334 million
2. United Nations, $21,174
3. General Electric, $19,735
4. Procter & Gamble, $19,171
5. Exxon, $8,350
6. Texas Municipal, $7,500
7. University of California, $4,501
8. Citigroup, $3,800
9. Prudential Insurance, $3,400
10. Eastman Kodak, $3,100

Source: *Pensions & Investments*, Top 1,000 Funds (annual), January 25, 1999, p. 56.

★3449★
TOP PUBLIC PENSION FUNDS*
Ranked by: Assets, in millions of dollars. **Number listed:** 10

1. California Employees, with $133,525 million
2. New York State Common, $99,739
3. California Teachers, $82,625
4. Florida State Board, $77,525
5. New York State Teachers, $71,077
6. Texas Teachers, $69,464
7. New Jersey, $63,324
8. New York City Retirement, $55,160
9. Wisconsin Investment, $50,991
10. Ohio Employees, $47,456

Source: *Pensions & Investments*, Top 1,000 Funds (annual), January 25, 1999, p. 39.

★3450★
TOP UNION PENSION FUNDS*
Ranked by: Assets, in millions of dollars. **Number listed:** 10

1. Western Teamsters, with $20,854 million
2. Teamsters Central States, $17,122
3. National Electrical, $8,485
4. UMWA Health & Retirement, $6,025
5. Operating Engineers, $5,461
6. Boilermaker-Blacksmith, $5,027
7. 1199 Healthcare Employees, $5,000
8. Sheet Metal Workers, $4,669
9. Bakery & Confectionery, $4,658
10. UNITE, $4,380

Source: *Pensions & Investments*, Top 1,000 Funds (annual), January 25, 1999, p. 39.

★3451★
TOP UNION TAX-EXEMPT PENSION FUNDS, 1999*
Ranked by: Assets, in thousands of dollars. **Number listed:** 1260

1. Teamsters, Western Conference, with $20,800,000 thousand
2. Teamsters, Central States, Southeast & Southwest Areas Pension Fund, $18,900,000
3. National Electrical Benefit Fund, $8,494,000
4. United Mine Workers of America Health & Retirement Funds, $7,666,648
5. Engineers, Operating, International, $5,745,047
6. Boilermakers-Blacksmith National Pension Trust, $5,444,533
7. Retail, Wholesale Union, Local 1199, $5,200,000
8. Health & Human Service Employees Union, Local 1199, $5,147,000
9. Bakery & Confectionery Union & Industry International Pension Fund, $4,942,562
10. Sheet Metal Workers National Pension, $4,362,233

Source: *Money Market Directories*, Money Market Directory of Pension Funds and Their Investment Managers (annual), 1999, p. 1425+.

Pension Plans--Europe

★3452★
TOP EUROPEAN PENSION FUNDS BY CHANGE IN NUMBER OF PENSION MANDATES, 1998
Ranked by: Change in number of pension mandates from 1997 to 1998. **Remarks:** Includes number of pension mandates for 1997 and for 1998. **Number listed:** 26

1. ING Investment, with 100
2. Robeco Institutional, 69
3. Lombard Odier, 46
4. Morgan Grenfell, 35
5. Achmea Global Investors, 27
6. Capital Intl, 21
6. Fidelity Intl, 21
8. Metzler Investment, 16
8. State Street Global, 16
10. Credit Suisse Asset, 14

Source: *Pensions & Investments*, February 22, 1999, p. 18.

★3453★
TOP EUROPEAN PENSION FUNDS BY CHANGE IN VALUE OF PENSION MANDATES, 1998
Ranked by: Change in value of pension mandates, in millions of U.S. dollars ($). **Remarks:** Includes 1997 and 1998 values. **Number listed:** 26

1. Schroder Investment, with $16,899 million
2. Barclays Global, $12,315
3. Achmea Global, $11,035
4. Robeco Institutional, $10,613
5. Merrill Lynch/Mercury, $10,414
6. Morgan Grenfell, $9,562
7. Fidelity Intl, $6,544
8. ING Investment, $5,448
9. State Street Global, $5,422
10. Phillips & Drew, $4,554

Source: *Pensions & Investments*, February 22, 1999, p. 18.

Pension Plans, International

★3454★
WORLD'S LARGEST PENSION FUNDS, 1997
Ranked by: Assets, in millions of U.S. dollars ($). **Number listed:** 300

1. California Public Employees (U.S.), with $127,656 million
2. Stichting Pensioenfonds ABP (Netherlands), $114,324
3. Association of Local Public Service Personnel (Japan), $98,986
4. New York State Common Retirement Fund (U.S.), $95,812
5. General Motors (U.S.), $90,600
6. California State Teachers (U.S.), $78,900
7. Allmanna Pensionsfonden (Board 1,2, & 3) (Sweden), $76,374
8. National Public Service Personnel (Japan), $73,895
9. Florida State Board (U.S.), $71,940
10. New York State Teachers (U.S.), $68,738

Source: *Pensions & Investments*, Top 300 (annual), August 24, 1998, p. 16.

Perfumes

★3455★
BEST-SELLING MEN'S FRAGRANCES, 1998
Ranked by: Sales, in millions of dollars. **Remarks:** Includes lead advertising agency and media expenditures. **Number listed:** 5

1. Stetson (Coty), with $47.3 million
2. Old Spice (Procter & Gamble), $46.3
3. Brut (Univlever), $31.8
4. Aspen (Coty), $24.9
5. Preferred Stock (Coty), $23.5

Source: *Brandweek*, Superbrands: America's Top 2,000 Brands (annual), June 21, 1999, p. 534.

★3456★
BEST-SELLING WOMEN'S FRAGRANCES IN DRUG STORES, 1998
Ranked by: Three-outlet sales, in millions of dollars. **Remarks:** Includes percent change and dollar share. **Number listed:** 10

1. Calgon, with $38.3 million
2. Body Fantasies, $36.6
3. Healing Garden, $23.2
4. Vanilla Fields, $20.9
4. Sarah Michaels, $20.9
6. White Diamonds, $20.0
7. Vanderbilt, $16.3
8. Jovan Musk for Women, $15.9
9. Jovan White Musk, $14.6
10. Charlie, $12.6

Source: *Drug Store News*, June 7, 1999, p. 202.

★3457★
BEST-SELLING WOMEN'S FRAGRANCES, 1998
Ranked by: Sales, in millions of dollars. **Remarks:** Includes lead advertising agency and media expenditures. **Number listed:** 5

1. Body Fantasy (Dial/Sarah Michaels), with $34.9 million
2. Calgon Body Mists (Coty), $34.2
3. The Healing Garden (Coty), $21.0
4. Vanilla Fields (Coty), $20.6
5. White Diamonds (Unilever), $18.5

Source: *Brandweek*, Superbrands: America's Top 2,000 Brands (annual), June 21, 1999, p. 534.

Periodical Publishers and Publishing

★3458★
COMPANIES SPENDING THE MOST ON MAGAZINE ADVERTISING, 1998
Ranked by: Ad expenditures, in millions of dollars. **Remarks:** Includes number of ad pages purchased. **Number listed:** 20

1. General Motors, with $459.3 million
2. Procter & Gamble, $407.3
3. Philip Morris, $383.5
4. Chrysler Corp., $354.6
5. Ford Motor Corp., $291.3
6. Time Warner, $180.0
7. Toyota Motor, $173.8
8. Unilever PLC, $169.6
9. Sony, $143.7
10. RJR Nabisco Corp., $135.2

Source: *Adweek*, Hottest Magazines (annual), March 8, 1999, p. 42.

★3459★
TOP MAGAZINE PUBLISHING COMPANIES BY REVENUE, 1998
Ranked by: Revenue, in millions of dollars. **Remarks:** Includes percent change in revenue, number of 1998 ad pages, and percent change in number of ad pages. **Number listed:** 36

1. Time Inc., with $2,935.4 million
2. Conde Nast, $1,215.1
3. Hearst Magazines, $1,140.0
4. Hachette Filipacchi, $960.7
5. Meredith Corp., $808.2
6. Gruner Jahr, $593.3
7. Parade Publications, $517.1
8. Ziff-Davis, $468.1
9. News America Corp., $461.7
10. Newsweek Inc., $400.0

Source: *Adweek*, Hottest Magazines (annual), March 8, 1999, p. 42.

★3460★
TOP MAGAZINES ADVERTISING CATEGORIES, 1998
Ranked by: Expenditures, in millions of dollars. **Remarks:** Includes percent change in revenue. **Number listed:** 20

1. Automotive, with $1,730.5 million
2. Direct reponse, $1,616.2
3. Computers, office equipment, $940.4
4. Drugs and remedies, $807.9
5. Travel, hotels, and resorts, $644.8
6. Financial, $607.1
7. Toiletries and cosmetics, $594.1
8. Publishing & media, $585.7
9. Misc. merchandise, $507.8
10. Apparel, footwear, accessories, $504.5

Source: *Adweek*, Hottest Magazines (annual), March 8, 1999, p. 42.

★3461★
TOP MAGAZINES IN AD REVENUE, 1998
Ranked by: Ad revenue, in millions of dollars. **Remarks:** Includes percent change in revenue. **Number listed:** 60

1. *People Weekly*, with $626.6 million
2. *Time*, $561.7
3. *Sports Illustrated*, $554.9
4. *Parade*, $517.1
5. *TV Guide*, $453.5
6. *Better Homes and Gardens*, $410.1
7. *Newsweek*, $400.0
8. *Business Week*, $361.6
9. *PC Magazine*, $314.2
10. *USA Weekend*, $274.5

Source: *Adweek*, Hottest Magazines (annual), March 8, 1999, p. 40.

★3462★
TOP MAGAZINES IN PAID CIRCULATION, 1998
Ranked by: Paid circulation. **Remarks:** Includes percent change in circulation. **Number listed:** 60

1. *Modern Maturity*, with 20,402,096
2. *Reader's Digest*, 14,675,541
3. *TV Guide*, 13,085,971
4. *National Geographic*, 8,783,752
5. *Better Homes and Gardens*, 7,616,114
6. *Family Circle*, 5,005,084
7. *Ladies' Home Journal*, 4,521,970
8. *Good Housekeeping*, 4,517,713
9. *McCall's*, 4,239,622
10. *Time*, 4,124,451

Source: *Adweek*, Hottest Magazines (annual), March 8, 1999, p. 40.

★3463★
TOP MEDIA COMPANIES BY MAGAZINE REVENUE, 1997
Ranked by: Magazine revenue, in millions of dollars. **Remarks:** Includes magazines as a percent of all media revenue, 1996 figures and percent changes. **Number listed:** 25

1. Time Warner, with $3,070.9 million
2. Hearst Corp., $1,460.3
3. Advance Publications, $1,283.0
4. Reed Elsevier PLC, $1,268.6
5. Thomson Corp., $937.0
6. Primedia, $859.1
7. Reader's Digest Association, $811.1
8. International Data Group, $786.5
9. Ziff-Davis Publishing Co., $747.6
10. News Corp. Ltd., $673.2

Source: *Advertising Age*, 100 Leading Media Companies (annual), August 17, 1998, p. S10.

Periodicals

See also: **Black Periodicals**

★3464★
BEST-SELLING MAGAZINES*
Ranked by: Audience gained, in thousands. **Number listed:** 10

1. *Vibe*, with 2,105 thousand gained
2. *Men's Fitness*, 1,177
3. *Men's Health*, 1,130
4. *Martha Stewart Living*, 1,073
5. *Inc.*, 856
6. *Golf Magazine*, 672
7. *Child*, 586
8. *Gourmet*, 553
9. *Fitness*, 545
10. *Sunset*, 491

Source: *Advertising Age*, March 8, 1999, p. 55.

★3465★
TOP BUSINESS/FINANCE PUBLICATIONS, 1997
Ranked by: Revenue, in thousands of dollars. **Number listed:** 11

1. *Business Week*, with $268,860 thousand
2. *Forbes*, $239,915
3. *Fortune*, $220,041
4. *Money*, $165,540
5. *Inc.*, $81,716
6. *Barron's*, $79,314
7. *Entrepreneur*, $70,176
8. *Kiplinger's Personal Finance*, $54,602
9. *Smart Money*, $49,920
10. *Institutional Investor*, $39,839

Source: *Folio*, Folio 500 (annual), July, 1998, p. 62.

★3466★
TOP BUSINESS, HEALTHCARE, FARM AND COMPUTER MAGAZINE CLASSIFICATIONS, 1998
Ranked by: Revenue, in millions of dollars. **Remarks:** Includes ad revenue, ad pages, circulation revenue, paid circulation, number of magazines, top magazine, 1998 revenue and percent change in total revenue from 1997. **Number listed:** 10

1. Computer/Internet (special class), with $2,568.4 million
2. Electronic engineering, $303.9
3. Travel, retail, $205.9
4. Medical & surgical, $145.8
5. Product design engineering, $106.9
6. Restaurants & food service, $102.6
7. Diversified farming & farm home, $80.7
8. Advertising & marketing, $80.6
9. Science, research & development, $63.0
10. Travel, business conventions & meetings, $61.9

Source: *Advertising Age*, Ad Age 300 (annual), June 14, 1999, p. S18.

★3467★
TOP BUSINESS MAGAZINES, 1998
Ranked by: Paid circulation, in thousands of dollars. **Remarks:** Includes circulation revenue, 1997 figures and percent change. **Number listed:** 15

1. *Successful Farming*, with $475,793 thousand
2. *Journal of Accountancy*, $358,746
3. *Aopa Pilot*, $329,353
4. *ABA Journal*, $322,547
5. *Progressive Farmer*, $290,881
6. *Fast Company*, $256,348
7. *Journal of the AMA*, $244,038
8. *American Medical News*, $225,621
9. *New England Journal of Medicine*, $225,364
10. *Farm Journal*, $174,203

Source: *Advertising Age*, Ad Age 300 (annual), June 14, 1999, p. S22.

★3468★
TOP COMPUTER CONSUMER PUBLICATIONS, 1997
Ranked by: Revenue, in thousands of dollars. **Number listed:** 9

1. *PC World*, with $160,158 thousand
2. *PC Computing*, $119,186
3. *Windows Magazine*, $99,906
4. *Macworld*, $70,065
5. *Home PC*, $34,715
6. *PC Gamer*, $34,492
7. *Internet World*, $27,698
8. *Computer Gaming*, $27,391

9. *Wired*, $29,499

Source: *Folio*, Folio 500 (annual), July, 1998, p. 72.

★3469★
TOP COMPUTER/INTERNET/ELECTRONIC GAME MAGAZINES, 1998

Ranked by: Paid circulation, in thousands of dollars. **Remarks:** Includes circulation revenue, 1997 figures and percent change. **Number listed:** 15

1. *PC Magazine*, with $1,182,181 thousand
2. *PC World*, $1,147,034
3. *PC/Computing*, $1,044,252
4. *Windows Magazine*, $818,972
5. *Computer Shopper*, $560,267
6. *Wired*, $511,478
7. *Home Office Computing*, $501,090
8. *Macworld*, $476,200
9. *Yahoo! Internet Life*, $453,433
10. *Family PC*, $401,163

Source: *Advertising Age*, Ad Age 300 (annual), June 14, 1999, p. S22.

★3470★
TOP COMPUTER TRADE PUBLICATIONS, 1997

Ranked by: Revenue, in thousands of dollars. **Number listed:** 10

1. *PC Magazine*, with $359,106 thousand
2. *PC Week*, $181,332
3. *Computer Shopper*, $178,393
4. *InfoWorld*, $169,996
5. *Computer Reseller News*, $148,190
6. *Computerworld*, $125,072
7. *Information Week*, $114,157
8. *Network World*, $67,011
9. *Network Computing*, $57,823
10. *Byte*, $49,000

Source: *Folio*, Folio 500 (annual), July, 1998, p. 80.

★3471★
TOP CONSUMER MAGAZINE CLASSIFICATIONS, 1998

Ranked by: Revenue, in millions of dollars. **Remarks:** Includes ad revenue, ad pages, circulation revenue, paid circulation, number of magazines, top magazine, 1998 revenue and percent change in total revenue from 1997. **Number listed:** 15

1. News-weeklies, with $5,176.6 million
2. Women's, $4,218.8
3. General editorial, $3,213.8
4. Home service & home, $2,067.1
5. Business & Finance, $1,899.6
6. Men's, $1,025.3
7. Sports, $659.6
8. Automotive, $556.7
9. Travel, $433.0
10. Parenthood, $377.6

Source: *Advertising Age*, Ad Age 300 (annual), June 14, 1999, p. S18.

★3472★
TOP CONSUMER MAGAZINES, 1998

Ranked by: Subscription revenue, in millions of dollars. **Remarks:** Includes paid circulation, 1997 figures, and percent change. **Number listed:** 15

1. *TV Guide*, with $525.3 million
2. *Reader's Digest*, $306.3
3. *Sports Illustrated*, $258.8
4. *People*, $228.4
5. *Time*, $226.6
6. *National Geographic*, $158.1
7. *Better Homes & Gardens*, $137.0
8. *Newsweek*, $123.1
9. *Consumer Reports*, $108.1
10. *Cable Guide*, $100.1

Source: *Advertising Age*, Ad Age 300 (annual), June 14, 1999, p. S22.

★3473★
TOP EPICUREAN PUBLICATIONS, 1997

Ranked by: Revenue, in thousands of dollars. **Number listed:** 9

1. *Cooking Light*, with $58,923 thousand
2. *Gourmet*, $58,762
3. *Bon Appetit*, $53,146
4. *Food & Wine*, $50,957
5. *Wine Spectator*, $22,292
6. *Eating Well*, $17,857
7. *Pillsbury Classic Cookbooks*, $17,547
8. *Vegetarian Times*, $17,474
9. *Saveur*, $15,618

Source: *Folio*, Folio 500 (annual), July, 1998, p. 76.

★3474★
TOP MAGAZINE AGENCIES*

Ranked by: Specific ranking information not provided. **Remarks:** Includes top magazine in agency. **Number listed:** 24

1. Richards Group, Dallas (in-house)
2. Y&R Advertising
3. Fallon McElligott
4. Fallon McElligott
5. D'Arcy Masius Benton & Bowles
6. Della Femina/Jeary & Partners
7. Better Homes & Gardens (in-house)
8. Warwick Baker O'Neill
9. Partners & Simons
10. Draft Worldwide

Source: *Advertising Age*, March 8, 1999, p. S22.

★3475★
TOP MAGAZINE PUBLICATIONS BY REVENUE, 1997

Ranked by: Revenue, in thousands of dollars. **Remarks:** Includes frequency, total circulation, percent change from 1996, paid subscriptions, subscription price, cover price, 1997 ad pages, percent change in ad pages from 1996 and ad page rate. **Number listed:** 500

1. *TV Guide*, with $1,125,400 thousand
2. *People Weekly*, $827,688
3. *Time*, $581,558
4. *Sports Illustrated*, $553,928
5. *Reader's Digest*, $536,358
6. *Better Homes and Gardens*, $454,700
7. *Newsweek*, $404,946
8. *PC Magazine*, $359,106
9. *Parade*, $352,526
10. *Good Housekeeping*, $292,156

Source: *Folio*, Folio 500 (annual), July, 1998, p. 62+.

★3476★
TOP MAGAZINES BY GROSS REVENUE, 1998

Ranked by: Revenue, in millions of dollars. **Remarks:** Includes headquarters location, 1997 to 1998 percent change, ad revenue, ad pages, subscriber revenue, newsstand revenue, paid circulation, and parent company. **Number listed:** 300

1. *TV Guide*, with $1,170,810 million
2. *People*, $1,078,027
3. *Sports Illustrated*, $850,057
4. *Time*, $814,300
5. *Reader's Digest*, $563,105
6. *Better Homes & Gardens*, $559,124
7. *Newsweek*, $547,164

8. *Parade*, $517,116
9. *Business Week*, $416,922
10. *PC Magazine*, $378,607

Source: *Advertising Age*, Ad Age 300 (annual), June 14, 1999, p. S22.

★3477★
TOP MAGAZINES, 1998
Ranked by: Adweek Performance Index. **Number listed:** 10

1. *In Style*
2. *Bon Appetit*
3. *Architectural Digest*
4. *Martha Stewart Living*
5. *Family Fun*
6. *VIBE*
7. *Fortune*
8. *Men's Journal*
9. *Marie Claire*
10. *Fitness*

Source: *Adweek*, Hottest Magazines (annual), March 2, 1998, p. 34+.

★3478★
TOP REVENUE-PRODUCING BRAND EXTENSIONS*
Ranked by: Ranking based on a poll of 54 b-to-b publishers. The named businesses ranked highest in terms of revenue production. **Number listed:** 10

1. Classified advertising
2. Trade shows
3. Buyer's guides
4. Custom publishing
5. Special issues
6. Newsletters
7. Literature reviews
8. Reprints
9. Direct mail
10. Product marts

Source: *Folio*, November 15, 1998, p. 34.

★3479★
TOP UP-AND-COMING MAGAZINES, 1998
Ranked by: Adweek Performance Index. **Number listed:** 10

1. *Fast Company*
2. *The Source*
3. *Yahoo!*
4. *House & Garden*
5. *This Old House*
6. *The Sporting News*
7. *FamilyLife*
8. *Weight Watchers*
9. *Mirabella*
10. *P.O.V.*

Source: *Adweek*, Hottest Magazines (annual), March 2, 1998, p. 38.

★3480★
TOP WOMEN'S PUBLICATIONS, 1997
Ranked by: Revenue, in thousands of dollars. **Number listed:** 10

1. *Better Homes and Gardens*, with $454,700 thousand
2. *Good Housekeeping*, $292,156
3. *Woman's Day*, $288,193
4. *Family Circle*, $275,515
5. *Ladies' Home Journal*, $253,146
6. *Cosmopolitan*, $230,415
7. *McCall's*, $171,492
8. *Glamour*, $171,462
9. *Vogue*, $163,364
10. *Martha Stewart Living*, $146,075

Source: *Folio*, Folio 500 (annual), July, 1998, p. 68.

★3481★
WORST-SELLING MAGAZINES*
Ranked by: Audience lost, in thousands. **Number listed:** 10

1. *National Enquirer*, with 2,356 thousand lost
2. *Sports Illustrated*, 2,200
3. *TV Guide*, 2,163
4. *Consumer Reports*, 1,749
5. *Star*, 1,688
6. *Field & Stream*, 1,595
7. *People*, 1,559
8. *Newsweek*, 1,481
9. *Hot Rod*, 1,328
10. *Country Living*, 1,308

Source: *Advertising Age*, March 8, 1999, p. 55.

Periodicals--Advertising

★3482★
TOP BUSINESS MAGAZINES BY AD PAGE GROWTH, 1998
Ranked by: Ad page growth, in percent. **Remarks:** Includes number of advertising pages and one-time black & white page price for 1997 and 1998. **Number listed:** 15

1. *Design News*, with 41.8%
2. *Successful Meetings*, 26.6%
3. *Furniture Today*, 21.5%
4. *Nation's Restaurant News*, 20.7%
5. *Farm Journal*, 19.9%
6. *Journal of Accountancy*, 19.2%
7. *Drug Store News*, 19.0%
8. *Restaurants & Institutions*, 18.7%
9. *Chronicle of Higher Education*, 14.0%
10. *Travel Agent*, 13.0%

Source: *Advertising Age*, Ad Age 300 (annual), June 14, 1999, p. S20.

★3483★
TOP BUSINESS MAGAZINES BY AD REVENUE GROWTH, 1998
Ranked by: Ad revenue growth, in percent. **Remarks:** Includes ad revenue and number of ad pages for 1997 and 1998. **Number listed:** 15

1. *Electronic Component News*, with 48.9%
2. *Design News*, 45.4%
3. *Successful Meetings*, 32.2%
4. *Nation's Restaurant News*, 32.0%
5. *Successful Farming*, 30.7%
6. *EE Times*, 22.5%
7. *Drug Store News*, 22.2%
8. *Meetings & Conventions*, 21.2%
9. *Architectural Record*, 21.0%
10. *Chronicle of Higher Education*, 20.5%

Source: *Advertising Age*, Ad Age 300 (annual), June 14, 1999, p. S20.

★3484★
TOP BUSINESS MAGAZINES BY AD REVENUE, 1998
Ranked by: Ad revenue, in millions of dollars. **Remarks:** Includes number of ad pages, ad revenue for 1997 and percent change. **Number listed:** 15

1. *EE Times*, with $116.3 million
2. *Travel Agent*, $101.7
3. *Travel Weekly*, $78.2
4. *Electronic Buyers' News*, $56.8
5. *Design News*, $48.4
6. *Nation's Restaurant News*, $46.8

7. *Electronic Design*, $45.6
8. *EDN*, $44.5
9. *Advertising Age*, $38.6
10. *Machine Design*, $38.3

Source: *Advertising Age*, Ad Age 300 (annual), June 14, 1999, p. S20.

★3485★
TOP BUSINESS MAGAZINES BY NUMBER OF AD PAGES, 1998
Ranked by: Number of ad pages. **Remarks:** Includes one-time black & white page rates, 1997 ad pages and percent change. **Number listed:** 15

1. *Travel Weekly*, with 5,800.00 pages
2. *Travel Agent*, 5,533.00
3. *EE Times*, 5,525.71
4. *New England Journal of Medicine*, 5,481.00
5. *Journal of the AMA*, 4,454.00
6. *Chronicle of Higher Education*, 4,231.09
7. *EDN*, 3,991.00
8. *Design News*, 3,808.91
9. *Nation's Restaurant News*, 3,695.81
10. *Electronic Buyers' News*, 3,682.11

Source: *Advertising Age*, Ad Age 300 (annual), June 14, 1999, p. S20.

★3486★
TOP COMPUTER/INTERNET/ELECTRONIC GAME MAGAZINES BY AD PAGE GROWTH, 1998
Ranked by: Ad page growth, in percent. **Remarks:** Includes one-time black & white page price and number of ad pages for 1997 and 1998. **Number listed:** 15

1. *Official U.S. PlayStation Magazine*, with 85.8%
2. *Yahoo! Internet Life*, 49.5%
3. *CIO*, 31.0%
4. *GamePro*, 20.6%
5. *Electronic Gaming Monthly*, 19.1%
6. *Interactive Week*, 18.6%
7. *Information Week*, 15.6%
8. *VARBusiness*, 6.5%
9. *Computer Gaming World*, 4.2%
10. *Network Computing*, 1.8%

Source: *Advertising Age*, Ad Age 300 (annual), June 14, 1999, p. S20.

★3487★
TOP COMPUTER/INTERNET/ELECTRONIC GAME MAGAZINES BY AD PAGES, 1998
Ranked by: Number of ad pages. **Remarks:** Includes one-time black & white page price for 1997 and 1998 and percent change. **Number listed:** 15

1. *Computer Reseller News*, with 7,776.28 pages
2. *Computer Shopper*, 6,524,75
3. *Information Week*, 5,591.46
4. *PC Week*, 5,447,22
5. *PC Magazine*, 5,385.84
6. *InfoWorld*, 4,709.51
7. *VARBusiness*, 3,061.17
8. *Computerworld*, 2,862.30
9. *PC World*, 2,766.53
10. *Network Computing*, 2,629.50

Source: *Advertising Age*, Ad Age 300 (annual), June 14, 1999, p. S20.

★3488★
TOP COMPUTER/INTERNET/ELECTRONIC GAME MAGAZINES BY AD REVENUE GROWTH, 1998
Ranked by: Ad revenue growth, in percent. **Remarks:** Includes number of ad pages for 1997 and 1998 and percent change. **Number listed:** 15

1. *Official U.S. PlayStation Magazine*, with 119.8%
2. *Yahoo! Internet Life*, 115.3%
3. *Interactive Week*, 51.3%
4. *CIO*, 43.8%
5. *PC Gamer*, 37.0%
6. *GamePro*, 32.9%
7. *InformationWeek*, 27.3%
8. *Computer Gaming World*, 25.0%
9. *Electronic Gaming Monthly*, 19.1%
10. *PC World*, 17.2%

Source: *Advertising Age*, Ad Age 300 (annual), June 14, 1999, p. S20.

★3489★
TOP COMPUTER/INTERNET/ELECTRONIC GAME MAGAZINES BY AD REVENUE, 1998
Ranked by: Ad revenue, in millions of dollars. **Remarks:** Includes number of ad pages for 1997 and 1998 and percent change. **Number listed:** 15

1. *PC Magazine*, with $314.2 million
2. *InformationWeek*, $193.9
3. *PC Week*, $193.7
4. *InfoWorld*, $183.7
5. *Computer Shopper*, $167.5
6. *Computer Reseller News*, $160.7
7. *PC World*, $147.9
8. *Computerworld*, $107.9
9. *PC/Computing*, $102.3
10. *NetworkWorld*, $83.1

Source: *Advertising Age*, Ad Age 300 (annual), June 14, 1999, p. S20.

★3490★
TOP CONSUMER MAGAZINES BY AD PAGE GROWTH, 1998
Ranked by: Ad page growth, in percent. **Remarks:** Includes number of ad pages and one-time black & white page rates for 1997 and 1998. **Number listed:** 15

1. *Fast Company*, with 50.3%
2. *This Old House*, 47.4%
3. *InStyle*, 44.7%
4. *Elle Decor*, 36.0%
5. *Hot Rod*, 35.7%
6. *Esquire*, 35.2%
7. *Mirabella*, 33.9%
8. *The Source*, 30.9%
9. *Bon Appetit*, 30.7%
10. *Travel Holiday*, 27.5%

Source: *Advertising Age*, Ad Age 300 (annual), June 14, 1999, p. S22.

★3491★
TOP CONSUMER MAGAZINES BY AD PAGES, 1998
Ranked by: Number of ad pages. **Remarks:** Includes one-time black & white page rates, 1997 ad pages and percent change. **Number listed:** 15

1. *Hemmings Motor News*, with with 9,250 pages
2. *Forbes*, 4,733.70
3. *Business Week*, 4,167.29
4. *People*, 4,038.08
5. *Fortune*, 3,898.59
6. *Bride's Magazine*, 3,669.82
7. *New York Times Magazine*, 3,173.69
8. *TV Guide*, 3,087.72
9. *Modern Bride*, 2,983.62
10. *The Economist*, 2,841.00

Source: *Advertising Age*, Ad Age 300 (annual), June 14, 1999, p. S22.

★3492★
TOP CONSUMER MAGAZINES BY AD REVENUE GROWTH, 1998
Ranked by: Ad revenue growth, in percent. **Remarks:** Includes number of advertising pages and advertising revenue for 1997 and 1998. **Number listed:** 15

1. *Fast Company*, with 121.7%
2. *This Old House*, 71.9%
3. *InStyle*, 70.9%
4. *Esquire*, 66.0%
5. *The Source*, 61.6%
6. *Hot Rod*, 51.3%
7. *Crayola Kids*, 47.5%
8. *Conde Nast House & Garden*, 41.8%
9. *Elle Decor*, 41.3%
10. *Weight Watchers*, 38.7%

Source: *Advertising Age*, Ad Age 300 (annual), June 14, 1999, p. S22.

★3493★
TOP CONSUMER MAGAZINES BY AD REVENUE, 1998
Ranked by: Ad revenue, in millions of dollars. **Remarks:** Includes number of advertising pages, 1997 revenue and pages and percent change. **Number listed:** 15

1. *People*, with $626.6 million
2. *Time*, $561.7
3. *Sports Illustrated*, $554.9
4. *Parade*, $517.1
5. *TV Guide*, $453.5
6. *Better Homes & Gardens*, $410.1
7. *Newsweek*, $400.0
8. *Business Week*, $361.6
9. *USA Weekend*, $274.6
10. *Forbes*, $265.3

Source: *Advertising Age*, Ad Age 300 (annual), June 14, 1999, p. S22.

Periodicals--Great Britain

★3494★
TOP ACTIVELY PURCHASED MAGAZINE TITLES BY CIRCULATION, 1998
Ranked by: Circulation. **Remarks:** Includes circulation for 1997 and percent change. **Number listed:** 20

1. *What's on TV*, with 1,765,369
2. *Radio Times*, 1,400,331
3. *Reader's Digest*, 1,302,659
4. *Take A Break*, 1,273,820
5. *TV Times*, 850,282
6. *FHM*, 751,493
7. *TV Quick*, 740,800
8. *Woman*, 711,133
9. *Woman's Own*, 654,473
10. *Bella*, 610,843

Source: *Marketing*, Magazine ABCs, February 18, 1999, p. 16.

★3495★
TOP CIRCULATION DECREASES BY YEAR-ON-YEAR PERCENT CHANGE, 1998
Ranked by: Year-on-year change, in percent. **Remarks:** Includes circulation and circulation decrease for 1998. **Number listed:** 20

1. *PlayStation Solutions (US)*, with -75.8%
2. *Total 64 (UK/US)*, -47.3%
3. *Debenhams*, -46.2%
4. *Total 64 Group*, -46.0%
5. *Total PlayStation (German)*, -44.8%
6. *Total 64 (German)*, -42.6%
7. *Glory Glory Man United*, -40.5%
8. *Big!*, -39.6%
9. *Babycare and Pregnancy*, -38.0%
10. *Cake Decoration*, -35.9%

Source: *Marketing*, Magazine ABCs, February 18, 1999, p. 19.

★3496★
TOP CIRCULATION INCREASES BY YEAR-ON-YEAR PERCENT CHANGE, 1998
Ranked by: Year-on-year change, in percent. **Remarks:** Includes circulation and circulation increase for 1998. **Number listed:** 30

1. *Essential PlayStation*, with 300.7%
2. *PlayStation Power*, 123.7%
3. *Bargain Pages Group*, 96.8%
4. *Play*, 93.4%
5. *Official PlayStation Mag*, 84.9%
6. *OK! Magazine*, 76.9%
7. *N64*, 68.0%
8. *Total PlayStation (UK)*, 60.9%
9. *Pregnancy*, 56.5%
10. *Powerstation*, 51.0%

Source: *Marketing*, Magazine ABCs, February 18, 1999, p. 19.

★3497★
TOP CONSUMER MAGAZINES BY CIRCULATION, 1998
Ranked by: Circulation. **Remarks:** Includes circulation for 1997 and percent change. **Number listed:** 30

1. *AA Magazine*, with 4,084,522
2. *Sky TV Guide*, 3,403,912
3. *Safeway Magazine*, 1,997,063
4. *Cable Guide*, 1,860,622
5. *What's on TV*, 1,765,369
6. *Radio Times*, 1,400,331
7. *Reader's Digest*, 1,302,659
8. *Take A Break*, 1,273,820
9. *Somerfield Magazine*, 1,177,307
10. *Debenhams*, 1,109,902

Source: *Marketing*, Magazine ABCs, February 18, 1999, p. 16.

★3498★
TOP HOME INTEREST MAGAZINES BY CIRCULATION, 1998
Ranked by: Circulation. **Remarks:** Includes circulation for 1997 and percent change. **Number listed:** 10

1. *Safeway Magazine*, with 1,997,063
2. *Homebase Living*, 598,500
3. *House Beautiful*, 288,452
4. *BBC Homes & Antiques*, 213,571
5. *Your Home*, 201,607
6. *Ideal Home*, 200,070
7. *Homes & Ideas*, 192,127
8. *Country Living*, 181,096
9. *Homes & Gardens*, 171,556
10. *House & Garden*, 163,313

Source: *Marketing*, Magazine ABCs, February 18, 1999, p. 20.

★3499★
TOP MEN'S LIFESTYLE MAGAZINES BY CIRCULATION, 1998
Ranked by: Circulation. **Remarks:** Includes circulation for 1997 and percent change. **Number listed:** 14

1. *FHM*, with 751,493
2. *Loaded*, 457,318
3. *Maxim*, 321,947
4. *Men's Health*, 283,359

5. *Sky Magazine*, 132,480
6. *GQ*, 132,185
7. *Esquire*, 108,284
8. *Wallpaper*, 102,158
9. *Bizarre*, 95,167
10. *Face*, 71,381

Source: *Marketing*, Magazine ABCs, February 18, 1999, p. 23.

★3500★
TOP MUSIC MAGAZINES BY CIRCULATION, 1998
Ranked by: Circulation. **Remarks:** Includes circulation for 1997 and percent change. **Number listed:** 5

1. *Q*, with 210,765
2. *New Musical Express*, 90,626
3. *Mojo*, 74,968
4. *Select*, 71,302
5. *Melody Maker*, 40,349

Source: *Marketing*, Magazine ABCs, February 18, 1999, p. 23.

★3501★
TOP TEEN MAGAZINES BY CIRCULATION, 1998
Ranked by: Circulation. **Remarks:** Includes year-on-year increase. **Number listed:** 12

1. *JazzyBooks (Group)*, with 799,800
2. *JazzyBooks (Secondary School)*, 600,325
3. *Sugar*, 451,696
4. *Top of the Pops*, 437,090
5. *It's Bliss*, 337,188
6. *Smash Hits*, 295,061
7. *TV Hits*, 269,061
8. *J-17*, 242,516
9. *Live & Kicking*, 165,248
10. *Shout*, 159,338

Source: *Marketing*, Magazine ABCs, February 18, 1999, p. 19.

★3502★
TOP WOMEN'S GLOSSIES BY CIRCULATION, 1998
Ranked by: Circulation. **Remarks:** Includes circulation for 1997 and percent change. **Number listed:** 18

1. *Debenhams*, with 1,109,902
2. *Cosmopolitan*, 476,288
3. *Marie Claire*, 445,289
4. *Good Housekeeping*, 400,063
5. *Company*, 290,402
6. *New Woman*, 261,681
7. *B*, 231,612
8. *She*, 226,079
9. *Vogue*, 202,321
10. *Elle*, 200,436

Source: *Marketing*, Magazine ABCs, February 18, 1999, p. 20.

★3503★
TOP WOMEN'S WEEKLIES BY CIRCULATION, 1998
Ranked by: Circulation. **Remarks:** Includes circulation for 1997 and percent change. **Number listed:** 10

1. *Take A Break*, with 1,273,820
2. *Woman*, 711,133
3. *Woman's Own*, 654,473
4. *Bella*, 610,843
5. *Woman's Weekly*, 594,680
6. *That's Life*, 540,003
7. *Hello*, 510,552
8. *Best*, 501,205
9. *Chat*, 497,731
10. *People's Friend*, 438,980

Source: *Marketing*, Magazine ABCs, February 18, 1999, p. 20.

Periodicals--Subscriptions

★3504★
TOP SUBSCRIPTION GENERATION TECHNIQUES*
Ranked by: New subscriptions made, in percent. **Number listed:** 19

1. Insert cards, with 96.1%
2. Direct mail, 89.2%
3. Internet, 88.2%
4. Special events promotions, 66.7%
5. Inbound telemarketing, 53.9%
6. Direct mail subscription agencies, 51.0%
7. Double postcards, 49.0%
8. Field agents, 48.0%
9. Outbound telemarketing, 43.1%
9. Public place distribution, 43.1%

Source: *Folio*, May, 1999, p. 50.

Perquisites

★3505★
MOST PREVALENT EXECUTIVE PERQUISITES, 1998*
Ranked by: Percentage of companies offering perquisite. **Number listed:** 10

1. SERP (Supplemental Executive Retirement Plans), with 60.4%
2. Leased automobile, 57.4%
3. Automobile allowance, 45.6%
4. Mobile phone, 45.0%
5. Free medical examinations, 44.3%
6. Change-of-control arrangement, 43.0%
7. Financial counseling (individual), 38.9%
8. Employment contracts, 34.2%
9. Country club membership, 33.6%
10. First-class airline seating, 30.2%

Source: *Compensation & Benefits*, September/October, 1998, p. 13.

Personal Care Products

★3506★
BEST HEALTH AND BEAUTY AID BRANDS ACCORDING TO DISCOUNT SHOPPERS*
Ranked by: Percent of discount shoppers naming brand as best. **Number listed:** 10

1. Crest, with 13%
2. Charmin, 9%
2. Pantene, 9%
2. Secret, 9%
5. Colgate, 6%
6. Gillette, 5%
6. L'Oreal, 5%
6. Sure, 5%
9. Mennen, 4%
10. Revlon, 4%

Source: *Discount Store News*, Top Brands Consumer Survey, Part II (annual), September 7, 1998, p. 25.

★3507★
BEST PERSONAL CARE APPLIANCE BRANDS ACCORDING TO DISCOUNT SHOPPERS*
Ranked by: Percent of discount shoppers naming brand as best. **Number listed:** 10

1. Conair, with 22%
2. Braun, 19%
3. Norelco, 17%
4. Vidal Sassoon, 11%
5. Remington, 6%
5. Black & Decker, 6%
5. Clairol, 6%
5. Panasonic, 6%
5. Water Pik, 6%
10. Sunbeam, 4%

Source: *Discount Store News*, Top Brands Consumer Survey, Part II (annual), September 7, 1998, p. 20.

★3508★
GEOGRAPHIC AREAS WITH THE HIGHEST HEALTH AND BEAUTY AIDS SALES*
Ranked by: Sales, in thousands of dollars. **Number listed:** 321

1. New York, NY, with $3,665,153 thousand
2. Chicago, IL, $3,649,008
3. Philadelphia, PA, $3,179,113
4. Los Angeles-Long Beach, CA, $3,146,384
5. Washington, DC, $2,541,974
6. Detroit, MI, $2,253,721
7. Tampa-St. Petersburg-Clearwater, FL, $2,180,131
8. Atlanta, GA, $2,015,973
9. Houston, TX, $1,932,629
10. Boston-Lawrence-Lowell-Brockton, MA, $1,887,943

Source: *Sales & Marketing Management*, Survey of Buying Power & Media Markets (annual), August, 1998, p. 192.

★3509★
LEADING CHEMICAL PROCESS INDUSTRIES BY SALES OF TOILETRIES AND COSMETICS, 1998
Ranked by: Sales, in millions of dollars. **Remarks:** Includes percent change from 1997, net income, profit margin, capital ratios, shareholder returns, prices and assets. **Number listed:** 6

1. Gillette, with $10,056 million
2. Avon Products, $5,213
3. Alberto-Culver, $1,835
4. Block Drug, $863
5. Carter-Wallace, $662
6. Del Laboratories, $275

Source: *Chemical Week*, Chemical Week 300 (annual), May 12, 1999, p. 54.

★3510★
TOP HEALTH AND BEAUTY AID CATEGORIES BY DOLLAR VOLUME SALES*
Ranked by: Sales dollar volume, in billions of dollars. **Number listed:** 60

1. Analgesics/internal, with $2.58 billion
2. Cough/cold/allergy/sinus remedies, $2.44
3. Feminine hygiene, $1.83
4. Shampoo, $1.63
5. Dentifrice, $1.60
6. Antacids/stomach remedies, $1.58
7. Deodorant, $1.55
8. Vitamins/mineral supplements, $1.36
9. Hair coloring, $1.10
10. Eye/contact lens care, $1.04

Source: *MMR*, September 21, 1998, p. 29.

★3511★
TOP HEALTH AND BEAUTY AID CATEGORIES BY UNIT VOLUME SALES*
Ranked by: Unit volume sales, in millions of dollars. **Number listed:** 60

1. Dentifrice, with $687.6 million
2. Deodorant, $680.7
3. Feminine hygiene, $637.4
4. Shampoo, $629.7
5. Cough/cold/allergy/sinus remedies, $561.0
6. Analgesics/internal, $555.5
7. Antacids/stomach remedies, $361.4
8. Hair conditioner, $360.6
9. Hair spray/spritz, $309.4
10. Toothbrushes, $308.4

Source: *MMR*, September 21, 1998, p. 29.

Personal Computers

See: **Microcomputers**

Personal Income

See: **Income**

Pesticides Industry

★3512★
TOP MANUFACTURERS OF PESTICIDES, 1997
Ranked by: Sales of agricultural chemicals. **Number listed:** 10

1. Novartis, with 4,170
2. Monsanto, 2,965
3. AstraZeneca, 2,650
4. DuPont, 2,555
5. AgrEvo, 2,350
6. Bayer, 2,180
7. Dow Chemical, 2,140
8. Rhone-Poulenc, 2,135
9. American Home Products, 2,120
10. BASF, 1,785

Source: *Chemical Week*, June 9, 1999, p. 13.

Pet Food

★3513★
TOP PET FOOD MARKETERS, 1998
Ranked by: Market share, in percent. **Remarks:** Includes 1998 estimated sales and 1997 estimates. **Number listed:** 10

1. Ralston Purina, with 15.4%
2. Friskies PetCare (Nestle), 12.4%
3. Heinz, 11.9%
4. Hill's, 7.6%
5. Doane (Windy Hill), 7.4%
6. Iams, 5.0%

7. Kal Kan (Mars), 4.9%
8. Nutro, 2.7%
9. Sunshine, 2.6%
10. Others, 32.9%

Source: *Petfood Industry*, Top 10 Pet Food Marketers, January/February, 1999, p. 42.

Pet Food--Germany

★3514★
TOP TYPES OF CAT FOOD IN GERMANY, 1997
Ranked by: Sales, in millions of U.S. dollars ($). **Remarks:** Includes 1995 sales. **Number listed:** 3

1. Moist, with $788 million
2. Dry, $138
3. Snacks, $74

Source: *Pet Food Industry*, 1998, p. 20.

★3515★
TOP TYPES OF DOG FOOD IN GERMANY, 1997
Ranked by: Sales, in millions of U.S. dollars ($). **Remarks:** Includes 1995 sales. **Number listed:** 3

1. Moist, with $387 million
2. Dry, $291
3. Snacks, $213

Source: *Pet Food Industry*, 1998, p. 20.

Pet Supplies

★3516★
TOP HOLIDAY GIFTS FOR PETS ACCORDING TO PETSMART, 1998
Ranked by: Gifts sold, in percent. **Number listed:** 10

1. Doggie holiday stockings, with 60%
2. Plush dog and cat beds, 58%
3. Fleece toys, 49%
4. String cat toys, 39%
5. Cat chase toys, 29%
6. Talking fleece toys, 18%
7. Dog sweaters, 11%
7. Aquatic Christmas ornaments, 11%
9. Christmas design hamster chews, 8%
10. The Princess Puppy Jacket, 7%

Source: *Pet Product News*, February, 1999, p. 10.

Petrochemical Industry

★3517★
TOP R&D SPENDERS IN CHEMICAL/ PETROCHEMICAL/MATERIALS, 1997
Ranked by: R&D spending, in millions of dollars. **Number listed:** 10

1. EI Dupont de Nemours, with $2,526.5 million
2. Monsanto, $933.6
3. Dow Chemical, $768.6
4. Exxon Corp., $529.8
5. Goodyear Tire & Rubber Co., $386.9
6. PPG Industries Inc., $250.6
7. Corning Inc., $246.4
8. Mobil Corp., $237.1
9. Rohm & Haas Co., $201.6
10. Shell Oil Co., $200.0

Source: *Research & Development*, Giants of R&D (annual), October, 1998, p. S-14.

Petroleum Industry

★3518★
LEADING CHEMICAL PROCESS INDUSTRIES BY SALES OF PETROLEUM AND NATURAL GAS PROCESSING, 1998
Ranked by: Sales, in millions of dollars. **Remarks:** Includes percent change from 1997, net income, profit margin, capital ratios, shareholder returns, prices and assets. **Number listed:** 22

1. Exxon, with $100,697 million
2. Mobil, $46,287
3. Texaco Inc., $31,707
4. Enron, $31,260
5. Chevron, $26,187
6. Shell Oil Co., $15,451
7. Phillips Petroleum, $11,545
8. Atlantic Richfield, $10,303
9. Sunoco, $8,413
10. Williams, $7,634

Source: *Chemical Week*, Chemical Week 300 (annual), May 12, 1999, p. 52.

★3519★
MOST ADMIRED PETROLEUM REFINING CORPORATIONS, 1998
Ranked by: Scores (1-10) derived from a survey of senior executives, outside directors and securities analysts. **Remarks:** Respondents rated companies in their own industry on 8 attributes of reputation. Also notes previous year's rank. **Number listed:** 10

1. Exxon, with 7.60
2. Mobil, 7.38
3. Shell Oil Co., 7.22
4. Chevron, 6.99
5. BP America, 6.86
6. Texaco Inc., 6.43
7. Amoco, 6.21
8. Phillips Petroleum, 5.90
9. Atlantic Richfield, 5.73
10. USX, 5.59

Source: *Fortune*, America's Most Admired Corporations (annual), March 1, 1999, p. F-4.

★3520★
TOP OIL AND GAS COMPANIES BY ASSETS*
Ranked by: Assets, in thousands of dollars. **Remarks:** Includes revenue, net income, stockholder's equity, and capital and exploratory spending. **Number listed:** 200

1. Exxon Corp., with $96,064,000 thousand
2. Mobil Corp., $43,559,000
3. Chevron Corp., $35,473,000
4. Amoco Corp., $32,489,000
5. Shell Oil Co., $29,601,000
6. Texaco Inc., $29,600,000
7. ARCO (Atlantic Richfield Corp.), $25,322,000
8. Enron Corp., $23,422,000
9. Conoco Inc., $17,479,000

10. Occidental Petroleum Corp., $15,282,000

Source: *Oil & Gas Journal*, Oil & Gas Journal 200 (annual), September 7, 1998, p. 68+.

★3521★
TOP OIL AND GAS COMPANIES BY CAPITAL, EXPLORATORY SPENDING*
Ranked by: Capital and exploratory spending, in thousands of dollars. **Number listed:** 20

1. Exxon Corp., with $8,811,000 thousand
2. Texaco Inc., $5,930,000
3. Chevron Corp., $5,541,000
4. Mobil Corp., $4,689,000
5. Amoco Corp., $3,943,000
6. Shell Oil Co., $3,131,000
7. ARCO (Atlantic Richfield Corp.), $2,985,000
8. Conoco Inc., $2,771,000
9. Enron Corp., $2,357,000
10. Phillips Petroleum Co., $2,043,000

Source: *Oil & Gas Journal*, Oil & Gas Journal 200 (annual), September 7, 1998, p. 54.

★3522★
TOP OIL AND GAS COMPANIES BY NET INCOME*
Ranked by: Net income, in thousands of dollars. **Number listed:** 20

1. Exxon Corp., with $8,460,000 thousand
2. Mobil Corp., $3,272,000
3. Chevron Corp., $3,256,000
4. Amoco Corp., $2,720,000
5. Texaco Inc., $2,664,000
6. Shell Oil Co., $2,104,000
7. BP (USA), $2,025,000
8. ARCO (Atlantic Richfield Corp.), $1,771,000
9. Conoco Inc., $1,068,000
10. Phillips Petroleum Co., $959,000

Source: *Oil & Gas Journal*, Oil & Gas Journal 200 (annual), September 7, 1998, p. 54.

★3523★
TOP OIL AND GAS COMPANIES BY STOCKHOLDERS' EQUITY*
Ranked by: Stockholders' equity, in thousands of dollars. **Number listed:** 20

1. Exxon Corp., with $43,660,000 thousand
2. Mobil Corp., $19,461,000
3. Chevron Corp., $17,472,000
4. Amoco Corp., $16,319,000
5. Shell Oil Co., $14,878,000
6. Texaco Inc., $12,766,000
7. ARCO (Atlantic Richfield Corp.), $8,680,000
8. Enron Corp., $5,618,000
9. Phillips Petroleum Co., $4,814,000
10. Occidental Petroleum Corp., $4,286,000

Source: *Oil & Gas Journal*, Oil & Gas Journal 200 (annual), September 7, 1998, p. 54.

★3524★
TOP OIL AND GAS COMPANIES BY TOTAL REVENUE, 1998*
Ranked by: Total revenue, in thousands of dollars. **Number listed:** 20

1. Exxon Corp., with $137,242,000 thousand
2. Mobil Corp., $65,906,000
3. Texaco Inc., $46,667,000
4. Chevron Corp., $41,950,000
5. Amoco Corp., $36,287,000
6. Shell Oil Co., $28,959,000
7. Conoco Inc., $21,410,000
8. Enron Corp., $20,273,000
9. ARCO (Atlantic Richfield Corp.), $19,272,000
10. BP (USA), $16,310,000

Source: *Oil & Gas Journal*, Oil & Gas Journal 200 (annual), September 7, 1998, p. 52.

★3525★
TOP OIL AND GAS COMPANIES BY U.S. LIQUIDS PRODUCTION, 1998*
Ranked by: U.S. liquids production, in million bbl. **Number listed:** 20

1. Exxon Corp., with 204.0 million
1. ARCO (Atlantic Richfield Corp.), 204.0
3. BP (USA), 202.0
4. Shell Oil Co., 179.0
5. Texaco Inc., 145.0
6. Chevron Corp., 125.0
7. Mobil Corp., 89.0
8. Amoco Corp., 84.0
9. USX-Marathon Group, 42.0
10. Phillips Petroleum Co., 34.0

Source: *Oil & Gas Journal*, Oil & Gas Journal 200 (annual), September 7, 1998, p. 56.

★3526★
TOP OIL AND GAS COMPANIES BY U.S. LIQUIDS PRODUCTION, 1998*
Ranked by: U.S. liquids production, in million bbl. **Number listed:** 20

1. Exxon Corp., with 204.0 million
1. ARCO (Atlantic Richfield Corp.), 204.0
3. BP (USA), 202.0
4. Shell Oil Co., 179.0
5. Texaco Inc., 145.0
6. Chevron Corp., 125.0
7. Mobil Corp., 89.0
8. Amoco Corp., 84.0
9. USX-Marathon Group, 42.0
10. Phillips Petroleum Co., 34.0

Source: *Oil & Gas Journal*, Oil & Gas Journal 200 (annual), September 7, 1998, p. 56.

★3527★
TOP OIL AND GAS COMPANIES BY U.S. NET WELLS DRILLED, 1998*
Ranked by: Number of U.S. net wells drilled. **Number listed:** 20

1. Texaco Inc., with 1,160.0 wells
2. Chevron Corp., 710.0
3. ARCO (Atlantic Richfield Corp.), 660.0
4. Burlington Resources Inc., 596.8
5. Union Pacific Resources Group Inc., 566.0
6. Enron Corp., 520.4
7. Anadarko Petroleum Corp., 493.9
8. MCN Investment Corp., 461.0
9. Pioneer Natural Resources Co., 404.1
10. Sonat, 323.0

Source: *Oil & Gas Journal*, Oil & Gas Journal 200 (annual), September 7, 1998, p. 54.

Petroleum Industry, International

★3528★
TOP OIL AND GAS COMPANIES BY U.S. LIQUIDS RESERVES, 1998*
Ranked by: U.S. liquids reserves, in millions of barrels (bbl). **Number listed:** 20

1. BP (USA), with 2,840.0 million
2. Exxon Corp., 2,377.0
3. ARCO (Atlantic Richfield Corp.), 2,131.0
4. Shell Oil Co., 1,965.0
5. Texaco Inc., 1,767.0
6. Chevron Corp., 1,196.0
7. Amoco Corp., 1,080.0
8. Mobil Corp., 935.0
9. USX-Marathon Group, 609.0
10. Phillips Petroleum Co., 366.0

Source: *Oil & Gas Journal*, Oil & Gas Journal 200 (annual), September 7, 1998, p. 56.

★3529★
TOP OIL AND GAS COMPANIES BY WORLD LIQUIDS PRODUCTION, 1998*
Ranked by: World liquids production, in millions of barrels (bbl). **Number listed:** 20

1. Exxon Corp., with 567.0 million
2. Chevron Corp., 391.0
3. Mobil Corp., 339.0
4. Texaco Inc., 317.0
5. ARCO (Atlantic Richfield Corp.), 234.0
6. Amoco Corp., 216.0
7. Shell Oil Co., 215.0
8. Conoco Inc., 136.0
9. Occidental Petroleum Corp., 101.0
10. Phillips Petroleum Co., 100.0

Source: *Oil & Gas Journal*, Oil & Gas Journal 200 (annual), September 7, 1998, p. 56.

★3530★
TOP OIL AND GAS COMPANIES BY WORLD LIQUIDS RESERVES, 1998*
Ranked by: World liquids reserves, in millions of barrels (bbl). **Number listed:** 20

1. Exxon Corp., with 6,174.0 million
2. Chevron Corp., 4,506.0
3. Mobil Corp., 4,105.0
4. Texaco Inc., 3,267.0
5. ARCO (Atlantic Richfield Corp.), 2,699.0
6. Amoco Corp., 2,417.0
7. Shell Oil Co., 2,181.0
8. Conoco Inc., 1,624.0
9. Phillips Petroleum Co., 1,189.0
10. Occidental Petroleum Corp., 900.0

Source: *Oil & Gas Journal*, Oil & Gas Journal 200 (annual), September 7, 1998, p. 56.

★3531★
TOP OIL AND GAS COMPANIES OUTSIDE THE U.S. BY PRODUCTION, 1998*
Ranked by: Production, in millions of barrels (bbl). **Number listed:** 20

1. Saudi Arabian Oil Co., with 3,021.1 million
2. National Iranian Oil Co., 1,322.0
3. Petroleos Mexicanos, 1,245.0
4. China National Petroleum Co., 1,171.7
5. Petroleos de Venezuela SA, 1,162.5
6. Royal Dutch/Shell Group, 850.0
7. Nigerian National Petroleum Corp., 834.8
8. Kuwait Petroleum Corp., 767.6
9. Abu Dhabi National Oil Co., 708.1
10. National Oil Corp. (Libya), 519.0

Source: *Oil & Gas Journal*, Oil & Gas Journal 200 (annual), September 7, 1998, p. 78.

★3532★
TOP OIL AND GAS COMPANIES OUTSIDE THE U.S. BY RESERVES, 1998*
Ranked by: Reserves, in millions of barrels (bbl). **Number listed:** 20

1. Saudi Arabian Oil Co., with 259,000.0 million
2. Iraq National Oil Co., 112,500.0
3. Kuwait Petroleum Corp., 94,000.0
4. Abu Dhabi National Oil Co., 92,200.0
5. National Iranian Oil Co., 89,700.0
6. Petroleos de Venezuela SA, 71,668.9
7. Petroleos Mexicanos, 47,822.0
8. National Oil Corp. (Libya), 29,500.0
9. China National Petroleum Co., 24,000.0
10. Nigerian National Petroleum Corp., 16,786.0

Source: *Oil & Gas Journal*, Oil & Gas Journal 200 (annual), September 7, 1998, p. 78.

★3533★
TOP OIL COMPANIES BY MARKET CAPITALISATION, 1999*
Ranked by: Market capitalisation, in billions of dollars. **Number listed:** 10

1. Mobil/Exxon, with $247.61 billion
2. BP-Amoco, $146.35
3. Royal Dutch/Shell Group, $151.31
4. Chevron, $52.80
5. Eni, $49.21
6. PetroFina/Total, $36.49
7. Elf, $28.67
8. Texaco Inc., $27.48
9. Arco, $19.64
10. Repsol, $16.54

Source: *Financial Times*, January 22, 1999, p. 28.

★3534★
TOP OIL COMPANIES BY MARKET CAPITALISATION, 1999*
Ranked by: Market capitalisation, in billions of dollars. **Number listed:** 10

1. Mobil/Exxon, with $247.61 billion
2. BP-Amoco, $146.35
3. Royal Dutch/Shell Group, $151.31
4. Chevron, $52.80
5. Eni, $49.21
6. PetroFina/Total, $36.49
7. Elf, $28.67
8. Texaco Inc., $27.48
9. Arco, $19.64
10. Repsol, $16.54

Source: *Financial Times*, January 22, 1999, p. 28.

★3535★
WORLD'S LARGEST CRUDE OIL MINING COMPANIES BY REVENUE, 1997
Ranked by: Revenue, in millions of dollars. **Number listed:** 3

1. Pemex (Mexico), with $28,566 million
2. Broken Hill Proprietary (Australia), $17,540
3. Rag AG (Germany), $14,403

Source: *Fortune*, The Global 500: World's Biggest Corporations (annual), August 3, 1998, p. F-22.

★3536★
WORLD'S LARGEST PETROLEUM REFINING COMPANIES BY REVENUE, 1997
Ranked by: Revenue, in millions of dollars. **Number listed:** 31

1. Royal Dutch/Shell Group (Britain/Netherlands), with $128,142 million

2. Exxon (U.S.), $122,379
3. British Petroleum (Great Britain), $71,193
4. Mobil (U.S.), $59,978
5. Texaco Inc. (U.S.), $45,187
6. Elf Equitaine (France), $43,572
7. ENI (Italy), $36,962
8. Chevron (U.S.), $36,376
9. PDVSA (Venezuela), $34,801
10. SK (South Korea), $33,816

Source: *Fortune*, The Global 500: World's Biggest Corporations (annual), August 3, 1998, p. F-23.

Petroleum Refineries

★3537★
TOP CORPORATIONS IN THE PETROLEUM REFINING INDUSTRY, 1998
Ranked by: Revenue, in millions of dollars. **Remarks:** Also notes profits and investment figures as well as number of employees. **Number listed:** 20

1. Exxon, with $100,697 million
2. Mobil, $47,678
3. Texaco Inc., $31,707
4. Chevron, $26,801
5. USX, $24,754
6. Atlantic Richfield, $13,195
7. Tosco, $12,022
8. Phillips Petroleum, $11,845
9. Ult. Diamond Shamrock, $8,347
10. Coastal, $7,125

Source: *Fortune*, Fortune 500 Largest U.S. Corporations (annual), April 26, 1999, p. F-65+.

Petroleum Refineries--Europe

★3538★
TOP PETROLEUM REFINING AND RELATED INDUSTRIES COMPANIES IN EUROPE
Ranked by: Financial size, in millions of European Currency Units (ECUs). **Remarks:** Also notes number of employees and overall rank among European businesses. **Number listed:** 17

1. RWE-DEA AG Fuer Mineraloel U.Chemie, with ECUs14.138 million
2. Total Raffinage Distribution SA, ECUs10.642
3. Dea Mineraloel AG, ECUs10.570
4. Agip Petroli Spa, ECUs10.560
5. Repsol Petroleo SA, ECUs8.507
6. Elf Antar France, ECUs8.005
7. Neste Oyj, ECUs7.617
8. Veba Oel AG, ECUs6.144
9. Compania Espanola de Petroleos SA, ECUs5.970
10. Petroleos de Portugal SA, ECUs3.984

Source: *Dun & Bradstreet*, Dun's Europa (annual), 1999, p. 244+.

Philadelphia County (PA)--Industries

★3539★
LARGEST PRIVATE-SECTOR EMPLOYERS IN THE PHILADELPHIA METROPOLITAN AREA, 1997
Ranked by: Number of local full-time employees. **Remarks:** Also notes number of part-time employees, 1997 revenue, number of offices, description of business and CEO. **Number listed:** 25

1. University of Pennsylvania, with 16,325 employees
2. Allegheny Health, Education and Research Foundation, 12,087
3. CoreStates Bank, 5,803
4. Thomas Jefferson University Hospitals, Inc., 4,764
5. Bell Atlantic Corp., 4,611
6. Independence Blue Cross, 4,264
7. US Airways, 4,161
8. Cigna Corp., 3,476
9. Thomas Jefferson University, 3,415
10. Frankford Hospital, 2,928

Source: *Philadelphia Business Journal*, Book of Business Lists (annual), December 25, 1998, p. 94.

★3540★
LARGEST PUBLICLY HELD COMPANIES IN THE PHILADELPHIA METROPOLITAN AREA, 1998
Ranked by: Revenue, in millions of dollars. **Remarks:** Includes phone and fax numbers, web address, net income/loss, total assets, market value, return on equity, number of employees, fiscal year ended, ticker symbol, description of business and chief executive. **Number listed:** 150

1. Cigna Corp., with $21,437 million
2. AmeriSource Health, $8,668.804
3. Sunoco Inc., $8,413
4. Crown Cork & Seal Co. Inc., $8,300
5. Unisource Worldwide Inc., $7,417
6. Unisys Corp., $7,208.4
7. Campbell Soup Co., $6,696
8. Ikon Office Solutions Inc., $5,629
9. Peco Energy Co., $5,210.4
10. Comcast Corp., $5,145.3

Source: *Philadelphia Business Journal*, (annual), May 21, 1999, p. B12.

Philippines Stock Exchange

★3541★
LARGEST LISTED COMPANIES ON THE PHILIPPINES STOCK EXCHANGE, 1997
Ranked by: Market value, in billions of pesos. **Number listed:** 20

1. Ayala, with PP129.72 billion
2. Ayala Land Inc., PP115.93
3. San Miguel Corp., PP95.97
4. Philippines Long Distance Telephone, PP95.68
5. Manila Electric Co., PP86.31
6. Metropolitan Bank & Trust, PP61.32
7. SM Prime Holdings, PP59.58
8. Bank of the Phil. Islands, PP50.01
9. Petron, PP31.41
10. Benpres Holdings, PP27.44

Source: *SSB Guide to World Equity Markets*, (annual), Euromoney Publications, 1998, p. 399.

★3542★
MOST ACTIVELY TRADED SHARES ON THE PHILIPPINES STOCK EXCHANGE, 1997
Ranked by: Turnover value, in millions of pesos. **Number listed:** 20

1. Philippines Long Distance Telephone, with PP30,388.71 million
2. Metropolitan Bank and Trust, PP29,369.54
3. Manila Electric, PP28,465.59
4. Belle, PP24,901.19
5. San Miguel, PP18,758.09
6. Ayala Land, PP17,547.78
7. Philippines National Bank, PP12,844.51
8. Empire East Land Holdings, PP12,383.29
9. Bank of the Philippine Islands, PP11,395.18
10. SM Prime Holdings, PP11,059.52

Source: *SSB Guide to World Equity Markets*, (annual), Euromoney Publications, 1998, p. 399+.

Photographic Industry

★3543★
TOP FILM BRANDS ACCORDING TO CONSUMERS, 1998
Ranked by: Percent of consumers naming brand as best. **Remarks:** Includes demographic profile of those surveyed. **Number listed:** 4

1. Kodak, with 84%
2. Polaroid, 12%
2. Fuji, 12%
4. 3M, 1%

Source: *Discount Store News*, Top Brand Consumer Survey-Pt. II (annual), September 7, 1998, p. 18.

Physician Practice Management Firms

★3544★
TOP PRIVATE PRACTICE MANAGEMENT COMPANIES, 1997
Ranked by: Revenue, in billions of dollars. **Number listed:** 5

1. MedPartners, with $6.30 billion
2. FPA Medical Management, $1.20
3. PhyCor, $1.10
4. Concentra Managed Care, $.46
5. Coastal Physician Group, $.43

Source: *Business and Health*, September, 1998, p. 47.

Physician Practice Management Firms—Philadelphia Metro Area

★3545★
LARGEST PHYSICIAN GROUPS IN THE PHILADELPHIA METROPOLITAN AREA, 1998
Ranked by: Number of physicians. **Remarks:** Includes phone and fax numbers, web address, number of patient visits, specialties, hospital affiliations, major health plans accepted, owner and top local executive. **Number listed:** 23

1. University of Pennsylvania Health System Physicians, with 1,147 physicians
2. MCP/Hahnemann Clinical Practice Groups, 600
3. Jefferson University Physicians, 495
4. Temple University Medical Practice, 365
5. Cooper Physician Association, 297
6. Einstein Practice Plan, 200
7. Temple Physicians Inc., 100
8. Fornance Physician Services Inc., 65
9. West Jersey Clinical Associates, 56
10. J.E. Wood Clinic, 50

Source: *Philadelphia Business Journal*, (annual), February 5, 1999, p. 17.

Picture Frames

★3546★
LEADING RETAIL OUTLETS FOR PICTURE FRAMES, 1998
Ranked by: Market share, in percent. **Number listed:** 10

1. Mass merchants, with 32%
2. Department stores, 17%
3. Chain drugstores, 15%
4. Craft/floral stores, 9%
5. Home/lifestyle stores, 6%
6. Supermarkets, 5%
7. Camera stores/photo labs, 4%
8. Card/gift stores, 3%
8. National chains, 3%
10. Other, 6%

Source: *HFN*, December 14, 1998, p. 4.

★3547★
TOP PHOTO FRAME RETAILERS
Ranked by: Specific ranking information not provided. **Number listed:** 10

1. Wal-Mart
2. Kmart
3. Target
4. May Corporate
5. Federated
6. Kohl's
7. Rite Aid
8. Walgreens
9. Eckerd Drugs
10. Michael's

Source: *HFN*, December 14, 1998, p. 10.

Pigments, International

★3548★
TOP WORLD MARKETS FOR PIGMENTS, 1998*
Ranked by: Market share, in percent. **Number listed:** 9

1. Western Europe, with 32%
2. North America, 29%
3. Asia, 13%
4. Japan, 8%
5. Eastern Europe, 6%
6. Central & South America, 5%
7. Mideast, 3%
7. Africa, 3%
9. Oceania, 1%

Source: *Chemical Week*, August 12, 1998, p. 22.

Pipeline Companies

★3549★
MOST ADMIRED PIPELINE CORPORATIONS, 1998
Ranked by: Scores (1-10) derived from a survey of senior executives, outside directors and securities analysts. **Remarks:** Respondents rated companies in their own industry on 8 attributes of reputation. Also notes previous year's rank. **Number listed:** 9

1. Enron, with 8.11
2. Williams, 7.63
3. El Paso Natural Gas, 6.65
4. KN Energy, 6.12
5. Dynegy, 6.00
6. TransMontaigne Oil, 5.71
7. Sonat, 5.61
8. Equitable Resources, 5.44
9. Western Gas Resources, 5.02

Source: *Fortune*, America's Most Admired Corporations (annual), March 1, 1999, p. F-4.

★3550★
TOP CORPORATIONS IN THE PIPELINE INDUSTRY, 1998
Ranked by: Revenue, in millions of dollars. **Remarks:** Also notes profits and investment figures as well as number of employees. **Number listed:** 9

1. Enron, with $31,260 million
2. Dynegy, $14,258
3. Williams, $7,658
4. El Paso Energy, $5,782
5. KN Energy, $4,388
6. Sonat, $3,710
7. Equitable Resources, $2,413
8. Western Gas Resources, $2,134
9. Transmontaigne Oil, $1,968

Source: *Fortune*, Fortune 500 Largest U.S. Corporations (annual), April 26, 1999, p. F-66.

Pizza

★3551★
LEADING PIZZA RESTAURANTS, 1997
Ranked by: Sales, in millions of dollars. **Remarks:** Includes rank in 400. **Number listed:** 32

1. Pizza Hut, with $7,300.0 million
2. Domino's Pizza, $3,200.0
3. Little Caesars, $2,100.0
4. Papa John's, $867.6
5. Round Table Pizza, $362.6
6. Godfather's Pizza, $265.9
7. Chuck E. Cheese, $263.3
8. Piccadilly Circus Pizza, $241.6
9. Pizza Inn, $206.0
10. California Pizza Kitchen, $187.3

Source: *Restaurants & Institutions*, Restaurants & Institutions 400 (annual), July 15, 1998, p. 100.

★3552★
TOP PIZZA CHAINS ACCORDING TO PATRONS, 1999*
Ranked by: Percent of respondents rating chain above average or excellent. **Remarks:** Also notes scores based on food quality, menu variety, value, service, atmosphere, cleanliness, and convenience. **Number listed:** 8

1. Pizzeria Uno, with 46
2. Papa John's, 38
3. Pizza Hut, 36
4. Godfather's Pizza, 31
5. Chuck E. Cheese, 30
6. Domino's, 28
7. Little Caesars, 27
8. Sbarro, 26

Source: *Restaurants & Institutions*, Choice in Chains (annual), March 1, 1999, p. 90.

★3553★
TOP PIZZA CHAINS BY NUMBER OF UNITS, 1998
Ranked by: Number of units or franchise operations. **Remarks:** Includes principal executive, city, state, year established, units franchised, international units, number opened in 1998, gross sales and percentage of delivery/take-out/dine-in business. **Number listed:** 100

1. Pizza Hut, with 12,285 units
2. Domino's Pizza, Inc., 6,219
3. Litte Caesars Pizza, 4,300
4. Papa John's International, 1,885
5. Sbarro, 898
6. Godfather's Pizza, 550
7. Round Table Pizza, 548
8. Pizza Inn, Inc., 513
9. Papa Murphy's Take 'n' Bake Pizza, 402
10. Hungry Howie's Pizza & Subs Inc., 400

Source: *Pizza Today*, Hot 100 Pizza Companies (annual), June, 1999, p. 60+.

Planned Communities

★3554★
TOP FEATURES DESIRED IN A PLANNED COMMUNITY, 1999*
Ranked by: Percentage of respondents interested in buying at master-planned or age-restricted community. **Number listed:** 9

1. Swimming pool, with 28.1%
2. Security features (gate-guarded entry, neighborhood watch patrol, etc.), 24.4%
3. Hiking trails, 17.1%
4. Bicycle trails, 16.4%
5. Clubhouse, 16.1%
6. Golf course, 11.8%
7. Retail shops, 9.0%
8. Boating/sailing, 8.0%
9. Tennis courts, 7.1%

Source: *Professional Builder*, May, 1999, p. 59.

Plastics--Additives, International

★3555★
TOP PLASTICS MANUFACTURERS, 1997
Ranked by: Market share, in percent. **Number listed:** 7

1. Ciba, with 15%
2. Akzo Nobel, 12%
3. Elf Atochem, 11%
4. Great Lakes, 8%
5. Witco, 7%
6. Rohm & Haas Co., 5%

7. Other, 42%

Source: *C&EN*, October 5, 1998, p. 22.

Plastics Industry

★3556★
LEADING USES FOR THERMOPLASTICS, 1997
Ranked by: Market share, in percent. **Number listed:** 8

1. Packaging, with 29%
2. Construction, 15%
3. Consumer products, 14%
4. Exports, 13%
5. Transportation, 5%
6. Furniture, 4%
6. Electrical, 4%
8. Other, 16%

Source: *C&EN*, October 5, 1998, p. 17.

★3557★
STATES WITH THE MOST PLASTICS ESTABLISHMENTS, 1996
Ranked by: Number of establishments. **Number listed:** 10

1. California, with 2,155
2. Ohio, 1,231
3. Texas, 1,023
4. Michigan, 993
5. Illinois, 977
6. Pennsylvania, 782
7. New York, 734
8. Florida, 714
9. Indiana, 653
10. New Jersey, 627

Source: *Business Facilities*, February, 1999, p. 28.

Plastics Industry--Export-Import Trade

★3558★
STATES WITH THE MOST PLASTICS EXPORTS, 1997
Ranked by: Exports, in dollars. **Number listed:** 10

1. Texas, with $1,899,191,015
2. California, $1,578,340,424
3. Ohio, $1,070,662,953
4. Illinois, $865,566,094
5. South Carolina, $810,318,854
6. Michigan, $728,353,642
7. New York, $682,915,656
8. Florida, $601,683,665
9. North Carolina, $600,151,115
10. Pennsylvania, $441,176,115

Source: *Business Facilities*, February, 1999, p. 37.

Plastics Industry, International

★3559★
TOP CORPORATIONS IN THE PLASTICS INDUSTRY, 1997
Ranked by: Market share, in percent. **Remarks:** Includes acetal, liquid-crystal polymers, nylons, polyarylate, polybutylene, terephthalate and polycarbonate. **Number listed:** 7

1. GE Plastics, with 22%
2. DuPont, 12%
3. Ticona, 11%
4. Bayer, 9%
5. BASF, 5%
6. Mitsubishi Gas, 4%
7. Other, 37%

Source: *C&EN*, October 5, 1998, p. 20.

★3560★
WORLD'S LARGEST RUBBER AND PLASTIC PRODUCING CORPORATIONS BY REVENUE, 1997
Ranked by: Revenue, in millions of dollars. **Number listed:** 3

1. Bridgestone (Japan), with $17,936 million
2. Michelin (France), $13,654
3. Goodyear Tire, $13,155

Source: *Fortune*, The Global 500: World's Biggest Corporations (annual), August 3, 1998, p. F-25.

★3561★
WORLD'S LARGEST RUBBER AND PLASTIC PRODUCING CORPORATIONS BY REVENUE, 1997
Ranked by: Revenue, in millions of dollars. **Number listed:** 3

1. Bridgestone (Japan), with $17,936 million
2. Michelin (France), $13,654
3. Goodyear Tire, $13,155

Source: *Fortune*, The Global 500: World's Biggest Corporations (annual), August 3, 1998, p. F-25.

Pollution

★3562★
TOP CHEMICALS, 1996
Ranked by: Number of releases and transfers. **Remarks:** Includes percent of total. **Number listed:** 20

1. Methanol, with 241
2. Zinc compounds, 207
3. Ammonia, 193
4. Nitrate compounds, 164
5. Toluene, 127
6. Xylenes (mixed), 83
7. Carbon disulfide, 73
8. n-Hexane, 72
9. Manganese compounds, 71
10. Chlorine, 67

Source: *Chemical & Engineering*, July 6, 1998, p. 20.

★3563★
TOP POLLUTERS, 1999*
Ranked by: Amount, in millions of pounds. **Remarks:** Includes location. **Number listed:** 5

1. PCS Nitrogen, with 32.2 pounds
2. Solutia, 27.2
3. DuPont, 23.5
4. Cytec, 20.9
5. BASF, 16.5

Source: *Chemical Week*, May 26, 1999, p. 16.

★3564★
TOP RELEASES FOR CHEMICALS, 1996
Ranked by: Share, in percent. **Number listed:** 5

1. Air, with 50%
2. Underground injection wells, 25%
3. Surface water, 12%
4. Land releases, 9%

5. Disposal transfers off-site, 4%

Source: *Chemical & Engineering*, July 6, 1998, p. 19.

Pollution--Mexico

★3565★
TOP PRIORITIES IN THE MEXICAN ENVIRONMENTAL MARKET, 1998
Ranked by: Priority, in millions of dollars. **Number listed:** 7

1. Wastewater, with $1,768 million
2. Air pollution, $599
3. Solid and hazardous waste, $464
4. Municipal, $325
5. Industrial, $102
6. Hospital, $37
7. Other, $39

Source: *Business Mexico*, September, 1998, p. 49.

Polyamides, International

★3566★
TOP SUPPLIERS OF POLYAMIDE RESIN, 1998*
Ranked by: Global capacity, in thousands of tons. **Remarks:** Excludes fiber capacity. **Number listed:** 8

1. DuPont, with 550 thousand ton
2. BASF, 285
3. Rhodia, 210
4. Allied Signal, 150
5. Solutia/Dow, 130
6. Ube, 80
7. DSM, 75
8. Bayer, 65

Source: *Canadian Business*, November, 1998, p. 8.

Polycarbonates, International

★3567★
TOP MANUFACTURERS OF POLYCARBONATES, 1998
Ranked by: Capacity, in billions of pounds. **Number listed:** 6

1. General Electric, with 43%
2. Bayer, 29%
3. Dow Chemical, 12%
4. Teijin Chemicals, 7%
5. Mitsubishi Gas, 3%
6. Other, 6%

Source: *C&EN*, December 21, 1998, p. 20.

★3568★
TOP USES FOR POLYCARBONATE
Ranked by: Global consumption, in percent. **Number listed:** 7

1. Consumer goods, with 16%
2. Automotive, 15%
2. Glazing/sheet, 15%
2. Transportation, 15%
5. Compact discs, 12%
6. Appliances, 10%
7. Other, 17%

Source: *C&EN*, December 21, 1998, p. 20.

Polymers

★3569★
TOP POLYMERS FOR EXTERIOR COATINGS, 1997
Ranked by: Market share, in percent. **Number listed:** 5

1. Epoxies, with 30%
2. Urethanes, 16%
3. Alkyds, 15%
4. Acrylics, 12%
5. Other, 27%

Source: *C&EN*, October 12, 1998, p. 61.

Polypropylene

★3570★
TOP END USES FOR POLYPROPYLENE, 1998
Ranked by: Share, in percent. **Remarks:** Includes 1998 U.S. demand. **Number listed:** 6

1. Injection molding, with 48%
2. Fibers, 33%
3. Film extrusion and coatings, 10%
4. Sheet, 4%
5. Blow molding, 3%
6. Other, 2%

Source: *Chemical Week*, June 2, 1999, p. 27.

Population, International

★3571★
LARGEST COUNTRIES BY POPULATION SIZE, 1998
Ranked by: Population, in millions. **Number listed:** 20

1. China, with 1,255 million
2. India, 976
3. United States, 274
4. Indonesia, 207
5. Brazil, 165
6. Pakistan, 148
7. Russia, 147
8. Japan, 126
9. Bangladesh, 124
10. Nigeria, 122

Source: *The Futurist*, February, 1999, p. 39.

Port Authorities

See: **Port Districts**

Port Districts

★3572★
LEADING PORT AUTHORITIES FOR 1996 TO 2000 BY TOTAL CAPITAL EXPENDITURES
Ranked by: Capital expenditures, in thousands of dollars. **Number listed:** 10

1. Port of Los Angeles, with $1,330,992 thousand
2. Long Beach, $1,232,400
3. Seattle, $484,654
4. Georgia Ports Authority, $447,303
5. Houston, $311,377
6. Port Authority of New York/New Jersey, $231,302
7. Miami, $203,275
8. Everglades, $197,932
9. Tacoma, $195,892
10. New Orleans, $193,696

Source: *Traffic World*, October 5, 1998, p. 29.

Ports

★3573★
LEADING U.S. FISHING PORTS BY VOLUME, 1997
Ranked by: Volume, in millions of pounds. **Number listed:** 10

1. Dutch Harbor, Unalaska, with 587.8 million po
2. Reedville, VA, 491.9
3. Empire-Venice, LA, 395.9
4. Cameron, LA, 389.6
5. Seattle, WA, 336.1
6. Kodiak, AK, 277.5
7. Intercoastal City, LA, 270.8
8. Morgan City-Berwick, LA, 222.9
9. Los Angeles, CA, 168.2
10. Pascagoula-Moss Point, MS, 164.7

Source: *National Fisherman*, November 1, 1998, p. 16.

★3574★
TOP U.S. PORTS BY VALUE OF FOREIGN TRADE, 1997
Ranked by: Specific figures not provided. **Remarks:** Includes ranking for 1992. **Number listed:** 10

1. Long Beach, CA
2. Los Angeles, CA
3. New York/New Jersey
4. Houston, TX
5. Seattle, WA
6. Hampton Roads, VA
7. Charleston, SC
8. Oakland, CA
9. Tacoma, WA
10. Baltimore, MD

Source: *Governing*, December, 1998, p. 44.

★3575★
TOP U.S. PORTS BY VOLUME OF FOREIGN TRADE, 1997
Ranked by: Specific figures not provided. **Remarks:** Includes ranking for 1992. **Number listed:** 10

1. Houston, TX
2. South Louisiana
3. New Orleans,LA
4. Hampton Roads, VA
5. New York/New Jersey
6. Corpus Christi, TX
7. Long Beach, CA
8. Baton Rouge, LA
9. Texas City, TX
10. Port Arthur, TX

Source: *Governing*, December, 1998, p. 44.

Postal Service, International

★3576★
WORLD'S LARGEST PACKAGE AND FREIGHT DELIVERY SERVICE COMPANIES BY REVENUE, 1997
Ranked by: Revenue, in millions of dollars. **Number listed:** 8

1. U.S. Postal Service, with $58,216 million
2. United Parcel Service (U.S.), $22,458
3. Japan Postal Service (Japan), $20,741
4. Deutsche Post (Germany), $15,654
5. La Poste (France), $15,535
6. Nippon Express (Japan), $14,513
7. FDX (U.S.), $11,520
8. British Post Office (Great Britain), $10,106

Source: *Fortune*, The Global 500: World's Biggest Corporations (annual), August 3, 1998, p. F-22.

Potato Chips

★3577★
TOP BRANDS OF POTATO CHIPS BASED ON SUPERMARKET DOLLAR SHARE, 1997
Ranked by: Dollar share, in percent. **Number listed:** 10

1. Lay's (Frito Lay), with 24.7%
2. Ruffles (Frito-Lay), 19.8%
3. Pringles (Procter & Gamble), 11.7%
4. Private label, 7.6%
5. Baked Lay's (Frito-Lay), 7.5%
6. Lay's Wavy (Frito-Lay), 3.4%
7. Utz, 2.4%
8. Herr's, 2.2%
9. Wise (Borden, Inc.), 2.1%
10. Jays, 1.7%

Source: *Distribution Channels*, March, 1999, p. 54.

★3578★
TOP BRANDS OF POTATO CHIPS, 1998
Ranked by: Sales, in millions of dollars. **Remarks:** Includes unit sales. **Number listed:** 10

1. Lay's, with $798.4 million
2. Ruffles, $385.4
3. Lay's WOW, $128.6
4. Wavy Lay's, $104.2
5. Ruffles WOW, $102.4
6. Utz, $54.4
7. Wise, $50.6
8. Herrs, $42.5
9. Ruffles The Works, $40.9
10. Jays, $35.0

Source: *MMR*, February 22, 1999, p. 24.

★3579★
TOP OUTLETS FOR POTATO CHIPS, 1997
Ranked by: Market share, in percent. **Number listed:** 8

1. Supermarkets, with 46.7%
2. C-Stores, 13.5%
3. Mass merchandisers, 9.2%
4. Grocery Stores, 8.8%
5. Warehouse Clubs, 4.9%
6. Vending, 4.7%
7. Drugstores, 3.9%
8. Other, 8.3%

Source: *Distribution Channels*, October, 1998, p. 47.

Poultry Industry--North America

★3580★
LARGEST MEAT AND POULTRY COMPANIES, 1998
Ranked by: Sales, in millions of dollars. **Remarks:** Includes location, chief officer, sales for 1996, fiscal year end, number of plants, number of employees and number of subsidiaries. **Number listed:** 100

1. ConAgra Inc., with $16,510 million
2. IBP, Inc., $13,300
3. Cargill Meat Sector, $9,000
4. Tyson Foods, Inc., $6,400
5. Sara Lee Packaged Meats, $4,300
6. Smithfield Foods, Inc., $3,870
7. Farmland Foods, Inc., $3,700
8. Hormel Foods Corp., $3,256
9. Gold Kist, Inc., $2,500
9. Oscar Mayer Foods Corp., $2,500
11. Perdue Farms Inc., $2,480

Source: *Meat & Poultry*, Top 100 (annual), July, 1998, p. 24+.

★3581★
MEAT AND POULTRY COMPANIES WITH THE BIGGEST DOLLAR GROWTH, 1998
Ranked by: Sales growth, in millions of dollars. **Remarks:** Includes 1996 and 1997 sales, percent change and comments. **Number listed:** 9

1. Smithfield Foods, Inc., with $1,486 million
2. ConAgra Inc., $1,323
3. IBP, Inc., $761
4. Gold Kist, $500
5. Seaboard Corp., $381
6. Colorado Boxed Beef Co., $360
7. Hormel Foods Corp., $157
8. Greater Omaha Packing, $144
9. Pilgrim's Pride Corp., $139

Source: *Meat & Poultry*, Top 100 (annual), July, 1998, p. 38.

★3582★
MEAT AND POULTRY COMPANIES WITH THE BIGGEST PERCENTAGE GROWTH, 1998
Ranked by: Sales growth, in percent. **Remarks:** Includes 1996 and 1997 sales, dollar change, and comments. **Number listed:** 9

1. Colorado Boxed Beef Co., with 54%
2. Smithfield Foods, Inc., 38%
3. Seaboard Corp., 34%
4. Greater Omaha Packing, 32%
5. Maple Lodge Farms Ltd., 30%
6. Buckhead Beef Co. Inc., 23%
6. Fletcher's Fine Foods, Ltd., 23%
8. Gold Kist, 20%
9. Rose Packaging Co. Inc., 18%

Source: *Meat & Poultry*, Top 100 (annual), July, 1998, p. 38.

★3583★
MEAT AND POULTRY COMPANIES WITH THE GREATEST DOLLAR LOSSES, 1998
Ranked by: Sales losses, in millions of dollars. **Remarks:** Includes 1996 and 1997 sales, dollar change, and comments. **Number listed:** 7

1. Cargill Meat Sector, with $-200 million
2. Tyson Foods, Inc., $-100
3. Champion Boxed Beef Co., $-65
4. Bob Evans Farms, Inc., $-57
5. H&M Food Systems, $-33
6. Gerber Agri, Inc., $-30
7. Thorn Apple Valley Inc., $-27
8. L&H Packing Co., $-15
8. Norbest, Inc., $-15

Source: *Meat & Poultry*, Top 100 (annual), July, 1998, p. 40.

★3584★
MEAT AND POULTRY COMPANIES WITH THE GREATEST SALES LOSS IN PERCENT, 1998
Ranked by: Sales loss, in percent. **Remarks:** Includes 1996 and 1997 sales, dollar change, and comments. **Number listed:** 7

1. Champion Boxed Beef Co., with -87%
2. Bob Evans Farms, Inc., -36%
3. Gerber Agri, Inc., -25%
4. H&M Food Systems, -16%
5. Norbest, Inc., -10%
6. L&H Packing Co., -9%
7. GoodMark Foods, Inc., -5%

Source: *Meat & Poultry*, Top 100 (annual), July, 1998, p. 40.

PPOs

See: **Preferred Provider Organizations**

Prague Stock Exchange

★3585★
LARGEST LISTED COMPANIES ON THE PRAGUE STOCK EXCHANGE, 1997
Ranked by: Market capitalization, in millions of koruna (Kc). **Number listed:** 20

1. SPT Telecom, with Kcs86,996.5 million
2. CEZ, Kcs58,714.9
3. Komercni Banka, Kcs24,801.4
4. Unipetrol, Kcs18,039.1
5. Tabak, Kcs15,118.2
6. Ceska Sporitelna, Kcs14,836.6
7. Cokoladovny, Kcs12,772.9
8. IPB, Kcs11,078.9
9. C Radiokomunikace, Kcs9,818.0
10. SPIF Cesky, Kcs7,619.4

Source: *SSB Guide to World Equity Markets*, (annual), Euromoney Publications, 1998, p. 157+.

★3586★
MOST ACTIVELY TRADED SHARES ON THE PRAGUE STOCK EXCHANGE, 1997
Ranked by: Turnover value, in millions of koruna (Kc). **Number listed:** 20

1. SPT Telecom, with Kcs52,405 million
2. Komercni Banka, Kcs40,570
3. CEZ, Kcs32,877
4. Vertex, Kcs7,143
5. Skoda Plzen, Kcs6,554
6. Elektrarny Opatov, Kcs6,344
7. RIF, Kcs5,868
8. Ceska Sporitelna, Kcs4,756
9. C Radiokomunikace, Kcs4,147
10. Chemopetrol Group, Kcs3,793

Source: *SSB Guide to World Equity Markets*, (annual), Euromoney Publications, 1998, p. 158.

Prefabricated Building Industry

★3587★
STATES WITH THE MOST MANUFACTURED HOUSING, 1998*
Ranked by: Number of manufactured housing shipments. **Remarks:** Includes 1991 figures. **Number listed:** 10

1. Texas, with 37,154
2. North Carolina, 33,318
3. Georgia, 21,412
4. South Carolina, 20,062
5. Florida, 18,971
6. Alabama, 17,323
7. Tennessee, 15,393
8. Michigan, 11,836
9. Kentucky, 11,723
10. Mississippi, 10,809

Source: *Builder*, September, 1998, p. 86.

★3588★
TOP BUILDERS OF HUD-CODE MULTI-SECTION MANUFACTURED HOMES BY DOLLAR VOLUME, 1998
Ranked by: Dollar volume. **Number listed:** 25

1. Champion Enterprises, with $1,427,315,000
2. Fleetwood Enterprises, $993,013,000
3. Oakwood Homes, $749,543,702
4. Palm Harbor Homes, $464,465,208
5. Clayton Homes, $410,000,000
6. Cavalier Homes
7. 403,000,000
8. Skyline Corp., $400,955,000
9. American Homestar, $331,952,436
10. Horton Homes, $224,097,586
11. Fairmont Homes, $200,873,000

Source: *Mobile/Manufactured Home Merchandiser*, Top 25 Mobile/Manufactured Home Builders, June, 1999, p. 28.

★3589★
TOP BUILDERS OF HUD-CODE MULTI-SECTION MANUFACTURED HOMES BY NUMBER OF UNITS, 1998
Ranked by: Number of multi-section homes. **Number listed:** 25

1. Champion Enterprises, with 43,006 homes
2. Fleetwood Enterprises, 37,274
3. Oakwood Homes, 22,274
4. Clayton Homes, 13,217
5. Cavalier Homes, 11,957
6. Palm Harbor Homes, 11,616
7. Skyline Corp., 11,182
8. American Homestar, 8,827
9. Horton Homes, 6,655
10. Patriot Homes, 5,738

Source: *Mobile/Manufactured Home Merchandiser*, Top 25 Mobile/Manufactured Home Builders, June, 1999, p. 28.

★3590★
TOP BUILDERS OF HUD-CODE SINGLE-SECTION MANUFACTURED HOMES BY DOLLAR VOLUME, 1998
Ranked by: Dollar volume. **Number listed:** 25

1. Fleetwood Enterprises, with $550,012,000
2. Champion Enterprises, $414,181,000
3. Oakwood Homes, $262,452,919
4. Clayton Homes, $242,000,000
5. Cavalier Homes
6. 239,000,000
7. Skyline Corp., $131,939,000
8. Southern Energy Homes, $87,636,498
9. Palm Harbor Homes, $87,198,320
10. American Homestar, $79,419,755
11. Horton Homes, $68,957,947

Source: *Mobile/Manufactured Home Merchandiser*, Top 25 Mobile/Manufactured Home Builders, June, 1999, p. 22.

★3591★
TOP BUILDERS OF HUD-CODE SINGLE-SECTION MANUFACTURED HOMES BY NUMBER OF UNITS, 1998
Ranked by: Number of single-section homes. **Number listed:** 25

1. Fleetwood Enterprises, with 28,948 homes
2. Champion Enterprises, 25,258
3. Oakwood Homes, 15,963
4. Clayton Homes, 15,212
5. Cavalier Homes, 12,430
6. Skyline Corp., 6,104
7. Southern Energy Homes, 4,345
8. Palm Harbor Homes, 3,736
9. American Homestar, 3,546
10. Horton Homes, 3,460

Source: *Mobile/Manufactured Home Merchandiser*, Top 25 Mobile/Manufactured Home Builders, June, 1999, p. 26.

★3592★
TOP BUILDERS OF NON-HUD CODE MANUFACTURED HOMES BY DOLLAR VOLUME, 1998
Ranked by: Dollar volume. **Number listed:** 25

1. All American Homes, with $130,282,358
2. Excel Homes, $67,385,000
3. Champion Enterprises, $62,401,522
4. Muncy Homes, $57,489,279
5. Nanticoke Homes, $55,000,000
6. Oakwood Homes, $53,035,909
7. American Homestar, $47,090,209
8. Crestline Homes, $40,383,033
9. New Era Building Systems, $35,000,000
10. Ritz-Craft Corp. of PA, $31,603,000

Source: *Mobile/Manufactured Home Merchandiser*, Top 25 Mobile/Manufactured Home Builders, June, 1999, p. 32.

★3593★
TOP BUILDERS OF NON-HUD CODE MANUFACTURED HOMES BY NUMBER OF UNITS, 1998
Ranked by: Number of non-HUD code and park models homes. **Remarks:** Includes individual breakdown of non-HUD homes and park models. **Number listed:** 25

1. Excel Homes, with 3,550 homes
2. All American Homes, 2,511
3. Champion Enterprises, 2,095

4. Muncy Homes, 1,514
5. Cavco Industries, 1,459
6. New Era Building Systems, 1,363
7. Oakwood Homes, 1,100
8. American Homestar, 895
9. Ritz-Craft Corp. of PA, 811
10. Chariot Eagle, 807

Source: *Mobile/Manufactured Home Merchandiser*, Top 25 Mobile/Manufactured Home Builders, June, 1999, p. 30.

★3594★
TOP MANUFACTURED HOME BUILDERS BY TOTAL HOME PRODUCTION, 1998
Ranked by: Total number of homes. **Remarks:** Includes dollar volume. **Number listed:** 25

1. Champion Enterprises, with 68,264 homes
2. Fleetwood Enterprises, 66,222
3. Oakwood Homes, 38,237
4. Clayton Homes, 28,429
5. Cavalier Homes, 24,387
6. Skyline Corp., 17,286
7. Palm Harbor Homes, 15,352
8. American Homestar, 12,373
9. Horton Homes, 10,115
10. Fairmont Homes, 8,954

Source: *Mobile/Manufactured Home Merchandiser*, Top 25 Mobile/Manufactured Home Builders, June, 1999, p. 22.

★3595★
TOP MANUFACTURED NON-HUD AND HUD-CODE HOME BUILDERS, 1998
Ranked by: Dollar volume. **Number listed:** 25

1. Champion Enterprises, with $1,865,546,000
2. Fleetwood Enterprises, $1,547,925,000
3. Oakwood Homes, $1,065,032,530
4. Clayton Homes, $652,000,000
5. Cavalier Homes, $642,000,000
6. Palm Harbor Homes, $551,663,528
7. Skyline Corp., $542,053,000
8. American Homestar, $458,462,400
9. Horton Homes, $300,110,452
10. Fairmont Homes, $262,853,000

Source: *Mobile/Manufactured Home Merchandiser*, Top 25 Mobile/Manufactured Home Builders, June, 1999, p. 24.

★3596★
TOP PARK MODEL MANUFACTURERS BY DOLLAR VOLUME, 1998
Ranked by: Dollar volume. **Number listed:** 5

1. Cavco Industries, with $21,639,278
2. Chariot Eagle, $15,120,798
3. Skyline Corp., $9,159,000
4. Champion Enterprises, $5,301,522
5. Fleetwood Enterprises, $1,547,925

Source: *Mobile/Manufactured Home Merchandiser*, Top 25 Mobile/Manufactured Home Builders, June, 1999, p. 34.

★3597★
TOP PARK MODEL MANUFACTURERS BY NUMBER OF UNITS, 1998
Ranked by: Number of park models. **Number listed:** 5

1. Cavco Industries, with 1,255 models
2. Chariot Eagle, 764
3. Skyline Corp., 563
4. Fleetwood Enterprises, 245
5. Champion Enterprises, 180

Source: *Mobile/Manufactured Home Merchandiser*, Top 25 Mobile/Manufactured Home Builders, June, 1999, p. 34.

Preferred Provider Organizations

★3598★
LARGEST PPO DOCTOR NETWORKS BY NUMBER OF PRIMARY CARE PHYSICIANS IN NETWORK, 1998*
Ranked by: Number of primary care physicians in network. **Number listed:** 10

1. National Preferred Provider Network Inc., with 127,757 primary
2. CAPP CARE Inc., 114,672
3. CIGNA HealthCare, 110,679
4. Mutually Preferred PPO, 108,707
5. Private Healthcare Systems Inc., 104,720
6. Pro America Managed Care, 103,360
7. UnitedHealth Group, 94,400
8. CorVel Corp., 90,964
9. Preferred Care Inc., 90,000
10. The First Health Network, 88,141

Source: *Business Insurance*, December 28, 1998, p. 1.

★3599★
LARGEST PPO ENROLLMENT BY NUMBER OF ENROLLEES, 1998*
Ranked by: Number of enrollees. **Number listed:** 10

1. CCN, with 31,890,100
2. MultiPlan Inc., 23,000,000
3. The First Health Network, 14,800,000
4. CorVel Corp., 6,530,000
5. Private Healthcare Systems Inc., 5,630,000
6. National Preferred Provider Network Inc., 5,078,576
7. Aetna U.S. Healthcare, 4,018,640
8. CAPP CARE Inc., 3,400,000
9. CIGNA HealthCare, 3,100,000
10. Blue Cross of California, 2,782,791

Source: *Business Insurance*, December 28, 1998, p. 1.

★3600★
LARGEST WORKERS COMP PPOS BY WORKERS COMP ENROLLMENT, 1998*
Ranked by: Members enrolled in workers comp. **Number listed:** 5

1. CCN, with 25,800,000 enrol
2. AnciCare, 10,000,000
3. CorVel Corp., 6,500,000
4. Armada, 2,500,000
5. Interplan Corp., 600,000

Source: *Business Insurance*, December 28, 1998, p. 1.

Preferred Provider Organizations--Chicago (IL)

★3601★
CHICAGO'S LARGEST PPOS, 1998
Ranked by: Annual healthcare, in millions of dollars. **Remarks:** Also notes percent change from previous year, enrolled subscribers and percent change from previous year, year plan founded, affiliated hospitals and physicians, and largest clients. **Number listed:** 15

1. Blue Cross Blue Shield of Illinois, with $1,800.0 million
2. Private Healthcare Systems Inc., $887.8
3. HFN Inc., $808.9
4. Healthstar Inc., $800.0
5. Health Marketing Inc., $414.2
6. United Healthcare of Illinois Inc., $356.0

7. First Health, $340.0
8. Epiqual/CCN Healthcare, $249.4
9. Wellmark Healthnetwork Inc., $191.3
10. Humana Health Plans, $130.0

Source: *Crain's Chicago Business*, Top Business Lists (annual), June 30, 1998, p. 159+.

Preferred Provider Organizations--Florida

★3602★
TOP PPOS IN FLORIDA, 1998
Ranked by: Enrollment. **Remarks:** Also notes number of physicians, affiliated hospitals, counties served, accrediting organizations, senior executives, and year founded. **Number listed:** 24

1. Blue Cross and Blue Shield of Florida, with with 935,735 enr
2. Beech Street Corp., 908,216
3. Oral Health Services Inc., 739,198
4. MultiPlan Inc., 653,052
5. American Dental Plan Inc., 650,000
6. Alignis, 650,000
7. Dimension Health Inc., 648,692
8. BayCare Health Network Inc., 641,212
9. CCN, 640,908
10. Managed Care Inc., 485,100

Source: *Florida Trend*, TopRank Florida (annual), 1999, p. 61.

Preferred Provider Organizations—Philadelphia Metro Area

★3603★
LARGEST PPOS IN THE PHILADELPHIA METROPOLITAN AREA, 1997
Ranked by: Number of local subscribers. **Remarks:** Also notes total number of members, member physicians, member hospitals, employer groups under contract, local service area, parent company, local administrator and operation date. **Number listed:** 18

1. Davis Vision Inc., with 1,200,000
2. Devon Health Services Inc., 837,000
3. Mental Health Consultants Inc., 750,000
4. Preferred Care Inc., 560,055
5. InterGroup Services Corp., 526,694
6. MultiPlan Inc., 246,752
7. Horizon Behavioral Services, 136,125
8. Capp Care Inc., 53,820
9. Great-West PPO/New England Financial PPO, 27,674
10. Admar's Med Network, n/a

Source: *Philadelphia Business Journal*, Book of Business Lists (annual), November 27, 1998, p. 18.

Prescriptions

★3604★
TOP NEW AND REFILL PRESCRIPTION DRUGS, 1998
Ranked by: Total number of new or refilled prescriptions dispensed in community pharmacies, in thousands. **Number listed:** 200

1. Premarin Tabs (Wyeth-Ayerst), with 41,316 thousand
2. Synthroid (Knoll), 34,709
3. Trimox (Apolthecon), 31,281
4. Hydrocodone/APAP (Watson), 30,747
5. Prozac (Lilly), 23,835
6. Prilosec (Astra), 23,586
7. Zithromax (Pfizer), 22,965
8. Lipitor (Parke-Davis), 21,575
9. Norvasc (Pfizer), 20,8383
10. Claritin (Schering), 20,031

Source: *American Druggist*, Top 200 Rx Drugs (annual), February, 1999, p. 42+.

★3605★
TOP NEW PRESCRIPTION DRUGS, 1998
Ranked by: Total number of new prescriptions dispensed in community pharmacies, in thousands. **Number listed:** 100

1. Trimox (Apothecon), with 29,335 thousand
2. Hydrocodone/APAP (Watson Lab), 24,759
3. Zithromax (Pfizer), 22,044
4. Amoxicillin (Teva Pharm), 16,487
5. Augmentin (SK Beecham), 15,463
6. Cephalexin (Teva Pharm), 15,286
7. Premarin Tabs (Wyeth-Ayerst), 12,127
8. Cipro (Bayer Pharm), 11,544
9. Acetaminophen w/Cod (Teva Pharm), 11,443
10. Synthroid (Knoll), 11,242

Source: *American Druggist*, Top 200 Rx Drugs (annual), February, 1999, p. 44.

★3606★
TOP REFILL PRESCRIPTION DRUGS, 1998
Ranked by: Total number of refilled prescriptions dispensed in community pharmacies, in thousands. **Number listed:** 100

1. Premarin Tabs (Wyeth-Ayerst), with 29,188 thousand
2. Synthroid (Knoll), 23,466
3. Lipitor (Parke-Davis), 14,462
4. Norvasc (Pfizer), 13,996
5. Lanoxin (Glaxo Wellcome), 13,875
6. Prozac (Lilly), 13,466
7. Prilosec (Astra), 13,425
8. Prempro (Wyeth-Ayerst), 12,372
9. Zestril (Zeneca), 11,265
10. Vasotec (Merck), 11,137

Source: *American Druggist*, Top 200 Rx Drugs (annual), February, 1999, p. 46.

Printing Industry

★3607★
FASTEST GROWING PRINTERS, 1998
Ranked by: Sales growth from 1996 to 1998, in percent. **Remarks:** Includes key market niches, sales growth dollars, number of employees and year founded. **Number listed:** 50

1. Copyright Printing, Inc., with 357%
2. Primary Color Printing, 183%
3. Earth Color Group, 174%

4. Contmeporary Color Graphics, 167%
5. Coordinated Graphics, Inc., 133%
6. Cunningham Graphics, 129%
7. Compu-Print Inc., 126%
8. St. Joseph Corp., 125%
9. Mailway Printers, 120%
10. Foremost Graphics, LLC, 117%

Source: *American Printer*, Top 50 Fastest Growing Printers (annual), June, 1999, p. 36+.

★3608★
TOP PRINTING COMPANIES BY ABSOLUTE DOLLAR GROWTH, 1998
Ranked by: Absolute dollar growth, in millions of Canadian dollars. **Number listed:** 10

1. Wallace, with C$494.0 million
2. St. Joseph Corp., C$135.0
3. Chapman Printing Co., C$57.0
4. Rhodes Printing Co., C$50.0
5. Henry Wurst & Co., C$35.0
6. Earth Color Group, C$33.0
7. Cunningham Graphics, C$30.0
8. Integra Color, C$21.0
9. Webcom Ltd., C$18.0
10. Copyright Printing, C$15.0

Source: *American Printer*, Top 50 Fastest Growing Printers (annual), June, 1999, p. 34.

Printing Industry--Detroit Metropolitan Area

★3609★
LEADING PRINTING FIRMS IN THE DETROIT METROPOLITAN AREA, 1997
Ranked by: Revenue, in millions of dollars. **Remarks:** Includes 1996 revenue, percent change, number of local and worldwide employees, number of presses, maximum sheet size, types of presses and specialties. **Number listed:** 20

1. Valassis Communications Inc., with $675.0 million
2. American Speedy Printing Centers Inc., $185.0
3. Edwards Bros. Inc., $67.0
4. Tweddle Litho Co., $65.0
5. E&G Printing Service Inc., $42.7
6. Malloy Lithographing Inc., $40.4
7. McNaughton & Gunn, $30.0
8. Northwestern Printing Co., $28.0
9. Thomson-Shore Inc., $27.7
10. Wintor Swan Associates LLC, $21.0

Source: *Crain's Detroit Business*, October 26, 1998, p. 12.

Printing Industry--Europe

★3610★
TOP PRINTING, PUBLISHING AND ALLIED INDUSTRY COMPANIES IN EUROPE, 1999*
Ranked by: Financial size, in millions of European Currency Units (ECUs). **Remarks:** Also notes number of employees and overall rank among European businesses. **Number listed:** 97

1. Bertelsmann AG, with ECUs11.367 million
2. Reed Elsevier PLC, ECUs5.042
3. Reuters Holdings LTD, ECUs4.252
4. Pearson PLC, ECUs3.383
5. United News & Media PLC, ECUs3.343
6. Rexam PLC, ECUs2.954
7. Axel Springer Verlag AG, ECUs2.241
8. Daily Mail & General Trust PLC, ECUs1.770
9. Heinrich Bauer Verlag, ECUs1.477
10. De La Rue PLC, ECUs1.133

Source: *Dun & Bradstreet*, Dun's Europa (annual), 1999, p. 240+.

Printing Industry, International

★3611★
WORLD'S LARGEST PUBLISHING AND PRINTING COMPANIES BY REVENUE, 1997
Ranked by: Revenue, in millions of dollars. **Number listed:** 4

1. Bertelsmann (Germany), with $14,006 million
2. Lagardere Groupe (France), $11,655
3. Dai Nippon Printing (Japan), $10,889
4. Toppan Printing (Japan), $10,461

Source: *Fortune*, The Global 500: World's Biggest Corporations (annual), August 3, 1998, p. F-24.

★3612★
WORLD'S LARGEST PUBLISHING AND PRINTING COMPANIES BY REVENUE, 1997
Ranked by: Revenue, in millions of dollars. **Number listed:** 4

1. Bertelsmann (Germany), with $14,006 million
2. Lagardere Groupe (France), $11,655
3. Dai Nippon Printing (Japan), $10,889
4. Toppan Printing (Japan), $10,461

Source: *Fortune*, The Global 500: World's Biggest Corporations (annual), August 3, 1998, p. F-24.

Printing Industry--North America

★3613★
TOP PRINTERS BY SALES, 1998*
Ranked by: Sales, in thousands of dollars. **Remarks:** Includes sales previous year, percent change, number of employees, sales per employee, primary sites, primary products and CEO. **Number listed:** 101

1. R. R. Donnelley & Sons, with $4,800,000 thousand
2. Quebecor Printing Inc., $3,483,199
3. Moore Corporation, $2,600,000
4. World Color Press, $1,981,000
5. Deluxe Corp., $1,919,366
6. Big Flower Press, $1,376,706
7. Wallace Computer Services, $1,300,000
8. Banta Corporation, $1,202,000
9. Quad/Graphics, $1,042,000
10. Standard Register Co., $965,674

Source: *Graphic Arts Monthly*, GAM 101 (annual), September, 1998, p. 50+.

Printing Industry--New Jersey

★3614★
TOP PRINTERS IN NEW JERSEY BY REVENUE, 1998
Ranked by: Revenue, in millions of dollars. **Remarks:** Also notes number of employees, year founded, specialties and president. **Number listed:** 25

1. Webcraft Technologies Inc., with $244 million
2. Sandy Alexander, Inc., $120
3. The Lehigh Press, $119
4. L.P. Thebault Co., $90
5. MacNaughton Litho Company, Inc., $80
6. Cunningham Graphics, Inc., $43.6
7. Federal Business Products, $41.7
8. Howard Press, $36
9. Pictorial Offset Corporation, $34
10. Scott Printing Corporation, $32

Source: *New Jersey Business*, Book of Lists (annual), 1999, p. 38.

Printing Industry--Philadelphia Metropolitan Area

★3615★
LARGEST COMMERCIAL PRINTERS IN THE PHILADELPHIA METROPOLITAN AREA, 1997
Ranked by: Number of local employees. **Remarks:** Also notes number of salespeople, 1997 sales, types of presses, specialties, notable clients, services offered and chief executive. **Number listed:** 25

1. Brown Printing Co., with 600
1. Webcraft Technologies Inc., 600
3. Quebecor Printing Inc., 400
4. Hippographics Inc., 395
5. Evergreen Printing and Publishing Co. Inc., 240
6. Lehigh Press Inc., 235
7. Baum Printing House Inc., 210
8. Braceland Inc., 200
8. Packquisition Corp. t/a Packard Press, 200
8. Smith Edwards Dunlap Co., 200

Source: *Philadelphia Business Journal*, Book of Business Lists (annual), December 25, 1998, p. 144.

Prints

★3616★
TOP ART SUBJECTS, 1998*
Ranked by: Specific ranking figures not provided. **Number listed:** 10

1. Landscapes
2. Wildlife
3. Florals
4. Abstracts
5. Impressionism
6. Marine
7. Traditional/Representational
8. Americana/folk art
9. Historical (non military)
10. Western

Source: *Art Business*, November, 1998, p. 1.

Prisons--Food Service

★3617★
LEADING CORRECTIONS OPERATIONS, 1997
Ranked by: Food and beverage purchases, in millions of dollars. **Remarks:** Includes population, number of facilities, production units and daily meal cost per inmate. **Number listed:** 12

1. California Department of Corrections, with $145.0 million
2. Federal Bureau of Prisons, $87.3
3. Texas Dept. of Criminal Justice, $70.0
4. New York State Dept. of Corrections, $48.0
5. Ohio Dept. of Corrections, $43.0
6. Florida Dept. of Corrections, $42.0
7. Michigan Dept. of Corrections, $39.0
8. Illinois Dept. of Corrections, $37.0 (estimate)
9. Pennsylvania Dept. of Corrections, $36.0
10. Virginia Dept. of Corrections, $30.0 (estimate)

Source: *Restaurants & Institutions*, Institutional Giants, September 15, 1998, p. 94.

Private Brands

★3618★
TOP OVER-THE-COUNTER PRIVATE-LABEL CATEGORIES IN DRUG STORES, 1997
Ranked by: Sales volume, in dollars. **Remarks:** Includes 1997 share and unit share. **Number listed:** 10

1. Vitamins, with $358.9
2. Internal analgesics, $226.5
3. Cold/allergy/sinus (Tablets/Lozenges), $162.2
4. Laxatives, $92.3
5. First aid treatments, $90.9
6. Adult incontinence, $71.1
7. Feminine needs, $48.1
8. Cold/allergy/sinus (liquids), $47.3
9. Cough syrup, $44.3
10. Antacids, $42.6

Source: *Drug Store News*, November 9, 1998, p. 54.

★3619★
TOP PRIVATE LABEL GROCERIES, 1997
Ranked by: Volume, in billions of dollars. **Number listed:** 20

1. Milk, with $6.2 billion
2. Fresh bread & rolls, $2.1
3. Cheese, $2.0
4. Fresh eggs, $1.6
5. Ice Cream/Sherbet, $.9844
6. Carbonated Soft Drinks, $.8953
7. Frozen plain vegetables, $.7194
8. Sugar, $.6736
9. Refrigerated juice/beverages, $.6721
10. Vegetables, $.6693

Source: *IGA Grocergram*, October, 1998, p. 9.

★3620★
TOP SUPERMARKET DEPARTMENTS FOR PRIVATE LABELS, 1998*
Ranked by: Dollar share. **Remarks:** Specific figures not provided. **Number listed:** 8

1. Dairy
2. Bakery
3. Frozen
4. Deli

5. Non-edible groceries
6. Edible groceries
7. HBC
8. General merchandise

Source: *Distribution Channels*, July/August, 1998, p. 47.

Private Corporations

See: **Closely Held Corporations**

Private Placement

See: **Securities--Privately Placed**

Products, New

See: **New Products**

Promoters

★3621★
TOP PROMOTERS IN THE AMUSEMENT BUSINESS, 1998
Ranked by: Total gross, in dollars. **Remarks:** Includes total attendance and number of shows and sellouts. **Number listed:** 10

1. TNA International Ltd./TNA USA, with $238,437,323
2. Universal Concerts, $168,792,108
3. Pace Concerts/Pace Entertainment/Pace Touring, $122,554,507
4. Cellar Door, $115,623,161
5. Delsener-Slater Enterprises, $102,458,446
6. Bill Graham Presents, $61,581,581
7. Jam Prods./Tinley Park, $59,658,043
8. Metropolitan Entertainment, $53,484,549
9. Magicworks Entertainment, $48,764,767
10. Belkin Prods., $44,175,493

Source: *Amusement Business*, Amusement Business (annual), December 28, 1998, p. 12.

Propane

★3622★
TOP PROPANE FIRMS BY NUMBER OF ACQUISITIONS, 1998
Ranked by: Number of acquisitions. **Remarks:** Includes number of gallons. **Number listed:** 50

1. Cornerstone Propane (Watsonville, CA), with 20
2. Independent Propane (Irving, TX), 14
3. MFA (Columbia, MO), 13
4. All-Star Propane (Lebanon, MO), 10
4. AmeriGas (Valley Forge, PA), 10
6. Heritage Propane (Tulsa, OK), 8
7. Star Gas (Stamford, CT), 7
8. Atmos Propane (Franklin, TN), 5
8. Suburban Propane (Whippany, NJ), 5
8. Aeropres Propane (Shreveport, LA), 5
11. Ferrellgas Partners, LP (Liberty, MO), 4

Source: *LP/GAS*, February, 1999, p. 18.

★3623★
TOP U.S. RETAIL PROPANE MARKETERS*
Ranked by: Retail sales, in gallons. **Remarks:** Includes other company information. **Number listed:** 50

1. AmeriGas Partners, LP, with 785,300,000 gallons
2. Ferrellgas Partners, LP, 659,932,000
3. Suburban Propane Partners, LP, 530,000,000
4. Cornerstone Propane Partners, LP, 304,405,000
5. Thermogas Company, 262,648,700
6. Heritage Propane Partners, LP, 170,443,000
7. National Propane Partners, LP, 155,000,000
8. Star Gas Partners, LP, 110,738,000
9. All Star Gas Corp., 95,000,000
10. Agway Energy Products, 89,300,000

Source: *LP-GAS*, Top 50 U.S. Retail Propane Marketers, January, 1999, p. 22+.

Psychiatric Hospitals

★3624★
HEALTHCARE SYSTEMS OPERATING THE MOST PSYCHIATRIC HOSPITALS, 1998
Ranked by: Number of staffed beds. **Remarks:** Includes number of beds for 1997, number of hospitals for 1998 and 1997 and number of states. **Number listed:** 52

1. Charter Behavioral Health Systems, with 7,610 beds
2. Behavioral Healthcare Corp., 3,537
3. Universal Health Services, 2,074
4. Columbia/HCA Healthcare Corp., 1,843
5. Brown Schools, 1,108
6. Sun Healthcare Group, 648
7. Children's Comprehensive Services, 585
8. Catholic Health Initiatives, 496
9. Tenet Healthcare Corp., 459
10. New York Presbyterian Healthcare Network, 442

Source: *Modern Healthcare*, Modern Healthcare 500 Multi-Unit Providers Survey (annual), May 24, 1999, p. 44+.

Public Relations Firms

★3625★
LARGEST PUBLIC RELATIONS FIRMS BY U.S. FEES, 1998
Ranked by: U.S. net fees. **Remarks:** Also notes U.S. number of employees, total fees and percent change from 1997. **Number listed:** 17

1. Burson-Marsteller, with $141,996,000
2. Fleishman-Hillard, $136,272,000
3. Hill and Knowlton, $113,000,000
4. Edelman PR Worldwide, $101,868,218
5. Ketchum, $101,485,000
6. BSMG Worldwide, $97,779,130
7. Shandwick, $91,485,000

8. Porter Novelli International, $85,235,570
9. Weber PR Worldwide, $57,866,543
10. Ogilvy PR Worldwide, $54,457,700

Source: *O'Dwyer's Directory of Public Relations Firms*, (annual), J.R. O'Dwyer Co., Inc., 1999, p. A17.

★3626★
LEADING ADVERTISING AGENCY-ASSOCIATED PUBLIC RELATIONS FIRMS, 1998
Ranked by: Net fees. **Remarks:** Also notes number of employees and percent change from 1997. **Number listed:** 44

1. Burson-Marsteller, with $258,417,000
2. Hill and Knowlton, $206,000,000
3. Porter Novelli International, $183,050,000
4. Shandwick International, $170,291,945
5. Fleishman-Hillard, $160,692,000
6. Ketchum, $125,248,000
7. BSMG Worldwide, $118,963,000
8. Weber PR Worldwide, $83,166,000
9. GCI/APCO, $79,667,957
10. Ogilvy PR Worldwide, $77,927,000

Source: *O'Dwyer's Directory of Public Relations Firms*, (annual), J.R. O'Dwyer Co., Inc., 1999, p. A15.

★3627★
LEADING GAINERS AMONG THE PUBLIC RELATIONS FIRMS IN THE TOP TEN, 1998
Ranked by: Percentage change in fee income from 1997 to 1998. **Remarks:** Also notes 1998 net fees and number of employees. **Number listed:** 8

1. BSMG Worldwide, with 93.0%
2. Weber Public Relations Worldwide, 36.2%
3. Ketchum, 29.6%
4. GCI/APCO, 28.4%
5. Porter Novelli International, 23.6%
6. Fleishman-Hillard, 19.1%
7. Edelman PR Worldwide, 18.1%
8. Hill and Knowlton, 8.9%

Source: *O'Dwyer's Directory of Public Relations Firms*, (annual), J.R. O'Dwyer Co., Inc., 1999, p. A19.

★3628★
LEADING GAINERS AMONG THE PUBLIC RELATIONS FIRMS RANKED 11TH THROUGH 30TH, 1998
Ranked by: Percentage change in fee income from 1997 to 1998. **Remarks:** Also notes 1998 net fees and number of employees. **Number listed:** 10

1. Ogilvy PR Worldwide, with 40.8%
2. Schwartz Communications, 37.4%
3. Cohn & Wolfe, 34.1%
4. Copithorne & Bellows, 23.9%
5. SCIENS Worldwide PR, 21.2%
6. Waggener Edstrom, 20.3%
7. MWW Group, 19.9%
8. Manning, Selvage & Lee, 19.6%
9. Morgen-Walke Associates, 18.6%
10. Cunningham Communication, 18.0%

Source: *O'Dwyer's Directory of Public Relations Firms*, (annual), J.R. O'Dwyer Co., Inc., 1999, p. A19.

★3629★
LEADING GAINERS AMONG THE PUBLIC RELATIONS FIRMS RANKED 31ST THROUGH 50TH, 1998
Ranked by: Percentage change in fee income from 1997 to 1998. **Remarks:** Also notes 1998 net fees and number of employees. **Number listed:** 10

1. Hawthorn Group, with 65.5%
2. Kemper Lesnik Communications, 61.2%
3. Hoffman Agency, 49.1%
4. Earle Palmer Brown PR, 36.0%
5. Chandler Chicco Agency, 34.0%
6. Cramer-Krasselt, 33.4%
7. Blanc & Otus, 25.9%
8. Nelson Communications, 24.0%
9. Kratz & Jensen, 23.7%
10. Wilson McHenry Co., 20.7%

Source: *O'Dwyer's Directory of Public Relations Firms*, (annual), J.R. O'Dwyer Co., Inc., 1999, p. A19.

★3630★
LEADING INDEPENDENT PUBLIC RELATIONS FIRMS, 1998
Ranked by: Net fees. **Remarks:** Also notes number of employees and percent change from 1997. **Number listed:** 164

1. Edelman PR Worldwide, with $157,840,530
2. Ruder Finn, $51,199,000
3. Waggener Edstrom, $40,900,000
4. Morgen-Walke Associates, $23,258,300
5. Cunningham Communication, $20,437,000
6. MWW Group, $17,220,267
7. Powell Tate, $15,656,880
8. Schwartz Communications, $15,019,646
9. Lois Paul & Partners, $13,482,032
10. Kamber Group, $12,215,000

Source: *O'Dwyer's Directory of Public Relations Firms*, (annual), J.R. O'Dwyer Co., Inc., 1999, p. A9+.

★3631★
LEADING PUBLIC RELATIONS FIRMS IN AGRICULTURE, 1998
Ranked by: Net fees. **Number listed:** 18

1. Gibbs & Soell, with $7,111,600
2. Fleishman-Hillard, $7,086,000
3. Shandwick, $5,689,000
4. Rowland Worldwide, $3,591,000
5. Bader Rutter & Associates, $3,500,000
6. Morgan & Myers, $2,792,919
7. CMF&Z PR, $1,635,000
8. Edelman PR Worldwide, $1,545,074
9. Dudnyk PR, $1,052,165
10. Charleston/Orwig, $737,419

Source: *O'Dwyer's Directory of Public Relations Firms*, (annual), J.R. O'Dwyer Co., Inc., 1999, p. A27.

★3632★
LEADING PUBLIC RELATIONS FIRMS IN BEAUTY AND FASHION, 1998
Ranked by: Net fees. **Number listed:** 26

1. Edelman PR Worldwide, with $7,794,929
2. GCI/APCO, $5,853,624
3. Rowland Worldwide, $4,718,000
4. Shandwick, $4,198,000
5. DeVries PR, $3,320,425
6. LaForce & Stevens, $2,998,278
7. Cairns & Assocs., $2,906,371
8. Porter Novelli, $2,824,000
9. Manning, Selvage & Lee, $2,281,000
10. Ogilvy PR Worldwide, $1,453,200

Source: *O'Dwyer's Directory of Public Relations Firms*, (annual), J.R. O'Dwyer Co., Inc., 1999, p. A27.

★3633★
LEADING PUBLIC RELATIONS FIRMS IN ENTERTAINMENT AND CULTURE, 1998
Ranked by: Net fees. **Number listed:** 31

1. Shandwick, with $14,994,000
2. Edelman PR Worldwide, $9,704,015
3. Porter Novelli, $7,304,000

4. Dennis Davidson Associates, $5,489,027
5. Ruder Finn, $5,250,000
6. Golin/Harris International, $4,971,162
7. Bender/Helper Impact, $4,797,011
8. BSMG Worldwide, $4,270,000
9. Bragman Nyman Cafarelli, $3,662,039
10. GCI/APCO, $2,059,664

Source: *O'Dwyer's Directory of Public Relations Firms*, (annual), J.R. O'Dwyer Co., Inc., 1999, p. A27.

★3634★
LEADING PUBLIC RELATIONS FIRMS IN ENVIRONMENTAL ISSUES, 1998
Ranked by: Net fees. **Number listed:** 28

1. Ketchum, with $25,100,000
2. Porter Novelli, $21,156,000
3. Fleishman-Hillard, $15,146,000
4. Shandwick, $9,322,000
5. Edelman PR Worldwide, $6,312,669
6. Ogilvy PR Worldwide, $4,774,200
7. Ruder Finn, $4,500,000
8. BSMG Worldwide, $3,584,000
9. GCI/APCO, $2,437,473
10. Kamber Group, $2,100,000

Source: *O'Dwyer's Directory of Public Relations Firms*, (annual), J.R. O'Dwyer Co., Inc., 1999, p. A27.

★3635★
LEADING PUBLIC RELATIONS FIRMS IN FINANCIAL PUBLIC RELATIONS AND INVESTOR RELATIONS, 1998
Ranked by: Net fees. **Number listed:** 56

1. Fleishman-Hillard, with $58,115,000
2. BSMG Worldwide, $39,612,000
3. Edelman PR Worldwide, $31,646,315
4. Porter Novelli, $31,311,000
5. Shandwick, $27,017,000
6. Morgen-Walke Associates, $23,258,300
7. Ludgate Comms. of WPRW, $19,116,229
8. GCI/APCO, $16,916,000
9. Manning, Selvage & Lee, $13,687,000
10. Ketchum, $12,925,000

Source: *O'Dwyer's Directory of Public Relations Firms*, (annual), J.R. O'Dwyer Co., Inc., 1999, p. A27+.

★3636★
LEADING PUBLIC RELATIONS FIRMS IN FOOD AND BEVERAGE, 1998
Ranked by: Net fees. **Number listed:** 50

1. Ketchum, with $25,123,000
2. Shandwick, $20,041,000
3. Fleishman-Hillard, $18,623,000
4. Porter Novelli, $17,770,000
5. Edelman PR Worldwide, $16,426,369
6. BSMG Worldwide, $14,153,000
7. Manning, Selvage & Lee, $12,926,000
8. GCI/APCO, $10,278,599
9. Golin/Harris International, $10,224,427
10. Ogilvy PR Worldwide, $6,952,400

Source: *O'Dwyer's Directory of Public Relations Firms*, (annual), J.R. O'Dwyer Co., Inc., 1999, p. A29.

★3637★
LEADING PUBLIC RELATIONS FIRMS IN HEALTHCARE, 1998
Ranked by: Net fees. **Number listed:** 77

1. Porter Novelli, with $40,227,000
2. Ketchum, $30,075,000
3. Edclman PR Worldwidc, $28,636,063
4. Burson-Marsteller, $27,890,000
5. Manning, Selvage & Lee, $24,332,000
6. Ogilvy PR Worldwide, $23,591,300
7. Fleishman-Hillard, $23,582,000
8. Ruder Finn, $21,430,000
9. BSMG Worldwide, $17,482,000
10. Shandwick, $14,200,000

Source: *O'Dwyer's Directory of Public Relations Firms*, (annual), J.R. O'Dwyer Co., Inc., 1999, p. A29.

★3638★
LEADING PUBLIC RELATIONS FIRMS IN HIGH-TECH, 1998
Ranked by: Net fees. **Number listed:** 84

1. Porter Novelli, with $54,981,000
2. Shandwick, $48,911,000
3. Edelman PR Worldwide, $41,139,676
4. Waggener Edstrom, $40,900,000
5. Fleishman-Hillard, $31,989,000
6. Copithorne & Bellows, $26,705,427
7. Weber Group of WPRW, $26,633,215
8. Ogilvy PR, $24,829,400
9. Ketchum, $22,988,000
10. Manning, Selvage & Lee, $22,811,000

Source: *O'Dwyer's Directory of Public Relations Firms*, (annual), J.R. O'Dwyer Co., Inc., 1999, p. A29+.

★3639★
LEADING PUBLIC RELATIONS FIRMS IN HOME FURNISHINGS, 1998
Ranked by: Net fees. **Number listed:** 16

1. Shandwick, with $6,231,000
2. Golin/Harris International, $2,417,297
3. L.C. Williams & Assocs., $1,558,146
4. Edelman PR Worldwide, $1,545,494
5. Ogilvy PR Worldwide, $1,341,600
6. Lou Hammond & Associates, $855,790
7. Gibbs & Soell, $670,500
8. DeVries PR, $627,263
9. LobsenzStevens, $600,000
10. BSMG Worldwide, $473,000

Source: *O'Dwyer's Directory of Public Relations Firms*, (annual), J.R. O'Dwyer Co., Inc., 1999, p. A31.

★3640★
LEADING PUBLIC RELATIONS FIRMS IN SPORTS, 1998
Ranked by: Net fees. **Number listed:** 22

1. Edelman PR Worldwide, with $7,576,243
2. Ketchum, $4,893,000
3. Alan Taylor Communications, $3,649,007
4. Shandwick, $2,715,000
5. GCI/APCO, $1,597,552
6. Fleishman-Hillard, $1,593,000
7. Rowland Worldwide, $1,137,000
8. Kamber Group, $1,100,000
9. Ruder Finn, $975,000
10. Kamer-Singer, $812,139

Source: *O'Dwyer's Directory of Public Relations Firms*, (annual), J.R. O'Dwyer Co., Inc., 1999, p. A31.

★3641★
LEADING PUBLIC RELATIONS FIRMS IN TRAVEL, 1998
Ranked by: Net fees. **Number listed:** 36

1. Shandwick, with $7,489,000
2. Porter Novelli, $7,474,000
3. GCI/APCO, $6,469,931
4. BSMG Worldwide, $6,000,000
5. Edelman PR Worldwide, $5,157,330
6. Fleishman-Hillard, $4,558,000

7. Ketchum, $4,022,000
8. Zimmerman Agency, $2,714,964
9. Lou Hammond & Associates, $1,977,170
10. Middleton & Gendron, $1,859,521

Source: *O'Dwyer's Directory of Public Relations Firms*, (annual), J.R. O'Dwyer Co., Inc., 1999, p. A31.

★3642★
LEADING PUBLIC RELATIONS FIRMS, 1998
Ranked by: Net fees. **Remarks:** Also notes number of employees and percent change from 1997. **Number listed:** 50

1. Burson-Marsteller, with $258,417,000
2. Hill and Knowlton, $206,000,000
3. Porter Novelli International, $183,050,000
4. Shandwick International, $170,300,000
5. Fleishman-Hillard, $160,692,000
6. Edelman PR Worldwide, $157,840,530
7. Ketchum, $125,248,000
8. BSMG Worldwide, $118,963,000
9. Weber PR Worldwide, $83,166,000
10. GCI/APCO, $76,667,957

Source: *O'Dwyer's Directory of Public Relations Firms*, (annual), J.R. O'Dwyer Co., Inc., 1999, p. A15.

Public Relations Firms--Atlanta (GA)

★3643★
LEADING PUBLIC RELATIONS FIRMS IN ATLANTA, 1998
Ranked by: Net fees. **Remarks:** Also notes number of employees. **Number listed:** 13

1. Ketchum, with $14,304,000
2. GCI/APCO, $5,330,170
3. Ogilvy PR Worldwide, $4,986,200
4. Cohn & Wolfe, $4,231,499
5. Fleishman-Hillard, $3,616,000
6. Manning, Selvage & Lee, $2,494,000
7. Golin/Harris International, $1,674,000
8. Jackson Spalding, $1,510,110
9. Edelman PR Worldwide, $1,458,698
10. Weber PR Worldwide, $1,184,048

Source: *O'Dwyer's Directory of Public Relations Firms*, (annual), J.R. O'Dwyer Co., Inc., 1999, p. A23.

Public Relations Firms--Boston (MA)

★3644★
LEADING PUBLIC RELATIONS FIRMS IN BOSTON, 1998
Ranked by: Net fees. **Remarks:** Also notes number of employees. **Number listed:** 25

1. Brodeur Porter Novelli, with $15,942,000
2. Schwartz Communications, Waltham, $15,019,646
3. Weber PR Worldwide, Cambridge, $14,954,134
4. Lois Paul & Partners, $11,965,627
5. Miller/Shandwick Technologies, $7,151,000
6. Copithorne & Bellows, $7,060,856
7. Regan Communications, $5,000,000
8. Golin/Harris International, $4,585,000
9. Cone Communications, $4,504,000
10. Cunningham Communication, Cambridge, $4,120,000

Source: *O'Dwyer's Directory of Public Relations Firms*, (annual), J.R. O'Dwyer Co., Inc., 1999, p. A23.

Public Relations Firms--California

★3645★
LEADING PUBLIC RELATIONS FIRMS IN THE SILICON VALLEY, 1998
Ranked by: Net fees. **Remarks:** Also notes number of employees. **Number listed:** 21

1. Cunningham Communications (Palo Alto), with $11,326,000
2. Weber Public Relations Worldwide (Palo Alto), $8,709,139
3. Miller/Shandwick Technologies (Redwood Shores), $8,213,000
4. The Hoffman Agency (San Jose), $6,514,271
5. Copithorne & Bellows (Irvine), $6,469,913
6. Wilson McHenry Co. (San Mateo), $6,425,752
7. Nelson Communications Group (Sacramento and Irvine), $6,167,551
8. Ketchum (Redwood City), $5,967,000
9. Edelman PR WW (Palo Alto), $5,290,482
10. Eastwick Comms. (Redwood City), $4,702,170

Source: *O'Dwyer's Directory of Public Relations Firms*, (annual), J.R. O'Dwyer Co., Inc., 1999, p. A25.

Public Relations Firms--Chicago (IL)

★3646★
LEADING PUBLIC RELATIONS FIRMS IN CHICAGO, 1998
Ranked by: Net fees. **Remarks:** Also notes number of employees. **Number listed:** 30

1. BSMG Worldwide, with $29,930,749
2. Edelman PR Worldwide, $29,457,562
3. Golin/Harris International, $18,790,000
4. Burson-Marsteller, $17,339,000
5. Kemper Lesnik Communications, $7,083,514
6. Ketchum, $6,938,000
7. Ogilvy PR Worldwide, $6,765,000
8. Hill and Knowlton, $6,400,000
9. Fleishman-Hillard, $5,232,000
10. Porter Novelli, $4,701,000

Source: *O'Dwyer's Directory of Public Relations Firms*, (annual), J.R. O'Dwyer Co., Inc., 1999, p. A21.

Public Relations Firms--Dallas (TX)

★3647★
LEADING PUBLIC RELATIONS FIRMS IN DALLAS, 1998
Ranked by: Net fees. **Remarks:** Also notes number of employees. **Number listed:** 12

1. Fleishman-Hillard, with $7,114,000
2. Cunningham Communications (Austin), $4,991,000
3. BSMG Worldwide, $4,523,882
4. Publicis Dialog, $4,017,400

5. Edelman PR Worldwide, $2,887,023
6. Dawson/Duncan Communications, $1,982,668
7. Levenson Public Relations, $988,431
8. Ketchum, $900,000
9. Lois Paul & Partners (Austin), $474,515
10. Hadeler White PR, $405,396

Source: *O'Dwyer's Directory of Public Relations Firms*, (annual), J.R. O'Dwyer Co., Inc., 1999, p. A25.

Public Relations Firms--Florida

★3648★
FLORIDA'S LARGEST PUBLIC RELATIONS FIRMS, 1998
Ranked by: Number of full time employees. **Remarks:** Includes phone number, address, number of Florida clients, number of offices, senior executive and title, and year founded in Florida. **Number listed:** 23

1. Weber/RBB, with 50 employees
2. Burson-Marsteller, 47
3. Fleishman-Hillard, 35
4. Continental Capital & Equity Corp., 32
5. Wragg & Casas Public Relations Inc., 27
6. Citigate Gordon Diaz-Balart, 24
7. Bitner.com, 22
8. Zynyx Marketing Communications Inc., 21
9. Clarke Advertising & Public Relations, 20
9. Backus Turner International, 20
11. CBR PR: Carlman Booker Reis PR, 18
11. Public Communications Inc., 18

Source: *Florida Trend*, TopRank Florida (annual), 1999, p. 70.

Public Relations Firms--Great Britain

★3649★
TOP BUSINESS-TO-BUSINESS PUBLIC RELATIONS FIRMS IN GREAT BRITAIN, 1998
Ranked by: Business-to-business income, in British pounds. **Remarks:** Also notes total income. **Number listed:** 50

1. Countrywide Porter Novelli, with £11,464,000
2. Citigate Dewe Rogerson, £9,685,000
3. Shandwick International, £8,787,000
4. Medical Action Communications, £7,520,000
5. Hill & Knowlton, £7,221,000
6. Text 100, £6,029,000
7. Burson-Marsteller, £5,375,000
8. Ketchum (including Life), £4,420,000
9. Charles Barker/BSMG Worldwide, £3,851,000
10. Brodeur A Plus, £3,839,000

Source: *Marketing*, Top Agencies (annual), May 27, 1999, p. 50.

★3650★
TOP CONSUMER PUBLIC RELATIONS FIRMS IN GREAT BRITAIN, 1998
Ranked by: Consumer marketing earnings, in British pounds. **Remarks:** Also notes total income. **Number listed:** 50

1. Hill & Knowlton (UK), with £11,880,000
2. Shandwick International, £6,202,000
3. Freud Communications, £5,734,000
4. Ketchum (including Life), £4,612,000
5. Burson-Marsteller, £4,479,000
6. Countrywide Porter Novelli, £4,478,000
7. Grayling Group, £4,046,000
8. Harrison Cowley, £3,200,000
9. Jackie Cooper Public Relations, £3,101,000
10. Biss Lancaster, £3,042,000

Source: *Marketing*, Top Agencies (annual), May 27, 1999, p. 65.

★3651★
TOP CRISIS MANAGEMENT PUBLIC RELATIONS FIRMS IN GREAT BRITAIN, 1998
Ranked by: Crisis management earnings, in British pounds. **Remarks:** Also notes total income. **Number listed:** 15

1. Countrywide Porter Novelli, with £3,403,000
2. Biss Lancaster, £1,159,000
3. Shandwick International, £1,034,000
4. Hill & Knowlton (UK), £932,000
5. Text 100, £773,000
6. Grayling Group, £728,000
7. Fishburn Hedges, £699,000
8. Government Policy Consultants, £640,000
9. Ketchum (including Life), £480,000
10. The Shire Hall Group, £422,000

Source: *Marketing*, Top Agencies (annual), May 27, 1999, p. 57.

★3652★
TOP FINANCIAL SERVICES PUBLIC RELATIONS FIRMS IN GREAT BRITAIN, 1998
Ranked by: Financial services income, in British pounds. **Remarks:** Also notes total income. **Number listed:** 25

1. Citigate Dewe Rogerson, with £14,726,000
2. Shandwick International, £4,135,000
3. Hill & Knowlton (UK), £2,795,000
4. Weber PR Worldwide, £2,697,000
5. Lansons Communications, £2,616,000
6. Fishburn Hedges, £2,046,000
7. Edelman Public Relations Worldwide, £1,787,000
8. College Hill, £1,640,000
9. GCI/APCO (include. Focus Comms.), £1,484,000
10. Charles Barker/BSMG Worldwide, £1,252,000

Source: *Marketing*, Top Agencies (annual), May 27, 1999, p. 55.

★3653★
TOP HEALTHCARE PUBLIC RELATIONS FIRMS IN GREAT BRITAIN, 1998
Ranked by: Medical earnings, in British pounds. **Remarks:** Also notes total income. **Number listed:** 25

1. Medical Action Communications, with £7,520,000
2. The Shire Hall Group, £4,222,000
3. Hill & Knowlton (UK), £3,028,000
4. Shandwick International, £2,584,000
5. Ketchum (including Life), £2,498,000
6. CPR Worldwide, £2,079,000
7. Holmes & Marchant Group, £2,005,000
8. Grayling Group, £1,780,000
9. Cohn & Wolfe, £1,566,000
10. Lowe Fusion Healthcare, £1,478,000

Source: *Marketing*, Top Agencies (annual), May 27, 1999, p. 62.

★3654★
TOP INFORMATION TECHNOLOGY PUBLIC RELATIONS FIRMS IN GREAT BRITAIN, 1998
Ranked by: Information technology earnings, in British pounds. **Remarks:** Also notes total income. **Number listed:** 50

1. Text 100, with £7,729,000
2. Shandwick International, £5,944,000
3. Brodeur A Plus, £4,228,000

4. Firely Communications, £4,020,000
5. Hill & Knowlton (UK), £3,494,000
6. Weber PR Worldwide, £3,344,000
7. Edelman PR Worldwide, £2,859,000
8. Harvard Public Relations, £2,799,000
9. Kaizo, £2,601,000
10. Citigate Dewe Rogerson, £1,857,000

Source: *Marketing*, Top Agencies (annual), May 27, 1999, p. 59.

★3655★
TOP INTERNAL COMMUNICATION PUBLIC RELATIONS FIRMS IN GREAT BRITAIN, 1998
Ranked by: Internal communications earnings, in British pounds. **Remarks:** Also notes total income. **Number listed:** 15

1. Shandwick International, with £2,067,000
2. Countrywide Porter Novelli, £1,970,000
3. Burson-Marsteller, £1,792,000
4. Charles Barker/BSMG Worldwide, £866,000
5. CPR Worldwide, £728,000
6. Barkers PR (Birmingham and Scotland), £601,000
7. Hill & Knowlton (UK), £466,000
8. Key Communications, £443,000
9. The Shire Hall Group, £422,000
10. BRAHM Public Relations, £413,000

Source: *Marketing*, Top Agencies (annual), May 27, 1999, p. 56.

★3656★
TOP PUBLIC RELATIONS FIRMS IN GREAT BRITAIN, 1998
Ranked by: Income, in British pounds. **Remarks:** Includes 1997 income, percent change, current staff and previous staff, and income per head. **Number listed:** 25

1. Citigate Dewe Rogerson, with £26,533,000
2. Shandwick International, £25,843,000
3. Hill & Knowlton (UK), £23,295,000
4. Burson-Marsteller, £17,917,000
5. Countrywide Porter Novelli, £17,913,000
6. Weber PR Worldwide, £10,786,000
7. Charles Barker/BSMG Worldwide, £9,627,000
8. Ketchum (including Life), £9,608,000
9. Edelman PR Worldwide, £8,934,000
10. The Grayling Group, £8,091,000

Source: *Marketing*, Top Agencies (annual), May 27, 1999, p. 39+.

Public Relations Firms--Houston (TX)

★3657★
LEADING PUBLIC RELATIONS FIRMS IN HOUSTON, 1998
Ranked by: Net fees. **Remarks:** Also notes number of employees. **Number listed:** 6

1. Vollmer PR, with $3,496,785 employees
2. Miller/Shandwick Technologies, $2,713,000
3. Pierpont Communications, $1,946,132
4. Fleishman-Hillard, $1,149,000
5. Ward Creative Communications, $673,577
6. Gibbs & Soell, $640,500

Source: *O'Dwyer's Directory of Public Relations Firms*, (annual), J.R. O'Dwyer Co., Inc., 1999, p. A25.

Public Relations Firms--Los Angeles County (CA)

★3658★
LEADING PUBLIC RELATIONS FIRMS IN LOS ANGELES COUNTY, 1998
Ranked by: Net fees. **Remarks:** Also notes number of employees. **Number listed:** 34

1. Hill and Knowlton, with $12,300,000
2. Fleishman-Hillard, $11,939,000
3. Shandwick, $11,899,000
4. Manning, Selvage & Lee, $11,666,600
5. Golin/Harris International, $7,765,000
6. Rogers & Assocs., $7,109,203
7. Stoorza, Ziegaus & Metzger (L.A. and San Diego), $7,047,261
8. BSMG Worldwide, $6,457,207
9. Burson-Marsteller, $5,547,363
10. Bragman Nyman Cafarelli, $5,488,429

Source: *O'Dwyer's Directory of Public Relations Firms*, (annual), J.R. O'Dwyer Co., Inc., 1999, p. A21.

Public Relations Firms--Midwestern States

★3659★
LEADING PUBLIC RELATIONS FIRMS IN MIDWEST CITIES, 1998
Ranked by: Net fees. **Remarks:** Also notes number of employees. **Number listed:** 14

1. Fleishman-Hillard (Kansas City and Milwaukee), with $14,533,000
2. Bader Rutter & Associates (Brookfield, WI), $4,494,843
3. Manning, Selvage & Lee (Detroit), $3,988,200
4. Cramer-Krasselt (Milwaukee), $2,510,000
5. Charleston/Orwig (Hartland, WI), $2,383,963
6. CMF&Z PR (Des Moines, IA), $2,348,000
7. Barkley Evergreen (Kansas City), $2,305,285
8. Laughlin/Constable PR (Milwaukee), $2,069,837
9. Shandwick (Detroit), $1,953,000
10. Morgan & Myers (Milwaukee), $1,816,041

Source: *O'Dwyer's Directory of Public Relations Firms*, (annual), J.R. O'Dwyer Co., Inc., 1999, p. A25.

Public Relations Firms—Minneapolis/St. Paul Metropolitan Area

★3660★
LEADING PUBLIC RELATIONS FIRMS IN THE MINNEAPOLIS/ST. PAUL METROPOLITAN AREA, 1998
Ranked by: Net fees. **Remarks:** Also notes number of employees. **Number listed:** 7

1. Shandwick, with $16,165,000
2. Padilla Speer Beardsley, $6,599,594
3. Tunheim Santrizos Co., $4,816,144
4. Fleishman-Hillard, $3,171,000
5. Karwoski & Courage, $2,750,000
6. Morgan & Myers, $1,157,548

7. Westmoreland, Larson (Duluth), $122,821

Source: *O'Dwyer's Directory of Public Relations Firms*, (annual), J.R. O'Dwyer Co., Inc., 1999, p. A25.

Public Relations Firms--New Jersey

★3661★
LEADING PUBLIC RELATIONS FIRMS IN NEW JERSEY, 1998
Ranked by: Net fees. **Remarks:** Also notes number of employees. **Number listed:** 4

1. MWW Group (East Rutherford & Trenton), with $9,200,519
2. MCS (Summit), $2,570,197
3. Gillespie (Princeton), $1,892,049
4. Star/Rosen Public Relations (Cherry Hill), $1,066,000

Source: *O'Dwyer's Directory of Public Relations Firms*, (annual), J.R. O'Dwyer Co., Inc., 1999, p. A23.

Public Relations Firms--New York (NY)

★3662★
LEADING PUBLIC RELATIONS FIRMS IN NEW YORK, 1998
Ranked by: Net fees. **Remarks:** Also notes number of employees. **Number listed:** 54

1. Burson-Marsteller, with $61,743,000
2. Edelman PR Worldwide, $41,213,135
3. Ruder Finn, $40,510,000
4. Ketchum, $28,734,000
5. BSMG Worldwide, $28,390,632
6. Porter Novelli, $24,921,000
7. Hill and Knowlton, $23,100,000
8. Fleishman-Hillard, $19,119,000
9. Manning, Selvage & Lee, $18,216,500
9. Morgen-Walke Associates, $18,216,500

Source: *O'Dwyer's Directory of Public Relations Firms*, (annual), J.R. O'Dwyer Co., Inc., 1999, p. A21.

Public Relations Firms--Ohio

★3663★
LEADING PUBLIC RELATIONS FIRMS IN OHIO, 1998
Ranked by: Net fees. **Remarks:** Also notes number of employees. **Number listed:** 6

1. Dix & Eaton (Cleveland), with $8,400,069
2. Edward Howard & Co. (Cleveland, Akron, Columbus & Dayton), $5,792,029
3. Northlich Stolley LaWarre (Cincinnati), $3,627,500
4. Dan Pinger PR (Cincinnati), $2,155,721
5. BSMG Worldwide (Cleveland), $1,909,748
6. McKinney Advertising & PR (Cleveland), $1,619,903

Source: *O'Dwyer's Directory of Public Relations Firms*, (annual), J.R. O'Dwyer Co., Inc., 1999, p. A25.

Public Relations Firms--Philadelphia (PA)

★3664★
LEADING PUBLIC RELATIONS FIRMS IN PHILADELPHIA, 1998
Ranked by: Net fees. **Remarks:** Also notes number of employees. **Number listed:** 6

1. Tierney Group, with $6,306,592
2. Dorland Sweeney Jones, $2,877,000
3. Earle Palmer Brown, $2,188,625
4. Dudnyk PR, Horsham, $1,156,000
5. Tattar Cutler-LD&B PR, Horsham, $819,146
6. Toplin & Assocs., Dresher, $675,111

Source: *O'Dwyer's Directory of Public Relations Firms*, (annual), J.R. O'Dwyer Co., Inc., 1999, p. A23.

Public Relations Firms--Pittsburgh (PA)

★3665★
LEADING PUBLIC RELATIONS FIRMS IN PITTSBURGH, 1998
Ranked by: Net fees. **Remarks:** Also notes number of employees. **Number listed:** 3

1. Ketchum, with $7,787,000
2. Burson-Marsteller, $4,859,000
3. Skutski & Oltmanns, $1,657,399

Source: *O'Dwyer's Directory of Public Relations Firms*, (annual), J.R. O'Dwyer Co., Inc., 1999, p. A23.

Public Relations Firms--St. Louis (MO)

★3666★
LEADING PUBLIC RELATIONS FIRMS IN ST. LOUIS, 1998
Ranked by: Net fees. **Remarks:** Also notes number of employees. **Number listed:** 3

1. Fleishman-Hillard, with $40,349,000
2. Shandwick, $4,045,000
3. Vandiver Group, $874,518

Source: *O'Dwyer's Directory of Public Relations Firms*, (annual), J.R. O'Dwyer Co., Inc., 1999, p. A23.

Public Relations Firms--San Francisco (CA)

★3667★
LEADING PUBLIC RELATIONS FIRMS IN SAN FRANCISCO, 1998
Ranked by: Net fees. **Remarks:** Also notes number of employees. **Number listed:** 27

1. Ketchum, with $12,809,000
2. Copithorne & Bellows, $8,454,797
3. Niehaus Ryan Wong, $7,731,041
4. Fleishman-Hillard, $7,076,000
5. Ogilvy PR Worldwide, $6,341,800
6. Access Communications, $6,215,000
7. Golin/Harris International, $5,497,159
8. GCI/APCO, $5,323,289

9. BSMG Worldwide, $5,272,081
10. Edelman PR Worldwide, $4,741,773

Source: *O'Dwyer's Directory of Public Relations Firms*, (annual), J.R. O'Dwyer Co., Inc., 1999, p. A25.

Public Relations Firms--Seattle (WA)

★3668★
LEADING PUBLIC RELATIONS FIRMS IN SEATTLE, 1998
Ranked by: Net fees. **Remarks:** Also notes number of employees. **Number listed:** 8

1. Shandwick, with $5,711,000
2. MWW Group, $4,704,107
3. Publicis Dialog, $4,018,300
4. The Rockey Company, $3,996,209
5. GCI/APCO, $2,045,000
6. Imagio Technology Adv. & PR, $1,349,009
7. Richmond PR, $934,224
8. Copithorne & Bellows, $592,545

Source: *O'Dwyer's Directory of Public Relations Firms*, (annual), J.R. O'Dwyer Co., Inc., 1999, p. A25.

Public Relations Firms--Southeastern States

★3669★
LEADING PUBLIC RELATIONS FIRMS IN THE SOUTHEAST, 1998
Ranked by: Net fees. **Remarks:** Also notes number of employees. **Number listed:** 13

1. Dye, Van Mol & Lawrence (Nashville), with $5,242,264
2. Charles Ryan & Assocs. (Charleston, WV), $4,364,620
3. Price/McNabb (Charlotte, NC), $4,012,368
4. McNeely Pigott & Fox (Nashville), $4,006,334
5. Shandwick (Louisvill), $3,325,000
6. Brodeur Porter Novelli (Raleigh, NC), $2,746,000
7. Gibbs & Soell (Raleigh, NC), $2,432,000
8. Guthrie/Mayes (Louisville), $1,976,439
9. James Fyock & Assocs. (Winston-Salem), $1,641,514
10. Ruder Finn (Raleigh, NC), $749,000

Source: *O'Dwyer's Directory of Public Relations Firms*, (annual), J.R. O'Dwyer Co., Inc., 1999, p. A23.

Public Relations Firms--Washington (DC)

★3670★
LEADING PUBLIC RELATIONS FIRMS IN WASHINGTON, DC, 1998
Ranked by: Net fees. **Remarks:** Also notes number of employees. **Number listed:** 35

1. Burson-Marsteller, with $32,875,000
2. Hill and Knowlton, $27,000,000
3. Fleishman-Hillard, $19,648,000
4. Ketchum, $18,946,000
5. Porter Novelli, $17,517,000
6. Ogilvy PR Worldwide, $16,229,000
7. Powell Tate, $15,656,880
8. GCI/APCO, $14,295,000
9. Shandwick Public Affairs, $12,899,000
10. Edelman PR Worldwide, $12,267,146

Source: *O'Dwyer's Directory of Public Relations Firms*, (annual), J.R. O'Dwyer Co., Inc., 1999, p. A23.

Public Relations Firms--Western States

★3671★
LEADING PUBLIC RELATIONS FIRMS IN THE WEST, 1998
Ranked by: Net fees. **Remarks:** Also notes number of employees. **Number listed:** 10

1. Waggener Edstrom (Portland, OR and Bellevue, WA), with $37,260,000
2. Karakas, VanSickle Ouellette (Portland, OR), $6,100,000
3. MGA Communications (Denver), $2,800,000
4. Ogilvy PR Worldwide, $2,348,100
5. Brodeur Porter Novelli, SLC, $1,923,000
6. Carl Thompson Assocs. (Louisville, CO), $1,813,985
7. Cramer-Krasselt (Phoenix), $1,580,000
8. KMC Group (Bellevue, WA), $1,240,212
9. Publicis Dialog (Salt Lake City), $731,900
10. Bremer PR (Salt Lake City), $594,125

Source: *O'Dwyer's Directory of Public Relations Firms*, (annual), J.R. O'Dwyer Co., Inc., 1999, p. A25.

Public Utilities

See also: **Electric Utilities**

★3672★
TOP CORPORATIONS IN THE GAS AND ELECTRIC UTILITIES INDUSTRY, 1998
Ranked by: Revenue, in millions of dollars. **Remarks:** Also notes profits and investment figures as well as number of employees. **Number listed:** 64

1. PG &E Corp., with $19,942 million
2. Duke Energy, $17,610
3. Texas Utilities, $14,736
4. Utilicorp United, $12,563
5. Entergy, $11,495
6. Houston Industries, $11,488
7. Southern, $11,403
8. Edison International, $10,208
9. Pacificorp, $9,443
10. Unicom, $7,151

Source: *Fortune*, Fortune 500 Largest U.S. Corporations (annual), April 26, 1999, p. F-71.

★3673★
TOP UTILITIES BASED ON EFFICIENCY SCORE, 1996
Ranked by: Number of times used as peer. **Remarks:** Includes returns to scale, holding company code for efficient peers and two closest peers. **Number listed:** 23

1. Idaho Power Co., with 55
2. Ohio Valley Electric Corp., 54
3. Montana Power Co., 30
4. American Electric Power Co., Inc., 24

5. MidAmerican Energy Holdings Co., 12
5. Washington Water Power Co., 12
7. Central & South West Corp., 9
7. LG&E Energy Corp., 9
9. Western Resources Inc., 7
9. North Central Power Co. Inc., 7
10. Duke Energy Corp., 6
10. Pacificorp, 6

Source: *Public Utilities Fortnightly*, September 1, 1998, p. 28.

★3674★
TOP UTILITY COMPANIES IN THE S&P 500, 1998
Ranked by: Each company is ranked by 8 criteria: one-year total return, three-year total return, one-year sales growth, three-year average annual sales growth, one-year profit growth, three-year average annual profit growth, net profit margins, and return on equity, with additional weight given to a company's sales. A company's composite rank is calculated using the sum of all its ranks. **Remarks:** Overall score not provided. **Number listed:** 37

1. AES
2. Duke Energy
3. FirstEnergy
4. PP&L Resources
5. Peco Energy
6. Entergy
7. Columbia Energy Group
8. Texas Utilities
9. New Century Energies
10. PG&E

Source: *Business Week*, Business Week 50: Top Companies of the S&P 500 (annual), March 29, 1999, p. 166.

Public Utilities--Florida

★3675★
FLORIDA'S LARGEST ELECTRIC UTILITIES, 1998
Ranked by: Number of customers. **Remarks:** Includes phone number, address, number of full-time Florida employees, 1997 Florida revenue, company ownership, year founded and senior executive. **Number listed:** 25

1. Florida Power & Light Co., with 3,600,000 customers
2. Florida Power Corp., 1,300,000
3. Tampa Electric Co., 528,000
4. Gulf Power Co., 345,377
5. Jacksonville Electric Authority, 335,463
6. Orlando Utilities Commission, 152,500
7. Withlacoochee River Electric Cooperative, Inc., 146,439
8. Lee County Electric Cooperative Inc., 137,505
9. Clay Electric Cooperative Inc., 123,773
10. Lakeland Electric, 104,786

Source: *Florida Trend*, TopRank Florida (annual), 1999, p. 104.

Public Utilities, International

★3676★
WORLD'S LARGEST ELECTRIC, GAS AND UTILITIES COMPANIES BY REVENUE, 1997
Ranked by: Revenue, in millions of dollars. **Number listed:** 16

1. Tokyo Electric Power (Japan), with $42,997 million
2. RWE Group (Germany), $40,233
3. Electricite de France (France), $36,673
4. Enel (Italy), $22,181
5. Kansai Electric Power (Japan), $21,666
6. Chubu Electric Power (Japan), $18,311
7. Duke Energy (U.S.), $16,309
8. PG&E Corp. (U.S.), $15,400
9. Korea Electric Power (Korea), $14,064
10. Tohoku Electric Power, $13,017

Source: *Fortune*, The Global 500: World's Biggest Corporations (annual), August 3, 1998, p. F-26.

★3677★
WORLD'S LARGEST ELECTRIC, GAS AND UTILITIES COMPANIES BY REVENUE, 1997
Ranked by: Revenue, in millions of dollars. **Number listed:** 16

1. Tokyo Electric Power (Japan), with $42,997 million
2. RWE Group (Germany), $40,233
3. Electricite de France (France), $36,673
4. Enel (Italy), $22,181
5. Kansai Electric Power (Japan), $21,666
6. Chubu Electric Power (Japan), $18,311
7. Duke Energy (U.S.), $16,309
8. PG&E Corp. (U.S.), $15,400
9. Korea Electric Power (Korea), $14,064
10. Tohoku Electric Power, $13,017

Source: *Fortune*, The Global 500: World's Biggest Corporations (annual), August 3, 1998, p. F-26.

Public Utilities, New Jersey

★3678★
TOP UTILITY COMPANIES IN NEW JERSEY, 1998
Ranked by: Number of customers. **Remarks:** Includes year founded, chief executive officer, URL address and counties served. **Number listed:** 22

1. Public Service Electric & Gas Co., with 2,100,000 customers
2. United Water Resources, 1,300,000
3. New Jersey - American Water Company, 1,100,000
4. Conectiv, 1,000,000
4. GPU, 1,000,000
6. Joint Meeting of Essex & Union Counties, 500,000
7. New Jersey Resources, 383,052
8. Atlantic County Utilities Authority, 366,500
9. Rahway Valley Sewerage Authority, 303,500
10. South Jersey Gas Co., 264,000

Source: *New Jersey Business*, Book of Lists (annual), 1999, p. 42.

Public Utilities--Securities

★3679★
TOP BOND COUNSEL FOR UTILITIES, 1997
Ranked by: Amount issued, in thousands of dollars. **Remarks:** Also notes number of issues. **Number listed:** 10

1. Fulbright & Jaworksi, with $2,086,900 thousand
2. Nixon Hargrave Devans & Doyle, $1,989,800
3. Orrick, Herrington & Sutcliffe, $846,000
4. Excamilla & Poneck, $767,900

5. Wickliff & Hall, $735,500
6. O'Melveny & Myers, $696,100
7. Robinson & Pearman, $650,000
8. Haskell, Slaughter & Young, $597,200
9. Vinson & Elkins, $574,400
10. McCall, Parkhurst & Horton, $533,800

Source: *Bond Buyer Yearbook*, (annual), 1998, p. 137.

★3680★
TOP BOND ISSUERS FOR UTILITIES, 1997
Ranked by: Amount issued, in thousands of dollars. **Remarks:** Also notes number of issues. **Number listed:** 25

1. New York City Municipal Water Finance Authority, with $1,525,600 thousand
2. San Antonio, TX, $767,900
3. Houston, TX, $735,500
4. Southern California Metropolitan Water District, $650,000
5. Jefferson County, AL, $555,500
6. Detroit, MI, $508,300
7. Massachusetts Water Resources Authority, $451,100
8. Texas Water Development Board, $450,000
9. Dade County, FL, $437,200
10. California Department of Water Resources, $356,600

Source: *Bond Buyer Yearbook*, (annual), 1998, p. 137.

Publishers and Publishing

★3681★
MOST ADMIRED PUBLISHING AND PRINTING CORPORATIONS, 1998
Ranked by: Scores (1-10) derived from a survey of senior executives, outside directors and securities analysts. **Remarks:** Respondents rated companies in their own industry on 8 attributes of reputation. Also notes previous year's rank. **Number listed:** 10

1. Tribune, with 7.50
2. New York Times Co., 7.24
3. Gannett, 6.71
4. Knight-Ridder, 6.50
5. Times Mirror, 6.47
6. Dow Jones, 6.41
7. McGraw-Hill, 6.37
8. R.R. Donnelley & Sons, 6.24
9. American Greetings, 6.02
10. Reader's Digest Association, 4.86

Source: *Fortune*, America's Most Admired Corporations (annual), March 1, 1999, p. F-5.

★3682★
TOP CORPORATIONS IN THE PUBLISHING AND PRINTING INDUSTRY, 1998
Ranked by: Revenue, in millions of dollars. **Remarks:** Also notes profits and investment figures as well as number of employees. **Number listed:** 22

1. R.R. Donnelley & Sons, with $5,900 million
2. Gannett, $5,121
3. McGraw-Hill, $3,729
4. Times Mirror, $3,291
5. Knight-Ridder, $3,100
6. Tribune, $2,981
7. New York Times Co., $2,937
8. Reader's Digest Association, $2,634
9. World Color Press, $2,357
10. American Greetings, $2,212

Source: *Fortune*, Fortune 500 Largest U.S. Corporations (annual), April 26, 1999, p. F-66+.

★3683★
TOP PUBLISHING AND BROADCASTING COMPANIES IN THE S&P 500, 1998
Ranked by: Each company is ranked by 8 criteria: one-year total return, three-year total return, one-year sales growth, three-year average annual sales growth, one-year profit growth, three-year average annual profit growth, net profit margins, and return on equity, with additional weight given to a company's sales. A company's composite rank is calculated using the sum of all its ranks. **Remarks:** Overall score not provided. **Number listed:** 13

1. Gannett
2. Comcast
3. McGraw-Hill
4. Tribune
5. Clear Channel Communications
6. New York Times Co.
7. Meredith Corp.
8. Time Warner
9. Knight-Ridder
10. MediaOne Group

Source: *Business Week*, Business Week 50: Top Companies of the S&P 500 (annual), March 29, 1999, p. 162.

★3684★
TOP PUBLISHING COMPANIES BY FULL YEAR AD REVENUE, 1998
Ranked by: Total PIB, in percent. **Remarks:** Includes 1997 PIB, percent change and number of ad pages. **Number listed:** 25

1. Time Warner, with 11.8%
2. Conde Nast/Advance Pub., 11.1%
3. Hachette Filipacchi Magazines, 8.4%
4. Hearst Corp., 7.0%
5. Times Mirror Magazines, 5.2%
6. Ziff-Davis, 4.2%
7. Primedia, 3.8%
8. Meredith Corp., 3.1%
9. Gruner & Jahr USA Publishing, 2.6%
10. New York Times Magazine Group, 2.4%

Source: *Advertising Age*, Top 10 Publishing Companies (annual), February 8, 1999, p. 73.

Purchasing Departments

See: **Purchasing, Industrial**

Purchasing, Industrial

★3685★
TOP INDUSTRIAL PURCHASING DEPARTMENTS, 1997
Ranked by: Expenditures, in millions of dollars. **Remarks:** Includes sales figures. **Number listed:** 250

1. Ford Motor, with $81,422 million
2. General Motors, $70,000
3. Chrysler, $40,500
4. IBM, $39,220
5. General Electric, $30,886

6. Hewlett-Packard, $17,587
7. DuPont, $17,348
8. Exxon, $17,133
9. Boeing, $16,800
10. AT & T, $15,978

Source: *Purchasing*, November 5, 1998, p. 48+.

Quality of Life

★3686★
LEAST LIVABLE METRO AREAS 1999
Ranked by: Results of the Federal Reserve Bank of St. Louis/ U.S. Census data measuring the net migration of people in the 59 metro areas with over 1 million people. **Number listed:** 5

1. Los Angeles, CA
2. New York, NY
3. San Jose, CA
4. Miami, FL
5. Orange County, CA

Source: *Business Week*, May 10, 1999, p. 6.

★3687★
MOST LIVABLE METRO AREAS 1999
Ranked by: Results of the Federal Reserve Bank of St. Louis/ U.S. Census data measuring the net migration of people in the 59 metro areas with over 1 million people. **Number listed:** 5

1. Las Vegas, NV
2. Atlanta, GA
3. Phoenix, AZ
4. Austin, TX
5. Raleigh-Durham, NC

Source: *Business Week*, May 10, 1999, p. 6.

★3688★
STATES WITH THE HEALTHIEST POPULATION 1998
Ranked by: Results of research undertaken by Arundel Street Consulting Inc. Researchers used 17 statistical measures including disease, lifestyle, access to health care, occupational safety and disability and mortality. **Number listed:** 10

1. Minnesota
2. New Hampshire
3. Colorado
3. Utah
3. Wisconsin
6. Massachusetts
7. Washington
8. Hawaii
8. Iowa
8. Virginia

Source: *National Underwriter Life & Health/Financial Services*, October 19, 1998, p. 3.

★3689★
STATES WITH THE LEAST HEALTHY POPULATION 1998
Ranked by: Results of research undertaken by Arundel Street Consulting Inc. Researchers used 17 statistical measures including disease, lifestyle, access to health care, occupational safety and disability and mortality. **Number listed:** 12

1. Mississippi
2. Louisiana
2. Arkansas
4. Nevada
5. West Virginia
5. Tennessee
5. Oklahoma
8. South Carolina
9. New Mexico
10. Florida

Source: *National Underwriter Life & Health/Financial Services*, October 19, 1998, p. 3.

Radio Advertising

★3690★
LARGEST NATIONAL SPOT RADIO ADVERTISERS, 1997
Ranked by: National spot radio advertising expenditures, in millions of dollars. **Remarks:** Also notes figures for previous year and percent change. **Number listed:** 25

1. MCI WorldCom, with $52.9 million
2. Viacom Inc., $29.8
3. Bell Atlantic Corp., $25.9
4. SBC Communications, $25.4
5. CompUSA, $24.8
6. U.S. West Inc., $24.7
7. News Corp. Ltd., $24.3
8. General Motors Corp., $21.5
9. GTE Corp., $18.8
10. Montgomery Ward & Co., $17.8

Source: *Advertising Age*, Leading National Advertisers (annual), September 28, 1998, p. S45.

★3691★
LARGEST NETWORK RADIO ADVERTISERS, 1997
Ranked by: Network radio advertising expenditures, in millions of dollars. **Remarks:** Also notes figures for previous year and percent change. **Number listed:** 25

1. Chrysler Corp., with $43.8 million
2. Sears, Roebuck & Co., $37.4
3. Chattem, $35.2
4. Warner-Lambert Co., $29.9
5. William Wrigley Jr. Co., $23.7
6. Procter & Gamble, $22.4
7. Reading Genius Home Study, $21.7
8. AT & T, $19.7
9. Tandy Corp., $18.3
10. General Motors Corp., $18.0

Source: *Advertising Age*, Leading National Advertisers (annual), September 28, 1998, p. S44.

Radio Advertising--Europe

★3692★
TOP RADIO ADVERTISERS IN GREAT BRITAIN, 1999
Ranked by: Network radio advertising expenditures, in millions of British pounds. **Remarks:** Also notes figures for previous year and percent change. **Number listed:** 10

1. Central Office of Information, with £6.08 million
2. BT, £8.51
3. Carphone Warehouse, £8.06
4. Vodafone, £6.79
5. Dixons, £6.14
6. Coldseal Windows, £6.08
7. Ford, £5.40
8. Renault, £5.37

9. Coca-Cola, £4.39
10. HEA, £3.66

Source: *Director*, March, 1999, p. 45.

Radio Broadcasting

★3693★
TOP MEDIA COMPANIES BY RADIO REVENUE, 1997
Ranked by: Radio revenue, in millions of dollars. **Remarks:** Includes ratio as a percent of all media revenue and 1996 figures. **Number listed:** 15

1. CBS Corp., with $1,187.0 million
2. Capstar Broadcasting Partners, $570.0
3. Chancellor Media Corp., $548.9
4. Jacor Communications, $503.4
5. Walt Disney Co., $450.0
6. Clear Channel Communications, $402.9
7. American Radio Systems Corp., $374.1
8. Cox Enterprises, $199.6
9. Sinclair Broadcasting Group, $66.6
10. Tribune Co., $65.5

Source: *Advertising Age*, August 17, 1998, p. S10.

★3694★
TOP RADIO COMPANIES BY REVENUE, 1997
Ranked by: Radio revenue, in millions of dollars. **Remarks:** Includes number of stations. **Number listed:** 5

1. Chancellor Media, with $1,600 million
2. CBS, $1,500
3. Jacor, $614
4. Clear Channel, $452
5. ABC/Disney, $299

Source: *U.S. News & World Report*, September 7, 1998, p. 50.

Radio Stations

★3695★
TOP HISPANIC RADIO STATIONS, 1998
Ranked by: Estimated ad billings, in millions of dollars. **Remarks:** Includes format, location, owner, percent Hispanic-owned and 1997 gross billings. **Number listed:** 10

1. KLVE-FM, KTNQ-AM, KSCA-FM, with $64.66 million
2. WSKQ-FM, WPAT-FM, $36.00
3. WAMR-FM, WRTO-FM, WQBA-AM, WAQI-AM, $32.00
4. WRMA-FM, WXDJ-FM, WCMQ-AM, WCMQ-FM, $25.50
5. WOJO-FM, WIND-AM, WLXX-AM, $19.00
6. KCOR-AM, KROM-FM, KXTN-FM, $16.87
7. KKHJ-AM, KBUE-FM, KWIZ-AM, $16.55
8. KLAT-AM, KLTO-FM, KOVE-FM, KRTX-FM, $15.33
9. KQQK-FM, KXTJ-FM, KEYH-AM, $14.00
10. KLAX-FM, KXED-AM, $13.10

Source: *Hispanic Business*, December, 1998, p. 62.

Radio Stations--Los Angeles Metropolitan Area

★3696★
TOP RADIO STATIONS IN THE LOS ANGELES METROPOLITAN AREA, 1997-1998
Ranked by: Audience share in percent. **Remarks:** Includes audience share for 1996-1997 and summer 1998, revenue in millions, format, station owner, profile and sales managers. **Number listed:** 15

1. KLVE-FM, with 5.9%
2. KSCA-FM, 5.2%
3. KPWR-FM, 4.2%
4. KFI-AM, 4.1%
4. KKBT-FM, 4.1%
6. KRTH-FM, 3.7%
6. KIIS-FM, 3.7%
6. KOST-FM, 3.7%
9. KTWV-FM, 3.4%
10. KROQ-FM, 3.3%

Source: *Los Angeles Business Journal*, October 12, 1998, p. 33.

Radio Stations--New York Metropolitan Area

★3697★
TOP RADIO STATIONS IN THE NEW YORK METROPOLITAN AREA, 1998
Ranked by: Arbitron audience share, in percent. **Remarks:** Includes previous year's share, average quarter hour audience, average quarter hour share morning drive, average quarter hour share evening drive, station cume and format. **Number listed:** 12

1. WSKQ (Spanish Broadcasting System Inc.), with 5.9%
1. WLTW Lite FM (Chancellor Media Corp.), 5.9%
3. WQHT (Emmis Communications Corp.), 5.6%
4. WHTZ (Chancellor Media Corp.), 5.1%
5. WCBS (CBS Corp), 4.6%
6. WRKS (Emmis Communications Corp.), 4.3%
7. WKTU (Evergreen Media Corp.), 4.2%
8. WXRK (CBS Corp.), 3.8%
9. WINS (CBS Corp.), 3.2%
9. WABC (Disney), 3.2%

Source: *Crain's New York Business*, September 28, 1998, p. 18+.

Radio Stations--Philadelphia Metropolitan Area

★3698★
TOP RADIO STATIONS IN THE PHILADELPHIA METROPOLITAN AREA, 1998
Ranked by: Arbitron quarter hour share. **Remarks:** Includes program format, wattage, full-time and part-time employees, owner, general manager and station's parent company. **Number listed:** 12

1. KYW News Radio-AM 1060, with 52,000
1. WBEB-FM 101.1, 52,000
3. WDAS-FM 105.3, 44,500
4. WYSP-FM 94.1, 36,900
5. WUSL-FM 98.9, 36,700

6. WOGL-FM 98.1, 35,600
7. WJZZ-FM 106.1, 32,600
8. WXTU-FM 92.5, 31,100
9. WMGK-FM 102.9, 29,900
10. WPEN-AM 950, 29,500

Source: *Philadelphia Business Journal*, September 18, 1998, p. B8.

Radiology, Medical

See: **Medical Radiology**

Railroads

★3699★
MOST ADMIRED RAILROAD CORPORATIONS, 1998
Ranked by: Scores (1-5) derived from a survey of senior executives, outside directors and securities analysts. **Remarks:** Respondents rated companies in their own industry on 8 attributes of reputation. Also notes previous year's rank **Number listed:** 5

1. Norfolk Southern, with 7.71
2. Burlington Northern Santa Fe, 6.91
3. CSX, 6.63
4. Kansas City Southern Industries, 6.09
5. Union Pacific, 5.63

Source: *Fortune*, America's Most Admired Corporations (annual), March 1, 1999, p. F-2.

★3700★
TOP CORPORATIONS IN THE RAILROAD INDUSTRY, 1998
Ranked by: Revenue, in millions of dollars. **Remarks:** Also notes profits and investment figures as well as number of employees. **Number listed:** 5

1. Union Pacific, with $10,553 million
2. CSX, $9,898
3. Burlington Northern Santa Fe, $8,941
4. Norfolk Southern, $4,428
5. Kansas City Southern Industries, $1,284

Source: *Fortune*, Fortune 500 Largest U.S. Corporations (annual), April 26, 1999, p. F-67.

Railroads, International

★3701★
WORLD'S LARGEST RAILROADS BY REVENUE, 1997
Ranked by: Revenue, in millions of dollars. **Number listed:** 7

1. East Japan Railway (Japan), with $20,487 million
2. Deutsche Bahn (Germany), $17,575
3. SNCF (France), $16,653
4. Union Pacific (U.S.), $11,014
5. CSX (U.S.), $10,621
6. Central Japan Railway (Japan), $10,414
7. West Japan Railway (Japan), $10,013

Source: *Fortune*, The Global 500: World's Biggest Corporations (annual), August 3, 1998, p. F-24.

Random Access Memory

★3702★
DRAM WORLDWIDE MEMORY MARKET SHARE, 1997
Ranked by: Market share. **Remarks:** Figures confirmed through IC Insights. **Number listed:** 7

1. DRAM, with 67%
2. SRAM, 13%
3. Flash, 9%
4. EEPROM, 4%
5. ROM, 3%
5. EPROM, 3%
7. Other, 1%

Source: *Purchasing*, July 16, 1998, p. 140.

Random Access Memory, International

★3703★
TOP DRAM SUPPLIERS, 1997
Ranked by: Revenue, in billions of dollars. **Remarks:** Also includes 1996 revenue and percent change. **Number listed:** 10

1. Samsung, with $3,610 billion
2. NEC, $2,265
3. Hyundai, $1,905
4. Hitachi, $1,846
5. Micron, $1,650
6. LG Semicon, $1,465
7. Texas Instruments, $1,440
8. Mitsubishi Corp., $1,215
9. Toshiba, $1,167
10. Siemens, $1,020

Source: *Purchasing*, July 16, 1998, p. 140.

★3704★
TOP DRAM VENDORS WORLDWIDE, 1997
Ranked by: Revenue, in billions of dollars. **Number listed:** 10

1. Samsung, with $3.6 billion
2. Micron, $3.1
3. NEC, $2.3
4. Hyundai, $1.9
5. Hitachi, $1.8
6. LG Semicon, $1.5
7. Mitsubishi Corp., $1.2
7. Toshiba, $1.2
9. Siemens, $1.0
10. Fujitsu, $.9

Source: *Electronic Business*, September, 1998, p. 72.

★3705★
TOP RAM VENDORS WORLDWIDE, 1998
Ranked by: Revenue, in millions of dollars. **Remarks:** Also includes 1998 percent share and 1997 rank. **Number listed:** 9

1. Samsung, with $3,350 million
2. Hyundai, $1,480
3. Micron, $1,301
4. NEC, $1,155
5. Siemens, $1,010
6. Mitsubishi Corp., $1,005
7. Hitachi, $916
8. LG Semicon, $885
9. Toshiba, $725

Source: *Electronic News*, March 15, 1999, p. 16.

★3706★
TOP SELLER REQUESTS OF REAL ESTATE BROKERS, 1998
Ranked by: Percent of home sellers responses. **Number listed:** 7
1. Find a buyer, with 30%
2. Price competitively, 28%
3. Sell within time frame, 26%
4. Help with paperwork, inspections, settlements, 5%
4. Negotiate/deal with buyer, 5%
4. Advise on fixing up home to help it sell, 5%
7. Help find another home to buy, 1%

Source: *Real Estate Outlook*, September, 1998, p. 6.

★3707★
TOP SRAM VENDORS WORLDWIDE, 1997
Ranked by: Revenue, in millions of dollars. **Number listed:** 14
1. Samsung, with $565 million
2. Mitsubishi Corp., $460
3. Hitachi, $435
4. Toshiba, $340
5. IBM, $330
6. Motorola, $314
7. NEC, $288
8. Cypress, $274
9. Sony, $250
10. IDS, $244

Source: *Electronic Business*, September, 1998, p. 74.

Real Estate Brokers--Detroit Metropolitan Area

★3708★
LEADING RESIDENTIAL BROKERS BY GROSS SALES, 1997
Ranked by: Gross sales, in millions of dollars. **Remarks:** Includes top executive, sales for 1996, number of residential transactions, number of licensed brokers and registered sales reps., number of offices and average sales per office. **Number listed:** 20
1. Real Estate One Inc., with $1,452.8 million
2. Century 21 Town & Country, $1,078.2
3. Coldwell Banker Schweitzer Real Estate Inc., $911.9
4. Century 21 Associates, $758.7
5. Prudential Chamberlain-Stiehl Realtors, $617.4
6. Max Broock Inc., $356.0
7. Century 21 Today Inc., $330.2
8. Edward Surovell Co., $300.6
9. Charles Reinhart Co., $300.2
10. Century 21 Kee, $298.2

Source: *Crain's Detroit Business*, Crain's Book of Lists Detroit (annual), December 28, 1998, p. 106.

Real Estate Brokers--Florida

★3709★
TOP COMMERCIAL REAL ESTATE COMPANIES IN FLORIDA, 1997
Ranked by: Total commercial volume, in millions of dollars. **Remarks:** Includes 1997 volume sales leasing/mgmt, 1997 square feet sold and leased, number of offices, senior executives, titles and year founded. **Number listed:** 24
1. CB Richard Ellis Inc., with $1,450.0 million
2. Cushman & Wakefield of Florida Inc., $898.5
3. Highwoods Properties Inc., $806.0
4. Holliday Fenoglio Fowler L.P., $802.0
5. Sonnenblick-Goldman Co., $623.0
6. Trammell Crow Co., $503.9
7. Codina Bush Klein-ONCOR Intl., $420.0
8. Continental Real Estate Cos., $340.0
9. Keyes Co., $337.8
10. Merin Hunter Codman, $331.0

Source: *Florida Trend*, TopRank Florida (annual), 1999, p. 32+.

Real Estate Brokers--Long Island (NY)

★3710★
TOP COMMERCIAL REAL ESTATE BROKERS ON LONG ISLAND, 1997
Ranked by: Number of licensed agents. **Remarks:** Includes CEO, phone, fax, web address, e-mail and number of offices. **Number listed:** 22
1. Manheim Realty, with 54
2. Grubb & Ellis/Island Realty, 35
3. Breslin Realty Developers, 25
3. Island Associates Real Estate, 25
3. Oxford & Simpson Realty, 25
3. Sutton & Edwards, 25
7. Insignia/Edward S. Gordon Co of LI, 21
7. Prudential LI Commercial Realty, 21
7. Soundview Property Mgmt., 21
10. United Realty, 20

Source: *Long Island Business News*, LI Book of Lists (annual), 1999, p. 99.

★3711★
TOP RESIDENTIAL REAL ESTATE BROKERS ON LONG ISLAND, 1997
Ranked by: Number of licensed agents. **Remarks:** Includes CEO, phone, fax, web address, e-mail and number of offices. **Number listed:** 24
1. Prudential Long Island Realty, with 1,197 licensed agents
2. Century 21 Real Estate, 1,052
3. Coldwell Banker Sammis, 500
4. Daniel Gale Real Estate, 357
5. Coach Realtors, 301
6. Hough Guidance Realty, 280
7. ERA Hamlet Realty of Islip, 200
7. National Homefinders, 200
9. Allan M. Schneider Assoc., 125
10. Homes America, 50

Source: *Long Island Business News*, LI Book of Lists (annual), 1999, p. 101.

Real Estate Brokers--Los Angeles County (CA)

★3712★
LARGEST COMMERCIAL REAL ESTATE BROKERS IN NEW JERSEY, 1998
Ranked by: Total square feet sold or leased. **Remarks:** Includes number of employees, year established, president and CEO. **Number listed:** 25

1. Cushman & Wakefield of New Jersey Inc., with 20,400,000 square footage
2. George Mintz & Company Inc., 14,560,000
3. SBWE Inc., 9,975,863
4. Murray Construction Company Inc., 7,500,000
5. McBride Corporate Real Estate, 7,264,484
6. CB Commercial Real Estate Group Inc., 7,116,672
7. Insignia/Edward S. Gordon Co., 6,275,000
8. Charles Klatskin Company Inc., 6,200,000
9. Resource Realty Inc., 6,025,828
10. Eric Bram & Co., 5,738,000

Source: *New Jersey Business*, Book of Lists (annual), 1999, p. 10.

★3713★
TOP RESIDENTIAL REAL ESTATE BROKERS IN LOS ANGELES COUNTY, 1997
Ranked by: Residential sales volume, in millions of dollars. **Remarks:** Includes 1996 sales volume, units sold, residential services, areas of specialty, profile, marketing contact and top local executive. **Number listed:** 15

1. Coldwell Banker Jon Douglas Co., with $10,110.3 million
2. Fred Sands Realtors, $4,804
3. RE/MAX Beach Cities/Westside Properties, $1,350
4. John Aaroe & Associates, $1,196.5
5. Dilbeck Realtors - Better Homes & Gardens, $896
6. Shorewood Realtors Inc., $891
7. RE/MAX Palos Verdes Realty, $769.8
8. Podley Doan Inc., $569
9. Realty Executives Santa Clarita, $530
10. RE/MAX of Valencia, $447.1

Source: *Top Residential Real Estate Brokers*, October 19, 1998, p. 25+.

Real Estate Brokers--New York Metropolitan Area

★3714★
LARGEST REAL ESTATE BROKERS IN THE NEW YORK METROPOLITAN AREA, 1998
Ranked by: Property sales, in millions of dollars. **Remarks:** Includes 1997 sales, number of units sold, percent of transactions where firm represented, number of units and number of agents. **Number listed:** 15

1. Douglas Elliman, with $1,869.0 million
2. Corcoran Group, $1,320.0
3. Brown Harris Stevens, $850.0
4. Greenthal Residential Sales, $750.0
5. Halstead Property Co., $685.0
6. Bellmarc Realty, $633.0
7. William B. May, $451.6
8. Coldwell Banker Hunt Kennedy, $387.0
9. Gumley Haft Kleier Inc., $239.0
10. Leslie J. Garfield & Co., $98.0

Source: *Crain's New York Business*, March 1, 1999, p. 38.

Real Estate Brokers—Philadelphia Metropolitan Area

★3715★
LARGEST COMMERCIAL REAL ESTATE BROKERS IN THE PHILADELPHIA METROPOLITAN AREA, 1998
Ranked by: Number of brokers. **Remarks:** Includes number of local offices, total number of offices, head of local office, additional services and year founded locally. **Number listed:** 25

1. Jackson-Cross Co - Oncor International, with 58
2. Grubb & Ellis Co., 45
3. Trammell Crow Co., 41
4. Cushman & Wakefield of Pennsylvania Inc., 34
4. Colliers Lanard & Axilbund, 34
6. CB Commercial Real Estate Group Inc., 32
7. LaSalle Partners Management Services Inc., 28
   Metro Commercial Real Estate Inc., 24
   GMH Realty Inc., 22
   Binswanger Intl./CBB, 21

Source: *Philadelphia Business Journal*, Book of Business Lists (annual), 1999, p. 43.

★3716★
LARGEST RESIDENTIAL REAL ESTATE BROKERS IN THE PHILADELPHIA METROPOLITAN AREA, 1998
Ranked by: Number of brokers. **Remarks:** Includes 1997 sales, number closed, percent of listings sold, local property listed in 1997, additional services, head of local office, parent company and year founded. **Number listed:** 13

1. Prudential Preferred Properties Inc., with 1,950
2. Fox & Roach Realtors, 1,700
3. Weichert Realtors, 1,400
4. Century 21 Lesniak Coulston & McKinney, 91
5. Coldwell Banker, Realty One, 68
6. Kurtiss Real Estate, 54
7. RE/MAX Action Associates, 40
8. Plumer & Associates Inc., 29
9. Quinn & Wilson Inc., 22
10. Dan Helwig Inc., 20

Source: *Philadelphia Business Journal*, October 16, 1999, p. 20.

Real Estate Development--Detroit Metropolitan Area

★3717★
LEADING DETROIT AREA NON RESIDENTIAL DEVELOPERS, 1997-1998
Ranked by: Square feet of construction, including renovations. **Remarks:** Includes name and title of top local executive, dollar value of current projects, type of project and major projects. **Number listed:** 10

1. Taubman Centers Inc., with 3,090,000 square feet
2. Walsh Group, 2,200,000
3. Ashley Capital, 2,175,000
4. Farbman Group, 1,880,000
5. Jonna Realty Ventures Inc., 1,290,000
6. Redico Management Inc., 1,000,000
7. First Industrial Realty Trust Inc., 779,340
8. Etkin Equities, 766,000
9. Hines Interests L.P., 400,000

10. DeMattia Development, 382,800

Source: *Crain's Detroit Business*, Crain's Book of Lists Detroit (annual), December 28, 1998, p. 110.

★3718★

LEADING DETROIT AREA RESIDENTIAL DEVELOPERS, 1997-1998

Ranked by: Square feet of construction, including renovations. **Remarks:** Includes name and title of top local executive, dollar value of current projects, and major projects. **Number listed:** 7

1. Pulte Corp, with 32,838,800 square feet
2. Crosswinds Communities Inc., 1,750,000
3. Silverman Cos., 1,491,280
4. Village Green Cos., 1,386,100
5. Robertson Bros. Co., 538,000
6. Lockwood Group L.L.C., 506,440
7. Phoenix Land Development, 340,000

Source: *Crain's Detroit Business*, Crain's Book of Lists Detroit (annual), December 28, 1998, p. 110.

Real Estate Development--Florida

★3719★

TOP COMMERCIAL REAL ESTATE DEVELOPERS IN FLORIDA, 1997

Ranked by: Square feet developed. **Remarks:** Includes address, phone, number full time employees, cost of developments, senior executive, title and year founded. **Number listed:** 25

1. Codina Development Corp., with 3,590,000 square feet
2. Michael Swerdlow Cos., 3,280,000
3. Stiles Corp., 2,146,363
4. Tambone Real Estate Development Corp., 1,550,000
5. Catalfumo Construction & Development Inc., 1,400,000
6. Central Florida Investments Inc., 1,000,000
7. Trammell Crow Co., 997,959
8. Pro Logis Trust, 817,898
9. Vestcor Cos., 674,000
10. Pattillo Cos., 600,000

Source: *Florida Trend*, Top Rank Florida (annual), 1999, p. 36.

Real Estate Development--Los Angeles County (CA)

★3720★

TOP COMMERCIAL REAL ESTATE DEVELOPERS IN LOS ANGELES COUNTY, 1997

Ranked by: Square feet developed. **Remarks:** Includes address, number of projects developed & owned, current projects, current renovations, fee work in progress, profile, contacts and top local executive. **Number listed:** 25

1. Majestic Realty, with 33,282,175 square feet
2. Trammell Crow Co., 26,000,000
3. Kilroy Realty Corp., 25,100,000
4. Macguire Partners, 18,134,567
5. Overton Moore & Associates Inc., 13,000,000
6. Watson Land Co., 10,000,000
7. Center Trust, 6,513,982
8. Catellus Development Corp., 5,887,479
9. Insignia Commercial Group, 5,400,000
10. J.H. Snyder Co., 5,080,000

Source: *Los Angeles Business Journal*, Book of Lists (annual), 1999, p. 78.

★3721★

TOP RESIDENTIAL REAL ESTATE DEVELOPERS IN LOS ANGELES COUNTY, 1997

Ranked by: Units sold. **Remarks:** Includes address, units built, revenues, developments, price range, headquarters and top local executive. **Number listed:** 25

1. Lennar Homes, with 452 units sold
2. Kaufman & Broad Home Corp., 336
3. S & S Construction Shapell Industries Inc., 271
4. William Lyon Homes, 238
5. Western Pacific Housing, 232
6. Centex Homes, 202
7. Lewis Homes Group of Cos., 171
8. Catellus Residential Group, 148
9. Shea Homes, 138
10. Richmond American Homes, 126

Source: *Los Angeles Business Journal*, Book of Lists (annual), 1999, p. 88.

Real Estate Development--New Jersey

★3722★

TOP REAL ESTATE DEVELOPERS IN NEW JERSEY, 1997

Ranked by: Total square feet owned or controlled. **Remarks:** Includes total staff, year established, president and CEO. **Number listed:** 25

1. Hartz Mountain Industrics, with 32,000,000 squarc foot
2. Gale & Wentworth L.L.C., 17,100,000
3. Mack-Cali Realty, 14,000,000
4. Heller Industrial Parks Inc., 8,500,000
5. Matrix Development Group, 8,000,000
6. Frank A. Greek & Son, 7,500,000
6. Murray Construction, 7,500,000
8. Charles Klatskin Co. (Foresgate Industries), 7,000,000
8. Vornado Realty Trust, 7,000,000
10. Reckson Morris Industrial, 6,000,000

Source: *New Jersey Business Journal*, Book of Lists (annual), 1999, p. 20.

Real Estate Financing

★3723★

TOP FINANCIAL INTERMEDIARIES, INCLUDING MORTGAGE BROKERS AND FINANCIAL FIRMS WHICH ARRANGED OR FACILITATED TRANSACTIONS, 1999

Ranked by: Dollars arranged, in billions. **Remarks:** Includes officers. **Number listed:** 21

1. Holliday Fenoglio Fowler L.P., with $10.1 billion
2. L.J. Melody, $7.0
3. Northwestern Mutual Life Insurance Co., $3.0
4. Legg Mason Real Estate, $2.4
5. First Union Real Estate Capital Markets, $2.43

6. Greenwich Group Intl., $1.25
7. Cohen Financial, $1.04
8. Bankers Mutual, A Division of FMAC, $1.0
8. Johnson Capital Group, $1.0
8. American Realty & Financial Services of California Inc., $1.0

Source: *National Real Estate Investor*, Top Lender Survey (annual), April 1, 1999, p. 70.

★3724★
TOP INTERMEDIARIES, 1998
Ranked by: Amount arranged/retail. **Remarks:** Includes officers, offices, major projects financed and amount arranged/committed by region. **Number listed:** 13

1. Holliday Fenoglio Fowler L.P., with $2,480 million
2. L.J. Melody, $2,290
3. USA Funding Inc., $830
4. Northland/Marquette Capital Group Inc., $663
5. Ackman-Ziff Real Estate Group Ltd., $430
6. Sonnenblick-Goldman Co., $400
7. Johnson Capital Group Inc., $329
8. Capital Network Advisors Inc., $100
9. David Cronheim Mortgage Corp., $99.25
10. Aztec Group Inc., $72

Source: *Shopping Center World*, Top Retail Lenders (annual), April, 1999, p. 60.

★3725★
TOP LENDERS INCLUDING FIRMS WHICH HAVE COMMITTED DIRECT LOANS, CREDIT LINES, CMBS LENDING AND OTHER FORMS OF MORE DIRECT INVESTMENT, 1999
Ranked by: Dollars committed, in billions. **Remarks:** Includes officers. **Number listed:** 59

1. Lehman Brothers, with $29.0 billion
2. Fannie Mae, $15.0
3. Credit Suisse First Boston, $12.0
4. GMAC Commercial Mortgage Corp., $10.0
5. GE Capital Real Estate, $9.4
6. First Union Real Estate Capital Markets, $8.2
7. Bank of America, $7.6
8. Keybank National Assn., $7.2
9. Capital, $6.0
9. Fleet Bank, $6.0

Source: *National Real Estate Investor*, Top Lender Survey (annual), April 1, 1999, p. 47.

Real Estate Investment Trusts

★3726★
METROPOLITAN AREAS WITH LARGEST REAL ESTATE INVESTMENT TRUST OWNERSHIP, 1998
Ranked by: Value of properties, in millions. **Remarks:** Includes number of properties and percent of all properties. **Number listed:** 20

1. Chicago, with $16,943 million
2. Atlanta, $16,692
3. Washington, DC, $15,630
4. Los Angeles, $12,426
5. Dallas/Fort Worth, $12,183
6. Houston, $8,951
7. Midtown Manhattan, $8,832
8. Boston, $8,604
9. Orange County, CA, $7,382
10. Philadelphia, $7,255

Source: *CB Richard Ellis Global Research & Consulting: North American Index*, Fourth Quarter, 1998, p. 14.

★3727★
TOP REAL ESTATE INVESTMENT TRUSTS, 1999
Ranked by: Implied market cap, in millions. **Remarks:** Includes symbol, property focus, April 1999 price, 1 year total return and equity market cap. **Number listed:** 50

1. Equity Ofc. Property Trust, with $7,249.75 million
2. Simon Property Group, $6,186.71
3. Equity Residential Property Trust, $5,379.85
4. Public Storage Inc., $3,050.49
5. Vornado Realty Trust, $3,030.82
6. Crescent Real Estate Equity Co., $3,028.22
7. Archstone Com. Trust, $2,799.99
8. Boston Properties Inc., $2,729.32
9. Apart Investment & Management Co., $2,530.41
10. Spieker Properties Inc., $2,484.48

Source: *National Real Estate Investor*, 5, 1999, p. 26.

Real Estate Management--Chicago (IL)

★3728★
LARGEST PROPERTY MANAGEMENT FIRMS IN CHICAGO, 1997
Ranked by: Commercial square feet managed, in millions. **Remarks:** Includes percent change from 1996, square footage 11-county, number of Chicago office employees and top clients. **Number listed:** 25

1. U.S. Equities Realty Inc., with 50.5 square feet
2. Lasalle Partners Inc., 35.2
3. Hamilton Partners Inc., 21.1
4. Centerpoint Properties Trust, 18.6
5. Cushman & Wakefield Inc., 18.0
6. Urban Retail Properties Co., 17.1
7. John Buck Co., 16.8
8. CB Richard Ellis Inc., 16.6
9. Hiffman Shaffer Associates Inc., 13.0
10. Insignia/ESG Inc., 12.6

Source: *Crain's Chicago Business*, Top Business Lists (annual), December 7, 1998, p. 115.

Real Estate Management--New York Metropolitan Area

★3729★
LARGEST COMMERCIAL PROPERTY MANAGERS IN THE NEW YORK METROPOLITAN AREA, 1998
Ranked by: Square footage managed, in millions. **Remarks:** Includes address, head of office, square foot managed in 1997, percent change, third party square foot managed, number of office employees, national headquarters and key clients. **Number listed:** 25

1. Cushman & Wakefield Inc., with 44.8 square feet
2. Newmark & Co. Real Estate Inc., 30.0
3. Insignia/ESG Inc., 27.4
4. Jones Lang LaSalle Inc., 23.1
5. Grubb & Ellis Management Services Inc., 20.0
6. Tishman Speyer Properties, 19.1
7. GVA Williams, 14.8
8. Colliers ABR Inc., 14.7

8. Mendik Co, a Division of Vornado Realty Trust, 14.7
10. Helmsley-Spear Inc., 13.3

Source: *Crain's New York Business*, June 7, 1999, p. 30+.

Real Estate Management—Philadelphia Metropolitan Area

★3730★
LARGEST COMMERCIAL PROPERTY MANAGERS IN THE PHILADELPHIA METROPOLITAN AREA, 1998
Ranked by: Square feet managed, in millions. **Remarks:** Includes address & phone, number of properties managed, type of space managed, type of management, major local properties managed, property management employees, head of property management and head of local office. **Number listed:** 25

1. Cushman & Wakefield of Pennsylvania Inc., with 14,800,000 square feet
2. Liberty Property Trust, 14,000,000
3. Compass Management & Leasing Inc., 11,000,000
4. Insignia/ESG Jackson-Cross, 10,000,000
5. Colliers Lanard & Axilbund, 8,600,000
6. Kravco Co., 8,304,568
7. Pennsylvania Real Estate Investment Trust, 7,980,261
8. Brandywine Realty Trust, 7,969,137
9. Grubb & Ellis Management Services Inc., 7,160,000
10. Trammell Crow NE Inc., 6,000,000

Source: *Philadelphia Business Journal*, July 10, 1998, p. 17.

Real Estate Managers--Detroit Metropolitan Area

★3731★
TOP NON-RESIDENTIAL PROPERTY MANAGERS IN THE DETROIT METROPOLITAN AREA, 1998
Ranked by: Square feet under management, in millions. **Remarks:** Includes address & phone, top executive, total square feet of nonresidential property 1997, total square feet of nonresidential property inside and outside Metro Detroit, total number of nonresidential properties under management and major properties. **Number listed:** 25

1. Taubman Centers Inc., with 31,418,000 square feet
2. LaSalle Partners Inc., 15,000,000
3. Farbman Management Group, 13,288,506
4. First Industrial Realty Trust Inc., 10,435,329
5. Real Estate Development and Investment Co., 9,300,000
6. Etkin Equities L.L.C., 9,043,068
7. Hines Interests L.P., 7,500,000
8. Schostak Bros. & Co. Inc., 7,000,000
9. Malan Realty Investors Inc., 6,638,593
10. Grubb & Ellis Management Services, 5,221,000

Source: *Crain's Detroit Business*, Crain's Book of Lists Detroit (annual), December 28, 1998, p. 108.

Real Estate Managers--Los Angeles County (CA)

★3732★
LARGEST PROPERTY MANAGEMENT COMPANIES IN LOS ANGELES COUNTY, 1999
Ranked by: Square feet managed, in millions. **Remarks:** Includes address, other types, contracts won in 1997, percent owned, services, number of employees, profile and top local executive. **Number listed:** 25

1. Tooley & Co., with 15.3 square feet
2. CB Commercial/Koll Management Svcs., 12.4
3. Charles Dunn Co., 10.3
4. Cushman & Wakefield of Calif. Inc., 8.8
5. Insignia Commercial Group Inc., 7.0
6. LaSalle Partners, 6.2
7. Prentiss Properties Ltd. Inc., 6.0
8. The Carlson Co., 5.9
9. Transwestern Property Co., 5.6
9. The Voit Cos., 5.6

Source: *Los Angeles Business Journal*, Book of Lists (annual), 1999, p. 84.

Real Property--Valuation--Los Angeles County (CA)

★3733★
HIGHEST ASSESSED PROPERTIES IN LOS ANGELES COUNTY, 1998
Ranked by: Total assessed value, in millions. **Remarks:** Includes address, primary use, profile and owner. **Number listed:** 25

1. J. Paul Getty Center, with $1,715.6 million
2. Chevron Refinery, $1,208.3
3. Mobil Refinery, $1,080.7
4. Arco Refinery, $997
5. Anheuser Busch Brewery, $763.5
6. Universal Studios, $541.2
7. Ultramar Refinery, $535.7
8. University of Southern California, $508.6
9. Universal Studios Hollywood/City Walk, $462.5
10. Cedars Sinai Medical Center, $458.8

Source: *Los Angeles Business Journal*, Book of Lists (annual), December 28, 1998, p. 26.

Refrigerated Trucks

★3734★
TOP REFRIGERATED TRUCK COMPANIES, 1997
Ranked by: Revenue, in thousands of dollars. **Remarks:** Includes net income, operating ratio, net profit margin, tons, and figures for previous year. **Number listed:** 10

1. Prime Inc., with $345,423 thousand
2. C.R. England Inc., $315,010
3. Rocor International, $302,842
4. KLLM Inc., $244,085
5. FFE Transportation Services, $241,173
6. Marten Transport, $172,412
7. Dick Simon Trucking, $168,137
8. Stevens Transport, $143,442

9. Midwest Coast Transport, $121,896
10. Transcontinental Refrigerated Lines, $114,833

Source: *Transport Topics*, Book of Lists (annual), August 10, 1998, p. 21.

Refrigerators

★3735★

BEST SELLING REFRIGERATORS, 1998

Ranked by: Market share, in percent. **Remarks:** Also notes 1993 market share. **Number listed:** 6

1. GEA, with 36%
2. Whirlpool, 28%
3. Electrolux, 16%
4. Maytag, 13%
5. Goodman, 7%
6. Others, 0%

Source: *Appliance Manufacturer*, April, 1999, p. 19.

Refuse Compactors

★3736★

BEST SELLING COMPACTORS, 1998

Ranked by: Market share, in percent. **Remarks:** Also notes 1993 market share. **Number listed:** 3

1. Whirlpool, with 89%
2. Broan, 11%
3. Others, 0%

Source: *Appliance Manufacturer*, April, 1999, p. 19.

Regional Banks

★3737★

MOST ADMIRED SUPERREGIONAL BANKS, 1998

Ranked by: Scores (1-10) derived from a survey of senior executives, outside directors and securities analysts. **Remarks:** Respondents rated companies in their own industry on 8 attributes of reputation. Also notes previous year's rank. **Number listed:** 10

1. Norwest, with 7.43 points
2. NationsBank, 6.95
3. First Union, 6.90
4. U.S. Bancorp, 6.87
5. Banc One, 6.41
6. Fleet Financial Group, 6.32
7. BankAmerica, 6.28
8. BankBoston, 6.26
9. PNC Bank, 6.14
10. Wells Fargo, 6.12

Source: *Fortune*, America's Most Admired Corporations (annual), March 1, 1999, p. F1.

★3738★

MOST PROFITABLE LARGE REGIONAL BANKS BY NONPERFORMING ASSET RATIO, 1998

Ranked by: Nonperforming asset ratio, in percent. **Remarks:** Includes 1997 figures. **Number listed:** 14

1. North Fork Bancorp, with 0.32%
2. First Security Corp., 0.35%
3. Zions Bancorp, 0.39%
4. Synovus Financial Corp., 0.41%
5. First American Corp., 0.47%
6. First Tennessee National Corp., 0.51%
7. Hibernia Corp., 0.52%
8. Compass Bancshares Inc., 0.55%
9. AmSouth Bancorp, 0.60%
10. Commerce Bancshares, 0.64%

Source: *American Banker*, Performance of Top Banking Companies (annual), March 11, 1999, p. 9.

★3739★

MOST PROFITABLE LARGE REGIONAL BANKS BY RETURN ON ASSETS, 1998

Ranked by: Return on assets, in percent. **Remarks:** Includes 1997 figures. **Number listed:** 14

1. Synovus Financial Corp., with 2.14%
2. North Fork Bancorp, 1.66%
3. TCF Financial Corp., 1.62%
4. Associated Banc-Corp., 1.48%
5. Marshall & Ilsley Corp., 1.45%
6. Commerce Bancshares, 1.43%
7. Citizens Financial Group, 1.41%
8. Hibernia Corp., 1.39%
9. First Tennessee National Corp., 1.35%
9. AmSouth Bancorp, 1.35%

Source: *American Banker*, Performance of Top Banking Companies (annual), March 11, 1999, p. 9.

★3740★

MOST PROFITABLE LARGE REGIONAL BANKS BY RETURN ON EQUITY, 1998

Ranked by: Return on equity, in percent. **Remarks:** Includes 1997 figures. **Number listed:** 14

1. First Tennessee National Corp., with 22.70%
2. North Fork Bancorp, 20.50%
3. Synovus Financial Corp., 20.43%
4. AmSouth Bancorp, 18.56%
5. Associated Banc-Corp., 18.33%
6. TCF Financial Corp., 17.34%
7. Old Kent Financial Corp., 17.08%
8. Zions Bancorp, 16.38%
9. First Security Corp., 16.21%
10. Compass Bancshares Inc., 15.93%

Source: *American Banker*, Performance of Top Banking Companies (annual), March 11, 1999, p. 9.

★3741★

MOST PROFITABLE MEGABANKS BY NONPERFORMING ASSET RATIO, 1998

Ranked by: Nonperforming asset ratio, in percent. **Remarks:** Includes 1997 figures. **Number listed:** 14

1. SunTrust Banks Inc., with 0.37%
2. Fleet Financial Group, 0.41%
3. National City Corp., 0.43%
4. J.P. Morgan & Co., 0.48%
5. U.S. Bancorp, 0.51%
6. Bank One Corp., 0.53%
7. PNC Bank Corp., 0.58%
8. First Union Corp., 0.62%
9. KeyCorp., 0.65%
10. BankAmerica Corp., 0.77%

Source: *American Banker*, Performance of Top Banking Companies (annual), March 11, 1999, p. 9.

★3742★
MOST PROFITABLE MEGABANKS BY RETURN ON ASSETS, 1998
Ranked by: Return on assets, in percent. **Remarks:** Includes 1997 figures. **Number listed:** 14
1. U.S. Bancorp, with 1.85%
2. First Union Corp., 1.66%
3. Fleet Financial Group, 1.56%
4. PNC Bank Corp., 1.49%
5. National City Corp., 1.34%
6. Key Corp., 1.32%
7. Bank One Corp., 1.30%
8. SunTrust Banks Inc., 1.18%
9. Wells Fargo & Co., 1.04%
10. Chase Manhattan Corp., 1.01%

Source: *American Banker*, Performance of Top Banking Companies (annual), March 11, 1999, p. 9.

★3743★
MOST PROFITABLE MEGABANKS BY RETURN ON EQUITY, 1998
Ranked by: Return on equity, in percent. **Remarks:** Includes 1997 figures. **Number listed:** 14
1. First Union Corp., with 22.81%
2. U.S. Bancorp, 21.90%
3. PNC Bank Corp., 20.81%
4. Fleet Financial Group, 18.07%
5. KeyCorp, 17.97%
6. Chase Manhattan Corp., 17.30%
7. SunTrust Banks Inc., 17.21%
8. Bank One Corp., 15.90%
9. National City Corp., 15.40%
10. Citigroup, 14.00%

Source: *American Banker*, Performance of Top Banking Companies (annual), March 11, 1999, p. 9.

★3744★
MOST PROFITABLE SUPERREGIONAL BANKS BY NONPERFORMING ASSET RATIO, 1998
Ranked by: Nonperforming Asset Ratio, in percent. **Remarks:** Includes 1997 figures. **Number listed:** 14
1. Harris Bancorp, with 0.20%
2. State Street Corp., 0.25%
3. Northern Trust Corp., 0.26%
4. Fifth Third Bancorp, 0.29%
5. Union Bank of California, 0.37%
6. Comerica Inc., 0.39%
7. Wachovia Corp., 0.40%
8. LaSalle National Corp., 0.41%
9. Summit Bancorp, 0.42%
10. Mellon Bank Corp., 0.44%

Source: *American Banker*, Performance of Top Banking Companies (annual), March 11, 1999, p. 9.

★3745★
MOST PROFITABLE SUPERREGIONAL BANKS BY RETURN ON ASSETS, 1998
Ranked by: Return on assets, in percent. **Remarks:** Includes 1997 figures. **Number listed:** 14
1. MBNA Corp., with 3.38%
2. Bank of New York, 1.89%
3. Mellon Bank Corp., 1.81%
4. Comerica Inc., 1.74%
5. Fifth Third Bancorp, 1.67%
6. HSBC Americas Inc., 1.60%
7. Union Planters Corp., 1.58%
8. BB&T Corp., 1.55%
9. Union Bank of California, 1.53%
10. Summit Bancorp, 1.51%

Source: *American Banker*, Performance of Top Banking Companies (annual), March 11, 1999, p. 9.

★3746★
MOST PROFITABLE SUPERREGIONAL BANKS BY RETURN ON EQUITY, 1998
Ranked by: Return on equity, in percent. **Remarks:** Includes 1997 figures. **Number listed:** 14
1. MBNA Corp., with 36.91%
2. HSBC Americas Inc., 24.93%
3. Bank of New York, 24.25%
4. Comerica Inc., 22.54%
5. Mellon Bank Corp., 20.70%
6. Northern Trust Corp., 20.47%
7. State Street Corp., 20.20%
8. BB&T Corp., 19.73%
9. LaSalle National Corp., 18.42%
10. Summit Bancorp, 17.50%

Source: *American Banker*, Performance of Top Banking Companies (annual), March 11, 1999, p. 9.

Rehabilitation Centers

★3747★
LARGEST HEALTHCARE SYSTEMS OPERATING REHABILITATION CENTERS, 1998
Ranked by: Number of beds. **Remarks:** Includes number of beds previous year, number of hospitals and number of states. **Number listed:** 44
1. HealthSouth Corp., with 7,938 number of beds
2. Sun Healthcare Group, 650
3. Catholic Health Care Network, 305
4. Tenet Healthcare Corp., 270
5. HealthEast Care System, 264
6. Brown Schools, 249
7. Allied Services, 219
8. Baylor Health Care System, 199
9. ProMedica Health System, 186
10. Detroit Medical Center, 155

Source: *Modern Healthcare*, Modern Healthcare Multi-Unit Providers Survey (annual), May 24, 1999, p. 50.

Reinsurance

★3748★
LARGEST U.S. REINSURERS, 1998
Ranked by: Net reinsurance premium written in 1998. **Remarks:** Includes previous years figures, policyholders surplus, net income, losses & loss adjustment expenses, loss ratio, underwriting expenses, expense ratio and combined ratio. **Number listed:** 20
1. General Reinsurance, with $2,707,368 thousand
2. Employers Reinsurance, $2,665,739
3. American Reinsurance, $2,276,153
4. Transatlantic/Putnam, $1,257,332
5. St. Paul Reinsurance, $1,056,229
6. Everest Reinsurance, $1,017,766
7. Berkshire Hathaway, $986,000
8. Zurich Reins. (N.A.), $852,503
9. Swiss Re America, $728,044
10. Hartford Re Co., $710,577

Source: *Business Insurance*, April 26, 1999, p. 49.

★3749★
LEADING REINSURERS WORLWIDE BY NET PREMIUMS WRITTEN, 1997
Ranked by: Net reinsurance premiums written, in U.S. dollars. **Number listed:** 20

1. Munich Reinsurance Group, with $12,474,589 thousand
2. Swiss Reinsurance Group, $11,114,948
3. Employers Reinsurance Group, $7,866,000
4. Berkshire Hathaway/General Reinsurance, $7,500,400
5. Generali, $6,424,723
6. Hannover Reinsurance Group, $3,733,810
7. Zurich Group-Reinsurance, $2,727,306
8. Gerling Global Re, $2,648,802
9. SCOR Reinsurance Co., $2,348,172
10. Lincoln Reinsurance, $1,335,300

Source: *Business Insurance*, August 31, 1998, p. 3.

Reinsurance, International

★3750★
LEADING PROVIDERS OF NON-LIFE REINSURANCE IN THE U.S., 1997
Ranked by: Assumed premiums, in millions. **Remarks:** Includes 1996 figures, percent of growth, market share, principal operating unit and S&P rating. **Number listed:** 100

1. General Reinsurance Group, with $3,028.1 million
2. Munich Group, $2,879.9
3. American International Group, $2,548.0
4. General Electric Group, $2,449.2
5. St. Paul Cos., $1,086.1
6. Everest Reinsurance Holdings Group, $997.9
7. Zurich Insurance Group, $990.9
8. CNA Insurance Group, $902.8
9. Hartford Insurance Group, $896.7
10. Swiss Reinsurance Group, $892.5

Source: *National Underwriter Property & Casualty/Risk & Benefits Management*, March 29, 1999, p. 10.

★3751★
LEADING REINSURANCE BROKERS WORLDWIDE, 1997
Ranked by: Gross revenues, in U.S. dollars. **Remarks:** Includes percent change from 1996, number employees and percent treaty. **Number listed:** 10

1. Aon Reinsurance Worldwide Inc., with $590.0 million
2. Guy Carpenter & Co. Inc., $502.0
3. Willis Faber Reinsurance, $241.0
4. Benfield Greig Group PLC, $148.9
5. E.W. Blanch Co., $124.7
6. Jardine Lloyd Thompson Reinsurance Holdings Ltd., $69.3
7. Towers Perrin Reinsurance, $44.8
8. Lambert Fenchurch Group PLC, $44.2
9. Am-Re Brokers Inc., $23.3
10. John P. Woods Co. Inc., $22.3

Source: *Business Insurance*, November 9, 1998, p. 3.

★3752★
LEADING REINSURANCE GROUPS BY REINSURANCE PREMIUMS WRITTEN, 1997
Ranked by: Reinsurance premiums written, in U.S. dollars. **Number listed:** 25

1. Munich Reinsurance Group, with $12,272,044 thousand
2. Swiss Reinsurance Group, $11,042,354
3. General Reinsurance Corp., $6,545,021
4. Employer's Reinsurance Corp., $4,545,000
5. Zurich Reinsurance Group, $3,954,400
6. Hannover Reinsurance Group 2, $3,705,083
7. Assicurazioni Generali SpA, $3,629,968
8. Lloyd's 6, $3,585,000
9. Allianz Group, $3,323,291
10. SCOR Reinsurance Co., $2,281,000

Source: *National Underwriter*, August 31, 1998, p. S-5.

★3753★
MARKET SHARE OF GLOBAL REINSURANCE INDUSTRY, 1996
Ranked by: Country. **Number listed:** 9

1. Germany, with 31%
2. United States, 26%
3. Switzerland, 14%
4. Other, 7%
5. France, 6%
6. United Kingdom, 5%
6. Italy, 5%
8. Bermuda, 4%
9. Australia, 2%

Source: *National Underwriter*, July 20, 1998, p. S-7.

Religious Organizations

★3754★
LEADING AMERICAN RELIGIONS, 1999
Ranked by: Number of congregations. **Number listed:** 24

1. Southern Baptist Convention, with 40,565 congregations
2. United Methodist Church, 36,361
3. National Baptist Convention USA Inc., 33,000
4. Roman Catholic Church, 22,728
5. Church of God in Christ, 15,300
6. Churches of Christ, 14,000
7. Assemblies of God, 11,884
8. Presbyterian Church USA, 11,328
9. Church of Jesus Christ of Latter-day Saints, 11,000
10. Evangelical Lutheran Church in America, 10,396

Source: *Brookings Review*, Spring, 1999, p. 12.

Relocation of Employees

See: **Employees--Transfer**

Research

★3755★
LEADING RESEARCH ORGANIZATIONS BY NON-U.S. RESEARCH REVENUE, 1998
Ranked by: U.S. Research Revenue. **Remarks:** Includes 1997 rank, headquarters, 1997 research revenue, percent change and worldwide research revenue. **Number listed:** 25

1. A. C. Nielsen Corp., with $1035.0 million

2. IMS Health, $671.7
3. Research International, $290.3
4. NFO Worldwide, $270.0
5. Gartner Group, $183.0
6. Millward Brown Intl., $154.6
7. Video Research, $149.0
8. United Information Group, $123.0
9. Information Resources, $114.3
10. VNU Marketing Information Services, $85.0

Source: *Advertising Age*, May 24, 1999, p. S4.

★3756★
LEADING RESEARCH ORGANIZATIONS BY U.S. RESEARCH REVENUE, 1998
Ranked by: U.S. Research Revenue. **Remarks:** Includes 1997 rank, headquarters, 1997 research revenue, percent change and worldwide research revenue. **Number listed:** 100

1. IMS Health, with $412.3 million
2. Nielsen Media Research, $401.9
3. Information Resources Inc., $397.0
4. A. C. Nielsen Corp., $390.4
5. VNU Marketing Information Services, $343.0
6. Gartner Group, $311.7
7. Westat, $206.0
8. Arbitron Co., $194.5
9. NFO Worldwide, $180.0
10. Maritz Marketing Research Inc. (MMR), $126.8

Source: *Advertising Age*, May 24, 1999, p. S2.

Research, Industrial

★3757★
CORPORATIONS SPENDING THE MOST ON RESEARCH AND DEVELOPMENT, 1997
Ranked by: Research and development expenditures, in millions of dollars. **Remarks:** Includes headquarters, SIC, percent of sales and change from 1996. **Number listed:** 60

1. General Motors Corp., with $8,413.6 million
2. Ford Motor Co., $6,538.0
3. IBM Corp., $4,327.2
4. Lucent Technologies, $4,119.0
5. Hewlett-Packard Co., $3,134.9
6. Motorola Inc., $2,743.2
7. El du Pont de Nemours, $2,526.5
8. Intel Corp., $2,329.6
9. Johnson & Johnson, $2,167.8
10. Microsoft, $2,141.0

Source: *Research and Development*, Giants of R&D (annual), October, 1998, p. S-4.

★3758★
LEADING RESEARCH COMPANIES BY RESEARCH REVENUE, 1997
Ranked by: Research revenue, in millions of dollars. **Remarks:** Includes percent of revenue and total revenue. **Number listed:** 50

1. IBM, with $4,877.0 million
2. Hewlett-Packard, $3,078.0
3. Lucent Technologies, $3,032.0
4. Motorola, $2,748.0
5. Intel, $2,347.0
6. Microsoft, $1,925.0
7. Texas Instruments, $1,536.0
8. Xerox, $1,079.0
9. Digital Equipment, $1,014.0
10. Sun Microsystems, $848.9

Source: *Research Industrial*, Top 100 R&D (annual), November, 1998, p. 70.

★3759★
LEADING RESEARCH ORGANIZATIONS BY NON-U.S. RESEARCH REVENUE, 1996
Ranked by: Total research and development spending, in millions of dollars. **Remarks:** Includes breakout of spending in life sciences, engineering, physical sciences, chemistry, math and computer sciences, environmental sciences and other sciences. **Number listed:** 30

1. Johns Hopkins University, with $798.7 million
2. University of Michigan, $468.9
3. University of Wisconsin, $412.5
4. University of Washington, $406.5
5. Massachusetts Institute of Technology, $380.7
6. University of California, San Diego, $371.6
7. Texas A & M University, $367.0
8. University of California, Los Angeles, $354.6
9. University of Minnesota, $341.2
10. Cornell University, $339.6

Source: *Chemical & Engineering News*, Facts & Figures for Chemical R&D (annual), October 19, 1998, p. 74.

Research, Industrial--Foreign

★3760★
TOP FOREIGN CORPORATIONS SPENDING THE MOST ON RESEARCH AND DEVELOPMENT, 1997
Ranked by: Research revenue, in millions of dollars. **Remarks:** Includes headquarters, SIC, percent of sales and change from previous year. **Number listed:** 50

1. Toyota Motor, with $6,468.3 million
2. Siemens AG, $4,618.6
3. Nissan Motor, $3,597.5
4. Hitachi Ltd., $3,427.4
5. Daimler-Benz AG, $3,403.4
6. Matsushita Electric, $2,830.3
7. Fujitsu Ltd., $2,761.4
8. ABB-Asea Brown Boveri, $2,657.8
9. NEC Corp., $2,630.0
10. L.M. Ericsson, $2,482.0

Source: *Research and Development*, Giants of R&D (annual), November, 1998, p. S-18.

★3761★
TOP RESEARCH USES OF THE INTERNET, 1997
Ranked by: Percentage of research users. **Number listed:** 18

1. Find technical information, with 90%
2. Find new product information, 83%
3. Communicate via email, 73%
4. Find science/technical news, 61%
5. Find business information, 54%
6. Find technical information from science journals, 52%
7. Research other organizations, 51%
8. Download software, 49%
8. Source/purchase equipment, 49%
10. Find conference information, 40%

Source: *Research and Development*, November, 1998, p. 21.

Restaurants

★3762★
FASTEST GROWING RESTAURANT CHAINS BY GROWTH IN SALES, 1997
Ranked by: Sales growth, in percent. **Remarks:** Includes sales dollars. **Number listed:** 400
1. Joe's Crab Shack, with $234.3% million
2. Einstein Bros. Bagels, $136.3%
3. Rainforest Cafe, $125.4%
4. Rio Bravo Cantina, $92.3%
5. On The Border Cafes, $77.6%
6. Logan's Roadhouse, $76.2%
7. Maggiano's Little Italy, $72.7%
8. Mr. Hero, $72.3%
9. Tumbleweed Mexican Restaurant, $65.4%
10. Mrs. Fields, $62.2%

Source: *Restaurants & Institutions*, July 15, 1998, p. 64.

★3763★
FASTEST GROWING RESTAURANT CHAINS BY HIGHEST AVERAGE UNIT VOLUMES, 1997
Ranked by: Average unit volume, in thousands. **Remarks:** Includes 1997 units. **Number listed:** 400
1. House of Blues, with $14,600.0 thousand
2. Rainforest Cafe, $13,000.0
3. Dave & Buster's, $12,900.0
4. Caesars World, $11,000.0
5. Planet Hollywood, $10,000.0
6. Cheesecake Factory, $9,851.0
7. Maggiano's Little Italy, $9,000.0
8. New York Restaurant Group, $7,300.0
9. Buckhead Life Restaurant Group, $6,000.0
9. Claim Jumper Restaurants, $6,000.0

Source: *Restaurants & Institutions*, July 15, 1998, p. 66.

★3764★
FASTEST GROWING RESTAURANT CHAINS BY SALES, 1997
Ranked by: Sales, in millions of dollars. **Remarks:** Includes units and percent change over previous year. **Number listed:** 400
1. McDonald's, with $33,638.0 million
2. Burger King, $9,800.0
3. KFC, $8,200.0
4. Pizza Hut, $7,300.0
5. Wendy's, $5,226.0
6. Taco Bell, $4,900.0
7. Hardee's, $3,526.0
8. Subway Sandwiches & Salads, $3,300.0
9. Domino's Pizza, $3,200.0
10. Dairy Queen, $2,540.0

Source: *Restaurants & Institutions*, July 15, 1998, p. 73.

★3765★
METROPOLITAN AREAS BY PER CAPITA EBI (EFFECTIVE BUYING INCOME), 1997
Ranked by: Per capita EBI (Effective Buying Income). **Number listed:** 321
1. Bridgepot-Stamford-Norwalk-Danbury, CT, with $32,686 million
2. Naples, FL, $25,391
3. West Palm Beach-Boca Raton, FL, $24,037
4. Seattle, Bellevue-Everett, WA, $23,714
5. San Francisco, CA, $23,527
6. Middlesex-Somerset-Hunterdon, NJ, $23,275
7. Washington, DC, $22,621
8. San Jose, CA, $22,304
9. Trenton, NJ, $21,919
10. Newark, NJ, $21,253

Source: *Restaurant Business*, Restaurant Growth Index (annual), October 1, 1998, p. 74.

★3766★
METROPOLITAN AREAS WITH THE HIGHEST EATING PLACE SALES, 1997
Ranked by: Sales, in thousands of dollars. **Number listed:** 321
1. Chicago, IL, with $7,734,859 thousand
2. New York, NY, $6,588,152
3. Los Angeles-Long Beach, CA, $6,489,436
4. Washington, DC, $5,185,130
5. Atlanta, GA, $4,698,332
6. Detroit, MI, $4,257,365
7. Boston-Lawrence-Lowell-Brockton, MA, $3,746,223
8. Houston, TX, $3,742,284
9. Philadelphia, PA, $3,662,964
10. Phoenix-Mesa, AZ, $3,629,759

Source: *Restaurant Business*, Restaurant Growth Index (annual), October 1, 1998, p. 62.

★3767★
METROPOLITAN AREAS WITH THE HIGHEST PER CAPITA EATING PLACE SALES, 1997
Ranked by: Per capita sales. **Number listed:** 321
1. Myrtle Beach, SC, with $2,822 million
2. Flagstaff, AZ, $2,244
3. Santa Fe, NM, $2,053
4. Boulder-Longmont, CO, $1,651
5. Panama City, FL, $1,605
6. Wilmington, NC, $1,595
7. Naples, FL, $1,593
8. Albuquerque, NM, $1,520
9. Orlando, FL, $1,506
10. Barnstable-Yarmouth, MA, $1,505

Source: *Restaurant Business*, Restaurant Growth Index (annual), October 1, 1998, p. 69.

★3768★
METROPOLITAN AREAS WITH THE HIGHEST PER CAPITA RESTAURANT SALES, 1997
Ranked by: Per capita sales. **Number listed:** 321
1. Myrtle Beach, SC, with $1,665 million
2. Flagstaff, AZ, $1,271
3. Santa Fe, NM, $1,263
4. Naples, FL, $1,133
5. Barnstable-Yarmouth, MA, $1,124
6. Panama City, FL, $935
7. Boulder-Longmont, CA, $921
8. Missoula, MT, $845
9. San Francisco, CA, $841
10. Orlando, FL, $833

Source: *Restaurant Business*, Restaurant Growth Index (annual), October 1, 1998, p. 69.

★3769★
METROPOLITAN AREAS WITH THE HIGHEST RESTAURANT GROWTH INDEX (RGI), 1997
Ranked by: Restaurant activity index. Number of points indicates an area's tendency to patronize restaurants. **Number listed:** 321
1. Bloomington-Normal, IL, with 140
2. Jackson, TN, 131
3. Dallas, TX, 127
4. Myrtle Beach, SC, 126
4. Kankakee, IL, 126
4. Indianapolis, IN, 126
4. Lafayette, IN, 126
8. Nashville, TN, 125
9. Champaign-Urbana, IL, 123

9. New York City, NY, 123

Source: *Restaurant Business*, Restaurant Growth Index (annual), October 1, 1998, p. 66.

★3770★
METROPOLITAN AREAS WITH THE HIGHEST RESTAURANT SALES, 1997
Ranked by: Sales, in thousands of dollars. **Number listed:** 321

1. Chicago, IL, with $3,619,342 thousand
2. New York, NY, $3,552,460
3. Los Angeles-Long Beach, CA, $3,224,068
4. Washington, DC, $2,466,137
5. Atlanta, GA, $2,103,344
6. Boston-Lawrence-Lowell-Brockton, MA, $1,921,680
7. Detroit, MI, $1,888,254
8. Philadelphia, PA, $1,836,820
9. Phoenix-Mesa, AZ, $1,691,063
10. Houston, TX, $1,635,865

Source: *Restaurant Business*, Restaurant Growth Index (annual), October 1, 1998, p. 62.

★3771★
TOP EATING AND DRINKING PLACES, 1998
Ranked by: Sales, in thousands of dollars. **Number listed:** 321

1. Chicago, IL, with $7,953,221 thousand
2. New York, NY, $6,686,983
3. Los Angeles-Long Beach, CA, $6,644,200
4. Washington, $5,076,975
5. Atlanta, $4,557,550
6. Detroit, $4,360,391
7. Boston-Lawrence-Lowell-Brockton, MA, $3,841,131
8. Philadelphia, $3,838,910
9. Houston, $3,788,218
10. Phoenix-Mesa, AZ, $3,602,754

Source: *Sales & Marketing Management*, Sales & Marketing Management Survey of Buying Power (annual), August, 1998, p. 24.

★3772★
TOP INDEPENDENT RESTAURANTS, 1998
Ranked by: Sales, in millions of dollars. **Remarks:** Includes number of seats, dinner check and number of people served per year. **Number listed:** 20

1. Tavern on the Green, with $34.200 million
2. Windows on the world, $31.870
3. Smith & Wollensky, $24.446
4. Bob Chinn's Crab House, $21.78
5. Sparks Steakhouse, $20.400
6. Joe's Stone Crab, $19.035
7. '21' Club, $17.289
8. Fulton's Crab House, $16.000
9. Four Seasons, $15.083
10. Lobster House, $14.954

Source: *Restaurants & Institutions*, April 1, 1998, p. 50.

Restaurants—Chain and Franchise Operations

See also: **Fast Food Restaurants--Chain and Franchise Operations**

★3773★
FASTEST GROWING RESTAURANT CHAINS BY INCREASE IN SALES, 1997
Ranked by: Percentage increase in sales. **Remarks:** Includes 1996 and 1997 sales and average unit volume. **Number listed:** 50

1. Joe's Crab Shack, with 146.7%
2. Coco Pazzo, 140.7%
3. Country Pride, 137.9%
4. Rainforest Cafe, 124.0%
5. Fazoli's, 121.2%
6. Einstein Bros./Noah's Bagels, 107.4%
7. Carabba's Italian Grill, 103.9%
8. On the Border, 77.6%
9. Rio Bravo Cantina, 70.9%
10. Logan's Roadhouse, 67.4%

Source: *Restaurant Business*, July 15, 1998, p. 64.

★3774★
FASTEST GROWING RESTAURANT CHAINS BY INCREASE IN UNITS, 1997
Ranked by: Percentage increase in sales. **Remarks:** Includes 1996 and 1997 sales and average unit volume. **Number listed:** 50

1. Joe's Crab Shack, with 188.2%
2. Coco Pazzo, 166.7%
3. Country Pride, 158.3%
4. Rainforest Cafe, 116.7%
5. Rio Bravo Cantina, 83.3%
6. Fazoli's, 81.8%
6. Casa Ole', 81.8%
8. On the Border, 80.0%
9. Einstein Bros./Noah's Bagels, 75.9%
10. Maggiano's, 75.0%

Source: *Restaurant Business*, July 15, 1998, p. 69.

★3775★
LARGEST RESTAURANT CHAINS BY REVENUE, 1997
Ranked by: Revenue, in million dollars. **Remarks:** Includes 1996 sales, percent change, total outlets, Detroit area outlets and total number of employees. **Number listed:** 10

1. Domino's Pizza Inc., with $3,200.0 million
2. Little Caesar Enterprises, $1,780.0
3. Elias Bros. Restaurants Inc., $750.0
4. A & W Restaurants, $282.0
5. Hungry Howies Pizza and Subs Inc., $157.0
6. Tastee-Freez International Inc., $114.0
7. C.A. Muer Corp., $70.0
8. Kasapis Bros. Inc., $45.0
9. Olga's Kitchen Inc., $39.0
10. Papa Romano's Inc., $33.0

Source: *Crain's Detroit Business*, Crain's Book of Lists Detroit (annual), December 28, 1998, p. 76.

★3776★
LEADING ASIAN RESTAURANTS, 1997
Ranked by: Sales, in million dollars. **Remarks:** Includes ranking within top 400. **Number listed:** 6

1. Panda Express, with $168.7 million
2. Benihana, $160.0
3. Manchu Wok, $76.0
4. Yoshinoya Beef Bowl Restaurants, $60.0
5. Sizzling Wok, $50.0
6. Leeann Chin, $46.4

Source: *Restaurants & Institutions*, Restaurants & Institutions 400 (annual), July 15, 1998, p. 103.

★3777★
LEADING BREAD/BAKERY CHAINS, 1999
Ranked by: Satisfaction index score. **Remarks:** Includes rating in food quality, menu variety, value, service, atmosphere, cleanliness and convenience. **Number listed:** 2

1. Einstein Bros., with 44
2. Bruegger's Bagel Bakery, 43

Source: *Restaurants & Institutions*, Choice In Chains (annual), March 1, 1999, p. 90.

★3778★
LEADING BURGER RESTAURANT CHAINS, 1999
Ranked by: Satisfaction index score. **Remarks:** Includes rating in food quality, menu variety, value, service, atmosphere, cleanliness and convenience. **Number listed:** 14
1. In-N-Out Burger, with 42
2. Sonic Drive-In, 40
3. Wendy's, 39
4. Steak 'n Shake, 35
5. McDonald's, 32
6. Burger King, 31
7. Whataburger, 29
8. Checkers, 27
8. White Castle, 27
8. Jack In The Box, 27

Source: *Restaurants & Institutions*, Choice In Chains (annual), March 1, 1999, p. 90.

★3779★
LEADING CAFETERIA/BUFFET RESTAURANT CHAINS, 1999
Ranked by: Satisfaction index score. **Remarks:** Includes rating in food quality, menu variety, value, service, atmosphere, cleanliness and convenience. **Number listed:** 5
1. Luby's, with 52
2. Old Country Buffet, 48
3. Home Town Buffet, 47
4. Picadilly Cafeterias, 46
4. Morrison's, 46

Source: *Restaurants & Institutions*, Choice In Chains (annual), March 1, 1999, p. 90.

★3780★
LEADING CHICKEN RESTAURANT CHAINS, 1999
Ranked by: Satisfaction index score. **Remarks:** Includes rating in food quality, menu variety, value, service, atmosphere, cleanliness and convenience. **Number listed:** 4
1. Chick-fil-A, with 40
2. Popeyes, 31
3. KFC, 30
4. Churchs, 25

Source: *Restaurants & Institutions*, Choice In Chains (annual), March 1, 1999, p. 90.

★3781★
LEADING DINNER HOUSE RESTAURANT CHAINS, 1999
Ranked by: Satisfaction index score. **Remarks:** Includes rating in food quality, menu variety, value, service, atmosphere, cleanliness and convenience. **Number listed:** 11
1. Romano's Macaroni Grill, with 56
1. The Olive Garden, 56
3. T.G.I. Friday's, 50
4. Bennigan's, 48
5. Black Eyed Pea, 47
6. Applebee's, 46
6. Chili's Grill & Bar, 46
8. Ruby Tuesday's, 46
9. Ground Round, 43
10. Fuddruckers, 39

Source: *Restaurants & Institutions*, Choice In Chains (annual), March 1, 1999, p. 90.

★3782★
LEADING DINNER HOUSES, 1997
Ranked by: Sales, in million dollars. **Remarks:** Includes ranking within top 400. **Number listed:** 59
1. Applebee's, with $1,818.5 million
2. T.G.I. Friday's, $1,291.0
3. Chili's Grill & Bar, $1,259.7
4. Ruby Tuesday's, $650.0
5. Bennigan's, $457.0
6. Hooter's Restaurants, $349.0
7. Planet Hollywood, $342.7
8. Red Robin, $292.0
9. Houlihan's, $262.0
10. Hard Rock Cafe, $250.1

Source: *Restaurants & Institutions*, Restaurants & Institutions 400 (annual), July 15, 1998, p. 100.

★3783★
LEADING DOUGHNUT/COOKIE/COFFEE CHAINS, 1999
Ranked by: Satisfaction index score. **Remarks:** Includes rating in food quality, menu variety, value, service, atmosphere, cleanliness and convenience. **Number listed:** 6
1. Starbucks, with 44
2. Krispy Kreme Doughnuts, 42
3. Dunkin' Donuts, 35
4. Cinnabon, 32
5. Mrs. Fields, 30
6. Orange Julius, 23

Source: *Restaurants & Institutions*, Choice In Chains (annual), March 1, 1999, p. 90.

★3784★
LEADING FAMILY DINING CHAINS, 1997
Ranked by: Sales, in million dollars. **Remarks:** Includes ranking within top 400. **Number listed:** 46
1. Denny's, with $1,900. million
2. Boston Market, $1,200.0
3. Shoney's, $1,100.0
4. IHOP, $903.1
5. Cracker Barrel, $863.1
6. Coco's, $730.0
7. Perkins Family Restaurants, $711.0
8. Big Boy, $697.0
9. Friendly's, $682.0
10. Waffle House, $612.0

Source: *Restaurants & Institutions*, Restaurants & Institutions 400 (annual), July 15, 1998, p. 100.

★3785★
LEADING FAMILY DINING RESTAURANT CHAINS, 1999
Ranked by: Satisfaction index score. **Remarks:** Includes rating in food quality, menu variety, value, service, atmosphere, cleanliness and convenience. **Number listed:** 15
1. Cracker Barrel, with $58 million
2. Bob Evans Farms Inc., $49
3. Marie Callender's, $45
4. Fazoli's, $44
5. Bakers Square, $41
5. Perkins, $41
7. Village Inn, $40
7. Shoney's, $40
9. Country Kitchen, $37
9. Boston Market, $37

Source: *Restaurants & Institutions*, Choice In Chains (annual), March 1, 1999, p. 90.

★3786★
LEADING ICE CREAM/YOGURT CHAINS, 1999
Ranked by: Satisfaction index score. **Remarks:** Includes rating in food quality, menu variety, value, service, atmosphere, cleanliness and convenience. **Number listed:** 5
1. Baskin-Robbins, with 42
2. Haagen-Dazs, 40
3. TCBY, 35
4. Dairy Queen, 33

5. Carvel, 31

Source: *Restaurants & Institutions*, Choice In Chains (annual), March 1, 1999, p. 90.

★3787★
LEADING ITALIAN RESTAURANTS, 1997
Ranked by: Sales, in million dollars. **Remarks:** Includes ranking within top 400. **Number listed:** 18

1. The Olive Garden, with $1,400.0 million
2. Sbarro, $463.4
3. Romano's Macaroni Grill, $294.2
4. Fazoli's, $277.0
5. Pizzeria Uno Chicago Bar & Grill, $261.5
6. Mazzio's, $180.0
7. Bertucci's Brick Oven Pizzeria, $134.4
8. Papa Gino's, $115.0
9. Old Spaghetti Factory, $86.0
10. Il Fornaio, $65.5

Source: *Restaurants & Institutions*, Restaurants & Institutions 400 (annual), July 15, 1998, p. 103.

★3788★
LEADING MEXICAN RESTAURANT CHAINS, 1999
Ranked by: Satisfaction index score. **Remarks:** Includes rating in food quality, menu variety, value, service, atmosphere, cleanliness and convenience. **Number listed:** 2

1. Chi-Chi's, with 44
2. Taco Bell, 33

Source: *Restaurants & Institutions*, Choice In Chains (annual), March 1, 1999, p. 90.

★3789★
LEADING PIZZA CHAINS, 1999
Ranked by: Satisfaction index score. **Remarks:** Includes rating in food quality, menu variety, value, service, atmosphere, cleanliness and convenience. **Number listed:** 8

1. Pizzeria Uno, with 46
2. Papa John's, 38
3. Pizza Hut, 36
4. Godfather's Pizza, 31
5. Chuck E. Cheese, 30
6. Domino's, 28
7. Little Caesars, 27
8. Sbarro, 26

Source: *Restaurants & Institutions*, Choice In Chains (annual), March 1, 1999, p. 90.

★3790★
LEADING SANDWICH RESTAURANT CHAINS, 1999
Ranked by: Satisfaction index score. **Remarks:** Includes rating in food quality, menu variety, value, service, atmosphere, cleanliness and convenience. **Number listed:** 5

1. Schlotzsky's Deli, with 39
2. Subway, 38
3. Arby's, 33
4. Blimpie Subs, 28
5. A & W, 24

Source: *Restaurants & Institutions*, Choice In Chains (annual), March 1, 1999, p. 90.

★3791★
LEADING SEAFOOD RESTAURANT CHAINS, 1999
Ranked by: Satisfaction index score. **Remarks:** Includes rating in food quality, menu variety, value, service, atmosphere, cleanliness and convenience. **Number listed:** 3

1. Red Lobster, with 52
2. Captain D's, 36
3. Long John Silver's, 31

Source: *Restaurants & Institutions*, Choice In Chains (annual), March 1, 1999, p. 90.

★3792★
LEADING STEAK/BARBECUE RESTAURANTS, 1997
Ranked by: Sales, in million dollars. **Remarks:** Includes ranking within top 400. **Number listed:** 33

1. Outback Steakhouse, with $1,246.0 million
2. Golden Corral, $770.9
3. Sizzler, $677.9
4. Ryan's Family Steak Houses, $635.6
5. Ponderosa, $630.2
6. Lone Star Steakhouse & Saloon, $585.3
7. Tony Roma's Famous for Ribs, $350.9
8. Western Sizzlin', $318.0
9. Quincy's Family Steakhouses, $283.6
10. Stuart Anderson's Black Angus, $264.0

Source: *Restaurants & Institutions*, Restaurants & Institutions 400 (annual), July 15, 1998, p. 102.

★3793★
LEADING STEAKHOUSE RESTAURANT CHAINS, 1999
Ranked by: Satisfaction index score. **Remarks:** Includes rating in food quality, menu variety, value, service, atmosphere, cleanliness and convenience. **Number listed:** 11

1. Outback Steakhouse, with 57
2. Stuart Anderson's, 54
3. Tony Roma's, 51
4. Ryan's Family Steakhouse, 48
4. Steak and Ale, 48
6. Lone Star, 46
7. Golden Corral, 45
8. Western Sizzlin', 40
8. Ponderosa, 40
10. Sizzler, 34

Source: *Restaurants & Institutions*, Choice In Chains (annual), March 1, 1999, p. 90.

★3794★
LEADING THEME RESTAURANT CHAINS, 1999
Ranked by: Satisfaction index score. **Remarks:** Includes rating in food quality, menu variety, value, service, atmosphere, cleanliness and convenience. **Number listed:** 3

1. Rainforest Cafe, with 52
2. Planet Hollywood, 44
3. Hard Rock Cafe, 43

Source: *Restaurants & Institutions*, Choice In Chains (annual), March 1, 1999, p. 90.

★3795★
TOP GROWTH RESTAURANT CHAINS BY SYSTEMWIDE SALES GROWTH, 1997
Ranked by: Percent change, in millions of dollars. **Remarks:** Includes company fiscal year end and growth over previous year. **Number listed:** 10

1. Chartwells, with $102.38% million
2. Fine Host, $90.49%
3. Papa John's Pizza, $40.12%
4. Starbucks, $36.7%
5. Schlotzsky's Deli, $33.49%
6. Romano's Macaroni Grill, $30.87%
7. Eurest Dining Services, $25.00%
8. Fazoli's, $24.83%
9. Outback Steakhouse, $22.52%
10. Blimpie Subs and Salads, $20.21%

Source: *Nation's Restaurant News*, A Year in Review (annual), December 21, 1998, p. 98.

★3796★
TOP GROWTH RESTAURANT COMPANIES BY SYSTEMWIDE REVENUE, 1997
Ranked by: Systemwide revenue, in millions of dollars. **Remarks:** Includes company fiscal year end and growth over previous year. **Number listed:** 10
1. CKE Restaurants Inc., with $111.08 million
2. Fine Host Corp., $90.49
3. Boston Chicken Inc., $89.94
4. Compass Group PLC, $86.61
5. RTM Inc., $59.85
6. NPC International Inc., $54.10
7. Avado Brands formerly Apple South, $48.04
8. Papa John's International, $47.71
9. Tosco, $38.89
10. The Cheesecake Factory, $35.62

Source: *Nation's Restaurant News*, A Year in Review (annual), December 21, 1998, p. 104.

★3797★
TOP RESTAURANT STOCK GAINERS, 1998
Ranked by: Percent change. **Remarks:** Includes ticker symbol, price at close 12-31-97 and 11-30-98. **Number listed:** 10
1. Brinker International, with 60%
2. Tricon Global Restaurants, 57%
2. Back Bay Restaurants, 57%
4. McDonald's, 47%
5. Ruby Tuesday's, 45%
6. Rare Hospitality Inc., 37%
7. Logan's roadhouse, 34%
8. PJ America Inc., 30%
9. CEC Entertainment, 29%
10. Cheesecake Factory, 28%

Source: *Nation's Restaurant News*, A Year in Review (annual), December 21, 1998, p. 104.

★3798★
TOP RESTAURANT STOCK LOSERS, 1998
Ranked by: Percent change. **Remarks:** Includes ticker symbol, price at close 12-31-97 and 11-30-98. **Number listed:** 10
1. Il Fornaio Corp., with -49%
2. Lone Star Steakhouse & Saloon, -56%
3. Einstein/Noah Bagel, -62%
4. Santa Barbara Restaurant Group, -63%
5. Famous Dave's, -66%
5. Landry's, -66%
7. Rainforest Cafe, -68%
8. Fresh Foods Inc., -71%
9. Planet Hollywood, -78%
10. Boston Chicken, -90%

Source: *Nation's Restaurant News*, A Year in Review (annual), December 21, 1998, p. 104.

★3799★
TOP U.S. RESTAURANT CHAINS ABROAD BY INTERNATIONAL SALES, 1997
Ranked by: International sales, in thousands of dollars. **Remarks:** Includes total system sales, share of sales, percent sales growth and 1996 sales. **Number listed:** 50
1. McDonald's, with $16,513,000 thousand
2. KFC, $4,330,000
3. Pizza Hut, $2,525,000
4. Burger King, $2,042,410
5. Tim Hortons, $749,901
6. Domino's Pizza, $680,000
7. Wendy's, $625,000
8. Baskin Robbins, USA, $500,000
8. Subway Sandwiches, $500,000
10. Hard Rock Cafe, $425,000

Source: *Restaurant Business*, Top U.S. Chains Abroad (annual), November 1, 1998, p. 37.

★3800★
TOP U.S. RESTAURANT CHAINS ABROAD BY INTERNATIONAL UNITS, 1997
Ranked by: International sales, in thousands of dollars. **Remarks:** Includes total system sales, share of sales, percent sales growth and 1996 sales. **Number listed:** 50
1. McDonald's, with $10,752 thousand
2. KFC, $5,117
3. Pizza Hut, $3,836
4. Burger King, $2,060
5. Baskin-Robbins U.S.A., $1,927
6. Subway Sandwiches, $1,851
7. Domino's Pizza, $1,521
8. Tim Hortons, $1,499
9. Dunkin' Donuts, $1,386
10. Yogen Fruz/Paradise/Java, $1,300

Source: *Restaurant Business*, Top U.S. Chains Abroad (annual), November 1, 1998, p. 38.

Restaurants--Los Angeles County (CA)

★3801★
LARGEST RESTAURANT CHAINS IN LOS ANGELES COUNTY, 1997
Ranked by: Revenue, in million dollars. **Remarks:** Includes average check, weekly meals served, number of employees, dept. of health grade, cuisine, profile and top local executive. **Number listed:** 25
1. Gladstone's 4 Fish, with $13.8 million
2. Gladstone's Universal, $10.5
3. Lawry's, the Prime Rib, $10.3
4. Jerry's Famous Deli, West Hollywood, $8.3
5. Sagebrush Cantina, $8.0
6. Jerry's Famous Deli, Studio City, $7.8
7. Bistro Garden at Coldwater, $7.0
8. Broadway Deli, $6.5
9. Ivy at the Shore, $6.3
10. Junior's, $6.2

Source: *Los Angeles Business Journal*, August 31, 1998, p. 18.

Retail Stores

★3802★
PHOTO AND WALL FRAME MARKET SHARE, 1998
Ranked by: Sales, in percent. **Number listed:** 10
1. Mass Merchants, with 32%
2. Department Stores, 17%
3. Chain Drugstores, 15%
4. Craft/Floral Stores, 9%
5. Home/Lifestyle Stores, 6%
5. Other, 6%
7. Supermarkets, 5%
8. Camera Store/Photo Labs, 4%
9. Card/Gift Stores, 3%
10. National Chains, 3%

Source: *HFN*, December 14, 1998, p. 10.

★3803★
TOP CHILDREN'S WEAR RETAILERS, 1998
Ranked by: Sales, in million dollars. **Remarks:** Includes location, store type and number of doors. **Number listed:** 100
1. Wal-Mart, with $4,800 million
2. Kmart, $2,300
3. J.C. Penney, $1,860
4. Target, $1,450
5. Sears, $1,400
6. Federated Department Stores, $1,260
7. May Company, $1,000
8. J.C. Penney-catalog, $830
9. TJX, $800
10. Kids ''R'' Us, $770

Source: *Children's Business*, Focus 100 (annual), May, 1999, p. 12+.

★3804★
TOP ELECTRONIC STORES, 1997
Ranked by: Sales, in million dollars. **Remarks:** Includes store type. **Number listed:** 25
1. Circuit City, with $5,837.5 million
2. Best Buy, $5,500.0
3. CompUSA, $5,070.0
4. Sears, $3,437.9
5. Radio Shack, $3.119.2
6. Office Depot, $3,083.3
7. Kmart, $2,869.0
8. Staples, $2,719.5
9. Wal-Mart, $2,500.0
10. Office Max Inc., $1,920.0

Source: *HFN*, July 20, 1998, p. 84.

★3805★
TOP HISPANIC RETAILERS, 1998
Ranked by: Revenue, in million dollars. **Number listed:** 10
1. Sedano's Supermarkets, with $294.00 million
2. Navarro Discount Pharmacies, $108.00
3. Gaseteria Oil corp., $97.00
4. ElDorado Furniture Corp., $59.50
5. Gracious Home, $35.00
6. King Taco Restaurant Inc., $28.68
7. La Pizza Loca Inc., $27.00
8. Norsan Group, $26.56
9. Holman's Inc., $24.50
10. Business Travel Advisors Inc., $23.60

Source: *Hispanic Business*, Hispanic Business 500 (annual), June, 1999, p. 100.

★3806★
TOP HOME GOODS RETAILERS, 1997
Ranked by: Sales, in million dollars. **Remarks:** Includes percent change from 1996, total retail revenue, number of stores and store type. **Number listed:** 200
1. Wal-Mart (including Sam's Club), with $16,956.46 million
2. Sears, $12,677.90
3. Circuit City, $7,560.00
4. Kmart, $6,399.59
5. Best Buy, $6,250.00
6. Home Depot, $6,039.00
7. CompUSA, $5,070.00
8. Target, $4,888.30
9. J.C. Penney, $4,109.35
10. Radio Shack, $3,112.17

Source: *Home Furnishings Directory*, Focus 100 (annual), July 20, 1998, p. 12+.

★3807★
TOP HOUSEWARE RETAILERS, 1997
Ranked by: Houseware sales revenue, in million dollars. **Remarks:** Includes store type. **Number listed:** 25
1. Wal-Mart, with $6,226.6 million
2. Kmart, $2,719.4
3. Costco Wholesale, $1,890.6
4. Sam's Club, $1,777.4
5. Target, $1,700.0
6. Sears, $1,362.8
7. Service Merchandise, $879.1
8. Williams-Sonoma, $840.0
9. CVS, $823.5
10. Ace Hardware Corp., $600.0

Source: *HFN*, July 20, 1998, p. 65.

★3808★
TOP MAJOR APPLIANCE STORES, 1997
Ranked by: Sales, in million dollars. **Remarks:** Includes store type. **Number listed:** 25
1. Sears, with $5,100.0 million
2. Circuit City, $1,199.5
3. Best Buy, $756.0
4. Montgomery Ward, $643.7
5. Lowe's, $611.0
6. Wal-Mart, $386.0
7. Costco, $270.0
8. P.C. Richard & Son, $230.0
9. ABC Warehouse, $215.0
10. Heilig-Meyers, $132.29

Source: *HFN*, July 20, 1998, p. 10.

★3809★
TOP PHOTO FRAME RETAILERS, 1998
Ranked by: Sales. **Number listed:** 10
1. Wal-Mart
2. Kmart
3. Target
4. May Corporate
5. Federated
6. Kohl's
7. Rite Aid
8. Walgreens
9. Eckerd Drugs
10. Michael's

Source: *HFN*, December 14, 1998, p. 10.

★3810★
TOP PUBLICLY HELD RETAIL CHAINS, 1997
Ranked by: Sales revenue, in thousand dollars. **Remarks:** Includes headquarters, main retail segments, 1996 revenue, profits, number of stores and comments. **Number listed:** 100
1. Wal-Mart, with $117,958,000 thousand
2. Sears, Roebuck & Co., $41,296,000
3. Kmart, $32,183,000
4. J.C. Penney, $29,618,000
5. Dayton Hudson Corp., $27,757,000
6. Kroger, $26,567,348
7. The Home Depot, $24,156,000
8. Safeway, $22,483,800
9. Costco, $21,874,404
10. American Stores Co., $19,138,880

Source: *Chain Store Age*, Top 100 (annual), August, 1998, p. 3A+.

★3811★
TOP RETAIL INDUSTRY EXECUTIVE COMPENSATION, 1997
Ranked by: Total cash compensation, in million dollars. **Remarks:** Includes executive, title, 1996 & 1997 salary, 1996 &

1997 bonus, percent change in cash compensation, percent change in stock price and potential realizable value. **Number listed:** 50

1. Dayton-Hudson, with $4,285,024 million
2. Kmart, $3,015,600
3. Office Depot, $2,640,000
4. Consolidated Stores, $1,800,000
5. TJX, $2,333,313
6. Wal-Mart, $2,265,846
7. Consolidated Stores, $1,800,000
8. Wal-Mart, $1,661,700
9. Best Buy, $1,586,750
10. CompUSA, $1,581,395

Source: *Discount Store News*, September 21, 1998, p. 21.

★3812★
TOP RETAILERS BY SALES, 1998
Ranked by: Revenue, in billion dollars. **Remarks:** Includes location, lead agency location and media expenditures. **Number listed:** 20

1. Wal-Mart, with $137.6 billion
2. Sears, $41.30
3. Kmart, $33.6
4. J.C. Penney, $30.5
5. Home Depot, $30.2
6. Kroger, $28.2
7. Safeway, $24.5
8. price/Costco, $24.3
9. Target, $20.4
10. Acme, Jewel, Lucky, Osco, $19.9

Source: *Superbrands: America's Top Brands*, June 21, 1999, p. S62.

★3813★
TOP TOY RETAILERS, 1997
Ranked by: Distribution of dollar sales. **Remarks:** Includes 1996 sales. **Number listed:** 20

1. Toys ''R'' Us, with 18.4%
2. Wal-Mart, 16.4%
3. Kmart, 8.2%
4. Target, 7.1%
5. Consolidated Stores, 6.1%
6. J.C. Penney, 1.5%
7. Hills, 1.2%
8. Service Merchandise, 1.1%
8. Ames, 1.1%
8. Meijer, 1.1%

Source: *Playthings*, July, 1998, p. 22.

Retail Stores--Food Service

★3814★
LEADING RETAIL STORE FOOD SERVICE OPERATIONS RANKED BY SALES, 1997
Ranked by: Sales, in million dollars. **Number listed:** 6

1. Wal-Mart, with $454.0 million
2. Kmart, $183.0
3. Target, $137.0
4. Nordstrom, $103.5
5. Dayton Hudson Department Stores, $95.0
6. Neiman Marcus, $31.5

Source: *Restaurants & Institutions*, Restaurants & Institutions 400 (annual), July 15, 1998, p. 103.

Retail Stores, International

★3815★
TOP RETAILERS IN THE WORLD, 1997
Ranked by: Sales, in million dollars. **Remarks:** Includes number of stores, number of formats and number of countries. **Number listed:** 25

1. Wal-Mart, with $111,829 million
2. Metro, $43,030
3. Ito Yokado, $40,099
4. Auchan, $33,348
5. Kmart, $32,183
6. Rewe Group, $32,015
7. Intermarche, $31,672
8. Sears, $31,495
9. Carrefour, $29,923
10. J.C. Penney, $28,685

Source: *MMMR*, September 21, 1998, p. 13.

Retail Trade

See also: **Department Stores**

★3816★
MOST ADMIRED GENERAL MERCHANDISERS IN RETAILING, 1998
Ranked by: Scores (1-10) derived from a survey of senior executives, outside directors and securities analysts. **Remarks:** Respondents rated companies in their own industry on 8 attributes of reputation. Also notes previous year's rank. **Number listed:** 10

1. Wal-Mart Stores, with 7.66
2. Dayton Hudson, 7.18
3. Nordstrom, 6.89
4. May Department Stores, 6.56
5. Federated Department Stores, 6.32
6. Sears Roebuck, 6.27
7. Harcourt General, 5.75
8. J.C. Penney, 5.33
9. Dillard's, 5.32
10. Kmart, 4.38

Source: *Fortune*, America's Most Admired Corporations (annual), March 1, 1999, p. F-3.

★3817★
TOP AMERICAN MICRO-CITIES IN RETAIL SALES, 1998
Ranked by: Per-capita income. **Number listed:** 10

1. Vero Beach, FL, with 28,977 income
2. Torrington, CT, 25,912
3. Key West, FL, 25,160
4. Concord, NH, 24,734
5. Carson City, NV, 24,422
6. Newport, RI, 22,465
7. Columbus, IN, 22,464
8. Salina KS, 21,785
9. Elko, NV, 21,785
10. Muscatine, IA, 21,742

Source: *GSB*, August, 1999, p. 13.

★3818★
TOP CORPORATIONS IN THE GENERAL MERCHANDISING RETAIL TRADE INDUSTRY, 1998
Ranked by: Revenue, in millions of dollars. **Remarks:** Also notes profits and investment figures as well as number of employees. **Number listed:** 20

1. Wal-Mart Stores, with $139,208 million
2. Sears Roebuck, $41,322
3. Kmart, $33,674
4. Dayton Hudson, $30,951
5. J.C. Penney, $30,678
6. Federated Department Stores, $15,833
7. May Department Stores, $13,413
8. Dillard's, $8,012
9. Saks, $6,220
10. Nordstrom, $5,028

Source: *Fortune*, Fortune 500 Largest U.S. Corporations (annual), April 26, 1999, p. F-60.

★3819★
TOP RETAIL SALES IN METROPOLITAN AREAS, 1997
Ranked by: Dollars spent, in thousands. **Number listed:** 300

1. Chicago, with $73,714,948 thousand
2. Los Angeles-Long Beach, $67,227,510
3. New York, $53,062,839
4. Philadelphia, $48,187,372
5. Washington, $46,921,312
6. Detroit, $43,953,411
7. Atlanta, $40,167,751
8. Houston, $37,825,115
9. Boston-Lawrence-Lowell-Brockton, $37,719,249
10. Dallas, $32,176,713

Source: *Sales and Marketing Management*, Survey of Buying Power (annual), August, 1999, p. 19.

★3820★
TOP RETAILING TRENDS, 1999
Ranked by: Top emerging consumer trends. **Number listed:** 10

1. Interactive Technology
2. New Lighting Techniques
3. Integrated Marketing
4. Multi-Dimensional Store Fronts
5. Flexible, Cost-Effective Graphics
6. Family Entertainment
7. Flexible Fixtures
8. Growth of Home/Lifestyle Products
9. Branding/Co-Branding
10. Neighborhood Retailer Returns

Source: *Craftrends*, March, 1999, p. 24.

Retail Trade--Asia

★3821★
LARGEST QUOTED COMPANIES IN THE RETAIL AND WHOLESALE TRADE INDUSTRIES IN ASIA, 1997
Ranked by: Sales, in thousands of U.S. dollars ($). **Remarks:** Includes profit as percent of sales and activity codes. Top 10 are in Japan. **Number listed:** 100

1. Mitsui & Co., with $131,103,869 thousand
2. Mitsubishi Corp., $119,069,318
3. Marubeni Corp., $102,099,678
4. Sumitomo Corp., $94,082,073
5. Nissho Iwai Corp., $75,245,112
6. Tomen Corp., $39,208,952
7. Nichimen Corp., $28,815,950
8. Kanematsu Corp., $24,354,371
9. Daiei Inc., $23,677,080
10. Ito-Yokado Co. Ltd., $23,425,067

Source: *Asia's 7,500 Largest Companies*, (annual), E.L.C. Publishing Ltd., 1999, p. 87+.

★3822★
MOST ADMIRED COMPANIES IN THE RETAIL/ CONSUMER GOODS INDUSTRY IN ASIA, 1999
Ranked by: Score. **Remarks:** Includes previous year's score, overall rank and change in rank. **Number listed:** 10

1. Jollibee, with 8.32
2. Coca-Cola, 8.22
3. Unilever, 8.21
4. McDonald's, 8.08
5. Nestle, 7.95
6. Carlsberg, 7.79
7. Shoemart, 7.65
8. San Miguel Corp., 7.61
9. Guinness Anchor, 7.49
10. Procter & Gamble, 7.46

Source: *Asian Business*, Most Admired Companies in Asia (annual), May, 1999, p. 29.

Retail Trade, International

★3823★
WORLD'S LARGEST GENERAL MERCHANDISERS BY REVENUE, 1997
Ranked by: Revenue, in millions of dollars. **Number listed:** 13

1. Wal-Mart Stores (U.S.), with $119,299 million
2. Sears Roebuck (U.S.), $41,296
3. K-Mart (U.S.), $32,183
4. J.C. Penney (U.S.), $30,546
5. Dayton Hudson (U.S.), $27,757
6. Daiei (Japan), $25,882
7. Federated Department Stores (U.S.), $15,668
8. Pinault-Prientemps (France), $15,280
9. Mycal (Japan), $15,006
10. Karstadt (Germany), $13,720

Source: *Fortune*, The Global 500: World's Biggest Corporations (annual), August 3, 1998, p. F-20.

Retail Trade--Japan

★3824★
LARGEST RETAIL CHAINS IN JAPAN, 1997
Ranked by: Sales, in billions U.S. dollars. **Remarks:** Includes percent change, net profit/loss and number of outlets. **Number listed:** 10

1. Daiei, with $17.6 billion
2. Ito-Yokado, $11.0
3. Jusco, $8.9
4. Mycal, $8.1
5. Takashimaya, $7.8
6. Seiyu, $7.1
7. Uny, $5.3
8. Mitsukoshi, $5.2
9. Seibu, $4.5
10. Marui, $3.6

Source: *MMR*, March 22, 1999, p. 11.

Retirement Communities

★3825★
LARGEST HEALTHCARE SYSTEMS OPERATING CONTINUING-CARE RETIREMENT COMMUNITIES, 1998
Ranked by: By total number of communities. **Remarks:** Includes 1997 figures. **Number listed:** 25
1. Evangelical Lutheran Good Samaritan Society, with 76
2. Life Care Services Corp., 54
3. Advocat, 52
4. Extendicare Health Services, 44
5. Beverly Enterprises, 34
6. Catholic Health Initiatives, 21
7. Catholic Health East, 20
8. Life Care Centers of America, 18
9. Lutheran Health System-La Crosse, 15
10. ServiceMaster Diversified Health Services, 15

Source: *Modern Healthcare*, Modern Healthcare Multi-Unit Providers Survey (annual), May 24, 1999, p. 58.

Risk Management Consultants

★3826★
LARGEST INDEPENDENT RISK MANAGEMENT CONSULTANTS, 1998
Ranked by: Revenue, in millions of dollars. **Remarks:** Also notes total clients and risk management professionals. **Number listed:** 10
1. Pricewaterhouse Coopers, with $60,840,000 million
2. Arthur Andersen, $54,647,759
3. Deloitte & Touche, $54,300,000
4. EQE International, $42,300,000
5. Ernst & Young, $31,038,000
6. Tillinghast-Towers Perrin, $28,356,000
7. Dames & Moore Group, $11,500,000
8. KPMG, $11,000,000
9. Milliman & Robertson, $9,487,000
10. J.H. Albert International, $6,800,000

Source: *Business Insurance*, March 15, 1999, p. 3.

Rubber Industry

★3827★
MOST ADMIRED RUBBER AND PLASTIC PRODUCT CORPORATIONS, 1998
Ranked by: Scores (1-10) derived from a survey of senior executives, outside directors and securities analysts. **Remarks:** Respondents rated companies in their own industry on 8 attributes of reputation. Also notes previous year's rank. **Number listed:** 10
1. Goodyear Tire & Rubber, with 7.76 points
2. Rubbermaid, 7.15
3. Cooper Tire & Rubber, 7.10
4. Tupperware, 6.93
5. GenCorp., 6.91
6. First Brands, 6.89
7. M.A. Hanna, 6.74
8. Mark IV Industries, 6.54
9. Bridgestone/Firestone, 6.51
10. Carlisle, 6.14

Source: *Fortune*, America's Most Admired Corporations (annual), March 1, 1999, p. F-5.

★3828★
TOP CORPORATIONS IN THE RUBBER AND PLASTIC PRODUCTS INDUSTRY, 1998
Ranked by: Revenue, in millions of dollars. **Remarks:** Also notes profits and investment figures as well as number of employees. **Number listed:** 10
1. Goodyear Tire, with $12,649 million
2. Rubbermaid, $2,554
3. Sealed Air, $2,507
4. M.A. Hanna, $2,286
5. Mark IV Industries, $2,210
6. Cooper Tire & Rubber, $1,880
7. Gencorp, $1,737
8. Carlisle, $1,517
9. Foamex International, $1,250
10. First Brands, $1,204

Source: *Fortune*, Fortune 500 Largest U.S. Corporations (annual), April 26, 1999, p. F-67.

Rubber Industry--Europe

★3829★
TOP COMPANIES IN THE RUBBER AND MISCELLANEOUS PLASTIC PRODUCTS INDUSTRY IN EUROPE, 1997
Ranked by: Revenue, in millions of U.S. dollars ($). **Remarks:** Includes employees. **Number listed:** 106
1. Continental AG, with $5,673 million
2. Manuf Franc Pneumatiq Michelin, $3.090
3. Freudenberg & Co., $2,731
4. Ruetgers AG, $2,620
5. Kodak Ltd., $1,916
6. Dow Deutschland Inc., Sweigniederlassung Stade, $1,853
7. Agfa-Gevaert NV, $1,438
8. Neumaticos Michelin, S.A., $1,420
9. Michelin Reifenwerke-Kg Auf Aktien, $1,388
10. Hepworth P.L.C., $956

Source: *Dun & Bradstreet*, Duns Europa (annual), 1999, p. 245.

Rubber Industry, International

★3830★
NEW RUBBER PRODUCTS CONSUMPTION BY GLOBAL REGION, 1998
Ranked by: Regional consumption, in metric tons. **Remarks:** Includes 1997 figures as well as projections for 1999 and 2000. **Number listed:** 8
1. Asia & Oceania, with $4,724 metric tons
2. North America, $4,512
3. Western Europe, $3,752
4. China/Asia CPEC, $1,613
5. Latin America, $960
6. Central Europe, $505
7. Commonwealth of Independent States, $460
8. Middle East & Africa, $427

Source: *Rubber World*, 1999, p. 14.

Rum

★3831★
LARGEST RUM MARKETS BY CASES SOLD, 1997
Ranked by: Sales, in thousands of 9-liter cases. **Remarks:** Also notes previous year's sales, percent change, and cumulative share. **Number listed:** 51
1. New York, with $1,516,470 thousand cases
2. Florida, $1,331,280
3. California, $1,307,930
4. Texas, $613,820
5. Illinois, $605,360
6. New Jersey, $598,970
7. Michigan, $565,250
8. Pennsylvania, $468,310
9. Massachusetts, $447,120
10. Minnesota, $389,030

Source: *Adams Liquor Handbook*, 1998, p. 145.

★3832★
LARGEST RUM MARKETS BY CASES SOLD PER THOUSAND ADULTS, 1997
Ranked by: Sales, in thousands of 9-liter cases per 1,000 adults. **Remarks:** Also notes previous year's sales. **Number listed:** 51
1. New Hampshire, with 218.9 thousand cases
2. District of Columbia, 201.3
3. Nevada, 165.4
4. Alaska, 146.5
5. Hawaii, 129.8
6. Florida, 125.4
7. Minnesota, 119.7
8. North Dakota, 119.3
9. Delaware, 117.4
10. New York, 117.3

Source: *Adams Liquor Handbook*, 1998, p. 146.

★3833★
LARGEST RUM SUPPLIERS, 1997
Ranked by: Market share, in percent. **Number listed:** 5
1. Bacardi-Martini USA, with 55.8%
2. Others, 22.1%
3. Seagram Americas, 14.3%
4. IDV North America, 4.0%
5. Jim Beam Brands, 3.7%

Source: *Adams Liquor Handbook*, 1998, p. 148.

★3834★
LEADING BRANDS OF RUM, 1997
Ranked by: Sales, in thousands of 9-liter cases. **Remarks:** Also notes previous 5 years sales and percent change. **Number listed:** 11
1. Bacardi, with $6,600 thousand cases
2. Captain Morgan, $1,670
3. Castillo, $960
4. Malibu, $536
5. Ronrico, $503
6. Myer's, $275
7. Monarch Rum, $155
8. Mount Gay, $118
9. World Famous, $82
10. Ron Matusalem, $80

Source: *Adams Liquor Handbook*, 1998, p. 148.

★3835★
TOP METROPOLITAN AREAS FOR RUM SALES, 1997
Ranked by: Sales, in thousands of 9-liter cases. **Remarks:** Also notes market share. **Number listed:** 50
1. New York, NY, with $783.8 thousand cases
2. Chicago, IL, $389.1
3. Washington, DC, $349.0
4. Los Angeles-Long Beach, $341.0
5. Boston-Lawrence-Lowell-Brockton, $323.2
6. Nassau-Suffolk, $307.1
7. Detroit, $284.1
8. Minneapolis-St. Paul, $251.9
9. Philadelphia, $248.0
10. Tampa-St. Petersburg-Clearwater, $223.9

Source: *Adams Liquor Handbook*, 1998, p. 139.

Rum--Advertising

★3836★
RUM BRANDS WITH THE GREATEST ADVERTISING EXPENDITURES, 1997
Ranked by: Advertising expenditures, in thousands of dollars. **Number listed:** 9
1. Bacardi, with $24,487.1 thousand
2. Captain Morgan, $9,060.4
3. Puerto Rican Rums, $4,556.8
4. Malibu, $1,749.8
5. Mount Gay, $1,517.3
6. Ocumare, $123.9
7. Ronrico, $85.2
8. Fernandes 19, $31.4
9. Gosling Black Seal Rum, $27.9

Source: *Adams Liquor Handbook*, Adams Media Inc., 1998, p. 150.

★3837★
RUM BRANDS WITH THE GREATEST MAGAZINE AD EXPENDITURES, 1997
Ranked by: Magazine ad expenditures, in thousands of dollars. **Number listed:** 7
1. Bacardi, with $21,727.3 thousand
2. Captain Morgan, $6,195.0
3. Puerto Rican Rums, $4,556.8
4. Malibu, $1,749.8
5. Mount Gay, $1,500.8
6. Ocumare, $52.0
7. Gosling Black Seal Rum, $27.9

Source: *Adams Liquor Handbook*, Adams Media Inc., 1998, p. 150.

★3838★
RUM BRANDS WITH THE GREATEST NEWSPAPER AD EXPENDITURES, 1997
Ranked by: Newspaper ad expenditures, in thousands of dollars. **Number listed:** 3
1. Captain Morgan, with $40.0 thousand
2. Fernandes 19, $31.4
3. Bacardi, $9.3

Source: *Adams Liquor Handbook*, Adams Media Inc., 1998, p. 150.

★3839★
RUM BRANDS WITH THE GREATEST OUTDOOR AD EXPENDITURES, 1997
Ranked by: Outdoor ad expenditures, in thousands of dollars. **Number listed:** 5
1. Captain Morgan, with $2,825.4 thousand
2. Bacardi, $1,134.3
3. Ronrico, $85.2
4. Ocumare, $71.9

5. Mount Gay, $16.5

Source: *Adams Liquor Handbook*, Adams Media Inc., 1998, p. 150.

Rum--Export-Import Trade

★3840★
LEADING DESTINATIONS OF U.S.-EXPORTED RUM, 1997
Ranked by: Sales, in thousands of proof gallons. **Remarks:** Includes previous 2 years' sales. **Number listed:** 6

1. Canada, with $1,147.3 thousand
2. Bahamas, $1,009.8
3. Columbia, $375.5
4. Japan, $320.2
5. Netherland Antilles, $237.1
6. Other, $992.4

Source: *Adams Liquor Handbook*, 1998, p. 219.

★3841★
LEADING RUM EXPORTERS TO THE U.S., 1997
Ranked by: Sales, in thousands of proof gallons. **Remarks:** Includes previous 2 years' sales and percent change. **Number listed:** 11

1. Barbados, with 195.5 thousand
2. Jamaica, 116.8
3. Dominican Republic, 32.9
4. Venezuela, 28.5
5. Canada, 20.7
6. Mexico, 19.6
7. Guyana, 16.5
8. Trinidad, 12.8
9. Bermuda, 10.3
10. Haiti, 7.4

Source: *Adams Liquor Handbook*, 1998, p. 219.

Sales Promotion

★3842★
TOP PROMOTIONAL PRODUCTS SALES, 1997
Ranked by: Percent of sales. **Number listed:** 17

1. Wearables/Apparel, with 27.2%
2. Writing Instruments, 11.8%
3. Glassware/Ceramics, 9.4%
4. Calendars, 7.3%
5. Desk/Office Accessories, 5.6%
6. Recognition Awards/Clocks/Watches, 5.5%
7. Textiles, 5.3%
8. Buttons/Badges/Stickers/Magnets, 4.4%
9. Automotive Accessories, 3.3%
10. Other, 3.2%

Source: *Potentials*, October, 1998, p. 12.

Sales Promotion Agencies--Great Britain

★3843★
TOP BRITISH SALES PROMOTION CONSULTANCIES, 1996-1997
Ranked by: Gross profit, in British pounds. **Remarks:** Includes percent change, number on staff and gross profit per head. **Number listed:** 66

1. Carlson, with £17,511,000
2. IMP, £10,778,000
3. Homes & Marchant Group, £10,629,000
4. KLP Euro RSCG, £10,050,000
5. Grey Integrated, £9,072,000
6. Marketing Store Worldwide, £8,646,000
7. Tequila London, £6,595,000
8. Triangle Comms, £6,394,000
9. Claydon Heeley International, £6,109,000
10. Interfocus Network, £6,064,000

Source: *Marketing*, Top Sales Promotion Companies (annual), October 29, 1998, p. 41.

★3844★
TOP GROWTH OF BIGGER CONSULTANCIES, 1996-1997
Ranked by: Percent change in gross profit. **Number listed:** 10

1. Claydon Heeley Intl., with 69.72%
2. Black Cat, 55.98%
3. Interfocus Network, 44.72%
4. Perspectives, 43.21%
5. Dynamo, 42.98%
6. sth stretch the horizon, 35.10%
7. Clarke Hooper Consulting, 33.09%
8. Tequila London, 32.83%
9. ZGC Group, 31.36%
10. The Marketing Store Worldwide, 29.17%

Source: *Marketing*, Top Sales Promotion Companies (annual), October 29, 1998, p. 39.

★3845★
TOP GROWTH OF SMALLER CONSULTANCIES, 1996-1997
Ranked by: Percent change in gross profit. **Number listed:** 10

1. Fleming Arthur, with 408.22%
2. Milton PDM, 145.98%
3. Marketing in Action, 120.78%
4. Spearhead Marketing, 108.47%
5. Manifesto, 81.33%
6. Positive Thinking, 68.71%
7. The Russell Organization, 68.34%
8. Ignition Marketing Group, 54.79%
9. Biggart Donald, 53.94%
10. GCAS Sales Promotions, 53.57%

Source: *Marketing*, Top Sales Promotion Companies (annual), October 29, 1998, p. 39.

Salesmanship

★3846★
COMPANIES WITH THE BEST SALES FORCE, 1997
Ranked by: Criteria created by a panel of more than 100 experts including business school professors. Panel and editors selected the 25 best. **Remarks:** Includes revenue and percent change. **Number listed:** 25

1. GE Capital
2. Cisco

3. Frito-Lay
4. Dell
5. Physician Sales & Service
6. Lear Corp.
7. Northwestern Mutual Life
8. Halliburton
9. Pfizer
10. Enron

Source: *Sales & Marketing Management*, Best Sales Force Top 25 (annual), July, 1998, p. 33.

Sand and Gravel Industry

★3847★
TOP INDUSTRIAL SAND & GRAVEL PRODUCERS IN THE U.S., 1996
Ranked by: Total output. **Remarks:** Includes number of active plants and states. **Number listed:** 10

1. Calmat Co.
2. Cornerstone Construction & Materials, Inc./Hanson Industries
3. CSR America Inc.
4. Redland Aggregates North America
5. Granite Construction Co.
6. Texas Industries
7. Martin Marietta Aggregates
8. Peter Kiewit Sons
9. Camas America Inc.
10. Lonestar Northwest Inc.

Source: *Sand & Gravel Industry*, January 14, 1998, p. 1+.

★3848★
TOP SANDWICH CHAINS, 1997
Ranked by: Sales, in millions of dollars. **Remarks:** Includes top 400 rank. **Number listed:** 35

1. Subway Sandwiches & Salads, with $3,300.0 million
2. Arby's, $2,060.0
3. Blimpie Subs & Salads, $350.0
4. A & W Restaurants, $280.0
5. Schlotzsky's Deli, $270.0
6. Einstein Bros. Bagels, $237.1
7. Au Bon Pain, $199.0
8. Bruegger's Bagel Bakery, $199.0
9. Miami Subs Grill, $148.1
10. Wienerschnitzel, $141.9

Source: *Restaurants & Institutions*, July 15, 1998, p. 105.

Santiago Stock Exchange

★3849★
LARGEST LISTED COMPANIES ON THE SANTIAGO STOCK EXCHANGE, 1997
Ranked by: Market value, in millions of U.S. dollars ($). **Number listed:** 20

1. CTC-A, with $5,770.60 million
2. Endesa, $4,706.14
3. Copec, $4,410.00
4. Enersis, $3,762.47
5. Chilectra, $2,266.30
6. Fatabella, $2,153.38
7. Chilgener, $1,971.76
8. Chile, $1,943.90
9. Santiago, $1,866.48
10. Cervezas, $1,769.37

Source: *SSB Guide to World Equity Markets (annual)*, 1998, p. 130.

★3850★
MOST ACTIVELY TRADED SHARES ON THE SANTIAGO STOCK EXCHANGE, 1997
Ranked by: Trading value, in thousands of U.S. dollars ($). **Number listed:** 20

1. Endesa, with $1,116,590 thousand
2. Chilgener, $864,616
3. CTC-A, $623,514
4. Enersis, $617,467
5. Copec, $160,69
6. Labchile, $158,780
7. Chilectra, $145,723
8. Soquimich B, $131,009
9. Sta Isabel, $114,506
10. D&S, $113,601

Source: *SSB Guide to World Equity Markets (annual)*, 1998, p. 130.

Sao Paolo Stock Exchange

★3851★
LARGEST LISTED COMPANIES ON THE SAO PAOLO STOCK EXCHANGE, 1997
Ranked by: Market value, in millions of U.S. dollars. **Number listed:** 20

1. Telebras, with $35,028.98 million
2. Electrobras, $26,834.66
3. Petrobras, $21,074.56
4. Telesp, $14,106.49
5. Bradesco, $9,261.35
6. Vale do Rio Doce, $7,511.00
7. Eletropaulo, $6,949.92
8. Sabesp, $6,604.63
9. Cemig, $5,287.68
10. Itaubanco, $5,221.15

Source: *SSB Guide to World Equity Markets (annual)*, 1998, p. 99.

★3852★
MOST ACTIVELY TRADED SHARES ON THE SAO PAOLO STOCK EXCHANGE, 1997
Ranked by: Trading value, in millions of U.S. dollars ($). **Number listed:** 20

1. Telebras (nominative preferred), with $78,826.49 million
2. Petrobras (nominative preferred), $7,694.17
3. Eletrobras (nominative common), $5,741.15
4. Telebras (nominative common), $5,432.85
5. Eletrobras (nominative preferred class B), $5,185.59
6. Telesp (nominative preferred), $3,400.38
7. Cemig (nominative preferred), $2,984.41
8. Vale do Rio Doce (nominative preferred), $2,623.34
9. Brahma (nominative preferred), $1,792.11
10. Bradesco (nominative preferred), $1,635.27

Source: *SSB Guide to World Equity Markets (annual)*, 1998, p. 100.

Sausage

★3853★
TOP MANUFACTURERS OF REFRIGERATED DINNER SAUSAGES, 1997
Ranked by: Sales, in millions of dollars. **Remarks:** Includes percent change, dollar share type, unit sales, percent change from previous year and unit share type. **Number listed:** 16

1. Hillshire Farm, with $289,561,568 million
2. Eckrich, $83,574,216
3. Private Label, $48,995,120
4. Bryan, $35,432,288
5. Thorn Apple Valley Inc., $33,696,736
6. Johnsonville, $28,092,764
7. Bryan Smoky Hollow, $19,546,154
8. Healthy Choice, $19,147,560
9. Mr. Turkey, $15,729,978
10. Butterball, $14,597,670

Source: *National Provisioner*, July, 1998, p. 38.

Savings and Loan Associations—Detroit Metropolitan Area

★3854★
DETROIT'S LARGEST SAVINGS AND LOAN ASSOCIATIONS, 1997
Ranked by: Assets, in millions of dollars. **Remarks:** Includes prior year assets, earnings, total loans, non performing assets, percent return on average equity, and percent return on average assets. **Number listed:** 6

1. Standard Federal Bank, with $16,414.6 million
2. Flagstar Bancorp, $1,901.1
3. D&N Financial Corp., $1,815.3
4. Sterling Bank & Trust F.S.B., $1,027.1
5. Dearborn Federal Savings Bank, $221.5
6. Home Federal Savings Bank of Detroit, $25.5

Source: *Crain's Detroit Business*, Crain's Book of Lists Detroit (annual), December 28, 1998, p. 146.

Savings and Loan Associations--Great Britain

★3855★
GREAT BRITAIN'S LARGEST SAVINGS AND LOAN ASSOCIATIONS, 1998
Ranked by: Assets, in millions of British pounds. **Number listed:** 20

1. Nationwide, with £46,302
2. Britannia, £12,620
3. Yorkshire, £9,294
4. Portman, £5,565
5. Coventry, £5,231
6. Skipton, £4,269
7. Chelsea, £4,018
8. Leeds & Holbeck, £3,171
9. Derbyshire, £2,441
10. West Bromwich, £2,156

Source: *Investor's Chronicle*, May 28, 1999, p. 36.

Savings and Loan Associations--New Jersey

★3856★
NEW JERSEY'S LARGEST SAVINGS AND LOAN ASSOCIATIONS, 1999
Ranked by: Total assets, in millions of dollars. **Remarks:** Includes total deposits, number of branches, CEO and URL address. **Number listed:** 25

1. Hudson City Savings Bank, with $7,313,999 million
2. Investors Savings Bank, $3,331,544
3. Provident Savings Bank, $2,060,205
4. Columbia Savings Bank, $1,617,081
5. Ocean Financial, $1,510,900
6. Penn Fed Financial Service, $1,475,500
7. First Source Bancorp, $1,049,300
8. Spencer Savings Bank, $944,517
9. Kearny Federal Savings, $776,792
10. IBS Financial Corp., $734,700

Source: *New Jersey Business*, Book of Lists (annual), 1999, p. 8.

Savings and Loan Associations—Philadelphia Metropolitan Area

★3857★
PHILADELPHIA METROPOLITAN AREA'S LARGEST SAVINGS AND LOAN ASSOCIATIONS, 1999*
Ranked by: Local deposits, in thousands of dollars. **Remarks:** Includes total assets, total deposits, net loans, net income, number of offices, chairman and president. **Number listed:** 24

1. Beneficial Savings Bank, with $1,255,488 thousand
2. Commonwealth Bank, $1,146,640
3. Firstrust Bank, $865,896
4. Sovereign Bank, $494,894
5. Farmers & Mechanics Bank, $475,358
6. Fox Chase Federal Savings Bank, $430,713
7. Third Federal Savings Bank, $345,661
8. First Savings Bank of Perkasie, $345,141
9. Willow Grove Bank, $309,727
10. Progress Financial Corp., $300,685

Source: *The +Business Lists*, Philadelphia Business Journal (annual), October 2, 1999, p. 18.

School Bonds

★3858★
TOP BOND COUNSEL FOR EDUCATION, 1997
Ranked by: Amount of issues, in thousands of dollars. **Remarks:** Includes number of issues. **Number listed:** 10

1. Chapman and Cutler, with $2,876,300 thousand
2. Orrick, Herrington & Sutcliffe, $1,927,900
3. Squire, Sanders & Dempsey, $1,888,700
4. McCall, Parkhurst & Horton, $1,681,900
5. Fulbright & Jaworski, $1,455,400
6. Hawkins, Delafield & Wood, $1,397,400
7. Thrun, Maatsch & Nordberg, $1,377,000
8. Kutak Rock, $1,163,400
9. Sherman & Howard, $932,300
10. Vinson & Elkins, $912,000

Source: *Bond Buyer Yearbook (annual)*, 1998, p. 113.

★3859★
TOP EDUCATIONAL BOND ISSUERS, 1997
Ranked by: Amount of issues, in thousands of dollars. **Remarks:** Includes number of issues. **Number listed:** 25

1. New York State Dormitory Authority, with $1,187,900 million
2. Chicago School Reform Board of Trustees, IL, $1,000,000
3. Ohio, $723,800
4. North Carolina, $645,000
5. California State Public Works Board, $622,900
6. Los Angeles Unified School District, $617,400
7. Cincinnati Student Loan Funding Corp, OH, $555,000
8. California Educational Facilities Authority, $442,100
9. Denver School District No. 1, CO, $384,200
10. Virginia Public School Authority, $372,300

Source: *Bond Buyer Yearbook (annual)*, 1998, p. 113.

School Food Service

★3860★
LEADING SCHOOL DISTRICTS IN FOOD PURCHASES, 1997-1998
Ranked by: Total purchases, in millions of dollars. **Remarks:** Includes value of commodity, number of schools, enrollment, number of meals served, percent of breakfast and brands. **Number listed:** 10

1. New York City Board of Education, with $127.5 million
2. Los Angeles Unified School District, $86.0
3. Chicago Public Schools, $70.5
4. Dade County Schools, $37.1
5. Philadelphia School District, $25.2
6. Detroit Public Schools, $16.0
7. Broward County Schools, $18.8
8. Hawaii Statewide School System (Honolulu), $34.0
9. Hillsborough County Schools (Tampa, FL), $18.0
10. Dallas Independent School District, $15.0

Source: *Restaurants & Institutions (annual)*, Institutional Giants, September 15, 1998, p. 78.

School Supplies

★3861★
TOP PLACES CONSUMERS SHOP FOR SCHOOL SUPPLIES, 1998
Ranked by: Shoppers, in percent. **Number listed:** 6

1. Discount Stores, with 76%
2. Office Superstore, 30%
3. Drugstores, 23%
4. Wholesales Clubs, 16%
5. Supermarkets, 15%
6. Other, 20%

Source: *Discount Store News*, November 9, 1998, p. 113.

Scientific Instruments and Apparatus

★3862★
TOP CORPORATIONS IN THE SCIENTIFIC, PHOTOGRAPHIC, AND CONTROL EQUIPMENT INDUSTRY, 1998
Ranked by: Revenue, in millions of dollars. **Remarks:** Also notes profits and investment figures as well as number of employees. **Number listed:** 11

1. Minnesota Mining & Manufacturing, with $15,021 million
2. Eastman Kodak, $13,406
3. Applied Materials, $4,042
4. Tektronix, $2,086
5. Polaroid, $1,846
6. Beckman Coulter, $1,718
7. Perkin-Elmer, $1,531
8. Teradyne, $1,489
9. Varian Associates, $1,422
10. EG & G, $1,408

Source: *Fortune*, Fortune 500 Largest U.S. Corporations (annual), April 26, 1999, p. F-68.

Scientific Instruments and Apparatus, International

★3863★
WORLD'S LARGEST SCIENTIFIC, PHOTOGRAPHIC, AND CONTROL EQUIPMENT CORPORATIONS BY REVENUE, 1997
Ranked by: Revenue, in millions of dollars. **Number listed:** 3

1. Minnesota Mining & Manufacturing (U.S.), with $15,070 million
2. Eastman Kodak (U.S.), $14,713
3. Fuji Photo Film (Japan), $11,226

Source: *Fortune*, The Global 500: World's Biggest Corporations (annual), August 3, 1998, p. F-24.

Scotch

★3864★
BEST-SELLING BRANDS OF SCOTCH, 1997
Ranked by: Number of 9-liter cases sold, in thousands. **Remarks:** Includes previous 5 years' sales and percent change from 1996. **Number listed:** 6

1. Dewar's, with 1,445 thousand cases
2. Johnnie Walker Red, 895
3. J&B, 644
4. Chivas Regal, 500
5. Johnnie Walker Black, 485
6. Cutty Sark, 320

Source: *Adams Liquor Handbook*, (annual), Adams Media Inc., 1998, p. 92.

★3865★
LEADING METROPOLITAN AREAS FOR SCOTCH BY SALES, 1997
Ranked by: Number of 9-liter cases sold, in thousands. **Remarks:** Includes percent share of total sales. **Number listed:** 50

1. New York, NY, with 655.3 thousand cases
2. Los Angeles-Long Beach, CA, 404.3
3. Chicago, IL, 268.3
4. Nassau-Suffolk, NY, 256.4
5. Washington, DC, 245.6
6. Boston-Lawrence-Lowell-Brockton, MA, 227.7
7. Tampa-St. Petersburg-Clearwater, FL, 178.8
8. Newark, NJ, 168.9
9. Philadelphia, PA, 167.0
10. Miami-Hialeah, FL, 156.0

Source: *Adams Liquor Handbook*, (annual), Adams Media Inc., 1998, p. 91.

★3866★
TOP MARKETS FOR SCOTCH BY CASES SOLD PER THOUSAND ADULTS, 1997
Ranked by: Number of 9-liter cases sold, per thousand adults. **Remarks:** Also notes 1996 sales figures and ranking. **Number listed:** 51

1. District of Columbia, with 180.1 thousand cases
2. New Hampshire, 180.1
3. New Jersey, 106.2
4. New York, 97.2
5. Nevada, 96.5
6. Florida, 96.5
7. Delaware, 76.0
8. Connecticut, 75.4
9. Massachusetts, 71.8
10. California, 65.7

Source: *Adams Liquor Handbook*, (annual), Adams Media Inc., 1998, p. 90.

★3867★
TOP MARKETS FOR SCOTCH BY SALES, 1997
Ranked by: Number of 9-liter cases sold. **Remarks:** Includes 1996 sales figures, percent change, 1997 share and 1997 cumulative share. **Number listed:** 51

1. California, with 1,440,970 9-liter cases
2. New York, 1,256,170
3. Florida, 1,024,360
4. New Jersey, 608,410
5. Texas, 552,210
6. Illinois, 372,670
7. Massachusetts, 321,530
8. Pennsylvania, 260,470
9. Georgia, 233,000
10. Maryland, 207,150

Source: *Adams Liquor Handbook*, (annual), Adams Media Inc., 1998, p. 90.

★3868★
TOP SINGLE MALT SCOTCH BRANDS, 1997
Ranked by: Number of 9-liter cases sold, in thousands. **Remarks:** Includes sales figures for previous 5 years and percent of change from 1996. **Number listed:** 19

1. Glenlivet, with 175 thousand cases
2. Glenfiddich, 105
3. Macallan, 52
4. Glenmorangie, 27
5. Balvenie, 23
6. Lagavulin, 15
7. McClellands, 14
8. Glen Deveron, 13
9. Dalmore, 12
10. Aberlour, 12

Source: *Adams Liquor Handbook*, (annual), Adams Media Inc., 1998, p. 92.

Scotch--Advertising

★3869★
SCOTCH BRANDS WITH THE HIGHEST MAGAZINE ADVERTISING EXPENDITURES, 1997
Ranked by: Total magazine advertising expenditures, in thousands of dollars. **Remarks:** Also notes newspaper, outdoor and total advertising expenditures for previous year. **Number listed:** 17

1. Dewar's, with $9,127.9 thousand
2. Johnnie Walker Black, $5,402.1
3. Chivas Regal, $5,059.1
4. The Glenlivet, $3,782.9
5. Johnnie Walker Red, $2,962.6
6. Glenfiddich, $1,889.3
7. The Macallan, $919.8
8. Cutty Sark, $838.4
9. Classic Malt - UD USA, $819.8
10. Johnnie Walker Blue & Gold, $659.8

Source: *Adams Liquor Handbook*, (annual), Adams Media Inc., 1998, p. 95.

★3870★
SCOTCH BRANDS WITH THE HIGHEST NEWSPAPER ADVERTISING EXPENDITURES, 1997
Ranked by: Total newspaper advertising expenditures, in thousands of dollars. **Remarks:** Also notes magazine, outdoor and total advertising expenditures for previous year. **Number listed:** 7

1. The Macallan, with $1,035.0 thousand
2. Dewar's, $800.1
3. Chivas Regal, $177.7
4. J&B, $171.2
5. Johnnie Walker Black, $73.3
6. Famous Grouse, $71.9
7. Glenfiddich, $4.5

Source: *Adams Liquor Handbook*, (annual), Adams Media Inc., 1998, p. 95.

★3871★
SCOTCH BRANDS WITH THE HIGHEST OUTDOOR ADVERTISING EXPENDITURES, 1997
Ranked by: Total outdoor advertising expenditures, in thousands of dollars. **Remarks:** Also notes newspaper, magazine and total advertising expenditures for previous year. **Number listed:** 17

1. Johnnie Walker Red, with $811.0 thousand
2. Chivas Regal, $414.2
3. Classic Malt - UD USA, $375.0
4. Dewar's, $228.4
5. Scotch - UD USA, $211.3
6. Johnnie Walker Black, $46.0
7. Cutty Sark, $11.3
8. Buchanan, $9.9
9. J&B, $9.0
10. The Glenlivet, $3.8

Source: *Adams Liquor Handbook*, (annual), Adams Media Inc., 1998, p. 95.

★3872★
SCOTCH BRANDS WITH THE HIGHEST TOTAL ADVERTISING EXPENDITURES, 1997
Ranked by: Total advertising expenditures, in thousands of dollars. **Remarks:** Also notes magazine, newspaper, outdoor and total advertising expenditures forrevious year. **Number listed:** 17

1. Dewar's, with $10,156.4 thousand
2. Chivas Regal, $5,975.7
3. Johnnie Walker Black, $5,524.0

4. The Glenlivet, $3,786.7
5. Johnnie Walker Red, $3,773.6
6. Cutty Sark, $2,487.3
7. The Macallan, $1,954.8
8. Glenfiddich, $1,893.8
9. Classic Malt - UD USA, $1,194.8
10. Johnnie Walker Blue & Gold, $659.8

Source: *Adams Liquor Handbook*, (annual), Adams Media Inc., 1998, p. 95.

Seafood

★3873★
LEADING SEAFOOD RESTAURANTS, 1997
Ranked by: Sales, in millions of dollars. **Remarks:** Includes rank in the top 400. **Number listed:** 15

1. Red Lobster, with $1,900.0 million
2. Long John Silver's Seafood Shoppes, $846.2
3. Captain D's, $464.4
4. Joe's Crab Shack, $134.1
5. Landry's Seafood House, $120.7
6. Legal Sea Foods, $80.3
7. Shells Seafood Restaurants, $74.9
8. C.A. Muer Corp., $67.5
9. The Crab House, $56.3
10. Rusty Pelican, $45.0

Source: *Restaurants & Institutions*, July 15, 1998, p. 103.

★3874★
TOP SEAFOOD RESTAURANTS BY EACH CHAIN'S SATISFACTION INDEX, 1997
Ranked by: Satisfaction index score based on response to survey. **Remarks:** Includes breakdown of score into categories. **Number listed:** 3

1. Red Lobster
2. Captain D's
3. Long John Silver's

Source: *Restaurants & Institutions*, Choice in Chains (annual), March 1, 1999, p. 90.

Seaports

See: **Ports**

Securities Exchange of Thailand

★3875★
LARGEST LISTED COMPANIES ON THE SECURITIES EXCHANGES OF THAILAND, 1997
Ranked by: Market value, in millions of U.S. dollars ($). **Number listed:** 20

1. PTT Exploration and Production, with $2,689.94 million
2. The Bangkok Bank, $1,822.82
3. Thai Airways International, $1,585.18
4. Advanced Info Service, $1,148.95
5. The Thai Farmers Bank, $1,015.87
6. BEC World, $812.69
7. Electricity Generating, $706.0
8. Siam Cement, $609.52
9. Delta Electronics, $507.93
10. Bangkok Expressway, $435.92

Source: *SSB Guide to World Equity Markets (annual)*, Euromoney Publications, 1998, p. 493.

★3876★
MOST ACTIVELY TRADED SHARES ON THE SECURITIES EXCHANGES OF THAILAND, 1997
Ranked by: Trading value, in millions of U.S. dollars ($). **Number listed:** 20

1. Thai Farmers Bank, with $3,103.46 million
2. The Bangkok Bank, $3,047.10
3. Industrial Finance Corp. of Thailand, $2,258.02
4. PTT Exploration and Production, $774.41
5. Telecom Asia Corporation, $752.79
6. Phatra Thanakit, $752.34
7. Siam Cement, $751.20
8. Safari World, $710.25
9. Advanced Info Service, $635.26
10. Siam Commercial Bank, $600.54

Source: *SSB Guide to World Equity Markets (annual)*, Euromoney Publications, 1998, p. 493.

Securities--Initial Public Offerings

★3877★
BEST INITIAL PUBLIC OFFERINGS IN ELECTRONICS, 1997
Ranked by: Proceeds, in millions of dollars. **Remarks:** Includes location and description of business. **Number listed:** 50

1. Amkor Technology Inc., with $388.0 million
2. J. D. Edwards & Co., $363.4
3. Celestica Inc., $360.5
4. Hypercom Corp., $180.0
5. L-3 Communications Holdings Inc., $132.0
6. Arm Holdings PLC, $114.1
7. Stoneridge Inc., $102.4
8. Software Systems Inc., $100.1
9. Excel Switching Corp., $94.5
10. QAD Inc., $86.3

Source: *Electronic Business*, 9, 1998, p. 52.

★3878★
BEST UNDERWRITERS FOR TECHNICAL INITIAL PUBLIC OFFERING, 1998
Ranked by: Proceeds, in millions of dollars. **Remarks:** Includes market share and number of issues for current and previous year. **Number listed:** 15

1. Morgan Stanley Dean Witter, with $1,116.9 million
2. Goldman, Sachs, $755.5
3. Salomon Smith Barney, $700.5
4. BankBoston, $298.3
5. Deutsche Bank, $228.8
6. Bankers Trust, $225.5
7. Merrill Lynch, $150.4
8. Bank of America, $139.8
9. Lehman Brothers, $105.6
10. Hambrecht & Quist, $97.3

Source: *Investment Dealers' Digest*, February 8, 1999, p. 20.

Securities—Initial Public Offerings--Great Britain

★3879★
BEST INITIAL PUBLIC OFFERINGS BY COMPANIES IN THE U.K., 1998
Ranked by: Global amount, in millions of U.S. dollars. **Remarks:** Includes offer date and book manager. **Number listed:** 10

1. Thomson Travel Group PLC, with $2,786.9 million
2. Computacenter Ltd., $486.6
3. Coca-Cola Beverages, $374.4
4. Amdocs Ltd., $252.0
5. New Look, $211.9
6. IT Net PLC, $206.2
7. Lloyd's of London Press (LLP), $150.3
8. Shire Pharmaceuticals Group, $121.1
9. ICO Global Communications, $120.0
10. ARM Holdings PLC, $114.1

Source: *Investment Dealers Digest*, January 25, 1999, p. 32.

Securities—Initial Public Offerings, International

★3880★
BEST INTERNATIONAL INITIAL PUBLIC OFFERINGS, 1998
Ranked by: Value, in billions of U.S. dollars. **Remarks:** Includes percent of share. **Number listed:** 10

1. Goldman Sachs, with $18.89 billion
2. Warburg Dillon Read, $12.78
3. Morgan Stanley, $9.54
4. Merrill Lynch, $7.37
5. Credit Suisse First Boston, $6.13
6. ABN AMRO, $5.56
7. J. P. Morgan, $5.19
8. Paribas, $4.81
9. Salomon Smith Barney International, $3.84
10. Deutsche Morgan Grenfell, $3.65

Source: *FT*, December 31, 1998, p. 13.

Securities--Privately Placed

★3881★
TOP ACQUISITION-RELATED PRIVATE PLACEMENT SECURITIES MANAGERS, 1998
Ranked by: Amount, in millions of dollars. **Remarks:** Includes percent and number of issues as well as figures for 1997. **Number listed:** 15

1. Credit Suisse First Boston, with $702.1 million
2. Morgan Stanley Dean Witter, $468.3
3. J.P. Morgan, $383.7
4. Merrill Lynch, $338.7
5. BankAmerica Corp., $223.9
6. Goldman, Sachs, $220.0
7. Chase Manhattan Corp., $186.0
8. Greenwich/Gleacher Natwest, $172.2
9. CIBC Wood Gundy Sccuritics, $169.0
10. Warburg Dillon Read, $165.5
11. ABN AMRO, $165.5

Source: *Investment Dealers' Digest*, Private Placement Sweepstakes (annual), March 15, 1999, p. 22.

★3882★
TOP DIRECT PRIVATE PLACEMENT INVESTORS, 1997
Ranked by: Total direct investments, in millions of dollars. **Remarks:** Includes percentage of portfolio. **Number listed:** 15

1. The Prudential Insurance Co. of America, with $2,886.0 million
2. John Hancock, $561.5
3. Teachers Insurance, $499.0
4. Travelers Insurance Co., $390.0
5. The Northwestern Mutual Life Insurance Co., $360.9
6. New York Life Insurance Co., $316.0
7. Hartford Investment Management Co., $232.0
8. Metropolitan Life Insurance Co., $200.0
9. Pacific Life Insurance Co., $133.0
10. The Principal Financial Group, $112.0

Source: *Investments Dealers' Digest*, Private Placement Investors' Survey (annual), August 10, 1998, p. 20.

★3883★
TOP EQUITY PRIVATE PLACEMENT SECURITIES MANAGERS, 1998
Ranked by: Amount, in millions of dollars. **Remarks:** Includes percent and number of issues as well as figures for 1997. **Number listed:** 15

1. Merrill Lynch, with $23,348.3 million
2. Donaldson, Lufkin & Jenrette, $17,790.0
3. Salomon Smith Barney, $7,204.0
4. Credit Suisse First Boston, $5,273.8
5. Morgan Stanley Dean Witter, $3,726.3
6. J.P. Morgan, $3,706.0
7. BankAmerica Corp., $2,781.7
8. Bank of Tokyo-Mitsubishi, $2,500.7
9. Goldman, Sachs, $2,436.5
10. Bankers Trust, $2,000.7

Source: *Investment Dealers' Digest*, Private Placement Sweepstakes (annual), March 15, 1999, p. 21.

★3884★
TOP HIGH YIELD PRIVATE PLACEMENT SECURITIES MANAGERS, 1998
Ranked by: Amount, in millions of dollars. **Remarks:** Includes percent and number of issues as well as figures for 1997. **Number listed:** 15

1. Salomon Smith Barney, with $11,226.9 million
2. Chase Manhattan Corp., $10,607.4
3. Morgan Stanley Dean Witter, $9,680.6
4. Goldman, Sachs, $9,164.0
5. Donaldson, Lufkin & Jenrette, $9,097.2
6. BankAmerica Corp., $7,374.9
7. Bankers Trust, $6,485.5
8. Merrill Lynch, $6,362.4
9. Lehman Brothers, $5,144.7
10. Credit Suisse First Boston, $4,908.8

Source: *Investment Dealers' Digest*, Private Placement Sweepstakes (annual), March 15, 1999, p. 19.

★3885★
TOP INVESTORS IN PRIVATE PLACEMENT SECURITIES BY VOLUME, 1997
Ranked by: Volume, in millions of dollars. **Remarks:** Includes expected volume, actual vs. expected volume, expected volume for 1998, volume for 1996, actual vs. expected volume for 1996 and 1997 and total portfolio. **Number listed:** 40

1. The Prudential Insurance Co. of America, with $6,021.0 million

2. John Hancock, $5,663.8
3. Teachers Insurance, $4,850.0
4. Hartford Investment Management Co., $3,400.0
5. The Northwestern Mutual Life Insurance Co., $3,370.0
6. New York Life Insurance Co., $3,173.0
7. CIGNA Investment Management, $2,749.0
8. Metropolitan Life Insurance Co., $2,560.0
9. American General Corp., $2,419.0
10. The Principal Financial Group, $2,293.8

Source: *Investments Dealers' Digest*, Private Placement Investors' Survey (annual), August 10, 1998, p. 17.

★3886★
TOP NON-CONVERTIBLE PREFERRED PRIVATE PLACEMENT SECURITIES MANAGERS, 1998
Ranked by: Amount, in millions of dollars. **Remarks:** Includes percent and number of issues as well as figures for 1997. **Number listed:** 15

1. Merrill Lynch, with $3,560.5 million
2. Lehman Brothers, $2,858.3
3. Goldman, Sachs, $1,894.0
4. Salomon Smith Barney, $1,180.2
5. Morgan Stanley Dean Witter, $982.2
6. Bankers Trust, $969.3
7. Donaldson, Lufkin & Jenrette, $914.1
8. J.P. Morgan, $561.9
9. First Union Corp., $420.0
10. Credit Suisse First Boston, $338.1

Source: *Investment Dealers' Digest*, Private Placement Sweepstakes (annual), March 15, 1999, p. 20.

★3887★
TOP PLAIN-VANILLA DEBT MANAGERS, EXCLUDING FUNDS AND TRUSTS PRIVATE PLACEMENT SECURITIES, 1998
Ranked by: Amount, in millions of dollars. **Remarks:** Includes percent and number of issues as well as figures for 1997. **Number listed:** 15

1. BankAmerica Corp., with $8,798.3 million
2. Merrill Lynch, $4,275.7
3. Salomon Smith Barney, $3,439.4
4. J.P. Morgan, $3,324.2
5. Credit Suisse First Boston, $3,301.6
6. Goldman, Sachs, $3,013.4
7. Chase Manhattan Corp., $2,888.6
8. Morgan Stanley Dean Witter, $2,342.6
9. Bank One Corp., $1,863.7
10. Lehman Brothers, $1,835.3

Source: *Investment Dealers' Digest*, Private Placement Sweepstakes (annual), March 15, 1999, p. 20.

★3888★
TOP PLAIN-VANILLA DEBT MANAGERS, INCLUDING FUNDS AND TRUST PRIVATE PLACEMENT SECURITIES, 1998
Ranked by: Amount, in millions of dollars. **Remarks:** Includes percent and number of issues as well as figures for 1997. **Number listed:** 15

1. BankAmerica Corp., with $8,798.3 million
2. J.P. Morgan, $6,194.9
3. Lehman Brothers, $5,586.4
4. Merrill Lynch, $4,275.7
5. Salomon Smith Barney, $3,569.4
6. Credit Suisse First Boston, $3,301.6
7. Goldman, Sachs, $3,013.4
8. Chase Manhattan Corp., $2,888.6
9. Morgan Stanley Dean Witter, $2,342.6
10. Bank One Corp., $1,863.7

Source: *Investment Dealers' Digest*, Private Placement Sweepstakes (annual), March 15, 1999, p. 20.

★3889★
TOP PLAIN-VANILLA EQUITY PRIVATE PLACEMENT SECURITIES MANAGERS, 1998
Ranked by: Amount, in millions of dollars. **Remarks:** Includes percent and number of issues as well as figures for 1997. **Number listed:** 15

1. Merrill Lynch, with $22,667.5 million
2. Donaldson, Lufkin & Jenrette, $17,206.0
3. Salomon Smith Barney, $6,407.8
4. Credit Suisse First Boston, $4,573.4
5. Morgan Stanley Dean Witter, $3,444.9
6. J.P. Morgan, $3,122.7
7. BankAmerica Corp., $2,573.9
8. Bankers Trust, $1,830.8
9. Goldman, Sachs, $1,500.9
10. Chase Manhattan Corp., $1,344.2

Source: *Investment Dealers' Digest*, Private Placement Sweepstakes (annual), March 15, 1999, p. 21.

★3890★
TOP PRIVATE PLACEMENT SECURITIES MANAGERS EXCLUDING MTNS, 1998
Ranked by: Amount, in millions of dollars. **Remarks:** Includes percent and number of issues as well as figures for 1997. **Number listed:** 15

1. Merrill Lynch, with $50,887.5 million
2. Donaldson, Lufkin & Jenrette, $35,115.4
3. Lehman Brothers, $34.478.3
4. Credit Suisse First Boston, $34,375.5
5. Salomon Smith Barney, $32,417.4
6. Morgan Stanley Dean Witter, $28,961.9
7. Chase Manhattan Corp., $27,440.8
8. Goldman, Sachs, $26,055.2
9. BankAmerica Corp., $25,835.7
10. J.P. Morgan, $19,770.9

Source: *Investment Dealers' Digest*, Private Placement Sweepstakes (annual), March 15, 1999, p. 18.

★3891★
TOP PRIVATE PLACEMENT SECURITIES MANAGERS EXCLUDING SELF FUNDING, 1998
Ranked by: Amount, in millions of dollars. **Remarks:** Includes percent and number of issues as well as figures for 1997. **Number listed:** 15

1. Merrill Lynch, with $50,744.7 million
2. Salomon Smith Barney, $32,289.1
3. Donaldson, Lufkin & Jenrette, $32,289.1
4. Morgan Stanley Dean Witter, $30,418.8
5. Chase Manhattan Corp., $27,935.0
6. Goldman, Sachs, $27,091.0
7. BankAmerica Corp., $26,031.6
8. Credit Suisse First Boston, $25,943.8
9. Lehman Brothers, $21,916.5
10. J.P. Morgan, $19,924.6

Source: *Investment Dealers' Digest*, Private Placement Sweepstakes (annual), March 15, 1999, p. 18.

★3892★
TOP PRIVATE PLACEMENT SECURITIES MANAGERS, 1998
Ranked by: Amount, in millions of dollars. **Remarks:** Includes percent and number of issues as well as figures for 1997. **Number listed:** 15

1. Merrill Lynch, with $55,864.6 million
2. Credit Suisse First Boston, $41,159.3
3. Lehman Brothers, $36,871.9

4. Donaldson, Lufkin & Jenrette, $35,125.4
5. Salomon Smith Barney, $34,906.9
6. Goldman, Sachs, $34,751.6
7. Morgan Stanley Dean Witter, $31,231.7
8. Chase Manhattan Corp., $28,215.4
9. BankAmerica Corp., $26,031.6
10. J.P. Morgan, $20,004.2

Source: *Investment Dealers' Digest*, Private Placement Sweepstakes (annual), March 15, 1999, p. 18.

★3893★
TOP RULE 144A EQUITY PRIVATE PLACEMENT SECURITIES MANAGERS, 1998
Ranked by: Amount, in millions of dollars. **Remarks:** Includes percent and number of issues as well as figures for 1997. **Number listed:** 15

1. Morgan Stanley Dean Witter, with $3,701.3 million
2. Salomon Smith Barney, $3,418.6
3. Merrill Lynch, $2,392.2
4. Goldman, Sachs, $2,252.7
5. BankAmerica Corp., $1,967.8
6. Donaldson, Lufkin & Jenrette, $1,228.6
7. Credit Suisse First Boston, $1,132.5
8. Lehman Brothers, $985.9
9. J.P. Morgan, $850.9
10. Schroder Group, $712.4

Source: *Investment Dealers' Digest*, Private Placement Sweepstakes (annual), March 15, 1999, p. 24.

★3894★
TOP RULE 144A EXCLUDING SELF FUNDING PRIVATE PLACEMENT SECURITIES MANAGERS, 1998
Ranked by: Amount, in millions of dollars. **Remarks:** Includes percent and number of issues as well as figures for 1997. **Number listed:** 15

1. Morgan Stanley Dean Witter, with $28,877.9 million
2. Goldman, Sachs, $26,825.7
3. Salomon Smith Barney, $26,774.2
4. Merrill Lynch, $24,852.5
5. Credit Suisse First Boston, $21,636.7
6. Chase Manhattan Corp., $19,979.6
7. Lehman Brothers, $19,190.7
8. BankAmerica Corp., $16,695.5
9. Donaldson, Lufkin & Jenrette, $15,265.4
10. J.P. Morgan, $15,245.0

Source: *Investment Dealers' Digest*, Private Placement Sweepstakes (annual), March 15, 1999, p. 23.

★3895★
TOP RULE 144A HIGH YIELD PRIVATE PLACEMENT SECURITIES MANAGERS, 1998
Ranked by: Amount, in millions of dollars. **Remarks:** Includes percent and number of issues as well as figures for 1997. **Number listed:** 15

1. Salomon Smith Barney, with $11,156.9 million
2. Chase Manhattan Corp., $10,362.4
3. Morgan Stanley Dean Witter, $9,680.6
4. Goldman, Sachs, $9,144.8
5. Donaldson, Lufkin & Jenrette, $9,097.2
6. BankAmerica Corp., $7,374.9
7. Bankers Trust, $6,470.5
8. Merrill Lynch, $6,079.3
9. Lehman Brothers, $5,094.4
10. Credit Suisse First Boston, $4,863.8

Source: *Investment Dealers' Digest*, Private Placement Sweepstakes (annual), March 15, 1999, p. 23.

★3896★
TOP RULE 144A NON-CONVERTIBLE PRIVATE PLACEMENT SECURITIES MANAGERS, 1998
Ranked by: Amount, in millions of dollars. **Remarks:** Includes percent and number of issues as well as figures for 1997. **Number listed:** 15

1. Lehman Brothers, with $2,487.6 million
2. Merrill Lynch, $2,090.5
3. Goldman Sachs, $1,894.0
4. Salomon Smith Barney, $1,180.2
5. Morgan Stanley Dean Witter, $982.2
6. Donaldson, Lufkin & Jenrette, $721.1
7. First Union Corp., $410.0
8. J.P. Morgan, $407.1
9. Tokai Bank, $333.3
10. Fuji Bank, $320.0

Source: *Investment Dealers' Digest*, Private Placement Sweepstakes (annual), March 15, 1999, p. 25.

★3897★
TOP RULE 144A PRIVATE PLACEMENT BY FOREIGN ISSUERS SECURITIES MANAGERS, 1998
Ranked by: Amount, in millions of dollars. **Remarks:** Includes percent and number of issues as well as figures for 1997. **Number listed:** 15

1. Goldman, Sachs, with $14,630.9 million
2. Credit Suisse First Boston, $14,039.9
3. Merrill Lynch, $8,657.5
4. Morgan Stanley Dean Witter, $7,611.8
5. Salomon Smith Barney, $7,381.5
6. Lehman Brothers, $6,059.1
7. J.P. Morgan, $5,098.8
8. Chase Manhattan Corp., $3,935.4
9. CIBC Wood Gundy Securities, $3,479.2
10. Donaldson, Lufkin & Jenrette, $3,135.5

Source: *Investment Dealers' Digest*, Private Placement Sweepstakes (annual), March 15, 1999, p. 24.

★3898★
TOP RULE 144A PRIVATE PLACEMENT BY U.S. ISSUERS SECURITIES MANAGERS, 1998
Ranked by: Amount, in millions of dollars. **Remarks:** Includes percent and number of issues as well as figures for 1997. **Number listed:** 15

1. Morgan Stanley Dean Witter, with $22,079.0 million
2. Lehman Brothers, $22,000.3
3. Goldman, Sachs, $19,763.1
4. Salomon Smith Barney, $19,392.7
5. Merrill Lynch, $18,991.6
6. Credit Suisse First Boston, $16,342.5
7. Chase Manhattan Corp., $16,108.7
8. BankAmerica Corp., $14,356.3
9. Donaldson, Lufkin & Jenrette, $13,936.2
10. J.P. Morgan, $10,225.9

Source: *Investment Dealers' Digest*, Private Placement Sweepstakes (annual), March 15, 1999, p. 24.

★3899★
TOP RULE 144A PRIVATE PLACEMENT SECURITIES MANAGERS, 1998
Ranked by: Amount, in millions of dollars. **Remarks:** Includes percent and number of issues as well as figures for 1997. **Number listed:** 15

1. Goldman Sachs, with $34,394.1 million
2. Credit Suisse First Boston, $30,382.4
3. Morgan Stanley Dean Witter, $29,690.9
4. Lehman Brothers, $28,059.4
5. Merrill Lynch, $27,649.1
6. Salomon Smith Barney, $26,774.2
7. Chase Manhattan Corp., $20,044.1

8. Donaldson, Lufkin & Jenrette, $17,071.7
9. BankAmerica Corp., $16,695.5
10. J.P. Morgan, $15,324.6

Source: *Investment Dealers' Digest*, Private Placement Sweepstakes (annual), March 15, 1999, p. 22.

★3900★
TOP SECONDARY PRIVATE PLACEMENT INVESTORS, 1997
Ranked by: Total direct investments, in millions of dollars. **Remarks:** Includes percentage of portfolio. **Number listed:** 15

1. Hartford Investment Management Co., with $974.0 million
2. John Hancock, $352.0
3. American General Corp., $287.0
4. The Principal Financial Group, $250.0
5. CIGNA Private Securities, $210.0
6. Great-West Life & Annuity, $209.9
7. Lincoln Investment Management Inc., $194.0
8. New York Life Insurance Co., $174.0
9. Pacific Life Insurance Co., $170.0
10. ING Investment Management, $139.6

Source: *Investments Dealers' Digest*, Private Placement Investors' Survey (annual), August 10, 1998, p. 20.

★3901★
TOP SECURITIZED PRIVATE PLACEMENT SECURITIES MANAGERS, 1998
Ranked by: Amount, in millions of dollars. **Remarks:** Includes percent and number of issues as well as figures for 1997. **Number listed:** 15

1. Credit Suisse First Boston, with $18,111.1 million
2. Lehman Brothers, $17,379.8
3. Merrill Lynch, $10,224.3
4. Chase Manhattan Corp., $9,833.5
5. Morgan Stanley Dean Witter, $8,654.4
6. Goldman, Sachs, $7,353.4
7. Salomon Smith Barney, $6,127.8
8. CIBC Wood Gundy Securities, $5,399.2
9. Bear, Stearns, $4,756.3
10. Donaldson, Lufkin & Jenrette, $4,560.4

Source: *Investment Dealers' Digest*, Private Placement Sweepstakes (annual), March 15, 1999, p. 21.

★3902★
TOP STRAIGHT DEBT PRIVATE PLACEMENT SECURITIES MANAGERS, 1998
Ranked by: Amount, in millions of dollars. **Remarks:** Includes percent and number of issues as well as figures for 1997. **Number listed:** 15

1. Credit Suisse First Boston, with $35,547.4 million
2. Lehman Brothers, $32,792.0
3. Goldman, Sachs, $30,421.2
4. Merrill Lynch, $28,955.8
5. Chase Manhattan Corp., $26,562.6
6. Morgan Stanley Dean Witter, $26,523.3
7. Salomon Smith Barney, $26,522.7
8. BankAmerica Corp., $23,038.8
9. Donaldson, Lufkin & Jenrette, $16,421.4
10. J.P. Morgan, $15,736.2

Source: *Investment Dealers' Digest*, Private Placement Sweepstakes (annual), March 15, 1999, p. 19.

★3903★
TOP TRADITIONAL PRIVATE PLACEMENT SECURITIES MANAGERS, 1998
Ranked by: Amount, in millions of dollars. **Remarks:** Includes percent and number of issues as well as figures for 1997. **Number listed:** 15

1. Bank of America, with $7,420.7 million
2. Credit Suisse First Boston, $1,945.0
3. Merrill Lynch, $1,782.0
4. Chase Manhattan Corp., $1,707.4
5. Bank One Corp., $1,697.5
6. Lehman Brothers, $1,660.3
7. Salomon Smith Barney, $1,235.4
8. J.P. Morgan, $1,217.9
9. Greenwich/Gleacher Natwest, $1,208.0
10. Warburg Dillon Read, $1,187.9

Source: *Investment Dealers' Digest*, Private Placement Sweepstakes (annual), March 15, 1999, p. 19.

★3904★
TOP YANKEE PRIVATE PLACEMENT SECURITIES MANAGERS, 1998
Ranked by: Amount, in millions of dollars. **Remarks:** Includes percent and number of issues as well as figures for 1997. **Number listed:** 15

1. Credit Suisse First Boston, with $21,322.4 million
2. Donaldson, Lufkin & Jenrette, $16,134.8
3. Goldman, Sachs, $14,818.7
4. Merrill Lynch, $13,710.0
5. Salomon Smith Barney, $10,285.4
6. Morgan Stanley Dean Witter, $7,686.8
7. J.P. Morgan, $7,042.1
8. Lehman Brothers, $6,275.0
9. BankAmerica Corp., $5,394.1
10. Chase Manhattan Corp., $4,831.0

Source: *Investment Dealers' Digest*, Private Placement Sweepstakes (annual), March 15, 1999, p. 22.

Security and Investigative Services—Long Island (NY)

★3905★
LARGEST GUARD AND PATROL SERVICES ON LONG ISLAND, 1998
Ranked by: Number of employees. **Remarks:** Includes address, contact, phone, fax, web address, e-mail and services. **Number listed:** 34

1. APC Corporate Security, with 625
2. Unico Security Services, 600
3. Wells Fargo Guard Services, 500
4. Wackenhut Security, 453
5. Empire State Loss Prevention Ltd., 450
6. Pinkerton Security & Investigation, 450
7. Dale System, 427
8. Watchdog Patrols, 375
9. Suburban Security & Investigation Agency, 367
10. Garrison Protective Services, 300

Source: *Long Island Business News*, Long Island Book of Lists (annual), 1999, p. 71.

★3906★
LARGEST SECURITY SYSTEM FIRMS ON LONG ISLAND, 1998
Ranked by: Number of Nassau-Suffolk employees **Remarks:** Includes address, contact, phone, fax, web address, e-mail and services. **Number listed:** 29

1. Slomin's Inc., with 500
2. ADT Security Services, 160
3. Sentry Detection, 110
4. World Wide Security, 100
5. Electronix Systems Central Station Alarms, 84
6. Wells Fargo Alarm Services, 76
7. Lowitt Alarms & Security Systems, 75

8. Alarms Unlimited, 70
9. Universal Security Systems, 66
10. Visiak Security Systems, 55

Source: *Long Island Business News*, Long Island Book of Lists (annual), 1999, p. 86.

Security and Investigative Services—Los Angeles County (CA)

★3907★
LARGEST SECURITY GUARD FIRMS SERVING LOS ANGELES COUNTY, 1999*
Ranked by: Number of L.A. County security personnel. **Remarks:** Includes address, number of companywide personnel, security services, type of investigations, security systems, profile and top local executive. **Number listed:** 25

1. Inter-Con Security Systems Inc., with 3,402
2. Wells Fargo Guard Services, 3,000
3. American Protective Services, 2,700
4. Burns International Security Services, 2,650
5. Shield Security Inc., 2,450
6. Pinkerton's Inc., 1,900
7. Guard Systems Inc., 1,750
8. American Commercial Security Services, 1,500
9. Argenbright Security West Inc., 1,343
10. International Services, 1,300

Source: *Los Angeles Business Journal (annual)*, January 18, 1999, p. 34.

Security Dealers

★3908★
TOP CORPORATE AND OTHER TRADING FIRMS IN COMMERCIAL PAPER, 1998
Ranked by: Bond managers survey. **Number listed:** 5

1. Merrill Lynch & Co.
2. Goldman, Sachs & Co.
3. Lehman Brothers
4. Credit Suisse First Boston
5. J.P. Morgan

Source: *Institutional Investor*, Top Fixed-Income Trading Firms (annual), November, 1998, p. 132.

★3909★
TOP CORPORATE AND OTHER TRADING FIRMS IN HIGH-YIELD CORPORATE BONDS, 1998
Ranked by: Results of a bond managers survey. **Number listed:** 5

1. Merrill Lynch & Co.
2. Donaldson, Lufkin & Jenrette
3. Salomon Smith Barney
4. Bear, Stearns & Co.
5. Goldman, Sachs & Co.

Source: *Institutional Investor*, Top Fixed-Income Trading Firms (annual), November, 1998, p. 132.

★3910★
TOP CORPORATE AND OTHER TRADING FIRMS IN INVESTMENT-GRADE CORPORATE BONDS, 1998
Ranked by: Bond managers survey. **Number listed:** 5

1. Merrill Lynch & Co.
2. Morgan Stanley Dean Witter
3. Salomon Smith Barney
4. Goldman, Sachs & Co.
5. Lehman Brothers

Source: *Institutional Investor*, Top Fixed-Income Trading Firms (annual), November, 1998, p. 132.

★3911★
TOP FIXED-INCOME TRADING FIRMS, 1998
Ranked by: Bond managers survey. **Remarks:** Includes 1997 rank. **Number listed:** 20

1. Merrill Lynch & Co.
2. Lehman Brothers
3. Salomon Smith Barney
4. Goldman, Sachs & Co.
5. Morgan Stanley Dean Witter
6. Bear, Stearns & Co.
7. Credit Suisse First Boston
8. J.P. Morgan
9. Donaldson, Lufkin & Jenrette
10. PaineWebber

Source: *Institutional Investor*, Top Fixed-Income Trading Firms (annual), November, 1998, p. 131.

★3912★
TOP GOVERNMENT/AGENCY TRADING FIRMS IN AGENCY PAPER, 1998
Ranked by: Bond managers survey. **Number listed:** 5

1. Merrill Lynch & Co.
2. Lehman Brothers
3. Salomon Smith Barney
4. Goldman, Sachs & Co.
5. Credit Suisse First Boston

Source: *Institutional Investor*, Top Fixed-Income Trading Firms (annual), November, 1998, p. 135.

★3913★
TOP GOVERNMENT/AGENCY TRADING FIRMS IN INTERMEDIATE AND LONG-TERM TREASURY NOTES, 1998
Ranked by: Bond managers survey. **Number listed:** 5

1. Merrill Lynch & Co.
2. Salomon Smith Barney
3. Goldman, Sachs & Co.
4. Lehman Brothers
5. Morgan Stanley Dean Witter

Source: *Institutional Investor*, Top Fixed-Income Trading Firms (annual), November, 1998, p. 135.

★3914★
TOP GOVERNMENT/AGENCY TRADING FIRMS IN MUNICIPAL BONDS, 1998
Ranked by: Bond managers survey. **Number listed:** 5

1. Salomon Smith Barney
2. Merrill Lynch & Co.
3. Lehman Brothers
4. Goldman, Sachs & Co.
5. PaineWebber

Source: *Institutional Investor*, Top Fixed-Income Trading Firms (annual), November, 1998, p. 135.

★3915★
TOP GOVERNMENT/AGENCY TRADING FIRMS IN REPURCHASE AGREEMENTS, 1998
Ranked by: Bond managers survey. **Number listed:** 5

1. Goldman, Sachs & Co.
2. Morgan Stanley Dean Witter
3. Lehman Brothers
4. Credit Suisse First Boston
5. J. P. Morgan

Source: *Institutional Investor*, Top Fixed-Income Trading Firms (annual), November, 1998, p. 135.

★3916★

TOP GOVERNMENT/AGENCY TRADING FIRMS IN SHORT-COUPON TREASURIES AND BILLS, 1998

Ranked by: Bond managers survey. **Number listed:** 5

1. Merrill Lynch & Co.
2. Salomon Smith Barney
3. Lehman Brothers
4. Goldman, Sachs & Co.
5. Credit Suisse First Boston

Source: *Institutional Investor*, Top Fixed-Income Trading Firms (annual), November, 1998, p. 135.

★3917★

TOP GOVERNMENT/AGENCY TRADING FIRMS IN TREASURY STRIPS, 1998

Ranked by: Bond managers survey. **Number listed:** 5

1. Merrill Lynch & Co.
2. Salomon Smith Barney
3. Lehman Brothers
4. Goldman, Sachs & Co.
5. Credit Suisse First Boston

Source: *Institutional Investor*, Top Fixed-Income Trading Firms (annual), November, 1998, p. 135.

★3918★

TOP SECURITY FIRMS BY NON-RESIDENTIAL INSTALLATION VOLUME, 1998

Ranked by: Number of systems installed. **Number listed:** 50

1. Protection One Inc., with 16,000 systems
2. Edison Security Services, 5,000
3. Bay Alarm Co., 4,500
4. Interface Security Services, 3,600
5. Guardian Alarm Co., 3,050
6. AFA Protective Systems, 3,000
7. SMC (Sonitrol Management Corp.), 2,259
8. SSD Systems/Kern Security Systems, 2,011
9. Per Mar Security Services, 2,000
10. American Security Systems Inc., 2,000

Source: *Security Distributing & Marketing*, SDM 100 (annual), May, 1999, p. 62.

★3919★

TOP SECURITY FIRMS BY RECURRING ANNUAL REVENUE, 1998

Ranked by: Recurring annual revenue, in millions of dollars. **Number listed:** 66

1. ADT Security Services, with $1,100.00 million
2. Protection One Inc., $454.80
3. SecurityLink from Ameritech, $432.00
4. Brink's Home Security Inc., $181.20
5. Edison Security Services, $84.00
6. Bay Alarm Co., $33.29
7. Guardian Alarm Co., $32.50
8. Slomin's Inc., $30.57
9. Guardian Protection Services Inc., $29.35
10. AFA Protective Systems, $22.20

Source: *Security Distributing & Marketing*, SDM 100 (annual), May, 1999, p. 64.

★3920★

TOP SECURITY FIRMS BY RESIDENTIAL INSTALLATION VOLUME, 1998

Ranked by: Number of systems installed. **Number listed:** 50

1. Protection One Inc., with 304,000 systems
2. ADT Security Services, 210,00.
3. Brink's Home Security Inc., 113,000
4. Edison Security Services, 70,000
5. Slomin's Inc., 31,000
6. SLP Ventures LP, 22,100
7. Guardian Protection Services Inc., 19,197
8. Protect America Inc., 19,000
9. Smith Alarm Systems, 11,000
10. SCANA Security, 8,373

Source: *Security Distributing & Marketing*, SDM 100 (annual), May, 1999, p. 62.

★3921★

TOP SECURITY FIRMS BY REVENUE, 1998

Ranked by: Revenue, in millions of dollars. **Number listed:** 50

1. ADT Security Services, with $1,330.0 million
2. SecurityLink from Ameritech, $482.0
3. Protection One Inc., $421.1
4. Brink's Home Security Inc., $203.6
5. Honeywell Inc., Home & Building Control, $200.7
6. Edison Security Services, $90.0
7. Slomin's Inc., $67.8
8. Checkpoint Security Systems Group Inc., $55.2
9. Bay Alarm Co., $50.0
10. Guardian Alarm Co., $45.0

Source: *Security Distributing & Marketing*, SDM 100 (annual), May, 1999, p. 54.

★3922★

TOP SECURITY SYSTEM INTEGRATORS, 1998

Ranked by: Revenue, in millions of dollars. **Number listed:** 14

1. Security Technologies Group Inc., with $95 million
2. Pinkerton Systems Integration, $64
3. Kastle Systems, $45.6
4. MSI Security Systems Inc., $29
5. RFI Communications & Security Systems, $25.5
6. NAVCO Security Systems, $24.4
7. Chubb Security Systems Inc., $24.4
8. Delmarva Systems Corp., $12
9. Deterrent Technologies Inc., $12
10. Interface Security Systems L.L.C., $12

Source: *Security Distributing & Marketing*, Top System Integrators (annual), July, 1998, p. 52.

★3923★

TOP TRADING FIRMS IN ADJUSTABLE-RATE MORTGAGE OBLIGATIONS, 1998

Ranked by: Bond managers survey. **Number listed:** 5

1. Lehman Brothers
2. Bear, Stearns & Co.
3. Goldman, Sachs & Co.
4. Merrill Lynch & Co.
5. Salomon Smith Barney

Source: *Institutional Investor*, Top Fixed-Income Trading Firms (annual), November, 1998, p. 135.

★3924★

TOP TRADING FIRMS IN ASSET-BACKED SECURITIES, 1998

Ranked by: Bond managers survey. **Number listed:** 5

1. Lehman Brothers
2. Merrill Lynch & Co.
3. Morgan Stanley Dean Witter
4. Credit Suisse First Boston
5. Bear, Stearns & Co.

Source: *Institutional Investor*, Top Fixed-Income Trading Firms (annual), November, 1998, p. 135.

★3925★

TOP TRADING FIRMS IN COLLATERALIZED MORTGAGE OBLIGATIONS, 1998

Ranked by: Bond managers survey. **Number listed:** 5

1. Salomon Smith Barney
2. Lehman Brothers
3. Bear, Stearns & Co.

4. Goldman, Sachs & Co.
5. Morgan Stanley Dean Witter

Source: *Institutional Investor*, Top Fixed-Income Trading Firms (annual), November, 1998, p. 135.

★3926★
TOP TRADING FIRMS IN COMMERCIAL MORTGAGE SECURITIES, 1998
Ranked by: Bond managers survey. **Number listed:** 5

1. Morgan Stanley Dean Witter
2. Lehman Brothers
3. Merrill Lynch & Co.
4. Nomura Securities
5. Donaldson, Lufkin & Jenrette

Source: *Institutional Investor*, Top Fixed-Income Trading Firms (annual), November, 1998, p. 135.

★3927★
TOP TRADING FIRMS IN FIXED-INCOME OPTIONS, 1998
Ranked by: Bond managers survey. **Number listed:** 3

1. Merrill Lynch & Co.
2. Goldman, Sachs & Co.
3. J.P. Morgan

Source: *Institutional Investor*, Top Fixed-Income Trading Firms (annual), November, 1998, p. 135.

★3928★
TOP TRADING FIRMS IN FIXED INCOME SWAPS, 1998
Ranked by: Bond managers survey. **Number listed:** 4

1. Merrill Lynch & Co.
2. Goldman, Sachs & Co.
3. J.P. Morgan
4. Deutsche Morgan Grenfell

Source: *Institutional Investor*, Top Fixed-Income Trading Firms (annual), November, 1998, p. 135.

★3929★
TOP TRADING FIRMS IN MORTGAGE AND PASS-THROUGH SECURITIES, 1998
Ranked by: Bond managers survey. **Number listed:** 5

1. Salomon Smith Barney
2. Lehman Brothers
3. Bear, Stearns & Co.
4. Goldman, Sachs & Co.
5. Merrill Lynch & Co.

Source: *Institutional Investor*, Top Fixed-Income Trading Firms (annual), November, 1998, p. 135.

★3930★
TOP TRADING FIRMS IN U.S. DOLLAR-DENOMINATED EMERGING-MARKETS DEBT, 1998
Ranked by: Bond managers survey. **Number listed:** 5

1. J.P. Morgan
2. Merrill Lynch & Co.
3. Chase Securities
4. Goldman, Sachs & Co.
5. Salomon Smith Barney

Source: *Institutional Investor*, Top Fixed-Income Trading Firms (annual), November, 1998, p. 135.

★3931★
TOP TRADING FIRMS IN YANKEE BONDS, 1998
Ranked by: Bond managers survey. **Number listed:** 5

1. Merrill Lynch & Co.
2. Morgan Stanley Dean Witter
3. J.P. Morgan
4. Salomon Smith Barney
5. Goldman, Sachs & Co.

Source: *Institutional Investor*, Top Fixed-Income Trading Firms (annual), November, 1998, p. 135.

Security Underwriting

★3932★
LARGEST BANK UNDERWRITERS, 1998
Ranked by: Premium, in millions of dollars. **Number listed:** 9

1. Hartford, with $3,808 million
2. American General Life Cos., $2,043
3. Nationwide, $2,035
4. Allstate, $1,014
5. Safeco, $964
6. Aegon, $706
7. Transamerica, $657
8. GE Companies, $653
9. Keyport, $643

Source: *National Underwriter Life & Health*, April 19, 1999, p. 1.

★3933★
LARGEST UNDERWRITING FIRMS BY AMOUNT EARNED, 1997
Ranked by: Total gross spread, in millions of dollars. **Remarks:** Also lists number of issues, 1996 rank, amount and issues. **Number listed:** 50

1. Salomon Smith Barney Holdings, with $24,932,200 million
2. Goldman, Sachs & Co., $21,962,300
3. PaineWebber, $21,664,700
4. Merrill Lynch & Co., $18,048,600
5. Lehman Brothers, $17,232,700
6. Bear, Stearns & Co., $10,826,000
7. J.P. Morgan Securities Inc., $8,752,700
8. Morgan Stanley Dean Witter, $7,267,000
9. Bank of America, $5,309,400
10. Prudential Securities Inc., $3,835,900

Source: *Financial Shelves*, Bond Buyer Yearbook (annual), July, 1998, p. 38.

★3934★
LEADING CONVERTIBLE TECHNICAL UNDERWRITERS (PUBLIC + 144A), 1998
Ranked by: Proceeds, in millions of dollars. **Remarks:** Also includes market share and number of issues. Excludes Biotech & Communications. **Number listed:** 11

1. Bear, Stearns, with $14,344.1 million
2. Merrill Lynch & Co., $2,366.8
3. Morgan Stanley Dean Witter, $2,298.7
4. Donaldson, Lufkin & Jenrette, $1,200.0
5. Goldman, Sachs & Co., $825.0
6. Salomon Smith Barney Holdings, $770.0
7. Bank of America, $190.0
8. Lazard Houses, $125.0
9. Prudential Securities Inc., $100.0
10. Deutsche Bank, $90.0

Source: *Investment Dealers' Digest*, February 8, 1999, p. 23.

★3935★
LEADING TECHNICAL UNDERWRITERS FOR STRAIGHT DEBT ISSUES, 1998
Ranked by: Proceeds, in millions of dollars. **Remarks:** Also includes market share and number of issues. Excludes Biotech & Communications. **Number listed:** 14

1. Merrill Lynch & Co., with $6,475.30 million
2. Morgan Stanley Dean Witter, $4,761.20
3. Goldman, Sachs & Co., $3,298.50
4. Salomon Smith Barney Holdings, $2,009.50
5. Credit Suisse First Boston, $1,897.10
6. Lehman Brothers, $1,841.80
7. Chase Manhattan, $1,743.00
8. J.P. Morgan, $1,380.30
9. Bear, Stearns, $1,155.80
10. Donaldson, Lufkin & Jenrette, $189.5

Source: *Investment Dealers' Digest*, February 8, 1999, p. 22.

★3936★
LEADING UNDERWRITERS FOR COMMERCIAL BANKS BY FULL CREDIT TO BOOK MANAGER, 1998
Ranked by: Debt and equity issued, in millions of dollars. **Remarks:** Also includes percentage of total, number of issues, debt and equity. **Number listed:** 25

1. Merrill Lynch & Co., with $76,802.0 million
2. Salomon Smith Barney Holdings, $50,882.0
3. Morgan Stanley Dean Witter, $40,375.0
4. Chase Manhattan, $38,780.8
5. Goldman, Sachs & Co., $37,696.4
6. Credit Suisse First Boston, $28,473.1
7. J.P. Morgan, $17,883.7
8. Lehman Brothers, $15,145.7
9. Bank of America, $10,373.6
10. First Union Corp., $8,022.9

Source: *U.S. Banker*, Top Underwriters for Commercial Banks (annual), February, 1999, p. 72.

★3937★
LEADING UNDERWRITERS FOR COMMERCIAL BANKS BY FULL CREDIT TO EACH MANAGER, 1998
Ranked by: Debt and equity issued, in millions of dollars. **Remarks:** Also includes percentage of total, number of issues, debt and equity. **Number listed:** 10

1. Merrill Lynch & Co., with $89,836.9 million
2. Salomon Smith Barney Holdings, $68,504.5
3. Morgan Stanley Dean Witter, $49,953.1
4. Goldman, Sachs & Co., $46,379.4
5. Chase Manhattan, $45,999.5
6. Credit Suisse First Boston, $44,929.5
7. Lehman Brothers, $31,821.0
8. J.P. Morgan, $21,682.8
9. Bank of America, $16,717.4
10. Bear, Stearns, $14,984.6

Source: *U.S. Banker*, Top Underwriters for Commercial Banks (annual), February, 1999, p. 72.

★3938★
LEADING UNDERWRITERS FOR THRIFT INSTITUTIONS BY FULL CREDIT TO BOOK MANAGER, 1998
Ranked by: Debt and equity issued, in millions of dollars. **Remarks:** Also includes percentage of market share, number of issues, debt and equity. **Number listed:** 18

1. Credit Suisse First Boston, with $2,324.0 million
2. J.P. Morgan & Co., $1,655.1
3. Merrill Lynch & Co., $930.0
4. Goldman, Sachs & Co., $827.5
5. Greenwich/Gleacher Natwest, $597.0
6. Lehman Brothers, $381.7
7. Salomon Smith Barney Holdings, $349.9
8. Bear, Stearns & Co., $349.0
9. Morgan Stanley Dean Witter, $233.3
10. Chase Manhattan Corp., $214.0

Source: *U.S. Banker*, February, 1999, p. 74.

★3939★
LEADING UNDERWRITERS GARNERING THE MOST FEES, 1998
Ranked by: Gross spread, in millions of dollars. **Remarks:** Also includes percentage of total, number of issues and average fee. **Number listed:** 15

1. Merrill Lynch & Co., with $1,499.3 million
2. Morgan Stanley, $1,251.2
3. Goldman, Sachs & Co., $1,097.9
4. Salomon Smith Barney Holdings, $921.8
5. Lehman Brothers, $515.4
6. Donaldson, Lufkin & Jenrette, $491.8
7. Credit Suisse First Boston, $389.1
8. J.P. Morgan & Co., $374.1
9. Bear, Stearns & Co., $298.7
10. Bankers Trust, $252.2

Source: *Investment Dealers' Digest*, February 1, 1999, p. 20.

★3940★
LEADING UNDERWRITERS IN AGENCY ISSUES BY FULL CREDIT TO BOOK MANAGER, 1998
Ranked by: Amount of high-yield straight debt, January 1 to December 31, 1998, in millions of dollars. **Remarks:** Also includes number of issues and percentage of market. **Number listed:** 15

1. Morgan Stanley Dean Witter, with $25,670.6 million
2. Merrill Lynch & Co., $24,339.2
3. Salomon Smith Barney Holdings, $23,152.6
4. Credit Suisse First Boston, $20,968.7
5. Lehman Brothers, $20,258.7
6. Prudential Securities Inc., $12,468.9
7. Bear, Stearns & Co., $11,708.8
8. Chase Manhattan Corporation, $10,768.5
9. J.P. Morgan, $8,794.0
10. Goldman, Sachs & Co., $8,061.2

Source: *Investment Dealers' Digest*, Underwriter Rankings (annual), January 11, 1999, p. 33.

★3941★
LEADING UNDERWRITERS IN ALL COMMON UNDERWRITING FEES, 1998
Ranked by: Gross spread, in millions of dollars. **Remarks:** Also includes percentage of total, number of issues and average fee. **Number listed:** 15

1. Morgan Stanley Dean Witter, with $697.3 million
2. Merrill Lynch & Co., $627.6
3. Goldman, Sachs & Co., $585.8
4. Salomon Smith Barney Holdings, $382.4
5. Donaldson, Lufkin & Jenrette, $302.9
6. Credit Suisse First Boston, $202.8
7. Bankers Trust, $191.4
8. Lehman Brothers, $173.1
9. J.P. Morgan & Co., $160.3
10. Prudential Securities Inc., $147.9

Source: *Investment Dealers' Digest*, February 1, 1999, p. 24.

★3942★
LEADING UNDERWRITERS IN ASSET-BACKED DEBT, 1998
Ranked by: Gross spread, in millions of dollars. **Remarks:** Also includes percentage of total, number of issues and average fee. **Number listed:** 15

1. Lehman Brothers, with $50.6 million
2. Credit Suisse First Boston, $45.2
3. Merrill Lynch & Co., $44.5
4. Morgan Stanley Dean Witter, $33.5
5. Salomon Smith Barney Holdings, $27.0
6. Goldman, Sachs & Co., $26.2
7. Bear, Stearns, $19.7
8. Chase Manhattan, $18.2

9. J.P. Morgan, $15.2
10. Bank of America, $6.4

Source: *Investment Dealers' Digest*, February 1, 1999, p. 25.

★3943★
LEADING UNDERWRITERS IN ASSET BACKED SECURITIES BY FULL CREDIT TO BOOK MANAGER, 1998
Ranked by: Amount of high-yield straight debt, January 1 to December 31, 1998, in millions of dollars. **Remarks:** Also includes number of issues and percentage of market. **Number listed:** 15

1. Morgan Stanley Dean Witter, with $25,670.6 million
2. Merrill Lynch & Co., $24,339.2
3. Salomon Smith Barney Holdings, $23,152.6
4. Credit Suisse First Boston, $20,968.7
5. Lehman Brothers, $20,258.7
6. Prudential Securities Inc., $12,468.9
7. Bear, Stearns & Co., $11,708.8
8. Chase Manhattan Corporation, $10,768.5
9. J.P. Morgan, $8,794.0
10. Goldman, Sachs & Co., $8,061.2

Source: *Investment Dealers' Digest*, Underwriter Rankings (annual), January 11, 1999, p. 31.

★3944★
LEADING UNDERWRITERS IN COLLATERALIZED SECURITIES BY FULL CREDIT TO BOOK MANAGER, 1998
Ranked by: Amount of high-yield straight debt, January 1 to December 31, 1998, in millions of dollars. **Remarks:** Also includes number of issues and percentage of market. **Number listed:** 15

1. Lehman Brothers, with $81,557.9 million
2. Salomon Smith Barney Holdings, $71,007.2
3. Merrill Lynch & Co., $58,541.6
4. Bear, Stearns & Co., $45,413.5
5. Credit Suisse First Boston, $45,357.1
6. Morgan Stanley Dean Witter, $44,513.5
7. PaineWebber, $37,938.0
8. Donaldson, Lufkin & Jenrette, $34,797.7
9. Goldman, Sachs & Co., $32,438.6
10. Greenwich/Gleacher Natwest, $19,036.5

Source: *Investment Dealers' Digest*, Underwriter Rankings (annual), January 11, 1999, p. 31.

★3945★
LEADING UNDERWRITERS IN COMMON STOCK BY FULL CREDIT TO BOOK MANAGER, 1998
Ranked by: Amount of high-yield straight debt, January 1 to December 31, 1998, in millions of dollars. **Remarks:** Also includes number of issues and percentage of market. **Number listed:** 15

1. Morgan Stanley Dean Witter, with $19,346.1 million
2. Merrill Lynch & Co., $18,355.2
3. Goldman, Sachs & Co., $15,855.2
4. Salomon Smith Barney Holdings, $8,521.3
5. Donaldson, Lufkin & Jenrette, $8,234.4
6. J.P. Morgan, $6,012.7
7. Credit Suisse First Boston, $4,424.1
8. Bankers Trust, $4,146.4
9. Lehman Brothers, $3,927.8
10. Bear, Stearns & Co., $3,677.0

Source: *Investment Dealers' Digest*, Underwriter Rankings (annual), January 11, 1999, p. 33.

★3946★
LEADING UNDERWRITERS IN CONVERTIBLE UNDERWRITING FEES, 1998
Ranked by: Gross spread, in millions of dollars. **Remarks:** Also includes percentage of total, number of issues and average fee. **Number listed:** 15

1. Merrill Lynch & Co., with $88.7 million
2. Lehman Brothers, $76.3
3. Goldman, Sachs & Co., $41.6
4. Salomon Smith Barney Holdings, $36.4
5. Donaldson, Lufkin & Jenrette, $30.1
6. Bankers Trust, $14.8
7. Morgan Stanley Dean Witter, $13.4
8. Bear, Stearns, $10.0
9. Edward D. Jones, $5.4
10. ABN Amro, $4.3

Source: *Investment Dealers' Digest*, February 1, 1999, p. 25.

★3947★
LEADING UNDERWRITERS IN CORPORATE DEBT, 1998
Ranked by: Gross spread, in millions of dollars. **Remarks:** Also includes percentage of total, number of issues and average fee. **Number listed:** 15

1. Morgan Stanley Dean Witter, with $325.9 million
2. Merrill Lynch & Co., $306.6
3. Salomon Smith Barney Holdings, $304.5
4. Goldman, Sachs & Co., $287.9
5. Lehman Brothers, $152.2
6. Donaldson, Lufkin & Jenrette, $143.8
7. J.P. Morgan, $121.9
8. Credit Suisse First Boston, $105.6
9. Bear, Stearns, $72.7
10. Chase Manhattan, $69.0

Source: *Investment Dealers' Digest*, February 1, 1999, p. 25.

★3948★
LEADING UNDERWRITERS IN HIGH-YIELD STRAIGHT DEBT EXCLUDING SPLIT-RATED ISSUES BY FULL CREDIT TO BOOK MANAGER, 1998
Ranked by: Amount of high-yield straight debt, January 1 to December 31, 1998, in millions of dollars. **Remarks:** Also includes number of issues and percentage of market. **Number listed:** 15

1. Donaldson, Lufkin & Jenrette, with $21,489.0 million
2. Morgan Stanley Dean Witter, $19,221.8
3. Salomon Smith Barney Holdings, $18,603.8
4. Merrill Lynch & Co., $11,619.1
5. Goldman, Sachs & Co., $11,120.8
6. Chase Manhattan Corporation, $9,096.1
7. Bankers Trust, $8,376.3
8. Lehman Brothers, $7,568.8
9. Credit Suisse First Boston, $7,547.3
10. Bear, Stearns & Co., $6,815.8

Source: *Investment Dealers' Digest*, Underwriter Rankings (annual), January 11, 1999, p. 30.

★3949★
LEADING UNDERWRITERS IN HIGH-YIELD STRAIGHT DEBT (PUBLIC + 144A) BY FULL CREDIT TO BOOK MANAGER, 1998
Ranked by: Amount of high-yield straight debt, January 1 to December 31, 1998, in millions of dollars. **Remarks:** Also includes number of issues and percentage of market. **Number listed:** 15

1. Donaldson, Lufkin & Jenrette, with $21,637.7 million
2. Salomon Smith Barney Holdings, $19,626.4

3. Morgan Stanley Dean Witter, $19,259.5
4. Merrill Lynch & Co., $12,512.6
5. Goldman, Sachs & Co., $11,320.8
6. Chase Manhattan Corporation, $9,096.1
7. J.P. Morgan, $8,476.0
8. Lehman Brothers, $7,917.5
9. Credit Suisse First Boston, $7,896.7
10. Bear, Stearns & Co., $6,815.8

Source: *Investment Dealers' Digest*, Underwriter Rankings (annual), January 11, 1999, p. 30.

★3950★
LEADING UNDERWRITERS IN INITIAL PUBLIC OFFERINGS BY FULL CREDIT TO BOOK MANAGER, 1998
Ranked by: Amount of high-yield straight debt, January 1 to December 31, 1998, in millions of dollars. **Remarks:** Also includes number of issues and percentage of market. **Number listed:** 15

1. Merrill Lynch & Co., with $9,595.0 million
2. Morgan Stanley Dean Witter, $9,455.9
3. Salomon Smith Barney Holdings, $3,458.5
4. Goldman, Sachs & Co., $3,418.9
5. Credit Suisse First Boston, $1,900.4
6. PaineWebber, $1,675.7
7. Prudential Securities Inc., $1,612.8
8. Donaldson, Lufkin & Jenrette, $1,609.9
9. J.P. Morgan, $1,541.1
10. Bear, Stearns & Co., $1,126.9

Source: *Investment Dealers' Digest*, Underwriter Rankings (annual), January 11, 1999, p. 34.

★3951★
LEADING UNDERWRITERS IN INITIAL PUBLIC OFFERINGS EXCLUDING CLOSED END FUNDS BY FULL CREDIT TO BOOK MANAGER, 1998
Ranked by: Amount of high-yield straight debt, January 1 to December 31, 1998, in millions of dollars. **Remarks:** Also includes number of issues and percentage of market. **Number listed:** 15

1. Morgan Stanley Dean Witter, with $7,855.9 million
2. Merrill Lynch & Co., $7,111.5
3. Goldman, Sachs & Co., $3,418.9
4. Salomon Smith Barney Holdings, $2,473.4
5. Credit Suisse First Boston, $1,900.4
6. J.P. Morgan, $1,541.1
7. Prudential Securities Inc., $1,425.3
8. Donaldson, Lufkin & Jenrette, $1,209.9
9. Bear, Stearns & Co., $1,126.9
10. Friedman, Billings, Ramsey, $950.7

Source: *Investment Dealers' Digest*, Underwriter Rankings (annual), January 11, 1999, p. 34.

★3952★
LEADING UNDERWRITERS IN INVESTMENT-GRADE DEBT BY FULL CREDIT TO BOOK MANAGER, 1998
Ranked by: Amount of high-yield straight debt, January 1 to December 31, 1998, in millions of dollars. **Remarks:** Also includes number of issues and percentage of market. **Number listed:** 15

1. Merrill Lynch & Co., with $208,075.7 million
2. Goldman, Sachs & Co., $135,177.7
3. Salomon Smith Barney Holdings, $134,078.3
4. Morgan Stanley Dean Witter, $129,386.4
5. Credit Suisse First Boston, $77,106.8
6. J.P. Morgan, $72,351.6
7. Chase Manhattan Corporation, $55,014.3
8. Lehman Brothers, $54,910.3
9. Bear, Stearns & Co., $33,157.1
10. ABN AMRO, $16,491.7

Source: *Investment Dealers' Digest*, Underwriter Rankings (annual), January 11, 1999, p. 30.

★3953★
LEADING UNDERWRITERS IN INVESTMENT GRADE DEBT, 1998
Ranked by: Gross spread, in millions of dollars. **Remarks:** Also includes percentage of total, number of issues and average fee. **Number listed:** 15

1. Merrill Lynch & Co., with $351.4 million
2. Morgan Stanley Dean Witter, $313.7
3. Salomon Smith Barney Holdings, $308.7
4. Goldman, Sachs & Co., $308.1
5. J.P. Morgan & Co., $181.7
6. Lehman Brothers, $142.2
7. Credit Suisse First Boston, $111.2
8. Bear, Stearns Cos., $80.7
9. Chase Manhattan, $59.4
10. ABN Amro, $37.1

Source: *Investment Dealers' Digest*, February 1, 1999, p. 24.

★3954★
LEADING UNDERWRITERS IN IPOS, 1998
Ranked by: Gross spread, in millions of dollars. **Remarks:** Also includes percentage of total, number of issues and average fee. **Number listed:** 15

1. Morgan Stanley Dean Witter, with $416.7 million
2. Merrill Lynch & Co., $330.2
3. Salomon Smith Barney Holdings, $195.5
4. Goldman, Sachs & Co., $585.8
5. Donaldson, Lufkin & Jenrette, $302.9
6. Credit Suisse First Boston, $202.8
7. Bankers Trust, $191.4
8. Lehman Brothers, $173.1
9. J.P. Morgan & Co., $160.3
10. Prudential Securities Inc., $147.9

Source: *Investment Dealers' Digest*, February 1, 1999, p. 24.

★3955★
LEADING UNDERWRITERS IN JUNK BONDS, 1998
Ranked by: Gross spread, in millions of dollars. **Remarks:** Also includes percentage of total, number of issues and average fee. **Number listed:** 15

1. Donaldson, Lufkin & Jenrette, with $114.8 million
2. Morgan Stanley Dean Witter, $90.4
3. Goldman, Sachs & Co., $50.5
4. Salomon Smith Barney Holdings, $48.9
5. Lehman Brothers, $42.0
6. Merrill Lynch & Co., $29.5
7. Credit Suisse First Boston, $29.2
8. Bankers Trust, $27.7
9. Bear, Stearns, $17.6
10. J.P. Morgan & Co., $16.9

Source: *Investment Dealers' Digest*, February 1, 1999, p. 24.

★3956★
LEADING UNDERWRITERS IN MORTGAGE BACKED SECURITIES BY FULL CREDIT TO BOOK MANAGER, 1998
Ranked by: Amount of high-yield straight debt, January 1 to December 31, 1998, in millions of dollars. **Remarks:** Also includes number of issues and percentage of market. **Number listed:** 15

1. Lehman Brothers, with $61,229.3 million
2. Salomon Smith Barney Holdings, $47,854.7
3. Merrill Lynch & Co., $34,202.3
4. Bear, Stearns & Co., $33,704.8
5. PaineWebber, $32,785.9
6. Donaldson, Lufkin & Jenrette, $31,697.9

7. Credit Suisse First Boston, $24,388.4
8. Goldman, Sachs & Co., $24,377.4
9. Morgan Stanley Dean Witter, $18,872.9
10. Greenwich/Gleacher Natwest, $17,433.2

Source: *Investment Dealers' Digest*, Underwriter Rankings (annual), January 11, 1999, p. 32.

★3957★
LEADING UNDERWRITERS IN NON CLOSED-END COMMON UNDERWRITING FEES, 1998
Ranked by: Gross spread, in millions of dollars. **Remarks:** Also includes percentage of total, number of issues and average fee. **Number listed:** 15

1. Morgan Stanley Dean Witter, with $633.3 million
2. Merrill Lynch & Co., $621.6
3. Goldman, Sachs & Co., $585.8
4. Salomon Smith Barney Holdings, $334.4
5. Donaldson, Lufkin & Jenrette, $282.9
6. Credit Suisse First Boston, $202.8
7. Bankers Trust, $191.4
8. Lehman Brothers, $173.1
9. J.P. Morgan & Co., $160.3
10. Bear, Stearns, $140.7

Source: *Investment Dealers' Digest*, February 1, 1999, p. 24.

★3958★
LEADING UNDERWRITERS IN NON CONVERTIBLE PREFERRED PUBLIC STOCK BY FULLCREDIT TO BOOK MANAGER, 1998
Ranked by: Amount of high-yield straight debt, January 1 to December 31, 1998, in millions of dollars. **Remarks:** Also includes number of issues and percentage of market. **Number listed:** 15

1. Merrill Lynch & Co., with $14,695.2 million
2. Goldman, Sachs & Co., $7,319.0
3. Salomon Smith Barney Holdings, $5,652.1
4. Morgan Stanley Dean Witter, $4,979.5
5. Lehman Brothers, $2,179.2
6. Bear, Stearns & Co., $1,295.0
7. Donaldson, Lufkin & Jenrette, $843.0
8. Chase Manhattan Corporation, $597.5
9. PaineWebber, $487.5
10. ABN AMRO, $416.7

Source: *Investment Dealers' Digest*, Underwriter Rankings (annual), January 11, 1999, p. 32.

★3959★
LEADING UNDERWRITERS IN NON-CONVERTIBLE PREFERRED UNDERWRITING FEES, 1998
Ranked by: Gross spread, in millions of dollars. **Remarks:** Also includes percentage of total, number of issues and average fee. **Number listed:** 15

1. Merrill Lynch & Co., with $357.5 million
2. Salomon Smith Barney Holdings, $118.5
3. Morgan Stanley Dean Witter, $102.8
4. Goldman, Sachs & Co., $85.7
5. Lehman Brothers, $31.2
6. Bear, Stearns, $28.7
7. PaineWebber, $14.3
8. ABN Amro, $13.1
9. A.G. Edwards & Sons, $6.3
10. Chase Manhattan, $6.3

Source: *Investment Dealers' Digest*, February 1, 1999, p. 25.

★3960★
LEADING UNDERWRITERS IN SECONDARY COMMON UNDERWRITING FEES, 1998
Ranked by: Gross spread, in millions of dollars. **Remarks:** Also includes percentage of total, number of issues and average fee. **Number listed:** 15

1. Goldman, Sachs & Co., with $391.2 million
2. Merrill Lynch & Co., $297.4
3. Morgan Stanley Dean Witter, $280.6
4. Donaldson, Lufkin & Jenrette, $203.3
5. Salomon Smith Barney Holdings, $186.8
6. Bankers Trust, $127.9
7. Lehman Brothers, $121.1
8. J.P. Morgan & Co., $112.1
9. Credit Suisse First Boston, $105.6
10. Bear, Stearns, $69.0

Source: *Investment Dealers' Digest*, February 1, 1999, p. 24.

★3961★
LEADING UNDERWRITERS IN U.S. CONVERTIBLES (PUBLIC + 144A) BY FULL CREDIT TO BOOK MANAGER, 1998
Ranked by: Amount of high-yield straight debt, January 1 to December 31, 1998, in millions of dollars. **Remarks:** Also includes number of issues and percentage of market. **Number listed:** 15

1. Merrill Lynch & Co., with $5,966.2 million
2. Morgan Stanley Dean Witter, $4,682.6
3. Goldman, Sachs & Co., $4,091.8
4. Donaldson, Lufkin & Jenrette, $3,945.6
5. Lehman Brothers, $3,321.2
6. Salomon Smith Barney Holdings, $3,010.6
7. Credit Suisse First Boston, $2,273.1
8. Bankers Trust, $1,125.0
9. Bear, Stearns & Co., $1,030.0
10. Warburg Dillon Read, $625.0

Source: *Investment Dealers' Digest*, Underwriter Rankings (annual), January 11, 1999, p. 35.

★3962★
LEADING UNDERWRITERS OF CONVERTIBLE SECURITIES, 1998
Ranked by: Proceeds, in millions of dollars. **Remarks:** Also includes market share and number of issues. **Number listed:** 10

1. Merrill Lynch & Co., with $4,236.5 million
2. Lehman Brothers, $2,641.2
3. Goldman, Sachs & Co., $1,759.3
4. Salomon Smith Barney Holdings, $1,693.5
5. Donaldson, Lufkin & Jenrette, $1,158.5
6. Morgan Stanley Dean Witter, $984.0
7. Bankers Trust, $775.0
8. Warburg Dillon Read, $350.0
9. Bear, Stearns, $250.0
10. 1ABN AMRO, $171.7

Source: *Investment Dealers' Digest*, December 21, 1998, p. 23.

★3963★
LEADING UNDERWRITERS WHO PAID THE MOST, 1998
Ranked by: Gross spread, in millions of dollars. **Remarks:** Also includes percentage of total, number of issues and average fee. **Number listed:** 15

1. Federal National Mortgage Assn., with $243.5 million
2. Federal Home Loan Banks, $168.3
3. Conoco Inc., $158.1
4. Federal Home Loan Mortgage, $154.9
5. Infinity Broadcasting Corp., $97.6
6. Fox Entertainment Group Inc., $95.2
7. Niagara Mohawk Power Corp., $68.9
8. Van Kampen American Capital, $64.0
9. Republic Services Inc., $52.8
10. Premier Parks Inc., $50.3

Source: *Investment Dealers' Digest*, February 1, 1999, p. 20.

★3964★
TOP COMANAGER UNDERWRITERS FOR DEVELOPMENT, 1997
Ranked by: Amount issued, in thousands of dollars. **Remarks:** Also lists number of issues. **Number listed:** 25
1. Goldman, Sachs & Co., with $1,233,900 thousand
2. Morgan Stanley Dean Witter, $762,400
3. PaineWebber, $648,000
4. Bear, Stearns & Co., $498,800
5. Samuel A. Ramirez & Co., $462,700
6. Merrill Lynch & Co., $421,400
7. Prudential Securities Inc., $391,100
8. Artemis Capital Group Co., $366,500
9. J.P. Morgan Securities Inc., $359,000
10. Lehman Brothers, $357,500
11. Raymond James & Associates Inc., $350,600

Source: *Financial Shelves*, Bond Buyer Yearbook (annual), July, 1998, p. 168.

★3965★
TOP COMANAGER UNDERWRITERS FOR EDUCATION, 1997
Ranked by: Amount issued, in thousands of dollars. **Remarks:** Also lists number of issues. **Number listed:** 25
1. Salomon Smith Barney Holdings, with $9,796,600 thousand
2. PaineWebber, $6,934,200
3. Merrill Lynch & Co., $6,122,100
4. A.G. Edwards & Sons Inc., $5,512,300
5. Goldman, Sachs & Co., $4,898,500
6. Morgan Stanley Dean Witter, $4,576,000
7. Dain Rauscher Inc., $4,405,000
8. Lehman Brothers, $4,394,600
9. Prudential Securities Inc., $4,092,000
10. Bear, Stearns & Co., $3,965,800

Source: *Financial Shelves*, Bond Buyer Yearbook (annual), July, 1998, p. 112.

★3966★
TOP COMANAGER UNDERWRITERS FOR ELECTRIC POWER, 1997
Ranked by: Amount issued, in thousands of dollars. **Remarks:** Also lists number of issues. **Number listed:** 25
1. Goldman, Sachs & Co., with $4,358,800 thousand
2. Salomon Smith Barney Holdings, $4,279,500
3. Bear, Stearns & Co., $3,218,100
4. PaineWebber, $2,571,600
5. Merrill Lynch & Co., $2,431,200
6. Morgan Stanley Dean Witter, $2,380,300
7. J.P. Morgan Securities Inc., $2,154,900
8. Lehman Brothers, $2,149,700
9. Seattle-Northwest Securities Corp., $1,245,200
10. Prudential Securities Inc., $787,400

Source: *Financial Shelves*, Bond Buyer Yearbook (annual), July, 1998, p. 176.

★3967★
TOP COMANAGER UNDERWRITERS FOR ENVIRONMENTAL FACILITIES, 1997
Ranked by: Amount issued, in thousands of dollars. **Remarks:** Also lists number of issues. **Number listed:** 25
1. Goldman, Sachs & Co., with $2,924,900 thousand
2. Salomon Smith Barney Holdings, $2,134,400
3. Merrill Lynch & Co., $2,124,600
4. Morgan Stanley Dean Witter, $2,106,300
5. Lehman Brothers, $1,779,500
6. PaineWebber, $1,543,700
7. Bear, Stearns & Co., $1,429,500
8. First Albany Corp., $1,274,900
9. J.P. Morgan Securities Inc., $1,219,100
10. A.G. Edwards & Sons Inc., $825,400

Source: *Financial Shelves*, Bond Buyer Yearbook (annual), July, 1998, p. 160.

★3968★
TOP COMANAGER UNDERWRITERS FOR HEALTHCARE, 1997
Ranked by: Amount issued, in thousands of dollars. **Remarks:** Also lists number of issues. **Number listed:** 25
1. Salomon Smith Barney Holdings, with $6,005,400 thousand
2. Merrill Lynch & Co., $5,909,300
3. PaineWebber, $3,617,000
4. Bear, Stearns & Co., $2,966,300
5. Goldman, Sachs & Co., $2,765,100
6. J.P. Morgan Securities Inc., $2,329,000
7. Morgan Stanley Dean Witter, $2,070,000
8. A.G. Edwards & Sons Inc., $1,791,600
9. Ziegler Securities, $1,586,900
10. PNC Capital Markets, $1,548,900

Source: *Financial Shelves*, Bond Buyer Yearbook (annual), July, 1998, p. 120.

★3969★
TOP COMANAGER UNDERWRITERS FOR HOUSING, 1997
Ranked by: Amount issued, in thousands of dollars. **Remarks:** Also lists number of issues. **Number listed:** 25
1. Merrill Lynch & Co., with $7,423,700 thousand
2. Goldman, Sachs & Co., $6,760,700
3. PaineWebber, $6,477,800
4. Lehman Brothers, $5,794,200
5. Bear, Stearns & Co., $5,646,500
6. Salomon Smith Barney Holdings, $5,073,700
7. John Nuveen & Co., $3,329,200
8. Samuel A. Ramirez & Co., $2,636,800
9. M.R. Beal & Co., $2,300,700
10. E.J. De La Rosa & Co., $2,092,900

Source: *Financial Shelves*, Bond Buyer Yearbook (annual), July, 1998, p. 144.

★3970★
TOP COMANAGER UNDERWRITERS FOR PUBLIC FACILITIES, 1997
Ranked by: Amount issued, in thousands of dollars. **Remarks:** Also lists number of issues. **Number listed:** 25
1. Salomon Smith Barney Holdings, with $3,725,500 thousand
2. PaineWebber, $2,626,500
3. Morgan Stanley Dean Witter, $2,597,200
4. Merrill Lynch & Co., $2,080,800
5. Bear, Stearns & Co., $2,078,700
6. Prudential Securities Inc., $2,074,200
7. Lehman Brothers, $2,008,200
8. A.G. Edwards & Sons Inc., $1,781,900
9. J.P. Morgan Securities Inc., $1,676,300
10. Goldman, Sachs & Co., $1,505,900

Source: *Financial Shelves*, Bond Buyer Yearbook (annual), July, 1998, p. 152.

★3971★
TOP COMANAGER UNDERWRITERS FOR TAXABLE ISSUES, 1997
Ranked by: Amount issued, in thousands of dollars. **Remarks:** Also lists number of issues. **Number listed:** 25
1. Salomon Smith Barney Holdings, with $5,847,800 thousand
2. Merrill Lynch & Co., $5,586,700
3. Goldman Sachs & Co, $5,488,000
4. Bear, Stearns & Co., $5,163,900

5. PaineWebber, $5,146,900
6. Lehman Brothers, $5,073,200
7. Morgan Stanley Dean Witter, $4,128,500
8. M.R. Beal & Co., $3,661,600
9. First Albany Corp., $3,001,400
10. William E. Simon & Sons Municipal Securities Inc., $2,986,400

Source: *Financial Shelves*, Bond Buyer Yearbook (annual), July, 1998, p. 184.

★3972★
TOP COMANAGER UNDERWRITERS FOR TRANSPORTATION, 1997
Ranked by: Amount issued, in thousands of dollars. **Remarks:** Also lists number of issues. **Number listed:** 25

1. Goldman, Sachs & Co., with $14,028,700 thousand
2. Lehman Brothers, $13,793,500
3. PaineWebber, $12,782,800
4. Salomon Smith Barney Holdings, $11,211,700
5. Bear, Stearns & Co., $10,854,600
6. J.P. Morgan Securities Inc., $8,855,800
7. Merrill Lynch & Co., $7,615,600
8. Bank of America, $6,501,100
9. Morgan Stanley Dean Witter, $5,933,100
10. First Albany Corp., $5,329,600

Source: *Financial Shelves*, Bond Buyer Yearbook (annual), July, 1998, p. 128.

★3973★
TOP COMANAGER UNDERWRITERS FOR UTILITIES, 1997
Ranked by: Amount issued, in thousands of dollars. **Remarks:** Also lists number of issues. **Number listed:** 25

1. PaineWebber, with $7,712,500 thousand
2. Salomon Smith Barney Holdings, $7,609,700
3. Merrill Lynch & Co., $5,676,400
4. Artemis Capital Group Co., $5,139,300
5. Goldman, Sachs & Co., $5,110,700
6. Morgan Stanley Dean Witter, $4,913,800
7. Bear, Stearns & Co., $4,734,300
8. J.P. Morgan Securities Inc., $4,462,500
9. Lehman Brothers, $4,396,200
10. A.G. Edwards & Sons Inc., $4,100,600

Source: *Financial Shelves*, Bond Buyer Yearbook (annual), July, 1998, p. 136.

★3974★
TOP SENIOR MANAGER UNDERWRITERS FOR DEVELOPMENT, 1997
Ranked by: Amount issued, in thousands of dollars. **Remarks:** Also lists number of issues. **Number listed:** 25

1. Goldman, Sachs & Co., with $860,200 thousand
2. PaineWebberInc., $461,400
3. Morgan Stanley Dean Witter, $436,400
4. Stone & Youngberg, $319,500
5. Bank of America, $269,100
6. Citicorp Securities Inc., $219,000
7. Mesirow Financial Inc., $214,600
8. J.P. Morgan Securities Inc., $204,500
9. First Chicago Capital Markets Inc., $184,300
10. Miller & Schroeder Financial Inc., $171,600

Source: *Financial Shelves*, Bond Buyer Yearbook (annual), July, 1998, p. 168.

★3975★
TOP SENIOR MANAGER UNDERWRITERS FOR EDUCATION, 1997
Ranked by: Amount issued, in thousands of dollars. **Remarks:** Also lists number of issues. **Number listed:** 25

1. Salomon Smith Barney Holdings, with $3,945,600 thousand
2. PaineWebber, $3,414,900
3. Goldman, Sachs & Co., $3,016,900
4. Lehman Brothers, $2,133,700
5. Dain Rauscher Inc., $2,072,500
6. Bank of America, $2,060,300
7. Merrill Lynch & Co., $1,935,100
8. A.G. Edwards & Sons Inc., $1,748,300
9. First Union Capital Markets Corp., $1,008,600
10. Morgan Stanley Dean Witter, $934,300

Source: *Financial Shelves*, Bond Buyer Yearbook (annual), July, 1998, p. 112.

★3976★
TOP SENIOR MANAGER UNDERWRITERS FOR ELECTRIC POWER, 1997
Ranked by: Amount issued, in thousands of dollars. **Remarks:** Also lists number of issues. **Number listed:** 25

1. Goldman, Sachs & Co., with $1,982,100 thousand
2. Bear, Stearns & Co., $1,390,900
3. J.P. Morgan Securities Inc., $865,500
4. Lehman Brothers, $649,200
5. Salomon Smith Barney Holdings, $560,620
6. Merrill Lynch & Co., $442,700
7. Morgan Stanley Dean Witter, $212,000
8. PaineWebber, $170,000
9. J.C. Bradford & Co., $61,800
10. Prudential Securities Inc., $52,100

Source: *Financial Shelves*, Bond Buyer Yearbook (annual), July, 1998, p. 176.

★3977★
TOP SENIOR MANAGER UNDERWRITERS FOR ENVIRONMENTAL FACILITIES, 1997
Ranked by: Amount issued, in thousands of dollars. **Remarks:** Also lists number of issues. **Number listed:** 25

1. Goldman, Sachs & Co., with $1,738,400 thousand
2. Salomon Smith Barney Holdings, $1,128,400
3. Merrill Lynch & Co., $970,100
4. J.P. Morgan Securities Inc., $807,300
5. Lehman Brothers, $740,900
6. Morgan Stanley Dean Witter, $600,800
7. PaineWebber, $484,500
8. Bear, Stearns & Co., $437,300
9. Citicorp Securities Inc., $414,200
10. Dillon, Read & Co., $195,000

Source: *Financial Shelves*, Bond Buyer Yearbook (annual), July, 1998, p. 160.

★3978★
TOP SENIOR MANAGER UNDERWRITERS FOR HEALTHCARE, 1997
Ranked by: Amount issued, in thousands of dollars. **Remarks:** Also lists number of issues. **Number listed:** 25

1. Salomon Smith Barney Holdings, with $4,342,600 thousand
2. Merrill Lynch & Co., $3,191,000
3. PaineWebber, $2,607,100
4. Goldman, Sachs & Co., $1,832,400
5. Bear, Stearns & Co., $1,726,100
6. Ziegler Securities, $1,144,800
7. Cain Brothers & Co., $925,000
8. J.P. Morgan Securities Inc., $820,700
9. Lehman Brothers, $750,000
10. Morgan Stanley Dean Witter, $712,400

Source: *Financial Shelves*, Bond Buyer Yearbook (annual), July, 1998, p. 120.

★3979★
TOP SENIOR MANAGER UNDERWRITERS FOR HOUSING, 1997
Ranked by: Amount issued, in thousands of dollars. **Remarks:** Also lists number of issues. **Number listed:** 25
1. Goldman, Sachs & Co., with $2,498,500 thousand
2. Bear, Stearns & Co., $2,483,900
3. PaineWebber, $2,440,300
4. Merrill Lynch & Co., $1,956,100
5. Lehman Brothers, $1,647,600
6. Salomon Smith Barney Holdings, $1,069,800
7. George K. Baum & Co., $880,700
8. Newman & Associates Inc., $530,100
9. William R. Hough & Co., $464,200
10. Dougherty Summit Securities L.L.C., $355,600

Source: *Financial Shelves*, Bond Buyer Yearbook (annual), July, 1998, p. 144.

★3980★
TOP SENIOR MANAGER UNDERWRITERS FOR PUBLIC FACILITIES, 1997
Ranked by: Amount issued, in thousands of dollars. **Remarks:** Also lists number of issues. **Number listed:** 25
1. Salomon Smith Barney Holdings, with $1,749,700 thousand
2. PaineWebber, $1,427,900
3. Merrill Lynch & Co., $771,500
4. Lehman Brothers, $738,100
5. Bank of America, $606,000
6. A.G. Edwards & Sons Inc., $483,200
7. Bear, Stearns & Co., $465,500
8. Morgan Keegan & Co., $299,500
9. George K. Baum & Co., $274,500
10. Goldman, Sachs & Co., $212,800

Source: *Financial Shelves*, Bond Buyer Yearbook (annual), July, 1998, p. 152.

★3981★
TOP SENIOR MANAGER UNDERWRITERS FOR TAXABLE ISSUES, 1997
Ranked by: Amount issued, in thousands of dollars. **Remarks:** Also lists number of issues. **Number listed:** 25
1. Merrill Lynch & Co., with $3,443,500 thousand
2. Paine Webber Inc., $2,005,800
3. Goldman, Sachs & Co., $1,623,900
4. Bear, Stearns & Co., $749,200
5. Lehman Brothers, $648,600
6. Salomon Smith Barney Holdings, $507,300
7. William R. Hough & Co., $363,000
8. Morgan Stanley Dean Witter, $304,200
9. Banc One Capital Corp., $204,700
10. Citicorp Securities Inc., $167,500

Source: *Financial Shelves*, Bond Buyer Yearbook (annual), July, 1998, p. 184.

★3982★
TOP SENIOR MANAGER UNDERWRITERS FOR TRANSPORTATION, 1997
Ranked by: Amount issued, in thousands of dollars. **Remarks:** Also lists number of issues. **Number listed:** 25
1. Lehman Brothers, with $4,798,600 thousand
2. Salomon Smith Barney Holdings, $4,773,400
3. PaineWebber, $3,738,500
4. Goldman, Sachs & Co., $2,620,600
5. Merrill Lynch & Co., $1,795,200
6. Bear, Stearns & Co., $1,627,700
7. Morgan Stanley Dean Witter, $981,600
8. J.P. Morgan Securities Inc., $728,700
9. Bank of America, $372,200
10. Dillon, Read & Co., $350,000

Source: *Financial Shelves*, Bond Buyer Yearbook (annual), July, 1998, p. 128.

★3983★
TOP SENIOR MANAGER UNDERWRITERS FOR UTILITIES, 1997
Ranked by: Amount issued, in thousands of dollars. **Remarks:** Also lists number of issues. **Number listed:** 25
1. Paine Webber Inc., with $4,061,000 thousand
2. Salomon Smith Barney Holdings, $3,001,800
3. Morgan Stanley Dean Witter, $1,199,500
4. J.P. Morgan Securities Inc., $921,100
5. Merrill Lynch & Co., $807,200
6. Goldman, Sachs & Co., $773,100
7. Raymond James & Associates Inc., $764,200
8. Bear, Stearns & Co., $642,900
9. Prudential Securities Inc., $411,400
10. A.G. Edwards & Sons Inc., $378,300

Source: *Financial Shelves*, Bond Buyer Yearbook (annual), July, 1998, p. 136.

★3984★
TOP SHORT-TERM UNDERWRITERS, 1997
Ranked by: Amount issued, in thousands of dollars. **Remarks:** Also lists number of issues, 1996 rank, amount and issues. **Number listed:** 50
1. Lehman Brothers, with $6,582,900 thousand
2. Salomon Smith Barney Holdings, $4,924,900
3. Goldman, Sachs & Co., $3,341,300
4. Fleet Securities Inc., $2,621,900
5. Merrill Lynch & Co., $2,533,600
6. Morgan Stanley Dean Witter, $2,434,400
7. J.P. Morgan Securities Inc., $2,079,400
8. Piper Jaffray Co., $2,013,400
9. Bear, Stearns & Co., $1,849,400
10. BT Alex. Brown, $1,628,900

Source: *Financial Shelves*, Bond Buyer Yearbook (annual), July, 1998, p. 52.

★3985★
TOP UNDERWRITERS FOR THRIFT INSTITUTIONS WITH FULL CREDIT TO EACH MANAGER, 1998
Ranked by: Debt and equity issued, in millions of dollars. **Remarks:** Includes percentage of market share, number of issues, debt and equity. **Number listed:** 10
1. Credit Suisse First Boston, with $2,824.8 million
2. J.P. Morgan & Co., $2,736.6
3. Salomon Smith Barney Holdings, $2,083.6
4. BankAmerica Corp., $2,028.7
5. Merrill Lynch & Co., $1,629.1
6. Goldman, Sachs & Co., $1,429.4
7. Lehman Brothers, $1,326.6
8. Bear, Stearns & Co., $1,076.7
9. Keefe, Bruyette & Woods, $615.2
10. Friedman, Billings, Ramsey & Co., $613.8

Source: *U.S. Banker*, February, 1999, p. 74.

Security Underwriting, International

★3986★
LEADING UNDERWRITERS OF INTERNATIONAL DEBT WITH FULL CREDIT TO BOOK MANAGER, 1998
Ranked by: Proceeds, in millions of dollars. **Remarks:** Also includes percent of total and number of deals. **Number listed:** 15

1. Merrill Lynch & Co., with $110,268.9 million
2. Goldman, Sachs & Co., $72,711.2
3. Morgan Stanley Dean Witter, $70,975.4
4. Warburg Dillon Read, $66,087.2
5. Salomon Smith Barney Holdings, $61,296.1
6. Credit Suisse First Boston, $54,513.0
7. J.P. Morgan, $43,782.5
8. Deutsche Bank, $42,548.2
9. ABN Amro, $41,778.3
10. Paribas, $38,889.6

Source: *Investment Dealers' Digest*, January 25, 1999, p. 39.

★3987★
LEADING UNDERWRITERS OF WORLDWIDE OFFERINGS WITH FULL CREDIT TO BOOK MANAGER, 1998
Ranked by: Proceeds, in millions of dollars. **Remarks:** Also includes percent of total and number of deals. **Number listed:** 15

1. Merrill Lynch & Co., with $356,575.5 million
2. Salomon Smith Barney Holdings, $250,474.3
3. Morgan Stanley Dean Witter, $249,075.2
4. Goldman, Sachs & Co., $236,601.4
5. Lehman Brothers, $168,203.4
6. Credit Suisse First Boston, $162,832.9
7. J.P. Morgan, $128,346.5
8. Bear, Stearns, $91,653.8
9. Warburg Dillon Read, $83,336.9
10. Chase Manhattan, $78,523.5

Source: *Investment Dealers' Digest*, January 25, 1999, p. 38.

★3988★
LEADING UNDERWRITERS OF YANKEE BONDS WITH FULL CREDIT TO BOOK MANAGER, 1998
Ranked by: Proceeds, in millions of dollars. **Remarks:** Also includes percent of total and number of deals. **Number listed:** 15

1. Merrill Lynch & Co., with $64,233.1 million
2. Goldman, Sachs & Co., $38,247.4
3. Salomon Smith Barney Holdings, $37,490.9
4. Morgan Stanley Dean Witter, $32,193.6
5. Credit Suisse First Boston, $23,024.8
6. Chase Manhattan, $20,311.9
7. Lehman Brothers, $7,420.6
8. J.P. Morgan, $6,940.4
9. Warburg Dillon Read, $2,431.0
10. Bank of America, $1,561.0

Source: *Investment Dealers' Digest*, January 25, 1999, p. 39.

Self-Storage Garages, Warehouses, etc.

★3989★
TOP SELF-STORAGE COMPANIES BY SQUARE FOOTAGE, 1998
Ranked by: Space, in square feet. **Remarks:** Includes number of facilities, number of units and percent of total square footage. **Number listed:** 50

1. Public Storage Inc., with 67,782,234 square feet
2. Storage USA, 29,500,000
3. U-Haul, 26,100,000
4. Shurguard Storage Centers Inc., 22,100,000
5. Storage Trust Realty, 12,242,00
6. Sovran Self Storage Inc., 11,000,000
7. U-Store-It, 6,500,000
8. Storage Inns, Inc., 5,000,000
9. Derrel's Mini Storage Inc., 4,738,486
10. Morningstar Group, 3,900,000

Source: *Mini-Storage Messenger*, Top 50 (annual), September, 1998, p. 38.

Semiconductor Industry

★3990★
MOST ADMIRED ELECTRONICS AND SEMICONDUCTOR CORPORATIONS, 1998
Ranked by: Scores (1-10) derived from a survey of senior executives, outside directors and securities analysts. **Remarks:** Respondents rated companies in their own industry on 8 attributes of reputation. Also notes previous year's rank. **Number listed:** 7

1. Intel, with 8.37
2. Texas Instruments, 7.29
3. Applied Materials, 7.29
4. Analog Devices, 6.60
5. LSI Logic, 6.00
6. Advanced Micro Devices, 5.01
7. National Semiconductor, 4.68

Source: *Fortune*, America's Most Admired Corporations (annual), March 1, 1999, p. F-6.

★3991★
TOP CORPORATIONS IN THE SEMICONDUCTOR INDUSTRY, 1998
Ranked by: Revenue, in millions of dollars. **Remarks:** Also notes profits and investment figures as well as number of employees. **Number listed:** 7

1. Intel, with $26,273 million
2. Texas Instruments, $8,460
3. Advanced Micro Devices, $2,542
4. National Semiconductor, $2,537
5. Amkor Technology, $1,568
6. LSI Logic, $1,491
7. Analog Devices, $1,231

Source: *Fortune*, Fortune 500 Largest U.S. Corporations (annual), April 26, 1999, p. F-68.

★3992★
TOP RESEARCH & DEVELOPMENT SPENDERS IN THE SEMICONDUCTOR INDUSTRY, 1997
Ranked by: R&D expenditures in millions of dollars. **Number listed:** 15

1. Intel Corp., with $2,329.6 million
2. Texas Instruments, $1,527.5
3. Applied Materials Inc., $606.5
4. National Semiconductor, $539.7
5. Advanced Micro Devices, $470.2
6. Micron Technology, $233.4
7. LSI Logic, $228.7
8. Analog Devices, $205.7
9. LAM Research Corp., $202.2
10. Novellus Systems, $201.7

Source: *R&D Magazine*, Giants of R&D (annual), October, 1998, p. S-15.

★3993★
TOP SEMICONDUCTOR COMPANIES, 1998*
Ranked by: Segment revenue, in millions of dollars. **Number listed:** 20

1. Intel, with $21,309.5 million
2. Texas Instruments, $8,092.5
3. Motorola, $7,150.6
4. Applied Materials, $4,546.2

5. IBM, $3,925.4
6. Lucent Technologies, $2,986.1
7. National Semiconductor, $2,592.9
8. Advanced Micro Devices, $2,356.4
9. Micron Technology, $1,833.6
10. Rockwell International, $1,582.6

Source: *Electronic Business*, Top 200 (annual), July, 1998, p. 95.

Semiconductor Industry, International

★3994★
TOP COMPANIES IN DYNAMIC RANDOM ACCESS MEMORY (DRAM) SALES WORLDWIDE, 1998
Ranked by: Worldwide sales, in millions of U.S. dollars ($).
Remarks: Includes 1997 sales, rank and percentage change.
Number listed: 10

1. Samsung, with $2,985.0 million
2. Hyundai, $1,590.0
3. NEC, $1,321.0
4. Micron, $1,301.0
5. LG Semicon, $1,164.0
6. Siemens, $1,010.0
7. Mitsubishi Corp., $1,005.0
8. Hitachi, $935.0
9. Toshiba, $685.0
10. Fujitsu, $570.0

Source: *Electronic Business*, Top 20 (annual), May, 1999, p. 90.

★3995★
TOP COMPANIES IN FLASH MEMORY SALES WORLDWIDE, 1998
Ranked by: Worldwide sales, in millions of U.S. dollars ($).
Remarks: Includes 1997 sales, rank and percentage change.
Number listed: 10

1. Intel, with $726.0 million
2. Advanced Micro Devices, $479.0
3. Fujitsu, $270.0
4. Atmel, $214.0
5. Sharp, $160.0
6. STMicroelectronics, $100.0
7. Mitsubishi Corp., $75.0
8. SST, $69.5
9. Samsung, $65.0
10. Texas Instruments, $52.0

Source: *Electronic Business*, Top 20 (annual), May, 1999, p. 92.

★3996★
TOP COMPANIES IN GATE ARRAY SALES WORLDWIDE, 1998
Ranked by: Worldwide sales, in millions of U.S. dollars ($).
Remarks: Includes 1997 sales, rank and percentage change.
Number listed: 10

1. NEC, with $591.4 million
2. Fujitsu, $477.0
3. Hitachi, $333.8
4. Toshiba, $322.7
5. LSI Logic, $285.0
6. Texas Instruments, $206.0
7. STMicroelectronics, $109.2
8. Samsung, $88.2
9. S-MOS/Seiko, $81.8
10. Mitsubishi Corp., $35.0

Source: *Electronic Business*, Top 20 (annual), May, 1999, p. 95.

★3997★
TOP COMPANIES IN MICROPROCESSOR UNIT (MPU) SALES WORLDWIDE, 1998
Ranked by: Worldwide sales, in millions of U.S. dollars ($).
Remarks: Includes 1997 sales, rank and percentage change.
Number listed: 10

1. Intel, with $19,627.6 million
2. Advanced Micro Devices, $1,402.7
3. Motorola, $1,088.4
4. IBM, $823.5
5. Sun, $275.0
6. Cyrix/National Semi., $233.5
7. SGI/MIPS, $210.0
8. Hitachi, $194.7
9. Integrated Device, $61.3
10. Fujitsu, $51.3

Source: *Electronic Business*, Top 20 (annual), May, 1999, p. 92.

★3998★
TOP COMPANIES IN SEMI-CUSTOM ASIC SALES WORLDWIDE, 1998
Ranked by: Worldwide sales, in millions of U.S. dollars ($).
Remarks: Includes 1997 sales, rank and percentage change.
Number listed: 10

1. IBM, with $1,827.7 million
2. Lucent Technologies, $1,655.0
3. NEC, $1,551.0
4. LSI Logic, $1,526.0
5. Texas Instruments, $931.3
6. Hitachi, $738.6
7. VLSI Technology, $652.5
8. Altera, $613.6
9. Toshiba, $591.9
10. Xilinx, $590.7

Source: *Electronic Business*, Top 20 (annual), May, 1999, p. 95.

★3999★
TOP COMPANIES IN STANDARD CELL SALES WORLDWIDE, 1998
Ranked by: Worldwide sales, in millions of U.S. dollars ($).
Remarks: Includes 1997 sales, rank and percentage change.
Number listed: 10

1. IBM, with $1,742.8 million
2. Lucent Technologies, $1,554.5
3. LSI Logic, $1,241.0
4. NEC, $893.6
5. Texas Instruments, $697.3
6. VLSI Technology, $601.7
7. Hitachi, $401.9
8. STMicroelectronics, $298.8
9. Alcatel Micro., $260.0
10. Toshiba, $243.8

Source: *Electronic Business*, Top 20 (annual), May, 1999, p. 92.

★4000★
TOP COMPANIES IN STATIC RANDOM ACCESS MEMORY (SRAM) SALES WORLDWIDE, 1998
Ranked by: Worldwide sales, in millions of U.S. dollars ($).
Remarks: Includes 1997 sales, rank and percentage change.
Number listed: 10

1. Samsung, with $640.0 million
2. NEC, $410.0
3. Mitsubishi Corp., $380.0

4. IBM, $350.0
5. Toshiba, $325.0
6. Integrated Device Tech., $315.3
7. Motorola, $265.0
8. Hitachi, $255.0
9. Cypress Semiconductor, $251.8
10. Sony, $235.0

Source: *Electronic Business*, Top 20 (annual), May, 1999, p. 90.

★4001★
TOP COMPANIES IN USER-PROGRAMMABLE LOGIC SALES WORLDWIDE, 1998
Ranked by: Worldwide sales, in millions of U.S. dollars ($). **Remarks:** Includes 1997 sales, rank and percentage change. **Number listed:** 10

1. Altera, with $613.6 million
2. Xilinx, $590.7
3. Lattice Semiconductor, $206.2
4. Vantis, $204.5
5. Actel, $153.5
6. Lucent Technologies, $100.1
7. Cypress Semiconductor, $41.5
8. Atmel, $34.5
9. Quicklogic, $25.5
10. Philips, $20.1

Source: *Electronic Business*, Top 20 (annual), May, 1999, p. 92.

★4002★
TOP SEMICONDUCTOR COMPANIES WORLDWIDE, 1998
Ranked by: Worldwide sales, in millions of U.S. dollars. **Remarks:** Includes 1997 sales, rank and percentage change. **Number listed:** 20

1. Intel Corp., with $22,092.0 million
2. NEC, $7,527.0
3. Motorola, $7,300.0
4. Toshiba, $6,125.0
5. Texas Instruments, $6,000.0
6. Hitachi, $5,455.0
7. Samsung, $4,567.0
8. Philips, $4,502.0
9. STMicroelectronics, $4,248.0
10. Siemens, $3,867.0

Source: *Electronic Business*, Top 20 (annual), May, 1999, p. 90.

★4003★
WORLD'S LEADING CHIP MANUFACTURERS, 1998
Ranked by: Worldwide sales, in millions of U.S. dollars ($). **Remarks:** Includes 1997 sales, rank and percentage change. **Number listed:** 10

1. Intel, with $22,784 million
2. NEC, $8,135
3. Motorola, $7,086
4. Toshiba, $5,869
5. Texas Instruments, $5,820
6. Hitachi, $4,620
7. Samsung, $4,595
8. Philips, $4,445
9. ST Microelec., $4,197
10. Fujitsu, $3,826

Source: *WSJ*, June 1, 1999, p. B4.

Service Industries

★4004★
TOP SERVICE INDUSTRY COMPANIES IN THE S&P 500, 1999*
Ranked by: Companies are listed, not ranked. **Remarks:** Includes market value, sales and profitability figures. **Number listed:** 14

1. Omnicom Group
2. Paychex
3. Interpublic Group
4. Enron
5. IMS Health
6. W.W. Grainger
7. Genuine Parts
8. Service Corp. International
9. Waste Management
10. Cendant

Source: *Business Week*, Business Week 50: Top Companies of the S&P 500 (annual), March 29, 1999, p. 162+.

★4005★
TOP SERVICE INDUSTRY COMPANIES ON THE HISPANIC BUSINESS 500, 1998
Ranked by: Revenue, in millions of U.S. dollars ($). **Number listed:** 10

1. Pan American Hospital, with $156.00 million
2. McBride and Associates Inc., $140.00
3. Molina Medical Centers, $135.00
4. Physicians Healthcare Plans Inc., $131.00
5. AIB Financial Group Inc., $121.00
6. Collazo Enterprises Inc., $117.00
7. Gonzalez Design Group, $99.90
8. Plaza Group Inc., $94.00
9. Spanish Broadcasting System Inc., $86.77
10. Oaks Group, $80.03

Source: *Hispanic Business*, Hispanic Business 50, June, 1999, p. 102.

Service Industries--Europe

★4006★
TOP MISCELLANEOUS SERVICE COMPANIES IN EUROPE, 1997
Ranked by: Sales, in thousands of U.S. dollars ($). **Remarks:** Also lists location of headquarters, industry codes, percent change in sales and percent change in local currencies. **Number listed:** 300

1. Shell Transport & Trading, with $45,922,137 thousand
2. Deutsche Telekom AG, $37,696,428
3. France Telecom, $26,123,139
4. BT Plc., $25,800,065
5. Internationale Nederlander Groep NV, $24,258,195
6. Telecom Italia spa, $16,683,491
7. Legal & General Group Plc., $15,569,778
8. Telefonica SA, $15,567,206
9. Deutsche Post AG, $15,142,857
10. Poste(La), $13,838,025

Source: *Dun & Bradstreet*, Europc's Thousand Largest Companies (annual), 1999, p. 688+.

★4007★
TOP OTHER SERVICE COMPANIES IN EUROPE, 1997
Ranked by: Sales, in millions of European Currency Units (ECUs). **Remarks:** Also lists overall rank and number of employees. **Number listed:** 543
1. W.P.P. Group PLC, with ECUs10,752 ECUs
2. AMB Aachener U. Muenchener Beteiligungs-AG, ECUs8,034
3. Cordiant Communications Group PLC, ECUs6,084
4. Granada Group PLC, ECUs6,036
5. Ladbroke Group PLC, ECUs5,631
6. Aegis Group PLC, ECUs5,389
7. Axa Colonia Konzern AG, ECUs5,252
8. Millenium Overseas Holdings Ltd., ECUs4,497
9. Philips GMBH, ECUs4,392
10. ICL PLC, ECUs4,304

Source: *Dun & Bradstreet*, Duns Europa (annual), 1999, p. 289.

★4008★
TOP TRANSPORTATION, COMMUNICATION, POWER GENERATION AND DISTRIBUTION SERVICE COMPANIES IN EUROPE, 1997
Ranked by: Sales, in millions of European Currency Units (ECUs). **Remarks:** Also lists overall rank and number of employees. **Number listed:** 374
1. Deutsche Telekom AG, with ECUs31,988 ECUs
2. Electricite De France, ECUs28,227
3. British Telecommunications PLC, ECUs23,078
4. France Telecom, ECUs20,712
5. Deutsche Bahn AG, ECUs15,326
6. Deutsche Post AG, ECUs13,541
7. British Airways, ECUs12,334
8. Centrica PLC, ECUs11,571
9. British Gas Trading Ltd., ECUs11,045
10. Deutsche Lufthansa AG, ECUs10,580

Source: *Dun & Bradstreet*, Duns Europa (annual), 1999, p. 260.

Service Stations

See: **Automobile Service Stations**

Shampoos

★4009★
TOP BRANDS OF SHAMPOO BY MARKET SHARE, 1997
Ranked by: Market share, in millions of dollars. **Remarks:** Also lists market share for 1996 and measured advertising. **Number listed:** 10
1. Pantene, with $15.4 million
2. Head & Shoulders, $8.3
3. Suave, $7.2
4. Pert Plus, $7.2
5. Clairol, $6.8
6. L'Oreal, $4.2
7. Finesse, $4.0
8. Neutrogena, $3.8
9. Johnson & Johnson's, $3.4
10. Salon Selectives, $3.3

Source: *Advertising Age*, September 28, 1998, p. 31.

Shanghai Stock Exchange

★4010★
LARGEST LISTED B SHARES ON THE SHANGHAI STOCK EXCHANGE, 1997
Ranked by: Market value, in millions of U.S. dollars ($). **Number listed:** 10
1. Shanghai Lujiazui Development, with $283.92 million
2. Zhejing Electricity Power, $222.18
3. Eastern Communications, $181.80
4. Shanghai Dazhong Taxi, $151.69
5. Heilongjiang Electricity, $137.88
6. Shanghai Jinqiao, $72.50
7. Erdos Cashmere (Inner Mongolia), $71.40
8. Jinan Qingqi Motorcycle, $70.84
9. Shanghai Zhenhua Port, $68.80
10. Shanghai Outer Gaoqiao, $65.31

Source: *Euromoney Publications*, SSB Guide to World Equity Markets (annual), 1998, p. 138.

★4011★
MOST ACTIVELY TRADED B SHARES ON THE SHANGHAI STOCK EXCHANGE, 1997
Ranked by: Market value, in millions of U.S. dollars ($). **Number listed:** 10
1. Shanghai Lujiazui Development, with $1.45 million
2. Zhejing Electricity Power, $1.36
3. Eastern Communications, $0.70
4. Erdos Cashmere (Inner Mongolia), $0.59
5. Shai Dazhong Taxi, $0.53
6. Yitai Coal, $0.50
7. Sh Zhenhua Port, $0.49
8. Heilongjiang Electric, $0.48
9. Jinan Qingqi Motorcycle, $0.44
10. Shanghai World's Best, $0.42

Source: *Euromoney Publications*, SSB Guide to World Equity Markets (annual), 1998, p. 138.

Shavers, Electric

See: **Electric Shavers**

Shenzhen Stock Exchange

★4012★
LARGEST LISTED B SHARES ON THE SHENZHEN STOCK EXCHANGE, 1997
Ranked by: Market value, in millions of U.S. dollars ($). **Number listed:** 10
1. Shanghai Konka Electric, with $166.09 million
2. Guangdong Electric, $151.53
3. Hainan Donghai Tour, $146.87
4. China International Marine, $142.11
5. Shenzhen Fandga, $115.07
6. Chong Qing Changan, $100.52
7. Bengang Steel Plates, $88.95
8. China Southern Glass, $84.29
9. Guangdong Prvl. Expr., $83.26
10. Shandong Chenming, $81.33

Source: *Euromoney Publications*, SSB Guide to World Equity Markets (annual), 1998, p. 138.

Shipping--Asia

★4013★
MOST ADMIRED COMPANIES IN THE SHIPPING AND TRANSPORT INDUSTRY IN ASIA, 1998
Ranked by: Score. **Remarks:** Also lists previous year's score, overall score and change in rank. **Number listed:** 11

1. DHL, with 7.34
2. Federal Express, 7.28
3. Saha Union, 7.06
4. Natsteel Electronics, 6.79
5. United Parcel Service, 6.66
6. Berli Jucker, 6.40
7. East Asiatic, 6.35
8. Keppel Corp., 6.25
9. Hanjin Shipping Company, 6.09
10. Surnitomo Corp., 6.03

Source: *Asian Business*, Most Admired Companies in Asia (annual), May, 1998, p. 29.

Shoe Industry

★4014★
TOP CITIES OF FOOTWEAR SALES IN APPAREL STORES, 1997
Ranked by: Sales, in thousands of dollars. **Number listed:** 321

1. New York, NY, with $1,242,694 thousand
2. Chicago, IL, $1,170,563
3. Los Angeles-Long Beach, CA, $1,020,244
4. Washington, DC, $762,559
5. Philadelphia, PA, $735,133
6. Atlanta, GA, $614,683
7. Detroit, MI, $606,665
8. Houston, TX, $597,237
9. Boston-Lawrence-Lowell-Brockton, MA, $572,744
10. Dallas, TX, $496,211

Source: *Sales & Marketing Magazine*, Survey of Buying Power (annual), August, 1998, p. 195.

Shopping Centers

★4015★
STATES WITH THE MOST SHOPPING MALL SPACE, 1998*
Ranked by: Leasable square feet, in millions. **Remarks:** Includes number of malls and mall space per resident. **Number listed:** 7

1. California, with 171.9 million
2. Florida, 105.6
3. Texas, 99.4
4. New York, 93.5
5. Pennsylvania, 88.0
6. Ohio, 85.9
7. Illinois, 82.5

Source: *Governing*, September, 1998, p. 66.

★4016★
STATES WITH THE MOST SHOPPING MALL SPACE, 1998*
Ranked by: Total number of major shopping malls. **Remarks:** Includes total mall space and mall space per resident. **Number listed:** 7

1. California, with 253
2. Florida, 185
3. Texas, 136
4. New York, 152
5. Pennsylvania, 167
6. Ohio, 147
7. Illinois, 148

Source: *Governing*, September, 1998, p. 66.

★4017★
TOP INTERMEDIARIES, 1998
Ranked by: Total dollar amount committed or arranged, in millions of dollars. **Remarks:** Includes address, phone numbers, officers, major projects financed, amount arranged/committed by region and lending goal. **Number listed:** 10

1. Holliday Fenoglio Fowler, L.P., with $2,480 million
2. L.J. Melody, $2,290
3. USA Funding Inc., $1,200
4. Northland/Marquette Capital Group Inc., $663
5. Ackman-Ziff Real Estate Group LLC, $430
6. Sonnenblick-Goldman Co., $400
7. Johnson Capital Group Inc., $329
8. Capital Network Advisors Inc., $100
9. David Cronheim Mortgage Corp., $99.25
10. Aztec Group Inc., $72

Source: *Shopping Center World*, Top 25 Retail Lenders (annual), January, 1999, p. 60+.

★4018★
TOP MANAGERS OF STRIP SHOPPING CENTERS BY TOTAL GROSS LEASABLE AREA OWNED, 1998
Ranked by: Gross leasable area owned, in square feet. **Remarks:** Includes address, phone numbers and officers. **Number listed:** 50

1. Kimco Realty Corp., with 45,600,000 square feet
2. CB Richard Ellis, 42,382,607
3. Developers Diversified Realty Corp., 34,321,294
4. Anderson Development Co., 33,850,000
5. Trammell Crow Co., 26,036,051
6. New Plan Realty Trust, 22,000,000
7. Weingarten Realty Investors, 19,494,237
8. Simon DeBartolo Group, 18,501,254
9. R D Management Corp., 18,417,974
10. Regency Realty Corp., 18,400,000

Source: *Shopping Center World*, Top Strip Center Managers and Owners Survey (annual), January, 1999, p. 61+.

★4019★
TOP OWNERS OF SHOPPING CENTERS BY TOTAL GROSS LEASABLE AREA OWNED, 1998
Ranked by: Gross leasable area owned, in square feet. **Remarks:** Includes address, phone numbers and officers. **Number listed:** 50

1. Simon Property Group, with 136,044,894
2. General Growth Properties, 71,536,695
3. Westfield Holdings Ltd., 60,800,000
4. Kimco Realty Corp., 60,623,975
5. Richard E. Jacobs Group Inc., 40,362,198
6. Developers Diversified Realty Corp., 40,356,118
7. New Plan Excel Realty Trust, 37,369,587
8. The Macerich Co., 35,000,000
9. Benderson Development Co. Inc., 33,272,000
10. The Cafaro Co., 32,169,933

Source: *Shopping Center World*, Top Owners Survey (annual), January, 1999, p. 70+.

★4020★

TOP OWNERS OF STRIP SHOPPING CENTERS BY TOTAL GROSS LEASABLE AREA OWNED, 1998

Ranked by: Gross leasable area owned, in square feet. **Remarks:** Includes address, phone numbers and officers. **Number listed:** 50

1. Kimco Realty Corp., with 45,400,000 square feet
2. Benderson Development Co. Inc., 33,850,000
3. Developers Diversified Realty Corp., 31,883,464
4. New Plan Realty Trust, 22,000,000
5. Weingarten Realty Investors, 18,588,635
6. R.D. Management Corp., 17,257,887
7. Inland Real Estate Corp., 14,422,119
8. Simon DeBartolo Group, 14,410,299
9. Regency Realty Corp., 13,400,000
10. Glimcher Realty Trust, 13,400,000

Source: *Shopping Center World*, Top Strip Center Managers and Owners Survey (annual), January, 1999, p. 66+.

★4021★

TOP RETAIL LENDERS, 1998

Ranked by: Total dollar amount committed or arranged, in billions of dollars. **Remarks:** Includes address, phone numbers, officers, major projects financed, amount arranged/committed by region and lending goal. **Number listed:** 25

1. Lehman Brothers, with $5.0 billion
2. Credit Suisse First Boston, $4.0
3. Bank of America Corp./NationsBanc Montgomery Securities LLC, $2.3
4. TIAA, $1.98
5. First Union, $1.8
5. Wells Fargo Bank, $1.8

GMAC Commercial Mortgage, $1.39
CIBC World Markets, $1.3
KeyBank National Association, $1.26
Goldman, Sachs & Co., $1.11

Source: *Shopping Center World*, Top 25 Retail Lenders (annual), January, 1999, p. 54+.

★4022★

TOP SHOPPING CENTER BUYERS

Ranked by: Number of purchases. **Number listed:** 10

1. Simon DeBartolo Group
2. Macerich Co.
3. Excel Realty Trust Inc.
4. General Growth Management Inc.
5. Zamias Services Inc.
6. Urban Retail Properties Co.
7. Westfield Corp. Inc.
8. Prime Retail LP
9. Colonial Properties Trust
10. Burnham Pacific Properties Inc.

Source: *Shopping Center World*, October, 1998, p. 44.

★4023★

TOP SHOPPING CENTER SELLERS

Ranked by: Number of purchases. **Number listed:** 10

1. Heitman Retail Properties
2. Equitable Real Estate Investment Management
3. Met Life Insurance Co.
4. U.S. Prime Property Inc.
5. California Public Employees Retirement System
6. Corporate Property Investors
7. Prudential Insurance Co. of America
8. Horizon Group Inc.
9. ERE Yarmouth
10. The Rouse Co.

Source: *Shopping Center World*, October, 1998, p. 44.

★4024★

TOP SHOPPING MALLS IN THE U.S. BY NUMBER OF MALLS, 1998*

Ranked by: Number of major shopping malls. **Remarks:** Includes total mall space and mall space per resident. **Number listed:** 7

1. California, with 253
2. Florida, 185
3. Pennsylvania, 167
4. New York, 152
5. Illinois, 148
6. Ohio, 147
7. Texas, 136

Source: *Governing*, September, 1998, p. 66.

★4025★

TOP SHOPPING MALLS IN THE U.S. BY TOTAL MALL SPACE, 1998*

Ranked by: Number of major shopping malls. **Remarks:** Includes total mall space and mall space per resident. **Number listed:** 7

1. California, with 171.9 million
2. Florida, 105.6
3. Texas, 99.4
4. New York, 93.5
5. Pennsylvania, 88.0
6. Ohio, 85.9
7. Illimois, 82.5

Source: *Governing*, September, 1998, p. 66.

Shopping Centers--Design and Construction

★4026★

TOP RETAIL CONTRACTORS OF INTERIOR SPACE

Ranked by: Shell construction square footage. **Remarks:** Includes address, phone numbers and officers. **Number listed:** 50

1. Fisher Development Inc., with 19,260,954
2. EMJ Corp, 18,857,272
3. The Whiting-Turner Contracting Co., 15,055,575
4. R.A.S. Builders Inc., 13,732,455
5. Walbridge Aldinger, 12,430,045
6. Miller Building Corp., 11,841,433
7. Vratsinas Construction Co., 9,900,000
8. Shrader & Martinez Construction Inc., 9,227,750
9. S.D. Deacon Corp., 9,045,975
10. Gallant Construction, 8,750,210

Source: *Shopping Center World*, Top Contractors Survey, July, 1998, p. 56.

★4027★

TOP RETAIL CONTRACTORS OF SHELL SPACE

Ranked by: Shell construction square footage. **Remarks:** Includes address, phone numbers and officers. **Number listed:** 50

1. The Whiting-Turner Contracting Co., with 20,074,100
2. EMJ Corp, 19,761,566
3. Walbridge Aldinger, 15,824,539
4. Miller Building Corp., 11,801,433
5. Bovis Inc., 11,490,700
6. L.F. Jennings Inc., 10,315,000
7. Vratsinas Construction Co., 10,200,000
8. Keene Construction Co., 9,972,090
9. Beaver Builders Ltd., 9,600,000
10. S.D. Deacon Corp., 8,925,497

Source: *Shopping Center World*, Top Contractors Survey, July, 1998, p. 60.

Shopping Centers--Detroit Metropolitan Area

★4028★
DETROIT'S LEADING MULTITENANT RETAIL PROPERTIES
Ranked by: Gross leasable area in square footage. **Remarks:** Includes address, occupancy percentage, center type, owner, leasing agent, number of stores and anchors. **Number listed:** 20

1. Northland Center, with 2,200,000
2. Oakland Mall, 1,500,000
3. Fairlane Town Center, 1,484,000
4. Lakeside Mall, 1,474,000
5. Great Lakes Crossing, 1,400,000
6. Summit Place Mall, 1,380,713
7. Somerset Collection, 1,350,000
8. Eastland Center, 1,300,000
9. Twelve Oaks Mall, 1,224,000
10. Westland Shopping Center, 1,017,222

Source: *Crain's Detroit*, Crain's Detroit Business (annual), September 21, 1998, p. 27.

Shopping Centers--Florida

★4029★
TOP SHOPPING CENTERS IN FLORIDA, 1998
Ranked by: Gross leasable square feet. **Remarks:** Includes address, number of stores and parking spaces, owner, management company, anchors, leasing agent, phone and year opened or renovated. **Number listed:** 25

1. Sawgrass Mills, with 2,350,000 square feet
2. Aventura Mall, 2,100,000
3. Pompano Square, 1,421,329
4. Boynton Beach Mall, 1,401,229
5. Dadeland Mall, 1,400,000
6. Regency Square Mall, 1,400,000
7. Pembroke Lakes Mall, 1,358,760
8. Gardens of the Palm Beaches, 1,350,000
9. The Avenues, 1,300,000
10. Town Center at Boca Raton, 1,300,000

Source: *Florida Trend*, Top Rank Florida (annual), 1999, p. 30.

Shopping Centers--Los Angeles County (CA)

★4030★
TOP SHOPPING CENTERS IN LOS ANGELES COUNTY, 1998
Ranked by: Gross leasable square feet. **Remarks:** Includes address, anchor stores, property owner, number of stores, screens and restaurants, history, general manager and leasing agent. **Number listed:** 25

1. Del Amo Fashion Center, with 3,000,000 square feet
2. Lakewood Center Mall, 1,805,489
3. Northridge Fashion Center, 1,573,687
4. Glendale Galleria, 1,364,000
5. Los Cerritos Center, 1,309,129
6. Media City Center, 1,259,000
7. The Plaza at West Covina, 1,236,344
8. Fallbrook Mall, 1,200,000
9. Puente Hills Mall, 1,200,000
10. Santa Anita Fashion Park, 1,122,188

Source: *Los Angeles Business Journal*, Book of Lists (annual), 1999, p. 92.

Shopping Centers--Management

★4031★
LEADING SHOPPING CENTER MANAGERS, 1999*
Ranked by: Total gross leasable area managed, in square feet. **Remarks:** Includes address, phone numbers and officers. **Number listed:** 50

1. Simon Property Group, with 164,919,363 square feet
2. General Growth Properties, 98,820,695
3. CB Richard Ellis, 64,200,000
4. Westfield Holdings Ltd., 60,800,000
5. Kimco Realty Corp., 60,623,975
6. Urban Shopping Centers Inc., 53,672,000
7. Trammell Crow Co., 51,390,251
8. Developers Diversified Realty Corp., 42,793,948
9. The Richard E. Jacobs Group Inc., 41,942,126
10. The Macerich Co., 38,000,000

Source: *Shopping Center World*, Top Managers Survey (annual), March, 1999, p. 40+.

Shopping Centers--Philadelphia Metropolitan Area

★4032★
LARGEST PHILADELPHIA-AREA ENCLOSED SHOPPING MALLS, 1998*
Ranked by: Total gross leasable area managed, in square feet. **Remarks:** Includes address, percent occupied acres, parking spaces, stores, anchor stores, year opened, year renovated, manager, owner and leasing agent. **Number listed:** 25

1. The Court & The Plaza at King of Prussia, with 2,900,663 square feet
2. Franklin Mills, 1,587,130
3. The Gallery at Market East, 1,348,000
4. Cherry Hill Mall, 1,286,000
5. Montgomery Mall, 1,274,248
6. Oxford Valley Mall, 1,142,730
7. Echelon Mall, 1,055,000
8. Deptford Mall, 1,040,000
9. Granite Run Mall, 1,035,700
10. Neshaminy Mall, 1,027,000

Source: *Philadelphia Business Journal*, Book of Business Lists (annual), December 25, 1998, p. 126.

Silver Mines and Mining

★4033★
TOP SILVER PRODUCING NATIONS, 1997
Ranked by: Ounces produced, in millions of dollars. **Remarks:** Includes 1996 figures. **Number listed:** 10

1. Mexico, with $86.2 million
2. Peru, $66.8
3. U.S., $53.3

4. CIS, $45.5
5. Canada, $39.0
6. China, $37.9
7. Australia, $35.6
8. Chile, $35.1
9. Poland, $33.8
10. Bolivia, $12.4

Source: *Jewelers' Circular Keystone*, July, 1998, p. 82.

Singapore Stock Exchange

★4034★
LARGEST LISTED COMPANIES ON THE SINGAPORE STOCK EXCHANGE, 1997
Ranked by: Market value, in billions of Singapore dollars (S$). **Number listed:** 20

1. Singapore Telecom, with ¥47.88 billion
2. Daimler Benz, ¥46.18
3. SIA, ¥10.39
4. OCBC, ¥9.70
5. Hong Kong Land, ¥8.40
6. UOB, ¥8.30
7. DBS, ¥7.23
8. Jardine Matheson, ¥6.45
9. City Developments, ¥6.19
10. SPH, ¥5.83

Source: *Euromoney Publications*, SSB Guide to World Equity Markets (annual), July, 1998, p. 431.

★4035★
MOST ACTIVELY TRADED SHARES ON THE SINGAPORE STOCK EXCHANGE, 1997
Ranked by: Trading volume, in millions of shares. **Number listed:** 20

1. Hong Kong Land, with 1,168.12 million shares
2. Singapore Telecom, 960.55
3. DBS Land, 722.04
4. Hotung, 684.25
5. IPC Corporation, 637.53
6. AFP, 626.98
7. Tianjin Zhong Xin, 477.61
8. FHTK Holding, 458.18
9. Keppel Corporation, 448.58
10. Natsteel Ltd., 401.28

Source: *Euromoney Publications*, SSB Guide to World Equity Markets (annual), July, 1998, p. 431.

Skin Care Products

★4036★
TOP FACIAL CLEANERS, 1999*
Ranked by: Sales, in millions of dollars. **Remarks:** Includes unit volume. **Number listed:** 10

1. Biore, with $140.8 million
2. Pond's, $104.5
3. Noxzema, $58.3
4. Clean & Clear, $49.2
5. Neutrogena, $44.8
6. Oil of Olay, $34.3
7. Sea Breeze, $23.2
8. St. Ives, $21.9
9. Cetaphil, $20.6
10. Freeman, $15.0

Source: *MMR*, May 3, 1999, p. 42.

★4037★
TOP FACIAL MOISTURIZERS, 1998
Ranked by: Sales, in millions of dollars. **Remarks:** Includes unit volume. **Number listed:** 9

1. Oil of Olay, with $146.2 million
2. L'Oreal Plenitude, $86.8
3. Pond's, $65.0
4. Neutrogena, $57.9
5. Alpha Hydrox, $21.0
6. Visage, $20.6
7. Almay, $18.3
8. Sudden Change, $9.8
9. Fa Li, $9.7

Source: *MMR*, May 3, 1999, p. 38.

★4038★
TOP HAND & BODY LOTIONS, 1998
Ranked by: Sales, in millions of dollars. **Remarks:** Includes unit volume. **Number listed:** 10

1. Vaseline Intensive Care, with $120.5 million
2. Jergens, $71.7
3. Suave, $54.9
4. Lubriderm, $54.3
5. Curel, $43.8
6. Nivea, $41.2
7. Eucerin, $39.0
8. Keri, $23.0
9. Neutrogena Norwegian Formula, $19.2
10. Jergens Ultra Healing, $17.5

Source: *MMR*, May 3, 1999, p. 44.

★4039★
TOP SUNTAN PRODUCTS, 1998
Ranked by: Sales, in millions of dollars. **Remarks:** Includes unit volume. **Number listed:** 10

1. Coppertone, with $62.7 million
2. Banana Boat, $52.8
3. Neutrogena, $40.1
4. Hawaiian Tropic, $24.4
5. Bain de Soleil, $20.9
6. Coppertone Sport, $20.7
7. No-Ad, $19.2
8. Coppertone Water Babies, $17.4
9. Coppertone Kids Colorblock, $14.1
10. Banana Boat Sport, $10.1

Source: *MMR*, May 3, 1999, p. 42.

Skin Care Products--International

★4040★
TOP SKIN CARE MARKET WORLDWIDE, 1998*
Ranked by: Sales, in percent. **Number listed:** 7

1. Western Europe, with 52%
2. Asia, 19%
3. Japan, 12%
4. North & South America, 7%
5. Rest of Europe, 5%
6. Pacific, 3%
7. Africa, 2%

Source: *MMR*, October 5, 1998, p. 4.

★4041★
TOP SKIN CARE PRODUCTS WORLDWIDE, 1999*
Ranked by: Sales, in percent. **Number listed:** 6
1. Other, with 64%
2. L'Oreal, 9%
3. Shiseido, 8%
4. Kanebo, 8%
5. Beiersdorf, 6%
6. Estee Lauder, 5%

Source: *Global Cosmetic Industry*, February, 1999, p. 18.

Small Business

★4042★
BEST SMALL COMPANIES, 1998*
Ranked by: Criteria includes profitability and growth. **Remarks:** Includes sales, net income, market value, EPS, P/E and recent price. **Number listed:** 200
1. American Locker Group
2. Syntel
3. Abacus Direct
4. Datastream Systems
5. Pre-Paid Legal Services
6. Anchor Gaming
7. National RV Holdings
8. Kaynar Technologies
9. Micrel Inc.
10. Media Arts Group

Source: *Forbes*, Small Growth Companies (annual), November 2, 1998, p. 86.

★4043★
FASTEST GROWING PRIVATE COMPANIES, 1993-1997
Ranked by: Sales growth between 1993 and 1997, in percent. **Remarks:** Includes 1993 and 1997 sales, profit range, number of employees and year founded. **Number listed:** 500
1. Justice Technology, with 26,899%
2. Power Lift, 16,988%
3. NexCycle, 14,332%
4. Heritage Communities, 13,991%
5. Adams Golf, 12,684%
6. Commercial Financial Services, 12,277%
7. Cybertech International, 11,682%
8. Charter Communications, 10,761%
9. Jade Systems, 10,432%
10. Gaiam, 9,653%

Source: *Inc.*, Inc. 500: America's Fastest Growing Private Companies (annual), October 20, 1998, p. 81.

★4044★
FASTEST-GROWING SMALL BUSINESSES BY EARNINGS GROWTH, 1997-1999
Ranked by: Earnings growth over a 3-year period, in percent. **Number listed:** 5
1. Brass Eagle, with $1,620.2% million
2. LHS Group, $286.7%
3. Cotelligent, $232.4%
4. Funco, $229.1%
5. Qlogic, $225.1%

Source: *Business Week*, Small Growth Companies (annual), May 31, 1999, p. 87.

★4045★
FASTEST-GROWING SMALL BUSINESSES BY EARNINGS, 1998
Ranked by: Earnings, in millions of dollars. **Number listed:** 5
1. Linear Technology, with $189.6 million
2. Centex Construction Products, $77.3
3. Citrix Systems, $74.6
4. Kaydon, $69.0
5. Anchor Gaming, $68.6

Source: *Business Week*, Small Growth Companies (annual), May 31, 1999, p. 86.

★4046★
FASTEST-GROWING SMALL BUSINESSES BY MARKET VALUE, 1999*
Ranked by: Market value, in millions of dollars. **Number listed:** 5
1. Linear Technology, with $8,360 million
2. VISX, $3,750
3. Citrix Systems, $3,663
4. Total System Services, $3,590
5. Vitesse Semiconductor, $3,560

Source: *Business Week*, Small Growth Companies (annual), May 31, 1999, p. 87.

★4047★
FASTEST-GROWING SMALL BUSINESSES BY RETURN ON CAPITAL, 1997-99
Ranked by: Average annual return on capital over a 3-year period. **Number listed:** 5
1. Specialty Equipment, with 47.5
2. Plantronics, 44.7
3. Landauer, 44.7
4. Duff & Phelps Credit Rating, 44.1
5. Metro Information, 42.6

Source: *Business Week*, Small Growth Companies (annual), May 31, 1999, p. 86.

★4048★
FASTEST-GROWING SMALL BUSINESSES BY SALES GROWTH, 1997-99
Ranked by: Average annual growth over a 3-year period, in percent. **Number listed:** 5
1. Friede Goldman Intl., with 186.5%
2. Citrix Systems, 159.5%
3. Brass Eagle, 159.3%
4. Advanced Tech. Products, 149.4%
5. International Network Services, 122.1%

Source: *Business Week*, Small Growth Companies (annual), May 31, 1999, p. 86.

★4049★
FASTEST-GROWING SMALL BUSINESSES BY SALES, 1998
Ranked by: Sales, in millions of dollars. **Number listed:** 5
1. Linear Technology, with $498.2 million
2. Specialty Equipment, $495.6
3. Wet Seal, $485.4
4. RemedyTemp, $465.0
5. Friede Goldman Intl., $459.3

Source: *Business Week*, Small Growth Companies (annual), May 31, 1999, p. 86.

★4050★
FASTEST-GROWING SMALL BUSINESSES, 1999*
Ranked by: Criteria including market value, current stock price and annual sales. **Remarks:** Includes current sales & earnings, 3 year averages and investment data. **Number listed:** 100
1. Friede Goldman Intl.

2. Brass Eagle
3. Salton
4. Media Arts Group
5. Apex PC Solutions
6. Bebe Stores
7. Funco
8. Metro Information Services
9. Kroll-O'Gara
10. ASI Solutions

Source: *Business Week*, Small Growth Companies (annual), May 31, 1999, p. 100.

Small Business--Finance

★4051★
FUNDING SOURCES FOR SMALL BUSINESSES, 1999*
Ranked by: Funding, in percent. **Number listed:** 8

1. Owner Equity, with 27.1%
2. Bank Loans, 19.9%
3. Trade Credit, 17.0%
4. Other Debt Sources, 15.4%
5. Equity from Friends & Family, 13.2%
6. Angels, 4.9%
7. Venture Capital, 2.4%
8. Credit Cards, .2%

Source: *Business Week*, June 7, 1999, p. 8.

★4052★
START-UP CAPITAL NEEDED FOR SMALL BUSINESSES, 1998*
Ranked by: Percent of capital needed. **Number listed:** 4

1. Less than $5,000, with 37.9%
2. $10,000 to $50,000, 27.3%
3. $5,000 to $10,000, 21.2%
4. More than $50,000, 13.6%

Source: *Journal of Accountancy*, July, 1998, p. 12.

Small Business Loans

★4053★
TOP SMALL BUSINESS LENDERS, 1998*
Ranked by: Overall loans, in millions of dollars. **Number listed:** 10

1. Wells Fargo & Co., with $5,751 million
2. Bank One Corp., $4,262
3. NationsBank Corp., $4,078
4. First Union Corp., $3,851
5. Norwest Corp., $3,758
6. Chase Manhattan Corp., $3,724
7. American Express, $3,505
8. KeyCorp, $3,464
9. U.S. Bancorp, $3,316
10. Fleet Financial Group, $3,227

Source: *US Banker*, November, 1998, p. 12.

Small Business Loans--Detroit Metropolitan Area

★4054★
LARGEST SBA GUARANTY LOANS DISBURSED IN THE DETROIT METROPOLITAN AREA, 1998
Ranked by: Loan amount, in thousands of dollars. **Number listed:** 25

1. Dequindre Properties Inc., with $2,700.0 thousand
2. New Center Stamping Inc., $2,500.0
3. New Pattern Inc., $2,200.0
4. Great Lakes Color Printers, $1,700.0
5. H&K Inc. & Stephieco Inc., $1,700.0
6. Vogue Furniture/Perspectives in Laminate Inc., $1,585.0
7. Baby N Kids Bedrooms, $1,559.0
8. Childers Print & Graphic Inc., $1,520.0
9. Insync Interactive Communications Inc., $1,300.0
10. Fire Academy, $1,225.0

Source: *Crain's Detroit Business*, Crain's Detroit Business (annual), November 9, 1998, p. 13.

★4055★
TOP SBA LENDERS IN FLORIDA, 1997
Ranked by: Volume, in dollars. **Remarks:** Includes number of loans, average loan amount, senior SBA executive and year founded. **Number listed:** 50

1. The Money Store Investment Corp., with $37,130,841 million
2. 1st United Bank, $31,740,350
3. AT&T Small Business Lending Corp., $25,537,700
4. Heller First Capital Corp., $23,189,303
5. NationsBank NA, $15,616,949
6. GE Capital Small Business Finance Group, $15,236,000
7. Emergent Business Capital Inc., $13,247,500
8. Admiralty Bank, $12,552,000
9. AMRESCO Inc., $9,762,500
10. Barnett Bank N.A., $9,244,685

Source: *Florida Trend*, Top Rank Florida (annual), 1999, p. 18+.

Small Business Loans--Los Angeles County (CA)

★4056★
LARGEST SBA LENDERS IN THE LOS ANGELES METROPOLITAN AREA, 1998
Ranked by: Loan amount, in millions of dollars. **Remarks:** Includes number of loans, minority loans, loan size, headquarters, and top SBA executive. **Number listed:** 25

1. Bank of America, with $73.1 million
2. Bank of Commerce, $67.2
3. Wilshire State Bank, $45.4
4. California Statewide C.D.C., $43.4
5. City National Bank, $34.2
6. Heller Financial, $29.1
7. Bank of Yorba Linda, $27.0
8. Hanmi Bank, $25.3
9. Nara Bank, $25.0
10. GE Capital Small Business Finance, $21.7

Source: *Los Angeles Business Journal*, November 9, 1998, p. 12+.

Small Business Loans--New York Metropolitan Area

★4057★
LARGEST SBA GUARANTEED LOANS IN THE NEW YORK METROPOLITAN AREA, 1998
Ranked by: Loan amount, in dollars. **Remarks:** Includes SBA share, loan type, participating lender, purpose of loan and industry. **Number listed:** 30
1. West Point Realty Inc., with $4,140,700
2. Red Hook Realty, $3,300,000
3. Bifal Corp., $3,000,000
4. Chemicraft International Inc., $3,000,000
5. Kaylu Realty Corp., $2,301,000
6. Eva LIC Realty Associates, $2,250,000
7. Olympia Mortgage Corp., $2,200,000
8. Rockland Standard Gear Inc., $2,100,000
9. Felix Storch Inc., $2,060,000
10. MJ's Supper Club, $2,000,000

Source: *Crain's New York Business*, Top 30 SBA Lenders (annual), February 8, 1999, p. 20.

★4058★
LARGEST SBA LENDERS IN THE NEW YORK METROPOLITAN AREA, 1998
Ranked by: Number of loans. **Remarks:** Includes amount of loans, minority loans and nonminority loans. **Number listed:** 30
1. Chase Manhattan Bank, with 496
2. Citibank, 241
3. Banco Popular de Puerto Rico, 130
4. Marine Midland Bank, 88
5. Commercial Capital Corp., 67
6. Broadway National Bank, 60
7. AT&T Small Business Lending Corp., 52
8. Fleet Bank, 42
9. GE Capital Small Business, 33
10. Key Bank of New York, 31

Source: *Crain's New York Business*, Top 30 SBA Lenders (annual), December 14, 1998, p. 24.

Snacks

★4059★
LEADING SNACK CAKE BRANDS BY DOLLAR SALES, 1998
Ranked by: Dollar sales, in percent. **Number listed:** 6
1. Little Debbie, with 31.4%
2. Hostess, 31.0%
3. Others, 15.5%
4. Tastykake, 9.0%
5. Drake, 7.7%
6. Private Label, 5.4%

Source: *Milling & Baking News*, June 30, 1998, p. 10.

★4060★
LEADING SNACK CAKE BRANDS BY UNIT SALES, 1998
Ranked by: Unit sales, in percent. **Number listed:** 6
1. Little Debbie, with 45.2%
2. Hostess, 20.7%
3. Others, 16.3%
4. Tastykake, 7.3%
5. Private Label, 5.5%
6. Drake, 5.0%

Source: *Milling & Baking News*, June 30, 1998, p. 10.

★4061★
TOP MEAT SNACK DISTRIBUTION BY OUTLET, 1997
Ranked by: Percent of total distribution. **Number listed:** 8
1. C-Stores, with 43.4%
2. Mass merchandisers, 16.6%
3. Supermarkets, 10.6%
4. Warehouse Clubs, 9.2%
5. Other, 8.9%
6. Grocery Stores, 6.7%
7. Drugstores, 3.1%
8. Vending, 1.5%

Source: *Distribution Channels*, October, 1998, p. 47.

★4062★
TOP MEAT SNACK FLAVORS, 1996
Ranked by: Percent of supermarket pound volume. **Number listed:** 7
1. Regular, with 33.3%
2. Hot & Spicy, 20%
3. Smoked, 17.3%
4. Other, 14.2%
5. Teriyaki, 10%
6. Meat & Cheese, 4.9%
7. Barbecue, .3%

Source: *U.S. Distribution Journal*, July, 1998, p. 20.

★4063★
TOP PRETZEL BRANDS, 1999*
Ranked by: Total sales, in millions of dollars. **Remarks:** Includes unit sales and percent change in dollar and unit sales from previous year. **Number listed:** 14
1. Rold Gold, with $145,067,616 million
2. Snyder's of Hanover, $111,765,552
3. Bachman, $21,646,932
4. Combo's, $17,406,806
5. Gardettos, $16,979,288
6. Old Tyme, $16,906,870
7. Herrs, $14,008,996
8. Utz, $11,830,743
9. Air Crisps, $11,589,763
10. Rold Gold Crispy, $10,929,523

Source: *Milling & Banking News*, April 27, 1999, p. 35.

★4064★
TOP SALTED SNACK BRANDS, 1999*
Ranked by: Total sales, in millions of dollars. **Remarks:** Includes lead agency and media expenditures. **Number listed:** 5
1. Lay's, with $1,039 million
2. Doritos, $785
3. Tostitos, $682
4. Ruffles, $557
5. Pringle's, $478

Source: *Brandweek*, Superbrands: America's Top 2,000 Brands (annual), June 21, 1999, p. S46.

★4065★
TOP SNACK BARS, 1998
Ranked by: Dollar sales, in millions of dollars. **Number listed:** 10
1. Kellogg's Nutri-Grain, with $149.7 million
2. Chewy, $119.9
3. Kellogg's Rice Krispies Treats, $102.9
4. Snackwell's, $80.0
5. Kudos, $46.6
6. Nature Valley Granola Bars, $37.5
7. Sunbelt Granola Bars, $33.5
8. Power Bar, $30.3

9. Golden Grahams Treats, $29.5
10. Entenmann's Multi Grain, $25.4

Source: *MMR*, August 3, 1998, p. 16.

★4066★
TOP SNACKS BY POUND VOLUME SHARES, 1998
Ranked by: Total pound volume shares, in percent. **Number listed:** 10

1. Potato Chips, with 31.0%
2. Tortilla Chips, 22.8%
3. Pretzels, 11.5%
4. Snack Nuts, 7.0%
5. Microwavable Popcorn, 6.8%
6. Extruded Snacks, 5.7%
7. Corn Chips, 3.8%
8. Ready-to-Eat Popcorn, 2.7%
9. Party Mix, 2.0%
10. Others, 6.7%

Source: *Discount Merchandiser*, October, 1998, p. 3.

★4067★
TOP TORTILLA CHIP DISTRIBUTION BY OUTLET, 1997
Ranked by: Total sales, in percent. **Number listed:** 8

1. Supermarkets, with 46.0%
2. C-Stores, 12.4%
3. Mass merchandisers, 10.4%
4. Grocery Stores, 8.7%
5. Other, 8.6%
6. Warehouse Clubs, 7.6%
7. Vending, 3.4%
8. Drugstores, 2.9%

Source: *Distribution Channels*, October, 1998, p. 47.

Soap Industry

★4068★
MOST ADMIRED SOAP AND COSMETIC CORPORATIONS, 1998
Ranked by: Scores (1-10) derived from a survey of senior executives, outside directors, and securities analysts. **Remarks:** Respondents rated companies in their own industry on 8 attributes of reputation. Also includes previous year's rank. **Number listed:** 10

1. Procter & Gamble, with 8.10
2. Gillette, 7.75
3. Colgate-Palmolive, 7.39
4. Estee Lauder, 7.02
5. Clorox, 6.97
6. Unilever U.S., 6.51
7. Avon Products, 6.46
8. International Flavors & Fragrances, 6.38
9. Alberto-Culver, 5.57
10. Revlon, 5.55

Source: *Fortune*, America's Most Admired Corporations (annual), March 1, 1999, p. F-3.

★4069★
TOP BAR SOAP SALES, 1999
Ranked by: Sales, in millions of dollars. **Remarks:** Includes percent change and share. **Number listed:** 10

1. Dove, with $269.5 million
2. Dial 1, $192.1
3. Lever 2000, $136.9
4. Irish Spring, $120.6
5. Zest, $113.9
6. Caress, $94.3
7. Ivory, $94.1
9. Olay, $69.0
10. Safeguard, $48.2
11. Coast, $43.3

Source: *Chemical Market Reporter*, February 1, 1999, p. FR16.

★4070★
TOP BRANDS OF SOAPS AND BODY WASHES, 1999
Ranked by: Dollar sales, in millions of dollars. **Number listed:** 5

1. Dove, with $271.2 million
2. Dial, $193.0
3. Lever 2000, $137.5
4. Irish Spring, $121.2
5. Zest, $114.6

Source: *Brand Week*, Superbrands: America's Top 2,000 Brands, June 21, 1999, p. 552.

★4071★
TOP CORPORATIONS IN THE SOAP AND COSMETICS INDUSTRY, 1998
Ranked by: Revenue, in millions of dollars. **Remarks:** Also notes profits and investment figures as well as number of employees. **Number listed:** 9

1. Procter & Gamble, with $37,154 million
2. Colgate-Palmolive, $8,972
3. Avon Products, $5,213
4. Estee Lauder, $3,618
5. Clorox, $2,741
6. Revlon, $2,252
7. Alberto-Culver, $1,835
8. Dial, $1,525
9. International Flavors & Fragrance, $1,407

Source: *Fortune*, Fortune 500 Largest U.S. Corporations (annual), April 26, 1999, p. F-68.

★4072★
TOP CORPORATIONS IN THE SOAP, DETERGENT & OTHER CLEANING & POLISHING PRODUCTS INDUSTRY, 1998
Ranked by: Dollar sales, in thousands of dollars. **Number listed:** 7

1. Procter & Gamble, with $37,154 thousand
2. Colgate-Palmolive, $8,972
3. Clorox, $2,741
4. Ecolab, $1,888
5. NCH, $784
6. Church & Dwight, $684
7. Enesco Group, $451

Source: *Chemical Week*, May 12, 1999, p. 54.

★4073★
TOP LIQUID SOAP SALES, 1999
Ranked by: Sales, in millions of dollars. **Remarks:** Includes percent change and share. **Number listed:** 10

1. Softsoap, with $123.1 million
2. Dial 1, $61.1.
3. Private Label, $30.4
4. Clean & Smooth, $25.7
5. Ivory, $14.5
6. Jergens, $13.1
7. Suave, $7.0
8. Irish Spring, $1.4
9. GoJo, $1.4
10. Level 2000, $.028

Source: *Chemical Market Reporter*, February 1, 1999, p. FR16.

★4074★
TOP SHOWER GEL BRANDS, 1999
Ranked by: Sales, in millions of dollars. **Remarks:** Includes percent change and share. **Number listed:** 12
1. Olay, with $80.9 million
2. Dove, $53.4
3. Herbal Essence, $45.1
4. Caress, $35.1
5. Softsoap, $35.0
6. Lever 2000, $25.2
7. Jergens, $23.7
8. Suave, $20.9
9. Dial 1, $18.0
10. Whiterain, $10.6

Source: *Chemical Market Reporter*, February 1, 1999, p. FR16.

Soap Industry, International

★4075★
WORLD'S LARGEST SOAP AND COSMETICS CORPORATIONS BY REVENUE, 1997
Ranked by: Revenue, in millions of dollars. **Number listed:** 3
1. Procter & Gamble (U.S.), with $35,764 million
2. L'Oreal (France), $11,843
3. Colgate-Palmolive (U.S.), $9,057

Source: *Fortune*, The Global 500: World's Biggest Corporations (annual), August 3, 1998, p. F-24.

Soda Ash, China

★4076★
TOP SODA ASH PRODUCERS, 1997
Ranked by: Output, in thousands of m.t. **Remarks:** Includes province. **Number listed:** 8
1. Tangshan Soda, with Yu679 thousand
2. Shandong Marine (Weifeng), Yu640
3. Lianyungang Soda Plant, Yu620
4. Dalian Chemical Industries, Yu482
5. Tianjin Soda Plant, Yu475
6. Qingdao Soda, Yu467
7. Hubei Shuanghuan, Yu314
8. Zigong Honghe, Yu218

Source: *Chemical Market Reporter*, October 28, 1998, p. 37.

Soft Drink Industry

★4077★
TOP MARKET SHARE OF CARBONATED DRINKS, 1998
Ranked by: Total market share, in percent. **Number listed:** 4
1. Coca Cola, with 37.0%
2. Pepsi Cola, 33.5%
3. Dr. Pepper/7 Up, 16.4%
4. Other, 14.1%

Source: *Financial Times*, November 13, 1998, p. 21.

★4078★
TOP MARKET SHARE OF NON-COLA DRINKS, 1998
Ranked by: Total market share, in percent. **Number listed:** 4
1. Dr. Pepper/7 Up, with 35.2%
2. Pepsi Cola, 21.6%
3. Coca-Cola, 21.5%
4. Other, 21.7%

Source: *Financial Times*, November 13, 1998, p. 21.

★4079★
TOP SOFT DRINK BRANDS, 1998
Ranked by: Total sales in millions of dollars. **Remarks:** Includes company name, location, lead agency, and media expenditures. **Number listed:** 10
1. Coca-Cola Classic, with $2,037.5 million
2. Pepsi-Cola, $1,399.8
3. Diet Coke, $851.8
4. Mountain Dew, $665.1
5. Sprite, $651.8
6. Dr. Pepper, $599.4
7. Diet Pepsi, $529.7
8. 7 Up, $210.9
9. CF-Diet Coke, $210.9
10. Minute Maid, $121.5

Source: *Superbrands*, Superbrands: America's Top 2,000 Brands, June 21, 1999, p. S28.

★4080★
TOP SOFT DRINK PARENT COMPANIES, 1998
Ranked by: Total gallons, in millions of gallons. **Remarks:** Includes market share, growth, industry growth factor and 5-year growth. **Number listed:** 10
1. Coca-Cola, with $6,764.4 million gallons
2. Pepsi-Cola, $4,207.7
3. Dr. Pepper/Seven Up, $2,135.5
4. Cott, $391.3
5. National Beverage, $291.0
6. Royal Crown, $180.2
7. Monarch, $101.8
8. Double-Cola, $63.9
9. Seagram's Mixers, $39.8
10. Big Red, $36.8

Source: *Beverage World*, June 21, 1999, p. 37.

★4081★
TOP SOFT DRINKS, 1998
Ranked by: Total gallons, in millions of gallons. **Remarks:** Includes market share, growth, industry growth factor and 5-year growth. **Number listed:** 10
1. Coca-Cola Classic, with $3,122.1 million gallons
2. Pepsi-Cola, $2,199.2
3. Diet Coke, $1,303.4
4. Mountain Dew, $1,017.6
5. Sprite, $992.8
6. Dr. Pepper, $899.1
7. Diet Pepsi, $759.6
8. 7 Up, $316.4
9. Caffeine Free Diet Coke, $272.8
10. Minute Maid, $189.4

Source: *Beverage World*, June 21, 1999, p. 37.

Soft Drink Industry--North America

★4082★
TOP SOFT DRINK BOTTLERS IN NORTH AMERICA, 1997
Ranked by: Sales, in millions of dollars. **Remarks:** Includes address, number of employees, sales per employee, 1996 rank, key executives, and vital statistics. **Number listed:** 25
1. Coca-Cola Enterprises, with $11,278.0 million
2. Pepsi-Cola Bottling Company, $7,156.0
3. Pepsi-Cola General Bottlers, $1,557.5
4. Coca-Cola Bottling Company (Herb Group), $935.0
5. Honickman Affiliates, $870.0
6. Coca-Cola Bottling Company Consolidated, $802.1
7. Dr. Pepper Bottling Company of Texas, $709.0
8. Beverage America, $492.9
9. Delta Beverage Group, $450.0
10. Coca-Cola Bottling Company United, $449.0

Source: *Beverage World*, Top 25 Bottlers in North America (annual), September, 1998, p. 62+.

Soup--Europe

★4083★
TOP SOUP COMPANIES BY EUROPEAN MARKET SHARE, 1998*
Ranked by: European market share, in percent. **Number listed:** 5
1. Nestle, with 32.4%
2. Best Foods, 23.9%
3. Heinz, 4.8%
4. Campbell, 6.6%
5. Others, 32.3%

Source: *Financial Times*, August 8, 1998, p. 21.

★4084★
TOP WET SOUP COMPANIES BY EUROPEAN MARKET SHARE, 1998
Ranked by: European market share, in percent. **Number listed:** 5
1. Campbell, with 31.7%
2. Heinz, 22.7%
3. Best Foods, 4.6%
4. Nestle, 0.6%
5. Others, 40.4%

Source: *Financial Times*, August 8, 1998, p. 21.

Spanish Periodicals

★4085★
MOST ADMIRED SPECIALTY RETAILERS, 1999*
Ranked by: Scores (1-10) derived from a survey of senior executives, outside directors and securities analysts. **Remarks:** Respondents rated companies in their own industry on 8 attributes of reputation. Also notes previous year's rank. **Number listed:** 10
1. Home Depot, with 8.19
2. Costco, 6.69
3. Lowe's, 6.50
4. Limited, 6.40
5. Office Depot, 6.28
6. Circuit City Group, 6.06
7. Best Buy, 5.95
8. TJX, 5.94
9. Republic Industries, 5.68
10. Toys ''R'' Us, 5.30

Source: *Fortune*, America's Most Admired Corporations (annual), March 1, 1999, p. F-3.

★4086★
TOP HISPANIC MAGAZINES, 1998
Ranked by: Circulation in thousands. **Number listed:** 5
1. People en Espanol, with 200 thousands
2. Latina, 175
3. TV y Novelas, 160
4. Readers' Digest Selecoes, 133
5. Cristina, 92

Source: *Discount Store News*, October 26, 1998, p. 112.

Spanish-Speaking Market

See: **Hispanic Market**

Sport Utility Vehicles

★4087★
BEST-SELLING LUXURY SPORT UTILITY VEHICLES, 1997
Ranked by: Percent share of market. **Number listed:** 10
1. Jeep Grand Cherokee, with 12.1
2. Ford Expedition, 9.9
3. Toyota 4Runner, 5.9
4. Chevy Tahoe, 5.7
5. Chevy Suburban, 4.6
6. Nissan Pathfinder, 3.4
7. GMC Suburban, 2.0
8. GMC Yukon, 1.9
9. Mitsubishi Montero/Sport, 1.8
10. Lincoln Navigator, 1.2

Source: *Advertising Age*, September 28, 1998, p. S12.

★4088★
TOP SPORTING GOODS BRANDS ACCORDING TO DISCOUNT SHOPPERS, 1998
Ranked by: Percentage of discount shoppers naming brand as best. **Number listed:** 10

1\. Spalding, with 21%
2\. Top Flight, 10%
2\. Coleman, 10%
4\. Nike, 9%
4\. Wilson, 9%
6\. Remington, 7%
6\. Titleist, 7%
8\. Rawlings, 4%
9\. Adidas, 3%
9\. Finwick, 3%

Source: *Discount Store News*, Top Brands Consumer Survey Pt. II (annual), September 7, 1998, p. 22.

Sports

★4089★
TOP MOST POPULAR SPORTS IN THE U.S., 1997
Ranked by: Participated in more than once annually, in millions. **Number listed:** 10
1. Bowling, with $53.3 million
2. Basketball, $45.1
3. Free Weights, $43.2
4. Billiards, $42.2
5. Freshwater Fishing, $42.1
6. Tent Camping, $41.2
7. Treadmill Exercise, $36.1
8. Stationary Cycling, $34.8
9. Fitness Walking, $33.2
10. Running/Jogging, $32.2

Source: *Home Care Magazine*, February, 1999, p. 60.

★4090★
TOP PARTICIPANT SPORTS, 1997
Ranked by: Participated in more than once annually, in millions. **Number listed:** 57
1. Exercise Walking, with $76.3 million
2. Swimming, $59.5
3. Exercise with Equipment, $47.9
4. Camping, $46.6
5. Bicycle Riding, $45.1
6. Bowling, $44.8
7. Fishing, $44.7
8. Billiards/Pool, $37.0
9. Basketball, $30.7
10. Hiking, $28.4

Source: *Boating Industry*, February, 1999, p. 16.

Sports Drink Industry

★4091★
MOST POPULAR SPORTS DRINKS/ISOTONICS, 1998
Ranked by: Dollar sales. **Number listed:** 10
1. Gatorade, with 66.2
2. Gatorade Frost, 14.2
3. Powerade, 9.8
4. All Sport, 5.9
5. Private Label, 1.4
6. SoBe, 0.6
7. 10K, 0.6
8. Twinlab, 0.2
9. Red Bull, 0.2
10. Snapple Refresher, 0.1

Source: *U.S. Distribution Journal*, January, 1999, p. 43.

Standard and Poor's--Stock Price Index

★4092★
LARGEST COMPANIES IN THE S&P 500, 1998
Ranked by: Percentage of S&P 500. **Number listed:** 10
1. General Electric, with 3.18
2. Microsoft, 2.41
3. Coca-Cola, 2.26
4. Exxon, 2.03
5. Merck, 1.63
6. Pfizer, 16.1
7. Wal-Mart Stores, 1.44
8. Royal Dutch Petroleum Co., 1.40
9. Intel, 1.36
10. IBM, 1.32

Source: *Business Week*, July 13, 1998, p. 121.

State Data (for individual states)

★4093★
CITIES WITH THE HIGHEST STATE/LOCAL TAXES, 1997
Ranked by: Tax amount, in thousands of dollars. **Number listed:** 10
1. Bridgeport, CT, with $21,790 thousand
2. New York City, NY, $15,030
3. Newark, NJ, $14,756
4. Portland, ME, $13,785
5. Milwaukee, WI, $12,095
6. Providence, RI, $11,738
7. Philadelphia, PA, $11,464
8. Louisville, KY, $11,390
9. Baltimore, MD, $11,296
10. Boston, MA, $11,191

Source: *Site Selection*, October, 1998, p. 834.

★4094★
STATES WHERE IMMIGRANTS ARE CONCENTRATED, 1998*
Ranked by: Number of immigrants, in millions. **Number listed:** 7
1. California, with 8,074,000
2. New York, 3,602,000
3. Florida, 2,351,000
4. Texas, 2,169,000
5. New Jersey, 1,208,000
6. Illinois, 1,100,000
7. All Others, 7,279,000

Source: *Southwest Economy*, July, 1998, p. 2.

★4095★
STATES WITH THE HEALTHIEST POPULATION, 1998*
Ranked by: Specific figures not provided. **Number listed:** 10

1\. Minnesota
2\. New Hampshire
3\. Colorado
3\. Utah
3\. Wisconsin
6\. Massachusetts
7\. Washington
8\. Hawaii
8\. Iowa
8\. Virginia

Source: *National Underwriter Life & Health/Financial Services*, October 19, 1998, p. 3.

★4096★
STATES WITH THE HIGHEST ENERGY CONSUMPTION, 1995
Ranked by: Consumption per capita, in millions of BTUs. **Number listed:** 10
1. Alaska, with $1,139 million
2. Louisiana, $879
3. Wyoming, $846
4. Texas, $559

5. North Dakota, $546
6. Kentucky, $459
7. Alabama, $455
8. West Virginia, $449
9. Indiana, $447
10. Montana, $435

Source: *Governing*, February, 1999, p. 97.

★4097★
STATES WITH THE HIGHEST LOCAL AND STATE TAXES, 1999*
Ranked by: Tax, as percent of income. **Number listed:** 50

1. Hawaii, with 14.19%
2. New York, 13.60%
3. Wisconsin, 13.52%
4. Maine, 13.34%
5. Minnesota, 13.13%
6. Connecticut, 12.85%
7. Utah, 12.70%
8. New Mexico, 12.38%
9. Mississippi, 12.34%
10. California, 11.99%

Source: *Journal of Accountancy*, January, 1999, p. 71.

★4098★
STATES WITH THE HIGHEST PERSONAL INCOME, 1997
Ranked by: Per capita personal income. **Number listed:** 10

1. Connecticut, with $36,263 dollars
2. New Jersey, $32,654
3. Massachusetts, $31,524
4. New York, $30,752
5. Delaware, $29,022
6. Maryland, $28,969
7. Illinois, $28,202
8. New Hampshire, $28,047
9. Colorado, $27,051
10. Minnesota, $26,797

Source: *New Jersey Business*, July, 1998, p. 60.

★4099★
STATES WITH THE HIGHEST QUALITY OF CARE RANKING, 1999*
Ranked by: Quality of care. **Number listed:** 5

1. Arizona
2. Colorado
3. Washington
4. Oregon
5. Florida

Source: *Crain's New York Business*, April 5, 1999, p. 4.

★4100★
STATES WITH THE LOWEST ENERGY CONSUMPTION, 1995
Ranked by: Consumption per capita, in millions of BTUs. **Number listed:** 10

1. Vermont, with $256 million
2. Florida, $248
2. New Hampshire, $248
4. Massachusetts, $246
4. Arizona, $246
6. Connecticut, $240
6. California, $240
8. Rhode Island, $237
9. Hawaii, $216
10. New York, $215

Source: *Governing*, February, 1999, p. 97.

★4101★
STATES WITH THE LOWEST QUALITY OF CARE RANKING, 1999*
Ranked by: Quality of care. **Number listed:** 5

1. Maine
2. New Jersey
3. New Hampshire
4. New York
5. Hawaii

Source: *Crain's New York Business*, April 5, 1999, p. 4.

★4102★
STATES WITH THE MOST FATAL TRUCK ACCIDENTS, 1997
Ranked by: Truck driver deaths. **Number listed:** 10

1. California, with 81
2. Texas, 40
3. Florida, 40
4. Pennsylvania, 36
5. Illinois, 33
5. Kentucky, 33
7. Tennessee, 32
8. Georgia, 28
8. Indiana, 28
8. Virginia, 28
11. Arkansas, 25
11. North Carolina, 25
11. Ohio, 25

Source: *Traffic World*, December 14, 1998, p. 19.

★4103★
STATES WITH THE MOST GOLF COURSES, 1998*
Ranked by: Number of courses. **Number listed:** 5

1. Florida, with 1,170
2. California, 942
3. Michigan, 906
4. New York, 838
5. Texas, 838

Source: *Hotel & Motel Management*, September 7, 1998, p. 32.

★4104★
STATES WITH THE MOST MANUFACTURED HOUSING, 1997
Ranked by: Number of manufactured home shipments & single family building permits. **Number listed:** 10

1. Texas, with 37,154
2. North Carolina, 33,318
3. Georgia, 21,412
4. South Carolina, 20,062
5. Florida, 18,971
6. Alabama, 17,323
7. Tennessee, 15,393
8. Michigan, 11,836
9. Kentucky, 11,723
10. Mississippi, 10,809

Source: *Builder*, September, 1998, p. 86.

★4105★
STATES WITH THE WORST CHILD PEDESTRIAN CASUALTIES, 1992-1996
Ranked by: Collisions per year involving children. **Number listed:** 10

1. New Mexico, with 36.2
2. Arizona, 69.2
3. Florida, 195.8
4. District of Columbia, 6.6
5. Nevada, 18.2
6. Louisiana, 63.4
7. North Carolina, 80.6
8. Delaware, 8.0

9. South Carolina, 42.0
10. Texas, 218.8

Source: *The Economist*, August 15, 1998, p. 22.

★4106★
STATES WITH TOP HIGH-TECH EMPLOYMENT, 1996
Ranked by: Number employed. **Number listed:** 10

1. California, with 723,976
2. Texas, 343,075
3. New York, 307,510
4. Illinois, 198,899
5. Massachusetts, 197,491
6. Florida, 184,456
7. New Jersey, 168,059
8. Pennsylvania, 151,366
9. Virginia, 137,596
10. Ohio, 123,356

Source: *New Jersey Business*, July, 1998, p. 6.

★4107★
STATES WITH TOP TOURISM BUDGETS, 1998*
Ranked by: Tourism budget, in millions of dollars. **Number listed:** 10

1. Illinois, with $35.3 million
2. Hawaii, $27.7
3. Texas, $25.1
4. Florida, $23.0
5. Pennsylvania, $19.4
6. Virginia, $18.3
7. New York, $18.1
8. Massachusetts, $17.4
9. Louisiana, $15.1
10. Michigan, $14.7

Source: *Association Management*, July, 1998, p. 23.

★4108★
STATES WITH TOP TRANSPORTATION FUNDS, 1998*
Ranked by: Transportation funds, in billions of dollars. **Number listed:** 10

1. California, with $2,407 billion
2. Texas, $1,888
3. New York, $1,351
4. Pennsylvania, $1,306
5. Florida, $1,209
6. Ohio, $897
7. Illinois, $885
8. Michigan, $825
9. New Jersey, $676
10. Virginia, $671

Source: *Metal Center News*, July, 1998, p. 31.

★4109★
STATES WITH TOP TRANSPORTATION FUNDS, 1998*
Ranked by: Transportation funds, in billions of dollars. **Number listed:** 10

1. California, with $2,407 billion
2. Texas, $1,888
3. New York, $1,351
4. Pennsylvania, $1,306
5. Florida, $1,209
6. Ohio, $897
7. Illinois, $885
8. Michigan, $825
9. New Jersey, $676
10. Virginia, $671

Source: *Metal Center News*, July, 1998, p. 31.

★4110★
TOP CYBERSTATES, 1996
Ranked by: Number of high tech workers per 1,000 private sector workers. **Number listed:** 10

1. New Hampshire, with 84
2. Colorado, 78
3. Massachusetts, 76
4. California, 65
5. Vermont, 59
6. Minnesota, 57
7. New Jersey, 56
8. Virginia, 55
9. Arizona, 54
10. Oregon, 53

Source: *Area Development*, September, 1998, p. 42.

★4111★
TOP HISPANIC POPULATED STATES, 1998
Ranked by: Millions of people. **Number listed:** 11

1. California, with $11,090.4 million
2. Texas, $6,235.9
3. New York, $2,868.4
4. Florida, $2,333.6
5. Illinois, $1,284.4
6. Arizona, $1,116.8
7. New Jersey, $1,026.3
8. New Mexico, $759.5
9. Colorado, $600.0
10. Massachusetts, $386.5

Source: *Telephony*, May 17, 1999, p. 112.

★4112★
TOP STATES FOR ALL TERRAIN VEHICLES (ATV'S) RETAIL SALES, 1997
Ranked by: Total sales. **Number listed:** 20

1. Texas
2. North Carolina
3. Louisiana
4. Kentucky
5. Arkansas
6. Mississippi
7. Pennsylvania
8. Georgia
9. Tennessee
10. Michigan

Source: *Agri Marketing*, February, 1999, p. 46.

★4113★
TOP STATES FOR BOAT SALES, 1998
Ranked by: Total sales, in thousands of boats. **Number listed:** 20

1. Florida, with $475.7 thousand
2. Michigan, $334.3
3. Texas, $302.4
4. Minnesota, $300.0
5. California, $293.0
6. Wisconsin, $232.9
7. Louisiana, $195.0
8. New York, $178.1
9. North Carolina, $170.5
10. South Carolina, $167.3

Source: *Boating Industry*, February, 1999, p. 13.

★4114★
TOP STATES FOR PLASTIC ESTABLISHMENTS, 1996
Ranked by: Total establishments. **Number listed:** 10

1. California
2. Ohio
3. Texas

4. Michigan
5. Illinois
6. Pennsylvania
7. New York
8. Florida
9. Indiana
10. New Jersey

Source: *Business Facilities*, February, 1999, p. 28.

★4115★
TOP U.S. COAL PRODUCING STATES, 1997
Ranked by: In thousand short tons. **Number listed:** 10

1. Wyoming, with 281,647 short tons
2. West Virginia, 172,954
3. Kentucky, 155,859
4. Pennsylvania, 73,232
5. Texas, 53,722
6. Illinois, 41,956
7. Montana, 41,016
8. Virginia, 36,389
9. Indiana, 34,515
10. Ohio, 30,654

Source: *Coal Age*, August, 1998, p. 10.

Stationery

★4116★
BEST STATIONERY BRANDS ACCORDING TO DISCOUNT SHOPPERS, 1998
Ranked by: Percent of discount shoppers naming brand as best. **Number listed:** 6

1. Bic, with 44%
2. Mead, 19%
3. Pentel, 9%
4. Crayola, 8%
5. Paper Mate, 7%
6. Parker, 6%

Source: *Discount Store News*, September 7, 1998, p. 23.

Steel--Cold Working

★4117★
TOP MARKETS WHERE COLD-FINISHED BARS GO, 1997
Ranked by: Percent of market share. **Number listed:** 7

1. Automotive, with 42%
2. Machinery, 31%
3. Agricultural Equipment, 7%
4. Electrical Equipment, 4%
5. Construction Goods, 3%
6. Commercial Equipment, 3%
7. Other, 10%

Source: *Purchasing*, October 8, 1998, p. 32B11.

Steel Industry and Trade

★4118★
LEADING CHEMICAL PROCESS INDUSTRIES BY SALES, 1998
Ranked by: Sales, in millions of dollars. **Remarks:** Includes profits, profit ratios, full year per share data and assets. **Number listed:** 5

1. USX-U.S. Steel, with $6,184 million
2. Bethlehem Steel, $4,478
3. LTV, $4,273
4. Ryerson Tull, $2,783
5. Armco, $1,707

Source: *Chemical Week*, May 12, 1999, p. 54.

Steel Industry and Trade, International

★4119★
WORLD'S LARGEST STEEL-PRODUCING COMPANIES, 1998
Ranked by: Crude steel output, in millions of tons. **Number listed:** 10

1. POSCO (South Korea), with $25.6 millions of tons
2. Nippon Steel (Japan), $25.1
3. British SteelHoogovens, $22.5
4. Arbed (Luxembourg), $20.1
5. Usinor (France), $18.9
6. LNM/Ispat (Britain), $17.1
7. Thyssen Krupp (Germany), $14.8
8. Riva (Italy), $13.3
9. NKK (Japan), $11.5
10. USX (United States), $11.0

Source: *The Economist*, June 5, 1999, p. 60.

Stereophonic Sound Systems

★4120★
IMPORTANCE OF STOCK OPTIONS FOR ATTRACTING & RETAINING EMPLOYEES, 1999*
Ranked by: Opinion of 150 executives at large companies, in percent. **Number listed:** 5

1. Somewhat Important, with 48%
2. Very Important, 37%
3. Somewhat Unimportant, 11%
4. Not at all Important, 3%
5. Don't Know/No Answer, 1%

Source: *Journal of Accountancy*, June, 1999, p. 12.

★4121★
LARGEST SELLERS OF AUDIO RACK SYSTEMS, 1997
Ranked by: Market share, in percent. **Number listed:** 7

1. Sony, with 25.10%
2. Pioneer, 24.50%
3. Technics, 20.0%
4. Kenwood, 11.20%
5. JVC, 5.00%
6. Soundesign, 2.00%
7. Other, 12.20%

Source: *Dealerscope Consumer Electronics Marketplace*, August, 1998, p. 22.

Stock Options

★4122★
IMPORTANCE OF STOCK OPTIONS, 1999*
Ranked by: Importance, in percent. **Number listed:** 5
1. Somewhat important, with 48%
2. Very important, 37%
3. Somewhat unimportant, 11%
4. Not at all important, 3%
5. Don't know/no answer, 1%

Source: *Journal of Accountancy*, June, 1999, p. 12.

Stockholm Stock Exchange

★4123★
LARGEST LISTED COMPANIES ON THE STOCKHOLM STOCK EXCHANGE, 1997
Ranked by: Market value, in billions of Swedish kronas (Skr). **Number listed:** 20
1. Ericsson, with SKr292.2 billion
2. Astra AB, SKr224.7
3. Volvo, SKr93.9
4. ABB AB, SKr88.0
5. Investor AB, SKr73.8
6. Svenska Handelsbanken, SKr65.3
7. Hennes & Mauritz, SKr63.9
8. ForeningsSparbanken, SKr63.5
9. Skandinaviska Enskilda Banken, SKr58.9
10. Sandvik AB, SKr58.5

Source: *Euromoney Publications Financial Services*, SSB Guide to World Equity Markets (annual), 1998, p. 469.

★4124★
MOST ACTIVELY TRADED SHARES ON THE STOCKHOLM STOCK EXCHANGE, 1997
Ranked by: Trading value, in billions of Swedish kronas (Skr). **Number listed:** 20
1. Ericsson, with SKr226.2 billion
2. Astra, SKr160.6
3. Volvo AB, SKr73.1
4. ABB AB, SKr58.0
5. Nokia AB Oy, SKr55.7
6. Autoliv Inc., SKr42.4
7. Skandinaviska Enskilda Banken, SKr38.2
8. Pharmacia & Upjohn Inc., SKr37.6
9. Electrolux AB, SKr32.5
10. Hennes & Mauritz AB, SKr25.7

Source: *Euromoney Publications Financial Services*, SSB Guide to World Equity Markets (annual), 1998, p. 469.

Stocks

★4125★
COMPANIES THAT DELIVERED THE MOST FOR INVESTORS BASED ON THE 500 LARGEST COMPANIES IN TERMS OF REVENUE, 1999*
Ranked by: Barron's formula, a combination of stock-market returns and returns on invested capital, in percent. **Remarks:** Includes revenue, revenue rank, 1998 total return and return on investment. **Number listed:** 500
1. America Online, with 299.65%
2. Dell Computer, 155.45%
3. Best Buy, 125.80%
4. EMC, 116.05%
5. Apple Computer, 113.50%
6. MediaOne Group, 110.90%
7. Lucent Technologies, 101.15%
8. Lexmark International, 100.55%
9. The Gap, 92.60%
10. Unisys, 90.15%

Source: *Barron's*, Barron's 500 (annual), March 22, 1999, p. 34+.

★4126★
MOST WIDELY-HELD COMMON STOCKS AMONG INDIVIDUALS AND INVESTMENT CLUBS, 1999
Ranked by: Number of investment clubs holding stock. **Remarks:** Includes rank by total share held, number of shares held by NAIC members, rank by total value of share held, total value of share held by NAIC members on 12-31-98 and investor contact. **Number listed:** 100
1. Intel Corporation, with 12,423
2. PepsiCo, 11,446
3. Merck & Co. Inc., 8,581
4. Lucent Technologies, 7,959
5. The Home Depot, 7,136
6. Cisco Systems, Inc., 7,130
7. AFLAC Incorporated, 6,926
8. Diebold Incorporated, 6,913
9. Motorola, 6,894
10. Clayton Homes, Inc., 6,311

Source: *Better Investing*, Top 100 (annual), April, 1999, p. 38+.

Stocks, International

★4127★
BEST PERFORMING SHARES, 1998
Ranked by: Percent change in U.S. dollar terms. **Number listed:** 10
1. Olivetti, with 553%
2. Colt Telecom, 504%
3. Dell Computer, 255%
4. Nokia, 249%
5. Apple, 211%
6. Finmeccanica, 200%
7. EMC, 199%
8. National Bank of Greece, 195%
9. NIDEC, 182%
10. Lucent Technologies, 181%

Source: *Financial Times*, January 4, 1999, p. 20.

★4128★
WORST PERFORMING SHARES, 1998
Ranked by: Percent change in U.S. dollar terms. **Number listed:** 10
1. Citic Pacific, with -45%
2. Cendant, -46%
3. Deere, -46%
4. Healthsouth, -46%
5. Toys ''R'' Us, -47%
6. Citra, -49%
7. Sumitomo Trust, -50%
8. Peoplesoft, -51%
9. Baker Hughes, -60%
10. Petrobras, -64%

Source: *Financial Times*, January 4, 1999, p. 20.

Stocks--Price Indexes and Averages--Germany

★4129★
FTSE "TOP 100" BEST PERFORMERS, 1998
Ranked by: Percent change on year. **Number listed:** 100
1. Colt Telecom, with 481.7%
2. Orange, 164.6%
3. Telewest Communications, 147.9%
4. Vodafone, 122.3%
5. British Telecommunications, 89.2%
6. Compass, 83.9%
7. Securicor, 75.9%
8. Hanson, 75.1%
9. Rentokil Initial PLC, 70.9%
10. Imperial Tobacco, 67.7%

Source: *Investors Chronicle*, January 8, 1999, p. 10.

★4130★
WORLD'S BEST PERFORMING SHARES, 1998
Ranked by: Value of holdings at December, 1998. **Number listed:** 11
1. Daimler-Chrysler, with 156.8
2. Allianz, 144.6
3. Deutsche Telekom, 136.9
4. Mannesmann, 71.3
5. Munchener Ruck, 70.1
6. Siemens, 68.5
7. Deutsche Bank, 59.0
8. HypoVereinsbank, 54.0
9. Hoechst, 43.2
10. DB Investor, 42.5

Source: *Financial Times*, December 17, 1998, p. 24.

Stocks--Prices--Great Britain

★4131★
FTSE "MID 250" BEST PERFORMERS, 1998
Ranked by: Percent change on year. **Number listed:** 250
1. RM, with 190.6%
2. Powderject Pharmaceuticals, 176.9%
3. London Bridge Pharmaceuticals, 153.2%
4. Logica, 125.7%
5. Nester Healthcare, 114.9%
6. FI, 111.4%
7. CMG, 100.0%
8. Somerfield, 91.2%
9. Sage, 89.2%
10. Iceland, 78.7%

Source: *Investors Chronicle*, January 8, 1999, p. 10.

★4132★
FTSE "MID 250" WORST PERFORMERS, 1998
Ranked by: Percent change on year. **Number listed:** 250
1. British Borneo Oil & Gas, with -76.4%
2. JJB Sports, -64.3%
3. Premier Farnell, -64.0%
4. LASMO, -63.8%
5. BICC, -59.0%
6. Monument Oil & Gas, -57.4%
7. Scapa, -56.9%
8. Charter, -56.4%
9. Devro, -54.6%
10. Pilkington, -53.5%

Source: *Investors Chronicle*, January 8, 1999, p. 10.

★4133★
FTSE "TOP 100" WORST PERFORMERS, 1998
Ranked by: Percent change on year. **Number listed:** 100
1. Imperial Chemical Industries, with -45.2%
2. BRT, -34.6%
3. Marks & Spencer, -31.2%
4. British Airways, -27.6%
5. Billiton, -23.6%
6. Reed International, -23.0%
7. United News & Media, -21.0%
7. Schroders, -21.0%
9. EMI, -20.9%
10. Siebe Plc, -20.7%

Source: *Investors Chronicle*, January 8, 1999, p. 10.

Store Fixtures--North America

★4134★
LARGEST FIXTURE MANUFACTURING FACILITIES, 1998*
Ranked by: Area, in square feet. **Number listed:** 17
1. L.A. Darling, with 2,600,000
2. Lozier Corp., 2,300,000
3. OSF Inc., 2,200,000
4. Madix Store Fixtures, 2,000,000
4. RHC/Spacemaster, 2,000,000
6. Syndicate Systems Inc., 1,500,000
7. MEG, division of Steelworks, 1,200,000
7. MET Merchandising Concepts, 1,200,000
9. Nashville Display, 1,000,000
10. Excell Store Fixtures, 800,000
10. Hamilton Fixture, 800,000

Source: *Visual Merchandising and Store Design*, Top 50 Fixture Manufacturers (annual), October, 1998, p. 62.

★4135★
TOP FIXTURE MANUFACTURERS, 1997
Ranked by: Gross sales, in millions of dollars. **Number listed:** 50
1. OSF Inc., with $192.0 million
2. Madix Store Fixtures, $160.0
3. Oklahoma Fixture Co., $78.0
4. Hamilton Fixture, $65.0
5. Ready Fixtures, $60.0
6. MII Inc. Fixture Group, $50.0
7. Goer Manufacturing Co., $48.0
8. Econoco Corporation, $43.0
9. Dan Dee Display Fixtures, $42.0
9. J.D. Store Equipment Co., $42.0
11. HMG Worldwide In-Store Marketing Inc., $40.0

Source: *Visual Merchandising and Store Design*, Top 50 Fixture Manufacturers (annual), October, 1998, p. 39.

Stores

See: **Clothing Stores Computer Stores Department Stores**

Stoves

★4136★
LEADING ELECTRIC RANGE MANUFACTURERS, 1999
Ranked by: Market share, in percent. **Remarks:** Includes 1993 market share. **Number listed:** 6

1. GEA, with 46%
2. Whirlpool, 20%
3. Maytag, 18%
4. Electrolux, 9%
5. Goodman, 7%
6. Others, 0%

Source: *Appliance Manufacturer*, April, 1999, p. 19.

★4137★
LEADING GAS RANGE MANUFACTURERS, 1999
Ranked by: Market share, in percent. **Remarks:** Includes 1993 market share. **Number listed:** 6

1. GEA, with 39%
2. Maytag, 26%
3. Electrolux, 17%
4. Goodman, 12%
5. Whirlpool, 6%
6. Others, 0%

Source: *Appliance Manufacturer*, April, 1999, p. 19.

★4138★
LEADING RANGE HOOD MANUFACTURERS, 1999
Ranked by: Market share, in percent. **Remarks:** Includes 1993 market share. **Number listed:** 4

1. Broan/Nutone, with 69%
2. Rangaire, 16%
3. Watertown Metal Products, 10%
4. Others, 5%

Source: *Appliance Manufacturer*, April, 1999, p. 19.

Sun Care Products

★4139★
LEADING BRANDS OF SUNTAN LOTION AND OIL, 1997
Ranked by: Sales in millions of dollars. **Number listed:** 10

1. Coppertone, with $61.6 million
2. Banana Boat, $51.7%
3. Private Label, $33.2%
4. Neutrogena, $27.0%
5. Hawaiian Tropic, $24.9%
6. Bain de Soleil, $21.1%
7. Coppertone Sport, $19.6%
8. NO-AD, $19.3%
9. Coppertone Water Babies, $17.4%
10. Coppertone Kids, $11.4%

Source: *Drug Store News*, September 7, 1998, p. 72.

Sunscreens

See: **Sun Care Products**

Suntan Lotion

See: **Sun Care Products**

Supermarkets

See also: **Grocery Trade**

★4140★
BEST SELLING FROZEN/DAIRY/REFRIGERATED PRODUCTS OVER $200 MILLION BY PERCENT CHANGE IN SALES, 1997
Ranked by: Change in sales, in percent. **Number listed:** 10

1. Sausage, with 34.9%
2. Entrees, Dinner, 32.0%
3. Prepared Fish Entrees, 19.1%
4. Puddings/Desserts, 16.0%
5. Creamers, 14.0%
6. Salads, Refrigerated, 12.9%
7. Poultry, 12.2%
8. Ice Cream/Sherbet, 12.0%
9. Party Snacks/Lunches, 10.2%
10. Pizza, 9.7%

Source: *Progressive Grocer*, July, 1998, p. 28.

★4141★
BEST SELLING GROCERIES BY PERCENT OF DOLLAR CHANGE IN SALES, 1997
Ranked by: Change in sales, in percent. **Number listed:** 10

1. Prepared foods, with 4.3%
2. Coffee & tea, 4.1%
3. Candy & gum, 3.9%
4. Nuts & dried fruit, 3.6%
5. Snacks, 2.5%
6. Pet foods, 1.9%
7. Desserts & toppings, 1.6%
8. Juice, 1.5%
9. Sauces & dressings, 1.2%
10. Pasta, 1.1%

Source: *Progressive Grocer*, July, 1998, p. 28.

★4142★
BEST SELLING GROCERY AND PERISHABLE PRODUCTS UNDER $200 MILLION BY PERCENT CHANGE IN SALES, 1997
Ranked by: Change in sales, in percent. **Number listed:** 10

1. Soup, Frozen, with 55.0%
2. Drinks, liquid concentrate, 32.7%
3. Salads, 30.0%
4. Candles, 17.3%
5. Lemonade, 12.0%
5. Oriental dishes, canned, 12.0%
7. Cleaners, glass, 8.9%
8. Toppings, refrigerated, 8.6%
9. Orange juice, 8.5%
10. Cheesecake, frozen, 8.5%

Source: *Progressive Grocer*, July, 1998, p. 28.

★4143★
BEST SELLING GROCERY PRODUCTS OVER $200 MILLION BY PERCENT CHANGE IN SALES, 1997
Ranked by: Change in sales, in percent. **Number listed:** 10

1. Grape Juice, with 29.4%
2. Bagels (pkg,), 13.5%
3. Ground/Wholc-Bcan Coffcc, 11.3%
4. Still Water, bottles, 10.5%

5. Wine, 9.5%
5. Candy, Holiday Specials, 9.5%
7. Instant Potatoes, 8.5%
7. Pies (pkg.), 8.5%
9. Breads, Rolls, Biscuits, Muffins (pkgs.), 8.2%
10. Green Beans, 7.5%

Source: *Progressive Grocer*, July, 1998, p. 28.

★4144★
BEST SELLING PERISHABLES BY PERCENT OF DOLLAR CHANGE IN SALES, 1997

Ranked by: Change in sales, in percent. **Number listed:** 5

1. Deli, with 5.9%
2. Produce, 5.5%
3. In-store bakery, 4.6%
4. Frozens, 4.1%
5. Bakery foods, pkg., 2.9%

Source: *Progressive Grocer*, July, 1998, p. 28.

★4145★
ITEMS MOST FREQUENTLY SHOPLIFTED, 1999*

Ranked by: Percent of items shoplifted. **Number listed:** 7

1. Cigarettes, with 33%
2. HBC, 27%
3. Liquor, 8%
3. Meat, 8%
3. Analgesics, 8%
6. Baby Formula, 7%
7. Other, 9%

Source: *Supermarket Business*, May, 1999, p. 83.

★4146★
LEADING CONSUMER PURCHASING PATTERNS IN SUPERMARKETS, 1998

Ranked by: Percent of households buying. **Number listed:** 17

1. Dinners/entrees, with 83.9%
2. Plain vegetables, 83.4%
3. Desserts/toppings, 75.5%
4. Pizza, 64.0%
5. Potatoes/onion rings, 61.3%
6. Poultry, 58.3%
7. Breakfast foods, 56.7%
8. Juices, 56.6%
9. Meat, 53.3%
10. Seafood, 52.8%

Source: *Progressive Grocer*, October, 1998, p. 86.

★4147★
TOP AMERICAN CHEESE BRANDS, 1998

Ranked by: Sales, in millions of dollars. **Remarks:** Includes percent change from previous year, dollar share, unit sales and percent change from previous year. **Number listed:** 10

1. Private Label, with $430.9 million
2. Kraft Velveeta, $347.3
3. Kraft Singles, $332.9
4. Kraft, $143.5
5. Kraft Deluxe, $140.0
6. Borden, $127.5
7. Kraft Free, $63.9
8. Kraft Velveeta Light, $46.4
9. Land O'Lakes, $21.4
10. Crystal Farms, $14.2

Source: *Dairy Field*, August, 1998, p. 26.

★4148★
TOP CANNED AND BOTTLED TEA BRANDS, 1998

Ranked by: Sales, in millions of dollars. **Remarks:** Includes percent change from previous year, dollar share, unit sales and percent change from previous year. **Number listed:** 10

1. Lipton Brisk, with $107.3 million
2. Nestea Cool, $77.3
3. Snapple, $66.3
4. Arizona, $54.3
5. Diet Snapple, $39.5
6. Lipton Brew, $24.8
7. Nestea, $22.6
8. Lipton Iced Tea, $13.3
9. Private Label, $8.5
10. Ssips, $7.5

Source: *Dairy Field*, August, 1998, p. 38.

★4149★
TOP CONSUMER PURCHASES IN SUPERMARKETS, 1999

Ranked by: Percent of households buying. **Number listed:** 16

1. Soap, with 63.7%
2. Shampoo, 50.0%
3. Hair conditioners, 33.1%
4. Hair spray/spritz, 25.8%
5. Hand and body lotions, 25.1%
6. Skin care, 24.5%
7. Nail cosmetics, 18.7%
8. Facial cosmetics, 18.5%
8. Hair styling gel/mousse, 18.5%
10. Hair coloring, 14.0%
11. Bath fragrances/bubble bath, 8.2%
12. Suntan products, 7.9%

Source: *Progressive Grocer*, June, 1999, p. 42.

★4150★
TOP COTTAGE CHEESE BRANDS, 1998

Ranked by: Sales, in millions of dollars. **Remarks:** Includes percent change from previous year, dollar share, unit sales and percent change from previous year. **Number listed:** 10

1. Private Label, with $287.6 million
2. Knudsen, $61.0
3. Breakstone, $51.9
4. Light n' Lively, $24.2
5. Dean's, $19.3
6. Friendship, $18.8
7. Light n' Lively Free, $13.5
8. Prairie Farms, $11.4
9. Knudsen Free, $10.34
10. Kemps, $9.7

Source: *Dairy Field*, August, 1998, p. 20.

★4151★
TOP DEPARTMENTS FOR PRIVATE LABEL, 1998

Ranked by: Dollar share. **Number listed:** 8

1. Dairy
2. Bakery
3. Frozen
4. Deli
5. Non-edible groceries
6. Edible groceries
7. HBC
8. General Merchandise

Source: *Dairy Field*, July, 1998, p. 47.

★4152★
TOP FROZEN NOVELTIES BRANDS, 1998

Ranked by: Sales, in millions of dollars. **Remarks:** Includes percent change from previous year, dollar share, unit sales and percent change from previous year. **Number listed:** 10

1. Private Label, with $263.9 million
2. Klondike, $98.5
3. Drumstick, $93.2
4. Popsicle, $92.8
5. Haagen Dazs, $59.4
6. Dole Fruit & Juice, $46.0
7. Eskimo Pie, $44.2

8. Dove Bar, $38.3
9. Blue Bell, $33.2
10. Wells' Blue Bunny, $32.6

Source: *Dairy Field*, August, 1998, p. 30.

★4153★
TOP ICE CREAM BRANDS, 1998
Ranked by: Sales, in millions of dollars. **Remarks:** Includes percent change from previous year, dollar share, unit sales and percent change from previous year. **Number listed:** 10

1. Private Label, with $824.4 million
2. Breyers, $408.7
3. Dreyer's/Edy's, $363.4
4. Blue Bell, $181.9
5. Haagen Dazs, $157.0
6. Ben & Jerry's, $122.7
7. Healthy Choice, $100.7
8. Dreyer's/Edy's Grand Light, $86.6
9. Turkey Hill, $80.0
10. Wells' Blue Bunny, $70.2

Source: *Dairy Field*, August, 1998, p. 30.

★4154★
TOP ITEMS BOUGHT ON DEAL, 1999*
Ranked by: Percentage of category dollar purchases. **Number listed:** 30

1. Low Calorie Carbonated Soft Drinks, with 46.1%
2. Frozen Pizza, 41.8%
3. Heavy Duty Liquid Detergent, 41.5%
4. Carbonated Soft Drinks, 40.8%
5. Layer Cake Mixes, 39.7%
6. Combination Shampoo, 39.6%
7. Cameras, 38.9%
7. Frozen Pies, 38.9%
9. Canned Fruit Drinks, 38.2%
10. Bulk Ice Cream, 37.3%

Source: *Supermarket Business*, March, 1999, p. 18.

★4155★
TOP ITEMS BOUGHT WITH A COUPON, 1999*
Ranked by: Percentage of category dollar purchases. **Number listed:** 30

1. Denture Cleansers, with 21.7%
2. Soluble Flavored Coffee, 20.6%
2. Cooking Sprays, 20.6%
4. Refrigerated Dinner Rolls, 20.5%
5. Freezer Bags, 20.1%
6. Toilet Bowl Cleaners, 18.8%
7. Refrigerated Cookies & Brownies, 18.5%
7. Laundry Soil & Stain Removers, 18.5%
9. Plastic Wrap, 18.3%
10. Automatic Dishwasher Compounds, 17.8%

Source: *Supermarket Business*, March, 1999, p. 18.

★4156★
TOP MARGARINE BRANDS, 1998
Ranked by: Sales, in millions of dollars. **Remarks:** Includes percent change from previous year, dollar share, unit sales and percent change from previous year. **Number listed:** 5

1. I Can't Believe It's Not Butter, with $211.5 million
2. Shedds Country Crock, $196.5
3. Parkay, $111.1
4. Private Label, $108.9
5. Blue Bonnet, $108.7

Source: *Dairy Field*, August, 1998, p. 37.

★4157★
TOP NATURAL SHREDDED CHEESE BRANDS, 1998
Ranked by: Dollar share in percent. **Remarks:** Includes sales, percent change from previous year, unit sales and percent change from previous year. **Number listed:** 10

1. Private Label, with 39.2%
2. Kraft, 28.7%
3. Sargento, 13.7%
4. Healthy Choice, 3.3%
5. Crystal Farms, 2.6%
6. Sorrento, 1.5%
7. Kraft Free, 1.4%
8. Churny Provincia, 1.2%
9. Sargento Preferred, 1.1%
9. Sargento Double Cheese, 1.1%

Source: *Dairy Field*, August, 1998, p. 26.

★4158★
TOP REFRIGERATED BUTTER BRANDS, 1998
Ranked by: Sales, in millions of dollars. **Remarks:** Includes percent change from previous year, dollar share, unit sales and percent change from previous year. **Number listed:** 10

1. Private Label, with $404.3 million
2. Land O'Lakes, $305.8
3. Challenge, $38.0
4. Breakstone, $23.6
5. Land O'Lakes Light, $19.0
6. Kellers, $16.1
7. Crystal Farms, $13.0
8. Hotel Bar, $12.0
9. Tillamook, $11.2
10. Grassland, $9.0

Source: *Dairy Field*, August, 1998, p. 36.

★4159★
TOP REFRIGERATED DIPS BRANDS, 1998
Ranked by: Sales, in millions of dollars. **Remarks:** Includes percent change from previous year, dollar share, unit sales and percent change from previous year. **Number listed:** 10

1. T. Marzetti, with $50.2 million
2. Private Label, $44.3
3. Dean's, $32.7
4. Kraft, $20.6
5. Heluva Good, $13.2
6. Calavo, $6.2
7. Rite Tribe of the Two Sheiks, $6.1
8. Rite, $5.7
9. Imo, $5.3
10. Bison, $4.7

Source: *Dairy Field*, August, 1998, p. 21.

★4160★
TOP REFRIGERATED YOGURT BRANDS, 1998
Ranked by: Sales, in millions of dollars. **Remarks:** Includes percent change from previous year, dollar share, unit sales and percent change from previous year. **Number listed:** 10

1. Private label, with $246.0 million
2. Dannon Light, $178.7
3. Yoplait, $168.3
4. Dannon Fruit On The Bottom, $108.9
5. Yoplait Light, $95.8
6. Breyers, $59.1
7. Yoplait Custard Style, $56.3
8. Dannon, $53.2
9. Dannon Blended, $48.4
10. Yoplait Trix, $47.2

Source: *Dairy Field*, August, 1998, p. 20.

★4161★
TOP SNACK CONSUMPTION BY REGION, 1997
Ranked by: Average pounds per person. **Number listed:** 7

1. West Central, with 24.5
2. East Central, 24.3
3. New England, 22.4
4. Southwest, 22.3

5. Mid-Atlantic, 20.3
6. Southeast, 19.7
7. Pacific, 19.6

Source: *Distribution Channels*, March, 1999, p. 55.

★4162★
TOP SOUR CREAM BRANDS, 1998
Ranked by: Sales, in millions of dollars. **Remarks:** Includes percent change from previous year, dollar share, unit sales and percent change from previous year. **Number listed:** 10

1. Private Label, with $152.1 million
2. Breakstone, $74.5
3. Knudsen Hampshire, $38.2
4. Daisy, $25.3
5. Land O'Lakes, $16.6
6. Daisy Light, $13.2
7. Land O'Lakes Light, $11.2
8. Naturally Yours, $10.0
9. Knudsen Nice N'Light, $8.9
10. Dean's, $8.6

Source: *Dairy Field*, August, 1998, p. 21.

★4163★
TOP SUPERMARKET RETAILERS OF HOME FURNISHINGS, 1997
Ranked by: Sales, in millions of dollars. **Remarks:** Includes percent of change. **Number listed:** 15

1. Fred Meyer, with $642.96 million
2. Albertson's, $383.43
3. American Stores, $251.61
4. Supervalu, $238.39
5. Ahold USA, $198.18
6. Kroger Co., $183.05
7. Safeway, $170.76
8. A&P, $142.22
9. Food Lion, $141.28
10. Publix, $135.23

Source: *Supermarket News*, September 7, 1998, p. 54.

★4164★
TOP SUPERMARKET SALES, BY CATEGORY, 1998
Ranked by: Sales, in dollars. **Number listed:** 17

1. Dinners/entrees, with $4,557,905,920 dollars
2. Pizza, $2,037,020,416
3. Plain vegetables, $1,673,446,784
4. Poultry, $1,384,256,384
5. Juices, $1,135,079,680
6. Breakfast foods, $864,301,952
7. Seafood, $853,435,136
8. Potatoes/onion rings, $836,121,920
9. Desserts/toppings, $732,085,120
10. Meat, $702,097,536

Source: *Progressive Grocer*, October, 1998, p. 84.

★4165★
TOP SUPERMARKET VOLUME SHARE BY CATEGORY, 1998
Ranked by: Volume share by category. **Number listed:** 13

1. Dry Grocery/Food, with 26.30%
2. Meat, Fish, Poultry, 14.45%
3. Produce, 11.27%
4. Dry Grocery/Nonfoods, 9.47%
5. Service Deli, 7.05%
6. Dairy, 6.20%
7. Frozen Foods, 5.47%
8. GM, 4.61%
9. HBC, 4.48%
10. Instore Bakery, 3.63%

Source: *Supermarket Business*, September, 1998, p. 22.

Supermarkets--Chain and Franchise Operations

★4166★
TOP RETAIL & WHOLESALE SUPERMARKET CHAINS, 1998
Ranked by: Sales, in billions of dollars. **Remarks:** Includes top executive and stores owned. **Number listed:** 75

1. Kroger Co., with $43.1 billion
2. Albertson's, $35.7
3. Wal-Mart Supercenters, $32.0
4. Safeway, $25.0
5. Ahold USA, $19.7
6. Supervalu, $17.8
7. Fleming Companies, $15.1
8. Winn-Dixie Stores Inc., $13.9
9. Publix Super Markets, $12.1
10. Loblaw Cos. Ltd., $11.0

Source: *Supermarkets News*, January 25, 1999, p. 8+.

★4167★
TOP SUPERMARKET CHAINS BY SALES, 1998
Ranked by: Sales, in billions of dollars. **Number listed:** 20

1. Kroger, with $28.2 billion
2. Safeway, $24.5
3. Ahold USA, $16.2
4. Albertson's, $16.0
5. Fred Meyer, $14.9
6. American Stores, $13.8
7. Winn-Dixie, $13.6
8. Publix, $12.1
9. Food Lion, $10.2
9. A&P, $10.2
11. Loblaws, $8.3

Source: *MMR*, Annual Report of the Mass Market Industries, May 3, 1999, p. 87.

★4168★
TOP SUPERMARKET CHAINS BY STORE COUNT, 1998
Ranked by: Store count. **Number listed:** 20

1. Safeway, with 1,497
2. Kroger, 1,410
3. Food Lion, 1,207
4. Winn-Dixie, 1,168
5. Loblaws, 1,065
6. Ahold USA, 1,031
7. Albertson's, 983
8. A&P, 894
9. American Stores, 807
10. Fred Meyer, 781

Source: *MMR*, Annual Report of the Mass Market Industries, May 3, 1999, p. 8+.

★4169★
TOP U.S. GROCERY CHAINS, 1998
Ranked by: Sales, in billions of dollars. **Number listed:** 10

1. Albertson's, with $36.0 billion
2. Kroger, $27.0
3. Wal-Mart, $25.0
4. Safeway, $22.5
5. Ahold USA, $18.5
6. Fred Meyer, $15.0
7. Winn-Dixie Stores Inc., $13.2
8. Publix Super Markets, $11.1
9. A&P, $10.3
10. Food Lion, $10.2

Source: *Wall Street Journal*, August 4, 1998, p. A3.

Supermarkets—Chain and Franchise Operations--Drug and Cosmetics Departments

★4170★
LEADING SUPERMARKET COMPANIES BY PHARMACY SALES, 1998
Ranked by: Sales, in millions of dollars. **Remarks:** Includes 1997 pharmacy sales, percent of sales from pharmacy, number of stores with pharmacies and number of pharmacies added. **Number listed:** 50

1. Kroger Co., with $1,800 million
2. Safeway, $1,200
3. Albertson's Inc., $625
4. Giant Food Inc., $572
5. Fred Meyer Inc., $570
6. H.E. Butt Grocery Co., $413
7. Publix Supermarkets Inc., $320
8. Pathmark Stores Inc., $264
9. Randall's Food Markets Inc., $219
10. The Stop & Shop Supermarket Co., $201

Source: *Annual Report of the Drug Chain Industry*, April 26, 1999, p. 64.

Supermarkets—Chain and Franchise Operations, International

★4171★
LEADING FOOD RETAILERS, 1998
Ranked by: Sales, in billions of U.S. dollars. **Remarks:** Includes number of stores, countries of operation and top executive. **Number listed:** 25

1. Wal-Mart Stores, with $139.33 billion
2. Metro Group, $49.83
3. Kroger Co., $43.0
4. Rewe Zentrale, $34.61
5. Albertson's, $34.57
6. Promodes, $34.54
7. Ahold, $34.3
8. Intermarche, $33.02
9. Edeka Group, $31.14
10. Tesco PLC, $29.78

Source: *Supermarket News*, May 17, 1999, p. 14.

Tableware

★4172★
TOP BRANDS IN GLASSES AND DISHES, 1998*
Ranked by: Percentage of discount shoppers naming brand as best. **Number listed:** 6

1. Corning/Corelle/Visions, with $53% million
2. Libbey, $15%
3. Pyrex, $11%
4. Rubbermaid, $7%
5. Anchor Hocking, $5%
6. Tupperware, $1%

Source: *Discount Store News*, Top Brands Consumer Survey Pt. II (annual), September 7, 1998, p. 28.

★4173★
TOP DINNERWARE 20-PIECE SETS, 1998
Ranked by: Sales. **Number listed:** 20

1. Corelle Callaway Pattern
2. Corelle Abundance Pattern
3. Corelle Summer Blush Pattern
4. Corelle Rosemarie Pattern
5. Pfaltzgraff Tea Rose Pattern
6. Corelle Blue Velvet Pattern
7. Corelle Sand Art Pattern
8. Int'l China Appletime Pattern
9. Interiors Fantasia Pattern
10. Pfaltzgraff Ocean Breeze Pattern

Source: *HFN*, January 11, 1999, p. 59.

★4174★
TOP STAINLESS STEEL FLATWARE, 1998
Ranked by: Sales. **Number listed:** 20

1. Oneida Easton Pattern
2. Oneida Flight Pattern
3. Oneida American Ballad Pattern
4. Oneida Daydream Pattern
5. Oneida Juilliard Pattern
6. Gorham Studio Pattern
7. Oneida Together Pattern
8. Oneida Gold Juilliard Pattern
9. Oneida Cassandra Pattern
10. Oneida Colonial Boston Pattern

Source: *HFN*, January 11, 1999, p. 59.

Tableware Industry

★4175★
TOP TABLETOP RETAILERS, 1997
Ranked by: Revenue, in millions of dollars. **Remarks:** Includes store type. **Number listed:** 25

1. Service Merchandise, with $116.0 million
2. Macy's West, $114.0
3. Macy's East, $109.2
4. Ross-Simons, $95.0
5. Dayton Hudson, $78.6
6. Fortunoff, $75.0
7. Dillard's, $70.5
8. Mercantile Stores, $66.0
9. Robinson's/May, $60.0
10. Hecht's, $59.0

Source: *HFN*, Top 25 Retailers (annual), July 20, 199, p. 58.

Taiwan Stock Exchange

★4176★
LARGEST LISTED COMPANIES ON THE TAIWAN STOCK EXCHANGE, 1997
Ranked by: Market value, in billions of Taiwan dollars (NT$). **Number listed:** 20

1. Cathay Life Insurance, with NTs506.47 billion
2. TSMC, NTs297.27
3. United Micro Electronics, NTs263.54
4. First Bank, NTs246.30
5. China Develop, NTs242.83
6. Hua Nan Bank, NTs236.84
7. Chang Hwa Bank, NTs223.10
8. Shin Kong Life Insurance, NTs188.00
9. China Steel, NTs181.75
10. Nan Ya Plastic, NTs170.40

Source: *SSB Guide to world Equity Markets*, 1998, p. 484+.

★4177★
MOST ACTIVELY TRADED SHARES ON THE TAIWAN STOCK EXCHANGE, 1997
Ranked by: Trading volume, in millions of shares. **Number listed:** 20
1. United Micro Electronics, with NTs20,828 billion
2. TSMC, NTs13,690
3. China Steel, NTs13,669
4. Hualon-Teijran, NTs13,539
5. Acer, NTs12,373
6. Winbond Electronics Corp., NTs12,326
7. Mosel Vitelic, NTs11,179
8. Macronix International, NTs10,981
9. ASE, NTs9,367
10. BES Engineering Corp., NTs7,180

Source: *SSB Guide to world Equity Markets*, 1998, p. 485.

Take-Out Service

See: **Food Service--Take-Out Service**

Tank Trucks

★4178★
TOP TANK TRUCK COMPANIES, 1997
Ranked by: Revenue, in thousands of dollars. **Remarks:** Includes 1996 revenue, percent change, net income, operating ratio, net profit, and tons. **Number listed:** 6
1. Chemical Leaman Tank Lines, with $262,135 thousand
2. Montgomery Tank Lines, $252,943
3. Matlack Inc., $194,700
4. DSI Transports, $159,212
5. Groendyke Transport, $118,289
6. Bulkmatic Transport Co., $113,335

Source: *Transport Topics*, Annual Report, August 10, 1998, p. 22.

Taxation

★4179★
STATES WITH THE HIGHEST LOCAL AND STATE TAXES, 1999*
Ranked by: Tax as percent of income. **Remarks:** Includes rank in overall states. **Number listed:** 50
1. Hawaii, with 14.19%
2. New York, 13.60%
3. Wisconsin, 13.52%
4. Maine, 13.34%
5. Minnesota, 13.13%
6. Connecticut, 12.85%
7. Utah, 12.70%
8. New Mexico, 12.38%
9. Mississippi, 12.34%
10. California, 11.99%

Source: *Journal of Accountancy*, January, 1999, p. 71.

★4180★
STATES WITH THE LOWEST LOCAL AND STATE TAXES, 1999*
Ranked by: Tax as percent of income. **Remarks:** Includes rank in overall states. **Number listed:** 50
1. Alaska, with 6.09%
2. New Hampshire, 6.52%
3. Wyoming, 7.89%
4. Tennessee, 8.61%
5. Alabama, 9.47%
6. Louisiana, 10.20%
7. Virginia, 10.32%
8. Texas, 10.52%
9. South Dakota, 10.62%
10. Florida, 10.65%

Source: *Journal of Accountancy*, January, 1999, p. 71.

Tea Industry

★4181★
TOP CANNED AND BOTTLED TEA BRANDS, 1998
Ranked by: Sales, in millions of dollars. **Remarks:** Includes percent change from previous year, dollar share, unit sales and percent change from previous year. **Number listed:** 10
1. Lipton Brisk Tea, with $107.3 million
2. Nestea Cool, $77.3
3. Snapple, $66.3
4. Arizona, $54.3
5. Diet Snapple, $39.5
6. Lipton Brew, $24.8
7. Nestea, $22.6
8. Lipton Iced Tea, $13.3
9. Private Label, $8.5
10. Ssips, $7.5

Source: *Dairy Field*, August, 1998, p. 38.

★4182★
TOP INSTANT TEA BRANDS, 1998
Ranked by: Sales, in millions of dollars. **Remarks:** Includes percent change from previous year, dollar share, unit sales and percent change from previous year. **Number listed:** 10
1. Lipton, with $105.4 million
2. Private Label, $74.9
3. Nestea, $45.4
4. Crystal Light, $14.5
5. 4C, $10.8
6. Tetley, $6.5
7. Nestea Decaf, $3.7
8. Nestea Free, $2.5
9. General Foods International, $1.6
10. Nestea Suntea, $1.3

Source: *Beverage Industry*, July, 1998, p. 10.

Technology

★4183★
COUNTRIES WITH THE HIGHEST TOTAL TECHNOLOGY SPENDING, 1997
Ranked by: Percentage of total world technology spending. **Remarks:** Data includes computer hardware, software and services and telephone equipment and services. **Number listed:** 10

1. United States, with 35.8%
2. Japan, 17.6%
3. Germany, 6.6%
4. Britain, 5.7%
5. France, 5.1%
6. Italy, 2.8%
7. Canada, 2.6%
8. Brazil, 1.9%
8.Australia, 1.9%
10. China, 1.6%

Source: *The New York Times*, May 11, 1999, p. 1.

Tel Aviv Stock Exchange

★4184★
LARGEST LISTED COMPANIES ON THE TEL AVIV STOCK EXCHANGE, 1997
Ranked by: Market value, in millions of U.S. dollars. **Number listed:** 20

1. Bank Hapoalim, with $2,958 million
2. Teva, $2,951
3. Bank Leumi, $2,376
4. Bezek, $2,023
5. Koor Industries, $1,762
6. Israel Chemicals, $1,625
7. IDB Development, $1,103
8. Bank Discount, $972
9. Clal Israel, $914
10. IDB Holdings, $903

Source: *SSB Guide to world Equity Markets*, 1998, p. 259.

★4185★
MOST ACTIVELY TRADED SHARES ON THE TEL AVIV STOCK EXCHANGE, 1997
Ranked by: Trading value, in millions of U.S. dollars. **Number listed:** 20

1. Bank Leumi, with $674.28 million
2. Koor Industries, $575.47
3. Teva, $571.29
4. Bank Hapoalim, $539.28
5. Israel Chemicals, $366.01
6. Bezek, $352.79
7. Bank Discount, $327.05
8. Discount Investment, $279.73
9. Formula, $231.71
10. Super-sol, $221.28

Source: *SSB Guide to world Equity Markets*, 1998, p. 260.

Telecommunications

★4186★
MOST ADMIRED TELECOMMUNICATIONS COMPANIES, 1998
Ranked by: Scores (1-10) derived from a survey of senior executives, outside directors and securities analysts. **Remarks:** Respondents rated companies in their own industry on 8 attributes of reputation. Also notes previous year ranking. **Number listed:** 10

1. Sprint
2. Tele-Communications
3. Bell South
4. Ameritech Corp.
5. Bell Atlantic
6. SBC Communications
7. AT & T
8. MCI WorldCom
9. GTE
10. U.S. West Inc.

Source: *Fortune*, America's Most Admired Corporations (annual), March 1, 1999, p. F-6.

★4187★
TELECOMMUNICATIONS COMPANIES SPENDING THE MOST ON RESEARCH AND DEVELOPMENT, 1998
Ranked by: Research and development expenditures, in millions of dollars. **Number listed:** 10

1. Lucent Technologies, with $4,119.0 million
2. Motorola, $2,743.2
3. MCI Communications Corp., $1,548.7
4. AT & T, $758.9
5. Sprint, $754.6
6. Bay Networks Inc., $702.1
7. Alltel, $564.5
8. 3Com Corp., $472.9
9. Worldcom Inc., $459.1
10. DSC Communications Corp., $378.5

Source: *Research & Development*, Giants of R&D (annual), October, 1998, p. S-15.

★4188★
TOP CORPORATIONS IN THE TELECOMMUNICATIONS INDUSTRY, 1998
Ranked by: Revenue, in millions of dollars. **Remarks:** Also notes profits and investment figures as well as number of employees. **Number listed:** 21

1. AT & T, with $53,588 million
2. Bell Atlantic, $31,566
3. SBC Communications, $28,777
4. GTE, $25,473
5. BellSouth, $23,123
6. MCI WorldCom, $17,678
7. Ameritech Corp., $17,154
8. Sprint, $17,134
9. U.S. West Inc., $12,378
10. Tele-Communications, $7,351

Source: *Fortune*, Fortune 500 Largest U.S. Corporations (annual), April 26, 1999, p. F-69+.

★4189★
TOP TELECOMMUNICATIONS COMPANIES IN THE S&P 500, 1999
Ranked by: Each company is ranked by eight criteria: one-year total return, three-year total return, one-year sales growth, three-year average annual sales growth, one-year profit growth, three-year average annual profit growth, net profit margins and return on equity, with additional weight given to a company's sales. A company's composite rank is calculated using the sum of all its ranks. **Remarks:** Overall scores not provided. **Number listed:** 17

1. SBC Communications
2. Tellabs
3. Airtouch Communications
4. Ameritech Corp.
5. BellSouth
6. Bell Atlantic
7. Lucent Technologies
8. Sprint Fon Group
9. AT & T
10. Alltel

Source: *Business Week*, Business Week 50: Top Companies of the S&P 500 (annual), March 29, 1999, p. 164.

Telecommunications--Asia

★4190★
MOST ADMIRED COMPANIES IN THE TELECOMMUNICATIONS AND MEDIA INDUSTRY IN ASIA, 1999
Ranked by: Score. **Remarks:** Includes previous year's score, overall rank and change in rank. **Number listed:** 10
1. AT & T, with 7.86
2. Singapore Telecom, 7.56
3. Indosat, 7.43
4. ABS-CBN Broadcasting Corp., 7.36
5. Post Publishing, 6.97
6. Dacom, 6.61
7. Globe Telecom, 6.34
8. Telekom Malaysia, 6.26
9. Hongkong Telecom, 6.20
10. Nissan Motor, 4.95

Source: *Asian Business*, Most Admired Companies in Asia (annual), May, 1999, p. 29.

★4191★
TOP INTERNATIONAL TELECOMMUNICATIONS CARRIERS, 1997
Ranked by: Outgoing minutes, in billions. **Remarks:** Includes country. **Number listed:** 10
1. AT & T, with $10.3 billion
2. MCI, $5.9
3. Deutsche Telekom, $5.3
4. BT, $3.7
5. France Telecom, $3.5
6. Sprint, $2.8
7. Telecom Italia, $2.4
8. Swisscom, $2.2
9. C&W Communications, $2.1
10. Stentor, $1.8

Source: *Telecommunications*, January, 1999, p. 33.

Telecommunications, International

★4192★
WORLD'S LARGEST TELECOMMUNICATIONS COMPANIES BY REVENUE, 1997
Ranked by: Revenue, in millions of dollars. **Number listed:** 22
1. Nippon Telegraph & Telephone (Japan), with $76,984 million
2. AT & T (U.S.), $53,261
3. Deutsche Telekom (Germany), $38,969
4. Alcatel Alsthom (France), $31,847
5. Bell Atlantic (U.S.), $30,194
6. France Telecom (France), $26,854
7. BT (Great Britain), $26,294
8. Telecom Italia (Italy), $25,130
9. SBC Communications (U.S.), $24,856
10. GTE (U.S.), $23,260

Source: *Fortune*, The Global 500: World's Biggest Corporations (annual), August 3, 1998, p. F-25.

Telemarketing

★4193★
LEADING INBOUND TELEMARKETERS, 1997
Ranked by: Number of hours of calls taken for credit card issuers. **Remarks:** Includes number of 1996 inbound calls. **Number listed:** 30
1. Matrixx Marketing Inc., with 10,000,000
2. ITI Marketing Services Inc., 9,015,045
3. TSYS Total Solutions Inc., 8,028,811
4. Signature Group Telemarketing, 7,331,707
5. ATC Communications, 7,141,000
6. SITEL Corp., 5,800,000
7. Telatron Marketing Group Inc., 2,490,000
8. IDRC, 2,283,606
9. West TeleServices Corp., 1,502,253
10. Ron Weber & Associates, 1,000,000

Source: *Credit Card Management*, July, 1998, p. 66.

★4194★
LEADING OUTBOUND TELEMARKETERS, 1997
Ranked by: Number of hours billed to card issuers. **Remarks:** Includes number of 1996 outbound hours, work sites and work stations. **Number listed:** 50
1. Signature Group Telemarketing, with 4,060,165
2. ACI Telecentrics
3. SITEL Corp.
4. TeleSpectrum Worldwide Inc.
5. IQI Inc.
6. APAC TeleServices
7. IDRC
8. DialAmerica Marketing Inc.
9. ITI Marketing Services Inc.
10. FutureCall Telemarketing West Inc.

Source: *Credit Card Management*, July, 1998, p. 64.

★4195★
TOP OUTBOUND SERVICE AGENCIES, 1999*
Ranked by: Company size as measured by the number of minutes each agency was billed by each of its phone companies for telephone service. Specific figures are not given. **Remarks:** Includes location, phone/fax numbers, year started, size of projects, type of calling, specialization, and number of call centers. **Number listed:** 14
1. West TeleServices Corp.
2. APAC Customer Services
3. Dial America Marketing Inc.
4. SITEL Corp.
5. Aegis Communications Group Inc.
6. IDRC
7. TeleSpectrum Worldwide Inc.
8. Convergys Corp.
9. ICT Group Inc.
10. Precision Response Corp.

Source: *Call Center Solutions*, Top 50 Service Agency Ranking & Industry Profile (annual), March, 1999, p. 96.

Telemarketing--Great Britain

★4196★
LEADING COMPANIES FOR INBOUND AUTOMATED LINES, 1997
Ranked by: Total automated, British in pounds. **Remarks:** Includes total inbound, automated interactive and automated passive. **Number listed:** 15

1. Scottish Telecom, with £23,375,000 pound
2. Broadsystem, £16,917,000
3. IMS Group, £14,438,000
4. BT CiB, £8,040,000
5. Greenland Interactive, £7,880,000
6. Sitel Corporation, £4,633,000
7. 7C, £4,400,000
8. Teleom Potential, £4,142,000
9. Telecom Express, £3,240,000
10. Newstel Information, £2,625,000

Source: *Marketing*, Direct Marketing League Table (annual), April 15, 1998, p. 47.

★4197★
LEADING CONSULTANCY COMPANIES, 1998*
Ranked by: Consultancy, in British pounds. **Remarks:** Includes 1998 turnover. **Number listed:** 15

1. Sitel Corporation, with £4,504,000 pound
2. Brann Contact, £2,047,000
3. BT CiB, £2,010,000
4. BPS Teleperformance, £1,132,000
5. InTelMark, £659,000
6. Greenland Interactive, £598,000
7. 7C, £550,000
8. Telecom Potential, £455,000
9. Access 24, £334,000
10. Oxygen Communications, £281,000

Source: *Marketing*, Direct Marketing League Table (annual), April 15, 1998, p. 51.

★4198★
LEADING FULFILLMENT COMPANIES, 1998*
Ranked by: Fulfillment, in British pounds. **Remarks:** Includes 1998 turnover. **Number listed:** 20

1. SSL, with £6,768,000 pound
2. Spark Response, £6,175,000
3. BT CiB, £3,350,000
4. Brann Contact, £3,070,000
5. McIntyre & King, £2,806,000
6. Omega Marketing Services, £2,298,000
7. InTelMark, £2,108,000
8. Response Analysis & Mailing, £2,048,000
9. Sitel Corporation, £1,930,000
10. Broadsystem, £1,611,000

Source: *Marketing*, Direct Marketing League Table (annual), April 15, 1998, p. 51.

★4199★
LEADING INBOUND PERSONAL CALLING TELEMARKETING COMPANIES, 1997
Ranked by: Personal answering, in British pounds. **Remarks:** Includes total inbound. **Number listed:** 30

1. SSL, with £63,379,000 pound
2. BT CiB, £45,560,000
3. Sitel Corporation, £33,973,000
4. Scottish Telecom, £19,125,000
5. Serco On Line Services, £9,193,000
6. The Merchants Group, £8,835,000
7. Brann Contact, £7,736,000
8. Broadsystem, £7,250,000
9. InTelMark, £4,638,000
10. Telecom Potential, £3,728,000

Source: *Marketing*, Direct Marketing League Table (annual), April 15, 1998, p. 46.

★4200★
LEADING OUTBOUND TELEMARKETING COMPANIES, 1997
Ranked by: Outbound, in British pounds. **Remarks:** Includes total turnover. **Number listed:** 30

1. The Merchants Group, with £22,224,000 pound
2. Sitel Corporation, £19,303,000
3. BT CiB, £8,040,000
4. Scottish Telecom, £7,500,000
5. Brann Contact, £6,753,000
6. Broadsystem, £6,445,000
7. InTelMark, £4,612,000
8. Teledynamics, £3,551,000
9. BPS Teleperformance, £3,397,000
10. SSL, £3,384,000

Source: *Marketing*, Direct Marketing League Table (annual), April 15, 1998, p. 48.

★4201★
LEADING TELEMARKETING BUREAUS, 1998
Ranked by: Turnover, in British pounds. **Remarks:** Includes 1997 turnover, percent change, pretax profits, percent change, staff and maximum lines. **Number listed:** 50

1. SSL, with £75,201,000 pound
2. BT CiB, £67,000,000
3. Sitel Corporation, £64,343,000
4. Scottish Telecom, £50,000,000
5. Broadsystem, £32,223,000
6. The Merchants Group, £31,524,000
7. IMS Group, £22,638,000
8. Brann Contact, £20,465,000
9. InTelMark, £13,177,000
10. 7C, £11,000,000

Source: *Marketing*, Direct Marketing League Table (annual), April 15, 1998, p. 39.

Telephone Answering Devices

★4202★
LEADING TELEPHONE ANSWERING DEVICE COMPANIES, 1998*
Ranked by: Brandshare, in percent. **Number listed:** 12

1. AT & T, with 34.00%
2. GE, 18.50%
3. Bell South, 14.00%
4. Phonemate, 8.50%
5. Southwestern Bell, 6.00%
6. Conair, 5.00%
7. Panasonic, 3.50%
7. Radio Shack, 3.50%
9. Sony, 2.50%
10. Uniden, 1.00%
10. Unisonic, 1.00%
12. Others, 2.50%

Source: *Dealerscope Consumer Electronic Marketplace*, August, 1998, p. 23.

Telephone Companies

★4203★
LEADING TELECOMMUNICATIONS BRANDS/ COMPANIES, 1998
Ranked by: Total sales in billions of dollars. **Remarks:** Includes company name, location, lead agency and media expenditures. **Number listed:** 10

1. AT & T, with $53.2 billion
2. Bell Atlantic, $31.5

3. MCI WorldCom, $30.4
4. SBC Communications, $28.7
5. GTE, $25.4
6. BellSouth, $23.1
7. Ameritech Corp., $17.1
8. Sprint, $16.0
9. Alltel, $5.1
10. Frontier, $2.5

Source: *Superbrands*, June 21, 1999, p. 564.

Telephone Companies, International

★4204★
LEADING INTERNATIONAL TELEPHONE COMPANIES, 1998
Ranked by: Total per-minute call interconnection fees, in cents. **Number listed:** 7

1. Telmex, with $7.11 cents
2. CTC, $3.85
3. Nynex, $3.03
4. NTT, $2.93
5. Telefonica d'Espana, $2.78
6. Bell Atlantic, $1.65
7. BT, $1.13

Source: *Wall Street Journal*, July 16, 1998, p. C1.

Telephone Directories--Yellow Pages

★4205★
TOP YELLOW PAGES COMPANIES, 1997
Ranked by: Yellow pages revenue, in billions of dollars. **Number listed:** 9

1. Bell Atlantic, with $2,298.0 billion
2. SBC Communications, $2,111.0
3. BellSouth, $1,934.0
4. GTE Corp., $1,507.0
5. U.S. West Inc., $1,197.0
6. Ameritech Corp., $681.5
7. Don Tech, $426.1
8. Sprint, $330.0
9. Reuben H. Donnelley, $130.0

Source: *Advertising Age*, 100 Leading Media Companies (annual), August 17, 1998, p. 59.

Telephone Switching Systems—Digital Switching International

★4206★
TOP DIGITAL SWITCH SUPPLIERS, 1998*
Ranked by: Ports, in millions. **Number listed:** 5

1. Alcatel, with $200.6 million
2. Lucent, $156.6
3. Siemens, $138.2
4. Nortel, $134.8
5. Ericsson, $128.5

Source: *Telecommunications*, October, 1998, p. 22.

Television

★4207★
TOP TELEVISION, VCR, AND TAPE SALES, 1997
Ranked by: Sales revenue, in thousands of dollars. **Number listed:** 321

1. Chicago, IL, with $953,685 thousand
2. Los Angeles-Long Beach, CA, $820,933
3. Tampa-St. Petersburg-Clearwater, FL, $784,900
4. Washington, DC, $584,093
5. New York, NY, $515,690
6. Atlanta, GA, $512,605
7. Detroit, MI, $446,736
8. Philadelphia, PA, $438,708
9. Houston, TX, $387,583
10. Minneapolis-St. Paul, MN, $361,956

Source: *Sales & Marketing Management, Survey of Buying Power*, Media Markets (annual), August, 1998, p. 198.

Television Advertising

★4208★
TOP NETWORK TV ADVERTISERS, 1997
Ranked by: Expenditure, in millions of dollars. **Remarks:** Includes 1996 revenue and percent change. **Number listed:** 25

1. General Motors Corp., with $819.3 million
2. Procter & Gamble, $662.2
3. Johnson & Johnson, $473.7
4. Phillip Morris Co., $464.3
5. Ford Motor Co., $341.9
6. Diageo, $324.8
7. Chrysler Corp., $301.4
8. McDonald's, $295.5
9. Walt Disney Co., $263.9
10. Tricon Global Restaurants, $258.2

Source: *Advertising Age*, 100 Leading National Advertisers (annual), September 28, 1998, p. S38.

★4209★
TOP SPOT TV ADVERTISERS, 1997
Ranked by: Expenditure, in millions of dollars. **Remarks:** Includes 1996 revenue and percent change. **Number listed:** 25

1. Chrysler Corp., with $427.6 million
2. General Motors Corp., $373.8
3. Phillip Morris Cos., $217.0
4. Toyota Motor, $197.8
5. Procter & Gamble, $197.5
6. Honda Motor Co., $189.9
7. Tricon Global Restaurants, $189.6
8. Ford Motor Co., $182.9
9. General Mills, $181.4
10. McDonald's, $144.5

Source: *Advertising Age*, 100 Leading National Advertisers (annual), September 28, 1998, p. S41.

★4210★
TOP SPOT TV CATEGORIES, 1998
Ranked by: Spot TV ad spending, in millions of dollars. **Remarks:** Includes 1997 figures. **Number listed:** 10

1. National Restaurants, with $1,226.0 million
2. Car & Truck Dealer Associations, $813.0
3. Cars, Asian, $517.0
4. Local Government & Politics, $496.0
5. Light Trucks, $485.1
6. Furniture Stores, $481.0

7. Cars, Domestic, $406.0
8. Motion pictures, $373.3
9. Business, Personal, Residential Phone Services, $349.1
10. Food Stores & Supermarkets, $330.2

Source: *Advertising Age*, May 10, 1999, p. 12.

★4211★
TOP SYNDICATED TV ADVERTISERS, 1997
Ranked by: Expenditure, in millions of dollars. **Remarks:** Includes 1996 revenue and percent change. **Number listed:** 25

1. Procter & Gamble, with $186.4 million
2. Johnson & Johnson, $96.5
3. General Motors Corp., $94.5
4. Diageo, $86.5
5. Umilever, $83.3
6. Kellogg Co., $75.6
7. Phillip Morris Cos., $69.4
8. Hershey Foods Corp., $58.2
9. McDonald's, $57.9
10. Walt Disney Co., $55.9

Source: *Advertising Age*, 100 Leading National Advertisers (annual), September 28, 1998, p. S43.

★4212★
TOP SYNDICATION TV CATEGORIES, 1998
Ranked by: Syndicated TV ad spending, in millions of dollars. **Remarks:** Includes 1997 figures. **Number listed:** 10

1. Long Distance, with $179.2 million
2. National Restaurants, $131.0
3. Motion pictures, $128.4
4. Candy & Mints, $112.4
5. Pain Remedies, $76.0
6. Cars, Domestic Factory, $69.4
7. Cereals, $66.0
8. Computer Games, $54.0
9. Shampoos, Conditioners & Rinses, $49.0
10. Cold & Sinus Remedies, $47.1

Source: *Advertising Age*, May 10, 1999, p. 14.

Television Broadcasting

★4213★
TOP MEDIA COMPANIES, 1997
Ranked by: TV revenue, in millions of dollars. **Remarks:** Includes 1996 figures, percent change and TV as percent of all media revenue. **Number listed:** 25

1. NBC TV, with $4,803.0 million
2. Walt Disney Co., $4,122.0
3. CBS Corp., $3,652.0
4. News Corp. Ltd., $2,730.0
5. Tribune Co., $861.0
6. Gannett Co., $653.1
7. A.H. Belo Corp., $536.7
8. Univision Communications, $459.7
9. Cox Enterprises, $450.0
10. Sinclair Broadcasting Group, $449.9

Source: *Advertising Age*, 100 Leading Media Companies (annual), August 17, 1998, p. S6.

★4214★
TOP TV BROADCASTING GROUPS, 1999*
Ranked by: Percent points of national coverage. **Remarks:** Includes all affiliates. **Number listed:** 25

1. Fox Television Station, with 35.3%
2. CBS Stations Inc., 30.8%
3. Paxson Communications Corp., 29.2%
4. Tribune Broadcasting, 27.6%
5. NBC, 26.6%
6. ABC, 24%
7. Chris Craft Television Inc., 18.3%
8. Gannett Broadcasting, 16.3%
9. Hearst-Argyle Television Inc., 16%
10. USA Broadcasting, 15.4%

Source: *Broadcasting & Cable*, Top 25 TV Groups (annual), January 25, 1999, p. 44+.

★4215★
TOP TV LOCAL MARKETING AGREEMENTS, 1997
Ranked by: Gross revenue, in millions of dollars. **Remarks:** Includes number of LMA's and percent of local market revenue. **Number listed:** 15

1. Sinclair Broadcasting Group, with $167.5 million
2. Raycom, $43.5
3. Clear Channel, $34.7
4. Media America, $19.0
5. LIN Television, $16.0
6. Hearst-Argyle, $15.0
7. News Corp. Ltd., $12.0
8. Capitol Broadcasting, $11.5
9. Viacom, $8.0
10. A.H. Belo Corp., $7.6

Source: *Broadcasting & Cable*, December 14, 1998, p. 22.

Television Broadcasting--Children's Programs

★4216★
TOP TV BROADCASTERS WHERE KIDS ARE TUNING IN, 1999*
Ranked by: Percent share of total viewership. **Number listed:** 10

1. Nickelodeon, with 50.1%
2. Cartoon, 28.4%
3. Fox, 6.2%
4. Family, 4.5%
5. Syndication, 4.0%
6. WB, 3.0%
7. ABC, 2.3%
8. UPN, 0.5%
9. CBS, 0.4%
10. All Others, 0.6%

Source: *Broadcasting & Cable*, March 1, 1999, p. 22.

★4217★
TOP TV SHOWS FOR TEENS 12-17, 1999*
Ranked by: Average rating. **Number listed:** 10

1. Family Guy, with 9.7
2. Sabrina-Teenage Witch, 9.6
3. Simpsons, 8.6
4. Boy Meets World, 8.4
5. Brother's Keeper, 7.7
6. Guinness World Records, 7.4
7. Dawson's Creek, 7.3
8. That 70's Show, 7.0
9. Friends, 6.9
10. Two of a Kind, 6.9

Source: *Mediaweek*, May 10, 1999, p. 6.

Television Broadcasting--Local News

★4218★
TOP LOCAL NEWS AGENDA, 1998*
Ranked by: Number of stories. **Number listed:** 19
1. Crime, with 3,397
2. Weather, 1,838
3. Accident/Disaster, 1,557
4. Soft News/Human Interest, 1,271
5. Health Issues, 1,265
6. Business/Economy, 1,239
7. Sports, 1,208
8. All Others, 914
9. Campaign '96, 754
10. Foreign News, 630

Source: *Public Management*, August, 1998, p. 22.

Television Broadcasting--News Magazines

★4219★
TOP BRANDS AND THEIR AD SPENDING ON ABC'S 20/20, 1997
Ranked by: Ad spending, in billions of dollars. **Number listed:** 10
1. McDonald's Restaurants Ltd., with $5,328,600 billion
2. Merrill Lynch Financial Services, $2,125,600
3. U.S. Postal Service, $1,871,300
4. Nissan Automobiles-Altima, $1,859,600
5. Sprint, $1,502,600
6. Discover Card, $1,479,500
7. Target, $1,295,500
8. MCI, $1,211,300
9. Sears Department Stores, $1,210.100
10. Home Depot Home Center, $1,131,400

Source: *American Demographics*, October, 1998, p. 34.

★4220★
TOP BRANDS AND THEIR AD SPENDING ON CBS'S 48 HOURS, 1997
Ranked by: Ad spending, in billions of dollars. **Number listed:** 10
1. McDonald's Restaurants Ltd., with $860,000 billion
2. Nissan Motor, $673,600
3. Nissan Automobiles-Altima, $670,700
4. Chrysler Corporation, $609,200
5. Campbell's, $583,300
6. True Value Hardware Stores, $572,200
7. Ultra Slim Fast, $511,200
8. U.S. Postal Service, $474,900
9. KFC Restaurant, $446,400
10. Zocor Cholesterol Rx, $398,200

Source: *American Demographics*, October, 1998, p. 34.

★4221★
TOP BRANDS AND THEIR AD SPENDING ON CBS'S 60 MINUTES, 1997
Ranked by: Ad spending, in billions of dollars. **Number listed:** 10
1. United Parcel Service, with $2,786,400 billion
2. Dollar Rent-A-Car, $2,553,800
3. Nissan Automobiles-Altima, $1,629,400
4. Nissan Motor, $1,621,800
5. Charles Schwab, $1,497,000
6. Merrill Lynch, $1,421,200
7. Wausau, $1,358,600
8. MCI Communications Corp., $1,353,000
9. Chrysler Corporation, $1,263,100
10. U.S. Postal Service, $1,256,300

Source: *American Demographics*, October, 1998, p. 34.

Television Broadcasting--Syndicated Programs

★4222★
TOP SYNDICATED SHOWS, 1999*
Ranked by: 30 second ad price, in dollars. **Number listed:** 10
1. Friends, with $140,000 dollar
2. Seinfeld, $137,000
3. Entertainment Tonight, $105,000
4. Home Improvement, $102,000
5. Frasier, $93,000
6. X-Files, $89,000
7. The Simpsons, $69,000
7. Wheel of Fortune, $69,000
9. ER, $66,000
10. Extra, $65,000

Source: *Advertising Age*, January 18, 1999, p. S2.

Television, Color
See: **Color Television**

Television Receivers

★4223★
TOP COLOR TV'S, DIRECT-VIEW (OVERALL), 1997
Ranked by: Brandshare, in percent. **Number listed:** 15
1. RCA/Pro Scan, with 16.60%
2. Zenith, 13.40%
3. Phillips/Magnavox, 12.20%
4. Sony, 9.50%
5. GE, 6.20%
6. Sharp, 5.0%
7. Panasonic, 4.50%
8. Toshiba, 4.0%
9. JVC, 2.50%
10. Mitsubishi Corp., 2.40%

Source: *Dealerscope Consumer Electronics Marketplace*, August, 1998, p. 19.

Television Sets
See: **Television Receivers**

Television Stations--New York Metropolitan Area

★4224★
TOP TV STATIONS IN THE NEW YORK METROPOLITAN AREA, 1998
Ranked by: Average Nielsen rating. **Remarks:** Includes address, channel, phone, top executive, Nielsen late news and number of employees. **Number listed:** 8
1. WNBC/General Electric Co., with 7
2. WABC-TV/Disney, 6
3. WPIX/Tribune Broadcasting Co., 4
3. CBS 2/CBS Corp., 4
5. WNYW/Fox Broadcasting Co., 3
6. WWOR/Chris-Craft Industries, 2
6. Univision 41 WXTV/Univision Television Group, 2
8. WNET/Educational Broadcasting Corp., 1

Source: *Crain's New York Business*, September 20, 1998, p. 20.

Temporary Help Service Agencies

★4225★
MOST ADMIRED TEMPORARY HELP CORPORATIONS, 1998
Ranked by: Scores (1-10) derived from a survey of senior executives, outside directors and securities analysts. **Remarks:** Respondents rated companies in their own industry on 8 attributes of reputation. Also notes previous year ranking. **Number listed:** 9
1. Robert Half International, with 7.23
2. Interim Services, 6.16
3. Manpower, 5.34
4. Kelly Services, 5.32
5. Norrell, 5.27
6. Accustaff, 5.19
7. CDI, 4.89
8. Volt Information Sciences, 4.56
9. Olsten, 4.20

Source: *Fortune*, America's Most Admired Corporations (annual), March 1, 1999, p. F-2.

★4226★
TOP CORPORATIONS IN THE TEMPORARY HELP SERVICES INDUSTRY, 1998
Ranked by: Revenue, in millions of dollars. **Remarks:** Also notes profits and investment figures as well as number of employees. **Number listed:** 9
1. Manpower, with $8,814 million
2. Olsten, $4,603
3. Kelly Services, $4,092
4. Modis Professional Services, $2,622
5. Interim Services, $1,890
6. Robert Half International, $1,793
7. Volt Information Sciences, $1,709
8. CDI, $1,541
9. Norrell, $1,411

Source: *Fortune*, Fortune 500 Largest U.S. Corporations (annual), April 26, 1999, p. F-70.

Temporary Help Service Agencies—Detroit Metropolitan Area

★4227★
TOP TEMPORARY STAFFING SERVICE FIRMS IN THE DETROIT METROPOLITAN AREA, 1997
Ranked by: Revenue, in millions of dollars. **Remarks:** Includes 1996 revenue, percent change, average daily employment for 1996 and 1997, number of W-2 forms issued, number of offices in metro Detroit, annual payroll for 1996 and 1997 and percent involved in staffing industry segments. **Number listed:** 20
1. Kelly Services Inc., with $3,852.9 million
2. Manpower of Detroit Inc., $104.5
3. Olsten Staffing Services, $87.0
4. Arcadia Services Inc., $78.0
5. The Bartech Group, $67.0
6. TAC Automotive Group, $65.0
7. Acro Service Corp., $47.0
8. Robert Half International, $43.9
9. Entech Personnel Services Inc., $42.0
10. Adecco - The Employment Services, $41.6

Source: *Crain's Detroit Business*, November 30, 1998, p. 22.

Temporary Help Service Agencies--Florida

★4228★
TOP TEMPORARY STAFFING AGENCIES IN FLORIDA, 1997
Ranked by: Number of average weekly temps. **Remarks:** Includes number of permanent employees, number of Florida offices, senior executive, title and year established. **Number listed:** 25
1. Interim Services Inc., with 26,242
2. Kelly Services Inc., 12,995
3. ProStaff, 12,000
4. Olsten Staffing Services, 9,548
5. AccuStaff Inc., 9,000
6. Western Staff Services, 7,000
7. Manpower, 6,748
8. Adecco Employment Services, 5,350
9. Norrell Services, 4,896
10. Labor Finders International Inc., 3,230

Source: *Florida Trend*, TopRank Florida (annual), 1999, p. 97.

Temporary Help Service Agencies—Los Angeles County (CA)

★4229★
TOP TEMPORARY EMPLOYMENT AGENCIES IN THE PHILADELPHIA METROPOLITAN AREA, 1997
Ranked by: Number of workers placed each week. **Remarks:** Includes address, phone number, total hours billed, number of local locations, benefits offered, services offered and training offered. **Number listed:** 23
1. TAC Staffing Services, with 3,000
2. Careers USA, 2,125
3. Protocall Business and healthcare Staffing, 2,000
4. Kaye Personnel Inc., 1,836
5. Manpower Inc., 1,800

6. Placers, 1,122
7. London Personnel Services, 900
8. CoreStaff Inc., 600
9. Snelling Personnel Services, 500
10. McCallion Staffing Specialists, 300

Source: *Philadelphia Business Journal (annual)*, February 12, 1999, p. 20.

★4230★
TOP TEMPORARY PLACEMENT SERVICES AGENCIES IN LOS ANGELES COUNTY, 1997
Ranked by: Revenue, in millions of dollars. **Remarks:** Includes number of employees, number of temporary workers placed per week, average hourly wage, profile, services offered, and top local executive. **Number listed:** 25

1. Manpower, with $118.2 million
2. Apple One Employment Services, $81.0
3. Volt Temporary Services, $77.5
4. Kelly Services, $77.0
5. Adecco Employment Services, $50.0
6. Interim Services Inc., $49.4
7. Remedy Intelligent Staffing, $45.1
8. CDI Corp., $45.0
9. Chipton-Ross Inc., $26.5
10. Westaff Inc., $23.0

Source: *Los Angeles Business Journal*, October 5, 1998, p. 42+.

Tender Offers (Securities)

★4231★
SUCCESSFUL CONTESTED TENDER OFFERS THAT ARE PENDING, 1998
Ranked by: Purchase price, in millions of dollars. **Number listed:** 4

1. AlliedSignal Inc. (hostile suitor), AMP Inc. (target company), with $9,676.0 dollar
2. Nationwide Mutual Insurance Co. (hostile suitor), Allied Group Inc. (target company), $1,626.4
3. Abbott Laboratories (hostile suitor), International Murex Technologies Corp. (target company), $216.2
4. Allmerica Financial Corp.(hostile suitor), Citizens Corp. (target company), $197.1

Source: *Financial Services Shelves*, Mergerstat Review (annual), 1999, p. 40.

Tequila

★4232★
CONSUMPTION OF TEQUILA RANKED BY STATE, 1997
Ranked by: Sales of 9-Liter cases, in thousands of dollars. **Remarks:** Includes 1996 figures, percent of change, share and cumulative share. **Number listed:** 51

1. California, with $1,172,770 9-liter cases
2. Texas, $683,440
3. Florida, $315,140
4. Illinois, $216,810
5. Georgia, $204,300
6. Colorado, $187,860
7. New York, $187,050
8. Arizona, $187,840
9. Washington, $159,270
10. Nevada, $141,320

Source: *Adams Liquor Handbook*, 1998, p. 159.

★4233★
LEADING BRANDS OF TEQUILA, 1997
Ranked by: Number of 9-Liter cases sold in thousands. **Remarks:** Includes 1992-1996 figures and percent of change. **Number listed:** 15

1. Jose Cuervo/1800, with $2,686 9-liter cases
2. Montezuma, $627
3. Giro, $390
4. Sauza, $360
5. Juarez, $308
6. Pepe Lopez, $175
7. Rio Grande, $153
8. Torada, $90
9. Two Fingers, $80
10. El Toro, $56

Source: *Adams Liquor Handbook*, 1998, p. 162.

★4234★
LEADING METROPOLITAN AREAS FOR TEQUILA SALES, 1997
Ranked by: Number of 9-Liter cases sold in thousands. **Remarks:** Includes percent of share. **Number listed:** 25

1. Los Angeles-Long Beach, CA, with $372.9 9-liter cases
2. Houston, TX, $174.1
3. Chicago, IL, $159.7
4. Phoenix, AZ, $149.0
5. Dallas, TX, $145.4
6. Atlanta, GA, $133.9
7. Orange County, CA, $123.9
8. Las Vegas, NV, $122.1
9. Denver, CO, $115.9
10. San Diego, CA, $112.6

Source: *Adams Liquor Handbook*, 1998, p. 153.

★4235★
TOP MARKETS FOR TEQUILA BY CASES SOLD PER THOUSAND ADULTS, 1997
Ranked by: Sales of 9-Liter cases, in thousands of dollars. **Remarks:** Includes 1996 figures and ranking. **Number listed:** 51

1. Nevada, with $133.3 9-liter cases
2. Colorado, $72.8
3. New Mexico, $67.6
4. District of Columbia, $63.8
5. Arizona, $58.5
6. California, $54.7
7. Texas, $53.8
8. Alaska, $52.0
9. New Hampshire, $47.8
10. Oregon, $47.7

Source: *Adams Liquor Handbook*, 1998, p. 160.

★4236★
TOP SUPPLIERS OF TEQUILA, 1997
Ranked by: Market share in percent. **Number listed:** 6

1. IDV North America, with 45.6%
2. Domecq Importers, 12.5%
3. Barton Inc., 11.4%
4. David Sherman, 5.1%
5. Brown-Forman Beverages, 2.9%
6. Others, 22.5%

Source: *Adams Liquor Handbook*, 1998, p. 163.

Terrorism--Foreign

★4237★
COUNTRIES WITH THE MOST TERRORIST ATTACKS
Ranked by: Number of attacks. **Number listed:** 20
1. Colombia, with 667
2. Algeria, 380
3. Sri Lanka, 268
4. Pakistan, 209
5. India, 192
6. France (Corsica-119), 132
7. Mexico, 97
8. Spain, 89
9. Burundi, 85
10. Russia, 78

Source: *CFO*, August, 1998, p. 58.

★4238★
TERRORIST GROUPS COMMITTING THE MOST ATTACKS, 1988-998
Ranked by: Number of attacks. **Number listed:** 10
1. PKK, Kurdistan Workers Party, with 3,575
2. Armed Islamic Group, Algeria, 2,067
3. National Liberation Army, Colombia, 1,817
4. Islamic extremists, Algeria, 1,794
5. Shining Path, Peru, 1,364
6. FARC, Colombia, 1,329
7. ETA, Spain, 1,140
8. Irish Republican Army, Britain, 1,125
9. Dev Sol, Turkey, 530
10. Tupac Amaru, Peru, 446

Source: *U.S. News & World Report*, March 1, 1999, p. 40.

Textile Fabrics

★4239★
TOP FABRIC CONVERTORS
Ranked by: Revenue, in millions of dollars. **Number listed:** 5
1. Richloom, with $201 million
2. P/Kaufmann, $200
3. Covington Industries Inc., $150
4. Ametex, $90
5. Lanscot-Arlen Fabrics Inc., $87

Source: *Furniture Today*, Top 5 Fabric Convertors (annual), May 31, 1999, p. 16.

Textile Industry

★4240★
MOST ADMIRED TEXTILE CORPORATIONS, 1998
Ranked by: Scores (1-10) derived from a survey of senior executives, outside directors and securities analysts. **Remarks:** Respondents rated companies in their own industry on 8 attributes of reputation. Also notes previous year ranking. **Number listed:** 7
1. Unifi, with 7.14
2. WestPoint Stevens, 6.94
3. Interface, 6.93
4. Mohawk Industries, 6.76
5. Shaw Industries, 6.64
6. Springs Industries, 6.52
7. Burlington Industries, 6.35

Source: *Fortune*, America's Most Admired Corporations, May 31, 1999, p. F-5.

★4241★
TOP CORPORATIONS IN THE TEXTILES INDUSTRY, 1998
Ranked by: Revenue, in millions of dollars. **Remarks:** Also notes profits and investment figures as well as number of employees. **Number listed:** 7
1. Shaw Industries, with $3,542 million
2. Mohawk Industries, $2,639
3. Springs Industries, $2,180
4. Burlington Industries, $2,010
5. WestPoint Stevens, $1,779
6. Unifi, $1,378
7. Interface, $1,281

Source: *Fortune*, Fortune 500 Largest U.S. Corporations (annual), April 26, 1999, p. F-70.

Textile Industry--Asia

★4242★
LARGEST COMPANIES IN THE TEXTILES, CLOTHING, AND FOOTWEAR INDUSTRY IN ASIA
Ranked by: Sales, in thousands of U.S. dollars. **Remarks:** Includes country, profit as percent of sales and activity codes. **Number listed:** 100
1. LG International, with $13,079.311 thousand
2. Toyobo Co. Ltd., $3,594,393
3. Ssangyong Corp., $3,088,543
4. Unitka Ltd., $2,639,169
5. Nisshinbo Industries Inc., $1,798,270
6. Onward Kashiyama Co. Ltd., $1,709,086
7. World Co. Ltd., $1,493,330
8. Gunze Ltd., $1,435,411
9. Formosa Chemicals & Fibre Corporation, $1,401,057
10. Wacoal Corp., $1,272,208

Source: *Dun & Bradstreet*, Asia's 7500 Largest Companies (annual), 1999, p. 81.

Textile Industry--Europe

★4243★
TOP TEXTILE MILL PRODUCTS MANUFACTURERS IN EUROPE, 1999
Ranked by: Sales, in millions of European Currency Units (ECU's). **Remarks:** Includes overall rank and number of employees. **Number listed:** 94
1. Coats Viyella PLC, with ECUs3,480 million
2. Coats Patons Ltd., ECUs2,393
3. Courtaulds Textiles Holdings Ltd., ECUs978
4. Total Group PLC, ECUs892
5. Tarkett Regulan GMBH & Co KG, ECUs684
6. DLW AG, ECUs600
7. Manifatture Lane Gaetano Marzotto & Figli S.P.A., ECUs572
8. Handelsges Heinrich Heine GMBH, ECUs507
9. Coats Viyella Clothing Ltd., ECUs505

10. IPT Group Ltd., ECUs462

Source: *Dun & Bradstreet*, Duns Europa (annual), 1999, p. 235.

Textile Mills

★4244★
TOP FABRIC MILLS
Ranked by: Non-automotive revenue, in millions of dollars. **Number listed:** 12

1. Joan Fabrics, with $630 million
2. CULP, $487
3. Microfibres, $250
4. Quaker Group, $225
5. Burlington House Upholstery Fabrics, $220
6. CMI Industries Inc., $169
7. Johnston Industries, $156
8. Blumenthal, $118
9. Hoffman, $115
10. Valdese, $80

Source: *Furniture Today*, Top 15 Fabric Mills (annual), May 31, 1999, p. 16.

Thailand Stock Exchange

See: **Securities Exchange of Thailand**

Theft

★4245★
TOP TYPES OF THEFT IN THE U.S., 1999*
Ranked by: Basis for ranking not specified. **Number listed:** 10

1. Motor Vehicles
2. Jewelry and precious metals
3. TV's, radios and stereos
4. Currency notes
5. Clothing and furs
6. Office equipment
7. Household goods
8. Firearms
9. Consumable goods
10. Livestock

Source: *Jeweler's Circular Keystone*, June, 1999, p. 160.

Theme Parks

See: **Amusement Parks**

Thrift Institutions

★4246★
TOP CORPORATIONS IN THE SAVINGS INSTITUTION INDUSTRY, 1998
Ranked by: Revenue, in millions of dollars. **Remarks:** Also notes profits and investment figures as well as number of employees. **Number listed:** 7

1. Washington Mutual, with $12,746 million
2. Golden West Financial Corp., $3,100
3. Golden State Bancorp, $3,026
4. Charter One Financial, $1,972
5. Dime Bancorp, $1,946
6. Sovereign Bancorp, $1,461
7. Astoria Financial, $1,285

Source: *Fortune*, Fortune 500 Largest U.S. Corporations (annual), April 26, 1999, p. F-67.

★4247★
TOP THRIFT HOLDING COMPANIES, 1998
Ranked by: Total assets, in millions of dollars. **Remarks:** Includes per change, total deposits, net income, employees, branches, ROA, and ROE. **Number listed:** 100

1. Washington Mutual Inc., with $165,493.3 million
2. Golden State Bancorp, $54,580.2
3. Golden West Financial Corp., $38,468.7
4. Charter One Financial, $24,467.3
5. Dime Bancorp, $21,913.9
6. Sovereign Bancorp, $21,913.9
7. Astoria Financial Corp., $20,587.7
8. Bank United, $14,791.5
9. GreenPoint Financial Corp., $13,970.3
10. Commercial Federal Corp., $12,178.3

Source: *American Banker*, May 22, 1999, p. 6.

Thrift Institutions--Chicago (IL)

★4248★
TOP THRIFT INSTITUTIONS IN CHICAGO, 1998
Ranked by: Assets, in millions of dollars. **Remarks:** Includes percent change, earnings, net worth, total loans outstanding, and loan types. **Number listed:** 25

1. LaSalle Bank FSB, with $11,672.1 million
2. St. Paul Federal Bank for Savings, $4,468.0
3. Mid America Bank FSB, $3,475.6
4. Household Bank FSB, $3,471.9
5. Liberty Federal Bank, $1,547.1
6. Superior Bank FSB, $1,349.9
7. Financial Federal Trust & Savings Bank, $1,245.7
8. Regency Savings Bank FSB, $917.6
9. Avondale FSB, $609.3
10. Liberty Bank for Savings, $578.5

Source: *Crain's Chicago Business*, Top Business Lists (annual), March 31, 1998, p. 70.

Thrift Institutions--Florida

★4249★
TOP THRIFT INSTITUTIONS IN FLORIDA, 1999
Ranked by: Total deposits, in thousands of dollars. **Remarks:** Includes assets, return on assets and return on equity. **Number listed:** 47

1. BankAtlantic, FSB, with $1,765,091 thousand
2. BankUnited FSB, $1,440,698
3. First Bank of Florida, $1,269,933
4. Fidelity FSB, $873,490
5. First of America Bank-Florida, $859,517
6. Harbor Federal Savings Bank, $936,168
7. Peoples First Community Bank, $670,414
8. Community Savings, $566,197
9. FirstSouth Bank, $448,546
10. First Federal S&L Association of Florida, $433,868

Source: *Top 50 Thrifts*, 1999, p. 24.

★4250★
TOP THRIFT INSTITUTIONS IN THE NEW YORK METROPOLITAN AREA, 1997
Ranked by: Total assets, in millions of dollars. **Remarks:** Includes earnings, net worth, total loans outstanding, percent change, and loan type. **Number listed:** 25

1. Dime Bancorp Inc., with $21,848.0 million
2. GreenPoint Financial/GreenPoint Bank, $13,083.5
3. Astoria Financial Corp./Astoria Federal Savings & Loan Association, $10,528.4
4. Emigrant Bancorp Inc./Emigrant Savings Bank, $6,077.5
5. Long Island Bancorp/Long Island Savings Bank, $5,900.0
6. Apple Bank for Savings, $4,474.0
7. Independence Community Bank Corp./Independence Savings Bank, $3,857.8
8. T.R. Financial/Roosevelt Savings Bank, $3,836.0
9. Roslyn Bancorp Inc./Roslyn Savings Bank, $3,601.1
10. New York Bancorp/Home Federal Savings Bank, $3,244.2

Source: *Crain's New York Business*, Top Business Lists (annual), 1999, p. 58.

Thrift Institutions—Philadelphia Metropolitan Area

★4251★
LARGEST THRIFT INSTITUTIONS HEADQUARTERED IN THE GREATER PHILADELPHIA AREA, 1998*
Ranked by: Local deposits, in thousands of dollars. **Remarks:** Includes total assets, total deposits, net loans, net income, total offices and chairman/president. **Number listed:** 24

1. Beneficial Savings Bank, with $1,255,488 thousand
2. Commonwealth Bank, $1,146,640
3. Firstrust Bank, $865,896
4. Sovereign Bank, $494,894
5. Farmers & Mechanics Bank, $475,358
6. Fox Chase Federal Savings Bank, $430,713
7. Third Federal Savings Bank, $345,661
8. First Savings Bank of Perkasie, $345,141
9. Willow Grove Bank, $309,727
10. Progress Financial Corp., $300,685

Source: *Philadelphia Business Journal*, Book of Business Lists (annual), December 25, 1998, p. 31.

Timesharing (Real Estate)--Caribbean Region

★4252★
ISLANDS WITH THE MOST TIMESHARES IN THE CARIBBEAN, 1999
Ranked by: Percentage of timeshare units on each island. **Number listed:** 6

1. Aruba, with 30.4%
2. St. Maarten, 18.3%
3. Dominican Republic, 13.3%
4. The Bahamas, 11.3%
5. U.S. Virgin Islands, 6.1%
6. Other, 20.6%

Source: *Hotel & Motel Management*, May 3, 1999, p. 16.

Tire Industry, International

★4253★
TOP TIRE MANUFACTURERS, 1997
Ranked by: Sales, in millions of U.S. dollars. **Number listed:** 7

1. Goodyear Sumitomo, with $22.6% million
2. Bridgestone, $18.6%
3. Michelin, $18.3%
4. Continental, $6.3%
5. Pirelli, $4.4%
6. Yokohama, $3.4%
7. Other, $26.4%

Source: *The Economist*, February 6, 1999, p. 65.

Tissue Paper

★4254★
BEST SELLING BRANDS OF FACIAL TISSUE, 1999
Ranked by: Sales, in millions of dollars. **Number listed:** 4

1. Kleenex, with $648.0 million
2. Puffs, $346.0
3. Private Label, $159.2
4. Scotties, $64.8

Source: *Brand Week*, Superbrands: America's Top 2,000 Brands (annual), June 21, 1999, p. S56.

Titanium Dioxide, International

★4255★
TOP WORLDWIDE MANUFACTURERS OF TITANIUM DIOXIDE, 1996
Ranked by: Global demand by segment, in thousands of metric tons. **Number listed:** 7

1. Paint, with 1,909 metric tons
2. Plastics, 606
3. Paper, 449
4. Inks, 107
5. Fibers, 58
6. Ceramics, 51
7. Other, 121

Source: *Chemical Market Reporter*, September 21, 1998, p. 18.

Toasters, Electric
See: **Electric Toasters**

Tobacco Industry
See also: **Cigarette Industry**

★4256★
MOST ADMIRED TOBACCO CORPORATIONS, 1996
Ranked by: Scores (1-10) derived from a survey of senior executives, outside directors and securities analysts. **Remarks:** Respondents rated companies in their own industry on 8 attributes of reputation. Also notes previous year ranking. **Number listed:** 5
1. Phillip Morris, with 8.51
2. UST, 6.74
3. Universal, 6.49
4. Standard Commercial, 5.91
5. DIMON, 5.60

Source: *Fortune*, America's Most Admired Corporations, March 1, 1999, p. F-3.

★4257★
TOP CORPORATIONS IN THE TOBACCO INDUSTRY, 1998
Ranked by: Revenue, in millions of dollars. **Remarks:** Also notes profits and investment figures as well as number of employees. **Number listed:** 5
1. Philip Morris, with $57,813 million
2. Universal, $4,287
3. Dimon, $2,563
4. Standard Commercial, $1,493
5. UST, $1,397

Source: *Fortune*, Fortune 500 Largest U.S. Corporations (annual), April 26, 1999, p. F-70.

★4258★
TOP MOIST SNUFF BRAND, 1996
Ranked by: Dollar share, in percent. **Number listed:** 12
1. Copenhagen, with 29.9%
2. Skoal Fine Cut Wintergreen, 11.8%
3. Kodiak Wintergreen, 9.5%
4. Skoal Long Cut Wintergreen, 9.4%
5. Copenhagen Long Cut, 7.2%
6. Skoal Long Cut Straight, 5.9%
7. Skoal Long Cut Mint, 4.4%
8. Skoal Long Cut Cherry, 2.9%
9. Skoal Bandits Wintergreet, 2.2%
10. Skoal Long Cut Classic, 2.0%

Source: *Tobacco International*, February, 1999, p. 25.

Tobacco Industry--Europe

★4259★
TOP TOBACCO MANUFACTURERS IN EUROPE, 1998
Ranked by: Sales, in millions of European Currency Units (ECU's). **Remarks:** Includes overall rank and number of employees. **Number listed:** 7
1. Reemtsma Cigarettenfabriken GMBH, with 5,635
2. Tabacalera, SA, 5,393
3. British American Tobacco Investments Ltd., 4,019
4. Batig Ges Fuer Beteiligungen MBH, 2,881
5. Ste Nat Exploit Industri Tabacs, 2,575
6. Rothmans International Ltd., 429
7. A Michailidis - Kapniki S A, 73

Source: *Dun & Bradstreet*, Duns Europa (annual), 1999, p. 235.

Tobacco Industry, International

★4260★
WORLD'S LARGEST TOBACCO COMPANIES BY REVENUE, 1997
Ranked by: Revenues, in millions of U.S. dollars. **Number listed:** 3
1. Philip Morris, with $56,114 million
2. Bat Industries, $26,802
3. Japan Tobacco, $14,125

Source: *Fortune*, The Global 500: World's Biggest Corporations (annual), August 3, 1998, p. F-25.

★4261★
WORLD'S LARGEST TOBACCO FIRMS, BY STICK SALES, 1998
Ranked by: Stick sales in bn. **Number listed:** 9
1. Chinese National Tobacco, with 1600
2. Philip Morris, 1000
3. BAT-Rothmans, 950
4. RJ Reynolds, 350
5. JTI, 300
6. Reemtsma Cigarettenfabriken GMBH, 150
7. Tabakprom, 130
8. KT&GC, 110
9. Tekel, 100

Source: *Marketing*, January 21, 1999, p. F13.

Tokyo Stock Exchange

★4262★
LARGEST LISTED COMPANIES OF THE TOKYO STOCK EXCHANGE, 1997
Ranked by: Market value, in billions of Japanese yen. **Number listed:** 20
1. Toyota Motor, with 14,219 yen
2. Tokyo-Mitsubishi Bank, 8,412
3. Nippon Telegraph & Telephone, 6,168
4. Sumitomo Bank, 4,680
5. Honda Motors, 4,667
6. Sony, 4,665
7. Matsushita Electric Industrial Co., 4,034
8. Seven-Eleven Japan, 3,847
9. Sanwa Bank, 3,830
10. Nomura Securities, 3,415

Source: *SSB Guide to World Equity Markets*, 1999, p. 283.

★4263★
MOST ACTIVELY TRADED SHARES ON THE TOKYO STOCK EXCHANGE, 1997
Ranked by: Trading value, in billions of Japanese yen. **Number listed:** 20
1. Sony, with ¥3,251 yen
2. Toyota Motor, ¥2,693

3. Nippon Telegraph & Telephone, ¥2,438
4. Bank of Tokyo Mitsubishi, ¥2,060
5. Honda Motors, ¥1,932
6. Fujitsu, ¥1,736
7. Canon, ¥1,603
8. Matsushita Heavy Industries, ¥1,550
9. Tokyo Electron, ¥1,507
10. Matsushita Electrical Industrial Co., ¥1,431

Source: *SSB Guide to World Equity Markets*, 1999, p. 284.

Toothpaste

★4264★
TOP BRANDS OF TOOTHPASTE, 1997
Ranked by: Percent share of market in millions of dollars. **Remarks:** Includes 1996 percent share and measured advertising for 1996 and 1997. **Number listed:** 10

1. Crest, with $24.5% million
2. Colgate, $21.3%
3. Aquafresh, $11.7%
4. Mentadent, $11.2%
5. Arm & Hammer, $7.2%
6. Rembrandt, $3.5%
7. Sensodyne, $3.3%
8. Listerine, $2.6%
9. Closeup, $2.1%
10. UltraBrite, $1.7%

Source: *Advertising Age*, September 28, 1998, p. S18.

Toronto Stock Exchange

★4265★
LARGEST LISTED COMPANIES ON THE TORONTO STOCK EXCHANGE, 1997
Ranked by: Market value, in millions of Canadian dollars. **Number listed:** 20

1. Mobil Oil Corp., with C$94,873 million
2. Citicorp, C$76,172
3. General Motors, C$65,135
4. Amoco Corporation, C$60,491
5. Chrysler Corporation, C$41,096
6. Northern Telecom, C$33,036
7. BCE Inc., C$30,288
8. British Gas plc ADS, C$28,631
9. Thomson Corp., C$23,831
10. Royal Bank of Canada, C$23,302

Source: *SSB Guide to World Equity Markets*, 1998, p. 116.

★4266★
MOST ACTIVELY TRADED SHARES ON THE TORONTO STOCK EXCHANGE, 1997
Ranked by: Market value, in millions of Canadian dollars. **Number listed:** 20

1. Northern Telecom, with C$9,864 million
2. Newbridge Networks Corp., C$9,835
3. Barrick Gold, C$8,882
4. Alcan Aluminum, C$7,206
5. Inco Ltd., C$6,039
6. Canadian Pacific Ltd., C$5,754
7. Placer Dome, C$5,708
8. Petro Canada C/V, C$5,510
9. Seagram, C$5,490
10. BCE Inc., C$5,161

Source: *SSB Guide to World Equity Markets*, 1998, p. 117.

Tortillas

★4267★
TOP SELLING TORTILLA CHIP BRANDS, 1998
Ranked by: Sales, in dollars. **Remarks:** Includes percent change and unit sales. **Number listed:** 10

1. Doritos (Frito-Lay), with $1,828,833,920 dollar
2. Tostitos (Frito-Lay), $526,189,184
3. Baked Tostitos (Frito-Lay), $118,258,104
4. Doritos Wow (Frito-Lay), $71,865,872
5. Sanitas (Frito-Lay), $54,625,376
6. Mission, $37,353,584
7. Padrinos (Granny Goose), $24,799,274
8. Tostitos Wow (Frito-Lay), $20,680,602
9. Old Dutch, $10,572,884
10. Chi Chi (Mesa Foods), $10,380,115

Source: *Milling & Banking News*, April 27, 1999, p. 32.

Tourist Trade

★4268★
TOP CITIES REINVESTING TAXES IN TRAVEL AND TOURISM, 1999
Ranked by: Dollars reinvested, in percent. **Number listed:** 10

1. Reno, NV, with 77.8%
2. Houston, TX, 67.6%
3. Riverside, CA, 60.6%
4. Las Vegas, NV, 59.8%
5. Dallas, TX, 57.7%
6. Detroit, MI, 57.1%
7. San Antonio, TX, 54.7%
8. Indianapolis, IN, 54.6%
9. St. Louis, MO, 51.4%
10. Austin, TX, 50.0%

Source: *Travelware*, 1999, p. 16.

★4269★
TOP STATE TOURISM BUDGETS, 1998*
Ranked by: Budget, in millions of dollars. **Number listed:** 10

1. Illinois, with $35.3 million
2. Hawaii, $27.7
3. Texas, $25.1
4. Florida, $23.0
5. Pennsylvania, $19.4
6. Virginia, $18.3
7. New York, $18.1
8. Massachusetts, $17.4
9. Louisiana, $15.1
10. Michigan, $14.7

Source: *Association Management*, July, 1998, p. 23.

★4270★
U.S. CITIES WITH THE MOST FOREIGN VISITORS, 1998
Ranked by: Number of visitors, in millions. **Number listed:** 10

1. New York, NY, with $5.0 millions
2. Los Angeles, CA, $3.9
3. Miami, FL, $3.3

4. San Francisco, CA, $2.9
5. Orlando, FL, $2.8
6. Honolulu, HI, $2.5
7. Las Vegas, NV, $2.1
8. Washington, DC, $1.4
9. Boston, MA, $1.1
9. Chicago, IL, $1.1

Source: *Expo*, March, 1999, p. 50.

Tourist Trade, International

★4271★
WORLD'S TOP TOURISM DESTINATIONS, 1997
Ranked by: International arrivals, in millions. **Remarks:** Includes percent change from 1996. **Number listed:** 10

1. France, with $66.8 million
2. United States, $49.0
3. Spain, $43.4
4. Italy, $34.1
5. United Kingdom, $25.9
6. China, $23.8
7. Poland, $19.5
8. Mexico, $19.3
9. Canada, $17.6
10. Czech Republic, $17.4

Source: *Travel Industry World Yearbook: The Big Picture*, 1996, p. 6.

★4272★
WORLD'S TOP TOURISM EARNERS, 1997
Ranked by: Tourism earned, in millions of U.S. dollars. **Remarks:** Includes percent change from 1996. **Number listed:** 10

1. United States, with $75,056 million
2. Italy, $30,000
3. France, $27,947
4. Spain, $27,190
5. United Kingdom, $20,569
6. Germany, $16,418
7. Austria, $12,393
8. China, $12,074
9. Hong Kong (China), $9,242
10. Canada, $8,928

Source: *Travel Industry World Yearbook: The Big Picture*, 1996, p. 6.

★4273★
WORLD'S TOP TOURISM SPENDERS, 1996
Ranked by: Tourism expenditure, in millions of U.S. dollars ($). **Remarks:** Includes percent change from 1995. **Number listed:** 10

1. Germany, with $50,815 million
2. United States, $48,739
3. Japan, $37,040
4. United Kingdom, $25,445
5. France, $17,746
6. Italy, $15,516
7. Austria, $11,811
8. Netherlands, $11,370
9. Canada, $11,090
10. Taiwan, $9,895

Source: *Travel Industry World Yearbook: The Big Picture*, 1996, p. 7.

Toy and Game Industry

★4274★
AVERAGE RETAIL PRICE OF THE TOP ACTION FIGURE BRANDS, 1998
Ranked by: August, 1998 sales. **Number listed:** 7

1. Star Wars, with $8.20 dollar
2. Power Rangers, $9.00
3. Transformers/Beast Wars, $9.71
4. Batman, $7.61
5. Godzilla, $10.37
6. WWF, $6.36
7. Starting Lineup, $9.18

Source: *Playthings*, November, 1998, p. 20.

★4275★
BEST SELLING TOY BRANDS, 1998
Ranked by: Total sales, in millions of dollars. **Remarks:** Includes location, lead agency, media expenditures. **Number listed:** 5

1. Mattel, with $4.7 million
2. Nintendo, $4.0
3. Hasbro, $3.3
4. Sony, n/a
5. Sega, $2.5

Source: *Adweek's Marketing Week*, Superbrands: America's Top 2000 Brands, June 21, 1999, p. S68.

★4276★
BEST SELLING TOYS INTRODUCED IN 1998
Ranked by: August, 1998 sales. **Remarks:** Includes date introduced and average retail price. **Number listed:** 15

1. Talking Teletubbies Asst.
2. Holiday Barbie
3. Small Soldiers Asst.
4. Flip 'N Dive Barbie
5. Hot Wheels Mechanix Vehicle Asst.
6. Flashlight Fun Stacie Doll and Pooh
7. Winnie the Pooh Bounce Around Tigger
8. Power Wheels Extreme Machine
9. Teletubbies Plush Asst.
10. Cool Blue Barbie Doll

Source: *Playthings*, November, 1998, p. 16.

★4277★
BEST TOY BRANDS ACCORDING TO DISCOUNT SHOPPERS, 1998
Ranked by: Scores (1-10) derived from a survey of senior executives, outside directors, and securities analysts. **Remarks:** Respondents rated companies in their own industry on 8 attributes of reputation. Also notes previous year ranking. **Number listed:** 10

1. Mattel, with 37%
2. Fisher Price, 21%
3. Playskool, 8%
3. Lego, 8%
5. Tonka, 7%
6. Hasbro, 5%
7. Milton Bradley, 4%
7. Parker Bros., 4%
7. Little Tikes, 4%
10. Matchbox, 3%

Source: *Discount Store News*, Top Brands Survey (annual), September 7, 1998, p. 26.

★4278★
TOP ACTION FIGURE BRANDS BY SALES, 1998
Ranked by: August, 1998 sales. **Number listed:** 7

1. Star Wars

2. Power Rangers
3. Transformers/Beast Wars
4. Batman
5. Godzilla
6. WWF
7. Starting Lineup

Source: *Playthings*, November, 1998, p. 20.

★4279★
TOP ACTION FIGURE BRANDS BY UNITS SOLD, 1998
Ranked by: August, 1998 unit sales. **Number listed:** 7

1. Star Wars
2. Power Rangers
3. Transformers/Beast Wars
4. Batman
5. WWF
6. Starting Lineup
7. Godzilla

Source: *Playthings*, November, 1998, p. 20.

★4280★
TOP CORPORATIONS IN THE TOY/SPORTING GOODS INDUSTRY, 1998
Ranked by: Revenue, in millions of dollars. **Remarks:** Also notes profits and investment figures as well as number of employees. **Number listed:** 2

1. Mattel, with $4,782 million
2. Hasbro, $3,304

Source: *Fortune*, Fortune 500 Largest U.S. Corporations (annual), April 26, 1999, p. F-70.

★4281★
TOP SALES OF TOYS BY TRADE, 1998*
Ranked by: Sales, in percent. **Number listed:** 6

1. Independent toy stores, with 31%
2. Hypermarkets, 19%
3. Department stores, 18%
4. Toy store chains, 13%
5. Mail order catalogues, 8%
6. All others, 11%

Source: *Playthings*, September, 1998, p. 58.

★4282★
TOP TOY RETAILERS, 1997
Ranked by: Distribution of dollar sales, in percent. **Number listed:** 20

1. Toys R Us, with 18.4%
2. Wal-Mart, 16.4%
3. K-Mart, 8.2%
4. Target, 7.1%
5. Consolidated Stores, 6.1%
6. JC Penney, 1.5%
7. Hills, 1.2%
8. Service Merchandise, 1.1%
8. Ames, 1.1%
8. Meijer, 1.1%
11. Caldor, .9%
11. Price Costco, .9%
13. Sears, .7%

Source: *Playthings*, July, 1998, p. 22.

Toy Industry

See: **Toy and Game Industry**

Trade Unions--Pension Plans

★4283★
TAX-EXEMPT FUNDS, 1999
Ranked by: Assets, in thousands of dollars. **Number listed:** 1260

1. Teamsters, Western Conference, Seattle, WA, with $20,800,000 thousand
2. Teamsters, Central States, Southeast & Southwest Areas Pension Fund, Rosemont, IL, $18,900,000
3. National Electrical Benefit Fund, Washington, DC, $8,494,000
4. United Mine Workers of America Health & Retirement Funds, Washington, DC, $7,666,648
5. Engineers, Operating, International, Washington, DC, $5,745,047
6. Boilermakers-Blacksmith National Pension Trust, Kansas City, KS, $5,444,533
7. Retail, Wholesale Union, Local 1199, New York, NY, $5,200,000
8. Health & Human Service Employees Union Local 1199, Pension Fund, New York, NY, $5,147,000
9. Bakery & Confectionery Union & Industry International Pension Fund, Kensington, MD, $4,942,562
10. Sheet Metal Workers National Pension, Alexandria, VA, $4,362,233

Source: *Money Market Directories*, Money Market Directory of Pension Funds and Their Investment Managers (annual), 1999, p. 1425+.

Trading Companies--Europe

★4284★
EUROPE'S LARGEST TRADING COMPANIES, 1997
Ranked by: Sales, in thousands of U.S. dollars. **Remarks:** Includes country, headquarters, industry, percent change in sales and percent change in local currencies. **Number listed:** 3750

1. Glencore International AG, with $39,824,224 thousand
2. Rewe Group, $34,363,839
3. Shell International Petroleum Co. Ltd., $33,380,897
4. Edeka Group, $33,147,321
5. Metro AG, $31,718,750
6. Tengelmann Group, $29,218,750
7. Carrefour, $28,212,910
8. Tesco, $27,139,557
9. Koninklijke Ahold NV, $25,041,339
10. Tesco Stores Ltd., $23,944,242

Source: *Dun & Bradstreet*, Europe's Thousand Largest Companies (annual), 1999, p. 499+.

Trading Companies, International

★4285★
WORLD'S LARGEST TRADING CORPORATIONS BY REVENUE, 1997
Ranked by: Revenue, in millions of dollars. **Number listed:** 19

1. Mitsui (Japan), with $142,688 million

2. Mitsubishi Corp. (Japan), $128,922
3. Itochu (Japan), $126,632
4. Marubeni (Japan), $111,121
5. Sumitomo (Japan), $102,395
6. Nissho Iwai (Japan), $81,894
7. Veba Group (Germany), $43,881
8. Tomen (Japan), $43,400
9. Nichimen Corp. (Japan), $31,362
10. Viag (Germany), $28,581

Source: *Fortune*, The Global 500: World's Biggest Corporations (annual), August 3, 1998, p. F-25+.

★4286★
WORLD'S LARGEST TRADING CORPORATIONS BY REVENUE, 1997
Ranked by: Revenue, in millions of dollars. **Number listed:** 19

1. Mitsui (Japan), with $142,688 million
2. Mitsubishi Corp. (Japan), $128,922
3. Itochu (Japan), $126,632
4. Marubeni (Japan), $111,121
5. Sumitomo (Japan), $102,395
6. Nissho Iwai (Japan), $81,894
7. Veba Group (Germany), $43,881
8. Tomen (Japan), $43,400
9. Nichimen Corp. (Japan), $31,362
10. Viag (Germany), $28,581

Source: *Fortune*, The Global 500: World's Biggest Corporations (annual), August 3, 1998, p. F-25+.

Traffic Accidents

★4287★
CITIES WITH THE HIGHEST RATE OF FATAL RED-LIGHT CRASHES, 1992-1996
Ranked by: Deaths per 100,000 people. **Number listed:** 10

1. Phoenix, AZ, with 8.11
2. Mesa, AZ, 7.08
3. Memphis, TN, 5.45
4. Tucson, AZ, 5.1
5. St. Petersburg, FL, 4.95
6. Dallas, TX, 4.89
6. Fresno, CA, 4.89
8. Birmingham, AL, 4.80
9. Albuquerque, NM, 4.77
10. Louisville, KY, 4.40

Source: *Governing*, July, 1998, p. 13.

★4288★
METROPOLITAN AREAS WITH THE HIGHEST PEDESTRIAN DANGER INDEXES, 1996
Ranked by: Combined federal data on pedestrian deaths and serious injuries with data on percentage of commuters who walk to work. **Number listed:** 10

1. Orlando, FL, with 95
2. Tampa/St. Petersburg/Clearwater, FL, 87
3. Miami/Ft. Lauderdale, FL, 78
4. Providence/Pawtucket/Fall River, RI-MA, 65
5. Phoenix,AZ, 63
6. Houston/Galveston/Brazoria, TX, 56
7. Atlanta, GA, 55
8. Los Angeles/Anaheim/Riverside, CA, 54
9. Buffalo/Niagara Falls, NY, 50
10. Charlotte/Gastonia/Rock Hill, NC-SC, 48

Source: *Governing*, October, 1998, p. 15.

★4289★
STATES WITH THE HIGHEST NUMBER OF FATAL ACCIDENTS, 1997
Ranked by: Number of truck drivers death. **Number listed:** 15

1. California, with 81
2. Texas, 75
3. Florida, 40
4. Pennsylvania, 36
5. Illinois, 33
5. Kentucky, 33
7. Tennessee, 32
8. Georgina, 28
8. Indiana, 28
8. Virginia, 28
11. Arkansas, 25
11. North Carolina, 25
11. Ohio, 25

Source: *Traffic World*, December 14, 1998, p. 19.

★4290★
STATES WITH THE WORST CHILD PEDESTRIAN CASUALTIES PER 100,000 CHILDREN, 1992-1996
Ranked by: Collisions per year involving children, per 100,000. **Number listed:** 10

1. New Mexico, with 36.2
2. Arizona, 69.2
3. Florida, 195.8
4. District of Columbia, 6.6
5. Nevada, 18.2
6. Louisiana, 63.4
7. North Carolina, 80.6
8. Delaware, 8.0
9. South Carolina, 42.0
10. Texas, 218.8

Source: *Economist*, August, 1998, p. 22.

Transportation

★4291★
TOP HISPANIC OWNED TRANSPORTATION COMPANIES, 1998
Ranked by: Revenue, in millions of dollars. **Number listed:** 10

1. Herman/Miles Trucking Inc., with $24.30 million
2. Pan American Express Inc., $19.62
3. McLean Cargo Specialist Inc., $15.80
4. La Rosa Del Monte Express Inc., $15.20
5. Public Inc., $14.00
6. Casas International Brokerage Inc., $11.00
7. Nu Trans Inc., $11.00
8. Leticia Inc., $10.10
9. MCO Transport Inc., $8.85
10. Mac Aerospace corp., $8.07

Source: *Hispanic Business*, Hispanic Business 500 (annual), June, 1999, p. 104.

★4292★
TOP TRANSPORTATION COMPANIES ON THE S&P 500, 1998
Ranked by: Each company is ranked by eight criteria: one-year total return, three-year total return, one-year sales growth, three-year sales growth, one-year profit growth, three-year profit growth, net profit margins and return on equity, with additional weight given to a company's sales. A company's com-

posite rank is calculated using the sum of all its ranks. **Remarks:** Overall score not provided. **Number listed:** 11

1. Southwest Airlines, with 55
2. FDX, 84
3. Burlington Northern Santa Fe, 109
4. Delta Air Lines, 123
5. AMR, 147
6. US Airways Group, 192
7. Laidlaw, 264
8. Norfolk Southern, 375
9. Ryder System, 378
10. CSX, 419

Source: *Business Week*, Business Week 50: Top Companies of the S&P 500 (annual), March 29, 1999, p. 164.

Transportation--Asia

★4293★
LARGEST COMPANIES IN TRANSPORT AND ALLIED SERVICES IN ASIA, 1999
Ranked by: Sales, in thousands of dollars. **Remarks:** Includes country, profit as percent of sales and activity codes. **Number listed:** 100

1. East Japan Railway Co. Ltd., with $18,823,405 thousand
2. Nippon Express Co. Ltd., $13,334,303
3. Japan Airlines co. Ltd., $11,838,016
4. Central Japan Railway, $9,568,525
5. All Nippon Airways Co. Ltd., $8,087,619
6. Nippon Yusen, $8,071,541
7. Kinki Nippon Railway Co. Ltd., $6,854,670
8. Mitsui OSK Lines Ltd., $6,249,094
9. Yamato Transport Co. Ltd., $5,623,929
10. Odakyu Electric Railway Co. Ltd., $4,258,188

Source: *Dun & Bradstreet*, Asia's 7500 Largest Companies (annual), 1999, p. 89.

Transportation--Equipment and Supplies

★4294★
TOP CORPORATIONS IN THE TRANSPORTATION EQUIPMENT INDUSTRY, 1998
Ranked by: Revenue, in millions of dollars. **Remarks:** Also notes profits and investment figures as well as number of employees. **Number listed:** 4

1. Brunswick, with $3,945 million
2. Trinity Industries, $2,473
3. Harley-Davidson, $2,064
4. Polaris Industries, $1,176

Source: *Fortune*, Fortune 500 Largest U.S. Corporations (annual), April 26, 1999, p. F-70+.

Transportation--Equipment and Supplies--Europe

★4295★
TOP COMPANIES IN THE TRANSPORTATION EQUIPMENT INDUSTRY IN EUROPE
Ranked by: Sales, in millions of European Currency Units (ECUs). **Remarks:** Includes country, employees, rank, volume and page. **Number listed:** 196

1. Bayerische Motorenwerke AG, with ECUs26,506 millions of ECUs
2. Renault, ECUs24,098
3. Robert Bosch GMBH, ECUs20,867
4. Automobiles Peugeot, ECUs15,489
5. Adam Opel AG, ECUs14,368
6. Ford-Werke AG, ECUs13,390
7. Man AG, ECUs10,829
8. British Aerospace PLC, ECUs10,723
9. Ford Motor Co. Ltd., ECUs10,492
10. Automobiles Citroen, ECUs9,818

Source: *Dun & Bradstreet*, Duns Europa (annual), 1999, p. 258+.

Transportation--Europe

★4296★
LARGEST TRANSPORTATION COMPANIES IN EUROPE, 1997
Ranked by: Sales, in thousands of U.S. dollars. **Remarks:** Includes 1996 rank, country, headquarters, industry, sales, percent changes in sales and percent change in local currencies. **Number listed:** 300

1. Deutsche Bahn AG, with $17,001,116 thousand
2. British Airways, $14,256,021
3. Deutsche Lufthansa AG, $12,917,968
4. Filal af Delta Air Lines, Inc. USA Delta Airlines, $9,857,083
5. Peninsular & Oriental Steam Navigation Co., $9,761,794
6. SairGroup AG, $8,672,068
7. SNCF-Ste National des Chemins de Fers Francais, $8,656,255
8. Koninklijke Luchtvaart Maatschappij NV, $6,617,807
9. Cie Nationale Air France, $6,523,792
10. Schenker AG, $5,636,160

Source: *Dun & Bradstreet*, Europe's Thousand Largest Companies (annual), 1999, p. 662.

Transportation--Securities

★4297★
LARGEST TRANSPORTATION BOND ISSUERS, 1997
Ranked by: Value of bonds issued, in thousands of dollars. **Remarks:** Includes number of issues. **Number listed:** 25

1. Metropolitan Transportation Authority, NY, with $1,950,800 thousand
2. Massachusetts Turnpike Authority, $1,764,400
3. Port Authority of New York & New Jersey, $1,634,100

4. San Joaquin Hills Transportation Corridor, CA, $1,448,300
5. New York State Thruway Authority, $1,304,100
6. E-470 Public Highway Authority, CO, $822,300
7. Denver, CO, $719,000
8. New Jersey Transportation Trust Fund Authority, $703,900
9. Massachusetts Bay Transportation Authority, $669,200
10. Florida, $550,800

Source: *Bond Buyer Yearbook (annual)*, 1999, p. 129.

★4298★
LEADING COUNSEL FOR TRANSPORTATION BOND ISSUES, 1997
Ranked by: Value of bonds issued, in thousands of dollars. **Remarks:** Includes number of issues. **Number listed:** 10

1. Hawkins, Delafield & Wood, with $3,521,200 thousand
2. Mintz, Levin, Cohn, Ferris, Glovsky & Popeo, $2,778,300
3. Krokidas & Bluestein, $2,433,600
4. Jeffrey S. Green, Esq., $1,634,100
5. Kutak Rock, $1,606,500
6. Stradling, Yocca, Carlson & Rauth, $1,448,300
7. Saul, Ewing, Remick & Saul, $1,359,900
8. Hogan & Hartson, $1,071,900
9. Vinson & Elkins, $823,700
10. Greenburg Traurig Hoffman Lipoff Rosen, $794,300

Source: *Bond Buyer Yearbook (annual)*, 1999, p. 129.

Trash Compactors

See: **Refuse Compactors**

Travel Agencies

★4299★
STATES WITH THE HIGHEST NUMBER OF TRAVEL AGENCIES, 1997
Ranked by: Number of agencies. **Number listed:** 51

1. California, with 6,911
2. New York, 4,076
3. Florida, 3,217
4. Texas, 3,193
5. Illinois, 2,762
6. New Jersey, 1,976
7. Pennsylvania, 1,873
8. Massachusetts, 1,722
9. Ohio, 1,597
10. Georgia, 1,556

Source: *Travel Industry World Yearbook: The Big Picture (annual)*, 1998, p. 51.

★4300★
TOP TRAVEL AGENCIES BY AIR SALES, 1998
Ranked by: Air sales, in thousands of dollars. **Number listed:** 50

1. American Express, with $9,700,000 thousand
2. Carlson Wagonlit Travel, $3,500,000
3. WorldTravel Partners-BTI, $2,750,000
4. Rosenbluth International, $2,381,000
5. Maritz Travel, $1,883,188
6. Navigant, $1,760,844
7. Sato Travel, $1,088,668
8. McCord Travel Management, $623,000
9. Omega World Travel, $570,000
10. Travel and Transport, $514,000

Source: *Business Travel News*, Business Travel Survey (annual), May 31, 1999, p. 4.

★4301★
TOP TRAVEL AGENCIES IN THE U.S., 1997
Ranked by: Gross sales, in millions of dollars. **Number listed:** 10

1. American Express, with $10,400 million
2. Carlson Travel Network, $6,300
3. Rosenbluth International, $2,810
4. BTI Americas, $2,300
5. Maritz Travel, $1,759
6. Navigant, $1,513
7. Liberty Travel, $1,320
8. Sato Travel, $1,075
9. Travel One, $916
10. World Travel Partners, $820

Source: *Travel Industry World Yearbook: The Big Picture (annual)*, 1997, p. 149.

Travel Agencies--Los Angeles County (CA)

★4302★
LARGEST TRAVEL AGENCIES IN LOS ANGELES COUNTY, 1997
Ranked by: Number of county employees. **Remarks:** Includes sales, profile, services, area specialties, marketing contact, and top local executive. **Number listed:** 25

1. American Express, with 450
2. Pleasant Travel Service Inc., 350
3. American Tours International Inc., 301
4. Uniglobe Travel (USA) LLC, 206
5. Hoffman Travel, 201
6. Travel Store, 186
7. Montrose Travel, 163
8. AAA Travel Agency, 102
9. Rosenbluth International, 91
10. Japan Travel Bureau, 87

Source: *Los Angeles Business Journal*, Book of Lists (annual), 1997, p. 95.

Trinidad and Tobago Stock Exchange

★4303★
LARGEST LISTED COMPANIES ON THE TRINIDAD AND TOBAGO STOCK EXCHANGE, 1997
Ranked by: Market capitalization, in millions of Trinidad and Tobagoan dollars (TT$). **Remarks:** Includes percent of market. **Number listed:** 5

1. Republic Bancorp Inc., with TT$3,596.9 million
2. CIBC(WI) Holdings, TT$3,403.6
3. Royal Bank, TT$2,720.1
4. ANSA McAl, TT$1,784.9
5. Bank of Nova Scotia, TT$1,589.8

Source: *SSB Guide to World Equity Markets (annual)*, 1998, p. 500.

Truck Freight Service

See: **Trucking Industry**

Truck Industry

★4304★
BEST SELLING CLASS 8 TRUCKS, 1998
Ranked by: Number sold. **Remarks:** Includes percent of market share and 1994 through 1997 sales. **Number listed:** 9

1. Freightliner, with 64,307
2. Navistar, 38,583
3. Mack, 26,801
4. Volvo, 24,064
5. Kenworth, 22,347
6. Peterbilt, 21,168
7. Sterling, 8,318
8. Western Star, 3,017
9. Other, 878

Source: *Traffic World*, March 29, 1999, p. 24.

Truck Plants

★4305★
TOP TRUCK ASSEMBLY PLANTS
Ranked by: Actual hours per vehicle. **Number listed:** 10

1. Nissan Smyrna, with $18.27 hours
2. Ford Louisville, $19.54
3. Ford Kentucky, $19.98
4. NUMMI, $20.10
5. Ford Twin Cities, $20.82
6. Ford Edison, $21.82
7. Ford St. Louis, $22.80
8. Ford Kansas City, $22.93
9. Ford Norfolk, $23.34
10. Ford Oakville, $23.50

Source: *Ward's Auto World*, August, 1998, p. 24.

Trucking Industry

★4306★
AMERICA'S MOST ADMIRED TRUCKING COMPANIES, 1998
Ranked by: Scores (1-10) derived from a survey of senior executives, outside directors and securities analysts. **Remarks:** Respondents rated companies in their own industry on 8 attributes of reputation. Also notes previous year ranking. **Number listed:** 10

1. CNF Transportation, with 6.53
2. Ryder System, 6.49
3. Yellow, 5.97
4. US Freightways, 5.84
5. J.B. Hunt Transport Services, 5.83
6. Consolidated Freightways, 5.65
7. Roadway Express, 5.53
8. Landstar System, 5.49
9. Arkansas Best, 4.95
10. Amerco, 4.78

Source: *Fortune*, America's Most Admired Corporations (annual), March 1, 1999, p. F-2.

★4307★
HEAVY SPECIALIZED TRUCK COMPANIES, 1997
Ranked by: Revenue, in thousands of dollars. **Remarks:** Includes 1996 revenue and percent change, net income, operating ratio, net profit margin, tons, and miles. **Number listed:** 2

1. Trism Specialized Carriers, with $193,509 thousand
2. Ace Transportation, $133,273

Source: *Transport Topics*, Annual Report, August 10, 1998, p. 22.

★4308★
LARGEST TRUCKING COMPANIES IN THE U.S., 1997
Ranked by: Revenue, in thousands of dollars. **Remarks:** Includes type. **Number listed:** 41

1. United Parcel Service, with $15,730,318 thousand
2. Roadway Express, $2,577,328
3. Schneider National, $2,512,000
4. Yellow Freight System, $2,509,537
5. Consolidated Freightways, $2,187,801
6. RPS Inc., $1,581,754
7. Con-Way Express Carriers, $1,359,550
8. J.B. Hunt Transport, $1,351,007
9. Ryder Integrated Logistics, $1,298,408
10. ABF Freight System, $1,136,402

Source: *Transport Topics*, Annual Report, August 10, 1998, p. 12.

★4309★
TOP CORPORATIONS IN THE TRUCKING INDUSTRY, 1998
Ranked by: Revenue, in millions of dollars. **Remarks:** Also notes profits and investment figures as well as number of employees. **Number listed:** 9

1. CNF Transportation, with $4,941 million
2. Yellow, $3,112
3. Roadway Express, $2,654
4. Consolidated Freightways, $2,238
5. C.H. Robinson Worldwide, $2,038
6. J.B. Hunt Transport Services, $1,842
7. U.S. Freightways, $1,835
8. Arkansas Best, $1,651
9. Landstar System, $1,342

Source: *Fortune*, Fortune 500 Largest U.S. Corporations (annual), April 26, 1999, p. F-71.

★4310★
TOP MOTOR VEHICLE TRUCK COMPANIES, 1997
Ranked by: Revenue, in thousands of dollars. **Remarks:** Includes 1996 revenue and percent change, net income, operating ratio, net profit margin, tons, and miles. **Number listed:** 5

1. Allied Systems, with $256,900 thousand
2. Active Transportation, $218,400
3. Leaseway Motorcar Transport, $207,565
4. Cassens Transport Co., $176,212
5. Morgan Drive Away, $146,154

Source: *Transport Topics*, Annual Report, August 10, 1998, p. 22.

★4311★
TOP THIRD PARTY LOGISTICS COMPANIES, 1998
Ranked by: Estimated net revenue, in millions of dollars. **Number listed:** 23

1. Ryder Integrated Logistics, with $1,439 million
2. Schneider National, $910
3. Penske Logistics, $600
4. Tibbett & Britten, $572

5. Fritz Companies, $558
6. Air Express International, $490
7. Excel Logistics North America, $441
8. Caliber/Federal Express, $424
9. Customized Transportation, $337
10. UPS Worldwide Logistics, $307

Source: *Transport Topics*, October 12, 1998, p. 13.

★4312★
TOP TRUCKING COMPANIES BY NET PROFIT MARGINS, 1997
Ranked by: Revenue, in percent. **Number listed:** 10

1. Pitt Ohio Express, with 12.6%
2. New Penn Motor Express, 12.4%
3. Crete Carrier Corp., 12.3%
4. Prime Inc., 11.4%
5. Southeastern Freight Lines, 9.7%
6. Contract Freighters, 9.3%
7. Stevens Transport, 9.2%
8. Estes Express Lines, 7.8%
9. New England Motor Freight, 7.1%
10. AAA Cooper Transportation, 6.5%

Source: *Transport Topics*, Annual Report, August 10, 1998, p. 24.

★4313★
TOP TRUCKING COMPANIES BY REVENUE GROWTH, 1997
Ranked by: Revenue growth, in percent. **Number listed:** 10

1. Dick Simon Trucking, with 46.6%
2. U.S. Xpress Inc., 38.8%
3. Smithway Motor Xpress, 28.1%
4. Estes Express Lines, 27.4%
5. Swift Transportation Co., 26.9%
6. Jevic Transportation, 23.3%
7. R&L Transfer, 22.6%
8. Watkins Motor Lines, 22.5%
9. Rocor International, 22.4%
9. Atlas Van Lines, 22.4%
11. M.S. Carriers, 22.2%

Source: *Transport Topics*, Annual Report, August 10, 1998, p. 24.

★4314★
TOP TRUCKING COMPANIES RANKED BY SALES, 1997
Ranked by: Revenue, in millions of dollars. **Remarks:** Includes web address, phone number, union or nonunion and public or private. **Number listed:** 10

1. United Parcel Service, with $22,500 million
2. Roadway Express Inc., $2,600
3. Yellow Freight System, $2,540
4. Schneider National, $2,500
5. Consolidated Freightways, $2,000
6. Penske Truck Leasing, $1,800
6. Ryder Integrated Logistics, $1,800
8. RPS Inc., $1,700
9. Con-Way Transportation, $1,600
10. J.B. Hunt, $1,554

Source: *Inbound Logistics*, Top 75 Motor Carriers (annual), September, 1998, p. 50+.

★4315★
TOP TRUCKING COMPANIES WITH THE BEST OPERATING RATIOS, 1997
Ranked by: Operating ratio, in percent. **Number listed:** 10

1. New Penn Motor Express, with 79.4%
2. Pitt Ohio Express, 86.4%
3. USF Bestway, 86.8%
4. Prime Inc., 86.9%
5. Estes Express Lines, 87.3%
6. Crete Carrier Corp., 87.6%
7. Contract Freighters, 88.0%
8. Con-Way Express Carriers, 88.6%
9. USA Truck, 89.0%
10. RPS Inc., 89.5%

Source: *Transport Topics*, Annual Report, August 10, 1998, p. 24.

★4316★
TOP TRUCKING FIRMS RANKED BY REVENUE, 1997
Ranked by: Revenue, in thousands of dollars. **Remarks:** Includes carrier type, 1996 revenue, percent change and operating ratio. **Number listed:** 10

1. United Parcel Service, with $15,730,318 thousand
2. Roadway Express, $2,577,328
3. Schneider National, $2,512,100
4. Yellow Freight System, $2,509,537
5. Consolidated Freightways, $2,187,801
6. Roadway Package Service, $1,581,754
7. Con-Way Transportation Services, $1,359,550
8. J.B. Hunt Transport Inc., $1,351,007
9. Ryder Integrated Logistics, $1,298,408
10. ABF Freight Systems, $1,136,402

Source: *Commercial Car Journal*, August, 1998, p. 48.

★4317★
TOP TRUCKING GROUPS IN THE U.S., 1997
Ranked by: Revenue, in thousands of dollars. **Remarks:** Includes 1996 revenue and percent change, ownership, and operating units. **Number listed:** 41

1. CNF Transportation, with $4,266,801 thousand
2. Yellow Corp., $3,348,868
3. Roadway Express, $2,670,944
4. Consolidated Freightways Corp., $2,299,075
5. UniGroup Inc., $1,749,444
6. Arkansas Best Corp., $1,643,678
7. US Freightways Corp., $1,565,249
8. J.B. Hunt Transport Services, $1,554,292
9. Landstar System, $1,312,704
10. NFC North America, $1,289,493

Source: *Transport Topics*, Annual Report, August 10, 1998, p. 1.

★4318★
TOP TRUCKLOAD CARRIERS ACCORDING TO DISTRIBUTION, 1997
Ranked by: Revenue, in thousands of dollars. **Remarks:** Includes 1996 revenue and percent change, net income, operating ratio, net profit margin, tons, and miles. **Number listed:** 4

1. Ryder Integrated Logistics, with $1,298,408 thousand
2. Customized Transportation, $296,172
3. Penske Logistics, $238,725
4. Penske Transportation Services, $175,341

Source: *Transport Topics*, Annual Report, August 10, 1998, p. 12.

★4319★
TOP TRUCKLOAD COMPANIES, 1997
Ranked by: Revenue, in thousands of dollars. **Remarks:** Includes 1996 revenue and percent change, net income, operating ratio, net profit margin, tons, and miles. **Number listed:** 41

1. Schneider National, with $2,512,000 thousand
2. J.B. Hunt Transport, $1,351,007
3. Werner Enterprises, $772,095
4. Swift Transportation Co., $713,638
5. Landstar Ranger, $456,322
6. M.S. Carriers, $415,933
7. Landstar Inway, $386,940

8. U.S. Xpress Inc., $371,030
9. Crete Carrier Corp., $298,520
10. Builders Transport, $288,145

Source: *Transport Topics*, Annual Report, August 10, 1998, p. 20.

Trucking Industry--Canada

★4320★
TOP TRUCKING GROUPS IN CANADA, 1997
Ranked by: Revenue, in thousands of Canadian dollars. **Remarks:** Includes 1996 revenue and percent of change, ownership and operating units. **Number listed:** 13

1. Trimac Transportation System, with C$446,070 thousand
2. Vitran Corp., C$358,137
3. Westminster Holdings, C$230,000
4. Mullen Transportation, C$228,522
5. Clarke Inc., C$207,298
6. TST Solutions, C$145,000
7. Cabano Kingsway, C$116,575
8. Contrans Corp., C$113,067
9. TNT North America, n/a
10. Day & Ross Transportation Group, n/a

Source: *Transport Topics*, August 10, 1998, p. 18.

Trucking Industry--Small Shipments

★4321★
TOP LESS-THAN-TRUCKLOAD (LTL) COMPANIES, 1997
Ranked by: Revenue, in thousands of dollars. **Remarks:** Includes 1996 revenue and percent of change, net income, operating ratio, net profit margin, tons, and miles. **Number listed:** 31

1. Roadway Express, with $2,577,328 thousand
2. Yellow Freight System, $2,509,537
3. Consolidated Freightways, $2,187,801
4. Con-Way Express Carriers, $1,359,550
5. ABF Freight System, $1,136,402
6. Overnite Transportation Co., $945,968
7. American Freightways, $870,319
8. USF Holland, $711,137
9. Watkins Motor Lines, $650,896
10. Viking Freight, $475,094

Source: *Transport Topics*, Annual Report, August 10, 1998, p. 19.

Underwriting of Securities

See: **Security Underwriting**

Unit Trusts

See: **Mutual Funds**

United States Occupational Safety and Health Administration

★4322★
MOST FREQUENTLY CITED OCCUPATIONAL SAFETY AND HEALTH ADMINISTRATION STANDARD SECTIONS, 1998
Ranked by: Number of alleged violations. **Number listed:** 10

1. Written Program, with 2,288
2. Unprotected Sides, 1,675
3. Guarding Methods, 1,378
4. Protective Helmets, 1,211
5. Information, Training, 1,202
6. Fall Protection, 1,104
7. Protective Systems, 1,039
8. OSHA Log, 1,008
9. Worker Instruction, 929
10. Safe Conditions, 882

Source: *Signs of the Times*, May, 1999, p. 14.

★4323★
TOP OCCUPATIONAL SAFETY AND HEALTH ADMINISTRATION SERIOUS VIOLATIONS, 1998
Ranked by: Amount of violations. **Number listed:** 10

1. Scaffolding, with 5,539 violations
2. Fall Protection, 3,862
3. HazCom, 3,274
4. lockout/Tagout, 2,537
5. Machine Guarding, 2,266
6. Power Presses, 2,230
7. Mechanical Power, 2,151
8. Electrical-Wiring, 1,902
9. Excavation, 1,399
10. Machine Guarding-Abrasive Wheels, 1,338

Source: *Safety & Health*, December, 1998, p. 49.

★4324★
TOP OCCUPATIONAL SAFETY AND HEALTH ADMINISTRATION VIOLATIONS, 1998
Ranked by: Total number of violations. **Number listed:** 10

1. Hazard Communication-General Industry, with 7,505 violations
2. Scaffolding-Construction, 6,239
3. Fall Protection-Construction, 4,369
4. Lockout/Tagout, 3,532
5. Electrical-Wiring, etc., 2,990
6. Mechanical Power Presses, 2,868
7. Machine Guarding, 2,576
8. Mechanical Power-Transmission, 2,387
9. Personal Protective Equipment, 2,101
10. Electrical Systems Design, 2,060

Source: *Safety & Health*, December, 1998, p. 49.

Universities

See: **Colleges and Universities**

Utilities, Public

See: **Public Utilities**

Vacations

★4325★
EXECUTIVES TOP AUGUST VACATION PLANS, 1998
Ranked by: Reasons cited by executive for their August vacations, in percent. **Number listed:** 5
1. Visit friends/relatives, with 34%
1. Entertainment, 34%
3. Outdoor recreation, 21%
4. Business, 8%
5. Personal/other, 3%

Source: *Sales & Marketing Management*, August, 1998, p. 14.

Vacuum Cleaners

★4326★
BEST-SELLING VACUUM CLEANERS, 1998
Ranked by: Market share, in percent. **Remarks:** Also note 1993 market share. **Number listed:** 10
1. Hoover, with 37%
2. Eureka, 22%
3. Royal, 13%
4. Matsushita, 9%
5. Kirby, 4%
6. Bissell, 5%
7. Iona, 4%
8. Electrolux, 2%
9. Rexaire, 2%
9. Others, 2%

Source: *Appliance Manufacturer*, April, 1999, p. 21.

Variable Annuities

★4327★
LARGEST VARIABLE ANNUITY SALES BY COMPANY, 1998
Ranked by: Sales by company, as of Sept. 30, 1998. **Remarks:** Also notes 1997 sales for same period, sales ratio, and 1997 rank. **Number listed:** 10
1. Hartford Life Insurance Co., with $7,577,499,000
2. TIAA-CREF, $6,085,156,459
3. Nationwide Life Insurance Co., $4,191,932,465
4. American General Corp., $4,175,696,924
5. Equitable Life Assurance Society of the U.S., $3,986,652,649
6. American Skandia Life Assurance Corp., $3,114,404,099
7. Anchor National Life Ins. Co., $2,817,788,002
8. Prudential Insurance Co., $3,585,049,399
9. Allmerica Financial, $2,480,830,000
10. Lincoln National Life Ins. Co., $2,473,795,000

Source: *National Underwriter-Life & Health Financial Services Ed.*, November 30, 1998, p. 1.

★4328★
TOP PERFORMING BALANCED VARIABLE ANNUITIES, 1998
Ranked by: Twelve-month return, in percent. **Remarks:** Also notes inception date, value as of May 31, 1998, three-year return, annual fee, fund/insurance expense, surrender charge, and telephone. **Number listed:** 10
1. MONYMaster Enterprise Managed, with 24.53%
1. MONYMaster Enterprise Managed (NY), 24.53%
3. Prudential Disc Select Group Q OCC Managed, 22.67%
4. Great American Reserve Maxiflex VA-FP Asset Alloc, 24.89%
5. Providian Life Marquee A-Units OCC Managed, 21.58%
6. Pruco Life NJ Discover Select OCC Managed, 20.87%
6. Prudential Discover Select OCC Managed, 20.87%
8. MONY ValueMaster OCC Managed, 21.07%
9. ReliaStar Select Annuity II OCC Managed, 20.97%
10. CIGNA Accru VA OCC Managed, 20.95%

Source: *Top Performing VA (annual)*, Dow Jones Investment Advisor, July, 1998, p. 78+.

★4329★
TOP PERFORMING CORPORATE BOND VARIABLE ANNUITIES, 1998
Ranked by: Twelve-month return, in percent. **Remarks:** Also notes inception date, value as of May 31, 1998, three-year return, annual fee, fund/insurance expense, surrender charge, and telephone. **Number listed:** 10
1. Great-West Life FutureFunds Maxim Corp. Bond Q, with 11.72%
2. Venture Variable Annuity Manu Inv Tr Strategic Bond, 8.26%
3. New England American Forerunner Series Strat Bond Opp, 9.14%
4. Manulife Vent Vantage Manu Inv Tr Strategic Bond, 8.10%
5. Venture Vision Manu Inv Tr Strategic Bond, 7.99%
6. AUL Variable Annuity Janus Flexible Income Q, 12.34%
6. AetnaPlus Janus Aspen Flexible IncomQ, 12.34%
8. New England Zenith Accumulator Strategic Bond Oppor, 8.76%
8. New England American Growth Series Strategic Bond Oppor, 8.76%
10. Life of Virginia Commonwealth/Janus Aspen Flex Income, 12.22%

Source: *Top Performing VA (annual)*, Dow Jones Investment Advisor, July, 1998, p. 79.

★4330★
TOP PERFORMING GOVERNMENT BOND VARIABLE ANNUITIES, 1998
Ranked by: Twelve-month return, in percent. **Remarks:** Also notes inception date, value as of May 31, 1998, three-year return, annual fee, fund/insurance expense, surrender charge, and telephone. **Number listed:** 10
1. Minnesota Mutual Megannuity Advantus NtGvBd 10 Q, with 22.85%
2. Minnesota Mutual MultiOption Select Advantus MtGvBd10, 21.51%
2. Minnesota Mutual MultiOption A Advantus MtGvBd 10, 21.51%
4. Franklin Valuemark Zero-Coupon 2010, 20.16%
5. Franklin Valuemark-IV Zero-Coupon 2010, 20.05%
6. Minnesota Mutual Megannuity Advantus NtGvBd 06 Q, 16.38%
7. First Investors Variable Annuity C Target Mat 2007, 16.84%
8. Amer Gen/VALIC Port Dir 2 Q Vanguard L/T US Treas, 16.23%
9. Minnesota Mutual Megannuity Advantus Mtg Secs Q, 9.68%

10. Minnesota Mutual MultiOption Select Advantus NtGvBd06, 15.12%

Source: *Top Performing VA (annual)*, Dow Jones Investment Advisor, July, 1998, p. 79.

★4331★

TOP PERFORMING HIGH-YIELD BOND VARIABLE ANNUITIES, 1998

Ranked by: Twelve-month return, in percent. **Remarks:** Also notes inception date, value as of May 31, 1998, three-year return, annual fee, fund/insurance expense, surrender charge, and telephone. **Number listed:** 10

1. Equitable Income Manager VA 97 Alliance High Yield, with 15.15%
2. Touchstone Advisor Variable annuity Income Opp., 6.64%
3. Equitable Accumulator Alliance High Yield, 14.92%
4. Touchstone Variable Annuity Income Opportunity, 6.06%
5. Equitable Momentum High Yield Q, 15.31%
5. Equitable Equi-Vest Ser300-400 High Yield, 15.31%
5. Equitable Equi-Vest Ser100-200 High Yield, 15.31%
8. Equitable Accumulator Select Alliance High Yield, 11.97%
9. Schwab Investment Advantage Invesco High Yield, 16.81%
9. Schwab Variable Annuity Invesco High Yield, 16.81%

Source: *Top Performing VA (annual)*, Dow Jones Investment Advisor, July, 1998, p. 80.

★4332★

TOP PERFORMING INTERNATIONAL BOND VARIABLE ANNUITIES, 1998

Ranked by: Twelve-month return, in percent. **Remarks:** Also notes inception date, value as of May 31, 1998, three-year return, annual fee, fund/insurance expense, surrender charge, and telephone. **Number listed:** 10

1. Anchor National Advisor Worldwide High Income, with 9.30%
1. Anchor National Polaris I/II Worldwide High Income, 9.30%
1. First SunAmerica Polaris Worldwide High Income, 9.30%
4. Alliance Gallery AIG Life, 4.63%
5. Alliance Capital Navigator Global Dollar Gov., 4.62%
6. Alliance Gallery AIG Life North American Gov. Income, 5.42%
7. Alliance Capital Navigator North American Gov. Income, 5.41%
8. GT Global Allocator Strategic Income, 5.87%
9. Travelers Vintage VA G.T. Global Strategic Income, 6.00%
10. Travelers Universal Annty/G.T. Global Strategic Inc, 5.91%

Source: *Top Performing VA (annual)*, Dow Jones Investment Advisor, July, 1998, p. 80+.

★4333★

TOP PERFORMING INTERNATIONAL STOCK VARIABLE ANNUITIES, 1998

Ranked by: Twelve-month return, in percent. **Remarks:** Also notes inception date, value as of May 31, 1998, three-year return, annual fee, fund/insurance expense, surrender charge, and telephone. **Number listed:** 10

1. Aetna VA Acct D MAP V Lowest Margin Janus Asp Wrld Gr, with 33.14%
1. AARP Variable Annuity Janus Aspen Worldwide Growth, 33.14%
3. Schwab Variable Annuity Janus Worldwide Growth, 33.15%
4. Commodore Enhanced Nauticus Janus Worldwide Growth, 33.01%
5. Great American Reserve Maxiflex VA-FP Janus Worldwide Growth, 32.94%
5. Privileged Assets Select Annuity Janus Worldwide Growth, 32.94%
7. Commodore Americus Janus Worldwide Growth, 32.62%
7. Commodore Nauticus VA Janus Aspen Worldwide Growth, 32.62%
9. AUL Variable Annuity Janus Worldwide Growth Q, 32.61%
9. AetnaPlus Janus Aspen Worldwide Growth Q, 32.61%

Source: *Top Performing VA (annual)*, Dow Jones Investment Advisor, July, 1998, p. 82.

★4334★

TOP PERFORMING SPECIALTY FUND VARIABLE ANNUITIES, 1998

Ranked by: Twelve-month return, in percent. **Remarks:** Also notes inception date, value as of May 31, 1998, three-year return, annual fee, fund/insurance expense, surrender charge, and telephone. **Number listed:** 10

1. MFS/Sun (US) Regatta Gold Utilities Series, with 31.44%
2. CIGNA Accru VA MFS Utilities, 30.99%
3. Allegiance Variable Annuity MFS Utilities, 31.01%
4. Ameritas Overture 3-Plust MFS Utilities, 30.90%
5. Jefferson-Pilot Alphaflex MFS Utilities, 30.88%
6. Ameritas Overture 3 MFS Utilities, 30.83%
6. Ameritas Overture 2 MFS Utilities, 30.83%
8. GT Global Allocator Telecommunications, 24.32%
9. Golden American GoldenSelect Real Estate, 14.42%
10. Amer Gen/VALIC Port Dir 2 Q AGS Science & Tech, 9.75%

Source: *Top Performing VA (annual)*, Dow Jones Investment Advisor, July, 1998, p. 82.

★4335★

TOP PERFORMING VARIABLE ANNUITIES BY AGGRESSIVE GROWTH, 1998

Ranked by: Twelve-month return, in percent. **Remarks:** Also notes inception date, value as of May 31, 1998, three-year return, annual fee, fund/insurance expense, surrender charge, and telephone. **Number listed:** 10

1. Jack White Value Advantage Plus Safeco Growth, with 56.18%
2. Safeco Life Resource B Growth Q, 54.77%
3. AUL Variable Annuity SAFECO Growth Q, 54.64%
4. Safeco Life MainSail Growth, 54.54%
4. Safeco Life Spinnaker Q Growth, 54.54%
6. Allegiance Variable Annuity JPVF Capital Growth, 36.36%
7. Safeco Life MainSail Wanger US Small Cap Advisor, 36.54%
8. Travelers Universal Annuity/Travelers Capital App, 33.74%
9. Principal VA Aggressive Growth, 32.92%
10. Kemper Passport Small Cap Growth, 30.47%

Source: *Top Performing VA (annual)*, Dow Jones Investment Advisor, July, 1998, p. 78.

★4336★

TOP PERFORMING VARIABLE ANNUITIES BY GROWTH & INCOME, 1998

Ranked by: Twelve-month return, in percent. **Remarks:** Also notes inception date, value as of May 31, 1998, three-year return, annual fee, fund/insurance expense, surrender charge, and telephone. **Number listed:** 10

1. Nationwide DCVA Nationwide Q, with 39.01%
2. MFS/Sun Compass G Mass Investors Trust Q (US), 30.24%
3. Hartford DCPlus American Century Income & Growth, 34.31%
4. MFS/Sun Compass 1 Mass Investors Trust Q (US), 30.18%
4. MFS/Sun Compass 1 Mass Investors Trust Q (NY), 30.18%
6. Diversified Investors Growth & Income Q, 34.86%
7. MFS/Sun Regatta Gold Conservative Growth Series (US), 30.58%
8. Northwestern Mutual Select VA FL Index 500 Stock, 29.97%
9. Vanguard Variable Annuity Plan Equity Index, 29.95%
10. Amer Gen/VALIC Port Dir 2 Q AGS Social Awareness, 29.05%

Source: *Top Performing VA (annual)*, Dow Jones Investment Advisor, July, 1998, p. 80.

★4337★
TOP PERFORMING VARIABLE ANNUITIES BY GROWTH, 1998
Ranked by: Twelve-month return, in percent. **Remarks:** Also notes inception date, value as of May 31, 1998, three-year return, annual fee, fund/insurance expense, surrender charge, and telephone. **Number listed:** 10

1. Nationwide DCVA Mass Investors Growth Stock Q, with 42.70%
2. MFS/Sun (US) Compass G Mass Investors Growth Stk Q, 42.37%
3. MFS/Sun (US) Compass 1 Mass Investors Growth Stk Q, 42.29%
3. MFS/Sun (NY) Compass 1 Mass Investors Growth Stk Q, 42.29%
5. Amer Skandia Adv Choice, 38.81%
6. First SunAmerica Polaris Alliance Growth, 37.28%
6. Anchor National Polaris 1/11 Alliance Growth, 37.28%
6. Anchor National Advisor Alliance Growth, 37.28%
9. Amer Skandia Axiom/AST JanCap Growth, 38.35%
10. Jack White Value Advantage Plus Alliance Premier Gr, 38.40%

Source: *Top Performing VA (annual)*, Dow Jones Investment Advisor, July, 1998, p. 79+.

★4338★
TOP VARIABLE ANNUITY CONTRACTS BY PRODUCT SALES, 1998
Ranked by: Total, in millions of dollars. **Remarks:** Also notes 1997 rank, sales, and sales ratio. **Number listed:** 25

1. TIAA and CREF Retirement and Suppl. Ret. (TIAA-CREF), with $7,863.4 million
2. The Director (Hartford), $5,713.1
3. Portfolio Director (VALIC), $5,093.2
4. Putnam Hartford Capital Manager (Hartford), $3,588.6
5. POLARIS/POLARIS II (Anchor), $3,021.2
6. Discovery Select (Pruco), $2,742.6
7. PREFERENCE PLUS Account (MetLife), $2,647.7
8. Equitable Accumulator (Equitable), $2,583.7
9. The BEST OF AMERICA America's Future (Nationwide Life), $2,426.6
10. EQUI-VEST (Equitable), $2,297.8

Source: *National Underwriter-Life & Health Financial Services Ed.*, Top 25 Contracts, February 22, 1999, p. 4.

Venture Capital

★4339★
TOP INDUSTRIES RECEIVING VENTURE CAPITAL, 1998
Ranked by: Amount invested, in billions of dollars. **Remarks:** Also notes percent of total. **Number listed:** 3

1. Software and information, with $4.55 billion
2. Communications, $3.95
3. Health care, $1.10

Source: *Entrepreneur*, May, 1999, p. 38.

Venture Capital Companies

★4340★
MOST ACTIVE VENTURE CAPITAL FIRMS IN ELECTRONICS, 1998
Ranked by: Fund amount, in millions of dollars. **Remarks:** Also notes location and contact information. **Number listed:** 30

1. Starmedia, with $80.0 million
2. Avici Systems, $52.3
3. Somera Communications, $51.8
4. Commerce One, $34.4
5. Talk City, $34.0
6. Unwired Planet, $33.0
6. U.S. Internetworking, $33.0
8. Argon Networks, $26.5
9. Nexabit Networks, $25.0
9. Pros Strategic Solutions, $25.0
9. Teralogic, $25.0

Source: *Electronic Business*, March, 1999, p. 66.

Venture Capital Companies—Los Angeles Metropolitan Area

★4341★
LARGEST VENTURE CAPITAL FIRMS IN LOS ANGELES COUNTY, 1999*
Ranked by: Capital under management, in millions of dollars. **Remarks:** Also notes contact information, investments, preferred industries, and top executive. **Number listed:** 15

1. William E. Simon & Sons LLC, with $1,000 million
2. Brentwood Venture Capital, $720.5
3. Domain Associates, $500
4. Enterprise Partners, $425
5. Levine Leichtman Capital Partners LP, $417
6. Pacific Mezzanine Investors, $350
7. Forrest Binkley & Brown, $305
8. Mellon Ventures, Inc., $270
9. Trident Capital Inc., $260
10. Media Technology Ventures, $200

Source: *Los Angeles Business Journal*, March 8, 1999, p. 32.

Venture Capital Companies--New Jersey

★4342★
LEADING VENTURE CAPITAL FIRMS IN NEW JERSEY, 1999*
Ranked by: Assets under management. **Remarks:** Also notes contact information, year founded, and managers. **Number listed:** 23
1. Nassau Capital, with $1,500,000,000
2. William E. Simon & Sons, $1,000,000,000
3. Healthcare Ventures, $475,000,000
4. AT&T Ventures, $348,000,000
5. BCI Advisors, $250,000,000
6. Domain Associates, $241,000,000
7. Edison Venture Fund, $200,000,000
7. Geocapital Partners, $200,000,000
7. Sycamore Ventures/CitiGrowth Funds, $200,000,000
7. The Telmarc Group, $200,000,000

Source: *Book of Lists*, New Jersey Business Journal, 1999, p. 44.

Venture Capital Funds

See: **Venture Capital Companies**

Veterinary Drug Industry, International

★4343★
LARGEST ANIMAL HEALTH MARKETS, 1998
Ranked by: Percent of market. **Remarks:** Also notes 1998 total sales figure. **Number listed:** 6
1. North America, with 32%
2. Western Europe, 29%
3. Eastern Asia, 17%
4. Latin America, 12%
5. Eastern Europe, 7%
6. Rest of World, 3%

Source: *International Veterinary Drug Industry*, May 31, 1999, p. 12.

★4344★
LARGEST VETERINARY HEALTH PRODUCTS FIRMS WORLDWIDE, 1998
Ranked by: Sales, in millions of dollars. **Number listed:** 15
1. Merial, with $1,495 million
2. Hoffman-La Roche, $1,379
3. Pfizer, $1,314
4. Bayer, $984
5. American Home Products, $799
6. BASF, $795
7. Rhone Poulenc Animal Nutrition, $668
8. Schering-Plough, $647
9. Novartis, $321
10. Elanco Animal Health, $614

Source: *C&EN*, May 31, 1999, p. 12.

Video Cassette Recorder Industry

See: **Video Tape Recorder Industry**

Video Games

★4345★
BEST-SELLING VIDEO GAMES, 1998
Ranked by: Unit sales. **Remarks:** Specific figures not given. Also notes platform, publisher, and retail price of game. **Number listed:** 20
1. Goldeneye 007
2. Legend of Zelda: The Ocarina of Time
3. Gran Turismo Racing
4. Banjo-Kazooie
5. Super Mario 64
6. Resident Evil 2
7. WCE/NWO Revenge
8. WWF Warzone
9. Crash Bandicoot 2
10. Madden 99

Source: *SN*, February 8, 1999, p. 10A.

Video Stores--Chain and Franchise Operations

★4346★
VIDEO STORE CHAINS WITH THE MOST RENTAL SELLTHROUGH REVENUE, 1998
Ranked by: Rental sellthrough revenue, in millions of dollars. **Remarks:** Also notes number of stores, percent of revenue from new vs. used sales, sales inventory per store, and data for previous year. **Number listed:** 100
1. Blockbuster Entertainment, with $2,816.7 million
2. Hollywood Entertainment, $662.9
3. Suncoast Motion Picture Co., $357.27
4. Video Update, $259.8
5. Movie Gallery, $240.56
6. West Coast Entertainment, $107.88
7. Family Video, $70.55
8. Video City, $49.14
9. Tower Records/Video, $43.23
10. Easy Video, $18.59

Source: *Video Store 100 (annual)*, Video Store, March 14, 1999, p. 15+.

Video Tape Recorder Industry

★4347★
BEST-SELLING VIDEOCASSETTE RECORDERS, 1998
Ranked by: Market share, in percent. **Remarks:** Also notes 1993 market share. **Number listed:** 15
1. Thomson, with 18%
2. Matsushita, 12%
2. NAP, 12%
4. Emerson, 7%
5. JVC, 6%

5. LG Electronics (Zenith), 6%
5. Sony, 6%
8. Sanyo Fisher, 5%
8. Sharp, 5%
10. Hitachi, 3%
10. Mitsubishi, 3%
10. Samsung, 3%
10. Toshiba, 3%

Source: *Appliance Manufacturer*, April, 1999, p. 22.

★4348★
TOP VIDEOCASSETTE RECORDER RETAILERS BY BRAND SHARE, 1998
Ranked by: VCR sales, in percent. **Number listed:** 20

1. Wal-Mart, with 16.90%
2. Circuit City, 11.90%
3. Best Buy, 9.70%
3. Appliance/TV Store, 9.70%
5. Sears, 9.30%
6. Discount Department, 6.10%
7. K-Mart, 5.50%
8. Montgomery Ward, 3.60%
9. Warehouse Clubs, 3.30%
10. Target, 3.00%

Source: *Dealerscope Consumer Electronics Marketplace*, August, 1998, p. 21.

Video Tapes--Renting

★4349★
TOP MOVIE VIDEOS BY RENTAL REVENUE, 1998
Ranked by: Revenue. **Remarks:** Also notes weeks in release. **Number listed:** 10

1. *As Good as It Gets*, with $64.2 million
2. *Air Force One*, $61.3
3. *Conspiracy Theory*, $56.7
4. *U.S. Marshals*, $52.0
5. *Good Will Hunting*, $51.7
6. *The Devil's Advocate*, $51.0
7. *Kiss the Girls*, $49.2
8. *The Wedding Singer*, $48.1
9. *I Know What You Did Last Summer*, $48.0
10. *The Game*, $47.9

Source: *Research Alert*, February 19, 1999, p. 8.

★4350★
TOP VIDEO MOVIE GENRES BY RENTAL TURN, 1992-1997
Ranked by: Market share, in percent. **Number listed:** 12

1. Comedy, with 23.4%
2. Thriller, 21.4%
3. Action, 19.2%
4. Drama, 17.3%
5. Adventure, 3.6%
5. Family, 3.6%
7. Erotic Thriller, 2.1%
8. Romance, 2%
9. Suspense, 1.9%
9. Sci-Fi, 1.9%

Source: *Video Store Magazine*, July 12, 1998, p. 17.

Vienna Stock Exchange

★4351★
LARGEST LISTED COMPANIES ON THE VIENNA STOCK EXCHANGE, 1997
Ranked by: Market value, in millions of Austrian schillings. **Number listed:** 20

1. OMV, with AS47,250 million
2. VA Technologies, AS28,770
3. Erste Bank St, AS27,925
4. CA St, AS23,247
5. EA-Generali, AS23,233
6. Weinerberger, AS21,053
7. Verbund Kat A, AS20,236
8. Bank Austria, AS20,210
9. EVN, AS18,924
10. VA Stahl, AS16,071

Source: *SSB Guide to World Equity Markets (annual)*, Euromoney Publications, 1998, p. 657.

★4352★
MOST ACTIVELY TRADED SHARES ON THE VIENNA STOCK EXCHANGE, 1997
Ranked by: Turnover, in millions of Austrian schillings (Sch). **Number listed:** 20

1. OMV, with AS40,311 million
2. VA Technologie, AS34,908
3. EVN, AS26,573
4. Boehler-Uddeholm, AS17,740
5. VA Stahl, AS16,918
6. Verbund Kat. A, AS16,472
7. CA VA, AS15,930
8. Wienerberger, AS15,642
9. Flughafen Wien, AS13,500
10. CA St, AS10,414

Source: *SSB Guide to World Equity Markets (annual)*, Euromoney Publications, 1998, p. 66.

Vodka

★4353★
LEADING BRANDS OF DOMESTIC VODKA, 1998
Ranked by: Sales, in thousands of 9-liter cases. **Remarks:** Also notes supplier name, 1997 sales, and percent change. **Number listed:** 10

1. Smirnoff, with 5,970 thousand cases
2. Popov, 2,330
3. Gordon's, 2,040
4. McCormick, 1,418
5. Barton, 1,290
6. Total Kamchatka, 1,047
7. Wolfschmidt, 1,000
8. Skol, 960
9. Gilbey's, 732
10. Skyy, 697

Source: *Beverage Dynamics*, May, 1999, p. 18.

★4354★
LEADING BRANDS OF VODKA, 1997
Ranked by: Sales, in thousands of 9-liter cases. **Remarks:** Also notes sales from 1992-1996, and percent change. **Number listed:** 27

1. Smirnoff, with 5,787 9-liter cases
2. Popov, 2,577
3. Gordon's Vodka, 1,955

4. Barton Vodka, 1,279
5. McCormick Vodka, 1,268
6. Total Kamchatka, 1,054
7. Wolfschmidt, 1,032
8. Skol Vodka, 924
9. Gilbey's Vodka, 777
10. Aristocrat Vodka, 605

Source: *Adams Liquor Handbook*, (annual), 1998, p. 132.

★4355★
STATES WITH THE HIGHEST CONSUMPTION OF VODKA, 1997
Ranked by: Consumption, in 9-liter cases. **Remarks:** Also notes previous year's consumption and percent change. **Number listed:** 51

1. California, with 3,806,680 9-liter cases
2. Florida, 2,876,320
3. New York, 2,168,680
4. Illinois, 1,559,900
5. Texas, 1,432,550
6. New Jersey, 1,355,240
7. Michigan, 1,276,380
8. Pennsylvania, 1,216,660
9. Georgia, 995,690
10. Massachusetts, 912,620

Source: *Adams Liquor Handbook*, (annual), 1998, p. 129.

★4356★
STATES WITH THE HIGHEST VODKA CONSUMPTION PER CAPITA, 1997
Ranked by: Consumption, in 9-liter cases. **Remarks:** Also notes previous year's consumption. **Number listed:** 51

1. District of Columbia, with 545.2 cases
2. New Hampshire, 525.3
3. Nevada, 452.7
4. Delaware, 313.9
5. Connecticut, 298.1
6. Florida, 270.9
7. Colorado, 240.3
8. South Carolina, 237.5
9. Wisconsin, 236.9
10. New Jersey, 236.6

Source: *Adams Liquor Handbook*, (annual), 1998, p. 130.

★4357★
TOP METROPOLITAN AREAS FOR VODKA SALES, 1997
Ranked by: Sales, in thousands of 9-liter cases. **Remarks:** Also notes previous year's sakes. **Number listed:** 50

1. Chicago, IL, with 1,114.4 thousand cases
2. Los Angeles-Long Beach, CA, 1,038.3
3. New York, NY, 964.3
4. Washington, DC, 760.8
5. Detroit, MI, 639.7
6. Boston-Lawrence-Lowell-Brockton, MA, 625.1
7. Philadelphia, PA, 623.3
8. Atlanta, GA, 565.4
9. Phoenix, AZ, 536.3
10. Minneapolis-St. Paul, MN, 494.4

Source: *Adams Liquor Handbook*, (annual), 1998, p. 134.

★4358★
TOP SUPPLIERS OF VODKA, 1997
Ranked by: Market share, in percent. **Number listed:** 6

1. Others, with 36.7%
2. IDV North America, 27.5%
3. Barton Inc., 11.3%
4. Seagram Americas, 10.5%
5. Jim Beam Brands, 8.1%
6. United Distillers, 5.9%

Source: *Adams Liquor Handbook*, (annual), 1998, p. 133.

Vodka--Advertising

★4359★
MOST ADVERTISED VODKA BRANDS, 1997
Ranked by: Total advertising expenditures, in thousands of dollars. **Remarks:** Also notes 1996 figures. **Number listed:** 22

1. Absolut, with $27,731.3 thousand
2. Smirnoff, $13,309.6
3. Stolichnaya, $7,845.3
4. Skyy, $3,816.8
5. Gordon's, $2,471.8
6. Finlandia, $2,414.4
7. Tanqueray Sterling, $2,306.9
8. Taaka, $237.0
9. Georgi, $156.7
10. Fleischmann's, $137.5

Source: *Adams Liquor Handbook*, 1998, p. 136.

Vodka--Export-Import Trade

★4360★
COUNTRIES IMPORTING THE MOST VODKA, 1997
Ranked by: Proof gallons, in thousands. **Remarks:** Also notes 1995 and 1996 figures. **Number listed:** 10

1. Sweden, with 6,382.6 thousand gallons
2. CIS a, 2,197.5
3. Netherlands, 741.2
4. Finland, 723.7
5. Poland, 378.6
6. United Kingdom, 311.3
7. Denmark, 179.5
8. France, 55.5
9. Austria, 40.0
10. Canada, 38.7

Source: *Adams Liquor Handbook*, Adams Media, 1998, p. 223.

★4361★
LARGEST IMPORTERS OF U.S. VODKA, 1997
Ranked by: Proof gallons, in thousands. **Remarks:** Also notes 1995 and 1996 figures. **Number listed:** 5

1. Taiwan, with 474.3 thousand gallons
2. CIS, 355.3
3. Germany, 156.8
4. Netherlands, 150.8
5. Japan, 138.7

Source: *Adams Liquor Handbook*, Adams Media, 1998, p. 219.

★4362★
LEADING BRANDS OF IMPORTED VODKA, 1998
Ranked by: Imported vodka, in thousands of 9-liter cases. **Remarks:** Also notes 1997 figures and percent change. **Number listed:** 5

1. Absolut, with 3,650 thousand cases
2. Stolichnaya, 1,230
3. Ketel One, 450
4. Finlandia, 220
5. Tanqueray Sterling, 180

Source: *Beverage Dynamics*, May, 1999, p. 20.

Voice Mail Systems

★4363★
LEADING VOICE MAIL SYSTEMS
Ranked by: End-user revenue, in millions of dollars. **Remarks:** Also notes market share. **Number listed:** 10
1. Octel Communications, with $471.5 million
2. Lucent Technologies, $401.9
3. Nortel, $276.7
4. Active Voice, $135.0
5. Comverse Technology, $127.7
6. Centigram Communications, $115.3
7. Siemens, $88.8
8. Toshiba, $55.8
9. Applied Voice Technology, $55.7
10. others, $606.4

Source: *Electronic News*, September 14, 1998, p. 10.

Wages and Salaries

★4364★
TOP HIGHEST-WAGE CITIES/METROS, 1998*
Ranked by: Average wage, in dollars. **Number listed:** 10
1. New York, NY, with $45,028
2. San Jose, CA, $44,819
3. San Francisco, CA, $40,016
4. Middlesex-Somerset-Hunterdon, NJ, $39,631
5. New Haven-Bridgeport-Stamford-Danbury-Waterbury, CT, $39,488
6. Newark, NJ, $38,886
7. Trenton, NJ, $37,598
8. Jersey City, NJ, $36,833
9. Washington, DC-MD-VA-WV, $36,383
10. Kokomo, IN, $34,779

Source: *Site Selection*, August/September, 1998, p. 620.

★4365★
TOP LOWEST-WAGE CITIES/METROS, 1998*
Ranked by: Average wage, in dollars. **Number listed:** 10
1. Jacksonville, NC, with $17,534
2. Yuma, AZ, $18,213
3. Myrtle Beach, SC, $18,551
4. McAllen-Edinburgh-Mission, TX, $18,928
5. Brownsville-Harlingen-San Benito, TX, $19,056
6. Visalia-Tulare-Portersville, CA, $19,768
7. Yakima, WA, $19,780
8. Laredo, TX, $20,388
9. Grand Forks, ND-MN, $20,476
10. Enid, OK, $20,629

Source: *Site Selection*, August/September, 1998, p. 620.

Warehouse Clubs

★4366★
BEST-SELLING WASHERS, 1998
Ranked by: Market share, in percent. **Remarks:** Also notes 1993 market share. **Number listed:** 5
1. Whirlpool, with 51%
2. Maytag, 23%
3. GEA, 15%
4. Electrolux, 8%
5. Goodman, 3%

Source: *Appliance Manufacturer*, April, 1999, p. 19.

★4367★
TOP WHOLESALE CLUB OPERATORS BY NUMBER OF OUTLETS, 1998
Ranked by: Number of outlets. **Number listed:** 3
1. Sam's Club, with 451 stores
2. Costco, 301
3. BJ's Wholesale Club, 96

Source: *Mass Market Retailers*, Hybrid Formats (annual), May 17, 1999, p. 22.

★4368★
TOP WHOLESALE WAREHOUSE CLUBS BY SALES, 1997
Ranked by: Sales, in millions of dollars. **Remarks:** Also notes 1996 sales, percent changes, number of stores and average store size. **Number listed:** 5
1. Costco, with $21,484 million
2. Sam's Club, $20,668
3. BJ's Wholesale Club, $3,226
4. Smart & Final, $1,453
5. Megafoods Warehouse, $193

Source: *Discount Store News*, Discount Industry Annual Report (annual), July 13, 1998, p. 80.

Warehouses

★4369★
TOP WAREHOUSE NETWORKS, 1999
Ranked by: Shortest average distance to the U.S. population, in miles. **Remarks:** Includes number of warehouses in the network. **Number listed:** 10
1. Terre Haute, IN, with 859 miles
2. Chillicothe, OH; Fresno, CA, 490
3. Allentown, PA; Paducah, KY; Fresno, CA, 378
4. Caldwell, NJ; Cincinnati, OH; Dallas, TX, 322
5. Summit, NJ; Macon, GA; Gary, IN; Dallas, TX; Stockton, CA, 268
6. Summit, NJ; Macon, GA; Gary, IN; Dallas, TX; Alhambra, CA; Oakland, CA, 241
7. Summit, NJ; Macon, GA; Gary, IN; Dallas, TX; Alhambra, CA; Berkeley, CA; Tacoma, WA, 222
8. Summit, NJ; Asheville, NC; Lakeland, FL; Chicago, IL; Dallas, TX; Alhambra, CA; Berkeley, CA; Tacoma, WA, 204
9. Summit, NJ; Gainesville, GA; Lakeland, FL; Chicago, IL; Dallas, TX; Denver, CO; Long Beach, CA; Berkeley, CA; Tacoma, WA, 189
10. Newark, NJ; Gainesville, GA; Lakeland, FL; Akron, OH; Chicago; Dallas; Denver; Long Beach, CA; Berkeley, CA; Tacoma, WA, 174

Source: *Ioma's Report on Managing Logistics*, April, 1999, p. 10.

Warsaw Stock Exchange

★4370★
LARGEST LISTED COMPANIES ON THE WARSAW STOCK EXCHANGE, 1997
Ranked by: Market value, in millions of U.S. dollars. **Remarks:** Also notes business sector. **Number listed:** 10

1. Handlowy, with $832.4 million
2. KGHM, $739.9
3. Elektrim, $649.1
4. BPH, $539.6
5. BSK, $513.9
6. PBK, $454.8
7. BIG-BG, $416.9
8. BRE, $394.7
9. WBK, $346.6
10. Debica, $337.8

Source: *SSB Guide to World Equity Markets (annual)*, Euromoney Publications, 1998, p. 405.

★4371★
MOST ACTIVELY TRADED SHARES ON THE WARSAW STOCK EXCHANGE, 1997
Ranked by: Total turnover, in millions of U.S. dollars. **Remarks:** Also notes percent of total. **Number listed:** 10

1. Elektrim, with $698.8 million
2. Handlowy, $570.8
3. Universal, $545.6
4. KGHM, $541.5
5. Mostostal-Export, $488.4
6. BRE, $450.5
7. BSK, $408.1
8. Optimus, $369.9
9. Budimex, $365.3
10. Okocim, $294.2

Source: *SSB Guide to World Equity Markets (annual)*, Euromoney Publications, 1998, p. 405.

Waste Management Industry

★4372★
TOP CORPORATIONS IN THE WASTE MANAGEMENT INDUSTRY, 1998
Ranked by: Revenue, in millions of dollars. **Remarks:** Also notes profits and investment figures as well as number of employees. **Number listed:** 4

1. Waste Management, with $12,703 million
2. Browning-Ferris Industries, $4,746
3. Allied Waste Industries, $1,576
4. Safety-Kleen, $1,185

Source: *Fortune*, Fortune 500 Largest U.S. Corporations (annual), April 26, 1999, p. F-72.

Water Heaters

★4373★
BEST-SELLING ELECTRIC WATER HEATERS, 1998
Ranked by: Market share, in percent. **Number listed:** 5

1. Rheem, with 31%
2. State, 23%
3. American, 20%
4. A.O. Smith, 15%
5. Bradford-White, 11%

Source: *Appliance Manufacturer*, April, 1999, p. 20.

Water Parks

★4374★
TOP WATERPARKS, 1998
Ranked by: Attendance. **Remarks:** Also notes percent change from 1997 and comments. **Number listed:** 15

1. Wet 'N Wild, FL, with 1,300,000
2. Blizzard Beach at Walt Disney World, FL, 1,280,000
3. Typhoon Lagoon at Walt Disney World, FL, 1,100,000
4. Schlitterbahn, TX, 877,000
5. Raging Waters, CA, 760,320
6. Water Country USA, VA, 650,000
7. Six Flags Hurricane Harbor at Six Flags Over Texas, 600,000
8. Adventure Island, FL, 550,000
9. Noah's Ark, WI, 500,000
10. White Water, GA, 450,000
10. Wet 'N Wild, NV, 450,000

Source: *Amusement Business*, December 28, 1998, p. 78.

Wealth

See also: **Billionaires**

★4375★
TOP BILLIONAIRES IN AMERICA, 1998
Ranked by: Net worth, in billions of dollars. **Number listed:** 25

1. Bill Gates, with $58 billion
2. Warren Buffett, $29
3. Paul Allen, $22
4. Michael Dell, $13
5. Steven Ballmer, $12
6. Helen Robson Walton, Jim C. Walton, John T. Walton, Alice Louise Walton, S. Robson Walton, $55
7. John Kluge, $9.8
8. Barbara Cox Anthony, $7.1
9. Anne Cox Chambers, $7.1
10. Gordon Moore, $7

Source: *Forbes*, 400 Richest People in America (annual), October 12, 1998, p. 166+.

★4376★
WEALTHIEST COMMUNITIES IN THE U.S., 1998
Ranked by: Median home price. **Remarks:** Includes population. **Number listed:** 47

1. Jupiter Island, FL
2. Aspen, CO
3. Atherton, CA
4. Hillsborough, CA
5. Belvedere, CA
6. Mountain Village, CO
7. Rolling Hills, CA
8. Snowmass Village, CO
9. Los Altos Hills, CA
10. Rancho Santa Fe, CA

Source: *Worth*, June, 1999, p. 115.

Wealth--Los Angeles County (CA)

★4377★
WEALTHIEST PEOPLE IN LOS ANGELES COUNTY, CA, 1998
Ranked by: Net worth, in billions of dollars. **Remarks:** Includes age, source of wealth and residence. **Number listed:** 50

1. Garry Winnick, with $6.2 billion
2. Marvin Davis, $4.7
3. Eli Broad, $4.3
4. David Geffen, $2.3
5. A. Jerrold Perenchio, $1.9
6. Ronald Burkle, $1.8
7. Franklin Otis Booth Jr., $1.6
7. Charles Munger, $1.6
7. Steven Ferencz Udvar-Hazy, $1.6
10. Steven Spielberg, $1.5

Source: *Los Angeles Business Journal*, May 24, 1999, p. 291.

Websites

★4378★
BEST BUSINESS-TO-BUSINESS MARKETING WEB SITES, 1998
Ranked by: Composite score based on company web site staff size, age of site, number of site redesigns, how sites are advertised and functions of sites. **Remarks:** Specific figures not provided. **Number listed:** 50

1. Marshall Industries
2. Cisco Systems
3. Bay Networks
4. Dell Computer Corp.
5. Compaq Computer Corp.
6. Federal Express Corp.
7. IBM Corp.
8. W.W. Grainger
9. 3Com Corp.
10. First Union Corp.

Source: *NetMarketing 200 (annual)*, Business Marketing, August, 1998, p. 32.

★4379★
ELEMENTS RANKED "VERY IMPORTANT" BY VISITORS TO MOVIE WEB SITES, 1999*
Ranked by: Important elements, by percent. **Number listed:** 5

1. Show times, with 59%
2. Plot, 55%
3. Video & sound clips, 32%
3. Reviews, 32%
5. Still photos, 26%

Source: *Brandweek*, February 8, 1999, p. 46.

★4380★
MOST POPULAR NON-ENGLISH LANGUAGES ON THE INTERNET, 1998*
Ranked by: Percent. **Number listed:** 7

1. Spanish, with 24%
2. Japanese, 22%
3. German, 13%
4. French, 10%
5. Chinese, 6%
6. Dutch, 4%
6. Italian, 4%

Source: *Bank Marketing*, November, 1998, p. 52.

★4381★
TOP AIRLINE WEB SITE BY NUMBER OF VISITORS, 1999*
Ranked by: Number of unique visitors, in thousands. **Number listed:** 10

1. Southwest Airlines, with 1,903 thousand
2. American Airlines, 1,635
3. Delta Air Lines, 1,299
4. United Airlines, 1,130
5. Northwest Airlines, 1,100
6. Continental Airlines, 967
7. US Airways, 871
8. Trans World Airlines, 568
9. America West Airlines, 384
10. AirTran Airways, 222

Source: *MediaWeek*, May 17, 1999, p. 60.

★4382★
TOP FINANCIAL MANAGEMENT WEB SITES, 1999*
Ranked by: Market share, in percent. **Number listed:** 8

1. America Online, with 32.5%
2. Intuit, 13.5%
3. Yahoo, 10.8%
4. Charles Schwab, 6.1%
5. Fidelity, 3.5%
6. Microsoft, 2.9%
7. Nasdaq, 2.6%
8. Other, 28.5%

Source: *American Banker*, April 28, 1999, p. 16.

★4383★
TOP WEB SITE DESIGN COMPANIES IN METROPOLITAN PHILADELPHIA, 1998
Ranked by: Number of web designers. **Remarks:** Also notes contact information, number of employees, fees, clients, and local executive. **Number listed:** 24

1. Brockwood Media Arts Inc., with 14 web designers
2. Kingswood Interactive, 12
3. CompuWeb Inc., 10
3. Skyhigh Information Technologies, 10
5. Interactive Graphics Inc., 8
5. Media Resource, 8
5. Mindbridge Inc., 8
5. Peec.com, 8
9. Clearlogic Inc., 7
9. I-Site, 7
9. Lorel Interactive, 7
9. World Wide Web Communications, 7

Source: *Philadelphia Business Journal*, April 2, 1999, p. 19.

Whiskey Industry

See: **Liquor Industry**

Wholesale Trade

★4384★
MOST ADMIRED WHOLESALERS, 1998
Ranked by: Score. **Remarks:** Also notes 1997 rank. **Number listed:** 10

1. Cardinal Health, with 7.74
2. Ingram Micro, 7.08
3. McKesson Corp., 7.02

4. Sysco, 6.92
5. Supervalu, 6.46
6. Arrow Electronics, 6.19
7. Bergen Brunswig, 6.08
8. AmeriSource Health, 5.63
9. Bindley Western, 5.59
10. Fleming, 5.07

Source: *Fortune*, America's Most Admired Corporations (annual), March 1, 1999, p. F3.

★4385★
TOP CORPORATIONS IN THE WHOLESALE TRADE INDUSTRY, 1998
Ranked by: Revenue, in millions of dollars. **Remarks:** Also notes profits and investment figures as well as number of employees. **Number listed:** 58

1. Ingram Micro, with $22,034 million
2. McKesson HBOC, $20,857
3. Supervalu, $17,201
4. Cardinal Health, $15,918
5. Sysco, $15,328
6. Fleming, $15,069
7. Bergen Brunswig, $13,720
8. Tech Data, $11,529
9. Amerisource Health, $8,575
10. CHS Electronics, $8,546

Source: *Fortune*, Fortune 500 Largest U.S. Corporations (annual), April 26, 1999, p. F-72+.

★4386★
TOP WHOLESALERS BY REVENUE, 1998
Ranked by: Revenue, in millions of dollars. **Number listed:** 10

1. Precision Trading Corp., with $155.00 million
2. Government Micro Resources Inc., $112.00
3. Northwestern Meat Inc., $111.20
4. Eagle Brands Inc., $91.79
5. Ramos Oil Co. Inc., $85.00
6. Refricenter of Miami Inc., $78.46
7. Pharmed Group Corp., $72.50
8. Suram Trading Corp., $64.00
9. TSN Inc., $60.90
10. Mendez Dairy/Tropical Cheese Co. Inc., $60.42

Source: *Hispanic Business*, Hispanic Business 500, June, 1999, p. 106.

Wholesale Trade--Europe

★4387★
TOP EUROPEAN WHOLESALE TRADE-DURABLE GOODS COMPANIES, 1999*
Ranked by: Financial size, in millions of ECUs. **Number listed:** 10

1. J. Sainsbury PLC, with ECUs21.395 million
2. Tesco PLC, ECUs20.491
3. Tesco Stores Ltd., ECUs19.142
4. Preussag AG, ECUs13.519
5. Franz Haniel & Cie. GMBH, ECUs12.789
6. Karstadt AG, ECUs12.195
7. Marks & Spencer PLC, ECUs12.163
8. BTR PLC, ECUs11.938
9. Otto-Versand, ECUs10.673
10. Carrefour France, ECUs10.649

Source: *Duns Europa*, (annual), Dun & Bradstreet, 1999, vol. 4, p. 265+.

★4388★
TOP EUROPEAN WHOLESALE TRADE-NON-DURABLE GOODS COMPANIES, 1999*
Ranked by: Financial size, in millions of ECUs. **Number listed:** 10

1. Gehe AG, with ECUs10.865 million
2. Aral AG, ECUs10.090
3. Stinnes Vermoegensvervaltungs-AG, ECUs9.288
4. Edeka Zentrale AG, ECUs8.218
5. Repsol Comercial de Productos Petroliferos SA, ECUs8.164
6. Kloeckner & Co. AG, ECUs7.796
7. Booker PLC, ECUs7.768
8. Spar Handels-AG, ECUs6.629
9. Raab Karcher AG, ECUs5.321
10. Stinnes AG, ECUs4.636

Source: *Duns Europa (annual)*, Dun & Bradstreet, 1999, vol. 4, p. 278+.

Wholesale Trade, International

★4389★
WORLD'S LARGEST WHOLESALE TRADE CORPORATIONS BY REVENUE, 1997
Ranked by: Revenue, in millions of dollars. **Number listed:** 9

1. McKesson Corp. (U.S.), with $20,857 million
2. Supervalu (U.S.), $17,201
3. Franz Haniel (Germany), $16,907
4. Ingram Micro (U.S.), $16,582
5. Fleming (U.S.), $15,373
6. Sysco (U.S.), $14,455
7. Bergen Brunswig (U.S.), $11,660
8. Cardinal Health (U.S.), $10,968
9. Edeka Zentrale (Germany), $9,887

Source: *Fortune*, The Global 500: World's Biggest Corporations (annual), August 3, 1998, p. F-26.

Wine Coolers

★4390★
LEADING BRANDS OF WINE COOLERS, 1997
Ranked by: Sales, in thousands of 9-liter cases. **Remarks:** Also notes sales for 1993-1996. **Number listed:** 10

1. Bartles & Jaymes, with 13,000 thousand cases
2. Seagram's Coolers, 12,000
3. Zima, 4,500
4. Bacardi Breezer, 3,000
5. Jack Daniel's Country Cocktails, 915
6. Tropical Freezes, 700
7. Purple Everclear Passion, 145
8. Jim Beam Classic Cocktails, 135
9. Caribbean Classic, 95
10. Sun Country, 50

Source: *Adams Wine Handbook*, (annual), Adams Media, Inc., 1998, p. 57.

★4391★
STATES WITH THE HIGHEST CONSUMPTION OF WINE COOLERS, 1997
Ranked by: Consumption, in 9-liter cases. **Remarks:** Also notes previous year's consumption and percent change, 1997 share, and cumulative share. **Number listed:** 51

1. California, with 773,500 cases
2. Texas, 512,300
3. Illinois, 380,500
4. Florida, 438,300
5. New York, 287,600
6. Georgia, 215,700
7. North Carolina, 204,300
8. Arizona, 201,000
9. Colorado, 166,300
10. Virginia, 165,100

Source: *Adams Wine Handbook*, (annual), Adams Media, Inc., 1998, p. 55.

★4392★
TOP METROPOLITAN AREAS FOR WINE COOLERS, 1997
Ranked by: Sales, in thousands of 9-liter cases. **Remarks:** Also notes market share. **Number listed:** 50

1. Chicago, with 387.6 thousand cases
2. Los Angeles-Long Beach, 232.2
3. Phoenix, 142.3
4. New York, 131.5
5. Houston, 125.5
6. Atlanta, 121.6
7. Minneapolis-St. Paul, 113.5
8. Washington, DC, 106.4
9. Dallas, 105.8
10. Denver, 96.5

Source: *Adams Wine Handbook*, (annual), Adams Media, Inc., 1998, p. 51.

★4393★
TOP STATES FOR WINE COOLER CONSUMPTION BY CDI (CATEGORY DEVELOPMENT INDEX), 1997
Ranked by: CDI number. **Number listed:** 51

1. Arizona, with 215
2. Colorado, 210
3. Minnesota, 174
4. Hawaii, 161
5. Illinois, 158
6. Vermont, 155
7. Maine, 154
7. Delaware, 154
9. New Mexico, 144
10. Georgia, 142

Source: *Adams Wine Handbook*, (annual), Adams Media, Inc., 1998, p. 54.

Wine Coolers--Advertising

★4394★
WINE COOLER BRANDS WITH THE HIGHEST SPOT TV ADVERTISING EXPENDITURES, 1997
Ranked by: Spot TV advertising expenditures, in thousands of dollars. **Number listed:** 2

1. Seagram's Coolers, with $558.9 thousand
2. Tropical Freezes, $321.4

Source: *Adams Wine Handbook*, (annual), Adams Media, Inc., 1998, p. 60.

★4395★
WINE COOLER BRANDS WITH THE HIGHEST TOTAL ADVERTISING EXPENDITURES, 1997
Ranked by: Total Advertising expenditures, in thousands of dollars. **Remarks:** Also notes 1996 figures. **Number listed:** 2

1. Seagram's Coolers, with $561.2 thousand
2. Tropical Freezes, $335.3

Source: *Adams Wine Handbook*, (annual), Adams Media, Inc., 1998, p. 60.

Wine Industry

★4396★
LARGEST WINERIES IN THE U.S., 1998*
Ranked by: Number of gallons produced, in thousands. **Remarks:** Also notes number of plants. **Number listed:** 75

1. E. & J. Gallo Winery, with 341,000 thousand gallons
2. Canandaigua Wine Co., 261,300
3. The Wine Group, 72,000
4. Vie-Del Company, 59,200
5. JFJ Bronco, 57,400
6. Golden State Vintners & Golden State Vintners Napa, 52,800
7. F. Korbel & Bros., 45,394
8. Delicato Vineyards, 40,412
9. Robert Mondavi, 27,000
10. Sutter Home Winery, 26,300

Source: *Wines & Vines Statistical Issue (annual)*, Wines & Vines, July, 1998, p. 46.

★4397★
METROPOLITAN AREAS WITH THE MOST VERMOUTH SALES, 1997
Ranked by: Sales, in thousands of 9-liter cases. **Remarks:** Also notes market share. **Number listed:** 51

1. Chicago, IL, with 184.7 thousand cases
2. New York, NY, 105.8
3. Los Angeles-Long Beach, CA, 99.5
4. Boston-Lawrence-Lowell-Brockton, MA, 68.5
5. Washington, DC, 51.2
6. Philadelphia, PA, 43.5
7. Nassau-Suffolk, NY, 40.3
8. Tampa-St. Petersburg-Clearwater, FL, 34.0
9. Orange County, CA, 32.0
10. Newark, NJ, 31.7

Source: *Adams Wine Handbook*, Adams Media Inc., 1998, p. 97.

★4398★
METROPOLITAN AREAS WITH THE MOST WINE SALES, 1997
Ranked by: Sales, in thousands of 9-liter cases. **Remarks:** Also notes market share. **Number listed:** 50

1. Los Angeles-Long Beach, CA, with 12,629.0 thousand cases
2. New York, NY, 8,833.0
3. Chicago, IL, 8,080.0
4. Boston-Lawrence-Lowell-Brockton, MA, 6,012.4
5. Washington, DC, 5,208.6
6. Orange County, CA, 4,246.0
7. San Diego, CA, 3,948.0
8. Riverside-San Bernardino, CA, 3,822.5
9. Oakland, CA, 3,618.1
10. Nassau-Suffolk, 3,394.5

Source: *Adams Wine Handbook*, Adams Media Inc., 1998, p. 25.

★4399★
STATES WITH THE HIGHEST VERMOUTH CONSUMPTION, 1997
Ranked by: Consumption, in 9-liter cases. **Remarks:** Also notes figure for 1996 and percent change. **Number listed:** 51

1. California, with 317,300 cases
2. Illinois, 248,300
3. New York, 204,600
4. Florida, 196,700
5. New Jersey, 115,700
6. Massachusetts, 89,400
7. Pennsylvania, 80,100
8. Texas, 57,000
9. Connecticut, 49,700
10. Ohio, 48,700

Source: *Adams Wine Handbook*, Adams Media Inc., 1998, p. 95.

★4400★

STATES WITH THE MOST DESSERT & FORTIFIED WINE SALES, 1997

Ranked by: Sales, in 9-liter cases. **Remarks:** Also notes previous year's sales and percent change. **Number listed:** 51

1. California, with 1,679,700 cases
2. Illinois, 1,045,400
3. North Carolina, 835,800
4. New York, 662,700
5. Pennsylvania, 493,400
6. Ohio, 470,500
7. Michigan, 450,700
8. Texas, 444,000
9. New Jersey, 362,900
10. Louisiana, 340,000

Source: *Adams Wine Handbook*, Adams Media Inc., 1998, p. 81.

★4401★

STATES WITH THE MOST TABLE WINE SALES, 1997

Ranked by: Sales, in 9-liter cases. **Remarks:** Also notes previous year's sales and percent change. **Number listed:** 51

1. California, with 35,609,700 cases
2. New York, 15,418,600
3. Florida, 13,471,600
4. New Jersey, 8,730,500
5. Illinois, 7,940,800
6. Texas, 7,876,700
7. Massachusetts, 7,311,700
8. Washington, 5,690,100
9. Virginia, 4,910,500
10. Pennsylvania, 4,694,800

Source: *Adams Wine Handbook*, Adams Media Inc., 1998, p. 37.

★4402★

TOP MARKETS FOR WINE BY SALES, 1997

Ranked by: Sales, in 9-liter cases. **Remarks:** Also notes previous year's sales and percent change. **Number listed:** 51

1. California, with 41,443,300 cases
2. New York, 17,714,300
3. Florida, 15,151,500
4. Illinois, 10,914,800
5. New Jersey, 9,870,600
6. Texas, 9,497,000
7. Massachusetts, 8,133,200
8. Washington, 6,259,900
9. Pennsylvania, 5,715,000
10. Michigan, 5,693,700

Source: *Adams Wine Handbook*, Adams Media Inc., 1998, p. 18.

★4403★

TOP METROPOLITAN AREAS FOR DESSERT WINE, 1997

Ranked by: Sales, in thousands of 9-liter cases. **Remarks:** Also notes market share. **Number listed:** 50

1. Chicago, IL, with 766.1 thousand cases
2. Los Angeles-Long Beach, CA, 524.1
3. New York, NY, 337.9
4. Philadelphia, PA, 237.2
5. Boston-Lawrence-Lowell-Brockton, MA, 213.4
6. Detroit, MI, 198.5
7. Washington, DC, 177.2
8. Orange County, CA, 172.3
9. Charlotte-Gastonia-Rock Hill, NC, 165.5
10. Greensboro-Winston Salem-High Point, NC, 158.1

Source: *Adams Wine Handbook*, Adams Media Inc., 1998, p. 83.

★4404★

TOP METROPOLITAN AREAS FOR TABLE WINE, 1997

Ranked by: Sales, in thousands of 9-liter cases. **Remarks:** Also notes market share. **Number listed:** 50

1. Los Angeles-Long Beach, CA, with 10,736.4 thousand cases
2. New York, NY, 7,676.6
3. Boston-Lawrence-Lowell-Brockton, MA, 5,428.9
4. Chicago, IL, 5,753.1
5. Washington, DC, 4,628.8
6. Orange County, CA, 3,645.5
7. San Diego, CA, 3,405.2
8. Riverside-San Bernardino, CA, 3,285.0
9. Oakland, 3,124.8
10. Seattle-Bellevue-Everett, WA, 2,957.4

Source: *Adams Wine Handbook*, Adams Media Inc., 1998, p. 39.

★4405★

TOP PER CAPITA MARKETS FOR TABLE WINE, 1997

Ranked by: Sales, in 9-liter cases per 1,000 adults. **Remarks:** Also notes previous year's sales. **Number listed:** 51

1. District of Columbia, with 2,544.4 cases
2. Nevada, 1,975.0
3. New Hampshire, 1,770.1
4. Massachusetts, 1,633.6
5. California, 1,624.0
6. Connecticut, 1,619.5
7. Oregon, 1,538.4
8. New Jersey, 1,524.2
9. Delaware, 1,516.0
10. Rhode Island, 1,497.1

Source: *Adams Wine Handbook*, Adams Media Inc., 1998, p. 38.

★4406★

TOP PER CAPITA MARKETS FOR WINE BY SALES, 1997

Ranked by: Sales, in 9-liter cases per 1,000 adults. **Remarks:** Also notes previous year's sales. **Number listed:** 51

1. District of Columbia, with 3,010.0 cases
2. Nevada, 2,263.8
3. New Hampshire, 2,007.7
4. California, 1,890.0
5. Massachusetts, 1,817.2
6. Connecticut, 1,806.9
7. New Jersey, 1,723.2
8. Delaware, 1,691.4
9. Rhode Island, 1,680.3

10. Vermont, 1,670.2

Source: *Adams Wine Handbook*, Adams Media Inc., 1998, p. 19.

★4407★
TOP STATES FOR DESSERT & FORTIFIED WINE CONSUMPTION BY CDI (CATEGORY DEVELOPMENT INDEX), 1997
Ranked by: CDI number. **Number listed:** 50

1. North Carolina, with 281
2. Nevada, 271
3. District of Columbia, 226
4. Illinois, 225
5. Louisiana, 207
6. Alaska, 147
7. California, 136
8. Rhode Island, 133
9. Delaware, 121
10. Missouri, 119
10. Michigan, 119

Source: *Adams Wine Handbook*, Adams Media Inc., 1998, p. 80.

★4408★
TOP STATES FOR VERMOUTH CONSUMPTION BY CDI (CATEGORY DEVELOPMENT INDEX), 1997
Ranked by: CDI number. **Number listed:** 51

1. District of Columbia, with 657
2. New Hampshire, 403
3. Illinois, 305
4. Nevada, 215
5. Connecticut, 212
6. New Jersey, 204
7. Massachusetts, 202
8. Vermont, 194
9. Florida, 187
10. Maine, 181

Source: *Adams Wine Handbook*, Adams Media Inc., 1998, p. 94.

★4409★
TOP SUPPLIERS OF WINE, 1997
Ranked by: Sales, in millions of dollars. **Remarks:** Also notes number of cases, sales volume and market share. **Number listed:** 12

1. E. & J. Gallo Winery, with $1,428 million
2. Canandaigua Wine, $614
3. The Wine Group, $426
4. Beringer Wine Estates, $279
5. Brown-Forman Beverages, $260
6. Robert Mondavi, $252
7. Schieffelin & Somerset, $247
8. IDV Wines, $233
9. Sebastiani Vineyard, $213
10. Sutter Home, $198

Source: *Adams Wine Handbook*, Adams Media Inc., 1998, p. 101.

★4410★
TOP WINE BRANDS, 1998
Ranked by: Total U.S. sales, in millions of dollars. **Number listed:** 10

1. Franzia, with $19.0 million
2. Carlo Rossi, $10.2
3. Livingston Cellars, $9.6
4. E&J Gallo Vineyards, $8.3
5. Almaden, $7.6
6. Sutter Home, $7.1
7. Inglenook, $6.1
8. Woodbridge, $4.7
9. Beringer, $4.4
10. Vendange, $4.3

Source: *Superbrands: America's Top 2,000 Brands*, Brand-Week, June 21, 1999, p. 526.

Wine Industry--Advertising

★4411★
DESSERT AND FORTIFIED WINE BRANDS WITH THE HIGHEST TOTAL ADVERTISING EXPENDITURES, 1997
Ranked by: Advertising expenditures, in thousands of dollars. **Number listed:** 8

1. Cockburn's, with $539.8 thousand
2. Dry Sack, $277.7
3. Dubonnet, $248.8
4. Grahams Port, $201.5
5. Sandeman, $153.9
6. Dows, $54.0
7. Fonseca, $43.9
8. Taylor Fladgate, $19.8

Source: *Adams Wine Handbook*, Adams Media Inc., 1998, p. 89.

★4412★
TABLE WINE BRANDS WITH THE HIGHEST CABLE TV ADVERTISING EXPENDITURES, 1997
Ranked by: Advertising expenditures, in thousands of dollars. **Remarks:** Also notes other advertising media expenditures in 1996 and 1997. **Number listed:** 15

1. Fetzer, with $3,330.9 thousand
2. Franzia, $2,725.8
3. Nathanson Creek, $2,182.6
4. Gossamer Bay, $1,460.4
5. Bolla, $1,431.8
6. Turning Leaf, $1,431.3
7. Sutter Home, $1,406.4
8. Concha y Toro, $1,139.9
9. Meridian, $851.6
10. Inglenook, $559.8

Source: *Adams Wine Handbook*, Adams Media Inc., 1998, p. 48.

★4413★
TABLE WINE BRANDS WITH THE HIGHEST MAGAZINE ADVERTISING EXPENDITURES, 1997
Ranked by: Advertising expenditures, in thousands of dollars. **Remarks:** Also notes other advertising media expenditures in 1996 and 1997. **Number listed:** 47

1. Ecco Domani, with $2,923.4 thousand
2. Gallo, $2,392.6
3. Woodbridge, $2,200.3
4. Beringer, $2,055.4
5. Riunite, $2,024.5
6. Forest Glen, $1,275.6
7. Bordeaux, $1,058.3
8. Santa Margherita, $537.1
9. Banfi Wines, $333.7
10. Turning Leaf, $330.5

Source: *Adams Wine Handbook*, Adams Media Inc., 1998, p. 47.

★4414★

TABLE WINE BRANDS WITH THE HIGHEST NETWORK TV ADVERTISING EXPENDITURES, 1997

Ranked by: Advertising expenditures, in thousands of dollars. **Remarks:** Also notes other advertising media expenditures in 1996 and 1997. **Number listed:** 5

1. Turning Leaf, with $8,585.3 thousand
2. Gossame Bay, $5,924.1
3. Nathanson Creek, $1,352.7
4. Cook's Varietals, $464.2
5. Columbia Crest, $283.0

Source: *Adams Wine Handbook*, Adams Media Inc., 1998, p. 48.

★4415★

TABLE WINE BRANDS WITH THE HIGHEST NEWSPAPER ADVERTISING EXPENDITURES, 1997

Ranked by: Advertising expenditures, in thousands of dollars. **Remarks:** Also notes other advertising media expenditures in 1996 and 1997. **Number listed:** 13

1. Folonari, with $394.2 thousand
2. Gallo, $378.0
3. Louis Jadot, $231.6
4. Tessera, $210.4
5. Beringer, $169.4
6. Robert Mondavi, $145.3
7. Vina Santa Carolina, $101.9
8. Ecco Domani, $98.9
9. Wente Brothers, $97.9
10. Sonoma-Loeb, $79.9

Source: *Adams Wine Handbook*, Adams Media Inc., 1998, p. 47.

★4416★

TABLE WINE BRANDS WITH THE HIGHEST OUTDOOR ADVERTISING EXPENDITURES, 1997

Ranked by: Advertising expenditures, in thousands of dollars. **Remarks:** Also notes other advertising media expenditures in 1996 and 1997. **Number listed:** 8

1. Chateau Elan, with $69.0 thousand
2. Opici, $54.6
3. Delicato, $35.1
4. Fetzer, $13.2
5. Geyser Peak, $7.7
5. Monterey, $7.7
5. Sebastiani, $7.7
8. Clos Du Bois, $0.8

Source: *Adams Wine Handbook*, Adams Media Inc., 1998, p. 47.

★4417★

TABLE WINE BRANDS WITH THE HIGHEST SPOT RADIO ADVERTISING EXPENDITURES, 1997

Ranked by: Advertising expenditures, in thousands of dollars. **Remarks:** Also notes other advertising media expenditures in 1996 and 1997. **Number listed:** 15

1. Corbett Canyon, with $5,557.2 thousand
2. Talus, $1,708.7
3. Coastal, $1,000.4
4. Santa Margherita, $818.8
5. Vendange, $576.4
6. Vichon, $493.8
7. Georges Duboeuf, $263.5
8. Bolla, $222.0
9. Tessera, $124.0
10. Folonari, $95.2

Source: *Adams Wine Handbook*, Adams Media Inc., 1998.

★4418★

TABLE WINE BRANDS WITH THE HIGHEST SPOT TV ADVERTISING EXPENDITURES, 1997

Ranked by: Advertising expenditures, in thousands of dollars. **Remarks:** Also notes other advertising media expenditures in 1996 and 1997. **Number listed:** 20

1. Sutter Home, with $3,133.8 thousand
2. Meridian, $2,219.0
3. Gallo, $2,169.9
4. Fetzer, $1,867.9
5. Talus, $488.2
6. Ecco Domani, $357.7
7. Nathanson Creek, $240.4
8. Turning Leaf, $105.7
9. Franzia, $94.8
10. Elmo Pio, $84.8

Source: *Adams Wine Handbook*, Adams Media Inc., 1998, p. 48.

★4419★

TABLE WINE BRANDS WITH THE HIGHEST TOTAL PRINT ADVERTISING EXPENDITURES, 1997

Ranked by: Total print advertising expenditures, in thousands of dollars. **Remarks:** Also notes other advertising media expenditures in 1996 and 1997. **Number listed:** 57

1. Ecco Domani, with $3,022.3 thousand
2. Gallo, $2,770.6
3. Beringer, $2,224.8
4. Woodbridge, $2,200.3
5. Riunite, $2,024.5
6. Forest Glen, $1,275.6
7. Bordeaux, $1,058.3
8. Folonari, $648.7
9. Santa Margherita, $537.1
10. Robert Mondavi, $337.4

Source: *Adams Wine Handbook*, Adams Media Inc., 1998, p. 47.

★4420★

TOTAL ADVERTISING EXPENDITURES FOR VERMOUTH, 1997

Ranked by: Total advertising expenditures, in thousands of dollars. **Number listed:** 2

1. Martini & Rossi Vermouth, with $1,589.3 thousand
2. Lillet, $31.5

Source: *Adams Wine Handbook*, Adams Media Inc., 1998, p. 100.

★4421★

WINE BRANDS WITH THE HIGHEST CABLE TV ADVERTISING EXPENDITURES, 1997

Ranked by: Advertising expenditures, in thousands of dollars. **Number listed:** 15

1. Fetzer, with $3,330.9 thousand
2. Franzia, $2,725.8
3. Korbel, $2,440.4
4. Nathanson Creek, $2,182.6
5. Gossamer Bay, $1,460.4
6. Bolla, $1,431.8
7. Turning Leaf, $1,431.3
8. Sutter Home, $1,406.4
9. Concha y Toro, $1,139.9
10. Meridian, $851.6

Source: *Adams Wine Handbook*, Adams Media Inc., 1998, p. 121.

★4422★
WINE BRANDS WITH THE HIGHEST MAGAZINE ADVERTISING EXPENDITURES, 1997
Ranked by: Advertising expenditures, in thousands of dollars. **Number listed:** 15
1. Freixenet, with $3,815.4 thousand
2. Ecco Domani, $2,923.4
3. Gallo, $2,392.6
4. Woodbridge, $2,200.3
5. Beringer, $2,055.4
6. Riunite, $2,024.5
7. Forest Glen, $1,275.6
8. Bordeaux, $1,058.3
9. Taittinger, $943.3
10. Perrier-Jouet, $792.8

Source: *Adams Wine Handbook*, Adams Media Inc., 1998, p. 115.

★4423★
WINE BRANDS WITH THE HIGHEST NEWSPAPER ADVERTISING EXPENDITURES, 1997
Ranked by: Advertising expenditures, in thousands of dollars. **Number listed:** 15
1. Moet & Chandon Champagne, with $448.8 thousand
2. Folonari, $394.2
3. Gallo, $378.0
4. Louis Jadot, $231.6
5. Tessera, $210.4
6. Beringer, $169.4
7. Dry Sack, $154.2
8. Robert Mondavi, $145.3
9. Vina Santa Carolina, $101.9
10. Ecco Domani, $98.9

Source: *Adams Wine Handbook*, Adams Media Inc., 1998, p. 116.

★4424★
WINE BRANDS WITH THE HIGHEST SPOT TV ADVERTISING EXPENDITURES, 1997
Ranked by: Advertising expenditures, in thousands of dollars. **Number listed:** 15
1. Sutter Home, with $3,133.8 thousand
2. Meridian, $2,219.0
3. Gallo, $2,169.9
4. Fetzer, $1,867.9
5. Moet & Chandon Champagne, $1,277.3
6. Martini & Rossi Vermouth, $1,044.7
7. Korbel, $980.6
8. Nathanson Creek, $240.4
9. Turning Leaf, $105.7
10. Franzia, $94.8

Source: *Adams Wine Handbook*, Adams Media Inc., 1998, p. 121.

Wine Industry, International

★4425★
PER CAPITA CONSUMPTION OF WINE BY COUNTRY, 1996
Ranked by: Per capita consumption, in gallons. **Remarks:** Also notes figures for 1993-1996, and ratio. **Number listed:** 45
1. Portugal, with 16.0 gallons
2. France, 15.9
3. Luxembourg, 15.3
4. Italy, 14.5
5. Switzerland, 11.4
6. Argentina, 11.2
7. Greece, 9.0
8. Uruguay, 8.5
9. Austria, 8.3
10. Spain, 8.0

Source: *Adams Wine Handbook*, 1998, p. 162.

★4426★
WINE BRANDS WITH THE HIGHEST TOTAL TV ADVERTISING EXPENDITURES, 1997
Ranked by: Advertising expenditures, in thousands of dollars. **Number listed:** 15
1. Turning Leaf, with $10,122.3 thousand
2. Gossamer Bay, $7,399.7
3. Fetzer, $5,198.8
4. Sutter Home, $4,540.2
5. Nathanson Creek, $3,775.7
6. Korbel, $3,421.0
7. Meridian, $3,070.6
8. Franzia, $2,820.6
9. Gallo, $2,169.9
10. Martini & Rossi Vermouth, $1,589.3

Source: *Adams Wine Handbook*, Adams Media Inc., 1998, p. 121.

Women Executives

★4427★
TOP PUBLIC COMPANIES FOR EXECUTIVE WOMEN, 1998
Ranked by: Various criteria for formula ranking. **Remarks:** Specific figures not given. Also notes founding date, company phone number, and highest ranking woman. **Number listed:** 25
1. Avon Products
2. Fannie Mae Corp.
3. Pitney Bowes
4. Procter & Gamble
5. Gannett Co.
6. Scholastic
7. Gap
8. Knight Ridder
9. Nordstrom
10. Sallie Mae

Source: *Working Woman*, Top 25 Public Companies for Executive Women (annual), September, 1998, p. 53+.

Women in Business

★4428★
TOP WOMEN MORTGAGE BROKERS, 1998
Ranked by: Sales volume, in millions of dollars. **Remarks:** Also notes firm and location. **Number listed:** 12

1\. Terri Caffery, with $113.2 million
2\. Susan Suminski, $110.8
3\. Mary Bane, $62
3\. Mary Glavin, $62
5\. Judy Blackburn, $60
6\. Laurie Vree, $50
7\. Tamera Blaylock, $46
8\. Katy Motlatch, $38
9\. Sherry Windfield, $33
9\. Brenda Harden, $33

Source: *US Banker*, March, 1999, p. 92.

Women-Owned Business Enterprises

★4429★
TOP WOMEN-OWNED BUSINESSES, 1999
Ranked by: Revenue, in millions of dollars. **Remarks:** Also notes owner, title, number of employees, and type of business. **Number listed:** 500

1. JM Family Enterprises, with $6,200 million
2. Fidelity Investments, $5,195
3. Golden West Financial, $3,100
4. Carlson Companies, $2,700
5. Raley's, $2,193
6. Washington Post, $2,110.4
7. Little Caesar Enterprises, $2,100
8. Ingram Industries, $2,000
9. Warnaco Group, $1,950.3
10. Albert-Culver, $1,834.7

Source: *Working Woman 500 (annual)*, Working Woman, June, 1999, p. 62+.

Women-Owned Business Enterprises--Chicago (IL)

★4430★
TOP WOMEN-OWNED BUSINESS IN COLORADO, 1998
Ranked by: Gross revenue, in thousands of dollars. **Remarks:** Also notes previous year's rank and revenue, chief officer, business description and contact information, and percent woman-based ownership. **Number listed:** 100

1. Ralph Schomp Automotive, with $131,044 thousand
2. Hach Co., $128,058
3. DSP Builders Inc., $52,900
4. Corporate Travel Services, $50,000
5. Pratt Properties, $40,000
6. Packaging West Inc., $34,000
7. Travel by Dana, $30,000
8. Carik Services Inc., $28,000
9. Travel Connections Inc., $26,300
10. McClain Finlon Advertising, $23,500

Source: *Colorado Business*, Top 100 (annual), May, 1999, p. 28+.

★4431★
TOP WOMEN-OWNED FIRMS, 1997
Ranked by: Gross revenue, in millions of dollars. **Remarks:** Also notes chief executive, 1996 revenue, percent change, number of employees, years of operation, years under majority woman ownership, and type of business. **Number listed:** 25

1. Frank Consolidated Enterprises Inc., with $1,022.0 million
2. Pampered Chef, $418.0
3. Chas. Levy Co., $360.5
4. Corporate Travel Management Group, $220.0
5. DSC Logistics, $205.0
6. Turtle Wax Inc., $152.0
7. Harpo Entertainment Group, $150.0
8. Gerber Plumbing Fixtures Corp., $102.1
9. Caravelle Travel Management Inc., $65.0
10. Marketing Innovators International Inc., $60.4

Source: *Top Business Lists (annual)*, Crain's Chicago Business, 1999, vol. 21, p. 47+.

Women-Owned Business Enterprises—Detroit Metropolitan Area

★4432★
LEADING DETROIT-AREA WOMEN-OWNED BUSINESSES, 1997
Ranked by: Revenue, in millions of dollars. **Remarks:** Also notes contact information and majority owner, previous year's revenue, percent change from previous year, number of employees for both years, type of business, and percent woman-owned. **Number listed:** 25

1. Troy Motors Inc., with $388.1 million
2. Jerome-Duncan Inc., $113.5
3. Continental Plastics Co., $99.0
4. Thomas Madison Inc., $90.0
5. Hubert Distributors Inc., $47.2
6. Michigan Rivet Corp., $43.0
7. Entech Personnel Services Inc., $42.0
7. Motor City Stamping Inc., $42.0
9. Systrand Manufacturing Corp., $39.5
10. Northwestern Dodge Inc., $37.5

Source: *Crain's Book of Lists Detroit (annual)*, Crain's Detroit Business, December 28, 1998, p. 46.

Women-Owned Business Enterprises--Florida

★4433★
TOP WOMEN-OWNED BUSINESSES IN FLORIDA, 1999
Ranked by: Number of employees. **Remarks:** Also notes number of female employees, as well as revenue in 1997, type of business, percent of business women-owned, owner, senior executive, and year founded. **Number listed:** 24

1. Michael Saunders & Co., with 400 employees
2. The Abkey Cos. Dba Fuddruckers, 300
3. J-Bar of North Florida, 167
4. Chappell Child Development Centers, 139
5. Supreme Janitorial Service, 121
6. Eastern Metal Supply Inc., 110
7. Investment Equity Corp., 102
8. First Coast Systems Inc., 97
9. A.W. Industries Inc., 89
9. River City Security Services Inc., 89

Source: *TopRank Florida (annual)*, Florida Trend, 1999, p. 112.

Women-Owned Business Enterprises--Long Island (NY)

★4434★
LARGEST WOMEN-OWNED FIRMS IN LONG ISLAND, 1999
Ranked by: Number of employees in the Nassau/Suffolk area. **Remarks:** Also notes contact information, year founded, and products and services. **Number listed:** 33

1. Prudential Long Island Realty, with 1,197 employees
2. The Lemon Tree, 500
3. Better Home Health Care Agency, 350
4. National Wholesale Liquidators, 310
5. Natural Organics, 300

6. The New Huntington Town House, 275
7. Cedar Graphics, 200
7. Love & Quiches Desserts, 200
7. Petite Fleur Nursing Home, 200
10. TXX Services, 175

Source: *Long Island's Book of Lists (annual)*, Long Island Business News, 1999, p. 43.

Women-Owned Business Enterprises—Los Angeles County (CA)

★4435★
LARGEST WOMEN-OWNED FIRMS IN LOS ANGELES COUNTY, 1998
Ranked by: Company-wide revenues, in millions of dollars. **Remarks:** Also notes contact information, number of employees, percentage women-owned, description, year founded, and top local female executives. **Number listed:** 100

1. Don Kott Auto Center, with $336.1 million
2. American Tours International Inc., $136
3. Montrose Travel, $83.9
4. ACT 1 Personnel Services, $80
5. W.I. Simonson Inc., $74.5
6. Chipton-Ross Inc., $49.7
7. Pacific Pioneer Insurance Group, $49.1
8. The Individual Group, $39
9. K T Kitchens Inc., $32.6
10. Ralee Engineering Co., $27

Source: *Los Angeles Business Journal*, March 1, 1999, p. 43+.

Women-Owned Business Enterprises—Philadelphia Metropolitan Area

★4436★
TOP WOMEN-OWNED BUSINESSES IN THE PHILADELPHIA AREA, 1997
Ranked by: Number of local full-time employees. **Remarks:** Also notes total number of employees, revenues, company description, majority owner, percent women-owned, and contact names. **Number listed:** 50

1. Wetherill Associates Inc., with 378 employees
2. Peirce-Phelps Inc., 162
3. Kingsbury Inc., 131
4. Harmelin Media, 101
5. Central Security Agency, 100
6. Frame's Motor Freight Inc., 96
7. J&B Software Inc., 90
8. City Cleaning Co. Inc., 87
8. RSI Data Processing Solutions, 87
10. All Secure Inc., 80

Source: *Book of Business Lists (annual)*, Philadelphia Business Journal, December 25, 1998, p. 117+.

Women's Apparel Industry

See: **Clothing Trade**

Work Environment

★4437★
LEADING CHANGES WORKERS WOULD LIKE IN THEIR WORKSPACE, 1998
Ranked by: Percentage. **Number listed:** 4

1. More storage, with 27%
2. Better technology, 18%
2. More privacy, 18%
2. More comfortable chair, 18%

Source: *Incentive*, July, 1998, p. 9.

★4438★
LEADING WRITERS OF WORKERS' COMPENSATION, 1997
Ranked by: Direct premiums written, in thousands of dollars. **Remarks:** Also notes premium change, market share for 1995-1997, adjusted loss ratios for 1995-1997, and percent of company premiums. **Number listed:** 100

1. Liberty Mutual Companies, with $1,947,175 thousand
2. American Intern Group, $1,670,815
3. CAN Insurance Group, $1,614,341
4. Travelers PC Group, $1,399,453
5. Kemper Insurance Companies, $1,186,365
6. Hartford Insurance Group, $1,113,914
7. Nationwide Group, $840,915
8. Zurich Insurance Group, $825,793
9. Fremont General Group, $738,830
10. Allianz of America, $658,463

Source: *Best's Review, Property Casualty ed.*, Four Property/Casualty Lines (annual), September, 1998, p. 98.

Workers' Compensation

★4439★
TOP WORKER'S COMPENSATION INSURERS, 1995
Ranked by: New written premiums, in billions of dollars. **Remarks:** Also notes figures for 1980. **Number listed:** 10

1. Liberty Mutual, with $1.9 billion
2. CNA, $1.7
3. AIG, $1.6
4. Travelers, $1.3
5. Hartford, $1.2
6. Kemper, $1.1
7. Nationwide, $0.9
8. Zurich, $0.7
8. Fremont, $0.7
10. Fireman's Fund, $0.6

Source: *National Underwriter Property/Casualty*, July 27, 1998, p. 3.

★4440★
TOP WORKERS' COMPENSATION INSURERS, 1997
Ranked by: Direct premiums, in millions of dollars. **Remarks:** Also notes percent growth and market share. **Number listed:** 50

1. Liberty Mutual Insurance Group, with $1,975.2 million
2. American International Group, $1,707.8
3. CNA Insurance Group, $1,615.3
4. Kemper National Companies, $1,241.0
5. Citigroup, $1,135.8
6. Hartford Insurance Group, $1,115.5
7. State Compensation Insurance Fund, $1,035.8

8. Zurich Insurance Group, $978.4
9. Nationwide Group, $873.6
10. Fremont General Group, $738.8

Source: *Business Insurance*, April 26, 1999, p. 48.

Workstations (Office Automation)

★4441★
TOP WORKSTATION VENDORS, 1998
Ranked by: Market share, in percent. **Number listed:** 7

1. Sun, with 51.9%
2. Hewlett-Packard, 15.5%
3. IBM, 10.9%
4. SGI, 9.3%
5. Digital, 2.5%
6. Compaq, 2.0%
7. Others, 7.9%

Source: *Appliance Manufacturer (annual)*, April, 1999, p. 23.

World Wide Web (Computer Network)

★4442★
TOP USERS OF ONLINE FINANCIAL SERVICES, 1998*
Ranked by: Users, in millions. **Number listed:** 6

1. Online users, with 41.5 million
2. Online financial users, 17.1
3. Gathered financial info, 9.3
4. Online stock trading, 4.6
5. Online banking, 4.2
6. Online insurance, 3.2

Source: *Cable World*, October 19, 1998, p. 1.

Yogurt

See also: **Frozen Yogurt**

★4443★
TOP REFRIGERATED YOGURT COMPANIES, 1998
Ranked by: Sales, in millions of dollars. **Remarks:** Also notes percent change from previous year, and unit sales. **Number listed:** 5

1. Dannon Co., with $573 million
2. General Mills, $488
3. Private label, $253
4. Kraft Foods, $175
5. Stonyfield Farm, $40

Source: *Dairy Fields*, January, 1999, p. 18.

★4444★
TOP YOGURT BRANDS, 1998
Ranked by: Sales, in millions of dollars. **Remarks:** Also notes percent change from previous year and dollar share. **Number listed:** 10

1. Private label, with $246.0 million
2. Dannon Light, $178.7
3. Yoplait, $168.3
4. Dannon Fruit on the Bottom, $108.9
5. Yoplait Light, $95.8
6. Breyers, $59.1
7. Yoplait Custard Style, $56.3
8. Dannon, $53.2
9. Dannon Blended, $48.4
10. Yoplait Trix, $47.2

Source: *Dairy Fields*, August, 1998, p. 20.

Zimbabwe Stock Exchange

★4445★
LARGEST LISTED COMPANIES ON THE ZIMBABWE STOCK EXCHANGE, 1997
Ranked by: Market value, in millions of Zimbabwe dollars (Z$). **Number listed:** 20

1. Delta, with Z$10,117.32 million
2. Ashanti Goldfields, Z$4,322.38
3. Meikles Africa, Z$3,210.65
4. Barclays Bank of Zimbabwe, Z$3,146.87
5. Hippo Valley Estates, Z$1,730.82
6. TZI, Z$1,484.15
7. Zimbabwe Sun, Z$1,382.43
8. Portland Holdings, Z$1,150.11
9. Zimbabwe Sugar Refinery, Z$1,110.38
10. Edgars Stores, Z$901.65

Source: *SSB Guide to World Equity Markets (annual)*, Euromoney Publications, 1998, p. 564.

★4446★
MOST ACTIVELY TRADED SHARES ON THE ZIMBABWE STOCK EXCHANGE, 1997
Ranked by: Trading value, in millions of Zimbabwe dollars (Z$). **Number listed:** 15

1. Delta, with Z$1,549.64 million
2. TZI, Z$665.36
3. Meikles Africa, Z$643.73
4. National Merchant Bank, Z$363.20
5. Zimbabwe Papers, Z$301.34
6. Interfresh, Z$181.48
7. Barclays Bank of Zimbabwe, Z$177.71
8. TA Holdings, Z$173.22
9. Zimbabwe Sun, Z$165.70
10. Hippo Valley Estates, Z$154.41

Source: *SSB Guide to World Equity Markets (annual)*, Euromoney Publications, 1998, p. 565.

Zurich Stock Exchange

★4447★
LARGEST SWISS COMPANIES ON THE ZURICH STOCK EXCHANGE, 1997
Ranked by: Market value, in millions of Swiss francs. **Number listed:** 20

1. Novartis N, with SFr147,697.52 million
2. Roche GS, SFr101,906.72
3. Nestle N, SFr86,297.08
4. CS Group N, SFr59,675.95
5. UBS I, SFr44,836.24
6. Rueckv N, SFr39,942.28
7. SBV N, SFr35,541.22
8. Zcurich N, SFr32,644.72
9. Novartis I, SFr15,568.48

10. ABB Ag I, SFr14,972.63

Source: *SSB Guide to World Equity Markets (annual)*, Euromoney Publications, 1998, p. 476.

★4448★

MOST ACTIVELY TRADED SHARES ON THE ZURICH STOCK EXCHANGE, 1997

Ranked by: Trading value, in millions of Swiss francs. **Number listed:** 20

1. Novartis N, with SFr103,976,426 million
2. Roche GS, SFr81,067,827
3. UBS I, SFr80,850,856
4. CS Group N, SFr63,447,179
5. Nestle N, SFr56,573,807
6. Rueckv N, SFr32,883,438
7. SBV N, SFr30,020,362
8. Zuerich N, SFr30,262,776
9. ABB Ag I, SFr15,070,794
10. Alusuisse N, SFr13,208,027

Source: *SSB Guide to World Equity Markets (annual)*, Euromoney Publications, 1998, p. 476.

Index

A

Index

B

Index

Index

Index

C

Index

Index

D

E

Index

F

Index

G

Index

H

Index

Index

I

J

K

Index

M

Index

N

O

Index

Q

R

Index

S

Index

T

Index

Index

U

V

Index

W

X

SIC Index

Agricultural Services

Forestry

Metal Mining

Coal Mining

Oil & Gas Extraction

Nonmetallic Minerals Except Fuels

General Building Contractors

Heavy Construction Except Building Construction

Special Trade Contractors

Food & Kindred Products

Tobacco Products

Textile Mill Products

Apparel & Other Textile Products

Lumber & Wood Products

Furniture & Fixtures

Paper & Allied Products

Printing & Publishing

Chemicals & Allied Products

Petroleum & Coal Products

Rubber & Miscellaneous Plastics Products

Leather & Leather Products

Stone, Clay & Glass Products

Primary Metal Industries

Fabricated Metal Products

Industrial Machinery & Equipment

Electronic & Other Electrical Equipment

Transportation Equipment

Instruments & Related Products

Miscellaneous Manufacturing Industries

Railroad Transportation

Local & Interurban Passenger Transit

Trucking & Warehousing

Water Transportation

Transportation by Air

Pipelines Except Natural Gas

Transportation Services

Communications

Electric, Gas & Sanitary Services

Wholesale Trade—Durable Goods

Wholesale Trade—Nondurable Goods

Building Materials & Garden Supplies

General Merchandise Stores

Food Stores

Automotive Dealers & Service Stations

Apparel & Accessory Stores

Furniture & Homefurnishings Stores

Eating & Drinking Places

Miscellaneous Retail

Depository Institutions

Nondepository Institutions

Security & Commodity Brokers

Insurance Carriers

Insurance Agents, Brokers & Service

Real Estate

Holding & Other Investment Offices

Hotels & Other Lodging Places

Business Services

Automobile Repair, Services & Parking

Motion Pictures

Amusement & Recreation Services

Health Services

Legal Services

Educational Services

Social Services

Museums, Botanical & Zoological Gardens

Membership Organizations

Engineering & Management Services

Services Not Elsewhere Classified

Executive, Legislative & General

Justice, Public Order & Safety

Environmental Quality & Housing

Nonclassifiable Establishments

SIC to NAICS Conversion Guide

Agriculture, Forestry, & Fishing

0111 Wheat ***See*** NAICS 11114: Wheat Farming
0112 Rice ***See*** NAICS 11116: Rice Farming
0115 Corn ***See*** NAICS 11115: Corn Farming
0116 Soybeans ***See*** NAICS 11111: Soybean Farming
0119 Cash Grains, NEC ***See*** NAICS 11113: Dry Pea & Bean Farming; NAICS 11112: Oilseed Farming; NAICS 11115: Corn Farming; NAICS 111191: Oilseed & Grain Combination Farming; NAICS 111199: All Other Grain Farming
0131 Cotton ***See*** NAICS 11192: Cotton Farming
0132 Tobacco ***See*** NAICS 11191: Tobacco Farming
0133 Sugarcane & Sugar Beets ***See*** NAICS 111991: Sugar Beet Farming; NAICS 11193: Sugarcane Farming
0134 Irish Potatoes ***See*** NAICS 111211: Potato Farming
0139 Field Crops, Except Cash Grains, NEC ***See*** NAICS 11194: Hay Farming; NAICS 111992: Peanut Farming; NAICS 111219: Other Vegetable & Melon Farming; NAICS 111998: All Other Miscellaneous Crop Farming
0161 Vegetables & Melons ***See*** NAICS 111219: Other Vegetable & Melon Farming
0171 Berry Crops ***See*** NAICS 111333: Strawberry Farming; NAICS 111334: Berry Farming
0172 Grapes ***See*** NAICS 111332: Grape Vineyards
0173 Tree Nuts ***See*** NAICS 111335: Tree Nut Farming
0174 Citrus Fruits ***See*** NAICS 11131: Orange Groves; NAICS 11132: Citrus Groves
0175 Deciduous Tree Fruits ***See*** NAICS 111331: Apple Orchards; NAICS 111339: Other Noncitrus Fruit Farming
0179 Fruits & Tree Nuts, NEC ***See*** NAICS 111336: Fruit & Tree Nut Combination Farming; NAICS 111339: Other Noncitrus Fruit Farming
0181 Ornamental Floriculture & Nursery Products ***See*** NAICS 111422: Floriculture Production; NAICS 111421: Nursery & Tree Production
0182 Food Crops Grown under Cover ***See*** NAICS 111411: Mushroom Production; NAICS 111419: Other Food Crops Grown under Cover
0191 General Farms, Primarily Crop ***See*** NAICS 111998: All Other Miscellaneous Crop Farming
0211 Beef Cattle Feedlots ***See*** NAICS 112112: Cattle Feedlots
0212 Beef Cattle, Except Feedlots ***See*** NAICS 112111: Beef Cattle Ranching & Farming
0213 Hogs ***See*** NAICS 11221: Hog & Pig Farming
0214 Sheep & Goats ***See*** NAICS 11241: Sheep Farming; NAICS 11242: Goat Farming
0219 General Livestock, Except Dairy & Poultry ***See*** NAICS 11299: All Other Animal Production
0241 Dairy Farms ***See*** NAICS 112111: Beef Cattle Ranching & Farming; NAICS 11212: Dairy Cattle & Milk Production
0251 Broiler, Fryers, & Roaster Chickens ***See*** NAICS 11232: Broilers & Other Meat-type Chicken Production
0252 Chicken Eggs ***See*** NAICS 11231: Chicken Egg Production
0253 Turkey & Turkey Eggs ***See*** NAICS 11233: Turkey Production
0254 Poultry Hatcheries ***See*** NAICS 11234: Poultry Hatcheries
0259 Poultry & Eggs, NEC ***See*** NAICS 11239: Other Poultry Production
0271 Fur-bearing Animals & Rabbits ***See*** NAICS 11293: Fur-bearing Animal & Rabbit Production
0272 Horses & Other Equines ***See*** NAICS 11292: Horse & Other Equine Production
0273 Animal Aquaculture ***See*** NAICS 112511: Finfish Farming & Fish Hatcheries; NAICS 112512: Shellfish Farming; NAICS 112519: Other Animal Aquaculture
0279 Animal Specialities, NEC ***See*** NAICS 11291: Apiculture; NAICS 11299: All Other Animal Production
0291 General Farms, Primarily Livestock & Animal Specialties ***See*** NAICS 11299: All Other Animal Production
0711 Soil Preparation Services ***See*** NAICS 115112: Soil Preparation, Planting & Cultivating
0721 Crop Planting, Cultivating & Protecting ***See*** NAICS 115112: Soil Preparation, Planting & Cultivating
0722 Crop Harvesting, Primarily by Machine ***See*** NAICS 115113: Crop Harvesting, Primarily by Machine
0723 Crop Preparation Services for Market, Except Cotton Ginning ***See*** NAICS 115114: Postharvest Crop Activities
0724 Cotton Ginning ***See*** NAICS 115111: Cotton Ginning
0741 Veterinary Service for Livestock ***See*** NAICS 54194: Veterinary Services

0742 Veterinary Services for Animal Specialties ***See*** NAICS 54194: Veterinary Services
0751 Livestock Services, Except Veterinary ***See*** NAICS 311611: Animal Slaughtering; NAICS 11521: Support Activities for Animal Production
0752 Animal Specialty Services, Except Veterinary ***See*** NAICS 11521: Support Activities for Animal Production; NAICS 81291: Pet Care Services
0761 Farm Labor Contractors & Crew Leaders ***See*** NAICS 115115: Farm Labor Contractors & Crew Leaders
0762 Farm Management Services ***See*** NAICS 115116: Farm Management Services
0781 Landscape Counseling & Planning ***See*** NAICS 54169: Other Scientific & Technical Consulting Services; NAICS 54132: Landscape Architectural Services
0782 Lawn & Garden Services ***See*** NAICS 56173: Landscaping Services
0783 Ornamental Shrub & Tree Services ***See*** NAICS 56173: Landscaping Services
0811 Timber Tracts ***See*** NAICS 111421: Nursery & Tree Production; NAICS 11311: Timber Tract Operations
0831 Forest Nurseries & Gathering of Forest Products ***See*** NAICS 111998: All Other Miscellaneous Crop; NAICS 11321: Forest Nurseries & Gathering of Forest Products
0851 Forestry Services ***See*** NAICS 11531: Support Activities for Forestry
0912 Finfish ***See*** NAICS 114111: Finfish Fishing
0913 Shellfish ***See*** NAICS 114112: Shellfish Fishing
0919 Miscellaneous Marine Products ***See*** NAICS 114119: Other Marine Fishing; NAICS 111998: All Other Miscellaneous Crop Farming
0921 Fish Hatcheries & Preserves ***See*** NAICS 112511: Finfish Farming & Fish Hatcheries; NAICS 112512: Shellfish Farming
0971 Hunting, Trapping, & Game Propagation ***See*** NAICS 11421: Hunting & Trapping

Mining Industries

1011 Iron Ores ***See*** NAICS 21221: Iron Ore Mining
1021 Copper Ores ***See*** NAICS 212234: Copper Ore & Nickel Ore Mining
1031 Lead & Zinc Ores ***See*** NAICS 212231: Lead Ore & Zinc Ore Mining
1041 Gold Ores ***See*** NAICS 212221: Gold Ore Mining
1044 Silver Ores ***See*** NAICS 212222: Silver Ore Mining
1061 Ferroalloy Ores, Except Vanadium ***See*** NAICS 212234: Copper Ore & Nickel Ore Mining; NAICS 212299: Other Metal Ore Mining
1081 Metal Mining Services ***See*** NAICS 213115: Support Activities for Metal Mining; NAICS 54136: Geophysical Surveying & Mapping Services
1094 Uranium-radium-vanadium Ores ***See*** NAICS 212291: Uranium-radium- vanadium Ore Mining
1099 Miscellaneous Metal Ores, NEC ***See*** NAICS 212299: Other Metal Ore Mining
1221 Bituminous Coal & Lignite Surface Mining ***See*** NAICS 212111: Bituminous Coal & Lignite Surface Mining
1222 Bituminous Coal Underground Mining ***See*** NAICS 212112: Bituminous Coal Underground Mining
1231 Anthracite Mining ***See*** NAICS 212113: Anthracite Mining
1241 Coal Mining Services ***See*** NAICS 213114: Support Activities for Coal Mining
1311 Crude Petroleum & Natural Gas ***See*** NAICS 211111: Crude Petroleum & Natural Gas Extraction
1321 Natural Gas Liquids ***See*** NAICS 211112: Natural Gas Liquid Extraction
1381 Drilling Oil & Gas Wells ***See*** NAICS 213111: Drilling Oil & Gas Wells
1382 Oil & Gas Field Exploration Services ***See*** NAICS 54136: Geophysical Surveying & Mapping Services; NAICS 213112: Support Activities for Oil & Gas Field Operations
1389 Oil & Gas Field Services, NEC ***See*** NAICS 213113: Other Oil & Gas Field Support Activities
1411 Dimension Stone ***See*** NAICS 212311: Dimension Stone Mining & Quarry
1422 Crushed & Broken Limestone ***See*** NAICS 212312: Crushed & Broken Limestone Mining & Quarrying
1423 Crushed & Broken Granite ***See*** NAICS 212313: Crushed & Broken Granite Mining & Quarrying
1429 Crushed & Broken Stone, NEC ***See*** NAICS 212319: Other Crushed & Broken Stone Mining & Quarrying
1442 Construction Sand & Gravel ***See*** NAICS 212321: Construction Sand & Gravel Mining
1446 Industrial Sand ***See*** NAICS 212322: Industrial Sand Mining
1455 Kaolin & Ball Clay ***See*** NAICS 212324: Kaolin & Ball Clay Mining
1459 Clay, Ceramic, & Refractory Minerals, NEC ***See*** NAICS 212325: Clay & Ceramic & Refractory Minerals Mining
1474 Potash, Soda, & Borate Minerals ***See*** NAICS 212391: Potash, Soda, & Borate Mineral Mining
1475 Phosphate Rock ***See*** NAICS 212392: Phosphate Rock Mining
1479 Chemical & Fertilizer Mineral Mining, NEC ***See*** NAICS 212393: Other Chemical & Fertilizer Mineral Mining
1481 Nonmetallic Minerals Services Except Fuels ***See*** NAICS 213116: Support Activities for Non-metallic Minerals; NAICS 54136: Geophysical Surveying & Mapping Services
1499 Miscellaneous Nonmetallic Minerals, Except Fuels ***See*** NAICS 212319: Other Crushed & Broken Stone Mining or Quarrying; NAICS 212399: All Other Non-metallic Mineral Mining

Construction Industries

1521 General Contractors-single-family Houses ***See*** NAICS 23321: Single Family Housing Construction
1522 General Contractors-residential Buildings, Other than Single-family ***See*** NAICS 23332: Commercial & Institutional Building Construction; NAICS 23322: Multifamily Housing Construction
1531 Operative Builders ***See*** NAICS 23321: Single Family Housing Construction; NAICS 23322: Multifamily Housing Construction; NAICS 23331: Manufacturing & Industrial Building Construction; NAICS 23332: Commercial & Institutional Building Construction
1541 General Contractors-industrial Buildings & Warehouses ***See*** NAICS 23332: Commercial & Institutional Building Construction; NAICS 23331: Manufacturing & Industrial Building Construction
1542 General Contractors-nonresidential Buildings, Other than Industrial Buildings & Warehouses ***See*** NAICS 23332: Commercial & Institutional Building Construction
1611 Highway & Street Construction, Except Elevated Highways ***See*** NAICS 23411: Highway & Street Construction
1622 Bridge, Tunnel, & Elevated Highway Construction ***See*** NAICS 23412: Bridge & Tunnel Construction
1623 Water, Sewer, Pipeline, & Communications & Power Line Construction ***See*** NAICS 23491: Water, Sewer & Pipeline Construction; NAICS 23492: Power & Communication Transmission Line Construction

1629 Heavy Construction, NEC ***See*** NAICS 23493: Industrial Nonbuilding Structure Construction; NAICS 23499: All Other Heavy Construction
1711 Plumbing, Heating, & Air-conditioning ***See*** NAICS 23511: Plumbing, Heating & Air-conditioning Contractors
1721 Painting & Paper Hanging ***See*** NAICS 23521: Painting & Wall Covering Contractors
1731 Electrical Work ***See*** NAICS 561621: Security Systems Services; NAICS 23531: Electrical Contractors
1741 Masonry, Stone Setting & Other Stone Work ***See*** NAICS 23541: Masonry & Stone Contractors
1742 Plastering, Drywall, Acoustical & Insulation Work ***See*** NAICS 23542: Drywall, Plastering, Acoustical & Insulation Contractors
1743 Terrazzo, Tile, Marble, & Mosaic Work ***See*** NAICS 23542: Drywall, Plastering, Acoustical & Insulation Contractors; NAICS 23543: Tile, Marble, Terrazzo & Mosaic Contractors
1751 Carpentry Work ***See*** NAICS 23551: Carpentry Contractors
1752 Floor Laying & Other Floor Work, NEC ***See*** NAICS 23552: Floor Laying & Other Floor Contractors
1761 Roofing, Siding, & Sheet Metal Work ***See*** NAICS 23561: Roofing, Siding, & Sheet Metal Contractors
1771 Concrete Work ***See*** NAICS 23542: Drywall, Plastering, Acoustical & Insulation Contractors; NAICS 23571: Concrete Contractors
1781 Water Well Drilling ***See*** NAICS 23581: Water Well Drilling Contractors
1791 Structural Steel Erection ***See*** NAICS 23591: Structural Steel Erection Contractors
1793 Glass & Glazing Work ***See*** NAICS 23592: Glass & Glazing Contractors
1794 Excavation Work ***See*** NAICS 23593: Excavation Contractors
1795 Wrecking & Demolition Work ***See*** NAICS 23594: Wrecking & Demolition Contractors
1796 Installation or Erection of Building Equipment, NEC ***See*** NAICS 23595: Building Equipment & Other Machinery Installation Contractors
1799 Special Trade Contractors, NEC ***See*** NAICS 23521: Painting & Wall Covering Contractors; NAICS 23592: Glass & Glazing Contractors; NAICS 56291: Remediation Services; NAICS 23599: All Other Special Trade Contractors

Food & Kindred Products

2011 Meat Packing Plants ***See*** NAICS 311611: Animal Slaughtering
2013 Sausages & Other Prepared Meats ***See*** NAICS 311612: Meat Processed from Carcasses
2015 Poultry Slaughtering & Processing ***See*** NAICS 311615: Poultry Processing; NAICS 311999: All Other Miscellaneous Food Manufacturing
2021 Creamery Butter ***See*** NAICS 311512: Creamery Butter Manufacturing
2022 Natural, Processed, & Imitation Cheese ***See*** NAICS 311513: Cheese Manufacturing
2023 Dry, Condensed, & Evaporated Dairy Products ***See*** NAICS 311514: Dry, Condensed, & Evaporated Milk Manufacturing
2024 Ice Cream & Frozen Desserts ***See*** NAICS 31152: Ice Cream & Frozen Dessert Manufacturing
2026 Fluid Milk ***See*** NAICS 311511: Fluid Milk Manufacturing
2032 Canned Specialties ***See*** NAICS 311422: Specialty Canning; NAICS 311999: All Other Miscellaneous Food Manufacturing
2033 Canned Fruits, Vegetables, Preserves, Jams, & Jellies ***See*** NAICS 311421: Fruit & Vegetable Canning
2034 Dried & Dehydrated Fruits, Vegetables, & Soup Mixes ***See*** NAICS 311423: Dried & Dehydrated Food Manufacturing; NAICS 311211: Flour Milling
2035 Pickled Fruits & Vegetables, Vegetables Sauces & Seasonings, & Salad Dressings ***See*** NAICS 311421: Fruit & Vegetable Canning; NAICS 311941: Mayonnaise, Dressing, & Other Prepared Sauce Manufacturing
2037 Frozen Fruits, Fruit Juices, & Vegetables ***See*** NAICS 311411: Frozen Fruit, Juice, & Vegetable Processing
2038 Frozen Specialties, NEC ***See*** NAICS 311412: Frozen Specialty Food Manufacturing
2041 Flour & Other Grain Mill Products ***See*** NAICS 311211: Flour Milling
2043 Cereal Breakfast Foods ***See*** NAICS 31192: Coffee & Tea Manufacturing; NAICS 31123: Breakfast Cereal Manufacturing
2044 Rice Milling ***See*** NAICS 311212: Rice Milling
2045 Prepared Flour Mixes & Doughs ***See*** NAICS 311822: Flour Mixes & Dough Manufacturing from Purchased Flour
2046 Wet Corn Milling ***See*** NAICS 311221: Wet Corn Milling
2047 Dog & Cat Food ***See*** NAICS 311111: Dog & Cat Food Manufacturing
2048 Prepared Feed & Feed Ingredients for Animals & Fowls, Except Dogs & Cats ***See*** NAICS 311611: Animal Slaughtering; NAICS 311119: Other Animal Food Manufacturing
2051 Bread & Other Bakery Products, Except Cookies & Crackers ***See*** NAICS 311812: Commercial Bakeries
2052 Cookies & Crackers ***See*** NAICS 311821: Cookie & Cracker Manufacturing; NAICS 311919: Other Snack Food Manufacturing; NAICS 311812: Commercial Bakeries
2053 Frozen Bakery Products, Except Bread ***See*** NAICS 311813: Frozen Bakery Product Manufacturing
2061 Cane Sugar, Except Refining ***See*** NAICS 311311: Sugarcane Mills
2062 Cane Sugar Refining ***See*** NAICS 311312: Cane Sugar Refining
2063 Beet Sugar ***See*** NAICS 311313: Beet Sugar Manufacturing
2064 Candy & Other Confectionery Products ***See*** NAICS 31133: Confectionery Manufacturing from Purchased Chocolate; NAICS 31134: Non-chocolate Confectionery Manufacturing
2066 Chocolate & Cocoa Products ***See*** NAICS 31132: Chocolate & Confectionery Manufacturing from Cacao Beans
2067 Chewing Gum ***See*** NAICS 31134: Non-chocolate Confectionery Manufacturing
2068 Salted & Roasted Nuts & Seeds ***See*** NAICS 311911: Roasted Nuts & Peanut Butter Manufacturing
2074 Cottonseed Oil Mills ***See*** NAICS 311223: Other Oilseed Processing; NAICS 311225: Fats & Oils Refining & Blending
2075 Soybean Oil Mills ***See*** NAICS 311222: Soybean Processing; NAICS 311225: Fats & Oils Refining & Blending
2076 Vegetable Oil Mills, Except Corn, Cottonseed, & Soybeans ***See*** NAICS 311223: Other Oilseed Processing; NAICS 311225: Fats & Oils Refining & Blending
2077 Animal & Marine Fats & Oils ***See*** NAICS 311613: Rendering & Meat By-product Processing; NAICS 311711: Seafood Canning; NAICS 311712: Fresh & Frozen Seafood Processing; NAICS 311225: Edible Fats & Oils Manufacturing
2079 Shortening, Table Oils, Margarine, & Other Edible Fats & Oils, NEC ***See*** NAICS 311225: Edible Fats & Oils Manufacturing; NAICS 311222: Soybean Processing; NAICS 311223: Other Oilseed Processing
2082 Malt Beverages ***See*** NAICS 31212: Breweries
2083 Malt ***See*** NAICS 311213: Malt Manufacturing
2084 Wines, Brandy, & Brandy Spirits ***See*** NAICS 31213: Wineries
2085 Distilled & Blended Liquors ***See*** NAICS 31214: Distilleries

2086 Bottled & Canned Soft Drinks & Carbonated Waters ***See*** NAICS 312111: Soft Drink Manufacturing; NAICS 312112: Bottled Water Manufacturing

2087 Flavoring Extracts & Flavoring Syrups NEC ***See*** NAICS 31193: Flavoring Syrup & Concentrate Manufacturing; NAICS 311942: Spice & Extract Manufacturing; NAICS 311999: All Other Miscellaneous Food Manufacturing

2091 Canned & Cured Fish & Seafood ***See*** NAICS 311711: Seafood Canning

2092 Prepared Fresh or Frozen Fish & Seafoods ***See*** NAICS 311712: Fresh & Frozen Seafood Processing

2095 Roasted Coffee ***See*** NAICS 31192: Coffee & Tea Manufacturing; NAICS 311942: Spice & Extract Manufacturing

2096 Potato Chips, Corn Chips, & Similar Snacks ***See*** NAICS 311919: Other Snack Food Manufacturing

2097 Manufactured Ice ***See*** NAICS 312113: Ice Manufacturing

2098 Macaroni, Spaghetti, Vermicelli, & Noodles ***See*** NAICS 311823: Pasta Manufacturing

2099 Food Preparations, NEC ***See*** NAICS 311423: Dried & Dehydrated Food Manufacturing; NAICS 111998: All Other Miscellaneous Crop Farming; NAICS 31134: Non-chocolate Confectionery Manufacturing; NAICS 311911: Roasted Nuts & Peanut Butter Manufacturing; NAICS 311991: Perishable Prepared Food Manufacturing; NAICS 31183: Tortilla Manufacturing; NAICS 31192: Coffee & Tea Manufacturing; NAICS 311941: Mayonnaise, Dressing, & Other Prepared Sauce Manufacturing; NAICS 311942: Spice & Extract Manufacturing; NAICS 311999: All Other Miscellaneous Food Manufacturing

Tobacco Products

2111 Cigarettes ***See*** NAICS 312221: Cigarette Manufacturing

2121 Cigars ***See*** NAICS 312229: Other Tobacco Product Manufacturing

2131 Chewing & Smoking Tobacco & Snuff ***See*** NAICS 312229: Other Tobacco Product Manufacturing

2141 Tobacco Stemming & Redrying ***See*** NAICS 312229: Other Tobacco Product Manufacturing; NAICS 31221: Tobacco Stemming & Redrying

Textile Mill Products

2211 Broadwoven Fabric Mills, Cotton ***See*** NAICS 31321: Broadwoven Fabric Mills

2221 Broadwoven Fabric Mills, Manmade Fiber & Silk ***See*** NAICS 31321: Broadwoven Fabric Mills

2231 Broadwoven Fabric Mills, Wool ***See*** NAICS 31321: Broadwoven Fabric Mills; NAICS 313311: Broadwoven Fabric Finishing Mills; NAICS 313312: Textile & Fabric Finishing Mills

2241 Narrow Fabric & Other Smallware Mills: Cotton, Wool, Silk, & Manmade Fiber ***See*** NAICS 313221: Narrow Fabric Mills

2251 Women's Full-length & Knee-length Hosiery, Except Socks ***See*** NAICS 315111: Sheer Hosiery Mills

2252 Hosiery, NEC ***See*** NAICS 315111: Sheer Hosiery Mills; NAICS 315119: Other Hosiery & Sock Mills

2253 Knit Outerwear Mills ***See*** NAICS 315191: Outerwear Knitting Mills

2254 Knit Underwear & Nightwear Mills ***See*** NAICS 315192: Underwear & Nightwear Knitting Mills

2257 Weft Knit Fabric Mills ***See*** NAICS 313241: Weft Knit Fabric Mills; NAICS 313312: Textile & Fabric Finishing Mills

2258 Lace & Warp Knit Fabric Mills ***See*** NAICS 313249: Other Knit Fabric & Lace Mills; NAICS 313312: Textile & Fabric Finishing Mills

2259 Knitting Mills, NEC ***See*** NAICS 315191: Outerwear Knitting Mills; NAICS 315192: Underwear & Nightwear Knitting Mills; NAICS 313241: Weft Knit Fabric Mills; NAICS 313249: Other Knit Fabric & Lace Mills

2261 Finishers of Broadwoven Fabrics of Cotton ***See*** NAICS 313311: Broadwoven Fabric Finishing Mills

2262 Finishers of Broadwoven Fabrics of Manmade Fiber & Silk ***See*** NAICS 313311: Broadwoven Fabric Finishing Mills

2269 Finishers of Textiles, NEC ***See*** NAICS 313311: Broadwoven Fabric Finishing Mills; NAICS 313312: Textile & Fabric Finishing Mills

2273 Carpets & Rugs ***See*** NAICS 31411: Carpet & Rug Mills

2281 Yarn Spinning Mills ***See*** NAICS 313111: Yarn Spinning Mills

2282 Yarn Texturizing, Throwing, Twisting, & Winding Mills ***See*** NAICS 313112: Yarn Texturing, Throwing & Twisting Mills; NAICS 313312: Textile & Fabric Finishing Mills

2284 Thread Mills ***See*** NAICS 313113: Thread Mills; NAICS 313312: Textile & Fabric Finishing Mills

2295 Coated Fabrics, Not Rubberized ***See*** NAICS 31332: Fabric Coating Mills

2296 Tire Cord & Fabrics ***See*** NAICS 314992: Tire Cord & Tire Fabric Mills

2297 Nonwoven Fabrics ***See*** NAICS 31323: Nonwoven Fabric Mills

2298 Cordage & Twine ***See*** NAICS 314991: Rope, Cordage & Twine Mills

2299 Textile Goods, NEC ***See*** NAICS 31321: Broadwoven Fabric Mills; NAICS 31323: Nonwoven Fabric Mills; NAICS 313312: Textile & Fabric Finishing Mills; NAICS 313221: Narrow Fabric Mills; NAICS 313113: Thread Mills; NAICS 313111: Yarn Spinning Mills; NAICS 314999: All Other Miscellaneous Textile Product Mills

Apparel & Other Finished Products Made From Fabrics & Similar Materials

2311 Men's & Boys' Suits, Coats & Overcoats ***See*** NAICS 315211: Men's & Boys' Cut & Sew Apparel Contractors; NAICS 315222: Men's & Boys' Cut & Sew Suit, Coat, & Overcoat Manufacturing

2321 Men's & Boys' Shirts, Except Work Shirts ***See*** NAICS 315211: Men's & Boys' Cut & Sew Apparel Contractors; NAICS 315223: Men's & Boys' Cut & Sew Shirt, Manufacturing

2322 Men's & Boys' Underwear & Nightwear ***See*** NAICS 315211: Men's & Boys' Cut & Sew Apparel Contractors; NAICS 315221: Men's & Boys' Cut & Sew Underwear & Nightwear Manufacturing

2323 Men's & Boys' Neckwear ***See*** NAICS 315993: Men's & Boys' Neckwear Manufacturing

2325 Men's & Boys' Trousers & Slacks ***See*** NAICS 315211: Men's & Boys' Cut & Sew Apparel Contractors; NAICS 315224: Men's & Boys' Cut & Sew Trouser, Slack, & Jean Manufacturing

2326 Men's & Boys' Work Clothing ***See*** NAICS 315211: Men's & Boys' Cut & Sew Apparel Contractors; NAICS 315225: Men's & Boys' Cut & Sew Work Clothing Manufacturing

2329 Men's & Boys' Clothing, NEC ***See*** NAICS 315211: Men's & Boys' Cut & Sew Apparel Contractors; NAICS 315228: Men's & Boys' Cut & Sew Other Outerwear Manufacturing; NAICS 315299: All Other Cut & Sew Apparel Manufacturing

2331 Women's, Misses', & Juniors' Blouses & Shirts ***See*** NAICS 315212: Women's & Girls' Cut & Sew Apparel Contractors; NAICS 315232: Women's &' Cut & Sew Blouse & Shirt Manufacturing

2335 Women's, Misses' & Junior's Dresses ***See*** NAICS 315212: Women's & Girls' Cut & Sew Apparel Contractors; NAICS 315233: Women's & Girls' Cut & Sew Dress Manufacturing

2337 Women's, Misses' & Juniors' Suits, Skirts & Coats; NAICS 315212: Women's & Girls' Cut & Sew Apparel Contractors; NAICS 315234: Women's & Girls' Cut & Sew Suit, Coat, Tailored Jacket, & Skirt Manufacturing

2339 Women's, Misses' & Juniors' Outerwear, NEC ***See*** NAICS 315999: Other Apparel Accessories & Other Apparel Manufacturing; NAICS 315212: Women's & Girls' Cut & Sew Apparel Contractors; NAICS 315299: All Other Cut & Sew Apparel Manufacturing; NAICS 315238: Women's & Girls' Cut & Sew Other Outerwear Manufacturing

2341 Women's, Misses, Children's, & Infants' Underwear & Nightwear ***See*** NAICS 315212: Women's & Girls' Cut & Sew Apparel Contractors; NAICS 315211: Men's & Boys' Cut & Sew Apparel Contractors; NAICS 315231: Women's & Girls' Cut & Sew Lingerie, Loungewear, & Nightwear Manufacturing; NAICS 315221: Men's & Boys' Cut & Sew Underwear & Nightwear Manufacturing; NAICS 315291: Infants' Cut & Sew Apparel Manufacturing

2342 Brassieres, Girdles, & Allied Garments ***See*** NAICS 315212: Women's & Girls' Cut & Sew Apparel Contractors; NAICS 315231: Women's & Girls' Cut & Sew Lingerie, Loungewear, & Nightwear Manufacturing

2353 Hats, Caps, & Millinery ***See*** NAICS 315991: Hat, Cap, & Millinery Manufacturing

2361 Girls', Children's & Infants' Dresses, Blouses & Shirts ***See*** NAICS 315291: Infants' Cut & Sew Apparel Manufacturing; NAICS 315223: Men's & Boys' Cut & Sew Shirt, Manufacturing; NAICS 315211: Men's & Boys' Cut & Sew Apparel Contractors; NAICS 315232: Women's & Girls' Cut & Sew Blouse & Shirt Manufacturing; NAICS 315233: Women's & Girls' Cut & Sew Dress Manufacturing; NAICS 315212: Women's & Girls' Cut & Sew Apparel Contractors

2369 Girls', Children's & Infants' Outerwear, NEC ***See*** NAICS 315291: Infants' Cut & Sew Apparel Manufacturing; NAICS 315222: Men's & Boys' Cut & Sew Suit, Coat, & Overcoat Manufacturing; NAICS 315224: Men's & Boys' Cut & Sew Trouser, Slack, & Jean Manufacturing; NAICS 315228: Men's & Boys' Cut & Sew Other Outerwear Manufacturing; NAICS 315221: Men's & Boys' Cut & Sew Underwear & Nightwear Manufacturing; NAICS 315211: Men's & Boys' Cut & Sew Apparel Contractors; NAICS 315234: Women's & Girls' Cut & Sew Suit, Coat, Tailored Jacket, & Skirt Manufacturing; NAICS 315238: Women's & Girls' Cut & Sew Other Outerwear Manufacturing; NAICS 315231: Women's & Girls' Cut & Sew Lingerie, Loungewear, & Nightwear Manufacturing; NAICS 315212: Women's & Girls' Cut & Sew Apparel Contractors

2371 Fur Goods ***See*** NAICS 315292: Fur & Leather Apparel Manufacturing

2381 Dress & Work Gloves, Except Knit & All-leather ***See*** NAICS 315992: Glove & Mitten Manufacturing

2384 Robes & Dressing Gowns ***See*** NAICS 315231: Women's & Girls' Cut & Sew Lingerie, Loungewear, & Nightwear Manufacturing; NAICS 315221: Men's & Boys' Cut & Sew Underwear & Nightwear Manufacturing; NAICS 315211: Men's & Boys' Cut & Sew Apparel Contractors; NAICS 315212: Women's & Girls' Cut & Sew Apparel Contractors

2385 Waterproof Outerwear ***See*** NAICS 315222: Men's & Boys' Cut & Sew Suit, Coat, & Overcoat Manufacturing; NAICS 315234: Women's & Girls' Cut & Sew Suit, Coat, Tailored Jacket, & Skirt Manufacturing; NAICS 315228: Men's & Boys' Cut & Sew Other Outerwear Manufacturing; NAICS 315238: Women's & Girls' Cut & Sew Other Outerwear Manufacturing; NAICS 315291: Infants' Cut & Sew Apparel Manufacturing; NAICS 315999: Other Apparel Accessories & Other Apparel Manufacturing; NAICS 315211: Men's & Boys' Cut & Sew Apparel Contractors; NAICS 315212: Women's & Girls' Cut & Sew Apparel Contractors

2386 Leather & Sheep-lined Clothing ***See*** NAICS 315292: Fur & Leather Apparel Manufacturing

2387 Apparel Belts ***See*** NAICS 315999: Other Apparel Accessories & Other Apparel Manufacturing

2389 Apparel & Accessories, NEC ***See*** NAICS 315999: Other Apparel Accessories & Other Apparel Manufacturing; NAICS 315299: All Other Cut & Sew Apparel Manufacturing; NAICS 315231: Women's & Girls' Cut & Sew Lingerie, Loungewear,& Nightwear Manufacturing; NAICS 315212: Women's & Girls' Cut & Sew Apparel Contractors; NAICS 315211: Mens' & Boys' Cut & Sew Apparel Contractors

2391 Curtains & Draperies ***See*** NAICS 314121: Curtain & Drapery Mills

2392 Housefurnishings, Except Curtains & Draperies ***See*** NAICS 314911: Textile Bag Mills; NAICS 339994: Broom, Brush & Mop Manufacturing; NAICS 314129: Other Household Textile Product Mills

2393 Textile Bags ***See*** NAICS 314911: Textile Bag Mills

2394 Canvas & Related Products ***See*** NAICS 314912: Canvas & Related Product Mills

2395 Pleating, Decorative & Novelty Stitching, & Tucking for the Trade ***See*** NAICS 314999: All Other Miscellaneous Textile Product Mills; NAICS 315211: Mens' & Boys' Cut & Sew Apparel Contractors; NAICS 315212: Women's & Girls' Cut & Sew Apparel Contractors

2396 Automotive Trimmings, Apparel Findings, & Related Products ***See*** NAICS 33636: Motor Vehicle Fabric Accessories & Seat Manufacturing; NAICS 315999: Other Apparel Accessories, & Other Apparel Manufacturing; NAICS 323113: Commercial Screen Printing; NAICS 314999: All Other Miscellaneous Textile Product Mills

2397 Schiffli Machine Embroideries ***See*** NAICS 313222: Schiffli Machine Embroidery

2399 Fabricated Textile Products, NEC ***See*** NAICS 33636: Motor Vehicle Fabric Accessories & Seat Manufacturing; NAICS 315999: Other Apparel Accessories & Other Apparel Manufacturing; NAICS 314999: All Other Miscellaneous Textile Product Mills

Lumber & Wood Products, Except Furniture

2411 Logging ***See*** NAICS 11331: Logging

2421 Sawmills & Planing Mills, General ***See*** NAICS 321913: Softwood Cut Stock, Resawing Lumber, & Planing; NAICS 321113: Sawmills; NAICS 321914: Other Millwork; NAICS 321999: All Other Miscellaneous Wood Product Manufacturing

2426 Hardwood Dimension & Flooring Mills ***See*** NAICS 321914: Other Millwork; NAICS 321999: All Other Miscellaneous Wood Product Manufacturing; NAICS 337139: Other Wood Furniture Manufacturing; NAICS 321912: Hardwood Dimension Mills

2429 Special Product Sawmills, NEC ***See*** NAICS 321113: Sawmills; NAICS 321913: Softwood Cut Stock, Resawing Lumber, & Planing; NAICS 321999: All Other Miscellaneous Wood Product Manufacturing

2431 Millwork ***See*** NAICS 321911: Wood Window & Door Manufacturing; NAICS 321914: Other Millwork

2434 Wood Kitchen Cabinets ***See*** NAICS 337131: Wood Kitchen Cabinet & Counter Top Manufacturing

2435 Hardwood Veneer & Plywood ***See*** NAICS 321211: Hardwood Veneer & Plywood Manufacturing

2436 Softwood Veneer & Plywood ***See*** NAICS 321212: Softwood Veneer & Plywood Manufacturing

2439 Structural Wood Members, NEC ***See*** NAICS 321913: Softwood Cut Stock, Resawing Lumber, & Planing; NAICS 321214: Truss Manufacturing; NAICS 321213: Engineered Wood Member Manufacturing

2441 Nailed & Lock Corner Wood Boxes & Shook ***See*** NAICS 32192: Wood Container & Pallet Manufacturing

2448 Wood Pallets & Skids ***See*** NAICS 32192: Wood Container & Pallet Manufacturing

2449 Wood Containers, NEC ***See*** NAICS 32192: Wood Container & Pallet Manufacturing

2451 Mobile Homes ***See*** NAICS 321991: Manufactured Home Manufacturing
2452 Prefabricated Wood Buildings & Components ***See*** NAICS 321992: Prefabricated Wood Building Manufacturing
2491 Wood Preserving ***See*** NAICS 321114: Wood Preservation
2493 Reconstituted Wood Products ***See*** NAICS 321219: Reconstituted Wood Product Manufacturing
2499 Wood Products, NEC ***See*** NAICS 339999: All Other Miscellaneous Manufacturing; NAICS 337139: Other Wood Furniture Manufacturing; NAICS 337148: Other Nonwood Furniture Manufacturing; NAICS 32192: Wood Container & Pallet Manufacturing; NAICS 321999: All Other Miscellaneous Wood Product Manufacturing

Furniture & Fixtures

2511 Wood Household Furniture, Except Upholstered ***See*** NAICS 337122: Wood Household Furniture Manufacturing
2512 Wood Household Furniture, Upholstered ***See*** NAICS 337121: Upholstered Household Furniture Manufacturing
2514 Metal Household Furniture ***See*** NAICS 337124: Metal Household Furniture Manufacturing
2515 Mattresses, Foundations, & Convertible Beds ***See*** NAICS 33791: Mattress Manufacturing; NAICS 337132: Upholstered Wood Household Furniture Manufacturing
2517 Wood Television, Radio, Phonograph & Sewing Machine Cabinets ***See*** NAICS 337139: Other Wood Furniture Manufacturing
2519 Household Furniture, NEC ***See*** NAICS 337143: Household Furniture except Wood & Metal) Manufacturing
2521 Wood Office Furniture ***See*** NAICS 337134: Wood Office Furniture Manufacturing
2522 Office Furniture, Except Wood ***See*** NAICS 337141: Nonwood Office Furniture Manufacturing
2531 Public Building & Related Furniture ***See*** NAICS 33636: Motor Vehicle Fabric Accessories & Seat Manufacturing; NAICS 337139: Other Wood Furniture Manufacturing; NAICS 337148: Other Nonwood Furniture Manufacturing; NAICS 339942: Lead Pencil & Art Good Manufacturing
2541 Wood Office & Store Fixtures, Partitions, Shelving, & Lockers ***See*** NAICS 337131: Wood Kitchen Cabinet & Counter TopManufacturing; NAICS 337135: Custom Architectural Woodwork, Millwork, & Fixtures; NAICS 337139: Other Wood Furniture Manufacturing
2542 Office & Store Fixtures, Partitions Shelving, & Lockers, Except Wood ***See*** NAICS 337145: Nonwood Showcase, Partition,Shelving, & Locker Manufacturing
2591 Drapery Hardware & Window Blinds & Shades ***See*** NAICS 33792: Blind & Shade Manufacturing
2599 Furniture & Fixtures, NEC ***See*** NAICS 339113: Surgical Appliance & Supplies Manufacturing; NAICS 337139: Other Wood Furniture Manufacturing; NAICS 337148: Other Nonwood Furniture Manufacturing

Paper & Allied Products

2611 Pulp Mills ***See*** NAICS 32211: Pulp Mills; NAICS 322121: Paper Mills; NAICS 32213: Paperboard Mills
2621 Paper Mills ***See*** NAICS 322121: Paper Mills; NAICS 322122: Newsprint Mills
2631 Paperboard Mills ***See*** NAICS 32213: Paperboard Mills
2652 Setup Paperboard Boxes ***See*** NAICS 322213: Setup Paperboard Box Manufacturing
2653 Corrugated & Solid Fiber Boxes ***See*** NAICS 322211: Corrugated & Solid Fiber Box Manufacturing
2655 Fiber Cans, Tubes, Drums, & Similar Products ***See*** NAICS 322214: Fiber Can, Tube, Drum, & Similar Products Manufacturing
2656 Sanitary Food Containers, Except Folding ***See*** NAICS 322215: Non-folding Sanitary Food Container Manufacturing
2657 Folding Paperboard Boxes, Including Sanitary ***See*** NAICS 322212: Folding Paperboard Box Manufacturing
2671 Packaging Paper & Plastics Film, Coated & Laminated ***See*** NAICS 322221: Coated & Laminated Packaging Paper & Plastics Film Manufacturing; NAICS 326112: Unsupported Plastics Packaging Film & Sheet Manufacturing
2672 Coated & Laminated Paper, NEC ***See*** NAICS 322222: Coated & Laminated Paper Manufacturing
2673 Plastics, Foil, & Coated Paper Bags ***See*** NAICS 322223: Plastics, Foil, & Coated Paper Bag Manufacturing; NAICS 326111: Unsupported Plastics Bag Manufacturing
2674 Uncoated Paper & Multiwall Bags ***See*** NAICS 322224: Uncoated Paper & Multiwall Bag Manufacturing
2675 Die-cut Paper & Paperboard & Cardboard ***See*** NAICS 322231: Die-cut Paper & Paperboard Office Supplies Manufacturing; NAICS 322292: Surface coated Paperboard Manufacturing; NAICS 322298: All Other Converted Paper Product Manufacturing
2676 Sanitary Paper Products ***See*** NAICS 322291: Sanitary Paper Product Manufacturing
2677 Envelopes ***See*** NAICS 322232: Envelope Manufacturing
2678 Stationery, Tablets, & Related Products ***See*** NAICS 322233: Stationery, Tablet, & Related Product Manufacturing
2679 Converted Paper & Paperboard Products, NEC ***See*** NAICS 322215: Non folding Sanitary Food Container Manufacturing; NAICS 322222: Coated & Laminated Paper Manufacturing; NAICS 322231: Die-cut Paper & Paperboard Office Supplies Manufacturing; NAICS 322298: All Other Converted Paper Product Manufacturing

Printing, Publishing, & Allied Industries

2711 Newspapers: Publishing, or Publishing & Printing ***See*** NAICS 51111: Newspaper Publishers
2721 Periodicals: Publishing, or Publishing & Printing ***See*** NAICS 51112: Periodical Publishers
2731 Books: Publishing, or Publishing & Printing ***See*** NAICS 51223: Music Publishers; NAICS 51113: Book Publishers
2732 Book Printing ***See*** NAICS 323117: Book Printing
2741 Miscellaneous Publishing ***See*** NAICS 51114: Database & Directory Publishers; NAICS 51223: Music Publishers; NAICS 511199: All Other Publishers
2752 Commercial Printing, Lithographic ***See*** NAICS 323114: Quick Printing; NAICS 323110: Commercial Lithographic Printing
2754 Commercial Printing, Gravure ***See*** NAICS 323111: Commercial Gravure Printing
2759 Commercial Printing, NEC ***See*** NAICS 323113: Commercial Screen Printing; NAICS 323112: Commercial Flexographic Printing; NAICS 323114: Quick Printing; NAICS 323115: Digital Printing; NAICS 323119: Other Commercial Printing
2761 Manifold Business Forms ***See*** NAICS 323116: Manifold Business Form Printing
2771 Greeting Cards ***See*** NAICS 323110: Commercial Lithographic Printing; NAICS 323111: Commercial Gravure Printing; NAICS 323112: Commercial Flexographic Printing; NAICS 323113: Commercial Screen Printing; NAICS 323119: Other Commercial Printing; NAICS 511191: Greeting Card Publishers
2782 Blankbooks, Loose-leaf Binders & Devices ***See*** NAICS 323110: Commercial Lithographic Printing; NAICS 323111: Commercial Gravure

Printing; NAICS 323112: Commercial Flexographic Printing; NAICS 323113: Commercial Screen Printing; NAICS 323119: Other Commercial Printing; NAICS 323118: Blankbook, Loose-leaf Binder & Device Manufacturing
2789 Bookbinding & Related Work ***See*** NAICS 323121: Tradebinding & Related Work
2791 Typesetting ***See*** NAICS 323122: Prepress Services
2796 Platemaking & Related Services ***See*** NAICS 323122: Prepress Services

Chemicals & Allied Products

2812 Alkalies & Chlorine ***See*** NAICS 325181: Alkalies & Chlorine Manufacturing
2813 Industrial Gases ***See*** NAICS 32512: Industrial Gas Manufacturing
2816 Inorganic Pigments ***See*** NAICS 325131: Inorganic Dye & Pigment Manufacturing; NAICS 325182: Carbon Black Manufacturing
2819 Industrial Inorganic Chemicals, NEC ***See*** NAICS 325998: All Other Miscellaneous Chemical Product Manufacturing; NAICS 331311: Alumina Refining; NAICS 325131: Inorganic Dye & Pigment Manufacturing; NAICS 325188: All Other Basic Inorganic Chemical Manufacturing
2821 Plastics Material Synthetic Resins, & Nonvulcanizable Elastomers ***See*** NAICS 325211: Plastics Material & Resin Manufacturing
2822 Synthetic Rubber ***See*** NAICS 325212: Synthetic Rubber Manufacturing
2823 Cellulosic Manmade Fibers ***See*** NAICS 325221: Cellulosic Manmade Fiber Manufacturing
2824 Manmade Organic Fibers, Except Cellulosic ***See*** NAICS 325222: Noncellulosic Organic Fiber Manufacturing
2833 Medicinal Chemicals & Botanical Products ***See*** NAICS 325411: Medicinal & Botanical Manufacturing
2834 Pharmaceutical Preparations ***See*** NAICS 325412: Pharmaceutical Preparation Manufacturing
2835 In Vitro & in Vivo Diagnostic Substances ***See*** NAICS 325412: Pharmaceutical Preparation Manufacturing; NAICS 325413: In-vitro Diagnostic Substance Manufacturing
2836 Biological Products, Except Diagnostic Substances ***See*** NAICS 325414: Biological Product Manufacturing
2841 Soaps & Other Detergents, Except Speciality Cleaners ***See*** NAICS 325611: Soap & Other Detergent Manufacturing
2842 Speciality Cleaning, Polishing, & Sanitary Preparations ***See*** NAICS 325612: Polish & Other Sanitation Good Manufacturing
2843 Surface Active Agents, Finishing Agents, Sulfonated Oils, & Assistants ***See*** NAICS 325613: Surface Active Agent Manufacturing
2844 Perfumes, Cosmetics, & Other Toilet Preparations ***See*** NAICS 32562: Toilet Preparation Manufacturing; NAICS 325611: Soap & Other Detergent Manufacturing
2851 Paints, Varnishes, Lacquers, Enamels, & Allied Products ***See*** NAICS 32551: Paint & Coating Manufacturing
2861 Gum & Wood Chemicals ***See*** NAICS 325191: Gum & Wood Chemical Manufacturing
2865 Cyclic Organic Crudes & Intermediates, & Organic Dyes & Pigments ***See*** NAICS 32511: Petrochemical Manufacturing; NAICS 325132: Organic Dye & Pigment Manufacturing; NAICS 325192: Cyclic Crude & Intermediate Manufacturing
2869 Industrial Organic Chemicals, NEC ***See*** NAICS 32511: Petrochemical Manufacturing; NAICS 325188: All Other Inorganic Chemical Manufacturing; NAICS 325193: Ethyl Alcohol Manufacturing; NAICS 32512: Industrial Gas Manufacturing; NAICS 325199: All Other Basic Organic Chemical Manufacturing
2873 Nitrogenous Fertilizers ***See*** NAICS 325311: Nitrogenous Fertilizer Manufacturing
2874 Phosphatic Fertilizers ***See*** NAICS 325312: Phosphatic Fertilizer Manufacturing
2875 Fertilizers, Mixing Only ***See*** NAICS 325314: Fertilizer Manufacturing
2879 Pesticides & Agricultural Chemicals, NEC ***See*** NAICS 32532: Pesticide & Other Agricultural Chemical Manufacturing
2891 Adhesives & Sealants ***See*** NAICS 32552: Adhesive & Sealant Manufacturing
2892 Explosives ***See*** NAICS 32592: Explosives Manufacturing
2893 Printing Ink ***See*** NAICS 32591: Printing Ink Manufacturing
2895 Carbon Black ***See*** NAICS 325182: Carbon Black Manufacturing
2899 Chemicals & Chemical Preparations, NEC ***See*** NAICS 32551: Paint & Coating Manufacturing; NAICS 311942: Spice & Extract Manufacturing; NAICS 325199: All Other Basic Organic Chemical Manufacturing; NAICS 325998: All OtherMiscellaneous Chemical Product Manufacturing

Petroleum Refining & Related Industries

2911 Petroleum Refining ***See*** NAICS 32411: Petroleum Refineries
2951 Asphalt Paving Mixtures & Blocks ***See*** NAICS 324121: Asphalt Paving Mixture & Block Manufacturing
2952 Asphalt Felts & Coatings ***See*** NAICS 324122: Asphalt Shingle & Coating Materials Manufacturing
2992 Lubricating Oils & Greases ***See*** NAICS 324191: Petroleum Lubricating Oil & Grease Manufacturing
2999 Products of Petroleum and Coal, NEC ***See*** NAICS 324199:All Other Petroleum and Coal Products Manufacturing

Rubber & Miscellaneous Plastics Products

3011 Tires & Inner Tubes ***See*** NAICS 326211: Tire Manufacturing
3021 Rubber & Plastics Footwear ***See*** NAICS 316211: Rubber & Plastics Footwear Manufacturing
3052 Rubber & Plastics Hose & Belting ***See*** NAICS 32622: Rubber & Plastics Hoses & Belting Manufacturing
3053 Gaskets, Packing, & Sealing Devices ***See*** NAICS 339991: Gasket, Packing, & Sealing Device Manufacturing
3061 Molded, Extruded, & Lathe-cut Mechanical Rubber Products ***See*** NAICS 326291: Rubber Product Manufacturing for Mechanical Use
3069 Fabricated Rubber Products, NEC ***See*** NAICS 31332: Fabric Coating Mills; NAICS 326192: Resilient Floor Covering Manufacturing; NAICS 326299: All Other Rubber Product Manufacturing
3081 Unsupported Plastics Film & Sheet ***See*** NAICS 326113: Unsupported Plastics Film & Sheet Manufacturing
3082 Unsupported Plastics Profile Shapes ***See*** NAICS 326121: Unsupported Plastics Profile Shape Manufacturing
3083 Laminated Plastics Plate, Sheet, & Profile Shapes ***See*** NAICS 32613: Laminated Plastics Plate, Sheet, & Shape Manufacturing
3084 Plastic Pipe ***See*** NAICS 326122: Plastic Pipe & Pipe Fitting Manufacturing
3085 Plastics Bottles ***See*** NAICS 32616: Plastics Bottle Manufacturing
3086 Plastics Foam Products ***See*** NAICS 32615: Urethane & Other Foam Product Manufacturing; NAICS 32614: Polystyrene Foam Product Manufacturing
3087 Custom Compounding of Purchased Plastics Resins ***See*** NAICS 325991: Custom Compounding of Purchased Resin
3088 Plastics Plumbing Fixtures ***See*** NAICS 326191: Plastics Plumbing Fixtures Manufacturing

3089 Plastics Products, NEC *See* NAICS 326122: Plastics Pipe & Pipe Fitting Manufacturing; NAICS 326121: Unsupported Plastics Profile Shape Manufacturing; NAICS 326199: All Other Plastics Product Manufacturing

Leather & Leather Products

3111 Leather Tanning & Finishing *See* NAICS 31611: Leather & Hide Tanning & Finishing
3131 Boot & Shoe Cut Stock & Findings *See* NAICS 321999: All Other Miscellaneous Wood Product Manufacturing; NAICS 339993: Fastener, Button, Needle, & Pin Manufacturing; NAICS 316999: All Other Leather Good Manufacturing
3142 House Slippers *See* NAICS 316212: House Slipper Manufacturing
3143 Men's Footwear, Except Athletic *See* NAICS 316213: Men's Footwear Manufacturing
3144 Women's Footwear, Except Athletic *See* NAICS 316214: Women's Footwear Manufacturing
3149 Footwear, Except Rubber, NEC *See* NAICS 316219: Other Footwear Manufacturing
3151 Leather Gloves & Mittens *See* NAICS 315992: Glove & Mitten Manufacturing
3161 Luggage *See* NAICS 316991: Luggage Manufacturing
3171 Women's Handbags & Purses *See* NAICS 316992: Women's Handbag & Purse Manufacturing
3172 Personal Leather Goods, Except Women's Handbags & Purses *See* NAICS 316993: Personal Leather Good Manufacturing
3199 Leather Goods, NEC *See* NAICS 316999: All Other Leather Good Manufacturing

Stone, Clay, Glass, & Concrete Products

3211 Flat Glass *See* NAICS 327211: Flat Glass Manufacturing
3221 Glass Containers *See* NAICS 327213: Glass Container Manufacturing
3229 Pressed & Blown Glass & Glassware, NEC *See* NAICS 327212: Other Pressed & Blown Glass & Glassware Manufacturing
3231 Glass Products, Made of Purchased Glass *See* NAICS 327215: Glass Product Manufacturing Made of Purchased Glass
3241 Cement, Hydraulic *See* NAICS 32731: Hydraulic Cement Manufacturing
3251 Brick & Structural Clay Tile *See* NAICS 327121: Brick & Structural Clay Tile Manufacturing
3253 Ceramic Wall & Floor Tile *See* NAICS 327122: Ceramic Wall & Floor Tile Manufacturing
3255 Clay Refractories *See* NAICS 327124: Clay Refractory Manufacturing
3259 Structural Clay Products, NEC *See* NAICS 327123: Other Structural Clay Product Manufacturing
3261 Vitreous China Plumbing Fixtures & China & Earthenware Fittings & Bathroom Accessories *See* NAICS 327111: Vitreous China Plumbing Fixture & China & Earthenware Fittings & Bathroom Accessories Manufacturing
3262 Vitreous China Table & Kitchen Articles *See* NAICS 327112: Vitreous China, Fine Earthenware & Other Pottery Product Manufacturing
3263 Fine Earthenware Table & Kitchen Articles *See* NAICS 327112: Vitreous China, Fine Earthenware & Other Pottery Product Manufacturing
3264 Porcelain Electrical Supplies *See* NAICS 327113: Porcelain Electrical Supply Manufacturing
3269 Pottery Products, NEC *See* NAICS 327112: Vitreous China, Fine Earthenware, & Other Pottery Product Manufacturing
3271 Concrete Block & Brick *See* NAICS 327331: Concrete Block & Brick Manufacturing
3272 Concrete Products, Except Block & Brick *See* NAICS 327999: All Other Miscellaneous Nonmetallic Mineral Product Manufacturing; NAICS 327332: Concrete Pipe Manufacturing; NAICS 32739: Other Concrete Product Manufacturing
3273 Ready-mixed Concrete *See* NAICS 32732: Ready-mix Concrete Manufacturing
3274 Lime *See* NAICS 32741: Lime Manufacturing
3275 Gypsum Products *See* NAICS 32742: Gypsum & Gypsum Product Manufacturing
3281 Cut Stone & Stone Products *See* NAICS 327991: Cut Stone & Stone Product Manufacturing
3291 Abrasive Products *See* NAICS 332999: All Other Miscellaneous Fabricated Metal Product Manufacturing; NAICS 32791: Abrasive Product Manufacturing
3292 Asbestos Products *See* NAICS 33634: Motor Vehicle Brake System Manufacturing; NAICS 327999: All Other Miscellaneous Nonmetallic Mineral Product Manufacturing
3295 Minerals & Earths, Ground or Otherwise Treated *See* NAICS 327992: Ground or Treated Mineral & Earth Manufacturing
3296 Mineral Wool *See* NAICS 327993: Mineral Wool Manufacturing
3297 Nonclay Refractories *See* NAICS 327125: Nonclay Refractory Manufacturing
3299 Nonmetallic Mineral Products, NEC *See* NAICS 32742: Gypsum & Gypsum Product Manufacturing; NAICS 327999: All Other Miscellaneous Nonmetallic Mineral Product Manufacturing

Primary Metals Industries

3312 Steel Works, Blast Furnaces , & Rolling Mills *See* NAICS 324199: All Other Petroleum & Coal Products Manufacturing; NAICS 331111: Iron & Steel Mills
3313 Electrometallurgical Products, Except Steel *See* NAICS 331112: Electrometallurgical Ferroalloy Product Manufacturing; NAICS 331492: Secondary Smelting, Refining, & Alloying of Nonferrous Metals
3315 Steel Wiredrawing & Steel Nails & Spikes *See* NAICS 331222: Steel Wire Drawing; NAICS 332618: Other Fabricated Wire Product Manufacturing
3316 Cold-rolled Steel Sheet, Strip, & Bars *See* NAICS 331221: Cold- rolled Steel Shape Manufacturing
3317 Steel Pipe & Tubes *See* NAICS 33121: Iron & Steel Pipes & Tubes Manufacturing from Purchased Steel
3321 Gray & Ductile Iron Foundries *See* NAICS 331511: Iron Foundries
3322 Malleable Iron Foundries *See* NAICS 331511: Iron Foundries
3324 Steel Investment Foundries *See* NAICS 331512: Steel Investment Foundries
3325 Steel Foundries, NEC *See* NAICS 331513: Steel Foundries
3331 Primary Smelting & Refining of Copper *See* NAICS 331411: Primary Smelting & Refining of Copper
3334 Primary Production of Aluminum *See* NAICS 331312: Primary Aluminum Production
3339 Primary Smelting & Refining of Nonferrous Metals, Except Copper & Aluminum *See* NAICS 331419: Primary Smelting & Refining of Nonferrous Metals
3341 Secondary Smelting & Refining of Nonferrous Metals *See* NAICS 331314: Secondary Smelting & Alloying of Aluminum; NAICS 331423:

Secondary Smelting, Refining, & Alloying of Copper; NAICS 331492: Secondary Smelting, Refining, & Alloying of Nonferrous Metals
3351 Rolling, Drawing, & Extruding of Copper ***See*** NAICS 331421: Copper Rolling, Drawing, & Extruding
3353 Aluminum Sheet, Plate, & Foil ***See*** NAICS 331315: Aluminum Sheet, Plate, & Foil Manufacturing
3354 Aluminum Extruded Products ***See*** NAICS 331316: Aluminum Extruded Product Manufacturing
3355 Aluminum Rolling & Drawing, NEC ***See*** NAICS 331319: Other Aluminum Rolling & Drawing
3356 Rolling, Drawing, & Extruding of Nonferrous Metals, Except Copper & Aluminum ***See*** NAICS 331491: Nonferrous MetalRolling. Drawing, & Extruding
3357 Drawing & Insulating of Nonferrous Wire ***See*** NAICS 331319: Other Aluminum Rolling & Drawing; NAICS 331422: Copper Wire Drawing; NAICS 331491: Nonferrous Metal Rolling, Drawing, & Extruding; NAICS 335921: Fiber Optic Cable Manufacturing; NAICS 335929: Other Communication & Energy Wire Manufacturing
3363 Aluminum Die-castings ***See*** NAICS 331521: Aluminum Die-castings
3364 Nonferrous Die-castings, Except Aluminum ***See*** NAICS 331522: Nonferrous Die-castings
3365 Aluminum Foundries ***See*** NAICS 331524: Aluminum Foundries
3366 Copper Foundries ***See*** NAICS 331525: Copper Foundries
3369 Nonferrous Foundries, Except Aluminum & Copper ***See*** NAICS 331528: Other Nonferrous Foundries
3398 Metal Heat Treating ***See*** NAICS 332811: Metal Heat Treating
3399 Primary Metal Products, NEC ***See*** NAICS 331111: Iron & Steel Mills; NAICS 331314: Secondary Smelting & Alloying of Aluminum; NAICS 331423: Secondary Smelting, Refining & Alloying of Copper; NAICS 331492: Secondary Smelting, Refining, & Alloying of Nonferrous Metals; NAICS 332618: Other Fabricated Wire Product Manufacturing; NAICS 332813: Electroplating, Plating, Polishing, Anodizing, & Coloring

Fabricated Metal Products, Except Machinery & Transportation Equipment

3411 Metal Cans ***See*** NAICS 332431: Metal Can Manufacturing
3412 Metal Shipping Barrels, Drums, Kegs & Pails ***See*** NAICS 332439: Other Metal Container Manufacturing
3421 Cutlery ***See*** NAICS 332211: Cutlery & Flatware Manufacturing
3423 Hand & Edge Tools, Except Machine Tools & Handsaws ***See*** NAICS 332212: Hand & Edge Tool Manufacturing
3425 Saw Blades & Handsaws ***See*** NAICS 332213: Saw Blade & Handsaw Manufacturing
3429 Hardware, NEC ***See*** NAICS 332439: Other Metal Container Manufacturing; NAICS 332919: Other Metal Valve & Pipe Fitting Manufacturing; NAICS 33251: Hardware Manufacturing
3431 Enameled Iron & Metal Sanitary Ware ***See*** NAICS 332998: Enameled Iron & Metal Sanitary Ware Manufacturing
3432 Plumbing Fixture Fittings & Trim ***See*** NAICS 332913: Plumbing Fixture Fitting & Trim Manufacturing; NAICS 332999: All Other Miscellaneous Fabricated Metal Product Manufacturing
3433 Heating Equipment, Except Electric & Warm Air Furnaces ***See*** NAICS 333414: Heating Equipment Manufacturing
3441 Fabricated Structural Metal ***See*** NAICS 332312: Fabricated Structural Metal Manufacturing
3442 Metal Doors, Sash, Frames, Molding, & Trim Manufacturing ***See*** NAICS 332321: Metal Window & Door Manufacturing
3443 Fabricated Plate Work ***See*** NAICS 332313: Plate Work Manufacturing; NAICS 33241: Power Boiler & Heat Exchanger Manufacturing; NAICS 33242: Metal Tank Manufacturing; NAICS 333415: Air-conditioning & Warm Air Heating Equipment & Commercial & Industrial Refrigeration Equipment Manufacturing
3444 Sheet Metal Work ***See*** NAICS 332322: Sheet Metal Work Manufacturing; NAICS 332439: Other Metal Container Manufacturing
3446 Architectural & Ornamental Metal Work ***See*** NAICS 332323: Ornamental & Architectural Metal Work Manufacturing
3448 Prefabricated Metal Buildings & Components ***See*** NAICS 332311: Prefabricated Metal Building & Component Manufacturing
3449 Miscellaneous Structural Metal Work ***See*** NAICS 332114: Custom Roll Forming; NAICS 332312: Fabricated Structural Metal Manufacturing; NAICS 332321: Metal Window & Door Manufacturing; NAICS 332323: Ornamental & Architectural Metal Work Manufacturing
3451 Screw Machine Products ***See*** NAICS 332721: Precision Turned Product Manufacturing
3452 Bolts, Nuts, Screws, Rivets, & Washers ***See*** NAICS 332722: Bolt, Nut, Screw, Rivet, & Washer Manufacturing
3462 Iron & Steel Forgings ***See*** NAICS 332111: Iron & Steel Forging
3463 Nonferrous Forgings ***See*** NAICS 332112: Nonferrous Forging
3465 Automotive Stamping ***See*** NAICS 33637: Motor Vehicle Metal Stamping
3466 Crowns & Closures ***See*** NAICS 332115: Crown & Closure Manufacturing
3469 Metal Stamping, NEC ***See*** NAICS 339911: Jewelry Manufacturing; NAICS 332116: Metal Stamping; NAICS 332214: Kitchen Utensil, Pot & Pan Manufacturing
3471 Electroplating, Plating, Polishing, Anodizing, & Coloring ***See*** NAICS 332813: Electroplating, Plating, Polishing, Anodizing, & Coloring
3479 Coating, Engraving, & Allied Services, NEC ***See*** NAICS 339914: Costume Jewelry & Novelty Manufacturing; NAICS 339911: Jewelry Manufacturing; NAICS 339912: Silverware & Plated Ware Manufacturing; NAICS 332812: Metal Coating, Engraving, & Allied Services to Manufacturers
3482 Small Arms Ammunition ***See*** NAICS 332992: Small Arms Ammunition Manufacturing
3483 Ammunition, Except for Small Arms ***See*** NAICS 332993: Ammunition Manufacturing
3484 Small Arms ***See*** NAICS 332994: Small Arms Manufacturing
3489 Ordnance & Accessories, NEC ***See*** NAICS 332995: Other Ordnance & Accessories Manufacturing
3491 Industrial Valves ***See*** NAICS 332911 Industrial Valve Manufacturing
3492 Fluid Power Valves & Hose Fittings ***See*** NAICS 332912: Fluid Power Valve & Hose Fitting Manufacturing
3493 Steel Springs, Except Wire ***See*** NAICS 332611: Steel Spring Manufacturing
3494 Valves & Pipe Fittings, NEC ***See*** NAICS 332919: Other Metal Valve & Pipe Fitting Manufacturing; NAICS 332999: All Other Miscellaneous Fabricated Metal Product Manufacturing
3495 Wire Springs ***See*** NAICS 332612: Wire Spring Manufacturing; NAICS 334518: Watch, Clock, & Part Manufacturing
3496 Miscellaneous Fabricated Wire Products ***See*** NAICS 332618: Other Fabricated Wire Product Manufacturing
3497 Metal Foil & Leaf ***See*** NAICS 322225: Laminated Aluminum Foil Manufacturing for Flexible Packaging Uses; NAICS 332999: All Other Miscellaneous Fabricated Metal Product Manufacturing
3498 Fabricated Pipe & Pipe Fittings ***See*** NAICS 332996: Fabricated Pipe & Pipe Fitting Manufacturing
3499 Fabricated Metal Products, NEC ***See*** NAICS 337148: Other Nonwood Furniture Manufacturing; NAICS 332117: Powder Metallurgy Part

Manufacturing; NAICS 332439: Other Metal Container Manufacturing; NAICS 33251: Hardware Manufacturing; NAICS 332919: Other Metal Valve & Pipe Fitting Manufacturing; NAICS 339914: Costume Jewelry & Novelty Manufacturing; NAICS 332999: All Other Miscellaneous Fabricated Metal Product Manufacturing

Industrial & Commercial Machinery & Computer Equipment

3511 Steam, Gas, & Hydraulic Turbines, & Turbine Generator Set Units ***See*** NAICS 333611: Turbine & Turbine Generator Set Unit Manufacturing
3519 Internal Combustion Engines, NEC ***See*** NAICS 336399: All Other Motor Vehicle Parts Manufacturing; NAICS 333618: Other Engine Equipment Manufacturing
3523 Farm Machinery & Equipment ***See*** NAICS 333111: Farm Machinery & Equipment Manufacturing; NAICS 332323: Ornamental & Architectural Metal Work Manufacturing; NAICS 332212: Hand & Edge Tool Manufacturing; NAICS 333922: Conveyor & Conveying Equipment Manufacturing
3524 Lawn & Garden Tractors & Home Lawn & Garden Equipment ***See*** NAICS 333112: Lawn & Garden Tractor & Home Lawn & Garden Equipment Manufacturing; NAICS 332212: Hand & Edge Tool Manufacturing
3531 Construction Machinery & Equipment ***See*** NAICS 33651: Railroad Rolling Stock Manufacturing; NAICS 333923: Overhead Traveling Crane, Hoist, & Monorail System Manufacturing; NAICS 33312: Construction Machinery Manufacturing
3532 Mining Machinery & Equipment, Except Oil & Gas Field Machinery & Equipment ***See*** NAICS 333131: Mining Machinery & Equipment Manufacturing
3533 Oil & Gas Field Machinery & Equipment ***See*** NAICS 333132: Oil & Gas Field Machinery & Equipment Manufacturing
3534 Elevators & Moving Stairways ***See*** NAICS 333921: Elevator & Moving Stairway Manufacturing
3535 Conveyors & Conveying Equipment ***See*** NAICS 333922: Conveyor & Conveying Equipment Manufacturing
3536 Overhead Traveling Cranes, Hoists & Monorail Systems ***See*** NAICS 333923: Overhead Traveling Crane, Hoist & Monorail System Manufacturing
3537 Industrial Trucks, Tractors, Trailers, & Stackers ***See*** NAICS 333924: Industrial Truck, Tractor, Trailer, & Stacker Machinery Manufacturing; NAICS 332999: All Other Miscellaneous Fabricated Metal Product Manufacturing; NAICS 332439: Other Metal Container Manufacturing
3541 Machine Tools, Metal Cutting Type ***See*** NAICS 333512: Machine Tool Manufacturing
3542 Machine Tools, Metal Forming Type ***See*** NAICS 333513: Machine Tool Manufacturing
3543 Industrial Patterns ***See*** NAICS 332997: Industrial Pattern Manufacturing
3544 Special Dies & Tools, Die Sets, Jigs & Fixtures, & Industrial Molds ***See*** NAICS 333514: Special Die & Tool, Die Set, Jig, & Fixture Manufacturing; NAICS 333511: Industrial Mold Manufacturing
3545 Cutting Tools, Machine Tool Accessories, & Machinists' Precision Measuring Devices ***See*** NAICS 333515: Cutting Tool & Machine Tool Accessory Manufacturing; NAICS 332212: Hand & Edge Tool Manufacturing
3546 Power-driven Handtools ***See*** NAICS 333991: Power-driven Hand Tool Manufacturing
3547 Rolling Mill Machinery & Equipment ***See*** NAICS 333516: Rolling Mill Machinery & Equipment Manufacturing
3548 Electric & Gas Welding & Soldering Equipment ***See*** NAICS 333992: Welding & Soldering Equipment Manufacturing; NAICS 335311: Power, Distribution, & Specialty Transformer Manufacturing
3549 Metalworking Machinery, NEC ***See*** NAICS 333518: Other Metalworking Machinery Manufacturing
3552 Textile Machinery ***See*** NAICS 333292 Textile Machinery Manufacturing
3553 Woodworking Machinery ***See*** NAICS 33321: Sawmill & Woodworking Machinery Manufacturing
3554 Paper Industries Machinery ***See*** NAICS 333291: Paper Industry Machinery Manufacturing
3555 Printing Trades Machinery & Equipment ***See*** NAICS 333293: Printing Machinery & Equipment Manufacturing
3556 Food Products Machinery ***See*** NAICS 333294: Food Product Machinery Manufacturing
3559 Special Industry Machinery, NEC ***See*** NAICS 33322: Rubber & Plastics Industry Machinery Manufacturing; NAICS 333319: Other Commercial & Service Industry Machinery Manufacturing; NAICS 333295: Semiconductor Manufacturing Machinery; NAICS 333298: All Other Industrial Machinery Manufacturing
3561 Pumps & Pumping Equipment ***See*** NAICS 333911: Pump & Pumping Equipment Manufacturing
3562 Ball & Roller Bearings ***See*** NAICS 332991: Ball & Roller Bearing Manufacturing
3563 Air & Gas Compressors ***See*** NAICS 333912: Air & Gas Compressor Manufacturing
3564 Industrial & Commercial Fans & Blowers & Air Purification Equipment ***See*** NAICS 333411: Air Purification Equipment Manufacturing; NAICS 333412: Industrial & Commercial Fan & Blower Manufacturing
3565 Packaging Machinery ***See*** NAICS 333993: Packaging Machinery Manufacturing
3566 Speed Changers, Industrial High-speed Drives, & Gears ***See*** NAICS 333612: Speed Changer, Industrial High-speed Drive, & Gear Manufacturing
3567 Industrial Process Furnaces & Ovens ***See*** NAICS 333994: Industrial Process Furnace & Oven Manufacturing
3568 Mechanical Power Transmission Equipment, NEC ***See*** NAICS 333613: Mechanical Power Transmission Equipment Manufacturing
3569 General Industrial Machinery & Equipment, NEC ***See*** NAICS 333999: All Other General Purpose Machinery Manufacturing
3571 Electronic Computers ***See*** NAICS 334111: Electronic Computer Manufacturing
3572 Computer Storage Devices ***See*** NAICS 334112: Computer Storage Device Manufacturing
3575 Computer Terminals ***See*** NAICS 334113: Computer Terminal Manufacturing
3577 Computer Peripheral Equipment, NEC ***See*** NAICS 334119: Other Computer Peripheral Equipment Manufacturing
3578 Calculating & Accounting Machines, Except Electronic Computers ***See*** NAICS 334119: Other Computer Peripheral Equipment Manufacturing; NAICS 333313: Office Machinery Manufacturing
3579 Office Machines, NEC ***See*** NAICS 339942: Lead Pencil & Art Good Manufacturing; NAICS 334518: Watch, Clock, & Part Manufacturing; NAICS 333313: Office Machinery Manufacturing
3581 Automatic Vending Machines ***See*** NAICS 333311: Automatic Vending Machine Manufacturing
3582 Commercial Laundry, Drycleaning, & Pressing Machines ***See*** NAICS 333312: Commercial Laundry, Drycleaning, & Pressing Machine Manufacturing
3585 Air-conditioning & Warm Air Heating Equipment & Commercial & Industrial Refrigeration Equipment ***See*** NAICS 336391: Motor Vehicle Air Conditioning Manufacturing; NAICS 333415: Air Conditioning & Warm Air Heating Equipment & Commercial & Industrial Refrigeration Equipment Manufacturing
3586 Measuring & Dispensing Pumps ***See*** NAICS 333913: Measuring & Dispensing Pump Manufacturing
3589 Service Industry Machinery ***See*** NAICS 333319: Other Commercial and Service Industry Machinery

3592 Carburetors, Pistons, Piston Rings & Valves ***See*** NAICS 336311: Carburetor, Piston, Piston Ring & Valve Manufacturing
3593 Fluid Power Cylinders & Actuators ***See*** NAICS 333995: Fluid Power Cylinder & Actuator Manufacturing
3594 Fluid Power Pumps & Motors ***See*** NAICS 333996: Fluid Power Pump & Motor Manufacturing
3596 Scales & Balances, Except Laboratory ***See*** NAICS 333997: Scale & Balance Manufacturing
3599 Industrial & Commercial Machinery & Equipment, NEC ***See*** NAICS 336399: All Other Motor Vehicle Part Manufacturing; NAICS 332999: All Other Miscellaneous Fabricated Metal Product Manufacturing; NAICS 333319: Other Commercial & Service Industry Machinery Manufacturing; NAICS 33271: Machine Shops; NAICS 333999: All Other General Purpose Machinery Manufacturing

Electronic & Other Electrical Equipment & Components, Except Computer Equipment

3612 Power, Distribution, & Specialty Transformers ***See*** NAICS 335311: Power, Distribution, & Specialty Transformer Manufacturing
3613 Switchgear & Switchboard Apparatus ***See*** NAICS 335313: Switchgear & Switchboard Apparatus Manufacturing
3621 Motors & Generators ***See*** NAICS 335312: Motor & Generator Manufacturing
3624 Carbon & Graphite Products ***See*** NAICS 335991: Carbon & Graphite Product Manufacturing
3625 Relays & Industrial Controls ***See*** NAICS 335314: Relay & Industrial Control Manufacturing
3629 Electrical Industrial Apparatus, NEC ***See*** NAICS 335999: All Other Miscellaneous Electrical Equipment & Component Manufacturing
3631 Household Cooking Equipment ***See*** NAICS 335221: Household Cooking Appliance Manufacturing
3632 Household Refrigerators & Home & Farm Freezers ***See*** NAICS 335222: Household Refrigerator & Home Freezer Manufacturing
3633 Household Laundry Equipment ***See*** NAICS 335224: Household Laundry Equipment Manufacturing
3634 Electric Housewares & Fans ***See*** NAICS 335211: Electric Housewares & Fan Manufacturing
3635 Household Vacuum Cleaners ***See*** NAICS 335212: Household Vacuum Cleaner Manufacturing
3639 Household Appliances, NEC ***See*** NAICS 335212: Household Vacuum Cleaner Manufacturing; NAICS 333298: All Other Industrial Machinery Manufacturing; NAICS 335228: Other Household Appliance Manufacturing
3641 Electric Lamp Bulbs & Tubes ***See*** NAICS 33511: Electric Lamp Bulb & Part Manufacturing
3643 Current-carrying Wiring Devices ***See*** NAICS 335931: Current-carrying Wiring Device Manufacturing
3644 Noncurrent-carrying Wiring Devices ***See*** NAICS 335932: Noncurrent-carrying Wiring Device Manufacturing
3645 Residential Electric Lighting Fixtures ***See*** NAICS 335121: Residential Electric Lighting Fixture Manufacturing
3646 Commercial, Industrial, & Institutional Electric Lighting Fixtures ***See*** NAICS 335122: Commercial, Industrial, & Institutional Electric Lighting Fixture Manufacturing
3647 Vehicular Lighting Equipment ***See*** NAICS 336321: Vehicular Lighting Equipment Manufacturing
3648 Lighting Equipment, NEC ***See*** NAICS 335129: Other Lighting Equipment Manufacturing
3651 Household Audio & Video Equipment ***See*** NAICS 33431: Audio & Video Equipment Manufacturing 3652; NAICS 51222: Integrated Record Production/distribution
3661 Telephone & Telegraph Apparatus ***See*** NAICS 33421: Telephone Apparatus Manufacturing; NAICS 334416: Electronic Coil, Transformer, & Other Inductor Manufacturing; NAICS 334418: Printed Circuit/electronics Assembly Manufacturing
3663 Radio & Television Broadcasting & Communication Equipment ***See*** NAICS 33422: Radio & Television Broadcasting & Wireless Communications Equipment Manufacturing
3669 Communications Equipment, NEC ***See*** NAICS 33429: Other Communication Equipment Manufacturing
3671 Electron Tubes ***See*** NAICS 334411: Electron Tube Manufacturing
3672 Printed Circuit Boards ***See*** NAICS 334412: Printed Circuit Board Manufacturing
3674 Semiconductors & Related Devices ***See*** NAICS 334413: Semiconductor & Related Device Manufacturing
3675 Electronic Capacitors ***See*** NAICS 334414: Electronic Capacitor Manufacturing
3676 Electronic Resistors ***See*** NAICS 334415: Electronic Resistor Manufacturing
3677 Electronic Coils, Transformers, & Other Inductors ***See*** NAICS 334416: Electronic Coil, Transformer, & Other Inductor Manufacturing
3678 Electronic Connectors ***See*** NAICS 334417: Electronic Connector Manufacturing
3679 Electronic Components, NEC ***See*** NAICS 33422: Radio & Television Broadcasting & Wireless Communications Equipment Manufacturing; NAICS 334418: Printed Circuit/electronics Assembly Manufacturing; NAICS 336322: Other Motor Vehicle Electrical & Electronic Equipment Manufacturing; NAICS 334419: Other Electronic Component Manufacturing
3691 Storage Batteries ***See*** NAICS 335911: Storage Battery Manufacturing
3692 Primary Batteries, Dry & Wet ***See*** NAICS 335912: Dry & Wet Primary Battery Manufacturing
3694 Electrical Equipment for Internal Combustion Engines ***See*** NAICS 336322: Other Motor Vehicle Electrical & Electronic Equipment Manufacturing
3695 Magnetic & Optical Recording Media ***See*** NAICS 334613: Magnetic & Optical Recording Media Manufacturing
3699 Electrical Machinery, Equipment, & Supplies, NEC ***See*** NAICS 333319: Other Commercial & Service Industry Machinery Manufacturing; NAICS 333618: Other Engine Equipment Manufacturing; NAICS 334119: Other Computer Peripheral Equipment Manufacturing; Classify According to Function; NAICS 335129: Other Lighting Equipment Manufacturing; NAICS 335999: All Other Miscellaneous Electrical Equipment & Component Manufacturing

Transportation Equipment

3711 Motor Vehicles & Passenger Car Bodies ***See*** NAICS 336111: Automobile Manufacturing; NAICS 336112: Light Truck & Utility Vehicle Manufacturing; NAICS 33612: Heavy Duty Truck Manufacturing; NAICS 336211: Motor Vehicle Body Manufacturing; NAICS 336992: Military Armored Vehicle, Tank, & Tank Component Manufacturing
3713 Truck & Bus Bodies ***See*** NAICS 336211: Motor Vehicle Body Manufacturing
3714 Motor Vehicle Parts & Accessories ***See*** NAICS 336211: Motor Vehicle Body Manufacturing; NAICS 336312: Gasoline Engine & Engine Parts Manufacturing; NAICS 336322: Other Motor Vehicle Electrical & Electronic Equipment Manufacturing; NAICS 33633: Motor Vehicle Steering & Suspension Components Manufacturing; NAICS 33634: Motor Vehicle Brake System Manufacturing; NAICS 33635: Motor Vehicle Transmission & Power Train Parts Manufacturing; NAICS 336399: All Other Motor Vehicle Parts Manufacturing
3715 Truck Trailers ***See*** NAICS 336212: Truck Trailer Manufacturing
3716 Motor Homes ***See*** NAICS 336213: Motor Home Manufacturing
3721 Aircraft ***See*** NAICS 336411: Aircraft Manufacturing

3724 Aircraft Engines & Engine Parts ***See*** NAICS 336412: Aircraft Engine & Engine Parts Manufacturing 3728; NAICS 336413: Other Aircraft Part & Auxiliary Equipment Manufacturing
3731 Ship Building & Repairing ***See*** NAICS 336611: Ship Building & Repairing
3732 Boat Building & Repairing ***See*** NAICS 81149: Other Personal & Household Goods Repair & Maintenance; NAICS 336612: Boat Building
3743 Railroad Equipment ***See*** NAICS 333911: Pump & Pumping Equipment Manufacturing; NAICS 33651: Railroad Rolling Stock Manufacturing
3751 Motorcycles, Bicycles, & Parts ***See*** NAICS 336991: Motorcycle, Bicycle, & Parts Manufacturing
3761 Guided Missiles & Space Vehicles ***See*** NAICS 336414: Guided Missile & Space Vehicle Manufacturing
3764 Guided Missile and Space Vehicle Propulsion Units and Propulsion Unit Parts ***See*** NAICS 336415: Guided Missile and Space Vehicle Propulsion Unit and Propulsion Unit Parts Manufacturing; NAICS 54171: Research and Development in the Physical, Engineering, and Life Sciences
3769 Guided Missile Space Vehicle Parts & Auxiliary Equipment, NEC ***See*** NAICS 336419: Other Guided Missile & Space Vehicle Parts & Auxiliary Equipment Manufacturing
3792 Travel Trailers & Campers ***See*** NAICS 336214: Travel Trailer & Camper Manufacturing
3795 Tanks & Tank Components ***See*** NAICS 336992: Military Armored Vehicle, Tank, & Tank Component Manufacturing
3799 Transportation Equipment, NEC ***See*** NAICS 336214: Travel Trailer & Camper Manufacturing; NAICS 332212: Hand & Edge Tool Manufacturing; NAICS 336999: All Other Transportation Equipment Manufacturing

Measuring, Analyzing, & Controlling Instruments

3812 Search, Detection, Navigation, Guidance, Aeronautical, & Nautical Systems & Instruments ***See*** NAICS 334511: Search, Detection, Navigation, Guidance, Aeronautical, & Nautical System & Instrument Manufacturing
3821 Laboratory Apparatus & Furniture ***See*** NAICS 339111: Laboratory Apparatus & Furniture Manufacturing
3822 Automatic Controls for Regulating Residential & Commercial Environments & Appliances ***See*** NAICS 334512: Automatic Environmental Control Manufacturing for Regulating Residential, Commercial, & Appliance Use
3823 Industrial Instruments for Measurement, Display, & Control of Process Variables; & Related Products ***See*** NAICS 334513: Instruments & Related Product Manufacturing for Measuring Displaying, & Controlling Industrial Process Variables
3824 Totalizing Fluid Meters & Counting Devices ***See*** NAICS 334514: Totalizing Fluid Meter & Counting Device Manufacturing
3825 Instruments for Measuring & Testing of Electricity & Electrical Signals ***See*** NAICS 334416: Electronic Coil, Transformer, & Other Inductor Manufacturing; NAICS 334515: Instrument Manufacturing for Measuring & Testing Electricity & Electrical Signals
3826 Laboratory Analytical Instruments ***See*** NAICS 334516: Analytical Laboratory Instrument Manufacturing
3827 Optical Instruments & Lenses ***See*** NAICS 333314: Optical Instrument & Lens Manufacturing
3829 Measuring & Controlling Devices, NEC ***See*** NAICS 339112: Surgical & Medical Instrument Manufacturing; NAICS 334519: Other Measuring & Controlling Device Manufacturing
3841 Surgical & Medical Instruments & Apparatus ***See*** NAICS 339112: Surgical & Medical Instrument Manufacturing
3842 Orthopedic, Prosthetic, & Surgical Appliances & Supplies ***See*** NAICS 339113: Surgical Appliance & Supplies Manufacturing; NAICS 334510: Electromedical & Electrotherapeutic Apparatus Manufacturing
3843 Dental Equipment & Supplies ***See*** NAICS 339114: Dental Equipment & Supplies Manufacturing
3844 X-ray Apparatus & Tubes & Related Irradiation Apparatus ***See*** NAICS 334517: Irradiation Apparatus Manufacturing
3845 Electromedical & Electrotherapeutic Apparatus ***See*** NAICS 334517: Irradiation Apparatus Manufacturing; NAICS 334510: Electromedical & Electrotherapeutic Apparatus Manufacturing
3851 Ophthalmic Goods ***See*** NAICS 339115: Ophthalmic Goods Manufacturing
3861 Photographic Equipment & Supplies ***See*** NAICS 333315: Photographic & Photocopying Equipment Manufacturing; NAICS 325992: Photographic Film, Paper, Plate & Chemical Manufacturing
3873 Watches, Clocks, Clockwork Operated Devices & Parts ***See*** NAICS 334518: Watch, Clock, & Part Manufacturing

Miscellaneous Manufacturing Industries

3911 Jewelry, Precious Metal ***See*** NAICS 339911: Jewelry Manufacturing
3914 Silverware, Plated Ware, & Stainless Steel Ware ***See*** NAICS 332211: Cutlery & Flatware Manufacturing; NAICS 339912: Silverware & Plated Ware Manufacturing
3915 Jewelers' Findings & Materials, & Lapidary Work ***See*** NAICS 339913: Jewelers' Material & Lapidary Work Manufacturing
3931 Musical Instruments ***See*** NAICS 339992: Musical Instrument Manufacturing
3942 Dolls & Stuffed Toys ***See*** NAICS 339931: Doll & Stuffed Toy Manufacturing
3944 Games, Toys, & Children's Vehicles, Except Dolls & Bicycles ***See*** NAICS 336991: Motorcycle, Bicycle & Parts Manufacturing; NAICS 339932: Game, Toy, & Children's Vehicle Manufacturing
3949 Sporting & Athletic Goods, NEC ***See*** NAICS 33992: Sporting & Athletic Good Manufacturing
3951 Pens, Mechanical Pencils & Parts ***See*** NAICS 339941: Pen & Mechanical Pencil Manufacturing
3952 Lead Pencils, Crayons, & Artist's Materials ***See*** NAICS 337139: Other Wood Furniture Manufacturing; NAICS 337139: Other Wood Furniture Manufacturing; NAICS 325998: All Other Miscellaneous Chemical Manufacturing; NAICS 339942: Lead Pencil & Art Good Manufacturing
3953 Marking Devices ***See*** NAICS 339943: Marking Device Manufacturing
3955 Carbon Paper & Inked Ribbons ***See*** NAICS 339944: Carbon Paper & Inked Ribbon Manufacturing
3961 Costume Jewelry & Costume Novelties, Except Precious Metals ***See*** NAICS 339914: Costume Jewelry & Novelty Manufacturing
3965 Fasteners, Buttons, Needles, & Pins ***See*** NAICS 339993: Fastener, Button, Needle & Pin Manufacturing
3991 Brooms & Brushes ***See*** NAICS 339994: Broom, Brush & Mop Manufacturing
3993 Signs & Advertising Specialties ***See*** NAICS 33995: Sign Manufacturing
3995 Burial Caskets ***See*** NAICS 339995: Burial Casket Manufacturing
3996 Linoleum, Asphalted-felt-base, & Other Hard Surface Floor Coverings, NEC ***See*** NAICS 326192: Resilient Floor Covering Manufacturing
3999 Manufacturing Industries, NEC ***See*** NAICS 337148: Other Nonwood Furniture Manufacturing; NAICS 321999: All Other Miscellaneous Wood Product Manufacturing; NAICS 31611: Leather & Hide Tanning & Finishing; NAICS 335121: Residential Electric Lighting Fixture Manufacturing; NAICS 325998: All Other Miscellaneous Chemical Product Manufacturing; NAICS 332999: All Other Miscellaneous Fabricated Metal Product Manufacturing; NAICS 326199: All Other Plastics Product Manufacturing; NAICS 323112: Commercial Flexographic Printing; NAICS 323111: Commercial Gravure Printing; NAICS 323110: Commercial Lithographic Printing; NAICS 323113: Commercial Screen Printing;

NAICS 323119: Other Commercial Printing; NAICS 332212: Hand & Edge Tool Manufacturing; NAICS 339999: All Other Miscellaneous Manufacturing

Transportation, Communications, Electric, Gas, & Sanitary Services

4011 Railroads, Line-haul Operating ***See*** NAICS 482111: Line-haul Railroads

4013 Railroad Switching & Terminal Establishments ***See*** NAICS 482112: Short Line Railroads; NAICS 48821: Support Activities for Rail Transportation

4111 Local & Suburban Transit ***See*** NAICS 485111: Mixed Mode Transit Systems; NAICS 485112: Commuter Rail Systems; NAICS 485113: Bus & Motor Vehicle Transit Systems; NAICS 485119: Other Urban Transit Systems; NAICS 485999: All Other Transit & Ground Passenger Transportation

4119 Local Passenger Transportation, NEC ***See*** NAICS 62191: Ambulance Service; NAICS 48541: School & Employee Bus Transportation; NAICS 48711: Scenic & Sightseeing Transportation , Land; NAICS 485991: Special Needs Transportation; NAICS 485999: All Other Transit & Ground Passenger Transportation; NAICS 48532: Limousine Service

4121 Taxicabs ***See*** NAICS 48531: Taxi Service

4131 Intercity & Rural Bus Transportation ***See*** NAICS 48521: Interurban & Rural Bus Transportation

4141 Local Bus Charter Service ***See*** NAICS 48551: Charter Bus Industry

4142 Bus Charter Service, Except Local ***See*** NAICS 48551: Charter Bus Industry

4151 School Buses ***See*** NAICS 48541: School & Employee Bus Transportation

4173 Terminal & Service Facilities for Motor Vehicle Passenger Transportation ***See*** NAICS 48849: Other Support Activities for Road Transportation

4212 Local Trucking Without Storage ***See*** NAICS 562111: Solid Waste Collection; NAICS 562112: Hazardous Waste Collection; NAICS 562119: Other Waste Collection; NAICS 48411: General Freight Trucking, Local; NAICS 48421: Used Household & Office Goods Moving; NAICS 48422: Specialized Freight Trucking, Local

4213 Trucking, Except Local ***See*** NAICS 484121: General Freight Trucking, Long-distance, Truckload; NAICS 484122: General Freight Trucking, Long-distance, less than Truckload; NAICS 48421: Used Household & Office Goods Moving; NAICS 48423: Specialized Freight Trucking, Long-distance

4214 Local Trucking with Storage ***See*** NAICS 48411: General Freight Trucking, Local; NAICS 48421: Used Household & Office Goods Moving; NAICS 48422: Specialized Freight Trucking, Local

4215 Couriers Services Except by Air ***See*** NAICS 49211: Couriers; NAICS 49221: Local Messengers & Local Delivery

4221 Farm Product Warehousing & Storage ***See*** NAICS 49313: Farm Product Storage Facilities

4222 Refrigerated Warehousing & Storage ***See*** NAICS 49312: Refrigerated Storage Facilities

4225 General Warehousing & Storage ***See*** NAICS 49311: General Warehousing & Storage Facilities; NAICS 53113: Lessors of Miniwarehouses & Self Storage Units

4226 Special Warehousing & Storage, NEC ***See*** NAICS 49312: Refrigerated Warehousing & Storage Facilities; NAICS 49311: General Warehousing & Storage Facilities; NAICS 49319: Other Warehousing & Storage Facilities 4231 Terminal & Joint Terminal Maintenance Facilities for Motor Freight Transportation ***See*** NAICS 48849: Other Support Activities for Road Transportation

4311 United States Postal Service ***See*** NAICS 49111: Postal Service

4412 Deep Sea Foreign Transportation of Freight ***See*** NAICS 483111: Deep Sea Freight Transportation

4424 Deep Sea Domestic Transportation of Freight ***See*** NAICS 483113: Coastal & Great Lakes Freight Transportation

4432 Freight Transportation on the Great Lakes - St. Lawrence Seaway ***See*** NAICS 483113: Coastal & Great Lakes Freight Transportation

4449 Water Transportation of Freight, NEC ***See*** NAICS 483211: Inland Water Freight Transportation

4481 Deep Sea Transportation of Passengers, Except by Ferry ***See*** NAICS 483112: Deep Sea Passenger Transportation; NAICS 483114: Coastal & Great Lakes Passenger Transportation

4482 Ferries ***See*** NAICS 483114: Coastal & Great Lakes Passenger Transportation; NAICS 483212: Inland Water Passenger Transportation

4489 Water Transportation of Passengers, NEC ***See*** NAICS 483212: Inland Water Passenger Transportation; NAICS 48721: Scenic & Sightseeing Transportation, Water

4491 Marine Cargo Handling ***See*** NAICS 48831: Port & Harbor Operations; NAICS 48832: Marine Cargo Handling

4492 Towing & Tugboat Services ***See*** NAICS 483113: Coastal & Great Lakes Freight Transportation; NAICS 483211: Inland Water Freight Transportation; NAICS 48833: Navigational Services to Shipping

4493 Marinas ***See*** NAICS 71393: Marinas

4499 Water Transportation Services, NEC ***See*** NAICS 532411: Commercial Air, Rail, & Water Transportation Equipment Rental & Leasing; NAICS 48831: Port & Harbor Operations; NAICS 48833: Navigational Services to Shipping; NAICS 48839: Other Support Activities for Water Transportation

4512 Air Transportation, Scheduled ***See*** NAICS 481111: Scheduled Passenger Air Transportation; NAICS 481112: Scheduled Freight Air Transportation

4513 Air Courier Services ***See*** NAICS 49211: Couriers

4522 Air Transportation, Nonscheduled ***See*** NAICS 62191: Ambulance Services; NAICS 481212: Nonscheduled Chartered Freight Air Transportation; NAICS 481211: Nonscheduled Chartered Passenger Air Transportation; NAICS 48799: Scenic & Sightseeing Transportation, Other

4581 Airports, Flying Fields, & Airport Terminal Services ***See*** NAICS 488111: Air Traffic Control; NAICS 488112: Airport Operations, Except Air Traffic Control; NAICS 56172: Janitorial Services; NAICS 48819: Other Support Activities for Air Transportation

4612 Crude Petroleum Pipelines ***See*** NAICS 48611: Pipeline Transportation of Crude Oil

4613 Refined Petroleum Pipelines ***See*** NAICS 48691: Pipeline Transportation of Refined Petroleum Products

4619 Pipelines, NEC ***See*** NAICS 48699: All Other Pipeline Transportation

4724 Travel Agencies ***See*** NAICS 56151: Travel Agencies

4725 Tour Operators ***See*** NAICS 56152: Tour Operators

4729 Arrangement of Passenger Transportation, NEC ***See*** NAICS 488999: All Other Support Activities for Transportation; NAICS 561599: All Other Travel Arrangement & Reservation Services

4731 Arrangement of Transportation of Freight & Cargo ***See*** NAICS 541618: Other Management Consulting Services; NAICS 48851: Freight Transportation Arrangement

4741 Rental of Railroad Cars ***See*** NAICS 532411: Commercial Air, Rail, & Water Transportation Equipment Rental & Leasing; NAICS 48821:

Support Activities for Rail Transportation
4783 Packing & Crating ***See*** NAICS 488991: Packing & Crating
4785 Fixed Facilities & Inspection & Weighing Services for Motor Vehicle Transportation ***See*** NAICS 48839: Other Support Activities for Water Transportation; NAICS 48849: Other Support Activities for Road Transportation
4789 Transportation Services, NEC ***See*** NAICS 488999: All Other Support Activities for Transportation; NAICS 48711: Scenic & Sightseeing Transportation, Land; NAICS 48821: Support Activities for Rail Transportation
4812 Radiotelephone Communications ***See*** NAICS 513321: Paging; NAICS 513322: Cellular & Other Wireless Telecommunications; NAICS 51333: Telecommunications Resellers
4813 Telephone Communications, Except Radiotelephone ***See*** NAICS 51331: Wired Telecommunications Carriers; NAICS 51333: Telecommunications Resellers
4822 Telegraph & Other Message Communications ***See*** NAICS 51331: Wired Telecommunications Carriers
4832 Radio Broadcasting Stations ***See*** NAICS 513111: Radio Networks; NAICS 513112: Radio Stations
4833 Television Broadcasting Stations ***See*** NAICS 51312: Television Broadcasting
4841 Cable & Other Pay Television Services ***See*** NAICS 51321: Cable Networks; NAICS 51322: Cable & Other Program Distribution
4899 Communications Services, NEC ***See*** NAICS 513322: Cellular & Other Wireless Telecommunications; NAICS 51334: Satellite Telecommunications; NAICS 51339: Other Telecommunications
4911 Electric Services ***See*** NAICS 221111: Hydroelectric Power Generation; NAICS 221112: Fossil Fuel Electric Power Generation; NAICS 221113: Nuclear Electric Power Generation; NAICS 221119: Other Electric Power Generation; NAICS 221121: Electric Bulk Power Transmission & Control; NAICS 221122: Electric Power Distribution
4922 Natural Gas Transmission ***See*** NAICS 48621: Pipeline Transportation of Natural Gas
4923 Natural Gas Transmission & Distribution ***See*** NAICS 22121: Natural Gas Distribution; NAICS 48621: Pipeline Transportation of Natural Gas
4924 Natural Gas Distribution ***See*** NAICS 22121: Natural Gas Distribution
4925 Mixed, Manufactured, or Liquefied Petroleum Gas Production And/or Distribution ***See*** NAICS 22121: Natural Gas Distribution
4931 Electric & Other Services Combined ***See*** NAICS 221111: Hydroelectric Power Generation; NAICS 221112: Fossil Fuel Electric Power Generation; NAICS 221113: Nuclear Electric Power Generation; NAICS 221119: Other Electric Power Generation; NAICS 221121: Electric Bulk Power Transmission & Control; NAICS 221122: Electric Power Distribution; NAICS 22121: Natural Gas Distribution
4932 Gas & Other Services Combined ***See*** NAICS 22121: Natural Gas Distribution
4939 Combination Utilities, NEC ***See*** NAICS 221111: Hydroelectric Power Generation; NAICS 221112: Fossil Fuel Electric Power Generation; NAICS 221113: Nuclear Electric Power Generation; NAICS 221119: Other Electric Power Generation; NAICS 221121: Electric Bulk Power Transmission & Control; NAICS 221122: Electric Power Distribution; NAICS 22121: Natural Gas Distribution
4941 Water Supply ***See*** NAICS 22131: Water Supply & Irrigation Systems
4952 Sewerage Systems ***See*** NAICS 22132: Sewage Treatment Facilities
4953 Refuse Systems ***See*** NAICS 562111: Solid Waste Collection; NAICS 562112: Hazardous Waste Collection; NAICS 56292: Materials Recovery Facilities; NAICS 562119: Other Waste Collection; NAICS 562211: Hazardous Waste Treatment & Disposal; NAICS 562212: Solid Waste Landfills; NAICS 562213: Solid Waste Combustors & Incinerators; NAICS 562219: Other Nonhazardous Waste Treatment & Disposal
4959 Sanitary Services, NEC ***See*** NAICS 488112: Airport Operations, Except Air Traffic Control; NAICS 56291: Remediation Services; NAICS 56171: Exterminating & Pest Control Services; NAICS 562998: All Other Miscellaneous Waste Management Services
4961 Steam & Air-conditioning Supply ***See*** NAICS 22133: Steam & Air-conditioning Supply
4971 Irrigation Systems ***See*** NAICS 22131: Water Supply & Irrigation Systems

Wholesale Trade

5012 Automobiles & Other Motor Vehicles ***See*** NAICS 42111: Automobile & Other Motor Vehicle Wholesalers
5013 Motor Vehicle Supplies & New Parts ***See*** NAICS 44131: Automotive Parts & Accessories Stores - Retail; NAICS 42112: Motor Vehicle Supplies & New Part Wholesalers
5014 Tires & Tubes ***See*** NAICS 44132: Tire Dealers - Retail; NAICS 42113: Tire & Tube Wholesalers
5015 Motor Vehicle Parts, Used ***See*** NAICS 42114: Motor Vehicle Part Wholesalers
5021 Furniture ***See*** NAICS 44211: Furniture Stores; NAICS 42121: Furniture Wholesalers
5023 Home Furnishings ***See*** NAICS 44221: Floor Covering Stores; NAICS 42122: Home Furnishing Wholesalers
5031 Lumber, Plywood, Millwork, & Wood Panels ***See*** NAICS 44419: Other Building Material Dealers; NAICS 42131: Lumber, Plywood, Millwork, & Wood Panel Wholesalers
5032 Brick, Stone & Related Construction Materials ***See*** NAICS 44419: Other Building Material Dealers; NAICS 42132: Brick, Stone & Related Construction Material Wholesalers
5033 Roofing, Siding, & Insulation Materials ***See*** NAICS 42133: Roofing, Siding, & Insulation Material Wholesalers
5039 Construction Materials, NEC ***See*** NAICS 44419: Other Building Material Dealers; NAICS 42139: Other Construction Material Wholesalers
5043 Photographic Equipment & Supplies ***See*** NAICS 42141: Photographic Equipment & Supplies Wholesalers
5044 Office Equipment ***See*** NAICS 42142: Office Equipment Wholesalers
5045 Computers & Computer Peripheral Equipment & Software ***See*** NAICS 42143: Computer & Computer Peripheral Equipment & Software Wholesalers; NAICS 44312: Computer & Software Stores - Retail
5046 Commercial Equipment, NEC ***See*** NAICS 42144: Other Commercial Equipment Wholesalers
5047 Medical, Dental, & Hospital Equipment & Supplies ***See*** NAICS 42145: Medical, Dental & Hospital Equipment & Supplies Wholesalers; NAICS 446199: All Other Health & Personal Care Stores - Retail
5048 Ophthalmic Goods ***See*** NAICS 42146: Ophthalmic Goods Wholesalers
5049 Professional Equipment & Supplies, NEC ***See*** NAICS 42149: Other Professional Equipment & Supplies Wholesalers; NAICS 45321: Office Supplies & Stationery Stores - Retail
5051 Metals Service Centers & Offices ***See*** NAICS 42151: Metals Service Centers & Offices
5052 Coal & Other Minerals & Ores ***See*** NAICS 42152: Coal & Other Mineral & Ore Wholesalers
5063 Electrical Apparatus & Equipment Wiring Supplies, & Construction Materials ***See*** NAICS 44419: Other Building Material Dealers; NAICS 42161: Electrical Apparatus & Equipment, Wiring Supplies & Construction Material Wholesalers
5064 Electrical Appliances, Television & Radio Sets ***See*** NAICS 42162: Electrical Appliance, Television & Radio Set Wholesalers
5065 Electronic Parts & Equipment, Not Elsewhere Classified ***See*** NAICS 42169: Other Electronic Parts & Equipment Wholesalers

5072 Hardware *See* NAICS 42171: Hardware Wholesalers
5074 Plumbing & Heating Equipment & Supplies *See* NAICS 44419: Other Building Material Dealers; NAICS 42172: Plumbing & Heating Equipment & Supplies Wholesalers
5075 Warm Air Heating & Air-conditioning Equipment & Supplies *See* NAICS 42173: Warm Air Heating & Air-conditioning Equipment & Supplies Wholesalers
5078 Refrigeration Equipment & Supplies *See* NAICS 42174: Refrigeration Equipment & Supplies Wholesalers
5082 Construction & Mining Machinery & Equipment *See* NAICS 42181: Construction & Mining Machinery & Equipment Wholesalers
5083 Farm & Garden Machinery & Equipment *See* NAICS 42182: Farm & Garden Machinery & Equipment Wholesalers; NAICS 44421: Outdoor Power Equipment Stores - Retail
5084 Industrial Machinery & Equipment *See* NAICS 42183: Industrial Machinery & Equipment Wholesalers
5085 Industrial Supplies *See* NAICS 42183: Industrial Machinery & Equipment Wholesalers; NAICS 42184: Industrial Supplies Wholesalers; NAICS 81131: Commercial & Industrial Machinery & Equipment Repair & Maintenence
5087 Service Establishment Equipment & Supplies *See* NAICS 42185: Service Establishment Equipment & Supplies Wholesalers; NAICS 44612: Cosmetics, Beauty Supplies, & Perfume Stores
5088 Transportation Equipment & Supplies, Except Motor Vehicles *See* NAICS 42186: Transportation Equipment & Supplies Wholesalers
5091 Sporting & Recreational Goods & Supplies *See* NAICS 42191: Sporting & Recreational Goods & Supplies Wholesalers
5092 Toys & Hobby Goods & Supplies *See* NAICS 42192: Toy & Hobby Goods & Supplies Wholesalers
5093 Scrap & Waste Materials *See* NAICS 42193: Recyclable Material Wholesalers
5094 Jewelry, Watches, Precious Stones, & Precious Metals *See* NAICS 42194: Jewelry, Watch , Precious Stone, & Precious Metal Wholesalers
5099 Durable Goods, NEC *See* NAICS 42199: Other Miscellaneous Durable Goods Wholesalers
5111 Printing & Writing Paper *See* NAICS 42211: Printing & Writing Paper Wholesalers
5112 Stationery & Office Supplies *See* NAICS 45321: Office Supplies & Stationery Stores; NAICS 42212: Stationery & Office Supplies Wholesalers
5113 Industrial & Personal Service Paper *See* NAICS 42213: Industrial & Personal Service Paper Wholesalers
5122 Drugs, Drug Proprietaries, & Druggists' Sundries *See* NAICS 42221: Drugs, Drug Proprietaries, & Druggists' Sundries Wholesalers
5131 Piece Goods, Notions, & Other Dry Goods *See* NAICS 313311: Broadwoven Fabric Finishing Mills; NAICS 313312: Textile & Fabric Finishing Mills; NAICS 42231: Piece Goods, Notions, & Other Dry Goods Wholesalers
5136 Men's & Boys' Clothing & Furnishings *See* NAICS 42232: Men's & Boys' Clothing & Furnishings Wholesalers
5137 Women's Children's & Infants' Clothing & Accessories *See* NAICS 42233: Women's, Children's, & Infants' Clothing & Accessories Wholesalers
5139 Footwear *See* NAICS 42234: Footwear Wholesalers
5141 Groceries, General Line *See* NAICS 42241: General Line Grocery Wholesalers
5142 Packaged Frozen Foods *See* NAICS 42242: Packaged Frozen Food Wholesalers
5143 Dairy Products, Except Dried or Canned *See* NAICS 42243: Dairy Products Wholesalers
5144 Poultry & Poultry Products *See* NAICS 42244: Poultry & Poultry Product Wholesalers
5145 Confectionery *See* NAICS 42245: Confectionery Wholesalers
5146 Fish & Seafoods *See* NAICS 42246: Fish & Seafood Wholesalers
5147 Meats & Meat Products *See* NAICS 311612: Meat Processed from Carcasses; NAICS 42247: Meat & Meat Product Wholesalers
5148 Fresh Fruits & Vegetables *See* NAICS 42248: Fresh Fruit & Vegetable Wholesalers
5149 Groceries & Related Products, NEC *See* NAICS 42249: Other Grocery & Related Product Wholesalers
5153 Grain & Field Beans *See* NAICS 42251: Grain & Field Bean Wholesalers
5154 Livestock *See* NAICS 42252: Livestock Wholesalers
5159 Farm-product Raw Materials, NEC *See* NAICS 42259: Other Farm Product Raw Material Wholesalers
5162 Plastics Materials & Basic Forms & Shapes *See* NAICS 42261: Plastics Materials & Basic Forms & Shapes Wholesalers
5169 Chemicals & Allied Products, NEC *See* NAICS 42269: Other Chemical & Allied Products Wholesalers
5171 Petroleum Bulk Stations & Terminals *See* NAICS 454311: Heating Oil Dealers; NAICS 454312: Liquefied Petroleum Gas Dealers; NAICS 42271: Petroleum Bulk Stations & Terminals
5172 Petroleum & Petroleum Products Wholesalers, Except Bulk Stations & Terminals *See* NAICS 42272: Petroleum & Petroleum Products Wholesalers
5181 Beer & Ale *See* NAICS 42281: Beer & Ale Wholesalers
5182 Wine & Distilled Alcoholic Beverages *See* NAICS 42282: Wine & Distilled Alcoholic Beverage Wholesalers
5191 Farm Supplies *See* NAICS 44422: Nursery & Garden Centers - Retail; NAICS 42291: Farm Supplies Wholesalers
5192 Books, Periodicals, & Newspapers *See* NAICS 42292: Book, Periodical & Newspaper Wholesalers
5193 Flowers, Nursery Stock, & Florists' Supplies *See* NAICS 42293: Flower, Nursery Stock & Florists' Supplies Wholesalers; NAICS 44422: Nursery & Garden Centers - Retail
5194 Tobacco & Tobacco Products *See* NAICS 42294: Tobacco & Tobacco Product Wholesalers
5198 Paint, Varnishes, & Supplies *See* NAICS 42295: Paint, Varnish & Supplies Wholesalers; NAICS 44412: Paint & Wallpaper Stores
5199 Nondurable Goods, NEC *See* NAICS 54189: Other Services Related to Advertising; NAICS 42299: Other Miscellaneous Nondurable Goods Wholesalers

Retail Trade

5211 Lumber & Other Building Materials Dealers *See* NAICS 44411: Home Centers; NAICS 42131: Lumber, Plywood, Millwork & Wood Panel Wholesalers; NAICS 44419: Other Building Material Dealers
5231 Paint, Glass, & Wallpaper Stores *See* NAICS 42295: Paint, Varnish & Supplies Wholesalers; NAICS 44419: Other Building Material Dealers; NAICS 44412: Paint & Wallpaper Stores
5251 Hardware Stores *See* NAICS 44413: Hardware Stores
5261 Retail Nurseries, Lawn & Garden Supply Stores *See* NAICS 44422: Nursery & Garden Centers; NAICS 453998: All Other Miscellaneous Store Retailers; NAICS 44421: Outdoor Power Equipment Stores
5271 Mobile Home Dealers *See* NAICS 45393: Manufactured Home Dealers
5311 Department Stores *See* NAICS 45211: Department Stores
5331 Variety Stores *See* NAICS 45299: All Other General Merchandise Stores

5399 Miscellaneous General Merchandise Stores ***See*** NAICS 45291: Warehouse Clubs & Superstores; NAICS 45299: All Other General Merchandise Stores

5411 Grocery Stores ***See*** NAICS 44711: Gasoline Stations with Convenience Stores; NAICS 44511: Supermarkets & Other Grocery Stores; NAICS 45291: Warehouse Clubs & Superstores; NAICS 44512: Convenience Stores

5421 Meat & Fish Markets, Including Freezer Provisioners ***See*** NAICS 45439: Other Direct Selling Establishments; NAICS 44521: Meat Markets; NAICS 44522: Fish & Seafood Markets

5431 Fruit & Vegetable Markets ***See*** NAICS 44523: Fruit & Vegetable Markets

5441 Candy, Nut, & Confectionery Stores ***See*** NAICS 445292: Confectionery & Nut Stores

5451 Dairy Products Stores ***See*** NAICS 445299: All Other Specialty Food Stores

5461 Retail Bakeries ***See*** NAICS 722213: Snack & Nonalcoholic Beverage Bars; NAICS 311811: Retail Bakeries; NAICS 445291: Baked Goods Stores

5499 Miscellaneous Food Stores ***See*** NAICS 44521: Meat Markets; NAICS 722211: Limited-service Restaurants; NAICS 446191: Food Supplement Stores; NAICS 445299: All Other Specialty Food Stores

5511 Motor Vehicle Dealers ***See*** NAICS 44111: New Car Dealers

5521 Motor Vehicle Dealers ***See*** NAICS 44112: Used Car Dealers

5531 Auto & Home Supply Stores ***See*** NAICS 44132: Tire Dealers; NAICS 44131: Automotive Parts & Accessories Stores

5541 Gasoline Service Stations ***See*** NAICS 44711: Gasoline Stations with Convenience Store; NAICS 44719: Other Gasoline Stations

5551 Boat Dealers ***See*** NAICS 441222: Boat Dealers

5561 Recreational Vehicle Dealers ***See*** NAICS 44121: Recreational Vehicle Dealers

5571 Motorcycle Dealers ***See*** NAICS 441221: Motorcycle Dealers

5599 Automotive Dealers, NEC ***See*** NAICS 441229: All Other Motor Vehicle Dealers

5611 Men's & Boys' Clothing & Accessory Stores ***See*** NAICS 44811: Men's Clothing Stores; NAICS 44815: Clothing Accessories Stores

5621 Women's Clothing Stores ***See*** NAICS 44812: Women's Clothing Stores

5632 Women's Accessory & Specialty Stores ***See*** NAICS 44819: Other Clothing Stores; NAICS 44815: Clothing Accessories Stores

5641 Children's & Infants' Wear Stores ***See*** NAICS 44813: Children's & Infants' Clothing Stores

5651 Family Clothing Stores ***See*** NAICS 44814: Family Clothing Stores

5661 Shoe Stores ***See*** NAICS 44821: Shoe Stores

5699 Miscellaneous Apparel & Accessory Stores ***See*** NAICS 315: Included in Apparel Manufacturing Subsector Based on Type of Garment Produced; NAICS 44819: Other Clothing Stores; NAICS 44815: Clothing Accessories Stores

5712 Furniture Stores ***See*** NAICS 337133: Wood Household Furniture, Except Upholstered, Manufacturing; NAICS 337131: Wood Kitchen Cabinet & Counter Top Manufacturing; NAICS 337132: Upholstered Household Furniture Manufacturing; NAICS 44211: Furniture Stores

5713 Floor Covering Stores ***See*** NAICS 44221: Floor Covering Stores

5714 Drapery, Curtain, & Upholstery Stores ***See*** NAICS 442291: Window Treatment Stores; NAICS 45113: Sewing, Needlework & Piece Goods Stores; NAICS 314121: Curtain & Drapery Mills

5719 Miscellaneous Homefurnishings Stores ***See*** NAICS 442291: Window Treatment Stores; NAICS 442299: All Other Home Furnishings Stores

5722 Household Appliance Stores ***See*** NAICS 443111: Household Appliance Stores

5731 Radio, Television, & Consumer Electronics Stores ***See*** NAICS 443112: Radio, Television, & Other Electronics Stores; NAICS 44131: Automotive Parts & Accessories Stores

5734 Computer & Computer Software Stores ***See*** NAICS 44312: Computer & Software Stores

5735 Record & Prerecorded Tape Stores ***See*** NAICS 45122: Prerecorded Tape, Compact Disc & Record Stores

5736 Musical Instrument Stores ***See*** NAICS 45114: Musical Instrument & Supplies Stores

5812 Eating & Drinking Places ***See*** NAICS 72211: Full-service Restaurants; NAICS 722211: Limited-service Restaurants; NAICS 722212: Cafeterias; NAICS 722213: Snack & Nonalcoholic Beverage Bars; NAICS 72231: Foodservice Contractors; NAICS 72232: Caterers; NAICS 71111: Theater Companies & Dinner Theaters

5813 Drinking Places ***See*** NAICS 72241: Drinking Places

5912 Drug Stores & Proprietary Stores ***See*** NAICS 44611: Pharmacies & Drug Stores

5921 Liquor Stores ***See*** NAICS 44531: Beer, Wine & Liquor Stores

5932 Used Merchandise Stores ***See*** NAICS 522298: All Other Non-depository Credit Intermediation; NAICS 45331: Used Merchandise Stores

5941 Sporting Goods Stores & Bicycle Shops ***See*** NAICS 45111: Sporting Goods Stores

5942 Book Stores ***See*** NAICS 451211: Book Stores

5943 Stationery Stores ***See*** NAICS 45321: Office Supplies & Stationery Stores

5944 Jewelry Stores ***See*** NAICS 44831: Jewelry Stores

5945 Hobby, Toy, & Game Shops ***See*** NAICS 45112: Hobby, Toy & Game Stores

5946 Camera & Photographic Supply Stores ***See*** NAICS 44313: Camera & Photographic Supplies Stores

5947 Gift, Novelty, & Souvenir Shops ***See*** NAICS 45322: Gift, Novelty & Souvenir Stores

5948 Luggage & Leather Goods Stores ***See*** NAICS 44832: Luggage & Leather Goods Stores

5949 Sewing, Needlework, & Piece Goods Stores ***See*** NAICS 45113: Sewing, Needlework & Piece Goods Stores

5961 Catalog & Mail-order Houses ***See*** NAICS 45411: Electronic Shopping & Mail-order Houses

5962 Automatic Merchandising Machine Operator ***See*** NAICS 45421: Vending Machine Operators

5963 Direct Selling Establishments ***See*** NAICS 72233: Mobile Caterers; NAICS 45439: Other Direct Selling Establishments

5983 Fuel Oil Dealers ***See*** NAICS 454311: Heating Oil Dealers

5984 Liquefied Petroleum Gas Dealers ***See*** NAICS 454312: Liquefied Petroleum Gas Dealers

5989 Fuel Dealers, NEC ***See*** NAICS 454319: Other Fuel Dealers

5992 Florists ***See*** NAICS 45311: Florists

5993 Tobacco Stores & Stands ***See*** NAICS 453991: Tobacco Stores

5994 News Dealers & Newsstands ***See*** NAICS 451212: News Dealers & Newsstands

5995 Optical Goods Stores ***See*** NAICS 339117: Eyeglass & Contact Lens Manufacturing; NAICS 44613: Optical Goods Stores

5999 Miscellaneous Retail Stores, NEC ***See*** NAICS 44612: Cosmetics, Beauty Supplies & Perfume Stores; NAICS 446199: All Other Health & Personal Care Stores; NAICS 45391: Pet & Pet Supplies Stores; NAICS 45392: Art Dealers; NAICS 443111: Household Appliance Stores; NAICS 443112: Radio, Television & Other Electronics Stores; NAICS 44831: Jewelry Stores; NAICS 453999: All Other Miscellaneous Store Retailers

Finance, Insurance, & Real Estate

6011 Federal Reserve Banks ***See*** NAICS 52111: Monetary Authorities-central Banks
6019 Central Reserve Depository Institutions, NEC ***See*** NAICS 52232: Financial Transactions Processing, Reserve, & Clearing House Activities
6021 National Commercial Banks ***See*** NAICS 52211: Commercial Banking; NAICS 52221: Credit Card Issuing; NAICS 523991: Trust, Fiduciary & Custody Activities
6022 State Commercial Banks ***See*** NAICS 52211: Commercial Banking; NAICS 52221: Credit Card Issuing; NAICS 52219: Other Depository Intermediation; NAICS 523991: Trust, Fiduciary & Custody Activities
6029 Commercial Banks, NEC ***See*** NAICS 52211: Commercial Banking
6035 Savings Institutions, Federally Chartered ***See*** NAICS 52212: Savings Institutions
6036 Savings Institutions, Not Federally Chartered ***See*** NAICS 52212: Savings Institutions
6061 Credit Unions, Federally Chartered ***See*** NAICS 52213: Credit Unions
6062 Credit Unions, Not Federally Chartered ***See*** NAICS 52213: Credit Unions
6081 Branches & Agencies of Foreign Banks ***See*** NAICS 522293: International Trade Financing; NAICS 52211: Commercial Banking; NAICS 522298: All Other Non-depository Credit Intermediation
6082 Foreign Trade & International Banking Institutions ***See*** NAICS 522293: International Trade Financing
6091 Nondeposit Trust Facilities ***See*** NAICS 523991: Trust, Fiduciary, & Custody Activities
6099 Functions Related to Deposit Banking, NEC ***See*** NAICS 52232: Financial Transactions Processing, Reserve, & Clearing House Activities; NAICS 52313: Commodity Contracts Dealing; NAICS 523991: Trust, Fiduciary, & Custody Activities; NAICS 523999: Miscellaneous Financial Investment Activities; NAICS 52239: Other Activities Related to Credit Intermediation
6111 Federal & Federally Sponsored Credit Agencies ***See*** NAICS 522293: International Trade Financing; NAICS 522294: Secondary Market Financing; NAICS 522298: All Other Non-depository Credit Intermediation
6141 Personal Credit Institutions ***See*** NAICS 52221: Credit Card Issuing; NAICS 52222: Sales Financing; NAICS 522291: Consumer Lending
6153 Short-term Business Credit Institutions, Except Agricultural ***See*** NAICS 52222: Sales Financing; NAICS 52232: Financial Transactions Processing, Reserve, & Clearing House Activities; NAICS 522298: All Other Non-depository Credit Intermediation
6159 Miscellaneous Business Credit Institutions ***See*** NAICS 52222: Sales Financing; NAICS 532: Included in Rental & Leasing Services Subsector by Type of Equipment & Method of Operation; NAICS 522293: International Trade Financing; NAICS 522298: All Other Non-depository Credit Intermediation
6162 Mortgage Bankers & Loan Correspondents ***See*** NAICS 522292: Real Estate Credit; NAICS 52239: Other Activities Related to Credit Intermediation
6163 Loan Brokers ***See*** NAICS 52231: Mortgage & Other Loan Brokers
6211 Security Brokers, Dealers, & Flotation Companies ***See*** NAICS 52311: Investment Banking & Securities Dealing; NAICS 52312: Securities Brokerage; NAICS 52391: Miscellaneous Intermediation; NAICS 523999: Miscellaneous Financial Investment Activities
6221 Commodity Contracts Brokers & Dealers ***See*** NAICS 52313: Commodity Contracts Dealing; NAICS 52314: Commodity Brokerage
6231 Security & Commodity Exchanges ***See*** NAICS 52321: Securities & Commodity Exchanges
6282 Investment Advice ***See*** NAICS 52392: Portfolio Management; NAICS 52393: Investment Advice
6289 Services Allied with the Exchange of Securities or Commodities, NEC ***See*** NAICS 523991: Trust, Fiduciary, & Custody Activities; NAICS 523999: Miscellaneous Financial Investment Activities
6311 Life Insurance ***See*** NAICS 524113: Direct Life Insurance Carriers; NAICS 52413: Reinsurance Carriers
6321 Accident & Health Insurance ***See*** NAICS 524114: Direct Health & Medical Insurance Carriers; NAICS 52519: Other Insurance Funds; NAICS 52413: Reinsurance Carriers
6324 Hospital & Medical Service Plans ***See*** NAICS 524114: Direct Health & Medical Insurance Carriers; NAICS 52519: Other Insurance Funds; NAICS 52413: Reinsurance Carriers
6331 Fire, Marine, & Casualty Insurance ***See*** NAICS 524126: Direct Property & Casualty Insurance Carriers; NAICS 52519: Other Insurance Funds; NAICS 52413: Reinsurance Carriers
6351 Surety Insurance ***See*** NAICS 524126: Direct Property & Casualty Insurance Carriers; NAICS 52413: Reinsurance Carriers
6361 Title Insurance ***See*** NAICS 524127: Direct Title Insurance Carriers; NAICS 52413: Reinsurance Carriers
6371 Pension, Health, & Welfare Funds ***See*** NAICS 52392: Portfolio Management; NAICS 524292: Third Party Administration for Insurance & Pension Funds; NAICS 52511: Pension Funds; NAICS 52512: Health & Welfare Funds
6399 Insurance Carriers, NEC ***See*** NAICS 524128: Other Direct Insurance Carriers
6411 Insurance Agents, Brokers, & Service ***See*** NAICS 52421: Insurance Agencies & Brokerages; NAICS 524291: Claims Adjusters; NAICS 524292: Third Party Administrators for Insurance & Pension Funds; NAICS 524298: All Other Insurance Related Activities
6512 Operators of Nonresidential Buildings ***See*** NAICS 71131: Promoters of Performing Arts, Sports & Similar Events with Facilities; NAICS 53112: Lessors of Nonresidential Buildings
6513 Operators of Apartment Buildings ***See*** NAICS 53111: Lessors of Residential Buildings & Dwellings
6514 Operators of Dwellings Other than Apartment Buildings ***See*** NAICS 53111: Lessors of Residential Buildings & Dwellings
6515 Operators of Residential Mobile Home Sites ***See*** NAICS 53119: Lessors of Other Real Estate Property
6517 Lessors of Railroad Property ***See*** NAICS 53119: Lessors of Other Real Estate Property
6519 Lessors of Real Property, NEC ***See*** NAICS 53119: Lessors of Other Real Estate Property
6531 Real Estate Agents & Managers ***See*** NAICS 53121: Offices of Real Estate Agents & Brokers; NAICS 81399: Other Similar Organizations; NAICS 531311: Residential Property Managers; NAICS 531312: Nonresidential Property Managers; NAICS 53132: Offices of Real Estate Appraisers; NAICS 81222: Cemeteries & Crematories; NAICS 531399: All Other Activities Related to Real Estate
6541 Title Abstract Offices ***See*** NAICS 541191: Title Abstract & Settlement Offices
6552 Land Subdividers & Developers, Except Cemeteries ***See*** NAICS 23311: Land Subdivision & Land Development
6553 Cemetery Subdividers & Developers ***See*** NAICS 81222: Cemeteries & Crematories
6712 Offices of Bank Holding Companies ***See*** NAICS 551111: Offices of Bank Holding Companies
6719 Offices of Holding Companies, NEC ***See*** NAICS 551112: Offices of Other Holding Companies
6722 Management Investment Offices, Open-end ***See*** NAICS 52591: Open-end Investment Funds
6726 Unit Investment Trusts, Face-amount Certificate Offices, & Closed-end Management Investment Offices ***See*** NAICS 52599: Other Financial Vehicles
6732 Education, Religious, & Charitable Trusts ***See*** NAICS 813211: Grantmaking Foundations

6733 Trusts, Except Educational, Religious, & Charitable ***See*** NAICS 52392: Portfolio Management; NAICS 523991: Trust, Fiduciary, & Custody Services; NAICS 52519: Other Insurance Funds; NAICS 52592: Trusts, Estates, & Agency Accounts
6792 Oil Royalty Traders ***See*** NAICS 523999: Miscellaneous Financial Investment Activities; NAICS 53311: Owners & Lessors of Other Non-financial Assets
6794 Patent Owners & Lessors ***See*** NAICS 53311: Owners & Lessors of Other Non-financial Assets
6798 Real Estate Investment Trusts ***See*** NAICS 52593: Real Estate Investment Trusts
6799 Investors, NEC ***See*** NAICS 52391: Miscellaneous Intermediation; NAICS 52392: Portfolio Management; NAICS 52313: Commodity Contracts Dealing; NAICS 523999: Miscellaneous Financial Investment Activities

Service Industries

7011 Hotels & Motels ***See*** NAICS 72111: Hotels & Motels; NAICS 72112: Casino Hotels; NAICS 721191: Bed & Breakfast Inns; NAICS 721199: All Other Traveler Accommodation
7021 Rooming & Boarding Houses ***See*** NAICS 72131: Rooming & Boarding Houses
7032 Sporting & Recreational Camps ***See*** NAICS 721214: Recreational & Vacation Camps
7033 Recreational Vehicle Parks & Campsites ***See*** NAICS 721211: RV & Campgrounds
7041 Organization Hotels & Lodging Houses, on Membership Basis ***See*** NAICS 72111: Hotels & Motels; NAICS 72131: Rooming & Boarding Houses
7211 Power Laundries, Family & Commercial ***See*** NAICS 812321: Laundries, Family & Commercial
7212 Garment Pressing, & Agents for Laundries ***See*** NAICS 812391: Garment Pressing & Agents for Laundries
7213 Linen Supply ***See*** NAICS 812331: Linen Supply
7215 Coin-operated Laundry & Drycleaning ***See*** NAICS 81231: Coin-operated Laundries & Drycleaners
7216 Drycleaning Plants, Except Rug Cleaning ***See*** NAICS 812322: Drycleaning Plants
7217 Carpet & Upholstery Cleaning ***See*** NAICS 56174: Carpet & Upholstery Cleaning Services
7218 Industrial Launderers ***See*** NAICS 812332: Industrial Launderers
7219 Laundry & Garment Services, NEC ***See*** NAICS 812331: Linen Supply; NAICS 81149: Other Personal & Household Goods Repair & Maintenance; NAICS 812399: All Other Laundry Services
7221 Photographic Studios, Portrait ***See*** NAICS 541921: Photographic Studios, Portrait
7231 Beauty Shops ***See*** NAICS 812112: Beauty Salons; NAICS 812113: Nail Salons; NAICS 611511: Cosmetology & Barber Schools
7241 Barber Shops ***See*** NAICS 812111: Barber Shops; NAICS 611511: Cosmetology & Barber Schools
7251 Shoe Repair Shops & Shoeshine Parlors ***See*** NAICS 81143: Footwear & Leather Goods Repair
7261 Funeral Services & Crematories ***See*** NAICS 81221: Funeral Homes; NAICS 81222: Cemeteries & Crematories
7291 Tax Return Preparation Services ***See*** NAICS 541213: Tax Preparation Services
7299 Miscellaneous Personal Services, NEC ***See*** NAICS 62441: Child Day Care Services; NAICS 812191: Diet & Weight Reducing Centers; NAICS 53222: Formal Wear & Costume Rental; NAICS 812199: Other Personal Care Services; NAICS 81299: All Other Personal Services
7311 Advertising Agencies ***See*** NAICS 54181: Advertising Agencies
7312 Outdoor Advertising Services ***See*** NAICS 54185: Display Advertising
7313 Radio, Television, & Publishers' Advertising Representatives ***See*** NAICS 54184: Media Representatives
7319 Advertising, NEC ***See*** NAICS 481219: Other Nonscheduled Air Transportation; NAICS 54183: Media Buying Agencies; NAICS 54185: Display Advertising; NAICS 54187: Advertising Material Distribution Services; NAICS 54189: Other Services Related to Advertising
7322 Adjustment & Collection Services ***See*** NAICS 56144: Collection Agencies; NAICS 561491: Repossession Services
7323 Credit Reporting Services ***See*** NAICS 56145: Credit Bureaus
7331 Direct Mail Advertising Services ***See*** NAICS 54186: Direct Mail Advertising
7334 Photocopying & Duplicating Services ***See*** NAICS 561431: Photocopying & Duplicating Services
7335 Commercial Photography ***See*** NAICS 541922: Commercial Photography
7336 Commercial Art & Graphic Design ***See*** NAICS 54143: Commercial Art & Graphic Design Services
7338 Secretarial & Court Reporting Services ***See*** NAICS 56141: Document Preparation Services; NAICS 561492: Court Reporting & Stenotype Services
7342 Disinfecting & Pest Control Services ***See*** NAICS 56172: Janitorial Services; NAICS 56171: Exterminating & Pest Control Services
7349 Building Cleaning & Maintenance Services, NEC ***See*** NAICS 56172: Janitorial Services
7352 Medical Equipment Rental & Leasing ***See*** NAICS 532291: Home Health Equipment Rental; NAICS 53249: Other Commercial & Industrial Machinery & Equipment Rental & Leasing
7353 Heavy Construction Equipment Rental & Leasing ***See*** NAICS 23499: All Other Heavy Construction; NAICS 532412: Construction, Mining & Forestry Machinery & Equipment Rental & Leasing
7359 Equipment Rental & Leasing, NEC ***See*** NAICS 53221: Consumer Electronics & Appliances Rental; NAICS 53231: General Rental Centers; NAICS 532299: All Other Consumer Goods Rental; NAICS 532412: Construction, Mining & Forestry Machinery & Equipment Rental & Leasing; NAICS 532411: Commercial Air, Rail, & Water Transportation Equipment Rental & Leasing; NAICS 562991: Septic Tank & Related Services; NAICS 53242: Office Machinery & Equipment Rental & Leasing; NAICS 53249: Other Commercial & Industrial Machinery & Equipment Rental & Leasing
7361 Employment Agencies ***See*** NAICS 541612: Human Resources & Executive Search Consulting Services; NAICS 56131: Employment Placement Agencies
7363 Help Supply Services ***See*** NAICS 56132: Temporary Help Services; NAICS 56133: Employee Leasing Services
7371 Computer Programming Services ***See*** NAICS 541511: Custom Computer Programming Services
7372 Prepackaged Software ***See*** NAICS 51121: Software Publishers; NAICS 334611: Software Reproducing
7373 Computer Integrated Systems Design ***See*** NAICS 541512: Computer Systems Design Services
7374 Computer Processing & Data Preparation & Processing Services ***See*** NAICS 51421: Data Processing Services
7375 Information Retrieval Services ***See*** NAICS 514191: On-line Information Services
7376 Computer Facilities Management Services ***See*** NAICS 541513: Computer Facilities Management Services
7377 Computer Rental & Leasing ***See*** NAICS 53242: Office Machinery & Equipment Rental & Leasing
7378 Computer Maintenance & Repair ***See*** NAICS 44312: Computer & Software Stores; NAICS 811212: Computer & Office Machine Repair & Maintenance

7379 Computer Related Services, NEC ***See*** NAICS 541512: Computer Systems Design Services; NAICS 541519: Other Computer Related Services

7381 Detective, Guard, & Armored Car Services ***See*** NAICS 561611: Investigation Services; NAICS 561612: Security Guards & Patrol Services; NAICS 561613: Armored Car Services

7382 Security Systems Services ***See*** NAICS 561621: Security Systems Services

7383 News Syndicates ***See*** NAICS 51411: New Syndicates

7384 Photofinishing Laboratories ***See*** NAICS 812921: Photo Finishing Laboratories; NAICS 812922: One-hour Photo Finishing

7389 Business Services, NEC ***See*** NAICS 51224: Sound Recording Studios; NAICS 51229: Other Sound Recording Industries; NAICS 541199: All Other Legal Services; NAICS 81299: All Other Personal Services; NAICS 54137: Surveying & Mapping Services; NAICS 54141: Interior Design Services; NAICS 54142: Industrial Design Services; NAICS 54134: Drafting Services; NAICS 54149: Other Specialized Design Services; NAICS 54189: Other Services Related to Advertising; NAICS 54193: Translation & Interpretation Services; NAICS 54135: Building Inspection Services; NAICS 54199: All Other Professional, Scientific & Technical Services; NAICS 71141: Agents & Managers for Artists, Athletes, Entertainers & Other Public Figures; NAICS 561422: Telemarketing Bureaus; NAICS 561432: Private Mail Centers; NAICS 561439: Other Business Service Centers; NAICS 561491: Repossession Services; NAICS 56191: Packaging & Labeling Services; NAICS 56179: Other Services to Buildings & Dwellings; NAICS 561599: All Other Travel Arrangement & Reservation Services; NAICS 56192: Convention & Trade Show Organizers; NAICS 561591: Convention & Visitors Bureaus; NAICS 52232: Financial Transactions, Processing, Reserve & Clearing House Activities; NAICS 561499: All Other Business Support Services; NAICS 56199: All Other Support Services

7513 Truck Rental & Leasing, Without Drivers ***See*** NAICS 53212: Truck, Utility Trailer & RV Rental & Leasing

7514 Passenger Car Rental ***See*** NAICS 532111: Passenger Cars Rental

7515 Passenger Car Leasing ***See*** NAICS 532112: Passenger Cars Leasing

7519 Utility Trailer & Recreational Vehicle Rental ***See*** NAICS 53212: Truck, Utility Trailer & RV Rental & Leasing

7521 Automobile Parking ***See*** NAICS 81293: Parking Lots & Garages

7532 Top, Body, & Upholstery Repair Shops & Paint Shops ***See*** NAICS 811121: Automotive Body, Paint, & Upholstery Repair & Maintenance

7533 Automotive Exhaust System Repair Shops ***See*** NAICS 811112: Automotive Exhaust System Repair

7534 Tire Retreading & Repair Shops ***See*** NAICS 326212: Tire Retreading; NAICS 811198: All Other Automotive Repair & Maintenance

7536 Automotive Glass Replacement Shops ***See*** NAICS 811122: Automotive Glass Replacement Shops

7537 Automotive Transmission Repair Shops ***See*** NAICS 811113: Automotive Transmission Repair

7538 General Automotive Repair Shops ***See*** NAICS 811111: General Automotive Repair

7539 Automotive Repair Shops, NEC ***See*** NAICS 811118: Other Automotive Mechanical & Electrical Repair & Maintenance

7542 Carwashes ***See*** NAICS 811192: Car Washes

7549 Automotive Services, Except Repair & Carwashes ***See*** NAICS 811191: Automotive Oil Change & Lubrication Shops; NAICS 48841: Motor Vehicle Towing; NAICS 811198: All Other Automotive Repair & Maintenance

7622 Radio & Television Repair Shops ***See*** NAICS 811211: Consumer Electronics Repair & Maintenance; NAICS 443112: Radio, Television & Other Electronics Stores

7623 Refrigeration & Air-conditioning Services & Repair Shops ***See*** NAICS 443111: Household Appliance Stores; NAICS 81131: Commercial & Industrial Machinery & Equipment Repair & Maintenance; NAICS 811412: Appliance Repair & Maintenance

7629 Electrical & Electronic Repair Shops, NEC ***See*** NAICS 443111: Household Appliance Stores; NAICS 811212: Computer & Office Machine Repair & Maintenance; NAICS 811213: Communication Equipment Repair & Maintenance; NAICS 811219: Other Electronic & Precision Equipment Repair & Maintenance; NAICS 811412: Appliance Repair & Maintenance; NAICS 811211: Consumer Electronics Repair & Maintenance

7631 Watch, Clock, & Jewelry Repair ***See*** NAICS 81149: Other Personal & Household Goods Repair & Maintenance

7641 Reupholster & Furniture Repair ***See*** NAICS 81142: Reupholstery & Furniture Repair

7692 Welding Repair ***See*** NAICS 81149: Other Personal & Household Goods Repair & Maintenance

7694 Armature Rewinding Shops ***See*** NAICS 81131: Commercial & Industrial Machinery & Equipment Repair & Maintenance; NAICS 335312: Motor & Generator Manufacturing

7699 Repair Shops & Related Services, NEC ***See*** NAICS 561622: Locksmiths; NAICS 562991: Septic Tank & Related Services; NAICS 56179: Other Services to Buildings & Dwellings; NAICS 48839: Other Supporting Activities for Water Transportation; NAICS 45111: Sporting Goods Stores; NAICS 81131: Commercial & Industrial Machinery & Equipment Repair & Maintenance; NAICS 11521: Support Activities for Animal Production; NAICS 811212: Computer & Office Machine Repair & Maintenance; NAICS 811219: Other Electronic & Precision Equipment Repair & Maintenance; NAICS 811411: Home & Garden Equipment Repair & Maintenance; NAICS 811412: Appliance Repair & Maintenance; NAICS 81143: Footwear & Leather Goods Repair; NAICS 81149: Other Personal & Household Goods Repair & Maintenance

7812 Motion Picture & Video Tape Production ***See*** NAICS 51211: Motion Picture & Video Production

7819 Services Allied to Motion Picture Production ***See*** NAICS 512191: Teleproduction & Other Post-production Services; NAICS 56131: Employment Placement Agencies; NAICS 53222: Formal Wear & Costumes Rental; NAICS 53249: Other Commercial & Industrial Machinery & Equipment Rental & Leasing; NAICS 541214: Payroll Services; NAICS 71151: Independent Artists, Writers, & Performers; NAICS 334612: Prerecorded Compact Disc , Tape, & Record Manufacturing; NAICS 512199:Other Motion Picture & Video Industries

7822 Motion Picture & Video Tape Distribution ***See*** NAICS 42199: Other Miscellaneous Durable Goods Wholesalers; NAICS 51212: Motion Picture & Video Distribution

7829 Services Allied to Motion Picture Distribution ***See*** NAICS 512199: Other Motion Picture & Video Industries; NAICS 51212: Motion Picture & Video Distribution

7832 Motion Picture Theaters, Except Drive-ins. ***See*** NAICS 512131: Motion Picture Theaters, Except Drive-in

7833 Drive-in Motion Picture Theaters ***See*** NAICS 512132: Drive-in Motion Picture Theaters

7841 Video Tape Rental ***See*** NAICS 53223: Video Tapes & Disc Rental

7911 Dance Studios, Schools, & Halls ***See*** NAICS 71399: All Other Amusement & Recreation Industries; NAICS 61161: Fine Arts Schools

7922 Theatrical Producers & Miscellaneous Theatrical Services ***See*** NAICS 56131: Employment Placement Agencies; NAICS 71111: Theater Companies & Dinner Theaters; NAICS 71141: Agents & Managers for Artists, Athletes, Entertainers & Other Public Figures; NAICS 71112: Dance Companies; NAICS 71131: Promoters of Performing Arts, Sports, & Similar Events with Facilities; NAICS 71132: Promoters of Performing Arts, Sports, & Similar Events Without Facilities; NAICS 51229: Other Sound Recording Industries; NAICS 53249: Other Commercial & Industrial Machinery & Equipment Rental & Leasing

7929 Bands, Orchestras, Actors, & Other Entertainers & Entertainment Groups ***See*** NAICS 71113: Musical Groups & Artists; NAICS 71151: Independent Artists, Writers, & Performers; NAICS 71119: Other Performing Arts Companies

7933 Bowling Centers ***See*** NAICS 71395: Bowling Centers

7941 Professional Sports Clubs & Promoters ***See*** NAICS 711211: Sports Teams & Clubs; NAICS 71141: Agents & Managers for Artists, Athletes, Entertainers, & Other Public Figures; NAICS 71132: Promoters of Arts, Sports & Similar Events Without Facilities; NAICS 71131: Promoters of Arts, Sports, & Similar Events with Facilities; NAICS 711219: Other Spectator Sports

7948 Racing, Including Track Operations ***See*** NAICS 711212: Race Tracks; NAICS 711219: Other Spectator Sports

7991 Physical Fitness Facilities ***See*** NAICS 71394: Fitness & Recreational Sports Centers

7992 Public Golf Courses ***See*** NAICS 71391: Golf Courses & Country Clubs

7993 Coin Operated Amusement Devices ***See*** NAICS 71312: Amusement Arcades; NAICS 71329: Other Gambling Industries; NAICS 71399: All Other Amusement & Recreation Industries

7996 Amusement Parks ***See*** NAICS 71311: Amusement & Theme Parks

7997 Membership Sports & Recreation Clubs ***See*** NAICS 71391: Golf Courses & Country Clubs; NAICS 71394: Fitness & Recreational Sports Centers; NAICS 71399: All Other Amusement & Recreation Industries

7999 Amusement & Recreation Services, NEC ***See*** NAICS 561599: All Other Travel Arrangement & Reservation Services; NAICS 48799: Scenic & Sightseeing Transportation, Other; NAICS 71119: Other Performing Arts Companies; NAICS 711219: Other Spectator Sports; NAICS 71392: Skiing Facilities; NAICS 71394: Fitness & Recreational Sports Centers; NAICS 71321: Casinos; NAICS 71329: Other Gambling Industries; NAICS 71219: Nature Parks & Other Similar Institutions; NAICS 61162: Sports & Recreation Instruction; NAICS 532292: Recreational Goods Rental; NAICS 48711: Scenic & Sightseeing Transportation, Land; NAICS 48721: Scenic & Sightseeing Transportation, Water; NAICS 71399: All Other Amusement & Recreation Industries

8011 Offices & Clinics of Doctors of Medicine ***See*** NAICS 621493: Freestanding Ambulatory Surgical & Emergency Centers; NAICS 621491: HMO Medical Centers; NAICS 621112: Offices of Physicians, Mental Health Specialists; NAICS 621111: Offices of Physicians

8021 Offices & Clinics of Dentists ***See*** NAICS 62121: Offices of Dentists

8031 Offices & Clinics of Doctors of Osteopathy ***See*** NAICS 621111: Offices of Physicians; NAICS 621112: Offices of Physicians, Mental Health Specialists

8041 Offices & Clinics of Chiropractors ***See*** NAICS 62131: Offices of Chiropractors

8042 Offices & Clinics of Optometrists ***See*** NAICS 62132: Offices of Optometrists

8043 Offices & Clinics of Podiatrists ***See*** NAICS 621391: Offices of Podiatrists

8049 Offices & Clinics of Health Practitioners, NEC ***See*** NAICS 62133: Offices of Mental Health Practitioners; NAICS 62134: Offices of Physical, Occupational, & Speech Therapists & Audiologists; NAICS 621399: Offices of All Other Miscellaneous Health Practitioners

8051 Skilled Nursing Care Facilities ***See*** NAICS 623311: Continuing Care Retirement Communities; NAICS 62311: Nursing Care Facilities

8052 Intermediate Care Facilities ***See*** NAICS 623311: Continuing Care Retirement Communities; NAICS 62321: Residential Mental Retardation Facilities; NAICS 62311: Nursing Care Facilities

8059 Nursing & Personal Care Facilities, NEC ***See*** NAICS 623311: Continuing Care Retirement Communities; NAICS 62311: Nursing Care Facilities

8062 General Medical & Surgical Hospitals ***See*** NAICS 62211: General Medical & Surgical Hospitals

8063 Psychiatric Hospitals ***See*** NAICS 62221: Psychiatric & Substance Abuse Hospitals

8069 Specialty Hospitals, Except Psychiatric ***See*** NAICS 62211: General Medical & Surgical Hospitals; NAICS 62221: Psychiatric & Substance Abuse Hospitals; NAICS 62231: Specialty Hospitals

8071 Medical Laboratories ***See*** NAICS 621512: Diagnostic Imaging Centers; NAICS 621511: Medical Laboratories

8072 Dental Laboratories ***See*** NAICS 339116: Dental Laboratories

8082 Home Health Care Services ***See*** NAICS 62161: Home Health Care Services

8092 Kidney Dialysis Centers ***See*** NAICS 621492: Kidney Dialysis Centers

8093 Specialty Outpatient Facilities, NEC ***See*** NAICS 62141: Family Planning Centers; NAICS 62142: Outpatient Mental Health & Substance Abuse Centers; NAICS 621498: All Other Outpatient Care Facilities

8099 Health & Allied Services, NEC ***See*** NAICS 621991: Blood & Organ Banks; NAICS 54143: Graphic Design Services; NAICS 541922: Commercial Photography; NAICS 62141: Family Planning Centers; NAICS 621999: All Other Miscellaneous Ambulatory Health Care Services

8111 Legal Services ***See*** NAICS 54111: Offices of Lawyers

8211 Elementary & Secondary Schools ***See*** NAICS 61111: Elementary & Secondary Schools

8221 Colleges, Universities, & Professional Schools ***See*** NAICS 61131: Colleges, Universities & Professional Schools

8222 Junior Colleges & Technical Institutes ***See*** NAICS 61121: Junior Colleges

8231 Libraries ***See*** NAICS 51412: Libraries & Archives

8243 Data Processing Schools ***See*** NAICS 611519: Other Technical & Trade Schools; NAICS 61142: Computer Training

8244 Business & Secretarial Schools ***See*** NAICS 61141: Business & Secretarial Schools

8249 Vocational Schools, NEC ***See*** NAICS 611513: Apprenticeship Training; NAICS 611512: Flight Training; NAICS 611519: Other Technical & Trade Schools

8299 Schools & Educational Services, NEC ***See*** NAICS 611512: Flight Training; NAICS 611692: Automobile Driving Schools; NAICS 61171: Educational Support Services; NAICS 611691: Exam Preparation & Tutoring; NAICS 61161: Fine Arts Schools; NAICS 61163: Language Schools; NAICS 61143: Professional & Management Development Training Schools; NAICS 611519: Other Technical and Trade Schools; NAICS 611699: All Other Miscellaneous Schools & Instruction

8322 Individual & Family Social Services ***See*** NAICS 62411: Child & Youth Services; NAICS 62421: Community Food Services; NAICS 624229: Other Community Housing Services; NAICS 62423: Emergency & Other Relief Services; NAICS 62412: Services for the Elderly & Persons with Disabilities; NAICS 624221: Temporary Shelters; NAICS 92215: Parole Offices & Probation Offices; NAICS 62419: Other Individual & Family Services

8331 Job Training & Vocational Rehabilitation Services ***See*** NAICS 62431: Vocational Rehabilitation Services

8351 Child Day Care Services ***See*** NAICS 62441: Child Day Care Services

8361 Residential Care ***See*** NAICS 623312: Homes for the Elderly; NAICS 62322: Residential Mental Health & Substance Abuse Facilities; NAICS 62399: Other Residential Care Facilities

8399 Social Services, NEC ***See*** NAICS 813212: Voluntary Health Organizations; NAICS 813219: Other Grantmaking & Giving Services; NAICS 813311: Human Rights Organizations; NAICS 813312: Environment, Conservation & Wildlife Organizations; NAICS 813319: Other Social Advocacy Organizations

8412 Museums & Art Galleries ***See*** NAICS 71211: Museums; NAICS 71212: Historical Sites

8422 Arboreta & Botanical or Zoological Gardens ***See*** NAICS 71213: Zoos & Botanical Gardens; NAICS 71219: Nature Parks & Other Similar Institutions

8611 Business Associations ***See*** NAICS 81391: Business Associations

8621 Professional Membership Organizations ***See*** NAICS 81392: Professional Organizations
8631 Labor Unions & Similar Labor Organizations ***See*** NAICS 81393: Labor Unions & Similar Labor Organizations
8641 Civic, Social, & Fraternal Associations ***See*** NAICS 81341: Civic & Social Organizations; NAICS 81399: Other Similar Organizations; NAICS 92115: American Indian & Alaska Native Tribal Governments; NAICS 62411: Child & Youth Services
8651 Political Organizations ***See*** NAICS 81394: Political Organizations
8661 Religious Organizations ***See*** NAICS 81311: Religious Organizations
8699 Membership Organizations, NEC ***See*** NAICS 81341: Civic & Social Organizations; NAICS 81391: Business Associations; NAICS 813312: Environment, Conservation, & Wildlife Organizations; NAICS 561599: All Other Travel Arrangement & Reservation Services; NAICS 81399: Other Similar Organizations
8711 Engineering Services ***See*** NAICS 54133: Engineering Services
8712 Architectural Services ***See*** NAICS 54131: Architectural Services
8713 Surveying Services ***See*** NAICS 54136: Geophysical Surveying & Mapping Services; NAICS 54137: Surveying & Mapping Services
8721 Accounting, Auditing, & Bookkeeping Services ***See*** NAICS 541211: Offices of Certified Public Accountants; NAICS 541214: Payroll Services; NAICS 541219: Other Accounting Services
8731 Commercial Physical & Biological Research ***See*** NAICS 54171: Research & Development in the Physical Sciences & Engineering Sciences; NAICS 54172: Research & Development in the Life Sciences
8732 Commercial Economic, Sociological, & Educational Research ***See*** NAICS 54173: Research & Development in the Social Sciences & Humanities; NAICS 54191: Marketing Research & Public Opinion Polling
8733 Noncommercial Research Organizations ***See*** NAICS 54171: Research & Development in the Physical Sciences & Engineering Sciences; NAICS 54172: Research & Development in the Life Sciences; NAICS 54173: Research & Development in the Social Sciences & Humanities
8734 Testing Laboratories ***See*** NAICS 54194: Veterinary Services; NAICS 54138: Testing Laboratories
8741 Management Services ***See*** NAICS 56111: Office Administrative Services
8742 Management Consulting Services ***See*** NAICS 541611: Administrative Management & General Management Consulting Services; NAICS 541612: Human Resources & Executive Search Services; NAICS 541613: Marketing Consulting Services; NAICS 541614: Process, Physical, Distribution & Logistics Consulting Services
8743 Public Relations Services ***See*** NAICS 54182: Public Relations Agencies
8744 Facilities Support Management Services ***See*** NAICS 56121: Facilities Support Services
8748 Business Consulting Services, NEC ***See*** NAICS 61171: Educational Support Services; NAICS 541618: Other Management Consulting Services; NAICS 54169: Other Scientific & Technical Consulting Services
8811 Private Households ***See*** NAICS 81411: Private Households
8999 Services, NEC ***See*** NAICS 71151: Independent Artists, Writers, & Performers; NAICS 51221: Record Production; NAICS 54169: Other Scientific & Technical Consulting Services; NAICS 51223: Music Publishers; NAICS 541612: Human Resources & Executive Search Consulting Services; NAICS 514199: All Other Information Services; NAICS 54162: Environmental Consulting Services

Public Administration

9111 Executive Offices ***See*** NAICS 92111: Executive Offices
9121 Legislative Bodies ***See*** NAICS 92112: Legislative Bodies
9131 Executive & Legislative Offices, Combined ***See*** NAICS 92114: Executive & Legislative Offices, Combined
9199 General Government, NEC ***See*** NAICS 92119: All Other General Government
9211 Courts ***See*** NAICS 92211: Courts
9221 Police Protection ***See*** NAICS 92212: Police Protection
9222 Legal Counsel & Prosecution ***See*** NAICS 92213: Legal Counsel & Prosecution
9223 Correctional Institutions ***See*** NAICS 92214: Correctional Institutions
9224 Fire Protection ***See*** NAICS 92216: Fire Protection
9229 Public Order & Safety, NEC ***See*** NAICS 92219: All Other Justice, Public Order, & Safety
9311 Public Finance, Taxation, & Monetary Policy ***See*** NAICS 92113: Public Finance
9411 Administration of Educational Programs ***See*** NAICS 92311: Administration of Education Programs
9431 Administration of Public Health Programs ***See*** NAICS 92312: Administration of Public Health Programs
9441 Administration of Social, Human Resource & Income Maintenance Programs ***See*** NAICS 92313: Administration of Social, Human Resource & Income Maintenance Programs
9451 Administration of Veteran's Affairs, Except Health Insurance ***See*** NAICS 92314: Administration of Veteran's Affairs
9511 Air & Water Resource & Solid Waste Management ***See*** NAICS 92411: Air & Water Resource & Solid Waste Management
9512 Land, Mineral, Wildlife, & Forest Conservation ***See*** NAICS 92412: Land, Mineral, Wildlife, & Forest Conservation
9531 Administration of Housing Programs ***See*** NAICS 92511: Administration of Housing Programs
9532 Administration of Urban Planning & Community & Rural Development ***See*** NAICS 92512: Administration of Urban Planning & Community & Rural Development
9611 Administration of General Economic Programs ***See*** NAICS 92611: Administration of General Economic Programs
9621 Regulations & Administration of Transportation Programs ***See*** NAICS 488111: Air Traffic Control; NAICS 92612: Regulation & Administration of Transportation Programs
9631 Regulation & Administration of Communications, Electric, Gas, & Other Utilities ***See*** NAICS 92613: Regulation & Administration of Communications, Electric, Gas, & Other Utilities
9641 Regulation of Agricultural Marketing & Commodity ***See*** NAICS 92614: Regulation of Agricultural Marketing & Commodity
9651 Regulation, Licensing, & Inspection of Miscellaneous Commercial Sectors ***See*** NAICS 92615: Regulation, Licensing, & Inspection of Miscellaneous Commercial Sectors
9661 Space Research & Technology ***See*** NAICS 92711: Space Research & Technology
9711 National Security ***See*** NAICS 92811: National Security
9721 International Affairs ***See*** NAICS 92812: International Affairs
9999 Nonclassifiable Establishments ***See*** NAICS 99999: Unclassified Establishments

Bibliography

ABA BANKING JOURNAL
Simmons-Boardman
Publishing Corp.
345 Hudson St.
New York, NY 10014-4502
(212)620-7211
Fax: (212)633-1165
Monthly
Subscription Rate: $18.50
ISSN: 0194-5947

Special Issue:
Banking's Top Performers (annual)

ABA JOURNAL
American Bar Association
750 N. Lake Shore Dr.
Chicago, IL 60611-4497
(312)988-6010
Fax: (312)988-6014
15x/year
Subscription Rate: $66
ISSN: 0747-0088
URL: www.abnet.org

ACCOUNTANCY
Institute of Chartered Accountants in England and Wales
40 Bernard St.
London WC1N WLD England
44-171-833-3291
Fax: 44-171-833-2085
Monthly
Subscription Rate: £65
ISSN: 0001-4664
www.accountancymag.co.uk
Special Issue:
International Edition

THE ACCOUNTANT
Lafferty Publications Ltd.
420 Lexington Ave., Ste. 2531
New York, NY 10170-0002
(212)557-6726
Fax: (212)557-7266
Monthly
Subscription Rate: $599
ISSN: 0001-4710

ADAMS LIQUOR HANDBOOK
Adams Media Inc.
1180 Ave. of the Americas, 11th Fl.
New York, NY 10036-8401
(212)827-4700
Fax: (212)827-4720
Annual
Price: $350
ISSN: 1046-8250

ADAMS WINE HANDBOOK
Adams Media Inc.
1180 Ave. of the Americas, 11th Fl.
New York, NY 10036-8401
(212)274-7000
Fax: (212)431-0500
Annual
Price: $265

ADVERTISING AGE
Crain Communications Inc.
711 Third Ave.
New York, NY 10017-0436
(212)210-0100
Fax: (212)210-0110
Weekly
Subscription Rate: $119
ISSN: 0001-8899
www.adage.com

Special Issues:
100 Leading Media Companies (annual)
100 Leading National Avertisers (annual)

Ad Age 300 (annual)
Agency Report (annual)

ADWEEK
Eastern Edition
BPI Communications, Inc.
1515 Broadway
New York, NY 10036
(212)536-5336
Fax: (212)536-5353
Toll Free: (800)722-6658
Weekly
Subscription Rate: $140
ISSN: 0199-2864
www.adweek.com/magazine/adweek.asp

Special Issues:
Agency Report Card (annual)
Hottest Magazines (annual)

AGRI FINANCE
Doane Agricultural Service Co.
11701 Borman Dr.
St. Louis, MO 63146-4199
(314)569-2700
Fax: (314)569-1083
9x/year
Subscription Rate: $36
ISSN: 0002-1180

AIPSO (Auto Insurance Plans Services Office)
302 Central Ave.
Johnston, RI 02919-4995
(401)946-2310

AIR CARGO WORLD
Journal of Commerce
2 World Trade Ctr., 27th Fl.
New York, NY 10048-0298
(202)783-1148
Fax: (202)783-2550
Monthly
Subscription Rate: $58
ISSN: 0745-5100

AIR TRANSPORT WORLD
Penton Publishing Co.
1350 Connecticut Ave. NW, Ste. 902
Washington, DC 20036-1702
(202)659-8500
Fax: (202)659-1554
Monthly
Subscription Rate: $55
ISSN: 0002-2543
www.atwonline.com

Special Issue:
Top 25 (annual)

AMERICAN BANKER
American Banker-Bond Buyer
1 State Street Plaza, 26th Fl.
New York, NY 10004-1549
(212)803-8200
Fax: (212)843-9597
Daily (except weekends and holidays)
Subscription Rate: $795
ISSN: 0002-7561
www.americanbanker.com

Special Issues:
Performance of Top Banking Companies (annual)
Top 50 in Mortgage Investment (annual)
Top 50 U.S. Bank Holding Companies (annual)
Top 75 Credit Unions
Top 100 Bank and Thrift Companies in Home Equity Loans and Lines of Credit (annual)
Top 100 Firms in Discretionary Trust Assets (annual)
Top 100 Originators of Residential Mortgages (annual)
Top Community Banks (annual)

AMERICAN DEMOGRAPHICS
American Demographics, Inc.
11 River Bend Dr., S.
PO Box 4294
Stamford, CT 06907-0294
(203)358-9900
Fax: (203)358-5812
Monthly
Subscription Rate: $69
ISSN: 0163-4089
www.demographics.com

AMERICAN DRUGGIST
Press Corps
444 Park Ave. S, Rm. 402
New York, NY 10016-7321
(212)686-8584
Fax: (212)686-9098
Monthly
Subscription Rate: $44
ISSN: 0190-5279

Special Issue:
Top 200 Rx Drugs (annual)

AMERICAN PRINTER
Primedia Intertec Publishing Co.
29 N. Wacker Dr.
Chicago, IL 60606
(312)726-2802
Fax: (312)726-3091

Monthly
Subscription Rate: $65
ISSN: 0744-6616
www.americanprinter.com

Special Issue:
Top 50 Fastes

Growing Printers (annual)

AMUSEMENT BUSINESS
BPI Communications
Amusement Business Division
49 Music Square W.
Nashville, TN 37203-3213
(615)321-4250
Fax: (615)327-1575
Toll Free: (800)561-5681
Weekly
Subscription Rate: $129
ISSN: 0003-2344
www.amusementbusiness.com

Special Issues:
Amusement Business Annual
Amusement Business Annual Year-End Issue

APPAREL INDUSTRY MAGAZINE
Shore-Varrone, Inc.
6255 Barfield Rd., Ste. 200
Atlanta, GA 30328-4300
(404)252-8831
Fax: (404)252-4436
Monthly
Subscription Rate: $61
ISSN: 0192-1878
www.aimagazine.com

Special Issue:
AIM 100 (annual)

APPLIANCE MANUFACTURER
Business News Publishing Co.
5900 Harper Rd., Ste. 109
Solon, OH 44139-1835
(440)349-3060
Fax: (440)498-9121
Monthly
Subscription Rate: $55
ISSN: 0003-679X
www.ammagazine.com

AREA DEVELOPMENT
Halcyon Business Publications, Inc.
400 Post Ave.
Westbury, NY 11590
(516)338-0900
Fax: (516)338-0100
Toll Free: (800)753-2732
Monthly
Subscription Rate: $65
ISSN: 0004-0908
www.area-development.com

ART BUSINESS NEWS
Advanstar Communications, Inc.
19 Old Kings Hwy. S
Darien, CT 06820-4526
(203)656-1976
Fax: (203)656-3402
13x/year
Subscription Rate: $39
ISSN: 0273-5652

ASIAMONEY
5/f Printing House
6 Duddell St.
Central, HK
(852)2912-8018
Fax: (852)2810-8417
10x/year
Subscription Rate: $325
ISSN: 0958-9309

Special Issue:
Asiamoney Stockbrokers' Poll (annual)

ASIAN BUSINESS
Far East Trade Press Ltd.
Kai Tak Commercial Bldg., 2nd Fl.
317 Des Voex Rd.
Central, Hong Kong, China
545-7200
Fax: 544-6979
Monthly
ISSN: 0254-3729
web3.asia1.com.sg/timesnet/navigatn/ab.html

Special Issue:
Most Admired Companies In Asia (annual)

ASIA'S 7,500 LARGEST COMPANIES
E.L.C. Publishing, Ltd.
109 Uxbridge Rd.
Ealing
London W5 STL England
0181-566-2288
Fax: 0181-566-4931
Annual
Price: £160

ASSOCIATION MANAGEMENT
American Society of Association Executives
1575 I St., NW
Washington, DC 20005-1168
(202)626-2740
Fax: (202)408-9634
Monthly
Subscription Rate: $30
ISSN: 0004-5578
www.asaenet.org/Publications/Amcurrent/index.html

ATI (AMERICA'S TEXTILES INTERNATIONAL)
Billian Publishing, Inc
(770) 955-5656
Fax: (770) 952-0667
Subscription Rate: $43

AUTOMATIC MERCHANDISER
Johnson Hill Press, Inc.
1233 Janesville Ave.
PO Box 803
Fort Atkinson, WI 53538-0803
(920)547-7377
Fax: (920)568-8305
Toll Free: (800)547-7377
Monthly
Subscription Rate: $60
ISSN: 1061-1797
www.amonline.com

AUTOMOTIVE INDUSTRIES
Cahners Business Information
201 King of Prussia Rd.
Radnor, PA 19089-0001
(610)964-4876
Fax: (610)964-6042
Toll Free: (800)274-2207
Monthly
Subscription Rate: $74
ISSN: 1099-4130
www.ai.online.com

AUTOMOTIVE NEWS
Crain Communications Inc.
1400 Woodbridge St.
Detroit, MI 48207-3187
(313)446-1679
Fax: (313)446-1679
Weekly
Subscription Rate: $109
ISSN: 0005-1551
URL: www.automotivenews.com

Special Issue:
S/I Top 150 OEM Parts Suppliers (annual)

AVIATION WEEK & SPACE TECHNOLOGY
McGraw-Hill Cos.
1221 Avenue of the Americas, 40th Fl.
New York, NY 10020-1095
(212)904-2000
Fax: (212)512-2930
Weekly
Subscription Rate: $82
ISSN: 0005-2175
www.aviationweek.com/aviation

BAKERY PRODUCTION & MARKETING RED BOOK
Cahners Business Information
1350 E. Touhy St.
Box 5080
Des Plaines, IL 60017-5080
(847)635-8800
Fax: (847)390-2779
Toll Free: (800)323-4958
Annual
Price: $255
ISSN: 0005-4127
www.cahners.com/mainmag/bpm.htm

BANK MARKETING
Bank Marketing Association
1120 Connecticut Ave., NW
Washington, DC 20036
(202)663-5378
Fax: (202)828-4540
Toll Free: (800)433-9013
Monthly
Subscription Rate: $120
ISSN: 0888-3149
www.bmanet.org

BANK SYSTEMS & TECHNOLOGY
Miller-Freeman Inc.
1 Penn Plaza
New York, NY 10119
(212)869-1300
Fax: (212)575-5136
Toll Free: (800)950-1314
Monthly
Subscription Rate: $65
ISSN: 1045-9472
www.banktech.com/banktech/
homepage.htm

THE BANKER
Financial Times Business Information
Maple House
149 Tottenham Court Rd.
London W1P 9LL United Kingdom
44-171-896-2525
Fax: 44-171-896-2586
Monthly
Subscription Rate: $295
ISSN: 0005-5395
www.thebanker.com

Special Issues:
Asian Top 200 (annual)
Europe Top 500 (annual)
Global Banking (annual)
Top 100 African Banks - By Country (annual)
Top 100 Arab Financial Institutions (annual)
Top 100 Central Europeans (annual)
Top 100 Japanese Banks (annual)
Top 100 Latin American Banks (annual)
Top 100 Russians (annual)
Top 100 Financial Institutions (annual)
Top 500 African Banks-By Country (annual)
Top 1,000 Banks-By Country (annual)
Top 200 U.S. Banks (annual)
Top Arab Financial Institutions (annual)
World Top 1,000 (annual)

BANKERS' ALMANAC WORLD RANKING
Reed Information Services Ltd.
Windsor Ct., E. Grinstead House
E. Grinstead
W. Sussex RH19 1XA England
01342-335-962
Fax: 01342-335-977
Annual
Price: $229

BANKING STRATEGIES
Bank Administration Institute
One N. Franklin, Ste. 1000
Chicago, IL 60606-3421
(312)553-4600
Fax: (312)683-2426
Toll Free: (800)655-2706
Bimonthly
Subscription Rate: $59
ISSN: 1091-6385
Special Issue:
M & A Forum (annual)
Top 50 Banking Companies (annual)

BANKRUPTCY YEARBOOK & ALMANAC
New Generation Research
2254 Friend St., Ste. 801
Boston, MA 02114
(617)573-9550
Fax: (617)573-9554
Toll Free: (800)468-3810
Annual
Price $175
ISSN: 1054-9463
www.turnarounds.com

BARRON'S
Dow Jones & Co., Inc.
200 Liberty St.
New York, NY 10281-1003
(212)416-2700
Fax: (212)416-2829
Weekly
Subscription Rate: $119
ISSN: 1077-8039

Special Issue:
Barron's 500 (annual)

BEST'S REVIEW LIFE/HEALTH EDITION
A. M. Best Co., Inc.
Ambest Rd.
Oldwick, NJ 08858-0700
(908)439-2200
Fax: (908)339-3296
Monthly
Subscription Rate: $25
ISSN: 0005-9706
www.ambest.com

Special Issue:
Accident & Health Premiums (annual)
100 Leading Life Companies (annual)

BEST'S REVIEW PROPERTY/CASUALTY EDITION
A.M. Best Co., Inc.
Ambest Rd.
Oldwick, NJ 08858-0700
(908)439-2200
Fax: (908)339-3296
Monthly
Subscription Rate: $25
ISSN: 0161-7745
www.ambest.com

BETTER INVESTING
National Association of Investors Corp.
PO Box 220
Royal Oak, MI 48068-0220
(248)583-6242
Fax: (248)583-1984
Toll Free: (800)275-6242
Monthly
Subscription Rate: $20
ISSN: 0006-016X
URL: www.betterinvesting.org
Special Issue:
Top 100 (annual)

BEVERAGE DYNAMICS
Adams Business Media Inc.
1180 Ave. of the Americas, 11th Fl.
New York, NY 10036-8401
(212)827-4700
Fax: (212)827-4720
9x/year
Subscription Rate: $35
ISSN: 1088-7504

BEVERAGE INDUSTRY
Stagnito Communications Inc.
1935 Shermer Rd., Ste. 100
Northbrook, IL 60062-5354
(847)205-5660
Fax: (847)205-5680
Monthly
Subscription Rate: $55
ISSN: 0148-6187

Special Issue:
Top 100 (annual)

BEVERAGE WORLD
Strategic Business Communications
355 Park Ave., S.
New York, NY 10010-1789
(212)822-5930
Fax: (212)822-5931
Monthly
Subscription Rate: $55
ISSN: 0098-2318
www.beverageworld.com

Special Issue:
Top 50 (annual)
Annual Beverage Market Index
Top 25 Bottlers in North America (annual)

BLACK ENTERPRISE
Earl G. Graves Publishing Co.
130 5th Ave., Fl. 10
New York, NY 10011-4399
(212)886-9567
Fax: (212)886-9610
Monthly
Subscription Rate: $21.95
ISSN: 0006-4165
www.blackenterprise.com

Special Issue:
Top 100 Black Businesses (annual)

BOATING INDUSTRY
National Trade Publications, Inc.
13 Century Hill Dr.
Latham, NY 12110-2113
(518)783-1281
Fax: (518)783-1386
Monthly
Subscription Rate: $30
ISSN: 0006-5404
www.boatbiz.com

BOND BUYER YEARBOOK
American Banker-Bond Buyer
1 State St. Plaza, 26th Fl.
New York, NY 10004-1549
(212)803-8200
Fax: (212)803-2223
Annual
Price: $49
ISSN: 1075-3710

BOOK OF LISTS
BIV Publications Ltd.
500-1155 W. Pender St.
Vancouver, BC V6E 2P4 Canada
(604)688-2398
Fax: (604)688-1963
Annually
Subscription Rate: $30

BOTTLED WATER REPORTER
International Bottled Water Association
1700 Diagonal Rd., Ste. 650
Alexandria, VA 22314
(703)683-5213
Fax: (703)683-4074
Bi-monthly
Subscription Rate: $50

BOTTOM LINE/BUSINESS
P.O. Box 58415
Boulder, CO 80322-8415
(203)625-5900
Fax: (203)861-7442
Semimonthly
Subscription Rate: $130
ISSN: 1082-457X

BRANDWEEK
BPI Communications Inc.
1515 Broadway
New York, NY 10036-8901
Fax: (212)536-5084
Toll Free: (800)722-6658
Weekly
Subscription Rate: $130
www.brandweek.com

Special Issue:
Superbrands: America's Top 2,000 Brands (annual)

BROADCASTING & CABLE
Cahners Publishing Co.
245 W. 17th St.
New York, NY 10011
(212)645-0067
Fax: (212)337-7028
Weekly
Subscription Rate: $139
ISSN: 1068-6827
www.broadcastingcable.com

Special Issues:
Top 25 TV Groups (annual)

BROOKINGS REVIEW
Brookings Institution Press
1775 Massachusetts Ave., NW
Washington, DC 20036-2188
Toll Free: (800)275-1447
Fax: (202)797-6004
Quarterly
Subscription Rate: $15
ISSN: 0745-1253

BUILDER MAGAZINE
Hanley-Wood, Inc.
1 Thomas Circle NW, Ste. 600
Washington, DC 20005
(202)452-0800
Fax: (202)785-1974
13x/year
Subscription Rate: $29.95
ISSN: 0744-1193
www.builderonline.com
Special Issue:
Builder 100 (annual)

BUILDING DESIGN & CONSTRUCTION
Cahners Business Information
1350 E. Touhy Ave.
Des Plaines, IL 60018-3358
(847)390-2650
Fax: (847)390-2152
Toll Free: (800)323-4958
Monthly
Subscription Rate: $108.90
ISSN: 0007-3407
www.bdcmag.com

Special Issue:
Design/Construct 300 (annual)

BUSINESS & HEALTH
Medical Economics Co.
5 Paragon Dr.
Montvale, NJ 07645-1735
(201)358-7200
Fax: (201)722-2490
Toll Free: (800)526-4870
14x/year
Subscription Rate: $99
ISSN: 0739-9413

BUSINESS FACILITIES
Group C Communications, Inc.
121 Monmouth St.
Red Bank, NY 07701-1110
(732)842-7433
Fax: (732)758-6634
Toll Free: (800)524-0337
Monthly
Subscription Rate: $30
ISSN: 0746-0023
www.busfac.com

BUSINESS FORMS, LABELS & SYSTEMS
North American Publishing Co.
401 N. Broad St.
Philadelphia, PA 19108-1001
(215)238-5300
Fax: (215)238-5427
Semimonthly
Subscription Rate: $95
ISSN: 1044-758X
www.bfls.com

BUSINESS INSURANCE
Crain Communications Inc.
740 N. Rush St.
Chicago, IL 60611-2590
(312)649-5398
Fax: (312)280-3174
Toll Free: (888)446-1422
Weekly
Subscription Rate: $87
ISSN: 0007-6864
www.businessinsurance.com

Special Issue:
Top Environmental Risk Management Consultants (annual) *Lloyd's of London (annual)*
Standard & Poor's Top Global Business Insurers (annual)

BUSINESS MARKETING
Crain Communications Inc.
740 N. Rush St.
Chicago, IL 60611-2590
(312)649-5200
Fax: (312)649-5462
Monthly
Subscription Rate: $42
ISSN: 1087-948X
www.netb2b.com

Special Issues:
Top 100 (annual)
Business-to-Business Agency Ranking (annual)
NetMarketing 200 (annual)

BUSINESS START-UPS
Entrepreneur Media
2392 Morse Ave.
Irvine, CA 92614-6234
(714)261-2083
Fax: (714)755-4211
Monthly
Subscription Rate: $10
ISSN: 1069-5818

Special Issue:
Business Mexico 100 (annual)

BUSINESS TRAVEL NEWS
Miller Freeman Inc.
1 Penn Plaza
New York, NY 10119-1198
(212)714-1300
Fax: (212)279-3947
Toll Free: 950-1314
29x/year
Subscription Rate: $95
ISSN: 8750-3670
www.btnonline.com

Special Issues:
Business Travel Survey (annual)
U.S. Hotel Chain Survey (annual)
Corporate Travel 100 (annual)

BUSINESS WEEK
McGraw-Hill Cos.
1221 Ave. of the Americas, 40th Fl.
New York, NY 10020-1095
(212)512-2000
Fax: (212)512-6111
Weekly
Subscription Rate: $54.95
ISSN: 0007-7135
www.businessweek.com

Special Issues:
Annual Survey of Executive Compensation
Business Week 50: Top Companies of the S&P 500 (annual)
Global 1,000 (annual)
The Best (annual)
The Best B-Schools (annual)
Growth Companies (annual)
Small Growth Companies (annual)
Top 100 IT Companies (annual)

CA MAGAZINE
277 Wellington St. West
Toronto, ON M5V 3H2 Canada
(416)204-3250
Fax: (416)204-3409
Monthly
Subscription Rate: $72
ISSN: 0317-6878

CABLE WORLD
Cowles Business Media
1905 Sherman St., Ste. 1000
Denver, CO 80203-1149
(303)837-0915
Fax: (303)837-0915
Toll Free: (800)775-3777
Weekly
Subscription Rate: $74
ISSN: 1042-7228
www.cableworld.com

CALIFORNIA MANUFACTURERS REGISTER
Database Publishing Co.
P.O Box 79924
Anaheim, CA 92825-0024
(714)778-6400
Toll-free: (800)888-8434
E-Mail Address:
sales@databasepublishing.com
Annual
Subscription Rate: $190 (Canadian), $229 (foreign)
ISSN: 0068-5739
URL: www.databasepublishing.com

CALL CENTER SOLUTIONS
Technology marketing Corp.
One Technology Plaza
Norwalk, CT 06854
(203)852-6800
Fax: (203)853-2845
Toll Free: (800)243-6002
Monthly
Subscription Rate: $49
ISSN: 1521-0774

CALLAHAN'S CREDIT UNION DIRECTORY
Callahan & Associates, Inc.
1001 Connecticut Ave., NW, 10th Fl.
Washington, DC 20036
(202)223-3920
Fax: (202)223-1311
Toll Free: (800)446-7453
Annual
Subscription Rate: $135
ISSN: 0888-8671

CANADIAN BUSINESS
777 Bay St.
Toronto, ON M5W 1A7 Canada
(416)596-5100
Fax: (416)596-5003
Bi-weekly
Subscription Rate: $34.95
ISSN: 0008-3100
www.canbus.com

Special Edition:
Performance 2,000 (annual)

CARD INDUSTRY DIRECTORY
Faulkner & Gray, Inc.
11 Penn Plaza, 17th Fl.
New York, NY 10001
(212)967-7000
Fax: (212)967-7155
Toll Free: (800)535-8403
Annual
Price: $425
ISSN: 1051-6778

CANDY INDUSTRY
Stagnito Communications, Inc.
1935 Shermer Rd., Ste. 100
Northbrook, IL 60062-5354
(847)205-5660
Fax: (847)205-5680

CARD MARKETING BUYER'S GUIDE
Faulkner & Gray
Eleven Penn Plaza
New York, NY 10001
(212)967-7060
Fax: (212)967-8269
Toll-Free: (800)535-8403
Price: $465

CASUAL LIVING
Columbia Communications, Inc.
1015 Seven Oaks Ln.
Mamaroneck, NY 10543-4720
(704)253-9299
Monthlyh
Subscription Rate: $20
ISSN: 0740-8285

Special Issue:
Top 100 Retailers Report (annual)

CATALOG AGE
Intertec Publishing
11 River Bend Dr. S
Box 4949
Stamford, CT 06907-0949
(203)358-4253
Fax: (203)358-5812
Toll Free: (800)775-3777
13x/yr.
Subscription Rate: $74
ISSN: 0740-3119
URL: www.catalogagmag.com

Special Issue:
The Catalog Age 100 (annual)

CB RICHARD ELLIS GLOBAL RESEACH AND CONSULTING: NORTH AMERICAN INDEX
CB Richard Ellis
1840 Century Park E
Los Angeles, CA 90067-2108
(310)550-2500
Fax: (310)203-9624

CFO
CFO Publishing Corp.
253 Summer St.
Boston, MA 02210-1114
(617)345-9700
Fax: (617)951-9306
Monthly
Subscription Rate: Free
ISSN: 8756-7113
www.cfonet.com

CHAIN STORE AGE
Lebhar-Friedman, Inc.
425 Park Ave.
New York, NY 10022
(212)756-5252
Fax: (212)756-5270
Monthly
Subscription Rate: $105
ISSN: 1087-0601
www.chainstoreage.com

Special Issue:
Top 100 (annual)

CHEMICAL & ENGINEERING NEWS
American Chemical Society
1155 16th St. NW
Washington, DC 20036-4899
(202)333-9511
Fax: (614)447-3671
Weekly
Subscription Rate: $125
ISSN: 0009-2347
pubs.acs.org/cen/

Special Issues:
Facts & Figures for Chemical R & D (annual)

CHEMICAL MARKET REPORTER
Schnell Publishing Co., Inc.
2 Rector St., 26th Fl.
New York, NY 10006
(212)791-4200
Fax: (212)791-4313
Weekly
Subscription Rate: $99
ISSN: 1092-0110
URL: www.chemexpo.com

CHEMICAL WEEK
Chemical Week Associates
888 7th Ave., Fl. 26
New York, NY 10106-0001
(212)621-4929
Fax: (212)621-4831
Weekly
Subscription Rate: $129
ISSN: 0009-272X
www.chemweek.com

Special Issue:
Billion-Dollar Club (annual)
Chemical Week 300 (annual)

CHILDREN'S BUSINESS
Fairchild Publications Inc.
7 W 34th St., Fl. 3
New York, NY 10001-8100
(212)630-4230
Fax: (212)630-4580
Subscription Rate: $24
ISSN: 0884-2280

COAL AGE
Intertec Publishing
11 river Bend Dr. South
P.O. Box 4294
Stamford, CT 06907-0294
(913)341-1300
Fax: (913)967-1860
Monthly
Subscription Rate: Free
ISSN: 0009-9910
www.coalage.com

COLORADO BUSINESS
Wiesner Publishing Co.
7009 S. Potomac St.
Englewood, CO 80112-4029
(303)798-1274
Fax: (303)794-2466
Monthly
Subscription Rate: $24
ISSN: 0898-6363

Special Issues:
Colorado's Private 250 (annual)
Colorado's Top Public Companies Top 100 (annual)

COMMUNICATIONS NEWS
Nelson Publishing
2504 Tamiami Trail N
Nokomis, FL 34275-3482
(941)966-9521
Fax: (941)966-2590
Monthly
Subscription Rate: $79
ISSN: 0010-3632
URL: www.asaenet.org

COMPENSATION & BENEFITS REVIEW
American Management Association
1601 Broadway
New York, NY 10019-7420
(212)903-8069
Fax: (212)903-8083
Toll Free: (800)262-9699
Bimontly
Subscription Rate: $197
ISSN: 0886-3687
URL: www.amanet.org/periodicals/cbr

COMPUTERWORLD
Computerworld Inc.
500 Old Connecticut Path
Framingham, MA 01701-4574
(508)879-0700
Fax: (508)626-2705
Toll Free: (800)343-6474
Weekly
Subscription Rate: $48
ISSN: 0010-4841

Special Issue:
Top 10 IT Job Markets (annual)

CONVENIENCE STORE NEWS
355 Park Ave. South
New York, NY 10010
(212)979-4800
Fax: (212)979-7344
16x/year
Subscription Rate: $85
ISSN: 0194-8733

Special Issue:
Top 50 Convenience Store Companies (annual)

CQ WEEKLY
Congressional Quarterly, Inc.
1414 22nd St. NW
Washington, DC 20037-1096
(202)887-8500
Fax: (202)728-1863
Toll Free: (800)432-2250
Weekly
Subscription Rate: $1395
www.cq.com
ISSN: 0010-5910

CRAFTRENDS
741 Corporate Circle, Ste. A
Golden, CO 80401
(303)278-1010
Fax: (303)277-0370
Monthly
Subscription Rate: $26
ISSN: 0897-6341
www.craftrends.com

CRAIN'S CHICAGO BUSINESS
Crain Communications Inc.

740 N. Rush St.
Chicago, IL 60611-2590
(312)649-5200
Fax: (312)280-3150
Weekly
Subscription Rate: $109
ISSN: 0149-6956
www.crainschicagobusiness.com

Special Issues:
Chicago's Top Employers
Top Business Lists (annual)

CRAIN'S DETROIT BUSINESS
Crain Communications Inc.
1400 Woodbridge St.
Detroit, MI 48207-3187
(313)446-6000
Fax: (313)393-0997
Weekly
Subscription Rate: $45
ISSN: 0882-1992
www.crainsdetroit.com

Special Issues:
Crain's Book of Lists Detroit (annual)

CRAIN'S NEW YORK BUSINESS
Crain Communications Inc.
220 E. 42nd St., Ste. 1306
New York, NY 10017
(212)210-0259
Fax: (212)210-0799
Toll Free: (800)678-9595
Weekly
Subscription Rate: $62
ISSN: 8756-789X
www.crainsnewyork.com

Special Issues:
Fortunate 100
Fastest Growing Co. (annual)
Largest Foreign Banks in New York City
The Private 250
Top Business Lists (annual)
Top310 SBA Lenders (annual)

CREDIT CARD MANAGEMENT
Faulkner & Gray, Inc.
11 Penn Plaza, Bsmt. 22
New York, NY 10001-2006
(212)967-7000
Fax: (212)967-8269
13x/yr.
Subscription Rate: $98
ISSN: 0896-9329
ccm.faulknergray.com

Special Issue:
CCM's Credit Card Industry Annual Report

CREDIT UNION MAGAZINE
Credit Union National Association, Inc.
5710 Mineral Point Rd.
Madison, WI 53705-4454
(608)231-4088
Fax: (608)231-4370
Monthly
Subscription Rate: $38
ISSN: 0011-1066
URL: www.cuna.org

DAIRY FIELD
Stagnito Communications, Inc.
1935 Shermer Rd., Ste. 100
Northbrook, IL 60062-5354
(708)205-5660
Fax: (708)205-5680
Monthly
Subscription Rate: $48
ISSN: 1055-0607

Special Issue:
Top 100 U.S. Dairy Companies (annual)

DAIRY FOODS
Cahners Business Information
1350 E. Touhy Ave.
Box 5080
Des Plaines, IL 60017-5080
(847)390-2916
Fax: (847)390-2445
Toll Free: (800)323-4958
Monthly
Subscription Rate: $70
ISSN: 0888-0050
www.cahners.com/mainmag/df.htm

Special Issues:
Annual Ice Cream Report
Top 20 Dairy Companies In Europe (annual)
Top 80 U.S. Canadian Dairy Companies (annual)

D.C. GREEN MINORITIES
Black Enterprise
Earl G. Graves Publishing Co.
130 Fifth Ave., 10th Fl.
New York, NY 10011-4399
(212)242-8000
Fax: (212)886-9618
Monthly
Subscription Rate: $21.95

DCI
Advanstar Communications, Inc.
7500 Old Oak Blvd.
Cleveland, OH 44130-3343
(218)723-9299
Fax: (218)723-9377
Monthly
Price: $32
ISSN: 1096-4819

DEALERNEWS
Advanstar Communications Inc.
7500 Old Oak Blvd.
Cleveland, OH 44130
(440)243-8100
Fax: (440)891-2727
Frequency: Monthly
Subscription Rate:

DEALERSCOPE CONSUMER ELECTRONICS MARKETPLACE
North American Publishing Co.
401 N. Broad St.
Philadelphia, PA 19108
(215)238-5300
Fax: (215)238-5412
Monthly
Subscription Rate: $79
ISSN: 0011-7218
www.dealerscope.com

DEFENSE NEWS
Army Times Publishing
6883 Commercial Dr.
Springfield, VA 22151-4202
(703)642-7330
Fax: (703)642-7386
Weekly
Subscription Rate: $99

ISSN: 0884-139X
www.defensenews.com

Special Issue:
Top 100 Firms (annual)

DIRECT MARKETING
Hoke Communications, Inc.
224 Seventh St.
Garden City, NY 11530-5771
(516)229-6700
Fax: (516)294-8141
Monthly
Subscription Rate: $56
ISSN: 0012-3188

DIRECTORY OF COMPUTER AND CONSUMER ELECTRONICS RETAILERS
(formerly Directory of Computer Retailers, Dealers, & Distributors)
Chain Store Guide Information Services
3922 Coconut Palm Dr.
Tampa, FL 33619
(813)627-6800
Fax; (813)927-6882
Toll-Free: (800)927-9292
Annual
Subscription Rate: $290
URL: www.csgis.com

DIRECTORY OF FOOD SERVICE DISTRIBUTORS
Chain Store Guide Information Services
3922 Coconut Palm Dr.
Tampa, FL 33619
(813)627-6800
Fax; (813)927-6882
Toll-Free: (800)927-9292
Annual
Subscription Rate: $290
ISSN: 0271-7662
URL: www.csgis.com

DIRECTORY OF REGISTERED INVESTMENT ADVISERS
Money Market Directories
320 E. Main St.
Charlottesville, VA 22902-5234
(804)446-2810
Fax: (804)979-9962
Annual
Price: $380
ISSN: 1059-7433

DISCOUNT MERCHANDISER
Macfadden Holdings Publishing
233 Park Ave.
New York, NY 10003-1606
(212)979-4860
Fax: (212)979-7431
Monthly
Subscription Rate: $35
ISSN: 0012-3579
www.discountmerchandiser.com/dm.html

Special Issue:
Head Turners

DISCOUNT STORE NEWS
Lebhar-Friedman, Inc.
425 Park Ave., 6th Fl.
New York, NY 10022-3549
(212)756-5106
Fax: (212)756-5125
Toll Free: (800)4-LEBHAR
Biweekly
Subscription Rate: $99
ISSN: 0012-3587
www.discountstorenews.com

Special Issues:
Discount Industry Annual Report
Top Brands Survey (annual)

DISTRIBUTION
Cahners Business Information
201 King of Prussia Rd.
Radnor, PA 19089-0001
(610)964-4000
Fax: (202)463-6456
13x/year
Subscription Rate: $65
ISSN: 1066-8489

Special Issue:
Distribution's Logistic Annual Report

DISTRIBUTION CHANNELS
American Wholesale Marketers Association
1128 16th St. NW
Washington, DC 20036-4802
(202)463-2124
Fax: (202)467-0559
Toll Free: (800)482-2962
10x/year
Subscription Rate: $36
ISSN: 1083-9313

DRUG STORE NEWS
Lebhar-Friedman Inc.
425 Park Ave., 6th Fl.
New York, NY 10022-3549
(212)756-5000
Fax: (212)756-5125
27x/yr.
Subscription Rate: $99
ISSN: 0191-7587
URL: www.drugstorenews.com

Special Issue:
Annual Report of the Drug Industry

DRUG TOPICS
Medical Economics Co.
5 Paragon Dr.
Montvale, NJ 07645-1735
(201)358-7200
Fax: (201)358-7250
Toll Free: (800)526-4870
23x/year
Subscription Rate: $61
ISSN: 0012-6616
www.drugtopics.com

DUN & BRADSTREET
Dun & Bradstreet
1 Diamond Hill Rd.
Murray Hill, NJ 07974-1218
(908)665-5000
Fax: (908)665-5418
Toll Free: (800)879-1362
Bimonthly
ISSN: 1088-9604

DUN'S EUROPA
Dun's Marketing Services
3 Sylvan Way
Parsippany, NJ 07054-3805
Fax: (201)605-6920

Annual
Price: $495
ISSN: 0957-5812

THE ECONOMIST
The Economist Bldg.
111 W. 57th St.
New York, NY 10019
(212)541-5730
Fax: (212)541-9678
Weekly
Subscription Rate: $125
ISSN: 0013-0613
www.economist.com

EDITOR & PUBLISHER MARKET GUIDE
Editor & Publisher Co.
11 W. 19th St., 10th Fl.
New York, NY 10011-4234
(212)675-4380
Fax: (212)691-6939
Annual
Price: $100
ISSN: 1082-0779
URL: www.mediainfo.com

ELECTRIC PERSPECTIVES
Edison Electric Institute
701 Pennsylvania Ave. NW
Washington, DC 20004-2696
(202)508-5595
Fax: (202)508-5759
Bimonthly
Subscription Rate: $50
ISSN: 0364-474X

ELECTRONIC BUSINESS
Cahners Business Information
275 Washington St.
Newton, MA 02158-1630
(617)558-4555
Fax: (617)558-4470
Monthly
Subscription Rate: $65
ISSN: 1097-4881
www.eb-mag.com

Special Issues:
Top 20 (annual)
Top 25 North American Electronic Component Distributors
Contract Manufacturers Top 200 (annual)
Electronic Component Distributors
Top 100 R&D

ELECTRONIC NEWS
Cahners Business Information
475 Park Ave. S, 2nd Fl.
New York, NY 10006
(212)736-5125
Toll Free: (800)323-4958
Weekly
Subscription Rate: $69
ISSN: 1061-6624
www.sumnet.com/enews

EMERSON'S DIRECTORY OF LEADING U.S. ACCOUNTING FIRMS
The Emerson Co.
12342 Northrup Way, Ste. 103
Bellevue, WA 98005-1956
(425)869-0655
Annual

EMPLOYEE BENEFIT PLAN REVIEW
Charles D. Spencer & Associates, Inc.
250 S. Wacker Dr., Ste. 600
Chicago, IL 60606-5834
(312)993-7900
Fax: (312)993-7910
Toll Free: (800)555-5490
Monthly
Price: $75
ISSN: 0013-6808

ENR
McGraw-Hill Cos.
Two Penn Plaza, 9th Fl.
New York, NY 10121
(212)512-2500
Fax: (212)512-6630
Toll Free: (800)525-5003
51x/year
Subscription Rate: $74
ISSN: 0891-9526
www.enr.com

Special Issues:
ENR Top Owners (annual)
Top 500 Design Firms (annual)
Top 400 Contractors (annual)
Top Specialty Contractors (annual)
Top 225 International Contractors (annual)
Top CM Firms (annual)

ENTREPRENEUR
Entrepreneur Media
2392 Morse Ave.
Irvine, CA 92614-6234
(714)261-2325
Fax: (714)755-4211
Monthly
Subscription Rate: $19.97
ISSN: 0364-7218
www.entrepreneurmag.com

Special Issues:
Entrepreneur Annual Franchise 500
Top 50 Business Service Franchises
Top 101 Homebased Franchises

EQUITIES
Equities Magazine Inc.
160 Madison Ave., 3rd Fl.
New York, NY 10016-5412
(212)213-1300
Fax: (212)832-7823
Toll Free: (800)237-8400
7x/yr.
Subscription Rate: $36
ISSN: 1053-2544

Special Issues:
Fastest Growing AMEX Companies (annual)
Annual NASDAQ 1,000

EUROMONEY
Euromoney Publications PLC
Nestor House
Playhouse Yard
London EC4V 5EX England
(212)501-8181
Fax: (212)501-8926
Toll Free: (800)717-2669

Monthly
Subscription Rate: $420
ISSN: 0014-2433
Special Issues:
Intersec 250 (annual)
Latin American 100 (annual)
Latin American 50 (annual)
SSB Guide to World Equity Markets (annual)

EUROPE'S 15,000 LARGEST COMPANIES
E.L.C. Publishing Ltd.
109 Uxbridge Rd.
Ealing
London W5 5TL England
44-181-566-2288
Fax: 44-181-566-4931
Annual
ISSN: 0800-0638

EXPO-THE MAGAZINE FOR EXPOSITION MANAGEMENT
Expo Magazine Inc.
11600 College Blvd.
Overland Park, KS 66210-2785
(913)469-1185
Fax: (913)469-0806
Toll-Free: (800)444-4388
10 issues/year
Subscription Rate: $48
URL: www.expoweb.com

FAR EASTERN ECONOMIC REVIEW
Review Publishing Co. Ltd
G.P.O. Box 160
Hong Kong, People's Republic of China
852-2508-4300
Fax: 852-2503-1549
51x/year
Price: $205
ISSN: 0014-7591
URL: www.feer.com

Special Issue:
Review 200 (annual)

FINANCIAL MANAGEMENT
Financial Management Association
University of South Florida College of Business
2404 E. Fowler Ave., Ste. 3331
Tampa, FL 33620
(813)974-2084
Fax: (813)974-3318
Quarterly
Subscription Rate: $80
ISSN: 0046-3892

FINANCIAL PLANNING
Securities Data Publishing
40 W. 57th St., Fl. 11
New York, NY 10019-4001
(212)765-5311
Fax: (212)765-6123
Monthly
Subscription Rate: $79
ISSN: 0746-7915

Special Issues:
Annual Broker Dealer Survey
Equity Fund Survey (annual)
Mutual Funds Survey (annual)

FINANCIAL TIMES
14 E. 60th St.
New York, NY 10022
(212)752-4500
Fax: (212)308-2397
Toll Free: (800)628-8088
Daily (except Sundays & holidays)
Subscription Rate: $184
ISSN: 0884-6782
www.FT.com

FISCAL STRESS MONITOR
National Municipal Research
PO Box 3437
Church Street Station
New York, NY 10008-3437
Monthly
ISSN: 1520-7277

FLOORING
Douglas Publications Inc.
2807 N. Parham Rd., Ste. 200
Richmond, VA 23294-4410
(804)741-6704
Fax: (804)750-2399
Monthly
Subscription Rate: $37
ISSN: 0162-881X
URL: www.flooringmagazine.com

FLORIDA TREND
Florida Trend Magazines, Inc.
490 1st Ave. S, 8th Fl.
St. Petersburg, FL 33701-4204
(813)821-5800
Fax: (813)822-5083
13x/year
Subscription Rate: $30
ISSN: 0015-4326
www.FlTrend.com

Special Issue:
TopRank Florida (annual)
Florida's Top 250 Companies (annual)

FOLIO: THE MAGAZINE FOR MAGAZINE MANAGEMENT
Intertec Publishing
P.O. Box 10571
Riverton, NJ 08076-0571
(203)358-4239
Fax: (203)358-5812
Annual
Subscription Rate: $96
ISSN: 0046-4333
URL: www.mediacentral.com

FOOD PROCESSING
Putnam Publishing Co.
301 E. Erie St.
Chicago, IL 60611-3059
(312)644-2020
Fax: (312)644-7870
Monthly
Subscription Rate: $30
ISSN: 0015-6523

Special Issue:
Top 100 Food Companies (annual)

FOODSERVICE EQUIPMENT & SUPPLIES
Cahners Business Information
1350 E. Touhy Ave.
Des Plaines, IL 60018-3358
(847)635-8800
Fax: (847)635-6856
Toll Free: (800)323-4958
13x/year
Subscription Rate: $65
ISSN: 1097-2994
URL: www.fesmag.com

FORBES
Forbes Publishing Inc.
60 Fifth Ave.
New York, NY 10011-8882
(212)620-2200
Fax: (212)620-2332
Biweekly
Subscription Rate: $59
ISSN: 0015-6914
URL: www.forbes.com/forbes

Special Issues:
Annual Report on American Industry
Celebrity 100 (annual)
Entertainers Making the Most Money (annual)
Forbes ASAP
Forbes 500s (annual)
Forbes Foreign Rankings (annual)
Global Billionaires (annual)
Largest Private Companies in the U.S. (annual)
Small Growth Companies (annual)
Super 40 (annual)
Technology's 100 Wealthiest (annual)
400 Richest People in America (annual)

FORTUNE
Time Publishing Ventures, Inc.
Rockefeller Center
1271 Ave. of the Americas
New York, NY 10020-1393
(212)522-1212
Fax: (212)765-2699
Toll Free: (800)621-8000
Biweekly
Subscription Rate: $49.94
ISSN: 0015-8259
URL: www.fortune.com

Special Issues:
America's Most Admired Corporations (annual)
Fortune Fast 100 (annual)
Fortune 500 Largest U.S. Corporations (annual)
Global 500: World's Biggest Industrial Coporations (annual)

FOUNDATION DIRECTORY
Foundation Center
79 Fifth Ave.
New York, NY 10003-3076
(212)620-4230
Fax: (212)807-3677
Toll Free: (800)424-9836
Annual
Price: $215
ISSN: 0071-8092
URL: www.fdncenter.org

FURNITURE/TODAY
Cahners Business Information
PO Box 2754
High Point, NC 27261-2754
(336)605-0121
Fax: (336)605-1143
Weekly
Subscription Rate: $129.97
ISSN: 0194-360X
URL: www.furnituretoday.com

Special Issues:
Top 10 Rental Dealers (annual)
Top 100 (annual)
Top 25 Furniture Manufacturers (annual)
Top 25 Retailers (annual)

FUTURES
Financial Communications Co.
250 S. Wacker Dr., Ste. 1150
Chicago, IL 60606
(312)977-0999
Fax: (312)977-1042
Monthly
Subscription Rate: $39
ISSN: 0746-2468

FUTURIST: FORECASTS, TRENDS AND IDEAS ABOUT THE FUTURE
World Future Society
7910 Woodmont Ave., Ste. 450
Bethesda, MD 20814
(301)656-8274
Fax: (301)951-0394
10 issues/year
Subscription Rate: $39
ISSN: 0016-3317
URL: www.wfs.org.wfs

GIANTS OF R&D
Research and Development
National Safety Council
1121 Spring Lake Dr.
Itasca, IL 60143-3201
(630)285-1121
(630)775-2285

GLASS MAGAZINE
National Glass Association
8200 Greensboro Dr.
McLean, VA 22102
(703)442-4890
Fax: (703)442-0630
Monthly
Subscription Rate: $34.95
ISSN: 0747-4261
URL: www.glass.org

Special Issue:
Annual Survey of America's Top Glazing Contractors

GLOBAL FINANCE
Global Finance Media, Inc.
1001 Ave. of the Americas, 21st Fl.
New York, NY 10018
(212)768-1100
Fax: (212)768-2020
Monthly
Subscription Rate: $255
ISSN: 0896-4181
URL: www.gfmag.com

Special Issue:
CFO Compensation Survey

GOVERNING
Congressional Quarterly
1100 Connecticut Ave. NW, Ste. 1300
Washington, DC 20036
(202)862-8802
Fax: (202)862-0032
Monthly
Subscription Rate: $39.95
ISSN: 0894-3842
URL: www.governing.com

GRAPHIC ARTS MONTHLY
Cahners Business Information
245 W. 17th St.

New York, NY 10011
(212)463-6836
Fax: (212)463-6530
Toll Free: (800)637-6089
Monthly
Subscription Rate: $94.90
ISSN: 1047-9325
URL: www.gammag.com

Special Issues:
Top Spenders on Advertising and Printing (annual)
GAM 101 (annual)

GSB CHICAGO
University of Chicago Graduate School of Business
5801 S. Ellis
Chicago, IL
(773)702-7431
Fax: (773)702-2473
Quarterly
Subscription Rate: free to qualified recipients
URL: www.uchicago.edu/news/gsbchicago

HARRIS INDIANA INDUSTRIAL DIRECTORY
Harris InfoSource International
2057 E. Aurora Rd.
Twinsburg, OH 44087
(330)425-9000
Fax: (330)425-7150
Annual
ISSN: 0888-8175

HFN
Fairchild Publications
7 W. 34th St., 3rd Fl.
New York, NY 10001
(212)630-4000
Fax: (212)630-4837
Weekly
Subscription Rate: $99
ISSN: 1082-0310

Special Issues:
Top 200 Home Goods Retailers (annual)
Top 25 Retailers (annual)

HISPANIC BUSINESS
Hispanic Business, Inc.
360 S. Hope Ave., Ste. 300C
Santa Barbara, CA 93105-4017
(805)682-5843
Fax: (805)563-1239
Toll Free: (888)447-7282
Monthly
Subscription Rate: $37.40
ISSN: 0199-0349
URL: www.hispanstar.com

Special Issues:
Hispanic Business 500 (annual)
Hispanic High Tech Companies (annual)
Top 10 Hispanic Radio Stations
Top 50 Exporters

HOMECARE
InterTech Publishing
(800) 543-4116
Fax: (310) 337-1041
Monthly
Subscription Rate: $48
PO Box 8987
Malibu, CA90265-8987
URL: www.miramar.com

HOME FURNISHINGS EXECUTIVE
National Home Furnishings Association
305 W. High St., Ste. 400
High Point, NC 27260
(910)883-1650
Fax: (910)883-1195
Toll Free: (800)888-9590
Monthly
Subscription Rate: $48
ISSN: 1073-5585

HOSPITAL & HEALTH NETWORKS
1 N. Franklin
27th Fl.
Chicago, IL 60606
(312)440-6800
Fax: (312)422-4500
Semimonthly
Subscription Rate: $80
ISSN: 1068-8838
URL: www.hhnmag.com/hhn-home.html

Special Issue:
Health Care 250 (annual)

HOTEL & MOTEL MANAGEMENT
Advanstar Communications, Inc.
7500 Old Oak Blvd.
Cleveland, OH 44130-3343
(440)243-8100
Fax: (440)826-2833
Toll Free: (800)225-4569
Semimonthly
Subscription Rate: $35
ISSN: 0018-6082

Special Issues
Top 25 Management Companies (annual)
Top 25 Design Firms (annual)
Top 100 Hotel Companies (annual)

INBOUND LOGISTICS
5 Penn Plaza, 8th fl.
New York, NY 10001-1810
(212)629-1560
Fax: (212)629-1565
Monthly
Subscription Rate: Free
ISSN: 0888-8493
Special Issue:
Top 75 Motor Carriers (annual)

INC.
Goldhirsh Group Inc.
38 Commercial Wharf
Boston, MA 02110-3801
(617)248-8000
Fax: (617)248-8090
18x/year
Subscription Rate: $19
ISSN: 0162-8968
URL: www.inc.com

Special Issue:
Inc. 500: America's Fastest Growing Private Companies (annual)
Inner City 500 (annual)

INCENTIVE
Bill Communications Inc.
355 Park Ave. S
New York, NY 10010-1789
(212)592-6200
Fax: (212)592-6459
Monthly

Subscription Rate: $55
ISSN: 1042-5195
URL: www.incentivemag.com

INCOME OPPORTUNITIES
Essence Communications, Inc.
1500 Broadway
New York, NY 10036-4015
(212)642-0600
Fax: (212)921-5173
Monthly
Subscription Rate: $18
ISSN: 0019-3429

Special Issue:
Platinum 200 (annual)

INDUSTRIAL DISTRIBUTION
Cahners Business Information
275 Washington St.
Newton, MA 02458-1630
(617)558-4564
Fax: (617)558-4327
Monthly
Subscription Rate: $10/copy
ISSN: 0019-8153
URL: www.inddist.com

Special Issues:
Top 100 (annual)

INDUSTRY WEEK
Penton Publishing, Inc.
1100 Superior Ave. E
Cleveland, OH 44114-2543
(216)696-7000
Fax: (216)696-7670
Semimonthly
Subscription Rate: $65
ISSN: 0039-0895
URL: www.industryweek.com

Special Issue:
Industry Week 1,000 (annual)

INSTITUTIONAL INVESTOR
488 Madison Ave.
New York, NY 10022
(212)303-3300
Fax: (212)303-3592
Monthly
Subscription Rate: $425
ISSN: 0020-3580
URL: www.iimagazine.com

Special Issues:
All-America Fixed-Income Research Team (annual)
All-America Research Team (annual)
All-Europe Research Team (annual)
Best Hotels Worldwide (annual)
The Euro 100 (annual)
Institutional Investor 300 (annual)
Institutional Investor Ranking (annual)
Top 25 (annual)
Top Fixed-Income Trading Firms (annual)
World's Largest Banks (annual)

INSTITUTIONAL INVESTOR INTERNATIONAL EDITION
488 Madison Ave.
New York, NY 10022
(212)832-8888
Fax: (212)224-3171
Monthly
ISSN: 0192-5660

Special Issues:
All-Asia Research Team (annual)
All-Europe Research Team (annual)

INSURANCE ADVOCATE
CCG, Inc.
25-35 Beechwood
PO Box 9001
Mt. Vernon, NY 10552-9001
(914)699-2020
Fax: (914)664-1503
50x/year
Subscription Rate: $49
ISSN: 0020-4587

INTERAVIA
Aerospace Media Publishing SA
Swissair Center
31 Route de l'Aeroport
Box 56
CH-1215 Geneva 15, Switzerland
41-22-788-2788
Fax: 41-22-788-2726
Monthly
Subscription Rate: $130
ISSN: 1423-3215

INTERNATIONAL GAMING & WAGERING BUSINESS
GEM Communications
888 Seventh Ave., 27th Fl.
New York, NY 10106
(212)636-2960
Fax: (212)636-2961
Toll Free: (800)223-9638
Monthly
Subscription Rate: $48
ISSN: 1066-145X

Special Issue:
Annual Study on Performance Executive Salary Update (annual)

INVESTMENT DEALERS' DIGEST
IDD Enterprises
2 World Trade Center, 18th Fl.
New York, NY 10048
(212)432-0045
Fax: (212)321-2336
Weekly
Subscription Rate: $625
ISSN: 0021-0080

Special Issues:
Fees (annual)
M & A Rankings (annual)
Municipal Rankings (annual)
Private Placement Investors' Survey (annual)
Private Placement Sweepstakes (annual)
Underwriter Rankings (annual)

INVESTORS CHRONICLE
Financial Times
One Southwark Bridge
London, SE1 9HL England
44-171-873-3000

Fax: 44-171-407-5700
Weekly
ISSN: 0261-3115
URL: www.investorschronicle.co.uk

IOMA'S REPORT ON COMPENSATION & BENEFITS FOR LAW OFFICES
Institute of Management and Administration
29 W 35th St.
New York, NY 10001
(212) 244-0360
Fax: (212) 564-0465
Monthly
Subscription Rate: $249
URL: www.ioma.com/ioma
ISSN: 1068-4239

ISSUES IN ACCOUNTING EDUCATION
American Accounting Association
5717 Bessie Dr.
Sarasota, FL 34233-2330
(941) 921-7747
Fax: (941) 923-4093
Quarterly
Subscription Rate: $30

IVEY BUSINESS JOURNAL
Ivey Publishing
Richard Ivey School of Business
The University of Western Ontario Ivey School of Business
London, Ontario, Canada
N6A 3K7
(416) 620-0116
Fax: (416) 620-1302
Quarterly
Subscription Rate: $45
URL: www.ivey.uwo.ca

JOURNAL OF ACCOUNTANCY
American Institute of CPAs
Harborside Financial Center
201 Plaza III
Jersey City, NJ 07311-3801
(201)938-3292
Fax: (201)938-3329
Monthly
Subscription Rate: $56
ISSN: 0021-8448
URL: www.aicpa.org/pubs/jofa

JOURNAL OF BUSINESS STRATEGY
Faulkner & Gray, Inc.
11 Penn Plaza, Bsmt. 22
New York, NY 10001-2006
(212)967-7000
Fax: (212)695-8172
Bimonthly
Subscription Rate: $98
ISSN: 0275-6668

JOURNAL OF PROPERTY MANAGEMENT
Institute of Real Estate Management
International Headquarters
430 N Michigan Ave.
Chicago, IL 60611-4090
(800) 337-0706
Fax: (312) 329-6039
Bi-monthly
Subscription Rate: $41.95
http://www.irem.org

KENTUCKY DIRECTORY OF MANUFACTURERS
Kentucky Cabinet for Economic Development
Capital Plaza Tower
500 Metro St., 23rd Fl.
Frankfort, KY 40601
(502)564-4886
Fax: (502)564-0023
Annual
Subscription Rate: $79

KEYSTONE COAL INDUSTRY MANUAL
PRIMEDIA Inc.
745 Fifth Avenue
New York, NY 10151
(212)726-2802
Fax: (212) 745-0199
Annual
Subscritption Rate: $110
ISSN: 0450-1772

LIMOUSINE & CHAUFFEUR
Bobit Publishing Co.
2512 Artesia Blvd.
Redondo Beach, CA 90278-3295
(310)533-2400
Fax: (310)533-2500
Monthly
Subscription Rate: $28 (U.S.); $38 (Canadian); $50 (foreign)
ISSN: 8750-7374
URL: www.limousinecentral.com

Special Issue:
Top 50 Livery Companies

LODGING HOSPITALITY
Penton Media, Inc.
1100 Superior Ave.
Cleveland, OH 44114
(216)696-7000
Fax: (216)696-0836
14x/yr.
Subscription Rate: $65
ISSN: 0148-0766
URL: www.LHonline.com

Special Issue:
Lodging's 400 Top Performers (annual)

LONG ISLAND BUSINESS NEWS
Long Island Business News
2150 Smithtown Ave.
Ronkonkoma, NY 11779-7348
(516)737-1700
Weekly
Subscription Rate: $59
ISSN: 0894-4806

LOS ANGELES BUSINESS JOURNAL
Scripps Howard Business Publications
5700 Wilshire Blvd., Ste. 170
Los Angeles, CA 90036-3659
(213)549-5225
54x/year
ISSN: 0194-2603

Special Issues:
Book of Lists (annual)

LP/GAS
Advanstar Communications Inc.
7500 Old Oak Blvd.
Cleveland OH, 44130-3343
(218)723-9299
Fax: (218)723-9377
Monthly
Subscription Rate: $30
ISSN: 0024-7103

Special Issue:
Top 50 U.S. Retail Propane Marketers (annual)

MANAGEMENT REVIEW
American Management Association
1601 Broadway
New York, NY 10019-7420
(212)903-8063
Fax: (212)903-8083
11x/year
Subscription Rate: $49
ISSN: 0025-1895

MANUFACTURED HOME MERCHANDISER
RLD Group, Inc.
203 N. Wabash Ave., Ste. 800
Chicago, IL 60601-2411
(312)236-3528
Fax: (312)236-4024
Monthly
Subscription Rate: $36
ISSN: 1047-2967

MARKETING
Maclean Hunter Publishing, Ltd.
777 Bay St., 9th Fl.
Toronto, ON M5W 1A7 Canada
(416)596-5858
Fax: (416)593-3170
Weekly
Subscription Rate: $59.50
ISSN: 1196-4650

Special Issues:
Direct Marketing League Table (annual)
Magazine ABCs
Top Agencies (annual)
Top Sales Promotion Companies (annual)

MARKETING NEWS
American Marketing Association
250 S. Wacker Dr., Ste. 200
Chicago, IL 60606-6313
(312)648-0536
Fax: (312)993-7542
Biweekly
Subscription Rate: $75
URL: www.ama.org/pubs/mn/pub2.html

Special Issues:
The Honomichl 50 (annual)
The Honomichl Global 25 (annual)

MASS MARKET RETAILERS
See: *MMR*

MEAT & POULTRY
Sosland Publishing Co.
4800 Main St., Ste. 100
Kansas City, MO 64112-2513
(816)756-1000
Fax: (816)756-0494
Monthly
Subscription Rate: $75 U.S.
ISSN: 0892-6077

Special Issue:
Top 100 (annual)

MEDIAWEEK
BPI Communications, Inc.
1515 Broadway
New York, NY 10036-8901
(800) 722-6658
Fax: (212) 536-5353
Weekly
Subscription Rate: $130
ISSN: 0155-176X

MEDICAL ECONOMICS
Medical Economics Publishing Co., Inc.
5 Paragon Dr.
Montvale, NJ 07645-1735
(201)358-7200
Fax: (201)722-2667
Toll Free: (800)526-4870
Biweekly
Subscription Rate: $99
ISSN: 0025-7206

MEDICAL MARKETING & MEDIA
CPS Communications
7200 W. Camino Real, Ste. 215
Boca Raton, FL 33433-5597
(407)368-9301
Fax: (407)368-7870
16x/year
Subscription Rate: $85
ISSN: 0025-7354
URL: www.cpsnet.com/PubsOnline/

Special Issue:
Healthcare Advertising Review (annual)

MEETING NEWS
Miller Freeman, Inc.
1 Penn Plaza
New York, NY 10119
(212)714-1300
Fax: (212)714-1313
18x/year
Subscription Rate: $65
ISSN: 0145-630X

MERGERSTAT REVIEW
1930 Century Park West
Los Angeles, CA 90067
(310)553-8871
Fax: (310)553-2173
Toll Free: (800)455-8871
Annual
Price: $249

METAL CENTER NEWS
Cahners Business Information
191 S. Gary Ave.
Carol Stream, IL 60188
(630)320-7000
Fax: (630)320-7105
Monthly
Subscription Rate: $89
ISSN: 0539-4511
URL: www.chilton.net/metalctr/index.htm

Special Issue:
Top 50 Metal Companies (annual)

METAL STATISTICS
Institutional Investor
488 Madison Ave.
New York, NY 10022
(212)630-4000
Fax: (212)224-3171
Annual
Price: $88
ISSN: 0076-6658

METRO MAGAZINE
Bobit Publishing Co.
2512 Artesia Blvd.
Redondo Beach, CA 90278-3210
(310)533-2400
Fax: (310)533-2500
Bimonthly
Subscription Rate: $25
ISSN: 1057-8196
URL: www.transit-center.com

Special Issues:
Largest 100 Transit Bus Fleets (annual)
Largest Private Motorcoach Fleets (annual)
Metro Rail Survey (annual)

MILITARY MARKET
Army Times Publishing Co.
6883 Commercial Dr.
Springfield, VA 22151-4202
(703)750-8109
Fax: (703)658-8314
Monthly
Subscription Rate: $84
ISSN: 0026-4067

MILLING & BAKING NEWS
Sosland Publishing Co.
4800 Main St., Ste. 100
Kansas City, MO 64112-2513
(816)756-1000
Fax: (816)756-0494
Weekly
Subscription Rate: $116
ISSN: 0091-4843

MINI-STORAGE MESSENGER
Mini Co., Inc.
2531 W. Dunlap Ave., No. 201
Phoenix, AZ 85021-2704
(602)824-6864
Fax: (602)861-1094
Monthly
Subscription Rate: $60
ISSN: 0273-5822
URL: www.minico.com

Special Issue:
Top 50 (annual)

MMR
Racher Press Inc.
220 Fifth Ave.
New York, NY 10001-7708
(212)213-6000
Fax: (212)213-6106
22x/year
Subscription Rate: $81
ISSN: 1080-0794
Note: Formerly *Mass Market Retailers*.

Special Issues:
Annual Report of the Mass Market Industries

MODERN BREWERY AGE
Business Journals, Inc.
50 Day St., Ste. 5550
Norwalk, CT 06854-3100
(203)853-6015
Fax: (203)852-8175
64x/year
Subscription Rate: $85
ISSN: 0026-7538

Special Issue:
MBA Statistical Study (annual)
Micro & Specialty Beer Report (annual)

MODERN HEALTHCARE
Crain Communications Inc.
740 N. Rush St.
Chicago, IL 60611-2590
(312)649-5350
Fax: (312)280-3183
Weekly
Subscription Rate: $125
ISSN: 0160-7480

Special Issues:
Contract Management Survey (annual)
Design and Construction Survey (annual)
Modern Healthcare Multi-Unit Providers Survey (annual)

MONEY MARKET DIRECTORY OF PENSION FUNDS & THEIR INVESTMENT MANAGERS
Money Market Directories
320 E. Main St.
Charlottesville, VA 22902-5234
(800)446-2810
Fax: (804)979-9962
Annual
Subscription Rate: $975
ISS: 0736-6051

MUSIC TRADES
Music Trade Corp.
80 West St.
PO Box 432
Englewood, NJ 07631-0432
(201)871-1965
Monthly
Subscription Rate: $14
ISSN: 0027-4488

Special Issue:
Top 100 Music Retailers (annual)
Global 200 (annual)

MUTUAL FUNDS
Institute for Econometric Research
2200 SW 10th St.
Deerfield Beach, FL 33442-7622
(954)421-1000
Fax: (954)570-8200
Monthly
Subscription Rate: $15
ISSN: 1079-0039

NATIONAL FISHERMAN
Diversified Publications
121 Free St.
Portland, ME 04112-5602
(207) 842-5662
Fax: (207) 842-5603
Monthly
Subscription Rate: $22.95
ISSN: 0027-9250

NATIONAL PROVISIONER
Stagnito Communications, Inc.
1935 Shermer Rd., Ste. 100
Northbrook, IL 60062-5354
(847)205-5660
Fax: (847)205-5680
Weekly
Subscription Rate: $38
ISSN: 0027-996X
Special Issue:
The Provisioner Top 200 (annual)

NATIONAL REAL ESTATE INVESTOR
Primedia Intertec Publishing Corp.
9800 Metcalf
Overland Park, KS 66202-2215
(770)955-2500
Fax: (770)955-0400
Monthly
Subscription Rate: $70
ISSN: 0027-9994

Special Issue:
Top 25 Senior Housing Owners & Managers (annual)

NATIONAL UNDERWRITER LIFE & HEALTH/FINANCIAL SERVICES
National Underwriter Co.
505 Gest St.
Cincinnati, OH 45203-1716
(513)721-2140
Fax: (513)721-0126
Weekly
Subscription Rate: $76
ISSN: 0893-8202

Special Issues:
Top 25 Contracts (annual)
Life & Health Statistical Review (annual)

NATIONAL UNDERWRITER PROPERTY & CASUALTY/RISK & BENEFITS MANAGEMENT
National Underwriter Co.
505 Gest St.
Cincinnati, OH 45203-1716
(513)721-2140
Fax: (513)721-0126
Weekly
Subscription Rate: $79
ISSN: 1042-6841

Special Issue:
Top 25 Highest-Paid Executives (annual)

NATION'S BUSINESS
U.S. Chamber of Commerce
1615 H St. NW
Washington, DC 20062-0002
(202)463-5650
Fax: (202)463-3178
Monthly
ISSN: 0028-047X

NATION'S RESTAURANT NEWS
Lebhar-Friedman Inc.
425 Park Ave., 6th Fl.
New York, NY 10022-3549
(212)756-5132
Fax: (212)207-1947
Weekly
Subscription Rate: $40
ISSN: 0028-0518

Special Issue:
A Year in Review (annual)

NEW JERSEY BUSINESS
New Jersey Business & Industry Association
310 Passaic Ave.
Fairfield, NJ 07004-2523
(973)882-5004
Fax: (973)882-4648

Monthly
Subscription Rate: $20
ISSN: 0028-5560

Special Issue:
Book of Lists (annual)

NEW YORK STOCK EXCHANGE FACT BOOK
New York Stock Exchange
11 Wall St.
New York, NY 10005
(212)656-3000
Annual
Price: $10

NEW YORK TIMES
New York Times Co.
229 W. 43rd St.
New York, NY 10036-3959
(212)556-1234
Fax: (212)463-1544
Daily
Subscription Rate: $401.10
ISSN: 0362-4331
URL: www.nytimes.com

NIGHTCLUB AND BAR MAGAZINE
Oxford Publishing, Inc.
307 W. Jackson Ave.
Oxford, MS 38655
Tel: (800) 247-3881
Fax: (601) 236-5541
Monthly
Subscription Rate: $30

NONWOVENS INDUSTRY
Rodman Publishing Corp.
17 S. Franklin Turnpike
PO Box 555
Ramsey, NJ 07446-2545
(201)825-2552
Fax: (201)825-0553
Monthly
Subscription Rate: $55
ISSN: 0163-4429

OCCUPATIONAL HAZARDS
Penton Publishing, Inc.
1100 Superior Ave. E
Cleveland, OH 44114-2543
(216)696-7000
Fax: (216)696-7658
Monthly
Subscription Rate: $45
ISSN: 0029-7909

O'DWYER'S DIRECTORY OF PUBLIC RELATIONS FIRMS
J. R. O'Dwyer Co., Inc.
271 Madison Ave., Ste. 600
New York, NY 10016-1001
(212)679-2471
Fax: (212)683-2750
Annual
Price: $145
ISSN: 0078-3374

OECD OBSERVER
Organization for Economic Cooperation & Development
2001 L St. NW, Ste. 650
Washington, DC 20036-4910
(202)785-6323
Fax: (202)785-0350
Bimonthly
Subscription Rate: $25
ISSN: 0029-7054

OFFICE WORLD NEWS

Bus Publishing
366 Ramtown Greenville Rd.
Howell, NJ 07731-2789
(732)785-8300
Fax: (732)785-1347
Monthly
Subscription Rate: $50
ISSN: 0164-5951

OIL & GAS JOURNAL
PennWell Publishing Co.
1421 S. Sheridan Rd.
Tulsa, OK 74112-6619
(918)835-3161
Fax: (918)831-9295
Weekly
Subscription Rate: $79
ISSN: 0030-1388

Special Issues:
Oil & Gas Journal 200 (annual)
OGJ Special

PAPERBOARD PACKAGING
Advanstar Communications, Inc.
7500 Old Oak Blvd.
Cleveland, OH 44130-3343
(216)243-8100
Fax: (216)891-2833
Toll Free: (800)225-4569
Monthly
Subscription Rate: $30
ISSN: 0031-1227

PENSIONS & INVESTMENTS
Crain Communications, Inc.
220 E. 42nd St., 9th Fl.
New York, NY 10017-5806
(212)210-0114
Fax: (212)210-0114
27x/year
Subscription Rate: $205
ISSN: 1050-4974
www.pionline.com

Special Issues:
Largest Money Managers (annual)
Master Trust/Global Custody: Special Report (annual)
Scorecard for Pension Managers (annual)
Special Report: Mutual Funds (annual)
Top 1,000 Funds (annual)
Top 300 (annual)
Defined Contribution Providers (annual)
Watson Wyatt World 300 (annual)

PET FOOD INDUSTRY
Watt Publishing Co.
122 S. Wesley Ave.
Mt. Morris, IL 61054-1497
(815)734-4171
Fax: (815)734-4201
Bimonthly
Subscription Rate: $36
ISSN: 0031-6245

Special Issue:
Top 10 Pet Food Marketers (annual)

PHILADELPHIA BUSINESS JOURNAL
MCP, Inc.
400 Market St., Ste. 300
Philadelphia, PA 19106-2501
(215)238-1450
Weekly
Subscription Rate: $52
ISSN: 0744-3587
URL: www.amcity.com/phildelphia/

Special Issue:
Book of Business Lists (annual)

PIZZA TODAY
ProTech Publishing & Communications Inc.
PO Box 1347
New Albany, IN 47151-1347
(812)949-0909
Fax: (812)941-9711
Monthly
Subscription Rate: $30
ISSN: 0743-3115

Special Issue:
Hot 100 Pizza Companies (annual)

PLAYTHINGS
Geyer-McAllister Publications, Inc.
51 Madison Ave., 28th Fl.
New York, NY 10010-1603
(212)519-7200
Fax: (212)683-7929
Monthly
Subscription Rate: $32
ISSN: 0032-1567

POTENTIALS MAGAZINE
Bill Communication
Circulation Dept.
50 S. Ninth St.
Minneapolis, MN 55402.
(800) 707-7776
Fax: (612) 333-6526
Monthly
Subscription: $24

THE PRACTICAL ACCOUNTANT
Faulkner & Gray, Inc.
11 Penn Plaza, Bsmt. 22
New York, NY 10001-2006
(212)967-7000
Fax: (212)967-7162
Monthly
Subscription Rate: $65
ISSN: 0032-6321

Special Issue:
Regional Rankings (annual)

PREPARED FOODS
Cahners Business Information
1350 E. Touhy Ave.
PO Box 5080
Des Plaines, IL 60017-5080
(847)635-8800
Fax: (847)390-2445
Toll Free: (800)323-4958
Monthly
Subscription Rate: $94.90
ISSN: 0747-2536
URL: www.preparedfoods.com

Special Issues:
The Global 250 Food Companies
New Products Annual

PROFESSIONAL BUILDER
Cahners Business Information
1350 E. Touhy Ave.
Des Plaines, IL 60018-3358
(847)390-2155
Fax: (847)635-9950
Toll Free: (800)323-4958
7x/year
Subscription Rate: $89.90
ISSN: 1072-0561
URL: www.probuilder.com

Special Issue:
Annual Report of the 400 Housing Giants

PROGRESSIVE GROCER
Progressive Grocer Association
23 Old King's Highway S
Darien, CT 06820
(203)655-1600
Fax: (203)656-3800
Monthly
Subscription Rate: $99
ISSN: 0033-0787
URL: www.progressivegrocer.com

Special Issues:
Annual Report of the Grocery Industry
Progressive Grocer's Marketing Guidebook (annual)

PUBLIC UTILITIES FORTNIGHTLY
Public Utilities Reports, Inc.
8229 Boone Blvd., Ste. 401
Vienna, VA 22182-2623
(703)847-7720
Fax: (703)847-0683
22x/year
Subscription Rate: $119
ISSN: 1078-5892

PUBLISHERS WEEKLY
Cahners Business Information
249 W. 17th St.
New York, NY 10011-5300
(212)463-6824
Fax: (212)463-6631
Weekly
Subscription Rate: $139
ISSN: 0000-0019

PULP & PAPER
Miller Freeman, Inc.
600 Harrison St.
San Francisco, CA 94107-1370
(415)905-2200
Fax: (415)905-2240
13x/year
Subscription Rate: $90
ISSN: 0033-4081
URL: www.pulp-paper.com

PURCHASING
Cahners Business Information
275 Washington St.
Newton, MA 02158-1630
(617)558-4291
Fax: (617)558-4327
Semimonthly
Subscription Rate: $80
ISSN: 0033-4448

Special Issues:
Purchasing Top 250 (annual)
Top 100 Electronics Distributors (annual)
Top 100 (annual)

R & D MAGAZINE
Cahners Business Information
1350 E. Touhy Ave.
Des Plaines, IL 60018-3358
(847)390-2343
Fax: (847)390-2618
Toll Free: (800)323-4958
Monthly
Subscription Rate: $45
ISSN: 0746-9179

Special Issue:
Giants of R & D (annual)

REAL ESTATE FORUM
Real Estate Forum, Inc.
111 8th Ave., Fl. 1511
New York, NY 10011-5201
(212)563-6460
Fax: (212)967-1498
Monthly
Subscription Rate: $65
ISSN: 0034-0707

REAL ESTATE OUTLOOK
National Association of Realtors, Research Group
700 11th St. NW
Washington, DC 20001
(202)383-1137
Fax: (202)383-7568
Monthly
Subscription Rate: $95

RENTAL EQUIPMENT REGISTER
Miramar Communications, Inc.
23815 Stuart Ranch Rd.
PO Box 8987
Malibu, CA 90265-4897
(310)317-4522
Fax: (310)317-9644
Toll Free: (800)543-4116
Monthly
Subscription Rate: $75
ISSN: 0034-4524
URL: www.rermag.com

RESEARCH ALERT
EPM Communications, Inc.
160 Mercer St., 3rd Fl.
New York, NY 10012-3208
(212)941-0099
Fax: (212)941-1622
Semimonthly
Subscription Rate: $369
ISSN: 0739-358X

RESELLER MANAGEMENT
Cahners Business Information
275 Washington St.
Newton, MA 02158-1630
(617)558-4723
Fax: (617)558-4757
14x/year
Subscription Rate: $60
ISSN: 1042-7325

RESTAURANT BUSINESS
Bill Communications, Inc.
355 Park Ave. S
New York, NY 10010-1789
(212)592-6200
Fax: (212)592-6650
18x/year
Subscription Rate: $79

ISSN: 0097-8043

Special Issues:
Restaurant Growth Index (annual)
Top 50 Franchisers (annual)
Top 50 U.S. Chains Abroad (annual)

RESTAURANT HOSPITALITY
Penton Media Inc.
1100 Superior Ave.
Cleveland, OH 44114
(216)696-7000
Fax: (216)696-0836
Monthly
Subscription Rate: $65 (individual); $85 (Canadian); $135 (foreign)
ISSN: 0148-0766

RESTAURANTS & INSTITUTIONS
Cahners Business Information
1350 E. Touhy Ave.
Des Plaines, IL 60018-3358
(847)635-8800
Fax: (847)635-6856
Toll Free: (800)446-6551
Semimonthly
Subscription Rate: $132.90
ISSN: 0273-5520
www.rimag.com

Special Issues:
Restaurants & Institutions 400 (annual)
Choice in Chains (annual)

ROCHESTER BUSINESS JOURNAL
55 Saint Paul St.
Rochester, NY 14604-1314
(716)546-8303
Weekly
Subscription Rate: $55
ISSN: 0896-3274

RUBBER WORLD
Lipincott & Peto, Inc.
1867 W. Market St., No. 5451
Akron, OH 44313-6901
(330)864-2122
Fax: (330)864-5298
16x/year
Subscription Rate: $29
ISSN: 0035-9572

SA BANKER
Institute of Bankers in South Africa
17 Harrison St., 9th Fl.
PO Box 61420
Johannesburg 2107, South Africa
Quarterly

SAFETY AND HEALTH
National Safety Council
1121 Spring Lake Dr.
Itasca, IL 60143-3201
(630)285-1121
Fax: (630)285-1315
Monthly
Subscription Rate: $56
ISSN: 0891-1797
www.nsc.org

SALES AND MARKETING MANAGEMENT
Bill Communications, Inc.
255 Park Ave. S
New York, NY 10010-1789
(212)592-6200
Fax: (212)592-6499
Toll-Free: (800)821-6897
13 issues/year
Subscription Rate: $48 (individual); $29 (corporate); $62 (Canadian); $77 (foreign)
www.salesandmarketing.com

SALES AND MEDIA MARKET
Bill Communications, Inc.
355 Park Ave. S.
New York, NY 10010-1789
(212)592-6200
Fax: (212)592-6499
Toll-Free: (800)821-6897
13 issues/year
Subscription Rate: $48

S & P 500 DIRECTORY
Standard & Poor's Corp.
25 Broadway
New York, NY 10004-1010
(212)208-8000
Fax: (212)208-1161
Annual
Price: $185
ISSN: 1088-8926

SDM (SECURITY DISTRIBUTING & MARKETING)
Cahners Business Information
1350 E. Touhy Ave.
Des Plaines, IL 60018-3358
(847)390-2116
Fax: (847)635-9950
Toll Free: (800)323-4958
13x/year
Subscription Rate: $82
ISSN: 0049-0016
www.sdmmag.com

Special Issues:
Top Systems Integrators (annual)
SDM 100 (annual)

SECURITIES INDUSTRY YEARBOOK
Securities Industry Association
120 Broadway
New York, NY 10271-0002
(212)608-1500
Fax: (212)608-1604
Annual
Price: $125
ISSN: 0730-5796

SECURITY DISTRIBUTING & MARKETING
See: *SDM*

SHESHUNOFF BANK QUARTERLY
Sheshunoff Information Services, Inc.
505 Barton Springs Rd., Ste. 1200
Austin, TX 78704
(512)472-2244
Fax: (512)305-6575
Toll Free: (800)456-2340
Quarterly
Subscription Rate: $495

Special Issue:
Largest U.S. Banks in Selected Categories

SHOPPING CENTER WORLD
Primedia Intertec Publishing Corp.
9800 Metcalf
Overland Park, KS 66202-2215
(770)955-2500
Fax: (770)955-0400
Monthly
Subscription Rate: $60
ISSN: 0049-0393

Special Issues:

Top Managers Survey (annual)
Top Owners Survey (annual)
Top 25 Retail Lenders (annual)

SIGNS OF THE TIMES
ST Publications
407 Gilbert Ave.
Cincinnati, OH 45202
(513)421-2050
(513)421-5144
Monthly
Subscription Rate: $36
ISSN: 0037-5063

SITE SELECTION
Conway Data Inc.
35 Technology Pkwy. S, Ste. 150
Norcross, GA 30092-2900
(770)446-6996
Fax: (770)263-8825
Bimonthly
Subscription Rate: $75
ISSN: 1080-7799

SMARTMONEY
959 8th Ave.
New York, NY 10019-3737
(212)492-1300
Monthly
Subscription Rate: $15
ISSN: 1069-2851

SN (SUPERMARKET NEWS)
Fairchild Publications
7 W. 34th St., 3rd Fl.
New York, NY 10001-8100
(212)630-3770
Fax: (212)630-3768
Weekly
Subscription Rate: $30
ISSN: 0039-5803

SOUTHWEST ECONOMY
Federal Reserve Bank of Dallas
2000 N. Pearl St.
Dallas, TX 75201-2272
(212)922-5254
Fax: (212)922-5268
Bimonthly

SUCCESS
733 Third Ave., 10th Fl.
New York, NY 10017
(212)883-7100
Fax: (212)949-7002
10x/year
Subscription Rate: $20
ISSN: 0039-4424

Special Issues:
Franchise Gold 100 (annual)
The Hot 100

SUPERMARKET BUSINESS
Bill Communications, Inc.
255 Park Ave. S
New York, NY 10010-1789
(212)592-6200
Fax: (212)592-6499
Monthly
Subscription Rate: $85
ISSN: 0196-5700

SUPERMARKET NEWS
Fairchild Publications
7 W. 34th St., 3rd Fl.
New York, NY 10001
(212)630-3770
Fax: (212)630-3768
Weekly
Subscription Rate: $30
ISSN: 0039-5803

Special Issue:
World's Biggest Food Retailers

SURVEY OF BUYING POWER
Claritas Corp.
53 Brown Rd.
Ithaca, NY 14850-1247
(607)257-5757
Annual
Price: $150

TELECOMMUNICATIONS
Horizon House Publications, Inc.
685 Canton St.
Norwood, MA 02062-2610
(781)769-9750
Fax: (781)769-6334

TELEPHONY
Primedia Intertec Publishing Corp.
9800 Metcalf
Overland Park, KS 66202-2215
(913)341-1300
Fax: (913)967-1868
Weekly
Subscription Rate: $87
ISSN: 0040-2656
www.internettelephony.com

TEXTILE WORLD
Intertec Publishing
6151 Powers Ferry Rd., NW, Ste. 200
Atlanta, GA 30339-2959
(770)955-2500
Fax: (770)618-0393
Monthly
Subscription Rate: $42 (individual); $21 (corporate); $42 (Canadian); $97 (foreign)
URL: www.textileworld.com

TOBACCO INTERNATIONAL
Lockwood Trade Journal Co., Inc.
130 W. 42nd St., Ste. 1050
New York, NY 10036-7800
(212)661-5980
Fax: (212)827-0945
22x/year
Subscription Rate: $25
ISSN: 0049-3945

TRAFFIC WORLD
Journal of Commerce, Inc.
529 14th St. NW, Ste. 741
Washington, DC 20045-1701
(202)383-6140
Fax: (202)783-2550
Weekly
ISSN: 0041-073X

TRAINING AND DEVELOPMENT
American Society for Training and Development
1640 King St.
Box 1443
Alexandria, VA 22313-2043
(703)683-8100
Fax: (803)683-8103

Monthly
Subscription Rate: Free with membership ($85, individual or corporate)
ISSN: 1055-9760
URL: www.astd.org

TRANSIT FACT BOOK
American Public Transit Association
1201 New York Ave., NW, Ste. 400
Washington, DC 20005-6141
(202)898-4000
ISSN: 0149-3132

TRANSPORT TOPICS
American Trucking Association, Inc.
Trucking Information Services
2200 Mill Rd.
Alexandria, VA 22314-4686
(703)838-1978
Fax: (703)683-9751
Weekly
Subscription Rate: $69
ISSN: 0041-1558

Special Issue:
Annual Report

TRANSPORTATION & DISTRIBUTION
Penton Publishing Inc.
1100 Superior Ave. E
Cleveland, OH 44114-2543
(216)696-7000
Fax: (216)696-4135
Monthly
Subscription Rate: $50
ISSN: 0895-8548

TRAVEL INDUSTRY WORLD YEAR-BOOK: THE BIG PICTURE
Child & Waters Inc.
PO Box 610
Rye, NY 10580-0610
(914)921-0988
Annual
Price: $92
ISSN: 0738-9515

TRAVELWARE
Business Journals, Inc.
50 Day St., 7th Fl.
Norwalk, CT 06854
(203)853-6015
Fax: (203)852-8175
Monthly
Subscription Rate: $32 (individual); $60 (foreign)
ISSN: 0747-475X
URL: www.travelwaremag.com

UNITAS
Union Bank of Finland
Economic Research Dept.
FIN-00020 UBF, Finland
Fax: 358-0-657-2898
Quarterly
Subscription Rate: Free
ISSN: 0041-7130

U.S. BANKER
Faulkner & Gray, Inc.
11 Penn Plaza
New York, NY 10001-2006
(212)967-7000
Fax: (212)695-8172
Monthly
Subscription Rate: $38
ISSN: 0148-8848

Special Issues:
Community Banking Rankings
Top 200 Mid-Sized Banks
U.S. Banker Top 100 (annual)

U.S. DISTRIBUTION JOURNAL
BMT Publications
750 Lexington Ave., Ste. 1600
New York, NY 10022-1262
(212)759-4505
Monthly
ISSN: 0897-1315

U.S. NEWS AND WORLD REPORT
1050 Thomas Jefferson St., NW
Washington, DC 20007
(202)955-2000
Fax: (202)955-2049
Weekly
Subscription Rate: $44.75
ISSN: 0041-5537
URL: www.usnews.com

Special Issues:
America's Colleges & Universities (annual)
America's Best Graduate and Professional Schools (annual)
America's Best Hospital (annual)
Best Mutual Funds (annual)

VIDEO STORE
Advanstar Communications, Inc.
201 Sandpointe Ave., Ste. 600
Santa Ana, CA 92707-5778
(714)513-8400
Fax: (714)513-8403
Weekly
Subscription Rate: $135
ISSN: 0195-1750

VISUAL MERCHANDISING & STORE DESIGN
ST Publications
407 Gilbert Ave.
Cincinnati, OH 45202-2220
(513)421-2050
Fax: (513)421-5144
Monthly
Subscription Rate: $39
ISSN: 0745-4295

Special Issues:
Top 50 Fixture Manufacturers (annual)
Top 50 Retail Interior Design Firms (annual)

VOLUME OF FUTURES TRADING
Futures Industry Association
2001 Pennsylvania Ave. NW, Ste. 600
Washington, DC 20006-1807
(202)466-5460
Fax: (202)296-3184
Annual

URL: www.fiafii.org

WALL STREET JOURNAL
Dow Jones & Co., Inc.
200 Liberty St.
New York, NY 10281-1003
(212)416-2000
Fax: (212)808-6866
Daily (except weekends)
Subscription Rate: $175
ISSN: 0099-9660
URL: www.wsj.com

Special Issues:
Annual Global Ranking
Shareholder Scoreboard (annual)

WARD'S AUTO WORLD
Ward's Communications Inc.
3000 Town Center, Ste. 2750
Southfield, MI 48075-1212
(248)357-0800
Fax: (248)357-0810
Monthly
Subscription Rate: $47
ISSN: 0043-0315
URL: www.wardsauto.com

WINES & VINES
The Hiaring Co.
1800 Lincoln Ave.
San Rafael, CA 94901-1298
(415)453-9700
Fax: (415)453-2517
Monthly
Subscription Rate: $32.50
ISSN: 0043-583X

WORKING WOMAN
MacDonald Communications
135 W. 50th St., 16th Fl.
New York, NY 10020
(212)445-6100
Fax: (212)599-4763
Monthly
Subscription Rate: $12
ISSN: 0145-5761

Special Issue:
Working Woman 500 (annual)

WORLD AIR TRANSPORT STATISTICS
International Air Transport Association
2000 Peel St.
Montreal PQ H3A 2R4 Canada
(514)844-6311
Annual
Price: $55
ISSN: 0084-1366

WORLD TRADE
Freedom Magazines Inc.
17702 Cowan, Ste. 100
Irvine, CA 92614-6035
(714)798-3500
Fax: (714)798-3501
11x/year
Subscription Rate: $24
ISSN: 1054-8637

Special Issue:
World Trade 100 (annual)

WORTH
Capital Publishing
575 Lexington Ave.
New York, NY 10022-6102
(212)223-3100
Fax: (212)223-1598
10x/year
Subscription Rate: $15
ISSN: 1060-5967

YOUR MONEY
Consumers Digest Inc.
8001 N. Lincoln Ave.
Skokie, IL 60077
(847)763-9200
Fax: (847)275-7273
3x/year
Subscription Rate: $15.97
ISSN: 1057-123X

Special Issues:
Internet Broker Scoreboard
Top 400 (annual)